BETWEEN A LAUGH AND A TEAR

BETWEEN A LAUGH AND A TEAR

Joy L. Esterby, Editor

THE INTERNATIONAL SOCIETY OF POETS

Between a Laugh and a Tear

Copyright © 1996 by The International Society of Poets
as a compilation.

Rights to individual poems reside with the artists themselves.
This collection of poetry contains works submitted to the Publisher by individual authors who confirm that the work is their original creation. Based upon the authors' confirmations and to the Publisher's actual knowledge, these poems were written by the listed poets. The International Society of Poets does not guarantee or assume responsibility for verifying the authorship of each work. Address all inquiries to Jeffrey Franz, Publisher, Poets House, Cremers Road, Dolphin Park, Euro Link Estate, Sittingbourne, Kent ME10 3HB.

All rights reserved under International and Pan-American copyright conventions. No part of this book may be reproduced, stored in a retrieval system or transmitted in any form, electronic, mechanical, or by other means, without written permission of the publisher.

ISBN 1-57553-179-8

Printing and Binding by
BPC Wheatons Ltd, Exeter, UK

Editor's Note

The caverns of the human mind are extraordinarily difficult to excavate, yet the results are infinitely rewarding. Humans are complex beings who experience a broad array of emotions, even several at the same time. Parents cry at their children's weddings, though they may very well be ecstatic. Often anger in addition to sadness is felt after the death of a loved one. In certain relationships love and hate battle each other in people's minds for ultimate expression. Understanding our own feelings can prove a daunting task.

Poetry has long served as a release for such strong, often dichotomous emotions. Indeed, writing poetry can help poets discover new things about themselves and others, just as the finished poem enlightens its readers. Phillip Aiken's "Funny How Poetry" (p. 323) aptly describes one of poetry's purposes:

> *pauses explaining*
> *imaginative thought*
> *run unashamed*
> *where we cannot*
> *expressing the secrets*
> *we dare not reveal*
> *for fear of rejection*
> *to things that we feel*

Where emotions are concerned, it is usually easier to write than to communicate orally those things we do not understand or may not want to admit. And when we convert our ideas and emotions into words, they become more tangible, and perhaps more manageable as well. The universe surrounding us certainly provides a plethora of topics to explore; however, the depths of each human mind contain equally fascinating insights into the human condition. Perhaps the emotion you are trying to define within yourself is somewhere *between a laugh and a tear*.

Alisoun Ward's "To M____. In Absentia" (p. 227) struggles to voice the emotions which plague the persona since somehow losing a loved one. By intentionally avoiding the specifics of the relationship involved, Ward allows her readers to identify easily with the experience:

> *My room will never be the same again*
> *Now you've moved out. It thought I could reclaim*
> *The space, the time, be mistress of myself,*
> *Be mine. But items that I thought I owned*
> *Have come through use to be your own....*

The structure of Ward's poem is also important. Though there is a definite rhyme and rhythm to the verse, each sentence does not necessarily start at the beginning of a line, nor does it conclude at the end of a line, and each rhyme occurs within the poem's body instead of at the ends of two lines. This lack of structure serves as a subtle indication of the persona's fragile, unbalanced condition. Finding it difficult to express her true emotions, the persona talks of her furniture, and "reading between the lines" the reader discovers those emotions:

> *...hollows*
> *In the cushions show where head, and legs and*
> *Arms should go. When I ease my frame against*
> *The back the fabric sags, I only feel*
> *My lack....*

On the surface, the persona is uncomfortable in her well-worn chair, while what she "lacks" more importantly is her loved one's presence.

Another poem which conveys emotion through poetic structure is Bryan Borgeat's "Sea Music" (p. 28). In this piece the poet recreates the "music" he hears when by the ocean. Borgeat's verse fairly dances with excitement:

> *There's a splashing and a lapping and a tapping on the shore,*
> *As the shells are humming mutely with the muffled ocean's roar.*
> *I hear breakers, music makers, I hear shifting rolling stones,*
> *As a spirit winging leeward stirs my antiquated bones.*

Throughout "Sea Music", Borgeat expresses the joy of his renewed spirit, the fear of life's powerful storms, and the melancholy of "old shanties drifting sadly from a million watery graves". In effect, the poem is an opera of words instead of music.

Other poets use original syntax within their descriptions to catch their readers off-guard and allow them to experience time-worn emotions anew. In "Clouds" (p. 324), Sioux Davey creates the feeling of awe encountered when observing the clouds in the sky. The piece is further energised by Davey's use of alliteration:

> *Mare's tail artwork,*
> *dark, dusty feathering,*
> *soft grey blanket*
> *or thundered black billowing.*

Davey's highly imaginative phrases form immediate pictures in the mind. Later the clouds are "Jitterbug petticoats" which eventually "[smooth] to persian purring / before they gently wisp away", and the reader can feel the excitement and then the peace.

Catherine Beer's "Esmerelda" (p. 223) uses similar techniques to evoke a cat owner's love for her pet and then joyful pride when her feelings seem to be returned:

> *Suddenly it pleases her to place an embellished purr*
> *Pinked like the edge of a chorister's ruff upon my curling ear....*
> ....
> *Her life, released in song, throbs for her and me and her*
> *While I inhale the pot-pourri of rain-brushed herbs in fur.*

Esmerelda is transformed into an exquisite portrait of beauty and grace and mystery by this poet's pen. The simple act of purring takes on new meaning when expressed through metaphor and a feeling of affection and peace result.

Simon Judd's "Birth of a Scientist" (p. 474) successfully builds a feeling of fear and suspense as it comments on the future of the world as it seems to be progressing. The poem is separated into three stanzas which end the same way: "And we accepted that". The first stanza talks about the birth of a human as early scientists discovered it began, with the union of the male's sperm and the female's egg. The second stanza speaks of today's new technology which allows scientists to build cells outside of the woman's womb. The third stanza delivers the poem's unsettling message:

> *And then one day, we heard the wail of a child*
> *Kicking and screaming -- the first new birth,*
> *And we looked, and we cowered from this blathering mass,*
> *Knowing that if we offered our fingers for it to suck*
> *It would rip them off.*
> *And we accepted that.*

Though perhaps we may not share the belief that human life produced through scientific means rather than natural means will result in this "blathering mass" which would rip our fingers off, the message of the poem is still effective. Judd is warning his readers that people may be too blindly accepting of scientific progress. He shows us that scientists may not fully understand what they are capable of creating, and thus might do well to reconsider the direction which their work is taking.

Other noteworthy poems are Gregory Bartnik's "Highgate Cemetery" (p. 71); "Cradle Song" (p. 225) by Frances Mawnam-Smith; and Rosemary Greenfield's "Pigeon Lady" (p. 46).

There are many other outstanding poems displayed within the pages of *Between a Laugh and a Tear*. I invite you to delve deeply into the pages that follow and enjoy all the different topics, styles, and themes as I have. All of the poets who have been published here should be proud of their accomplishments.

I would also like to say a special thanks to those who have made *Between a Laugh and a Tear* possible. The editors, assistant editors, graphic designers, and customer service representatives have all brought their talents to bear on this project and I sincerely appreciate their assistance.

Joy L. Esterby
Editor

Featured Poetry

Still Some Time

I walk down the street and look up at the sky.
I see the gases and dust breathed by you and I.
You hear discussions about what should be done.
The rate we are going we don't have long.
The solutions we have are not enough.
The destruction we create is because of greed and lust.
The greedy get rich, the poor get poorer.
The Earth is running out of time and we still ignore
It's not too late, there still is time to repair the damage
and pay for our crimes.
Time to stop talking, time to stop thinking, make a stand
and keep on living.

Arun Sharma

Separation

Bells ringing.....
Clear, carried by hawks' wings across separating peaks,
Below, a swirl of saffron, gold, rich blood red,
Dotted figures assemble in lulled space.

Bells ring.....
Searching the peace of pastoral realms,
Arable separation carries green tipped remnants of memory.

Bells ring....
For centuries submerged in aquamarine graves,
Separated skywards in quiet mackerel rayed evening light.

Bells ringing within, head bells....
That high pitched ring,
Presager of intimate awareness,
The body's alarm,
Attracting etheric particles
Being inside, yet lifted to bat-like acuteness,
Through twilight's separating arms
Out into the deep blue sward of night,

Bells ringing for eternity.

Jackie Sowerby

Pebbles

I picked up pebbles from the shore and held them tight in my hand,
Each one more beautiful than the last, a gift from the sea to the land.

Too soon my arms were laden with jewels from the sea's crown,
My heart was warm and contented and wearily I sat down.

My eyes gazed around me taking in the painted view,
Till my eyes rested on a rock and my interest in it grew.

I was oblivious to the water licking my naked feet,
The tide rose up gradually nearly reaching my sacred seat.

I stared at this marvellous stone and took in its flawless shell,
Of all the pebbles I'd found today this truly was the belle.

I reached to pick up the gem to add it to my set,
But I dropped all the others and they fell face down in the wet.

The tide came in and took them away, including the special stone,
I had lost all for the want of one, like a dog with more than one bone.

Caroline Turner

Persistence Of Memory

It was time to say good-bye
A dark shadow and darker memories to forget

But he will always be my sweetness

Aching tears and hurting bruises melt away
In a smile to end all summers
Remembering every intoxicating breath of him

I can forgive him now
Bad secrets
With these old bruises
is love and
No regrets

Christina Hughes

Morning's Arms

There's a calm atmosphere around me,
a cool inviting aroma of the sea,
I feel a stillness that says so much,
as I stand on a rock with my
arms stretched out,
I touched hands with the wind,
that steadied me from falling,
I know God is with me,
I hear his voice speak through
the waves,
As I watch the sun go down,
I find the night long and lonely,
In my sleep I wait for morning
to wake me, I open my eyes,
peeping through my fingertips,
and to my surprise,
there's no more dark shadows of
the night,
there's only sun in my eyes,
and I'm in morning's arms.

Elizabeth Ann Firn

Heartbreak

If only I could be where moss and fern and lichen be,
and heather that coloureth the grassy slopes,
and blackthorn that shadeth God's miracles.
It is there I would lie and dream,
and dream of thee and all the love thou gave to me,
and dream that God in all His mercy,
would give thee to me and me to thee
and love for all eternity.

Jim Mortell

Renewal

The grey day slowly opens up its doors
Admits me to a world of damp
And stillness in the morning haze
No birds, no sounds to brighten air
And lighten fear that's born of loneliness.
Mud and dank weeds entrap my slippered feet
So go barefoot and let the dewy grass
Cleanse from my ageing skin
All blemish, sore and mark
'Til youth renewed I find that I can run
Towards that blinding light
And opening door.

Carol Rickard

Through The Eyes Of Another

Through the eyes of another one can see
a beautiful rainbow—a bumble bee,
stretches of emerald green and undulating hills,
scores of tiny birds perched on window sills.

Through the eyes of another one can see
parched deserts and a withering tree,
land when there wasn't land,
dying creatures sinking in the sand.

Through the eyes of another one can see
victims of war dying in front of me,
thousands of bodies being thrown about by the waves,
tearful families putting flowers on graves.

Through the eyes of another one can see
depravation and poverty,
hungry mouths and desperate faces,
poisonous fumes that are destroying all races.

Through the eyes of another one can see
the world collapsing in front of me,
scientists struggling to rectify errors,
to protect all men from their darkest terrors.

Francis Anderson

Heaven Waits

Lonely lady - As I passed by I spoke to you, but by then your time was due. Angels came to carry you away - no more time would they delay. Gone now dear soul is all hurt and pain - in this cruel world you'll never suffer again. To seem alone is sad I know - but Jesus felt it time to go. God's spirits bring you sweet release - near to Jesus you will find true peace. Absent loved ones - they found bliss - you'll see them again soon through God's heavenly mist. Throughout the vigil of each lonely night - watched those unseen shadows - hid from sight. The touch that you felt upon your cheek - that was our Lord, so happiness seek. Alleviate your dreams - visions in your conscious Mind - Joy and rapture soon once again you will find. God waits there, your sadness to erase - to hold your tranquil body close to him - and safe. Enchanting - bright new world above - no place on earth ever held so much love. Look down soon lady and know that someone did care - when you died I said a prayer. If I could I'd have held your hand while the angels prepared you for the promised land. Drink in love with your eyes - heaven holds so much surprise! Arms of love around you curl - hidden day dreams now unfurl. To express right words is so hard to do - but sweet soul - may God bless you. You need not be afraid to care for in God's heaven - real love lies there.

Jackie Hills

Romance Of Lake And Mountain

No corner of England is surpassed by the striking grandeur of Lakeland
With its beauty to lift one's spirit, giving hope for renewal of faith.
The dramatic peaks and crags offer wondrous links with the past and
the lakes and the tarns reflect memories of a shifting medley of life.

There's a creative power in the scenery which varies as the sun rotates,
from the repressive awe of shadow to the expectancy of day's full light.
Braided sunbeams, or haunting vapours, enhance the changing scene,
giving depth and a true understanding for our minds to feed upon.

Lofty edges stand before us as the mountains come into view;
An eerie stance that threatens yet draws on to the mystic heights.
The challenge is ever present to compete with nature's work
And stand on high with clear vision, and marvel at the wonders of God.

Vast stretches of water move silently in the first peaceful rays of day,
reflecting the valleys' clear raiment in an expectant, emotive way.
The rich pastures of lowland dwelling provide a contrast to the heights above
and the traditions of a lifelong inheritance set seeds for the years to come.

From these mystic heights and lake sides, the surroundings paint a memory,
to enrich our true perception of the land we're entrusted to share.
To look down on receding horizons, or up to the peaks beyond
gives tranquil moments of insight to distance our daily care.

Christine W. F. Birchall

Ted

The autumn leaves of russet and gold
A blanket make, to keep "Ted" from the winter's cold
A voice had whispered, "Come on Ted, don't be slow.
Your work's done, it's time to go,
Let it not be said you ran a good race
But there waits another dog to take your place."
Come spring, "Ted" will rise and stand
To keep watch over the newborn lambs
By the light of the moon he'll guard the flock
Ever vigilant for the scavenging fox
Close to the moor over which he did freely run
Shaded by the trees from the summer sun
The lambs grown and full of zest
Now "Ted" can return to his well deserved rest

Harold W. Bundey

Untitled

My day began as all good days.
A bright red sun, set in a golden haze
Swirls of colour reach my heart.
To start my brand new day.
Fields of clover dotted white.
Makes my day oh so bright.
Flying swallows, soaring high, diving
Swiftly, playing freely within my sky.
How I love my brand new day.
The mighty oak, she stands so tall,
To guide me on my way.
Fields of colour swaying gently in the
Morning light.
How bright the flowers, that dot my
Path.
I thank you Lord, for my Brand
New day.

Anthony Bell

The Elephant

A life begins, beneath the cobalt sky,
A calf is born, as the dawn overtakes the starlit night,
Gazing at the world with blinking, innocent eyes.
A child of Africa, his fate uncertain,
Standing still, as the sun grows warm, haloed in its light.

The years go by, the seasons turn, and turn again,
The calf grows to maturity beneath the African sun.
Lord of the Serengeti, master of the plain
A grey colossus astride a continent,
King of the herd, defying all, and fearing none.

A life is ended, cloaked by an African night.
A premature death, undignified, the giant brought to his knees
The herd taken refuge in panic-stricken flight.
But none can fight the bullet, the deadly executioner;
When Man pursues, none can hide, nowhere to flee.

An African sunrise, the Eastern sky tinged with red,
The shame of Man on show for Heaven and Earth to see.
The vultures circle slowly, hovering overhead,
The King lies dead, killed for profit
For his Royal crown, his curse, his ivory.

Linda Pilgrim

'Oh, Didn't You Know?'

Oh, didn't you know the world was flat?
  A child of two could have told you that!
    For how could the sea stay there at all
      On a big round ball?

Oh, didn't you know the sky at night,
  Is paper waiting for God to write?
    He pricks the paper a time or two,
      And a star shines through!

Oh, haven't you seen when the sun is red?
  He dips in the sea to cool his head,
    Then up he comes with his face all white,
      And he shines all night!

Oh, isn't it sad when a child is grown?
  He loses a knowledge that's all his own,
    The earth, the sky, and the blazing sun,
      Oh, they're all such fun!

Brenda Baker

A Special Kind Of Love

A love so strong, so special and free
A love that's given only to me
A love from a mum so warm and so safe
A love that lights up the whole of my face
A love that's unconditional, a love that's for me
A love from my mum sent only to me.

Laura McGeoch

Grief's Release

Without a choice, I became, without
a choice, to strive and suffer, without a choice.
Into the light, I strove to lean, into
the light, to finally see, no choice to be had.
Dreams and schemes flow like the tide,
But still are dashed, by fate's design board.
Comforts small, or, not at all,
were had and lost, with no choice at all.
With no desire, no long last wish,
I carry on, down the dusty path.
Signs and turns, sights that blind,
tastes that burn, and smells that sting.
Into the dark, to lunge and touch, and find the path, the dusty path.
In the end, it's all the same, go or stay, for hell's reward.
To be found without a search.
When it's done, who will know
what that thing will spawn, on hell's doorstep.
To bring it down, in one fell swoop,
hearts will melt, and liars frown,
For all will know their game's amiss, when all are found by Nemesis!

Jerry Layne Rogers Sr.

Creator God?

In life it is very difficult to see
A clear and absolute philosophy.
Science indicates no God, yet,
In our thinking we can hardly forget
That all things must have a cause
Especially the big bang that once was.
However long ago we may date her,
Surely even she had a creator,
And therefore It would seem rather odd,
If we didn't call this being, almighty God.
Maybe our doubts are a bit of a test,
And one day all turns out for the best.

John Albert Smith

To Walk With God

To walk with God will lift my eyes to beauty
A clear blue sky the ripple on a lake
And from a tree the sound of sweet birds singing
The countryside alive and so awake.

The grass so green sweet fragrance of the flowers
God's beauty seen within an artist dream
I lift my eyes to see the light of summer
And now that I have walked in peace
Where God has been.

Who walks with God the lowly or the mighty
No one can say to each the right to pray
But where love lies then God will be there dwelling
Within a friend or in a child at play.

To each his own he will whisper that he loves you
His voice you will know and answer when you can
He understands and waits for us so patiently
To walk with God in peace his gift to everyone.

Betty Stenhouse

Silence

i thought you'd listened

but did you hear;

or did I only scream the words in my mind.

Jenny Baskerville

Suffolk

A place of beauty from where I stand,
A colourful scene - this lovely land.
Where seasons come and seasons go
Through misty dawns, and freezing snow.
The waving corn on Summer days
Seen through a warming shimmering haze
Delights the eye, and makes hearts swell,
To know that all is doing well.
The rivers flow, at such great speed
And after showers they take no heed
Of floods that may befall us all -
The animals scared - begin to call!
Autumnal colours, such a sight!
A shame when darkness brings the night
To put the sights and sounds to bed
But bring the stars and moon instead.
I love it all, this glorious place
Suffolk has such gentle grace.

Gwen Ives

" Texas Pete "

Texas Pete was six years old,
A cowboy, through and through
He loved the West, and all their ways,
And nothing else would do.
He had a pair of cowboy boots,
A big hat, and six gun.
He'd shoot the dog, and scalp the cat,
And then, he'd lasso mum.
I'll fill my gun, one last time,
With water from the tap,
And when I see those injuns,
I'll give them rat-tat-tat.
It's time for bed, cried Peter's Mum,
To sleep, and rest, and dream
Of cowboy days, and cowboy nights,
And things that might have been.

John McCann

Road Train, Australia

Huge monster that roars and growls through the night.
A creature that sweats and strains on the hills.
Its twenty orange eyes blink out a warning to lesser vehicles.
Curled up in its belly a small, white, frail creature.
How many coffees have you drunk?
How many steaks, chips, hamburgers have you eaten?
All served by dull women in plain smocks.
In road houses you sit, with plastic flowers,
plastic tables, and harsh neon lights.
Back then to your monster, to devour miles
of road, to travel on forever, never to be satisfied.

Carole Shaw

Breakfast For Two

The old man pulls back the curtains
a crisp white splendour greets his gaze.
Trees and shrubs stand erect
fleecy white coats without a spec.

The old man's heart feels light
with pleasure.
As the Robin swoops in
looking for treasure.

Soon both are busy
breakfast is here.
Crumbs for one
toast for another.

How blessed I am
the old man stutters.
To share this meal with you
where once there were others.

Keith Furner

At The Pale Turning Of The Year

At the pale turning of the year
a distance fell between them, and their lives
were bounded by no ordinary silences.
A cold sun gleamed in the sky,
evenings lengthened inexorably.
Gardens stood defenceless in a green mist.

That was the moment when
the sun-splashed vision faded, silver trumpets
shrilled no longer high above tree-lined streets
un-peopled now by saints, emptied of angels.
That was the moment when
they paused, un-willing to accept
the innocent moon's betrayal,
the heart's denial.

Chilled, uncertain, searching for some sign
they lay curled close for comfort, yet apart:
Held for that moment by their corporate pain,
bewildered by the individual hurt.

Keith Styles

The Storm

A storm is threatening. The skies darken black.
A distant rumble, silence, then a lightening crack,
a fork of light, sharp and angry, that brightens the sky.
A lengthening silence follows. Is the storm passing by?
But no. A rumble that emerges into an almighty roar,
a continuous crashing that will be followed by more.
Now sudden rain lashes down, soaking the ground,
rushing, gushing, making pools that whirl round.
A frightening glare, the sky is lit up bright white
as electrical tongues lick the earth from great height.
Rumbling, crashing, banging, the storm rages on.
A blustering wind howls, clouds roll along,
trees strain and bend, branches bow down,
leaves fly, falling, swirling to the ground.
Monsters are wakening, it seems at a glance,
as flashes of light cast evil shadows that dance.
But wait. The sound of thunder is fading away.
The battle of the skies is giving up for today.
Darkened clouds are replaced by a sky clear and blue.
At last, peace now, and silence, the storm is all through.

Gail Busuttil

War Time Poetry

A little girl's mum sits there in pain,
A soldier is pleased with what he has gained.
The little girl sees sadness and badness.
And when she has dreams, she sees terrifying beams of bombs
A man in the hall is being beaten near the wall
A mother is crying because her little child is dying.
And that's what war time's about.

Lotis Bautista

Dedicated To The Victims Of The Docklands Bombing, 9th February 1996

Last Friday evening just after seven
A dream of peace was broken
The bomb that exploded in London
Mocked all the words that had been spoken
So many people — so much to fear
Their lives will never be the same
Why is it these innocent people
Are the victims of a "Terrorist Game"
We all saw the pictures on television
The carnage and ruin left behind
How can anyone ever justify
This atrocity to their fellow mankind
In a world already full of sadness
Just how much more can we take
Please stop this mindless killing
If not for us — for our children's sake.

Jane A. White

Love And The Rose

Love is like a rose in bloom
A fragrance which anoints the room
You love the scent of the rose so fair
But wonder why the thorns are there

You touch it gently and recoil
A drop of blood falls to the soil
This rose of beauty, flower of joy
Has turned out more than just a toy
Like some dark secret, full of tricks
Pain and pleasure intermixed

And now you view it with suspicion
To conquer it becomes a mission
You hate the pain but love the pleasure
Precious moments always treasure

Shy away from getting hurt
Keep your distance, then revert
To the fateful masochistic
In love with love and rose artistic

Lyndon T. Wall

Longing

Our love, mon amour, is a special elation,
A fusing of hearts and minds, a combination
Of a myriad feelings and fires,
A love transcending base thoughts and desires.
In the long silent watches of the night, my dear,
I'd give a thousand kingdoms to have you near,
To reach out and touch your lovely face.
The very thought makes my heart quicken apace.
Day takes an eternity to arrive.
With mounting impatience I strive
To will the clock onward through the hours
Till we meet. The bliss! The imagined scent of flowers!
All too quickly time has flown.
We part again. Quelle triste chanson!

Harry Grainge

Untitled

For you I wish for many things,
A life of joy where laughter rings
For health and happiness supreme,
A life to full and yet serene,
To you my son I lay with love,
That I am blessed from up above,
And to your Mum this I will lay,
Thank you Dear for my greatest day,
One thing more then I'm done,
Bless you Darling for my wonderful son.

Don Overbury

Brotherly Love

My brother is a tall, twisted tower;
A lanky dreamer with his head in the clouds.
He thinks I am our kitchen door;
Something to kick when he's in a mood.
He haunts me like a rowdy rap song,
An annoying parrot that never shuts up.
He sees me as some pure orange juice,
Which can be sweet but it's mostly sour.

My brother is a playful pup;
Can be comical but beware he bites!
To him I'm just a restless spider;
Able to do eight things at a time.
I see him as a sheet of sandpaper;
Rough, ready and able to scrape.
He sees me as a big grey cloud,
That covers his beams when he wants praise.

My brother is a dandelion; he sprouts up almost anywhere.
To him I'm just a dandelion too
And both sun and rain I'm glad to share.

Andrea Dever

Children Of War

The promise of love,
A gift promised but not yet received...
Tears from war,
Oceans of tears overflowing in our hearts...
Happiness stolen,
Left crying. Left dead. Left alone...
Cry of hope,
A cry, a message, a plea. Empty hearts...
Belief in the world,
Drained from them along with their lives...
A dreadful end,
There are no more tears left...

Lucy Hawker

Paper Moon

Into the deep end I fade, like many others before me, holding on for a glimmer, a brief sign of love from our chosen loved ones lost and foolish in the hope they gave, lost in something we never work out, we never understand, lost in unbroken circles and stubborn dreams, it helps me forget where I am, how I wish to be so far away or even with you, just anywhere instead of today, we lean on each other, we swear ourselves to strict secrecy, we can never help ourselves or stop ourselves from falling into love so hopelessly. In the past we laughed, scared of nothing, sailing on the suspense, but those songs and words of long ago don't seem so cold and now make so much sense, could we ever go back or even be the same? It hurts to think we have really changed; what do you think of when you turn out the light? Do you dream like me and believe in love at first sight? All of those times when I was prepared to be hurt for you, so we could carry on, so we would always come through, a heart in two parts, how could this ever be right? Any small time now feels like forever, I always thought no matter what, we'll be in this thing together, but her perfume and scent fades from my clothes but the heartbreak and hurt never ever goes, there is nothing left for me to give away, for all has been done, all has been said, with all this damage which has been caused, we have to let it go with this day.

Kenneth Hughes

The Forgotten Friend (God's Work Or Coincidence?)

An empty void, depression deeper than the sea,
A hate of the world. Jealousy.
Every turning closed
And every mind diverted.

No way out, no view of the end,
Until I remembered the forgotten friend.
All the wasted time, He'd watched and waited,
And through all my negligence
He showed not anger nor hatred,
But patiently waited
Then listened and guided,
So when you're alone, then
Pray, like I did.

Jane Elizabeth Henning

The Time Will Come

We live in strange and troubled times
Great changes to alter our consciousness and way of thinking will occur
Difficult hurdles lie ahead of us all
Thus have been shown various signs.
Inklings of the beginning of a new world will within us gradually stir
We all have to wake up to what is going on.

Our minds will open to other realities
We, in the Universe, are not alone
In all of our history, we never have been!
Greater beings have constantly watched over us
We are spiritual beings who will never die
But the way things are now, nothing divine can ever be won
We have to rid this planet of all its evilness!

Jacqueline M. Eldridge

For My Loved One

This Oak is planted in memory of you,
A history for it to live, up in the sky so blue,
Its roots to grow and soon to spread,
Amongst the rich earth and soily bed,
To stand secure within God's land,
For he will protect it with his hand,
He'll teach the tree to learn to live
On moisture the clouds so kindly give,
To absorb the rays the sun lays down,
Upon the heat it will not frown,
There's so much love in the air around,
A healthy future for this Oak is bound,
But just like you, only God decides,
If in this life, this tree survives,
But we are luckier than this tree,
For we have something you cannot touch or see,
It's memories of you which we have each day,
Each to our own never to be taken away,
So whether the tree lives, we have to wait and see,
Whilst you remain in our thoughts and in our hearts you'll always be.

Mrs. Belinda Pothecary

Ode To Sarah

S - is for Sarah, sweet and sincere,
A - is for ardent — one that's so dear.
R - is for righteous, reason and rare,
A's for angelic — she has a fine air.
H - is for humour, she has lots of this,

M - stands for mystical — she's heaven, sweet bliss.
Y - is for years, where we've shared so much love,
  yonder and yearning, like a white-coated dove.

L - is for loving. We are friends, we shall glide
O's ostentatious, to always abide.
V - is vivacious, to be always with me,
I's for intrepid, like a bird she is free.
N - stands for natural, like a soft, curling wave,
G - is for gentle, like a child that was saved.

S - stands for soul, forever we'll be,
I's for inspired, in sweet harmony.
S - is for song — we've shared many a tune,
T - is for triumph, you're treasured, a boon.
E - is for earnest, she's oh very true,
R - stands for richness, I shall always love you!

Andrea C. Watson

Life Times

A Springtime promise of new life born,
A family complete, together drawn.
With girlish dreams, and runny ice-creams,
Just a childhood of innocence
And laughter, it seems.

Blossoming now in the Summer sun,
Wedding day bliss, and apple-pie fun.
Baby's asleep, toys in a heap,
Just a life of fulfilment
And feelings so deep.

So now the Autumn sun sets low,
A time to reflect, a time to go slow.
Grandchildren play, tea on a tray,
Just enjoying the moments,
"Content", as they say.

The Wintry days come icy cold,
How did I get to be this old?
With snow-kissed hair, and rocking chair,
Just a lifetime's fond memories
For loved ones to share.

Kathryn Craven

The Seat Of Power

There he sits in his ivory tower,
  a man drunk on delusions of power.
He peals out his orders like many bells chiming,
  but lacking truth, sincerity or timing.

He looks to his soul but finds he has none,
  which serves to explain why he thinks he has won.
He lives in a world so completely his own,
  as one rules from some titanic throne.

He looks at his subjects with both of his faces,
  each of them lacking the poorest of graces.
One face makes promises kind as can be,
  the other he hides lest the truth you should see.

To sum up the man, he is shallow and rude,
  his outlook outrageous, his manner crude.
He is blind, deaf and dumb to all but himself,
  yet he has the command, the power and stealth.

George M. Talbot

Day

Atop the stony rooftop world
A mountain soars through snow
Dark in the cloudy night, ice and rock
A pinnacle stretches forward for the sun

Leaping, Clawing, a silver spirit rises
Slinking past his moonlight shadow
An aged wolf pauses to sense the floating air
His grey muzzle lowers, move on, the time is near

Circling, gliding, above the frozen tops
A proud eagle surveys the icy pedestal
Cries shriek out into the broken night
As a crawling shadow mounts the pinnacle

Stars wink at the twilight scene below
Startled moon heeds the messengers cries
Wolf howls echo atop the frozen white post
As bold eagle dances circles in the night sky

Time draws close as the cries increase
Morning ritual nears a wintry end
Fire will soon dawn to lick the mountain tops
As talons flashing will slash the break of a new day.

Andrea Hawkes

Holistic Visions

You stand in the desert of existence and wonder at your journey
A small spirit growing bigger with each step
— You progress.

Where water now bathes your lips, its simple sweetness filled with hope
For years your life was a fantasy and a whisky bottle, which enabled you
— Not to live.

The mind bends like a willow branch and now, with rose sap in your eyes
stare back at the cactus people, see a woman with flowers on her breast
— And thorns in her heart.

And now look forward and see yourself in the mirage, sacrifices to come?
A person trapped in the desert who will not drink the sweat
— Of their dying companion.

Grab the moment, release the past and thirst for the future
Seeing the sunshine birds flapping their wings
— To a million heart beats.

At your feet a skull in the dust, unknown
Its brains the sands of knowledge stretched over a million years.
Fate blowing forever
— In the whirlwind of time.

Geoff Ringham

The New Beginning

A new beginning
A new day dawns
Flowers are opening
Offering themselves to the bees
All around us the earth is stirring
New sights of wonder to behold
The heavens are filled with joyous singing
As birds on high above are winging
Their way as scenes are changing
Day gowns herself in golden light
The new sun so beautiful and bright
Was never a birth so gentle
The birth of a new day
A day that holds so much promise
Until evening shadows gently start to flow
As shades are tenderly drawn
Pushing back the rays of the sun
As if to the earth it did shun
Every dawn is a new beginning

Joan Parkinson

Earth, Wind And Fire

Earth is like a big round ball
a place to live together large and small
human being's, insects and tree's
animal's, flowers and fish in the seas
as sure as day and night takes a turn
the world will change as we learn

Wind whistles around and never ends
sending seeds in the air as nature intends
blowing leaves from dying trees
making waves on the raging seas
a spinning tornado races across the land
picking up debris in her hand

Fire with flames dancing high
Flickering burning reaching for the sky
Destroying everything in its path
Leaving nothing but a charred aftermath
and yet these wonders we stand and admire
These basic elements earth, wind and fire

Celia Law

The Raven

Upon a gnarled and twisted tree,
A Raven sat and stared at me,
The mist of morning swirled around,
It just looked down and made no sound.
It cocked its head for me to speak,
Was it my soul that it did seek,
The wicked thing I'd done last night,
Was it for love or just for spite,
My younger sister fair and sweet,
Now lay bleeding at my feet.
She aroused my lover with her charms,
He slowly drifted from my arms,
Now night has gone and it is day,
Was it I who sinned, or was it they.

Amanda Penty

Peace

Peace, what does it mean to you and me?
A moment of tranquillity,
Beside a gently rippling stream,
Somewhere to pause, a time to dream,
A place where everything is safe,
Contentment in a loved one's face,
How wonderful the world would be,
If everyone had liberty, freedom, and security,
With no more fear of bombs and strife,
The wicked waste of human life,
Soon we hope that all can say,
Peace at last is here to stay.

Joan Murch

Mixing It

A cuddle or a coffee cake?
A roll or piece of pie?
What a choice I have to make!
Dilemma! Me? Oh my!

She stands against the table pressed,
As beaten eggs submit.
Her milky skin with flour caressed,
And hand all firm to grip

And work the lucky spatular
In whirls of creamy marge.
I'm glad I'm not a bachelor,
All free, and lone at large.

She bends below the larder shelf,
Her store of fruit she picks,
And licks and tips and empties self
Into the stirring mix.

Round and round with little sound
My dreams and sighs do follow.
The elixir is oven-bound;
My love waits 'till the morrow.

David Robshaw

The Futility Of War

And then it came, the telegram,
A small yellow envelope, clutched in the hands of a trembling boy
Who stuttered, "B B Brown it's for you."

She felt the blood drain from her body,
Hands shaking she took the oblong object and closed the door.
She swayed and eased herself into a chair. His chair.

She stared in disbelief, and time stood still
As she sat startled, stunned, her hands moved clawing at the paper.
She read the words, 'Missing, Presumed Dead.'

More words on strips of paper, eyes too blurred with tears
Savagely shed. "Bloody war, what for?" She screamed.
"Not yet nineteen, and to be killed doing his duty."

"What duty? To be brave, to have courage, to be dead."
"To be dead, to be dead," Words echoed in her head,
No medals for those heroes, only a boy, not old enough for a door key

Mature enough to carry a weapon and be killed by one.
Now gone, earth fertilised by his blood,
Rose petals lie on her table, blood red, like drops of blood.
His blood, shed for what? The futility of war.

Gloria Levy

A Walk In The Forest

Stress!
A small business headache!
Oh for a break
A walk in the forest.

Off to Grizedale, an hour away, up the motorway.
Entering south of the Lakes
Begin to relax; slow down; calm at last.
Park and walk, slowly, take in the air.

A Robin escorts us on our way
Pecking the still-frozen ground
Searching for food, but not stressed,
Only busy.

Look skyward, are they Buzzards or maybe a pair of Red Kites?
Soaring gracefully, high above, relaxed, calm flight,
Suddenly! Wings folded drop to earth, searching for food
Just hungry.

Robin again, or maybe another
Close to us, unafraid.
Escorts us to the edge of the forest
Ah well! Back to Business!

Jenny Matthews

Stoat

I saw him first; moving across the open glade.
A streak of russet brown - and into the ferns.
We held the moment in case he should return.
And while turning to each other in the warm June afternoon,
There he was again returning whence he came.
And in between the warmth we gave each other,
He went across our vision eight times no less.
We watched this little creature, intent on carrying
His litter from one ferny side to the other.
We rose from the stile to look closer for its home.
I crossed his track. "You've broken his scent.
He won't come back," she cried.
We sat a moment. A hedge-cutter came.
We quietly wandered into a leafy lane going Flaunden Way.

Ian Woodward Smith

Thoughtstream

Every night as I lay on my bed
a stream of thoughts goes rushing through my head.
I fear I'll sink in the whirlpool of my mind,
answers to my questions I can't find.
Like broken bottles smashed against a wall,
most of my thoughts don't matter here at all.
'Cos one thought keeps on coming back to me,
in Jesus you can be completely free.
I heard it when I saw the preacher man,
he said I should believe but here I am,
still swimming in the whirlpool of my mind,
and answers to my questions I can't find.
Maybe I should receive.
Oh Lord I will believe.
Now every night as I lay on my bed
a stream of worship flowing through my head,
I'm flowing in the river of his grace,
as I see my lovely saviour's face.
Now this one thought keeps coming back to me,
in Jesus I am completely free.

David G. King

Remote Control

I sit and watch the late night news
A tear leaks from my eye
As I see a helpless Mother grieve
Another child's goodbye.
It makes me mad to see such pain
In a land that claims it's free,
Bombs crashing throughout its town
With no thought for morality.

Have we really got so used to the pictures
That rage has passed us by,
Implicit in our train of thoughts
That we no longer hear the cries?
We shake our heads and watch the bullets
Flying through the air,
Then turn the channel over
From the comfort of our chairs.

C. J. Sharp

A Voice From Heaven

Let there be peace on earth,
A voice from heaven says,
Let there be harmony and love from day to day,
Enjoy all of life's blessings,
And be grateful for all of these,
So let there be peace on earth,
And be thankful day by day.

Let there be love in the world,
A voice from heaven says,
Remember what I taught you, to honour and obey,
Let there be light in your life,
And diminish all of your evil,
So let there be love in the world,
And respect all of my people.

Elizabeth Anne Fimognari

Broken Spirit

I was born spirit of youth,
A thoroughbred not coarse or uncouth,
My younger days spent with others in play,
During my prime I did race until the fateful day,
What's this pain and why have I been withdrawn,
With no other use, to me a foal is born,
Again and again I am covered and have no more,
To some my useful days are gone that's for sure,
I've given my all and now I must wait,
For a distant uncaring master to seal my fate.
Left in a field some say put to pasture,
All I have now is memories to nurture,
Through time and the elements is this the end,
Hello, a stranger comes in, be a friend.
I'm caressed and fondled though still young I look old,
One good thing, at last I'm brought in from the cold,
What's this, no new home, another miserable day,
I know he loves me, what's the delay?
The owner wants to give me to an unseen for a favour,
Could I still be dogmeat and if so what flavour?

Colin G. Foster

The Oil Slick

We can see the Isle of Man, from the window facing north,
A vast expanse of Irish sea, tankers sailing back and forth,
A place of natural beauty of which we are possessive,
And of nature's gifts around us, we really feel protective.

"Have you seen it then" my husband roared. "Just take a look through these."
Handing me the binoculars and pointing out to sea.
"You'll have to phone the coastguard before it spells disaster,
It's definitely an oil slick, and it's moving pretty fast here.
With that he left, without a word, expecting me to do his dirty work.

To me it looked like flotsam or jetsam or whatever,
Who was I to argue? So I picked up the receiver.
"Hello? Hello? Coastguard? There's an oil slick out at sea,
Location? I'm not really sure, 'twixt the Isle of Man and me.
How fast it's moving? I'm not versed in knots,
But since I've picked the phone up — it's gone behind the rocks!
It's making for Llandudno, I think it came from Cemaes."
"Well thank you Ma'am for phoning, we'll contact the emergency service."

With bated breath I waited, peering out to sea for action,
I could have saved a thousand birds — a medal, commendation?
The telephone rang,"Coastguard here, in answer to your query,
Your oil slick was some seaweed — on the way to Tipperary."

Lowri Rhiannon Hughes

Wishing Well

I made a wish in the wishing well,
a wish that I could never tell,
a special dream I could not share,
or maybe no one would ever care.

Perhaps my dreams were misted by fears,
or washed away by endless tears;
still emotions like cold, clear ice,
running, hiding like fields of mice.

Pools of colour light the sky;
swirling clouds asking why;
whispering trees, they must not tell
the secrets of my wishing well.

Fears fading like melting snow;
flame burning a tiny glow;
emotions flowing like liquid gold;
my heart no longer empty and cold.

Dreams escaping like falling rain;
water glistening like sweet champagne;
could this be my wish come true
in finding all I want in you?

Lorraine Williams

Things We Used To Know

I look into my mirror and see a different me
a woman, not a child, where can that child be
That child believed in magic, in fairies in the yard
that life was always wonderful, not meant to be hard
Believed shadows could be monsters, sometimes a best friend
that life was an adventure, a story without end
Now I am a woman with children of my own
no longer believing in magic now that I am grown
But I won't forget that girl, the child I used to know
I'll see her in my children as I watch them grow
Through their eyes I will see again the magic I once knew
and sometimes for a little while I'll be a child too
What a pity we forget how good our lives can be
taken in the simple form, accepting what we see
Through children's eyes life's wonderful, a shame we have to grow
into adults who forget somehow the things we used to know

Dawn Chew

Frost

What's that sparkle I can see
A wondrous sight for you and me
Of diamonds shining on the ground,
Of fairy lights flickering all around.
A sprinkle of the nighttime air
Lying there for us to share.
This lovely sight on bush and tree
That seems to reach to eternity,
It fills our days with peace and joy,
A pleasure that all can enjoy.
Oh for the power to make that pleasure
A continuous part of work or leisure.
To have that joy within our being,
To take that beauty for inward seeing,
Then we will all be one with God
And His wondrous painting on the sod.

Iris Peck

'Busy Day'

On walking home about five past nine,
A wondrous stillness enclosed me at twilight time.
The awesome silence between night and day,
Pierced only by distant murmurs of motorway,
And, above and around, birds in full throat-away.
There's a magical majesty about this time,
Before nature's sleep descends and rewards their prime.
A time that echoes in a timeless way,
Spending, ending, in the dull lit grey
The dusty, husty, bustle of another busy day.

Alan Hartwell

Nicola

I couldn't believe it when you said
about the feelings for me in your head
You don't know how happy you made me
For once my dream started to become reality

You made me feel special so warm inside
We went for a walk just give minutes to hide
from the people you thought wouldn't take it well
but they knew, I didn't have the heart to tell

Hand in hand but had to let go
as we approached the people who weren't to know
with them we stood close but far apart
It didn't matter your smile was in my heart

Later you spoke of your worries of becoming two
you'd found out that the others knew
their our friends but do go on
If you do things different to everyone

We spoke again but you're not sure
if you and I will become anything more
Now I'll just have to see
If that dream becomes reality.

Ian Tattershaw

A Death In The Family

The other day I was thinking, of people I've loved and lost,
About the hurt and pain and just how much death costs.
We take people for granted because they're always there.
It's only when they're taken away, you really know you care.
But no-one lives forever, this I understand, but if you've lived
a long full life it's easier to stand
But what if it's a baby or even a little child, what about the
family who loved that child so mild.
My sister had a baby, a beautiful baby boy and in the five months
of his life he brought us so much joy, his giggles and his laughter
his smiles and his love, his baby skin as soft to touch as the
feathers of a dove.
But five months is nothing in which to live and grow, to learn
to talk and walk he had so far to go. That's what makes me
angry, that's what makes me sad, for someone to die so
young, and life to be all bad.
The thing that I don't understand is why it happened to him,
a lovely bouncing baby with lots of love to give.
But now he cannot give and we cannot receive. I know that
he is with us in our minds of make believe
He will always be our baby and always in our hearts
and maybe in another life, he'll get a proper start!

Abbe Sterland

Breathe And Begin

We were talking —
about the space that is between us,
and people who hide behind illusion!

We were talking —
about the love we could share,
if and when we really find it!

With some love —
we may save ourselves,
if we only understood it!

We were talking —
about the desire that was one within you,
or were you, within you? Who can tell?

We were talking
about a love that's gone cold
try some warmth!
When you've seen beyond yourself
you'll find peace to free your mind!

We were talking
about how we never really talk —
Breathe and Begin!

Anthony Davies

The Ultimate Betrayal

No one knew what I felt inside
All my sad feelings were masked with a smile
To the left of my thoracic, my heart was pierced through
My emotional fulfilment had been ruined by you

The relationship we had had been oh so strong
When we were together, no one else belonged
What baffled me most is that I couldn't understand
Why when it came to marriage, you took someone else's hand

She never could feel what I felt inside
When I lay in my bed each night and cried
Tears of hurt, memories, tears of pain
One year and some months, all down the drain

She must have been good to have stolen you away
A relationship that lasted one week and a day
To totally obliterate all that we had
After one week of bliss is terribly sad

But you never can imagine the thoughts in my mind
How I blame myself for being so blind
As I cried each night in the bed where I lay
I was a woman alone, rejected and betrayed.

Grace Ama

Fat Lady

Her swollen ankles,
above on oversized foot in a child's shoe.
She managed to dress today, in yards of
nondescript material, hanging over multitudes
of flesh and stretch marks.
Below the chin didn't matter, deny the body
and live another day were the rules she lived by.
Tolerated were bodily functions, as a guilty
murderer tolerates prison.
Her only role model, a china doll she was allowed
to love as a child.
Hours and hours spent perfecting her make up
and lipstick in the dolls image, a face
she had kissed at lease a thousand times.
She had become that doll, a face without a soul,
the only difference, a broken body.

Julie Hope

A Path In The Wind

There's nothing like the freedom of the hills
Above the distant valley down below,
To watch the buzzard fly, and prey encircle,
To see the path on which the river flows.

As eyes take in the landscape that's prevailing
The steeple of the village church stands proud,
Vast amount of green stands out in wonder
With patterns made from shadows of the cloud.

To walk among the heather, fern and gorse
Silent, but for trickling water spring,
In the air the fox aroma lingers
The distant echo sound of curlews sing.

So walk upon the hills that stand in grandeur
Enjoy the view that nature calls its own,
Be thankful for the countryside around us
The freedom of the places we can roam.

Dawn Poole

Autumn

Tall shadows stalk in silent stealth
   across an uncut lawn.
High Geese in gaggles gather
   at early dusk and dawn.
Trees shed and spread their mantle,
   the cycle circles on.
The summer — long awaited — too soon
   has been and gone.

Frost's fingers paint new colours
   and sculpt in fog and ice.
Roses cry pearl teardrops
   while the hedge is veiled — so nice.
The elements and nature
   as one God did ordain.
Each season has its cherished charm;
   it's Autumn once again.

Frank McArthur

A Trillion Grains Of Sand

Hearts that are shattered.
A thousand lotus petals scatter reality
into a trillion grains of sand.
Glimpse the fleeting face in the palm of a hand,
Blood that courses through our veins
The river Nile that flows,
Clutching ever tightly we release the reins.
Sounds of the gods empower an empty space
Harmonics rise and fall with grace; as
Seeded by the starlight we emanate the sound.
For ancient is the memory, eternal path is found.
Levels seven, sweet sisters seven surrender to the light.
No permission needed, the planet to unite.
Infinite was the love of his beloved Queen
How sublime the consciousness, allowing us to dream...

Annie Lucas

Storms

Thunder rolls, lightning roars
Across the land down to the shores,
Tempests rage, the sky is grey
Is it night or is it day,
Birds are silent, they will not sing
In the raging storm none can take wing,
Rain comes down in scalding showers
It seems to last for hours and hours,
No let up in the storm and rain
Water pours down every drain,
Rivers swollen beyond belief
For this ravaged land is there no relief,
At last a glimmer in the sky
The raging storm begins to die,
A calming force now holds sway
As the dark recedes and we see the day,
The storm is spent, it's lost its hold
Clouds fill the sky, the wind is cold,
But the storm no longer is in charge
All anger spent and calm at large.
Brenda M. Daubney

Fairies

Tiny fairies tiptoe fast,
across the shining dew dropped grass.
Trying hard to make no noise,
so as to wake little girls and boys.
They find a place to rest their heads,
on the soft and comfy flower beds.
Gail Adams

Anticipation

Expectancy runs before the result, enhancing ultimate pleasure,
Adrenalin flows when the mind races on,
Looking forward to things we all treasure.

The great guessing game of looking ahead
Can give joy, or end in remorse,
Silver linings are few at the end of the day,
But to hope is a natural course.

To foresee what is hoped for, to consider before,
and decide to enjoy in advance,
To anticipate is a subconscious thrill,
Well known to us all, as just chance.
John W. Smith

In My Thoughts And Wonderings

I sometimes sit and wonder what life is
  all about,
The will to take and not to give, the cruelty
  and doubt,
The blessings which we had when young are
  frowned upon today,
The good, the kind, the gentlefolk, are lost along
  the way,
But soon I hope we'll realize the love which
  on us showers,
If only we'd appreciate what's yours, what's mine,
  what's ours.
Kathleen M. Gaskell

Political Fires

Political fires burning in our hearts,
All turned to hate
Going to tear us all apart
I have rights to my views as much as they,
Why isn't it my mind powering you all today?
The selfishness of the leaders
But you all stay and bow
Lead us to heaven, they promise
But lead us and leave us in hell!
Kathryn Summer

African Politics

At midnight, the new government was born. They call it democracy!
After the explosion of that historical fuming volcano
In a bloodless coup, the so-called liberators emerged!
Suspension of the one-man's charter soon followed.
   That is African Politics!

Yes, the awaited polling day came. And we "chose" our leaders.
They vowed to serve us. In the city, in the slums and villages
Economic reform! End of hunger and thirst. They campaigned!
No brutality and detention without trial! They preached.
Better working conditions for the common man!
   No corruption and nepotism. They shouted!

Votes were counted amidst intimidation of cannons
Yes, "our men" had won! Some applauded.
Slogans were chanted, drums heard everywhere and trumpets sounded.
"Victory" — they called it and jeered at the losers!
   Oaths of allegiance followed: "For God and My Country"
they chorused.

Next day, ministers were appointed: Mineral and Water
   Resources, Lands and Surveys.
Ministry of Internal Affairs, Justice, Labour, Social Welfare,
   Foods and Agriculture etc.
But alas! What a shame! The cry of the hungry hangs in the air.
So do the ones of the poor, oppressed workers
Prosperity for the elected, misery for the common man!

They call it "democracy!" That is "African Politics" some conclude.
Charles Lwanga Ssenkungu

" Finding Me "

Flowing, encircling, filling smoothly; and then oozing Outwards.
Again, and Again, and Again;
Drifting slowly deeper; moving Inward.

You are within yourSELF.
A foreigner. A friend.
Made aware of its presence, you are in awe.
Its silence and unobtrusiveness has seemingly given power to
its fecundity.
The silence of its omnipotence makes it all the more sure;
its sureness all the more sublime.

Creator within the created. God within the atheist.
FIXED, ATTACHED, UNMOVING, FIRMLY ROOTED:
PERMANENT.
Nourisher on which we refuse to feed.
Sage whom we refuse to trust.
Refuge in which we refuse to hide and gather strength.

I see clearly now; my vision is fresh and accurate.
Yet,
I am uneasy with your closeness. I am uneasy with myself.
I cower at my own power;
unwilling to see it as part of me;
perhaps thereby preserving its sanctity.
Leonie Jacobs

Birmingham

By night, a space city, diamond-lit,
Against the ink-dark sky.

By day, a meeting place for beetles,
Creeping down their well-routed spaghetti,
Twining wide concrete ribbons into
Finer thread, for underground fluorescent
Tunnels, spiralling down at their peril,
To the city's undoing.
A blinded place,
Like the monorail's stunted race
Shuttles back and forth, driver-less,
Aimless, and unattended.
And underneath this sloping labyrinth,
Two men stir stiffly in their sleep
And dream of life's soft verges.
Christine N. Gray

Thought For Today

Our homes consist of bolts and bars,
alarms and theft locks guard our cars:

This is the age we're living in,
an age of rape, mugging and sin.

Can someone explain where we went wrong?
Nothing is safe! O how I long

For days gone by, when I recall
open doors, a welcoming hall

"Just come on in" was the usual reply
as you called to a neighbour when passing by

Now, you have to knock, and wait for alarm release
and security gate

If you decide to take a walk lock your windows,
don't dare talk

If you are asked, "Where do you live?"
"Hell's" the answer you might well give.
Betty Binns

" Corridors Of Time "

The room was large and full of life, logs on the fire burnt no strife.
All around me familiar faces, smiling and chatting of common places.
Exchanged expressions understood, laughter and banter in
brotherhood.

The open door revealed the past, a corridor of time, archives amassed.
Floating down, each door ajar, revealed set times from afar.
Friends and relations passed before, some were now on
heaven's shore.

No sign of hurts existed therein, as shelved and padlocked,
   vacant chairs remain.
Absent were the slander mongers, who tried to blemish
   friends and lovers.
Gone was threat of violent spite, into the sea of forgetful night.

One final door ahead came close, approached with care,
   but calm response.
An outreached hand was not required, it opened to reveal what
   I desired.
In calm and studious repose, my father sat studying a rose —
dried and pressed within a book, held in his hands, a loving look.

"Come sit with me, don't be distressed" lovingly said "My Princess".
Elenor Milne

The Bently

She stood there so clean,
All chrome and green.
Her four litres handled her gently,
This lady of mine, my very first love,
The lady I know as the Bentley.

I remember the day, we were far up North,
I'd been casting a line or two gently.
My Landlord said "Sir I do like your fish".
But his eyes reflected the Bentley.

We've sped through the night,
A ghost, green and bright.
We've climbed up the Royal rivers bent.
Come up with the dawn over the downs
And growled through the hamlets of Kent.

So now I'm abed and grey in the head
And I still love your gran so intently.
But I must tell you my boy, They fill me with joy
These gifts that heaven has sent me.
The loves of my life, you and your gran,
And the lady I know as the Bentley.
Antony A. Rushworth

Humble Snowdrop

You are a lovely little flower, so humble yet so bright,
All dressed up for an evening ball in your little gown of white.

Such beauty, so virginal, you bow your tiny head,
In honour of our Maker, I have heard it said.

With your brothers and your sisters you make a pretty bunch.
Gathered all together for some shelter and for warmth.

Beneath the trees and shrubs you seem to like it best.
When twilight comes you close your tiny petals for a rest.

In bleak dark days of January when nothing is in bloom.
We look for you to show your head and hope it will be soon.

A dead emigrant brought home for burial to this land.
His grieving mother placed a bunch of snowdrops in his hand.

This simple flower of purity and this act of love.
A sad farewell and hope for a heavenly home above.

I savour this time when I look at your face so clear.
With hope that you will come along and cheer us all next year.
Jean Armstrong

November '95

And so, the year is coming to its close,
All clad in leaves of gold the great oak glows.
The evening sky with Autumn's colour blends.
Ah! with what gorgeous pageantry it ends.
In burnished copper, beeches tall conspire
With maples' flame to set the woods afire.
In clearest yellow silver birches gleam,
And painted leaves make patterns in the stream.
Springtime confetti, petals pink and white
Along the roadside fill us with delight.
But now, the circle turns, vibrant and bold,
And Autumn's bridal paths are strewn with gold.
Hedgerows are thick with berries, red as blood
And God, Creator, sees that it is good.
Lena Brewe

Take A Ride

Queuing for a ride on the ghost train?
A journey through a world of horror and pain,
Shocking the mind, tricking the brain,
The big wheel turns again,

Children sit helpless in the middle of it all,
Upon wooden horses that rise and fall,
A lucky kiss on the coconut ball,
Another miss for a 'no prizes' call,

A magician tries to break through the trance,
But the fortune teller sees, only won'ts and can'ts,
The fruit machines need their money in advance,
And the waltzer, could be the last dance,

An intricate juggle by a group of clowns,
A world, the stencil, for their painted-on frowns,
Dizzy from all the merry-go-rounds,
But reality is out of bounds.
Gary Michael Harris

Dartmoor

If I am born will you shun me?
An unborn child of nature unfettered still
Free with my own free will

Bleak has been my birth
Lonely and cold
Mother Nature in her mirth
Has made me strong and bold

Now my form is showing beauty
Heather, bracken, gorse clothe me
Creatures big and small I see
Mother Nature, now I thank thee
Jean Sinclair

A Plea To A Dying Husband

Don't leave me, darling, please don't leave me.
All earthly joys are here.
Put aside your pain, come alive again, for the sake
  of the things you hold dear.

Your loved ones are pained, your garden neglected,
How can I go alone? I am sad — I'm rejected

Be damned to the cancer — ignore it, and then it will go away,
Those wonderful men in white coats told us so,
Please darling — don't call it a day.

But I know that I've got to be stronger and come down to
earth; if I must?
So have no fear, I promise you dear, I will always
  honour your trust.
I shall keep an eye on your garden and tend
  to the flowers with love,
I will talk to them, explain there's no problem
You could be watching them bloom from Above.

Wait for me, darling, wherever you are, for when my life's
  journey is thro'
We will be side by side, in heaven abide,
And our love affair we can renew.
   Barbara Jennings

'Night'

I wish sleep would envelop me like a warm duvet,
All I can see are shadows of objects,
My eyes are perceptive to the light now.
My family are spinning around me,
Like horses on a merry-go-ground.
Making me dizzy.
They talk, but the words are not heard.
Their expressions tell a story,
Of both happiness and sadness.
I see my reflection in the glass of the window.
It is a face that holds many memories, of good and bad.
The evil words which have tormented me,
Would be heard even by the deaf.
Slowly my family fade from vision.
My teddy is held tightly,
And slowly, slowly, I drift into another world,
Where if anything hurts me, it's erased,
When the morning light shines through my
  bedroom window once more.
   Hayley Parish

Personal File

Remember it well, he sniffed, and still filed,
all the difficult days when we started.
My memories stay warm, a haze guards the child,
untroubled still, before we all parted.

Not always like this, the current carping,
nor the different viewpoints strong grasped.
Life's small wounds accumulate, wrapping
the whole in a file of hurt, harshly rasped.

No, he said, much better for us this norm.
Three's a crowd, isn't it? We're better alone.
I nod and watch his wood-carving take form,
the ninth rocking-horse he'll lovingly hone.

The boy's gone, I said, can't you accept it?
The wood's being wasted, your toys not needed.
My words float over his file to hit,
but he still hummed and filed, nothing conceded.

Think of me, or think of him, I pleaded,
short life, incomplete, like wood unbeaded.
He wept and filed, stroking each wood blemish.
Personal file, he said, for our lost wish.
   Jim Easton

All My Living Days

You are the promised, a breath of spring time
All the loveliness it brings
You are the hush of early morning
And the early birds that sing

You are the cosy blush of summer
Its flowers, birds and bees.
You are the glowing sun just setting
All its beauty one can bring

You are the touch of early autumn
Its warm and fiery hue
You are all its dazzling wonder
That lingers all day through.

You are the sunlit days of winter
That peep through clouds of grey
You are all these things so precious
And will be, all my living days.
   Joan Barker

Reality Is Too Final

What do you do when a myth becomes reality?
All the mystery, all the intrigue vanishes.
I've caught the Loch Ness Monster, I've caught a myth.
As she twists and turns, so do I
One to escape, one to control.
Do I want to enter the realms of fantasy,
To be a legend?
One legend usurping another.
How long would I last before I were destroyed too?
Men may search, but do we really want to find?
She would die, the legend would die, what then?
Reality is too final.
We examine, dissect, then desert.
What shall I do?
If I prove her existence, I destroy her.
If I let her go she will live forever.
She is immortal as long as she swims
She needs the myth to keep living,
We live with the myth.
Go free, my friend, we are not ready for you yet.
   Belinda Hastie

Days Of War

A flower blooms then wilts with fear,
An unsure future which once seemed clear.
Search for your freedom up in the skies,
Restore all the peace before everyone dies.
A dump site of a world, as if nothing mattered,
All of our dreams which seem almost shattered.
The life that once was no longer exists,
The image of war and anger persists.
The mirage of world peace which holds in our mind
Can be solved with some help when together we bind
If we all start anew and put behind us our strife,
The flower which dies may spring back to life.
   Linda Thompson

Fire

It's in our hearts as passion grows,
An unyielding love from head to toes,
Found in hatred as tempers flare,
A moment of weakness logic up in the air
It tears our emotions denying common sense
Leaving us bitter distraught and tense
Ever present as we strive to achieve
Strengthens our faith our quest to believe
It's in our bellies as we struggle through life
In hate and evil it's always rife
Red when out of control it proves too much
Eternally burning the core of the earth
From Lucifer's chamber it rose from birth
   John A. Stirling

The Battle Lost

The battle scars reflect in her eyes,
All the pain, all the sorrow
Her mournful cries.
A burning ember once burned so bright
Has left her now like a bird in flight
Perhaps her love like the blackbirds song
Full of promise and beauty in his
Springtime song.
And in the darkness of winter
No song can be heard.
On the battle ground
Just a broken bird
The silence so deafening lonely and long
Please carry her swiftly through
Loves sad song.

Deirdre French

The Quest

To search is to seek, discovery knowledge divine
All the talents of the Ages, I wish I could combine
For I seek a world that beyond us all so pure
I can conceive no quest in mortal life so truer.
To stand safe in the all embracing bosom of love
Shrouded in the warmth of heaven from above,
To lie in green pastures in the Courtyard of Truth
Dwelling with the poet who called himself swain uncouth,
Learning the magic arts from poets and prophets gold
Absorbing the power of knowledge only they behold,
Castle Joyous within the soul of the Bower of Bliss
The Garden of Adonis where hate is but fountain piss.
I am but an unknown poet of Youth who knows no bounds
My works are but thoughts in my mind which swirl around,
Never surfacing, for I have no skill on rhyme nor verse
Who can express nought, and for a poet nothing is worse.
I must search to seek, that must always be my quest
I must not stop nor expire, for it is my soul test.

John P. Heginbotham

Hugh MacDiarmid A Tribute

Write me a poem about Scotland's sons,
All those who suffered at the hands of English guns,
Before your pen their blood runs,
Sing me a song about border reiver,
Words were your loom,
And you were the weaver,
The English Edward the bold deceiver,
You pounded out your patriotic missile,
You! O son of thistle,
To English ears your Stern Epistle,
How Scotland suffered at their hands,
Cry! The wasted, wasted lands
From Cullodens Moors to Highland Clearance,
Your work brooked no interference,
From Flodden Fields to Cheviot Tup,
The bile spilled over from your cup,
Sir Walter Scott was not your graven image,
But more like Burns your stately visage,
So lets usurp the English bastard now,
Like an aged horse dies before the plough.

Alan Pow

Vampire's Hair

It was the dead of night,
All through the village,
No-one's moving,
Nobody's stirring,
Not a sound is heard,
But high above the village,
A castle stands.
A vampire stirs.
Suddenly it swoops over the houses,
Everyone awakes to a piercing scream,
They are glad they're alive but tomorrow is
    Another day!

Charlotte Cougill

I Still Need You

Mother, I'm in fear of getting older,
Allow me to rest my head on your shoulder.
Sadness is such a mixed feeling...
Explain, please, what does it all mean?
It's my life. But I still need you.

I'm lost, like one word in a book,
Never given a chance, a second look.
If someone were to hold me close again,
Would the tears fall down like rain?
It's my life. But I still need you.

Sorry, I was lost within my thinking,
Fingers snapped, I must have been dreaming.
But life seems so much more appealing,
When you're lost in deep sleeping.
It's my life. But I still need you.

David Brealey

Dolphins

Shattery brilliant sunset, till misty dawn awakes
alone or pairs.
They've been around centuries before, let's hope for
Centuries more. Beautiful creatures of the sea,
Swimming around, making pleasure abound,
Sleek of body, wise of mind, too fast, too
Intelligent for human kind.
One swish of tail, one dorsal fin, one sad,
Yet hopeful eye, they dive deep, then up
They go, out of water way up high,
One last look, straight down again,
Splash!
Now they've gone.
Still there's always tomorrow,
Isn't there?

Leigh J. Fisher

Untitled

From Weybridge I come, as a boy we had fun
Always I remember, not necessary November
But yes I remember the plot
for one day a year those gates I fear
were closed, no entry behind it were gently
Titles and money champagne with honey
Dad had beer and skittles sad no titles
The Brig General manned those gates told me my fates
You over there in hoyle I spare
You with Errand Boy Bike you and alike
Will Errand Boys be, he said with glee
Are the Hills of St Geuise inside there's money they Guise
Give me that cream a Trojan I seem
The lady will set no title regret
But wealth she has, has they, a friend I say
Weybridge born you said with that oap on your head
Not from the gutter thames I will utter
So bugger off now we will not row
Tomorrow these hills will be alive with music!

George A. Rowland

My Prince, My Father

His smile thrilled me, his frown terrifying,
all bad things forgotten when enrobed in his
huge arms,
No one or nothing could harm me when he held
my hand,
Spoilt yet swallowed up in love,
My childhood was a fairy tale,
My prince, my father,
This love grew with me, although in his
eyes I'm still his little girl
His need to shield me from the world is
sometimes welcomed, sometimes not.
Still a strong man, still there for me,
But now I am there for he,
My prince, my father.

Lisa Batten

Delightful Pentayia

Delightful Pentayia, oh how I long to be
amongst your beautiful sights to walk along
your narrow streets and smell the citrus fruit aroma.

How I long to be with you Pentayia this coming
Christmas, to be in Ayios Nicolas church
witnessing Christ's birth and rejoicing along
with all my friends from the Turkish
Occupation Pentayia your freedom.

How I long presents to be taken to all the sick
in your hospital on New Year's Day and in your
beautiful square games to be playing.

How I long to be with you Pentayia this coming
Christmas and to be celebrating the return of all
your GREEK children to their Homeland the
land of our fathers.

Constantina S. Kouspoyenis

Buchan Bachelor

I aince wis' a strappin' gweed-lookin' chiel
An' a' the lasses lo'ed me weel.
An' when Leap Year did come roon,
The postie's bag wis wechted doon.
I got proposals frae far and near.
An' ilka one began wi' 'Darlin' or 'Dear'.
Darlin' one said, " I've a big hoose and siller".
If ye mairry me and tak'alang ma mither
Noo ae woman in a hoose micht work awa
But I draw the line at bidin' wi' twa.
So I just made them a' the same
Nane o' them hid tae change their name.
Tae keep a wife and dress her aye braw
My siller wid shortly wear awa.
I think I'll just bide wi' ma mither.
We've been richt happy baith the gither
An'if in the winter, I am could in my bed,
She'll gie' me a het water bottle instead.
I am noo growing auld and short o' breath
Tae mairry noo micht be my death.

Ethel Willox

Golden Partners

This longing for a baby, how can it be expressed.
An empty hollow feeling, an aching in one's breast.
It's not just wanting children, but the giving of a life.
Instead, this hollow heartache and turning of a knife.

We look back at the passing time and childless years gone by.
Then meet our partner's loving glance and heave a thankful sigh.
For where would we be without support, of love and humour bright.
They bring us into sunshine and out of gloomy night.

Barbara Buist

Complicator

Forever making what could be
A simple existence complex,
Forever exploring my life,
Guessing what'll bring the pain back next.
Always pointing out a million
Points of myself to hate,
Always remembering I've got a good side,
But remembering too late.
I torture myself for my small mistakes,
For what I do or say,
My punishment gives me the right to exist,
Keeping death away.
I think too much,
I blame myself for all the pain I see,
I think too much,
It drives my hatred, my hatred points at me.
I think too much,
It hurts so much, a tear spills from my eye,
I think too much,
But I won't stop thinking until the day I die.

Barry Alan Saunders

HOPE

HOPE is ever eternal, for every one of us,
An entity to call on, when we feel we must.
We always HOPE for a healthy life, to all newly born,
Then HOPE their childhood is enjoyed, as it follows on.
There's always HOPE for their success during their school studies,
Giving further HOPE towards a good career, with seldom any worries.
We HOPE they'll meet someone to love, and HOPE they'll also marry,
To bring fresh HOPE everyday, from children crying "mummy".
There's always HOPE from everyone, for others in distress,
For without HOPE, what would we do, when we're in a mess?
There's HOPE for peace and HOPE for joy, also tranquillity.
There's always HOPE for everyone, until eternity.

John White

Elborada (Spanish, For Dawn)

Night time goes, Daylight grows,
An ever growing lustre to the night.
As it glows, o'er the hills.
Day, tapping gently on the door of night.
Blushing Dawn, Night forlorn,
as her sleepy glow leaves reluctant bed of Night.
Changing into day attire, as we watch her Dawn boudoir,
Shy beauty, on her lovely face.
Suffused glow, sets me afire,
with yearnings of suppressed desire.
To share myself with this wonder of the Dawn;
Lifting my soul.
And my heart's on a higher plane,
I don't want to step on earth again,
Just drift, on the soft beauty of a cloud
tinged with the sun's awakening rays.
Loving feelings have set my heart ablaze,
as I watched the soft unfolding of the Dawn.
As I watched the Sun kiss the Night goodbye,
in the boudoir of the Dawn.

Derek Asker

Life

Life is a pleasure, and not a curse,
An immeasurable treasure, that cannot be bought with
any purse,
Even when it seems to be full of pain,
It can be turned around to yield great gain,
In every misfortune, a lesson learned,
And in time you'll see what patience you've earned.

Helping the helpless, loving the unloved,
Like God's kind of love, which comes from above,
As you reach out, to make someone else's day,
True fulfilment, will come your way,
Then with me, you'll say in verse,
Life is a pleasure, and not a curse.

Edwin Oludotun Shadare

Old — Not Cold

What do you see when you look at me?
An old man of seventy or eighty maybe...
This suit is the one I wore when I got wed,
The same one I'll wear on the day that I'm dead.
I don't smell too good and I shuffle when I walk,
Young people pass by me, they've no time to stand and talk.
But look in my eyes and you'll see,
They have smiled
Look and remember that I was once a child.

What do you see when you look at me?
An old man who dribbles when he drinks his tea....
This hat is the one I wore when I got wed,
The same one I'll wear on the day that I'm dead.
My fingernails are dirty and my face is lined with years,
Young people pass by me, they've no time to see my tears,
But look in my eyes and you'll see,
They have smiled
Look and remember that I was once a child.

Carol Kravis

The Caterpillar

Munching its way through a fresh green leaf,
An ugly type worm with razor sharp teeth,
A long slim body and stumpy shaped legs,
With silky type skin it eventually sheds,
Hanging upside down on a single thread,
A crispy formed shell that seems to be dead,
Have you ever believed in reincarnation?
As time goes by to your fascination,
A change takes place and forms within,
A new life is created and starts to begin,
Wiggling and fighting to escape from its shell,
It hasn't gone to heaven, it hasn't gone to hell,
As this ugly bug you thought would die,
Now emerges as a butterfly.
   Brian Johnson

The Little Boy In The Supermarket Trolley

Crouched over a frozen pizza steering wheel
And a celery gear stick,
He roars down the aisles,
In his rear-engined one-mothered-powered trolley,
Sponsored by Sainsbury's,
The three year old Damon
Sweeps past the four hundred horse power
Of Schumacher.
Formula One, just like the detergent.
He swings through the hairpin by the bacon,
Accelerates down the straight past the soap,
Slows distractedly by the sweets,
And weaves majestically through the traffic
At Frozen Chips Corner.
The bottles of champagne are on special offer
To celebrate victory at the Grand Pris-Unic.
It's all such fun.
But it cannot last.
The check-out
Is the pits.
   Adam Wilson

Gertrude

She lay in the hospital led, a bag of bones
And a face so distorted by life.
None of us knew if she was a spinster, or a
mother or wife.
No visitors ever came to see her, these was no
sign of a family.
She lay there for weeks in deaths shadow,
hardly caring to notice or see.
Then Janet appeared before her, like a
magical and friendly light
Perhaps for a few precious moments her
Life became decidedly bright
She row had one good friend in this cruel
world, a girl who brought her gifts and
warmth and love.
Goodbye then, dear old Trudy, we hope you
are with the Lord up above.
   Alan Heath

Empty Feeling

An empty space with no floors
An empty space with no walls
An empty space with no ceiling
There are no corners for one to creep in

It has no darkness
It has no light
It has no turning, horizontal or vertical sight

To touch it misses
To smell it passes
To catch it lapses
So it is passive
   Joy Patricia Johnson

Ode To Sandra

A first grandchild comes into the world
And a never-to-be-repeated experience is unfurled

A feeling of awe knowing baby is part of you but not your own
Your son — now a man — in stature has grown

He'll soon know the responsibilities and worries you had
As he faces those of his own as a dad

A baby is precious — a new generation
And grandparents should be treated with great veneration!

They give unconditional love and are there when they're needed
But, of course, their advice often goes unheeded

Adjusting is needed to be "Mum" and "Dad"
And sometimes events can make you a little sad

But just say thanks for this new creation so small
And as parents and grandparents stand proud and tall
   Jean Symonds

The Revenge Of The Fleshcrawl

Amid the smoke infested sewers of life, lies hatred
and agony, a creature hungry,
waiting to come out.

Can you smell the blood, clotting, rotting, spreading
depression, court in session,
"I think I'll kill again".

It's so easy to forget about yourself as life slips
through your fingers, death still lingers,
nail the coffin shut.

Welcome to my own private hell, it's a world full
of failure, society's traitor,
do you really care.

"So I'll make the little angels pay,
rape your f***ing minds".
killing binds,
the devil in disguise.
   David Lunt

The Insomniac's Prayer

When darkness and stillness around me prowl
And all the world sleeps with a tranquil peace,
Wakeful lie I, hearing every hoot-owl
Through turbulent thoughts which never know cease.
Around... around, like a mouse in a cage,
They scramble, scrabble, and chase away sleep,
Making me fretful or fuming with rage
Till dawn roses out with the sun's first peep.
Help me, dear Lord, in this my affliction,
Enable me, please, to find peace and rest;
Let sleep, deep sleep, become my addiction,
With Morpheus, sweet Morpheus, my nightly guest.
Grant me, O Lord, this small dying each night
That morn's resurrections come as delight.
   Cynthia Stewart

My Heart Attack

How can I ever hope to convey,
All that is in my heart to-day,
Five months have passed since that dreadful day,
When my life so nearly ebbed away,
You took my heart, dear Lord,
And with it, my very life,
But I will live with a heart that's strong,
And serve you faithfully each day long,
To thank you for all you did for me,
When I was as sick as I could be,
The world has become a lovelier place,
My heart is light and full of grace,
I thank my Lord for his love and care,
Which I can see just everywhere,
On bended knee I bow my head,
And thank my God, I am not dead.
   Freda Allan

The Photograph

"Who's the man in the photo, Nan?" A small boy asked one day.
And as she held the photograph, the long years slipped away.
She saw a man in uniform and, standing at his side,
The image of her youthful self so keen to be his bride.

How could she tell this little boy about that awful war
That took her soldier from her more than forty years before?
And then she'd married grandpa 'on the rebound' as they say,
And though their lives had been fulfilled, some thoughts don't go away.

They'd had their sad and happy times, but often in between
She'd dreamed about her first love and the life that might have been.
It would have been so different; the many things they'd planned
She couldn't share with anyone. They wouldn't understand.

The question in its innocence had caught her by surprise,
And with rekindled memories the tears welled in her eyes.
"Who is it, Nan?" He prompted as the tears began to show.
With winsome smile she answered, "Just someone I used to know."

Dennis Turner

Untitled

Dear Darren,

Our hearts are truly broken
And can never be repaired,
There will always be a piece missing
Now that you're no longer there.

But if pain and tears could build bridges
To heaven where we're sure you abide.
We could cross that bridge tomorrow.
To be there by your side.

Then our hearts that are truly broken
Could be mended and freed from pain
We could hold you in our arms once more
And know happiness again.

Delise Carter

" Boy Youth, And The Girl, Life "

The girl wore a star upon her hair
And danced like the merry moon upon the sea,
A sylvan elf, with all that she did wear
She held your heart and would not let it free.

She caught your eyes, deep as the forest pools,
And played with them a game of light and shade,
I heard the years of Wisdom call you fools
For you, not she, are one with things that fade.

Boy, she broke the beauty from your eyes
And danced the dawn beneath imperious feet,
Your dream were desolate dreams of winter skies
Hopeless little urchin of the street!

Jean Mary Orr

Winter Morning

The frost lies crisp upon the ground,
A silver blanket all around,
The sharp fresh air is bitter cold,
Now the year is growing old.

So quiet, so still the world is now,
It's quite a perfect sight somehow,
There's not a sound that can be heard,
Except the shrill song of a bird.

I squeeze my toes to keep them warm,
And watch a robin on the lawn,
He hops around, pecks here and there,
Then flies off to a nest somewhere.

Now I'm left alone to meet,
The winter morning at my feet,
But soon, the world will stretch and yawn,
And yet another day will dawn.

Kim Driver

Dark Thoughts Of Need

As sunlight fades upon the moor
And darkness shadows reclaimed tracks,
In an endless stand of Alder Carr,
Where moonlight strives to pierce the black.
The icy autumn winds converge
To cast the golden leaves below
Upon the sodden woodland floor,
To shimmer in the water's flow.

There flooded marsh of rancid soil,
Attired in nature's patchwork shroud,
Concealed the frenzied savagery
A summer's day had once allowed.
Hastened to a shallow grave,
Where heavy rains, in part, exhumed.
Her silent sleep is tortured still,
As time defiles where beauty bloomed.

The strange companion can't relent,
Dark thoughts of need come pulsing back
To shatter faith and innocence
Once more, along a lonely track.

Howard Long

Bygone Gratitudes

Take not for granted what God has given,
And dismiss not the wonders of life's true rhythm.
For when their enjoyment you're unable to take,
Life may seem dull, and all for no sake.

Soak up every moment of every walk,
And every word that is spoken or thought.
Remember the moon shining down from above;
Its reflections from pools, and personified love.

Take not for granted being able to walk,
Or having a real friend with whom you can talk.
Remember the games you played as a child;
The running and jumping, a shout in the wild.

Watch with diligence the turn of the tide,
And the forming of buds along the roadside.
Remember your hopes when life was still new,
But regret not those dreams that haven't come true.

Take not for granted the sights and the sounds,
Of life in abundance, and pleasures abound.
For God's gift of remembrance is great joy indeed;
Accept it with love, as part of your need.

Christine Campbell-Sturgess

Untitled

The seasons change with rapid measure
  and each one gives a special pleasure.
Seems strange how just a while ago
  the furthest thing away was snow.

It seems like only just last week
  we sat in sunshine, basked in heat.
But winter came around this morning
  crept up softly, gave no warning.

Shorts and t-shirts put away
  replaced with warmer clothes today.
No sandals, sun hats, cotton dresses
  but woolly jumpers, scarves and wellies.

Snowflakes dance and whirl about
  but never will you hear them shout.
They come to settle on the leaves
  make spiders' webs a sight to see.

Huddle close around the fire
  watch the winter world grow whiter.
Warm your hands and feet and hearts
  and wait again 'till springtime starts.

Linda Eley

Old Age — A View On Him

With customary dread, I tap on the door
And enter, murmuring how glad I am to see him
With a note of forced civility I almost shout
How well he is looking.
I see that flicker across his face — he nearly smiles
A cynical look, as though he's recognized my lie!
He stares at me — and I feel a blush
Ashamed of my automatic conversation
I enquire if he has eaten lunch and he nods 'yes'
Then that long silence resumes and lingers — pointless

I get up and move across the room
Commenting on the fine view he sees,
Then I recall his sight is poor —
And I pray his hearing is too.

His eyes so judgmental — the shame I feel
But he couldn't have lived with us.
Now no reason can stop his sorry tears,
And they will haunt me for the rest of my years.
Coral Glover

The Final Frontier

The Solar wind through space it flies
And enters into earthly skies.
The Aurora Borealis with colours bright,
Twists and turns in the Arctic Night.

Comets too come into sight,
On their voyage through that same dark night.
The Hubble telescope with clear vision
Observes there will be no collision.

Man's earthly struggle to reach the stars
Will begin with a visit to the Planet Mars.
Onward and forward to the Milky Way,
To the nearest galaxy the experts say.

To seek out new life they boldly go,
Through asteroid belts moving to and fro.
Deeper into that dark abyss
The thrusting engines give a flaming hiss.

What will they find, no one knows,
Courageously onward the human spirit goes.
On a no-name planet together they will stand,
"In the name of peace we claim this land."
Glynis Stuart Thomson

For Charlie

Welcome little fellow, your life has just begun
And every family knows, it's good to have a son

The world is ever changing, and puts us to the test
You must find your place within and strive to do your best

And when you've tried and mastered some new-fangled toy
The rest of us will shout with pride three cheers for Charlie boy!
Brenda Clark

Sadness

Come walk with me
and feel the silence of the night.
No sound is heard,
No winged beat in flight:
The silence like a velvet cloak
Surrounds my form.
I wait alone to contemplate
The Dawn.

Rain falls, leaving tree trunks gleaming
White;
But still the silence stays,
No moon tonight?
Is this the way that life is meant
to be?
No sun, no moon,
But darkness in the trees.
Kathleen Hearn

To Open A Closed Mind

This poem should make you wake up
And give your mind a shake up
For a head that's closed and sleeping
Leaves the soul tired and weeping

This adventure called life is fun
So let your imagination run
Stay on the well trodden track
Look forward as well as back

Poetry is a door to the soul
To open it is a poetic goal
With blank verse, sonnets and rhyme
Spirits are lifted all the time

By reading a poem you'll see
It's as good as its author is free
From the shackles and chains of reality
To the realm of imagery

As I finish I hope you will start
To take an active part
And think poetically every day
To discover the poet's way
Derek Morgan Lockwood

You And Me

You guarded me in the night
And greeted me in the morning light
Through a troubled veil thrown across
Dark corners concealed from me
Of mind stealing to infinity
Uncontained by flesh alone
But stretching out to life unknown

We cannot give a name
Like raindrops on the ocean
A single one cannot contain
Beyond the wide horizon
The rainbow's new domain
Unknowing of the reason.

For the journey is of trust
That night shall follow day
And hope one minute meets the next
To help us on the way.
So morning came and in the quick of time.
We were here in tune and rhyme
At one with eternal mind.
David Arthur Evans

Remembrance

Gaze gently at the flowers of the field,
And every blade of grass,
Multitudes of marvellous memories do they yield,
Of lives from ages past.

In silence do they sweetly sway,
And scent the heavenly air;
All through the slowly changing day,
Their loveliness they wear.

Flies and bees and butterflies,
Flutter and fly around;
The wind with sounds of humming sighs,
And whispers to the ground.

All, long ago, their lives they lived,
As we, in turn, today;
Their marvels, and the things they willed,
The world now does display.

From earth we rise and are slowly weaned,
And back to the earth we pass;
Gaze gently at the flowers of their field,
And lightly tread the grass.
Elwyn Williams

Yosemite

When fall comes to Yosemite, Arts' brush is dipped most generously and hands that sculpted waterfalls paint colours on the leaves and walls of granite, sheer, upwardly stretched, tall, sliced and tabled, finely etched, now daubed with pastel sunlit strokes, creation's artist has evoked a scene of Lordly majesty, the mountains of Yosemite.

Huge boulders line the trackers path and roaring streams declare their wrath but dwindle low in Summers week and bumble gently down each creek. Great firs like mighty arrows soar, deep roots held fast to valley floor with reddened bark, jig-sawed and crazed, myriad shaped and roughly raised to speed the feet of living things while birds find rest for tired wings

Sierra bears that sleep on high were here before white men drew nigh when Indians roamed and lived as one with valley, beast and ripening sun, where Mirror Lake and Bridal Fall would listen to their haunting call. Now striped racoon, coyote and deer have nothing from each guest to fear but wander with impunity at Nature's Park, Yosemite.

Frances C. Jakeway

Shaft Of Darkness

Coal is black and shiny
and hard to get sometimes.
I still glisten with sweat
as I dream of dust and grimes.
The sudden drop of cage leaving light
with cramped bodies breathing in unison.
Thuddingly bumping to a halt
at the dripping shafts station.
Voices activated by the safe arrival
at the pit bottom electrically lit.
Instructions received, oil lamps checked,
head for the darkness, this is it.
Beams of light glisten the rails
as we walk on sleepers evenly spaced.
Towards the face that has many features
whose injuries have made bodies defaced.
A brief rest, a swig, stripped for action,
tools come to life in expert hands.
I'm there again giving roof support
to a gone by life that had such plans.

Kenneth J. Williams

Home

A Palace or a Cottage small,
A Hovel or Baronial Hall
Where'er you live, that place you call
Your Home,

Where all your joys and treasures shine,
A comfy chair that fits your spine,
A Wife, A Child, whose love divine
Makes Home,

A place wherein your wildest dreams
Are filled with hopes, ambition beams,
And life is always what it seems,
At Home.

Where'er you are, whate'er the plan,
Try finding better if you can,
There's no place quite as good to man,
As Home.

Charlie Boy Smith

Grandma's New Life

Although my grandpa has gone to heaven,
and my grandma is all alone,
I hope that she can live a normal life at home,
But I see her dressed in black, with tears in her eyes,
always remembering the day when my grandpa died.
Slowly she's accepting her new way of life,
and learning how to live without him by her side.

Ivan Robba

There's A Boy I Like

There's a boy I like
and he likes me
but the problem is my mum doesn't agree.
I told her it wasn't like that
but she didn't care it wasn't the fact.

She told me that he was bad,
that made me really sad.
I wish I could see him forevermore
but for her he was out the door.

As I see him in the street
I put my head down to my feet.
I want to raise my head to say hello
but for he was not a descent fellow.

He will always be in my mind
for her she will never find.

I want to see him again in time
but my chances will be forever to come
'cause his heart will be completely gone
for mine will still be hanging on

Lisa Denyer

Turn Off The Night

Oh how long the night is
and how long before the dawn begins.
Seeing, hearing the wakening birds
and then how long before the sun
lifts silently to witness the world.
The shadows came and filled my mind
and giant fears abound my being.
Stillness and darkness walk hand in hand
I dread the long hours, as I sit and wait for light.
All manner of things grow in my mind
and I shrink in fear of senseless thoughts,
the imagination rules mightily as reason
slips into darkness and pain increases.
My body shakes, chills and shivers take hold
but yet still I feel the heat.
Oh but then the dawn is here,
the birds sing, and the chorus begins a new day is borne.
Then, sleep invades my relaxing body.
The sun warms my soul, and black thoughts
disappear back into the night.

Lesley Croft

The Loss Of A Husband

My John has gone to Jesus
And I am left alone,
My life seems dull and empty
And home's no longer 'Home!'

For home is where the heart is
And my heart's gone with John,
He waits for me in our heavenly home
Where we'll meet again when I pass on.

But Jesus brings me comfort
And gives me strength to live each day,
He is my constant companion
And guides me through life's way.

I trust in him completely
I could have no better friend,
I pray he'll stay with me forever
Until I reach life's end.

Then to live with him in glory
Sharing in his light and love,
Reunited with our loved ones
In our heavenly home above.

Lilian Heach

The Speed Of Time

Another year has just gone by
And I didn't see it go
I wonder if it's just my age
for they used to go so slow
I'm sure as we grow older
There becomes a new dimension
Must sort this out when I get time
and give it my attention
But if I give time to things like this
The time will go more fast
I wonder what's the remedy
to make tomorrow last
I try to keep an hour or two
tucked up within my sleeve
But when I glance down at my watch
I swear my eyes deceive
for there it is the day has gone
it's time to go to bed
but tomorrow may last longer
If I don't wake up dead

Euphemia McKillop

The Dream Train

Now in the dark the dream train jerks and rolls
And I embark upon that nightly quest
The soul-fired engine huffs and puffs and pulls
Its roller coaster, grumbling to the crest,
Then, whoosh — the flimsy craft abruptly falls
Down slopes of sleep and thunders on headfast
Into that chasm, black with doubt and fear,
Where chaos lurks and devils hiss and jeer.

Wise men who probe the mysteries of life
Deny there is existence after death,
Suggesting death means peace, no care, no strife,
Just sweet oblivion after that last breath.
Surely they wonder as they wake from sleep,
Trying to grasp the fleeting, fading dreams,
Before they slide into the sub-conscious deep
Whether the dream experience mocks their schemes.

What if the terrors which our fears ignite
Refuse to end in that unending night.

George Waldron

A Child In Thought

I love to lie and watch the sky
And see the great clouds rolling by
Then the sun goes down behind
Something that looks like a dark blind.
It is a rain cloud o'er the trees
But still the sun shines overseas,
With little children saying grace
In every Christian kind of place.

Joan Britton

Sonnet To Youth

Time was, when youth and joy were fresh and sweet
And morning dawned with confidence and trust,
The daily path quite firm beneath our feet,
Giving faith to accomplish what we must.
No disillusions yet to mar our dreams
Of reaching out to claim our heart's desire,
The senses all indulged to far extremes,
Ambitious then to set the world afire.
We knew it all when "crabbèd age" advised,
In love and truth, another path to tread,
Curtly spurning the course that they apprised
And pursuing our wilful way instead.
Youth seemed eternal as the stars above,
Considering the world well lost for love.

Joan Weston

Untitled

The Lord said, "There, behold, that is your task"
And I looked up, and saw a mountain vast.
I cringed, and cried, "My Lord, this cannot be —
It is too great a climb you wish of me!"
And thus I sat and stared with mounting fear
And prayed to God that it would disappear.
But it refused to vanish from my sight
And there remained to mock me in my fright.
Such agonies of mind I then pursued
And following each dark and bitter mood
The very depths of Hell I felt I trod
Until, at last, I pleaded with my God.
He promised me the strength to start the climb
But said that every effort must be mine.
With timid heart I started the ascent
And on the Mighty Hand of God I leant.
It seemed to me I struggled on for years
But when I reached the end, with grateful tears,
I looked behind, and saw to my surprise
The mountain now appeared of mole-hill size!

Christina Clark

Reflection

If we were young again
And in love as we used to be
We might swim again in the trout-filled stream
With Mac and sweet young Jean.

We might stroll again in the woods
Under beaches and oaks and elms,
And Marok decide which would burn best
Not smoke in the chimney breast.

Blind Prince would run along-side
Chasing Susie the Road-Island hen;
While we, in a pie-dish pickled strawberries-wild —
Along the high-banked glen.

The laughter of our old folk
Might chime as we came back home —
To the smell of mushroom-fry
As it wafted the circle of home.

Now we stay home by the fire
And welcome the young as they come
To visit the old homestead —
And be with us — till we move on!

Agnes Michie

The Descent

Consciousness flows into other streams
    and night gives rise to invention,
    Pouring forth an ocean of dreams
    from the depths of imagination.

Some spirit of malevolence,
    Or mechanical dispensation,
    Stirs memory and conscience;
    the nexus of persecution.

That monstrous incubus, from Thought's abyss;
    Dread phantasm of most cruel propensity,
    Broods in the disfigured darkness;
    it's chosen or fated territory.

For all is doom-laden certainty,
    And I bear mute witness
    To an incommunicable tyranny,
    and means to madness.

With the gradual disordering of perception,
    The will is submerged and drowned.
    I may not define the condition,
    Since reason is overturned!

Jeffrey Donoghue

Reflection

I am with you always, and forever,
and in my eyes lies your destruction
My love alone is ice and burning fire:
without it you are nothing. A shell.
All is futility: nothing you can do.
Nothing to escape me. I am endless.
I envy your fragile, vivid dreams
for dreams are hopes and echoes of hopes
and I am eternally a creature of despair.
I watch you forever on the border of reality
and my darkness touches your soul.
Like a black breeze blowing, I reach out
and I claim your heart as my own.
Like the cold, pale moon in the night
reflects the living light of the sun,
my life is in the balance of your dreams,
in your destiny. I am your reflection.

Lucinda Hallowes

The Carousel

I sat beside the carousel,
And it went rolling 'round,
Its painted horses on their poles,
That fuzzy fairground sound.

Still children love its simple fun,
As mine did years ago,
For me those years rolled by too fast,
For them they went too slow.

Written on a visit to Barry's, Portrush, 9/8/'87

Joseph Kennedy

Autumn Leaves

I watched the leaves falling onto the grass,
And knew that the Summer had silently passed,
The trees were shedding crisp leaves to the ground,
A golden brown carpet stretched out all around,

A little breeze hurried the leaves on their way,
And Autumn seemed golden that glorious day.
The leaves that had sheltered and draped every tree,
Now lay on the soft grass in all their beauty.

I could not help but marvel at this Autumn sight,
It made such a dull day seem really quite bright,
Nature had showed me a glimpse of her year
Her beauty each season is perfectly clear.

And now as the light fades and darkness draws round,
I will know that the carpet's still there, by its sound,
The beauty of Autumn leaves falling that day,
Is engraved on my mind in its own special way.

Janet L. Hennem

The Homeless

As I sit by my fire, with my nourishing (food)
And know I have a comfortable bed, which is (good)
I have no worries, as each day goes (by)
But when I think of the homeless, I want to (cry)
Poor souls, who walk the streets, at (night)
Or live in cardboard boxes, it's not (right)
Who hardly eat, or sleep, as each day (passes)
Young and old, there's always (masses)
It's a very cruel world, we live in (today)
If only some-one would help, in some (way)
Sometimes, it is no fault of their (own)
But we have a cheek, to sit, and (moan)
And stop them begging at the (door)
I pray to God to help them (soon)
And keep them safe from midnight until (noon)
To keep them warm, as the winter winds (blow)
And give them hope, when they're feeling (low)

Catherine M. Balmain

" It "

The woman next door's got it all in 'er arm
And last week it was all in 'er thigh.
The week before that, it was all in 'er back
And I thought of our poor Aunt Vi
She'd 'ave it everywhere — all at once,
From the top of 'er 'ead to 'er toes,
But just what "it" was, she never would say,
And to this day nobody knows.
"I've got it all in me leg" she'd say with a wince,
"And Fred's got it all in 'is neck.
It started last week and 'e 'asn't slept since
Now 'e looks like a physical wreck."
What can it be, this "it" thing
That's affecting the human race?
I've just seen the woman next door again,
Now she's got it all in 'er face.

David Luton

The Thief

He came, not by night, but in the afternoon
and left a footprint on my windowsill.
Whilst I was out, my home he cooly ransacked
and carried out the task with skill.

He took small trinkets he could carry easily,
unwanted bits discarded on the ground.
Grandmother's brooch and Mother's rings he fancied.
My Father's watch and chain he also found.

The Police were very sympathetic, but no help!
The perpetrator of the crime they knew
but catching him, that was a different matter;
their records for arrests were, sadly, few.

My house is now a fortress, barred and bolted.
My cat still hides when people come to call.
And I daily curse the thief who knew no better
and cares not that my life's forever spoiled.

Joy Harman

If (It Could Be)

If you can scan your life in one broad sweep
And lend a hand to those who stumble on their way,
If you can pull the mighty from the deep
And do your best to clear your conscience every day,
If you can help to right a wrong and still
Hold in good stead the unfortunate,
If you can rise to the occasion,
Enjoy your part and never deal in hate,
If you can see the moon and count the stars
And hold the hands of those who cannot see,
If you can pass the moon and carry on to Mars
You'll lead the foolish to eternity.
If you can calm the raging waters of the heart
And lull the mind to tranquil harmony,
If you believe and always play your part,
You'll stand steadfast upon that highest balcony.

Beryl Aldous

A Winter's Day Ago

In days gone by, in times of coal
  and life was very cheery,
    We used to huddle by the fire,
  do you remember, dearie?

We'd watch the smoke and flames go up
  and listen to its crackle.
    We'd think of summer fishing
  like sorting out the tackle.

Those were the days I used to love
  and in my heart will cherish.
    Oh! Put another bar on
  before my poor feet perish.

Brian Greig

Tranquillity

I sit here by the sandy shore,
And look to the horizon beyond,
A mirror of stillness as far as I can see,
As the sky and the sea merge as one,
The air is filled with tranquillity,
A sense of calm surrounding me,
As the sea glistens in the warmth of the sun,
Wavelets merging from this mirror of blue,
Dancing happily to their own sweet tune,
Rippling gently towards me,
Lapping softly onto the golden shore,
Softly Softly
Until they are no more.

Annabel Barrett

Heidi

I treated you with tenderness,
And lots of loving care,
Now my heart is broken,
Because you're no longer here,
Oh! Heidi, how I loved you,
Right from the very start,
When as a tiny puppy,
You crept into my heart.
You were my loyal and loving friend
Happy and faithful right up to the end,
I'd rub my face into your fur.
And whisper sweet nothings into your ear.
As the weeks and months roll by,
I often think of you and cry,
It was the worst day of my life
When I had to say goodbye.
God bless my faithful Heidi until we meet again.

Joan Gooch

On Reaching Eighteen Years

The days of youth are going fast
And manhood, it is here to last
Gone are the halcyon days of school
Where one just followed the Golden Rule;
You are entering the world of hopes and ambitions,
Schemes and Schedules and Snap Decisions,
Appointments to keep, all Struggle and Strife;
Don't let the Computer shape your life.
Don't trust to luck or live by Perchance
Just keep a cool head — think well in advance.

Congratulations on having got this far.
May Good Health and Good Fortune be your guiding Star.
Steer your own course — don't just follow the crowd
And for what you achieve be justly proud.
Ah yes, there are times when you will make a Bloomer
But above all else — Keep a Good Sense of Humour.

Charles Keswick

Never Ending Questions

In our world we all ask,
And from night till morning we're awake wondering
About the past and the future,
Why do we wonder.

What makes the rolling thunder,
What are stars and planet Mars,
What will happen next, what will not exist,
A new computer or planet Jupiter.

How did the first human get to be on this earth,
And was it a baby boy or baby girl,
And how did they grow and survive,
Are we gullible because we believe in God.

I know we will never stop wondering,
So while we live we must do our deepest best,
Remember we must do our heartily best,
Have a smile and come together as we strive
To make our world a better place, then we can wonder as we rest.

Gary Haro

Voices

Here comes this other person again
And my head is hurting quite bad
Please — Don't stay too long this time
When you're gone — I'm always so glad

I can't help what I'm doing
Don't listen to what I say
Will you ever stop coming to see me?
I pray you will — some day

The pain gets stronger as you retort
I'll never leave your side
You see — I am your twin spirit
And you'll never be able to hide

The doctors, they can sedate you
Making you drowsy with every pill
But one thing that will never change
I'll be with you — I always will

Don't you think you're different!!
This world — you have no part in it
But let me tell you — everyone here
Has their own — "EVIL TWIN SPIRIT"

Carys Mortlock

She

Sometimes when life has got me down
And my soul lies beaten and bruised on the roadside
She comes to me and tells me everything is alright
She makes me strong again so I can lift my head up high.
When all I see is sorrow all around me,
When I just can't seem to get back up and fight
When I've taken all I can from the world around me
Her eyes speak to me softly and tell me it's alright.
When I've given all I've got and they still want more
When I'm broken, bloodied, hurt and scarred
She comes to me and lifts me up, she gives her love to me
I know I'm only human and there's only so much I can do
She comes like a spirit of protection, like a blanket she comforts me.
She makes me feel like a hero instead of a battle-scarred fool.
I know my battles don't seem like much to an outside view,
And my scars are seldom and quite few.
But to know she's there amazes me,
When she say's the words "I love you".

Brian Mason

" Reflections "

I'd like to come to terms with all I've written,
And not look back in anger at the things I've done.
Go on and make myself a better person,
And wake each day, just thankful for the sun.
To walk with head held high amongst my peers,
And know true friendships I'd count dear.
That I could thank the folk who taught me long ago,
With not an enemy to hate or fear.
To look upon all men as equals,
Which in God's eyes this we all are.
Then I'd be glad I'd sojourned here.
And place my principles upon the highest star.

Joan Gilliver

The Shadow

A shadow passed in front of the sun
And for a moment I stood uncertain.
Was that really me that I could see
Or was I a different person...

The winds of change were in the air;
Discontent wore an ever changing disguise.
The torment and turmoil wrangled inside
And, in turn, gave nothing but sorrow and sighs.

The shadow is fading; the day shines brightly;
Will sensibility ever return;
For once in my life I've seen the light
I thought I'd never learn.

Kate Sherratt

Ethiopian Child

Those dark, sad eyes, bereft of hope,
and parchment skin, hung on your tiny frame.
The only things you've known in your short years,
are hunger, deprivation, death and pain.

Born to a world devoid of care,
and endless days when hunger gnaws,
but desperation soon becomes despair,
when no-one out there seems to heed your cause.

No food or shelter, only heat and flies,
and flesh that now has melted down to bones.
The hopelessness that each new morning brings,
the wretched sorrow that no-one atones

Who understands the awful aching grief?
When in a tiny bundle at your feet,
there lies your Mother and your guiding strength
but life denies you energy to weep.

LIFE, WHAT LIFE, you only just exist!
A living torment, born and doomed to die.
We Mothers everywhere reach out to you,
and long to ease your pain and question 'WHY'?

Elaine Creswell

Untitled

I gazed at the house on that cold Winter's morn
And my eyes filled with unshed tears
For this was the house in which I'd been born
And spent my childhood years

I heard once again the laughter and shout
Of children happy at play
But there was no-one at all about
On that cold Winter's day

The rooms were all empty, silent and bare
Neglect and decay all around
Ghosts of the past enveloped the air
But never making a sound

The memories returned of days long ago
When I was just a wee lad
And I lived in this house which I love so
Together with Mum and Dad

I knew there and then what I must do
And the reason why I had come
I'd restore it and make it good as new
And once more I would call it my home

Jean Grinsted

A Childhood Memory

There's an island that is far away from Scotland,
And I heard it oft described, and as a child
I lay in bed and fancied I could see it,
So barren, grey, with seas around so wild.

And then my parents took me, and it wasn't
As I'd imagined, not at all.
I gazed with wonder as we sailed towards it,
This island off the coast of Donegal.
It seemed to rise so gently from the ocean,
With patchwork fields of gold and brown and green,
And little white-washed cottages were scattered here and there,
Flowering banks of fuchsia hedges in between.

There were people waiting patiently around the old grey pier,
Shy, sweet faced, shawl-clad women, children too,
And as 'Jack the Glen's' white motorboat, with us, drew ever near
Rugged island men strolled down to help the crew.
As I turned to gaze across the bay at the lovely silver strand
At the turf smoke curling upward in the fragrant, balmy air,
The magic of that dear place stole into my heart and soul,
Though a child I knew I'd always love Ireland.

Kathleen Brady

She

She, with the golden sunshine in her hair,
and peace and warmth in her eyes —
such eyes,
that played upon my soul
like a thousand silent angels,
playing harp and chiming song.
My world stopped —
and happiness' flame danced before me
as peace fell like diamond rain;
She was the sun, which,
for one golden moment,
my world revolved around.
Her soul, pure and sheer and free of taint,
touched me like the breeze —
as, in one lost moment of peace and joy
destined to haunt me evermore:
She took the stage, a graceful goddess;
when time stopped —
  and she was everything.

Damion Brown

Our World

If we did not dump all our rubbish,
and pick it up, and throw it away
and don't say you will start next year or next month,
just tell yourself I'll start today.

Can't you see the world's not going to last forever,
if we keep on acting like we are
so everyone, let's pull together,
and make each one of us a star.

If we can keep up all our good work,
the world will be a wonderful place, and it will last much longer
than if we sat at home in disgrace.

Think of oil spilt into the sea, killing every fish, every bird,
and shout about what you have done to stop this
loud enough so everyone will have heard.

If we can start to recycle,
like making compost out of vegetable peel
it would do a great deal.

So if you help, together we will stay alive;
also we will help the world to survive.

Kelly Wrenn

The Man With A Cat On His Head

Manchester Fine Art Fair ninety four was all pretty pictures
and pink champagne but one leapt off the wall and belted me
between the eyes. A man with a cat on his head, I thought.
No thought can trouble by unwholesome pose titled the artist,
who posed riddles in tempera and gouache. I bought it.
They were watching balefully, silent and still,
but they spoke and I heard.
The same night I dreamed of a colourful circus wittily presented
by the cat, until the entertainment seductively metamorphosed,
became sinister, it was like a fragment of my unconscious meeting
a darker soul. So I woke, I knew I could not exorcize our Demons.

Kim Kennedy

The Robin's Song

"Oh, the sun on the thatch, and the green on the tree,
And the hush'd happy fields that were rapture to me!
Oh, the flags in the water, the blue of the sky!
Was it one summer since, or have ages slipped by.

"Now the snow lies in drifts, there is ice on the eaves,
On the brown moaning beech flicker three russet leaves;
And I sob, singing dule, on a fence in the snow,
Was it centuries back, or a summer ago?"

Pretty fool, singing dule, quit your sorrow, and sing,
How the snow'll turn to snowdrops, how seasons will bring
The blithe sun to the thatch, the glad green to the tree,
And the summer once more to the world, you, and me.

Friar John D. DeMontalt

A Sleeping Child

As I enter the room to wake her
and place a loving kiss
a sleeping little angel
a dainty, pretty miss.

My heart does a little flutter
what a beautiful child she is
but now I must bend and wake her
wake her with a kiss.

She'll turn, she will stretch and she'll murmur
at last she's beginning to stir
she's probably been in fairyland
if I know anything about her.

What a lovely sight, a sleeping child
looking innocent and small
it makes one feel so meek and mild
that God so loves us all.
Joyce Hammond

Party Meeting

It was 'next business'
And 'point of order'.
Democracy was a brash rubber ball
To be batted into oblivion,
While stubbled aggression lurched forward
To confront the barbed wire of capitalism
And bayed for the means of production,'
Amongst the rancid smoke.

Huddled desperately;
Comrades in concert applauded
Violent rhetoric, while some shuffled feet,
And spectres roamed amongst the hard benches
Implanting their heretical seed
To clutching minds.
Cloth caps are warped anachronisms
Of the struggle, but spirits survive
And somehow paddle the movement
Through the mine fields of logic.
Eddie McGonnell

Spring

Spring! The very breath of heaven
And promise of the joy to come
Descends upon us now and gives us hope;
The soaring creatures of the air
Bring with them rapture, love,
And fresh new thoughts of warmer days,
Of peace and revelling in the sun.
Come quickly now and cheer us with your breath
We long to feel your comfort and your gentle touch,
The roaring winds of winter and the frosty days are past,
The sombre nights and chilly morns
Are long since gone
And mildness fills the air,
Stay with us yet awhile to gladden now our souls
And rescue us from deep despair.
Brenda Evans

Obituary For A Care-Taker

She cared
    And put her time into caring.
She sacrificed her own comfort
    Because she believed in something
And one day,
    She learned to enjoy herself.

She set herself high standards
    And hated to fail.
She stood up to be counted
    And learned more by letting go.
She learned
    That she had cared too much.
Catherine Mason

Wimbledon

They travel there from far and near
And queue for hours to clap and cheer
Their favourite tennis star on court
Playing what used to be a sport
But now alas it's money, money
Nothing there remotely funny
Showbiz it is, a travelling circus
Two weeks a year, to amuse the workers
Racquet strings and tempers frayed
Each seven games new balls arrayed
"Fault" or "out" the linesman cries
"You must be mad" the server sighs
The royals beam and clap politely
The players bow or curtsey slightly
Never were such jamborees
Champagne galore with strawberries
And then at last comes finals day
The winners collect their inflated pay
More than workers earn in years
But they pay for it to watch poor dears
Len S. Wade

Friends At War

The Moon saw the Sun,
And said with a sigh,
You are the day,
And I am the nigh',
You are the light,
And I am the dark,
You are the tree,
And I am the bark.

The sun replied, shining bright,
You're more important than you'll ever know,
I be the arrow,
And you be the bow,
Alone I am weak,
With you I am strong,
Alone life is short,
With you it is long.

A star then twinkled,
And told the two,
My friends you are even,
The world needs you.
Daniel Thompson

Untitled

Liquid watermelon sky
and salmon stripes
quickly fading
    fading fading.....
Into the monotone of the city of gloom
The greens of tree and reds of roof
darken into shadows
    into grayness, then to blackness

This is where the lovers hide
In matching camouflage
Unseen to the naked eye
or wary passer-by

Song is carried on the wind
The voice of someone lost
in the strangeness of the night
Singing of some far gone place and an ancient plot

Feed me — Feed me more
before I die — before I join the worms
As I lay entwined in thoughts and
tiny swimming sperm.
Kerry Boettcher

Snow On Christmas Morning

I looked out on christmas morning
And saw a wonderful sight
Rooftops, gardens, and pathways all covered in white
I bounced and yelled hooray Paul
Lets go out and snowball
Throwing snowballs is such fun
Hiding, ducking and having to run
We built a snowman round and fat
And on its head we put a hat
We rolled in the snow
Until our cheeks did glow
The snow was frosty and so cold
But we didn't come in when we were told
We made a sleigh and started sleighing
And not until dinner did we stop playing.
Joyce McKendry

"Sunrise," "Sunset"

When I awake in the morning,
and see the light in my room,
what a lovely pleasant feeling,
as if to dispel all gloom.

I walk across to the window,
gaze eastward, and watch you move,
to where I can see your reflection,
as you slowly move out of your groove.

Your movement; so slow and tenacious,
as you saunter across the sky,
the warmth from your glow, touching my face,
such a lucky person am I.

Then; in the pale of the evening,
you slowly sink in the west,
first the yellow, the orange, then the deep red,
this is what I like best.

The artists dream in the making,
an exquisite scene, and yet,
the supreme joy of it all, I am sure you will agree,
is the lovely; beautiful; "Sunset."
Doreen Michael

The Perfect World

To awake in the morning and look outside
and see the perfect world will fill you with pride
To see the grass so green and flowers at their bloom
To see the sky so blue and your sun filled room

Then when you step outside there's people all around
They greet you and smile, their heads never to the ground
To see adults so friendly and adults so caring
To see children full of love and children that are sharing

As you walk up the street left open are the doors
Inside are teenagers helping parents with their chores
To see families so happy and not a row or a fight
To see doors left open is a very pleasant sight

Then when evening arrives the streets are so calm
Everyone in bed and no one causing harm
To see peace all around and the stars up above
To see a perfect world is a world full of love.
Jill Brown

From The Cradle To The Grave

I once had a son who sparkled with love
and shone with a glow that came from above.

I once had a son who possessed the power
to bring out the sun in the midst of a shower.

Now that son has gone, and with him my love,
nothing but darkness falls from above.

Now my world is empty, the sky's never blue,
My life has no meaning, my son, without you!
Anne Le-Britton

New Life

When orchards blossom in early spring
And so with it new life begins
Pink flowers will bloom and fruit
Young saplings make healthy root
Daffodils will stand so bold
They've survived the winters cold
The willow turns a shade of green
Young lovers talk of their dreams
Hours of light takes on the dark
The land is waking with new heart
Life is growing on land and sea
I'm so happy you're next to me
The morning sun that shines so clear
Telling us all, summer is near
Babies from the pram will walk
And many more will start to talk
Life is growing at a rapid pace
Can't you just see it, in the face.
David B. Black

" The Other Side of the Mirror "

What life of man's contrivance does use 'my' eyes with which to see
and stares with glazed-emotion into my soul, so cryptically?
How can such a warm and mortal vision so coldly mimic me
with every smile and frown and teardrop, reflect impassively?
The whole-world turns within a mirror and through it destiny
Look beyond its misty-lustre and read life's book, in POETRY!
Barry Howard

Forgotten Skies

When the sun no longer shines
And stars have fallen from your eyes
It's come the time, when you must turn
and leave it all behind.

If the dancing wind turns colder
Or the trees turn grey and bare,
You can only turn back and remember
What used to be there.

If the laughter of every day
Shrivels up and dies.
Brings a shadow over sunshine
with dull, forgotten skies;

Then it's time to seek new pastures
Where life is fresh and bright.
Until those dull forgotten skies
Have vanished out of sight.
Kathleen Knecht

" Yester-Year "

I remember Bath-night when I was small
And the Big Zinc Bath that hung on a wall
The "Set-Pot" or boiler provided the heat,
For lots of hot water for friday night's treat

In front of the fire, with its flickering flame
The Bath would be placed like the start of a game
And filled with a ladle, a pan, or a pot
With just enough water to not waste a lot

We undressed ready and waited our turn
On the rug by the fire, and watched the coal burn,
In its warmth and its light the room seemed to glow,
And the hiss of the gas-light that burned soft and low.

The soap was "White Windsor," or a hard yellow block
And sometimes "Carbolic" that smelled quite a lot
A towel has hung on a "maiden" nearby
Then being scrubbed pink, we were ready to dry

So dressed in our "nighties" and ready once more
We left the warm room for the wood staircase door
A cold icy blast would come down the stairs
Then by our Brass-Bed we knelt for our Prayers.
Beatrice Ford

The Coming Of Spring

What joy, when the winter days are o'er
And the birds commence to sing,
What is it? That comes knocking at your door,
Why the coming of spring,
Are not all eager to indulge in the
Thought of what the approaching time will bring
When the song of the lark which forever cares nought,
Will come with the coming of spring.

Ada Melville

Glad Or Sad

I can hear the silent whispers of the leaves,
and the darkness of their shadows makes them
seem like they are waving to me.

I can hear the sweet music of the birds
and the gentle flutter of their wings makes
it seem like I am in paradise.

I can see the small buds of the flowers
slowly awakening to the sunlight of the
morning, and it makes it seem so beautiful.

I can smell the freshness of the air
around me, and it makes me appreciate the
countryside and be glad that I am British.

I can feel the frustration of others
which makes them hurt and steal and riot
in our streets. I can't feel proud of them.

It makes me sad that I am British!

Heather Hill

Greed Destroys, There Are No Winners In War, Only Awful Memories

Call me when it's over
   And the daylight comes around,
I'm sleeping through the torment
   How I hate the guns sound.

My house cannot protect me
   The soldiers have broken through,
Some of the village people
   Running without shoes.

Streets with littered, broken human beings
   Death and dying lay about
Too late to withdraw, when lives have ended
   All this for greed, the old woman shouts!

Call me when it's over
   And the daylight comes around,
I'm sleeping through the torment
   How I hate the guns sound.

Now that it is over
   and the daylight has come around
Sleeping is a nightmare,
   For I still can hear the guns sound

Carol Trevett

Untitled

As I recall those first few words
And the smile as you spoke to me,
I often wondered how it would be
If we had never met,
Perhaps there would be no sunny days
No starry nights casting long,
No one to care what the future brought
Or be there if things went wrong,
All the things I remember,
But the one thing I'll never forget,
That love in your eyes
That captured my heart
The glorious day that we met.

Donita Lois Guile

In The Days Of Sail

When your ship reached up to Africa, along the tropic zone,
And the old Atlantic madness dropped to a heavy swell —
And the gulls came out to meet you —
A whispering breeze, from a million trees,
Brought a prehistoric smell;
For a league away, above Freetown Bay — lay rotting Sierra Leone.

In those days in time so distant, when they really sailed the seas,
And steamships hadn't ventured into ports which had no coal,
The white man's grave — they called it,
And the skippers of the clippers, dropped their anchors at the bar,
Dreading pestilence and heat,
And rank water and foul meat —
And malaria — which felled you to your knees.

The port's one street was bare of folk, in the hot hours of the day —
They were lying in the shadows — for the sun was overhead
And a shelter from its burning, common need,
Then at six o'clock about — almost sudden as a shout —
The dusk fell as a blanket, as sol dived the deep Atlantic,
And silence succumbed to the jungle drums,
Sounding distant through the trees.

Harrydan Howard

Peace

The land is silent now,
And the planes lie dormant in their hangars,
Weary from their long and endless journey.
The old air shelters stand empty,
Empty, yet full of memories of laughing children who knew no fear,
And the faces of the old who lost everything and gained nothing.
No guns sound now,
Only the beating of broken hearts
And the whisper of words afraid to be spoken.
The bombs fall no more, just the tears from saddened eyes
that have seen the terror and hatred, scarring their minds forever.
The sirens sound the end of an era,
And the sun up high casts its shadows on the debris of life,
While the rain tries fruitlessly to wash away the pain and the suffering.
The rainbow above shines on through the day
Spelling out its message of peace.
The war is over, but in our hearts it lives on.

Lynne Groves

The Swing

Oh! I am so lonely when winter is here
And the snow is on the ground
Only the wind blows me to and fro'
There is not a child to be seen around

But when the summer sun is out
And flowers blooming are to be found
There are laughing Children jumping about
Sending me to and fro'
And I am not lonely now

If only it was summer all the time
And the weather always fine
The children would keep me swaying to and fro'
And I would never be lonely anymore

Iris A. Davidson

Sweet Memories

All our yesterdays
are so vivid, it takes
time to organize and remember things as they were.
Especially the happy days with the children
in those days to see the happy faces of children
enjoying themselves, it's quite the pecton to see
their faces, time marches on, those were happy days
then, the days were long, but one was never lonely
there was so much to think of in those days
that lonely was a thing of the past, so I sit and
I dream of those happy days, and everything is just as it was.

Florence Hawes

Sea Music

There's a swishing and a shushing and a hushing from the sea,
And the waves are foaming palely while the gulls are flying free.
I hear trebles on the pebbles, I hear singing from the sand,
With the shingle drumming softly like a military band.

There's a splashing and a lapping and a tapping on the shore,
As the shells are humming mutely with the muffled ocean's roar.
I hear breakers, music makers, I hear shifting rolling stones,
As a spirit winging leeward stirs my antiquated bones.

There's a surging and a sifting and a drifting 'neath the swell,
While the skies are dark'ning swiftly to the danger warning bell.
I hear thunder up and under, I hear rumblings t'ward the strand,
And thick purple pulsing channels blight my tightly knuckled hand.

There's a lashing and a crashing and a flashing in the sky,
Now the clouds are gath'ring closely while the sea-birds shoreward fly
I see lightning stark and fright'ning, I see raindrops on the beach.
And the dimpled patterned grains slip slowly out of reach.

Soon the pounding and the pelting and the belting storm throes cease,
And the dark is graying slowly and the mist is bringing peace.
I hear noises, I hear voices, I hear choirs o'er the waves,
And old shanties drifting sadly from a million watery graves.

Bryan Borgeat

Uncle Wyn's Paintbox

White is the colour of a blossom at spring,
And the winter's moon in the winter's sky,
Maybe a lamb which has just learn't to run,
Or a shower of snow on Christmas eve.

Black is the colour of a spider leg,
And the bleak reflection on city walls at night,
Maybe the colour which flows round the planets,
Or the colour of the deck of the darkest ship.

Orange is the colour of the sun in the sky,
And the daffodils that have just had birth,
Maybe the colour of a lantern at night,
Or a planet looking far away.

Blue is the colour of the sky when it's clear,
And the bell of a plant that grows in the wild,
Maybe the colour of the roughest ocean,
Or the gentle look in someone's eye.

Red is the colour of rubies that glisten,
And the sky on a warm summer night,
Maybe a rose lying in a flower bed,
Or the colour of the purest heart.

Kevin John Parry

Antonio

He dived deep down below the waves
And there he sees the thing he craves
A large seashell on the ocean's floor
Surfaces, takes breath until he can no more,
And dives deep down through the ocean's spray
Hands outstretched to catch his prey
Grasps it hard, surfaces without delay
How wonderful the treasures of the deep
He knows that it's something he will always keep
His toil was hard, for it he longed
Once in the seabed's vastness
Now to Antonio belonged.

But when he saw her waiting there
Again he wanted his love to declare
So his most precious gift he gave
To the girl he would give his life to save
She smiled and wondered at the prize
And at the love light in his eyes
And clasped it to her breast.

Daphne Pierce

The Price Of Freedom

When will people realize that freedom isn't free?
And there will always be 'The Casualty'.
There are some funds from assorted sources who will help
Injured Forces. Funds which weren't available before.
You can ask the old Gent who lives next door.

Sad to say, today. Greed has taken over where pride used to be.
I hear you say 'What right have you to say all this?'
Being married to someone in the Armed forces.
For too often we have had that 'Parting Kiss',
Whilst wondering if he will come home the same as this.

Every night he is home is a bonus.
Every moment a gem.
You tell me, how can you put a price on them?

I knew a casualty of war.
The truth to tell, He really should have died.
Like so many from 'The First World War' he had his last rights and more.
He suffered each day he lived with no grumble of the agonizing pain.
Though 'one look' at his gentle face and it was plain —
THE PRICE OF FREEDOM.

Jane Ayer

The Clouds

I lie and daydream in the grassy lea
and watch the clouds drift by
shapes take form, they seem to be
like royal chariots in the sky

The Cirrus soft and touched with gold
to flocks of sheep they change
straggling home to reach the fold
across the heavenly range

Soon they melt and float away
to make but yet another scene
teams of stallions, white and gray
gallop where the flocks had been

A sudden change of coming gray
The nimbus clouds appear.
Blotting out the sun's last ray
the sky now dark and drear

The blacker clouds spread over
and with the first few drops of rain
my reverie breaks, I run for cover
and wait for the magic clouds again

Olive Woodhouse

The Crying Stops

I see my son contented and loved,
And weep for those who cry and cry,
Nobody comes to cuddle and rock,
The crying stops! The child is spoiled.

A room full of cots. Babies with AIDS.
I turn away. Distressed! Distressed!
A woman dying, babe by her side,
Forget! Forget! Put out of mind.

Where do you begin to put it right?
Greed seeps in its blackness crawling.
I want to give, but to those who need,
So far away, what can I do?

Children unwanted, neglected, left,
The system's there to care for these.
Headline news, official inquiry,
The system failed, a child is dead!

What can be done, is sometimes hindered,
Red tape, rules and regulations.
Sight is lost of the important thing,
We must look after our children.

Dianne Elizabeth Whitley

Landscape With Tower

Thin branches scribbled algebras equate
and unify bole, cloud, soil, foetus leaves.
Meshed sun conducts its luminous debate
flecks sodden grass. A flash dark alternate

catches still rain. The cooling tower relieves
itself of sullen vapours, flares its sleeves
tapering concrete, firm and temperate
the spare geometry that mind achieves.

Cock pheasant minces bright beside the wall,
head swivelled lightly, golden-oiled and sleek,
The beck, replete, to river swirls and speeds,
bustles at stones and flattens water weeds,
impatient past the wood, as though to seek
some last equation that resolves it all.

Andrew Hunter

" When Time Began "

Was there e'er a time when time was not?
And were there dreams so long forgot?
And did the sun shine in glory...
And was there truth in heaven's story?
And did the opening clouds reveal
A grandeur fantasized as real?
Or is within itself a dream,
All humanized to make it seem
That grasping hands can shake a star
And bring it near from very far?
Then will our eyes see future's plan
And break the seal of history's span
To realize that 'now' is 'then,'
And 'always was' will be again...?
So... time's own meaning has no end
Where dreams and stars will surely blend
Into a void no deeper than
The one we dreamed when time began.....

Ken Allen

The Bird House

We built a house, so small you see
And yet so large, my aviary.

A simple base, branches to roof,
Amid a tree, and not aloof
From nature and the natural things,
The blackbirds song, the beat of wings.

The food and drink the birds find there,
In their pleasure we do share.
We watch them as they come and go,
Unrestricted, friend and foe.

At home they seem part of the scheme,
Shrubs, bushes, flowers and trees,
Blending in accessories.

I think of Eden long gone by,
And free one day I know I'll fly.

John Vincent Michael Heach

Attitude

Attitudes to this and that
Are often faulty I'm sure you'll agree;
It helps to angle all you see —
Look at the view from every side,
Reason plays a vital role
In understanding of the soul
Don't bully, bruise or crush each other
In an attempt to prove your point,
Don't be too sure of your opponent —
There's more to him than meets the eye ....
Never underestimate the potential of this other Guy.
Is it your ego you over-rate ....
Then heed this warning before it's too late ....

Dorothy Williams

The Mighty Spurs At The Lane

Kick off lies with Man United,
Andy Cole falls flat on his head.
Chris Armstrong's astonishing run,
Speeds down the wing like the bullet of a gun.
He knocks it on to Ruel Fox,
Who crosses peacefully and deadly into the box.
Behind Dean Austin comes Andy Cole,
Who very unwisely heads into his own goal.
The mighty, "Hotspurs," once again,
Go one-nil up at the Lane.
The Tottenham fans stand up and cheer,
While the men from Old Trafford sit down in fear.
The director of football at the Lane,
Swears they will never lose again.
All the whites stand proud and tense,
kept away from the players by a large steel fence.
The Ref. blows for full time,
And United fans shout, "Just about time!"
The fields of white in the Tottenham stall,
All stand and cheer as Fox gets the match ball.

Garry Manley

A New Life

In my belly, a brand new life
Another creation by man and wife.
From a tiny flutter, to a good hard kick.
So you feel quite tired and a tiny bit sick.

Who cares you're fat, it's all worthwhile.
To hold your baby and see her smile.
Through teary eyes, we look at each other.
Hello baby, I'm your mother.

We'll make a promise to give you the best
But just for now, we need a rest.
I close my eyes and hope it's not a dream,
Then remember my stitches and want to scream.

The emotional rush is oh too much,
I hold out my hand for you to touch.
Not just a parent, but your best friend
Someone on whom you can always depend.

Christine Stephenson

Daydreams

I glance through the window and float away far into the clouds
Another world surrounds me now away from madding crowds
A thousand thoughts whirl through my head as I drift far away
Don't stop me now as my mind's set free to wander and to play.

What's it like to be a bird flying high and free?
And if I were a flower would people admire me?
A butterfly with colours true, a beauty to behold
Is beside me in my secret world, out here there is no cold.
The sun is warm, the breeze is soft as it whispers past my face
I'm flying in a new free world far from the earthly pace.

Slowly falling back to earth my secret world is gone
But all those gentle daydreams, in my mind will linger on.

Barbara Casey

Mistresses

"It's in my genes!" I heard him say,
As he walked in late from work one day
Admitting he had had an affair,
And seeming like he did not care.

Well I cared, and I screamed and gave a shout,
And I packed his bag and I chucked him out.
He'd married me 'till death do us part
But death seemed far away, so he found himself a tart.

What gives him the right to stray away?
He took away that option on our wedding day.
Marriage is for life, a commitment to each other,
Not to man and wife and his mistress and his lover.

Clare Barton

When The Dead Wake Up

When the dead wake up there'll be no hiding place
Apocalypse upon us the end of the human race

They'll outnumber us by tens against the one
How many years before the whole sad episode is done?

Fight for survival keep them out if you can
In the end it will be pointless, goodbye to man

No sleep, no pain, no needs, no fears...
The whole of mankind awash in a sea of tears

Imagine a world populated only by the dead
The last living creature bid goodnight and put to bed

No fishing, no walking, no going down the pub
No more social gathering, the dead form their own club

No good days, no bad days, no more long weekends
No more summer holidays and following new trends

Say goodbye to the people, say goodbye to the human race
No one left alive at all upon this earthly face.

Gary Newson

The Cuckoo's Song

I woke up to the cuckoo's song one tulip,
    April morning
And list'nd enraptured, lest his song should
    vanish without warning.

On hearing his perennial tune, I knew that
    daffodils would bloom
And all the merry sounds of May would promise
    soon a summer's day.

And what sheer beauty in this certainty
That fills glad hearts in you and me.

We know each year the grass will grow;
That we can reap just as we sow;
That summertime will follow spring
And bring fresh joy to everything.
That summer seas will bid us 'come'
To dapple toes in morning sun —
And fields of ripening harvests bear
The joyous truth: that God is there.

Hannah Yates

Confusion

As I went up, I was going down.
As I walked straight, I was going round.
As I searched, I could not find.
As I was nasty, I was kind.
As I went in, I was coming out.
As I was sure, I had a doubt!

Katie Hickman

Earth Song

I know a place where bluebirds dance,
And sweet wild primrose grows.
Where the scent of heather fills the air,
Where the fierce and wild wind blows.

It's heaven sitting there alone
With nature as your friend.
Just watching sparkling streams flow by
To where the waters bend

Listening to sweet natures song
And the rhythms of the breeze.
The chime of distant chapel bells
And the humming of the bees

They say that heavens up above
For sure, some day we'll know.
But I'm content believing
That heaven's here below.

Letizia Alfieri

" Snowflakes "

Our friends we know,...from times before,
are here yet again,...to visit once more,
Inevitable...in drawing our stare,
we accept the memories, we know they will bear.
They swirl and they dance in silent chaos,
...like children they follow...fearful
of loss. Reaching the ground, they are at
one with their Kin, close and secure, and settled therein.
Deserving care, and gentle thought...
walking through, we crush...should we
ought! We look all around, with
magnetic gaze,...and breath in times
gone through shimmering haze.

Our eyes again...do close up tight,
failing to cope, with reflection so bright.
Then... finally when, there's dark and
no light,... we look down and hope
they survive the cold night

Alan Lockwood

On The Line

Where are you now, if only I knew
Are you thinking of me or somebody new
Do you think of the times when we laughed and we cried
Tell me, my darling, our love hasn't died
When all alone in your room at night
Who do you think of to make you feel right
Would it be me with my heart on the floor
Or a stranger in lust who'd make you want more
Who would you be with and who would you throw
Please tell me your answer 'cause this I must know
My loyalty is always I want nothing to change
So why do you insist on acting so strange
Make your decision and make it fast
Shall we call it a day or make this thing last
Clearer the picture I need it to be
So just say the word so that I can see
If you're not too genuine just let me know
My case will be packed and off I will go
If on the other hand you want me around
Pick my heart up off this cold lonely ground.

Daniel Moynihan

From Dawn To Dusk

From dawn to dusk I think of thee,
As from a leaf you create a tree,
You have changed like to love within me.

You have created a bush from a single rose,
Have opened wide the door I had closed,
And everything dead, in your heart still grows.

You give me the strength when I am so weak,
Somehow glorify each word that I speak,
Throw sunshine on my world that was bleak.

You are the sun and the rainbow too,
That always manages to shine through,
And put right the wrong that I do.

In your heart there is no despair,
Only the love that you want to share,
And in your soul the words "I care."

Helen Christine Sheldrake

A Father's Love

Here I sit all alone chewing on my chicken bone,
As I gaze upon the wall I often think I had it all,
With pictures here and pictures there, my little
Children are everywhere,
As I wonder what went wrong, for my children I'll be strong,
For my children I love so much, once a week our
Hearts will touch.

Alan Hudson

Pussy Cat

Pussy cat, pussy cat, as you lie there,
Are you thinking what to do and where.
Are you dreaming of chasing mice or rats.
Or dreaming of snugging with little she cats.

As you lie sleeping, I sit and watch you,
You fill me with interest, through and through
Some of your antics, as you lie and dream,
Favour the pussy cat who swallowed the cream.

Then suddenly your fangs are on full show
You're springing on some hapless rat, I know.
Then just as suddenly, you stretch out,
With a pleased little wiggle, of your snout.

Mission accomplished, your expression doth say,
I leave the rest, for another day,
So go on dreaming my pussy cat, and then,
When night falls, you can start the hunt again.

Lily Needham

Catastrophe

Arthur was a tom cat, Arthur was a creep
Arthur spent the daylight curled up fast asleep

Arthur in the moonlight made a frightful din
Till an irate neighbour put him in the bin

Arthur didn't like it so he called up to his mates
Who all came out together and bawled from every gate

The noise was so appalling it set off fire alarms
And started dogs a-barking from all the nearby farms

Then police from all directions came rushing to the scene
With all their sirens blaring, the noise was quite obscene

And there was poor old Arthur still locked up in the bin
But on his scheming crafty face there was an awful grin

Until his irate missus came screaming to a halt
"You stupid moonstruck numbskull, it's your blooming fault"

Anne Stuart

Peace Not Fear

Love can be constant,
As constant as time.
Peace should be growing,
And showing, in the faces that shine.
People are living in fear and hate,
If only they would stop, and wait,
To look around at the poverty and waste,
And use up their energy, to make the
world a better place...
There would be no more hate, and no more fear,
But lots of happiness without pain or tears

Heather Louise Kay

Beauty Bleak

A bleak wilderness of rocks and stones
As far as the eye can see,
Miles of vast space where horse and sheep graze,
Where the wind blows free howling with no grace,

Legends of bronze and iron age
Lost forests on granite did grow
Now only the winding waters flow,

To walk and explore forgotten tracks
Tramped by pilgrims long ago
On trodden carpets of mosses and peat
That fuelled the fires of time
And preserve any relics left behind,

A yellow blaze of glory when the gorse comes into flower,
The picture of natural beauty can be seen from afar
Then the smothering mist swallows up the land
As like the dark cloak of night
They sometimes walk hand in hand.

Andrea Axworthy

Runaway

Into a different world he stepped,
As from the coach he leapt.
The boy that day had travelled miles,
Unaware of coming trials.

London's streets were hard and hot,
Full of drunks, dirt and rot,
As on the streets he begged,
A cup of tea, a slice of bread.

Sex and drugs were part of the scene,
Life was harder than it had ever been.
Food was scarce and had to last.
Sleeping in bed, a thing of the past.

If only he could ring his Mother,
(She always got him out of bother).
But his Father beat him hard,
Threw him out, his life scarred.

Help arrived in a nick of time,
The charity man treated him fine,
Into care, a home was found,
Where he could grow, safe and sound.

Jean Everest

Goodbye My Friend

I sit watching these hard won seconds
As holding your limp passive hand
I know that life is in the slowing phase
Seeking its exit from this earthly land

I think of the words we have spoken
Of belief in God who is true;
The hopes and dreams sadly broken
And how it will be, missing you.

If you must leave us alone with our tears
Then with much love, now go on your way
Freed from indignity pain and your fears
Slipping away peacefully as you pray.

"Where are you now?" I do ponder
As 'twixt life and death you reside.
There's a look on your face full of wonder
That speaks of much struggle defied.

My friend, what an honour to know you,
To be here and meandering a while
With one who has fought the last battle
And departs from this place with a smile.

Gerry Savage

The Countryside

The countryside is a pleasant place
And trees are gently swaying in the breeze
The fields are gaily decked with flowers
And children play around for hours

The lambs are frisking in the fields
Where a stream gently ripples along
The church bells merrily ringing
And all the people are singing

There's an old country pub
Where the people go for a drink
With a park and swings near by
And the children are playing happily

The cows and horses are grazing
And the farmers are ploughing the fields
Some are busy sowing their wheat
And people are talking in the street

The little friendly village shop
Stands on the village green
The village hall where people meet
And the little school in the street

Doris Robey

Bittersweet Lovejoy

Bittersweet lovejoy streams down my cheeks
As I count and lament the number of weeks
That it has been since I last laid eyes on you
Held you or touched you
Burning tears
And reddened eyes, thank God that it has not been years
Because each day seems like one without you
And so they would seem a lifetime without you
Love, true love, my love could never die
That is why I sit here and cry
While I wait on you, wait on you to return
The tears in my eyes do burn
As I yearn
For your return
As I anticipate
And cannot wait
The day I will see you and hold you in my arms again
Again, and again
But till then, bittersweet lovejoy will stream down my cheeks.

Egya Appiah

The Doctor's Waiting Room

The doctor's waiting room was crowded with patients of all kinds
As I sat there, I'm sure the same thoughts were in our minds
The silence was oppressive as we sat staring into space
Wishing we were well away in a much more pleasant place.

Suddenly the door opened and a woman came rushing in
Sat on the only vacant chair, looking around with an infectious grin
Then started to chat to her neighbour who answered in likely vein
While the rest of us listened eagerly, forgetting our aches and pains.

Gradually she brought us all into the lively conversation
Soon we were laughing and joking without any reservation
I don't think we will meet again, just like strangers in the night
But for that short period, our meeting had brought delight.

The time passed so quickly, soon it was my turn to go through
To get my blood test, so sadly I bade my new friends, adieu
Especially to that woman who had cast away our gloom
That never-to-be-forgotten day, in the doctor's waiting room.

Jane Osborne Clachrie

Eclipse

The lightning strikes above your home,
as I sing to the moon,
St. Catherines Hill is lit by thee,
the light of Luna's love but soon,
she disappears in shadow of the earth,
herself part of the mother's breath,
the mist of secrets kept;
until we meet on you hill,
above the heath cliff.

Douglas T. Newman

Life

Life is like a motorway
And our bodies are the cars
Our souls are the drivers
keeping us on the road
The journey we do take as life
Differs for everyone
The journey may start well and smooth
But bumps we soon shall meet
The journey may be long and hard
But we shall succeed
We fight the hardships
And win the wars
And goodness shall prevail
And when we've reached our destiny
We step out from our cars
Doctors come and tow them away
And our souls unchained and free
Happiness we will receive for eternity.

Leanne Pennick

The End

Every day feels like a million years
as I sit in silence in the bastille;
no sounds, no movements do I hear
except the beating of a drum
taking prisoners to their execution.
I dread the day when it will be me
walking next to the drum beat.
I fear the sights that I see
watching friends die by the guillotine:
Soon it will be my turn to die;
I will see friends who used to be.
Who can I turn to in my hour of need?
Only God I see.

Joy Norman

Easter Parade

Can it be Easter again
As I stand close by my window pane
Has winter's cold and icy blast
Gone at last
Will those sweet birds come back to me
That flew to warm lands across the sea
Glad to rest
And build their nest
In my heart I feel such a thrill
To see my first daffodil
Then come to a stop
To see my first snowdrop
I will be sending my warm regards
To friends with their Easter cards
Things to be made
For a happy Easter Parade

Iris Heale

October Gave, October Took

October 1963 a cold and bitter day, you cradled me you little girl
    as in your arms I lay.
My head was resting gently upon your warming palm, I was
    so very tiny but you kept me safe from harm.
With tenderness you raised me, you taught me right from wrong.
You chased away my nightmares; I lay in your sleeping song.
Stories you have told us my memories hold dear. "Tell us a
    story Daddy" is all you seemed to hear.
You guided and protected me, stepped back and let me grow,
into the mould you set for me so very long ago.
You taught me 'RICH' was family, friends, love and laughter,
    to give, to care, to comfort for now and ever after.
You listened with your wisdom, you talked with such concern,
Older I grew, so did you and then it was my turn,
to comfort and to hold your hand to chase away your fears
to be strong in case you heard us and to save my aching tears.
18 days so bravely fought so as not to let us down, you didn't
    want to leave us, you tried to stay around.
But you cannot fight forever, it was time to say goodbye,
you stepped into a peaceful sleep; we came unto your side.
A love so strong and comforting mere death can never part,
for you'll always be beside me in my memories and my heart.
October gave, October took you in heaven with my twin.
It's now her turn, soon she will learn, you're the best dad
    there's ever been.

Jenny Birchall

Untitled

Lace upon white is what she wore
    As she appeared through the innocent door
Sweetness is possessed from her very core
    Now, then, and before
From her soul did kindness pour
    She, the most beautiful to adore
Being in her presence, you may hear the oceans roar
    The serenity of time would breeze through
    her hair as though she had wings and soon to soar
The happiness of deep within is what she bore
She is what I wish to be, and more.

Jacqueline Tavis

Untitled

I sat and stared at the turbulent sea
As it drifted onto the sand
My mind was filled with wonder
At the power of that unseen hand
Was there a message there for me
In the sound of those oncoming waves
I am just a nonentity
Yet for me this life He gave
The waves turned around and rolled forward
To teach another shore
They were obeying a heavenly command
To which I listened no more
I have been given these ears to hear
These eyes and this voice to use
Why oh why had it taken the sea
To tell me that I should not refuse
To listen, and obey when He speaks
And know that He's in command
He will be there when I need Him
And He will take hold of my hand.
Helen Knott

View From The Tor

On sunlit days the clear views draw the breath,
as miles around sweet Devon's mantle spreads.
Textured, patchwork fields,
and sparkling rivers thread
their babbling paths towards the open sea.

High in the cloudless skies,
a throatsome lark song drifts.
The untrained eye quite blind to a ghostly songster.
Yet his winsome song permeates the golden air.

As evening shadows creep,
Nibbling silently at each straw filled field.
Soft mists drift as haloes round the tors.
Natures necklaces, girding the throats
of granite outcrops, sleeping dragons.
Cynthia Byrnes

Sleep

Fast fell the eventide,
As mist crept through the darkened air,
And captured every shadow's side
With heavy slumber, not a care.

Then slept the woods in dark debris
Awaiting the morn to waken once more,
Sleek shadows of tall timber trees
Stand still, subdued, a darkened door.

Flowers, heads hanging beneath the clouds,
Sleep silently upon the grassy green ground,
Dreaming of sunshine to lift their heads proud,
But on realization, is darkness all around.
Jean Bennett

1990's

Tensions through these muscles
    and these membranes.

Pressures through these thoughts
    and these minds.

Affliction in our times, these lives
    this world, our words.

Heartbeats through our sinews
    bleeding on the screens.

Conflicts in our minds, on our streets
    powerful men sleep at night.

Societies build a lie, each man by himself
    and woman too, alone.

Selfish blindness we have all embraced
    binding ourselves within the lie.
Claire Dobson

Stepping Out

Stiletto, low or medium, well heeled or even down;
As one before the other, they stroll around the town.
They're laced, zipped up or buttoned, or maybe highly strung;
With soft and easy brogues, or long and silver tongue.

Seductive straps are courted, unless the toes are square;
And many rounded toppers will peep without a care.
While climbing, running, walking or learning how to dance;
Their lovely styles and colours will flatter and enhance.

In plastic, suede and leather, in canvas, cloth or hide;
And "Once Upon A Time" in glass, a prince put on his bride.
Some people step into them quick, and then wish they had not;
For corns and nails ingrowing, are vesicant and hot.

The beauty of the wearing is helped by "horns" and "trees";
With buffing cloths and brushes, all working hard to please.
So find the pace for comfort, the choice is up to you;
It's down to earth, yet versatile, the sole of fun "The Shoe."
Joy M. Bartlett

Letting Go

My love for you was as deep as the ocean,
As powerful as the sunset, as infinite as the sky.
You were like a magic potion,
The cure for my sickness, without you I would die.
But then you left me, weak and alone,
Crying and useless, I was on my own.
I contemplated suicide, you unhinged my mind.
Although you had left me, our souls were still intertwined.
Then I improved, my heart grew stronger.
I thought of you rarely, I wept for you no longer.
Now you walk in my door and back into my life.
You say that you've changed but I have also.
You cut me deeper than if with a knife,
But I loved you, I grieved for you, then I let you go.
Elizabeth O'Hara

Country Walk

Today he fell in love with nature
As she took him in her sweetest arms
And nuzzled away those terror years.

Not so, as a child some glorious summer dream
But a bubbling brook that let loose some grumbling sounds
And empty walks that led to nowhere else but truth.

Oh! To escape that damp and squalid flavour.

Yet here, under each gloss and glitz of grass, there is a
    deeper shaft of joy,
That sweeps ten thousand off their feet and slips a ring
    upon his lonely finger.

It's here that God flies above to herald his intent,
For fleeting moments one holds to his existence
As a drowning peace to a blade of grass.
Clare Whitehead

Betrayal

The days and nights are cold and meek
as I sit here awaiting the love I seek.
The wind is whistling above my head
as I lie here waiting in my bed.
As I lie here wondering why he left
determined and shaken by an unpleasant
guest. He'd never admit that he'd spoken
with her, as it was brought up it caused a stir.
His baby is here crying he's farther
he awaited in his cradle he wonders
why mummy and daddy aren't by his side.
One day he'll find out the mistakes
he made. I often hear his
voice from afar, Danniella, he called
her the Witch Dunbar.
Joyce Johnson-Conley

A New Beginning

Time to start afresh and begin anew,
as the sunlight glistens on the early morning dew.
Remove all traces of bloodshed and war,
endorse a new treaty of Mother Nature's law.
A future of joy and hope, not sorrow and pain,
within our hearts we can begin again.
Remembering love before dawn and of children still unborn.
The rich and fullness of the heart,
The world as one never to be torn apart.
The hopes and dreams of a perfect place,
Not of hate or an empty space.
Freedom for all mankind, leave troublesome times far behind.
Bloodshed forgotten, let us all live as one.
All races united, endless peace has begun.
  Helen F. Gate

Lost At Sea

The grey clouds scurry across the sky,
As the tide of love rises and falls,
Cruelly the north wind sweeps across the mainland,
Bearing promises of the storm ahead,
And I am lost.

The waves of pain wash over me.
As the current boils into a fury.
The unsuspecting swimmer ventures into waters
Which are no longer serene,
And I recognize myself.

Slowly engulfed by the raging surf,
I feel myself captured, helpless,
In the callous current of love,
And the waters break viciously against the rocks,
Leaving the naive
Bruised,
Battered,
Drowned.
My body and mind in Harmony — at sea.
  Gail MacDonald

Inner Peace

Inner Peace comes with the flush of sunrise
The kiss of early morning dew
The fragrance of herbs as evening falls,
and the glow of the Moon when it's new

Inner Peace comes with Church Bells in the morning
The hoot of an owl at night
The wind moving through the trees,
a flock of geese in flight

Inner Peace comes with an open fire
whilst rain lashes against the panes
Cows quietly dozing in an ancient byre,
or weaving through country lanes

Inner Peace is in the soul
There to be found and cherished
Inner Peace is in us all,
if we can but keep it nourished.
  Amanda Wheler

What Is A Memory?

It's remembering the good times,
As well as the bad,
All the happy times,
As well as the sad.
It's growing up from young to old,
With different stories yet to be told,
To reminisce your childhood days,
The friends you had,
The games you played,
To find a love to have and to hold,
To join as one, as memories unfold,
A family to love, the pleasures to gain,
And yes, the memories still remain.
  Beverley Richard

When You Have Not Got The Guts To Say How You Feel Send A Note Like This And Your Dreams May Become Real....

I looked in your eyes and I remember hoping you felt the same
As the world suddenly brightened when into my life you came
I think of you in the morning, I think of you last thing at night
I can only dream and wonder what it feels like to hold you tight

I feel as if I've known you all of my life and more
When you're by my side I know I love you, of that I am 100% sure
I want to hold your hand and always be by your side
The day I did not tell you the truth I felt my heart rip open as if it knew I lied

I regret a thousand times the words I never had a chance to say
I hurt all over when I think of the love I could give every night, every day
I want to scream and shout exactly what I feel for you
Because I deeply, truly love you and I think you feel the same way too

Please give me a chance to show you the real me
There's a whole world to discover for us to taste and see
Take my hand and let me show you the meaning of love
Because when you and I met, I'm sure someone was smiling above
  Julie Keogh

The Reason Why

A father's smile, a mothers look of love and great relief,
As they gaze at their little girl in awe and disbelief,
While hands are held and bonds are forged a tear runs from their eyes,
For what's the real reason, and what's the real why.

See will grow like all the rest and play and laugh and cry
Not knowing of the real truth and the real reason why,
Early years come and go, like ripples on a lake,
Oblivious of the present path and the road that she must take.

Childhood years diminish and maturity it brings,
Her thoughts have change from toys and dolls to wedding bells and rings,
But now another card is dealt from life's uncertain deck,
She plays her hand the best she can, but fate still wins the bet.

The wedding day is in the past and motherhood is here,
She looks a mother's loving look, then wipes away a tear,
For with a somewhat heavy heart she knows the reason why,
Her little girl like all of us is simply born to die.
  George A. Griffiths

The Circle Of Life

A father's smile, a mother's of love and great relief
As they gaze down on their little girl in awe and disbelief.
As hands are held and bonds are forged, a tear runs from their eyes.
For what's the real reason and why's the real why.

She will grow like all the others, and play and laugh and cry,
No knowing the real truth and the reason why.
Early years come and go, while education's pumped through every pore.
Oblivious of the road that she must take,

Play and abandonment diminish and adulthood it brings,
With thoughts of responsible behaviour and of wedding bells and rings
Now another card is dealt from life's stacked deck,
She plays her hand the best she can, yet fate still wins the bet.

Finally fulfilment and motherhood arrives.
And she gazes at her own daughter and she looks deep into her eyes,
And with a somewhat heavy heart, she now knows,
The real reason why the circle of life
Revolves so fast, we are born to simply die.
  David Harrison

No More Proverbs, Please!

If life's a bowl of cherries,
As they state in certain homes,
Pray tell young pup why I end up
Holding all the stones?

One stitch in time could save us nine,
As taught by those who know.
That may well be, but don't tell me,
I never learned to sew.

Is life really what we make it,
As suggested by some chap?
For if that's true, I'm telling you,
I've made a pile of crap.

Does every dog have its day,
As once read on a sign?
I must confess I'm in a mess,
Perhaps I slept through mine.

Such proverbs leave me empty,
At least for now desist.
From where I stand, a bird in hand
Leaves nought but muck on the wrist!
Andrew J. Kenyon-Smith

Perpetual Motion

The moon watches over earth
As it moves slowly along
Hanging in orbit
A satellite in outer space
Distinguished in elevation, in revolution
In its element of gravitation
Sending light that does not burn
Splendour as it circles in the empyrean
Stands out among the rest
A planet, a million miles away, yet looks so near.

Its distance men have achieved
Walked its surface
In awe of what they find
A heavenly body of a different kind
Its dust unique, unparalleled.

Lovers gazed to see its beauty
As they embraced, transfixed to see the power of light
Night becomes day by this satellite
Its environ encompasses us all
Leaving us all enthralled.
John W. Follett

Children Of A Summer's Dream

Eyes that open with a gleam
Are children of a summer's dream
Upon a gentle breeze then lie
Adrift beneath the summer's sky

In children thoughts like fairies seem
Damsel flies on a gentle stream
Dreaming under the summer sky
And afternoon in warm july

In innocent eyes of wonder seen
Are daisy chains in fields of green
With buttercups and daffodils
And baby birds with open bills

As birds sing all your fears to cease
In natures silent song of peace
Like moving pictures in the sky
A flock of clouds go floating by

With smiles that gleam like a warm sunbeam
The earthly angels that they seem
Are children of a summer dream
John Eaves

Fight For Our Earth

We fight for our rights,
As women, as blacks, as handicapped.
Why should we struggle are we not life,
born to be free to live as we like.

The poor fight for more,
refugees fleeing, want an open door,
Some people want land,
Nobody helps no one lends a hand.

We don't want our children fighting like us,
let's join together let's have some trust.
Will this ever be or is it a dream,
destined to be shattered by blood lust and greed.

Bitter tears they should fall,
for the waste of it all,
All of this fighting could all have some worth,
if we all fought together to save our earth.
Jennifer Rigby

Obsession

When the lights go out and no-one sees who you are
and obsession becomes nothing
in the velvet dark there is only a soul
that thinks and breathes and loves
and makes beautiful noise
because obsession is gone
and sight is gone
and all you are is you
and the life inside
that is only yours
and never shows
in light.
Because the world becomes obsessed
with the vision you make or the way you smile
or blink
and if the world was one midnight place
it would see so much more
see everything invisible
through this bright mask of obsession
or light.
Carrie-Ann Rhodes

Earth Spirit

The earth's soul cries out in pain
As we thoughtlessly dig quarries
Leaving scars on her body and pain in
    her heart.

Humans have souls, so why shouldn't the earth.
The earth is alive — a living planet.
We must stop killing her,
destroying her trees
polluting her seas
choking her to death.

The earth spirit loves us all
But it can't help us unless we help ourselves
We must unite to save her with love
Because love is the ultimate goal.
Claire Cameron

Racism

If you judge me by the colour of my skin,
You'll never get to know the beauty within,
You really don't seem to understand,
That this isn't just you own land,
I have a right to live here too,
So stop all the cruel things, you say and do,
If only we all learned how to show
That being at peace is better than war,
I would not have to cry myself to sleep every night,
Wishing that I could be pure and white.
I could be proud of who I am,
And we could all be together, living hand in hand.
Pamela K. Ware

Untitled

You walked into my darkness
And brought with you light

Now you are gone, darkness is mine

Together we were light
Apart we are free to shine strong and bright

Whilst, out of my darkness, you still are my light

D. F. McLaughlin

Untitled

Whatever you choose to excuse what you've done
you've to live with yourself — be deluded by none
as you run from yourself bet you never surmised
that you'd envy the victim whose death you devised.

Tho' a friend may sustain you as long as he's there
Maybe share in the guilt you no longer can bear
When he's gone you will find as the torment begins
there's a price to be paid by your mind for your sins

For remorse is the punishment you've to endure
as you try to escape from it — prove there's no cure
or you may in your grief utilize every breath
crying out for relief for your very own death

Ostracized from society thus you remain
once you've branded yourself with the dread
'mark of Cain'

S. Kelly

Older, But Wiser

Age no longer holds such fear for me,
Youth with all its fun, I did not see.
Happiness I have learned comes in time,
Honest earned.
Patience, I have found the key
is understanding, liking me.

T. Moy

For You... Jane...

You're my Sunshine on a Stormy Day
You're my star that shines so Bright
You're my wind and rain, my Snowflake
You light up all my life
At night you are the Sandman
Who comforts me to Sleep
As day breaks through my Curtains
You awake me from the Deep.
If Daytime could be longer
Although not long enough
And all the stars up in the Sky
Could shine both Day and Night
I wish that I could give You
My Dreams to all come True
You're worth your weight in Gold
So precious to me... that's You.

D. J. Wild

Ode To A Joyrider

Are you a joyrider who seeks a thrill,
You steal someone's car with a risk to kill.
Spoil someone's life, and get one last thrill,
All this for a chance to test your skill.
You see the blue light, a voice shouts stop,
You must keep on going you know it's a cop.
Step on the gas there's a road block ahead,
Just a few more seconds and bang you're dead,
Remember the people you called Mam and Dad,
They wait for the child that they once had,
They don't know you lie on a mortuary slab
Cause of death certified by a hospital lab.
Your soul hovers above you caught in a spell
Which way is it going is it heaven or hell??

Sylvia Sanders

Chains On My Soul

You dog my heels like a black cloud on a sunny day.
Your unwanted presence makes me shiver like
a rat before a snake.
My body quivers at the thought of the inevitable
For, one day I will be the unwilling guest at your table.

To forget you is to forget what tomorrow may bring.
I search within and without
Yet you evade me like that shadow of mine.
Fear grips my heart like a steel vice.
For I know not when you cometh for me.

You appear in my dreams,
To hear the frenzied beats of my pulsating heart.
To smell the sweat of my fear.
To mock me with your tasteless humour.

If I could talk to you
I would ask when it is.
I would beg that our paths never collide.
For I know not what lies beyond.

Toheeb Dosunmu

The Pike

I watch you with unblinking eye
Your silver beauty flashing by
You turn and speed into the light
To catch a fly that fell in flight

Gracefully, you take your meal and glide back down
And glide back down like
Polished steel

You flick your tail without a care
And do not see
Me lying there

Your beauty still enthrals my eye,
But I must eat
And you must die.

Suzanne Perris

" ASK "

Ask, says the word of God, then ask indeed.
Your prayer may be but falteringly expressed
Ill-framed, perhaps ill-timed, and your request
May not be for the very thing you need.

Yet persevere — it is the vital link
With him who knows your being through and through
And all your inmost need, with power to do
Far above all that you can ask or think.

And never, though your faith be tried, forget
His love for you, so great, so plain to see
Throughout that lowly path to Calvary.
Ask, and your need will certainly be met.

D. Downey

The Love I Lost

My love was like a never ending stream
Your love was like a bright and shining star,
My friends all thought I was lost in a dream
But you are still with me, I know you are.

We spent our time together, having fun
Those hours we spent I thought that they would last,
Your love will shine on like the brightest sun
I'll not forget you and the love that's passed.

I knew that one day I would lose your smile
The life that lay ahead you could not take,
But now you rest, you've walked the golden mile
At one time I was sure my heart would break.

I will keep a place in my heart for you,
You'll be missed forever, by all you knew.

Rebecca Mainstone

Thoughts

I shall think about the good times,
Your laughter and your smile.
Then at our shattered lives,
How could it turn so vile.
And when I turn around you'll not be there.

I shall think about your face,
And the colour of your hair.
You could have been more honest,
You could have been more fair,
And when I turn around you'll not be there.

I shall think about the arguments,
The storms that brought the rain,
Of all the things that happened,
The joys and all the pain.
And when I turn around you'll not be there.

I shall look back in the future,
Not in anger nor in tears,
But with a kind of sadness,
For all the wasted years.
Because in my heart I know that you were never there.

Roz Parker

Words

You said you loved me very much,
Your heart tingled at my touch.
If only I would be your wife
You would look after me for life. WORDS

For me you'd buy a lovely home,
Work your fingers to the bone.
Of this you never would tire,
To give me all that I desire. WORDS

I spend my life in a tower block,
With three children for my flock.
By day you say you have to think
And at night you need a drink. WORDS

When off you go to draw the dole
I look and ask, "Where is your soul?"
You could sweep the road or drive a lorry.
Then when I'm sad, you say you're "sorry". WORDS

Even though I love you still
I've just about had my fill.
Next time round I'll find a man
Whose actions speak louder than WORDS.

Sylana

Cindy Doll

Beautiful lady, dressed in blue,
Your golden mane compliments you.
Steel grey eyes piercing out;
Succulent lips, when you pout.

A button nose adorns your face;
Each item in its perfect place.
A graceful neck with no slack,
Superb body with flawless back.

Your arms were sculptured by a mason;
Your soul, I know, you have kept chasten.
Slim fingers that could charm a saint;
A visage every artist would paint.

Your legs so firm and, oh, so long;
Not a thing about you could be wrong.
Your feet so cute, with beauteous toes.
I look at you and my heart glows.

The whole of you is just ideal;
Please tell me that you are real.
I wish I could share with you this joy,
But, alas, you're just a Cindy doll toy.

Paul Cook

Your England, My England

Bad vibes... passed tuts and sighs.
Your England's green, full of high hopes,
mine is grey with low self esteem.

Conscious of hostility festering around,
aimed at the mixture of guises;
drowning in phobia in the western frontier,
sickened by window reflection.

Envy the freedom angels possess
the joy, arrogance, laughter;
Shield intact against verbal cannons
not one of the sheep in the line.

Soul in sombre stasis, veto approved
enduring, the constant private talks;
judged and packaged before I arrive,
eaten up by pity inside.

Boxed in animal, identity interned,
anxiety lingers in cold pseudo-concern;
Stuck in stoical swaggering behind callous
transparent doors and yet the stardust in
the veins is the same as runs through yours.

Nathan McGuire

Grandmother

Oh Grandmother dear are you watching me
Are you guiding me through my life
Were you there that day to witness me
Take the vows that made me a wife

Oh Grandmother dear were you with me
On the day that my daughter was born
Did you see how perfectly formed she was
As they lifted her out of my womb

Oh Grandmother dear are you out there
Can you see inside my heart
Will you always be near when I need you
To show me where to start

Oh Grandmother dear I implore you
Keep loving me now as I grow
Guide me through a happy life
When I falter show me the road

Oh Grandmother dear are you listening
Do you hear my thoughts and see
That I wish I could be near you
As you are always near me.

Carole Anne Thomson

The Shoemender's Dream

What will people do when the petrol runs dry.
And cars are stacked as high as the sky.

With weeds growing up through the motorway road.
And the train breaking down with the weight of the load

Sure there'll be some for emergency use
But certainly none for total abuse

We striped nature bare, to create this invention
And all drove around with the best intention

One in a car in the traffic jam
With the bus standing by saying here I am

Neighbours don't talk, they seem so remote
And all dash around in a steel overcoat

Fumes from the back burst the ozone bubble
Scientists say this can only mean trouble

But I know a man who's jumping with glee
It's the shoemender saying, "There's a future for me".

Brian Ponder

A Deathly Habit

In discos and pubs, in dance halls and clubs
Young people go out seeking fun,
They drink and they eat, and dance to the beat
Of guitar, and cymbal, and drum.

You young girls and boys adore all this noise,
But one thing you don't understand,
As you dance and you sway, you are gullible prey
To substances which have been banned.

For certain young thugs will be there "pushing" drugs,
And tell you they give you a thrill,
They charge such a lot for a tablet or "shot",
But don't say these substances kill.

You'll rarely find "pushers" addicted to drugs,
They know it is very unhealthy,
But they do know, of course, you're a wonderful source
Enabling them all to get wealthy.

So don't be absurd, there is one little word
You MUST use, and be ready to show
These evil young thugs that you won't buy their drugs,
And tell them, Emphatically, NO!!!

A. E. Lyes

Walking

Walk along a country lane,
You'd be surprised at what you'd gain,
Just about how much you'd see,
And happier you would ever be.

Under the hedgerows, deep in the vine,
Hunting for morsels, that they may find
Field mice dodging here and there,
To feed their families, fair and square.

Across the field, the rabbits run,
Weaving about, just for fun,
They always are a joy to see,
For all and sundry, not just me.

The skylark, on the wing so high,
Singing sweetly, and, by and by,
She swoops right down to find her nest,
To feed her young and take a rest.

Enjoy your walk, take great care,
For you never know what may be there.
What could be better, fresh air too,
Look in at nature, it's so good for you.

D. Cook

I Am

Listen to the wind sighing through the trees,
You will hear my voice carried soft upon the breeze.
When the playful wind caresses your cheek,
be sure to listen, for you will hear me speak.
Turn and greet the wind with a smiling face
for it is only me and my fond embrace.
Lift up your face to the gentle rain
and I will help to wash away your pain.

Look out at the sparkling, dancing sea and quietly think of me.
I am every wavelet gently lapping, I am every lazy swell,
Listen, you will hear me softly murmur, be at peace for all is well.
I am the soft and gentle hush before dawn is shrilly spoken.
Watch for the cheeky robin, the gentle wren, because for you
they are my token

I am of the earth and of the sky,
I am every rook and seagull's cry
I am every colour in all the Autumn leaves
I am close beside you when silently you grieve.
I am in soft scented woods and the salty sea breeze
Remember,...... I am each and every one of these!

Sadie Freeman

MUM AND DAD

You were there for me when I was born, the day I came about
You were there for me when times got rough and you would
bail me out
You were there for me when as a child I cut myself or fell
You were there for me when I got sick or wasn't feeling well
You were there for me to guide me through those difficult
teenage years
You were there for me to mend my heart and overcome my tears
You were there for me whatever time, be it night or day
You were there for me to help me on when I went wrong
in any kind of way
You were there for me when I felt down and often feeling sad
Thanks for all you've done for me, my loving Mum and Dad

Dedicated to Joan and Sid
Pièrre Raymond

To A Mouse Badly Caught In A Trap

Poor wee mouse with stricken eye,
And heaving heart by terror bound,
Did I but know the way to cry,
With tears I'd bathe thy fearsome wound.

More fearsome sight I ne'er have seen
Than this which here confronts me now,
Of thee with stark perplexity
Arraigned with pain upon thy brow.

And in this pain 'tis plainly writ,
The sum of man's iniquity,
That he could such vile deed inflict
On tender morsel such as thee.

Yes, you're gone you poor wee thing,
No more I'll ever see thee out,
And still thee to thy supper cling — thy last,
DECEITFUL LAID, I shout.

George S. C. Davis

Rescuing Goannas

There are some goannas in my back yard,
And they wriggle about and play,
I'm sure that you will laugh a lot
When I tell you what happened today.
They were playing in the lower part
of the yard, near my back door —
And then it rained, and rained and rained,
'Till it could rain no more.
Oh! what a pool, where the ground was low
And what to do, I did not know.
For goannas can't swim —
And it sure did show.
So I opened up some sardine tins
To strap upon their feet
So they could water-ski to land
Just to see it was a treat.
It really was a funny sight
I'm sure that you agree,
And I'm so glad the sardine tins
Didn't have to fit on me!

Kaylea Fallon

Power Of Love

Oh power of love, oh power of love
You came to me as a beautiful dove
You made me as happy as man could be
When we met, my dear, by the pale blue sea
But now you are back in heaven, my love
Passing back to all that wonderful love
We can all now receive your love from above
That power of love you shower on us
From heaven above, but soon my love
I will join you there then will I do
My heavenly share that power of love
That power of love you send from heaven above

A. R. Knight

Together

You feel the need to care
You want to be able to share
Feeling lost and lonely
Surely that one and only is out there
Then one day you stand and stare
You meet that person stood right there
Your heart feels warm
Your mind is torn
And you know that you've been reborn
A new feeling grows around you
A life for living and giving
Has found you
A fulfilment of love and joy
Surrounds you in this life that binds you
There's laughter and tears throughout the years
You create a life
And as a family you are right
You grow old and grey but together you play
You've lived your life until today
And that's the way it will always stay

Rebecca R. Close

Memory Lane

The sunlight on your hair so soft, sweet laughter in your eyes,
You stood upon the hillside, beneath the bluest skies!
I hear your voice — a tinkling sound, you gently call my name.
I turn around — you wave to me.
I'm back in memory lane.
That song we hummed together upon the golden sands,
Our love was young and beautiful, and gaily we held hands.
When winter came I see you yet, in snow and wind and rain,
Running laughing — hair a'flying.
I'm back in memory lane.
The sun's gone down, it's darker now, so homeward we are bound,
A glowing fire, a cosy room — nought sweeter could be found.
I see your face in sweet repose.
Beside the firelight's flame — sweet contentment always.
I'm back in memory lane.
We shared so many lovely things, each one I still recall,
The quiet and the sad times, but the laughter most of all.
I turn the music on now, such a haunting sweet refrain,
I feel the tears upon my cheek,
As I walk from Memory Lane.

Veronica Gibney

Remembrance

I walk with you in silence for you have left this earth
You smiled so bravely through your pain
Oh that we could have shared more years, but this was not to be
For I had left your English shores, Welsh mountains and countryside
I travelled west to find a life away from war-torn years.

I walk with you in silence on England's Western shores
The great Orme reaching upwards, the narrow country lanes,
The roads we walked together refreshing in the rain
I walk with you in silence, but death shall not deter
The love for you within my heart, though you have left this earth.

E. Wilkinson

Autumn

Autumn leaves begin to fall,
You see red, yellow, brown
As they all flutter down.
Coating the ground beneath your feet
They crackle in a steady beat,
Someone's walking by.
When the beat fades away
There's silence in the wood.
Until the sound of falling leaves
Rustling to the floor,
Proves that autumn's really here,
Knocking on winter's door.

Susan Hall

Valentine

You never sent a Valentine,
You never sent me flowers,
You never complimented me on my domestic powers.
But every day for thirty-five years you made my morning tea,
You helped with kids and broken nights,
You shared all chores with me;
Confided thoughts and doubts and hopes,
As husband, helper, friend,
So through the years, the message was, love I could comprehend.
You never sent a Valentine,
Remembered special days,
But every day you showed you cared in very special ways.
You never sent a Valentine,
And sometimes I got mad.
But what's a piece of cardboard compared to what we had?

M. Martin

Getting Older!

As the years go by
You may stop and ask why?
Why do people think life slows down,
Or stops as you get older
After all your age is just a number
When people say
"You can't turn back the hands of time"
They are wrong
If you keep memories of special times in your heart
You will always feel young and alive!

Sarah Skinner

Cease Fire

Steal away into the darkness of the day
You masked men with miner-like eyes
Appearing through gaping holes,
As does the blood from your victim's wounds.

Cemeteries bear testimony to your deeds
As the seed you sow is fruitless
And a pall of anguish etched in grieving eyes
Mirrors a legacy of misguided ideologies.

Lay aside your arms I implore thee
As a writer of verse addressing that which is perverse
The tongue and pen are mighty weapons too,
No sword or gun has ever silenced these.

Our fires must burn with coal
Wrestled from the earth by sweat and ingenuity
And our wars ought to be fought across tables
Crafted like the peaceful words of Jesus the carpenter.

Like a burning passion I am engulfed by the flame
Of love for all that lives on planet earth
That the reader is fuelled and consumed by this — the bright light
Is why the poet digs deep — and deeper still.

Tom McGrath

I Loved You When I Saw You

I loved you when I saw you
Your face as pure as pearl,
The raven hair upon your head
Dark midnight's wing unfurled.
I loved your eyes, as wells of laughter deep and bright,
Your face and smile, kind as the summer light:
I loved you, love, I loved you, loved you all,
Yet best of all I loved your lovely soul.

Now time has passed and we have both grown old
And left all hopes and dreams far in the past.
So much, where we raged hot, we stand so cold,
So much we yearned for first that fails at last.
And only ghosts and shadows now remain to scorn
That beauty by your haggard face once worn.
Yet evermore I love you, love you more,
forevermore I love your lovely soul.

Richard Osborne

Carrying

We walked side by side
You looked to me for my hand,
I was waiting for your request,
A moment meant so much
That cannot be compared.

On one walk you went for miles,
But I was ready to carry you home,
With arms outstretched and pointing upwards,
For me to collect;
I gently cradled you.

You rested comfortably in my embrace
You were no burden,
I still carried you,
The ache in my arms
Confirming the love I have for you.

Pausing briefly to kneel and rest
Your singing softly in my ear,
Made me smile of your request,
You will only be an infant for a short while,
I knew — so I carried you.
Steven Clark

Lonely

Being lonely makes you feel old and bitter.
You long for love and friendship to
make you feel alive and needed,
to make your life feel full and
bright, and keep the darkness from your soul.
Lying alone in bed and listening to
your tears, your heart empty and aching.
Close your eyes and dream of a
better life, a life of love to fill
your life of meaning and hope.
But wake up screaming and crying.
WHAT'S THE POINT! WHAT'S THE BLOODY POINT!
What's the point of being alive and
alone, thinking of ways to end it all.
But realizing there maybe someone
out there who needs my love and friendship.
There is some hope left in you.
P. Rippingale

The Lottery

I thought I'd buy a card that itches
You know, the ones that you scratch
You have to get three sevens in a line
I can't get mine to match

I'll try the other kind then now
I've got two thousands and two ones
I only need another one of either
It's two tens, that's it done

All that's left now is the lottery
I can't wait for eight o'clock
I haven't got even one number
I might as well take a walk
Margaret C. Rae

Why

There's millions of people in this world
yet some are still alone,
Every where you look there are buildings
but still people are without a home.

There's food on every grocery store shelf
yet still starving people die,
There's so much money in this world
but so many poor people, why!

Why does every body suffer
and through their lives have so much pain,
After all nobody asked to come here
although it's said we'll come again.
D. Goodall

My Love For You And Copperas Hill

Though your love for me has withered,
You know I love you still,
But I know you will return my love,
Once more to Copperas Hill.

To be with you once more my love,
Then sit and reminisce,
Of things we did in days gone by,
Then seal it with a kiss.

I hope you will return my love,
To Copperas Hill once more,
Where I picked for you the primrose,
And the sea shells from the shore,

Your love I know has ebbed for me,
Just like the Solway Tide,
Where from my boat I fished my love,
And you fished by my side.

But although it's ebbed and ebbed,
I will wait for you until
You return to me once more my love,
Where we first met on Copperas Hill.
F. Burns

A Wedding Toast

Health, wealth and happiness to you both evermore.
You have found the key, so now open that door,
To the future you both have forever to share.
To the love and affection for you always to care.
Behind that door, you'll find waiting there
All the good things in life, things so rare.....
As faith, trust and honesty and love reigns supreme,
I do hope together life will remain one long dream.
To live together in peace and harmony forever and a day.
To always have each other on your long way.
The journey is hard and could be quite tough.
But together, I know your love will be more than enough!
Marlyne A. Millen

My Mum... My Best Friend

You have always been there from the day I was born
You have always been there from dusk until dawn,
You are always there to kiss goodnight
You are always there to hold me tight,
Whenever I am down you pick me up
Give me a smile and one of your looks,
You are always there to hold my hand,
To pull me through and to understand,
You see the sun when I see the rain
You help through the tears and you help through the pain,
You've given your all in the years that have passed
As I haven't been perfect, it's been shown in the past,
I could be much further than a million miles
But I would always see your loving smile.
Nicola Dolby

Someone Awaits!

You have a lot to eat and drink.
You have a lot to use and spend.
Look, someone near you is needy and hungry.
Give him your crumbs, it will be a feast for him.

You have a lot to make you smart and warm.
You have a lot to make you attractive.
Look, someone on the street is cold, shabby in rags.
Give him a few of your clothes, you will have made his day.

You have a lot of friends and company.
You have a lot of free time, spent in nice places.
Look, someone not far from you is sick in hospital, lonely in prison,
has no one to talk to.
Your word of "Hello there" will be a Queen's visit to him.

To be a friend in need is to be a friend indeed.
Richard Mark Ssajjabbi

Betrayal

Seductively, with venomous snipers eyes persisting,
You hand me a death-filled gift with cold fingers,
Your bloody smile strangling my mind.
Temptations accepted, I open it.

Pain. Sudden excruciating pain shrieking maniacal fury
Soars through my existence, an overpowering masterpiece of envy.
Panic smashes my ship-wrecked soul into shark-filled waters
of despair,
Terror now a prisoner, within.

Fading away, a cinder of your destruction,
I inhale the crisp, dry fumes of defeat.
Lethargy engulfs me, my mind beholds monotony, boredom,
Embracing futile belief.

But somewhere, in the pits of my logic,
The awakener has touched the light,
And hope transpires once more,
Through darkness.
Tahira Akram

To Lose Someone

How do you feel when you lose someone close to your heart,
You feel like the world is upside down and torn apart,
You don't understand and can't answer why?
That the one you love happened to die,

The pain and trauma that hits you hard,
When through the post arrives a sympathy card,
It brings everything to life and seems so real,
You just want to be left alone to know how you feel,

You feel sad and empty and something is missing,
You need someone there, someone listening,
You cry all night and let emotions flow,
It is not understandable why this world let them go,

You always want them back lying next to you,
But you have to accept that what has happened is true,
But you won't get them back and you must carry on,
And just remember that memories of them forever live long.
Sally-Ann McDuff

Well Dressings

You should visit Derbyshire in the summer season
You don't need an excuse, I'll give you a good reason
For many towns and villages take part
In a unique traditional folk art
Of dressing the wells with biblical scenes
In the high streets and on the village greens.

A framework is placed over the well
A designed board with a message to tell
The picture is drawn on the clay
And when it gets close to the day
It is filled in with Mother Nature's supply
Of petals, leaves, moss and berries, all found nearby

The effect is beautiful to behold
The picture and story it does unfold
And when the wells are finally dressed,
The local vicar sees they are blessed
In short it's a thank you for the springs
That provide us with water each well brings
Shirley Travis

Alone And Unwanted

He's gone from my life, he doesn't really care,
yet I still want him. But he isn't there.
I cried and cried such endless tears,
hoping that one day I'll have happy cheers.
Night after night I sit and weep,
when all my children are asleep.
Maybe tomorrow, I always say.
After all, tomorrow is another day.
Susan James

" The World Situations "

If you sit and think, in the dark, or the light,
you can think of the world and its pitiful plight.
What on earth can be done, so that peace may resume
instead of the hatred and darkness and gloom.
The answer is war some people may say,
to banish the darkness and brighten the way,
giving us hope for the future instead
of hearing of millions, homeless or dead.
Perhaps in the future, a great change will take place
and life will slow down to a much slower pace,
we may all be prosperous, or again we may not,
This isn't in our life, it's in the year dot, dot, dot.
R. T. Williams

The Telephone

It's a wonderful invention, the telephone.
You can speak to people from the comfort of home.
You need never be lonely. Pick up the receiver set,
And you can speak to someone you've never even met.
When I was young the world was really vast;
Now that conception is a thing of the past.
I can contact people miles over the sea
And listen to their voices speaking back to me.
There's birthdays, Christmas, yes almost everything.
Just lift the telephone and give them a ring.
There's certainly some snags when you're waiting a call,
Then the phone rings, it's not that person at all.
Friends and family whom you love very much
Just lift up the phone and keep in touch.
Though miles separate us over land and sea,
They are there at my side talking to me.
I'll put down the receiver in its cradle in the hall
And just sit in my chair and relive it all,
And always feel happy that all is well,
So here's to its inventor Alexander Bell.
A. Douglas Preston

Life's Lament

With his protection it is told,
You can find love and wealth untold;
And as we wonder of what to ask,
It could be better to ponder our task;
Temptation beguiles us to take the hay,
Do your worst, while you may.

I decided, this way looked best,
Who needs anyone to pass this test;
The path was easy, I gained much treasure,
But to my surprise it gave no pleasure;
So at last I gave it away,
S'late for salvation, T'late for sway.

Being no piker I'll not grumble,
When it's time for my earthly tumble;
This tale is about, you still have choice,
You can decide whether to roll the dice;
Myself, it's clear towards end of day,
All I can do, is pray.
T. L. Bonham

To My Sick Friend

You are better, dear friend, and there's joy in my heart
You can always tell when God's played his part.
I asked him to help you when all seemed in vain
He answered my prayer and eased all your pain
But now you are well, but not out of the wood.
Please do be careful, and try to be good,
Don't overdo things and think that you're strong.
For the way back to health may be uphill and long.
Be patient and tolerant and keep smiling through.
Say 'Thanks' be to God, and the rest
 Up to you!
A. Bentley

Love To Stevie

Myself and offspring all alone,
You came to us and made it home,
Though all of us were bruised and blue,
You stood by us, and saw us through,
Old spouse and kin had ruled the day,
That he would see you far away,
But you stood firm and showed to me,
That love would win, but nor would he,
And all his anger he had shown
To us, no longer! No more alone,
Now all our fears have gone away,
No longer will he rule the day,
And you my love will always be,
The offspring's father, and husband to me!
M. J. Chambers

The Love Song

I love you, my darling Angel
You are the sweetheart of all my heart.
Never let us be apart.
Although you were meant to be
My Valentine Sprite, you came a few days later,
In the dead of night,
Then smiling upon me
In the morning light.

You were the joy of my heart
From the start,
Your beautiful black eyes
So kindly and wise.
I will be happy for
The rest of my life
Through trouble and strife.

The old lady said nothing
Sitting by,
Shed a tear from her old eye,
As she heard the bombers
In the distant sky.
Zelia E. J. Barrett

True Love!

Your lips are red like fire,
You are my one desire,
Your body drives me crazy,
You make my mind go lazy,
I've seen too many things,
But it's you that makes my heart sing.
I see you in the morning light,
The emotions I get feel so right,
All I want to do is hold your body tight,
Each and every night.
You know just what to do,
While other girls haven't got a clue,
So I hope we can be man and wife,
For the rest of my natural life.
C. A. Smith

Too Late For The Sun

You were never as old as I am now,
Yet it was I had youth enough to spare.
My life touched yours for such a little while,
But time enough for love to spark and flare.
Now, my magician gone, enchantment fled
I have no silver wand that I can raise;
No miracle will bring your voice again,
No loved hand will soothe the weary days.
Sometimes an echo of the time passed by
Whispers to me and you are near once more.
Then I can smile and face the world anew -
Remember happy days long gone before.
Too late for the sun we enjoyed the moon.
I came too late, my love. You came too soon.
Natalie Thomas

Parting

We grew up together
You and I
And from a small pine tree
You have become a giant
Will you reach for the stars
After I am gone?
Your branches like angel wings
Move with such grace and majesty
I love to see you in full swing
Swaying in the wind; You are a sanctuary
A paradise for birds
Often have I dreamt of faraway places
Just gazing at you
Now is the time for us to part
And it breaks my heart
You have shared my joys and my sorrows
An evergreen solace
Throughout the seasons
Pulsating with life
You have been a friend
Marie Rachel

Nightmare

Something's pursuing me, my way to freedom, the hungry sea.
Y'on bridge, wood slats lashed with rope, offer me my only hope.
Scrambling o'er the slimy tracks, can't go on, I'm being pulled back.
Panic stricken I break free, mouth parched, heart thumping, swiftly I flee.
Hollow echoes, my feet pound, terror grips, I hear a sound.
Heavy footsteps to my rear, lungs gasp for breath, they're getting near.
Foot slips, onto the slats I crash, with outstretched hand, grabbing at lash.
The turgid torrent swirls around, my foot is caught, it drags me down.
Choking, retching, once more I rise, can't see clearly, brine scalds my eyes,
A ghostly figure in distance appears, my blood runs cold, the shadow nears.
'Tis my dearest father, long since died, beckoning me from t'other side.
Snarling waves engulfing me, clawing wildly, as the bridge tears free.
Futilely threshing despair rises anew. I try to scream, I cannot do.
Father's strong arms tight around me, slowly, we sink beneath the sea.
Down to Davy's locker of dread, as we're about to touch the bottom, I awake, I'm still in bed.
Patricia A. Mythen

Moorland Bounty

Strolling in a woody dell, or on a moorland hill,
You'll find more things to cheer the heart,
Nature's beauty to impart,
Your wildest dreams fulfil,
Pretty flowers of every kind,
Peace and quiet prevail.
A rippling brook, a shady nook,
Along the moorland trail.
Little nooks and crevices,
Their treasures to unfold,
Tiny buds, ferny frond,
Cheer you as you stroll along,
With wealth, worth more than gold,
Heathers, daisies, bluebells, rue,
Heads heavy with the morning dew,
Brighten paths, and woodlands green,
No finer sight was ever seen.
Or ever will, I know that's true.
On moorland hill, or woodlands stream,
Its beauty will shine through.
M. Hanson

Togetherness

You love each other and live as one,
yet without compromise, nothing can be done.
You bicker like children but think you're mature,
you have everything, but seem to want more.
The everyday relationship between woman and man,
hoping you can make it work like everyone else can.
Controlling the anger, living with the pain
because without each other, it wouldn't be the same.
Another aspect of life, a new lesson to learn,
love is one module, another corner to turn.
It may be hard and it may take time,
but every relationship has a bump, somewhere along the line.
So do not give up, without a good fight,
because the day will come when regret it you might.
You only get one chance and there's no turning back,
so put into your future what your past did lack.
Agree to differ but promise to forgive,
and a happy long life together you'll live.

Paula Gillingham

Life's Too Short

Life's too short to quarrel — this is what we say.
Yet we forget this saying — nearly every day.
We are so quick — with hurtful remarks to make,
Never willing to give an inch — demanding to take,

If only we could stop and think — before we speak,
If only we could find peace — and not trouble seek,
There would be an end to wars — no trouble round about,
Life would be so good — no one would shout.

The world would be a better place — for all of us to live,
We could stay together — each other help we'd give,
But this is just a dream — but we can play a part,
It always takes two people — for a quarrel to start.

K. J. Havard

A Wreck Of A Woman

Today I look upon the world to see what's in store for me,
Yet to day I'm filled with sadness,
So lonely, so desperate, so out of touch that's me,

No friends to go with-or some one to love,

My heart has forgotten the need to be wanted,
Since "He" the one I loved, left me for someone else,

Now I cry all the time, happiness has gone from my life,
That man I loved-woke me to find dawn,

A new day arisen-yet what do I see;
A wreck of a woman,
That person is me,

Rachel Smith

Alone

And now he is gone, no longer a part of my life.
Yes, he is here still
But, no longer shall I see the twinkle
In his eyes that was known only to us;
The unseen brush of his body against mine
When we were not just two;
No longer shall we laugh, at secret, childish jokes
Were it not for her, we would be one.
How I despise her,
She who took away my Greek God.
She who is like an invisible wall,
Forever separating us from what we want.
Why should time strengthen his feelings
For her and not me?
We had only seven days and nights;
they passed like the blink of an eye.
But they were good, they were heavenly.
Why can she not free her captive to me
And enmesh someone worthy of herself?
Not one who she keeps by female tricks.

Simone McEvoy-Morris

The War Widow

My weeping now is a silent thing
Wrung from my heart with tears of blood,
Would that the gun had killed me too
The gun that killed my love.
I turn my head and see my child,
Bonny, happy, unaware,
Too young to feel the loss of love
That fathers have for son and heir.
He too may cry his silent tears,
In later years — on parents day
When fathers play his team
And only mother's there — he will compare
And conjure up a father in his dreams.
Not killed I just wounded — such a wound!
There will be no repair,
This ache for him will be forever there.
What will the future bring?
How will I raise his son?
With God's help?
To this I must cling, and now — my learning must begin.

Victoria Haines

A New Day Begins

The air is filled with silence
Wrapped in shrouds of mist.
No sight, no sound escapes
As moisture forms in damp and dreary skies
And touches on the face of Mother Earth.
How still until the wind begins to stir
And, tantalizing, dances through the air
Until it gathers up and sweeps away
All signs of cold and murky grey.

High above the sun breaks through.
Shafts of brilliant sunlight creating patterns
With golden rays stretching down
To spread their warmth upon the grassy banks
And raise the heads of dainty flowers,
Their gentle fragrance pervading the air
Whilst humming bees on borage blue
Gather pollen from flower upon flower
Day long, arduous hour upon hour.

World awaking, morning breaking
Once more to a fine sunny day.

Margery Brazier

Somewhat Different!

You can't lay blame for the way you feel
You can't lay blame for the way you are
You've created and evolved into what you are
No other person has lasted this far!

You've begged, stolen and borrowed people
Stolen their views, their likes, their feelings
Begged and borrowed all of the meanings
Messed them all around and created you!

Influenced, impressed, involved, ignored
Every feeling has another counter-feeling
You're still moulding the sculpture of you
Understating, undermining, understanding!

Joy and happiness and sorrow, but never love
Just skating around the icing of life
Never looking too deeply into anything
You have a deep fear of what you may find!

The clock of life keeps ticking by
You sit and fret, and worry and analyze
Looking through your nostalgic glasses
Indecisive about where your future lies!

Roland Guy

A Week To Remember

Growing up time for him — just nineteen. She, three years older,
worldly wise. He, eager for adventure, she in control.

They took the boat train from Calais. Linked to the Gare de Lyon.
Silly chap missed the connection.

Followed in frustration, till he caught the "Blue Train.'
Just as it moved out of the station then she saw him — then
he found her, United again!

She cradled him for an hour... While they planned their next day.
Panic ceased — relief took over, Young love triumphant.

South to La Napoule — home of "La Mere Terrat", renowned fish
restaurant where diners listened to the guest violinist playing
music of the sea.

Meagre means — forced to budget, an anonymous B&B where they
found life heavenly in slovenly rooms,
Ate croissants, drank
comforting coffee on the beach.

Seven short days romance. Fantasy. Illusion.
She returned to her
deluded family. He to his own disillusion.
Was that IT?

Paul Lucas

Nineties Addiction

Still need your job, but you hate it,
work till the weekend, then your money's wasted,
go shopping. Can't wear the same as last week
new trousers, shirt and shoes for your feet.

You've searched this town, up and down,
looking for some wicked sounds,
dancing all night, is the feeling in your mind
adrenaline flowing. You're one of a kind.

Money's no object in the pubs, and at the nightspots,
music, girls and rhythm, now it's really getting hot.
Bills are forgotten, till the light of day,
don't care if they take your possessions away.

Money flows through your hands both day and night,
loud Hi-Fi's and CD's take over your life.
The music puts you in a world of your own,
you don't want it to end, you don't want to go home.
Lack of sleep, makes you angry and frustrated,
you tell your girlfriend, "It's work related".
Can't wait to cut the groove at the next party,
you're addicted to the fast lane of the nineties.

Peter D. Plant

Under The Sea

I love the thought of under the sea
with all the fishes swimming with me,
The coral grows more great each day,
Until one day it is washed away.
The sorrow grows all over the sea,
And splashing waves come all over me.

Sarah-Jane Connolly

Tear Of Sadness

Here you sit all alone
Wondering why you're on your own,
The baby you want has gone away
No one knows why it happens this way,
How it's made you sad and grey,
Now it's time to be happy and glad,
Because you have four beautiful lads,
They think you are the world's best Dad,
And never want to see you sad,
They make you laugh, they make you cry,
They never want to say good bye.

Tracey Baker

No Words Are Spoken

Silent is the voice not spoken,
Words whispered into vast openness,
Pray for contentment within a haunted soul
Heed not the temptation of sin,
cry freedom freedom yet there is no
forgiveness for EVIL.

Silent is the voice not spoken,
Into the emptiness of long ago.
And gone is the fear of yielding,
to the spirits of the past.
Carnage and despair cry in a
wilderness of empty souls.
Listen listen to words unspoken,
Of cherished memories long ago,
To war men went slain in anger,
Hate not of fellow man.
Silent words are spoken within
an emptiness of so long ago.

Thomas H. Preece

Christmas

Turkey, Christmas Pud and Mince Pies
Wonderment in the Children's eyes,
Santa Claus, Rudolph and his sledge
Icicles hanging from the hedge

A Holly Wreath hanging in the hall
A Snowman stands against the wall
Christmas presents under the tree
Some for all the family

Friendly visitor's glasses of Port
Their visits are welcomed however short
Merriment and laughter, Carol singers
mmm... the smell of Brandy sauce lingers

This is Christmas in every way
But also remember it's Christ's Birthday

C. A. Beardmore

Newborn Babies

Newborn babies, a brand new birth.
Wonderful creations that join this earth.
Giving pleasure to mum and dad
Never doing anything bad.
Giggling and burping when they are fed.
Sleeping content when laid in bed.
Dreaming of life that is to come.
Waking up then screaming for mum.
Washed and changed then being well fed.
Laid down again to rest their heads.
One last giggle and one last burp.
They sleep again who joined this earth.
Beautiful babies wonderful to hold.
Soft and cuddly so we are told.
Newborn babies, a brand new birth.
Wonderful creations that join this earth.

Richard Sylvan

Blessed Gifts

My children are everything to me
Without them I am nothing.
Should they cease to exist
So too would I stop living.
I gave them life from my body
Their bodies gave me a purpose to live.
They are a part of me - within me
I do not own them
They do not belong to me
And yet they are mine.
Mine to love, to care for.
Their dependence on me
Gives me a reason to live.
Without them I am nothing.

Toni Kemp

True Love

You to me are the very essence of life itself,
Without you I would cease to be.
You bring the sunshine into my life,
Without you my days are dark and dismal.
You banish the gloom and the grey skies
And light up my world like a rainbow on a dull day.
You are my best friend and reason for living,
And I wonder how I managed without you in my life.
You are always in my thoughts and dreams,
You share in my joys as well as my sadness
We share so much that I wonder how we manage to live apart.
To imagine a time without you is something
I care not to do, so I don't!
My love for you is so vast that I know it will last forever.
You are my FRIEND, my COMPANION, my LIFE and my LOVE,
For now and forever.
N. T. James

'Am I Awake'

In the night she comes
without word, with such calm
and stands by my bed in the moonlight.

Such white skin and soft curls.
So small yet so real
A vision of beauty dressed in white.

Am I awake or only dreaming.
Is she searching to be free,
for I know not this vision
that stands before me.

Only when I'm alone does she
Stand at my bedside
Alone in my thoughts of dreams that may be
Tell why does she come
For no words are spoken.
L. F. Regan

The Nobody

No one cared when the 'nobody' was born,
   Without love, no money, just hardship forlorn.
The same throughout life, as it was at school,
   No shoes, torn clothes, life's very own fool.

The years pass by, he's still just a flop
   Still at the bottom, no nearer the top.
The World has no time for people like him,
   Simply ignored, thrown out on a limb.

In Life no one cared, the same in Death,
   No one bothers when he draws his last breath.
There he lies — a penniless knave,
   Buried by the State in a pauper's grave.

Standing at the Gate, Saint Peter did stare
   "That's strange", he muttered, "There's nobody there.
Must be a fault in the Gateway Bell
   Or some lost soul on his way down to Hell."

This troubled Saint Peter, who gave it much thought,
   Then from Hell to Heaven the 'nobody' he brought,
Saying "Throughout life you missed on good things
   But here we're all equal, from 'Nobodys' to Kings.
Richard G. North

The Landscape Grey

I look across the landscape grey
With earth and trees all torn away
No more will children laugh and play
For war alas has passed this way

If you think all war a sin
Sometimes perhaps a political whim
When once it starts we hear the din
Let's prey the whole world won't join in.
Ramon Leeves

Homeless - Within A Home

Can I have a normal life,
without all this hassle and strife!
I would like to do some laundry,
hang it in the sun, blowing till it's dry,
To be able to look out my kitchen window,
while washing up, to see the birds.
To put newly laundered sheets on the bed,
and plump up pillowcase, but instead,
I have to fumble beneath plastic sheeting,
just to find a dry patch to sleep in.
Among the cardboard boxes, packed the last five years.
Are hundreds of my possessions, I can still see through my tears.
Money hungry developers, too rich to afford any morals,
come in with their bulldozers, tearing down birches and laurels,
fifteen, luxury riverside apartments,
just who's is this department.
My house, is on the riverside,
they cannot build, beside,
while I'm there, at the riverside,
unless, a closing order is made.
Saira Thompson-Scrivener

End Of The Line

Majestic she stands, polished and painted,
within two score years she'll lie idle and tainted.
To hell with King George and cries of Sir Harry,
this monarch before me will be rusting in Barry.
Today is yours, you wondrous creature,
you may even be preserved as a historical feature.
Heaped with coal the engines tender,
ammunition for the fireman ready to send her.
She knows the route well, every milepost and junction,
fresh from the works each part will function.
All seats are taken, some people must stand,
the guard blows his whistle, green flag in hand.
Grey white smoke belching from her funnel,
Engulfing the coaches as we enter Severn Tunnel.
Arriving in Cardiff somewhat a facade,
ten miles southwest is Woodhams scrapyard.
With welsh coal afire deep inside her belly,
she leaves in her wake Neath, Swansea and Kidwelly.
Fishguard Harbour beckons she's gathering speed,
the fireman works in unison to sate her need.
L. Hollier

I Give You

I give you the oceans in calm and storm,
   With waves that dance in the air;
I give you the showers and the winds
   And summer days, warm and fair.
I give you the rainbow that springs from the sun,
   The clouds that drift slowly by;
I give you the vision of anger and peace,
   With beauty to feed the mind's eye.

I give you the buzz of the insects,
   The drone of a plane overhead;
I give you a night beneath the stars,
   Another snuggled warm in a bed.
I give you the flowers, the bushes and trees,
   The birds and the beasts of the field;
I give you a crop of wishes and dreams
   With the pleasures each harvest will yield.

I give you a heart to fill up with love,
   The chance of a life free from cares;
All these things I gladly will give,
   If you will give Me your prayers.
May Park

Pigeon Lady

She limps, being awkward. Ten loaves are hard to carry
With the plastic bags so bulky, and a little ripped.
You cannot manage living quite so easily
When you're seventy-six, and rheumatics have you gripped
But once on the bench, the pigeons take her over,
Bounce landing on her head, her arms, her sloping lap.
Their feathers sighing round her ears are shielding her
From outrage. "Disgusting! Tell the Social! All that crap!"
She bows her head, and smiling, with her knotted bones,
Feeling on one finger the clutch of feet close-curled,
Struggles to break white Hosts for their Communion.
Later, after the cell door slams, birds, wings furled
Alight on the barred window's sill. Now vainly, for bread
Her hand fumbles. And wings whirr, beat-beating inside her head.

Rosemary Greenfield

The Elusive Picture

The Lochs, Rivers and Burns are all frozen over
With the life underneath all cocooned
Reflecting views of skies, trees and hills
With glitter and icicle patterns festooned.

The grasses and trees are all white dancers
Making beautiful scenes no one can capture
Because sometimes a glimpse of sun peeps through
The picture becomes transformed too
Changing the scene minute by minute
As bits of ice melt there are no limits.

No artist can catch a landscape so changing
For before his eyes, like a mirage fades
The scene becomes all kinds of shades
As shadow and light come and go
Sometimes fast, sometimes slow.

Before he can put a brush stroke in
It may have changed from bright to dim
So with our eyes and memories too
We must all treasure the beautiful scenes that we view.

C. Dennett

The Profound Dream

From the steps of my redoubt
   With questing gaze cast about
Seeking source of light and song
   Then I behold the celestial throng.
And with bounding joy then I see
   My dearly beloved approaching me
From their midst with ethereal grace
   Hastening to our trysting place
Encircled in her warm embrace
   A loving smile upon her face
One tender kiss, she then moves on
   Beyond the shores of Rubicon

Willie Aistrop

War

Dark was the sky on the thousand plane raid,
With planes full of brave men who were really afraid,
Their cargo so deadly, their targets obscure,
Destination, Hamburg, Cologne or the Ruhr,
The mission, full of dangers, crews would be lost,
Such a waste of young lives, but that was the cost.

The oceans, an enemy in their own right,
Came into the equation as a part of the fight,
The sailors from both sides all knew the score,
Of the two pronged attack of this bloody war.
Fighting the enemy as well as the waves,
Sent many young men to their watery graves.

War fought on land is the worst kind of all,
To stand there and watch as both friend and foe fall,
To be with your best friend as he breaks down and cries,
Or to kill another young man as you look into his eyes,
The death of a soldier in a field far away,
Just one of so many to die on that day.

Terry Jones

The Locket

I stood at the window one dull, cloudy day,
With nothing to do, watching children at play,
I turned and noticed an old jewelry box,
Picked it up slowly and opened the locks.
In a small dark corner, trying to hide,
I found an old locket with pictures inside,
The locket was gold, the engraving worn,
Parts of the pictures were tattered and torn.
They stared out at me, this girl and this boy,
The boy young and smiling, the girl rather coy,
My eyes misted ever, remembering with pride
Coming down the aisle with this young man at my side.
The locket, a birthday gift, many years ago,
From the boy in the photograph — time passes so!
Just then, a knock, a shout at the door
Brought me quickly back to the present once more.
Our children were here, with their children too,
I called to my husband — something to do!
I smiled to myself as I opened the locks
And returned the locket to my old jewelry box.

Virginia Beryl Ayre

The Times Of Past And Present

Times have been hard for you and I
With nothing to do but sit and cry
No food on the table for us to eat
Oh to give the kids a treat
Bread on tick at the corner shop
No shoes on the feet of our little lot
Covers to come from off our backs
To lay on the bed called anoraks

How time flies you can hear them say
Tomorrow will be a better day
No more tick from the corner shop
You have what you have or you have not
Now we have made it you and I
No more scrimping trying to buy
All the things that others have
At last the times are not so bad

Now you ask would I go back
To the days when covers were anoraks
I smile at you and softly say
I much prefer the better days.

Y. Taylor

With-Out You Dad

   Since you went away, my heart has broken in two, my cheeks are wet with teardrops, tears I cry for you. I know that I can't bring you back, for you are sleeping a deep sleep, but the pain I feel is so very real; I can't let you go, I never will.

   Your face was so lovely, your eyes were of pale blue, your smile was of an angel, an angel I always knew. Your nature was one of kindness, truthful and just; and in my times of trouble, although they were few I could always come to you and you would tell me what to do.

   It is so very hard to say goodbye to you, you've always been part of my life. You held me as a child, and gave me away as a bride. I was so very proud of you in your navy suit; and when your pale blue eyes met mine, this is when I knew I would always be a little girl, the one you loved so dear.

   In time you grew weak and fell very ill, and there was nothing anyone could do. I would sit with you and hold your frail pale hand and try to nurse you the best way I could. You died in my arms, my pain was so great. Also I gained, a great strength for I thought I had lost you, but this was not true, for I am not with-out you. You are very near in everything you taught me and the memories I hold so dear.

D. West

Memories Of A Childhood

I remember, walking in the snow
With my favourite best coat
Bright red, with velvet on the collar,
To keep me from the cold.
With beautiful fur mittens
To keep my hands warm.
The snow deep and crisp
That glowing feeling,
That makes you sleep.
To awake next day, to again go sliding down the hill

Building a man of snow,
Dressing him with eyes of coal,
A nose made of stick, a mouth made of leaves,
Only to find next day,
The sun had melted him away
And all that remains —
Is heaped in one great puddle
The sticks, the coal, the leaves,
Like so many things in life
They disappear, and just memories are left...
Mary Wright

Our Yesterdays

Our yesterdays are bygone days,
With memories bright and gay,
The treasures that's enshrined in them
Time gently fleets away.

We recollect,
And we reflect,
The pleasantness and joys.
We revel in those happy hours,
Those bygone days of yore.

Those reveries
How sweet they are?
If only we could bring them back,
Re-living all past joys.

But the future lies ahead of us,
And we should not look back.
Remember what befell Lot's wife!
Look forward, and not back.
Victor S. Barrett

London

Is London really paved with gold
With majestic buildings bright and bold?
Is London truly the place to be
From Kensington to Battersea?
With West End shows always on
Like Cats, Oliver and Miss Saigon.
Fast transport can be found
Through the London Underground.
Pigeons flock to Trafalgar Square
From Park Lane, Bond Street and Mayfair.
Tourist, worker and resident
Or even a visiting president
Will always find London to be
A place of versatility.
As its marvels, mysteries and wonders unfold
Yes — London's streets are paved with gold!!!
Sharon Housden

Epitaph, 20.11.1991

This morning a blue tit crashed into the balcony window.
Wildly flying,
Sudden dying,
Gently laid
In leaf-strewn shade.
I hear God's word
Encompassing
One small bird.
Mary Wilson

'Horace'

'Horace' is my little car
With lots of love, he'll take me far
Treat him right, and he'll respond
First time we met, I felt the bond.

He's such a lovely shade of blue
We'll never part, we'll stick like glue
I know he's not perfect - the odd spot of rust
But he'll do nicely - I'm not fussed.

How did we survive without one another
I'm like his sister, and he my brother
But, alas, one day, I'll have to say "bye"
To my horace, when he goes, to the scrapyard in the sky.
Marie Hinsley

Death On A Welsh Hillside

Against a blue and bannered sky
with joy we trod the heather down,
and searched among the rocky clefts.
for orchis and the cotton grass.

And near the wall, surprisingly,
we came upon a hastening stream
that coursed with clamour through the rocks
to join another further down.

And as it swept to turn about
the rough-clad hillside parted there
to make a hollow chamber; there
a lamb was held in silent world
caught in some tangle of the rocks.

Like some sweet symbol on a banner worked,
aloof and perfect prototype, it stayed
sheltered from winds, the only sound the urgent water;
imprisoned in the falling stream like fly in amber.
I stayed, a raucous child, to gaze
and death, in mild guise, took hold
and said "Behold".
P. D. Salmon

Fruiting Bodies

The dreaming flower blooms
With its iridescent light
that flows from within,
Revealing and reflecting the awe and wonder,
Unravelling its own energies
of discovery,
Channelling a pathway within and without,
Keeping rooted to Mother Earth
As the mind flows into the infinite beyond,
Creating as it does,
Constant, and witnessing changes,
Reflecting Heart, Soul, and metaphysical matter,
Seeking true Love
That is waiting in us
to bear eternal fruit
Direct from God through the Self
In the language of Nature and her Symbols
of divine communication
That always exists,
Emerging
Scott Seeley

Melpomene

A kindly lady firm but fair,
with comely looks and eyes that care,
with character so very rare,
and her own special brand of flair.
When He looks down from His heavenly shrine
and sees me in my grief supine,
I pray He'll grant my wish sublime
to meet her at the end of time.
C. E. Lord

A Lifetime

Just six weeks old he moved my heart
With him I vowed I would never part
In return he gave to me
His friendship, love and loyalty.

Following me by day, sleeping close at night
With his bark so bold and brown eyes bright
He shared my life, he was my world
Knowing every move, understanding every word.

He knew him, I would never abuse
Confident, I could never refuse.
In time as the years crept up on him
I watched with dread those brown eyes dim.

A lifetime my friend had been by my side
Thoughts of life without him I tried to hide
Then he left me one day, alone to cry
Although ours was not a permanent goodbye

I had made a vow from the very start
With my little Tramp, I did not really part
Wrapped warm in memories, he lives contented I know
In the heart he once moved, seventeen years ago.

Margaret Thompson

Bury Me Not

Bury me not, in the churchyard ground,
With all those dead people lying around,
For I have not died, but have been set free,
My soul's been unlocked with that final key.

Bury me high, where there's gentle breeze
With the sound of songbirds among the trees.
Surround me with flowers, still held by their root,
Where the crispness of Autumn I will hear under foot.

Bury me high where the rivers run by,
Where they laugh and they chatter, with never a sigh,
Where dragonflies call with their hesitant flight,
Where moonlight's reflected, on a magical night.

Bury me high, where sounds of children I will hear,
I will share in their laughter, and feel every tear,
I will sing such sweet music, I will dance in the sky,
I will lie with them quietly as summer dreams by.

Bury me high, so I can gaze at the sea,
Hear its mood changing sounds, feel its waves around me,
If this you can do, you'll swap sorrow for glee,
For this place is heaven, where God awaits me.

Sally Annette Parker

Progress

Oh for the peace of yesteryears,
With a single plane droning on high,
Amid cottonwool clouds 'gainst azure blue,
In a calm and peaceful sky.

Today, all is noise, and hustle and speed,
Jets screaming overhead;
Time was when we could stand and stare,
But now — faster! faster! — is the creed.
The roads are full of potential death,
With all kinds of vehicles crammed,
The pedestrian seeking to cross the road
Interrupting the flow, is dammed.

I know it's called PROGRESS, and machine-wise, it is,
But not for the likes of us,
We enjoyed our lives at a slower pace
Without so much bother and fuss.
Although we find pleasure in T.V. and such,
And have gadgets that do their work well,
There are days when we wish all this PROGRESS
Was not such a noisy HELL!

Maisie Sell

Advice To The Bride

Faithfully always love each other,
With a love both deep, and true,
Lovingly ever do your best to see,
The others point of view.

Generously share things with your partner,
Yet respect his private rights,
Never Oh never resort to tantrums,
Nor indulge in sulks and spites.

Warmheartedly have a sense of humour,
And enjoy a joke and a laugh,
Courageously bear it without malice,
Should it sometimes turn to chaff.

Tenderly cherish one another,
Both in sickness and in health,
Carefully regulate your spending,
In accordance with your wealth.

Joyfully realise that marriage
Is a case of give and take,
Continually ask the Lord to help you,
And a success of it to make.

I. Griffiths

Beyond Love

Here before me she lies,
with a glow that never dies.
She dreams of loss and sorrow,
and of the love she can now only borrow.
Her face not having a happy day,
since I left and passed away.
But her face begins to rearrange,
as her dreams interchange.

She wakes with a smile,
so I will stay and watch a while.
But her smile is soon out like a flame,
leaving me knowing I'm to blame.
She's thinking how she would have enjoyed the coast,
if it hadn't have left her with this ghost.

She shall stay there alive,
as long as here I thrive.
I will stand my ground,
against any danger found.
Fighting to keep her,
from my victor the grim reaper.

D. Holdcroft

Untitled

Give me a mossy bank and rippling stream
Where beauty reigns supreme
A place of exquisite peacefulness
A paradise made to dream.
Where cares and trials are lost from sight
It's a haven in which to rest
Oh lucky am I in this England fair
For this is our heritage
No stately mansion do I have
But the simple things of life
Where soul and body rest content
In nature's wonderment.

V. Cambridge

The Precious Gift

Wherever there is darkness, there's always something light.
Whenever there is sadness, there is gladness and delight,
Whenever you're downhearted and in depths of despair,
A ray of hope will suddenly fill the air,
When people all around you seem to be there for the taking,
And you can't make them realise the mistakes they are making,
That the treasures and the pleasures you find when you can give,
Are the greatest feelings you can have and life's most precious gift.

Denise Oates-Smith

Circles of Time

Time stood within present encounters
Wishes seemed dry emotionless empty
Little upward warm breezes lifted shining
Dark clouds rolled gathering speed
Wisely high walls seem to tower
No way round slippery slopes

Look up above search the way
See before you endless circles of time
Reach hoping stopping tired tracks
Smooth rippling sunshine ideas caressed
Smiles everlasting just test the deepness

Robert O'Hara

The Ridgeway

As I look back at the twisting track
winding its way to the valley floor
pitted and scarred by countless feet
that have walked this way before,
the lark's song overhead
accompanies each step I tread
past avenues of standing stones
like bones picked clean by time.

Past ancient hill fort lookout posts
where ghostly roman soldiers drill
waylands hammer strikes the iron
and when the evening's still,
the ferrous sparks fill the night
like a million coloured stars in flight
and a white horse as pale as chalk
runs across the hill.

Richard James

The Sea Gull

Looking seawards, dark clouds rolling by,
wind rustles, bushes, sweeping the grass,
as if by one, big hand,
surf breaks on the sand,
There, in the wind, surveying it all,
A one legged seagull stands.
One wonders, what in life,
has happened to thee,
There you stand, as strong as the rest,
looking about, surveying the land,
Then, on one leg, balanced,
takes off in flight,
Perfectly.
As ever the same, with grace and ease, fly's.
A lesson to all, perhaps,
to carry on, in life,
Whate'er befalls.

Patricia Caldwell

The Master's Reign

Was I happy in those days that passed?
Will it ever be feasible to say
That they regarded me as a companion?
They say 'no'
Without realizing its implications.
Trivia becomes an important state of mind.
Obsessed by a pretty face
And a nice behind.
They were never really concerned about life.
Life, or sincerity?
The two are now the same.
And now the time has come
To crush this hypocritical reign.
They think they've driven me
To the brink of life.
But they don't know that I've always dreamt
Of being stabbed in the back
By a poisoned knife!

Simon Oakley

Long Meadow

Long meadow is a special place
Wild flowers, sweet grass, adorn her face,
A little stream that gurgles by
Froggie rests on mushroom stool
And trout abound in darkened pool
The lark sings merrily on high
circling, climbing, clear blue sky
Black sings with out thrust souls to rest

D. Harrill

Getting Old

Why was it her?
Why wasn't it me?
We both lived the same
As happy as can be

She had a good mind; not like me
She was loving, caring and helpful to me

She was sixty four when she passed away
It shouldn't have happened; it wasn't her day

Now I am old, and scared to be free.
Why isn't she here to comfort me?

I'll be in a home soon,
It's not fair to me.
I'm not as dumb as they think, you see.

Soon it's my turn, I hope it will be.
Then we'll be together, in complete harmony.

Paul Mead

Winter

Why do we have to have winter
Why not just summer, autumn and spring,
Window shopping's no fun when your feet have gone numb
But in summer your heart starts to sing.

Why do we have to have winter
When even the trees look so bare,
Not a leaf can be found except those on the ground
And faces look glum everywhere.

Why do we have to have winter
Often I've heard these words said,
There's nothing out there; the streets are quite bare
I'd rather stay home in my bed.

Why do we have to have winter
When everything turns into ice,
There skating I know, but I'd rather go
Where everything's warm and so nice.

Why do we have to have winter
When no sense in it I can see,
The Kiddies adore it, but me I abhor it
I'd rather have summer or spring.

M. Kay

Bitter Sweet Memories

As a child so innocent and so defenceless
you learn by every day,
you have memory as you get older
of the times of fun and play.

memories of my sister's before being
put into care
I know how most feel of the lost
memories they didn't share.

when in care all was not up hill,
abuse mental torture is all I could feel.

We were lucky three out of five went home,
to rebuild lost memories gone by.
But strong I have been from then to this
day and you know what all I did was try.

L. Fagg

For No Man

Oh time!
Why is it, we worship you most dearly,
Is it a shrine? somewhere to stand.
To watch; as the seconds tick away,
Lost in a moment never to return.

If only!
That what they always say:
If only!
The water does not pass under the bridge,
Will times remembered come flooding back;
Deep: from recluseless channels of the heart.

As these flood gates open;
This hidden recess, from with-in the millpond pool:
So still; statically calm, oozing with pressure.
As the stallion; straining at the reins ready for release:

Integrated together; contrasting thoughts of gushing eddy's,
Smashing too and throw!
Like a pendulum of a time-piece;
Never ceasing to stop,
Not for no man!
   S. P. Warren

'Why God'

Why God allow us to suffer so much,
Why God allow us to have so much hurt
Why God allow us so many failures
Why God are our lives in turmoil and confusion
Piously and faithfully we always said our Prayers
Artificially, now we know
God is real to us now and always
Because we realize that we were always asking and never
understanding
Thank You, Lord, God
We can see again and know that each moment is a thankful one.
   Ruben Pillay

Why

Why do I love you?
Why does my foolish heart miss
Whene'er you smile
And skip each time we kiss?

Why does the earth spin
And stars leap from the reeling skies,
Whene'er I see
The love light in your eyes?

Why when we're apart,
The sun and moon refuse to shine?
And then I see you
And all the world's divine.

Why, my heart asks,
And as I wonder what to do
You come to me
And then I know.
I love you because you're you.
   J. C. A. Abatagelos

Things To Come

How fortunate are we, born this progressive age,
   Who witness British history turn yet another page,
Oh lucky generation when man and brain create,
   Give praise for ingenuity on this historic date.
This project now accomplished, a dream now come true,
   Hail! to thee all Europe, Great Britain welcomes you.
Accept you, this forerunner of great things yet to be,
   Strengthen chains of friendship with this link beneath the sea.
Rejoice mankind this happy day, give thanks to all who planned,
   We greet you not by sea alone, but also over land.
Praise also be to God, may this union hold the key,
   That this land of Hope and Glory ever keeps man free.
   R. S. Morton-Holmes

Why Do We Live?

School to work to pension to grave,
Why do we live this life God gave.
I've seen friends and family pass away,
Throughout generations I wish they could stay.

But why do we come and why do we go?
It's a pointless life and full of woe.
The rich and the poor are happy and sad,
I look at the rest and it makes me feel glad.

No job, no money, no real great life,
All that you face is trouble and strife.
So why am I here? I wish I knew,
How did we get here, just out of the blue?

No-one knows why or where we came from,
But all of a sudden we die and we're gone.
   Sabrina Ramm

A Cry For Help

The world keeps turning, spinning round space,
why do people destroy this beautiful place?
Green lush pastures spread across the land
mountains kiss the horizon vast and grand.
Flowers grow and blossom in spring,
tall high branches where birds like to sing.

Our atmosphere has a really huge hole,
caused by pollution and aerosols.
We must recycle all our trash,
ban leaded petrols and C.F.C. gas.

Whales and dolphins swim happy and free,
this is how the world should be.
Tranquil countries like England and Greece.
Stop all fighting, leave the world at peace.
   S. H. Weaver

When All Else Fails

When all else fails —
Why do I lift my eyes to the hills?
Because their majestic mass offers
Stability in this transient world.

When all else fails —
Why does the mighty roar of the ocean
Excite in me a passion and a hope
That re-vitalizes my spirit?

When all else fails —
Why do the frail petals of a flower
Touch such a tenderness in me
That I feel love stir?

He, who made these wonders,
Is there for me with constant love.
This gives me comfort
When all else fails.
   Mary Mayo

The Silent Heart

My heart from all disturbing depths
Would ask to be made free.
So peaceful lies the quiet heart;
As tranquil as the sea
When fiercest storms their rage have ceased
To grant the billows ease.
For now they gently, gently swell,
Caressed so by the breeze.
Merciless were the elements, the
Waves were nigh o'erwrought
But ah the calm and oh the peace
Dear breeze lend me your thought
For mind and heart so tempest toss'd
Are wearied by the storm
But all the gentle breeze will come
A gentler scene to form.
   M. Ellinger

Why Victimized Child

Why do eye feel so cold inside?
Why are these crazy thoughts in my mind?
Why am eye all alone?
Why is this fire burning in my soul?

Why do eye feel this crippling pain in my heart?
Why did this war have to start?
Why has my world fallen apart?
Why such a swift and sudden fall?

Why have my dreams been shattered?
Why do eye feel as if eye have been battered?
Why has my life been destroyed?
Why is it hard to believe that eye was once a happy boy?

Why is this violence making me drown?
Why have my hopes crumbled down?
Why can't eye breathe?
Why does nobody really give a damn?

If we pull together we can save the human race.
It's not like eye can't explain what's going on.
Eye know my god hasn't given up on me.
Peace now that you are here please don't disappear

Mansur Mahmud

Poor Old Mum

Oh what can it be that is getting me down
Why, an army of germs, of that I'll be bound
It sent me to bed not an hour ago
When I found all I did was becoming quite slow.

Now my head is all fuzzy and my nose is red raw
And a box full of tissues lays strewn on the floor,
The doorbell is ringing — oh who can that be?
I wish they could make me a nice cup of tea.

There is laundry to do, a huge pile in the bin
If I left it there smelly — would they think it a sin?
And the mending has grown to a heap on the sill
Oh why do I have to be lying here ill.

My hungry young men — pretty soon, with a roar
Will come bursting in hungry, like bulls through the door
A shoe kicked off here... another one there
And coats on the banister — what an untidy pair!

Oh why must this happen to me, I must ask
As I creep from my bed and put on a brave mask
There is too much to do, I just mustn't give in
So I'll shake this old cold and appear with a grin!

Sarah Woolley

Unemployed Days

Dumped by a sudden twist of fate
Who's to blame, who's to hate
Will I get invited back?
Or have I lost a mate?

Taking yesterday's stride
Flowing through the human tide
Manoeuvring into a bar
Where I plan and hide.

Entering the battle plains
Full of enquiry's and packed out lanes
Will it be different?
No, just the same.

They make me feel ashamed when I sign on
They look at me as if I've done something wrong
At least I know it's not my fault
The way it's brought my life to a halt.

How far do I have to stray to get my pay?
Will it be like this until I lay?
Or can I ever reach the final day?
It will be another year in May.

Nicholas Hughes

Watch The World Argue!

Who is wrong, and am I right?
Who wins this worldwide fight?
We sit and listen to a chosen few,
and we all watch this world argue.
No fortunes in peace, we make war,
count the profits and keep the score.
I want action and talk is cheap,
they discuss whilst the widows weep.

Money is wasted, millions are spent,
houses are empty but none for rent.
Hospital wings are closing down,
and work's getting harder in this town.
As fewer things are working out,
don't you want to scream and shout?
It's time to clean up this world's mess,
who will do it and do you care less?

R. F. DeBono

WHO?

Who was the first one I saw on earth?
Who was the one who gave me birth?
Who, when I was helpless, nourished and dressed me?
Who kept me safe from all that distressed me?
Who taught me to talk, taught me to walk?
Who showed me where it was safe to go?
But sometimes said 'naughty' sometimes said 'no'
Who, when I was bigger, took me to school,
And was proud of my learning when I did well,
But when I failed, who loved me still?
Who stayed by my bedside when I was ill?
Who, when I grow older, will love me still?
Who, when I'm an adult, will still be there,
With me to share every pleasure and care?
Now is the time to show how I love her —
Today I say "thank you" and "God Bless You — Mother"

M. Edwards

Untitled

Once there was a girl of three
who used to sit upon my knee,
golden hair with a lovely hue,
and two big brown eyes
that would look at you.

Then all of a sudden you look around,
and that little girl nowhere can be found.
I look and what do I see,
a young teenager looking at me.

I turn around once more,
and see a young lady going out of the door.
I wonder if I look some more,
if I see another generation like before.

Whatever happened to that girl of three,
that was contented to sit on my knee.
Going on quite happily,
being a mother just like me.

C. Britton

Listen, can we hear the wind whisper

Listen, can we hear the wind
Whisper to the trees
Gently tossing their new spring leaves
Listen to the wind
Whispering to the trees.
Spring will come round again and
bring with it fresh hope, as we
watch our world going round in cycles
The seasons change, so do our lives,
giving us the time to reflect on our mistakes.
Picture if we can the wind
blowing around the world
stirring us before it's too late
Listen to the wind
Whisper to the trees.

S. M. Parks

My Meeting Up With My Lord Jesus Christ

I had a pain in my chest, I called upon my doctor
Who turned me away from his door as an impostor
He did not know even his own roster
It was he that was the real dangerous impostor

As six hours later I had a burst ulcer
My doctor was sent for, but he would not muster
He left me lying in nothing but a cluster
Two days later he was sent for as I muster
Have a doctor for another eruption cluster

He sent me to the royal victoria infirmary to order
Where the professor said you are over the border
As your doctor has neglected your general order
All I can do is give you a bed without any order

I was left there all night to fight the good fight
With all my might and all my very own sight
New day came the vicar without any right or might
I died at that point against all my might
I was taken to my Lord Jesus Christ, he looked deep into my eyes
That were like great mince pies at the sight of his eyes
Of his great lordship and magnificent eyes
  F. Scott

The Brightest Star In Heaven

He came to us, a tiny scrap.
Who took our hearts and held them tight.
We were so proud of this little one.
Who struggled hard but lost the fight.
We cannot see him, touch him, hold him
But we're glad that he was given.
Although he touched this earth so briefly
He is now the brightest star in heaven.
  P. R. Smith

Our Shadow

I am alive like the ghost who haunts you,
Who smiles through all his pain.
You try to imbibe his darkness,
But your aspiration is all in vain.

His pale face is unmodulated.
His smile is only skin-deep.
His glassy eyes are void,
Worn away from the times he weeps.

His chains of thoughts are tangled,
You struggle to set them in rows,
You're the sower who plants good seeds,
But odium is all that grows.

I lock him with his affliction,
I drown him in his pain.
I blame him for eternal hate,
Could blame him for the rain.

He is the ghost of the future,
Whose strength you've yet to see,
Black-strength which grows on lasting sorrow.
He, the ghost, is me.
  Sophia Gill

Fallen Idol

You were the masterpiece I did create
Who grew to charm, disarm and then to hate
You were my moon, my sun, my night and day
My shining idol wearing feet of clay
You were the dawn of all my happy days
The love that I can never now replace
You were the brightest figment of my mind
Proof if required that love is ever blind
In you I saw each virtue well displayed
Listened with love to every word you said
What is the pain that holds me in its thrall?
The discovery that I knew you not at all
  May McCabe

Shooting Fancy

If I should die think this of me,
Who fixed the fence under the tree,
And made a gate to wheel bikes through,
And shovelled up the doggy poo;
That somewhere now above this earth,
With fattened and ungirded girth,
There sails an angel, not quite white,
Smiling down upon the sight
That fertilizing doggy poo
Has made the fence branch shoots anew!
  J. Edwards

While Thousands Pass

Who knows what life-line led them into this chasm of degeneration?
Who cares where tomorrow leads them when sad humanity
  has sunk so low?
What sorrow or what happiness has been part of their journey,
  since that small beginning?
What endless slide has culminated thus, in undergrounds,
  dark doorways, wasted spaces?

You see them, (if you look), oh yes you see them,
Old raincoat long decayed, old trousers, gloves, attempt to
  keep the cold from wasted limbs.
You'll find them (if you try), you'll surely find them,
Ferreting around in filthy dustbins for some discarded bite to
  soothe the belly.

So what? So, what of others better placed whose circumstance
  has kept them up, up higher?
Just watch for some small sign, some indication of sorrow or
  of sadness as they pass.
There's one or two who care, a tiny few, who aid the plight of
  suffering mankind
What better place we'd live in, would we not, if others only
  seemed as though they mind?
  Stephanie Manuel

"Viewed From My Window"

Tall evergreens touch the sky,
Wispy clouds float gently by.
A squirrel hunts in the copper beech
For something tasty out of reach.

A blackbird sits on the electric cable,
While doves coo softly from a nearby gable.
A small dog waits in a parked car
And motors pass from near and far.

From my bed I can see
Several faces in each tree.
Some are thin and some are fat,
One smart lady wears a hat.

Another is like the Prince of Wales,
An odd one out is a ship with sails,
A child with curls, a man with a beard,
And many more that are really weird.

When the wind was very strong
They all seemed to go quite wrong.
I feel that I can truly say
I'd miss them if they "went away".
  A. Toley

The Fishermen

To be, or not to be, that is the question,
Whether to be quiet, or full of action,
Whether to reap the harvest, of the day,
Or let things flow, along life's way.

It's a wiser man, who patience gains,
For he's at one, with nature's ways,
The secrets of the universe, he'll find out.
Of this, there is no doubt,

To be, or not to be, that is the question.
  B. Kerfoot

The Sailor

The sailor had a morbid life
which well you may tell by his looks
but morbid yet is the life he'll get
if his ship sails without any books

A book is the sailor's salvation
he will read whatever he may get
from Peter Cheney to Rudyard Kipling
or even the London Gazette

But yet you will find he is of a kind
whose whims and fancies are small
Keats, Woodhouse, Longfellow
you will find he has read them all

And when the toil of the long day is over
and down to his cabin he'll go
he may pick up a book on science fiction
or another by Daniel Defoe

His knowledge of books will amaze you
as his actions most often do
and the best book in his collection
is the Testaments Old and New.

A. E. Rendell

Encouragement

Encouragement is something
Which we all need
To face up to the difficulties in life,
And without it very few people will succeed.

Today so many of our young people's lives
Are in such a mess,
For lack of love and encouragement,
To help them towards success.

Tell someone that they are useless,
And that is exactly what they will be,
But tell them they are wonderful,
And watch their face light up with glee.

A word of praise
Can make all the difference
Between failure and success,
Especially when it brings with it happiness.

So be not stinted in your praise,
And give it with a smile,
Words of encouragement can enrich our own lives,

While making someone else's life seem more worthwhile.

Mary Daly

Easter Reply

Oft did she ask with serious mind,
"Where will I be when this be shorn;
Will this be the all there is?"
The questions left her quite forlorn.

She left at last her earthly frame,
And that, which was the one, we thought,
Passed into the holy ground,
Which she and husband Sam had bought.

Easter! And to the holy ground,
We pilgrimaged, but heavy stepped.
The grave was vibrant with the blooms,
But what came next — her doubt was swept?

Daffodils heralding the day,
But one stood out on longer leg,
With trumpet reaching for the sky
And showing us a blackbird egg.

We left the scene with lighter heart,
And slipped into the car, and said
How wonderful this day had been,
When two white doves flew overhead.

Rhys Clement

What Is Its Name?

This restful, placid, peaceful game,
Where we are told, (when shown its aim),
"Don't bowl it heavy, bowl it light!"
"Don't fire the bowls with dynamite!"
"Don't bowl it long!" "Don't bowl it short!"
(We TRY to do what we are taught!)
"Don't bowl it here!" "Don't bowl it there!"
Some days we simply stand and stare,
Wondering for a moment or so,
"Where DID my PERFECT bowl just go?"

What is its name, this gentle game,
Where swearing language brings us shame?
That gets us worked up every end,
When curving bowls we cannot send?
When each time the match is o'er,
We go home, then come back for more!
Don't let the pressure get to you
When not a winner, start anew
'Cos after all, it's only a game!
AH! INDOOR BOWLS, yes, that's the name!

Sheila P. Wright

The Sky

Where birds upon the wing do fly
Where upon the breeze the clouds hang high, and low
And change their shape,
As they go by
Such a place is the sky

Where thunderstorms brew,
And lightning flashes, when it strikes the trees they turn to ashes,
And painlessly die
Such a place is the sky

Where old flyers' dreams
Have come true, thinking of when in machines
They once flew,
Upon the air up high
Such a place is the sky

Where eagles soar
At break of day, searching for their intended prey
As only they can,
With an eagle eye
Such a place is the sky

Raymond M. Cowin

Gorillas In The Mist

In the mist of the hills
Where the water runs clear
The brink of extinction is so near
To guard their territory is all they know
A hand for an ashtray just for show
All God's creatures have the right to exist
High in the hills, gorillas in the mist

N. Appleby

Why?

Why do I have to be what I'm not,
Why do I have to pretend,
Why do I have to be someone else,
Just to be your friend.

Why do I have to be what I'm not,
Why do I always get blamed,
Why do I have to change my life round,
Just so you're not ashamed.

Why do I have to be what I'm not,
Why do I have to change,
Why does it feel I'm performing,
Forever in a cage.
Why do you have to be ashamed,
Why can't I be your friend
Why can't I be set free
And why does it never end.

Suzanne Physick

Sleepers Garden

Gentle sleeper in your silent garden
where the grass grows long and deep
I walked through your silent kingdom
in the bareness of my feet.

I heard the song of the nightingale
how sweetly she did sing
on a branch high overhead to keep
to tune with the wind.
Where the dainty heads of wild flowers
sway in the passing of a breeze
where tall grandfather oaks are the
guardians of the trees.

The headstones tilt and lean in the
mischief of winter's gale below the sleeping
night, below a silent moon so pale
O gentle sleeper, sleep on through time
and time that's yet to come, sleep soundly
in your kingdom of silence, your paths in
life are run.

G. W. Charles

My Garden

My Garden's somewhere nice to know
Where I can feel at ease,
Watching the lovely flowers grow.
In the shadow of the trees,

No noise, no sound, it's really grand
To leave my cares behind
Almost as if some unseen hand
Bears them on a gentle wind.

Each rosebush means a lot to me
Given by a special friend.
Now I bloom for all to see
Just how the colours blend.

The plant I cherish most of all
My passion flower great and glowing
Climbing slowly up the wall.
Now oblivion in all its glory.
Search the earth and scan its girth.
It's clear for me to see
Never while I've lived on earth
Have I been closer, Lord, to thee.

Vera Lewis

Souls

Take me to another place,
where only souls can embrace.
Up where the truest hearts entwine,
and lovers let lose their inner minds.
Take me where they cannot stop,
the lightning fire that burns white hot.

Souls burn within this heat,
passions inflamed through the body's beat.
Salted sweat how sweet the taste,
as we writhe in deep embrace.

Now we fall our love all spent,
in damp wet pillows, a heady scent.
Then from deep within the bodies cry,
is heard the hearts breathless sigh.

Yet, with loves dark secrets who can tell,
is this heaven or is this hell.
To be in love with one so close,
the hurt is strong but it gives the most.

So, was it here we touched the soul,
by shaded darkness on a night so cold.

Maurice Hessey

The Simple Things Of Life

Sitting in the cornfield —
    where did the poppies go?
getting freckled by the sun,
    wearing a 'sloppy jo',
I thought of all the people who
    care not for simple things,
like gentle rain, and butterflies,
    and birds, and 'fairy' rings.

Of swaying trees, and nodding flowers,
    of apples picked from trees,
of droning bees, and scudding clouds,
    and hair swept in the breeze.

Of gently lowing cattle,
    and bleat of baby lambs,
of blackberries and strawberries —
    and the resultant jams!
How much they miss, these people
    who just let time go by —
but they will never learn, will they?
    They only sit — and sigh.

J. Hockley

No Reason To Live

A tear drop rolls down a once rosy cheek,
Where now pale flesh prevails,
And smile lines seldom show themselves,
They are hidden behind the tales.
Where light once shone, a healthy glow,
There is now a shadow so dull,
And hair hangs long and greasy,
Over a once well cared for skull.
Below are clothes that looked so nice,
That looked so handsome and gay,
But now the dirt just gathers,
More each passing day.
The shoes once new and polished,
Are now tatty and torn,
Scuffed and uncared for,
Looking too well worn.
The person, once a healthy man,
Has lost his love, his wife,
He now no longer sees why,
He has to live his life.

Suzanne Henwood

Awaiting My Lord

Thank you for the life you've given
and your goodness, when I'm driven
awaiting my Lord, for thee
Thank you for the good and bad
also for the life I've had, sometimes sad.
Awaiting my Lord, for thee
Thank you in sickness and in health
for my family, that's my wealth.
Awaiting my Lord, for thee
Thank you for an angel, now at rest
I know I did not always
do my best.
Awaiting my Lord, for thee
Lord, when it's time, my eyes to close
Thank you for the faith I chose.
Awaiting my Lord, for thee

Thank you when it's my time to go
my mind and soul you do know.
Awaiting my Lord, for thee

John D. Ainsley

Pictures On The Wall

It was Varga Girl calendars, back in those dark days,
When young men left home for the war,
Saucy, appealing, though not *too* revealing,
We'd seen nothing like them before.

There were film stars as well, such as Turner and Grable,
To brighten the old barrack-room,
High heels and swimsuits, legs that seemed endless,
The start of the glamour-girl boom!

In more peaceful times there was magic Monroe,
Her like again we'll never see,
Then our sons had a crush on Lusardi and Fox,
And the others who posed for Page Three.

But the times are a'changin', say calendar-makers,
The pin-up girl's losing her way,
The nation's gone green, wants the pastoral scene;
Meadow and woodland, lakeland and bay.

So... let 'em print landscapes, and seascapes,
And badger and deer, if they must,
But with no pretty frame, it won't be the same,
And the calendar trade could go bust.

Raymond Kingston

Memories

Dear father, we recall the day in nineteen sixty-three
When you were called to heaven's rest
You'd given of your very best
Through days of hardship, war and peace
Your every effort did not cease
To build a home with truth and love
Complying with the one above
Who cares for you now you have gone
Although your memory lingers on
And will forever and a day.

The memory of you, father dear
Will keep and guide us on our way
For with the thoughts of you to guide
Our efforts cannot be denied
And we shall strive to lead a life
Upon the pattern you did make
Endeavouring through toil and strife
To be able to of good things partake
Until we take the final test
Before we too are laid to rest.

J. E. Cooper

God's Little Angel

They say you're in pain,
You cannot love
You cannot feel
You live in a world all of your own
Your eyes look far away
They say walk away
Live your life a different way
But not me, all I say
I look into your eyes through the windows of your soul
I see the flickers of love you once knew
I see your outstretched hand reaching out to me
I am the sun and warmth that make you live another day,
They say why adopt you, you'll only be here for awhile then go away
I just smile and say, God's little angel is meant to be mine
And when I shed a quiet tear I hear a little voice say,
Don't cry, mummy, I have a voice now.
Heaven not so bad.
Now I can turn and say,
Your love was worth your short stay.

Maria Price

Release

Did you laugh, or did you cry
When you viewed yourself before your shower?
Did you smile, or did you sigh?
To remember a once delicate flower.
When you splashed 'neath the temperate spray,
Did your memory come into play?
You live over again that special day?
That followed a night of compounded rapture, and delight
When you had no doubts, and knew it was right.
Yet that had only been the beginning
So what went wrong
To stop your heart singing?
Then alone, the days have been long,
And the nights always longer.
It has taken time to recover some,
But taking stock, you feel less glum.
You like what you see and feeling stronger,
'Tis a pleasure to be
So before your date, 'tis good to be free.

R. Elsworth

Men

Everything's perfect, everything's great,
When you think you've found the ideal mate,
You're happy and gleaming with this wonderful life,
Then he'll use you, ditch you, and go home to his wife,
No one knows what you're going through,
unless they've been there
And you put on this act that you don't really care
But deep down inside you're going through hell,
And wiping the tears so that no one can tell,
You go through each day and do nothing but cry
Think the only way out is to curl up and die.
But a lot of people say that's not what you do,
You must get a life and find someone new!
We know it's hard and they say time heals,
But most women know exactly how it feels
To sit there waiting, watching the phone
So the best thing to do is stay on your own
Then you'll never have worries about who there with
Go back to being happy, and start to relieve,
But try to keep up this sad brave face
As there a waste of time and a waste of space!

Sharon Wiseman

I Can See The Blood

I can't help it and I've tried
When you swing your arms
so casually, so carefree
When you walk with a bounce in your step
When you turn and smile at friends,
I see the blood.

I see the blood
as if the jacket was newly ripped from your back
as if the shoes had just been stripped from your bones,
I don't wear leather ... anymore.

I can't help it and I try
When you fill your trolley
so casually, so carefree
When you cook your meals with glee in your eyes
When you turn and smile with family,
I see the blood.

I see the blood
as if you ran through the shop trying to escape
as if you had been killed in that very kitchen,
I don't eat meat ... anymore.

Tracey Jones

The Open Sea

Gone are the worries and cares of the land
when you leave the harbour and are outward bound
peace and tranquillity then enter your soul
filling your body it makes you feel whole
and the freedom I give no other could bestow
as you roam across the ocean far from the land you know
just like a caring parent your character I mould
giving you self confidence and patience that's controlled
all these things you get from me and all are given free
for I am the Mother of Mothers and called the Open Sea

Life's nursery was born in each passing wave
and the salt in all blood is that which I gave
my beating heart are the tides that don't die
caused by the moon that hangs in the night sky
and from my safe womb I produced and gave birth
to the beginning of life that now populates earth
Eternal Mother, I try to behave
but sometimes my cradle turns into a grave.

Mike Buttery

Let's Talk About It

When you're feeling sad and down
When you don't even like the sight of a clown,
When you can't even raise a smile,
Let's talk about it.

When you have a tear in your eye
When you want to have a cry
When you want to be alone,
Let's talk about it.

When you want a great big hug
When you want a great big cuddle
When you want a whisper in your ear,
Let's talk about it.

When your mum puts her arm around you
When your mum kisses you better
When you can now raise a smile,
Let's talk about it.

Tom Harrison

Yesterday

Yesterday is today, yesterday I thought had gone away
When will today be my day, I long to leave my yesterday
I look for peace within each hour, I want to chase
The rainbow after rain, I look for cloud's that have
No darkness, the inner peace that brightness brings
The sun warm upon my face, the grace and favour of lovely days.

The turmoil and darkness and inner strife leave
Me to find my strength for a little while
Yesterday oh yesterday how I long for you to go
Stay in the past were you belong and let
Today stay like a song.

Mary Morris

Father Of Mine

Father, dearest father, what a joy you are to me.
When we are together I'm as happy as can be.
You know how much I love you for your kind and loving ways
Your care and deep devotion throughout my childhood days.
Now we both grow older and our love still stays the same
These twilight hours that we now spend forever will remain.

Father, dearest father, I cherish all the days
You showed me joy and laughter and all life's rightful ways.
Each day brings back fond memories of good times past and gone;
Your once proud form so sadly bent, your dear face tired and wan.
Those kindly eyes no longer see as your arms reach out to welcome me.
I never can repay you for the good you've always done.
I'm proud of you, dear father, there is not a finer one.

Vera Otto

Optimism

Times past seemed brighter than today
When those I loved were still at hand
It seems the best is over now
Their lives run out, like shifting sand

Some days the memories bring a pain
And emphasize the loss I bear
Until my heart reminds me of
The luck I've had, that they should care

I turn away from rainy thoughts
And face towards the years ahead
Then, silently, the sun appears
And brings me peace of mind, instead

The corner's turned and, even though
We'll meet no more along life's way,
I know they're there, in all I do
They made me who I am today

Life still is sweet, though different now,
With new-made friends, and things to do
I see a world of hope and joy
At last my heart can sing anew

Patricia Vincent

Josh

There comes a time in people's life,
When they have to cope with grief and strife.
We are told that Jesus only takes the best,
So in His arms Josh will safely rest.
A little boy people took to heart,
His illness he fought right from the start.
With so much courage he bore the pain,
With the support of his family again and again.
He set an example to all of us,
Who, when we feel unwell, make such a fuss.
But Josh did not die in vain,
For from it we hope people will gain.
Dear God, take care of Josh with love,
As he lives with you in Heaven above.
Life without him will be hard each day,
But the loving memories we have of him
Will always stay.

Ruby Hall

Spring

How can I express the feeling of re-birth
When so many famous poets have written on the theme
How can I aspire to match their soulful worth
When they verbally paint a picture of a scene.

The wondrous feeling of lightness when March days dawn
A kaleidoscope of colours bathe the land
Warm with the sunshine, feeling re-born
All of nature hand in hand

See the fresh green creeping through the hedgerows
Trees getting ready to burst into bloom
The animals, birds, insects all wild life knows
That it's time for the re-opening of natures womb.

A. J. Johnson

England In Spring

How lovely is the month of May,
When skies are blue, no touch of grey,
When lilac is in full bloom,
With lovely smell of its perfume,
How lovely is the May on the trees,
The blossoms pink that dance with the breeze,
Daffs, tulips and flowers colourful and neat,
That grow in gardens in every street,
England in spring is hard to beat
Nowhere on earth that can compete.

G. Gale

What Is A Day Dream?

I think most people have experienced this state of mind
When they have gone into a trance that leaves worries behind.
This imagination can come over you at any time of day,
Especially if you are wishing a boring time away;
Your mind goes berserk when ideas fill your head
A new car flashes by, perhaps you'll chose one in red
Or you may be on a liner cruising to a distant land
You could be at the proms listening to a military band.
On the other hand an aeroplane flight may be your wish
Or dining in a top hotel sampling some exquisite dish.
You may be the owner of a thatched cottage and garden
With lots of gnomes talking in a country jargon.
A party, a dance wearing an Alice blue gown
Or some other excuse to be making whoopee in town.
Wherever these flights of fancy make you take you
They are only daydreams but one day may possibly come true.
A new lease of life has been given to the mind.
To help cope with the stress of the everyday grind.
A ring on the doorbell is the end of all dreams
And you are transported back to earth by some magical means.

M. Jackson

Space Above The Clouds

Once a year,
when the sky is clear,
and the stars are shining bright,
there's an ethereal mist, an eerie feel and a white resplendent light.

A comet's tail had left a trail
of smouldering crimson hue,
the shooting stars enhance this view,
in a sky of prussian blue.

Meteorites were everywhere, unusual chunks of granite,
I know not where they came from,
except another planet.

Much later I viewed Jupiter it was a wondrous sight,
encircled by the moon,
both lost within the night.

The magic of this cosmic world,
and all that it enshrouds, to live a life so blissfully,
in space above the clouds.

Warrick G. Wincup

Poetic Grief

There's no tears from the eyes like a poet cries,
When the heart is broken in two.
For no one despairs like the poet,
Never knowing what we go through.

There is no grief like a poet's grief,
No wound that goes half as deep,
The searing fate of the poet.
It's no wonder I sit and weep.

Inspiration homes in, for my heart is raw!
As my loved one slowly dies.
So he can't see the depth of pain
In this poet's misty eyes.

As the evil consumes his body,
The words from my heart overflow,
For there's no lament like a poet's,
It's something that only we know.

As I head towards a labyrinth,
I pray that I'll find an end,
When I suffer the wrath of bereavement,
After losing my husband and friend.

Patricia-Mary Gross

Morning Rose

When a teardrop is falling, you know you have hurt
When she pulls, oh so gently, the words have been curt.
When her hands are a-twisting, with fingers entwined
Her pain is with her, her future is blind.
When the distance between you is too much to bear
Entice her, caress her, tell her you care.
'But what can he know of her feelings so fraught?'
She twists and she turns with the pain of her thoughts.
He sees all her passion, her senses so strong
But lays in her hand, a rose with stem long.
He'd picked it that morning, when dawn was just peeping
Knowing his loved one was tenderly weeping.
No words had been spoken at that dewy hour
When for once in his life he'd gathered a flower.
In her palm lay the rose, its beauty so healing
Her hair gently swaying, when she was then kneeling
Praying softly for guidance to understand life.

M. K. Mason

The Passing of Time

"Remember in the beginning
when love was an endless flame?"
'Rising' in the height of passion
'living' — 'burning' felt no shame.
Time seemed to pass so slowly
patience fraught till we'd meet again.
But pass it did, continuously
summer — winter — spring,
bad and good times, infinite thrills.
Sometimes we would hurt, laugh, cry or sing,
in each other's arms time stood still.
Then suddenly like the end of time — love died,
the flames extinguished — intolerance burned,
time waits for no one, it comes and goes,
passing on forever, never to return.
time heals "does it?" who knows!

M. Lambie

Childhood

It's easy to think of my childhood
When the sun used to shine every day.
And the pavements were warm to the touch of bare feet
And the streets were safe places to play.
We'd draw a few squares on the pavement
Play hopscotch with an old baccy tin
And constantly pricking our fingers
We'd sew bags to keep marbles in.
Then later we'd sit on the doorstep
Telling stories of ghosts and the dead
And then after frightening ourselves half to death
Lie quaking with fear in our beds.
We didn't need money in those days
To have fun and have a good time
Life was just one big adventure
In that wonderful childhood of mine.

E. J. Kilcoyne

" Life "

Life is not always a bed of roses, as many of us know,
when we are failing, ailing, lonely, then our moral gets low;
we moan and groan about the burdens we have to bear,
and with these problems around us, we give way to despair;
days and nights seem long and dreary, many things are all wrong,
the trouble is that our hearts, are not in tune with life's song;
but if we accept the rough with the smooth, then much can be done,
so let us put aside our troubles, and go looking for the "SUN;"
days of sunshine and days of rain, important parts they play,
to bring forth the SPRING flowers, together with blossoms in "MAY."
As we walk in the garden, or long some country lanes,
see the beauty of nature, we shall then forget our aches and pains;
give a thought for other, who have heavier burdens to bear,
offer a helping hand, speak a gentle word, just to show you care;
within this world of ours today, so much trouble and strife,
we all need that love and understanding, for a better "LIFE."

A. E. Wetton

Do You Dream Of Our Love

My love, do you dream of our love
When in slumber, you rest this day,
Or perhaps some far distant shore;
Some distant shore, wishing to explore.
Do you tire, grow weary of your way,
Longing to discover pastures new.
Are bless'ed days ever unceasingly,
Ever unceasingly, trapped in time perpetuity.
Content, the summer years yearn I,
For thyself, my greatest passion,
Have I no commanding goal than this bequest,
This bequest, unobtainable as is your rest.
My heart, my life, my meagre existence
Offer no more, for no more have I.
Must you depart; go now, follow your quest,
Your quest, for I stop you not and be blessed.
But when you are in slumber, my love,
My love, do you dream of our love.
Michael Cooper

Last Year's Summer

Deep into the winter
When I'm worn down with the grind,
Thoughts of last year's summer
Drifts into my mind.
Sat beside the river
In the grasses deep and long,
The hum of last year's summer
Starts to sing my daydream's song.

When bat thwacks ball, the cheers ring out
Home team is full of smiles.
These memories waft across to me,
Across my daydream miles.

I recall the haze of summer
The pavilion lending shade
The lazy buzz of insects
As the light begins to fade.
Voices calling "Well done, son!"
And "Bravo! Run some more!"
Thoughts of last year's summer
Start to open daydream's door.
E. L. King

Me And My Garden

Now gardening's the thing that I love the best
When I'm working in wellies, old shorts and string vest.
When I'm up to my elbows in fishbone and peat,
I'm out in all weathers, the cold and the heat.

Pansies and daffodils, the tulip and rose
Wheelbarrow, spade, shredder and hose.
The frost in the winter, the thaw in the spring,
The ladybirds, greenfly and bumble bee sting.

The lawn in the summer before drought turns it brown,
The winds in the autumn when leaves tumble down.
Yes I love my garden, a nice place to rest
After working in wellies, old shorts and string vest.
Ray Wicks

A Childhood Lost

I have moved no further from this place,
Where evil things I had to face.
I can't go forward, I can't go back,
Suspended in time, everything black.
Who is this man who comes for me,
A child abuser, no face I see.
Just a heartless shape, who will not hear,
My cries of terror, my cries of fear.
Why must I still endure the pain,
So many years reliving all over again.
Will I ever be free from this awful shame,
From the man who took my innocence,
and left me only pain.
V. C. Blake

My Childhood

My name is Will I was but three,
When I went to my grannies by the sea.
Dad sent us there when our Mam died.
I remember the day, how hard he cried,
When he parted with Rose, Owen, Jim and Me.
Sending us to live at the cottage by the sea.

It must have been a mammoth task,
To take us in no questions asked.
Dad stayed in the valley to work underground,
To my granny each week he sent a few pound.
She made sure we went to school every day,
Walking the fields, three miles, one way.

We spent many hours on the seashore,
Sometimes great fun, very often a chore.
Picking seaweed off the rocks,
And packing it carefully into a box.
Charlie the donkey and his cart took us to town,
To sell our seaweed for Half a Crown.

As we grew older no work could be found,
We had to return, To Work Underground.
C. A. Stradling

Hand Held

The sky is grey, I really like it blue
    When I come to film a lovely view,
However, it may well clear,
    And through the clouds, a hole appear,
So lovely sun comes shining down,
    My beaming face replaces frown.
What is this O-zone that we hear about,
    Is it nay a hole in heaven letting sunshine out?
The O-zone and heaven are here with me,
    It's the oh! I exclaim when this beauty I see.

Leaving Rat-Race town do I begrudge?
    Where its noisy busy streets I'd trudge,
Oh no! This lovely amble, ramble, leisurely stroll,
    Through woodland glade, thicket bramble, revives my soul.

These pathways which I tread, this sod,
    Have, and has, been trodden today by God,
He's surely walked this way, his glory I see, in grandiose array,
    Why! I think he even holds the hand of me today.
Peter W. P. Turner

Remember

Remember me in Springtime
When earth becomes young once more,
When daffodils star beneath old stone walls
When sap in the greenwood begins to rise
And the welcome cuckoo now calls.

Remember me in Summer
When white horses ride the seas,
When our dappled rivers shimmer with heat
When shade in the greenwood shelters from sun
And at tennis and boats we meet.

Remember me in Autumn
When fruit ripens on the trees,
When harvest Thanksgiving is in our minds
When leaves in the greenwood colour and drop
In the Fall see where our path winds.

Remember me in Winter
When the snow rests on the ground,
When the dark bleakness is everywhere
When trees in the greenwood are Tempest tossed
Remember me, remember where.
Maureen Newsham

New Life

Spring is the best time of year for me,
when buds shoot forth from every tree.
And bulbs peek through from mother earth,
pushing upwards for all they're worth.

Blue skies replace old winter's grey,
chasing snow and frost away.
And soon it seems that overnight
the gloom has changed to colours bright.

Do we ever wonder how
each new shoot springs forth from bough?
Or how, with every passing hour
new blossoms form on every flower?

Don't wonder how it came to be,
Just gaze and take in all you see,
and marvel at God's living 'store'
and know that spring will come once more.

Sheila Feeney

Marie — The Usher

At bow county court you made your name
When an usher you became
In your black gown you look refined
Although they are not well designed
Sorting lists and taking names
To many folk this looks a game
Calling cases and being polite
Hoping there will not be a fight
Running here and running there
Answering buzzers in despair
Come this way and take a seat
Better ushers you will not meet
If I'm not back go straight in
That bloody buzzers off again
As a team we are second to none
But most of all our work gets done
At 65 you've passed the test
And now deserve a well earned rest.

Rita Brown

Why?

Why does sorrow knock upon some people's door
　when all their world seems desolate,
their happy dreams depart.
Why is it only agonies and fears breathe
　within their troubled heart.
Why are some people blinded by self doubts and deep distress.
Find no contentment, sweet simplicity or taste the joys of happiness.

Why do some people mourn and live with deep regret
　even with the passing of time,
their inner soul does not forget.
Their heart's red wounds are never healed
their journey's never end,
they stumble on the road of life
　their weary path ways twist and bend.
Never finding a smoother path
Were they can walk with ease,
Or strolling in the sunshine of life
Entranced at were the paths may lead.

P. Brown

Untitled

How lovely to have these few moments of peace,
When all the noise around me cease.
To close my eyes and float away,
And dream again of yesterday.
Days in the sun with skies of blue,
Holding hands as we used to do.
Watching the fish in the skimming stream,
Walking on grass so fresh and green.
To have a cool drink in the shade of the trees,
Many a day we had like these.
Memories are very precious that's true,
How lovely it was to have shared them with you.

B. M. Booth

A Fighting Man

What makes a man want to fight?
What's in himself that gives him the right
to inflict pain, without remorse,
But only when the fight is in its course.

Well I'll tell you why, it's in his eye.

He'll tell you all so you can see
the contract's set, 'It's you or me.'
With skill and precision, he's clinically bound
And all you can hear is that fightin' sound.

Try and remember this in times to come
When there's chance to fight or chance to run.
If his eyes are cold, whether young or old,
And his mind's got that strength of power and will,
Be careful boy, that man can kill.

So take heed of what I've told and said,
'Cos without that look you could end up dead.
Beat him if yer can. — yer fighting man

Richard Penarski

" LOVE "

There is "love" in every "season,"
Whatever they may bring,
There is "love" in everyone's minds,
With the exchanging of "gold rings,"
But, the greatest "love" of all
We can find within ourselves
Is the "love" we give to others,
Without "question," "greed" or "doubt,"
For "love" overcomes all obstacles,
Whether "great" or "small,"
And the "love" you have within
Your "hearts" is the greatest
　"Gift" of all.

Sheila Salter Phillips

Lost Horizons

Yesterday made me think.
What would we do without ink.
What would we do without paint or glue
I haven't got a clue, have you?

Some long while ago it was
That man made things of wood.
Now that all the forests have gone.
How has that happened and not taken long?

Tell me why man is in a rush.
Everything seems to be pull and push.
Ever forward, just not looking.
Hey don't ask what nature's cooking.

Look no further than dried up land.
Please give it a helping hand.
Save that paper, save that can.
Save that forest and Save Man.

W. Moore

Untitled

It was a Saturday night of 87
when I gazed over and thought I had gone to heaven,
She looked at me and gave me a smile
there was only one thing on my mind to walk down the isle.
She had on a pink top and denim skirt.
To ask her out and she say no would have hurt.
I plucked up the courage to ask her for a date.
She looked at me said yes and I couldn't wait.
I asked her to marry me when I gazed in her eyes.
She said yes to my amazing surprise.
She got pregnant and had a baby boy.
All I could do was jump for joy.
I told her I hope we never ever part
because if we did was almost certainly break my heart.
We have been together for nine years.
And I told her I would always be her's.

Peter Harding

Putting On A Face

Draw back the curtains on the new day
What will it bring today
The sun, the rain, the wind, the snow
Each needed in its own way

Will it be a good day?
Only time can tell
Some days good, some days bad
Sprinklings of red letter days as well

Faces we show to this new day
Seem self assured and brave
This is what the world expects
A correct way to behave

But when the day is over
The curtains drawn for the night
Our guard can drop, the pretence all gone
We see ourselves in a different light

Alone with our thoughts of days gone by
A future we cannot see
As we sit and muse in the fire light
Thinking what will be, will be

Peggy Hunter

Past Eighty

What are you thinking now, old man,
What passes through your mind,
Pardon my curiosity, old man,
Do you think of years behind.

Do you see a lovely wife, old man,
With hair, all gold and wild,
Slippers warming by the hearth,
And curly headed child.

Did you bend your aching back, old man,
And shrug away the pain,
And worry about the sack, old man,
And little monetary gain.

Rest a peaceful while, old man,
In the winter of your year,
For days and friends long lost, old man,
Perhaps you shed a tear.

Did you drink life to the full, old man,
Or with gentle, careful sips
What mark will you leave on the world, old man,
When death has sealed your lips.

G. H. Bryant

My Friend Jack

Come dad, look and see
What I've found under the tree,
It's all long, hairy and black,
I think I'll call him my friend Jack.

I'll show him my pals,
They'll think I've gone nutty,
When I promise to put him on my sister's butty.

She'll shriek and scream and hide behind mum,
I'll laugh out loud,
Oh! What fun.

Mum will chase me with the wooden spoon,
I'll grab hold of Jack,
And dash out of the room.

And in the garden there's lots of space,
I can hide Jack all over the place,
I'll make him a home out of leaves and mud,
And build him a roof out of stones and wood.

And if he escapes he'll soon be back,
Because after all,
He's my friend Jack.

Margaret Walker

Innocence

A child is born, new life begins,
What does such innocence know of sins?
A world of strife — division deep,
Too young to understand and weep.

The hapless infant in a shawl,
What will destiny on it befall?
Uncertain time may tell the tale,
To see it through, or death prevail.

With loving care, and hope eternal,
With cherished dreams, and love maternal,
You will survive when day is done —
The night endured, you'll see the sun.

With lisping prattle and childish glee,
These wonder years will surely be
An innocence that is sublime,
Outshines the stars of space and time.

May your tender years be filled with light,
And darkness flee like shadows flight,
These precious times you can't recall,
But the guiding hand will tell it all.

Patrick Smith — Padraig

Loneliness

It's quiet, the morning's grey
what can I do today

I'm alone, made many cups of tea
I wonder, will anyone call to visit me

I go to the shops, something to do
hoping the hours will pass, only a few

I put the TV on, voices to hear
because no-one calls, no-one comes near

I've washed my cup, just the one
Cooking for me just isn't fun

It's evening now, and it's still grey
no-one called at all today

The silence shouts, seems to scream
but only the lonely know what I mean

Susan Rosemarie Chandler

Help Save The World

Are you worried about the world's population?
What about the rain forest's deforestation?
Is it just that people don't care?
Or don't they watch TV, are they unaware?
In a while many species will be lost forever,
Our fate could be changed if we all work together.
Will the world be left to decay?
With all of its resources wasting away.
The decision is up to this generation.
Help save the world, without hesitation.

Sarah Gurl

A Day At The Seaside

A day at the seaside, the grandkids and me,
What a good time we'll have, a jolly good spree,
A ride on the donkeys, a cone of ice cream,
Watching the sailboats, drifting all serene
Making sand pies, and castles so grand
'Twill be lovely, just to laze on the sand,
And think of the times, when I was still young,
Of the happy days I had with my Dad and Mum,
It will be lovely to see the kids having fun,
Being careful not to get too much sun,
I hope when they're older
They remember with glee,
The days they were happy
Days spent by the sea.

E. B. Brown

Lady Of The Night

Lady of the night with your face painted bright
What are your secret thoughts when you're alone?

Do you remember when a child
On the long summer nights
You played hopscotch with the little boy next door
They were carefree happy days
Fun and seaside holidays
Do you think of all these things when you're alone?

Do you remember growing up
Loving the boy next door
He gave you your first kiss, you were so shy
How the sun and moon did shine
Feelings heady just like wine
And nothing ever quite the same again

Do you remember that sad day
When he had to go away
Knowing in your heart it was forever
You had a child to care for
Rent man knocking at the door.
With heavy heart you walked into the night.

B. D. Tremblin

The Cat's Poem

He loves the night
What an awesome sight,
To mice or birds you see,
He is little, he loves you and me,
Feed him twice a day,
He will kill for his pay,
Are they good or bad,
If they're bad why should I be sad,
I mean the birds or mice,
This time round who throws the dice,
He knows the difference between bad and good,
The bad ones have fear and so they should,
They have laughed for 6000 years,
Now he will say you will pay my dears,
He wants to be free all day and night in my garden,
Now the cat is free of his burden,
So he can keep away the company of satan,
The tide has turned for certain,
He is proud he is from the house of cat,
So you have the choice wether or not to believe that.

Robert John Quinlan

Little Coloured Boy

Hello there, little coloured boy,
What's this I see?
Tears in your dear little dark eyes,
What can the matter be?

Come-on now, little coloured boy,
Was there something said?
Tears in your dear little dark eyes
Mean your heart just bled.

I love you, little coloured boy,
And though you may not see,
All the fighting over you and yours,
Someday will make you free.

Free to play with all the other kids.
Free to call a place your home,
Where no-one will hate and call you names,
And no-one will try to make you roam.

So dry your eyes, little coloured boy,
For soon you will agree,
That this world is a mighty fine place indeed.
When everyone is free.

E. J. McNally

The Cellar

Here in the dark I lie,
Wearied beyond sleep, pained beyond relief.
Few months ago I lived to struggle, now I struggle to live.
Blurred faces and voices surround me,
Deft hands work quickly over me,
I am not alone, others lie huddled here beside me.
The fearsome barrage rides overhead.
I haven't the strength to fear,
But I bless these damp earthy walls and blessed soft darkness
which enfold me.
I touch them as other hands have touched,
They are the bulwark which has withstood the passing of time,
And which will survive to serve other purposes
When my short day has blended into night and I have gained
Eternity and peace.

D. M. Conceprio

Trials And Smiles

A mother-daughter relationship has its ups and downs,
We wear our smiles, share our graces, yet often
Wear our frowns,
For though, yes, often close, we sometimes near the
Blows,
I, of course, the youthful foe, and you just
"One who knows".
Yet in the context of this truth, the aggression, yes,
Does end,
And in the times when anger reigns, to each other
Still a friend,
So fear not Mum, I assure you now, friends we'll
Always be,
So it seems that I am stuck with you, and you, yes,
Stuck with me.

Sarah Hinton

I Require Autonomy

Your government said lay down your arms, we're ready to negotiate
We want you all round the table for a lengthy debate
For generations many a bloody battle has raged at our doors
Would we have been different had religion not reached our shores
They said hand in all your weapons, keep none, don't you dare
We lost our friends and family, they don't know because they
  weren't there
As the processions passed hear the snipers' bullets thud
Leaving another mother's child lying face down in the mud
We broke into their homes with our guns and hood
We'd found them guilty so shot them where they stood
Our weapons have been with us since cradle, to the Virgin's
  loving care
The peace keepers don't know because they weren't there
It's the innocence that suffer the children, mother and wife
They've got to hold the family together, throughout all the strife
I offer my hand in peace, you say, how come
I offer only one hand, I need the other to hold onto my gun
My generation was brought up with a violence that didn't cease
How can they expect us to accept this conditional peace
Surrender all your weapons, or the peace process can wait
If they can't be more flexible, we'll return to our program of hate.

M. J. Streatfield

Homeless

Still there are homeless attempting sleep,
Under open sky, newspaper their sheet,
Cardboard boxes their encasements,
In tunnels, hideaways and basements.

May society never be content,
To see humans lie this trench,
Ever show determination to help,
Needing more than distribution of wealth.

Let love rule head and heart,
Care, share your immediate part,
Actions overrides all promises made.
Never let need for homeless your memory fade.

M. J. Evan-Yates

We Thank Thee Lord

We thank thee for thy presence, Lord,
   We thank thee for thy love,
We thank thee for thy gifts, oh, Lord,
   Brought to us from above.

We bless thee for thy birth, oh, Lord,
   In such a stable born,
We bless thee for thy loving care,
   Brought to us every morn.

We thank thee for the power of prayer,
   And for the gift of hope,
We thank thee for thy light, oh, Lord,
   And for thine aid to cope.

We bless thee for the means to live,
   Each and every day,
We bless thee for thy guidance, Lord,
   To help us on our way.

We praise thee for thy keeping, Lord,
   In thy constant care,
And trust that thou watch over us,
   In what we do and share.
    Margaret R. Bromham

Winners And Losers

Saturday at eight o'clock,
We players sit silent and hushed,
Whilst on T. V. the button is pushed,
And tears of laughter and of shock,
As the numbers fall from the big wheel's spin,
And an ordinary man has a lottery win,

Some ten pounds and some much more,
And one or two the jackpot score,
but most of us will not smirk,
For Monday we'll return to work,

Next week,
We will bet again,
Along with all the others,
Then,
At eight o clock we'll sit once more,
Hoping this week,
Is the week we'll score
    R. Mitchell

Mediumistic Doors

Divine Spirit, Heavenly Father
We lift up our eyes to Thee
And as we look beyond this world
Our eyes begin to see

Begin to see a world full of love
A world full of life and beauty
A world in which our spirit friends live
And return to remind us of our duty

A duty not only to ourselves
But to all who dwell on this planet
So that as we express the highest within
Love, Knowledge, Wisdom and Truth, will span it

A duty not only to every Man, Woman and Child
But to the Animals that share this Earth
To exploit, To test drugs, To eat, we are advised
Was not the reason for their birth

So it is with reverence Dear God
That we thank You for Your Natural Laws
That allow Love, Knowledge, Wisdom and Truth
To stream through Mediumistic Doors
    Rodney George Priest

Ancient Winter To Modern Spring

Winter this Year was Cold and Severe, Winds from the Steppes did Blow
We Hurried Home and to Fight the Cyclone, became part of Winter's Glow.
At the Change of the Pelt as the Winter Snows Melt,
We look forward to Oncoming Spring.
Man has Changed Breeding Plans, so that Dear Little Lambs,
Can Appear at the Push of a Thing.
Veterinarian as a Father, Oh What a Palaver, please learn from Time Now Gone By.
To Refuse Natural Behaviour, will Not be the Saviour, for Farming or Children at Knee.
But at least they Still See, As they Walk Safe and Free,
Bluebells and Primrose a Plenty.
If Restraint is Not Shown, The Museums Will Own, these Carpets in Years Maybe Twenty.
The Refreshment of Spring, May then Be a Thing, Cast into a Bygone Age.
If Deprived of this Charm, Who Can Measure the Harm,
To Minds Possessed By T.V.
Will all Natural Acts Be Decided By Fax, Or will this Word Now Be Heard.
By those Who Can Change, What Has Now Been Deranged.
Or Will a Protest be Quite Absurd.
    Raymond Lang

Mother Earth

Oh Mother Earth, on whose bosom lie
We humans like a horde of ants,
Beneath an ever changing sky,
Seasons of change bring a rainbow glow,
Colours of green, gold and silver, gleam,
Where mighty oceans and rivers flow.

Hills, mountains and forests of green,
Lie in the foreground.
Oh what a beautiful scene,
Treasures of wealth buried so deep.
Gold, silver, and diamonds, shine,
Rivets of veins hidden away from
The eyes of mankind
Ready for the valiant to reap.

When you are angry you rumble and roar,
Fire, and ash, to the atmosphere soar,
Hurricanes, typhoons attack with force
Like spirits in the night from
Some unknown source,
Oh Mother Earth, jewel of the universe.
    C. Matthews

Liberation

It's fifty years since that great day
We heard sir Winston Churchill say:
"Our dear Channel Isles will now be free
The war is won — it's victory"

Those five long years at last were over
No more air raids, or taking cover
When the planes flew over their bombs to drop
Those awful sirens at last would stop

For those who stayed - it meant their freedom
From years of fear, frustration, boredom
Instead of Jackboots marching on the street
Some friendly faces they soon would greet

We think with pride all those thousands
Who left their loved ones and their homelands
To fight for country, liberty and peace
So that all wars and strife would cease

Many were young and had no training
They went without question or complaining
They were brave, some with their lives had to pay
For our tomorrows they gave their today
    Maud Falla

Robin (My February Friend)

Icy February, with some snow;
We have homes but where can you go
Little round ball of fluff?
Haven't you had enough
Of the permafrost in the ground
And the freezing wind all around!
Yet you are singing a song from the heart
As if you and I would never part!
Nothing moves only your throat
As it trills each tiny note!
So tame you are and very bold
With feathers fluffed against such cold!

Veronica Twells

Snowman

The snow was very crisp and white,
We had a snowman built that night,
We put some stones upon the top so
You could see what a face he'd got,
You couldn't hold him close to you
because the snow would melt right through.
So when the snow comes thick and fast,
you'll know a snowman's made to last.

K. J. Watson

" Hopes For Tomorrow ".....

Many illnesses, horrific at that, exist in our world today
We can't sit back in the hope that they'll just quietly fade away
Instead we must research them, in the hope to find a cure
Experimentation is all well and good, but the results are often poor.
Scientists spend hours and hours, performing test upon test
In the hope of discovering the miracle drug, to stop cancer of the breast
Or other such dreaded illnesses, such as AIDS and HIV
All of which are so commonly heard of, but treated unsuccessfully
It's through no fault of our hospitals, the doctors try to save
Lives of those who're terrified they may die, but try their hardest to be brave

Relief may be provided, but pain still affects the mind and soul
Victims try to overcome their illness, to get better is their goal
Whether they do or not — it seems — the choice isn't ours to make
But the reality of it is eternally with us, when we go to sleep and when we wake
Only fortunate ones recover — for others — such hopes seem far away
They keep up their spirit, as their condition deteriorates, more each day
Their treatment becomes ineffective — and the inevitable draws near
Their days now numbered — they've got six months left — if they're lucky it could be a year.
So perhaps then for some it's all over, but those who remain must fight on 'til they find
A revolutionary drug to cure all ills, and instill in us all — peace of mind.

Rachael Hughes

Complacency

When others boycott meetings, go on strike
We show our disapproval, then forget
When lovers of our heritage protest
By climbing trees to stop another road
We dub them radicals and hooligans
(Despite the local people in their midst)
We rightly ostracize the terrorists
Yet cheerfully accept a national call
To take up arms in some far foreign land
(Especially if our oil supply's at risk)
As long as our backyard is not involved
We'll criticise the others as they fight
Against contamination of our land
We shouldn't fear subversion from a few
Complacency of many is the foe.

L. C. H. Long

On The Birth Of S.R.M. Jones

Your name is Jones, young sir? Ah well,
We cannot all have names that knell and thunder to eternity.
Perhaps a hyphen? No. I see.
What boots it anyway if yours is just one more of many scores
Of Joneses sounding all the same.
But pray have you another name?

Sebastian! Ah, now I see! Your parents were ahead of me.
Sebastian falls on the ear like clashing swords, a buccaneer,
A man to reckon with, a dash
Of dauntless confident panache.
Will Robert, balanced, cool, inspire
A temp'rance in Sebastian's fire?

And Maxwell too! Young sir, you need
No sympathy from me. No creed
Can half endow you like your name
To guarantee success and fame.
Those nine fine syllables ensure
That in a century or more
Some abbey proud will guard your bones,
Sebastian Robert Maxwell Jones

Richard Need

Rhythm Of Life

There's a never failing rhythm in the world which God has made;
We can sense it all around us in the universe displayed.
There is rhythm in the sunset, in the evening and the dawn,
In our wakening from healthful sleep to greet another morn.

There is rhythm in the kettle when we put it on to boil;
The appearance of the flowers after winter in the soil.
There's the rhythm of the planets ever spinning down the years.
Keeping always to their courses to the music of the spheres.

Sometimes the tempo's slower when the world seems full of care,
When the burden seems too heavy, and there's no-one there to share.
But there's rhythm in the mystery surrounding life and death,
Repeated in the pattern of our rising, falling breath.

There's the grand and glorious rhythm of the waves upon the shore.
They were there in the beginning, and will be forevermore.
But the great conductor has the elements in His control,
And can quieten the mighty winds which blow from pole to pole.

Then the rhythm of our heartbeats, never ceasing all life long
Will accentuate the rhythm as we praise His name in song.

Marjorie Gardner

Goblin O Goblin

Goblin o Goblin where are you now?
We besiege you to tell us how to bewitch
you now.
You come, you go but how.
So bring a bit of magic to me now.
I see you now out yonder in the wood sitting on
A log made of wood.
I only wish you could be good.
So we could play in the mud.
Goblin o Goblin please be good if you would.

K. Robinson

Ready Steady Go

A family stood at the pavement's edge,
Waiting to cross the road.
"Watch for the green man" the father said,
"When he lights up we can go."

"Why are those people not doing the same?"
The children asked. "Why do they cross
When the man is still red? Who would be to blame
If they fell whilst running across?"

"It would be a great shame if this happened of course",
Said dad, "But what you need to know
Is, don't copy others. Do what is right.
Look! The man has turned green. We can go."

M. Pollock

Hope

Sometimes loved ones have to leave;
We are left to cry and grieve.
God takes them for a reason,
When they have lived out all their seasons.
It's not for us to question why
We are all born to live and then to die.
There is another place where we meet again,
Free of anguish and all pain,
A lovely place full of love,
Beautiful gardens and virgin white doves.
It's said if you have glimpsed it you won't want to return,
And we are only on this earth for a short time to learn,
And when all that learning is finished,
Our pain and sorrow will be diminished.
Our loved ones have gone first to prepare us a place;
They will be waiting for us with such joy on their face.
There will be angels singing and bells ringing,
Separated again never,
Just tranquillity and love forever and ever.

R. I. Pratchett

King Coal Is Dead

I was old before I grew up.
We all were. Old people living
In an old valley, near an old town.
Forgotten. Sad-eyed children frolicking
Over once vibrant entities we called pits.
Buried souls, and buried bones where
Once men toiled, and some despoiled. Again.
Only a ghostly echo of migrated spectres.
Nothing is precious here anymore.
Not even the cricket pitch.

It is Midwinter, bleak and barren.
I am no hero, just an aberrant phantom
Returning to haunt my ancestors,
And mourn the loss of a dear friend.
He was an emperor of this desolate domain.
Tall, proud and strong, a colossus of the
cricket pitch, the colliery and the pub.
Even the graveyard echoes wistfully
With his nobility, courage and humility.
A defiant valediction no one can deny.

Neal Wilford

Michael

My son Michael — tall and straight,
Waving Goodbye at the garden gate.
Joining the Air Force to see the world,
Starting a new life with dreams unfurled.

The weeks flew by to his "PASSING-OUT",
Where we heard the Sergeant's orders shout.
To left and right he did march and drill,
While the pride in our hearts our eyes did fill.

Then home at last for a few day's leave,
With silver wings on his smart blue sleeve.
On Sunday morning — by his side,
We walked to Church and were filled with pride.

Then he brought home a girl so sweet;
With dimpled smiles and dainty feet.
Eyes of brown and hair so fair,
And a voice that was soft with a Suffolk burr.

"We want to get married" we heard him say;
And swiftly dawned their Wedding Day.
And the love in their eyes made the day more bright,
Than the sun shining down on the happy sight.

Marian D. Dobbins

Winter's Hold

Icy fingers have touched the land, all has become and frosty,
Water suddenly runs no more, it lies silent and solid.
Icicles hang down like long frozen fingers,
where once water trickled gently over stones.
Trees seem almost unable to move, like all else they seem
   frozen in time.
Winter has its hold on everything, yet it is only biding its time.
Time to cover everything in a different shade of white.
The white of snow, that flutters down so peacefully,
So peacefully, that it seems like twinkling pieces of lace,
Yet on the ground it covers all,
Like a heavy blanket, cold, and foreboding.
The bleak sun tries its very best, but its weak rays can do
   nothing,
Nothing but wait and bide its time.
Winter holds everything, but it will not always do so,
Soon it must release its grip, and quietly disappear.
Disappear that is, until the following time,
When it will again be in control, and all will freeze and shiver,
And wait for springs turn, and life to again come once more.

Penlee A. Sowerby

Slumbering

The House is slumbering, still, watching windows silent vigil keep.
Watching, waiting, beckoning to curious eyes, come, enter, for I
   sleep.
Enticed, enthralled, on trembling threshold the curious now stand.
And then, upon the yielding door, a pushing, probing, curious hand.
Voices rising to crescendo, drift carelessly on still - hung air.
Footsteps echo, stamp and stride; fear forgotten, seeking
   secrets here and there.
Laughter, words and whispers rustle dust - dried walls that
   gently sigh,
As silent shadows stir, awakened by that shrill, sharp, human cry.
Misty maelstrom slowly swirls, as captive flies within its dusty
   clouds collide,
And dank, dark waters swell, erupt round stumbling feet by
   terror tied.
Putrid, reeking emanations stifle, sting their streaming, blinded
   eyes;
As burning throats scream silently their horror - anguished cries.
Screaming, sobbing, entwined, flailing, threshing bodies safe
   sanctuary seek;
But tortured, slaughtered, are cast carelessly into obscene
   oblivion, bodies broken, meek.
The House moans rapturously, its savage presence feeding,
   devouring flesh and pain.
At last appeased, its ancient, bestial, ravening needs now
   sated once again.
Now silent, spectral shadows soothe its dark, demonic halls.
Until the next awakening, a slumbering crypt and sepulchre
   within its silent walls

P. A. Fox

Peaches And Strawberries And Pears, Pick Me

Is she vexed?
and tired withered eyes,
and staring blindly,
and peaceful and
content and full of
things to come,

In old treasure chests
and through a moonface
in a burning flame
and a face not
yet touched and
Jackets and dresses
and novels,

With a still thoughtless
mind and fragile
speeches and peaches
and strawberries
And pears, pick
me.

Eleanor Murdoch

Ode To Being Deaf

I sit on the sand, knees bent, head in hand
watching the wavelets trickle to my feet.
I see great liners passing by carrying people
to other lands. I see them where sky and sea meet.
I see but I do not hear.

I see white sea horses playing atop the waves
gambolling playfully with the creatures of the sea.
I feel the throb of engines from the boats passing by.
I wave to the people, as they wave across to me.
I see but I do not hear.

I see the swooping sea gulls herding in a fishing boat.
The other day, the sea brought in a green glass fishing float.
I gazed into the sea green glass, all I saw were ships that
pass, to places I have never been.
I see but I do not hear.

I would like to go to those foreign lands,
where the oceans and sea gulls visit,
I sit, I see, I wonder if I did so
they could understand, and talk to me using just their
hands. I see but I do not hear.

Sylvia Colebourne

What Have They Done?

I'm gazing at the ocean
Watching the shadows dancing by,
As I peer at the tides in motion
Wishing and wanting things to change.
This oily black endlessness
We'd do anything to exchange.

The cold ebb of the tide
Along this beautiful welsh coast,
We wish that the sludge would subside
Our beaches are now covered in oil
Young and old help in the clean up
The locals trying hard through toil.

Black, motionless, animals are what we see
These limp creatures were our wildlife
Who like the fisherman, depend on the sea.
Do the ones who are to blame realize
The harm that has been done?
Damage so great, we don't have to surmise!

C. M. Scone

The Joy and Sadness of Winter

I sit at my window on a cold winter's day,
Watching the birds as they take nuts from the tray,
One by one they fly away,
I say to myself, I wish you could stay.
Then I smile as I see the children at play,
I listen to their squeals as they slide down the bray,
And think to myself once I could have got up that bray.
Now I can only watch from my cosy little patch,
I laugh as they roll the snow to a ball,
I can tell it's going to be quite tall,
I guess you all know what they are building with snow,
Oh how they cheer as they add eyes, nose and a bow.
It saddens me as I see them get ready to go,
A wave and a smile as they pass my front wall,
Now they are gone, unaware of the pleasure they have given.
They have brightened my day and I yearn for yesterday,
As all I can do is to stare at my wall and pray,
Yes, I pray for a summer's day,
So I can get out for a day,
And to the garden I'll go and watch the flowers grow.

Rosemary Splaine

Purr

Pussibly cute with claws,
Utterly adorable with paws,
Resting contented with ears alert,
Ruffling my fur and cleaning my shirt.

D. R. Sharpe

All In The Mind

Come on Chip, let's go for a stroll
Watch out lad, don't fall down that hole
Come here boy, don't get in a fight.
You know darned well it gives me a fright.
You've jumped over the stile with ease.
I've got stung right up to my knees
Come on lad, stop racing around
Or you'll tire yourself out, I'll be bound
Now then lad, stop messing about
Let's finish our walk whilst the sun's still out.
If you carry on sniffing around
We'll get soaked to the skin, I'll bet you a pound.

All these thoughts are just in my mind
Only a few will know how much I've pined
I'm walking alone in the field today
But I feel he's still with me, my dear little stray

Peggy Edwards

This Year

This year won't be like the others
Wasting time searching for meanings.
Digging for reasons just smothers
More abstract and artistic leanings.
No more soul-searching and delving
No longer with life will I race.
I'll make my mind neat racks and shelving
And keep every thought in its place.

I used to think destiny measured
With not much allowance for wrong.
Your childish ambitions were treasured;
The words of a long written song.
I now feel there's no point in trying.
It's already known what occurs.
A flash to the past — has it shown you at last?
But memories soon become blurs.

I'll tell to myself as a chorus
Repeat it again and again
If everything's preordained for us
Why should we suffer the pain?

Rosalyn Nancarrow

Mum

For a every special mum,
Whose time alone with dad has come.
She wanders round the house so bare,
reminiscing about all the happenings there.
The shouting the laughter, the tears, the joy, and
the running around of her little girls and boy.

It's hard for a mum when her chicks have flown,
they've all got bigger and now have lives of their own.
Be rest assured they'll always need you still,
as they battle their way up that lifelong hill.

The bond between us all is so very great,
but it's mother who now has a big space on her plate.
Now is the time to go and do everything you wish,
go do lunch, to the spa and eye up that dish!!!

Then come home and meet our dad,
go out to the movies, for a drink and don't be sad.
Because no matter how far those chicks have flown,
there'll be nothing as welcome as visiting mum and dad at home.

Theresa Chambers

The Butterfly

Do not leave me yet awhile, stay a little longer.
Until the sunshine dries your wings and your legs grow stronger
Soon you will be flying as your wings gain power,
Over fields and meadows, visiting each flower.
Today a miracle, before my eye unravels.
Goodbye little butterfly, good luck on your travels

Phyllis Sandiford

Plum Blossom

I, a bottle without a ship
Washed up on far away shores
Without papayas
Flower necklaces, haunting drums or cannibals
Was nonetheless pleased to see plenty of curious natives
curiously pleased to see me
These Japanese, who aim to please
Welcoming with cherries, pines, with mountains tongued by mist
Offering a world newly carved and tinted — so much sculptured
sashimi on a lacquered dish
Miso and McDonalds, manners, mobile telephones
K.F.C. and kimono, strains of koto drowned out with traffic's
Not the ocean's hum
I asked myself was this why I had come?

But then in a Kyoto garden
By a temple shrugging off the crude insinuations of a cold
February sun
Drenched in blossoms that knew nothing of the rose, lavender,
old violets of my grandmother's dresser drawer
The skin remembered salt that memory forgot
And knew my ship, in a branch of plum.
Tracey Gannon

Dogwood

A new nightgown for now
was what I'd wanted,
a little sun, the oldest cover,
a meeting with the other.

More naked than before,
unmet, uncovered,
a succubus staring,
I've stayed myself, have lacked the other.

Now I clothe myself more surely,
know my colours, poise the feelings,
proud my hips.
I'll bear myself this spring,
no other.

This spring I'll note more clearly
the dogwoods' veil, children's beauty, and
all defects of age in thought and thing.
This spring I'll lay bare and comic
all I learn.
As others I am:
naked with, and naked without, another.
Mary Dyson

Alfred Archibald Percy Maghee

Alfred Archibald Percy Maghee
was the scourge and curse of his form class 'C'.
His teacher Miss Pym said he really was wild.
A spotty, myopic, detestable child.

His talent for mischief was blatantly dire.
As the boss of his gang he was there to inspire
which he did every Friday behind the bike shed.
If you dared not to show you'd be basically dead!

His exploits were legend, incredulous, ghoulish.
To turn a blind eye would be seriously foolish.
The locals all trembled and shook at his name,
such was the impact, the power of his fame.

He terrorized teachers and grannies and all
if they wouldn't give in, if they wouldn't play ball.
His tantrums were noisy and messy and mega,
his face turned to purple the 'orrible beggar!

But for all of the battles and criminal wiles,
the tribulations and terrible trials,
and though his misconducts were awfully bold,
he's just like other four year olds!
L. Baldwin

Memories Of Summer

Awaken at dawn to a chorus of birds
  Warm sunlight on my pillow,
Cumulus clouds in a cerulean sky
  Fields of golden wheat below.

The buzzing of a Honey Bee
  As it passes by unseen,
The distant sound of a cricket game
  being played on the village green.

A graceful flight of Swallows
  Soaring high above the trees,
The fragrant scent of Lavender
  Carried by a summer breeze.

A picnic with my loved one
  Eating strawberries in the sun,
The peaceful sound of a Blackbird singing
  When the day is done.

All these fond memories of summer
  Seem to help me in a way,
When the weather's cold outside
  On a frosty winter's day.
Paul Vincent Brown

Rock 'N' Roll Band

Where were you when we were getting high?
Walking in these corridors, slower than we remembered and
faster than a cannonball.
You stepped outside, we were on the stage, in the light of glory,
in a man made heaven, having the time of our lives.
Who was that in the shadows?
Amplifiers sing with discordant voices and guitars feature
heavily in bass solos. Drums echo the inflated roar of the crowds.
In electronic kingdoms, we're the land of milk and honey.

Now, Strat silence, on a distant playing ground, no more electronic
information to tamper with your soul.
The show is over, take a bow.

And let me ask,
Weak as I am, was I too much for you?
Suzy Louise Watson

'A Rainy Day'

Raincoats on backs,
Umbrellas held high,
This is no time to linger and sigh —
Faster and faster the rain tumbles down —
Splish, Splosh,
All over the busy town.
Sheila Matthews

The Man

He shuffles along, with a hole in his shoe.
Wrapped up in many layers.
Dirty vests old jumpers,
anything to keep him warm.
People look at him with disgust on their face.
They don't see the man. Only the tramp.
They don't see the man he used to be,
A man who had respect,
A man who had a family.
He looks in to the bin for something to eat.
Anything to fill this hole.
This emptiness that has crept into his soul.
He is empty with hunger, and empty of love.
He sits on the road and sighs.
Puts his head in his hands and openly cries.
Where are his family? where did they go?.
He can't remember he doesn't want to know.
Too painful the memories, of them killed in the crash.
Too painful to live life, so he let's it all pass.
Shirley Lockey

The Faithful Wanderer

I've tramped o'er windswept heath and moor,
Walked wooded vales and hills that soar
To mountain crags whose peaks appear
Above the very clouds.
Down ancient highways I have strode,
Cool leafy lane and rough-hewn road,
To flag-stoned streets whose pavements teem
With faceless, madding crowds.

O'er timeless seas my mind has strayed,
At sacred shrines my lips have prayed
To ancient gods whose mystic powers
Are hidden in the past.
And yet, for all my wanderings,
For all my wild imaginings,
I've always come back home to you,
My darling love, at last.
Peter P. Balshaw

Requiem

I have travelled this life with its ups and downs,
Walked through memory's meadows where golden buttercups
   abound,
Trodden the highways of difficulty too,
Sometimes felt weary, anxious and blue.
But always my loved ones and friends have been there
To lift up my spirit when burdened with care.
So when life for me on earth is no more
And I enter the portals of death's beckoning door,
Then, dear Lord, please let me be
Among all those loved ones who once loved me
And let me find they love me still
As I pass through the valley and out over the hill
And Lord, let me feel their warm embrace
And with you in Paradise take up my place.
V. R. Charlish

Lincolnshire

Lush green fields and golden sands,
Walk together hand in hand,
The air is sweet, but yet is keen,
Tranquillity felt, tranquillity seen.

Villages scattered far and wide,
Neat and tidy, full of pride,
Lambs and calves skip through the air,
Playing happily without a care.

Silence so great it can almost be heard,
Broken at random by songs from the birds,
Rabbits seen playing as a matter of cause,
Pheasants strut by for their evening walk.

Crimson sunset slips over the wolds,
Nighttime is falling all nature is told,
This place where all my hopes and dreams aspire,
This earthy, loamy, Lincolnshire.
R. R. Spittle

The Wall

I lie awake each night
Waiting for the morning light
Thinking of the day before
That was the last time my love I saw
Feeling her body next to mine
How I wish that she was mine
Holding, caressing, stroking her hair
Feeling her love instead of despair
Life is cruel, it's just not fair
Can it last, this love affair
Daylight comes, I hear the birds
I listen to their call
But the thing I long for most of all
Is my love beyond that wall.
William Beswick

Hit And Run

Flickering windows, bloodstained floor.
Vomit on the pavement, the slam of a door.
Shuttering steel, broken glass.
The homeless sleep in Hotel Underpass.

Desolate Metro, beggars and strays.
Under a footbridge, adolescent runaways.
Yesterday's papers, fast food slowly eaten.
An ambulance rescues the bottled and beaten.

Drunken drivers trying to be sober,
Read the next day that the boy they ran over,
Wasn't a hedgehog going under the Ford,
But a f***ed up cabbage on a life support.

"He'll come 'round," says the man at the wheel,
"He'll get sympathy and money and a record deal.
With luck the surgeon will make a mistake,
On a three day shift and he's barely awake."

"And the folks will get millions in compensation,
And then they can have that Caribbean vacation,
No more worries 'bout the bills to pay,"
"Yeah," He says, "they'll probably thank me one day."
Mark Ritchie

A Butterfly

Today I saw a butterfly
Virginal white against blue sky
It fluttered by without a sound
Travelling on to where it was bound

The tranquil elegance of its flight
Stirred my soul with much delight
Returning me to when a child unperturbed
I too played in serenity undisturbed

The beautiful thoughts of my child mind
Allowed me freedom of every kind
No restrictions no confines
A butterfly-child flying no set lines

A wonderful time never forgotten
But only the once ever begotten
Too soon it's just a memory passed by
Until you see a butterfly!

I felt a little sad as it left the scene
Yet glad to have recalled moments serene
The gossamer beauty flew free and bright
'Good luck' I whispered as it left my sight
G. A. Hopkins

A Plea For Their Planet

Before man placed corrupting hands
Upon these rare created lands
How wonderful they must been
Their beauty only ever seen
By creatures who had no intent
To rape their own environment
Who only killed so they could eat
And in so doing helped complete
The plan which nature had decreed
To raise no more than earth could feed.

But then God made His one mistake
And in His wisdom? man did make,
Man whose everlasting greed
Cares nothing for what others need,
Man who takes at any cost
And never sees what he has lost.
Man's arrogance is just obscene
Dear God, why don't You intervene?
Can you not rid this place of man?
And let Your good earth start again.
Maggie Allen

A Father's Love

He walks along the country road
Upon his homeward way.
He's milked the cows and fed the pigs
And gathered in the hay.

His work-worn hands swing by his side
In rhythm with his tread,
His old brown jacket open wide,
His trilby on his head.

His face lights up with happiness
As he hears our hurrying feet.
As we race and chase each other
To be the first he'll greet.

No father ever showed more love
Or had more tender care,
Whenever we were in trouble
He was always there.

But now he has gone, his memory will
Forever with me stay,
His loving smile and gentle voice
Will guide me on my way.
Sarah E. Roberts

Divorce

We hear the word "divorce" these days and never really care,
Until it comes into our lives and stays forever there,
It's not just the wife who is left with pain,
Her family and friends all feel the strain,
For the daughter you thought of as happily wed,
Now sleeps alone in a single bed.
Your granddaughter too has her life shattered
For she obviously wasn't the one who mattered,
Her Dad's last words were "I need some space"
Which seemed to her like a slap in the face.

From a nice family home, where things appeared great,
To a two bedroom flat on a council estate,
And the friends they once had are no longer there,
For they had been friends that they knew as a 'Pair'.
But when you're a social security mum,
Old friends walk on by you as though they were dumb,
And the daughter who once used to sing and to dance,
Just gets on with life as though in a trance,
That's when you finally realize,
Divorce is a thing that ruins many lives.
T. M. Devaney

Life?

Birth. The striking of a match.
Bringing a new light into the world;
A small flame in a world of darkness.

A surge of energy in the young flame,
Eager to experience life and love,
Gulping at its fuel to make it strong.

Rising, growing bigger and bolder,
Then shrinking,
As the desire to grow older disappears.

Glowing embers rekindle fond memories,
But haunting shadows from previous years
Flicker menacingly.

The inevitable journey to death
Which began at birth is only now realized.
Regrets and lost opportunities cannot be resolved.

Bridges have been burnt and there is no way back.
Oxygen can no longer revive the flame.
Only ashes are left.

The ashes are thrown away and forgotten
And more matches are manufactured.
Lorna Hale

Life In The '90s

Life's pleasures taken one by one
until eventually there's none
The devastating disease tearing him apart
destroying his body, but never his heart
The ugliness of AIDS appeared
after living with HIV for several years
Physically destroyed, struggling with pain
drained emotionally, praying to stay sane
Looking haggard, feeling old
and lonely in the cold
Another life fading away
so desperately wanting to stay
So much joy you brought us all
feeling so helpless as you call
Weight dropping by the stone
facing death all alone
No known cure has been found
more news of deaths circling round
J. Cook

Deathtrade

We chase them and we hunt them till there's nowhere left to hide,
until all they can hear is their heartbeat, the measure of their stride. The single ones are lucky they have a chance to run but mothers stand in fear in a bid to protect their young.
They make an easy target one shot and they are gone, leaving behind an orphan looking for life in a carcass where there is none.
Many lives have been taken for the sake of ivory or fur, to be worn by an ignorant person who never had to care.
They didn't have to hear the cries of one alone as it nuzzled death for life, as it wasted away slowly eternal sleep an escape from strife.
The hunters triumphant shouts echo again and again as they leave the scattered dying oblivious to the pain.
They just don't understand the drastic change they bring, the full that they leave empty the slaughter of true kings.
Tania Woolcock

England Today

There are dragons out there on the streets,
Untamed, and free to roam.
Frightened folk remain at home
For lack of hunters on their beats.
The forked tongue and slimy skin
Display the evil deep within.
Gestating from the deep morass
Where prophets perished long ago
They stalk the streets en masse
Without restraint, free from foe.
The man who tries to overthrow
Is stricken with a murderous blow.
How many saints will they devour
Before it is St. George's hour?
E. Carlton

Love

Dearest Mum and Dad
When you're near me your love for me is like a bright light
Shining through the darkness
You bring me joy with everything you do and say.

You gave me everything you could
You put up with the bad things I did and my rebellious ways
You even put up with all the trouble I got into

Even though were so far apart now, I still think about you
And love you more with each passing day.
If you had to go away and leave me my whole world
Would fall apart and my life wouldn't be worth living anymore.

But deep in my heart I know you'll always be there for me
And you will never ever leave me
So I pray to God each night to thank Him
For sending me two angels for my parents
And I will always love and cherish you.
M. Needham

Scotch Katie

In her innocence and youth
unpretend and truth.
With stars in her eyes of promised prize that on
the other side the grass greener grew.
Only to make a foolish mistake, that one day she came to rue.
From a far away place quite near to a lake, by the
sea of brilliant blue.
She packed her bags addressed her tags and into
England flew.
Away from the fresh air on a wing and a prayer
and away from the folks that she knew.
To a city of old, with streets paved with gold
This she thought to be true.
Only to find her dreams unwind, here in a
little old flat, where the neighbours won't chat
with her mangy old cat, here her dreams came to rot.
So to this very day her thoughts drift
away to the spot she left behind by
the sea, and as for her now she's a
cranky old cow, who's always ready for a good row.

P. McGuinness

Moon-Gem Seduction

You guard your territory well.
Unobtrusive in amongst the pebbles, rocks
and lots of insignificant debris that is
washed up by the swell.

You use the light to lure them.
Twinkling in seductive manner
you wave your little diamond banner,
a provocative little Moon-gem with
your dark side hidden well.

The snare is set.
The silken net is cast to bring them to your lair
as they walk past.

Reaching for
what they perceive as treasure on the beach,
you seize your chance to
put a little colour on your cheeks.

You lie and wait, and hide your head
at the limit of their reach and
while their hands start to caress
you stain their skin blood red.

Roy Frankland

Night By Orinoco

Stars trip,
up, down,
Always lonely.
Lusciously meandering your long, obsessive venture

Everywhere tiring in awe.

Marie Louise Andrew

The Birthday

She looked in the mirror and sighed,
What was different about her tonight?
Her skin was still good; her figure still trim.
When happy, her eyes were still bright.

She knew she had blessings and riches,
She led a very contented life.
Her house and her garden were precious to her,
She knew she was loved as a wife.

Why then, was she feeling so restless?
Why did she feel so sad and alone?
She had a husband, a family and friends,
Yet she felt she was adrift on her own.

She shrugged at her thoughts as she left,
For some moments she suffered real fear.
She smiled at them all as her husband said,
'Happy sixtieth birthday, my dear.'

Moyra Crandon

Torn Apart

The day has come for me to go
Unfortunately this is so
My body is weak, my thoughts are strong
I feel this will carry on and on

The days have passed
Only four in total
It seems like months
I feel that emotional

The two of us had fun together
and I'd hoped it would be forever
The future was discussed just so
but now....Oh I just don't know

I'd not a thought in my mind
That I'd be gone in a matter of time
It makes no sense, we were so happy
He must have gone a little scotty

Tanya Hudgell

A Marriage Tribute

For Susan and Gerry

S haring your destiny, that was your desire
U nderstanding and forgiving is all you require
S uccess you will find it you count up to ten
A nd this truth you will know but only then
N o one is perfect we are agreed.
+
G iving and taking is all that you need
E verlasting happiness you will surely find
R emember your promises and try to be kind
R esolve to be true through trouble and strife
Y ou are then sure to find a wonderful life

S incerely we wish you all of the best
H appiness, contentment and all the rest
E verything we wish you comes straight from the heart
P lease accept our best wishes just for a start
H ealthy and wealthy we hope you will be
E leven bonny babies we hope soon to see
R emember to be faithful together, stand fast
D epend upon each other and your happiness will last.

C. G. Walker

Untitled

You kiss my cheeks as the snowflakes fall
Brushing my hair as the gentle breeze that blows
Warming my soul the glow of light that love in a beam —
Need I want more?
You whisper in my ears through the sound of the water's stream
Energy flowing through the branches of the trees
You whisper in my ears
The clouds float by as there is not time
Rhythmic, colourful, projecting their images.
They float by, up, up, up there high
Need I want more?

Christina Hellebrandt

Miss Amelia Pouch

Miss Amelia Pouch was a most unfortunate name,
But all of a sudden she came to fame,
For an aged aunt who thought her quite plain and truly tame,
Had bequested to her a most handsome claim.

And now Miss Amelia Pouch found herself,
Much to her surprise and pleasure,
Adored and called on, and even given the title of Dame.

However, as time passed daintily on,
And Wealth became the tool to maim,
She decided for a new and a biting surname,
Which was to be, and soon became widely known
As the grand, the demure,
The Dame Amelia Sham.

Ayesha Akhter

A Mother To Her Child

When I look at you and see you smile, and when you're fast asleep,
your breaths are slow and even, your lashes rest upon your cheek.
I pray you'll always have that peace, feel safe, not toss and turn,
but I know as you get older, like us all, you'll have to learn.

You'll have some disappointments and I hope that they'll be few.
You'll meet people who will hurt you, maybe things that frighten you.
And I will try my very best to soften every blow,
To be there for you night and day, to protect you as you grow.

And when you're down I'll remind you that, the world's not as bad as it seems,
that there's a new ambition born out of every shattered dream
That there are more than seven wonders, in this planet where we live,
the wonder of books, of music, the capacity to give.

The beauty of art and laughter, the miracle of space,
and the wonder of the love I've had for you,
Since first I saw your face.

Tracey Anne Murphy

Why

Why are they fighting in Bosnia
Why are they fighting this war
Why are they fighting in Bosnia
is it worth dying for

The carnage, the suffering
A child's shattered life
How can we help ease their pain
Knowing tomorrow will be safe for us
But for them it all happens again

Schools and houses can all be repaired
In spite of all the damage
How do you mend a child's mind
How can we stop the carnage

Why are they fighting in Bosnia
Why is there all so much hatred
When will the world take a lesson from this
That all human life is sacred

Ron Lambert

" Dreamtime "

Shadows are creeping, time you were sleeping

Mummy is waiting on you —

Soon you'll be waking; when dawn is a breaking
your dreamtime will be through!

Dreamtime is coming in again, my love, sleepy land
is just around the corner

So put your toys away, it's the end of another day
and night was made for dreaming, so they say.

Angels will be watching round your bed, gently
smiling as you slumber.

So dream your little dreams, 'cause you'll be grown
up too soon, it seems.

So make the most of your dreamtime now —

Dream on, little one, it's dreamtime NOW!!!

W. P. Folkard-Garratt

Tiger

The striped carnivore that stalks its prey
Beneath the cover of darkness.
A cat feared by animals
But obviously not by man.

Creatures murdered daily
For their bone, flesh and coat.
Would you kill a person
Because you want his clothes?

Lisa Faulkner

Wedding Of The Seven Rainbows

I sit on a mountain boulder in Glen Brittle
Yonder are the majestic Cuillin, a veritable jewel carved by
Nature on Scotland's Isle of Skye.
I love the bright sun; the showers I do not mind.
Suddenly, lo and behold; I am entranced by a sight never
beheld by man or beast.
Seven rainbows, yea, seven! float along the glen in stately
procession.
Eagerly, like a schoolboy I watch them. Will they touch the
silvery burn racing down opposite?
I hold my breath! Yes, oh yes! The left arch of the first rainbow
bestows a nuptial kiss on the burn. (Where is the pot of gold?)
And the second, third, fourth, fifth, sixth, and seventh, one
after the other.
Ah! What a tremendous sight to gladden heart and soul.
Alas! The show is soon over.
The rainbows journey on to the sea loch.
The drops rejoin the waters from whence they came.

Raymond Japhet

Life's An Illusion

Life goes on around me, I'm happy people think
What's in my head is different life really does stink

Sitting on the outside, always looking in
Being part of a group would really feel like a sin

Nobody knows this feeling, its lonely being me
Always there for others, it's the real me they fail to see

Perhaps one day I'll crumble, and shout just what I feel
but I doubt it somehow, as life never seems quite real

Putting on an act, no worries, cares or woes,
Never dwelling to much or everyone becomes a foe.

So I'll keep this happy mask on, it's easier somehow
Never thinking too far ahead, living and coping for just now

I'll be that happy person, jolly and always there
Totally reliable, without a single care

But you and I know different now, a black side lingers on
Never to see the light of day but then life is just a con.

J. A. Fletcher

Starlight Starbright

Glimmering, shimmering bright,
up high amidst the sky at night.
Shining such a luminous white,
there's no such sight as twinkling starlight.
Billions upon billions floating way up above,
to many of us they're a sign of God's love.
Come the night and gone the day,
they guide our path when we've lost our way.
For all of mankind including me and you,
they keep on blinking shinning through,
those clouds that gather as they do.
Glimmering, shimmering bright,
that magical, mystical, starlight.

Phillip N. Dawson

Life Gets Harder

What to do next is a hard choice
Watch a video or play with my toys
Go to school, see my friends
Or pretend I am ill, till it ends

Mummy goes to work, daddy does too
Nana looks after me, well, someone must do

I want a brother or a sister named Sue
But mummy says no way, I am like two
I get told off when I am naughty
You see daddy's no patience he's nearly forty
When I grow up I'll be a train driver
Or maybe a postman or fire fighter
Life gets harder, so I'm told
So I think I'll remain, at four years old

K. W. Mayoh

The Hungry Hawk

The hawk is in a fierce flight,
At every move she gains in height.
She peers down with her sharp red eyes,
Seeing no food she gently sighs.

But she still dives on, swooping with ease,
She lands in her nest upon the trees.
Her young look around but see no food,
So they all start calling in a terrible mood.

But the hawk in the tree does not know,
That there is a small rodent in the bushes below,
And the small rodent cannot see,
That there is a predator in the tree!

Amy Oates

For The Animals Of The World

All the animals of the world cry out,
At man's inhumanity and clout.
Can't they see the suffering they cause,
That goes on and on without even a pause?

The lonely hours they endure,
Must it go on forevermore!
Has man lost his compassion, for greed?
Haven't we all enough for need?

The cages, the pens, for pigs and for hens,
The pain and the cramp, till they don't know when
No hope! Despair!
What have they done! It's so unfair.

The sheep and the lambs crammed into vans,
For hours on end while man fights for plans,
Man's dreadful greed comes before need,
When will we ever learn?

The pictures they churn on T. V. each night,
We see and we hear of their dreadful plight,
Sad eyes pleading for help, miseries beyond compare.
When will we ever learn? It's so unfair!

Joan W. Needham

Tabernacles

I look forward to each Sunday, when people come to pray.
At my house of worship, it is a lovely day.

Everyone in Sunday rest, the children clean and neat
Adults on best behaviour, they gather there and meet.

The people with their tellies listening to the hymns.
It's grand to think they love me so, my heart it fairly sings.

However one must bear in mind, as just it was my plan.
Not to have such gandy shows, that I would come to man.

He only has to offer prayer, his best love for me save.
and I will travel anywhere, to house, or flat, or cave.

Although I love each Sunday, when people have more time.
I'm on call each and every day, I'm always on the line.

And every prayer I answer, you may not think this so.
You must remember sometimes that my answer will be no.

Gladys Richards

Richard

I looked upon his smiling face, I could not ask for more,
At nine months old, he's perfect, the grandson I adore,
He looks so much like Alan but with a sweetness which is Anne,
I wonder what the future holds for this precious little man.
Will he be tall and handsome, will he be clever and bright?
Do these things really matter when it comes to judging life.
To appreciate the countryside and all that grows around,
To have a love of nature and the peace that does abound,
To be an upright citizen and love his fellow man
To respect the other's point of view and do the best he can.
These are the things I wish for him as he grows big and strong,
Then I know that he'll be happy and life will be a song.

Lesley Fotheringham

The Seed Of Hope

The plant it sheds another leaf
At one time so grand
It stood upright and full of life
Fed by a loving hand

With extra love and tender care
Less solemn it would be
But the leaves have lost their glossy shine
The plant, I feel, is me

When new life starts in fresh new soil
With tender care it thrives
Without that special caring touch
In time this new life dies

If tendered in the best surround
And kept that way for life
The plant will flourish, make its roots
Then show itself with pride

If all the leaves fall to the ground
And shows but just the stem
Then we must plant new seeds hope
And form that love again.

Diane Richards

Highgate Cemetery

:Pure place:
at the cross-roads
of two mighty rivers
that calm each other into
this
:pure place:
cut out inside chaos
by brick wall

Where if not here, were we children
for a while
and where if not here, will we grow up perhaps
to take the pain we give away
Mum.

I'd come here in fever
but I got cold
fountains of ivy flow their green blood
into shelters, arbours, chapels, graves

I'd come here broken
but the ivy invaded me and now it is climbing up
my hard spine like monks building cloister on a lonely crag

Gregory Bartnik

So Much Silence

Her unsmiling face, glimpsed
at the window, meant goodbye.
For, at the late home-coming
to locked doors and a darkened house,

she lay on the kitchen floor,
head on a cushion
placed inside the oven's dragon-mouth;
all now deathly cold.

Dark uniforms came
in a clamour of lights
and took the body away;
leaving behind one shoe

and, stained with vomit,
that terrible cushion:
her only comfort —
that I couldn't wait to burn.

Almost worse was her letter
read after the verdict —
its scalding accusations
never to be answered.

John Younger

Seasons — Autumn Leaves!

Branches swaying in the breeze,
Autumn leaves begin to blow,
Here and there, everywhere,
Now is the time to say I care,
Golden brown they all fall down,
Floating and toppling through the air,
It just makes me want to stare,
The season has changed yet again,
Tipple, topple, those drops of rain
Glistening in the light so bright,
Making the season feel just right,

Forty one years have passed me by,
Every year these seasons do fly,
Winter, Spring, Summer and Autumn,
They can never be forgotten,
Reminders of our lives so precious,
Each coming day always brings new pleasures,
Open eyes so lucky to see,
The Autumn leaves swaying in the breeze.

Diana C. Rek

Memories Of Village Life

Peace, tranquillity, all is at ease
Away from the turmoil of modern living,
The birds for company up in the trees,
What sweet harmony is their singing
Villagers recall the days now past
When annual fetes were held
In the Vicarage garden, where there were stalls
And teas were served on the lawns

A concert there was, out of doors
The schoolmaster sang
And a lady too, with her lovely voice
Made everyone rejoice.

Pleased with financial success
And the company of friends,
The helpers all tired,
The busy day ends.

Homeward bound now, moments to recall
Smiles and laughter, joys galore
Friends look forward to another year
In faith and happiness, self assured

Edna F. Pine

A Lost Cat

Bagcat was searching and all alone
Bagcat was seeking a good new home.
He pattered round on stealthy feet
And sat in the gardens down the street.

Bagcat was pretty both honey and white
His face was jolly his eyes were bright
The patterns of his coat a delicious sight,
Although he had scars from many a fight.

Bagcat had chosen you and me
But he got shut in and couldn't get free.
Bagcat was rescued a little too late
He was carried away to meet his fate.
In the home of his choice he quietly lay
But by the morning he drifted away.

Bagcat lives on a lovely pet
Who never quite made it, but is with us yet.
Memory is not of sadness and fear
It is the realm of enchantment of what we held dear
Say but his name and Bagcat is here.

Gladys Eileen Brunell

Healing Of Nations

Mutilated ground
Bare and hostile with the fading suggestion of life;
Life filled with pain and hunger
The harsh breezes moan out to darkening valleys;
Naked and scattered with bones.
The blackened sky looms, thick with menace,
Suffocating the light.
Then like the swipe of a tapered sword
Blinding glory of something billions of times greater
　　than our star
Cracks the quilt of cloud.
Spears of flame, golden, yet clear as glass and
　　shimmering with rainbows
Echo off deathly rocks and spiral towards the realms of infinity.
The river of life cascades joyfully through the once destructed
earth, restores life and fills souls with hope.
Cries of laughter float upon the sweet air like music
And nourish new life until the whole kingdom is resonating
with beauty.
Trees flourish and bear the succulent fruit of knowledge;
Their leaves shall be the healing of nations.

Heather Thomas

Harvest Moon

Opalescent light,
Bathe thine body tonight,
Long shadows stretch out, caress and distort,
Turgid reflections that we never sought,
A crunching of stubble underneath foot,
Pushing cut stems into the sole of my boot,
Sweet heady smell, the horses' sweat,
Malevolent paths to travel yet,
Snorting and moaning the horses pull
Cart loads of wheat past the moon so full,
Flickering candlelight by house and inn,
Clandestine lovers entwined within,
Darkened churches where heads once bowed in prayer,
Now the pews are so bare,
Take thee bales so that we may lay,
On a bed filled with sweet musky hay,
Thistledown soft we search for each other,
The wife and her messidor lover.

Jill Whitchurch

While My Eyes In Darkness Stare

While my eyes in darkness stare.

In the shadows of my mind, and
Bear the burning spears, that bind
My thoughts to a darkened world.
My lamp is of a thousand stars, that
Light my cell, to free the bars
From my prison of winter night.
And escape my fate of sunless eyes,
That deafen me, my cries of silent pain.
But I will ride the plains and
Climb my spirit to its majestic
Heights, and sit upon my throne
Of faith, and judge not
the lightened world.

George T. Hurley

Halloween

On Halloween you can dress up as a mean Queen.
Dracula or Frankenstein, a mummy with no spine!
Trick or treaters come to your door.
Sometimes people give them a penny or more.
Sometimes they say a thank you rhyme like "The sky is blue,
the grass is green, thank you for the penny on Halloween".
Then they run off but other children come and they say,
"Please may we have a penny or more?" Nasty people just
slam the door; kind people give them — one pound!

The Halloween pumpkin lights up the room puff!
It goes out but we will light it up soon.

Charlotte Baetul

Just Musing

When I delve into the back of my mind
Beautiful pictures I know I will find
Of golden sands and sea so blue
In a country so old and yet so new

I see run tanned bodies and happy faces
They don't need to dream of far away places
There is sailing, surfing and barbecues as well
And dozing old timers have their stories to tell

Nearby a koala sits high in a tall gum tree
Munching tender leaves as happy as can be
On the ground an old goanna is having his fun
Lazily sleeping in the mid-day sun

When the kookaburra laughs just about noon
It's a sign it will probably rain quite soon
Parakeets and budgies burst forth into song
And cockatoos and galahs join the happy throng

Palms and giant tree ferns are beginning to loom
And jacaranda and wattle will soon be in bloom
One country I love best on this earth
Is you Australia, dear land of my birth

Joan Thomas

Daughter, Dear Daughter

Angel-like you are, so fair in face,
Beauty dark in long locks, hair yet so out of place,
Lips, like heart shaped, sweet of red rose colour,
Pale complexion fine like glass, perhaps a little fuller,
Tall and sleek in height, I cannot match you,
So like the Venus of the sea, your eyes of blue,
Eyes that shine like stars showing such inner magic,
Wide and full of innocence of fine quality, majestic,
I once watched this little one grow like flowers in the field.
And this Goddess like all seeds began to yield.
Each breath, each move so graceful,
Each movement watched so peaceful,
Mine eyes have witnessed miracle upon a mother's life,
I my child have witnessed, happiness, hardship, strife
Oh, grow like God's earth grows, spread your wings and fly,
I will watch, smile at you, and inside I will cry,
Locked in the heart of hearts is the tenderness of I.
You, oh Goddess, Venus of all Women, I your mother sigh.
   Breathlessly at you?

Irene L. Latham

Don't Look Down — Look Up

When you are alone in grief and despair
Because someone you love has gone from your life
When friends turn away rather than say hello
Leaving you feeling rejected, lost and forlorn
Don't look down — look up, Jesus's comfort and love is there
When laughter goes on and you're standing alone
And you feel like an alien from a planet unknown
When darkness and sorrow is all that you see
And you walk in a grey mist with no love of your own
Don't look down — look up, Jesus's unseen arms are holding you near
When your world falls apart and there is no light in the sky
And you silently scream for you cannot face a new day
Don't look down — look up, Jesus is smiling in greeting this day
When you want to run back down yesterday's path
In search of the love you have lost on the way
And you are crying inside for you have lost all hope
Don't look down — look up, and you will see a bright road
That stretches ahead full of vales and hills and laughter and tears
For at the end of the road is a beautiful light
Where Jesus is waiting with your Love at His side.

Ilona LaBouchardiere Fisher

The Solway Firth

The wild cold marshes of the Solway Firth
Beckon the geese to swoop and land
To eat their fill which the sea throws up
Then rest in the hillocks and down on the sand
Only the sheep give scant recognition
To the barnacle geese, the mallard and swan
Then down with their heads oblivious thereafter
The job in hand cropping the sparse and salty land
As the year slowly opens, the blinkered world
Throws off its mantle of sombre grey black
A world is appearing in colours anew
When the sun creeps over the rim of the east
It bathes the globe with bright daylight
But always shining bravely when rain mars its sight
As evening approaches the shadows lengthen
The marshes mysterious, take on majestic hues
Then the sun displays its mastery with palette
Far out and beyond the sea its canvas stretches
Then slowly and graciously the curtain falls
On the firth of the Solway till the morning light calls.

Helen Wood

The Carpet Man

Walk through the door into his world and you will think that you've been hurled.
Onto a magic carpet ride, time forgotten as you glide.
And as his wondrous tales are told, each piece he picks up to unfold
Will take you to a far off place, nimble fingers, peasant's face,
That wove his wonderful treasures then, in years gone by, in lands of Zen.
He'll show you knot, he'll explain weave, you'll find that all your senses leave.
When you look into his eyes, his story transports you through the skies.
Topkapi, Kum, the Caspians shore, long gone tribes and Gypsy lore.
He'll show you piles of wool and silk and you'll have never seen their ilk.
History unfolds with every story, as he talks of Khurd and Persian glory.
He talks of dyes and of years spent, on tree-made looms, of Beduin tent.
Russian Kazak, or silk Bokhara, Kashans, by camel across Sahara.
Of ancient carpets hidden away, from Western eyes, in Mosques today.
You'll learn of these and more beside, if you will only step inside,
and with me come and join the van, of Ilyas, "Magic Carpet Man".

Jim Cruickshank

Long Lost Love Of Mine

Oh! what horror, there they are twirling and turning
Before my eyes.
Like two snakes together sharing only one skin.
He all in black and her looking so trim.
How can he do this, hard of the heart and so unkind.

A flash of the ring as they glide past
Not giving me so much as a glance.
As I stand transfixed in the middle of the floor
Knowing I'll have to endure
Seeing again this lost love of mine.

My partner's not special but he'll have to do
While they keep on smooching in full view.
Me with my brave face and a smile or two.
Find a replacement, that's what I'll do.

To forgive and forget, I have no choice
I must rise above this sordid affair,
But until then it's more of the same.
Ah! here comes a new partner, handsome too,
Now they shall see, this could well be
A new love of mine.

Hazel Blackwell

Kilkenny Castle Echoes

Beneath the banner of Ormonde,
Behind grey limestone walls,
Built upon Strongbow's marital bond,
Beside the rushing river Nore,
Meandering centuries are recalled,
Steeped in silent rocky pores.

The well-laid slabs where Normans trod,
Hard set in Irish mud,
While exercising an iron rod,
Suppression of a bold, free heart,
Dipped deep in Celtic Blood,
Unoccupied, unconquerable rampart.

Mauled by voracious maw,
Proud bearer of battle scars,
A casualty of rapacious war,
Rest now and count the cost
Of excessive dalliance with Mars,
Whence your soul was lost.
Andrew Burford

Chameleon Joker

Peel away — disregard the painted mask,
  behind the painted flesh —
Ingrained with contradictory smiles,
  stretching for endless miles
across your face.

For who would deem broken wings
  could carry you for miles,
Until strength seems to sap like honeycomb wax.
  Collected into glass jars;
  helplessly trapped!

Hear the Joker laugh —
  for the insane Man he is!
Caught between worlds in a bath of dry tears.

The stripes he adorns on his own,
  All forlorn,
Shall not bend to the weave of his life.
And the jangle of brass bells upon his hat,
  shall never awake the jumbled mind
inside an empty head.

Clowns are clever... but fools just wither.
Lisa Jane Izatt

Untitled

I can't believe it
Believe what I have seen.
There walked an angel
She walked right up to me.

Sometimes the way that someone lights a cigarette
can tell a story.
I read every page.

There can never be enough stars
Won't you come with me?
Fingertip to Fingertip
Anthony Macciolo

For My Children

My love, my heart, my very soul
Belongs to you, each one,
From the early dawn of every day
To the setting of each sun.

You mean so very much to me
My love grows day by day.
I try to tell you with each deed
As the words are hard to say.

Life's precious gifts I'd give to you
If they were mine to give,
But I can only give my love
Through all the years I live.
Beryl Egan

The Wayside Shrine

Beside the dusty road Our Lady stands,
Beneath an angled arch of weathered wood,
Once wrought by loving hands that travellers
Might both be cheered as they pass by each day
And remember and honour the Mother of the Way.

Through storm and sunshine smiles that gentle face,
Serene and still beside the dust and noise:
Sometimes a peasant lays aside his load
And kneels before that sculptured gentleness
And in the soft sweet eyes, feels the curved hands' caress.

And children place their posies at her feet
And on the dewy flowers gathered wild
From airy mountain sides and meadows still
And brought by little hands in childish love,
Looks down in tenderness the Holy Mother mild.

In the pale dawn she waits all gemmed with dew,
Greeting the early traveller on his way,
And in the noon she hears the Angelus:
Dimly she stands amid the evening mist
And through the midnight keeps her constant tryst.
Daphne Foreman

Rooftops

A view across rooftops, a certain kind of magic holds,
Beneath each one, what diverse tales of intrigue unfold?
Rooftops, slates, tiles, reds, greens, dingy greys,
Steeped in history, yet yielding to our modern days.

Rooftops above attics, concealing dusty family treasures,
A rooftop view is surely one of life's simple pleasures;
Rooftops, steep, stark, outlined against threatening sky,
Covering, protecting, keeping our precious dwellings dry.

Rooftops sparkling in the rain, water sliding down,
Shelter for those tired souls, hurrying home from town;
Rooftops, clad with snow, and glistening purest white,
So strangely changed after just one cold frosty night.

Rooftops in summer, creaking, expanding 'neath midday heat,
Rooftops in the fall, shrouded in mist, shapes incomplete;
Rooftops in spring, reaching up for air, fresh and clean,
A land of rooftops, a world set apart for that special dream.
Jan Falla

Innocent Nudity

He followed her to the quiet valley
Beneath the spreading trees,
And on the river bank she disrobed
Unbutton'd her soft silk shirt,
Unclipped her long straight skirt.

Follow me Oh! My love she called
As into the deep she stepped,
And shyly viewed her nudity bold
Mirror'd within the watery glass,
And when she rose, her silver'd hair wet,

Her eyes were opened to a shining mass,
A naked form lying on his back
Silver'd by the moon's bright rays,
Lay floating on the silent waves
Rippling an etching for the artists page.

Infinity held in that short spell
As bodies meet beneath the deep,
Bursting passion in this place of usage
Afore resigned they rise, abandon the moonlit creek
Enchanted! The rose of Dawn to greet.
Elisabeth Corica

The Snow

I delight in the beauty of the snow, in the glory of the scene it does bestow
In the sparkle of the sunlight in the crystal flakes, in the untouched wilderness it creates
And in this wilderness I find wonder, in this new land rejoice to wander
Where no human foot has trod, no other soul explored
And seeing the tracks of wildlife in the snow, we discover the secrets of where they go
And marvel at the architecture of the drifts and the elegance of their shapes
In the excitement of this novelty, in the brilliance of this view
When snow lies all around me, virgin chaste and new
When the moons beams gleams astound me, when the stars are shining bright
When the heavens vastness thrills me, I drink deeply on such sights

James Brownlee

Untitled

Friendship is a special bond
between two people who care
Someone you will do anything for
And who's joys and troubles you will share

Someone who knows you better then you do
And who will do anything you ask
for them no matter what it may be
it will never be too large a task

Someone to tell your nightmares to
or even share your dreams
trust and tell your secrets to
only they know how much that means

Friendship is also all about
a relationship that works both ways
when all you have to do is listen
and hear just what the other one says

To be a best friend has no limits
you just have to learn to trust
and do and care and worry for
to have a best friend is a must.

Catherine A. MacDonald

God's Covenant

Upon the wind, doth sail the Sycamore,
Black Bryony, the passing season blooms,
And resting tranquilly upon the floor,
The tired fingers of the naked Broom.
Majestically, mighty Cedars climb
Relentlessly toward the dimming light,
As dancing Daisies, daintily do mime
Beneath the falling shadows of the night;
And cooling breezes, hesitantly blow
The wand'ring clouds across the open skies,
As jewels of the golden sunset, glow,
Like ornamental palaces on high:
   And, here, I marvel at such wonderment,
   As all is held within God's Covenant.

Graeme Leslie Jennens

No Tears

I am denied tears,
else others will know my fears,
so I lie still, and gaze into the blue, blue sky.
Realization sets in, there is no possible cure,
how confident I was — how positive I was and sure,
but that was yesterday, and now it's today
Today I sort out the remnants of my feelings.
Dismay, disappointment, I must sweep them all away.

Courage, faith, determination must be my goal,
I must pray hard for guidance deep in my soul
My love and trust in God will help me fight my fears.
Laughter, new ideas... but no tears.

Gita Landau

" Colours Of My Mind "

Blue is the colour I feel today,
Black is the night that watches me pray,
Red is the devil that haunts my mind,
And gives me this phobia that is so unkind.

Green is the envy I feel inside,
As I see people who don't have to hide,
A rainbow of colours these people see,
They're so lucky, so calm, so free.

White is the colour I long to see,
When my mind and thoughts so clear will be,
I will be so glad to conquer my fears,
No more hiding, no more tears.

This grey cloud hanging one day will be gone,
And all I'll see is the yellow sun,
Burning bright in a clear blue sky,
Then I can walk with my head held high!
Social Phobia, Bye, Bye!!!

Catherine Cobham

THE DESPAIR OF THE MOON

Looking at the sombrely clouded misty lake ensconced by
                      black and even blacker rocks.
The rippling waves and smaller whirlpools swirling and curling
                      not to mock.
Tall pine cladden trees surrounding this surreal like scene
O'er the moss-edged shore the thundery overhead in greys lit
                      up by lightning,
A yellow zig-zagged course it took.
Down fell the cloud burst so mighty it shook.
The little narrow wooden boat anchored by the bull rushes green.
An oar fell out and o'er the lake did splash
Into an Eternal Heaven it had met its match.
Looking up at this greying mass suddenly the moon appeared,
The only visual light as if it feared
Opposition to this bereaved world,
Betook by the very elements of nature revealed.
A travesty it had met its match,
Until the storm covered clouds had obliterated no more to watch
The nightmare of a midnight world
Bereft of an enlightened soul.
Not in all this darkened without solace land
No more in time Begot by Man.

Dulcie Veronica Fricker

Distant Muses

Burst clouds popping in my conscience.
Bleary eyed I stare to the heavens.
Thoughtless and distant,
I fly between the chilled flakes of winter.
Hands absent from mind,
Scribbles appear on a mache page,
as I long for the one I have lost.

Carol Thomas

Two Autumns

When leaves begin to glow orange, red and yellow, and the noise beneath even the lightest foot becomes apparent, we know that the season of autumn is upon us. At this point the world within our vision begins to die. Melancholy thoughts of blue flesh, and rattling teeth disturb the embers of months before, when all was warm, bright, glad and free. Selfish indeed is the air of autumn when breathed by the adult mind.

When leaves begin to glow orange, red and yellow, and the noise beneath even the lightest foot becomes apparent, we know that the season of Autumn is upon us. At this point the world within our vision takes on new dimensions of sight, sound and smell. A fragrant, fresher atmosphere tears up the hot, green, stuffiness of months before, with eager thoughts of days ahead. Innocent indeed is the air of Autumn when breathed by a child's mind.

David Crane

THE BIRTH

4.55 P.M.; it was 19th day of April 1975, when the silence broke.
Blood and water flowed as one.
Commotion hither and thither, it's time to leave!
A pushing force followed a wanting cry.
I felt a touch, a touch of life.
A pushy pull; and I was out, to see my kind of existence, the existence of my kind.
As I sniffed the earth and all that was in it, I cried, just like a baby, that I was.
Smiles all around, as my bearer smiled her cry to laughter.
An atmosphere of delight for all who understand.
Faces read "cry your own cry".
I cried on, for comfort and understanding. "Where am I"?
From blood to light. The light of life? Or from blood to light.
The light of death?
Like Sirius — the piercing star; through all there was, the light shone.
And peaceful air pleased my breath. "Would this last"? I wondered, pondered and considered.
Time spoke; the moon rose, night falls, and the glass at sight responded.
There, I saw me, staring at myself.
Weeh-weeh... I cried.
Like a congregation in worship, they gathered, with faces saying, "We are with you".
".....With me always"? I asked. My words unheard, my questions unanswered.
As the likeness of the dead lowered to dust; Alone, I have come.

Kazeem O. Adio

Hourglass

Throwing sand to the wind,
blowing through the face of time.
On which side shall the grain fall?
Can we chose the second at which it lands,
the second to where we wish to be.

I wish to throw a memory,
forever blowing in time,
away from my awakening.

I wish to feel free
of the burden of time.
I wish to pluck my mind
of memories — haunting,
to throw them aside
and start afresh.

To be reborn into an oasis of nonchalance,
to be dragged from the abyss.

I need to be cleansed.
I need to live.

Andrew Alexander O'Henley

My Rainbow Poem

What is blue?
Blue is the sparkling silent sighing sea.
Blue is when my friends leave me out.

What is red?
Red is the erupting steaming volcano
Red is the boiling lava from a hot volcano.

What is green?
Green is the grass dew and as good as new.
Green is the scaly body of a reptile that's slimy.

What is black?
Black is the grim, dark, misty, mysterious room.
Black is the creepy howling hound on a silent night

What is gold?
Gold is a solid happy thought.
Gold is a moment when someone is joyful and happy.

What is pink?
Pink is the tender soft skin of a person.
Pink is the romantic touch of a married couple.

Adam Bush

Nature's Song

Trees stand tall and gently sway.
Blue skies peep through their leafy way
Grasses rustle gently in shades of gold and green
Flowers sing their scented tune.
Nature's gift for all to see.
"Lovers' whispers" fly away,
With the birds' "Melody",
And nature's gentle breeze.
Life's Jewels are the simple things
We take for granted,
Until fate clips our wings,
A gentle reminder of all these lovely things

Joan Anne Curley

Spring

Spring has arrived
Bluebells a-ringing
Daffodils swaying
Rabbits are playing away.
Lambs jumping, bleating out loud.
Far distant cuckoo awakening us all.
Streams trickle above and beneath.
Grass whispers too silent to hear.
Branches are blooming, ready to burst.
Oh what a season, our beautiful spring.

Elizabeth Ann Glover

A Perfect Love

A perfect love, all loves transcending,
Born of dreams from heavenly spheres,
A love eternal, never ending
Clouds of gold and angels' tears.
A perfect love of mystic beauty
Glowing with a rainbow's hue,
A love that ever knows a duty,
Sacred vows once more renewed.
A perfect love beyond description,
Rivalling all earthly dreams,
A love that is a benediction,
A gift that has no measured means.
A perfect love of heaven's divining,
Blessed are they beneath its light,
A love forever softly shining
Through the ever darkening night.

Jennifer Anne Butler

Life

Conceived, in all-embracing passion and joy
Born, with undying love, be it girl or boy
Baby, brings sleepless nights, oh so demanding!
Toddler, climbing, falling, walking, wanting
Infant, forming friendships, full of life
Youngster, pressure's mounting, worries and strife
Teenager, a revolutionary kid with a hate
Adult, more mature, willing to wait
Old, are forgotten, a burden, a bore
Death, is everlasting sleep, to be broken no more.

Graham D. Terry

Light Of Day

Let darkness fade
Bring forward the light of the world
Let peace wander into our open hearts
Let evil be transformed into nothing but ashes
Ashes from the burning fire
Lost and forgotten
Make the world gleam with beauty
Make love fall from the skies
Like petals from a flower
Let life never end
Let each day follow another
Until the end of time is upon us.

Claire Jones (Age 10)

Dream Away

Sweet scented flowers all around,
Bringing a heavenly fragrance
To those they surround
Dream on peaceful lady, dream on.

Float away
Taking with you the perfume,
Like clouds drifting on a summer's day.
Dream on lovely lady, dream away.

Let the clouds transport you
To the land of dreams.
On a magic carpet travel
Through peaceful skies,
And watch below
The world rush by.

Speed kills the moment
So hold tight.
Savour it while you may.
Tomorrow is another day.

Jean B. Scott

The Turning

Perhaps I could welcome winter.
Brisk cold to clear mind;
Grey days to quieten soul.
Longer sleep to heal body.

Seasons roll; year made whole;
Find winter at the end — or is it beginning — of the year?

No! No!
Spring is better
Life returning
But summer!

Summer best of all, sun burning energy into my eager being.

Such energy!
Autumn beautiful, sad.
Yet not so bad as winter, come too soon
Again

Joan Southern

The Whale

With a crash the wave rolls back to sit on the calmness.
But the movement of life below splits the surface,
And with a surge of power the Whale lifts through the sea and sky.
The water falls off its back as it glides elegantly
back towards the ring pools below.
Again the Whale splits the surface of the sea,
as it disappears once more through the door of the water.
The watchers can no longer see the grace
and beauty of the Whale.

Lisa Yates

Our Hearts Are Set In The Heavens

A pale hawk slides across my vision.
Beautiful it is,
The colour of nature's eyes.

Fly deep into the ravine, pull me free.
My spirit magnetized, pull me free.
Your shape takes my breath away,
Your skill forever stays with me,
Play out nature's song, remind me I still belong

Soft eagle perched over me, soft eagle watch over me
The earth sends its song
Nature takes me along.

My heart swells to bursting,
My mouth turns up at the edges,
A smile forms across my heart
That place is still there
deep inside
and invincible.

Daniel Manning

Courage

Broken arrow, broken bow
broken string, broken woe
broken pain barrier.
Weak, exhausted, frightened, cold
Where to find the rebuild mould?
Deep, deep inside, in heart somewhere
lies the map Intensive Care
unroll it gently, step by step
here's the first one, do it, yep
rest awhile and then proceed.
Compost on the planted seed
water, wind, sun and moon
combine to make a happy tune,
strength is passing to the seed
soon it will be strong indeed.

Geoffrey M. Gardiner

D-Day 1944

The D-day landings of forty-four
Brought home to us all the sorrow of war
Never to be forgotten in our memory
The sacrifices made for you and for me
Their courage and bravery will never be known
So many young men so lost and alone
Straight into battle as they waded ashore
The strong the meek the rich and the poor
All had one aim to get the job done
To fight to the end when the battle was won
Thousands of lives were lost that day
On a Normandy beach so far away
As we look back over fifty years
With a lump in our throat and eyes filled with tears
We must remember with the greatest pride
That our boys fought together side by side
Never to be forgotten by each generation
The love in our hearts and pride in our nation.

Joyce Carey

My Harmony Does Blossom

Harmony is her name.
Brought to being,
peaceful in every way.
Soft and tender, with long flowing locks,
eyes that glisten, then retreat
Harmony sweet harmony
My harmony.

Sweet flower of love,
I call, she hears,
but choosy she is through her life long years.
This trickle, then spring became a fountain.
Like strong winds, she does move me
Singing, still that sweet sweet tune
"O' swoon o' swoon"
That's my sweet harmony.
My harmony.

Don Spencer Fields

It's Harvest Time Again

The spring-time came and with it life anew,
Bringing forth flowers of every shape and hue.
Making us forget the winter stillness as the snow lay deep.
Living things were not dead but only fast asleep,
Now as the days start getting warmer and brighter,
We know it's summer and our hearts feel lighter.
Each day the farmer prays that the sun will shine,
To help ripen his wheat and corn; then all will be fine.
Now at last the time has come to gather it in,
For to waste any of it would be a sin.
To show our gratitude to the great reaper above,
We decorate our church to express our love.
And offer up our thankful prayers,
As Jesus shows us he really cares.
One more harvest is safely gathered in,
And we all know we owe thanks to him.

Carol Diane Milne

Jealous Tree

During the Summer I'm fat and bold,
But barren and empty I stand in the cold,
Having followed the sun over the sea,
Gone are the birds who flocked in me.

To all of my cousins known as a Fir,
The same sad thing doesn't occur.
Inside them lives a permanent guest,
Lovingly known as Robin Red Breast.

When to the humans Winter calls,
Their branches are adorned with balls.
Do they know how lucky they are,
To be crowned with a Christmas star?

While out in the snow I creak and sway,
With bright lights they're dressed all gay.
Just for once I'd like it to be
ME the children come running to see.
   Donna June Clift

Forward Thought

Yesterday's memories last,
But don't look back, it's in the past.
Yesterday has been and gone.
It may have hurt, but life goes on.

It's only natural for mankind,
To stop and take a look behind.
When you're desperate, lost and lonely,
You can't help but think 'if only.'

Though this is simply going to let,
You go through life with much regret.
The rest of your life has just begun
There's time to do what you haven't done.

Yesterday may be full of sorrow,
But we still have today and tomorrow.
The past has gone, so let it go,
And when you do, you'll come to know;

If something is to be unseen,
Dwelling on what could have been
Is painful, bare and self destructive.
Life is fact and not inductive
   Gillian Meek

I Don't Believe

I don't believe in God,
But have you looked at the sky on a frosty night?
The stars! The silence! The majesty!
The mystery!
Pretty serious splendour, I think.

I don't believe in God,
But have you felt the warmth of the sun,
The breeze bringing summer scents,
The leaf-laden trees?
Wondrous stuff, I feel.

I don't believe in God,
But have you felt heart-glow
When a child smiles into your eyes,
Or an old man chuckles?
Pure joy, it gives.

I don't believe in God,
But have you witnessed the season-change,
The colours! The diversity! A Presence!
No, I don't believe in God,
And Yet...?
   Brenda Tucker

All By Myself

So many took something from me when I was young you see
But I pushed it all to one side
And blamed it onto myself
I thought someone hated me up in heaven but I was wrong
I took it upon myself and said that it's all up to me
Then I put my life in order
This I did all by myself

I know that someone up there really cared for me as I was told
But I yet didn't know who or if it was really true
until I accepted him into my life
For then my life was taken up by the Lord Jesus Christ
my life revolves around him now
For I took him into my life and did it all by myself
   Geraldine Perkins

Our Little Monster

Now it's ever so hard, with a baby on the scene,
But isn't she just a little dream?
Even when she's awake all night,
And kicks and screams with all her might.
Now finally, she's fast asleep,
Softly, slowly, we try to creep,
Out of her room and into our bed,
Our eyes so heavy, like pieces of lead.
Tomorrow is another day;
It will start and end, in much the same way.
But, because our love is ever so strong
We just keep plodding on and on.
   Elaine Dalton

Mad Dogs And ....

Not too many nubiles, not too many sylphs,
But lots of Auntie Ada's and several Uncle Wilf's.
Quite a few with freckles, some an awful sight
Showing acre upon acre of flabby cellulite.

Happy is the Briton out in the midday sun.
However painful sunburn is, he thinks he's having fun.
In silly hat and baggy shorts, he lounges by the pool,
Thinking "What a dashing lad", not "What a silly fool".

He waddles off into the pool preceded by his belly,
Watched by his skinny, tight-lipped wife who'd rather watch the telly.
She knits and reads and moans and whines and carps about the dinners.
She doesn't like the nudity, thinks cruisers are all sinners.

Happy is the Briton out in the noon-day sun.
He's paid his debt to human kind, now he's the only one.
He's pleased himself, he's had his way, he's cruising with the toffs.
He lights his seventh fag that day, then coughs and coughs and coughs.
   Judith Wilson

Being

Oh, how I long to be alone in the quietude of my being
But no, they follow wherever I go, looking but never seeing
I grasp and I try to make some sense
Clawing away until my mind is all spent
My thoughts they chatter, on and on they go
The noise that they make, it deafens me so
Oh! what is the use? Who cares anyway?
How I live my life, be it years or a day
I do, I hear, then thoughts please disperse
Just let me sit at the centre of the universe
This and that, distracting, misleading
Living my life without any meaning
Shh, I hear something, I am sure that I did
That tiny voice from within my head
All is now quiet, I am focusing well
I am one with the universe, the universe is myself.
   Heather Grounds

Times

When I was young my values were true.
But now I have grown,
And these values are challenged.
All the thoughts and desires
Have been soiled with experience.
To reach those far gone years
Would be every human's desire.
The life that would start so sweet
And end so beautifully.

For all the torment, sorrow and despair,
Life will start and finish the same way,
With a blissful ignorance.
I may go on or I may disappear,
But I know that the present will help,
It will guide me through.
Laughter, smiles and happiness,
These will be my encyclopedia for life,
And for every smile in my life
My presence on this earth will be extended.
I thank whoever for these attributes.

Jo Sale

Cold Feet

Preparing a meal was always plain sailing
But now it just has me ranting and railing:
These kilos are driving me wild.
Conversion to pounds by me is quite hazy,
It isn't stir-fry, it's simply stir crazy.

A dozen red roses, ah, that was the fashion
For every young man declaring his passion.
"Send ten" doesn't have the same ring.
I don't want to change, but I'm given no choice,
Nobody listens to my little voice.

Some pretty new curtains to brighten the room,
The thought brings no joy, only gloom.
The length and the width I must measure,
Then sit down with slide rule and pencil and paper.
Please, somebody, find me an old-fashioned draper.

I just won't accept these terrible metres:
I'll still buy my petrol in gallons, not litres,
And measure my carpet in yards.
But it's just too late now for inches and feet:
O.K. metric, you win, I admit to defeat.

Bernice Bastin

Guilty Secrets

His hands were upon her, she recoiled at his touch,
but she knew he cared not for what she was feeling,
his satisfaction was all that he cared for
while he bruised her deeply, she stared at the ceiling.
Relief as he left her, but guilt filled the spaces,
she covered up well and hid them from view.
The sight of her body disguised, displeased her
the degradation that nobody knew.
Again and again, he'd find her and use her,
laugh at her humiliation and mock.
He forced her to lie each time he abused her,
her mind in confusion, her heart hard as rock.
His conquests he boasted and rubbished her daily.
She kept them inside, guilty secrets untold.
They'd call her a liar, reject her, then maybe
Banish her from their lives, from their souls.
The burden of shame burrowed deeper and deeper.
Was buried and though she covered it well,
Grew heavy and caused such pain that it pierced her,
Tormented and tortured and put her through hell!

Julie Mills

Tribute

My blood from yours, I am your daughter.
But that's not enough, there's more to it, because:
You were my champion, my hero
even in my darkest hours,
I closed my eyes and felt the comfort of your arm around my shoulder.
And I could be strong too.

My heart from yours, I am your daughter.
But that's not enough, there's more to it, because:
You were the first great love I knew,
whenever the world frightened me,
I listened to the words you used to say.
And I could be brave too.

My mind from yours, I am your daughter.
But that's not enough, there's more to it, because:
You were always able to understand,
every time I felt alone,
I thought of you and of the day you would be back.
And I could believe it would get better.

Karen Jane Cartwright

No Rights For Us

We're headed in and out,
   But we cannot shout.

We're sprayed with horrible stuff,
   Till we've really had enough.

We're bought and sold, stamped so bold,
   Then we're left to graze.

We may be shipped abroad,
   Cramped together on board.

Long after long, kind people only see our eyes.
   If only we could cry
When knowing it's goodbye.

Then they may have pity on us,
   The men who do all this,
We're too stupid to rebel,
   Against the human race.
When will it ever stop,
   Solutions must be found,
If only we could keep ourselves,
   Firmly on the ground.

Christine Miller

Not Enough Time (For Paul)

We didn't see enough of you
but we soon put that straight.
We hadn't said "I love you",
until it was almost too late.
We thought that we would have more time,
Alas it wasn't so.
We tried so hard to keep you here.
We didn't want you to go.

We think that you were very brave
to endure what you went through.
You never gave up fighting.
We were fighting with you too.
Like a carousel ride;
one day up, the next day down.
If there was a token for bravery
you would wear the crown.

We'll miss you more than words can say.
Words cannot describe the pain.
You'll be in our thoughts and memories,
until one day we'll meet again.

Diane Fackerell (nee Spicer)

My Worth

I have a name, a place of birth, I have dependents and a life,
But who am I and what's my worth, whilst on this planet, earth?
I sleep, I wake, I laugh, I cry, I walk and talk, but who am I?
Who is this person, deep within, with complex mind?

'Twould seem maturing years have caused this searching of my soul,
when young ones now are fully grown, noise no longer fills the home.
Too many hours feel unfulfilled, demand no longer pushing me,
an eagerness to do things right, for that was how it used to be.

Now, who am I and what's my worth, as mid-life now descends?
A life that held so many dreams, 'twas a lane with many bends.
That eagerness to make things right and share my thoughts
with all around
so much to give and gladly too - 'twas a satisfying battleground!

Am I to fade, to take the role of an ageing earthly soul -
with aching legs, with brittle hair and concentration hard to hold -
with ageing skin and lessening sight, who notices my inner plight?

For worth is measured by one's life and self-belief, a must,
maturing years hold hopes and fears, 'tis so for all of us.
The dawning of another day, and so the final scene -
for I still have a zest for life and will prove my self - esteem!

Angela Jarvis

Watch Me Swim, I Can Win

The media named me Glenys, others call me the common dolphin,
But you see I'm really Delphinus Delphis,
In the sea I'm in; Yes that's me,
Watch me swim I can win.
My back is dark brown, my belly white,
My sides yellowish grey in the natural light,
Watch me swim, I can win.
Graceful, gracious and trim, that's me
In the sea, watch me swim I can win.
I'm racing Tuna! It's such fun under the blazing sun,
I can catch them, I can pass them, I can beat them
Watch me swim I can win.
Where am I now? I'm caught in this thing, but how?
I'm tossing and turning, I want to get out,
Can't they hear me shout, Please let me out,
I want to swim, I can win,
I'm out of the sea, That's me caught in this thing,
The light is fading,
I'm not moving, I'm not stirring, I'm not swimming
But I wonder.....DID I WIN?

Anna Jenkin

Those We Have Loved

The Tragedies we read about over the years
Bring to us a few silent tears
But after a few mournful days pass by
We wipe the tears out from our eye

Unless these things touch us directly
Affect our Husbands, Kids or Wives
We hear the news and then forget them
It never really touched our lives

Not so the Victims, whatever race
Theirs is a life sentence in every case
We ask our God, "How can this be?
Why does this happen? Explain to me."

Our God replies, "An answer I cannot give,
But all the Sufferers have come to live
With me on high, now a shining star
That those they left watch from afar

A Star that twinkles, an eternal light
So look to the heavens and see the sight
Of those you loved, who went away
Now with me here, to hear you pray"

Eva Stanley

A Perfect Love

The love that missed the marriage bed
By death, word or deed
In every captive heart
Will plant a tiny seed

The perfect love will flourish
Untouched by selfish need
Fed, watered, nourished
Perfection guaranteed

No argument could threaten
Love's sweet secret lent
Nor would time diminish
A passion never spent

Linda Smedley

Message To Mr. "X"

Only one God created us all
By giving us a body and soul.
Of course with a message to love one another
And be like sister and brother,
But not far away, just behind my wall
There is a single man with a rotten soul.
He doesn't even try, he doesn't want others to see
How nice and valuable a person he can be,
He is looking for crime and always for war,
He has no feelings, he has a rotten soul.
Look at yourself and search for your soul,
Stop this silliness and stop that war!
Yes Mr "X" it is you
I am talking to.
I know that you are lost, feeling like nobody loves you,
But you are wrong, because I do
And there are many people like me
Just wait and you shall see.
Believe me we can make peace together, because I love you
And I am sure that soon you will love me too.

Ewa Demus

Are Visited On The Children

For all the evil done before
By our fathers' sins, our mothers wore
The cloth of ashes; then our babes were born
Into the world, their future torn
Into shreds, because we are their past
And debts must be repaid at last!
But, for their sake, shouldn't we once more
Delve, beg and implore
The truth be told, no matter what
Comes from the past? We did not
Dream our futures could be cast
So certainly, until the very last
Breath we take! Today, deeds we commit
Are visited on our children as we sit,
Silently watching, helpless, numb,
As wounded victims they become!
One day far on, should they incline,
To try and make it right next time,
They'll learn forgiveness, and then forget
All bitter hatred and regret.

Lauren Perfit

Passing

One who takes without being invited is an enemy,
Camouflaged as something less,
gradually identifying its form.
Death is my enemy, but also my saviour.
You weep for me, but weep only for yourself,
it is you that must suffer living.
Drifting, immersed in peace, happiness, love,
your tears upon me devour the last fleeting embers.
Eternal immortality enters.

Amanda Jayne Rowse

Somebody Died

I got knocked back each time I tried
By puerility personified,
to tell or guess, or even see
that somebody died and it could have been me.

And that puerility was you.
And every lie I told was true.
But we were both too blind to see
somebody died and I think it was me.

So let your bones tear through your skin,
when you submit and your world caves in.
I think you'll find it's in life you're free
somebody died and I hope it was me.

Death would alter you not it seems
so unconscious you sleepwalk even in dreams
I didn't die-no, it was you
when you tore my perfect world in two.
Alexandra Downes

The Showdog

With swishing tail and pride in stride
By stylish glamour, he commands the scene
Away to the front, out and around the side
A racing glide, lines swift and clean

Aloof, he scorns the watchful throng
Cock confident of the treasured goal
Sports gleaming coat and head held strong
To catch the eye and snatch the soul

Harmonic vision, a pure spirit forth
Blithe spectacle of divine creation
Epitome of the true breed worth
Bold symbol for his generation

The prospect firmed, the prize in hand
The victor bounds his exultant lap
The judge pens notes as the finalists stand
The ringsiders sound their ultimate clap

No humans attain their own perfection
They learn their failings, accept the strife
But honour to those who, by a different election
Seek to nurture ideals through another life
John Ellis

An Old Lady

An old lady sitting in her chair,
by the window there.
Dreaming of the days when she
was young,
when she went to school.
Dancing round a big hall,
now she's old she's sometimes very cold,
she has no money to buy some coal,
she has a cat, he's all black
he sits on her lap.
No one comes by and says hello or
even goodbye.
She sits by the window once more
hoping to see children at her door.
Linda Gannon

Bye Old School

Bye, old school, it's time to go
Bye, old school, I will miss you so
I need to tell you I'm moving on; that's why I shall tell you this song
My best meal was pizza and chips; then I would go outside
and play with my skips
Does the school ever end
I suppose I am leaving with a friend
I will remember the Teachers that told me why
But now I shall have to cry
Bye, old school, it's time to go.
Linsey Sarah Ellis

A Summer Evening

Standing on shore I look out to sea,
Calm today and I cannot tell
Where ocean ends and sky beings.
The sea reflecting soft the sky,
End of the day pink, gold and blue.
I listen, I hear, ssh! be quiet,
It's the sound of the waves as they kiss the shore.
I can hear the sea gulls circling for home,
Sailboats coming in to their moorings,
Children being called to bed,
Now it's time for the sun to set.
Sea's now red, indigo and gold,
Soon the moon will rise in the east,
Lighting romantic paths in the sea,
Just enough light for lovers to see.
Tonight's so quiet, hardly a sound,
Still I can hear, ssh! be quiet,
The sound of the waves as they kiss the shore.
Iris Ballard

Our Vacation

Let me tell you of the way I'd choose to spend a holiday.
Camping sites; flying kites.
Golden sands; grubby hands.
Roller-blades; loud arcades.
Seaside fair; tousled hair.
Pony rides; water slides.
Fishing net; soaking wet.
Sleepless nights; pillow fights.
Midnight feast - one at least.
Mum and dad have their idea of how we'll all have fun this year.
Open spaces; friendly faces.
Endless walks; cosy talks.
Country pub; home-cooked grub.
Hire a car; drive too far.
Ocean views; midday news.
Taking tea; Monopoly.
Window shopping; starting, stopping.
Candlelight; early night.
Mustn't groan, I realize. Happily I compromise.
Angela Moore

Danablu

He tried to be a poet once.
Can once, though, ever be enough?
Once too he tried so hard to please
a woman who, scorning his verse,
polished her silver, fed him cheese.
He her silver reflection, she his Danablu.

Poetry and cheese: his soft poems
mirrored her blue-veined cheese
and other food that exercised
his poetic digestion; his lyrical enzymes
transmuting her carnal profferings
while she contemned his protean offerings.

He her unmade bed; she his maker
whispered how to create
blue poetry on blue sheets, blue pillows,
the colour of her sighs.

Now alone, he ruminates on his Danablu,
but no more sates her Danish thighs
deriding his ecstatic lies.
He her Danablu, she his blue reflection.
Bernard Sharp

Crawl

Silently, with purpose, across the
ceiling he crept, sending tangent
shadows darting to corners,
intent in direction...
...On a silk thread he mindfully lowered
himself toward the dark maw of the
slumbering giant.
Aaron Marque Soan

Tribute To James Bulger

Dear little James how sweet you are
Cared for by Jesus in a place not far,
Playing with the Cherubs as the clouds roll by
Laughter and chuckles as they teach you to fly.

God bless you dear James not long did you live
And now you're with Jesus all His love He will give.
Here on God's earth you are in our memory
You've taken the hearts of each and every.

Though you don't know us, we will surely know your name,
When that day comes when we all meet again
The dearest little angel Jesus took by the hand.
And led him into Heaven to join the peaceful land.

June Baden

A Peaceful World

War is evil and solves nothing
Causing horror, death, and pain,
Buildings reduced to dust and rubble
What on earth is there to gain.

Young and old are innocent victims
Fleeing from their land of birth,
Peace makers risk their lives to save them
To stop war spreading on this earth

We all are guilty of some atrocity
It's a part of evil war
We must forgive for peace and freedom
No more war for ever more

Let us put the past behind us
Those who want war are insane,
Go forward build a better future
Let prosperity be our aim

Now two generations onward
It's time the flags of peace unfurled
Together try to live in harmony
In a Civilized peaceful world.

Edna Nation

'A Tail Of Woe'

I write this poem to show my disgust,
Changing dirty pants is a must.
Once a week is not enough
They form a thing just like a crust.
Something like this should not be seen,
Because I think it's too obscene.
I pick them up with paper towel.
Should I bury them with a trowel?
He wears them even in his bed,
He's fond of them now it could be said.
Do others have my 'tail' of woe
On things unclean that do not show!
Will husband change, oh not a jot,
Do I like him this way, well, not a lot.

Clare Bright

The Four Seasons

In Spring, flowers open wide,
Children laugh and play outside.
In Summer, people go to the beach,
And feel the sand run through their feet.

In Autumn, leaves fall from the trees,
In that cold and windy breeze.
In Winter, we might have snow,
Some people want it to last, some to go.

After all that happens,
It starts all over again.
Will it all be different,
Or the same?

Laura Corradi

The Christmas Message

Yes, it's almost that time of year,
Christmas day is almost here.
They're more concerned with their presents,
And decorating the tree, they don't seem to care at all for me.
Why do they think I died on the cross?
Most of them think that it's no great loss.
They give me the odd prayer if they must,
But most of them think, "What's all the fuss?"
They criticise those who worship me,
I died for you all, Can't they see?
Well I'm sorry to ruin everyone's plan,
But the real meaning of Christmas is
God becoming man.

Jessica-Donna Marie Saddler

Solitude

Sitting beside a rippling brook
Closed eyes at the page of an open book,
Water and the sound it makes
Fish will follow in the wake,
Trees whispering in the sunny air
Just enjoy without a care.

No matter what the time of day
On your own in a pleasant way
Relax and see closing your mind
How wonderful to unwind.

Forgetting your cares for a while
Coming to with a smile,
All is good from this interlude
Relishing the solitude.

Ivy E. Baker

Whispering Grass

Whispering grass, the swaying trees.
Colourful flowers, a gentle breeze,
the honey bees fly from flower to flower,
pollen to collect, every daylight hour.

Spiders weave artistic webs.
Between whispering grass,
flowers nod their heads,
the fire fly has wings of gold,
silhouetting at night,
like a small light bulb,

The moon above, looks down while we sleep,
an owl has seen a mouse for a feast.
The stars depart when the dawn breaks through,
the spiders' webs, covered with dew,
the fragrant perfume fills the air,
the whispering grass so debonair.

Audrey Cooper

God Nights

Was in the Troodos mountains,
under a pine dressed night,
our souls staggered, drunk, momentous.
Above stars flashed, then fell, some smiled wide as opium,
besotted in their inky prayer — Lovers
torn in splendour, review the moon drenched lake, later
they wander down to her choir side.
Mellifluous secrets flow.
She shimmers finest silk, her scent is wild thyme — Divine
embryonic depths, dream haunting mosaics, compassion reflects.
Trees, aside stumble, ascribe in ancient voice.
Ghostly shadows crawl, exaggerate a move.
A chorus manipulates when wind strikes time, vibrations run.
Miracles of silence grow,
Lovers nurse hot thermals, idle, dumbfounded.
Gods drag clouds for tomorrow's rain, mountains yawn.
The lake sleeps, for tomorrow's August heavy with
passion and rage.

Simon J. Veal

'Paper Floo-ers'

Mither it's misses Broon f'ae up the stair
Come oan in, you'll ha'e tae sit oan the flair
Ma', man's at a flittin' in the next street
He'll be roon' shortly wi' a three piece suite

Mither! here's faither wi' Uncle Tam
They've got the three piece suite oan the top o' a pram
Enter oor character by the name o' Sanny Doyle
At the fishin' boats in Ayr does toil

Noo Sanny likes a laugh an' a joke
An' some o' his habits wid gie ye' the boak
Wi' mocket haun's he'd go fur a pee
Then share his fish supper wi' you an wi' me.

Aroon' the pubs in Ayr he'd roam
Then fa' oan the bus an' head fur home
Askin' his wife, "Whit's your caper?"
We are makin' floo-ers oot o' toilet paper

Floo-ers, floo-ers,
Floo-ers oot o' toilet paper
Christ that's a farce
An' we're usin' newspaper tae wipe oor arse.

Jean Brown

Cowards In The Shadows

You callous cowardly murderous men
Come on out into the open
Give and take must be made
Honest policies must now be laid
All the talking has gone on too long
Giving promises not fulfilled; this is wrong
All parties must get round the table
Get things back to normal and stable
You almost ruined your land with carnage and murder
You must stop it at once, take it no further
For eighteen months comparative quiet
Then on Friday night of the 9th we all got a fright
The London dockland bombing gave us a shock
The carnage it caused made us all rock
We hope the troubles are not starting over again
When element started this and who will take the blame
Think of your beautiful country going to waste
Sit down and think; don't do things in haste
Come on, let's stop all this fighting
Let's all get together and start uniting

David Forteath

The Journey

You arrive at the platform, it's six people deep
Commuters keep pushing, they shuffle and creep
Their way to the front, get a foot's length ahead
"Watch out for the gap" swims around your dazed head
Then along comes the train, there are groans of despair
Through the misted glass windows, the glum faces stare
People writhing and twisted, bags become linked
Faces squashed beneath elbows and armpits that stink
The doors slowly open, not many alight
Won't deter the platformers from fighting the fight
Squeezing and forcing their way through a gap
To a seat that they spotted five people back
It's a battle of wills, a fight for the brave
It's for who gets there first, no concern for age
As the elderly stagger and steady their stance
The victor won't turn for a cursory glance
The doors now are shutting, the air becomes thin
Our ears grow accustomed to the familiar din
Of muttering and tutting and the ringing of phones
My nightmare continues, a journey with clones!

Liza Green

A Chess Match

I am now in motion. I am now ready.
Confidence has become belief.
All outside drifts into nothingness as I sit behind my army of
   black chessmen.
The clock is pressed, a handshake, and he starts.
The Queen's pawn comes to the fourth rank; King's Indian.
He follows Samich; I pursue.

My father read the news he needs. The battle proceeds.
Igniting, I seize the initiative.
As subtlety begins to take a hold, he sees me.
He knows I know but won't admit it. No one else knows.
The naivety I knew has not completely gone.
It is different now, and serves simply to set my play on fire.
Inhale me.

An error? We will see.
One thing you may be sure of is the all knowing, all conquering
   truth of destiny.
So worry I welcome you, compliment you, and indeed challenge you.
Moreover, we both know I have devoured you.
Today I won a chess match.

Ben Griffiths

A Passing Storm

An eerie silence, an angry frown,
   Conflict in the sky.
Magnetic light, thundering hooves,
   The Devil passes by.

One tear is dropped, eruption follows,
   To drench the arid ground.
Supreme He reigns and stands aside,
   And utters not a sound.

Rampaging rain assaults the ground,
   Lightning shows its power.
Thunder roars in frightening tones,
   More awesome than the tower.

"Enough," He cries "On your way,
   My children are afeared,
Satan's hold must be weak,
   Not to be revered."

The sun reflects a dozen hues,
   Peeping through the rain.
Steam ascends bewildered earth,
   God is here again.

Ann Ede

Life Gets Harder

What to do next is a hard choicePeople Say.....
That prostitutes should be stopped
Walking the streets with hardly any top
Wiggling their bums with a slight shake
Walking the streets till it's almost late
But that's all red-tape
Think how many people
Are arrested for rape
And the children
Who are used and abused
And the police haven't always got someone to accuse
Prostitutes help keep down sexual attacks
By simply making a living
On their backs
This is not fiction, it's facts
Good girls go to heaven
Is what they say
She replied
Bad girls go all the way.

Ronnie Mitchell

The Washing Machine

Converter of homes to factories;
Continuous thunderous vibration;
A churning turning mass of metal,
Serviceable by man's creation.
Fabric is forced through open jaws
In water-bubbled detergent,
Revolving; tumbling; regurgitating,
Successful digestion is urgent.
An airy lathery slippery foam
Bubbles and froths like well whipped cream.
A fascination to those awaiting,
And answering a woman's dream!
Elizabeth Hunter

Ode To The Weeds

O ye groundsel and chickweed, you'd better watch out
'Cos Gladys and Edna will soon be about
Down the path, looking, with trowel in hand.
They'll terrorise you, they're the best in the land.
Try keeping your heads down, you might stand a chance
But, out you will come, If you dare sneak a glance
P'raps, when the sweeping and dead heading is done,
They'll take a rest, on the seat in the sun.

And put up their feet and forget about you
Whilst puss plays and birds bathe, in leaves of brown hue.
Down in the shrubbery all looks so bright,
So groundsel and chickweed do stay out of sight.
Doreen Buchanan

Without You

Without you I'm nothing and that's no jest,
'Cos you and me together are always the best,
When we're together the sun always sets,
If we're apart it feels cloudy and wet.

Without you I'm just the world without air,
The sea without water, and world without care,
When you're not around I'm an empty space,
With no-one to hold me or stroke my face.

You make me feel warm from deep down inside,
Sometimes it's so great I've even cried.
I want to be with you forever and ever,
You think I'll stop loving you? I will say never,
I want to see grey hairs, pot bellies and wrinkles
And to look in your eyes and see memories twinkle,

You may think this corny and made up for the day,
But I wrote this to tell you I feel this way.
I send you my heart wrapped up in me,
Just look into my eyes and love you will see.
Jeneane Easterlow

The Memory

She emerged from the mud baked hut
wispy grey hair, tied back in a bun.
Faded cotton dress. Brown sandled toes
face burnt by the African sun.
Where she had come from nobody knows.
She reached for the old wooden stool.
Placing it on the hot white sand.
And sitting, held out her hand.
Slowly from the scattered huts,
The children came, their eyes
So wide, their legs so thin,
Protruding stomachs — fretful cries
So hungry yet so very brave,
to listen to the words, that somehow
gave them hope. She could not give
them food, she'd none to give, so head
bent low, she prayed — and
hoped that they would find
the will to live.
La Jones

Ode To Christchurch

Christchurch is a lovely town, two rivers running through,
Curved Stour and the Avon bring calm beauty to the view.
The millstream flows past Castle ruins by the Priory,
Flowing on to pass the yachts and greet the swannery.

Twynham, was the old town's name, from times long past away
When smugglers transferred booty to boats waiting in the bay.
Fair Saxons, Vikings and the Romans, wrought their iron-will,
Even after all these years, the echoes linger still.

Quaint cottages and shops as if cars should not be there,
Just ladies in their crinolines, with time to stop and stare.
Walk past the Parish-Church, then such delight before your eyes,
The Harbour scene and wildlife give one a grand surprise.

Rivers meet to join the run through to Mudeford Quay,
A picturesque hamlet, with a sea-fishing industry.
Lobster-pots and tangled nets to mend, drying in the sun,
Children catching crabs to let them free again for fun.

Salmon leap the harbour mouth, so wanting to be free,
You can walk along the shore and see swans upon the sea.
Ten minutes pleasant stroll away, a golden sandy beach,
With the New Forest waiting within an easy reach.
Iris Barker

The Gardener

Carefully he plants the seeds,
   Cuts the hedges, destroys the weeds.
Sweeps away the garden leaves,
   Prunes the bushes, welcomes the bees.
Knows the name of every flower and shrub,
   Created by our Lord above.
Bending back aching, but on he goes,
   Content in his work he loves and knows.
Working outdoors in all kinds of weather
   His hands and his face tanned like leather.
The love from hands continues to flow,
   As his busy green fingers are kept on the go.
Kneeling in garden there, tending the soil,
   Each task he does with infinite care.
Working quietly alone but unaware,
   Our Lord was resting in the garden there.
Ivy Balch

Springtime

Where once the earth was cold and bare,
Daffodils are nodding there,
Greeting us with a sign of Spring,
With all the beauties it will bring.
Nature goes her own sweet way,
Bringing surprises day by day,
Everything seems to come alive,
Like busy bees working in their hive,
Buds bursting on apple, plum, and pear,
Fruiting later for all to share,
Birds flit from tree to tree,
Young lambs gambol, oh so free,
In pastures green, Country serene.
Beatrice May Scofield

Children

Little and inconsequential children walk
children talk
children hear
Little and inconsequential they see
they imagine
they vision
Little and inconsequential they want
they ask
they get
but that's okay
little and inconsequential they pretend to be.
Camilla Thomas

Unlike The Fur

Purist clear solid light your motley aura dwelt long
dark centuries in cramped despair,

Most resolute of beauties exposed to air.

Elaborate measures minds villainous preen, the craved
of pleasure depraved of scheme, not paid in pennies nor
paid in gold, but chance, to possess your petrified soul.

Bring me everlasting trips of gleam to meditate,
the fugitive flicker of fiery beams from gem through eyes
to mesmeric dream.

Just one link from precious mould and you are chained
to vanity's finger.

Who will fight your cause? Your bed of years goes
unheeded yet a fur takes just one generation to grow, how
many mink have born and died in your evolution?

None will quench your fire, so shine my unmelting piece
of ice, shine, as true to be seen as your truth in my dream.

Trouble me no more with foolish toys, I wish this
stone for all its joys.
Daniel C. Smith

Weathering Life

Since before time, before the dawn of mankind, before the light
of the day showed us the way.
The dark of the night, a silent twilight, gave way to the rise of
the sun.
Life had begun.
The sunshine of love, sent from above, bathed a sea of
enchantment.
Offered peaceful contentment.
But as the sands of time enveloped our minds, a fog of
confusion with no solutions
Settled over the ocean of life, so between man and wife,
a mist of mistrust, unbelievable just,
drenched us with a reign of sorrow
It saddened tomorrow and our ocean of life, living and loving,
was covered by the snow of foreboding.
We were angry and loathing, as the frost of deceit froze our
icy retreat
To the winter of hate, negativity's gate.
But with a sky of blue our horizon's renewed, blown by the
winds of change.
So different and strange, with a new understanding between
me and you.
A positive reaction, with no fond adieu, the days of together,
week, month, yearly forever, mean that the sands of time, will
part us never.
David Shaun Aston

Alien Thoughts

The past has gone the future is now
Daylight is closing I must take a bow
Walking life's treadmill for a number of years
Sometimes with laughter many times with tears

Looking through life's mirror I look at the past
Bad reflections fade quickly, Happy ones they last
So on we go all through life's throws
Thorns pierce my palm from the bloody red rose

My tongue remains silent, my thoughts run wild
When I think of the past when I was a child
Coldness and darkness surrounded my fears
Something I grew out of over the years

I'm not who you think I am
I don't even know myself
I came here many light years ago
In search of grandeur and wealth

Goodbye to the world and all that has passed
Man's been to the moon, I'm going to mars
I am an alien just passing by
Look at your world, it's not much different to mine.
Brian Kenneth Weston

A Soldier's Thought

Too many conflicts
Dead beaten bodies
Shadows of crosses
And acres of bumps
Souls with lustre revenge in their eyes
Screaming with hatred of people they despise
Whose blood did I dishonour?
The world's or my own
With contemptuous lies and unprofitable war.
Anthony Paterson

Ocean Silence

Quiet is all around me,
Deafening my senses and numbing my responses.
The silence engulfs me,
The loneliness in my heart is growing,
I do not know where I begin....

And this silent underworld ends.
Some may say this isolation does not really exist,
But the ocean of loneliness, in which I drown,
Is becoming colder now.
The people near me are like ripples in the water....

They touch me, then leave me,
Nobody listens to me, nobody really tries to shed my loneliness.
I do have friends who care, and parents who love me,
But I also have loneliness as vast as any sea.
I can't control the situation around me....

They are of a higher force than me.
The quiet is still all around me,
And no light from above passes below to guide me.
I can't do this alone.
I have never had to learn to sink or swim.
Lorraine Wilson

" Each Soul Is Important "

The niche carved for you generations ago
Decided the pattern, the way you could go,
So, whatever your sin — the situation
you are in is the pathway in which you must go.
You learn as you travel many truths on the way,
For the wrong that you do — many others will pay.
No one knows the full mysteries of the mind and the brain,
why the sins of our fathers will haunt us again.
We are not alone in the evil we've done,
for no-one is perfect under the sun,
so can we not try to place there
a shield between evil,
and I know each soul is important, and all that we do,
we do to our children, the answer's with you.
Jean Hunaban

The Miners

The miners trudge to the small cramped shaft,
Behind them, with a slam, they shut the
door fast.
They travel deeper and deeper where no
light is found.
It is cold and dark deep under the ground.
The miners work all of the day,
Earning money for their pay.
At the end of the day the miners are
black.
They go home tired with aching backs.
As they crawl around on the ground,
They hear a loud sound,
They think it's a gun,
But it's an explosion.
No longer will the miners have to dig and
delve,
No longer will the horses have to be fed,
For all the miners, on that day,
Lay on the floor — still and dead.
Anna Cook

Cock - O - The North

Proudly they marched with heads held high
Defying the clouds in a rain filled sky
The Pipers played and the kilts swung by
As a tear trickled down from the onlooker's eye.

In silence they watched as their hearts slowly bled
For the death of a Regiment
And to what lay ahead
None finer a soldier this land ever bred
No longer a Gordon but a 'Highlander' instead.

Annie McKimmie

Bloodshed And Tears

What can reduce a grown man to tears?
Deprive their offspring of happy childhood years,
Force woman to grieve, through the blood and the tears,
As they wait in torment, to realize their worst fears
Their husbands, their sons, are maimed and for what?
A fight amongst brothers, their souls left to rot.
All return tired, limbless or worse,
At death's door because of a war:
It's a curse!
Man can put his fellow man on the moon,
Keep babies alive, that are born too soon.
Build waggons and trains, fast wheels for the road,
Invent medicines that help men grow old.
On one hand he helps prolong life for his brother,
And then, on the other, takes child from his mother,
It's such a great pity that one simple task,
Like living in peace, is too much to ask.
Deep down in their hearts, they must not pretend,
Throw down the weapons,
This bloodshed must end!

Kathryn Susan Shaughnessy

Life After Death

"Why him?" you ask, but no-one really knows how to explain,
Desperately you try to understand, your answer — but a
  nagging, lonely pain,
Death is so unfounded, but then so again is life,
God sends these things to try us... pain, upset and strife,
A fist full of emotion, a heavy heart that wants to break,
Your father is at peace now and would want you to shake
Off the pain, erase the sadness from your face,
Wipe away the tears — etch a smile in their place,
Look beyond your veil of doubt and his love will live through you,
Your life is just beginning and live it you must do!
Remember all the good things, the fun you had together,
This will guide you through the storm, and help you to weather
All the pain, the sorrow and regret,
Your Dad, Your father, Your icon — it's his life you'll not forget.

So pray to him if you want to, talk to him out loud,
To talk will clear your head and disperse that doubtful cloud
Of darkness, and in its place the sun will shine,
And as time goes on, the pain will go, you will find it easier,
And through life you will begin to sail,
Your strength and ability to laugh will return, and happiness
  will prevail.

Emma Morrison

The Second Millennium

Crucify! Crucify!
Do you hear the savage cry echoing across two thousand years?
Hide your head and turn away — 'not my fault' I hear you say,
Leave it and it's bound to go away!
What's it got to do with me? I can't help the blind to see,
Nor give limbs to those who now are lame.
And the poor, what's all the fuss? They will always be with us
He told us that when first on earth he came!
Selfish, thoughtless, cruel man... nothing's changed since time began,
Still refuses to accept the blame!

Christina Kempster

Untitled

Oh! Weak, weak man, when will you stop
destroying all that God had wrought?
To interfere with his plan here adds chaos,
frantic searchings through the years
of unlinked parts, now lost in space,
a threat to all the human race;
His scheme of things no longer fits; the
future lacks,
Perhaps, the best-hewn parts, which
alone, the continuing structures strong
Find necessary builders, corner stones,
to support the weak,
Continuity retain and hope, life at
its best, renew again.

Are we too late? Perhaps, not yet,
To heal and mend the feeble parts,
To tender thoughts to future years
instead of self indulgence, fears.

Henrietta Walker

The Colours Of Peace

An unexpected return to a familiar atrocity
Devastating in its surprise and velocity
Lips that are moving, yet no words are spoken
Promises made, where hope is broken.

A beautiful landscape made ugly by war
Streams salty with tears, earth putrid with gore
How can it end when it's always beginning?
There are no losers as nobody's winning.

Men of steel, yet with razor blade hearts
A bumper war volume of many parts
While leaders in their ivory towers will sleep
The poor man, endangered, on the street will weep.

For both sides to talk, such a simple task
People crying out: "is that too much to ask?"
An ocean between us, yet it's laden with bullets
'Pull this switch for peace', but no one will pull it.

Let's put colour back into the people's lives
Though splattered with red, by strength they'll survive
Reveal a morn as yellow as corn, end this lengthy campaign
Let London's streets be golden once more, and Ireland green again.

Andrea J. Delaney

Silent Armageddon

The veiled, black deep of leader's minds
conceals an iron - cast shark,
the enemy propels a path of
threat in the murky dark.
Death lies in wait in a hard case of steel,
the hunter turns with stealth,
and slips the tide of a secret war
as a sonar screams for wealth.

Leviathan has fled in fear;
cold ripples shade the lands.
With walls of waves a silent
Armageddon stalks the sands.

Emma Unsworth

Pill (Pretty Intelligent Life Losted)

Location drug ward
Dead at scene an eighteen year old
has been
Died for a thrill not a tablet but pill.
Pretty intelligent life losted only ten
pounds that's what it cost
Raised well and taught good
Died in the style of Hollywood
Her life saved seven
Let's hope she's safe now and in heaven.

Jeffrey Coppin

Cathedral

'Twas once part of the firmament of clay,
dispersed in natural element it lay,
no form that would attract the human eye,
untouched, unsought, it would forever lie,
but man, with strength and tool did excavate
with thought in mind of thing more intricate,
assembled thus, this mass to shape and mould
a building so ornate, of splendour to behold;
and man in his good time will thus create
a cathedral, magnificent, and great;
base earth, man's skill and artifice transform,
a church, that will environment adorn,
as man to God his work will dedicate
a temple made with hands to illustrate,
reflected in this architecture fine
man's monument, his tribute to Divine.
  Arthur George Carter

Do I?

Do I pay the rent
Do I buy some food

When the tally man comes
The children must lie on the floor
A game of silence until he goes away
A game to be replayed when he comes next day

Do I pay the TV licence
Do I risk going to jail
Do I buy my kids some shoes

Do I wait for the bastard their father
Of whom there is no news

Do I give up smoking
Burning moments of calm
Taking away my appetite
In the depths of worry-balm

Money won't buy happiness
Money is a curse
Money is an evil

What joy an empty purse
  Denny Bradbury

Thoughts

Why do we get lost in our own world?
Do we even know right or wrong
How many questions can we ask ourselves, or do we carry on
without question
Is the answer his or hers or the young or old
How many times a day are we lost
Should we ever worry about cost or not
Health or ill health, richness or poverty
We don't really know or do we?
  John O'Donnell

What Do You See...?

What do you see when you look at me?
Do you see a frown where a smile should be?
Do you see lines on a careworn face
Or do you see style, beauty and grace?

When you hear me talk do you hear what I say?
Do you listen intently or just turn away?
Do I interest you, or am I a bore
Do I repeat the same things I've said before?

Old age creeps up on you like a thief;
It may steal a layer, but not what's beneath.
I don't have my looks, stamina or good health
But I have my memories, they're more important than wealth.

I've lived a full life, seen many wonderful things
I've experienced the joy a loving family brings.
Don't worry, I've finished my rumination!
But what do you see — wisdom or stagnation?
  Beverley Burrows

Storm Of Night

Wind howling through the rafters — creaking window panes
doors squeaking at their hinges
Lashing icy rain
Force six gale is blowing — wrenching at the roots
of trees about to topple
while men in rubber boots
attempt to reach a stranded flock — marooned on yonder hill
Unexpected storm tonight
A farmer's bitter pill
Roads awash like rivers — running wild and free
gushing through the farmyard gate
makes one large muddy sea
Sirens of fire engines — rescue close at hand
Lone crow sits on a chimney stack
surveys the oozing land
Storm force wind exposes — weakness of mankind
while nature's might seems to delight
in chaos left behind
  Bruce Davies

Shattered Dreams

Oh dreams forlorn, where are you now,
Dost thou not see the sweat, upon my brow,
The dreams I cherished, so long ago,
When I first met my darling Beau
They held such love, those dreams of mine,
But they forgot, with passage of time,
They could be broken just like mine,
My dreams they did turn around,
And now lay shattered on the ground.
Around life's bend I'd failed to see,
What cruel fate held in store for me,
The BEAU I did love so, then,
Became an Ogre in its den,
And oh, how I do loathe him now,
He caused the sweat upon my brow,
And as I lay me down to sleep,
I dream of dreams, I could not keep.
  Dorothy Morris-Hague

Winter Weekend Break

Staffordshire moorland, the edge of the Peak District,
Dotted with farms and its closely-knit hills;
Dry stone-walled fields lying bare to the elements,
Exposed to a wind that incessantly chills.

Climb up to a field to see four sturdy horses,
Racing to greet us as we stop at their gate;
They'll be looking for crusts or even some sugar-lumps,
Our stay quickly passes and tea-time won't wait.

So it's back down the hill for the warmth of the farm house,
We'll run all the way to see who will be first;
Then get inside quickly, sit round in a huddle,
Eating toast by the fire-side and quenching our thirst.
  Guy Cockerton

Time Flies

Day breaks, morning comes
Daily chores, some please, some bore

Noon arrives, is it bright or dull
Will the sun shine, or the rain fall

Will it make us happy, or bring us to a halt
What we're preparing in our thoughts

Work or relax, do what we may
Life's passing us by each day

Evening is here, our family needs to be fed
Clear the dishes, it's nearly time for bed

Life's what you make it as you know
But oh how quickly does it go
  Iris Molyneux

The Holiday

We went on a trip, just Buba and me,
Down to Lyme Regis to be by the sea,
To walk on the shore, to sit in the sun,
Watching children having fun.
We went for a sail, took a ride on a train,
But when we got off it started to rain,
We went back to the hotel, as fast as could be,
To change our wet clothes, and be ready for tea,
We sat in the lounge, feeling quite glum,
Wondering why we had bothered to come,
But then we decided it was rather fun,
Sitting there in the dry, watching people go by,
Splashing in puddles, umbrellas held high,
And maybe tomorrow, the sun will come out.
And we will see children out and about,
And perhaps we will walk, just Buba and me,
Through the park down to the sea.
   Happy Holiday.
   Emily Morosoli

The Visitors

I can see the river from my first floor window, over the rooftops
dozens of gulls, men in boats delivering their catch, buoys afloat.

The ferry awaits, large and looming, another set of visitors to
Deliver to the island beyond, across the river.

The horn blows, away she glides in a southerly route
people stand on deck, waving to those who care to look.

Soon they will stand down, find a seat and take in the joy of this
wonderful feeling, the ferry so large smoothly crosses the
water, the smaller boats left reeling.

The journey is over, it saddens a few, at disembarkation
excitement is rife; there is the island, their new life.

The ferry turns tail and returns for more visitors to take to the
place where life can be enjoyed at a slower pace.
To leave this hell on earth to the land where life is easy
is the desire of all who live and breathe.
I can see the river from my first floor window, over the rooftops
the dreams of men and women like the buoys — afloat.
   Catriona Dunstan

The Spring

The grey, brown earth turns slowly green,
Drab birds now dance in brightness.
Then hibernates creep out, are seen,
Heavy skies turn again to lightness.

The promise, the tryst of Persephone is here,
An imprint of flowers depicts her way.
Little lambs gambol all unaware,
Longer and brighter grows the day.

Sounds sweet, this season of hope,
But the night is still damp and cold.
Mist hangs over all like a rope,
A cord tied to winter of old.

Where is the hope of warm summer sun,
When there is no place to go,
And nowhere yet to run?
Yet ever on we search to find the rainbow.
   Cynthia A. Price

O Silent Flight

Each time I hear an aircraft engine roar
Dread feelings tighten hand and heart,
Each time I know the fear I knew before
When in a war I unwillingly took part.

Childhood memory of air raids come again
Burning fear I knew by day and night,
Lost relations, home and searing pain
This echo will fade with silent flight.
   Gwen Mason

Winning Mania

A holiday of any description
Draws me to enter a competition.
It might not be where I want to stay
But at least, it's a break away.
They say a breaks as good as a rest
Why can't I win their simple contest.
A weekend break is all I ask
Surely not an impossible task.

To lie on a beach with nothing to do
And not go to work for a day or two
No chores to be done, no grocery shopping
Let someone else do all of the cooking
Oh how glorious just to be lazy
If I don't win I think I'll go crazy.

I've found a different way to compete
With only a few days left to complete
An original poem, what shall I write?
I really will have to get this right
To win the money, what bliss that would be
Do you think I can write winning poetry?
   Lynette Wheatley

Dreams

Dreams are beautiful, beautiful thoughts,
Dreams can never, ever be bought.
Dreams of magic, of things beyond means,
Dreams of places which might never be seen.

Dreams of yesterday, when care we had none,
Dreams of words and things we've not done.
Dreams of weddings and the ringing of bells,
Dreams of the feelings unable to quell.

Dreams of babies all well and content,
Dreams of the love with which they were sent.
Dreams of attaining the things that we wish,
Dreams for some of becoming quite rich.

Dreams of a long and healthy good life,
Dreams of the partner, the husband or wife.
Dreams when we sit at the end of the way,
Dreams just to be able to have one more day.

Dreams are a must for all of our pleasure,
Dreams for things past and lost that we can treasure.
   Alwyn Hall

Morning Mists

Through the night it appears
drifting through valleys and trees
feeling the earth with feathery finger
seeming to hesitate and linger
Before moving on over river and stream
softly, silent, as if in a dream
with early dawn comes birdsong
muted among the early mist
the green fields kissed
With early morning dew
like crystal droplets on a new
velvet gown
   Kathleen Fox

'Blind To The World'

Searching through life, searching for love,
Finding nothing and giving up.
Once a child, sweet and innocent,
Nursery rhymes and nanny's treats.
Those deviant days have passed me by,
I look at the world and sit and cry.
We earn the money to pay for the bread
And keep a shelter above our heads.
Who lives in a cottage made of sweets?
Who can afford to eat and eat?
"When I grow up I want to be..."
The start of a fairy tale, far from reality.
   Catherine Hughes

Dawn Of A Silent Spring

This planet will surely become a lifeless place,
Due to greed and demands of the human race,
No wild animals prowling, no birds to sing,
We are heading towards a silent spring.

Government demand economies to expand,
Putting more pressure on our precious land,
This human folly will surely bring,
A barren wilderness, a silent spring.

People of all colour, religion, and creed,
Must slow down demand, cut out their greed,
To all branches of nature, humans must cling,
To halt the progress of a silent spring.

Why must man, just for capital gain,
Destroy the forests, produce acid rain,
In his quest for power, man will be king,
Of a lifeless landscape, a silent spring.

The seeds we are sowing of self-destruction,
Will be more disastrous than any volcanic eruption,
Leaf-less trees, no bird on the wing,
Can we survive a silent spring.

Graham Longden

Destiny

Flowers died and skies turned grey,
duty called, we had to part.
Our souls were joined by an invisible thread,
our destinies etched on both our hearts...

One last look, one last kiss,
a short embrace, one last wish.
Would we ever meet again,
would love last through thick and thin.

Flowers bloomed and rivers flowed,
Willows swayed and hedgerows glowed,
White clouds wandered, waves rolled and floundered,
Life passed by, but we remembered.

Our love survived, our two souls twined,
Our spirits await the fate of time.

Agnieska Norris

For Baby Kylie

My darling I'll remember you
each and every day,
I know that in my heart of hearts
you'll never fade away.
Kylie you were my everything
you made me laugh and sing,
I cry for you, I sigh for you
my darling everything.
Your smiling face, your dancing grace.
Your laughter and your cry.
Kylie, my darling,
I will never say goodbye.

Denyse Hancock

A Mother's Death (From Her Child In Bed)

Lonely by nature, silent from cause
Consciously feeling totally lost
Candles glowing dimly, depict the scene
Hot embers cast shadows to the ceiling.

Eyes that are staring into redness
Sleep with dreams will eventually come
Peace at last from outward elements
Comforts the body like warming sun.

Brightness from the next day's dawning
Streams delicately into the room
The dark tunnel that engulfed there
Opened its doors to let out the gloom.

Kathleen McKenzie

Nature's Clock

Nature's wondrous clock never fails us and amaze,
Each and every season tends to make us stop and gaze.
Honour please these seasons, that are sent without fail,
The rain, the sun, the snow and raging winter gale.
His universe and seasons are sent for all to enjoy,
Sent for everyone, man, woman, girl and boy.
Sent also for each animal that grazes from the land,
God will intervene stop man's interfering hand.
Man may do such damage even this He will put right,
God and his seasons He'll protect with Godly might.
Take great care not to harm the seasons for our kin,
Without God's wondrous seasons what a devastating sin.
God will always rectify all man made damage done,
Protecting for us the seasons, each and every one.
You will find once again wild flowers will surely bloom,
Wild flowers picked by children again will scent the room.
Laughter of children as they gambol like tiny lambs,
In God's world of seasons that are safely in His hands.
Let nature's clock go ticking on with Him at the helm,
He will continue sending down His ever healing balm.

Evelyn Slade

Christmas In England

We are lucky to live in a country like this,
Each Christmas holiday is filled with bliss,
Our parents, the turkey, the Christmas tree,
The warmth from the fire, but best, we are free.

Think of the children in countries afar,
Where nothing matters but hunger and drought,
Or hiding from the guns of war.
Someone should listen to their cries of pain,
And give them peace and hope again.

Free them from their lives of fear,
Thank God it doesn't happen here,
Our Christmas is spent with our Fathers and Mothers,
Our families around the Christmas tree,
The warmth of the fire, but best, we are free.

Leanora Pawley

Imagine

Imagine living in a world, where people were all the same
Each person just a replica, No pleasure or no pain.
No variety of colour, or differences in shape and size
No changing of emotions, or expressions in our eyes.
No one tall, no one short, No one fat or thin
No one first, no one last, No one to lose or to win
Imagine living in a world, where individuality did not show
If ever one were conforming, Then 'self' no one ever would know
No discrimination, No violence and no crime
No more inequality, No more yours and mine
No one ever happy, yet no one ever sad
No one ever angry, No one ever mad..
Never any different thoughts, No knowledge learned or gained
No more goals to strive for, Nothing left to change
So however different we may feel, However hard it seems
Just think if we were all the same, what that would really mean.
There would never be any growing, for we would not have ourselves to share
There would never be any beauty, for there would be nothing with which to compare
There would never be the sense of achievement, at overcoming the problems life gives
There would never be any wishes or dreams, or any purpose for which we should live.

Jacqueline Maria Shepherd

"Dreams"

In the quiet of morning when the earth is still
Dreams and plans are made.
Ideas (in anticipation) wait
Eager to explode into fate.
A second cup of tea...
Oh! I'm going to be late,
So — 'goodbye' to my dreams 'till morning.

Edith Daniels

A Chance

Is there a chance, of our lives to enhance,
Each Saturday night, I sit in a trance,
In front of the television, I await to see
If the Lottery Balls come right for me.
What I would do, if fate was kind,
So many things I have in mind.
To the animals first of all I would give,
They have such a short time to live.
And then the blind, who miss so much.
They only live, by smell, and touch.
Little children, so shamefully abused.
I want them never again, to feel used,
To the old people, who we owe so much
Help, and encouragement give quality as such.
Then of course family and friends,
So much pleasure in store for them.
All this of course, if wishes come true.
This by my life I pledge to do.
With hope I await next Saturday night.
Then only fate will know if I'm right.

Constance E. S. King

The Unknown Soldier

They stand in their thousands to honour the dead
each with a memory filling the head,
The grave of an unknown bedecked by the wreaths
lain down by the faithful whose lives had been freed.

I walk in the midst of the salt from their tears
and know of their sorrow, the grief through the years,
In my silence I touch somebody's hand
a gesture unnoticed whilst on plays the band.

I reach out to embrace a tormented soul
torn apart by death's grip that none can console,
I tenderly wipe a watering eye
the response is only a heaving sigh.

Heads bowed in silence
in deep memory
of the unknown soldier
and I am he!

Adele V. Garner

The Verdict

Drugs can cure, and drugs can kill,
Ease the mind, or destroy the will,
A body punctured with tiny holes
A life akin to that of moles.
    Digging, always digging.

So when imagination turns to false delight,
And followed by darkness as black as night,
Winding their way through tunnels dark,
Always the needle leaving its mark,
    Tunnelling, always tunnelling.

Until death raises its ugly head,
The doctor's verdict, this one's dead.
And on the streets is the nameless man
Bartering his drugs to whomever he can,
    Dying always dying.

Delphia Beer

2012

The Pleiadian Sun, it twirls and spins.
Entering the great Aquarian Age.
The photon band will bring mournful din.
As the Sun it doth encage.

The sun will sing a sad tune.
A sad tune it will sing.
The primitive one will think of doom.
To the great one, Joy it will bring.

Juliet Louise Pyke

Dedicated To Ruth

The empty shell of her body lies dormant,
Encased by a crisp white sheet.
Immense sadness, a black cloud casts over the room,
Her maker she has left to meet.
We all stand silent, for a while,
No words we can find to say.
The beauty of her aged face, that gentle smile,
As her life is taken away.

We fight back the tears, our hearts fit to break;
Then a feeling of 'hush' like after a storm,
Realizing her body will no longer ache.
The softness of her listless hair, there should be life?
Her hand still warm - no, her soul is no longer there.
A better place we know she has found,
Where wrinkles fade and youth returns.
We have to leave, to turn around,
A goodbye kiss to place upon her head.
The cloud does lift and the tears do flow
But eternity will unite us, one day, we know.

Amanda-Louise Webster

Another Chance

No hope, best to destroy
End his life, this beautiful boy?
I buy, I love, I care, I try,
but most of all I pray.

This is the happiest day.
My beautiful boy runs through
The meadow, fit and strong again
Tossing head and glowing mane
Yes my boy's a horse.
Now fit and well and full of life.
I call him Reilly, we're friends him and I.
I thank my God as I look to the sky.

Joyce Tremble

Untitled

On a high, flying through the sky, dreaming away another endless day, hoping that soon I'll hit the moon, but coming down, I hit this town and wear my frown, like a thorny crown.

Then I hit the brown and laugh, like a mad, demented clown, without any tears, at all those yesteryears, when all I had were fears.

And I awake in a wedding cake and coil out, like a slippery snake, by the side of a misty, stench ridden lake and oh how my whole body does surely ache.

Then I catch sight of the ferryman, ringing his bell, letting me know that it's time for hell, but I don't want to go, I had so many years left to grow.

Christopher Harrison

Nefertiti

The line that's drawn around the eye
enhances what the name describes,
and precious mouth and priceless crown
are far removed from such as I.
Pleasant evenings on my own
will dream me to another land,
where hands that worked you were not mine
but belonged to some unknown.
Though fame that was statue-deep
is known to millions such as I,
your face is his, and his alone
for whom Tell-El-Amarna keeps no memory of thought alive.
So when the crowds subside,
and words of hate no longer heard,
I will be there where you reside with other images;
preserved only in alien eyes.
Take away the wolfline gasps and leave, at least, your blinking
So simple, this feast of seduction
will stop all vicious thinking.

James Norman Anttoni Hyslop

A Battle

Anorexia, all alone,
Entering into an unknown zone.
A world of darkness, fears and scares,
A road of rocks, holes who dares.

A ball of thoughts all mixed and jumbled,
Absorbed in the mind and the body crumbled.
Distorted, tangled turned inside out,
Tears and disaster, is what it's about.

I'm failing fast, all out of control,
I haven't the courage to play the role.
The enemy, the devil, before your eye,
Your strength is needed, where does it lie?

Those questions and answers I'm always challenging,
Myself and loved ones I know I'm damaging.
I want to stop; but I hesitate,
My fears and pain I must designate.

For on the horizon there's a new tomorrow,
With hopes and dreams that no more I borrow.
Created and whole I come reborn,
Into a life that once was forlorn.

Linda Gibney

Hazel And Dick's Retreat

Their garden is a real delight
Especially when the sun shines bright.
Flowers in every nook an cranny,
All varieties, and oh so many.

Trees and shrubs all neat and trim,
Rainwater butt filled to the brim.
Fishpond with lilies, shading the fish,
A drink for the hedgehog in a dish.

Elves and gnomes, frogs and a fox,
And a big white stork stands on a box.
While the weeping willow in the breeze blowing,
Everything is really glowing.

A conservatory overlooks all this,
To sit in there is really bliss.
Just to watch the birds and bees and a butterfly,
Or follow the white clouds across the sky.

There's the cabin for doing what takes your mood,
Modelling, or painting or making things out of wood.
It's so private and tranquil, there's no-one about,
They're just living in peace, the mad world shut out.

Amy F. Childs

" Fiat Justitia, Ruat Caelum " For A Hero

I have perpetual honours for my brave deeds in my country,
eternal and lapidary remembrance, my white black statues,
national and luminous museum, my poor small house,
ecstatic and charming myth, my flourishing grave.

I have perpetual curses for my crimes on the other side,
countless cenotaphs look like wild looking Cerberuses,
historical books relate the outrages of my soldiers,
horrible anathemas dart for the hostile general daily.

I supplicate my gravemates of my worm-eaten body
rainwaters, cold winds, mold soil and flashes of midnight
to give the solution. And you, the lovers of my Soul,
the love and the hate, decide who will be married in the
infinite temple of the Harmony.

Celestial hierophants echoed that the rose-water said:
"Both unwritten and written laws are in conflict".
Delphian and Dodonian pythias sent me enigmatic oracles:
"Son of the uncreated, you were balsam of the wounds
of the old maid earth in vain looking for her starmate".
"Son of the uncreated, you were bigamous in the teleological
Fair of the Colosseum of the seven soul earth".

Georgios A. Mertzios

The Human Race That Changed The World

The world could be a better place,
evaluating the human race.
Looking back over the years,
making accusations of the past.
Serving rights, votes, politics, and
serving man kind.
Humans are people with thoughts, and
fears, with desires and troubles, seeking
their minds.
International society's around the world,
helping the lives of the rich, and poor.
People, and children on the streets, cold,
begging for food at your feet.
Humans have different subjects, and
styles, the world is exclusive, organizations
are supplied, to receive, and re-supply.
The world is unfortunate, in many
ways, people and the environment suffer
all because of the selfish man kind.

Kellie Thatcher

Winter

A mystical being has painted every tree and branch,
even every blade of grass - not a single one escaped.

Beautiful arachnid doily's more lovely than anything
lace makers could craft, among the hedgerows draped.

Whilst the world slept he worked with glistening frosted dew
and transformed until all gloom and grey was lost.

Oh! So breathtaking a morning such as this; so pure, so clean,
all drabness gone, so white shrouded in virgin frost.

The sun touches all this beauty with its light and warmth,
enhancing and reflecting every crystal jewel.

But as it does, the illusion melts away - all begins to revert
to gloom and grey. Just like real life it's really rather cruel.

Gill Oakes

Sorrow

The pain I feel now, oh how I have cried
Even more than when mum and dad died.
All of our family have been greatly deceived,
Sorrow for husband and father not even bereaved.

Another woman has taken him away from me
Straight longish hair and barely forty,
Two years older than our eldest daughter,
I cannot bear to think that now he will court her.

It is not only me that has lost everything
He has lost three daughters by his great sin,
They cannot bear to see the state their mother's in,
Lost nearly a stone and getting very thin!

Two darling grandchildren just cast aside,
You pretended you loved them but they knew that you lied,
Steven and Daniel saw how their own mummy did cry
They thought Nanny had cancer and was going to die.

We have different values for why we are living,
You only took whilst I did the giving,
The person you loved once you said was so kind
So why desert me now and leave all that behind?

Daphne Smith

Dew On A Spider's Web

Dew on a spiders web is a wonderful sight,
Early morning finds what has been created at night.
Lovely designs spun so nice,
Without a pattern or device,
Looking at a mat of lace,
Shows how long it takes to place.

Dorothy Snow

Why?

You once stood tall, mature and glorious,
Evidence of God who created you.
Your branches, with their sticky buds, waiting patiently for Spring,
Were suddenly cut down by man's barbaric act.
You lived in trust, what could you do?
Defenceless, unable to resist.
I mourn for you, I grieve for you.

No more will your buds reveal large, hand-shaped leaves,
And flowers, like candles, until they fall
To make a carpet of pink or white.
In Summer heat you gave a canopy of green
To cool us or protect us from the rain.
On Autumn days your leaves of yellow and brown
Swayed to and fro and rustled in the wind.
Your shiny conkers came tumbling all around,
Followed, for this last time, by your leaves.

Now in the Spring the other trees will dress themselves in green,
And you will stand; your trunk and stumps are maimed.
I mourn for you, I grieve for you.
Angela Macdonald

Towards The Light

Often I have pondered the meaning of life
Evolution, creation, husband and wife,
And the seed born between them
That creates, peace, wisdom or strife.

I walk thro' the forest, in awe of the trees
But the might of the jungle just cannot appease
My thirst for knowledge of things yet to come

The gurgle of water, the blue of the sky
The smell of the fresh grass
Bring a tear to my eye.

Then I feel a power, so gently divine
It urges me, leave "the old world" behind
And come to a land where paradise is free
Then the glory of life and creation you'll see.

Soon I'll know the wonder of
This beautiful land,
And that a maker-creator
Holds it all in His hand!
Alistair Brown

" Uncle Hughie "

The family name is Mitchell — nine of them in all
except for Uncle Geordie, the men were all quite tall,
they must have been a handful and what a motley crew,
the cheekiest of all of them being my "Uncle Hugh".

To know my "Uncle Hughie" — you need to know his lady,
she's only wee but very strong and her name is 'Auntie Sadie',
she brought up the five kids and kept the ship from sinking
whilst 'Uncle Hugh' went missing — for his hobby was his drinking!

My Uncle had a near miss, in fact he had a few,
he wasn't always healthy but his heart was always true.
pay day was his favourite — Auntie Sadie knew it risky
for instead of buying messages, he'd be out there buying whisky!

I'm related to my Uncle because my mother is his sister
and sometimes when he'd had a few, he'd phone to say he missed her,
they didn't see each other much, as all they did was row
and I guarantee if he was here — they'd do the same right now!

And now he's gone I feel it's time to sit and wonder why
that the only time I'll see him is the time when I shall die,
I know that in my next life I shall meet him again
and hear his booming Scottish voice ask "how you doin', hen?"
Lesley Stewart

Living With A Smile

If life is for living, and money for giving,
excuse me whilst I stand in line,
If tears are for crying, and questions for why-ing,
to me that may well be fine,
But in all said and done, why am I the only one,
That wants a really good laugh,
Just what does it take, for a comedian to wake,
and give me a chuckle by half,
Hour after hour, there I have sat, waiting for a giggle to rise,
Oh' please will it come, as I wait for the pun,
and then for the big surprise,
To laugh and laugh, until no-more, my sides aching with pleasure,
I'd give all that I've got, to have a great laff,
give all that I really do treasure,
but no, no such luck, what do I do, to have a really good giggle-ish
well, I've just found out, and without a doubt,
I'm laughing because I am tickle-ish.
Carol Roberts

Snow

Slowly, silently, the large white feathery flakes
fall gently from the grey, heavily-laden sky
onto all in its midst, disguising all but simple shape
and leaving a ghostly evidence of crisp white snow.
The village is asleep still, save for a few birds
ruffling their feathers to keep warm.
A rabbit scuttles at speed across the snow
leaving its telling prints for all to see. Beware of hungry foxes!

Suddenly, there is a shriek of laughter from
happy children. They have spotted the blanket of
snow beckoning them tantalizingly towards the
wonderland sitting like a Christmas card outside.
The quiet landscape turns into a battlefield
as the children throw snowballs with squeals of joy.
Gone is the smooth carpet of glistening snow
as children whistle down the slippery slopes on sledges.
Nightfall arrives, and once again, the land
is still as the snow falls quietly from the sky undisturbed.
Bryn Lloyd

The Amber Leaf

As I watched the amber leaf
fall gently to the ground
I thought of all the other trees
shedding their leaves without a sound
I stood beside the railings
reflecting nature's thrill
as she stripped her trees in winter
dressing them as she will
In spring she puts on gowns of green
the likes of which you've never seen
  In Autumn amber leaves appear
   like golden strands so pure and sheer
    those trees were old
  when I was small
yet here they stand so proud and tall
I was the stranger whose time was brief
not the lovely amber leaf
Brigid Whyte

Nam Et Ipsa Scientia Potestas Est

Test followed by exam followed by degree.
Gainful employment followed by the anonymity of retirement.
I hold these certificates of perceived knowledge,
Yet I can never answer the question: why?

Until then, I am a nobody, a nothing,
A statistical number in the cogs of
The mathematical wheel of fortune. Luckily, my
Answer will be given when I meet the

All-knowledgeable, all-powerful: when?
Charles Bettinson

As The Year Is Ending

Red and gold, the gentle tints of autumn
Fall softly to the ground.
Mist rising over quiet fields,
Sherbet sky slowly turning
To glorious azure,
Crisp and clear.
My favourite time of year.

Smoke curling from garden fires
Drifting lazily above the roofs.
That certain scent, all their own.
Damsons and apples, all nature's bounty
Picked and stored.
I love this time of year.

Now, a cold wind ruffles the lake
Wild birds wander, forlorn.
The sun hides his face behind grey curtains.
But a child comes, running, with cheeks ablaze,
Carrying bread.
The other side of autumn;
Winter is near.

Silvia Ann Mansell

Autumn

The sky grows dark, it's heavy with rain. Autumn is calling once again.

The swallows are preparing to fly over land and seas. Leaves are falling from many trees.

The woods where foxes have made their den, are covered by mist so thin.
They are afraid to come out, I afraid to go in.

A nesting box in a tree so tall, lay damp and forgotten as autumn calls.

Beside the river on the bank, thunder rumbles, a lightning flash, a dog barks, a duck quacks. The river roars, tumbling over the weir.

Summer has gone, autumn is here.

Betty Ashton

The Missed Childhood

Dying, starving and what for?
Famine, draught? No civil war
10-year-old boys growing up too soon
Their orphaned childhood is one of sadness and gloom
Gun in hand he goes to kill his friend
Hypnotized by a mad dictator, whose pocket he defends

Ethnic cleansing a Race is culled
A child is given a grenade to throw and a trigger to pull
On this young soldier no stars or strips will be found
Tomorrow he will be shot, while sightless and bound
He is now just another missing child
Who never got to laugh, grin or smile

John Pringle

Ribbons Of Love's Pastiche

'Tis like a whispering repose,
Echoes of love's chosen rose.
These dancing facets in mind's eye,
Questioning the reasons why?

Like gossamer leaves paying mistral spent.
The chambers of my mind hath sent.
What is this treasure your heart desires?
A nugget of gold cannot aspire, or hold such bounteous pleasures.

How do I then, What, Where must they seek these things I speak.
Nor err a chalice can hold within love's truest potion
Search, surrender the charism of your heart.
Drink the mead of its chantry.
Float, and rest in its hammock of contentment.

Kay Alexander

Play On

If music be the food of love, play on
Famous words from one who's long since gone
And on through time they've echoed in our ears
To stir imagination, down the passing years.

For music has a power, no other sound can beat,
It moves our senses to a state, where heart and mind will meet,
And memories come flooding back, to haunt our waking hours.
They come, then fade, then die away, like softly falling flowers.

The sweet sound of a lullaby, in the flickering candlelight,
When sandman and a whispered prayer helped us through the night
The morning brought the song of birds, so full of joy and cheer,
And life was good when we were young, and there was naught to fear.

When couples met and pledged their love, as the dance-band played
A waltz by Strauss, a melody, to which we all then swayed,
And then there was the Wedding March, we walked the aisle with pride,
Two people starting out in life, to share it side by side,

And so through time our memories are linked with sounds like these,
Until the Hymns of Requiem, when joy and gladness flees,
But memories are precious, and these I'll dwell upon,
If they bring solace to my heart, I'll say, Play On, Play On.

Esther Barry

Eunice Has Gone

Eunice has gone to a place
far beyond,
where my eyes can see.
When I come home, not thinking
I call out her name.
I struggle alone doing the housework.
Hope she can't see me, but
I can hear her laughing!
Together, as a family, we were everything;
now, sitting alone, I am nothing.
I shed tears, thinking of her courage
and dignity showed fighting cancer.
When friends came,
"I don't want any tears" she would say.
She kept her pecker up
until the end at five past nine
"What time is it?" she had kept asking.
Eunice was not going to be late
for her next life.
She deserves another life — free of pain. God Bless

Frank Dawson

Imprisonment

Baby lies in the palace
Feathers and frills enfolding
Softly breathing sweet and scented air
Fed from Nature's finest fruits
In a silk and satin world reflected in her shining hair.
Through open windows the sounds creep in
Of humanity living its life
Distant, muffled, foreign to Royal few
Guarded, shielded, protected from public view
The baby sleeps, by Protocol imprisoned.

Baby cries in the Ghetto
In filthy rags enveloped
Choking on a mildewed atmosphere
Black bread her food of luxury
To starve skeletal form and nurture a feverish tear.
Through gaping walls the stench seeps in
Of humanity living its life
Sticky, stifling, close to suffocation
Unkempt, neglected, a disgrace to a nation
The baby weeps, by Protocol imprisoned.

Jacqueline M. Johnson

The Last Goodbye

Where once was happiness and life and warmth as well, where once was feeling, sorrow, touch and pain, all melted now and just an empty shell, nevermore to have or hold again. To comprehend that nowhere on this earth will sight nor sound be ever spotted now; a life, much more than life itself is worth, gone to who knows where and out of reach. This mystery no human mind can solve, or reach out, touch, or travel to that place. Communication severed as of now; wrinkled smiles stolen from this face.

To clutch that hand and reach his destination; to travel with him to where his journey ends, Life, love, and distance know no limitation. To be with him and hold him 'till the end. The graveside flowers shimmer in the snow: the vista fresh; the rolling pastures wide. To visualize his body there below yet know the spirit no longer rests inside. No pain he feels, no weight of heavy earth, no sorrow now, perhaps his heart no love admits. At peace with all he lies for evermore and lets the world drift on without his pain, nevermore to bear the strain of life or let its cruel ways hurt with yet again.

The lessons learnt were hard and never he forgot the wicked wiles of life; too tough for him they proved. Deceit and selfishness he knew them not but for honour and integrity he stood. The cold and hard exterior he showed, so foreign to his real self alone; eventually the love and warmth exposed to show an inner person rarely known. A lifetime filled with bitterness and lies; no wonder trust was difficult to find. A sadness round his lips and in his eyes; an inner heartbreak never cured by time.

Joy Langley

My Daughter And I

Nobody here but you and I
Feeling the presence of each other
And the presence of nature
We hold onto our love as nature surrounds us
I appreciate love
I hope you do mine
Love surrounding us
With complete peace wonderful
Thank you love
For the peace and quiet we feel
The peace giving me the thoughts to write
No talking, breath saved
For the writing of the poem
You picked the flower for me
With your love
I picked one for you
There is a part of a forest
Which we pass which is in my thoughts
Noise passing us, taking us away from peace

Cynthia Osborne

Mothers' Precious Jewel

I love the pen and pencil on my three piece suite.
Felt tip and wax crayon make the pattern more complete.
Chocolate on my telly! Crisps crunch underfoot,
Jam smudged on my curtains that's why they're never shut.
C.D.s in the washer! Socks are missing too,
Potpourri floating in the sink, my toothbrush down the loo.
Books have lost their covers, pages ripped and worn,
Scratches on my table top, photo's bent and torn.

My home was once a haven, tidy clean and neat,
A place of tranquillity, a welcoming retreat.
Books slept in their covers, Videos in their case,
bags were in a cupboard now bulge on my face.
Silicon didn't beckon but now I'm not so sure,
What once was firm is flabby, size 12 will be no more.

Please don't be mistaken goodness not mislead,
I enjoy being up all night than fast asleep in bed!
I've never been so contented, life's so wonderful,
My daughter's gorgeous and mischievous, no day is ever dull.
Momentous are stuck in scrap books, in case the memories fade,
Of my adventures of the good old days, of a Mum to Amber Jade!

Gaynor Tomblin

The Festive Season

Time to go shopping for presents and food.
Fill up our baskets... get in the mood!
Roll up... roll up... forget the pain,
The starving people of the world,
In prisons, or in corners curled,
In foetal position waiting to die,
Perhaps too old, or too weak to cry.

Sit at the table and eat and eat,
'Til our seams are bursting, our eyes are bleak.
Everything in a hazy glow,
Beside the fire... outside the snow.

But in other countries far away, this is not a special day.
Children's bellies swollen there, because there is no food to spare.
People are flogged and people are shot...

My what a lot to things I've got!
Look at my present from Auntie Jane, from Uncle Tim I've got the same.
Everyone laughing and talking and drinking..

But somewhere else... tortured and stinking,
A Soul cries out "Mercy!"... I almost hear it!

Why am I such a hypocrite?

Joy Paton

New York

The Big Apple, well, well, yes it's New York,
Filming, producers, there's many a thought,
Elegant buildings such as twin and trump towers,
People walk the city for 24 hours.

Beggars on corners, asking for a few cents,
Trains underground, whistle by under the vents,
Yellow cabs are there for all to see,
Sirens sounding, hooters blasting, all near me.

Steam pipes blowing upwards against the cold,
The sales are on — in Macy's, most are sold,
A trip down Broadway, then to Times Square,
The atmosphere's bursting, people and lights everywhere.

Liberty, an elegant lady standing there,
Empire State, to the top, you do stare,
Brooklyn Bridge and then there's Queens, we do see,
A walk in Central Park, just my boyfriend and me.

Tall buildings shoot upwards towards the sky,
The Avenues are long, the streets, by and by,
New York's the place we do adore.

Averil A. Perkins

The Man In The Goal

The man in goal
Did he ever blackmail
Or is it an excuse for the law
To lock the doors along with the pops

Can a prisoner really be guilty?
Whether if he said the truth or if he had fiddled
And if he's a prisoner without a blame
How d'you think you'll give him back those wasted times again?

Or d'you pretend you'll change his past
By saying, 'Oh, I'm sorry but it was really a mistake'
Then don't you think he'll have the right to say
'So you don't mind if your life I'll take!'

How many prisoners wait for their doomsday?
But will the goal change these humans someday?
Or is it a waste of time and lives
To live in a dungeon with tiny mice

Some prisoners say 'I'm in a cell and eat free
When I was out I never possessed a family tree
There in the jungle goal I watch a colour T.V.
So d'you really care if I want to die like a flower?'

Carmen Horth

Fire Around Me

Fire around me; am I dead?
Fire around me; it's in my head.
I call for help
but no one's there.
Will I survive?
Does no one care?

Fire around me;
I crawl to the floor;
can't get near to the door.
What about all the people I saw before?
They weren't on the floor.
They weren't in the fire.
But I am! - this isn't what I desire.

Fire around me;
I reach for the phone. I'm all alone.
I dial; it rings, noise in my ears,
bringing all my fears and the tears.
As the sound vibrates in my ears.
I wake up and find myself all tangled up.
There's no fire around me; it's just my FEAR.

Leanne Brent

Summer Heat

Shimmering dragonflies
flickering iridescent,
across the surface
of water incandescent
with haze.
In humid caldron of steamy stillness - summer days.

Bees languid drones,
and wood-pigeons tones,
lone fishermen
quiet, half - sleeping.
Shaded below
graceful willow,
trailing ripples, sadly weeping.

Biting mosquitoes
crowding thickly.
Heady, perfumed
flowers sickly.
Scent of decay,
as white - hot day, turns to moonlight.

Jennifer D. Wootton

Walk Tall

Well here I am stuck in bed
Doing what the Doctor said
I've been here since Tuesday week
Which makes me feel rather sick!

I've taken tablets till I rattle
And still I haven't won the battle
I can't run, walk or dance
But hope to have another chance

My spine is causing all the trouble
It seems that it is starting to crumble
I miss you all and wish you well
When I will see you, who can tell

To stretch my leg they might try
And if that works then I'll get by
Until another time I fear
And then it is straight back here

I play music and dance in my mind
But it's not the same I find
So a happy new year to one and all
And remember, walk tall.

Jean Stewart

'Magic'

Yesterday, the rain and I shed a tear,
Flooding our souls with memories and thoughts,
We cried a waterfall of love
And made a pool of dreams

Today, the clouds and I drifted together,
Filling the sky with hopes and fears,
We rained the past
And made a heaven of destiny

Tonight, the stars and I wished for happiness,
Lighting each other's silent prayers,
We held each other close
And made a beautiful moon

Tomorrow, the sun and I will shine as one,
Waiting, seeking a new future of light,
We shall create
A wonderful colour-filled sunset of fire
And watch it descend to another man
As we make a twilight for something new.

Angela Scott

Autumn Footsteps

Colours are changing, brown, red and gold,
Flowers are dying of the cold,
Summer has gone,
Autumn is here,
It's getting cold and winter is near.

The year's growing old,
The season is cold,
Look forward to Christmas and a happy new year,
Time goes on, remember summer is done,
Goodbye to the old year,
Hello to the new one.

Ellen Marie Quayle

Free Spirit Horse

A beautiful shine on a soft satin coat,
Flowing tail and mane,
Strong body, thundering hooves,
No two horses ever the same.

A velvet muzzle, intelligent eyes,
Large questioning ears.
Humans given implicit trust,
Providing joy, faithful throughout the years.

A friend when one is needed,
Used in sport, ridden for pleasure.
Not to be taken for granted,
Loyal, noble, a lifelong treasure.

As wild as the wind in winter,
Powerful, yet ready to flee,
Never forget a horse is a free spirit,
Not just a slave for you and me.

Carole Benjamin

Enchanted Worlds

Kites twisting pulling on your arm
Flying through the air
Like graceful Eagles
With pictures of prancing horses
And castles with Knights
Or maidens fair haired
Or funny faces with ribbons round their faces
Or just pretty patterns
Or meadows in a frame of sheep
around the kite
Or sails in fields with masts
Like an imaginary little world
When wind dies down we all go home
with enchanted worlds in our heads.

Christopher Smart

The Pain And Joy Of Leaving

Three weeks have passed by and he's leaving today
For cold offshore waters and I hope and I pray
The wind won't blow strong and the sea will keep calm
He'll stay safe, be well and come to no harm

A job on the rigs can be lonely and tough
But the sea is his life, nothing else would be enough
So I hold him close and hug him so tight
I'm dreading him going, I'm dreading tonight

Tomorrow I'll feel better, I'll keep busy all day
It's just at bedtime when on my pillow I lay
Oh the night is so long, lonely and cold
And I stare in the darkness at my band of gold
Then I feel his love just as if he were there
I remember I'm special, I'm one of a pair

Three weeks will soon go and I'm lucky you see
For when he gets back, it's a second honeymoon for me
Three weeks together, what heaven, what bliss
The pain of the parting is what leads to this.

Dianne Anderson

Hillside Home

Dear land, I must leave your lakes and hills so high,
for foreign pastures new, as to distant shores I roam,
but there, in timeless patience, ever in mind's eye,
will always be that precious hillside, which is home.

That hillside fine lived on, oft recalled in exiled mind,
unchanging, yet changing as each new season dawned,
kept by those who stayed, in summer sun and winter wind,
to labour hard and tend that hillside, which is home.

This land is ours, its freedom won by those who stayed
and fought, and prayed I'd one day safely come, to roam
again the stone walled fields in which we'd played,
and kindle warm the fire, on that hillside which is home.

Their prayers are answered, and the exiles back once more,
to make again the ever open door for all with will to come
for welcome true and warm, so all those who've gone before,
may look down and bless this hillside, which was home.

I left my love far off, as though my own sins to atone,
to make my peace where old walls crumble and brambles come
to claim their own, and do as much as one can do alone,
to make fine again this blessed hillside, which is home.

John Durkin

Mourn For Me Oh Lord

Mourn for me oh Lord
For I have surely sinned
For when I awoke this day
I did spy a dark shadow upon my soul.

Mourn for me oh Lord
For I shall surely die within the week
Last night a black carriage passed me by
And from inside a white hand did beckon me.

Mourn for me oh Lord

For I have climbed aboard
Where to I asked?
But Death just smiled and turned away.

Mourn for me oh Lord
For I am on my way
Soon destined to meet my fate
Will it be Heaven or Hell?

Oh Lord I have arrived
Arrived at your door
You have welcomed me in
I am at peace at last.

Linda Garry

Dreams

Suddenly I woke and let out a scream
For I had a nightmare a very bad dream
I dreamt I was paralysed and I couldn't walk
So I started to shake and tremble in shock

I felt like a needle stuck in a groove
And just like that needle my legs wouldn't move
I shouted for help but no-one came near
I shouted again was there no-one to hear

I was then in a wheelchair and people walked by
When I asked them for help they only said why
It wasn't just strangers but people I knew
As I held out my hand they quickly withdrew

So from that moment I felt so alone
With no-one to help I was all on my own
I felt like a stranger alone in a crowd
And no-one would hear me if I shouted out loud

My hands still shaking, a cigarette I did light
I thought it might help me to get over the fright
I kept telling myself that this wasn't true
But what if it was? Just what would I do?

Daniel Carr

A Father Of Flanders

Where is my father a boy enquired,
For I have seen him not.

With tear filled eyes and reverent voices,
A mother did reply.

A soldier was your father son,
In Flanders field he lays.

He gave his life in battle son,
That our lives be free this day.

In hope no strutting tyrant comes,
To conquer and enslave.

Don't cry my son, he sleeps my son,
Red poppies shade his grave.

Now should the call to duty,
Ever come again.

Go forth my son, be proud my son,
You have your father's name.

Leslie Price

How Sleep The Dead?

Never wake the dead!
  For if ever they should find
  The legacy they've left behind,
They'd view their past with dread.

The evils some have bred,
  Although mistaken deeds of might,
  Are too long past to put aright.
So never wake the dead!

Whole nations have been bled.
  The continents are red with blood,
  While millions die for want of food;
So, do not wake the dead!

Yet we may think we've led
  A blameless life in all we've done;
  Dare someone lift our troubled stone
To wake us up when dead?

When we in graveyard bed,
  For all our many wrongs need sigh,
  Shall we not also deafly cry,
'Please, never wake the dead!'

Leslie Green

The Language Of Love

If I could have a wish come true it would not be for gold,
For if I held it in my hand, my heart would soon grow cold.
It would not be for diamonds no matter how they shine,
For they wouldn't mean a thing to me, if you could not be mine.

But my tongue remains dumb and lifeless, as I at times feel too.
And my wish seems so faraway
To be able to say that "I love you."

Do you know that I care?
And can you really understand
The funny way I express myself
By the movement of my hands.

If you do then I am grateful
That the good Lord's not taken from me
These two hands that are my language
And these eyes that help me see.

Angela Wood

" Jesus Within Our Families "

Now is the time when we should pray
For love and kindness in the world today.
Then God will surely find the way
To put Jesus within our families.

We don't seem to talk much anymore
We've lost the contact we had before
So think of a way that will open the door
We need Jesus within our families.

If you want to get your priorities right
Then join together your thoughts at night
It's the only way we can win our fight
It keeps Jesus within our families.

Life is something that should always be
Full of goodness for you and me
Love is the one thing that holds the key
And brings Jesus within our families.

So lift up your hearts and sing out loud
To show the world that we are proud
For we have joined God's own crowd,
That has Jesus within our families.

David Perry

Happiness

Happiness is a stage we all go through.
For many it may stay, but to a few
It fades away; what should we do, where should we go?
I've searched this world high and low,
And still I'm left feeling incredibly sad,
Because of the joy I once had.
People see me, I try to smile;
I know it's only for a short while.
All too soon it fades away,
But there'll always be another day.
Yesterday gone, tomorrow will soon be here;
Will it be another lost and lonely year?
Happiness will come, of that I'm sure.
So I'll just wait, you never know,
Because there's nowhere left to go.

Caroline Troke

New World

The human race must take the blame
For wars, the killings, the cause of pain,
The destruction of beauty all around
The pollution of the sea's and ground,
So it's time to take another look
At the human race and the history book,
To turn a page-to start again
To do away with grief and pain.

Edward B. Pugh

Why

Why does there always seem to be a strip of fiercely fought for territory
For no matter whether it be rich soil or desert sand
He shall find no joy in victory, or welcome home again party
The man who lays his life down for that land

So why should a soldier fill his gun to kill a father or a son
And leave a woman or a child in misery
Why can't we teach him to have fun, something's lost and nothing's won
If the world can't learn to live in harmony

Why should a sailor board his ship to fire a broadside so explosive
It turns a calm sea into one that's so angry
Why can't he make it a pleasure trip, stop somewhere and take a dip
Without the fear of any lurking enemy

Why should an airman climb into his plane to drop down bombs like pouring rain
And perhaps wipe out some innocent family
If he stood his ground and refused to aim, would we see in him no list of blame
Or try to rob him of his pride and dignity

And why should countries always fight, each leader claim to be in the right
Why can't they see we would sleep more peacefully
If they themselves stepped on that strip of land, shook each other by the hand
And swore by God to keep any new treaty

Lawrence Greenhow

Peace

Tell me why countries fight one another,
For power, religion, or hate for the other?
Or maybe they've forgotten the reason,
Please tell me why countries fight.

Look at the face of a child of war,
The face of innocence in so much pain,
It's the children who will pick up the pieces,
If only they're given the chance to live.

For the sake of your child, learn how to love,
For the sake of your child, forget the past,
For the sake of your child, look to the future,
For the sake of humanity -
Find a way to restore peace.

Diane F. Lee

Harmony

I suppose music is the only place
For scales of love,
Where major and minor
Work well side by side.
Where notes of varying degrees congregate
To make melodious sounds.

I suppose music is the only language
Understood universally,
Where endless combinations of notes,
Equal or diverse, sustained or depressed,
Amalgamate, to trigger all emotions.

It would take little effort to
strike a chord with one another.

Christopher Scott

Faith

With all my heart I thank you Holy God
For that great gift you deigned to give to me
The gift which holds my very life in being
The gift that outstrips all the world for me
Without this gift my life would hold no meaning
The joys I have would be an empty sham
Pain and sorrow'd be beyond all bearing
But for the faith I have in just one Man

Janet Cash

The Battle Of Britain

We salute you Boys of Britain
For the brave deeds you have done
For the blood and sweat you gave for us
That the battle could be won
We're proud of you Boys of Britain
For the task that you fulfilled
For the courage and devotion to duty which you skilled
We thank our Gallant Allies too.
Side by side they fought with you
You gave your life without a care
For you were masters of the air
Deep in our hearts lies a heavy pain
For those who did not return,
We mourn our boys
Who died for us.
For them our hearts still yearn,
Let nations fly the flag of Liberty
"The spur to future unity"

Irene Parker

Not Long

I grieve for I'm waiting to leave
for the days that were given are ending
at the end of each day
I don't know if tomorrow's beginning
days now are empty the mind it is cloudy
the body so heavy
but I'm thankful for all of those days that I've had
when I could see clear hear well and move quick
I've loved and I've laughed seen beautiful things
enjoyed life on earth and all that it brings
still much unanswered still much unseen
so many places where I've never been
just wish I could stay so much longer.

Jean Read

Love From Three Cats

Happy birthday we miaow today, to one that we love so —
For the devotion she's so ready to give
and the care she's so willing to show.

When we hear her steps coming down the stairs
and the can-opener going, for us it means the start of
the day of the love she's always showing.

She talks to us as she prepares our food, placed on bone
china plates; and never squirms as she empties our tray,
and re-litters without showing distaste.

We are always well provided for when she has to leave
each day; for we have a cat door to go in and out, and
can decide to eat, or sleep or play.

And it seems as if we know the time as we patiently sit
and wait for the sound of her car as it comes round the
bend. We hope she'll not be late!

Then it's our favourite time of the day when she takes
each of us up in turn to sit on her lap and lovingly pat,
and we'll purr and her affection return.

Dena Hamlin

Advent

High birds fly south, a migrant thread,
Formatting on necessity;
Patterned in arrows, surely aimed,
Unquestioning their destiny.
Such goings, though, take on instead

An air of cold foreshadowing:
The leaves have gone. So, too, the days.
Those wings are beaten blindly by
Resistless seasons. Nothing stays
What is bitterly approaching.

Antony Gordon Clark

Who Is She?

When I look in my mirror, who do I see?
For the person reflected is surely not me!!
Who is that woman, so plump and so grey?
When did her youth slip so quickly away?

The young girl inside me, full of laughter and fun,
Can't remember when all of this change was begun!
Surely, last week I was running up hills —
When for my heart did I start taking pills?

The trips up and down to the school every day
With my four little lads, seems so far away.
For now, twice a week it's become a fast rule,
To take the grand-children to nursery-school!!

Did I go to sleep, or temporarily die?
Or did twenty years pass, like the blink-of-an-eye?
I can't not believe it, though I would like to try,
But my head tells my heart that my mirror can't lie!!

Jeannette Jones

A Song For Tomorrow

Listen, my friends, to the songs I sing,
For they speak of all our yesterdays;
They speak of miseries and of anguished hearts,
They speak of sadness and frustrated hopes.

Listen, my friends, to the songs that your children sing,
For they sing of their coming tomorrow;
They speak of their aspirations,
And of their stifled hopes for tomorrow.

Tell me the songs that your children sing,
And I'll tell you the future for them;
Tell me all their dreams they carry,
And I'll bring the realities for them.

Music is the same, tunes are the same,
But the message they bring sounds so different;
For the day after tomorrow, the songs they sing,
Will be the songs of yesterdays, like the songs I sing.

That which is now in the past was once in the future,
And that which is for tomorrow will, in turn, be in the past;
A child was born millenniums ago, to bring peace on Earth,
The symphony still remains unfinished, and a new millennium arrives.

Anil Vyas

Nostalgia

Why do we long for what has been,
For things we've done, and things we've seen,
For years gone by, and Friends of Yore,
Why do we never close that door?

Why is the Present not as good
As the "Glorious Years of Our Lost Youth"
When everything was fresh and new
When days were warm with Skies of Blue?

Why does the Future seem to hold
Less promise than the years of old?
Remorseless Time — with ceaseless tread
Puts willing feet into shoes of lead.

Eileen A. Appleby

He Died Alone!

Begging in the streets, cardboard box his home,
Frozen in the winter's night-he died alone!
Not enough to eat, hair for years uncombed,
No one there for him at night-he died alone!
 Alone! His life expired. Just another statistic
 In the homeless file.
  Just another space for another cardboard box,
  In the 'cardboard city mile.'
Begging on the streets, looked for kindness shown,
Frozen, he gave up the fight-he died alone!

Alan Wright

Freddie

To Battersea in Eighty-Three, with good intent went I
For to find a little dog, for the apple of my eye
Not huge, nor fierce, was needed
Adept in tooth and claw
But just a friend, his life to spend
Now who could ask for more...
I picked him out from all the rest
It was not hard to do
For he was just a Rag — a Muff, and I was Forty-Two
But innocent and unaware of what I had, was I
A long haired Jack, who'd snarl and bite
And cock his leg from morn till night
And never would comply
And so the years have hurried on and Freddie still prevails
But mellowed some and prone to sleep
I know that soon, a time to weep....
And most would say, a lucky dog, yes, you'd agree
Methinks
The lucky ones are we.
Jan Bailey

" From The Moment "

From the moment I saw your smiling eyes, I wanted to give
you my soul
For you to take and do as you please, to make my life feel whole
A longing and a yearning that impossible to suppress
Those tingling feelings in my head as I yield to your caress.

From the moment I saw your smiling eyes, I wanted to give
you my mind
For you to share my innermost thoughts, be they mundane,
cruel, or kind
To let you search all of me and take everything that you can
Our thoughts entwined, our thoughts as one, a universal plan.

From the moment I saw your smiling eyes, I wanted to give
you my love
To hold you tightly in my arms and enter you from above
To take you to a different plane and fill you with my fire
A smile, a hug, a lingering kiss, whatever you desire.

From the moment I saw your smiling eyes, I wanted to give
you my heart
For you to have and open up every single part
To let you see the way I feel and all that I want to share
To lie together and love together, to feel how much I care.
Kevin Parker

The Mancunian Way

Not much happening here — so I'm off to Manchester Town.
First I'll pay a visit to the market underground.
The smokers put a choke on me — I arose for air and wandered
'round.
Put on my personal stereo, stepped back and forward to the sound.
I looked up, seen people laughing — eyebrows raised to frown.
But I always come here, just happy wasting time.
Tapping feet to many rhythms — the homeless inspire my rhymes.
I may be penniless one day — who said soup kitchens are fine?
This is all downtown, my town, your town.
I sit and watch the passing strangers and listen to crowds.
In this fairground of dodgems the buskers are most loud.
Sometimes a strange atmosphere — always the Saturday tension.
The kids are playing, now they're stuck climbing barbed wire fencin'
Slowly, the sky turns a dimmer blue, oh and the crowd is going too.
People ejected from a gamblin' house, these men don't like to lose.
Bag ladies change their shift — their only pay is a bottle of booze.
This is all downtown, my town, your town.
It's tough old Manchester Town — be sure, I'll see it other days.
All these characters in this crazy place.
When falling down, they still stand tall — it's the Mancunian way.
Michael Lambe

The Strange Crop

Supercilious Jane, so sanguine
Forgot one day her brain to bring
Did it matter — not much
Remnants left from the previous day
Were swept into a bag and thrown away
Then senses reeled when a crop appeared
To heighten the intellect or just one for the pot?
So until one quite ordinary fellow feels inclined
To test his new found acumen on Mastermind
Or inspired to comfortably manage
A creditable performance on University challenge
We shall not know if cabbages will remain
The humble veg allowing cauliflowers to keep us sane.
Elizabeth Simpson

Prayer

To all those that have touched my life,
formed part of my existence,
then gone.
I pause and send to them a silent thought.

To all those that have left their mark,
added to my make-up, made me,
then disappeared.
I pause and send them silent thanks.

To all those that have changed my thinking,
modified my attitude,
then vanished.
I pause and shed a silent tear.

To all those that tore into my life,
all noise and joy,
then died.
I pause and say a silent prayer.

Within me you will live forever.
Ivan J. Peck

Slugs And Snails Or Dining Out At The Cavern

The old witch in that dark retreat
Found plenty there for her to eat.
A gruesome dish of roasted cat,
A jar of slugs and pickled rat.
Some sifted grubs all in a bowl
And jellied snails that smelt most foul!
An earwig trifle very nice!
Quite thickly strewn with ground wood lice
A plate of mouse tails dipped in brine,
And cooked in caterpillar wine.
At last with sharp teeth like a ferret's
She chewed a few owls' cast off pellets.
Then off upon her broomstick flew,
To think about a spell or two.
Leonora Simpson

LIFE —

A voice within cries out so silently yet damns the coming night.

Feelings fade and blood congeals, cell walls close in, unseen so real,
Forcing halting bursts of breath, raging still, defying death.

Memory gnaws at shrivelled thoughts, once whole now crudely strewn,
Spirit, soul and mind are crushed, pulse, heart, senses, hushed.
Nature finely wrought, distorts within life's room.

Desperate slivers of tedious reason tear,
Tear at the darkness, gouge thinning air,
Spill gall for all to see, to know,
Essence, being, all must go.

Bones, sinews vainly grasp —
Bless'd release at last?
Mind's eye sightless,
Still, flightless,
Lifeless
LESS?
Linda Hunt

Mirrors of Time

Candles flicker through moments of joy,
Founded in bosoms of bright gold,
Marinated in flavour of the male kind,
With curls of brown and eyes of blue I want him forever
my polished toy,
Clouds of dust hang over the great grey city of failure,
While fat flies grow quickly and the daylight forms me paler.
Playing in groups is humanly fine,
But when feelings become a menstrual thought something
to claim which is bodily mine,
fishing through limbs entwined but easy to undo
He looks over the atlas of my body's view,
As my teeth become wrapped in a duvet of red
My lips the pillow for such a delicate head,
camped upon my site of heavenly seduction
He devours the coolness, the purity, me the food,
freckled, fresh, young, contemptuous, raw and nude.
oh how sweet those notes do sound,
finally I can rest deep in soil amongst the shadows in the ground
  Joanne Sutton

Our Weekly Family Gatherings

My Mum had a big family
   Four girls, and five boys,
The clothes we wore were hand-me-downs,
   And we had no expensive toys.

But that never really bothered us,
   We were content with what we had,
Tho' we were poor, we never complained,
   And we showed respect to Mum and Dad.

Saturday nights were party nights,
   When all our relations would call,
And when they all did their "Party-Piece,"
   So we really "had a ball".

The children got to stay up late,
   To join in all the fun,
And we all had a plate of Mother's soup,
   Or sampled her Home-made bun.

The entertainment cost us nothing,
   And it really makes me think,
Why young folk today can't enjoy themselves,
   Without taking Drugs, or Drink.
    Jean Hendrie

Window Of Hope

Cautiously stepping through the threshold of a year so new;
From times of sadness and of pleasures few,
One's own life's dreams scythed down in betrayal,
Left empty in a world which is troubled, grey and pale;
So weakened and chilled in a cold winter of disillusion;
Endless dark nights, floundering in a sea of confusion.

I glance in the hedgerow as I walk along;
Huddled, cold and wet, lies a thrush without song;
What wealth still hidden, or left sodden in the wet winter mud:
The splendid beauty of a flower, snugly cocooned in its own
   mother bud;
Shoots bursting forth from the darkness of their wild flower bed;
Nature slowly giving birth, all around and along, these paths
   that I tread.

I no longer fear what the New Year brings;
The dawn of springtime waiting in the wings;
My very soul stripped, as naked as a leafless branch on some
   windswept tree;
Through the open window of hope, a ray of sunlight reflects
   warmth on me;
Enticing me through the door of trust, into the New Year's
   virgintime;
Precious are the hours, days, weeks, and years, not yet soiled
   by the misuse of mankind.
    John F. Shelley

Maybe

Alone and middle aged

Alone loneliness, emptiness, sadness,
frightened. A ship without an anchor,
lost, a half of once a whole.

Going about the daily business, talking, laughing,
acting, pretending, keeping pretty, keeping active,
keeping fit.

Inside the soul is screaming, needing, looking,
hoping desperately of finding a new love, aching,
longing, desperate to be spoilt, to be held, to share,
to give, to take, to be complacent, satisfied, safe
in loving arms, to be desired, to be wanted.

To open the door on fullness, living breathing life
at the end of the day, not echoing rooms of nothingness,
untrue dreams, dark long nights, reaching out,
remembering, crying, dying. Waiting for the next day,
another hard day, another long day, but a new day
of hopefulness.

Maybe today, just maybe will be "the day"
   Linda MacPherson

Weep Away

Look at me through undefined beams
From a wavering spot of damned reverie.
Look at me and shout out, cry out,
Open your brilliant, sarcastic snout,
Subject me to your tormented dreams.

No agitated declaration of hatred
To awaken my silent banshee vehemency.
No sparks burning from ephemeral holes,
Just ill-timed nothing, wet, blackened coals
Once vitriolic that flashed and created.

Look at me now and wallow in your tears
With your damned entombed lack of decency.
Look at my droplets annihilate our life,
Our binding, melting words of "man and wife."
A second to death, weep away, mock our years.
   Alison L. Compitus

Shaping The Future

Polluting the earth is very cruel,
From pipes, petrol and from fuel,
It kills us, animals and the trees,
So do not pollute, please, please, please.

Extinction of animals will soon come true,
Extinction of plants and rain forests too,
Trees in the rain forest help us to breathe,
So do not pollute, please, please, please.

The ozone layer will get destroyed,
From men, ladies, girls and boys,
We don't want to kill the birds or the bees,
So do not pollute, please, please, please!
   Jo Hatt

Geraniums

Burning pink, irradiant
From the twilight and the flower
Details, part only of the whole.
Yet just as relevant of Nature's power as their dying,
Or our coming to.

Both dark and sun make up the normal bower.
The deep untested at the end
Is but a part and parcel of the hour
That holds the start and finish,
Fear and friend.

Is not the warmth and brightness of the colour
More real than shadow?
Less trivial than the pain?
   Cherry Luxton

How Long

How long now,
from the beginning until now?
How long now,
from now until the final meeting?
Will the end come swiftly and painfully?
Or will it creep up slowly
until we are half remembered whispers in the corners of our minds,
Remembered with an inward laugh and with joy.

For every time we meet,
it marks the passing of time.
Age is mercilessly creeping on,
and age is against us now.
And so every time we meet I die a little.
No longer looking to the next time with tingling excitement and hope
But rather will this be the last time.
And so I die a little.

Hettie Duff

The Raising Of The Titanic

Now he sits waiting to be uplifted,
from the decaying weeds that strangle him.
The birds flock like elephants in great herds,
fantasy, futuristic, fish fly like birds.
Empty galleries and dance-floors seem blank.
The once strong, great and mighty long steel bars.
Now left only an ageing large liner,
The enthusiasm now leaves this oath.

But not, cables are sent to the oceans floor,
these form bubbles which lifts the drowned ogre.
Sweeping the clumsy giant off his feet,
looming him back to the surface and life.
Bubbles bounce off his surface climbing high
to the oceans roof, which he has nearly reached.
Now he's up, water gushes down his sides,
the old forgotten sailor is now born again.

Jack Hamilton

The Mask Of Grimley Ash

It's all so close to closing in
From top, to bottom, to side
I can't face up to this all on my own
I need a mask so behind I may hide.

Too hard to cope with all that surrounds
Too hard to handle all by myself
So if I cannot take all on my shoulders
Could I become somebody else?

Can I act? Can I really act?
Could I really invent another me
Become someone who is so much stronger
So much stronger than I ever could be.

I can make it, I will build it
I do not know how long my mask will last
But while it lives, I will name my new face
It will be known as Grimley Ash.

Andrew Whitelaw

No Change

One day there will be no tomorrow,
For the day will come that's your last.
You will think of the things that have been,
Far away, long ago, in the past.

Things could have been, oh so different,
If only you'd stopped now and then,
To see which way you were going,
But you knew best, like all men.

One day there will be no tomorrow,
And you will ask for just one more chance,
But it's too late, time has run out,
And she won't even give you a glance.

Alan G. Priddle

The Catch

I hear them laugh and a tide of sorrows suppresses me
From turning to see what incident has caused
    such happiness and joy. . .
For one laugh is false and one is overcome with awe;
And I despise it.
For the laugh that is false is for my ears only
And it pierces to my very heart, and there
it twists and slashes restlessly,
    and will not stop, because the sender seethes...

With an apparent serenity she relishes my silent cry,
And continues so gently to grind me
Lethe-wards, from whence she came so fair and calm
With countless admirers to welcome her with love.
Her innocence is her venom.
The awesome laugh can't see me; it is transfixed upon the ideal.
And as she departs to hold another's hand, he smiles
    and has a light heart, while I, with green eyes
Reflect on the Friend,
    who knows me too well.

Grainne Nolan

A Visit

Death came to the house today,
Furled his cloak, stole a loved one away.
Wrapped her close, he coveted her so,
Left the place bare where she once lay,
Gathered her to him and sped away.

Silent as night, he trod the stair,
Went with the prize deep into his lair,
Cherished his burden, garnered too soon.
We, left alone, bereft of her bloom;
We, left alone, o'erfull of care,
Though we pursue, the act cannot repair,
Limping and lame, cannot keep with his pace;
Learn to accept with dignified grace.

Nothing but memory remains in her room.
Out there in the darkness, only thought can roam
Of the life that was taken 'ere it was spent,
Of the soul rent from us, for a short time lent;
Can catch in the mind echoes drawn from the past,
Echoes that now th'eternal loam holds fast.

Gillian Davey

The Cry For Peace

Go tell the people of the world,
Go tell them, everyone.
They're so busy making war,
When they should be having fun.

Your lives are slipping by you,
While you're causing grief and pain.
Each day that dawns of this useless fight,
Will never come again.

You've worked so hard at hating,
Couldn't you work that hard to love,
Then, just maybe there would be a chance,
To save this world for us.

Hilda J. Bibby

Solitude

When one's alone, with time to think
Try hard to find the missing link,
So many blessings to be counted,
Our health, we really take for granted.
We look up to the Lord and pray,
And thank him for another day,
A day to try and make amends,
To make, not enemies, but friends,
But Satan we have near us all,
And we do listen to his call,
Redeemer of mankind and healer,
Forgive me, Lord, I am a sinner.

Wenvis Martin

Times Gone By

To see the sunlight through smiling eyes, for in her
Garden beauty lies, and just beyond the old wooden
Fence are fields of yellow gold brown and green as she
Sits in her garden and gently dreams,
Her mind runs wild as she sits and ponders, oh through
Those fields I'd love to wonder, with wind and rain
Upon my face, and soft grass beneath my feet, if only
I still had my youth and my heart a steady beat,
But looking down at her tired old frame, she'll never
Run through those fields again,
with wind and rain upon her face,
She'll sit in her garden and gently gaze, thinking of
Times in her younger days,
Turning her head unto the sky, she sits and thinks of
Times gone by.
Ian Hudson

Country Carnival

Make your way to the Village Square, bright colourful floats are gathering there.

Vibrating air embracing the crowd, drummers drumming, sometimes too loud.

Cameras clicking, music strumming, dogs barking, children running

Expressive bright faces, sheer delight as the buoyant clowns tumble out of sight.

Is that a fleeting glimpse of fear? for the winner's float is now quite near

Hats, tall and pointed, black as night, leering witches, an awesome sight.

Happy folks smile, throw money, they care, for the magical carnival at the quaint Village Square.
Jean Parish

And Angels Listen

My love,
gentle and rare as a snowdrop
in a ruined city.
Strong, proud lion
encircling my heart.
Your roar sends love around the universe
and angels listen.

My love,
good knight, hold me in your arms
and with a sword of flame
protect me from dark shadows.
I follow close behind you with my
lighted candle
that softly illuminates our path.
Have faith, our love's a song in heaven
and angels listen.
Eleanor Malcolm

Growing Poverty

On a bench in the pouring rain,
Getting wet and drenched again,
All my comrades lying there, in cardboard
Boxes and nothing to wear, with brown paper
Bags and scraggily hair,
Trying to beat the cold night air,
You've got to admit that life isn't fair,
We see the toffs walk through the park,
They point and stare and have a laugh,
I often wonder what they would be like,
Down on their luck and barely alive,
Maybe one day they'll find it out,
And laugh on the other side of their
faces no doubt.
Barry O. Connor

My Prayer

As life takes me along its paths,
give me the strength and courage
to forget the laws and conspiracies,
which fail to chain me down
to a low-life of self importance.

Help me search, not out-with, but with-in.
To find the love and peace which is in my heart.
Disentangle me from this unfair system,
so I can recognize and understand the energy of my spirit
and that of others.

Let me forget not the hopes and dreams of my past.
Allow me to hold the eternal torch
of love, truth and knowledge,
so I can light and guide my way.
When working hard to build a brighter future.
Dawn Shaw

Did We Make It Home?

When the walk to your chair, and the length of your hair,
give you a glint in your stare, and take you back over there.

Dressed in black, and ready to fight,
he was farmer by day, and our enemy at night,
We smoked to get high, and to believe the lie,
that the good old U.S. of A were gonna save the day,
and blast communism away.

And now as I sit here alone,
I think back of the guys, of the blood, and the lies,
my God I can still hear their cries.

Hueys fade away, but will be back again today,
and as I break out in a sweat, I realize I'm a vet,
who can never free myself of the Vietnam debt.
John Adam Grey

My Heaven!

A valley, sodden from the latest downpour
  gleams dew, as the sun awakens and smiles
   her long arms stretch to the sky and touch forever

Dirt tracks lead from here to there and beyond,
  climbing the mountains and hills,
   leading me on to follow.
The trees all standing to attention,
And foxglove waving in the cool, satisfying breeze,

There seems no sign of life as such.
I'm alone to witness the beauty which surrounds
  and cradles me,

Staring, feeling,
The earth belongs to me today, it's all mine
  I selfishly wish,

I want this place to be a secret, my secret,
  a place to visit when I feel alone,
  and want to be alone,
  and am alone.
Hayley Taylor

Golden Sands

Golden sands on a dark night,
Glowing like crystals in the Moonlight,
As the stars hang in the sky,
The crystal like sands light up the shore,
Like a host of angels on high,
The dawn now strikes the
Crystal sands,
And the hanging stars are
Hidden from land,
And the host of angels
Are seen no more,
As the golden sands lie
Before the shore.
Alyson Sian Jones

"He's Not Worth A Light"

"Dirty old thing, he's not worth a light".
"Go on, toss him a penny, I don't think he'll bite".

A mangy mane, half hidden beneath a worn out cap
A face far too thin with deep lines in the skin
they hang almost as baggy as the clothes on his body
decayed and degenerated from his daily drunken old rage.

In the downtrodden gutter where he lies, as sly as a fox,
he secretly sips from a brown coated box
and waits 'til the moon is high in the sky
believing the stars will show him the way

He staggers to find a place nearby
where there's a pint to warm his insides
then spends the night creating a scene
so everyone will holler and scream

Tossed out on the street, down on his luck
he pleads for a penny from anyone who cares
but they're oblivious to the mud-caked man with stony grey eyes
so he only has time for mutters and sighs

"Hurry away, useless thing, he's not worth a light.
Quick, he'll bite".

Cheryl Karen Diglis

"The Miracle"

I look through the window and what do I see,
God's magical world looking at me.
The oak, the ash, the chestnut tree,
Branches outstretched blowing in the breeze,
The sky so blue, and the grass so green,
The dew in the morning, everything so fresh and clean,
With masses of flowers standing so serene.
The English rose with its fragrance so rare,
It's just like a dream growing there.
The birds singing up in the trees
The sparrow, the thrush, the robin, the lark.
Their singing awakes you in the morning when it's dark.
Yes God created some beautiful things
Like hills, and valleys, mountains, and streams.
Bright sunny skies, and a nice cool breeze.
Raindrops falling to fill the reservoirs and streams.
Sometimes we don't appreciate God's precious gifts,
And the love He gave to all of us, after all when he made man,
He created the earth to put us upon, we take for granted all of this
But if you stop-think-and-listen, He performed "A Miracle" for us.

Jennie Howe

Susannah

I've never seen a child so fair,
Golden sand is in your hair.
Beautiful, and full of laughter,
Were you, an answer to a prayer?

A dainty child, without a care,
So fairy like, and sweet and rare,
With golden curls that flow so tree,
I know, that God's been good to me.

When you twirl round that garden tree,
The little birds sing happily,
They know they're safe, because you're sweet,
And little cats, sit at your feet.

A little star that shines at night,
With eyes so bright, and full of light,
Your pinkish tosses, covered in dew,
I never tire to look at you.

A little dancer, in the snow,
A precious stone that's all aglow,
My love for you, you'll never know.
What would I do? if you should go?

Julia Ann Holliday

Seasonally Yours

You do for me, like rainfalls for spring,
Breathing new life, each raindrop caressing,
Nothing left dry, every inch of me drenched,
And I like a flower take you up deep within.

You do for me, what the sun does for summer,
Showing me light with its rays softly soothing,
Warms me inside, every inch of me shines,
And I like a rainbow thrive off your strength.

You do for me, like a windstorm in autumn,
Clearing a path, blowing cobwebs away,
Helping butterflies fly, soaring high in the sky,
And I like a cloud am taken with you.

You do for me, like the cold does in winter,
Brings inspiration and everything's pure,
Going through me so softly,
Sending chills down my spine,
And I like a snowflake am alive 'cos of you.

Fiona McGinty

Children Of Tomorrow

Children of tomorrow, what planet will they see
Full of toxic poisons no longer blue and green
If the day should ever come that greed can be suppressed
Will the planet have enough time to save itself from death
Poisons in our rivers flowing to the seas
Soon all the fish will be dying full of mutations and disease
What will be left of the forest as they chop down all the trees
A bleak and barren desert shall be our only legacy
The politicians give speeches full of empty rhetoric
Cowering below big business who might see their profits slip
We must stand up for the planet the rain forest of Brazil
The Rhino in Africa we must no longer let its blood be split
Don't let me stand alone when I give my battle cry
Or the tears of our children will mark well our passing by.

Duncan R. Carthy

'Arsonist'

With petrol and paper, matches and rags,
Fire and taper, hope there's no snags!

You've paid me the readies, my balance is swell,
My hand's they are steady, won't end up in a cell!

Fully gutted, or a frazzle, maybe just a singe,
Whatever, it's no hassle, though many would cringe!

In through the back door, and into the hall,
Dousing the ground floor, and even the wall!

The flint it is lighted, there's A Flickering Flame
All is well ignited, you'll soon make your claim!

Front page of the paper, a mishap or a crime,
Some kids and a caper, they'll find out in time!

Geoff P. Cook

The Sound Of Her Music

The sound of music grabbed my soul,
Follow you I shall.
The sound of your music reminds me
Of a world destined to be.
A seventh heaven behold,
All that glitters is truly gold.
I look beyond the horizon,
What do I see?
A world, a world which was meant to be,
I hear the sea beckoning me.
My love, I am in paradise.
I listen to your music,
In a world that belongs to you and me,
My one and only fantasy.
My love, you are my world.
Your music has captured my soul,
Your music has captured my soul.

Jason Vinodh Nair

Decisions

Some say you must ignore your head and listen to your heart,
But the courage to do this is a very fine art.
You cannot decide in which direction to go,
But just listen to your heart and soon you will know.

For deep down inside you know what is right,
And if you'd just open your eyes, it's there within sight.
The journey may be fraught and full of pain,
But persevere — for you have so much to gain.

People may scorn and many will mock,
Your confidence will take one hell of a knock.
But rise above this and keep walking tall,
For in this equation you are the most important element of all.

You are an individual; so learn to break free.
To your own destiny, only you hold the key.
Only you can decide on which route you must take,
And if you only listen to your heart, you know you'll never make a mistake.

Jan Bradley

Eternal Longing

We are drowning in our sorrow,
But your love will guide the way.
You will light all our tomorrows,
As you shone through yesterday.

A father, there to nurture us, and lean on,
As we grow,
The aching of your absence in our lives.
You'll never know.

The anguish wells within me,
Fills my soul with cold despair,
That my children will not have the privilege,
Of your unconditional care.

Now your strength, your joy, your dignity,
Forevermore a dream,
We will follow that sweet dream of you,
Until we meet again.

Beverley Radley

Beauty Of Each Season

Joy of joys, spring awakes anew
Every little flower and leaf becomes unfurled
Majestic and stately trees don gowns of grandeur
The breathing hope of this precious world.

Long summer days shed warmth
and light upon the land
O'er babbling brooks, vast silver seas.
And stretches of golden sand.

Fresh whispering scented breezes
Bring Autumn dressed in best attire
Flaunting her glorious display
A festival of colour and fire.

December transforms the bleak dark days
Delicate filigree, jewelled sculptures bright
Crowning winter's earth in glory.
Mystic magic, a mantle of purest white.

Greta Craigie

Untitled

The verdant pastures sprawl languidly
'Twixt the coastal waters on this isle
On which there is an uncanny affinity for myself.

Amidst them dishevelled hedgerows riotously
Charge fed by brooks and burns that meander untamed.

Where am I?

Composed on returning to his homeland on 9th Feb 1996

Mark D. Chandler

Life Is So Precious

Life is oh so precious, so guard it while you may,
For you might end up regretting it one fine day,
Don't think about the bad times just about the good
Or stand around and think 'I only wish I could',
Just look around at nature, the trees and the flowers,
Look forward to another day, not count away the hours
Gaze into a baby's eyes and see the trust that's there,
Pick him up and love him, show that you really care,
If you find you are alone find someone to talk to,
There is a lonely neighbour who would be glad to see you,
Try to give a friendly smile to everyone you meet,
Whether you are in a crowd or walking down the street,
Some may not return it and you may wonder why,
But don't give up for many of them won't let you pass by
Without returning your smile, you'll really make their day
And they will smile at others as you go on your way,
So get rid of the hate and fill your heart with love,
And for each precious day of life, give thanks to God above.

Christine Brown

Colours Of Winter

Bright, watery rays from the sun so low,
Trees and houses all aglow.
Lights twinkle and dance on the river's tide,
The muddy banks are the water's guide.

Blue-green hues turn black and grey
As clouds pass over the River Tay.
Soaring over Discovery's mast,
Darker and darker, light fading fast.

Snowflakes drifting in the breeze,
Gently floating to the trees.
Branches soon bow to the ground,
The weight of snow on these abound.

Everything covered heavily white,
Darkness drifting into night.
Silence hovers with the final flake,
Snow like icing on a cake.

Dawn breaks across this virgin sight,
Blue sky and water slice the white.
Golden rays of the early sun
Fall playfully on the river's run.

C. J. Halliday

Mysteries In My Mind

Memory wells of cells are spawning, resurrecting without warning,
Forgotten times erupting, waking, through my recollections raking.
Fragments surfacing unsought, in and out of conscious thought,
Unknown faces, places, flashing, into my amnesia crashing.

A tantalizing glimpse is seen on the very edge of dreams,
Splintered images piercing, pushing,
    through my puzzled mind's eye rushing.
Out of nowhere thoughts are jarred prompting memories quite bizarre.
A snatch of music heard again re-kindles flames of joy and pain.

Intangible dream bitter sweet, unfamiliar and incomplete.
Evoked by a word heard by chance,
    inspired by a splash of past fragrance.
Separated from truth by time, another life perhaps not mine,
Appearing like the scattered shards of a precious shattered vase.

Confused feelings for a faded past, or imagined in my dreams
    perhaps,
Thrust into view by a simple taste or maybe a phrase
    or a distant face.
Are these mysteries in my mind curious shreds of childhood times?
Or has my sanity surrendered to these dreamings half remembered?

Jane Desforges

" Hopefully Inspiration "

March 88, I look back now, was not a good year for me
Two parts of my body, were taken away you see.

Into a hospital ward I'm booked, My life in their hands now
I prayed, "Lord show me, please show me how?"

Silently I asked his help, alone, afraid and sad
O.K. my boobs weren't perfect, but they're the only ones I had!
I signed upon the dotted line, my heart was grave within
For I knew "he" loved another, and now I'd never win.

With my mutilated body and my husband now gone
At last I'm given courage to want to carry on.

Finally I made it, and found a strong new me
And with a man to love again, as happy as can be.

However desperate, don't give up, life can begin for you
For I was "there," and can assure you, I nearly gave up to!

H. Robinson

Eternity

Twin souls who can't exist apart,
Two hearts must join, to make them start,
To beat together for our lives,
We'll be together all our lives.

And after that who knows what place
Will find us hand in hand to face
Another lifetime, can we dare,
To hope that on and on we'll share
Eternity forevermore,
For surely we have loved before.

The mists of time are but a veil,
To curtain hearts that never fail,
To recognize each other when
We join together once again.

Then hand in hand just as before,
We'll walk once more through passion's door,
And though we die, our love survives
We'll be together all our lives.

Valerie Carol Holland

Autumn

Brown trees and golden leaves
Twisting, turning in the breeze
The fields of grain are safely stored to make the
Bread in our cupboards.
The birds migrating with their chatter
And the tractor with its clatter help bring in the harvest.
Smoky bonfires all ablaze
Make it one of those autumn days.

Victoria Brew

Autumn's Dawn

Autumn's cast, Autumn's dawn
twisting shadows of an unfriendly foe.
Still shadows on a weary lake,
the wind emerges, the stillness breaks.

Crinkled leaves cringe and wither,
the air is cold, it makes one shiver.
Dark water, dark sky — blankets of rain
that seem to cry.

Morning dew, and a sigh of a discerning breeze,
two legged animals hustle and sneeze.
Turbulent clouds, that float hastily on,
Dropping their inflated water until it's all gone.

Dark sombre nights, and bright speckled lights;
starlight that glitters in Autumn's gaping bite.
Coloured leaves of rusty reds, and sunlight
yellows, descend to the ground to paint an
Autumn meadow.

For Winter's shadow is near at hand,
the wet, the cold, that permeates the land.

Paul Downie

Betrayal

Who betrayed and on you cast a blight?
'Twas Judas, in the Garden, that night.

Who pushed that stone, knowing it was right?
'Twas the Angel, in the dead of night.

Who saw you first and then turned to stone?
A woman true who grieved at your tomb.

Who denied you when the deed was done?
Peter, the rock on which the church was born.

   Doubters, traitors and charlatans
   With the learned, preachers and puritans
   Since then, have transmuted your verse
  From the Aramaic to the Greek
   Into the tongues of Babel, too prosaic,
   Not caring for your style, always terse.

   Thy many mansions chant Thy glory,
   But the world is sinking, still gory.

Have we misread The Mount's clear-cut Call?

Suzanne Harris

The Passing Of Time

Watching footage on the box
Turning back all the clocks
It makes you wonder why we're here
Is it just a stopping point for greater things to come
Or has man created something totally wrong

As I watch the stars at night shining all so bright
I think of other persons watching that same light
From a different world better than our own
When we die, perhaps we fly
To that planet in the sky

The thought of rotting in the ground or sitting in a pot
Doesn't bring much comfort when it's time to stop your clock
When I walk the churchyard looking at the stones
I read, Charles Dine, 1809
To think he walked the earth long before my time
But in a different world to mine

To think one day a young boy just like me
Will read my name and date and say
To think he walked the earth long before my time
But in a different world to mine.

G. Milsom

To My Father

I would not call you back again
To walk the long dark avenue of pain.
But oh! My heart drips tears of grief
For you have left a blank beyond belief.

Dear Father, shall all your wisdom wit and mirth
No longer be upon this earth,
All your integrity and faith
Is it to vanish like a wraith?

This shall not be. My child will know
And his child too the way to go,
For I will teach them as you taught me
To value life's simplicity.

In them I will instill your creed
Of a helping hand to those in need
And to the future I'll impart
Your loving and most generous heart.

So though your earthly body lies
In some drear grave your spirit flies
Unfettered now, joyous and free,
And with us to Eternity.

D. L. Gates

Perfection

I would gladly live my life a pauper,
Turning away a king's ransom for your love.
Pearls, diamond tiaras, the finest silk look drab in comparison
To your beauty. Scented roses, the sweet smell of lavender lose
Their dew, coming off a poor second best in your presence.
Gladly I would die a thousand deaths for an exchange of a dazzling
Smile, from those perfect lips, a twinkle in your eye meant for me
And me alone. It would be impossible to eliminate an imperfection
From your being. Simply as God is my witness you have none.
You are my life, my very soul, I am proud to be recognized in
Your presence. Surely one day you will reap your just reward.
For my part I would spend an eternity in your shadow never once
Complaining. Feelings I cannot control devour me from head to toe,
In an overwhelming desire to hold you tight.
What wiser wisdom do we know than the ultimate wisdom of love?
You arrived in a picturesque painting from a mist of light.
Gazing upon your beauty, I have no known antidote at my disposal.
You neither condone nor patronize laziness, yet your communication
Is remarkable bordering on the spectacular.
Conclusions are reached with a common sense rare to your breed.
Finally I wish to be engulfed in a sea of your eternal love.
  Robert Watts

From Aber Ithy

Fieldfare and wren in dimming phalanx and fleet
Turn on the last
Sunlight where purple trackways through the wheat
Unweave the past.
Swarm to the night, rise to the nightly dim
Rain pelted on fields,
Mist poured on hills; the lash at the sea's brim
When no rock shields.
Fall to a day that has no dawn, no gold
Gives to the earth
Whose sodden stooks grudgingly take their cold
Unwelcome birth.
Sunlight is broken; you battle like the leaf
No branch can save,
And in the dikes your summer sun and grief
Float to the grave.
  V. Gwynn

" Non Basta Una Vita! "

Out of the darkness comes creeping one small faint glimpse of
  the truth.
Hid in this frame, there lies sleeping one once-ambitious small youth!
Then in my blood there ran coursing dreams and desires unsaid,
All of them somehow enforcing ideas to flood through my head;
Ideas that never can flourish now that the years have rolled on;
Ideas I still faintly nourish, grasp at, and then they are gone!
Life has just slipped through my fingers. What have I done?
  What achieved?
Still the old ambition lingers to be famous, and well-received!
There's an Italian true saying, minted through lives that were tough
Useless one's hoping and praying, "One life is just not enough!"
  R. H. Gimi Jordan

Sweet Sorrow

I dreamed of sunlit waters
Tranquil seas in tropic lands
I watched a golden sailing ship
Saw the shifting sands.
The clouds, they gathered overhead
Grew leaden grey with threat,
Felt menace in the soft breeze's breath
Sweet sorrow Life's regret.
I held a crystal rainbow
Fragile beauty so divine
Heard spoken words of lying eyes
Made wanton this foolish heart of mine.
For though I loved you freely
It's time for me to fly,
I must return to another
Bid our secret love goodbye.
  Margaret Ann Cookney

Blessings

Count not your blessings in what you possess,
True love is a blessing that has no redress,
Your heart may be happy or the tears may flow
But true love stays with you, wherever you go.

Its comfort will guide you through all of life's sorrow,
Its joy will continue with each tomorrow,
God gave us love, to cherish not spurn.
And the richness of love is what each of us yearn.

When true love comes, don't count the cost,
Just count your blessings, that to you, love is not lost.
Hold on to that love, its richness to treasure
And peace in your heart, you will find there forever.

Love's not for the old, it's not for the young;
Love has a melody that cannot be sung.
True love is forever in every way.
True love is from meeting, till judgement day
  Norman Russell

A Quiet Walk

Going out alone for a quiet walk,
Tramping through the glades, no more talk,
Listening to the trees rustling in the wind,
Birds perched on branches trying to sing.

Looking at the flowers all out in full bloom,
Smelling, breathing in their sweet perfume,
Look at all the busy bumble bees,
Working so hard and trying to please.

Look at the grass ever so green,
I'll sit amongst it all and just daydream,
I'll lie quite still and stare at the sky,
Just to watch all the fluffy clouds go by.

Look at the sun ever so yellow,
He is warm and such a happy fellow,
I'm so happy and content being here,
It is after all the best time of year.

I will now stroll by the stream,
See how the water glistens and gleams,
Rushing on its merry way,
So must I, I cannot stay.
  Shirley Pedlow

Meander

A Wealth of experience and a turn of phrase,
tongues between teeth and faces burning,
we are renowned for endlessly learning,
in the university of life.

The strange, undertones of wisdom and charm,
with the words unsaid but considered
and a look both fierce and withered,
we who shall decide.

We do not take what we need from life,
only what we feel we deserve, and yet,
who can decide who wins the bet,
and if the starting price is fair.

For this is how we love and live,
with others asking why we make a fuss,
soon there will be too many of us,
and few to teach what we have learned.

Movements ebb as the feelings flow,
the patience of time and tide is known,
families created, nurtured and grown,
have flown the communal nest.
  Philip R. Clark

My Lonely Days In Greece

I had this ambition to work out in Greece,
To work in some stables, for 6 months at least.
I wasn't very happy, in fact I was sad,
'cause I missed my mum and friends really bad.

I had been there two months, but it felt like forever,
It was too hot to work, I prefer the English weather.
I cared for eight horses, two dogs and one cat,
I loved them all dearly, I miss them now I'm back.

There were Albanian men living in the flats next door,
I was told that they were all very poor,
They looked and stared when they saw you outside,
It gave me the creeps, so it was best to just hide.

The end of July I came back home,
So then I no longer felt all alone.
It will be some time before I'm ready to leave here,
And put myself through the loneliness and fear
Of being miles away and feeling so sad,
the whole two months had been really bad.

Paula Best

" Spring "

What clear young voice is this that's heard,
To wake the countryside, howbeit o'er each grassy verde,
Its import doth betide, such wealth of joy, such praise to sing,
Such soft, such varied hue?
'Tis Spring, 'tis Spring, is on the wing,
And life bursts forth anew.

What merry laugh is this that trills,
Upon the still, chill air,
Is't strange the feathered throat it fills,
With song, so wondrous rare?
Not so, when silent glens do ring,
With echoes of the jolly sound,
'Tis Spring, 'tis Spring, is on the wing,
And beauty doth abound.

What sprite is this with airy tread,
Traverses waiting earth, what magic touch is this to shed,
Such brilliance, such mirth?
What fragrant breath forthwith to bring!
Not least response from man — This Dove
Is Spring, is spring, 'tis on the wing, Dear life, 'tis Thee we love.

G. H. Farquhar

Untitled

Friend Death, you wear the mask of life,
To tread the earth and scorch the light;
Your beryl shadow fear souls of sin;
And on Pluto's scaffold many steps attend.

My Friend, you will not catch me with your call,
Though brushed we once along that hall,
Your faceless phantom swirling by
Seeing all with sightless eyes.

I fear you not, my faithless friend,
As travel I to my journey's end.
For happy would my spirit be to roam
Along with beloved astral's who led me home.

My soul with knowledge must fulfil,
As steady climb I, up that hill,
With breathless presence now often feel,
I, alone, will turn life's wheel.

Sightless one, forever by my side,
From you alone I cannot hide,
Fearing none, you feel no pain,
Even sinners you came to tame.

Maureen L. Handy

Resolution

Away! Faint heart, where fear and doubt contrive
To undermine the will and take control,
Where cowardice and weakness both connive
To stem resolve and overlook the goal.

Initiative is lost by hesitation,
No battle's ever won without attack,
No cause upheld by indetermination,
No end achieved by ever turning back.

So though your heart be filled with apprehension,
The odds against your winning though seem slight,
Do not betray your ultimate intention
And fight unto the death for what is right:

Prepare to give your life to win the race,
Then if you fail you'll fail without disgrace.

Reginald Miles

The Garden

Where the gold rays descend, oblique,
To the seclusion of cool bowers,
In steady ranks as if to seek
Gay rendez-vous with lovesick flowers,
Where memory tries to ensnare
Scents of dead roses, ghosts of bees,
In human brains, so as to share
December's gloom with May time revelries,
A young man and a girl walk alone hand in hand
Through the nascent upsurge of an awaking land.
Yet they are not alone, the unborn and the dead
Are forever with them in the peace of the garden,
And they walk by their side, resolute, unafraid,
Seeking neither revenge nor impossible pardon.
The young man and his girl are the symbol eternal
Of a life that is doomed, yet eternally vernal,
In the aeons of time that the future encloses,
In a future that knows neither death nor decay,
In the flow without end of our loves and our roses,
In the unending round of our endless today!

R. Wilkinson

In Praise Of Atheism

If you believe you have the right to pray
To your God in the manner of your choice;
But you believe yours is the only way
And other Gods speak not with a true voice;
If you believe as many others do,
That foreign faiths are basically flawed,
Then be you Christian, Muslim, Sikh, Hindu,
Or any cult or creed that's fiercely warred
'Gainst them whose faith is other than their own,
Think twice before you kneel in earnest prayer,
Be you in Church, Shrine, Temple or alone,
That, if about humanity you care,
'Twere better p'raps that all religion cease,
For thus the world may then find lasting peace.

Peter Williams

A Prayer For Growing Old

As I grow old Lord, may I find
tranquillity and peace of mind
Be thankful for the joys I found
And never burden those around.

To be tolerant of youthful ways.
As I remember my own young days.
And when health fails as fail it must.
In you Lord may I put my trust.

Not to whine or to complain
To the brave enough to bear my pain.
To forget hurts, the doubts and fears
And travel gently through the years.
As I grow old Lord may I find
Tranquillity and peace of mind.

S. C. Bray

Love

To love is there and being gone
To sweet emotion, fire night shone
Empowering angels of bitter sweet name
Wash away but still feel the pain
Burning fields unto new life born
Rose's mist so once forlorn

Shining protection and bitter perfection
The greater power of star-full connection
Of ambition forsaken and things undone
Words unspoken and songs unsung
All dust to gold and then beyond
And still in rags a new cape donned

All things all and all things will come
A familiar rhythm from an ancient drum
On all the trials to base the find
So pure the end, on healing dined
Love is love of many lives
In all confusion still survives

A. C. Weaver

The Cat's A Fly Yin

She pauses an' poses an' poises her paws.
to strike at a stroke, with her deadly cat's claws.
She watches an' waits, with an unblinking eye,
Woe beside her poor foe, it's an unknowing fly

She stealthily creeps, from table to chair.
Never once loses sight o' that flea in the air.
The flea never knows from where the cat comes.
The only sign o' attack is her wagglin' bum.

The fly finally settles on a fireside tile,
The cat pounces and strikes, but she misses a mile,
She's up her hind legs swiping fresh air,
But by that time the insect's far away up the stair

Matthew Welsh

The Plough Horse

A plodding horse behind a plough,
Turning the earth so heavy now,
I see his breath upon the frosty air
And stand and watch, but he's unaware.

He plods along so big and strong
I'm sure he sings a happy song
I know he is happy in his work
His step is so light upon the earth

I see him no more that trusty friend
For the life of the plough horse is at an end
You will only see him at country fairs
But I see him still in my heart of hearts

He never broke down for lack of fuel
As the modern machine does now
He just flicked his ears if things went wrong
Oh where is that horse and plough now gone.

Muriel M. Boomsma-Williams

Spring 17

March again
the spring surge careers abandoned
in its flush of newness
thrusting green devours the ground
populates our eyes and dreams
madness wears disguise of blooms
all is frightening, wounding, new
as venomed sweetness cants abroad
we are at home with spring's caress
sensing not its ruthlessness
we disturb the crest of spring's taut wave
as much as garlands can outlast the grave

A. M. Ward

New Years Resolution 1996 (Condensed Version)

The time of year has come to dispose of all my sins,
To stop smoking and stop drinking, and to lose my double chins,
But the thought of this new life style fills me with no fear
Actually, it's a piece of cake, I did it all last year.

So I discard my guiness for a nice cup of black tea,
And chocolate bars, and fresh cream cakes, they're really not for me,
But this drastic change of life style, on close ones, takes its toll,
With regard to heath and fitness as their virtues I extol.

Well, now it's time for work, and seeing as it's not far,
In accordance with my life style, I'll walk, not take the car,
And for lunch, no pub, a quick swim, a sauna and a spa,
And jog back to the office, well 5 miles isn't far!

So now my way of life is set, and has been for some while,
But although I'm fit and slimmer, I've forgotten how to smile,
To look and feel athletic is generally quite nice
But as with all things in life, there always is a price.

So, what the heck, it's down the pub, for a pint and Burger Roll,
What a lovely feeling, now this helps to lift the soul,
It's down to quality of life, and as I was saying to my wife
I can honestly say that they were the worst 2 days of my life!

C. J. Wright

Christmas Day Invitation

It's such a pleasure to receive loving invitation,
 to share this very special day celebration.
Exchange warm greetings, kiss under the mistletoe,
 open kind gifts, wrapped with a neat little bow.

Turkey dinner, stuffing, piled high on a plate,
 Mince pies, Xmas pud, piece of Christmas cake.
Laughter and jokes, pull a cracker with you,
 play the piano, have a sing-a-long too.

Rowdy and boisterous, party whistles to blow,
 beneath paper hats, silly faces aglow.
Dominoes, cards — Snap, Trumps and Old-Maid,
 drinking neat Brandy, Martini 'n' lemonade.

Sit by the fire.... relax.... and unwind,
 Peace and goodwill to all mankind.
For born today, our Lord Saviour, a King,
 time to rejoice, to be merry and sing.

Now the day's over, and evening is nigh,
 everyone's happy, and spirits are high.
Merry Christmas, Happy New Year everyone,
 it's been a wonderful day, I did have fun!

Lucy Jordan-Meadows

A Lifetime

Time is like an ever-turning mill
To test the endurance of our will
A bright new sun revives each day
To keep us fresh and ripe as hay

From seed to youth we quickly grow
The happy years which gently flow
Then suddenly in confused array
We face the world as naked prey

Amidst a mighty holocaust of sound
Through life's tumbling stream we bound
Our ageing body stoops low and ails
Until we cannot mend the sails

Courage then from our hopes we must draw
To rejuvenate our will once more
From silent thoughts we must devise
A path once more to mould our lives

Inside we hold our feelings inert and still
Lest we should show our grievous fill
Oh time please give me a minute more
That I may have one last long roar

Martyn J. M. Hough

Tantalus

O Tantalus, thine agony were bliss compared with this —
To see my love and hear his voice yet never know his kiss.
I sought my love through half the world I wandered
   far and wide
Then turned to home and found him here who should be
   by my side.
For some brief hours we know the bliss of perfect soul
communion
With harmony in every part to justify our union.
But man made law divided us whom love had made divine
So thine eternal agony, Tantalus, now is mine

C. M. Viney

Three Wishes...

I wish they were here, to watch me grow,
To see me through the highs and lows,
To guide me along with their hand and their love,
Instead they watch from their home up above.

I wish they were here, for me to tell,
For them to listen and to wish me well,
To be proud to see what I achieve,
For me to show, and them to believe.

I miss you Nanna, and you Grandad
I miss you Grandma, but I won't be sad,
Because in everything that I do,
You love me, and I still love you.

Teri Williams

Do You Care?

Anguish, tears and scars seem
to roll into one large blur,
They wondered, they pondered at
what made their world turned upside down?

   Their despair and dilemmas
   few will ever understand or feel
   they hog the limelight
   but for a moment, then
   back once more into the abyss
   their predicament dismissed, forgotten.

Can you share with them this journey
so full of pain and strife?
Needles misery and suffering
are their share of adult care.

   Life's joy is at best elusive
   can it blossom amidst
   trying circumstances?
   Well, ...

Yin Heng Wong

The Sea

Here I sit watching waves roll in, restless and anger seething within,
boats toss and turn with strength from the sea, putting a show on especially for me.
Force of the waves against the sea wall, gulls dip and dance on wing with a call, today the wind blows with fun and such force, surf strips the beach with no thought, no remorse,
Sands lay still, shining and clean, shells peep out, perhaps never seen, children once played and danced in the sun, paddled and surfed, freedom and fun, bright coloured deck chairs, ice-cream galore, once strewn the beach, the pebbled sea shore,
Sand castles gone, built with small hands, pleasurable memories of fun in the sands, buckets and spades no longer scattered, seaweed lies tangled, torn and tattered, summer has gone, winter unfolds, gives the sea an excuse to be strong and bold, the sea has no rules, no law to abide, cannot be tamed or set aside, it has hidden secrets in darkness blue, with stories and legends it holds for you, one moment it's peaceful and gentle within, next moment it's angry, as if the devil is kin.
Remember, remember it's wild and free, please, please remember to respect the sea...

Carol Hobbs

Equs

Once freedom of spirit, body and mind
To roam the hills and plains of a land man-free.

To feel unfettered the wind through flying manes,
The earth strong and firm beneath our pounding hooves.

To feed upon the richness of the land,
To live, breathe and die upon the gift of our inheritance.

Then man, a creature with the power to inflict torture and pain
The need to dominate and break the spirit of our very being.

What threat were we, to be treated thus,
Our bodies racked in agony as man fought to imprison our very soul.

But gentle hands will reach out with compassion and love,
To make us one with man, harnessed together in mutual love and respect.

The world will soon be changed by the power of light and love,
And we shall breathe again the very essence of our unfettered lives.

Sue Kerr

Speech!

Unaccustomed as I am,
To public, speaking, private Too.
Normally I'm like a clam,
Wouldn't speak to he nor you.
I'll write it short, but speak it long,
As I go on and on;
To praise you with sincerity,
In a non-stop eulogy;
Showing my vocal repertoire,
As I go on, blah! and blah!
My speech I'll make with style and force,
A most superior discourse.
I'll waffle with pomposity.
And meandering loquacity,
With dialogue at gathered speed,
Building to a daunting screed.
Just as your tea you think you'll miss:
I'll stop with laryngitis!

Michael John-Gwelf Marshall

The Concrete Jungle

The beast roams the concrete jungle and trails of tarmac laid,
to prey on helpless victims that a depraved society raised.
Not for food to feed its young, whose bellies empty are,
but for videos and tellies or someone else's car.
He stalks the night like cowards do
and with this blanket, evil he doth strew.
He shies away from any light and surveys the concrete jungle.
We must keep our children young and sweet,
from the animals that roam our streets.
No more to roam our countryside or local parks where evil hides.
No more our doors to open wide, the welcome mats all locked inside.
Locked and bolted turn that key,
"FREE!" no isolating me.
When authority apprehend do-gooders him on holiday send.
Problem solved a miracle cure for the beast that we call, "MAN".

T. F. Nabbs

'Only Crosses Remain'

Only rows of regimental crosses remain,
to remind us of all the anguish and pain,
of fledglings thrown into a nightmarish hell,
wasted by bullet bayonet and shell,
left fallen and twisted, as one with the earth,
so far from home and their place of birth,
blood stained and twitching, death rattle groans,
thoughts of mother's mourning simple headstones,
fading sight, grinding of teeth,
pitiful death throes, more poppies for the wreath.

D. D. Lloyd

Love In A Recession

Money, who needs it? We do.
To pay the bills, to pay for thrills,
Without it what are we? Lost.
We pay the cost in worry, how to cope,
The kids need shoes, I shed a tear
The mortgage is due, will we lose this house we
hold so dear? Is that time coming? It seems so near.
But wait, there must be answers, we're still a pair,
We have our children and love still surrounds us....,
So what if life deals out hard blows,
If we make mistakes along the road,
As long as we come through with dignity and self respect
And care for our children without neglect,
Together we'll fight the oncoming tide,
And together we'll win, still side by side.

Valerie Fay

" If Only Man Could See "

Let man clasp hand from land to land
To live and love, let peace come flowing through,
With gentleness comes happiness.
Be alive, we have eyes to behold
Let the beauty of our world unfold

The green promise of spring
With the busy birds that sing.
Summer is a tapestry of flowers
With warm sun and shady bowers
All alive by sunny showers
The silver stream all summer gleams.

Golden autumn, cooler now
With bounty's harvest on the bough.
Winter fun in silvery snow
Children playing, rosy cheeks, aglow.

Look up and gaze at the blue blue sky
Beyond is the galaxy,
Yes, this is heaven on earth
If only man could see.

Mabel Melvin

Night Ride

O hands of time please rest awhile, and leave me to my sleep,
To lie within this emptiness, to sink into the deep.
O hands of time please wait until I've had my chance to dream,
To float into infinity before you show your beam.

O darkness that surrounds me, enfold me through the night,
Just let me lose myself in you until the morning light
O sleep that overcomes me, erase my troubled mind
Just welcome me with sweet delights, my sorrows leave behind.

O dreams that bring confusion of happiness, then grief,
Release me from this torment, and bring me sweet relief.
O shadows all around me that change from black to grey,
Is this the coming of the dawn into another day?

O hands of time I thank thee for bringing me your light.
You woke me from my darkest hour,
Released me from the night.

Olga Horpe

Haunting My Soul

While I try to escape the battlefield of my mind,
time and time again you return to haunt my life.
And as I shudder at the pain which is building up inside,
you dig into my heart again to find a place of death within.
And as you climb into the grave you force me to see,
into shadows of memories of who I used to be.

In my heart you have died chained to my soul,
along with the memories which will not let me go.
Although you're with me, I still feel I'm on my own
and though fate walks through life beside me,
my dreams still walk alone!

Rowan Stephens

Love

Love's a tender gift to get,
To hold and love and never forget.
Feel the coldness on your skin.
Feel the love rush within.
When it comes, don't let it go,
For life's too short and time's not slow.
If love is strong, hold it tight.
Never let go the right to fight.
When together think not of tomorrow
For tomorrow may bring us meaningless sorrow.
Tender love we hold in our hearts
Will always fill in the missing parts.
Our dreams and hopes will never crumble
When we give them to love to humble.
My heart and soul in one combine.
When I see love, I know it's mine.
When lightning strikes across the sky,
I know love's there to hear my cry.
When thunder pounds, love finds the key,
For man and woman are bound for eternity.

E. C. Jones

Clouds

These thin, dark clouds, teased out by following winds
To fragile scarves that pattern the pale sky;
That fly beside the tall, white castle-clouds
Whose summits catch the glitter of the sun;
Enhance such glories by their slaty-grey.
This mute procession, harried by the wind,
Calls me to join its solemn, painted flight:
Assume inconstant shapes of mist and rain
And fly, in changing patterns, free and light.

Noele Mackness

" High "

I don't need drugs, to give me a "high"
I've only to see the sun's first glint in the sky,
to hear the first birds sing their sweet songs.
And if I step out at the dawn of a new day,
the world seems so peaceful and calm.
The flowers newly waking, dripping with dew,
everything seems, to have had a shower.
The air is so fresh, and free for the taking,
I slowly inhale, till my lungs are aching.
What could be more wonderful?
There is the distance, a gift from above,
the arc of rainbow, its colours a haze,
How long did I stand there and gaze?
If people took time, just now and again,
to savour the gifts of a fresh new day,
with a surge of new hope, and a feeling of "high",
how could anyone want to deny
this wonderful world, or even abuse our own gifts of life?

G. M. Uttley

Musician Manqué

The urge to play lies deep, a constant need
  to share his love of music, feel the glow.
Acclamation feeds him. Wood and reed
  together, like the water's ebb and flow.
The dragging pull of other duties tires
  him, drains from him all sympathetic tones
for ageing patients. Humbly they reply
  as querulous he probes their aching bones.
He's torn apart. Opposing forces dare
  to hold him, chained and patient, listening to
the stream of painful tales, which though he cares,
  no longer move him as they used to do.
Musician? Doctor? Could he rearrange
priorities, and cope with such a change?

Susannah Hayward

Self Realization

The pain is there, but refuses to be recognized.
To fall apart would be to give in.
Protecting myself, the wall rises and I suffocate in silence
　And the realization is, I have realized.

My denial and negativity have gone beyond the stage of saving
It has taken little time for this to occur in my existence,
　although many memories to acknowledge it have been
　here within.

Now accustomed to this feeling, I have no choice, but to be
　the entertainer for the unwelcome, uninvited guest.
It pulsates the blood near my soul,
　stealing the last drops of positive energy.

Slowly fading, I see my few hours beyond, holding only
　loneliness, the want to be truly happy, to be me as
　I once was, is no longer in reach.
No one heard my past cry for help.
　Susannah Jensen

Thank You God

Dear God above, send down your love
To earth where all men live,
And spread the truly gospel news
Not to receive, but to give.

The poor and sick require your help
As they live from day to day
They have no say, how the world is run
Just happy to live in peace and pray.

"The Children", whom we all adore
Make such a lovely formation,
We must take special care of them
For they are our future generation.

"The Animals" all belong to God
And require to live a full life
Just like any decent husband
Who adores his beautiful wife.

The governments all around the world
They try to make things right,
To help the poor and hungry
And ease their heavy plight.
　William McCairn

Dreamchild

He had dreamt a thousand dreams
To destroy those things he feared
But on looking high to the enclosed sky
His dreams had disappeared

They were carried off, far away
On the back of an unkind breeze
Blown for miles, releasing no smiles
Over land and foreign seas

The boy would not be defeated
He went home and dreamt some more
Dreams of glee at being free
And bringing an end to war

He packaged together each dream
And sent one to every nation
To Kings and Queens and world supremes
Each with an invitation

Please come to a magic party
And celebrate a sacred birth
Our world depends on us being friends
Wrote the boy who saved the earth.
　Simon Vanstone

For a Birthday

It is your birthday. Here are flowers
To cheer those unrepeated hours
And wish you, all the years you live,
Gladness no longer mine to give.
No brake on time's swift wheel has stayed,
These fresh, young blooms are bound to fade
Before a week is out; but then,
All lovely things that comfort men
Sooner or later go that way —
The sun that warms the longest day,
Sweet music heard alone at night
And words that stir the heart's delight;
And children's voices on the green;
And friends; and being seventeen.
　Michael Oakley

God's Blanket

Flowers are God's blankets,
To cheer and keep us warm.
Flowers are sent from Heaven,
The world, they do adorn.
To look at one single flower,
Is for all of us to see.
That the one who lovingly made them,
Made also you and me.
So sleep all those who've passed away,
In the beds where you now lie.
And may the flowers keep you warm,
Till in turn they also die.
"For after all, what is a bed
Without its blankets."
　Marion Brown

Anorexia

Hatred of food in the mind is bound,
to breed depression, terror and fear,
But still!
The battle of mind suppressing the will,
Spins round in circles of turmoil real;
So in confusion, guilt is large,
You may wind up on a suicide charge.

Crazy it sends the spirit high,
Bringing makes it hard to try;
But in!
All this the will is just to cry,
Yet still no tears for them to ask why?
Because the price of pain is to lie.
　Stephanie Davies

The Black Forever

To be entombed, to choke on desperation,
To be strangled with fear for the future.
The only comfort is black, darker than the darkest black,
To curl up into a ball, to climb into oneself,
To fight your way into the very depths of despair,
To find comfort somewhere in the deep recesses,
in a corner, untouched, not yet found,
To go deeper and deeper, to burn with a sick,
sick, stomach-churning sadness.
Not to have the will to save yourself, not
to care anymore.
To climb out of oneself, into the light, to be free
into the light of your soul.
Yet you are gripped, stopped dead in your tracks.
The Black has returned, taken over, become your
lover, your friend, you embrace it with all
your heart.
Yet through love there can be true salvation
you climb again,
higher and higher you go...
　Mark Morris

Winter's Dawn

As I look at the night sky
Tiny snowflakes floating by
Slowly covering all around
Drifting softly, earthward bound
As darkness fades and turns to light
The children in the street will fight
Snowflakes fly and shouts of glee
What fun well have, my friends and me.
  Wendy J. Collins

Touchstone

Through time so troubled and tangled
Times of restless urgency,
Times of wondering, wandering
Through a haze of half hopes
Dreams and schemes,
A crooked clock ticks out, teasing time,
Clawing precious hours away.
Time that seemed so distant
Is now part of yesterday.
It dares you to blink an eye
And leaves you breathless as it all slips by.

But you, you break all the rules of time.
  You are my touch and tingle,
  My tiny piece of tenderness,
  The touchstone of my senses
  In this throw away, tear it up,
  Rush around, take for granted,
  Walk away world.
  A. G. Pengelly

An Affair Of The Heart

This torture in my heart still grows,
Time wasted waiting for you,
The next time we meet no-one knows,
It's always left up to you.

But now I'm anxious, I can't stand any more,
I need to find out why,
Your hugs and kisses you're keeping from me,
I'm trying hard not to cry.

So how do you feel? You never tell,
Can't cope with this frustration inside,
Oh it's bottled up, I need to yell,
"Please don't push me aside".

But we both know it can't go on,
There's too much in life at stake,
So help me cope with this hurt I feel,
And give up this life that we fake.
  Weeney

" Love "

Love, like a glove, a snug hug from above,
Fills me then spills me and drinks my drunk blood,
Without, filled with doubt as deep as my shout,
With, I can't live if I can't let it out.

Spinning me, spiralling, cunning wind tripped me,
helpless has lamed me, bitten then ripped me
My skeleton quakes till my heart shakes then breaks,
But room in my womb heals the gloom love won't take.

Sweetly like harmony, symphony inside of me,
Crescendoing the core of me, please take some more of me,
floating on ripples, a pool for a strawberry,
Drowning and crippled if not in your company.

Please, oh may, could I, regardless of should I,
Pour my glass full of you, overflow would I,
Drown in your puddle reflecting the sunshine,
Whistling while drifting on cloud number nine.
  Lorna Merrick

Whispers Of Time

Time speaks of impending fortunes
Time speaks of days gone by
The statutes of our past will all crumble
The architects of the present build again

Echoes of laughter from the old ruins
There days spent searching fallen walls
For lost worlds and hidden meanings
In a vain pursuit of the present's smile

Tears of a nation collect in a huddle
The rivers swarm with the grief of old
Rudderless boats toss their captives
Turbulent times swept into the sea

Our very foundation littered with intrigue
Leaders and rulers burnt at the stake
Speeches spoken and feelings stifled
Revolutions crushed by the grip of a hand

Questions answered and answer questioned
The heartbeat of time starts anew
Knowledge gained and meaning explained
Whispers we hear come from caverns we've seen
  B. Fawcus

Flying Time

When I was young I was told
Time goes faster when you're old.
Now I'm old I find it's true
Time rushes by for me — not you.
It's not as if I live a whirl of social life and partying.

I jog along from 6 a.m.
Flick the dust and sometimes sweep,
Shop and read and get the meals,
Do the garden, have a sleep,
Walk the dog and watch TV.
Yes I'm content — dull you say?
But quietly as I pass the day
Still the dates go running past.
No sooner Jan. than Feb. is here
No sooner '95 than '6.
I know I haven't many years
So I'm not in a hurry
And if it isn't me then why oh why
As I get older do the minutes, hours, day and years
Ever faster go?
  Pam Garner

Maybe, Maybe Not

Life is like a clock,
ticking all the time,
one day it'll stop,
then I too shall cross the line,

We breathe and drink similar air and water.
and our biology is the same,
yet we may still kill and slaughter
just to clear or blacken someone's name,

These days people seem to always fight,
but every time there are no winners,
however no one can blame black or white,
for he who does, must to be a killer.

The darkness of the lonely night,
gets brighter as together we dance,
for we are not in a shadow, but the light,
and as we're young, I must take a chance,

But of course, this is a dream,
and is not reality,
for as I wake, I may scream,
throughout my mentality.
  Roger Wetton

The Exam

Waiting for the exam to begin, nerves start to tingle,
Tick tock goes the clock.
Time to begin your exam.
Open paper, take a deep breath, tick tock tick tock.
Finding questions to do, tick tock tick tock.
Twenty minutes are passed and questions done are none!
Panic takes over, face starts sweating.
Tick tock tick tock.
Wait a minute you know the answer to this one.
Rush! rush! rush!.
Relaxation and confidence take over.
Here's another question you know and another.
Tick tock tick tock.
You've finished with ten minutes spare.
At the ceiling and paper you stare.
Oh no!
You've only answered three out of a needed six.
Rush! rush! rush!
Tick tock tick tock, time up!
Out of your eye comes a tear, oh well there's always next year!

S. V. Sewoke

" Growing Old "

How soon one's lifetime passes
through the laughter and the tears
we have had our spring and summer
now we are in our autumn years.

The spring in our step in days gone by
when learning about all life
we are wiser now but our pace has slowed
after years of toil and strife.

These are times for recollections
through those days of yesteryear
when once our youthful bodies danced
now we've aged with greying hair.

Lives well spent. Achievements gained
and for most a family too
now soon our second generation
will all come shining through.

We can look now to our futures
where we can mingle with our peers
gone maybe spring and summer
we will enjoy our autumn years.

Terry Thompson

For King And Country

In scarlet fields they fought and fell,
through mud and blood and fires of hell.
Choked back were tears of mournful sorrow,
to live today, to die tomorrow.
The air still sweet with death's decay,
as the bugle calls the ranks to play.
The whistle blows, the game begins.
Just simple pawns for regal sins.
'Over the top' with gun in hand,
we trudge our way through no-man's land.
Left and right my peers are falling,
the dead lie dead, the dying calling.
A few more yards through pit and wire,
we'll never gain, for shell and mire.
A glimpse around where friends once stood,
now nothing stands and nothing could.
The guns have stopped the cannon quiet,
a lark surveys this futile riot.
No more poppies, no more trees,
just lingering souls on a summer breeze.
And now we sleep in grave terrain,
the bugle sounds for us again.
With bayonets fixed and gas masks on,
we haunt the gauntlet called 'the Somme.'

Nathan R. Edwards

The Void

Perhaps you'd rather wander
Through life in an aimless way
So you've closed your eyes to the wonders
Of the beauty of this world today
You prefer to be blind to the beauty
And only your sights to maintain.

But soon comes the day of reckoning
Much sooner than you had surmised
Your world is covered in darkness
No sounds penetrate the skies.
You've no roses to gather in winter
No bird song to lighten the gloom

But Jesus is all forgiving
If repentance is sincerely made
And you may yet hear the music
Of the wonderful song of God's word.

So go forth today with a purpose
A purpose both loud and clear
To tell and show others of Jesus
And the wonderful word that's here.

Mary Rennie

Dreaming Or Thoughts

Oh, how I would like to wander
Through and over the green fields yonder
And see the birds building nests
It would seem an island blest
The king cups yellow and gold
As they face the wind so bold
The lady's-smock and harebell too
Pick up the hue of a sky so blue
Under the hedgerow as I pry
Celandine and violet catch my eye
The oak and ash are beginning to unfurl their leaves of green
What a wonderful sight there is to be seen
The river gurgling on its way
Into each and every newborn day
All these show the creator's glory
Unfolding like a giant story
So I go happily on my way
Down the road I tread with pleasure
With the thoughts I will always treasure.

H. P. Wesson

" Hauling Done "

The trucks they head toward me, by day and then by night.
To see their lights approaching is a fearsome, terrible sight.
Their engines they are roaring, their exhausts a-belching smoke
"Get that barrier open mate, my gearbox is broke."

With a shudder of the trailer and a screeching of their brakes
Oh! please, I ask, let them stop, for all of our sakes.
"I'm just back from Verona, from Rome and from Turin,
Got any room left there, pal, to fit another small one in?"

From all over the continent these artics do appear,
Always, at ten thirty there's one who's bringing up the rear.
"The customs, they have stopped me and I've come so very far,
Book me in quick as you can guv., and I'll just catch the bar."

Now the motors, they are silent, their drivers are at rest.
They've showered, shaved and fed, but this part is the best.
"I want four pints of Murphy's, two lagers and one beer.
Move on down the bar, lads, let a thirsty man get near."

"No driving for me tomorrow, son, I've come to a stop.
Now's my turn to tipple; the grape, barley and the hop.
But when I'm out there driving, I drink in only the road,
The only tip I'll touch out there is when I'm tipping off my load."

Terence J. Stacey

Enchanted Way

A long remembered walk
Through a leafy glade,
Treading on dew damp moss,
Sun rays cast a beauteous glow,
Magical to the beholder.
Quiet a deathly hush at the grave,
Which has long since been forgotten,
The spider spins his web already wet with dew,
Now awaits his victims who venture this way.
The sudden scurry of a rabbit bustling on his way,
Startling the robin busy feeding his squawking hungry chicks,
Primroses dazzling in the sunlight,
Bouquets such like nature's natural way.
Blue are the bells for us to see,
In harmony the blue of the violets, heavy-scented perfume,
Daises hanging their heads as if in shame.
All too soon, as if a figment of my imagination,
Perchance the wonders we have seen.
A. Clapton

Homeless

I was walking by
Three men sleeping
In their cardboard homes.
The filthy pavement was their carpet
The starlit sky their roof.

The street was their world
The sound of traffic their music
Other people's rubbish their diet
Other peoples lives their dreams.
You could call it second hand living.

The lights were up for Christmas
Everyone I knew was happy.
My light had gone out and could not be relit
Till the homeless people in all the world
Have their lights lit in a proper home.
Seke Chimutengwende

God Bless

I waited for the car to come,
Thoughts twisting through my mind
The feelings pumping in my heart
My eyes, the tears could find.

Memories, sweet seemed like yesterday,
A child I was just then.
The days of us all together
It's not hard to remember when.

The long chats we had, the sensible words,
She always knew what to say.
Whether, much younger, I took notice then,
The memories of them, always have stayed.

As I say my final goodbyes and God Bless,
The sadness full in my heart
I know that joined together they are,
Now they will never have to part.
K. Hurst

Untitled

I knitted thae' baffies
Tho' I was half deid
A crazy wee notion, cam in tae ma heid
So oot cam the wool
It delighted the kitten
She tugged and she pulled
But I kept on knittin'
Ye may think, that thae 'shoes'
Are for dancin a jig
But it's just that ma pins
Were twa' sizes ower big
The colour's no lemon, no yella, but maize,
How long did they tak me?
Twa nichts' and twa days!!
E. Rooney

Yesterday Girl

The hurt will never go away
thought of you so many times
went to work..my mind did stray.
Dreamtime over...then five o'clock chimes
day went quick..well, just another day.

Separated but still in love
had regrets..often wonder why
I think o my god and look above
can't see much for the tears in my eye
still look around..where are you my love.

Not as all other women are
is to my soul so really dear
her thoughts and fancies come from afar
beneath the silver evening star
yet her heart is always near.

Really hoping you might call
try my best before we are out of fashion
memories of that we had a ball
entwined in all that smouldering passion
we loved each other...do you recall?
S. J. Hutchinson

Untitled

I've lost my youth, oh where has it gone. I've though and
    I've thought but I'm no further on.

I look in the mirror and what do I see? — This middle aged
    woman is looking at me.
She's fat and has wrinkles, so this is not me.
Well who is this woman who's looking at me?

Oh, wait just a minute, now let me see. Yes I do know this
    woman, she's a Mother of three.
Two Daughters and a Son, who love her so much.
She's one lucky lady the dear old Dutch.

She's also a Gran to two little boys, who fill her head and her
    house with noise.
And when sometimes they come to stay, they keep her young
    with their fun and play.

This woman, she must feel like a millionaire, with a family who
    love her, a family who care.
She's certainly lucky, of that there's no doubt and
    she's not really fat — just a wee bitty stout.

Yes, the middle aged woman in the mirror can stay — Who
    was that gawky looking kid anyway?!
Mary Cochrane

Woman

I must be walking through heaven itself
Though grey the day and winter snows left to melt
I must be walking through the brightest skies
Wherever I go I cannot hide

No eyes could be more pensive
And smiles, not brighter is a flash of lightning
No hair could be so coloured right
And skin softer than daylight.

Like a stone around my neck
Your leaving footsteps do bedeck
Like children's laughter on my lips
When I feel your tender kiss

Each time I see you, I live and die
In the cafe, or wherever you go by

Hanging onto the arms of time
To make this moment forever mine
Your beauty turns a room into a world
One brief moment forever could not remove.
Mark Anthony Adamson

That Boy, Is Mine

That boy, with excitement in his eyes, is mine!
Those two dark laughing pools
That overflow to his lips,
Are my most precious jewels.

That boy, with tears in his eyes, is mine.
He's just found a bird, almost dead, not quite,
It died as he held it,
Though he prayed with all his might.

That boy, with bravery in his eyes is mine.
"Don't dare hit my sister you little brat",
Says Sir Galahad by her side,
"I'm the only one who's allowed to do that".

That boy, with mischief in his eyes, is mine.
"Wash your face and neck" I say,
And backing quickly out the door, he laughs,
"I did it yesterday."

That boy, with sleep in his eyes is mine.
Yawning, he sinks into his bed,
Murmurs "Goodnight Mummy,"
As I kiss the tousled head.

Mary Maguire

Viola (Da Braccio)

Your delicate shape in space contained
Those crevices that crave the senses
Besotted by your voice that gained
The love that shouts in many tenses
The bridge that opens a million sighs
Supporting lust that knows no bound
Your body that beguiles the eyes
And heart from asiatic sound
I need to caress your slender neck
To move my hands round sensuous hips
To coax you to everlasting pecc
And seek close message from your lips
Age will not wither your timeless frame
Nor years of loving will ever defile
Your belly smooth will stay the same
Enchanting lovers with no guile
Alas I must leave but you will remain
To tempt with love from nature's phial.

Peter Blackburn

Epping Forest (After The Gales)

The forest is crying, the forest is sad;
Those beautiful trees — the best that we had,
Are lying around so broken and torn;
The forest is muddy, old and careworn.
The splinters and shards stand stark to the sky;
It's cruel to think our forest might die.
The fallen trees do now block our way;
Our walks in the forest are different today;
The wildlife is silent, the birds do not sing,
So please let us pray for a happier spring.

M. K. Glozier

Life Or Love

Born from love, a beautiful thing
This child of mine that's so divine
In this new life, he must find
The love of his, to feel sublime
Through thick and thin, he shall begin
Into the unknown, as life begins
In life he'll seek for greater things
In love he'll look for similar things
He'll find that life's not what it seems
And so must take what life gives out to him
And face the future with a grin
With love and care, life's only hope
For that future that's made out for him
True love in life eternally

Sadie Parkes

Destructive Greed

This world so green,
This world so fair,
Very soon this world so bare.

We cut the tree,
We pull the weed,
This to satisfy a human greed.

The open hands of thoughtless greed,
Green is the money we use to feed,
The humans of destroying greed.

The forests are gone, the animals too,
Does this matter?
There's still the zoo.

With our children choking on factory smoke,
The ice caps melting,
Too warm to float.

What will save this planet now?
Humans of greed,
Act wisely now!

Michael Horth

Cosmos

Beyond the horizon of existence
This world reflects her mirrored images
Captured from the silhouette of life.
And though each glorious setting of the sun
Lends darkened shadows to each night,
New dawns incipient gleam, excels its light
As constant as the sands of time
How infinite this orbital acclaim,
Rejoices constantly - for the worlds magnitude
And its survival.

S. Gartside

The First Spring Day

The orangy glow, the birds' dawn chorus,
This wonderful day is breaking before us.
The morning air so crisp and light,
The breaking of dawn, what a wonderful sight.
The sparkling stream swiftly flows,
Beneath the trees the fierce wind blows.
The floral display of splendid colour,
This fierce wind causes all to flutter.
A quick look up through sparse leafed trees,
A flock of birds is all she sees.

The day is young but will get old,
What further beauty does this day hold.
The wild trees slice through open land,
Their new spring colour reduces all that is bland.
A sudden shout, a sudden cry,
The warning sound as blackbirds fly.
She turns around and to her surprise,
A kestrel swoops before her eyes.
For food this bird will always chase,
Displaying power and elegance with such grace.

Rebecca Corns

An Hour Upon The Stage

"Where did it go?" they say, "How quickly Time flies!"
They talk of "making hay while the sun shines".

Memories of all we've had are all that we can hold,
Whether they are good or bad, for our fate, it is foretold.

Almost forgotten now, it was so long ago —
Ecstasy, Bliss, Joy — emotions riding high.
Life was lived on the crest of a wave.
All that I had to give, I gave.

We must remember all the best — leave Sorrow in the past.
After all, Life is but a jest and only the Earth was made to last.

P. Reeves

My Son

I pace the floor, my senses reeling,
This waiting is a dreaded feeling,
How much longer will it be?
I think I've drunk a gallon of tea!
If there were anything that I could do,
Don't they know, I'm anxious too,
To hear the words, "You have a son,
Congratulations sir, well done"
The door swings open, I hear my name,
Oh God, I pray she's not in pain,
Come right this way, the nurse calls out,
And see what your wife is so happy about,
At last, I cry, oh let me see
With arms outstretched she smiles at me,
Thank God it's over and you're all right
We have a son, oh, what a night.

V. Vincent

When Love Has Died

I look in your eyes, the love has gone;
This truth you cannot hide.
A smile can't hide the feeling
Of your emptiness inside.
Without your love, our future's doomed,
The two of us no more.
My heart's now broken, this is true
'Cause you're whom I adore.
My love for you will never wane;
I know you wish to leave.
I'll not make a fuss, or beg you to stay;
When I'm alone I'll grieve.
Before you go, please tell me this,
Just when did your love die?
The years together for me were good;
I love you, good luck, goodbye.

H. Grey

This Noble Planet That Man Called Earth

This noble planet that man called earth,
This sacred place that gave us birth.
What is its value, what is its worth
This noble planet that man called earth.

Gunshots firing in every direction,
Breaking families, stealing affection.
There's no joy, no valid mirth,
From this noble planet that man called earth.

Children living their lives in fear,
Trying to hold on to those that are near.
The future is bleak, there's nothing beneath
This noble planet that man called earth.

There's no hope for peace ever after,
No newborn joy or blissful laughter.
Man has blown it, replacing flowers with wreath,
On this noble planet we now call earth.

There's disaster in every nook of the land,
Danger in holding a friend by the hand.
What is its value, what is its worth,
This noble planet that man called earth.

C. Hall-Baker

Peace Not War

Upon the golden sands of old
The jewels lay of clustered gold
They be not gems or precious stones
But souls of men who died in vain
They roam the sands with the wind
And tell mankind of what's to come
Take heed, I pray, of what they say
Or our own souls may join theirs someday.
The message is very clear to all
To keep the world in one piece

Mary Anne Ratcliffe

Egypt

Long ago, a land forgot and lost in time,
This place of mystery I wish were mine.
The treasures, the wealth, bold colour and myth,
This wonderful land, mysterious Egypt.
Such strong blue skies and sands of gold,
Oh the temples and monuments of old.
Time stands still in this magical land.
Modern day items not always to hand.
Peace and tranquillity the way of life,
Rarely trouble, rarely strife.
How far away this land now seems,
The land and valley of the kings and queens.
But I shall return so very soon,
Listen, he calls you, the king,
    Tutankhamoun.

Pauline Giles

Stranger In The Mirror

Our eyes have met,
This mortal shell, stranger in the mirror
Where in a woman's womb my soul conceived
We grew, laughed and cried together
Yet dimly knew a time would come,
When each must grow apart.
I saw despair cloud his eyes,
Felt the fearful beating of his heart
Gently I touched the glass,
Our finger tips did meet,
We'd shared this life, from boy to man.
Now we sense the cosmic plan.
He must die that I may grow,
Into the eternal cosmic flow,
And be, both God and man.

Percy Sheppard

Pure Heart

When we give love and never do wrong
This is when our spirit is strong
Never to spite or speak in malice
Then we'll drink from the heavenly chalice

Our hearts will be filled with God's pure grace
Never again to feel shame or disgrace
We can walk the earth, free of all pain
And do good deeds, without thoughts of gain

We can rid our hearts of sadness and sorrow
And joy and contentment must surely follow
And if we allow God into our heart
There can be no fear when we depart

For a heavenly messenger will take our hand
And lead us into his promised land
With a spirit so pure and full of love
Through the light we'll walk, to God above.

G. Witherington

Requiem

When I vanish —
    Think of me — only this,
It was not a banish —
    But an earth-free search for bliss.

And again, the immortal powers that be,
    In their great and holy wisdom,
Will have certainly sent for me;
    Perhaps to meet my past and aged Mom.

I have no fear of what becomes of me,
    I've feared not the many lives I've led,
And many more indeed must be,
    Until I'm "777" times dead.

Only then may I go to Utopia,
    Being a very far distant planet,
Many light years from Europa,
    And meet her again — dear Janet.

A. Geoffrey Stedman-Polehampton

Souvenirs

Souvenirs are treasures, fond memories of the past.
Things we keep forever, our love will hold them fast,
Photos of a bygone age, that seemed so long ago,
Letters that were written to some-one dear to know.
Little drawings that we did, when we first went to school.
Comic cuts, when we dressed up, and tried to play the fool.
All secured with ribbon, and fastened in a bow.
Looking rather faded, but still sets hearts aglow.
Some tiny pearls that grandma wore, to decorate a dress
The imprint of doggies paw, that still looks quite a mess.
A locket with a tiny curl, just neatly placed inside.
Two photos of dear Mum and Dad, they are my special pride.
But nothing can replace the love, a souvenir can bring.
For they are priceless in themselves, that goes for everything.
And as the years go rolling by, they always will remain.
'Cause even though the world may change — they still will be the same.
Mollie Sage

Legacy

She was — this, and she was — that
 They will say when I am gone.
The sudden shock might make them stop
 In shopping queue, or fireside chat
They could recall the things I have done.
 These memories might bring a sigh
Or break long silence with a cry that they are now alone.

For as my life has been so plain
 And not endowed with brilliant mind.
What legacy is mine to leave.
 No loud applause did greet my name,
No treasures for the world to find
 Invaluable in the years to come.

Yet I have walked the earth with pride
 And kept my standards high and true.
Drying your tears with smile, have tried
 To give comfort when sympathy was due.
So, my friends, it must be love
 The gift that I leave behind for everyone I've known.
D. M. Smith

And Cucumber Sandwiches?

They've opened "buck House" to the public,
They want to make a quick "Bob" or two.
There's things to be done at "Windsor"
They want it to look "good as new".
They've had lots of response, and their bookings
Are a sell out 'till late' ninety six.
Prince Edward's preparing to sell souvenirs,
And the corgi's are learning new tricks.
"Guards" in "bearskins" will take your tickets,
While they keep you strictly in line,
To relieve the monotony of waiting,
The "Drill Sergeant" will make you "mark time."
I doubt if you'll be able to see much,
You'll be in and out in an hour,
And if you should stray, from the well defined way,
Chances are you'll wind up in "the tower"
No doubt they'll charge you extra.
T. J. Trew

Duncker House

At Duncker house
There is a beat
You can hear the pitter patter of barefoot feet
Dancing through the tunnel of freedom
Seeping out through the cracks in the wall
They fall slowly
Disintegrating upon the surface of reality
No more shall I buy it, no more shall I bite it,
We were born free and uninhibited
And so we shall remain
Free and uninhibited
With the world at our feet.
Mairead Hassett

Yet Another Report From Biosphere 1

Here brain washing is legal
They start on us quite early
Their eyes peeled like the eagle's
Watch over us, Frightfully
Their messages distinct like the bugle's
Through mountains and empty valleys
Echoing in our unreachable minds
The highways without signs
The incomprehension which binds and keeps us in their lines.

Tiny puns in their game
Play soldiers of a faith
Administrators of a way
We are taught to love, with hate
Spread the hopeful message with the invisible Cane
Hope is only possible with pain
Crime, only reasonable in His name
If your flesh deny, you maim
We are made to believe in the way
The authority being what they say
And we wait for a certain day to receive our pay.
O. A. Quadri

Trees

Nobody ever stops to ask, 'Do trees think or feel?'
They see them standing there so tall and perhaps not real.

They stand there all alone
each one different in its own way,
Looking down as we walk by
each and every day.
Their colours are so beautiful,
in Autumn brown and gold.
In Winter they still stand there proud
but perhaps quite cold.
Then comes Spring and once again
their leaves start to appear.
How tall they stand there through the seasons
Each and every year.
In Summer they are happy now
with the sun and the warm rain,
to keep them in their splendour
until Autumn comes again.

So do please think about the trees and really start to care
For without these beautiful, quiet things, our world look quite bare.
Susan Thompson

I Love White Dresses

"I'll be an angel, a candle even, in a white dress", I said.
They said, "You are a narrator and your dress is red".
So, I read as a narrator.

"I'll be Cinderella, a fairy Godmother, a ghost even, in
a white dress", I said.
They said, "You'd be better as witch", which I was.
"I'll be painted in a field of poppies standing in a white
dress", I said.
They said, "Don't be silly; it wouldn't suit you".
So, I painted the fence instead.
"I'll wed in white, all misty, a `Snow Queen'", I said.
They said, "You've been unchaste, you'll wed in haste".
So, I settled for something sensible that covered up my sin.
I'll have a white dress to go to heaven in.
Marie B. King

Falling Over Frontward

If a hammer was stick and a stick a hammer
The hammer would hit and the stick would clamour.
Now if you had a stammer, used the stick on a wall
You could walk with the hammer so you wouldn't fall.
If you used a punch for support - crutches would punch out
Holes in paper, it's a thought, to see through no doubt.
And when you'd done all this to see what you'd really like
You could jump over backward and disappear from sight!
A. J. Venter

The Rainforest

The trees in the forest
They long for the rain
The branches are limp, crying in pain.
The tractors, the noise
The workmen they shout
In less than a day
The trees are wiped out.
The fire in the sky
It lights up the night
The land burning and dying
Such a pitiful sight.
The last tree it falls
It lays dead on the ground.
The men and machines gone
There is no more sound.

Marie Weir-Burrows

Men Oh! Men!

Men are animals! Don't you agree?
They have not evolved like woman — you see!
That's why they rape, maim and kill.
They don't seem to know they are animals still!

The way they gather in packs and groups
Makes them feel safe and cock-a-hoop.
Because they know there is more of their kind
Lurking about — who could attack — from behind.

How can there be a God? I don't understand!
How can he give this world into the hands of man?
We all know about Adam! It fills us all with shame.
But even after all this time it's Eve who gets the blame.

Man invented the bow and arrow
The bullet and the gun
And every other weapon
Under-neath the sun!

Man has had his chance! He blew it all away!
And now it's time for woman — to try and save the day
Man has one saving grace
After that! We will take his place and reign supreme!

M. Banham

Wishing

Sitting by the window the cars and wagons whizz by,
They go so fast they make me gasp, it's almost as if they could fly
Housewives doing their shopping, children run here and there.
Would that I could, I would join them, but who will push my wheelchair?

Nighttime now is falling, boys and girls go out on their dates.
If they haven't got a partner then they go out with their mates,
To the pub then on to dancing, all I can do is stare
Would that I could, I would join them, but who will push my wheelchair?

For pleasure I have my day dreams, or else I read my book
Does anyone know I am lonely, will they be bothered to look?
Will they give me a nod or a pleasant smile, or simply show that they care.
If only they would, then I know that I could feel happier about my wheelchair.

Sheila Love

" Loneliness "

Loneliness I know, is a sad thing to all,
There's no one around, if you happen to fall.
No one to talk to, or tell of your fears,
Sometimes you feel you could burst into tears.

Please someone come, lift me from this state,
Before something happens, and it's too late.
If one person was with me, I would feel duty bound,
Loneliness would be gone, with a companion around.

Bill Rowsell

Looking Back

We played "Blind Man's Bluff" at chapel one night
they covered my young eyes with a scarf so tight,
spun me round and round, no way could I see.
I grabbed at the teasing arms that I could not quite hold
they teased and laughed at my mad tantrums bold.
"'Ah' but then I struck" — I had hold of one too bold.
He gave a protest shout then rolled.
But I clung on with a two hand hold.
Then all hell broke loose, my feet jerked off the floor
flung I was at arm's length around the room with screams galore
load voices "Gerim Off" but with vice grip I held on the more
I shall never forget that thing I held so tight
Like a Bobby's truncheon — but warmer — not quite right
then came my dad's booming voice "get off you silly lad"
accompanied by a clout that made my head spin bad.
They took away the scarf from around my blind eyes.
There beside me lay "Big Bill" a man of six foot size
Bill lay still and white — his eyes blood shot wide,
his tongue lay out;
he groaned aloud; a doctor was called to bring him round.
A trapped nerve in the "ovaries gonads" that were cricket ball size.

Tom Timms

Central 11:17

A million lights burn for my convenience
They are the last objects my yawning eyes desire.
A seat of comfort my homecoming carriage
Is not the want of my wasted limbs.
Raging metropolis reaches with offerings of
Tempting vices,
My need lies not there
I flit from its grasp.
Hours burnt in labour for physical substance
Yet my heart lies wasted, craving.
Surrounded by mortal companions
But so alone am I taking solace in my thoughts
Of you
Miles away
Yet only minutes apart.

Martin Ashley Jones

Active Mind

Pass me a pen, lest I forget
these word's that go round and round,
I cannot sleep when they are forming
brimming over and over in my mind.

Sleep it did betray me
and I could not rest
until on paper I had wrote
and my head found emptiness.

Soon morn will escape from darkness
and a bright new day will begin,
the songbirds will chirp there chorus
and my writing, I'll start again.

Sally Moreton

Autumn Song

The wintry nights, the stormy days,
The grey and brooding sky,
All fill my heart with loneliness
And song becomes a sigh.

The towering branches bare and stark,
The empty earth below
Seem cold and lifeless to the eye;
The wind will bring the snow.

But underneath the snowy scene
The birth of spring will start,
And little shoots will push their way
Through Winter's cold, cold heart.

Mariann Walker

To Our Little Ones

Can anyone tell me why
These little ones should die... when
    The membrane and the womb
    Become the death shroud and the tomb.

God alone in Heaven
Knows the choices we are given... when
    The membrane and the womb
    Become the death shroud and the tomb.

Lord enfold them in your care,
Just cradle them up there... when
    The membrane and the womb
    become the death shroud and the tomb.

How foolish we can be
When beyond that moment we fail to see... and
    The membrane and the womb
    Become the death shroud and the tomb.

Forgive us Lord above
Surround us with your love... when we've made
    The membrane and the womb to
    Become the death shroud and the tomb.

Pauline Aarons

The Skiers

They climb higher beyond Bad Hartzburg town,
These Christmas-tide sportsmen, cloth'd all in white.
Colder, brighter, nearer the winter sun
They go, to places only Brocken's witches know,
And taste the pure, clear iced wine air,
That gives them strength before they dare
The mad pursuit, with cheeks aglow, o'er gleaming snow,
Bringing them back to lowly earth again,
Where goblins, sprites and witches never roam.
Where winds blow softer through forests of fir.

The course is done, there's a prize to be won
By the log fire in the house in the vale.
So wearily, happily on they plod
Beneath the trees, their branches bowed low with white flakes,
Very soon the sky in the West
Breaks up as the sun goes to rest.
Now bars of crimson and gold paint the lowland lakes,
While pink fingers creep through the forest trees.
Night falls and they see no more that cold, clear,
Classical beauty — winter's heritage.

A. R. Barnes

The Gates Of Hell

Are these the gates of hell? He whimpered at his birth
These are the gates of life. The life you'll live on earth
Are these the gates of hell? He said outside the school
No behind these gates you'll learn the golden rule

Are these the gates of hell? He cried in youthful dread.
These are the factory gates. Where you will earn your bread
Are these the gates of hell? He gasped with his last breath
That only you will know for these are the gates of death

A. L. Price

Toys

Castles and kites, teddies and bikes
These are our children's favourite likes,
A bucket and spade to play on the sand
What could be finer, more pleasant or grand?

These pleasures we take sometimes for granted
Our prayers we hope will always be answered,
But what of our cousins in far distant lands
Do they have these toys to hold in their hands?

Next time we shout or holler and scream
For things we see on the T.V. screen,
Perhaps we should think of a special thought
For children worse off, who've never been taught.

Carol P. Smith

I Wish That I

Many years have passed us by, since my dad passed away,
There's still so many things I feel, I wish that I could say,
Just how much I love him, and miss him every day,
Remembering the hours we spent, the games that we would play.

I wish that he was with me now, with my children, that he'd love,
Although I feel he's watching us, somewhere up above,
I wish that I could cuddle him, the way I used to do,
I wish that I could talk to him, to laugh and joke now too.

I hope someday, when my time comes, to leave this earth one day,
My dad will be there waiting, to guide me on my way,
But now my family are my life, they are precious that I know,
Although my dad will always be, in my memory even so.

I know that he will guide me, and show me what is best,
My memories will comfort me, and my heart will do the rest.

Rhonda King

Feelings

Those bridges have been crossed, the barriers are down.
There's no need to hide your feelings, for love has been found.
The feelings that you locked away, someone has now freed.
So they can grow just like the trees, from their tiny seeds.
When you're sick and need some caring, I'll nurse you back to health.
Love and attention you need to get well, you can't give yourself.
Only you can smile like that, and always make me sigh.
This love, it has to be for real, it's something you can't buy.
Forever I'll be yours, I hope you will be mine.
Getting closer day by day, until the end of time.
That day I fell in love with you, you were the one for me.
Together, forever always, until eternity.

Sylvia Warnes

A Dying Sentimentality

Keeping the family in touch is a struggle,
There's always so much I need to juggle,
My husband and son provide loving care,
But of mother and sisters I'm in despair.
I do my best to keep in touch,
I write, I phone, I worry so much.
They're all too busy, is the reply
Before you know it a year's gone by!
Birthdays forgotten, promises broken,
I never did learn how to be outspoken
Perhaps this is where I have gone wrong,
Putting up with it all for too long,
Too well behaved and too soft-hearted,
Too forgiving when "sorries" are started.
It's hard to be tough when you want to stay friends,
But I guess in the end, it all depends
On whether I can live and learn
To train myself to less concern,
Or let them drift away as they please,
And reconcile it as a life of ease!

Sharon Blevins

Always

For all the love you give me
For all the times when you were there
For all the words of wisdom
For all your loving care
For all the holidays you gave me, for all
The times by the sea
For all the childhood memories, for all
You gave to me
For all the kindness you have shown
For all the pride you give me still
For all the feelings of belonging
For all the love that time cannot steel
For all the times when I was a child
For all the times you spent with me
If I could be the perfect parent
Then I would be half as good
As you.

Joanne Wisdom

The Dreamer

Open wide the porthole, enter if you dare
There's a world of mystic wonder waiting over there.
Enter at your bidding, for you alone will know
Just exactly how and when or where you choose to go.

The magic of this journey will take you far away
It may happen in the dead of night, or in the light of day.
There's no restriction on admission, for you possess the key
The door is easily opened, but only you can see.

When securely locked within this strangely hypnotic state
We're numb to this world's corruption, violence and hate.
We have the power to summon happiness, build castles in the air
A knight in shining armour, instead of dungeons of despair.

Allow yourself to travel along its gentle, tranquil sea
Release your inhibitions, imagination flowing free,
And enjoy the transition through this far off, unknown land
'Cause therein perfection dwelleth, and you're always in command.
Romaine Kane

The Mangle

My mother often told us
There was one thing that she craved.
But when we heard just what it was
This item was then waived.

But someone must have heard her prayer
For trundling up the street,
A handcart (not that that was rare)
And the patter of many feet.

There was pushing and some grunting,
But finally — at an angle
With a little bit of shunting
Stood a large, old, iron mangle.

It wouldn't fit into the kitchen
(It would have gone right through the floor)
But that didn't matter a smidgen,
And it couldn't have been cherished more.

So it stayed where it was in the backyard,
It was used for a good many years,
But turning the handle became a mite hard
'Cos the rain has rusted the gears.
Marjorie Johnson

Fears Of Childhood

Things that creak and rattle
Things that go bump in the night
Tucked up in the bed-clothes
Heart bumping in fright
Gently stretch your hand out
To feel the cat is there
Close your eyes, all is well
The cat begins to purr.

The sandman comes to scatter sand
Into your tired eyes
Then sleep creeps in to fill your dreams
With wonderful surprise
Prams and dolls and aeroplanes
And swiftly moving trains
Then mum comes in to kiss you awake
It's morning time again.

Have you had a wash
And eaten breakfast, you hear your mother say,
Then watch the road and do take care
When you go out to play.
Richard A. Lee

Football

I hate football yes I do
There must be better things to do
Men dressed up in pretty shirts
And getting kicked just where it hurts

Pushing and shoving and arguments
To me it doesn't quite make sense
To get that ball into the net
A more stupid game, I've to see yet

Men cost a fortune I don't know why
Unless they think their going to die
From tearing around like lunatics
Chasing a ball while the fans have fits.

I suppose money's insurance
For men such as these
I wonder how much
They pay referees?
R. Wigmore

Secret Land

By the soft and golden sand
There lies a youngsters secret land.
Of golden shells and silver waves
Deep remains of sea creatures graves

To the child this is a treasure chest
Of sorrows she has laid to rest
All that was way in her past
Sitting here her youth will last.

When she sits down by the shore
She hears the waves they crash and roar
As if the sea has come to talk
With the child in her lonely walk.

Wishing she could be much more
Than a girl alone on a sandy shore
She has no friends to guide the way.
For she's by herself each lonely day.

If you saw her as she stands
Looking around at promised lands
No more would you feel that life was steep
As feelings of pity for her are deep.
Margaret Owens

War " No Rhyme No Reason "

A baby cries, a child weeps,
　There is no peace for them to sleep.
　　The soldier cradles his mother's head
　　　It makes no sense that she is dead,
　　"War" they fight for pieces of land
　　They cannot stand hand in hand
　　Now it is finished, what is left?
　　　Anger, hatred and homelessness.
A. J. Howard

Coloured Dreams

If God has given the gift of sight
Then you can see day from night
Try to explain the colour green
To someone who has never seen

He feels the sunshine the cool of shade
The chill of ice the sharp of blade
But when he sleeps can he see
In dreams of colour like you and me

Don't take for granted your gift of sight
The magical beauty of birds in flight
A sweet red cherry, a rose in bloom
The stars at night, the big round moon
All the precious things around
And all he has is touch taste smell and sound
Susan J. Haley

Heart Of Wishes

The heart within can sometimes feel,
There is no blood just cold of steel,
To know not love but nor how to give,
It beats for life nor how to live.

With love of all held deep inside,
Emotions lost and warmth denied,
To care for child, for pain and loss,
For love of Christ, upon the cross.

I wish to be, I wish to love,
To be as one like hand in glove,
And cry a tear for those unknown,
Their pain to share with heart, not stone.

Please let this heart of ice be free,
To turn from self and think of thee,
Its melting surface warm to touch,
Allowing all to mean so much.

Maybe the day will dawn and find
That thoughts of love possess my mind,
And I will let my heart be true,
In giving, loving, wanting you.

Stuart Robey

The Sun And The Moon

In every single heart, in every single room,
there is always a sun set, and always a moon.
Some nights they will rise together but only in my dreams,
a place where she has ruined and ripped at the seams,
I thought my dreams were safe locked inside my head,
but when I fall asleep I remember every word she said,
my dreams always turn to nightmares when I think of the
bad times we had, and everything goes horribly wrong and
I wake up feeling sad.

Maria Holohan

Man's Folly

God planted a garden called Ireland.
There He put Man He had formed
to share life's joys, and to prosper
midst mountains and rivers, sun warmed.

But Man had misused all these blessings
to riot, to rage and to fight
their Church, their friends and their neighbours
The streets now with blood run red bright.

God planted a garden called Ireland,
but Man has a battlefield formed
to fight and to kill one another
midst mountains and rivers sun warmed.

E. Sussex

Winter Scene

In our parks and gardens
There comes a busy man,
  To paint our trees and bushes white
Is his yearly plan.

  He stealthily creeps upon us
As the sun goes down and darkness falls.
  Roads and paths become a risk
Whilst he gaily marks our gates and walls.

  He means no harm, as he moves his brush,
There is even beauty for those of us
  Who gaze through windows in early morn.
On which pictures and maps have been skilfully drawn.

  The sun comes out to end his play
Heralding a cold, but cheerful day.
  Jack Frost is his name, we all know,
When Winter is over, away he must go.

Rose B. Whiting

Imprecation Of A Soul

Stay still, your head reclined on my breast, o sweet!
There can't be to this night a tomorrow to meet;
Banish all thoughts from your mind, think of the present,
For genial issues in the Soul are latent.

Let the Sky tumble down dragging Universe,
Let the Oceans Creations into abysmal depth immerse;
Let Chaos arm-in-arm with Havoc blend,
Rid putrid Humanity of its predicament.

Only then, O my Soul, you can break your cage to witness
a world to a new Life reborn and Humanity bless,
Revelling in the joy to see wishes come true
Faith, love, our hearts filled with, until Eternity I and You.

Z. Gizman

" Unspoken Words "

Dedicated to a dear brother "Graham"

If I'd known that he was leaving —
  There are words I would have said.
I was sure he would recover,
  For I felt no sense of dread.

Believing there was ample time
  to voice how much he meant,
To reminisce on happy days
  The good times we had spent.

The love we shared spanned many years.
  My brother — best of mates!
Did he know he had a journey?
  Were his thoughts on Pearly Gates?

Always there for one another —
  The miss of him now great.
Regretting those unspoken words
  We should not leave too late!

Rosemary Pearson

" Reflecting "

It was just another illness they said — nothing more
Then they told me I was going to die.
Time to reflect?

I stare into space and think what a waste;
Do I rush to fill the time I have left,
Whatever that may be?
All the books I didn't read,
The people I never met.
The places I've never seen, or maybe
That book I'd write one day, and yet
still reflecting.

Was it worth holding onto that childhood
Dream, when sometimes in the night I
Quietly scream? Who would hear?

Does respective change? Maybe for now,
I look at flowers as they bloom and next
year they will be twice as good —
How do I know this, and no longer cry?
Because I do not yet choose to die.

A. V. Cleaver

Refreshed

A stormy day, a cloudy sky
The streets awash with rain
The trees all bend beneath the wind,
That shrieks as though in pain,
Then clouds glide by, the blue sky peeps
Around the pall of grey
The wind dies down, the rain is stilled
The storm has blown away.
A rainbow steals across the sky
All sparkling fresh and new
Reminding us that after storms
Our world can bloom anew.

Margaret Sawdon

The Steam Train

It starts with a whistle then with a blow.
Then starts to move very slow.

Moving along the metal track,
Making a sound like clickety clack.

Wheels turning round and round,
The soot and steam floating all around.

Picking up speed as it goes along,
The driver starts to sing a jolly song.

Pile on more coal until the fire burns bright.
Oh how it makes a lovely sight.

The train slows down as it reaches its destination.
There's the inspector waiting at the station.

The people get up and out of the train.
It's the start of the journey once again.
Thomas D. Hunt

Baby's First Snowman

Standing by the window looking into space.
Then snowdrops falling from the sky bring a
  smile to his little face.
Daddy puts his coat on, then his woolly hat.
Climbing into his wellies, which are standing
  on the mat.

Out into the garden, with gloves on his little
  hands.
He starts to pile up all the snow, to build
  a little man.
Daddy gets three acorns, to use for his
  nose and eyes
Mummy's best scarf around his neck,
  won't she be surprised.
The final touch a plant pot, which
  makes a smashing hat.
Last of all for a walking stick, his
  daddy's cricket bat.
M. Fiddes

He Played At Being God With Me

He played at being God with me,
Then he tried to be Christ with me,
Only he could not see,
I was not fooled at all by he.

The reason was it simply could not be,
I really had God with me,
If only he could really see,
He would not say he was God to me.

Now who but a criminal would claim to be
anything he could not see,
While all the time I roamed free,
In hell it was he said he be.

I had to break the law said he,
He even tried to make me flee,
If only he had been able to see,
At the end it was only me.
Victor Parratt

The Loss Of A Son

My life must go on without my eldest son
The emptiness inside without my eldest son
The tears fall free for my eldest son
The sun still shines for my eldest son
The days go on without my eldest son
The joy of the birth of my eldest son
Is it really no more for that eldest son
For at the end of the day we were nearly one
My one and only my first born son.
Rosemary Rainbird

Remember, Remember

The Doctor's mad, the nurses, they're crazy
Their words are so sterile and their meanings hazy
"I'm sorry. Your Wife will not last the night."
Oh No! "Hang on, this can't be right."

We've been together for, "How long now dear?
You know I always forget the year!"
Now let me think. "Was it Thirty One
Cup Final day, when West Bromwich won."

"I never remember but anyway
We had the most wonderful Wedding Day."
She was a beauty, an English Rose,
Dark and fragile with a turned up nose.

"She walked up the aisle with grace and charm
I was so proud to have her on my arm"
A bonny young woman and gentle lover
This was love at first sight, for me no other.

"You see, I can't explain all these things I feel
But what you say just cannot be real"
This dying woman is not only my wife
This dying woman is the whole of my life.
Ruth Adams

Word Blown

I labour slowly over words,
their elusive meanings such a haze.
Most of these are read and heard,
and some are oh, so very vague.

I trawl my dictionary, far and wide,
because of the skills and lack,
Among the labyrinth of verbiage I ride,
for the meanings of words to track.

The many definitions there to find,
are mind boggling, in their scope.
The more I delve, the more I mind,
that I should at school, have coped.

Those verbs and consonants cause me to moan,
grappling with vowels, I give a groan,
I am really as dense as a little stone,
as I negotiate those verbs and tones.

With consonants, it is quite as grim,
to be so very, very, dense and dim,
And when I deal with antonyms and synonyms,
I am completely, word blown, out on a limb.
L. Owen

Scavenger

With shining eyes and bushy tail
The young fox starts from his den
He raises his head and begins to wail
And call his foxy brethren

Together they travel down the hill
Flecks of fire in the green
At the bottom they summon all their will
To run through shadows in the street.

Along the track and under the gate
In their merry and playful mood
By now the time is growing late
To go and catch their food

In the curling, misty morning light
The prey tonight are few
But these scavengers do now take flight
It's a human they pursue

A pile of scraps lies in the grass
The cubs then feast with glee
And as they see their enemy pass
They know that they must flee.
Samantha Board

" The Loneliness Of Old Age "

I don't know where the time has gone
The years have just flown by.
Not long ago it was all to come
And now I wait to die.

There's not much to get up for,
I've nothing left to do
Except worry about how to pay the bills,
And what to leave to who.

Though I've many many memories,
Some good, and some sad,
Up to now I have enjoyed, for most,
The life I've had.

I cannot get around much,
My body is slowing down,
But my brain is still quite active
And I very rarely frown.

I'd just like a visit,
From a neighbour or a friend,
Someone who can spare some time,
For someone near their end.
Susan O'Brien

Meditation

The sea is yellow and the sky is green.
The world is empty, mankind cannot be seen.
The gulls are circling, crying.
The waves beat on the shore.
And I am here no more.
My existence has become a state
Where there exists no pain or hate,
No past, no future seeing.
Just being.
Not emptiness, but being filled.
Happening, but not self-willed.
As the unending universe extends,
It embraces me, like a friend.
This eternal moment filled with joy and peace
Is mine, at once with all, no one can take.
The moment passes and brings release,
And in the true, pure love I wake.
By what I do, I push the love away; I have not learned,
That it is mine always, and need not be earned.
G. Patterson

A Poem Is A Multitude Of Words

A poem is a multitude of words relating to a theme,
The words are thoughts, feelings, even fantasies it may seem.
The theme, of course, is anything central to the writer's ideal
Of life, of love or things material as the writer may feel.
Most themes relate to worldly things, of countries or their style,
Relating them to politics, the theatre, or matters that beguile.
The scenery, if coastal, might then relate to sea,
The countryside like farmland, could centre on a tree.
Animals that live and breed, their tenders or their brand,
The farmer or his wife maybe, or just the farmyard hand.
Many things on this fine earth, so readily come to mind;
And the mind's no need to travel far, its riches there to find.
The clouds above the landscape, the trees upon the ground.
With birds on wing, the horse on hoof, life surely does abound.
All life on earth abounds with much colour and delight,
When then put into words, translate to all things bright.
The climate does indeed dictate the stature of most life,
With frost and snow, with rain and sun, is surely nature's wife.
Every aspect of word used, be it animal or mankind,
Such love of life indulges all in matters of the mind.
Ramon H. Clarke

Summertime In Sussex

Southwards Ho! to the green Sussex hills,
The winding rivers, sea and old windmills,
to the warm summer sun and cool sea breezes,
Chanctonbury walks, the high gulls' screeches.

Blue sky and orchids among the grass,
Chalk Hill Blues, in colour full pass,
views over Bramber the Adur Vale,
stories of Monks, their deeds we hail;

The Legions of Rome came this way,
a settlement at Bignor they did lay,
a palace at Fishbourne they began too,
Please can you tell me, where's the Loo?

Yes! Sussex is the county for me,
beautiful green hills, by the sea,
history and legend in time honoured way,
where young lovers kiss, in the Summer Hay!!!!
Robert Cary

The Streets Are Quiet Now

The streets are quiet now,
The wind is howling,
Across the streets at night,
Whilst children sleep at night.

The streetlights shine,
Through the curtain's at night.
The sky so black you can see the stars,

Looking like diamonds,
Shining bright in the night.

The streets are quiet now,
How strange it seems at night.
Not a sound to be heard.
Till morning breaks.
How peaceful it sounds,
Outside at night.
A. Fletcher

A Bit Of Nonsense

The nights are drawing in, my dear, and I am growing old,
The weather is not so warm now, in fact it's downright cold.
It's nice to sit here by the fire when the wind is blowing wild,
I often think of nights like this when I was just a child.
I loved listening to the rain at night while I was snug and warm,
I loved to watch the lightening flash, whenever it did storm.
The thunder did not frighten me and neither did the dark,
I'd often walked alone at night through woods or in the park.
But I am rather lazy now and find other things to do,
Like watching programmes on T.V., knitting and reading too.
My life is very full these days, I'm busy as a bee,
But now I must put down my pen and go and make some tea.
I. Buckley

Life (Just Too Much)

As I gaze upon the dawning day,
The waking sun eases the night away,
The morning dew glistens in all its
splendour, the swallows sing so
sweet, so tender.
The night so calm, peacefully and still
shattered by the days we are
forced to fill,
    filled with families, work and
careers, these monotonous tasks
which bring me to tears,
with the day comes normality, suffering and
despair, is this the reason for life
does anybody care?
As I sit just watching the mid-morning
sky, a solemn cloud drifts slowly by.
To waste away the days, striving
for the night, the normality of
life is out of my sight.
T. Moseley

The Pits Are Closed!

The wheels and cogs have stopped turning
The valleys they are stilled,
The silence is deathly quiet
In the countryside they killed.

Now we have our peace and quiet
But what a price this is to pay,
The valleys now are empty
All the families have moved away.

There are no jobs now
Since the order is so tall,
When they closed down our heritage
This started a sad time for us all!

C. Way

Nightmare

The bells of ivy mould the chains of grief,
The unrequenting fire burns blackthorn bright,
The raven trails the walls of castle keep,
The never-ending, ever-waking night.

The spheres arc massive, grey, relentless,
Echoing, grinding, crushing, screeching.
Intersecting lifeways to destruction,
The musty scent of crying souls beseeching.

The dungeons of the mind in darkness dripping,
Rustling, crawling, gnawing, choking.
Enticing madness stalks the encircling darkness,
The razor's edge ahead the end evoking.

Alarm bells sound — the dreaded hour is nigh,
The 'Teasmade' calls the tune — no time to die!

Paul V. Davis

The Burning Mountain

The flames leap high on Moel Gilau (Mole Geeli) mountain,
The trees are black and burnt and dry.
Oh why did not the rain come earlier,
When they could have spread their branches to the sky.

What has happened to the wildlife
Have they run to save their lives,
A thoughtless act that caused this fire.
So stupid it was tinder dry.

The firemen work all day and night,
To save our heritage that is our right.
Oh let the rain fall in mighty streams
And let our grass and trees grow green.

G. M. Ashton

" The Girl Child "

Our hearts bleed for the girl-child,
The treatment meted out to her,
It's not only among the Slum-dwellers,
But with the upper-class too, we fear.
Some time ago we daily witnessed,
The most shocking cruelty,
Both physical and mental
To a baby girl of three!
Her mother would repeatedly slap her
For no good reason we could see,
Till the child's fair, and chubby cheeks
Were as red as red could be,
The father too, not to be outdone
His girl-child he'd pick up,
And make as if to throw her,
Into a near-by garbage dump;
By the terror-stricken look on her face,
She knew this could not be fun,
Such cruelties they would not enact,
If their girl-child was a SON!!

Vera M. Jennings

Hidden Cries

A wandering soul alone and in pain,
The torment and cries turning insane,
Frustration and loneliness hurting once more,
Still standing are problems which people ignore.

The world is changing whilst still turning,
The fires of anger still alive and burning,
Darkness if forming covering the sky,
I see my soul travelling ready to die.

Beside me rush the blue waters flowing,
Deep in my heart I feel it glowing,
I feel the time to curl up and leave,
I'll leave now without having to deceive.

I ask for the secret in which I need,
To open the door for my dream to lead,
A force lies beside me pulling back,
Holding away the good I lack.

I'm left to inherit that care and love,
I ask for peace flown by the dove,
Is happiness here yet to be shown,
Or will I die having not known.

Natalia Watts

Ben In Green Glasses

The child anticipated with little joy,
The tinge of sadness — a male child — a boy,
His mother a mother but not yet a wife,
In a pale plastic box he fought for his life.
And we prayed with our hearts he would still be on earth
As we travelled with haste to the place of his birth.
But his eyes were bright and we knew he would fight
And use all his endeavour to stay in the light.
And so we kept watch as day followed day
Until someone answered and said he could stay.

But now I must lose this child of my heart
Grown tall and strong though so weak at the start
He entered this world with unbridled haste
With energy he thrives and no time to waste
And wherever he goes as he happily passes
They smile at the boy in electric green glasses
As fate has decreed that we must be apart
I will carry this image locked deep in my heart
And though we will see him whenever we can,
The moments are precious from boyhood to man.

Patricia Andrew

Nowhere Left To Run...

Well there's no use trying to explain to me
The things that I already know
Because I know that soon we'll be going there
To a place I don't want to go
Well there ain't no sun a-shining, only dark black sky
Only children whining but no one hears their cry
   The sky is dull, the clouds are full
   And the rain it starts to pour
   But I ain't gonna run for shelter
   Because there ain't no use me running anymore

Well there ain't no use living when there's nowhere left to live
And there ain't no use giving when there's nothing left to give
Should I just sit back and watch my life drift by
Or hide my eyes, fall on my knees and then begin to cry
Can you hear the wind a-howling and the thunder in the sky
The echoes throb inside my head then drift away and die
   The sky is dull, the clouds are full
   And the rain it starts to pour
   But I ain't gonna run for shelter
   Because there's nowhere left to run to anymore.

Sean Robinson

Chip Off The Old Block

She's as old as the hills people say,
the things she does in her funny ways,
she can be wicked at times — especially at night,
tell her it's time for bed, well she goes light,
bed at seven, asleep by ten,
up the next morning and it all starts again.
She twists and she winges, she kicks and she screams,
I know that sounds awful but it's not as bad as it seems,
she can be quite a sweetie in her own little way
but I still look forward to the end of the day.
Apparently it's God's way of paying me back
because when I was young, sleep I did lack,
I would stay up all night cutting things out,
until 2 a.m. when my big sister would shout.
I was a horrible kid, now need I say more
but I've now got a daughter who I simply adore...
Tina Ramshaw

My Distant Love

This week my love, is slowly passing by
   The tears of sadness forming with in my eyes.
I wonder what you are doing my love and
   Hope your thoughts are at me, so far away.
For, I miss the sparkle of your eyes
   And that warm and caring smile.
Your manly scent, I yearn to smell —
   It's so sweet yet savage and wild.
But most of all my love, I miss your tender touch.
   The warmth of your hands, the heat of your lust.
My heart aches more and more --
   As the days go on and on.
It awaits you home-coming and the cuddle,
   That shall release my tears of sadness.
And turn them into tears of happiness.
Stephanie Bones

Emotional Compassion

O God my love I pray for you,
The tears and heartache you suffer,
For on the day you see my face,
Your heart will begin to flutter,

The tears of joy, the tears of pain,
As the gate of freedom opens,
Then our lives together are filled again,
With happiness and laughter upon us,
And love and kisses forever.
Michael Bromley

Untitled

Carbolic soap, and the jingle jangle of keys on chains.
The swish of black veils, sweet smell after the rain.
Carbolic soap, and the rattle of rosary beads on chains.
The whiteness of wimples, the smell of incense remains
Embedded in my memory, as some faces are.
People, places, circumstances,
All seen from a far off hilltop
On a bright sunny day.
People and their faces, fading away.
True love, old love, no love at all.
Wash basin of plastic in the dormitory hall.
Prayers in the morning, noon, and night,
Candles and vestments shining, bright.
The big girls so proper, and cold as ice,
Try as they may, they couldn't be nice.
Carbolic soap, and the smell of fresh flowers in the chapel.
The silence of the red stone hallways broken only by the
   sound of a bell.
A monotonous clang, resounding over again.
Calling us to our prayers and saying,
Only nine years old, and already grown.
Melvina Mary Thompson

Life's Dream

Billowing clouds like white fluffy powder puffs
The sun's rays trying to break through
Buds of trees and bushes coming into leaf
And plants and flowers of every hue
Nesting birds emitting various calls
Frolicking lambs beyond dry stone walls.

Away the noise and dirt of nearby towns
Away the crime and violence of the world
Begone all the hatred and greed of man
And let a perfect peace be unfurled
Each living in harmony with their neighbour
Never letting our trust and common sense waver.

Life is short, oh so short
Never realized till too late, why waste it
Think of the goodness that could be done
Don't drown like others in an endless pit
Imagine a place of flowers and lambs
Walks in the country and no traffic jams.
M. E. Thompson

The Squirrel And The Acorn

One day as I was walking down a quiet country lane,
The sun went in behind a cloud and it began to rain,
I ran beneath a great oak tree with branches spreading wide,
And as I lent against its gnarled trunk this is what I spied,
Sitting on a bough with eyes inquisitive and bright
Was a bushy tailed squirrel, and I smiled in sheer delight,
For in his paws he held an acorn so big and golden brown,
Then to my dismay he darted away and dropped it on the ground,
I bent and picked that acorn up it really was a size,
And as the sun came out again I could feel those watchful eyes,
I took that golden acorn and planted it that day
At the bottom of my garden, where now I'm glad to say,
There grows a little oak tree, that someday may provide
Food and shelter for small creatures, and a squirrel's hide.
Margaret Harvey

Sunset Over The Lake

Peeping out behind the shadowy trees
The sun sets over the lake,
As the dark water reflects the orange light,
Which ripples in the breeze,
All that is above is seen below,
In this glorious reflection of the coming night
Streaks of pink and grey mingle with the golden hue,
and gently fade away.
The light almost gone, the lake is eerie,
Sounds of waterfowl screech out,
At last, all is silent except for the sound of the trees,
brushing about in the breeze,
And the gentle lapping of water.
Patricia Mary Knight

Love Is A Journey

Each star in the heavens was given its place,
Thoughts by design from a higher grace
With the seeds of love were dispersed through the ages,
To be reaped on a plain, with a pale moon and pledges.

The road I chose, there was but two,
Was also the one chosen by you.
A journey began that was to encompass
Life's loves, seasons and expectations.

A love like this has been before,
Spoken of through history and told in folk-lore.
Do our slumbering recessive thoughts hold the key
To the answers I seek, why you? why me?

I've learned to master the measure of time,
The custodian's purpose to separate riddle from rhyme
What can two weary travellers hope to find
At the end of the road, a rainbow? or another mile?
Marlene Lynas

Springtime

I wake up in the morning,
The sun is shining bright,
I Look out of the window,
To a rare and wonderful sight.

The daffodils are swaying,
Gently in the breeze,
Blue bells forming circles,
Round the bottom of the trees.

The tulips standing straight and tall,
A colourful array,
I realize then that spring is here,
It's a lovely sunny day.

No more wintry snowstorms,
or winds blowing from the north
Only pleasant days ahead,
with sunshine bursting forth.

I look forward to the springtime,
The birds have flown the nest,
Everything has come to life,
Awakened from a winter rest.
Marie Barrett

Motorway Piste

Driving along on a cold winter's night
The sun has gone in and it isn't so bright

With deep snow around, car slipping and sliding
Makes me just wish that I wasn't driving

The skating vehicle now has its own mind
Others just starting have this yet to find

What a long journey, all stop and go
Making each going home, so tediously slow

Some thrashing their engines they slowly get stuck
I just keep going trusting to luck

Samaritans with spades digging us out
Pushing and shoving and sliding about

Muscles and mind all stressed and strained
Teeth grinding, drivers looking quite pained

Lumping and bumping mile after mile
I turn the last corner, then start to smile

The car slides to a standstill the journey is done
Let's hope by the morning the snow has all gone
Vera Harries

The Unexplained

The universe is a phenomenal mystery,
The stars fascinating chemically,
The planets orbiting gravitationally,
The earth and its intriguing geology.

The existence of life began simply,
Every age gained complexity,
The start of something extraordinary,
Evolved from sheer simplicity.

A life of great superiority,
That functioned purely psychologically,
Invented laws that were proved scientifically,
And included themselves in that category.

But the mind works supernaturally,
What we would consider paranormality,
Like psychic predictability,
Is what it does systematically.

The human mind is a phenomenal mystery,
Incredibly complex psychologically,
How can we limit its capability,
When we have yet to discover its full capacity?
Radmila Topalovic

Hands Of Friendship

In this world of ours today, life is sometimes tough.
The struggle for survival can be so very rough.
Traumatic daily problems, they just never cease,
Few things ease the worries, they just all increase.
On days like this switch off, and share
Your thoughts, with friends for whom you care.
Friendship for me is certainly
A thing to treasure, a special pleasure.
Nothing lasts forever, life slips quickly by,
As we tread life's weary road, no matter how we try
We just can't cope with all the loads, so backs will start to bend,
That's why it's so important to have a special friend,
One who will be always there, one who will be always fair,
One whom in the rain or shine, always makes things turn out fine.
Friends, like hands, have no doubt,
You just cannot do without.
Pauline Harmer

Night

Like precious jewels in a heavenly crown
the stars that are set on a navy blue gown,
the birds are all resting the world is asleep
the night is around us a glorious peace,
just a faint rustle now and again
a far off hoot from the owl can be heard
but most things are silent and all things
asleep even the tick tock of the clock
seems to cease, the moon starts to come
up a beautiful pearl, she rides over the
skies her beauty unfurled,
it finger of light starts to light up the sky,
then all of a sudden the night sky has died,
the dawn starts to break the sun comes
up too, another day dawning and everything
moves, the dark night has gone her
peace has gone too, another day starting
with every thing new.
D. McIntyre

The Combat

Parading round and round
The stags sum up one another.
Both are strong and both
Are anxious for superiority.
The younger, the challenger,
The elder, the champion of last time,
Pawing the ground and grunting; then silence.

Staring across the empty space,
Heads down and charge.
The clatter of antlers echoes through the forest
Like a wooden sword fight.
The challenger determined not to be beaten.
The champion not yet ready for defeat.

Both are getting weary but,
Only one will know that he's weaker, and retreat.
The battle over; the unbeaten champion
Reigns for another year.
The challenger staggers away to
Await the time when he will be stronger,
And superior.
Annette Jarvis

A Sight To See

Cars are parked along the frosted streets
The pavements glowing with the footprints of feet
Condensation forming on the faces of glass
People staring around as they pass

The tide is low with its sunken boats
And seaweed entangled around dilapidated floats
The masts that are swaying as cold breezes blow
May soon be covered with the whiteness of snow

All that surrounds will soon disappear
But we'll remember it still as we saw it so clear.
Colette Alcobi

What A Change

The sun is fading
The sky is clear.
Out come the stars,
In numbers too numerous to count,
Flickering faint and bright
To cheer our hearts,
To say tomorrow will be another glorious day.
But alas, at dawn no clear sky,
Our hopes dashed with clouds.
We wait to see if we can anticipate
A day to gladden our hearts,
But a storm is looming
We wait inside — shutters closed
To keep us safe from the howling winds.
M. Goodliffe

A Coming Event

Springtime seems so far away
The skies are grey
We shiver and say
Perhaps tomorrow, we'll have a fine day.
The promise is there
If we stop and stare
Birds are singing in the trees
They are pairing, and preening
On lawns that need seeds
The snowdrops are showing
The crocus are growing
The tree buds are there
Just waiting for warm air.
The daffodils, beneath the soil
A golden harvest, waving in the breeze
A lovely sight for the eyes to see
Spring is not a fantasy
It is there for all of us to see
Count your blessings, one by one
Springtime is sure to come.
A. Stella Woods

" Another Day "

I hear the silence —
    the silence of the night before the dawn.
I hear the silence
    I hear the silence of a world asleep, and waiting to be born.
A gentle glow is creeping all around,
    and then a sound,
A sound of many sounds —
    a deep sigh.
Now I can see the outline of the sky, the distant hills,
    the first ray of the sun.
A solitary thrush sings her first notes
    on the clear air.
The lights that twinkled like the stars,
    have vanished one by one.
Silence has gone!
    Another day has begun.
Frances Hall

" Silent Darkness "

The sound of the birds in the early morn,
The rise of the sun at the beginning of dawn,
Are wonders of nature for most to behold,
As silvery mists from themselves unfold.

The birth of the day so new and so young,
When shimmering cobwebs from the branches are hung,
Sparkling like jewels in the light of the sun,
Only to fade when the day is done.

Yet sadly a thought is crossing my mind,
The loss of these pleasures by the deaf and the blind,
If only we all had the eyes that could see,
And ears that could hear the buzz of the bee.
J. P. Eldred

Lesliekins

My brother-in-law has been taken away.
The shock of that day will always stay.
So unsuspected, it's hard to bear.
It breaks my heart because I care.
So many questions as to why.
I cannot hide the tears I cry.
Anger, frustration and deep despair,
Why was he taken? Life's so unfair.
So full of hurt, the pain is strong
How to cope, to carry on,
Words of sorrow are never enough
For a special man who was loved so much.
Since I was four, he has always been there
Twenty-three years my sister and he did share
But for only twelve weeks she was his wife
Where is the reasoning, why take his life?
I will always miss Les not being here
I'll smile at his memories and shed a tear.
For he was a unique and very loved man
No one could match Leslie William German.
Trudy Carpenter

Experienced

I think that's it now — the storm has passed;
The sea is calm now, there's peace at last.
I hear the wind, no longer cold —
My future clear now and my past been sold.
What once was real is now behind me,
I hear laughter now and my eyes can see.
Seven plus ten and my mind is sharp,
I have vision, can see, and have offered my heart.
Life is new and fresh, but for my part,
I have learnt it hard and will not forget the pain
I've caused and the youth I've scarred...
E. H. Randall

Memories

A whiff of familiar after-shave
The scent of your favourite flowers
A stranger whistling 'our' special song
Stirs memories of times long gone

A clip on TV of an old fashioned dance
The sight of our son in look alike stance
A man in the street in a similar shirt
Makes my heart skip a beat and brings back the hurt

A John Wayne movie with horses and cattle
Sheep on a back road still narrow and metal
A late night repeat of the days big test
Our youth in the outback, the time we loved best.

Darling you'd just love our only grandson
He's handsome, he's fun, he's so like you
Kind folk keep saying, 'time eases the pain'
But honey I'd give anything to see you again.
Patricia Williams

" My Islands "

Today a cloud passed over, the rising sun of peace
The reign of peace had such a short lease.
The bomb blew and London was awake
The talks, the silent times were fake.
The I. R. A. our freedom, trust, does try to take
But love is strong for peace and quiet.
So go, you evil men and may your soul remain in hell a light.
No need to murder, damage, maim;
For God's sake let peace remain.
People need to live and love and feel their Islands are secure
Not defiled by a dangerous few
What is to be gained, by inflicting such horror and pain?
Let all sides bend and messages only of peace be sent.
All may rest and know the best was done.
To beat the men who held the gun because it blurred God's sun.
Margaret Brogan

Thoughts Of Christmas

The flames are crackling warm in the hearth,
The punch is bubbling warm in the glass.
The snow is dropping cold on the path,
Oh I am so glad it's Christmas.
The days are long and cold and bleak,
But God has given us a treat,
Of holly green and berries red,
Icy ponds and Robin red
Oh I am so glad it's Christmas
Children sitting round the tree,
Singing christmas carols for you and me,
Little noses cold and red,
Now it's time to go to bed,
Oh I am so glad it's Christmas.
Nicoli Thompson

The True Britain

We saw the best of Britain
The pre-war working class
We had fun and frolics
   though we never had much "brass"
We could do our window shopping
At midnight if we cared
And we never saw a mugger
Not one even dared.
We set our clocks by buses
And trains too were precise
If those old days could but return how nice!
They think today is paradise
But those are just the fools
Whose main professions seem to be
To try to break the rules.
We ran the world in our day.
Now we cannot run ourselves
Because we seldom see our goods
Displayed upon the shelves.
Why ponder over reasons
When it only needs one guess
It's greed and 'I'm all right Jack'
That's got us in this mess.
F. Carter

And So It Came To Pass

"I wash my hands."
The powder-blue eyes pierced his pounding heart
Those awful eyes
In condemnation yet in compassion
For a coward
Who killed through irresponsibility
The Saver of man
Sent as a chance by a great Forgiver.
No more chances.

Through the jeering streets a brown beam he bore.
Lustful eyes laughed: His laughed back and they knew
Then it was too late to save their sad souls.
Iesus Nazarenus Rex Iudaeorum.

Little they knew, blind fools nailing that man.
Couldn't they see, mirrored in His pained face,
The love of their Creator — their last chance?
The mortal frame shuddered: with it died everyman.
Steve Sharp

Untitled

Bleak! Bleak!
The caw, caw, of the weather
As the trash lies matted and dead.

Not like a dead bird,
Not like the humus, half decayed, half frozen.
Half frozen hands reaching for soup cans.
But the opener is rusted, half rusted;
It cries caw, caw, piercing the tin,
But there's decay within,
Matted and dead.
Richard Byford

Peace Is Come!

It is well, peace is begun.
The peoples of the earth plain
Heed the words of logic — at this time.
Divine light envelops all peoples o'er the land.
Would that mankind could continue in harmony,
Man with man and all creatures of this world.

Wars bring sufferance to the children
The misery is for all to see, whosoever seeks knowledge.
Men of Ignorance see nothing, they feel not the pain of the afflicted.
Power causes claims to reverence, but they fool only themselves;
Their greed will overcome them and end their glory.
Supreme powers (from above) engulf the meek and mild
Strengthen spirits, heal pain when none else seem to care.

Blessed are they, the spirit of God protects all
Who turn to him in their anguish.
Peace be on this earth from this day forth!
Patricia E. Weir

The Clock of Life

Tick Tock. Tick. Tock.
The pendulum swings beneath the clock
With every swing and every sway
Ticking your very life away
The first third of your life is spent preparing and growing
For all the seeds that you will be sowing
The second third filled with lots to do
Work and fun and family too
Ups and downs, good times and bad.
Tears of laughter and tears when sad
Into the last third growing older
The swinging pendulum sounding louder
Swinging towards the last decade
As your speed and strength begin to fade
You and your partner side by side
Enter old age with a sense of pride
At what you have done to enrich the ride
Through time and trouble until you knock
On the last door before He stops the clock.
J. Hampton

Untitled

The world rode out to meet me in a dream
The patterns of the day were mixed with grey
The golden shafts of sunlight danced away
And life had nothing lovely left to deem.

I walked along the strand our usual way
Remembering the way our life had been
The edges of the waves were laced with cream
Now sadness laced the edges of the day.

I stopped and wrote your name upon the sand
The waves they came and washed the words away
I spoke but there was nothing left to say
I stopped and wrote his name upon the sand.
J. Munn

Despair

The pit of despair is very deep,
The path to the top is very steep,
We clutch at straws along the way
And hope to see a brighter day.
We take one step up and two steps back
And ask ourselves is it courage we lack,
But if we're lucky and reach the top,
Let's not forget that others are there,
Still in the pit of deep despair.
So lend a hand as they struggle on,
And give them courage to carry on,
For if we help a friend in need,
And try to sow a tiny seed,
And if you show them that you care,
You'll lift them out of this deep despair.
M. Thompson

Granny's Parlour

Stiffly folded into place
The parlour curtains edged with lace
Forbade a touch of this small hand
But oh the yearning, just to hang and swing
on silken cords that hold
These lofty sentries in their folds.

They frown at me beneath their fringe
Conspiring to make me cringe,
Their daunting presence overpowers the urge to shout
Or hurl the flowers
That dried and dusty, sit and stare at me,
Oh if I'd only dare.

M. A. Rogers

Love Is The Keeper

From the depths of my mind
The pain is entwined,
Like a thorn, torn deep in my side.

Blissful ignorance reigned supreme.
'Til startling awakeness destroyed the dream!
Glistening cobwebs once woven in stitch,
Hung, torn and tattered, no longer rich.

Confusion of thought is all that is left.
Within this deep, dark chasm of emptiness.
If there's one thing I've learnt about love
That is true,
It will never be kept,
But will be the keeper of you!

J. Prentice

Hallowe'en

I kick the leaves which whisper in the dark,
The owl above me screeches in despair;
A film of misty rain clings to the bark
Of bare-ribbed sycamores, and damps my hair.

The greying moon gropes through the hazy sky;
The road a dull grey beam into the night;
All Hallow's Eve the time for joy to die,
A dismal, weary way, without much light.

This last October's night I am forlorn.
Uncertain way ahead, a life behind —
A certain midnight comes — long gone the dawn;
The obscure dark blots out bright day in mind.

Along a garden path I turn, to where
The sounds of children's voices, mask-bedimmed
Lance out into the dark to conquer care
With dancing, sparkling lights illumined.

I kick the leaves which whisper in the dark,
But now they tell of spring, not autumn rain.
A footprint in the sun is childhood's mark —
I kick the leaves and am a child again.

Phillip Mallpress

Equanimity

The magistrate peered sternly at the poor wretch in the dock,
The only sound that could be heard was the
ticking of the clock,
Your learned counsel tells me you're a
man of diverse mood,
Sometimes very bad but quite often
very good,
Deciding on a sentence has greatly
stretched my wit,
It's not easy to be just to a
personality so split,
You're obviously two people but I am
duty bound,
I hereby sentence both of you to a
fine of fifty pounds.

Thom Broadbent

Love Lies

What is life to mean to me?
The only reason seen to be
is love I say;
but what? Such a notion lies.
It only proves to tear my dimming soul,
once so heightened, sinking low.
The days grow old, the tedium of my solemnity
clawing, not with anger, but with a void
so deep as to encase a thousand foes.
His hair so flaxen, once I could caress,
now only a memory, a turmoil to lay to rest.
This anger whirring in my womb,
a feeling now I can't consume.
But as I look upon a world that hates
me, in perspective naivety and I are
dainty and only shows the pettiness
and futility that is me, and only then
can the lonely see.

Verity Courtney-Thomas

Night-Fall

Soft, style, short along the way
The old cuckoo sang out his day
Willowed down the tree sagged heavy
Done the day and all was steady

Slumber now the saplings curl
Swift the sunset downing hurl
Yellow shades amongst the shadows
Night-time here in darkest gallows

Broad light beaming down — the dawn has riz
And sadness no more is 'the biz'
Drifting by the wafting swallow
Hidden deep in tree trunk hollow

Life alive — and all is well
Sing out loud and ring the bell
Song thrush turn and dance your tune
Night-time comes but all too soon.

Marion Langton

Zipolite   Mexico December 1995

Tribal rhythm, badly beaten by a western hand,
The ocean feeds
Foreign bodies lying naked in the burning sand.
The ocean sees
With waves of fury
Fearful play:
A multi-storied waterway,
Through rock and mountain guardians of retreating land,
The ocean weaves.

Soothing sun on salty-misted shore,
The ocean shares
A coat of lightest blue, lines shaded raw.
The ocean wears
Preying seabirds,
Leaping fish:
A silver-plated wilderness.
Who can conceive the power in nature's law
The ocean bears..?

J. B. Kluk (Currently teaching English in Colombia)

To A Wildcat

Wild, wilful, wandering;
The cold milk of the moon in your veins,
In your belly the fire of the sun.
Sharp as the claw of winter,
Fearless as spring,
Dappled by summer clouds,
Thistledown fall.
Wild through the centuries,
Hard as the boulders' shelter,
Molten with the vent of the earth;
Snarl then as you pass
Like the wind on grass.

E. J. Macdonald

Walking Memories

On a cold summer's day,
The north wind did blow,
I walked through the meadow,
That lay by the shore.
And I thought of the day,
That we both said goodbye,
And the wind blew the grass in the meadow.

So please, my love, don't forget
What I said to you,
I will be waiting for you to return.
The sun, it glowed in the sky
Just like my heart did burn...
And the wind blew the grass in the meadow.

Marie Carrons

Speech

There is nothing better than life! (They say who?)
The next best thing is love!
Or is it just a state of mind friendship is the key to love.
To check out the person who holds it.
To understand, to give, to receive

Or is it is just state of mind

Where and when does it begin
Will it end.... and begin again. Only to begin again

To know someone will you be someone
To know someone is to know yourself.
To know 'someone' is to be 'someone'
If you are someone will you be someone
If you are someone will someone want you.

I think life is a giant crossword puzzle
You're given a clue - find the answer
It could be a few things! how do you know?
If you find the answer does it help
Move to the next clue eventually fini
Are you satisfied or do you crave to do some more
Is it just a state of mind?

N. O. Watt

Camelot 1996

Where once were woods and magic lands
The newsagent in the Highstreet stands.
For Galahad the Grail — the mystic gleam,
Now the glittering Jackpot is the dream.
No striving now through stream and thicket,
Just queuing up to buy the ticket.
No dark enchantment bars the way,
Just the inability to pay.
No calls on Merlin, now he slumbers,
For tracing out the magic numbers
Ah, well this is a rational era,
But still each chases his chimaera.

S. P. Osley

Stripped Bare

There is a death
The news has spread fast
Even before the body is cold
The scavengers and vultures descend
Coming out of nowhere
Picking out tasty morsels
Helping themselves to what they want
Claiming what they think is due to them
Leaving nothing behind
They fight each other
And get what they deserve
They come in different shapes and sizes
Some on two legs
Others on four
The story is familiar
Human beings and animals are different
Or are they?

Michael Leonard

A Moving Story

Boxes piled high, filled to the brim
The moving man's coming; his face looks quite grim.
His back is aching from lifting each load
he'd be glad to be back in his lorry on the road
there's great excitement filling the air
are the neighbours saying "Look at that daft pair!"
with great energy and gusto everyone rushing about
they're going to their new house and taking nowt
'cept their belongings and ornaments that they treasure
and perhaps a flower or two just for good measure
The van's finally full and nothing is left
except the feeling, one of bereft
now comes the sad part they are leaving their nest
the last few years have put to the test
all their strengths put together behind hidden smiles
at last! A short journey of only a few miles
for memories anew to flood through the doors
maybe they should write it in its own clause
opening the new door and carrying her through
here's to the new home of 'Tony and Sue'.

S. J. Winter

Gethsemane

Gethsemane! You saw the Saviour weep!
The moonlight filtered through the olive trees;
He was alone; His friends had gone to sleep.
He turned away and fell upon His knees,
Praying again that this dread cup would pass
And laid His lovely head upon the grass.

He saw me then, laden with all my sin
And all its filth I flung on His pure soul;
And then he knew His Passion would begin.

He took it all; it was His Father's will
That He should bear my sins and on the morrow
Carry them all upon a road of sorrow
And nail them to a cross on Calvary

Yet, had He not been whipped and slapped and nailed,
I would one day have had to stand alone
Before the purity of God's great throne.
Justice, not Mercy, would have then prevailed,
And I, in sorrow shut away from Heaven.
But Jesus faced that dreadful hour for me
and took my burden in Gethsemane.

Mary Hunt

Mary's Waiting

There's a richness in waiting, but also great pain.
The long hours are graced with the saviour's reign.
We seldom can see beyond the cloud that's around,
That God's choicest blessings always abound.

In the life journey of Mary, we see waiting graced,
With a heavenly strength — her reality faced.
Troubled, bewildered, whatever the news,
The sure presence of God shaped all her views.

With her tribe in Juda she awaited in prayer
For the coming Messiah, their burden to share,
In that mystery was hidden the when, where and how.
Did she ever dream, that the coming was now?

This holy waiting was the pattern of her life,
Pregnant with God's love, for nine months a silent wife;
Powerless her spouse's anxiety to relieve,
Awesome in expectation her Messiah Son to receive,

Her commitment was firm, the outcome concealed.
How long would be the waiting, 'till His secret be revealed?
She prayed in the darkness awaiting the mystery to be told;
The depth of its meaning has still to unfold.

Sister M. Catherine Quane

Ode To The Innocent

From Death, there came a promise from
the men who held
their heads in shame's mask
We shall give way,
their leaders say,
give our demands is all we ask.
A simple land for simple folk,
not guns and bombs and murders provoke.
But see, we can entice to come,
for peace in Jesus, find you some.
For Kin folk from Emerald Isle,
kill innocence,
burn Children's smiles.
Political views of Sympathize,
could never match a baby's eyes.

P. A. Hutt

Untitled

My name is Ken, I'm the Wheelie Bin King,
The man in charge of this magnificent thing,
It stands in the garden serene and so bright,
To get it emptied, me you must fight,
7.30 am on the Kerb it must stand,
Above sea level and on firm land,
"Can't take it," I'll say if the lid is up,
I don't want to see all your household muck,
If it's too heavy there it must stay,
I won't be taking that bin today,
Complain to the Council? You'll get no joy,
'Cos I'm their informer, number one boy,
I've been on the mobile reported in,
Told them the story about your bin,
You'll not catch me out I'm right on the ball.
I'm the Wheelie Bin King and I'll give it my all.

Marylynn Bolwell

Spring

Who can describe the coming of spring?
The magic we see on earth's awakening.
First come the snowdrops, their green spears erect
Then crocus and primrose, the shy violet.

The daffodils form a carpet of gold
We forget dull winter — the frost, snow and cold,
The countryside becomes green and lush
With new buds appearing on tree and bush.

New lambs are frolicking in the fields
The birds are building their nests
Of all the seasons of the year
Surely this is the best.

New life surrounds us — new hope for the future
We could learn a lot from old Mother Nature
Things that appear dead — lie dormant for ages
Can often awaken — then blossom and flourish.

Jean Kelly

Eternity

Eternity: the endless future of everything we know.
The long 'forever' where past, present, all
   tomorrows spin away
Where thoughts and words and feelings
   must inevitably go.

Where all we've ever done, for better or for worse
Goes on and on, like smaller fading echoes.
And kindness, harshness, love and hate all mingle
Where music goes when human ears hear it no more.

There, riches have no value
And people feel no pain
Eternity, as vast as space, forever and forever
Eternity, where only God shall go.

Wyn Long

The Joys Of Spring

We scrambled down the hillside, with
the lush green grass springy below
our feet. The sun shone down on
the two of us, reflecting the blondness of
our hair. We walked into the village,
hearing shouts of laughter. Birds
twittered in the trees, singing
the joys of spring. Cheerful
greetings came our way, from the
friendly villagers. Children happily
played in the street, laughing
and shrieking in delight.

How wonderful that scene appeared
to us, after the bleakness of the
winter months. Spring was a much
brighter time, but summer was
yet to come.

Martine Lara Daniel

Clovelly

Clovelly on a Summer's day I shall remember
The little harbour nestling on the strand
With tiny houses clinging to the cliff-face
The battered coast — the sea — the sand.

The white beached row-boats lying on the pebbles
Receding tide beside the granite wall
Buttressed by tree-logs that once graced the forest
Above the shore-line standing green and tall.

A place of peace where time has slowed its passing
From our mad worldly rush of mortal greed
Giving us time to sit and gaze in wonder
Brief relaxation — from our urgent need.

Until we climb again the ancient High Street
That travesty of road — that cobbled lane —
On which we slip and struggle to the car park
Knowing that we shall try and come again.

L. T. Coleman

War

Eyes stricken with terror,
the little boy waits listening in the little shelter
he's grown so well to know.
All around the earth shakes,
as bombs drop from high above down on his
little world he once loved.
From beneath in the shelter, the little boy
asks the same puzzling question he's asked
many times before.
How long will it last?
Screams of terror echo all around,
as houses are crushed to rubble
or burnt to cinders leaving only the remains
of dead bodies amongst the debris.
But still the little boy asks from below
in the shelter,
How long will it last?

Stephanie Burns

Storm

On a cold, dark, stormy night,
There was a ... CRASH! of light.
CRASH! BANG! Lightning struck the town,
And the rain came pelting down.

My face began to sting,
And the church bells began to ring.
I wished my head was on my pillow,
As the leaves fell off the willow.

The wind was blowing,
And it was even snowing.
The lightning CRASHED!
And the thunder BASHED!

Rachel A. Hampton, age 10

'Til The Next Show Lifts Its Veil

Ha ha! (ha ha!). He he! (he he!). Look look! The clown is here!
The laughing fellow beams with glee and loves it when we cheer.
(See him stumble. Hear the drum rumble.
Why so silent now? O dear!)

But now you see he's up again, with bright red curly hair.
His great big, whacking, floppy shoes look far too big to wear.
(Give three cheers now! Wipe a tear now!
Help! he's fallen down the stair.)

Yes yes! He's up! He's up and glad! So glad he isn't hurt.
His gorgeous, laughing face peers out. But watch! He's going to squirt.
(Oh disaster! "Run, run faster!"
Now he's wet his own blue shirt.)

Ha ha! (ha ha!). He he! (he he!). The laughter fades away.
We're happy now. The clown we hope will play another day.
(He has cheered us, kindly steered us,
Brightened up our dreary day.)

But poor old clown, alone and sad, is really very frail.
No children are close by to help. They do not know his tale.
(Sadly grieving, no relieving,
'Til the next show lifts its veil.)

Marjorie E. Norton

The Older Woman's Prayer

Oh dear Lord, you who makes the blind to see,
  The lame to walk, the deaf to hear;
You can also raise the dead, and take away our fear.
  Can you with infinity, look upon me — with pity?

Please bless my organs of reproduction!
  Endow me with life anew —
Please, oh please complete my seduction,
  And allow me a baby or two.

Please refurbish my tubes and womb, and my ovaries,
  And revitalize my aching breast,
And see clear to bless me!
  I'm sure we could do the rest.

Oh dear Lord, I've hesitated to ask this of you,
  As I've been taught "others first, and self last,"
And I agree with this point of view.
  I've always been mindful of this in the past.
(But it's not for me — 'tis for he) —
  That now dear Lord I beseech you!!

Please, dear Lord... glove this darling man.
  You know I'm sure — that I'm his loving lady!
Oh please, oh please — let it be in Your plan,
  To allow us our own darling baby.
          AMEN.

D. M. Phillips

Big Brother

Airdrie had video cameras installed.
The police were more easily called.
The barmen were 'bugged' — their customers were mugged.
The 'neds' were unaware of
  BIG BROTHER.

It was decided to extend the new test.
Glasgow was chosen for V.H.S.
The experiment proved to be a success.
If you're a mugger or a thief
do not be up to mischief.
As the waiting, watching,
whirring eyes are secretly recording.
  BIG BROTHER

Orwell's 1984 was correct.
Watched at a protest march — organized fete.
Breach of civil liberties? You bet.
Their eyes are fixed like glue.
Just who is watching you?
  BIG BROTHER

Thomas Carroll

Togetherness And Love

Love is doing things together and being together
The knowing you are the love I have searched for
Having you by my side in good and bad times
Just being there for me
To share each others experiences
Together watching our children grow into adulthood
Love and togetherness most of all is always
Being there for each other

S. Muxlow

The Poppy Fields

Imbued with dreams of Germanic might,
the Kaiser cast his ghastly dice.
A swift manoeuvre of massive force
soon became a European holocaust.
That blighted wasteland of the Flanders fields,
such futile slaughter, yet none would yield.
Bewildered generals dressed in their colours and plumes
spent a generation of lives from aloof map rooms.
Through potholes, craters and tangled barbed wire,
they sent wave after wave over that deadly mire.
Attacks were thwarted as masses fell in vain,
still those stubborn old men tried again and again.
As stalemate prolonged, both continued the fight,
men filled with awe and the air with cordite.
For those comrades in arms who dwelled in a trench
there was lice-ridden, rat-infested decaying stench.
Generations have passed and the soldiers have gone,
but history will tell of Verdun and Somme.
The blood has dried up and the wounds have now healed
but mankind must remember, always — the poppy fields.

Stuart Jackson

Together As One

Making love,
  The interlocking of two souls
As bodies become entwined,
  In a feverish pitch of desire,

The dominance of man,
  Sharing his need with his submissive female,
Slaves of passion,
  To their wanting

Together they explore
  The unfathomable depths of ecstasy,
As two souls become flooded
  By drowning waves of love.

Paul Warwick

Alter Boys

In silence we walk
The Incense smells sweet,
People in Pews
Eyes at their feet,
Father in front Prayer Book in hand
At the Alter he stops, by his side we stand
Blessings are passed, Congregation reply
A signal is passed by the flick of an eye,
To the Pews we float
The Organ sounds grand
In unison we sing Hymn Book in hand
More Blessings are passed and Hymns abound
The congregation transfixed by the beautiful sound
Down from the Pulpit Father descends
From Pews we glide - the Service it ends,
Back down the aisle in silence serene
watched by OUR LADY - THE HEAVENLY QUEEN
In years to come I'll remember with pride
The years I served the LORD by Fathers side.

Thomas Edwin Clarke

A Whisper Of Love

Never again will life be the same,
the hurt the realization and solitary pain,
And as sleep evades me deep into the night,
Your sweet name I keep calling but no answer to my plight.

For the heartache and sorrow was never meant to be,
As you were taken so cruelly from me,
I long to hear you speak my name,
Or to say daddy first would be the same.

No sleepless nights or teething problems,
And children dreams with ghosties and goblins.

For God keeps you now in his warm embrace,
And I keep the memory of your dear little face,
So sweet dreams my baby until we meet again,
For ours is a bond that we need not explain.
Sharon Goldsmith

Elephants

In life we are faced with many 'elephants',
The huge, dull grey barriers that every so often trample you down,
Problems herded up in your head and
Thudding thoughts that make your heart ache

But like everything in the world that has its own special place,
The 'elephants' of life must be experienced
So that the brighter, better things can be fully appreciated,
Then one day, the herd will pass over and the thudding will dull,
and it will be a long time before you're trampled down again

So even though the huge grey 'elephants'
in your life may sometimes seem overwhelming,
Put them down to an experience —
A page in a chapter of a very long book that hasn't yet
been fully written,
and remember only you are the author.
Miranda Hodder

Hello My Darling

He walks in the house and drops his coat,
the "hello my darling" is a crying joke.
There is no love in this house that can consist,
just a shameful routine that can't be fixed.

She is the cook, the mother, the maid,
he is the provider, the foundation that was laid.
He chased and romanced his princess bride,
he then used her, destroyed her and slowly she died.

She was once a beauty, an elegant queen,
a confident lady with a handful of dreams.
Now she complies to her husband's demands,
so unsure with shaking hands.

She cries at night, slowly she tries,
shaking the bottle with the poison inside.
Her mouth slightly open waiting to be filled
She slowly dies with the memories that killed.
Sara Mitchell

Time To Share

May we all have time to share
the happiness and friendships that
surround us everywhere.
Time to help each other, as we go along
life's way, and stop to give the busker a
coin from your pay.
Time for making children happy and helping
them to share, so to grow up with a kindness,
knowing that they really care.
Share the joy of Christmas with everyone
around, no matter where we all may be,
we'll share the chocolates on the tree,
sharing troubles, sharing fun
making people happy is how we
must live on.
Margaret H. Marshall

Death

Death portrays a figure clothed entirely in black
The grim reaper of an ending we each do not lack

Death is the mourning of one passed on
And is the lonely silence that lingers so long

Death can be frightening, sudden and quick
But to those who suffer this road they may pick

Death is the pathway from this world to our fates
This belief many keep faith with, in reaching heaven's gates

Death is relief from a body tired, old and worn
It is the be all and end all of each human born

Death of a life to some, is not the final end
But the release of the spirit, for which God does send

"Do not waste the time you have", death is a reminder to us all
As the years pass by quickly — like seasons change and fall

In time before you realise, the one life that you were given
The reaper takes away the life that you have liven.
Maria Patricia Nash

The Precious Gift

'Twas at the age of twenty-three,
The gift of love was sent to me,
This precious gift in tiny form,
To me a darling son was born.

At three days old he nearly died,
It broke my heart, I cried and cried.
I hoped and prayed that he should live,
That God would spare my precious gift.

My prayers were heard and so he grew,
But didn't do as others do,
At ten months old, my little chap
I was told was handicapped.

What lay ahead? God only knew,
How would I cope, what would I do?
The years they passed, he's now a man,
Run nor walk, no he can't.

He's never said, "I love you mum"
But brought me joy and so much fun.
My special gift made with love,
Was surely sent from heaven above.
Margaret Gale

Cathedral Woods

Frosted snow encrusted, bending low,
The laced branch and weighted bough.
Blue canopied heaven stretching above
This is my cathedral that I love.

Crisp the white carpet o'er which I pass.
Gleaming pure the aisle of snow.
Bird song fills the air above,
In this cathedral that I love.

The snow has gone and spring has come
Now the canopy has changed to green.
Star spangled grass with flowers shine
In this woodland cathedral of mine.

Birds build their nests in leafy fold
Of oak, ash, sycamore and beech.
Sturdy trunks in stately line
In this great cathedral of mine.

Autumn's glow of sun-beamed arch.
Full thronged the path with fallen leaves
Gold, red and rich the carpeted way
That to my cathedral leads me every day.
Mary Dale Hellawell

The Choice

I had a dream last night, and in that dream
The golden days of youth returned once more.
Things long-forgotten flashed upon the screen
Of memory, and I could see before
The vision changed the faces of old friends.
How gloriously we viewed the future then!
What dreams of paradise that never ends
When we had set the world to rights again!
The flame of our ambition quickly died
From lack of kindling. Though we still believed
Life's little pleasures tempted us aside.
We made the choice, but what have we achieved?
And time remains the constant enemy
Unyielding, in man's efforts to be free.
Patricia Anne Woodhouse

Words

Words so small and yet so powerful.
The first words of a baby — what pleasure they bring.
The last words of a dying person — the remembrance of everything.
Words can influence the young and the old — the three
  little words "I love you", what a magical
  command over people they can hold.
Words can give comfort, happiness, laughter and joy,
  but sometimes they cause tears and long lasting fears.
Words of the clever lawyer can make white look black
  and black look white in his endeavour to get
  things right.
Words printed in large type or small, so necessary for
  communication, do not always bring elation.
Politicians may bawl, but as no one is perfect, they
  should guard against their own downfall.
So choose your words with care, my friend, because
  their influence for good or bad, can have no end.
Hilda Care

" I Am The Bright And Morning Star "

As Day's last rosy glow dies in the West,
The first pale star gleams on the cloak of Night.
While slow hours pass, the quiet sky is blessed
With galaxies of soft ephemeral light.
Through endless years these teeming galaxies
Have guided traveller, shown Truth to Sage;
To questing dreamer have brought ecstasies;
And never-dying faith to every age.
But as the Night stars fade, the loneliest
And last shines forth — the glorious Morning Star.
In pearly Dawn it reigns — the loveliest
Translucent herald of the day — by far
The rarest jewel in the diadem
Of Him who leads us to our Bethlehem.
Marjorie E. Rayment

The Finality Of Death

He is dead, he is dead,
The final state beyond recall.
Could not I just once more,
Please hear his foot-steps in the hall?

Once more to hear him say,
"Chop, chop, I'm home again my dear",
And while he drank his soup,
His endless stories I would hear.

Once more to hear his voice,
To see again his kindly face.
Just one more time, please, please,
To snuggle in his warm embrace.

Once more to see his smile,
But it can never, ever be.
I could live forever,
But nevermore could I see thee.
C. M. McLean

The Best Things In Life Are Free

The best things in life are free,
The first catkins to appear on the willow tree
Our winter robin singing high on the bough,
Summer has gone — it's winter now.
We've had our first fall of snow,
The traffic on the roads was go, stop, go.
As usual chaos reigned — once again,
As heavy snow fell when it should have been rain.
All our calves and bullocks eat more each day,
Straw, silage, cake and some sweet-smelling hay.
It's lovely in the barn when all have been fed,
And the floor littered up to make a nice bed.
It costs us nothing to be friends and talk,
It costs us nothing to go for a walk.
To see the birds soaring high above
Reminds us of the freedom which we all love.
Christmas can be a simple time.
Jesus came to earth to give us a sign,
He came here simply, no fuss and pageantry,
But born quietly in a stable for all to see.
Susan Jury

Seasons

The year is divided into seasons of four
The first being spring which I truly adore
It is the sign of new life all over the land.
Plants and bulbs start to grow and require gentle hands
To clear away debris of the winter past and encourage
  new life after a period of fast.
Then along comes summer all of a sudden and
  the warmth of the sun makes the heart gladden.
To see gardens ablaze with such wonderful colours
  and trees bearing fruit to eat at our pleasure
Autumn arrives at a leisurely pace
Toning down colours to softer shades
The reds, orange and brown try their best not to go
But something tells them to make way for snow
Winter soon comes round huffing and puffing
Making lives miserable and causing long suffering
He casts his spells of frost wind and rain
Turning snow into ice which brings lots of pain
At last he is tired and the snow starts to thaw
Making future refreshment to keep in store
For the time coming soon will make our hearts sing
  yes you guessed the return of spring
Mollie Crawshaw

Rambling

As I walk over hills and dale,
The fields stretch out, like a green vale,
A rabbit there, sits up to stare,
Its nose a-twitching in the air
Paws go up to wipe his face,
He sees me, and scurries off at a hurried pace.

The birds chattering and singing in the trees,
Mild perfume of flowers on the summer breeze,
There on high a skylark sings,
The beauty of a butterfly's wings

It never ceases to enthral,
The wonder of it all,
It fills me with such delight,
To see a sparrow hawk in flight,

Rippling of a hillside stream,
The sparkle of the sunlight's beam.
All these things colourful and bright,
How I thank God for my sight.
Rita Spooner

Waiting For Mother

The strain I fought, the energy zapped,
The feelings felt, the emotions tapped,
The fears, the worry, the sleep I lost,
The days, the nights, the hours it cost,
The courage it took, the strength I needed,
The looking, the crying, the people I pleaded,
The praying, the wishing, the nurses I sought,
The questions, the answers, the feelings i fought,
The times I laughed, the times I wept,
The visions I saw, the company kept,
The things that I did, the lights which were lit,
The eyes that were sore, the lips that were bit,
The pain, the hurt, the power, the glory,
The relief I felt at the end of the story,
The father, the son, the sister and brother,
These things I felt while I waited for...
MOTHER...

If I had just one wish, then that wish would be,
For mother to wake and change places with me.
Phillip S. Clarke

War

All in the shelter safe and sound
the family crouch deep under the ground
far from the bombs and guns and noise
far from the lines where the soldiers poised.

The dead lay on the fields in the morning sun
the young boys only armed with a knife and a gun
the houses were all trashed and burnt
children full of violence for that's all they have learnt.

The funerals each week a young boy each time
the tears that were cried, families just like mine
losing young lives there's no justice at all
pointless deaths each day even more.

When the war finally ended when it came to an end
the lives pieced together, so much left to mend
the memories still there stuck in people's minds
for the boys who fought so much, together on the lines

The ones who survived brave all the way through
left with the nightmares but glad feelings too
the friends they made the friends they lost
but in a war, simple lives don't have a cost.
Nicola Lampard

The Broken Peace

The bombs blasted, the bullets whistled,
The dead were buried, the people bristled,
Twenty five long years we lived in fear,
We marched, we prayed, was there no one to hear.

Hope remained as our only light,
It was often dashed on the rocks of despair,
One man ignored many a slight
He pursued the path of peace without care.

The sides dug in as ever before
Each blinded by the myths of folklore,
He spoke with his enemies with calm persistence
And slowly broke down their fearful resistance.

The semtex was silent, the bullets stopped flying
No more the women and children were crying,
The peace that needed such nurturing and trust
After seventeen months of preconditions, now lay in dust.

Are we to wait for three thousand more to go to the grave
O, where are the unionist and nationalist so brave,
To walk the short distance in open embrace
Both to live on the island with peace and good grace.
Patrick Tierney

Untitled

Beauty is in the eye of the beholder.
The eyes in the mirror see me getting older.
Betrayed by my body fast losing a face.
The me that I was can feel the disgrace.
Too tired to feel different, too weary to care.
It's hard to see past the deep lines of despair.
I'm living in a body I can't stand to see.
My reflection an image I don't want it to be.
Insecure awareness was there at the start.
Jokes and unkindness shot through the heart.
Childshapes in form don't look right with age.
Needing to be different only fuelled up the rage.
Repulsion brought tears I thought wouldn't dry.
But then into limbo where pains never cry.
The festering scars thrive somewhere so deep.
That only new wounds cause poison to seep.
How do you mend damage with no sense of pride.
I can't run from myself, I've got no-where to hide.
Ruth

The Lost Reality

Waves tumbling together on cold and stormy nights,
The ember perpetually shining like a star,
Harmonious is the moment,
that smells so aromatic.

Enchanted looking into space,
Hear the music,
I've lost the pace,
Deserted wandering in a foreign place.

Gazing at the smashed reflection,
Water running through my hands,
Burning fires growing,
Destroyed.
Shireen Kasraie

The Guardians

Hush now hush now hush....

Settle yourselves, calm your souls
The earth is ours, it was foretold
In future eons we shall be
Almighty majesty on land and sea.
No more the poisonous minions play
Ravaging the earth, bringing decay
In the mists of despair, a place of peace
The land is weary it needs release.
All will be well, all will be light
The sunny days, the moonlit night.
The grass, the trees will rise anew
Resplendent in their green garbed hue.
We shall bide our time, we will survive
Long have we waited, it will arrive
Freedom from the burden we bear
Our hearts are strong, little they care
It will come to pass, have no fear
Salvation for all we hold dear.....
Sylvia Rose

Peace At Long Last

There's peace here at long last
The guns have stopped and the bombs don't blast.

But how long must we wait
Until the politicians get rid of their hate.

For twenty five years we've been at war
I'm glad to see the end of gore.

So many men, women and children have died
But we must never forget how we cried.

I'll thank God each day we're at peace
And always remember the poor man in the street.

We need all the people to get together and vow
To make our dear country a better place *now*.
Mary Gordon

The Crocus And The Snowdrop

December we were buried alive, with one burning ambition to survive.
The earth is dark I cannot see, hold my hand, stay close to me.
We will patiently await the glow of light, until then stay
   close - good night.

January our heads are green, but hardly recognized or seen.
Oh no, open up your eyes the gardener's coming use your disguise.
Will we be seen amongst the weeds and grass? Just keep
   quiet and hope he'll pass.

February we are so alive, and pleased to show we did survive
Our colours a brilliant yellow and white, acknowledged by all
   as a beautiful sight.

March brought along rain and wind. Did we deserve this, had
   we sinned?
Weary after being battered about, a rest was needed without a doubt.
Desirous of protecting our drooping heads we retired exhausted
   to our comfortable beds.
   M. Lineham

Crete

I came to Crete late in the year,
The days were warm, the skies were clear-
The seas were a calm and wondrous blue,
Michalis came by saying 'How do you do?'

I came to Crete late in the year,
I walked through the mountain villages here-
The potter's wheel spun, with a lazy sound,
Michalis was there when I turned around.

I flew from Crete late in the year,
Trying to hide an errant tear-
As I took my leave of sun and sand,
Michalis appeared and shook my hand.

Now in Crete it's spring again,
The mountains are washed with snow and rain-
Flowers abound in every hue,
Oh! Michalis, I dream of you.

I came to Crete late in the year,
Wistful, wondering, full of fear-
I flew like a bird to sun and sand,
Michalis appeared, and held my hand.
   Marion John

The British

This country of ours, this fair Isle
Has taken some knocks in these years
For wars in their fury have taken their toll
And brought worry, doubts and fears.

Once ours was greatness, supreme and sublime
We ruled the water, the earth, the sky
Now we have slipped from the position we held
Now our name is mud you cannot deny.

Out there abroad our soldiers few
Stand guard at troubled spots
They are spat on, sneered at, sniped on too
Blamed for others' failures, that's all the thanks they got.

In this Isle too there's been a call
For home rule so they say
To split this fair land into four
Though there has been no affray.

So if you're challenged, here or abroad
Don't be shy, belligerent or uppish
Just stand upright, look them straight in the eye
And with dignity say I'm British.
   Doreen Mooney

Hands Of Time

The years seemed just like days
The days as minutes past
Like the hands upon a clock
Our life together seemed to go so fast

Did we do all those things?
Have our children, see them grown
All the years went sweeping by
And suddenly I'm left alone.

I can't believe it went so quickly
Only yesterday I was a bride
Now I awaken every morning
Without you darling by my side.

When my end comes, will you be there
Waiting as I am for you.
Lead me to a new beginning
To start again in pastures new
   Veronica Barnett

Winter Thoughts

Riding through the valley at the dawning of a winter day
The dark-cast mountains far away look cold, forbidding, bleak today
It seems like an eternity 'til spring again will come to me
New life, new growth, so much to see, as I go on my way
I picture summer in my mind, with warmth, light, laughter deep
   entwined
But I've left summer far behind, and I scowl as I go on my way
Today, snow lies on the ground, stifling colour, dampening sound
Makes stark the landscape all around, as I shiver on my way
Oh, that I could simply sleep, pass these cold months in
   slumber deep
Beneath thick furs, a cosy heap, until the next warm day
A small, dry cave, beneath a hill, within, without, all quiet, still
No need to face this awful chill, I'd sleep the winter away
And dream of warmest autumn gold, of Nature's treasures,
   rich and bold
Maturing as the world grows old, and I drift on my way
For I know winter doesn't last, this cold will one day be the past
My spirit then won't be downcast, and I'll smile as I go on my way
   Patrick Corcoran

An Element Of Emotion

The orange-pink skies,
The clear blue crystal of the sea,
Soft as a feather, warm as the sun,
Joyful as a harmony of a favourite song,
Free as a bird, as high as a cloud,
As beautiful as a sunset, peaceful as the dove,
A rainbow of colours, from black to white,
A rose amongst many thorns.

Yet, a thorn itself,
As bitter as the cold, cruel as the wind,
The stormy skies,
The crashing of the sea against rocks,
A stab in the heart,
Sharp as a knife, as ruthless as war,
As wicked as the death of a close someone,
Sad as a prisoner, lonely as a tear,
Love.
   Tina Brennan

Facade Of The Bourgeoisie

An infinity of street lamps twinkled and glittered,
grinning like idiots from every hilltop, every valley,
and every leafy suburb.
The barricade of chintz curtains and paper doilies
Kept hidden from prying eyes the mounting terror within,
the empty brick shells where perversity, despair
and depravity reigned,
eating away like consumption at the will to live,
corroding away the structure like a burning acid.
Unperturbed, the lights shone on.
   Elizabeth Wren

A Touch Of Nostalgia

What has happened to God's beautiful world?
The carefree world we knew,
Where we could walk about in peace,
And people were good and true.

The country lanes we used to stroll,
The fields where we could play,
The wild flowers and the hedgerows,
And the smell of new mown hay.

We did not crave for money,
Nature was our delight,
No door was ever closed to us,
And the future looked so bright.

But now we dare not venture far,
Our lives are ruled by fear,
Behind locked doors we have to stay,
And life gets very drear.

Today it is all technology,
And hard to understand,
Oh why has our beautiful country
Got so completely out of hand?
C. Whyles

I Remember

I remember sunlight on my face,
the burning amber warming up my heart.
I remember cooling waves around my feet,
deep and reassuring but giving me a start.

I remember feeling frost at winter,
and seeing snow, crested on the trees,
like icing on the cake upon my birthday,
sweetest smelling fondant which would please.

I remember gazing to the stars,
looking for my brother in the moon,
climbing trees and singing with the birds,
staying there and waiting till high noon.

So let the angels take him by the hand,
and lead him to a better, peaceful place,
where he can walk along the shore of life,
and feel the waves of heaven at his grace.
Myfanwy Ann Cope

Be Like Them

The brave soldiers are there,
The brave heroes are already fighting,
Every day they wake up, they realize
They may face their death today.
Don't you want to be like them?

When they meet their friends,
They are able to boast about how
They helped to save the country
In its time of need,
Don't you want to be like them?

When their children say to them,
How brave were you in the war?
How many people's live did you save?
And he can reply with pride,
Don't you want to be like them?

When they come home from the war,
The greetings they will get.
Their wives giving them a warm welcome,
Being treated like heroes
Now it's too late to be like that.
Philippa Green

The Documentary Said Nothing
(About The Bosnian War)

Minarets in pieces, buildings smashed to smithereens,
The boy was killed instantly, he's only in his teens,
We've tried to understand, tried to understand this war,
The documentary said nothing, I still don't know the score

The knot was tied so tightly, the sin locked within
The dead, they lay in bundles, beside their next of kin,
Can you smell the stench of sorrow? Can you really see their tears?
Did we know in our complacency this was brewing up for years?

From the suburban living room we've seen the blood, the rape, the grief,
But the truth about the Balkans is beyond our belief,
Have we tried, tried to understand this war?
The documentary said nothing, we still don't know the score.
Sandra Wells

The Flute Player

The sun was shining brightly,
The birds sang oh so sweet,
I rested my head on the window sill,
And listened from my window seat.

I heard the children playing,
They laughed and ran around,
Then all at once I heard the flute,
It was a lovely sound.

I remembered when I used to play,
I always loved my music,
And when my sight was getting worse,
I hoped I wouldn't lose it.

Now all the things I hear and touch,
I picture in my mind,
The flute I loved I cannot play,
Because I now am blind.
A. J. Monger

Satisfaction

Rising early, refreshed from sleep
The birds in the trees their dawn song keep,
With the sun just rising over the hill
Of the morning air, I take my fill.
A scent of applewood, burning near
As coffee and bacon help to cheer
The dew on the grass, sparkling bright
With fruit trees laden, a glorious sight
Mushrooms nestling in dew-drenched grass
Awaiting an eager gourmet to pass.
The boxes stand ready, for fruit from the trees
With a bevy of workers, eager to please.
No time to stop and stare, boxes of apples everywhere.
The smell of the fruit, luscious and firm
As the warmth of the sun begins to burn.
Blue skies above, and a sense of delight
To sit on the boxes, for a rest, and a bite.
Nowhere on earth such joy can lend
To a rewarding day with money to spend.
C. King

Wife's Birthday

Today's the day I celebrate
the day that you were born.
Without this day my life would be forlorn.
You bring a wealth of feeling, happiness and joy,
That makes me glad that I was born a boy.
With every morn the sun comes up,
I give thanks that you are here.
It makes life more bearable
to know that you are near.
Though aches and pains beset you
a smile is there to see,
it spreads such happiness around
I'm glad that I am me!
Ron Stuart

The Rest

My youth was good as I recall
Good at sport and knew it all
OR so I thought until one day
My sturdy feet turned into clay,
For my child was born a handicapped boy
My life I thought he would destroy,
No way would he be good at sport
The very thought made me distraught.
But through the years I've lost my pride
Ah yes I know I've often cried
Though not for me but for my son
Because of things he's never done
For he deserves the very best
For he stands tall amongst the rest,
Included in "the rest" is me for he has shown and made me see
That winning is not the major aim
But to participate in the game, in this I mean the game of life
With all its trials and deep down strife,
So Graeme in sport is just a dream
But in life I know he stands supreme.

Fred Stansfield

A Special Gift

Little baby lying there
Greatest gift that we could share
Lying there so peaceful and warm
We will love you and keep you from harm
You are so beautiful to my eyes
Little voice, demanding when you cry and
Eyes so blue, like the midnight sky
Face like an angel, so soft and pink
Cute little nose, your mum's I think.

Another babe was lying there, in a manger
Filled with straw
He was sent to give us hope and worship from afar,
But this little babe is all our own
No kings in shepherd's fleece
What a joy you are to us, my little grandson Reece.

Eunice Bower

Pride And Prejudices

Drab grey houses back to back, pollution gushing chimney stacks,
Grim faced women, scarves on heads, scruffy kids fed jam and bread,
Cobbled streets no sign of gold, folk who die before they're old.
Loud mouthed yobs with beer bellies, would they recognize a deli?
Basic diet of chips and pies, grey, cloud-laden, rain-soaked skies.
Millions of people with no jobs, it's their own choosing, enjoy being yobs. No get up and go, it got up and went,
Now all their empty days are spent on bingo, gambling, down the pub, spending cash that is meant for grub.
Flat caps, watch fobs, walking sticks, kids in shops nick pick 'n' mix,
Turban-clad wives, fag in mouth, nagging at their drunken spouse,
Backstreet dustbins, roaming dogs, lifeless workers in heavy clogs.
Redundancy, debt, empty days, what can they do to change
   their ways?
'Get on your bike', move down south, learn to speak with
   plum in mouth,
Go on a diet, go macrobiotic, get healthy, happy, busy, erotic.
You'll still be at risk from sickness and stress, smoggy air,
   fumes on your chest,
They'll mock your accent, tell friends you're queer, don't fit in,
   belong down here.
No peace of mind, or quality of life, all work and travel, idea for
   strife.
Don't be judgmental, keep your mind free, listen and learn,
   believe what you see.
Good health, love, peace and laughter, these are the things
   that truly matter.

Linda Cannings

Roger

Seven o'clock french time you made your wife a coffee.
Happy and smiling you were about to complete your dream.
Then suddenly you slipped away and peacefully fell asleep.
The shock left us devastated, it was like a cruel blow.
You were our son. Oh how we loved you so
We ran around in circles: Grief and disbelief
How to get to you, so many miles across the sea
They laid you out in state, mourned you like a brother.
Said: One pair of hands — skilled they had seen no other.
We shall never forget that lovely face.
You seemed to be asleep;
The hands now still that made music talk.
Pride would make me weep
The school children of Naizin
Showered rose petals as they laid you down to rest
They took you into their hearts, to them and us you were the best.
Though the sea divides us, you'll awake with us every day,
God knew your body was tired and took you in heaven to rest,
You loved us so dearly, as we loved you too.
Goodnight, sleep tight, God Bless and have a well deserved rest.

Lilian Rose Palmer

Precious Globe

I close my eyes and I can see,
Happy, smiling people, and that's how it should be.
Our beautiful globe, which has so much to give
We just stand there divided, watching our dreams,
Like sand, falling through a sieve.

My heart is heavy, and it hurts too much,
So many people with power, yet everything touched, turns to dust.
Life is precious, you only get one chance,
Stop going in reverse, go forward, ADVANCE.

We must reconcile our differences and see what we can save.
As for fighting over land, at the end,
all it takes is a nine foot deep grave.
It doesn't matter how important or ordinary you are
Your very being, your existence, swells the repertoire.

Your role in life is precious to whatever vicinity you are in,
So don't discourage the other folk,
Let them help, don't reject them, that's a sin.

So, COME ON, do this beautiful big globe proud,
Show this lovely lady we appreciate everything we've been
   endowed.
PEACE is first, LOVE comes next,
Put these two together, there's nothing that can't be fixed.

Diava Cairns

Tomorrow?

What will the future bring?
Harmful days and other things,
This is a result of man's ignorance,
The world is bare when once it was abundant.

Destruction is pointless, a cause of hate,
We've destroyed the planet, now it's left to fate
What will happen to us, we just don't know
For the next generation, there's new seeds to sow.

If we stop all the waste, pollution, and such,
We might have a chance, and that means so much
A chance that our children can grow and survive
A chance that our world can stay alive.

If we choose to forget and refuse to see,
What the effects they just could be
Then we're ruining hope and dreams of all of the young
When their lives have only really just begun.

Is it too late perhaps? Even to try
The world and the hope are beginning to die
Slowly and surely destruction has begun
Is it too late? Is the harm done?

Lindsay Curnow

Mother Earth

Ho, wonderful planet earth, mortal man
Has wound you badly. Are you now beyond
Recovery? Your wounds are not healing
them-selves anymore. You once recovered
so rapidly from man's folly. Are you now
losing the will to carry on, producing your
treasures? That gives all life? Thee abuse by
man of your gifts to him, that made you his
mother earth. A wonder of our own
universe, the diamond of the stars, now
alas being ravaged, by the life that you willingly
blessed the most. Of all the life on your
wondrous planet, mother earth, the
human is the child of your home, but
sadly a delinquent that is unable to change.

Dennis Thomas

The Caravan Holiday

Four teenage girls festooned with bags and bulging cases tied
  with string,
Haul their belongings to the caravan—a battered blue tin thing.

Tired but eager, pile through the door. Then puzzled to each
  other call;
"There's no water." "Is that a stove?" "Where are the beds?"
  "It's all so small."

Unpacking. Shoes, jeans, tops, skirts are strewn around. Are
  they here for weeks?
Chaos reigns. The floor is littered, drawers bulge and every
  cupboard creaks.

Then shopping, still a novelty. Fish fingers, biscuits, bread
  and beans;
A tricky choice as they can't cook and have very limited means.

Dusk brings the gas mantle challenge. "Perhaps a match?"
  The flash of white
Crumples to black dust. Failed once, twice—they're only lit by
  torch that night.

Blocked sink, attacked with coat hanger tool, frees debris
  which rushes through;
Those inspecting bucket end are showered in brown liquid—
  greasy—pooh!

Curtains drawn, nighties on. One needs the loo, the rest say,
  "Go, it's dark."
But she zooms back in froth of pink, "There's frisbee players
  in the park!"

Next day at dawn, the birds feet clatter loud—they stroll on
  top the van;
Shocked girls leap up, all wide awake. "What now?" "Let's
  swim!" So off they ran.

Splashing fun. Return cold, damp and—oops!—locked out.
  All wail, "Don't blame me."
Smallest grabbed, shoved through window slit, lands upside
  down but finds the key.

A happy week soon passes and frenzied tidying marks the way
For rubbish clearance, souvenir hunts—the end of the holiday.

Hester Shier

An Elegy

The old man sits alone in pensive mood,
He sees the children playing on the shore,
The sea gulls hover low in search of food,
A speedboat leaves the harbour with a roar.

Some men are fishing from the harbour wall,
They rest awhile whilst waiting for a bite.
The tide is coming in, waves rise and fall,
The beach is slowly vanishing from sight.

The old man stirs and looks up to the skies,
The day is nearly o'er, the sun sinks low,
The pain of loneliness shows in his eyes,
And rising with a sigh he turns to go.

Edna Fendick

The Price Of Peace

Can peace at last
Have come unto this troubled land
Whose war-torn soul
For years has scarred its heart?
Where human suffering and misery
Were every day of life, a part?
Whose children born a few years ago
Knew nought but fear, both night and day?
It's hard to realize how many lives
The price of peace has had to pay,
But will man ever learn to count the cost
Of all those lives that have been lost?
Maybe, one day much wiser men
May rule this earth
A new awakening of life be given birth.

Jean Edmonds

Number One?

What has become of the human race?
Have we lost our purpose, lost our place?
Reached number one on the evolution scale,
But the pictures and stories tell a much different tale.

Cattle and sheep jammed tight in a truck,
A wealthy young squire shooting pheasant and duck,
The hare might escape, but he's got to be quick,
A helpless young seal pup, clubbed to death with a stick.

A pup on the streets, his coat caked in mud,
A harpooned whale floats on a sea red with blood,
A fox in a cage, but what do we care?
A lovely fur jacket for the lady to wear.

A pony neglected, so weak it may die,
I just want to shout, I just want to cry,
One day soon Nature might turn on her heels,
Then maybe us humans will know how it feels.

Julie Lee

My Brother

My Bother is different without a doubt
He cannot talk, he cannot shout
He cannot read or write or spell
What he thinks about, we cannot tell
But, I don't want my brother changed
Because I know he's not deranged
I know, he knows what's going on
And he loves everyone

When I lie in bed at night
I think of him, my little light
I hear his laugh, I see his eyes
I think of how he really tries

I can smell his breath, I can feel his love
His pureness is like a thousand white doves
I can see his face and his smiles
His happiness goes on for miles
Jamie is a handicapped boy
But to me and my family he is pure joy.

Katie Cowin

The Happy Alcoholic

He looked at me, slowly, with shaking
hand reached for the whisky at his side,
"Cheers"
He said.

With loosened tongue he muttered on of
days gone by, crying, laughing, bursting into
feeble song, picked up the bottle, eased the
pain, then started muttering again.

Pulling the weathered coat around his
bloated body, he rubbed his swollen hands
to keep them warm, took another swig of whisky.
Laid down upon the bench.
He was gone.

Jill Barratt

The Folly Of Man

God created the earth, sea and sky
He endowed it with forests and mountains, towering on high
Creatures wild and roaming free
And birds sang joyful melodies.

For many years there was peace in the land
Then greed and enmity took a hand
In the form of man, who was also given life
For many a long year, there was nothing but strife.

Nation fought nation throughout the ages
But still they don't learn from history's pages
Man creates his own hell here on earth
When it could have been so different, the land of their birth

When will it cease, all of this slaying?
Man killing man, with no thought of paying
The ultimate price, as finally, they wend
To face their maker, at journey's end.

Elsie Gallagher

Boy

You ask me, "What does he look like?"
He has blonde hair and deep blue eyes, like a wild sea."
You ask me, "When do you see him?"
"I see him on Saturdays, for hours on end."
You ask me, "Do you fancy him?"
"Yes, I have for some time. I quiver when he is near."
You ask me, "Have you asked him out?"
"No, every time I see him, I feel nervous, and I can't speak to him."

Louisa Howison

" The Highs And The Lows "

He saw not the morning sunrise,
  He heard not the sounds of dawn;
The music of springtime fell hollow,
  As nighttime gave way to the morn.

For his mind and his soul were despondent,
  Sunk in a world of their own,
He could not believe there were folk worse than he,
  He convinced himself he was alone.

Then a voice close beside him spoke softly
  "Please follow me close where I go,
I will show you the beauties of nature, tho' perhaps it is all in the mind,
  The colours that glow, the whiteness of snow,
For you see my dear friend — I am blind!"

Another voice said "I will play you such music that's sweet to the ear
  Ah illusion perhaps, for ne'er in my life,
Have I ever been able to hear."

There's a lesson to learn from this story
  Or perhaps 'twas a dream, whose to know;
But remember there's always a someone out there
Far worse off than you are, you know.

Eileen Barbara Berry

Soldier Boy

Once I knew a Para, Michael was his name.
He loved a girl called Annemarie,
But fighting was his game!

He went across the water, to Ireland's Crossmaglen!
His Barracks suffered mortar fire,
But still it churned out men!

His letters home were full of cheer..
Masking fear and dread..
Of nights spent in the NAAFI downing pints of beer..
Erasing dreams of Para mates... long since dead!

That Para has a mother...
MINE!!
He is my brother...

Christine Foulkes

Horace The Welterweight

Like holding reigns of a galloping horse
He is a worthy champion of formidable force
With sinews of steel and nerves to match
He's the welterweight that's hard to catch

With zest to his stride and loping motion
Carrying forth his pride and devotion
He bounds ahead to achieve his task
As defender protector with the woeful mask

As he snorts his way through the heather
He nuzzles undergrowth for his pleasure
With a gape expressing his sprightly spree
Dangling tongue depicts exuberant glee

With powerful paws that are velvet gloves
With an affectionate gaze his master loves
Returning he sits and waits till the morrow
For the escort befriended to uplift his sorrow

Dennis Peter Nicolle

" The Lord I Love "

The Lord I love is a friend from on high,
He keeps me warm and comforted inside.
We walk together, along life's way,
Together we stand, never to stray.
Our shadows entwined as we tread the path,
Through life here on earth, as we sit by the hearth.
We sit and we talk, as I read His true word.
He's teaching me wisdom, through readings that I've heard.
He's telling me stories of tales long ago,
Of times when He walked on the earth, here below.
His company was twelve, with thousands to hear,
As He sat on a rock, up high on a hill,
Teaching the Word, to those who sat still.
The Word is now written, it's now in a book,
All we have to do, is read and take a good look.
Look at the Words, they all come to life,
They paint a true picture of Our Lord Jesus Christ.

Jill Munday

To Be Or Not To Be

Pretty flower, tell me, as each pulled petal falls,
He loves me or he loves me not.
If love, why then uncertainty; if not, why sweet relief.
Speak my fate as you fall.
Dying at my feet.

Back and forth and tick and tock, in time my pendulum.
Chime the hour, was that for love
Chime that half, or was it not.
Time my fate as you go,
swinging back and forth.

High and low by moon's decree, the tide does ebb and flow.
Silvery calm — serenity.
Rampant storm — unsurety.
Which sea will seal my fate?
Boiling rage or calm.

Love with me, or not with me, and laugh or cry or sigh.
Still the thoughts that wreck my peace.
Relief at last, to find my ease,
When chains are bound or broke.
Together or alone.

Carol Assam

What Is A Dog

A dog is uncomplicated.
He loves you for what you are,
You don't have to dress up for him,
Or even drive a car.
You don't have to put on grace and airs.
He doesn't know what they mean.
As long as you love and care for him,
He will follow you everywhere.

Irene Holder

What My Lover Has To Say

He tells me I was born for him
He only had to wait for twenty years
He says no matter how long
He would have had to wait
He would still have waited for me

And now it's almost twenty years of love
He's proud we're still together
And our loving is stronger
Our love will last forever
He says it will never end

He tells me when he's dead and gone
He will still go on loving me
His soul will watch over me
His heart will be waiting for me
His love will never fade

I'm glad he tells me
What I need to know
Because our love can grow and grow
A day never goes by, without the words
"I love you", passing from his lips.

Christine Richmond-Bate

Our Dog

We have a lovely sheepdog, he's coloured black and white
He really is a special pet, that guards us day and night
Whenever we are playing, he's always by our side
And if we go out walking, he'll roam the country wide.

We've had him since he was a pup, we found him, cold and thin
No-one seemed to own, so my brother took him in
We thought he'd only stay a while, but that was years ago
Now we wouldn't be without him, because we love him so.

We called him Shep — and Laddie — and both names seemed to fit
When we couldn't make our minds up, he didn't mind a bit
Now he'll come for either name, as if he should have two
We think there's no-one like him, and if you saw him, so would you.

Eithne Ryan Lima

Untitled

Once upon a time there was a bird who did not have a coat.
He said to spider, "Will you lend me one of your feathers?"
"If I did I would not have enough to invite flies in."
The bird was fed up. No room for under pants.
He fell into a mash. This was a sort of a coat.

Chinyere Mbadiwe

Keiko

Keiko is a killer whale, but now so gentle and mild,
he should never have been taken from the wild,
people took him from the sea, hoping to gain a fee,
they put him in a water tank too small,
learnt him to do tricks to perform for the whole world to see.
Take pity.

They have made a film about Keiko being set free,
but that is not how it became to be, he's still in his tank,
his eyes deepened and his heart sank,
how unhappy he must be, taken from his family,
for us to watch him do his tricks in captivity,

I can hear his whispering cries, echoing into the night,
travelling over the sea to his family,
if you listen very hard deep into your hearts, you will
hear his wailing cries that he makes in the dark,
wanting, waiting, to be with his elders, in the great deep
waters of the sea.

Help Keiko to be set free, like all animals should be,
no animals should be taken from the wild and kept in captivity,
they should be let to live their lives wherever that may be.
BUT FREE.

Kathryn Hamill

The Thrush

The Robin's song is a chime of bells,
He sings best in the fall,
The Thrush pours out his song of hope,
And I love him best of all.

The Cuckoo tells us spring is here,
Oh, what a joyful call,
The Thrush still sings of joys to come,
And I love him best of all.

The Blackbird sings with exuberance,
He's always on the boil,
But the gentle Thrush still sings of peace,
And I love him best of all.

The Greenfinch asks for bread and cheese,
Up there in the treetops tall,
And the Thrush pours out his heart with ease,
And I love him best of all.

The Nightingale sings, I love you,
At dusk you hear him call,
But the Thrush just says, I love you too,
So I love him best of all.

Doris Hardy

Grant

He stood alone and watched her die.
He stood alone...couldn't even cry,
for tears, nor fears could quite express the pain of being motherless.

She'd held him tight,
yes, all the while she'd held him tight and tried to smile,
but those sweet words through shallow breath still couldn't
hide the face of death.

He'd seen it then as he sees it now;
he'd seen it then in his dreams somehow.
Yet, though he'd know the pain was there, the final sight he
couldn't bear.

He buried her up on the hill.
He buried her but she lives on still;
for though in body she'll never be here, he always knows he
has nothing to fear.

She looks back down as he walks away.
She looks back down as he starts to pray.
In every light that shines on him, there's a tiny flicker of Her within.

So now he sleeps and he knows she's there;
so now he sleeps without a care;
for deep inside he knows up high there's a bright star burning
in the sky.

Brigitte May

Summer Days

Its early morning birds are whistling
The dew upon the grass is glistening.
The farmer starts his busy morning.
The rooster gives his early calling.
Bees are busy coming to and fro.
Back to beehives with their pollen go.
Fields are ploughed and seeds are sown.
The last of winter's winds have blown.
Hedges and trees are full of colour,
Apples and berries grow riper and fuller.
The sky is cloudless beautiful blue.
Wall to wall sunshine all day through.
Fishes rise in rivers and streams
Catching flies dancing on sunbeams.
Cows are munching their lush green grass.
Endless summer days come and pass
The day is closing, the sky turns red.
All the animals bedded down and fed.
Happy days of fun and laughter.
Fairy tale ends of happy ever after.

Raymond Birch

My Life

His face devoid of emotion
he stretched the surgical gloves to fit his hands.
Hands which were soon to become weapons.

I could hear the clinical clink of the cold chrome.
My secure bubble was my only resistance.

"Bubble, bubble, toil and trouble" the Shakespearean witches chant.
I toiled in vain to escape the forthcoming army
of steel, as cold as the soldiers' faces.

As I now perceive the world I should have owned,
I foresee the discovery I would have made,
the suffering I would have alleviated.
Alas the bubble's burst.
Bernadette McCluskey

Untitled

Toby Jug was a little jug who wished he was a cup,
He wished that someone would brew some tea,
And come and fill him up,

How tired he was of standing there,
On that dusty shelf in pride of place,
A twisted grin enamelled on his face,

When visitors called they would exclaim,
Oh we've a jug in our china cabinet just the same!

The china set on the bottom shelf,
Were all in pottery blue,
How pretty they looked full of tea,
Shining and practically new.
Toby Jug his day when the vicar called to tea,
Toby's heart sang when he heard the vicar enquire...
Whose is that charming jug?
I would prefer it to a cup!
The vicar then duly drank a steaming pint of tea,
While the china set of the bottom shelf,
Hung their handles miserably...
Carol Latham

My Hero

He lay there with a worried stare, although to me it was plain,
He would never admit to all the pain.
Frightened to upset us more
It was enough to see the sight we saw.
Whether or not he would get well,
Whilst lying there going through what must be hell,
Was not what he was worried about.
It was us, with him could we manage without.
But that was typical of him, a considerate man.
Never a sin did he ever commit,
And this was his benefit.
How he was he would never mention,
Talking of home, anything to ease the tension.
About the time he would be home again,
Just as if it was all a game.
He knew just as we did he would live,
But the bid that he would walk again was low.
How he survived completely I will never know.
His determination and courage was great,
That is why my Fathers name is the top of my hero's slate.
Denise Randall

" The Song Of Pan "

Noble spirit of the wood, with breath of steam and hoof of dew,
Hearn the hunter calls upon the lifeforce that's within you,
Gentle faun of the glen, proud king with antlers high,
Though man has sought to harm you, your race shall never die.

For Oberon has made a pact upon this woodland feast,
That man shall pay a penance if he harms the favoured beast,
So man with gun who harms the hart, your soul is already sold,
For Oberon has traded it with "Him Below" for gold.
Janine A. Smith

Two Beaches

That is a great shell beach —
Heaped with banks of cockle fans
Flame-orange, lemon-yellow, jet-black, plum-purple
Crackling underfoot among the oyster hulls,
So thick you can't fit a bare foot between them.
Crimson carpet-patterned plates of scallop-fans
Bounce to dog paws.
Cart away whole big buckets full
You leave that beach none the sandier.

Here on this beach, shells don't leap to sight
Just grey waves, weed, a crying gull,
But sit down awhile.
Sift your fingers through the sand
And you see its grains are trochus cones,
Sunrise-pink trumpets, rice-white bubbles of cowrie,
Minutely perfect shining shells
Cradled in your great big hand.

Back at that beach, crouch down and find
Among the flaring cockle fans,
There too, seashells small as sand.
Judith Hanna

Winter Friends

Good morning! Robin Redbreast,
Hello! sweet Jenny Wren,
Hi there! cheeky Blackbird,
It's good to see you once again.

I look forward to your visits,
As cold winter comes around,
I've topped up with your seed and nuts,
There's plenty here, you've found.

I won't forget your special treats,
Currants, fruit and fat,
To keep your little bodies warm,
Because you have no hat.

Greenfinch, Jackdaw, Bluetit, Dove,
Chaffinch, Sparrow, Magpie, Thrush,
Chirping, chasing, pecking about,
Who found the apple core? Oh! what a fuss.

It gives me so much pleasure,
To care for the feathered few,
I am glad my garden's a small one,
Or I would probably start a Zoo.
Dorothy L. Garlick

Forgive To Forget

Sitting, watching the stars go by
Hearing the sound of a little child cry
Seeing how we are blinded by destruction
Telling me, get out of my sight, in the confusion
Working, so if you can get a second look-in
Forgive the best, for they will deal you a lucky number seven

Hoping, that don't notice the dome of sinners
Ringing, to get in some King's home place
Wearing some clothes to hide out the person
Looking, to jump to another dimension
Wishing the world would mind their own business
Forget the past, for tomorrow is a new day.

Missing, the yester-years of days gone by
Stitching the time to stay alive
Drinking, to quench the thirst of depression
Coughing, to bring up the memories of a right mess-in
Breathing to say a last goodbye
Forgive the rest, for they are soon going to die.
Kamla Thaper

The Cobweb

Transient thing of beauty suspended in the air
Held by slender, silken cords woven with great care
I just chanced to see you as the sun rose in the sky
A few bright glistening dewdrops caught my wandering eye
They had floated to you just as the sun came up
They'll foil the spider's purpose, if they don't dry up.

For though a thing of beauty you appear unto my eye
You're really there to catch some poor hapless fly
A lovely work of art, your beauty makes me sigh
Yet no human eyes have seen it save my sister Nan's and mine
And she would not have seen it, had I not said "Look"
The web, a thing of beauty before the fly you took.

A thing of gossamer splendour, attractive to the fly
Who soon within the web is caught, the spider sitting by
He will spring to action, Oh! poor hopeless fly
I will hasten on my way; I cannot watch you die.
This evening you will be away; the spider, wise is he.
He will spin another web where I cannot see.

Jean Downs

Feelings

A very big thank you for being so kind,
Helping to sort things out in my mind.
The time you have given in seeing me through,
When life had no meaning and what should I do.
The importance of having someone to listen,
When friends and relations were all very distant;
The comfort I felt in just having you there,
Letting go of my feelings being able to share.
You understood deep inside my suffering and sorrow,
The support gave me strength for a brighter tomorrow.
All of these things I just wanted to say,
With all my thanks in my own special way.

Christine Hammond

Mummy Dear

In all her glory standing tall and bold,
Her anger rises, we shall be told,
The orders come out loud and clear,
To us the ones she loves so dear.
Why is it she can never be wrong,
When shouting loud I want her gone,
Each day the same thing, nag, nag, nag,
We love her, hate her, the old bag.
But in our hearts we know she's right,
Without her in our lives, it wouldn't be so bright,
She's always there during our laughter and pain,
For what she asks is not her gain,
We expect it and love it, as she is the best,
She'll tell you she's; a cut above the rest,
Whatever I say and do, you must always know,
My love for you is like an eternal glow.
Of course at times I wish I were right,
But hey, one day I'll be as bright!
But you'll then be nagging gran,
As history repeats- That's where it all began.

Kim Stewart

Autumn Splendour

The Autumn in the misty morn,
Has beauty, even though forlorn,
The dancing leaves, red, russet and gold,
Paint a picture of splendour, a delight to behold.

The bright red berries on the trees,
The copper-gold leaves dancing along with the breeze,
Caught up in the merriment of a great gale blowing,
Showing nature's loveliness with all their colours glowing.

So here the melancholy Autumn dwells,
Misty and magical, casting her spells,
Across the shadows of the plain,
Until she disappears,
But do not be sad, because she will return
In all her beauty once again.

Annette Barker

You

You believed that the rainbow once poured
Her colours into the heart of every flower
 and made them beautiful.
Then as the breeze gently swayed their stems
 and caressed their petals, they whispered
The words of poets to your listening ears - I remember you.

You saw the world as an enchanting mystery
 and captured its secrets upon your canvas.
And in seeing the sorrow of your dearest,
 you consoled them softly with your loving eyes - I Deeply miss you.

You journeyed with the ageless grace of the warrior
 and sought a place for everlasting peace.
My thoughts for you shall never tire,
 and until my last breath, shall never cease - I Think of you.

I pray you are eternal,
 for the Heavens have wept Angel tears for you.
I see you in each solitary star enlivening the darkest night,
 and feel your warmth in the rays of yellow dawning light
  I shall always love you.

Claire Horton-Rackstraw

A New Life

This is the moment, this is it,
her heart beats fast.
Driving up the road, screaming like mad,
a feeling that she's never had.
To the maternity ward, on the bed.
Looking at her leg's, 'please spread'.
Open wide, push hard,
screaming out, 'this is bad'.
Out comes a head, pushing and pushing,
resting on the bed, crying and crying.
Out comes an arm, then another.
Out comes the body, she's going to be a mother.
Out comes the leg's and the feet.
Looking at him, he's so sweet.
Handing him to his mother,
he's so beautiful.
The father holds him,
"He's wonderful,"
our own little boy to cherish and love,
just thank the Lord up above.

Helen Jones

Times Have Changed

The moon shines behind their shadows,
her shadow used to be mine.
He used to sit and talk about the future,
but he never mentioned her.
She ran her fingers through his hair.
That was my job, I thought to myself.
Her hair twinkled in the sparkling light.
He turned his head and wished.
I closed my eyes, I couldn't bear
the thought of another kiss.

Danielle Smurthwaite

The New Widow

I hear a quiet voice at my side,
"He's just left us."
But I knew a second before, when that
last week pulse throbbed beneath my hand.
Kind nurse who didn't speak that final word.
And I, unable to think, no longer whole
because of your going.
One half of that sweet partnership
that is no more.
I stand on the edge of a chasm
of loneliness and silence
that your dear voice can no longer dispel.
My friend, my love, my anchor, my husband.

Jean Dorey

Mutability

Grey-blue solemn shrouds of smoke,
Heralding an early autumn,
Draw a fine and hazy mesh
Through disintegrating leaves
Spreading incense through the air;
Brought from life into cremation,
Burning with nostalgic sweetness
Curling into fantasy;
Upwards spreading through the branches,
Curtaining the shades and colours,
Merging one into the other.

Caught by sudden springing breezes
Flames become the devil's helpmate,
Grasping, twisting violently,
Changing spirals into belches,
Turning sweetness into odour,
Substituting fear for beauty.
One thing cancels out another
As if it were the law of Nature
Destined to be so for ever.

Irene J. Goldsmith

The King Of The Beasts

That golden fur, that fiery mane
Here comes the king of the jungle
The fearsome beast that everyone fears
Who can bring them bitterness and tears
Get out of the way! Get out of the way!
As he roams through the jungle, green
Never a care if he is seen
He can roar whenever he likes, ROAR, ROAR.
Suddenly all the majestic sense in him
Seems to crumble away
As a mind of an angry dragon seems to get in the way
His eyes flash red
His mouth lets out a roar
And then he pounces...
His prey is no more!

Leagh Cliffe

What Price Peace

The light dawns on yet another day
Here in this land of mine and countries far away
Some children open their eyes and see a mother's love
Some children open their eyes and see the sky above
 What Price Peace

Some men sit down to eat with their families each day
Some men have no family, theirs were blown away
 What Price Peace

A mother lifts her child up at the dawning of each day
Another lays hers in the ground, their will be no joy for her today
 What Price Peace

There should be no segregation
No war, no aggravation
It brings only devastation
And the price we pray for peace

Bronwen Forsythe

Adam To Eve — Religious Rape?

There is an infinite river running,
horizontally to the ocean of psychedelia,
Ecstasy it brings throbbing and screaming,
To the surface, taking prisoners,
from innocents to the whores of life,
stealing their pureness, devouring
their prey like hungry serpents,
screaming like Adam and Eve,
offering their necks to a lusty vampire,
From God to 'The Other Side',
Where the blood is redder.

Katy Race

Man

Man is a creature that's hard to understand,
He's cunning, crafty and cheats his fellow man;
His envy and avarice baffle the mind,
But then again he can be tender and kind.

He's callous, cruel and wants to dominate,
To keep him in check we have laws made by the state;
His temper is vile and he always wants to fight,
But to save a loved one he'll use all his might.

He's keen to conquer other people's lands,
On everything he sees, he wants to get his hands.
To the ills of others he is often blind,
But sometimes he's gallant and noble of mind.

This enigmatic being rules the whole sphere,
And exploits everything that he can get near.
He has explored the seas, the air and the land,
Now on other planets he wants to get his hands.

Bridget Machin

The " Macho " Man

My husband thinks he's one of the so called 'macho men,'
He's five foot eight, but imagines he's six foot ten!
He's into 'pumping iron', kendo, judo, and such;
Has it improved his physique? Not very much!
When asked to wheel out the refuse bin,
He puffs and pants like anything!
On Saturday morning he's off to the 'gym,'
Does he come back looking dashing and trim?
Not on your life! He's practically on his knees!
And could be knocked over by the slightest breeze!
Is he like 'Big Arnie?' he certainly is not!
Does this bother me? Not a lot;
If he looked like him, I wouldn't have a chance!
A real 'macho man' would lead me a dance!
So my little fellow will do me just fine!
And I'll be sure he's mine all mine!

Flora Divers

A Levantine Escape

The sea is tossed an emerald green
Hiding its secrets from prying eyes,
A cave of treasures guarded by hordes
If seaweed riding bareback upon the tide.

A lone crab scuttles across the dunes
Till swept away on a magic carpet ride,
Over the domed roofs of the barnacles
With their sleeping occupants safe inside.

A sea gull calls the flock to prayer
As a fish lies helpless on the sand,
Then swoops down headlong through the air
Like a scimitar to a thieving hand.

The wind lets out a heathen sigh
While a pale sun fails to lift the gloom,
But yonder in an Eastern sky
Shines brilliantly the crescent moon.

Though the chilling breeze makes me weak,
My thoughts crusade and take to flight,
To a land of a mirage and mystique
To a sea of faraway delight.

Gavin Doyle

There Is Someone Special In My Life

He's tall but not dark
His hair is a fluffy ball on his head
I know him but he does not know me
I wish one day we could meet
I dream every day of him
You never know how much people have in common
He doesn't go to my school
But I wish he did
There's someone special in my life
And I love him very much

Emma Weatherley

Growing Wisdom

Grey mist hangs mockingly over the town
Hiding the urban life, hoping to drown
Industry, commerce, the day's ebb and flow
Heedless and menacing lingers below.

Revealed now in greyness man's sombre strength
Spanning the city with concrete in length,
Knitting together bold patterns in mesh,
Railways and roadways and frail human flesh.

Bound up so tightly in a maze of regrets
Did the man with the slide rule really forget?
Glimpsing, then grasping, before it's too late
Hoping to muffle the clang of the gate.

Building and growing are two separate plights
Man's aspirations are mixed with man's rights.
Gillian Lewtas

Stealing Apples

Oh! the joy of stealing apples
high above the garden wall.
Though the climb was fraught with danger
never did I fear the fall.

It seemed to me an invitation —
One which I could not resist
Though the wall was high above,
I had no choice — I must persist

Driven on by unknown forces
waking from my sleeping soul,
I was the puppet of my passions,
almost losing self-control.

The treasure of the orchard beckoned
willed me on to scale the height,
I felt the joy of stealing apples
and knew the bliss of that first bite.
Irene Smith Wilson

Lofty Pursuits

Catholics and Christians are a passing phase;
Hinduism, Buddhism, just some religious craze.
There is a God who will change your life in oh so many ways
And all is for the better if you just do what he says
But what, I hear you ask, 'is this new sensation.'
So let me introduce you to... the God of loft insulation

Oh God of loft insulation, please hear my prayers
I offer up my house to you for central heating repairs
I have not always followed you but I can't get any dumber
So as a gift from me to you, I sacrificed the plumber.
Andrew Stafford

Friday The Thirteenth

As he entered at the cemetery gate,
His heart it skipped a beat,
His body shaking like a leaf,
From his head down to his feet,
He saw the yard in front of him,
Grave stones as dull as thunder,
Covered in cobwebs—spoilt and rotting,
Haunted by what lies under.
He looked up in the gloomy sky,
Grey and filled with sin,
Clouds as deep and black as midnight,
Eerie and frightening.
He walked on through the graveyard,
Hearing spooky howls,
Demons playing vicious games,
Roaring and creepily rattling chains,
And the sounds of angry growls.
What happened next is classified,
But now the lad's dead and buried beneath,
He was just another victim of Friday the Thirteenth.
Kevin Fieber

Chasm Of Love

The way he always looked at her, to wipe away her fears,
His firm yet modern outlook, throughout his countless years.
She loved him more than life itself, a love beyond belief,
Family so in harmony, now one bears all the grief.
I've tried so hard to fill the gap, which grows each passing day,
Sometimes that gap's a chasm, that never goes away.
So often have I knocked the door that shuts across your mind,
Always when you open it, such sorrow there I find.
You miss him and you mourn him so, all this I understand,
Father daughter partnerships, forever hand in hand.
Dad watches over you from high, his love is all around,
Day and night, at work, at home, to keep you safe and sound.
So open up that door of yours, and wedge it open wide,
Let your sorrow now escape, and feel his love inside.
Your dad is always there for you, to mould your every thought,
Let him show you what to do, whenever you're distraught.
His loving words to cherish now that dad has moved along,
"Here I am" to comfort you, as if he'd never gone.
David Wilcox

Prometheus

In stealth-etched secrecy,
His sparing steps shed preciously,
Prometheus' dark theft
Of specious wealth was deftly fetched.
Beneath a sky cocooned in cloud,
Feet creeping eagerly between fierce
Strife inebriated idols, he,
Primeval hero, swelled aflame
In gleeful freedom reached
'Till blazed in furnace brilliant dazzle,
Prometheus' sudden arc of fire exploding
Scarred the frayed and vacant battlescape
In blind-baked light.
Sparked clamorous choirs pierced
Scriabin's bright climactic icon
Of orchestrated crescendo's scream
With cries of glorious acclamation
Clawed into a single-word command;
"Create!"
Gordon Vale

The Unexpected

William shuffles with a stumbling gait,
His thoughts preoccupied, his movements slow.
Not once had he thought this would be his fate,
To him it is a very bitter blow.
In youth, his strength was equal to the job,
Not specially strong like some, but strong enough.
Now Parkinson's, from him, his strength will rob,
And nothing can he do as a rebuff.
He tries to think of other pleasant things,
Of writing, music, cooking, eating, love,
But all serve to remind him, and each brings
Its own sweet, sharper memories which prove
That youth its opportunities should take,
And not stand waiting for a better break.
Ivor F. Standen

Stamp Collector

My husband,
He's a stamp collector
Where they come from doesn't matter
He drives me mad with his boring patter
Fact I'm not interested doesn't matter

From countries no longer in existence
Mergers and Independence

Changes of flag
And even colour

Prices soar to post a letter
Pen friend writer I would be
If he'd give a stamp to me
Christine Gould

"Just A Guitar"

A boy with dreams of going far
His type of music, and a guitar
Bright lights calling, long way to go,
Will he make it, does he know.

Time flies onwards, what happens now
Success followed dreams, then that row
Why was he stubborn, he wasn't mean
Those angry words, shattered his dream.

He reminisces, what does he see
Things he thought were meant to be
Phantom music plays in his mind
Guitar strings of a special kind.

Looking back, what has he got
Nothing at all, life gone to rot.
Beautiful music, gone, a crying shame
Those angry words, they are to blame

There lingers a shadow on the wall
Of an object, three feet tall
There sits a shape, no dreams to bar.
A lonely man, with just a guitar.
Anne E. Gardiner

The Weeping Giant

He stands on the hill, his head in his hands,
His wrinkled old skin as old as the sands,
My lifelong friend is filled with despair,
For soon he will die, and will no-one care?
So graceful he stands, in sun and in storm,
Mother earths creation, uncared for, forlorn,
In springtime his fresh new coat will unfold,
The autumn brings colours of red, flame and gold,
In summer his shade gives coolness to all,
An oasis for creatures both great and small,
In winter his boughs embrace frost and snow,
Up high in a branch sleeps an old crow,
He stands on the hill, his head in his hands,
My lovely old playmate as old as the sands,
His branches are bare, inside he is weeping,
Through the soil and his roots deadly poisons are seeping,
"I need to live, I need to survive,
Not only for me, but for all forms of life,"
"My friend," he said, "Why can't they see?"
"That our world will end, along-side of me."
Emily Potts

Interlude Remembered

Along the lane we walked and ran;
Hither and thither the ball would go,
In play all thought of distance gone,
With shout and laughter in progression.

Thatch cottages around the bend discerning,
Frontal gardens, flowers in riot with delight,
Protected by fences painted bright;
Bordering a sward of grass so small.

Healthy smell of country air absorbing,
Scent of growing things embraced us;
Up the track, into the woods we went,
Birds all a-flutter wild things a-scurrying.

No harm was meant as we passed;
Bluebells in profusion spread,
Like a carpet on which we dare not tread,
En masse beneath tree and bush.

In reverence we moved, difficult it was,
A fleeting tranquil moment of peace;
Reliving again a lovely experience,
Acquiring an urge to re-visit again.
Clifford G. Luck

One Precious Moment

Hold back the heartache, save it for a rainy day.
Hold back the sorrow, you cannot chase the blues away.
But you can give him a moment, one precious moment.
If you love him, like you say you do,
You'll let go of him now, like he wants you to.
Don't hold him so close when the feelings wrong
Because there's nothing to breathe, all the freshness has gone
He's hurting inside, from the pain in your eyes
And the blame that he sees when he looks at you now.
So give him a moment, one precious moment.
When he opens the door for the last goodbye
Don't hurt him more by letting him see you cry.
Put a smile on your face and wish him well
And make him feel that you're happy for him
For the love that he found, for the love that he feels.
Hold back the heartache, save it for a rainy day
Hold back the sorrow, you cannot chase the blues away.
But you can give him a moment, one precious moment
To remember you by in the years to come
When you've walked through the rain and come out into sun.
Edna Hodgson

A Week For Bereaved At Worth

Worth was the place to find,
Hoping for some peace of mind,
Leaving all our cares behind.
In our group we number six
And find we are a good mix.
From the South of France there's Terry
Nearer home is Ann from Surrey.
But by far the greater number
From Kent are Patience, Margaret, Heather.
Before we go into assembly
Don't forget Bridget from Wembley.
Willing helpers there are many
Chief-in-charge is friendly Debbie.
In the evening an added bonus
When the monks descend upon us
Just to have a friendly chat
You know about this and that
And before the close of day
A few moments just to pray.
Ann O'Keeffe

Questions

Why do I work? I work to live.
How do I live? From day to day.
What do I do? I do my own thing.
What is my thing? Walking around.
Doing what? Looking at things I cannot buy.

What does he do? Works on and on.
And leisure time? Football on Saturday.
Without me of course. I am an extra. Existing.

Tears come. They sting my face
And drip down on to the paper.
'Count your blessings', they say.
How can I count what I cannot find?
People worse than yourself. Look all around.

On the dole. No pressure of work.
In mental institutions. No worry there.
In prison. Time for leisure.

Leisure? What does that mean?
Time. To do your own thing.
Friends? Where are they? Gone!
When I am gone, the questions remain. Unanswered.
Elaine Hilditch

Ode To Tom Upon The Occasion Of His Mid Quindecile

Ah, Tom!
How doest thy disposition like Good Wine mature
Adding to Yre Sanguine nature, more of the
Ageing sage or Savant's strange allure.
What, wit!
Flavour'd with Observance and a literate Spirit
Transposed to paper, Spiced 'gainst fancy
With a mien entirely empiric.
Long may you live good Friend t'enjoy
Your leisurely and iconoclastic Years,
Nurtured in the estimable bosom of your Spouse
Astute to the Substance of how a Thing appears,
Benignly chuckling at the Affairs of men
Till, bored with Discourse, 'tis time to pour
Another glass of Waitrose gin. Again.

Bruce Abrahams

A Child's Lament

Mum, dear Mum and Dad of mine,
How sad I am for such a long time.
You fought and quarrelled, decided to part,
And left me to struggle with my broken heart.

You want to be happy — you just had to part,
But what about me? I'm too young to depart.
There are two different homes, you found a new life,
But what good is that, folks? My life's full of strife.

Stepmother resents me, and stepfather too.
I am sad and bewildered. Don't know what to do.
There's nothing I can do. I just have to wait
Until I grow up, to put my life straight.

And so in the meantime I come and I go
Between my two homes, full of sadness and woe.
So, mothers and fathers when you separate,
Try to think of the children before it's too late.

E. Staunton

If Only...

Why was it that when you were here I often failed to say
How very much I loved you, mum: And so I write today
Of the many times I reminisce of years so long ago
When I was small and timid just how you loved me so.
You cared for me when I was lost along life's bumpy road.
You always shared my trouble and so lightened up my load.
You laughed with me,
You cried with me,
You scolded here and there
But even in your anger, you picked your words with care
To let me know that without spite you disagreed with me;
Allowing us to sort it out in fairness, now I see.
And now, here in my middle years, since you have passed away;
The sadness in my aching heart gets heavier every day.
Regretting how I sometimes failed to put my arms round you.
Regretting that I didn't show how much I loved you too.

Barbara Sims

The Sparrow

Walking in the park on a hot sunny day,
I caught the quizzical look from a sparrow,
It made me want to laugh, with interest I
saw it only had one leg.

I admired my new friend, it had no wooden
splints, nor an artificial leg, I thought
As it flew away, you have done it my
friend, how I do not know.

It must have been a hard thing to do,
land and hop on one leg, yet in flight
you could not tell.

Goodbye my new friend, wish I had
a crumb of bread.

J. M. Garbett

My Valentine

I treasure each day you touch my life
How you walk and laugh and sing,
You and me fit together like clockwork
For you I'd do anything.

I keep all the letters you gave me
In a little box in my mind,
The lock's key I keep close to my heart
So I know it's easy to find.

We belong to the morning's whisper on the moors
Held in the balance of the wind together,
Clinging to our souls on a lover's breath
Loving forever and ever.

The memories we've shared have been our best creation
As they last longer than a shooting star,
Speeding through our picturesque black sky
Nothing can compare to what we are.

You have filled my life with such happiness
Bringing the Sun to each and ev'ry day,
Your promises, your poetry, your devouring embrace
I wouldn't have it any other way.

Kate-Emily George

Our Friends

How does an ant behold the world?
Huge, enormous, frightening too!
How about an elephant-what does it see?
Chained to a circus or brought down with the trees?
Not much of a future for me, says he.

How does an abandoned stray dog look at life?
With desperation, I'm sure.
Where is his next meal?
Where can he stay?
NOBODY CARES.
He won't live much longer — he's only a stray.
Still, NOBODY CARES.

Glancing at goldfish in polythene bags....
people passing by, nobody blinks an eye!
Three darts. There's a winner -- does he know that it's cruel?
Probably not. What a fool.

These are but a few of our many varied friends,
In differing situation from endangered to risk-free.
Why can Man be so ignorant? When will Man's lesson be learned?
Somehow I think it's never to be.

Glen Sayers

Won't You Buy My Pretty Flowers

I have Forget-Me-Nots blue, Marigolds too
Hyacinths purple and white.
Sweet Snowdrops peep out, surrounded about,
With Primroses' pastel delight.
Red roses share with pinks delicate flair,
To bring a blush to a maiden comely.
In this basket I store magic galore,
In fancy we roam to the sea.
Behold the green of the fern, as the ocean does turn,
Spraying garlands of pearl coral bells,
Majestic green stalks take marathon walks
Bending leeward as grass on the fells.
Each small sailing ship bobs and it dips
And flutters its sails in the breeze.
Smell the salt of the spray, and the blossoms of May,
In your hand hold the fruit of the trees.
Leave noise and the grind, leave the city behind,
Come away to wild woodland bowers.
Please sir, if I may, once more I will say,
Won't you buy my pretty flowers.

Gwyniris Semmens

" The " Pirate

Ahoy! my handsome pirate, my traveller of the seas
I am so sad they caught you, and threw away the keys

Yet, had it not been for your ill fate, that day five years gone by
We would not be conversing 'cross the universal sky

You tell of your adventures, and I am in awe
of your fearless spirit, and your courage
This is so

I write to you of trivia, but yet you still reply
And in the darkness of the night
There's a twinkle in my eye

Your spirit is amazing, your resilience so bright
Your soul, so full of kindness, no matter of your plight

Ahoy! my handsome pirate, my hero of the pen
Goodnight brave one, sleep sweetly, until we write again

Lesley Bowler

Bonding With Baby

He's lying asleep in his own little bed,
I bend down to kiss him on his small perfect head,
He stirs just a little, then moves his wee hand,
Then he's off in his dreams to the new baby land.

In one hour he'll wake up and look round for me,
To feed him and change him, and lie on my knee,
Then he'll want cuddles and kisses as well,
He can't speak in words yet, but I know, I can tell.

My baby and I have a real special bond,
It's wondrous, it's magic, and I don't need a wand,
I just need to hold him and cuddle him tight,
And he senses he'll never be far from my sight.

And when he's all grown up, the bond still in place,
I'll know how he feels by the look on his face,
He'll still come to me with his worries and strife,
He just hopes I'll be there for the rest of his life.

Elizabeth Blue

Air Raid

I can see that my house has been bombed
I can hear aeroplanes overhead and I can hear bombers blowing up
I can smell smoke form the burning houses
I feel frightened a lot.

I can see aeroplanes and I can see people dead
I can hear people screaming of terror
I can smell smoke from the burning fires
I feel sick.

I can see fire engines putting out the fire
I can hear my mum calling me
I can smell home sweet home
I feel that there are no more bombs and I feel
that the war is over.

Craig Applegate

The Undecided Dreamers

I know not what to write about,
To sing for joy, or wail or shout.
I never can decide just what to do,
To laugh or cry, or mourn for you.
The dream of dreamers not in sleep,
Bewildered minds in thoughts so deep.
Thoughts that linger for the past.
Or will the future whisper - peace at last.

The studious do not think or frown.
They scribble hard and get things down.
Not for them the undecided,
Only the dreamers are unguided.
The day has passed, the hour is late
So lay your brow and rest with fate.
See what tomorrow holds for you
No more dreams, well - just a few.

P. M. Raby

Endless Night

Let my heart sleep.
I cannot endure another night of turmoil,
Of anguished dreams, of endless quests
For unseen things.

Let my heart sleep,
My body rest, contented,
Peaceful as the night ticks by,
Oblivious to the conflicts of my mind.

Let my heart sleep,
Deeply...
That I may have the strength
To follow the path it leads me down.

Let my heart sleep,
Gently...
That I may gather courage
To fight for what is right,
Destroying the horrors of the night.

Let my heart sleep,
That I may rest my weary soul,
To rise refreshed upon the morrow.

Claire Milne

A Cheesy Tale

Whilst strolling through a shopping mall,
I chanced upon a cheesy stall,
Displayed before my eyes to see,
Were cheeses of high quality.

From there I chose to choose a cheese,
Which I thought would my palate please,
How surely it did prove me right,
That cheese was strong, but sheer delight.

There's an old wife's tale that's often told,
A tale which I shall now unfold,
To eat strong cheese quite late at night,
Your dreams will end up fraught with fright.

If truth be told straight from the heart,
I sure did waken with a start,
For I had eaten late that night,
The cheese I'd relished with delight.

From the old wife's tale that I've just told,
A learn-ed lesson does unfold,
To slumber on in sweet repose,
You must not choose the cheese I chose.

Arch P. Fisher

Goodnight Lover

It was all so simple then.
I could feel your passion, whether you were near or far.
We could talk to each other, smile and laugh together,
And you were perfect in every way, I wish you still were.
Now I cannot feel your warmth and love,
And the look in your eyes is cold and unsettled.
What did I do? What was the cause?
The way you act deserves applause.
Do you not remember the feelings we shared?
Not so long ago.
When you said I was the best thing you had.
I believed you, ignorant and foolish.
You were there to hold me close.
What is my crime?
What is my fight?
Did I not scream loud and long, in dead of night.
When you used my body,
Pushed feelings and my legs aside. No more!
I want to be, dream to be, need to be strong...
I am leaving, sweet lover.. sleep well.. and sleep long!!!

Fiona McDonald

The Lights Flickered

There was a time when I thought
I could make everything wait for me
Time would stand still
Whilst I proved to myself what I could be
Then the lights flickered
And for a moment time stood still
Whilst I journeyed back and forth to hell

Positive thoughts, friends and family pulling me through
All telling me what I must do
The journey seems long
My road ahead
But I must believe what has been said
I must fight to make time stand still
Whilst I mend this mind and body from these malignant cells

I will win, I must, to survive
To prove to myself that I am very much alive
The lights only flickered
They did not go out
Time has just stood still
I hear my body shout
Linda Davis

" Missing You "

Sitting in your room last night, I thought of you and wept
I could see you lying there, in the place where you once slept.
I felt you very near me, smelling the aroma of your pipe
Again I heard your laughter bringing more tears for me to wipe.

The sound of your bed creaking echoed across the room
I then began to realize you had left me far too soon.
I remembered the night you shouted me, calling out my name
I should have known that moment, life would never be the same.

In my mind I felt you touch me, my vision blurred for I was crying
You looked at me and smiled: you knew that you were dying.
Hour upon hour I spent with you, never leaving your side
You told me of the light you saw, I held you in my arms and you died.

A day does not pass by me as I wonder where you are
Is the breeze your hand on my face or are you that beautiful star?
When I take flowers to your resting place, it always seems to rain
Like tears of sorrow that you are gone and my heart is full of pain.

Now you sleep forever, but no longer in your room
I'll go on missing you endlessly, like the sky would miss the moon
You cannot ever return to me, from this world you had to depart
Memories of you go on living for they are locked within my heart.
Beverley Ann Bracken

My Lifelong Friend

When I was young I had a friend
I could talk to every night
Beneath the covers on my bed
Small hands pressed together tight

Although I couldn't see him
I knew that what I said he would hear
And if he thought it right to help
I would feel his presence near.
As I grew up as a young man
That friend I did neglect
His presence was never far away
Because in all I did it would reflect.
Then came the time when trouble brewed
On whom could I rely
I thought of him my lifelong friend
As I gazed up to the sky.

What right had I to ask for help
Or guidance in any way
But I knew deep down he would hear my prayer
And still does every day.
Dennis J. Ward

The Birthday

Today is my son's birthday,
I don't know what to get,
I have thought of every thing on earth,
Come up with nothing yet,

Yesteryear it was so easy,
Roller skates or Dinky cars,
Balloons and birthday party,
Crackers and chocolate bars.

Shirts he's got in hundreds,
Hankies and socks galore,
Then I had a brain wave,
A load of manure.

May be he will not like it,
Won't give him such a buzz,
but if he does not need it,
The garden surely does.
Joan Boss

Wings Of Love

Gazing through my empty mind
I dream of love and all mankind
Looking through my lazy head
I smile for the living and weep for the dead

Is this life worth all its prevails
Wings of love crushed holes in sails?
Not knowing quite which boat to row
Traffic lights say stop, but you just want to go!

Looking for something that just isn't there
Life's like a fairground, go on the rides if you dare
You think you've found happiness and true love
Only to find a raven, but where is your dove?

So tread carefully on the sodden ground
And maybe one day your heart will be found
Until such a day, you can but dream
Instead of a lonely river, you'll find a beautiful stream!
One Day!
Alison Jarwood

I Remember

I remember when I was a kid
The things we had and what we did
We didn't have salmon or even ham
On our bread we only had jam
We couldn't afford posh toys from the shops
Instead played in the street with our whips and tops
There was no pocket money, it didn't seem fair
We went tater picking, had nits in our hair
At Christmas we made our own decorations
We didn't ask for much, no high expectations
Although, as I've said, there wasn't a lot
Santa Claus always came, he never forgot
We were happy back then, me and my friend
It seemed the long summers never would end
But we had to grow up, go our separate ways
Oh Yes, I remember those good bad old days.
G. Garner

Dreaming

I must be dreaming, for I know no fears,
I have found a way through this vale of tears,
A peace of mind I've never known,
A love at last to call my own.

Soft and gentle, the noise of night,
Captures the magic of loves perfect flight,
Wispy thoughts that are never real,
But, oh, is that the touch of your hand I feel.

If I am dreaming, let me sleep,
These fleeting moments I long to keep,
That when I wake, sweet memory's clear
Of your lovely face, I hold so dear.
Alan J. Phillips

Shattered Dream

I had a dream; it didn't last.
I dreamed the bombings in the past.
Heard children's laughter in the air
To your shame
It didn't linger there.
The bombs they come louder than before
On peace you'd firmly closed the door.
In your righteousness do you see
God's throne before you.
Or do you
destruction strewn within your path
Fear God's mighty wrath,
And do you upon the Sabbath Day
on bended knee devoutly pray
Forgiveness for your sins?
The laughter died; the children cry,
The bombs so loud you do not hear.
It's peace we want
not more fear.
Let us pray.
Lorraine Heenan

Untitled

The midnight sky, I question why,
I feel a desperate urge to fly,
If I don't I'll surely cry, or else I'll feel an urge to die.

One single star, seen from afar,
sacrificed on time's altar,
mirrored though I'm sure we are, we're nothing but a shooting star,

Of purple time, we hear a chime,
of I am yours and you are mine,
and you and I will surely dine, on love's sweet crimson holy wine.

A lonely cloud, I shout out loud,
it's blocked our star out from the crowd
I'm on my knees and I am bowed, underneath the lonely cloud,

The sun has come, seen but by some,
now it's time for day to come,
it's a shame our star has gone, seen by only seldom some.
Gary Pickup

Golden Days

The warmth seeps into my lifeless being
I feel for the first time
It's dark in my bed, no light am I seeing
but awaken I must, and upward climb.

My journey is long, with rewards at the end
I quiver with expectation at this time of my birth
slowly upwards my shoots I'll send
pushing their way through the warm damp earth.

At last the time has come!
I move the final clod
my shoots now grow quickly towards the sun
leaving behind the damp chill sod.

My head bent, as in silent praise
I stand tall now, erect and strong
my golden trumpet opens, my head I slowly raise
and join my companions in spring's silent song.
Josephine Ann Stewart

Nobody Wants Me

I roam around every town
I walk every street, and find another dead end
I'm on my own, all alone
I need someone
Someone, somewhere just waiting for me
I'm running free but I don't want to be
My feet are tired from walking
I need someone
To help me find my way
I've got to get out of this town
Before I do I'll take a last look around.
John Eagle

Begging Pennies

The cold seeps through my feet,
I feel no warmth, I feel no heat.
A cardboard box, a daily paper
I hate this lousy homeless caper.
Begging pennies from the passing few,
who seem to think they're better than you.
There but for the grace of God,
'Oh thanks a lot you stingy sod'.
It's not the way I'd like to live,
depending on what people give.
So what's the choice, I ask you, please!
Do you think I like to sit here and freeze?
But who the hell's going to give me a chance,
no-one even takes a second glance.
I'm just another bum on the street,
begging pennies at your feet.
Janis Melville

Untitled

You have really and truly messed me up,
I feel so hurt,
that you have treated me like about dirt
I feel like dying,
and I would be lying,
if I tried to deny that fact.

I feel used and abused,
torn and worn and all alone.
I like to pretend that it can't be the end.
But deep in my heart
I know it is and all have
to learn to live with this.
I really miss the way you kiss
when I felt down it give me a lift.
Just for your lips to touch mine
but maybe in time,
I'll get used to the fact that
they will meet again.
Colette Owens

Lonesome

I sit and watch the clouds go by
I feel so sad that I could cry

How bad it is to feel alone
I should be glad I have a home

Many hours alone I spend
No one to call my own true friend

A trust you find will never end
Then you have found your one true friend

No more to watch the clouds go by
No more to feel that you could cry
Linda Williamson

A Rose Petal

A petal fell off my rose today
I felt your pain in my tears
The hazy sunshine lost its way
through the darkness of your fears.
A soul trapped beneath the stormy sea,
the spirit found its way to the tide,
a dove's wings to set you free
and love and courage on your side.
The innocence of your sweetness
cuts me to the heart,
I remember my mother's tenderness
your beauty leaves a mark.
The faith of your love
brings blessings from above,
your petals shall heal in the dew
and I cherish this rose just for you.
Charles Forrester

The Waves Live On

As the tide creeps toward distant sands,
I gaze on outward, blankly staring.
My woes escape me, free from binding hands,
Feelings vanish, 'tis life long past caring.

Why don't the waves sleep under the moon?
They carry on turning, continuing momentum.
Like the beat of one's heart, as ever too soon —
Comes morning — the wake of life's mere motion.

Pray, what be the purpose? What be the way?
Fulfilling one's dreams, an eternal struggle.
Never-ending worries, dawn on to break of day.
An unexplored mind, like the depth of a puddle.

Must be trodden, tried, on till the last.
Its significance felt, its importance measured.
How does one know life's future, till it be passed?
Except day by day, precious moments treasured.
Harriet Lewis

Charlie

Slow and graceful he wakes and turns to me,
I gently stroke his coat of black and white.
The quietness of the moment is broken softly,
By his blissful purring in the morning sunlight.

Now fully awake he jumps down from the bed,
Awaiting impatiently for me to follow.
Quickly down the stairs into the kitchen I am led,
Once breakfast is devoured outside he will go.

A miaow is heard until I open the front door,
Then a cautious sniff of the morning air.
No danger is established so he is off to explore,
Happy, healthy and without a care.

Outside he will stay until the weather turns bad,
Or maybe hunger will strike, it has gone past five!
In which case forgotten is the breakfast that he had,
At the glass front door his face soon arrives.

Darkness falls as the night draws in,
But it's far too cold to go out for a roam.
So he snuggles on my lap as I tickle his chin,
And basks in the love and warmth of his home.
Fiona Allett

Feelings

You've now kicked my life into touch
I guess this is because I don't deserve that much
I now have lost the power to give
I may as well lose the will to live

To me my life has been full of giving
to lose this power is to lose a living
but I can't be sad and I can't be blue
'cause life is hard and this is true

life is unfair
I've found that out
'cause people don't care
which makes me shout

But you should know
from the job you do
make Love not War
that's people for you
Cheryl Dix

The Artist

In solitude he craves the crowd,
In throngs seeks isolation.
Beneath the Bodhi Tree he sits,
Awaiting inspiration,
Thoughts, tiny sparks, the dancing quarks
From which all seeds of art grow,
Notes, brush strokes crafted by man's skill,
To make our hearts and minds glow.
Alan Swift

Highland Clearances

Homes are being ruined,
I have been split up from my family.
Glowing in the light of one sun,
Hills are glowing like the light of a torch.
Loving memories of my childhood are gone,
All my future is gone.
Now my heart is burning like a flaming torch,
Dawn is rising and the ashes glow,
Crofts are burning in the distance.
Lived here all my life.
Everywhere crofts are burning,
A crackling sound behind me,
Raining on my burned down croft.
All my friends break down and cry.
Now my heart is breaking.
Could this be the end?
Everyone is sad,
Sellar ended my future.
Emma Stirling

Enigma

Unbearable yet familiar jealousy delivers,
I have only delusion, knowing is only a slither,
malignant is the domination, I represent,
Fear, trust and love are my opponents,
Enemies surround me, all mere mortals,
Loneliness is my destiny if awakening dawdles.
Julie Hope

Birds' Territorial Tricks...!!

Little Jenny Wren,
I hear your anxious chittering call
from the bird box on the laburnum tree,
a sanctuary by the fern covered wall.

You scold Cock Robin for being so bold,
up to territorial tricks
Perched at your door, how can you ignore
his envy, as thatched straw he plucks and unpicks.

No need to hide from the mischief
in those petulant eyes.
Cock Robin and his ego
are too big to Squeeze inside.

Robin Shoo...!!
Catch a worm or enjoy a bath
Inside the bird box I decern
Jenny Wren's chittering, Triumphant laugh.

Neighbours, neighbours - starling debate your brawling.
Harmonize your songs
Let lilting calls, great with joy
Spring's new dawning.
Joanne Manning

Christmas Fayre

I'm a Christmas pud with a cherry on top.
Holly leaves and berries to decorate me.
Hidden inside a nice surprise,
a penny for you or me.
Eat me up, I'm nice to have at Christmas time
Quick! Before your brother eats me.

A mince pie to die for!
Nice with ice cream, heaven with cream.
When you're cold, you should hold a plate with me on.
Lovely as a snack; or to pack
inside your lunch box to take to school.
I'll fill your tum at Christmas time

Ask your Mum to bake you Christmas cake.
With Santa on top and a sack full of toys.
Just right for hungry girls and boys.
Marzipan snow, every good child knows;
To bake a cake as nice as this; it would have to be on time.
Christmas in the kitchen.
Hannah Ford

Home

As I said goodbye streams of tears filled my eyes
I hope to return again someday; I'm leaving the sun
Those clear blue skies
The coolness of the water I'll leave behind.

Oh land of my birth my soul cries out to you
The cool evening air
The sound of steel band in my ears
Children playing, people singing
Oh land sweet land of home.

As I cast my eyes to the hills above
On this beautiful island that I love
I may travel far across the sea
But thoughts of my island
Will always remain with me.

Sitting on the steps in the old backyard
I know sometimes life was hard
But my grandmother always did the best she could
Gathering food and firewood
And when the moon and stars came out at night
My little island, you gave me light.

Jacqui Hepburn

Ode To Kurt Cobain

When I heard about Kurt
I just felt totally hurt
There was no way to describe the pain
Of never seeing him again

Think of Dave and of Kris
Who I'm sure that Kurt they'll miss
Think of Courtney and little Frances Bean
Who'll never be seeing him again

Nirvana music will always be around
With loud guitars and acoustic sound
"Smells Like Teen Spirit" and "In Bloom"
They could help anyone who's feeling the gloom

Kurt's life was short and sad
Though really it couldn't have been all bad
For he had a kid and a lovely wife
So really why did he take his life?

It was because of drugs he did take
He didn't realize his life was at stake
They led him to depression and suicide
And so in the end, he had nowhere to hide

Laura Miller

Who Cares

Whilst sitting, waiting, on standby in my room
I know the I.R.A will weave their evil loom,
They're trying to kill a soldier, at any time
Making us close ranks in a tighter line.

Why should they get there evil way
To kill and maim on this, or any other day,
Let there be justice, not a dead face in the dust,
Don't let the I.R.A carry out their blood lust.

Suddenly there's a blast and a flash
Broken glass and buildings crash,
Another bomb blowing people away
Why are they doing this the I.R.A.

Peace is what we are looking for
But innocent children stand at their door,
They look out with tears in their eyes
At their mummy and the way she dies.

When my tour is over, yes I will still care
Though I've done my bit for the people out there,
I'm alive and will soon rest in the arms of the one I love
I wonder? Does he really care? The Almighty God above.

Kevin Wildish

Tranquillity

Across the meadow and down by the stream,
I lay on the bank and started to dream,
I dreamt away the restful hours,
just lying amongst the lovely flowers.
To many people they are just weeds,
because they're not grown from packets of seeds.
These beautiful flowers have life, they are living.
Just think of the joy that they are giving,
when the cold weather's gone, and along comes the spring.
To people like me a joy they do bring,
they push themselves bravely up through the sod,
all lovingly put there and cared for by God.

Anne McWilliams

Summer

Summer, summer, boiling hot,
I like it such a lot.
Buttercups, strawberries, blueberries too,
Gathered in the morning dew.

Summer is my favourite season.
Now, I will tell you the reason.
Watching cats play in the sun,
Chasing bees and having fun.

Playing games and feeling jolly,
While I eat my cold ice lolly.
Splashing in the paddling pool,
In the garden, keeping cool.

Emma Victoria Martin (Age 7)

Trafalgar Spirit

Don't grieve for me now I have gone,
I lived my life, though not for long,
as full as possible for me,
my spirit fought and now is free.

From happy childhood, sun-filled days
I grew to manhood and my gaze
sought far horizons, lands anew,
a sailor with ambitions few.

The battle ensigns, flying proud
appeared to touch the passing cloud,
the roaring canon, heaving sea
living hell was home to me.

I fought with Nelson by my side,
I stood by as my Captain died,
he gave his orders, we obeyed,
and by that gallant's side we stayed.

My spirit also fled that day,
Trafalgar took my life away,
Twenty summers, a life so brief,
I chose my path, please, feel no grief.

Don W. Rowse

My Special Friend

You did not stay for very long, but I felt I knew you well,
I longed for you to tell me, the things you longed to tell,
The thoughts that filled your head, the feelings never shared.
As you lay locked in silence, did you know how much I cared?

I'd sit there at your bedside, and hold your tiny hand,
Giving the attention that you could not demand.
I sat and talked, you never spoke, but if you could have, you would,
For even now you've gone. I believe you understood.

Your ears, they heard no voices, alas you never talked
Your eyes, they saw no faces, your legs, they never walked
Your dreams were left unuttered, your tales were left untold
But inside your tiny body, beat a heart of solid gold.

And sometime in the future, our paths will meet again.
And I will hear my special friend, call me by my name.

Annamay O. Donnell

Am I Really Fifty?

Fifty now, how time has passed.
I look upon my sons,
In teens they're both 6 ft and strong,
My daughter married, life goes on.

It goes so fast, it won't slow down,
So much to do, I fly around.
Two part-time jobs plus home and hubby,
Two Grannies, the shopping, the washing and scrubbing,
The committees, the wining, the dining and dancing.
Help, I can't stop, there's so much to do, still running around after all.
Yes it's true.

The biggest battle of life I feel
Is the computer — it makes me reel,
The learning, thinking and trying to cater, with Modem, Internet, Word and Data
Hubby says that what I need
is logic thoughts, to give me speed.

I can't believe I'm really fifty, I multi-function in a jiffy.
Did I ought to slow life down,
Stop and stare and look around?
I think the answer here is YES, but not just now,
so when, and how?
Jill Carroll

Untitled

I once knew a man who I truly loved,
I looked in his eyes and saw all his love,
He made me so happy for a short while,
The man that I love with the lovely smile.

We made many plans for our lives together.
Growing old, having fun in all kinds of weather.
I tried all I could to make him happy and proud
And loved him so much I'd like to shout it out loud.

The man that I love, he phoned me one day,
He made me cry as he took his love away.
I cry every night and wonder inside,
Why the man that I love made me want to die.

My life seems so empty and lonely without
the man that I love and that's no doubt.
I love my two sons who are happy and proud,
they make days worth living but night's so sad.

So is this true love of something inside.
Hey, the man that I love, have you something to hide?
Yes, the man that I love, I need you so much,
This pain in my heart needs your tender touch.
Debra Doyle

Simon

I looked at his photograph, it made me cry,
I looked into those deep blue eyes
There was just a phone call to say he was dead
No one held me or uttered a word.
Standing there, I fell to my knees
He was dead, I would see him no more.
In my mind I saw his face so clearly,
His image embedded in my heart
Precious became those moments we had shared.
Over and over, I felt the pain, the loss.
No anger did I feel inside, no one was to blame.
Only silence befell my ears as the tears did fall,
Leaving a torn heart, a shattered soul.
Memories and emotions bore into my heart,
My soul cries out with pain.
My heart full of disbelief.
Those priceless moments to be cherished,
Of my loved one who perished.
A kindred spirit had been set free.
Linda R. Parks

My Sisters

My three big sisters
I looked up to them all,
When it was my turn
They had all been to the ball.

A brother separates you all from me,
A fourth sister in our particular tree.

Always trying to keep up
Making a mess,
I wish I had known
What would be the real test.

Feeling left out, boring and sad,
Going over the top totally bad.

Now I need you all
Like never before
I knew you would never
Show me the door.

I am so proud of my sisters
For giving me strength,
To be here for my three daughters
Whatever the length!
A. Gillett

Yorkshire Dales

I love to holiday in the Yorkshire Dales
I love the smell of old hay bales
Smiling faces in riding hats
Is better than the sight of high rise flats
The lorries at home stink of diesel
and they don't look nice upon my easel
The flowers in Yorkshire make me smile
after I have walked a mile
I like to relax and eat a scone
I think of the presents I have sent home
I feel perplexed my case is packed
The place I love I'll have to leave
The taxi's here, I'll have to go.
Jenny Dunkley

Everyday Bustle

I love to climb upon a hill on a lovely summer's day,
I love to watch the sea gulls as they fly across the bay,
I love to watch the cars and buses that go by every day,
Lorries and coaches and motorbikes as they all go on their way.

I love to look across the fields and the smell of new mown hay,
I love to see the horses and cows, sheep and the little lambs at play,
The scent of flowers, such lovely hues, all glistening with dew.

I love to hear the chirping of the birds up in the trees,
And watch the leaves all dancing in the summer breeze,
I love to hear the buzzing bees all busy in their hives,
With all these lovely things to see it's great to be alive.
Helen Barwood

The Art Of Marriage

Talking things through and remembering to say,
'I Love You Dear' at least once a day.

Holding hands without thinking you're too old,
Snuggling up together when you're feeling cold.

Being able to forgive and forget,
Saving a little never getting in debt.

Not going in the huff when you've had a fight,
Never going to bed angry or upset at night.

Giving each other the space to grow,
Boosting their confidence when they feel low.

Marrying the right person is hard it's true,
But being the right partner can be bloody tough too.
Lynda Anne Smoult

To My Husband

Once I was your little girl cherished every day,
I loved the way you brought me gifts and made me happy in every way,

You started to get distant more and more each day,
I thought it just a phase of you and it would go away,

Something happened recently I always will regret,
You spent sixteen nights away from me, sixteen nights I won't forget,

The loved and cherished little girl left upon her own,
The little girl has disappeared, a woman now full grown,

I mourn the little girl in me, killed dead over night,
I don't want to be a grown up yet, it doesn't feel quite right,

I cry myself to sleep at night, no one seems to hear,
A woman's cry is not so sweet, a little girl's is dear,

Where is my husband, that sweet gentleman I knew,
He loves his beautiful babies, why can't he love me too,

He says that I am wicked and never help him out,
He says I make him want to hurt me, and all I do is shout,

I lie at night beside him, his heart as cold as ice,
If only he could know the secret; it's being loved that makes me nice.

Alison Roberts

Dying Man

Once I was young and running free,
I once went to beaches and swam in the sea,
once I was happy, healthy and well,
"you've a whole life in front of you," my mother did tell,
I looked on my life as one big dream,
discos and parties and cinema screens,
time passed me by as the older I got,
a few years later an illness I fought.

Soon I felt lonely, unhappy and old.
I recalled and I thought of the stories mum told.
I thought of that story, I said it's a lie,
a whole life in front of me,
but soon I would die.

Where have they gone to, all those years;
why does death fill me with sorrow and fears,
for I've done no wrong up to this day
but I've got cancer the doctor did say
but before I die, to God I do pray
that I'll go to heaven and there I will stay.

Glenn Campbell

Hands Of Time

The old man fumbling with his watch
his fingers bent and trembling thick
head bent down intent on task
but hands cannot reflect this wish.

The old man sighs. A simple thing
to hold the watch and turn the spring
but old gnarled fingers have no skill
to wind the watch and obey his will.

Does he, I think, recall the time
when those old hands were strong and firm
when farmhorse held by loving touch
furrowed straight along the line?

Strong and firm those hands once were
guiding straight the plough through field
working hard throughout his life
clasping tight when knelt in prayer.

I think that when his days are done
when he is gathered to his Saviour's fold
our Lord will gently take his hands
and very softly make them whole.

Edna Waring

" It's Good To Talk "

When I'm a little sad, lonely or blue
I pick up the phone and talk to you
It may only be some small "chit-chat"
But it brings me closer to you for all that
A little joke to induce a smile
The response of laughter makes it all worthwhile
You may talk to family, friend, or other
Eager to share your views with another
Feelings, emotions, memories, sometimes sad
But, more often they're happy and glad
Down memory's lane we stroll together
And in our minds do intertwine and discover
How much in common we have with each other
So no matter in which direction we walk
Remember as the advert says "It's good to talk"

Granville Angell, Lord of Cannock

Goodnight, God Bless My Special Child

As you sleep peacefully in your bed,
I place a kiss upon your head,
I love to stand and gaze awhile,
Awake or asleep you make me smile.

I love to stroke your hair, so soft and fine,
And thank the Lord that you are mine,
So special to me, you were from heaven sent,
And all my love for you was meant.

Your hand in mine I gently hold,
The sweetest child my eyes behold,
So peaceful in your resting sleep,
I ask the angels to safely keep

From my eye a single tear,
For to me you are so very dear,
The love and joy you bring with you,
I treasure you, sweetheart, and cherish you too.

Delphine Tyrrell

Through The Eyes Of A Child

As I gazed across the desolate Moor,
I reached out my hand to further explore,
And took hold of the child who stood at my side,
So her inspiration could become my guide.

And now for the first time I could see,
Fairies and elves dancing in front of me,
One sat on a stone and played his pipe,
As others ate apples green and ripe.

And the hundreds of Fairies that sat in the trees,
Were preparing for autumn by painting the leaves,
And as they called up the wind with their magical spell,
I knew this was a secret I never could tell,

And that is why our imagination slows,
When we grow old and our innocence goes,
So break down the barriers, let yourself be beguiled,
And take a look at the world through the eyes of a child.

Alison Gorton

A Quiet Reflection

I sat all alone and viewed my old home
   I remembered the good times
     Along with the sad times

I can hear laughter
   I can see tears

I must turn away
   Not think of those years

I think of the love
   The joy and the peace

I count myself lucky
   Those memories won't cease

Constance Hall

On The Wings Of Morning

On the wings of morning
I rise to see the view.
Under clouds of wishes
The breathtaking blue.

As the veil of dawn is lifted
A shimmering light is revealed
Golden horizons announce their arrival
Nothing can be concealed.

Lloyd Prideaux Richards

The Rose

At the break of dawn, all covered in dew,
I saw a rose, and compared it to you;
It opened its petals, and reached to the sky,
I knew I would love it, till the day that I die!!

The rose in the garden was fairest of all!
If I fell in love, for you both I did fall!!
While looking at the rose, I saw your beautiful face,
So shapely, so slender, with honour and grace.

Its leaves and its foliage were bright, full of sheen,
Just like your eyes that are emerald green;
The rose like your cheeks was red in full bloom,
With a fragrance so lovely, a heady perfume.

But all I can offer is affection and care,
And a shiny blue ribbon, to tie up your hair;
I could face all my troubles, with you at my side!!
With a sweetheart like you, I'd be full — full of pride.

John V. Morris

My Daughter

Before she was born I knew her,
I saw her face, and her beauty,
I saw her smile, and her tears,
I saw her pain, and her anguish,
I saw her blush of her womanhood,
　And the hope of future years.

And when she was born, I knew her,
I recognize her face, and her beauty,
I recognize her smile, and her tears,
I recognize her pain, and her anguish,
And in time, I recognized the blush of womanhood,
And the promise of future years.

And when she died, I did not know her,
But they asked, was it her,
And then I remembered, before she was
　born I knew her, and I answered,
"Yes it is her".

Brian Barrett

Laughter

There are sounds of laughter and singing,
I see cheerful children coming and going,
and when wholesome laughter fills the air
loneliness and unhappiness depart
for laughter lifts us way above despair,
and is a strong tonic to cheer the heart.

Laughter can give communication
and joy to the deaf or the blind,
a strong and invisible conversation
that can be shared by mankind,
no matter what colour, race or creed,
good infectious laughter is a common need.

Laughter can spread joy in all directions,
weaving magic spells of true affection
to show love and care to humanity,
spreading sunshine when its wild and stormy,
lifting us up from anxiety and strain,
giving us hope to try and try again.

Lavinia Brown

Shadows

Transforming shape from dawn to dusk,
I see the characters slide about,
From all dimensions, figures explore,
A chilling scenery without a doubt.

In the dark shadows, the temperature drops,
And objects are masked to people around,
Darkened by light and travels through day,
Move so slowly without any sound.

Eyes watch from the misty grey,
Embedding my mind in a shadowy sea,
Mystical windows from hidden lands,
Ghostly people staring at me.

Chilling whispers caress my ears,
I gaze at the depth of the colourless shade,
Like elastic stretching, moving about,
Watching the images gradually fade.

Jenny Orr

Ripples In A Pool

My child, you see a drop in the ocean.
I see the ripples in a pool;
Spreading, spreading, wider, wider;
Encircling that drop far beyond its vision.
　People watch the drops downward plunge;
　Beautiful for a moment, catching a brief sparkle of the sun.
　Momentarily sad when it is quickly submerged into the whole,
　They turn and walk away,
　Mind, remembering the brief glimpse of a jewel.
　Vision, dulling by the second.
　Eyes, searching for the next moment of joy.
　Or, sit, looking into the depths;
　Trying to retain that momentary thrill.
　Seeing; yet not seeing at all; the ripples in the pool.
But I see them; swaying the grasses,
Startling the fish into taking a new watery pathway,
Causing the frog to leap; the dragonfly to spread his wings and fly.
Patterns on that pane of glass; growing more and more;
Till, edges reached, they caress, gently, the bank;
Their FINAL shore.

Christina Fowler

'Dreams'

I see you when awake.
I see you when I close my eyes.
You're in my thoughts and dreams,
I can feel your hurt and your sorrow.
What do you see when you look at me?
At me. In me. Do you see a woman? Do you see a child?
I feel like a child, but long to be a woman.
I want to tell you things, my innermost secrets.
Longings, fantasies.
What do you dream of when you sleep?
Dream of soft pillows.
Dream of floating clouds and blue skies.
I dream. I hope. I wish you everything you desire.

Joy Rankine

" When I Was Small "

When I was small, my world was bright,
I loved each dawn with all my might.
My days were warm and full of glee,
What on earth has happened to me?

I grew and grew, until I could see
All the darkness of the days to be.
The wars and hates of my fellow man
The greed and the grasping, to grab what they can.

The day and grey and people were crying,
For love in their lives, was that not worth trying?

They grew and grew, until they could see,
The light was coming and not just for me.

Angela Marie Smyth

Insanity

Just when I thought my life was set free
I sense that something is following me.
My heart beats fast, could this be?
Someone's invading my privacy
For I've entered the house in my head.

The dreams in my sleep didn't warn me of this,
Somehow my sanity must have given it a miss.
I can't stay here just for death's kiss
So I'm leaving the house in my head.

I can't think from where these fears creep.
My feelings lie dead in a muddled heap
And I'm trapped in the house in my head.

Will nobody hear my strangled screams?
I'm dying in the house in my head.

Insanity's a lonely thing.

Kate Chandler

Memory Of A Dream

To where I fled from out of fright, to solitude
I shall return, I shall lose myself in the forest,
The naked roots of ancient trees will be my pillow,
Their dead leaves my cover; I shall fast and wait
To hear the grass singing to the sleeping birds,
The ghosts of the forest dancing in white circles
To the tune of a thousand flutes, breath of dreaming trees,
Now a hymn and a prayer and now a lament;
Sleepless I shall listen to the birth of pearls
At the shores of moonlit lakes.
Farewell my love, a salty wind wakes up
A dead sailor's soul nestling in my chest,
A yearning for the open sea, its fertile solitude,
Overpowers me, directs my will to the quest
Of what lies beyond my grasp; my only guide,
The memory of a dream, a creature of fantasy,
A premonition of another world.

Antonis Modinos

Birthday Blues

It's my birthday today, I'm 16 years old;
I should have been happy, instead I feel cold.

My mother's just died, I feel all alone;
I've still got my father so I'm not on my own.

She died last night, it was a surprise,
But she knew she was ill, I could tell by her eyes.

Katie called round, she's been my best friend for years;
She held me so tightly as I shed my tears.

"It's not fair", I cried, "It should have been me.
This is not meant to happen, it's not meant to be"

She listened intently as I shed my woes;
I'm numb from this crying, from my head to my toes.

I fall fast asleep, right there in her arms.
I dream of my mother and feel ever so calm.

The funeral's on Friday, that's three days away.
This is my worst birthday ever, I can honestly say.

Emma Walters

Man As Beast

As I lie in solitude I'm thinking back
I was just nineteen when I made that attack
I was a nice boy clever at my work
Then something inside me began to lurk
That poor old lady had done nothing to me
But in my eyes she became by enemy
All I can remember, is she lay at my feet
Like a broken old doll lying in the street
I am now in prison serving my time
   for that dreadful deed...oh! that awful crime.

Gayle Wilkinson

Your Name

I wake in the morning and call your dear name,
I sleep through the night but in dreams it's the same —

When I first heard it or from whence it first came
Long since is forgotten, it's there just the same —

That name now repeated again and again
Invades my whole being, incessantly deep.

It echoes with constant monotonous beat,
Now part of my living, awake or asleep.

How strange you should suddenly enter my life,
An unknown maid, neither sweetheart nor wife —

Your face and your name then so fixed in my mind
That respite from you I no longer can find.

I've relinquished all hope I'll ever be free
Unless you break the spell you've cast over me.

Laura Edwards

My Tomorrow

A Christmas tree so tall and green
I stand amid a snowy scene
I know one day my chance will come
To join the happy Christmas fun.

I stand as proud as proud can be
Chosen by a special family
To decorate in colours bright
While the smell of pine evades the night.

My slender branches bow and lean
As twinkling stars light up the scene
Bright coloured baubles and toys abound
With tinsel shining all around.

Little eyes in wonder gaze
Faces sparkle for many days
While Mums and Grans share memories
Of distant childhood Christmases.

My Christmas task will soon be done and I have shared in all the fun
So spare a thought and waste me not but plant me in the vegetable plot
Another year through wind and hail so I can live to tell the tale.

Jean Padmore

Our Planet

What are we doing to this planet of ours?
How much longer will we view the stars?
Polluting the rivers, the seas and the sky,
Holes in the ozone, it's their fault, not mine.

Nuclear testing, hotter summers, big freeze,
Vacuums to suck the fish from the sea.
Whales are culled to feed foreign lands,
The blood is there, but not on my hands.

Newspaper reports tell of another war,
Another tanker has been grounded ashore.
Chop down the forests for big industry,
We've demanded the paper, yes, you and me.

We have tried to contact life from the planets,
Will they reply in some way, I doubt it.
They have seen us make a mess of our earth,
They will stay well clear, for all they're worth.

We have looked at the problems, and blamed one another,
It's time for people to sit up and bother.
This is a beautiful world, let's enjoy it while we can,
Before the question becomes, who will save man?

Andy Gill

Untitled

As I sit on the grass at the top of the cliff over looking the sea
I think of all the times we used to stop and share each others company,
The birds fly above us as they cry the wind through our hair blows
Among the clouds we also fly high as the whole world for us slows,
On the deep waves there comes a breeze that sends shivers down our spine
Our love so true as every thing around us sees now I really know you're mine,
As I sit here alone and admire the view of the beauty that's stretched ahead
The sea and sky meet in an endless blue or do I dream it all in my bed,
The words that you said that meant so much to me you'll never know
The days of bliss that we spent no one ever doubted us though,
I hear a car approach near as I shut me eyes and wish
That you were with me just here as I speak all you say is sshh,
As we sit on the grass at the top of the cliff over looking the sea
Holding in each others arms we stop and share each others loving company.

Amanda Jane Harding

Daisy Chains

As I walked along my village road
I turned down memory lane.
I saw some playmates standing by,
I was a child again.

We skipped and played the 'Alley O.'
Made daisy chains and more,
Our feet danced whither they would go,
Outside my old front door.

I heard my mother sing inside,
I smelled a good beef stew.
Next, the door swung open wide,
Was that really you?

That 'nowty' lad who lived next door
And used to pull my hair
But when I fell and my leg was sore
You always would be there.

As I walk down my memory lane
Your shadow's by my side
For although I never took your name,
My love has never died.

Gillian Lloyd

Health Is Wealth

Of all the things in this whole world,
I value most my health,
Without it I just could not cope,
My health it is my wealth.

Sure I am happy with my lot,
Health, happiness, love and peace,
Each of these, they cost me not,
Thank you Lord, don't let me cease.

For eyes that see, and ears that hear,
For a heart that's kind and true,
No amount of money would,
These God-given gifts outdo.

There are some folk, who just crave wealth,
Indeed what would it be,
If they were maimed in any way,
That wealth could go to sea.

For a love that comes from God alone,
For a peace of mind contented,
I would not change my life at all,
For all the world's invented.

Kathleen Blanchfield

Time Passing

When I was young and filled with dreams
I walked with leisured stride,
Loitering in Life's morning sun
While time was at my side.

And Time said, "Stay. No need for haste
To climb Life's rugged hill."
Oh, happy were those golden hours
When Time and I stood still.

I dreamed of fame and fortune
As noontide came, and went.
Still Time's unspoken promise shone
On endless merriment.

Now Twilight's here, how Time has changed,
False friend he's proved to be.
Time now runs by on swifter feet
And will not wait for me.

Barbara Rowley

Child's Eyes

I want to see the world through a child's eyes
I want to believe that nothing ever dies
I want to walk in my field of dreams that never ends
I want to feel free and innocent, I want to pretend
That when I touch your face, we will fall in love
Into your love that will lift me to the sky above
Then you'll ease me down into the soul of your arms
And once again I'll fall in love with your blue eyes of charm
Then you'll put your lips to mine and know I'll want more
So take me down, give love like you have never before
I want to make the sun shine and never bring rain
I want to feel the pureness of love without pain
I want to lie in a field that's upon fields, without a sound
I want to share with the sky of peace, the love we've found
This feels so right, peaceful, so warm and true
Just look through a child's eyes and you'll feel it too
I'll walk you through this dream that has no lies
And has no reason to feel pain or a need to cry
You can feel young and innocent and feel a love that never dies
All you have to do is see the world through a child's eyes.

Kelly Gibson

Casualty

A thousand pains running through my soul,
I want to leave but I cannot go
Faces of anguish all around
So many souls, so little sound
Murmurs solemn and concerned
How little waiting have you earned?
The aching shoots right down my spine
And penetrates deeper every time
It seems a million hours away —
Will I get to be seen today?
How much longer will I wait,
Before they let me through the gate?
It is the thought that I'm not the one
Whose waiting has but just begun
I know there's others worse than me,
But the pain is so great
I find it hard to believe.

Ana-Maria Rey

Dentists

George oh George, let me tell you the truth,
If you don't go to the dentist you'll have problems with your tooth,
So don't be silly, don't be a berk,
Or you will have to have time off work.
I've been brave, very brave you see,
I had to have my B.C.G.
I'm a little girl and I've been brave,
So go to the dentist and your tooth he will save.
I don't like you to be in pain, you see,
So go to the dentist just for me.

Kelly Allen

Memories Of Galloway

At sunrise, I saddled and mounted the mare,
I wanted to get away — and free from care;
We galloped thro' fields, and over the drills,
To my favourite spot, in the Galloway hills.

On top of the ridge, overlooking the Bay
Across to Glenapp — a few miles away;
The heather reflected its purple glow,
In the clear, blue water of the Loch below!

What a glorious feeling — the wind in my hair!
I used to spend hours alone up there
And sometimes, I waved to the Irish boat
When it sailed to Stranraer — its final port.

The gathering mist, I watched in the Glen,
So hauntingly beautiful, I remember it then;
Where once I fished without a reel
And caught, in the burn — a monster eel!

And I'll never forget the deer on the hill;
Those regal creatures, I can see them still
Silhouetted, against a crimson sky —
At sunset, when the end of the day was nigh.

Irene Telfer

" Green Fingers "

Plucked fresh and firm from the vegetable plot
I was growing quite happily and now I'm not
I've been nurtured and loved in his own special way
Watered and fed at least three times a day.

I'm placed wrapped in paper on a comfortable bed
In his barrow of wood with a bag on my head
He whispers very quietly I'm not to be seen
And transports me gently to his moving machine.

He sits in the front and chortles with glee
He should win something with a specimen like me
He starts up the engine and off we go
Full steam ahead to the annual vegetable show.

I've been cleaned and polished and placed on a stand
My owner waits eagerly duster in hand
Judges go past, they've looked at me twice
To win a rosette would be terribly nice.

The results are announced, I've won first prize
You should see the deep emotion in my owner's eyes
I love my dear owner, he's very special to me
And to celebrate our win, it's stuffed marrow for tea!

Claire Smith

The Good Old Days

The good old days were the best days.
I wish they would come back.
The old never went cold the neighbours would see to that.
  'Cause they lived in a back to back.
The old days were the best days although many people were poor.
You could walk out at night, without having a fright.
  And you never locked your door.

The old days were the best days
When beer was tuppence a pint, and a shilling would last all night
Put on the pot, the Lord will fill it, my mother used to shout.
With meat and veg and tatties, and we never went without.

People worked hard in the good old days
They took a pride in what they did
No family allowance to bring up your kid.
Now it's all grab or you're a scab, TV, cars, and the like.
If you don't do as you're told, you're out on strike.

Strikes and scabs, hatred and greed.
People not quite human, violence, drugs and muggers
Who rob and maim all for gain.
I wish the good old days were back again.

Jean Tombs

Regret

She took me to a small and quiet place;
I went and saw you lying all alone,
Just covered by a sheet — except your face,
so still, just like a statue made of stone —

Or maybe marble for you looked so white,
your skin so smooth as if you'd shed some years,
I tried to speak but try hard as I might,
My words were lost and mingled with my tears.

I wished that she would go and leave me there,
For while she stayed I really felt too shy
To kiss your cheek or touch your thin grey hair,
To say "I'm sorry" and then say "Goodbye".

I missed that chance and that is my regret;
Though years have passed, I never will forget.

Eve Goldstein

That Look In Your Eyes

That look in your eyes, the look of love that I can see
I wish that it could always be that look in your eyes.

That look in your eyes of sadness and regret
I've tried so hard to ease your pain and yet
it's still there, that look in your eyes.

That look in your eyes, the look of joy and happiness,
try not to ever transgress from that look in your eyes.

That look in your eyes, the look of sorrow and discontent,
you're not happy, that's evident; take away that look in your eyes.

That look in your eyes, the look of terror and fear,
but it will pass quite soon, my dear, so take away
that look in your eyes.

That look in your eyes brings back the look of love, my dear,
and you'll be happy, have no fear, forever keep that look in
your eyes.

Eileen Neal

Last Visit

Going home last night
I wished that I had listened more.
Trite words and gossip were the order
of the day
And yet they covered many things that
I would like to say.
It's easier to forge ahead
Covering reality with trivial things
And yet it wasn't you, but me,
Who was afraid.
You have a strength about you
It fills the room
And if my words were trite and light
They only hid how much I care
and feel for you.

Joy Elizabeth Temple

Never Alone

I know that I am not alone
I know that you are here, I feel your presence in the room,
I know that you are near.

You were very young when you had to depart,
You went so sudden, It broke my heart,
I had so much love I had to give,
If you were given the chance to live.

You have a grandson, I know you'd love,
I know you see him from above,
Why did you have to leave that way,
I wish you could be here today.

Heaven to you, is now your home,
Among Gods children you will roam,
This empty space makes me very sad,
You will always be my mum and dad.

Elsie Elliott

" Wistful Thinking "

If I could peer into my body
I wonder what I would see;
Would the first thing be my conscience
Trying so hard to hide from me?
Or, would it be shame and sorrow
For things I have done, or said;
Not malicious, or even spiteful
Just ideas that came into my head?
I feel sure I would notice some envy
Which at times I have felt secretly
Then, as quickly regretted the feeling
Arising from deep jealousy.
Apart from these traits, I hope I would find
Some traces of loving and caring;
Of kindness and thought, sense of humour,
Finding time, too, when troubles need sharing.
Above all let there be my own recipe
Not to sleep, when there's wrath in my heart;
To forgive and forget, without any regret
As I wait for a new day to start.

Kitty Hayward

The Mirror

As I look in the Mirror I see you Dad
If I were to smile, I smile like you Dad
If I were to cry, I cry like you Dad
As I breathe, I breathe you Dad.

You give strength and encouragement
Even though you are not here
It is through your Daughter
This shines through.

The Mirror is like a picture
A picture of Time
I stand looking in the Mirror
As Time goes by.

Once I walk away from the Mirror
There I still stand
Not as a reflection Dad
But as a figure of Time.

Time will only tell Dad
If we live our lives to the full
But as long as I know you're still within me Dad
I'm not sure but I'm certain we all will.

John Miller

" I Will Be Here When You Awake "

Maybe I could find the words to say
if loving you is wrong I will never be right.
When you fell into a deep sleep I too became tired,
don't expect me to walk away
because you cannot, that I could never do.
You gave me your heart and asked
me to take care of it forever,
I said "it would be my pleasure"
Now that you can no longer dance in my arms
the way you used to,
I would rather not hear another music play,
without you hearing it too.
God made you for me and he said,
"I have moulded your lady the way she should be,
love her with all your heart deeply
but most of all tenderly,
don't ever let the sun go down
without your arms around her secure,
and remember to tell her,
"I will be here when you awake and that you can be assured."

Jennifer B. Small

Night Prayer

If only the sun would stop shining,
If only the sea wasn't blue,
If only the birds would stop singing:
Then I would be home, and with You.

If only the waves would stop pounding,
If only a sound could just cease,
If only the wheel would stop turning:
Then I'd be with You, and in peace.

The noise on my radio - buzzing,
The swirl of these currents of air
Distracts me from You and Your Voices,
And leads me away in despair.

O speak to me, Darling, of colours,
Remove the thin film from my eyes:
That I may see You in Your Glory,
Away from this human demise.

For You are with me on all levels,
In storeys, upstairs, on all floors,
So give me the key, Dear Almighty
Until I'm with You and All Yours.

Cath Boden

Look To The Future

This planet Earth is soon to be doomed,
if people don't respect it.
Pollution, bombing, nuclear testing,
destroying it bit by bit.

Mother Nature's getting drained every day,
of oil, coal and gases.
Like a body being drained of blood,
becoming dryer as each day passes.

It's not just the Earth, it's the animals too,
being hunted, poached and culled.
Elephants, rhinos, even our seals
will soon be extinct from the world.

The planet itself will soon be extinct,
if something isn't done fast.
Wake up to yourselves before it's too late,
THIS WORLD HAS GOT TO LAST!

Gypsy Carkett

Lines On A Mixture Of Races

Child of mixed races, there's no need to weep
If prejudice sets one aside in the sheep!
Our shepherd who cares for us, each one and all,
Was concerned if even a sparrow should fall.
So be not ashamed of religion or race
(And who knows the colour of our MASTER'S FACE?)
For should you arrive at the gates of heaven
Think you HE will ask if you ate bread unleaven?
Do you think HE will care about colour of skin?
No! Greater value HE'LL set on the person within!
Accept this plain truth; may you hold your head high
Be as good as the best; look the world in the eye.

Helen Smyth Thomson

Only The Wind

When you're not here
I hear only the wind
And the creak of expanding materials.
The house is as silent
As the compartments of my mind
Where my spirit cannot settle
But drifts from room to room
Looking in all the places
Where you might have been,
But knowing that you're not there.
I miss you
Wishing you were here.

Edi Clack

The Fire Brigade

An important service, the fire brigade,
If you want to join a life-saving trade,
A dangerous job, as everyone knows,
But very rewarding, and here's how it goes,
Building on fire, it's well ablaze,
Visions of people, through the smoke haze,
The brigade has arrived, the engine goes by,
The fireman are running — adrenalin high,
Child's face at the window, oh so clear,
Screaming so loudly, she's full of fear,
Up goes the ladder, so very fast,
As all the smoke, goes swirling past,
The ladder goes up, the fireman moves in,
Lying on the bed, is the little girl's twin,
He lifts them both with loving care,
And brings to the ground this lucky pair,
Down in the kitchen, their mother is found,
So grateful her children are both safe and sound,
She thanks the firemen, one and all,
Then they're off to the station to await their next call.
Florence J. Gillanders

Why

Wondering why is a waste of time
If you're looking for reasons
You will always miss the why
If you're using all your time looking for the sign
You will wait and never try
Benjamin MacLeod

" God's Roses "

If I get to heaven before you
I'll whisper a word in God's ear
And ask him to send you roses
One for each month of the year.
The first rose will be a red one,
A symbol of love that is true.
The second, a rose tinted yellow
For peace a remembrance are there,
A white rose will be
For the power of prayer and
Pink for a friend, when you need a friend's care.
All other roses of different hues
Will be in the bouquet of God's gift to you.
But the rose you will see stand out from the rest
Will be your favourite, by far,
The 'fairest rose' from heaven will be sent
On the wings of an angel's star.
Beryl LLoyd

Killer

He stalked his victim down into the park
His mind so warped as he planned in the dark

The body was found, brutally mutilated in death,
Just dumped, so cruelly on the heath

An investigation the police did lodge,
But which the killer did manage to dodge

Finally, when he was caught
Insane, he definitely was not

A respected member of the public in fact
For which he was shown a great deal of tact

It was put before the court
When four years imprisonment was all to report

An eye for an eye was the old fashioned way
But it's not done like that today

The death sentence is what he should face
Maybe it would deter others and help keep us safe.
Louise D. Carle

Untitled

Oh Jesus! What is this I feel
I'm a killer but why is it such a big deal
Teenage emotion, a girl and a boy
I committed a murder, a fire I did destroy
I the tormentor, it is such a scandal
I the big twister, I feel like a vandal
One day it will happen, I feel it in my blood
But for now it really stinks and is the colour of mud
Everything gone, in me a great vacuum
Everything gone, swept up by a broom
I know where you live, I've lodged there before
I know how you live, real painful and sore
Yesterday I could have been you
A pearl in your eye
After tomorrow I will have seen you
And inside I'll cry
I know how you feel, your respect is sincere
But what is respect — but another word for fear...
Keith Moon

My Recluse

He's getting worse you know, even by the day,
I'm frightened, scared and lonely because I know he'll send us packing. My father was never like this, sure, he'd sometimes say, "I'm going out for a bit" but he'd always come back, and we didn't mind the smacking. He'd kiss our mum; there was so much fun. But those days are now far away.

When he walks around the house the furniture quakes with his feet, I stay very quiet while a light goes off here and a fire down there, "God! Don't let the child sit in his seat."
So we creep around, otherwise he'll say we're always in his hair, Put the child to bed; silently kiss her head. Now I'm terrified we'll meet. You must understand he wasn't always like this, it was better when he went to work but now he works from home, he was funny and charming, those are days I miss. But nowadays he even growls at the phone. He's irritated by people; any really. Do you suppose we'll ever make up and kiss.

I'm not allowed our friends and family here now, he will simply moan And say he needs his peace. (Why can't he drop dead then?) I so much want to talk it out but he'll just sigh and groan. I don't want to leave, but I know I have to agree we'll "go away", when the words I'd love to hear the most again are, "We want to be alone".
Delia Mary Anne Bruton

Feelings

I cry as I hold myself, I try to sleep at night
I'm frightened, so frightened of the world outside
Trouble outside my window, people shout and fight
I feel the need to run away but there's nowhere to hide

I try and bite hard on the bullet of silence
As the streets outside bleed hatred and violence
Loneliness and solitude and total isolation
Are a price I pay, to stay away from people's violation
Not just that we had many years of lowly unemployment
Staying in night after night with only T.V. for enjoyment
A sad, useless, futile, pathetic life just wasting away
There's no reason to existence when your being is just
    nothing day after day
A prisoner, a victim, I'm doing hard time
Loneliness, penniless, and friendless, that's my crime
the streets appear empty but they're full of fear
I don't wonder the suicide rate is high around here
Crying, screaming, dying, but nobody hears
Crying, screaming, dying about the wasted years.
Andrew Norris

June's New Wellies

Hip hip hooray, hip hip hooray
I'm going shopping to Mansfield today
I need some new wellies, my others both leak,
So off to the shoe shop, some wellies to seek
My feet are all wet, in fact they are sodden,
'Cos down in the yard in the sludge I have trodden,
But all that is finished now, I'm pleased to say,
I bought my new wellies in Mansfield today.

My friend Jean only eats margarine
It sells in the name of "Flora"
It works like a treat, for her figure is so neat,
And all the boys "Adora"

Think of all those years ago
When our love was new, our eyes aglow
Now look at us, we're old and grey
And bicker and argue every day.
June Gibson

Habit Of A Life-Line

Don't you love me Mummy?
I'm here, inside your tummy,
And I'm trying every day, to breathe and grow.
But there's something on my mind,
Are you cruel, or are you kind?
Why do you try to choke me? I don't know.
If I've been naughty, no one told me,
Oh Mummy, please don't scold me,
Or you won't see or hold me,
Will you?..... Mummy.
Jeff McCue

The Dangle Doll (The Rejected Toy)

I'm the Dangle Dolly, I haven't got a name,
I'm just like the others, we all look just the same.
I'm the Dangle Dolly, I'm hung up on a string,
I'm stuck here all day long, I never do a thing.

My life is such a sad one, but my mouth is made to smile,
I'd rather be down on the floor, next to the Lego pile.

I'm the Dangle Dolly, my hair's like golden corn,
I've only got one eye, my dress is ripped and torn.

For as long as I remember, I've been upon this nail,
My make-up's fading by the hour, I'm looking rather pale.

I'm the Dangle Dolly, I try to be so glad,
But you must admit that really, my story's very sad.
Danyele L. Thorpe

" Raisons De Poesie "

Some write in verse to please their mate
I'm not averse to that
And others write of well loved pets
Their hamster or their cat

Much doggerel is often found
In poems such as these
But it is hard to be a bard
If experts you would please

Some pen long lines, like columbines, that string their words together
Some gain their inspiration from peculiar sorts of weather

A limerick is often used
To tell a dirty joke
A lass from Yorkshire doing summat
To a Yorkshire bloke

Some write from dungeon dark and grim
In hope to gain remission
But I am writing this to try
To win a competition
Douglas J. O'Neale

A Day In The Life Of Dudley

Please let me out, it's almost dawn
I'm sure there's something on the lawn,
Please let me go, 'twill soon be light,
I have been good, stayed in all night

I'm out at last, I've been released,
Anticipation has increased,
A cat! It's black — and so serene
Must be a girl — oh! Love's young dream!

My mistress thinks I've gone astray
She's hunted everywhere all day!
Why all this fuss and consternation?
She knows I've had the operation

By ten, she quite thought I was dead,
So master took himself to bed.
When no-one's looking, in I'll creep
And curl-up tight, and go to sleep
Relief — when they find me alive —
I'll get them up again at five!
My lovely girl-friend will come back,
'Cos I'm a moggie-ginger cat!
Diana Hickman

Secure For A Moment

Her arms held out
I'm taken in,
Protected from the harsh world wind.
The warmth and softness of this place
Smothers all my day's disgrace.
Covered with love in this surround
My feet no longer feel the ground,
I'm held, suspended, in the air
Relieved, secure in trust and care.

My embryonic state will break,
The minute daylight strikes I wake.
All the tenderness is gone.
Yet again, I stand alone.
Elizabeth A. Sorbie

Reflections Of The Unknowable God

When we have fears that we may cease to be,
In a cosmos whose purpose we cannot see,
In a life without reason or rhyme,
Though we try to put meaning to time,
When all deeds are swallowed by the great abyss
And intentions, meaning, hopes become remiss,
Then in that abyss, where love is just a dream,
Is Man's defiance sensed, in its silent scream.

An echo of a shadowed essence, long forlorn
Shall, with joyful wisdom, smile upon the years unborn;
For in the twilight of idols and their kingdoms demise,
From ashes in ashes, therein shall arise —
Man's muted spirit defiant, like a last trumpet call —
A new god, The True God! — for love conquered all.
James Hale

Bridegroom Speech

Now the bond is set between me and my wife,
I want you all to witness it's intended for our life.
To love each other dearly more and more each day,
Sticking close together, strong against the fray.
We thank you all sincerely, we're glad you could attend,
To all you here now gathered, warm greetings we extend.
With your gifts we are delighted, overcome and quite excited.
Best man, bridesmaids, groomsmen too,
we give our thanks to all of you.
Thanks to our parents seated at our side, we hope this special day of
Ours has filled your hearts with pride.
And now at last in ending there's one thing left to say:
Thank you, dearest Kathleen, for being my bride today.
Chas E. Thompson

Andrew

I saw my boss Andrew the other night
In a dream — he said to me "it's alright."
He rushed round the corner in his usual way
As if it was just an ordinary day.
I worried the others might see him and cry
Or think that their eyes were telling a lie.
Perhaps he didn't know he shouldn't be there
He'd died in a car crash as we're all aware.
Perhaps he just came to say his goodbyes
Though to think of him still brings tears to our eyes.
Chris Keys

The Ballad Of Asda's Explosions

The quiet area was shattered
In April ninety four
When the floors of Gosport rumbled
Like they'd never done before

People were running around their houses
Shouting out in their fear
"My God, it's the gas cylinders
Behind our houses here!"

High up go the explosions
With a ball of flame
Some people saw two boys run off
Are they the ones to blame?

No one ever thought that it
Would get onto the news
They think it was those boys to blame
But the police are finding new clues
Amanda Adams

Dilemma

Life and time move ever on
In constant waves of crest and fall,
Ours did with realistic flurry
Until the day that came for Louis.
Too soon, too soon, now he is gone.
I lived, he died, his waves ran on
To nothing on the sands of life.
Dilemma wrapped itself around
And in a dank and dreary place
I floated free of feeling.
Voices calling, wake now wake, it's time to go.
Cars arrive, black all black, I hide my face.
Too bright the sun slanting through the window,
Glasses help, their darkened lens concealing
Tears and doubt from neighbours prying.
Return. People talking drinking, how they stare,
It's cold and empty, you are not there.
Dilemma, a hard choice, the sage will say.
I've tried, I've tried and am still trying.
To me it simply means I've lost my way.
Betty Smith

Dad

My words couldn't tell you how much I love you so
The feelings that I have inside, I tried so hard to show.
You were a dad in a million, simply the best,
And now on Monday, we're laying you to rest.

Help us get by in this time of need,
Throughout your life you did your good deed,
Help us with your courage, guide us with your love,
Now you're at peace, just like a dove.

You were loved by all, you'll be missed as much,
We'll never hear your voice again, nor ever feel your touch,
You'll always be with us in our minds and our thoughts,
You always loved us with all of our faults.

Now the time has come for you to go,
Rest in peace, Dad, I love and miss you so,
Rest peacefully, Dad, I hope you can,
'Cos all through my life, you were a wonderful man.
Tracey Banks

Frost In Spring

The frost his wonders will perform,
In darkness and alone.
With magic strokes he works unseen,
Mysterious powers will change the scene.

His silent gift, artistic flair,
In spring will catch us unaware.
His work begins before the dawn,
We wake to see our world transformed.

With strokes of skill he paints the trees,
Lightly touching flowers and leaves.
A fairy glen his paradise,
Deceiving us with power, he tries.

The gentle flowers of Spring will fail,
To trust or understand.
This swiftly moving stranger,
With deft and powerful hands.

When the morning sun's warm rays,
Will touch his work of art,
They vanish like a stranger,
Who works alone when dark
Dorothy Wales

God's Presence

God's presence is all around us,
In everything we see.
The shy and tiny violet,
and mighty forest tree.

A woodlands leafy glade,
The sparkling mountain stream.
And towering peaks, that to heaven point,
In sunlight's bright golden gleam.

In the glowing colours of the sunset,
Or the rosy pink of dawn.
The cry of a lonely curlew,
So sad and so forlorn.

The gentle murmur of the waves,
On a distant sandy shore,
Or crashing down upon the rocks,
With a cruel, and savage roar.

All these things will tell
Of his presence, ever near.
To comfort, and reassure us,
And free from our darkest fear.
Ernest Scott

Childhood's End

Darkness is not my friend.
  In it my teddy bear cries and I lie dry-eyed,
  Trembling, curled in a ball,
  Willing it not to happen tonight,
  Please, oh please...

Darkness is not my friend.
  I wish Daddy would come and make me safe,
  But Daddy isn't Daddy in the dark.
  I love my Daddy.
  Please, oh please...

Darkness is not my friend.
  A monster with Daddy's voice hushes me,
  Its fingers, Daddy's fingers, touching me in funny ways,
  In funny places. I'm frightened.
  Please, oh please...

I will be six years old tomorrow,
  And Daddy says he will give me a special birthday present.
Jeanne M. Cahill

Destiny

I closed my eyes and I went to sleep.
In my mind I went down deep.
Deeper and deeper I travelled inside.
Trying to find the things I hide.
I journey on without any fear
I've gone so far, I must be near.
At last I find what I'm looking for
It's hidden deep behind a door.
I reach this door, and as I turn the knob,
I heard a cry, a faintly sob.
I wonder what I'd probably see.
A ghostly future, ahead of me.
I ask myself, "Is this the way
This door could lead to my dismay?"
I closed the door and shut it tight
It is my choice. I hope I'm right.
I travel back up my mind.
Leaving my destiny way behind.
So, waking up I realize
Knowing your future is not wise.

Kevin Dunn

Ave Maria — Rosa Mystica

O lady, they write about roses in song
In poetry, music and art
But there's one fragrant rose that they know not about
The rose, who is queen of my heart.

Innocent and untouched, you were chosen by God
To enclose in your womb His own Son
For from all Adam's daughters, no other was found
Who would give Him pure love but this one

Though a sister and mother to many through love
No creature but Him came from you
For purity it was the dress that you wore
Virginity, your own virtue.

In these times when e'en priests despise this great wealth
As they seek once again poisoned fruit
We will hold up your beauty for all eyes to see
Your chaste love in our hearts will take root

So, Mother, cultivate all your virtues in us
For your children have known bitter blows
Make us blossom and grow in earth's garden for God
And for you, our sweet mystical rose

Frances Anne Doogan

The Clover Field

To wake in peerless sunny June
In that month's lovely morning
To walk through fields of clover bloom
Dew kissed in early dawning
A fragrant memory in time
A small bliss to be treasured
Timely reminder that such joys
Are neither bought nor measured.

Doris A. Birke

A Dream

One day I dream of being far away,
In the countryside where the lambs play,
where the valleys are green and the skies are blue,
I can only dream that one day it will come true,
where the horses and the cattle feed,
in the fields of grass
with the cool breeze and the shining
Sun, I hope it will just last and last,
As I lay here dreaming of the place I want to be,
with the streams of water and the hills so high,
I wish I was a bird so I could fly,
as I could see my dream from the sky,
As I lay here so far away.

Kerry Davis

Words

There are no words here,
In the dark pathways of everything I know
Years of education come to this
You are wonderful, indescribably so,
Inexplicable, you are,
My feelings are a mystery even to myself
Only I have never felt like this before
I need only you, and no one else.
I once thought I had mastered words
But now they came to nothing
But still, only sentences, missing something
Only this is what I'm sure of
There is no doubt, no pain, no fear
For you are somehow something more
Than any of the words that are written here
So what is beyond words?
If words are mortal, my feelings must be raised above,
Embedded in the depths of my very soul,
Eternal, everlasting love.

Heidi E. Mercalfe

The Cat Sat On That Mat (Feline Philosophy)

The cat sat on the mat, contented with his lot.
In the friendly, flickering firelight caring not one jot,
For that hostile world outside, all jungle tooth and claw,
Was left behind forgotten after coming through the door.
O fluffy furry feline, what is your secret, tell
To me that I may also share and with such bliss can dwell.
Then speaking without saying a word! He turned his head with affection
"If you appreciate what you have, what you have is perfection."

Ken Harvey

The Prostitute

She walked along the village street,
In the glare of light to offer her treat,
Their eyes looked out from curtains drawn,
They were cunning and wished it was dark.

Her legs were shapely like her face,
The swerve of her body could hold you in disgrace,
Lust and must not was in many a stare,
How to catch her in your imaginary snare.

From bedroom windows they looked down in forlorn mood,
And instead of contact they settled for food,
They imagined the grasp of her waist,
And the willingness of her body to the caress.

With wife they lived in nagging doubt,
And in silence they sought this prostitute out,
One moment of bliss they found in between trees and hedges bare,
She kindled the fire of passion and left them to stand and stare,

Now woeful Nell walked the village through the day,
Not one of her clients will want to recognize her this way,
But when darkness creeps through the half lit streets,
They will remember Nell and her treats.

John Cusack

The Birth Of Spring

As I gaze from my window into winters dark gloom
in gardens and hedges are the promise of blooms
Since their conception seems a long time ago
I wait with excitement for blossoms to grow

While springtime is slumbering there seems no great haste
Snowdrops and primrose are warmly encased
Deep in the earth, nature is stirring its seeds
Like embryos growing in blankets of leaves

In underground darkness the quietness prevails
We all watch and wait for those first fragile pearls
Then with calmness and beauty struggling through Mother Earth
These gentle sweet flowers have at last given birth

Georgina Bond

Footsteps

Through the waving grasses our footsteps whisper still,
In the glow of morning and the evening chill,
Among the rustling branches our voices murmur on,
And drifting on the night breeze the echo of a song.

Hear you not our laughter, gentle as before.
Turn your head and listen then to this sweet encore
Of our beings moving through another dream,
Timeless as a distant star or a fleet sunbeam.

Think you all is lost, because you see us not,
Can you lose a memory that will not be forgot,
Cast away all boundaries of your human thought,
Open up your vision, forget all you were taught.

Seek out the space in which to breathe,
Tread lightly through the air,
Look far beyond the fretting throng
and you will find us there.

Enid Brewer

Coming To Terms

An empty chair at the table, a hat on the stand
   in the hall
Rob sits and waits by the doorway, with his
   lead, a stick and his ball
Alert for the sound of a footstep and for his
   name to be called;
For him no more walks with his master - can't
   believe this has happened at all

Rob will still have his outings and bury his
   ball in the sand
I will stroll by the seashore to think of all
   we had planned
But the days will seem so much longer without
   the warmth of his hand;

If I feel that each day has no purpose and
   that my life is going nowhere
I'll reflect on all that was lovely - of all
   the times we would share
And be thankful for so many fond memories
   As Rob sleeps in his master's old chair

Anne Goodale

Laburnum

The day... the memory ... dust motes dancing
In the sun's rays — bold colours romancing,
Fresh like the Very First Day — unmuted,
Dawning untouched, unmarr'd, unpolluted,
Shining brightly... clean, clean... undistorted.

Heat hazy on the open road, the rich smell
Of sweet-mown hay, carried on the wind to dwell
Forever treasur'd, well-remember'd — and more,
Insinuating subtly on mem'ry's store,
Penetrating... deep, deep... your very core.

The road winding, winding to the blue sea, hedg'd
By a terraced hillside... at the ocean's edge,
A bank of golden rain growing, there adorning,
Slight fragrant pendulous blooms deeply glowing,
Like a cascade... down, down... softly flowing.

Gwen Douglas

Memories

Laughter filled the house so still
In memory stored, to hear at will
The silent house, no laughter here
These thoughts were from a yesteryear
When children played, their happy sounds
The house with laughter knew no bounds
But only silence now is heard
Except for thoughts that can't be shared
But they can fill the house once more
With laughter, like it was before

Ann Muir

Shades Of Autumn

Shades of autumn all around,
In the trees and on the ground,
Rustic colours tinged with yellow everywhere
And the leaves they set the scene
For the season that is queen
As she reigns o'er all the colours
In her care.

And autumn leaves beneath my feet make me recall
The times we walked together when the leaves did fall,
For like the leaves that leave the trees
When parted by the autumn breeze
My love she wandered far from me
And left me like some leafless tree

When the autumn days are gone
And the winter days are born
Shades of autumn I'll engrave
Within my mind,
And I'll picture me with you
In the autumn days we knew,
And my lost love in my mem'ries I shall find.

Alex J. Lawson

" The Lonesome Soldier "

As I lie here upon my bunk,
In this forsaken place,
England rushes back to me,
With all its love and grace,

Take me back to those isles I love,
To those shores I surely miss,
Oh! let me go home to the comforts of home,
And the warmth of my Mother's kiss.

Maybe a day, a month or a year,
When I will be set free,
I'll look back on this place with a smile
It will be just a memory.

Elsie M. Hellon

Dave On, 'Children Of Hope'

I rarely cry or shed a tear,
In this war-torn world of strife and fear,
Where many exist on a paucity of pleasure,
And a dream of unearthing some hidden treasure.
But suddenly from a great abyss,
Can erupt a source of peace and bliss,
That restores your faith, restores that smile,
Restores that glow for at least a while.
I found a treasure right out of the blue,
When 'Jack and Beanstalk' I was asked to view,
Performed by children with loss of hearing,
With hearts so big and so endearing.
So much was given by so few,
A performance of class and courage too,
Inspired by staff with sheer devotion,
Combining to produce pure sweet emotion.
And the effect of tears running down my face,
Suddenly gave me hope for the human race.
Now when I feel sad, down or worse,
I just think of the children that inspired this verse.

Dave Elliott

Lovers

The frozen fragrance of sweet love thrives
intimately amongst nostalgia.
Sensitized lips of entanglement are placed
carefully on celluloid grains.
Infectious moments of observations tend to be
influenced by intense passion.
Bringing closer inconceivable fragments of
affection.
Standing sexposed for the world to see.

Kurt Clegg

'Unrequited Love'

Today, your birthday once again
In thought I'm with you all the day,
I live again the joys we knew
My heart is full of times so gay.

So many miles between we two
I long to see your face once more,
To touch your hand and be content
To walk with you as long before.

September days, October nights
With stars ablaze and moon-bright skies,
Though I spoke naught of love to you
Deep happiness was in my eyes.

I loved you well, but I was young
Too young and gay to know just then,
How, through the years my love would grow
And burn inside with endless pain.

For you are far from me, my love
And I can only dream of thee,
Until such time when I shall come
To tell you that my soul is free.

Barbara Oldfield

A Valentine To E.C.D.

E ileen, thou sweetest lover of my heart,
I n thy fair arms my heaven on earth is found.
L ingering there with loving bands fast bound
E ver I'd be but I must needs depart.
E ver to be with thee — no separation,
N o other joy could be so full of bliss.

C ould I but order all the whole creation,
L overs would never know a parting kiss.
A nd yet, of course, they'd lose the joy of meeting,
R eturning after many moons away,
I nstantly dispelling, by their greeting,
C ares, troubles, gloom that spoil the sunny day.
E aster and April now are drawing near,

D arling, and that means we shall be
I n ecstasies of joy. We are united!
F or that is happiness for you and me.
F ain would I come to you at this fair season,
E ven this day of holy Valentine.
Y es, 'cause I want to hear you whisper

That for eternity you will be mine.

Leonard Griffiths

Market Day

What hurry, what scurry, all in a hurry,
In town on a market day.
What pushing, what heaving, coming and leaving,
One dare not stop or stay.

Such crowing, such lowing, strong words a flowing,
As folk start to sell and to buy
The peals of squeals as pigs come on wheels
And four-legged beasties draw nigh.

Such excitement I vow, but I'll hie me right now
Back where the fields are all green.
Where no one need hurry or scurry or flurry
And never a soul may be seen.
Where crowing and lowing are part of the morning
And soft words, not harsh echo by.

Although folk may chaff me, or even strafe me.
Or may be just call me a fool.
Oh! fie me, I'll hie me back to the country
To brooks that are clear and cool
And I'll never, no never again go to stray
In town, on a market day.

Irene Ryder

Navy Life

Let me escape from this rabble and noise —
Indifferent matelots and foul-mouthed boys,
Who went through the war —
(So they say) —
And learned nothing more
Than the price of a whore,
And then wrote, as before,
"To my girl in U.K."
And the chaps who signed on
Whose ambition is gone,
Who soon gave up thinking —
For drinking.

David M. N. Scott

Holiday Home

Milestones represented by this one place.
Infinite in the mind though transient in reality,
a retreat, a world apart, a breathing space
wherein to pause, to put life into neutral
and, for an instant, timelessness embrace.
I dwell for a moment, linger, sit
upon the terrace and become a part
of this breathless, dreaming landscape. Tit,
taunting woodpecker, foraging squirrel start
and end their lives here but I must quit;
gather the pressed flowers of the mind,
wondering if these memories will be the last.
I leave for home without a glance behind,
knowing this spot is unaware of past
or present; undemanding — blind.

Brian Smith

A Unique Discovery Of Creation

Creation arose through one man's work
inspired by images and dreams
devoid of the impracticality
of ambitious, inconceivable themes.

Scrutinization of various concepts
attitudes of behaviour and growth
became almost incomprehensible
when studying the emotions of them both
for one emotion was quite inexplicable
its power and indestructible tie
such strength of affection and loyalty
for which people were willing to die
that pure enchantment of man
unbiased, determined and true
increasing in hearts day by day
affecting people like me and you
one delicate part of creation
concealed like a hand in a glove
a unique bond between two people
the security and devotion of "Love".

Julie Taylor

A Snowman's Life

I am a snowman, cold and white.
I stand all day and stand all night.
The children who made me
just leave me to melt,
here in the winter sun, slowly I smelt,
down — down — further I go
until one day I'm not even snow.
Can nobody help me
from this terrible slaughter?
Oh no, you're too late
I've turned into water
Down the long drains
on into the sea,
there I am free,
and I can see
many a snowman
just like ME.

Emma Kilduff

On Finding Love

Out of the darkness and into the light;
Into the sunrise from the depths of the night;
Out of the coldness and into the warm;
Into the harbour, safe from the storm.

From the petrified forest to the leafy glade;
From the burning desert to the welcoming shade;
From the raging torrent to the tranquil stream;
From the darkest nightmare to the sweetest dream.

Where once flew a vulture there now flies a dove;
Where once there was loneliness now there is love;
Where once was a vacuum there now beats a heart,
Pierced at long last by Cupid's rare dart.

Now that I've met you my life's not the same -
Now there is pleasure where once there was pain;
Now there is joy where once there were tears;
Now there are hopes where once there were fears.

If you give me your love and banish my sorrows
I have nothing to offer but all my tomorrows.
If you give me your love, not in part but the whole,
I have nothing to give but my heart and my soul.

Anthony J. Marston

Red Rose, Red Of Love

I feel how the distance
is cutting our veins,
I feel how the air
is taking our memories,
Ploughing the sea,
moving the mountains,
dying without me....

I imagine you loving the eternal frame
of my picture,
spelling each letter of my name,
thinking that the Red Rose
only loved in vain.

Red Rose, Red of Love
Queen of roses,
decipher the blue enigma
in the sea, hidden.

Rose of Love, Queen of Roses,
you told me that love was art,
Red Rose, Red in the Distance,
I've lost my heart.

Joanna Mireles Romero

Night Time

It's getting dark, the time I dread,
Is going to bed
I have to go upstairs all by myself
I'm really scared because it's very dark

Oh no! There's a noise behind me!
Phew, it's all right — mum's dropped her keys
I'll run upstairs as fast as I can,
Maybe there's nothing up there?

I brush my teeth, my heart is racing,
The light is on until I fall asleep
Into bed I snuggle down
Under the blankets I feel quite safe

Bang, bump, what is that?
I can't see because it's pitch black
I sweat and shake for a long time
My dreams scare me until the light wakes me up

At last it's night, time to get up
Everyone sleeps but I'm awake
I pick up the book that fell off the bed,
Every night is filled with dread.

Jennifer McAlpine

Friendship

The funniest thing about special friends
is hoping the friendship never ends,
enjoying the time together, that you share,
it's good to know there's some-one who cares.

Two sides are needed to being a friend:
feelings are involved, there's rules to bend,
accepting each other just the way that we are,
no matter whether you're near or far.

Abuse such trust, and caring you lose
for it's simply up to you to choose,
lovers — they may come and go,
true friends are forever, for you to know.

There are many types of love that one can feel,
the love of a friend you don't need to conceal,
that special bond, you can share for years,
throughout your life, your happiness and tears.

Caroline Knowles

Joanne — You Have My Blessing

Where is the Mum that used to be,
Is it something to do with me?
This question from my daughter stays,
Forever in my mind for days.
Have I changed — am I afraid,
To lose the love that we have made.
The years fly by — I knew that day
Would come, but not so soon, I say.
Only on loan, so I am told,
They have to go — so don't keep hold.
If only she knew I wish her well,
My heart just will not let me tell.

Carol Robins

The Problem

Greatest of all the great creations
Is resumptive man,
Who is too often quite unaware
Of his own great architectural plan.
Built from two tiny cells to spring
Into one complete full blooded,
Living, thinking, human thing.

With all this art great universal mind
In which we have our being,
Reveal, Oh please reveal to us
The Chemistry of reason.
Unlock, Oh please release the key
To the unknown essence of our mental chemistry.

How can we watch men fresh with glorious prime,
Go forth to slay or die,
Leaving behind a trail of limbless corpses
And half dissected children on their way,
Lest we on reaching some preeminent shore
Corrupt it, and destroy ourselves forevermore?

Georgina James

An Unrequited Love

Each minute of every hour that goes past
Is an eternity since I saw you last.
My wishes softly spoken are of you.
My dreams and my heartache are nothing new.
You never seem to notice how I feel.
This love and this need are very real.
If only you could see what's inside.
This love for you I have to hide.
To hear your voice and know you're near.
Alone at night I shed a tear.
I wish you felt as I do.
If only you would love me too.
My only hope, a silent cry.
Just one kiss before I die.

Janis Johnston

'Just Wishful Thinking'

To lay wrapped in your arms all night
   is something I long to feel,
to wake up beside you every morning
   would be wonderfully unreal.

To look into your eyes each day
   would be my dearest wish come true,
my second wish, just a simple one
   to hear you say 'I love you,'

To kiss your lips and hold you tight
   and make love each day with you,
I dream of doing all these things
   from dusk till morning dew.

You're on my mind every single day
   when I'm eating, sleeping and drinking,
but we both know that in reality
   this is all 'just wishful thinking'.

Annette Warnes

Our Lunch At Orsett Hall

A day in my life I will always recall,
Is the day we had lunch at Orsett Hall,
With me were Dennis, Arthur and Jean,
As well as Phyllis, and our dear Friend Jan,
It was so nice to be together, we chatted and laughed,
We spoke of the present, we recalled the past,
We admired the decor, and lovely surroundings,
The view through the windows was really astounding,
For a moment my thoughts went back to Sir Francis
And his Lady, and of King George V planting an Oak tree
In these lovely grounds, so beautiful and pleasant,
And inside the Hall, of History and of treasures.
The staff were so courteous, and kind, the food was
Delicious, the champagne superb, of a better place I have
Never heard. We came home elated, so full of good cheer,
Surprised at the cost for this day and year.
"Cheers to all, Management, and Staff of Orsett Hall;
We shall return without fail. Warm thanks to you all."

Doris A. Clark

The Gift Of Life

The greatest gift that you can give
Is the gift of life, to breathe and live
You had a difficult choice to make
You refused your treatment for babies' sake
Your loved ones stood by you with pride
Your husband proud by your bedside
Nine months have passed, the time has come
In return for your pain, a newborn son
What price death and family strife
A gift so precious, the gift of life.

Colin Henderson

On Faith

Your eyes searched deep into my own, and then —
"Is there a God for you?"
The answer, in the air before I spoke,
Brooked, surely, of denial — as you knew!

You did not judge, but gently, speaking soft,
Told of your God of love,
And of the son I had not time to name,
Whose pure, unblemished soul He guards above,
Of other sons who stride across this Eden
In consequence of me,
Of faith and life and courage fresh discovered,
By those with eyes that are prepared to see.

If God resides with beauty and in truth,
And through them shows the way,
And since, with you, these graces are confided,
Then, in that room, He was with me, that day.

Leslie J. Butt

Untitled

I'm 38 years old, what on earth am I doing?
Is this really a dream, that I am pursuing?
My heart beats a lot faster my body is shaking,
A fool of myself, is that, what I'm making?

Questions I ask of myself, as I make my journey,
Is this desire to achieve, after all, really for me?
Perhaps I should stay at home, it's where I belong,
I'm much too old to compete against the young.

My struggle will be fierce, it's a young person's thing,
If I did succeed, just exactly what would it bring?
The work will be intense, will I be able to manage?
Will it reflect on my family, causing untold damage?

Will I earn the friendship and respect of my peers?
These uncertainties I have, concerning my fears,
Such negative thoughts whirling around my brain,
But if I don't at least try, what then, will I gain?

With the support of my family and the love I take with me,
I will go to college, and try to get my degree,
Will I succeed or fail? The answer I do not know,
Of one thing I am certain however, I'll have a go!

Jennifer Ann Anderson

Parents

There is a light, I see it clear.
It becomes apparent the time is near.
There are people shouting, push, yes push.
Oh hold your horses; what's the rush?
O.K. now let us part.
I guess it's time, my life should start.

Yes I'm here, oh what an entry.
Have I entered the land of gentry?
Does it matter? No I don't mind.
The man looks happy, the lady kind.
In their arms they hold me tight.
I'm tired now; it must be night.

My life is racing; I'm growing fast.
I've found my feet; I'm having a blast.
They gave me life, a chance to dream
They're the greatest, what a team!
They make me happy when I'm sad.
Thank you so much, Mum and Dad.

Linda Wood

Wishes For The World

'Twas the night before Christmas and all was still
Is that Santa's sleigh coming down the hill
The children in bed awaiting the dawn
They'll open their presents with the coming of morn

If only all cares the people could shed
If fighting could cease, the world have peace
No youngsters in doorways to sleep in the cold
No stories of violence newspapers unfold

God has given us all that we need
So much has been spoiled by hate and greed
Man makes his own hell on life's pathway
But God's light will always brighten his way

So shine on the light of the Bethlehem star
So carry on Santa, keep travelling far
So sleep on you children in beds safe and warm
With faith in these things, we can weather all storms

The sky may be dark because it is night
But the stars and the moon give us bright light
Good thoughts and hope always come through
Remember that someone will always love you

Chrissy Thompson

Dalesman's Epitaph

As I sit amongst these hills so wild
It brings back thoughts of when a child.
Then, all that mattered was to chase a dream,
And remember every mystic scene.
But youth is quickly passed by age
And all too soon our life must change.
No more to climb these hills so high,
To reach the top and touch the sky.
The spirit's strong, but the body's weak,
Never again can I climb that peak.
Now I sit here, old and grey,
Nearing the end of my earthly stay.
I am not sad, nor will I cry,
For I still walk these Dales in my inner eye.

Anthony Horrell

I Saw A Star

I saw a star, it was very bright
It came from God, I know that's right
He is with me all the while
And even now he makes me smile
I see Jesus come to me
Makes me happy as can be
They give me peace and contentment too
They take away all my blue
And mother God is there as well
She will always ring a bell
She will guide me all the way
To the land where all is day
And where no pain ever will be
I will love them all eternally
And on the road there I'll wind
And take brothers and sister's to be my friends

Alma Hindson

Heidi

This sweet haven, is my garden.
It holds my memories and tells many stories.
Crawling ivy reminds me,
The luscious grass tells me of my past.

I used to be a daisy,
Raising my dew-painted lips to the sky.
But now I feel like a dandelion,
If the wind blows roughly, my petals will scatter.
I feel my soul belongs on the mountainside,
In the gentle breeze and tall fern trees.
On sunkissed slopes and quiet glens,
Where whispers echo by even pools.

I long to be the heather,
Wild and free.
But my one true love,
He prefers the English Rose to me.

You cannot hold a moment,
They become but gentle dreams.
The night is growing cold,
I'll protect my heart with my leaves

Heidi E. Metcalfe

" Just For You "

If I could catch the dawn, the rising sun, the morning dew,
I would keep them "just for you",

If I could catch a rainbow, I'd tie it in a bow,
And wrap around a raindrop, and keep it "just for you".

I would hold on to the bird song, the
    awakening of the land.
The burning golden sunsets, I'd put them in your hand.

These are the things I would give to you,
More precious than money or toys.

For these are the things throughout your life,
That will bring you endless joys.

June McCabe

Poems

That have the shape and sound of music.
It is my own voice
You will reply.

That catch the elusive moment in a phrase.
This was my purpose
You will sigh.

Limned with the briefest brush strokes.
Just what was intended
You imply.

That capture fugitive feelings and the pain.
This was what I hoped for
You will cry.

That tremble on the edge of a discovery.
These are my dreams
You will reply.

That presage home-coming by land, sea and sky.
That this is your destination
You can't deny.

John Roland Haynes

The One Love I Ever Knew

Where are you now my love?
It is not for you, my dear, my darling dear
that I live and you die, my love
It is for us that you have paid the price
My heart is aching, my heart is aching
for the one love I ever knew

My heart is aching, my heart is aching
for all the good things you always did
God knows what I'll do without you now
If only you knew how much I miss you
My heart is aching, my heart is aching
because I loved you so, did you know

Gone are the days when two lovers met
Gone are the nights, when two hearts beat
Gone are the moments we sat and sighed
Gone are nights I'd look into your blue eyes
Gone are the moments when you laid down and died

Until my beautiful, my love divine
Calm is the slumber as an infant sleeps
and man who is on borrowed time is called to rest in peace.

Agneta Hughes

The Tonsillectomy

Can I cope with this vigil I've made,
It is something I cannot evade.
You must be brave and strong little Spike,
You and your daddy are so much alike.

Down to the theatre, we are going at last,
will come for you when the hour has passed.
Time moves slowly, I feel so alone,
My stomach is churning, must not moan.

The nurse calls me, it's all over now?
I hear you shouting, sounds like a row.
Into the lift and back to the ward.
With this grandson, who's so much adored.

Restlessly sleeps for most of the day.
I wish he were well and wanted to play.
Passed four o'clock, Spike opens his eyes.
He's awake at last, and then he smiles.

It is good, Spike will now be alright,
'Daddy will come to see you tonight'.
I must leave now, my vigil is done.
'Goodbye for now', my little grandson.

Jean Stinson

Enigmatic Thoughts

Poetry is a comfort in a world so insecure,
It is the soul writing the pages, releasing the impure.
It acts as a religion and makes one look within,
At facing our mortality and recognising sin.
It purges doubt and disbelief within the human frame,
Putting things in perspective when the ego's hurt and lame.
The mind is strengthened in resolve, to face each cruel jolt,
As sham is ever present where it was thought there was no fault.
Tears stream within to wash away the anger one can feel,
When analysing hurt and letting deep wounds heal.
The scars, called "experience", are made of endless toil,
Waning only on the day we shuffle off this mortal coil.
Each day is one step nearer that end, whate'er it be,
When the struggle is all over and the soul is really free.
It is an enigma, wondering why during life's short span,
Man cannot be more honest towards his fellow man.
   Dennis V. Clough

Peace

How peaceful, how white,
it is today.
The tall trees in my garden,
the grass, the bushes,
all around is white....white....,
so peaceful....
   The snow is falling slowly, slowly,
   the beauty of the moment,
      the enchanted second...
      peace, nothing but peace....
For this moment,
for the snow falling slowly,
for allowing me to be here,
for allowing me to be at peace
with myself and at peace
with everything around me
thank you good Lord.
   Helena S. Armstrong

Love's Journey

Love is elusive but ever present
It quickly darts in and out of the minds of men
Love cannot remain at any one time or place
As all gifts have to be appreciated
Love is worthy of man's constant search
And as man searches so love searches man

If a man is of truth and sincerity
His share of the love force will remain with him
To warm his soul and body
For love was born to abide in all life
And only wanders to share its beauty and grace
With those who seek its everlasting force

Love is to be cherished and kept warm
But is an entity which exists for itself
For if it did not, man would have lost love long ago
   Jacqueline Butler

My Rainbow

I saw a lovely picture, a rainbow after a storm
It seemed to be so peaceful, as if all the wrong was gone
It had a sense of honesty with sunshine all around
As if this thing of beauty was too pure to touch the ground

But then the storm restarted, more violent than before
It caused my rainbow so much harm it cut it to the core
I ran to seek some shelter from this most fierce-some storm
But on turning back to see my rainbow its colours were all gone.

I started questioning myself, why did I run away?
If e'er I meet that storm again, I'll face it come what may.
And with my newfound courage I questioned all the more
Until I asked my maker, the truth was what he bore.

He sent me forth a message which was sadly told to me
I had not realised before, but that rainbow once was me.
   Grainne Moore

Whilst Sitting On A Creative Seat

I sit and stare down at my shoes,
it seems I've got the toilet blues.
Seated here for such a long time
I've even compiled this awful rhyme.

I can't do a poo, I don't know why,
it just won't come, as hard as I try.
With clenched muscles and bowels it's really not fair,
all I can manage, is smelly old air.

Beginning to get pins and needles in my legs,
oh, if only I hadn't eaten — so many eggs.
Concentrate now — I think there's a sign,
I just need to squeeze -- one more time.

I can do a poo, I know that I can,
one last squeeze and it plops in the pan.
More slides down the side, and sticks to the bottom.
Don't know what I've eaten, but it must have been rotten.

Wondering why it just wouldn't give,
next time I'll take a laxative.
I learned all this stuff from my silly old tutor.
What a wonderful place to use a lap-top computer.
   Brian H. Reeman

The Late Kevin Carter Or Conscience Of Africa

In the paper a photo shot
It seems the man who took it never forgot
For later he took his own life

Ultimate atonement? Call it what you will
That same picture haunts me still
And always will.

Yes he won the pulitzer prize,
But afterwards did he realize
What matters most are human lives?

It said he chased the vulture away
The tragedy was he let the little girl stay
dying in the sand.

People condemned him, I did too
Until I read what he had been through
Who to leave who to save,
What a decision to have to make.

He did not lack compassion's touch
He was only the man, who they said,
   saw too much
   Hilda Atchison

Thanksgiving

Autumn is the time of fulfilment,
It is the time of harvest,
After the months of preparation, and development,
A time of reward, storing, and thankful feast.

Around us a profusion of glorious colours to see,
Ripening fruits, vegetables, corn and wheat,
Beautiful richly-hued flowers,
And fallen leaves, kicked and crunched by children's feet.

Harvest suppers, festivals, thanksgiving,
The cleaning, sorting, thinking, decoration and displaying,
Apples, oranges, pears, grapes, pomegranates arriving,
Harvest loaves, communion Set, the Bible on white cloths gleaming.

Flower arrangements done with zest and flair,
The largest pumpkin that's ever been grown,
Long inscribed vegetable marrows handled with care,
All the produce of field and garden, from the miracle of seeds sown.

The Preacher has come, the choir is ready,
The organist strikes up a harvest hymn,
Children bring in their gift baskets, slow and steady,
Walk back to their seats, let the service begin.
   Doreen Dower

Ritual

Jacob is waiting for his collar:
   It shows that he is mine,
I slip my watch upon my wrist:
   It shows I'm bound to time.

Bare oak and chestnut, sycamore,
   Lent lilies waving past,
And who went this way yesterday,
   What scents left in the grass?
Jacob bounces, trots and canters,
   Keeps an eye on me,
He greets his friends, two-legged and four-
   And spreads his joie de vivre.

We wind our way by woodland track -
   A ritual blessedness,
Then home again for coffee time
   Dear Jacob wouldn't miss.
Charlotte Golding

Some Times

To waste it is a moral crime,
It started to direct mankind,
It controls the working day,
Called to halt our evening play,
Consuming tasks that take too long,
To spend it well is never wrong,
If you're not on it people scoff,
You're frowned at if you have it off,
Fictitious heroes travel through it,
Criminals if caught must do it,
If out of it you cannot win,
Conform to it, direct your sin,
Created as killer bomb,
Hail! Modern master, freedom

Gone

In writing poems, I must confess,
I'd like some of them to be it less.
Catherine Burgess

What Is Love

Love is something you can't define,
It strike at will but the feeling is divine.
It matters not what age you are,
You fall in love and there you are.
Love is like a bowl of primroses all yellow and bright,
It warms the heart and makes everything right.
You can't buy love with riches and money;
All I know is I love you honey.
My eyes are no longer dull and wet with tears;
They focus on Rome in the coming years.
You call me handsome, which I'm not,
It's because you love me such a lot.
You are my queen and I'm your knight;
I'm willing to serenade you every night.
Our eyes sparkle, the adrenaline flows,
People smile because it shows.
Kenneth Merchant

Smiling A Smile

A smile has a lot of value, it is a priceless thing
It's amazing how much happiness a smile can bring
A smile is a gift, which everyone can give
A smile makes the world a better place to live
a smile cannot be taken, or ever given away
life will be much better if you show your smile each day
A smile can make it easier to bear problems that you face
If you keep on smiling, you'll feel quite safe
A smile expresses how you feel, it can mean so much
It keeps you shining through the day, and holds that loving touch
I know we all feel blue, once in a while
But cheer ourselves up, all we have to do is....
SMILE!
Emma King

" Te Amo "

It vibrates in my head, runs down to my toes,
It takes me on journeys where no one else goes,
It lifts up my spirits like a bird when it flies,
It stirs my emotions, brings tears to my eyes,
Like a bolt of electric, that starts with a spark,
It's the surge in my veins,
It's the light in my dark,
An ecstatic sensation, that stays in my mind,
So hard to let go of, yet so hard to find,
It's the vibes that I feel, when I hear the right note,
And the lyrics when added, bring a lump to my throat,
It's the cause of my body to feel every beat,
It squeezes the pulse that starts tapping my feet,
It's a feeling we all have somewhere in our hearts,
And everyone's triggered by a different spark,
But if you have a close look at my sparks you will see,
That what I'm describing
IS MUSIC IN ME.
Delia Hampton

They Say...?

Dedicated to James Tyrell

'They say' it will get better, but what do they know?
It takes time 'they say' and then it will go,
Cry a few tears, have a cup of tea,
Come out with the girls
But it's awkward with three...

'They say' it was painless and you're now in peace,
But don't they know I want you to feel pain,
at the very least,
So you too can feel the pain I hold inside,
the pain 'they say' will one day die.

How dare you leave me, so alone and blue
I hate you for going, why can't I come too?

Life goes on, or so 'they say',
Time will heal...
Oh, I just wish they would go away,
Just leave me alone, just like you did too,
Just let me live each day without being reminded of you.

Don't they know, can't they see,
These people that say,
Don't they know the price those left pay?
Katie Gill

Football Game

One spring, during May,
It was a warm, bright, sunny day,
Me and my friend, Jon was his name,
Went to the park for a football game.
I put on my boots and got my ball,
A 'Mitre Delta' I recall.
We walked to the park and it began to rain,
But we were almost there so we didn't complain —
We got on the pitch — it was a raging storm,
Really quite different from early this morn!
My mum had told me "Keep clean today!"
So we decided to wait 'til we began to play.
We went under some trees away from the wet,
It reached 5 o'clock and it hadn't stopped yet.
Under the trees we were kicking the ball,
Until my friend Jon lost control.
The ball rolled off along the grass,
I chased, I slipped, I made a splash,
Right in a puddle! What would my mum say?
But then I decided — "I might as well play!"
David Thomas Sutton

The Glitter Snow

I watched the snow fall down gently.
It was like cotton wool dropping from the sky,
a burst pillow with all the feather falling down,
or bits of scrunched up paper just floating up and down.
The circles twirl with glittering pride.
It stopped, and people went out in their cars.
It sounded like crunching an apple or snapping of a twig.
Its sheet covers the land leaving it blank,
as it slowly pushes itself gliding away.

Laura Blundell

Such Joy

The first time we met, I fell for you,
   It was such a shock, what could I do?
Right at the back, you sat there,
   On me your shining eyes did stare.
Until that day, I was really frightened,
   You have now my life enlightened.

Loving you is not so very hard,
   When going out, I say, "Stay, guard".
Your favourite time is the weekend,
   Going out with your best friend.
Down to the shop is your caper.
   You carry home the daily paper.

As "Dad" gardens, with spade and harrow,
   You love to ride in the wheelbarrow.
When at home, just you and me,
   We enjoy a biscuit with our tea.
You are our "Baby", "Dad's" and mine,
   Our Tibetan terrier, pet dog, "Shine"

June F. Allum

5-4-3-2-1

It all started when a spaceship was launched
It was to visit mars and the silver stars
Months went by and it turned into years
Laughter stopped and turned to tears
Other ships went up to check
But it was found there was no-one on deck
The news said all the people had died
But later we found out they had all lied,
As from nowhere the ship came back
And gave all the engine-makers the sack
People still live to tell the awful advent
And now no more rockets are sent.
But if you keep looking up to the sky
One day you night see a rocket fly by.

Carol McLaren-Gibbs

Footsteps

The field is warm and bright,
it welcomes me with open arms,
the trees sway contentedly,
and leaves flutter to my feet.

I walk slowly in a daze
towards the lake,
the water glistens and shines
and is clean.

Memorized by this happiness,
I sit down in the long soft grass,
the sky above me is shades of pastel blue,
and the reflection of the sun on the lake smiles at me.

So many times I've feared being alone,
and yet this is like a dream, so soft and gentle,
like a silk blanket it wraps around me
and comforts me.

Like a child, I cling to this happiness,
I long for life to always be this simple,
to never be unhappy again,
and then I hear footsteps and realize I'm no longer alone.

Donna Booton

Jumble Sale

I went to a Jumble Sale — what a disaster,
It's a wonder my leg didn't end up in a plaster.

Elbows in face, push chairs in knees,
Heaving, shoving, "Do you mind, please!"

Well, I'd come for the bargains (Emmanuel at least),
But found only ark models, and even they were creased.

Feeling dejected, I screamed, "Show me those labels",
Then all the clutter fell off from the tables.

"And that wouldn't suit you", was some smart aleck's cry,
True, me in rust crimpelene — I would rather die!

At 30p a time I said, "Hold on a min,
Most of this stuff's only fit for the bin."

"We need new tents", some helper retorted.
"Too late", I cried, "this rubbish's been sorted".

Now, I'm immune, and if such craving prevails
I say, "blow the Scout Hut, I'm off to the sales!"

Gail Walker

Life

Life is but a mere journey
Its beauty locked in the splendour
of each accomplished moment
Its pain gathered in the wreckage of
our bleeding hearts
Its glory driven along the road of our
desired success
Life chooses its followers
Day by day
To endure this journey in the silence of
the wilderness which we must now
carry until the end....
When our destiny withdraws the essence
of a life we can only hope brings us to
understanding the strength that lies
within.....

Amanda S. K. Mohammed

Life

As I lay down in my bed at night, and try and go to sleep,
I think of all the many people who don't have such a treat.
No warm bed to lay down on,
No clothes upon their backs,
A good hot meal inside them is very very rare.
And as I try and fall asleep
I think life just isn't very fair.
Then I think of all the rich
In their houses standing tall
and of all their fine clothes;
They couldn't possible wear them all.
And then I think of all their food,
they just don't seem to have a care.
And as I try and fall asleep,
I think life just isn't very fair.

Elizabeth Chapman

Beauty Comes

Beauty comes with the morning
Slowly on silent feet
But man with reluctant sighs awakes
As life returns to the street.

Beauty comes with the noonday
And laughs in the evening sun
But man only wipes the sweat from his brow
Relieved that his work is done.

Beauty comes with the twilight
For those with the gift of sight
But man goes to bed all unheeding still
As beauty comes with the night

L. Y. Saxon

The Beech Tree

A burnished crown of gleaming copper
framed against a turner sky
Galleon clouds all gaily scudding
silently as they sail by

A jackpot cascade flutters earthward
at the bidding of the breeze
A crinkled carpet crisply settles
deep enough to reach our knees

Confetti crisps, our footfall crunches,
Brittle leaves bedeck the ground
Little boys arrive in bunches
Look for conkers - can't be found.

And I give thanks - all praise to thee
who thought it through to wield a spade
The man who knew to plant this tree
and put his fellow man here..in the shade.
Don Lynch

My Land

Meadows gone; and all that nature paints so wild.
Hedgerows gone; the greens and browns that I loved as a child.
The little lane meandering under leaf and bough,
The noise of sheep and of the friendly cow
The kestrel swoops, to live his prey must die;
Man exists, and all of this is in his way.

The little inn; the farmhouse lit in early dawn.
The morning sun; the cockerel crows, new day is born.
Of mighty oaks, and ash, and beech, and elm,
Where have they gone, what now stands in their place.
The little lanes are now wide tarmac strips
Where once stood birch a lofty building sits.

And all my fields of green and brown are gone
A growing town spreads like a fire amongst the corn
Destroying all; that we were born to love and understand
In this once green and pleasant land.
Alan V. Jones

The Hand Of Friendship

In trouble or in peace,
The hand of friendship will never cease,
The road may be hard, long and drear,
But the hand of friendship is always near.

When skies are black and overcast,
And friends forsake and turn their backs,
Do not despond or despair,
The hand of friendship is always there.

The world is full of sin and strife,
Your neighbours cut you like a knife.
Laugh and smile,
The hand of friendship is with you all the while.

Trust and have faith,
For with God you are safe,
And the hand of a friend
Is there to the end.
E. Woodward

To Pat My Love

Like the ever rising sun -
  That gives the morning light
Like the brightly shining star -
  Up in the heavens at night
Like the fragrant attracted flower -
  That blossoms in the spring
Like the gently falling rain -
  That flows on endlessly
All these things and more, dear Heart -
  Are like my love for thee
E. P. Morse

Never Any Time

Never any time to hold me
To whisper of hopes, or sometimes fears,
Never any time to kiss me
Or wipe away the everlasting tears.

I lie and watch the dawn light up the leaden sky,
I lie alone, and wonder why
If there's twenty four hours in a day,
Why there's never any time for you to stay.

My love is like a tender blossom
Its hold on life as fragile as can be,
It needs the warmth and love surrounding
But there's never any time it seems to me.

And so I've made myself a cross,
That only I can bear,
And the culmination of my love will never be
'Cos there's never any time for us to share.
Rowena P. Carpenter

Sarina's Song

What can I give you, sweet grandchild of mine
To show that I care each second of time
I can give you my heart, my body and soul
But these precious things you have already stole

You took them away on the day of your birth
And they're yours to keep for what they are worth
They are worth every ounce of the love I can give
To my beautiful grandchild as long as I live

What more can I give you, sweet grandchild of mine
To show that I care each second of time
I can give you a hug each time that you're near
And give you a kiss to dry up a tear

Whenever you're scared I can hold you real tight
And sing you a lullaby to bid you good night
I would give you the moon and the stars up above
But they're not mine to give, so I'll just give my love
M. Southerton

" El Diablo "

I would like to take you on a journey to places far and wide,
I'll open up a dark oak door and help you step inside.
The images that you will see, you may have never seen before,
I'll take you deep down underground, and sink you in the core.
I'll touch you with a velvet glove and stab you with a thought,
And when you've seen from within my eyes, you'll wish to see some more
I'll show you truths and feed you lies, on which you'll surely feast,
I'll lock you in a realm of hatred, and then unleash the beast.
The pain will teach you to respond and serve its every need,
You'll beg forgiveness and cry redemption, with each drop of blood you bleed.
On wooden crosses I'll break your will, and shatter your beliefs,
The only saviour you shall seek, is the evil inside me.
I am the son of nothing holy and Christ shall surely fall,
For the devil hides inside and is waiting for your call.
Kevin Ryland

The Path To The Moon

Across the bay a fiery glow lights up the sky,
The ascending red moon means evening is nigh.
Fisher Folks' lights wink at me on the shore.
As its beams beat a path straight to my door.

The red ball changes to a bright yellow glow.
Are you harvest or hunter? My father would know.
Oh brilliant moon, shining bright, shining clear,
If I follow your path shall I disappear?

Night hours pass, widening your beam 'til I wake,
Brightness gone now, fading fast, towards day-break.
And now in the place where the moon rose before,
So the fiery red sun beats a path to my door.
Melvene Stirk

Happy Birthday

Sitting in a cheerless room
the bearded man watches the sun rise
Another day in a long lonely life
Depression and despair his only companions

His world is one but full of dreams
Too many chances missed
Too many doors left unopened
Waiting for this special woman
to make his dreams become reality

Reflections of the past come back to haunt him
Stolen moments of happiness to fill a lifetime
Old age wiping out all hopes
Too much past and no way forward

Night draws in bringing welcome relief
He survives yet another day of birth
Praying only this the last shall be
spent alone in his dying world
N. M. Langdon

The Sounds Of Summer

The rustle of the willow as it stands beside the green,
The babble of the water as it tumbles down the stream,
The cry of birdsong overhead, the buzzing of the bees,
These are the sounds of summer that are carried on the breeze.

Across the green a family, are walking in the sun,
A Mother, Father and their child, their closeness is as one,
They see the swaying of the trees, and colours in the stream,
They watch the sunshine kiss the waves and dazzle with its gleam.

Among this green and pleasant stage, with beauty all around,
The child turns to her Mother, and she speaks without a sound,
Her fingers moving swiftly, and her head bobs up and down,
To emphasize a point she makes when Mother starts to frown.

The father looks up the birds that circle round on high,
He bends to pick the child up, and he points into the sky,
The family gaze up at the birds, their faces quite bereft,
The sounds of summer don't exist, for every one is deaf.

Take away the rustle of the willow on the green,
Take away the babble of the water in the stream,
Take away the birdsong and the buzzing of the bees,
The sounds of summer don't exist for people such as these.
R. G. Burman

The New Beginning

The sky so blue
The air so crisp
The dew now gone
Just a touch of mist

The baby lambs who love to play
In fields so fresh amongst the hay
The little birds they sing their song
Spring is here, it took so long.

Children dance and play around
A new found happiness they have found
I love this time of year so much
Everything so new so young to touch

A rabbit scurries down a hole
As a mother gently caresses her foal
Spring is a time to be together
I want to cherish this moment forever.

So many flowers I never have seen
The humming bees descend so keen
As the old church bells start ringing
I know it's come the new beginning.
Natalie Blomfield

A February Morning Scene

This morning was intensely cold,
The air was calm but keen,
The frost so white upon the grass,
Enhanced the wintry scene.
The tall trees stood 'mongst the slight haze,
Thin broken clouds passed by,
The lazy sickly pallid sun,
Showed in the wintry sky.
Along the hedgerow base I found
Plants were awakening here,
The dainty snowdrop blooms were now
Spreading their special cheer.
Then as I progressed down the lane,
'twas a great joy to hear,
Our little song birds twittering,
Insisting spring draws near.
William Porter

Untitled

The sun goes in, the warmth goes too,
The air is chilled like a storm is due
Lightning flashes and the thunder roars
Raindrops splatter on the floor
The road gets wet and people too
Some umbrellas go up, to protect the few
The sound of running feet go by
As I shelter in a doorway, keeping dry
Water flows fast to the nearest drain
Hope they're not blocked or it's floods again
I want to move on, though I know I'll stay
Hope it lets up, then I'll wend my way
'Cos I hate getting wet, and soaked right through
I'd rather have sun, than rain, wouldn't you?
So the only water, I like you see,
Is the boiling type for my pot of tea
Sheila Rayner

Duty

People say a woman's work is never done,
It is our duty, but it sure isn't fun.
We work from the minute we get out of bed.
We see to the kids, then make their beds.
We do the shopping when we go into town.
The weight of the bags just gets us down.
You get back home and put it away.
Six hours have gone, that's a typical day.
The kids come home, and it starts again.
You get dinner ready, when will this end?
It's noisy when the kids are about.
All they do is fight, argue, and shout.
As time goes on and bedtime draws near.
To get rid of the kids is your only cheer.
Then when you're sat watching T.V.
You plan the next day, "Now what shall I do for tea?"
Gaynor Turner

Give Thanks

Give thanks to the wind
That blows away
The cobwebs of a dying day;
To the rain
That falls upon the ground,
Giving sweetness and life to things around;
To the stars
That shine on high,
Lighting up a blackened sky;
To the moon
That shines to show the silent world asleep below;
To the sun
With its golden light,
For lifting the darkness of the night;
For the one, who made it so,
Takes us home when it's time to go.
C. S. Bartholomew

Walking Through The Seasons

Long days, short days we do see,
that's my two dogs accompanying me
On daily walks to and fro,
We see the seasons come and go.
Winters snow and ice domain,
then washed away by the ardent rain.
Trees undressed without their coats.
Winds that rattle round the moats.
Then spring pops up around the hills
brings forth the crocus and the daffodils
Buds on trees, are bursting through
shining in the morning dew.
Without a blink the summer's here,
trees and flowers, in colourful gear.
Sky so blue, way up above,
soaring high the gentle dove.
So quickly it's past, and autumn's nigh,
again the trees let out a sigh.
Their golden leaves fall to an end,
as winter's waiting round the bend.

Patricia Ellen Barge

Solitude

The sunshine was blinding,
that's good, felt great.
Then the darkness sets in...
no room to morn.
Warmth from this little being,
makes it worth the while.
Then the darkness sets in...
no room to morn.
Drowning now, can't see,
choking, feel to explode;
the pressure simmering. It's calm, yet not.
Still the darkness sets in, more and more.
There's no room to morn.
Men speak from the box in front of me,
don't understand a word they say.
Where is this world that looks so clear,
wish I could go there,
they seem to care.
The silence, the darkness: It's still there.
Not fair.

Margaret Edwards

Lying In A Field Of Dreams

The grass are the jokes on a thousand tongues,
That sway and caress in teams
Laughter stepped up a thousand rungs,
Lying in a field of dreams.

Ascending fluffy seeds are the sweetest thoughts,
Drifting on a memory stream
Up escaping just to get caught,
Lying in a field of dreams.

Warmest rays are the smiles of sunshine,
He'll not be seen serene
Sharing your joy, what's yours is mine,
Lying in a field of dreams.

Cotton bud clouds are the tissues of sorrow,
Evenly spread, spaces in between
And squeezed now and then, today and tomorrow,
Lying in a field of dreams.

The bees are the future, the direction to take,
As in all life it seems
The soul outside will never wake,
Lying in a field of dreams.

Natalie Morgan

Commitment

I never will forget,
That year of '91,
The moment that we met,
A summer of endless fun.

And over the following years,
Through all our troubled weather,
We have cried such bitter tears,
But our hearts grow stronger together.

The plans we are making,
Are so long overdue,
The step I am taking,
Is down the path to you.

I can't predict the future,
My darling, my best friend,
But one thing that's for sure ... is
My love will never end.

J. Hathway

The Dove Of Peace

When will they ever learn that war is not a game
That whoever pulls the trigger is not the one to blame
The men that tell them what to do, for freedom they shout
What is the purpose, or the reason, what are they fighting about
A slice of land, a mountain top, to be taken at all cost
No one caring, no one counting, how many lives are lost.
A whisper of peace, fulfilled dreams, turmoil will be no more
The dove of peace, released throughout this land to soar
Then another killing, a father dead, the body just left to lie.
A wife, a son, a daughter, in the darkness, no one hears their cry.
Shattered dreams, misplaced hopes, broken as they die
Like the dove of peace, body torn, bloodied,
No more allowed to fly.

Margaret Jean Wright

WHEN

When did it happen? I only wish I knew
that very special moment when I fell in love with you.
I was independent, all women were the same,
when suddenly without warning into my life you came.

Was it only yesterday, or was it long ago,
Or was it in some other age, I really do not know.
Time without you has no meaning, time spent with you is ecstasy.
Since the moment you stole into my heart,
and became a part of me,

I still do not know just when it was
I am not sure even why,
but one thing that I am certain of
I will love you until I die,
and if there is life after that, the only heaven for me
is to be close to you my love,
throughout all eternity.

A. R. J. Mitchell

The Stream

I gazed with joy upon the stream,
That through the village gently flows,
So crystal clear, so full of life,
Making sweet music as it goes.

It brought to thought the living stream,
Where, all mankind may find,
Refreshment for the thirsty soul,
Peace for the troubled mind.

Symbolic of the stones of life,
Are those the waters overlie,
Protected, cleansed and purified,
Assurance of His love close by.

"Believe on me," the Saviour said,
And from thirst your soul set free,
For I am the living fountain,
Now, and eternally.

A. Huggins

Spring

The cherry tree
That stands so tall
With blossoms pink
Against the wall

Because I know once more it's spring
But when the wind's begin to blow
The blossom falls. Just like snow
I often stand and look around.
At the soft pink carpet on the ground.

Underneath the cherry tree
Golden daffy's smile at me.
Snowdrops. Crocus. Primrose too.
Make a most exciting hue.

Oh, what a lovely time in spring
When all the birds begin to sing
And build their nest up in the tree.

To rear their young.
Until they flee.

H. Brown

Love...

Love is but a tender seed
That only grows with care
With sunshine and with raindrops too
Not with stormy days, but fair

It must be nurtured carefully
Just like a tiny flower
The seedling must be good and strong
If you're to build a bower

Through its life, you must tend it true
With soft hands and soft words
Sweet music will help it grow up strong
As the trilling of the birds

Seeds have to work their way 'round stones
That are strewn down in their path
When they do, they're stronger, yet
They pray for kinder earth

From tiny bud to flower full blown
Only days or hours may be
But love tended with the greatest care
Will span eternity

Sheila Clapham

Untitled

What would you do if I should say "Love is a devils's charm,
That leaves behind it hopeless, and can do only harm."

Some would agree, and some would not. You would answer
    from your heart
And when it came to make a choice, it could tear you apart.

"I have been hurt too much," would answer some - whose
    hearts were torn in two,
"I just cannot - I will not care." They would answer, sad and true.

And some would say - "Oh, all love me!" who could not understand
Their arrogance eclipsed the truth, as they raised their empty hands.

Then there are those - still innocents - despite toil through
    fear and pain,
Who still believe in love's own truth, and so shall find it again.

For love can dwell in all the hearts that beat on this fair earth,
And if allowed, through dark storm clouds, all people can find mirth.

For laughter is a part of love, an integral part and true,
And the Devil can only curse because, that is found in me and you.

So he can take the ones we love, but never steal their souls,
For a part of us of reach, and so shall never grow cold.

Michelle O'Brien

Time

What is this thing called time
That masters all our lives on Earth.
The sun comes up after we have slept
And another day begins anew.
Minutes, hours and days go by,
The sun sets in the west, and it is night.
The minutes, hours and nights go by,
But each new day and each new night
Never meet, yesterday's gone,
Tomorrow is to come.
But what of today? Where does it go?
Time chases time but never catches up
One day with another.
Night falls and stays alone.
The previous night has flown
And so it goes on forever and ever.
Time? There is no time,
Only we think there is.

Marjorie Joan Hudson

Memories

There is a bridge of happy memories
    That leads from earth to heaven above
It keeps you near to me, it's called
the bridge of love,
    One day I'll cross and find you
Then we'll forget the sorrow and all
the pain,
    I'll see your lovely laughing face.
We'll be together again
    Till then, dear Lord above,
Please let Eddie hear my prayers of love
    God bless you, my sweetheart,
I love you forever.

J. Paget

If Only

I often dream of life when I had a quiet minute
That is when I get a minute
"Can I have this can I have that"
You will have to go without
"What would I be doing now."
To think work is the peace and the quiet.
Sounds as though I regret it
No not for a minute or an hour or two-
Laughter and fun we have at times
Everyone gets frustrated but only for a minute.
When time is rather short-
That's all my minutes spent
But time is precious when there are four-

E. Yardley

So, This Is Love

The first time you spoke to me, I knew
That special moment when your eyes met mine, I was sure
That here was the man I was to spend the rest of my life with
So, this is love.

When your lips found mine in the longest kiss imaginable, I knew
When you held me close for so long, I was sure
This was what I had been waiting for all my life
So, this is love.

This was the beginning of everything,
the beginning of the rest of my life.
I would not have cared if that moment had been
all there was going to be
So, this is love.

Thirty years on I still feel that it is the beginning,
Still feel there is everything to look forward to
Though many years have passed and our children are grown
I feel just the same as I did that moment so long ago
So, this is love - yes, this is love.

Tina Wells

Bottom Of A Glass

The bottom of the glass can tell,
That I am now living in hell,

No happy life, or even strife,
And all because, I've lost my wife,

Just me to blame,
For involving an old flame,

An answer to my prayers,
Really, just intoxicated affairs,

That initial feel good rush,
So I can hear the sound of hush-hush,

These scars inside,
Is the only thing, I can hide,

If only I could keep dry,
That will be, my only high,

Live day by day,
Very easy for people to say,

Promises made, promises spoken,
To be left with a heart, that's broken,

Now I am split and cut into a sliver,
Left only with, cirrhosis of my liver.
Steven Monks

To A Man...

A man always thinks that he's the best
That he's a cut above the rest
God's gift to women that's what he thinks
Full patter which always stinks

Many names to him I'd give
From macho man to chauvinistic pig
He works hard and he has fun
But a woman's work is never done

He's waited on hand and foot
His pockets always lined with loot
Always making plenty of noise
Claiming he's one of the boys

Out on the town painting it red
Comes home late at night to bed
Turns to his wife and expects his right
Whether it's morning, noon or night

After having this my say
I wouldn't have it any other way
Until some day the human race
Finds something else to take his place
P. A. Dolan

Looking Down

Looking down upon the Earth I see such wondrous things.
That God has made for man the trees, the birds, and animals.
The flowers all shining bright.
Why is man destroying this planet so beautiful to see.
Why is man so blind to all the wondrous things we love,
That God created everything for us to see, to smell and touch?
I look down, and feel so sad
That one day all things will be gone.
Someday they will remember what they had, and lost.
But it will be too late, and God will only know.
For God created the Earth for man,
And everything for man to love.
So while I am looking down,
I thank God I am here in Heaven above.
Where everything is bright.
For one day they will be with me.
Looking on their Earth below so brown, and grey, and empty.
They will be sad like me.
For the Earth is very beautiful, and everything is free.
For God created everything with love for me.
G. Reynolds

The Monster In The Living Room

There's a monster in the living room,
That eats at such a pace,
I know it's very ugly,
but I can't quite see its face,
I glimpse a long and bony snout,
with nostrils that flare,
and a finger that goes up it,
in search of what is there.
It lets off gas in such a way,
that its bottom emits a squelch,
and from the deepest of its stomach,
it makes a ponging belch,
I pluck up courage then I say,
'Are you feeling Ok mister?'
It turns to look me in the eye,
'Help, it's my little sister!'
Sarah Beech

Untitled

It tears you limb from limb, this pain
that comes from deep within.
It fills each corner of your mind, this scream
Time and time again.
Nothing prepared me for this,
But lighthearts pay a fee,
God came down and took my son, I blinked,
He ceased to be.
Life?..... It stretches,
With endless days to pine,
There will be no silver linings, where once
There was bright sunshine.
Pamela Jackson

This Frightful Thing Called War

My mind is weary, my thoughts are caught of wars through the years that come to nought. Politicians of countries play a game with you and me. What is their aim? It's as though like children when they were small, they saw a map upon the wall. Who is at peace and working well, let's change it all, let's break the spell. Let's set man against man. Where is the harm, does it matter, if he looses an arm, if he looses his friends, his mind, his pride? If he was left at home he would still have died. He's someone's son, brother and friend, does it really matter how his life will end? When their words ring out, "Let's go to war", when they think of victory, how do they score? Is it by counting the dying, the dead and the maimed, who wins? How is it claimed? Let all politicians and people that kill wear the uniform of war, their dreams to fulfil. Let them march and see at first hand the blood and the killing, see what they planned. Let them shoot it out till the end of the day, let them get maimed and slaughtered — Yes — let them pay. Let's hope a "War to end Wars" is a thing of the past. Let's walk together, let happiness last. It can be done, so let us try, no more battlefields where we will die. One day we all will die, in the autumn of our lives, until then — let's be happy; that should be our prize. Let happiness be for everyone, young, old, rich and poor. Communicate — Love one another. We don't need to go to war.
P. A. Porter

Trees From My Window

As I look through the window they are there —
Tall, stately, lovely and proud,
Their bearing upright and their branches unbowed.
Their colours a cascade of green, red and yellow,
Their movement now gentle, so softly they whisper,
Of things too precious for mere humans to hear.

The mood changes, their whispers become thunder,
And I watch as it rumbles and rumbles,
And murmurs and murmurs away into — peace.
M. Barron

Magic Moments

There is no emotion greater for man and wife,
Than to give birth and give life,
So tiny and tender to touch,
Oh! We love him so very much.

Dainty hands and tiny feet,
Tucked under a clean white sheet,
In a pram all warm and cosy,
A visit from the park leaves cheeks all rosy.

There have been songs of love and emotion,
And some of great devotion,
But God's most precious gift of all
Is when My name he does call.

As I grow old and wise,
He still will never cease to surprise,
That enormous big smile upon his face,
Will fill your heart with love and grace.

School and the dreaded first day,
How did I ever drag myself away,
The tears I had when I closed that door,
But on returning he still wants to play some MORE!

Mandy Coker

The Admirer

Stranger, my admirer —
Tell me why you do haunt me with your love
There is a lane I walk along, where I see all
the trees are brown, the grass is green —
The skies are blue, the sun always shine —
I can see your face, I imagine your kisses sweet
You are always in my mind —

As you stretch fort to caress
Your love is good, your kisses sweet —
You are always in my thoughts
Those strong arms that are so firm
The thoughts of you do fill my mind —
Your arms are open wide with love —
That makes a fire that burns inside
and fill's me with desire —
No thoughts of mine could be so real, as I walk along that lane
I imagine your lips telling of many things —
Stranger, my Admirer, you are always on my mind —

Viola I. Delgaudio

Untitled

You ask me what I need from you.
"Tell me, my love, what do you need", you say?
I do not need your constant declaration.
Love can be easy.
All to often just an easy word.
I need your conversation, your consternation.
Some days to be the first one in your thoughts.
Not every day.
In little ways.
Taking the time for small important things.
Important, not to you, but meaningful to me.
I try to see the way you look at life.
And understand.
And if I cannot always see, then let me be.
I need to share the lightness and the laughter.
I'm always here.
And if you're needed, I need to know you are aware.
Wanting to be there.
I do not need the words.
I need the care.

Yvonne Brayshaw

Lake Konstanz

Lake Konstanz, Lake Konstanz I know you not, but I understand you can tell a lot of stories that are both new and old, of stories that are left untold.
You know the faces of passers-by of leaping frogs and dragon-flies
They dash and dart along your edge and dice all day with life and death.

I've seen your picture a fleeting look, all put together in a big fancy book
In places you appear quite mild, in others you seen rather wild
So wild you toss the sailing boats that struggle just to stay afloat
Shall I meet you, do I dare to take a look and maybe share
my Secret in your watery deep another secret for you to keep

Lake Konstanz, Lake Konstanz, I don't know you yet, but I've seen you flirting with the red sun-set
I've seen your brilliance, I've seen your shine, you're an excellent host for those with time
Oh Time Lake Konstanz I haven't, so I'm hoping you can help with a quandary of mine that's so deeply felt
Tell me Lake Konstanz, am I really to blame, will I ever be the same?
You know the answer, you're old and wise, your wisdom gained beneath the skies

Until we meet Lake Konstanz, I wish you well and then I hope you can cast away this spell
that's kept me enchanted for such a time and kept me walking the borderline
Or make a portion strong and new from your hidden depths that are so blue
Bind this spell and make it last for time is running out so fast
I need a potion that's really true, Until we meet Lake Konstanz, I think of you....

Wendy Eisenschmid

The Green Valley

Across the down's not far away
Tall grasses slowly start to sway
Hidden lies a valley deep
Peace and quite, like eternal sleep
Slowly sunlight starts to recover
Awaking the call of the plover
Horses, cows, rabbits and deer
Oh so far, yet so near.
Flowers wild, colours bright
Scattered throughout like stars at night
Midday perfumes fill the air
Grass, flowers, wood fires under care
White cotton clouds floating by
Glittering streams where silvery trout lie
A simmering sun starts to set
Another day over, not quite yet
Skylarks singing high above
See, it's there, this place I love
   My green valley.

J. W. Young

Blind, Deaf, Mute... And I

I paint pictures for those who cannot see
The beautiful colours of this world that give joy to you and me
To those who live in darkness and have never seen any light
To those who have been destined never to gain sight.

I sing songs to those who cannot hear
To the people far away in a land beyond the frontier
In a world of their own, where noise is not a threat
And the peaceful sound of silence is all they'll ever get.

I make music for those who cannot speak
To those who have no voice to give the answers we always seek
To those we often neglect for not uttering a single word
To those whose only friends are the sun, moon, stars and birds.

In all these things I do there are many things I realize
That in this world there are many people with many unheard cries
And that you and I are still lucky, we're still very blessed
So we should share the things we can, and that shouldn't be a guess!

Marbill De Gracia

Passing Years

Oh where is the youth with the laughing eyes
Tall and lithe who captured my heart?
Where, where, is the mischievous smile
Of the lad who winked as we walked down the aisle?
Gone, gone with advancing years,
Now a bald crown where bright curls have been,
Limbs have stiffened and lines of care
Have furrowed the brow with the worries we share,
Oh, make the most of the youthful years,
For days may come when flow the tears.
Life is short and time ebbs away,
May we have courage to face each day!

Sheila King

Friendship

The tree that caught my eye was the oak
tall and firm, its leaves covering like a cloak.
So majestic and proud it stood, the tallest tree in the wood.
My thoughts were taken back in time, to friends and dear ones
long since gone, and then my thoughts began to wander on.

There stands the old oak tree as firm and solid as friendship
should be.
It weathers the storms and gales of life that come with every season,
knowing deep down inside there has to be a reason.
For true friendship like the tree will gather roots and cling firmly.

Patricia Millen

Veiled Threat

Death hides behind its gossamer shroud
Talking in whispers, never out loud
Always with us, but never quite there
Forever waiting for lack of care.

We run a race we never can win
And it matters not if freed from sin
For the good die young (or so they say)
But you never know when comes the day.

Robert D. Archer

Drugs Poem: A Parent

I see people in the streets,
  Taking drugs as much as they want.
They don't care what might happen,
  They don't care what it does.

My daughter died by taking drugs,
  It was her first and the last.
She knew what they would do,
  But her friends said they wouldn't hurt.

I hope they are happy,
  Killing a loving, intelligent, helpful girl.
Her life is over because of drugs,
  Why do they take them?
That's what I want to know.

Martina Waller

Moon Over Malaya

The moon was shining o'er Malaya
Stars were twinkling down from up above
Girls in their sarongs and Cobias
In their compongs, sing their songs of love
Trambulan and old Serena
Songs their mothers sang in days gone by
From Penag to Ipoh and Molacca
you can hear those enchanting lullabies

Guitars were strumming in the moonlight
The echo of their tron-shons never die
For the moon was shining o'er Malaya
'Twas there we loved and kissed and
  said good-bye

J. H. Coleman

Welcome To Our World

Welcome to our world, please walk this way
Take a good look around, would you care to stay?
And if you can shed a tear then shed them on us
As that's the only water that will ever settle the dust.

This world is empty of food although rarely cold
Many of us die young, no time to grow old
Our families are few but we share each day
Before they too, just simply, fade away.

Babies crying, their empty bellies hurt and swollen too
Our hearts are heavy as we just don't know what to do
To help relieve their pain so that they need not suffer again
But maybe, just maybe, tomorrow it will finally rain.

Do we have a future when all we know is our past
And will we still be here to see another year last?
Has the rest of the world really chosen to forget?
Oh, how we wish we could also share their sunset.

So as you settle with those you love for yet another night
Think of us as we start another day, another fight
And if you can remember us, if you can spare the time
As we have so little left, before the end of our line...

Rosemary A. Rogers

Whirlwind

It came in the night with force and with vigour,
Swirling and whirling, getting bigger and bigger.
A slow little whine that grew into a wail,
Starting with raindrops that turned into hail.
Up came the trees that for time had stood firm;
Slates from the rooftops came crumbling intern.
Travelling wood buildings ended up invert;
River banks broken that had stood before inert.
In explicable to our lands this mystery of nature,
At dawn our eyes inflicted with human rancour.
Death and destruction was all over the place,
A lesson to be learned for the human race.
The mighty had spoken in ways unexplained,
The more we fight, the less we retain.
We shall have to go back to the days of respect,
Perhaps then our lives will go on to resurrect.

V. A. Marshall

A Memory Of The Malvern Hills
(Or The Whisper Of Nature)

The supple limbs of the young saplings
Sway unresistingly to the gentle nudges of the light summer-breeze.
A rustling ripple creeps gently across the leafy ocean,
An undulation of alternating greens.
Nature's whisperings caress the receptive ear,
And secrets revealed to those who deeply listen.
Stem the chattering of the mind; be still!
Then clearly a secret message will be heard.
It cannot be phrased in words,
For such are mere reflections.
Thoughts have to be discarded,
Completely abandoned and surmounted.
Then, and only then, does Nature's oracle
Dispense its blessing to the humble one,
Awaiting in simplicity for that message
Which opens the door to ecstasy.

Roy Harris

The Consequence Of War

Amidst the lingering murk that
swathes the lonesome soul
there is no feeling.
Within the depths of solitude where
pain taunts, hissing sweetly
there is no laughter.
Where ghostly shadows echo in darkness
with reminders of yesterday
there is no tomorrow.

Malcolm Custerson

To Love And Serve My Country

I was born on a island,
Surrounded with sky blue water,
With other little neighbouring islands
Just as beautiful as mines,
This I am happy to be part of.
I have lots and lots of memories,
They are of happy and sad ones to,
A way from my island in the sun
I have come to realize
What a beauty I have left behind.
It is the simplest little things with in
That makes it such a paradise.
This is why I will try to do my best
Towards my fellow country men and friends
Who remains behind to keep it well,
For this my island in the sun.
  Veronica J. Greenfield

In Memory of Child

A tiny girl lies helpless in a dimly lit room
surrounded by her loved ones dressed in misery and gloom.
Her lifelight fading slowly.
Distance growing in her eyes.
A look of heartfelt pleading, a veil of Death's disguise.

So soon she takes the journey
            we all must make one day,
but with her goes our love
            to help her on her way.
Across the void 'tween life and death Victoria must go alone,
but soon to join the shining angels beneath the Lord God's throne.

Weep not for your little one who's left us all behind,
for she will find a wondrous place, pain free, loving and kind.
Be happy for her final peace.
Be happy she's at rest.
Be thankful for the time you shared,
            consider it the best....
  T. G. Foley

Written On A Sunny Day In Belfast

O' bastard drum and f***er fife in the
    sunny summer heat,
Whipping up the passion with that non-stop
    hate-filled beat.
You think not of the future
    you care but for the past.
A riot, a shooting
    or just a few stones cast,
All to you are satisfaction, someone's answered your call.
Marches and parades, I say f*** them all!
  Patrick McArdle

Contr-addictions

A sea of strange faces in a familiar crowd
Suffering in silence while screaming out loud
Living to die yet dying to live
In a condemning world that will always forgive

One hour of ecstasy for two of despair
A universal problem that no-one can share
Sinking so low just to climb high
Crawling in the gutter to float in the sky

Searching for an exit while hopelessly trapped
The fantasy of illusion becomes reality of fact
No intention to rely on, now somehow dependant
Maybe not guilty but on a life sentence

The shaking comes easy while the shaking is hard
In a pack full of aces the joker's your card
A state of confusion where all is so clear
Life feels so cheap, but the price is so dear.
  Martin James Woodfine

The Worker Bees

The worker bees hover from flower to flower
Sucking up the nectar with such power
They gather the pollen into their baskets
The nectar and pollen are brought to the nest.

They shape the wax into a waterproof honeycomb
This colony is queen bee's new home
They do all the chores for the queen bee
Preparing for her new family.

They pack the pollen above and beside the nest
The nectar above that, for the honey is next
They flap their wings like little fans
keeping the hive cool and fresh as they can.

In winter they gather over the cells in a cluster
Their wings produce heat as they all flutter
The queen bee's eggs are pearly white
the lava that crawls out is just a mite.

It's fed on bee bread when it is three days old
It then becomes a pupa as it unfolds
It later develops into a worker bee
Then it's off to work on another colony.
  Rose Bell

Perch Lake

Hidden scenery, on private land
Such quite presence kept from public gaze
Yet I stumbled upon this magical scene
By pure co-incidence, left in a daze
Rhododendrons all around this lake
With tall tree's looming in there wake.
Blue still waters with ducks upon
Suddenly flap by man's sight, and then fly on,
No damage brought by public detection
Has left this scene a pure induction,
Of peace, tranquillity, and Gods own grace
Perch lake is such a memorable place.
  P. Daniels

Contentment

A suckling babe in loving arms,
Such honeyed sweetness all around.
Two lovers lying side by side;
Dew-drenched stars upon the ground.

A mountain tall against the sky
And valley below with tinkling streams.
A lonely train that snakes its way
Up the track to vales of dreams.

A sun-kissed field with lazy drone
And horses gambolling in the grass.
A cottage ceiling long and low,
Big black grate and shining brass.

A rippling pond with graceful swans
so silently they glide along,
Whilst swaying branches fan the air
And birds trill out their heartfelt song.

A church that stands upon a hill
Its solid building age defies.
And all around is peace and love;
That's where contentment really lies.
  Rosaleen G. Cole

" For You "

I can offer you not material things,
Such as gold and silver or diamond rings.
My gifts are simple, hence not very grand.
Only words of advice or the skill of my hand
Or bring to your notice the things that please me -
The song of a bird or the sweep of a tree.
But I pledge you my life and whatever beyond.
True friendship and love for eternity bond.
  C. R. Spillett

Drive In The Country

Driving along the roads of Briton,
Such a lot about them's been written,
Of the fields, the sky, the lanes and trees,
So I would put forth my humble pleas;
To write of the animals in the fields close by,
The pigs and the piglets in their sty,
Those horses galloping across the field,
The cows contentedly chewing to build their yield,
And lambs all frisking about,
Their mothers bleating and saying nought,
The pride in us it does arise,
And makes us thankful to belong
To this island that has endured for (so long).
Violet Carter

Thoughts Before A First Operation

Just a year since my dear wife
Succumbed before the surgeon's acolytes
Now, I too, entrust my life
To that same surgeon and his knife.

Ever must mankind beware
Carcinoma, you are there
Could I, should I, ought I pray?
That God might me in mercy spare?

Nurse and Sister's ward behaviour
Can be nought but my sweet saviour
When at last I home return
Let me only patience learn.

Now's the time to make a stand
And with a loving partner's hand
Prepare for future better years
Begone despair and morbid fears.

The way ahead is now quite clear
I vow to cherish all those dear to me.
And so with good intent
Show what their love for me has meant.
D. J. S. Waterhouse

War Cemetery

Here stand the stones that stream away in military rows
Straight and erect
As if held by the men in everlasting sleep
Under where the green grass grows

Holding forth their names as if to say, remember me

As I remembered you when I was asked
To walk the aisles into the terrible unknown
Where tides of men died in war's horrific sea.

Now here flowers grow under the peaceful skies
Darkened now and then by tears
And the birds sing their songs
To the men who lie and watch with empty eyes
W. A. Cook

Adoption — The " Adopted Child "

I'm suffering again, I suffer each day, but you got your wish,
I'm staying away.
I've tried shutting you all right out of my mind, still searching for answers, so very hard to find.
You're still hiding the truth and living a lie, I wish you could look me straight in the eye.
So young, the family pressure they put on you, swept under the carpet, all those years ago.
A sister, two brothers, they don't know about me, someday your secret will surely break free.
You must know that one day it will all come out, this child born through your love wants to stand up and shout.
So why can't you admit that I really exist, I'm no longer just a number on some old list.
I know things can't change, I don't want this to be, all I want is for you to know the real me.
J. V. M. Edwards

Listen To Me.....

Hey you, listen to me, listen to what I say,
Stop putting me down, shoving me round,
Listen to what I say.

Forty-nine, you've had a rough time, why take it out on me.
If I step out of line, it's no big crime,
Why take it out on me?

So I'm different to you, what's the big deal,
why do you hate me so much?
You're my dad, my old man, my number one fan,
Why do you hate me so much?

Looking back on my life, I'm sick of the strife,
it's time to call it a day.
I give up on you now, step out with a bow,
And accept you won't hear what I say.

Hey you, listen to me, listen to what I say,
Stop putting me down, shoving me round,
Listen to what I say.
H. A. Smith

Diverse Melancholy

My life is like a shattered glass,
Still sparkling, yet in fragments of blades like grass.
Sometimes dull like the grass without sunshine,
But in my heart I know, I'll be just fine!

Depression is a melancholy condition,
My prohibitions are now an inhibition.
For I long for a lover to open my soul to,
But my life would not be uncomfortable, merely taboo!

My bed I have made to lie on,
"Oh", sometimes — I just want my mom!
I must smile and continue this begotten saga,
For I belong in the kitchen by the "AGA"!

Life goes on and my head is held high,
I really could drink a whiskey and "RYE".
Spring is yet near and I am alive,
"Hello, Everybody. Can you hear my cries?"

Sometimes I feel like a silhouette,
But I won't stand for it, I won't be celibate.
St. Valentines day has been and gone,
"WHAT?" — NO RED ROSE — I'll just have another "Bourbon"!
Azure

The Rainbow

I stood alone in wonder, and gazed at the sight with awe,
Stark in its coloured detail, circled from shore to shore.
Saw sunlight reflections gleaming clear thro' the crystal rain,
Just where the clouds were darkest, the covenant bow remained.

I watched the shades harmonizing, just for a moment or two,
Red, orange and yellow emerging, green, indigo, violet and blue.
Thought, where's there an artist to rival, in what perfection so lush,
With the darkest of clouds for a canvas, and the rays of the sun for a brush?

Pondered, who was this master artist, who painted the sky with light,
And in such incredible manner created this wonderful sight?
But the one who created the Heavens, and flung the stars into space,
Who promises mankind salvation, to save the whole human race.

I went home, but the promise went with me, so clear as never before,
That if I'm alone and despairing, and sad to the very core,
If storm clouds gather about me, and my life seems filled with rain,
I must look for the rainbow, the certain sign that the sun will shine again.
Percy Webb

The Days Of Wine And Roses

It occurs to me as I cross the street
Staring down at two saturated feet,
That these youthful hours of smiles and poses
Might become the days of wine and roses.

This collection of rain-soaked, tea-stained days
Filled with debt, and badly written essays,
Damp filled houses and everything on toast,
The sudden absence of the Sunday roast.

Perhaps these are the best days of my youth,
Of being embarrassing and uncouth,
And the endless hours of smiles and poses
Will become the days of wine and roses.

Maia Bishenden

Prehistoric Times

When giant monsters once ruled our land
Standing strong and powerful and yet so grand
Never fearing their friend or their foe
A towering strength that moved quite slow

With Volcanos erupting for years every day
Throwing out their molten and fiery spray
A Tyrannosaurus Rex is now roaming the wood
Your guess as good as mine he's up to no good

He comes face to face with a massive Dinosaur
Yet he stands his ground with a frightening roar
Then a fight begins, this Dinosaur has no fear
Tyrannosaurus strikes, ripping Dinosaur's left ear

Dinosaur then turns with a mighty lash of his tail
Tyrannosaurus lies dead, a fatal wound within his scale
There's a thunderous sound as the Dinosaur walks on
Completely unaware he's stalked by a big Ptyronadon

The Mountainous peaks almost touching the sky
High altitudes where Pterodactyls fly
Now we live upon this land, those Monsters, they do not
Just their buried bones remain... in a land that time forgot.

S. Arrowsmith

The Sea Birds Toll

Sad, stricken sea birds
Standing on that distant
Slimy beach. Necks cricked and
Skewered in dejection. Too
Stunned to call a cry,
Sleek proofed feathers congealed and awry.
Sharp beaks corroded, quick eyes dimmed.
Oil. Mankind's new life-blood -
Stagnated blood of constellations of organisms,
Spurted from earth's severed arteries
Shipped in dinosaurian tankers
Spines racked and split on turbulent
Seas, oozing black entrails into
Stunned oceans, dulling the glistening fish,
Stultifying the sonorous sounds of the
Sea, whilst short-sighted men steer new disasters.

Maureen Davies

Oh Home A Home

The grass is there, but the Stadium is bare.
Stand in the car park if you dare
and remember the time when Rovers was there.
Goodnight Irene was the roar of the
crowd, believe it or not it all started there.
It's ten years now since leaving the ground,
no home of our own, when will we come home.
The floodlights are on as the dogs run around,
it's hard to just stay and look around,
Oh how I wish it was still the Bristol Rovers ground.

Craig Ford

Food For Thought

Lift not your eyes to the heavens, if what you're building
 cannot stand.
It's not just bricks and mortar, for good rules always stand.
The rule of thumb, which some are using, to others it's not clear.
Perhaps we're ever changing, by day, and even years.
To others it don't matter, as they don't count the cost.
Yet children keep on learning, at quite an awful cost.
The mule cannot be happy, when he takes up his load, for he hopes
to find contentment, some day, without a load.
Now people are always chasing, just what they want to do.
Let's hope by sense and reason, we don't make one great stew.
Our world could feed its beggars, same earth can feed the horse.
We could be better builders, let nations take the torch.
To be a better builder, I venture to decree.
The power of wisdom's mighty, much bigger than any tree.
Let's stop this hanky-panky, to stand and look around.
Where Britain stands impressive, there's law and order found.
Don't ask me where it started, it's just not on the ground.
Let's be proud but very friendly, to all that seem around.
It's not quite always easy, to be a better man.
Whilst woman knows this better, there's hope, in every man.

P. B. Finney

Freedom On The Sea

Day after day I watch the young boy
Stalwart limbs arched in jubilant joy
Racing his speedboat across the blue bay
His prowess on water a dynamic display.

Duties and burdens are left far behind
Freedom and power the thoughts in his mind
Waves crashing round him, the sun blazing down
His golden skin glows like a diamante crown.

Another boat joins him criss-crossing his path
A maelstrom of currents makes the youth laugh
Intent concentration etched on his face
He outwits his opponent with a fast cracking pace.

He approaches the shoreline his friends shout and wave
Droplets of water around him cascade
Myriads of rainbows sparkle and gleam
Fleetingly caught in the sunlight's beam.

Red rays herald dusk at the end of the day
Harbour lights twinkle many miles away
Night shadows descend and the boy turns for home
He beaches his boat euphoric and windblown.

Yvonne Glikzeliger

The Rite Of Spring

At last Old Winter's grip has thawed,
Spring's soft, sweet kiss has melted his cold heart.
Her warm embrace has stirred his sleeping soul,
Once more he will surrender to her touch.
All spent, Old Winter weeps for his sweet Spring
But she is gone, no backward glancing,
For Zepher's wing she waits, on pointed toes,
So light of foot she steals the centre stage
To dance, her own sweet dance of life reborn.

S. W. Nicholson

Daffodils

Gently swaying to and fro,
Spring's first soldiers to the front do go.
Nodding heads in agreement say
Go away winter, take your blues away!

Golden heads and slim straight stalks,
Trumpets resounding along country walks.
The joys of Spring are in their sway
Awake they say, come alive today!

Yellow and gold, white and green
Adding beauty to the country scene,
Rejoice and live, there trumpets say
On this God's ever beauteous day.

Phyllis Tutton

Oak Tree

Rooted in the ground,
Splaying forth with determined
strength,
Arms outstretched to touch the sky.

Twisted and gnarled where
time has engraved its name.
It stands there a being of majesty,
Not like any other before or after.

Dressed or naked it holds its dignity,
unveiling different sides to its character.
Ever constant and ever changing,
I breathe in the life it breathes out
and give thanks.
Sara-Jane Thompson

Nocturnal Traveller

Silvery moonlight bathed the country scene,
Sparkling the frosty surrounds in its gleam,
The night, lying still in Winter's arms,
Enraptured one with moonlight's magical charms.

Suddenly! ... So suddenly it came...
Out of the moonlight... I couldn't give it a name!
It hung like a lantern in the starry skies,
Right there before my very eyes.

It spun, and twisted... did all sorts of gyrations,
Fascinating this mortal with its friendly actions,
Whilst I — amazed — could only stare and wonder,
What is this thing, this strange nocturnal traveller?

It zoomed so close to me, its speed was swift,
And with a 'salute' of lights began to lift,
Then with a final, impressive display,
It showered jewel-bright starlets as it sped away.

Sceptics would, probably, question — a dream, imagination?
But on that frosty moonlit-night 'I know'
That I had a close encounter with a 'UFO'...!
Winifred Davis

If Only

If a deaf person could hear the birds, it would
sound like a Symphony.
If a blind person could see his garden, it would
look like the most breathtaking landscape.
If a person with no legs could take but one step,
It would be like running a marathon.
If a person with no arms could hug the one they love,
It would be like holding the most precious moment.
If a person who takes such gifts for granted could
appreciate them more, it would be like living in a whole new world.
Carol Willes

Man's Best Friend

They say that dogs are man's best friend
That's true in every way.
Their loving face and smiling eyes
Light up the darkest day.

They always make you welcome.
And greet you and at the door.
They get oh so excited, they skid across the floor.
They help us through the good times.
They help us through the sad.
They may have been the best friend
That one has ever had.

It's oh so sad when they grow old.
And with them we have to part
But they'll have left a special place
Imbedded in our hearts.
And if there's a doggy heaven
I'm sure that's where they'll go
But all of us they have left behind
Will never ever know.
S. Cowlin

Never Ever

Is there somewhere I don't know,
Somewhere where I can't go,
Much more wonderful than all of this,
But within reach of illusion and myth.

Is it just that I am mortal,
Unable to pass through a superhuman portal
That defines the genius from the mild,
Fired by the imaginations of a child?

Is Avalon in all our minds,
Behind a great oak door waiting to be unlocked,
And why are the people who hammer and wait
Scoffed at, laughed at, and used as bait?

Is it perhaps the fourth dimension,
Whose untold powers of ascension
Can lift us up to that mystic level,
Where white witch and warlock can only revel?

Or am I destined for all my days,
To strain and strive against my mortal ways,
That somehow trap my inner being,
And stop myself from really seeing?
M. J. Hazard

Devon

From Malmsmead to Meddon, Tamar to the Lym,
Somerset to Cornwall, Dorset to the Plym,
English Channel Southwards, Bristol Channel North,
Encompassing my county, the finest on God's Earth.

Wild and windswept Exmoor, gorse and purple heather,
Granite tors of Dartmoor, sculptured by the weather,
Swiftly running rivers, rushing to the sea,
Rugged, rocky coastline, cliffs and estuary.

Unspoilt sandy beaches, pretty rocky combes,
Miles of open foreshore, bounded by the dunes,
Gentle tidal rivers, through wooded valleys flow,
Stippled by the sunlight, calm waters come and go.

Patchwork quilted meadows, of greens and reds and browns,
Picture postcard villages, bustling market towns,
Wild deer in the forests, sheep graze on the hills,
Salmon in the rivers, trout in sparkling rills.

Friendly, honest, country folk, who know just what it's worth,
To dwell in this, their paradise, which God has put on Earth,
A little piece of England that's fallen down from heaven, this
magic piece of wonderland, that we call, "Glorious Devon."
Roy B. Franks

Friends

Friends are, someone to share with,
Someone to care with,
Someone to sort out problems with,
Someone to cry with,

Someone to buy your first gown with,
Someone to go to town with,
Someone to take the big step with,
Someone to buy cosmetics with,

Someone to look at men with,
Someone to double date friends with,
Someone to help you when you break your heart,
Someone to get you back on your feet,

Someone to walk down the aisle with,
Someone to laugh and smile with,
Someone to help you in a divorce,
Someone to pick up the pieces,

Someone to draw your pension with,
Someone to sit in the park and talk with,
Someone to live and cry with,
Someone to wake up and die with.
Nicola Russell

I Remember

I hear my name whispered low, or is it the breeze?
Someone taps on the window, but no-one's there.
I hear soft footsteps and a gentle sneeze.
When the door opens I stay silent, in my chair.

No-one comes in and I close the door again.
I sit down, the wind is howling now.
I draw the curtains, and see it's beginning to rain,
I close my eyes and feel a hand upon my brow.

A kiss so soft it's like thistledown on my face,
Someone is sighing, but I think that must be me.
An arm around my shoulders, a touch as soft as lace,
A little hug, just like it used to be.

You are not here, you fell in love and went away,
I just sit dreaming and remembering our love,
You forgot your vows and our happy wedding day.
You can't see my tears as I pray to God above.

I pray that you will miss me and come back.
Please love me as I know you used to do.
I still love you and so does our son Jack.
He misses his Daddy and surely you miss him too!

Pamela Bryant

A Marriage Made In Heaven

A marriage that's happy with someone so special
Somehow seems doomed — doomed from the start,
You feel something will happen, to one or the other,
and then it does, and you have to part

Oh why does it hurt so, especially in Springtime
with snowdrops and daffodils, crocuses too,
Folk hand in hand, walking out in the country,
my thoughts always turn, my darling, to you.

How we loved to wander, way back in the old days
admiring the countryside — animals — flowers
I wander alone now, I miss you so much
without you I spend long lonely hours

I picture your face as I walk down a lane
I hear your voice — whisper your name
and remember with love all our happy years
as I wander alone — blinded by tears.

V. K. Scott

Someday...

Someday ... we will stand before the sun as it sets,
Someday ... we will stand together at the end of the rainbow,
Someday ... we will see the silver lining of every cloud,
Someday ... we will fly across the planet and look down on
            our wonderful world,
Someday ... love will reign over all the Earth,
Someday ... we will live in perfect harmony with each other,
Someday ... we will triumph over hate,
Someday ... all the people of the Earth will understand one
            another,
Someday ... we will all be at one with the Earth,
Someday ... we will dance to the music of eternal peace,
Someday ... I hope this dream will become a reality.

Rachel Stroud

" Some Friends "

Some friends are for helping one another,
Some friends are for keeping you out of bother,
Some friends are for telling a secret or two,
Some friends are for showing affection to you,
Some friends are good company all of the time,
Some friends are always so very kind,
Some friends are often full of chat,
Some friends are always cheerful and that's a fact,
Some friends are caring in every way,
Some friends are forgiving, come what may,
Some friends are a comfort in times of sadness,
That's why some friends are filled with gladness.

Miriam Jean Goodacre

The Essence Of Love

Some say it is the food of life,
Some say it is a spell,
Some say that it's but trouble and strife,
I say that it is hell.

Some say it is the rarest wine,
Or a wonder of the seven.
Some say it's good food on which to dine,
I say that it is heaven.

Some say it is a blessing,
Upon favoured men from God,
Until I revealed my secret love,
When upon my heart he trod.

For love is only happiness
When the one you love loves you.
And though I wish I could love him less,
To my heart I must be true.

Marie Bruce

'The Train'

People waiting, standing and queuing, some coughing and
sneezing some in a rush, coats flying, as they run down the
station at the sight of the train.
Pushing and shoving, babies crying in mothers' arms, some
standing on others' feet as they fight to get a seat.
Climbing hills, faces at windows, pale and worn. The train
travels on passing factories and mills. Stopping and starting at
stations as some people get on some get off.
I'll be glad to reach my destination back at the station.
The cleaners come in, talking and smoking, with dusters and
polish to make my windows shine.
Men with buckets of hot water to wash off the grime.
Wheels gleaming, shiny and black, ready to start another day.
Tomorrow they'll be back, hot breath steaming the windows,
tickets dropped on the floor, polluting the air with their cigarettes.
Out in the country, cows stand and stare, chewing the cud as
we go by, wheels turning, pulling and grinding, twisting round bends.
I'll be glad when we stop, the engine's hot.
It's getting quite dark, thank God at last, another day is past.

Valerie Kempster

Changes

Life brings many changes,
Some good, and some bad.
Some that make us happy
And some that make us sad.
Some we do not like at all.
Some that give us quite 'A ball',
Some we feel we could do without.
Some - we wonder what it's all about?
Yes, life brings many changes,
And it's right it should.
For it usually turns out, for our very own good.

Q. Smith

Life?

There is this thing called life
That was given to us by Christ
Some of us love it, and some of us hate it
and sometimes it cuts like a knife

Its heart is full of emotions
its soul is full of search
For the endless question of what is life?
and why it breeds on earth.

This life it lives, this life it dies
It is happy yet it cry's
Some people take it, some give it back
Some of us treat it like a beaten track.

It's yours to use to your best
It's yours to put to the test
You set your destiny out yourself
To seek and search for life itself.

Melodie Lunn

A Childhood Fear

Nobody knows quite how he got there, right out there,
Solitary figure in the middle of that ploughed field.
Maybe it was only a secret that darkness itself may yield.
An eerie silhouette against a setting sun beckons goodbye to the day,
Welcomes the night whence ghouls and demons from the other side come out to play.
From afar should anyone be brave or foolish enough to watch or stare, like a statue does he stand,
no footprints, tracks, not even a clue is left behind on that freshly tilled land.
Only with the elements does he share his secrets, sometimes the faintest of whispers as the winds provide an ear,
maybe an overactive imagination can play the cruellest of tricks,
images, fantasy, reality entwine making real my fears.
As midnight approaches the fullest of moons bathes an unnatural light as far as the eye can see, miles and miles,
"You don't scare me Mr Scarecrow", I say mockingly from my bedroomwindow, that wise old man of string and straw, opens his eyes and smiles
  Michael Hartshorne

Twinnie Bobs

Two pairs of eyes, all velvety brown,
Solemnly eyeing you up and down,
Two small faces, alike as two peas,
Which one is which, they tease.

Dressed alike, with bob caps on,
Only Mummie knows which one,
Nannie gets them right, mostly,
Granddad has to look more closely.

The teachers I bet, have a bit of trouble,
Trying to sort out this double.
Name badges swapped with a giggle,
Hey, are you two doing a fiddle.

Of course, when poorly, they are more bother,
They come down with the bugs one after the other.
And if to one Mum gives a slap,
The other one defends him, just like that.

But when they are in bed, and all is calm,
You pray to God to keep them from harm,
What a wonderful gift, hard work though they seem,
These two little boys, KEIRAN and DEAN.
  R. Barber

Soldier Boy

The beaches of Dunkirk are never at rest.
Soldiers who died there were amongst the best.
Letters they sent home to wives, sons, daughters.
They spoke of the trenches, deep in mud, swamps, and dreadful stenches.
Lord, they found the burden of war hard to carry.
To all british mothers. All our soldier lads are our sons.
We admire them all, and love every one.
As I kneel in the village churchyard, by my soldier boy's grave,
My eyes fill with tears for his life he gave.
I was a young girl then, when this war was on.
Now all these lonely years since I kissed you have passed on.

There is not only one hero in war.
Many thousands have marched on before.
Many poppies have grown upon your grave,
Reminding us of the lives our soldier boys gave.
And I just want to say, I still love you, my hero,
In remembrance, we honour all lives what were lost.
Red on the poppy reminds us of the blood what was shed.
Black in the middle tells us to respect the dead.
  Marie Graham

A Zoo Remembered

Black-backed jackals, dingoes wild;
Soft eyes sorrowing in frustrated hunger
For half-remembered freedom.
Brave lion heart in your cemented cell
And meals on time
And you, baboon — swinging on your dunlop
What do you know of freedom, performing for your oranges to ignorant cheers.
And fish, your prison no wider than you
That you swim around in circles — obeying the geometric glass.
My poor cheetah — no more running with the wind
Your silent longing for your graceful speed
Will remain a dream forever — until you die.
Oh my friends — how can we make amends
For what we have done to you?
For something good for us is bad for you.
We are free to stand and stare at your unnatural submissiveness.
Goading you to some strange action
For our own selfish pleasure.
  Christine Aitken

Time

Time stands still for no man woman or child;
  So why in this life is time pushed aside?
Rushing, pushing, watching the clock,
  It's all we have, it's all we've got.
So don't push time aside; it is after all our lives.
  What does go on inside? Tic Toc Tic Toc, we all live by the clock...
  Rushing, pushing, hurrying around, no one has any time.
Just slow down and look around;
  Time is all we have; it's all around.
Don't rush it, push it all away.
  Take your time to love, play, work and relax.
Remember time is your friend; it's all you have.
  Have time for everyone and everything, make time for people you don't often see, make time for yourself to enjoy your life.
  Time lasts forever if you'd just relax and try.
  Mandy Bancroft

Shades Of Autumn

With shades of orange, red, yellow and brown,
So the earth does shed her bright summer gown;
Paper thin leaves floating down to the ground,
Blown to and fro', soft whispering around.

Lofty skeletons are now standing bare,
Robbed of a life that was not so long there;
Revealing gnarled old bough, and naked bark,
No more a hiding place for thrush and lark.

As summer moves on, no wasp sting to fear,
Now chilly winds declare autumn is here;
Farewell to warm evenings with cool soft breeze,
Longer light days fade away with such ease.

Sweet scents of summer once wafted this way,
Bright coloured petals, awake during day;
Birds on the wing, gliding by on warm air,
Their homes now repossessed, no longer there.

Grey evenings draw in, blue skies are no more,
The squirrel has gathered his winter store;
Summer has passed by but will, without fear,
Like a faithful old friend, return next year.
  Margaret Settle

In Memory Of My Dog Lady

Lady! you were my baby and best friend,
So sadly your life has come to an end,
You showed so much love every day,
Now! to God's Land, you have gone to stay,
But my love for you will never stray,
Though I know you have gone,
In my heart, you will always belong.
  Vie Jones

My Cat In The Summer Garden

My cat long haired shades of white, grey and brown,
so relaxed in the garden with the sun shining down,
even with the sound of the song thrush she doesn't stir,
she knows her meal will be ready, when she gives a purr,
the rockery bed is comfortable and dry,
with only an ear twitching, to the setting touch of a fly,
the stream trickles and bubbles over the rocks,
gently splashing on her paws, and little white socks,
her feet are gradually easing over the rockery into the stream,
as she dreams it's Sunday, with helpings of double cream,
then suddenly an aeroplane thunders overhead,
and her dreams are shattered, as she jumps up from the flower bed,
she races up the winding path into the house,
finding comfort attacking an old woollen mouse,
her owner gives her a pat on the head, and a dish full of cream,
now life is wonderful, just like the dream,
Teddie the cat climbs into her basket to bed,
the day is complete, now she has been fed,
it's back to the land of dreams,
which do come true, for a cat it seems.

Patricia Anne Spriggs

In A Mining Vale

All the unpleasant scars
So prominent by day
Are magically beautified by night.
Even the hill of slag that mars
A landscape once unblemished green,
May reveal a hidden splendour,
And delight the observant eye.
But, like the comet's transient flight
Its beauty is not permanent
And, with the unfolding rays of dawn
I reluctantly witness the event
Of day's disfigurement reborn
In ugly nakedness, bearing wounds
That heal, and vanish with the night's return.

Richard Towyn Jones

Through The Park At Dusk

As the light fails so does its life,
so precious and dear for everything.
The birds slow down, oh enchanting song,
now disappearing in the wind.

The petals close to say goodnight,
it's been a long day so warm and bright.
It's time to sleep and rest in sorrow,
before those bee's attack tomorrow.

As the light fails, life comes to some,
as badgers scurry for food in twilight.
They come and sit all sullen and hollow,
to fish the night until the morrow.

The stars come out as though to play,
they stay and pose all proud and bright.
Hoot, hoot, it sounds as if to say,
goodnight one and all until a new day.

Stephen Cooke

The Four Seasons Poem

Spring flowers all in their bloom
spread themselves out and have plenty of room.
Summer sun showing its glow,
bees buzzing around, always on the go!!
Autumn with many windy days,
leaves of many colours fall to the ground,
without making a sound.
Winter with drifting snow, children making snowmen,
and off they go!!
These are the four seasons, so special and unique,
so look outside and take a peek!!

Rebecca Owen

To My Daughters

You have to work your own lives out
So please be sure what you're about
Be always thoughtful, always kind
And scandalous tongues please never mind
Help the helpless, help the poor
What you can do is so much more

Keep you mind and your body clean
A paragon of virtue you'll be seen
Walk in the light keep out of the shade
The way you are is what you made
So keep heart pure, keep eyes bright
You'll always know what's wrong, what's right

Keep God within your heart and soul
And only then your life is whole

F. Shelvock

Growing Up

Little one awakening, questioning, starry eyed,
so much to see, discover, do. . .
this tired world looks good on you.

Let us keep silent, stand aside
no disillusionment must steal
youth's indefatigable zeal.
Leave them to dream, build castles in the air,
to probe, investigate, search everywhere.

Success and failure, both are meet,
we need the bitter and the sweet.
Life in full measure drains the cup.

Gladly we gave while you learned how to live,
now you demand your turn, your right to give,
to take the helm when storms are blowing up,
and stand alone — because you're growing up.

Moyra Platts

Looking Back

You should be glad, they say, to be so old
So many happy thoughts and memories to hold.
They cannot understand the sorrow that I feel
Because so much has gone for time to steal.

Looking back on my long life is sad,
Not because me memories are bad.
Those memories are happy, joyous, clear
But sad because they are no longer here.

Looking back and thinking how it was
Cannot make me happy now because
I want much more than memories allow
I do not want it then, I want it now.

Winifred Johnson

An Hour In The Night

It's three in the morning and I can't sleep
So I get out of bed and down I creep
Moving as quietly as I could
I hear an owl hoot in the nearby wood
As I look from the window into the night
And gaze at the stars shining and bright
Is there anyone else out there can't sleep
Or is it just me and the owl and sheep
Thoughts are swimming round in my mind
Of the jobs to be done I'm certain to find
But first in the morning when it's bright and sunny
I'll have jam on my toast or maybe some honey
When a branch on the tree moves without warning
I'm startled and jump, it soon will be morning
As I look round the room all safe and secure
The doors are all locked, of that I am sure
Nothing can be done now it has to be said
So I'll go back upstairs and get into my bed
I sneak in beside the warm love of my life
He hasn't missed me for an hour in the night.

S. Truda Watson

Untitled

Most of my life has been lived now
So I feel quite qualified to say
That the world is a wonderful place to live in
When everything's going our way
To compromise is part of the secret
To happiness, contentment and joy
Discuss things that are not agreeable
Don't argue, blaspheme or annoy
Time is well spent if considering
That the other side could be right and not you
Then young folk with these thoughts in mind now
May see all future dreams coming true
Rosemarie K. Brace

" My Daughter "

It's so hard to imagine, as I look at you now
So grown up, looking so self-assured
As I try to re-capture, in my mind's eye
All the years that have gone by before!

From the first time I saw you, in your mother's arms
I was such the proud father, you see
That I telephoned everyone, with the news
Back in nineteen seventy-three!

If ever there was a storm in the night
Of one thing, we were certainly sure
We would listen for the patter of your tiny feet
As you'd make your way to our bedroom door!

Long gone are the days, when you played with your dolls
And would make sand castles, down by the sea
And you used to dash in, after playing with friends
Shouting, "Hey Mum, what's for my tea!"

Now in the place of our once little girl,
An elegant, and confident, young lady we see,
But oh how we long for those long bygone days
When you used to fall asleep on our knee!
D. Fishwick

" Spiders "

The void of October creeps in through the curtain,
Snuggling up to the glowing fire and soft music
The feeling of deep security wafts around me;
I retreat into the pages of my book.

Pale night light magnifies everything
Out of the corner of my eye I spy a huge, grotesque,
twitching monster,
Legs hairy like tentacles,
Eyes like double jointed crabs,
It gets bigger nearing the light of the lamp.
Thoughts of my book drift away,
An eerie skin crawling repulsion steals over me,
I feel hundreds all over my body as I scramble from the carpet

The creature runs out of the light into reality,
Into a world where it does not look so fearsome.
Scuttling towards the door I ponder the existence of such life
I wonder if it too is afraid;
Afraid of me.
Sarah Butt

Spring

Spring is in the air, in the early morning dew
Snowdrops and crocuses are just peeping through
Dew covered cobwebs glisten in the sun
Daffodils appear, spring has just begun
Take a walk through the woods and you will find
Blossoms on trees, wild flowers of all different kinds
Primroses, bluebells, and when they start to appear
It is the most beautiful sight now that spring is here
R. Underwood

" Raindrops "

I saw you in the frozen wastes, did I not? Drifting snowflakes
in the snow, blizzards, icepacks, icebergs; to thaw, ascend,
then to return to us below.

I saw you in the rising mist, did I not? one early summer morn,
then later on that too returned as rain another dawn.

I saw you in a raincloud, did I not? when you brought life to
the barren ground, and now in my juicy apple, that shower in
Spring I've found.

I saw you in falling water, did I not? as you ran from the
mountain high-high above the mountains, raindrops in the sky.

I saw you in cavern, did I not? raindrops dripping to the floor,
building stalagmites for years to come, 'til then one day — encore.

I saw you in a rainbow, did I not? peeped through the sun one
showery, sunny day, then an arc of pretty colours, told me
raindrops were on their way.

I saw you in a sleeping pool, did I not? caring pondlife, weeds
and spawn, through sleep 'tis not the end of all, but where
evolving life is born.

I saw you in a teardrop, did I? which said sadly, this really is
the end, then a raindrop, a holy raindrop, gave me faith,
and a continuation of that 'end'.
R. R. Pammenter

The Awakening

Eve tasting the fruits in the garden
Smelling the flowers, feeling the leaves
Filling her memory with new life
Living in ease and tranquillity.

She shivered at the forbidden tree
God made everything good, what use was this?
She had to be wise, know right from wrong
But God said — She didn't want to die.

'You won't die.' That voice was always there.
'Its use has been proved over aeons,
By all creation from plants to primates,
All knowing the good, discarding the evil'.

'They're seeking the best for their species.
What judgement can you make — you alone,
Independent of God your Maker?
Eat, and self motivating you'll be'.

She stretched out her hand. It was very good.
Suddenly aware of her form and beauty,
She raced to share with her mate.
And afterwards they were sad, and hid.
R. Swann

To Die

I die,
Is there nothing?
No love, no laughter.
Does the earth not move at my passing
Will the wind that carries my soul, not pause,
Allow a second glance.
A chance to reflect.
No! we journey on.
Is that an angel? or just a passing cloud that turns the mind
to heavenly view.
Heaven? a reality, an imagination.
Alone, lost the soul that travels on.
Vast horizons, no end, no beginning.
Is life and death but a mirror image of what or might have
been, is to be?
Does it matter, our reality of life, be it lost in deaths obscurity?
Has life really ended in death?
Or is death but another chapter of life.
Enid Bale

Why Are They Homeless?

The noise of the metal forks hitting the table,
smacked the small young boys,
the hostel filling with hungry, cold people,
starving, struggling in from the streets.

Many of these people have fled from home,
many orphans, old and young, cold and alone,
there's no light in the tunnel, no voice on the phone,
for the hungry, lonely people will never go home.

The richer people walk the streets,
not looking at their lonely, bloodshot eyes,
they hold out their hands, begging for money,
to buy some food or a cheap form of booze.

Each of these people has a secret,
to why they have ran away,
but no one else will hear it,
as they find themselves alone.
Natalie Hooper

The Magic Of The Dawn

A light peeps o'er the horizon,
Slowly spreading its arc,
The sky like a shroud of black velvet,
Furls its margins back.
Timid at first as a candle glow,
Barely creasing the night.
Then rising out from the shadows,
exploding to brilliant light.
The earth breathes a sigh all around me
and the flowers open their eyes,
The birds begin to sing their song,
as a new dawn lights the sky.
Some old life gone, some new reborn.
Some night life passes to sleep.
And as the sun caresses me,
I feel my spirits leap.
The dawn indeed is a magical scene,
breathing life into this world,
And the black velvet cloak of darkness,
Is now completely furled.
Margaret Nimmo

The Meeting

He lay there, unaware of the world
Sleeping soundly, silently I tiptoe
Sneaking a look at him, a new child,
a stranger to me, and yet I know him

I know him well, not by sight nor by
sound, but by touch, I felt his kick,
caressed the curve of her tummy,
as her soothing voice read to us.

Now he has come, now he too can
see her face. She gathers him close
his eyes stare intently, drinking in
each line and curve of her face

Feasting on her features, a frown
breaks across his brow, she turns him
round in my direction. We meet now.
Unfocused eyes strain to see the shape.

The shape I see is that of things to come.
Sara Jones

Desperation

Stuck in deep, dark, black despair,
Surrounding and pounding everywhere,
No way to escape the smothering cloud,
Desperate to elude this cloaking death shroud.

All hope of light has blown away,
Leaving pungent, seeping dense decay.
Into spiralling madness I am being sucked,
Save me Jesus, before I self destruct.
Nicola Bird

Wind By Night And Day

The wind doth blow night is long
Sleep wont come and day is gone
It bends the trees strange shapes
To make
That play in the light and keep you awake.
Sometimes it's frightening when it
Howls at night
After endless hours at last its light
The wind still as strong seems less
Fearsome at day
Falling leaves make a pattern and seem to play
As I watch from my window not a sole in sight
No dog or cats no birds in flight
Early morning sunshine and the day is still
Suddenly the wind rises the calm to kill
It spoils the pleasures of a country amble
And to wear a hat is really a gamble
Wind is no mans friend, but some would say
A breathe of wind would be welcome
On a hot summers day.
Sandra Witt

The Wood

Spaniel days in long sunlit lanes,
Skittering over verges for sticks,
So eager to please; your wet-nosed brain,
Whiffling, chases bracken-hid chicks.

Burrowing into Dog-Rose briars
Pink petals tumbling, wood pigeons flee.
Wagging your tail, springing up higher,
Scattering Foxgloves, Dog's Mercury,

Flushing out rabbits, sparrows and voles,
Anticipation heightening fun;
Lolloping tongue laughs down a fox-hole,
Flapping long ears, all Goosegrass, undone.

Cracking undergrowth opens into
A mystical misty, gladed dream
Clearing to shimmering heat on dew,
Dragonflies waft through magic unseen.

How could you know this Bower of Bliss
Deep in the woods, a guarded secret?
Swiftly clouding, scenery changes,
Shrinks and dwindles to your panting breath.
Suzanne J. Price

Gran-Ma

A little old lady with silver hair
Sitting there in her favourite chair,
No one wants her now she is old
"I love you Gran" she is seldom told.
Crippled with arthritis, unable to hear,
She sits with composure, sometimes a tear.
The lady opposite is ninety years old,
And still her life stories she can unfold.
A twinkle comes to her jaded eyes,
A smile upon her wrinkled face,
As thoughts go back down memory lane.
A fun-loving husband she tried to tame,
Five precious children, they gave heartbreak and joy,
Four were girls, and one a boy.
She has suffered pain, and quietly wept,
But is thankful for her memories kept.
When in bed, she prays at night,
She knows the end is now in sight,
And puts herself in her maker's hands,
Knowing for her, "His love still stands."
E. D. Shaw

My Easter Poem

At Easter time we do rejoice
Sing Alleluias, as with one voice,
That Christ has risen from the dead
No more that cross on which he bled
And died for me.

Happy are they that love the Lord,
Who listen intent to hear his word,
Read from the book, the deeds he has done,
Millions of hearts he already has won,
And he died for us.

Cruel his death, so long ago,
Short was his life, so long ago,
But now, he lives, and Easter shows
How best we live, and Jesus knows
We live for Him — Alleluia.

Phyllis Olley

A Bi-Centenary Tribute To Robert Burns 1759-1796

Two hundred years and more have gone
Since Rabbie Burns has aye passed on,

His Life and works immortal are
Continuing like a Shining Star,

Nae just the Scots keep faith but
Sassenachs and others too
From near and far his works to view,

His love of creatures great and sma'
Is an example to us a',

So here's a toast to one and all
As on his Birthday, we recall,
With haggis, pipes, a dram or two
"A' the Best of Health to you."

D. L. McFall

Winter, My Friend

Blue pastel sky cradles the moon.
Silver the sixpence I can see from my room.

Ice cold the morning that waits for the sun.
Grey clouds whispering, he might not come.

It seems so long since Autumn did call.
Leaving you only a brown paisley shawl.

'Tis little against those long angry storms
And pathetic to see such bleak wretched forms.

O Winter, my friend, stripped to the bone.
Heard in the wind is your sorrowful groan.

But I see your beauty and know of your love,
As you patiently wait, for Spring's warm glove.

Sharon C. Richards

Your Words

Words like water from a tap
Slip so easily out of your mouth,
Splashing hard on the ground
Or trickling without a sound
Like a tree losing its sap.

It's the life you take when you speak;
Harsh words that crush like rushing water,
Knocking me clean out of my socks
Dashing my heart on these rocks
Showing me how really I am weak.

Then words come soothingly, like fresh rain,
They wash over me and calm.
You bring me up again to the norm
And I forget the torrents of the passing storm
And everything is sweet again.

Susanna Miller

The Autumn Leaves

Swirling softly, round and round,
Silently, without a sound,
Suddenly the leaves awake,
Trembling slightly, starting to shake.
In the Autumn breeze as though in a trance,
One by one, they start to dance,
Higher and higher, faster and faster,
Tip-toeing lightly, each leaf its own master.
Unexpectedly it comes to a pause,
Our ballet leaves smile at the applause.

Tasneem Mueen

The Last Tear

I sit, I wait, and as the dawn of a new day unfolds "I pray". Silently and without movement through bloodshot eyes, I sense two faces looking at me; they are my guardians watching, waiting for any sudden move I make. But what can I do locked in a square room with barred windows, like a captive animal I'm "trapped", I want to scream. But no, I am a lady, a woman of well being. They will not know that they have won.

HARK! What was that, footsteps outside, a key in the lock. I turn and my guardians turn too. Come! a smiling face whispers and then louder, only to another room my dear. OH my God thank you, thank you to be spared a few more minutes. The guardians grip my arms. I, I feel so weak that my legs can hardly walk. But somehow they can just to get to the other room for a few more minutes to live.

What I should have done, could, would have done, all this runs through my mind, until a huge locked door stares me in the eyes. OH NO! No, No, I'M numb as my hands are tied behind my back and they walk me through the door and out onto the platform. Then and only then do my tears fall silent, as the hood comes down over my head and I cry my last tear.

Sheila Watts

" Memories "

The cottage stood serene and still on the
silent side of a winding hill,
Legs trembling from the long cycle ride from
my village far on the other side.
I was there to stay for a week and a day
with my Grandpa and Nan in their treasure chest
of tassled clothes and dark decor what child could
ever ask for more.
Fetching the milk in shiny tin cans straight from
the churn, warm to the hands.
Onto the heath from the garden gate, the
rabbits running as if they were late, the grasshoppers
too were making a din, singing, hopping without and within.
How oft I ponder of things that were, happy and
joyful without a care.
I'll never forget and remember still, my
Grandparents' cottage that stood on a hill.

K. V. Breach

When Love Hurts

One of the nicest things in life is when you grow up and have someone to love, to be happy, and to have children. But sometimes this is not to be. You may find that you are with child, you are so happy with your partner, then something goes wrong and you lose the baby. It is so hard to come to terms with. Or, you may have the baby and all is well for so many years then things are not what you thought. There may be an accident or the child takes ill and passes over to spirit. All life becomes hard, no one can say what you want to hear, perhaps that your child is alright, and the hurt overcomes you like a heavy weight. It would be hard for you, but if you could speak of the child with love in your heart the pain would gradually ease for you. We all think that we will grow to be old but it is not always the way. Our Father God gave us life. When it is time for us to go back to him it is hard and it hurts so but if we can know that love never dies and we love on in God's House it will not be so hard and the pain gets eased.

M. Catterson

Inner Beauty

Where there is darkness of the soul,
Show to all My light.
Where there is sorrow and sadness,
Show to all the beauty of existence.
Where there is hatred and enmity,
Show to all the joy of life.
Where there is destruction and chaos,
Show to all true creation,
Not of earthly structure, but of The Spirit.
For without creating a place of inner beauty,
One is bound to dwell in the darkness of the mind.
And this I say to you...
To those who reach out and search,
Much shall be given to them.
For My storehouse abounds with many treasures of The Spirit.
Come, take what you desire.
Wilma Hogg

He Rules My Heart

Important, grand, certainly king of The Land,
Shoulders square, confidence of a bear.
Magnificent, majestic, tame and domestic.
Terribly smart... he rules my heart.

Long black coat, short white waistcoat,
Pure white shoes — got to be a virtue,
Or could it be? Long white boots for he.
Terribly sleek... he rules my heart.

Curiously mystical, undoubtedly egotistical,
A brush of his tail, the feel of his detail.
He's heaven to hold, body so warm, nose so cold.
Terribly kind... he rules my heart.

He's a best friend, no I lie, he's a Godsend.
He comforts, he waits, peace he makes.
He's quiet and still, he watches from the windowsill.
Terribly loved... Smutty cat rules my heart.
Valerie Green

Waterfall

Picture a cool clear crystal cascade
Shimmering over a rocky span,
Like an eternal supply of lemonade,
Poured from an ice cold ring pull can.

And from that watery stew,
Touched by virgin light,
Stripes appear of every hue,
A kaleidoscope so bright.

You feel that gentle spray,
As a breeze breaks its formation,
The colours merge in great array,
What perfect transformation.
J. Wilshaw

Time

Time was forever when we were young
Time for learning exploring and fun
Laughing days in cowslip fields
Counting the hours on the dandelion clocks.

Time was our time when first we loved
Time to feel and touch and know
Days full of longing nights too slow
Counting the hours until we met again.

Time became master as the years moved on
A time for caring and working and living
Days full of children who stole our time
Counting the hours of their childhood dreams.

Time has became our precious time
Each day to be savoured and stored away
Memory recalling our special years
Counting the hours dispelling our fears.
Pamela Westley

The Bag Lady

The old and frail woman just sits and begins to cry,
she's walked these streets for many years,
her life has passed her by.

No one knows her reasons, no one knows her pain.
Does anybody really care, or is it just a game?

Her clothes are all in tatters, her feet are soiled and bare.
Does anyone know where she is heading,
will anyone be there?

Her belongings are not many, the bags are all that's left,
and yet she will not leave them
for they contain her Sunday best.

For Sunday is her special day when memories allow
to remember all the family and where they may be now.

She likes to believe they'll come for her,
and yet she knows they won't,
for her family gave up long ago — CARE — well they just don't.

So if you see her sitting there, crying on her own,
just spare her some of your time, for at least you have a home.
S. M. Brown

Fay

There is a girl I work with
she's a leading hand in fact
she's a jolly sort of person
but just a little fat
she gets on well with people
that is except for one
she's always having a go at her
you would think she was her mum
at times she can be very nice
and also very witty
but most of the time she shouts at her
and that really is a pity
I feel sorry for this girl
So gentle, quiet and shy
I wonder what makes her take it
there must be a reason why.
I suppose it's because they are really friends
and it's all in fun you see
because the girl that she keeps picking on
believe it or not is me
Margaret Reeves

The Wonders Of Springtime

Those winter months are over, we have the first signs of spring,
Shrubs are growing shoots of green, as the birds begin to sing,
The snowdrops and the crocus, have suddenly burst into bloom
Next come the daffodils and tulips, they follow on quite soon.

Newborn lambs are frolicking, in the meadows oh so green,
You get so many memories, from this rustic countryside scene
Watching the birds of the air, find their partners for mating,
And after all their rituals, build nests for the mothers in waiting.

The May blossom is so pretty, mauve, red, pink and white,
Nature produces these colours, such a magnificent sight,
There are primula and pansies, multi-coloured primroses as well,
Beneath the weeping willow tree, are clusters of scented bluebell.

The crystal clear pond in the meadow is sheltered by a big old oak,
And from the reeds along the side, a bullfrog lets out a croak,
Two beautiful swans have returned; they come here year after year,
For breeding it is a safe haven, they know they have nothing to fear.

Farm fields and house garden soil, are prepared and seeds are sown,
The meadows they are left untouched, but all the lawns are mown,
After the early morning dew, we are blessed with hours of sunshine,
These beautiful things for all to see are the wonders of springtime.
Wenn the Pen

Mothers Day

We all have, or have had a Mother
She was the one who gave us life
The person who carried us for nine whole months
Very often through struggle and strife

A Mother is a person who cares for us
Who nurtured us with milk from her breast
Who changed our nappies, cleans up our mess
And gives us all that is best

As we start to grow up choices have to be made
What playgroup, nursery or school
A Mother has to be so many things at once
Whatever she is, she is no fool

Not a day goes by when thoughts are not present
In every Mothers mind
Of how each child will grow and progress
And if they will be good and kind

Today is known as Mother Day
A tribute to Mothers one and all
An opportunity to say "Thank you"
For giving your children your all.
   Stella Evans

Child Of Quietness

Sitting alone is she there, a child of quietness.
She very seldom speaks a word.
There is an air of tenderness.
Each new day is an experience,
New things to learn and do,
She embraces these with a softness
An ability beyond her years.

She gives her love so freely to those for whom she cares.
Time has no meaning, for one so young in years.
Her presence is so comforting
Peaceful company she provides.
The quietness within her shows in her eyes.
Whenever you shall meet her, unattached is she.
Adding to her character an air of mystery.
Some will say it cannot be,
Some will not understand.
They will only look and see a young person in an
adult land.
But you and I will softly smile,
Knowing the peace that sleeps inside, quietness in a child.
   Susan Matthews

My Wife

She starts my day with a kiss,
She is my heaven of which is bliss

She is my light in my darkest hours
She is my field which is filled with beautiful flowers

She is my shoulder to cry on
She is the one most person I solely rely on.

She is a mother loving, kind and gentle
To our children she is their angel.

She is always there when I come home at night
She is my one and only true delight

She is the woman I only live for
She is the only woman I care for

She builds me up when I am down
She makes me feel like a king, then I become her clown

She is my heart, she's in my thoughts
All the day while I'm at work.

Washing, meals, dishes and lovingly she does do
She works and toils the whole day through

She means more to me than my life
She, of course, is my wife!
   Philip R. White

Our Dear Little Grand-Daughter

Our grand-daughter is such a dear.
She has pale blue eyes and short blonde hair.
She's three years old and very sweet.
She's three feet tall, with dainty feet.

With her mischievous smile,
with her tongue in her cheek.
We see her regular three times a week.

As she plays, she's quiet as a mouse,
with her books, toys and a small dollies house.

Dressing up she likes to do,
with an old grey coat and a floppy hat too.
Over her eyes, the hat does fall,
nothing in sight could she see,
but her ball under her arm,
pair of brown boots on wrong feet.

As the day goes by,
she will often say,
"Thank you Nan for a lovely day!"
She's so loving and very sweet
then she lies down and goes to sleep.
   S. J. Thompson

The Unapproachable

Languid and lazy, graceful and small
She covered the scene from her place on the wall.
That dog with the scowl that matched the face of his master,
He could run fast but she could run faster.

Then there was Bandit - the scourge of his race,
A feline so evil, you avoided his face.
A permanent hiss and claws open wide,
When he appeared you looked for somewhere to hide.

But Beauty, so high-bred, with refinement so rare
Was far too well-mannered to stay round and stare.
She spent much of the day from her place in the sky
Watching the people, and things, passing by.

In a lazy and hazy world of her own,
Beauty found interest in movement alone.
A peer in her class, with an owner to match,
The boys stood in awe of such an elegant catch.

They would have loved to have asked her to come out for the day,
But one withering glance always kept them at bay.
And Beauty just looked at them waiting below,
The lady who smiled but always said "No".
   Ronald Moore

The Weather Lottery

Tomorrow's weather forecasts will they all come true,
Shall the sky be sombre grey or a sunny blue!
Snowstorms, hailstones, floods galore, lightning
And the thunders roar, can the soft snow turn to ice,
Perhaps we all should toss a dice;
Shall I wear a raincoat or one of my
wind breakers, scarfs, gloves and woolly hats
All combine to make good heaters.
Hope for the best is what I pray,
But you could set four seasons in one day,
Try to be all I can, I could never be a weatherman.
   C. Stephen

Wedding Day Expectations

As Mark and Julie make their vows
   on this September day,
Lord help them and inspire them
As they travel along life's way.

And as they reach their rainbow's end
And reflect on all that's been.
I pray their memories will be sweet.
And enshrined on their hearts,
   "Love's young dreams"
   Olive E. Barber

Tempting Flame

What is this flame so near, so far?
Shall I reach out, my life to char?
How bright it flickers before my eyes
Is it the truth, or just more lies.

With fascination I watch it burn
What happens flame, if I should turn.
Just as a magnet draws me near,
Appears so warm, I still sense fear.

Oh what the hell, I'll make a grab.
My God, it hurts, the burn is bad.
Time will heal my broken skin
But wound is deep, the scar within.

The candle burns as life is long.
But all flames end like every song.
When all is dark, last glow of light.
I'll reach again, should I?, I might..

Sandra Elizabeth Lee

It's Alright, Ma...

Darkness at the break of noon
Shadows even the silver spoon.
The handmade blade, the child's balloon
Eclipses both the sun and moon.
To understand, you know too soon
There is no sense in trying.

So many masters making rules
For the wise men and the fools —
With nothing, Ma, to live up to... I'm one more person crying.

Drained, you stand with no one near.
You lose yourself... You reappear.
Then suddenly there's no more fear....
A trembling, distant voice — unclear,
Startles your sleeping ears to hear
That someone yearns to find you.

So do not start if you should hear
A foreign sound at your ear.
It's alright, Ma... it's only me... the tears have dried... I'm sighing.

And it's alright, Ma... I'll make it.

Robert G. Smith

Earth

As I open my eyes upon God's wondrous show,
Shadows dance like angels, a warm Autumn glow,
The dew drops look warmed to the start of the day
I look to my lover and know why people pray.

The Summers are longer the Winters grow short.
Untruths and injustice are ours to abort,
Wars that mankind could afford to of missed,
The innocent dying, a full reaper's list.

Our forests of green grow smaller each day
Animals poached when protected they say
With a hole in our ozone for our children to find,
Educate well save our earth for mankind.

Paul McGarry

Elizabeth I

Elizabeth I is coming to town
She will come in a carriage
And wear a golden crown
Her hair is red
Her eyes are green
She is more beautiful than any other queen
She loves jewelry
Also very clever indeed
She is bright and intelligent too
She never got married
But I don't know why
She is proud of England
And so am I.

Shari Louise Chapman

At Two In The Morning

At two in the morning, softly in the gloom,
Seven new friends, on safari in the dunes,
Four girls, three men, making for the sea,
Two feeling love, the others loose limbed free.
The early blood-red sun had dipped and lost its bloom,
Now all of us were shadows in the West Wales moon,
Four score years for me, she not two point nine,
Had found each other's souls in Harlech sands of time.
At two in the morning, naked on the beach,
Seaweed strewn, the ocean out of reach,
We stand and shyly stare, where legs and bodies join,
As warm fingers of air grip hidden spastic loins.
Five mirrored images rush out to the moon black view,
While our rhythmic bodies kiss, on Harlech Beach at two.

Martin Greason

Mother

Mothers are angels, without any wings,
Sent to sing us lullabies, softly like hymns.

Mothers are gifts, sent from afar,
To teach us how precious and wonderful we are.

Mothers are inspirations of love, and of life
Sent to guide us, through tunnels of doubt to comfort and light.

My mothers an angel full of wisdom and care,
With her smiles, from above, none can compare!

I love my mother with all of my heart,
Yet I know some day heaven will call,
And we will have to part...
Being an angel she will look out for me,
And because of her, I know that the sun will always shine, on me.

V. L. Benton

Island Life

Ocean winds, bereft of trees to bend,
Send salty scouts to scour the hills.
And miles inland, where the ocean is but a whisper,
Sea plantains taste the salt and wonder where they are.

From wavelets of countless calmer days,
The sea, when in the mood,
Builds great hills of water,
To lean upon the land.

The tidal pendulum inside the sea,
Compliant servant to the moon,
Moves to and fro, yearning to stay,
Turning only to return.

The thieving waves, failing to intimidate the land,
Scatter in disarray then reassemble,
Bruised but undeterred,
Content to pilfer cliffs a fragment at a time.

Trevor Norton

God's Fault?

Things are going wrong in the world, is God to blame?
That people are allowed to suffer, it really is a shame
Killings and wars, we vent our anger and outward cry
Please God stop this but you don't, we don't know why.
But maybe those who have died are in a better place
Because no more pain and suffering of this world they have to face.
God could have made us like robots and controlled our strings
But He gave us freedom of choice to do our own things.
If we chose to ruin His creation and then when nature rebels complain,
We use our talents to create weapons but then shout when they cause pain.
Perhaps we should look in the mirror and see us in our own true light,
And just be glad God is there to help us whatever our plight.
So please stop and let us by our mistakes be taught,
And realize that the bad things in life are not really God's fault.

B. Clarke

Freedom

What intolerance and bigotry
Self interest and hypocrisy
Is guised in the names of freedom.
Shall I be free when freedom means
The yoke upon my brother.
Can I be free when the price
Is slavery for another.
Such freedom bought with another's pain,
Tho' it may bring some transient gain,
Makes a mockery of freedom.

And now Ulster torn with strife
Where brothers in the name of freedom
Threaten brothers, homes and life
And at the urging of self-seekers
Who hope to rise upon the chaos
Impose their will upon the meeker,
And with gibes of freedom flay us
Destroy the lifeblood of their land
With misery on every hand
All in the name of freedom.
Robert I. Barton

Untitled

The Sun, setting in a golden glory,
Sees the world, but knows not what it sees:
Gracious light illumines ev'ry storey,
Of ev'ry man, when the world's at ease.

And, like the sun, so many people tread,
The long path through life and never look,
On either side, where sadness, lurking, dread,
Lies in waiting, with bait and hook.

They've burned their candles much too fast,
No time at all to spend in learning;
And, when they reach the sacred gates at last,
They stand outside and gaze with yearning.

Within, the gayest colours, dances, tunes,
Gather to delight their eyes and ears.
But they have wasted many precious moons,
And, too late, they cry for wasted years.
Roger Wrenhurst

The Castle On The Hill

I see this castle on the side of the hill
Set amidst green yews so dark and still.
Its beauty is wondrous to view from afar.
And when touched by moonlight it is something so rare
From this life which seems made up of turbulent care.
But alas, when I draw near this castle so white
It seems to repel me with all its might.
Some walls are crumbling and lying in ruins,
Makes me turn away quickly
From this sad sight ensuing
That this dark and dead castle
With its past now behind.
The enchantment is only so much in the mind.
Morfydd Davies

War

Why do people wish to make war
Something which is horrid and vile to the core
We were not born to fight and to kill
For fellow humans blood to spill
Yet people kill, for peace, they say
For peace they murder and the innocent slay
And when the sun brings forth the dawn
Many for their loved ones mourn
Peace is only found perhaps
When we leave this earth and its baited traps
To seek our refuge and peace of mind
And leave this troubled world behind
From high above we can view this scorn
And pray for those who are yet to be born.
L. Bates

Newbury

I have lived for more than a hundred years,
Seen my body move up towards the sky,
As young couples below kiss, make love, and move away in tears,
And spring, summer, autumn, and winter go ceaselessly by.

Now is written a new page, and with it another age,
Where my lungs are congested by smoke pollution,
As a mechanical monster takes over from horse and stage,
Will there ever be a solution?

Yet today there is a great affray,
Protestors march with banners, stop the heavy "plants,"
But my time is measured only by days,
Even those who climb, sit in my bows, are forced away
by the seat of their pants,

Uprooted and pulled down my life has been sapped,
To make way for the new idol that saves time,
The old route, they say, is better lapped,
Whilst the planners celebrate with opened bottles of wine,

They have, though, offered to make amends,
Lining the way with young seedlings,
On them, all that live, depends,
Can this make up for these feelings?
Terry Morris

Time's Wanderer

I can but walk among mortal men.
Seeking solace in misery, purpose in despair.
Following the cries from he who dares
Defy all in actions pure.
Dead to the four winds but destined to remain,
I can but forge the guarded remnants of righteousness.

For he whom is destined has no rest,
Ever onward need being my wont.
For darkness may not fall when all is good in men's minds,
The lighted torch of illumination burned in men's hearts.
But alas, ignorance devours hollow existence.
Barren, fickle selves justly enslaved.
Freedom is but a thought away.
J. Lauder

Love Renewed

There go the lovers drifting apart,
Seeking new interests and affairs of the heart.
Words of recrimination and anger are said;
Their love is dying, their lonely hearts bled.

Love has grown cold, Cupid has had his day.
Discontent and unhappy, they go their own way.
Unable to live while far apart,
Cannot find new love, where do they start?

Meet in the street, interest renewed,
Undisguised glances, their old love reviewed.
Unite them in love once more to be one,
A new love so tender, and Cupid, this time make it fun!
Sylvia Roberts

Oil Slicks

As I walk along the beach
Seeing dead birds at my feet,
I wonder who put the oil into the sea,
Who can these murderers be?
They may make a lot of money
But killing birds is not funny.
Perhaps someone should make a rule
That stops humans from being so cruel
Then some day the world will be
A better place for all creatures to be.

If that were you lying there,
In the oil totally bare,
You will think how bad oil can be,
For all creatures in the sea.
Matthew Thorpe

Nature's Awakening

Seeds so tiny, I need glasses to see,
Seeds as big as a bean or a pea,
I read on the packet, sow from March to June,
Then if you're like me, you'll pray that soon,
Healthy shoots, will peep above the earth,
Life giving rain, has Quenched their thirst,
Sun's warming rays has given them birth,
Springs well advanced, Birds on their nests,
Feeding fledglings, they know what's best,
This year's new story, awakens God's earth.
It was not just by chance, that the Prince of Light,
Was killed on a tree, taken from sight,
At the time of the year, when seeds lay buried,
They too like Him, had to rise from the dark,
For the Glory of God on the cross, in the tomb,
Is the Good News of rebirth's, first steps to Heaven.

A. Brookes Reid

Let's Look At Life

Man's strength you say;
See what with bricks and mortar built
A sacred edifice
Ah yes there's the rub, it lasts, the flower wilts
'tis but the clock that tells the time
Man adds no single stroke
Watch then the sun go down,
Mark then the calendar
   And proudly say,
Now has the sun gone down
In summer longer stay
Now has the Winter come
Man but the pattern makes;
Not from choice does he grow old
   Over length of life has he no control
   But all the pleasures give
   And no care to share but care.

S. Wilson

Africa

Heat! Liquid fire in a hot, blue sky
Scorching vast plains of waist-high scrub.
A ridge of peaks, colours burnt and dry
And the plaintive mew of a lion cub.

Torrid air, drowsy with mosquitos;
Tall grass — almost motionless but not quite —
Moved by a soft, warm breeze as it blows
And chases fireflies in the night.

In the shimmering distance on far horizon
The endless mountain chain spans its way
Through the hazy, golden dawning
And the brightening break of day.

Pounding hooves of frightened wildebeest
As thunder rolls and lightning streaks the skies.
Rainfall! Dark clouds pouring rain without cease
As hovering birds beg shelter with their cries.

B. M. Hanna

" The Night Sky "

The sky at night is a lovely sight
Scattered with billions of glittering stars,
They seem to be happy at that height,
Some sprinting about with bright tail light.

Disco time, the sky is darker,
A couple of stars with their partner
Dancing, not close, through the night,
It will be over before morning light.

Tonight the sky is grey and dull,
The shutters are down, I cannot enjoy
Another night of glitter and twinkling,
New moon is out with heavy cloud, it's
  raining.

M. Allen

Time

Time is a special thing, we should not waste.
Savour the moment, enjoy the taste.
Look forward with pleasure, but remember the old.
Memories are sweet, from them stories are told.
Some may be happy, some may be sad.
To live each, we all should be glad.
From each little thing, lessons we learn.
Knowing right from wrong, and which way to turn
Time goes so fast, from cradle to coffin.
We take time for granted so very often.
That we miss all the good things, big and small.
The earth's green grass and the trees so tall.
And the flowers that grow and the birds that sing.
To many of us they are no big thing.
But we are wrong to ignore these treasures.
Because they are the doorway to many more pleasures.
Just stop for a moment and look around.
On this great earth treasures abound.
So if the moment be big or small,
Waste not time, enjoy it all.

Pauline R. Melbourne

A Mother's Grief Of Loss

A Mother sits alone and weeps,
rye red her eyes that find no peace in sleep.
She mourns the loss of her beloved son,
whose life was vanquished by a faceless assassin's gun.
These tears shed by this devoted mother are shared by all,
The cream of England's youth are slain.
Don't let their deaths be in vain.

Their sacrifice in a golden book will recall,
foreign the earthy beds they sleep, in peace and gentle repose.
Called to stand proud in God's heavenly army each one chose.
Tears shed by all Mothers measured, would be a raging tide,
Until mankind in all its guises and faults finds eternal peace.
Love for all time.

Then Mothers of the world, united in grief,
will lift their eyes to the sky,
And thank God and know
that no more sons of England will ever have to die.
No more a Mother sitting alone to weep,
no more her eyes rye red.
Her inner self finds peace.

D. Rundle

Wings Of The Angel

The grimy child in the alley
Sees the angel's shining eyes,
Feels the warmth of his wings
And the soft brush of bright hair to dry his tears.

The angel moves on, upwards,
Sensing another soul in pain;
The brink of eternity is here
At the top of this building,
On this ledge,
For the man who is drowning
In the River of Life.

Gentle wings close round him,
But the warmth is torn away in the wind's chill;
Whispered words of comfort
Fall unheard in the tumult of torment.

No! The sky screams as the man jumps.
The angel turns away in horror,
A shadow of grief dims the radiant face.
Where hearts are too heavy for wings to lift,
Even angels lose sometimes.

W. Musker

Garden Of Dreams

Roses in a garden fair, roses here and roses there —
Roses, roses, ev'rywhere, in the garden of my dreams.
I have no garden of my own, no roses bless my humble home,
But lovely roses I have grown, in the garden of my dreams.
Let me dream of lovely roses that are blooming ev'rywhere —
Let me dream of lovely roses that demand no special care:
Let me slumber on in peace, where fragrance fills the balmy air,
Do not wake me while I'm dreaming of my garden fair.

Roses are my heart's delight, I see roses ev'ry night,
Crimson, yellow, pink and white, in the garden of my dreams.
When winter comes so dark and drear and gardens have no
    rose blooms there,
I see my roses bright and clear, in the garden of my dreams.

When I am about to die, my hands I'll lift to the sky —
I'll ask God to let me lie, in the garden of my dreams,
And when the songs of Angels sound, and I see roses all around,
I'll know at last in Heaven I've found that rose garden of my dreams.
  Walter N. Blake

The Smiling Magician J.F.K.

Onto the magic screen,
Rides the smiling weaver of dreams.
With symbolic words and images you stream,
Down the flickering electric screen.

To share with the watcher.

Into a close up, the screen glides,
Catch the gaze of the president's eyes.
What could you see, in a breath,
Brilliant fires of atomic death,
Invisible doom for generations yet unborn?

And in those final seconds,
Did you hear the muffled drum?
Hear the last heartbeat, America's son?
Death winged in on Dallas heat,
Destiny had you meet.
The price of eternal fame, life to part,
Your final journey on a cannon cart.

Watcher, switch off the screen,
Turn out the power, of the magician's dream.
Put out the light,
Return him to God or eternal night.
  Peter R. Dyer

The Cat

Thistle-down tabby with shot silk fur,
Reverberating, ingratiating happy purr,
Eyes coloured topaz in full sunlight,
Glowing emerald green in depths of night.

Me-owing voice well known to all,
Seductive tones of mating call,
Chirruping greeting so full of charm,
Diabolical war shrieks that cause alarm.

Furtive, noiseless padded paws,
Disguised sheaths for hidden claws,
A mobile tail, upright or curled,
Signalling moods to the outside world.

Deceptively tranquil in repose,
With switched on ears, and twitching nose,
But hint of alien scent or sound,
Limbs spring to action with a bound.

A poem of grace, tame yet wild,
Immaculate, haughty, yet loving and mild,
A creature of character, and because of all that,
Fortunate are you, if owned by a cat.
  Winifred Roberts

Sweet Singing Bird

I saw you yonder on a leafy branch, sweet singing bird,
Rich scented blossoms to your tune did dance, lone winging bird,
The air was filled with whisperings of delight, the purest heard,
I stood enchanted; 'twas the morning light and all things stirred:
And as I held you rapturous in my sight, most joyous bird,
The sun did glisten on your trembling breast of song and word
And crescent waves of scintillating sound, now up, now down,
Spread like bright burning bursts of fire to everything around;
The melody sublime rose in the air high on the breeze
And gathered up the dust of dreams unused, and tenderly
It lifted off this cloak of worldly care, o blessed relief,
And chased away my melancholy gloom and gave me peace:
Though long time gone your song remains unchanged and
    e'er preserved,
To treasure and to love for all my days, sweet singing bird.
  Maibrooke Willis

Our World

The world goes around in perpetual motion,
Revolving the land, the sea and the ocean,
Dawn and daylight, dusk and night,
Dappled with sunshine and silvery moonlight.

Round and round with never a stop,
First barren land, then luscious crop,
Hungry children full of woe,
Chubby cherubs with faces aglow.

This world is such a magnificent creation,
With something special in every nation,
So why have we wars and terrible greed,
When we have such beauty and all we need.

Isn't it a crying shame,
That all the world's people aren't the same,
Happily having plenty and some to spare,
With peace and contentment everywhere.

If we could only share the good,
All our land and all our food,
What a lovely place this world would be,
For simple people like you and me.
  Molly Beare

" Oh To Be Lonely "

Smiling pleasantly as people passed by,
Saying nothing but now one new why
The roads where busy, noisy, and full,
But no one acknowledged her as she stood alone,
Why oh why has the world changed so,
Please can't you see I am all on my own,
No family no friends I feel unwanted and low,
With my eyesight failing and my hearing gone
I stand at my window just wishing for one,
Just one person to look, stop or wave,
Before it's too late, please let the world change.
  C. Eagles

Dedicated to Paddy S.

Deep in your mind, where are you now?
Sailing blue seas, 'neath bright blue skies?
Your desire ....

Do you fall and rise quilted in thoughts?
Ridiculed troubles, memories..... as plain as
the nose on your face!

Does your calm smile hide all your worries,
Though your actions speak louder than words?

Are you struggling to express? To be understood?
Struggling to take only one step... Yet,
Go a long way?

Calm that stormy mind! Be patient.
For your greatest treasure is your mind.
Be wise, search and find.....
  Marni Harris

The Tryst

He strutted down towards the park his head held high and proud
Revelling in the sunshine as it peeped out from a cloud

He wondered if she'd be there as she used to be each week
Lying underneath the oak, so beautiful and meek.

He'd made this journey every week, since first they met last year
The fact that she'd not been there for six weeks, filled him with fear.

There hadn't been an argument, in fact they'd never rowed
They'd always spent their weekly trysts strolling in the crowd.

He never knew from where she came, nor she know his address
It added to the mystery of their meetings nonetheless.

His breath now came in gasps as he neared their sacred place
He stopped and blinked to make quite sure whilst gazing at her face.

For lying there she was as though she'd never been away
Looking oh so beautiful, this was a wondrous day

He slowly stepped towards her to ask of where she'd been
She stretched and smiled seductively, she looked a bit more lean.

Then everything was answered as her new born pups so sad
Ambled quickly forward to finally meet their dad.

So side by side they left the park, two beagles, sons and daughters
To see if they could find somewhere to set up married quarters.
Sandra Kathleen Still

Lest We Forget

Lest we forget the fallen ones; our freedom their dying breath
Resurrection of our hopes arose from their very death
Think not of them as history, for the present owes them deep
Far from home they shall rest, far from where their widows weep
For a painful yard of land they fell; each one somebody's son
For a cause they gave their lives, before it had begun

Lest we forget the living, whose ears still hear the blast
For they shall live each new day, with their souls half mast
Medals upon their chest they wear for the ones they left behind
A tear shed as their brothers in battle go marching through
   their minds
We must protect the dove of peace they won so fragile in our hands
For we know upon its death, will bring another destruction of
   the lands

Lest we forget where they fell; The Somme, Alamein and Verdun
Rangoon, Gallipoli, Normandy and Arnhem to the land of the
   rising sun
Lest we forget any man buried on a foreign shore
And lest we forget the epitaph; their name liveth forevermore.
Terence Craig Currie

The Promise

As she lay in her sick bed, sleep far away,
Restless, in the still of the night,
Stars twinkled brightly, as she watched a while,
Through the window, a beautiful sight.

Was that the rustling of the wind in the trees?
Then an eerie owl hoot far away.
Moon and clouds casting shadows around the room,
Making patterns of ghostly array.

Her thoughts went back to three years ago,
When she nursed Darling Dave, who lay dying.
He had made her a promise that he would return,
"If only My Love", she thought sighing.

Then a voice she knew gently called her name,
And a brilliant white light around him shone.
She saw him there with outstretched arms,
Beckoning softly, her life on earth done.

How willingly she took both his hands,
And stepped into his spiritual light.
He had kept his promise to her to return,
Then together for God's Heaven, they took flight.
Madeline Kavanagh

Travelling Through Time

The candle that glimmers in the corner of the room,
Removes all darkness and the gloom.
In silence she sits, for a noise to break,
Tensed and motionless whilst she waits.

Five minutes go by,
She begins to cry,
Maybe she'd care,
If she was all there.

No reason,
People think it's the change of season.
I laugh so I do,
As if only they knew.

I feel desolate in my own space,
Where all they can do is look at my face.
A place where people surround me,
With looks of anxiousness and curiosity.

Paranoia sets in,
And so it begins.
Time travel it seems the first for mankind,
Replenishes the soul and enlivens the mind.
Michelle Hobbs

Remember....

In the still small hours of morning, do not weep because I'm gone
Remember how I loved the morning, dry your tears and carry on
When the day seems long and lonely, when you long for company
Do not bow your head in sorrow - relive the times of you and me
Times we filled with love and laughter, times we spent in quiet grief
They're the times you must hold onto with open heart and
   strong belief
For I'm in the morning stillness, feel my presence ever near
My smile is in the golden sunshine, you my love must never fear
You'll hear my laughter in the wind that rumbles round our
   loving home
And you will know within your heart that though I'm gone
   you're not alone
See me in the lovely things, the flowers and rainbows bright
See me in the beauty of a dark and starlit night
For I loved the simple things, the beauty of a garden small
The way the birds build strong safe nests and how the leaves
   know when to fall
I'm in each raindrop falling softly, in each drop of glistening dew
For you know I loved all these things and you know that I loved you
I'm not dead but only sleeping, this is just a passing thing
I know you're sad but just remember after winter comes the spring
God will keep you safe and happy with the family we have made
And through them my life continues and memories will never fade...
Nicola Woodley

Never Look Back

Do you ever wish you could turn back the years,
Regretting the past that's gone by,
Heartbreaks and failings, decisions and fears,
The wrong path of life brings sadness and tears.
We tend to find a listening ear and wallow in sympathy,
We get bogged down with crying and pain,
Never seeking out sunshine amongst the clouds and the rain.
We must never look back but look forward,
It's the only way to go, as we reach the crossroads,
Think carefully, think twice, go slow.
We can learn from little children, happy on a sandy shore,
They work to build their castles bigger than ever before,
The tide destroys what they've achieved, washing their castles away,
But it doesn't stop them building another one next day.
Perhaps we can help each other! We've nothing to lose but to gain,
Let's open our eyes with courage, find the right path once again.
We must keep on hoping and trying, wear a smile instead of a frown,
Keep our balance in the dark of night, when things will pull us down,
Beyond every darkening shadow, a light is shining through,
Brightening up our confidence, our hopes, our dreams come true.
Margaret Roscoe

Autumn Mists — Summer Song

The autumn leaves are changing fast,
Red, yellow and gold,
Pronouncing summer has past,
Mists linger over the rivers and ponds,
Migrating geese flap their wings and flee —
Oh where, oh where are those cloudless summer days,
Hazy, lazy days I do so adore,
Come winter snows, come fast,
Then spring will blossom and soon after, soon after,
my beloved summer will return,
With majestic trees covered in leaves,
Sweet smelling blossoms that linger on the night air,
Velvet carpets of green everywhere,
But until then it is just a dream, as I gaze across the misty river
and long to hear the summer song,
The summer song.
Patricia Summerfield

Proposal

I walked along the path in the park,
realising I was late for it was getting dark,
trying to keep under the light of the moon,
hurrying along for I had to meet my girlfriend soon.

The restaurant was booked; we were going out to dine,
A candle-lit table and a bottle of white wine,
the moment I was waiting for all of my life,
about to propose to her and make her my wife.

But I had to hurry and find the park gate,
for she would be quite upset if I turned up late.
Once in the restaurant I asked the waiter the time,
then in walked my darling as usual in her prime.

As we finished off our dinner it came time to propose,
I gave her a ring and a single red rose.
for she would look lovely in a white wedding dress,
I gave a sigh of relief as my sweetheart said " Yes".
William McLuckie

Complexions

White lies are falling in misty grey rhymes,
Reaching, riding, this tangle webbed mind.
People, faces, screaming their right.
Turning, churning, my days into night.
Deeds left undone keep searching for space,
But too many thoughts have taken their place.
From whence do I come? To where shall I go?
The answers withheld — I'm glad I don't know!
Humour's still mine, though I laugh on my own,
At these crazy complexions I seem to call home.
Am I victor, the winner, with my prize happiness?
Am I valour, the trier, with my eye on success?
Am I? — I am — victim, by my hand I so choose,
The loser of all in a land called confused.
So now you may laugh, a laugh full of scorn,
At this child of derision from ignorance born.
Laugh long, laugh loud, laugh well — for there
forever I fear I shall dwell.
Yes! Laugh long, laugh loud, laugh well,
let merriment and mirth be my sustenance in hell!
Peter Karrie

A Tribute To A Mother

Her virtues are many, whilst her deeds become commonplace,
Quite often you miss seeing the angel, in your mother's face.
Seldom do you hear her grumble, doing tasks with no thought
  to complain.
Even when her weary body is suffering from severe pain.
She's no union to defend her, when things don't seem to be right,
Like gently soothing fevered brows through many a sleepless night.
Much love, help and guidance, she'll willingly give her child
  to the end,
Because when God created a mother He intended she'd be
  your dearest friend.
Muriel Ross

Memory Of Childhood

Early morning, sleepy head
Quiet voice by the bed.
Are you coming, be quiet and quick
Hot tea, wellies, a good stout stick.

Chilly morning, upturned collars
Words echoing through silent streets
Lane at last, the meadow and the grass
Dewy patches, making patterns with our feet

Our stile the search begins
First pet's look for fairy rings
Careful moving of the grass
Go back over, where once we passed

A, whoop of joy, the first one found
Wee white head peeping through the ground
Searching then, more intensely still
Our buckets soon we hope to fill.

Homeward, now almost running
Weary, chiffy, but oh so proud.
A lively fire, a loving greeting
Breakfast, porridge, a taste of our - mushrooms.
Norma G. Huntington

'My First Childhood Holiday'

It was not so long ago that I was a child
Quiet and innocent but sometimes wild

When my brothers and sister and family as one
Decided to go on holiday to the sun

All of us together having lots of fun
Trying to remember all the things we'd done

We went for walks and took a trip to the zoo
Where there were lots of other children and families too

We'd have ice-cream and sweets and laugh all day
Mam and Dad giving us all our own way

It was such fun being a child
Doing what we wanted and being wild

We would never listen to Mam saying 'that's wrong'
But scared of Dad because he was strong

Typical children being a pain
Running around playing games

Sat in the sun, playing in the sand
Splashing water all holding hands

Then back to the caravan, we wished we could keep
All falling down tired and asleep.
Tina Taylor

Hung Quarter

Blessed spring snatches the
pulse and heart, tugs weary
the mortal from winter's depth,
from whence we came in previous cold.

Undeterred by memory of changing
seasons past, we revel again in
euphoric glee. Optimism high! As the
sap in the willow pushing forth leaf.
To grace once more this earth.

Daffodil open and yellow, to mind
she sits in two seasons, firmly
on the cusp. Bloomed in winter's
embers, thrived in shade of cloud.

By name only spring presents her
first day. Expectation dashed with
grey sky courting chill wind, we
stand garbed against elements
reluctant to conform.

Blessed spring, blessed herald,
Blasted cold!
P. G. Josling

Herald Of Spring

It battles forth through ice and snow,
Pushing; piercing; steadfast and slow,
Undaunted; unhurried gaining in height,
Bulging; straining seeking the light.

Then at last with crown uncurled,
A colourful beauty complete: unfurled,
Selected yellows of delicate hue,
Gasps of joy from of those who view.

Aloof; serene this herald of spring,
With golden head in rhythmic swing,
No sound comes forth, no lilting shrill,
From the noble trumpet daffodil.

J. A. Kent

Snowdrops For A Lady

Figureheads of green,
   Push through the frozen soil,
To face the enemy,
   In splendid battle royal.
"Heralds" of Springtime forces, so they stand
   Opposing winter's onslaught,
— 'cross the land
   As they grow strong,
And sun begins to rise,
   Such visions of loveliness
March on, before our eyes.
   Like graceful swans with slender necks,
These blooms, the winter's earth bedecks.
   Living, so they give love,
— As mother nature to her baby,
   What joy to see,
— My "Snowdrops for a Lady!"

T. G. Bloodworth

Supreme

Self-butchering, puny mortal, you dissemble,
Pursuer of all material, yet nothing,
Self-creator! The pattern is his design,
Evolution His fleeting whim,
Stumbler through Earth's galaxy, speck at His foot rotting,
Look upwards — see His face and tremble!
The Day of Reckoning is held by Him.

As serrated tongue of fire, whiplash of the Maker,
Blinding, brilliant, fells forest giant,
Screaming, tortured, groaning, crashing,
Through rippling, searing flame purified, pliant,
Returns to Earth, the giver and the taker;
Will monstrous wave, massive flood,
Purge poisonous Earth and Man,
Drown foul air, disease, destruction, death,
Shape the supreme plan?

In terrible cataclysmic burst will human inhumanity end,
Piecemeal, dispersed — in time the Universe can lend?
The Infinite, supreme, alone may give,
If pleased in peace, can Man live?

Sydney Oates

Dying Embers

There he sits as the fire-light gleams,
Smokes his pipe, dreaming his dreams.
Memories pass before his eyes,
Hear his chuckles, hear his sighs,
Thoughts of those long past gone,
Faces appear, then pass on.
Their names are re - called, one by one,
His loves, companions, and his son.
He then reviews the paths he trod,
And all the times when he called on God.
The embers flicker, then slowly die,
From his lips there comes a sigh,
His head droops gently to his breast,
He also has found eternal rest.

C. R. P. Morgan

Master

Without thought the careless giant, master
Puppeteer, drops the strings, heeds not the call.
Collapsed skeleton in a corner
The motionless freak leans against the wall.

His limbs hang loose, his outsize head bows down,
Still resigned, he slouches, even though
A comic expression betrays the clown
In him and suggests happiness below

The cross to which he owes animation.
This life-giving cross bears the weight of all
His troubles and takes the blame for his sin.
It gathers him up, causes him to fall;

It controls his movements to great applause
But still he remembers the attachment,
The bearer of life he can't leave because...
That judging cross and the laws heaven sent.

Thomas Ferrington

Pushing Your Luck

Some will play these deadly games
Pumping drugs to their brains.
Some will live, some will learn
You play with drugs your body will yearn.

Taking drugs, they think it's hip
Some are looking for that trip
The buzz, the high to reach the sky
Why all their loved ones stand and cry.

Some, they take the funny pill
The one they call the ecstasy thrill
Dancing all night out of their heads
When they should be in their beds.

Where did the world go wrong?
It's gone on now for far too long.
We need to stop this dangerous craze
Before it sends us up in a blaze.

Belafonte

Violet

The road to her house is here, normality rules, another Sunday.
Pulling up, I confidently go to the door; it's locked.
I knock, I know she's there. No sound. Blackness greets
   me through the letter box.
Knock again and shout, nothing! — but the roar of silence.
Broken window to gain access, rushing ambulance, skating police.
All helter-skelter in the snow; to remove what once was
   and is no more.
Return to surrounding, unknowing life, dreadful in its complacency.
All that remains is the impression of her head on a pillow,
and sweet memories of my mother gone forever.

J. Colin Smith

On Looking At The Sky

Even your clouds, Lord, are beautiful:
Puffs of smoke from panting trains,
Fancy puffs for ladies' boudoirs,
Monsters in a blue world;
Sometimes moving gently into lines,
To draw for us an image that we know,
And then to fall away mis-shapen.
Oh! the dreams there, Lord, when we were young;
All the glory and ventures yet to come
Passed across in promises foreseen;
But now, Lord, the old see nothing there,
Except the few who hope for things
Not found in years gone by,
But know a wonder as they gaze,
For clear to misted sight is seen
A host of angels resting on the clouds
Singing of a dream for them come true.
Will it be like that, Lord, for me.........with you?

Marie Sanders

Willow

The cat with the question mark tail,
procrastinates and contemplates upon which waters to sail.
The river of life with tempestuous seas,
or quietly to drift on the river of sleep?
With wondering eyes, decisions fail,
for the cat with the question mark tail.

This ebony feline is proud,
he tolerates, but less of late, his peers within the crowd.
Will he be so tiresome when late in his years,
as slow or as wistful as they now appear?
With wondering eyes, decisions fail
for the cat with the question mark tail.

The cat with the wisdom of years,
whose tail is straight and compensates for his dark and
deepest fears.
If requiring an answer has seldom to seek,
for puzzles are solved whilst he is asleep.
No wondering eyes or thought to fail,
all cats once had a question mark tail.

Vanessa Hinkley

Untitled

Hands that touch across the table
pour scorn, on those that are unable,
To feel as lovers often do
Looking, touching, across at you,
Light that shines on dear fair hair
your arm in mine, let them all stare,
They probably think, that I'm too old
to kiss your cheek, so ever bold,
Your hand in mine, in sweet repose
you look even better, in those clothes,
White you very often wear
soft, white, bow holds back your hair,
You wear the little brooch I bought
not expensive, it's but the thought,
In five short days, you've taken me
From total hell, to ecstasy,
What's in a name, we did but ask
together, in the sun, we bask,
A tear again, upon your cheek
it's been a beautiful, long, hot, week.

G. D. Moore

Christmas Wonder

Turkeys are bought and chestnuts too,
presents for her, and him and you.
But stop a minute and let us ponder,
there are people who don't have this Christmas wonder.
They are the old folk, who have only their past.
Sadly they think that each Christmas is their last,
grown old and weary, families all gone.
Remembering times, when young and strong.
In their eyes there is longing, and secrets of life.
We could learn from their knowledge, struggles and strife.
Shouldn't we listen to them, and memories share?
give them love and protection, show them we care?
Christmas is not just for eating and gift bringing,
it's to give love and kindness, be thoughtful and giving.
The Christ child came to show us the way,
so that love would be here, on Earth to stay.
To show us that we must all humbler be,
Please look into the eyes of the aged and see.
See! that they are people with hearts that beat,
help them and give them a special treat.....

Valerie M. Bacon

Hush My Baby

Hush my baby, don't you cry,
Poppa's gonna sing you a lullaby,
A song so sweet you'll long to hear,
Come let me dry your soul sad tear.

Your Momma's meek and oh so mild,
You're Momma's one and only child,
She also loves you just as I,
And cannot bear to hear you cry.

The moonbeams shine, the stars are bright,
There's none to fear on this calm night,
My arms are strong, my heart so warm,
I'll cradle thee 'till early morn.

There now, both blue eyes are closed,
In peaceful rest you now repose,
Relaxed and sleeping with a sigh,
As Poppa keeps a watchful eye.

Now morning breaks, a cool fresh dawn,
A smiling face, a lazy yawn,
The sun is risen, gold morning spell
Hearts are happy, all is well.

Philippa C. Benacs

Family Clocks — Louise And Jane

When we are from this world gone
Pray help Louise to carry on,
Ticking away the Godly time
And cheering you with melodious chime.

A hundred years have come and gone
But Louise proudly carries on.
She will repay your loving care
By giving pleasure beyond compare.

Think of all the joy and tears
Louise has witnessed through the years.
Maybe, perhaps, you once a while
Will recall past owners with cheerful smile.

Jane, too, a splendid piece of work;
Still carrying on and does not shirk.
Looking so elegant and with style
I trust she will grace you long awhile.

Although poor Jane must weary get;
Being older than Louise, but tasks still met.
Keep her going as long as you can
But I know she's had a goodly span.

E. F. J. Smith

You Are You And I Am Me

You are you and I am me.
Poles apart we seem to be.
Different notions, different looks.
One likes dancing, one likes books.
You've been here and I've been there,
yet many avenues we share.
Different pathways we have walked
but when we've sat and really talked
we find we've both had joy and pain
and like encounters in the main.
I cannot feel the way you do.
You cannot know my feelings too,
but if we learn to recognize
each other's needs and hidden cries
Then you can share a part of me
and I can walk your path with thee.
Together we can learn and grow,
uplifting, caring and we'll know
that different though we'll always be,
I'm part of you. You're part of me.

Wendy Deakin

Betrayal

The spoken words lay heavy
pointing the finger — at whom?
No name given.

Where did he acquire his information
to which he had no right?
Over whose coffee table
did such betrayal take place?

Into which envelope
shall I place thirty silver coins,
and to whom my offering make?

Sylvia Coward

Moonbeams

Oh lovely moon, when next you shine
Please tell that little girl of mine,
Of all the wondrous things I've seen;
Of chipmunks, squirrels and fairy queen.
And tell her how I miss her so,
And pray for all the days to go,
Until she'll soon come here to me;
Then I'll be happy as can be.

Each night as she lies fast asleep.
Gently through the window peep,
And tightly kiss her sleeping head.
So keep her from all fear and dread.
Then as you shine unto the west,
You'll shine on me while I'm at rest
There I'll receive the fond caress
You bring from her, to seal my bliss.

R. Wolstenholme

Based On The Gulf War

People are crying because of the war,
Please stop the war, they will cry no more.
Please stop the fight,
Saddam will go as fast as light.
Please stop the war,
Nobody will cry anymore.

Aircraft bombing on the land,
Go away Saddam from Kuwait,
Don't try to stop us; we're not too late.
We'll get you back to Iraq,
Come on you others, we've gotta attack.

The children here at home they cry,
"Oh look, is that my daddy flying in the sky?
But why is my daddy up there and not at home?
I'm standing here waiting for him, it's as if I'm a garden gnome.
I love you, and don't want you to die,
Please come back, I don't want you to say goodbye".

Stephanie Udall

Old Black And Gold

I'm dressed in Black and Gold, my nose so wet and cold,
Please look my way, have I done wrong today,
Why do you look away, and whisper I'm too old,
I'm fit to run all day, Old Black and Gold.

I feel there's something wrong, and yet I'm big and strong,
Please look my way, if I must go today,
Is there no other way, remember times we had,
I beg you to let me stay your bonny lad.

Before the sun goes down, let me look around,
And one last time, I'll kiss those friends of mine,
They've been so good to me, from birth through puberty,
But what must be must be, it's time to go.

Farewell and all the best, my whole life's been blessed,
Please look my way, remember me today,
When feelings you can't hide, put your hand by your side,
And feel those silky folds, of Black and Gold.

Scott Selkirk

O Lord

O Lord I pray I pray to you,
Please don't ever let me go.
I give you my heart
I give you my soul
O Lord please don't let me go

I pray each night, I pray each day,
O Lord please don't turn me away.

I've committed no crime
No crime that I know
I've committed no sin, that I've been told
My heart I give, I give to you.
My soul I give to you as well.

N. J. Hennessy

Voices

Voices screaming out abuse,
Please can't you find someone else's brain to use.
I am so tired and weary,
They send me into a rage and fury.
Death is all they speak to me,
Please can't you help me?
My heart feels so heavy,
Life's troubles make me weary.
They make me feel unworthy,
As a Mum, Sister, Wife and Aunty.
Don't stand there looking in at me,
Come in, embrace me and say you care,
And don't go away and leave me in despair,
I need your support and caring,
As I am falling into a pit of despairing.
Lower a rope of hope for me,
To help lift up my soul to be,
A caring person once again,
Come snow, sun and falling rain.

Susan Meager

Nature

Scent from magnificent roses, in the sunlight, drifting my way,
Perhaps this unsolved nature, is having words to say.
There is no need to ponder and worry at this special glory,
Just look around and everywhere you peep, you'll find a story.
Buds breaking into perhaps, so many star-like flowers,
Brightening and showing off our gardens, in the passing hours,
Purple clematis, creeping gently over an old tiled roof,
No doubt in their natural beauty, showing us the proof.
That nature is perfection, fascinating in shape and looks,
Like a panorama designed for our nature books,
And also in her world, colourful treasures we will always seek,
Viola, hibiscus, hydrangea, a tulip or a daisy — so meek,
We thank her for her beauty, that sprinkles us with pleasure,
So we can relax and drink it in, during these moments of leisure.

W. G. Jackman

A Special Day

To-day for two happy hours my little
room was transformed and not by one
so very big. My coffee table became a
ship a sailing on the sea. My favourite
chair a big red bus and it was I who
rang the bell, and it was I who looked
for sea serpents, fishes from the deep.
For the driver of the bus was also the captain
of the ship. Now alas all is still within
my small room, my table stands on four legs
once more and the little shoe that could
not be found lies inside the cupboard door.
The biscuit crumbs all swept away and
my chair beside the window stands where
I will sit and wait looking out on the
street below, until this day comes around
once more I shall hear an eager knock
and a voice I love call, "It is me and I have
come to see you, Nannie."

Nannie Norfolk

A Silent Tear

Why is life so full of fear?
Perhaps the riches were too high for my possessions or deserving.
What freezing days I have felt and darkest days never ending.
Sometimes in sleep I dream of love's involvements,
only to hide the guilty feelings of my sensual awakenings.
The birds still sing their songs, so why the gentle gloom?
We have to put aside this fear for in our lives there is no room.
Heaven and hell still lurks to yield our fate,
but still I know my heart is full of love not hate.

Pam Justice

Who Cares!

Our world is in danger of being destroyed
peoples greed for power and money is taking
precedence over lives.
How much more can the world take, wars,
famine, natural disasters.
No thoughts or love for common man
complacency is room for a nuclear bang.
One person alone cannot fight the
devastation and sacrifices of countries,
diseases, terminal illnesses, hatred all these
should be a warning.
God alone is supreme rules over this land
we are here for a purpose though we don't
understand.
One chance on earth is all we get
love your brother, even the ones you
have not met.

L. Williamson

Receding

The image of people who die,
People you could not believe you would never see again,
recedes slowly.
It loses its sparkle and its crispness,
and slowly it goes, back into the mists of memory,
until the face you believed you would never cease to know
dims and is only remembered at times.
Those who you thought you would still meet
looming down a city street,
make this a sad impossibility.
Yet still you would not be surprised
if you came upon them.
One part of your soul will never believe they went.

Pamela C. Porter

Untitled

All around the mixed up war of muddled words and phrases.
People strive to understand with vacant stares and gazes.
Faces furrowed deep in thought going through the paces,
leaving none to wonder why they lost in all the races.

Steady hands that hide the fear of times they could not cling to.
Working boots on aching feet, no more tunes to sing to.
Times will change and people die, the world will keep progressing.
Now the ever-spinning void balanced on obsession.

H. Tracey Finn

Laughter

Like the babbling of the brook
or the shuddering of the trees
or you thought it was the thunder as it echoed through the hills
and you pause to think and murmur......
   that's laughter

There's another kind of laughter
you can hear from yonder house
It's the children playing happily, no doubt,
you can listen to the other sounds
but none compares with this.........
   it's laughter.

Olga Saville

Does It Matter?

Different creeds and religions, from people down to pigeons,
People say don't matter, a steel tray to a silver platter,
But it does matter, as you know people chatter.
Black, white, orange, green,
Why are people so God darn mean, Catholic, Christian, Jews
Why should people have to choose.
When it comes down to it we're all the same
So why do we try to push the blame,
On to the colour of our skin,
Or on to how the earth did begin.
Does it matter what people believe,
as long as it makes no-one else grieve,
and don't try and turn someone else the way they want, be yourself
Let your soul free, don't let anyone else decide what you're
going to be, Colour doesn't matter,
It's the person that counts,
Why should it matter if you're different outside
we're all the same inside,
We were all born the same way,
and were all put here for a purpose, whatever it may be.

Melanie Willmore

A Step Into The Unknown

I entered the school,
People like trees, tall and older than me,
People I recognized, people I didn't.
A mass of bodies, swarming around like ants,
They were a lot louder than trees
And a lot more lively.

People tight together like blades of grass,
People in a hall, square like a field.
We were looked upon by the Head teacher
Like the sun on a clear day.

People put into classes, like seeds in a flower bed.
People excelling or not, like flowers, flourishing or dying.
Teachers helping us to grow in knowledge
Like raindrops helping all vegetation to grow.
People like trees growing, getting strong only to die.

Matthew J. Haughey

Opposing Voices

I can hear shouting, screaming, bricks crashing and
People banging their hands against the walls.
The noise is tremendous,
It is deafening to my sensitive hearing.
I don't understand this chaos and I am afraid.
From this metal prison, there is
No escape.

The truck is trying to enter the gate.
The police have formed a human wall.
A guard opens the gate, we rush forwards.
A desperate attempt to stop
The injustice.

I slide back the bolt, the truck accelerates past me.
I sympathise with these people and their cause.
I don't decide, yet I receive abuse.

I hang upside down in a cold, dark room.
Trickles of red liquid flow from my neck,
Dripping quietly onto the floor.
I am dying.

Serena Bader

The Passing

Soul, flying free at the moment of our death,
Pause, 'ere you fly into eternity.
View those on earth who loved you,
And mourn your passing with their tears,
Your memory held close for all their future years,
Eyes bright with tears, and faces dulled with sorrow,
Comfort with hope to meet you on the morrow.

Vivienne Greenwood

A Friend

A friend of mine sat alone each night,
Pen in hand he tried to compose the poem,
The poem he had written a hundred times in his head,
The poem whispered by lovers on moonlit nights,
The poem to make Amor weep.

The words he searched for echo on a Summers breeze,
The whispers of poets vanished and gone,
He would have gladly sold his soul to find the words
And lived his life with Shakespeare and Mozart underground.
A life of misery for a few memorable words.

However, Janus, the god of beginning gave him his inspiration,
With a new chapter added to the book of his life.
A woman more precious than any gem,
A woman more delicate than any flower,
A woman sculpted by Aphrodite herself.

My friend still sits alone each night, but know the poem is written,
The poem has been delivered and read.
My friend, my heart, now beats to a new rhythm.
My friend now belongs to someone else,
My friend now belongs to you.
Paul Cox

The Magic Of Scotland

Mystic mountains clear and stark,
Patterned green and shadowed dark.
Green sward sweeping from your height
To the valley swathed in light.

Majestic guard o'er lochs you keep
Mirrored lochs with secret deep.
Swaying, Murmuring lacy trees too
Pay homage from below to you.

Your peaks take drink from misty clouds
Which fold around you like a shroud.
Your thirst then quenched you now supply
Cascades of water to the valleys dry.
To gently flowing winding rivers
Where reflected sunshine gleams and shimmers.

Oh, mighty mountains great and high
Silhouetted against the sky,
Your powerful strength is our gain
To us small mortals on lower plain.
G. Lawrence

Chalk Talk

Outline the entity that is you,
  pastel your passions, place them on view,
  blend softly the yellows, the reds and the blues,
  humbly collecting the revenue...

Cast from the peoples that pass unaware
through the days of your life as you colour them there.
They give and they go but rarely they look,
at how much they gave or how much they took.
"Ignorant bliss," you excuse their neglect
remember the booty you're there to collect.
And those that do stop and linger a while
in time will move on with ambiguous smiles.

The faces that stay rarely give of their wealth,
but acknowledge the splendour you give of yourself.
They indulge you but ultimately give nothing you crave
like the brief interaction of the others that gave.
At dusk as the footsteps erode you draw
you ponder which group has given you more.

Over their heads or below their feet,
Tomorrow, again you draw in the street.
Robert M. Fowles

Torrent Tossed On Life's Ocean

Cascading on life's ocean clear, a torrent raged from year to year,
Passions fraught with changing scene, cascading shadow near complaining
Of, I wished as I dreamed, for the inspiration of shadow,
Light or dark for none can tell,
Where begins the light that shineth, darkness where you feel all is well.

Ought I stop? When torrent tossed, brings to me the darkest night,
Casing over darkest canyons, blocking out all daylight bright,
In my darkness come rays of light, to light the dark,
For nought can stop the light, from piecing deep within, the darkest night.

So cast off conflicts of souls sorrow, weep no more for all seems bright,
Grasps the smallest ray of brightness, travel down the pit no more,
Tell of love that triumphs, over, darker shades of grey,
Tell of brightness love, and laughter, paint the dark clouds, shade them gay.
H. E. Wylde

The Love Garden

I entered the love garden — in full bloom with
Passion-flowers, forget-me-nots and bumble-bee kisses;
But the love garden was not a bed of roses.
Roses fade, forget-me-nots forget and
Bumble-bees find gardens with more exotic blooms.

In the love garden was a weeping willow
Trailing its lashes in a stream of tears.
Its high fence could be breached. After all
The bumble-bee found no obstacle, so why
Not climb the rambling rose and escape?

It would be a thorny journey, not without
Some bleeding and trepidation:
But then — who would tend the seedlings still
Young and tender, secure in their love garden
And its faithful gardener?

So I stay in the love garden watching
My seedlings grow. And the roses growing
In the bed which I made for them
Are mainly of the cabbage variety.
J. M. Barton

A Spirit Love

A love of mine so close and dear
Passed over, when things became so clear.
It was his time, his body weak from
Stress and pain from which he reached his peak.
The angels took him by the hand,
To take him to the promised land
Where flowers bloom from day to day,
His weary bones we put to lay
Into the ground to rot away.
But I know different, his spirit lives
It comes from love, that we can give.
Patricia Stoneman

From An 81-Year-Old

To me and people of my age,
Poems should rhyme and scan:
Yet often at this present stage
Poems too often ban
The use of rhyme and often time
Are almost without scan.
And often they are meaning short,
Not like the ones that we were taught.
Bring back the days of lilting lays,
Of sentences of sense
Away with gloom and deadly doom
And all the feeling tense
So often found in poems now
Of joy in life there's none, I vow.
F. M. Laughton

The Cottage

I heard you below
Parting curtains and telling rabbits
Where to go.
I caught your laughter
As they defied your window tap
Inviting you after.

Later you stood
And watched the bluetits flit
'Neath skull-cap hoods,
And then affirmed,
In dancing breathless words,
That the deer had returned.

And I loved you
In the swelling tide of morn',
With a love simple and true,
As you lifted up the day
To hand me in your eyes
And drove night fears away.
Robert French

The Bored Secretary

In the nineteen sixties, what a lot of fun
Paris in the Springtime, nothing there was glum

Croissant in the morning, coffee hot and steaming
It all gave life such tremendous meaning

Getting slightly older, wiser and defeated
How I would just love to repeat it

Sitting in an office, feeling very low
Not a job to do, what an awful blow

Days are long, evenings bleak
I really feel such an awful freak

Got a lot to offer, but they do not care
It's just another "aggro" I'll have to bear

All that lovely freedom, all that lovely air
Just sitting here, it really isn't fair!!
Philippa Phillips

Malaise

Food waste composted
Paper re-cycled
Led free petrol — less pollution

Locality surveyed;
Slums gone, now rejuvenated
White tarmac and concrete effervesce,
Stark and lonely spaces.

Nature trails, picnic sites,
Invaded by empty cans and cigarette stubs,
No one comes to the rescue
To make wholesome again.

Soil cultivated conifers dominate.
Hedgerows obliterated from the limelight,
Insects enjoy their last fling.
Minnie Fenton

Seldom Seen

A seat among the hills so green
Overlooking mountain stream
Beyond Glencoyne a sight supreme
A view of Ullswater seldom seen

The stream tumbles down from the same mountain ridge
Flowing down to the lake through the old Glencoyne bridge
A leafy glade in majestic ravine
This is the splendour that's seldom seen

Seek the path from which to gaze,
Look o'er the vale where sheep still graze
Find out then just what these words mean
Discover the beauty that's *Seldom Seen*.
Norman Fairley

Forgotten Heroes

Skilled with arms and weaponry they stride
over a mass of cold, numb, senseless bodies.
Beating to earth that fellowship hate
that reigns over a sea of brown mud.
Those soldiers who fought,
took with them both honour and pride.
For us, they lived a life of torment,
striving to keep the breath, the reality of a hellish life.
They fell like men built from china,
brittle and fragile, they turned to dust.
To keep them happy, the people at home.
Those senseless humans who bear no names.
Some returned. But it wasn't many,
and nobody wanted to hear their tales.
They locked them up in their tormented minds,
to live their horrors for a second time, until,
they finally died.
Sarah Jane Fairnington

Jumpers

Slip one, knit one, pass the slipped-stitch
Over.
Goodbye, slipped-stitch.
You were once on my needle,
But,
According to the pattern
I had to let you go...
Shelagh Watson

Prince

I opened the gate and you were gone,
Out into the world all alone.
You seem quite happy to be there,
Because you've not come home.
I only wish I knew where you were,
Because I miss you and wish you'd return,
To sit next to me and listen and learn.
I can remember when you first came
Into my life with nothing but a name.
I gave you a home kennel and food,
A friend for life is for what you became good.

You lived with us for four or more years,
And when you left there were many tears.
All memories of you are still in me,
Your different expressions I can still see.
Although I mayn't have shown it all of the time,
I was proud when asked if you were mine.
With your glossy black coat and your big paddy paws,
You broke all the rules and made your own laws.
But fate intervened and you had to go,
I just hope you're OK 'cos I loved you so........
Nicola Brandon

Life

Life's too short for falling out
Tempers frayed and such
Life's too short without a doubt
And life can mean so much

Angry words that are not meant
Spoken without thought
Life to us is only lent
And life can be so short

We all should think before we speak
As along life's path we walk
Sometimes we have to keep tongue in cheek
And listen to others talk

Life's far too short to be unkind
We should live it day by day
Don't let things play on one's mind
And let sleeping dogs just lay
J. Power

The Bomber

It was just after midnight and it was time to go
Out into the night to make the old building blow
I hurried stiffly and huddled across the crisp winter snow
And considered the consequence if my footprints were shown

My cheeks are stinging as I wait in the street
Waiting for a lad who I am yet to meet
My feet become restless as the cold wind blows
And I bury my face in the lapel of my coat

A figure approaches and nods his head
And I pick up his pace as he moves on swiftly ahead
We'd arrived at the building and I took a glance at my watch
It is 1 a.m. read the hands on the clock.

I paced up and down to check that nobody was around
While the lad made an entry hardly making a sound
I followed him in and I wiped my brow
Then I uncovered my parcel and laid the contents on the ground

My mind started racing and my heart thumped in my head
As I thought of all the people laid tucked up in bed
As there was enough dynamite here to blow up us all
And there they are thinking that they are all safe and secure

Nicola Dymond

" The Battle Of Britain "

The Battle of Britain was fought in the sky,
Our brave fighter-pilots were willing to die,
For Hitler wanted to invade our shores —
"The Few" were ready to fight! "The Few" were ready to fight!

Now the German Air Force (Luftwaffe) had thousands of planes,
Our few hundred fighters would have famous names,
We had hurricanes, we had spitfires, too —
These fighters took to the sky! These fighters took to the sky!

For our brave young men knew that they had to win,
As failure would let Hitler's Nazis come in,
He'd conquer the world if he had his way —
The Fuehrer had to be stopped! The Fuehrer had to be stopped!

Now the Heinkels, Dorniers, Junkers, Messerschmidts,
They came over Britain, but were shot to bits,
They just could not break the proud R.A.F. —
The R.A.F. were to win! The R.A.F. were to win!

Yes, our homeland was saved by the boys in blue,
They'll not be forgotten — those immortal few,
Although 1940 is now long ago —
Still, we remember that time, when we stood defiantly free!

B. T. Lewis

Contemplation

I came to Oxford
   one summer morning,
     and found by chance, a corner
      of the heart of God.

A tributary
   of the River Thames,
     where the bright yellow kingcups
      and wild iris grow.

Banks of willow line
   slow moving water,
     private cool dim hollows where
      lily-trotters hide.

Majestic swans glide
   between bull-rushes,
     gnats dance in the sun above
      the dazzling eddies.

The ducks are busy
   paddling and diving,
     as if they were sole owners
      of this paradise.

H. M. Partington

My Cat

Sometimes I wonder whether I own a cat,
Or whether the cat owns me.
It seems I'm forever at her beck and call
And that I must never be
Too busy to gratify her every whim,
To pet her and always be
Prepared to drop everything at her command
Or else she will turn from me,
Or gaze with reproachful, amber eyes,
In a very haughty way,
Reminding me she's superior to me —
That she can always stray
To a better home where they'll appreciate
Her ancient mystery —
Cosset her and fuss her most befittingly.
I think the cat owns me.........!

Nora H. Munro

Why

Why do people stand and stare,
   or rush on past and pretend you're not there.
If ever our eyes often do meet
   there eyes, always drop to my feet
What do people really think?
   That we are all mad, and we really can't think.
I am the same as all human beings,
   I have the same thoughts and feelings.

I'll go to the pub for a drink and some grub,
   will I get chatted up? Oh I wish would.
They get out of there minds drink after drink
   then they come over, I'm lucky you think.
For the very next day, when there all sobered up
   they never give you a second look.
There is nothing wrong with my mind
   it's my feet that don't work that you will find.
So when you see people in a wheel-chair
   Just forget that it's not really there.
Come over for a laugh and a chat
   we really will be thankful for that!!!

J. White

Looking For Freda

I'll think of you every time I hang a Busy Lizzy in a tree,
Or have a picnic in the woods, the children running free,
I'll see you through an open door that hides a garden fair,
With flowers of every shape and hue, and know that you are there.
I'll feel you on a winter's night, warm, snug, and heart content,
When deep in book and printed verse, and thoughts of wonderment.
I'll find you in an antique shop, in a work box hidden there,
With pins and lace and sealing wax, all saved with loving care.
I'll hear you on a summer's breeze, when beneath that garden tree,
I'll dream of times not so long ago, Busy Lizzies, you and me.

M. E. Nichols

Knowing And Caring

Do you know how many stars are in the sky
or can you count the clouds that are moving by,
Do we care for the endless children who cry
or have we any thoughts for the reason why?

Do you know, how many trees grow on this earth
or can you count the women who give birth,
Do we care about the world's biggest dearth
or have we any thoughts for all it is worth?

Do you know how many birds are flying with ease
or can you count the animals that still run free,
Do we care, about the people who disagree
or have we any thoughts for why they don't agree?

Do you know how many rivers each year overflow
or can you count the flowers that in the parks grow,
Do we care about the day when we get overthrown
or have we any thoughts for the end of the unknown?

Margret Foulger

A Battlefield's Legacy

The Poppies bloom and grow blood red
one hundred thousand men are dead.
They fought a war, their lives the price,
like the Poppies bloom, it was gone in a trice,
The seed of man like the Poppy grows,
how it will end, nobody knows.

Man's aim, like the Poppies, is to procreate
but for me, it is too late.
My life at Flanders was cut short.
freedom for you was my only thought.
My blood has mingled with the Poppy seed
so you will not forget my last brave deed.
   Susan Elizabeth Anderson

" Unspoken Words "

If I could only share with you
Once more the fruits of yesterday,
Could I forget un-spoken words
The changing colours of your ways.

I can still see you standing there
Holding my hand, begging not to go,
Don't hide the tears, I'm crying too
It doesn't matter, you must know

I'm always with you by your side
Watching over you, feeling every pain
Hold your head high, think of me there
I'll soon be with you once again.
   Wayne M. Gleave

Sort It Out

It all depends on what you think
On whether elephants are pink,
Or whether pigs can really fly
And leopards spots are just plain dye.

You think of these, it troubles you
Now how can you decide it's true,
The elephants have just been dyed
And leopards are, well pink outside.

And as for pigs, well you don't know
So pigs will simply have to go
That leaves the elephants of blue
And one dyed leopard I think, don't you.

One dyed leopard gone away
He will be back another day
So elephants in suits of blue
If that's the case it must be true.
   B. Smedley

I Remember

I remember the mandarin sun beating down,
On the innocent coterie of tourists.
I remember the ice-cream trickling,
Leaving its own trail of frustration.
I remember the polluted smoke from nearby factories
Proceeding on its own journey.
I remember the long sultry afternoons
With just a whisper of a breeze.
I remember the women down by the lake,
Washing clothes whilst revealing their life stories.
I remember the gypsies travelling door to door,
To bring prosperity, in a bid to enhance their social life.
I remember the envious eye of an adult, wishing life was so simple.
As the street callers pack away
And the women go home to participate in another chapter of their
lives, I remember children, uprooting the stumps,
Realizing dinner was an hour ago.
Night falls and the crickets come out to play their own game,
Delhi is covered in a blanket of hush, only the crickets dance
the tune of joy.
   Mandip Bhogal

March The First

March the first dawned bright and clear,
On the crisp and frosty air.
Larks sang blithely in the blue,
Singing songs of hope anew.
The sad laburnham hung its head
With tears of ice hard pressed to check.
The pyracantha defied the cold
And shone with diamonds bright and bold.
"I'm here beside my friend the tree
To guard her from the winter freeze".
"And so am I the crisp grass said;
I shield her feet you guard her head".
In the dykes the ice did melt,
For the touch of Spring was felt.
O'er the fields of sparkling snow,
The sun said warmly, "You must go!"
"Your work is done upon the earth,
Away! and let the flowers give birth!"
   D. M. Chatwin

The Power Of The Universe

The foam-flecked breakers crash and roar
On Scotland's rocky western shore;
Black clouds race in a storm-rent sky,
And a wild wind hurls the spray on high.

This is a night when devils ride,
And laugh with glee at the boiling tide;
When a shrieking wind in bitter rail
Sends far inland the Atlantic gale.

Far off in the glens men bolt their doors,
And creep to bed as the torrent pours;
The mariners have long since sought
The sheltered cove or fishing port.

But here on the cliffs at the midnight hour,
Where the jagged rocks rise tower on tower,
The voice of a mighty power is heard,
And man stands awed by His dreadful word.

For in the wild wind's frantic cry,
In the gushing tears of the storm-racked sky,
In the crashing roar as the seas disperse,
Is the throb of the Heart of the Universe.
   R. H. Hodgskin

Irish Thoughts

Oh let me cross the sea again
On rocky ship or silver plane
So I'll discover once again
Your broad magnificence

To see again your western coast
Where oft my mind fleets like a ghost
And cast my eyes upon your most
Rugged elegance

To hear again your Celtic charm
Where ancient songs relate a yarn
For angry years can never harm
Your unique eloquence

Oh let me cross the sea again
To breath the air and taste the rain
For there's no way I can explain
All nature's affluence

And when this life has gone from me
And I am just a memory
Then let my spirit be set free
To Ireland's reverence
   Terry A. Tuvey

The Sea Empress

Tears of black seep from Her bows; the dying Days of Sea Empress.
On rocks She dies, fighting wind and rain from the skies!
Pushing tugging surface craft fight. Sea Empress's final plight?
Onshore people gaze, T.V.s send their super Rays.
Beaches morning black costume. Its normal creatures now presume.
In the Sky Man's Dakota's fly... Not the place for bird's to fly!
CRY Come to Sanctuary Porpoise, Seals, Fish and Eels?
FOOD for many.. POISONED not any..
DIE. Bird, Clam, Starfish too.
All the rest of you.. You can DIE too..
Man makes good Man makes bad OH OH NO CRY. It's so SAD.
Come to me my dying friend air sea rescue's our best friend!
A new found trend, it will never mend..
Don't worry it will all soon END...?

Peter Martin

A Holiday Romance

A holiday romance, they say, can't last.
On Jersey Isle we met, as strangers meet,
No longer young we were, both widowed long,
Alone and shy, but yet a tryst, a troth.
Romance, from love affair, to marriage vows,
With friends and families, and bridesmaids too,
Young granddaughters, long since full women grown.
But all things have to end, though love remains.
Alone, I turn my head, I reach my arm,
I hear a step, a voice, but no one's there.
A holiday romance, they say, can't last,
But this romance was love until the end.

Phil Richards

My Dad

Fifteen years since my Dad passed away...
On His Grandson's Twenty-First birthday.
A little family celebration
Turned quickly to a sad occasion.

Lying there with all life gone,
All through my life his presence had shone.
For a long long time I could not cry...
"Why Oh Why did he have to die?"

A working class background, He had no life of ease
Commitment to his family did never cease.
Of material wealth he hadn't a lot.
But what he had we always got.

Passing of time eases the pain
Life without him will never be the same.
Memories I have, both happy and sad.
I'll always think a lot of MY DAD.

M. Hemingway

The River Gleanor

The river tidemark stretches.
On forever on the shore.
The lady comes from o'er the stile.
To glean the mark for many a mile.

Peering searching in the jumble
From which young crabs profusely tumble.
Seaweed, Bottles, all are there.
With wood, and shipboard things disregarded
O'er the side at sea.

Still she searches ever onward.
Finding bits and pieces still.
Placed in bag at her disposal,
To scan later at her will.

Now the bag is getting heavy
Time to turn and head for home,
Back down tide mark.
To the stile field.
Till another tide is born.

Peter Orr

" Letting Go "

October fifth nineteen seventy-seven,
One minute in hell, the next in heaven.
This tiny person now in my arms,
Brings flutters to my heart and sweat to my palms.

How will I cope with all the feeds,
With sleepless nights and endless needs.
The years fly by, I watch you grow,
Everything you learn has been mine to show.

You're eighteen now, your wings have grown,
Time to let go, make a life of your own.
The teenage years have been just like people said,
One minute best friends, the next sheer dread.

We've coped quite well, with all the stress,
From teenage views and bedroom mess.
You're my first daughter, it's hard to let go,
But that's what I must do, I now know.

My wishes for you are sincere, with love too,
May all your dreams and plans come true.
Good friends I hope we'll always be,
And now my dearest Amanda, "You're Free."

A. Hardman

Time

Time melts away so quickly,
One life is all we have,
No time to sit around and wonder if times
Are going to be good or bad.
It's up to us to create our own destiny,
To ensure our dreams come true,
Because when our bodies are old and tired,
Sweet memories will be all we have.
Do not despond when things go wrong,
Challenges will arise,
Take optimism by the hand and look on
To brighter days ahead.
The world has so much to offer us,
Riches and knowledge to share,
It's our future that we should be concerned with,
As our lives reflect what we have learned.

Samantha Dinner

The Track

The Track is my master I hate it for that, making me rise when I've only just sat, beckoning me up from my chair in the morn, never thinking to wait 'til I've finished my yawn! Remorseless, relentless, it goes on its way, Cab after Cab — day after day, if only it would stop; if only it would cease; if only I could have just a few minutes peace, but it won't, and I can't, because the Track is my master and there are rumblings afoot it has yet to go faster! But how can I possibly give any more? When it's already ground me into floor, with its incessant demand upon that which sustains all the life in my body — well that which remains, and yet it's so different first thing in the morning, I arrive for my shift just as daybreak is dawning, I look up at the Track, it's so peaceful, so serene, I glance at the clock; it says seven fifteen, the Track looks so resplendent in this motionless state, as pretty as any picture that's hung in the Tate, but nice as it is, the moment's just fleeting as the Track and I will soon be competing, this thought alone makes by body quiver, my stomach is churning, I'm all of a dither, like a condemned man who waits for his last, I sit and I wait as the minutes go past, I open my paper but don't really see — I even miss the girl they put on Page Three, then a chain's started up and though we're not rolling yet, I can already feel my palms starting to sweat! Then a buzzer sounds out — I jump up with a burst, and my mate says sit down — it's only the first, my nerves are now frayed, I have difficulty controlling, for I know in five minutes the Track will be rolling, it's as if I'm falling down some bottomless well, I'm a slave to its rhythms, I'm under its spell, yes! The Track is my master — I hate it for that.

R. Haury

Rocking Chair

Echoes, memories of tears once shed,
Old lady through silent waters led, she rocks in the stillness,
her youth, unheard laughter, deaf!
This forgotten face, too old to dry,
time passes, like love passes, by!
Too old, silent waters, tears to cry,
tired heart, alone tonight, left behind.
Rocking chair, her souvenir of life,
grief, loss of friends, arthritic side,
her pain is much, it's there —
but nothing like the echoes in her rocking chair.
Moulded to its padded back, wooden and worn the tapestry flap.
Alas! she alone controls the picture shows,
as she sits in the freezing winter cold.
Empty within, without those little cries,
photo's of the lost, her child.
Gone, she smiles, rocking chair, and
laughs she, at love with such despair.
And friends, the voices, everyone's gone.
Rocking chair, I believe you creak at the memories you keep!

S. Fardon

Sleepy-Head

The alarm rings in the morning - 7 o'clock - time to get up
   Oh what a drag!
I'm glad I'm not a smoker needing that first fag.
Breakfast is very simple, cereal, tea and bread,
But I still wish that I could go back to my bed.
The birds start to sing but I would like them to stop their
   Early morning chorus - they make such a din.
The day is getting brighter, the watery sun is breaking through,
It's now 8 o'clock and the man on the radio tells me to start
   The day anew.
I don my coat and gloves and tell him to go away, he must know
   I'm a sleepy-head, but I must start work today.
Out I trip, bag and keys in hand. If the sun shines wouldn't
   It be grand?
But if it turns to wet and wintry weather, back to bed I go,
   Even the weather man says it might snow!

B. Halliday

Burning Heart

Beat, oh beat, with the rhythm of my blood -
   Oh heart of mine.
Comfort the tearing of my soul,
   quench the dry thirst that parch the
   depths of my desire.
Find me a cure for my ills and reach out and touch
   the core of this love I require.

Faster, faster, oh heart of mine,
   reach a tempo so strong, ready to explode like a volcano.
Sweep me away with a rush of fire.
Burn, burn till only ashes remains.

Melford Fearon

Sheriff Muir (Near Sterling)

A ramble on sheriff muir one day,
Raised my spirits, blew my cares away.
Far from the city where crowds were looming
The peace and quiet was all consuming.
The plaintive cry of the curlew rang
While a cheerful ditty the skylark sang.
There, polecats and rabbits frisked together
Romping and racing through the heather.
Sheep and cattle roamed free, at ease,
And stared, quite rudely, if you please.
A playful wind tossed my hair,
As if it, like me, was happy there.
This tranquil scene in my mind is stored,
No more will I feel downcast or bored,
For now, at will, I can go in spirit
To Sheriff Muir — and the peace within it.

Mary Stack

Love is Magic, Love is Sweet, Love. . .

Love is magic, love is sweet,
Love should thrill you, to your feet,
It warms you, on a winter's night,
It comforts you, and holds you tight,
There is no substitute for love.
And you should thank the stars above,
That heaven sent someone for you,
Someone who'll love you, sure and true,
So count your blessings, every day,
And never hesitate to say
The words you mean, from a heart so true,
My Darling, I really do love you.

John R. King

Loving Is Knowing

It's sad when there's no one there to say I love you — no loving arms to hold you in your time of need — no goodbye kiss or welcome hug — no special one to care. The days are long but the nights are longer — loneliness is hard to bear. When darkness falls into the warm enfolding arms of night we creep and treasured memories with loving thoughts give comfort while we sleep. Then it seems as though in silent meditation we are told — hold fast to faith, another day is dawning and the sun will once more shine; — Your loved one's love has never left you, and God's love is also thine.

Eve de Silk

The Gentle Panther

In the solitude of the silent jungle,
Lurks a cool, calm, clever cat.
At first sight, with his mouth open wide,
Showing crystal white teeth,
He looks quite awesome and ferocious.
Yet he's only yawning, like you and I.
When he lifts a heavy ebony paw,
Flexes his razor-sharp claws,
He's only playing with an emerald leaf,
That fell on his pretty satin nose.
He may softly brush by you,
To reach the turquoise and quartz river,
Lapping the foaming waters with a peach-coloured tongue.
He then may leap up on his shining, smooth rock,
Turn quickly as if to pounce, instead he lies down,
His coat turning ginger in the golden sunlight,
He'll close his peridot eyes,
Twitch his snake-like tail,
Then settle into a silky slumber, purring,
The gentle panther.

Christina Benjamin

It Could Just Be

What has happened to England's green and pleasant lands,
Lush green fields and golden sands,
Where children could walk with laughter and bliss,
Lovers could stroll safely and share a kiss.

What now we ask, what can we do,
families together are so few,
Children roam streets alone by night,
Homeless people are a regular sight.

Just take this world and shake it well,
You never know and who can tell,
In its making it might just have happened,
That this world of ours just got misshapen.

Maybe if it's taken into hand,
People might once again understand,
That it takes love and sharing to make it whole,
to give our living and world a soul.
So please take heart, make a new start,
Make a new world,
Make a new year,
Where a child can walk without any fear.

Brenda Ann Moore

Trip To Bali

The bustle of a packed fairground
its familiar noises.
'Three darts for ten p.
shooting for prizes'
(An aside -
'Did you pipe one on your way in?'
lured gullibles to my stall.)

She appeared from nowhere - tall, slim,
silent: joined me for an evening meal.
Later - within the confines of my room
we took an unbridled, exotic trip to Bali
where muted eastern bells sounded a strange
repeated rhythm all night long.

Jeff Sabner

Gossip

As the years go by I have found
It's gossip that makes the world go round
Rich or poor, young or old
There is always a story to be told
In the office the workers are at a loss
Why is the secretary so long with the boss?
The typist with her skirt so short and tight
Looks as if she doesn't know wrong from right
She flirts with the new man in sales all day
But he is not interested, could he be gay?
The supervisor is pregnant, her husband is glad
If he found out about the manager would he go mad?
At home it's no better, the gossip is the same
The neighbours, the tradesmen, they are all fair game
The curtains twitch and the heads they shake
The comments flow out, what harm do they make?
No one will stop it but just bear in mind
Next time that you gossip don't be unkind
What you say about others they say about you
So make sure it's not vicious or totally untrue.

Gill Pummell

" Limbo "

I write my life away so many hours a day,
It's hardly worth the paper for all I have to say.
I wonder how I did it, lived this life so long,
I've never really done anything very wrong,
I've never been so lonely as what I am to-day,
I feel I have the plague and everyone's staying away.
Or maybe it's finally happened, the bomb has hit this land
All around is silence and here alone I stand,
How long I've been in limbo, God only knows,
In my reflection in the mirror, the horror certainly shows
Something dreadful's happened, and I've just realized,
How could I let it happen, let me die before my eyes.

Ann Craig Duncan

Dinky

There was a dog called Dinky, his coat long black and slinky,
Out he ran into the road! By came a lorry with a heavy load,
"Come back", "Come back" the owner cried,
But Dinky ran on and there he died,
The owner lifted him eyes filled with tears,
his Dinky's dead after all these years,
I warned you Dinky everyday, that on the road you cannot play,
The owners heart thumped on his
breast as poor Dinky he put to rest.
Five little girls loved Dinky too, this
brush with death the first they knew
Their mum came home from work that
day "Oh mum"! They cried Dinky's gone away.
Their mother choked at their dismay
brought them close and began to say,
Come now girls listen to me, Dinky's not dead he's alive and free,
He lives in a world just a thought
away and when you sleep he comes to play,
They lifted their heads and smiled with
glee so glad in the knowledge that Dinky was free.

Marina Vaughan

Demons

I have never felt such an intense pain
it's neither mental, or physical, but from deep within the soul.
    Like in a dream — when I stretch the sinews
      to the point of tearing — reaching desperately to touch you,
      my fingertips are ready to brush and caress you,
      but alas you are not within my grasp, instead,
      every time, just a little beyond — is this not torture?
Yes, again I am taunted and dallied with, mocked —
my love for you is mocked by you!
    No! I cannot believe it!
What hurts I have endured, those that I've cast aside —
I feel they have not yet gone — but have festered,
waiting for their moment, to come back and haunt me,
demons to cause such fear and anguish.
    Is it not a cruel joke indeed —
      played by the subconscious mind.
      I think you can replace the torments with peaceful joy
for when you are here, my love,
my fingers will caress your flesh —
    so real.

Kirstin Helen Smith

Depression

Depression and boredom are two in one,
it's not like being under the nice hot sun.
Depression could lead to madness or even death,
this could mean taking your last breath.
"Cheer up woman! life is fun,
everyone's different, big bum or tum.
Proud of yourself that's what you should be,
either through looks or personality!

Kiran Lyall

A Thought For Today

Necessity they say is the mother of inventions
It's said as well the road to hell
Is paved with good intentions
Pride goes before a fall
So look before you leap
He who hesitates is lost
And still waters run deep
Don't look a gift horse in the mouth
It's liable to spit in your eye
A stitch in time saves nine
And you don't miss the water
Till the well runs dry.

Helen B. Muir

The Dark Power

Grey, cold, the cement memorial stands upon the moor,
Its shadow dark'ning life beneath yet lighting all the world.
It has an eerie silence, this man-made soul,
Yet what comes forth gives voice to melody and word.

It is a statue dedicated to an age that's still to come,
Its unknown power harnessed within the reinforced walls
Of fear and ignorance, of petty falsehoods and intolerances
That fail to give it credence or a chance.

The tamed but vibrant energy motions engines into life,
The submarine to swim, the rocket to fly, the turbine to spin,
This miracle of science, this fusion of the elements
Is a consequence that has evolved to help man-kind.

The glowing warmth that emanates from deep within
Banishes winters from our doors, brings spring into our hearts.
Yet once we're enlightened as to which way to go,
What happens to the force that's spent and died?

Can Einstein's theories ever replace gas, oil or coal?
Can ordinary men ever see this physics mystery as safe?
It's awesome, powerful, frightening yet magical.
This unseen, odourless, non-polluting saviour of the earth.

Jenny Care

Time

Time is so precious, though it never stands still,
It's the one thing that no one can stop.
Since this world began, it has gone marching on,
And is shown by the hands on your clock.

When you're feeling so good doing things that are nice,
It seems to go faster than light,
But when you're feeling sad, with worry and pain,
Time seems slow, days are long, endless night.

Our life's span is short and in time it's minute,
So enjoy it, this poet has said,
For when you have gone, there's no coming back,
Time stands still, only when you are dead.
Kenneth McGovern

Earth Spirit

There's a rumble in the still night air.
It's the spirit of the earth, telling us to be aware.

This world and its nature is so innocent and pure,
let us treat it gently, let us nurture it, let us give it more.

Treat every living thing as though it were we,
with kindness and love and harmony.

All of nature — animals or plants — have a spirit of their own,
see each new leaf, see little insects making their homes.

They have a right to live on this planet earth.
Don't destroy the spirit of life, enjoy, be tender and see the worth.

Everything here on earth is for a reason.
Understand all that is and of nature, don't commit treason
Beth Rogers

Halloween

Halloween, halloween
It's the time of year that makes you scream.
Trick-or-treaters stalk the streets
Knocking on doors and asking for treats.
They knock on your door late at night,
Dressed like vampires ready to bite.
If you choose a treat
Then you have to give the kids some sweets.
But if it's a trick that you choose
a lot of trouble can be caused by these youths.
So beware, beware on halloween night
when wolves, witches, ghouls and ghosts will fight.
To see who's the strongest of them all
Why don't you choose out of the terrible four.
Louise Palfrey

Ruthless Survival

Hustle, bustle, stress and strain,
  It's called the nineties survival game.
Technology booming, surfing the net.
  Pen and paper are tools to forget.

High power bosses more ruthless than ever,
  Pay rises pending on the never, never
Promotion "you'll be lucky" it's tough at the top,
  Redundancy more likely, or a wage drop.

Young single mothers — what can be done?
  Ruthless survival will cut off their fund.
Make the rich richer as the poor fight to exist,
  Always just a number on another list.

What else is there in this nineties age?
  Drugs awareness, ecstasy rage.
Overcrowded prisons, famine and war,
  No rest for the homeless, those abused and the poor.

But people keep smiling and living in hope,
  For happier times, when they're able to cope.
"I'll put a £1 on the lottery", fingers crossed that I win,
  Then face the problems the money will bring.
Claudine Aaron

Natural Love

Wherever you look
It's there to see
The picture of beauty
Which glues nature together
That which combines to show all things in love

As a sight of perfection
Created by the universal maker
He who knows all things
And to whom we should all show thanks
Yes a thanks for the natural love we
  are given in abundance.
Donald E. Smith

The Smile

Have you noticed the smile of a Yorkshire lass?
It's warm, it's bright, not bold as brass.
It can light up your day, turn grey skies blue.
Tinge your mood with a rosy hue.

It must be inherited from hard working stock.
Passed down through the genes, a chip off the old block.
It leaves you so peaceful, you never want to part,
From that wonderful smile that glows with health
Nothing can buy it, not the lands greatest wealth.

If you pass through Yorkshire one of these days,
Remember my words as you wind on your way.
Stop for a chat, linger a while,
You will be happily given that beautiful smile.
Lilian Roundhill

Dreamtime

I've tried the genie of the lamp, and moonbeams in a jar.
I've climbed the ladder to the sky, and polished every star.
I've even rode a unicorn around the town at night,
I've even played with fairies, now that's a pretty sight,
I've even done the baking, for the queen of hearts one day.
I've even shown a crocodile how to smile and swim away,
I've helped some little spiders to spin a yarn or two,
I've rode upon old Moby Dick into a sea of blue,
I've even been to wonderland, met everybody there,
I've tickled Mona Lisa, and put her smile there,
I've even rode on Rudolf, with Santa on his sleigh,
I've turned the grey skies upside down, to make it rain one day,
I've done the rounds with sandman to help you sleep at night,
I've never been to dreamland, so I will say goodnight.
Jean Freeman

Apoplexy

Get out of my space, I'm trying to breathe
I've got this claustrophobic sense of unease
And the vein, to my brain, has left a gap for the entering rain
I don't know, I'm not sure
If my legs are still moving or they're pinned to the floor
Oh God I feel, half diseased
I've got an annoying itch but I'm in a state of apoplexy

Do you know what it feels like, when you know you want to die,
The whole world is running around you,
But you're stuck to the frame that feeds your insides.

Get out of my room, I want to move
You said, I'll be alright, you've got a nerve
It's the hole, in my soul, that pours out bad feelings as I
  slowly grow old
I can't feel, no, I can't see, if it's my heart or machines that
  pump fluid around me
Oh Lord I am, all disease
I've still got that itch but I'm in a state of apoplexy

Do you know what it feels like, when you're empty inside,
The whole world is neglecting you,
But the ruptured vein is stopping your screaming I've died.
Derek Salisbury

Hidden Love

You fill my thoughts both night and day,
I've never loved in such away.
If only you would notice me,
Yours forever I would be.
To dream of being in your arms
And falling deeply for your charms,
Makes my poor heart skip a beat
With you my life would be complete.
But you don't know I'm even there
To see how much I really care.
My love to you I send with wings
To me you are my everything.

Carolyne Hudson

The Bridesmaid

I want to be your bridesmaid,
I've waited all this time,
I haven't been a bridesmaid,
Since nineteen fifty nine!

I had a lovely dress then,
All blue and very long,
It wouldn't look too bad now,
If I could only get it on!

On second thoughts I've changed my mind
You are the bride you see,
And I would look so ravishing
They'd all be watching me!
I do not want to spoil your fun,
It is your special day
So I'll decline the offer
And put my dress away,

Now, anyone who is a bride,
And wants a maid of honour
Please make it quick and contact me,
Before I am a goner!

Catherine E. Mansford

Ivory Towers

Little linnet in your gilded cage;
Ivory towers up on high engage
Your tiny frame, yet with a song so sweet,
Inside my heart a tuneful note does meet.
Oh linnet, how I'd love to set you free,
To open up the door and watch you fly
Out through the window over treetops high,
For that is also where I'd like to be:
But how can I set free my thoughts within
These bars of my own making and then win
The prize of freedom and gain heavenly peace,
Where gilded bars and Ivory Towers cease.
Oh little bird, you are much luckier than I
For one day soon, you'll soar away up to the sky.

Jill Barker

My Mother

My mother is as the sea,
Power to nurture or destroy.
Her solid uplifting arms
Guiding my buoyant journey.
Those pure soft fluid arms
Have caught my failing falls,
Waves of strength and passion
Carried me to unexpecting shores.
Always near, sometimes far,
Giving me air to breathe,
Thoughts of her, droplets from her soul
Float through me, absorbing into warmth.
Without mum, I am nothing,
For as water is partly sea,

She is within me.

Michelle Kemp

Running Stream

Running stream, please wait for me, let me share your
journey to the sea.
I sit and watch you hastily taking with you life's history.
Where did you begin?
Where do you end?
Tell me your secrets, I'm your friend
I'll close my eyes and just pretend it's you
and I on a journey's end.
Take me to a heavenly shore where hatred and
evil are no more.
Running stream, please wait for me, take me with
you across the sea, where little children never
die, and soldiers run free.
To a place shimmering in gold and people never
ever grow old.
Running stream, please wait for me, no one will
ever know you've taken me.
Take me to your sanctuary,
Let me too run free.

Gillian Burton

Untitled

The morning breaks — bright, eternal
Just as though a mantle of light was spreading over the sky.
I wake from slumber, pleasant thoughts fill my mind.
I hear the song of the bird, the gentle rustle of the leaves on
    the trees.
My heart with thankfulness faces the new day...
And then realization comes — of the night past, of sadness,
    of grief and devastation...
Once again those dreadful words — "There's been a bomb!"
Lives ended, limbs broken, mothers, fathers, wives and
    children heartbroken, mourning.....
The happiness is gone, the joy of the new dawn turns to sadness
To fear, to dread, to choking back the tears — to cry for peace,
    to yearn for a better way.
What will it take to make them see — the evil of their ways.
How dare they? Oh! how dare they take it all from us.
The peace, the joy, the coming together of the past months.
It was fragile, just like the white dove soaring in the sky.
But we held on, hoping against hope, that it would grow,
    would blossom
And our children would know a brave new world.
We can't go back, we must strive with all our strength to carry on
To pray that hearts and minds will be transformed
To welcome love instead of hate — to understand and not conflict
Then a bright new morn will dawn — and right will reign eternal.

Grace McGaffin

" Little Star "

To see your little face so bright,
Just fills me with so much delight,
Your sparkle shines and brings a tear,
And all my sorrows disappear.

With each new days there's something new,
Discovering tasks which you can do
You learn with versatility,
And develop a personality.

Your laughter and loud hearty screams,
Are you own way of fun it seems,
A vivacious child you really are,
My one and only Little Star.

Elaine Wood

Brewed Tea

She could capture your heart in the palm of her hand
Once you've tasted her blood red flesh
Lay waste to your whole being in the blink of an eye
Lead you in conversation with the muse of a 1000 is
Till words pour from your mouth
Like perfectly brewed tea
But then again maybe it's just me
With a man eater such sweet liberty

J. Paul

Never Will I Know

Alone I trudged on the 'Dalton Road', not a living soul in sight,
Just the whisper of a gentle breeze on a cool bright moonlight night.
Suddenly the picture changed before my very eyes,
A blinding flash, and an echoing sound, took me by surprise.
Rooted to the spot, stricken down with fear, some unknown apparition was getting very near.
Eerie sounds of muffled hooves stopped me in my track, as the moisture from my pores trickled slowly down my back.
Through the gathering mist on a fiery steed through the bracken and the heather, a phantom on his fiery steed was going hell for leather,
Pursued in haste with evil intent, he seemed desperate with fear, with deadly foe in hot pursuit coming from the rear.
Suddenly a beam of light flashed across his face, that phantom on his fiery steed went hurtling into space.
I stood erect, aloft I gazed not a living soul in sight,
Just the whisper of a gentle breeze on a cool bright moonlight night.
I made my way to the Toby Inn to tell them of my plight, I was greeted by unseeing eyes that vanished in the night.
I hastened on my weary way as fast as I could go,
What happened on the fateful night, 'NEVER WILL I KNOW'

John Bray

Requiem For Wholeness

If you must consent to being broken and pain-filled
Kindness may wash over you like a river,
Bearing small boats filled with relatives, friends,

And people you've never met before
Bringing unfamiliar cargo.
That exotic plant you yearned for
Those expensive flowers; you may have them now
In exchange for hobbling awkwardly from room to room
Unable properly to trust the damaged leg,
Days spent reclining, frustrated.
Yet remembering those whose plight is even worse.

Lilian Cadoux

Airs And Graces

The day of departure is finally here.
Kinsfolk rush madly, some shed a tear.
On the road to the airport we set out at last,
Driving with tension and needlessly fast.
The lounge in the airport is stuffy and warm,
No hint on the speaker of turbulent storm.
But up through the clouds we eventually break.
The view good enough for one's breath to forsake.
With a squeal of the tyres and faint puff of smoke
We land with a bump yet nobody spoke.
We debark from our aircraft with half nervous smile.
The aircrew mouth softly, "We'll see you awhile."

Jonathan Mapp

The Four Seasons

Nature awakes with the breath of Spring
Lambs in the field and birds that sing
Daffodils bloom, birds build their nest's
Nature comes to life, after Winter's rest

Summer arrives with a burst of colour
Leaves on the trees, buds in flower
Sunshine, scenery, sand and sea
Is always there, for you and me

Autumn comes with the Fall
A carpet of leaves from the trees so tall
Squirrels collect nuts for to store
As we gather in fruit and harvest galore

Winter comes with snow so deep
Fires aglow, while nature sleeps
Children's laughter while sleighing down the hill
As Mister Snowman is composed and still

Doris Lambert

Help Is At Hand

What a beautiful Country you had,
Land of plenty and healthy folk,
Then it happened and War broke out,
You call it ethnic cleansing,
Do you really remember what it was all about?

Thousands have died in your Country,
Land turned to war-torn grounds,
It stops and starts as often as the sun dares to go down,
Misery covers your land,
Why don't you please let someone give you a hand.

Your Country is being slowly destroyed,
Gun shots reign through the air,
Smell of human blood has stained the earth,
People's hearts are aching for peace,
Isn't it time to let the dead rest
And start rebuilding a new peaceful land.

Beverley Marie Orrey

Goodbye

Driving in a sports car,
Landscapes so brightly coloured,
Animals running free,
What paradise,
A wall rising out of the solid ground,
I'm floating through the blue sky,
And then I landed on the crisp grass,
Thistles growing all around me, holding me down,
Black paint dripping,
Dripping over the blue sky,
Flowers shrivelled, animals ran into the dark woods,
I'm floating again, no worries, just happy,
Light pushing through the dark,
A box, a house with no roof,
Colours beaming,
I float towards it, now I'm inside,
The ceiling is coming down,
The walls are closing in,
I close my eyes, and say goodbye.....Goodbye

Alexandra Richardson

Woodland Day (Michael's Song)

Lying on our backs just looking at the sky, Daphny and I.
Languid days, married's of dappled shades, and butterflies,
Lazy bumble bees suck the nectar from honey dew flowers,
Gentle breezes, fresh scented grass, and dandelion showers;

Of white gossamer seeds floating up to the clouds,
Lazy hanging black cherries all ripe and proud.
To feel her lips in the hollow of my throat,
Gently kissing, fills me with so much happiness I seem to float,

In a sensual world where no sadness can survive.
Makes me feel that it is so good to be alive.
Rocking gently with our arms and bodies entwined,
Soft breathing, sweet breath and a pleasure oh so fine.

Woodland days, lying close together my love and I.
We don't need fast cars, expensive clothes, a jet to fly.
What we have can't be bought, it is given to us by love,
Love passed down from far beyond the clouds above.

Allan Glassbrook

The Storm

The house was all in stillness
On the dark and stormy night
When my dog just started howling
Filling me with fright
The lightning flashed around the room
Reflecting on the stair
Was it my imagination
Or was there someone standing there
My heart it started pounding
And I tried so hard to scream
When then I was awakened
And found it all a dream

Rosina Dian Speed

The Reluctant Cynic

Last summer's leaves have now all fallen,
Last summer's sun has ceased to shine.
The laughter that then echoed loudly
Now has a dismal hollow sound.
The remembrance of cruel words spoken,
Words that there should not have been,
Has pierced the heart
And scarred the mind.
For man 'tis true, is less than decent,
And his motives are much less than kind.
The scars of time engrave themselves upon our faces,
And disbelief in human virtue
Becomes daily more our sole belief.
And all those things we once held sacred
Are the shattered dreams of vanished innocence.
Last summer's sun shall never burn so brightly,
And the sky shall never seem so blue.
For as the sands of time slip by inexorably,
They grind us down
both me and you.
Anna E. Miller

What The Handicapped Have To Endure

Stared at,
Laughed at,
Pointed at,
Whispered about,
Sneered at,
Jeered at,
Roared at.

This is what happens when they go outside.
Some want to face the world, but most want
to hide. Society won't accept them as special
human beings. They don't go by inner beauty,
they go by what they're seeing. Someday
they'll be accepted, they will not have to hide.
People will realise that looks don't count,
but the person deep inside.
Eileen Black

Swan Song

Now the music sings; I offer you my hand,
Lead you to a waltz, played by a long forgotten band.
Two lovers still dreaming, while sunset is gleaming,
For love that keeps dreaming will not fade or die.

Dancing in the dusk, lovely moments fly away,
Soon our day will die, all gold will turn to grey.
Our two hearts are meeting, yet two lives are fleeting,
And soon the glory shall fade from our sky.

Now the music stops. All our world is dark and cold.
Light has left our sky, we know we're growing old.
Remember our story, remember the glory,
For love that dreams will never die.
George J. Butler

Brotherly Concern

The picture of you lying in that bed
Just haunts me like no other thought and stays inside my head.
You look so well and yet deep down I know
That life will go on forward now but not so fast — more slow.
Machines and wires check to see all's well,
But they can't feel inside or see the pain that I can tell.
Now by your side, I too must bear the cost,
To help you live again and deal with time you may have lost.
A warning sign, sent down from God above,
A warning to be heeded, a reminder of His love.
With those around protecting — ever near,
With many times ahead of you, although not very clear.
This life, so precious, live until the end;
This life, so precious, live it now,
Much better with a friend.
Alan J. McGregor Dearie

Yet Kindly

Turn from the sight with dreary heart,
Leave sickening sounds behind.
In darkened streets and homes abounds
An ugliness of mind.

The plastic bags flap thinly there,
The fallen bins behind.
Outpourings from their depths reveal
The refuse of mankind.

Draw back the curtains to the moon,
Behold with better sight
The scattered bins a glistening throng,
A waterfall of light.

Like goodness struggling through the gloom
To point the way to go,
For the yet-kindly feet of man,
Soft as forgiveness, falls the snow.
Helen Kardar

Where Sunbeams Flicker

Sunbeams come, then go. Like a rainbow from its heavenly glow. Leaves are green by a mystic touch. With branches so brown, as the leaves down. Making a carpet of brown. When Autumn has flown then, the snow descends sweet robins appear. Delightful to behold, in their majestic array. All is silent. Then as if by magic, when the months have passed, the buds appear, like a tear, the rain drops full. Then the sun breaks through, touching each bud, as they burst into flower. Then it gathers up its rays then sweeps it along, with birds all chirping, their sweet songs. Up up like shining stars, to tree tops high. Where the leaves have curled, in the heat of the day. The sun beams flicker. Soon the moon beams will come, so all will be sleeping. Away into shadows even quicker. Then the magic comes at the dawn of day, like a spirit hand took it away. To fields of green, to start a new day. No children play. It's only meant for nature, where swallows fly. Fascinating to be hold. Waiting with the door mouse, with eyes so large and black, finding things to feed on till the sun comes back. MAKING nests in tree holes, then curl up, and sleep. Lost in another world, we shall leave, these creatures, great and small. To mark another day perhaps, some where perhaps. When the rainbow appears. Quickly disappears. Floating away on some bellowing clouds, high up to heavens above. A golden thread descends, caught up in the hands of time. To bring again another day, sunbeams, that come out to play. Then flicker, to meet another day.
D. J. Brent

To Peter

We expected you in August but little did I know as I sat soothing your kicks and loving you as you grew bigger and heavier within me, that you would arrive early.

You arrived very quickly on the last day of June, a tiny scrap, weighing only three pounds. Your arrival heralded by a sixty mile an hour dash and a blue flashing light.

For a moment I heard you cry as you came into the world, I watched your tiny bruised face as wires and tubes were fastened to you. I felt so proud, a tiny son. I saw panic on their faces, "He's too sick to cuddle," they said. I was in Heaven and Hell. This is a nightmare, it must be! Voices asked, "What are you going to call him?" "Peter", I answered and then I thought Peter our rock.

For two whole weeks you fought to stay. We held your hand, we talked to you, we loved you. Then one day, heartbroken, I watched the priest christen you. You needed surgery, I needed to cuddle you but tubes, wires and a glass box denied me.

We saw you before they took you. You held my hand so tight, you looked so beautiful. I know you knew your Dad and I and then you had to go. You never came back and we never saw you again.

We were so proud of you, we loved you and we will remember you forever. Your tiny body left us but your great spirit will fill our hearts for as long as they beat.
Lynn Dryden

The Fox And The Pheasant

The fox a-hunting he did go,
   Leaving footprints in the snow.
South, North, West, and East
   He's not looking for a feast,
Just some food to keep him going.
   When oh when will it stop snowing?

He trotted off across the lea,
   Then spied a pheasant in a tree.
Staring in the poor bird's eyes
   The fox soon had him mesmerized.
The pheasant's eyes rolled round and round,
   Without a sound it hit the ground.

On falling down, he cracked his head,
   And was by now, quite truly dead.
The fox pounced upon its prey
   And ate his first meal of the day.
He settled down, and ate and ate,
   Then took the rest back to his mate.
Now the wind has started blowing
   When oh when will it stop snowing?
   Florice Capewell

Attention!

Heads front.
Left, right, left, right.
The long black car rolls slowly along,
anxious for it to be over, wishing it had never begun.
Unable to see the end of the procession.
Looking forward with an unbelievable realization.
Thank you all for coming.
Thank you all for caring.
He is surely missed,
He is truly the best.
We'll get by, it'll work out.
He has taught us well.
It comes to all,
only the good die young.
He has left his mark, four of us,
to continue his name,
to continue his life,
We'll miss you
   Ian McGrath

Request

Please, don't grow old without me,
   Let me share with you the years that are left
   Come, before time tells another act of theft,
And takes away an opportunity.

Please, let us travel side by side,
   Together let us step into the years that wait
   Where winters and springs rendezvous with fate,
All along Life's ebbing tide.
   Jean F. Skinner

Step Out Of Reality

Step out of reality and into a dream,
Let your mind fantasize for a while.
Imagine a place, imagine a scene,
Somewhere to make you smile.
Forget your humdrum, busy life and let your mind explore,
The things that are always beyond your reach,
The things you have always 'longed' for.
A paradise island, with powder white sand;
And seas of crystal blue.
Imagine the warmth of the sun on your face,
Picture the breathtaking view!
No noise around, except for the sound,
Of the rustling of the towering palm trees;
The occasional whistle of a tropical bird,
Or the whisper of a gentle breeze.
Dreams allow us to escape, into another world;
So take time away from the stresses of life,
Relax: Let your mind be unfurled.
   Louise Riley

There Is More Than Seven Wonders In This World, Just Look And You Will See

Let me look and let me ponder,
Let me think and let me see,
Let me gaze out yonder,
Onto the brilliance of the sea.

See the waves, how they are rolling,
On that mighty sea she's a foaming,
In the sky the gulls are gliding,
As ships, sails full of winds, are gracefully sailing.

See out there on that vast horizon,
Now the sun she's slowly beginning to start her new day arising,
Reflecting her golden rays on the crests of the shimmering waves,
As I stand on the shore taking all in such a wondrous gaze.

See all the men along the shore,
Just a bite or two, they want no more,
Cobbles in the depths are trawling their vast nets they have cast,
Displaying skills which they have mastered.

To feel that fresh sea breeze on my face,
Our coastline is such a picturesque place,
Oh God we thank thee with all our grace,
For the beauties of this wondrous place.
   John N. Birtley

Cardboard City

Don't go until you hear what I have to say,
Let us take a walk down cardboard city today.
Don't be afraid to meet the lost and the lowly,
For some can't remember their names they are faces only.
Don't ignore the lost, don't think you are too grand,
Try to show love and compassion, try hard to understand.
Don't just walk on by, don't turn the other cheek,
Look into the eyes of these strangers, tired and weak.
Don't pass judgment, don't condemn a life you can't comprehend,
Instead try to understand these lonely souls need a friend.
Don't say this could never happen to people like me,
But for the grace of God, this could well be.
Don't try to make apologies for what we have not done,
Try to help, remember, this is someone's daughter or son.
Don't make wild statements saying, there is nothing you can do,
It only takes a helping hand, or a smile from you.
Don't think you can't brighten up their forlorn forsaken day,
Your helping hand, your smile, will remain forever and a day.
Don't go down cardboard city without you bearing in mind,
They wait for God, a stronger faith you will never find.
   Doreen Sheriff

The Panoramic Decline Of Nature

Broad leaved grass like a green and silver sheet,
Joined sky and horizon where all must meet.
Urged by the breeze which followed behind,
It bowed from my feet, as I searched to find
My old friends of the wild, I used to greet.

I had nurtured the thought of coming back,
It seemed so long since I walked this track,
But sadness came in cruel scenic change,
What now lay before me, was treeless range.
No white gates in sight, to welcome me back.

Gone the trimmed hedgerows where songsters hid,
Torn from the earth at the farm tractor's bid.
Who would need to take the windbreaks away?
To win a few grains, or a bale of hay.
This desert of land tells me someone did.

I disturbed not the dozing hare so shy,
Nor heard hovering larks sing in the sky,
As I walked the sheet of silver and green,
To the skyline, where once a copse had been,
Seeing not bee, nor the pretty butterfly.
   Colin A. J. Billups

Snowdrops

When January's icy blast, and February's frequent snow
Lie thick around the ground at night, little do we know
Of nature's constant growing pains, of dormant bulbs unseen
Disturbing sods of clay and earth, to push up in between.

Those first green shoots, that signify a stronger being than ours,
That create beauty out of sight, before our waking hours
To rise and see such slender buds, withstanding gales and rain
In ones and twos, and little clumps, all flowering once again.

Where 'Man' has left them undisturbed, or singled, as his wont,
To fill his borders, flowers worth, or left in nature's haunt,
That precious snowdrop, virgin white, with dropping head so frail,
So calm amidst a world of strife, just like a wedding veil.

An outward mask of barren earth, a radiant face unseen,
Who stoops to see your slender buds? Who knows just where you've been?
For only those who beauty seek, will only beauty find,
And as the spring leaps far ahead, the snow drops way behind.
Ian Boddy

A Search For Love

A Bouquet of death rises in a mushroom cloud
Life embalmed in a sea of mud
Immortalized souls imprisoned in those who remember
While the aroma of burned flesh fills the air

Accept my love from a forgiving god
Let the nucleus in atoms start anew
From out of dust clay forms a city
A jungle of concrete points to a sky

Lest we forget that boom of light
The bodies that walked, no skin or hair
Only agony in faces from tears of pain
A nation we saved from insanity and lies

But, mushrooms grow in a dark abyss
In hearts of men who search for peace
Fungi breeds power, domination over another
When will we learn to love our foreign brother
Alec Fearnside

" Something Beautiful Happened Today "

Just when I thought
Life held no more surprises,
No more joy on wonderful days,
Into my world comes a special some-one,
Something beautiful happened today

My step is lighter, my eyes are brighter.
My life not dull or a little grey.
The grass is green, the sky is blue,
The birds' song sweeter
Because of you.

When you are with me, I can be
Whom or whatever I want to be,
A fairy princess, or even three bears,
In the secret, pretend games we share

And in the magic of the words
"Come play with me, Grandma."
Bernadette McCormick

Do You Know Why I Love You?

Do you know why I love you?
It's the way you make me smile.
When we are in a room together, you wink at me once in a while.
You tell me silly stories and you whisper in my ear.
And I know that without looking, you are standing near.
You sense when I am happy, you know when I am sad.
You make me feel such happiness, more than I've ever had.
You teach me how to share my life, you show me how to care.
I have no wish to do anything, without you being there.
I can't predict the future, but if we should ever part.
I will always, always, love you for waking up my heart.
Jo Turner

A Day, Any Day

A day, any day has a Million feelings, feelings from my life.
Life is what I see through my eyes, eyes that search and ponder,
Pondering for those thoughts that run through my head
Looking for an escape, escaping from my heart to yours.

A day, any day has a million hearts, hearts that pump the blood of emotions, emotions that lift my spirits and raise my heartbeat
Expecting my love to search for its lair,
A lair for your love, a lair for my life, living for your love.

A day, any day has a million tears, tears of joy, tears of sadness,
Sadness at the prospect of losing my love
Losing such happiness that is here and now,
Happiness is you and your love.

A day, any day has a million gifts, the gifts of sight to see your smile, the gift of speech to talk of love, the gift of hearing to hear your laughter, to hear you is to be.

A day, any day has but one thought, the thought of my life before,
A life I cannot forget
Where were you, my love?
My love is my thoughts.
Adrinia Steel

Forgive, And You Will Find

They could not bear to be apart for any length of time,
Life to them was wonderful, just like matured wine,
Their love so beautiful, deep and strong, it reached up to the sky,
A solid partnership made in heaven, that money could not buy.

Lying still in unbelief she stares into deep space,
The pain of knowing he had left, was shown upon her face,
Cold emptiness she felt within, and in her distress she sighed,
Heartache crushed her spirit so, she wished that she had died.

As if floating on the clouds of time, she struggled to start again,
Her mind in turmoil still, her body etched with pain,
She made a final effort to rebuild her life once more,
Then HE came back and renewed her strength, as he walked in the door.

Would it ever be the same again? she thought in disbelief,
Remembering how it was, through heartache, pain and grief,
Maybe one day the wound would heal, enabling her to live,
A broken heart takes a while to mend, and a long time to forgive.

He held her hand and gazed into her eyes,
He looked so sad, the sight of him was much to her surprise,
She touched his cheek, and kissed his lips and pressed against his chest,
Then knew at once, the time had come. It was the start of happiness.
Joan Yvonne Matthews

Sit And Smile

I don't much care for rush and bustle
Life's too short to always hustle
Don't be late, no one can wait

Yet there is so much to do
Places, tasks, plans to make
Faster, faster, release the brake

Will nothing be left undone
Will you look back and say with pride
I did it all before I died

Just think before you're laid to rest
All you wish will not be done
Places missed however fast you run

So sit and look around
Let others rush and run about
Discovering more but gaining nowt

Do the things you want to do
Take time out just for you
Rest awhile, sit and smile
Lewis Hawke

Wreck

An angry sea on a stormy night,
Lifted a trawler to a tremendous height.
On rocks below the ship was tossed,
Bravely men fought, but lives were lost.

They clung to pieces floating past,
And prayed to God for help at last.
Quite soon a lifeboat came in view,
To help with the bodies and pick up the crew.

On shore were groups of people waiting
For news of loved ones, afraid and hating
The terrible sea for what it had done,
Dragging men up the beach, slowly one by one.

Sad were the faces as they looked down,
To see these brave souls as they lay on the ground.
An ambulance carried survivors away,
Some others sank down on their knees to pray.

Beulah Thompson

The Tower

It was greenery, greenery, all the way
Light in the windows
Children at play
Until they built the tower block
And gave us all a nasty shock.

A great big ball on the end of a chain,
Knocked all the houses
Right down the drain
Next, little gardens all in a row
Were then ploughed up, so the money could grow.

The local council had done its best
To put the people's
Minds at rest,
Housing for all they said it must be
But it wasn't for you and it wasn't for me.

The playground was concrete; the lift was the toilet,
I thought they said
Nothing would spoil it.
Very soon after, walls started to crack
And everyone wanted their houses back!

Barbara M. Stratton

Artist's Landscape

From here the town is barely seen
   Light red with blue is it? Or green?
I pause a moment at the doubt,
   Then leave it out.

Hardby, the six-lane by-pass runs
   With squared-up grey pantechnicons,
But at the river's edge the blue
   Of shadow has electric hue,
And on the far hillside the snow
   Is touched with mauve and indigo.

And here am I and there's the sky
   Translucent lapis lazuli.

Gordon Hereward Hales

Treasures

Uncle Tom's box stood under the stairs
Like the tall ticking clock
It had always been there!

My cousin Mary, older than I
Said inside the box
A great treasure did lie.

From uncle Tom's room, I took down the key
And crept down the stairs
The great treasure to see!
Some letters, a locket, a strand of red hair
Uncle Tom's treasure
I left lying there.

Alan Burns

The Dawning Of The Light

Sunlight dancing on the window sill,
Like a nymph of spring, gay and bouncy,
Light of touch and body, then still,
Enthral, bright and yet piercing.

Rainbows of light on the walls,
Hues of blues, gold and pink,
The brightness makes my eyes blink;
After the winter grey and darkness.

The heavy frost of the night before,
Its mark leaves patterns on the floor
Of the garden, cold and icy,
Yet with a chilling, silvery beauty.

The awakening of the spirit and life
Of the smallest bud on the mighty tree,
All things of emotion and love,
The thawed water of life ever flowing forward.

Carole Elizabeth Lawrence

'To That Special Someone'

Without you my life would be worthless
Like a soul trapped within an empty existence
My sun would cease to shine
Light is destined to fade to nothingness

Your smiling face is rich with the soft glow of a candle
Your body a magnificent temple
Eyes so deep depicting the rippling of waves
Crashing against distant shores.

The gentle seductiveness of your voice
Caressing my soul with your every word
Your strong defined character
Blessed with a heart so warm and loving
Filled with an endless love for everyone you know.

My friend but yet my love
The one of whom I trust
Without you I'm sure to fail
You're my life.

James Leyland

Eloquence

True oratory is like unto a flame,
Like flame she demands fuel to sustain her.
Like flame she is stimulated by movement.
Which in turn gives light,
Only when she burns.
True eloquence is alight.
But like a flame when derived of air, she dies,
Oh; rhetoric flame spread thy light
To all the world its scholars bright.

James J. Connolly

Eyes Of India

Driftwood fires, long shore lights.
Like her, fire and air, eyes of India.
Gypsy soul, charcoal hair.
Our eyes weave words unsaid, oh my love leave,
Your breath on my pillow, your heartbeat in my bed.

The pub wise dare, under acid stares.
You and I, ask the reasons why.
Our skins speak colours, our hearts the same,
girl bear my name.
My love will never fall,
from hollow of heart bleeding by pub walls.

Weeping willow, cries for free,
Like her, broken bare, eyes of India.
Torn apart, heart in tear.
The sitar sings a strange lament, out ride the storm.
Raging in the elements, we're children of the dawn.

Leaving soon nights of neon blue, only us two.
Twilight on snow dunes, all my love lives in you.
Lay bare, beauty born rare, light of dawn.

Duncan Thorburn

October Rose

The rose stood forlorn in a sea of petals,
Like markers on graves.
The last of a dying breed
Like a lone warrior against an army.
Its petals were once rich in colour and strength.
Now they are faded,
Washed out as if they were cleaned too ferociously by the weather.
The petals feel elasticated and highly drawn.
The scent is fresh but a sense of death is nearby.
The thorns stand rigid.
Soldiers protecting the stem until the very end.
The stem is tarnished.
This is a ruthless time — a time of change — nothing is constant.
The sun is warm, caressing the rose and all around it.
The wind has a bite as sharp as an icicle
Cutting through the rose like an unseen murderer.
Still the rose sways.
Like a dancer in an endless waltz.
Always living in hope.
Carol Solley

Africa

The sounds of Africa soak into one's mind
Like scenery immense, backdrops of a kind.
For the echoes that support the images and thoughts
Like a lesson not learned, but purely self taught.
It used to be one could sit beneath the velvet sky
And listen to the many calls, to try and identify
From dusk to dawn they escalate on boundless different scales
They touch the senses, tense the nerves, the wonder never fails
The urban jungle screams and spreads its thickset roots
It stamps on life regardless, like dying rotten fruits
So civilization takes its toll and strain
With lack of space and the awesome acid rain
How will we describe in later times
The rustle of life in its natural clime
With no fences or wire, not even a gate
Are we the privileged few, is it too late
To hear Africa's call to try to contrive
A land of hope and the will to survive?
Lynda Musgrave

Misty Memories

My hopes lie scattered in fragments on the ground
Like the blood-red petals of a dying rose.
The part of my heart which remains ever yours
Withers and weeps, and aches for you.
My shoulders are heavy with the burden
Of the pain I know you suffered.
In my mind float the misty memories
Of times when I could see you
When I was near you,
The diamond-precious time when I held you...
But now you are out of reach.
You slipped away with shocking abruptness;
One minute, here; the next — nowhere.
There is nothing more painful
Than a parting with no goodbye.
If I had never believed in eternity
I would have to believe in it now,
For if I truly felt you had gone forever
And I could never reach you again:
I would die.
Helen Charlotte Hill

A Winter's Scene

A snowy white blanket has covered the ground,
Little robin redbreast roaming around.
Houses with beautiful snow-covered roofs,
People say they can see reindeers' hooves.
All the bushes are covered in snow,
A thick creamy blanket just like dough,
But it's all a gift from heaven above,
It shows a token of God's perfect love.
Joanne Tinker

Liquid Assurance

Collision directed by physical crash
listening images make thy sense
be gone by faith allow with splash
bless become, forth come your allowance
breath spontaneous by ice reflections
I am thee confusion with particle silence
control by diluting thy pleasures
be strong to divert false humour
produce hearts of texture pure
melting moments design for sure

Allow responses admit thy time
smile yearly through, it may inflict
encourage thy nature, be reckless
questions arise, answers, capsize
voted acquaintances trial your world
story dead or alive, honesty is sense
torment is often asked upon
peace is what you accomplish
name thy flavour, I shall convince
thyne I bequest an unusual substance
Allyson Barrass

Paradise

Paradise is where I would like to be,
Living like a bird, simple and free.
Where the skies are clear and very blue,
And the sun always shines on you.

Everyone moving at a steady pace,
Life for living and not a race.
Harmony being the name of the game,
Everyone equal, everyone the same.

Sleeping safely in bed every night,
No burglars giving anyone a fright.
Walking the streets much at ease,
And doing exactly as you please.

No fighting, no need to make amends,
Living together as inseparable friends.
Starvation and poverty, words from the past,
Universal peace that will definitely last.

What I am looking for, I may not find,
As all I really want is peace of mind,
To be allowed to do as I did before,
And live in paradise forevermore.
Jean Hardie

Untitled

His golden coat is covered in spots
loads and loads of little black dots,
In Africa or Asia he can be found
roaming and hunting all over the ground.
He's a big cat, with a long thin tail
a little bigger in body, if an adult male,
He prowls along the plains
each defenceless victim he slays
Have you guessed what I am?
A predator of man.
Anne Small

" You Are "

You are my reason, my life, my love,
Lodged in my soul like a hand fits a glove,
I think of you every minute of each hour,
And from the ground grows the most beautiful flower,
Like I've never seen in all my years of living,
And through the blur of tears that are welling,
In my eyes, my happiness I cannot disguise,
While feeling like this,
A single beat my heart just missed,
But my heart is warm, like the warmth of that glove,
Remember, you are my reason, my life, my love...
Karen G. Hall

Earth — Are You There?

Small blue sphere, floating in the void black of space,
Locked within your realm where occult mysteries take place.
We who call from distant galaxy
Seeking tactile minds, despair of thee.
Engendered by your perfect post relating to the sun,
All that we have gathered speaks of joy; continuum.

Almost at the spiral tip; beautiful and blue
Within young aeons of time we filter past you.
Respond if you are there and we will stay
And talk with you whilst closing; a few light years away.
Radio wave, if you are there, constantly we try,
Do you have wave congestion, causing messages faint... to die?

Once we tried a laser beam with tidings to relate.
Did that also fade and die — or did an early warning activate?
Subliminally, we offered love — friendly mind to friendly mind.
Did warlike thoughts obscure receptive senses, so to blind?
Or is the Earth a private world, heading for a fall?
Perhaps again, we have it wrong — there's no-one there at all!

Brian W. Drew

Freedom

In winter I look outside,
lonely and lost in the big grey sky.
In winter I look outside, sad and frightened,
locked away like a prisoner in a dark foreboding cage.
My tears are in the rain.

With aching arms I reach to the sky,
longing for the warmth of the sun,
wrapping itself like a cloak around me.
I sit in my cage and close my eyes
and all of a sudden, I hear a thousand voices calling me.

I get to my feet.
The moment has arrived.
Like a knight in shining armour
Spring has come to save me from my loneliness.
My cage crumbles to the ground and I am free.

With wild freedom I take to the sky.
Like a soaring eagle looking for its prey,
I look for the beauty and happiness
I have been waiting for.
Nothing can lock me up again for I am free.

Christy Pearson

War

Destruction, disasters, everything in tatters
loss of lives, loss of homes, of everything that matters
dust and rubble. Metal and wood, window frames and bricks
furniture like tables and chairs reduced to a pile of sticks
how can there be such evil. In countries that could be free
all it will do is destroy everyone and leave them in poverty
boys being men, before their time, leaving their youth behind
not knowing what their going to see, not knowing what they will find
men who are laying scattered around, trying to catch their breath
some who were sent to come home safe, some who were
sent to their death.

Diana Colling

The Smile

My first grandchild, three months old,
Looking at me with quiet appraisal;
Candid eyes searching for sincerity;
We smiled at each other, man to man:
My smile, shaped by the harvest of my years;
His smile, melting my heart with its warmth;
An innocent, guileless, penetrating sunbeam,
That reached the corners of my dusty heart:
Touching neglected springs of hope and trust
Part frozen by the hoary hand of time:
Little David; mightier than myself
For all my strength and manhood: I've grown weak;
But get my strength back in a baby's smile

Alexander K. Sampson

Look At Me

You walk past me,
Look at me, in disgrace
Because I have no job, no home,
You don't see beyond my face.

You don't see what's behind my eyes,
Don't know what I've been through,
What pain and suffering that I have seen,
The things I've had to do.

To you I'm just a nothing,
Make streets look so untidy.
You don't want to think life's like this,
So you dismiss as you walk by me.

Next time take a look,
Look long and hard at me.
I'm the truth of what life is like,
It's not how I want to be.

I have no place I can call my own,
Except the doorway of a shop.
I plead and pray that soon one day,
Homelessness will stop.

Jasmin Croft

The Last Straw

They were going on Safari
Looking forward to the trip
They ignored the poor old camel
He was just a desert ship

They piled on luggage and refreshments
And passengers galore
And lots of little trinkets
Till they couldn't manage more.

The camel wasn't worried
He took it in his stride
He was always overloaded
When he took them for this ride.

Soon everything was ready
The sun was really hot —
When a lady on his back cried out —
"Stop, there's something I forgot"
"Please pass me up my straw hat
I need it on my head"
This really was the last straw
And the Camel fell down dead!

June Ball

The Dawning Of A New Day

Our children are lost in a maze,
 Looking, searching, not finding;
Because those who would be their teachers,
 Are also lost themselves.

So much suffering and pain inflicted,
 By those who are "doing their best",
Damage that breaks hearts and wills,
 Until even the body gives in.

Yet there is an answer in friendship,
 There are people who really care,
They dare to be honest and loving,
 They bring you out of despair.

In the compassion of others,
 You see God at work in Himself,
And realize that just as He lives in them,
 He can come and live in you as well.

So let go of the pain and the past,
 Accept all that was given or taken,
Walk forward with spirited steps,
 Cast away self and welcome new life — awaken!

Kazimiera Krzyworaczka

Imperfect Present

Let me be, let me go, let me out
loose me from the suffering and grief
deny the earth its sting of death
deny it its cruelty
deny impossibility
or let me inhabit another world
let all persons grace its grass
let love be the sole gesture word
flowers the only offering
let a smile mean that all is love
let love mean that all is a smile
let all who face the well of life know
one must love all to drink
let lesser lovers love less where
suffering and grief exist
loose me from the suffering and grief
let me be let me go let me out
Alastair Marshall

Love

Ceaselessly caring from morning 'til night
Love flames for ever, so clear and so bright.
True love knows no bounds, or near or far,
For love is the Morning and the Evening Star.

Love is unstinting and grudges nought
Can never be traded, or sold or bought.
Not of the head, but of heart and soul,
Offering not part, but giving the whole.

If perfect love is to be the prize
The cost is a lifetime of sacrifice.
Yet if all is given, and all is received
The paradox of love Entire is achieved

As the first and the last in the heavens afar,
So love is the Morning and the Evening Star.
Jessie Edwards

" Universal Love "

LOVE is the Sunshine upon your face,
LOVE is a friend, in a lonely place,
LOVE is a small trusting hand in yours,
LOVE is the word that opens doors,

LOVE is the answer, when you're lost,
LOVE is the ocean upon which dreams are tossed,
LOVE grows with feeding, from strength to strength.
LOVE is a cord of endless length.

LOVE is what we need, in order to survive,
LOVE is the food that keeps us alive,
LOVE costs you nothing, but gives more pleasure than gold,
LOVE is freedom, which cannot be bought or sold.

LOVE is the knowledge that you're part of the whole,
LOVE is at home when it touches the soul.
LOVE is the fountain of wisdom and youth,
LOVE in the end, is the only truth.
Anita West

An Apology

Life is confusing
Love is blind
Feelings are powerful
Reality — so difficult to find
Fantasy — my other world
One of which I've been hiding within
You are my only true friend
I am the plant and you are the sun
I am the water, you are my land
My only wish is that time would turn back
To when love and hate meant the same
Then your hate for me would be desire
A poem always says something important
This one says — I'm sorry.
Leanne Sollis

Love Is Grand

Love is holding someone's hand,
Love is when you understand,
A gentle kiss, a longing touch,
Loving someone means so much.

The feelings that you feel inside
Are whirled around your body and mind,
Love is priceless, but sometimes blue,
Love can make your dreams come true.

Sharing and companionship become a part of Love,
Cupid's up there shooting with his arrows far above,
Fun and laughter fill the air
Love is when your love is there.
Laura Thurley

Out Of The Clouds

Midget channels from the top
Made noiseless speed with every spot
As crystal pear-drops plopped on plop.

Stainless on the shimmering pane
A'wash as nature's generous rain
Sent globules down with rapid gain
And heedless joy, which was quite plain!

When out of the clouds a beam appeared
Which said 'no more', and the rain just cleared!
In its place a gleaming hue
Spread out across the mighty blue.

A rainbow was born
Which grew and grew
As sun shone through
The draining few.
Barbara Voss

All Kinds Of Love

True Love — Spirit of the Heart,
Magical emotion which can tear one's world apart,
Eternal devotion — tender and true
Caring, unbelievable, treasuring you!
Love for a woman or maybe a man,
Love for a child — since the world first began.
Love for God's creatures, furry and small,
The sea and the mountains and wild birds call.
Love of the flowers, the trees and the sky,
Love just of living as time passes by.
The Stars in the heavens sparkling and bright
Reflect in the eyes which shine with love's light.
The love and the passions of youthful dreams,
Turn to gold embers where aged ones lean.
But forget not our Maker and answer his call
For He gave unto us the greatest love of them all.
Enid Hewitt

A Name

A name is but a name
Make of it what you will
A name is what charts our progress through this world
From our birth unto our death
From the cradle to the grave
Be the name great or be it small
Be it linked to great richness or great poverty
Be it belonging to a famous family or to the most humble of beginnings
A name is what, and most importantly who, you are
And make of it what you will
For it is you who must seize the day
Make your mark upon this earth
For when we mere mortals are but dust
It is our name that is our marker, our monument
And remember a name is but a name
Make of it what you will..
David Davies

Friendship

Friendship is a treasure that
makes you comfortable and
comfortable to be with.
It feels good.
If you have to rearrange your life for
a friend, then you are not
comfortable and it's not your
true self.
Being comfortable with your self
and your friends is when hesitation
does not exist and comfort
takes over.

Angela Meja

The Forest Cries

The wind softly blows its branches to and fro,
Making the tree seem to bend.

Men with horrible axes and saws cut the tree,
So it can't mend.

The forest wakes up in the morning, calling
For help, it says,
"Help us trees, we are dying."
But the world, can't hear it, for the world
Is crying so loud.

While our forests are dying, no one hears them crying,
"Is there nothing on earth that can be done?"

Katie Jayne Mythen

Requiem

A battle raged that summer day
Man killed man, face to face;
Each believing in his own creed and race
Until silent was that bloody place.

No priest came to bless the slain or house the dead
Looters came with cart and dray;
Pillaged, divided, then drove away
The poor bones lay.

Carrion with beak and claw ripped and tore,
Rain washed the blood away;
Ice coffined them, snow covered
in sure embrace.

Spring brought soft green grass and flowers,
Curlew called, mate to mate;
Hares chased the hours away
in amorous ecstasy.

The plain was vibrant with noisy life
and they, their bones sunk deep into clay,
No noise make they.

Enid Parkin

Sea Killing (Hong Kong, The Philippines)

A land once free
Many leagues to see
The pulse of rosette
Coral; poisons grate,

Wreathes of flittering
Light flowering, glittering
Life, once mysterious.
In human agony, perilous.

The mindless beast
Would feast
On these, not the least,
From West to East.

Even if he die from
Gluttony obscene and long gone
The forests of the nether world:
The beauty in Being there unfurled.

John Amsden

Words Unspoken

Many words have remained unspoken,
Many times my heart has been broken.
I wish I had the courage to express
    the warmth and tenderness I feel for you.
Bottled up inside of me are words that will not come easily.
If I had accepted just one kiss
You would have understood all this, and words would not be
needed.
God knows I've tried to hide my emotion
Thinking it for the best.
But now you have seen through that ocean of heartache and
emptiness.
Together we have learned to accept the memory of a
    secret kept deep within our hearts.
Now all we have to remain
Is time to heal the pain.

Julia Sladden

Loss

I have lost a sand quarry
Martins swooping sharply on the wind
Now it's a green desert
The memories are buried beneath the grass.

I have lost a stone quarry
Veined with quartz, mysterious depths
Of water. Divers with derring-do.
They've buried the place of my first kiss

I have lost a bronze ring
Given to me only because I admired it.
Someone else did too.
A sweet girl, but forgetful.

I have lost my mother, my brother,
Sundry friends, to death
And now, mugged, robbed, violated,
I have lost my sense of invincibility.

My innocence... For what that's worth

Aiden Connolly

A Dream of a Garden

A man who does not fear the world
May not be loved at all,
On the merriest heart can love not care,
Not in the meanest, smallest soul.

Must a dream be lost of precious time?
For men can love but in short space,
Man is gone too long in death,
In the perished water's oppressive face.

Of men who do not love of fortune,
Can they love with honest part,
Who care not for their brother's failure,
A Mother's pleasing in their heart?

On the wings of time fly troubled sinners,
May they wash in laboured love,
Can a fool who would gain a garden,
Find a peace in past life above?

Dorothy Iris Pearson

The Magpies And The Daffodils

March, the beginning of newness, of rebirth,
Magpies, dancing in the fresh green grass,
the sweet smell,
Makes us feel good to be alive.
I see nature start to live again,
This makes *me* want to do the same,
The feeling of warm sunlight,
Cuts across my face,
I feel contentment in my shattered soul,
And hope grows from the heart I own,
Like daffodils in the magpies' grass.

Ian G. Forster

Hidden Feelings

Maybe he's old, maybe he's slow,
Maybe a face I don't know.
Sometimes it lights up, without a frown,
Sometimes a little dim, as though the
Lights have been turned down.

Maybe he's warm, maybe he's kind,
Maybe loving him, I don't mind.
Sometimes a little cold, as though his
True feelings have been put onto hold.

Lines of deep impressions furrow his face.
Years of hard living have taken its place.
Yet beneath his tawny rough skin,
Truly, is a man who loves all his kin.
Dorothy Ann Gibson

Lottery Lot

I buy a ticket every week
Maybe I will get a winning streak
All week I dream of what I will do
When I win a million or two
Help the homeless, buy a horse
A trip around the world of course
My house of dreams, a thousand schemes
The way it would look, the garden nook
My family made secure for life
No more worry, or strife
Saturday comes, and the numbers are drawn.
There I am a sitting prawn.
Once again luck has passed me by
Oh well. it was only pie in the sky.
Havis Bakhurst

Media Views!!

No more news for me
Media views or T.V.
Population, disasters, oil slicks
And camera tricks
Bring back beauty, silence and harmony

Stop spoiling and oiling
Our daily toiling
Bring back peace and
Cease the environmental lease

No more birds in oil
To spoil our soul
Please oh please
Bring back beauty, silence and harmony
Christine Jones

Menage A Trois (Unholy Trinity)

"Menage a trois", he said to me on a sultry day in June
Menage a trois? I looked bemused, was this a melodious tune?
And as we sat in the meadow sweet, beside the holy Gave
He spoke of lusts and fetishes and just what he thought of love.
I'd spent the year in bed so sick, lonely and afraid
I'd spent the year in hospitals where I'd constantly prayed.
Not once he wrote, no card he sent, as he propped up a Dublin bar
and as I looked into his azure eyes he said 'menage a trois'.
'Menage a trois' he sang his tune in the meadow holy
Menage a trois, I repeated his words, did he think me so very lowly?
For I only played the game of truth although I knew I'd fail
I felt like Christ upon the cross stigmata'd by those nails.
No pleasure could I ever get from playing the game of cheat
I sacrificed ego and truly preferred to wash my enemy's feet.
The game of pain, can it produce some good or just a jealous desire?
Are the dice loaded with seeds of truth or flames of tormenting fire?
... So I missed my time of heaven on earth, a time of prayer and love
I felt deprived and cheated by the one who rules from above.
If I'd been well, if only Lourdes wasn't quite so very far
If only there'd been a sweet kiss goodbye... but he just said
'Menage a trois'.
Elaine Pomm

A Remembered Place

Fluids exchanged in the throws of adult passion
Metamorphosis into a connection,
A unison developed by a vanquished omnipotence,
These pink thermal walls
Pulsate,
Each tremor retracts and reverses unremittingly,
A confused buoy floats in
Amniotic ecstasy
Unidentifiable, oblivious of individuality
It trusts, convinced of its protective oneness.

The journey begins,
Its tumultuous exit into a cruel alien sphere,
Cries echo endlessly,
Piercing the sterility
Whilst optimism throbs in a mother's breast,
The persistent evolution of life,
Makes us harken to that,
Remembered place,
The pink humming sanctuary we call
Home.
Caroline Hardwick

Winter Nights

Sun sets with blood streaked eyes
Moon rise opposing sky
Spinning turning, rolling spheres
Witness the wonder with glistening tears.

Colour, shapes in great profusion
Is it nought but grand illusion?
Feel it, solid, movement, certain
Rain beats down a beaded curtain

Wind and seas swish and blow
Sometimes quick. Sometimes slow.
Tripping falling through the jumble
Must those thunder clouds above so rumble

Climate change to winter white
A blanket stretches out of sight
Crisp and clean with tingling touch
Pregnant stillness holds so much

Dark shapes lengthen, snow turns grey
Night time deepens, shadows sway.
Quiet now for all is still
Creeping claw marks scratch the hill
Arthur Capenhurst

I Remember

The voice whispers devour it, devour it all,
like a recurring dream
I remember, I remember, I remember it all

Go away, go away the voice screams inside,
so we can be alone
I remember, I remember, I remember it all

The rest is a blur as I devour, on and on,
lacking all self control
I remember, I remember, I remember it all

Now I'm in control, the voice whispers inside,
let it out, let it out
I remember, I remember, I remember it all

You hold out your arms and tell me it's fine
I remember, I remember, I remember it all

Don't let them in, it's our little secret I recall
mustn't tell, mustn't tell
I remember, I remember, I remember it all

The voice starts to fade and I hold out my arms
Yes, I tell them it's fine
I remember, I remember, I remember it all
Deborah Hanley

You, Through My Eyes

Bush of gold and flame of red upon a pedestal of immense knowledge
Moon with lagoon crevasses, decrease with constant cheshire
Love radiated from the inner core
External, beautiful subject emits soul.
Unearthed pyramid
Bull powerful torso verses digits masterly in control.
Stock of steel and intrinsic air, ever growth of amour.
Projections, tree like woodiness, extremes to that of ice,
   hard and grand
Inquisitive hemisphere of understanding and sensitivity
The core of my life and sanity
Lisa Anderson

Ocean Song

Sun dancing on the surface,
moon's reflection on the shore.
Hypnotic rolling of the surf,
like a magnet I am drawn

I sit and stare in silent wonder,
bewitched upon the shore.
The sea so gentle, so beguiling,
yet so dangerous and exciting.

Beneath the tranquil surface life sustained,
as in a womb.
Through the storm its wrath incurred,
it becomes a living tomb.

I have felt its delicate caress,
upon my mortal flesh.
I have felt its might and power,
take my every breath.

Still I sit in silent wonder,
Transfixed in total awe.
Ocean song so dangerous, so exciting,
yet so gentle and inviting.
Juliet Osborne

War Cries

As the war machine shifts into gear,
Mother's children flee in fear
From promises it won't happen here
Though once again they lied
The soldiers once triumphant cry
Lies buried in the sand.

The guns of arrogance and pride
Rage through the months from side to side.
Till there's no place for men to hide
And no place to call home
No God to pray, to end it all.
Heart broken, now "He's" gone.

A wife, a mother sits at home,
her heart primed ready by the phone.
Waiting; has he lost or won?
Willing him to survive
While piece by piece she dies herself
To keep her son alive.
Ian F. Robertson

I Trust The Lord

In avail, I trusted the man.
My friends, blood relatives and companions
Stand against me.
I need nothing in them anymore.

Yea, I need the Lord Jehovah only.
He is the only one I trust.
His love endures forever.

He darts off hot arrows aimed at me.
I will fear no more for his love sealed my trust.
He will never ever leave me alone.
I will enjoy his security for me on the land forever.
Davison Mathonsi

Washed By The Ebb Tide

Pensive reflections, that weathered face
Moving images, mirrored through time
Pain is etched there now
Transmitting its effect to mine.

Why should I care and be so moved?
Desertion, separation, uncaring situation
Not yet from memory removed;
But recollections, long submerged, of
Happy loving times persistently emerge.

How can one sustain an angry heart
Towards the helpless, hapless, hopeless?
Bitterness is lifeless, sadness, pointless
Worn away by time and present compassion.

Was that a flicker of a smile, I ask —
Contentment — that shows he knows?

Becoming sustained, certain, through a loving look
A tranquil, special, all knowing moment —
Changing to fixity?
John L. Wilkins

A Poet Born?

I was a child awakened by a storm
my cat was heard crying outside forlorn,
and when my mother would not heed my plea
by letting my pet back inside with me
My frustrations I vented out in rhyme
the poet inside me was born, aged nine.
That moment I've remembered through the years
still using verse to show my joys or fears.
This option gives freedom for thoughts to fly
above all else like a bird in the sky.
Sometimes the words just flow straight from the heart
but others they stumble right from the start.
Myself I lose while sorting what I feel
and writing it down makes it very real.
The gift of expression is there to use
be it in prose or verse I'm free to choose.
That's part of the challenge of poetry,
finding out individuality.
When I write poems they make me feel whole
because they are me and come from my soul.
Linda Bagnall

The Golden Pathway

As I lay stretched upon the sands
My eyes were filmed with shimmering bands
And then the ringing in my ears
Took me from these present years.

A golden pathway led me where
Sounds of music, strange and rare
Drew me through a cloudy way,
Violet, rose and blue and grey.

Sweet perfume filled the sacred air
Flowers blossomed everywhere.
Creatures frolicked in the light.
It was a truly awesome sight.

Then, down the path, I saw perfected
The world on which I've oft reflected
Where peace and love forever is,
All people one, united — bliss!'

Then quite soon I was awake,
My sandy clothes I had to shake.
Gone was the ringing in my ears
And I was back in present years.
June Relph Roberts

To My Dear Mother

The phone-call came from Cavan that you hadn't long to go
My family and I we rushed out to Heathrow,
We caught a plane to Dublin, it was a lonely flight
And then we drove to Cavan at high speed through the night.
We prayed that we would make it just to say a last Goodbye
You spoke to us and told us that you were going to die
And then you asked for 'something' to try and ease the pain
The injection it was given and you never spoke again.

The sidewalks of the streets were lined with cars along the way
As we drove behind your coffin on that sad and dreary day
We took you past that winding lane which to your home did lead
But your dying wish to go back there, alas! we could not heed.
We took you to the chapel where fifty years before
You and Dad so lovingly your wedding vows had swore
We knelt beside your coffin all your family
Where five weeks before you had knelt with us
For your "Golden Jubilee".

Christina McGuire

Sixty Plus

Now, we've been married for sixty-odd years,
My goodness, just how time has flown.
We've shared lots of laughter, as well as tears,
In this, I don't think we're alone.

Life has been good to us, that's what I say,
And my spouse just thinks the same too.
We do have our quarrels, but then — each day
We make up, that's just what we do.

There's one thing we've learned — it's never to say,
"It's too late to make up anew".
It makes good sense at the end of the day
To remember — you vowed to be true.

So look to the future with hope, and say,
"Things are not as bad as they seem".
If we stick together, in work, and in play
Life will pass, just like a good dream.

John Jardine

The Inner Ear

When I remember my early years
My Grandma's philosophy rings in my ears,
"Look to the future Love, never look back,
What's done is done, so try not to lack
The visions, the programme of future endeavour,
Sparkle with hope and be negative never,
Be led by your instinct and when you're unclear,
Wait for instruction from your inner ear.
It was there before birth, it's the role you must play,
Mapped out and planned for each single day.
It's in tune with your head and more with your heart,
It tells you when to stop then spurs you to start
Up again, on again, all through your life,
Try not to panic through periods of strife,
You'll be guided along, if you listen intent
To the voice in your heart, and when your life's spent,
You will judge yourself on how well you heard,
And how you applied it and how much you cared,
And if you helped others to play out their role,
Because they are you, we're all part of one soul.

Brenda Brookes

Two Beacons

Flames dance and hearts sing but not for me today
My world has sank so very low and that you both can see
You give me hope, you spur me on, how wonderful you are
In you both there shines a light for me, our ever hopeful star
The beacons that show the way, that say I will come through,
And should I fall along this path, you'll pick me up that's true
So should you ever need me with my shoulder for your heart.
I'll take your hurt and pain away, as you've done from the start
Our friendship means so very much, on that we all agree
Strong in roots just like the oak, indestructible like we three.

Joanna Wedderburn

To A Friend

He'll always be there in my hour of darkness,
My hand he will hold when I lose the path,
My listener he will be when I need to speak.
Through rough times and good times he'll be my strength,
My guide he will be when I am unsure,
My comforter he will be in times of sorrow.
In the darkest night he will be inside my soul,
My fears he will ward off with his love,
My tears he will dry when I am scared.
In return I will give all that I can to him,
My love when he is lonely,
My arms to hold him when he is sad.
I will do my best for him as he does for me,
My time I will give when he needs me,
My advice when he is lost or confused.
I may not always do well enough to help but I'll be there,
As long as I still have life,
As long as he wants me to be there.
We have an everlasting partnership.
He is my friend.

Katharine Simmonds

'I Walked At Morn'

Welcome Spring, to thee my heart doth sing,
my happy feet caressed in the scented grasses pressed
far from the hum of life's harrowed drum of woe
I walked at morn to great the sun and fill my heart aglow

I seem to hear a murmur from the endless
winding stream, she alone knows the secret how
to catch a sunlight gleam.
In a moment all is hushed for human feet
to tread, the fairy looms are silent in the yellow covered bed.
Above the lark doth treble notes bursting close to heaven's gates,
the verdant rosebud shyly peeps while Mother Nature waits
Here I am, queen of all I see, here with the mirth-filled music
in my ear, Want there is none to find a myriad of song
so I caught the happy light as I walked at morn.

Janet Simpson

Sonnet

I cannot write poetry, though I often try.
My head filled with flowing observations
On life and love, I reach for my pen ready to tap the vein,
Create myself that from which I derive such pleasure.
But alas, I am destined never to be the dying swan,
Only the humble rose thrower.
The power in placing those few words
Like a sculptor moulding beauty from limited clay,
An artist positioning light and colour.
How I revel in metaphor and simile,
Wallow in the sound of spoken sensation.
I have my consolation: Reciting sonnets in the bath.
My tiled haven echoes with undulating appreciation,
Mine to love, just not my personal creation.

Loraine Anderson

Kaleidoscope

Pattern, colours, interacting,
   Moving shapes — expanding — contracting.
    Ever changing,
Constantly re-arranging,
   Mirroring life,
Reflecting rainbow hues,
    Yellows, red, greens, blues.
   Always vivid, always bright.
An optical delight,
   Colouring life.

I'm transported from my gloom,
Within the confines of my room,
   You show me a rainbow without the rain,
  Giving me hope
   To try again.

Brenda Faruque

Life's Blessings

It came to me softly or so it did seem
My life flashed before me one night in a dream
A child about three with black curly hair,
And a brother just two, so blonde and so fair
Life was so happy and so full of love
Then god took our mother to heaven above.

As the years travel on, our father, he wed
Our life changed from love to a feeling of dread
As I look through the haze and into the light
I see a young bride, her groom by her side
Love has returned to a life that had none
Now we've been blessed with a daughter and son

As I move through the years I see them both wed
I know they are happy, a few tears I shed
Our children have grown and are with us no longer
But the love that we share grows stronger and stronger
All the gold in the world could never replace
The love of your family or just an embrace,
To show that they love you and that love in return
Is just your life's blessings all rolled into one.

Anne Burnett

What Ever Happened To The Sun?

What ever happened to the sun?
My life has only just begun
Yet as I lie here in the dark night
I wonder who decided to take all my fun,
It's cold and dark, a lonely place
I hide away won't show my face,
Then it starts it just won't stop
Over and over oh please make it stop,
And then silence, I rush to the door
Turn on the light and look for him,
He smiles at me with a pure undying love
My tiny son, my precious son
Suddenly it's light so very bright,
And as I hold him in my arms I know,
That my joy and fun have only just begun.

Justine Vallis

Love, Just A Word

Love, just a word
My love said before he died.
In my heart I knew what he meant.
One word could not describe the feelings felt,
The wonderment of ever having met.
The sheer joy and lightheartedness of being together
The passions shared, so strong,
Like a physical pain.
Never to be felt again.
For death came along
And with one fell swoop
Changed these emotions
To utter desolation and despair.
A deep and hungry longing for a touch, a final look
Or feel his breath upon my hair
All these feelings caused by just a word called love.

Jeanette Black

Negative Mind

I sit and stare into nothing,
My thoughts capturing my mind and destroying it in their coils,
My emotions have entwined themselves around me,
I'm left with a mass of painful thoughts that never go away.

My positive mind has crumbled to dust,
The negative takes the triumph,
No more happy thoughts just miserable sorrow,
The self esteem has taken flight.

As the days go on the negative thoughts breed,
But I bravely fight on though the war,
The negative mind has won I think but I will carry on.

Clare Freeman

February In North Devon

As I walk along the tracks and lanes
My mind reflects on many things.
Heavy rain showers in the night
Turn to sunshine at crack of light.
The wet and warmth aid man's toil to raise his crops
May they be wheat, barley, oats or hops.
The raging torrent soon becomes a babbling brook
As the water tumbles o'er the pebbles, on its way
To join the sea in some far off bay.
The yellow hazel catkins bounce with ease
As their boughs sway in the gentle breeze.
The birds all chirp and sing
Knowing that winter will soon turn to spring.
The glint of the sun plays shadows on the trunks of trees
As lichen and moss sap energy from their barks.
Soon to be heard are the call of larks
As they wheel and hover o'er moor and lea.
But none of this would occur in course
Were it not for an unseen divine Force.

Jenny Scales

There's No Such Thing As Monsters

"There's no such thing as monsters",
my mummy had said,
but what's this thing lurking
from under my bed?
It isn't my teddy, I have him right here.
It isn't the dolly that sits on my chair.
It isn't a mouse,
it's too big for that.
What do you think? It could be a rat!
Maybe a snake or a speckly old frog
or something disgusting brought in by the dog.
I crept my hand under
and got such as shock,
when I pulled out my 'Monster',
a fluff covered sock.

Linda M. Tyldesley

Vic's Story

My legs don't work, I'm wheelchair bound.
My name's as old as this century
I have to ask for simple things,
For toilet, books, bath, food, T.V.

On summer days, I'm parked outside
The sea-side home that's all I know.
But this frail shell still holds a mind
As fresh and sharp as years ago.

So, though you see me as I am,
Just think of how I used to be
I was so strong, and fit and tough
The young girls loved to flirt with me.

Young girls with names like Phylis, Glad,
And lovely Peg with sun-kissed face,
Are they now dead, or do they sit
In some sparse room, in some bleak place?

So as I sit, with fag and rug
And think of days forever past.
Don't think that I am less than you.
I was you once — youth does not last.

Lynda Shaw

My Poems

My Poems are my sense of release.
My stress and tension they turn to peace.
I'm not the sort to rant and rave.
I'm not that strong... I'm not that brave.
When storm clouds brew and want to rage
I turn spoken word into written page.

Christine C. Stevens

Depression

When he died my strength and tolerance died with him.
My patience went and feelings gone forever
There is no reason to live, it's gone, things will never be the same.
Life is empty nothing is important. No point.
Just try to get the children to a reasonable age to live a normal life
It's hard.
Have to carry on as long as I can, don't show too much how hard it is
Sometimes it really becomes difficult. Sometimes I wish it were over.
I laugh and play and try to show everyone how I love living, but,
Deep down I have no reason.
Each day becomes a mountain which seems harder to climb
and I don't know if I have the strength to continue.
I know I have to try for just a few years more. I will do it.
I will battle on for as long as I have to.
But please understand when it's done, I will go.
I'm not sure how yet, but although I know life is beautiful
There comes a time when life is pointless and the struggle just
becomes too much.
   Jo Fountain

Horses Of The Skies

Noble, enduring, hard working too.
My soul agonizes what this world has
done to you.
The fire spread so quickly, in the stable you
called home.
You and your companions were frightened
and alone.
Perhaps a higher power comforted and calmed.
Set your spirit free, it was just your body that
was harmed.
Maybe someone came to guide you, through the
mist to this other plane.
Someone oh so gentle, to wash away your pain.
I'll see your tossing halo in every golden sunset;
your sheerness when clouds are flying high.
Be happy and contented, my horses in the sky.
   Julia Pledge

Exile's Dream Of Home

As I lay beneath a burning sun in a land so stark and bare
My thoughts were of my homeland and its beauty beyond compare
Where flowers come to greet me gently nodding in the breeze
With trees' great branches sighing like ships on stormy seas
The Kaleidoscope of colour, predominantly green
The trilling of a skylark whose nest cannot be seen
I heard the cattle lowing as lazily they roam
And the clip-clop of the horses wearily wending home
I saw the richness of the earth newly turned to the sun
I heard the whistling of a farmer's boy, his work nearly done
Children's voices echoing merrily across the sky
Full of the joy of living, no cares for you or I
The gently sloping hillside, fields of golden corn
The beauty of each sunset, the kiss of each new morn
Who could wish for better mistress, or friend so true and rare
Than this our island homeland with its beauty e'er so fair

   Wherever I go on land or sea
   No matter where I roam
   Your memories live within my heart
   "England my Island Home"
   Albert H. Gormley

Reflections

Cowslips in the meadow,
Plaited golden hair,
Daisy chains, buttercups, dandelions fair,
Woven fields of summer,
Bluebell scented haze,
Frogspawn jelly diamond bright,
Childhood, carefree, maze,
Laughter, blushing innocence,
Simple, harmless pleasure,
Mirrored in the pools of life,
Reflections last forever.
   Eileen Brown

Life In The Library

I'm an educated book-worm and my home is in a book,
My vocabulary's stunningly superb.
Having wriggled through the first page with its copy-righted date,
I've consumed some definitions and a verb.
From adjectives and pronouns I have reached pronunciation
Then carried on to origins of words.
I have tackled prepositions, on abbreviations dined
And chewed on what the alphabet affords.
In the Oxford dictionary, starting with the letter A,
Three thousand A4 pages, more or less;
For a tiny, short-legged insect it's a long exhausting hike;
If I manage to get through to the letter S,
My performance might be listed in another sort of book
As the fattest, longest living of my clan.
Should you find it not recorded in the Guiness book, you'll know
I've been swatted, spotted by a crossword fan.
   Howard Cooke

Remember Me With Laughter

Do not go to silent fields full of marble stones
Names carved in cold precision by strangers.
My empty body shell may lie in that field with others
My dancing spirit lives on wherever you are.
The dark field is not familiar to me.
Sadness you feel leaves my spirit static and dull,
I long for you to be in places where we had fun
You cared for me, my parent, and it will always count.
Please leave this quiet place where darkness grows,
Go to the classroom where my picture hangs still
Through you and with you we will laugh together.
No one will know except the special ones
that I am with you still. Please take me there.
I touch your cheek trying to tell you I am happy
There is so much love now around me. Why be sad?
You must laugh again with those still close on earth.
Too soon we will meet again, you have my promise.
I was young, still a child when I left you suddenly
Now I am wiser even than my parents, and so loved.
My Father in heaven cares for me now;
he will love you too if you let him.
   Eileen Fry

Haunting

Trapped in a world of no reconciliation,
Needing is the only treasure.
Pictures are locked away,
Far from any actual pleasure.

The feeling is increasing.
No breaks of glass,
Or noise through jealousy,
Will stop the world from turning,
Or the lines from rolling.

Nothing can break the boundaries in this way.
There has to be another thought.
Another game.
Something to free the prisoner,
And its heartfelt fear.

Maybe then the haunting will stop.
Maybe then the doors will open,
The windows will open,
And the path can be cleared.
   Claire Elizabeth Kelly

Esmerelda

Suddenly it pleases her to place an embellished purr
Pinked like the edge of a chorister's ruff upon my curling ear.
Now is the time for nature's facial scrub, as skin on skin
I'm hooked like velcro cleaving to her vibrant rasping thrill.
Her life, released in song, throbs for her and me and her
While I inhale the pot-pourri of rain-brushed herbs in fur.
   Catherine Beer

The Killer Whale's Last Storm

There are two killer whales happy in the calm sea,
Neither has met but they both know each other.
One has a problem, he is slowly dying,
The other is sad for she's losing touch
With what she can see in her mind.
The bond between them is slowly breaking.
The storm is starting to thrash against them
As they rise to the surface to breathe.
The gentle giants are pushed together by the storm,
They embrace in their own special whale way.
As soon as they touch the storm subsides.
The killer whales knew in their hearts
It was destiny that brought them together at last.
The sun is now shining, the clouds have moved away.
The male whale is gone, but still two remain.
Their love now lives on in the calf that they made.
Claire Foxall

Riches

What are these riches they talk about
never having had any,
Yet my life as rich as I feel
as I see the sun shine,
feel the earth beneath my feet.
See the raindrops with so much splendour
buds blossom in the spring,
as if from nowhere.
These are my riches I feel
I touch, I smell, I see.
My heart fills with delight
when I hear all the good news
so this I write, of all the riches,
that fill me with so much pleasure.
Open your sights to the treasure
of the riches that are all around,
don't be so blind that you cannot see
what is really before you.
Laura Sorrell

Untitled

Stroppy moods bouts of shouting
never trusting always doubting
tempers flaring no reason apparent
to me I see you as transparent
but I'm still here while you chastise
pleasure is frail while it laughs it dies
A breath of wind from the wings of madness
passed over me today causing sadness
am I being deceived well
or choose this hell?
I only know that summer once sang
but sings no more since all this began
hope is disappointment postponed
with happiness loaned
known by the wise
so I open my eyes
my tears bleed
and I concede.
Kathy Gray

Morning Mist

The silence of the morning mist,
No sound to break the peace
Remnants of a peaceful night,
Still remain, as shadows cease.
With the coming of the dawn,
Shafts of lights stream though the sky.
God's gift of yet another day,
As the early sunrise finds its way.
Gentle is the mist that shrouds above the trees,
Softly caressing freshly budding leaves,
Its ghostly shape that swirls around,
Through gossamer webs, without a sound,
In the morning light, will slip away,
To return again, on another day.
Adrienne Davies

First Born

You plan a family that's the norm
Next you know the child is born
The nappies and the sleepless nights
You sometimes wonder is this right?

And then the baby begins to walk
The next you know it starts to talk
It wants to touch all precious things
you never knew this life would bring
you running in an endless ring.

But then your child is fast asleep
you go upstairs and take a peep
you look down on its angel face
your worn out day there's not a trace
that love you feel deep down inside
makes up for all those sleepless nights

I love you Darling, you do say
I worship every God sent day
Jean Elizabeth Hollings Grant Ross

Moonlight And Strangers

A crisp cold night
no bird in flight
I throw a gaze of vigour
Lace filled air
with twinkle tear
absorbs a distant figure.

The darkened face with cold night pace
has coventry and speed like cat
he walks first here and then goes there
passes, then lowers his hat.

With bolstered breath
which cuts the cold to here the sound of water
I rest on pine with winter vine
to smell, savour then saunter

As cold prevails like cockleshells
on beaches as long as time
I hurry home that wishful thought
through cold translucent moonshine....
Andy Rosser

" Ode To Marriage "

We fall in love and give one heart to someone hoping never to part
Never to cry, never to frown, never to let that someone down
But life is not the way it seems, things are real, not like in dreams
So when the pain gets hard to bear, we close our minds like
  we're not there

We marry young, we marry old, it's still the same story that's told
For love is hard when things go bad and no-one means to end up sad
Still feelings seem to get confused and someone always has to loose
But it shouldn't matter who's to blame, for we've already
changed our name

So when our marriage stakes are down, we ought to take a
  look around
Forever though we feel unruly, there's certain things that still
  are pure
Our children mean the world to us, we shouldn't let them loose
  their trust
So don't give in without a fight, there'll always be another night

We loved each other at the start so that's good reason not to part
Far fields may seem to be more green, but things aren't always
  as they seem
For when we're old and all alone we may start thinking about home
Those we hurt and threw away may mean much more to us someday.
Jacqui King

'Same Difference'

Laughter is the same in any country
No matter what the colour or the creed
So the secret is, be fluent in every language
And a happier person you will be, indeed.

Tears, they fall like rain in every country
Just water droplets falling from the eye
They don't have any class or creed distinction
And everybody knows that word called "cry".

Birth is birth, in animal or human
All over this whole world, it's just the same
If you see it happen in a foreign country
You'll know it, if you never hear the name.

Death, it is the one thing we're all sure of
No matter who we are, or what we know
If we're millionaires, or we don't have a penny
When the good Lord calls our name, we have to go.

So why are we all fighting with our neighbours?
Why do we take another person's life?
At the beginning, and the end, we are all equal
So please, try to end this universal strife.

Charles C. Devine

" Remembering Rambo "

No more cups, and no more shields
No more walks in Platt fields
No more grooming, and that's quite rare
No more bobbles in my hair
No more rides in John's car
No more shows near or far

Nothing more for me to prove
Oh how good that I could move
With John, we were as one
But really, truly, we had some fun
And with Terry, I was a mummy's boy
In fact, I was her pride and joy

Now it's time for me to go
So I say to all, "Cheerio"
I'll spend my days where I can play
I've lived life full all my days
You must agree I've done my best
Now I'm home for my final rest

John Simmonds

" A Desperate Plea "

No make-up upon my face, just painted lines of hope, no sunlight in my eyes, no paid exotic places where sunburnt bodies lie. No luxury materials, no silk liquids for my hair, just a dusty dirty body and eyes with tears but no one cares.

No elegant attire, just cloth to keep me cool. No one to teach me better, no books so I'm a fool. No shoes upon my feet, just mud and soil beneath them, that will be my food to eat.

I have a smile, I do have a smile, I just need a reason, please give me a reason, I desperately need a reason. Tell me why I shouldn't cry, tell me that I will not die, tell me that I'll live to see another day, tell me that this nightmare will eventually go away.
Please bring me into your world, your world of food and water.
Please bring me into your world where I might feed my sons and daughters.

Take me from this awful world, even if with my life.
Take me from this mad world, this crazy world, this "Third World",
Take me from it, help me from it, please take me from it....

Elle Pearson

An Atheist's Prayer

No poetry, no pain, no pleasure.
No touch, no sight, no sound, no smell.
My creed is nothing for tomorrow,
Forgetfulness in void and vacant hell.
I cannot win the argument religious
My best is stalemate, black night over all
For faith escapes me tantalizing.
I cannot find belief beyond recall.
It's comforting to lay the blame and credit
And live in certainty of afterlife relief.
To know beyond a doubt that there's hereafter
Lord, if you're there, please help me to believe.

Alan Barlow

I Want To...

Tower blocks and bridges with man-made, stone-clad, hard-core edges.
No wonder mankind splutters! It even causes me to stutter —
for which there cannot be a cure
by the th-ther-therapist or doctor.

And me, the daughter of a procurator fiscal, living in a place that's dismal! Breeding rats and then contempt.
I wish I was safe in my new (refurbished) tenement, where the window boxes flourish with some violent coloured blooms that make all homes seem more than they are!

I speed up in my car to inspect the mansions of the richest.
While my mind is being made at home in the dirtiest of ditches
I wonder to myself, as I speed along the highway, passing through the normal by-ways to rich and luscious destinations, if the lottery is mine this week!

Fiona McCormick

Precious Moments

We stroll along hand in hand, footprint patterns in the sand. No words we say, a silent embrace, hearts entwined in our magical place. The chiming bells, an array of white, the union of love a beautiful sight. The vows exchanged, an April day, cherry blossom confetti, around us lay.

The paper's signed, the house is ours, a quaint garden full of flowers A bit run down, new skills a must, paint-streaked hair, plenty of dust. The morning sickness, baby is due, nursery's painted pink and blue. Three years pass, another patter of feet, with this addition the family's complete.

A lovely home, the children small, money's tight but all in all, We are content, our little nest, surely these years are the very best. The music's loud, times are tense, we're now on the other side of the fence. As hormones race and spots extrude, a grey hair exchanged for an adolescent mood.

Time has passed, birds have flown, after many years we are on our own. The pages turn, a chapter new, moments precious, the years are few. We stroll along hand in hand, hotel booked, close to the sand. Our idle chatter, a steady pace, hearts entwined in our magical place.

Jenny Mason

Cradle Song

The child touches smooth wax stillness,
Recoiling at the after-life repose.
Cradled in satin, your winding sheet shawl
Holds you in a history of pain relieved.
No harsh breath breaks the silence
As you sleep free from our tears
And all those vain remedies we used,
To keep you there beyond the bearing.
Still the people you became
Live on the lips of those who call you
Daughter, wife, mother, dearly beloved,
And like whispers echo softly
In the empty rooms, needing and fearing
To detain you, except in the quickening of time.

Frances Mawnam-Smith

The Best Time Of Life

Life is fantastic when you are young,
No worries, no fears, just songs to be sung,
As you grow older things start to change,
You cry for things that are out of your range,
Before it was sweets and pencils for colouring,
Now it's for cars, computers and bigger things,
And as we grow older and start to mature,
We now look for bigger things, like love that is pure,
This time of life is the hardest of all,
For this is the time you take life's hardest fall,
For if the love you find isn't true,
This will surely be the end of you,
But if the love you find is real,
There are no word to explain the emotions you'll feel,
And now that your life is full of love,
Along comes a gift from heaven above,
A new life, so precious, so young,
No worries, no fears, just songs to be sung.

Bushra Iqbal

Nobody Sleeps

Nobody sleeps by Night or by Day.
Nobody trusts burglars by Night or by Day.
No country trusts each other by Night or by Day.
War is an Event in which nobody wins.
When it comes to War no Country
in the World is civilized.
So let us one day sleep peacefully
by Night and by Day.

Daniel Enticknapp

Hospital Visit

The still, dread silence does not quiet my thoughts.
Nor yet the laid out form with countenance leaden,
Tired, worn, disappointed.
I want to shriek, "Don't dare to shroud this con
with silence, masquerading as respect
and so deny the question, "Why?"
"Why?" needs no answer. Why should it?

In such moments all is certainty.
Certain chaos: Certain shambles
Ashes to ashes — that's all it ever was.
Random disintegrate particles. That is certain.
But then disturbing doubt intrudes
as moving from mortuary to maternity, my certainty is shaken.

A primal cry penetrates my chaos,
And bubbling, gurgling, laughter
brings my shambles certainly to order.
A tiny hand entwines my fingers,
And destined though, like me, to die,
sufficient is its clasping trust to reassure me
and dismiss my massive, pompous, "Why?"

Canon D. Mackay

The Old Shawl Seller

The old lady sits in her chair and knits
Not a care in the world
Her needles click and clack
Her bony fingers hardly move, just her wrists
She is lonely as she sits there
Staring at nothing in particular
The clock ticks on but she doesn't care
At last she rises absent-mindedly
But then sits down as if someone has told her to
Without warning she rises again
And makes for the kitchen so bare
Shakily she pours a mug of tea
The old lady weakly climbs the stairs
To the bedroom where she lights a candle
Then slips into bed and stares at the ceiling
Slowly but surely her eyes droop
She soon is in a deep dreamless sleep.

Clare Fowkes

Seizing The Opportunity

I became unemployed at Yuletide
Not the present I liked on my tree
Work I have searched for far and wide
But out of work seems the situation for me.

I have always enjoyed reading poetry
Never realizing the monetary gain
More satisfying than doing the lottery
So here I am trying to pen it in vain

You have to have a sense of humour
Regardless of one's own plight
So please do not believe the rumour
That everything is not alright

As long as you have love and health
And a good woman to stand by you
You really have much more than wealth
This is certainly my point of view

Your prize is a very good offer
And to write for it I feel I must
It would certainly fill up the coffer
Though given the chance is as good-I Trust!

Lorn Gaston

What Distance Cannot Take Away

Perfection, in love, it's so beautiful and so true,
nothing else matters, just me always being with you.
All my burdens and pain you have taken away,
no more sadness, just sunshine, clear skies all the way.

Over with forever? As I depart feeling so sad, and blue,
nothing else could ever mean more to me than my time with you.
All the happiness you've given me, distance threatens to take away,
no longer any sunshine, my skies are forever grey.

Shattered, apart, so alone, and so regretful too,
how could we break up, we were meant to be — me and you.
Reunited, our happiness returns, our inhibitions slip away,
the sunshine has never shone brighter than it does today.

Adele-Marie Clough

Retirement

What have I got to do today —
Nothing that matters, it won't run away.
Retirement is such a wonderful thing
Get up when you like, walk around with a grin
But unless you've thought all this out before
It can become rather a bore
Busy workers have no time to chat
The social scene is adding the 'vat'
So if you'd like to be part of the scene
Plan well ahead, don't sit and dream.

Cora Fixter

A Hedgehog Died Today

I found a dead hedgehog today.
Nothing unusual in this you might say.
It's a common enough sight, on any road
Where the car is the usual travel mode.
There was something quite odd about this one though,
He'd met his death in a different way.

His jaws were prised wide open and like a horses bit between,
was a plastic ring seal. Like the sort you would find,
to hold in place, the top, off a bottle of pop.

This picture....... I assure you, was obscene.

Caught too, by the spines at the back of his head
It would be a long, long, time before he was dead.
Deprived of food and water, his had been an awful death.

So let me tell you one and all,

Don't leave litter ... no matter how small!

Linda J. Allen

" Rainbow Hues "

Colours of the day depict your moods in every way,
Now take this very morning — the sun was
breaking through, the air was crispy too,
so I take from my drawer a soft scarf of a rosy hue.

Tomorrow may be grey, my mood of gloomy
sorrow, so take a scarf to suit the day,
perhaps a lovely yellow.
But if birds are singing, air is clear
a different colour does appear
a splendid Lavenda affair.

If rain is falling a thousand jewel
colours fill the air,
Blues, greens, pinks, lemons
of every creamy hue,
so as we cannot outdo that
a plain white will do.

So make the day a kaleidoscope
a colourful array, and beat
those awful moods that
try and ruin some of our off days.

Lal Hall

As You Were

Old woman, old woman, what are your thoughts
now that your lips are unable to tell of the pain
and discomfort that old age has brought?

It's difficult trying to smile and be happy,
when all that you want is release from that state of indignity,
and all that you ask for is peace.

Old woman, old woman, look at me now,
were you not as selfish and thoughtless, and how is it
that you think me different from you when your skies were blue?

The body that once was lithe as a kitten,
with hair that would shine as morning dew,
when once your youth would seem never-ending,
but suddenly life has caught up with you.

Be in peace, old lady, and try to remember
that autumn is known to begin in September,
and after the fall there is only the winter.

Be not afraid when it's your turn to enter
that place we know nothing of, save what we're told,
where sadness is silver and loneliness, gold.

Grace Barber

To M____. In Absentia

My room will never be the same again
Now you've moved out. It thought I could reclaim
The space, the time, be mistress of myself,
Be mine. But items that I thought I owned
Have come through use to be your own. Your mug,
Though chipped and less than smart, refuses
From my shelf to part, and waits in vain your
Lips to claim, and squats amid my porcelain.
Your chair's been moved, from here to there, and back.
Its future tense, it was quite perfect in
The past. Each curve and contour flaunts the space
Once filled with you; that knot reveals the place
Your fingers idly used to trace, hollows
In the cushions show where head, and legs and
Arms should go. When I ease my frame against
The back the fabric sags, I only feel
My lack. The very air describes, in part,
The negative you gave my heart. Empty
Of you, my couch and rug in turn conspire
To bring to mind your absence, my desire.

Alisoun M. Ward

Whose Future?

With all the problems in the world today
Nowhere for my future children to play
The streets all cluttered up with litter
Thinking of my future makes me feel bitter
With people drunk stood on the street
Because of the drug addictions they want to beat
With rapists, burglars, robbers walking free
Cant anyone for once just stop and think about me
I'm afraid to walk the streets at night
Maybe one day the dark will turn to light
But until that day I'll sit in my house
As scared as a small defenceless mouse
Sat all huddled in my room
While next door's music pumps BOOM BOOM
One day the murderers will stop the pain
The day the acid leaves the rain
The day the IRA finish the fight
Then maybe I'll feel safe at night.

Louise Waite

A Victorian Valentine

My heart is soaring like the lark,
O'er glade and copse and woodland park,
It sees the calm serenity
That its repose could find with thee.
My happiness would be complete
If our hearts one day should meet,
And like the grapes in summer sun
The juice would mingle and o'er run
Into a life that precious few
Will find, unless they too have you.
I beg you sweet Sir Valentine
Come hither dear, be mine.

Chrissie Davis

Promised Land

High above the shaded lanes
    o'er wheat fields swaying gold,
A swallow soars on tremulous wings
    his poetry to unfold.
Where sunbeams dance on a pool of jet
    in dazzling rainbow showers
And summer's breeze gives tongue to dreams
    that whisper through the emerald hours.

Skylarks sing from a cloudless sky
    to the music of the river as it rushes by,
And beneath, the corn as it sways and dips,
    is brushed by the scarlet poppies' lips.
Where dragonflies hover in a mist of blue
    and field mice play 'mid the sparkling dew,
Here in this spot near to God's right hand
    lies the home of my soul — the Promised Land.

Cheryl Ann Morrison

Cold Chicken Surprise

I had a dream the other night
    of a chicken minus its plume,
already cooked, so delicious it looked,
    till it got up and ran round the room.

Then sheer chaos broke out as the folk ran about,
    all trying to chase their dinner,
someone cried, "Oh catch it quick —
    before we get any thinner!"

But the bird was a canny master of arts
    giving all of them the slip,
I couldn't resist the tug of a smile,
    beginning to pull on my lip.

Eventually, the tasty dish
    landed upside down in the bath,
their expressions of shock nearly split me in two
    and I awoke as I started to laugh.

Angela Abrey

Just Dreaming

Dreaming dreams of many things,
Of birds flying high,
With outstretched wings,
FREEDOM! - That's what they have,
For which many people, crave and starve,
Oh how wonderful, to be free as a bird,
But in this real life,
That's just absurd.

The human race has crosses to bare,
And many people just don't care.
The lies, the cheating, deceit and corruption,
One day this earth will die in ERUPTION !
With chemical waste and all the pollution,
Wars, and Death, - Is there no solution.

Earth and life are such precious things,
Lets work together, We could all have wings.
Wings to fly, to the highest of highs,
The future may hold much brighter, blue sky's.
Elizabeth Harrington Clark

Blue-Tits

I love to see the swooping flight
Of blue-tits in the apple-tree.
They dart in scalloped loops of light,
Then pause to give me time to see
Their shades of green and blue and black,
Their dainty heads, their clinging feet,
As upside-down, like acrobat,
They dab and stab to glean the meat
Of fat and seeds and glossy nut
That lurks within their feeding-bell
Hung in the branches we have cut,
To give them perching stands as well.

They've gone! And oh! How empty now
My apple-tree with leafless bough!
Arma Cochrane

'No More The Child'

A poem about the progression
of child into adulthood...

Brilliant is the day, that it blinds me with sentiments of youth,
childhood friends and the games we'd play
Lush summer meadows and amber filled skies,
ringing out with song of bird.
Leaping through streams into worlds of dreams.

Today is the day that the rains will fall with such plenteousness it
will wash away my youth forever, cleaning me for the shackles
of responsibility.
Without warning the bitter winds of shattered ideals will sweep in,
no more shall we tread those wonderful world of dreams.

Tomorrow is the day I'll meet the future...
Dawn awakens hope and a new direction
The fruits of life shall blossom once more, until the day...
I'll be no more.
Faizan B. Kent

My Younger Days

I wonder if you would remember if I told you
Our pathways now in bloom.
With snow drops and plants
We planted when the moon
Rose up before the April sun.
Had scarcely time to set.
I try to remember what made us laugh
Was it some thing I said
The poor birds won't know it to sing or
go to bed
But I am along way from that time
And you will never see
The flowers I picked for you
When we were twenty three.
J. Parker

The Empty House

A house that once rang with noise
Of children at play with their toys
Now stands empty, as it has before,
Waiting for newcomers to open the door

Sun through grimy window gleams,
Motes dancing in golden beams,
The only sound of time passing by
The drowsy hum of a wandering fly

Unused hinges clog with rust,
Fine mosaics are hidden by dust
Pendant cobwebs in corners hang
Loose shutters in stray draughts bang

Ghosts of memory walk the rooms
Talking, dancing, wielding brooms
A phantom figure sits reading a book
Shadowed people through windows look

Outside, weeds with flowers entwine
Mute Testimony to the passage of time
Since, green fingers, with loving care,
Planted a flower here, pulled a weed there.
Barry Dugmore

Fading Light

They sat there, by the fireside, softly talking
of days gone by and the times they had known.
Fifty years had now passed since saying, "I do."
Yet still, to each other, their love was shown.

They talked of the hard times, and some of the sad.
The winter of 47, and how their baby girl had died.
How the drought had taken an entire year's crop.
Their eldest son killed, three weeks she had cried.

There were happy times too, they talked of these.
Their children's weddings, the gaiety and the joy.
How Robert had been found, after three days in the snow,
and the thrill of the first grandchild, such a fine boy.

They mused on their life together, sorrows and joys,
agreeing that through it all, an experience not to be missed.
For the joys and blessings far outweighed the sad parts.
Looking into each other's eyes, they smiled, and tenderly kissed.

Old Tom felt the tears rising at the back of his eyes.
He knew this woman he loved was gently slipping away.
His strength also, slowly subsiding, in time with hers.
He prayed that together, forever, they may stay.
James A. Wilson

The Curate's Toast

Our curate has a special way
Of eating buttered toast,
Acquired, no doubt, from men of faith,
Who love the 'middles' most.

They hold their toast 'tween fingertips,
Then with a sudden thrust,
They reach the tasty middle bits
By nibbling off the crust.

This genteel way of eating toast,
Encouraged now en masse,
Is born of urban scholarship
And mostly middle class.

There is another way I know,
Long practice recommends;
One lays one's toast across one's palms
An' folds it from the ends.

The middle bits are then exposed
To eat without delay,
And crusts, left square and centre-less,
Can then be thrown away.
Jack Scott

Shattered Dreams

We had made such plans for the years ahead,
Of just how it would be, it all had been said,
This was our dream, our future before us,
Two birds on a wing, united in chorus.

We'd live in a cottage down Devonshire way,
With a beautiful garden, a sunshiny ray,
A brook would be gurgling and dancing about,
In such an idyllic setting we'd be so hard to rout.

In our mind's eye we'd feel the happiness there,
See the beauty of nature, devoid of all care,
A haven of laughter, too beauteous to measure,
That we would succour and joyfully treasure.

We'd invite friends to come and enjoy what we had,
Give them an insight as how not to be sad,
We'd replenish their souls; reupholster their lives,
Bestowing on them sweetness as from the beehives.

But our dream was shattered, as illness appeared,
Our lives were in tatters, it was what we feared,
As my love was taken, the emptiness welled,
In a heart that was broken, so cruelly felled.

Anne Richardson

Time

The glow from the street lights cast shadows on the walls,
of monsters roaming empty halls.
The halls they stalk are the shadow of my mind,
of memories lost with the passing of time.
Nameless faces, and faceless names,
friend or foe the images wain.
A girl walks out of the mists,
her name escapes me as the drift,
taken by the flow of time.
I call out to the face I knew so well
"please take me from this living hell,
back to how it used to be,
to run in the fields, to play, to be free."
As I watch the face turns to dust,
I feel a wind a chilling gust.
It swirls and eddies down the ancient halls,
stripping memories from grey stone to walls.
I wake once more from the shadows of my mind,
and live in fear of the passing of time.

Ian Williams

I Know How You Watch Me

I sleep in your arms but I dream of the days
Of a love long, long gone by.
You hear me breathe, and you do not know
That I know how you watch me lie.

So I hear your words in my head at night,
(For you think you know me well)
How your plans for love have all come true,
But for me they sound the knell.

For a love, for a love that cries once more
To be remembered, felt, endured;
A love that was buried, lies cold and old,
Yet daily fresh immured.

And in the day, cold light of day,
Such thoughts are kept at bay;
But in your arms, each dreaded night,
The memories hold sway.

So I sleep in your arms, but still dream of the days
Of a love long, long gone by;
You think you know all there is to know
But I know how you watch me lie.

Alex Wilde

Escape To The Hilltop

Shadows creep, under oblivious clouds, over the roof tops,
Of rows of houses down below, it's cold and unreal.
Eyeless windows, curtained, hiding family squabbles,
Children play, grown-up affairs, hidden problems,
Never noticed, like boxes, still unsealed.

Climbing ever higher into sunlight, heading for the top.
Out of breath, each step, one nearer to heaven.
From heather, gorse, to stubble, rock-edged mountainside.
It becomes Everest in the mind, resting here and there,
And giving no quarter, the steepness intensifies.

Skylarks rise in the quivering air, complaining at intrusion.
Springy turf, and rocky outcrop, with lichens and small flowers.
The air, like wine, the wind is singing in my hair.
I reach the summit, and dream-like, enter another world.
Away from it all, my Shangri-La is here.

Gwyneth Pritchard

The Invite

My breathless gaze caresses the shadows
of sleeping valleys kissing fields of grain.
Dawn-cried teardrops are wept on the meadow
as the cracked farm bird crows to ease the pain.
The cloudless skies absorbed by the hillside.
Mother Nature's face wakes to melt the moon.
Pegasus spreads his wings to a gallop;
Sown from a forest the candlelight blooms.
Streams trickle slow like the blood in my veins,
relaxed to a heartbeat pumping in time.
Cradled in beauty, goblet shaped mountains
encourage the tasting of blue sky wine.
Tears wept of sadness for what was conserved:
My table is laid and dinner is served.

Kate Chapman

Dawn

Night now has passed, and soon the grey
   of the sky changes to the blue of day
And, as if all nature with the dark
   Loses her fears, high in the sky, a lark
Starts the hymn of praise
   that the myriads of songsters raise
To God, at the beginning of each new day
   Each tiny voice, in its own way
Pours out its soul in a burst of song
   whose wonders will last long
With the hearer, causing him to pause
   and fling wide the doors
Of his own soul. So may there be
   a song of praise raised to God
for all eternity.

Dorothy Ventris

Swift As A Kiss

If I close my eyes and reminisce,
Of years gone by swift as a kiss,
Blackpool's tower reaching for the sky,
I can see it all in my mind's eye,
Summer days of long ago,
As the tide they ebb and flow,
Donkeys ambling along the sand,
Castles that look so very grand,
Kiss-me-quick hats above a smile,
Each one bought on the golden mile,
Pleasure beach with its rides on shore,
Thrills and delights by the score,
Crowds of people thronging past,
Happy folk, smiling at last,
Theatre lights twinkling in the night air,
What they had seen, nothing can compare,
Morning sun in a bright blue sky,
I can see it all in my mind's eye,
If I close my eyes and reminisce,
Of years gone by swift as a kiss.

Jean Ventress

Untitled

I wish I could take the pain from you
Oh how I wish with all my heart
Knowing that special friend of yours
Is soon from you to part.

Try to remember the good times
You shared with one another
And you must always remember
He wouldn't want you to suffer.

This world is full of evil things
But he will feel no pain
He'll go to doggie heaven
And have everything to gain.

We don't know what kinda life he had
But this you know is true
You gave him everything you could
In the short time he had with you.

Don't fret my love, don't fret no more
He will soon be fast asleep
And all those treasured memories
Are forever yours to keep.

Amanda Gray

Street Of Hell

Walking along the street with rain turning to sleet
On hearing this loud shout, I looked all about
A girl with wet hair cried "look over there!"
Silhouetted in the shop lights were these horrid sights

Oh look! A man, he falls, soaked to the eyeballs
Snow was pelting down, maybe he was trying to drown
Water streamed past his head looking like he was dead
He struggled to his feet and declared "No defeat!"

Hearing this wailing sound I turned my eyes around
Looking like a refuse tip I walked towards a skip
A body began to appear. It was full of fear
A child in a box. Oh my God! It's got pox

What's that terrible smell, it's no channel
From where it was seeping look what was sleeping
Four girls in a sack like cards in a pack
Skin pierced with bones, all I could hear were moans

Why are these persons marooned to a life so doomed?
Living in a cardboard house not fit for a mouse
People take no notice of these bodies of ice
All they just say "Summer is on the way".

Alan Stanley

Dilemma

If I were a farmer I would have two farms;
One for bread and butter, one for nature's charms.
Milking parlour, hens in a row,
In clinical perfection-
And poppies where they should not grow
In every wild direction!

We cannot do these things by halves
For somebody may crate my calves,
And chickens surely feel the stress-
So - mushroom beds and watercress?

But stay, there are so many factors,
And harmless mice are crushed by tractors.
I'm wasting all my skills; besides,
The thrush succumbs to pesticides.

But then when all is done and said
The children cry for daily bread.
Be still, my heart, and no more panics
I'll take a course in these organics.

I trust this is the better way
And hope the flat-worms stay away!

John Urwin

Cries For Mercy

People don't realize what goes
on in this world,
They don't see beyond their nose.
There is hatred and war,
People are bitter and raw.
Fighting doesn't solve anything,
but a dead body in a grave,
It will be too late for the mistakes
you've made.
Bereaved and angry people won't accept,
your cries for mercy,
and make you feel
you're not worthy.
So end this spiteful place,
you will have no last chance,
no judge, no appeal,
I rest my case.

Juliet Elisabeth Scott

Hunter

I used to be touched by the sad ship's eyes
On the last day of Ramadan
And was ashamed like the weak rusty tooth
In a big devouring mouth.

Wanting to comfort unhappy dolphins
In their last swim in Elsan
I sent them songs (like a rose) with no mourn
Keeping tight on my chest its horn.

Then I saw the blood on my brother's shirt
On the last day of motor shells
And crushed like a fat gallon of red wine
On the silent threat of a mine.

These days some see me as a piece of dirt
On my real-fur coat their anger falls
Looking so comic they are shouting
Like a drop of snow melting to nothing.

Amna Oruc

Don't Play With Fire

Do you know the night it is
On which we can have fun?
November fifth,
That's the night for bangers rockets, guns.

Potatoes baking in the fire,
Lights flashing all around;
Animals within the byre,
You know they hate the sound.

What must we as children do
If this night we'll enjoy?
Take heed of grown ups, who
Have our good in their minds.

Fireworks are not to play with!
In fact, they can be
Really dangerous!
Especially for child like me!

Alice McCarroll

Soliloquy

I am one with the fall of the Autumn leaf
One with the wind in the ripening sheaf
I am the sweep of the swallow's flight
And the quiet that follows the storm racked night
I am the morning song of the thrush
I am there in the drowsy evening hush
I am the strength of the tidal surge
And I the eternal vernal urge
I am the trail for the stars ascending
Angels' song and the never ending
I am all Man can ever be
One fleeting breath in eternity.

Claude H. Bigg

Verbal Tea

Once upon a time
Once upon a rhyme
Lived a man who owned nothing
Neither crown, nor kingdom, nor palace
Yet, all around his birthplace
he was considered as a king.

His power was beyond belief
So anyone who came to grief
Soon would rejoice, forget the pain
Lulled by his purely enchanting style.
A broken face would brighten and smile
A broken heart would beat again.

Once upon a time
Once upon a rhyme
Lived a man somewhat heroic
Neither God, nor genius, nor prophet
Yet the crowd worshipped that poet
Whose language reached absolute magic.
Laurence Canham

Memories

Family memories are taken for granted
One day they'll just slip away
Contrasting moments of happiness
And sadness we deal with every day

Our lives are shaped by many influences
Not the least of these are great
But nothing in the world is better
Than the love that we create

Life brims over with plenty of feeling
Never encountered before
One year builds upon another
And love builds more and more

Where our arms do not reach
There are our dreams that will
No matter what we accomplish
There will be another hill

Love is an affirmation of our hope
And an adventure of always and never
But all our special memories
Will stay in our hearts forever.
Andrea Smith

Our Day Out

Thank you Dave for being such a rave,
On our day out at Draton Manor Park,
For without Dave and Stella it couldn't have been better,
Because they are definitely game for a lark.

The log flume was great although I did hesitate,
Well wouldn't you if everyone was coming off ringing wet,
The parachutes turned my tummy and Dave didn't think they were funny,
Stella gave this one a miss while talking to other people she had met.

Dave was very brave by riding the ultimate shock wave,
Rather him than me I think you all would agree,
then there was Buffallo Bill, well he gave us all a thrill.
Then it was time for lunch and a nice cup of tea.

There were Anthony and Bradley who of course were very happy,
Well wouldn't you be if you were a little boy in paradise,
The mini dragon was fun then off to the carousel we did run,
and the train that toured the park was nice.

The pirate adventure we all thought was very clever,
Although we still got a little bit wet,
The rapids were a scream as we were careening down the stream,
So did we get wet again, YOU BET!
Irene Partridge

There Can Only Be One

Here we are the final eight
 One hundred meters will seal my fate
All my dreams I hold in my hand
 To be the fastest in the land
Seven men share my dream
 Seven men that I must beat

Here we stand in a stadium of light
 looking at that burning light
All the crowd silent in wait
 To see who'll break the line of white
Who will hold that medal of gold
 Who will hear their anthem play

Here we stand in a line of eight
 Three to my left, four to my right
All my hopes ten seconds away
 No past, no future, just ten seconds to play
Now we wait for that fateful gun
 Knowing there can only be one.
Leslie De Ath

Mini-Ode To A Poet

Odious acronyms littering my thoughts and scuffing your pen, poet;
Only you can eloquently scud through them — avoid their fall-out.

Soothe me beyond the fuzz words to euphonic euphoria with your
Talent and gentle skills.

Opiate my weary ears
Score-through the staccato politically-correct prosaic headline oaths

And once again let your sweetly hand-held words
Embalm my soul.

Ah, even as my eyes embrace your form
My heart smiles with your Attic wit
My tongue drawls with languorous leisurely harmonized syllables
And I pause to think awhile —
To wonder at your inherent unsophisticated unsimulated ability
To make today splendid, again.
Lynette King

The Elements

From the Earth, everything grows,
Only to be covered by a carpet of snow.

The Fire burns and destroys all in its path,
The flames flicker and crackle, seem to laugh.

Water engulfs, and rises to steam.
Black ashes remain, like in my dream.

The invisible air, there all the time,
Carries away all secrets of mine.
Carol Brown

Sleigh Ride

Oh what a view, oh what a sight,
Oh what a feeling, such a delight.
Over the rooftops, way up in the sky,
Just like a bird flying up high.

Very tall mountains, covered in snow,
Out in the darkness, oh how they glow.
Snowflakes are falling, fluffy and white,
I'm flying much higher, higher than a kite.

I'm starting to slow down, spinning right round,
Swooping and diving I head for the ground.
But please do not worry, don't have a fright,
I'm not going to crash out here on this night.

I head for the houses all covered in snow,
And pick up my sack and shout Ho, Ho, Ho.
I deliver the presents and then I will leave,
And it's back on my sleigh till the next Christmas Eve.
Deborah Harker

The Chosen Ones

Who's involved, do we all care,
Or are we all frightened of this AIDS scare.
Frightened we may be, love and care a fallacy.

Education and learning the country is yearning,
Communication and skill, the youth worker will.

A matter of acceptance may be
This AIDS scare, not for me.

Misunderstanding, guilt and blame,
All taken in AIDS' name.

Lost friends, relatives too,
Maybe there is a new friend for you.

'Rivilin Valley' is a beautiful place,
A tranquil setting for our careers to face.

Isolation, loneliness and despair,
Make us all realize this AIDS scare.

Love and affection, we all need,
Makes our careers a very special breed.

Joan Cuffling

Dying Leaves

Where'er I tread the leaves are red,
Or brown, or gold, but all are old.
They're crisp and dry, beneath a sky of sunny blue, with golden hue;
And piles so neat surround my feet.
The leaves are tired, they'll soon be fired,
And gardeners keen will all be seen
Stoking the fires, to smoky spires;
A single bird can still be heard
On leafless tree, singing so free.
I love the 'fall' — it tells us all
That winter's rest will bring the best
Of bud and leaf to spring's new sheaf;
The trees so bare will stand and stare
At frosty skies, but how time flies
Before we know, after the snow, the brave new year will soon appear.
We'll see again after the rain, the blooming flower just like a shower.
The birds will sing to hail the spring.
So sit and dream — this autumn scene,
Is set out here, our hearts to cheer;
Spring will return — so let leaves burn!

Joan G. Greenwood

When Will It Be Over?

"The terrorist attacks are over"
Or so we were led to believe,
No more bombings, killing people
Which leave loved ones to grieve.

Buildings, where only yesterday
Everything was running well,
Now all that remains
Is just an empty shell.

I can't see any reason to it
Can you?
Who gets pleasure from seeing this happen?
Who? Tell me who.

We were told the attacks had stopped
So why did they start again?
They don't fill people with happiness
Only with pain.

Will we finally get the truth
Out of the IRA?
Will they actually stop the terror
And give us all peace one day?

Belinda Faulkner

Untitled

Is it the colour of your hair,
　or the way it is cut.
Perhaps it's the freckles,
　from head to foot.
Maybe it's the mischief
　that plays upon your face.
Or could it be the laughter
　you've brought into this place.
I think it's just the sound of your voice
　yes definitely, the way you talk.
No, I know what it is
　it's just the way you walk.

Ann Boults

No Mores

No more aches and no more pain
Or the worry that I may go insane
No more wrinkles or worn out bones
Or people listening to my moans and groans
No more worry if my ticker should stop
Or the vein in my head will suddenly pop
No more hobbling from room to room
Or trip over something and head for doom
No more worry about the way I smell
Or other stains that people can tell
No more worry about my water works
Or any illness that suddenly lurks
No more worry of losing my sight
Or other things you have to fight
No more worry of losing sound
Or mislaying things that's never found
No more worry about getting old
Or losing teeth and going bold
No more worry to get out of bed
No more anything because I am dead.

John Masters

A Father's Truest Love

Some of us love money and the power that it brings,
Others love possessions and other material things,
But me I love my children because in their eyes I see,
A very special twinkle when they say that they love me.

I guide them and protect them with such a love unbound,
I'd even go to hell and back to keep them 'safe and sound,'
When they fall I pick them up and show them that I care,
And tell them that no matter what "Your daddy's always there."

It gives me untold pleasure to be with them every day,
And show them that I love them in daddy's special way,
I hug them and I kiss them, I love them through and through,
I do it with the knowledge that my children love me too.

My time with them I cherish for one day soon I fear,
I'll turn around and they'll be grown, then they will disappear,
But that is in the future and until then I know,
The feelings that I have inside grow and grow and grow.

I wish I could explain to them this love and joy they bring,
The happiness I feel inside makes my heart want to sing,
But these feelings running through me, I really can't express,
That more than all those earthly things my children I love best.

Christopher John Evans

A Present From My Sister, A Book With Blank Pages

When I am gone, this lovely book will linger on
Perhaps some future relative will write upon
　These virgin pages which I love so dear
　And which my own so poor attempts will now appear.
I love to write, I love my life, I love my God
　who made me so.
He brought me through my Heaven and Hell
　And back to Peace — He knows me well;
And when He takes me Home, I wonder,
If I shall still be writing
　there, up yonder!

Hazel Templar-Smith

Our Black Struggle

Every day we struggle,
Our black struggle,
We argue and fight,
From day 'till night,
For we must stand up for our rights.

We work under interrogation,
Forever we fight ugly discrimination,
Others look down on us,
But we stand proud with our heads held high,
We'll never give in,
No, we'll never say die,
For our black struggle will continue,
And we will be free,
Because that's how our God meant it to be,
For all eternity.

Angela D. Anderson

Untitled

When we are children we don't worry at all,
Our soul aim in life is to have a good time.
The woes of the world, they pass us by,
Our childhood, just one long nursery rhyme.

As we get older, so problems we find,
At home and at school then later at work.
The stress and strain begin to tell,
And behind a facade of normality we lurk.

Frightened to change the life that we have,
The unknown more terrifying than the life we know.
To take those steps to change our ways,
A path down which we're frightened to go.

Decisions to make, choices to take,
Do we have the courage to make the change.
Dare we settle for second best,
Or make a move to a life that's strange.

Denise M. Almond

Barriers Within

Casualties of circumstance,
Our spirits perform their lonely dance.
Never touching, separate, alone.
Forgotten feelings that should have grown.
Different tongues, not communicating.
Shared hopes not integrating.
Needs ignored, or misunderstood.
Affection repressed that could make good.
Hands that reach out but never find.
Thoughts that scream out for a receptive mind.
Eyes that plead for recognition.
Hopes that die without fruition.
Indifference grown so manifest.
Basic desires never put to the test.
Lost souls searching in the dark
Groping, hoping, for some spark,
And emotional scars litter the scene;
The graveyard of 'what might have been'.

Bryan Davies

Remembrance

When you're standing in judgement so firm and so strong,
Please don't forget what it's like to be young.
We've so much to do, and so little the time,
And the road to the top is a frightening climb.
So please understand if we happen to stray,
And put off till tomorrow affairs of today.
When you were a juvenile, long long ago,
Were your parents impatient when progress was slow,
Did they demand loyalty, how you should work,
Can you honestly, truly say you didn't shirk?
There must have been times when the world was all wrong,
So please don't forget what it's like to be young.

Lillian Leeming

Tides Of Change

The beautiful power of the sea,
Our strong friend,
Is a hostile God,
Suffocating at random,
Brave Warriors,
I've seen the Earth,
And the soft undulating flow of the Land,
And we in our rigid structures,
Digging the dirt,
Going against Nature in itself,
In all its innocence and purity,
The damage is in us and around us,
Bleeding money trees dry,
In our desperately controlled lives,
Longing to fly but closing the eyes of infinite wisdom,
Fearing the bearers of truth.

Louise Stocker

The Passing Of Time

As we grow old with the passing of time,
Our thoughts often stray through the years,
To times of joy and happiness,
To times of pain and tears.

Oft times we wish, that we could return,
To the golden days, once we knew,
To days of love and friendship
To last our whole life through.

Could we but stop the clocks of time,
And return to our yester-years,
To put right schemes, that once went wrong,
And dispel, our doubts and fears.

Loved ones and friends, will grow old together,
And the days will go swiftly by,
We can only watch, the passing of time,
Until the day we shall die.

We may change plans throughout our life,
Our desires and ways to fulfil,
But we cannot stop the passing of time,
Because time; will never stand still.

John Hill

Untitled

Great wings of light
Our weary bodies hold,
Supporting us with love and hope
Until our lives unfold.

The path of life is never clear
Until we find our rest,
All we can do along the way
Is just our very best.

Look only to the love we find,
Breathe in its light with joy,
Release that breath, spread out the love
To all who pass you by.

Libby Parr

Do They Have To Eat Meat

They go out to lunch and sit round the table
out comes the food all piled up so neat.
They eat and they eat as much as they're able
Until someone shouts "Can I have some more meat"
If only they'd think and just shout for more veg,
The animals we love would stay behind the hedge.
In the fields where they belong looking healthy and strong
Not on plates in the dinner making a pong!
The smell of the flesh just makes me heave
If I had to sit at that table I'm afraid I'd leave.
Would they eat their pet dog or cat I ask
I think even to them that would be a task.
So stop eating meat I'm asking you to
and start eating things like vegetable stew.

Eleanor M. Morris

The Bubbling Of Dublin

Today a bubble floated down O'Connell Street,
Over the Liffey, past Trinity
And on to St. Stephen's Green.
And as the rainbow orb passed it saw below
Other bubbles floating up;
Bubbles of words, drifts of speech, snatches of talk,
Laughter, tears, cries,
Swear words, words of joy and surprise,
Murmurs, rumours, truth, lies;
Swirling and stirring, twisting and turning,
Rising from the streams of people meandering below.
Bars of music flowing from musical bars,
Strings of notes from pavement players.
Cars and bikes, roaring and ringing,
Noise from everywhere, inside and out,
A constant outpouring of sound.
Like the Liffey always moving onwards,
The bubbles keep floating up,
Bubbles from the suburbs, bubbles from the centre,
The bubbling and frothing mass that is Dublin.

Caroline Coker

Secrets Of The Deep

Oh come with me and we shall see what secrets lie beneath the sea
Over the side with cutlass drawn,
And another gallant ship goes down

Down, down fathoms deep, who shall we find who lies asleep there down below
Since time began the sea has won and conquered man

Will we find a galleon that sailed the Spanish Main — or a pirate ship that plundered all who crossed her lanes
Sending them down to Davy Jones, never to be seen again

Aye down to Davy Jones who guards the treasures of the deep
A thousand secrets he could tell of how men died, and in his keep so shall they sleep

Will we see the Jolly Roger blowing in the mist or hear the cry of the Buccaneers as they go to keep their tryst

You and I will never know what really lies far down below

Eleanor Rule

Pain

Pain stings like a wasp in an apple.
Pain burns inside my soul where it hides away.
Thoughts turning in my mind
Another time, another day.
Somewhere a fortress, some earthy place.
Travellers' dreams lost in space.

Back to earth it's the place to be.
With the landscape of the hills and trees.
Loving memories I will always treasure,
Always giving the greatest pleasure.
Happy! No time for tears or pain.
As thoughts turn to a different plane.
   Without an apple.
   Without pain.
The sting moves on and is lost again.

Hazel Faulkner

The Swimmer

Iridescent waters still, cascade blue and white reflections,
Lighting, gleaming all around, the warm air silent
until the sound of entry echo's,
Splashes, whirring, shushing, like beads on glass,
Moving on, the race begun, iridescence gone,
Sharp, slide, pull, as flesh cuts through the liquid,
Caressing every contour,
Bubbling, white, foaming, over and turn, smooth glide
Silent as lung breaks air,
Stretch, stretch, through to cold smooth ceramic,
Touch from silence to glory.

Karen L. Webb-Jones

The Rose Garden

In the spring roses bloom,
pale and silvery in the moon.
Drops of dew adorn as pearls,
sliding from the petals in the early morn,
as the birds chorus and wake them at dawn.
Standing proud and gay for all to survey,
they climb and clamber in close array.
From gold and yellow, to pink and red,
they sprout open and unfurl their head.
Butterflies stop to admire and drink them in,
to cut them down would be an unforgivable sin.
Alas, the gardener is master here,
He doesn't like the colour of this little rose, I fear.
With the shears gleaming in the light,
He mercilessly prunes the little rose with all his might.
And now the petals lie on the ground,
the poor little thing makes not a sound.
Spring is over, Spring is gone,
and now not one rose grows in the garden....not one!

Anne-Marie Hopkin

To Trevor

When you or I are reduced to a pale face
Above the tight white sheets of a hospital bed,
And some young intern has said,
"There's only hours in it"
Then I'll know the desperation that
There *are* only sixty seconds in every minute.
And as one of our lives flickers into history,
Why you ever chose to love me
will still remain a mystery.

Karen Boult

On Seeing Vandalism

I entered through the front door
Paper and rubbish littered the floor,
I felt cold and began to shake
How could people such chaos make?
What pleasure did they derive from this?
In their lives, is something amiss?
I went from room to room and saw
Destruction, that cannot be halted by any law.
A fire ripped out of a wall
Glass and metal strewn over all.
In each room they had left their mark
To me, it was like wandering in the dark.
I could not believe what my eyes were seeing,
Done surely by an animal and not a human being.
Here for an eon this building had stood
And for the community provided only good,
Vandalized, in a modern day and age
Because man against fellow man still must rage.

Audrey Twiss

The Butterfly

It's free to roam, this flighty thing,
Paper-thin upon the wind.
Soul flying high with timeless wing,
Seeking redemption for all who've sinned.

Will it pay the price and meet the cost,
This filigree symbol of innocence?
Or, will mankind bow to the hopeless lost,
This mindless mirage of incandescence.

Don't fly too close to the sun, little one,
To singe your wings would render you flightless.
Little one, you need to have fun,
Bring laughter to the sad and depressed.

Raise hearts high above the plains.
Spirits lifted, weightless, without substance,
Devoid of suffering and pains.
It is gone in an instance.

Gillian M. Thomson

The Sound In The Night

Wearily wondering what it could be,
Pausing, I posed:
A plea it should be.
The volume of echo drains and darkens
My whisper of wisdom, as the night harkens.
Rolling and racking my head for response,
The answer, I ask,
My thoughts will ensconce.
The completeness of silence brings nothing back
From where it went to answers I lack.
Tiredly trying to steal any sound
Away from a
Source that I haven't found.
The rasp of soft tones crescendoed the clamour,
Hoping I'd hear the request of a stammer.
Aurally ambling toward my tense mind:
A quizzing so quiet, I would fail to find,
The mystery of melody that seems so slight.
A noise perplexing:
The sound in the night.

James Kerr

Letters From Home

His letters were few and far between,
Penned in his bold yet elegant hand,
The same hand that held me as a child.

I can still picture him with pen poised
To form immaculate characters,
Words written with painstaking slowness,
Strength and tenderness steeped in his script.

His letters came unexpectedly,
Finding me in college or bedsits,
A stark reminder of his absence.

I opened them eagerly and read
News from home enriched with his humour,
Gentle reprimands for not 'phoning
Belying his fatherly concern.

He can no longer send me letters,
But I've kept those he took pains to write:
An indelible testimony
Of his unerring paternal love.

Liz Rowlands

The Beauty Of Nature

Snowcapped mountains standing majestically proud,
Peaks of snow reach to kiss the cloud.
Valleys below lie in pastures lush and green,
A carpet of colour, the like of which I have never seen.
A man and his dogs wander close to the stream,
Smooth ripples kiss the shore, the sun catches the gleam.
The sparkling waters running fast and free,
Going where I ask, It whispers "Follow me."
Flowing leisurely to distant shores,
Down by the valleys, the hills and the moors.
The eagle flies lazily above my head,
Swooping, searching for a way to be fed.
He hovers in mid flight, what has he seen!
He dives very fast, Skimming the stream,
As he sores into the sky trophy held high,
His shadow becomes a blur in the sky. The sun goes down, its
golden glow fading, the valleys and trees fall into dark shading.
It's time to go, it's such a shame, to leave this valley I must
come again. The beauty of nature is ours to behold,
in pictures and words this will always be told.

Lynda Fraser

When Is It Going To End

When is it going to end,
   people are dying, suffering.
Men leaving their wives and children
   never seeing them again
Children evacuating, leaving
   their parents behind, probably
Never seeing them again
   Germans were bombing our ships
   that were bringing us food
People were not only dying
   because of bombing but of starvation.
Children having to wear horrible
   sweaty gas masks to learn in,
They were probably horrible to wear but safe.
Bombs being dropped by the
   minute people dying getting
   hurt, the sky was black with smoke
Most buildings wrecked, most people dead.
   We have won victory
   The war has ended

Hollie Mulreay

Time Of Day

Six thirty the alarm bell rings
Outside, the whistling wind, it sings
Snuggle down and hide away
alas — I can't, I must go play.

Eight o'clock the traffic buzzes
Radio 1 hisses and fuzzes
Turn the corner, left then right,
past the children in my sight.

Eight thirty-five, yet more bells,
the start of the day it falsely tells.
The noise in the room, the eyes that stare,
"Good morning children" in my care.

Two forty-five it rings again.
You'll find no one here who will complain.
Learning, working, making, doing.
Minds developing, knowledge brewing.

Ten o'clock, oh how time flies,
marking the hopes of a child that tries.
Time to relax, but my mind is still working
I know the six thirty alarm is there lurking.

Denise Carpenter

Our Dying Breeds

The beauty of a beast will hold
My heart, until its death turns cold
For all is man, a cutting race
Who keeps the earth right in its place.
The hurting of all things unborn,
Could make me sad in silent scorn.
I'm not alone as these thoughts bring;
A picture of each screaming thing.
For others feel it's such a shame,
And turn upon all those to blame.
Through battle, never out of touch
Shielding wild, who need so much
Their actions made straight from the heart;
If only I could be a part.
I love this world and what it gives,
For us, and all that meekly lives.
As man treads down on creatures so
I thank the Lord that they don't know.
The human race is all for kill
And yet we few are dreaming, still.

Julie Slater

A Day's Work Done

Beneath the dome of a blue sky,
people move to and fro in one big pie,
'Tis five p.m. at a roar.
Nottinghill gate station groans,
nothing till late stirs.
A sudden rush of bodies
erupts from the underground, a leash, to
tired limbs and mental death,
as zombies to be met,
an atmosphere of rush, rush, rush
to sausages and mash,
till tomorrow a repeat tryst,
one of life's journeys,
endless days of reminiscences
stumbling to the inevitability.

Anno C. DeSilva

Love — Is It Worth It?

One-sided love is the hardest of all,
Phone calls made, but all you get
Are excuses and coverings
Which drive you mad.
Asking yourself questions like:
'Why can't he tell you his true feelings,
Instead of leading me on?'
The one in love is hurt most of all,
Dreaming about what could've and should've been.
Vowing never to be 'taken in' again
And making sure that the next time,
It will be two-way love,
Which never happens.
So life carries on, taking you with it,
Clinging onto every little thing you can get.

Claire Martin

A Space In The Race

Sitting here silent surveying the scene,
Pink sprout the lilies from pads smooth and green.
The fuchsia looks pale from too little wet,
Water line's dropping and I start to sweat.

The breeze feels so cool, it rustles the fern
But it does not last; the grass starts to burn.
Pond skaters skating and Damsels that fly
Rabbits and squirrels, the birds in bright sky.

.....Hustle and bustle heard from afar,
Shouting of voices, the drone of a car.
How dare they enter my mind in this place!
Cruelly disturbing the peace and the place.

I don't want to leave, but I know it's time
To rejoin the world of business-like minds.
This can't go with me; 'least not physically,
But it can live on in my memory.

Andy Shaw

Lost Love

Dear God, I am in torment, I don't know what to do
Please come close and tell me, is this a lesson too?
My mind just feels that it will blow, my heart feels it will break
Why does this have to happen, how much more must I take?

I loved him very much you know, but he can't seem to see
That all I want is his happiness and for him to just love me
And yet it seems impossible, for he's not with me at all
But far away in another world, as if he can hear you call.

If happiness is for him to be without me anymore,
Let him remember me sometimes, but be with you forevermore,
For he has worked so hard for you, and deserves to have your love.
I'm not quite sure what I deserve, perhaps a little from above.

So keep him safe and free from harm, and happy from within,
Let his days be full of love, and know that he will win.
That your great love and light will shine, and that he will always be
Safe within your loving arms for all eternity.

June Margaret Avery

A Day At The Market

Early to bed, early to rise,
Pitch up stall with bleary eyes.
Council stipulates terms and rules,
Market life and licensed stalls.
Wind, rain, no distraction,
Get it up before the action.
Stand on crates, stall up and sound,
Morning milkman! on his round.

Stragglers drift from different roads,
Where they come from no one knows.
All laid out professional job,
Cup of tea for a couple of bob.
Unpack boxes fluff up gear,
Get set out before crowds appear.

Punters coming thick and fast,
Money changing hands at last!
Socks, rompers, dresses, vests,
Everything for the little pests.
End of day panting and puffing,
You can rig a kid out for next to nothing!!!

Graham Peter Childs

The Good Things In Life

There are so many things that are
    pleasant in this world of worry and strife,
Take the flowers and the trees
    the birds sing to please the
        music of church sounding bells,
The sheep with their lambs,
    the cows with their calves so happy
        all grazing in grass,
They haven't a care, the whole
    world is theirs, they sit
        and let daylight pass,
The mother's with babies all
    cuddly and warm, a lullaby when time for bed
With dreams of their toys
    or playing with the boys
How happy when resting at last,
The breeze on the trees, the clothes
    on the line all white and refreshed as the dew,
It may be hard work but see the results
    and family will always thank you!

Dympna Slattery

Share A Tear

Don't sit there crying by yourself.
Please, come and cry with me.
You shouldn't have to cope alone.
We both need company.

But if you feel that I'm intruding.
Don't hesitate to say.
I'd hate to think I've made things worse.
I'd rather walk away.

When I saw you sitting there.
I couldn't help but see
Your tear-filled eyes, that's when I knew.
You're feeling just like me.

Sadness is a burden that most of us must bare
It sometimes helps to overcome
If only you can share

So if you need a shoulder to help you see things through
Please let me stay.
What I'm trying to say.
Is I need a shoulder too.

Kenneth B. Roffey

The People Who Don't Care, Rivers Flowing Down To The Sea

Rivers flowing down to the sea
polluted with chemical waste,
the fish struggle to breath
as they gasp their cries are not heard
by the people who do not care.

Traffic flowing, ever increasing
belching out its toxic pollution
as the children gasp and wheeze
sucking on their ventalin to ease their plight
their cries are not heard by the people who don't care

Power stations spewing out carbon dioxide
into the atmosphere causing acid rain to fall
on forests many miles away,
Trees dying, crying out to mankind, you're killing the planet
there will be nothing to leave behind,
but their cries are not heard by the people who don't care.

Leonard Wilson

My Soul Sister

My soul sister, not bound by blood unyielding all the same
Predestined together as if surely written,
I feel her pain as it were mine
Yet still I cannot stop it.

She perceives me when no-one else can,
Gives me strength and courage when I have none
We know the other's thoughts without query
What is this that joins us?

So alike in every way as if one person in two bodies,
But when we do go astray, we always find our way back in the end —
To that special friend.
Strong is the bond, it feels we will be in unison to the end.

I do not know what I would do, if she were to go and leave me
on my own all alone in this big world.
I do know I would never find this kind of friendship again,
A friend like you, you only find the once.
Friendship is a special kind of love.

Jane Elizabeth McCann

Good Will Always Triumph Over Evil

Murderer, mugger, rapist, thief,
Pretty soon you're gonna come to grief.
Remember, scum, you just can't win
You're gonna pay for your damn sin.

Wife-beater, bully, junkie, crook.
We'll never let you off the hook,
Drug dealer, terrorist, pedophile, perv,
You're gonna get what you deserve.

We'll hunt you down, photofit your face,
We'll track you down, we'll win the race,
You won't succeed, the law and we will,
For good will always triumph over evil.

Bill Forbes

Schizophrenia

Where did you go, my love, that awful day,
Oh yes! You're with us for now but will you stay,
Our lives go on, but oh the change,
It isn't you — this man who is so strange.
The children ask me why you've altered so,
How can I answer, when I don't really know?
This dreadful illness that so affects the mind
The doctors try to help, but still no cure can find.
If this is life I wonder for how long
That I, weak as I am, can go on being strong.
I try to understand, sometimes I fail it's true,
But still I go on hoping, loving you — and praying
That with each passing day
You will get better — yourself again,
And back with us — to stay.

Irene Rice

Autumn Years

Time steps by, youth is gone,
Priceless gift was your carefree song,
Endless dreams that didn't come true.
Sadness sometimes that shows the true you
Life's joy and pain show in your face
Slows you down to a slower pace.
Autumn of life, winter yet to come
You think of things you've left undone
Words left unsaid play on your mind,
Memories, some sad, some sweet and kind,
Loving words said and actions too.
Some dreams that maybe could have come true,
Winter nearly here, another day to dream,
Thinking of things that may have been,
Seek comfort in the wisdom of your years
Strive to be happy and forget the tears,
Count your blessings one by one.
Live out each day as it may come.

Ann Dowding

Escapism The Traffic Jam

Encapsulated in this metal structure
Protected from the outside world, from nature's force.
Unable to touch and feel life, or be touched by it.
Absolute power over a destiny which you may not even reach.
Each driver aiming towards a different place.
Yet, from one move of a fellow being this ambition is shattered.

In front someone overtakes,
For this one moment they think they are special,
They will disturb the monotonous pace ahead,
Sacrifice others' destiny for their own,
But will they be let back in.
Or drive forever on the outskirts, never content?

All plodding along the same route
To reach very different destinies.
Looking around seeing frustration, anger, and boredom.
While some give up and change direction,
Others continue, determined to reach their destiny.

Alice Blamey

Who Is This Man?

Who is this man called "King of the Jews"?
Read all about him in the "good news".
No princely robes had he to wear,
no jewelled crown, his head was bare.
He was so gentle, and so kind,
A closer friend you would never find.
He healed the sick, made cripples to walk,
The people gathered to hear him talk.
The crowds just followed him everywhere,
On him they placed their every care.
But why do they call this man a king?
Why do so many people his praises sing?
This man died and rose again,
soon will come his glorious reign.
So who is this man called
   "King of the Jews"?
His name is "Jesus".

Lilian Nolan

Monday Night Blues

Reality has passed me by,
Reality is a week away,
I am feeling weak, the future is looking bleak,
Is it only me at their lowest ebb?
My downcast soul is near its death,
Morbid minds make mine alive,
An active mind is in the mind's eye,
I am deranged, devoid of emotion,
A locomotion that has fallen in the ocean,
I try, I really do try,
So why, please tell me why.....
....you won't let me die.

Gary Scott Beazleigh

Window Pane Between

A patchwork cover thrown over the hills.
Pure sunlight and long dark shadows lengthen
Into square green patterns beneath bird trills.
Such country scenes my spirits strengthen.
Under patchwork duvet of my sick bed,
Sewn snips of memory, in stripes and dots.
Soft colours that are pleasing for my head
Remind me of parties and flower pots.
Lovely sights to reflect upon, I see.
Parsley trees, spinach leaf fields and oat path,
Bluebell sky, white mallow clouds float-free!
Then — fondant colours — after purple wrath
of loud storms — to radiant rainbow hoop!
I pull my white feathers round me so cosy,
Safe in my room — as if a chicken coop!
Cottage curtains blow, showing a posy,
Sweet, scented flowers arranged to dream of.
I close my eyes; cool air past glass wafts in.
The tabby cat pads down the tiled roof.
She's warm outside — I am sun-kissed within!

Joan S. Childs

He's Coming Ever Closer...

The signal crayfish — Saddam of the sea,
Rampages on the land, as well as even on the quay —
The Killer, colonizing watery wastes —
With the freedom of a spree.
Encroaching mile on mile — up hill down dale —
He cannot fail..
Voracious snapping of the jaws — at anything he sees,
Inclusive of the crayfish prized of yore —
But now — of course — extinct.
What answer is there? None...
Except for quickly chomping through the beast.
At least it's not a chore — and truth is — it's delicious...
Just match his might — and grab him tight...
Until he knows no more!
Then cook him — eat him and be quick!
As on the move's an ARMY of these Saddams —
All awaiting confrontation..
And finally — to think — that 'Yes' they'll grace the table:
Dear GOD, it's just as good as any fable!

Elizabeth Laing

Is There A Place?

Is there a mountain that I could climb with its shrouded peak
  reaching for the sky,
A place where I would be all alone and out of sight, where
  tears have never fell, a place where I could cry,
There I could shout and scream into the wind so it can carry
  my voice loud and clear,
Carry my voice to the one I have lost and let her know that I
  am here,
Invisible wind you have no form but you can scream and pass
  me by,
Can you carry my message through the hills and dales on
  your way searching from the sky.
Blow across the deserts and cover the wounds and scars with
  sand,
Just like the falling snow that covers the desecrated land,
When the gale force wind blows and drives the ships that soil
  the waters upon the rocks as if to clean the sea,
Could it blow the pain and sorrow from my broken heart to
  give me strength and give new life to me.

Lewis E. Baunton

Surprise

Pulling back the curtains and seeing all the snow, it's
like a sheet of whiteness which covers all I know. I'm
watching the little Robin; he's flying to the ground now
hastily picking at the food we've left scattered all
around. I can see him watching, but oh he's off with
such a start, maybe he saw me watching him with an
anticipated heart. Goodbye little Robin, until you visit
me again.

Yvonne P. Dyson

The Cobweb

Morning sunlight sends long fingers
Reaching out towards the trees
In a sunlit sheltered corner
A dew kissed cobweb rides the breeze.

With each breath it shakes and shimmers
Masking well the hidden threat
For behind such fragile beauty
Its creator's trap is set.

The hidden spider sits unmoving
Clinging to a silken strand
Waiting for the slightest movement
From its victims as they land.

So it is that natures beauty
Woven by our cunning friend
Traps within, the unsuspecting
To a quick untimely end.

Anita Larraine Moss

The Silent Friend

Oh gloriously proud old mountain
Rearing your summit so high
What secrets do you hold of days gone by?
When girls were shy
And boys, as always, bold when night was nigh
If you could speak, what would you say
of what you've seen on summer's day?
Children playing on your side
As up they'd climb and down they'd slide,
Skimming away!
Or lovers vowing to be true
Then next day they're with someone new —
Bright and gay
Majestic mountain, secrets you enfold
That never will be told by you
For you are everybody's friend
And will be — to the end
For when all else has passed from earth's domain
You will remain — ever true.

Joan Armstrong

The Town I Grew Up In

The town that I grew up in,
Recalls memories of my past.
Some just fade away,
But some of them last.

Some of my friends seek adventure,
Some chase dreams.
Like a tributary tumbling down a mountain,
In ever changing dreams.

The town that I grew up in,
No-one can replace,
The buildings, such tall structures
In so confined a space.

The town that I grew up in
Holds memories of smiles and tears of joy
And sadness,
And frustrations,
Mingling with my fears.

Anthony Thorpe

Spring Joy

My garden in Spring
Is a place that will bring
A riot of colour and sound
Of bell-like notes from the Blackbird's throat
And the crimson hue of the Robin's coat
As he hops along the ground
Nowhere on earth can be found such a worth
Of colour, song, and form
As Nature gives birth, and reclothes the earth
A piece of God's Heaven is born

Nan Gosling

Peace

I don't know why, people fight,
Just for a piece of Land,
I think weapons and gases should be banned.

Parents and Teachers,
Are all in despair,
But the Soldiers and Officers,
They just couldn't care.

This World,
Has turned upside down,
Ever since Hitler hated the colour brown.

I don't see why,
Innocent children should have to Die,
While their Mother cries.

One day all Wars will Cease,
So come on,
Let's all pray for peace.
Roselynne Spray

Dawn Chorus

In the solitude of dawn
just before the silvered threads of spiders' webs break
and mist creeps slowly, veiling lawns,
before trees shed their delicate cloaks of crystal drops
the blackbird heralds the dawn.
Uplifting song uplifts weary hearts
and as if on cue a noisy mob of sparrows
breaks into a scrum.
People arise, children shout, traffic roars into life
shattering the glass-like delicacy of the spell that
the blackbird has woven.
With one last melodious chord he flies,
leaving dawn behind, just a memory.
J. Gillions

Christmas

Christmas is a time for happiness,
Joking and laughing and things,
I will always remember the real reason,
It's not presents and parcels and things.

The real reason for Christmas is Jesus,
Happiness fills the air,
I'll always's remember at Christmas,
Jesus will be there.

Christmas is a time for everyone,
For carols and songs of praise,
We should always be thinking of Jesus,
And following in his ways.
Nevenka Markac

Hasta Pronto — See You Soon

I've travelled the world, I've seen the sights
I've walked on beaches on balmy nights
I've held your hand, you stole my heart
We vowed to each other we wouldn't part
The hours and days soon became a week
Our time together is over, I weep
I wish I were rich, I wouldn't have to go
I don't want to leave, I love you so
So many words are left unspoken
I get on my plane and my heart is broken
I'm working hard to plan a vacation
So I can be with you, my vocation
But I need proof that you still really care
I'd come back with a whisper, if I knew you were there
So please be a darling and write very soon
To let me know I'm not reaching for the moon
Just two little words, I'm waiting to hear
As you taught me in Spain, when I was still there
You said "Te Quiero" which means "I Love You"
"Hasta Pronto", "See you soon".
Toni-Marie Benton

Curtains

A thousand eyes all peer at me
In different ways
Sad, unkind, evil, happy
Different eyes on different days.

Faces roll as if dead
Faces smirk
Faces peek from the flower bed
Do such faces truly lurk?
Or only in my lonely head?

Signs written in the green stem's curl
Lines wriggle and lines unfurl
A face that knows the riddle
In its sly glance I hear it giggle.

Movement
A draught from the window
As you fall asleep
The curtains cast another shadow
And in dreams
It is the knife that's drawn.
Nigel Crofts

Dead Elms, 1978

Stark, staring skeletons of leafless time,
In desolation bare,
Pointing their naked fingers to the empty air,
As in derision.
Leprous scales from off the trunk,
Lie fallen at its base.
The pale dead patches, white, they stare
And the eye catches the disgrace of death.
This timber does not rot away,
Man has reserved it for his final end.
This is the canopy that cloaks his clay,
When it's required that we should send,
Ashes and dust to dust.
All are returned to earth, this way.
Pam Harvey Richards

One Last Chance

From this dark place bereft of light,
In confused bewilderment I write,
The pain of parting brought great sorrow,
For with it there is no to-morrow.

In love we spent those happy days,
Enjoying life in many ways,
But now we've reached a great divide.
A chasm, with you and I each side.

Please hear this plea and give me strength,
To build a bridge ne'er mind its length,
For all we've known I plead one last chance,
To prove that I will, our love enhance.
G. Barrie

Castles In The Air

Oh you Dreamer, we have need of you.
In a world lost in the race for money,
We have forgotten how to lift ourselves
Into castles built of coloured smoke and
Light moulded by our hope for beauty.

When magic drains from this world where is hope?
Heroes are lost in the quest for greed,
Who will heed the Dragon's call to ride the wind
Building towers of distant dreams for you and me?
Have you the courage to sing the song that lifts?

I have walked the high path of imagination,
Living in worlds that are real to the mind,
Seeing the beauty of this sad place reborn,
questing for the love of the land which is the grail
In the Isle of the Mighty.
J. Burges Watson

Bread And Wine

The faithful guests are welcomed in,
Spread the cloth of linen fine;
The mystic feast shall now begin,
Break the bread and drink the wine.

Hear — as He lifts the chalice up,
Pledging kinship by such sign —
"Ye who would drink with me this cup,
All I am shall now be thine".

Thus was ordained that man should be
Through love's alchemy divine
Arrayed in robes of majesty
By transmuted bread and wine.

But now the paling mist of years
Dims the sight and hides the sign,
Still fall the falsely contrite tears
While we kneel for bread and wine.

Now harken to the cock's shrill cries
As the bullets sing and whine,
Where trampled deep in mud there lies
Broken bread, and crimson wine.

Andrew Cole

It's A Dog's Life

I am a border collie
A blue-merle actually
That means I'm multi-coloured
So good looking - naturally

I've been a little devil
(In my time you know)
Like when I ate the carpet
And had to then lay low!

I also have a fetish
With socks of any kind
I rifle through the ironing
'Til I find one - no-one minds!

I go to bed quite early
But sometimes get quite mad
As I have to move right over
Because of mum and dad

They tell me 'on your own bed'
But my baskets not the same
So I wait until they're snoring
And sneak on up again!

Amanda Morton

'For Margaret'

Life is like a garden
A place you think you know
In patches there are weeds and thorns
In others all things grow.

You nurture plants as best you can
With tender loving care
But you have no power to prevent
Effects of cold brash air.

And when you wake one sunny morn
To check they're all alive
'Tis devastating to discover
That one did not survive.

Then you feel great sorrow
And anger may be felt
What kind of hand has old fate
To this subject dealt.

Yet moments which have been so warm
Precious memories and days
Nothing can ever take those away
They are with you always.

Jacqueline A. Hackley

A Spell in the Heather

Lying in the heather
A breeze,
A very gentle breeze
softly breathes on your ears
next to silence.
But for one other sound, just one —
The ceaseless quiet rumble
Of a distant waterfall.
Then, that breeze gets stronger,
Starts the heather whistling
Now soft sighing to the ears
Becomes a chill around the neck
The spell now broken
For me to be on my way.

John Adshead

Fear

I lie in bed and think what's that?
A bump in the night
What a fright
What a sight
There's a DEMON on my door!
A MONSTER on my floor!
Mum! I shout
I'm scared
On comes the light
Oh, it's alright
The demon is my dressing gown
The monster is my light

Clemmie Wisdom

Hounded For Life

It's early in the morning
(A cup of teasmade tea)
Already the beagles are howling
To greet the dawn and me

In unpolluted air
That lasts about two hours
We walk the lanes and meadows
Of sun, lush scent and flowers

The dogs pull here and there
Showing me what they've found
Tasty vetch, rabbit or cowslip,
A fox that's gone to ground

When we've bathed in transient goodness
That natural pleasures bring
Fresh air, sun and the awareness
That invites the birds to sing

We wander home to breakfast
With the memories that remain
It's never a chore walking beagles
Tails wagging through snow, mist and rain

Geoffrey Ingle

A Rainbow In Winter's Time

Yes, it was January 1992
a man felt alone
so the rain came turning the
world, cold to touch.
As the clouds gathered for a
three day stay
the colour blue remained.
So the man felt the rain, never
revisiting a memory of utopia days.
Why did he act so old?
Why couldn't he let go?
So picture this a rainbow in
winters time.
A miracle for the refugees souls
why feel so alone.

Andrew Ryan

A Flowering Of Crimson

A flowering of crimson,
a Daffodil Spring,
toward the shimmering sun.
Forever hopeful,
what you might bring.
Wild Damson bride,
for nature to sing
Fortitude stampeding,
flowing through my side.
As the moon swept over
this wild mountain scene,
towards the naked sun,
enchanted as it gleams.
Such a strange kind of being,
as the moon eclipsed reality.
To watch the spirit fly,
a distant voice from afar.
Stark, still, so incomprehensible,
to touch a majestic star.

Chris McIntosh

The Stranger

Alone, deep inside myself,
A familiar stranger resides.
She moved in a year since,
Took my name,
Proclaimed it as her own.
Talked with my tongue,
A voice that was not mine.
Soaked my soul in her essence
Until it was no more.
I have long since given up
The fight and left my home
As she ordered,
Leaving behind the merest
Hint of a memory
That I ever lived there at all.
Now my best days are acted out
In someone else's mind...
Inside my life the shadows flicker,
She's laughing at me
For she knows she's almost won.

Lucy Victoria Sell

"Rain"

A clash of clouds,
A flash of light,
And rain begins to spread the night.
As it falls it dances on roofs,
Slides down drainpipes, under
Pavement grooves, cleans the
Streets, dampens dust, turns iron
To a fiery rust, drips from
Leaves to pavement stones,
Down umbrellas, shivers your bones.
Floods rivers, overflows streams,
And sometimes dampens a lover's
dreams.

Gerard Woods

Your Cue Next

There's a gleam in my eye
And I'll tell you for why
Although I'm alone
Just sitting at home
A middle aged matron like me,
Has been out and had fun
By beating my son
Playing snooker, not bad for old me,
Well you live and you learn
To-night was my turn
'Cos you don't need no physical skill,
And I put down those balls
With no trouble at all
Well next time will be up to him.

Joan Ingham

Afterdeath

I want to know if death's the end
a friend of mine is gone
I hear his whispers but pretend
that I can hear no one.

Is there a heaven and so a hell
please tell me so I know
or do souls stay on earth to dwell
please tell me where they go.

I like to think there is some place
we race to after death
we cannot go without a trace
after our final breath.

Many theories have been guessed
the best of which is mine
I truly think that all the rest
are scared to cross the line.

They lie to keep us from our fear
we hear and believe
but death forever brings a tear
deep down we're not naive.

Daniel Buxton

A Leader!

We seek him here, we seek him there,
A leader for today.
Unsullied and untarnished,
But he is hid away!
Not one in the Palaces.
Not one to be found
In all the world's Parliaments,
Not one to be crowned!
Not one in the churches —
Too many gods around!

Must we give up searching
And leave wide open ground
To crooks and wrong doers,
Cranks and sleazy hounds?
Or to all those false prophets
Who suddenly appear,
Promising salvation
If we give them our ear?

Woe betide us if we do!
Have we forgotten and now ask, who?

Claude A. Knight

The Clock

Just a face upon a wall.
A plain face I suppose.
Not completely featureless,
But without eyes, or mouth, or nose.
Dictating when it's time to come.
And when it's time to go.
Blamed for being advanced sometimes,
Accused, of being slow.

You stare at me, quite frequently,
In that disbelieving way.
Question my ability,
I'm slowing down your day.
Along guidelines, tried and tested.
Doing all within my power.
Whilst at night, I'm never right
I'm rushing through each hour.

With due respect, I don't detect
Tween kings, and queens, or fools.
Wait's for no one, the tide and I.
But did not make the rules.

Kenneth A. Porter

The Wise Man

This used to be the Wise Man's seat,
A ragged armchair in a public street,
Displaced;
Rendered a throne by his thoughts
As he held lonely counsel
To indifferent subjects,
His words hanging
Like threads on their breeze

I saw him last an age ago,
Fiery life in ice-thin clothes,
Half-mad eyes lowered
To bandage-dripping feet.
He wore a sign around his neck,
It screamed injustice.
And he was helpless,
Smelled of blood and dirt,
And I was helpless,
Soon forgot,
His brave words invisible.

Jody Ball

A Lost Soul

A lost soul, a soul without love.
A sad and dark, dismal place.
I stand abandoned and alone,
Like a child without a home
I cry out for peace
For no one can see
The anguish deep inside of me.
The deep despair and fear,
Swell within me, dear.

Carole Baker

Timeless

An eye perceives
A sinking sun
Beginning and end
Mesh into one

Who walked before
The footprints fade
Of ages past
The sand is made

A voice has spoken
But heard no more
A world unfolds
In old folklore

Eternity lingers
In age old eyes
The future is heard
In a baby's cries

What was before
Has come and gone
An endless night
Begins the dawn.

Lisa Peters

The Seeds Of Time

As breezes flutter and lift
All those seeds and let them drift,
Far and wide they sow their crop,
Flowers bloom where they drop.

Busy bees move in and out,
Pollen floating all about,
Meadows bloom in a yellow haze,
Trees and hedgerows join the phase.

As seasons come and seasons go,
Will the seeds no longer sow?
As years drift by and times alter,
The "Seeds of Time" will never falter.

Doreen M. Coppin

The Vision

Last night as I lay asleep dear,
A vision appeared unto me.
It vanished when I awoke dear,
I wondered what could it be?

Was it you in all your glory?
My love, my Queen so divine,
I'm sure it was,
For your sweet face I saw.
Your lips they were pressing on mine.

Alas I must have been dreaming
'Twas then that I suddenly awoke.
I called your name but you'd gone dear
That kiss the vision had broke.

But some-day we'll both be together,
No dreams no visions there'll be,
For I'll be beside you my darling.
No more to be parted from thee.

Gladys Small

" Goodbye "

As I watch my love sleeping,
A voice seems to say,
'Forget what you're dreaming
And leave right away.'
  Despite what he says
  He never will be
  The husband you've longed for,
  Your children's daddy.
Disregard all his words,
What he'll make you believe,
His heart's just not in it
And you'll start to grieve.
  Forget his tough image,
  This is only a ploy,
  As he always will be
  His mum's little boy.
Although it seems hard
Being alone again, free,
The future's important for somebody —
Me.

Elaine Jackson

Tears Of War

Draw up a seat and watch it
A war for all to see
Gather round, keep the score
Of battles on TV
No more can man plead ignorance
Of his brother's pain
Watch the news at evening time
It's coming round again
How sad to see the little ones
Not knowing what is wrong
The guns of war are booming
No birds will sing its song
The old ones wander all alone
No hand to hold in fear
Silent prayer on still lips says
Please let peace be near
We sit and watch each agony
The world, it does not care
With hand on heart each of us say
Thank God! We are not there

C. Haughey

Quatrain

Nacreous sunlight of late October.
I no longer recognize my face.
Here comes your liver-spotted future,
Urine tickling down the leg.

Geoffrey Minish

Idealist

He seeks perfection,
Abstract and precise.
Intervals of the octave
Are measured in his thoughts,
The structure of a ship
Is clearly planned
Clouds, waves, hills
Form a complete design
And may not deviate.
All must conform
To this celestial scale —
Concord of line and form,
Perfect proportion
Of waste and arm,
The symmetry of a goddess
Is demanded —
But not found,
So, always seeking
The unobtainable
Restless and alone forever.

Ian S. MacPhail

Martyr Of The Chinese Folly

The shots rang out,
Acrid smoke filled the air.
Death all around
In Tiananmen Square.
Innocent eyes,
Wide,
Aghast,
The tanks rumbled on,
Ignoring the damage,
The hurt they had done.
One boy stood his stance,
Chaos around.
He never heard it;
He stood his ground.
This land's my home,
It's mine,
I'll fight,
In front of the tank
I'll stand and dare them to
Mow me down in Tiananmen Square.

Catherine Mitchell

The Elegy Of The Damned

Alas my life is at an end
All joy and love has flown
No migrant hope could apprehend
The pain of being alone
The talons of love have torn my heart
Its wings have passed me by
Its seething beak (razor sharp)
Has cut apart my life
The future stands before me
My life within my hands
My dismay reflecting sombrely
The elegy of the damned.

Lee Maling

The Tiff

These flowers of mine
Express a love so divine.
No words can match your charm.
As your beauty abounds
To capture our minds.
No words can express
Your beauty so enshrined.
These flowers are mine
To capture your mind
With words I could not find.
These flowers of mine
To help the mind
Understand my love so divine.

David Bruce Moffatt

What Has Happened To This World?

What has happened to this world?
All this fighting and war,
Just because people want their ways.

Aren't these people human beings,
Dying of hunger and thirst?

So what do we care,
As long as we live in luxury,
So let the people die?
Do we really care?

Aren't these people human beings,
Just like you and me?

What will happen in the future?
What will remain of this world?
Or will it be just be a lump
of unwanted place?

Farooq Mulla

The Clowns

One up, one down
along came the clowns
all brightly coloured
walking upside down

The audience laughed
the roars cried out
legs like jelly
one with a wobbly wellie
but then they are the clowns

Alexandra Louise Breare

Frozen Life

The fallen sedge like a lazy sea
Along the train embankment lay;
A-frozen into deathly white:
Catacombing furry life.

Cattle graze in famine fields.
Sheep cry out for a spring-like day;
Fleeces yellowed against so white:
Black lambs' tails a-showing life.

Through soupy fog no eye can see
Beyond where those dark cedars stay;
Solid bulwarks against the light,
Camouflaging antlered life.

How still the earth, and all the fields!
Patchwork white mid walls of grey:
Pink painted house into the light!
A smouldering chimney — human life!

Helen Spellman

Confessions Of The Lake

The white lady swims
across the lake
of an everlasting love
of the silver glow
of the lake
as the moon beams its light

Upon the shadows
of romance
where reasons disappear
and desire's strength
within the seas
of higher waves

That none can be found
where crosses of pain
that none can bear
alone at night of confession
only to be deceive one's self
of being a fool in love

Helda Nissan

The Tramp

Nobody lives there anymore.
An empty shell, breathing
But not living.

How could you define the
Death of a spirit?
A person living?
A person dying?
A person dead?

How could you respond to eyes
That looked at you,
In you,
Through you,
But never saw you.
Eyes that endlessly sought,
  but never found.
Eyes that had no life
Or light behind them.
A person condemned to live.

Nobody lives there anymore.
An empty shell, breathing,
But never living.

Helen Tuton

Traces

Mirror, self-forsaken.
An image that is me.
When all my dreams have scattered,
And all I have left is a belief,
No tangible denial,
Nor moods to grip my soul,
In cobweb dances of history,
An emptiness for goal.
Photographs in these eyes,
of human-trails, of lifetimes,
of flickering firelit faces,
I reach to touch these images,
Expecting to find them real,
yet beneath my questing fingers,
There is nothing I can feel.
I wipe away those images,
They're but a trick of light,
There are no cobweb memories,
Just darkness... and the night.

Hazel Deborah Hopes

T.G.I.F.

Friday afternoon, won't work late
An urgent job? Sorry, mate.
I'm dead meat
if we don't reach
the game reserve gates by sunset.

Speed along the North Coast road
then turn inland to Eshowe,
Melmoth, Nqutu...
"I'm staying in front of you!"
The sugar cane lorry derides me.

At last the turn-off, end of tarmac,
red dust in the sinking sun.
Acacia and sisal
majestic in silhouette,
scarlet fires from distant kraals beckon.

The ranger salutes as we enter the kingdom
where wild animals reign supreme:
spot a family of warthogs,
wildebeest, kudu, impala
Goodbye, cruel world —
Hello African dream!

Beulah Felstead

A Shiny Star

A sparkle in the sky,
And a person who has died,
Always feel lonely inside.

But then there is a shiny star,
That sparkles in the sky once more,
Over the head of a woman's bed.

So, sparkle in the sky again
And let me flow, and flow away.

Kerrie Bennett

A Hope For Peace

When all is said and done
And battles lost or won
All hopes of peace to rise again
And trample down the gun.

The children's faces say it all,
"Please let the torment end"
In silent prayer you hear them say
"To us a saviour send."

"We want to live our lives in calm
And beautiful surrounds
Not hiding every time we hear
Shells and rockets hit the ground."

So give the children half a chance
I'm sure they'll find a way
To bring about the end of wars
And have peace from day to day.

David Duff

Promenading By The Sea

There's rollers and skateboards
and bikes though forbidden;
punks with freak hair,
their clothes from a midden?
Youths wearing high heels,
the girls in 'flats',
their faces made up
like the players in 'Cats'.

Then there's stylish old ladies
and all sorts of men and couples
who walk hand in hand:
all ages and stages it
seems quite the trend!
Are they sweethearts or lovers
on a 'dirty weekend'?

As I sit in my beach hut
drinking my tea,
almost all give a look in —
laughing at me?

Gertrude A. Somerville

For Yvonne

I have at last found
a place on this earth,
next to you,
your hand in mine
without you I would miss
out on so much;
laughing in the rain,
holding hands on the beach,
the constant clowning of true lovers,
doing everything together
I have faced the trials
of the heart and won.
Your troubles are mine,
and mine shared with you.
You are the keeper of my heart,
earthmother, lover and friend.
Always and longer shall
I love you!

Dave Newton

Healing World

I watch the sky as darkness rises
and bright the stars shine!
It's quiet and peaceful.
Here on this little world of mine!
On a beach just looking up
with a cold breeze of sea air!
I look at planets
I wonder, if anyone is there.

Murder and distraction are destroying
this world of mine!
This once was a planet filled with
things that were as divine!
I wonder if other planets are
the same as on earth!
No planet wants to be like us,
it's more than life is worth.

We need to heal the problems here,
to make my planet fine!
I want to live in happiness
in this big world of mine.

Janet Bayliss

Sleep Forever

When pain cuts too deep,
And guilt bleeds out,
I feel I want to sleep forever,
And forget the pain I've caused.

Is it my fault?
Did I do something wrong?
Surrounded by crowds,
Why do I feel so alone?
Surrounded by Daylight,
Why is it all so dark?
Surrounded by love,
Why am I in pain?
Even when I'm awake,
Why do I want to sleep forever?

If I could just close my eyes,
And forget all that's happened.
If I could just fall asleep,
And find it's all a big dream,
I only hope you'll still be there
When I wake up again.

J. E. Teather

Youth, Priceless Gold

Youth, priceless gold
lost in the deep blue abyss
like a white tiny dove.

I wonder where could you be
I wonder how could you feel,
if you just told me....

I imaging you sailing by sea,
caressing the foaming waves,
now too far away from me.

Youth, priceless gold,
lost in the oblivion of my eye,
please do not move.

I imaging you as the eternal frame
of a picture,
as the sparkling glimpse of a tear
if it were not just a game,
can you whisper in my ear,
why did you leave with a tear?....

Bruce Richard Baker

Only One

Place a snowflake in your hand
And it will fade away,
Gaze at the brightest star at night
Twill fade at break of day,
Hold you then the sweetest rose
Its wondrous scent inhale,
Enjoy its fragrance whilst you can
For slowly it will fail,
Will you my friend then wonder why
This lovely flower will surely die
Follow you a rainbow
Try to reach its end
You won't succeed, however hard you try
It's just refracted light, my friend
Listen to the song bird on a summer's day
Enjoy each note it sings for you
For soon 'twill fade away
So is there anything that will never never end
Of course there is, there always is
The true love of our friend.

James R. Randell

The Dying Rooms

You tie them up
And leave them there,
They have no life
Their world is bare.

Think of the children
And how they feel,
They've never had
A decent meal.

A baby is tied to a chair
It has no food
No water,
But you don't care.

In my perfect future world
Those poor children in china,
Would be treated
Much, much kinder.

Jennifer Horn

Never To Learn By Talking

If gossiping causes concern
And listening helps you to learn
Then thousands of people's ears
Are all about to burn.

If the truth causes pain
And telling lies causes shame
Then really
By talking
It leaves you nothing to gain.

Kyle Mail

Now

Tomorrow, today will be gone
And made one of those yesterdays
So let's make the most of the moment
While we sit and gaze
At the roses in bloom
The bird on the wing
Life is so sweet
Birds realize this and sing
Why oh why can't we be like them
And be satisfied
Give love and affection to the
Child that cries
In giving a little comfort and care
We can begin to learn how to share
This wonderful world God gave us to live in
Because that's what it is if man didn't sin

Jean M. Dansie

There's A Lion On The Stairs

There's a lion on the stairs
And no one cares.
There's a lion on the stair
And he's giving me a glare.
There's some lions on the stairs
And they're not like teddy bears.
There's a lion on the stair
And he's not giving me a glare.
There's a lion on the stair
And he's my teddy bear.
Claire Green

April's Song

I listen to a black-bird sing
and robin pipes his song
the forest-roof brings forth new leaf
this is April's song

See those daffodils in bunches
those red, and yellow tulips
blue bell clusters
this is April's song.

I touch the softness of the dew
see diamonds on the lawn
crystals hang in morning mists,
this is April's song.
Jean De Voy

The Rainbow

I look out through my window
And see a rainbow there
A curve of perfect colour
A sight for all to share
The red upon the outside
Is my poppy by the wall
The blue is my delphiniums
Standing straight and tall
The purple and the mauves there
Is the lilac on the tree
And in the pink so delicate
My roses I can see
The green and yellow blending
Is the daisies on my lawn
Primroses and buttercups
That come out with the dawn
The orange like my lilies
So fragrant in the morn
And as I stand here quietly
I'm thankful I was born.
Joyce Clifford

Freedom

I once sat in the desert
 and smelt the golden air
Only the grains of shifting sand
 knew of my freedom there.

I wandered over the desert
 to an oasis silent and cool
I felt the night approaching
 and the air becoming chill.

I wandered into the desert
 a dwelling came into view
I sheltered in its fading warmth
 and thought my thoughts of you.

No longer I wander the desert
 that dwelling now my home
My thoughts are still about you
 but my freedom is here alone.
Anna Harrison

Yorkshire

The Yorkshire hills are many
And some are monstrous high,
They do enhance the landscape
For all the passers-by.

Those winding roads so serpent-like
Creep over hill and dale
Surprise round every corner
Like drawing back a veil.

The hillsides ooze spring water
That gathers at their feet
Trickling, rushing, roaring
Where strong streams meet.

Those still lakes in the sunshine
Twinkle and glitter full free
Of garbage and undesirables
Beauty for all to see.

The view from all high places
Show beauteous country side
Threading walls can't be forgotten
For they are Yorkshire's pride.
Georgina Whitfeld

The Power Of Love

An Angel crossed my path one day
And stepped into my heart.
I knew that this was perfect love
Right from the very start.

Tall and dark and beautiful,
His hair as black as coal,
His eyes of grey looked into mine
And found my very soul.

Of all earth's wonders I'm aware,
The moon, the stars above,
But none perceived more beautiful
Than through the eyes of love.

Now although he's gone from me,
A blessed comfort I can find:
I close my eyes and him I see
In the pictures of my mind.

'Tis said our destiny in shaped
By Divine power from above.
I only know that I was shown,
And felt, the power of love.
Doreen Murphy

Is There Anybody There?

Another ice cold day,
and still no sign at all,
if there's no one about tomorrow,
we really must go and call.

There's two pints of milk,
on the door stop stands,
tomorrow we'll see if she needs
an extra pair of hands

The papers hang out of the letter box,
I suppose we should have known,
she might just have needed us,
instead she was all alone.

We put it off until tomorrow,
there was no one enough to care,
and now we're filled with grief,
was there anybody there?
Kirsty Garwell

To My Valentine

Another year has just gone by
And still we are together
With all the love I have for you
The storms we'll always weather

Our special day has come again
With luck it always will
Until the end of time itself
I'll always love you still

As a wife you deserve the best
You've made our home a little nest
And in it there are lovebirds two
Me my love and darling you

Your present hasn't arrived this year
I've not had time to look
You know you'll get one when I can
My heart's an open book

We're not as young as we once were
But we're not as old as most
We're just in time to enjoy our prime
Let's have another toast
Albert Simpson

"The Proposal"

"The winter's nearly gone, my dear
And time I found a bride",
Chirped hopeful mister blackbird
With his head held on one side.

His coat was very shiny black,
His beak a golden yellow,
And, certainly, to blackbird hen,
He seemed a handsome fellow.

"Mid February's here you know,
The day most birds are wed.
I cannot be the only one
Without a bride", he said.

"Oh! Ours will be the cosiest nest
That birds did ever feather.
We'll build it in the hawthorn hedge
Protected from the weather".

"Then soon we'll teach our baby birds
To sing and then to fly,
And watch them as they soar away
Into the azure sky".
Lilian Kitchin

Gratitude

I am grateful for so many things
And to name but just a few,
For each bright sunny morning
And the fallen dew.

I am grateful too for friendship
Of people good and kind,
I am grateful for most anything
That gives for peace of mind.

I am grateful for love and beauty
The grass flowers and the trees,
The gracefulness of Butterflies
And the sight of busy Bees.

I love to put my thoughts in verse
Moreso if they should rhyme,
I love to hear sweet music
And bells that gently chime.

And so dear Lord I thank you
For everything that's good,
And pray all treat our neighbours
Just how you meant we should.
Derrick Alan Day

One Day In Arabia

Today I drove three hundred miles
and visited a dozen desert rims,
edge darkened by date palms.
It was a bright day,
quietened by thin cloud and dust.
One strange thing about this quiet
and interesting day
is that you were there, everywhere
I went.
You were everywhere I went,
at each dead end to desert,
in the midst of shady palm groves
in dusty Arab villages,
looking in from the vastness,
making it a quiet and a beautiful day.

Alan Farrington

"The Opening"

You look into my eyes
and what do you see,
My life, my destiny.
Like opening a book
and turning the pages,
finding out my past
in different stages.
Digging, deeper and deeper
into my mind,
these are the secrets
I want to leave behind.
With help and kindness
you brought me thro'
you gave me health, life,
and I owe all this to you.

Lois Sweetman

Untitled

You know, what's falling down
And what is going up.
You know what is to lose,
and you know how to choose.

Don't say you don't remember,
Don't say that you forgot.
Those feelings stay forever,
So never let them go.

Keep going on and on.
Don't listen to the things they say.
Keep still, don't say that's right,
To those who think you're wrong.

The last thing I am saying,
remember you have friends,
Who still can live and love,
so everything from you depends.

Laura Podlipskaite

Poets

Some people say that poets
Are dull and utterly bore
Especially if the lines don't rhyme
After the ones before,
Some poets have a certain style
They write them all the same
Hoping that the ones they write
Might fetch them some fame.
Poets are a different breed
They are a little strange
Maybe your next door neighbour's one
Who knows?
You see this poem is different
You thought line twelve would rhyme
It shows that not all poets
Are predictable all the time.

Andrew Wade

Standing Alone

They gave you an opening.
And you saw a space.
You used your talent
to make a stand
and you changed the land.

It was clear to you
and simple then.
You reflected, introspected,
created and tasted
like a tool you used your pen.

It grew on you.
You grew through the blue.
Expanding and landing the pinnacle
you found your place.
Standing alone is what you had to face
standing alone with your place.

Alan Brett Smith

Change

Today is a special day
Another chance
To live God's way
If you can change
Anything at all
No matter what
Big or small
Nothing bad
Comes from trying
The change you feel
Is strange at first
It's only removing
The outer rust
A precious diamond
Is waiting inside
To shine one day
Sparkling and refined.

Kim McKellar

The Storm

A bleak and misty morning,
Another day is dawning.
The mist is rolling in from the sea.
Believe you me,
The day is cold and still.

The day is dull,
The dock is full.
A ship is tossed at sea.
Believe you me,
The day is cold and still.

A bleak and misty morning,
The next day is dawning.
The mist is rolling in from the sea.
Believe you me,
The day has ended.

Kelly-Emma Dawson

One Winter's Day

Outside it's cold
and white with snow
Time goes by very slow
as I sit here in the fire glow
I warm my toes
by the blazing logs
and listen to the
gentle snoring of my dog
She reaches up and licks my hand
because she knows I understand
Although she's growing old and grey
she still likes to run about and play
She will be faithful
until the end
Penny, my dog and best friend

Delia Gibson

Untitled

So something has gone wrong
Another problem you cannot face
A trial too hard to cope with
A cross too heavy to bear
In your frustration, in your anger
You shake your fist at me
You blame me for what has happened
For the cruel words that hurt
The letter that rejected you
The friend that betrayed you
All have become thorns
Behind each one I'm there
Ready for you to lean on
To pick you up and draw you near
All I ask is that you don't cut me off
That you don't push me aside
Don't use me as a punch-bag
And then walk away
Turn back to me, stay with me
Only I can help you.

Anne-Marie Fox

To Tara — My Border Collie

A small bundle of fluff
Appealing eyes

All teenage legs
Curious eyes

Try and catch me
Mischievous eyes

Am I doing it right?
Puzzled eyes

Adulthood gained
Happy eyes

I enjoyed that walk
Sleepy eyes

What is happening to me?
Bewildered eyes

My back legs won't work
Unhappy eyes

Do you love me still?
Worried eyes

I love you
Warm eyes

Joan Cutner

Tapestry

We all control our destinies
As down life's path we wend
Planning out the patterns
And hoping we can blend

All the discoveries
We make upon the way
All the things we'd like to achieve
Travelling from day to day

Life is a blank tapestry
For us to work upon
Weaving the colours skilfully
Making a pattern form

Filling in the colours
Some pale and others bold
Finishing the picture
Our story has been told

Enid Grace

Forgotten Memory

The sight that the eyes behold
As I gazed across the glen
Long before beheld a sight
I can ne'er recall again
As I walk along the rocky ridge
A memory comes and then
Tears like the mountain mist
Begin to fall again
The bracken and the heather
Like a carpet to the fen
Now only shadows of a past
I can ne'er recall again
The warble of the songbird
No more fills the glen
And once again those misty tears
Begin to fall again
I wander now along the path
That leads to only then
And once again the memory
I can ne'er recall again

Jean Allan

Unknown Entity

I am so small, so very frail
As I kneel at the foot of my life
And gaze to the future so far away.
Yet I'll take a step, my first step
Though no doubt I will stumble
Oh yes, I know I will fall
But I will climb upward, onward
As I strive to reach my goal.
There will be no one beside me,
No gentle arms to soothe
Nor calm my inward fears
For the guiding hand of a mother
will be absent throughout my years.
I will never know what her love is
Or, what I could become,
For she will always, ever be
A shadow, a hovering host
Of an unknown entity.

Elizabeth Saunders

War Cry!

I am uncontrollably crying
As I know I am dying!
I am too young to die
And that's why I cry!

My whole life flashes by.
All I can do is sigh.
I have had no life,
Only this strife!

My family I will never see.
A father I will never be!
Why was I born
For my body to be torn?

I am holding on in desperation.
I am a soldier of the nation.
I can no longer run.
My life is done!

I can't see!
Is this really me?
Death, here I come reluctantly.
Welcome a speck from the earth triumphantly.

Jennifer Bainbridge

Untitled

Love me,
as I need to be loved
as I love you.
Give me your hand, your heart;
share your soul with me.
Let us join together
our lives, souls, minds, hearts.
We are special together my love —
let us create a life,
a reflection of our love.
Love me,
that in our loving
we will know the wonder
of true bonding —
love that knows no end,
that lives forever.
Hold me my love,
never let me go.

Allison E. P. Fung

A Golden Moment

The sun rays came through the window,
As I sat alone in my room,
Outside was bright and beautiful.
While inside I felt full of gloom,
Then, suddenly, I saw you standing,
In the middle of the floor,
I'd been given a wonderful chance,
To see you again, once more,
You held my hand, and kissed my brow,
And said, "I love you Mum"
Then my 'Golden Moment' was gone,
As you were there no more,
But I know we'll meet again my son
And walk on God's Beautiful shore

Cathie McCall

Confusion

The sun shines
as I shine
the moon becomes entangled
with the stars
with the sky
Daylight sings
through the windows of complexity
and reality knocks on my door

And moonbeams shine
and star light shines
and raindrops patter in my head

And behind my eyes
the thunder and lightening
reign in my brain

And the window of complexity
Become a rainbow mixed with dreams

Denise Sellen

A Fancy

I heard a sound the other morn
As if some spirit, heaven-born,
To earth had strayed
And, seeing there
The glory of the dawn, had played
Upon his pipe a song.
In rapture, loosed from earthly ties,
It soared aloft and from the skies
In echoes came;
It rose and fell,
The theme was ever yet the same,
A joyful fount of praise.
I thought to glimpse that Spirit fair
That warbled such a wondrous air,
But this was all that I could see —
A blackbird in an apple tree.

Geoffrey H. Jackson

Just One...

Just one little tear
as noiseless as a deer
falls smoothly down my face
just as soft as lace.

Just one small sigh
as shattering as a cry
escapes from my throat
coming out as a different note.

Just one wrong word
said so loud that everyone heard
the pain in my heart was sealed
the looks in their eyes said it couldn't
be healed.

Just one lonely girl
left in a whirl
by myself in my fear
to carry on with another year.

Elizabeth Jones

Withered

Red rose dropped its royal head
As rain soft fell from sky,
Deep within my darkened grave
Mud buried dreamer's clay,
Sodden soil to sink my soul
And rainbows brightly fled,
Muffled fall of earthen soil,
Dead rose upon my head.

Elaine McGoff

The Widow

Envy not the widow
As she sits and drinks her coffee
And remembers — the happy
Days of long ago!!

Envy not the widow
She has not long to go
Till she too joins, the man
She lost, not so long to go.

And like the old song says
If heaven is kind — she'll wait
There to find — those two eyes
Of blue — still Smiling Thro' —
"At Me".

Catherine Browning

Nessie ("The Twist In The Tale")

We Nessie's ma name,
As you all know,
I live in the loch,
Somewhere below.

I know you've no seen me,
But that's no ma fault,
I've even jumped out the water,
And done a summersault.

I come up now and again,
For a look at the castle,
But every time a pop ma heed out,
Awe a get is hassle.

Noo am away back to the deep,
For a wee bit peace and quiet,
And maybe a wee sleep.

Noo a know you've no seen me,
So just think what you've missed,
'Cause I've been watching you,
While you've been reaching this.

David Head

The Aftermath

The love that you so highly held,
As you marched away,
Then in one moment of madness,
It was cruelly cast away.

Harsh words and recriminations,
To us were all in vain,
For what we had and threw away,
In one moment of lost restraint.

Hindsight and intervening years,
Do not erase the pain,
Things would be done so differently,
If we could relive that time again.

The parting caused such sorrow,
Not only to ourselves,
In the broken lives around us,
Lay hearts like empty shells.
Evelyn Cleghorn

Lost

I feel so utterly dead
At least inside my head
All day long
I sit
Thinking
Day after day
Where do all the pieces fit
Where did I go wrong
Where do I belong
Nowhere!
Lesley Cox

A Spider's Web

Oh gossamer thread from garden shed
Attached to nearby tree
A finer piece of tapestry
My eyes will never see.

So intricately woven
In a web of such delight
With dewdrops glistening on the rim
All sparkling and bright.

Oh what a busy spider
To weave a web so fine
Its silky threads all interspersed
In crissing crossing line.

And when your work is over
You sit there patiently
Awaiting unsuspecting flies
Who you will eat for tea.
Barbara Hampson

Summertime

Now that winter's cold has gone
And early spring is also done
At last the summer is here
sun, grass and trees are dear
To see the children in the park
And the dogs so joyous bark
Here today to see the lake
Ducks and sways to feed with cake
Beds of flowers in colours fine
Roses, bushes and trees of line
Beauty around we see so much
How grand life is when we go Dutch
Time in, time out we look for it
Picnic people on grass they sit
How grand the days on sunshine now
with birds a singing on the bough
Our days of summer warmth employ
Those happy feelings to enjoy
June Fury

Without A Single Doubt

Sometimes I wonder,
Back into the past.
My mind a show of pictures,
Racing back so fast.

My eyes, waterfalls,
Gushing with anger and pain.
And all the hatred I felt back then,
Haunts me over again.

Each picture tells a story,
They make me stop and think.
Somehow concealed inside them
Is a very important link.

A message? A moral?
I don't know what.
Like many pieces of string,
All tied up in a knot.

But maybe someday,
I'll work it all out.
My mind will be so very clear,
Without a single doubt.
Laura Waugh

Hold Me

I need to hold you in my arms
Because I love you so much
To savour all your charms
Slowly and not rush

Because I love you so much
I will be gentle and tender
Slowly and not to rush
Soft kisses I will render

I will be gentle and tender
Because I know it is your first time
Soft kisses I will render
Hoping you will be mine

Because I know it is your first time
I will put you at your ease
Hoping you will be mine
And that I will please

I will put you at your ease
To savour all your charms
And that I will please
I need to hold you in my arms
Joseph Doyle

My Favourite Thing

My favourite thing is a lemon,
Because, it allows me to indulge
In all the lovely food to eat
And yet control the bulge,
I take this in my morning tea
To help reduce the fats,
I find stains will soon disappear
When into my hands I pat.
I know when making strawberry jam
To obtain a better set,
I add the juice of a lemon
My palate it too does whet!!
What about those summer drinks
That make me feel so cool?
A slice with a gin and tonic
Oh!! What a talkative fool,
Now, am I a fool?
I know the answer - a lemon!!!
Dorothy Ashby

Hatred

I hate this girl
Because she's so perfect
She is so pretty
She is so slim

I hate this girl
Because of her figure
Because of her
Long, blonde hair

The man that I loved
Went to a disco
Guess who was there?
She who's so perfect
She with the hair

The things that I like
About the girl that I hate
Is her unshaped nose
And her bad personality
Dawn Fotheringham

Anuran Amour

How many frogs do I have to kiss
before I find my prince?
Human lips would sure be bliss.
How many frogs do I have to kiss?
Maybe snakes? Oh no! They hiss,
perhaps I need a few more hints.
How many frogs do I have to kiss
before I find my prince?
Annette Robinson

" Last Thoughts "

From birth to death,
beginning to end,
the good times,
... the bad,
Laughter and tears,
moaning and groaning,
As I near to my death,
life's gone by, with
troubles and joys
my desire to live
for just once more,
is blackened out
forevermore,
now that the end
is drawing near
praying silent prayers
"God bless me forever"
I'm fighting for life
but destined to doom!
Geraldine Green

Through My Window

Through my window, I can see
Birds, grass, flowers and bees,
Blooming Roses what a sight,
Shooting stars through the night,
Morning dew on the grass,
I see this through the glass,
Morning dew on the web,
On a spider's home or bed.

Roses drop their weary heads,
And sink down in the flower beds,
When winter comes the snow does fall
And lands upon the garden wall,
Then the snow of course does melt,
And then the rain begins to pelt,
The rain then stops and out comes the sun,
Letting us have some fun,
Through my window this is what I see,
Children playing happily.
Caroline McGuigan

Voices

Once was strong but now is weak
Black death working through the week
Fire shalt not keep away
The black death at his cruel play
Saddened eyes no future be
Only death the people see
Voices from the heaven's call
The children at their feet they fall
Weak and tearful was their life
Black death killing man and wife
Every tear that children shed
Sent them home with weary head
Even if they hadn't been clever
They would know they'd rest forever
Every bell that rang out loud
Would wave good-bye the ghostly crowd
Of children, husband, man and wife
One more hope but no more life
Off to heaven safely glide
On your heaven guarded ride
And when you reach the promised land
God will hold out his right hand

Emma Salmon

" Scarlet Tears "

Poppies swaying in the breeze,
Blood-red silent,
Ill at ease!

Symbolic, thus, of long lost love,
Love that lasted but a while —
Love that did my heart beguile!

Are they shedding tears for me?
Those Poppies standing silently...
Heads bowed low in sad repose...

Or is it rain that gently flows —
As such my tears do fall!

The pain returns within my heart,
As year by year,
Their petals fall
Upon the ground below.

For such a little while they stand,
Blood-red, silent,
Straight and tall!
Those scarlet Poppies —
They say it all!

Freda Ringrose

Somewhere

You are somewhere
breathing air.
Living, thinking, moving.
I wish I were there.
And in this somewhere,
I wander what you do.
Thinking of my thoughts,
The all and only you.
I want to tell,
but I wouldn't dare.
I want to be with you,
I want to be somewhere.

Deborah Murison

Contradiction

Darkness comes and with it light,
Day has dawned and here comes night,
Ugliness and beauty too.
So many gifts and yet so few.

Joy and goodness,
Life and death,
Peace and anger,
Stillness breath.

Christine Cliff

Childhood Remembered

We were so poor in the thirties
but everyone was alike
Lucky if we had roller skates
never dreamed of having a bike.

What happened to the whip and top
Hopscotch and Squashed Sardines
Hide and Seek, the skipping rope
games we played till our early teens.

We'd play for hours with marbles
Have fun with a bat and ball
Most cost only coppers
And some cost nothing at all.

Now the kids have video games
computers portable tellies
expensive trainers on their feet
where he had only wellies.

But I wouldn't swap my childhood
or my teenage years
for all the kids have got today
just don't outweigh their fears.

Elsie Wroe

Miracles In Our Midst

We don't see trees or babies grow
But grow they do
The miracle wonder
We should ponder
We don't see God
But He's everywhere
Never letting us walk alone
We don't see flowers grow
But grow they do
They sleep like us
Wake up like us
All aroma and trust
The sky is full of birds
Singing for pleasure and us
Their speciality the dawn chorus
We see the sun-moon-stars and rain
Flooding the world
With wonderful light-heat and drink
Let's praise God and keep alive
All those miracle wonders.

Katie Kent

Consider The Lilies

"Consider the lilies", once he said,
clothed in raiment white,
"And yet they labour not nor toil
God fills them with His light."

"Behold the birds of air," He cried.
"That neither sow nor spin,
And yet God watches over them
And they are fed by Him."

And if He cares the sparrows small
Arrays the lilies so,
What depth of love and tenderness
Will He not on us bestow.

If all our striving we would cease,
Cast (missing word it was cuts)
and trust in Him with all our hearts
Then He would be our guide.

For surely He who made the world
And every tiny seed,
Sees what's best for all of us
Knows our every need.

Kate Smith

Gilbert

So very old in years he was
But he carried those years with grace
And no-one un-informed could guess
From looking at his face
That he had a further problem
His sight so nearly gone
For in his look was wisdom
His eyes with interest shone

His mind was filled with knowledge
And memories of the past
His understanding perfect
His answers apt and fast
There was patience in his stillness
For all his friends to see
And, oh, I was so very glad
That one of them was me!

Helen Bruce

Hard Tears

It hurt, it hurt deep inside,
But I knew I couldn't cry,
I couldn't show my emotions,
Why, why did she have to shout?
What was she feeling?

I closed my eyes, tight shut,
But I felt a drip roll down my face,
I could taste the bitter salt in it,
I tried to stop, but it was no use,
I couldn't hold it in any longer,

The tears just kept on coming,
Until there were none left,
But what now?
Would she shout again?
I wouldn't know, I couldn't know.

But now it was she who cried,
I could feel her tears,
As if they were my own,
I held her close and tight,
Never would I let her go.

Leane Bottomley

My Love

The cold grey sea laps on the shore
But my dear love I'll see no more
Far out in the savage anguished deep
My dearest love is fast asleep

My love was young and brave and fair
Of charm and beauty he'd good share
But lost forever his smile so gay
Nor will my heartache go away

'Twas Christmas day he sailed away
My heart was sad he could not stay
The wind blew hard and harder still
The cruel sea was out to kill

My love, my love, I long for you
To hear your voice in accents true
To see your eyes and smile so gay
To have you kiss my tears away

G. Wilson

Springtime

Snowdrops, crocuses and daffodils,
Array the garden with all their will.
New shoots are appearing everywhere,
To show springtime is really here.

In the fields; now a sea of green,
New born lambs scamper free.
Everywhere now seems alive,
To show springtime has arrived.

Karen Faulkner

Miscarriage

You kick around inside of me
But no one knows of you
I haven't told my mam and dad
They haven't got a clue

I don't know what to do anymore
I dread to go to school
My childcare lessons mean everything
All of this is because of you

3 a.m. I woke up startled
I knew something was wrong
I couldn't feel you moving
I knew that you had gone

I'm lying here in hospital
I can't stop thinking of you
Would you have been a boy or girl
I just don't have a clue

My mom said she would have let you stay
It's too late now you're gone
I hope you're happy where you're at
You won't be lonely for long.

Catherine Hepton

" Dead Flowers "

Why not throw them out
Can't be bothered.
Why
No reason to
It doesn't matter now
Not much does
Such a feeling of sadness,
On the table
They are usually pretty
Fresh flowers in a bowl
Arranged with pleasure
By me
Cut from the garden
No one to notice
Just me
So, why bother anymore
Leave the dead ones there
Like the dead love.

Joyce Mastin

Cats

Cats in my bedroom
Cats in the hall.
Cats in the kitchen, but
The bathroom not at all.
Meowing in the morning,
Purring in the day.
Scratching at the door post,
Going out to play.
Sleeping in the washing,
Licking out the fish bowl.
Lapping cream,
Chasing paper in and
Around the house.
Rubbing at my legs,
Jumping on my shoulder.
Meowing, meow, meow.

Lee Stuart Bunce

A Manager's Paradox?

It seems to be,
at least to me
In times of strain and stress.
That to be alone is desirable,
Where the 'pace' of life is less.

Yet when achieved that aim, it seems,
is not the ideal solution.
Thoughts and wishes of hectic times
is the obvious evolution.

John Tattum

Shame

The thick black clouds loom,
Church bells boom,
The sounds of doom.

A candle light flame,
Hides the ones to blame,
When they hang their heads in shame.

They know what they've done
And it's too late to run,
After their harmless act of fun.

Their plan never worked
Now their faces smeared with dirt,
Realize that someone is hurt.

They think it could have been their mate
As they stare at the sorry state,
And await their forthcoming fate.

Hayley O'Riordan

Postcard

A postcard came.
"Ciao" it said.
No "Wish you were here."
No "Miss you" message.
A rushed word,
Hardly worth,
The bother.

Julie Palmer

What Is A Valentine

A valentine is someone you hold
close to your heart
Someone who makes you feel special
right from the start
He makes you feel warm inside
and holds you so tight
The one you always dream of
in the darkness of night
He is someone who cares
and loves you for you
Will always stay faithful
and never untrue
He is someone you share
everything with
He doesn't just take
He always gives
He's someone you fit with
just like a glove
The person you care for
The person you Love!

Emma Wall

To A Special World Champion

We were told to expect nothing
But a cabbage in a chair,
If we'd listened to the experts
We'd be in despair.

We struggled on regardless
Hoping they were wrong,
And watched our lovely daughter
Grow alert and strong.

Each little bit of progress
We greeted with great glee,
We felt we had a bonus
If only they could see.

Twenty years just flitted by
Our pride and joy unfurled,
Special sport seemed worth a try
Now she's Champion of the World.

Jane Spicer

Out Of Darkness

Out of darkness
Comes early break of dawn,
Time for complacency
"Peace" for thee,
As early morn, you see,
Time for solitude
While the world sleeps,
Quietness, serenity,
Tranquillity, being unperturbed
Feelings of not being disturbed
Brings us sheep closer
To the herd,
As we know
Of his "awareness",
And senses of his word.

John Barry Robinson

Untitled

There goes the baby
Crying again
If he keeps this up
I might just go insane

It's never in the morning
Always at night
As if he seems to know
Now the time is right

But no one else will help
They all stay in bed
"We never heard him"
That's what they said!

So, again I'm up
To make his bottle hot
And I can hear him laughing
While laying in his cot.

Linda Hare

Summer Balm

Light the summer breeze,
Dancing as she pleases
Drifting through the green boughs
Shimmering oaken leaves,
Basking through the grasses —
After cooling showers,
Flustering the flowers
To shake their skirts so dear,
Sending poppies bowing
Blushing at her coaxing
To kiss the golden corn
Shocking oaten ear;
Over ponds and water
She plays with ripples clear.
Happy dragonfly skims upon the breeze —
Adding to the gifts
She brings of summer cheer.

Angela B. Vanes

Smile

A smile is something we all have,
But don't always feel like giving,
Although it costs us nothing,
It can change our way of living.
For if you smile at someone,
It can open up their heart,
So they will smile at someone else
And that is just the start,
Now we have started the ball rolling,
As we merrily go along.
You smile at them, they smile at you.
You're ready for a song.
Although I cannot sing, myself,
I like to wear a smile,
So that it can make others feel
That life is still worthwhile.

Georgina Bertram

Catch The Chaser

Can you catch the chaser?
Dashing after dreams.
Invisible illusions,
All's not what it seems.

She sees a fleeting fancy.
Beauty to behold.
Its wealth is wisdom,
Not silver or gold.

Her livery's like lightning,
Designed by life itself.
It utters words of urgency,
Don't be left upon the shelf.

What magic might materialize,
Or could it disappear.
Catch the chasers heartbeat,
Listen whilst it's clear

Lesley Wells

Sadness

The sadness envelops my soul
deep in the dark abyss
where my heart once was
now is a shattered realm

My eyes look but they don't see
my mind wanders amid clouds
searching for a better place
willing myself onwards

My body suffers silently
housing a broken dream
too many illusions wrongly diagnosed
but not enough to end heartbreak

I feel the empty space
where my heart used to beat
with every pull of my senses it widens
the fissures are irreparable

So many feelings, so much pain
maybe tears will help ease heartache
time is a good healer so they say
but then time is infinite

Hayley Stones

Night Slayer

Pain, kill, torture.
Destroy the light,
Blight out existence
Nothing the same.

I want to die,
In a world where men cry,
Love is lust and hate is
A gorging of one's self.

Beautiful people rape
The cold corpses of their shadows,
I want to die on a planet,
That does not exist.

Take me, God, if you be,
To a place of magic and mystery,
To a hole in the ground where toads
Vomit and blood boils,

So heavenly black.

Kill me if you can,
Beast from the sky, I want out,

Yesterday.

Andrew Knell

Lost Youth

Doom and gloom
Destruction, despair
I stand alone
I do not care
Empty pocket
Stolen locket
Eyes red rimmed
I stand and stare

Youths rebel
They shout and yell
As wise men lead
Them into hell
No work, no pride
No self esteem
There's nothing left
They can redeem.

Elaine Roberts

Now That I Know....

Now that I know —
Do not allow me to infuse you,
and do not let me attempt to fill you

You are already saturated
— with her love —
Plump, sodden.
And I am still brimming, belching,
vomiting this forth
Like an incurably sick child....

Emma Caves

Departed Friend

My best friend's gone away,
Don't know how long it will be,
Before the tears stop flowing,
One year, two or three,
I know I'll never forget her,
Or all the things that she did,
The smiles, the love and laughter,
She gave when I was a kid,
And when I was all grown up
Still she was there for me,
Understanding and forgiving,
And as gentle as can be,
My friend's gone to heaven,
I miss her every day,
The memories never fade,
With me they'll always stay,
I know life's not forever,
One day my time will come,
And she'll be there to meet me,
My friend, my life, my mum.

Dianne Keeble

Edge

Falling
Down to an invisible Edge:
The cold, still heart,
White precipice of destruction.
Plains of indifference
Cushion the finality
Of passing the screaming-place
Silently.
None can return from the Edge
Without knowing the landmarks
But they are blown like sand
And learning is useless...
Better to stay near an oasis of tears
Than go on through the pain
To the Edge
Of no pain.

Julia Bishop

Dreaming On

I'm in my bed in a deep sleep
dreaming in a faraway land,
going through the woods as I speak
to a person who I don't understand.

Walking through a village,
knocking at a house,
finding out where I am
there comes a squeaking mouse.

Feeling hungry, feeling cold,
looking for a sign,
there comes an old lady
with her washing line.

Walking through the gardens,
sitting on a bench,
looking at the blazing flowers
I wonder where time went.

Julia Orr

Help I Am The Victim

I woke up sweating and in a daze,
dreaming you killed me in a maze.
And now your life is so protected
I feel my body has been infected.

People say "You're coping well,"
but they don't see what's inside this
shell, a shaking heart a mixed
up mind, and a loss of trust for
Those who are kind.

Not for a moment in this tiny day
Will thoughts of survival go away.

Lindsay Clair Hulme

Springtime

Lambs gambolling, fledglings cheeping.
Spring is here!
In greener grass, Daisies peeping,
Dandelions appear;
Bluebells streaming through the woods,
Misty blue arrayed;
Trilling brook reflects the mood
Of an April day.

Earth aroused from winter's sleep,
Feels the warmer sun,
Man walks tall on lighter feet,
Gardeners get work done.
Opening blossoms on the bough
Wait for buzzing Bee;
Hear the Cuckoo calling now!
Spring fulfils all needs.

Kathleen D. Netherton

End Of The Crocodile

Twenty years of silence,
except for the steady ice drip
of marital disharmony.
'He' is back again,
latching on the end of
a family crocodile.

Of course he paid his entrance fee
disinterest demanded it.
The years of knowing him
are bright with menace.
Time has made his venom harmless,
pity creeps in like a slow toad.

The Devil has told me
he always stashes cash.
Who am I to deny
his underprivileged children
death's eventual entitlement?

Constance Johnson

Lovers

I love my life with you,
Each and every day,
All the things you seem to do,
In your own special way.

I love you in the morning,
When the sleep is in your eyes,
I love the look upon your face,
When I give you a surprise.

I love the way you smile at me,
When you're relaxing in your chair,
And when I reach out to touch you,
I know you're always there.

I love the little things you do,
To please me in your way,
And how you always seem to know,
The very words to say.

I know I'll always love you,
And with you I'll be content,
Because I know the love we share,
Has been heaven sent.

Doreen Southall

Vandals

Breaking glass and running feet,
Echo down an empty street,
Crime and evil sows a seed,
For this is where the vandals breed.

Dirty curtains, walls with bugs,
Sniffing glue or 'shooting' drugs,
Drunken father, streetwise ma;
Rob a shop, or steal a car.

'Mug' an old man, or his wife,
Beat with stick or slash with knife.
Hate and greed are all you know,
In all the world, no place to go.

If only you could see, it's true.
That youthful beauty, belongs to you,
But there's no hope, these ones are hard,
Destined for the Prison Yard.

Lorna A. Tweedale

Dawn

Through the haze of misty light
   eloquent with sleep,
   and the velvet night,
Floating on a bed
   of cotton wool clouds,
Come soft dreams
   that escape the day.
Tranquil thoughts
   that belong in a world
   of magic moments
The flush of dawn
   creeps over the sky,
Changing the blue
   to a golden glow
A cascade of colour
   now touched with pink
Bringing a new day.

Emily Bowden

Untitled

Snowflakes falling to the ground,
Flying, twirling all around,
Big and small they dance and skip
Run and leap and slowly dip
To the earth, all gleaming white.
Snowflakes falling through the night.

Doreen Landon

Autumn

Frosted communities
Estranged
Congealed
Eyeballs
Calling
Beak
Breast
Small hand collectors
Suicidal leaves
Pasted
Printed
Folded as envelopes
By second class mail.

Anna Geatches

My Lucky Night

I sit in front of the telly.
Every saturday night,
Waiting for the numbers,
That will change my life.
My numbers are coming out
One by one.
My minds racing of the things
to be done.
Champagne dinner's.
Parties in town.
Presents for the family.
Perhaps a silky sexy gown,
A Holiday for Mom,
A new red car, for my brother John.
I'll buy a house, and live by the sea.
No more struggling, to make
ends meet.
But it all comes to an end
As I wake from my sleep.

Joyce Langford

Freedom

With the toss of his mane,
Eyes flashing bright,
This fiery young colt
Takes off into the night.
He lengthens his stride,
Hoof hitting stone,
The icy cold air
Cuts quick to the bone.
On he gallops,
Purpose in his stride,
Nostrils flared out,
Smelling the tide.
At last he is there,
Where he longs to be,
One of the wild white horses
Of the sea.

Alanna Allen

All Alone

A flower with no petals.
A bee with no sting,
A street with no cars,
A bird with no wing,

A shop with no customers,
A dog with no tail,
A cat with no claws,
A boat with no sail,

Loneliness,
How I feel,
A fishing rod,
Without a reel,
Like one part,
Missing the other,
That's how I feel,
Without my mother.

Cheryl Gray

Snowfall

The silence is deafening,
Falling —
On listening ears.
Snow blankets the Earth,
Quietly.
Transforming ugliness to beauty,
Darkness to silver,
Sparkling.
Nothing is moving, all is silent,
Lying undisturbed —
Is pure white snow.

Elizabeth Camp

State Of Mind

Falling deeper in despair
Falling, falling,
Deeper there
Is the bottom now in sight?
Will I hit it, will I fight?
Could my heart with
Feelings stir?
Upwards, upwards,
To the air
If my soul's desire took flight
I should once again delight
In endless day, not endless night
Perhaps I will just pause a while
Thinking, thinking,
Could I smile?
Leaving fear and dread behind
Loving, loving,
With all my mind.

Linda Potter

Goodbye To Winter

Winter days, dismal days,
Feeling rather low,
Oh, what's this I see
Peeping through the snow?
The dainty snowdrop proudly stands
It's the first little flower to show.

I feel my heart just leap with glee,
For it's brightened up my day.
Now we know that very soon
Spring is on the way.
Crocus, tulips daffodils
Are pushing through the earth.
Trees and bushes sprouting buds
For all that they are worth.

So winter's nearly done
And soon the sun
Will bring smiles to our face
With happy laughter all around
To brighten up the place.

Doris Fletcher

Aspirations

tree
fir
tall, heaven
seeking, upward
and inward, gently
moves branches, softly
releasing sweet scent
but never, O never, enfolds me;
scent sweet releasing
softly branches move
gently inward and
upward, seeking
heaven, tall
fir
tree

David Nelson

Sharon

Fair of hair and green of eye
Firm of breast and thick of thigh
Round of hips, a passionate lover
Faithful, kind a gentle mother
Understanding, slow to rage
Always funny, wise like sage
Athletic, friendly ever deep
What secrets doth thy heartbeat keep?
Your taste upon my lips doth linger
What price that ring upon thy finger?
Saintly, true with so much pride
To thee my heart on wings hath flied
To me you give your heart, your time
I was empty 'til he made thee mine
To me from thee a child was given
To be like thee so oft I've striven
Thou art mine, and I am true
Dearest Sharon, I love you.

Kevin George Curry

Untitled

You are just a little thing
Five feet and an inch or two
The moment I caught you in my eye
I fell madly in love with you
When I heard the music of your voice
I became your willing prisoner
I really had no choice
Oh darling I'm so happy
As hand in hand we walk
It is like a love song
When I hear you talk
We need not walk or talk my love
I know that sounds absurd
Our hearts are so in unison
We need not say a word
Just to hold you in my arms
And love you sweet paradise, sweet bliss,
No bee's ever made honey
Sweeter than your kiss.

Anthony Tortolano

Summer Evening

Red and gold the closing day,
Flame of fire the setting sun,
Shadows, purple, stretch and play
Upon the earth when day is done.
Stand and listen, smell and hear
All you miss when day is clear.
-Listen to the insects' whirr,
Song of river, creak of tree,
Sway of grass and kitten's purr.
-Smell the scent of new-cut grass,
Flowers in a hedgerow sweet,
Heather in a mountain pass,
Sea and soil and drying peat.
-Listen to the rustling leaves,
Pull of waves along the shore.
-Stand, and let the evening's peace
Wash away the stress of day.
Then refreshed, your footsteps turn,
Walking home in setting ray.

Jane Waite

Outside My Window

The birds flying up and up, oh how
I would love to fly,
bees, bluebottles, wasps and more
don't even have to touch the floor,
just flap their wings and up they go
flying looking down below.
Over the clouds away they go
beneath the sun I'd love to go.

Alice Marie Dixon

Candle Light

The string with its blade
flickering in the dark.
The wax dripping and hardening
Its solid liquid gas.
Your light sings me a lullaby softly
With your kind voice.
You glow up my paper
When I am writing.
Candles are victorian lights.
But be careful
They can be dangerous.
So BE AWARE.

Lucy Dumbrill

Pittsburgh University

Hail to thee dear Alma Mater
  For all thou didst for me.
Your warmth and erudition
  Were there for all to see.

Where else exists the coupling
  Of Professors who really teach
Yet are flexible in their tactics?
  A goal not many can reach.

Professors heavy with learning
  Yet unable to explain a thing
Alas, are people we've all met
  But 'tisn't of them I sing.

I sing of well rounded learning
  In a setting of beauty supreme
Surrounded by sportsmen unequalled
  Of what more can one possibly dream?

Dorothy Miller

Married Bliss!

For richer, for poorer,
For better, for worse,
As I lay there at night,
These lines I rehearse.
I toss and turn
In time to the shaking.
My nerves are on edge
With the constant vibrating.
What would it measure
On the Richter scale?
Or how many I wonder
In decibels?
I reach for my earplugs
From the bedside drawer,
As I lay there listening
To that constant snore.
With the force of my elbow
I give him a dig,
With the stark realization,
I've married a pig!

Diane Mary Watt

Sweet Repose

She gathered a petal
For each silent tear
Shed in her loneliness
Silence and fear
Just one tiny petal
For long lonely hours
And felt herself drown
In a carpet of flowers
She scattered them upon her bed
And made a garland for her head
On her breast she placed a rose
Then she lay down to sweet repose.

Barbara Pitter

What About The Children

If we could learn the lesson,
from mistakes we made before.
There would never be a reason,
to start another war.

When you gaze upon the country,
where the bullets fly around.
You're sure to find the victims,
lying dead upon the ground.

But what about the children,
who are standing there all crying.
With fear and desperation,
as they watch their parents dying.

Their eyes are full of sadness,
and their bodies shake with fear.
Whenever there's a stranger,
who tries to get too near.

The children are the losers,
at the end of every day.
Can anybody tell me,
why the children have to pay?

John Griffiths

Prayer For Peace In Northern Ireland

O Lord in Heaven I cry to Thee
From strife and war my country free,
My heart is torn with grief and pain
O let my country live again.

For many years we've lived in fear
With bombs and bullets ever near;
Our land is weary of its pain
O let my people smile again.

Let men of violence cease to kill
Remorse and sorrow their hearts fill;
In repentance humbly bow their knee
Ask Jesus from their sins to free.

Lord, You are merciful and kind
You save, forgive, grant peace of mind;
From our wilful ways we must first depart
Ask Your forgiving love to cleanse our heart.

Grant courage dear Lord I humbly plea
For my trembling lips to speak up for Thee;
In this dear land may Your will be done
And all glory given to Your Son.

Edith Kennedy

Bereft

I took a vow of poverty
Gave away my property
Silver and gold I sold
Nothing remained Tear-stained
Bereft of all I possessed
Depressed I wanted you

I took a vow of chastity
Denounced all my curiosity
Never to conspire with desire
Goodbye vanity Hello banality
Bereft of all that obsessed
Transgressed I desired you

I took a vow of obedience
Denying self and confidence
No choice No inner voice
Now compliant and not defiant
Bereft of all things expressed
Distressed I needed you

Austen A. Penlington

That Grassy Hilltop

Luscious leafy greens
Glisten in the light,
Never have I seen
One so burly and bright,
Towering above the village,
As high as the eye can see,
Luscious leafy foliage,
Can this really be?
Upon that grassy hilltop,
'Tis rooted and shall stay,
A century is not a lot,
To an Oak, 'tis but a day!
But go they say it must,
For fall someday it may,
And downhill roll towards the ground,
Where children laugh and play,
So early one dawn when we heard the sound,
An angry thundering and crashing down,
We knew it had to be one to go,
'Twas either the children or the tree.
Aasia Bibi

Aspects Of Love

I stand in pools of watery stars
Glistening on God's wondrous chain
Where heaven meets mighty mars
Taking me up on his flowing mane

Lovely flower you catch my eye
I long to caress your slender waist
Sweet nectar from your lips sigh
Filling my cup with a wanton taste

A storm rose and swore at me
Bright berry on a mountain ash
A distant sky lark sang in my lea
Till the rain spilled with a flash

I touched a wandering butterfly
Anointing her serene and silken face
My tears rose and fell to lie
In the beauty of her lace

Her eyes like poppies set in silent rosary
Lift my heart on a golden stem
To my troubled brow sweet rosemary
A blessing for the growing day, Amen
John Crofts

Doggie

Doggie, Doggie don't bite me,
I'm not a tree,
I'm not a bee,
I'm not a toy nor a boy.
I'm just myself, not anyone else.
Catherine Himer

Love You, Love Me

Hammer in your head
Gun against your heart
Tied against the bed
Used right from the start
All your days are black
Maybe it's all over
All your dreams are broken
Your life's going nowhere

Caught amongst the flames
Passion doused by water
Nothing but to gain
Jesus walked on water
And you can't find a way
The sun has clouded over
Can you make life pay
Can you say you love her
Ian Hall

Be Happy

My dear where do you
go to when the day is done
like flotsam floating
on a stream
Do you sail on and on
my darlings, why do
you cry, is life so full
of woe
My dears, be happy
dream a dream
and knowing a blue
star is yours to reach
out for.
Float on a cloud
look down to
meet the stream
be happy basking in
its warmth
go on.
Cynthia Arnett

Evening Over Dhaka

Dusk creeps slowly across the sky,
Gold streaked clouds
Rose-pink wondrous light of sunset
Enchanting shades of evening.
Lengthening shadows, and
Late — the last birds hurry
Home to their roosts
Dancing, flittering fireflies,
Noises of the night.
From the City of Mosques,
The call to evening prayer
Floats on the cooling air, from
Across the river —
Flowing softly, leisurely
Towards the wide Bay of Bengal.
Averil Jones

The Fourteenth Of February

Bunches of florists
Haunt office-block alley-ways:
Prudent receptionists
Place buckets near the doors.
Despite the cold,
Office-girls wear short skirts
And hopeful expressions.
Even the Sun shines
On this transplanted spring day.
In Napoli and Firenze
Lovers kiss in sunshine streets,
While we, no longer cold
Though oblivious to an ice-blue sky,
Surreptitiously snuggle in restaurants
and cafés...

*On this star-crossed lovers' day
Have another glass of wine,
Become so sloshed that you will say
You'll be my Valentine.*
David J. Davies

The Glade

In the green and leafy glade
I sat alone cold and afraid
As the deer silently leapt
I turned my head and slowly wept
I knew I was no more alone
and that my heart had been as stone
Give me a heart of flesh I pray
So I may help others on their way
Thank you for that leafy glade
Where alone I sat and prayed
for there my heart became like new
and my life was given back to you.
Karin Field

Endless Pounding Haze

We who have lived
Have also died
For our memories still remain
Of the sorrow, and the pain
And we live them everyday
Through this endless pounding haze
Our sorrow will last long
From day to day that goes on
But there's nothing left to do,
No one can help us get through
For we have seen the cry of death
That lingers on through this
Endless pounding haze.
Bernie Jay Jordache

Children

Many daughters and many sons
Have been taken by the hand of man
And delivered into the hands of God.
Distraught parents left on earth
Are told by the cloth of God
That their offspring
Is in a better place.
Where is this place
That can care for our loved ones
Better than we?
God is life?
We need to die?
Where is God in all of this?
His son was killed by a loving kiss;
He was the lucky one.
Death allowed him home
To live together with the love of his father.
John Lambert

Untitled

When God made the world
He gave us the trees
We were blessed with the sunshine
And a cool summer breeze

He sent forth the seasons
The rain and the snow
The flowers of springtime
And rivers that flow

He sent us the creatures
That inhabit our lands
The fish in the sea
And the soft yellow sands

He sent forth the bluebird
To soar from above
Then looked down with passion
And gave us his love

But of all God's Creations
One compares with no other
The miracle he sent
Whom I call my dear mother
Andrew Paul Vanviere

Felix

So calm, slender, erect and proud.
He sits before me.
His ears alert in case of danger.
He listens tentatively.
His coat, like velvet covers him.
Magnificently worn.
Emerald eyes shine like glass.
Observe the world with scorn.
You are a magnificent beast indeed,
So solemn, quiet, yet strong.
Handsome little cat.
To no-one do you belong.
Jenny Crisp

The Soldier

With helmet reflecting the evening sun
He surveyed the field of death
The cries of anguish, fear and pain
The rattle of man's last breath

Stench of death from man and horse
The battlefield was filling
Pike and sword, axe and flail
Had done their task of killing

Whether the cause was justified
Was not of his deciding
He only knew that friend and foe
Were now with God abiding

His limbs were aching, his mind confused
Yet somehow he felt strangely at peace
This time he'd survived to fight again
The honours of battle were his

Think not too deeply of what you see
Just thank God it's yours to survey
The eyes that have closed, will never reopen
They have seen their last break of day

Kenneth Helm

Out Of Season

Autumn days, skies are bleak
Hear the wind howl and shriek
See the cliffs, orange red
Scale the heights, dizzy head
Screaming gulls, fishing catch
Quayside bustle, open hatch
Fish and chips, seaside fare
Crunching pebbles, wind in hair
Along the front, take a ride
Watch the boats catch the tide
Pier is closed, arcades shut
Absent deck chairs, padlocked hut
Choppy seas, green and blue
Evening skies a crimson hue
Closing shutters, early nights
Setting sun, twinkling lights
Wending home, parting ways
Fond thoughts of autumn days.

David Johnstone

Rescue

Network of friends saved me,
Held net so taut
I bounced back.

Gail Longrigg

Sorrowful Thoughts

If insecurity were collateral
I could buy the earth
If treated a little better
I would know my worth

If being hurt by someone
Meant a guiding light
The times I've been degraded
Would only be a slight

If weakness were a strength
I'd be very strong indeed
If being frightened were an asset
I'd be sure to succeed

A person without thought
What a waste of space
Dare I consider myself
Part of the human race

People say I should be
To them I'm worth a deal
But if you're nothing to yourself
How can they think you're real?

Beverly Balderstone

Spirit's Reflection

I hear the tolling of the bell,
hollow senses follow;
in close proximity - I note
the mourners bid to come
and pray that I stay out of hell.

I see a steeple tall and straight
and windows of stained glass.
The gravestone's silent testament,
inscription bold and true,
the final words confirm my fate.

Chanting the hymn - a mournful dirge
by organ's reedy tune;
the sound of voices - not too strong,
vague memory of me.
Is this the sound my soul to purge?

Now - the cleric ceases praying,
formalities are done.
Alone to enjoy all quietness -
reflect on life that's gone.
Ah! Farewell - I'll not be staying.

Helen Reynolds

Untitled

I've sat here all night,
hoping that you are alright.
And here I wait,
Waiting for you to open the gate.
Outside I see rain,
And hope you would come in and
   ease my pain,
But deep inside I really know,
that you will not be back again.

Charlene Stevenson

Abused

Lying there, like a dinosaur
How could you, as I grew,
I never knew what to do.
There was no lollipop woman
No bull in a field
Except the one made of china
Reflected by the mirror.
Framed, the art of loneliness.
Portrayed, fragile and dismayed
A lifetime's array.
No time to joke, or play.

Iain Codona

Red Rose

I am delicate as the petal,
I am strong as the stem,
I am sharp as the thorns,
I am sensitive as the scent,
And my name ... Red Rose,

My eyes behind the veil are shy,
Like the opening of a new bud,
I count the minutes,
That are shown on the clock,
And see the brave day sink
Into the darkness of the night,

I stand alone in the night,
Longing to hear you say the words,
I ... Love ... You,
Those heavenly words from your lips,
Are like the fountain in my garden,
Which contains the spring of my
Everlasting eternal love,

As the beauty of the red rose never dies,
My love for you, my darling, will never die.

Anbarasi Horajoo

The Snowdrop

At the foot of a tree
   I chanced to see,
To my delight, a snowdrop white.

Her head was bowed
   But she was proud
For she had braved
   Chill winds that raved.

To bring her tidings,
   Loud and clear,
And tell us all
   That spring is here.

Albert W. Holliday

I loved you and you left

I loved you and you left
I dreamt about you and you came,
But that was just a dream,
Nothing more.

I loved you and you left.
I searched for you and found you,
But I didn't let you know,
I knew.

I loved you and you left.
I hurt you and you cried,
But I left you there,
To die.

I loved you and you left.
You hurt me and I shouldn't have cared,
But I did and yet,
Not now.

Cathryn Smith

The Life Of A Toaster

My place is next to the microwave.
I have a pleasant view...
... of the kitchen.

They think
   My purpose in life
   is
      to toast.

It is not.

I am the reincarnation of
   Ginger Rogers.
I waltz with the whisk.
Fox-trot with the fork.
   Maybe's not.

I was really a wedding present.

Joanne Costello

Black Jack

I have a friend who is black,
his name is Jack.
Yes, you have guessed!
He is a cat.

Looks so cunning,
sitting on the mat,
waiting for porridge doused in milk,
7:30 a.m. at that.

In a devious way he talks,
purr, meow, purr, meow,
paws nudge, claws come out,
only being playful is his pact.

Green eyes pierce me through,
seem to say, look after me,
because after all is said and done,
I am your friend, black Jack.

Kathleen Gosling

Helen

I wrote this poem just for you,
I hope you like it, as much as I
like you.
With your beautiful looks and
engaging smile,
I hope one day you will be mine,
don't give up on me yet, as I've
still got plenty of zest,
me and you, could be the best!

Keith Huntington

Mum

Mum I miss you, please come back,
I know you would, but can't.
There are times I really need you,
to hear me be a part.
I need to hear you talk to me,
to share and talk things out.
Only you would understand.
and help me work it out.
I've tried to tell some people,
explain just what it's like,
they just can't understand me
or what I'm all about.
You told me once I'd miss you,
I never understood.
I miss you Mum and love you,
you knew I always would.

Karen Luff

The Change

Your love for me is changing
I see it in your eyes
No more loving glances
I'm waiting for goodbye

You used to take me places
And shower me with gifts
Now bickering is all we do
We call them lover's tiffs

You love me with your body
I love you with my heart
Yet when you hold me close
We seem so far apart

We used to talk of many things
But all that now is dead
The only thing we've kept alive
Is making love in bed

Someday soon the change will come
And one of us will say
We cannot go on like this
It's time to walk away

Colin S. Webb

Waiting

We are waiting
For the
Mysteries of self
To reveal
Their secret mysteries!
The joyous union.
We unite in waiting.

Ancient are the supple movements
Our universe!
Gels as one.
And our dreams
Are like old origins
Of our selves
Origins we cannot find!
Like the frozen children on the beaches
of time
Acting out memoirs from our minds

John Ennis

Autumn In The Valley

Looking up over the valley
I see many shades of green and brown,
rust and gold
Gold like treasure, which unfolds
before my eyes, in unending pleasure.
Under the chalk pyramids
that stand high in the breeze,
the multitude of squares
which I thought were fields
on closer scrutiny reveals
the curling tops of trees.
Oh how I wish I could paint
all this beauty I see,
The halo of houses, caressing the hills,
Tree tops of russet hues
Such magnificence to which the mind thrills
Many horizons, going up, going down,
In the midst of which
is LEIGHAM — NOT FAR —
from Plymouth town.

Joan Dubicki Matthews

I Can See

I can see the sky clear
I see the clouds white
I see the grass green
and a sun that shines bright.

I can see the sky turn dark
I see the stars twinkle
I see the frost glisten
on the grass in the park.

I can see the sky turn dull
I see the rain fall hard
I see a cat hiding,
in someone's backyard.

All of this as this is life
but what would we do
if we had no sight?
We'd have to listen, we'd have to hear
and touch for a clue to all that is near.

A world of darkness, And yet so bright
for your memories stay
when you loose your sight.

Beryl Joanne Losits

I Love You, Mum

Even though you're not here anymore
I still sit here thinking of you.
Wondering what will happen to me now.
I try to carry on but it's hard to.

I watch each day pass me by,
Living each day of my life, alone.
It's harder than I expected
But there is nothing I can do now.

I have many memories of you.
I know I'll never let them go.
We all remember the good times
Even some of the bad times.

I know there is my life left
But I wish you were here as well
Helping me through the good and the bad
Although I know this will never happen

My life is not the same anymore
But I have to carry on for your sake
I only have one thing left to say, that is:
I still love you, Mum.

Georgie Bail

New Age History

Around the corner,
I turn and watch
The people huddled together
Too scared to speak or cry out,
What is happening,
Red faces, loud voices.
No way out, no corner to turn,
Pitiful screams, bottles crash,
The Red, White, and Blue Army.
Out on the street.
Such hatefulness and sorrow,
Could this be the new tomorrow.

We cheer in the street
And walk together.
Forever a dream, we see,
Pictures in our faces,
Of blood and fears.
No more dreams, no more united
struggle
To find our freedom within.

Loretta Lathwood

An English Friend

Happy birthday, Lawrence
I wish you well
Whether Wales beat England
Only time will tell

Watch out for young Arwel
The new number ten
He's mean and his cunning
A new breed in Welshmen

The dragons are hungry
There's so much pride within
And that will be the big difference
On Saturday when we win

Don't take it too personal
Just have a nice day
Drown all your sorrows
And get Lindsey to pay

Cynthia Davies

So Unfair

If I had my Dad
I would not feel so sad

If I had my Mum
I would not feel so mad.

In the depths of despair
It seems that no one cares.

People all around you but
You're not sure who you are

No-one to turn to
No-one that matters anyhow.

Feelings so strong encase you
Life and living without your parents
is nearly too much to bear.

Karen Brent

Earth Awakens

Mother earth stirs and smiles
Ice caps melt above the clouds
Running into flowing streams
Birds build nests in budding trees
A watery sun lights the sky
The warm breeze passes by
It shakes the spider web of pearls
Plants are growing in the earth
In bluebell woods the wildlife play
Spring is surely on its way

Doreen Atterton

Sarah's Retreat

If I had a wish for just a day,
I would wish to get away.
A room will do with just a bed,
Maybe a pillow for my head.
No clocks, no phone, no radio or T.V.,
Just a door that has a key.
I would like a window too,
That maybe has a country view.
Then I could sit and dream all day,
Or even sleep my time away.
But after this I'll be alright!
You see I like my busy life,
So if you know of just the place,
where I could go and get some space,
Or is it really such a feat,
To find for me a quiet retreat....

Brenda Wibberley

My Dream

If I could win the Lottery,
I'd want the world to see,
I'd give up a percentage,
To my favourite charity.

I'd buy a house, a nice fast car,
I'd even buy a yacht,
I'd phone up friends and relatives,
And say, "look what I've got".

My wardrobe would be full of clothes,
My shoes, (a pair a day),
I'd go to theatres near and far,
And take a holiday.

But now my dream has ended,
All thoughts of greed must cease,
This world does not need money,
But love and hope and peace.

Debbie Browning

Whisper A Prayer

Whisper a prayer for me,
If nothing else,
I long to know that you'll remember.
Hold my hand one day,
To comfort,
To ease my sadness.
Listen as you have before,
And understand
For that is all I ever ask.
But alas, do none of this
Unless your heart permits it;
For my soul cannot accept
Forced feelings of compassion,
And my heart cannot bear
Understanding that flows
From pity.
So whisper a prayer for me,
But only if God will listen.

Elizabeth Raven

Feelings

I'm sorry if I hurt you
If you thought I didn't care
But in my heart I loved you
Even though I wasn't there
Now you're gone I miss you
More than any words can say

The pain I feel inside for you

Won't ever go away
I'm glad for the time we had together
The love we shared
No other love in the World
Can ever be compared

Carol Tuckett

Little Imp

I sometimes sit and ponder
If you are a girl at all,
Or if you are the devil
Disguised and made so small.

Sometimes you make me happy
Sometimes you make me sad,
Sometimes you make me love you
But mostly make me mad.

You torture and torment me
And make my life a living hell,
But then you have a change of heart
For why, I still can't tell.

Then you're like a little angel
With a smile so sweet and gay,
You lift your little arms to me
And that just makes my day.

You tell me that you love me
As I hold you on my knee,
How can I stay so mad at you
When you are only three.

David H. Rogers

The Viewers View

Whilst watching couples on the box,
I'm bored by all the bed!
The woman strips and then the man
And all the clothes are shed,

Then we get full frontals
And watch the writhing start,
I just sit there waiting
For the story line, next part.

I'm sure it was much nicer
When couples just held hands
And closed the bedroom door on us,
Whilst waves rushed on the sands.
We got the love and meaning,
Without sweat and eating kiss
Love seemed more mysterious
And surely kinder bliss.
Or is it on the modern stuff
That I'm not really sold.
And the reason I'm complaining
Is that I'm just getting old.

Flora Passant

Unfulfilled

My heart grows sad
I'm feeling lost
Is it all worth it
Or will it cost?

A mother of two
One more on the way
I'm tired, exhausted
At the end of the day.

In a four bedroom house
Is where I live
I have so much
Yet not much to give

I feel I am nobody
Being told I'm 'just a mum'
Everyone believes
That us mums are so dumb

Is it that I
Am brought here by fate
Or have I missed out
And now it's too late!

Denise Cooper

The Gunner's Lament

I'm gunner do this
I'm gunner do that
I was gunner do all sorts under
This artillery hat

I'm gunner go to exotic places
I'm gunner fight in all the wars
I'm gunner sort out Ireland and
End all these bloody tours

Sometime soon I know
What I'm gunner do
I'm gunner retire and wish
"A good gunner farewell
To all of you"

John W. Cookson

Relevance

Her soul screams out
in bewilderment,
Her voice lost,
Questioning her identity.

Through the dark void
of insanity,
she seeks to find
her escape.

The mist of imbroglio
Shadows everything
with doubt.

Emma Lee Cooper

My Dad

If we could only walk awhile
In fields of grass so green
Poppies, Daisies, Buttercups
Some new as yet unseen

If we could only talk awhile
With arms linked as we stroll
Our laughter soon would fill the air
Above the clouds would roll

If we could only sit awhile
In all these pastures green
Our silence would absorb the wonder
Of nature's work as seen

If only dear friend you had not gone
To pastures, fresh and new
We could walk awhile and talk awhile
With me, just beside you.

Julie Lees

Overweight?

Slumped back
In the chair
Watching neighbours
Enjoying an eclair

Thinks she's fat
So don't want a date
I ask myself
What's overweight?

Is it twenty stone?
Maybe eleven?
For a small person
It could be seven.

If you feel comfortable
With what you weigh,
Then you should be able
To enjoy your day.

Whose idea was it
To choose I wonder?
What weight's over!
And what weight's under!

Emma Bowden

Dedication

I have loved you
in the dawn of time
as woman needs man
passionately and sensually
but now,
I will love you
till the end of time
and past eternity
when our flesh can no longer join
but our souls can meet.
Grace Agyapoma Nkansa

Winter Silence

Muffled silence all around
In the trees and on the ground.
Houses icing-covered lie
Shining out against the sky.
Crunching footsteps thick and deep
On the ground which lies asleep.
Frozen pond and waterfall,
Blanket covered hedge and wall.
Icicles drip in the glow
Of the winter sun, to show
That she is still giving heat
Though the coldness chills our feet
Soon the snow will melt away
Bringing on a warmer day.
Kathleen Mitchell

Each...

Each has a world
in which to contend.
To recall when it started
ponder when will it end.

Each world so unique,
yet each one the same.
With sadness and weeping —
a lonely heart to blame.

Each heart will feel sadness,
be broken and shattered.
But always beats strongly
for that which has mattered.

Each heart has the power
to strive 'til at last.
Each beat pushes sad times
into memories of the past.

Each had a world
in which to contend.
Where lows can be raised
knowing each has a friend.
Eliza

Idle Dreams

Let me sit
In winter time,
And relive memories past of mine,
Among the books I treasure most,
In this room I love so much,
Dimly lit;
While outside the lives of
Others carry on,
Their ways of which are many.

Let me sit
In summer time,
On this grass so bright and green,
Among the flowers that I love,
Beneath these trees with leaves
Of sheen,
And once again,
I'm glad this earth
Is mine to live upon.
Janet Elizabeth Weaver

I Miss You

I miss you Nan, sitting there
in your chair.
Your warm hug, your kiss,
I miss.
The stories of old
you told.
Your reddening face
by the fireplace.
The delights you'd cook
everyone had a second look.
You gave such loving care
I now know this is rare.
You gave me a key, the door to find
my own mind.
I miss you Nan, from deep within my heart
You and I know, we'll never really part.
You gave much, to many
You were rich without a penny.
I hope now your infectious laughter
fills the heavenly hereafter.
Karen Hayes

Daughter

Giving birth to a daughter
Is a dream come true
The face of an angel
Her eyes are dark blue
As you watch her grow up
And play with her toys
You will know quite soon
She will be ready for boys
The ribbons have gone
She's growing up fast
In a few more years
She will be married at last
She will borrow your clothes
And your make-up too
The years have gone by
You know your works through
But when she walks down the aisle
With her husband to be
Take time to think
Who's a proud mum (Me).
June Trayner

Thirty Something

Becoming thirty something
Is a real drag
Grey hair starts appearing
Things begin to sag

Becoming thirty something
Is a real pain
You remember being eighteen
In your mind you feel the same

I look into the mirror
Is that really me in there
Middle age is spreading
All those tyres going spare

My bikini days are over
A one piece is a must
It's just such a shame now
My stomach is bigger than my bust

Still life begins at forty
Hold that thought because
There's only one thing to look forward to
It is the menopause.
Anne Cross

Devotion

To see you well again
Is all I'm hoping for,
To walk with you, talk with you
And hear you laugh once more.
I sit at your bedside
Watching as you sleep,
Trying to hide my silent tears
You must not see me weep.
All I can do is comfort you
For just a little while;
I hold your hand and talk to you
Hoping to see you smile.
I never once hear you complain
About your suffering and pain.
I shall do anything I can do;
I will give all I have for you.
There is no doubt, I will cope,
Because in my heart there is always hope
You will get well again.
Caroline Hill

Loving Thoughts

My love for you
Is as the day is long
My love for you
Keeps me here, where I belong

Your love for me
A gift you freely give
Your love for me
I hope will last as long as I live

Our love for each other
Keeps our hearts entwined
Our love for each other
Weathers the sands of time.
Lynn Rose

Our World

The world in which we live
Is indeed a very strange place
Or is it the people in it
Or indeed the constant pace

To keep up with the Jones's
Is the phrase we've often heard
That would be quite something
If only anyone cared.

The breed they call the human race
Is slowly going down hill
Self first is all they think about
Sex, debauchery, or the pill

One cannot read the newspapers
Or even switch on the telly
Without the tale of murder and rape
Gods built world turned into jelly
Kathleen B. Counihan

Zoo Animals

When I went to the zoo,
I saw a monkey go oo oo.
I saw him eating a banana
In his pyjamas.

I saw a lion roar,
his bottom was sore.

A seal had a chill,
it felt quite ill.

I saw a penguin,
pretending to be mending,
something bending.

I will say bye for now,
see you next time at the zoo.
George Lindop

Love Has Passed

The silence of you here
is not the pleasure of my heart
Your sweetness now too far
to recall your sudden smile
At breeze rippled lakes we walked
our hands to feel
The trees have bent to wind
our love the fallen leaves.

Christopher Irwin Poynter

Nostalgia

Sitting here watching the TV
Is that all we do
We've become so lazy
Hour by hour wasted away
We must be crazy

People used to gather
Around the piano
For a sing along
And later have a natter
Round the hearth

They used to have discussions
With one another
You'd stand alongside
Your brother
And listen to your mother

Now we're all divided up
Miles apart
In our little sections
All going in our own
Different directions

Kathryn Longley

My Future Husband

I am sending this letter,
It can only get better,
Now that you're about,
Without a doubt,
You're driving me crazy.
No, I am not lazy
Day in, day out,
Finally it's come true,
It's just me and you.
In love and in bed
We never see red,

You're simply the best
You know the rest,
Change you I'll never
Forever and ever.
I will love you forever.

Joyce Nicholson

To Him The Glory

Can you feel the excitement,
it's like electric in the air,
how great the presence of our Lord,
we feel him everywhere.

We feel his love surrounds us,
as we sing and praise his name,
our hearts are full to bursting,
with this love we can't contain.

How blessed we are that he chose us,
to serve him out of love,
to be used as an instrument,
through whom his works are done.

For as we seek to do his will,
all will plainly see,
the likeness of our Lord and king,
who dwells in you and me.

Linda Bleach

Love...

Love has to be given,
It cannot be bought,
It comes from within you,
Cannot be taught.

Love has to grow,
Like corn in a field,
Love can protect you,
It can be a shield,

Love is a pleasure,
Love is a strain,
But love will guide you,
In sun and in rain.

Love is to obey
Honour and protect,
Love is to remember,
Never forget.

Love enters your heart,
Never asks why,
It makes you eternal,
Love will not die.

Louise Burks

Untitled

It came to me as night comes,
It did not make a sound,
It took my heart and crushed it,
Then scattered it around

It came to me as night comes,
As silent as the grave,
It took my heart and picked it up
And said your life I'll save

It came to me as night comes,
And now I could not doubt,
This thing called love consumed me,
It turned me inside out

It came to me as night comes,
I could not fight again,
I gave my heart,
My love,
My all
And surrendered to the pain

Bruce Watkins

Choices

My will to live has left me
It didn't have far to fall
And I hope you all will heed
The futility of it all

Because my love has turned and ran
And money's feeling tight
The more I think, the more I learn
That nothing turns out right

As Lady Luck's a tricky soul
Who knows your dreams and teases
She lets you have one sniff of joy
Then lets fate do as he pleases

The only way to win the fight
Is attack life at full force
Never stop or pause to think
Just let it run its course

So I guess I'll carry on
With choices made for me
You'll find my body's got no choice
But at least my mind is free

Andrew Jones

Untitled

To be in Devon in early Spring
It is a wondrous thing!
To walk beside the river Dart
Is joyous to the heart.
Clouds that scurry across the sky
As we wander by
In between the whispering trees
Bending in the breeze.
The water swirling in the stream
Turning froth to cream.
Nature's ever-changing scene
Now burgeoning in green.
It is God's gift renewing birth
To all of us on earth.

Hazel K. Lees

Memories

In the twilight of our life
It is sad that we must part,
Now you have gone, and left me
Alone, with an aching heart.

I know that you are in heaven,
Please keep a place for me,
And if we are re-united
How happy we both shall be.

I really truly loved you,
It was plain for all to see.
Your every word, deeds and smiles
Were 'all the world' to me.

I really truly loved you
My life with you was bliss,
But, little did I know then
There was sadness, such as this.

The sunshine from my life has gone,
As each day to God I pray,
That I may be fit to join you
In His paradise one day.

George Ferrier

Death Lottery

Brushing past your lips
It leaves your eyes no light
No prejudice to any being
No sense of timing right.

Age there is no preference
Nothing can prevent
Most I know will fear it
Borrowed time unspent.

Why pay to play the lottery
As from the time we breathe
We each receive a chance to play
Until the time we leave.

Dawn Clayton

A Rose

A Rose is a beautiful flower.
It looks up to the heavens above.
It symbolises an emotion,
And that emotion is Love.
It opens its intricate petals
Like the blinking of an eye,
With colours as soft as the rainbow
After a cloudburst sky.
Roses are like people
They need tender, loving care,
And break just like porcelain
Their meagre lives to share.
So stand in a garden of Roses
And smell the fragrant air,
Knowing they were sent from above,
With Love, for all to share.

Barbara Hellewell

The Conquering Hero

It creeps, it stalks
It picks its prey.
Icily moving on its way.

Tingling feeling
Down my spine.
Ghostly whisper
Say's you've mine!

Gyps even tighten
Holding me close
Locked in the arms
Of a silvery ghost.

I'm crying, I'm screaming
Huge waves of fear
Please listen to me.
Does nobody hear?

Nothing is forever,
Everything must pass,
Death is the conquering hero
at last.

Dee Evans

Untitled

Sadness comes often now
It waits in dark corners
And approaches when I am at my lowest
I find no peace in its presence
And never have
Lingering far too long
To be of any comfort
This unwelcome stranger
Whose face I never see
Calls often now
He brings me no peace
And leaves me with even less.

Lesley Hartley

The Flower

I gently grasped a flower
  Its beauty to behold
But as I stood and watched
  The colours they ran cold
The leaves turned pale and hard.
  So very hard...
The very sap of life drained
  Away down the stalk
And I wondered why?...
Why did God ever let me
Pick this beautiful thing
  And cause death?

Dafydd Marriott

Untitled

As I sit across the room from you
I see your serenity and your wisdom
Although you may not see it yet
It is there
And someday soon
you will find the space
to open your mind
and look inside
surprised by what you may see
you may turn away
and not believe
but it is there
Although the world may pass you by
in time you will learn to cry out
for many things you will see and learn
and though you may not use them yet
one day soon their time will come
just be patient
and remember to always hold on.

Ffyona Mitchell

It's So Different Now

It's so different now,
It's not like before,
My girlfriend has dumped me,
My job's such a bore.

It's so different now,
But I really don't care,
The telly don't work,
The cupboards are bare.

It's so different now,
My friends never come by,
I haven't upset them,
So I don't know why.

It's so different now,
The neighbours don't call,
All they ever do
Is tap on the wall.

I don't really know
Why this happened or how,
I just know that,
It's so different now.

Andrew Farthing

Life

Life can be sad
it can sometimes be rough
But when good happens
you can't get enough.

People who Bully
and make life a mess
don't know that the victim
come's out the best

Sisters and brothers we all hate
But never mind them being here
is just a twist of fate

The worst in the world
that makes you so sad
is someone dying like
your mum or your dad

The most important thing in life
is a good family or friend
to help you get over sad things
and put you on the mend

Denise Drewery

Discontent

I wish that I knew what to do,
I'd like to walk away from you.
I'd like the time to be myself,
Time to linger, look and browse.

I'd like to go and walk alone,
Along some beach far from home,
Amongst the waves and glistening sun;
It seems like years since we had fun.

I'd like to see what I could be
Without these ties strangling me.
Would I die or would I thrive,
Would I feel much more alive?

There's more to me than wife or mother.
Maybe I should take a lover
And try to capture years I've lost,
But would it all be worth the cost?

Would I in the years to come
Find that I had been outdone
By fantasies and misplaced dreams
Instead of living with 'what might have been'?

Jean B. Crabb

Wealth

What is wealth?
It's the mind's glad store
of precious memories,
the great outdoors.

I have wealth
in fields so green
a well of wealth
that goes unseen.

I know wealth
in trusting eyes,
in music and laughter,
a new sunrise.

Through divine providence
wealth is my guest,
intervening with fate
to ensure I am blessed!

Christine Whatley

My Way Out

I cannot hide away like this
It's too late to find the truth,
That lay behind my actions,
Of my very special youth.

Full of ideas now, remarks,
That are not to be listened to.
Pains of disgrace
That I had to go through.

Oh the torment and silence,
That my life was ruined with.
All the unanswered questions
That I had to live with.

You must now understand why I have to go,
And I shall keep on running forever.
With every thought so close to me
Of all the times we had together

Joanne Rogers

Video Viper

A serpent coiled tight around
Itself, long unwinding flame of
Colours, rainbow sharp
Sometimes a gliding, slow and
Sinuous tale perhaps of love
And gentle reminiscent lives

And there again with violent
Turn becomes a shocking
Frightening thing with bloody
Teeth and jaws of death
That bring the whole world's
Horror to your fireside

Hypnotic power of this
Tantalizing worm, gathers you
In to gorge your mind
With boa constrictor charm

Lyn Livingstone

Untitled

Are Wizards just a myth,
Just casting out their spells,
Well, a legend's not a story,
So the mouth of folk lore tells,
These myths they can be real,
Enchanting in their tales,
They are nature's safety net
Incase the present fails.

For what all this is worth
They are written from the heart
They are what I feel inside of me
And therefore play a part.

Jacqueline M. J. Cole

The Poor Man's Pendulum

Life,
Lead-weighted
Is like a pendulum
Imprisoned
Within the boundaries
of an old clock.
Life-force limited.
Rhythm-restricted,
Movement-monitored.
Left-right-tick-tock!
Left-right-tick-tock!
Left-right-tick-tock. In severed swing.
Fate's fickle hand then winds the spring
SO TIGHT
To test and fortune its patient strength
By—— slow ——— degrees ————
Allowing only minuscule moments of
movement
Interspersed with senile servitude
Invisibly measured
on an expressionless face.

Anita Crisp

Nutty

Up, down,
Leaves rustling,
Branches crunching
Under the weight
Of a bushy-tailed,
Bright-eyed
Squirrel.
Hiding, popping out,
Scared of me,
Preparing for winter
Two months early,
Getting ready
To hibernate
Through the long
Dark months.
Squirrel,
Collecting nuts,
Completely
Nutty.

Karen Hilton

Why Did Your Heart Stop Beating?

Why did your heart stop beating
leaving me numb with pain,
that day the sun was shining,
surely it should have rained.

I felt you move within me
each day your small form grew,
now all my dreams are shattered
I'd planned so much for you.

I held your tiny body
I kissed a perfect face,
born to this world still sleeping
your loss a tragic waste.

All I have left are memories
some photos within a frame,
why did your heart stop beating?
I had so much to gain.

Jean Pedder

Untitled

Life without you
Life without me
Only words?
Let's see.

Kevin Lee

Motorway

Wipers swishing, motor throbbing,
Lights glaring, wheels spraying,
Motorway in the rain.
Indicate, pulling out,
In the middle, overtaking,
Passing a lumbering crane.
Easing forwards, water flying,
Flashed in, lights answering,
Inside lane again.
Onward, climbing,
Down gears, changing,
Engine taking the strain.
In the cab, radio playing,
Heater on, warm and drying,
Ploughing through floods,
Never stopping,
The truck in its own domain.

Celia Sorrell

Pennine Winter Sunset

Brilliant Picasso painted sky
Lights up the winter masquerade,
Heralds ahead the reason why
Winter's fury has been delayed.

Silhouettes stand bold and clear,
Against this fiery back cloth drop,
Many still have cause to fear,
As snow and ice ensure no crop.

Nature, dominant to the last,
Does emphasize such human plight,
Man and woman forced to fast,
When crops do cease because of blight.

Enough for us to reason why
The canvas sky turns duller now,
The day concedes to evening's cry,
And darkness answers our last vow.

Harvey Mawston

Dragons And Nights

Daybreak snaps
Like a bone
With the sun searing pain
On the visual canal
Crescendo all voice
With reception unclear
And paralysed throat
Is unkind to reply.
The dragons have gone
But their footsteps
Still echo like thunderclap.
This battle was won
Though regroup and prepare
For they will return tonight
To fight
The perpetual war.

Jim Aitchison

Lost A Friend

Red rum's the one we all
loved best,
and now we're sad he's
gone to rest.
We put our money on the nose;
and now we can't even see his toes.
We all laid roses at his feet,
Then watched him on film as
a special treat.
All the roses he won
put end to end
lets us know, we all lost a friend.

Deneze Sudders

A Feather In The Wind

She could skip across the stage
like a feather in the wind,
the eternal ballerina who lives
her life now, in a dream.

Her twilight years so hard to bare,
as her mind slips from reality
to dreams,
life never to be, what is was,
it seems.

In her youth she'd danced for
kings and queens,
and was adored the whole world over,
her life it seemed was charmed,
covered then in clover.

Her elegance and grace still
shine through,
she walks as on a cloud,
this butterfly from the past,
of whom we're all so proud.

Jacqueline Le Stocker

The Rose

Nothing seems important,
Like all worries ta'en away,
I sense the peace here, deep inside,
And I wait the dawning day,

For the years,
And memories I have here,
Like the thoughts of you,
I'll keep them near,

I never really knew you,
Even though we were together then,
But together we're in heart now,
I shall never ask you when,

There's a rose,
Of dignity and truth,
The love you have,
Shall this sorrowed heart soothe,

I shall miss you,
And although we were not close,
I shall forever remember,
You are always, the rose.

Eyin Temple

Tainted Worlds

You want to fly,
Like birds on the wind
To go and seek
Where freedom reigns?

You wish to engender pleasant moods.
To be no longer denied aerial views,
Of mountain ranges, open seas,
Savannahs, plains, creation's whims

Instead you stumble
through streets of woe,
For there is no beauty
In our treeless jungle.

With so much toxins in the foul foul air
It's not even safe in the atmosphere.
No creature escapes the bane of infection,
For all breathe in our poisonous pollution.

Though you wish you could soar up high
To find escape in the dreamy sky,
Not even there does freedom reign.
You may even get shot for game.

Erskine James Paterson

Winter Magic

Everywhere is crisp and white
Like the icing on a cake
What a pretty Christmas card
This wintry scene would make.
Snowflakes falling softly
On the frozen ground
Yes, they fall so softly
You don't hear a sound
The moon above shines brightly.
Sending forth a heavenly light
Dancing on the snow and ice
It brightens up the night.
But soon the ice will melt away
And then it will be spring.
Trees and flowers will grow and bloom
And the birds begin to sing
Then it's 'goodbye' to winter
A new season has begun
Welcome to the springtime
Followed by the summer sun.
Janet Walker

Manic Depression

Who are these strangers
Lodging inside.
deep,
In my unconscious mind?
no matter where I try to hide,
they haunt me,
taunt me!,
me?
Through the ghosts of my past
a faint whispered echo,
a child's game of hide and seek,
my reality
shadows of what I used to be

You know,
Before,
when I was real and free.
Faye Chandler

To Fay

I'm on my own tonight, alone
longing to be with you
And dreaming of a week-end flown
Re-living moments through
Your loving eyes I see again
Saying that you will be
Always my darling, and remain
Ever as one with me
I hate the lonely life I lead
Without you, Fay, my love
The only one I'll ever need
Until I'm called above
I love you, Fay, there is no doubt
For since we've been apart
You're all that I can think about,
The one who fills my heart
George Elsmore

Reflections

Reflections echo,
  Memories fade,
Of love wary,
  Mistakes before made.

Feelings beckon,
  Emotions run wild,
Mind games playing,
  Fear of my find.

Accident or fate,
  hard to explain,
Love not hate,
  Maybe more pain.
John Thynne

Untitled

Clouds above worldwide skies
Looks of hate in People's eyes
Just because they have the might
Who's to tell them which is right

To rob the old and rape the young
Or steal a life that's just begun
Black or White, Red and Brown
What the hell is going down

Allah or Bhuda, Catholic and Jew
Who you believe in is up to you
Shinto or Christ, Jehovah and Sikh
Does it matter of which you speak

Young and old, colour or creed
Tolerance is what we need
End all fighting and all strife
Remember that "your God" gave life

Given for a special reason
To take or spoil is an act of treason
Live together as meant to be
All the same, in harmony
Jon Arrowsmith

Reflections

Where do we go from here?
Many a long day left ahead
No kisses, no cuddles
No tumbles in bed;
Where do we go now
The first flame of passion's dead.
What was it you said
When we first fell in love,
Oh yes, you said I was your life;
Not wanting a wife
Just a slave to cook and clean
Some old has-been
Can make the grade,
Now beauties fade
And feelings pass,
Where did she go
That cheerful lass,
Who turned to frump
And went to fat
Became the old worn out doormat.
Aureen McCrea

'A Feather's Tale'

Soft white feather on the air
Just drifting, to and fro
Twisting, turning, floating down
With no place far to go

It comes to rest upon the ground
Are days of drifting past?
When suddenly, a gust of air
It's off again, at last!

A gentle, upward flow of air
Now takes it on the breeze
The ebb and flow upon the wind
As waves upon the seas

A subtle, downward blow of air
Upon a tree, it rests
When suddenly a bird swoops down
And takes it for its nest

So proud he was for he had gone
To where good feathers go
To make a bed so soft and light
Where baby birds can grow
Julie Butler

Then All Is One

When the rocks
meet the sand
and the sand
meets the grass
and the grass
meets the snow
and the snow
meets the ice
and the ice
meets the river
and the river
meets the sea
and the sea
meets the sky
and the sky
meets the sun
then all is one!
beneath the sun
Carl R. Rehm

Seasons Of Love

Autumn, winter, summer, spring
Memories of you in everything
God gave us the seasons
I asked myself why
He gave us such beauty
Surrounded by sky
Yes, we know the pleasure
Just you and I
Enjoying each season as it passes by

Riches around us, sent from heaven
As precious to me as the love
you have given
What more could I ask for on
this dear earth
Only stay with me darling
And savour this worth
Barbara Ann Beacham

Poetry

Poetry's a special gift
  Like love it's from the heart,
When words just seem to fail you
  And you don't know where to start
Poetry just flows along the page
  It knows its way
It doesn't need a helping hand
  It says all you want to say.
If you're feeling down and miserable
  Just find yourself a pen
Jot down little phrases
  Number them from one to ten
Start at the beginning
  And very soon your page will be
Full of what you wanted to say
  In glorious poetry.
Lisa Reid

The One Who Cannot Decide

Once a heart has been broken
it's impossible to repair.

Once words have been for spoken,
it's obvious you don't care.

Many memories arise,
and bring a smile upon my face.

Many bring back cries,
of sadness I wish to erase.

You talk about confusion
but what help is that to me?

Wake up from your illusion,
and please let me be free.
Jessica Shepstone

The Dream

I once dreamt of you,
your radiant face
and dark brown eyes
looking down on me
in the still of night.
Your lips touched mine
not once, but twice,
and I was in ecstasy.
I breathed in your soul,
it became a part of me.
Together, forever,
the lovers we were,
till daybreak dawned.
The morning was cold,
I shuddered alone.
The dream had ended,
I faced the world once more.
Zahara Walji

" The Spiral "

"Try it, just once,"
"You'll love it", they said
One quick drag,
And you're out of your head
That one quick drag
Led to one small white dove
I spin around the floor
I'm oozing with love
Then a raging thirst
A panic attack
Lend me more cash
I'll soon pay you back
This spiral leads downwards
You scream and you yell
Don't flick that switch, it's too late,
See you in Hell.
Stuart V. Howells

Grandad

Over twenty two years
You showed me you cared,
I'll never forget
The friendship we shared.

You're such a lovely man
You mean so much to me,
And you'll always be
In my memory.

All that I hope
Now you're deceased,
Is that you are happy
And may you rest in peace.

One last promise
I'll do all that I can,
To be there forever
To look after Nan.
Tracy Crowe

Spring

The sun kissed the earth
with the promise of spring
The gentle wind
makes the daffodils swing
The trees are dressing in
shades of green
telling the world, this is spring
Blossoms of pink
Blossoms of white
Fields of green
to behold, to delight.
White candy clouds
in skies of blue,
This is nature
being renewed.
Sheily P.

Black Tears

They shouted
'You Paki go home,
We don't want you here'
I felt helpless, homeless.
They grumbled,
You black
You can't mix with us;
And I felt stripped, naked.
They laughed
At my language.
And I became dumb, speechless,
I wanted to cry
But terrified tears were frozen.
Also
I was overtaken
By a gripping fear
That my tears
Might be black.
Vidya Misra

" Beyond Your Dreams "

Beyond your dreams
You can find
The rest of your life
I have gone a bit of the way
There it is
Like a lovely bright sun
With my life waiting
For me to unlock it
Waiting for the right moment.
Tanya Page

Untitled

You are no longer with me,
yet I still feel you here.
Although I can't touch you,
your presence is near.
I still speak to you,
in the same old way.
And I know you are listening
to what I have to say.
I get such a feeling
of calm when you're here.
A feeling so peaceful
you take away all my fear.
But there's one thing I'm missing,
it's a dream I have had,
that once more I could hold you.
"Dreams come true; don't they, dad?"
K. Barnes

Runner's Day Dream

I've spent my life in darkness
yet all around is light,
Why, why I ask myself,
Why can this be right?

Factory walls a prison make,
And traps us here within,
How, how, I ask myself,
Can I escape this din?

The floor is hard trod underfoot,
And brightly does it gleam,
When, when, I ask myself,
Can I trod the grass so green?

The clock has struck, time has come,
To run out through the door,
Now, now, I tell myself
Now, I'll run for evermore.
Peter M. McCamley

Song

Have you seen Love walk by?
Yes, he came, dressed all in gold,
too dazzling to behold.

Have you heard Love sigh?
Yes, so soft a song
I could not listen long.

Have you felt Love try
to wound you with his dart?
Yes, too gently he awoke my heart.

Have you felt Love fly
into your soul?
No, I bade him go.

Have you heard Love cry?
Yes, so pitiful a song
I could not bear it long.

Have you seen Love die?
No, Love passed by —
it was a part of me that died.
Ruth M. Andrews

If I Said (Would You?)

If I said I was a singer,
Would you like to join my band?
If I said I needed assistance,
Would you lend a helping hand?

If I said I was an actor,
Would you share my starring role?
If I said I had a mission,
Would you like to share my goal?

If I said I was a loser,
Would you help me win the game?
If I said I was a hero,
Would you treat me just the same?

If I said I was a prisoner,
Would you come and set me free?
If I said that I was lonely,
Would you be a friend to me?

If I said I was a dreamer,
Would you make my dreams come true?
If I said that I loved you,
Would you say you loved me too?
W. C. Trace

Rainbows

You don't get a rainbow
Without any rain
I'm learning that now
My rainbow was heaven
But it wasn't meant to last

Then down came the rain
Gradually, at first
Then more, and more

The storm was next
It had to happen

Then quiet, silence
The calm after the storm
Tears were shed, I nearly drowned

Then lightning struck
I thought my world was over

But in time, the rain passes
The wounds from the lightning will heal
One day soon the sun will shine again

But for now, if I want that rainbow
I gotta put up with this rain
Rachel Wright

Friends

They say a friend is someone nice,
   With whom you feel at ease.
Someone who is right at hand.
   To cheer and help and please.
Someone who is quick to praise
   And very slow to blame.
One who over looks your faults
   And loves you just the same
I say a friend is all these things
   And many more things too.
And everyday you prove it all
   Just by being you.
Paula Willis

The War Plane Song

I'm a plane, a fighter plane,
With my wings I soar.
I'm like a bird, I can fly,
I go low, I go high.

I'm a plane, a fighter plane,
With my guns I go bang!
With their cannons they shoot,
So the home guards they salute.

I'm a plane, a fighter plane,
With my friends we blow up towns!
Then it's mostly ruins around,
It's so silent, not a sound.

I'm a plane, a fighter plane,
With my helicopter friends we fight.
We win the wars,
The soldiers applause,
And we rest throughout the night.
Robert Lindop

The Recipe Of Life

The melting pot is brimming,
   with harmony and joy.
The recipe is so unique,
   for every girl and boy.
Add the warmth of a loving heart,
   and watch the mixture swell.
Fold in happiness and laughter,
   they blend so very well.
Add love for every race and creed,
   and our land will flourish too.
Knead with tenderness and humour,
   and the world will smile with you.
Sprinkle seeds of compassion,
   so the rich give to the poor.
Especially add a spring of time,
   that's what we all hope for.
When ready to serve add the zest of life,
   for everyone large and small.
Garnish with peace and contentment,
   serve liberally to all!
Val MacFadyen

Winter Thoughts

I love the winter
   with frosts the snow.
Evenings by the fire side,
   Watching flames glow.
Shadows on walls,
   as evening tide falls.
Gathering our thoughts
   at the end of the day.
It's peaceful, still,
   Tranquillity comes to us all.
Margaret Brown

Heavenly View

When the sky meets the horizon
   with earth down below,
The fields could be filled
   with flowers,
     or even the winter snow.

Snowdrops peep through
   to God's Heavenly light,
And bow their heads sweetly
   at a wondrous sight

Dark comes quickly
   in a winter sky
But spring will come again
   to wave winter goodbye.
Margaret Balmbra

Soldier Boy

Young soldier boy,
With bloodshot eyes,
His face all scatched and drawn,
From nights in deep dark trenches.

While sparks are flying all around,
His thoughts of home,
Of Mum and sister Kate,
And Auntie Vi,
Oh for Mum's homemade
Apple pie.

With head hung low,
Rifle held high,
He fumbles for the trigger,
Hands so cold, feet so sore,
Please dear God,
End this war.
V. J. Foster

A Stray Bitch

She's a border collie
With a doleful eye
Sweet natured she is
And a friend of mine

An orphan, no owner
Just two years old
Picked up by the police
In Yarmouth I'm told

To Potter Heigham they took her
The R.S.P.C.A
Two thousand are gassed
Every week they say

We paid ten pounds
Just to save her life
But what a friend we have
Me and my wife.
Philip Knight

Autumn, Leaves

The wind it makes a mournful sound
whining, sighing all around.
Leaves are thrown in swift dilemma,
swirling, swaying, drifting ever.
Up and down in panic strewn,
surely rest must come and soon.
Greater now in fury rise,
higher, higher in the skies.
A sudden lull, a moment's rest,
renewed again, and at its best,
trees are stricken, bare, bereft.
And now upon my garden path,
leaves are strewn in aftermath.
Peaceful now, but not for long.
Must I sweep them, every one?
Shirley M. Megginson

Beggar And King

If you have a large mansion
With a crown on your head
Or walk underneath the starlight
With a box for your bed

Only God knows the purpose
And the reason he'd bring
To a world full of contrast
Both beggar and king

God who created the river
That rolls to the sea
And the little birds singing
On the solid oak tree

He gave us the moonlight
So cool in the sky
And the sun that is blazing
Yet we never know why?

He gave us sweet life
With the death it must bring
Eternal peace with no contrast
For both beggar and king
Thomas McTaggart

Winter

The leaves have gone from the lanes,
Wind has blown of what remains.
All is bleak and bare,
In this winter air.

The squirrel scamper not the bough
Nor does the song bird rouse
With song the call of spring.
For spring is far away.

The biting winds in coldest form
Sheep the hedgerows seek to warn.
Shepherd hurries with his dog.
To a warming fire another log.

The meadow grass no longer tall
Awaits the winter's snow to fall
The village clock echoes its time
While shadows deepen with each chime.

'Tis autumn gone left well
The country side is wrapped in shroud
Stripped of all its splendour proud
It breathes the dampening mist around.
E. V. Walkden

Two Years Kidnapped

After two years kidnap
Micaelas back in town
Her Mother and Father watch her play
It doesn't bring a frown

She was snatched from hospital
When she was just a tot
The trixer put her in her car
And drove off round the block.

Micaela cries for Nenna at night
The only Mother she knew
But then her Mother comes in
And says I'll stay with you

Now she's got company
For a little baby brother
They really like to play
From now they play with each other.

She's used to her home
She know's where she lives
And every time she goes to bed
She gives her mum a kiss
Amy Bulpin

The Beggar

I passed a man upon the street
Whose eyes were filled with pain.
A patch of dry ground at his side
Where last night he had lain.
All around was drenched by rain
But his protected spot.
To keep his tiny rest place dry
He didn't ask a lot.

No food had he, no hope of any.
He begged with passion,
Spare a penny.
Coppers for a cup of tea,
To warm my weary soul.
I'm only here and destitute,
Because they stopped my dole.
I'd love a job, a home, bed.
Spare some change the poor man said.

Margaret Malcolm

Gardener's Friend

When I'm working in my garden
Who should come along
But my friendly little robin
With his melancholy song

He hops up really close to me
And there he stands firm
Until I get my spade out
And dig him up a worm

I awaken to the tapping
On my window pane at dawn
Until I go downstairs and throw
Some bread upon my lawn

Some say it's only cupboard love
With this I don't agree
Because when he's eaten all he can
Why does he stay with me

One day I'm going to miss him
Sadly he will be gone
My friendly little robin
With his melancholy song.

Rita Brown

A Storm

Shining skies and a sunlit sea,
   White gulls wheeling, wheeling;
A soft wind, and the fisher boats
   Out from the harbour stealing.

Heavy clouds across the sun,
   Grey gulls wheeling, wheeling;
Swift for home the brown sails run,
   Hark! The thunder pealing.

Jagged lightning tears the sky,
   No more the gulls are wheeling;
Flash and crash the storm rolls by,
   How the boats are reeling!

Cruel rocks and a smiling sun;
   Again the gulls are wheeling;
By a battered form whose race is run
   A fisher lass is kneeling.

Winnie Mitchell

Untitled

You made my world a happy place,
with the love in your heart
and the smile on your face,
and you left me a memory
time cannot erase
of a Dad I am proud to call my own.

Winifred White

Decline

As conversation tapers,
Whispers plot,
And conspire silent,

Speeding heavily paranoid,
I lose ground,
My face behind my back
Lacks spirit,
Forever haunting my courage
To ask,

For this now irrational torment
Breaks silence, laughing,
Provoking untamed opinion —
The offended voice,
An unspoken retaliation — whimpering, caged,
The tiresome thoughts reasoning —
Unfairly,
My suspicion of conspiracy,

Broken, without option,
I resign.

Geoffrey Allan Eyre

In Memory of Rod

Sleep my little one, sleep
Whilst those around you weep
It is no surprise
I've got tears in my eyes.
When God's got your soul to keep.

Rest my little one, rest
He's only chosen the best.
You were honest and kind
But it's of no peace of mind
And now you're one of God's guests

Be still my little one, be still
My tears and grief I reveal
I may look distraught
But you're still in my thoughts.
Until I see you again, until.

To you my God, my God,
My little one was rather a sod.
He is safer with you
And happier too
Good luck, God bless, bye bye, Rod.
Amen.

N. Campbell

The Soldier

He lay still on the ground
Not a shudder or a twitch
The gunshots were still firing
Which rang in his head

He heard something behind
So he felt for his gun
Then turned around quickly
But it was only a bird

Why did he join the army?
It was so tough
To see everybody around you
Being killed or shot

The firing has stopped
Had it all ended?
He got up to see
But was shot in the arm

He felt dizzy
And very weak
He thought about his family
And then blacked out

Rudy Mashongamhende

Your Love

Your love will always reach me
wherever I may be,
bridging tracts of untamed lands
and many a turbulent sea.
It is a golden beacon,
A glow in the darkest night,
Calming fears that I may have,
reassurance all is right.
Your love is deep in feeling,
full of passion and of care,
Containing purity and goodness
I don't deserve to share.
I hope I'll hold this treasure
to cocoon me through this life,
my dear and precious darling,
my ever loving wife.

J. Carron

Reflection On Reflection

Leaning over the wooden bridge
Where the river backwater flows
I see my own reflection
in the water down below
silently I watch my shadowy self
looking back at me
which one of us is real
ask the shadow, that is me.
Clear thoughts in clear water
transmit by me to you
beneath the waters can you breath
as my reflection does for you
making faces waving my hand
your smile acknowledged me
I smile, you smile
two blue sapphires I see
looking down at the river bed
clouds sail by your head
when I leave, my shadow flees
on its voyage in transparent space.

Philip Anthony McDonnell

The Skylark

I stroll along the country path
Where it takes me to the place
The special skylark sings its song
With such beauty and such grace

Some other birds
May be boring
But the skylark sings and
Keeps on soaring
down towards or by my feet
To grab the food that he has to eat.

Sarah Savigar

My Baby

Ten little fingers and toes
Wisps of blonde hair that glows;
Chubby cheeks on a cute face
Eyelashes delicate as lace.

Deep blue eyes on pale skin
Within a body that's quite thin;
Skinny arms and skinny legs,
Sticking out like little pegs.

His body so perfect in every way
Whether laughing, running or at play;
He could be two or even twenty
I'll love, cuddle and play with him plenty.

He's my flesh and blood and will always be
He will always remain this close to me;
To teach him what's right I will endeavour
He'll be my baby forever and ever.

Dawn J. Davies

Morbidity

I have a dream, a fantasy
Where all men live in harmony
And end to pain and enmity
A new birth for humanity

Each day I wake reluctantly
And come back to reality
I look around in misery
And see the true insanity

A world ruled by brutality
Supported by complacency
We're in the grip of tyranny
Choked by our own misanthropy

The masses in obscurity
Condemned to live in poverty
A life of harsh severity
The cruellest immorality

Each day a new atrocity
Will reach new heights of cruelty
We're sinking into savagery
A slow death for humanity

P. G. S. Gibson

What Is Love?

Love is making up after a feud,
When you've argued with your partner
And you've both started to brood.

Love is going through the good
As well as the bad,
The highs and the lows,
The happy and the sad.

Love is admitting your mistake
When you know you've been wrong,
Having a slow advance in a nightclub
To a soppy love song.

Love is about sharing
Whatever you've got,
Even your last Rolo
If you haven't a lot.

Love is to love one another
However hard this may be,
So the world becomes a safer place
For all of mankind to see.

Phil Preston

Morning Tears

As I look into the silence
When the morn is touched with frost,
So early in the morning
Yet the beauty is not lost.

When daylight dawns to meet the sky
I watch its fingers touch
On everything this world creates,
At once I see so much.

Like diamante' filigree
Between so many flowers,
So busy are these little lives
As we sleep away the hours.

The gods have wept for joy again
The proof is all around,
The iridescent teardrops sparkle
Outside on the ground.

So hold this moment while it lasts
A precious time to keep,
Before the day begins again
Soon wakened from its sleep.

Stephanie C. Bridgford

No Regrets

Once upon a time
When the days were sunny
And life was simple and fun,
I met you
And you met me
And I thought you were the one.
But disappointment bloomed
And the days to follow
Turned gloomier hour by hour,
And before too long
The day was night
And even the air turned sour.
And though the grass is greener now
And night is once more day,
The air still has an aftertaste
And it is the taste of grey.
But I do not let it hinder me
For whilst living we must learn,
And though I have not loved yet
Soon shall be my turn.

R. Heath, no one special

Rapture

Nearer to a time
When the air was still,
A skylark
Echoed a sweet refrain
Above the meadow
Rich with the fragrance
Of your inner self.
Fresh like the dew
At the break of day.

Exquisite, like the
First flower of Spring-time,
Clothed in the
Beauty of the morning.

Ebullient water
Flowing in a steam of love.
Clear blue skies,
The sun shining through
The peace of the
Woodlands,
Resplendent
In the wild romantic air.

G. E. Burgess

Gwen

Who will make us smile
When outside the weather is vile
When she is gone

Coffee or tea served without fuss
But not by Gwen for us
When she is gone

Who will peel the spuds
And put their hands in suds
When she is gone

Thursdays will never be the same
Especially during the Bingo game
When she is gone

Who will bake the cake
For our special occasion's sake
When she is gone

Gwen, we wish you all the best
And hope you will enjoy a rest
After you've gone

F. W. C. Watts

Memories

It is so very sad,
When our loved ones have gone,
The heart ache we suffer,
When told we must carry on.

We reminisce with our memories,
Through heartache and pain,
And shed lots of tear drops,
Down memory lane.

Although time passes quickly,
And the years roll on by,
We often sit quietly,
And silently cry.

But our life must go on,
Through happiness and tears,
And we keep in our hearts,
Those memorable years.

Then when our time comes,
And the Lord takes us away,
We can take up into heaven,
Those happy memories to stay.

P. Rawlings

Will You Love Me When I'm Old?

Will you still love me when I'm old?
When my blood is thin and cold?
When my hands are gnarled and brown?
And my shoulders drooping down?
When I am no longer fair?
And I have no teeth or hair?
When my eyes are sunken in?
And my vision has gone dim?
When my mind has gone all blurred?
And I cannot still be heard?
Are you still so sure and bold?
To say you'll love me when I'm old?

M. R. Simpson

My Sons

Don't grieve for me
When I am gone,
'Tis where I want to be.
I've wanted for so long
To be at peace,
To sit at Jesus' knee.
To ask of Him
Why me? Why me?
My cross has been so hard to bear,
My heart so heavy,
Is no one there
My broken heart to share?
Eyes that weep no more,
No children, what a waste of life,
Theirs or mine? I ask.
A broken heart
A mother's task,
Oh, for what might have been
Or is that just a dream?

S. M. Dotchon

Jacarandas

Can it be from Fairyland
You come each year anew?
Wafting from those misty bells
A rhapsody in blue.
No mortal artist ever mixed
So glorious a hue.

With this enchanted loveliness,
Each gladsome spring you greet.
Then in your bounty haste to spill
Blue Heavens at your feet.

Sheila E. Charles

Why Is It Wrong?

Why is it wrong to love this man
When he's everything I need
Why is it wrong to want him so
He's the very air I breathe.

We should have met so long ago
Before our vows were taken
If we had met when we were young
My heart would not be breaking.

It started as a brief affair
No-one would ever know
But now he owns my very soul
And I mustn't let it show.

At night we meet and share our love
By day we're "Just good friends"
We live with guilt, we know it's wrong
But it's something we can't end.

His love means all the world to me
He makes my dark times light
It can't be wrong to love this man
When my heart tells me it's right.

Valerie Walton

A Tribute To My Mother

It started ninety years ago
When God first gave you life.
You grew up with your family
And later on became a wife.

Wally was the man you chose
Both of you in love did fall
Your family, two boys, two girls
Were Frank, June, Jean and Paul.

You gave to me your help and love
Sacrifices you always made
You gave to me your very best
As my path through life I paved

They say that life deals many hands
They talk of destiny and fate
I'm proud that you have been my mother
And that Dad was your lifelong mate

So the reason I am here today
Is because I wanted to come
To celebrate your ninety years
And to say thanks for being my mum

Paul Hyde

Belonging

In the quiet of the morning,
When all around is calm,
I heard a soft voice calling,
Come back where you belong.

You've been away for ages,
I'm here and I am strong,
To lift you once more to me,
To hold you, and to keep you,
To give you love, and guide you,
To lead you from that downward path
That you were heading for.

I turned around and I could feel,
His warmth upon my face,
Urging me to take that step
Once more to see the grace of Jesus
Christ, our
   mighty Lord, who never lets us go.

He lets you wander for awhile.
Then takes you by the hand.
He brings you back, then says to you,
Come back where you belong.

M. Lyon

Turmoil

Who am I
What do you see
Do you see
The tortured soul
Inside of me
The fight for good
Against the bad
Sometimes happy
Sometimes sad
It makes me feel
I'm going mad
Can you release my spirit
So I can be free
To release the tortured soul
Inside of me

G. R. Bennetts

An Advertisement Break

Wake up, Wake up,
Were under attack
Sound bite shrapnel
Photo image flock
Clandestine attrition
Incessantly so abstract intrusions
Wherever we go.
Sowing the seed so creating a need
Because the enemy know
You reap what you sow.

"Buy two get one free"
But do we need a trio
Did we ever need two
With just one we'll make do

Under the flag of contentment
Call a cease fire
Dispelling resentment
No more dreams on the pyre,
For satisfied souls and peace of minds' sake
It's time, Mr Advertiser,
We all had a break.

Roger Roge

Untitled

Hospitalized or Motorized,
We're akin to a car;
We are!
Health check: Screening.
M.O.T.; renewed.
Spare plastic parts:
Hips and hearts.
When too old and over the hill;
Leaving behind log-book or will!.
A waving of wand;
To the scrap yard, beyond.

D. H. E. Bradley

True Treasure

Simple are the pleasures
which truly last long
which enliven the heart
with a resounding joyous sound
of ways surely won
by inner flowing outwards
instead of outwards seeping in
now the difference I know
no longer do I worry
but celebrate the ways
I have trod along the journey
for a beauteous sight ignites
a flame within the soul
caressing the eye and mind
brightening the span of the man

D. Sowerby

My Town

Standing on the South - East Coast
Well equipped for playing host
It's the place I love the most
Brighton by the sea.

Seat of royal residence
Unashamed elegance
To amuse a regent prince
In Brighton by the sea.

Home of the commuters trains
Noted for its famous Lanes
Guided tours along its drains
That's Brighton by the sea.

Once a year by patronage
Motors from a bygone age.
Struggle southwards stage by stage.
To Brighton by the sea.

In its halls when autumn comes
Party members bang their drums
But they're all the best of chums
In Brighton by the sea.

Philip Howard Whitford

Seasons Of Life

The Magnolia blooms again bringing
welcome to spring,
life bursting forth from barren
ground with promises of summer.
Memories of seasons past return
on tides of tears, and thoughts of
walks we trod through nature's
warmth seem a distant dream.
A warm nature, yet so cruel to
part us brings only endless
winter to thoughts of spring
and walks with a faithful friend.

A. J. Bird

War

Buildings crashing,
Weapons slashing,
Children crying,
Soldiers dying,
Fathers fighting,
Missile sighting,
Mother's weeping,
No one's sleeping,
Aeroplanes flying,
People sighing,
Guts and gore,
This is war!

Rebecca Thwaites

April Wound

Your leaving wounded me.
Its sliver of glass
slit straight within,
ripping our love apart.
Like creamy crimson velvet
love poured forth and weakened
with its flow.
I paled and grew ice-cold.
Tucked numb and shut
like a re-folding bud,
but it was far too late.
Your leaving sliced too deep,
and after all this time
not scarred nor healed,
my life flow not congealed.
Your incision with its sliver
sticking out
still draws my blood.

Caroline Ellul Parody

Nature's Way

It only seems like t'other day
We used to sit and chat awhile
Nothing daft life holding hands
Just smiling and enjoying the day

We used to share a job or two
Like gathering wood to fill our shed
The smoke from our chimney curled
We were friends not married like

The old summer house
Empty bottles left on the shelf
When thrown down the throat
He said 'two's like a scarf round throat'

But now he's gone from me
For that old gate speaks no more
Strolling down the garden
Brushing away the tears

I hold the note he wrote whilst
At the bottom of the garden
A flower has pushed its tiny head
A snowdrop dear... I'm still here

O. M. Wolff

" Flames Of Love "

If for some unknown reason
We should ever part,
I want you to know
That the love that I feel for you
Comes straight from my Heart.
Wanting you near me,
The touch of your hand,
Warmth of your friendship.
The laughter, peace, your love.
Days to remember, you and I.
No one can ever take them away,
And we can't say goodbye.

P. Burroughs

A Plea For The Oppressed

O God of mercy, God of love,
We pray to you in heaven above
That you will comfort every nation
Who suffers from severe oppression.

Take away their yoke of burden,
Give them freedom from their pain,
May your love forever widen
Bringing peace and joy again.

Take away their fear of torment,
May they know the love you give,
Take away all unfair judgement,
Give them hope and strength to live.

May they always feel your glory
May their love be steadfast, true,
When they feel despondent, weary,
Give them faith and trust in you.

O God of mercy, God of love
Show us how to serve you best,
In our daily lives to prove
How we can help the sore oppressed.

Mary Stace

Early Morning

Just to sit and think awhile
When all the house is still
Just to sit and close my eyes
And dream my dreams at will
To hear the ticking of the clock
As the second hand ticks on
For soon I know the house will wake
And my dreams of quiet are gone.

Marion Hailstones

A Call For Love

We talked on the phone
We met in my town home
We passed by each other
My heart gave a flutter

I wasn't sure
but I knew there was more
We talked all day
Your smile took me away
My heart gave a whirl
as I saw in your eyes our baby girl

You stayed next weekend
Ben stayed with a friend
We used nothing but love
Someone blessed us from above

Now she is here
I have no fear
I love you both to eternity
You and beautiful Hannah Leigh

S. Tingley

The Cat Bag Hat

I got a cat
We didn't have
Cat is my pet
My cat is fat
No he not fat
Cat wear a hat
My top hat
Where is the cat
I call the cat
Where are you pet
There my hat
Not a cat, kitty cat
I call out loud, kitty kitty
Come out the bag
I let the cat out of the bag
You are the cat
Living inside the bag
No one see it, no one hear
You are my cat pet
Living inside the bag.

K. Bridson

July 1995

Ice melts and
water warms dusty in
this heat - gasping
you swallow hot air
like sawdust, tickling
bronchials and branching
through the brain. - A
terrible see-saw dangerous
heat that laughs at the
city madness it spreads and
hunts down the haunted
with those all or nothing plans
that leave small children murdered and
a little girl lost without a nightie.

Tania Jacklin

Until Then

Heaven's foundation
will shake
angels larynx
will shatter
earth's axis
will dissolve
The ocean's bed
will quake
when we
as one
fuse
in a cosmic eruption

Veda C. Rolle

A Broadland Experience

A peaceful stillness lies around
Water lapping, a gentle sound,
Night descends in a cloak of dark
Fingers of light a ghostly mark

A solitary bark of a lonely dog
Echoes across the marshy bog,
A lonely angler casts his line
Over the water you hear it whine

A spectre of mist creeps slowly by
Unseen by those who sleep nearby,
A time for those who hunt by night
Then hide again before dawn's light

How quickly dawn begins to break
Eager to welcome the world awake,
An early mist, so chill at first
Warming as the sun's rays burst

Time to rise and drink your fill
Of the picture painted by Nature's quill
So many pleasures here to see
No other place will do for me

Sheila Branch

Pastimes

My life is like an open book,
waiting to be read.
Happiness is in my pages,
but so is sadness, fear and dread.

There are times of calm and strife,
embossed upon my leaves,
full of magic and wonder,
trapped inside a single sleeve.

So take me, love me,
criticise me if you will,
though don't ever try to change me,
if your expectations I don't fulfil.

Stroke my spine with tenderness,
never shut me tight.
Read my words in adoration,
hold me close throughout the night.

My life is like an open book,
waiting to be read.
Without you I am nothing,
close me, and I am dead.

Nicola Lawrence

Cancer

She dwells within her prison,
waiting on death row.
No sin has been committed here,
but tears of sadness flow.
No barristers to set her free.
She must have been so good.
We know the saying is true now,
to reap this sad reward.

One gift is with this sentence,
the gift of love so strong.
A gift that opens up the eyes,
unknowingly closed so long.

Keep your face of vanity.
Keep your riches of gold.
The laughter and joy of children,
are the jewels that life beholds.

Enjoy your season tickets.
Enjoy sun, sea and sand.
Enjoy walks with vigilance,
till the Lord God takes your hand.

H. J. Whalley

The Bully

I was miserable,
Upset,
Petrified,
Of a person far bigger than me,
When she bullies,
It's unforgettable,
Upsettable,
We can't be friends,
Never again,
I am by myself alone,
I am lonely,
I don't want to go to that place called school,
Never,
She just picks on me because I am clever at maths,
Spelling and reading,
I can't be someone else.....
Or can I,
When I am older,
I will get my revenge......
Or will I?

Rebecca McLean-Brown
(age 9 years)

" Tales From Ziggy "

There are two cats a lazing
Upon my garden chair
The boy cat is telling
A tale of many dares

He talks of many ventures
And one to fear the most
Was coming face to face with
A large red coloured Fox

A chase he had to tell of
Was fraught with sudden thrills
When hunted by huge dog
Across the rugged hills

Of all his great adventures
He proudly did explain
Need never really happen
If you stayed in your domain

So listen little girl cat
And be advised by me
To stay inside your garden
In complete security.

Yvonne Dalby

The Man In The Street

What kind of person is he,
What does his future hold?
A product of his parents
He did what he was told.

He wakes up every morning,
Begins another day.
He makes an honest living
In his individual way.

A man should set his targets
And make his desires real
To give his life a purpose
And follow an ideal.

To love one's fellow creature
Is certainly no disgrace,
When people live in harmony
The world's a better place.

So may we all be happy
And show it with a smile.
It cost you simply nothing
And makes your life worthwhile.

Trevor Rogers

Short-Sighted Man

Why don't we open
up our eyes,
Then maybe we
will see the chaos
And devastation,
Created by inhumanity,
We fight at will,
We maim and kill,
But what is it all for,
Why can't we build
A better place instead
of pulling down,
Why obliterate a country
Why degrade a fellow man,
Let us all stand up together
And support each other,
While we can.

M. B. Sellen

Time Warp

I look at the photograph
up on the wall,
the girl is so young
so slim and so tall,
where has she gone
that young blushing bride,
she should be somewhere
hidden inside
the layers of fat
and soft wrinkled skin,
hair that's gone grey
and the large double chin.
When I look in the mirror
I know what I see,
that young girl has gone
I can only see me.

Kathy King

Never Will I Understand

Never will I understand,
Until my dying day,
Why people like to hurt each other,
with the things they say.

Never will I understand,
Until my time has come,
Why people like to tell and harm
With the things they've done.

Never will I understand,
Until my life is through,
What I've done to deserve
This hell on earth with you.

Never will I understand,
as I see the end is near,
The life I've had with you
Is all so crystal clear.

Never will I understand.
It seems I got it wrong.
It's not been so bad at all,
Just mole hills in the sand of time.

P. A. Ilott

Today

Today we start our life anew
Troubles in the past
Yes we've had a few
But now's the time to plan ahead
The hopes and dreams
Which are in our heads
Now onto paper we must write
To make the things in our life
Just right.

Pauline Haggett

The Reunion

Coming from the past,
Uncertain who they were.
Moving towards the future
Fearful who they may become.
Apprehensive in belief
Tenuous in relationships!
And retentive in prejudice.
Together by choice
Or ritual form
Genetically diverse
Habitually related
Who celebrates the moment.
Individual complexity computes the present,
Nostalgia yearns for yesterday,
Hope reaches for tomorrow
Today we pause
To recognize our ego.
In the morning
We step into the unknown.

G. Ballinger

Bedtime Reverie

How is it in this twilight hour
'Twixt bed and sleep I have the power
To re-live all the things I've done
The arguments I've lost and won

How do these cells within my head
Remember all the things I've said
The notes to all the songs I've sung
Or tried to sing when I was young

In this short hour I can remember
Awful times and moments tender
When half asleep I can run so fast
Oh how I wish this hour could last

But come the dawn I won't recall
Anything I've done at all
Or anything I've got to do
Does this happen yet to you?

It will one day when you are old
And start to feel the winter's cold
No more then the twilight planning
Tomorrow's jobs and work load manning

J. Derbyshire

The Devil And The Angel

I thought I saw the Devil,
'Twas in a London street,
A child lay dead beside the road
While people crowded round and wept.
And then I saw the Devil,
He smiled and went away.

I thought I saw an angel,
'Twas in a country lane,
The earth lay glittering with frost,
And trees all clad in diamonds fine.
A little bird began to sing,
And then I saw an Angel,
He smiled, and went away.

Marjorie B. Culmer

Reflections

You look in a mirror
Truth stares back
knowing everything
revealing nothing

Truth staring back
Boring deep into the soul
as soon as you turn
you carry on living the lie.

Paul Stubberfield

The Child's Night
Go quietly about the house,
Tread softly on the stair,
Do not disturb the little ones,
Who sleep without a care.
Watch carefully their faces,
They're in adventure land,
Riding flying horses
Building castles in the sand.
They're hunting pirates treasure,
And sailing oceans blue,
Exploring deep dark caverns
In lands so strange and new.
No wonder when they wake up,
Dreams fresh inside their head,
They want to close their little eyes
And climb back into bed.
Sharon E. Genge

She, The Snow
When the cold afternoons come,
together with the frozen air,
everything grows older,
and all is dyed in white.

The dry leaves,
the transparent rain,
the solemn trees...

As a big avalanche,
the snow is welcomed,
There, She comes,
SHE, all in white.

Unique, Majestic...
Impetuous....
All SHE,
She, the Snow, is WHITE.
Richard Ian Baker

The Glass Ring
If a stranger were to give
to you a jewelled ring,
would you not wear and admire
it for awhile?

Then just put it away with the
rest of your jewelry,
For to you it might as well be
made of glass.

Though if someone with love were
to give to you a glass ring,
would you not wear and admire that
ring always, as if it were a jewel.
Robert J. Feather

Evening Classes
Once again in the moving mass
Making our way to the evening class
Studying hard on our window display
Never a moment to look away
Material, dresses, coats and hats
The whole thing is driving us bats.

Polystyrene, paint and plaster
doing display can be disaster
Moving models shifting stands
You'd think we had two pairs of hands
Teacher is a heartless ruler
Expect nothing else of Mrs. Muller.

Tuesday night we are down a flight
But dearie me it's a terrible sight
Mr. Hardie is teaching us lettering
But for us there is no bettering
Drawing, painting, general theory
Oh my gosh we're drained but cheery.
Lorna E. P. Treasurer

A Distant Star
A light is flashing on my window
To touch the memories inside
Behind the shell I fear my life
A distant star is here tonight.

I'm heading for a distant star
To get to heaven if I can
I'm searching for a distant star
To catch my life in my hands.

I stand in the lamp light
At the corner of the road
A shooting star is falling down
To touch the wounds, I cannot heal.

A distant star that came to me
To help me breathe, to help me see
A distant star, a shooting star
A distant star.
E. M. Langford

The Winner
It's very hard to get him
To tidy his own room.
The thought of straightening his bed
Fills him full of gloom!
He never polishes his shoes
And leaves the Bathroom cluttered
And lots of things I'd like to say
I have to leave unlettered!
There she goes again" he cries.
And the Battle scarce begun
He throws his arms around my neck
And his Mother's heart is won
F. L. Sneddon

Things To Tell
Where do I begin
To tell you how I feel?
To tell you that my love for you
Is most sincerely real.

To tell you of my feelings
And the way in which they've grown,
To thank you for your friendship
And the kindness you have shown.

To tell you how I miss you
When I know you can't be there,
How I think of all the good times
And the laughter that we share.

To tell you of a special place
That's here inside my heart,
A place reserved for the times we share
To recall when we're apart.

And although I know it may never be
That we'll truly be together,
This love I have inside of me
Will remain, with you, forever.
P. A. Pendleton

Your Absence
If I could
warm your lips
with a kiss,
If I could
wash your cheeks
with my tears,
If only I could
whisper in your ears
how much I miss
the touch of your skin,
you would know
that your absence
is killing me.
Vicente Uceda

Belinda
Be still my darling daughter
To one I hold so dear
Even though we're far apart
I'll always keep you near

You're in my thoughts
You're in my heart
Time cannot keep us apart

My love for you will always be
Deep in my soul
Safe as can be

As I think of you today
Come whatever may
Be still my darling daughter
In my heart you'll always stay
To remain with me this day

My love
Always and Forever,
Mum
December 25th 1995
Margaret Bowley

Is It Wise To Fantasize?
When making love - is it a sin
   To indulge in some imagining
Whilst physically with your lover
   To picture yourself with another?

If we pretend for added bliss
   It is another that we kiss
Is it wrong to tell white lies
   Denying that we fantasize?

Would it really be a crime
   Or more likely just divine
If when some other arms entwine
   I was yours and you were mine?

Just consider you and me
   Locked in blissful ecstasy
So if only you'll agree
   Let me be your fantasy.
G. B. Rowe

I Forgot To Remember!
A visit to the shops I plan
To get some various items,
I know if I don't write them down
I'm certain to forget them.

I need a tube of yellow paint
And one of cobalt hue
A "(get well)" card to cheer a friend
Who's feeling somewhat blue.

I need some tea-bags, cat food too
And a reel of dark brown thread,
Some knitting wool, a magazine
(Must remember wholemeal bread).

I reach the shops, I feel quite smug
I really am most able,
But where's my list, that dratted list?
I've left it on the table!
Rose E. Gibbard

The Posy
Few gardens could ever make
the posy I was given today,
some yellow buttercups in bloom
brought by a child into my room,
clutched in small and loving hands
given with a kiss for me
secretly no one else to see.
They stand with pride upon my sill
a small bouquet of innocence.
J. Terry

Tuppy

My master's off to uni
To get himself a degree
I saw him packing all his things
And thought he was taking me

Posters came down off the wall
Our room was still and bare
My master was excited
He forgot that I was there

Then they loaded up the car
With his books clothes and C.D.'s.
The last thing was the computer
He wasn't taking me

I soon adapted without him
Although I missed our walks
But oh the fun when he came home
We had such lovely talks

He told me all about his life
The new friends he had made
I was so glad he missed me too
Our friendship had been saved

Sandra Gartside

Just A Dream

To breathe for once untainted air
To fill my lungs without a care
For lead and fumes and noxious gas
I dream that this could come to pass

To boil an egg and know it's true
That this small egg is good for you
With not a bug or other taint
To make you ill or make you faint

To drink clear water from a stream
I know that's just a fading dream
With sewage stuff and stagnant stink
There is no water fit to drink

There's meat to make your Sunday joint
Another thing at which to point
Does B.S.E. lurk there inside?
What other terrors does it hide?

To eat and drink just what I like
To breathe fresh air out on a hike
Just these small things let it be said
I'd like them now before I'm dead

Michael W. Moir

Betrayal

She and I
Walked together,
Deep in love
In sunny weather.

Making many promises
She waved in sacred,
Which I knew
May change in hatred.

My fear came true
When she compared my love
Against wealth and glitter,
Giving me the taste
Of dismay and bitter.

She left me alone
Crippled and empty,
In the unexplored
Depth of dark,
Leaving on my soul
A painful scar.

Ranjit Kanwar

Results Of Child Abuse

Sometimes I feel afraid
To face the world
And show who I really am
So I withdraw inside
Where space is timeless
And there is time to waste time.

Not so for my brother
He means the world no harm
Because he has no power
He tends to fight and harm
So when we're down and helpless
Say a prayer for us.
Behind the scenes
I'll scribble a verse
While he drinks to stop his hurting.

Margaret Irwin

My Love For You

I have a dream, a dream with you,
to be together through and through,
never to hurt or to dismay
I want you forever in any way,
I need you now, I need you more
not just in rich, but also poor.

You're my only love and my only life
without you, I'd have no wife,
my love for you is so strong
so never to part, for it's you I long,
never let our love be low
we are together for everyone to know.

Our love is strong, I tell no lie,
being without you, I'd rather die,
we've had a girl, as well a boy,
let's live as one and all enjoy,
don't let anything come between,
it's you I love, I sincerely mean.

Patrick Jordan

" Time "

Time, if we only had time,
Time to spare
Time to share
Time to talk to one another
Yes, when I have time, we say.
Maybe tomorrow, next week,
Next month, next year,
Yes, when I have time,
But, time comes and goes
And life goes on and still
We say, yes, when I have time.

Joan Evelyn Brown (nee Lees)

Her Room

Sun shone on the doll's house
Through the open door
Toys slippers ribbons
Strewn around the floor
Bookshelves packed with fairy tales
Alphabet hung on wall
Red transistor on the bed
Wicker basket, a baby doll
No secrets here
Just fun and games
Children's conversation
Using fictitious names.

Change will come
As the sun goes down.

Margaret Toppin

One True Friend

Many places I have flown,
through sun and rain with you,
Some people think I'm all alone,
Just think if they all knew.
Within myself there's company,
a spirit within my soul,
Whatever life has done to me,
I'm never left too cold.
Sometimes depression gets to me,
and tries to drag me down.
That's when my spirit lifts me free,
the one true friend I've found.

Paula Richardson

A Traveller's Tale!

I've climbed the hills of Katmandu
Thro' snow-capped mountain scene,
I've trod the dusty plains below
And India's millions seen.

I've watched the Bali sunset sink
In warm and wafting air;
In jungle and the Thailand Isles
What breathless beauty there!

I've been among the poor folk
Of China's teeming strong,
And crossed the sampanned harbour
Of the waters of Hong-Kong.

I've climbed in heat up Ayres Rock
And "cooled" in Alice Springs
Bemused by hopping Kangaroos
And where Koalas Cling.

Though I've never left these English shores
Like others have to roam
My nephews, nieces all have gone,
And brought back the world to me at home.

Mollie D. Earl

Beautiful Day

It's a beautiful day
Though the sun doesn't shine,
The birds are all singing,
The air is alive.
Thoughts rush, like water
That sparkles and glistens
And bubbles that linger
In streams, as you listen
To bees in the meadow
And rustling trees;
The clouds making shadows;
The feel of the breeze.
A wonderful feeling
Of freedom and peace,
Impressions of laughter
And joy never cease.
What a beautiful day
Though the sun doesn't shine,
A gift to be savoured
Of Nature's design.

K. Williams

Thank Heaven

When darkness hides
The ones I love
And nightmares plague my soul
I speed a prayer
To those above
And soon the world is whole
For sleep
Sheathes every dagger
And makes the lions purr
Till sparrows start to chatter
And daylight climbs my stair.

B. I. Brumpton

Far From Home

I picture in my memory
Those happy days I knew,
Before I sailed across the sea
To a land out in the blue
Away from England's Pleasant Shore
To a land of sand and sun,
To do my bit for England's cause
Till Victory is won!!
And so until my dreams come true,
I'm afraid I'll have to stay!
With all those loving thoughts of you
To help me on my way?.
And as we sit together dear
When my work is done!!
I'll tell you how I missed you
In the land of sand and sun.

R. T. Foskett

Solitude

With solitude I walk
this road,
her tender heart I win
The hand that softly guides
My way, is hers my kin.
The gentle touch, so kind and
soft, delays the
crowded world.
Upon my mind, to disrupt
I hide behind her shield.
As gently she allays my fears.
I quietly go my way.
With solitude, the morning mist clears
To invite another day.

T. L. Gee

Loneliness

Like the desert bare of wealth
this loneliness in me is felt.
Like when you sail upon the sea
nothing down below can see.
Like when you look up at the sky
can see no end there way up high.

Walk the streets at early dawn
not a sound one soul forlorn.
An empty room, four square walls
echo an empty echo call.
That's the feeling that it gives
this loneliness inside me lives.

J. Roberts

A Mother's Love

They say it is, they say it must be
They say you know it is
But no one said just how it would be
This love I have for you.

You're more than my world
You're bigger than my heart
Your well being envelopes my brain
This love I have for you.

You are the light of my life
The candle that burns eternal
The spark that lights my days
All is this, this love I have for you.

You are everything that's good
That extinguishes all things bad
You are everything that's right
That illuminates all things wrong.

You are always in my prayers
This wonderful and pure human being
This tiny scrap of mankind
My son, my darling son - love is you.

Nicola Rogers

The Wasp

People busy working,
They hear a buzzing sound,
Then quickly dive for cover,
As a wasp starts flying around.

Someone grabs a newspaper,
Then quickly takes a swing,
But the danger's not averted,
As they've missed the wretched thing.

The wasp then starts to settle,
It's what we've waited for,
Then they swing a second time,
Oh damn! They've missed once more.

The wasp flies out of the window,
And danger's passed away,
I'm sure another will return,
To pester us one day.

Steven Collett

Untitled

I know right now you're feeling blue,
There's not much I can say.
Except that I love you very much.
In a very special way.

You always know where I am
If you need a hug or a chat,
I'll be there to see you through
Just always remember that.

Now I had better go
I send this with a kiss
Cheer up Mel
My darling pretty sis.

H. Parish

Dreams

The walls of fear gloom above you
There's no escaping, but through
your heart there's an opening
Those walls of dread are growing
higher
You are now surrounded by your
own desire
Do you dare to look back on those
fears you have created?
Turn away, hide your head
for soon it will be but a dream
The fears of your own heart are
no more than a fantasy

Philippa Louise Robinson

Untitled

Friendship is important
To such as you and I
We strive to give everything
No matter, do or die.

We do things for each other
No questions do we ask
For we receive some pleasure
With each and every task.

May the trust we give each other
Never ever be breached
As we'll stand and fight together
For the friendship we have reached.

May we stay friends forever
Never cause each other pain
As friends who stay together
Have everything to gain.

E. J. Moss

Untitled

From the dark
There was light
From the light
There was hope
From the hope
There was opportunity
From the opportunity
There was reward

From the dark
There was no reward
From no reward
There was no hope
From no hope
There was only the dark

N. Hartigan

Trees

The scars of humanity
There to be seen,
Stripped of its bark
And denied of its sheen.

Acid raindrops
Corroding the land,
The devil it seems
Now has the upper hand.

Roots searching deeper,
No food to be found.
Infertile soil all around,
Denied of all food
And pelted by rain.
The scars are left
By this acid rain.

Stephen McGeeney

Nature Is So Cruel

They say that if you're poorly
Then all you have to do
Is take a look around you
As some are worse than you
But imagine you're a baby
Who's suffering every day
How do you ask a doctor then
To take your pain away
We're always told that nature
Is wonderful and kind
So if it is so wonderful
Then why do babies die
Although we have no children
It feels so nice to know
We both have niece and nephews
We'd like to call our own
but when they start their families
As some's already done
I hope they'll all turn out like them
As then will love each one

Merilyn Gulley

Invisible

Oh, how I wish I were invisible
to flit from place to place,
when I liked, and where I liked,
to feel the sun on my face.
No more to worry day to day
of other's moods and swings, and
fret about insecurity and what the
future brings.
Oh, how I wish I were invisible
to hear if I'm truly loved, but
then what would be the
point to it, I could never
ever be hugged!
(just the ramblings of a
silly housewife and mother)

Maureen Claxton

Gran

How shall I remember
The Woman in the dress,
The one she always wore for me,
The one I loved the best,

How shall I remember
The hugs she used to give me,
The love we shared together,
I never will forget her.

How shall I remember,
The day she said goodbye,
The way she walked away from me,
The tears in her eye

How shall I remember
All the memories that are there,
The ones that never go away,
The ones you like to share,

I realize now I'm Lucky,
She gave so much to me,
Rest now Gran,
But don't ever forget me.

N. Williamson

Feelings

Give me your hand and show me
The way for living good,
Give me your hand and guide me
Show me a simple mood.
Give me your hand and lead me
Along the path of life,
Give me your hand and let me
Pass the road of strife.
Give me your hand and tell me
The goodness that you are,
Give me your hand and hear me
Don't let me wander off far.
Give me your hand and see me
See me for what I am,
Give me your hand and hold me
As cosy as a lamb.
Give me your hand and touch me
Soft, and warm, and real,
Give me your hand and whisper
Tell me how you feel.

Pamela Cooper

The Gale

Dry leaves will dance in the Garden,
the tree's will bow their heads,
before the wind will gather
enough force to lift a shed.

Cattle all are standing
with backs against the hedge,
crowding close together
uneasy with lowered heads.

Leaves now leap and spiral;
papers swim around,
the old oak tree is groaning
crack! it crashes to the ground.

The clouds hang dark and threatening.
No birds are left on high,
in safety somewhere setting
to let the gale pass by.

With banshee howl, and thrashing wheeze,
another ash tree falling.
As the gale came it slowly leaves
distractive energy spending.

Rosalind Ing

Ode To Tiree

Glintingly, unstintingly,
The sun shone on the sea
As we travelled to the islands,
My dearest love, and me.

The sky was blue as heaven
And the waves as green could be,
As we stood on board the ship
Which took us nearer to Tiree.

The air was frosty on my face,
So how lucky then were we
To travel in such weather
In the month of Janu'ry.

We drew nearer to the island
With its lovely sandy shores,
And with such unspoiled beauty
I knew my heart was yours.

Glintingly, unstintingly
The moon shone on the sea,
As we left behind that island,
My dearest love, and me.

Rosemary Christie

Pleasure Around Us

An open book, a candle light,
The sun by day, the moon at night.
A baby rabbit, a tree in spring,
A rose, a bud, and birds that sing.

A dog that sits and then he begs,
A lady-bird on tiny legs.
The sun and snow and even rain,
A cottage with a weather vane.

A lamb, a ring and a baby seal,
A woman at her spinning wheel
A lawn that's cut, a bowl of rice,
And even sand and tiny mice.

A tiny child so small and fair,
Enjoying life without a care,
Open your eyes and look in leisure,
There's always something to give you pleasure.

D. E. Lee

After World

Carnal desire,
we both feel it too.
To the future we look,
with half hearted smiles.

Immerse me,
Immerse me.

Kaleidoscopes of emotion,
revolve through my mind.
Pulsating so true,
emerging so bright.

Immerse me,
Immerse me.

For now warm embraces,
till we meet again.
I see your next life,
when our love shines again.

This love will last,
forever (in chains).
Till we both fall and die,
when our love shines again.

Martin Stuckey

Beyond The Meadow

The green lies flat in the meadow,
The stream, it goes babbling by,
It does seem so happy,
    so shallow and lappy,
As it catches the sunlight,
In abundance and glow,
The hue of the trees in the coppice,
From a green to a lingering brown,
A leaf gently falls to the wayside,
A bird stops to look, and away,
Soon it will come Autumn,
A smell of woodsmoke, in the far above air,
As it twists from the chimneys of cottages,
And the fox, it returns to its lair,
The shadows are now into falling,
As the night is just on afar,
And as it gets near,
The owls all are here,
To sing all their praise until dawn.

Patricia Westwood

Unto You This Day Is Given...

From Life to Life
The Spark Divine
Goes ever onward
Into Time.
From Boy meets Girl
To Darby, Joan,
The Fire of Life
Is given On Loan.

On Loan is given
To pass along
From Old to Young
From Weak to Strong;
To Fashion, Shape,
Enrich, Increase,
Till Son of Man
Can live in Peace.

Reg Hunter

Travelling

The linen is changed,
The sink is clean,
But for my luggage
I might never have been
In this small room.

Soon the brilliant mirror
Will detect
Another journeying soul
And reflect
Their night's musing.

Thus is life.
In a little space,
A short stay
And no trace
When you are gone.

Joan Allen

A Promise Of Spring

The crocus in all its glory
Spreads out to greet the sun
Like people on a crowded beach
Where children love to run

The daffodils just toss their heads
As the gentle breezes blow
Bracing themselves in case
There is another fall of snow

The primroses scattered
Like small bouquets
Brighten up the mood
Of the cold Spring days

D. Grove

1st Day of Summer 18/3/79
For my precious daughter
Melanie E. Brown

The Cherry Tree And You!

The Cherry Tree was planted in 1967
The same year as Melanie was sent
      from heaven,
Like "her" the tree grows more
      beautiful each year.
But all year Melanie's beauty
      stays,
While the Cherry Blossom just
      lasts for days!

With love,
Patricia M. A. Brown

Untitled

The truth in a tear,
The purity of snow,
The promise of life,
Wrapped in the crystal case
of a raindrop.
Tease us with the dreams
we long to own.
Our life of lies,
encased in the nightmare of reality.
The dancing light of the sun,
Beckoning us to believe,
While the low black clouds
Captures our souls, and,
our cries for help
are lost in the wind.

T. J. Jenkins

Till Death Do Us Part

A dim light glows in the dark
The only sound his laboured breath
His love for me shall leave its mark
As I wait in sorrow for his death

He will often be in my thoughts
All around our lovely home
Are things he loved and bought
How shall I cope when I'm alone?

Our love for each other is strong
Our cares for each other unique
Even when things went wrong
We vowed our love week by week

And now the time is near
When we must be apart
For only a short time, dear
Soon I'll join you in soul and heart

Margaret Doyle

Lost Thought

I can walk for miles oblivious
To worldly affairs.
Thoughts totally lost on senses
And feelings of life's existence.
The formation of the earth in
Combination with atmospheric
Climatizations.
The organic shrubbery dancing
Between the fossilized insects
Embedded in solid formed rocks.
Rivers trickling over discarded
Debris of land forming and
Shaping the world as time
Takes its place in ageing
And rebirth of life.

C. M. Spillane

A Child's Love

Is that my brother's star, Mummy?
The one that's shining bright,
It seems to come from heaven
So I know I must be right.

Is that my brother's star, Mummy?
So high up in the sky,
Will Jesus put his arm round him
And tell him not to cry.

Is that my brother's star, Mummy?
That twinkles up above,
It's shining down upon me
And sending me his love.

Why did my brother die, Mummy?
I miss him oh so much.
I want to fly to heaven
Just to feel his gentle touch.

I said a prayer tonight, Mummy,
I asked the clouds to part,
And let my brother's star shine down
To mend my broken heart.

Sharie Cannan

Giuliana

The days are long
The nights are cold
Weekends far apart.
But you can be sure
That at all times,
I hold you in my heart.
The letter, the cards,
The phone calls too
All mean the world to me.
The times I treasure most of all
Are when you're close to me.
Your loving eyes, caring smile,
Welcome arms and warm heart
Are what I do admire.
To be with you, a dream come true,
You've set my heart on fire.
The searching has now ended,
In a relationship such as ours
I know I'll be contented.

Robert McKeague

What About Us?

In cities, towns and villages
The news soon filtered through
Peace had come to Ulster
What did this mean to me and you?

No searches while you're shopping
No checkpoints and long queues
To walk the streets in perfect safety
This is what it meant to me and you.

In cities, towns and villages
The news soon filtered through
A bomb had just exploded
What did this mean to me and you?

A return to grief and heartbreak
Terror stalking the streets at night
To endless, senseless funerals
This is what it will mean to me and you.

To all who take time to read this
We ask you to think and pray
To help turn this near disaster
And save the me's and you's.

Sam Dunbar

One In A Million

A tear falls freely,
The memories stay clearly,
Your smile,
Your face we loved.

Your body ached,
The pain you hid,
Your smile,
Your face, we loved.

Your fear of dying,
Your need to live,
Your smile,
Your face, we loved.

Your life has gone,
Your love lives on,
Your smile,
Your face, we loved.

Michelle Holley

Lighthouse

We look from the shore,
the lighthouse we see,
Standing alone, tall
and so free.

Men who manned
that great big light
To save the ships
who sailed the night.

Years have passed,
seas so rough,
The rocks are hard
but men are tough.

So glad that light
has shone so bright.
The birds that rest
there from their flight.

A pillar of hope
that lighthouse stands.
It saves the ships
and all their hands.

T. B. Rees

Beauty

I don't want to follow
The hungry marching of life,
I want to stop awhile
To gaze at the beauty
Wanting to be seen.

Beauty,
Has been too long forgotten,
For the minds of the marching
Seek more.
Though the soul
Seeks only the peace from beauty,
That nobody stops for anymore.

Rukhsana Aslam

First Love

In a class of forty-three
There was only you and me,
Abacus and building bricks,
We were mad in love at six.

Many schoolgirl crushes since,
To see them now makes me wince,
Think what would have been my fate,
They're well past their sell by date.

Horrible thought
You will agree,
They must think the same
Of me.

May Butler

The Prodigal Sons

Know not men the sacred source,
The genesis of our life force,
Yet see it fit that they divorce
Life spans from their natural course.

Creation within mankind flows,
Inventive thought that can oppose
Suffering, yet men compose
A symphony of death and woes!
Timothy C. Jefferies

Time

Time is the present
the future, the past.
Time is the future
that comes round so fast.

Yesterday, memories
of times now long gone,
Tomorrow, the sorrow
and joy yet to come,

Time ever moving,
moving so fast,
Today is right now
then yesterday's past.
Norma G. Hannan

The Coming Of Spring

The sun drinks the early morning dew.
The few clouds ride across the sky
like giant knights on their steeds.
The wind gently pushes the branches
of a nearby beech.
I grasp the scent of spring,
holding it, trapping it in my mind.
The rising young flowers
encircle me in an organic cell,
holding me, forcing me
to savour the taste of spring
and celebrate its arrival.
The start of a new season
and the start of a new life.
Spring belongs to me,
my heart belongs to spring

and my mind embraces the onset!
Michael Turner

Lost England

Oh how I long for England,
The England that we've lost.
The England that we fought for
At such a heavy cost.

No terrorists or muggers,
Drug addicts very few,
And well behaved school children,
Not bullies sniffing glue.

No litter in the hedgerows,
The people loved their land.
And a friendly local Bobby,
Always there to give a hand.

Not shocking riots in the streets
With violence and looting.
And if a burglar came to call,
There wasn't any shooting.

When I think of England
In those days before the war,
Nostalgia overtakes me,
And my heart is very sore.
Marjorie Hart

Untitled

The pain,
The death
I feel it hard in my heart.
The burning of tears,
The loss.

Every man must die,
Every soul.
But to lose our friends...

My tears go unnoticed by death,
Their fire does not touch him.
Comfort must be with the living,
The fleeting embrace of life.
Mhorag Duff

Wedding Day

Dear Lord, Let us remember
The day we were wed,
Not just the glitter
But the words that were said.

The plans we made together
From the moment that we met,
Will carry on throughout our life.
The pattern we have set.

From today we make our vows
And declare our love to you,
Knowing that the love we have
Will help us all life through.

Keep us loving in this way,
As through our married life
We share both the good and bad
As Husband and Wife.
Shirley Gibson

Candles On The Cake

It seems like only yesterday
the candles were so few,
My Mum had made a great big cake,
when she said 'blow, I blew.'

A teenage party, what a bore,
I had to kiss the boy next door,
My friends should all be home by ten,
The candles - didn't notice them.

I'm icing cakes for grand-kids now,
with candles five, four, three.
There's no U turn for middle age,
Time won't hold on for me.

In twilight years the cakes seem small,
so many candles now.
They'll keep me warm in my old age,
I'm out of puff - can't blow - can't blow.
P. J. Rigby

Childhood Friends

Oh, yes they're still there
The bubbles in my hair
The childhood dreams
Of kiss and dare.
Speaking with friends
In a language with no ends
Playing crazy games
And swimming gave the bends.
Watching and waiting
Until we got older
And the showers that we had
Got colder and colder.
Where are they now?
Those friendships of old
The ones that meant everything.
More precious than gold.
Martin Smith

Perculiar Names

We of'n played cricket,
the boys and I,
but more of'n than not,
We needed the girls
to make up the numbers. What else!
so in they came:

    One at short leg,
    another at silly point,
    a mug to fetch the ball,
    hit for four,
    time an' again,
    and short back-ward square;
    another of those perculiar names.

The late commer was
sent to stand-off.
"But that's n'rugger".
a voice was heard to say
Not surprisingly, it was all
a bit much too much
for the girls. So they left.
Michael Jaffeir

" Put Down "

          (By Order)

Dougal is dead.
The blue-wet road is spotted
    with yellow leaves!
Black Dougal is dead.
Problems overwhelmed —
    destiny expedited.
Life is indestructible —
    in the end.
But, Dougal is dead!
J. C. MacDonald

Lover's Journey

At last I've found
   the beat for my heart
     the one that's for you alone

I've searched, dreamt
   and now woken to find
     everlasting love
   in you and from you.

You are with me, always
   every thought and smile
     surrounded by happiness

Endless days with you
   infinite romance and friendship
     through laughter and tears
   my life is you.
Sue Lord

The Angler

At last it's here, it's Saturday,
The angler's on his way,
All week his mind's been planning
His tactics for today.

He is optimistic,
As are all his breed,
He'll even swear he lost one
When his line is snapped by weed.

His optimism does not dim
Though hours pass him by,
He'll cast to many places,
and different tactics try.

Alas, defeat he must concede,
As comes that time of day,
When he must pack his tackle up,
And journey on his way.
G. A. Loughlin

Watching

The stars twinkle brightly,
The air is cold and crisp.
The hedges rustle secrets,
That lie in dark's own mist.
The woods become enchanted,
The shadows take on form.
Sitting watching nature,
And waiting for the dawn.

P. Davies

An Englishman

Solid as an English oak,
That's how I see England.
Changing seasons, summer showers,
That's how I see England.

We all speak freely, without fear,
Rant and rave, or shed a tear.
For king and country,
Men have fought,
And died for love of England.

All the friends, I've ever known,
All the lessons, I've been shown,
We've laughed and learnt,
And played as one.
Each glad to be an Englishman.

Paul B. Hennessy

Abandoned...
"For Two Little Pups..."

Two balls of fluff...
That's all you were!
But I'm man enough
To show I care...
Your deep brown eyes...
Your dark brown fur
Your cute little paws...
It just ain't fair!
As I write this down
I know you're safe...
Together forever
'Cause I have faith...
Someone will come along,
Just as they do...
They'll see you're special
They'll rescue you
Things will work out right
Of this I know...
May God protect you both
Wherever you go...

Nik J. Tyrrell

Loving Words

How can you tell the ones you love
That you must go away
To look into those tear-filled eyes
Upon this fateful day.
No soothing words of comfort
For they don't understand
The reason why you're leaving
With a suitcase in your hand.
Though life is never easy
And there's nothing to prepare
For sorrow and the heartache
This pain we must all share.
Dear Lord in heaven help me
Please give guidance from above
To ease my heavy burden
To tell them of my love.
No more loving words were spoken
As I reached out for the door
Four words that were to change my life
Daddy, please don't go.

A. G. Evans

Life

Life is like a pathway,
That we all must walk,
We must learn to love and laugh,
But most of all just talk.

In the time that I have had,
It's pretty much quite sad,
I've loved and lost,
And now I find my man,
Was not that bad.

My children who are so, so, dear,
I love in every way,
I see them grow and laugh, and learn,
And play each and every day.

So I pray with all my heart,
The love that they will find,
Will be everlasting,
And treat them very kind.

Simone A. Prigmore

Creation

Tiny little hands,
That tug at my heart strings,
I couldn't imagine before,
The joy a child brings.

Little noises and giggles,
At night from her cot,
Make me realise,
What a treasure I've got.

What will she grow up to be
Model, film star or hostess,
But to me,
You'll always be my princess,

My wife and my daughter,
The two most important people to me,
Thank you both, my darlings,
For letting my heart soar free.

Mark Stange

Wishes

I wish that wishes would come true,
That the lottery was for me and you
That I would fly to Timbucktoo
Or even visit London Zoo.
I dream of Scottish glens so green.
Of English strawberries and cream
Of sunny Spain, the arid plain.
And the wonderful Italian train.
The Middle east I'd like to greet.
I've read so much about this treat.
The Chinese race are full of grace
I'd like to see the Monte Carlo race.
Gay Paris is just for me,
I'd love to be there on a spree.
If wishes were horses then beggars would ride
I could have flown and been inspired.

M. P. Booth

Provence

Oh calm sea of tranquil blue,
Oleanders, palms and you
Sunshine, be my friend forever
In this land of never never.
Warmness stealing over me
Solitude and peace will be
As I wonder by your shore
Let me stay for evermore.
I shall return perhaps one day
And see you once again so gay.

Rita Douglas

Home

Home is where the heart is
That is what they say
Whatever direction you take
Home is that way

Home is where you're happy
And where you can be sad
Home is where the love is
Whether you're good or bad

Home is where the family is
Brothers, sisters and parents too
Home is the best place to be
For me and all of you

Home is the best place
For comfort when you're ill
Home is where you laugh or cry
And where they test your will

Home is where I like to be
In the warmth of my family
Home is where I can smile
And I can just be ME!

Margaret Harrison

Love

Love is an emotion
That dwells beneath the soul,
The soul of every man and women
Like a dice it lives to roll.
The place of love
Is with anxiety and depression
It clasps ahold on either
As passion gathers by the second,
But the weight of love is not heavy,
It leaves you suspended in mid air,
With the feeling of radiating joy
Like a school boy at the fair.
The symptoms of love
Are loneliness, anger inside
With the experience of ambivalence
Followed by joy in body and mind.
Love is positively tangible,
You can touch the heart of it
Predictions are impossible.
Kismet.

Seth Adams

Pride — And Shame

It was for "our tomorrow"
That they gave "their today"
This was said of gallant men,
Who, long since, passed away.

They did not want to carry guns,
And march off into war.
But they had a common foe to fight,
As men had done before.

Some men carry guns today,
With murderous intent.
Or, on robbery with violence,
Think their time's well spent.

They can always find good reasons,
To justify their acts.
But they cover up their faces,
Hiding from the facts.

And when they face their Maker,
When it comes to Judgment Day,
Without their guns and face-masks,
What then will they say?

E. E. Waite

My Love

I know, my love,
That all of us
Have to go one day,
I never thought you'd go just yet,
And I would have to stay.

I thought we'd be together,
And do the things we planned.
I miss the simple gesture,
Like when I held your hand.

And all my worldly goods I'd give
If I could have you home.
I'd give away my silver,
I'd give away my gold,
And every day that I am here
Brings me closer yet to you.
And we will meet again, my love,
  I always will love you.
Susan Savage

" Tionance "

Communicative self destruction
Terminal incompetence

Turn a blind eye to corruption
Idealistic self defense

Attract attention with eruptions
Are you really "on the fence"?

Flattering with great distortion
Working up to an advance

Most achieved with great contortion
Working hard and try to dance

Environment denies abortion
But wouldn't given half a chance

Overacted satisfaction
Who am I to be the judge

Be assertive, cry for action
Even though the buck won't budge

Relationships that don't gain traction
Why must they always bear a grudge?
M. G. Higginbottom

Man

Man is a pinnacle
  tempered by fate,
Drawn from the cynical
  by kindlier mate.

Man is a depth
  by water made visible,
Hiding with stealth
  the reflection is miracle.

Man is a mix
  of autumn and spring,
Saved from his tricks
  by hearing us sing.

Man is a fortress
  more empty than cold,
Filled with vague weapons
  the emperor sold.

Man is a promise
  in grave clothes enshrouded,
The heartbeat of Thomas
  when daybreak he doubted.
Natasha B. Fleming

My Love

Hold me and caress me,
Tell me that you're mine,
Thrill me and test me,
Till the end of time.

I long for your kisses,
Your tender embrace,
To have you, to hold you,
To see your sweet face.

Your kisses are sweeter
Than the sweetest of wines,
Your touch is like magic,
Sends shivers down my spine.

To have you, to hold you,
To know that you're mine,
If you ever did leave me,
You'd leave emptiness behind.
M. Tourle

Shopping List

Crisps
Tea bags
Sliced Bread
Tomato soup
Cereal
Rice
Ex-mature Cheese
Butter
Milk
Lark's tongue in Aspic
Go to Library
T.V. License
Waterproof tape
Shelving brackets
Soft toy for Lucy's birthday
Pay deposit for world cruise
M. Woodcock

Sands Of Time

The drifting sands in the desert,
Swirling mist at dawn.
Lost, in that vast wide empty space
Tired and so forlorn.

Warm inviting sands,
Cruel and treacherous at times.
Moving, ever changing,
Yet golden and sublime.

The drifting sands of time,
Move swiftly, soft and sinking.
Mist will vanish, sun will shine.
New life already blinking.

What next, oh shifting sands,
Erotic are your moves
Let's lie awhile, make new plans
Your soft warmth, gently soothe
M. Ridgway

" My Tears "

Disaster has struck on
The Domestic front — sadness
And hurt... but amidst
The pain... words flow freely
Like rain... she will enter...
Again... and... again... hopefully
The words will flow again
With joy... and not this
Presently broken heart.
Please note change of
Address... please... wait...
The poetry will... soon...
Fly fast... and Furiously
Once more!
Meg Gaspar

A Mother's Love

A mother's love is a wondrous thing
sweeter than flowers
And birds that sing.

A daughter may take a husband
A son may take a wife.
But a mother's love is there forever
For the rest of your life.

A mother is always there for you
Loving, kind and true.
No other one in all the world
will be as true to you.

So if you have a mother
Then thank the Lord above.
No matter how poor or ill
you are,
She'll give you all her love.
I. Busley

Crock Of Gold

Colours arched, rainbow bright,
Sun etched cloud, rain is light,
End of rainbow, I can't see,
crock of gold, not for me.

Colours brighter, need a friend,
To go and find the other end,
Rainbow searching, in my mind.
Beautiful colour, so unkind.

Cloud has overwhelmed the sky,
All these colours, fade and die,
Darker now, I can't see,
Crock of gold, not for me.

Colours arched, rainbow bright,
I can see you, day or night,
All this colour, in my mind,
Need a friend, for I am blind.
Rob Diaper

"Existence"

If endowed with health
strive for harmony
Achieve harmony and you
may know happiness
Temper with wisdom and
you may know inner calm
Combined they may
motivate love
Should love enter your
life acknowledge a
priceless treasure
If prosperity be yours
make peace your aim
Acquire humility and
share with others less fortunate
Try never to abandon hope
nor for granted our planet take
Precious is every moment
of our existence
Moreen Cunningham

Mid-Day Wave

The breeze in the air
Softly numbs the hotness,
The fans a-blaze
Releases one's hair,
Whilst the mid-drift follicle
  - felt in between -
Of an Air Balloon's charge
Bellows outwards
Upon one's head,
Remaining stagnant,
'Til the next breeze flows.
Wendy Fairish

An Agnostic's Query

What do you see there?
Standing in your dusty pulpit
And looking out across
Endless centuries of earth.

What, where is eternity?
Can the light in your eye
To comprehension show the way
Conception of where it is and why?

Over all the durable substance
We see mainly change and fall,
Each and every apparent instance
Seems to indicate the end of all.

Which then is life's category;
Is it endless as you say
Or a perishable commodity,
In endless time a passing day?

Out in endless all of space
Does the answer lie?
Or is it here before our face;
Shall we live on after we die?

Thomas Anibal

Rejoice And Remember

Rejoice and remember
Spinning shells dropping on Earth.
Rejoice and Celebrate
The glorious devastation of homes,
And sublime carnage
That covered a claustrophobic land.

Rejoice and remember
The merciful Gestapo?
Rejoice and Celebrate
Their inhuman Wisdom,
That burnt holes in breasts,
And flogged legs as thin as the
branches they used.

Oh yes!
We will remember,
The thoughtless slaughter
Of naive minds,
And indescribable anguish
Of when the Hunger
Consumed man,
And left us in its wake.

Michelle Reid

Evocation

The heady scent of summer sweetness
Sunlit patterns in leafy glades,
Shadows of the past.

Of time stood still
Of scarce remembered days gone by,
Of things that might have been

Of long ago
When you were there
And unaware,
Of things that were
To be.

I loved you then - I love you now
With love so pure and free
That time cannot diminish it,
Nor ease the memory.

A sweet, sad fragrance
Permeates the breeze,
And shifting sunlight
Centres on the scene
Where you and I were one - and will yet be.

J. J. Sheen

Queries

Have you ever glimpsed in passing
Somebody who wasn't there?
Brushed against something or someone
When you climbed an empty stair?
Have you felt a presence near you
Knowing you are quite alone?
Felt the pulsing throb of being
Seeping from a wall of stone?
If you turn and look quite squarely
At the place it should have been,
There is nothing to decipher
Where the being should be seen.
Are we in the wrong dimension?
Are they spirits from the past?
When we pass that final gateway
Will we meet these wraith at last?

E. M. Reece

A Cat's Life

I see a pair of sparkling eyes
Some large white whiskers too,
And all at once a set of paws
Comes flying across the room.

The vision jumps upon my lap
And starts to wash its fur,
Then because I take no notice
Steadily starts to purr.

"Oh what is love", the feline says,
with face so prim and pure,
"Other than to adore you
And look so very demure?"

Oh to be as free as air,
Jumping and climbing everywhere,
After birds without a care,
And then to sleep in someone's chair.

Cynthia Beddow

Big House Hallway

Alone on a green floor
Soft shaped seats wrap around
Stillness in the air broken
By quizzing giggling sleepy voices
Pillars of sunlight streaming in
Flood the air with a warm glow
Doors open with squealing sounds
And creak shut with an eerie groan
Pictures stand like wall soldiers
Watching you watching them
Music quietly fills the still air
And thoughts of other places
Other times stream in
Feeling tingle with sensations
Of quiet peacefulness
Nice place
Nice time

Philip Mulcahy

This World!!

I am quite speechless
No words that I can say
How very sad I am
At the state of the world today

Has this world gone bloody mad
It looks that way to me
People do not seem to care
Not like it used to be

Some folk are like concrete
Getting harder every day
Not showing any humanity
as they go along their way.

E. Taylor

Top Twenty

Today we have top twenty
So pop groups we have in plenty
They don't do any harm
But they do kick up a charm
You need not be a pretty
A stone or just a ditty
Just have a little poise
And make an awful noise
There need not be any words
To get whistles from the birds
If your hair is long and scraggy
And your trousers they are baggy
Just shake it here and there
And the girls will do their share
And before you can say Bentley
They will have got you
In Top Twenty

P. Funcy

About The Birth Of My Daughter Sarah

So beautiful and sweet
So gentle and neat
Ten tiny fingers
Ten tiny toes
Bright little blue eyes
Pink shiny nose
So perfect in every way
A mother's love
A precious gift
from God above.

And now that you are growing
into a beautiful girl
although you do not have any curls
And your hair is kind of straight
you'll be my special lady
forever and a day.

I will love you so very much
It's very plain to see
That's why the Lord above
Has lent you to me.

Margaret Price

" I Think - I'm Almost Certain "

Now where is this dark place I'm in
So friendly and so warm
I feel a Stirring in myself
A shape I need to form

What is this ache I need to fill
A trembling in my thoughts
A greater sense of atmosphere
A presence my love's caught

I feel a growing, growing now
A surging up to light
A difference waking through my veins
A nearing power of flight

Where is this place, so good, so free
Who's giving me this power
I think - I'm almost certain - that
I am a perfect flower.

Mary Hulme

Winter Poem

The king on his throne
Sighing silver breath,
Icicles hanging from the ceiling
The silver crown on his head.
Swords on the wall
Cold, oh
So cold in the palace.

Magdalen Mannion Daniels, age 6

Loneliness

I'm like an ant
small and vulnerable.
I feel like an old book
neglected on a shelf.
People in groups laughing.
I want to join them.
I want friends.

I'm alone and helpless
Detached and afraid
Sad and solitary.
I could be in quarantine.
I might as well face it
I'm an outcast.

Steven Chapman

Black Beauty

Black, pulsating, vibrant beast
Sleekly clothed in velvet fur,
Softly sprawled in relaxation
Warm contentment in her purr.
Dignified and independent,
Ruthless with prospective prey,
Loyal and a staunch companion,
Claws withdrawn in friendly play.
Calling her from some fierce fight
I search the blackness of the night.
Howling banshee noises cease —
Quite indescribable, the peace.
Wider yawns the kitchen door
Yielding to her pushing paw.
Green orbs in the darkness shine —
So beautiful, this cat of mine.

Rosemary Gowans Smyth

Forgive Me

Forgive me twice
Should I seem slow and cold
Beneath this berg of ice
There beats a heart that's bold
And warm and true
I hesitate to show it all to you
For love released is love in pieces
Love discovered always ceases
Whilst in bondage love is whole
Does no damage save unto a soul
That selfish though it be
Accompanies that love so utterly
Forgivably sincere....
Forgive me dear

Judy Butler

My Fantasy

Axes and crossbows,
Shields and swords,
Monsters and witches,
Kings and Lords,
These are all parts of my fantasy.

Trolls and Goblins,
Giants and Elves,
Dwarves and griffons,
deep dungeon cells,
These are all parts of my fantasy.

Skeletons and Demons,
Magical Wizards,
Orcs and brave knights
and huge massive lizards,
These are all parts of my fantasy.

Dragons of all colours,
red, green and blue,
how I wish my fantasy
could be very, very true.

Nigel Chorlton

Protector

Venus is my defender
Shielding me from harm
And although I know I surrender
She is forever losing her charm
She keeps my faith from wavering
Re-stocking my mind in turn
With things to which I am clinging
But my mind just chooses to burn
She is always there before me
Listening to my every word
When others never seem to see
And even find somewhat absurd
My friend you are a liar
For all things in my head
You are just the supplier
Of things I'll find instead.

Sian Ross

Up To The Times

Ugly concrete monsters
Sheer blocks of masonry,
Towering above us
Everywhere to see.
Who is housed within them?
People by the score,
Must be like a prison
When they're behind their door.
No gardens for their children
Wherein they can play,
Tied to their mothers' aprons
Always they must stay.
Is this the way to progress?
Where is the human side,
And those cosy homes for people
Who have to live inside?

A. E. Surtees

Reaching Out

With the faith of a child
She shuts out the pain
As she reaches for the rainbow
That comes after rain
In the innocence of childhood
She hides away her fears
As she reaches for the sun
To dry away the tears
A little heart so innocent
Who knows she must not cry
Looks in awesome wonder
At stars up in the sky
A little child so trusting
Looks at the moon above
And holding out two little arms
She reaches our for love.

Sandra Douglas

Compline

At last the night has settled down:
The harshness of the day
Has crumbled into memories
Like fragments on display,

As if some archaeologist
Has dug them up for me
And laid them out as evidence
Of how I used to be.

My mind relaxed, prepared for sleep,
Unwilling to relate
To excavations that reveal
Its other, anxious state,

Prefers instead to put on file
And quietly forget
The recent past — and for a while
Exist without regret.

Mark Waberski

My Mother

In Spring the world received her
She grew, inspiring love
Maturing, even greater love
Was born of pain and joy

In Summer we assured her
There was no greater love
Perfection ill-prepared us
For the dark clouds up ahead

In Autumn with the scattered leaves
We learned of other love
We tested, dipped, committed
And were fluttered by the wind

In Winter with the frost and snow
She went too far away
For us to ever let her know
No princes walked this way.

Rosemary Phelan

The Forest

There's a forest by the railway
Seen by many as they go,
From the City, down the line,
To the tower blocks at Bow.

It's a still, haunted place,
With tall, tall trees,
And the paths that go winding
Are of several one sees.

But is it really a forest?
The council says a park.
And as we slow down to Bow,
Lamps give way to dark.

And on this clear Winter's evening,
As homeward bound we go,
You can see the dark creeping,
Up the ivy trees weeping,
On graves, lost and gleaming,
In the forest down by Bow.

E. J. Christmas

War Cry

Smouldering ashes, burning flesh,
Screams of tortured men,
Women dying, children crying,
Here they come again,
A whine of motors overhead,
The sirens' plaintive wail,
A noise like thunder, crashing down,
A flash, explosion, gale,
Dust and dirt, and acrid fumes,
A mushroom ball of smoke,
A million lives have gone today,
A million hearts are broke,
Must man kill man, to live in peace,
And innocently say,
What we achieve in war right now,
Will benefit some day.

Sandra Benson-Dare

Untitled

The wits of colours
 please do,
apply the paint,
take plants into your shower

Bring to me violets
allowing for my colour,
close to gold,
only now, can you show me a tower

Shona Hastie

Who

Who noticed the clouds meet
Saw the suns energy brake
Watched sky birds weave
Ready to mate

Who noticed the rain cloud
Felt the day begin to change
Who struggled home alone
Saw the robin following

Who knew in the hollow
Of your roof top
The swallow nesting

Who watched the caterpillar
Pass a dangerous road
Who picked it up to safety
To continue its new life through

Who saw a spirit every day
Helping guiding all who do
I saw the hay sway side ways
The wave scrape emotion
Off the shore

Simon Kelsey

Legend Man

Flowing in my mind
Salty tides of ancient times
Carving memories never lived
Young and fresh, but old and dead.

Spreading all over my face
Deep green wrinkles never felt
Never cried, never laughed
But rooted ivy shaped my eyes.

Blooming all around the space
Dreamy visions always there
Gods and heroes, knights and swords
Splashing back the legends' soul.

Toni Conesa-Ribera

" Mistletoe Winter "

Two green balls of mistletoe
Ride high above the car park
Mounted on bare winter trees,
A yellow-green and white
Glow of spring
Round like the Green Knight's head.
Heralding the year's start for Ywain.

In Christmas discarded shops
Are bundles of candles,
Beeswax honey brown,
Golden when lit
Like the nectar of summer's flowers
Frozen into long spires.

The pale winter sun
On reed beds and sea
Promises the upsurge of life to come,
Stirs in my home
A sleeping butterfly.

Shirley Mungapen

Stay Young And Innocent

A child's eyes
rewarding;
Not soon enough.

Speak out against
How?
Grow up, advance.
Why?

See what is obvious
Ignore all else.

S. J. Kerr

Decoraging

In front of me a bare, pink wall
Reminds me of my past;
A colour that once suited me,
But little girls grow fast.

Excitement at the prospect
Of a brand new bedroom shade,
The carefree pink of childhood
I never knew would fade.

An adult now, with grown-up thoughts,
Or so the people say,
And carefree pink must be replaced
By older, wiser grey.

A change of personality
As subtle as it's sure,
I wonder now, as years go by,
Will colours change once more?

In front of me a bare, pink wall
Reminds me of my past:
As grey laps over memories,
I know I'm old at last.

Sandra Gilliard

Global Warning

Violent homicide
Religious cult genocide
Civil war and political unrest
The U.N. put to the test
What is the sense in
All this ethnic cleansing
Hard core pornography
Child sex photography
Columbian cartel
With their drugs to sell
Snuff movie makers
Immigration passport fakers
Mafia 'Dons' notoriety
Break down in society
World leader's myopia
This is hardly UTOPIA

Flakie

Sea Fury

The wind and waves rising high.
Reflecting the colours of the sky.
What a glorious sight to see.
They're all there for you and me.

Giant waves crashing down.
Disturbing sand and pebbles round.
Making patterns in the sand.
Sea creatures forced to land.

The little ships so far away.
Hurrying back across the bay.
To shelter from those giant waves.
That crash and echo in the caves.

D. F. Silk

I Need An Answer

Clean, tall buildings standing by,
radiation in the sky,
giving out something I hate
right to Heaven's pearly gate
often now, you read or see
Leukaemia by the power station
nuclear power just had to be
but is it good for you and me
or is it killing off the nation.
Can there be a link with cancer
I have to know
I need an answer.

Maggie Moulder

Man Against Earth

Ball of blue on axis spinning.
Poor sick sapphire choking burning,
Earnest is the search for a twinning.
Spaceships leaving and returning.

Mankind doomed since creation,
Using tools making tools,
Nation striving against nation,
Engines belching burning fuels,

Automobiles, carriages of the masses.
Green lungs consumed in fire.
Atmosphere poisoned by deadly gases,
Nature lying on a funeral pyre.

Ecological terrorism is alive and well
In search of profit costing the earth
Starvation and hunger the living hell
Another oil spillage what is it worth?

Slow down this human race
Survival of all the world is the aim.
A smile on a long troubled face.
Save the world and end man's shame.

Robert R. Adams

Schizophrenia

Festering thoughts kept
plaguing my mind;
were they someone else's or
could they be mine?

Doctors and nurses confine
me to my thoughts,
chlorpromazine, my straight jacket
does nought.

They told me to kill them,
it was God's work they said,
but it's me, not them, that's
confined to this bed,

Demons and devils burdened
their souls,
they had to be freed or
so I was told.

But now I am here,
the voices have gone,
I hope they don't find another
to carry on.

J. Manning

Dancers

Every step a fantasy
performed in perfect harmony
defying the laws of gravity
creating the art of dance

Defining every sound
as the music spins them round
with arms and legs abound
as though locked into a trance

Interpreting the mood
choreography pursued
The dancer's attitude
in formation so complete

holds my jealous gaze
as I watch their every phrase
and willingly give praise
to their ever golden feet

Stan Jenkins

The Housewife

Cleaning the dirty dishes
Scrubbing pots and pans
The next time I'm here on earth
I hope I'll be a man

B. A. McClune

Song

I could tell thee of the quiet,
Peace enfolding,
Mountains, deep un-dreamed of lakes,
Silence holding.

I could tell thee of the spring,
Pain unheeding,
Cruel earth-wombs passionless,
Stone's cold breeding.

I could tell thee what the snow
Whispers falling.
What the bee hears, honey blind,
Of flowers calling.

Tell thee a tree's heart when the wind
Fingers through it,
I would tell thee of my love,
If I knew it.
J. Richardson

Own Back

I needed to get my
own back
The back that had
been pressed
against the mattress of
our love making
I loved mating
I loathed breaking
a mould I had
grown accustomed to.
Sarah Guppy

Change

Things don't change
overnight
One step at a time
is alright
like a scab you wait
for healing
scratch it off and you'll
be bleeding
Slowly - accept the change
give it time
It's O. K. you are divine.
Valerie Hare

Kids

Kids everywhere
Over here, over there

A blessing from God
so they say
For each one I pray

For as they smile, I see
fire in their eyes
A spark of true life eternal

It makes me feel paternal
Michael Wright

Hostility

He's shouting at me
Only to be sent to my room
She never sees my opinion
Two of them against me
If only they knew
Lies and deceit is all I hear
Inadequate is all I'm told
Together they stand, I'm alone
Yet they are happy, am I?
Stephanie Hall

" Goodnight Sophie "

Goodnight, Sophie,
Our thoughts are with you,
Our tears flow for you,
Dearest sister, cherished child,
Now at rest.
It was such a cruel death,
God grant you peace.
How could it be?
These words are your epitaph.

Sophie, Goodnight,
Our hearts are broken,
Prayers are said for you,
Heaven is home for you,
In your short life, you gave so much,
Everlasting joy be yours.
M. F. French

Memories Of Wartime

Evacuate! Evacuate!
Our Mums and Dads did speculate,
So off, with gas masks on string,
The kids all did bring,
To wait for a train,
In the pouring rain,
Oh! The poor little dears,
Trying to dry their tears,
Mummies little soldiers,
Had to keep back their shoulders
As off to a farm,
To keep from harm
They fought their war
On some distant tor!
Those little teenies
Were brave ovaltinees.
Valerie J. Cave

To The Peacemakers

Faceless and fearless
Our men
Have created a Sequoia
In our midst.
Like ripples in the water
the outer ring, when disturbed,
knows no bounds.
Our hands are tied with the
unseen threads of destruction.
We cannot use their machine
lest we should entwine ourselves
in the branches of their forest of fire.
Fight, we cannot,
Join, we dare not.
This whirlpool will engulf us all
Sooner or later
Unless we find the Seed and
form a new beginning.
Moira Lavery

Life

Sometimes we dream
Other times it seems,
Some days are good
Some days are bad,
Life just goes on
Even if it's wrong,
How nice it would be
If we could just see
What's on the line
Ahead of our time,
What changes we would make
Or chances we would take,
But life is a gamble
We take every day.
Valerie Morris

The Tramp

Once he was fair
Once he was young
He was some mother's darling
Some mother's son

Some mother rocked him
As a baby to sleep
Now he's a tramp
Lying drunk in the street
Margaret Black

Why

I have heard the song of thrushes
On the breeze so lightly borne,
I have seen the sun as it rises
In beauty with the dawn.

I have stood on the hillside
With the scent of nature's blooms.
And below me the silver river
Reflected the sun at noon.

Then why with all this beauty,
Must man contrive to find,
Excuse for war with blood and tears
Of man against mankind.
J. Cunningham

Horizons Of Summer

Sun stained grass
  On sand we tread
Our memories pass
  We dream instead
Of futures bright
  We know no less
We leave with all our might
  Progress
To wonders big
  What jewels that shine
Beneath our dig
  A silver line
That leads us forth
  To worlds that show
Our every worth
  Where lovers go
To find the truth
  Of happiness
We found in youth
  And friendliness...
Mark D. Darch

The World Today

There's many people in the world
Some are happy some are sad
Some are caught up in their fears
Caused by worries through the years

But life is hard it's plain to see
You have to fight to make it free
Or else you'll live a life of hell
Trapped inside a tiny shell

There's people in the world today
They have no food they have no say
They didn't ask to come this way
Where there's no laughter or no play

Then there are the other side
They live a life of hope and pride
Where money's falling everywhere
But do they really have a care

So next time life seems hard to beat
Think of those who hardly eat
Who cry for love someone to care
The world today is just not fair
R. Mazzuccato

Treasure (For Cally)

She gave me a book
On 'LOVE' as a gift.
I read it and
Indulged myself
In words of
Tenderness and sincerity.
She touched my heart
Nay, my very soul.
Deep inside me
Sending delicious
Ripples of Love
And wanting.
A fire inside me
Was lit but cannot
Be quenched
Ever again.
She is part of me
I am part of her.
Joined beneath our
Skin forever.

B. Thomas Ahearne

Leap Year 1996

Stand for a while
on a February night
to gaze on a rare couplet
of magical de-light.

A glowing half moon
a showing of Venus
stoically.. spotlighting the scene.
It invited a wish
of some secret desire
NOW.. is the time.. before you retire

Perhaps.. a romantic leap, into
partnership new
a lightening of stress..for
those, who are blue.

The tree's bare branches,
stretch .. to plea,

Please kindly moon, shed some
light on me

Phyllis D. Williams

The Happy Spider

I'd like to be a spider
on a brewery wall,
Before I went to bed at night
in the vat I'd crawl.

I'd have my fill of ale
then to my web I'd go,
stagger up my thread
singing as I go.

Every night I would party
in my endless supply of booze,
Drinking and singing all night long
then back to my web to snooze.

I suppose it would get boring
especially through the day,
eating flies and insects
and other kinds of prey.

On second thoughts I'd rather stay a man
and sit and drink in comfort,
have a laugh a joke with my pals
then home for tea and crumpet.

L. E. Gray

We, The Refugees

We, the victims
    of ethnic cleansing,
our lives exposed
    to untold horrors;
grief-laden,
    we cling to life
within the dark
    of these stone walls.
And overhead, the tanks roll on.

Refugees we,
    from power-seeking warlords.
(How cold these stones
    how dank this cellar!)
We ask no more, now, than
    the sigh of the stranger,
the rise and fall of the
    breast that is dear to us.
    And Silence —
    to nurture the dormant seed
        when the tanks cease to roll.

Venetia Carse

Celebration

O the clean, bare brightness
Of a sunny winter's day!
With a soft wind or an icy wind
That takes your breath away:

The clear, sharp detail
Of everything around,
From golden beads of gorse buds
To grass blades on the ground.

The glossy, spiky holly
And shining celandines;
Fine interlace of branch and twig
With ivy intertwined.

The rushing, gurgling brook — by field
Of bleached and fuzzy grass;
The unexpected snowdrops
That delight me as I pass.

And oh, the blessèd, welcome warmth
Of the downpouring sun!
Reminding me of summer
Now that spring has just begun.

Pat Gelling

I Long For African Soil

The harshness of their skins
Symbolic of their given land
Uniqueness of their ways
And sun that pelts upon the sand.

I wore what life for mine -
Was cast in their ways -
And years gone by begin to show -
I still dream of those days

The world I love -
It still exists
Beyond the seas -
Beyond the mists
One day my life will give —
To me -
The life I love -
Across the sea

These years seem long -
But I can wait
Regain my roots -
My African fate.

D. Morrison

Oil Slick

We had the wrecked oil rig,
    now we have on oil slick.
It lures the sea, the beach's birds,
    it makes one sick.
Why do we have to have oil
    at all? It is such a pest.
The fishermen, life boat men,
    will be to sea again, no rest

When the summer comes,
    tourists we will lack.
It clings to the rocks,
    makes a mess of everything.
The sea gulls, the Hawks, sand warblers
    have oil on their wings.
The children will paddle,
    will have oil on their feet
And we will all have to take our own seats

O. R. Quin

Un-Born Dream

The cord is cut
Now I am here
My mother's arms protecting me
Innocently
I stand naked before my life
No sin
Life's long path I shall tread
No fears
I see no evil
Feel no pain
No poverty
No enemy
No hatred in this world I see
Hope springs eternal from my mother's
bosom
If only
If only
Sadly an un-born dream.

Sylvia Sharon Brown

Untitled

Your eyes, they shone
Now dim they have gone
A heart that was so warm
Now bitter and so torn

Oh how those blue eyes
would shine
When I would draw your
lips to mine
Or was it the effect
of the 'Chivers' smiling
That worked and got your
body writhing

And so to sleep
But the memories I'll keep
Of my love I shared
And those times I cared

But of course to you it
was a game
That's left me sad and
to blame

Michelle King

A Geranium Called Gwen

Each morning when I wake,
On my window sill,
My eyes behold a sight,
That gives me such a thrill.
A burst of mauve cerise,
Upon a slender stem,
An orb of flowers hustle,
A geranium called Gwen.

Valerie Yvonne Tootal

'Tales Of Realisation'

I have only found
now
to-day.

There was a time when I would say
to-morrow
I will.

Next month
I'll stay.

Next year
I'll take a dream,
of clay.

But now
has come.
These moments
shall not tick away
before the fabric bonds
and knots.

On seconds
the mind
may play......

Joanne Young

The Storm

The night had started clear
Not a cloud was in the sky
But by the strike of midnight
Not a piece of earth was dry

The hail and rain had lashed
Everything in its path
Down the chimneys it blew
And landed on the hearth

It crashed on the rooftops
And through the open doors
It banged on the windows
And saturated the moors

The thunder and the lightning came
And just as quick was gone
But the short time it had lasted
The winds had been so strong

But when the sun came up
We opened up the shutters
The only signs of the storm
Were the overflowing gutters

Susan Stevens

Untitled

The rain, it raineth every day
Not a chance to "out and play".
It makes you browner than browned off
Enough to give you a death-cough.

I know full well about this "SAD"
And it will make me very glad
When we see the sun again
And say farewell to all this rain.

I know the need to top the ponds,
But surely it is not beyond
The wit of man to bleed-off streams
Or is that the stuff of dreams?

Ever since I was a child
I remember getting wild
To see rivers draining out to sea.
'Stead of being used for you and me.

One thought, that being privatised
'twould be better, but not surprised
Are we to find priorities wrong
And all our hopes like a lost song.

Ron Lane

Life

Live not for the future,
Nor dwell on the past,
For no action today,
No will, or way,
Can change the outcome —
Of yesterday's deeds.

Whilst sitting there wondering —
What could have been,
What should have been done,
And what tomorrow may bring,
Vital seconds just slip away.

It's today's achievements —
Which determine tomorrow's events,
So shut the door on the past.
For looking back will just hinder,
Whilst forwards not help,
So live each day as it comes.

Melanie Victoria King

Aloof Or Alone?

She does not talk
　nobody listens
Nobody to sob with
　so no tear glistens.
When she cries
　she cries alone
Dissolving the myth
　of her heart of stone.
The silence is deadly
　louder by night
With shadows of emptiness
　clouding her sight.
Nobody to laugh with
　nobody to share
She no longer looks
　for nobody's there.

Tanya Fowles

The Light

He is so unwell
no-one knew, no-one could tell.
We know that life is so dear,
Now that death is so near.
Can't understand why it
had to happen this way
he's so weak — in his
bed he does stay.
There is so much pain,
I know I will never see
him again.
Maybe soon he will
give up the fight
close his eyes and
see the light!

Naomi Pelling

My Dream Girl

She came to me
Not I to her
The time I can't forget
It seems so long ago
The memory lingers yet

I would she came
for one brief spell
a dream girl was
my only wish
That she would come
and leave me with a kiss
alas 'twas only in my dream
She came to stay
I would she were
here forever and a day

C. Collinson

An Arthritic On His Cross

Here I linger,
Nimble as a doubly broken finger,
Doomed to be
A breathing part of community;
A life cruelly nailed away;
Away from active living,
Denied the joy of sharing,
The joy of giving.

Gazing into a succession of faces
Which peer out at me unseeingly;
This multitude around me races,
While I, uncomforted, sit;
Touched not by their hands or hearts,
Solitary, wondering;
Relaxing now each aching limb,
Easing one pain out and another in.

And so linger!
Yet for their pains and sorrows must I feel,
Their agonies share,
With an understanding tear,
and a silent prayer.

Robert Bailey

Harvest Poem

Fruit and nuts and berries
Nice and ripe and sweet
Golden corn in the meadows
All for us to eat.

Rich food in its plenty
Picked and stored away
While others in their countries
Are starving every day.

Mothers in the market
Choosing what to eat
Perhaps a rich fruit pudding
For a special treat.

In heats of Ethiopia
Where little grows on land
A mother looks at the food for the day
Which only fills one hand.

In lands of drought and hunger
No more dear Lord we pray
Must mothers ask the question
Which child to feed today.

Susan Webb

I Am

Quietude. Hush.
No turmoil. No anguish. No rush.
Inhale. Exhale. Sweet the air.
Breath of life. So fragrant. Fair.

Relax. Unwind. Let go.
Allow the life to flow.
Let all thoughts subside.
The mind must open wide.

Rest. Silence. Peace.
Now gain a true release
From self. Relate to all
And break the iron wall.

The barrier's breached.
The sleeper's reached.
The love. The joy
Without alloy.

The healing grace
Within this place
I now bestow.
Be still and know.

Sylvia Bewers

Beloved Child

Lovely baby, pink and rosy
Nestling in your crib so cosy,
Engulfing me in Tides of Love,
A treasure sent from Heaven above.
Beloved child on dancing feet,
With gentle ways and smile so sweet,
Gave my life a golden glow.
Midst days of joy, how could I know
Although you were from Heaven sent
You were not mine but only lent.
When all too soon we had to part
You left me with a broken heart.
Bereft and torn apart with grief
And misery beyond belief,
Now I am old and still I pray
To God that on my dying day,
Sweet Jesus ever meek and mild,
Please give me back my darling child,
That when once more I see her face,
I'll rest content with God's good grace.
P. M. Forristal

The Crucible

Xeno, arisen, yawned,
Myriad tints, orbs of light,
Appeared to be spawned,
From the vastness of night.

Anti-matter resumed,
Transmission and data,
Network, almost presumed,
To be lost, in the strata.

Searching eyes scanned,
Spheres of the sun,
Life being spanned,
When the spiral was spun.

Linking circumstance,
Fluid rhythms croon,
In mystical dance,
Clasped by the moon.

Surfacing to skim,
Dimensions revealing,
An aurora's rim,
The crucible concealing.
Ruth Mary Hayes

Irony Of Life

My heart is sore
My spirit low,
Tell me, please tell me
where can I go?
I looked to my right,
Trouble and strife
I turned to my left
nothing was right.
The images of people
are of wanton and greed,
Help me, please help me,
just help me please!
I wanted to run,
run away and hide,
somewhere, where calm
and peace abide.
War, crime, hate, fear
are everywhere.
Please hide me, protect me,
from this irony of life.
M. Walker

My Mother

When I was a lively lass
My mum said I was slow,
Now, this used to bother me
Although she would not know.

When Ina peeled potatoes
To race her I would try
To fill the bowl before her
But sadly I would sigh.

When berry picking came around
And Lizzie was at her best.
I'd try so hard to beat her
But she was like the rest.

Now I'm a sprightly pensioner
My relations say to me
You remind me of your mother,
At last I've won, don't you see?
Violet M. Young

Taken

The rowdy voices of the past
My mind too often hears
The clouded thoughts, unspoken times
Yet understanding tears

A face, mirror, time to clock
The day that happened then
Reflective years that were to be
In memory, such a shock

To start at the beginning
My life my body tried
But to know the misconception
Of the secrets she had to hide

My memory of a love embrace
Now painful, yet so clear
She surely could have not yet known
My love I called you dear

The hours that we lost together
Heart echoes have no lies
But one last thing I pray to know
Was it you who had to die?
Tony J. Brown

Deep In Love

My life would be a waste,
My life would be no more,
My life would have no meaning,
If you walk out of my door.

My feelings for another,
Can never be so strong,
for in my eyes and in my heart,
It's with me that you belong.

You're the one I yearn for so much,
You're the one I can't live without,
You're the one I'd give my life to,
You're the one I love no doubt.

The sun is always shining,
for you brighten up my days,
And without you in my life at all,
My heart would just decay.

Let nothing ever part us,
In my heart you're always top,
My love for you my precious,
Like time will never stop.
Wai-Ling Yip

Our Robin

The Autumn leaves have fallen
The winter snows do fall
We wait to see if he comes back
To pay his usual call.

At last he visits our garden
His lovely breast a glow
He is the finest of all birds
Off that we know for sure.

His visits soon get shorter
We wonder when he'll go,
To somewhere far away from here
I guess we'll never know.

The long hard winters over
Off to pastures fresh and green,
We haven't seen him on the lawn
It's as if he's never been.
J. Welna

Rainbow

Majestic arc which spans the sky
Mysterious and marvellous to the eye
Following torrential rain
Heralding sunshine once again

Kaleidoscope of beauty bright
Misty hues of ethereal light
Entwined within a graceful band
Magnificently the earth is spanned

No artist's brush can capture quite
The beauty of this wondrous sight
That lifts the heart and mind
A gift from heaven to all mankind
Patricia Whittle

The Dance

The dance is short,
the tempo varied,
so too is the step.
Partners change with graceful ease,
the patterns never set.

Every dance is different,
though the rhyme
remains the same.
From the start, all take part,
till our destiny is met.

When their dance is ended,
partners bow, and fade.
Then it begins again,
all over.
In life's eternal serenade.
Mark Taylor

Lighten Our Darkness

Standing on the hilltop
On a starlit night,
Marvelling at the beauty
Of the Heavenly sight.

The sky like a velvet cushion,
Diamond studded, all-aglow,
Pouring forth a radiance
On the Earth below.

Each star a separate planet
Illumining the night,
Shining through the darkness,
So full of love and light.

I pray we all awaken
And fill our hearts with love,
That our dear Earth may twinkle
Just like the stars above.
J. M. Dobson

Musicians

M is for Musicians,
morning, noon and night,
U is for unsightly,
though sometimes they're bright!
S is for singing,
not always a good sight.
I is for inconsistent,
especially at night!
C is for carefree,
though some are polite.
I is for interpretation,
to what you might see!
A is for arrogance,
they always think they're right.
N is for 'Nose and Chin'
they think they can win,
S is for 'Salmon and Trout'
if you give them a kiss,
They'll buy you a stout!

Jacqueline Humfrey

Innocence

Father plays,
Mother plays,
Grandma sighs,
Bobby cries.

Without love,
Tasting fear,
Outstretched arms,
Never there.

Hollow minds,
Empty shells,
No surprise,
Innocence rebels.

Media flaws,
Government bites,
Society ignores,
Bobby fights.

Blackened thoughts,
Daunting times,
Hurt distorts,
Nothing rhymes.

Elizabeth Lawrie

Lonely...

I'm lonely. I'm lonely again.
Mum shouts at me.
Dad shouts at me.
My brothers shout at me.

Who do I turn to?
Who listens to me?
Who loves me?
Who cares?

Why am I alone?
Why am I crying?

Is it me? or
Is it you?

Who do I turn to?

Who gives me a cuddle now and then?
Who tells me that they love me?
Who's going to say "Everything's
going to be alright?"
Whose shoulder am I going to cry on?

A new day comes. Nothing's changed.
It's all the same.
I'm still lonely...

Haleema S. Mahmood

The Old Ash Tree!

The swing swings on
My dear children are gone,
as the swing swings on
the old ash tree,

Oh for the days
they sat on the swing,
as the childish song they would sing,

But these days they are gone,
And the swing swings on
that old ash tree in the garden,
now our children have grown

From home they have flown,
Some work on the buildings
Some went on the beat
Some sit in a office
Some have it great,

But the swing swings on
My darlings have gone,
As the swing swings on
the old ash tree!

Betty Woods

My Dad Ernie

My dad is my life, my soul, my being,
My friend, my protector, my hope.
He slipped away, one cold dark day,
And left our hearts so empty.
He tried his best to stay with us
To be with his family.
But he was needed somewhere else,
Where we cannot yet go.
My Dad Ernie, he was so brave,
No one will ever know
How much he loved, and cared for us,
Until he had to go.
Goodnight dad, and you take care,
We promise to be strong.
You're in our hearts, and in our minds
Until the End of time.

Lorraine Faulkner

What is the Answer?

My eyes are dim
My gait is slow
My mind is fickle
Is it time to go?
Time hangs heavily
When the body is slow
Long since gone
When Life was a glow

When life is boring
Why do we stay?
As time creeps upon us
Why the delay?

What is the answer?
For I'm not sure
And is Euthanasia
Really the cure?

George E. Arter

For You

My love for you is unprofound,
My happiness in you I've found.
For God my life it must be casting,
My love for you is everlasting.
So please be careful,
   please be kind,
Take good care o' this heart of mine.

Joanne Tonkins

Freezing In The Playground

I'm cold,
My hands and feet are numb,
I'd love a nice and sticky bun,
To go into my empty tum.
My nose is red,
I'd love to snuggle up in my bed.
My ears burn,
When will the wind learn...
To stop blowing,
Or I'm going!
My teeth are chattering,
My knees are wobbling,
At last,
We're all running so fast.
The bell has rung,
I've got a cold little tongue.
(And we're not looking forward
to lunch break!)

Kylie De Biasi

Alone

I came to work, it hurts
my head...
I got drunk last night,
real dead...
She finished with me,
again alone...
So I drank to forget,
at home...
I cried real hard to ease the pain
once again.
Then I got mad right to the core
Smashed the hell out of the kitchen door.
And as I said...
I hurt my head, it's bruised you see,
Just like my pride
Why do I leave myself open wide
I'd just like somebody by my side.

Anthony Robert Smith

One Man

Shaped into one man I've seen
My life so far as it has been,
And possibilities of what could be,
Eyes so blue they carried me
To places I have only dreamed.
And through the windows of his soul,
He let me briefly flee.
I saw in him my darker half.
I felt his gaze brush by my heart.
In the moonlight I faced my fears.
Dawn's rays brought forth my tears.
Time was my enemy, time ran out
Before I had chance to find out
If he was my destiny or fated to be
Just another some-one to me.
He's a shadow now at the back of my mind
For I still harbour hope he could be mine.

Claire Michelle Edwards

"A Moment Of Sadness"

I wake again, another day!
So dark and grey and sad,
So many things go wrong for me,
Are taken, that I had!

I miss my friend, my faithful friend,
He was always there for me,
And now I've lost my work as well,
How hard can my life be!

I want to wake and see the sun,
And hear another bark!
I hope it won't be long for me,
To climb out of the dark.

J. A. Wells

Silent Thoughts

As I sit here behind these walls,
My thoughts and dreams afar,
Of sunny places and haze faces
Oh life it is so hard.
Outside the skies darken
the trees are shaken
the flowers have all died.
The wars return, no gain but pain,
the parents cry, the children die,
And laughter passes us by.
Thoughts of peace and harmony
Still so far away,
But just for one minute
I see sunny places and hazy faces
In the place I live today.
For a second am I dreaming of
Peace, not war?
Or are my thoughts reality
And will there be sunshine anymore?

Linda Swinburn

Dad

I hold a rose to you my love
My very special Dad
Who inspired me so and gave me love
And left me very sad

You suffered more than anyone should
It really wasn't fair
To watch you fight the way you did
You inspired me beyond compare

I miss you Dad - it's not the same
Without your presence and care
You've gone away - I'm all alone
You're simply just not there

My life is empty; I feel alone
There's space - it's cold and bare
Until we meet again my love
At these four walls I'll stare

Jennie Moyes

Life...

A summer breeze
like a passing tide,
a glimmer of light
like the life of a child.

Life is a sequence
a time to be served,
full of opportune
but also of hurt.

Love is a feeling
an emotion deep inside
to be loved is a greatness
and to love is a pride.

Life is a series
of emotions, of pain,
to live out a life
is to live in a private domain.

Louise Telford

" Night-time "

"What way, what way,
Oh, I wish I knew where I was."
Bang, ouch "Oh that cupboard!"
Black, gloomy, misty and silent,
Spine chilling sounds.
Dull, grey, eerie and dreary.
Afraid to touch,
Terrified to walk,
"Oh, how I hate going to bed!"

Louise Hounslow

Retirement

The years go by relentlessly
My working days have passed.
Retirement I've looked forward to
Has come around at last.
My life will be much easier now
So why do I feel sad?
They told me "take it easy now
Your life won't be so bad"
I'm old and hardly needed now,
As a pensioner I'm not required.
I never knew it would be like this
The day that I retired
But wait, I think I've found my place.
The doorbell rings, I see a face.
"What do you think we'll do today?"
That's what my grandson Joe will say.
Now I've got lots of time to play!

Anne Moreland

Next Door's Cat

What do you think has happened
Next door has got a cat
I know what you'll be saying
There's nothing wrong in that
But I can't open my back door
'Cos in the house it creeps
And there upon the kitchen floor
I find a little heap.
I've tried and sprinkled pepper
My problem would it ease
So far I've not been lucky
It's only made me sneeze.
Now if I catch that little cat
I know what I will do
It won't be taken to next door
I'll send it off to you
And when it does its little act
Upon your kitchen floor
I'll say to you about that cat
There's really nothing wrong in that.

Agnes Spellman

" My Life "

My life is drifting on and on
No battles lost, no battles won,
What is the purpose of my soul
I need something to make me whole.
I wander down the paths of life
Gaining wisdom, facing strife,
but never is my heart at ease
and so I fall upon my knees.
Questions fill my head once more
What is it that I'm looking for,
Comfort, joy, hope or ease
Will someone give me answers please!
I know you live and then you die
You say hello, then say goodbye.
I hope my time will not be wasted
True fulfilment has not been tasted.
So once again the weeks roll on
With nothing ventured nothing done
I cannot try to think it out
I just don't know what my life's about.

Debbie Sollis

Untitled

So now you leave me all alone
no face to look at but my own
I never know when you'll appear
inside my head with garden sheers
to slice apart what is not there
you broke me once and left me bare
but now I'm strong and back again
to conquer over you my friend

Lorraine Robinson

To Marjorie

I have no rose, no perfect bloom
No handkerchief to cry on
Here I stand, and in my hand
A little Dandelion.

To me this is the sunshine
That brightens up the day
And when it dies, I blow the seeds
And watch them fly away.

The last time that I saw you
A Dandelion I gave
Now Marjorie, in memory,
I place one on your grave.

And when I'm in my garden
And that drop of gold I see
I'll pick it up with fondest thoughts
Of my friend, Marjorie.

From Billy (Aged 2), written by his Nanny, Carole Hunt

Love Remembered

You're here with me
No matter
I try so hard to let you go
I succeed
A song — a few words heard
Again you're here
The memory brings pain
Longing, aching, joy once known
So brief that joy
But such a glow, what happiness
It entered my life
Time stood still
No one but us
Words unspoken — no need
We looked — magic
Love a precious time
A memory
Locked in my heart.

Eileen Burroughs

It Must Be Lovely Being Dead

It must be lovely being dead
No more worries in your head
No getting up
No lying down
No staying in
No going to town
Yes,
It must be lovely being dead.

Anne C. Scott

Love Is Not For Sale

Love is not for sale
No price tag can justify
For doing the things we often do
Without a reason why

Love is not for sale
You either will or you won't
There is no compromise on this issue
You either do or you don't

Love is not for sale
There are different ways to explain
Why we sometimes lie
And sometimes cheat
And cause each other pain

What's the price of your love
But think about every detail
And when you have come to your conclusion
Tell me is your love for sale

Delores McPherson

Budgie

You were tiny when you arrived,
not a single word could you speak.
But after a while, and lots of love,
'Pretty boy' came from your beak,

You used to fly around the room
Without a single care,
Then you thought it would be fun
To land in someone's hair.

Your cage was always open,
You were allowed to roam,
Until the day you found the door
and never came back home.

You heard the call of other birds,
you had to go and see.
With wings spread wide, off you flew.
You knew that you were free.

And even though you left us
and my heart I have to mend,
It's in my heart you'll always be
My very special friend.

Geraldine Mathieson

The Battered Wife

Alone I stood, at the mouth of hell,
Not knowing which way to go
My body shook, my tears they flowed
Each movement pained me so.

I could not think, I could not feel,
Fear my only friend;
Each day that came bought no respite
No calm in this living hell,

No feelings left, emotions drained
I took a hasty flight,
I left behind my cruel mentor,
I ran into the night.

Some years have passed, freedom gained
No fear, no pain, no guilt,
The days are bright, the evening calm,
My soul is healed and light

I love, I laugh, I feel, I see,
What freedom's given me.
Never again will I ever lose
That special part of me.

Jane Tickner

The Arborist

I'll write about the darkness,
of star and stormy sea,
I'll write about the arborist,
who felled the maple tree.
This was a tree of beauty,
from spring unto the fell,
I thought of her creation,
if only she could tell.
Her foliage in summer
made us a lovely shade.
The dewdrops in the morning
the soft refreshing glade.
There came the final Autumn
her leaves lay on the ground,
green and red and russet gold dancing
all around.
I climbed up to her highest bough I
knew she had to go.
To make way for extension to the
bungalow below.
I thought of God's creation of sand and
stormy sea,
for man can do most anything, but only
God creates a tree.

John Duncan

The Lost Life

Where once stood a Tree,
Now all that confronts me
Is a memory.
Oh, how my heart cries.
No longer will I see
The beauty that surrounded me.
In spring to bud.
In summer to bloom.
In autumn to shed.
In winter lying waiting.
Oh, my soul is left
With a hologram
Of the life
That was around me.

John Quinn

A Little Memory...

My brother, dead these twenty years,
Now dies again, yet slower;
For I have forgotten the memories
That I pledged never to forget;
Giant pillars supporting my life
Have decayed beyond recognition.

This second death of forgetting
Is surely as final as the first:
It is decay by neglect.
I writhe in my helpless guilt
Nauseated by the taste of shame
Blinded by the invisible blood on my hands.

Even the remaining memories
I see now as an adult views children.
My cold, blue, unblinking eye,
Its fixed pupil
Frozen in the wind of time,
Stares without focusing into the past.

Bruce J.W. Evans

Heaven

I think heaven is like a world
of dreams
with gates of gold and lights that gleam
A world for life ahead
A place for the dead.
You will tread the skies up high
Has heaven really got the people
up there who despair from lives
down here?

Joanna Curtis

The Blind Beggar's Song

I sit among columns
of flesh and bones
And featureless faces
And I wonder....
At parallel thoughts
that never can meet
Of minds that cannot conceive
Of a heart that knows no reprieve
Seems like a passing dream
With the dimensions of a nightmare.

Men talk of a soul
that exists within
I believe them.
I can feel something within me
Restless as a bird in a cage
In agony like a fish out of water
Just waiting to be released
In a release I dare not name
Here I sit and wonder....

Azra Tezien-Devonshire

My Butterfly

Go little butterfly
    Of poetic utterance:
Dusty cocoon abandon
    Wings spread forth
Emerge glorious
    From your chrysalis
Incredible in colour
    Triumph of creation
Fly, little butterfly, fly
    To the ends of the earth
And bear me swiftly
    On your wings...
My butterfly.

Joyce Bridle

All, One And Who

Calmness settles, the separate place
of scenes of loss of human race.
A place, a time of futile hope
in towns of little surface slope.

A future lost, in past of now
famous belief, entrust and doubt.
Of mourning voice, of slowness poised
to empty, forgotten, submissive toys.

In crowds of hatred, fearful shout
restore a sense of poisoned doubt
to quell a spark of joy euphorious,
of life too glad, but why for all of us?

Compassion, thought and free to do
controlled, encouraged and changed by you
a thought, a scene, but once a view
corrupted by all of one and who?

Giles Checketts

Untitled

As I wander through the streets,
    of someone else's mind
Hoping against hope I seek,
    the truth one day to find
As I look at emptiness,
    in the face I see.
I wish that I could find the words
    that could help turn the key.

As I walk through corridors
    of sad and lonely souls,
I wonder what's behind the eyes
    that look like empty holes.
As I see them standing there,
    staring at the wall,
I ask what has life left them;
    it seems nothing all.

Eileen Tompkins

The Disease

A disease called money,
Spreads among us.
Greed the visible symptom.
Unseen the tumour grows within us,
Eating away inside our minds.
Pressing down,
Distorting our vision.
Cynicism and hate
Pervading through society.
Poverty it seems is the only crime,
A fate worse than death,
Sending us into decline.
Killing us slowly,
Passing on to our children.
Can we stop it
Before it destroys humanity?

F. Harrison

On Leave

Sights and sidewalks
Of the dust-licked city
Curdle and then crawl
Through his deadpan eyes;
Forty-eight hours
Of cardboard pleasure
While the metal sinews
Batter and spew
A silky elixir
From the sea-bed's stew.

Swilling cigarette smoke
Down granite alleys,
Catching his shadow
In karaoke bars;
He'll be there with the gang,
Fleecy-eyed at daybreak
As the waves muscle up
To the harbour wall,
Waiting for the chopper
To drop through the skies.

Alan Spencer

About Love

Dear one if I could tell all
of the love in sublime fall
which tears with all dew,
A love which lifts at your call
and I answer in ways small
all in wait for you,

If you could know of the fair
and bounteous gift as I swear
loyal love to be,
Ever burning in bright flare
as the sight of you in stare
sighs but deep in me.

But sweet one I cannot say
of the feelings all in play
as stifled must sleep,
Not to be plied in any way
as kept from the light of day
but laden with weep.

Anne Huntly

Dawn

The awakening
Of the next sleepy morning
Is rosy coloured,
Lovely as the flamingo,
In his plumage of beauty.

Lynne G. Winsborough

The Show

Prepare for the show
Night after night
Desperately trying
To get it right

As the night draws near
So does the fear
With nerves we laugh
And shed a tear

Don't be frightened
Don't be scared
Go out and enjoy
And let it be shared

The hard part is over
You've got through the worst
It's time to relax
And hear the crowd burst

More! More! More!

D. Woolford

US

Our youth was within us
Of time there was plenty,
Age never thought of
Time to infinity.

Lover, companion, friend
Wrapped all in one.
How time has flown
Now you are gone!

Joan E. Lewis

30th February 1999

Fields of green, pastures seen
Of what we may all have been
You and I
Blue blackened sky.

Thrust your truth upon me
I care not of what's meant to be
These push and pull strategies
Being born into yesterday's society.

Smoke, drink
Until the brink
Of your pre-recorded death
Number, token what's your worth?
The time and date of precious birth

Look out, look in
What's your sin?
The past, future or what you're in
Care not I for blue-blackened sky
For blindness beckons You and I

Aimee Hartley

Guilty

I'm always feeling guilty
off all the things I do
I shout at those who love me
for reasons I don't know

I'm such a wicked person
I hate myself inside
I'm up in arms over nothing
Then I just sit and hide

I really do love people
it's just something I can't control
if I could just find the answer
perhaps I'd feel quite whole

I know there's blue skies up there
the sun shine from above
If I could just see dearly
and stop hurting those I love

Delia Viola Mosquera

Child Of My Heart

Deep within, the secret lies,
Oh child of mine, no death defy,
Gone the years, the hope, the fun,
Once was here but now is gone.

Taking time to shed the pain,
In a corner of my heart remain,
Taboo subject, secret child,
Talk of you, so much denied.

Feel the need, to hold again
So raw at times, to go insane,
Memories linger, your smile so sad,
Release from pain, for that I'm glad.

Though people think, your time has gone,
My love for you, still lingers on,
Until that time, we're not apart,
I hold you close, child of my heart.

Deidre Gillian Mercer

My Poem

I met you in Amble
on a hot summer's day
and when I first saw you
it was love straight away
it made me skip a heartbeat
and then I couldn't breathe
as time passed by I knew
you had to leave,
it left me so empty
it left me so sad
and all I could dream
is the things that we had
so now this poem has
ended, and now I have to go
all I ask from you is to
go with the flow...

Laura Louise Holt

A Gift To My Children

When I was first born
on that January day,
that's when my mother
began to teach me to pray.
To trust in the Lord
and let my faith grow,
so throughout my whole life,
his love would I know,
so I learned to depend
on this gift called prayer,
I believed in the Lord,
and he always was there.
And when I grew up,
and with my children was blessed,
I promised to teach to pray
till I'm laid to my rest.
so they can live my life
long after I'm gone,
and through my grandchildren,
this gift will live on.

Bernadette Charlton

The Old Oak Tree

Big old oak tree
on the ground
I wonder why
they chopped you down.

You took so many
years to grow
I wonder why
you had to go.

To make a table
oh so fine
and chairs to match
that look divine.

It is for sure you'll
never look so fine
as standing tall
and in your prime.

Carole Waters

Birds Of Disaster

Hear them cry
See them fly,
To cliffs and o'er the sea.
Hear the news
See the abuse
And the worthy helpers plea.
Here them cry
See them die
How quick
How slick
The oil!

Eleanor Stephenson

My First Taste Of Wales

The beauty of Wales
on this September morn,
The clouds around the mountains
as the day did dawn.

The warmth of the sand,
the freshness of the breeze,
the coolness of the water
as it laps around your knees.

The children playing quietly
with their buckets and spades
as the ocean seems to play a tune
of some sweet serenade.

The sun lighting up
the ripples in the sea.
This wonderful secluded beach
means all the world to me.

Denise Pickersgill

My England

My dearest beautiful England,
Once again I must say goodbye,
You are the country of my birth
The country where my ancestors lie.
A land of ancient history,
So proud for all to see,
Your beauty and your seasons,
Are a special part of me.
The greenness of your valleys
Your rolling hills and dales,
The colours of the Autumn
Your winter snow and gales.
The magic of the Springtime
And your long lit summer nights,
Wherever I go, you always will be.
My dearest beautiful England
— my birthright —

Jay-Bee Crawford

Hidden Wealth

When hanging out my washing
one cold and frosty morn.
I could scare believe my very eyes
I saw jewels on my lawn.
Not one, not two, but thousands
all glistening in the sun.
Alas I knew that they'd be gone
before the day was done.
The sun and early morning dew
had given me my wealth.
I contributed nothing, but said,
Thanks for my good health.
Thanks for the eyes that let me see
those jewels on my lawn.
When hanging out my washing
on a cold and frosty morn.

Dorothy Parker

Especially For Two

Paul's musical melodies sound
  Proficiently sweet,

As he carefully considers the rhythm
  and beat,

Some favourite melodies he did not
  anticipate,

Come on mum, hurry, or we'll be late,

We have to get a pleasantly
  comfortable seat,

Especially for this extremely nice
  wonderful treat.

Lynne Charlton

Dear Mum

In times of doubt
One will always think,
My world will
Never be the same
In times of happiness
Not a second thought,
Will come against
The hopeful grain.

So in between these spheres
A period will arise,
Doubt and happiness may go away
Instead the love of life remains!

Your husband, children, fond ownership
Pride and strength found within,
Joy has passed your way
Sorrow has appeared equal too.

Yesterday, today, tomorrow also
May continue to beset your thoughts
What of the future question?
No-one today has trod tomorrow's dew.

Amy Hogan

" Miracles "

Do you believe in miracles?
Or are they only dreams,
The beauty that surrounds us
Often goes unseen.

The sunset on a Summer's eve,
That ends a perfect day.
Birds' early morning chorus
Promise of a brand new day.

Daffodils upon a hill
Swaying in the breeze.
God's majestic creations
Tall lovely trees

All these wonders in this world
Belong to you and me.
Many, many miracles
God's gifts for you and I to see.

Dorothy Bell

Northern Ireland

P is for the people
Of this green and pleasant land
Whether Catholic or Protestant
God holds us in his hand

E is for the enemies
We've lived with all these years
But if we pass on fear and hatred
Then expect to see more tears

A is for acceptance
Of each other one and all
We must leave the past behind us
And start to break down walls

C is for consolation
For the grief this land has borne
Let no other heart be broken
We've seen too many families mourn

E is for equality
As we learn to love our fellow man
We'll do away with them and us
Lets show the world we can

Put these letters all together
And the word you find is PEACE
So lets work things out together
And make sure the killings cease

Elizabeth Lennox

Searching

When we're a feeling down
or feeling blue
what the hell
are we supposed to do
we try for jobs
but there's no luck
what the hell
where's the work

There's pain and anger
all around
and jobs are thin
on the ground
so why not smile
instead of cry
at least we'll know
we really do try.

James McIlroy

" A Child "

Like the first rose of summer
Or the daffodils in spring,
There is nothing in creation
Gives the joy a child can bring

The trees in the forest
Or the flowers growing wild,
Just cannot be compared
To the beauty of a child.

Like the gentle flowing river
Or the summer breeze so mild,
In natures roll of honour
They are far behind a child

Even colours of the rainbow
And the dawning of the morn,
Cannot match the joy and wonder
On the day a child is born,

Jim Quinn

Snow

I woke early one morning
Outside the world was bright
I looked out of my window
And everything was white.

The trees had beards like Santa
I couldn't see the grass
Outside the world became transformed
By this swirling, white, soft mass.

I've heard of changes in the world
Oh! what a change last night
It looked as though the Angels
Had had a pillow fight.

I wonder what this white fluff is?
Is it friend or is it foe?
I asked the poor cold trees
And they whispered back, "It's Snow".

Frederick Wilson Rabjohns

It Will Ache

I love my green room
Opposite the lake.
The four walls are protecting me
From the shock - To awake.
The stuffy air is reliable,
Never putting me at stake
To breathe the cold of Reality.
And for this sake
I gaze at my lake,
I know it is fake.
It is deep and it is harmless.
The four walls can be so safe.
And as soon as I cross the lake
It will ache - THE REALITY.

Katrina Sadzhaya

Felis Tigris

Tiger tiger, Badua Bali
padding paw, curling claw
amber stripes jet black between
eyes that hypnotize the night
moving over forest floor
unseen spirit, father, brother.

Tiger tiger, Mahela Bali
padding softer, cubs beneath her
symmetrical through sun and shade
ears pointing, whiskers white
Bengal tiger hunting free
lithe and graceful is the mother.

Tiger Bangee with crooked leg
limps with pride, shortened stride
hides in shadows, seeks his brother
hunger sucks his belly limp
felis tigris looks for cover
dying, dappled, Asian cat.

Jennifer Fox

Pain of Life

Hurt is pain
Pain is hurt
Hurt and pain
cause hate
Hate Hate Hate
I hate to hate
But hate is all I know
I have been hurt
from the first to
my last
If I stay I'll grow
to be hurt and hate
NO!
If my Parents never met
I'd never have known
the word hate
I hate my Parents
I hate my life
but most of all I
hate hate.

Belinda Prince

'Flowers By The Roadside'

Tributes tied to fences
passing people quietly pray
flowers by the roadside
now that you have gone away

Tear stained notes on little cards
messages of sadness
flowers by the roadside
to mark the spot of madness

When the buds start to fade
the memories still live on
'though the flowers by the roadside
have wilted and have gone

Laid by family and by friends
strangers lay them too
flowers by the roadside
to say how they'll miss you

Lisa Turk

Untitled

Perhaps today I'll sail a yacht,
Perhaps tomorrow,
Perhaps not.

Perhaps today I'll see you again,
Perhaps tomorrow,
When?

Laira Turner

Life

Newborn baby
pink and warm
opens its eyes for the first time.

Fish gasps for breath
as it dangles on a line.

Clings to its mother.
As the hunters slaughter her!
The baby gorilla.

Newborn fawn
runs beside its mother,
and feels the grass beneath its feet.

The owl ruffles its feathers,
and hoots,
as it beckons in the night!

Kelly Oakley

Listen

O'er my grave he did softly tread
Placed a flower above my head
Breathed a sigh and then he said
I wish my love that I were dead
Evening shadows slowly falling
I think I hear you softly calling
Across the void to this empty heart
Why, my love did we have to part.

I felt his sorrow so cold a thing
As o'er the void did my spirit bring
And o'er my grave did I softly tread
Placed a hand upon his head
breathed a sigh and then I said
I wish my love I were not dead
But as evening shadows ever falling
There's a voice ever calling
And if you listen from the heart
Then my love no more will we part
I felt his love so warm a thing
As from the shell did his spirit wing.

Jean Allan

Please Don't Shout At Me!

As I like to read a book,
Please don't shout at me!
For unmade beds, dirty plates
And general anarchy.

As I like to write things down,
Please don't shout at me!
For dredging from within my depths
And shaping soulfully.

As I like to walk the hills,
Please don't shout at me!
For pounding upwards, breathing gone
Alone and solitary.

As I can't escape myself,
Please don't shout at me!
For blaspheming, swearing, shouting,
At the men who shaped me!

Jo Dewhurst

To A Dumplin'

I love yer Bonnie Sonsie face
  Yer lovely treckle innards
  I love yer skin
    Yer fruit within
      Noo lets eat a' yer gizzards
Fur a birthday yer a treat
  Oft wi' custard, you we eat
   Hot or cauld, a slice or a daud
    Or fried wi' ham
      Whit ur ye ca'ed —
      "A dumplin'"

Anne Wilson

Wailing Sirens

Two people, no
problems normally, can't
cope when
these machines are between.

Technology, it seems, not a
blessing but an
angry
insult to conversation.

Words, somehow mangled,
meanings warped between distance,
no face with smile,
or reassuring touch;
a menacing field of tone
fuzzy in comparison.

If only we two were telepathic, could
rid ourselves of such miserable makings;
yet we are not
and cannot
lest we'd cease to speak
at all.

Kirsty Clarke

Earthquake

A giant city once stood
Proud and tall.
Its indestructible buildings
Reaching for the sky
Its people in high spirits
Oblivious of impending doom.
Then came a rumbling
Deep in the earth.
Followed by the crumbling
Of future hopes and dreams.

A giant city now lies
In humble ruins
Its indestructible buildings
Just piles of masonry
Its people, spirits broken,
Traumatized by fear.
Then came the crying
Deep beneath the rubble
And a motive for trying
To rebuild future dreams.

Cynthia Murrells

Alarm

Red, amber, green,
Red, amber, green,
  All my life is...
Red, amber, green.

Josie Williams

Where Were You?

The distant rumble of thunder
Reminds me of you.
The bright flash of lightning
Splits my heart in two.

Why didn't you call
And say you'd be late?
The dinner I'd made
Was lying cold on your plate.

The sweet smelling candles
I'd lit at the start
Were now burning low,
Deep in my heart.

You could have picked up the phone,
And saved me this pain.
Are you gonna try,
To do this again?

Kirstie Faulds

IRA Ceasefire Breakdown

Hopes were held so high,
Right up to the sky
That peace had broken out,
Without there being doubt
From that bright August date,
There was much to celebrate,
Now the IRA
Was going peace's way
So put away the ration
And enjoy a celebration,
For now instead of war,
There would rather be jaw, jaw
For eighteen months it lasted,
Till Canary Wharf was blasted,
And now it's back to gloom
As IRA return to bomb.

John Albert Smith

Hillclimbing Motorsport Tension

Start the engine
Roll down the hill
Up to the start line
Oh, what an ordeal

Revving up the engine
Visor coming down
Sweating under cover
Green lights winking now

Round the first bend
Skidding as I go
Through the speed trap
change gear into low

Through the "S" bends
Finish all in sight
What can my time be
I hope it's alright

Charlotte Cock

Sight Beyond Seeing

Silence,
Rose of betrayal
With the fruits
Thy would hide
A deep and evil plan
Caprice covered love
Is what fools do see
When even fools are wise
Without greed.
A token of worldly things,
Laugh do I
Yes, I do
For the rose shall wither
Its fruits bitter
But life with me remain.

Edward Lee Crosby

" Defiance "

Bring forth all your artillery.
Run over me, the past.
Attack me from all angles.
Approach me slow, then fast.
Slay me down to size you may,
but I express no pain.
I stand here, in defiance,
Determined to remain.
That winter's gone, we'll clash again.
This triple-seasoned fight,
Returning to our trenches.
When cold days starve us light.
My blade, it cannot spurn you,
But my colour's to the mast
I state this day, "I'm here to stay".
    Hurrah, the blade of grass.

Ken Porter

Sea Of Love

If your words were like a ship,
sailing in the sea,
then they would be calm,
as calm as calm could be,
but if your words were
like a ship,
and mine the ocean,
deep and blue,
then you would surely drown,
when I say, that,
'I love you?'

Lora J. Parsons

Seeking

Look and you will see
Seek and you will find
The wonders of the Lord
Are hidden in your mind

Don't think you won't falter
It's hard at the start
God will not fail you
Be strong, faint heart

In the quiet of evening
And stillness of dawn
Ask God for his help
Anew you will be born

Your faith can move mountains
It can open the door
To a far, better future
You thought impossible before

Why don't you try it
What have you to lose
There's so much to gain
But only you can choose

Kathleen W. Heasman

Nico

Flaxen hair
Sensuous stare
Marble eyes
Parisian sighs
Pouting lips
Model hips
Warhol's baby
Velvets lady
Sultry tones
Morbid moans
Morrissey snaps
Nico adapts
Celluloid movie
Undergrounds groovy
    The End.

Carole Patricia Smart

The Last Dalmatian

Candy died on Christmas Eve.
She did not die alone.
I knelt beside her, loving her
and saw her to her home.

Oh what an empty feeling lies
deep in my grieving heart.
I try to think she's happy now,
but it's very hard to part.

Simon, Lady, Jane and Baron
all have passed away.
Candy joins them now at Christmas.
No more words are left to say.

Enid Gardner

" The Creature With The Fag "

Her name is Alison Hughes
She doesn't take long to blow a fuse
Her eyes go green
Her face goes red
The next thing she does
is bite off my head
With a fag in her hand
She sits and dictates
a running commentary
of my many mistakes
She always catches me
without a doubt
and never fears to roar and shout
I reckon,
all the staff should get together
buy her out, peace forever!

Katrina Cadger

Sleeping Beauty?

Upon pricking her finger,
She fell to the ground,
A hundred years later,
Only then, she was found.

The Prince Arrives

He saw her beauty fallen there,
And knelt beside his find,
Kissing her without a care,
No thought of caution in his mind.

The Princess Stirs

The lovely vision made upward gaze,
And to her feet did climb,
She stared into his longing face,
Yelling, "About Bloody Time!"

Katherine M. Gibbs

My Mum

She owns the shoulder to cry upon,
She has the arms to hold,
She comforts when all hope is gone,
And with her all problems unfold.

When life becomes a world of fear,
When only darkness is in sight,
She'll dry away every tear,
And make the future bright.

She'll soothe away the sorrow,
She'll blow away the pain.
And in the problems that follow,
She'll do it all again.

My mum's there for me every day,
There are no words to cover,
The one thing I would like to say,
How much I really love her.

Anne Wiltshire

After Sunrise

Orchestral winds
recall the tide.
Waves break into
regimental
lines of white foam,
slithering, spliced
by salted rocks.
After sunset
the sea recedes.
Moonlight mellows
bedraggled seaweed,
crabs half eaten
by gulls as sands
sigh for sunrise.

Celia Heathwood

Amber

I have a cat
She is quite fat
She loves her food
And is very good

She jumps upon my lap
When she wants a nap
But lies on my chest
When she wants a rest

I put out her fish
On her favourite dish
Giving her plenty
It is soon empty

My cat is a dream
She loves to lick cream
She does like to play
And has the last say
  My Amber.
Gwyneth Sturgess

Basic Understanding

"Can I have a computer, Dad?"
She shouts as I open the door
"Can I have a computer Dad?
I've asked a million times before."

"We've been learning BASIC, Dad
The mouse goes to and from
The school's got a computer, Dad
Fitted with a CD ROM."

"Can we have a computer Dad?"
She shouts when I'm in the bath
"Can I have a computer, Dad.
Please don't be filled with wrath!"

"Laura's got a computer, Dad
And she's only eleven
She's in her bedroom all night, Dad
And her parents are in heaven!"

"Yes, you can have a computer, Danielle
I can take a hint!
But you can't have one just now, Danielle
Me and Mum are Skint!"
Keith Stephen Fraser

Relative

She's not black
She's dark
He's not white
He's pale
She's not yellow
She's jasmine
He's not red
He's just another shade of flesh.
Time teaches us art imitates life,
Colour is relative to the picture
Only when it's understood
We're all related in our veins
By the colour of our blood.
Alene Kimm

Black Dog..... (For Dick)

Black dog sleeping
Silently in the sun,
Big paws twitching,
Dreams have just begun.
Chasing over meadows,
Through the bluebell wood,
Catch the cheeky rabbits,
If only you could!
Black dog sleeping,
I watch you as you lie,
My dearest friend forever,
Until the day I die!
Gabrielle Purves

Black Hole

Touched me in the soul
Shining bright, star unknown
See you move, glide alone
The heart of love, so whole

Ride an incline. This world of mine
Sleep from the rest. Parody of time

Wheel of motion, chicken's heart
Spin your spell, into my web
You took, you came — I gave
The only way out, I, a slave

Sail on my body in the sky
Hold me fast with your eye
Walk to cold, dark grateful town.
Tears of a Jack, dreamt by a clown
Jumping to move ahead
Move me to the unknown
Cast of the old, love me whole
We were once friends
Two loyal and bestowed
Gerol F. Williams

Winter

Gloomy, dark,
Sinister and cold,
The trees are all bare,
The year has turned old.

Fog lingers lowly,
Like spirits of death,
Their after-life worn out,
No human life left.
The rain drizzles quietly,
Not making a sound,
Each drop like a tear,
Hitting the ground.

The wind moans like voices,
Tormenting the night,
It claws at the tree tops,
Bending their height.

Everything dismal,
Everything cold,
The days seem worn out,
The year has turned old.
Lucy Barwick-Ward

Happy Nessy

Monster Nessy in the loch,
Sleeps inside a cave of rock,
She swims around and round all day,
It seems a lonely way to play.

So when the tourists stand and stare,
She pops her head up in the air,
They gasp and take a photograph,
And monster Nessy starts to laugh

She quickly dives and hides below,
Is she real? They'll never know.
Katie Heinson

The Drink Of Courage

The suckle sip of magic fluid
slithers down my throat
and grasps my heart
fighting to be freed.

Oh spiritual liquid race
round my body.
The engine is oiled,
now I can start being me.
Lucia Moya Gil

The Old Slouch Hat

There it hangs upon the peg
Slightly tattered around the edge
Once it was smart and handsome
Brand new and proudly worn
Now, its life is waning
Its future looks quite grim
The hat is old and battered
Sorely needing some new trim.
The battle scars it carries
Were earned for services rendered
But now the old slouch hat
Is left hanging unattended.
The Khaki is all faded
The badge is hanging off
Its owner never wears it
So it never gets to doff!
It has seen many changes
Since it first went off to war
Let's hope the thing it stands for
Doesn't happen anymore.
Kay F. Ruane

Jade A Precious Gem

Our daughter called Jade
So beautiful and bright
Smile so wide full for delights
Long brown hair
A beauty she's grown
Precious like a gem stone.
Looking around frightened sometimes
Helpless and scared
But she always knows I'm there.
Now you're twelve a young
lady she likes you to know
for my precious gem is Autistic
a strange word not many people knew.
Love and treasured
you will always be
Someone very special to me
Jacki Joyce

Fishes

I hate fishes
so boring and plain.
Swimming about like
an aeroplane.
Wagging their tails like
a dog on a mat,
but not much
like one, I can
tell you that.
Camilla Ohlsson

Time

Time is running out
So I must try to do
All the things I've wanted
But haven't found time to do
Whether to see the Taj Mahal
Or even the London Zoo
The Acropolis in Athens
Syon Park at Kew.

Time is running out
Still such a lot to do
Especially tell my loved ones
How much they mean to me
Put photos in the album
Finish my knitting too
Would like a trip on the river
And a day in the country too.
Betty Groves

Liquid Love

The glass of purest opalescence
so innocent it seems,
BUT
I, like many others,
have fallen victim to its dreams.
It promises so much you see,
Yet hides a deadly sin,
and no one plays the game and wins
you only fall straight in.
You know it never solves life's pain
but still you keep on drinking
until one day you realize, you're like a
ship that's sinking
You think that you are strong enough
and there's no need for panic,
BUT,
What was it that happened to the ship
named the Titanic?
So take another look at life
from behind your shiny glass,
You may discover that you too
are living life too fast.

Deborah Cassidy

Breakers Yard

Once a young man's fancy,
Once an old man's dream.
Then, the chrome and paintwork
With love and care would gleam.
Many times the young man
Would speed without a care,
The old man drove more slowly,
His speed, past fifty, rare.
The young man started speeding
At a speed to surely kill.
The old man started dreaming,
As old men sometimes will.
No power on earth could save them
As they crashed upon the hill.

Now neither young nor old man
Will ever drive again,
Their cars lie broken, mangled,
Rusting in the rain.
For both the young and old man
These, their epitaphs, remain.

Jill M. Kimber

It

There it sits before me
So majestic and serene
Yet its power and presence
Seem to dominate the scene.

Donated by a dear dear friend
Who thought I knew the score
It's idiot-proof I heard her cry
As she headed for the door.

With keen intent and firm resolve
To prove myself its master
I've tried so hard, I'm losing face
It's ending in disaster.

It stares at me with cold disdain
Cool, gleaming, and aloof
I know I whisper to myself
I know it's idiot proof.

With hanging head, and fevered brow
I'm now the sad possessor
It's got to be the only one
A Demon Word Processor.

Catherine Udenkwo Nee Griffin

Untitled

We saw you for just a moment
so small yet so sweet
our precious little baby
with little fingers and feet
our hearts you opened up
the love we share is gold
we only wish that you were
here with us to hold.

Helen Carroll

When Autumn Leaves

So loud, this sound of silence.
So still, the autumn trees.
A golden leaf falls near me
as grows a gentle breeze.
Not wanting to be removed from beech
its mighty branches span.
The life that it was given,
a part of nature's plan.
If only you could see this view
that's set before me now.
A pleasure it would be for me
to share with you somehow.
I'll tell you when it's spring again,
So you can share the new.
And don't forget to think of me,
as there's no forgetting you.

Adrian Hill

True Love

Waking in the early light
So troubled by the fear
That you, perchance, had left me,
I turn....but you're still here.
Breathing gently....sound asleep,
This time it is for real,
For I have never loved this way
Or felt the way I feel.
I touch your cheek so softly,
You stir....but happily....
You slumber on, regardless,
Perhaps to dream of me,
For I will always love you,
You will never be alone,
Even to the very end
When all my time has flown.....
But now the birds are singing,
A new day has begun....
And it's time that you were getting up
My darling baby son.

Anthony Hilton

Sister

You rush over to support me,
So typical of you,
To take my hand and ease a pain,
The like of which is new.

Thank you for your comfort,
As I say to him "Goodbye",
"I'm alright", I whisper,
My tears suggest a lie.

How can he have left me
A man who's always there?
Someone I rely on,
To guide, to love, to care.

Who is there to turn to
To share this ache inside?
You are here beside me,
Your father too has died.

Christine Hulme

Woman's Mould

Feel your flesh
So warm, glowing
Touch feel
Life inside you, growing
This inner beauty
Felt yet unseen.
Unexpected radiance,
Gift of woman
Life is coming born.
Beautiful feeling tiny a must.
Know with creating life
You rise in peril
Nature's gift of wonderment.
Would now you be without?
Your smile births spirit ecstasy
Silently whisper 'Mother'
The bonding of life
Flesh forever bound
It's a mother's love
This life borne.

Kathleen Anderson

The Snow

The snow, the snow is falling
 softly on the ground.
It covers everything in sight
 like a warm, white gown.

She wears her gown
 of fine white snow
that covers all the ground.
 The trees and flowers,
they've changed their colour
 from green to cold white snow.
But if only you could see
 the change of colour
just like me.

Joyce Margaret Turner

Who Cares?

Someone tonight will drink —
Someone tonight will die —
Someone tonight will anger —
Only God knows why.

They didn't even know him.
Who said he had to die?
Does the birth certificate say
"Twelve years" — and then, Goodbye?

Tonight a mother will wait,
Wait up, and wait in vain.
Will hear the awful message —

Forever feel the pain.

Anne Duncan

"Something Taps On My Window..."

Something taps on my window
Something scratches at my door
Is it my imagination
As I hear the thunder roar
Something moves towards my bed
A scary, creepy silhouette
Something tugs at my covers
To my relief it's baby brother
Eyes wide as he cries
Wet me in carowine
Lightening strikes blue and white
Little brother hugs me tight
Billy wind rattles doors
Once again the monsters roars
Then slumber takes us on a journey
To a sunny day — bright and early

Frank Howarth-Hynes

A Place (Somewhere)

At a place... not known to others
Somewhere no one else has seen
  I stand
    Hand-in-hand... with Freedom
For company — my thoughts of home.

Just a place... yet special to me
Somewhere no one else has been
  I hide
    Side-by-side... with Panic
As Awareness states I can roam...

Oh, a place... in which to break-out
Somewhere no one else can go
  I cry
    Why oh why... such silence
Whilst relishing moments alone...

To a place... I would love to live
Somewhere no one else can know
  I pray
    Day-by-day... such wishes
The location — "a place" unknown...

Gary Standen

The Cog Of Life

Time is moving on now
Soon I shall be gone
Just a book of memories
From which I once belonged.

I look in the mirror
And what do I see?
Life's long reflection
Still holding the key?

So write me a letter
Compose me a song
Do for me something
To remember me from.

Write it on paper,
Carve it on wood,
Make it cut deeply
Engraved there for good.

Lesley Durrant

He Who Is Jealous

He who is jealous
speaks through a tongue of poison.
His eyes are webbed with green envy
so thick he cannot see.
His ears hear nothing but praise,
praise he wishes for himself.
His mind doesn't control his body.
His jealousy does.

Heidi Newman

Hope

Hope is like a star
So near yet so far
So bright in the dark of night
Comes dawn
And hope is gone
The cold light of day
Hides its brightness away
Come twilight
And hope is still there
Waiting
For an earnest silent prayer
Evening
And hope shows its face
I thank you Lord
For life and faith
A telegram
My son is safe.

Joe MacLean

The Fear Within

The wheels of my mind,
spin around,
I close my eyes,
there is no sound,
I wake in the morning,
wide eyed, and yawning,
ready to face,
the new day
that is dawning.

The fear within me,
grows so deep,
faster, and faster, my heart leaps,
the day grows, never ending,
my knee's so weak
they're practically bending.

And so at last night time falls,
but the fear within my mind, still calls,
I close my eyes, and try to sleep,
and pray to God, I do not weep.

Donna Davenport

Dandelion Day

Sunbeams press against my face
Spreading warmly as they land.
My hair sparkles spectrum colours
And my eyelashes make big discs
Melting into a kaleidoscope.
More colours.

I inhale the sky
A suck of infinite blue.
Even with closed eyes
Red and yellow appear before me.

Bees hum to the beat of my heart
And the breeze whispers
Sweet nothings in my ear.

Tick, tick, says the dandelion clock
Swishing past
In a hurry to be nowhere...

Carole A. S. Sutherland

The Mirror

Here against the wall
Stands a silent witness.
Door of the past.
A cold clear eye,
Unyielding.
Priest of many confessions.
Receiver of the sly side glance.
Rehearser of the unrehearsed.
Patiently waiting
At a spot venerated
By many acts
Of private devotion.

Julie M. Boden

I Fly

I fly so high in the sky
Swoop down and catch my food
Glide up so high and fast I go
Through the trees look down below.

Fly over houses past the trees
Sit on rooftops me alone!
Then day becomes night I fly to bed
I close my eyes and comfort my head.

Now it is morning
I open my eyes
I flutter my wings and fly away
going to have a lovely day.

Kerry Ballantyne

Untitled

I could sit here for hours
Staring into space
Building stronghold towers
Against the human race.

I could dream myself a dream
Against life's bonds and ties
And use it as a beam
To fly where freedom lies.

I could do this and that
In my imagination
I could give tit for tat
In gross retaliation.

I could try to conquer hopelessness
I could try to change my mind
I could also try to care much less
And take what can I find.

But no, my heart has turned to stone
It is beyond repair
I just want to be alone —
Sit by myself and stare!

Ingrid Kemna

Flowers From Within

As March approaches and flowers
start to bloom,
people fill up their vases to
brighten their rooms.
The fragrance and the colours
seem to take away the gloom
of all the cold and winter months,
that tend to return so soon.
But if you are truly happy,
and live life to the full,
you will always have flowers,
because they will grow inside of you.
And the stems will have strength,
straight from your heart,
and the petals won't fall;
they will never part.

Joanna Marsh

Untitled

If I could only
stay as free
as walking in the rain;
I could love you then,
and laugh at all the leaves
now dying on the sidewalks
of the city

Janet Mortimer

Winter

Snowy carpet upon the ground,
still night air not a sound.
Birds in trees shivering cold,
cunning foxes stalk so bold.
Gently snowflakes softly fall,
Tawny owl her mate does call.
Snow flowing brook in the lea,
Oblivious of you and me.
Horses huddled in the field,
Barren trees no leaves yield.
Sheep move with leaden feet.
Break silence with a forlorn bleat.
Suddenly the still night air,
is wrecked with noises everywhere.
Flashing aircraft passing by,
like silver pinions in the sky.
A frosty moon looks on with scorn,
and slowly breaks another dawn.

John Hopkins

Mankind?

Nature's animals kill,
Stomach search of meat,
Necessity not thrill.
Death needed to eat.

One animal chosen, weak;
Outlook bleak,
But the herd breeds on,
The young feed on.

One animal kills for fun,
Invented gun,
Death to more than one,
Thousands on the run.

But, He kills his people,
Erects steeple,
Buried underground,
Never to be found.

Man calls it war
I say "What for?"
The future of the Earth?
Ironic Mirth.

Ken Voase

Lighted Candle

I light like a candle
Straight from the ground
Too hot to handle
So don't sit around

The looks on their faces
Are full of surprise
Would you like to change places
Before your own eyes

Christopher Peach

Love Eternal

And deep in my heart
Such love is calm,
A sure steady stream
Wide, boundless, warm.
And deep in my soul
Such love is free,
A universal
Eternity.
All swirling planets
Encompassed high,
Reflect directly
In my soul's eye.
Such is this - my love,
From high to small,
Perhaps a butterfly
On the wall,
Perhaps a snail
Upon a stone,
Maybe the ocean
And I'm alone.

Chris M. Hall

Another Rose

Deep seated is the thorn
That pierced the tender skin
Crimson flowed on white
Evoked a painful cry
My love is as that thorn
An encumbrance to the flesh
If I searched within
And found the dagger's route
A calm could spread anew
And time would heal the scar
But I am thwarted in this hope
The thorn sinks deeper still
When love should be such joy
Tears rend the heart of me

Anne Maudsley

Untitled

She roars out her call with
Such passion and power,
Her infinitive goal to, to and fro,
She is both lion and lamb,
Her depths are a secret beauty
a dimension to pursue,
She is subjected to torture by
human discard,
She draws forward, beckons, and
asks me why?
Do we violate her territory and
family?
I cry at her beaches, the garbage
portrayed
The traffic that shouts
Pollution rules O.K.

Respect our seas.
Jane B. Lambra

My Country Garden

Roses swaying in the breeze
Sun shining through the trees.
The green green grass comes up
To your knees
In my country garden.

You can see those Honey Bees
Make their nest among the trees.
You can smell those sweet sweet peas
In my country garden.

Cher Reynolds

At The Crossroad

We claim to be
Surrounded by silence
When we know well
that steamrollers grind
their solid way past us
rolling flat the tarmac
to guide us on our way.

As we burst
the tar bubbles
Why do we sense regret
When all we find is air?
Maybe just one day
We'll meet the man
Who died on the crossroad
or better still,
The man who made the car.

Brian Caton

August

August and salt sweat on lips.
Swallow babies squeak.
Hot winds fill sails of little ships.
Butterflies cling to buddleia tips.

August, Dahlias, Gaudy, Flaunting.
Phlox and tansy full in bloom
Frenzied bees gather honey and
Windows wide in every room.

August, and the streams are dry.
Darting dragonflies, holiday people
Champing horses hug the hedges
And a heat haze clouds St. Mary's
steeple.

August and the schools are closed.
Dogs lie panting on the grass
Whining mowers torment the evening.
Old men watch the steamers pass.

Florence J. Wayles

"A Celestial Prayer For Healing"

Rock me gently;
Sway me sweetly,
On cushions of clouds
Of ombre and tangerine.
Oh moon, bathe me in your stardust,
Draw me to your milky breast
And warm me with your glow.
Cradle me against the fearful nights
That torment my soul.
Hum the lullaby of the stars —
Diadems of light and music.
Infuse my soul newly wrapped
In moonglow and stardust,
Where once was ash and lead.
Transform my pain to joy
And restore my soul's own glory —
To sing and swim amongst
The moon and stars once more.

Frances L. Palau

Untitled

To the worn people
take all your time to say it
say it when it hurts your throat
it's best not to lubricate
stay pertinent and dry
when the gold's gone away
besides
I met an ape (no fools here)
he liked me (maybe)
he is me (but I forgot, definitely)
so with a mirror
I pulled
and felt (fact)
an angel was pulled
to the ground.

Ian Robb

Growing Up

Open your eyes little girl,
Take note of what people say,
They tell you wisely
Be on your guard for,
People around you can be hard,
Understanding has yet to come,
So heed the warning and,
Bite your tongue!

Carol Brown

Reflections

I know not where my journey ends
  take time to stop and stare,
From childhood to my ageing years
  of love, tears and care,
So peaceful are my thoughts of thee
  into a sea of mystery.

The world so upside down to me
Can dream of peace and tranquillity.

Eileen Scoates

Give Me Time

If I should sleep don't waken me
That I may dream on undisturbed
And never think the waking thoughts
That fill my mind and will be heard
Echoing memories through past years
Of happiness and blended tears
Where once was laughter love to give
Now the path ahead is grey
But tomorrow I must live
But tomorrow not today

Irene Herring

When The Clouds Have Gone

Dark days ahead
Tears fall like rain
Heartache despair
Hopelessness and pain.

This feeling of loss
Is the hardest thing to bear
I need so much to see you
Even though you are not there.

But time passes by
And life carries on
The sun's a little brighter
When the clouds have gone.

Memories can't be taken
They live on in my heart
I'll keep them there to treasure
And we'll never be apart.

I cannot help it sometimes
There's still a time to weep
As I tend to the flowers
At the place where you sleep.

Kym Pattison

Lots Of Things

There are the farmers
tending the cattle.
There are the knights
fighting out the battle,
And there are the men
Fighting over the crown,
And there is chocolate
all creamy and brown.

Jinny Wadsworth

I Wish

I wish that food was plenty
That all could have their fill,
I wish that we would share out bread
So hunger couldn't kill.

I wish the sad were happy
Had help with their affairs,
I wish the sparkle to come back
And care free days be theirs.

I wish we were more honest
And there was no mistrust,
I wish that we were more humane
And we were not unjust.

I wish that there were no more wars
That fighting was to cease,
I wish for everyone to be
Friendly, and at peace.

I wish nations were united
That we could all relate,
I wish our love was endless -
And there was no more hate.

Celia Dredge

My Love

A touch as soft as gossamer wings
That is his hand in mine
The feel of fluttering butterflies
just as his lips touch mine
The brightness of the morning sun
shines out from his blue eyes
And in his loving warm embrace
I know the world is mine.
To have shared a love like this
Must be Gods greatest gift
And so to him I give my thanks
For giving me his gift.

Joan Revell

The Revolution

Here is the shower
That claimed its victim.
Cleansed the father
And devoured him.

Here is the water
That's drained from the sink
Seizing the daughter
And pulling her in.

Here is the pillow
That smothered the dream.
Leapt on the mother
And swallowed her screams.

Here are the darts
In the train spotter's back.
(Pursued the brother
And punctured his anorak).

Here is the fire
That brought the solution.
Finished the house
And the revolution.

David Richardson

Man's Mistakes

Acid is the rain
That falls upon our heads,
Polluted is the air we breathe,
Often full of lead.

Our oceans are over-fished
As we trawl away,
Pollution and oil-spills
Happen every day.

The rain forests become basins
As we cut down the trees,
Conservationists we're not
We shouldn't be very pleased.

Environmentally friendly
That's how we ought to be,
Not killing off the universe,
The likes of you and me.

Animals become extinct
Because of our foolish ways,
Won't we learn by our mistakes?
It's life that always pays!!

Christine Jordan

Sky Watching

One of my favourite moments,
That of Sky watching by night.
A burst of stars to surround
The moon.

Me watching and they watching
Me, Nocturnal companions.
In a blink of my eye they may
Have moved.

Time passing but I'm never
Watchful of it, This collage
Seems to shyly freeze under
My stare.
I wonder if I can seduce them into
falling?

It's a perfect two-way affair,
Even on silver less nights.
I'm left thinking........
They've touched down or reclined
To their slumber or mine.

Anthony Baker

A Spring Day

I am walking in the woods,
The air is fresh and cool,
The winter gales are gone.

An old year is over,
A new one is beginning.

I am walking in the woods,
The flowers are in bud,
The Christmas fun is gone.

An old year is over,
A new one is beginning.

I am walking in the woods,
The sun is shining bright,
The snow and ice are gone.

An old year is over,
A new one is beginning.

I am walking in the woods,
The little birds are singing,
The winter blues are gone.

An old year is over,
A new one is beginning.

Karen English, aged 11

Trees

I walked in the park today,
The air was damp and grey
Not a soul was around
The leaves lay still upon the ground.

The trees like silent sentries stood,
Great guardians of wood
Neither leaf nor branch they stirred
Not a sound was to be heard.

I had stepped into another world,
Where time very slowly unfurled
And only the trees held sway
Over the passing of the day.

Far away the traffic roared,
And the world continued in discord
But the park seemed far removed
And I felt somehow soothed.

As I sat and contemplated,
The trees stood by and waited
As they have done in time past
And will, even after I have breathed my last.

Dominique Lechner

My Dad

I know my dad is sick
Or as I prefer 'not well'
Some people think he's thick
Of course they just can't ever tell

It's like we've got a different dad
One with a mixed-up brain
Who sometimes acts mad
To some he's just insane

But I would never think that way
Even though I sometimes wonder why
All those horrible words I say
Come tumbling out of me

I hope you can forgive me, dad
I know you understand
The pain that has no word
Watching the one I love fade away

I'd just like dad to know
Whether the light is bright or dim
That from my heart he'll never go
And that I'll never forget him

Catrina Clark

Changes

What's the world coming to?
The ancients all say
I don't understand
Not like this in my day

What's the world coming to?
I say to you
The things we held dear
Now have no value

What's the world coming to?
I hear your echo
It will all end in tears
The ancients say so

What's the world coming to?
I say again
It's the people who change
The world is the same

Eileen Cantwell

The Last Roses Of Summer

Petals fall
The aroma still lingers in the air
A sweet smell
Pastel petals of colour
Pink, Rosebud Red and yellow
Memories of a summers day past

I remember the day you gave me
the lovely bouquet my friend.
The roses die
But the friendship still blossoms
in my heart.

Winter covers my world
Cold white frosty fingers
Tapping against my window pane
My mind dreams of future summers
when I can smell the roses from
your garden again.

Anna Caroline Mercer

Gulf War

The oil lies heavy black and thick
The birds now either dead or sick
A remnant of a war gone by
No longer heard their plaintive cry

Vast lakes of oil across the sand
The migrant birds now look to land
No man can shift for many a year
Their journey now so full of fear

They struggle, sink and then inhale
As they try to preen to no avail
What can I do to help their cause
As still they come without a pause.

Barbara Sutcliffe

The Sea

I am the sea
that quenches the sand and rocks.

I feel the pain
of the poison that pierces
my skin

I cannot breath
with the oil choking
My lungs.

I cry for help
But no-one listens

I am afraid of
tomorrow...

Anthony J. Hicks

And The Dream Made It Worse

Dreaming awake.
The Butterfly flutters,
As the smell of toast
Wafts.
The Crow caws
In a dark morning sky
And the Dream made It worse.

Awake in your sleep
And the Blackbird flaps its wings
As it hurries away.
Checkmate;
My Queen to your King
As the first big drop of rain falls
And the Dream made It worse.

She runs through the
Narrow
Halls, and he sits there,
Imperiously, impassively.
And the Raven gives one last caw
And the Dream made It worse.

Heidi Jane Wirth

Alone

When friends have gone home,
The children are asleep.
The house is all quiet
I sit here and weep.
No one to talk to, no one to care
No one to love me,
Now, you're not here
My heart is still aching
My soul feels numb.
Now that you've left me
and, I've got no one.
I wish you were still here
Here by my side
Instead I feel empty, knowing you lied
You said that you loved me
and said that you cared
That we'd always be together
That you'd always be there
Now, though, you've gone, you've got someone new
So I sit here alone, not sure what to do.

Beverley Miller

The Race

Up high in the sky
The clouds float by,
They fly over the sea
Trying to catch up with me.
But I'm away with my dreams,
Far from the sea and the streams.
Running through a field of grain
I feel the first drops of rain,
As they gently touch my face,
I know the clouds have won the race.

Emma E. Fitzgerald

Shadows

In the shadows, men set off,
the dim street-lamps casting a soft
glow for those who quickly go.

Joe stands at his window
longing, and listening to the
sounds of those who have found.

The demoralizing monster
laughs in his face, taunts,
teases him without cease.

A man's broken spirit crowded
with worthlessness and shame —
work gives a smirk.

Carolyn Hall

Senility

'Tis strangely still:
The falsely bright who mill
About the ward have fled —
Relieved to find their duty done,
To sanity return.

And I remain:
Among the old, infirm, insane
Confined to chair or bed,
My next event a cup of tea:
Who would be me?

In shrivelled shell
Which once was strong and well
I'm all but dead.
By wondrous scientific feats
My heart still beats!

Elizabeth Allan

'Still Trying To Find Love'

Still trying to find love,
The feeling just won't stay.
I think I've got a hold of it,
But then you walk away.

I feel It in my heart sometimes,
I think I've found the key.
But when I look into your eyes,
You're just not loving me.

But please don't tell me that
  you love me,
Then just walk away,
You've got to feel it in your heart
To let the feeling stay.

Lynsey Kelly

Summertime

Once again it's summer,
the flowers are all in bloom,
the birds in tree and hedgerow
break forth in cheerful tune.

The cattle in the meadow
and sheep upon the hill,
with Collie and his master
performing wondrous skill.

The cart horse in the stable
has just produced a foal,
the vet just been sent for
to exercise control.

Alan F. J. Packett

Showing Prospective

High in the heavens,
the stars shed their light,
set on a black cloth,
of velvety night.

They twinkle and dance,
like candles afar,
and for every light,
there lies a star.

This void is enormous,
it's ever so vast,
like grains in the desert,
of sand, first to last.

Its beauty is endless,
no borders it's got,
with thousands of mysteries,
for us to plot.

So as you look up,
at the heavens tonight,
put yourself in prospective,
and your troubles seem light.

Kenneth McGovern

The Cold Fox

In the glistening snow
The fox starts to howl,
While the wolf starts to growl
The hunter is on his way
With a gun in his hand,
Fox skins on his back.
The snow comes gently down
on the hunter's trap
That will soon start to snap.
The hunter will pull back his gun
and the fox will be gone.
The bushy tail will not be bushy
anymore.

Dean Phillips (Age 8)

Blessed Are The Peace-Makers

An iron curtain made of stone
The human spirit all alone
Down with the wall!

Death on the wire
The Holocaust of fire
Bring down the wall!

Unite in the light
Eradicate spite
Remember the wall!

June Meader

Winter Joy

Every day,
The lonely old man
Looked at the hyacinth
Beneath his bed.
And then one day
   He knew the date
Two pink buds
Stared him in the face

You little dears he cried
And searched his memory for a phrase
And when it came
He looked both right and left.
And touched each one
With a grubby finger.
Yes - that's it.
Two little dears
Two little breasts.

Kate Trimmer

Disco

The lights, the sounds
The music drumming,
The tunes, the lyrics
The kids all humming,
Bums wiggling, skirts flowing
Mass hysteria to crescendo growing.
What's the meaning?
What's the score?
Insane oblivion — nothing more?

Youngsters hungry
For some action,
Objectively speaking
What's the attraction?
Glasses filled
Obliterating mind
Self deception — draws kind to kind.
No need to delve deeper
Nobody does,
I'd rather stay home
It's much less fuss.

Barbara Boulton

It's Up To You

If you get hurt and let it heal
The pain will go away.
But if you brood about that hurt
The pain is sure to stay.

Betrayal often leaves a scar,
But scars are just a sign.
Telling you what's happened
Not what's next in line.

If you're left with bitterness,
A passion to condemn.
Your feeling of resentment
Is another point to them.

To escape from shock misfortunes
There is little you can do.
But their effect upon their future
Is entirely up to you.

Alex Morrison

Ghost

The room was dark,
The room was cold.
There was a ghost here,
so I was told.
I looked in the cupboards,
and under the stairs.
I looked in the wardrobe,
but nothing was there.
Then I saw her,
a lady in white.
I could see right through her,
she gave me a fright.
There's no such things as ghosts,
everyone said,
Try telling that to someone who's dead.

Gemma Frances Reed

Blue

Blue is soft, it is natural,
The sky, the sea, the cold,
The deep blue sea,
The soft blended sky,
The chilling effect.

Blue is sad,
Used for feeling down,
Felt when you're by yourself,
The chilling loneliness,
Given off by icy thoughts.

Blue is FREE, it's on its own.
Blue is refreshing,
Just like the sea waving with might.
Blue is powerful, it sets you free,
it wakes you up, BLUE.

Graeme Elliott

Welcome The End

You're thinking far more
Than your slurred speech can say,
Your body immobile,
Your mind far away;
At the end of your life, came
A world of dismay,
With a conflict each second
A battle each day.

And what is it for?
Your fight for each breath?
Do you pray for the end?
For the calm of sweet death?
Rest in peace; do not struggle,
And fight on no more,
Let pain be forgotten,
Surrender the war.

Paul Hobson

" Reveille "

The beauty of a baby's skin
The softness of a feather
The swiftness of a passing cloud
That heralds in the weather

Rain that sparkles on a path
Snowflakes that make no sound
Tiny shoots that poke their heads
From way beneath the ground

All these things around us
Things that we should treasure
Things we need no money for
Just things that bring such pleasure

But do we see them you and I?
In this world of deceit and lies
When all we have to do my friend
Is open up our eyes!

Jeanne Clarke Heredge

Unforgettable Friend

In your eyes I see,
the tears that can never fall,
In my heart I feel,
the love we could not show.
In my thoughts I imagine,
you close to me every day.
In my ears I hear you,
whispering all that you do say,
although now to someone new.
Of the eternal love,
that I once shared with you.
Our love was never meant to be,
and now it is all so clear,
that your heart was with someone else,
all the time you were with me.
But I still love you deeply,
and I think I always will,
in my heart especially.

Angela Craig

Deep Down

Deep down in my soul,
The thunder roars,
The lightning strikes,
And the rain falls down.
But soon the wind will come,
And blow the storm away,
Yet, I know the thunder will return,
With the lightning and the rain,
Deep down in my soul,
The storm will brew again.

Hannah Tuson

Alone

Why are you alone
Sitting and weeping,
Did you know him,
Did you love him?

Why are you alone,
Sitting and cleaning,
A long forgotten grave,
Did you love him?

Why are you alone,
In an empty grave yard,
Run down and in Ruin,
Lost under a sea of grass?

Why are you alone,
Was he a brother,
Was he a lover,
Was he another?

Donna Arliss

If Only

"If only" all the world could see
The whole of mankind a family tree
What would we give, what is it worth
For eternal life and peace on earth

Dennis William Leslie Bocock

Strathmore

The long grass writhes as
   the wind's pull bends furiously.
Trees complain, exercising
   stiff joints.
The leaden rain reflects
   against a sullen sky
   rumbling displeasure.
Swollen river, driving forward,
   displays white-hot anger.
The huddled cattle bellow
   their fear as the river
   breaks its banks and
   lightning jabs a fencer's thrust.
Then suddenly, clouds
   disintegrate into blue and
   wary sunlight stretches
   fingers that dance upon the ground.
Nature forgives and bathes
   all in her warmth.
The land drifts back to sleep.

David Doig

A New Journey

Clouds pass over a crescent moon
Their shadow black the earth
The icy wind, blows from the north
It blows for all it's worth.

Your presence is never far away
Your memories are with me,
Day after day
Your love lies deep within my heart
Never to be forgotten,
Never will it part.

I look deep...
Deep into your eyes
They glistened,
As though they were stars
As you float beneath the moon lit skies
On moon beans of pure light
You have healed these gaping scars.

For when life's journey
Comes to its end
A new journey has just begun.

Colin Francis Hauxwell

This Bloody War

In our way, there lies ruin
There can only be deceit
This bloody war that's ragin'
Can only bring defeat.

In our path, there lies obstruction
Of our sight, a blinding light
The bombs that cause destruction
In this war we fight tonight.

There is pain, and there is glory
for the victor of this war
Do you ever stop to ponder?
I often stop in awe.

One day, there will be no ruin
One day, there will be no pain
The children of this brutal war
Will have so much to gain.

Anthony Fidler

Whisper Of Life

Time you will find is too short,
There is none to spare at all.
As before you have even started,
You can hear the final call.
So turn your back on yesterday,
With tomorrow still to be.
Open your eyes, staring wide,
Can you really see?
What is going on right here,
Is it all just a dream?
As your silent prayer for life,
Turns from a whisper to a scream.

Keith Evans

Clouds

Clouds are not loud.
They are silent and deep
And pass by your window
While you are asleep

What would they say
If they told all they see
I'm sure all the stories
Would shock you and me.

They travel the world
Not saying a word
As swift as the breeze
And as light as a bird

Wouldn't it be lovely
to be free from all worry
free as a cloud
And in no sort of hurry

Eileen Casey

Two Little Sisters

I have two little sisters,
They're not as nice as me,
They shout and squeal and squabble,
While I sit quietly.
My sister Kim's a beauty,
so small and so petite,
I'm not that bad,
but I do have smelly feet.
Lisa is our baby,
An angel good as gold,
But I was a nicer baby,
"Well that's what I've been told."

Kelly Ann Readman

Forward

Sitting here, so quiet, so still,
thinking of times gone bye,
I felt a tear fall from my eye,
and I began to cry.

I remembered all the good times,
as a child I had,
mingled with some sad times,
very rarely bad.

I think of people I have met,
places I have been,
and how the years have come and gone,
the things that I have seen.

I drift back to the present day,
with thoughts of times to come,
words I've left unsaid,
and the things I've left undone.

I dry my tears, think of my life,
and where I want to go,
Forward to the future,
and the days I do not know.

Lana Fulcher

She's A Piano So Grand

She's a piano so grand
This beauty is her key,
From B-flat to F-sharp
Inside she is a harp

With her rhythm she starts
The beats to my heart.
She plays out the blue's
And plays anew theme
She's a solo in my soul
She's a musical dream.

Jason O'Donnell

The Majestic Sea

The rise and fall of the ocean,
This tranquil easy motion
The sound of the sea, calls out to me
"STAY STILL, TAKE CARE, HAVE CAUTION".

I stand on my tall majestic cliff
Watching the waves rise and dip,
Caressing the rocks as they fall,
Like wrapping a baby in a shawl.

This wonderful movement of the sea,
A waft of affection it appears to be.
This vast ocean can always win.
Reaching out to greet the welkin.

The ocean waves now appear to care,
To form the curl of a maidens hair,
Gracefully waltzing with the breeze.
The sea is alive and appears to breathe.

The rise and fall of the ocean.
This tranquil easy motion,
The sound of the sea, calls out to me,
"STAY STILL, TAKE CARE, HAVE CAUTION."

Carol Bannister

Footprints In The Snow

I wonder where they go,
Those footprints in the snow,
They are made by different things
A man, a cat, something with wings.

To follow them I feel I must,
I look around the corner, but just
Then they come to a full stop,
As across the road they seem to pop.

My own footprints I like the best,
As the snow crunches beneath my step,
I wear my shoes that leave a swirl,
I walk, then run and do a twirl.

Down the road I can see,
Where a dog has done a wee,
"When you go you've got to go man"
Who said that, was it the snowman?

Helen C. Jackson

Nana

One minute she was here
The next she was gone
But what I didn't know was
How far or how long

At first I couldn't take it in
I blocked it out instead
But then I began to realise
My nana was dead

I wouldn't scream, I wouldn't shout
I would just lie in my bed and cry
But something I will never know
Is why my nana had to die

Linda V. Cramb

Tenderness

Whenever I look into your eyes
Though I do not wish to stare,
I see love without disguise
Humour, honesty without a fear.

Day by day this goes on
I hope it never ends,
I look away and I become
Beware of countless friends.

They always seem to be around
Whenever they are needing,
But they never can be found
To give a care for healing.

A word, a smile, a look of kindness
Would always help to cheer
A sad unbroken loneliness
That fills one with despair.

With you the opposite I find
No words have to be said,
A touch, a smile of any kind
And I gaze, don't move your head.

Eleanor Clarke

Beginning

I couldn't write my poetry
Till I'd experienced life,
Because I had so much to learn
From happiness and strife.

My poems may not be so free
As from a young one's pen,
When I was young I never thought
Of writing poetry then.

It seemed I needed experience
To taste the good and bad
Before I could translate my thoughts
Onto a writing pad.

I feel happy when I'm writing
And find a perfect peace,
I take myself through life again
The intrigues never cease.

So in middle years I wonder
How long I'll see this light
That shines and brings me poetry
And how long will I write.

Dorothy June White

Halloween

Halloween
Time for the dead
Old corpses rising
From an underground bed.

People screaming
At ghosts and foes
A whole night dreaming
Of what goes on down below.

Witches crying
Flying on brooms
Poltergeists trying
To scare people blue.

Bloodthirsty monsters
Rise from the ground
Gravestones are moving
No human to be found.

Leonard Goodliffe

Soulmate

Set your sails, love
   Time is short
      And the tide is rising
The moon has gone on ahead
     And the breeze has caught my hair
      My heart knows where to go
So if you wish
   Please follow ...

Christiane Roland

" Four Minutes "

Four minutes to go
Time passes quickly, not slow
Life has no meaning
Without radiation screening.

Mushroom clouds loom
Just waiting for the "big boom"
Three minutes, and counting
Much panic and shouting.

The West, The East
Swallowed alive, by a nuclear Beast
Two minutes more
Then the world shuts its door.

I look to the sky
"Lord, I don't want to die!"
Sixty seconds left
Billions of people — bereft.

The silence is deafening
All hearts are quickening
All hopes now shatter
Nothing more to matter.

Kim Wilson

Away

Our friend Ian went away,
to a distant land so far away.
Then we received a letter from
him to say
he didn't know if he should
return or stay.
Then on the grass he lay one day.
A pretty young lady passed
his way.
That was the day he decided to stay.
His name by the way was Ian Varlay.

Carole Taddeo

Watching My Chatterbox

I saw you before you had the chance,
To catch my eye.
Sweet man who speaks to strangers,
Always talking,
Yakitty yak.

I laughed inside as bubbling pride,
Filled my throat.
While you stood, incessantly talking,
Making days,
Yakitty yak.

Your precious gift is time for all,
They lap at it.
Streaming sunshine in gloomy tides,
Filling gaps,
Yakitty yak.

But when at last you've said and done,
In your own dreams,
I know you speak exclusively to me,
Sweet nothings,
Yakitty yak.

Josephine Cole

Sweet Memories Of You

I've lost you my love
To God above
And oh how my heart is sore
Because I will never see
Your smiling face
On this earth any more
My memories
Are a wonderful consolation
A consolation
Because our love
Was so sweet and true
You were the most perfect wife
Who give me the happiest years of my life
And a wonderful mother
For me there can be no other
So darling till we meet again
I will keep walking
Down memories lane

John Evans

The Innocent

An Innocent life taken and destroyed,
To help minimize your need,
One more small statistic,
In a world based on greed.

Demons fill her darkening hours,
Terror devours her days,
All her world is closing in,
Her once warm heart decays.

No locks or bolts upon her heart,
No chains around her soul,
So trusting and so vulnerable,
Your one malignant goal.

Her emotions gorged and consumed,
Leaving but flesh and bone,
And memories of frightening times,
Of feelings all alone.

Claire Rhodes

Laughter

I've listened to your voice,
To its many different sounds.
The nicest one of all,
Is when you laugh aloud

I suspect you laugh quite often,
But keep it deep inside.
Sometimes it bubbles over,
And takes you by surprise.

Laughter is a happy sound,
It comes from deep within.
Your tummy aches
When you try to hold it in.

My eyes they do water,
When I'm doubled up with mirth.
We ought to know more laughter
It's a sound not often heard.

Doreen Fraser

Coming To An End

When the light goes out
The darkness sets in
Melting, burning
The time passing
Racing and fighting
Trying not to flicker
When the light goes out
The end is almost near

Cathy Jones

"Seasons"

How I love the seasons
To know the flowers they bring
Daffodils and tulips
Bursting forth in spring.

To walk around my garden
On a lovely summer day
With the scent of roses
To guide me on my way.

The falling leaves of autumn
Scattered on the ground
And Jamie, my old labrador
Scampering around.

Then cold and snowy winter
Brings Christmas time to mind
I'm happy in this wonderful world
Even though I'm blind.

Dee Bull

The Loneliness Of Death

No choice for him
To live or die
No pillow for his head
And staring eyes
Transfix the one
Who comes to declare him dead.

Just stones and dirt
And grassy bank
What was his regiment?
What was his rank?
The pallor shows that he is dead
And still no pillow for his head.

Now moistness seeps
From shattered limbs
The sun goes down
And daylight dims
Grief-stricken comrades to sleep are dead
But still no pillow for his head.

Joan Farrell

Thyroid

Please be gentle, all's not well.
To look at me, you'd never tell.
That deep below this laughing face
Is a person! No one can place!

Please be patient, spare a thought
For one whose life seems overwrought.
I seem a mess, I quite agree.
I warn you now, stay clear of me.
Please be gentle. Don't get annoyed.
It's just my active — THYROID.

Carol Slaney

A Victorian Feeling

The class was dull and quiet,
not any noise around,
when she told us to speak,
it made a ghostly sound.

Teacher very, very strict,
tapping with her cane
made us feel very scared,
of the horrid pain.
She made me wear a dunces cap,
that made me very shy,
I wonder why she did that,
oh why, oh why, oh why.

We were happy the day was over,
the teacher made a fuss,
I hope she wasn't as bad to them,
as she was to us!!

Mansurah Malik

"So The Days Pass"

Dawn
  to my lawn
    brings a scatter of diamonds —
      dew on the grass.

Noon
  comes too soon
    the thirsty hours drinking
      the jewels as they pass.

Night —
  semi-light
    folds petals, folds wings —
      a soft lullaby sings.
Nature's asleep!

While it slumbers deep
life's silent birth pain
brings forth a new dawn
with its scatter of diamonds —
  dew on the grass.

Coral Connell

Poetry

Look at a blank page
To see an idea grow.
It's like watching winter rain
Melt the purest snow.

A story is there to be told.
Line by line a mystery,
That slowly unlocks
A world of magical history.

Pencilled into various shapes,
Curving round and straight.
Come together one by one
To reveal the writer's fate.

Nothing into wondrous script.
A marvel to read.
Pours out from the inky stick
Like a heart that bleeds.

Frank McGowan

Host

I want to live in my dream,
To see if it is all it seems,
Or if they're all just scenes.

The white dove on the battlefield,
The only river in deep heat,
The shadow at your front door,
The man you meet on the street.

I'm the only call-box for miles,
Your last cooked piece of meat,
I rotted your mouth to remind you,
All that is good is not always sweet.

The noise outside your window,
The invitation on the hall floor,
A gold medal awarded for bravery,
The man who asked you for more.

The madcap who took those big chances,
The outsider who pipped you to the post,
The man who finally cried "Freedom!"
The world that kindly played host.

Gordon S. Allen

Adolescence

There's a place where I go
When I want to be alone.
A place that no-one can invade.
This place where I hide,
That no-one else can find,
Is hidden
Deeply in my mind.

L. J. Sparks

Another Superstore

Hurrah! Another superstore
  To shorten workless week.
For unemployed and OAP
  A shelter and a goal.
On Monday, hike to Do-it-All
  And call at Leo's hall.
On Tuesday, spend the morn
  At Tesco, superstore.
On Wednesday, trek to Quicksave
  And jog to Woolworth old.
    On Thursday, swim the Avon
  To Safeway super new.
I'll call at Boots on Friday
  On Saturday, try the lot.
On Sunday, Holy Sabbath Day
  In Church I'll pray for work
Gi'ss a job, oh Lord, Gi'ss a job
  Amen

Gwyneth Thomas

My Best Friend

He's been gone two years
to somewhere beyond the stars.
I miss him so much;
he was my best friend.

He was fun to be with.
He won everyone's heart
with his big brown eyes.

I have no one to share secrets with,
no one to play with, and
no one to laugh with anymore.

I will never see him again,
only in photos,
but they aren't the same
as touching his shiny black coat
and his soft floppy ears.

People say, "He was only a dog";
but he was my dog.
He was my best friend.

Emma Kerr

A Valentines Day Message

An Ode
To the man I Love
Be my Valentine
Now and forever
For despite your
Winter 'Blues'
'SAD' in modern day news
I will love you
Through and through.
Soon the summer skies
Will light up your eyes
No longer will you shiver
As cupid takes up his bow
Your heart will be a quiver
Of arrows fleeting by
As you take your stance
And chance
Yourself, Oh! Prince
As my Valentine.

Linda Granger

The Snowdrop

Beneath the glittering carpet of snow,
Warmed by autumn's fallen leaves,
Fairy flowers start to grow
To bring us joy to darkened leaves.

A snowdrop lifts a fairy head
And is the first to smile,
They spread along a crispy bed
And stay with us a little while.

Lorna Moffatt

Our Love

Together we've shared the good times
Together we've seen some bad
Together now let's share the greatest
  gift anyone could have
Our baby son has now arrived
Together we created this brand new life.
Let's cherish each minute and watch
  him grow
And show him this love that we
  both know.
Charlotte Theobald

" A Mother's Love "

Never doubt a mother's love,
Treasure it with care,
As when there's no one else around,
Your mother will be there,
Many times when you were young,
She nursed you on her knee,
Gave you lots of cuddles,
And kissed you tenderly,
She had many a heartache,
You will never know,
Often she would turn away,
To let her tears just flow,
Someday, you may have trouble,
And you agree to part,
Remembering the one you leave behind,
For she will break her heart,
You will miss her love, and many friends,
Perhaps, you may find others,
Out of all the friends you left behind,
The best friend is your mother.
Alice Ibbetson

Snowflake

Snowflakes littering on the ground
Treetops glistening all around
Footprints in the heavy snow
People walking to and fro
Snowmen watching everywhere
Pinch his carrot if you dare
No leaves upon the trees
Snowflakes blowing in the breeze
People wearing hats and gloves
People wearing ear muffs
Children's teeth are all a chatter
But it's CHRISTMAS, so it doesn't matter!
John Collins

Summertime

Clouds go roaming in the sky,
Treetops jitter in the breeze,
Songbirds chirp, and twit, and cry.
In full mirth at summertime.

Petals blossoming and bloom,
Boast their colours in the sun
Giving splendour and perfume,
To make life bliss in summertime.

You dress casual every day,
No wellies, no winter coat.
You put on your shorts, and, hey!
You look so smart at summertime.

You have that lovely feeling
When summertime is here.
And there is no concealing,
Summertime is best of the year.

Before we know, it's all done
And we are back to grey skies.
So enjoy yourself, have fun,
While still there is the summertime.
James Richard Christie

War And Sound

I like the sound of the birds
Twittering in the trees.
I like the sound of the trees
Rustling with the breeze.

I dislike the sound of the bullets
Breezing through the hills.
I dislike the sound of my people
Dying with their shrills.

I am forever hearing the sound
of our leaders.
So listen now the ones that feed us
We are sick of the sounds of
our many dislikes.
How about more of the ones that we like.
David Wallis

Homeless People

In dirty streets they roam
Unhappy and alone
Young children, yet old in years
No food, no money, many fears

Cardboard boxes for their home
Drug addicts on the roam
Smelly, dirty
Ill and cold
Is this their life till they get old?

No food, no money
Life just isn't funny
For the people
Who have no homes.
Chris D. Boulter

Fival

I once rode a horse called Fival,
Until I found out he was sold,
But it was only last week
That I was told.
I used to shout his name
And to the door he'd come.
I don't know what it was,
But I felt like his mum.
I rode him every chance I got
And loads of sweets I bought
Just for him to munch and chew.
Oh Fival, why did she have to choose you?
I loved the way you cantered,
So soft and silky smooth,
Your mane flying high,
I love the way you moved.
When I think back on the times
We had together,
On the lessons, on the treks,
I'll forget you never.
Laura McDermott

The Gift

Thrown around, battered by the sea
until one day, you came to rest
on my seashore
freckled grey, like an egg,
flat, motionless, I caress you
I fondle you, like a child
with a gift, a secret
eyeless, toothless, deaf and yet
you project calm
I place you in a basket, along
with all the other pebbles
but you remain the best, my
tactile beauty
Lyn Barlow

Our Place

I must return to climb the path
Up the gentle hill
Where the little farm nestles
In the dip
And the old church
stands so still

In Spring the ewes with
Their babes abound
Despite the wind and snow
And the crisp oak leaves
Beneath the trees
Scatter and blow

It's a beautiful place
Where time's stood still
Our place on the hill.
Leslie Paus

The Beginning Of The End

When boredom looms
upon the human race,
and death and destruction
set the pace.
When bodies are rotting
for the world to see,
and the devil has come
to collect his fee.
And night time
causes insanity.
When you can't run for your life
because it's too late,
pain, misery and death
are now part of your fate.
For the end shall soon come,
encouraged by hate.
Now is the time
to pick up the pace,
as the world gets set
for the final race.
Jennilea Towse

Time

Time is our master,
We are its pawns,
We would like to stand still
but we must move on,
The future is pressing
progress or stagnate,
follow your heart
before it's too late.
Linda Steel

Terrorism

A thunderous roar the sky turns red
upon the living and the dead.
Falling masonry wood and glass
Spouting water smell of gas
Running people, flames of fire,
Broken standards trailing wire.
Emergency services reach the scene
Is this the end to a hopeful dream?
Has wrong now triumphed over right
And peace forever gone from sight?
Innocents from their families torn
Leaving loved ones, shocked, to mourn.
Can man no longer find a way
To solve the problems of the day?
Must life's blood be forever spilled
With children, men and women killed?
Is no solution to be found?
Surely there must be common ground
To end the suffering and the pain
So sanity can rule again.
Cyril Douglas Patterson

Winter

The snow descended silently
Upon the midnight air,
Covering the earth with beauty
And purity so rare.

The moon was bright,
And all around was bathed in
Peaceful light.

Tranquillity was o'er the land
And not a sound was heard
'Til dawn came, and in the
Distance was the singing of a bird.

This heralder of morning light
Brings joy to all who hear,
The night has crept away
And with it all our fear.
Amy G. Chapman

Morning Glory

Looking eastwards from my window,
Very early in the morning,
I can see the sky grow lighter,
I can see a new day dawning,
I can hear a gentle twitter
As the little birds awake,
Skylark, blackbird, thrush and cuckoo
Sing as dawn begins to break.
I can see a soft mist rising
In the valley down below,
And the tips of clouds grow golden
As the sun begins to show,
Rising slowly on the skyline,
Warm and golden, clear, and bright.
May the future, like the sunrise,
Be a peaceful happy sight.
Grace A. Batho

Table Manners

There are two cakes on the cake dish
Waiting for our tea.
One is for my brother,
The other one's for me,
I've studied them all afternoon
'Though identical they seem,
One is decidedly bigger
And has certainly got more cream.
Now we've been taught our manners
Both me and brother John,
And to choose the largest cake first
Is definitely not on.
So when it comes to tea-time,
I'll say politely 'After you,'
And hope our John remembers his manners
And picks the smallest of the two.
Eileen M. Pilkington

An Epitaph

A headstone stands
Weathered and worn
Who lies beneath?
When were they born?
What kind of life
Did they have on this earth?
Did they use every moment
To its full worth?
Questions unanswered
Float away in the air
Did someone love them?
Did someone care?
For now I stand here
Waiting all alone
Reading my name
Engraved on that stone
Diana Meek

Thought For Today

Soft is your pillow
Warm the Duvet covering
Pleasant are your dreams
So peaceful is your slumber
And with your new dawn
Sun rays come to offer you
A new day to live
Another day for dreaming
Oblivious of others

Whose pillow is hard
Withered skin their covering
With no time to dream
Tormented is their slumber
And with their new dawn
Sun rays come to torture them
A new day to live
No — A new day for dying
But that's no concern of yours
David Blaney

Life's Race

Time is our master
We live by the rules
Survival's our game
We're governed by fools

Are we not free
To do as we please
To take every day
And fill it with ease

Regulations and work
keep us in tow
If we didn't have these
Where would we go

It's easy to stray
From the path that you choose
You can gamble what you've built
Unless you're scared to lose

Discipline's the answer
It's installed when we're young
So parents hold the key
To what we will be.
Jane Wise

" Seasons Of Life "

We think back to our childhood
We re-live it through our own
And we warn them, and protect them
And we wish that they were grown.

Then suddenly they're adults
We compare our 'times' with theirs
And we talk about the 'good old days'
And when we had no cares.

Now hastily our middle years
Creep on us day by day
And we strive towards retirement
and look back to yesterday.

We watch our 'Children's' progress
As they climb another rung
And we worry for their future
And we wish that they were young!

And life passes through its seasons
Springtime birth to summer sun
And we want to stay in autumn
For come winter.... we'll be gone.
D'reen Wilshaw

What's Age Got To Do With It?

So now you're 65, they said,
We'll put you out to graze,
No more work for you, they said,
It's time for lazy days.

I want to work, I said,
I need no more time to play.
I'm no different now, I said,
Than I was yesterday.

My brain is still in working order,
My body seems quite fit.
Why do they make me feel as if
I've suddenly lost all my wit.

My hair is getting white, I know,
Lines on my face appear.
But don't help me across the road,
Or raise your voice and call me "Dear".

Don't count my years in number,
Look in my mind instead,
Let me stay young for longer-
I'll all too soon be dead!
Joan Scarisbrick

Can You See My Face?

Emotion.
What a great commotion.
Sometimes there can be revolution.

Escape;
Thought; Plan:
Need to work this out.
What are all my emotions about?
I want to release a certain sound
Of shout.

Escape: Not exultant.
Can you see my face?

Need to work this out,
So then I can somehow feel
Exultation.

Escape;
Compensate,—
Relate:
This is a 'heavy case'.
Can you see my face?
Eileen Daly

Some Other Time

"Some other time," the answer is,
Whenever I've some tale to tell.
There's tennis or a boxing match
And so the urge I have to quell.

Important news or trivia,
Whichever matters not a jot.
"Some other time," may come too late.
The moment's gone; the news forgot.

Commercial breaks some respite give,
Provided that the tale be short.
But moments brief do not allow
For stories of the longer sort.

Then, "Make it short," the answer comes,
In stern, indiff'rent or curt tones.
But stories told in brevity,
Are merely skeletons of bones.

And so postponement still goes on,
The answer always as before.
That "other time" may be too late.
The tale is lost for evermore.
Isma Munro

Whither

So simple it was
   when I was a child
I loved believed
   trusted and grew.
And then came the War
   and fear took control,
Faith melted away
   hope challenged and damaged.
Now I am old
   uncertain and frail.
Time's rushing by.
    Where are the answers?
   What is life all about?
Of one thing only I am sure.
   I'm not sure.
Bertha Snowman

Purple Heather

Have you seen the purple heather
When it blooms upon the brae?
Best in sunny weather,
Or at the closing of the day.

If you've seen its shimmering beauty
In the sun's reflected light,
Then you've seen a part of my Land
That should fill you with delight.

I must pick a bunch of heather,
Take it with me round the world
To remind me of that wee hoose
Where we danced and the bagpipes skirled.

When my travelling days are over
An' my banes are laid to rest,
Place that bunch of faded heather
On a once warm Scottish breast.

If I should go to heaven,
An' there's not much for me to do,
Let me roam among the heather
And see its beauty, tipped with dew.
Cyril Carter

Who Cares

A friend to Him you where
When no one else did care
You took Him in, no questions
Asked I think you knew who cared.

Alone you where parted from a wife
Who had once cared, to late now
To cast a doubt.

We shared a christmas you showed
such joy.
But then you vanished we knew
Not were, we worried silly
we still did care.

We went a searching and there you
were hanging just above the stairs,

To late now to show who cares.
Christine Maxwell

Whisper

Why do I whisper your name
Whisper, whisper always with me
Always there many sounds come
And many go
But you are there forever more
Although you died not long ago

Whisper, whisper breezes blow
Through grasses and meadows
Thunders sea's or softly falling snow
Your name your name only I hear
The whisper of your name.
Iona Mair Pearce

Laughter

How can you speak of laughter!
When so many cry,
How can you write of laughter,
As the innocents die.

Faces of young children,
Etched in tears and pain.
Their laughter has been stolen,
Do they weep in vain?

Cliffs washed over by the sea,
Are cleansed by waves no more.
Crude oil spilling, gushes free,
Polluting sands and shore.

Devastated by man's greed,
Helpless, with feathers oiled,
Lie seabirds, wildlife, all in need,
With their lovely plumage spoiled.

I can only write of sorrow,
My tears have been denied.
Will there be hope, tomorrow?
For today — the laughter DIED!!!
Lucie Montague-Thomas

What Price Freedom

In private moments of despair
When the caring takes its toll
I long for freedom, long to be
Not part of me, but whole

To come and go just as I please
Without the plans and worry
Visits friends, go to the shops
And never have to hurry

I dream of things we used to do
Before our lives were shattered
Simple joys, but shared with him
And that was all that mattered

But all the wishing in the world
Can't renew a life, like Spring
And freedom can only come for me
When he no longer needs my caring

No point in longing for freedom if it
means living my life on my own
Without him to love and to care for, no
sunshine, no laughter, no home

So I'll dry my tears and carry on and
pretend that I'm alright
For the price of freedom is too high and I
won't pay without a fight
Jan Horseman

Untitled

I feel so warm
When you're around
And when you're not
I always feel down

I love you, I love you
There's no doubt about that
I want us to be together
Forever and a day
For my love for you
Will never fade away

To have you and hold you
Close in my arms
I promise you one thing
To never do you any harm

That special touch
That only you hold
Makes you stand out alone
So proud and bold
Bryan Newman

Lindisfarne

What is it draws me to this place
Where hallowed saints once trod;
Where centuries of years were spent
In reverence to God?

What is it draws me year by year
To rest and bide awhile;
To drink the beauty and the peace
Of this holy isle?

It could be dunes of sand so soft
Upon the travellers' feet;
Or sight of bird and rabbit
Which one is sure to meet.

Perhaps the glow of setting sun
'Gainst castles, isles and hills;
All treasured things of beauty
With which my memory fills.

Yes, these are things that call me
O'er the causeway's mighty ford;
But most of all what draws me
Is the presence of the Lord.
Albert Ward

To Mac

You always skated on ahead
while I trailed along behind.
For fifty years you hurried,
till fate became unkind.
A firefly on broken wings.
Bright candle burning down.
Anchored to my slower pace.
as I carried you around.
But Mac, you managed one last time,
and from this world were gone.
Keep a space beside you, love,
Until I come along.
George Colla

Flashover

Raging, burning,
Whirring.
Senses spinning,
Reeling.
They leap - screaming-
Clawing at the darkest depths,
Searching for endless life.
Life and elements;
Raw, natural elements,
Most basic.
Most beautiful evil.
Death following-
Panting, begging.
They breathe.
Beverley Ann Smith

The Last Leaf Of Winter

I met you at the corner
where the march wind blew,
Helter-skelter rushing by
Quick, as though you knew
That Spring had come.
Then turning round and round
You danced for me,
A jig upon the ground,
Whirling your frail tattered cloak
Once more before my proving eye;
The next instant to be gone,
A leaf... a speck upon the sky
Charles Simpson

Utter Nonsense

There was a man
Who got out of bed,
Walked down the street
But left his head!

He marched back up
To put it on,
When he found
That it was gone!

After searching high and low
He yelled out "Good grief!"
And to his
Utter disbelief

He looked down where
His feet should be,
And it was
His own eyes staring back at he!

So he swapped them round
But gave a frown,
For he was walking
Upside-down!

Alison Devine

Eye Of The Beholder

Your eyes enable me to see
Who I am inside
Your touch makes me feel
Warm and alive
Your body moves
In unity with mine
My heart and soul
With yours entwine
A moment of love
Filled with grace
I see in the beauty
Of your face
Your lips are still
But your eyes speak to me
I fall into their depth
An eternal sea
Your arms embrace me
And my body is on fire
Your my heart and soul
My only desire.

Jacqueline Ang

The Man From Peru

There was an old man from Peru
Who liked watching Doctor Who
He said, oh sis!
I'm fed up of this
That Doctor who needs to be sued.

Amy Nyklewicz-Betney

" With Respect "

With respect those little homes
That step out of a dream
Children that are never heard
Nor hardly ever seen
All things are there in place
Bright and squeaky clean
Kitchenette like some advert
For a glossy magazine

The family never raise their voice
Somehow there is no need
There never is a dirty dish
Nor a garden weed
I am sure when they die
Their epitaph will read
"With respect" they never lived
But died "with respect" indeed.

S. Wylie

The Gardener

I knew a gardener once in France
Who loved to work away,
He loved each flower as his own
Until his dying day.

He'd dig his garden in the sun
He'd dig up worms and snails,
He'd dig it in the cold brisk wind
They all got up his nails.

No, nothing else he cared for more,
Not a wife he had in France,
Not a child to tell a secret,
Only flowers, trees and plants.

And when the winter came his way
And summer days were past,
He'd leave his warm place by the fire
To tend his garden fast.

But oh dear, now he's passed away
It's all become so dark,
You'll know why when I tell you that...
They've now built a car park!

Christina Le Pavoux

Cruel Sea

Oh for six brave fishermen
Who sailed the savage seas
Casting nets in waters deep
To feed their families

Raging storm, black clouds
Boat tossed from side to side
Smashed against the rocks
By the rolling tide

Waves ten feet high
White foam sprayed the deck
Ruffled feathers of gulls
Hover over the broken wreck

Speck of light from a flare
Last prayer for hope
As the boat keeled over
Hands slipped from the rope

Mighty ocean had won
From its powers we cannot flee
What more enemy of men
Than the cruel sea

Iris Smith

You

If love is joy
Why do I feel pain
If love brings us together
Why I am lonely
If love is protection
Why am I scared
If love is devotion
Why do I sense hatred
If love is sweet
Why do I taste bitterness
If love is a weakness
Then I know what love means
Inside of my heart I am helpless
I'm defenceless to the strength
Of the way I feel
If love is so good
Why does it hurt
If love means forever
I'm lost in confusion
I'm powerless to the mercy of you.

Clare Protheroe

Thoughts

Ever tried to clear your mind?
Why do they come from behind?
How do they get there?
Why do we think?
Is it a link
to the past, present or future?
Maybe... maybe not!
What?
Stop the questions
But why are you there?
Where?
Talking all the time
even whilst I try to Rhyme.
Listen!
Speak to yourself and you'll know
Why your mind isn't for show!

Aulfat Bi

Christopher

Sweet sweet brother of mine
Why ever did you go
Saturday mornings are empty now
you can't call here anymore.

I never got to say goodbye
I hope you understand
Illness kept me within these walls
completely out of my hands.

One day I know we'll meet again
and we can say hello
in the paradise I spoke about
a place to dwell forevermore.

So rest in peace my brother
until that lovely day
when your eyes will slowly open
and all the bad has gone away.

Joan Vincent

Ode To Spring

A scent of spring on air and sigh
Wild flower of my dreams and yet
A swallow swoops and sails away
O'er meadow green and lush
To dance with a butterfly

A scent of spring on air and sigh
A glistening through streams on rock
Nearby a humming is the bee
Glorious as sun on blue sky

A scent of spring on air and sigh
Abound the cooling morning breeze
That teases through the sweeping glade
While insects drink upon the well
Of pearly dew on leaf and fell

A scent of spring air and sigh
Long gone the chill of whitened glow
And bitterness of the wind
No ice topped pond and grey of sky
Now spring has sprung on the air and sigh.

Claire Johanna Percival

" Dragon In The Trees "

There's a dragon in the trees
Who always likes to sneeze
You'd think he had a cold
To unfold
Achoo! Achoo!
Do you dare to unfold
His cold.
I wouldn't
If I were you.

Joseph Bailey

When You've Got A Minute

When you've got a minute Mum,
Will you sew this button on,
When you've got a minute Mum,
Will you see that the bath is run.

Mum, have you got a minute,
I answer, oh, what now,
Will you catch this spider,
I don't know how.

Oh, Mum, have you got a minute,
I am rushing for the bus,
Will you iron my shirt,
It shouldn't need too much fuss.

Mum, when you've got a minute,
Will you get my school book out,
To glue these pictures in it,
It will only take a minute.

Then I thought to myself, when all these
jobs are done,
At the end of the week,
These minutes must turn into hours,
I should be having fun.

Bridget Ann Mitchell

A Witch's Story

I am the Witch!
With a black, pointed hat,
I ride my trusty broomstick,
With my little black cat.

I have a crooked nose,
And I wear a long black dress.
My hair, is black and knotty,
And I have to say... a mess!

People think I am very bad,
And on them, spells I cast,
But this was all, so long ago,
In our deepest, darkest past.

Now-a-days, we are very good,
Our spells are only fun.
And I know, we don't look pretty,
We make you scream and run!!

But be careful, little children
For, if you are bad or rude,
I may mix up a little spell...
And turn you into F O O D!!! eh! eh!

Diana Drew

Tragedy At Canary Wharf

Canary Wharf, the dock land
With a people far removed
From what the Irish conflict
Has meant for all these years

Once again the innocent mortals
Suffered loss of life or limb
Maimed and injured mankind
Creating confusion deep within

The shock, the pain to hear the news
The IRA cease-fire was at an end
Pulling down the shutters
Of the hope and faith been built

Quite oblivious to the plight
Of oppressed people of Ireland
Now these people share with us
This search for solid Peace

Optimism is in our hearts
Take heed and speak for Peace
Please gather round the table
Leave prejudices aside

Catherine O'Kane

Romance

Romance is love,
With a romantic dove,
Romance is grand,
It is no demand,
Romance takes time,
Then suddenly the bells chime,
Romance is happiness,
It is hard to confess,
When you're in love,
Your heart flies like a dove,
You're in a wonderful world,
Your heart is curled,
You're in a dream come true,
You're not with a captain's crew,
You're not mean,
Because you're in a dream,
You get carried,
Then you get married,
THAT IS LOVE,
WITH A ROMANTIC DOVE.

Harriet Tierney
(Pen name: Ann Beth)

Thoughts Of A Lame Child

Why was it that I could not play
With all the other girls and boys,
But always sat out of the way
With many kinds of different toys.

My parents said I was not strong,
But told me if I really tried
I would grow better before long,
And so my weakness I defied.

At first I felt it very much,
But then, as time went quickly by
I learnt life has a gentle touch,
And cares for children such as I.

All people were so very kind,
They helped me everywhere I went,
And soon I found I did not mind
When others were on pleasure bent.

There was so much I found to do
And many things I learnt to make,
That loneliness I seldom knew
Through all the hours I was awake.

Christina Winn

May

May, you come to grace my days
with pink and white blossom
and Lilac sprays,
Bluebells and Wallflowers,
your mild, humid ways;
may you come to me?
You certainly may!

Christine Anne Sherlock

Untitled

The sunlight bathes his features
With a mellow, morning glow.
Contentment wells within me
How could he ever know.
Should I try to make him understand
The wealth of which he brings
Security and happiness,
A host of other things.
He stirs a little, gently,
I bend to kiss his head.
Then cuddle up beside him
Content here, in our bed.

Carole Graham

Butterfly Day

Once, I saw a butterfly,
with hues of gold and blue,
floating on a summer breeze —
I marvelled at the view,
And as she fluttered by me,
I wished that she would stay
and wept when I remembered,
she would only live one day.
Who would share her beauty,
her fragility and grace?
Would she pass by silently,
disappear without a trace?
I whispered her a promise,
to ease away my pain,
I'd engrave her on my memory,
She would not live in vain.
And as I wiped away the tears,
I then began to see,
I was looking in a mirror
and that butterfly was me.

Evelyn Mouzo

" Memories "

How wonderful my life has been
With memories I've kept within
The springtime of my years I see
Of happy days, secure and free
The halcyon summer days so sweet
With children there around my feet
Of growing years and learning more
The Autumn days that I adore
When winter in my life begins
With memories I've kept within
And when I think the time is right
I'll share the riches of my life
The wondrous years, and precious times
Of memories within my mind

Jeanette Gaffney

October

October was a splendid month
with sunshine on the land
The autumn leaves began to fall
like people hand in hand

Each day gave new excitement
with an increased louder beat
And no-one else that mattered
was walking on the street

The parks they bloomed with happiness
and whispered to the skies
Informed them of the loveliness
that came into their eyes

When nights were getting longer
and daylight fading soon
The shadows in the evening
were kissed by harvest moon.

Beatrice May

" My Pride And Joy, My Boy "

My son he stands before me
  Waiting to greet his bride.
My boy so tall and manly
  Filling my heart will pride,
This lad so full of coverage
A soldier in battle he's been
Now taking his vows in marriage
Forgetting the horrors he's seen

I pray the lord will keep him safe
  when he returns to war.
God please protect him with your love
as no-one else could love him more my cry.

Dorothy Ann Williamson

You Taught Me How To Feel Love

I used to think that I could live
Without love, with none to give,
And then my love, you came my way,
And I knew I'd found a brighter day.

You made me feel I'd come alive,
That for heaven I could strive,
You taught me how to feel love,
And how to reach for the skies above.

As time passed by my love did grow,
And in my heart I did know,
That loving you so deep and true,
Is all I ever want to do.

In you my darling, I have found,
The one I'll always want around,
So together hand in hand,
Let us walk to love's sweet land.

You taught me how to feel love,
You taught me how to really care,
Now all I want to say, my love,
That just for you I'll always be there.

Alex G. Crewdson

Autumn

Silently it crept in,
Without warning, summer's wane.
Still the sun shone
But all the warmth was gone.
Trees cried silently,
Leaves fell as tears
In the gathering dusk.
We voiced all our fears
No more to lie,
Laughing in the heat
But to huddle for warmth
And watch the summer's retreat.
The sky has darkened,
The rain begins to fall;
Autumn has arrived
Now we hear winter's call.

Carole Blair

'Alive Amongst the Dead'

Alive amongst the dead,
Yet my soul stirs not.
All around is still, is quiet,
is not of this world.
I am unruffled,
I am alone.
You're not there,
though it's you I've come
to see;
It's you I long for,
for you I cry.
I lie back,
I'm here, I'm next to you.
Only stillness.

Kerry Webb

Water, like the mind

Water, like the mind
you are there, but not there
I feel but cannot grasp you
I see you and see through you.

Your pool shimmers in the breast
Through the limbs you ripple and run
Your mists rise like the breath,
caress and cloud me.

Ocean water is salty as blood.
In the current a million
Silver flashing dancers
Merge and emerge like thoughts.

Dido Dunlop

Friendship Unclothed

You listened
You believed in me
I feel unburdened
I feel light
The dark cloak of heaviness has gone
I am bathed in a clear white light
I have to clamour forward
Days of looking back are past
New directions beckon me
Confusions fading fast
Ambition is pulsating
Rushing through my veins
There really was a reason
For the anger, fright and pain
Tranquil waters calm me
Take me gently down the stream
Without a friend like you to care
I may not have found my dream

Denise A. Redford

Kisses

Go kiss the blarney stone
you blathering-tongued idjit,
one said to the other.
Go kiss the wailing wall
you blathering fool,
the other might have said
to the one's oi yoi yoi.

Entwined against the cries of another
who has nowt more concrete
to kiss than shadows,
one said to the other
here is encapsulated goodness,
saturated warmth.
I feel a poem coming on,
the other said
as the one thought it.

And the one kissed it to paper.

Lucy Rainbow

You

They say, you always want what
you can't have,
and maybe that could be true.
'Cos after all this time,
there's not a thought in my head
but you.
They say, when you find the one,
don't ever let go;
you could have been it, now we'll
never know
until it's too late,
then the love in my life to me,
I'll be blind
'cos you'll still be on my mind.

Clare Brandley

My Love

So sorry to see you leaving.
You've been so dear to me.
Someone I could depend on,
I thought for eternity.

They say, "everyone has a bad side",
Yours you never let me see.
They say, "no one is an angel",
Yet you seemed like one to me.

For someone who understands,
Cares and loves the way you do,
There's a special place in heaven,
Reserved for only you.

Ann Lowde

Bridge

Connector, ugly and physical,
You draw me over,
And put me down
the other side.

But in between
You spin my mind
And re-awaken my memory.

I see the far lights,
And smell the sharp air,
Physically dissolved.

In this heady atmosphere
My feelings wander, madly,
Searching for their ancestors.

They as descendants suffer
the constant evolution,
the cruelty of passing bliss.

Bridge, you uplift me,
beyond the urban chaos,
into further confusion.

Kelly J. Maher

My One And Only

My dearest one and only
You sooth my worried mind,
You keep me in contentment
My body you entwine

Your soft and gentle touch I feel
In need, you're always there,
To ease my worried mind and soul
I always know you care

So many years together now
So many nights we've shared
Through dark and dreary times as well
My heart to you I've bared

No matter what the day will bring
When every things been said,
You'll sooth away my ache's and pains
My soft, my gentle bed.

Joyce Moody

To My Gran

Although I did not know you well
You were always good to me,
I'm sorry that you've gone away
But now your soul is Free,
You're Free to watch the family grow
And help us if you can
I'll miss you in my own wee way,
from Charmaine to my gran.

Charmaine Dunbar

Richard, My Friend

He's only a small and friendly lad
With golden tousled hair,
A shirt tail flapping in the breeze
And socks not quite a pair!
He runs and plays like other boys
And kicks up quite a clamour,
But that is where the likeness ends,
He has his own quaint glamour.

He always has a helping hand
To stretch in my direction,
And tells me many a story too
With quite a real affection.
I'll miss him when the boy I know
Approaches days of manhood;
But just for now I'm thankful for
His cheery, friendly childhood.

Doris A. Bruce

Untitled

In a heartbeat
you were mine,
in the sun
I saw your eyes shine.

My soul was simply burning,
my passion was desperately yearning
to gain some peace of mine.

I have my room, some place to stay,
but I'm homeless everywhere,
for home is where my heart has a bay.

You play the piano,
I don't play the blues,
although I love
the girl in your shoes.

If you don't want kisses
be a muse to me.
Precious woman, beautiful misses,
I'd like to draw out a picture of thee.

So lovely Eva let us go
where the peaceful rivers flow.

Christian Daniel Lawall

A Broken Heart

You'd take away my sadness,
You'd add to all my gladness.
All my madness,
Just slipped away,
When I knew today,
I'd have my way.
Just to hear you call my name,
Then suddenly I had no shame,
And everything I had was to gain.
When you used to hold me dear,
I thought that you were sincere.
Because I was the song you were the rhyme,
I was the poem you were the mime.
But you chucked it all away,
I remember that sordid day.
Why? Together we were everything,
All for the sake of a pointless fling.
I hate the songs we liked before,
Just because you walked out that door.

Helen Collingborn

Forever True

Your touch is soft and meaningless,
Your eyes are filled with pain,
I want to help you to forget,
So you can love again.

Forget the love you both knew,
As it's now in the past,
Forget the times you spent together,
You knew it could never last.

I have to make you realize,
I have to make you see,
You'll never stand a chance,
Because all she wants is to be free.

If you need a shoulder to cry on,
Mine is here for you,
If you want someone you can love and trust,
Pick me, I'll be forever true.

Dawn Robertshaw

Isolation

I am your mother
your son
your egg
your seed.

I people my world with my plurality.

Elizabeth Bluck

Serenade

I am honoured by your presence
Your magic spanish dance
Toying with my emotions
Your personal private dance
Demanding my attention
Commanding the mood
You swivel me around
In your mental whirlpool
You gently sway me
Then spin me oh so fast
And catch me in your arms
Sealing the trance
Sensual sensations
Sweep through my mind
Driving me crazy
With excitement and pride
Love but a word
That hides many faces
Peek a little behind
Serenade the character the graces

Donna Johnson

What Is A Friend?

A friend is someone to share
your sorrows,
to have a laugh with through
today and tomorrow.

A friend will stick by you through
good times and bad,
and cheer you up when you're
feeling sad!

A friend will help you with work
when you get stuck,
and go shopping with
to buy the latest new look!

A friend is forever
and you never should part,
and a true friend always,
come straight from the heart!

Hayley M. Sutton

'S No Man

Snowman, snowman
You're not just any old man
You're big and fat
You wear a hat
You never sleep upon a mat
Your head is round
Your eyes are black
Sometimes, just sometimes
You have a sack.

Hey, stop,
Turn around
And with one bound
Jump at the snowman
But don't knock it down
We've done far too much for that
Now,
Let's get him a hat.

Liam Higginson

I Am

And I, being only me,
Would be the one whom you
As my only lover would
Wish for me to be.

I am me! True to myself;
Being only responsible to me,
And mine; who will love me
for who I am, not what they
Would wish that I would be.

Ann Metcalfe

Alone

Sitting here all alone,
No sound at all,
Not even a groan,
Just a tick-tock, tick-tock,
The sound of a chiming clock.
Christmas is coming,
It's getting cold.
Another year is passing.
I'm getting old.
Everyone's asleep.
Tucked up in bed,
Nothing to do,
Not a word to be said,
The clock ticks on.
It's gone midnight,
I'm all alone. So I'll say ...
   'Goodnight'.

Helen Berry

A Monkey

Why am I a monkey
Sitting in a zoo
You have crazy people shouting out
And steering up at you

I'm stuck behind these bars
With my food in a silly pail
I bet them people would not be happy
If they were locked in jail

I would rather be in the wild
Having lots of fun
Swinging through those trees
That shade us from the sun

But instead of that I'm in here,
Not feeling very well
But if only they could understand
A cage is really hell.

Shaun Goodson

Born On Death Row

Tears fall as I write
these words to you,
The ink runs like blood
from open wounds,
This page was once
without a mark,
Is stained with bloodshed
from unhealed scars.

The deepest cut
is this goodbye,
From a sentence passed
for an unknown crime,
The Hangman's noose
dormant for years,
Is unmasked as an illness
with no known cure.

Harjit Panesar

Let It Be

Let it be, Lord,
   my earnest prayer,
      that,
         when my times comes,
            I die
               Alone in this chair.

Here in this room
   of remembered things,
      content,
         causing no fuss,
            let me
               find death's wings.

Maisie McCall

The Bungee Jump (For Charity)

Standing on the bridge side
My legs tied by the rope
Will the butterflies stop fighting
Is there any hope
Of a last minute cancellation
To save my face of fear?
Step back in time
To change my mind
Not to volunteer.

How did I come to be here
Amid the frenzied cries
Above the silver river
On a bridge so high?
The drum continues beating
In my stomach pit
It's time to fly
To say goodbye
Here I go
SH—I—TTTTTTTTT——!

Michael Fay

My Toys

All my toys are brilliant
My kite, my teddy bears
I've got loads and loads of them
I really like them all

My kite, my teddy bears
My dolls and all the rest
I really like them all
But i like my teddy best

My dolls and all the rest
They are so furry and soft
But i like my teddy best
And nobody says they're not

They are so furry and soft
They are so cuddly and cute
And nobody says they're not
Because they have got them too

All my toys are brilliant
My kite, my teddy bears
My dolls and all the rest
They are so furry and soft.

Samantha Hitchins

Untitled

I sit here thinking out loud.
My head and hart above the cloud,
I live in hope from day today.
Praying that you're here to stay.
My life without you I cannot see,
as you mean all the world to me.

May K. Sheerin

Awareness

Death was a mystery when
My Granddad died, but when
My Nan died I became aware.

Death brought tears which
Had hidden away from me,
From inside my close family.

Death brought sorrow and
Mourners in black gowns,
Covering the holes in their hearts.

Death upset me, as did
The depression I witnessed,
Although they tried to disguise it.

Death brought peace for my Nan
And through her there was peace for me.
We loved each other and always will.

Stacey Coleman

No Music No Soul!

Tempo slow, or tempo fast
mournful, dull or gay,
It matters not the tune I hear
I listen, come what may.

Moods deter the songs I play;
my beating heart does stir,
Melodic sounds they do me good,
But why? I hear you say.

Emotions raw - senses alive,
my pulse keeps in bear to the sound,
Soul now on fire, I let it roam free
Such is the effect of music - profound

Music is the food of love,
'Tis true, I must agree
Yet must also be the food of life -
No music as fuel,
My soul would surely die.

May Lambie

Summer Breeze

The sky how blue in
morning dew life holds so
much wander. The giving of
life how flowers bloom.
The smell of sweet blooms,
the rippling streams of
sparkling dear waters, the
majestic wander of the
rolling hills. The trees how
they blow softly to and
fro. The birds how they
sing in melodies tones.
The fields of green laden
with a yellow carpet of
blooms swaying gently in
the breeze. The sun shines
down and gives life to all

B. Kirkbright

Miss You

A day comes, then goes by
month after month
year after year.
I miss you.

You took a life,
For this crime you must pay,
I'm sorry to say.
But I miss you.

Wife, husband, lover,
Maybe Mother.
 NO!
You, Yes You, are my
Brother.
And oh! How I miss you.

Penelope Heather Mary

Woven Dreams Into A Dark Night

Die on a soft pillow.
Mix into nothingness.
Who will notice
That you won't be there?
Isn't it strange?
Rain falls loudly on the windows,
Someone is trying to get in.
Won't someone come and keep me
warm?
Life frightens me.
Blanket dreams.
Fulfilled.
If only...
Solitude.

B. S. M. McNamara

Will I Ever See Them Again

The mountains beyond my reach
Meadows rolling down to the beach
In colours like a quilted bed
Lush green grass, cattle are fed
To watch the sun morning born
It's helping to grow the corn
Watch it become fiery red
Then go down smouldering dead
Daffodils that sway in the breeze
And tulips stand by in a freeze
Rose buds born in the warm sunshine
Pansies and stock on an incline
Excited children squeal and cry
As they run, jump and try
To hide from grandma and gramps
Who seek them around the trees
stumps.

G. Gunter

Soldiers

Soldiers marching, marching,
Marching to their deaths,
Singing songs of glory,
Yet marching to their deaths.
Now they're on the battlefield,
Stuck in mud and water,
Lice, blood and disease.
No longer songs of glory.
Friends killed and wounded;
Some are lost forever,
Lost in mud and slime.
No, no longer songs of glory.
Now they're marching back
To have a so called rest.
Looking like the dead,
No longer singing songs,
These men have all met death.

A. Simmons

Life's Long Highway

In every good atlas
Maps of life should appear,
A route could be planned
That avoided All Fear,
Sign posted destinations
Would be Happy and Joy,
With a by-pass for Sorrow,
Upset, and Annoy.
There'd be heavenly landscape
For mile upon mile,
And all fellow passengers
Wearing a smile.
Imagine travelling life
With no worry or strain,
Each day filled with sunshine,
No grey, slanting rain.
Would you reach Perfect?
No, you'd face a blank wall.
If you don't go through living
You have no life at all.

Pamela Fudge

Snowdrop

Snowdrop, snowdrop, with your pretty
Little white head, what a joyous
sight you are when we get out of
bed, you make us feel so good,
because you are the first signs
of spring, and we know there are
better things to come, with all
your family and friends beginning to
show their heads, it makes one
feel so good to see you all enjoy
the spring, and all the happiness
you bring.

Sally K. Jarvis

They Have No Respect For Others

Walking through the crowds I hear
many people's thoughts aloud.
As I look down, there on
the ground is an old man
looking for charity. I don't
mind as his hands are frostbitten
and he is living in poverty
How sad I think

Turning the corner only to hear
"Big issue! Big issue! Madam?"
Madam's looks can only speak,
as she walks away. There's
another one, only they act
upon charity. For I take in
what they wear, designer clothes
the best of gear.
For they have no respect for
others, and show no fear.
Monica R. Rehill

Tears Of A Clown

The man in disguise,
Made to make us all laugh,
As he falls from a building,
And lands in a bath.
But what is he inside,
It is this we don't see,
Is he as carefree as this,
Or hiding secret anxiety?
His emotions are suppressed,
As he enters the ring.
He puts on his act,
Conscious of the smiles he must bring.
But when the people leave,
And the benches are bare,
You see the clown sitting,
With his hands in his hair.
Now you see what he hides,
As he steps onto the stage,
He's tired and saddened,
As he changes with age.
Sneha Wadhwani

Yesterday And Today

Yesterday,
love was just a word
I'd never heard
before.

Yesterday,
love was just a thing
no-one would bring
to me.

Yesterday,
love was just a feeling,
so unrevealing
for me.

Today,
love is something new,
given by you,
forever.
E. J. James

Untitled

"Your heart I take and care for dearly
My heart I give so very clearly
For I will want the world to know
My love for you can only grow"

"I need your love so very much
The feeling of your tender touch
My life complete, you by my side
My love for you I cannot hide"
A. Marlow

Feathered Friends

As I'm sat here with my breakfast
looking through my window pane
I can see them all a'gathering
not all of them the same.

Some are sitting on the fence
some are in the tree
Some are on the clothesline
peering in at me.
I sit and watch them closely,
while I drink my tea.

There are brown ones, black ones
green ones too
so many different colours
all free for you to view.

All different shapes and sizes
gathered all around
if you just put some bread out
they'll sing, it's a lovely sound.
L. Read

Cry Of The Dolphin

Searching the depths
Looking for love
Finding nothing
I tunnel above.

Clear waters are my friend
Lower depths is where hell begins
Fighting evil isn't too bad
Fighting man, often makes me sad.

We should be friends
We breath the same air
You try to destroy us
That just isn't fair.

Why do you kill us
We mean you no harm
Please let us be friends
I'll show you my charms.
Our knowledge can help you
Teach you to love
Travel through your mind
Be free like a dove.
S. A. Davies

If Only

I sit here by my window
Looking down on the garden below
and as my mind drifts back in time
I see them as they were long ago
Playing in the garden
Squealing with delight
Playing games and chasing round
making such a lovely sight
If only I could pass through time
and be outside with them
and have them sitting on my lap
inside their little den
If only all those years ago
we knew what was in store
We'd forget about the housework
and enjoy our kids much more
and while I sit there looking
they start to laugh and scream
Oh mummy, mummy, please do come
But I can't, I'm locked in a dream.
Valerie Hebberts

Litter Litter

Litter here, litter there,
Litter litter everywhere.

Litter on the playground,
Litter in the woods,
Litter on the footpath
Litter in my boots.

Litter on the highway,
Litter on the beach,
Litter in the meadows
Litter at my feet.

Litter from my pocket,
Litter from my shirt,
Litter from McDonalds
Lands up in the dirt.

Litter all around us,
Litter needs to go,
Litter needs a place to rest,
In the bin it goes!
Selina Corradi

We Are The Same However...

I do not weep
Like you weep,
Silently,
The face hidden
In an handkerchief.

I cry out the pain
I cannot contain,
Loud,
My face exposed,
To allow the tears
From my eyes
    to
        drip
            down
To be myself.
Theodore Allo

S.O.S. (Save Our Sunblest)

In the evening of August
Like regimented soldiers they stood
   symmetrically
the light of the golden sun,
catching the golden hair,
bodies (stood) ram-rod straight.

In the distance, the grim reaper,
with its rotating blades
of death, advances,
designed to cut them down
with just the feet left in the ground.

The word 'Sunblest'
takes on a new meaning.
Stephen R. Harrison

Siesta

No concept of time
like falling feathers
weightless carefree
in soft white clouds
circles of birds
the singing of angels
and gentle fluttering
sailing through oceans
over fields and meadows
travelling a dimension
mind is briefly free.
Sharon Evans

Mother Volcano

Frustration stir,
like bubbling fire porridge.
She erupts,
strikes his innocent face.
No sweet smelling flowers.
Nothing
but black ash in her hand.
Can he live
to walk over
this bed of lava?

Margaret Muldowney

Tyger

The past comes at you
like a raging tiger

At you at me
or you and me

Is it the 'tyger of wrath'
Blake mentions

Or is it any old tiger
raging with hunger
looking for a meal
at random

Which just happens
to be

You
or me

Ursula Bayer

Loss

The pain of loss burns
  like a fire inside,
There is nowhere to run from it
  nowhere to hide.
Tears course down our cheeks
  rolling away,
Drowning in the fear of always
  living this way.
Yet we do live; we struggle
  on and by,
Searching for some small signs
  of normality.
Slowly days become weeks,
  months and years,
Gradually smiles and laughter
  replace the tears.
Our days continue, our journey
  goes on,
But there remains an emptiness
For that which is gone.

Sue Lund

Wind

Listen to the sound
Of the wind that blows
Hearing the leaves reply
No go away we want to stay
For another day

Listen to the sound
Of the wind that blows
Hear the reply of the waves
Stay we want to play

Listen to the sound
Of the wind that blows
Hear the birds reply
Go away we want to stay

Listen to the sound
Of the wind that blows
Hear the reply of the sails
Stay we want to play

A. S. Grieve

Beauty

She soars
Like a cloud in timeless flight:
Towards the sun,
She looks.

She moves
With the gracefulness of majesty:
All the world,
She sees.

She speaks
With the voice of an angel:
Sounds of life,
She hears.

She commands
By precision that no mortal can acquire:
From the sky,
She falls.

She kills
With the quickness and deftness of an artist:
She, is beauty,
The eagle.

Sylvia Doughty

Gentle As A Butterfly

Gentle as a butterfly's wing
Like a bird she does sing
Her beauty fills his empty heart,
He loved her from the very start,

Oh like a star
She did shine
Her beauty so divine

Come to me
My fair maid
on
Golden straw
We shall be laid

And see the moon
When it shall shine
Then, my dear, you'll
be mine

M. E. Long

Books

Books to the lonely man
Lighten slightly
time's gaping void,
Stretching on endlessly,
unstructured infinity.

Books capture a moment
slow down time hell bent,
between comma and colon.
Puts man there, in a season
and be-here-now present
short respite
from headlong descent.

B. J. Hunt

When

When your load is heavy
Lean on me
When no one listens
Talk to me
When you feel alone
Come to me
When you want to cry
Cry with me
When you need help
Ask me
When I'm asked any of these things
Please God help me.

S. A. Farmery

The Dawn

Dawn is breaking
Life is waking
Little feet a pitter patter
Little voices loudly chatter
Tiny fingers through my hair
Little arms so cold and bare
Tightly wound around my neck
As I move from my warm place
A rag doll falls upon my face
Then as I wake from slumbers deep
All I feel are two cold feet
Firmly placed upon my rump.
I'm wide awake with one great jump.
I turn around to face the scene.
Behold! My darling Bernadine.

Mary N. Herron

My Real Live Picture

The snow upon the mountain top
Lies sparkling in the sun,
The shaded hills all round about,
Is where I used to run.

The freshness of the morning dew
Invites me to admire
The beauty of those hills out there,
Of which I never tire.

The creator's handiwork is here
On these fair hills I see.
When dew bespattered crystal clear,
A real live picture for me.

Mary E. Cairns
(written at 15 years of age)

Flames

Flames a licking around the coals
Lends the room a cosy glow
Keeping out the winter cold
Cheering to the young and old
Casting shadows in the room
Off the walls great shadows loom
Long and tall, short and small
Eerie pictures on the wall.

The smoke gives off a musty smell
Of burning bracken, pine as well
Around the warm and friendly fire
Wondrous colours do aspire
Red and yellow gold and blue
It reaches out and welcomes you.

But when this friend becomes your foe
It's time to take yourself and go
For when the flame rages free
This is no place for you and me
The engines come their sirens wail
And this is where I end my tale

Susan Caile

Envy

A man beset by envy
Is a sad man to behold
He feels he's on the outside
Always in the cold.

Success you'll find in this world
Is not just a matter of course
Sometimes we lack motivation
Or we just don't have the resource.

So if you'll take stock
Of just what you've got
Forget the groans of lament
And then you may find
Your own peace of mind
And the bliss of being content.

W. Docker

Thoughts At Dawn

I went out into the morning,
Leaving the sleepers behind —
Heedless of day's new dawning,
Dreaming of things of the mind.

But I stood quite still and savoured
The taste of a fresh clear morn,
Feeling I was one of the favoured
Who watch when new things are born.

I saw night's dark hues turning
To the pinks of the rising sun,
Making mother of pearl clouds burning
With edges of gold, new spun.

The dewdrops took on a glitter
That rivalled a rainbow's hues.
I heard the early birds twitter
And the sound of a kitten's mews.

A breeze rustled leaves and grasses
And blew softly on my face,
As I turned to waken the lasses
To begin that day's rat race.
Una A. Stewart

Dreamer

Close your eyes —
lazily drift to the cushioned
world of dreamers.
Cares recede and are lost with ease
as sleep's tide runs deep towards
tranquillity.
Daylight streams thro' veils of grey
to the sound on the ear.
A touch of a breeze,
or was it the cold tears
in the trees that wakes the dreamer
to cold reality.
Wenda Miles

Untitled

In a quiet country church yard.
Lay a soldier in his grave
Mute unmoving, He tell a story
In his long and narrow grave

In the silence of the church yard
A stranger stop to read his name
Wonder if he fought in battle's
Shrug his shoulders and go on his way

But a soft breeze rustle past him
And he hear the soldier speak
Desert war's, tank battles
Valiant and glorious deeds

Then the soldier speak of his country
English towns and country lane's
Then his voice turn to sorrow
Of his wife and unborn child

So stranger as you go now
Home to your loving wife
Just think of those who died for you
And Remember me, remember me.
Reg Hammett

" A Caring Heart "

When we see some broken things
Just lying anywhere
Thrown away so worthlessly
Dispelled without a care
We may see a broken heart
Dispensed and broke in two
It only takes one caring heart
To collect and make as new
A. Abbott

Untitled

To someone special in my heart
knowing that we will never part
trust and love I have in you
my days will never be blue

You care for me when I am ill
and are always there with my pills
a pot of tea every hour
you are my strength and by power

Homemade wine and beer too
we sit'n laugh and have a few
tear's and laughter and lots of fun
remembering our holidays in the sun

Kisses and cuddles for my one and only
this is why I am never lonely
I love you more each passing minute
a few lines of poetry just for you is my limit

A caring man that you are
and always wished to play the guitar
the only strings that you have pulled
are the ones to my heart you fool
Mary Clark

Untitled

Never doubt this love you
 know to be yours,
For throughout our future together
It will remain,
And with time, deepen still.
Catherine Campbell

Whispers

Kiss the breezes, goodbye, love,
Kiss the whispers, goodbye, my love.
Blurry images walk softly by,
Shadows caress my every sight.
Careless whispers in my ear,
Sweet music or fear?
Nothing changes,
Forever.
Mix my destiny with light,
With every rhythm in my stride,
With every heart that despairs,
Never let it be again.
Daggers in every heart,
Scars that stay apart won't heal.
Life and death seem the same.
Cry in hope, mortal souls,
Caress every heart so blind, untold.
— Pain inflicts across every mind,
Breezes die in hoping minds,
Whispers lie, sweetly, kind.
Priti Indrayan

A Day At The Beach

The splashing waves
Splash over me
As I paddle in the sea,
The sizzling sun
Gives me a tan
While I hop and skip around,
Some seagulls cry and fly around
And some don't make
A single sound,
Some children play
And scream all day
While some sit down and
Eat and lay,
Lots of people buy ice-cream
And if some kids can't have one
They kick and scream and
Moan at their mums.
Nicola Kinch

Untitled

Let us part
Just be friends.
It breaks my heart
No way to make amends.

For all the tears
That we have shed.
For all the fears
That shared our bed.

There's no way back
For love to re-emerge.
A windswept track,
Weeds upon the verge.

If we could gather all our sorrow
Pile it in a heap to burn,
Then maybe there'd be hope tomorrow
And something still to learn.

That nothing else will last
From the lives we're living
Except the love that's passed
The only thing worth giving!
Yvonne O'Brien

My Home

Just a little bit of this country
just a little piece of land
I don't want nothing special
I don't want nothing grand
A place to lay my weary head
to ease my aching feet
A place to bring my friends
too so every one can meet,
don't give me any mansion
A little house will do
I don't care what it looks like
just as long as it has you.
Sally Young

My Dream Home

Roses round the doorway,
Ivy up the walls.
Crazy paving pathway,
Mini waterfalls.

Fountain in the sunlight,
Tinkling of a stream.
Pastel coloured roses,
Perfume like a dream.

Cherry blossom falling
On the grass below,
Forming a soft carpet,
Looks as soft as snow.

Smell of new bread baking,
Marmalade and jam.
Percolated coffee,
Really feels like home.

Floral chairs and curtains,
Beams are overhead.
Every room is cosy,
What more can be said?
Mary George

Autumn Breeze

Rustle, whip, whirl, twirl
I whisper, goes he and gamble.
Bronze, orange, lime, crimson
Autumn leaves.
Minuet and polka under
clear blue winter skies.
W. H. Staff

Jewels Of The Night

I love to watch the night-time sky
Its wonders to unfold,
The moon that shines with majesty
The stars such beauty hold,
Just like jewels in a crown
No one can ever steal
The wonders of the universe
So beautiful so real.

A passing cloud hides the moon
A second from my sight,
The hooting of a wise old owl
Breaks through the silent night,
As morning comes and night time fades
A new day has begun
I watch the stars all disappear
And vanish one by one.
Muriel P. Cooper

The Women Of Britain

The women of Britain
It's up to you
To help us win
And carry through
For it's on your courage
Us men depend
To fight this war
Until the end
When this war is over
And the British have won again
Don't forget, it was you
Who pulled us through the main
So smile, you women of Britain
Smile when you want to cry
For remember for you
Us men would die
E. Hodgson

A Daughter Lost

I had a dream that was absolute,
Its subject matter a daughter.
The dream was carried away from me,
My heart lay deep in slaughter.
In every clan I recognized
the bliss taken for granted.
My vacant stare not understood,
The woe inside decanted.
Should fate be heartless
to innocent souls?
Their lives unknown
Their measures untold.
To all who suffer this lament
Should know that she was heaven sent.
Stephen Bourge

The Denial

Should I appear a little flushed,
It's simply that the day is warm.
And if my heart is beating fast,
'Tis merely startled by the storm.
These are not tears within my eyes
It's just reflections from the skies.

And when your hand caresses mine
Although it feels delightful,
You mustn't think it means I care -
That really would be frightful.
We'll always be forever friends.
And that is where the story ends.

But should my body start to tremble,
And I should let you hold me near,
'Tis simply that the night is cold
And you are warm my dear.
And if my eyes shine starry bright
It's purely from the starry night.
Maggie Bode

My Treasure Chest

My Treasure chest is priceless
It's not made of silver or gold.
But holds some beautiful memories
That never will grow old.

My treasure chest lies open
Its contents all on show
I finger all the trinkets
They set my heart aglow
Some make me dream of childhood
It seams so long ago
All the beautiful memories
Will never lose their glow

Off all the things I treasure
My chest is far the best
No one will know its secrets
Until I go to rest.

My treasure chest is closed now
I'm very near the end
I cannot take it with me
I'll leave it to my friend.
Margaret Bell

What England Means To Me

The snow is falling
It's cold outside
There is a lot of things
Going on in my mind
Just think of the people
Out in the street
With nothing to drink and
Nothing to eat
But England's my home
I like it here
Where people go to the pub
And get a beer
The little thatched cottages
And the countryside
That's what's going on in my mind
Samantha Lee

Smoky Grey

In strictest contrast to the scene,
In the corner, on the right,
There sat a hackneyed figurine,
Quite unfit to fight,
A shadow of his former self,
His life was measured by the shelf,
Indifferent to his stand,
Smoky grey; his mind, his eyes,
Against a checkered world he cries,
This man, in no man's Land.
Sheila Tucker

A Single Rose

A single rose
is the symbol of my life
With Thorns
that represent all strife

The petals are red
beautiful and bright
They represent love
for which I fight

The stem is
what brings life to the flower
Just like hope
in my soul every hour.

Like all good things
the flower must die
And just like it
So will I
Ruth Packer

" Frustration "

I don't know how it gets there
It's a wonder to behold
But no matter how I try
It's always there in the bowl

I search and search to try and find
Where the little devil may be
But always it's the same old grind
It makes a fool of me

What is this thing that drives me mad
I go into a swoon
For when I've done the washing up
I always find a "spoon"
Valerie Moll

A Walk Down Memory Lane

The day I walked the Valley
It was on a stormy day
The hills were steep
The walk was good
I really did the best I could.

I called upon the home I knew
My feelings there I knew were true
The childhood days I did remember
My walk took place in late September.

My memories which are good and bad
I owe them to my mum and dad
Dad passed away some years ago
He'd walked those hills to and fro
He never failed to beat the weather
Walking through the deepest heather.

I took a friend to show the way
To me it was a happy day
I talked about the days gone by
It brought a tear into my eye.
Pat Clarke

Time

Time crept up behind me
It took me by surprise;
I looked at time between us,
When I saw it in your eyes.

Time passed by so quickly
It was never within my grasp,
There are things I want to tell you,
Things I need to ask.

Time stood still so briefly
As you devoured me with your passion,
I tried so hard to hold time still,
But it fled, without compassion.

Now, time is telling me to go,
To leave you far behind,
But in my heart I long for you
To want me, to love me, to be forever on your mind.
Susan Wise

Home

My home is so special
it means a lot to me
I love every corner
window and wall
Although the people inside it
I love most of all
To have your family around you
makes you shine with glee
My home is my home
and I like it.
Maria Osborn

A Welcome Arrival

Oh, the dreary winter,
It just goes on and on,
Days are grey and dismal,
The nights are dark and long.

Seldom do the birds sing,
As they search around for food,
Lack of flower colours,
Don't help my downcast mood.

Most trees have shed their leaves,
Their branches bare and brown,
The grass has lost its sheen,
In places trodden down.

Then without a warning,
Its head so pure and white,
The snowdrop has returned,
Nodding in sheer delight.

At last I can rejoice,
Now spring will reappear,
Winter will soon be gone,
For nearly another year.
Sylvia Mark

Waiting For Spring

Just another day for some,
It is cold and very grey.
No more waiting, my time has come,
It is such a lovely day.

I cannot wait for summertime,
It holds no joy for me.
Today is perfect to be sublime
A sight for all to see.

Winter has gone, my beauty is grand,
For spring is such a thrill,
I have grown again, here I stand,
A lonely little daffodil.
Philip A. Denham

Blinded

The heart races
it feels no pain
it's caught in that
dramatic situation again

Stuck in a time warp
doesn't progress
hasn't developed the
hurt and the stress

So, it is ignoring
its critical head
no time to stop
it's racing instead

But when it does notice
the love wasn't true
it is then struck
by the trauma that grew.
Sarah Louise Winch

Life Span

The snowflake is a fragile thing
It falls from way up high
In silence you can hear it sing
As it floats down from the sky
It settles on the cold harsh ground
Wrapped up in winter frost
Its happiness is soon to end
The life it knows, be lost
And every kind of life that's known
Will reach the same short end
And only the planet as it stands
Like the moon, be left, to mend!.
P. F. C. Fairhurst

Addicted

Alcohol is my chain
It constantly runs through my vein
But keeps me on a level plain
Although some think that I'm insane

My only comfort is to sleep
But this is only a short relief
As when it is time to wake
My body again begins to shake

The only answer is to drink
Because it helps make me think
And when I'm asked the question why
My only response is to cry
I don't know the reason why
I only know that I will die
Philip Glendinning

Despair

The sun is shining bright,
it burns into my soul,
I feel as though my body
is falling, beyond control.

I can't breathe, I'm drowning,
falling further,
I need air, I'm gasping,
someone help me, I'm falling deeper.

My mind is heavy, it feels like lead.
Am I alive? Am I dead?
There is no end to this despair,
someone, somewhere, hear my prayer.

My body is rising,
carrying me towards the light,
I feel air, I'm breathing,
I rise without a fight.

The sun is shining bright,
it burns into my soul,
I'm alive,
at last, I'm in control.
J. A. Harper

What Is

Trees of green
Is what we mean
Trees of grey
Is what I say
Skies of blue
Is that true
Skies of white
Is that right
Dark of night
No it's not right
It should be bright
The dark of night
What do I see
In front of me
Is it true
Or just a fantasy
M. E. Vansfield

Conviction

The confinement of peoples minds
Is what imprisons us
In the asylums,
Or by the kitchen sinks
Are they the same ones,
Or is it we as judges
Horribly convict ourselves
To our own madness
Without even knowing it,
Indifferent to the indifferent!
Michael F. Timmons

Love's Lesson Learned

Too soon the love that was forever
Is trodden underfoot,
By other needs and other lives,
Now more important, but the root

Is that the things we think we want
Assume a greater role,
And in so doing drown the love,
That was our heart, our soul.

Unique it seems to be to us,
And pure, but how short lived
When pride and avarice prevail,
To write loves' epitaph in pain
And feelings now like earth are sieved

Into a crumbling multitude
Of shattered, disconnected dreams
Reflections from a broken mirror thrown,
In all directions, and so it seems, to understand
When yesterday,
Reality was endless love,
Is that for wisdom, we must pay.
Robert A. Freeman

Their Puzzle

Many people are drinking tea
Many people are playing games
on tranquil lawns as the light
is slowly and quietly
flickering down over there

Hands are almost touching
the horizon that never
seems to meet the earth or the sky
in between to set the rules
and the impedimental distance

Sorry people have no tears
they roam streets which have
lost tarmac and names and abodes
Sorry people are lying there
in silent grief and rather quiet

Merry people always mingle with
Merry people who have serene
memories of the horizon
meeting the sky and setting the
rules for the Sorry people there
Mariana Gardner

My Thoughts Of You!

I look at you,
my eyes aglow,
my love so deep,
But still unknown,

My tears for you
Are really true,
So to fight for you
Is all I can do,

I think of you,
Both day and night,
I'm all alone
In this callous fight,

You need your space,
Your lonely sad face,
It breaks my heart,
While we're apart,

I remember your touch,
That makes me shiver so much,
I think of your smile,
And know it's all worthwhile.
N. Kelly

Snowdrops

Who said the age of miracles
is past?
Come walk with me down
my garden path,
And I will prove to you
without shadow of doubt,
They still exist if you
seek them out.

Just look at this tiny
snow-white flower
and marvel at the unseen
power
That causes it to emerge
each year
Through snow and ice, and winds
that sear
As if to us mortals a
message it brings —
This miracle of nature,
Harbinger of spring.

Winifred Lund

My Kitchen Window

My kitchen window
Is my universe to the world,

My base of independence
Behind these four walls enfurled

I lure to seek the magic
Entwined upon the skies

With every cloud embrace enfolded
Before my eyes,

I search to seek life's meaning
Behind this clever disguise.

Moira C. Hardie

The Bonnie Lass O'Fyvie

The Bonnie Lass O'Fyvie
Is known both near and far.
Her great gift and love of music
Is a pleasure for all to hear.

She is always there to listen
When things get us down.
It is really nice to know
We have got a friend like her around

When she has troubles of her own
She always has a smile.
Makes the world a better place
By just living up the town.

Always lends a helping hand
To people young and old.
That Bonnie Lass O'Fyvie.
Everyone's so proud to know.

Mary L. Ward

Never Give Up Hope

It's another day
In the kennels I lay
watching, waiting, listening

A car draws up
And I never give up
Thinking, hoping, wishing

My hopes are raised
After fourteen days
Missing, wanting, needing

The life I yearned
Has finally returned
Kissing, cuddling, loving

Tracey Williams

Where Is Love?

Where is love?
Is it hiding 'neath the hedgerows
Or behind the stack of hay?
Is it in the snow-capped hillside
Or river flowing into Bay?

Is it with the homeless
Asleep in Town's doorways,
Or with the caring few
Who minister to their needs?

Is it with the tiny babe
asleep in 'Bethlehem'?
He came to tell us Love is born
To save mankind from harm.
To show us Love
So we *give* love.

When the echoes of the heart tell us:
The simplest task becomes a joy
When it is done in love —
There is Love.

Robina Trevenelyn

Untitled

Faraway, past all understanding
Is a mind in a cage of steel.
It's the mind of an infant
Locked in an adult;
A pearl of price,
Tight in its shell.
But do we remember
The jewels inside them, the feelings
The wounds we cause when we reveal
That we really don't know
The person inside them.
We just look at the outside
And leave them alone.

Ruth Jackopson

Life's Pattern

Oh, what a pattern we can weave
　In three score years and ten!
And not one thread can we unpick,
　Or weave it in again;
The threads of happy childhood,
　Days filled with fun and joy;
Excitements, pleasures, ecstasy
　Of love when girl meets boy;
The knot within the pattern
　When promises are made
To have, to hold, to cherish
　With love that will not fade;
The golden threads of friendship
　We find along life's way,
The happiness that we can share
　With others day by day;
Kind memory stores these threads for us,
　That we might live again
The golden days, when we have spanned
　The three score years and ten.

Patricia McGavock

The Lake Is Weird

Fish, fish, in the lake,

What are you doing up so late?
Frogs are jumping up so high.
The sun is so hot they might fry.
Newts swimming so fast.
You should go on Slim Fast.

Bye bye from up in the sky.
Birds flying high higher into the sky.

Matthew Lewis

" Reflections "

I've seen so many changes,
In Three Score, plus some Years.
I've seen a lot of Happiness,
But also seen some Tears.

Look around the World today,
Not always a pleasant sight.
A question that so many Ask,
Just Why, do People Fight?

A thought so dear to many,
To Live in Perfect Peace.
If it were left to Children,
Hostilities would Cease.

Because Children throughout the World,
No matter what Colour, Race, or Creed.
Will always play together Happily,
"A LESSON HERE INDEED".

E. G. Johnson

The Weald

I'm a stranger here....
In the witchy woods
And thickets....
The chalk....
White
In the hidden hollows.

The green rolling ridges
In another time....
Another place.
Not quite England.
Sheltering sunny cotts....
Dreaming of the Downs
With white sea gulls
From the Cliffs.

Timeless Wartime places....
Forever under
The blustery
Wind driven clouds....
Blowing up
From the South.

Sian L. Haynes (c) 25/1/93

The Presence

Lord I feel your presence
In the quiet of the night,
And you're with me always
Sweet Saviour, be my light.

Enough strength you give to me
When my energy seems low
One look from you, oh Lord, and
I can feel the flow.

When such trials and temptation
Disturb my way of life,
I called to you, Lord Jesus
And with you I overcome the strife.

I dare not make a move without you
On my shoulder you place your hand,
I can still feel your presence, Lord, and
I know that you understand.

M. Joseph

My Dad

My Dad was Mr. S. Lyall
He was a nice man
And he was a nice Dad to me.
And he liked my family too.
And I loved him.
And he loved me
But his favourite was me.

Priya Lyall

Noises In The Night

Who's that banging on my window
in the middle of the night?
It's really very noisy and it gave me
such a fright.

Who's that rattling all the dustbins
and banging at the gate?
I wish that it would go away
it's really very late.

Oh! Now it's getting louder,
I think I want to scream
I don't know if I'm wide awake
or in a nasty dream.

Help! Now it's opening up my door,
I'll snuggle down and peep.
Thank goodness, it's my Daddy,
come to see if I'm asleep.

"Don't worry son," he gently says,
"there's nothing to this din,
I'll fasten all your windows up,
then you won't hear the wind."

Maureen Lake

Gossip

The idle gossip that is born
in the main street,
Rears its ugly head, like the smoke
that pollutes the air
Round the houses, above the town.
Each curtained window,
each doorstep, aproned women
with folded arms agree.
Milk bottles deposited at the gates —
Tinkle like the grapevine that
never fails to find a tale so long,
that when it reaches the ears
of the one concerned —
Its magnitude dwarfs reality.

Mary Josephine Devlin

Untitled

When I found no hope or faith
In the human race
Like an angel
You showed me the way

Faith, love and fathering
These three are you
So scared to loose you
Hope I don't drive you away
Is there more to life o wise one?
Maybe I'll go take another look

Just to be me
Is what you accepted
It doesn't sound like much
But it is my world
So glad you stopped to take a look, dad

Yasmin Taara Newman

The Hoover

Wide awake and ready to go,
I'm the machine that sucks and blows.
Some stand tall, some stand low,
Out I come and here we go.

The children's room is such a mess,
Here we go, I'll try my best.
Here's the bed, under we go,
Don't know why it's never on show.

Backwards, forwards over the dust,
This piece is done I'm ready to bust.
A bump down the step onto the stairs,
Oops, not again, there go my spares.

J. Hall

Is It Really You?

The grass that sways gently
  in the breeze,
The flowers so scented and sweet.
My heart so heavy and full,
  this does not appease.
Through the old and sagging gate,
I make my way on winding path,
Stopping, reading and wondering,
  then I hesitate,
For there in startling form,
So new and yet so true,
  your epitaph!

My eyes do not see,
They weep with no control
I feel hurt, anger, burning inside,
Why oh why did you leave me?
I sit awhile, my sobs subside,
A gentle, gentle butterfly
Helps me to decide,
Yes! My dearest one. This is really you.

L. F. Baker

Winter

The scene is set on chilly days
In hues of black and bluey greys
Trees that now are shed of green
Silhouettes against the sky are seen.

A few weeks on and Winter lays
her mantle o'er man's many ways.
The Farmer's horse in narrow lane
Slithers on and shakes his mane.

All God's creatures make for home,
Only the Robin dares to roam.
Field and hedgerow white with snow
The river seems to quicken its flow.

All around winter's icy hand,
Pushing children in happy band,
To frozen lakes across the lea,
Making such jolly company.

B. Shaw

I'm Going To Win The Lottery

I'm going to win the lottery
In a week or two
I know I'll win the lottery
My numbers must come through

I'm going to win the lottery
It has surely got to come
I don't want to win the jackpot
Just a tidy sum.

I'm going to win the lottery
It will not change my life
I'll move into a palace
But I'll probably keep my wife

I'll buy myself a guard dog
To protect my stately home
And if he does it really well
He'll get an extra bone.

W. M. Dawson

The Flame

Fire of passion
Die down
Snap crackle in another heart
Singe another's world
Crave in another man's soul
Fire of passion
Die down
Burn out quickly
But leave me the embers
Lest I forget the flame...

D. A. Barnes

A Cat's Tale

We three were born in an old M. G.
In a cold and draughty barn,
But one of us didn't make it —
It wasn't very warm.
I was only very little
Just half the size of my brother,
I knew that I'd have problems,
Without some love and succour.
Then came the day when we were moved
To the porch of the old Farmhouse,
My brother cuddled up to me —
Bet he thought I was a mouse!
I needed very special care,
My eyes were closed and sore,
But slowly they began to mend,
And I could see once more.
There are many, many people,
And this really makes me glad —
Who are very kind to Pussies,
One of them is my Dad!

Vera Hartley

Coping

Now that I'm old
I'm not so bold
Don't dash around
Might fall to the ground
Legs are stiff
Pain in the midriff
Is the kerb very near
I don't see so clear
To the shop I must get
It's quite a bit yet
Friends would save the trouble
But I'm not quite bent double
Shop keeper is good
Helps me get my food
We have some fun
Maybe over a sticky bun
There's always Jim or Jack
Who will help me back
So why need I mope
While I can still cape

J. Dell

" Scatterbrain "

My life seems topsy-turvy
I'm like a missing link
I can't believe the things I do
Wish I could stop and think.
It's off to work, I know I'm late
With fly spray on my hair
The flies I've sprayed with lacquer
They're all stuck to my big chair
My purse I need for bus fare
I'm sick of those four walls
My washers going round and round
With my purse among my smalls
I go half way round the corner
With slippers on my feet
I fed the dog a tin of steak
Instead of his dog meat

From day to day I plod along
Although I'm not insane
At least I get a laugh from life
I'm just a "Scatterbrain".

M. Summers

Stress And Strife

I'm nervous I'm restless
I'm anxious and insane
I need a hit with a needle
Will it rush rite through my arm

I'm stressed and I'm tensed
I'm down I'm feeling lost
I need a drug inside my head
Till it makes my legs feel like lead

My minds not rite
My head is full of thoughts
Too many causes frights
Too intense are my thoughts

I'm feeling down I'm lost I frown
My mind's not rite I frown I fight
I lose my rest
All through the night

My lust for life
Causes me stress and strife
I've lost my lust
I've lost my life.

Steven Hinds

The Angel

Have you got a headache mum
I'll get a cloth for you
maybe it's a tumour mum
or perhaps it's just the flu

Does your head feel dizzy mum
sit down and rest yourself
I'd get you a drink mum
if I could reach the shelf

I'll give you a cuddle mum
to make you feel much better
and then I'll get a biscuit for you
and fetch daddy's great big sweater

How do you feel now mum
after your carton of drink
I'm sorry I ate your biscuit mum
that was the last one I think

I'm going to sit next to you mum
to keep you company
and I'll think we'll have a sleep mum
then maybe watch T.V.

S. Hamill

A Snow Maiden's Prayer

Oh! Snowdrop fair,
with your head silently bent as if
in prayer.
How can I not but
hesitate, and at your
serenity stare.
I visualize you giving
thanks to mother earth
for your miraculous
rebirth.
And expressing gratitude
for the nourishment of
your roots.
Which enable you to
multiply and develop
new shoots.
Oh! Snowdrop fair,
you must feel proud
for God chose you to
cover the snow frozen ground.

Elizabeth Crellin

Dirty Needle

You're my heroin
I'd like to inject you
Make my blood warm up
Until it boils
You're my crack
I'd like to snort you
Make my senses
Blow my mind.

And now you've
Turned the other cheek
But I still find you so addictive
I am your dirty needle.

You're my AA session
Trying to poison my mind
I can't fight it
Never could
You're the spliff
I made earlier on
Like to roll you tight
Rouch your soul.

Trudy Wall

Owed to a Friend

Are you the billy morgan
I used to know so well?
Great sportsman, fisherman,
good friend as well.

Or are you the billy morgan
I knew so long ago?
Full of youth and spirit,
And energy galore.

I can remember back in time.
I can see us swimming in the bay,
Chasing after little fish,
and other games did play.

I am looking at you, billy morgan,
There lying in your bed,
And sorrow is with us to stay,
as your soul just passed away.

And at the graveside next morning
The priest was heard to say,
"God bless you, billy morgan,
we shall meet another day."

T. MacMahon

My Love

Each morning when I wake up
I thank God that I'm alive
For every day that passes by
My love is by my side

Deep down within my soul
Lies burning passion in repose
Yet my love we are but one
So like a fire it often glows

Caress my body, oh my love
Let our spirits reach the sky
Oh let this moment linger on
Nay never let this feeling die

With arms entwined our dips do meet
Our bodies touch and merge as one
A gentle rhythm to the beat
A kiss that lingers on and on

Forever I shall love thee
With every breath that I shall take
So never ever leave me love
Just be there always when I wake

Pamela E. Gill

Just For Love

Just for love
I stumble breathlessly,
Ready to fall
Never to be caught.

There are no hands helping,
Nothing but word of mouth advice;
Should optimism rule my mind?
Or pessimism, with its claws
In a state of eternal decay.

The food of love
Maggot-infested by every greedy bite.
The tentative nibbler starves
Every way on any day.

Moments of ecstasy
Coupled lovingly with your trivial
tragedies.
Jut for love, you know.

J. P. Holt

The Old Lane

As I wandered down the lane,
I stopped at the old church wall,
There stood a lady proud and tall,
She had very little to say
As I went on my way.

The next day we met again,
And stopped to pass the time of day
Before going on my way.
This went on for many a day
Until we walked together
To the end of the lane,
Never to part again.

Many years later we walked
Back down that old lane,
Until we came to the spot
Where I had stopped,
We fell in love all over again,

We held hands, and looked at each other
As we wandered on, to the end of our days.

K. A. Bourne

A Pain In The Gut

He stands there, brown.
I stand here, white.
His hands are rough
And mine are smooth.
His eyes are dull,
Yet mine are bright.
He has no car
But I have two.
His feet are bare
yet mine wear shoes.

But he and I
Have common ground.
His stomach is fat
And so is mine.
He breaks wind
And so do I.
His stomach aches
And so does mine,
But he never eats
And I never stop.

Phil Benz

An Ode To My Mom

When I was a little child.
I sometimes drove my mother wild
Wanting this, and wanting that
I'm sure I was a little brat
But mother loved me just the same.
And often played a childhood game,
Snakes and ladders tiddly winks
Lots of fizzy pop to drink.
Alack alas mums eighty six.
Sometimes quite well, but often sick
I no longer drive her wild
For I'm the mum, and she is the child
But I will love her all her life.
A wonderful mother, and loving wife,
I often wish I could turn back the clock
To when I was the child, and she was the rock.

J. Cunnah

Visions Of Life

When I look outside my window,
I see so many things,
the birds that sit upon a tree,
the children on their swings;

The people with their shopping,
the stars that shine above,
the traffic bustling to and fro,
the couples so in love.

And yet I never wondered,
the beauty there could be,
for my life has been in darkness,
since I was only three.

But now I look around me
and gaze up to the sky,
for now my blindness has been cured,
I'm so happy I could cry.

Ruth Doyle

Only Sister

I remember you being born,
I remember when you died.
You were taken to be God's angel,
He took you to the other side.
You watch over the children,
You came from a song,
A loving voice we hear.
Was this too young?
I remember you with so much love
When the sun is so hot in the
sky. But then a breeze will come
along. I hear you whisper, "I am here"
I remember you when the snow
falls white and clean. I know
you're here. But most of all
I remember you when the leaves
fall, for that was when you were
born and when you died.

Pauline Swales

Silhouette

I looked and saw it hanging there
I lost my thoughts to stop and stare
Red sun low down in crimson sky
That warmed my skin, my mind, my eye.

The world was bathed in waves of red
My life became a silhouette
Time eclipsed for just one second
No past or future, only present.

Oh to live like that forever
Perpetual light and problems never!
"Sun, your reds are fading lower
Won't you stay with me some more?"

Michael Aidulis

Waiting At Pause For Fast Forward

My eyes are dry, my skin is too
I miss the zing I used to feel
Dryness pervades right through
A twilight feeling surrounds me
I must cast this veil and
See more clearly, love myself
More dearly.

Count up all the things I have
Go walking in the rain.
Start laughing and living again.
For I am waiting at a pause
Before emerging at another stage
This larva state will end
When I accept that my
Journey must carry on and
I must be lenient with time's
Ravages and know that it's
Only a shell. Inside it's me
And always will be

In time all will be well

Sylvie Padwick

The Sea

As I walk along the beach
I look at the sea.
Shimmering, sparkling crystals
Looking back at me.
Calm as calm can be
Lapping, endlessly upon the sand.
Relaxed, peaceful, still.

Walking along the prom.
Violent waves lashing at me.
The waves, gloomy and dull
Thrash around wildly.
All the ocean seems disturbed.
Loud and cold
The sea seems furious,
Dark, dull, rough.

Sherlene Shevlin

Lovers Lost Paradise

As I sit here full of gloom
I look around the empty room,
The memories flood into my head,
But there is nothing to be said,
my soul is dull with emptiness
Of bygone days and happiness

My heart is torn in many pieces,
Sighs and tears are all it teaches,
Hurt and sorrow, bringing forth
   a lost tomorrow.
If I could change the sands of time
And drink with him a glass of wine
No tears would stain this face of mine.

B. Davis

If It Hadn't Been For You

If it hadn't been for you,
   if it hadn't took so long,
things could have been so different,
   they'd be right instead of wrong,
if somehow we'd foreseen,
   the road that lay ahead,
of the years that were between,
   of words that once we said,
then things would be so different,
   in the light of day,
and if it hadn't been for you,
   I wouldn't have learned to pray,
but I can't help looking back,
   to cherish what we had,
and I can't help being thankful,
   for the day that you came back.

Maureen Bell

Lost Love

If I don't see you
I know I won't cry
The days may seem longer
But I know I'll get by
And If I don't kiss you
A tear I won't shed
But I know I'll dream of it
As I lie in my bed
And if I don't hold you
I won't fall apart
I'll get back the pieces
That you took from my heart
You told me you loved me
But you just loved yourself
Was I.....A book you put back on the shelf
But some books are for keeping
You'll learn that someday
When someone tells you
They love you
Then walk's away.

Mark A. Jarrad

Nonsense

When I read about the contest
I just had to write to you
So in the toilet I went to think
And dropped the paper down the loo.

As I sat there, my mind went blank
And the paper it went down
This is all I need, I thought
And my face beheld a frown.

On what to write I couldn't think.
Could it be babies, girls or boys?
Then on the other hand
Should I write about the toys?

Now the paper's all dried out
So where do I begin
I think a whisky's what I need
Or better still a gin.

So all I got is daft ideas
And nonsense of which I'll send
So I've wrote it out in my neat hand
That's all, it's over, the end.

P. Wainwright

Open Up Your Window

If November days seem dreary
And there's not much sun about,
Just open up your window --
LOOK - THE WINTER JASMINE'S OUT.

If November skies are leaden
And the lawn looks bleak and bare,
Just open up your window —
THERE'S A LITTLE ROBIN THERE.

On a dreary Sunday morning
When the birds forget to sing,
Just open up your window —
YOU CAN HEAR THE CHURCH BELLS RING.

At Christmas when there's frost and snow
And the night is clear and fine,
Just open up your window —
SEE THE STAR OF BETHLEHEM SHINE.

So in the bleak mid-Winter
If your faith in God burns dim,
Open the window of your heart
AND LEAVE THE REST TO HIM.

Nellie Stanley Hodge

Brandy (Dog)

In the morning when I awake,
I hope to see your happy face.
But when I come down
And you're not there,
I feel so sad, and full of despair.
I loved you then, and I love you now,
I'll never forget your lovely frown.
Your ears were black,
Your eyes were brown,
Your white bushy tail,
Your little black nose.
I wish I were with you,
My little Red Rose.

H. A. Costigan

The Invisible Corner

Just around that corner,
I hear them say,
but I feel like a mourner,
Who's lost her way.

The road ahead,
Seems bleak and long,
and I've often said,
What went wrong?

The clouds hang low
The pain goes deep,
as I take another blow,
I begin to weep.

Each new day,
starts full of hope,
I sit and pray,
please help me cope.

But I'll proceed
till I reach my goal,
then I'll succeed,
and release my soul.

L. Insall

The Fieldmouse

Though I am just a fieldmouse
I have quite a lot to say
While I sit here in the field
Watching the farmer gather hay
He sits on a steel monster
Whose blades go round and round
So I have to keep a lookout
As my home is in the ground
You see I have children too
And I watch them night and day
So when he goes home at sundown
That's when they go out to play.

Margaret Wilson

A Happy End

Here I stand all alone
I wish I had a friend to call my own
no one knows how I feel
I don't make any deals

Here I am in a street
Looking at all the people I meet
In the rain, snow or sun
I don't have any fun

Here I stand in a room
the music going boom boom
I'm here listening to the beat
It's so hot, can someone turn down the heat

Here I stand and I'm not alone
Now I have friends to call my own
Here I am in the sun
now I'm having fun, fun, fun.

Sian Davies

My Promised Land

As the sun shines upon my face,
I find myself beside a gate,
The entrance to an unknown place,
To which I venture into straight.
A dangerland, it cannot be,
For once inside this fantasy,
Sees only scenes of harmony,
And feelings of security.
I glance above, the skies are blue,
I make a wish, it will come true.
-Thus now, I'm standing next do you,
And you must Love me, Yes you do!
I'm free from hurt, I feel no pain,
Within this world I only gain,
Where Love for you is not in vain;
So why do I feel such disdain?
Because my dream, I must forsake,
The end exists, there's no mistake.
Re-al-it-y will come to take-
-me back to life, I'll soon awake.

P. Tran

From Heartache To Happiness

My heart was aching,
I felt so alone
My relationship of 4 years
had left me hurt
and on my own
He saw fit
to have an affair
leaving me hurt, lonely
and full of despair
I have a baby daughter
who couldn't see my sorrow
but they say another day is tomorrow
Then I met Lewis
he's everything to me
everything to me
what a man should be
he's caring, loyal,
and as loving as can be
I hope we're together for eternity.

Suzanne Crumpton

A Moment In Time

When I received his letter
I couldn't think just why
He'd written to a stranger
A young girl such as I.

His letters grew more frequent
And soon I understood
That if he felt the same as me
Our future could be good.

The war was on — he was abroad
And leave was hard to get
But we just kept on writing
And then at last we met

Marriage followed later
With babies — in good time
And we were very happy.
I knew that he was mine.

But all too soon it ended
When he became so ill
And I was left with memories
The kind that linger still.

Sonia Lewis

Classroom Dreamer

Dreamily through the class window
I could see the gardener there
Squatting in corduroy trousers
Strung below the knee.
Rough calloused hands deftly moving
As he artfully clips a shrub
A tuneless whistle on his lips
Unheard above the classroom drone.

How I envied his freedom
His beloved garden lair
Not for him a stuffy classroom
But the fresh and open air.
Pausing for to fill his pipe
Glancing up he caught my gaze
Winked, grinned and thumbed me inwards
So snapped me from my daze.

Raymond Brett

Music

As I listen to the music,
I close my eyes and dream
Of swans as white as thistledown
Floating along on the stream.
Each note is pure like sunlight
On the waves that ripple by,
Each chord is full of beauty
Like the wings of a butterfly.

The music flows on around me,
I laze in the warmth it inspires,
My heart cries out with emotion
and love and hidden desires.
Gone is the world around me,
I drift like the swans on the stream,
Borne along with the music,
Lost in the world of the dream.

Renee Clegg

The Sea

"You're a eunuch,"
I challenge the wave
Seeing him rear his head
And then fall subdued
I swim triumphant in his swell

But under, down there
Where my legs dangle
What lurks beneath
Waiting to clutch and pull
Entrap and sting?

"Perhaps a shark
Little girl
A eunuch eh?"
The wave soars crashing white
Burying her down, down
Finally she falls
Prey to little fishes
And slow crawly things.

Rosalind Ash

Golden Autumn

Silent leaves so crisp and brown,
Falling so freely to the ground.
Birds seen migrating as they fly,
Disappearing towards the warmer sky.
Now that autumn is on its turn,
Of golden leaves and golden fern.

Farmers collecting crops they yield,
Out in the country and far afield.
The sun fades with little light,
As darkness falls into the night.
Golden autumn is well under way,
For we'll have another autumn day.

Nigel A. Webb

Pew Torr

As I look out from my window
I can see the top of pew,
It's not the highest of the torrs
But it has a mystic view.

The top is like a human face
Looking up into the sky,
The ragged rocks of centuries
Is where he wished to lie.

He has the sheep for company
The ponies from the moor,
The Adder coiled beneath his head,
The birds above him soar.

The silver grey of mist descends
To cover him for sleep,
The moon and stars shine down on him,
His nightly shroud complete.

Marjorie Horgan

In Dreams

In dreams with the Earth far below
I boldly go where no men go
The journey there I seem to know
But if asked I could show

In my secret world I find
The mental chaos left behind
All distracting thoughts they cease
As my body rests in peace

When the God of light appears
The golden fragments are unclear
My eyes more open than before
What I see I can't be sure

In resisting the temptation
For artificial stimulation
The mass will rise to form a nation
That will thrive on meditation

Kingdom come thy will be done
One by one they will succumb
The call they answer will be true
For they are the chosen few

Neil Lester

I Am

I am not my body.
I am not my feelings.
I am not my thoughts.
I am that which exists in an infinite
sea of glorious bliss.
Nothing may harm me here.
I am a pearl of wisdom
Encased in an unbreakable clam.
I am open only when
People wish to see me shine.
Here, at the centre of the universe,
I have a panoramic view of infinity.
Its waves of harmony gently wash
The tears of joy from my face.

Robin Sands

War

A mist hanging in the air,
Darkening people's hearts.
People in the streets,
Lying, crying, dying,
In indescribable pain.
The red carpet spreading,
Welcoming the host, death,
No-one without pain,
Survivors left with horrible scars,
Wishing they too,
Could have died.

Naomi Scott

Plants

Please take care of me,
I am a living plant.
I think you know the sign language
So please don't take a chance
I would like a drink at times
And just a glance or two,
To show you how I do my job,
To make it nice for you.
So remember when I bloom
I do it just for you
I'm used for love! Kindness!
And sorrow too!
So please don't let me die!

Shirley Mannering

Friendship

Kath, when I think of friendship
I always think of you
I know you'll always be my friend
No matter what I do
Caring thoughts, loving smiles
And also helping hands
Someone who is there when needed
Someone who understands
You never ask for anything,
    no matter what you've given
You make me feel so special,
    and you make my life worth living.
Thank you friend.

Sylvia Pigg

Dragonfly

Iridescent dragonfly
Hovering near us,
Darting by.
Red of rose,
Deep blue of sky
Caught on wings
Of dragonfly.

Bright ephemeral dragonfly,
Opaline
On summer's day
Shimmering
All care away.
Momentary,
Fleeting,
Heart's yearning meeting
Soul's voice lifting high.
Up and soaring
Dragonfly.

S. M. Windsor

Pathway To Love

A world beyond sight
Hidden from view by life's breath,
Awaits us one day.

A world of promise
Where pain and fear hold no place,
And only love abounds.

A land where we'll find
Man can walk free of all hate,
Greed and jealousy.

A kingdom of trust
Where all men will reign as King,
For all men ARE King.

And this world shall know
An abundance of colour,
Where rainbows are shamed

A world beyond sight
When mortal state is no more,
Awaits us one day.

Suzan Lawrence

My Pet

He's not very short
He's not very fat
He's not very tall
And he sleeps on the mat

He runs in the field
And likes to play ball
He likes to eat dinner
And when I want him I call

He's a very pretty dog
He's very strong
His eyes are brown
And his tail is long

His name is Tyg
He's as fast as a car
And if you race him
He'll beat you by far

He's my dog
And for him I care
And whenever I need him
He'll always be there.

Owen Good

The Tragedy Of Mankind

What's a tiger mummy?

Gosh that's an old book,
Here let me have a look.
Eyes that glitter in the sun,
Tell of a story that's just begun.

Swift, agile and graceful too,
Not one left, even in the zoo,
Coat that shines, sleek and healthy,
Long ago stolen, for the wealthy.

A face so bold, proud and strong,
Why did mankind do such wrong.
Those who cared tried to stop the slaughter,
While those who didn't, did it with laughter.

Not caring how many they killed.
Their coats, and bones, the buyers trilled,
Kill more and more, we want the cash,
Not caring that they were so rash.

Now for our children, their children too,
Only pictures remain. Thanks to you.

Sally Fountain

What's Your Poison

Here is my poison
Here in this glass
It's only cider
The head-ache will pass

Here is my poison
Here in this roll
It's marijuana
But I'm in control

Here is my poison
Here in my arm
I don't really need it
And it doesn't harm

I've got a bad liver
And a bad cough
AIDS from a needle
And I'm feeling rough

These are my Poisons
Now I'll take a pause
And ask you this question
Which one of them's yours?

Robert Hurcombe

"Mary"

She walks past me.
Her scent fills the air.
Catching my eye her form excites me.
A soft sheen on her lush lips,
Rays of sunlight glowing around her,
I wish she would look at me,
I know a thousand things about her,
I wish I knew this beauty's name.
Filling me with electricity,
Filling me with anticipation,
She looks my way,
Haunted eyes of brown,
Inscribed on my mind for all eternity,
Drawing me close to her.
We talk with no words.
She enters my soul.
I ask her name.
Mary, she softly replies.

Robert Pottinger

Mr. Cat

Mr. Cat is on my back,
Heavy like a coalman's sack.
Before, he sat out side my door,
Rain falling on his ruffled fur.
It was not pity
That makes him scrabble on my back,
He should have stayed out in the rain
Or under the shed,
So little do I care.
It is the argument next to me,
The twinned shouts next to me,
That send Mr. Cat,
Like an unwanted salesman,
To my back,
To dig his delicate pin thin claws
In me,
His pretty venomous teeth
Deep inside me.

Martin Forman

Thoughts

Lambs are leaping
Hearts are beating
Birds are tweeting
Stop weeping

Spring is coming
Please stop running
The sun is coming

Flowers will open
Birds fly high in the sky
So do not cry
Just give a little sigh
You could fly high up in the sky
So why cry
Life is such fun, why run
Go out into the sun and have some
Fun, don't run, sweetness will
Come, have fun in the sun

Mary P. Moore

Worries

All my deep worries,
Ebb and flow in great flurries.
I pray for the rain,
Soft calming of pain.
Raise my eyes to the light,
Long for everything bright.
Still I worry and fret,
Body rigid and set.
Why, Why, do I worry?
Heart racing with hurry.
WHY?

Vera Stanley

Lullaby Ode

Sleep child close your eyes
Hear the sweetest lullabies
Time to put away your fears
Teddy here will dry your tears

Sparkling magic dust drifts down
To grant you wishes now till dawn
Ready child to take their hands
Fairies here with magic wands

High adventures in the stars
Walk the moon or fly to Mars
Sail child the seven seas
Tall ships here to please

The world is yours to so command
Rule child wave your hand
Create peace where'er you go
Helpers here to make it so

And when the night draws to a close
You'll find the wonders you did choose
Can one day become very real
You child must set the seal

Shelley Diamond

Poppy Fields

His face is a stone wall.
He will not let me in.
For though I beat the door
With weapons of guilt,
I am but a crack,
On a smooth
And rounded shell.

I did not cradle him,
The inner child to stroke.
But spat out anger
My frustrations so to ease.
For love denied me,
Found no common ground,
But lay,
Amongst poppy fields.

Sarah Jane Luck

The Clown

The Clown was in the circus
He was loved by everyone
His funny feet his made up face
Made him a figure of fun.

He'd revel in the laughter
And at the children's glee
But deep inside he's thinking
Oh yes they're laughing at me.

He loved to see them happy
Why he couldn't say
He only knew he'd miss it
If he ever went away.

And so he carried on
Laughing all the while
And no-one saw him crying
Behind his painted smile.

Ronald William Miles

My Mother

Gentle eyes of green alight
Ever watchful through the night
When we hurt, she held us tight.
Singing lullabies until dawn's light
Rocked us gently to and fro
As the seasons come and go
Always in my heart she'll stay
Until memory fades away
There will never be another
So loving and caring as my mother.

Mary Riddick

Old Charlie

Old Charlie likes his snooker
He plays it once a week.
He's able to pot a ball or two,
He's average so to speak!

He watches the "Pros" on telly,
Thinks there's nothing to it!
But when he gets on the table,
He finds he cannot do it!

He tries the long and short shots,
He even tries the double,
He then miscues and goes in off.
And finds himself in trouble!

But Charlie has improved now,
Alas it is too late,
Time is now against him,
For he's nearly at the gate;

He'll dream one day
Perhaps in heaven,
Of that damned elusive,
One-four-seven!

F. T. Pagett

The Unbaited Hook

Porthos is my garden gnome,
He fishes in my pond,
I bought him with a fishing rod
But it's like a magic wand.

My pond was full of goldfish,
Who swam around all day,
I'd often sit and watch them
And while some time away.

Soon the fish were getting fewer,
Where were Cedric, James and Flook?
Somebody was stealing them
I'd have to find the crook.

Now Porthos had a big broad smile,
And seemed to have grown a bit,
But could he be the culprit,
Could the clues all fit?

Then finally his head turned grey,
That was the final clue,
A heron landed on his head
And did what herons do.

Peter Giles Heron

The Spirit

A spirit comes to our house
He doesn't say a word.
Or perhaps he speaks so quietly
That we have just not heard.
He brings a sense of well-being
A feel of peace and calm,
We're sure he's looking over us
To see we meet no harm.
We call him he, for we are sure
This spirit is a man.
He's tall and dark and gentle
As a real gentleman can.
He isn't here all the while
Sometimes he goes away,
And though he's gone for quite a time
We know he'll come some day.
We're not afraid to see him
It's nice to know he's there,
That we've got a guardian angel
Someone who seems to care.

Valerie Lloyd

The Flames

The flames of my desire
have died a rapid death
Left are the fragments
Of the life I knew so well

I will cry
I feel the pain
Will I break?
I have nothing to gain.

Nothing inside
desolation, emptiness
Nothing to hold onto
but sweet memories.

Incisions forming in my heart
Slowly it falls painfully apart
Will I find what I dream of?

Bring forth a new life
filled with spirit.
When beauty cries
the flames will die.
Maxine Walton

" Morning Sunshine "

A black still night
Hard frost of white
A glimmer of light
But the air full of bite

Routes without obstruction
Roads with no disruption
A covering of salt
With its rotting destruction

A clear mountain outline
Introducing our new day
A sky of gradual sunlight
Arriving for today

Fields of celtic green
Mountains of shivering snow
A light full of promise
Of that sunshine glow.
Ronnie Parry

Gentle Love

Your precious music in my ears,
hand to hold to still my fears,
loving footsteps in the night,
treasured hopes,
forever bright,
brightest love, gift from on high,
Gentlest sweetest lullaby,
Singing sweetest little song
my heart to yours will ever belong,
this final bond, this tie so sure,
from our love, so strong and pure,
Our love will always ever keep,
and as the magic stardust soars,
my heart is ever, always, Yours.
Margaret Beddoes

A Special Someone

He'll never feel sadness,
He'll never feel pain,
He'll never hear thunder
or the pitter patter of rain.

He'll never see sunshine,
He'll never see snow,
He'll never sing songs
or wail pangs of woe.

His voice is lost,
his body gone.
He was human thought,
a special someone.
Sinead Barrett

Dragon

Magical creature, portrayed as killer
Guarding the treasures of a kingdom.
Mystical, unknown.
Never really understood.
See him now, scaly and golden,
Majestical, sun glistening,
Wings like gossamer,
Fire spewing forth.

Beautiful creature, magical smile.
One bite could kill,
No harm, though, in his eyes.
Befriend him, he protects.
Graceful, intelligent, loyal.
Born to protect, destined to die.

For the love of his country,
A spear through the heart.
Last of a living legend,
One final turn, one final sign
Gone now forever,
Forever to the end.
Stephanie Rhodes

England

Rise up you England of St. George,
Great is the future you can forge.
Your strength will all time defy,
Your heart will never ever die.

Your fields are of the richest green,
Beauty many eyes have never seen,
An island set in a troubled sea,
A haven for the spirit free.

A gentle land, a calm retreat,
But inside a lion's heart doth beat,
With a pulse so steady and so strong,
Has defended this Isle so long.

Do not let internal strife prevail,
Where a thousand enemies would fail.
Join together you classes and creeds,
Throw aside your individual greeds.

An England united will never fall.
Work together now for the good of all.
In the fairest land there has ever been,
Created from a perfect dream.
J. V. Ford

Gambian Palm Tree Boy

Black skinned brother,
Great Africa your mother,
How your spirit moved me,
With your calm mentality

Possessions so very few
Whiteman's greed is not in you,
You opened my eyes and I saw
We're the ones whose souls are poor

With patience, strength and strife,
You treasure real values of life,
Family, friends, faith in God,
Make me like you if you could

Remember me, my black brother,
For you were really like no other,
Even though we're miles apart,
You're always close in my heart

Your inner strength glows like gold
Easy life makes ours grow cold
You understand what life is worth,
God to man and man to earth.
Susan Hopkinson

Loving You

You changed my life,
From bad to good,
By loving me each day!
I never expected you to leave!
Cause I thought you'd always stay.

But now you're just a memory,
That passes through the day,
I never thought that you would go,
And leave me in this way!

I often wonder if you'll be back!
And love me one more day,
Although you have your own life now,
I'll miss you day by day!

Before we part upon these terms,
I have one more thing to say,
I'll love you more tomorrow,
Than tomorrow's yesterday!
M. K. Todman

The Salmon

It is a silvery gleaming fish
From across the wide and open sea,
And having travelled thus so far,
Makes its way across the bar
Into its native estuary.

Then up the river deep and wide
With its cousins by its side,
The urge is strong to nature's call,
It jumps the thundering spuming fall.

There within the rippling stream
It makes its way as if in dream
Home at last in rocky pool in the water
deep and cool,
Finds its mate, and there they spawn,
The next generation soon are born.

The eggs are laid beside a stone
And there are fertilized one by one,
It lies content, its task is done,
And so beneath a silent sky
Its life is spent, it has come home
At last to die.
Margaret Fox

Untitled

Life's gloom descends in the morning,
Happiness is surely a lie,
Love is the inevitable killer,
My soul ascends as now I die.
C. G. Rich

Crazy

I do believe I'm crazy
I do believe I'm mad
My mind is a gibbering mess
Going from worse to bad
I see things moving
When they're still
I see a duck with a muzzle
When it's got a bill
I forget where I put things,
Forget where I am.
I put coffee on my toast
When it should be jam.
I hear people say things
I don't hear them right
I say "Hello, how are you?"
I think they want a fight!
I battle with sanity
The madness I am fighting
I do believe I'm crazy
I've forgotten what I'm writing......
Stephen Dent

" Wavelengths "

High on the hilltops,
Free as a bird,
Noises of silence,
Never a word.
Visions of emptiness,
Hidden rebirth,
Reason for living,
Heaven on earth.

Tune in your ears to the
Call of the wild,
Look at the world through the
Eyes of a child.
Hopes for the future,
Dreams of the past,
Body and spirit
United at last.

Maureen Roper

Tears Of The Fountain

In the shadow of the Sloan
Fountain the tramp sleeps.
A pillow for his head is a dog.
The only sign of life is a rabbit
chasing dream, with paws twitching
and itching to run the green grass
meadows of old.
The children run around, leaping
and jumping over the oblivious two,
their laughter mingling with the
hustle and bustle of the affluent.
Leave the man and his last loyal
companion to their dreams of times
gone by, accompanied by the
tears of the fountain.

Tina Kiddell

Natalie

Natalie, you are so dear
For your life, we did fear
As soon after you were born
Upon the doctors it did dawn

That your heart was not right
For your life you had to fight
Our little girl did not give in
Always on her face a lovely grin

Then came that dreaded day
To hospital you went on your way
How we hoped, how we prayed
As in the operating theatre you laid

Then it was over all complete
Now they said, she will sleep
Try not to worry, she is fine
Her heart now beats like yours and mine

Tears of joy we then wept
For Natalie, your life you kept
Now how we love to watch your play
Like other children, normal in every way

Sandie Patching

When

When will my dreams
   come true?
When will my fortunes
   change for the better?
When will Love
   come my way?
When will my
   gloom and blues go away?
Please tell me,
When will my life change
   for the better?

Mark Weedon

Peace In Our Time

We hoped and prayed
For grandchildren's future today
Are they to pay for mistakes made
Haven't we learnt anything
Fifty years on right from wrong
As the future generation.
To go through hell on earth
To satisfy man's right to kill
Destruction, bombing, lives lost.
We old ones know for what it's worth
That war years stole our Youth.
Peace must be the future outlook
Peace peace peace.

O. B. Pickford

What You Could Be

There's no room in this life
For
Racism
Sexism
Ageism

Distortions
Divisions
And self
Incisions

It's a state of mind that counts
We can leave behind the labels
And twisted fables
Of who
And what
You should be
And concentrate your will

On what you could be

When mind is set free.

Matthew Whatley

Recollections

As I sit beside the fireside,
Fond memories I recall.
The happy times I spent at school,
The sweetest days of all.

The snowflakes slowly falling,
The sparkling Christmas tree.
The children singing carols,
And my son upon my knee.

And now I watch my children grow,
I see their smiling faces.
Playing with their cuddly toys,
And they've been to many places.

The years have passed so quickly,
My friends have come and gone.
But I'll travel on regardless,
Till my earthly days are done.

Rose Ashe

Untitled

Twelve turned down beds;
Eleven laying vacant.
Speaking tongues
Having been expunged
Quietly recant.

Twelve turned in heads:
Five schizophrenes
Behind split screens,
Five controlled platonics.
One unglued catatonic,

Then me; who I have heard them say
Resembles Randall P. McMurphy.

Shaun Ryan

Orchestral Flight

A summer breeze between the trees,
Flowers bloom in tranquillity.
A running stream carrying a dream
To the ends of eternity.

Breath of nature free to roam,
In darkness and light, never alone.
Harmony in motion, Mustang and Deer,
Shed a tear in beauty, not fear.

Hearts of songs and hopes cherished,
Nourished soon to flourish.
Wings of patience strong and clear,
Soul felt dream is near.

As Autumn comes all above remains,
Rest easy as only the colours change.
When Winter comes all will sleep, but
Spring will wake.
So once again birds will sing,
In love and laughter it will bring.

Audra Ann Murphy

Looking On The Bright Side

I'm pleased I'm not old yet
feeling helpless and sad
I wake up each morning
ever hopeful and glad

As I greet God's new day
See the birds in the sky
and breathe the sweet air
Oh how lucky am I

So much to do
Maybe new friends I'll meet
A smile from a neighbour
As we pass in the street

I might take up a sport
Well, no, I'm just a bit weighty
But I've ten years to slim
Before I reach eighty

Yes, I'm glad I'm not old
That I'm here and alive
I know what I'll do
I'll learn how to live.

E. Curran

Rest In Peace

Soldiers laid to rest, in
Foreign Lands,
Did not hear the sound, of
Military Bands,

The sound of shells, and
Mortar Bombs,
Will never be heard, by those
that's gone,

Nor no more, the sound of
the Pipes,
Leading the Scots to Battle
and Fight,

Kilts and Sporrans, in full Swing,
as sounds of steel, in their ears did ring,

Bayonets flashing, in the Sun,
Chasing the Enemy, on the Run,

The Battle over, they add up the score,
How many's gone, how many to go,

Or Military Bands, they hear no sound,
As they lay in peace, below the Ground.

J. Burge

Untitled

The sun turns its skull-like
features to the wind. Blood seeps
from within its pores, the maidens
will not venture here anymore.

They run through the flowery
grasp of infancy, their long life's
trail before them. The days
wear on, the path gets shorter
their existence is only evident
in the dreams they fought for.

They dance in the meadow,
unaware of any pain or suffering,
a beautiful Utopia fuelled
only by innocence and love.
Despair can never enter this enclosed
paradise, nor hate, nor regret.
Oblivious to negative emotion,
they dance forever.

Michael Hall

Funny How Poetry

Funny how poetry
fanciful words,
metaphors flying
like colourful birds
pauses explaining
imaginative thought
run unashamed
where we cannot
expressing the secrets
we dare not reveal
for fear of rejection
to things that we feel.

For inanimate symbols
line upon line
don't crumble with sorrow
at reason or rhyme,
giving us bridges,
burning or crossed,
to face every vista,
windfall or loss.

Phillip Stephen Aiken

Untitled

Leafless, beech and oak latent stand,
Exposed to grey monochrome sky;
While under hard and frosty land
Progeny to their labour lie
Waiting; both tree and seed dormant
'Til jack has sung his lullaby.

Vic Jackopson

Retrospective

The sea was cold
Exhilarating.
Strong, westerly winds
Blew across the wide beach.
When the waves drew back
And my toes sank into the wet sand
I think I knew then
That you had already gone.

We held hands as we
Walked down to the river.
It was a wet morning
With the scent of autumn.
Your fingers closed around mine
Warm, yet without comfort
Though you were with me
I felt your absence.

Pat Wilks

Obsessions Of You

Why do I think about you,
Every minute of the day?
Why do I count the hours
when you are away?
Maybe,
Because I love you.

Why do I dream about you
every single night?
Why do I count the moments
until you hold me tight?
Maybe,
Because I love you.

Why do things remind me of you,
everywhere I go?
I see your face, your smile,
And somehow,
I know
It's because I love you.

E. J. James

Actors

Actors have a power,
Especially over me,
A chance to be just anyone,
An actress I would be.
For everyone there's someone,
On the screen, they think's ideal.
Performance is perfection,
In your heart they are for real.
Imagination is so potent,
Even though it's just a sham,
I know that I do build them up,
To be my Superman.
How does it feel to have this power,
To be in my very soul?
I know you're not for real.
You don't exist at all.
But I'll dream on regardless,
Because dreaming's part of me.
I'll think, and hope, and smile a lot
Even though you cannot be.

S. M. Harpham

My Seasons

The storms and snows of winter over
England's spring is here,
With flowers in abundance
As if to say 'Were Here.'
With fields and hedgerows glowing
Their blossoms fill the air,
With summers heady scents
Of roses everywhere.
Autumns spent in Canada,
Majestic trees are there
Displaying Red and Orange hues,
Dry leaves falling everywhere.
Winters spent in warmer climes,
In Southern Spain I stay
Beside the sea, on sunny beach I lie,
'How fortunate am I.'
No thoughts of Winter here
Palm trees swaying in the breeze
Blue waves rolling to the shore,
Soon, I'll be back home, once more.

Mary Whysall

Colour

Colour is a relationship
as in music,
a chord makes
one sound.

B. Battiscombe

Handel

Georgian
Echoes
Oft
Resounding
Greeting
Every
  Festive
  Round.
Ever
Dallying
Ever
Ranging
In
Celestial
  Keys of sound.
  Hearken
  Always
  Night and day
Evermore
Laudamus te.

T. L. Cahill

My Dream

People try to steal my dream
Each night I hear them pray
They whisper in the midnight hour
That my dream will fade away

If they wish they may use words
Which hurt me deep inside
They laugh, they try to make me cry
They say I have no pride

Still, I want to be a singer
and make everybody see
That I am unique and special
Why can't they believe in me

Now all my wishes and my dream
Lay deep inside my soul
So when people shout at me
My dream stays in my hold

I just want to be a singer
Sing my songs to everyone
I want the world to love me
Why is that so very wrong?

Vanessa Sanderson

" My God "

My God will keep and guide me
each day whilst e'er I live
He will always be beside me
his help and comfort give
To him I owe my happiness
each and every day
At night he will watch o'er me
and guide me on my way
I could not live without him
to him I owe my all
I love, respect and fear him
for he hears my every call
He is always standing by my side
to teach me right from wrong
Without his comfort and his cheer
the road would seem so long
Life is oh so barren
without a God to guide
So hurry up and find him
and place him by your side

Marjorie Blasdale

Drunk

Drink, I love it.
Drink, I drink it.
Drink, I've drunk it.
Drunk the drink have I.
I sunk the drink, I drunk.
Drink, drunk been sunk.
Sinking, drinking, drunking.
I have no drink, it's drunk.
Sunk, drunk as a skunk.
Drink, I think I'll have.
Have a think, I'll drink.
Drink, a think, I'll have.
My drink, where's.
Where's drink, my
Drink my, where's.
Stinking drinking, drunk.
Drunk, stinking drink.
I'm think, drink I.
Drunk I'm, a think.
I think, I'm drunk.
Neil Meadhurst

My Love

My love you awaken in me
Dreams I've never known,
Times I've never had —
Loves I've never experienced.

Times together are short
And filled with gentle longing.
Of caring, sharing and giving.
For a moment you are my life.

The minutes are like hours,
The hours are like minutes,
The minutes disappear —
And you are gone.

You will return again —
Some day, some time,
But you are not mine to keep,
Only for a moment — you are my love.
Sandra Mary Watt

Mas'querade

The devotee of life
Dreams even.
Propertier of the soul.
Rising terran winds.

The keeper of keys,
Each to its own destiny.
Unique in shape
Even in personality.

All gems sparkle,
Material insecurities.
Poverty has no effect
Selfishness arises in this no fixed abode.

The dessert sands shift
From moon to shine.
No-one ever knows
Whether they will...
Live or die.
Raman Kaur Sidhu

Where Does Love Lie?

Love is a power,
But where does it lie,
At the end of a rainbow,
Or moonlit sky,
Across a wide ocean,
Or heavenly high,
Love is a power,
But where does it lie?
Matthew Owen

To The Beach

Dry the sun the morning dew
Drawing rays across the day
Dwindling drowsy dreams away
While dressing up the singing birds.

Down by the valley a deer runs
Bending daffodils along the path
Windy wings on either side
To lead him where all rivers die.

This and that and there we are
Dancing sandy mounts aside
Drifting far to swim the sea
Where dolphins dive the ocean deep.
Toni Conesa Ribera

Down To The Sea

I carried your ashes
Down to the sea.
I held them close,
You were with me.

I sprinkled your ashes
Upon the blue sea.
I felt your warm breath,
You spoke gently to me.

I watched your ashes
Float upon the sea.
Your voice was clear,
You said you loved me.

I saw your ashes
Go under the wave.
Your hand in mine,
Made me feel so brave.

I carried your ashes
Down to the sea.
I let them go,
You stayed with me.
Pauline Hart

Highland Rhyme

I went doon to buy ma porage,
Doon in the toon one day.
I thanked the lady kindly,
and I took ma porage away.
I took it back up to ma croft,
And I ha it for ma tea.
But I could no help ma sel but think,
It tasted strange to me.
I looked upon the box,
and felt that I could kill her.
For it was no porage there at all,
but blasted polyfilla!
My God but it was terrible,
it rocked me to ma socks.
Can you imagine the agony,
of passing concrete blocks?
B. F. Moss

Clouds

Mare's tail artwork,
dark, dusty feathering,
soft grey blanket
or thundered black billowing.
Saltless foaming spray.
Rouge puff bubbles,
velvet mouthed, nibbling
the bright ice mountains.
Flickering phoenix flares.
Misty fish skin swirl.
Jitterbug petticoats.
Snowing power warriors
smoothed to persian purring
before they gently wisp away.
Sioux Davey

The Third World

Look hard...
do not turn away
gaze upon my haunting frame
"I"...
The Third world
of whom you speak
your promises
that drain my blood:
sap my strength,
in terror, pain, starvation.
You my brother... help too late
and watch a dying nation.
The need to act is sacrosanct.
Set my people free
Give to us our heritage

Forever... You are Me.
Mary Ratcliffe

The Grave

Do not cry for me
Do not shed any tears
You were not there when I needed you
You never shared my joys or fears
Put no flowers on my grave
Don't kneel, don't say no prayer
Don't be a two faced lover
Pretending that you care
I see you standing above me
As I lie here in my grave
Already you are thinking
It is time that you should leave
Go now, my two faced lover
Go now, my two faced friend
I know you will not visit
I know my grave you will not tend
But come you will for certain
When your life comes to end
And I will be waiting
My so called friend.
Rose Marie Clarke

Two Way Traffic

Like an angry rash over earth's face
diseased by its hollow victory
crossing over empty places
to corrupt each with the other.
Ground left bleeding, heaving,
twitching in the aftermath.

Vacant view through the glass
where once the scene kept shifting
green against the cloudy blue.
An unnatural river of grey
that feeds no living thing,
but the crow that grows fat.

Round motion replaces breathing step
metal over feather and fur.
Ego hungry human in a hurry
versus mate hungry, searching creature.
Two worlds debate for an instant,
and only one hunger is fed.
Sonia McGuire

The Harpy

Sharp, sharp eyes
Beneath a feathered crown,
The joyless monkey
She brings down,
Soft downy wings
Like whispered breath
Carrying forth
The talons of death.
E. R. Thwaites

Simplicity

Starlight and sunlight,
dewdrop and rainbow,
fleeting in time,
yet enduring in memory.
More than the world's cares,
- the concrete, the marble,
yes, even the glory.
These gifts are forever,
these glimpse of heaven,
for us to hold on to.

As we face the ending
we find the beginning.
Our works and our worries,
our hopes and our joys,
once ruling our passions
enslaved our existence.
All fade from the vision.
We take on the freedom
of starlight and sunlight,
and peace, going home.

Vivienne Bamber

Catch A Shadow

Catch a shadow in your hand.
Darkness falls softly and hides
Fleshy folds that will flow.

Catch a light in your hand.
Brightness falls softly and reflects
Lines and mounds that show.

Catch a warmth in your hand.
Heat falls softly and absorbs
In the nerves that will glow.

Catch a wind in your hand.
Breath falls softly and moves,
Awakes senses that will know.

Catch a sound in your hand.
Murmurs fall softly and hear
With an ear that sings low.

Catch an idea in your hand.
Thoughts fall softly and plant
In the mind and then grow.

A. Todd

Worlds Beyond

Unleash the silence
Darkness awakening
Voices from beyond this place
Lure you into the dream
Colours bright
Images sharpening
Slow motion frenzy
Caught in the spotlight's beam
Faces frozen
Blank eyes hold your gaze
Memories of the future
The past not yet known
Fragments flash by
Emotions ablaze
Others surround you
But here you're always alone

S. M. Gonsalves

Sitting In The Garden

Sitting in the garden
beneath the apple tree
The bees are buzzing
round their nest
the birds are singing joyfully
all is pleasant
all is calm
beneath the apple tree.

C. Fleming

Like...

The stars that lighten up the
   Dark sky at night
You have lightened up the
   Whole of my life.
The sunrise that starts
   A shining day
You have brought sunshine
   In your own sweet way
The moon that touches everything
   With a special sheen
You touched me and leave that
   Very same gleam
The sunset that finally ends
   A beautiful day
As is each day with you
   Is as beautiful.

Melodie Dean

Aspidistra

Triumphant British racing
curved open pointed in a shoe
horn slant, with sleekly spaced
vertically veined ribs, tracking
gently from arrow pointed tip to
feather tapered fold, down a fluted
straw stem
to an arid ancient
loamy mixed base
collected in a
spent bedpan
chipped, on
shadow's
dusted
life

A. Thompson

Storm In Cornwall

I watch the waves in a storm
Crash against the rocks
Covering everything in its path
The wind howls and moans
Around every corner
Huge black clouds accumulate
Out over the bay
Making wonderful angry shapes
The sea turns grey
White horses galloping
On its surface
Birds soar and screech
Shouting a warning
I stand on the cliff
Watching a storm in cornwall.

Sheena Best

After The Fire

The great, irrepressible sky
Hangs helpless
Across phosphorus limbs,
As they grab
Its transparent vastness
With knuckled silence.

Their demolition complete,
They weep morning dew
From peeling skins,
While in mourning
For the flesh of earth
Made parched and bare.

And upon the broken clay
They cling tenaciously;
Obstinate in death.

Robert Fox

On The Threshold

Slowly
Consciousness slips
Darkness all around
Heartbeat stops
Death

Light
Bright white
Joy and salvation
Floating towards
Heaven

Abruptly
Movement ceases
Distant voices call
Physical ties
Pull

Panic
Fighting doubt
All in vain
You return
Alive

Stuart George Parkinson

The Trippers

"It is time that we had a vacation"
Commented my wife yesterday
"Then will you select the location"
I said as I promised I'd pay

Then she did a wee spot of thinking
Then a big smile lit up her face
"I think this is a smashing idea
Would you like a trip into space"

When we arrived at the airport
A notice read rear seats for Mars
We selected a seat by a window
Which allowed us to study the stars.

As we were bypassing Venus
I whispered, "Would you like a drink"
And she replied, "That would be
welcome
They'll be open on Neptune I think"

So we spent a fortnight on Neptune
As guests on an animal farm
And then came a heart stopping clamour
I had not switched off my ALARM!!!

L. Gurr

This World

This world of ours
Given to us with love
Each day something more
Is set to destroy
Something of beauty
Something of life

The forests of grandeur
Wiped out by greed
The tons of toxic waste
Buried with speed
Polluting rivers and seas
Causing wildlife to suffer
Unmeasurable pain and torment

Why is man who is suppose to be
The most intelligent species
On this planet of wonder
Destroying everything even each other
Where will it all end
Or rather when will it all end

Tina Howe

Untitled

Old page pensioners advise
come all you old women
I hope you'll draw near
when you're lifting the
pension don't touch on
the beer
keep your purse in your
pocket where it won't be
seen, for he tell you what
happened the old crocked reen
she went up to the chapel
for to say a prayer, left the
purse in the cart unable
with care the share holder
blackguards arrived
on the scene and walked off
with the pound on the old
crock adreen.
Rose Green

Untitled

Suspended from a single strand of
cobwebbed frosted time,

Delicately falling, a tender memory
encrusted shine,

Surrounded by a deepness that echoes
from such height.

With a shadow that's engulfing the
silence of the night.

Fading in the distance like the
drawing of last breath

Coloured by a sadness and the
taste of recent death.

Its movement is so perfect like music
so sincere.

And its motion always steady with
out concern for hidden fear.

Reliable and trust worthy but melon
colic (how I know).

My heart, my heart, oh truly
How you've suffered with me so.
N. Price

Ruth's Birthday

Soon it will be March,
Clear crisp and gay,
Her anniversary arch
Her seventeenth birthday,

She came into the world,
And angry lusty bundle,
Did nothing but scold,
It was cold and she did grumble,

Form maternal warmth,
To march cold air,
She came to our family hearth
That was all loving care,

She screamed her disgust,
At her baptismal petting,
This world she did distrust,
Cared nothing for her setting,

Her milestone years,
She battled through,
Guarding all that was hers,
Solidly she grew and grew.
M. I. English

Christmas

Snowflakes are falling
Christmas at last
Another year dawning
Another year past

Season of plenty for some young
And old
For others a wish of a secret
They hold

Songs for the season
Presents for the tree
Smiling faces
All filled with glee

Joy for the season
Which will always last
For every year dawning
And every year past
Tracy Evans

The Spring

Spring is coming! Spring is coming!
Chirruped the Robin on the bough,
Thrushes, Linnets, busy warbling
Songs of Spring Time for us now.

Flowers from the earth are creeping
Snowdrop, primrose, violets new,
From their winters sleep are peeping
Sending forth their fragrant hue.

Frisky lambs are now appearing
And we hear their plaintive bleat,
Telling us that Spring is nearing
As they stagger to their feet.

Trees and shrubs are now preparing
Taking on another sheen,
Soon we'll see them all wearing
Foliage of brightest green.
Sheila Ormerod

Sunrise On A Country Lane

The sun rises in the sky,
catching the morning dew
like a highwayman's bag
of precious gems, sparkling.
A cool breeze blows,
gently encouraging the aroma
of ripe, wild strawberries
along the way.
Dragonflies, and butterflies
dart across, from hedgerow
to hedgerow.
The steady trickle of water
sounds like the soft strumming
of a harp.
The friendly chatter of the birds
greets you.
This is my favourite time of day.
Sunrise on a country lane.
Sarah Louise Spooner

Winter Song

Slanting rain and leaden skies
But we were in paradise.

Driving wind and stinging sand
We two laughing hand in hand.

Cold grey sea and flying spray
One must go and one must stay

As we said our last "goodbye"
Gentle snowflakes filled the sky.

All the love I'd ever know
Left behind me, with the snow.
M. C. Owen

Falling In Love

The beauty of one moment
Captured in your mind
Sudden sweet awareness
The world is left behind

The longing in another's eyes
Perfectly matched to yours
Love, in mirrored images
Opens up its doors

No touch, or human contact
Is needed here today
Words are unnecessary
There are no words to say

Minds and thoughts entangle
Spirits soar and fly
Lifts you into ecstasy
So sweet you want to cry

A feeling of true union
A love that soothes and calms
As the beauty of this moment
Enfolds you in its arms
Maureen Blanchard

Together Two People

Together two people
  Can have such fun,
Two worlds and two
  Hearts become as one,

The greatest joy
  That you can have
Is someone there to
  Hold and love,

To make you happy
  When you are sad,
Getting through the days
  That are good or bad,

To share your troubles
  And your fears,
And dry your eyes
  And kiss the tears,

What better pleasure
  Than holding them tight,
To begin the day
  And say goodnight.
Patricia Ann Moir

Dilemma

It isn't easy to be always right,
But worse to be always wrong.
It isn't easy to show who you are,
So you show another one.

Throughout the day you live a lie,
Being what you are not.
That inner voice you do deny,
Those instincts you do block.

I tell myself that this is how,
I should appear to be.
But it only makes my truer self,
Feel a deeper inferiority.

Perhaps I chase after rainbows,
And in doing so miss the sun.
Perhaps I should be as I am,
It could possibly be more fun.
Rosamund Jane Barker

The Lonely Lover's Ditty

Would you were
But with me now
At this,
Of all the
Loneliest
Hour
When sleep and passion
In the soul conspire.

Now I believe,
Yet cannot bear my faith
Alone.

Oh come, my love
To comfort me:
Help me elude
The ransom of desire.

Paul Eisler

Somebody Died

Somebody died
But the clouds kept on moving

Somebody's ill
But the sun keeps on shining

Somebody laughs
But the wars keep on raging

A wedding takes place
Everyone's happy

Somebody died
And the clouds keep on moving

Susan Eggleton

Just One Wish

So many things I wanted to say
But now it's all too late
My grandpa has been summoned
To those glowing pearly gates.

To tell him how I loved him
He wiped away my tears
Protecting, caring, sharing
Watching over me for years.

His love was unconditional
His heart so big and strong
A cuddle always there for me
Until his heart went wrong.

Now my life's so empty
No-one could fill the gap
If I could have just one wish
I'd like my grandpa back.

Michelle Harris

Pride Of Place

Subdued were we, by Anglo might,
But not without a merry fight.
It was not in the Celtic way
To give up 'neath the victor's sway.

So, though our mystic hills are clad
With castles that make Merlin sad,
'Tis said "To fight and run away"
Is better than to let them slay.

So perchance, if we just sing,
Of days gone by, when "DWR" was King
And every cot, and merry hearth
Rang with song, and sound of harp.

Bend we did like stalks of wheat,
Tho' not like slaves, bowed with defeat,
But showing homage to the earth,
Who truly knows our Celtic worth.

B. G. Metcalfe

The Wandering Mind

Pretend that you have felt success,
but living only in a mess
of mixed up thoughts and ideas;
working them out through the years.

The dreams of grandeur and success,
Crashing, crumbling through abyss.
Awaken from this dream of yours
and settle down to daily chores.

Mundane routine repeating work,
the golden thoughts, they still lurk
in distant dreams not yet fulfilled,
the castles in the air we build.

These dreams of ours are full of tales,
of things to come, when the ship sails
home with the harvest of riches untold.
Then life begins, life can unfold.

William I. Cleaton-Roberts

I Long For

Your kiss I long to feel
But I know I never will,
If I could only hear your voice.
How my heart would rejoice.

I long to hold you near
But when I do you disappear,
I feel my heart is going
  to break,
Will I never lose this ache,

I long to hold you close
But my dear you're just a
  ghost.

B. M. Fuller

Untitled

I see a tree out there, it is bare
but do not worry, soon my leaves
and flowers will be there,
Winter is past and spring has
come at last, I feel it is time now
To awaken and let the world
know this tree was not dead after all.

I will show pink and white blossoms
and aroma will send out perfume
That all who come near me will say
"True only God can make a tree as
beautiful as me that once was that
Bare tree!"

I hope again when autumn leaves
begin to fall I will be here watching
you standing tall, shedding once
again your golden leaves and flowers
blown away with a gentle
breeze into the sunset of another year.

Vera Hynes

The Act Of Love

Slowly the body is being caressed,
Clothes slowly being removed,
Bodies moving closer together,
The temperature rising fast,
A rhythm of movements is being taken,
The final climax begins,
The movement of his body over hers,
She slowly begins to move with him,
Looking at his face,
She feels security and love,
Feelings of a special act of love,
Finally the end is coming,
Two people lying there,
Quietly, in each other's arms,
Until the next time.

Maria Lazarou

Dreams Of Love

Sun, flowers, wind and rain
Bringing to me, my love again,
Love that was lost,
Yet kept on living,
Within my heart, forever giving,
Warm feelings to cherish,
my thoughts of you.

Sun, flowers, wind and rain,
When will we be together again,
Days gone by, lonely days,
Blue skies to come, and sunny rays
Warming my heart, and giving hope
That one day, the sun,
Flowers, wind and rain
Will come and take away the pain
Loving forever my love so true
Dreams to cherish
My thoughts of you.

C. Butcher

Old Father Time

Old Father Time as time be spent,
Both past and present is heaven sent,
'Tis but a moment without face,
Nor length of which one cannot trace.

Time is eternal, long or short,
Time just merely floats on thought,
Circumstance proves hard to bear,
When time is of the essence spare.

But when abundantly we hold,
This time we have must not unfold,
Not to squander without thought,
But seek to profit from time so brought.

Time cannot keep with lock and key,
God's precious gift won't wait for thee,
For once 'tis passed, 'tis passed forever,
Return it not, not now or ever.

Philippa C. Benacs

Just to say...

Your hair is like a golden flame,
blowing in the wind.
Your eyes they shine like diamonds,
your ears so beautifully pinned.

Your smile is such a pleasant view,
your lips like ruby wine.
And every time I see you
you're heavenly divine.

R. S. Chaggar

Our Cat

The black and white cat
"Blackie" to us all
With the ever active ears
Sits idly on the window sill.

Watches the world go by
With deep concentration
Her tail moves slowly or quickly
Depending on her prey.

Beautiful green eyes
Wide open so as not to miss
Whatever passes by.

Acknowledges that I'm there
Gets back to more important things
Looking at the birds on the tree
Will I be lucky this time

Tail waggles furiously
She's found her catch
Skilfully jump from the window
Misses by an inch.

M. Moollan

Untitled

I stand
Between insanity and pain
Blood, guts, all washed up
Fish stranded on a beach
Dying in the merciless sun
Desert sand blows into rocks
Creating form out of the formless
The knife-cut of reality
Droplets of red
Dancing in the midnight sun
Who's to define
What's normal and what's not?
I see beyond myself
Into my sulpiride jar
I take a tablet
To be accepted by vicious society.

Melanie Muende

Cats

Sinbar and Zenith purr
beside me
when summer's birch logs
crackle
in the open grate
and my kitchen window
frost etched
becomes a still life
of ferns
or some exotic jungle
of strange palms
from where
I expect to see
the eyes of the cat
stare out at me.

G. E. Sowerby

Sea of Hope

Take me on a journey
Beneath the sea of hope,
Where angels ride the dolphins
down life's awe-inspiring slope.

Where coral castles looming,
Inviting dreams to haunt
And whirlpool mind streams melt
into tornados, luck to daunt.

The mighty whale just watches,
Eternal wisdom dancing in his eyes,
The gentle dolphin holds the key
to man's existence in his cries.

Beyond the sands of time
Dimension's tide will carry Earth,
Can Gaia save her planet
for a peace-showered rebirth?

Take me on a journey,
That sea of hope to find,
Hiding in our future,
in the shadows of my mind.

Tina-Jane (Luna) Woodhouse

Panther By The Water's Edge

My calm awaits your wondrous gaze
As jet black eyes and silken coat
Crouch low, limbs tense;
To ponder thus your mighty power,
That I reflect from depths so still.
Your speed and grace is unsurpassed,
Respect you claim from all around;
Yet tender is your paw's soft touch
As you reach out to drink
The ripples of my mind.

Moira Patricia George

The Trap

We think we are lucky,
Because we are free,
We think we are happy,
Both you and me.

But don't be mistaken,
And don't be misled,
Because tomorrow everything,
Could be turned on its head.

People all over the world,
Once thought they were free,
Now most of them live,
In fear and poverty.

So don't take things for granted,
That we have all this splendour,
Because at the click of a switch,
It could all be ended.

Don't look on these people with scorn,
With hatred and abuse,
Because you could lose all one day,
Then this might be you.

J. Robinson

A Journey

She walked the path of angels,
Basked in the glory of the sun.
She raised her eyes to heaven,
Praised the day begun.

She walked through fields of poppies,
Scent of summer in the air,
A quiet breeze it whispered,
Gently touched her hair.

Her spirit wandered freely,
Searched high and low and long,
Through forests' soft, green foliage,
Cool waters' mellow song.

Until she reached the mountains,
And here she gave a sigh,
As she felt the wondrous beauty
Of heaven, earth and sky.

And there in hues of purple,
The journey nearly done,
Her spirit now at peace expired
With the setting of the sun.

Sharon Wyn Thomas

Cafe People

Cappuccinos and cigarettes
　chitchat and gossipers.
　　Sitting in the summer sun.

Short skirts and smiles,
　Yuppies and office talk.
　　Lovers gazing into
　　　each other's eyes.

Young men debating,
　Young girls giggling,
　　teasing with their looks.
　　　There's love in the air!

Well-groomed men.
　Prettily dressed women.
　　Discussing the trials and
　　　tribulations of life.

Sitting in the corner with a
　cappuccino, listening to chitchat
　　and other people gossip.
　　　In the summer sun.
　　　　Cafe people!

Mark Harrison

Civil Times

Come with me my little one,
Away from this beating drum,
Let the soldiers fight their way
You'll only die if you stay.

War, oh this bloody war,
Bodies lying across the floor,
Fine men they once were,
With tears, they became a blur.

Houses, fields, burn to ashes,
Looters, suffer leather lashes,
Shells shake this rocky ground,
With cries of pain, from all around.

The smell of cordite powder,
As the gun fire echoes louder,
Charge after charge, dulls the pain,
With inch by inch, of land they gain.

Let's go, let's flee this bloody war,
You won't suffer this no more,
Come with me my little one,
Before we, and this nobody war is done.

D. Honeysett

The Rabbit Chase

A spark of alert
awakens her chocolate eyes.
Ears pricked, hackles high,
what has she seen?

A doe rabbit,
lazing in the midday sun,
senses her agitation
and starts to run.

A pursuit begins,
hunter after prey,
each trying to outwit the other,
trying to get away.

Through riverside ferns they dash,
eyes glazed, but they persevere.
Finally the doe can run no longer
and in one bounding leap the dog is
upon her —
blinded by the desperate sense of a hunt —
and with one snap of her jaws
the doe is dead.

Sarah C. Thomas

Window

I look out of my window
at the sights that I behold.

I see trees with leaves that
are beginning to unfold.

I see dogs in back gardens
barking at birds in the trees.

I see cats in the sun
fun blowing in the breeze.

I see children on swings and
going down slides,
playing in paddling pools
throwing balls in the sky.

I see adults walking hand in hand
looking into each other's eyes.

I look out of my window and what
do I see?

I see a picture of the world.

The way it's meant to be!

Neal Byford

Tranquillity

As I looked out my window
At the garden down below
The sun was shining brightly
On buttercups, aglow
Birds were singing happily
Peace was all around
Butterflies were fluttering
Wings making no sound
Flowers swaying gently
In the morning breeze
Giving me a feeling
A warming sense of ease
Whatever could be nicer
For starting a new day
I closed my eyes, hung my head
And then began to pray
Who makes this happen
Don't let this feeling end
Whoever makes this happen
   AMEN
B. Hammond

This Tramp

People stare with contempt,
At an old man in rags,
He has nowhere to go,
With his life in his bags.

This tramp had a life,
Until his business went bust,
Then his wealth and riches,
All turned to dust.

His family soon went,
His friends didn't call,
The money disappeared,
The divorce look it all.

He stumbles and staggers,
Alone in the cold,
The pneumonia he suffers,
Has at last taken hold.

So it's goodbye to his life,
And a world he once forgave,
As he falls to the ground,
In a gutter for a grave.
Julie Hart

Lament Of A Sailor's Wife

You went away and left me
alone, and feeling blue.
You said you would always love me
and I know that it was true.
But war was a cruel master,
The sea an enemy.
The U-boats hunted and harried,
I prayed you'd come back to me.
But far, far away your life ended
before it had hardly begun,
I was left, a young widow
with a heart, not a life, that was dead.
M. Gunderson

Infinity

Son of mine
Behold of your life
Do what you will of it
Never is past so soon
Sense my spirit all around
When I am no more of body
      and know
That we are not parted
Susan Dixon

Child Of Visions

As the darkness falls about me
As your image fills my mind,
Tender kisses, carefree whispers,
Should I wish that you were mine.

Dancing shadows, flames that flicker
Mirror teardrops in your eyes,
Hold me close now, cry no longer
Cast away the fears you hide.

Take my hand and fly forever
Wear a flower in your hair,
Child of visions, sing your anthem
Touch your heart, I am living there.

Greet the sunrise, catch the rainbow
Be the eagle on the wing
Taste of freedom, not a captive
Lift your voice and let it sing

Child of visions, cry no longer,
I am with you, do not hide.
Tony Conlon

Millennium

Ship of Life — sail on
as the old century dies,
a new horizon beckons us
where the sea gull flies.

Escape the jaws of death
life's hanging by a thread;
preserve each living thing
or all Nature will be dead.

Last century's follies past;
accepted as a crime, hear
unborn human's silent screams
within the womb of time.
R. M. Evans

Love And Death

The dew lay on the meadow,
As the dawn began to light,
The birds awake and singing,
Ready for morning flight.
Nothing there to give away
The anguish in my heart,
None to see the tears I shed
Because we had to part.
I alone remember you and the
Joy you brought to me,
You were my one and only love,
But now I've set you free.
Be happy dearest one
Keep a smile upon your face,
For one day soon my darling
By your side I will take my place.
I will meet you in the wings of time,
And when that day is nigh,
I will leave this earthly life,
For the happy by and by.
P. White

Looking Forward

You must always look forward
At the new things to come,
The past is a memory
Of things that you've done.
Remember the bad
But cherish the good,
Learn from life
As always one should.
And when you feel lonely
With no one at all.
A friend's always there
Just give one a call.
B. Meale

Wait For Me Please

I placed my hand upon her head
As she lay dying in her bed.
And heard the voice of my sweet wife
Saying thank you for a wondrous life.

I heard her say "I love you,"
Then tears flowed from my eyes.
I tried to smile a gentle smile,
My feelings to disguise.

And then I whispered to her
The things she loved to hear.
With trembling lips I kissed her.
I knew her time was near.

"Wait for me, I beg you,"
I whispered to my wife,
"I cannot live without you,
I love you more than life."

She smiled her very special smile
And breathed "I love you too.
But I'll go first and prepare a home
Just for me and you."
W. Leonard

The Big 4-0 Looms

Does life begin at forty,
   as many seem to think?
Will I still feel as happy,
   and be feelin' in the pink?

Will I, in two years time,
   be really glamorous,
and make the men turn their heads,
   and begin to feel real amorous?

Will I have a zest for life,
   go buying all new fashions?
Will I be a sprightly young thing,
   and have heaps and heaps of passions?

Or, will I run a marathon,
   like Oprah Winfrey achieved?
Will I have zeal and power?
   this, I'd like to believe!!

Well, in two years from now,
   I'll have achieved the fatal 4-0,
if I'll then have all these things,
   that's good, 'cos I haven't now!!
Susan Woods

Torture Chamber

In torture rooms
Around the world
The echoes of dead men's throes
Live in the very walls.
Blood spattered, sweat stained

Here, man found the measure
Of man's tortured soul
Down to the bare bones
Where no one can hide
No kings, and no heroes

Just torturer and tortured
Damned and dying
Each hanging on
To the vain belief, they're right
And belief is worth sacrifice

No audience to witness
No referee to keep score
No escape, but the one way
All men shall one day exit
To see who judges then
Nigel Bangert

Jewels

The most beautiful of all jewels
   Are the drops of crystal dew,
Hung out in the morning early,
   And seen by so very few.

You find them in such strange places -
   On the tip of a blade of grass,
Or sparkling on the fern fronds
   As down country lanes you pass.

They dangle in great profusion
   From the leaves of all the trees
And, as the day advances,
   Scatter abroad with the breeze.

Oh, why, with such beautiful jewels
   Hung out for the eyes to see,
Are diamonds and rubies so precious,
   With dew-drops there for us, free.
E. Jepson

"Wintertime In Austria"

The mountains looking down on me
Are just like another dream.
I stand and stare, I look around —
Am I the only one that is about?

It is so quiet there is no sound —
No cars, trains, or planes around.
I walk and walk, I am all alone
And yet I know I am not alone.

I hear a bird, I see the trees
Swaying slightly in the breeze.
The branches are so full with snow,
Soon the wind will drop it all.

But that will be another scene,
Another season to be living in.
Spring will be here and all around,
Flowers will push through the ground.

It is so nice, this world of mine.
Why can't there be peace all the time?
H. Murray

Vicious Circle

Another bomb
another threat
another tear
another death

Anger and fear
where is the end
families apart
crying to cheer

Where does one start
to re-build the peace
bring joy in one's heart
and the bombing to cease

Let's talk and compromise
sit down together
stop all the violence
we're at the end of our tether.
Sinead Comerford

Untitled

There is a love,
a love so fine,
a love so sweet,
a love divine,
a love that's true,
a love that's mine,
you are my love,
to keep this time.
C. A. Arthur

The Quarrel

We niggle and chide
Anger wells up inside
Let our feelings be known
We have a good moan!

We bitch and shout
Got to get it all out
Each wanting to win
Not be the one to give in!

We sulk and feel hurt
Our retorts become curt
A stale mate is reached
Will the void ever be breached?

We feel sad and alone
Our behaviour none can condone
To bring back our love
We should hang up our gloves.
Philippa Walter

Kill Yourself

If you don't love animals,
And you love shooting them,
Then you're not a human at all,
And you got no right to say you are.
For I'm a human with a heart,
So you don't come close to me,
And I wouldn't want you near me,
So take your gun away,
And just walk away from the animals.
You may find it fun,
But it is cruel and sick.
We don't need you round here.
They're animals here that should be loved,
No animals here to be killed.
So if you want to kill something,
Just kill yourself.
S. L. M. Critcher

Distant Feelings (Across The Room)

One curt glance, eyes entwine,
   Fleeting,
Gentle hearts, rise in time,
   Beating,
Coursing blood, flows through veins,
   Rushing,
Sets wan and pallid cheeks,
   Blushing,
Bodies warmth rises to
   Burning,
Feelings well up inside,
   Yearning,
Both coy, too shy to start
   Flirting,
Watch romance walk away,
   Hurting.
D. T. Morgan

If Only

If only I could be your love
And you be my love too
My life would have much meaning
'Cos I'd belong to you

If only you could come around
And see me just one day
You'll want to hold me in your arms
And that would make my day

If only I were older
I know that you'd be mine
If only you were younger
My life would be divine
Marcia Celestina Lewis

People

They say that beauty's just skin deep
   And maybe that is true;
For God made all the angels
   But made some devils too;
So the wisest of selections
   Must come from me and you.

Just travel on life's journey
   And keep an open eye.
Check that all the pleasures
   Do not pass you by.
The good outweighs the evil,
   On that you can rely.

Now within the human race
   Some are cruel, some are kind;
So look beyond the average face
   And maybe you will find,
That hidden there's sincerity
   With a heart of gold behind.
G. Bleasdale

Policy Of Chance

I can see dreams within a dream
And lives within a life
I touch ecstasy in pain
And brought joy into strife
But I can't imagine
Why they do this to us
We're all just the innocent
In a world that's fit to burst
In traps left behind
On days of remembrance
So callously plain
Is the policy of chances
I have a dream in a dream
My life is in this life
Where no one has to fear
And no one sheds a tear
In a bomb of politics
And a war of religion
A dream I so hope
Is soon the beginning
Steve Baker

Love's Lament

I've grown weary, of waiting
And listening for your step,
Yearning! for your arms and yet!
My heart can never forget
How much you meant to me

The early morning mist
The sunlight of the day,
When lover's kiss and go their way.

Oh! fragile of all dreams,
Is love's first love
In tear-drops gleams
That higher love above.
M. Clifford

Today Or Tomorrow

I've been far away
And left you behind
But not in my heart at least
For when I was sad
I thought of your smile
That kept me so warm and at peace
So now I've returned
To claim what is ours
A love so strong and so sure.
As I kneel here before you
To give you thy ring
Please marry me, today or tomorrow.
Rodney Lawrence

Stranger's House

I'm here
And wonder why sometimes.
Why this house
Why this time

Who are you
You never say
I know your face
Your likes in life
I live here too
I am your wife

We're here we two
Like all the others
Wives, husbands, mothers, lovers

So here we stay
With strangers all
Never really knowing
And spend our time
Each day to day
With strangers
In their houses

Rosalind Caruso

Tears

What do they mean
and where are they from
What do they convey
when they have gone

Happiness and laughter too
sadness, despair and grief
They can last all too long
or be all too brief

Salty and silently running
down over our cheeks
Evoking sympathy or
derision for being weak

Whatever the cause
they cleanse the soul
Tears come to us all
whether young or old

Hot and burning
cool and quiet
Soaking our skins
way into the night

N. Parsons-Hann

Reflection

If I should have to ponder why,
and think upon my life,
And contemplate the time I die,
as just tormented strife.

Will I have used up to the full,
the years allotted me?
Or should I reach deep in my soul,
all wasted time to see?

Will it matter that I've been
and spent a little while,
Who will care what I have seen,
time spent in self denial.

Yet now in age I find I care
and wish to leave my heart.
The world should know that I was there
Before I must depart.

Too late I fear, the end is now
If only I had seen,
If only I had known just how
To let them know I've been.

S. A. Alcraft

Relax A Little

When life is a struggle
And the road seems uphill,

Your troubles are many
And you've had your fill.

Just rest for a while
Let everything go,

If you don't you will find
On your face it will show.

Just think of bright colours,
Of the sun's golden rays,

Of the way things were
On much happier days.

Breathe slowly and deeply,
Let your body wind down.

Then things will feel better
And you'll smile and not frown.

Margaret Langshaw

Imagine

Imagine the Sun, never to Shine,
and the rain, never to fall.

Imagine a voice shouting,
and no one to hear it call,

Imagine a flower, standing,
alone in a field of corn,

Imagine no birds, singing,
in the early morning Dawn,

Imagine having no teacher,
when you're trying to learn,

Imagine giving Love,
and have nothing, in return,

Imagine all this, you imagine me,
Full of emptiness, I cannot see.

K. E. Lake

Caring For A Carer

Thank you for your caring
And the kindness of your Heart
I never ever would accept
That we were worlds apart.

You showed me such compassion
And encouraged me to be
Interested — Motivated
Discovering the Real Me.

If fate had drawn a different hand
Our life journey to pursue
You could have been me, my friend
And I could have been You.

Shirley Davis

Time

Time has no boundaries,
And will never stay still
Time is a good healer
When you suffer from ills.
Time can be patient
If you are willing to wait
And can be a nuisance
When you turn up late.

But never look back
Or time will catch up
And then you will find
You are out of luck.
'Cause time stops for nobody,
So use it up and never
Look back, always look up.

Mark O'Donnell

Last Moments

I sit on the bench,
And stare at the walls
It's dark and it's damp
but I can't feel the cold.

I hear them coming and
I know that it's time
I've waited so long
That this moment is mine

I can hear them talking
But it's not going in
Now we are walking
Time to pay for my sin.

We're now in the room
Where it's going to happen
I'm tied and I'm bound
With a hood on my head

The tears run free
Oh why is it me?
There's suddenly no floor,
And I'm dropping to...

D. K. Newell

My Promise

When skies look grey,
And shadows are long.
Plus everything's gone wrong
I'll be there....

You feel no-one cares,
Others don't want to know
And your worries seem to grow
I'll be there....

If you're feeling low,
Don't know what to do
Let's talk it over, see it through.
I'll be there....

If you need a friend,
Help dispel your fears
Just remember through the years.
I'll be there.

P. Cooley

Witchery

I walked along a country lane
And paused beneath Milady's Tree,
Beguiled by bird with plumage black
Who ope'd his orange bill
And trilled a witching song to me

With breath all stilled I listened,
Thrilled, beneath Milady's Tree,
But he took wing, that bird so black,
Leaving but the echoing trill
Of the song that witched me

Again I walked along the lane
And paused beneath Milady's Tree,
Where leaned a youth, whose hair so black
And eyes so bright, filled
My heart with different witchery

Now years have passed, and in the lane
I pause beneath Milady's Tree,
Remembering bird with plumage black
Who fled, and the youth who still
Keeps my heart, with love he witched
from me.

Marie Wallis-Pattison

To Daddy

When you are lonely
And no one cares
You think of the past
And the troubles you shared

When the baby was born
And it didn't survive
I wanted to die
Not stay alive

But you were there
My sorrow to share
You helped me through
With a smile and a prayer

Daddy, I loved you
In so many ways
And I'll love you forever,
The rest of my days.

Joy Cosaitis

Dreaming

Dreaming of you, when shadows fall,
And night comes stealing down,
When stars are spangled in the sky,
To make the moon a crown,

Of arms that used to hold me close,
Of lips pressed tight to mine,
Of stolen moments, wild, and free
Yet never was I thine.

Oh! vain regrets, for what has been,
Will never be again,
I only wish, and long, and dream,
I had been, wholly, thine.

J. Cochrane

" Hope "

I was alone,
And left bereft,
No more tears
Had I left.
A robin — cocky — sure
Stood proudly at my back door
I threw a little crumb to him
Inviting him to come in,
He cocked his little head
But really wasn't after bread
In silent language, I said "Hi"
He never even blinked an eye —
With one swift movement
He was gone,
The seed of love had been sown
I no longer — was alone.

P. Young

Lover's Mask

A lover many masks doth wear
Beguiling charming one to snare
Tokens o'love and a silver tongue
Till a fair maid's heart is won

Now thy heart is mine to keep
Fair maid then begins to weep
Saying it was only lent
Never bought on what you spent

Once I was free as a bird
Silly cupid must of heard
Fickle arrows aimed at will
For a loving heart to kill

A heart on cupid did depend
O fickle love on thee pretend
And then cupid an arrow aimed
A heart to bruise 'n wound, 'n maim

Tomahawk

The Preternatural Hunter

I am the bitter enemy
and I want my sweet revenge
I'll scare you
I'll kill you
I'll frighten you to death
I'll haunt you in another life
until you are no more
I'll hunt you down
like a helpless fox
You'll wish you never dared
to cross my path
you dug your grave....
And as the hunter hunts,
The vampire loves to kill.

Marina Kyriacou

One Single Red Rose

One single red rose you gave to me
and I treasured it with all my heart,
it was a private and personal thing
but only to say we must part,
My rose it had a tear on it
Fresh from the morning dew,
Just like the one in my eye
As I said goodbye to you,
You know how much I loved you
But you could no longer stay,
But I still treasure the rose
That you gave to me that day,
I pressed it into a book
To remind me of a love so true,
And every time I look at my rose
It still reminds me of you.

Sharon Chittenden

The Mists Of Time

The mists of time are clearing
And I begin to see
A rocking chair with Grandmama
And I'm upon her knee
I loved you dearly Grandmama
That I can recall
But love was lost those years ago
You died when I was small
And now that I am ageing
And have children of my own
I wish for them to know the joy
Of love that I had known
And when they grow and live their lives
And if they feel inclined
Maybe they'll remember me
Within the mists of time.

Val Harvey

Percy

Percy is fine
And he is mine
He's always there
To hug and care
He'll be my guide
Right by my side
Those big brown eyes
Those gentle sighs
We'll walk together
Through fields and heather
He's lots of fun
He brings the sun
When things are down
He'll not frown
Who is Percy?
My loving Corgi.

Mary Loader

The Wild Dog Rose

Strewn across the boundary hedgerow
And hanging down in trusses
Along the lanes and by the meadow
In June the Dog Rose blushes
Pink and White like a maidens cheek
Suffused with pure clean colour
A tranquil beauty modest and meek
Borne on a wild rose bower
In sunshine when a new day breaks
With petals wide open and inviting
The honey bee full advantage takes
Of the nectar sweet and delighting
Amongst the blossoms the song birds build
Safe and sound under a thorny shield

G. Edwards

Band Of Gold

There's gold in the mountain
And gold in the sea
But the gold on your finger
It means more to me
It's to say that I love you
It's to say that I care
And when ever you need me
I'll always be there
Together for always
In your arms I'll be.
For the gold on your finger
Is more precious to me.
And when we grow old
And have nothing to do
We can remember the good times
And what we used to go through
Together forever for eternity.
With the gold on your finger
That I gave to thee.

F. Briggs

Hope

I have travelled a lonely road
   and found it long
With heavy heart and purpose lost
   wondered on.

The joy and wisdom of loved ones
   missed by me.
Will there be happiness
   for me and mine.

Now, a ray of sunshine
   steady we go.
Like a ship sailing to still waters.
   with new hope aglow

Mary Hughes

My Son

My son, you mean the world to me,
And everything you do
Will always be a part of me,
And I a part of you.

I pray that I have given you
The strength and love you need
To rise above your problems,
And the courage to succeed.

The bond we have together
Will last our whole lives through,
I love you son so dearly
And I know you love me too.

Just share that love with others,
And you will surely find
A life that's filled with happiness,
And stands the test of time.

H. E. Blewitt

Feelings

Time takes away the heartache
and evens out the score.
Memories will linger on
when love goes out the door.

New life starting, on your way,
tomorrow is another day.
Tears are gone, temper ceded,
were you ever really needed?

Passing shadows in the night,
afraid to walk alone.
Ever turning, backwards glancing,
always looking, back to home.

Alone in life, to start again,
heartache gone, still feel the pain.
Drowned of drink, and of sorrow,
will there ever be a tomorrow?

You stand alone, you stand erect,
that knowing union was your wreck.
Where to go to ease your pain?
Back to life, and start again.

G. R. Green

Destiny

I love the world for what it is
And do not wish to leave it,
For why should I decide to go
Or God decide it for me.
But I do believe it must be He
Who has the final right,
To say that I must live
Or pass away this night.
For it is He who says you stay
And directs you what to do.
He knows the pain of what He does
For He has known it too.
He knows that love can hurt you so
Although He introduced it.
But love that's true will come too late
For those whose destiny He made it.
I do not believe that love like this
Is against what He dictates,
For we are surely not to blame
As it was He who ignited up the flame.

Patrick Baron

Mother Nature

I walk along the garden path
And as I look around
I see the trees and flowers in bloom
And a carpet of green and brown.
The birds are flying in the sky
So graceful, wild and free
They perch upon the garden fence
All looking down at me.
The bees are working very hard
Buzzing from flower to flower
Collecting pollen as they go
I could stand and watch for hours.
A colourful butterfly in the air
Fluttering in the breeze
It looks so pretty as it lands
On the branch of a willow tree.
I walk along the garden path
The sun shines clear and bright
The work of mother nature
Is such a wonderful sight.

Shirley Gleaves

Autumn

Suddenly it's Autumn
And a chill is in the air.
Where is breakfast in the garden
And bronzing bodies, if we dare?
Sadly now these are just memories
In the album of our mind,
As we set our sights on weather
Of a very different kind.
But how nature compensates us
With the canvas that we see,
Gleaming gold and rust and scarlet
From the crown of every tree.
It's time to undress the garden
And move flowers from all the tubs,
Replacing them with chubby bulbs
Which in spring will burst in buds.
It all comes round so quickly,
Each season that we know
But to me the days of Autumn
Have a very special glow.

Primrose Tingey

The Rainbow Of My Heart

A rainbow made just for you,
An omen of a love so true,
Never to die and fade away,
Forever in our hearts to stay.
No pot of gold at its end,
But a broken heart that you did mend,
A heart that now belongs to you,
Yours forever, yours so true.
A rainbow made just for you,
It whispers sweetly that I love you.
Never forget these words of truth,
As they whisper sweetly above the roof.
Words to be heard only by you,
From my heart and so true
The rainbow of my heart is yours,
Now, always and evermore.

W. S. Cowans

Your Face

Your face in the sky,
amongst the dark clouds,
your face in my mind,
a vision, love at first sight.

Forever radiant,
forever eternal,
a light in the dark
is your face in my life.

A flower of passion,
a ripple of pleasure,
and there on the moon,
our two faces radiant together.

J. K. Steel

Yesterday

Photos which I have of you
Capture forever in them your smile.
My own photographic image
I hope you somewhere file.
I know I should kiss yesterday's now
    gone goodbye,
But if I said this I was going to do,
it would be a lie.
Wherever you are, please kiss me
Sometime, or she who is now me.
And if you are making love to her
think of us and how it used to be.
Then look across your shoulders;
I am always close behind.
Though you cannot reach my body,
you can always reach my mind.

Paula Marten

From Me To You!

Mum you held us so close,
all wrapped up warm;
You laid us down at dusk
'till dawn!
You brought us up with a
memory or two,
But my special memory is the
one of you!
A mum is someone who means
a lot,
A mum is one who is never
forgot!
I want you to know, I'm thinking
of you.
And just let me know when
you think of me too!
This is a message long overdue,
sent with love from me to you.

Maria E. Oldfield

God Cares

In a crowd
All alone.
Who knows me?
Who cares?

In my home
All alone.
Who visits me?
Who shares?

In the workplace
All alone.
Who supports me?
Who gives?

In my worship
All alone.
Who consoles me?
Who lives?

Pauline Turner

The Church

Who, what, why and where?
And what do you want with me?
For I'm not going anywhere
And that is plain to see.
My roots are founded sure and deep
With love and peace for all.
Then at His name just bend the knee
And for His mercy call.
My doors are always open wide
No change is made, so step inside.
Bend the knee and bow the head,
Go where His footsteps led.

Violet Cowley

Of A Ship-In-A-Bottle

A pirate ship no longer free
Condemned to sail a lifeless sea
A flag, three sails, in wonder stand
Still'd by the movement of a hand
No breeze has sent this ship away
To plunder, steal, for many a day
Becalmed she stands inside her cell
Corked, imprisoned by the spell
No more to sail the stormy main
Or proudly fly her flag again
That fearsome flag of black and white
Upholding wrong, condemning right
The last is, sure, the reason why
She sails a sea now wooden, dry,
Remaining always on that sea
Transfixèd for eternity.

Mary Edwards

The Prisoners

You and I are similar
Alike in many ways
We sit and think of many things
To try and fill the days

A letter to write
A crossword to do
Someone come and talk to me
It really does not matter who!

Both of us are locked away
You in your cell, me in mine
Staring at the four walls
Trying to pass the time

The difference is that I am free
Or so the people think
They do not know that each new day
May cause my heart to sink

My cell, it is one I have built myself, as only lover's can
My only crime - to fall in love, with this special man
Soon I hope we will both be free, I pray to heaven above
You, the prisoner of the state, me, the one of love!

H. Warne

How To Make A Healthy Body

Take a handful of salad and stir,
Add a litre of water and boil,
For ten minutes,
Meanwhile get a clean bowl,
Add to it a healthy heart,
Sprinkle over a litre of blood,
And let the heart soak in,
For five minutes,
Next take out the salad,
Give it a last stir,
Cut open the heart
Put in the salad
Then bake for an hour,
(if you want it strong store overnight)
Then mix in vital organs as well as the heart,
Throw those into a saucepan
As well as the leftover blood,
Cook these for an hour,
Next take out the bad parts
Like drugs and alcohol
Then you should have
  a healthy human body.

Sinead Hassett

Untitled

Here I lie, I am wide awake,
and I'm still learning.
Helpless in the passion of my
yearning, in amongst the
trees so wise.
I gaze of years and of
witches burning, mystics from
centuries past still linger in
the mind, casting shadows
over the eyes of the blind and
taunting the sight of the sane.
Freedom from the heart of my
desire, treacherous journeys
travelled into the inevitable
fire still haunt through the night.
The dawn returns
and healing sight, banishing
witches and mystics, cast
to the shadows in the darkness
of a hollow light.

V. Jones-Morris

Everything Has Something

A book has its words
A writer has his pen.
An artist has his brush
Poetry has its meaning
Music has its rhythm
Every flower has a scent
Every tree has a branch
The wind has its breath.
Every voice has an echo
Our heart has its beat.
Food has its taste
Water has its purity.
Animals have their families
Families have their love.
But only the dancers
Have themselves.

Patricia Lewis

A Harebell

A mere pencil-stroke;
A waif, wisp, whim;
Scarce registering colour;
Incapable of losing grace,
Though petals and leaves
Falter and fall,
Draping themselves
In elegant posturing,
Sinuous stems spilling
Into continuous fluidity,
Poise balancing counterpoise
With daring dalliance;
Such stammering advocacy,
Making so ineffable
An understatement.

Mavis Hanson

What Should I Do?

Do I listen to you,
  a voice of one.
Or do I go with my feelings
  of doubt.
And a bloody big choir?

A choir singing in loud voice...
  that you are being untrue to me.

I know what I will do -
I will turn down the volume
  of that choir
And listen to that voice of one.

  Because I want to believe you
  Because I love you.

J. Slattery

Vital Statistic

You're only a statistic,
A fact numerically,
Only one of many,
Collected systematically.

You're a splash in the ocean,
A lonely face in a crowd,
A straw in a haystack,
A wisp of a cloud.

But I would ride pillion,
With my man in a million,
Into the future unknown;
Only looking ahead,
Not a tear would I shed,
As we entered the twilight zone.

You may only be a statistic,
But it's plain for all to see,
Without you I'd be nothing,
You're a vital part of me.

Maggie Novotni

Fortitude

She's New!
A twinkle, but a fading star.
Not one to withstand procrastination
She'll cry
And when her tears dry
...As they will!
He'll sidle on back to me.
I am not fickle
As he would surely advocate.
It takes strength and determination
... to 'always' be there
When life's storms blow him off his feet
Again he'll find solace in my world.
When torment corrodes his thoughts
And desperation courses through his veins
He'll sit once more.... 'with me'....by the fire side
And presuppose that... 'this time'... I understand.

Marianne Bullen

A View Of The Past

Adjacent to my office door
A stable block that is now a store
The old clock tower
No longer chimes
A monument to bygone times
Of horses' hoofs upon cobbled stone
And carriage wheels
That bring you home
To the manor house
With a big log fire
A glass of punch
And then to retire
To a four poster bed
With curtains drawn
Then sleep away
The hours till dawn
A chorus of birds
To start your day
It's nice to think
That it was that way.

F. A. Waugh

Toy Soldiers

His fair tousled head bent low
Above the polished floor,
His leaden army skilfully placed
Were ready now for 'war'.

I smiled upon his happy face,
Maternal pride within me swelled.
Sweet innocence in God's fair world;
A seed of fear I quelled.

Long since those gallant little men
Within their box were laid,
Across the sandy desert wastes
A bloodier battle's played.

The fair hair now is tinged with grey,
Gone the childish glee.
"Please God", I pray, "forgive them
and bring him home to me."

The leaden army snugly smiles
Inside their metal tin.
The seed they'd sown so long ago
In men — had grown within.

E. Combellack

Blondie

I remember you with joy.
A plump and golden bundle,
A wild, engaging sprite;
A canine child.
Faithful playmate.

I remember you with love.
A beauty in your prime,
A free and fearless spirit.
An endless appetite!
Loyal friend.

I remember you with tears.
A strong, unceasing fighter
As age pursued its final path.
A dignified demise.
Beloved companion.

I remember you with pride.
A friend for life who left
A legacy of love for me,
As years go by.
Sweet memory.

D. Pamela Wills

The Modern Teenager

She was in her teens,
A girl of lowly means,
Her skin was like silk,
The colour of white mink.

She walked with a sway
That took one's breath away.
Her eyes shone like the stars,
As bright as the planet Mars.

She was a pleasure to be near,
Her patter was fine and clear,
She knew how to entertain,
All for fun and not for gain.

A happy-go-lucky girl,
Who had her friends in a twirl.
But the best part of her life
Was that she would make a good wife.

J. Leighton

Lovers No More

Alone I look
Alone I stare
He may glance back
But do I care
For many years
I loved you so
Now it's time
For you to go
Alone I'll be
Just like before
Do I care
Not anymore
For I know
Our love has died
Mistakes I made
Tears I cried
But now it's over
Time to part
With always a memory
Here in my heart

Tracey Bourne

Loneliness

Loneliness is isolation,
A feeling that isn't there,
An empty void of desolation,
No-one else can share.

Loneliness is dark and hollow,
A cave that leads to nowhere,
An aching path no-one can follow,
No-one else can share.

Loneliness is an empty space,
Big and black with room to spare,
It's ever vacant, there's no trace,
No-one else can share.

A huge dark chasm, black as night,
A winding tunnel cold and bare,
No sense of being or of light,
All alone - who wants to share?

Valda Teasdale

A Country Walk

Whilst walking down
A country lane
In England I did see
A really beautiful butterfly
As colourful as could be

It fluted over flowers
Where the sun shone so bright
I sat down in the meadow
To gaze at this wondrous sight
A hawk flew high above me
In a cloudless sky of blue
A rabbit ran across the meadow
Then disappeared out of view

A thought then came into my head
As I started to settle down
How lucky I was to be born
In the country, not in a town

Robert E. Bates

'Beloved'

I'd simply like to say 'Beloved'
A simple word that comes to mind.
Beloved, I've never found.
To search in vain and back again.
Beloved, where are you?

Reality, the break of day.
Our dreams now shut away.
My beloved appeared, I saw him
 Passing by.
Who was he? I cry.
Beloved, only a word
 I know.
So why am I searching so?
One life to find him;
 It's getting late.
Beloved, do you believe in fate?

Pamela Blackburn

The Real And Wayward Dreams

The real and wayward dreams,
A broken path of pleasure,
Confronts my waking mind,
Skeletons line in carpet
The path I seek to bind.

Uncertainly surrounds me,
But so the way of life,
An infant artist,
An unconscious exuberance,
The perverse I secretly entice.

Duel oppositions approach in unison,
Fighting for peace with each,
The true anima hides beneath the blood,
Narcissistic emotions naked on a beach.

Forbidden in reality,
The dark caves of the primal soul,
The lost murmurs of effrontery,
Tortured desires repressed explode.

Paul MacKenzie

A New Life

Where did you come from
 Were you a shining star
Twinkling in the distance
 Did you have to travel far?

Maybe you were the rainbow
 When the storm was gone
Giving us the hope and strength
 So we could carry on

Were you a drop of purest rain
 Landing in the desert plain
Or the warm sun on a winters day
 To help us along when the skies were grey

Perhaps you were the song bird
 That came to us at dawn
Waking us so gently from
 Our slumbers deep and warm

Where ever you came from we welcome you
 A precious life all brand new
A gift so rare, so pure, so sweet.
 You made our happiness complete

Evelyn Howard

The Gentle-Man

He gave me life, that gentleman.
 A gift that's made from love
As he held me in his arms
 God looked from up above.

I held his hand each step I took
 He showed me right from wrong
I know he was my hero
 So gentle yet so strong.

I feel him close beside me
 Wherever I should go
Still trying to teach me
 The things that I should know.

If I could only thank him
 For all the love I had
And tell him that I love him
 The Gentleman, my Dad.

D. R. Challis

Grandad's Gripes

"I just can't gerra roaad thru" says Grandad from his bed
Oh father stop your griping or you'll send me off me ead
Can't you think of summat else or play another tune
Yer at it early morning 'till late in't afternoon
"It's alreet tho for thee lass, I might `ave gorra stoppage"
Oh come on Father, don't be daft, just eat a bit more porridge
That'll help you on your way, I'm sure of it you'll see
But if it won't, don't worry, we'll find another remedy
Next morning dawns and Grandad's still as miserable as sin
"I've still not ad a roaad thru' lass" - Oh here we go agen
By this time mother's had enough and seeks medical advice
Back from the Doctor's surgery she's sure this will suffice
Nurse'll be here tomorrow, they think an enema's the answer
"Oh there's no need fer that lass, stop worryin', don't banter —
   I'm sure I'll be okay"
His attitude so quickly changed from that of yesterday
A few hours pass and Grandad seems to rapidly recover
The sound of toilet flushing
Peace at last — for Grandad and my mother
The moral of this story is "It's the thought that counts"
   P. M. Nutton

Progress

The look Ben gave was scathing, his voice a tortured sigh...
"Oh come on Gran," he muttered, "You've got to really try!"
"It's alien boy," I answered, "I haven't got a clue....
The guide book is just useless, I don't know what to do!"

Robert, younger by a year, just grinned and looked away.
"Will YOU help me?" I grovelled, "I'll get it right one day."
With a glance that mirrored pity, he went through it all once more
As my feeble brain ticked over, they bolted for the door.

Because time and tide and football, and roller blades and bikes,
were more important to them than teaching ancient types,
and loyalty to Granny... although the pull was strong,
paled into distant memory when play friends came along.

It took a four year old named Joe to lay it on the line.
"You press this, and you move that" - at least he had the time
to sit and show his Granny, who is desperate to learn the
technology and science on which the world now turns.

Inspired by his child-like trust that I wasn't really thick,
and driven on by husbands bet... "You'll NEVER master it!!"
They day came when Joe's work paid off, the stage was really set.
I booted up and logged on to, THE GLOBAL INTERNET!!
   K. R. Jones

Moon Dream Sequel

Yearn not my child for an unfinished dream
Of when Moon left you on that autumn night,
Deep in the forest, in the small folk's care,
You held to his cloak as he took flight,
Minus a rag end with dawn coming near.
   Fast fading the beam.
Though promises made are sometimes broken,
P'haps elven friends are expecting you soon,
Back where they helped you off silver-boat Moon.
But, can you return once you've been woken?

And did you not glean that when bright Moon beckoned
You, sleep-eyed, away on a late night ride,
He would be your boat, scimitar gleaming;
Unbreaking the sleep though your mind's open wide,
Making exciting this your first dreaming?
   Expecting a second.
Cherish all innocence — for a while yet.
Moon didn't deceive you. There was no mistake
But, whilst touching your sleep before day's break
He has taught wisdom before your ways are set.
   Richard B. Callum

Don't Stop Believing

Too many confused illusions
Of the way things ought to be
Do we stop believing in dreams
And face up to reality

Tomorrow is full of promise
Your fortune could lie inside
But it's just another day for many
Who are only there for the ride

Ambition can be hard work
If your goal is achieved it's worthwhile
For being happy with the thought of success
It's worth going that extra mile

Dissatisfied with living
Then death is your other choice
Never suffer in silence
Let God hear the sound of your voice
   Mosty Gaillard

Nostalgia

Were they real or did we dream
Of the homes that once we knew,
When we were young our homes were old.
   This alas was true,
I now perceive an empty space
Where once our houses stood,
And I sometimes wish we could rebuild
   the dear old neighbourhood,
The price of progress is so great
   and always aims to please,
yet I often like to reminisce
   among my memories
Now when at last my time comes
   and my memories are no more,
There will always be others who,
   themselves will have
   memories by the score.
   Thomas E. Irwin

Chess

The things in my head are a whirling mess
Of tangled up knots and a game of chess.
My part seems to vary, the piece never the same,
As I win, and then lose in this one long game.
A Queen for a minute, a pawn for a day,
'Til a knight comes along and whisks me away.
Each move that I make turns a page of my book,
Each role that I play gives me one more look;
A look at the inside and outside of me,
And people that surround, and things I can see.
But sometimes the pages get ripped or torn
'Til I turn to the next and my name is reborn.
I'll go endlessly on, playing who? I don't know
In an all-singing, all-dancing
One woman show.
I am the woman
I am the game
Trying to write my own name.
   Ruth Elisabeth Neilson

Soul Mates

We have lived on earth before
Not just one life, but many more,
I look into your eyes and find
My soul mate — one of a like mind
Death is our friend, not cruel fate
It would not such true love separate
We do not know when we began
Or of our journeys through the past
One day we'll know, in God's good time,
And we'll be home at last.
   Vera Prentis

The Tragic Tree

Whenever I walked past this tree, I was conscious of a strange sense
of sorrow and compassion which was singularly intense

I looked up at the foliage and saw one branch bare of sprig and leaf,
It was scarred and withered, and exuded shock and disbelief.

I spent an hour looking at the ground below this withered limb
spawned by this very ancient tree that spoke of past action grim

On going to the library I found a book on past and present history
and in particular this ancient heath, and reference to this tree

At last I found the cause of this tree's disturbing emanation,
it was the result of lynching, a foul misguided perpetration.

It transpired that a young female was murdered in eighteen
   forty three.
A local farm worker was falsely accused, and hung from this very tree.

When I researched the name of the man who from this bough
   was suspended,
it laid the ghost of my unease. From him I was several times
   descended.
   D. J. Webb

Early Bird

A Japanese exquisite scene
Of purest art on fine silk screen,
Artist's palette of barely blues
And softly greys — all pearly hues,
A confection of spun-sugar strands
Fashioned by unearthly hands?
'Tis but a spider's gossamer skill
His patient toiling frosted white,
Whilst half the world is sleeping still,
By will o' wisp in dead of night.
A sweet enticement to the eye
Of early risers such as I.
Then strident colours of the dawn,
Bleed through the canvas sky of morn.
Ethereal silks melt away
Before the coming of the day
And pre-dawn, fading, slips away.
   G. Y. Chestney

A Memory Made In Heaven

I have this picture of heaven, a free and peaceful fantasy,
Of pearly gates and gorgeous love a world in harmony,
This fantasy brings me joy like a warm embrace,
'Cause when I think of heaven I often see your face,
It's a kind of sad happiness that brings a tear to my eye,
For your peace I'm happy, for myself I cry,
Your life was long and plentiful, you lived it to your best,
But soon, your heart got tired and now you are at rest,
I still talk to you sometimes when life is hard to comprehend,
I feel a kind of comfort though my darkest night descends,
The times we spent so priceless something money just can't buy,
And though you're now in heaven I know my memories won't die,
Our memories were made in heaven, memories I'll never forget,
'Cause they bring a ray of hope to me though I feel upset,
But I'm missing you like crazy and it's tearing me apart,
But my dearest man you'll never leave this home here in my heart,
I love you so much, my sweet angel, in that I take console,
Forever in my loving thoughts God rest your beautiful soul.
   Theresa Elizabeth Hughes

Venus In Transit

Ovion stumbles, chained to the hunt
of brighter jewels or a darker night,
now time has made his weapons blunt
and forced the Gods to flight.

Around her we pass, the worlds rush on
in vain, unheeding that pale gaze
which illuminates the carved bone
of endless yesterdays.
   D. Shade

If Only You Could Hear Me

O children of the poorer lands who know
   of nothing else,
I look at things from where I live and
   cannot understand.

I sometimes think that we are lost in
   politics and grief,
But when I turn my thoughts to you
   it's somewhat disbelief.

I will never understand how you suffer
   in this way,
When people in the richer lands have
   plenty every day.

But we cannot choose our origin and
   therefore can't accept
Why some of us have everything and
   some have nil or less.
   Maureen Such

Lost At Sea

Crackle-faint the forecast,
Of lightning, winds gale-force.
"All hands on deck and anchor fast,
Before we're blown off course!"

The wind in blustery squalls,
And waves that lash the mast.
In heaving nets the fish are trawl'd,
And deckwards slither-cast.

Lashed fast to rope and line,
Together, we, as one.
The decks awash with blood and brine,
Of fish, ton after ton.

Appease the raging force!
Return to the sea a gift!
Before your boat loses course,
Before you run adrift.

Beyond familiar Quayside,
Your loved ones overwhelm.
Carried on the back of a high tide,
And no-one at the Helm.
   Verity Rosas

Autumn Days

The trees that sway in the gentle breeze
Red, gold and brown the coloured leaves
Like jewels in a crown that shine and glow
They flutter from the trees to the earth below

The ground is covered like a patchwork quilt
As summer plants start to die and wilt
Nuts and berries hidden in the leaves
By birds and squirrels are soon retrieved

Birds are singing their farewell song
As autumn ends they will be soon gone
The days get shorter, the nights are long
Migrating birds come join the throng

Small and large the creatures scurry
To prepare for winter is their hurry
Plants and animals go to sleep
Through winter when the snow is deep

Autumn winds begin to blow
To let you know that there will soon be snow
Farewell to summer, but new life will grow
As trees and plants their seed will sow
   Fay Stanton

A Father's Love

I remember soft images of childhood
Of fun and family and friends
River banks, tall bull rushes
Of peace and happiness
A time when these things ruled;
Being loved and wanted
Sharing and togetherness
Tender touches, tender guidance
Deep roots of care, of being the very special one
A foundation on which to build a wonderful life;
Through the ups and downs
Those memories have borne me through
Without me even knowing;
I sought a return to those feelings
Now seeing my son, I realize we are all children
Ever learning, ever erring, being hurt and hurting
Always growing, always changing
But always needing to be loved;
And although there's no love harder
There's no love greater than that of a man's father
   Paul Davies

The Magic Of Night

They know more than I of magical scenes
Of cauldrons bubbling with nasty things
they see more at night when I'm asleep
of magic places with secrets to keep

Under the purple black of moonlit skies
a dusting of stars and faraway cries
they find their way to a hidden place
where shadows dance with midnight grace

There, they hear in the dead of night
the chanting songs of sacred rites
that would chill us mortals to the bone
the ancient words once carved in stone

These feline creatures with eyes so wide
see many things they choose to hide
worlds enchanted and spells of old
legendary tales that some were told

My familiars then returns at dawn
by my side they stretch and yawn
then hide away their nightly powers
and wait once more for the witching hour.
   Paula Stedman

Fallen Petals

It started as a tiny bud,
O! such a thrill to watch it grow.
It blossomed to a deep deep red,
A ruby in a flower-bed.

The dew each morning kissed its face,
Its perfume wafted on the breeze,
What joy to have in one's collection
A flower of such pure perfection.

But like all things, as time went by
Its beauty had begun to fade,
Until there came that fated day
When on the ground the petals lay.

The jewel has left the flower-bed,
That lovely rose is now no more,
What sadness on the day you found
Those petals scattered all around.

And life can seem just like that rose
If you have lost your dearest love,
Those precious moments filled with pleasure,
Like fallen petals...gone forever.
   Marjorie Povey

The Mist Cleared

The scene was grey at the dawn of day,
Nowhere at all was a chink in the pall
Of Mist; as it swirled around, from the roofs to the ground
Covering everything from sight, that should have been light,
After the darkness of night.

Slowly as time passed, the grey became imbued
And opalescent hued, clearing in a blaze of light
The Mist; the rising Sun shone down so bright
On filmy cobwebs decorated with diamonds of moisture,
Decked with jewels were pasture, trees, flowers, all of Nature.

The Sun shone so bright, after the darkness of night,
With beauty rainbow hued, its beams a wondrous sight,
The Mist; clearly unsubdued, clung with might as a right
To the shadowed remnants of the night,
Before giving way to the Sun's mastery of day.
   Rita Yuen

Poor Arabella Fussell-Clowes

Once upon a time in our village you could buy freshly-baked bread
Now the Fussell-Clowes are here, there's pot-pourri instead

O Hunters and Barbours and saddle soap
All is not well, Arabella can't cope
Because, like the ill-fated tower of the Genisitic fable
Badly built was Coriander's stable

Now Arabella is in a bit of a to do
Mummy won't engage a tradesman and Tuck the handyman has flue

Then there's to be that beastly school trip to Norwich -
to the Noverre
To watch a film with sub-titles called Le Famine Pomme De Terre

Pity she couldn't just bugger off to London - to lodge
With her sister who works in the City at Barclay De Zante Hodge

But what then of the things she likes most to do
Hearing her favourite bands in Norwich,
at Kearney's Rendezvous
Big Girl's Blouse, Gallic Shrug, Mud On Road
Spending the night in North Walsham with hunky Nick Garrood

And she would miss helping mummy in her shop called
Paraphernalia
Selling Shaker furniture and artifacts and Driza Bones from Australia

O Hunters and Barbours and saddle soap
Things will soon improve for Arabella, we hope
   I. J. Duncan

Brave Commitment To The Moment Of Truth

All party on the tenth of June
Prospect of building, rather than ruin

Entrenched distrust must be put on hold
Political capital needs to be bold

The prize is so nearly within our grasp
Please be a dove and not an asp

Surely it is worth the extra mile?
To impede progress would be vile

Build bridges so solid they will never flounder
So slowly trust can then become rounder

The weightless wonder of freedom for all
Everyone trying so hard to walk tall

It has not been easy, is too simple to say
When lives have been lost, in the horror of the day

So learn the lessons of the past
And nail the flag of peace to mast.
   Rita Gardiner

Farewell Brother Dear

Brother dear, you've fought so well, against all odds you've stood,
Now it's time to face the end, somehow you knew you would,
I watched how hard you struggled, amazed how hard you tried,
Heard your hollow laughter, how helplessly you cried,
It's hard to say farewell, to let you rest at last,
The future bleak without you there, remembering the past,
If things could be different, and life could be replaced,
The bitter tears I cry for you, I'd never have to taste,
Please don't feel you stand alone, our hearts are joined as one,
And with the final breath you take, my life will come undone,
My brother, with each passing day, I know I'll miss you more,
Longing now to hear your voice, and see your face once more,
You've left so much behind you, so many things unsaid,
Words expressing how I feel keep passing through my head,
I can't help feeling like I do, I wish this pain would leave,
The feeling that my heart will burst, while deep inside I grieve,
The emptiness you left behind, will not be full again,
Memories of your life with us, I pray will ease the pain.
Paul Clark

They Can't Help It

Those little creatures used to suckle
Now in those crates their legs do buckle
Lost all dignity now known as veal
Just to provide an unneeded meal

Transported miles in some cramped death Lorry
For their hunger and thirst I feel so sorry
No longer in fields or with their mother
Now sentenced to a short life in which they'll suffer

I wish we could go back in time
For everyone to have an idea like mine
To set them free, to let them go
To watch nature and let them grow

Is it so important they adorn your plate
Please think of them for their sake
Are you prepared to make a stand
If we all did, this would be banned.
M. Colella

The Long Sleep, Maybe?

I've been laid here to rest
Now I'm with all the best
So I can concentrate on my sorrow
I look up to the sky
Remember times that go by
And wonder how much time I can borrow

Eyes closed I fight
Try as I might
All around me there's a crowd
I've been here so long
My friends are so strong
But upstairs the music's so loud

For the time that I long
But the light is so strong
The rector has returned to his home
For my journey I'm bold
The air has turned cold
The eternal, I lie here alone
Steven Hirst

Full Circle

When all is dry as dust, scorched and parched
No respite from the days and nights of heat,
What joy the rain, cool breeze and splashing rill
And ice cream such a blissful treat.

Then winter comes and snow and ice hold sway
Shivering, pinched, frost - nipped our ways
Such comfort then from heat in which to wallow
And long to live again the summer days.
E. R. Wollington

Solitude

I loved too well.
Now he has gone and I am left in
a vast abysmal pit to call my own.
"Life must go on", they say,
I live, I laugh, I love,
And the dismal facade of life goes by,
Until comes the great day,
When I hear his warm and magic voice:
"You are not there,
You are with me, my wife,
and we will walk again together, you and I."
B. E. Rivett

A New Dimension

It is not death I fear, but the manner of my decline
Now causes me to shed a tear for dignity that was mine.
Treat my body with affection for it has served me very well,
When I go to a new dimension and leave behind an empty shell.
Will velvet darkness enfold me, or shining light lead down a lane
Point the way and mould me, to suit some high or lower plane.
Perhaps I'll be the dog acquired the very day that I expired,
A bird with a lovely song to sing, a butterfly passing on the wing.
The subtle perfume of a bride's bouquet, a supernatural apport
Maybe a horse or even a flea, don't swat that fly, it could be me!
Ruth Lyne

Spring

Frost, snow and bitter winds have said goodbye
Now bleak grey landscapes slowly change to green
Each day there's something new to greet the eye

Like caterpillars hanging out to dry
Soft catkins on the willow tree are seen
Frost, snow and bitter winds have said goodbye

Small fledglings wobble as they try to fly
While cheeky starlings chatter as they preen
Each day there's something new to greet the eye

Sparse coated lambs from cold no longer die
White pearly blossom trembles on the gean
Frost, snow and bitter winds have said goodbye

A squirming squeeze of piglets fills the sty
Tired honey bees must tend and groom the queen
Each day there's something new to greet the eye

Chill spitting rain comes jetting from the sky
Fused rainbow colours show their opal sheen
Frost, snow and bitter winds have said goodbye
Each day there's something new to greet the eye.
Mary Rea

The Way Of Life

All alone on that dreadful day,
Nothing was spoken, no words to say,
Looking around that empty house,
Thinking about my lover, my spouse.
Thoughts in my mind of those lovely years,
My eyes are red, and full of tears,
Thinking of many ways in which I could die,
Just breaks me up, and makes me cry.
She said she loved me, but she could not stay,
She's gone with her lover, they've ran away,
I'm afraid to go out, I've lost my wife,
This damned woman is ruining my life
I realize now it wasn't meant to be,
My life has changed, it's so plain to see.
I've got so many friends, there's so much to do,
My life is full, there's no more feeling blue.
I've now met someone, someone completely new,
She makes me happy, she's so beautiful, so true,
I'm on a cloud, and floating above,
Now I'm so excited, and yes, I've fallen in love.
T. Austin

Peace

Will there ever be peace on earth
nothing could pay the price it's worth
Do the IRA know suffering and pain
is death and destruction their gain

How would they feel if their families were dead
if England planted bombs in Ireland instead
I'm sure they would be full of disgust and hate
I wonder how high killings would then rate

Blowing up buildings, buses and trains
innocent victims found in the remains
Guildford, Brighton, London anywhere they can
the dead include children, women and man

What is peace asks little girls and boys
what is playing safe in the streets with our toys
Is all our family safe for the day
how did they die, where do they lay

Please pray we get peace before we all die
let us live on this planet like clouds in the sky
Am I asking to much for my little plea
No bombing wars or fighting is what I'd like to see
   Tina E. Down

Mirror

I look in the mirror and what do I see?
Not you, him, or her but me,

I look in the mirror and what do I see?
Freckles, freckles, yes, yes, it's me!

My eyes are green,
Just tiny pins in the middle,
I don't look mean,
My teeth in a fiddle,

My hair is dark blonde,
My lips pale peach,
And my arms which reach right down to my feet,
And not forgetting my very sweet nose,
So when I look in the mirror, I'll be sure to see me!
   Yes me! only me!

If you look in the mirror,
You'll see your own face,
Just like everyone would in the human race.

No one else can look in the mirror and see me
'Cos we're all different and individuals you see.
   Natasha Coombes

A Child's Loving

As they gather round, the burials completed,
Not wanting to believe what's happened,
Not wanting to let go of his face,
Peoples smiles and happiness,
Blown away in the gentle wind.

Through all the mourning and sorrow,
A child stands there so still,
Holding on to the flowers,
Wondering why he's gone.

She has more sense than the adults,
Remembering what he was like,
Holding on to the good times,
Washing the bad out of sight.

She wonders why people fight
With their guns of pain and fright,
Piercing through hearts that were once warm and loving.

She knows this is not the first time,
She knows she'll go through it again,
But as she puts the flowers to her heart,
She remembers those bright summer days.
   Susan Anderson

"No One Can Own Her"

No one can own her, my Lovely Fiona,
Not me, who bore her with pain —
New life to begin,
   With horizons anew.
May there be more sunshine than rain.

No one can own her,
   My lovely Fiona,
Not even the husband so new.
She will love and adore him,
   do the impossible for him,
But to herself she will always be true.

No one can own her, my Lovely Fiona,
Not even the children she bears —
She will love and protect them,
   chastise and correct them,
Be the one who constantly cares —

Only one can own her, My Lovely Fiona —
That is God in his heaven above.
May his light shine upon her, as she travels along,
With her path filled with joy, and much love.
   Pamela Richards

Last Night

At the moment I feel nothing
Not love nor hate, pity or lust
Nothing except this unyielding empty void
that hungers deep within me.

Your devouring passions have sucked dry my emotions
and now, left for dead, scorching
in the hot arid sun of burning desire
I crawl on blooded stumps mile upon pain wrenched mile
without form or direction
inside this vast dark wilderness

My youth was lost in the high turbulent winds of time
then blown across the empty husk of virginal innocence

Disembowelled and consumed
The essence of my life stains red
The asylum's wall of reality

Then trickles, slowly

Into the cold blue abyssal of experience
Where I, drifting listlessly, feel only
the soft lapping waves of your memory
and the fathomed depths of your loss
   Trevor Garrud

The Unborn Child

We all are waiting expectantly
Not just the future mother, father,
but grandparents and other relations too
We long to welcome you into the world
To see your face, feel your soft cheeks
To hold you tight
And sing you to sleep at night.

We only have your pictures from the scanning machine,
a puzzle of black and white but no problem they said
But we see your shape now, you the unborn
with tiny limbs and rounded head.

You move gently in your warm and safe place
Making a flutter
But soon it will be a splutter
as you pass through
into the world
Where we all wait to welcome you.
   P. N. Jeffery

The Anniversary

By Edgehill field two men dared venture upon a scene,
not believing of those who had before been.
The air grew colder the closer they crept
and they began to wish that in bed they slept.

The mist formed silently amidst the trees,
the night creatures moved stealthily about at ease.
The silence was broken by a loud report
and strange shapes shifting formed ready for sport.

In the first flash of light the sabres shone bright,
the pikes were raised high and the horses did die.
The cannon roared loud, the muskets did score
and line after line the gallant ran fore.

Line after line they fell to the ground,
line after line their blood spilt around.
The wounded did cry and the valiant did die,
the hour seemed long and time was all wrong.

The two that had dared stood shaking and scared,
for the armies there led had long since been dead.
Next year they say, indoors they will stay.
The ghostly hour passed and the peace came at last.
Stuart G. Mountford

The Parting

I know not why you seem to me to be so much less fair,
Nor why those eyes no longer hold beauty hidden there
   In dark pools of loveliness.
Your face not long ago, I thought, held unsurpassed joys,
I know not why my love should fade nor why fair beauty cloys
   As poppies in loneliness.

Reproach me not to faithfulness, think not of me with hate,
I gaze for love and cannot find the beauty that of late
   I always found in you.
Though in your eyes where once shone joy, regret there I can see,
It will not mar the joy we knew — tomorrow cannot be
   A day that I will rue.

Let's call it a day, you and I, bid each other adieu —
We had our Heaven together till disenchantment drew
   Its veil with gentle pain.
What can I try to do or say in making my amends?
When we were all in all 'twould be trite to say be friends.
   No! — We will not meet again!
G. A. Edwards

" Optimism "

Love does not shudder at improbability,
Nor shrink from the unlikeliness.
But like a balloon filled with its own breeze
Floats —
Suspended on the hope of ever soaring upwards.
Wendy Parkyn

Reflexion

Nobody understand my feelings,
Nobody understand my thoughts;
In my laughter and my tears,
I find my consolation.....

For peace and love, I must try
and with my soul: To justice arrive.
Not looking back, with valour and courage,
my life deliver at last.....

I am a reflex of love;
through my veins run, the current of fear.
My heart is in my mind,
and my heaven is the perfection......

My body is the universe
My soul is the sun
My eyes the stars
and my mind is God......
Max Bruno

Lonely

Nobody to make the place untidy anymore,
Nobody to badger me with questions by the score,
Silence, like a monster, stalks about the house all day,
Everywhere's deserted. No friends have come to play.

The toys stand neatly, row on row; his bedroom still is tidy.
It's never been like that before, especially on Friday.
On Friday all the toys were out and Mark and John came round,
But now the house is quiet. Indoors there's not a sound.

There's no-one now to 'help' me as I peg the washing out,
There's no-one now to answer back when I get cross and shout,
No little hand in mine the way it used to be before,
No dirty little footprints on the just-washed kitchen floor.

"Bye Mum" he yelled and off he went and part of me went too,
The part that loves a little boy in spite of what he'll do.
I've forgiven all the tantrums and forgotten all the noise,
I'm lonely now he's gone to school with the other 'grown-up' boys.
Valerie Sutton

Kath

You are going on a journey, I don't know why
Nobody knows when but we all want to cry.
Because you've been with us all for such a long time
And to let you see how much we love you surely is no crime.
You've fought really hard for oh so very long
We've tried to cheer you up — to keep being strong
But the battle now is over and very soon you'll see
There'll be no more pain or suffering, at last you will be free
With a face that is happy, but for us it will be sad
When at last the way is open to go and meet your Dad.
The tears that we shed are because you've gone away
When in fact all that we wanted is to have you stay.
We don't want to lose you but deep within our hearts
We know you can't carry on; it's time for us to part.
Now we will watch as the tide slowly ebbs away
With the sun sinking down, quietly melts the day
Little by little your light is going down
Then soon all that you'll feel is love all around
And now the journey's over and you're on the other side
Your Dad will be there with his arms held open wide.
Sue Bonning

Untitled

In this world of broken dreams
nothing in life is as it seems
we do things that we should do
we leave things that we should do too
we take things for granted every day
both in our work and in our play
what a wonderful place
this world would be
if we all lived together in harmony
no violence or wars
that would be grand
then peace could reign
in this fair land
Peter Edward Waires Briggs

Priceless Gift

Humour, said the wise old man,
Now the right sort it be the spice of life.
There's the dry, the witty, and the sarcastic kind
The last one aims to wound like a knife.
This be the lower form of wit
Only big headed, small minded, insecure tribe use this
Making it a habit will gather many enemies no doubt
And to amazement find friends they are without
So take warning you who would practice lower wit
Lest one day no one's there to practice wit with
So if you want to be humorous, have friendship in mind
Forget about lower one
Use the brain God gave you
Pick one of the other kind
Winifred McCluskey

" The Horse "

I witnessed not, at the sweet birth, in stable rude and bare.
No warmth of horses' breath encompassed him, I was not there.
I who from time to time, have borne proud kings in pomp and state
and into battle charged that sealed whole nation's fate.
Though ox and ass and sheep all played a part

No horses were present at the coming of the king, no kin of mine
flexed sharpened ear to hear the angel sing. I bore no kings to
make their offerings fair of gold, frankincense and myrrh.

I did not gaze in awe upon the sleeping face, no room at inn
for theblest holy pair, no place for horse at miracle so rare, I
did not hear the glad hosanna's cry, while brother ass did take
the saviour by. No palm-strewn streets did mark my presence
there. I was not in the milling throng, that pushed and jostled,
with hatred in their hearts, that screamed the awful shout of
"CRUCIFY!" Yet when he staggered 'neath the awful weight
of cross not so, to ease the burden should they so command,
yet when 'twas over, and our saviour lifted from the cross,
to rest in cavern deep, I drew that precious load, the way was
long and steep. When the huge stone was by the open
entrance wide, I with my gathered haunches, pulled the stone
aside, and likewise sealed the cave. Sweet Lord, these deeds
endorse and let your blessing rest on me THE HORSE.

G. A. Mowat

The Mistress

Love, kindness, and tender words, no longer spark to flame,
No move or gesture holds him fast, his mistress is to blame.

Once young lovers, sighed and wooed,
 with treasures locked from sight.
But now they are left as memories, amidst angry words, and fights.

I cannot compare with raptures, that only she may bring.
For I bear love and tenderness, she brings bitterness and sin.

She steals him from his working day, and from my side at night.
Making foolish promises, with dreams of wild delight.

Gone is the man of vigour, his youth and boyish charm,
That once knew joy and generousness, sincerity, truth and calm.

Now frail and weak, no strength to fight, mistress in trembling hands,
He sips her beauty before my eyes, and begs me to understand.

I watch him slowly waste and die, I resign myself to pity.
I await his death, her work complete, the mistress's name was whisky.

D. E. Chanler

A Glimpse At Nature

Presenting to you live and clear
Nature at its very best.
The deep blue sky,
And fluffy white clouds
Are divine work that the earth admires.

The roses come in three shades
Of red, white and pink.
Jasmines put on their yellow cloak,
And lilies flaunt around in green.

The stately palm trees stand firm
Never bothering to look down,
But sway to and fro, when the wind says hello.

Apples and oranges, quite juicy indeed,
strawberries and blue ones too,
All hang from their trees.

The clear blue sea, so vast and wide
Breaks into waves, with every wink of the eye
And there's the bubbling brook rushing on ahead,
Inviting everything on its way,
To become its friend.

Yewande Lukan

Childlessness

Endless, childless, days and nights,
No little toddler saying "leave on the lights",
No babies' nappies, bottles, or pins,
No little bibs tied under their chins.

Endless, childless, weeks and months,
No little boys with daredevil stunts,
No tiny girls with tangled curls,
No toys, Teddy bears, or petticoat twirls.

Endless, childless, middle years,
No teenagers to drive me to tears,
No footballs, home-work, or untidy den,
No make-up, hair-dos, or scruffy young men.

O, how I've wished for all of those things!
A gang of wild children under my wings.
I would gladly swap my childless zone
For the chaos and confusion when kids come home.

Noreen Sloyan

My Friend

He came into my life, when I was only eight,
No flowers, treasures, or riches,
Or proof, of what, my fate.
No tender loving kisses, or father's gentle hugs,
Only the gift of life itself,
Sent from heaven above.

Yet as the years progressed,
From child to womanhood,
I soon became aware
Of the things not understood,
That this friend of mine was precious,
And priceless beyond degree;
He would always be there,
Walking every step with me.

The road I had chosen, not easy,
Unseen difficulties lay ahead,
Yet I gently put my hand in his,
knowing that by him I would be led.

Over the years, this friend has always been my guide,
And I will stay close beside him, and in his love abide.

Margaretta Rosewall

Pondering Its Meaning

Sitting alone on a chill winters night
No feeling of cold, no feeling of fright
Wondering what this world is about
Wanting to scream, wanting to shout
With all the frustration that's welled up inside
For there's no place to run, no place to hide
Thinking only as you do at the time
What can I do with this life that is mine
Knowing that all you have done has now failed
Knowing that all your pipe dreams have now paled
Concluding that life is a journey of trust
You do what you can and you do what you must
Beware of the dangers and dead ends that come
But do not give in, don't ever succumb
Enjoy all the good times for they are the best
Be happy with life and let fate do the rest

Vicki Ann Slater

Untitled

No act is without consequence.
No deed however small.
The walls we build on this day
Are tomorrow doomed to fall.
The dawning of each new day
Cause enough for a bird to sing.
The tranquillity of the garden is broken.
By the beating of a butterfly's wing.

Roger D. Mountford

The Third World

Stomachs that bulge, they cry out in pain,
No crops to eat, why doesn't it rain?
A pound to the poor, at a charity ball,
You've done your bit, so stand - - head up tall.

No feelings in your soul, you don't really care,
But supposing your fate made you live there.
How would you survive on one meal a week?
Just stop for a moment, their lives are so bleak.

Even the flies starve, they're hungry too,
How would you feel, if they fed on you?
How would you feel, if in their place,
The pain and the hunger, all over their face.

One night down the pub, would you really miss?
It doesn't take much, to make their lives bliss.
We worry about bills, for the phone and the car,
If we gave it all up, our souls would stretch far.

Things must be done, to change how they live.
If only people would be happy to give.
No one deserves to exist like they do,
You don't choose your parents, it could have been you.

Susan Evelyn Churton

Together

I recall well the day we were wed,
No church covered aisle for you to be led.
A cold office room, official and bare,
No wedding dress finery for you to wear.

Our lives together, our family grew,
As each of the children came there anew.
Together in harmony, with love and respect,
We lived in happiness, no more to expect.

To teach all our children what life was about,
Sometimes voices rising, but never in shout.
The values and duties we expect them to live,
With others about them, enjoined, and to give.

And when they had left us, all of them gone,
Out into the world, far away and beyond.
We cherished the memories and smiled at our thoughts,
Sure they had gained knowledge from all we had taught.

So now together, in peace and in bliss,
And our "good nights" are sealed with a kiss.
We know for certain our duties were done,
And together our battle with life has been won.

T. Lamden

Moments More To Go "Over The Top"

Singing and laughing, masking the truth,
No bed, no warmth, no shelter nor roof,
Trenches filled with vermin and mud,
Letters home to the ones you love.

Illness and death are everyday sights,
Scared, lonely and tear-stained nights,
Gun barrel and bayonet wink in the sun,
For tomorrow the dreaded order will come.

Torn from families, schooling and jobs,
Pulled by the romance to find there was none,
For king and country they must not stop,
As they dive into death "Over the top".

Snow, sleet, wind and rain,
Sacrifice and untold pain,
No hope, no hate, nor energy,
Yet still they'll face the enemy.

Tearing across No Man's Land,
Cut down steadily man by man,
The dead and dying left on the ground,
Agonized cries — the echoing sound.

Sarah Docker

" Desertion "

It ended abruptly, you left me for someone
new and I never realized I could feel
so blue, longing and yearning for a
reconciliation with you.

To make a go of it I really did try, and
now I feel so sad that I just want to die.

I thought we were compatible but
now think it laughable, because of
your desertion for somebody new.

My heart is now broken and no words
have we spoken, in years that have
passed since your very last.

All I have left now are dreams so
divine, and the hope that someday,
once again you'll be mine.

Although the memories so beautiful
haunt me day after day, all I can do
now is pray, pray and pray.

Patricia Anne Handel

Tribute To A Humble Electrician

A humble electrician he'd restore heat and light
Never wavered or grumbled if called out at night.
Always quipping and joking he'd say with a smile,
"Well you can't let bairns freeze in this winter's clime!"

When illness engulfed him, he continued to joke,
Lighting the lives of so many old folk,
But God in his wisdom said gently one night,
"Rest now my son in the warmth of MY light."

No, he wasn't a Bishop, an Earl or a King,
Yet the Church rafters ring with the praises they sing.
For they'd braved the cold winds, the sleet and the snow
To say farewell to a man they know
As Lenny the 'Lec.

Victoria Smith

You Are You

You are the splendour of the sun that will
never fade,
You are as precious as a teak-wood cabinet
filled with jade.
You are the tang of the salt breeze
from the sea,
You are all that I wish for that is dear
to me.
You are what love and I set out to
inspire,
You are the dream of my yearning heart's
desire,
You are the burning flame of love that's
kindled anew.
You are these things and more because
you are you.

William W. Dow

Afterwards

For a while, there were two inside this body
My little one and me
He didn't want a family
For us to be a three.

So the three I had imagined
Become just me and you
Now I'm back at one again
Farewell our little two.

My dreams of love were shattered
You were the broken part
And I am all alone again
But you are near my heart.

Naomi Weller

Neptune's Warning

Hark, can you hear the wind o'er the sea?
Neptune is angry, and well might he be,
Man in his wisdom has found a deep place
For dumping pollution of all the land's waste.

Oil spills from tankers, nuclear waste,
Tipped in our waters with furtive haste,
Bottles and plastic, sewerage and cans,
Dumped in the ocean by uncaring hands.

Roaring and crashing the waves hit the beach,
Spitting out rubbish far as they can reach.
Neptune's deep belly is getting its fill,
And back whence it came from it's starting to spill.
This dumping of refuse could stop if we wish,
Saving the lives of the birds and the fish.

The forces of nature will start to rebel.
So think on this problem, and think on it well.
The time is soon coming when man has to pay
For spoiling our planet, it's called "judgement day".

Hark, can you hear the wind o'er the sea?
No-one to listen, too late the plea.
Maureen Bevan-Jones

We Forget

Regardless of religion, be we coloured, black or white,
Nearly all of us are prejudiced, and believe that we are right,
So smug and self satisfied, with our noses held high,
We forget we're only mortal, that tomorrow we may die.

Have a stroll down through a graveyard, read the names upon the stones,
Underneath them lie their bearers, now reduced to dust and bones,
Of what consequence their opinions now? Does it matter what they said?
Who was listening when they said it? Who remembers now they're dead?

Ask a muslim, or a hindu, ask a christian, or jew,
They will tell you in all sincerity, only their beliefs are true,
Oh why must we all be identified by some colour, creed, or clan,
They're barricades across the highway to the brotherhood of man.

Think of all the little children, growing up so tall and strong,
What a tragedy for humanity, if we're teaching them all wrong,
Pride and prejudice, hate and bigotry, we must hope they rise above,
Teach them kindness and compassion, teach them tolerance and love.
Matthew L. Burns

Not Ready For The Scrap Heap

There was a time when I was young,
My zest for life was a joy to all.
Once I was the only one.
The hopes we had, my hand in yours,
I was complete. We were whole. I was woman!

But life is cruel.
We were torn apart, dreams shattered, a broken heart.
I'm no longer a woman,
Just a half.
Part time this part time that,
I'll get myself a part time job,
Learn to repair the broken parts.
I'll climb the ladder of success,
Reach up to the brightest star,
View the world from afar.
Mend my shattered broken heart
In spite of many years now past, erase the memories,
And forgotten pain, I will survive,
For I am woman! Once more I'll learn to live again.
Rose Younger

A Birthday Wish

Now that I have found the time
My thoughts to you I send in rhyme
To tell you all the little things
The pleasure that your company brings

The laughter, tears we both have shared
Knowing that you always cared
Being patient, being strong
Supportive, even when I'm wrong

Together now, for many a day
Together always, come what may
All the good times yet to share
With each other, always there

This birthday wish I make for you
May all your hopes and dreams come true
Come, take my hand and walk through life
My friend, companion, and my wife
H. McKay

" The Poet "

All thro' the day and sometimes in my bed
My marbles clink and chatter in my head.
And in the quietness of my humble den
Odd dribblings spurt from off my quivering pen.
Some are gay and some are sad,
And others, well, they seem quite mad.
But there I sit and scratch away
My marbles tell me what to say.
And in the silence of the night,
I sit and write and write and write.
This fearful urge that eggs me on
Gives thoughts of madness, off and on.
But Lo! this could not hap' to me,
Say I, "Tis Genius!', so let's be free
Of thoughts so dark,
And take a romp around the park.
L. H. West

The Victim

I am lonely, I have no friends
My life is a mess, I just wish it would end.
Every day, they come after me;
They take my money, and anything else I've got.
I just wish it would stop.

When teachers are around,
They are friendly. It makes me sick.
As soon as they're gone,
It starts again.
This went on for months
Until I got the courage
And did something about it.

Now I have got friends, I'm not lonely.
I just wish I had done something before;
Then, my life might not have been so bad.
But I went to hell and back
Just because of some silly children,
But now, I'm no longer 'the victim'.
Nicola Ray

Autumn

The splendour of Autumn is a joy to behold
Its mingling of colours, red, brown and gold
The shimmering of leaves as they fall from the trees
Or floating around, when blown in the breeze
A walk thro' the woods, with leaves 'neath your feet
Rustling and crunching with air which is sweet
No cars or pollution to poison the air
So saunter along or just stand and stare
Each season is blessed with its own special touch
So savour it wisely, it doesn't cost much.
Madeline Hill

Reflections

As I sit watching rainfall,
My life goes back to when I was small,
To when I was just an innocent,
Nothing had a precedent.
No objective, no reason to have one,
Learning about myself was fun on the run,
Until it shocked me, at the age of fourteen,
On the streets on my own, they were so mean.
Broken soul from a broken dream,
Trying hard just to keep my head clean.
Back home to mommy, trying to get back to reality,
Wanted to get on with the tribe, yeah my family.
Couldn't cope, thoughts of swinging on a rope,
Went full out, couldn't even do it with dope.
Tried to make it big on the crime scene,
Make me a million, that was my dream.
Thinking back now, I need a family, and
Somewhere to live that feels real homely.
C. M. Jones

'Waiting'

Into a bar I went to wait:
(my friend, of course, is always late!).
I sat down to drink my beer
And nobody noticed I was there;
Or if they did, no-one cared:
No conversation with me was shared.
'Anonymous' must be my name,
Which is really quite a shame,
'Cos I have many tales to tell;
Friends say I've been quite a 'gel'!
I'll listen too; tell me more;
I'll never make myself a bore.
Still, on my own I just sit here
And no-one sees my forlorn tear.
Everyone else in twos and threes:
Sitting here I mentally freeze.
Hoping some-one will 'break the ice';
A conversation would be so nice.
Ah! there now, I see my friend,
My loneliness is at an end!
H. M. Birch

Three Wishes

If I could have three wishes oh! I know what I would wish
My first would be to see again the loved ones sadly missed
To say once more "I'm sorry" for mistakes that I had made
To make amends for things done wrong
The word said in a rage.

My Second wish is something, maybe one day we'll take for granted
Food to feed the hungry, to see their barren lands planted
With grain enough for everyone, where famine is no more
Irrigation of the land, perhaps the answer that we're looking for?

And last of all, my third wish is that we may live in peace
In this land of ours we love so well, a love that will never cease
If we could just go back in time, before the bomb was invented
And spend the rest of all our days, fearless and contented.

To look into a future, that doesn't threaten a Nuclear war
The wisdom to talk things over, instead of violence to settle
 the score
Yes these are my three wishes and what a happy world it would be
If only they could just come true, for all of Humanity.
Margaret Butler Smith

The Snail's Trail

The slow, slippery, slimy, soft-bodied snail
moves gracefully across my veg patch, and starts
munching on a lettuce leaf. Sensing I am watching
him, he stops and curls up in his hard-like shell.
Feeling danger's passed, he moves off, leaving a
shiny trail behind him.
W. J. Hinton

Destiny

My destiny haunts me by day, my destiny haunts me at night.
My destiny speaks to me each morning, still I have not
understood what "Destiny" is.
My destiny keeps me up at nights pondering about "Destiny",
which I have heard so much about. Yet, I cannot find the
answer to my own destiny.
Seeing my fellow human it would appear that most of them
have found the secret to this destiny. But, some like myself
are still in search of our destiny.
My destiny suddenly came to light when I was near my end
through the path of life. And, it was at that point I became
aware that my tasks throughout my life were my destiny.
My destiny has been visible in my actions and audible in my
words during my life.
The failure to make contact with my destiny was none other
than lack of understanding.
Destiny beckons me with these words, "If you had known the
meaning of the word destiny, you would not have toiled so much".
That is your destiny.
W. Hull

My Favourite Bug

Green fly, black fly, caterpillar, blight
My arch enemies are in my sight
They and I, we wage a war
Squirting, spraying, killing galore,
They attack my flowers with all their might
Those green fly, black fly, caterpillar, and blight.

But under the stones, and pieces of wood,
There a little fellow I'd leave if I could
The cute little wood lice, so slow and old
They call them grandads
So I've been told.

They plod along and stop and stay
They don't hurry to get away
Their little bodies wobbling along
For they don't know they're doing wrong.

So if I can, and quite a lot
I leave them there just on the spot
Hoping they'll know of my good deeds,
And walk right past my garden seeds.
G. M. Bryant

Ellie's Passing

Her old eyes are cloudy
But that makes her pain clearer.
She still wants to please us
But her body can't cope.

We have to say "Goodbye, dear friend."
It's the only way now...
The only way we can thank you,
For all these happy years.

Time goes..... so quickly now
Because we want to stop it.
But... all too soon
Time comes.

Grief hangs heavy, and we try not to show her.
Don't cry, don't be afraid, don't let her sense it.

A pin prick, a cuddle, a tear slips onto her head...
A sigh that releases and she sleeps away.

Now our eyes are cloudy as tears well and fall at will,
But it makes our pain sharper and we need to feel.
Karen Law

Turmoil Of Separation

There I was sitting all alone,
Mustn't cry, mustn't moan,
It was my own doing, I cast her out,
Was this the right thing, there is a doubt,
Now I must get on with life
With or without the wife.

I wish her safe and well,
She doesn't deserve a life of hell,
She was too mixed up with thought,
Oh! the trouble it has brought,
I had my share of the dealings,
But what of others feelings;

My self I must blame,
Now I must live with the shame,
Sorrow now is not the cure,
Positive thinking is for sure,
Oh! that girl I will miss,
Not so much as a farewell kiss.

Richard Paul Collins

The Storm Last Night

The storm last night gave me a fright.
Mum came up and asked if I was alright.
I said 'no'. Mum said, "Oh, what's your problem, you little mite?"
"Mum, this is not a joke. Do you know I nearly choked!"
I will go and get my coat, and warm you up with some cocoa in a cocoa cup.
The storm last night gave me a fright; I screamed in my dreams with all my pain and might.

Nanette Chapman

Forever

If you can give me love
  Much more than I have known
    And always make me feel
      I'll never walk alone.

You'll make my life worthwhile
  Each moment that I live.
    By sharing every happiness
      That only you can give.

I'll wait until forever, dear
  For you're the love which always seems
    The one and only thing I know
      Will satisfy my dreams.

So when you share this love with me
  And I'm more than just a friend
    I promise that I'll always stay
      With you until the end.

William Henry Rawlings

Separation

How hard it is to laugh alone,
Much easier to sigh,
When hearts are heavy as a stone,
And loved ones say goodbye.
The days are long, the way ahead,
Is dark, and hope is gone.
Still when the bitter tears are shed,
Some faith will spur us on.
Though sadness stays, a way is found,
To keep us safe from Desponds mire.
Our eyes are lifted from the ground,
And moon and stars the soul inspire.
So vast the sky, so bright the sun,
When dawn from dark the day has won.
So from our darkness into light,
Each new day helps us win the fight,
For only time will heal the pain,
And let our lives begin again.

May Harrison

Life's Golden Ways

Life's golden ways are not of our choosing,
Much as we'd like it we cannot decree -
That our footsteps would never in darkness wander,
Or that sorrow we'd never be destined to see.

But if life were one long joyous endeavour,
Where sorrow and pain were hidden from view:
Would the rose that had basked all day in the sunshine
Not pine just a little for the soft balmy dew?

And yet as we pass on Life's golden journey,
The troubles and sorrows we meet on the way
Are nothing compared with the joys and the happiness
That crown the achievements we've conquered each day.

And they who've loved the dearest, the fairest, the truest,
As Life's long journey draws nigh to a close,
Will live in the hope of Life's crowning glory -
The happiness that lies in the soul's sweet repose!

B. McGinty

Oxford, My Cat

The sleek, silent shape moves,
Moving with planned precision,
It navigates across the floor,
The light catches its fur,
Shines rich ginger, thick as marmalade,
As his name suggests,
Its luxuriant stretch; its delicate yawn,
The cat's life is a happy life;
Pads among people, as it moves,
Smoothly, sleekly but so, so silent,
As it creeps from bed to chair,
Displaying perfect royalty, a regal air,
The most perfect animal,
Radiating shining superiority,
Looking at the world with deep disdain,
It settles carefully curling,
And dreamily, its perfect purr,
Rumbles through the room,
The king sleeps.

Paul Wooldridge

The Windy Breeze

The windy breeze
Moves through the trees,
Making them dance about
With elegance and grace.
The sun shines down
On leaves that are brown,
And everything just falls into place

The leaves turn to gold
As the wind takes hold,
The sunshine, with its rays so bright
The leaves dance about
There is no doubt
Like dancing jewels in
The warm sunlight.

Tina Brennan

The Scan

The beating heart that I saw on the screen,
Most wondrous thing I've ever seen.
Firm and strong
Like a burst of song
From the lungs of the Lord.
It made me feel humble,
And my own heart smiled
As I looked at the heart of my first grandchild.
And I blew a metaphorical kiss
To the little heart — the pulsating bliss.
One day I'll hold you in my arms.
One day you'll fill my life with charms
Until that day
I'll think of this — I'll think of this.

Sheena-Rose Martin

Sharing

Time won't stand still, while you ponder,
Minutes rush by, it's a wonder.
You don't grasp life, hold it tightly,
Filling your days, and quite rightly.

Make a good world, love and receive,
Remember some folk, don't give, but need.
Things in life shared, spread God's preaching,
Selfish people spend life reaching.

So take notice of what I say,
Help these people live through each day,
Giving, sharing and accepting,
Even minutes, no neglecting,
'God' rewards the ones who care.
Life's enjoyed by those who share.

Valerie J. Escandell

Girls In Summer Uniforms

Girls in Summer uniforms,
Mini skirts discarded for slacks,
Legs no longer the fashion,
But tight bottoms singing their own songs.

Tight jumpers over tight mounds,
Rigid like two concrete points,
Just an occasional plunge line,
Leases a feminine touch.

Girls aware of Summer smells,
Of sensual nuances in their walk,
Glancing at the men who pass,
Seeking assurance for their sex.

Girls aware of sensual joys,
Yet tight lipped at the men who gawp,
Only clothes and make-up exhibit
An all-embracing courting dance.

Girls walking through jungle glades,
Loin-clothed to hide their secret parts.
They're naked in a naked jungle
And there is poetry in every stance.

Stuart Plumley

Make It A Better Place

England, a place of spirit and glory
Millions of people with their lifetime story,
Landscaped fields with grass so green
The polluted town, more grey than it's ever been,
The golden sun, shining so proud,
And the storms, so strong and loud
Animals everywhere, in the park and zoo
We kill them, destroy their home, do we have to?
We fight other countries and have wars
We always have someone breaking the laws,
We have our freedom of speech
And have our next generation to teach
The world will never be completely good
But if everyone plays their part it could.

Melissa Gibbs

Getting There

Am I losing it I wonder, staring blankly into space.
Mild manic thoughts, energetically jostling for a place
To occupy my mind, with madness or delight;
God, what on earth is happening, I must look an awful sight.

Eyes bulging in their sockets,
Puss oozing out of pores
nails bitten down to nothing
who could ask for anything more.

Abandon thoughts of beauty or essence of stolen bliss,
the only element surrounding me, is the stench of day-old piss.

Look at all the old folks, shackled to the chairs, and wonder if
your life will eventually mirror theirs.

Margaret Bowman

In The Country

Annie sat in disbelief, not that she was lottery addicted
Merely that after years of hard work
She was in need of some relief

The numbers came up, the first, the second, the third
She sat quite still, not uttering a word

The fourth, oh my God, could this be
More than a tenner? Let me see — she got on the phone

How much for four? Sixty eight pounds!
And if you had one more
A couple of thousand, her uncle did roar

Oh I don't care, Annie thought to herself
This will do fine. Sixty-eight pounds is plenty
For a really good time

A short break in the country
That's what I'll do, to visit my friends Peter and Sue

Long walks — fresh air, then when it ends
Back to London to try once again

For six numbers this time and a chance to win
A cottage in the country called "Fortune's End"

P. O'Connell

" The Royal Scot "

Some years ago when railway trains were pulled by power of steam,
Men tried to make the services into the traveller's dream
They speeded up, they added diners, gave them names, the lot,
And one that I remember well, was called "The Royal Scot".

This express train left London town, each day at ten o'clock,
Up Camden bank, through Wolverton, the passengers took stock,
They saw the Midlands murky mills, and up through Lakeland pride,
They crossed the border, over Beattock, then down to the Clyde.

This train with such a Regal name was started years before,
By men like Webb and Pickersgill, who studied railway lore,
Right through the years it travelled on, through rain and sun,
    and snow,
And very rarely was it said to ever travel slow.

All through two major conflicts, it still did quite a lot,
And though its name was taken down 'twas still the "Royal Scot,"
When war was done, it carried on, but ending was in sight,
When diesels came, and 'lectrics too, the "Scot" had lost the fight.

Wilson Jefferson

The Tables Of Time

The times are churning, the tables are turning
More and more I look at the door
The door to where? Is the passage there?
The passage to what? Is it time we have forgot?

Time is a healer, a wheeler, a dealer
Of goodness and love sent from those above
They have a hand in our almighty land
Aiding our decisions without any derisions

They help us a lot in our undying plot
To do what is right in our forever plight
Plight of what you ask in our continuing task
To do as we always should in the hope that we could

After life on this Earth join Him in His mirth
To eventually help those in our lasting repose
Returning as best we can our thoughts, deeds and plan
To help the living man as they in their time ran

Our lives to His decree as peacefully as could be
Peace, love, sureness of mind, all this we will have with His
    eventual kind
Oh yes...The times are churning the tables are turning
More and more I look at the door

Marion Griffin

Life's Review

Lights in the window glistening bright
Memories and thoughts become clearer at night
Wishes and wants, good or bad
So often happy, but sometimes sad
Not all good, but hopes abound
Please take some time, I'll show you around
My innermost thoughts, hopes and desires
Time from you is all that's required
A cloud in the sky
More thoughts travel by
O where in my dreams does reality start
Try as I might and feeling apart
My life so much once ahead
But once all reviewed, mostly all said
To relive all the memories, present and past
My joy and laughter made to last
Stay a while longer in company of rhyme
Not much longer, just a little more time
Await the next time when lights glisten bright
More memories for rhyme becoming clearer at night
Suzy Watts

Me, You, Us, We, Free

How can you do this to me?
Me! the one who's loved you through it all,
Me, the one who helped you forget your miserable past,
Me, who actually made you become someone!

How can you expect to survive?
You! the one who's nothing without me,
You, so weak when you're alone,
You, the flower I made bloom!

What will you do without Us?
Us, who were so much in love,
Us, who never needed anyone,
Us, who would grow old together!

How can you be happy?
With just yourself for company,
And books and songs and poetry,
When you haven't got We?

Who can run forever, You?
I made you what you are
I own your soul, and you will see
That you can never get it free!
J. DeQuincey

The Corporation Dustbin Bags

We all took a trip to Alton Towers;
Me Mam didn't like the idea,
'Cos the rain it fell down in continuous showers,
And the fact we'd be soaked was her fear.
This soaking we'd get on her mind did nag;
Then suddenly she slapped on her thigh!
'You'll all wear a corporation dustbin bag!'
She yelled with a fiendish cry.
We looked at each other with fright;
We couldn't believe what we'd heard;
To be walking around looking a terrible sight
Was completely and utterly absurd!
But out came the scissors and out came the bags;
She cut holes for each of our legs!
Then pulled up the bags without any snags
And tied them just short of our heads!
With a satisfied grin she turned us both round,
And there for all to see,
Upon reaching our destination safe and sound
Were those unforgettable letters SMDC!
Pamela Hurst

Maybe

In another dimension, at some other time,
maybe then love would flourish, and you could be mine.
But in this life I'll never be the man for you.
No matter what I say, no matter what I do.

I've tried for so long to win over your heart,
but I'm still just a friend, so maybe I should depart.
If I were to leave, could I possibly forget,
my feelings towards you, or the fact we ever met.

I think back to the day your beauty caught my eye,
and my heart sinks so low it brings a tear I have to cry.
So much should be said when I'm there by your side.
But how can I reveal all the feelings that I hide.

I know you cannot see that I've fallen in love.
And there seems to be no future in the stars up above.
So I think I'll just stay here, hiding how I feel,
and dream of us together in a place that is surreal.

My heart will stay empty in the hope that one day,
you may grow to love me, and see me another way.
If that ever happens, I'll give all my love to you.
But for now I'll have to wait for my dreams to come true.
Simon Cox

My Son

His hair is blonde, his eyes are blue.
Mischievous things he likes to do.

He wakes every day at the crack of dawn.
I've never even seen his yawn.

I remember the first steps he took.
He used to get into every nook.

We built a fence five foot high.
But he climbed over it easy as pie.

He programs the microwave, video and all.
He'll pick up the phone and give you a call.

Today he sits upon my knee.
A lovely boy and just turned three.

It won't be long till he goes to school.
To hide the tears will be my rule.

But after all is said and done.
He'll always be my number one.
Jacqueline McGill

"Time"

If I could choose a special gift meant only to be mine,
or a wish that could be granted, then I know I would choose 'Time'.
Time to have and time to spare and use up as I please, to do those
endless little chores with special care and ease.
No need to rush or hurry because time is slipping by,
or say again those meaningless words, 'Hello, can't stop, must fly.'
Time to cook and time to sew and get the washing done, time
to do the gardening or sit out in the sun.
I would have time to watch the seasons change from Springtime
into Fall and appreciate the beauty and never care at all that
time was ever passing by — because with my gift so rare
I would simply use a little more and still have some to spare.
But then when I stop and think about this precious gift of mine
would it be so wonderful, this illusive thing called 'Time'?
Might it drag by so slowly with no-one else to share all my
extra hours, and would I then despair?
But what is the point of thinking of what can never be and I am
really far too busy to be writing poetry and wishing for the
things in life that never can be mine.
I am really just daydreaming — in fact — I am wasting 'Time'.
Jean Perry

An Enigma

I like to expose all things of beauty
Maybe I'm naughty, when I see something fruity,
I like that house; it's old and stately.
Focus right and record it for posterity.

Wow! That's a loving couple, catch that look.
Such warmth, such feeling, straight from romance books.
Must capture those children, romping with the dog.
Over there Quick! There's some playing leap frog.

This work I hate, these scenes of disarray
Mangled bodies and cars fill me with dismay
Lovely in white, veil flowing free, pages three.
Now I can cast my spell, a magic that is me.

I'm a camera, I cannot lie, they say.
With lens, viewfinder, I know the way,
To measure light, and expose the speed.
Eager to set the scene and do the deed.
J. Spencer

Welcome To The World

Dear little one, welcome to life's many paths.
   May your way be happy and long
With joy in abundance, sunshine and laughs
   may your journey through life be a song

I hope that your path has thousands of flowers
   as you, yourself, blossom and grow
That your life is filled with happy hours
   which will gather memories each step that you do.

You may sometimes come to a turning
   when it will be hard to know which way to go
But that's all part of life's learning
   and you'll be guided by love, this I know

Sometimes the ground will be stony
   and you may stumble and fall.
But you will never be lonely
   and will be very much loved by us all
S. V. Gilbert

For My Children

There's a little child in my house, he follows me around
Sometimes, he looks sad and doesn't make a sound,
Other times, I see him smile and life is not so bad
He jumps and plays and talks to me, I even hear him laugh

I hear his feet around the rooms,
and sense his warmth and need,
I feel the wetness of his tears
The roundness of his limbs

My children have grown up and gone and have no need of me,
so who is this little chap I have here constantly?
Is he just a ghost of all the years, a shadow of my life?
My conscience for all the things I did which were not always right?
So many things I cannot mend, and yet
from somewhere far away I still have a little friend.
Linda Barlow

The Wind

Whisper, gently whisper,
Stirring all the trees.
Bending flowers and grasses
With your gentle breeze.
Dancing with each butterfly,
Kissing lovers as they sigh.
Happily joining lambs at play.
Busy, busy, through the day.
Then throughout the night conspiring,
Roaring, soaring, never tiring.
Tearing leaves from trees and flowers,
Scented roses from their bowers.
Then, you with sighs, caress the garden,
Dying out and begging pardon.
Gladys Ramsay

Untitled

PINK the early morning sky,
MAUVE a little cloud floats by.
BLUE under the trees the bluebells show,
GREEN and the grass begins to grow.
BLACK the horse for Dick Turpin's ride,
YELLOW the primrose opens wide
WHITE the spume upon the shore,
GREY the rocks where the young seals snore.
GOLD are the curls on the baby's head
CREAM are the blankets on his bed.
BROWN the shoes that he wears to play,
RED the sky at the end of the day.
Roma C. Christian

A Winter's Tangent

The snow is lying heavy on your frozen brow,
Matted in your hair, the curls are blonde and white,
Your coat is fastened high, your boots stomp a definite path,
A path that has two forks,
One for joy and love, the other to hesitate for a moment,
"Who knows says the first, my hesitation is because of foresight,
As much as indiscretion and maybe I'll yield soon when the Season has changed,"
The other then intercedes "Pray do enjoy the coldness of winter,"
For without this bitter passing,
The shoots of spring would lose significance.
Simon Dincalp

Legacy

If I die what's left behind me?
Material possessions and memories
Thoughts of depression, feelings of hate
A job, a few friends, my parents and family
To go to what I don't know
The options aren't understood
No one speaks from experience
To experience is to die
Death is finality in this world
It's against all sense to know
What to expect beyond life
No one comes back to tell you
They come back, they're not dead
How can they possibly know?
You cannot be warned, told or defended
Death will always catch you unawares
What do you leave behind you?
The remains of your regime
For some other, unsuspecting entity to absorb
Death is their reward. One day.
Simon Blacknell

Demolition

They are knocking it down, that building you see
Once it was home for someone like me
A place to be cherished and cleaned every way
A refuge to return to at the end of each day

Tomorrow there will be nothing to see
Only an empty space where it used to be
Only dust in the air and rubble on the ground.
A lifetime of hope will be nowhere to be found

The people who lived there cared for that place
It was a haven to go to when they could not face
The trouble and worry in the world outside
This made it a wonderful place to hide

Those fallen walls cannot hide anymore
The love and the hope that they had to pour
Another building will rise from that empty space
And soon will be forgotten what was there in that place.
Cheridan Hughes

Welcome To Middle Age

Happy Birthday, have a great party,
   many congratulations,
     sure hope that being forty
   meets all your expectations.

For your age you're looking nifty,
   I'm sure you'll be the same at fifty,
     Pollyfilla used each day,
   helps to keep the wrinkles at bay.

But Mother Nature has got a cruel streak,
   muscles will stiffen and bones will creak,
     teeth will fall out — it's hard to chew,
   sorry if I'm depressing you.

It's really not all doom and gloom
   primrose oil can help you bloom,
     vitamin E and jars of honey
   will keep you frisky as a bunny.

Lift your chins up while your corns are soaking
   I am really only joking,
     treat yourself to a bottle of wine
   and pretend you're only thirty-nine.

Moira Sokolowski

Storm

Dark and menacing, cold, slate grey ocean
malignantly evil, with each and every sullen motion
titanic waves pound the bleak barren beach
and hoping thunderous waves cannot reach;
Small vessels sheltering behind the harbour walls,
Icy fingers of water, touch them thro' the howling squalls.

Through ominous rain-sodden clouds,
Eerie mists fall hauntingly like death shrouds.
Residents locked inside sit and pray
That they'll survive to see a new day.
Hushed and quiet in their form, huddled together from the storm.

One light shines, vainly to penetrate the pitch darkness,
Wailing foghorns moan, captured by the cold wind's harshness.
This punishment, as it seems to be, for this pair's alliance.
Trying to bring to safety, with their bold defiance
Any sailors who may be lost upon that seething foam.
Guiding those poor wanderers home.

After raging hour after hour, the torrent seems to lose its power.
As the storm twists and turns in its final death throes,
Through a break in the clouds, a shaft of light shows.

G. Ainsley

" Omnipresent God "

God is Love,
Love is God,
God is Truth
Unchanged and eternal

He is at our birth and death,
He is in our every breath,
He is in our laugher and cry,
He is in our deep despair and distress.

He is in the golden rays of dawn.
He is in the Fragrance of Blossoming Flowers.
He is in the splendours of the setting sun;
He is in the Silver living dark clouds.

He is in the stars, moon and sun
He is in the rising tide of ocean,
He is in running brooks and rivers,
He is in the Hills and mountains.

He is with the destitute and down-trodden,
He is with the tillers — tilling the fields,
God is embodiment of Love, Truth and Peace,
God is omniscient, Omnipotent and omnipresent.

Naren Makan Patel

At The Launderette

I am sorry to say this: but I think a great many people are slightly mad.
I am sitting in the launderette, listening to a young couple having an argument.

I know I am an elderly woman — past seventy. But I have always been balanced, controlled — and I am aware of it.
My washing is in Matilda — she is the second washer on the right, a good, conscientious girl.
Othello, the large dryer on the left is empty, waiting for my washing.
Matilda and Othello have an understanding which may lead to matrimony.

I am going back to my bed-sit. To preside at a wedding ceremony.
The small table is marrying the youngest table mat.
They interrupted a TV programme I was watching and told me of their love.
I'll drink sparkling orange at the wedding. I know the cushions will pretend it is cheap champagne, but the cushions are frivolous.
The couple are making up.
I am going to take my washing to Othello. Our private joke is that he will never make my washing black.
Then I must get back to the bed-sit. And preside over the wedding.

Margaret Hudspith

Summer

Dear summer — full of fickle waywardness,
Lures with passionate warmth the blazing sun,
Then turns her back with distant chilliness.
Tumble the flowers in glorious disarray:
While bees sip nectar with their greedy hum,
And birds, full-throated, give their song display.

The meadow grasses bend as in a dream,
Soft by the dew her tiny feet are kissed;
Sweet in her ear the murmur of the stream
Whispers to her alone — 'Please love me still'.
On quivering wings they also join the game
The pretty butterflies, so sweet and gay
Gather like moths around a candle flame.

With voice of thunder rendering the skies,
Caught in her web — the mighty Thor draws nigh,
Bright from his steeds the vivid light'ning flies;
While gathering clouds grown black, break down and cry.
Yet even as he bends to clasp her in his arms,
Coyly she smiles and bids the God be gone,
And turns, with brittle smile, to fresher charms

Marjorie Johanesen

Togetherness

Large limpid pools of brown
Loving eyes look up at me
Never changing their look of love
No matter what happens they stay the same
Unaffected by circumstances

Always a greeting never dimmed
An acknowledgement of my love
Enticement to play the sparkling eyes
A present offered for approval
Then capriciously taken away

Head on my lap entreating me.
A glance to the door then back again
One word is spoken and rapture abounds
And eruption of happiness greets the sound

Bounding here, bounding there
An ecstatic dance ensues
Kisses and licks say, now, please now
Out of the door with tense eager pulls
Scenting the air in anticipation

M. P. Huggett

Ace Of Hearts

Love is sharing, love is caring.
Love is when your heart is daring.
Love can die or love can grow.
No one knows where love can go.
Love can bring joy, it can bring pain.
It can end then start again.
True love never dies, true love never lies
there are no secrets,
there's no betrayal,
there's only trust,
you cannot fail,
you will know when love touches you,
it hits your heart you know it's true.
Then it blossoms like a tree,
Nurture kind and keep it free,
Like a burning flame in history,
Love will last all eternity.
Salima Hassan

Feelings Of Sound

Thou speakest to me of love yet love is not of words,
Love is of feelings like the cut of swords
The deepest pain is felt within my heart my love when we're apart
Yet ecstasy can know no bounds at the feel of cupid's dart.
Why wasteth then your breath on useless sound
When one sweet kiss would set my heart to pound,
Thou knowest not my love how your caress
Can fill my aching heart with sweeter tenderness.
There is no sound in this whole universe can bring such pain
As I reach for your love, yet reach in vain,
No word can fill my heart with feeling so sublime
As holding you for one sweet moment in this endless time,
Would that this time that passeth in a blink
Of one's eye could last forever, then I think
That words and pain would nevermore exist
And would I to your love submit, for I could not resist.
Then touch'eth me, my love, breathe not a word
Your message will convey though nothing heard,
And soaring like the flight of gentle dove
My heart will know that we have found true love.
W. Morley

" Love Is Life, Life Is Love "

Love is life, the universe, every living thing on earth.
Love is joy that comes to you, in all the good things you do.
Love is calm compassion care, in everything you touch that's there.
Love, it shines abundantly from every living thing you see.

Let's share this love, help it grow, give love to everyone we know,
To all the people all around for they need love that we have found.
Accept each other openly, to make this world more heavenly,
And soon this love will spread so fast, the more you give the
   more it lasts.
Soon this world will feel its joy, every man, woman, girl and boy.
Love that is that's what we need, for all our hungry mouths to feed.
Then peace will naturally form on earth, oh what a joy to take
   your birth
Nicola Brandrick

Thoughts

At night when I am alone in bed,
Many thoughts enter my head:
Questions, hopes, fantasies and fears.
These thoughts, they bring me many tears.
I think of the future, I think of the past,
I think of the present, how long will it last?

Are there other worlds and beings around?
Are they near and will they ever be found?
If there are, will this mean war,
A war of the worlds, an extreme uproar?
I've thought of the future, I thought of the past,
I've thought of the present, I hope it will last.
Stacy Drummond

Working Together

On the day you say "I do"
Love is easy when young and new.
Life's adversity you have not been through.
Trials that put love to the test,
patiently endure, give your best,
prove what the strength of love can do
when life is not a 'bed of roses' for you.

Work together to secure your nest
with the blessing of peace and happiness.
A stable base for young to grow,
love's reward, then rich will flow.
By giving more than you receive,
there is so much to be achieved.
When the road ahead blossoms anew,
Still working together 'Dreams come true'.
Sheila Burke

Definitions Of Love

Love can be happy
Love can be sad
We are all born with love
Love can be someone something somewhere
It's Love that makes us really care
Love can be selfish
Love can be kind
Love can sometimes make us blind
Love can be sweet
Love can turn sour
Love can be gone one day
Love can return back tomorrow
Love can hurt
Love can be seen
Love is what makes us all human beings
Margaret Green

Loud, So Loud

The birds are singing in the trees;
Loud, so loud I can't hear the bees;
Who gather pollen from sweet fresh flowers;
That gain their strength from April showers;
Which are fuelled by the earth's great rivers;
Whilst they over rock and ravines slither.

Children laughing in the park;
Loud, so loud I can't hear dogs bark;
Who jump around and play with sticks;
Thrown by people who live under brick;
Which is composed of earth and clay resources;
That's often churned by hooves of horses.

All this happens year after year;
But still for our existence I fear;
Earth pollution is just not on;
Take care of it now, before it is gone.
Mary-Ann Martin

Integration

Cloud, dark, deep, down.
No clarity within this shadow.
Could we but touch the force of
Archetypes and branch in all directions.

The shadow hangs endlessly
By force we seek to destroy.
To let the conscious, dominant branch
Rule supreme over that which is in cloud.

To force nature into repression invites eruption.
Branch after branch bursts forth demanding
An independent existence from these clouds,
And honesty demands that shadow stand side by side with sun.

Branch on branch blends and conflicts and
Cloud and sun are like a constantly shifting dance.
Insight reveals that shadow and 'I' make for duality;
A combined force of energy, face to face in friendship.
Helen M. Speer

Lotti Madness

Life is a lottery,
Lottery Madness,
Lottery tessa's savings, love, money galore,
Lotta bottle we must have,
Lotta things to do
Lotta to cope with in the great lottery of life.
Take the bottle
In your hand, and you will succeed
in the biggest lottery of all,
life.
Precious, demanding
Hard work.
The greatest gift,
The lottery of life.
Sally Davis

Planet Julie

Imagine life on planet Julie
lots of fun but nothing unruly
utopia in one person's brain
not finding the way would drive you insane
at the core of this planet is one hundred percent pure gold
with a warm glow that never goes cold
like all things delicate it needs treating with care
never to be neglected — that's so unfair
this is the place I would choose to live
not just taking but with plenty to give
Mark Tucker

Lost In Our Own Space

We were a generation who lived for the time we had, spaced out and lost in it. For long decades we seemed to drift, only to surface when a new generation found our music. A music that came and went like a breeze, soft and warm as if rising from the depths of our very soul.

Our values were what we could make them, the future was of our youth, and that was all about us. We lived for love and loved what we lived for, and time was so kind to give us so many good memories. For to feel as we do is to have lived a dream and only time can take that away.

The Beatles and the Stones drove us on, splitting us apart like two halves of an apple and yet keeping our collective will ever reaching for a dream or a wish of what. Will we ever know!

I am a child of that dream. A child of the swinging sixties, cry not for me when I am gone. For I made your time what it is and the freedoms you take for granted now, we created and we exploited them all to the full.

We did not suffer for the gains we made, well, not as our parents did but more we lived our lives to the full. Then with the passing years past these freedoms on, so you could live your lives to something approaching a gone but not forgotten time. Our time, The Swinging Sixties.
Richard Gwyn Dyer

The Hungry Furry Mouse

A furry mouse lay hungry, within his tiny home,
  no waiter there to serve him, he was all alone.
Decided he must wander, some nourishment to find,
  he must watch out, that fearsome cat seems always close behind.

Silent in the darkness, the searching made him weak,
  the smallest little snack would do, a feast he did not seek.
A morsel of a biscuit, a crumb upon the floor,
  perhaps a fallen cornflake, a wasted apple core.

But in sudden rich amazement, deliriously pleased,
  ripe before his eyes, there lay, a luscious hunk of cheese.
Mirage, or is he dreaming? this lump of grub so sweet,
  the furry little mouse surveys his long awaited treat.

Cunning, not his strongest point, although he wasn't green,
  the table he was dining on was a trap he hadn't seen.
Greedily he munched content, soon he would be fed,
  but the trap sprang into action and crushed his furry head!
Patrick Shortall

A Living History

You stand there centuries old
Looking so tall and strong.
What sites you must have beheld
Through the ages long
The creatures and animals that housed in your branches,
How many have there been?
The changes of buildings that encircled you,
What different changes you have seen.
In the midst of town you stand so bold
Watching daily life go on.
The people scurrying around from early dawn,
You have shared their laughter and their tears.
Generations come and gone,
From boy to man, girl to woman.
The seasons you have endured,
Of rain, wind and shine.
I hope you live for centuries more,
Or at least to survey these years of mine.
Patricia Crisp

My Last Hour

I stand here alone, surround by my inner thoughts,
Looking down on fields, many shades of green,
Children playing in valleys below,
A black cloud descends, threatening to shut out this mother earth.
The birds flying above, and yet not wanting to leave.
And still the black cloud descends.
All now is quiet in the valley below, the children's
Voices are gone forever, and the birds fly South for the winter
Now the black cloud descends shutting out this mother earth,
I now lie down in green pastures, shutting out this day
This day I shall not see again, through the eyes of a dying horse,
Respect it, cherish it,
So that you and others can keep the memories I have.
The black cloud now covers my life and dreams,
Dreams that can only be seen through your eyes.
Ronald Smith

I'm Happy Sitting In My Chair

Here I am! I'm sitting in my chair
  Looking at a sleeping man who's lost most of his hair,
Another friend is knitting while the rest all watch T.V.
  And me? I'm happy sitting with memories for company.

My bedroom is so cosy with central heating and warm bed:
  It's got views across the gardens, and I've got a roof above my head.
When I wake up every morning the sun warms my ageing bones,
  And I count my blessings that I live in a lovely Old Folks' Home.

The meals here are among the best though I eat less than I did —
  I don't need SIX meals a day like when I was growing kid!
But it's the little things I like the best as the years go ticking by;
  Like sunsets, bingo sessions, cat-napping, and apple pie!

I can't get about as I used to, my legs tremble when I walk,
  Though my mouth's O.K. (so my friends say) 'cos I talk, and talk, and talk.
I've had a long and happy life. I worked my fingers to the bone,
  And I'm happy sitting in my chair in this lovely Old Folks' Home.
Molly Lightowler

Love Your Life

Love your life and life will love you.
Look with your heart at everything you see
Your eyes are to look with, we know that is true
But your heart matters most, to you and to me.

If you can help someone, your day has been worthwhile
Harsh words can hurt, and often leave a scar
It costs so little to be kind and to wear a smile
But it means so much and can reach out so far.

Someone, somewhere, is waiting for that outstretched hand
Make that your aim as you begin every day
And you will find that in this green and pleasant land
Love is with you always and will never go away.
Rosemary Wright

Stars

Stars are alien souls which radiate with hope.
Look up at the sky and let your spirit climb the lightful rope.
Stars hold the answers to everybody's dreams.
Let your eyes absorb the vigour, the wisdom and
the innocence of the beauty in the beams.
Hold your stare and let the knowledge cleanse
your energy, your dying light.
Now pray to the celestial bodies, and share their insight.

Rachel Brown

A Rainy Day

Rain on the windows, pitter-patter, plop.
Look for a rainbow in every shining drop.
Water like a river gushes down a drain.
Sun gone for hours, will it ever shine again?

Grans hauling shopping stop to have a moan.
Mums pushing buggies hurry to get home.
Toddlers in red wellies splash in the rain.
Mud splattered clothes will never be the same.

Cars making waves, sail up the street.
Puddles on the pavement, shoes wet on feet.
Now dark clouds lighten, wrung-out of every drop.
Rain on the windows trickles to a stop.

J. Murphy

Untitled

My heart is open wide,
Longing for you by my side.
Emotions run high when you are near,
Your feelings for me are so unclear.
I wish you'd seen the moons above,
for the light they shine shows my love.

You'd feel the moonlight deep within,
as daylight fades and night draws in.
But now this moonlight shines elsewhere,
I wonder who will find it there?
Could it be you? I wish I knew.
It seems our chance took flight and flew.

So now I fear our end has come,
it's over now, all said and done.
But should you ever need a friend,
my help to you I will extend.
So goodbye, my friend, find someone who,
like me, shone moonlight just for you.

K. Lavin

Memories

Treasured memories, recalled with ease,
long summer days, hot summer breeze.
Carefree, happy, no worries or fears,
no way of knowing that heartache and tears
were looming, uncovered, waiting to strike,
to void us of hope, the very essence of life.
Love can be painful, when loved ones held dear,
fade from this life, from our sight disappear.
We're unable to exchange a touch or a glance,
unable to comfort, when fate takes its chance.

Feelings of loss remain in our hearts,
they stay forever and never depart.
So young ones, stay young, for as long as you can.
So often our lives go not according to plan.
So try to remember days of carefree play,
sadly they vanish; they're not here to stay.
Years can be cruel, without reason or rhyme,
so enjoy and be happy, whilst still in your prime.
There's a long road to travel with many hills to climb,
so forget not your happiness, or your memories sublime.

Val Noton

A Fenland Minister

For fifteen years the Fens have been my home:
... long roads, deep dykes that yawn around sleepy Fenland towns.
The land is flat and almost seems to touch the sky,
intertwined with spires and windmills.
This is my home: these are my people: this is my calling.

So here, almost within the sound of the Wash, parents bring
their babies for a blessing, people seek God in prayer and worship,
or they bring their loved ones to be laid to rest.

It's here I see the children in Village School,
visit homes and hospital, caring for young and old.
"Watcha Mate" they say,
but I think "Will they come and pray today?"

Here above all, true to my call,
and clear and bold,
I preach the Word of God — like a Fenland sower —
some seed by the grace of God falling on good ground.
For others the message in their minds becomes like Fenland mist
that clouds and passes in a while.

Oh Fens, with a beauty of your own — I'm drawn to you,
I love you — I cannot stay away.
"There's still much more to do" I hear God say.

Michael E. Haighton

Soil

Here I have been millions and millions of years.
Long before you were ever born.
Humans come and humans go
But I live on to tell the tale.
Your existence depends largely upon me.
The crops I nourish provide you with food.
Deep, deep down you find water
On my surface water too — rivers and seas.
You anchor huts, mansions and skyscrapers upon me.
So much you obtain from me:
Diamonds, silver, gold, aluminium.
Simple or sophisticated tools you use to till me
Such tedious toil I admire, then smiling say I,
"Toil on, toil on, till toiling days are done,
For some, anxiety piles high, about taking your flights in winter!
Whatever the clime, you will be fine.
Fear not, little ones, you are part of me.
Toil on, toil on, toil on.
One day tailing you will complete
Then you will come to be with me forever."

Vera Gregory

The Fall

That unmistakable tang of cordite remained
long after the last shots had died away.
True, the Monster's been put down,
but in ourselves something monstrous grows.

To defeat this Devil, we followed it down to hell,
turning evil upon itself a hundredfold.
Before our mailed fist spectral landscapes
lay shattered, centered; we emerged scorched,

But besmirched, our Galahad purpose soot-stained,
less pure. We had countenanced child murder,
bestiality, scapegoats sent to the oven
like yellow cordwood, collaboration with gangsters,

Whole cities burnt with lightning, lies, counter-lies,
crosses and double crosses. Above all, we thrust down
our revulsion at these ghastly crimes, we said,
"for Freedom's sake". To achieve Victory of the Good

We became one with Evil, vanquishing ourselves.
Still from its filthy pit beneath crossroads
thrice-staked, issue demon shrieks gibbering
promising more Devil's work and professional pride.

Victor West

"Your Sad Loss"

I didn't cry till late,
  long after the event,
when tears were dry,
  discussion stale,
the hopeless quest for rationalization
  abandoned in the dejection
  of miserable reality.
And then I cried:
  hot tears
  wrung from a contorted face
  that I could not control,
  nor sought to hide.

J. H. Burman

Loneliness

Silence is loneliness when you turn the key in the
lock to open the door, and there is nobody to greet you,
but a dark room, and the time going by as you hear
the clock ticking.

Silence is loneliness when I hear the sound of my
own voice, and I answer myself.
Silence is loneliness when there is no laughter
from children's innocent mouths

No one to kiss good night, just me crying myself to
sleep at night,
saying in a whispering voice, oh God help me out
of this lonely life I lead,
give me strength for my next lonely day that will follow.
Silence is loneliness when I wake up and
there's no one to say good morning.
Oh God please tell me what you have
in store for me, please, please, but there's
only silence and silence is loneliness for me.

D. R. Southorn

You Said, "Don't Cry"

Do not weep or mourn for me,
Live your life as it should be.
Make it useful, make it light
So my star shines ever bright.

How can I be useful?
How can I be light?
When the pain in my heart
Is so very tight.

The anger and the despair
Of not being able to see you are here,
To turn and see your beloved face
Or to touch your hand and feel your embrace.

If you will help me, then I will try
To think of the good things as time goes by.
I will try not to weep or to mourn,
And so make you happy.

V. J. Reid

It's 2 A.M.

I look at the clock, it is 2 a.m.,
listen to the noise, oh no, not them again.
Heavy footsteps running up the stairs,
do they always have to come in pairs?
As I pull the duvet right up to my nose,
they enter the room and start pulling at my toes.
Very quietly and quickly they move up the bed,
and end up sitting either side of my head.
I lie as still as a mouse with my eyes shut tight,
hoping against hope they don't start to fight.
They pump the pillow with their very large paws,
oh please don't use your claws.
But no, a rough warm wet tongue licks my cheek,
another playmate they have come to seek.
Cats will be kittens, Charlie and Kate are their names,
2 a.m. is when they want to play games.

P. Winyard

Legends

Through times long gone, times of legend
Little is known that we comprehend,
the dragons and pegasus, how did they fly,
And 'oh' the unicorns, why did they die.
Witches and warlocks, so misunderstood,
the sword of King Arthur that fought for good,
demons so hated, God's so adored,
all now gone from this ancient world,
giants and dwarves, the elven so bold,
Are only in stories, as a child, we are told.
The magic, the mystery and brave hero,
fade in the storm, as the wind doth blow.
The legends are there for all to unfold
but the magic will be gone as we grow old,
though, maybe not if we try to keep hold.

D. C. Jarvis

Countryside To City Dwellers

Look at that bird, sitting on the fence,
Listen to it singing, the sound is intense.
Look at that owl, perched in that tree,
Look at it staring, just watching me.
Listen to the wind, rustling the leaves.
Nature is wonderful, beauty beyond belief.
Listen to the rain, pattering on the ground,
Making little puddles, around and around.
Out comes the Sun, from behind the clouds,
Lighting the world, making the country proud.
Admire the fields, with flowers in bloom,
Waiting for insects, attracted by the perfume.
See herds of cows, grazing on the land,
Turning grass into milk, ah this is grand.
Out comes the farmer, tractor in tow,
Preparing more fields for new seed to grow.
A walk in the country you just cannot beat,
Sure as Hell better, than walking down the street.
These sights and sounds, are one in a million,
But then after all, this is just my opinion.

S. Wilson

Tíroma

There.... it comes again.... tumbling out of the season,
Lingering languidly on the palate of memory.
Turf-scented air, a strong bouquet,
Spiralling downwards on the damp evening dew.
Fusing with the aromatic certainty of
Breeze-stirred autumn leaves, brown and beige,
Dependable as the hour after the Angelus bell
When you would set the range afire,
Sending up puffs of smoke to chase away the swallows.
And the kettles bubbling on the hob
Would sing of love unspoken.

R. J. Devine

The Great White Shark

I'm sometimes angry, that I agree
and no one would ever dare fight me.
I am mighty, I am strong
but I do know right from wrong
I hate dance and music and song
for I am the Great White Shark

I am the strongest in the sea
so no one dares bother me
I swim along and fish all flee
as soon as one of them sees me
I hate laughter I hate happiness
for I am the Great White Shark

Even humans run when they see me
I come up for a laugh just to amuse me
all the people run away until the beach is blank
except for all the stones and sand and sometimes even a plank
sometimes I would get a leg or sometimes even two
but who knows next time I come up I might just get YOU.

Michael McClure

'Silent Thoughts'

Silence surrounds me.
Limbs sapped of strength
Lay soft and lifeless.

Thoughts create a pulse,
Course through hollow veins,
To meet an untimely end
In a forest of gutted nerves

Still smouldering from the recent blaze,
Still twitching, though raw and shattered,
Craving to show you
I am still within.

Your eyes expose the soul,
Tired and seeking release,
Slipping away, sinking into ether.

My heart weeps,
My soul weeps,
My thoughts weep,
As I sound the battle cry
And you call 'Surrender!'

Val Kolacs

Tinkling Cymbal Bells

I touch your body, your laughter tinkles out,
Like tinkling cymbal bells
Chiming gently in the breeze.
My touch should make me shout
"I love you", but I silently mouth
A concealed outburst of affection.
I want no deflection
From your girlish laughter
Because of the tinkle-bells sound
And the bells profound
In appreciation of you,
For you are wonderful,
I think you are supreme,
And all I ever want in any dream
Are tinkling cymbal bells.

M. Webber

The Silent Enemy

I threw a pebble in the brook, and rippled a memory there,
Likened to a day in time, when I was too young to care.
As that ripple quivered and expanded in the stream, I paused
for a moment to visualize the scene, a garden surrounded
with roses holding their heads to the sun, children happily
playing with their dolls, their tanks and their guns,
From behind a cloud a silent bug pounced like a bird of prey,
The crater it made was then to be the children's communal grave,
The roses bowed their heads in grief, their petals silently fell
And the happy little family was crushed beyond repair,
Where was their guarding angel on that tragic day?
Did it come with the V2 flying bomb to give life in another way?

Martie Lockington

A Soliloquy

I must tread like a whisper down the garden path — beyond the patio. For my pet lies sleeping and I keep weeping for the days of long ago. Through clematis bowers to a garden of flowers, past a velvet lawn emerald green, one can stroll any way, any time, any day... and feel watched by eyes unseen.

Oh! Pretty leaves, how you dance in the trees... adorned in Autumn hue. Do not harm my love, when you fall from above... just gently kiss the dew. Ah! Touch lightly the mound upon the ground where Puggy's laid to rest. And before you wilt, weave a patchwork quilt to cover his precious nest.

I will wander my way, and in silent dismay, plant a sapling somewhere close by. I'll inscribe your name in a little frame, and so often — will I sigh. When I brushed your fur and caressed your hair, your beautiful eyes would glow. Oh... our days would be long and full of song. My pet, I loved you so.

Iris Cazaly

Like Father, Like Son?

I often think that words of wisdom should be handed on
Like things I learned when I was young and passed on to my son.
Little things that matter, such as, what a man should eat,
And how to talk to ladies when he meets them in the street.

The best advice I ever heard was back in 'forty three,
A prisoner of war, he was, who came from Italy.
"Eat-a plenty spaghetti, boy, it-a make you very strong"
So I thought, well, he's big and tough, I'm sure he isn't wrong.

Well, I asked here, and I asked there, and I asked all around,
But of spaghetti there was none, it just could not be found.
Believe me, at that time I was a most unhappy lad.
There's just one man can help, I thought, I'll have to ask me dad!

"Don't touch that foreign muck," he said, "Don't let it pass
   your lips,
You're British through and through, my lad, so what you want
   is chips.
Eat a plate of chips a day, that's my advice to you
But make sure that they're British chips — those French fries
   just won't do!

So ever since that happy day, I've eaten chips galore,
And one plate, now, is not enough, I always ask for more.
I think, by now, I've eaten chips with every kind of dish.
But I must say, my favourite meal is good old chips and fish.

Jack Foster

The Sun

What is this fascination we have for the sun?
Like lemmings we flock to expose ourselves
whenever the sun finally deigns to appear.
What is this compulsion we have for pain,
and for looking ridiculous in ridiculous summer gear?
Grown men, with bodies that should be well-hidden
under voluminous layers of clothing,
appear in baggy shorts with baggy stomachs!
Arms with well-defined rings from tee shirt use,
bright red necks and swan-white chests.
These are the legacies of the summer sun,
and the summer sun-bathing madness,
while lobster-like we appear after a day outdoors.
Then comes the inevitable peeling, and the pain,
and the regret, and the untouchable shoulders,
and the sleepless nights and the uncomfortable days!
What is this "Cause" we suffer for?
Why do we overdose on self-inflicted pain?
I, truly, cannot understand this reasoning.
As, all I long for is gently refreshing rain!

Robert J. Thompson

All Together Now!

There's more life in the dead than the living
Little wormies are having a ball,
And the graveyard is very forgiving
As it swallows us up, great or small.

From the baron brought low by his uppers
To the pimp, down at heel, gone to pot,
High and low provide their own last suppers
Class to rank, every grade comes to rot.

Lamb and lion both lie down forever,
Foes repose though their stones still parade;
In the place where each race blends together
Very soon we are all the same shade.

Layabouts lazily leave their labours,
Chaste and chasers lie in the same bed,
Saint and sinner are the best of neighbours
Bearing grudges is hard when you're dead.

There's more life in the dead than the living
Little wormies are having a ball,
And the graveyard is very forgiving
As it swallows us up, great or small.

N. J. Hogben

The Sunday Dinner Saga

She had wanted to be a - 'proper cook'
Like...Delia Smith - "has a nice figure hasn't she dear?"
She married a - 'something or other'
She thought he looked waif like and had that hungry look.

Meanwhile - 'the girl with the nice figure'
Was currently enveloping a large kitchen chair.
Wallowing in greasy self pity
Another culinary creation had passed the hungry oven doors.

Countless Sunday dinners surrounded her - 'pretty figure'
Not quite Delia Smith proportions anymore.
She cried a few packets of 'sun dried' tears,
Parsnip fingers reach out for her pudding comfort,

The - 'proper cook' had eaten all her just deserts' for one life.

Rebecca Crowe

What To Do?

Sun sets on the horizon
Like an eternal flame going out,
I watch, then it's over,
Darkness.

Waiting at the water's edge,
The moon is rising high,
I can't believe it's over,
As I look up to the sky.

I remember when our love was first conceived,
The subtle look in your eyes.
I never would have expected
That now I'd have to cry.

Now as time ticks away
And memories fade to blue,
I find myself wondering
Not why, but what to do?

Mark D. Bradshaw

Farewell To A Child (Brain Damaged)

Though with us for but a little while
Like a ray of sun was your fleeting smile
Those lovely eyes that could not cry
Were surely made from a summer sky
Your rosebud mouth that had no speech
So soft and velvet like a peach
Shell like ears that did not hear
Never learnt of hate or fear
With shining hair like fairy gold
You were made from a angels mould
Whilst living in a world apart
You captured everybody's heart
So, darling, though we say goodbye
For you our love will never die
Your memory in our hearts will keep
As you sweetly lie in eternal sleep

Rosemary Coleshill

Country Scene

Moon and stars beam bright from above,
Lighting our darkness with heavenly love,
Sleepy sun awakes, over quiet green hills
Lending her beauty, as God wills,
Flowers all coloured a sight to behold,
Gracious their splendour, sweet scent unfolds
Full trees, their leafy heads do sway,
Arms outstretched as if to pray.

Cool, clear, fresh stream ripples, wandering alone
Searching and winding, dancing in foam,
Birds on high as chirping they play,
Swooping and turning, then darting away,
Sad, nature's dark blanket, night is near,
Day must end, do not fear,
We have the moon and stars above,
God be willing, all his love.

R. J. Cartlidge

" Rays Of Sunshine "

Rays of coloured light rushed through the door,
Lifting my heart as they danced round the floor.

In and out like lightning flashing,
Sparkling and beaming, really dashing.

Faces shining like the sun,
Always laughing, full of fun.

The hours have passed, it's time to say goodnight,
Yes! Grand-children are a pure delight.

H. T. Smillie

Life

Life's too short to quarrel, Life's too short to fight,
Life's too short to hold a grudge and demand one's always right.
Life's too short for hurting and giving others pain,
Surely giving happiness is much the better aim.
Life is a gift and is there for living,
Happy is the receiver but much happier in giving.
Life moulds our bodies and our brain,
Life moulds our face with lines of happiness and strain.
Life can have its good patches, life can have its bad,
The one is so enjoyable the other is so sad.
A life is individual for one to bare,
But is enhanced when with others happiness we share.
Life is about giving and not counting the cost,
And hanging on when treasures and loved ones are lost.
Life can be heaven, life can be hell,
Sometimes we fail miserably and sometimes do so well.
Life can be a challenge with such goals to be gained,
But at times when we're defeated we feel mentally maimed.
If I was asked to choose a life that I'd most treasure,
It's a life filled with so much love it would be impossible to measure.

Patricia Long

The Final Accolade

There is nothing left, it's all gone,
Life's last breath, beneath this skin,
I leaves this world - with no one,
And leave behind my kith and kin.

Death is so lonely - on one's own,
It's final, gone, to a new life,
There's nothing left, just bone,
There's nothing left, just strife.

Gone forever, no fear, no pain,
My duty done on this good earth,
They lay me down, as I have lain,
My body bound around my girth.

To God's good world, in peace, I go,
The angels waiting, just for me,
In peace I go, and I hope you know,
You'll join me soon, and then we will be,

A family once again.

J. E. Harper

Un-shed Tears

Have you ever had that feeling
of lagging behind
The rest of man-kind,
The world going quicker,
While you're feeling sicker
And wanting to shout,
To those still in doubt,
With no help to proffer,
Stop the world, I want to get off 'her'.
They say, it's old age catching you up,
And all I can say is, never give up.
You shouldn't despair —
For you've done your share.
And are deserving of leisure —
So just take care.
And enjoy it with pleasure.

Ernest D. Rowland

Body And Soul

The purpose of this journey I figure not
life's baffling mysteries elude me once more
My soul's desires release from this bodily knot.
Karma, absolution, perhaps the lore.

Eternal abuse my soul cries,
Grieved in pain and misery.
Striking chords of a hundred harps,
The spirit in vain flees for sanctuary.

Eternal bird in a cage,
Free-spirited, strong, and pure, a time gone.
Paging alone in captivity with silent rage
Wings of freedom, bound for eternity, till kingdom come

Enduring soul, flee not
Know thou the cycle of life.
Accompany me, desert me not
Till the end of this dangerous strife.

Your abode, this body, this vessel
Cannot be your conscious choice
What evil is this, so contemptuous of this body and soul
That slices like a million razors, with unanimous force.

Ruth Wheater

Spring Day

As the morning mist hugs the land, day break arrives to awake
life with a hand.
Wildlife stirs for a new days fight, for food and pleasures
with much delight.
Birds start singing there choruses to each other, young ones
awake and turn to there mothers.
Fathers go off to work for daily chores, because his love for
his family he adores.
The sun breaks through bright and yellow, flowers unfold
with perfumes some strong, some mellow.
The tree's look strong and very green, buds are born sunlight
they have never seen.
Mist and haze rise from the fields, the land is alive with
pleasures much to yield.
Strong sunshine breaths life to animals and flowers, with
beauty and colour for the day light hours.
The day was long warm and pleasant, evening draws in birds
asleep flowers resend.
This was one Spring day which closes to an end.

A. J. Masters

A Seal's Lament

I went swimming with my mama, not far from the shore
Life was good and we were happy, we never wanted more
We played around for hours, joked with dolphins passing by
The sea shone bright like crystal, beneath a clear blue sky

Disaster struck so suddenly, when tankers did collide
A slick spread far and fast, driven by the tide
Mama knew the danger, she pulled me on her back
Then swam towards our cove but the water turned jet black

I slid from her poor body, she could not carry me
Her flippers wouldn't move, her eyes they couldn't see
My mouth was filled with darkest slime, it tasted bitter sweet
Struggling hard to breathe, my heart just ceased to beat

Humans found and saved me, cleaning all the oil away
Though they were kind, I can't forget what happened on that day
No doubt they can be caring, these creatures from the land
Yet they kill and maim so needlessly, I'll never understand

I haven't found my mama, I fear she must have died
Our rock is cold and empty, I miss her by my side
No more will I know bliss again diving through the foam
Man's not content destroying his world, he's started on my home

C. Sutcliffe

" The Revellers "

We laughed and danced together,
Life was carefree; it was always summer then.
The grass was green, vegetation so thick,
It obscured our view of things to come.

There was no forecast warning at that time,
And so we kept up the laughter and the dance,
Until the hot winds came and blew over us,
Bending, breaking, searching with great force.

The laughter and the music stopped, became as a loud hush —
We shared the silence, afraid to speak,
And so the time to talk and reminisce, came and went,
Slipped away, now beyond our grasp.

There is an empty space, where you once stood,
It can be seen and is keenly felt.
And yet no one has come to say, I will fill the void,
For it is known, this can never be.

Shaw Taylor

Time Reveals All

The secret of the universe,
Lies finally in tomorrow's hearse,
Where renewal defies the cold, failed heartbeats.
No need to mourn, for mourning cheats
The trembling senses,
Multiplies the fretting memory cells,
And questions time's authority.
Ignore the doomsday preachers;
Instead, think of the knowledge gained
When confronted with the cosmic truth,
Which offers an inheritance infinite,
In a region of vivid, expanding light,
Where illumination casts no shadow,
Where science and philosophy are made redundant.
No clocks, no ticking death-watch beetles
Disturb the all-embracing peace.
However, earth's search for vengeance will not cease,
For we are but mayflies with mayfly needs;
And after a daytime flirtation,
We spiral down like sycamore seeds.

Raymond W. Seaton

Pride's Folly

Heavenward my hopes Zeppelin floated
Inflated with a hot, presumptuous pride,
'Til this heart by aspirations bloated
To my more sane and certain judgement lied.
Self-deception, tyrant blind of reason,
In soaring dreams you hid reality
Whilst self-rebuke fell as earthbound treason,
And counterfeited talents minted me.

B. M. Phillips

Ideal World

In an ideal world, this is how it would be,
No suffering, no pain, it would be perfect you see.
No old ladies battered, no children killed,
No animals mistreated, it would be just as God willed.

No hatred, no war, no starvation, no anger,
The world would be one happy place, free from danger.
It would be safe to go out, on your own after dark,
And let your children play with their friends in the park.

No murders, no rapes, no sorrow, no shame,
No crime on the streets, and no-one to blame.
In an ideal world, this is how it would be,
But it's just the opposite, because it's not perfect you see.

We live in a world, that is far from ideal,
Where the bad things in life are horribly real.
We are responsible for things being this way,
Only we can change things, let's make a start today.

Corrieanne Barr

Keep On Trying

Keep on trying and pushing
  Let no one deter
    To get where you're going
      You must have someone who cares

        To achieve the impossible
          It is quite a challenge
            To find that big ladder
              And climb to the top

                Well cast off those chains
                  And get one foot on the rung
                  For there is only twelve
                  Before you get to the top

                      Success is what you make it
                      No one said it was easy
                      To climb to the top
                        Only to find there is another

                            So do not be downhearted
                            You can never go back
                            For things seemed to look brighter
                            On the other side of the track

                                R. Glass

Love Thyself

To thee who are bound by chains of chastisement,
Let life expose its nudity,
Unabashed, waver not at crossroads of decisions
Nor be prevented in corridors of convoluted imaginations,
Housed in cranium of thoughts.

Be ye not bowed, as lash of whip,
Or scourge of tongue causes bones to melt.
Heave not from stench of copious decay,
Neither be ye choleric at expulsion of warm moist fluids
As bowels disband in attempt to overwhelm thee.

Cautiously debate, the platitude of thy oppressor
Weighed in reality of thine own world
Savour life's consequences
Ye cannot recant them.

Do not avert thine eyes, from flow of blood,
Or moribund of death
Elated, welcome ye the toll of bells
A mirror image of what thou shalt be.

To thee whom are bound by chains of chastisement
Be not recreant. Love thyself.
   Moreene Adessa Bennett

Your Mother

If you have a mother
Let her know that you love her
For there will never be another
Like your own dear mother

Just remember when you were small
And for you she did all
She'd wash your face, learn you grace
There is no one else can take her place

She was the one, when you were ill
Who put you to bed, and gave you a pill
She'd sit by your bed and softly sing
She was like an angel without wings

She was the one to whom you would go
When your heart was full of woe
She'd sit you upon her knee
Fill your heart with joy and slee

So if you still have your mother
Let her know that you love her
Don't forget her or neglect her
Just show that you love her, for she's your mother.
   Margaret McLachlan

Fallow Ground

On sudden impulse I walked away
leaving the drab and littered street
images of childhood stirred my mind
of poppy heads in fields of wheat
I passed the hoardings, the boarded shops
strewn empty cans and painted scrawl
as endless noise assailed my ears
I caught the train, away from all
there's peace and calm inside

The inn was just as I remembered
except the sign was red with rust
along the lane I chose to wander
to distant fields once green and lush
the hedge was chopped as if in battle
deep ruts beneath the slippery mud
tall nettles, docks and tufted grasses
alas no corn, no cows to chew the cud
there's only set - aside
   Margaret Green

Leaving

To travel to a far off place
Leaving no trace of the journey you take
Parting from family, friends and enemies,
Do you now miss what has been the past
The closeness, joy, sorrow and pain
Or is it all now forgotten
A new life, a future of dreams
Once dreamt, remembered.
   R. W. McPhail

Communique! Part One

Somewhere deep in the chambers of my mind,
Lay dormant the truth,
The truth of my being.
I shall attempt to unlock these chambers,
and discover what lies within,
I shall attempt to convey this truth to the world,
And for those of you that can understand
and relate to my every word,
I say Hallelujah, praise my creator.
For at last I'm no longer alone,
For we know what we see and feel are real,
And I rejoice to meeting you all again.
But until such time, I will jog your vision,
And for those of you who lack this knowledge of creation,
Then you have a long rocky road to take,
But it will get easier, as your soul will grow and learn,
Making up a very important part of this network,
this jigsaw puzzle called life.
I hope I can take you home.
Come fly with me, let's fly to the sun.
   E. J. Preston

A Day at the Seaside

I place my deck chair near a sheltered wall
Lay back in comfort and close my eyes
Just letting the sounds drift by
Children's laughter, a baby's cry
The sound of music, the bark of a dog
The shrieks of laughter that come from the sea
As bathers get wet from the spray
I open my eyes, I must have fallen asleep
People are passing with jugs of tea
Packs of lunch for a family
Glad I brought some lunch with me
All too soon it is time to go
Ah some people are waving, friends from the bus
I'll stop at that stall, buy some sweets and rocks
My grandchildren will expect some
Homeward bound in the evening sun
A pleasant journey has just begun
Back to Leeds and home.
   Esther Newton

Refugee

Look into my eyes and you will see grief
Keep on looking and you'll get no relief
Come on look deeper, deeper if you dare
My soul is open for all to stare

My land has been raped, torn and broken
what's left of life is just a token
Don't shed any tears, for anyone here
for what you see is really crystal clear

Starvation of hope and deprivation of faith
Believe me, I've seen the grim reaper's wraith
So I will pray to all of Humanity
About bloody war and all its stupid insanity

But voices in the wind, no one hears
Will always be said for years and years
So please help, help me in my Hie
To rest my head, lay down and die

A. J. Evans

Love

I've spent a lot of time
just thinking what you mean to me,
and come to the conclusion
that our love was meant to be.

We share even the simplest thoughts
we speak as if one mind,
a sweeter man in all the world
I know I'll never find.

Your sweet embrace, your tender touch
a love you never fake,
are strings that hold me to your heart
that I will never break.

I'll love you while I still have breath
to know that you are mine,
and then our souls will travel on
until the end of time.

N. J. Gilbert

" Rich Man, Poor Man, Beggar Man And Thief "

Indeed He was a rich man, He had a heart of gold.
Just read the Bible stories, the parables of old.
We know He was a poor man, in a stable born.
Ox and ass beside Him, on that happy morn.
Yes, He was a beggar, He begged that we might cease
All the world's evil ways, and strive for inner peace.
And He was a simple thief, He stole our hearts away
When they crucified Him, on that dreadful day.

Rich man, poor man, beggar and thief, our Lord was all of these.
He tried so hard to save the world, and everyone to please.
He told us of the righteous path, and how to seek the common good.
He whispered, "Father, forgive them", as they nailed
   Him on the cross of wood.

Olga Ramshaw

Let Us Cross The River Of Sorrow

Let us cross the river of sorrow,
Let us reach for the blue sky — the ocean of bliss,
Life is like a story, a book —
A bagful mix of weal and woe,
With tides flowing high and low.
This moment we have love,
Next moment the hurt of unrequited love,
Just as a good harvest is followed by drought,
And then comes floods to devastate all!
To heal the heat of summer, rain comes,
Sometimes assuming the fury of storms.
Spring is short, but makes us sing and dance,
Winter, like death, ends it all.
Let us cross this river of sorrow,
The blue sky beckons us for a blissful morrow.

Sunil Guha

Our Girls

Our darling little Hayley, how we all adored her,
just like our sweet baby, our darling little Laura.
We know you are together,
That's just how it should be, so we all still get together,
For your birthday tea. We all sing and blow the candles out,
At this time every year, we try to smile and hide the pain,
But always shed a tear. Every day we make us strong, to face the
Cruel blunt world, but in our hearts is an empty place,
Where we grieve for our little girls.
To have you back in our lives, bodily, would be a plus,
But we know that we will meet again, the day you come for us.
So with these words we send to you, in heaven way up high,
Our love and thoughts of days gone by, and still the question why?
Although we're sad and memories make us weep,
We know your pains have gone away, and you can softly sleep.
We do not fear, scents that appear, and do not make a fuss,
We appreciate it's both of you, come to visit us.
What more can we say through all these tearful showers,
But send our love to you and you,
And leave your favourite flowers.

C. Young

New Year's Day's Regrets

New Year's day has passed away, unlike this hangover
I've nursed all day.
My head still thumps, and I try to forget a
resolution I know I'll regret.
The things we say when full of cheer,
"Have another drink, Happy New Year"
We brag and boast to those just met,
"A week for ten pounds?" Yes it's a bet
Did that happen only last night?
Can I be wrong? No it must be right.
Now feel remorse, and here comes regret
but remember, remember that wager, damned bet.
The week crawls by; it's oh so drear.
But a cigarette I daren't go near.
Now at last that magic night is here.
Walk to the pub, slow down, don't sweat.
Open the door, all gazes met,
"Your ten pounds here, you won the bet"
You smugly drink but then start choking.
As he admits that all week long, he's been SMOKING.
Your only regret is you didn't choke Him!

T. M. O'Reilly

The Squeaking Rocking Chair

I have a little rocking chair and all it does is squeak,
It sits beside my unit, where my taps have sprung a leak.
The door bell rang as I began to fetch a can of oil,
"Oh" drat that bell and what's that smell
It's my stew that's on the boil.

"What do you want," I shouted through my open door,
"Sorry Love," a voice cried out (I'm collecting for the poor.)
"Oh" can't you see I'm busy (as I fumbled for my purse) and my
Rocking chair keeps squeaking and it's getting worse and worse.

"Don't" despair (It's just a chair) the voice it "Shrilled" with glee,
I'll take the rocker off your hands and that way you'll be free.
"But all it wants is oiling" I said to him all "gruff,"
"Please yourself then" he replied, and went off in a "Huff."

Now I needed not to be disturbed and set about the "chore,"
Trying to "oil" my squeaking chair that's become a dreaded bore.
I tried hard not to weaken as I gave the chair a "Poke,"
And realized that the "squeak" had gone —— cor' blimey,
it's no joke.
So all my efforts were in vain and "Frustration" left me weak,
Instead I should have mended — (Those old "Taps" that
sprung a leak.)

R. I. Jones

Voices On The Wind

I hear the soft voices on the wind gently vibrate
I've listened long enough to their murmured, magical, rhythm gyrate.
Whispering to me to return to my birth lands again.
A calling from the past of celts, gaels and clans of the
   Scottish Brave.
Of mystical stories, orotund of folklore and heroes our men
Sung to me songs, once, lone laments of their birth to the —
   Peaceful grave.
Voices on the wind in my ears render the call of the Highland Glens,
Of the past again, to freely roam in the springy moss
On the hills of purple heather, to climb amidst blue ascending Bens.
My barefoot again to tread the soil of home in Wester Ross.
Voices on the wind travel over, far distant miles
Remembered deeply my sad sigh of despair released to depart
   Forgotten Never!!!!
The intense tranquillity and beauty of the retiring sun sinking —
   Over my western Isles.
Given in to my yielded yearning —
To return home with eternal joy in my heart
Have you also yet to hear or listen to the
   Voices on the Wind?

   Yvonne Fraser

" Help Doctor "

Doctor! Doctor! Can you help me?
I've fallen out of an old oak tree.
First I slipped and then did slide,
then I landed on my behind.
I banged my head and it did hurt.
My mum will kill me if I've ripped my shirt.
On a branch I caught my knee,
now it's bleeding, can't you see.
I think I also tore my pants
just before landing in a nest of ants.

   G. Barnes

A Rebel

A rebel I could really be,
It's you that keeps me constantly aware,
of dangers unforeseen — that spring
to mind with vibrant flare
Red torch of fire, warning me.
To stand and stare.
To stop and think before I dare.

Soulmates my spiritual link.
Transfer thoughts so deep.
Quite impossible not to obey.
Their wishes and morals so to keep
Bad vibes can really fade away
It's red for danger every day.
Caution when you see the red light
out of the way.
Get out of sight.

   C. Baldam

A Forgotten Love Note

A forgotten love note gathers dust,
Its worthy author is dust too.
He once had breath to utter profound sayings.
Proficient in his assertions.
His mawkish love note is as he was -
A jumble of verbosity and vulnerability.
Pensive, poignant passions were printed in a heavy hand.

The note had declared his fixed worship of her vivaciousness.
It failed to mention intimacy, the warmth of love.
What momentous insight had he,
And the sagacity to write it.

The love note will still be gathering dust,
For it had lost its meaning,
Right from the beginning.

   Zarina Anwar

The Sea

I see it from my window,
It's turquoise, green and blue.
Each time that I look at it,
It shows a different hue.

It holds many deep, dark secrets,
It sees everything you know,
Secrets that it will not share,
Are buried deep below.

White horses roar across the top,
As if racing to the shore,
Although they've been there time again,
They still go back for more.

The summer view's quite different,
It shows another side,
Children play and paddle,
And surfers ride the tide.

I couldn't find a better place,
To make my little house,
Life really is quite sweet,
When you're a cabin mouse!

   Sian Mayers

Stop Worrying

Stop worrying, and enjoy every minute of every day,
It's the worrying that kills, is what the doctors say.
Half the time we worry, we don't know what it's all about
And it usually isn't important, as in the end we find out.

We worry about money, whether we've too much or not enough,
If it is the latter, we don't starve so why make such a fuss.
We worry about the car, if it's cold so will not start
Yet we weren't going anywhere, so why do we lose heart.

We worry about the garden, the lawn needs to be cut,
But it won't stop raining, and you feel you'll do your nut.
We worry about neighbours, if they've had a rotten day,
Are nasty when spoken to, and it hurts what they say.

We worry about bills, we know they must be paid,
But if we've got the money, it's a worry we have made.
We worry about a little pain we haven't had before,
Don't stop to think it's a muscle used that's just very, very, sore.

We worry about a wrinkle, when it appears on our face,
And most of all the aging bit, why not accept it all with grace,
We spend our lives a worrying, we really must be fools,
For in the end we realize, there was no need for it at all.

   R. F. Gilder

Progress

I used to sit here admiring the view
It's something I so often liked to do
With pastures green as emerald gems
And buttercups mimicking petticoat hems.
The daffodils reached tall up to the sky,
Yet I never once thought to ask them why.

Seasons fled, creatures came and went,
I befriended them all 'till their time was spent.
The snow would arrive, and make all appear right,
With its blessed cover of virgin white.
The problem though, was man came around,
And brought his diggers to cut the ground.

Times then changed, life moved on,
The fields ripped up, one by one.
All the animals had to leave this place,
Leaving me crushed with utter disgrace.
For 'twas my fellow man who demanded this change,
To a life of concrete, greed and rage.

   Rosemary Coulter

Egg

Into your cupped dry palm I dropped the smooth cool curve
of an egg;
its shell strong as the transparency of bone
behind eyes, cradling
the slick curd of brain.

thin as the skin of the frosted world in a blue space.

the curve of a face,
a cup,
the arc of a cool tower,
an aeroplane slingshot to heaven,
the blue horizon.

the rind of the lonely moon.

Within a viscous slop shaped by its casket.
Thin wet rounds turned to thick juice
pour out, not left to set,
harden as clay
and unpick the white cathedral membrane
from the inside.

Patricia Saunders

The Old Brown Jug

The old brown jug stood on the shelf,
Its shape was round and bulbous
Down the years it's been passed on...
and filled with flowers it's gorgeous!

Oh! what tales that jug could tell,
It's seen much joy — but also woe,
And maybe seen a kiss or two —
As Gramps watched Grandma roll the dough.

At Christmas-time the jug came down
from off its shelf, so comely;
And filled with holly berries bright,
My, it did look most homely.

J. D. Roberts

Your Eyes

When I look into your eyes I see nothing there.
It's not me you see in that vacant stare.
That look in your eyes gives it away,
I know it is not true, the things you say.
Your eyes are cold and your heart is too,
What did I do to cause this from you?
This broken feeling deep down inside,
But this emptiness from you I hide.
You hold me close, but you're so far.
Just leaving my heart with this painful scar.
Day by day I look at you,
Never knowing what to do.
Maybe one day those eyes will say.
And I will know either way.

Mia Towersey

I Am Not Alone

I walk through the trees
my feet crunching the fallen leaves.
I stop, touch, feel the barks.
The sun filters through,
morning dew
colours glisten.

Somehow I am lost;
I can't get in touch —
all seems so vast
and then
beneath my feet, between fallen logs
I see a face...
A tiny flower looks up at me
and I know that I am not alone in the vastness,
that there to share my smallness, littleness
is another of his tiny miracles.

Elizabeth Anne Greathead

On The 41 Bus

Four times a week I travel on the 41 bus.
It's my great day out without any fuss.
From my council flat to the other side of town.
Our bus driver's a kind man, he says, "Be Careful",
as you sit down, I look out the window to see small
children shouting, and laughing on swings as they go
up, down and round. Overhead a silver plane does
not make a sound. Its "Giant Tadpole" tail streams
across the sky. From "The Fish Shop" older children
stop to watch sea gull's fighting over a discarded
chicken pie. I notice councilmen putting new pipes
in houses for "The Gas Board", then a container lorry
goes by with its continental hoard. A police car, and
ambulance (hope no one's too ill), lovely gardens. A cottage
and a mill. A golf course (people playing). By a farm where
hens are laying. A white horse to bring me luck,
and put a sixpence under my foot. Help an old lady
on bus with bad knees, help young mum with baby, off
bit of a squeeze, "See You Tomorrow" as I come to my stop.
O 'Dear', I must not forget to buy a new mop.

Winifred Townsend

A Shift Worker's Lament

The radio blasts, from sweet sleep I am torn,
It's just 5 o'clock on a Monday morn,
I rub my eyes, try to clear my head,
what a struggle to get out of bed,
I stagger downstairs then turn on the light,
another day starts in the middle of the night.

The day's not over when we change shift at two,
when I get home there's still plenty to do,
no time to sit and put up my feet,
I'm off to do more jobs to help make ends meet,
then I really look forward to the weekend,
to do some overtime on which I depend.

Once more the night shift comes around,
I can't sleep through the day because of all the sound,
and during the night if there's chance for a break,
then I can hardly stay awake,
still, there is some hope for all shift men like me,
come Saturday I might just win the lottery.

D. A. Sainsbury

Temptation

The games began, you start the chase,
It's how we hurt the human race.
The cheating and the lies begin,
To play this game you have to sin.
You show no fear or any doubt,
You think that you won't get found out.
But should the one that's left behind,
Be hurt and treated so unkind.
You do not feel their hurt or pain,
Because you play this foolish game,
You think that life will be the same,
But what is left will surely change.
So if temptation knocks your door,
You'll say I won't play anymore.

A. L. Price

Without You

Learning to live without you,
Is something I could never do.
I want you here beside me,
Forever to love me, as much as I love you.
Tomorrow would mean nothing,
Without your warm embrace
Or your kind and gentle face,
As you make me feel secure,
In a world that s so unsure,
Of what life holds ahead.
My heart would surely break in two,
If I had to live my life without you.

J. L. McLeod

After-Thoughts Of The Damned

I fear not death, for peace it brings,
Its dark abyss, with long black wings,
My mind a deep blank void, full of rage and hate,
A sinner I am, and will always be,
For where there's light, there is also dark,
Both must exist, the good and bad, I've merely lived my part.
I knew no love as a child, fear and pain filled my heart,
And then one lonely darkest night, I held my knife and felt its power
The moon was full, the time had come,
To take their souls, and make them mine.
My knife I held, above his chest, no remorse did I feel,
His blood it flowed, it felt so right, it felt so good
My mother's face was bathed in sweat, her eyes were full of dread,
As I put my hand across her mouth, her throat I cut,
her life force spilled, but no pity did I have
They taught me well not to feel, no mercy did I give,
Many times have I killed, but I have no regrets,
Except but one, my time has come,
No longer will I feel the power of my knife.
   Shirley Smith

Belfast

Tonight, I look out over the city,
   It's a beautiful place.
Street lamps twinkle like countless stars.

You look peaceful and calm.
   People going home,
Quiet headlights on the carriageway.

From the hills I see no division
   No East, no West.
You hide your pain well.

I know how Jesus felt as He looked over Jerusalem,

"If you only knew ..."
   Oonagh Griffith

Lost In Prison

I feel lonely, useless, no good to anyone.
It wasn't really me, who says it's me.
You have no proof it's me.
This is terrible. I need someone to talk to,
someone who will understand me, my problems,
and prove my innocence.
Every day I feel upset, ashamed,
but what have I got to be ashamed about?
It wasn't me.
I'm scared! What's going to happen to me.
Maybe they will find out it wasn't me, or maybe then
it will be too late.
Every day I cry, cry, cry.
Sometimes it's hard to stop but sometimes it's no use.
It's just one big nightmare!
Nothing to stop it happening again,
You just have to face it, there's nothing stopping you,
Just face the facts of life...
You're stuck, till someone proves your innocence.
I just wish someone would open the door and let me free.
   Philip Meikle

Anger

Anger is black
It tastes of brussels sprouts
And it smells like rotten eggs
Anger looks like an explosion
and sounds like fireworks
Anger feels like acid that makes you burn
Love is red
and tastes of marshmallows
and smells of strawberries
and looks like pink champagne
and sounds like Pavarotti
Love is very soft, but it is strong
   Matthew Hart

What Next

We stood alone while Europe bled
It was our finest hour, he said.
Backs to the wall stood every man
Each proud to be an Englishman.
And now we've joined the E.E.C.,
And lost our pride and dignity.
For former foes hold us in sway
And tell us how to work and play.
"You can't fish there, you farm like this
Your money too must go.
As for your queen, she's not our scene"
Another body blow.
And now there's Maustrich telling us
Were being nationalized
It's then the old bulldog appears
To save our heritage and pride.
For being European is out
Though that's the Brussels plan.
We'll stand by what we've always been
And that's an Englishman.
   E. Yates

Liberation From A Despot

It was I that turned away,
It was I that said no more of this -
This inner turmoil, these anguished sobs.
So like a fledgling, I took those first uncertain steps.
The distance between us then widened.
It was I that rejoiced in my strength,
And in my invincible brooch of courage.

It was I that was bruised, bullied and scarred,
From the brisk, blunt blows that you freely dealt out.
But it was I who finally denounced your terrorist tactics.
It was I that moved on,
Advancing nearer and ever nearer to my piece of Heaven,
While you descended into the Pits of Hell.

It was I that was found in that fertile ground,
Wandering about in a state of grace and serenity,
For I was given my liberation from a despot.
   Marina Thorpe

My Grandmother

A stately lady who sat in her chair,
It was her throne to all who knew her.
Her heart full of love and understanding;
But if she was crossed, she would be very demanding.
Always ready with kind words in store,
Never a time when she would close her door.
Her hair of long and white;
Put up in a bun all neat and tight.
A smile and a hug was always there,
As she sat upon her stately chair.
Knitting needles clicked like hammers so small;
Endlessly making things for one and all.
Sewing too, often prevailed;
Never letting a mistake make her fail.
And still she sat upon that stately chair,
Often I wish she was still sitting there.
   Teresa Hudson

A Beginning

You totter forth with smile so wide,
It leaves a heavenly glow inside.
All hands clap as you pass by,
Your little head held proudly high.
Birds are singing in the trees above,
While the sun beams down its rays of love.
My little darling soft and sweet,
All the world is at your feet.
To-day is just for you a start,
Happy birthday — from my heart.
   V. P. Brown

Head Dress

This is my first trilby bought
It was for the first lady I court
Second cap black when she died
The tears soaked in it as I cried
Third bowler was my sister's marriage
They left the church in horse and carriage
Fourth a soldier's cap for a blind date
She turned up in uniform an hour late
Pretty, well spoke, and polite
I fell for her that very night
After wearing many hats over time
I proposed to her over a glass of wine
My fifteenth was a wedding hat
Oh my memories linger still of that
My sixteenth was a christening
Baby crying, family listening
Nowadays I wear an American cap
To play with grandchildren on my lap

B. Frost

Death

I just think about death and I get a cold chill,
it travels down to my spine and makes me stand still.
It creeps into my mind, like a sneaky black cat,
ready to pounce and take my life,
I don't like to think about that.

Death is a tornado that sucks people in,
and takes them away with its fast flowing spin.
They go to a world in the sky, where they drop on some scales,
to weigh up Heaven or Hell, or is that just fairy tales?

I've decided to end it here,
maybe my time is near,
well, I'll just have to see,
and wait for death to take me,
and steal away my shell,
and take away my life,
for someone else to tell the tale....

Toni Beadle

Strife Of Life

Is the beginning ending of past
My body is aching from wanting and rage.
If this existence just develops with age,
With what of my feelings such senselessness rage.
So what of my symptoms,
have I just a flu!
I have been waiting,
I know not, of due.
So why of the ending?
so dull and so blue.
I know not of that, if that's
even due.

With what of the last,
just simply a parce,
Is the ending — beginning
at last.

H. Smith

Bereavement Poem

There's a little place in heaven, just a mile or two,
It needed some baskets of flowers so God
sent for you.
He knew you were very special, and he knew
I loved so.
There's just one thing he's forgotten I
didn't want you to go.
But now that he has taken you he'll
take care of you for me,
I'll never ever forget you, in my heart
you'll always be,
I loved you so much mum.

M. Alldred

The Agony And The Ecstasy

I hear the key in the lock and my heart skips a beat, because I want it so much, have I imagined that sound?

The 'phone rings, a letter drops on the mat, and my first thought - is it you?

Each time I promise myself, this will be the last, surely the hurt can't be greater than these endless hours of watching, waiting, hoping, merely existing until our time comes round again.

But at long last our bodies entwine, hands clasped together we make love through our finger tips, and such sweet sensations pass from yours to mine, like mini electric shocks.

Our mouths touch, yet lips don't move, drowning in our emotions we act, think and breathe as one, for these few precious moments we are one.

Sue Desney-Hudson

Time

Time is indestructible and meaning different things,
It never stands still, but comes with chimes and rings.
Being good times or bad, a span, or a long duration,
'Once upon a time', was told with a long oration.

Lifetime is judged by a span of years; a human notion,
It is a kin to the heavens, an unstoppable motion.
For us it's a clock, with its hands and face,
With different numerals all over the place.

Tic-Tock! Tic-Tock! Go the clocks of Man,
Time progresses onward, to stop it no one can.
It is not regressive, only in Man's thought,
Time cannot be traded, and never could be bought.

We know of past and present, but the future is unknown,
Thinking back, we wonder where time has flown.
So do not even worry, it will be there when Man has gone,
Times that waits for nothing, will go on 'till anon.

W. L. Downes

A New Day

As a new day begins, a flower is born
It is with wonder, a perfect thing,
in a world war torn

The petals open, in sheer perfection
The world to view, for our delectation
Their perfumes are all too rare,
We just stand and smell the air

As the sun begins to set at night,
We are still in wonder at the sight.
Tomorrow is another day.
Let's hope we're here, we pray.

As the day draws to a close,
I liken it to a rose,
The petals fold, the night clouds roll-in,
Waiting, for a new day to begin

J. Farrow

A Child's Grief

Your life was too short, quickly you left
Leaving a child with a heart sharply cleft
Yet your love was so strong that you remain
Engraved on her soul in a secret domain.
With the warmth of a gentle midsummer breeze
The memories she holds help her heart to unfreeze
But the pain still remains and to this day
She can't understand why you were taken away.
She needs to believe to relieve her depression
That life where you are is a mere extension
And the love that you both knew and held so tight
Will continue to grow, and as day turns to night
You will caress her again in distant lands
Though not with your memory but with your hands.

Martin Oliver

The Cycle Of Seasons

When the ground recovers from the snow
It is Springtime and flowers start to grow
There are Snowdrops, Tulips and Daffodils
Growing in beds and wild on the hills
Then into the Summer more blooms can you see
Geraniums and Roses, Foxgloves for the bee
Lilies and Fuchsia and Canterbury Bells
Lavender and Honeysuckle with their lovely smells
But all too soon the tree leaves turn red
And most of the flowers soon will be dead
But even at this bleak time of year
Michaelmas Daisies and Golden Rod appear
And then it is Winter, the ground cold and bare
But in the trees the Holly Berries are there
Jasmine and Aconites they now appear
With Christmas Roses, until Spring is here
Then the cycle begins once more
With Snowdrops and Tulips and Daffodils galore.
   Sonia Gillings

Mother

"Twenty four years now you've been my Mother
It has to be said you're like no other
I've not made life easy you have to agree
But I hope my love for you you can always see.
Through the good and the bad you have always been there
I still search for ways to show you I care
I'm not good at emotion I'm sure that you know
But your love behind me has helped me to grow.
So with you by my side to help and to guide
I hope I can fill you with love and with pride
So thank you so much for all that you've given
And for all the times my spirits you've risen
So now as this ends I say 'I love you'
And a big thank you for all that you do."
   J. Newbery

My Life — Cry of a Refugee

You would not call mine a life
It has been hurt, humiliated with the sharpness of a knife
I have suffered misery, hunger and pain
It tormented me and almost drove me insane
I have witnessed violence, depression, and disdain
We were made to suffer with little to gain
Surrounded by gunmen, terror in the air and doom looming in the sky
Every minute passed with fear, and hope as high
People crowding even more
Food and space is even shorter now than before
Why have I ended up here, so far away from my homeland
With few to comfort me and lovingly hold my hand
People are dying of starvation and thirst
But to the fighters freedom comes first
I have lost everyone known to me and am now all alone
But then after all I am a survivor.
   Prachi Rajgarhia

Looking Forward

Sometimes when you feel unsure —
Maybe something made you sore,
Lift your face and feel the breeze,
Drink in the beauty of the trees.

Pause just now and ease hurt thought.
Wait for the peace that you have sought
To flow into your weary heart —
Let Man and Maker nothing part.

Refreshed, invigorated, start anew —
Plan ahead, fresh things to do.
Keep peace, tranquillity and hope.
Use these three to help you cope.

When life is at its darkest hour,
Give your cares to one whose power
Heals all hurt, and cleanses new —
There is always hope for you.
   Heather E. Cook

Heart Of Gold

When you were younger and took a fall,
It hardly seemed to bother you at all.
Now that you are aged and take a tumble,
I'm sure I hear your bones creak and grumble.
Your face that's always smiling and looks so kind,
Has become rather wrinkled and heavily lined.
Hair that once curled as it blew in the breeze,
Appears quite lifeless like last summer's leaves.
Your hands that used to gently dry my tears,
Have somewhat stiffened over the years.
Yet in that body that has grown so old,
There beats a heart that is full of gold.
It reaches to me when I'm in pain,
Enfolding me warmly until I smile again.
It lets me know that you still care,
And when I need you, you're always there.
It doesn't matter that you've grown old,
For you are my Mother, my friend, with a heart of gold.
   D. V. Bryan

Contemplation

What if I were a poet? Not great, just normal.
Is there such a thing? I think I meant informal!
Writing simple words that all people understand,
not long sophisticated poems we can't comprehend.
When I say "We" I mean ordinary people like me!
Is there such a thing? Are all people simply "We?"
Most people are okay, some are contrary, like me!
What if I were not a poet, what could I then be?
Such a stupid question, I can't be anything else!
I said I was contrary, sometimes I make no sense.
Is there such a thing, as people who are contrary?
Surely if there is then they can't be so ordinary.
Then they wouldn't like the simple things I write!
When I say "I write" what I mean is "What I might"
if I were a poet. But what if I were a writer?
The more I think the more the pen get's mightier!
   K. F. Adamson

Love

Love is like a flower, a rose,
Into life's challenges, it throws,
Its ups, its downs, no lover knows,
The wonder of love, and all it shows.
Life's a twisted path, be sure,
It's many secrets to explore.
But if your love is strong and true,
No obstacle will surpass you.
There are no bounds to where love goes,
Its trials, its errors, no one knows.
So happiness can just be found,
For love to make the world go round!
   P. R. Woodward

Season's Change

First flowers seen, new leaves of green
   Lambs playfully skip among the cowslip
Hedgehogs peep from their winter's sleep
   Birds build their nest — no time to rest.

All colours abound, birds' chirpy sound
   Insects fly in a clear blue sky
Children at play, hot sunny day
   Beaches, pools and holiday

Crisp frost in the morning, gives an early winter warning
   Leaves of orange, brown and rusty red fall to the ground
Bare branches, on the wind-blown bushes
   Through the rain everyone rushes

Evening comes much too soon
   Flowers lose their pretty bloom
Cats prefer to stay indoors
   Instead of getting muddy paws
Snow and ice on the path outside
   See the children slip and slide
   Kaye Andrews

The Troops Are Marching By

The Mother on the sidewalk, as the troops are marching by
Is the Mother of the flag that is waving in the sky.
Men have fought to keep it splendid, men have died to keep it bright,
But the flag was born of woman and her sufferings, day and night.
'Tis her sacrifice has made it, and once more we ought to pray
For the brave and loyal Mother of the boy that goes away.

There are days of grief before her, there are hours that she will weep.
There are nights of anxious waiting when her tears will banish sleep.
She has heard her country calling, and has risen to the test.
And has placed upon the altar of the nation's needs, her best.
And no man shall ever suffer in the turmoil of the fray,
The anguish of the Mother of the boy that goes away.

You may boast men's deeds of glory, you may tell their
 courage great,
But to die is easier service than to sit alone and wait.
But I hail the little Mother with her tear-stained face, and grave,
Who has given the flag a soldier. She's the bravest of the brave.
And that banner we are proud of, with its red and white and blue,
It's a lasting tribute holy to your Mother's love of you.

R. Angell

My Tribute To You, My Daughter

The Love my Daughter gives to me
Is Something I truly treasure,
Her caring ways and Kindness too
   She is so very special.

Throughout the years I have been alone
She has always been there for me,
She solves my worries, and my fears,
I thank my Lord, for my daughter dear.

Because she is a special gift,
Which has enhanced my life,
My prayers for her are peace and love,
From Christ, our Saviour, up above,
And I know well, I am certainly blessed
For a life, which has been destined,
To have been endowed with a daughter like you,
was meant, without any question.

N. Wilson

In The Mosaic Of Heaven

Each precious piece in Heaven's mosaic
   Is placed with loving care
The high and low, the rich and poor
   A common bond doth share.

A bond of God's infinite love
   That holds each piece in place
And keeps them ever by His side
   Encompassed by His grace.

And when He calls us to come Home
   And leave this earth's dark shore
He'll place us with our precious piece
   United, evermore.

W. B. Champion

The Silence Of Pain

The sudden sound of death;
Is light to us who understand.
Even though people say you're strange inside,
You disagree; but why try to hide?

They can't see the pain and sorrow you once had,
So they don't realize that's what made you so sad.
The tears in your heart; caused by pain,
Reflect to people as you being vain.

And now you've gone, far, far away,
Into a world where you shall stay.
And the silent screams inside your head,
Are now whispers, like you, which are both, forever, dead.

Melissa Davis

What Is Love?

Is it faith, is it hope, is it just being free
Is it whatever we make it or want it to be
Is it sharing our hearts with no reserve
Is it giving till there's nothing more to give
Is it a fleeting shadow on the wall
Is it the life that throbs within us all
Is it caring for an old tramp in the street
Is it smiling at the friends we meet
Is it the anguish for a moth hitting the light
Is it saying you're sorry when you know you're right
Is it the sunset glow of a happy heart
Is it knowing true lovers never part
Is it the lost sense of wonder that makes us say
"Oh" with awe at the beauty around us
Is it the searching of minds, will it change us or mould us,
Or will it leave us just as it found us
Is it the story you tell me to make me laugh
Is it the being a whole and not just a half
Is it me, is it you, is it really true
What is love? — it is me, and I am you.

Moya Gray Flockhart

Domestic

Fear, despair, pain, confusion,
Isolation, tears, false happiness and blood.
Is there no one to release me
From this never ending cycle;
Doesn't anyone notice, am I not understood

Is everyone blind
Or is it they just don't see.
Red, blue, yellow and green
These colours aren't natural
This can't be happening to me.

Embarrassment, humiliation,
When did my pride disappear.
Gone are my hopes, forgotten are my dreams,
Abandoned by life
Friends and family, too, it seems.

When did it start,
Why did it begin.
I have no identity,
Please help me.
I want my life back again.

S. M. Spriggs

Spring

Once again it will be spring,
It is the best season of the year,
Birds, their lovely song will sing,
Different shrubs, and flowers, will appear,

The cows, colours of brown, yellow, black and white,
Lying in meadows, so lush and green,
Calves, playing around their mothers in delight,
As the sun shines down, what a lovely scene,

The trees, some big and tall,
Will spread their leaves, to give
Shelter to birds, large and small,
Where in safety, they can live.

Rabbits, and their young will run
On the hilltops, or fields, so free,
Until they hear the sound of a gun,
Down into their holes, they will flee,

The farmers, working in the fields,
With the plough, and horse,
Getting ready for the summer yields,
So much work to be done, of course.

Pearce

What Is Love?

What is this mysterious thing they call love,
Is it really true, it comes from up above?
Some people believe that it might,
And sometimes, I think they are right.
It can take control of most any-one,
Even those who think they're strong.
It worms its way into your heart.
You may not notice at the start.
Before you realize, it's taken hold,
And increased its strength, fold by fold.
You hear about it in all the songs.
It lets you know just where you belong.
Occasionally, it's blissfully sweet.
It can sweep you off your feet.
It can also bring along despair,
When the one you love doesn't care.
You can fall in love with someone you shouldn't,
But even if you tried to, with others you couldn't.
Although it consists of ups and downs,
It's the most precious thing to have around.

M. Trigg

"Ad Astra"

Adventure in the seas of outer space
is calling men to wander 'mid the stars.
From far-off Venus, Jupiter and Mars
the challenge comes to all the human race.
Now nation vies with nation in the chase,
no more sufficient is the speed of cars,
of sound itself now broken are the bars,
and far beyond the clouds they rush apace.

What seek they, as beyond the earth they fly?
If Heaven beyond the heavens were but the goal
we humbler earth-bound mortals view the sky
to see the myriad wonders ageless roll,
and hope that peace will be the far-heard cry
which sends a world-wide hope to every soul.

J. G. Dougan

Without A Friend

Without a friend of any kind,
Invisible, visible or mankind,
Through the door of friendship you will find,
Happiness, and
Occupations of all kinds.
Under your skin and deep inside your heart, you
Trust and confide in your special friend,
And suddenly you break up with your friend, you fight,
Although you know all you really want to do is
Rebuild your friendship, hug and make up.
In class you sat alone, nobody to help you,
Envy strikes inside as everybody seems to take her side,
Nobody to trust or tell your secrets to, although you want to.
Deep inside you know you're alone, you don't like it, but who does?

Tara Penny Reeves

My Bar of Chocolate

When I was a child I saved my pennies
In the days of L.S.D.
But I always had to earn them.
They were never given to me.
And sometimes when I had 'tuppence'
I would run to the shop up the street
For a 'two ounce' bar of chocolate,
Always a special treat.
All my life I always found that
The two ounce bar was nice,
And always managed to buy one
In spite of the rise in price.
But now the chocolate is sold in grammes,
To me a stupid measure,
As I will always recall my two ounce bar
A memory to treasure.

S. J. Harrison

Forty Winks

Shady summer dreams
Invade the sanctuary of my sleep
And wrap me in their blessed warmth
Chastise the chill that bid'st me wake
And all around a million dreams are spread
The blanket of starry night
Puts enmity to rest.

And cherry petals fall
From Granddad Charlie's tree
And all about the orchard
We play hide and seek
Cold lemonade we drink
Through melting ice and straws
We chased the seasons round and round
To a war to end all wars.

And from the hazy corridors
That lie 'twixt wakefulness and sleep
I pass the cheery landmarks of my life
And rush to meet the embrace of my foes.

Paul Richards

On The Scent Of Treasure Island

Sweet the scent of Polynesia, hanging thick on breathless night.
Intoxicating frangipani, gently stirred by lantern light.
Drifting, misty, round the vale, fanned by wild banana leaves.
Feel it on the lips and nostrils, taste the mystery it weaves.
Mysterious as Tusitala, sitting scratching, spinning tales,
Of smelly, patched up, peg legged, pirates and of foggy
   highland dales
Beyond the palms the waves are breaking, phosphorescent on
   the sand.
Above, the lunar light is bathing silver shadows on the land.
The winking lights of nighttime fishers, in their double hulled
   canoes,
Set the scene for magic fables, nothing in their telling lose.
Is that the voice of Tusitala, husky in the heavy night?
Whispering of Bonny Scotland and her people put to flight.
Or is it only sun bleached palm trees, rustling, (though there's
   no breeze?)
Or rattle-bones of murdered sailors, lost in bloody mutinies.
A flash of sunlight on the water putting all the stars to flight,
Leaves the scent of Tusitala, inky, on a haunted night.

Roderick Porten

Lost Innocence

When I saw what had happened I couldn't stop crying
It was you that was gone, but it was me, that was dying
You had so much to live for, you were so young
Your life had just started, it had only just begun

You took it so calmly, when they said you were ill
It was me that was worried I couldn't keep still
I was your mother, from me you were born
So little time together I was shattered and torn

You were born a hemophiliac
You had many blood transfusions
To say this blood was killing you,
There must be some confusion

You were only seven a child so sweet and pure
They told me you had AIDS, a disease they cannot cure
The time you spent in hospital, you kept smiling through
I kept a smile on my face, I did it just for you

At least I was with you until the very end
You left your pain behind but my heart will never mend
I visit you daily, to your graveside I go
My darling little daughter, whom I'll never see grow

J. Giltnane

Grand Daughter I

Small child of beauty and grace
Innocence and purity all.
Smile at me, with doll-like face
Careful lest you fall.

Doll like features, cheekily grin
Tiny limbs in perfect miniature
Sometimes little devil within
Careful, don't bump into the furniture

'Oh' your fragrance, your pretty dress
Your hair curling like soft down
You fill me with such happiness
Every princess should wear a crown.

Peter Sharp

Jus Drivin

Say Mister Flat Cap where you sat,
In your car or on the sofa.
Say man are you squeezin the break,
Accelerate or jus move on over.
Sit down, turn on, tune in,
Does what you're doin matter?

Tell me! where are your wheels,
In the air or on the road somewhere.
Man where is your brain,
'Cos your mouth's already in fourth gear.
Head turnin from side to side,
Yes the view is very nice.

Acceleratin, movin up, movin on over,
Man, can I feel your disapproval.
Face red anger boilin over,
Too young, too fast, too hot, to be drivin.
Tell me! are you in control,
What screen have you be'n watchin?

Mandy Brown

Illusion

Sometimes a door opens and no one is there.
In the shimmering heat of summer afternoon
When the hawks are motionless above,
I turn suspecting your appearance,
But it is too soon.
Rather than contemplate my sadness,
I turn away from where you ought to be,
Locking tight the door of the room we once lived in.
Sometimes it's in a wood
Where the trees weave intricate patterns
And the sun searchlights a glade
That I see you standing, afraid,
Vanishing slowly with each step I take nearer
And I want to tell you that fear grows
Until, one day, I too will be afraid to go to the woods.

D. L. Lines

To A Snowdrop

Your call it is an early one, you come to make us glad,
In the morning of the year, when we were feeling sad.
Brave, modest little maiden, we salute you once again,
You are telling us that others will follow in your train.

Snowflakes are caressing you; is that why you hang your head?
They're making quite a blanket around your little bed.
Someone in the Autumn planted little bulbs just new,
Purchased in a garden shop, and now behold they're you.

Your coming gives us courage, symbol of hope are you!
As braving all the elements, you modestly peep through;
I expect our Heavenly Father knew we needed little you,
To brighten up the garden, when flowers are so few.

Fair little maid of February, your petals are not soiled,
All the mud around, you cleverly have foiled.
You teach us cleanliness and purity and modesty as well,
A message for this troubled world, you assuredly do tell.

Nan Downs

In The Darkest Hour

In the darkest hour
In the deepest pit of despair
Where there's no-one around to be loved by
Where no-one has time to care,

There's someone alone in the shadows
Crying out for someone to be there
A person afraid of the darkness
Alone in the dark monster's lair.

Something in the shadows starts moving
Instilling a deep-rooted fear
There's no-one around to protect them
From the shapes that begin to appear.

The need for someone grows stronger
With shadow creatures wicked and wild
Taking shape into ghosts, ghouls and goblins
Bringing a fear that began as a child.

There's no-one around to bring comfort
No-one special to hold them so tight
To give them a warm feeling of safety
Which always appears at first light.

Rachel Walker

CWM Pennant Haunted House

This ruin which once was man's treasure,
Is a desolate spot, the house gone to pot.
But oh! What infinite pleasure,
Rhododendrons, and bluebells, azaleas too
In colours of orange, wine red and blue.
The cuckoo sings gaily, the sun it shines brightly.
The mountains surround it, quiet pervades it,
Such quiet as only God can renew.

Now to add to my pleasure,
One of God's creatures has given me a treasure,
He was only a passing stranger
Who had gathered some beauties here showered
But seeing me empty handed,
Gave me a bouquet of these lovely flowers.

My heart is so delighted.
At the beauty which God has inspired,
And all his wonderful blessings,
And love that never expires.
It is now whilst realizing his wonders
I must share like the man with his flowers.

W. A. Bottley

Unwanted Faithfuls

Poor little ponies, caught in a pen,
life has gone so sour for them,
  all because of men.
Life, it has no meaning now,
they just stand and wait,
the end, it is a certainty,
it's a cruel and dismal fate.

Yet once they were happy, galloping and free,
with children laughing on their backs,
their joy was plain to see,
But children grow and leave the nest,
yet ponies stay the same,
now all they have is memories,
of the happy joyful games.

The hammer comes down, the ponies are sold,
we don't do this to human friends
when they grow too old.
The smell of death, it hits them all,
  the gun... the bang...
and then they fall...

Pamela Hodgskins

Reverie

At the dusk of dawn, every day
In the darkest night, there I lay
All the time I dream, dream a life
A life I always wanted, which is not my life
I wonder what it would be like
These things I think which shine so bright.

Is it wishes or is it hope?
Hope for the future, where I hold the ropes
A lifetime which looks so long
Yet is short, and wonder where is everything from
What is life? which everyone asks all the time
A future I cannot tell, would my life be fine.

Is it a dream or just an escape from reality?
Or is it in everyone's eyes, what they see,
Their dreams to show something within?
Are these dreams a sort of a sign?
Within me there lay an answer there.
Everyone's answer is different, depending on their insight.

Sai Kong Tsang

The Fisherman

Fearless are they who sail the seas
In search of food for all our teas
Strong in purpose, muscle and mind
They sail in weather of every kind

Not for them the fireside chair
As they chug on through the frosty air
A way from home for many a day
A 'safe' return is what we pray

Storm and tempest, snow and ice
Life is like a flick of the dice
They have braved natures worst
Home to port and a restful berth

Remember too when you eat your fish
Courageous are they who catch this dish
Natures bounty from the sea
Caught by them for you and me

Sidney Wilson

Innocence

Tell me about happiness
Of laughter and dreams
See children run, run, far into the distance
Through fields, green, tall enough to buckle knees
We stumble helplessly, helplessly into a world,
Of immaturity,
Innocent like the day we are born
We remain free, protected by our blood of fear
"Fear a friend in the time of need."
Now you tell me about sorrow,
Struck down and wounded by reality,
That sharp object which pierces us all,
Those who are born tonight I praise
To understand one present and future takes time,
Time that hangs over us all like the final call,
At a deserted station platform.

Mark Davies

Littleton Colliery Epitaph

Arm in arm, we grieved today.
I'm glad my brothers are gone,
Never seeing such destruction.
Our shaft winding wheels are none,
Our brave men folk all departed
No dirty faces blinking at the sun.

I'm glad my dad is dead.
I'm glad he never lived to see this day.
The whole of his life's work gutted,
They've take his soul away.
The Littleton Pit has gone.
Flattened back to clay.

Stephanie M. Spiers

Once Upon A Time

I remember the rubbery smell of a far off war
In our school drill when gas masks we wore
I remember the whistle of a falling bomb
And the drone of the German plane it came from
I remember the summers of thin cotton dresses
The fear of having nit laden tresses
The chapped knees caused by gymslips of serge
The scathing tongue of the teachers scourge
I remember the wise words of a caring gran
When chastised in tears to her I ran
"You must have done wrong for your mum to snap
Go say you're sorry, don't make such a flap"
I remember collecting the "charks" in the lane
These large ashes from old fires to burn again
I remember when snowdrifts were taller than hedges
Reaching above our bedroom window ledges
I remember when peace came, the beacons we lit
And soldiers returning after "Doing their bit"
In time the things I remember will be history
To be recounted perhaps in our family tree.

K. Ryder

Streets

I've walked the streets of many towns
In many countries too,
The things you see around the world
Are unbelievable, but true.

The streets you see in Singapore
With coloured lights at night,
The entrances to Teahouses
All full of joy and bright.

I've walked the streets of Hong Kong
Of Bengal and Peru,
I've seen the streets of Kure
And those at home in Lewes.

I've wandered up the streets of Crewe
And down the streets of Timbuktu,
The mountain streets of Tokyo
To visit shrines amid the snow.

But of all the streets I've walked along
My feet worn to the bone,
The streets that I remember most
Are those I left at home.

H. Coon

The English Abroad

He stumbles away from the seven four seven
In his ill fitting shorts he's looking for heaven
Carrier bulging with duty free booze
For a package of two weeks he's nothing to lose

He weaves into discos and wobbles through bars
Cursing and swearing and kicking at cars
His union tee shirt and tattoos say all
He's a brit on the bevvy and having a ball

The girls down the hallway keep showing their knickers
Can't stand the food so they're living off snickers
They party all night and then sleep on the shore
So they're all red as beetroots and feeling quite sore

With two point four children that can't take the sun
Family man is desperate for fun
But his wife is so tired she's flaked out in bed
So he goes to the pub and gets out of his head

At the end of two weeks they've all had enough
The girls are all peeling, the hardman feels rough
Family man is loaded with gear
The courier knows that they'll be back next year

Tony Hatton

The Flower Of Manchester

The flower of Manchester he has not died,
In his heavenly office he's gone to reside.
And when his teams playing, and there on the run,
If you look up to heaven you'll hear "Go on Son."

He planted his seeds, all over the land,
Not only his players but also his fans.
He didn't give orders, no only advice,
Thousands would listen, sir Matt was so nice.

The man never gave up, whatever went wrong,
Look on the bright side, forever his song.

Margaret Angela O'Brien

Hereford Castle Green

I stroll through the castle green
In footsteps of past kings and queens
Where fanfares played triumphantly
To splendour pomp and pageantry
And gallant knights and chivalry
On Horseback rode majestically.

Now it's but a village green
Quite sombre, solitary.

Where once the thundering cannon roar
Beat the pulse of civil war
And mighty iron cannon balls
Pepper'd and breached the towering walls.

Now the castle stands no more
Long has gone those granite walls,
'Cept for a gentle light that falls
On Nelson's column standing tall,
A symbol of another war.

Michael Hogg

To Geography

In temperate landscapes day follows night
In a small-scale cycle of darkness and light.
But the scale of the cycle's enlarged at the poles,
With perpetual darkness (resembling black holes)
Which is, at last, followed by six months of light
With the melting of ice caps — a wonderful sight.
So the interaction of time and space
Is the basis of Geography — here rests my case:
Way back in the past the vast glaciers flowed
And carved out our landscape, and volcanoes glowed
Before their eruption to form some new land,
And plate tectonics moved continents round.
The world, how it shook when the mountains were made,
Before weathering, which lowered them, began to fade
Into the present processes seen in our time —
The present is of the past but a mime —
For here in the present's the key to the past
And by using it now we can back — or forecast.
So will glacier, desert or water follow
to cover the England of tomorrow?

R. Jane Harrison

Give Yourself Time

Give yourself time to do as you please
In a field, dew-fresh, at dawn, there's ease.
Give yourself time to breathe the air,
Feel the breeze ripple through your hair.
Give yourself time to watch the trees
As sunlight filters through the leaves.
Give yourself time to watch a flower
Open its buds to sunshine or shower.
While all the things we eat, drink, or buy
Are raising prices way up to the sky.
These God-given gifts are yours for free
All you have to do is stop, listen and see.
If you give yourself time, you'll very soon find
You've a very much lighter, heart and mind

W. M. Swann

Death

Death, you creeping reaper, when uninvited you enter in,

With stealth you seek and carry off with speed, one or all with-in.

Others implore you to come pay them a call, they long for the release your freezing embrace will bring,

Yet often you totally ignore their warm deathly welcome, until it suits your contrary whim,

Grief and tears are the music you play to, not one of us is allowed to miss your final call,

The question is, 'When will you come with your invitation?'

That knowledge is thankfully spared most of us, but certainly not all.

Pauline Hamblin

Reflections

I saw a bird up in a tree,
I'm sure I saw him wink at me.
I saw a portrait on the stairs,
Whene'er I pass he simply glares.

I saw a cat go slinking by,
He looked at me with baleful eye.
I saw a squirrel flee up tree,
His eyes in fright look down on me.

I saw a fox one moonlight night,
Sly eyes reflecting moon's bright light.
I saw a lion in a cage,
He looked at me with helpless rage.

I saw a puppy frisking, gay,
His eyes inviting me to play.
When I sit down at night to dine
Two eyes with love look into mine.

D. M. Trewern

Man

Why can't mankind live in peace like God's intended plan
Instead of causing tragedies like only mankind can
God gave creation to us in every shape and size
And man just chose to question it and change it for his eyes
He kills his fellow human on grounds of race or creed
He leaves the poor to die from pestilence and lack of feed
He carves up all the forests to earn his dreaded cash
He desecrates the cities and bombs them into ash
He lectures that his aim is peace on Earth to everyone
And yet he makes his money by the selling of the Gun
Money is man's only God and one that he can trust
He's lost all sense of proprieties and considers wealth a must
Maybe He will seal our destiny and God will watch in ore
As He tinkers with atomics and sends this Planet into war
Then when it's blown to kingdom come and only dust remains
God will start His evolution plan and begin the World again.

Sheila Anderson

To Be Free

Day after day, hour after hour.
I'm forced to run, to run and cower,
It's above me, it's after me, it's coming this way,
Getting inside me, eating away.

It's paranoia. It's fear. Of what I don't know,
Its parasitic misery is beginning to show,
Isolated, I'm hiding again,
Battling to keep this ruined mind sane.

Come. Follow. Down into my head,
Find me here trembling. Naked. Under my bed,
The storm is above, stalking you and me,
So why do I cry alone that I want to be

Free?

Stuart Whellans

But Then....The Cloud Parts

I've got this joy deep down in my heart
I'm like a mountain climber
I have reached a peak
That I've been struggling to reach for along time.
I take in my surroundings and I spread out my arms
With a sense of victory, a sense of achievement.
But then...the cloud parts
And I see yet another peak,
I realize I still have a long way to go
I don't feel disappointed that I've not made that far
Because I have this strength,
This boundless energy.
I say to myself with a smile,
"I didn't know I would make it this far
But I have made it
I'm therefore determined to make it this far
Some day I'll reach that peak
And everyone will hear me speak
They won't go away
Until they have heard what I have to say"
Sheena J. Chisnell

The Return

My joy is immense but my sorrow is deep.
I'm glad to be home but my friend is dead.
I love my house, my kids, my wife. But
sorrow is strong my friend is dead.

This place is great, this place is kind.
But it is lonely my friend is dead. This
is hell sitting, waiting. Waiting for the
moment to end. This is the funeral for my
dead friend.

The quality of life has been lowered.
Although he is gone his wife still mourns
She sits around moping and crying. It must
be hell for her knowing he's dead. I know
how she feels. Although I'm not related, I
mourn just the same.

A year has passed it still feels the same.
Although he has gone I still feel the pain.
It's getting better the pain is easing but
he is still remembered. Little John the
Hobbit. A hero just the same.
Richard Hudson

" 1914 - 1918 "

They've fetched our black shire-horse today,
Old Gipsy is his name.
Them Army chaps have taken him,
And pushed him on a train.
He's only known our farm and ways,
It's really broken my heart,
I know we won't see him again,
'Twixt shafts of our milk cart.
We've had him here from just a colt,
And taught him how to 'go',
As well as many a fancy trick
Before he got too slow.
He's nigh on twenty years come June,
The same year we had Tom;
A Soldier now — somewhere in France,
Around a place named 'Somme',
Where's Gipsy going? We 'must' enquire,
But from this farm has gone,
A part that's best of English Shires,
Old Gipsy — and my Son.
Betty Holyland

My Culture

My hands are my Culture
Like the tree tops softly swaying, way above me
My Culture is like a mighty river
that never stops flowing
the colours of my culture from the seeing of my eyes
is the beauty of flowers growing in the wildness
the feelings of my Culture so deep inside of me
is like the so deep blue ocean. Swelling
the sound of my Culture is like the clouds in the blue sky
not a sound they make. As they roll on by,
like the lips of a silent pray saying,
My Culture is so rich.
Like a pearl, free from its shell
My life is like the light of a candle burning
lighting up, the darkness in me.
That is the Culture that God made for me
Like the freedom of the birds
Flying freely in the blue sky way above me
that's my Culture, my freedom, my life, my all
B. W. Curtis

Island

Pollution, noise, music in your head, gun shots, gang war, people dead.

The fruits of life are always rotten, alone on my own, but not forgotten.

A gentle breeze that cools the shores, people screaming, slamming doors.

A quite life that's what I long for. To get away from it all.

A lonely Island amid the seas, just me alone lost amongst the trees.

My Islands gone, alone once more, with the guns, the drugs, the slamming doors.

The homeless that line the dirty streets, the people that kill a man for the shoes on his feet.

If my Island was real I'd run away, it won't be a dream some day.
Adam Hole

Autumn

Autumn has come and leaves are falling
Making a carpet on the ground.
Crisp and thick — they fall like snowflakes
Yellow, orange, russet and brown.

Trees are beginning to look quite bare,
Frail branches stretch up to the sky.
Do they feel cold? — I see them tremble
As gusty winds go whistling by.

When skies are heavy and clouds are dark
And mist makes everything look grey
The world seems dull — the people too —
It's hard to chase those blues away.

But faces are happy that greet each day
On autumn days when skies are bright.
The world's a beautiful place again.
The joy of living is pure delight.
Margaret J. Mercer

Absent Love

Here I lie, on my bed, in my room,
staring out of my window and up at the moon.
I think of you while lost in the view,
with the hope that you're out there watching it too.
Although we're apart, we are sharing the sight,
And also the thought of being together tonight.
You've said it to me, now I want to tell you it too,
You're the one for me, and I do love you!
Kelly Clark

Vacillation

Householders resident in pre-war houses may
remark that their roof-top requires attention
having already permitted an elapse of months'
to a full year's extension possibly not being aware
of the old saying "A stitch in time saves nine"
which if acted upon immediately could possibly
have avoided further damage in time.

However better late than never, some qualified
slater ought now to be procured in order to
Thoroughly examine the roof to help one become
reassured that there is no possibility of
serious damage looming up ahead such as the
much dreaded wet or dry rot
Through either rotted wood or lack of lead.
Elizabeth G. Harris

Reasons

Is there magic around us. Thoughts that go on and on?
Repercussions of past lives....a plan laid before a song.

Is there meetings before we start and meetings at the end..
Is there guidance all the way till our time is spent.

Will I understand my reasons for what I am to do..
Will I awake while dreaming and light comes shining through.

I wonder do people come to me or do I go to them..
And am I casting pearls. Or gathering in the gems?

Can I think.. that I'll go on and on important to breath of
things...or will I fool myself and I'm only water within a .. spring..

Nothing to a person..nothing to the world..nothing to the
magic that gives me thought and love

Am I nothing to give me reason..am I only dust at the end..
Was there nothing at the beginning and nothing at the end...
Ann Edmead

Prelude Of Peace

To taste the tender wind
Rippling our hair.
The felicitous sun deliciously smiling
Igniting us with renewed hope
As we gaze over the battered streets,
The mangled mutilations of destruction.

To see the embittered land,
The exploding, agonized hearts
Of the blood-weary peoples; at last,
We can smile without weeping
While the scattered petals
Dance and glide.

To watch the silky ribbons of dove-white
Soaring high along the crest.
To be so blest
So liberated
So breathtakingly free.
Alix Hearn

Untitled

Stars twinkle tunes of magical dreams coming true
Sunshine smiles as tears of laughter rain.
Paradise is discovered.
The ultimate creation of our lives is love
Unveil the beauty the earth provides
Amidst the trees, creatures and fruits of life evolve.
Quakes divide but hearts continue to beat together
Seas devour but love lives on
Waves crash with soothing passion
Volcanoes erupt, smouldering glorious
blood red fire.
Hearts burn with raging desire
Fulfilled lives eternally survive.
Clare Barrington

Our Situation

From the moment of birth it seems we are fading,
Rise and decline, strong then infirm,
Programmed for life, But mortality dragging,
Yet out of the bud we smile at the worm.

For with spirit do we address our fate,
Joking and laughing while death's at the gate,
Bloodshed and toil afflict our existence,
Yet nothing on earth can halt our persistence.

For consider that it might not have been so
The loss of friends and onset of woe.
The daily grind, a weary routine,
But problem-free in life like a dream.

No heaven and hell, nor war and regimes.
No giving and taking or unfair extremes.
No cancerous growth or pain of deceit.
No bombing campaign or babe's cry for meat.

Still despite it all we embrace what we know
A workable greyness, not unreal allure
For rather than fading, from birth we shall grow.
And God is the genius who makes it all so.
Andrew T. Megson

Death

Once it would touch me rarely,
Rising briefly from a recess of my mind.
Unwelcome, unbidden, disbelief.
Fear.
Now, as time moves forward,
It comes into consciousness bidden,
Shaping thoughts, senses, emotions.
Near.

No longer its presence colours black.
But light. An end, a beginning.
Its coming heralds unburdening.
Release.
I travel now to that finality,
My companions weariness and pain,
Reaching out towards the freeing of my soul.
Peace.
Julie Williams

Endocrine Delower Hossan Monju

Feet changing road
Road stopped, under the pressure of feet
Groaning feet on the road.

Days
In the day dividing human stomach
Flower and Pollen,
Days groaning in days
Heart groaning in heart to heart.

Stony pedestrian
Mutually go on hiding
Mutually remain hidden.
Delower Hossan Monju

The Whales

We once were free
Roamed waves and sea
Together

But man's cruel heart and selfish will
Causes him to hurt and kill
Forever

We now are few and getting less
For massacre and bloody mess
Destroys us all

But beasts shall one day seek revenge
No more upon a man depend
And they shall fall
Alyson Hunter

Death Of An Animal Oblique Of Humanity
Dedicated to Julie Kirby

He hums beneath my touch; Ah! such pleasing murmurous fur
Robust and farm-bred spirit softened, unbestirred
Curls warmly by the windowpane's smoothly silent mire
Encased blackly with unearthly flow lurks feline glittering fire;
Brooding; tempestuous......drooling desire.

Embedded in their velvet surround, snap open twin jewelled orbs
Burning with furious intellect, foreboding violent discord.
From what grim knowledge looms forth this Ominous Threat
Of carnage quite dormant, and feverish fret?
An illusion of an allusion to a fate better to forget.

What of this fanciful animal dream;
Of its unease and anguish — to this race Supreme?
Pulsing warmly through the sorrows of the weary dying day
Who, with calm and reason, could read behind that burning gaze?
As with innocuous charm, a panther's shadow pads
Down winding Metropolitan ways....

Crushed beneath car wheels, all that remains
Of my domestic Messiah of Wrath
Is the trace of muddied paw prints — never from conscience erased
On the lip of my domestic bath.

Julie Campbell

Survival

Sea gulls, sea gulls squawking screeching swirling
round always looking to the ground for food
and tidbits to survive
"Oh it's good to be alive!
But what is this there's one above looking for
a God to love.
Far away from the madding crowd looking for
peace and love abound.
He knows that there's more to life than this
Squawking and looking for material gifts
In peace and love contentment he'll find a life
more wonderful the spiritual kind.
Soaring high above the wind nearer to God with peace
of mind he knows that he has found the answer
to all life's problems. Trust in Him who is above
and in Him you'll find true love, and everlasting
life. Pure and free away from the usual drudgery
of squawking and fighting to survive.
"Then God it will be good to be alive."

Jessie Knox

Fear

Fear is such a lonely place,
It stays there in your head,
It's there with you all through the day,
It follows you to bed.

People say "Don't think of it", "Don't worry", "Have no fear",
But when you're afraid and all alone
You shed a silent tear,

Fear is the silent enemy
You wish would go away
It finds a corner of your head
And slips in there to stay.

Many types of fear there are
All waiting to come round,
But if you have a loving heart
Comfort can be found.

The ones you love will help you through,
When everything seems grey,
And you will wake one morning
To a clear and fearless day.

D. Highfield

Keep Faith

"I'll bring no children into this world"
  said the Woman,
"Not to face the fear and horror of this
  polluted nuclear age!"
"The decision's not yours to make!"
  exclaimed the spirit of an unborn child,
"For God created man in His own image
  and with Freewill — a Precious gift,
Freewill to create or recreate, hopefully, for
  good, but could be evil,
man has faced the unknown and the fear
  of evil down the ages!"
"No! The future's ours, its problems ours
  to solve, the future, ours to live;
Good and Love will prevail, Keep Faith!!"

Arthur Renshaw

Alison

Alison was special, to me anyway, I know lots of people who felt the same way.
Pretty was she, freckles and fair, gorgeous blue eyes and curly brown hair.
Sometimes she smiled, oft times she cried.
I said she would laugh, and twice she tried.
Sleeping all day, awake half the night, nothing would change that, try as I might.
No words could she speak, no steps did she take, her hands did not reach out, nor mess did they make.
Strapped in a chair or on my lap she would sit.
Always supported, lest she should slip.
Her hearing was perfect, unlike her sight, no T.V. for her to bring some delight.
No grazed knees to bandage or tumbles down stairs.
Day-to-day worries, she had no cares.
Was she unhappy, I like to think not, everyone loved her, how could they not?
Innocent as the day she was born, never could she play on a lawn.
Six months they gave her, but she proved them wrong.
Twelve years she lived on, for she was quite strong.
That last night she battled, fought on and on, her strength finally left her and then she was gone.
Then one week later, at her service it proved, her life was not wasted, how could it be, when so many people whose lives she had touched, came to say goodbye to Ali, they loved her so much.

Carol Botterill

God Below

I hear the call
Saying the tides of my love will thrown all your
Sorrow'
But I was told the story about the boy who cried
'wolf'
You loaded away your secrets in cages of steel
But along with my burdens I set them free.
Your love was a mere concept of immorality
And the concept grew in shame,
Whilst your cups overflowed with the promises
You made.
You nurtured fields of humanity,
But I walked through barren desert lauds
And the choice was nine.
You became a pretence for what lay within,
And because of this,
Your throne,
At least in my palace,
Lies in dust.
Last is a concept of start reality.

Jag Khurana

Hills Of Home

And if upon these hills, shall the four winds
Scatter my powdered ashes, then some part of me
Shall be forever here, and if those earlier breezes
Retain the echoes of the voices, with whom
I had shared both laughter and endless conversation,
Then indeed I shall in eternal spirit dwell,
Forever amongst my friends.
But if by fate I shall depart this life,
In some far and distant land, to lie buried deep,
Beneath the desert sands, I shall be remembered,
Only by those, who pause awhile to recall
The times we had spent upon these rolling hills.
But alas, with them gone, the memory of me
Would die also, because no part of me would
Anymore be here, all but in dust and spirit.....
To float upon the wind.

Allan Orpin

Winning Shots

Bouncing here, bouncing there, always on toes, never on top,
Screaming plays, zooming past guards,
Keeping up, falling hard.
Everyone plays, "FOULED" but, still no call
Talent dribbling, past the point.
Badly shot
RICOCHET
"ALLEY OOP"
Lovely dunk, losing team begins to sulk,
Roars of pleasure, their team won,
Up and down their highly strung,
Losers feel like they've been cheated,
Easy shots but we're still beaten
Screaming Coach in locker room,
Atmosphere is full of DOOM!!!

Fraser Rose

Festival Finish

Where else to be than Cheltenham, now winter's done, they say?
Scudding clouds and icy winds — spring really on the way?
Collars turned against the blast, straining for a view,
Thousands waiting in the stands, the climax all but due.

The leaders now in line for home, from them there's not a sound,
Those strangely distant figures seem to float across the ground.
From the tannoy flows the commentary, tones clipped, precise and cold,
Then gradually, the cries go up, a hubbub's taking hold.

Up the straight towards the stands, the cries become a roar,
Forget about the tannoy — you can't hear it anymore.
There's two of them together, battling up the hill,
A flash of colour, bright and brave, ambition to fulfil.

The last fence now behind them and a hundred yards to run,
Ireland's best a length in front, the victory's almost won.
The whole place now in tumult as the leader finds no more
And the favourite runs on strongly — with luck he'll be 9-4.

The wall of sound subsides at once, just as it came to be.
Left, just a babble of excitement and the tannoy's 1-2-3.
It's another piece of folk-lore on another famous day —
Where else to be than Cheltenham, now winter's done, they say?

Ian C. Crawford

Ode To Twinkle — Our Beloved Cat 1969 - 1988

Aubretia was your chosen bed,
Summer swallows above your head,
Happy times we had together,
Hammock slung for times of leisure,
This is how we will remember,
Nineteen years of your shared pleasure,
Dear companion you taught us to love,
Could God recreate you for us above?
No soul the Bible promises for pets,
Yet nothing is impossible, so I will hope yet.

Kay E. Strange

The Garden

Sunlight kissed the Garden in sugared adoration.
Searching for her lover,
The faithful master.
Her eyes roamed the garden, hot-blooded jealousy;
Here was his life, of which she had no part.
Her tears fell bitter sweet.
Why did he spend so long in the garden?
Caressing the soil,
Lovingly, tenderly.
Longing to be the soil, she desired only touch.
Only death could kill his passion.
Her eyes could not see it
Blind to his devotion;
"I love you" written in roses, blatant on the lawn.
His simple act of love, the widow's mite.
Who now will nurture the garden?
In honoured commitment
Listen to the cries of a humbled garden
Now that the husband is gone.

Hazel Wright

Untitled

At the Zenith of our love, that soared on mighty Condor wings
Searching jetstreams fast and new, soaring mighty thermals high.
Higher than the Angels tread
Surveying from our lofty vantage inconsequential life below,
Pathetic trivialities of the world.
Who needs cocaine or opiate, for life's sensations old and new?
We fly higher than a crystal grain achieve amphetamine, hallucinogenic mind
Yes higher than the mighty Condor our love's horizons knew no bounds
Now the tear has left your cheek, the rivulet run dry
We stand alone amongst this torrid mass again,
Mere mortals where love is pain, whilst life so precious passes by.
Quick, grasp my hand and we will fly as one again.
Aloft above this stinking mire.

Christopher George Graham

Call Me From Another Planet

Telephone directories and yellow pages
Secretaries flying off in angry rages
Word processors, Fax machines and colour printers
Everyone racing like Olympic sprinters
Computers, typewriters and calculators
Business people looking for translators
Spell masters, lap top systems and digital planners
Where has everyone left their manners?

Drugs, big money and under hand dealing
Housebreaking, fraud and petty stealing
Wider motorways and faster cars
Soon we'll all be taking off to Mars
Have you got a second hand rocket?
Or a hand held computer in your pocket?
We could see aliens on the Internet
Or earthlings may appear of our planet set.

A fax from the moon would be very nice
But have you thought about the price
Maybe a call on a mobile phone
Whizz kids in space could call home.

Ann Copland

Her

Can you see her dark eyes and the whites
Shining in the moonlight,
And the touch of her silk-like skin upon my
chest, let love begin,
Sweet is the aroma from her fine brown hair
That whips my face with lustful grace,
And the erotic sighs from lips upon mine
gentle pleasures from her hands so kind.

David Bain Wilson

Destined To Fall

Khaki uniforms and hob-nail boots,
Shabby wardrobes with uninviting suits.
Fathers, Husbands, Sons, they're Men alright,
Too young to vote, but old enough to fight.
Weeping wives, with a final farewell,
As one by one in battle they fell.
Bodies and souls that were ripped apart,
By men conditioned to have no heart.
As their agony continued, so too for their wives,
No plans of a future for their shattered lives.
No Fathers for kids who were suffering too,
No Husbands for wives, whose days were too few.
No Sons for Mothers, whose gift was of life,
Who were enduring the pain of the twisting knife.
The people who mourn them, mourn them still,
Tho' they've picked up the pieces, they've had their fill.
Their names will live on in the halls of fame,
This Country must shoulder some of the blame.
But people, like me, can never recall,
The plight of the many, who were 'Destined to Fall'.
Jan Carling

Found And Lost

Never could a smile capture so much in a soul
Shadowed under the cross where Jesus' clothes were sold
Soft brown eyes alluring my capture to warmth
A smile that promised life from a broken birth
Private school, private lives taught me discipline, my body defiled
Graduate the therapy child, destroy my thoughts to be meek and mild.
To the streets of cold, reality's evasion got to run away from
Love to be, love to feel innocent, try to be someone.
I hid my scars as you fed me with your bread
A feast of fortune drinking Christ's blood as I fed
The Deity on the cross, bleeding, dying, saving my soul
His love your secret need to care with all its toil
But fleeting fancies wither and trepidation will grow.
God bless you, I cannot feel what I do not know
It hurts to be happy, to kill me with your kindness
This foreign feeling retreats me back to my land of sadness
Forbidding tears too proud to falter break for freedom down your face
Scarring its sweet nature, collapsing its resilient embrace
And praising the gift of life seems so shallow today.
When benevolence preaches no failure, but for the one that got away.
Alex Hawkins

'Before'

Before that night he was a man,
She a girl so gently bred.
After that night he was a fiend,
And she was dead.

They searched for her by night and day
And found her in a shed.
They tried so hard to give her life,
But she was dead.

They sought her killer far and wide,
They thought he must have fled.
But he was living deep in hell.
For she was dead.

"What have I done", he cried in grief
And to himself he said,
"I must be evil to the core,
I should be dead".

They found him hanging on a tree.
A note pinned to him read,
"I cannot live with such as me,
I'm better dead".
Helen West

The Nightingale

She is a friend very special,
She always has a smile,
She always takes the time
To stop and talk for a while.

When times got tough,
You would hear her sing a little tune,
And her smiling little face,
Would always wash away the gloom.

I feel quite sure throughout my life.
I could never wish to meet,
One who could begin such a simple friendship,
And turn sour into sweet.

So caring, and so giving of herself,
Sincerity, hope and trust,
What wealth!
The wealth of true friendship
Beyond compare!
Annie Atkins

Lost Cause

She is a gentle soul lost in the compulsion to give
She gives freely, wanting to love those lost in their need to lose

She is a needy soul lost in a compulsion to be gentle
She talks freely, wanting to be positively heard by those not wanting to hear

She is a generous soul lost in a compulsion to be needed
She listens carefully, wanting to experience all unfamiliar pains

She is a sensitive soul lost in the compulsion to be hurt
She argues, not wanting to be frustrated by those who will be depressed

She is a free soul, anxious for those who are trapped
She is lost with people who determine that happiness depends on others

She is alone but feels strangely at home
Kaelin Forder

" She "

She leads a sad and lonely life
She is a sad and lonely wife
She took abuse, she suffered lies
for wasted years this woman cries
but for two children bringing joy
a little girl and baby boy
She can't imagine life before
these children mean the world and more.
In spite of pain the marriage brought
she weakens at the very thought
of love once shared and love retrieved
before this tangled web was weaved
When children made from love were born
and insincere promises were sworn
A lonely life she may lead now
but that could change, she prays, somehow
her broken heart will mend and find
a lasting love sincere and kind
together with her children's love
the bad times she can rise above
Louise Fitzsimons

Going Dutch

"You buy the popcorn I'll buy the tickets"
She said, throwing back her hair.
Inside in the darkness
The price of the seats preyed on my mind.
But as we touched so gently,
Our hands entwined,
......I didn't care.
Jeff Spencer

"The Prisoner"

She sits at the window, just looking out,
She knows if she could, she would scream and shout.
Trapped like a prisoner, alone in her mind,
Body of vegetable and partially blind.
She longs for the day, when it will end,
To get rid of a body that will no longer mend.
She cries in her sleep, so no-one can hear,
Because they'd push and they'd prod, saying "Alright my Dear."
She knows they are kind and very good,
But it's hell being trapped and not understood.
For death would be a blessing and no-one should mind,
For death is not awful, but sometimes quite kind.
Charles Trail

Grandmas

My grandmama, I thought was very old.
She lived in solitude — the house too large and cold,
Of dark brocade, her gown was trim and neat,
Quaint lace-up boots concealed her tiny feet.
Grey plaited locks reflected Time's swift race;
Lost hopes and dreams were etched upon her face.

We called on her each Sunday to take tea.
Those visits were eternity for me!
In straight-backed fear, upon an upright chair,
[I still recall the scourge of black horse hair.]
Her strong hot tea was drunk, without a word.
For 'Children should be seen but never heard!'

Now all too soon the passing years have flown,
A small grandchild I welcome of my own.
Her squeals and chatter make a cheerful noise.
Each room besieged with many scattered toys.
A chocolate circled grin, a small hand on my knee;
"Please Grandma, is there ice-cream for my tea!"

"Oh! Grandmama, the cold conventions of your time
Deprived you of the love this child has brought to mine."
Lilian M. Ball

A New Life

The tiny seed began to stir
She moved her fragile roots,
Drank sweet water from the earth
And pushed out dark green shoots.
With trembling stem she found her way
Through damp and rich brown soil,
Then as she breathed the clean sweet air
She rested from her toil.
The kind sun warmed her baby leaves
The soft rain kissed her clean,
She looked around her in great awe
At the pretty garden scene.
The days passed by, she stronger grew
Her flowers blossomed fair,
And the scented beauty of this plant
Graced the garden there.
Carolyn Fraser

Enfolded

Cannot sleep, the small child thought
Said my pray'rs, as I was taught.
Counted sheep, it was no use,
Call my mum, make some excuse?
Maybe not, she may not come.
I try, sigh, then yawn — ho-hum!
Close my eyes, I shut them tight.
Think of stars that shine so bright.
Whirling, swirling through the night.
Swirling with them, me so small.
Whirling, whirling with them all.
Love enfolds me, love so deep.
Wrapp'd in wings, fall fast asleep.
Stars around me swirl and sweep.
Falling safely, fast asleep.
Amaqla Wood

A Tiny Tale

Miss Teeny Weeny suits her well
She stands just four feet high
And in her little stockinged feet
She's sunk in carpet pile

The wonder of her tiny feet
Those dainty ankles shod
She's dwarfed by men of normal height
Notwithstanding Mr. Plod

When hoeing with the garden rake
With six-inch heels in mud
We look around to find her gown
Upended in the spuds

Oh! Sharon is your end in sight
We've mistaken for a tater
My one and only son's delight
His little ripe tomater
Doris M. Jackson

"Twilight", (The Wanderers Dream)

Twilight is the grandest lady of all
She stands off the floor nearly eleven feet tall
She glides along all polished and smart
And everyone waves when it's time to depart

Twilight provides all the comfort you need
Home Sweet Home and more indeed
With a bed, bath and lounge there is nothing amiss
She even takes along her own satellite dish

Twilight will take us wherever we like
For cycling when there she carries our bike
When it is time to relax there's no need to despair
She has chairs on the inside and more in fresh air

Twilight is happy to go a long way
Maybe because she's from the U.S. of A.
When we fancy a trip we just climb aboard
And choose a point on the compass here or abroad

Twilight makes friends wherever she goes
Some of them caravans with hooks on their nose!
Be it Paris, Geneva, London or Rome
We would never be without our dear motorhome
Julie Adams

Lady

Lady was like Lassie the dog.
She was our hero from out of the fog.
It was a shame she had to die
I didn't even get to say good-bye.
She was an enjoyment for all of us.
It was a shame she had to catch the heavenly bus.
She was the item that brought us to-gether
we all wish we had her forever and ever.
Amy West

Poor Aunt Flo. (Deceased)

It's sad we can't mourn our Aunt Flo,
(she wasn't very nice to know)
But in a way we'll miss Aunt Flo.

We hardly ever saw her smile,
(she was, in fact, rather a trial)
But we will miss her once a while.

She'd say "I always speak my mind",
(adding "it's for your good, you'll find",
but it was often quite unkind.

Of course we all will send a wreath,
(for 'though we cannot feel much grief),
she'd lots of good points underneath.

And all of us have faults that we
(hope those whom we call friends don't see)
On this perhaps we all agree.
Joyce Higgs

Besotted, The Angel, Shattered His Crest

Cradling creatures there stands a great oak.
Sheltering life beneath emerald cloak.
Though you are of soft flesh you are as the tree,
Noble and handsome, protective you'll be.
On thundering hooves of a faithful old steed,
For king and for country you'll dutifully speed.
Brave knight as you charge with shimmering sword
At monsters of evil where blood they have poured
You think not of fear but just to protect,
The good, the helpless and those you respect.
Now slain are the dragons with fiery breath
that cursed the land with terrible death.
Leave your weapons, you've accomplished your quest,
and wicked were claws that tore at your chest.
The oak tree has fallen all burning and black.
Ferocious the beast that struck with a crack.
So lay gently down your head on my breast
Renounce your body, your soul now must rest.
Rise with my spirit on glorious wings,
of heavenly peace, a nightingale sings.

Debra Dowie

Our Susie

A bundle of mischief, of coppery gold
She's really still tiny and not very old
Two gleaming bright eyes and a dear little face
Such love and affection she's made her own place.

So full of life 'though young in years
No time to sit quiet when Susie appears
Out in the open she goes chasing around
Playmate or plaything must quickly be found.

When tea is served it would not be quite right
If you finished your treat and ate the last bite
That surprised little face seems to look up and say
"That was mine, you got plenty, just pass it my way"
She's a dear little dog, she's now done her part
For a tiny, wee doggie has captured our heart.

Jean Lawrie

The Unborn's Thoughts

I, the Unborn, heavy in your womb —
Shifting, growing, moulding features,
Following ancient genetic instructions
That will make Me what I am.

I, the Unborn can hear water lapping —
Surely I have left Creation's shore?
And all about an undulating film
Protects my unguarded movements.

I, the Unborn heavy in my capsule
Can hear the voice of Nature calling
Soon my time 'to be' draws hence
And my egg-shell world will break.

I, the Unborn — what will I be?
A leader of men, A god to mortals?
Or simply a man content to live
Until his span is run?

I, the Unborn, my time is nigh.....

Julie Parkinson

His Love

But do you love him,
Still,
After all this time?
You still have feelings for him? Yes.

Do you love him,
What, his love?

You can't call what you have been going through love,
It's hell, it's torment,
It's wanting love to be.
Be.

Heather J. Lewis

Jesus

Thank you Jesus for your light,
    shining on us day and night.
Thank you Jesus for being our guide,
    evil things cannot hide.

Jesus you are so great
    I trust you rather than fate.
Thank you Jesus for being my friend,
    when I die this is not the end.

Thank you Saviour for your love,
    your wonderful spirit, the holy dove.
Lord Jesus who is our King,
    Prince of Peace and everything.

He died on the cross for our sin,
    to save us, so we can be with him.
He rose from the grave,
    all people He wants to save.

Elizabeth DeMeza

Tangier

A cockerel's crowing, the mosque is wailing, day is coming to life.
Ships' horns blow from across the bay, fishes swim out of their path.
Early tradings in the harbour, trucks running in and out of port.
With public transport, departures and arrivals, imports and export.

Through the streets into medinas, winding into souks.
Filling up with djellabah clad men, and kaftan dressed women.
With only her eyes on show, their silence behind her veil.
Whilst going on all around her, is this hustle and bustle.

Earthenware pots, berber carpets, brass and silver, striking one's eyes
The stall holder, touting and punting for the best of price.
American express, Yankee dollars, German marks, or the
    English pound.
Anything you like, as long as it makes that till opening sound.

Sitting on this magic carpet, drinking herbal tea.
I'll take four hundred, no I'll give you three,
Settled for three fifty, and we'd Made A Deal.
That stall holder sure did give a whole lot of spiel.

'Twasn't long, before I was to experience some more.
When up to me, came this shoe shine boy.
Hadn't yet paid him his five, when from out the cornerstone
    came a tourist guide.
Now I'm sitting, reminiscing, intrigued, whilst I write.

John Langbridge

The Tree

Standing tall against the winter sky, its branches reaching high,
Silently and bare the three stands and waits.

Standing tall against the spring sky.
The tree stirs and comes to life,
Buds appear as the sap of life rises,
And the cycle starts anew.

Standing tall against the summer sky,
Clothed in all her beauty, of green and brown.
Birds sing on branches reaching towards the sun.

Standing tall against the autumn sky,
The tree now all gold, and brown,
The leaves one by one come tumbling down,
As the tree prepares to sleep.

Standing tall, the tree does not move,
But life is still within, sometimes sleeping,
Sometimes stirring gently, or bursting with energy,
How great is nature if we understand.

Man too is like the tree in all its seasons,
And if we understand the tree,
Then we have hope in understanding man.

George Aspinall

A Winter's Tail

She came upon a winter's night,
Shocked and trembling, sick with fright.

Missing brother, sister, mum,
In the garden tries to run.

Hates the collar, hates the home,
Hides in a corner to be alone.

When she found we meant no harm,
She hid her head beneath our arm.

Loving care and gentle voice,
She'll never go back given the choice.

A life of shouting, punches and kicks,
Bruises to heal, wounds to lick.

Now she's loved and fed too well,
We took her from a living hell.

Her fears still there, buried deep,
Her trust and love are ours to keep.

She came upon a winter's night,
Our pride and joy, our summer's light.

Elizabeth Brewer

Island Tweed Shop

Bales of hoarse tweed touch
shoulders here. Rough moor
is woven with peat,
a herringbone. Here, a mountain
burn falls in yards
upon the counter, and careful
scissors cut a bracken slope.
There, a loch's blue depths
are measured, and a mist-grey sky unrolled...

Outside, the real landscape waits.
Fresh rain falling
and a salt-marked shore.

Kath Barr

Romeo and Juliet... With a Difference!

"Romeo, Romeo where can you be?"
Shouts Juliet from the edge of her balcony
"Over here, you fool!" He shouts back in dismay
Wishing that she would just go away
For he was sitting reading an interesting book
On the nice, quiet bank of the peaceful little brook
Enchanted by the words leaping off of his page
He didn't notice Jule's approach in a terrible rage
"What are you doing?" she demanded at once
He stood up quite quick and his face she did punch
He hit back quite hard, but cry she did not
She went back to the terrace and back to her spot
Where this time her shout was not "Where can you be?"
But "Romeo, Romeo, come hither ye"
When no reply was given to her last roar
She ran away with the boy next door!

Julie Adams

'Seasons'

We pass through winter carefully
Snow, rain everything,
Yearning very restlessly
For that single sign of spring.
'Spring arrives with flowers
We feel good but yet it's true,
Our thoughts race on for summer
Hopeful skies of hazy blue.
Autumn follows quickly
Falling leaves, most blossoms are gone,
Shades of brown are common
We are heading to square one.

Janet Hall

A Field Of Silence

The bodies fill the fields for miles.
Silence!
Except for the weeping of the wounded
Like a field of crying wheat.
The wheat has changed to poppies
As red as blood!
Cries of birds calling for their friends.
Friends?
All I have is a half dead dog.
I hear a new sound
Like an earthquake!
I dive into a stream
A blood red stream!
Shiny boots charge past.
I stay as still a rock.
Then BANG!
A scream.

Daniel Walker

Moon-Struck

Lady Moon incandescently bright,
Silent, breathless, not even a sigh
Painting the landscape in silvery light
Eclipsing the stars in indigo sky.

Bright enchantress weaving your spell
Inviting lovers to drink of your light,
Confessor to secrets never to tell
Recipient of prayers murmured soft in the night.

Ethereal beauty commander of oceans
Earth and tide bow to your ardent desire,
Ensnaring and toying with mortals' emotions
Inspiring, conspiring, lighting their fire.

Mystical Moon spinning cobwebby shrouds
Lighting the owl on its soft feathered flight,
Hiding your face behind purple-banked clouds
Guardian to spirits and creatures of night.

Hazel Clifton

Autumn Beauty.......

What beauty in your forest Lord,
    silent, misty, wondrous beauty!
In it all your steps are traced;
    while dappled bracken, leaf and grass,
shine like crystal from your hand.
    Thank you Lord for treasures shared!

As I walk my golden path,
    may others find your beauty here
traced within my Autumn years;
    Dappled pain and joy enduring,
spreading God's love everywhere.
    Thank you Lord for treasures shared!

Josephine Payne

A Sailor Lad

Then came the peace. He
mingled with the aftermath
Coughing and pain, the Doctor came,
Too long below in the ship.
Long hours below, dot dash, dash dot,
Tuberculosis took him by storm.
His battle raged through choppy streams of red.

Someone said he was dead! His
sister came with children. "We
want to see Uncle," they cried.
They saw him from far fields.
This time he couldn't play — the bell
tolled, but not for him — this time.

He shouted at the red streams,
pushed away his pain. A hand
stretched down, pulled him up,
and saved him once again.

Gladys Llewellyn

Geezer In The Freezer

I'm looked on as curiously odd and unusual
Since I announced I don't want a funeral
'Cause unless I'm laid in the box upside down —
The fire will shrink me, turning me around
Or — the worms will crawl over my face and chin
Even worse — a while after my teeth fall in
I have willed my dead body to advance knowledge
To be carved and dissected at a medical college
A beneficial donation, a gift to modern science
Grand bare appearance to an intelligent audience
My new priorities are painted glossy toes
Eyebrows shaped — "perm" never outgrows
My family are cheering at the "dotty" request
Since they won't have to pay or even get dressed.
If I "cash in" at Xmas — inconsiderately
The doctors and students all away on holiday
— Alas my plan may never come to fruition
They can refuse me, it's their decision
So please delay the call — put me in the freezer
Squander the brass left by this odd geezer.

Dot Dillow, Biggin

Tomorrow

Do not cry for me when I die
Since my operation, it's been try,try,try.
I cannot talk or shout.
This is what life os partly about
I am not the man I was
But I will fight to the end, because
God made me a fighter
Talking to him the weight seemed lighter

I know I cannot smell the flowers
Or the green grass after showers
I can laugh but no sound is heard
But I can hear the song of the bird
Stand up man! Shoulders back
What's the saying. "I'm alright Jack"
Writing this poem has lifted my heart
Tomorrow you will see me make a new start.

John Weatherley

" A New Birth "

As each day dawns, it is for me a day of grace,
   Since now, I have two new eyes of faith
And may behold my Saviour's lovely face.
   For I live and tread the earth
As seeing him, who is invisible,
   Yet 'tis he who liveth now in me.
For without him how would or could I cope?
   Since he it is who promises through life
My hope in things eternal and divine.
   So for future days upon the earth
And later on in Heaven,
   Jesus is always mine.

Barbara Mason

The Top Of The World

I stand alone a-staring in the wan wood-light;
Shivers my shadow on the bank upright;
Shivers my heart as it cries aloud to thee.
My darling, I'm in hell for you, and you're in hell for me!

A single sprig of cotton-grass rears up toward the sky;
A single lonely lava field lies there for you and I.
Where have you gone? Where are you now?
Beyond the icy sea; beyond the wintry Iceland waves that
   sob aloud to me.
My darling, I'm in hell for you, and you're in hell for me!

High on the heights of Thule I stand and hear Earth's bowels roar,
They vomit rocks and boiling broth upon that dreary shore:
A power immense, incarnate hate, and wrath and grief and rage.
And havoc wreaked unmerciful upon a broken stage.
And thus my heart is torn apart, as I look out to sea;
My darling, I'm in hell for you, and you're in hell for me!

Jean Mary Edwards

Unemployed Miner

Forty years old, militant and uncompromising
Six feet tall, blue scarred and intimidating
Half his life spent under mountains shovelling,
Months since the lay off, 25 years to a full pension

Strong face, heavyweight shoulders
Salt and pepper hair, full frosted beard
Black cap and clothes, scuffed white black boots
Damp with sweat, ice and snow

He walks up to pithead most weeks over tips
To see mine agent for any job
He buses every second week to valley town
Signs on at joke centre and scans vacant boards

Survives week to week, savings gone
Like three thousand others in valley
On dry days picks coal from tips,
Teenage daughters can't understand

The warm glow of sleep envelops him;
Black and white dreams of abandoned coal faces
Brave comrades, alive and dead
Bad memories of rock falls, water and fire.

Alex Greenow

Sometimes

Sometimes I feel like it's
slipping away
A dream in the distance
as night steals the day
It's the only thing I've got,
this surreal ambition
A world needs a war
like a God needs tuition

But sometimes a loser wins
and sometimes a preacher sins
I've seen love break down the walls of hate
Tonight it's time to celebrate

Sometimes the rain will
beat down in spring
A fool will grow wiser,
a prince will be king
Look into your heart,
for it's there you will find
Don't peer through your eyes,
Or you'll only be blind.

Kevin Maher

The Life Of A Rose

A tiny rose that flowers and grows,
Small and sweet with petals so neat,
With daylight the petals open and bloom,
And darkness closes the rose with its gloom.

With a stem that grows so tall and strong,
Like a father whose strength stays all along,
And thorns to protect the rose from all foes,
Like a mother protects her child as it grows.

A symbol of love for Valentines day,
To express the feelings that words cannot say,
The rose will see the sun, snow and rain,
Not just once, but again and again.

The rose like a child, will grow year after year,
But one day will leave behind those who are dear,
Life after death? nobody knows,
Blessed to be born with the life of a rose.

Amanda Vince

Night Sounds

Scratching, sighing, tip toeing,
Snoring, prowling, hooting,
Whispering winds, trees making love, elements disputing
Darkness king of the night ruling.
Ghouls looking for a resting place.
Death stalking its prey defeating,
Earth creaking and sighing
From the weight of our woes.
Newborn babies crying for the security of the womb.
The slushing noise of life blood gushing from a stabbing
The swish of a bullet rushing to meet its victim.
The bang demonstrating the unbalanced mind
The tick of a clock our supreme ruler obeyed by all men.
Birds twittering in their sleep
As they gobble choice crumbs.
The click of high heels —
As women of the night display their wares,
The silent witness and the revealer,
Seeking pleasure to satisfy the outer man
And the inner man searching peace for his soul.
Bridget Cooper

Untitled

A woman's nature is deceiving
So be wary of believing
That the virtues you extol
Are truly mirrored in her soul,
The grace and poise and loving heart
She may have learned like any part
In any play — to please your sight
And yet, who knows? — you may be right

Perhaps the wise man would attend to
The one gift she can't pretend to,
And would recognize God's grace
In the beauty of her face.
James May

" Down And Out "

Demon Angels of doom battle in the skies above,
So evil they are devoid of love,
Stars don't seem to be glistening tonight,
The Atmosphere has no light,
'And eerie silence takes over'...
'It will soon be Morning'....

This poor pathetic Human will have to fight another day,
What cruel obstacles will stand in his way?
He is "Down and Out" and has no place to go,
Why has his life sunk so low?
His angular face is wrinkled and sad,
Maybe tomorrow won't be so bad,
Discarded food from here and there,
With the same result extreme despair,
A lifetime in this depressed state,
In this his eternal fate?
A bottle of meths and several pills
Could be the cocktail that death fulfils?
Christine Kitson

To The Children Of Smokey Mountain

Walk down streets of sadness, colder than the snow.
See the children crying but no one seems to know.
Sifting through the garbage, trying to find a meal,
With wounds that cut so deep, scars that never heal.
Hidden in the shadows they are crying out a prayer,
"Another one has passed away, doesn't someone care?"

No matter what I do, no matter what I say,
I'm just one person like I was yesterday.
Please don't turn away, I want you to understand.
Wasn't my intention, was not what I had planned.
Because I want to help, there is only one thing I see,
To heal the world of suffering, the change must start with me.
Amber Collins

" The Seasons "

A lot of snow fell in my garden last night,
so I look out today at a beautiful sight.
It's thick on the ground, the trees and the fence,
the birds can't find food because it's so dense.
I'm watching a robin, then suddenly see
three squirrels playing, up in a tree.

When the snow melts, soon spring will be here,
the bulbs will come up, to bring us all cheer.
Life will spring back to the trees that were bare
and wild flowers appear, without any care.
Then summer will come and it will get hot,
the daylight draws out, which we all like a lot.
The lawns and the flowers then grow very fast
and we hope that the summer is going to last.

Then comes the autumn and things start to die,
the leaves from the trees seem to fall from the sky.
Everything changes to browns and to golds,
the colours are lovely, as autumn unfolds.
We drive in the country at that time of year
to see all the beauty—before winter's here.
Anne Davis

The Old Codger

I ain't got a rhyme inside me old 'ead
So instead of thinking I goes to bed
It's the 'ard ground below an the black sky above
But I'se got fer me piller the England I love.

It's 'ard goin' up and it's 'ard goin' down
When yer old feets ache as yer tramp ter the town
An yer boots need a mend an yer 'eart stands still
When yer thinks yer won't make it over the hill.

There's no one ter listen ter grumbles and sighs
Yer can only curse at the earth and the skies
But it's comfort I gets when I 'ear old Ned
Braying his 'eart out but still quite content.

It ain't no use sighing and longing fer riches
An wishin' yer didn't 'ave ter sleep in ditches
I'm jist an old codger like poor old Ned
An we'll go tergither when it's time ter be dead.
Daphne P. A. Day

Sweet Thing

Hey sweet thing! — Remember me? I had a crush on you!
So long ago — remember when?
But no you don't! — Of course you don't!
I wrote to you such wondrous things!
I sang to you on golden wings!
I whispered out your name at night,
My heart beat faster at your sight!
Sweet thing — remember me? But no you don't! You couldn't do!
I had a crush on you — but never said!
I wrote of you, but never sent!
I sang of you, but no words went!
I whispered your name to myself,
And here I am, still on the shelf!
Hey sweet thing! — Remember me?
Discarded, old, and lonely me?
Of course you don't!
How could you?
I NEVER SAID!!
Colin Gander

My Little Man

He comes into the room, jumps into bed.
Snuggles down, takes all the bed,
Laughs and giggles, squirms about,
is this what it is all about?
Time to get up Grandma.
What shall we play?
The rest of the house sleeps on,
Grandma's here today.
Eileen Hallas

The Last Centurion

With head bowed low the soldier stood
So low he looked in shame
Around him lay the dead and dying
But he himself was not to blame.

His comrades had fought and hard that day
The enemy had been stronger
The blood that spurt from his wound
He could not live much longer.

Beside him lay a golden bird
An emblem he knew well
One last salute he gave
Then on earth no more to dwell.

Joyce Boast

Thoughts On Ireland

The innocent streets see so much shame,
So many fine flowers brought to the ground;
A few outgrow the pavement, leave for fame,
For fortune and hard stones confound
Them, dragging at their heels; pull back
The talent, bury genius for the lack
Of understanding; and common stones
Form common resting place for common bones.
The rendezvous disputes for pride of place
With barricades against a common race;
Streets know no creed, and stones have hues
Of blood, hand painted by such men as choose
Blood brothers' deaths, bodies in a gutter
To boon companions. The same tongues utter
Creeds as little different as one stone from another.
Walk safely down my street, my innocent brother.

Eric Chapman

A Lost Love

My darling, I love you through and through,
so much more than any man should do,
even if it's only been a short number of days,
I've missed you, in every possible way,
you are my dream, and my heart's desire,
always setting my heart and soul on fire,
with all the care and grace I receive,
I love you more than you can ever believe,
outside I smile as inside I cry,
slowly breathing a tearful sigh,
all these days that I endlessly pine,
finding that the sun no longer shines,
within my lonely heart, your thoughts lie,
without your love, I would wither and die,
do both our tender hearts beat as one?
Of any doubts, there is surely none,
an earthly treasure, you will remain,
keeping me content, and my thoughts sane.

Christopher Higgins

Tugging

I sink beneath the ripples
Of a river in my dreams,
The water pulling softly
As I wonder what it means?

The colours all reflecting
The depth and troubled mood,
The dark, the passionate, the foaming,
The inner battling feud.

The tide forever rising
Waiting for the dam to burst,
Releasing all the anguish
And quenching the ocean's thirst.

The debris on the surface,
The remains of a troubled mind
Floating gently with the current
As the scars are left behind.

Tracy Cavender

Neglect

The church stood upon the ground
So quiet with hardly any sounds
Dull and bleak with flaking paint
Never no sign of a heavenly saint.

The pews were empty, alone they stood
Broken and torn, made of old wood
So very still, the air was cold
Slimy walls green covered in mould.

No people were present, no prayers were said
Where had they gone, were they all a bed
Now the neglect was sad to see
Everybody absent like you and me.

This once bright cheerful church, once great
Where is everybody, do you all hate
It's sad to see this once holy place
Demolished soon as its sad fate.

Without thinking of times past or present
Never waiting even for the message
God loves us all, old, young or small
So he will forgive us, one and all

Janice M. Baker

Midnight Immortality

As the moon becomes a full,
So the wolves release their howl,
The breeze blows fresh and cool,
With every sound of an owl.

The trees surrender followed by their shadow,
Across a reflected moonlit lake,
All for the devil's sake.

So hush little children hush,
Say your prayer if you must,
At night run free do all lost little ones,
They are the ones to which all evil shall come,
The rustle of all wild things diminish,
If you're not careful, so shall your soul and spirit.

Now creeps in the beauty of dawn,
And so the little ones begin their mourn,
Their lost mortal soul, Gone forever the devil bestow,
Yet at night when the infant's shadow diminishes within the devil's,
And he sees them, and he charms them, and whispers,
"Suffer the little children to come unto me,
So come little children come unto thee".

Christina Pope

Widespread Notoriety

Flippant quips about life in Major's classless
society have only earned the Tories widespread notoriety

Crumbling school buildings, once proud industries
discarded, those who govern our lives are certainly
hard-hearted

The Health Service is safe with us was their cry,
but Market Forces mean that some poor patients die!

I voted for Maggie, now I rue the day that I
was naive and easy prey

Money and materialism was her rallying call, then
like Lemmings her Yuppies headed for a fall

But what about the Poor, the Weak and the Sick,
surely they fall by the wayside under this Yardstick

Grind those into the ground who can't keep up,
whilst those with the means drink from an over-flowing cup

Caring and compassion must win through, their days
are numbered, they're up for review

Let Blair and his visionaries show us a new way,
right now might must save the day

Ken Jackson

Daylight of Hope

As the hours of daylight are breaking
So the world of nature is awaking.
Upon trees growing so tall
Birds to their friends do give a call.
Lazy old cats would give a stretch.
Folks their alarm clocks would press.
All of a sudden the world is awake.
People rushing so as not to be late
Rushing here and there
With loads of worries and care,
If only people would slow
Down and think for a while
Maybe we would have a
World for us all
Full of happiness and smiles

John Emary

Getting Through The Tough Time

You live your life day by day
So unselfish is your way
Even when your day has been long
You always make time for everyone

I know you're having your share of pain
Smiling through when there's nothing to gain
Getting on with your life as best as you can
That's what makes you a good man

Although you've a big struggle ahead
Which will make your heart feel like lead
I know one day your pain will heal
And the winning card will be in your deal

But for now you will carry on getting by
One day all your tears will dry
Even though you are going through this sadness
You still bring people lots of gladness

The happiness you give is your wealth
So never hide away in yourself
At the end of the tunnel there is light
So John Harvey, your future looks bright

Jacqueline Hartley

A Story Of A Tree

I started as a tiny seed, implanted in a womb,
So warm and safe and snug inside, wrapped up in my cocoon.
I had to leave my dark surround by order of creation,
So struggled slowly through the ground with fear and hesitation.
As the years went rolling by, I stretched to reach above me,
I felt a need to touch the sky and lots of people loved me.
They left their mark upon by bark for all the world to see them,
Their written word a pact of love, I've wished that I could be them.
Also sorrow I have seen by lovers standing near me, and then
I've wished that I could talk and maybe they could hear me.
There's too much sadness in this world, sometimes it just astounds me,
If people took a closer look, there's beauty all around me.

Kathleen Brown

Flower Pot Men

My big sister and I decided to sow some seed,
So we went into our garden with packets of flower seeds,
And while we were there we met
Two wonderful little men, standing
In two of our flower pots behind our garden shed.
We asked them their names, and they
Looked up to us, and said, "We are
Bill and Ben, the Flower Pot Men.
Once we were famous on television."
Then they asked us politely for
Tea and toast,
And said in exchange, they would
Sow all of our seeds,
And keep all of our flower beds
Neat and tidy and free from weeds.

Len Pearson

Floods

Dank, dark days of dreary drizzle,
  Sombre skies that auger more grey,
Wild winds whipping up sheets of showers
  To billow and fall on beds of clay.

Reticent rivers reluctantly rise,
  Flooding fields and filling furrows.
Sodden streets streamlined with sandbags,
  Wildlife flees from homes and burrows.

Relentless rain is battling bravely,
  Barometer still staying low.
Goddesses are gulping gallons,
  Parishes praying winds will blow.

Bridges being built by army
  Open over sodden sod.
Southern sites seem doomed to drowning
  But for reign supreme of God.

Cherry L. Tompsett

Charlotte's Garden

I see so many faces in all the flowers that grow
Some are quite familiar, some I don't even know

All of them are smiling as they raise their pretty heads
Up towards the sunshine streaming down upon their beds

I see them all as children growing up so straight and tall
Some so bright and vivid, some almost no shade at all

I know there's a flower growing for every child on earth
New ones appearing daily to announce each baby's birth

So if I had to choose just one flower to fill my garden plot
It would be the one which grows especially for my lovely Charlotte

Each time I walk into my garden when the grass is wet with dew
I would smile and say "Good Morning" and my thoughts would be of you.

Dorothy Browning

Observations

Some folks are happy, some of us sad,
Some folks are good, and others are bad

Some people are fat — whilst others are thin,
Some people lose, and others just win,

Some feast all day, and some not at all
Some are quite tiny, and others quite tall,

Many are poor, and many are wealthy
Whilst some souls are sick and others are healthy.

We meet people arrogant — others are meek.
Some of us chatter — and others don't speak.

Some are so cheerful, and love each new day
They know how to live, and show others the way.

Kathleen M. Daniels

Waves

Triumphant as crested dragons, spitting foam and spume,
So the eternal waves roll home.
Each in its turn crashing to the beach,
Hesitating before a hissing retreat.
Sucking back in shingle hungrily,
Coke cans, crisp packets, drifting debris.
Floating miniature rafts of dropped lollipop sticks,
Launching ice-cream tubs and lost shoe ships.
Then heady and giddy with champagne elation,
They linger, fizzing in inlets and bottleneck places;
Stirring up the murky weed
Where the dark eels lurk and feed.

Tide running low, the breakers mellow,
Reining in across the shallows
To frolic like dolphins, chuckle and leap;
Until in translucent ripples - they tiptoe to the beach.

Catherine Curtis

Closing Time

Just the clinking of some glasses, in some down town smoky bar,
Some lonesome ho-bo strumming a tune on his guitar.
The ashtrays overflowing, empty bottles, empty chairs,
Cards strewn around the tables, money lost, nobody cares.

Moll has done her singing, her swan song has been sung,
Her golden days are over, she leaves them for the young.
A drop-out in the corner, he's got no place to go,
Where he will do his sleeping, nobody seems to know.

A dog is cowered by the fire, finding shelter from the cold,
Its battered frame is showing the signs of growing old.
Shadows forming pictures, silhouettes upon the wall,
The smell of oil that's burning, from the lamp lit in the hall.

Match sticks lie like soldiers, dead upon the floor,
A hat someone's forgotten, left hanging on the door.
The honkey-tonk piano has played its last request,
The barman's closed the shutters, the town has gone to rest.
Jacqueline Sanderson

Someone

Someone to hold me when the nights grow cold
Someone to love me when I grow old
Someone to look after me, someone to care
Someone who will always be there

Someone to share the good times and the bad
Someone to show me all the things I've never had
Someone to hold me when the day is light
Someone to hold on to in the silence of the night

Someone who understands and has a sympathetic touch
Someone who knows that a little love can mean so much
Someone who knows that we all have our little ways
Someone I can live with for the rest of my days

Someone who knows about hearts and flowers
Someone who likes to dodge the April showers
Someone who loves music, soft rock, jazz or even motown
Someone who loves to sit and watch the sun go down

Someone to sit with and play the blues
Someone to help me colour in life's many hues
Someone to stroll with through life, hand in hand
Someone to be part of my life that is not yet planned
Edina Harman

Untitled

The morning breaks — bright, eternal
Just as though a mantle of light was spreading over the sky.
I wake from slumber, pleasant thoughts fill my mind.
I hear the song of the bird, the gentle rustle of the leaves on
   the trees.
My heart with thankfulness faces the new day...
And then realization comes — of the night past, of sadness,
   of grief and devastation...
Once again those dreadful words — "There's been a bomb!"
Lives ended, limbs broken, mothers, fathers, wives and
   children heartbroken, mourning.....
The happiness is gone, the joy of the new dawn turns to sadness
To fear, to dread, to choking back the tears — to cry for peace,
   to yearn for a better way.
What will it take to make them see — the evil of their ways.
How dare they? Oh! how dare they take it all from us.
The peace, the joy, the coming together of the past months.
It was fragile, just like the white dove soaring in the sky.
But we held on, hoping against hope, that it would grow,
   would blossom
And our children would know a brave new world.
We can't go back, we must strive with all our strength to carry on
To pray that hearts and minds will be transformed
To welcome love instead of hate — to understand and not conflict
Then a bright new morn will dawn — and right will reign eternal.
Grace McGaffin

Nellie Bligh

"Murder-Murder" was the cry
Someone's killed old Nellie Bligh
Good Riddance too said barmaid bet
no one will miss the silly old get
poking her nose wherever she went
The silly old hag was surely bent.
How did she die asked one old goat
Someone went and slit her throat.
From ear to ear so I've heard said
and some say it near cut off her head
Much blood about? Asked pub crawler pete
sure enough — all over the sheet.
What a rotten way to die
still — who will miss old Nellie Bligh
Brian D. Cotterill

Just Another

The voice drones on, film stars arriving, the price of cars.
Someone's sitting up a pole and won't come down.
Yes dear, we'll have a cup of tea, and watch another film.
Perhaps I'll take a nice hot bath and drown!
The villain is stalking another girl, with rape and murder on his mind
The music is frenzied and now the deed is done
Should I buy the baby another toy, or meet with Jennie for yet
   another lunch
Perhaps I'll walk stark naked down the street and tell the Police
I did it just for fun!

Yes dear, the cat's put out, we'll go to bed. I'll take my book,
and leave the mundane world the light is out, the day is gone
With another just like it when I wake
I look over at a well known face, disgruntled me and wanting more
Then suddenly it's all in place
I'm filled with warmth and here I'm safe.
A kind strong hand, an open smile, a constant man with no demands
My comfort always comes first
The butterflies may have their brilliant moments in the sun.
But for me this warm cocoon is summer long.
Eve Mannings

Homelessness

As I'm walking through the streets, what can I see?
Something that is very clear, clear to you and me,
People in shop doorways, lying on the floor,
Lying on the concrete and blocking up the doors,
Coughing and sneezing all through the day,
These people must be ill, ill in every way,
Dying of starvation and dying of the cold,
Any object they possessed, they've taken to be sold,
No money and no food at all, nothing left to eat,
Even an apple or a plum would go down as a treat,
The things we take for granted, the things that are so small,
They are crying out for, oh can't you hear them call,
All that they will want tonight is just a place to sleep,
Instead of lying on the floor and lying in a heap,
Some crusty bread and butter, maybe with some jam,
It's not as if they're asking for turkey or roast ham.
So spare a little money, just to let them sleep,
In a place that is not on the floor and lying in a heap.
Emma-Jayne Anderson

I Danced With The Salt Prince

I dreamt that I danced with the salt prince
Somewhere in the middle of the sea
And large cakes surrounded me
I couldn't see his face clearly
Just his power protecting me
I lost my shoes in the process
I could feel the water run through my toes
It was warm and safe
I didn't need to breathe through my nose
It seemed to cleanse me within
And stimulate the senses
That cover my skin.
Jean Iona Johnson

Rich Man Poor Man

I am the filthy poor man, sleeping in your street
Sometimes dressed up as a tramp with no shoes on my feet
or begging on the corner when my family needs to eat
Hey man I'm your brother, that you don't want to meet.

You are the filthy rich man, adorn yourself in gold
surround yourself in falsity and things you love to hold
You house yourself in grandeur where your rooms are never cold
Brother, you're the shadow of the spirit that you sold.

I lead a simple lonely life, bad memories cut in deep
But what I have I'd share with you, yet what you have you keep
My possessions all fit in this case, my pillow while I sleep
Brother, it's the life I choose, for freedom don't come cheap.

Your money buys misery, your greed has turned you blind
To all your acts of selfishness that made you so unkind
My humble life's my fortune, that buys me peace of mind
Brother, you can keep your cash, I've got wealth you'll never find.
David Newton

Martha

Always there,
sometimes interfering.
That enigma called mother from whose loins
I sprung.

Gone so suddenly,
No goodbye.
She lies there lifeless, calm, at peace, so young.

Waves of grief,
untold regrets.
There was always tomorrow to get to know her.

Aching sadness, wasted years,
The gaping void when there's something I want to show her.

Did she love me?
Who can say.
Was there anything of me brought pleasure?

Was she happy?
Where is she now?
Has she memories to treasure?

Oh! For a minute back.....
Just a minute!
Linda MacPherson

The Time Share Toaster

Be careful if it's toast you need, the message it was plain;
sometimes it's white or brown or black, don't worry, try again.

'Twas obvious something was wrong, maybe the driver's dead,
there can't be many working parts, it only cooks damn bread.

A technician was called in, to assess and mend the thing —
he stripped down every little bit, down to the little "ping".

To start the operation he undid all the screws, then moved wires
and springs and other things, and parts you mustn't lose.

He scraped off all the crumbs and stuff and spread out all he found —
'twas really unbelievable that little coloured mound.

There were crumbs and rice and currants too, all nicely toasted black —
but on close examination cried out, "What's that at the back?"

"It's pasta I behold", he said removing all the fluff, fresh
toasted pasta might be nice but howd'ya spread the stuff.

He looked at all the pasta bits, and scratched his balding head —
"It's the flaming Common Market fault — it's got left hand thread."

The toaster's back and working now, so set at number three,
but if a second lot you want, try two — then make the tea.
Jim Pritchard

Padre

What mocking winds have sent you here to save this
  soul from mortal sin?
My heart is stirred within your sight, your chapel
  I yearn to enter in.
Yet furthest from my mind to pray, or listen to your homily,
Nor have you sermonize to me upon your vague tranquillity.
Who sent you here to preach within this barren land of ochre dust,
To have your skin burn from the sun, and instigate a maiden's lust?
If only I could share your faith, your succour and obedience,
Or are you just a picaroon awaiting holy recompense?
O loathsome, iniquitous desire which overwhelms my rectitude.
Sweet death please kiss your gift on me that I might lie in solitude.
Then he can lead in robes of black with crucifix held to the sky,
My phaeton drawn toward the tomb, therein forevermore to lie
Elizabeth A. Grant

Peace In Our Time

Do you believe in the non-violent dream?
Sounds so good but could
it ever be as good as it always seems?
They say you need to taste the bitter
before you know the sweet.
Will good things ever feel so good
if we do not feel the bad?
Can we ever be truly happy if
we never have been sad?
So many questions crowd the mind
— make me want to scream.
Thinking about the reality of
mankind's eternal dream.
But it feels good
to crowd the mind, leaving no room for pain,
the pain of knowing the world's a disaster
that would otherwise drive you slowly insane.
Amanda Nwanosike

Real Wishes

Life flows on like silver sand
Speckled with tiny flecks of gold
With every creature in the land
Possessing hopes and dreams untold

Some of these will be fulfilled
Others- remote, abandoned, forgotten
Like clothes out of fashion, on hold until
They're changed or altered - dyed like cotton

Dreams are fragile, but not dark shadows
That cast doubts upon tomorrow
Obscuring rainbows of today, as these
Blind life's treasures with their sorrow.
Linda Hardy

Edgar Allan Poe

Beauty and horror melded in night,
Spectral-formed visions, thin crosses of light.
Demon-powered breakers on gothic-bound shores;
Crenellate turrets, and worn dungeon floors.
Sharp scythes the pendulum, relentless the fall,
And scarlet the masked death that waits at the ball.
Phantom-bourn whispers from mould-marbled tombs,
Ice-sheeted laughter in candle-lit rooms.
For hell is a coffin, in trance sleeps the 'dead'
With fingernails broken; the soul not yet fled!
What embered secrets were owned by Lenore?
Memories erasure are words 'Nevermore.'

In dream-realms of sunlight, there lived by the sea
A free-born, child-goddess named Annabel Lee.
They loved beyond all love, and shared the same crown
Of water-drop diamonds, and shaded renown.
For love is a passion that lives between breath,
Is sleep only frozen, dark daughter of death,
In ecstasy's tortures souls shiver as one,
Dual shadows in twilight — last rays of the sun.
Christoper Rothery

The Revelation

Strong in heart though weak in limb sound in mind and far from dim
Spirits high though I quest not why heaven knows so oft I sigh
Against all odds from earth to sky blessed with power greatly pure
I can with hope and trust endure regardless of no promised cure
With renewed wisdom preciously rare in answer to my
   constant prayer
Yet oft in slight despondency apart from some discrepancy
Perhaps in time he will explain and comfort me from now until eternity
But what of the love for my family when only a miracle can set me free
And what of my soul will it remain or was my devotion so all in vain
'Behold' he may gently call me by name and softly whisper,
'Verily you shall indeed be fully restored and born again.'

Eleanor Haydon Sanderson

" From A Play "

The Drunkard Speaks:

"Sour before, beyond, after; sour the last sigh of mankind's makings,
Of truth before the gentle night stirs no more in a weeping man's
Blood. Sweet the waking not, the weeping not, the elegy of nought
Behind, the wasted breath of Hope. Nor wise men, the last trail
By, can whisper of Hope nor this to the Angel's sleepless dreams;
Nor good men, bred for good, try to teach the unborn dead of truth in
Light, life in light; nor wild men, blood of others deep with the
Blasphemes of the stations of the breath, yearn forgotten majesty's
Of burning Young man's death. Robed in nought lies children's
Whispers, weeping whispers, and empty be the plumes of Angel's Love
Dwelling beyond this weary withered while of nothing, of nothing..."

He turns saddened to 2nd Drunkard:

"Our prophet lies dead; withering in old man's rage, an
Old man's tears shed for dawn. Nor him nor our Young man's sage
Can speak of Pity beyond, for beyond he dwells not; for us
No food suffices but the food of Death;
The wept tears of the Dead be our elixir; the ceremony
Of breath and thought draws end of end.
After the first Death, there waits no other."

Gary Cole

Old And Lonely Highway

Across a tainted landscape, the battered highway rolls,
Sprawling in a splendid dereliction.
Marking out the lei lines — some still in contra-flo —
Of that last, great, Twentieth Century Religion.

Abandoned hamlets huddle, in the shelter
Of the underpasses,
Overgrown with undergrowth, and rancid grasses;
Still waiting for the traffic from the last millennium:
Where the side-roads slide away
Into oblivion.

And Time has hallowed, every relic that survives;
Turning every hoarding, and every hazard warning
Into a way-side shrine;
A place of wind-swept sanctuary,
For the lonely Travellers
  Of the Old M.63.

   June Lamb.
June Lamb

The Chrysanthemum

Tall and stately they stand.
Spreading joy throughout the land.
Heads erect, held up high,
Their creator draweth nigh.

He looketh proudly on the man,
Who worketh well within his plan,
The humble gardener works well and true,
Sowing and planting, God's work to do.

Heads gold as the sun, white as the snow,
Share God's love, for all to know,
Let praises to God be joyfully sung
For the elegant, beauteous chrysanthemum.

Ada Pickering

Springtime

When Winter passes by and
Springtime in her glory is once again restored
The earth shall then appear as if it's wed
To some old ancient custom of its own.

Things of long ago may change
and progress in her way may still continue on
Releasing new ideas in her wake
Another season then shall surely dawn.

Generations then must surely come and go
The citizens of yesteryear shall take their bow
Giving welcome to the seed so young
Wishing that the new life then shall grow.

Springtime looms amidst the year
Calling to the world of her own fate
Telling of her own most innate fear
"Coming soon" lest in her bridal suite be late.

The March winds howling song
Perhaps relate in some old distant voice
"Springtime now appears with Heaven's own bountiful
bouquet"
Married to the month of her own choice.

Louisa Prince Gould MacLachlan

Anger

Why is it when I'm angry and I really want to shout
Stamp my feet, rant and rave, and really let it out
I never even murmur, I do not say a word
And then everyone just looks at me as though I am absurd

I want to throw a paddy, I want to air my lungs
I want to make a noise that is louder than great guns
But it's not like me, to yell and really bawl
I'm not that kind of person, I'm not like that at all

Why is it everybody seems to let their feelings out
Screaming loud to tell the world just what it's all about
While I just sit and listen to all the row they make
About their own wrongdoing and all their own mistakes

I would not really mind if they were always right
But they seem to be just baiting until they get a bite
Why is it not possible for all the fights to cease
Then everyone could live their lives with happiness and peace

Denise Hammond

"Circle Of Memories"

Come to me, to the ring of stones
   standing guard over this never-never land;
Frost-rimmed sentinels pointing rudely
   to the star-spangled night;
Where the moon's halo speaks
   of ice-cold yet to come.
Two hares gambolling....
   you and I once gambolled
Among these stones....
   made love upon the altar;
Now the odour of decay assails my nostrils
   goes bobbing away
On the thin wind that wails in and out
   and through each grim monolith.
My cries are echoed by the sea's surge
   and the owls nearby....
I lie upon this stone
   so cold now, haunted by you,
Waiting to be sucked into the ice-rock,
   nothing left....

Joanne White

The Park At Dawlish

The shrubs the trees the weeping willow.
Stands a tree one hundred years
A little girl steps out so graceful
To feed the ducks she loves so dear.

The little bridge across the river
Flowers around of every bloom
Underneath the weeping willow
Are some sparrows eating food

As you wander up the river
Take a look the other side
You will see the grass is greener
Seats for you they do provide

By this time you may feel tired
There's a cafe you could try
Ground coffee it is lovely
And their cakes are never dry

Enid K. G. Wilcox

Neglected Old Cottage

Neglected old Cottage that's seen better days
Stands falling to pieces down a long country lane
Surrounded by trees planted a long time ago
By people who were proud to call this place their own
The undergrowth creeps ever nearer the walls
And the wind blows through windows as to each room it calls
The echoes of time in each place you look
Like the bricks that are missing from the old inglenook
Like the floorboards all rotting and the tiles from above
The paintwork all flaking once a labour of love.

The rustic old arches from the gate to the door
Lay smashed and broken, scattered all over the floor
Once it was cosy, comfy and warm
Now it stands empty, cold and forlorn
Perhaps someone nice will soon come along
And put all the things right that are horribly wrong
I'd like to believe that life once again
Will return to the cottage down the long country lane.

George Richard Long

Timelessness

Snow lay in lines marking the winter furrows,
Stark, black trees crowned the skyline.
A few noisy crows flew by
As we sat in the car and watched.
Spring was very late that year,
Early flowers were not even showing green,
Just a black and white scene,
Like some ancient pen and ink artwork.
There was a timelessness about it.
Our car, like a time machine,
Had taken us back to a medieval age,
And onwards into the future.
Interesting, I thought, mankind is nowhere to be seen.
Only Nature taking her relentless course
Unaided by the people sheltering in their homes
Believing that they are important.

Janet Collier

Your Time Is Up

According to convention, just before you die,
the important events in your life, all flash by.
Like a video play-back, recalled and reviewed,
the happy, the sad, best forgotten, the lewd.
Perhaps it is your story, your record, your worth,
a sum of your value attained here on earth.
Is there something, or someone, who's keeping a score,
adding up, plus or minus, or perhaps something more.
To be held to account for your words and your deeds
have you given, or taken, or just met your needs.
There's no evidence to prove that, my mind's being flighty,
but supposing it's true - Oh Lord God almighty!

Derek Brisco

Dead End

The sunset shimmers with golden light,
Stars and moon feed astrologers' delight.
The ocean waves caress skyline blues,
And watch passersby on a nighttime cruise.

The distant horizon dismays the watchful owl,
And the obedient cat ends its nightly prowl.
The last people home from their graveyard shift,
Pavements and roads disappear with a snowdrift.

Hedges and fences keep in or keep out?
A mother groans at a child's shout.
Creaking swing on an empty park,
Foisty smell of rotting bark.

Lonely drunk hobbles down a cobbled street,
Homeless man warms cold feet.
Doors close and whisper silence,
Burglar creeps, chanting violence.

Dawn Matthews

Chorus Of The Dawn

Suddenly a noise disturbed the silence of the night,
Startled I opened my eyes and listened hard,
A cockerel crowing heralding the dawn, was that all?
But no, as if by magic, other sounds filled the air —
The blackbird clear and distinct, thrush and chaffinch,
Robin and wren, their voices too, raised in song.
Then, unmistakable, the cuckoo's loud unvaried call,
Which, though not quite so spectacular,
Gave to me a thrill of spring here at last.
I sat up in awe — how could I sleep mid music such as this?
Quickly to open the window wide I ran —
I must hear more of these delightful sounds.
As daylight came the world was bathed in sunshine
The fragrance of the dawn was so appealing
Out there a world unknown to those still sleeping,
I longed to be a part of it — a sudden feeling.
Now wide awake, I dressed and went outside
To me no man-made music could compare
With nature's creatures in full-throated song
How wonderful it was — for me — just to be there.

Jeanne Woodward

Comfort In Words

Keep close beside me through the long dark night
Stay close beside till I reach the light
Help me dear God to ease the pain
Till my love one and I are together again

It's a long lonely road when you're left on your own
No sign post to point the right way home
I know there's light on the other side
Only thing is the gap is so wide

Just keep going there must be an end
It will not seem so long with the help of a friend
I pray each day but don't understand
Why God won't call and take my hand

Come dry your eyes a voice seems to say
Take one step at a time it's the only way
If you need some help God is always there
All it takes is a silent prayer

Louise Borowanski

The Wind

The wind, it whistles through the trees,
Takes your breath the strong, strong breeze.
Fences falling, bottles rolling.
Leaves rustling, hats a-blowing.
The wind, it blows you down the road,
As you struggle with your heavy load.
Slates that drop from roof tops,
Shutters swinging, banging, on windows and shops.
When will the wind die down to a gentle breeze?
Hush, hush, no wind, no sound, calm seas.

Janet Elizabeth Isherwood

Abervan 1966

O' why should fate with cruel twist
Steal those young ones from our midst
So many, so young were slain
Now only a few of them remain
They thanked God for their daily bread
And moments later they were dead
'Twas a monstrous mountain made by man
That brought tragedy to Abervan
O' God can you angry parents blame
If some may now renounce your name
It was man that came and built these things
Ignorant of the danger they'd bring
Was it really one of God's aims
For man to build such black mountains?
Was it really God's plan
To slay the children of Abervan?

Kenneth Strang

Treasured Love

How sweet the love I once knew
Still it remains a silver hue

Icy feelings have I not
Without your love I am forgot

What would it take to keep your affection
Anything would I do, save deception

Tears are bitter and full of sorrow
But I stop and smile there is always tomorrow

My friend be cool, be calm
And most of all, never lose your charm
Love is precious, indeed a treasure
So many find it but know not its measure

Cast not aside disdainfully
I know your heart so perfectly
Sincere these words, they are to me
Forever in my heart you'll be

Elizabeth McCutcheon

There Was A Lady Prim And Proper

There was a lady prim and proper, but when she talked, you couldn't stop her.
She'd prattle on and on and on from break of day to set of sun
Her husband gave up in despair, his words in edgeways were so rare
But when they lost friends, one by one, he felt it time something was done.

He thought and thought and racked his brain, she rattled on like an express train
What could he do to stop the flow; he'd ask his neighbours, perhaps they'd know
He asked his neighbours on the right and told them of his dreadful plight,
But he received no good advice, although they both were very nice.

They asked him in to have a drink and promised him they'd have a think.
So to neighbours on the left he turned to see what wisdom could be learned
They too were kind and said they'd try to be of help, but my oh my,
What a problem he had got, he certainly was in a spot.

He felt he couldn't stand much more when someone knocked upon his door
The man that stood there said that he had got a problem that could be
A help to both, if they just could get together, it might come good.
"I've heard about your wife today and think that I have found a way.

My wife just will not speak a word, her silences are quite absurd.
So why not swap for weeks about, a week of talking, a week of nowt."
The two shook hands upon the deal and now a secret I'll reveal
When they shook hands and then departed, that's when wife-swapping first started.

Ida Steele

Christmas In The Meadow

All mice and bunnies are tucked up in bed
Straining to listen for sounds of the sled
Out in the meadow snow covers the ground
Silently, sneakily, without a sound

A brilliant sun rises and shines boldly its rays
Through icicles glistening in glorious blaze
The chilled wisps of breath hang on the air
As bewildered young rabbits in wonder just stare

Exclaimed delight they gabble and shout
As they crunch through the field and slither about
The first snowballs fly, they laugh and they giggle
Icy cold paws they rub at and wiggle

Mama Rabbit pops out and calls to them loudly
Hurries them in, and grooms them all proudly
At the big laden table they sit down to munch on
Her elaborate and festive, fine Christmas luncheon

They cluster together by hearth's orange fire
Full from the feast and from playing they tire
To snuggle down close, to doze and to dream
On all of the wondrous sights they had seen.

Constance O'Brien

Wearily I Weave My Wandering Way

Wearily I weave my wandering way, through woods and streams of wanton golden solitude,
sensuously the silken shining sunrays glisten and dance between the leaves, intrude
and filter through my golden soften locks and tresses,
as I sit gazing languidly at my shadow in the stream, forgetting,
when you have forgotten how to love another,
when no girl wants to be your lover, You sit and sigh and sadly wish,
the silence hurts; and the broken leaves swish,
the hours drift and there is no-one there,
no-one in this world to share a care,
lazily, I languished lasciviously 'long side the limpid lagoon,
for hours, longing, dreaming, for poetic power,
like a ghost sliding silverily, shivering in the woods,
wanting so much to be understood,
the stream meanders just like my thoughts,
shall I 'give up' here, not missed, not sought?
My breath is gone, it gasps, it sighs, I may as well lay down and die,
wet Earth, brown soil, in you I must lie, my will has gone, my soul must fly.

Dennis Symons

King Of The Savannah

Slowly the giant leaned against the knurled Acacia tree
strength diminishing with each hard fought breath.
Small eyes reached out into the moonlight
scavenging Hyenas awaiting the Bull Elephant's death.

Occasionally the creature placed his gentle trunk into his mouth
attempting to alleviate the unreasoning pain in his broken jaw.
The legacy he had obtained from his meeting with man
two long agonizing weeks before.

The festering wound had taken its toll
the Bull quivered and fell to the ground.
The silence of the night was interrupted
Jackals and Hyenas hesitantly gathered round.

Perhaps Africa's drums will fall silent
and man's soul seek repent.
As the last Elephant falls dead
Ivory decorating the walls of the supposedly more intelligent.

The great regal creatures once roamed
rulers of the scorched savannah.
Now they face extinction due to 'Man'
'I apologize for us — O Loxodonta Africana'.

Garry I. G. Evans

Life Is A Colour

Blues and Yellows, hues of a Rainbow,
Stretching out, touching depths of the land.
Towering high, colouring the landscape,
I try reaching out so it touches my hand.

Earth is to nature, the sky is a mystery,
Day is to night, as life is to death.
Natural beauty is there if you find it,
Like a red blaze of sunset, cascading the depth.

The nighttime so black, the moon lifts its head,
A halo of light, twinkling stars gather forth,
The once angry sea now shimmering softly, as
The moon looking down lights it up like a torch.

Dawn brings the dew, the sun warms the earth,
Nature is stirring, the cycle resumes,
A quivering brook, idly drifting along
The soil seeps its moisture for flowers to bloom.

Waterfall glistening, cascading the rocks,
Frothing and swirling, devouring their paths,
Twisting and turning to find its way out,
Life, as the rainbow, changes colour, never lasts.

Christine McRae

Kentish Oak

This oak has grown to such a height
Stretching up to the sun so bright.
Showing quaint and varying features
Is natural home to many crawling and hopping creatures.
Its trunk with a girth so large
Would never float upon a barge
There are many more years to pass
Hopefully before it falls to grass.
The year of London's Great Fire
Commenced its birth in the mire.
Three centuries now have come and gone
Yet still it stands staunch alone.
Even two hurricanes that were sent
Never left its timber for ornament.
We look up to such beauty every day
And just know it's here to stay.

Iris E. Weller

A Walk On The Wild Side

O to be out walking it's such a joy to me
Strolling through the heather
Taking shade beneath a tree
The gurgling of the river
And the bleating of the sheep
The dizzy heights of freedom
That I dream about in sleep
Up and down the mountains round and round the hills
Peering over ledges going green around the gills
It's nice to be in England exploring in the Dales
Not understanding Wainwright
And getting lost along the trails
The farmers tending crops in their fields are clearly seen
And I just keep on walking over patchwork fields of green
My feet are like fat sausages my legs are heavy weights
And the blisters on my heels are just like two big plates
The scenery is stunning
But my body is quite shattered
I'll be glad to put my feet up
'Cos I'm just a bit cream-crackered.

Cynthia Lansdell

Christmas From Hell

Rows with the in-laws, ill and in bed.
Ten thousands indians banging drums in my head.
Too much turkey with food all around,
More festive noise, should be more silent sounds.
Kids too excited, you're feeling unwell.
You have to admit this is Christmas from hell.

Gina Hardstaff

The Salvation Coup D'Etat

Daily, peace was being negotiated.
Suddenly, the coup interrupted,
The dull pseudo-democratic game.
So clear the saviour's message came:
"Time has come for a positive change,
That will reach the longest range,
And bring salvation to all nations."
That was the declaration of intentions,
Which in their minds were nurtured:
To conquer and rule the 'pagan-natured',
And secure their 'safe haven' in heaven.
Out of their homes all were driven.
To safe havens some brave a journey.
But, there they all dwell in agony,
With divided families and attention,
Thinking of their kin in detention,
Who are daily being tortured,
Who are daily being pressured,
To confess their 'obvious' guilt,
Before they are abused and killed.

Deng Deng Hoc Yai

Therefore I Am!

I think of
Summer streams, shimmering in the light
you when I lay awake, alone at night

I think of
Sweet music floating in the air
living life without a care

I think of
Mountains covered with feathery white snow
and how I never want to let you go

I think of
The whine of the wind blowing through the trees
how you make me feel totally at ease

I think of
When I'm with you, for hours
and buying you a whole kingdom full of flowers

I think I think of love

Ian James Barker

The Huntsmen Of Scorne

On a crisp October morn, woken from their beds at dawn,
summoned by the hunting horn, came the famous Hunt of Scorne.
Some sip whisky, others port, warming up before the 'Sport,'
hounds a'baying, horses neighing, 'Tally Ho' and 'Off we go.'

As they race across the heather through the spinney up the hill,
hounds and huntsmen bound together by a maddened lust to kill.
See the vixen break her cover even though she's doomed to die,
trying to save her cub which cowers lying in the lair nearby.

Now the hounds have caught and killed her, huntsmen ride
back to the lair,
probing, digging, scraping, seeking, the helpless cup they
know is there.

Evilly they sacrifice him with a smile on every face,
were I but to sit in judgement, I would make them take his place.

Geoffrey C. Payne

A Sticky Tale

Sticky prints upon the wall
sticky prints that say it all
that sticky hands have passed this way
while eating bread and jam today

Sticky prints upon the door
sticky prints upon the floor
sticky prints not hard to trace
when once you see your sticky face

Deborah James

Vesuvius Waits

Villas clambering across the mountainous slopes, rise up to reach the sun, the lower stretching to meet the higher, only to be left in the shade the others shun. Flat white roof tops lazily sprawl, baring themselves to the shimmering heat that gently seeps amongst each crevice and bakes their stone as they try to retreat. Narrow lanes weave and wind, as they trickle towards the blue waters cool, where gulls cry out with a deafening echo as they screech to the fisherman returned with his haul. Now stillness of the daybreak broken, the once empty lanes fill with sound as traders prepare for another morning, trundling carts to their site of ground. Soon the streets will be full of many, villagers...tourists...and scooters racing, like fireflies caught by a night light, they'll dart around, then stand debating. The smells of strong coffee, pasta and sauces will fill the air as the chefs work their skills, in the brightly coloured cafes that litter the pathway, all ready to tempt you with their sumptuous meals. Whilst sweet music drifts in the air from a side street, a violinist serenades...con amour, and across the water from the hustle and bustle, in silence... Vesuvius watches it all.

Helen Chennell

Sunday Afternoons

I hate Sunday afternoons.
Sunday afternoons are family time
going out for a walk and tea and crumpet time
everybody else's time
not my time.
Most Sunday afternoons I sit at my desk
planning the lessons I shall teach
but Sunday afternoon intrudes
I get twitchy.
Sunday afternoons mock me
make me endure them
jeer at me
make me feel trapped
a long elusive tea time
rattling cups and smell of fresh-baked scones
for sharing
jam for tea
not me
O God
I hate Sunday afternoons.

Susan Shackleton

Fermin'— Or Is It?

The horses they were the first tae go, replaced wi' machines
 rarin' tae go.
They'd dae the work in half the time, and for a while, a'thin'
 was fine.
But next it wis the men tae go, there's no a lot o' work, so,
They were sent doon tae sign on the lines, they'd only be
 used at busy times.
Next it wis the fermer's pain, he wis telt tae cut doon on his grain.
The silos are packet oot tae the door, please dinna grow anymore.
And if yer coos ye have tae milk, poor it doon they new drains
 ye've jist built.
But better still, instead o' coos, turn yer ferms into zoos.
Instead o' sheep, get some llamas, their braw soft wool mak'
 fine pyjamas.
Instead o' coos, get some deer, they're easy tae keep, hive nae fear.
But better still, lay bare yer fields, ye'll no hae the worry aboot
 the yields.
We'll even pay ye tae dae this fer us, it'll cause a lot less fuss.
And dinnae worry aboot the stervin' west, let somebody else
 feather their nest.
Please Mr. Government Official, whit's tae happen tae the
 Scottish thistle
If this progress, ye can keep it, gie me the times when folk
 were needed
Wi' sheep and cattle, tatties and grain, please can ye no leave
 ferms alane!

Joyce Melville

An Austrian Village

An Austrian village is where I want to go
Sunshine sparkling on lovely soft snow
The snow birds sing their tinkling song
that is where I feel I belong

To hear the gentle hiss of my skis
the mountains bathe in shear beauty
the forest trees stiff and white
no drugs involved, but I'm high as a kite

The ice, the lake, balloons in the sky
Dreading the time I must say goodbye
if I could stay and remain there forever
I'm sure my life would become much better

Once every year, I go back there
Ice festivals and the fishing fayres
Every year my feelings get stronger
The time in between gets much longer

Maybe someday I'll be able to stay
I'd go right now if I had my own way
Instead I'll survive on memories alone
And wait the year out in my English home

Annette Crook

Loch Eck

Ah, Loch Eck! Living, vibrant testimony to Creation;
Superlatives all inadequate to describe your beauty.

In all seasons you charm and stupefy in equal measure;
A conjunction of moods and movement and mystery.
Not for you the bleakness of winter, but rather, on moonlight night,
Surrounded by snow-clad peaks caparisoned by rime-wrapped
 boughs,
You present a spine-tingling scene of splendour and majesty,
Of awesome intensity, near painful to behold.

Pulsing, alive, energetic and vital in spring;
Silvery cascades from streaming hills, in endless profusion
Tumble, bubbling and boiling into your deepness,
And sparkling effervescence thrills the exulted heart.
Yet summer is a tranquil time, a season for reflection;
A hazy, misty, mystic time for dream and meditation,
And still, your loveliness beyond compare.

Your autumnal tapestry of variegated hues is,
In sweet suffusion, richer than cloth of gold.
And flaming Aurora's cheeks, like sweating sun's at close of day,
Are mirrored blood-red, flushed upon your slender form.

Ah yes Loch Eck, peerless jewel of Cowal, 'tis joy to know you

George Newall

Peace

If there is no to-morrow,
That could mean a lot of sorrow,
No future to look forward to,
We will hope it's a dream that never comes true.

We have just one life to live,
And lots of love to give,
So why not have an aim in life,
To help each other and end the strife.

When we have so much to be thankful for,
We should try and open the closed door,
To those in need of help and care,
And we should not just stand and stare.

Perhaps we live in countries at war,
Or maybe in a far away shore,
Where homelessness is a way of life,
And the only future is war and strife.

If there is just a chance to dream,
Of peace on earth, like a flowing stream,
Lets come out of the stormy scene,
And build a long and lasting peace because we are so keen.

Beryl Sylvia Rusmanis

Morrar

Far away in the north there's a heaven I know
surely most picturesque in the land,
Where the babbling brooks all run into the sea
close by Morrar's silver sands,
Let me see once again the silver sands
where ripples the waves in the bay,
Of Morrar I dream, in the dread winter nights
'Tis there I would like to stay,
I've travelled the north, the east and the west
but there's only one place for me,
'Tis Morrar forever that will hold my heart
with its sands glinting close to the sea,
A boat flits so gently 'cross water so blue
the sun shining down from above,
'Tis the place of the north, the tang of the breeze
'tis Morrar, my only love...
Agnes Murray

Scotland

Scotland is so wonderful
surely the crown in the world's jewel

With the unpredictable weather
Spectacular Scottish heather
Jaggy thistles along with whistles
In the wild wind
Amidst the Scots mist
In the land our ancestors once fought
For hand and fist
Many magnificent meandering mountains
So very high
Voles crawling amongst each voluptuous valley
So very deep
In the land our people once fought
Tooth and nail to keep
The benefits of a heritage which we can now reap

So when you say you're a Scot be a little coy
For the mountains that are every other nation's envy
Can be your very own pride and joy.
Jacqueline Jordan

Untitled

I blow you kisses every day.
Sweet harbingers of joy are they
As summers warmth envelopes spring.
For as they float on sylphed wing,
Their every moment fills with bliss
The hills and vales they gently kiss
With blossoms sweeter than before.
Bright Songbirds, as they upward soar
With joyous trill do thrill the air,
Our secret happiness to share.
For nought they touch, but is enriched
upon their journey to your lips.
Then nestling close. Back to my heart
Thrice blessed, they joyfully depart.
Gerald William Botteley

Little Girl

For here lies all. Death's blackened rose,
Sweet nurturing, for this!
Thus danced a little angel once;
Betrayed now, with her kiss

To mourn the life we will not share —
Came this, her last goodbye;
Such words can't fill the silence left,
To live, yet choose to die.

Might I have tried to understand
Such feelings trapped inside?
These petals are my little girl.
We talked. And still, you lied.
Donna Prime

Blackberry

Surrounded by brambles you sit.
Sweet. Ripe.
I battle for your taste.
I battle for your taste, touch and smell.

Surrounded you sit.
Long, sharp, twisting barriers;
Their evil thorns dig deep in me
Puncturing my heart and shredding up my soul.
Are those long twisting arms trapping or protecting you?

Blackberry, my blackberry.
Is this the way it's meant to be?
Andie C. Dever

To The Young

Is my wisdom enough to make you wise?
Take all my words and live them,
Dearest Ones,

And keep me in your heart, where living lies,
For in my heart you live, and I in yours.

Are these my gifts to you of ample worth,
Or thoughts so deep, suffice to satisfy
My own desire with yours continuing forth,
Our mutual peace and bliss to multiply.

Unneeded words, although I love to voice,
Yet when I can no longer speak with sound,
Love will remain always with gracious choice,
Ever alive, unfettered and unbound.
Helen Wingate

Mystical Love

Come, be My beloved,
Take My arm and walk with Me,
Let Me lead you.
You are the fragrance of the lilac after a gentle shower of rain,
Let Me love you.
O come, My beloved,
Give to Me your hand
I will protect you.
For you are the summer rain that gently falls,
Refreshing My parched land.
You are the words of the poet
And I, the greatest Laureate of all.
O, sweet rose, how My heart yearns for your love.
Be My canvas
And I will paint your life into a thousand sunlit days,
Each one entwined around the other, never ending of their glory.
And as the sun sets from your eyes, we'll sit quietly.
I'll sing for you sweet love songs as you gently fade to rest.
Then I will wake you, My beloved,
As My bride.
Elizabeth T. Creagh

Motor Way

I watched the men the other day
taking all the earth away.
They cut the trees and tore the grass
and moved it out so very fast.
Where flowers once bloomed and birds did sing
There was no sign of anything
but the never ending dug out thing.
Which on one day the cars will race,
Driving at a dangerous pace,
bringing with them noise and fumes
instead of all the song birds' tunes.

How very sad it is today that concrete
takes the fields away.
You have to go so many miles
before you find the country stiles.
Edna Somers

The Searching Wind

I love to hear the stormy wind round corners blowing strong
Tap-tapping at the window panes throughout the night so long
It seems forever searching out a secret thing mislaid
With sudden fury rising then its strength begins to fade
Calling out to what it seeks with plaintive gentle cries
Whistling and caressing with frustration in disguise
Swishing through the leafy trees like sea upon a shore
Rattling like a madman on each and every door
And if I lie and listen hard I sense its frantic fear
That it will never find the secret thing held dear
Often on its journey its tears fall fierce and fast
Then spent by all its anger with one almighty blast
It slinks away to hide the failure of its work
To rest itself and gather strength within the nightly murk
Until its peace is shattered by an insistent inner guest
Who spurs again to action in its never ending quest.

Joan C. Brooks

Sometimes The Wind Blows

Dress me my angel in life's spoken dreams
Teach me the songs
So I know what they mean
Those that order me
And call me by name
Those that will replace me
And erode me by fame
Those that take from me, the desire to burn
And twist it, and tear it
And make it their own
I follow in anguish
No desire, no joy
I follow my victors
Like a child's clockwork toy
I come at their beckoning, I come at their call
With no peace of mind
With no mind at all
To stop this charade, their game of deceit
To take back what's mine
To succeed in defeat

Gareth M. Adams

Thank You

Thank you Lord for all my blessings,
Thank you Lord for what I've got.
Though I may not be completely happy, I am quite
content with my lot.
Now my life does have its moments when I've had just enough.
When my hair I feel like tearing and from my
Mouth comes lots of swearing.
There is one thing I have to say, and I say it every day.
Thank you Lord for all my blessings,
Thank you Lord for what I've got.
All these words that I say daily, I send them to
The Man above, and these words that are said gaily
Are absolutely crammed with love.
So I thank you Lord for all my blessings
I thank you Lord for what I've got!...

Dawn Overson

War Games

War is the game of tin soldiers and tanks,
That rages below the dining table,
Where men are murdered in order of rank,
Then brought back to fight ready and able.
The naval battles take place in the bath,
Where the boats hide behind iceberg bubbles,
Some boats are sunk and some broken in half,
But no one gets into any trouble.
"Adult war is different" so people say,
"And the children are only pretending",
So they carry on thinking war's the way,
But soon it'll be them we are sending.

Children today are adults tomorrow,
Don't educate them to spread war's sorrow.

Kirstie Baker

How Discontented?

Tears, idle tears, I know not what they mean
Tears from the depth of some divine despair
Rise in the heart, and gather to the eyes
I'm looking on the happy autumn fields
And thinking of the days that are no more
Is the view of isolation?
A view of self-righteous doctrine
The priest was passing by the church
Wearing the white flower of a blameless life?
Who dares to enter the doctrine of the church,
Too few, along this view
Maybe it's the weather
Not the happy Autumn fields
Or is there a mortal presence
beyond this discontentment, beyond
This melancholy, this view, this loss, this discontent.
La tout n'est qu ande at beaute — lives, calm et volupte.
Everything there is simply order and beauty,
Luxury, peace, and sensual indulgence.

Helen O'Neil

In The Name Of Peace

I switched on my telly this evening, only to hear the news reader tell.
Of an explosion that went off in London, of the suffering innocents felt.
We are told this is due to no peace talks, taking place amongst parties involved.
From people who rule by the bullet, demanding their problems be solved.
They say they want peace for their Country, a Nation United and Free.
Then sneak in the night like jackals, planting bombs as their only decree.
They care not who dies in the process, they care not of the pain that they cause.
For the temporary peace they agreed to, to them was just a short pause.
And now they've resumed back to violence, expecting the World to agree.
That their justified killing and maiming, with murderers roaming quite free.
They are unable to sit round a table, debating their views candidly.
Letting democracy be the ruler, heeding to the needs of the majority.

Christine Sandford

Nature

Soft blue sky, clouded white
Thank you for our daily light
Sun so sharp you dot our eyes
We're grateful that you choose to rise,

Wintry white, cold blue snow storm
You make us cold but feel so warm
You wrap us in your coat of flakes
'Til spring bounds down and your seam breaks,

Summer haze, blazing yellow sky
Shine my skin, make me dry
How glad we are to feel your heat
Golden fine sand hot on our feet,

Water clear, blue aqua sheen
Wetting, refreshing me, making me clean
Praise be to your cool ebb and flow
Your seas divide worlds above and below,

Natural the elements we use for free
Natural the life we destroy in the sea
Natural the atmosphere we pollute more each day
Natures destruction will happen our way.

Darin Lambton

Elemental Masters

Air is the gentle, cooling breeze,
That counters summer's heat,
It's the hurricane that brings us to our knees,
Sends us into retreat.

Water quenches mankind's thirst,
Rain cleans the grimy town,
It floods the rivers 'til they burst,
And leaves mankind to drown.

Earth bears the life that lets man live,
The soil is turned and ploughed,
But when it has no more to give,
The earth becomes our shroud.

Fire is the heat we try to tame,
The warmth in which we trust,
But when released, that glowing flame,
Reduces man to dust.

From the moment of humanity's birth,
To the future that is our death,
Water, fire, air and earth,
Have ruled our every breath.

Dan Ashton

I Wandered Lonely As A Cloud...

I wandered lonely as a cloud of smoke,
That floats low and high o'er kilns and stacks,
My contents stifling, for all to choke,
Trailing grimy despair, within my tracks,
Polluted air, where fresh once blew,
Grey descending, instead of crimson hue.

Carrying on, though desolation lay all around,
I came upon a host of golden bulldozers, dancing to man's tune,
Who ripped the daffodil bulbs from out the ground,
Ten thousand stomping boots, bowing peaceful glades to ruin,
The hills and vales were levelled as one,
A barren, bland landscape, the damage done.

To think that Wordsworth once had wandered here,
Leaving footprints placed unhurried,
And all the glories he then had spied,
Now under tarmac buried,
If his inward eye was now to flash a view,
In his grave of solitude, he'd surely turn a time or two.

Clive Blake

Imbalance

The rich man watches TV, harvesting pictures from the sky
The poor man, whose crops have failed, harvests nothing
His children die

Wealth breeds complacency, does nothing for the soul
Poverty breeds anger, global consciousness should be our goal

Harmony with each other and earth on which we dwell
Unity in a common aim — let our spirits gel

Chris Glover

No Word

No word no word I know exists
That can describe your tender kiss
No word no word can ever say
How sad I feel when you've gone away
No word no word can ever express
The feeling of your warm caress
No written word in any book
Can tell me why, with just one look
My body aches for one embrace
And to touch your lovely smiling face
If I could find the word to say
How much I care in every way
Then you would know, oh how you would know
How much how much I love you so
Till then my love through all our goodbyes
The word you'll find in my loving eyes

Alan Kilminster

From Cobwebs, Jewels And Spangled Stars

As I look around this room-cave
that has been a home to me
I see wondrous objects gathered round
delights and treasures that I've found
that beckon and welcome all of those
who care to come and see

Bright spangled scarves and golden stars
adorn the once-bare white-washed walls
and velvet fragments, beads, and half-forgotten cards
stare from their cobwebbed hiding places only to call
with their very own song of beauteous harmony
to those who would listen, linger and open their
half-closed eyes to see

Necklaces hang in silent rows, like jewelled webs they gleam
And dusty knitted dolls smile sweetly from the sturdy shelves
while faded flowers face again the daylight dream

Jackie A. Griffiths

Is It Really Worth The Kill?

There are many animals on this earth,
That have done no harm since their birth.
They have been killed for their skin,
All to please those young men.

Rabbits, Fox, Badgers and Deer,
All of these you should not fear.
Black, brown, white and grey,
All the colours that come your way.

Everyone says humans are boss,
My opinion is it's the animal's loss,
I just wish we could all be the same,
It's not as if the animals are to blame.

I know it's not going to happen that way,
Because we humans have all the say.
So although it may be less money in the till,
Is it really worth the kill?

Angela Radford

As One Gets Older

Spare a thought for the unfortunate ones,
That have to wear glasses when very young.
As one gets older it isn't much fun,
So spare a thought for the unfortunate ones.
If you haven't worn glasses up until now,
And your eyesight is failing, you're thinking 'Oh hell.'
Glasses are a nuisance, they smear up and fall down.
Lost them again. Where can they be found?
Oh what a bother, why can't I see?
Why, oh why has this happened to me?
Now think of the years you've been blessed with good sight,
And thank the good Lord for getting that right.
So, spare a thought for the unfortunate ones
Who have to wear glasses when very young.
Alas! Without glasses where would we be?
Thank God for our glasses,
At least we can see.

Doreen Griffiths

My Dream

I dreamt of you one foggy night,
That you were truly mine to-night.
And every time I saw your face,
You were there, smiling with grace.

My heart goes out to all to-night,
Who have to wait for broad daylight.
It will come soon,
And you will be on top of the moon.

This poem has a particular meaning,
That leaves me with a special feeling.
This feeling is magical, and will always be,
So I'll leave you now, so cheerfully.

Caroline McPeake

Love And Life

After my last love I swore
that I would never love again,
but each day more and more
I miss the tenderness and the pain.

What is life without love
but an empty ageing shell,
like the vulture and the dove
life is peaceful and threatening as well.

What is the point of life
if it's not lived to the full,
the usefulness of a knife
lessens, when the cutting edge is dull.

I should sharpen all my senses
refresh my thoughts and desires,
drop the guard on my defences
and rekindle old flames and fires.

Graham Roy Pillar

My Wish

I wish I were an octopus
That lived upon the land
I could do at least four things at once,
Wouldn't that be grand?

"Press my trousers, mum, be quick,
I'm in a hurry out."
"My shirt needs a button too."
My other son does shout.

"Have you seen the hammer, Dear?"
I've got a job to do,
In fact I need the glue as well,
The sole's come off my shoe."

"Is dinner ready yet, mum?
I'm really hungry now."
If this goes on much longer
There's going to be a row.

If I were an octopus,
And helping all in need.
Maybe I would really want
To be a centipede.

Constance Adair

Rebirth

Perhaps the dreamed imaginings,
That pollute my childlike brain,
Are more the seedlings of psychosis,
Than future glimpses of the sane.

Hard to accept, when all that's sound
Decays, dissolves or is banned.
When those who steer the sad machine,
All but rape this once proud land.

Yet the die is cast, the progression set.
What is shall come to be.
What fools alone cannot rebuild,
Shall yet come through technology.

With minds cleansed to purity,
Released potentials uplifted.
The unshackling of genius
Of the greatness and gifted.

To bathe in the unbounded knowledge,
Amidst the freedoms of the data flow.
To swim in the seas of the com net,
Where the billion minds, fuse in the know.

Hamilton C. Chant

What Is Love?

Love strikes a chord on a vibrant string
That quivers on air, and dying, lingers.
Ever an unpredictable thing —
Caresses and hurts with the same tender fingers.

Love knows no pride but the pride of belonging
Knowing no hurt, save the hurt of despair,
When trusting it gives, all soul and all longing
Then finds it destroyed and laid hopeless bare

Love knows no creed save the joy of believing
Implicitly trusting — eternally free —
Strong in its loving, fierce in its hating
Seeks only devotion and harmony.

But love stays the course over hurdles, true
It heeds not the dangers nor tricks so rife
For love is no fantasy, it's the joy to renew
The togetherness, the union; 'tis the Essence of Life.

Cecily Brandon

This Godless Generation

That drinks and smokes and drugs itself all around
That robs and knifes and bludgeons its old to the ground
That batters and bruises and shatters the bones of its babes
That lies with itself and rapes and gives others Aids.

It's T.V. Entertainment that is savagery and porn
Which corrupts not educates the child as soon as it is born
"Suffer the little Children" for yes indeed they do
As so-called wise grown-ups force on them their own sexual view.

Where are the voices calling in the wilderness, "Stay thy hand, Oh! Stay"?
Where are the voices shouting from the rooftops "This is not the way"?
Lost in the noise of explosions, rioting, mockery, greed and wrath
Lost in the lack of control and compassion for those caught in its path.

The Devil must be resting and laughing, truth to tell
He has no need to come up to earth in wickedness to dwell
The humans who are living here are doing his work so well
He can afford to sit back and wait for them to descend to hell!

Imp.

Your Rainbow

You paint my life with the colours
    that surround you;
Hues so beautiful to my eyes
    they could only be mirrored in
    the Summerlands.
And through this lucid spectrum
I glimpse a future swirling with
    the promise of endless breathless
    colours awaiting their debut.
Bring to me your palette
And I will drink in your iridescent colours
And they will shine
    in my very deepest heart
    forever
        any beyond.

Karen Speirs

The Game

The mighty lion gazed over his vast terrain.
The carcass of a wildebeest lay rotting in the midday sun.
The vulture hovered overhead, his gaze covering the rain-starved plains.
The cheetah started his attack in a blistering run,
His target, a startled gazelle whose life hung by a thread.
Death was imminent in this land of dread,
A bizarre lottery where life was rarely long, and
Survival only by the strong.
The lion, the King, was master of the plains,
The bull elephant was the only one to dispute this claim,
The rest were just pawns in this deadly game.

James Carl Savage

"Adam's Apple"

If I should die think only this of me
That there's some corner of an English field
Beneath an apple tree
Where lies a richer dust concealed
Buried deep and hidden among its roots
Yet rising radiantly rich from winter's sleep
Bursting with living leaves and shoots
Sight blossom white in Easter light.

In death how can we know or show
That passing on is change by which we grow?
That tree remains; continues to be fed
By transubstantiated daily bread.

And hearsay: — Hey!
An apple a day keeps the doctor away:
That's what my mother would say. She also knew (with a sigh),
That Adam and Eve understood about apples too. Could we say
If it weren't for "apples", you and I
Wouldn't be here today?

Is that obloquy or sobriquet?
Either way, it provides a thought for any living day.

John Miller

Elementary, My Dear

Some may say, we are strangers, you and I
That we never mix, never meet eye to eye.
But without you, I am nothing
As you are at a loss without me.

In our own ways we bring good, we bring bad
We bring life and death, both soft and hard.
You give warmth in the cold
I give my blood as it flows
Without you and I
Where would they be?

They have harnessed our power, bringing riches and power
They have used and abused us, hour by hour.
But you have shown you are not tamed
And I have shown them the same
Just enough fear
Let them know, we are here.

Some may say, we are strangers, you and I
But my brother, I know you, I hold you.
You, the fire that burns
Me, the water that calms...

Chris McConnochie

What Might Have Been

There is a blueness in this summer sky
   that seems to stretch forever ...
   into the blue
   of the identical sea.

I wonder at the oneness of it all;
   and in my mind's eye
   picture
   a perfect union,
   so absolute that no man can divide it.
   Yet can that ever be?

I thought we had that oneness, he and I;
   for so it seemed.
   But though our love reflected
   the beauty of our blue and cloudless youth,
   it faded in the changing face of autumn.
   He went away from me.

The winter sky and sea grow grey and lie
   as one in their devotion ....
   I wish that we
   could have grown grey together.

Carolyn King

School

Everybody hates school,
that's why they like to break the rules.
The teachers, well they boss you around,
they make you sit and make no sounds.
My favourite lesson is PE,
Because all you do is play games you see.
My favourite part of school is dinner time,
The first meal you've had since half past nine
going home is just like school,
Mum says "If you miss your homework you'll become
a thick fool.
There's not that many that do like school,
they're usually bluffing as to who likes to keep the rules,
those people, they don't want to become a fool,
So at home they work as well as at school.
I bet you don't know how much I hate school
But really I'm not thick, nor a fool

Lisa White

Boxer

"Happiness and love is the victory I crave
The acceptance of associates would give me joy
My hands are my words, and my wit,
Without my fists, my personality is destroyed,
Happiness and love is the victory I crave,
The search may soon lead me to my grave,

My mind is gentle, as soft as the spring rain
Though my hands may kill with the ferocity of the storm
The blood that entices me flows from my foe
These fists keep pounding when his heart says 'no more'
My mind is gentle, as soft as the spring rain,
Please don't let this fresh-faced boy be forever laced
with pain."

Gary Doyle

Together We Stand On Death Row

Here we stand alone,
the accused, the guilty, the deceased.
Is it worth the pain, to be standing here?
Right now seeing the torture,
seeing the result,
Is this worth the torment
of no repent,
the guilty without trial,
the tried without guilt?
are we guilty,
you'll never know.
Together we stand on Death Row,

You said it wasn't too late to deny it all,
You said it would show I loved you,
God I was a fool,
In the end it's my life on the line, not yours,
How many times do you want to play the system,
How many times do you want to play and lose?
Infatuation with death will end in tears,
No more love, no more fears.

Grace Ward

Still Life

The Earth still swings beneath the Sun,
The air is quick with dancing birds,
The trees throw flowery kisses all around,
And blue-bells jump up in the woods for joy.

Everything is light and warmth,
Why should a heart be cold?

The hills lie contented in the Sun's embrace,
The lake is a dream of Summer sky,
The bees visit drowsily amongst the flowers,
And the stream sings, lazy in its little bed.

To live is enough on such a day,
Despair must wait for darker hours.

Dorothy Millington

The Weeding

Can that lovely stranger be
The baby I once knew
The little girl with flaxen hair
And eyes of deepest blue
The years of caring laughing days
The good times we have known
It seems like only yesterday
How quickly time has flown
Dearly beloved, one and all we're gathered here today
The words are said, the deed is done
The couple kneel to pray oh God be good to them
Help them though their life
Watch over them and give her strength to be perfect wife
Give him understanding and a patient loving heart
They both have such a lot to learn
Today is but a start.
Whisper to him softly Lord, say we love her so,
We're trusting him to care for her
Our blessing's with them go.
   Ena Wright

Always Comes Spring

After winter always comes Spring
The birds building nests, the chorus they sing,
Snowdrops and primroses quietly appear
Up from the soil to the air so clear,
The daffodils yellow and glistening bright
And the buds and bulbs that appear overnight,
The lambs that are born white and clean
Now graze on the grass where snow has been,
The animals awake from their winter sleep
And the insects appear from the ground so deep,
The days seem longer for the evenings are light
And winter is fading from our mind and sight
What we thought had withered and often dies
Now the beauty unfolding before our eyes,
So if by chance we have dreary pathways
Look ahead with hope to brighter days,
Remembering in life whatever it may bring
After winter always comes Spring.
   Gillian Mary Probert

With You On My Mind

The warmth of the sun as it shone on my face
The blooms of the flowers as they stood full of grace
The trees as they swayed in the breeze to and fro
The sound of children's laughter on faces aglow
Afternoon tea, now that would be nice
Cucumber sandwiches, and cakes that are iced
Sweet playing music played by a band
With smart looking uniforms, and white gloved hands
Waves that crash on the beach nearby
While up in the air not a cloud in the sky
All of these things are happy and true
All of these things remind me of you!
   Loraine Ward

" Not Sickly Like Chocolate "

Never has been a day such as this,
That my heart o'erflowed with burdening bliss,
The sorrows and woes of days gone before,
All have eroded away from my shore,
The power of your smile and twinkling eyes,
Have taken away all those deafening cries,
The light I see, that you've given to me,
Has saved my soul from hell's eternity,
So please let me try to offer to you,
The taste of a love totally true,
Not sickly like chocolate, honey or wine,
But sweet as the sun and endless in time,
If never there is another today,
I'll always treasure the love that you gave.
   Carmen Nicola Nichols

My Son

Where is my wandering boy tonight?
The boy of my tenderest care
The boy that was once my joy and light
The child of my love and prayer.
Oh where is my boy tonight?
My heart over flows, I love him, he knows
Where is my boy tonight?
Once he was pure as morning dew
As he knelt by my knee,
No face was so knight, no heart more true,
And none was as sweet as he.
Why have you changed all you loving ways
Since manhood deigned you my son?
Give me once more as in days new past
Your sweet loving smiles once again.
Ah! Life was a merry chime
Go search your heart for my son tonight
My sonny with the summer smile
Remind him of his happier self
On boy of my tender prayer.
   Francesca De-Whomes

Year's End

I sit alone now to survey the view,
the breeze and blush of autumn hue.
I find in the colour and the leaf
a kind of hope that brings me real relief.

My breath sits hot upon the air
like mists that settle on the fields and dare
to sleep around the trees and near the rose,
and rise and wend without purpose.

Heart fires once lit I now forget
changed eagerly for scents that wind and set
my mind in reeling spin, my nose aflame
with colours, red and orange, viridian,
wood smoke spark of burning summer's lease.

The crackle on the air, the crispy leaf
brown brittle now torn down, an unseen thief
the wind blows cold upon my ageing cheek,
and winter waits, pale, shrouded sweet,
I fail too like dying leaf, free falling to release.
   Felicity Thompson

Spring: A Villanelle

The sun shines on the peaceful, sloping land.
The buds on trees show shades of spring-like green.
All nature wakened by a mighty hand.

The daffodils, they're yellow like the sand,
Burst open to reveal a golden scene.
The sun shines on the peaceful, sloping land.

While hyacinths, a mauve and purple band,
Are lovelier than the jewels of a Queen.
All nature wakened by a mighty hand.

The trees, majestic on the tow'ring rand
Are greater than the mightiest ever seen.
The sun shines on the peaceful, sloping land.

A tulip breaks the earth like slender wand,
More beautiful than poem has ever been.
All nature wakened by a mighty hand.

We thank you, Lord, for beauty never dammed,
But poured out with a splendour never mean.
The sun shines on the peaceful, sloping land.
All nature wakened by a mighty hand.
   Joyce M. Turner

"Memories"

When laughter dies, the tears they fall,
The candle burning, flickers and dies,
All thoughts and troubles all pour through,
No more cares of being with you.

The body drained of loving thoughts,
Can make or break a caring world,
Hold on to memories, Don't let them fade,
Keep hold of the life you both once made.

For when love is finished,
And laughter dies,
Only memories remain
Till the end of time.
Anita MacDonald

Bloody Friday

Promises were shattered at 7.01
The Capital rocked to the terrorists' bomb
Innocent were maimed as they passed
And homes, shops and offices stooped to the blast.

Hopes also foundered over the sea
The Province as outraged as you and me
For, for seventeen months thoughts of peace were alive,
Uneasy at first, but with a will to survive.
Troops were withdrawn and blockades brought down
Much safer trips could be made into town
A spirit of hope made its tentative way
Crossing barriers of creed and political sway.
Everyone prayed for the troubles to end
And from enemy once, some now made a friend
Then a heinous, cowardly act raised its head
Leaving ordinary people shocked, wounded and dead.
We remembered Tim Parry and Jonathan Ball
Did their precious young lives mean nothing at all?
For them and all victims of this tragic plight
Condemn hatred and violence — demand peace, it's your right!
Brenda Hedley

Ode To Philosophy

The evidence, the truth sustains
That what we get is what obtains.
In symbols on some disk celestial,
Our lives are writ, good, bad and bestial.

Can life's computer freely run,
Through megabytes of heavenly fun?
Or is there some great, grand design,
Which, though our lives are not benign,
Make all things right at journey's end,
When all the gods at last unbend,
And grant to us eternal rest
In paradise, forever blessed?

Or do they, with a byte of malice,
Proffer to us a poisoned chalice,
Re-run the disk, and set in train,
Once more, our journey through life's pain?
Bertrand Ewart

The Beautiful Rainforest

The tall palm trees swaying in the wind.
The little cubs playing the long green grass.

As I stand in the mighty rainforest.

The chirping of birds in the tall tall trees.
The buzzing of bees taking nectar from the blooms.

As I stand in the mighty rainforest.

The beautiful scent of plants growing,
The luscious limes as they fall off the tall tropical
trees and burst open.

As I stand in the mighty rainforest.
Carol McDonald

My Son

He looks at me with wondrous eyes
The chilly smile on his face soon dies,
But a longing is still in his heart.
He thinks loud and thin — cons a start
And clumsily mumbles his instilled part.

He looks at the moon and stars
With bewildered thoughts; forgets his scars
Of the day, dreams of unseen melodies,
Creates an unknown world of parties
Wandering aimlessly among the fairies.

The rainbow startles him curiously,
The cloud and the blue sharpen his wits.
His bitter enthusiasm grows furiously
When far and wild his reverie crumbles to bits
But yet looks at me with a derelict smile.

I look at him with careless eyes,
A cunning smile and devoted passion rise
But I am like him; he knows not —
Yet my sensuous mind reels hot
And devours my core, he knows not.
Daya P. Balla

Christmas Eve Peace

The candles are lit, the dishes are done.
The Christmas Eve battle is once again won.
Children in bed trying to sleep.
Secrets that everyone's trying to keep.
Christmas tree lights shining so bright.
This is a wonderful magical night.
Tomorrow is Christmas, a wonderful day.
The table is set for the lunch time fray.
Red serviettes and bottles of wine,
Crackers and candles, we're all set to dine.
Everywhere's hushed oh the Christmas Eve quiet.
But the kids will be up soon — then there'll be riot!
Now the turkey's been eaten, Great Grandma's asleep.
Dad quietly snoring — cheese and biscuits will keep.
The odd snore from Grandad, great Grandma still snoozing.
But where's Mum and Grandma? At the table still boozing!
The Christmas tree lights twinkle once more,
Paper and presents still litter the floor.
It's all quiet once more, there's peace in the lane,
And next year we'll do it all over again.
Christine Anne Storer

The Green Fields Of England

I remember the home where I lived as a child,
The church and the little village school;
They gave me all I'd need for the life I was to lead
In the England that I knew so long ago.

I remember the days by the little village stream,
The hours that we spent sitting there;
To catch the biggest fish was every schoolboy's wish
In the England that I knew so long ago.

I remember the birds that sang from the trees,
The creatures that roamed the woods nearby;
Their home was still their own and we left them all alone
In the England that I knew so long ago.

Now the village school has closed and the stream's disappeared,
There's a barbed-wire fence where hedges grew;
And though all these things have gone the memory lingers on
Of an England that I knew so long ago.

And shall we walk once again through the green fields of England,
Or stroll together down a country lane;
Will the autumn leaves return with their tapestries of gold -
Will we ever find our yesterdays again?
Anthony Rousell

Time Reaper

Tick tock tick tock
"The clock on the wall means nothing at all but time for me"
The ancient grandfather clock that has faithfully ticked and tocked
Great grandfathers his son my fathers and most of my life away
Ended his diligence with history last night
He stopped with an ear piercing silence
He's always been there
Standing his stately guard by the front door
But I never noticed him
We see but we don't observe
Grandfather clock grandfather clock earnest and tall
Who is the fabled of us all
I am he groaned tick tock
Time goes by we say
Now I know
Time stays
It's we who go
Tick tock tick tock

Anthony Hopkinson

Home At Last

The solitary bell sounds to welcome night,
The clouds move across the sea-like sky.
The silent houses keep their inner secrets.
The speakers within them laugh, talk and cry.
This Norfolk is the sky's ever splendid peak.
The village in silence speaks the past.
This sanctuary among the many changes
Keeps its flower-strewn dykes until the last.
Norfolk men, now following their fathers,
Guardians of the lands, crops sustaining,
Yearly the harvest of corn still gathers,
Heralding the plough to straw remaining.
Winter to spring, to summer into fall,
Seasons demanding man's work in the field,
Toil from ages past still encounters all.
Scythes to machines and modern ways will yield.
In truth, such scenes can be forever found
In this lovely place, given to peace.
In quiet happiness our days we pass
In clouds of calm, nature's balm will not cease.

Beryl Ferguson

Life Is No Holiday

There are songs of the islands, of their beauty to see,
The creations of God are magnificent, and free,
The mountains, the glens, the sea and the sky,
People gasp in delight while they're passing by.

They visit the islands near and far,
Either taking or leaving the family car,
One foot on an island and their vision is misted,
They imagine life off it never existed.

The breathtaking views have always been there,
Be it a day, a week, or a month anywhere,
A short time like that is never enough,
To find out and see what the inhabitants are worth.

Watching, prying, gossip and gab,
Annoying, destroying, take all they can grab,
As once a "White Settler", I know them well,
Fifteen years experience — There's much I can tell.

Island life is no retreat,
Crafty and sly are the folk you'll meet,
Where is this place on the west coast shore?
The name on the map is — The Isle of Lismore.

Eileen Wincentzen

My Dream

Closing of the eyelids as I rest my mind to peace
The darkness that endures me as I fall asleep with ease,

My mind begins to wonder floating, drifting off in space
Flashes, people, scenes and places I can't keep with this pace,

It rests now on a vision lightly scented all around
There is no sound or motion just a scene from days of past,

An old victorian lamp post grows dim as morning breaks
The scent was from the flower stall as bottom holes she makes,

Then I see a stranger a young man is in my dream
I can't quite make his face out but he's lonely just like me,

My visions growing dim now I try to hold on tight
The man I'm sure I know him but my dream has lost its fight.

I feel an arm slide round me, it's real now, not a dream
I open up my eyes to find my husband who's my dream.

Jacqueline Brockway

Summer Morning

Three o'clock the rooster crows
The dawn will soon be breaking,
To the sound of a beautiful melody
As all the birds are waking.

Through the haze of a summer morn I wandered,
Down a country lane,
In the air was the scent of a thousand flowers
Refreshed with gentle rain.

Dew drops sparkled on the ground
Like diamonds in the sun,
Covering up the strawberries lush
That grew in ripe profusion on the bush.

I climbed the stile to rest a while
Amidst the smell of a new mown hay,
As larks soared heavenwards to the sky
I heard the music from up high.

Hilda Jones

" Boots " My Cat

A Robin called on us that day
the day God took my cat away
and now each morning that he sings
I think of all the joy Boots would bring.

On winter night's he'd keep us warm
curled on our bed through ragging storm
and if by chance you felt unwell
he was there to guard and tell.

Sometimes now on darker nights
or when you just switch on the light
I'm sure I see him walking by
and then I have a lasting sigh.

But in my heart I know it's true
Boots is here watching all we do.

Julie Barker

Mother's Child

Mother and child share so much;
The joy, the laughter;
The warmth, the softness of their love.
Then the sorrow, the hatred, the quarrelling.
But always the happiness of the loving reunion.
From birth, they are inseparable;
The mother's child, the child's mother.
They have a bonding like no other.
Mother like beach; child like sea;
Always floating from security,
Always to return to serenity.
The storms are overcome by the radiant sun.
And forever is love shared by the child and mum.

Heidi Lewis

Motherhood

A strange and foreign land I entered,
The day I held her in my arms.
Fragile and weak, I watch her sleep.
Sleepless nights and days,
Bring me closer to her every day.
Death comes to mind, I face my mortality.
Being a Mum is strange to me,
Whoever said it came naturally?
Victoria, a small bundle of love,
A smile full of life,
Eyes that never cease to amaze me.
Beautiful you are to me, your presence
Fulfils me, and drains me at the same time.
How did we ever become?
Did you choose to come through me?
Become a part of me?
Sometimes I wonder...

Hala Di-Maio

The Lord Is Risen

I stood alone upon a hill,
The day was dark and very still.
Our dearest Lord had died for me
Upon the cross at Calvary.
Not just for me, but others too
Who loved him with a love so true.
For sinners who would break his heart,
He played his final role, his part.

Now suddenly the day grew bright,
The hill was filled with heavenly light.
A joyous feeling filled my breast,
Our Lord no longer lay at rest.
My heart felt glad, no longer grey,
For on this Happy Easter Day
I met him with a loud "Amen."
Our dear Lord has risen again.

Janet Short-Windsor

To Love Each Other Is To Love Ourselves

The weight of my world is like thunder
The depth of my feelings are true.
My heart is full of tears for the sadness of others in view
Weary from life's long journey, unable to cope with the pain
Lonely and feeling so wretched crying, "I'm going insane!"
"Where did my life go, what's happened?"
"Help me where do I belong?"
Still the same spirit inside me
Unable to join in the throng
What is life without someone to love me
To show that they really do care.
My hope and my saviour in heaven.
"OH GOD I DO HOPE YOU ARE THERE."

Dorothy Ann Williamson

Capturing The Ozone

Oh! What a mess we've made, our life
Sure to fade. How on earth can we
Condone, this destruction of our OZONE.

For centuries we've been looters, now
We've become our own polluters. Our
Ozone layer's crumbling, only few of us
Are GRUMBLING.

This message needs to get across,
Especially to those that are loss.
Forests like the Amazon set the tone,
These are our mainstay and BACKBONE.

So please everyone hear this call, go
Tell one, tell them all. None of this
Can we disown, we're all guilty of
  CAPTURING THE OZONE.

Lucita Allen

Untitled

No one understands the way I feel,
The despair inside I cannot reveal.
Worthless feeling, I have no cause,
This is no act, I don't want applause.

People around getting uptight
With the sad lonely person who's losing their fight.
No one to explain the numbness inside,
Just close out the world, find somewhere to hide.

It is funny how people surround you all day,
yet the loneliest girl is stood in their way.

The will inside to fight has vanished.
The life I had has now been banished.
Another tear runs from my eye,
Another breath turns to a sigh.

Darkness all around, no light in sight.
Permanent sadness through day and in night.
Annoyance of others makes it clear,
Maybe one day I'll disappear.

Lynn Anderson

Two Visits To Savannah, Georgia, U.S.A.

Savannah in the springtime, a wondrous place to be.
The dogwood out in blossom, and azaleas blooming free.
We went again in winter, more places for to see,
With guide who drove the trolley and, regaled its history!

A man sailed up the river, in seventeen thirty three.
He'd sailed the great Atlantic and found the place to be.
He drew the plans and started, a fine place there to build.
With grassy squares, and stately homes, and land which could be tilled.

He made friends with the natives who lived there in the bay,
Especially the Indian chief, who's honoured still today.
The town filled up with people, and as the years went by,
There came the revolution, and blood red was the sky.

Now looking back through ages of all the folks who came,
And settled down, from many lands, and some of them found fame.
The great Savannah river could tell so many tales;
Of ships with cargoes in full sail, of indigo, and cotton bales.

This town has always struggled against adversity,
Like hurricanes and civil war, but kept its dignity.
The cobbled streets and alleys and churches, oh so fair!
Not least of all I love the oaks, you see them everywhere.

Enid Gosney

Insolence

Insolence — I think it's called —
The cat does it.
She sits fast and looks bored —
Looking in front not listening
And I am calling — nerves bristling.
"Blow you then — stay out tonight
If you're cold serves you right!"
It's pointless to chase her, she flits away
She's had her food and her tray —
Got what she needs till next day,
But till then looks away.

A daughter does it
When to listen she refuses
She either talks too — or abuses
But mostly she looks the other way
Vacant and far away.
She knows it's true
And she should do
That's insolence too.

Betty Carpenter

Our Nature Reserve

It's peaceful and quiet at the lake
The ducks and fish swimming by
We sit on the seat and wait
And see the birds flying high
Swooping down on the water they dive
Swans and their cygnets are swimming by
At least they have all survived,
Fishermen are sitting very still
Hoping to catch what they will,
It might be Pike or Bream
They all go back in the stream,
Lilies in bloom everywhere,
The trees and bushes are now not bare,
The wardens keep the lake and sides clean
They work hard and are a good team,
Everyone can walk or sit and be peaceful there
And we all know they do care,
At our Nature Reserve.

Joy Hall

Scotland My Scotland

The stag roaring, echoing through the glen,
The eagle soaring, swooping, golden.

The mountains, craggy, threatening in their winter snow
Yet softened, beckoning in their spring green.

The heather, springy purple, a welcome bed to the clansmen of the past
Hiding in the mountains, gathering for war, rebellion.

The lonely windswept moors, the peat diggers, stackers
Toiling with thoughts of winter fires and whisky.

The bluebells, vivid carpets, the pale fern fronds,
The salmon leaping, glistening tirelessly upstream to spawn.

The waterfalls thundering down, the deep clear pools,
The lochs, mysterious, deep, ancient —

Ancient land, Scotland my Scotland.

Jean Scott Duncan

A Soldier's Scorn

We serve in Northern Ireland where bombs and bullets reign
The people throw the debris, the soldiers feel the pain,
The children grow in anger, spurned on by the lies
Suddenly a shot rings out and another soldier dies,
The man who did this killing soon receives his pay
He pops into his local to celebrate his day,
The wife back home in England, she soon receives the news
She cries herself to sleep that night for the man she had to lose,
People home in England think Ireland's just a game
They hear another soldier dies, to them it's just a shame,
So listen all supporters of the provisional IRA
Someday we'll find you paddy and then we'll make you pay,
And when we find you paddy no courts or jails for you
Just think of all those soldiers, then laugh as we shoot you.

Darren Paul Thomas

Ode To A Lovely Lady

The hands that firmly held the babe, tremble slightly now.
The eyes that shone so brightly then, are somewhat dimmer now,
But the heart that warmed, beats ever strong and her arms embrace me still, and love that came when we were young, still comes to warm the chill.
The kids have left and we're alone, but not for long you know,
The grandkids come and bring us cheer, oh how we love them so.
We're in the Autumn of our years, contented with our lot,
Our life's been like a garden, a very fruitful plot,
Sown with love and kindness and thoughtfulness and care,
The harvest has been bountiful, our cupboard is not bare.
And she still looks at me with those smiling eyes,
And I'll hold her sweetness in my heart, until my last goodbyes.
When I am laid beneath the earth, close by a tree that's shady,
She'll be near to cherish me; oh my LOVELY LADY.

Kenneth V. Jackson

Snow

With numbing chill and icy blasts,
The elements combine with awful
Leaden skies on the horizon,
To augur the onset of crystal fall.

An unseen hand then releases,
In ones, and twos, then in myriads,
White butterflies, that flutter down,
Like a swarm of itinerant nomads.

Quietly, slowly, a flight of snow
Petals the floor with a cloud of white,
Leaving for a moment a trail
Of journeys, before hiding them from sight.

But days that once were short and cold,
Grow longer, heralding a new sun
Metamorphosing white stillness,
Into a winding snake of liquid run.

That carpet of white purity,
Hid secrets of things that are to be
In nature's annual cycle,
That the warm breath of spring arrived to free.

David Rossington

Humanism...

Together in mind, in body we find,
The energy we need to lift mankind.
But there are those who cannot cope,
It's them that rob us of our hope.
Leave us gutted of our pride,
An empty feeling, the jilted bride.

Through heaven and earth little people dance,
Living their lives at a sudden glance.
Not knowing who they are, or what they could be,
Minds full of hope, they border insanity.

Why the hell is it, we destroy one another,
For earth means earthlings, sister and brother.
Should we listen to our dictator,
Issuing orders of hatred and murder.

Where is the harm in aiming for peace,
Submission of war, freedom released.
For within my time, I hope to see,
A world engulfed in tranquillity.
That people come, and races unite,
And colours go unnoticed, like day and night.

Danny Maher

M. E. And I

The feeling that life has been taken away,
The envy of seeing the children at play,
The once simple task of a walk down the street,
Has now become a difficult feat.

As I lie on my bed in total despair,
and think of the love of the people who care,
I feel the tears running down my face,
I'm living my life at a different pace.
I feel so tired but I just can't sleep;
The hole is so black, murky and deep.
I wake in the night sweating with fear,
waiting for the clouds to lift and clear,
perspiring from face, back and palms,
unable to move my legs and arms.
When I relax and realise I'm safe,
I soon recover and regain my faith.

The tunnel is windy with so little light,
but at the end I know the future is bright.
One has to learn, don't turn and run,
Just live with the illness until the battle is won.

James Arnold

Untitled

Love is not couples of women and men,
The fashion or form or the flight of a pen,
It does not exist in pre-planning or aim,
And nothing evolves from the strategy of a game.

When persons unite out of structure or trend,
Its value is only such as duty might lend,
Just the feeling of everything being in place,
Is the ultimate worth of a love of that face.

A meaningful love pays no mind to tradition,
The stylish approach or a standard position,
Equations are nought beyond plateaus of science,
And routine is stifled by feeling's defiance.

The reaction relates to the person alone,
Their personal self, and whatever its tone,
It's sparked from within by the nature implicit,
Requiring no more than what taste can illicit.

It's profound in its focus on everything real,
And derives nothing potent from general appeal,
It spurns in its simplicity all socially complex,
And discriminates neither in status or sex.

Di Wade

Peace

Although we're in peace, how long will it last?
The fighting must cease, we must forget the past.
The bombs were lethal and innocent were lost
Yet the bombers stood tall while we paid the cost.
Fighting has ceased, or so we are told,
But where are the arms which are still being sold?

Feeling hatred is wrong so don't let that grow
Among generations to come who don't have to know.
Religion should be free, like a bird in the sky
So please ensure us that peace isn't a lie.
United or not, violence is not the way,
Go to the table and there have your say.
Don't let your children grow up fearing the sounds
Of the shooting of guns or bombs in the towns.

In years to come,
Our children should be looked in the face
With peace in their eyes, knowing,
Northern Ireland is a safer place.

Lynne Cairns

Waiting For The Father

Sipping wine and sitting by the quayside
The old man gazes out to sea
Eating bread and sitting by the quayside
He waits so patiently.

Though ships may come and ships may go
Through the wind the rain the sleet and the snow
The old man's gaze is fixed endlessly
Far out across the blue turquoise sea.

Mothers, fathers wrap up against the cold
From afar you watch your children grow old
It's up to them the paths they take
It's up to them the mistakes they may make.

Now the old man is buried on the hill
But his soul is searching still
Like a statue stands guard on the quay
Watching, waiting for you and me.

Sipping wine and sitting by the quayside
I find myself gazing out to sea
My son sits quietly beside me
In his heart he's already free.

Lawrence Andrew Cade

Birds Last Song

Up high in the branches I sing my dawn song.
The first rays of sunlight tell me it's morn.
This morning in summer I wait for the heat.
To warm my cold body, it makes my heart beat.

The cat in the garden looks up from below.
I see in it's eye, that it's soon time to go.
So I flap my wings wildly and starting to rise.
Look back to the tree and see into his eyes.
The sun on his fur gives a beautiful shine.
I look once again and he's started to climb.

I fly and I fly right up in the air.
I look down again and can't see him there.
I swoop and I dive, the tree is all mine.
Land back on my branch, and see his eyes
SHINE...

Hazel V. Jackson

Beginning... End

We heard from her today
that a woman would come to see us,
to see if we fitted the silhouette,
that moment it began
my downfall,
though many believe that a life
of entertaining is glamorous
there lies behind it a dark hole which is ever
swallowing.
You don't realize till it's too late,
until you're trapped,
in a bottle or in a higher reality,
but you can break free
sitting, talking, revealing, unreeling.
It helps some, though not others
for me maybe if I had tried
but I didn't
I took the other way out.

Catherine A. Edwards

Untitled

In our last breath then perhaps we'll see,
The irony and futility of our fears.

In that last moment when fear grips
at the fabric of which we are made,
and all of me, Love, Regret, Pain, Happiness,
is there in one moment.

Then we will see,
I hope we will see,
Don't live for today,
Live for Eternity.

For Eternity is as long as you will live,
and what we do today,
We will remember for eternity.

Andrew Lockwood

A Reaction

He had to go because of me, my angry skin would never let
him be the jittery havoc in our little room, the fizzing life in our
domestic gloom; his ghost now settles at his favourite spot
and the silence speaks but forgives me not.

Taking his bones — shrink-wrapped-with-skin, we give him a
place to fatten in, where he found a voice through his ravaged
bleat and heroics in his foetal sleep; the very light of the room,
he became, stalking the shadows, giving them a name.

He sparkled from my partners' eyes, the games between them
hypnotized, skipping as she chased him across the floor and,
ever ready, he danced for more; I watched them sifting into
each other, the swaying drift of a child to mother.

And my livid skin would prickle and tease, the itch eluding my
clawing plea.

Gordon Wilkinson

Untitled

As I lay gently in the breeze
The flowers in my hair
Start to grow with the peace
Like a quilted tapestry of care

Love offers its hands open wide
Waiting for the embrace that combines
The deepness of the feelings I hide
And the love, so hard to define

The coffee, instant like feelings
Thoughts that flow of flowers in hair
The touch performing sensitive healings
On the bed of roses upwards I stare

The melodious guitar refrain
whistles through the air
As the pale dove flies upwards
towards harmony
Waiting for a time everyone has a
love share
Andrew Glasson

The Friends I Used To Know

I wonder where they are tonight
The friends I used to know,
We lived and laughed, loved and cried
But that was long ago.

I wonder if they stop to think
As I so often do,
Of dreams we dreamed, vows we made
Of friendships ever true.

Yes that was oh so long ago
And time has taken flight,
The promises once made have dimmed
Like shadows in the night.

But life goes round full circle
And new beginnings grow,
Still I wonder where they are tonight,
The friends I used to know.
Delia January

Battles

It's you again, it usually is,
The one who's wrong, the one they may not miss

It feels like a burning in your heart,
As if they're ripping your soul apart

You try to explain, for all that's been done,
But they won't listen, the battle's been won

You know you're loved and treated the same,
But when it comes to argue, you're out of the game

So what's the difference between them and you,
Why are they always happy, while you are always blue?
Julie Huckstepp

To The Moon

I lie here and I wait for you.
The pale moon rises, opens its mouth huge
and swallows my lantern in its luminous stare.
Trees spread spiky branches on the orange horizon.

My clock strikes slow, sloth-like, pendulous seconds.
Each atom open and expectant,
streaked across a multi-coloured sky
like the broken strings of an ancient violin.

This night sleeps on silently. Infinitely.
Burying my seed in the core of the universe,
I curl up in this quiet, navy womb
to watch your beginning eclipse my end.
Giuliana L. Fenwick

The Rite Of Spring, Then And Now

It is time for feasting, wild delights,
The garland spring of floral joy,
With gladsome days and loving nights;
Come nymph and with your rustic boy
Drink long and deep, your cup is full.
Now gentle Phoebe, take no chance,
Make sure that in the minuet
Or in the throes of longways dance,
You tread not on the broadsword edge,
Nor stub your toe against a skull.

It is time for rocking, wild delights,
Of springtime lust and Ecstasy,
With red-eyed days and jerking nights;
Come nymph and with your dreadlock stud
Drink hard and deep, your cup is full.
Now smooth-thighed Phyllis, take no chance,
Make sure that in that sinuous prance
You go not near the Semtex bomb
Some smirking leprechaun left here,
To turn a pretty head into a skull.
Laurence Millband

Steak And Cosmetics

i. In the insect midday warmth they lie
   The grass and sky reflections comply
   To the gentle, stolid, glassy eye
   Soon to blink an eternal good-bye

   This slope adorned with headstones
   This lea sprouts green from white bones
   Ears tune in to distant laughing
   To rooms prepared and blades for sharpening

   Your birth and life is born to this
   To fatten up on borrowed bliss
   Together they wander, to radio kill
   As finally the cattle come down the hill

ii. (A jungle abduction)
    The light of day stolen, worried eyes - desperate, swollen.

    The horror and fear, Today's rag revelation
    Of incisions, maternal and sense depravation

    Two monkey's in a cage
    Who held hands throughout the whole rampage
    From the trees of Vietnam chased
    To England, MY home, and laid to waste.
Alex Wallis

Beyond The Death Of Hope

This once magnificent life-giving planet, said long ago to have been the home of the great majestic Gods from above

Now metamorphosing from nature's gentle hand through corruption, greed and self-deprivation, to the hopeless disillusionment of love.

A spinning mass of warped tormented minds, aching with the longing yet futile promise of unfulfilled dreams.

An ever-growing cancerous quagmire of dark futility, pulling, tearing endlessly stronger at unseen moral seams.

What of pity, love, truth, honesty, and most of all hope, all gone, dead and forgotten, taken over by man's out and out all consuming greed.

Our only legacy now, total death and annihilation, as so often long ago foretold, and in ancient prophecies decreed.

For nothing foreseeable supports the future, how long then before the future becomes as dead as the past?

Or will nature first demand the ultimate retribution for all our deadly self indulgent crimes against her, and deservedly, make us pay to the very last.
Janet Mills

A November Day Begins — Or As We Were

The enshrouded morning comes at last with searing damp
The huddling birds by chimney tops make raucous cry
Then downward swoop with sudden vicious greedy croak
To gobble scattered crumbs or unsuspecting worms.
The shivering folk emerge unwilling from their beds
To quickly re-submerge in water's welcome warmth.
Then making their eager way where sound of sizzling pan
And rattling kettle lid and sparking, crackling fire
Tell of sustenance in comfort soon to come, they sit
At ease, receptive to the all-pervading smell
Of English breakfast on a dank November day
And meditate on inner joys while scanning news
Of Occident and Orient which shake the world.
That is but naught. A steaming plate has now arrived
Uplifting over all man's gastronomic soul.
The anticipatory dream is realized. Is this
Wherein the strength of England lies? Replete and warm
His erstwhile torpid mind astir, man rises, sighs,
Brimming with satisfaction now he turns to work
To face with fortitude the day - which has begun.
Lily Bailey

Ulster

Ulster needs permanent peace
The killings and bombing must cease
We're told we must do this and that
To get all round the table to chat

How can the talks make all things right
When there are those about who still want to fight
Too many have sores that just run too deep
And violence doth more violence reap.

I think that to talk may be good
But there are things that need understood
The terrorists must learn there's a right and a wrong
And forget about blarney and political song.

Destroy those weapons of war
And leave us all on an equal par
It's then that trust would build up
And we'd soon from the same cup sup.

The talks then could really bear fruit
And lead us all down a sensible route
Where with nothing to fear both sides could draw near
And expel the terrorist brute.
Drew Robinson

Early Summer In Lincolnshire

The wolds and fens, the great expanse of sky,
The lovely colours, 'tis impossible to try
to describe the shades of blue and green and brown,
So subtle, so restrained, and finely drawn.

O God, how lovely is this countryside of ours
Where grasses gently wave, among the flowers,
The flowers I've known and cared for all my life,
Pale cuckoo flowers, moon daises and Loosestrife.
And Kecksies, or as some say, Queen Anne's lace,
Bordering the wayside, with enchanting grace,

On mossy banks, mid leaves and tangled roots
In dappled sunshine are the pale green shoots
Of bracken, curling ere the fronds unwind,
And honeysuckle, with wild roses are entwined.
A spray of blossom, in the peat brown dell.
A bumble-bee exploring foxglove bells.

And in the hedge a blackbird sings for me
And pigeons coo together in the hawthorn tree:
When sun and flowers and music all are blending
With me in peace, which passes understanding.
Gwendolen M. Kent

The Mask

The mask, a face
The mask, a smile
Oh so sad tears, yet dry eyes
So many things the mask hides
Reality hides behind the mask
To keep it there is such a great task.
Every so often I escape through, revealing emotions to you,
My masked face hides away
Never tells you how it feels
People use you to take advantage
To make you a complete fool
To me the mask is never so cruel
It is my best friend, I never have to pretend.
My only cover, protection... it carries away the pain
So I won't suffer any rejection
The mask covers up everything inside
Everything inside that is me, If it wasn't for the mask
I don't know where the hell I'd be
Because I take it in my hands, put it to my face
Every feeling and emotion, disappears without a trace.
Kathrine Jones

Millennium 2000

Poetasters ev'rywhere, heed the times, beware, beware!
The millennium beckons — don't be perverse
Time to dispense now with Doggerel Verse
Soon a new century, soon a new you!
Two hundred decades scribing sky-blue with true!!
An epic now — a Homer, a Keats!
Think now of England, not of defeats
No bawdy limericks, no bar-room quip
To gain the odd flagon for your lyrical wit.
And 'Shame' quoting Kipling to augment your tippling
Is your pen poised for history! Or brainless whittling!
An Iliad now — an Auld Lang Syne,
A burning desire for much better times
No sonnets please from those lakeland bards
Yes, yes, we do recall Dickens when times were so hard
But forward now to earn your ovation
The nineteens, the twenties in 'grand' copulation
The exquisite moment, the birth of the century
Champagne and oysters now, on the inventory
But only of course — for the landed gentry!
Albert H. James

In The Dead Of Night

The stars are glistening in the sky,
The moon is shining bright,
All the world is quiet and still
In the dead of night.

The swans are bobbing in the bay,
An angler gets a bite,
You can only hear an owl hoot
In the dead of night.

A fox creeps through the farmer's field,
Caught in a beam of light,
A boat glides gently out to sea
In the dead of night.

I can hear an aer-o-plane,
There goes a meteorite,
I thought I saw a falling star
In the dead of night.

Everywhere is sparkling,
The frost is glittering white,
It's really very cold out here
In the dead of night.
Joan Guy

Winter Everywhere

The wintry air, the icy breeze,
The morning dew on frosty trees,
The sunset burns right through the sky,
The call of birds up way up high,
The earth's great creatures of the sky,
The earth, the sea and waters high,
They all adopt the fight for life,
To dodge the guns and spears and knives,
Listen as they cry for help,
The lions roar, the seal-pups yelp,
They wait in anger, deadly sore,
For what they know will come once more,
The beating of their very hearts,
Will match the hunters deadly march,
They hide in fear, for once again,
They can't take anymore deep pain,
Their dead, their gone and sleeping now,
In peace, they lie upon the ground,
For what was once the fight for life,
Is sleeping now as cold as ice!!!
Linda Spurway

Slighted

From dusk to dawn
The night forlorn
My body asleep, amidst the smell of corn
The harvest abashing.
The dogs dashing, to the sound of the horn
Summer came and brought the light
She stirred away the darkness of night
My body relaxed
My mind a haze.
Happy was I to sleep it by,
Too soon had autumn gone
The winter was upon.
Too soon to know just how long.
I see the world go by and heave a sigh
No more birds flying by.
Only the dragon chasing the sky.
Carole Anne Thompson Fisher

Death Of The Mill

An illness but nobody knows clickety clack clickety clack
The noise is there no one to care clickety clack clickety clack
There is work to do machines to run clickety clack clickety clack
Night and day to earn your pay clickety clack clickety clack
The sounds die down as times do change clickety clack
The illness strikes still nobody knows clickety clack
Progress comes the machines must go clickety clack
Four days three days two days a week clickety clack
The old men get older the young despair clickety clack
The mills are dying the trade is gone clickety clack
Empty shells both human and stone clickety clack
Silent are the looms dead is the mill
David Jackson

School Day

In memory, I can still recall
The grandeur of the odd school hall,
Echoing the footsteps of each small child
who walked across its polished tiles.
In regiments, the coat peg lines,
above each one a tag defines
the owner of each Duffle grey,
same sense of order, every day.

The classroom with its windows tall,
Alphabet letters adorn each wall.
For each child a desk, a suitable chair
and the sense of belonging is everywhere.
The smell of the chalk dust, the paints and the clay,
expected to learn and encouraged to play.
Time passes so quickly, yet all so clear
is the memory of that first school year.
Gill Garbutt

Why, Should I Live?

Am I alive, or am I dead?
The old man pondered alone on his bed.
For my life must have reason and my reason has gone,
And without a reason, I just can't go on.
He walked to the bathroom, his mind full with thought,
His heart numb with passion that yearned to be sought.
He reached to the sky with his arms stretched above high,
A small bead of water escaping his eye.

He turned off the bath tap, the water was warm
The ran his hand through it, but his feeling had gone.
He took down his razor and admired the craft,
Then as he entered the water he laughed.
He laughed and he laughed, as the razor bit deep,
And under the water his life's blood did seep.
He closed his weary, imageless eyes
His spirit floating, like a cloud through the skies.

His mind went blank, he felt himself go
Into the blood-stained water he slipped below.
A muffled cry, one last breath
He had no reason to live, he surrendered to death.
Debbie Gown

Ode To An Old Woman

I wonder what became of her
The old woman waiting for the train
Hours and hours she waited
Whether it be sunshine or rain
Day after day, year after year
Waiting, just waiting
But alas, her train never came

Was she waiting for a long lost love
Perhaps one already departed above
Maybe a soldier returning from war
Or even a sailor from some far-off shore
I hope she found peace in her lonely quest
Some day to put her mind at rest
Poor old woman, I miss her so
Sad old woman, with back bent low
Joyce Roberts

The Bus Ride

I'm sitting here far away,
The only sound hums like crying,
My eyes dart, my body shakes
This information rolling like skates.

Looking around, the eyes stare back
They feel like me under attack.
Soon the door will part, my teeth will unclench
The lights at the end, no more shall I relent.

The haze on the window, moulds my breath,
The slight breeze through the pane curls round my neck.
Stopping, starting, stopping, starting.
Fingers pressing, noise whirling
People passing; me, I'm uncurling.
Claudine Franklin

Come Hither

The darkness looms,
The pain enshrouds,
Mist shadows the heart,
Mortals weep.
The darkness forbidding yet comfortingly safe,
The pain is devoured into the dark,
Lifted from the soul.
"Come hither to the light..."
While mortals weep.
The darkness breaks,
A light descends,
"Come hither to the light, come hither."
Souls embrace the joy and the release,
Mortals weep for lost times.
Kelly Ladell

In The Ballroom

A once great mansion stands empty devoid of life.
The owners moved on to new and greater heights.
Inside a desolate ballroom, abides one lonely piece of furniture.
This thing of beauty; standing, lonely, abandoned,
waiting in wonder,
Quiet, listen, to the ghostly echoes of Mozart, Verdi, and Strauss
haunting, spinning a waltz along the corridors, daring to
dance into each empty room.
Room redolent of whispered secrets of seduction and lovers kisses.

Great works of art now removed leaving through nought but
dusty shadows.
Porcelain, china and precious crystal wrapped, carefully
packed and gone.
Drapes and hangings taken down and neatly folded away.

As night descends eerie shadows dance from window to window.
The undisturbed silence broken by the uncanny flutter of a
bat's wing.
Morning upon us sunrise brings in light, yet still alone it
stands bemused.
The suns ray shimmers over a thin covering of dust upon this
thing of beauty.
Suddenly the large front door creaks open breaking the silence.
A man enters, footsteps echo on the barren boards.
Standing casting a knowing eye over this beautiful piece he
sets about his work.
With the specialists gentle thoughtful touch, wrapped,
protected, bound, ready.
Now ready to be reunited with its caring owner and a new ballroom.
Carolyn Foggin

Nostalgic Regret

I sit alone, weep and regret
The passing of ones I can't forget
When they were here, life then was fun
Their absence now blots out my sun.
They did not fail to disagree
When to vain folly I did cleave
My losing footsteps caught in nets
Because of where my sights were set,
They tired to make me get things right
When folly blotted out the light
My mental processing was dimmed
By folly camouflaging sin.

The wasted years in madness spent
Will not undo the thing that went
Advice from loved ones cared have saved
And left me with a kitten name.
Though I cannot recall the past
Their memory will always last
Advice from those whom I hold dear
Still calls as did when they were here.
Katie Sarah MacDonald

Wrecks

Locked within their splendid coral cemeteries,
sunken wrecks,
peopled now by piscatorial squatters.

Captain and crew ride no more the broad oceans;
statue-like
they cleave to decks where mountainous seas had stormed.

Bridge, handrail, chartroom, cabins, foc'sle, decks,
all transformed
by the busy handmaidens of centuries.

Unconcernedly, the fish glide through tragedy;
their domain,
a man-made home, not a graveyard of the sea.

Time and tide ceased long ago for the sunken ones
fixed in youth,
but the denizens of the deep glide ceaselessly,
their sea-born lives untouched by the awful truth.
Leonard Saunders

Self Destruction

Rain-filled skies closing all around my head,
the path which I am taking would surely find me dead.
Pain cuts away my skin leaving me alone,
where do you begin when all that's left is bone.

Emptiness leaves me standing,
cold and in the rain,
every time I see your face,
I feel a stabbing pain.
The wind that lifts and carries me,
past your open door,
blows so strong from in my head,
that you may be no more.

Bringing pain upon myself,
a mental suicide,
if I could kill my inner thoughts,
I'd be very much alive.

The clouds that are surrounding,
came from in my head,
if I can't put these to one side
I will very soon be dead.
Ian Christopher Wilkinson

The End

Suddenly everything a bright white,
The mushroom clouding a clear night.
The wind demon howls its ghostly call
As it charges through the windows
and smashes down the walls

Knocked over the innocent fall
By the intense heat of the fireball.
In thousands their souls float away,
From the ghostly world to a place far away.

The silent sky black and dead.
World stained a deathly blood red,
Smothered by the fog of death.
Sun choked by the killers breath.

Days pass and few survive,
Eating corpses from the rubble to stay alive.
One by one they grow weak and die,
More food for the remaining to get by.

Over the darkened skies flies a dove
Symbolizing the end, the lack of love
Killing the world and it cries
As the last remaining survivor dies.
Julie Caswell

Bethlehem

The universe is silent; it lay undisturbed,
the night Jesus came to live on earth.

The newly born lay silently and innocently in the stable
where he lay amongst the hay.

Wise men came from the east, they came from the west,
they followed the star and that night were blessed.

They gave him gifts and all they had
but the Lord Jesus didn't need any of that.

He laboured as a carpenter's son while years passed by,
until on a cross he did finally die.

He spoke of Heaven as a place of rest,
and hell a place of torture,
he spoke the gospel, he spoke the truth
and for this he was crucified in disrepute.

There is a Heaven,
there is a Hell,
when you die will it be Heaven
or is it Hell?
B. A. Reynolds

Promises

The great wars end; they promise now a new beginning.
The people must begin again to build a bright
new future, for the offspring they will bear.
North Sea Oil and Gas they promise, new
work, more money for the poorer class
but what has happened to that dream, those
promises, they're gone for good it seems.
Young people have such sadness in their eyes.
The people cringe, the bombs still blast;
where is that bright new future? they all ask.
The old in fear sit behind their bolted doors,
the children that we love have turned to crime.
No work, no money, they all cry.
So knife will flash in drugged abandon and another body lies.
There dies the promise of a happy future.
Is this the end, just more despair, is there no one who
really cares
To make a fresh start and a new tomorrow?
Dorothy M. Neale

The Sound Of Silence

In a leafy glade so quiet, where
The perfume of bluebells fills the air,
I tiptoe softly on mossy leaves
Where no man walks, no roadway weaves,
And all I hear is the sound of silence.

Look! A lake of mirror'd perfection, where
My silhouette's a neat reflection there,
No reeds a-rustling, nor waves a-lapping,
No sound from the owl on phantom wing,
Only the eerie sound of silence.

Look! My empty childhood home, where
Memories force me to stand and stare,
Noises of laughter, of children singing,
In my mind and ears are ringing
Loudly, in the sound of silence.

Onward through the forest, hushed, where
To make one noise I would not dare.
I'm standing still and listening, now,
God made this haven, I know not how,
And I thank him for this sound of silence.
Christine Farmer

Broken Dreams

Are passions dead that one time ruled?
The promises made and yet were fooled,
For life's not always what it seems
And we are left with broken dreams.

Lost is the faith in which we were taught
Distant the battles in which we fought
The dead are forgotten — or so it seems,
And are left with their broken dreams.

Emotions run dry — no more tears to shed
We've betrayed our brothers and buried our dead
Dreams that we dreamt — now foolish schemes.
And we are left with broken dreams.

Where now is this brave new world
Into what new tomorrow must we be hurled?
A beckoning light but barely gleams.
Move quickly — or more broken dreams.

Dreams now mankind of future expansions?
"In my father's house are many mansions"
For life's not always what it seems
We could be left with broken dreams.
Allan Galsworthy

The Answer

Those who seek shall surely find
The reason why we sometimes fall
The purpose of life for all mankind
We care only for ourselves and not for all

We have that choice that freedom of will
I say these's things that you might gain.
That wonderful gift that Bears no ill
The lesson of life we need to obtain

In all the world people ask why
I can only say that when we pause upon our path
What really happens when we die
The journey continues it is not the last

The Path you take must be chosen well
A guide book and chart do not exist
It's not for me to show and tell
There are no signs, there is no list

It's within us each all mankind.
J. Cox

The Tree

Standing there beside that great big tree,
the rest of the world, the tree and me.

Large and strong with hidden strength,
grand to see in all its length.

In splendid majesty, branches outstretched,
a haven to many and truly blessed.

Overlooking the merrily babbling burn,
as it winds its way around every turn.

The seasons pass, they come and go,
for this tree time will smoothly flow.

The world changes gradually at its own pace,
bark and branches never change their face.

The path is wearing deep in this leafy land,
foliage and ferns growing tall and grand.

This sentinel of time I'm heartened to know,
will stand here long after it's my turn to go.
John Gibson

To Someone Not Yet Born

Spirit, Yes you! From somewhere there, beyond this life of mine.
Hear me as I call to you, from somewhere back in time.
Are you just the same as me, with failings human still?
Or has our evolution taken your free will?
Do you hold the heart of one to whom you are most dear
Do you know of happiness? Do you still shed a tear?
Do you feel the wonder of your sweet child's embrace?
Do you feel the sun and wind, and rain upon your face?
Do you still grow old with time, lines etched on your brow?
Are you still a human mould? If not, what are you now?
Penniluck Nicolson

Sonnet For Spring

Mighty Winter bowed and stepped aside beguiled.
His ermined cloak he'd laid before her feet.
Lifting her trailing rain soaked veil she smiled
as Innocent and wily veteran meet.
Dismissing him with gesture quite sublime
she will not brook his strong desire to stay.
In pique he doffs his cap of crystal rime
to scatter rattling hail across her way.
Daffodils and daisies in joyous scene
wave gold and pure white banners on the lea.
Tall beeches weave a tapestry of green
and chirp of sparrow vies with buzz of bee.
Spring has arrived, let all of us give praise
for life renewed and longer sunlit days.
G. R. G. Narramore

Transcension

As the tune plays, the red merges, blue too,
The head revolves from here to there, as the
grass is in unawares,
Of the tune and the rhyme, too.
Play do the parasites, mould and create
Plasticine landscapes.
  The inner ear croaks, releasing ghosts and
in my daze,
The Pony melts, his skin tenders,
Steak for the table, kiss the plate,
The dreams are laid,
Cast ambitions to the waves.
Tell the joke,
Foretell pacifists' tempers, still
Where are the Ponies now: Laid to waste,
upon the plate,
I see the tree fall, empathy resides,
The revolution's inside,
Hard and torn, a new soul is born,
But have I the heart to tell them?
Lee Freeman

Solitude

All alone, I hear the gentle hissing of the gas,
The flames inside the fire.
A train speeds quickly down the track,
Goes onwards, passes by us.
The sound of silence lingers in this place where no one talks.
Except the wandering of my thoughts encased inside my mind.
My private cellar, stored inside it lies my heart, so carefully
concealed. It hides behind my face, inside my smile so blind.
Feelings of my heart, my mind,
So empty sometimes sitting here.
The small clock ticking.
Marking time, it passes, progress!
So quiet and alone I stay.
Thinking and daydreaming timeless thoughts.
My own and others mingling in a cobwebbed maze.
A jungle fact and fantasy.
A fairy tale
My dreams
My cardboard memories
My plaster casted world.
Janice L. Williams

A Young Boy And His Kite

A swooping eagle tugs at the young boy's
heart with its string.
Wild, the eagle flits between
one instant of danger and another.
Its broken frame tumbles
from the pellet of an air gun to the concrete.
Wings shiver in the young boy's arms after its fall,
small, faltering hands smoothed over
fragments of torn feather tissue.
Sharon Gatfield

First Love

Week at the knees when he comes near.
Heart beating fast is what I hear.
First love will last many a year.

Through all the smiles and many a tear,
Memory of this love will never fade,
As the years go on and we both age.

First love is always the best,
This is the love you'll remember
Until the day you are laid to rest.
Maureen Jean Cogar

Untitled

I whispered for my love to be with me
I opened my eyes and thought that he was there with me
I felt and looked, and saw and said, who can my love be
He gave me the rain, the morning dew, the sea
and ever think that he resided there He gave unto me
I felt and I looked and I saw and said
who can my love be
I whispered for my love to be with me
My body became week and I felt him embrace me
He tenderly touched my breast with his embrace
I felt my soul drift into space
Who can my love be
I whispered for my love to be with me
Let's dance, he said to me
I felt his soul take mine into paradise and we danced
I whispered for my love to be with me
let's talk intimately about sex and we
how his voice echoed throughout the universe
I whispered for my love to be with me, let's sleep in bliss
He said unto me, I was not dreaming
Tina Hewitt

" Nana "

When my daughter's children look at me,
I often wonder, just what they see.
Someone who's always there for mummy to call
Someone to kiss them better should they fall.
Someone to mind them if mummy's at work
To teach them rhymes, to count, and to talk.
Someone who visits, and never misses.
Someone who always wants cuddles and kisses.
A lady who's handbag always contains a treat.
An apple, an orange, or perhaps a sweet.
Perhaps one day, when they have grown
And have grandchildren of their own.
They will remember how a Nana should be.
Loving and kind, head of the family.
Ron Foster

Life

As I wander along this road,
I often wonder if truth be told,
What lies ahead, around that bend?
Many heartaches that may not mend.
These things we cannot quite foresee,
Thank the Lord, between you and me.
Laughter and hope along the way
Let's just live our lives day by day.
Matty Jones

Family Ties

Sometimes when I sit alone,
I often think of times long gone,
When the children were so small,
I seldom had free time at all.

Now they have left the family home,
And all have children of their own,
To love and cherish, clothe, and feed,
See to everything they need.

I hope their children care like mine,
And for their parents find the time
To sit and talk, to hear their view
On what is best for them to do.

I do thank God for my good health,
We all got by without much wealth,
Family ties mean so much more,
Than any money held in store.

All my sons, and daughters too,
Although they have a lot to do,
Each finds the time to come and call,
And I must say, I love them all.
Sarah Magill

Miss — Perfection

My name's Sabrina I'm four years old,
I'm a perfect child and as good as gold,
I'm beautiful, brave and very bold,
a truer story I've never told.
I'm bright, intelligent and oh so witty,
I'm charming, cute and very pretty,
I can write my name and read a book,
There isn't a meal that I can't cook,
I can sing you songs all day long,
Not one verse will I get wrong,
There's nothing in the world that I can't do,
I'll make you laugh when you're feeling blue,
I'll do any chores that you want me to,
As long as you believe this poem is true!

S. Lawson

Ben — Where Does He Go?

"I'm just going out Mama squirrel" he cried
I'll have me some fun — I will run and hide.
Then I will visit that lady who gives me good food
She treats me with respect and is never rude.
Never grabbing at me or trying to catch
As I sit there quietly having a scratch.
I have seen her getting right down to my level
As I snatch the nuts — I'm a real little devil.
There are monkey nuts, filberts, large Brazils too
I will eat some and bury some — maybe dig up a few.
Then I will scurry off to my family
With my full fat tummy and they will see
That I have been o.k. and very well fed
But just in case anything is said
That I'm looking in the best of health
I'm keeping my adventures all to myself.

S. G. Holmes

One Holy Mess

If you exist then why persist in ruining our lives
If you are there then don't you care if this fragile earth survives
If you created man was it your plan to make him such a fool
To live his life in constant strife and breaking nature's rules
To murder trees and poison seas and forever go to war
And take his aim under your name is this the dream you saw
Is it you who sends the quake and flood, is it you who
 poisons all our blood
Is it you who sends the fire and drought to steal our food,
 leave us without
Is it you who makes us live in need, who fills our minds with
 hate and greed
Is it you who leads us blindly on until this planet's breath has gone
I don't believe in rich and poor, there's no such thing as a holy war
I don't believe in killing man because he follows a different plan
I don't believe that black and white is the same as saying
 wrong and right
I do believe in the power of love but I don't believe in you.

Ricky Silk

Thank You, Please, And Sorry

We all know three words that are used every day
If used in succession they cause such a stir
But use them in order; it really sounds nice.
Thank you, for the birds that sing
Thank you, for that long awaited ring
Thank you for being my friend

We could go on for a very long time
But we'll now go on that little word "Please"
We all want to do this, one way or the other
Remember these three words all came from our mother
Then there's "sorry", what a wonderful word
We feel so much better as soon as it's said
Now put the three together; what have we got?
Thank you — please and sorry!
The three most beautiful words in the dictionary.

L. Stephenson

A Mother's Broken Heart

Why did you break my heart?
If only I had known from the start
from the first time that I held you
I loved you with all my heart.
But you were to take it and tear it apart
From nought to five you were so lovable
From five to ten you were so troublesome
And then it began the worry and the sorrow,
the question would be what will happen tomorrow.
Those teenage years were full of worry
But I had to work to make some money
So I was not there when the police came knocking,
To give the news, that was so shocking.
You married at 20, it was so young
It did not last for very long
And so to drink and drugs and degradation
Oh what has become of this generation
And when I visit you in jail
I go home to weep and wail
Oh my son, why did you break my heart?

Margaret Thompson

My Dogs

My wonderful dogs, so faithful and true
If only I could give them more than I do,
But what more do they want than a walk each day,
My loving devotion and time to play.

C. Arnold

In My Wildest Dreams

If I could flee old London Town,
I'd travel as a Circus Clown!
Escape the trap of misery,
The dole queue and no equity;
And dressed in brightly coloured clothes,
Fantastic hats and velvet hose,
With friends and little dog in tow
A painted bus and magic show,
My unicycle and firesticks,
By spreading joy with simple tricks,
I'd visit Thailand and Peru,
Greece, Turkey, Guatemala too!
Then after one year on the run,
I'd end in Key West in the sun.
And on my journey, I'd collect
All kinds of head-dress from each sect,
Upon return, hat shops to run,
To fund a space for children's fun —
A circus workshop, wild and free,
Just like I dream that I can be!!

Rachel Caine

The Flame

Sitting in my darkened room
The flame provides me with light,
Revealing to me the things
That I cannot see with my own eyes.

Whenever I am cold
The flame gives me heat
As if an invisible sheet is laid upon me,
She gently embraces me from the cold.

Sometimes when I am alone
The flame dances to entertain me,
Accompanied by the following shadows
That bring my room to life again.

When I am in need of love
The flame caresses me with her warmth,
And as her affection gently surrounds me
I am taken in by her serenity.

Yet if this flame was to ever go out
I will have none of these things or you,
For this flame is you.

Jason Thomas

Winter Hedgerow

The sun shines down on frosty hedges
Icicles hang like crystal wedges
By the minute getting shorter
Turning ice back into water
Frozen cobweb in suspension
Far from spiders main intention
A relic of those warmer days
When spider had most devious ways
Blackbird through the hedgerow hurries
Seeking out the ripened berries
Testing Mother Natures larder
Winter days make feeding harder
If they could pray, they'd pray for spring
Time for nesting and time to sing
And to feeding a greater need
With all those extra beaks to feed.
Stanley Swann

Finding Favour

Matthew freezes: glacial as the teeth that grin with malice,
Ice-chipped words enclose him.
"Head Master wants to see you tomorrow."
'Why? What have I done? What have I done?'
Thoughts, like imprisoned birds, panic in his head.

Too terrified for tears, heavy heart and leaden feet lead him home.
'What will Mummy and Daddy say?'
They do not see the fear behind stark eyes in strained face.
Tea time — but he does not eat. 'Is he sickening?'
Early to bed; prayers; left alone. Pen to paper; last resort.

  Deer God, Plees help me. I am in trubel at skool.
  The edmarsta wonts to see me tumoro. Luv Matthew.

He posts it through the transome.

The wind wafts the precious paper to the ground.
The frost pinpoints it with sparkling precision.
The moon beams benevolence on five year old innocence
And spills pure light upon it.

Mother finds and understands: tears as sweet as morning dew
Fall on fair skin. They will face the fear together, hand in hand.

'Good work! Well done, Matthew! I'm moving you up.'
Patricia Green

Dear Father

Dear father you have been absent for so many years.
I wonder where you are, and if you are content.

Your character was that of such a splendid one,
but you left us behind so soon, and yet life still carries on.

You were such a kind man,
always thinking of others, never caring for yourself.

You were such a wonderful man,
who always gave and never expected anything in return.

People who did not even know you
said, that you were really someone rare,
because of the qualities you possessed and the man that you were.

No one knows how it feels when someone so close in your life
is gone.
But you have been my inspiration, the person who has kept
my strength for so long.

I know I will never find again the exact amount of love you
gave to me,
but those moments have been captured in my heart ever so
preciously.

If I had known you were to leave us in such a haste,
I would have been able to make every moment special,
they would not have gone to waste.

But you breathed the last breath of life before my very eyes.
You died right in front of me, something I will remember for the
rest of my life.
Mina Karim

The Year I Didn't Hear The Cuckoo

The year I didn't hear the cuckoo,
  I won the lottery of life;
The cuckoo didn't come that May,
  But one year later I heard it play.

Months had been long, and so intense,
  My hopes were up and down;
Family and friends prayed for me,
  That sunshine could be found.

As God looked down, and brought me joy,
  My tears flowed freely, I was not coy;
Birds were singing and flowers were seen,
  And I knew it was real, and not a dream.

The year I heard the cuckoo,
  I could not believe my luck;
Doctors and Nurses looked after me,
  And kept me in the book.
Peter Loughborough

I Wish

I wish that life was full of joy, for each and every girl and boy,
I wish that pain and sadness would cease and everyone could
  find some peace,
I wish there were no tears or sorrow, that I would have a
  bright tomorrow,
I wish the world was full of laughter, that we could live
  happily ever after,
But then my wishes are but dreams, that cannot be, or so it seems,
We just go round and around forever,
We may find peace, but maybe never.
D. C. Quinlan

My Lost Lover

I'll never forget the day you chased after me to steal my heart,
I wish I'd known at the time how you would tear it apart.

First you took away your tongue and magic lips,
Then you took away your breath-taking kiss.

Then you took away your loving fingers,
That gave my body all over the shivers.

Then from me you took away your body,
And left mine lost and feeling lonely.
Then I turned around and you were missing,
And I found out another you had gone back visiting.

Then your phone calls became less and less,
And then my life became such a mess.

I have seen the change in you as time went by,
you have lost that twinkle in your eye.

Gone is that smile that was always on your lips,
And gone more and more each day is the memory of your kiss.

Why did you want to hurt me so.
When all you had to do was simply let me go.
T. Tanner

Memories

A panoramic vision unfolded in my mind,
the magic and the trauma of a lifetime left behind.
Like big bold italics placed on paper with a die.
An existence gone forever was recaptured in mind's eye.
The screaming little boy being pried away from
mother, as she left to go to hospital to bear his baby brother.
The cold but tasty lollipop the man made
in his box, the hounds and reckless horsemen in
pursuit of frightened fox. The view from on the
mountain to the kraal across the plain, the grief
at loss of loved ones, the anguish and the pain.
They gathered there before me forming pictures
in my head, like a badly made B movie of the good, the bad, the dead.
These and many others intruded inner sky
I heard the sounds, I saw the scenes, but
was it really I, or my imagination which deceived me with a lie?
Ben Herbert Brumel

The Terrorist

Peace they said would come one day
I will not change my view and give way
Bomb, Gun, Bomb, stir up my hate
That's the way I intend to play
Care I not a jot, a coffin here or debris there
On your knees and say a prayer
What in the world do you call fair?
I make my mark, I keep my power
Fear and hatred grow tall as a tower
A Husband, A father, I may well be
This mask and gun truly changed me
In the dim light of a secret place
We work out our strategy of hate
My cause, my cause, it's always right
This is only and ever in my sight
Beware, man, child or beast
I will hold ahead my gun and bomb
When you call Peace
    Margaret Mitrega

To — My Legs

My legs would not climb up the stairs
I was taken unawares
They go up often two a time
Surely these cannot be mine
Opinions differ, one, two, three,
Osteo Arthritis of the knee
Wear and tear and growing old
Rheumatism and the cold
Come on legs, you've carried me
O'er mountain, hill and dale and lea,
A hundred thousand miles there be
Of roads and bikes and you and me
I'm not concerned about their views
What do they know of me and you
One day soon, I'll run upstairs
Again you'll take me unawares.
    Muriel L. Dale

The Victor

The curses rained down on my head,
"I was a fool, an idiot" he said.
"How could I not see the error of my ways
One day it could be serious" he said.
My lip trembled, I fought against the tears,
The lump in my throat grew, I had fears
Of choking. Standing my ground
Desperately searching for the lame excuse,
I felt such a goose.
So vulnerable, I wished that I were dead.
"I have only one more thing to say to you" I said
As he paused for breath. I knew that I had won.
"Only one more thing to say.
Your flies are undone!"
    V. Marlow

Fire Within Me

Thinking again tonight of you
I want to write your name
and tell you how I feel
But I must never name you
Yes, you have a name, Fire.

Fire, I have danced in your flames
Your flickering tongue licked my body
I felt the intense heat of your passion.
Have seen the warmth within you

I was drawn nearer and nearer
Was consumed, scarred forever
I played with fire
I was truly burned.
    Sheila Toms

Rebirth

I used to have a recurring dream.
I walked alone beside the sea,
I felt the wind on my face
And in my hair.

But each morning I awoke
To the dark limbo of another endless day.
I hovered, trembling, on the brink of the Styx
But the Ferryman did not come.
I walked through the Valley of Shadows,
Through the mists and out into the light.

Now I hear the sound of sea birds crying.
I step over rock pools, and see
The ebbing tide stretching the pebbles.
I walk in a living dream,
Feel the salt wind on my face,
Tugging my hair.
    W. Helen Tayler

Ole Cornwall

Cornish born and Cornish bred!
I walk the land my ancestors tread.
My forefathers have long since died,
But they'll never bid this land good-bye.
You can feel them all around you.
Both on land and by the sea,
For Cornwall has such mystery
And no-one holds its key.
I see visions of ancient Cornwall,
Of how it used to be.
Fisherman out fishing — wives waiting down the quay.
Ole tin mines are no longer used,
The men have long since gone.
But Cornwall holds the memories.
And the wind still plays their song.
    D. Dallimore

Homeland

Resting on the farmyard gate
I view our pleasant land
The distant fields are ploughed and bare
With glistening furrows dark,
While close at hand the tufted grass
May house a nesting lark.
In spring there's no more joyous sound
Than when the skylark leaves the ground
And climbs aloft, throat full of song,
Rising, falling, all day long.
The pastoral scene, set fair and wide
With close-knit hedges down each side,
The village green, the country church,
The massive oak and slender birch,
The pond where little children play,
Where swans may nest, and ducks display,
The primroses lane, the market town,
The white walled cottage, thatches brown;
This is our land, yours and mine.
May it be so 'til the end of time.
    B. C. Neave

" Dreaming "

Here I sit and wonder why...?
I try to smile but start to cry.
I've loved so hard and lost so much,
How I long for someone's special touch.
A sweet caress... a tender touch...
A loving kiss that means so much;
These things I wish would all come true,
Without them, here I am feeling blue.
I know I'll laugh... I know I'll weep...
I've tired so hard this "Love" to keep
And looking on I live in hope...
Of one day finding the perfect bloke!
    Rachel Dale-Patteson

Retirement

When I was still a working man, with quite a decent screw,
I used to wile some leisure hours rehearsing what I'd do
When I'd retired. I had a list much longer than your arm,
A mobile home, a sailing boat, perhaps a little farm,
A world-wide tour, a pad in Spain, a long cruise in the Med.,
A tramp through snowy wastes, where lesser mortals fear to tread,
Hot-air ballooning, paragliding over Garda's lake,
(Well, and why not? For I was fit enough, for goodness' sake).
To run the London marathon, and, what I longed for most,
To ride the crashing breakers on Australia's southern coast.
Then came the magic 65; retirement! pension! free!
Take one year off, and plan and plan — then face reality.
It's all no use; you have to be your own severest critic;
Re-tired, it seems, means "tired again"; besides, I'm too arthritic.

T. G. Freeman

The Dream

Alone to the end of the soulless queue
        I trudge.
One day to meet — one day to judge
        my judge.

William A. Smith

Infinity

Alone in a night of torment
I tossed on a bed of despair
Pounding the door of silence
Shrieking "Is anyone there?"
Till soft as dawn was breaking
The door slid back to show
A beauteous, brilliant, blinding light
A throbbing, pulsating glow.
Silent and stunned I watched amazed
But before I recovered my senses dazed
Somebody closed the door.

Mary Rosier

Snow

February is now here
I thought Spring was near
Then the winds did blow
And down came the snow
At first it looked a pretty sight
With the snow so white
A lorry came to grit the road
Then went back for another load
Cars go slow as they pass by
The elderly stay at home in the dry
Children happy to play with their sledge
And later gather snow from the hedge
To make snowballs for a fight
Whilst it is still light
The sky is now very grey
With more snow on the way.

Pamela Halligan

The Labour'd Of The Day

Though I see with dreaded calm,
the rising hackles,
and sweaty palm,
the moonlight shadows,
silent and bereft,
waiting to take my weary breath,
I struggle to waken my laboured limbs,
of weary oak and dainty trim,
but cannot resist the heavy ground,
as the ax-man's weapon brings me down.
Here I lie, alone in the dark,
the quiet mystic of the cricket's bark,
slowly dimming, running dry,
boughs all broken, no longer high,
as the night-time passes by.

Andy Ridge

"Hello Dad"

Hello dad, and how are you?
I thought I'd write a line or two.
We really miss your garden tasks.
It takes us ages to cut the grass.
The flowers now are really dead
So it must be nearly time for bed.
Mind you it's only half past eight.
Oh no, the clematis is banging at the gate.
The pansy's yelling, "Pack it in",
The fish is shouting, "The cat's coming",
The dog next door is barking mad
Because the cat's in our back yard.
The gnome is riding on the pig,
The cat is meowing, it's just been sick.
Fred the frog is hopping mad,
Because of the reactions in the back.
Cyril snail is full of joy as he made
Love to the tortoise.
I'm sure he's blind that he can't see
The tortoise has always been plastic.

Wenda Roberts

My First Pony

I always thought Rana was brill,
I think this very much still.
There comes a time in life when we have to part,
But I always know she will be in my heart.
Rana, Rana, pretty as ever,
I always thought we would stay together.
Never mind, I will see you soon,
If you want to remember me look at
the moon.
Remember your little stable room.
Remember I used to always wear Fruit-
of-the-Loom.
Rana, Rana, I will miss you always,
Remember all those brilliant days.
You always gave me a great big lick,
Oh why, oh why, did I have to grow out
of you so quick?

Rebecca Diane Topping

Picture, Picture On The Wall

As days go by
I think of you
As my dad, and best friend too
When I am low, I look at you
Your picture says it all for me
Your gentle eyes, and silver hair
The smile that says you really care
This poem I wrote is just for you
It's my way of saying, I love you too
I never said these words to you
So picture, picture on the wall
Keep me company, through Winter
Summer, Spring and Fall always.

M. D. Mello

If

If I could only see you as I know you really are,
If I could only shut love out with key or lock or bar,
If I could only tell myself the things I know are true,
If I could only make myself believe that I hate you.

And if I could do all these things
And let you go away,
Who'd welcome me when I come home
After each busy day,
Who'd look at me with pleading eyes
Sometimes wicked, sometimes wise,
Who'd bark and run and jump about
Asking to be taken out.
No, I couldn't part with you, my pup
So here's good health, bad dog, good luck.

Marjorie Sharpe

Shadows on the Grass

Between long shadows on the grass
I think I see the changing scenes long past
Your face appears before my eyes
your presence by my side I recognize
and all my sadness lifts awhile
thinking I see you, thinking I see you smile

You left without saying goodbye
and I have no more tears left to cry
I miss you all the whole day through
I try to find fresh things to do
I miss you when the morning breaks
but most of all, I miss you when day is done

Someday we'll meet again I know,
the very thought of this gives me a glow
So I will travel in your wake
until I see you through the break
and we will be together again
Oft times I wonder, oft times I wonder when?

Rita Atkinson

Our World Is God's World

As I look at this world from my window,
I think, and I wonder why
God gave us such a beautiful place,
He gave to you and I,
The song birds that sing,
The flowers in spring,
Enchantment of how it began,
Its magic, its splendour, unending adventure,
God gave to you and me.

Oh let it remain, this world of today,
Don't spoil it any more, or we may
Be sorry that all of those wonderful things
May fade as time passes away,
So let us wonder,
Slow down, while we may,
Stop, think, and then we will know
Why God gave us, such a beautiful place,
To live in peace, let us stay.

M. Bailey

After The War

While sitting here, I only can say thanks for being you,
I thank the Lord that in your life God's love shone through.
So though I'm going to miss your presence and your care,
I will remember, when I needed you, that you were there.

Put out your hand and in it take my own,
And with my inner eye I'll clasp it to my heart,
Rememb'ring all my past in which you were a precious part.

That day we said goodbye, we knew that distant bombs would fall.
Strong in your uniform, we heard your duty call,
Smiling at me with love, you spoke your parting prayer,
That while you were away, I should remain within God's care.

But as we said goodbye and kissed farewell,
I did not know that now and every future day,
My memories will be all I have of when you passed this way.

Sheila E. Harvey

The Sea

I am the Sea, the mighty one
I send my waves to thunder on
Beware ye mortals of the deep
For when sometimes I seem asleep
I can burst forth with mighty roar
Destroying all on ship or shore
I demand from all - respect
For failing that you shall be wrecked
No one to heed your piteous cry
As in my eerie dark you lie
I have no door, I have no knocker
But hold the key to Jones's locker.

J. J. S. Dixon

The Pain

The light seeps through a crack in the blind,
I stir from sleep with thoughts on my mind.
The pain is there, it's there every day,
I pray with time it will fade away.
The Lord watched over me throughout the night,
He knows I won't give in, not without a fight.
I put on my mask to help face the day,
Listening to the music I like to play.
The birds are singing — it looks cold outside.
The isolation and boredom I try to hide.
The days go on and the weeks fly by,
Being patient and strong, well — at least I try.
I am not very happy with my little lot,
I ask myself Why me? — Why not?

Valerie Clark

Lonely

Close to heaven, but not quite there,
I stand and face a village fair,
No one sees or hears me pass,
A distant figure with no second glance.
They're too busy parading around,
To notice me treading their ground.
Perhaps I'll stop just once more,
Better not I've a long way to go.
My feet so sore, bones so cold,
I've walked a long way to be this old.
Not much further my day will come,
I'll see the light then I'll be home.

Benjamin Richards

Malcolm

On this bleak November day
I sit here and dream away
Fond memories that time cannot fade
of a love that lasted over two decades

I remember you, young again
Jumping in puddles, laughing in the rain
My love for you I can never explain
For it caused others a lot of pain

My dark haired guy with the sparkling blue eyes
My life with you was one big surprise
I know we will never have those times again
but in my heart you will always remain

Sandra Lunnon

A Highland Picture

I will paint you a picture of Scotland my land
I will paint you a picture divine,
In this lovely picture the highlands you'll see
Dressed for each season, in gowns that are free.

In winter, the mountains are clad in snow white
The rivers rush madly and dance with delight
Come spring time, a gay time, a quick change of scene,
The rivers are sparkling, the valleys so green.

Drift into summer, so quiet and still,
The hills with heather aglow,
Reflecting this beauty in mirrors so clear,
Are the 'Lochs' sleeping soundly below.

Autumn appears with a sad little sigh,
The spring and the summer have gone,
But, as leaves start to fall, and the green turns to gold,
Her gown is the richest of all.

White, green and purple, and gold you have seen,
My painting is now complete,
Please take it, and frame it, in your memory
This picture of Scotland, so sweet

Violet M. Webb

The Gift Of Sight

Another dreary Sunday dawns, I stretch and waken with a yawn
I sit down in my dressing gown and through the window view
  the town.

Mid grey walls and dark grey slates, the smoke above the
  chimney waits
The lazy wind has overslept as daylight out of dark has crept.

My nose pressed to the window pane, I look but all I see is rain
A droplet stops and starts at will, another sledges to the sill.

The puddles merge into a pool, the children from the Sunday School
Splashing, laughing, all but one left standing hand in hand with mum.

With eyelids closed — but hearing bright, she never had the
  gift of sight
She smiles and nods as others play, she's never seen the light
  of day.

I watch that child, her happy face, her charm, her beauty and
  her grace,
And dismal though the day may be I thank the Lord that I can see.
  Myra Allan

Reflections

As the clock ticks slowly by
I sit alone and wonder why
In the past the office was the core
Alas, these days are no more
I reminisce and think of the work companions I now miss
Gone is the old life spiral
Replaced with the all too familiar retiral.
  A. C. M. Scott

Untitled

Saint Patrick, Sir; I see your isle,
I see your land so green.
Your island, where, since your time,
there no snakes have been.

Your fair land, though full of strife,
remains the emerald Isle.

Now revéred Saint; I wish that I
were you; and if I were I'd bow
my head and pray your land at peace.

Your beautiful but troubled land
is there for all to see, a heritage
for many folk, especially the wee.

The leprechaun, the little folk,
their lives so full of lore, whom,
when you catch one, grant those
wishes three.
And of those, please let this be
the fore:

The settled land!
  Philip Trevor Williams

My Love My Life

As I look around the world,
I see wars and hunger all around.
I thank the Lord that I can find tranquillity,
contentment and peace of mind.
Just to know that you are near,
helps me forget the things I fear.
Your love I need forever more.

To me it is the air I breath,
and as I look into your eyes,
I see ten million twinkling stars
in a midnight sky.
You see my love, to me you are the earth,
the moon and all I can ever desire.
You are my life my love forever more.
  P. W. Nelson

The Light In Me

Tumbling to my knees,
I saw a light shine down,
I felt my body rise,
As the brightness tugged and called.
In the dark I heard tears, with
The memory of all my fears crying and pulling,
Knowing that life was dark — and death was light,
I favoured the dark,
But the tug was more than the pull, and the
Light charmed and warmed my heart,
Hearing the cries of the living —
And feeling the warmth of the dead,
Slowly I turned my head,
Closer and closer I conveyed to the light,
No tear — no scream could stop me,
I found myself waving to my body and welcoming my soul,
And now forever in the light I'll be,
And you too someday,
Will see the light in me.
  Michael Gerald Christy

Flowers Know

Wide-Eyed Narcissi
I saw a crowd together.
All on a sunny slope
In the sunny weather.

Bland were their faces
Yellow ones and white
Their eyes turned sunwards
Smiling with delight

I saw the same narcissi
Beneath a sunless sky
Hope still brightened, each eager little eye,

Calm were their faces no vestige of despair,
Their eyes turned sunwards
Knowing he was there

Thank you narcissi for silent sermon given,
When dark clouds curtain the sun in his heaven,
Still look we sunwards
Through sorrow and through pain.
Knowing as you do he'll soon shine again.
  Marjorie Taylor

Life's Mysteries

If I had my life to live over
I wouldn't change a thing
I'd still wonder at the clear blue sky
And at the birds that sing

I'd still wonder why the grass is green
Why it shoots up from the ground
And why some animals live on top
Why some live underground

Why rivers flow into the sea
And day turns into night
Why the sun shines when it's light
And at night the stars are bright

I'd still wonder how flowers know
When it is time to bloom
Why winter comes at year's end
And it's summer time in June

I'd still wonder why trees grow tall
And mountains reach the sky
I'd still wonder at all these things
And still be asking why.
  Sheila Graham

Tribute To 'Eagle'

Oh little feathered friend of mine, I miss you so!
I remember when I brought you home many years ago,
You were beautiful and so small, feathers of lovely hue,
You brightened many a day for me, when I was feeling blue,
You were my companion and friend in good times and in bad
Though sometimes your screaming whistles near drove me mad!
You liked to be free and flew about all around the flat,
And I kept a lookout for our neighbour's stalking cat.
Your favourite perch was my shoulder, so you could nip my ear
So many memories of you I have, I cannot help but shed a tear,
You were so determined, and had the heart of an 'eagle' your name
In later years, still you flew, though now you were lame,
If as the good Lord said, many mansions there are above
And perhaps the good Lord knows of my great love.
Then, in a quiet corner, with the sun shining through,
There, to greet me, in a cage of God, will be you!

Maurice Chesterman

FREEDOM

As I sit at my desk waiting for the phone to ring,
I read, I doodle, sometimes I even sing.
I love my work, I love speaking on the phone.
I'm not despondent, I never feel alone.
I am grateful in this day and age, that I am still employed,
My work comes first, I do not shirk, whatever's put before me,
I like to feel I'm useful, and people don't ignore me
I've worked for someone all my life, but soon it's going to end,
I will retire gracefully and then I'll have to spend my time
at home doing things for me, making little cakes, helping family.
Will I be bored, oh no, not I, for then I'll have time to reach for
the sky.

V. Walker

The Dreams

I slipped the outstretched hand of time,
I raced back down the years,
To days when you and I were young
The days that held no fears, and
As time reached to grasp me,
With a laugh I swiftly flew and
The past reached out to clasp me,
To lead me back to you.
There for awhile, once more we roamed
The lanes of yesterday.
All the world our stage and
We the stars throughout the play,
Until the final curtain,
It was then the nightmare came
I awoke and knew our halcyon days
Could never come again.

Pauline Butler

Spiritual Journey

In quiet corners of the day, where time will linger as her ease,
I pause and find my thought's will stray, and wonder in which
   path they please,
So to relieve an aching mind where doubts and hopes will
   swell and fall
Like waves that in a restless wind pound against the harbour wall.
Once released, these faded shreds of fallen dreams and earth-
   born care,
Rush off, now unrestrained it seems, to feast on fruits of
   minds elsewhere
And so it is to you they fly on shimmering wings, sun-hugged
   with gold
Love plucks them colours from the sky and warm desire paints
   them bold.
There in a sphere of spinning senses, in deep communion
   shared by all,
Our thoughts combine and so condenses the sacred message
   of each soul
But now they come to kiss my head, while whispering through
   the mask of fear -
So at last is madness fled and peace of mind is drawing near.

Rosemary Capon

"Time Runs Out"

The concrete highways ever more encouraging speed
I pass by your crumpled, twisted body, never more to feed
Poor fox — no more to roam — your freedom cut short
At least you will not suffer the hunt and the sport.
Your hunting days were over when you searched for a meal
One hopes you've no young awaiting your kill.
As you lay at the curbside, glazed eyes to the sky
Still endless traffic goes thundering by
You join rabbits, birds and hedgehogs and other breeds
And man is the enemy, his "greed for speed."

Marion Withrington

Could That Be Me

I wander down the country lane, just my old dog and me
I often stop to gaze at the beauty of a tree
And then my thoughts start wandering and climbing up that tree
I see a laughing little girl
Could that be me

I see her running down that lane in gay abandon in the breeze
Carefree as the birds that sing, no one but herself to please
Could that be me

Happy as the day was long, no tears to dim her eyes
The great big world was made for her, hers not to reason why
Could that be me

I turn back in that country lane, just my old dog and me
I see a different picture now as I gaze up at that tree
Birds sing among its leaves that have turned from green to gold
Here and there a broken bough, she could not climb it now
No longer does she run along, her steps are slower now
Clouds have passed across her sky, it shows upon her brow
And so I pass along that lane, just my old dog and me
And wonder what it was all about, in my memory

Yes that was me

B. J. Neale

Through A Child's Eyes

I'm a little girl on a swing,
I never knew then what tomorrow would bring.

Ignorance is bliss, black and white is no issue,
those words are not used like a dirty tissue.

My elders I look up to and value what they teach,
I have the respect for them in what they preach.

Each person is an equal different in each way,
they still have thoughts and feelings which change each
   and every day.

To me we all have a beauty whether it's noticeably big or small,
you may have big blue eyes or be slender and tall.

I am innocent with no sense of spite,
I'm a little bird taking those steps towards my very first flight.

Now I have stepped out of that picture that I drew a long time ago
   and I'm no longer that little girl.
We are all guilty of abusing our freedom of speech,
after all, aren't we all as precious as an oyster that's captivated
   a pearl?

Sarah Holland

Awakenings

As the cool breeze washed over me on that hot summer's day,
I lay in silence and listened.

I heard the cool gurgle of the ocean
As its waves broke upon the rocky shore,
And I realized how small we are.

I heard the beautiful voice of the nightingale
As it sang its melody in the treetops,
And I realized how ugly we are.

As I lay there with that cool breeze washing over me,
I realized how enchanting the world is.

Richard Craig

My Dog Pepe

Why did you have to go away,
I miss seeing you everyday,
You were there for me when times were bad,
And now I am very sad.

You grew up to be part of the family,
I love you so much, oh can't you see,
But sadly you were twelve years old,
But you were very brave and bold.

Sadly you died at the vets,
Oh, you was a lovely pet,
I wish you was here with me,
But sadly it was not to be.

Nicola Walker

It's Just Not Fair

"It's mine" "No it's mine".
"I lost it" "And I found it".
"But you know that it's mine, and it's just not fair".
Sarah's mummy's always telling us that we've got to share.
"Mummy, it's Sarah, she's not playing nice".
"Paul I've already told you twice
To play together nicely, and share your toys.
Without all this fighting and constant noise".

"But it's not fair, you're always picking on me".
Just because I'm six and she's only three.
She says it's hers, but she's telling a lie,
So to get her own way, she just starts to cry.

It always works, it's always the same.
Anyway it's not fair, I'm not playing this game.
"Daddy's home, Paul, it's time for tea".
Oh it's not fair, I'll miss children's T.V.!

Susan Lesley Jacques

Remember

The gentle breeze soft upon my cheek,
I look out at the sea but cannot speak,
The clouds swirling in a violet haze
And thinking of some happier days.

The foaming sea travels in and out
I try to whisper — I try to shout,
I know what to say, but the words won't come,
It makes me unhappy and it makes me glum.

The rippling water flowing through the sand,
I try to reach out and hold your hand,
The sound of your voice and warmth of your smile,
I remember those times for a short while.

Like waves in and out of distant coves,
Your memory lingers and yet I suppose,
The past has gone as I heave a sigh,
I'll say God bless and our last
goodbye.

Ruth Bray

A Thought For Today

If I should die before I wake, will my problems still be with me?
If I should close my eyes, shut out the light, will I still be
    able to see?
If life goes on and time stands still, can we see the past?
If I can smile, doubt the pain, can my happiness last?

If clouds roll on and lightning strikes, will the sun still
    shed its beams?
If fear sets in, if insecurities bring doubt, can life really be
    what it seems?
If I can cry, if I really weep, yet dance on stage and smile.
Am I a book? revealed if read, with its own oblivious style.

If I should die before I wake, will the sun still warm my world?
If I could travel in my dreams, at the sky I shall be hurled.
If I could run and never wear and reach my wanted place.
Where would I be? and could I then, my problems really face?

Tracy Gilhooly

Childhood Memories

As I wearily walk down this long lonely road
I look back one last time at my humble abode.

All the memories come rushing back
Was I really born in that tumbling old shack?

Though musty and old it might have been
The warmth and love still comforts me.
Never quite enough food or coal for the fire,
But all the loving care you could ever desire.

All heavens riches or all the world's gold
Could never replace this rag doll that I hold.

Made from grandpa's best suit, full of
holes from the moths, a piece of fine lace
and some faded old socks.

The reason for this is easy to understand
It was made by my mother's warm loving hands.

Samantha Korczynski

Nature

Sitting in a tree looking around
I look at all that can be found
A cat comes stalking, I wonder why
I soon learn and off I fly
A dog comes barking, the cat starts to run
Off they go having all their fun
I fly and search for food to be found
There I spy it, bread on the ground
This luscious feast is nice to find
Placed there by mankind
These tit bits are scarce and rare
But when man comes, I fly off with a scare
Soon spring will be here, and summer too
But when winter comes, that's when we need you.

Sylvia Cann

Never On Your Own

A part of me feels caged upon this lonesome road,
I know it is my mind that never keeps control.
My feelings, deep down inside are bursting to be let outside.
I say my prayers intently and cry "I hope they are not unheard"
And then I do disturb my inner-self,
For I know my prayers are heard.

This is a Time for unfoldment to the outside world,
To awaken and let loose the spirit in us all.
Our soul and our guide shout out in loving glee,
At last, good child, you set us free.

From this time on along this long and winding road,
Remember, my child, you are no longer alone.
For your heart cried out and you can be assured
That you are always heard.
So you have nothing to fear as we are always near.

Michael J. Taylor

Children

The children they are growing fast
The peace of mind, it does not last
Away they go there breaking free
To the streets they take, corruption they see
You try your best to keep them in
But you know in your heart, that time has come
Here starts the worry, what are they doing now?
You can't keep asking questions, it ends up in a row
You try your best to trust them, you taught them right "you hope"
Then you suddenly realize, your daughter's started to smoke
You keep her in on punishment, your mind's at rest once more
But you can't keep her in forever, she's going through that door
You sit and try to tell, it's all for your own good
But you might as well be knocking on a piece of wood
No matter what we do or say,
So all we can do is sit and pray.
Pray they take the right road, the one we tried to teach
And not the road that leads to that lost pebble on the beach

Beverley Salt

The Office

There's a dinosaur at the bottom of my in-tray —
I just saw his tail disappear!
It's surprising he could find his way out —
There's an Amazon rain-forest around here.

There's a dinosaur at the bottom of my in-tray,
I think I glimpsed a mammoth as well.
They haven't seen daylight for many a year —
The in-tray's a bottomless well!

There's a dinosaur at the bottom of my in-tray.
Could he be the only one left?
It would be a great shame to take his home away,
And to leave him feeling bereft.

There's a dinosaur at the bottom of my in-tray.
He's probably quite safe for a while
For, try as I might, I can't see the day
When all the papers are put in a file.

There's a dinosaur at the bottom of my in-tray.
I wonder if he'd like to be set free?
What worries me most, thought I don't like to say —
He may think that his Mummy is me!!

Toni Romero

Our Little Amy

When she was born, she looked just like her sister
I held her so gently, and tenderly kissed her
A little bit bigger, but 1/2 an inch shorter
A real little gem was our precious daughter
On the day of her birth, a day of great gladness
But also for us, a day tinged with sadness
She should have been there to share our elation
To marvel and coo at our special creation
Now Grandma has gone but her memory lives on
And with it her name for our little one
Amy Patricia's a bundle of joy
A real little rascal, a proper tomboy
What she really enjoys is having a bath
Especially with Catherine who makes her laugh
What her sister likes best is watching her dance
The look of sheer pride you can see at a glance
For Mummy and Daddy, our joy is complete
Catherine and Amy are both loving and sweet
We are now the proud parents of two little girls
A gift far more precious than diamonds and pearls.

Janet Carter

Train Spotting

It's half past five, I've got five minutes
I haven't bought a ticket
Peak time, there's queues, only two serving
It's just not bloody cricket

Never mind, head down, run fast the guard
Straight on to platform two
If I'd have queued I'd miss the train
What else was I to do

Twenty minutes I've been stood here now
Collar of against the cold
A delayed incoming service
Means my train's been put on hold

Hang on, here's one coming now,
It must be mine, for sure
Oh bloody hell, the points have changed
It's gone to platform four

Thank God I haven't bloody paid
I'm fed up with all this fuss
Its late, I'm cold the trains are crap
I'm going for the bus.

Mark Birchall

'Memories'

So still. So still the night. But yet,
I hear the whispering of someone dear.
I hear the whispering, or do I hear?
I listen hard, but it's not so.

My heavy eyes do close their lids,
and whispers are no more. For clear
voices I do hear, and love ones dear
do greet me so. Together for a while,
deep in love and memories that we have shared.
How swiftly times goes by, and
morning light does shine upon my eyes.
And from that tranquil sleep I rise,
to start a fresh the day that comes.

Sonia Redfern

Sonnet

Blue days of loneliness are nothing new,
I have shared my soul with the sky before —
And spent many long hours thinking of you,
Wasting time, because I did not need it.
Poetry has flowed from my pen like wine,
To try to unravel all this madness —
To tell myself that you'll never be mine,
Smiling to know that in one way you are.
Secrets that we share can never be known,
To us alone they are whispered shadows,
And I have chosen, no, fate has shown
That I should number among those lone few
Who talk only to the dark, and believe
That they only have themselves to deceive.

Sue Berry

My School

My name is Tracey,
I go to Churchdown school,
We are supposed to do everything by the rule.
The teachers there are very nice,
Always there to give me advice.
Mr. Griffin makes me laugh,
I wonder if he does the same to the staff.
Why not look around
Listen to the sound
Of pupils rushing up and down.
Footsteps stomping all around,
Sometimes I wish there wasn't a crowd.
The bell has gone, it's time to move on, next
  lesson in here again.
I wonder what we've got to gain,
Never mind it will soon be tomorrow
  more of the same.
Churchdown school I find the best
Come and join all the rest......

Tracey Freeman

Forever In A Smile

As I walk through the path of life's tomorrows
I dream of yesterday
My heart is still racked by the pain and the sorrow
And disbelief that you've gone away.

Our love, it was mingled with laughter and love
Of pleasure united with pain
I sigh in my heart to the Lord up above
To give me the strength to remain.

Our future, a diamond that sparkled with light
A treasure so priceless and rare
Was taken away when you lost your great fight
Now for me only tears and despair.

Although you are gone and I can't see you there
As I trek through life's lonely miles
I know I can feel you and so I can bear
For Forever was one of your smiles.

Susan Calvert

The Windows Of My Mind

I gaze through the window of life, how do I feel and what do I see
I feel a great love for my creator, and a soul that yearns to be free,
By seeing the vision within me, and looking through physical eye,
There are family and friends around me, with a love that cannot die,
God has spoken to me so gently, in a way that is special to me,
The question I ask myself is this were I want to be,
The view from my window keeps changing as the years go racing past,
Is this a true reflection, have I discovered myself at last,
The level of wisdom and understanding, is worth its weight in gold,
Feeling God within us, we can be very bold,
We all face the joys and the tremors it makes us who and what we are,
For we are part of each other, and must live and love without any bars,
Always look to see the vision, and recognize your worth,
You are a special person, since you chose to come on earth....
Patricia Bray

Four Seasons

Partridge, pheasant, rabbits galore
I expect now it is spring, there will be a lot more
Cabbage are over, purple sprouting not ready
It needs warm rain, so we have to go steady

Summer will soon be here with plenty to do
Crops to be gathered and planting too
Working on the land is a wonderful life
Away from all the troubles and strife

We have what we earn with no fixed time
And enjoy the warmth of the summer sunshine
When winter arrives it's a different matter
Your feet get real cold and your teeth start to chatter

But we enjoy our work and are pleased to say
Fresh produce to sell at the end of the day
Vegetables packed and well displayed
Will be around to the end of the decade.
B. H. New

A Waterfall

I have heard you love another,
I dreamed of you both together
Then my tears eternal fall, by a waterfall.

To remember, beyond this life, your kind smile.
Forever love keeps burning in my heart.
More and more, true love grows
Shining on as the brightest star glows.
Oh! So lonely spirit of the waterfall.

As night follows day
So my love for you, has come to stay
The sun, the moon, shines as love
Always light, always love.

So tears continue to fall
There to mingle with the flowing water
Always leading back to... the waterfall.
Sandra Diana Rose

Mother-In-Law

She says she will give me anything,
I don't want things from her,
All I want is to spend some time with her,
She has spent time with the other girls,
I'd like to get to know her better,
It seems like she doesn't really care,
Sometimes I feel so hurt inside knowing that she doesn't care,
Deep in my heart I love her very much,
She will never know I feel this way,
Why does she make me feel like this,
I don't know which way to turn,
do I tell her how I feel or do I keep it inside,
I don't know a thing about her in all this time that's gone by,
I really want to get to know her,
I wish in time she will try to see how I feel.
M. J. Baxter

Goodbye

I've closed my eyes to you, covered my ears to you.
I don't want to hear from you, I no longer feel for you.
I gave you all my love, all you gave me was pain.
You broke my heart and drove me insane.

I bared you my soul and you tore it in half.
I gave you my tears and all you did was laugh.
You gave me false promise to get your own way.
I gave you my trust and you threw it away.

You played with my feelings and messed me about.
Toyed with my emotions and now I want to get out.
You say that you need me, but I don't need you.
You say you won't leave me but I'm leaving you.

I'm leaving your hurt and I'm leaving your pain.
I'm taking my life and I'm taking the reins.
From a girl that I thought was my best friend.
But she's not anymore, that's why this is the end.
Michael Stirton

A Promise

When I depart and travel on, it's only a transition
I don't get off the wheel of life, I merely change position
Whilst on this earth I need my hands, to touch and feel the way
My legs to travel to and fro, to run from day to day
My face it shows expression and helps me recognise
My smile can say "I love you" and tears can fill my eyes
My ears can help to keep me safe, from dangers that lurk near
They also listen to the birds, a sound I love to hear
These are but tools to do the job, there's also soul in me
I leave them here when I depart, no need for them you see
I leave my loved ones full of grief, but really don't despair
I am only just a step away, look round and I'll be there
Look hard enough and me you'll see, reach out and touch my hand
Just talk and I will answer you and you will understand
I'm trying to say I haven't gone and never will I go
There is no place that's up above and none that's down below
There's only here and only now, there's nowhere else you see
For we will always be as one — together you and me.
Michael Thomas Cheeseman

My First Poem

When I first put pen to paper, it was the strangest thing,
I did not know the words were there, they came from deep within
The words they could have jumbled, but instead they rhymed.
Can I put pen to paper? It seems the hardest thing,
Can I do this writing, I wonder if I dare
I close my eye's and before me see the words are waiting there.

When I put pen to paper, the words flowed sweet and light,
Like a prayer said at bedtime to see us through the night
The words they could have jumbled, but instead they rhymed.
When I put pen to paper the words were in my mind.
Marion Hatton

The Path Of Life

One day as I was walking,
I felt a presence near
It filled me with the greatest joy,
And banished all my fear.

The path that lay before me
Was narrow all the way,
With signs along the roadside
Warning not to stray.

I knew it would never be easy,
More often it would be tough
For the path of life is seldom smooth,
Like an ocean, the seas can be rough.

But let the rains fall on my features,
Let the storms lash on my brow
I will tread onwards unafraid,
For the Lord is with me now.
Mary C. Ritchie

Forgotten Dreams

As I look to my lost childhood
I cry to the wind.
My tears carried like raindrops,
Across the sky and back to a time
— Long forgotten

A laughter once echoed there.
Across Autumn breezes,
In the shadows of my mind, I
Hear that laughter still. I thought it
— Long forgotten.

Images of joy and wonder dance
Through April showers.
No complications I knew back then;
Only now. The true essence of life is
— Long forgotten.

The eyes clouded, the heart like stone.
The reason for it all? Now unknown,
— Long forgotten.
Peter Godden

" The Boss Is Watching "

I wouldn't swap jobs with God, not even for a day.
I couldn't cope with his workload, not even for more pay.
Well, would you know where to start to sort the business out?
I think that I would scrap the lot and leave the world with nowt.
It's being ruined anyway, counterproductive the Boss would say.
There's cheating, lying, lust and greed, grabbing things that
   we don't need.
"Give us more and more and more, helping others? That's a bore.
Things have gone from bad to worse, this world we work in,
   it's a curse.
"Whose fault is that?" The people cry, "Not mine, nor mine,
   I really try."
Well, anyway the Boss can see, He's busy watching you and me,
And when we line up for our pay, you know the thing called
   Judgement Day,
"There'll be no bonus." He will yell, "You've turned my world
   to living hell."
"I'll start again with just a few, those who are loyal and good
   and true."
"The rest of all mankind," says God, "Will die and rot beneath
   the sod."
Marilyn Faith Gunther

The Epitaph Of A Working Man

I did no wrong, I was born poor,
I committed no crime, yet I was sentenced
To a life of imprisonment
In a scheme where life goes on
without meaning.

I live from day to day, Hungry;
Not in body but in mind
I search for peace in vain
Is it only in death
That I will find rest.
I think my thoughts alone
they belong to me.

Although my mind is free
I cannot break the chain of circumstance
If only they could understand
It's not for riches that I strive.
My Son, give him a better chance than I.

I was born, I worked, I died
The epitaph of a working man.
Robert Pitt-Kelly

The Pigeon

Her wings beat on the window glass,
I clutched at her with friendly glance,
She looked at me and I at her,
We knew this meeting was not chance.

I carried her to open air,
She winged her way but not that far,
I realized that she lived quite near,
Just above my office door.

I've watched her now for two full years,
Her nest is an untidy heap,
The eggs fall down but tears are mine,
Yet still she struggles to survive.

This year she hatched a little chick,
A kestrel swirled and she took flight,
Amongst the other pigeon group,
She protected until nearly night.

I like her grace and simple mind,
I wish that mine was of that kind,
However, as we strive for nought,
The purest mind is often sought.
Rosanne Orr

Trapped

I can't speak ... yet I am not dumb.
I can't see ... yet I am not blind.
I can't hear ... yet I am not deaf.
For I am trapped in my own little world.

I'm locked away, deep down this fifty
foot well.
It's dark, it's cold, I'm all alone.
I want to cry! I want to shout!
I want to let all this anger out!
For I am trapped in my own little world.

I hide away like a disoriented cat.
Running away from this and that.
Not being able to express myself makes
me feel even less of myself.
For I am trapped in my own little world.

Yet in reality people think I'm fine.
As I smile and wish them goodbye.
But I am not for my whole life is tied
in a knot, I go on being trapped in my
own little world.
Mark Hammond

The Terrorist

Don't ask for mercy from such as me,
I cannot hear, I cannot see;
The birds, the trees mean naught,
For all my life's a battle fought.

I've killed, I've maimed; to terrorise.
To gain my ends, I've closed my eyes —
To the hell I've wrought on fellow man,
It could never end, what I began.

To leave a child without a dad —
I do not think that it is bad —
To make young innocence suffer so!
More death to others I will sow.

For what I want is my own way,
Don't let majorities have their sway,
They want to talk and bring back peace,
But I crave violence will not cease.

Born with hate within my soul,
Fuelled with ignorance from the call.
Futile kindness makes me sneer,
The only power I have is fear.
Philip Gillard

Mum

The time has come for me to write and let my feelings known
I cannot find the words to say how much my love has grown
When I was young, you were there, whatever I had done
But never did I stop and say 'Hey, she's great my Mum'.
Now with age I have learnt how valuable you are
How difficult it must have been to view me from afar
But never did you interfere or tell me what to do
Just gave advice and full support to start my life anew
You gave the best gift possible and are still giving now
For all those years I took for granted and never asked you how
You find the time to still be there and understand my strife
You'll always be a person who is a big part of my life
So finally I say to you in words that seem so small
Thank you Mum, you are the best, I love and owe you all.

D. Aitchison

Love

I am the purest and dearest gift that can be given.
I cannot be bought.   I cannot be changed.
Once I arrive I am here to stay.
I am cherished by young and old alike.
I am given at birth and taken to the grave.

I am exchanged between man and woman.
Lavished from Mother to Son.
Poured out to a daughter, for her to pass on.
I am a treasure passed on from the good Lord himself.
I have no sense of time.

They say there will come a time,
When all love will be spent.
But give me a chance to go roaming among mankind.
That is when peace will rule the land.
For I am Love

Margaret Coon

Growing Old

I sit there in the café, having a quiet cup of tea
I can feel their stares, as if stabbing right through me
Drinking my tea, I see what they can see
A frail little old woman, looking very weary
I see them laughing, thinking it's a game
But growing old is not a game
It's a shame
A shame how these young people nowadays,
just sit there and laugh

But if they only knew the truth
The truth of the thoughts which were hidden deep inside me
Their smirks would then fade away
and they would soon come to realize
That they'd be here one day
one day in my place
with nowhere to go, no one to talk to
with all their closest friends and family dead
sitting there with all these thoughts rushing through their head.
Wishing now, that they too were dead!!!

Michelle Meaden

Friends

Moving to a new estate
I came upon a garden gate
A little girl was swinging there
she had such lovely golden hair.

She asked if I would be her friend
to this I said — until the end.
We had a lot of fun together
using up our shoes of leather.

Playing — running — dancing — singing
all our thoughts of pleasure — bringing
happiness to both of us
Friendship — without too much fuss.

Peggy F. Steele

The Rose

This morning I went outside and plucked a rose.
I brought it in and placed it in a vase,
And remembered you.

This afternoon the scent of my rose filled the room.
The petals opened wide to show its heart,
And I remembered you.

Now my rose has withered quietly away.
I gather the petals and cup them in my hands,
And remember you.

Patricia Davies

A World Dream

To a world filled with fighting and sex and crime and hate,
I bring a whole world's wisdom and pray — can it really be too late?
To feed the starving millions and heal those wounded hearts,
To kneel in prayer to mother nature — to give us one last chance;

If we remove our language and colour — aren't we all the
    same inside?
So come and join hands together and put your principles aside,
Help to stop pollution — and the warming of the earth,
Open your eyes and listen, to that miracle called birth;

Picture a world with no more fighting or poverty or crime,
Hear your children's laughter and feel the sun begin to shine,
Dream of bright stars above a clean and powerful sea,
A world of love is where I'd like to live;
But the dream is up to us — that's right — you and me!!

Tammy L. Finch

Mother Earth

I am what you breathe, so! feel me,
I am what you eat, so! nourish me,
I am what you sleep, so! nurse me
I am your mother, with open arms I fill your life
with love and charms.
I give you nature, in an ultimate way, yet, you
crucify me.
You spill my dreams, then turn away.
I give you everything, so don't hurt me
in this way,
Turn off your ignitions and step outside.
I am a glorified ball of love and trust, stop!
Burning my crust, I beg of you — everyday, I
cry for my life.
I am fading away, so help me, my children
keep me safe — for I am your mother earth

Samantha Phillips

Animal Jail

I went to the zoo today
I felt sick and looked pale
I wanted to see beauty
All I saw was a jail

God created a jungle
Where the cheater could play and run
Man invented a net and tranquillizing gun

So across the ocean he fetches
For city folk to see
A wild cat of beauty
But now no longer free

His eyes now show sorrow
His heart heavy with pain
Walking around in circles
Slowly going insane

Tear down the blocks of concrete
The bars made of steel
Give back a little dignity
After all how would you feel.

J. J. Foster

What Is My Name

I am the breeze that gently kisses you at night
I am the summer daylight that fills the world with light
It's me that makes the sunshine refresh the tired soil
And give the human heart strength, from danger to recoil
You may find me in laughter, or see me in your dreams
Where everything your eyes see is not really as it seems
In many quiet moments or when man must go to war
I am the new tomorrows that knock upon your door
If you wonder what my name is, search within your mind
For I am there inside you, the creator of mankind

Maureen Turner

Myself As Something Else

I am a daisy all yellow and white.
I am sitting in the garden and sleeping at night.
Here I am a fluffy cream cat,
Singing to myself and purring like that.
Here I am a new bouncy chair,
Through the windows I do stare.
I am a salad. In salads you get different things.
Sometimes I am different, some days I am happy,
Some days I get mood swings.
Here I am a circle all shy and round,
Rolling round and round on the ground.
I am a pretty, light green room,
By my bed I have a brown broom.

Serena K. Thomson

My Own Poem

I may not be rich, but then again,
I am not poor, at times, I could do
with that little more.
What I have, I'll share with you,
so take it my friend, and be satisfied,
Because the Lord has been good to me
this Christmas tide.

W. M. P. Sweeney

Self-Inflicted Weapon

I will kill any being faster than anything on this earth.
I am a self-inflicted weapon,
I will hunt you down
and like a lamb to the slaughter
you will obey my every command,
as I take over your limp body
and add power.
Without even knowing it, your
body, mind and soul
will be mine.
And suddenly you're out of control.
And suddenly you're lonely.
And suddenly you're lying in a wooden box
awaiting the return of the bright light
when you think
what a waste
but it's too late.

Thomas Stuart

My Dog

My Lassie she is getting old,
I hold her paw she feels quite cold
she whimpers quite a lot these days
other times she happily plays
she sleeps and sleeps in her arm chair,
she misses me when I'm not there,
I call her but she does not hear,
I've had her since eight month's old,
She's been so good, done as she was told,
Suppose she'll stay asleep one day,
Let's hope she dreams
She's still at play.

Violet Smith

Dead Petals

Till the dead petals fall
I abide by your law
And wrap myself inside the cruel flower
Waiting for the pain of freedom
Reveal now your secrets unto me
Till we have secrets no more

And when the fire of life has turned to ash
I stand in the midst of time
And cup my hands against my face
Holding my breath attempting to fly
From this cold, immortal place

Sitting now quiet and still
Beckoning memories of your sallow skin
The warmth spent in ethereal passion
I weep now for one last embrace
Then close my eyes and hold the thought
Till the dead petals fall no more

Michael Jones

Monuments

Tall dark stacks against an empty sky,
Huge stones of granite now lie
Where beneath the ground, once sounds were heard
Now all that's left is the cry of a bird.

Once through the adits lamps did creep
Strong men died leaving women to weep.
All for the sake of the shining ore
Tin for the rich, death for the poor.

All covered now by furze and heather
Stone worn smooth by wind and weather.
Silent monuments reach to the sun
Each one a miner his life's work done.

Tony Webster

Life's Surplus

Everywhere the girls in desperation
huddle; unwanted. Not for them the joy
of life's air, to fill their lungs with giving gulps
of breath, clean and bright. Only numbers

Above the bare shared beds give identity
four two seven, four two eight; birth date unknown.
Discovered - Wuhan. Thrown away - Xian.
Refuse disposal, they cling to life.

Refuse to die. A faint cry goes unheard
and no one comes. Tiny bound feet echo
in sympathy along the corridors of
forgotten decades. No hope at all

For these market economy rejects.
A little one shudders and life slips away.
No torment, ill treatment; just no loving care
and quiet neglect is all that's required.

Wilhelmina Stratton-Dresser

Why Reality?

While escaping reality,
I climbed into insanity.
Feeling the need to be freed;
Wanting to be hurled off the earth.

Craving to fall, and fly high
but always a wall blocking the light.
Now, soaring through the sky needing it to be night,
so no one can see the real me.
Then, stopping deadly still and slowly
thoughts seep into the dark.

Wishing for a light to glow,
to guide the soul onto the path
to escape the insanity
while climbing back into reality.

Nicola George

Redundancy

I wake up lonely and full of fear.
How will I manage again next year.
Prices are rising faster and faster
All I see is I'm heading for disaster,
The bills keep coming, more and more
Now I dread the knock at the door.
The clock is chiming it's only three,
Not yet time to make the tea.
I wake up lonely, and full of fear,
How will I manage again next year.
The money gets less and the jobs get fewer,
I am feeling lower and lower.
The Government and the Bosses
Have no idea of the people losses
They just smile and say it's the economy thing.
It is world wide you know,
But, I can't laugh and I can't sing.
They are not the ones who wake up each night
So full of fear, so full of fright.
Shelagh R. Pile

Samson And Delilah

Judges tells of the strength of Samson,
  How the strength came from his hair,
  But others were curious as to where it came from,
    And encouraged Delilah to find out where!
  After question by question, he finally gave in,
    She caused him to sleep on her knees,
  So that others could come, and have his hair shorn,
    They then came and took out his eyes.
  But as time went on, Samson's hair grew,
    He was determined to avenge for his eyes,
  But to do this he knew, for to see it right through,
    He must wait for the occasion to arise.
  The opportunity came, when he was led out,
    To the Arena, to be made sport of,
  He requested to be, between pillars right by,
    called to God, give me strength, with them let me die,
  He bent down heavily — and with last breath,
    Heaved, and the people fell down, and with him met their death
  He brought buildings and all down, as he'd set out to do,
    And God was with him, all the way through.
D. Martin

The Hands Of A Priest

How precious are the hands of a priest!
how precious is the man!
heaven sent, heaven lent,
to be used in God's glorious plan.

Every time you see the priest on the altar
offer a silent prayer
for those hands that are blessed and anointed
have the power to bring Jesus there.

So rejoice, be glad, be happy for the sacrifice
of the Mass every day,
Jesus is truly present,
the priesthood has opened the way.
M. M. Forrest

Too Late To Say

When you were alive I could never say.
How much you meant in every way,
You shaped my life for future years
And many times you dried my tears,
When I needed you, you were always there,
No problem to small for you to share,
My haunted teens you guided me through,
I loved you so much and you never knew,
Now time has passed, and I've grown older,
You'll never know how I've missed your shoulder,
So kind and gentle and full of grace,
You loving arms, and laughing face,
How much I wished I'd told you Nan,
You made me who and what I am.
Sandra Roberts

Autumn

Autumn season lush and mellow
How I love the dress you wear
Rustling skirts of brown and yellow
Golden sunlight in your hair.

Lead me on and I will follow
To the forest secret place
Over hills and into hollow
Where the spider spins your lace.

Woodland folk their coats are growing
Comfort for the winter chill
Weary farmer stops his mowing
Trudges home his barn to fill.

Autumn season, won't you linger
Let me drink in your delight
Safe from winter's icy fingers
Colours all my dreams at night.
M. D. Baker

I Wonder.....

I often wonder, as a child,
How grasses grow so tall and wild,
Where seeds of dandelions come to rest,
How chirping chicks will leave their nests,
And where do sparrows sleep at night?
How does the wind hold up my kite?
When the rain falls where do bees stay?
Does anyone listen when I pray?

How many waves slip across the sand?
Will I ever hold a moonbeam in my hand?
Who put the treasure at the rainbow's end?
And what makes a river twist and bend?

I should ask the lady who lays out the snow,
And makes the sunflower and marigold grow,
Who makes the sun gleam and glow,
Because Mother Nature is sure to know.
Shireen Farkhoy

War Crime

You were my neighbour and once my friend,
How could it be that you would not bend.
The hand that held friendship now holds a gun,
It killed my husband, then my son.

Where once we laughed in the face of war,
You have me kneeling on the floor.
Oh please God, make them understand,
Is all this worth it just for land?

If this is freedom, give me chains,
Death right now would soothe my pains.
Just pull the trigger and have it done,
Released from suffering I shall have won.

Will there be justice when you have had your way?
Perhaps in heaven on judgement day.
I asked for mercy so you beat me more,
Then tore my dress and closed the door.
Rosalind Alexander

A Tea Towel To The Rescue

How do you tell your children that Dad was attacked at
  breakfast by his egg
They would laugh at you directly and think you'd pulled their leg
He put it in the frying pan and it spat straight back in his eye
He placed it into scorching fat, it took revenge and began to fly
Trying to turn the gas tap down was painful to his face
Fat flying from the frying pan was slowing down his pace
I thought about giving him an upturned chair to ward against the foe
But a brightly coloured tea towel was the thing I had to throw
He put the tea towel to his face, just like a training matador
Had it been a contest between Dad and the egg, the egg
  would have won the score.
L. A. Dedman

Deliverance

The woodland rings with tongue of hound,
Horses' hooves on frozen ground,
As Reynard Fox, strength ebbing fast,
Yet spirit unwavering to the last,
Summons up his last reserves,
Survival thrumming through his nerves.
Forever an hour, through field and wood,
Hedgerows, thickets, cloying mud,
He's evaded the ultimate brutal kill,
By inbred cunning and consummate skill,
Yet matched by his pursuers and despite all,
He feels the pack closing, the relentless horn call.
Heart pounding, breath gasping, he scents fresh sea air
And halts at the cliff edge, turning to glare.
Only yards separate them as he jumps to a ledge
And watches the pack pour over the edge,
Hears voices screaming, distraught with pain,
At the loss of the pack to the watery main.
Reynard lies hidden for many an hour,
Then jumps to the clifftop and home to his bower.

Michael Anthony Lindop

Hooked

Hooked on a drug, where there's no escape.
Hooked on a drug, which is going to rape
Your heart, your money, your soul, it's funny,
To think you found the goal you believe is so profound,
Condemning the few who really knew, you had your point of view.
You're hooked you said, as you roll out the same side of bed,
Hooked on a drug that's dragging you down,
Inject yourself with an eternal frown.
You're stuck in a room with no cracks on the walls
Walking down, walking down, walking down door-less halls.

Petals on a flower are starting to matter
But while you're hooked, you still continue to flatter
Yourself with knowledge of its meaning,
But now while the sun is gleaming,
While you're hooked, I've got that feeling,
I'm floating, I'm drifting, I'm beautifully reeling
Lead me on a hike across the moor,
Barren and bare and more and more,
Loving the way that children play.
Fondled and needled, and moulded like clay.

Stephen Gribble

Sister Demetria

She sat on a stool by my hospital bed
Holding my hand and cooling my head
A figure draped in white, with a gleaming black face
A sister of mercy — so full of grace
Her rosary beads touching the sheet where I lay
As she lowered her head each time she would pray
Sister Demetria (nee) Katherine Smith
A nun I shall remember as long as I live
Her American accent, her nursing and care
Her faith in the Lord was how I met her
From the United States to Liverpool
Until she left that day
I'm so glad I met Sister Demetria and I thank her for
  passing my way.

Rosa B. Gosling

I'm Watching You!

Its eyes sparkle,
Glance to a move,
Eyes are fixed,
Not to move,
Watch, watching you,
Stalk, stalking 'The sheep' that's you!
Watch its beautiful eyes,
Watching you.

Selena Bray

Graciously Ageing

A man sits pensive in the corner of the room
His face tells the story of two world wars
He cleans a clay pipe into the palm of his hand
Makes a non-angry fist over the ashtray's edge
And lets the residue of burnt tobacco
Slip through like the sands of time

He leans forward adjusting his seating position
Extending an arm towards a jug of stout
His eyes fixed on the dimplex distorted contents
As it begins its shaky journey to his goal
Lips meet glass in a halfway compromise
To complete his subdued satisfaction

His eyes now reflecting the log fire's warmth
He returns the ale to its place of rest
Lifting his head he observes youthful quaffers
Smiling gently as they acknowledge his presence
He thinks for a moment of what might lay ahead
Content in the knowledge that his hard work's done
No more anxieties and no more burdens
Just the process of graciously ageing

M. A. Brown

Farewell

An old man died in his stately bed
His death was more peaceful than the life he'd led
The family had gathered to witness his end
No more would the doctor attend his old friend
Ruth gently said, Mother, you must have some rest
My brothers will make the arrangements that's best
The family and friends stood round the grave
To say their goodbyes to a man who'd been brave
In two wars he'd served the best way he could
His wife did her share as he knew that she would
Together they'd made a home for a family of three
Now they are the roots of a large family tree
They gathered round when the will was to be read
After they'd got their fair share there was more to be said
Look after your mother and treat her with care just as if I were
  still there
Always be proud of all that you do, never bring shame to the
  name I gave you
There's no more advice for me to give; may God bless and
  keep you as long as you live.

Marion Hutchison

Thinking Of You Each Day

Thinking of you each day
How I long to be with you
Sat looking through the square window
Thinking of you each day

Thinking of you each day
Catch a train to take the strain
Was in vain didn't ease my pain
Holding back the tears
Thinking of you each day

Thinking of you each day
If you would write me a letter or something
Just to ease my pain
Thinking of you each day
The postman came and went
He said no letters post card today
The sadness I felt
Thinking of you each day

Thinking of you each day
How do I know you are there
Thinking of you each day.

Randolph Holder

Death Of A Clown

Grey-paled, the man leans frail against the wall
his cough is hacked and shakes the withered frame
of bones, beneath the mantle of his garb
yet no one cares the slightest,...least his name.

A name that once in lights, respect had held
enchanted crowds had flocked and queued the hours
to savour of his mirth and revelry
the clown of clowns, no more those winning powers.

Command-Performances he'd had his share
the thrill to 'Walk-the-boards' like treading air
but as a christian...now to higher claims
as gone, he'd slipped away to greater fare.

The clown within our midst has much to give
a tonic for our ills and troubled minds
his kind are sent to us that we may live
in warmth of heart, against the winter's winds.

So never take the clown to be a fool
'tis just an act within the sober man
accomplished first, his skills in other spheres
too few can expert, both do,....as he can.
    A. G. Clench

Kamikoche, A Mountain Idyll?

Up from the bustling, coastal plain,
High in the Alps where the air is pure,
To Kamikoche in sun or rain;
Young and old find its peace a lure.

The rippling stream — a silver vein
Giving succour to fish and fowl,
Washing the feet of the mountains,
Where demons, once, were thought to howl.

Then Weston came and scaled the heights,
Proved fiendish cries were just the wind.
No longer need anyone take fright;
How could people have been so blind?

Mountain pools mirror rocky peaks
That soar into a clear, blue sky,
Peaks that Nippon climbers seek
To test their skills — they're keen to try.

Top winds whine and scream as night falls;
Moonlight reflects from silver vein.
Can it be that Weston's ghost calls?
Have the demons come back again?
    Malcolm R. Wade

In Death We Are All Equal

There is the tramp with his shoes down-trodden,
His clothes all ragged and torn.
But he doesn't fret or worry:
He's had nothing since the day he was born.

Now there, the ladies in all their finery,
With dresses and clothes galore,
Are not as happy as the tramp who has nothing:
They are greedy and want more and more.

There the princes in their palaces
With plenty of money to spend:
But though they put on their airs and graces
Are no better than the tramp in the end.

In life they may think they are better
Than the tramp who is down and out.
But in death the tramp is equal —
Of that there is no doubt.

Because we all come into this world with nothing
And with nothing we have to go out.
    E. Dutton

Little Man

The little man, I used to know.
He's walking, where the bluebells grow,
The forest where he's walking at
Is where his daughter Susie sat.
Up above the sky was blue.
Down below the trees were green.
It was the greatest sight was ever seen.
He walked along the winding path
With dear Susie he did laugh.
As they walked around the bend,
He disappeared with a friend.
He disappeared up to the sky.
His friend and he were floating high.
This little man had left behind
His daughter Susie for me to mind.
As we walked this winding path,
I and Susie we did laugh.
This little man we used to know
Has left us both to walk below
In the forest where the bluebells grow.
    C. J. Bunch

Autumn

An artist's palette couldn't better match
His brush to the canvas, in trying to catch
The vibrancy of colour as the October leaves fall,
Emblazoning our memories which we can recall
When the snow is deep beneath our feet,
And the colours of Autumn beat a sad retreat,
Gold and yellow and deep rustic red,
Beware our feet lest they tread on
Spiky green cases split from head to toe,
A bright red chestnut shining and aglow
Peeps out of its shell at the awaiting scene,
Of upturned leaves where the children have been
Seeking a champion for the conker game,
And abandoning the hunt when twilight came,
Now so quiet the rustle of leaves is music to the ear
As the mantle of the evening sky draws near,
A sharp sweet smell pervades the air
As the branches undress and twigs are laid bare,
Above, hanging limply, a determined few,
As our ankles sink in a deep coloured hue
    W. Anne Harris

Many A True Word

Here's a toast to a really grand fellow
He's lived a quite turbulent life
He's made his war stories,
Survived under the Tories
And survived having me for a wife.

Raise a glass, to that jolly good fireman
Whose actions were daring and brave
He flinched not from danger
For many a stranger
From a flaming demise did he save.

As a driver for Wesht Midlands buses
He drove many a soul round the bend
Now he'sh finally retired,
Quite well liked and admired,
Let'sh drink to his future, my friend (Hic)

May hish hours fill with leisure and plaughter
May hish wallett be long, and his days fat
May we wish him good keer
May his chairs disappear
And I'll think another to drat (Hic)
    Ruth Rimell

Unconditional Love

There's a four footed friend that exists on this plane,
He's a kindly old soul and exists with restrain,
He's joyful, content with all that he's got,
He's willing to please and thankful for his lot,
A cuddle, kind word is all that he asks,
He's no major goals or difficult tasks,
He's just there to give joy to mankind.
The tasks he's allotted he never finds
Difficult to deliver, the joy he's brought to give,
He's just there to eat, sleep and live.
To please his Master, forgiveness in stride,
For any harsh word that might injure pride,
He just is loving and kind,
He just is of a SPECIAL MIND.

V. C. Sparkes

Spring

Snowdrops peeping through the earth
Heralds of the spring
Primroses and crocuses and birds upon the wing
Trees and shrubs all bursting forth
With faces to the sun
And daffodils so tall and straight
God made them, every one
The newborn lambs all gambolling
In the fields so green
All nature comes alive again
Where winter's chills have been
Dear Lord, you made the earth so fair
There is beauty all around us
We thank you for your love and care
And the blessings that surround us.

I. Garrod

Thoughts

Deep in the garden soil, the sleeping bulbs stirred,
Heralding the awakening of spring anew.
Songs of thrushes and blackbirds could be heard,
As tips of crocus and daffodils pushed through,
With each day, rays of the sun become stronger,
As birds hurry and scurry, a nest site to find.
Aware of the urgency as the days grow longer,
To build a nest so neat and carefully lined.
Becoming filled later with ever hungry offspring,
Never satisfied with gapes a wide filling the nest.
No matter how frequently their parents may bring,
Caterpillars and worms, and some things people detest.
Helping to retain nature's balance intact,
A close run thing in this day and age, it is true.
The sooner the better we realize this fact,
The future of our planet is ensured, for me and you.

H. G. Miles-Berry

Brown Eyes

At last she's here, her dazzling beauty here before him,
His love for her must be denied - but not through shame.
He has a love which cannot speak its name
He looks into deep brown eyes that are wide and clear
He knew her mother, not too well but for a long time
When, although they both had partners they were
both so lonely.
"My mother often spoke of you", she said,
"I feel I know you well."
(What had her mother said? What secrets now lay
beyond those perfect lips?)
And now the punishment.
The inability to share or show he cared.
"It's been so good meeting you and talking to you",
he heard himself say,
"Remember me to your father". (God, she is so beautiful)
"I will", she said as she turned,
And his daughter walked away.

Norman Beggs

Spellbound

My Country's old — though not to me!
  Her youth awakes for all to see
Her glories unsurpassed by Time:
  The Tundra, Redwood, towering Pine.

When flames of Autumn touch her leaves,
  They play, they float, down from her trees;
They dance their ballet — fast, now slow —
  On winds that bring the Winter's snow.

Rocky Mountains traced with gold,
  Conceal the wealth she seeks to hold;
Her Prairies vast — the Lakes the same —
  Those renegades Man tries to tame!

She did not sigh nor heed his gun;
  She waited there to greet the Sun:
For she has diamonds 'neath the ice,
  Which, if plundered, there's a price...!

For her they shine by Northern Lights,
  Those phantom neons of God's Might;
Half encompassed by the sea,
  My Country really baffles me . . . !

D. R. Payn Le Sueur

Waiting

She sits alone in her darkened room,
Her thoughts of years gone by,
Of her only love, who broke her heart,
And how he made her cry.

He was the one she worshipped so,
Until he took her hand,
Not to propose, as she had hoped,
There would be no gold band.

He told her there was someone else,
He loved and hoped to wed,
Her face went pale, she could not speak,
She turned from him and fled.

She remembers still in her ninetieth year,
Of the way she felt that day,
Still feels his hand as he broke the news,
And how she ran away.

There was no other love for her,
The tears begin to fall,
She hopes one day they'll meet again,
As she waits to answer God's call.

Terese Bell

A Mother's Joy

Anguish, pain, she must endure to hear her infant's cries so pure
Her child arrives just newly born, bursts into being through the storm

Tiny mite, such beauty formed, comes to greet us unadorned
Divinely sent from heaven above, deserved of our wondrous love

Tiny ears and button nose, scent more lovely than a rose
Eyes that sparkle like a stream, answer to a wishful dream

Tiny fingers, tiny toes, clustered in artistic rows
Small fat legs and wiggling feet, tears of joy on mother's cheek

Arms outstretched, hands in the air, seeking solace, gentle care
Nestled to its mother's breast, picture innocence at its best

Little mouth upon the teat, mother — child are now complete
Ecstasy, harmony and elation, symmetry of God's creation

Cradled through its childhood ills, cutting teeth and clashing wills
Such short time on mother's knee, gently nurtured by degree

Crawling, walking, run around, lots of games and fun abound
Time for school, time for learning, mother left confused and yearning

Soon it's adolescent youth, parties, music lifts the roof
Were we ever at this stage — rebellious, sulky, noisy age?

Of course we were, if truth be known, it's part of life ere we leave home
Then having joined the adult set, we still remain our mother's pet.

J. B. Ryan

Waiting

The cat sits silently, upright,
Her breast smooth and white as new fallen snow —
And as motionless.
She has ceased her reckless play at twilight's fall
Has taken up her vigil in soft grass by the woodbine's edge
And sits as if musing, comforting in her comfort
But her eyes do not dream — and small winged creatures
That fly to the scents above
Are not met with complete oblivion.
Diurnal dies, or sleeps — still bright the sky above
With light, with beauty
Ethereal cloud wracks stealing in
Yet how darkly the earth meets the eyes' return —
The trees are sharp silhouettes, no detail is defined —
The cat's striped flanks are blending with the grass
Her breast a pale glow in the darkness
An air of mystery hangs about her
I search blue twilight for the evening star
But she, nocturnal, is waiting for the night.

H. J. West

The Midnight Fox

The fox, that moves like lightning
Her black nose, her black coat tipped with white
Eager to protect her cub, eager to protect herself.

Midnight is when the fox hunts, midnight when the fox howls
Interested in people, intimidated by man
Determined to succeed, desperate to survive
Never looks happy, never looks sad
In the hen hut, in her den she feels indiscretion
Graceful when running, graceful when walking
Hoping for her cub, hoping food is plenty
Twinkles under the sun, termination under the moon.

Flitting here, flitting there, wherever you turn that fox is near
Often seen near the hen hut, often nearly shot
Extraordinary fox, extraordinary fox.

Richard Tindall

Switch Off

To ease the pain you have within.
Help you through the suffering.
Knowing the sorrow cuts like a knife.
Coping with this in the midst of life.
I may look alive lying there,
But the machine lies of life in here.
Asleep, now gone from this world,
We'll be united as the Bible foretold.
Conscious of nothing, I feel no pain.
In the resurrection, I'll see you again.
Turn the machine off, no more to be done.
A new day begins on the rising sun.
And life for you must continue on.

R. Jackson

He'll Be Home Soon!

She's sits in the living room, and looks at the clock,
He'll be home soon.
She sips coffee, and looks at the clock.
He'll be home soon.
She looks at the tablets, sees the end of the misery,
Looking in the mirror, she now sees what we see.
He'll be home soon.
Her eye is as black, as the bruises show, her heart is
as broken as the cups on the floor.
And he'll be home soon.
Her mouth still aching opens to receive the last taste
of freedom.
The tablet box now empty lies on the chair.
Her body now lifeless lies on the floor, her eyes wide open
looking up, on the mantel the clock ticks, and as she
slips away, her last thought as her eyes close
is he will soon be there. And he'll be home soon.

Tania Black

New Prayer For Peace Of Mind, Unbelievers And The Millennium

Dear Lord our God, if thou exist,
Help us through life's swirling mist,
Give us please, clarity of thought,
Help us find those things most sought.

Assist us through these darkening times,
Where stress causes not just facial lines,
But strain bears heavily upon the brain,
And all one's best efforts seem in vain.

Oh God, if faith be what is required,
To make me less afraid and tired,
To overcome this daily grind,
That so pervades our suffering mind.

Give us the strength to fight the fear,
That tomorrow may bring disaster near,
Repossession of house or loss of job,
So prevalent 'midst today's working mob.

New prayer for strength should God exist,
Get us clear of this all pervasive mist,
Not burdened, fraught, in perpetual hurry,
But enlivened, enriched, and free of worry.

Michael A. Smith

"Shadows"

Life is robust, yet not grand
Help me control a shaking hand.
Blindly I wander to pastures new
Yet again only thinking, thinking of you.

The upsurge of time, no longer mine,
Passions burnt out, this life to surmount.
Too much love and too much hate
Destiny is sure as fate.

Once again I am giving,
Almost dead yet still living.
Looking forward never back,
Help me down this beaten track.

Pocket dreams until tomorrow.
They will come, as will sorrow.
Perhaps tomorrow I will see;
A brand new life open to me.

Then the shadows of my mind
Like a tide will turn and find
Life and love. Expectation!
Never more a revelation!

Sylvia Ann Best

Nobody Wins A War

The world is fair or so they say
I think it's wrong in every way
people killing all the time
to me it's a terrible crime
the devil around us every day
he makes us evil in every way
these wars and killings can't be right
why each day must we fight?

Bring down the walls and let's be one
surely enough bloodshed has been done
so leaders of the world unite
all this heartache can't be right
there's no time for us to waste
it doesn't matter what it takes
the time for peace has arrived
it's what we need to survive
so put down your guns everyone
the time for solidarity has come
because there's only one thing that's sure
and that is that nobody wins a war.

Penny Boucher

Untitled

O sleepless night,
heavenly delight.
Why? Why?

Some of your subject feared to shut their weary eyes.
Are they afraid of dying in their sleep?
Or feared the obsessive nightmare
In their slumbering sleep.

Grant us peace. Grant us peace.
As we relaxed our head to sleep,
We surrender to the hours that you have rendered.

O sleepless night,
heavenly delight.

Here we are your subjects await,
Asking you not to keep us up too late,
In your remand we put our faith.

We do not fuss. We do not fight.
Give us this night.
Give us this night.
Give us this night.
And it will be alright come daylight.

M. I. Saleem

Untitled

Dance Salome, Queen of the seven veils,
Heathen, uncivilized, born to be wild.
Whore Jezebel — an innocent child.
Merlin's Ninian from a retreat in Wales,
Witch, enchantress, crazy woman.
Maiden, mother, long lost sister.
Seasiren wailing at the mistrals.
Adam's spare rib shapes Eve human.
Pussycat purring a breastful of milk.
Lioness stalking an immobile prey,
uninhibited prostitutes primeval ways.
Mermaids combing shimmering silk,
Samson's chopped by Delilah's revenge.
Acting the weak from physical forces.
Have we that power, Oh magic sorceress?
Gathered together his stories seem strange.

D. S. Witt

My First Love

My fist love I found and lost,
Hearts of gold and hearts of frost.
The passion we had I failed to keep
still lives inside as I cry to sleep.
I wake every morning lying alone
Looking around me I'm all on my own
No love around me, no kissing no more
Remembering the day he walked out the door.
I only wish that he could see how much he really means to me.
If I could have another try
mine and his love would never die.

Stacey Tyler

Faith

To find stillness in the
Heart of the storm
How deep within us if we can reach
Calling on it is the strength
A silent strength.
Gentle, unknowing manipulation
Powerful, loving guidance
Persuasive in forcing us to go forward
With calmness to cope with whatever
Is demanded of us at any given time,
To reach, stretch, grasp
The never ending lifeline...
We simply call faith.

Pauline Russell

Falcon

Your eyes are all fire
head full of pride and coquetry
and a deadly heartbeat

Meat from a gloved hand

Then with a cry you fly
the wings of an empire
taught in the burning sun

The desert is an altar

Casting death's shadow in the sand
you are all things sharp and difficult
there is no answer to you

Suddenly a hare

The earth stands still
establishing a tyranny of pain
you clutter the life out

You eat

Then you know the hooded lantern's peace
until the chiming hour of nature's clock
when you will rage and cut again.

Stephen Whitehouse

Lost Love

Of all the loves I've ever known
He was the best — the epitome
He came to me, a spirit free
And stayed to take the best in me
I gave him love, and oh so deep
My soul it was all his to keep
He was so strong, so full of love —
Each night a memory
And though I knew it could not last
He meant the world to me
We shared the moon, we shared the stars
We shared a love so true
And then one day he met his death
And with that I 'died' too
Of all the sorrows I have known
This was the worst — the epitome......

C. Hartley

The Pathway Of Life

He came upon me quietly — while walking through the grass
He was old — yes ancient — I moved for him to pass.
I had not seen him standing there — he just appeared to me
But as I raised my head and looked — for all the world to see
Was kindness strength, and courage — in those very gentle eyes
We gazed at one another — one ignorant — one wise.
His words came very softly — but then I saw his strength
Was in the wisdom of his words — which he said at length.
Child, do you see the pathway that winds up on the hill
Sometimes you'll find it hard to climb — but I'm sure you will
At every little turning — there will be something new.
Not always what you wish to find — but if your heart is true
Your faith will always carry you
Your legs will never stop
And you will find God's hand reach out
And lift you to the top.

Joyce Branford

My Big Brother

My big brother is very tall,
He makes me look like I'm very small.

My big brother is very smart,
Compared to me he pulls me apart.

My big brother is in his teens,
He's probably the biggest teen that I've ever seen.

My big brother, he's a big foot,
He's sometimes interested in a science book.

Rebecca Sleigh

Poem To A Punk

Sid vicious was the link in our society,
He took the rap, for all to see.
His friends will scorn to see he's gone,
But they are the ones that should have fled,
Not he — who now is dead.

The true punks are the ones who live
Off young and immature poor souls,
To clean their cars and spend their cheques,
Mow their lawns — they are the ghouls.

They live on, to find another guy
Who will bring sparkle to their eye.
There will be more fall in the trap,
With money as their gain, but no one
Says "You fool, you'll end up insane".

And so the poor and needless task
Of rising to fame
Will no doubt end up in the end
As quite inane.

I. R. Langston

Little Box, With Little Sticks

Frightened and alone
He sits in the corner just staring
He does not understand why she had to die.
He does not say a word
He reaches in his pocket
The matches he takes out
He stares, this little box, with little sticks
The matches which helped her to die.
He's left in the world
with no-one to care
He now understands
The little box, with little sticks
He'll never touch again.

Sharon Pearce

At War In Britain

Oh! that rotten father of mine,
He sent me to Britain the rotten swine,
I'm an alien in a faraway place,
I want to go home (it would be ace!)

Everyone here thinks I'm bad,
Hitler! he's worse than dad,
He started this war to get more land,
When he has all of Germany in his hand.

They think I'm Hitler's number one spy,
Work for Hitler (I'd rather die)
Its cold and damp it always rains
I can't live like his, full of pain!

Tommy Fox

Sunday School

When Tommy went to Sunday school
he larked about and played the fool;
then teacher pinned up pretty pictures
onto green felt on the wall.
A baby hidden in a cradle
in the bulrushes so tall
a big man in a lion's den
and fancy being swallowed by a whale.
A babe was born inside a stable
who grew into a kindly man
he healed the sick, fed the hungry
cured the lame and made the blind man see;
but what a sad, sad ending to the tale
when he was hung upon a cross with nails.
Tommy grew up and soon forgot
the good man nailed upon the cross
but mother knew he would recall
one day the pictures on the wall.

K. D. Smith

D. O. M. Plc.

I have an elephant, I call him Fred,
He lives down the garden in our shed.
It takes tons of hay to keep him well fed.
  every day.

I take him for walks at darkest night,
So no-one sees him and has a fright,
We can't meet other elephants for Fred to fight
  they're vicious.

He gives lots of manure for our vegetable plot,
For all town in fact, because he does a lot,
Too much for a spade, I hire a Drott
  (an excavator).

I'm starting a firm, "Dave's Organic Manure"
I'll do lots of business of that I'm sure,
Buy lots more elephants, stop being poor.
  Hurray.

On the stock market my firm will float.
I won't sit around counting money and gloat,
I'll travel the world by 'plane and by boat,
  Concorde and QE2.

D. Newsome

My Grandson

He is cute and he is cuddly, and oh so loving.
He is a bundle of laughs, and he is fond of hugging.
He's as bright as a button, as clever as can be,
He knows all his numbers, just you ask and see.

Show him a letter he'll say what it is,
It's just like uncorking a bottle of fizz.
Shapes are no problem, he'll know what they are.
Little James Thomas will certainly go far.

He knows all the colours that brighten our world,
A precious gift held when on a lap he is curled.
He's a gem, he's so lovely, a bit like the rest,
But, not quite, because he's simply the best.

J. Wain

The Good Companion

He's handsome yes, his coat's like silk
He gets the cream off all the milk
He's black and white and full of play
My long-haired Tomcat, just a stray.

I took him in, no more he'd roam
He turned my house into a home.
Of loneliness, I'd known good measure
So when he came I'd found a treasure.

He's neutered, has no lady friends
With love, I try to make amends
Because at heart I do lament
For having him made impotent.

As cat food prices soar and soar
We feel the pinch, like many more
And should inflation get too steep
All else may go, but him I'll keep.

The reason for this 'ere emotion
He's given me day by day devotion
And if I live to ninety-nine
I'll ne'er forget this cat o'mine.

M. I. Knaggs

Moments Lost, Moments Gained

Every single day spent without seeing you leaves me feeling
that I have lost part of my life.
Every single moment with you is one to be savoured and I
become completely alive.
I find life without seeing you can be hell. I hope therefore that
in your mind you also join me there sometimes.

J. W. Knight

One Dewdrop....

As the sweet nightingale sings
He gently flaps his wings,
I fall softly asleep
And the sweet music picks me up in one sweep....

I float away to a far off land
That nightingale's music is the hand,
My troubles are far, far away
As I wonder I feel like a castaway....

Suddenly the music comes to a stop
And all that is left
Is the nightingale and the sweet music is one dewdrop....
Nick Green

The Metaphorical Burglar

Dog tired, the cat burglar arrived back at his house
He crept through to the kitchen, as quiet as a mouse
As hungry as a horse and as greedy as a hog
He ate like a pig, then slept like a log

Though cunning as a fox and as strong as an ox
he was mild as a lamb to his wife and their tots
He was proud as a peacock of his wife and the children
And would fight like a tiger, if anyone illed them

He began his career to support his first daughter
And he took to it like a duck takes to water
His wife turned a blind eye to his illegal pickings
And she treated the children like a hen with her chickens

He was lively as a cricket while the children were little
And he genuinely felt he was as fit as a fiddle
Though stubborn as a mule to any thoughts of a change
He was wise as an owl, although this may sound strange

He was blind as a bat to his uncertain future
And at the time never considered agriculture
But as he grew older, the thought was alarming
So he decided to settle for animals and farming.
M. Rock

" Cor Man Bob "

I have a man, his name is BOB
He cleans carpets and hoovers ats his job
A lot of folk phone im bit he's nay aye in
And fin he's in his garage he makes an affa din
He likes a golf club and awa wee Doug
Bit dinna tell I'm a tilt ye
or hell skelp me in the lug
Hes an afa fine mani in he gings it see ma granny
So nobody better look down their noses
As we love Bobby in a his hoses
His wife loves him in his quine dis n a
This is fae Maureen an An-gel-a.
Maureen Cardno

A Blind Man Can't See

A blind man can't see, because he hasn't eyes,
He cannot see people, or look up to the skies;
He can only hear people, and hear their words;
He cannot see the flowers, the hills, or the birds.

He cannot see all that is around,
He can only listen, and hear its sound,
O what a blessing, that we have sight,
That I can see, all I see tonight.

Isn't it wonderful, God's wonderful love,
That we can have sight, from Him up above;
Isn't it wonderful, God's holy plan,
For God's made a body perfect for man!

O Father God, I really thank Thee
That I have sight, that I can see;
Bless those, Lord, who do not have sight;
Bless them by Your love, in Your wonderful light.
Neil Fitzgeorge

First Love, Lost Love

With a newspaper bag on his is light slender form
He assiduously walked on his way.
I tagged behind in sunshine or storm,
Proud to follow my hero all day.

So happy, so close, in our innocent love
It felt like a fantasy dream.
His touch on my hand made my crazy heart move,
And was soft as a gentle moonbeam.

In a wartime world with its stress and strife,
Our innocent trysts we so treasured.
My hero, my friend, my love — my life.
For me you cared and you pleasured.

This precious love, so pure, so shy,
Our parents thought errant — no less,
No time to kiss my darling goodbye,
We cried in our sad loneliness.

First love of my youth, first love of my heart,
Though other loves came and were sweet.
You have been in my soul from the time we did part
In a new world one day we may meet.
Sylvia Johnson

Shattered Thoughts

Footprints in the snow, where do you go
Have you gone to some warm, far and distant land
Where sunshine cast its rays upon your face,
And the beach is covered with a golden sand.
Where nighttime shadows below a silvery moon
Reflect upon the waters, by the shore
Where a warm gentle breeze against your skin
Brings a feeling of excitement to the fore.
Footprints in the snow, please take me with you
To a world where your mind can drift away
Let me feel the oriental breeze,
Blow softly now, forever and a day.
Footprints in the snow, you are no more
For it seems to me you've reached your journey's end
As I gaze into the chilling ice water,
My shattered thoughts of where you've gone, I can't pretend.
Were you sad to share this world of mine
Were your troubles far beyond repair
Footprints in the snow, are you happy now?
In my heart for you, I'll say a silent prayer.
Maureen Carlisle Dennett

Full Circle

Isn't it strange? Life I mean.
Have you ever noticed how its cycle returns full circle?
All the years spent in caring are never wasted.
Take it from one who knows by experience.
The time spent over many years in nurturing, have returned to me a thousandfold.
I lie here and know that at this moment, the roles have been reversed.
I look upon my beautiful girl, my Nickie, as she tenderly mothers me.
This child of mine, who not so long ago was a child herself
And here she is, so strong, so capable, so caring.
Loving me and gently nursing me back to health.
Pat Hanrahan

Watery Movement

Crystal and cantering, diamond and dancing,
Gushing unguided with an infinite force,
Sparkling and scampering over rock and stone.

Mature and murky, meandering mightily,
A life-giving liquid in total unity,
Running its race with the greatest of ease.

Basking in the bright sunshine,
Rippling carelessly at the pebbled shore,
Quietly numbing the swimmers' toes.
Sharron Claringbold

Spring Again

hate to stir myself from winter's wasteful cold
hate to meet the coming of the spring
and yet I could have missed it, had I not stirred
from lethal comforts that a modern age doth bring.
So I moved one morn to walk the trust
with ungracious step at being so disturbed
and yet I could have missed it, had I not stirred.
And there they were — waiting to greet me
Heads erect and standing proud
A carpet sea of bluebells in woodland glade.
Once more, they've come to meet and greet,
courtiers of anemones and primrose
and chestnut trees bursting forth with bud and stickle
beeches with a filigree of delicate green leaves.
What a joyous sight
This England in spring
   V. P. Thomas

Wrong Direction

You planted the bomb that shattered the peace
Hate in your heart and blood on your hands
Leaving death and devastation for persons unknown
No more fragile peace, just our broken bones
Mother and brother wept as peace faded away
A young victim who will never get to vote
We bury our dead, the piper plays your tune
Your struggle, our fear entwined for years
Use the ballot box, not the barrel of your gun
Let our children have a future, not just a dream
Evil in your heart, you took my precious life
Why are you going in the wrong direction
   Sue Williams

Shilstone Cottage

Sequestered haven amidst Devon's rural scene,
Harbouring peace and contentment, calm and serene.
Inherent is the welcome this cottage displays
Looking so attractive in the sun's golden rays.
Surrounded by farmland and a wealth of fine trees
That add their cool shade to the gentle summer breeze.
Over this tranquil scene old Shilstone Hill presides,
Neighbour for centuries, many secrets it hides.
Exmoor's superb, contrasting countryside is near,

Covert for the soaring buzzard and wild red deer.
Open moors, heather, native ponies, bubbling streams,
Tidy thatched cottages with old oaken beams.
The splendid coastline and deep wooded combes we view,
Appledore, Bideford, Instow, Torrington too.
Great though the appeal of this fine county may be,
Even greater the kindness of this family.
   Ron C. Davies

Evening Hush

Tranquil sky, a blood-red sun
Hangs suspended, day has run
Slipping now behind the hill.
Hush descends and all is still.
Throughout the day unceasing plough
Has turned the earth, criss-crossed each field
Preparing for next season's yield
And now silent, lies beyond the brow.
A wondrous time at creeping dusk
After every stalk and husk
Is baled and stacked, and land lies bare.
Twilight falls, and fills the air
With scents of evening, and each bough
Gentled by the wind's sweet sough,
Harbours creatures hidden close until
Dawn will bring their chorus shrill.
And with the rising of the sun
Another day will have begun.
What is this life, if unaware
Of simple joy, we cease to care?
   Pamela Kirby

Two Dresses

In my wardrobe at the back,
Hang two dresses one cream, one black,
I push the other clothes aside,
And look at those two dresses hanging side by side.

My fingers caress the dress of cream,
I close my eyes and then I daydream,
Of that happy day I wore that dress with pride,
The day I became my beloved's bride.

The dress of black I do not touch,
For memories still pain me too much,
Of that day of untold grief when we had to part,
And I was left with a broken heart.

I close the door on the clothes that hang in there,
If only the door of life was open our lives still to share,
Now within the sanctuary of my heart happy memories
are but dreams,
Especially the day I wore my dress of cream.

As I look back, oh how I wish life hadn't meant me to have
   that dress of black.
   Marjorie E. Morrow

Bonds Of Sisterhood

Bonds of sisterhood with unjudging family ties,
Hand in hand, but leading separate lives
Flecks of green amidst amber Iris, gently
   Hidden behind a cage of lashes,
You're a part of me that cannot be, but
   Together one efficacious entity
Secrets shared to the grave of forbidden passions,
With voiceless language of descriptive names
I stand among broken dreams, alone, but comforted it seems
Replacing each crash with embracing arms,
You counsel with harkening endurance then veracious charms
So much to give - nothing to take
A friend is a treasure a jewel to preserve
Until the time comes to be a friend in return
   Mandy Jane Gamble

A Burning Candle

A fire that glowed deep within
Had been a long time out.
With your love you rekindled it,
And now it glows in my heart.

Like a candle that drips with wax,
My heart pours with love.
That candle still burns and burns.

Not the strongest wind could put it out,
And if it should ever melt,
My heart would fade and soon be frozen,
Like a harsh, cold metal case.

But now there glows where once was darkness,
A flame, fuelled by love.
Generated by the strongest emotion, but only...
...A simple burning candle.
   Sylvia Maria Harlin

Derelict

The sound of creaking rafters that fill still night air,
Gives an eerie ghostly feeling that numbs your mind with fear,
A house that once held laughter now open to the rain,
Its damp and dismal bedrooms will never be the same.
Doors hanging on their hinges swinging to and fro,
waiting for that welcome hand that they never more shall know.
Windows banging constantly tell travellers in the night,
That this once loved and cherished place is now a sorry sight.
As winter slowly gives away to warm and gentle spring,
A new life is beginning on a broken window sill.
A family of feathered friends has made it home once more,
This derelict and lonely house will live again I'm sure.
   Valerie Helliar

'When God Made Our Mother'

From precious diamonds he made her eyes that sparkled like a star,
Guiding lights that watched us whether we were near or far.
From the blush of the rose he made her cheeks that glowed
  like a warm fire,
Nothing was ever too much trouble, our happiness was her
  only desire.
From tulips he made her delicate lips that kissed and spoke
  such words of care,
No matter what our problems, we always knew that she was there.
From music notes he made her voice, soft like that of the lark in spring,
With this she spoke with guidance and taught us to bear
  whatever life would bring.
From the colours of the rare rainbow he made her cherished smile,
Despite how short a mother's time she would sit and talk with
  us a while.
From the shells of the sea, God made her ears to listen and to share,
In our laughter when life was good, to our tears when it
  seemed unfair.
From the light wisps of fluffy clouds he made her soft brown hair,
So perfect did God make her he must have surely placed a halo there.
From the rays of the sun he made her heart, never was there
  one more gold,
So wonderful God made her he must surely have broken the mould.
From the wings of angels he made her arms to enfold, comfort
  and caress,
Yes, when God gave us our Mother he blessed us with more
  than the very best.
  Angela J. Brandon-Smith

Aconite

Little yellow aconite,
Green collar all around,
Lying so close to the deep-sleeping ground,
With hellebores, cyclamen,
And the white and purple ling -
What pleasure you do bring,
After the grim, dark days of Winter -
True harbinger of Spring.
  W. J. Sudworth

The Garden

Though June and Summer are here and flowers in sunshine bathe,
Grass and fallen beech leaves must suffer the shearing blade.
Plugged in, with safety cut-out, the mower blade rotates
And lifts across the lawn from plot to plot,
Like hovercraft from coast to coast.
Grass segments in all directions spray, rusty leaves leap.
Do my eyes deceive me or does that leaf stare at me?
The hovermower silent, I say, "Thank God, I missed that little frog."
  D. Gourlay

An English Oak

How high, mighty and magnificent you stand!
Grandest of this island's living things;
Casting your shadow across an acre of land,
Supping enormous draughts from subterranean springs.

A whole universe exists under your spreading canopy,
Countless birds roost within your shaded bowers;
Myriad insects thrive amongst your branches panoply,
While ruthless hawks command your topmost towers.

A great empire was founded on such as you,
Your ancestral forests yielded to the shipwright's saw,
Making ships to carry Drake and many a Devon crew,
Across uncharted seas, to annex an unnamed, distant shore.

Size alone tells us something of your history,
At least three centuries ago the acorn was sown;
To us unknown, the benevolent planter remains a mystery,
Unrecorded, the rustic who could claim you for his own.

I gaze upward through your emerald foliage, musing,
How cryptic is the thread in creation's plan.
One thought resolves from others, confused and confusing;
Compared to such a majestic work, how insignificant is man.
  A. F. Allen

Looking Through My Window

I look through my window and what do I see
God's creation staring at me,
Winter is here, the snow is so clear
The birds are all singing for all to hear.

A rare bird in my garden, at least near the house
A Jay and its mate sit quiet like a mouse,
On top of the bird table as proud as a lark
They give my garden a bit of a spark.

The diddy well, its bucket hanging
I hear a noise, what's all the banging,
A little bird so small and neat
Was in the bucket, but not to sleep.

A little Wren I do believe
Shot out the bucket, quick to leave,
She flew into a nearby tree
Without a thought it seems for me.

The Blue Tits small and hardly seen
Fly about unhindered, so serene,
They fly around checking nest boxes many
But rarely seem to go in any.
  H. G. Smith

Territories Closing, Diminishing World

Rosewood, rich red flanks,
Gleam in the bright morning glow.
Muscles tensed, ripples, flexing limbs,
Ears pricked, wide chocolate eyes.
Ready for the race, a true thoroughbred trembles.

Something moves, a sharp retort,
Could this be it, off in one.
Leaping, bounding, elegant and sure footed,
Startled eyes, focused ahead.
Remember the periphery, competition abounds.

Brash silver grey, threatening danger,
Closing in, it seems, from far and wide.
Confident, prolific, not blue-blooded,
Ancestry untrue you can trace no line
Of this, the foreign impostor.

Nerves of steel, the smaller red,
Carries on relentless, territories closing.
The grey pursues, no time for thoughts,
Of what is now a diminishing world.

From this, the grey, tormenting squirrel.
  Virginia Gibson-Barkess

Bobby

Slim, petite, dark hair bobbed
Giving voice to the nickname Bobby
So many heads turned in the street
To man and boy, the dream bequeathed
She was not, as some might say
A fool in love, must find a way

A million thoughts of her, in a single day
Never a one of anger
The madonna wrapped in mystery
Senses so dulled, once again awaken
Life has few rights, many reasons
Justice makes light of our claims

That slim figure, her dark hair bobbed
Hope, ever painting the spectrum anew
'Tis the way with rainbows
No ending plain to see
Just the distant "Fading"
Of the walkway in the sky
  D. L. Archer

Mindscape

The darkest corners of the mind,
Give rise to deepest despair.
As fate unleashed the demon kind,
To roam far from their lair.

The ghouls and ghosts that serve the night,
They come to trouble our sleep.
Disturb our rest before day's light,
Our souls they try to keep.

Throughout the night the dark holds sway,
And fear rules the mind.
For that unseen, we kneel and pray,
That solace we will find.

Banished back by sun's new light,
They hide away once more.
Until they can renew the fight,
Within the body's core.
Robert Selby

The Working Wife's Nightmare

It's the working wife's nightmare but nobody cares
Get your husband to work, drag the kids down the stairs.
Wash them and dress them while buttering toast
You look in the mirror, you're as pale as a ghost
Then the school bus departs and the silence descends
So you start on your hair, try to hide those split ends.
You get to work late and you sit down to find
That your trusty computer's gone out of its mind.
At lunch you nip out just to shop and pay bills
But the banks are full and there's queues at the tills.
So you wait in the line with your bread and your cake
As you get to the checkout she goes for her break.
After work you go home and you're dead on your feet
And you meet the school bus pouring kids on the street.
One's missing — you ask and you find that there's
Some hijackers holding him hostage upstairs.

After tea you sit back, send the kids up to bed
But your program's been cancelled, there's sport on instead.
Climb in bed, close your eyes, hope it eases the pain
Then the working wife's nightmare starts over again.
T. J. Evison

Nature's Smile

Hazy sunshine and a warming breeze
gently blew around me. I ambled across
the lush green meadow, buttercups and
daisy softly spreading under my footsteps.
The meadow rose steeply uphill pointing
towards the deep blue sky. Reaching the
top of the meadow, I stumbled upon an old
wooden stile. Deciding to linger for a while,
looking back in the distance, I could see a
very busy street, crowds of people. Hot
and tired, rushed off their feet, if only
they would slow down, linger just a while.
Perhaps they could discover and enjoy
nature's charming smile.
D. G. Thompson

The Birth Of Spring

Spring is here bringing fresh joys anew,
Gardens tipped with green in the morning dew.
Buds bursting on branches, the yellow daffodils,
The hope of promise banishes winter chills.

Nature renewing life all around,
Birds chirping merrily, the sounds abound.
No longer branches cold, dark and bare,
But clothed with green in the warm spring air.

What wonderful promise of life bursting forth,
To lift our spirits and give us cheer.
Wonderful spring is shouting I am here! I am here!
Look at me now, soon I shall disappear.
C. E. Atkinson

Redwings

What birds are these,
gardening on the playing fields?

Like large robins, with a thrush's
family jauntiness.

Their beaks snag into the broderie anglaise,
their wings are tipped with red like cycle clips.

Bird-children skating on developing ice,
I envy them their winter fun

And could cry 'Havoc' and let my setter loose
on one of his teeth-baring runs.

Remember the day of your father's funeral.
You saw a hawk, so adventitious,

And thought it was your father's ghost,
an omen or the emperor's Roman eagle.

When I die, let redwings do the offices,
summer gules on winter's dun livery.
Michael Henry

Untitled

I like the thrill of a rocking horse canter,
Galloping quickly away;
I could ride forever on my horse Prancer,
On a sunny May day.

The steady rock of my horse,
Is really definite and certain
When galloping over a race course,
When the wind blows out her mane.

With no effort at all,
We breeze along
Past the trees which are ten feet tall,
Racing the wind so strong.

Dodging rocks and trees as we go,
Jumping logs and streams too,
Now you can't say Prancer is slow,
Because she could surely outrun you.

As we gallop along,
All the trees are a blur,
Her feet hit the floor just like a gong,
And I know I can trust her.
Rebecca Higgs

The Song Of The Dawn

The scent of the morning peace
Hangs softly in the air,
Combined with the fragrance of fruit-trees,
Apple-blossom and pear.

The bottle-green grass
Shivers in the caress of the breeze,
While the early sun shines
Down on the whispering trees.

The exquisite and charming robin,
Who has a crimson breast,
Awakes from her peaceful slumber,
And sings with joy and zest.

Diadems of dew-drops
Adorn the satiny rose.
They are torn away by the laughing wind,
Who dances wherever he goes.

But gradually the sun climbs up,
The Day is here at last.
The trouble with the dawn is that
It goes so very fast.
Sarah Watton

Incarnation

I shall awake from barren sleep with dreams of death and
   fruitless gain,
Entombed in wasteland, cold as night, my promises I'll keep.
No frosty chains can hold me down, nor concrete coat of
   welded snow,
This heart of mine still beats within, too long I've been alone.

My aching limbs, so sore to touch, dry parchment face devoid
   of form,
I fight against the kiss of time, to die is just too much.
There stirs within my seeded womb, kept warm and fed by
   nature's life,
The promise of a better time to beat against my tomb.

The shroud of death is rent in two, the pain of birth composed
   its dirge,
A season's babe now gasps for air, and hands reach out anew.
My child's the song the elements sing with colour, warmth,
   sweet perfumed breath,
The joy that slept, awakes, bursts forth; this incarnation, Spring.
   Roy Bricknell

At Heavens Gates

When the referee came to the gate.
Gabriel stopped him and made him wait.
"What especially brave thing
Can you tell me you did?"
"I disallowed a goal
So Scotland lost it."
Gabriel checked his computer.
"I can't see it here, when was that then ref.
Maybe last year?"
The ref. looked at his watch and said:
"Oh dear me no. It was only I think just
5 minutes ago."
   Marja Goodwin

The Blitz

Panic, screaming everywhere,
Fumes and burning fill the air.
Aeroplanes always bombing the streets,
The German, Hitler and his fleets.

The smell of gas, death and fear,
Yes, it's true, the blitz is here.
Firing, yelling, crying, bombing,
Oh when will it end? I'm always longing.

"There goes my house,
Crackling away,
Those nasty Germans,
They are going to pay".

It doesn't end,
It's not going to stop,
I want to escape, forget the lot.

All those colours,
All those smells,
All I hear is shrieking yells.
   Natalie Luckham

Lottery Blues

O woe is me — such strife
Go quick — go hide the kitchen knife
   Gloom doom doom gloom
      Go open up the family tomb
After checking all tickets I almost wept
My guiding star must have overslept
Like an addict craving his drug
I feel as low as a garden slug
   Zim zam zoom gloom doom
      Go open up the family tomb
To fulfil my dream would be nice
To own a diamond full of fire... yet cold as ice
   No — no — wait, tomorrow is another day
      I'll get new numbers and play, play, play
   M. A. Teece

Blue Windflowers In A Hampshire Wood

Blue for the colour of the virgin's gown,
Full open petals in the April sun
That underline the gift God gave us
When he sent His only son
As sacrifice.

We were not good enough to hang
Upon the cross He had to bear,
For we, the thieves that hung with Him,
Were quite unfit to share the blue of Heaven.

We may have been through centuries
The sons of those beside Him then,
But thanks to Him at Easter time
Our downcast eyes can see some tint of Heaven's blue
Reflected in the eyes of men
From April flowers.

So praised be God for sky,
For virgin's gown, and blue anemones
That stand as hope for modern sons of thieves
Among the lately coppiced hazel wands
Beneath the trees.
   Patrick Gordon Duff-Pennington

Now Called Butterfly

I hear you,
Fulfil my appetite with generous words,
My senses are hungry.
I shall not judge, feel free,
Speak your heart's truths,
Tell tales of conquests and desires,
I hear you, speak on.

I look at you,
My eyes absorb your glory
As I behold your new form,
Radiant and magnificent
You emerge from the cobwebs
of the darkened past.

Awake, awake, reach tall,
Grasping breaths of life,
Simmering, readily awaiting
Your destiny
The journey has commenced,
Go forth now, fear nothing.

You are once born. Live.
   Melanie Wingfield

An Artist's Palette

With the gentlest brush stroke He splashes a peach pink blush
His tenderest touch paints a rosebud mouth

Soft blonde curls formed from His mixing of Gold and Brown
Damp like early morning Dew framing His picture
His ivory base complimented by thick dark lashes

Softly she stirs, she wakes, eyes now opened, shining cerulean blue
The rosebud opens, it folds gently back with a heaven sent sigh
Now appears the dusky pink, soft sweet tongue with six tiny
pearls adjacent

Like a race to capture the essence of an ever changing sunrise on a
Winter's morn His paint brush flashes, now darting
That sunbeam smile brightens all around

His palette has created more than a mere image, it has created Life
and it has created music

For as her smile widens, her eyes flash, full of innocent
wonder and unconditional love

She speaks .... "Mummy".
   Nicolle Cowles

Remembering

Holly Berries, Mistletoe,
Frost that made our faces glow.
Tiny toes and fingers tingled,
Bells that rang and bells that jingled.
Carols that were songs of praise.
The turkey lasted days and days.
Old folks sitting by the fire,
Listening to a children's choir.
All the family gathered there,
Father in his favourite chair.
Prayers that ended in Amen,
Peace on earth goodwill to men.
Greeting people with a smile
Seemed to make it all worthwhile.
Alas, those days just did not last
For that my friend was Christmas past

G. Silgram

Noise

Do you hear, do you hear, a mist on the mountain
From which comes the great waterfall
a small sound, only slight, from a primrose unfolding
or the ivy that crumbles a wall

In the night, listen now, small waves on the seashore
are turning rough boulders to sand
'Tis not noise, not just din, that
　makes great things happen
does a thunderbolt create new land

Be you quiet, be you still, O you
　child of the space age
And listen as never before
lest you drown, lest you stifle
the quiet sounds of your world
and are able to hear them no more

Pat Sperring

'Waking For Work At Five In The Morning'

When, soundly disconnected
From thoughts of tomorrow's trials and tortures,
when, buried beneath
the safely insulated citadel of blankets
reigning, peacefully unconscious in a kingdom of respite,

When, eyes are torn open
to the visage of cracked ceiling,
Flaking wallpaper,
the odorous stains of a working house,

When, yawning and scratching subside
and legs must leave
the carefully cultivated mattress warmth
to gingerly step within the day's maze,

The shrill stinging ringing
Of a tenacious clock
is no welcome siren
to slight slumber
and rudely rouses reluctant ears.

Seamus O'Hare

She Dances Like A Daydream

Shining with emerald.
From the trees she came.
Stepping out into the daylight.
While the sun tried to shine the same.
She radiated a nectar of sweet soundless music
That danced lovingly with the breeze.
A dazzling sunshower of diamonds appeared
A cloud had gone weak at the knees
Perfection hungrily clutched at her body
Beauty laid claim to her face.
As she danced just like a daydream
My emotions won the race.

Paul Tristram

Farmer's Working Days

A farmer's work is never done
From the rising to the set of sun
Ploughing harrowing the field
To produce at harvest a bountiful yield

Milking cows and tending the young
Making silage and spreading dung
Hedges trimmed, and livestock fed
Threshing wheat for our daily bread

He takes a break in the mid-day heat
To renew his strength, and a bite to eat
Duty Calls — and he's off with his dog
Through the meadows, to gather the flock

As the sun sinks in the West
He sets off home, for some quiet rest
His family gather at eventide
Listening to stories by their father's side

J. M. Luck

Special Delivery

By pilot-boat they came,
From the home-port of Tyne.

In the roads at midday our vessel lay,
Eyes intent towards the pierheads gazed.
Familiar launch — 'Hadrian' — a bone in her teeth
Brought a smile; She's on her way!

A waving hand, small behind the windshield's glare
Made certain the hope; She is there!

Upstretched hands from the heaving deck
Raised the token, as eyes met
And understood.
In plastic bag, with 'papers for the crew,
The floral blooms gave their message clear.

'I wanted to bring you something
You don't see on ships...'

Fresh flowers now the cabin grace,
In the shaving glass — the only place.
A gift of home, from Home.

T. J. Boult

Ghost

The letter. A memory like light peeps
from the blue envelope. Your lost voice speaks:
A regular echo from the page like
The thudding of soil on wood. The clouds burst.
Raindrops were the bullets you fired to pierce
my guard. Now tender, the water is your
presence rushing through me; I start to drown.
Memories form dreams of you. These dreams are
addictive diseases I run to catch.
My hand grips your letter: I still hold you,
but you are only words. Your ink is smudged.
You engulf my presence. Tears blur my
vision. I read no more. You hurt, but I'd
swim in your rippling soul forever.

Nadine Pittam

Red

Red as a colour, it's plain to see,
Has many uses for you and me,
Traffic lights, pillar boxes all use red,
If you ignore red signs you could end up dead.

Scarlet and crimson, it's sometimes said,
Make red a colour to fear and dread,
But our queen sleeps well at night in bed,
Knowing she's protected by soldiers in red.

Mars is a planet that's known as red,
And it's for sure and must be said,
If Martians came, would they be red?
Or orange, or purple, or green instead?

K. Maloy

The Diaries

Because I've read your diaries through,
From the beginning to the end,
I feel nostalgia for the past,
They brought back memories now grown dim,
Of how you pampered every whim.

You brought me flowers, cleaned my shoes,
Sat by my bed when I was ill,
You were so thoughtful, I recall,
Comforted me in times of sorrow
Until it seemed a bright to-morrow.

When we were parted, long ago,
You wrote me letters by the score,
Spoke of your dying love for me,
You were so lonely, husband dear,
For we'd been married not a year!

Though you've passed on, I feel you're near,
And if I could lead my life again,
I'd strive to be a better wife,
You loved but me, I know it's true,
Because I've read your diaries through.
Olive E. Leavold

Mandala

Life is a circle containing a cross within
From cradle to grave we have decisions to make
Travelling the long and weary road
Until we reach the next intersection
Be still. Consider what has gone before
And what yet lies in the womb of time
Journeying onwards knowing life is a game of consequences
Paying the price or receiving the benefits
Sometimes becoming entangled in our confusion
With each mile comes knowledge and understanding

Observe a weed, how resilient it is
Whether trod on, run over or cut down
It is not deterred
Rising again, standing tall, defiant and proud
Gardeners are ashamed of them, but still they grow
We should learn from this, suicide is no way out
When the circle of life is complete
The cross is our final tribute
Whether rich or poor, we end up equal
Lying in God's acre
Marie Musleh

Passing Temptations (1983-1993)

I glance over his face
forced into focus in a semi-blurred landscape

Strong brow, lickable jaws, full mouth, warm, out-going eyes
crowned by touch-me hair

And my throat swells, my breast blossoms and yearns
and my groin draws

But the pain in my heart
cardboard, cruel memory
that fills my throat with tears stuffed back, refused, denied
Echoes bad memories, in my head of reason

Though his hard thighs
agile limbs and taut buttocks
promise me much

My head of reason
reminds me of the promise
of ragged shreds of heart
that his personality will definitely
tear from me, with many uncertain fears

And my glance moves on
Ramona Sterling

Oblivion

I met him in a turmoil of confused thoughts.
From a doctor's lips he introduced himself.
This threatening stranger intruding into my world
Where I'd set no place for him.

His was the knock in the middle of the night,
The persistent salesman's foot in the open door.
"Close your eyes, he'll go away"
But my pained body denied this exorcism.

I came to accept his constant presence,
Unobtrusive by day, but close to me at night
Whispering gentle promises of peace
If only I would take his hand in mine.

He courted me with dreams of bygone days,
He freed my mind to wander distant hills
And when his soft seduction was complete,
I changed my name to his — Oblivion.
Then I knew no more.
R. Somerville

Youthful Freedom

There so helpless, alone so free
free sounds so good to you and to me
but loneliness and freedom
is too much to handle
especially when you're young
and have no light for your candle

There young so fragile
a feather breaks their heart
if they were to fly away
away would be too far
they can't even stand they can't use their head
but they do have feelings and use these instead

There lives are getting shorter
but still a long way to go
the days are going far too slow
there young but old
they need warmth not cold
but there helpless and free
nothing like me
Rachel Amanda Jones

Tree

Tree, oh
How amicable you are,
What a nice woody
self-supporting main stem you have,
Your branches expeditiously diverge,
deviate, oscillate and undulate
in the cool breeze,
Oh, I love your pompous leaves,
How seductively you drop em
and bear your embarrassment throughout
the cold winter,
Gallantly your roots rape and pilfer
the soil's nutrients,
How insolent your condescending heights make me feel,
Am I barking up the wrong tree?...
Mark Raybould

Our Winter Wonders

Snow has whitewashed all the ground,
Footsteps create a creaking sound.
Children catch snowflakes on their tongues
And rosie cheeks rush home to us Mums.
Sit by the fire and warm to a glow,
It's exhausting work to play in the snow.
Remember the fun and cherish the games,
To have to grow up is such a shame.
Wanda Monks

Jamie

Two little faces staring out, looking for trouble, of that there's
no doubt, found an innocent baby lad, who'd never been
naughty, never been bad.
They battered his body, tortured his mind, were cruel, evil,
impassive, unkind, eventually murdered by the two faces, left
in cold unfamiliar places.

Okay, now he's gone to a better place, with no pain on his
angelic face, but long before his time was up, and so overfills
our bloody cup.
So who is to blame for this wicked deed, this vile plan, how
did it succeed?
Which one of you turned so blind an eye? There were so
many passersby.

Now those two little faces as guilty as hell, who tales on each
other did tell, was it all a game which went so wrong, ending
little Jamie's song?
Yes, we can jeer and shout the blame, for it hides our own
immoral shame.
A world in which we ignore each other, and let the innocent
people suffer.

So sleep in peace little child, whose life has been so cruelly
defiled.
Gone — Yes — but not forgotten — You've left behind a
world that is rotten.

Tracy Green

Harold And William

Harold of England, brave man was he,
Fought all the Normans so gallantly,
Fought them at Hastings, close by the coast,
Said to his soldiers 'Fear not the host'.
The bowmen of William, hundreds were there,
Fired all their arrows up in the air.
Under the onslaught, Harold's men began to die.
He looked up himself — and caught an arrow in his eye.
'I cannot see now,' to his men he said,
'You must fight on though, even when I'm dead.
The battle must be fought exactly as I planned,
They must never capture our fair and lovely land.
Men, I beseech thee, strive main and might.'
But when he died, they soon gave up the fight.
William, he conquered — oh, what a wrench,
Some of us here are descended from the French.
Had the Normans landed further to the west,
Harold and his men would still have done their best,
They may have lost the fight, 'tis true, success exactly nil,
But William the Conqueror would be known as Portland Bill.

Terence W. Leat

The X-Perience (On Being Twenty Something)

Well the dawning of our generation pales into the night,
foundering on potholes that our parents left behind;
grafting us to values they once Loved against as Lies;
we spend our days rebelling from their own rebellious times.

Well the dawning of our generation's not like that before,
as those we call Our Fathers fought the jungle Commie war.
And who knows of the brothers we may have of Saigon whores?
But the Commies are our brothers now, and the jungles are our cause.

Well the dawning of our generation's not quite in control —
too slightly left of centre, of too radical a whole.
Conservatives strive endless for their partnerships and condos;
and no one left reads poetry, and fewer still write poems.

Well the dawning of our generation's here for all to see:
We came of age, attempted change, then crawled away to bleed.
Traditions built by ages don't fall easily it seems —
Perhaps we're a direction, not The Way that we perceived.

Well the dawning of our generation's not that grand a sight;
as once again we sit and watch the Boomers lose a fight.
But the stars over Sarajevo are the same as in my night,
but there's bare enough for us to read — what hope for
wisdom's light?

Simon Paterson

" A Breast-Fed Baby "

Do feed your baby on the breast,
For you will find, it is the best,
Your babe will thrive and be so good,
When it is getting nature's food.

The milk is clean, the heat just right,
but don't forget, no feeds through night,
If babe can't sleep the whole night through,
give cooled, boiled water — that will do.

You'll find your mind won't be at ease,
when some poor child has a disease,
don't worry if your child's breast-fed,
for they escape it — so it's said.

They know their mums, and love them too,
their smiling eyes prove this to you
do feed your baby on the breast,
for breast-fed babies are the best.

Sadie Dixon

Life's Mystery And Love

In life it was once said that it is never too late to try,
for to try is human and human is love.

Could it work, a great question of both Scientists and Poets,
the only way to find out is to try.

A love lost is a tragic thing,
it haunts one for all one's days.

But even though the Ghosts of life haunt us daily,
being human means we keep trying.

If there is doubt no matter how very small,
if there is hope no matter how very small,

To be human means we will try,
and tame that beast called love.

Robert Martin

Human Child

Don't play with the Gradys, Child,
For they're crawling.
The mother's a slut. The father a drunk.
The boodies they harbour are monsters.
Don't play with the Gradys, Child,
Don't play.

I'll play with the Gradys, Ma,
I'll play.
For they reek of the coals, the wilds and the bogs
and they speak in the talk of the traveller.
I'll play with the Gradys, Ma,
I'll play.
When you're not looking, Ma,
I'll play.

Yvonne Roche-Harth

A Castle In The Air

These walls were once strong,
For they had once been loved.
Time, nor sea, could corrode these walls.
With foundations set firm on earth,
Its turrets caressed the sky.
And when the seasons came and went,
Laughter echoed from these hallowed halls.

Now with turrets bare to sky,
The seasons stab at mortar,
Oh! How these once strong walls,
Without their shining knights have crumbled.
Now no-one walks within its garden,
And a sigh, such a mournful sigh
Can be heard by those who would listen.
But none will listen now,
Nor see what once stood here.
No children will play within my shade.

Roy C. Henderson

Caught With Fright!

I walked into the room and immediately froze,
For there he lurked in the dark shadows.
My heart skipped a beat and my stomach churned,
And it was my husband's presence for which I now yearned.
I could hear the steady ticking of the clock,
But I was still motionless in a state of shock.
I was certain now that he could see me,
Perhaps wondering if I would let him go free.
I took a step backwards towards the door,
My feet like leaden weights against the floor.
When suddenly he moved ever so slightly,
Which made my muscles tense more tightly.
I realised it was time to take heed of my senses,
And begin to think of my best defences.
So I dared to take a sideways look,
Whereupon I caught sight of an old heavy book.
In one swift movement I grabbed at it,
And with my face now quite alit,
I raised my arm as my eyes became wider,
Then... BANG... I squashed that big black spider!

Paula Gilbey

Ode To A Fallen Tree

A tree, in which the magpies sat,
For them a shady habitat.
For me, a bit of greenery,
To beautify the scenery.

Then one day the wind blew strong,
Its gusts went on for far too long.
The tree, grown now to such great height,
Crashed down to earth with all its might.

The magpies found a new abode,
And I can see right up the road.
But footpaths, rooftops, can't compare,
Without the tree it just looks - BARE.

Renee D. Radcliffe

The Gentle Breeze Of Summer

Even the sun can't outshine your beauty
For the shadow you cast is blessed
And the earth to which it lends itself
Is a home free for angels to rest
And how the stars your eyes do envy
As life your smile has always done
Yes you're the gentle breeze of summer
Every fragrant flower, and yet none

You're an emotion so far beyond words
Your presence a dream to be lived in
You're a fire whose taste is to touch
A million stories of stars never-ending
So much more than a mere Maud Gonne
So much more it's just too hard to say
Yes you're the gentle breeze of summer
The wonder of an everlasting day.

Tony Sullivan

Coniston Water

Through beautiful woodland to an open field,
Grey stone walls bare hands had to build,
Down to the lake crystal clear,
And Old Man of Coniston towering near.
Its dark peaks reaching up to the sky,
Brushed by the clouds as they pass by,
Standing here in the evening sun,
Seeing newborn calves having fun,
And colourful sailboats starting a race.
It's hard to believe this tranquil place
Was once the scene of a tragic fate,
When man and metal challenged the lake.
And when the metal failed the test,
The lake became man's place of rest.

Pat Lambourne

Ode To A Lady

Oh, please dear lady, do not give up.
For others mistakes please don't pay.
I know you've been ill for some time now,
But you cannot just dwindle away.

There are a few of us that find it disgusting,
What they've done to you for profit and greed.
Please don't give up the fight for your life,
Because a few of us still love you and know it's you that we need.

Gather your strength together.
A few will help you get well.
Then together when you are back on your feet,
We will banish the rest to hell.

You can sparkle with beauty again my dear lady.
You've the strength but have you the will?
If you haven't I can't say I blame you.
Do they realize who they've nearly killed?

As you lie there and fight for all you're worth,
I will help you as much as I can,
For I know if you die dear Mother Earth,
Then so will the whole of man.

S. C. Kennedy

" Growing Old "

I know that I am growing old
For my feet they really feel the cold
At night in bed the cramp I get
In my legs my back and also my neck
My bones they certainly do stick out
And I'm growing thinner there's no doubt
The gardening's getting too much for me
I've hardly the strength to go to pee

I see my hair is thinning on the top
And it's mostly silver threads I've got
My teeth have nearly all come out
And my hearing's so bad you have to shout
My eyes run when the wind blows cold
Ah well - these are the signs of growing old
But apart from all this my heart's quite strong
So if you like me to I'll sing you a song
For I'm happy when each new day comes around
Well there's lots to be thankful for I've found.

P. E. Salmon

First Touch, New Love

My journey now is almost o'er. This puffing train will puff no more for me at least. I have come home. No longer have I need to roam.

Gazing through the window pane, on this puffing jolting train, I see the stations whizzing by, as onward to my love I fly.

Pennsylvania, Ohio too. Indiana, on right through.
Illinois, Missouri, Kansas City flies past me.

Colorado, there we climb. Majestic mountains, train takes time.
Oh! Hurry train, please don't be late, on this my first important date.

Wonder what she will be wearing? Recognize her? Hell! Stop staring!
Only seen her photograph. Makes me cry, but want to laugh.

Emotions strange within my soul. Heart itself doth take its toll.
Legs feel weak. Head unclear. Keep your cool she's very near.

Utah next, and then Nevada. This is the state, not much farther.
Reno! Reno! Here it comes. Jeeze! My mouth feels full of plums.

Tongue is tied and legs like jelly. Got the cramps within my belly.
Don't be shy. Must be brave. Oh! There she is. Now just you wave.

Hi! Roxanne! Shout it loud. Now she sees you through the crowd.
Can't get to her soon enough. Now's the time for charming stuff.

Face to face, and very close. Stretch out hand. Put on pose.
Smile through tears and grip her tight. Very first touch. Now all is right.

T. Eccleston

Kismet

Where there is love, there is devotion,
For love is poetry in motion,
Total love, it's there to be found,
Is to experience, walking on enchanted ground.
Such a love began, in War-Time Ryde,
When at a distance I espied,
A vision of beauty, so fair of face,
The sight of which caused my heart to race.
This meeting, which appeared by chance,
Became the start of our romance.

It is my belief, I am bound to say,
That we were destined to meet this way,
The love we share has never wavered,
Life to the full, we both have savoured.
And now to the end of my well-spent life,
I know that my fate is bound up with my wife,
Not just on Earth, for a few years or more,
But throughout eternity, forevermore.

A. E. Lock

" A Warrior's Prayer "

So much to remember, let alone write,
for just one life.
How can I hope to recall a past life
spent, when I cannot remember why I've
been sent.

What purpose this short life
what should I know or what path should
I follow.
What help can I give, indeed sometimes I
question why I should live.

My life seems pointless and is hard to
bear, I'm so lost at times and often
despair.

I do not want another life until
I've learned to live this one right.

Perhaps I never will, but some force
within me tells me I should try even
up to the very second when I die.

S. Hallard

The Assassination Of Physic's Companion

to Steven Weinberg

(Nobel laureate in physics, who believes Metaphysics is dead)

Metaphysics trod time's highway, gazing to the Heavens,
for endless years a worshipped idol, oracle of men.
Then one day his ear caught Physic's gay and forthright song.
"Let's step together," Meta pressed, "and help each other along."
And gave to Physic as a sign, a casket for his gems.

Smooth the path till Physic came of age, as Modern Science,
and smarting, suffering wrongs and pain, he cast his friend aside.
"Charlatan, you're less than nought, you've lied and slandered me,
Religion too, what harm you've wrought." And with a might sweep
he threw his net o'er Heaven's domain — now his. Yet with
  this triumph,

alarmed and fearing, Physic traced his foe's continued power.
And so one chosen night he chased him up a creaking tower
"to squint into the past," he gushed, "my very latest art."
And with this trick he turned and thrust his hate through
  Meta's heart
and flung him to remotest space. But from his wounds spilled
down magic potions, kinds of lotions, charts and wizardry,
signs and tokens, curious notions, tables that foresee.
But Physic held his casket up: "Come see my wares," he said,
"my cryohope and isotopes and moonwalks and the Net."
But Web-ensnared his chest stayed closed — for Meta held
  the key.

Susan Biggin

At Peace From A Thousand Thoughts

This world known as reality has no meaning for me,
For I am a peach encaptured in moss.
The boundaries in which you perceive
Can only result in my loss.

A shadow of smoke from burning embers,
Means nothing to those who I seek.
And this is the guidance I live by.
Experience proves they are weak.

As for the question, in love?
Turmoil of self pity and hatred surpass,
An emotion so strong it deserves recognition.
A fear I have yet to grasp.

Because I am in love forever,
And pain is remembered each breath,
For I dare not to ask myself, why.
The Conclusion To That Is Through Death.

CKLE

Untitled

Mum, I wish to demonstrate to you appreciation.
For every moment of my life, you've given dedication.
You carried me and kept me warm, fed me strength to grow.
Defending and protecting me from all injurious foe.
Committed to your parenthood, attending with devotion.
A thoughtful mind and gentle hand, aiding with my emotion.
You gave compassion tenderly and raised me up with care.
And every trouble that I had, diminished, you did share.
Righteously you understand, so generous with forgiving.
I'm blessed with you, you sacrificed, to make my life worth living.

Sarah Burley

An Englishman Abroad

Father set sail for France one day,
For a quarter of nugget, and I've francs to pay,
"Nougât, mais oui" smiled the vendor and bowed,
"No, nugget", said father and he grimly frowned,
"Nugget I want — that's it just there"
"Nougât" said the Frenchman with a patronising air,
The Frenchman nodded and held out his wares,
"Nugget" said father, with a frosty stare,
His colour was rising, and so was his voice,
"Nugget, I said, and that is my choice,"
With outstretched hands, the Frenchman smiled,
That was the gesture that drove father wild,
"Nugget or nougât, I'll not have it at all,
I can buy it much cheaper on our market stall",
"So I'll bid you good day, and I'll not come back,
Just you learn to speak English, or you'll soon get the sack!"

J. Gant

Work

People think, oh no it's Monday,
Getting up early unlike on a Sunday,
getting up and out of bed,
It's very cold wishing it was warm instead,
going to work feeling very sleepy,
Walking about in the dark, it's very creepy,
Through the car park and up to the door,
what lies ahead you just can't be sure,
You're sitting there doing your job,
It's better than hanging about being a yob,
Tuesday, Wednesday, Thursday goes by,
It's Friday tomorrow my oh my,
Fridays arrive and you think it's great,
You can go out at night and come in late,
the weekend's ahead and there's lots in store,
It's time to party and lots lots more,
The weekend time soon flies by,
It's back to work with a great big sigh,
It all boils down to one true pact,
you need the money and that's a fact.

C. Green

Freedom For Foodies

It's very hard to diet, when everywhere I go
food is in abundance
it's very hard you know.
To browse along the Deli when you haven't had your lunch
so you open up the crispies and have a little munch.
Just look at all those savories
(sweet stuff leaves me cold)
except a malted milk at night, I must be getting old!
A plate of ham, cut off the bone, with crusty bread and cheese,
some pickle and a glass of wine
I'm not too hard to please.
I'll leave the lettuce to the folk who find the need more pressing
to fight the battle of the bulge without good oily dressing.
I'll use the yoghurt for a sauce, to compliment my pasta
that's tossed in garlic butter — parmesan is added after.
I'm better now that I've confessed about the way I feel
so I'm off to have sherry, before my evening meal.
Rosemary Hayward

My Darling Daughter

Oh, why did you go, so far away,
Flying across the sea on that sunny day
A new life you are seeking on far distant shores
My best wishes go with you for you and yours.
I sent you off with a smile and a wave
Although my heart was breaking I tried to be brave.
I gave you wings to fly away with
The hope that you will return, one day.
Maureen Lamb

Dream Trip. Love's A Drug?

Is love a drug? I ask as I slurp the dregs from my whisky
flask. Caught off her guard, a shrug, a mutter. My legs of lard.
You nutter, you're off your hinge. She ruined my ballad about
my trip into the gutter, stuck in the syringe. It made me cringe
on my final flip. A Bard on the binge. Stinking steam clouds
oozed from bubbling Mexican mud. Daylight, now hazy,
coloured in purple heart and Acapulco gold. Choking,
gasping and grasping, a sniffing and snorting stud, cavorting
in a Reefer. So bold. So old. So cold. Ecstasy speeds on,
chasing the dragon and making hash of magic mushrooms and
cold turkey from the cache.

Must dash. More cash. Lying on the grass, supping from a
pot of coke, the tragic heroin puffing tootsie roll, cracked a
joke. No point. Some joint. Withdrawal symptoms of a kind.
Hallucinations. Out of mind. Freaks out, no doubt. And then
my dream and tempo changed. Drugs had left me dis-ar-
ranged. Soliloquizing thus, maiden in floating petticoat or
sarong, consciously unconscious came along, on a wing,
delightfully laden. My antidote. Sensations, symbols and
dreams. Tools to unlock heart strings. Drool over wonderful
things. And Rings. That's the door bell. Oh Hell! He's
rocking the boat. Don't gloat. It's that man in a white coat.
S. G. Brian Clay

Clothes Don't Maketh The Man

I've met all sorts in my life
Good, bad, dull, sometimes bright,
But the clothes they wear never give a clue
As to what they are, only what they do,
Some wear tuxedo and look very fine
Study their character, they really don't shine,
They put on an act "Oh la de da"
And drive around in a great big car,
I've also met men, who use shovel and spade
Who wear woolly hats, their wives have made,
Some would help you if they could
Some really don't see why they should,
So all in all at the end of the day
It's not what you wear, or the size of your pay,
It's what's there inside
Not the make of your car
That makes you the man you really are
P. A. Lowe

Comfort In A Coal Fire

Coal scuttle's full upon the hearth
Flames winding up the chimney
Logs piled up high to stoke it with;
In winter, what a wonderful sight to see.

Glowing and warming, comforting too
After reaching its crescendo, once lit
There's not many a sight emitting such peace and calm
To the sofa or chair where I sit.

Moments stolen, as I sit all alone
Relishing the time to myself,
Shadows dance around the room
Bouncing off ornaments on the shelf.

Gazing deep and long into its core
I drift and I dream, and I stare
Creating pictures and countless images
Around me; what goes on, I don't care.

In time, but slowly, its mass dies down
Its heat turns to a glow,
Taking care to check the fire guard's up
Then wearily up to bed I go.
Susan Merrifield

Trees In The Wind

Tossing and waving to and fro
First to the left then the right,
Branches of trees in the wind do blow
Casting shadows in the half light.
Of the darkening day, as evening draws in
And night begins to fall,
Then imagination comes alive
The shadows make figures tall
Figures of demons, hobgoblins, witches,
As they sway in the wind a'moan:
Look — there's a fox, see how his tail twitches,
There's another, he's not alone.
There's a bird, there's a fish, a giant or two,
As those branches bend and sway:
Why here comes a ship with all its crew
Majestically sailing away.
Wondrous pictures before one unfold
Passing as dreams for the eyes
Yes, trees in the wind bring marvels untold
Each one a greater surprise.
N. Soppitt

Destiny

Weep, oh weep my soul,
for the child that was never born,
the child that you never wanted
then suddenly you did.

What was the morning of enlightenment?
That blinding flash of rapture,
of encompassing,
in the arms of a total love.

All encompassing, all fulfilling,
that seemed so complete.
Seven summers of rapture,
then sudden death.

And into that black ravine
flew the hidden child of your hidden desires.
The child you never knew you wanted,
until then.

And what now, oh my soul?
Hope beyond hope, endless naivete.
Irreplaceable joy.
Irreplaceable motherhood.
M. Ellis

Fred And Jupiter 1981

When Jupiter from 'Voyager' seen
First flashed upon Fred's TV screen
Fred gazed amazed and scratched his head.
"It's bloody marvellous," he said.
An unromantic soul was Fred,
And scarce profound was what he said,
But as in reverence he swore,
He opened wide a magic door
Upon the mystery of space,
And glory bathed his homely face

I didn't get a chance just then
To talk about it all. Too late!
For Fred has now passed on, and gone
In wonder through the golden gate.
I see him, gorged on heavenly pie
Winging his way across the sky,
Beaming at stars as he passes by.
Perhaps I'll join him when I die.

E. S. Howarth

Reality of War

A sniper crouches behind a wall
Fires a bullet — his victim falls
Death triumphant, bullet and gun

Symbol of war, bomb, bullet and gun
Devastation of city, town, and village
Slaughter, torture, rape and pillage
Green grass in meadow turning red
Soaked with life blood of the dead
Broken bones, pungent flesh around
Feasts for vermin and vultures abound
Death triumphant — bomb, bullet, and gun.

Symbol of peace, symbol of love
Olive branch, cooing dove
Sky above, song of the lark
Soldier sits on a bench in the park
Noise of children happily playing
Far off sound of dogs baying
Chirping birds in trees nearby
Soldier wonders with a sigh, oh why! oh why!
Right to live, not to die.

Richard Lloyd

Running For Pleasure?

A nervous glance around the corner,
Fingers crossed, excited now
She sees him running on the pavement,
Notices his furrowed brow...
His pace has slowed, his breath is laboured,
He bends a little, drops his head
She wants to give him all her courage.
Do his running, but she can't. Instead
She watches from her wheelchair, smiling,
Doing all she can to urge him on.
She sighs with relief as her Husband passes,
Now he's finished the Marathon!

Gillian Fogg

Untitled

I lie here dozing but my soul soars free,
Floating above me, lost in time and space.
Why am I here? What cause can there be?
Am I just another part of the human race.
If a race we be, then what is our goal?
People as far as the eye can see,
Millions of bodies, but what of our soul,
Are any on the point of discovery.
Perhaps as I age, my purpose will become clear,
I must make my mark to leave behind.
Something to show that while I was here,
I made something better for all of mankind.

S. C. Marsters

Old Acquaintance

Beeches tower the pathway to panacea, with outstretched
boughs fingering the sky,
Resounding secrets whisper through the breeze, centuries of
pilgrims utter, chased away,
Dedications to love, reflect in coloured glass, pastoral
obligations clear,
Flowers trodden, pashed by unknown crusaders,
seeking redemption,
Through the lych gate, consciences clear,
An old acquaintance awaits earth's acquittal.

D. L. Brown

The Coming Of Winter, St. Paul's Jarrow

Centre of learning, spiritual writing,
Festival year for you.
Great new improvements in your surroundings
Bring pilgrims and visitors too.

Benches to rest on; arbours for roses;
Graceful lamp standards; young trees;
Healthy herb garden colourful, scented,
Humming and buzzing with bees.

Winter approaches, leaves form a carpet,
Soft the path to the door,
Stark and forbidding yet beckoning, warm,
'The message' will always endure.

How we revere you venerable building,
Prayer and reflection inspired,
Braving all weathers, pillage and conflict
Your presence is ever desired.

M. E. Morton

Ireland

Ireland, beautiful land of dreams
Full of beauty, full of woe
Never again shall I see your hills
moonlit shores, or lovely streams.

You were never meant to be free
To much poverty, too much misery
I know now why there is so much rain
rain, and oh such pain.

I think the heavens are crying for you
Clouds of tears that freely flow
How I wish soon that God in his love
will reach out to your terrible plight from above.

Turn off your misery, turn off your pain
Let some light shine in there once again

Sarah Cramp

Brick Wall

'I have become a brick wall'
For, is it not for me to choose
What weapon I should use
Against the barbed sword of words
That others deem to inflect
To boost their own esteem, morale,
Who, being in their narrow world
Insist, there is no other interest to pursue
But theirs, and should you dare exceed
The rule, do what you would
Even venture a verbal opinion.
Expect retaliation, to crush, subdue, any
Form of enthusiasm that might outshine
Beyond their narrow world, their status
It is not my nature to fire verbal darts
Rather show an example, encourage potential
Be pleasant and kind, enjoy life, smile,
So that is why in the firing line
Of verbal ammunition whoever from
I have decided I am a brick wall.'

Mary Hunter

The River Trent

Like a great brown serpent searching for prey
The River Trent winds on her way,
A great brown snake through browns and greens
Fed by water from a thousands streams,
Looking lean at times, till gorged by the tide,
Then, a great sluggish monster with nowhere to hide
So eager to help any poor suicides
Who enter her depths, their faces to hide.
Ruthless, cruel, cold, so deep,
How many ride her tides in death's dark sleep?
For what is hers she will keep, a secret guarded,
'Till tired of playing, on mudbanks discarded,
Her toys she leaves, rotting, soiled.
An armada of craft on her great back ride
At the beck and call of her surging tide.
Listen her evil chuckle, smell her fetid breath,
Rotting vegetation, filth, decay, and death
As like a great brown serpent searching for prey
The River Trent winds on her way.

Geoffrey W. Pell

The Road To Heaven

The road to heaven is tortuous,
The road to heaven is long,
The road to heaven is the one true light,
Where right suppresses wrong.

But there are many roads to heaven,
(Not all roads lead to Rome),
Some tread that path in search of power,
While others seek a spiritual home.

In life you must take many roads,
But always note the signposts back,
In case the way you choose,
Is just another cul-de-sac.

Frank McKeown

Into The Depths Of Death

From the hillside I look down upon
The rows of stone surrounding the crematorium.
As silence echoes from chipped works of art,
Light reflects shadows, revealing a map of deathly charts.
An existence is etched onto the purposefully changed stone
So that the living will remember and the unwanted won't die alone.
Past the memorial statues enveloped with age.
Past the wind blown trees, twisted as though in a forgotten rage.
Standing abstract before a landscape of liquid heaven appears,
Serving a purpose to the dead, as the sea wells with ghostly tears.
From the hillside I tower over the burial site,
But am I invading their peace and surrendering my respect at
this immortal height?
Life is filled with carelessness, anguish and mistakes,
But death is filled with mystery, wisdom, secrecy and grace.

Deborah Lawlor

The Children Have Gone

Oh how I miss them when they've gone home!
From room to room I silently roam,
Picking up toys they have left around.
No sticky fingers to cling to mine
Or bright eyes with glee all a'shine,
No little legs on mischief bent:
It was "Goodbye, Nanny" and off they went!
No little arms to cuddle me tight
And whisper "Nanny may I stay up tonight".
No bundle of mischief to shoot me with his gun,
Then when I recover he starts to run.
No little girls saying "Nanny, may I bake some cakes"
And a cup of tea to eat with the things she makes.
There is nothing here now,
Gone all the fun,
For the children have just gone home to Mum.

Olga Duff

My Lovely Mum

It was a cold and wintry day,
The saddest day of my life, as next to mum I lay.
Still to mum I talk in prayer,
And praise her for all her kindness, love and care.

My dad was dying in hospital
So mum's bed I did share
For she was brokenhearted
And we hugged each other tight.
Sadly her heart broke and could no longer fight.

Then her heavy breathing increased, as her life ceased.
The doctor came,
And mum was still the same.
He pressed her chest,
She had gone to rest.

Tears are now swelling in my eyes.
My memory of mum is of love.
It will never fade
Due to her excellent impression on me she made.

I lost my best friend,
Miraculously, I was with my lovely mum to the end.

Janet Marian Burns

Across The Miles

Across the miles that separate us,
The seas that part us,
The race that divides us,
We feel your pain.

Your suffering becomes ours
And with each death part of us dies too.

We are one!
United by our humanity,
Yet torn apart by our human nature.

In your eyes, we see our guilt.
In your pain, our cruelty.
And in your death, our ultimate loss.

To do nothing!
That, in itself, condemns us.

Makes us one with the oppressor.
At peace with the aggressor.

Let our voice be heard across the miles, raised in protest.
Let our hands stretch over the seas to give you aid.

And let our differences become opportunities
To love each other more.

Helen Short

Black Gold

The sea glistens,
The sheen is everywhere,
The black waves lazily wallow
As the sun slants down its gold rich rays
Upon devastation.

The rugged cliffs await,
The threat comes ever closer
The rocks stand stoically proud
As black waters slop menacingly near
Ever relentlessly.

The birds wheel around,
The familiar rocks below look welcoming and grand,
The cries are quizzical and sad
As they drop to rest, to feed, to preen, to die
It is inevitable.

The stranded ship heaves clumsily,
The black gold leaks ever outward,
The greedy people watch from afar
As damage oozes forth and the sands of time march onward
Upon our natural world.

Dilys E. Cook

The Supermarket In Our Street

The supermarket in our street is colourful, bright and bold.
The shelves hold goods for everyone, for people young and old.
And once a week a window sign announces SPECIAL SALE,
Then all the people in our street buy cut price food and ale.

As daylight fades the shop doors close and everyone goes home,
Then Father shouts "Let's have a party, fetch the Gramophone".
The chairs and tables all are brought, and then before you know it,
The people in our street are saying "A party? Yeah, let's throw it!!"

Balloons and Poppers, Streamers too, and all the food and ale,
And Auntie Ada's famous punch in a giant milking pail.
The party swings throughout the night until the first cock crows,
Then everything is cleared away, and everybody goes.

Now everyone has jobs to do, some farm and some go fishing,
And for the next street party, everyone is wishing.
The housewives start their daily chores, and clean their front
    room carpet,
And as for me, ah well you see, I own the Supermarket!!
Chris J. Lilley

Evacuees

The muffled crying, the last farewells,
The shouts of anger. Negativity fills the air.
The thoughts of a new home, a new family,
Thrust upon me. A false identity.
All of these worries make me feel alone.
The clutching of hands, times never to be forgotten,
The whistle of a steam train, a piercing scream of abandonment,

The guard shouts his final warnings,
Children are crying, weeping, clawing for safety,
Watching the dull, drab buildings disappear,
Buildings that resemble home, happiness,
Memories are fading fast, a part of me is failing.
Home is no longer.
I am no longer.
Emptiness engulfs me.
Farewell, home.
Justine Allman

A Father's Thoughts

Then sun has risen and the sun has set while the moon rides high in the sky,
And yet, my dear, the time that has passed is nor but a blink of an eye.
And as my memory returns and returns to the day that you told of your love for the man in your life, who will share all he has with the girl he'll one day call wife.
And mother you'll be with all that name means, and God's blessing from me to you both.
For now I know that your love's ringing true to each other as well it may.
And blessed be the union that all built on love, and out from it's born such a gift, a child who will be more than heaven to see and spreading happiness now far and wide.
So God bless you, my dear, from the man who had tears but finds they are now wiped away.
Bryan William Whitfield

Free Spirit

I see you walking in the morning sun
the soldiers watch you and tighten their guns
I see you running so free so free
with no need for possessions seeking tranquillity.

I see you laughing sometimes through the day
untrapped by convention and all that persay
I see you crying saying suffer unto me
All God's little children isolated by their own captivity.

I see you sleeping when your toil is through
at the peak of the mountain still moist from the dew
when you awaken no more will you mourn
you will arise to the sunlight refreshed and reborn.
Joy Flynn

The Bomber

The smell of candy floss and sawdust,
The soft patter of darts intent on target,
The elation of screams from nearby machines,
The purr of the gypsy caravans.

In the corner stands the bomber,
Its long red arms guiding its captives,
Round in-senseless circles, delineating fear,
Shrills of uncanny pleasure fill the air.

Macho boyfriends standing at the gate,
Quite aware of their awesome fate,
As the cage twists in and out, up and down,
The waiting victims can only frown.

Soon dreadfully it becomes their turn,
Tender eyes watch, their egos burn,
It spins, it sways, time after time,
Appalling dreadful contortions on the spine.

Staggering off, deceitful wiles,
Give way to meaningless indecorous smiles,
About their flight they stand and gloat,
As their stomach ascends towards their throat.
Jason L. Danciger

Killer Whale

A big, dark silhouette outlined against
The soft, silky sky blue sea.
The power of the dark creature
Thrashes the water violently.
Destroying the peacefulness.

The dull moaning spreading further
Deadly, darkens the oncoming night
The wailing echoes around the world
As the sunset dies with the rising of the moon
And nature soundly sleeps.

The morning awakens, the sky grows bright
The large black and white mammal
Fighting to live another tomorrow
He devours his prey diabolically
Leaving the water fiery-red and rusty.

Dewy-eyed with disenchantment
The creature moves slowly in the still water.
Waiting like a young child to be loved.
Days and years go by like a quick flash
Yet still, the silhouette is formed.
Laura Walton

Majesty

Journeying eerily, deeper and deeper into the valley,
    Forced round ominous grey boulders
Skirting wide patches of springy, brown peat bog,
    Thickened mysterious mists, rolled forwards, backwards
Spiders webs clung slenderly to lichened trunks,
Gossamer threads, twinkling, scintillating, suddenly,
A wisp, a puff of wind blew, blew the mist away.

Clear air ridges on rocks, ascending in a long gradual haul
    Flanked by massive caricature stones, natural vaults,
        Little streams trickling, leaping, twisting
            Dancing silvery in heather and sun
Splashing with vociferous, abandoned gaiety into a raging Tyne
Heaving, leaving behind stalwart towering, brooding masses
    Of contemplative rock
        Ancient in antiquity, priceless, ageless
    Each calling to each, each throwing shadow to each
        Suppressing a thousand secrets
            Characteristically irregular, individual
                Intriguing in shape, size and capacity
                    Uplifted, perpendicular to the sky.
Nora M. Davidson

Release Of God

Children's laughter fills the air
The song bird's note is clear,
With your ear you cannot hear,
As your heart's weighed down with care.

The sun shines brightly through the raindrops
Clouds dance o'er the light in the sky.
The rainbow's beauty strikes the hillside
You are blinded to God's wonders on high.

His chords of love would draw you,
To set free from the things that bind.
As you trust Him with your troubles
New joy in life you will find.

You shall join with the children's shout of glee,
You shall see God's wonders in the sky.
You shall know a spiritual harmony
Drinking deep God's life from on high.
Grace Gilchrist

Spring

Oh how I love the wonder of spring
The sound of birds singing in endless rapture
The fragrance of flowers where bees cling
And like a book 'tis the beginning of a chapter

If only I could spread my wings and fly
Over the distant hills and calling seas
I would have no time to weep and cry
Like the trees mourn their falling leaves

The warmth of the sum upon my face
Creates a glow within my being
A gentle breeze offers a warm embrace
And fills me with a spiritual feeling

Trees full of bud soon to burst with new leaves
The gentle waves lapping round the cliffs
And as darkness creeps o'er the calm seas
The moon and stars appear to create a state of bliss

As I gaze up the bright starlit sky
My heart is so full I feel it will burst
Oh Dear God in the heavens so high
I thank thee for all the wondrous things on earth
Joanne Gill

Wild Night

The night is still
   the stars shine brightly
     above snow-covered pasture
no sound disturbs the air
    shadows are frost-bound dark blue

A vixen calls far off
   there is no answer, no sound
the village sleeps

The vixen calls again
   closer now and pads her way along the hedgerow
marking her footsteps in the freshly fallen snow

She calls close by
   we both wait listening
    no answering call comes back
slowly she returns
   alone the way she came

Long silence
   then one far-off shrill wild cry
    in the stillness

No more
Jane Bennet

A Dark Performance

The moon glows, its halo bright,
The stars shine their forgotten light,
The plum sky, the stage,
The dark clouds with no age,
The black silhouettes, a silent crowd,
The gentle wind seems too loud.

I watch from afar, nature's show,
At this moment I seem to know,
As I have done from the start.
In this play, I have no part.
Leigh Paul Cosgrove

Alice

Feathery ferns are frosted on the inside of the pane.
The steady tick-tock breaks the silence of another winter dawn.
An unrested soul, oblivious to the cold,
Pads across the lino from the chair to the sink.
Another pot of tea in isolation!
Night is often day, and she forgets.
And she says things over and over and over.
In her head it is clear.
Words just get tangled in her vocal cords.
Friends and family are afraid
When she doesn't make sense,
So they don't call any more.
"Best don't tell anyone".
A familiar picture.
A fading figure forgotten.
Anne Savan

Syzygy

Waxing and waning:
   the strained smile of her death caress
    is full and feminine in
     tortured beauty —
   flowing silk enfolds her,
   black and textured.
In starlit dimness
the pallid, grainy death mask face
reflects flashes of the knife edge:
   cold steel; discordant, sharply ironic
   in the dream sequence — hard, unyielding
and without sympathy among so many intangibles —
   Yet she is motionless, briefly;
   glimpsing her own cyclic nature — then —
Liquid, tidal,
   inevitable as sunrise over frosty Air:
Fire and Earth slice sinew and sever vessels.
In extremis, Unity — her and the moon...
   the knife falls
And Phoebe is supplanted by Thanatos
Kasy Pearson

My Motherland

So much corruption greed and starvation
The suffering is so much the pain the same
So we seek salvation

Oh such leaders without foresight
So blind they have turned our day to night
A bare feet kid working to school
Unknown to him what tomorrow brings

They invent strategies to suffer the common man
But one man's invention is another man's intervention
Three decades ago the 'biafran' war had destroyed the people
How could my people face this again
All the struggle over the past would be in vain

Home sweet home she is blessed with all mother nature
has to offer, yet she weeps in pain
as she fears everything is down the drain
And so where do we go from here
They say if it ain't broke don't try to fix it
But if it's shattered how do you fix it.
Enoh Agege

Summer Flowers

In a time, when the wind didn't blow and,
the sun didn't shine,
And all the will to survive had gone,
I sat desperately in search of what life
was all about,
And at that moment, "Skippety", "Hoppety," around
the corner came
A beautiful freshness, with all the sparkle
and innocence of fresh snow,
And eyes like large sparkling jewels, with
the energy of a young deer,
unburdened with the responsibilities of life,
flowing like a fresh mountain stream,
She gave me an answer, hope and inspiration,
Life should be fresh, loving and energetic,
innocent and full of sparkle,
I then realized, after months of companionship,
Life is full of "Summer Flowers",
To love is to live.

John Hyland

Summer

Summer has come 'oh my oh my'
The sun is shining in a clear blue sky
Brightening the lives of people confined
In the tower blocks so badly designed
Whoever designed them should be shot
Or better still lock up the lot.

I feel a dislike for the inconsiderate few
Whose legacy is a sad adieu.
The world out there being a wonderful place
Encompassing people of every race.

The trees blossoming bringing such joy
Growing beneath that wonderful sky
Wonderful of course when it doesn't rain
But we need to wash the earth now and then
Water being more precious than gold
When mixed with the right spirit so I am told!

Lee Lowsley

Beauty Is Within

I'll always be strong, when you're so near
The sunshine is out, when you are about
My heart it is not usually full of fear
My mind was never, ever covered with doubt
Each time I saw you, I was on cloud nine
My mind thought you were stylish and grand
Thinking that you are fantastic and divine
I would travel the distance of all lands.
Emotions run wild, going out of line
My heart is an ocean, the way that I feel
The beauty lies deep within your own mind
Blossoming outwards, they see me for real
We're not ugly, for beauty lies within
so please don't judge, with a smile and a grin.

Emma Harding

Paradise Lost

The tide had left the beach smooth again
The sand a perfect slope to the sea
Where miniature waves overlapped each other
Steps to eternity

The sun through the palms left their shadows on the beach
Reaching down towards the blue
A cool path for bare feet off the sun-scorched sand
But today, unused

Just one dark shape on the water's edge
Shows that he has died
Clothes folded neatly, now wet but drying
All else wiped clean by the tide

Emily Taylor

" Spring Time "

The spring sunshine is a beautiful thing
The trees burst into blossom and the birds they sing
And the glorious weather that is to come
Makes life worth living, and as for some
They tend their gardens, and plant their seeds
They plant their flowers, and dig out the weeds
But let's hope the rain will stay away today
But wants to come another day, but I must say
We can't do without it, that's for sure
The plants love it, it's lovely and pure
So let's not waste the beautiful water from above
It would be a sin, the water we love
Just think of the countries that don't get wet
And the crop they sow just does not set
And people starve because of their plight
Little children die, what a terrible sight
I wish we could send them some of our rain
To help them to drink and save them pain.
Oh please God, help them, is what I say
And let the little kiddies have the strength to play

K. J. Trickett

To My Aunt

The flowers had bent their stems down,
the trees had stopped their quivering,
I felt my heart contract
when you lay motionless
like a poor emaciated puppet.

I stroked your face for a long time,
I kissed you with love
and rearranged your thin, white hair
under the little comb
which held it.

And now I am weeping
and I love you as I did then
for everything has stopped
with your death...
and I still hold you in my arms.

Elisabetta Puglisi Gissara

Night Nature

The birds settle down to sleep,
the trees rustle good night.
Also the grass beneath my feet,
seems flat and wet and a sorry sight.

I stand and listen, and wait,
for more wonderful sounds.
And, as if like fate,
night animals creep around.

The foxes round about prowl
silently across the fields,
Looking around for maybe sleeping fowl
for her young cubs' meal.

Now dawn again has broken
so once again man moves.
Nature now has awoken.
As pigeons again begin to coo.

Joan Mavis Jenkins

The Rose

Every summer the Rose blooms so brightly,
The white rose is an enormous height,
As the winter comes all its petals fall off,
As I watch it die I hope that it blooms again,
When the petals fall into the water,
Its reflection is so dull,
The rose smells like my Mums perfume,
and I can smell it over and over again,
So in winter and autumn I can smell it,
As I smell it I think of summer and spring.

Gemma Paddock

Our Heritage

This heavenly countryside of ours
The trees, the shrubs, and wayside flowers
Roads that wind through hill and dale
Windswept trees from winter gales
Homesteads dotted here and there
Furrows ploughed with utmost care
As we pause! For blissful gaze
Church spire points through summer haze
River's flow to journey's end
Woodland, fields, and hedgerows blend
Herds and flocks create a scene
Castles left where kings have been

From planners' dreams there's no escape
They love to build, and so reshape
The landscape we have learned to love
Given to us from God above
We have a duty to our kith and kin
To keep this land and all within
Free for all who love to roam
To live in peace, this is our home

"This England"
Cecil Williams

Urban Oasis

Within the garden's fragrant cloistered calm
The trough, set square aside the curving path,
Nestles neath a white and pink starred cloud of London Pride,
Its edges chipped from laddies' winter sport
When ice resisted sticks and stones, and sparrows chirped unbathed.

Its greeny water now just wets the toes of tumbled stones
Once placed to bridge the wriggling taddies' ways
And daphnia and midge nymphs throng the shrinking pool,
Whilst black and yellow darting hoverflies alight upon
Its sun-warmed walls of brown and creamy weathered glaze.

A rusting pan lies near, a relic of the times when
Boys trawled, happy, in its murky mass,
And butterballs and bluebells spill colour round the bordered lawn
Where blackbirds hunt, head cocked,
Alert for hidden movement in the grass.

An orange flush of rosebuds overhangs the lichened sandstone wall,
And further back a fragrant froth of rhododendrons,
White, pink, and purple, is heavy with the drone of bees.

What need have I for all those things out there
When I have these?
Alan Ayre

Hard Case

One loving mother your perfect cover,
the truth is a sensitive thing.
You choose your own story,
Your trials, your glory,
the truth is a dangerous thing.

A picture of virtue and everyone knows,
the truth is a dangerous thing.
You tell your own story,
Your trials, your glory,
the truth is a dangerous thing.

It lived in a mirror that shattered for life
and everyone knows how you tried.
You tell your sad story,
Your trials, your glory,
abuse is a dangerous thing.

Nobody sees you and everyone loves you,
the truth, an invisible thing.
There's only one witness, your greatest of fears,
one lonely witness,
your hard case is here.
Lynne Olivia Luckhurst

Anthem To A Tiger

Majestic tiger, courageous and bold, whose genesis on earth is old,
The ultimate symbol of nature's worth, a glorious creature
  from the day of birth
Would that I could be with you, accepted and equal in all you do
Stopping the breath in the human throat at the sight of your
  eyes and regal coat
A gift of nature, a glorious design, I wish that your spirit
  could be drawn into mine
The finest of nature's gifts to the earth, a sovereign feline of
  incalculable worth.
You must survive and continue to be, to walk with grace, both
  proud and free.
You face the greatest hazard of your life, the need to succeed
  in your fight to survive
Humanity will be judged by the earth's creator on how it
  defends this miracle of nature
If mankind fails, we are all benefit for none other of your spirit
  on earth is left.
Evelyn Thorn

The War

I am so afraid, I feel so alone,
The war has caused me to loose my home.
My family have gone, my dreams have died
And all for the German Soldiers pride.
There's no one to turn to or no one I know,
I've no where to live or no where to go.
I pray to God that the war will soon end
And I can return to my family and friends.
Where everything was different and as once
Before the death and destruction caused
By the war.
Why am I involved in the war at all?
Why do the murderers still walk tall?
I ask myself time and time again
The war is driving me insane
Innocent people die every day
I wish the war would just go away!
Lianne Knighton

Wondrous Sea

I sit there listening to the rough, rough waves,
The water flooding into the dark, dark caves.
Winter sea dreaded with violent storms,
In the water imaginary patterns form.
When I listen to the sea,
I feel it strangely contacting me.
It's such a typical winter's day,
And to think that I sat here just last May,
Listening to a quiet and gentle sea,
With everyone on it pleased to be,
But now if it weren't for winter's rough waves,
I'd be sitting here, silently!!!
Emma Kirby

Reflections On Wagtails

In warm September sun we sat to gaze
From Iford's bridge of greyed and weathered stone
At water wagtails' yellow jasmined coats
By river's edge from where they first had flown.

They both had come from warm and creviced homes
Upstream from here where flight could make its start
When from fledgling down to richly coloured gown
Male sought the wing to win his love-filled heart.

For their life, their love, was all by water bound.
On glinting rocks by babbling scenic stream
They stood so peaceful, graceful, enclosed within
A perfect world that is for humans just a dream.

With blue-grey back and sparkling jewelled eye
Their mother nature laboured long in making such a gem.
For food they searched, together yet apart
And in love's ways, I saw ourselves in them.
B. J. Antell

Spare A Thought

Bikinis and ice-cream are far from my mind,
the weather is harsh, cruel and unkind.
As the wind whistles it speaks to me,
telling tales of the cold, the poor and unhappy.

The children build snowmen,
the cold is still biting,
families have snow fights,
the homeless lay numbing,
glances through windows,
the children are glad.
Some aged sit huddled. Too poor to be warm,
the naive bless the snowfall and the fun to be had
the chilled?
They sit, raw, benumbed, stiff and sad.

As the wind whistles it speaks to me,
it says, spare a thought this winter;
there are those less fortunate than you,
be thankful you are warm,
be glad you've a home to go to.
Lisa Pay

1980's

The Reds, they aim to conquer; the Blacks just power is sought;
The Whites are high and mighty; the Yellows overwrought.
So go the protest marchers, with banners on display.
Their destination, London; their shouts, "Stop World Decay!"

"Feed the starving, ban the bomb, buy your council house!"
 they say.
"How the heckers can we on the Social Service pay?
And what about our industries? Do they think we're so unwise
When they sell our country's riches out to private enterprise?

"Stop discrimination!" the angry marchers yell,
"Join the nation's dole queues, learn to live in bloody hell!
Who thinks about our miners in their present dreadful plight?
Confused and frightened tough men with no future and no right."

Can they really stop Ken Livingstone, now they've took the GLC?
Can't they see the people love him and will back him when need be?
Who'll ease the tired, aching feet and tend the poor man's pain?
Is there someone with an answer? Or do the marchers march in vain?
Kay McNeil

Untitled

Blue skies and sunshine
The wind and the rain,
The snow and the starlight,
moonshine on the plain,
God's gift to we mortals
To let us all know
He is the master of all, here below.
Dark clouds may gather,
And storms stir the tide
But never forget, he is there by your side
Keep faith and march onward
Tho' the road may seem long.
Hold your head up high, have faith, carry on!!
Lillian Graham

The Ships Sail By

The ships sail by the river mouth.
The yards are gone, lost forever.
The cranes stand in silent mourning for the spirit of better days.
The river banks that were once grey and black are cleansed,
Wiped clean of the grime and toil of ages past.
Wharfs and quays have only the river for company.
Garths stand their lonely watch over ghosts of yesteryear.
What hope do these lands have?
What hope for the 'wrights who built the ships?
What hope for the folk that sit idly watching
As the ships sail by the river mouth?
David Metcalfe

'The Natural World'

Out in the country all nature stirs
The wind in the willows, the song of the birds
Starlight recedes from a new morn, begun
With the freshness of dew and the dawning sun.

Awake, all you People, see the natural world
The greatness of all our God has unfurled
Green is the grass and buds on the trees
Birds flying swiftly with the soft gentle breeze.

Look out of your window, look into the sky
Watch the sun fading and clouds rolling by
Who was it said "There is no God"?
Could humans create the earth and the sod?

The flowers in the fields, the wildlife so free,
The sheep with their lambs, the small busy bee.
Our God the creator has not worked in vain
As Christians will praise him with so much to gain.

He gives us the love we have for each other
The beauty of nature for all to discover
To follow Christ is to understand
The mysteries created by God's mighty hand.
Eileen Chamberlain

" Into The Light "

From a union of passion a new life begins,
The wondrous miracle of life,
A seed that grows forming organs and limbs,
Shielded from stresses and strife.

A small human being, nurtured inside,
Then conveyed into an uneasy light,
No longer in that warm, safe place,
Seized from the peace of night.

Though traumatic the entrance will inevitably be,
The love there waiting holds on bounds,
A new security emanates from the dark,
New experiences, treading new ground.

With love enveloping as this life grows,
The independence of life has its fear,
No matter what befalls as time goes by,
Tenderness is forever near.

The definition of love is a question,
With many conflicting answers compiled
But the most profound of devotions,
Is the love of a mother for her child.
Avril Trotter

A Walk In The Winter Countryside

Snow lies all around me,
Flat, white and smooth,
Icicles hang from twigs and branches.
A lonely bird call breaks the silence,
A rabbit disturbed, scampers off.
A horse and rider trots down the
silent lane, the horse blows leaving
a cloud of breath in the frosty air,
I walk on down the frosty lane,
It starts to snow,
The air tastes crisp and fresh.
A man walks past me,
His old shabby over coat turned up
against the cold.
His dog shakes trying to rid his
coat of the flakes.
Red holly berries add colour to
the vast landscape,
I walk on leaving no trace of
my existence, only my footprints say I was there.
Roxanne Richards

Time

When we are young there is so much ahead,
The years stretch out and we can see no end,
Life is ours to do with what we will,
To us the joy and love will all transcend
What others have or ever hope to feel.
But as the years go by we find we learn
We're not the centre of the universe,
That love, joy and respect are there to earn.

Then, as the years move on we find their worth,
But time is rushing by with faster pace,
As humans we cannot control the tide,
Though there is now an end that we must face.
"Have I made greatest use of all my life?
Could I have loved or helped or given more?"
Perhaps we put our mind to better things
As we perceive the closing of the door.
Joyce Walker

Past And Present

Rock formation, rigid stand,
Their bases buried beneath sand,
Misshaped by pounding waves
whose gouging onslaught formed deep caves.

In caverns small and caverns vast
lie many clues to the past —
A history of a bygone age
awaits revelation's stage.

The inquisitive seek near and far
hoping to find where they are —
Each one working with Zest,
history's lost story to digest.
Ever curious, longing to find
clues to the origin of mankind.
Here in the present I clearly see,
mankind's betrayal of earth's stability.

Dangerous experiments, nuclear bombs
dispatched with nonchalant aplomb,
could undermine earth's natural thread,
so it and us wind up dead.
Audrey Luckhurst

Trees

The straight bringers of life stand
Their cold fingers grasping the earth,
A reward for their vital work.
Rain commences the sun's feeding
The walker runs seeking shelter
Under one of Nature's intensive care units.

The rain stops its refreshing downpour.
A man carrying a motorised death machine
Examines a white cross on the tree
With sadistic look on his face.
Teeth start to fly round his weapon
They tear into the helpless helper.

A bird flies away sorrowed by the loss
Of its nest of eggs.
The walker no longer has shelter,
A hole emerges in the forest canopy
Waiting for the next hundred boxes of matches
Thousand sheets of paper, ten planks of wood to grow.
James Douglas Grassick

Silent Tears

The tears rolled silently from my eyes,
There was no sob, no noisy cries,
No aching from deep inside my heart,
No pain from being torn apart.
The body was numb from taking enough,
But the outer layer just wasn't as tough,
So to release the feelings there were some leaks,
And the tears rolled silently down my cheeks.
Alison Wood

On A Picture Of The Nativity

The gentle ox and ass are standing there,
Their sad eyes watching, breathing low and deep
To warm the untouched hay, the freezing air
About the child born in the cold; asleep.

Sleep on most precious baby; stay with dreams
While angel-voices sing; while shepherds play
Their softest music; while the great star gleams,
Leading rich kings from fair lands far away.

Dream; before waking to the world where man
Has turned from love; where you must bear the pain,
The burden of all sin since time began,
By bitter death bring life to man again.

So, divine child, we worship you, we pray,
As Mary cradles you with infinite care;
Angels sing on and the rough shepherds play,
And humble ox and ass stand waiting there.
Diana Momber

Necessary Evil

Should we deny a place up high
Then blame is not ours
God knows we tried.
Unplug the phones, change direction
No prize for distraction
This surge is more than physical attraction,
Here we are with a pain to soothe
A thirst to quench.
Casting all reason
Casting all sense
As one we become a necessary evil.
Carol R. Barrett

Thoughts On A Hill-Top

I climb the hill, and reach the peak —
Then breathless sink upon the ground,
And as my eyes survey the view —
A deep contentment fills my soul.

Far below — a glorious scene —
A tapestry of colours strewn,
Corn and grass — trees and flowers —
Blend in perfect harmony.

High upon my lofty throne —
I feel as if I were a giant,
The cars in narrow winding lanes —
Like scurrying beetles now appear.

Mid cottages of mellow stone —
A church spire towers above the trees —
My heart will ever grateful be —
For hills to climb, and scenes like these.
Doreen Clayton-Fergusson

Just One Day

The day begins with sunny smiles
Four laughing bright blue eyes
It's no good lounging in my bed
I know I have to rise.

It's scamper to the kitchen quick
Must start the house a humming
I have to move my weary self
Before my twins start running

They've both been washed and fed and dressed
Oh don't they both look lovely
But as the day goes rushing by
Now did they get so grubby.

It's time for supper 'Jamas Bed
They've played and had a fight
But now they're glad to see their beds
And whisper sweet good nights
Patricia Margaret Price

Heartache

If you lose the one you have always loved,
Then your heart is going to ache
Though you hired someone to take his place,
Your heart is going to break.
A stroll 'neath the moon, his favourite tune
Will bring memories,
A seat in the park, a kiss in the dark
You are going to wish that you were his
If you lose the one you have always loved,
Then your heart is sure to break.
   Kathleen J. Gregory

Disillusion

Mother Nature's Crying,
There are oil slicks down her cheeks.
Could it be she hears her children crying,
Because they are so weak.
Could it be the random distraction,
of the sick and the meek
and all the innocent people,
tortured, afraid to speak,
and all the young lives taken,
Just to get a thrill.
It's no wonder Mother Nature,
Is feeling oh, so ill.
   Elizabeth Ann Condron

A Way Of Life In The Country

You can roam for miles in the country
   There are signposts to show you the way
Go down to the valleys and over the stiles
   Thru' tiny hamlets all greeted with smiles.

Climb up the mountains if you're that way inclined
   But as you get older, it's harder you'll find
There are footpaths to follow, just look for the signs
   If you're a hardnut, you will have to pay fines.

You don't need permission to cross the estates
   Remembering always to fasten the gates
You will find there are bins for your rubbish and such
   So please don't leave litter; it's not asking much.

You are free as a bird as you wander along
   With a good pair of lungs, you can burst into song
You can stop at your leisure to admire the scene
   Watch the bowling or cricket being played on the green.

When you meet with the locals, they'll hold out their hand
   And offer you friendship, the best in the land
You may think they are simple, but don't be mis-led
   You can't tell a book by its cover, it's said.
   David Livingstone

" Abigail "

She looks like a dream in her satin and lace,
The sunlight reflects on her beautiful face,
She knows she's admired
And piles on the charm,
She flutters her lashes to cause an alarm.

The ladies all know
That they can't compete,
With someone so confident and utterly sweet,
The audience give her admiring glances,
As around the room she cheekily dances,

Then clapping her hands
She suddenly spies,
One man in the room, for whom she's all eyes.
He wants the next dance,
With the girl dressed in blue.
Well, he is her daddy,
And she's only two.
   Gwendoline Kershaw

My Kitchen

There's a lovely smell in the kitchen today
There is no denying it's fish that is frying
The monks got the habit
And preferred it to rabbit

There's a lovely smell in the kitchen today
It's all very thrilling
For it's steak that is grilling.
It's a bit of a farce
In fact there's a teaser
The mushrooms alas
Are still in the freezer
There's an incomplete smell in the kitchen today.
   Charles Heanley

The Cow

Cows they chew all day in the field,
Their large bodies protect them like a shield,
They are milked twice a day and given hay,
Peaceful creatures in their own way.
Their large brown eyes so round, flies seem to attract,
They pester the poor cow, but it doesn't attack,
It just goes on chewing from morning to night,
And makes the milk so creamy and white,
They stand in the field swishing their tails,
And don't really care about rain or gales,
Slowly they walk by without a care,
But we ought to thank them sometimes for the milk they share.
   Elizabeth Bates

The Two Seasons

What purpose is life to end in death
There seems no meaning.
Why are we here to love each other
It's just the beginning.
To give of yourself as husband or wife
There is a reason.
To love your own child or any other
There is a season.

Now is the season for loving and giving
It feels like spring.
The season of death when it comes unexpected
Has a bitter sting.
Through dark skies of death the sun does shine
'tho we can't see it.
God help us through this winter time
Our faith renew it:::
   Anne R. Mayes

Public Transport Is Fun In The Indian Sun

When in India do as the Indians do,
They don't make a fuss, they all travel by bus,
Where they pack people in like prawns in a tin.
Three sit on a seat made for two,
If they are thin squeeze another one in.
Standing room only for thirty or more,
The last passenger hangs on with one foot in the door

Along the roadside can be seen,
Water-buffalo working in paddy fields green.
Indian Villages and small farms,
In the shade of towering coconut palms.
Native cattle in the street and shop doorways lie,
Rickshaw taxis and bullock carts pass them by.

Each time the bus comes to a stop,
Beggars' hands in through the windows pop.
Others tell that they have fruit and drinks to sell.
By the time your ride comes to an end,
You will have made another friend.
You'll walk away with a smile.
A bus journey is well worthwhile.
   Les Wood

Reflecting Truth

They talk of men from yesterday
There will be no better is what they say,
It's their written word, their brag, their boast,
But let us see, examine close,
If they from yesteryear should boast
Of strength and might and muscle toast.
Where are the ones of great success?
Where are the ones who say we're best?
The silence says there is no one
The truth displays that they're all gone.

The call of death they all obey,
Where are the men of yesterday?
Danny Churchill

Strange Days

These are strange days that we live in
   There's a tension in the air
Politicians are always talking
   Superficial words of care
Are they talking of global disasters?
   Or sharing a vision of peace?
Nothing is ever that easy
   Because the solution is always, just out of reach

These are strange days, that we live in
   There's a wind blowing hard, from the west.
Now all the walls have crumbled
   As the bear draws its very last breath
So who will lay the foundations
   When new foundations have to be laid?
And who will do the collecting
   When the debts have to be paid?
Kevin Wild

For Better Or For Worse

Life's ever changing, accept that as fact
There's no longer time for politeness or tact
Words that were commonly used in the past
Must go with the flow or like litter be cast
Gay's no longer happy, cool's not at all cold
And speed isn't fast when the brain goes on hold
A rod's not for casting a fly in the deep
And ram-raiders do not go out rustling sheep
But, dedication, that rings a bell
It's there on the cover of C.D.'s they sell
Money's no object, we go for the best
Just put a down payment and HP the rest
The clothes are designer, a must for the vain
With holidays in Portugal, Cyprus and Spain
Of time we have plenty, on patience we're short
All must be forthcoming or here's the retort
Give us our right, give us our due
Give us it now or we'll have to sue
Life's for the living, life's to be enjoyed
By the experts at keeping themselves — unemployed.
Betty C. Konradsen

Where?

As I journey down those lonely streets how winter makes them so bare,
Gives me time to recollect and to wonder where?
Where do all those past times go?
Now just memories deep in my brain,
Gone dissolved forever never to return again.

Or are they just all the better because they're in the past?
If time stood still forever, would these feelings really last?
Still these feelings are so real so deep beneath my stare,
These memories of such happy times make me wonder, where?

Tiny little moments that now stand out so clear,
Reflects themselves in sentiment and forces out a tear,
There's nothing wrong in remembering for to do so is to care,
The good times have not vanished, they're in our hearts that's where.
Stephen George White

Light Is Life

Darkness surrounds you, no glimmer of light,
There's no one to help you, they think you're alright,
They can't see the rot as it eats you away,
But then they're not with you each minute, each day,
They don't see you clawing away at the pain,
They don't know you're trying to live once again,
The longer you struggle, the harder it seems,
And life may be ending, you've only your dreams,
So on goes the battle, for dreams are at night,
When darkness surrounds you, no glimmer of light.

Please listen to someone who struggles in vain,
By loving another and changing your name,
You lose your identity, become just the same,
As the others who only dare cry in the rain,
Take hold of your life, while you still can,
Don't give all your love to an ungrateful man,
Be caring and loyal, if he does the same,
But be ruthless if need be, to prevent any pain,
And always remember to cherish the light,
Don't let dark surround you, then you'll be alright.
Ann McCabe

Untitled

How often have you heard it said that love you cannot buy,
These words are meant to sound profound but they are but just a lie,
Oh yes my friend we pay for love and the price we pay is dear,
The payment down, that first we make, is a payment down in fear.

Fear of what might happen and of things might never be,
Fear of oh so many things that the heart alone can see.
At first it seems but a tiny price for all love gives to share,
But greater grows the payments as deeper grows our care.

So we journey on our way sharing joys, smiles and tears,
But ever paying the debt we owe with ever growing fears.
And then one day with horror we awaken just to find,
That so much time has slipped away and youth is left behind.

But still with love we journey on each signpost pointing clear,
Towards the place that's the journey's end where no longer we'll know fear.

And then one day by a tiny spot we'll kneel and place a wreath,
The final payment then is met but this time paid with grief,
Oh yes my friend we pay for love, you might say pay with kind,
And the greatest price of all is paid by the one that's left behind.
Francis Liegaux

Choices

Fate holds the key to future events,
They are gifts to take that are heaven sent,
We have a choice in what we choose, some things we gain, some we lose,
It seems at the time we make the right choice - we listen to that
Inner voice - that seems to say this is what I need.

But always remember you must take heed - of the signs and warnings along the way,
You may hear again that inner voice say -
What am I doing with my life today -
Perhaps my problems will pass away -
They pass away when you break the ties
That bind you tightly to the life of lies.

The life of lies that you live each day
You know in your heart they won't fade away,
And so you think of past events, those little gifts that were heaven sent
And all the choices you could have made
Do you wish now that you may have stayed - on the path that Seemed so clearly laid,
The mistakes you made way back then, learn by them -
For the choice is yours you can begin again.
Jane Bruce

Sunday Morning People

I love Sunday morning people,
They are quiet and relaxed.
Women on horses ride the country
lanes and woods,
Wind-flushed faces turned to meet
the morning sun.
Men, contemplating Sunday roasts,
Walk dogs eager for strange smells and
canine friends.
In well-trodden paths joggers in
shorts puff happily and steadily along,
A patch of colour in the morning haze.
Old ladies walk, fasting, to church
to eat of the Body of Christ,
Prayer books clutched in gloved hands,
All wrapped in their own concerns.
The World is a different place on
Sunday mornings.
Fresh and clean and free of
hostility.

Gwendoline Alder

When Amy Came To Stay

Big eyes looking at me
They belong to Amy,
One look and she melts your heart
Of this family she's certainly a part.
This dear little angel with ginger hair
Makes one think life is so unfair,
Our Grandchild more precious than gold
Has brittle bones we've been told.
Nicola's her Mum and Dave her dad,
When she arrived they were oh so sad,
They were told she wouldn't last the night
It gave us such an awful fright.
But through the months they've loved and cared,
And many ups and downs they've shared,
With love and strength from up above,
They've shown what good parents are made of.
This precious bundle with a beautiful face,
No one else could take her place,
And their words at the end of the day:
"We're so glad Amy came to stay".

Joan E. Jones

Untitled

From coast to coast of many hues
They came to wear the navy blues
God loved these men who went to sea
To defend this land and keep us free
Their thoughts were not of a watery grave
When they sailed away, this land to save
But, many perished, as well we know
In conflicts from the enemy below
So let the winds subside and the seas be calm
let us give thanks and recall the psalm
For God loved these men who went to sea
And the land that bred them is still free

Bill Roberts RCNVR (deceased)

My Son

The day you were born I was so proud
They cut the cord, you screamed out loud
I held out my arms and kissed your head
The nurse interrupted — you needed weighed

A big boy you were, nearly eight pound
With lots of hair and a face so round
Nurses commented 'oh what a cutie'
How you have grown into my little beauty

Now you are four years old
Three feet tall, big and bold
With lots of hair and big blue eyes
You're still my baby in disguise

Jackie Harvey

Untitled

Some dreams were only dreamed for a time and if by chance
they did come true, then it was usually too late.
The time soon comes when dreams are done.
I dare not sleep for the dreams that come,
yet not remain awake for what unseen terrors are
hidden in the darkness.
Happiness doesn't come from doing this or that, or even from
thinking happy thoughts, happiness is what we are, inside.
It doesn't matter what I believe, it only matters what is.
Sometimes with sunrise and sunset, sky and
land are aflame with red and golden fire.
Even in times of darkness, there is time to dream of
love. Love is the most precious drug of all, let the
romantics debate its existence, but with every
awakening dawn love rises up and touches the
lives of all.

Alison Lawrence

Men!!!

Men!! — They bring out the Poet in Me
They enter my life
Inflict their damage
and then...
walk free

Each one — oblivious to the wrong he's done
He pursues me
Woos me
and then...
he's gone!

A slave to love unrequited
A fool to passions, excited
Then much too late
when apparent the fact!
A love he confessed turns out to be part of an act
and I am left
In pain, confused and bereft

Carol Dinham

Dreams

Our dreams are an illusion,
They give the spirit hope.
They help us through the lonely times,
When we no longer cope.
They also cause us great distress,
If none of them come true.
Perhaps we hope for far too much,
That's why we feel so blue.
But no one could survive today,
Without a fantasy.
It lifts us up, and leads us on,
Far from reality.
But, let us not be led astray,
Keep feet on solid ground.
We'll keep our hopes, and keep our dreams,
They're nice to have around.

Adrienne Howes

Happiness

No rarer Jewel could I find, than to give the sunset to the blind;
The sweet song of the little bird, I would give the deaf to be heard.
A golden voice I'd give, and teach, a dumb one turn thoughts
to speech;
I can talk...and hear... and see and realize without these three,
Life wouldn't be so sweet — would I have courage enough to greet,
The dawn of day... And still be gay?
Life must surely hold something more for those who have to endure —
They seem to have an inner light, that in us isn't quite so bright...
Perhaps if the truth were known, nearer to God they may have grown.
Maybe the blind can see much more of "Him" than you and me;
And I'm sure the deaf can hear words from one who is always near
A dumb one's prayers I know are heard, by one who listens to
every word,
I wonder who do possess the elusive happiness.

Doreen Dillon

A Comet's Tail

Some time ago, an early night, I asked the stars to grant me light
they grew like suns and harmed my sight,
I witnessed darkness that burned bright.
Before I blinked, my eyes were frail and blind to see a comet's tail.

I heard the sky tear wide apart revealing angels and an ode
high note pictures of my home, a paved-with-gold forgotten road.

They fluttered wings to start their flight, one brushed by me and
warmed the night. His halo fell and scattered light; I held it up;
It was so bright...above my head it made me cry as stars in
contrast chose to die...

My soul would scream, my corpse would lie, to live anew, it
took to die.
I wept and sought and came to hear; echoes of light in every tear.
The music played along my sigh; my wings I stretched and
looked up high.
Then blew the wind and what a feeling!
I flew at last to find my healing.

Lost in the air and nowhere bound, we swirled and flew the world
around. Amidst the clouds we loved and lay until the day he
went away...
he took the curse from Mida's hand; I cast the gold where
sunsets die,
the Horn Of Plenty fell and hid inside a sea's eternal sigh.

Although the journey healed my sight,
his wings at night still hold me tight.
He flutters; warms and burns the light;
when darkness falls his face is pale...

Reflecting dim a comet's tail....
Efrosini Moschoudi

The Ones We Have Loved And Lost

Why do people who we love have to die?
They leave us behind, we can't say goodbye.
There's so many things we forgot to say.
It doesn't get any easier day after day.
We wonder why they got chosen to go.
Is it because they're so special because we loved them so?
All we have left are their pictures and memories in mind,
Of how they were so loving, caring and kind.
Their Christmas's and birthday's as they pass us by,
Touch our hearts and our thoughts and we tend to cry.
Where have they gone to when they leave their shell?
Is there such a place as heaven and hell?
I hope they have gone to a far better place.
Where everyone cares for each other no matter what race.
I hope when I die I won't be alone.
That loved ones who've died will take me to my new home.
That's what makes us carry on when they go away,
That when it's time for us to die we will meet them
Again one day.
Clare Louise Heaton

The Wayward Tear

The heart's well is not so deep,
There's only so much one can keep inside,
Before the pain becomes personified.

I joined the race of inter-city slickers,
That faceless sea of city suits and limp newspapers,
With made-up face and smile to match,
Dapper clothes and filo-fax,
I took my place — I held the pace
Until, one day, 'Oh no — not here!'
So I spoke to the wayward tear,
That brimmed and threatened to divulge
The secret of the aching heart, to all the world.
But I need not have feared,
The cracking of the fine veneer,
For everyone looked, but no one saw,
The wayward tear spill from cheek to floor.
Jean Merrill

Empty Shells

All I have left are empty shells,
They litter the cold marble corridors of my mind,
A broken heart unable to mend,
The days and nights drift on a forever tide,
Like a vast deserted beach, loneliness is your
only friend,
The price you pay when love turns cold,
I think of you when I walk the shores,
Battered by the ice, wind and rain
I turn to see your face again,
You came to me in a summer's month,
I walk through the past mists of time,

Cold December days are here once more,
Empty rooms can only be found,
Filled with empty shells all around.
I will not believe that you have gone
And I am left to soldier on,
Must I forever march the beaches in my mind
For empty shells are all I can find.
Cristian Campisi

" The Highlanders "

The pipes, the drums, the sway of kilts,
They march so proud and tall.
The boy's from all the regiments.
We highlanders love them all.
Seaforth's, Gordon's, Cameron's, Queen's own,
They all used to be.
But now a highlander one and all
The greatest battalion we will see.
Our boys are not afraid to die
For queen and country proud.
They carry out their duties
And sing their songs out loud.
The Scottish Highlands is the best.
I know it pleases me
That I am a highlander born and bred.
Thank God for victory.
Three cheers for the highlanders.

Hip Hip Hooray
Hip Hip Hooray
Hip Hip Hooray
Alice Devita

Billy The Bus

I'm a Bus! What a fuss! I must leave on time.
   They fuel me up, check my oil, and wash away the grime.
My route is over hill and dale, until I reach the City.
   Where workers work, and shirkers shirk, and everyone is witty.

I'm a Bus! What a fuss! The children call me "Billy".
   Their teacher too, her name is Sue. I think it's rather silly.
My passengers, I know them all, they are a friendly lot:
   There's Sara-Jane, and Mrs. Layne, and even Colonel Mott.

I'm a Buss! What a fuss! My Driver's name is Bert.
   He welcomes all the girls aboard, he's really quite a flirt.
There's some in skirts, some in jeans, and some with bags of
shopping.
   With vegetables and meat and bread, and eggs which won't
stand dropping.

I'm a Bus! What a fuss! No wonder that I'm late.
   They're digging up the road again, the Gas man and his mate.
Last week it was the Water Board, and someone from the phones.
   The traffic waited half an hour, you should have heard the moans.

I'm a Bus! What a fuss! My day is nearly done.
   I'm going to the Depot now, I've had a lot of fun.
The Cleaners sweep me out and then, I'll try and go to sleep.
   Tomorrow is another day. Good night. God bless. Beep! Beep!
Clifford H. De Meza

They Tell Me To Write Poems About Small Things

"Don't be ambitious, the epic form is dead,"
They tell me to write poems about small things.

So I examine the stones in my wall,
But I only see in the wall: Big Things:

In the footings; the apex of an arch,
And over it a date; Fifteen sixty,
Here a lintel at perpendicular,
And sills and mullions but no windows,
There, a mason's mark, fractured, inverted...

I'd better find myself another wall,
That's small enough to squeeze into a poem,
One built of bricks, fresh fired, McAlpine laid.

But then I'd have to aerosol my words,
A curlicued history by solvent night.

No thanks, I'd sooner bang my head on stones,
And stick to my wall daubed with swallow's sh**,
Blue-lichened and quick yellow lizarded,
Answering the thunder word for word.

Graham Chadwick

Alone With Only Hope

People move in eerie circles about me — I alone.
They touch, they tease in erotic safe games — I observe.
Lover's laughter flows in melodic song — I absorb.

Why am I scared to join the game of life?
I BLAME YOU! The evil part of my history.
Two tall faceless men, that took my fledgling adulthood.
Your knife point blunter than that which penetrated my skin.
You broke my soul beneath your thrusts. Your greatest sin,
You let me live.

A real man would never have let them — I'm to blame.
None shall be permitted so close — I'm the shame.

My eyes weep no tears, my nose smells no perfume.
My ears hear no giggles,
The husk that lived may be born again.
If only I may mourn the man that died that day.
Two devils stole my soul, in the name of play,
All it takes is one angel to give it back.

Perhaps some girl will see beyond my bravado? — I pray.
She'll reach beneath my pain and gently care — I wait.
Will I have the strength to reach out and love? — I hope.

Keith Raynal

Waiting

Years ago
They waited for me to come,
For many months they waited,
Then came to joy of a birth.
My waiting began!
Waiting to grow up;
Waiting for exam results;
Waiting to leave school, find work.
Meeting the right man - waiting for the wedding day.
Waiting for our children, watching them grow.
When they were nearly grown
Watching him suffer and waiting for his death.
All life is one long wait, for happiness
Or for sadness.
Are we ever content,
Or is life just one long wait
For Heaven?

Anne Armitage

Once Upon A Time

Don't pretend you mean what you say
The story varies from day to day
You love me, but 'can't we just be friends'
I guess that's where the story ends.

Linda Galforge

The Gulf War

It's not the same without the boys
They're men and soldiers, not tin toys
They go to war to fight Saddam
The enemy don't care a damn
Our boys help to feed the same
The injured and those in pain
My boy was one of those
He said he's glad to come to blows
He's done his time in two wars
And hopes Raf don't find no more
Because he's coming home today
To care for the loved ones he adores
Please God look after them all
And thank you boys, God bless you all

Lily Rowland

The Challenge

The game is on, the die is cast,
They've got together now at last
Deep blue is white, Kasparov's black,
Who will win alas alack,
Gary then becomes one down
That's when he begins to frown,
The next one he will have to win
Or he will reckon it a sin,
He wins the next and all is level
Gary then begins to revel,
Then the next two games are draws
Now it's time to take a pause,
Kasparov then wins the next
Just like reading from the text,
Then he says "I'm not too late?
And after that announces "mate"!

Denis Briggs

" Jilted "

The groom stood alone, sheepish at altar
Thinking his bride is later than oughter
   A rustle from rear as bride enters church
Now he's so relieved, as she makes approach

Now both stand together with that silly grin
Vicar now saying, dear friends, let us begin
We're here before God, to wed these two
Now ask each other, will you always be true?

The ceremony goes well, again Vicar did ask
Are there any objections? If not, we will pass
   Bride gave a scream, said mate. I won't do
With sardonic laugh, said, I won't marry you

She turned with a flourish, and tucked up her dress
Groom ashen faced. Vicar croaked, I'll be blest
Groom is in a trance. Chorus cried, God it is sad
Soon groom livened up and exclaimed, I am so glad

The folk are all numb. One said, let's have a party
Now all tucked into goodies. All hale and hearty
   Questions are asked. Why did she not wed
Told she found another, with riches instead

John J. McCormick

Peace, Oh Perfect Peace

Primates, Politicians, People, Police.
Thinking, talking, all calling for peace,
The bandits, the bullets all veering away
Guns in one hand, the Bible the other
One minute a villain, the next a brother.
The prayers, the bombs, the crying of pain
Please give us our peace they call yet again
The leaders, the preachers don't hear what is cried,
They're too busy building their pie in the sky
Yet? Peace will prevail, people's prayers answered true,
Ireland and the Irish all born anew.

Claude Faull

Inner Pain

Hooded cloak — draped around darkness,
This does not disguise you.
I recognize you, even your darkness
As you tip-toe over God's bright colours,
Crushing beauty, menacingly moving nearer.
Many dark days, many black nights
Have helped conceal you.
I see you for what you are.
Now I know my enemy, I can fight.
God heard my anguish — many times,
You were there — listening, laughing silently.
My audience was vast — yet I stood alone,
Beware — now I know what you are.
My power is strong —
Be ready to flee — turn swiftly —
Let your cloak flow,
Run — run fast, I am close behind you.

Christine Bailey

Time

As time moves on, passing so slow
This endless time with nowhere to go.
It begins at the beginning, to the end
Time itself, itself must end.

Like flowing streams across the lands
Timing the sky, timing the sands
An unseen void, that knows its place
Yet time itself has no face.

It comes, it goes, we know not where
It moves, it stops, it doesn't care.
You stand and wait, it will pass you by.
Quick unseen as time flies by

It will fill your soul, it will fill your mind
Yet no one understands this thing called time
From the lowest depths, to the highest height
Unheard by the ear, unseen by the sight.

My page runs out, I must end my line.
I have to stop for this thing called time.

Andy Woodward

Untitled

This is my fantasy,
this is my dream,
the images that I cling to in quiet moments.
I see you and I entwined.
I see your eyes
and fall into the dark pools
that reflect my desire
and I drown.

I hear the caress in your voice,
whispers and hot breath against my skin,
on my face.
I feel your lips
and I swallow you.
I melt inside the moist warmth of your love.

Not real.
Nothing is real
but I shall dream on.

Corrinne E. Spencer

Bad Day

When I give it my all, and it's still not enough.
This way you behave when your day's been rough.
The thoughtless way you criticize
Makes salty tears sting in my eyes.
I wish I'd the nerve to call your bluff.
I'd like to show you you're not so tough.
The hurtful things you say in spite
The way you act good — it's just not right.
I'd like to see you cope with my day.
You think you'd manage — huh! no way.

Christine C. Stevens

Teardrops' Chalkmarks

Unlike the sky the message was clear:
This is where he died, just here,
inside these lines.

Unlike lots of other crimes
this one was solved. All wrapped up,
like him in the body-bag.

Just like teardrops
rain fell,
just like Teardrops,
so I ran for cover.

Alan Marston

My Son

He's been romping at his play today
　This little boy of mine,
And his hands were soiled and dirty
　And his shoes had lost their shine.
He made his mommy scold him
　For crying during tea,
But when it came his time for bed
　He climbed up on her knee.
He loved her, all forgotten
　Were the scoldings through the day
As he put his hands together,
　For he had prayers to say.
Now he's lying fast asleep
　Where he was when day began
And I thank God that we've got him,
　For He's made a better man.

Desmond G. McMahon

Tribute To Silver

He was so young when first he came
This little pony small and lame
He gave great pleasure o'the years
Fun and laughter, love and tears
Gymkana jumping he did his best
He always won and beat the rest
Bathing, grooming, he shone like snow
He certainly had far to go
He took most children to the top.
Now time has passed he has to stop.
His legs are tired, his pace is slow
How far I wonder has he to go
In grass so green he takes his rest
No more to beat the very best.

Joyce Watson

* * * * *

Foggy days — Drizzle days — Damp days

All of a sudden you remember
This means only one thing
Time is marching near
And brings again, a week-long thrill

The kids all demand to go
In fact, should not be allowed
To miss this yearly experience
Fair's on its way!

Frosty days — dull days — dark days

Hot dogs, toffee apples, chips
Candy floss, nougat, crisps
Careful now, you'll make yourself sick

Helter Skelter, Ghost Train, Big Wheel
Speedway, Caterpillar, Waltzers
Not one to be missed!

Is that all? Where have they gone?
Will they return? When?
Only 365 days to the next "**HULL FAIR**"!!

June Wightman

The Mirror In The Hall

Who was it that I saw
This morning in the mirror?
It wasn't me, I'm sure.
I was just passing by
The mirror in the hall.
The person that I saw didn't look like me at all.

Her face looked, oh so old!
Her hair was lank and grey.
Beneath the chin an ugly fold,
I didn't know her so I turned away.

Where is that pretty girl I know myself to be?
Whose eyes are bright; whose skin is smooth and clear.
Has all that beauty gone away and left that creature there?

There is no change inside
The mind is just the same.
The feelings are as strong, of love, of fear, of shame.

But the mirror in the hall
Says that life exacts a fee.
The mirror says it all.
That old lady there is me!

Ann Clark

Incantation (*Vogue la galère!*)

Mellifluous bile's entangling ooze, oh sweet suffuse
This welling essence of Mnemosynean progeny!
Disembogue this auspicating paraclete, inspiring
Rhapsodist insatiate and perspicacious visionary!

Infuse ichor, gilt weaving honeysuckle ore!
Maelstrom's epitome quicksilvering capillaries
Enharmonizing intricate mechanicals to draw
Converging distillate of quintessential spirits raw!

Ethereal fluid filoselle inviting lovers' fontanelle
Make Echo Narcissus repeat, assimilating great conceit!
Pandora's Box inlaid spinel where cameoed maenads revel
Wish bitter-sweet chimerical propitiating fates foretell!

Subliminal electric storm — peerless primrose's blue lymph warm:
Rubicon to Art Celestial, ush'ring lightning's dart terrestrial;
Confluent edulcoration, obviating exsiccation —
Crystallize as panels sliding, endless japonoise beguiling!

Elite Phantôme of Western Wynde, Ithuriel's spear Greatness excind
And mystic paragon infix, freezing ephemeron Phoenix!
In stasis bind Euphrosyne, captured in locket or etui;
Aglaia, Thalia join who'd flee — dispersed to fade in entropy!

Jonathan Little

Melancholy Sow

I think that I have several people in my head,
they share the day between them,
they use my body for their own ways,
their twisted, perverted, obscene fantasies,
I look in the mirror and don't recognize
the face staring back at me,
the greasy hair, the dead eyes,
chalk white face, who is this woman?
Do I know her?
She opens her mouth to speak but the
words do not fall from her lips,
the reality seizes the existence of this woman,
this human being,
pushing her down,
throwing a net over her and buckling her hands and feet,
hundreds of hands break through the
concrete floor and pull her under,
all that is left of her are the empty
words circling in he air,
looking for a voice...

Lisa Mortlock

" Knowing "

Sitting here doubt fills my existence,
This world around thee
Is I believe deceiving me,
All alone am I — no one questioning why?
Abandon, abandon I feel so much,
Not knowing where I'm heading,

Memories of my adventurous and tearful pasted,
Shrike me as that they will only be but that,
Do my pasted moments still crease to exist?
Is what I've experience now still reality?
Or is the present only what truly is?

Mistakes that I have unregrettably made,
Determine how wise a being I become,
Within thee deep I know unwantingly,
That my future is bound to what I do now,
Knowing is good — but I'm afraid!

Karenanne Nelsey-Brown

One Boy One Son

One boy, one son, the only one
Those big blue eyes looked up at me
The best thing a mum would see
I loved him from that day on
I knew one day he would be gone
He learnt to crawl; he learnt to talk
It wasn't long before he could walk
He sat there laughing; he cried in pain
It was those awful teeth again
He went to school; he learnt to swim
He had a go at everything
He's left school now and gone to college
I say, have a nice life
And gain more knowledge
I'm proud I am of my boy Sam
One boy, one son, my only one

Brenda Eyre

Everyday Folk

We stand outside their esoteric suffering,
Those doomed people television ambushes us with,
Whose pleas deafen us from the doormat.
It couldn't ever be us:
That once-weekly smiting of luck
That turns the most retiring into the most feted —
Astonishing misery, astonishing good fortune,
Both ignore us, and life creeps inexorably, unremarkably, past.
And yet ... No day dies without its glory:
First small, floundering, steps;
The miracle of getting a child asleep;
A cake rising in the oven;
Pages parting onto paradise;
A joke new-told;
A sky the colour of honey;
And, before eyes are halfway opened,
A blackbird communicating delight.

Jennifer Holland

Autumn Days

Oranges, russets, browns and reds
They lay on the floor like a great fiery bed
In the crisp autumn air it's a pleasure to walk
Through woods, fields and meadow, perhaps spy a hawk

The sun shining through the bareness of trees
Gives an ethereal feeling when there's a slight breeze
The squirrels are searching for nuts for their store
And birds start migrating for a far warmer shore

There's something poetic at this time of year
A feeling of peace and a hope of good cheer
So savour these moments for this season won't last
As winter comes round far too bitter and fast

Leila Caryll

How I Miss You Now In My Twilight Hour

Through the trampled corridors I walk
Those endless voices, still they talk
Each word haunting my every step.
Like them once through here I crept

Just a passenger passing through each term
Nor, they or I, thought would return
Now grey hairs are my disguise.
I wonder if he'll remember or recognize.

The last time we met he was so keen
To dish out so violent, on parts so lean
For I was that criminal of scribbled text.
"For the toilet wall," "This anger I'll vex."

Many times I chanced my arm
When caught, never saved by childish charm
White marks on black, justice he thought
Pain saved by a text book, he never sought.

Oh! how I loved my English days.
Many times by Keats, pain was saved
And now through here I pass again
Still in search of Utopia and the odd, lost, friend.

Garry Royston Weeks

Epitaph For A Swan

For many years I've wandered by
Those tranquil lakes
And wondered, at the snow-white dignity
Of Cob and Pen
Gliding along in silent majesty,
Feeding from friendly human hands,
And then, producing cygnets for us
All to share.
Grey fluffy things, that grew to be as fair
As they themselves.

No more will this pair breed,
And fill our lives with joy.
No more will they swim side by side, and wait
For food, serenely at the waterside.
Only the Pen remains, lost and bewildered
In her lonely state,
Bereft forever of her faithful mate.

Anne Dyson

To Those Who Come After

Make your day worthwhile, I hope mine has been.

Keep faith with that which is good and true, for my sake and those you love.

Those I love will weep, for they will ask, "why"?

"Why me?"

I reply, "Because I am here and that is enough!"

Enough to know that what I have done and what I am doing is building for the greater good.

So take this sacrifice and be proud to build upon it.

The tyranny which I seek to dispel must never taint the minds of those I love and seek to protect.

The guardianship of this I must leave to you and my fellow men, our offspring and their generations.

I am but a spent force, a mere spark in the fire of humanity.

A fire which I hope will burn brighter and fiercer as a result of my passing.

Do not forget me for I am your past, your history, which has enabled you to be what you are and do what you do.

Make your doing worthy of my remembrance and in so doing make your remembrance worthy also.

John Lee

" Mother's Rocking Chair "

I stare at mum's room, now empty
though memories still be there
and from time to time I often see
"Mother's rocking chair"
mother sits upon it knitting
rocking to and fro
her smiling face a picture
as pure as driven snow.
Please help me, son, says mother dear
please help me wind this wool
gently now, just gently
just ease it out, don't pull
mother's image then fades away
in the chilling cold, cold air,
that room again empty, 'cept memories
of "mother's rocking chair."

James Hope

" So Far... Away! "

When the love is in a different world
   Though you share the same moon, stars and sun,
When you feel your life has ended
   But a new chapter has just begun
When you remember the times and happiness
   The thoughts within, you try not to cry
Wanting so much just to touch them
   So far that you can't even try.

When every night they are there in your dreams
   You awake to find it's not true
These are the times that you miss them
   And the sky doesn't seem quite so blue.
As happy and content as you may be
   There is always that empty space
When you are looking forward to seeing them
   And you await for the look on their face.

Lucy Jane Elton Powell

Private Thoughts

A sad, sad sight, a sparrow dead
Thoughts come to me of words well read,
Of how God knows, when each should die,
How much I hope this is no lie,
Alas for me, a Thomas.

Gordon Neale

The Painting

The artists works.

He brushes misted shafts of early sunlight
Through a forest's dawn-damp trees;
Sprawls their bare arms across the canvas.
His oils sidelight rough bark
With a blessing of warm gold;
Bronze the umber pads of wet leaf
That still grip Autumn tree crowns.

The artists works.

He makes the forest very still,
Its depths suffused with smudged pinks of distant plant;
Its back cloth smoked grey with fog that sucks the earth's sediment;
Spreading fust to the eye.

In the foreground, he creeps the sunlight
Over mud and stones; leaves and burls;
Hides it in the walnut undergrowth;
Reanimates it in a humble pool of night rain
Like a burst of praise
Reflecting every colour of the forest;
Every nuance of his art.

Jo Noble

Tenandry

Dear River of mine as it flows down the glen
Through forest and moor Mountain and Fen
Its beauty is there for all to behold
Memories sweet, so many untold.

Oh Mountain of mine that we climbed to the peak
No better measure did we ever seek.
Than to climb to the top of Ban'y'vracke so clear and
View the white cottage we all loved so dear

The old winding road that leads onto there scenes
When the bairns were small, the grass ever green
Dear ones have gone but memories stay
Like the fragrance of flowers at the end of the day.
Jessie Morrison

Time

Withered is my soul — as I walk
Through the whispering shadows of the night
Their torturing echoes — as they stalk
My diminishing spirit takes no flight.

My head is a prison of confined memories
The tender promise of eternity
Now cuts through my mind so swiftly
And I so remember love's sweet rarity.

The silent wish for yesterday to become tomorrow.
But time has no essence, all the memories merge
Together to create only a feeling of sorrow
Too painful to put into words.

Every line may be re-written, when time has had its way
Nothing stays the same — everything must change.
Though gone are the echoes of sweet yesterday
There will be tomorrow — another page.
Kay Louise Robinson

Scribe

Trusted scribe tells the tale
through your vein words flow
words that would burn my throat
tumble from my quiet hand

Virgin page is scarred by you
with bitter truths and thoughts
like knives I fear my speech
it would cut my precious air

They are too strong to dormant lie
an escape through quill's disguise
blessed are you who read yet are blind
damned are we who hear yet cannot say

The fresh leaf to clear each day
like tonic to the dying man
hidden confession for all to see
released without trace of escape

Dear scribe my trusted friend
this silent touch will never end
you listen to all I have to spill
yet you cannot ease my heart
Agnes-Anne

Unseen Hand

From deep dark whirlpool, plucked at last
To cross the wandering eddying stream
That soothing, caressing, murmuring flow
Which hides our faltering steps
O'er unseen hidden slippery rocks
To reach the other side
There be immersed in purest pool
Or lie beneath cascading waterfall
Drenched, cleansed and purified.
Denis N. Holt

Sacrifice

The driftwood branches,
thrown by careless, wave to wave,
washed up to burn, on some remote and lonely haunted shore,
strange shapes in moonlight,
like lovers, for all eternity.

And I gaze at the endless sky
nature's cathedral of divinity
the swift winged ones fly shadows in the sun,
I am lost in the slipstream of their metallic wings,
the rainbow in my hands is none of these things.

But sometimes none of this beauty can reach me,
even if fair Hawaii could be seen from my very door,
for I have not the word
that so many speak of with unwise and foolish tongue
that I long for, I am a stranger, out of step
and I can only hear their marching feet
and can only hide invisible,
part of the rain, part of the air
for I have not the word, I am the branch left to burn,
in the cold light of moonlight, I am just a TREE.
Joan Paul

Bejewelled Stars

Bejewelled stars in the midnight sky
Thrown in place by God on high
Twinkling, glistening, shimmering rays
Held by our Father, the universe stays
God treads the high place, we walk on earth
Forever and only held, praise his birth
We can watch the stars that twinkle there
Bright in the distance, the universe shares,
So vast is the scope of mystery and power
We are told to wait for our Lord's coming hour
For out of the hand that made all things
Is our Father, worshipped with heavenly wings
For each star known by name says God,
This is my wonder, so far you have trod
For the stars that I threw, bejewelled too,
Can be seen by human eyes that view,
But the star of all stars in Bethlehem shone
Heralding in God's only Dear Son,
Your Father bejewelled your sky up above
Come now, give Jesus all your love.
Lillian R. Gelder

Tranquillity

Through the endless sandstorms of time,
Thrown up by relentless hammerings of wind like tomorrows,
Comes the realization of a mortality controlled existence.
A life, albeit minuscule in the vast wastelands of space,
Arrives from a collective, yet to be given experience.
To live and love, to be free inside oneself,
The hopes and pains, the joy and fears, to ponder and yearn.
Some of the dreams and imaginings are never to be.
But the cause? The question? The answer?
We strive from the moment that reasoning opens our souls,
To the moment that return to the collective is inevitable,
To demand to touch the elusive fabric of knowledge and certainty,
To know, which for eons the similar consciousness has striven for.
The tightly stretched gossamer thread that runs through the
    parallel existences
Binds, controls, causes us to question being.
In some, a glimpse of wonders endlessly needing to be set free,
Drift languorously to the surface, waiting to be realized.
Seize hold, embrace with the very existence granted,
The acceptance being offered from inside the hidden inner
    recesses of the soul,
There to soothe the rough waters of discontent into tranquil
    beginnings of tomorrows.
Donna Prow

Sacred Golden Rose

O yellow rose, whence camest thou —
Thy face so golden on the bough?
Was't kissed by the Sun, thy face so rare
While born of the Moon thy sister fair
And baptised by fire the red rose bright?

O yellow rose, what meanest thou —
Thy face so golden on the bough?
A white rose for love and purity,
A red rose for passion and beauty,
Art thou the sign of love eternal?

O yellow rose, who lovest thou —
Thy face so golden on the bough?
By Lancashire and England the red rose bright,
By Yorkshire and Athens the white rose light,
But, sacred golden rose, do all love thee?

Betty E. Cundey

Nature's Garden

Rainbow gems crown the Earth
tiara fashioned with blossoms wild
beautifully styled, they lazily nod
while kissed by summer's roaming breeze
to tease the petals, pastel borne
worn by meadows and leafy dales
on trails of yellow and lilac blue
with blushing pink and poppy red
pearls of dew coronet the head
of sleepy Mother Earth
her loveliness beguiles the morn
amidst the fields of cud and corn
festooned, each hill, as daisies spill
their milk of pretty petalled flowers
which never sours, yet drapes the days
in summer haze on emerald down
each view, a humble sparrow's glance
with nature's dance of silvery shower
sprinkling drops on fragrant stems
of rainbow gems that crown the Earth.

Elizabeth Wilson

Friend Or Foe

How proud you look with head held high
Tilted and pointing towards the sky,
Firm straight legs are set apart
Puffed out chest hides a strong brave heart.
In camouflage coat of bracken brown
As soft and warm as the lightest down,
Your crimson shield for all to see
Warning the foe "don't meddle with me!"
But now a question I must ask
And take the reader here to task,
Is this great warrior Wallace or Bruce?
A mythical God or mystical sooth?
He is neither the latter nor one of the rest,
He is my friend — the robin redbreast!

Evelyn Davidson Lindsay

Temptress

The temptress bares her morning breast,
To feed the babe upon her chest.
No reaching out for the hand that cries,
Which bathed the brow when pain did strike.
Pleasures proved, our love did find,
To sow the seeds for another life;
Now love is buried deep in root;
The seeds are sown — no love has shown.
Come caress my burning heart,
So long the time now we are apart.
Had future known how it would be,
Our love between us, not split three.
Come temptress, lay your head by mine;
The waiting spirit bears no more time.

Erika Maria Labancz

Wasted Pain

Held by a clamp around his neck
tiny electrodes are planted like flowers in his head,
and when the flowers kill the soil,
the cat will soon be dead.

Muscle spasms and electrified jolts
Lots of screws, nuts and bolts
Make sure he can never get away
And to 'thank' him for being 'helpful' in their 'invaluable' work
He gets a jab in the arm and is put to sleep.
His mind is blank, he cannot see
Oh where in hell can he be?
Voices, laughing, humiliation
He is still in captivity
Struggling, struggling to break free
Oh why, oh why can't he see?
The end.

Kelli Greenhalgh

Nurjahan

Dainty, tinsel-sprinkled laughter;
Tiny hands and feet, nails brightly painted
and all a-jangle with many bangles.
Long, oily black plait, delicately woven with
lilac and gold, silk ribbon, dances against
flashing purple and gilt-braided sari.

Eyes huge, like deep, black lakes, gazing
dolefully from between long, moist black
lashes, fluttering, like a fragile butterfly.
Lips, red and glossy, parting to reveal white,
even pearls.
Dark, smooth, oval face, lit by
crimson spot on forehead.

God's perfect, intricate design to
colour a culturally-diverse
globe, and to enrich the lives of
those whom He loves.

Jennifer Barclay

Winter

Winter, season of peace
Tired earth sleeps with her past
Taking with her the secret
of life and death
Moldering leaf, germinating seed
Snow lies thick on deserted fields
Streams flow under an icy cap
Leaving no trace of their passing
On the banks either side
Sun tints the ice.
And snow crisp earth crunches underfoot
A robin on a frosty twig
Puffs his feathers against the cold
A hedgehog hibernates in a leafy cocoon
The blurred sun dies, the moon shivers.
The leaden day escapes into darkness
Only the hoot of a barn owl
Shatters the silent peace.

Cindy B. Brewster

Deafness

Muted from the outside world
To see a sunrise but not to hear the morning chorus
To touch the water but not to hear the waterfall.
A closed up world of oneself.
To be alone around so many living people
To miss the message of life and yet to live
To fail to catch the beauty of music
To see the words that cannot be spoken
To see yourself without your name.

Claire Holsey

Untitled

Where to now, poor yearning soul?
'Tis surely the greatest task of all
To have found faith, yet still the pain
Can one still climb or must one fall?

What is this bitter fruit you seek?
This yearning ache that gnaws at you?
For if you are one with God and all,
What is this state you're striving to?

Where is this bliss of what you know
And are you really sure
That it exists right here on earth
Or is death the only door?

Anne Black

Reflections

Absence makes the heart grow fonder,
'Tis true, I know, for when I wander
Through the woodlands and the fields,
I find a spot to sit and smile
In solitude, I think a while — of you.

And as I watch the setting sun,
The birds sing out their evensong.
The fiery ball is sinking low,
Its burning reds and vibrant hues
Fill my heart and love exudes — for you.

My darling, stay within my heart,
And let us always be a part
Of one another's wildest dreams.
And I will pray those dreams foresee
Reality, my destiny — with you.

Anthea Dixon

Invisible

Rushing blackened swirling clouds
To a far off destination
Where to, perhaps nobody knows
Continually forced into changing shapes
Greyness stretches far across the cheerless sky
Invisibly the air in motion
Prepares the dying trees
Undressing their branches
From the dead and discoloured leaves
While evergreens caress the bough
Unwilling to release the colour they still hold
Even the birds fight
Seemingly against the sky
Rising and falling maybe even
Forgetting how to fly
In this invisible force we know as the wind

Jacqueline Nelson

Age And Youth

With age I have learnt to tolerate,
To accept, acquiesce, to understate
No more the need to fight the world,
With head held high and flag unfurled,
No more the passions, the wild desires
For Age has dampened down the fires,
No longer the dreams that reached for the moon,
Tender and fragile they faded too soon.
Yet, now and again, perhaps in the Spring,
When wild flowers bloom, and a lark may sing,
Just for a moment or two I have stood,
Where bluebells are beckoning deep in the wood,
And felt the old longings, the ache to achieve,
And Adventure's wild spirit has tugged at my sleeve,
With a conspiratorial gleam in his eyes,
Which says "Follow me, and we'll reach for the skies"
And nostalgia engulfs me with bitter-sweet pain,
And forgotten dreams I dream once again
Bewitched by the beauty, beguiled by the sun,
I am old, I am young, for the two are as one.

Freda Shackleford

Poetry Not Potion

To priestly virtues... our hearts repent
To an analyst... our minds torment
To physical ills... a physician's care
To poetry... sweet revelations.

Lend an ear to the poet's word
Soothing emotions into thoughts made clear
and words... into sweet rhyme.

Let their sensitive touch seduce
Tangled thoughts to slumber
Negative dreams pull asunder
Caress disruptive discord.

Let sorrow elude the awakening mind
From the sweetness of youth to the more refined
Setting grievance to verse.

Let freedom of spirit that poets achieve
Allow the heart once more to believe
In the darkest places on earth
Love can still be found.

Doreen Welby

In Days Of Old

In days of old I would run to my mother, her open arms a safe place to be
She'd wipe away the tears of my sorrow, her gentle voice sating my fears
As I grew older all my fears grew with me, fears that gentle words could not expel
And yet a distant feeling not quite buried, tells me that she could still make these things well
Oh how I wish that life could be that simple
The woes of life banished by a mother's love
But I know life can never be as simple as it once was to that small boy
So now I search for a new solution, to each problem that bars my way
No longer can I depend upon an answer, sometimes I cry, sometimes I pray
Once a child's robbed of his illusions, can he ever feel as free?
In days of old I would run to my mother, her open arms a safe place to be.

Christopher Grace

Untitled

You are all together now, one family like it used to be...
Although you have been laid to rest, your life still
Goes on in another world,
Hopefully now you can guide me through my life,
Like the guardian angel that you never see.
All the happy memories are treasured within our
hearts, and these cannot be taken away.
Someday we will meet again, this time face to face.
And the family will begin to grow again until the
circle is complete.
It's funny I can remember all those wise words
you all used to say.
They are all tucked away in the back of my
head like a little parcel all so neat.
I guess this is goodbye, not forever, just for
today.

Angela Bell

The Big Win

I buy a couple of lines every week.
To see what I could win I often think.
But when I don't win I always grin.
I wouldn't be happy with all that cash.
I would have to become upper class.
But now it's become part of my life
A small amount would be nice to be rid of some troubles and strive.

Hazel Cromie

Swear Off

One used to need some unction
To describe a bodily function
In a manner that was open and was frank;
But now you don't need daring,
Why, everyone is swearing.
If you object you're thought of as a crank.

Most letters of the alphabet
Now describe another set
Of words that I consider very rude;
But don't use the initial,
It's OK and official
To shout them out, even if they're crude.

On the advice of the constabulary
I limit my vocabulary
Avoiding the shocking and profane.
I suppose that I may bore us
With words from my thesaurus
But the sensitive among us don't complain.

David Walters

Untitled

When nations get together
to discuss the use of drugs,
The pusher goes on pushing
to the unsuspecting mugs,
Although the law is working hard
to put a stop to this,
More dangerous drugs are on the street
to tempt the younger kids.
Ecstasy, cocaine and speed,
Your life for these you'll pay,
So if you want to live tomorrow
Say 'no' to drugs today!

Geraldine Simmons

See You In Paradise

If I can borrow a little time,
to do and say some things.
I think I'll start by saying thanks,
to all the people that I know.

Thank you for being my friend,
and for being there for me.
Thanks for all the love I've been given,
to help me through my life.

You showed me happiness,
and how to be patient and kind.
I've enjoyed my time spent with you,
and I hope you have too.

But I can see the light coming near,
and time is running out.
I shall close my eyes and say goodbye,
and hope to see you in paradise.

Amanda Hillbeck

Love

Love is a rose, with soft, winding petals
To envelop, to caress, and to wind
Around two young people whose eyes are ensouled
In each other's in romance sublime.

Each day brings fragrance, enhancing delight
Bringing freshness and real joy untold
Each meeting adds richness towards their insight
Of maturity and faith to each mould.

Then as time winds on its endless pursuit
Love blossoms as flowers in spring
Courtship, then marriage, fulfilment to each
The blessings of suchlike then bring.

Barry Marshall

The Sense Of Sight

Awaken, in the morning, to the beauty of the dawn
To everything around us, to colour, shape and form
As overhead, a hazy sun creates a golden hue
Birds are gliding, lazily, across the skies of blue

Pause awhile, absorb the sight of such a wondrous scene
Of trees and shrubs and hedgerows, in many shades of green
In the depths of winter, snow lays shrouds of white
And puts a magic brightness into the black of night

Look at all the faces and the places that we know
A picture of tomorrow as our vision seems to grow
We have a gift, a precious gem, the eyes through which we see
And if we close our eyes to look, what then would we see?

Awaken, in the morning, to the chorus of the dawn
Harken to the song thrush, feel the dew upon the lawn
Take pleasure as the sun bestows its warmth upon the earth
Inhale the air, salute the day, as yet another birth

Through sight or sense we strive to be
In harmony with nature
If I were blind, then I would see
All that life has given me.

Deirdre Tuff

The Force

The elation as the seeds of love are sown and life blossoms from bud to flower!
to flower!
But there is a secret, a secret that nobody knows of.
And a secret which not even the host has a clear perception of.

I have another friend, not even a friend,
An accomplice with a hulk of primitive tendencies
And a less than understanding character.

Attention be paid to this monster of a thousand faces
With only one voice, one purpose and one desire:
The destruction of enchantment, the bursting of the bubble.

The beast stalks again, preying on that one moment
Which will break free his bonds and unleash an eternity of suppressed torment
As love grows in strength, strength is mutated to anger
The reluctant result of harmless acts which exaggerate in a fervent mind.

For every truth there is a lie,
For every life, a death,
For every love, a hate
And for every beauty, a beast with no princely destiny.

Graeme T. Crump

" Outside "

Outside as the light disappears with your laughter
Thoughts distil into the frisson of whispered candour
Sober and silent, we enter our blissful, secret room
Only tonight will I watch you undress
Soft snapping at your back, your breasts appear
Now you reach down and quietly step to stand, naked
You are all I can remember as you approach
I close my eyes and draw you to me, breathing your nuchal scent
Slowly reclining on the cold bed, we kiss
I will never be here or feel your skin this way again
Still, I am blank, lost in a breathless steadying of limbs
As you climb, arching and urgent
The metronomic delight of your gentle, languid rocking begins
Sustained to a tightening of cloying, gasping bodies
After, as we lie in passive languor, you look at me with
  implacable eyes
Then close them to my fearful stare and turn away to sleep
For a while I look at you as the light reappears
Steeling myself to abandon you until in slow haste I prepare to leave
A wish ungranted as I step outside
No stirring from you as I stand in the breeze

Daniel Thomas Cookson

To Suffer

I sometimes feel the urge in me
To help the starving refugee
Poor people caught up in someone's war
They don't know what they're fighting for.
I remember those violent scenes
Flashed upon our T.V. screens
It makes me wonder why it's done
When it's finally over, no-one's won.
Why don't they stop their fighting and killing?
Perhaps it's because they're just not willing
Children bleed and scream and cry
It's clear they're suffering, but why oh why?
Someone has power to make it cease
And give these people the right to peace.
Linda J. Cook

My Guardian Angel

My guardian angel must be working overtime
To keep me out of trouble everyday.
My guardian angel must be that good friend of mine
Who always helps to chase my blues away.

Still every time I see a chance I crash right in
I never stop to think my options through
I always tell myself that this time I might win
though I hope things may change, they never do.

I cross the road of life and don't look either way.
Yet always make it to the other side
I'm far to busy looking back at yesterday,
to ask myself what may tomorrow hide

Occasionally I wind up in life's fast lane
and end up feeling happy for a while.
But then I crash straight into trouble once again
it's then my guardian angel seems to smile

The fast lanes far more busy than it used to be
I'll wait here in life's layby for the night.
Until my guardian angel comes to rescue me
I'll dream sweet dreams and fear the morning light.
David Allan

The Seasons

The snow is God's great blanket
To keep the good earth warm,
Though 'tis hard to realize
When we suffer winter's storm.

So soon will come a sunny day
When nature says awake
The birds and beasts come out, for they
Their exercise must take

The world takes on her summer cloak
Of shining green, and flowers
And we are blessed with sunshine
On this grand world of ours

Then comes the autumn mists
The trees in reds and colds
Such beauty and such splendour
Yet another year unfolds
Lilian Smitherman

Searching

The time to grieve is over, I watched you fade away
To lose the very thing you love turns worlds to a dark grey
Lonely, long, so dark here, where everything stands black
Where I hope to find you wondering, so I may call you back
Each night I go far hunting into that deep dark space
Hoping that one day I'll find you in a lonely place
The wind around us fiercely raging, so desperate and true
All our Earthly knowledge could now be used anew
Every night I search, it leaves me worn and dead
Though this is all but nothing, to the pain of fear and dread
That one day I will find you, but you'll not know my name
And all my aching dreams of us are lost to time's cruel flame.
Loretta Chegwidden

The Church Hall Sale

She shuffles on along the busy street,
To make her way home from the Church Hall sale;
With aching back and corns upon her feet,
Against a wind that feels more like a gale:
Her solitary purchase clearly shown,
A teddy-bear, in a carrier bag, upside down.

No cars slow down to help her cross the road,
No one looks out to see she does not fall;
As she plods on towards her warm abode,
Not many people notice her at all:
It's lonely walking through a busy town,
With a teddy-bear, in a carrier bag, upside down.

If she gets home will anybody care?
Give her warm slippers and a cup of tea;
Will there be someone there with love to share?
She knows full well there will, and so do we:
The evidence is there in gold and brown,
The teddy-bear, in the carrier bag, upside down.
David Leonard Taylor

Alone

The pain inside I feel right now,
To make it go away, I don't know how.
No one knows how I feel,
To them it is no big deal.
Listen to what I have to say,
To try and explain, why I feel this way.
No one will listen,
Nobody cares,
For this pain of mine, no one will share.

On I drift, with this pain inside,
Trying to conceal the tears that I cry.
To understand exactly how I feel,
This, I know, nobody will.
Fiona Gibbs

Nightmares

Nightmares are a warning sign
To make you look back in time,
Back to when your childhood started.

Insecure and sometimes worried,
A hidden fear is often buried,
Deep within our sub-conscious mind,
Is locked away for all time.

But when it surfaces, as it will,
A childhood fear can make you ill,
But dealt with slowly over time,
Will reap the rewards of a healthy mind.
Helen Kelly

My Dad's Stroke

They called it a large low density infarction,
To me it was just a stroke.
At first my dad went weird,
And didn't recognize my mum,
But then he went all wobbly,
And fell down to his knees.
My mum then rang the ambulance,
Oh hurry, hurry please.
He couldn't feel his arm or leg,
I knew this was something bad,
I was blinking back tears, I couldn't lose my dad.

The ambulance only took
Seven minutes to come,
But to me it was lifetime all rolled into one.
My dad is getting better,
That one thing makes me pleased,
But the pain that is in all of us hasn't yet eased.
Elizabeth Hornby

Brave New World

You say the time has come when we must follow your elusive star,
to other regions from this place afar.
You take my hand and tell me to be unafraid;
your journey's end will far exceed the plans our youth had made.
This matters not to me —
You know if Lucifer himself called you to Hell below,
I still would take your arm, though warily I'd go!
For what is home if you're not there to warm it with your smiles?
It's just an empty shell, so what is distance but a few more miles?
So I will follow and leave this native ground as Ruth did
   those long centuries ago,
but if I tend to linger on that day, or leave with leaden
   step and slow,
you must forgive my sloth — the beauty of this place,
I'll carry with me as I go.
   Dorothy Brookes

" The Storm "

From far off Canada it came,
To our shores, with might and main.
The waves rose to a tremendous height
Scattering all within their sight.

Roads and houses flooded out,
Debris lying all about.
Water here and water there,
Water flowing everywhere.

The wind did roar the snow came down
Rain and hailstones beat the ground,
And then — calm — not a sound
The storm was over.
   Ella B. M. Nettlefold

Autumn

Autumn is the time of year
To reap the harvest in,
And all the fields are neatly ploughed
Ere Winter days set in.

When all the leaves begin to turn
A bronze and yellow hue,
It's nature's painted picture
From an artist's point of view.

And Autumn cues the creatures
To gather Winter food,
For hibernating soon begins
Their sleep of solitude.

The first morning mist of Autumn
And the birds begin to debate,
Nourished from the hedgerow fruits
As to when they will migrate.
   Audrey Beck

Friends

This is a poem from a friend to a friend
To remind you of all the times we have had to make amends.

The secrets we share and the fun we have had
Will hopefully continue through good times and bad.
I'm the kind of friend who just won't go away
The kind who embarrasses you every day.
Shopping the fashions, watching the boys
Are the things in this world we most enjoy.
Our biggest problem is when we are stressed
Is it really worth letting it get us depressed?
We are still in our teens, not old grannies yet!
Let's enjoy our life and our problems forget.
I hope this poem is not too silly or sad
I didn't write anything hurtful, so you can't get mad.

Friends I hope we will stay for a while
As friends like you are not found every mile.
   Jenny Moore

The Flame Of Life

If you touched the flame, would you burn?
To resist, would you burn any less?
As the flames from within burn out of control,
   this is the ultimate test.

If the flames burst forth, would you run?
Or yield to their searing caress?
As the flames dance still higher, uniting as one,
   this is the ultimate test.

If the flames of love burn, let them claim you.
To resist, you will forever regret.
If the flames live or die, you can only but try
   because love is the ultimate test.
   Helen Bartlett

Lettra

Almost painless, I peel away a fresh sliver of self
To slip it, still quivering,
Into a crisp envelope which
Boasts your name and hide-out.

Soon it shall lie in the belly
Of a metal bird, pregnant with precious hides —
Some dazzling like diamonds
Others with spikes that slash and tear
And still others pale and thin as shed snake-skin —
Tokens for lovers to hold close and kiss
Or memory-aids for distant friends
Offering whiffs of scent, flashes of colour
Recalling those younger days lived together
Of which we had far too few.

I wonder what you do with my rind
Once you've held it between your fingers,
Brushed it against your skin?
Do you combine it with earlier pieces
To build a little effigy?

Or do you simply throw me out break me up reduce me to dust?
   Daniel Humphries

Winter Of The Country School

The school bell cuts through the icy, unblemished air
To stop sharp, small delicate voices and so to hear
Leathered feet padding softly towards the cosseting warmth.
The sugared fields surrounding lay waiting patiently as they
   continue their silent, glacial vigil.

In time the excited voices return to build white sentinel friends
   with unseeing yet all-seeing eyes.
What gladness they have witnessed over each sleeping season.
Muffled shrieks of delight as multi-faceted
   crystals float effortlessly ground-wards obeying gravity's call
Accompanied by a fleeting glimpse of a Victorian past.
A mirror image of the present,
Of children playing with innocent happiness.

The delicate existence embracing the winter chill
Like a sphere of lightly packed snow destined to disintegrate on
   contact.
Hope as ever may bring a change of garments to clothe an
   uncertain future.
But for now, the warm glow of a contented past.
   Kay S. Kebby-Jones

Dreamworld

Somewhere in my Dreamland, there's a place that I can go,
To take me from my sorrow, whenever I feel low.
Something in my Dreamworld can take away the pain,
I see things in a different light, no solemn thoughts remain.
You need no reservation, you're guaranteed a place,
Come and go just as you like, dream on at your pace.
I'm suddenly awoken, back to reality,
But Dreamworld's always open, although it's fantasy.
   A. D. Beaumont

The Eyes In The Sky

I look up through the rain-streaked pane
To view the glimmering rocks placed in the ancient night,
Shining their bright light of wisdom
for many centuries past. They
hang motionless watching,
laughing at the polluted globe.

I see moving clouds drag the ones which lag,
over the clustered light hung
in the sky's bleak land. They wet my flame, I sizzle
out. Blinded by the moist haze drifting by.

I still am here when the Red Giant is out, where
his radiated rays no longer bounce, but
penetrate the Earth. I see the destruction of
my world and the toxins released. I choke.

I suffocate, contaminated
by my ruthless species, drowning
in the abyss of space. My euphoria
crumbles as I shrink, my prongs are blunt.
I wonder, maybe the eyes in the sky will fall.
One day.
  Emma Hutchinson

I Never Get Grapes When I'm Well

It's a comforting sight in the dead of the night,
To wake up and see 'neath the flickering light
A nurse... sitting quiet in a chair.
You awoke with a start, to a cough, or a fart,
A pain in your side like the stab of a dart,
Thank heaven the nurse is still there,

She comes with a smile, and sits for a while,
Flicking through notes in your medical file,
Checking your drip and your drain.
She makes sure you're not dead, smooths out your bed,
Lays a cool hand on your feverish head
And amazingly eases the pain.

With the coming of day, the nurse goes away,
The doctor comes round, has nothing to say,
Too busy to stop you can tell.
Then people drop by, some laugh and some cry,
But then when they're gone, I ask myself why
I never get grapes when I'm well.
  Bill Evans

Discontent

"Take what you have, and be thankful!
Think what many poor wretches endure!"
"Oh yes, yes indeed, I am thankful!
But still, there is so much more!"
"Look around you, and count your blessings!
And weep for what others endure!
Take what you have, and be thankful!"
  But the soul still cries for more.

There's an ache in my heart that I cannot quell,
There are tears that are suddenly welling,
A voiceless cry to the uncaring sky,
A yearning that surges, rebelling.
Sometimes that yearning will sleep like a stone
In deep water whose stillness is lulling,
Till stirrings and shiftings and movings and driftings
Awaken an unquiet feeling;
And then once again all the churnings return,
The longings that Life is not filling,
The ache in the heart, and the cry from the soul,
And the tears that come suddenly welling.
  Jean McCabe

Thrown from she you loved

Thrown from she you loved
To walk the lanes, lonely
With a freedom that spurns sharp edges
To cut all like her
Anyone that could remind you
Of that smile, the way she was with friends
Those memories jealous, that she could find happiness again
And not need to find your love for her
So close then, when inside, the joy to feel
Once inside, now pulled away
Find her somehow lost in history
And the pages burnt, the kind words turn
Of the pieces you read, those you repeat
Over in your mind, to force you to retreat
From anything she could possibly be
And anything that was
Must guard you from being burnt
By her touches that weren't
  Jason Diplock

The Sons Of War

The grieving mothers line the streets,
To watch with pride, their sons with feats
That hang upon their bloodied pleats,
Of Gods own cloth, adorned in heaven.

The screeching cries from fields afar,
Cannot explain the battle marks,
That stain grey tunics of grim war,
And scars the flesh of mothers torn.

For wings would have sheltered,
They would have knelt and honoured
Their men of peace and glory.
If only to have loved again,
To hold and behold their men of war
To leave the emptiness behind
And know sound sleep once more.

But no, not all who wait to meet,
Will see that happy faces greet.
For mot will spy dry bones galore,
Through cracks in boxes made for war.
  Andrew Jenkinson

World

Our world is but a pin prick in an unknown universe.
To what do we deserve a place so unique and diverse?
We hold an honoured privilege to live within this place,
And life would be so simple here without the human race.

Our world is one of plenty, yet many are denied.
Half the world is starving. How is it justified?
Computers aid our every need, the world is at our feet.
Whilst miles away but oh so near there's not enough to eat.

Why in our world of plenty is there hatred, hurt and spite?
Why do famines happen? And why do people fight?
Why burn the trees for selfish needs? Why hunt the carefree bird?
Such thoughtlessness and cruelty in this world should not be heard.

We never should have been allowed to rule this sacred land.
There's only so much harsh abuse this planet can withstand.
The world is far from perfect, however this is true,
It would be such a better place if we were all like you.
  Christine Meynell

Cliff Top

Sullen skies threaten thunderous applause.
Waves crashing widely against unmoving rock.
Blustering winds scream as clouds
dance madly across darkening skies.
Seagulls wail, swooping in disarray.
Children's laughter can be heard far below.
Lovers entwined, hoping no-one will see.
Birds hover in their play,
Whilst winds whisper, teasing the trees to sway.
  Georgina Irene Amelia Rook

Truths Behind Faces

Faces running to and fro and to
— to where?
To who cares?
No one knows what goes on
in that place that matters the most.
The most of all which is kept locked up under
protection of the host.

For want of security it's better to ignore.
The truth is what everyone is seeming to implore
Diplore. Impure: - God give us more
Than the guilt and the hate that you claim
to abhor

Not everyone can see this flaming truth
That comes from beyond this height of matter
Spilling its guts like a visual guru
And failing all else like it did our charter.
Cristina McKerchar

An Encounter With Yeshua

Who can describe such a moment of confrontation?
To whom is given the wit to define the beauty of His appearing?
For to define is to limit, and who may prescribe the Limitless?
Yet grace was given that I should stand within that awesome
presence and receive the precious gift that He bequeath to me;
His Very Self.

It was a meeting so profound. So exquisitely powerful.
My enthralled spirit, folded in Love's embrace, soared to
heights and dimensions unimaginable. What rapture! O ecstasy!
More tangible than physical perception proves and yet, so
intensely physical my mortal flesh could endure it but briefly,
or melt in the agonizing rapture of His nearness.

The encounter, fleeting, so fractionally brief.
Then, as in instant of radiant brilliance fades and disappears,
leaving an afterglow to mark its once spectacular appearing;
so the fragrance of Love's consuming presence lingered in an
effusion of sensuous wonder. So near, so close; yet His
withdrawal, deep sorrow. Such deep inconsolable mourning.
Douglas Raine

Ode To The Old Billingsgate Fish Market

Before the sun has risen the men are on their way,
To work beside the River Thames 'til middle of the day.

In and out the market, threading through the throng,
Porters by the dozen wheel the goods along.

Prawns and eels and shellfish, fishes by the crate,
Cod and plaice and haddock, salmon, whiting, skate.

Filling up the lorries, stacking on the vans,
Lobsters, crabs and herrings in overflowing crans.

The traffic is diverted to expedite the flow,
Half the lanes reserved for transport row on row.

Soon they will be finished, the fish all on the road,
Ice and water everywhere and nothing left to load.

Then homeward bound the fishmen, white coats put away,
Leave the streaming market until another day.
Eric Hanson

The Swansea Quadrant

The Quadrant is like a large biscuit tin
Waiting to be filled.
Rows of shops like a long line of soldiers.
Everything quiet like a mouse.
Darkness everywhere like a shadow of a shadow.
Lights come on like a flash of lightning,
Shutters go up like a clap of thunder.
Light shines in like a spotlight on a stage.
Louise Meller

After Death

Oh my love, my voiceless ghost,
to your next life I now must toast.
Where you will be next I do not know,
but I do know that you have to go.

This ghost I now frailly follow,
deprives me of my pain and sorrow.
In my mind I can hear you call,
and on the wall your shadow falls.

Your old haunts will pass away,
and I'll lose you more every day;
Yet I can't grieve whilst you're near,
but for you I need to shed a tear.

I'll remember you when you're gone,
and your face where laughter shone;
I'll not forget you like spilt wine,
and although dead you're always mine.
Gail Adams

Winter's Beauty

Aconites and Snowdrops blooming
together in moss and grass,
Carpeting the woods
Between tall trees stretching heavenwards,
Could heaven be more beautiful?

The bright yellow of the aconites turned gold
In the winter's sun,
Sharpened by the pure white of snowdrops
Their little heads waving in the breeze

The carpet spills over into the Churchyard
Elsie gathers twigs,
She treads carefully between the tombstone
So as not to hurt the flowers.

She loves sticking for her fire, especially
When freeing flowers
So they bloom to the greater glory of God,
And help others to see the miracle of creation.

People come from far and near to this quiet spot.
Hidden on the wolds,
It has other charms as the seasons change
Not only Elsie thanks God for its beauty.
Elsie Pescod

Looking For Change

Lurking, stalking, scheming with greedy almost needy eyes,
  transfixed
Toward turd clad, traffic soiled, latently lavish pavements,
Adorning untold riches, unseen diseases and tempting
  discerning dishonest thoughts
A moment interrupted by non-rhythmic clatters of street
  infested footwear
Growing louder and fainter during the day's dithering diversions
This street living element, assimilating with one eye, glimmering gifts
As they are reflected by shimmering pools of pollutant field streets
and probing with other eyes toward bulging back pockets worn, some
torn with age, preceded by claspless handbags, owned by generous
geriatrics who unwittingly invite a visit from this malice aforethought,
the product of impetuous pompous politicians who are
sh** scared of becoming like 'them' and so ballot their bereaved
brains at the expense of some poor pitiful bastards, who know only to
to make, to lie, instead of asking why? and if given perhaps a chance,
their own lives they'd one day enhance
Whether it be money found in streets or fortune found in life,
Can't we all try and change in order to curb our strife?
Donald E. Abbott

'The War'

People say I'm too young to remember the war,
Too young to understand what they fought for.
But I've seen the war in my Mother's eyes,
When she speaks of the memories that remain for life.

I've seen the house as a girl she called home,
Number 52, but now eight stand alone.
The others were victims of Hitler's 'elite',
Bombing the docks to try to destroy our fleet.

When our house caught an incendiary device,
It blew out the ceilings but didn't ignite.
Our family was moved out to the countryside,
Longing for the day when war would subside.

When that day came in 1945,
My mother said everyone laughed and cried.
A bonfire was built on Plymouth Hoe,
Everyone sang and danced with hearts aglow.

So when they say I'm too young to remember the war,
I say yes, but I understand what they fought for.
It was so you and I could forever be free,
To those who fought I will always grateful be.

Glenda Quirk

Music

Listen to the music of the falling rain, through the tree
tops green, listen to the music in the air, as the wind plays
with the trees so tall let it flow, let the music flow.

Listen to the music as raindrops fall to the earth below,
listen to the music in children's laughter, as they go wandering
by, playing with the falling leaves and raindrops from the sky,
let the music flow, let the music flow.

Music to the ear every where, listen to the music of a bird
in the sky, just as twilight falls, listen to the music of the
sea and stars, as on and on it flows in timeless quality, let
the music flow,

let the music flow, let the music flow let the music flow.

Listen to the music of a stream passing by, the gurgle of water
Over stones, listen to the music as on and on it rolls as the music
Swells in timeless quality, keep a song in your heart, let the
music flow, let the music flow.

See all the beauty of the rainbow, as the colours flow through
the music, Rivers play over stones, through valleys green, over
meadows on their journey to the sea, making music as they go,
Listen to the music of The falling rain, music is everywhere

Janet Middleton

'As the desert is, I am'

As the desert is, I am,
undiscovered, cold and lonely,
I long to feel soft breezes,
the freshness of a light shower,
the warmth of the sun's kiss...

...Instead, there is only a bitter wind,
with no water to quench my thirst,
no escape from the blistering heat.

Should I let you survive the journey,
stop pounding you with my elements,
lead you to drink from my oasis,
shade your weary form?

Or should I let you wander,
watch you trip and fall over and over,
let your once moist mouth crack,
see you kneel and pray for death to save you?

As you lay there, perfectly still,
I'll say goodnight and cover you...
with sands that move once every thousand years,
and know your sleep will be without end.

Jacqueline Richards

Tradition

Through generations, from year to year,
Traditional Values have been made.
From Parents to their youngsters,
Birth, of which they gave.

Engagements, Weddings, Children, Old Age,
A cycle of life of which to follow.
As years go by, new ideas inspired,
Traditions, get hard to swallow.

Church weddings are slowly dying,
Beach weddings are all the rage.
Or why should you even get married?
People don't do it in this day and age.

Who needs a wedding to say they're happy,
A ring, to have a child.
How many people remember Traditions,
Where have they gone?   Where are they filed?

Family values is what's considered,
If no-one cares then why should you.
Don't criticize the young generation
We all live our lives as we choose.

Lisa Perry

Compline... In Winter

Silence, and solitude, and time,
Transmuted to eternity;
The singers come in darkness, but
With shining points of clarity,
In their candled hands, they pause;
The music's pure economy
Fulfils its own perfection, breathes
Its richness in austerity,
Its quintessential probity,
Sweetly, through jangled senses, wreathes
Its peace within the restless heart;
And lucis ante terminum,
Lightens our inward darkness, and
Establishes our tranquillity
Of mind, upon a certain good:
Silence, and solitude, and time,
Transmuted to eternity.

Barbara Gadd

" Humble Recorder "

Mellow tones to move and haunt,
tunes to arouse and moodily daunt.
Melody of awakening pitch,
high notes, low notes they enrich.

Why engage the fingers four?
Music from mouth doth pour
Joyous and melancholy rhythm in mind
Written scripts of musical kind

Clever words made out through tune
Methodical breath to the mouthpiece strewn
Harmonization of blown order
Through the humble, hollow, recorder.

Karen Shrimpton

Little Robin Red-Breast

Little robin red-breast
Twittering in the trees,
Darting down to greet me
Gaily in the breeze.
Sitting on my spade
Hoping for a worm
Sometimes too big,
Never too firm.
"Robin red-beast he is called"
As he glorified our Lord,
Plucked a thorn from that painful crown
He dipped his breast in gore so red
Hence beloved bird forever blessèd.

Frances Grieve

Woman Child

This woman child so far away,
Unable to wish you a Happy Birthday
To touch or to hold is my greatest wish,
A word of "hi mum" would silence my miss
Just to know you are healthy and happy inside
To feel your deep down vibes
Telepathy is my only vine,
To this birthday woman, child of mine.

Janet Antonietti

The Adulteress

Going out for a walk was her excuse
Unashamed recklessness
Being loved was worth every adulteress minute
To be really cared about, to feel truly cherished
Floating on the warm thermals of the love she received
No longer feeling like a bird with clipped wings

Stolen moments with him were so precious
The tenderness of his love making
Totally possessed her heart, her emotions
He understood the pain, the web of deceit she was living
Time for her to hurry for the last bus

Not knowing when they could next snatch time together
Made the reality of it seem almost pointless at times
A heartful of love is a heartful of tears
They kissed and embraced like it was for the last time

Arriving home, putting the key in the door
She is warm and flushed but still she shivers
Back home to the suffocation and confines
Of a one way loveless marriage

Alison M. Craig

Remembering

I arrived, so nervous as I was on my own
Unbeknown at the time you were also there, alone
I sat with some old friends, for some time sipping wine
When I casually looked around and saw you staring at thine

You asked me to dance, I accepted, it felt good
We talked as we danced, slowly, smiling at each other
Knowing we felt comfortable, automatically as you should
I think this man could well be my lover

We had to say good night, you asked to see me again
I was delighted and flattered my heart raced so fast
I did not want to sleep that night for fear of losing sight of your face
But I did and dreamt of you, and longed to see you at last

We have seen each other every day since then
Have wonderful times remembering when
We fumbled as we danced, standing on each other's toes
We really are having a romantic life together as it goes

Helena Hutchings

Untitled

Far from real are words on paper
unless the moment, frozen, packaged
changes reader into taster
knifing forking at your offer

Orgasmic vulture; tearing skin
feeling in, devouring the tender meat.
Full. The words repeat,

And still, the few; experience of life denied?
Now hide, and say that certain words
do not belong in art; poetic.

Don't swear, to me you don't feel pain
I feel it. I choose my words. I express
even you! I will not judge you less.

Liz Wakefield

Snowdrop

A little snowdrop nestled in the ground,
Unseen, unseeing, darkness all around:
Close to the bosom of its mother earth,
Waiting the time appointed for its birth.

Every field and forest waited too,
With winter's bleak tracery still in view:
His frosty fingers lingered long this year,
It seemed that spring would never reappear.

Then one joyous morning all nature stirred.
"Come, greet the sunshine" sang one little bird.
Earth's moist cloak was asunder torn,
The first frail flower of the year was born.

Eleana Arnold

Inspiration

In the savage of my brain that lies
Unwinking in this moonless night;
A turgid thought unbends a narrow back
And fosters light to rub a minute dry.
Amorphous in the marrow of my dreams
Wherein the lifeless clay to mould
All this, I fear, will issue forth
Among the musty sheaves.

A spark illumes the foggy path,
Past the grey, deceiving mind;
And leads the famished blood to roost
Clinkered by the lowly bone.
Shafts of mem'ry point the whistling way
On toward the senile brain that dims
Half-witted in the evening flush.

No more! No more! In vain I rail
Racked and thumb-screwed
On the mattress of my fallow mind...

Charles R. Covey

Silvery Shadow

In midnight skies I look for inspiration,
up among the stars, and the moon's silvery shadow
That cause me to shiver with fascination and wonder

Watching moonlight dancing upon the water and into the woods,
so still but for the noises of the wild. Captivated by this
moon glow and the secrets of the dark, that entice me still,
to the realm of dreams and my window, where I watch the
stars and hope I catch a falling one to pin my wishes upon.

As my thoughts drift on into the right, I dream with
eyes wide open, at magic and mystery, and loves I have
lost, beginnings, endings, dreams and ambitions, whilst the
moon silently listens, weaving its web of intrigue, captivating
my mind, time after time, with its sweet silent music of
the soul

Heidi Newton-Edwards

Thoughts

Is my Guardian Angel cold
Up there in realms of light?
Send him some heat:
Pictures of the autumn's gold,
Leaves, grasses, trees,
Brown earth warmed by summer's sun
And the black cat stretching in the late sun's rays.

Joy! Gratitude! I turn to thank someone.
But why?
Has someone brought me a three-tier chocolate cake?

No, it is my Angel's thoughts
So close-knit with mine
To seem as if my own.
And I feel his wings outstretched
To warm me through.

Lorna King

I Wish!

I wish, I wish that I could fly,
Up, up, up in the bright blue sky.
Or if that wish did not come true,
There's a million things that I could do.

I could run away, far to sea,
But what kind of life would that be?
I could be a princess, beautiful and kind,
Or be an explorer, what wonders would I find?
I wish, I wish that I could love,
And be as gentle as a dove.
Or if that wish did not come true,
There's a million things that I could do.

I could ride a runaway horse,
On a track or on a course.
Maybe go mining and find some treasure,
But would that really bring me pleasure?

I wish, I wish that I could be,
I wish, I wish to be just me!

Gemma Booth

Living On The Edge Of A Dream

Asleep I dreamed of floating passions dancing
Upon sunny fields of gold, we lay, softly breezes kissed our lips
The smell of sweet perfume in the hay beneath us
Caresses growing stronger, into the heavens I gazed
Until that final moment satisfied we laid.

In a single moment darkness began to fall
This dream is now a nightmare, if only I could wake,
Wild Wind's embracing us, the heavens start to fall
Rain beating faster, faster, hearts tired we fall,
Trees falling, falling, calling, my man has gone.

I'm running faster, faster, getting no-where at all,
Screaming out in silence, no-one to hear me call
I've reached the edge of Hades, no end and no one living,
Looking up to the heavens, reaching the sky I began to fly
Away up high a new day was dawning, gone my man to the heavens

I awoke to hear just silence, peace and tranquillity
My eyes glanced beside me — an empty space be spread
Where once my husband laid with me upon this lonely bed
Suddenly I remembered, my darling, he was dead
This wasn't just a dream; it was reality that I had seen.

Jane Dewey

Lost Not Found

Who am I that lives and breathes
Upon this planet, ill at ease.
With Fate before me in whose hand
I lay my life, misunderstand
The path meandering all around
Which I am on — lost not found.

Found: all of life's great complications.
Lost: all my greatest expectations.
Lost love, lost hope, lost happiness
Found anger, rage, resentfulness.
The tears, the fears and cries of woe
That echo far on distant shore.

Lost I stand alone and fearing
Of the next life now appearing
In the distance grey and sombre
In the deepest darkest yonder.
An island floating out to sea
Awash with sadness, picture me.

Eleanor I. Magee

Your Heart's Desire

Go higher, flier, with desire slalom the sky
vehement fortitude speeds, needs of forty thousand deeds
racing, pacing, without spacing — never asking why.

Stars cluster, thoughts muster, shrieks form, without warn
spreading, heading, bending and sending — you don't even try.

White waves collide, roaring, soaring, sweltering and melting
become one, someone, on one, have fun and it will be done
it's all a meeting to the glory to the sun.

Pleasure seeker, holds life in a beaker, balancing act
glides, collides, all the rides — and how they react
when someone calls and the beaker falls on the short and the small.

It is the doing, between the to-ing and the fro-ing, while you're
growing not just the sowing, between a lust or a crust
that appears, endears, spears, enfolding whilst it disappears.

This conception of actuality to which you aspire
knowingly, in earnest that it concerns you
its fruits to fulfil your heart's desire.

Glyn Jones

Being A Parent

Like a seed that is planted in the garden, and struggles against the
  vermin of the earth, and eventually rises up like the Phoenix to
  tell the world of its birth.
I'm of a one-parent family, which can really be hard at times,
  sometimes it gets so bad, that I think I'm going out of my mind.
I have three children who are not really troublesome but who
  sometimes take over my head, sometimes I feel like a robot,
  I've even wished I was dead.

Then one day I was asked to do a parenting course. Me! I thought,
  what more was there to know, hadn't I really got first-hand
  knowledge on how to help my children grow.

So for six consecutive Thursdays, I went out in wind and in rain,
  and really looked forward to the next week, because none
  was ever the same.
I learned to communicate and listen, and hear what was said
  and what was meant, and that my children were humans like
  I was, they were a gift which was heaven sent.

I learned that I provide all my children, not so much with what
  they want as what they need, and as long as they grow up
  respectful and loyal, then I'll have really planted the seed.
So like the seed that was planted in the garden, and tended
  with rain as nature designed, I will rise and shoot up like the
  Phoenix, and be a parent, the best you can find.

Bernadette O'Connor

This Place

I stood here as I had stood before
Viewing all before me, from a
far and distant shore.

There was nothing to be seen
by a naked human eye,
No life, no difference, not even
between sea and sky.

There was no day and there was no night,
Just existence in a world of constant twilight
With tears in my eyes, I turned to go,
Stumbling in pain, and my efforts slow.

For there was naught but destruction and decay,
No-one left, no hope, no way.

My comfort was that death was near,
The sooner the better, I knew no fear
Almost to the second it was timed,
My last agonizing step, I! The last of mankind.

A breeze caressed his body, covered slowly by shifting sand,
Soon, there was nothing left to see, but a lonely outstretched hand.

Irene Smith

Dreams Twisted

Dreams twisted
Visions distorted
Frustration creeping in.
The path I've taken, becoming overgrown
Further I struggle, the scratches get deeper
Is it time to re-track or will the struggle find an
opening?
I dream of seeing a clearing
Where I will rest and relieve the pain of the past
battle.
And then continue the journey of my life.

Iain Moore

Deadly Seduction

Oh death come quickly, take this pain away
Visit me with tenderness, I'll let you have your day
I'll welcome you with open arms as a lover to my bed
I'll kiss you on your stone cold lips, so full and dark blood red

Oh death, how sweet you are, no torture in your ways
Your fingernails caress me at this ending of my days
Naked and seductive, you take my breath away
Your lips are wet, your touch is cool, your eyes a winter day

Oh death, you evil thing, for only now I see
As your arms and legs surround me, you crush the life from me
You visit as a lover and as love slides into hate
You leave me, grinning viciously, to find another mate.

David Campbell

Catching A Fish From The Sea

You hear the howling wind rushing,
Waiting, waiting for a fish to come.
You've eaten your crisps, you've eaten your dinner
Waiting, waiting for a fish to come.
The bait's gone quick, o' flip come quick
Waiting, waiting for a fish to come.
My rod struck once that's a sign
Waiting, waiting for a fish to come.
My rod is pulling tight
Reeling, reeling, reeling the fish in
It's coming, oh gosh! It's coming, oh gosh!
Reeling, reeling, reeling the fish in.
It looks like a cod, or maybe a bass
It's coming, it's coming, a very big fish
Hurry, hurry it's coming very quick
I can't look, oh gosh! It's coming in quick
What a whopper, a 4 lb cod,
I can't wait to show my Dad.

Lucas Grant Phillips

Flight In To Fantasy

Awake in the rainfall, watching the sky,
Waiting with patience for a unicorns cry.
A song on the wind, pain in the sky,
A thunder of hoof beats, a fearless cry.

The horned horses appear on the horizon afar,
Dancing to music from a distant guitar.
Over hills, over mountains, they run without fear,
Toward faraway futures, never shedding a tear.

A pony of silver, stars in his mane,
Child of the moonlight, the manhunters bane.
Running with darkness, escaping the sun,
Searching for hope away from man's gun.

A shot from the grave, disorder within,
A red glow in their eyes, man's deadliest sin.
The child becomes angry, man feels its wrath,
The world will have anguish 'till unicorns come back.

A moonbeam from heaven floats down through the sky
Freedom runs up it, the world starts to cry.
Awake in the rainfall, watching the sky,
Waiting with patience for a unicorn's cry.......

Erin-Marie Carrigan

My Best Friend

Walk beside me to the end,
Walk beside me ever more,
I will know you are always there
Walk beside me to the end.

In the woods where the blue bells grow
In the fields where the flowers bows
In the rivers where the water flows
Up the hills going slow.

You held my hand
Freedom was my gift
A gentle kiss a golden time
Another world, another life

No more pain no more tears,
No more heartache, goodbye pain
You're in a world no one hears
To see your sweetheart was your aim.

Until the golden hours when we meet again
Friends here, friends there, it's all the same
We shall meet love and laugh again,
Good night, God bless my best friend.

Caroline May

Realms

Every way you wanted the world to move I granted your dream,
Walk beside me for a while and listen to my thoughts.
With my help your world was formed lavished and adorned.

The future was bright and clear, no fear was never to near,
all our life together we worked and prayed, and in our hearts
we knew we had it made.

Purposely the ice cool wind of youth chilled your heart,
perhaps the thought of pastures new were an answer to a
question you never knew?

Left alone to go in circles with the pain, unbearable pain
wondering some days if I was indeed the one who was sane.
Colours went away beyond my sight to a corner of dwindling light
all my movements in the day were covered by the blanket of night.

When the fear of being alone and confused slowly evaporated away
clearer thought within the mind came to stay
Roses may be red, skies might be blue, but the world began to
look better without having you.

The dawn began to melt the dark shadows far, leaving the
crystal its colours beaming forth to touch and cleanse, this
dawn is still so young but still so sure, I feel as it awakes
more and grows to fill me with truth,
putting to rest the embers of unpredictable youth.

Gabriel Duffy

At The Foot Of The Cross

This restlessness — that ensnares me,
walks over me, squeezes me dry,
leaves me with thumping heart and aching head,
poises me for flight,
lashes me against the rock of my will.
This restlessness I offer to you, my Lord...
You take my restlessness,
my aching body, my trembling heart, my feverish brain...
my despair, my destruction...

This stillness — that is followed by restlessness,
like a deep, dark, impenetrably dark void, like an icy hell
envelops me, freezes my heart, mind, body, renders me null
and void,
when a silent scream of "I am not any more"
heralds finally an absolute zero, -273°C.
This deadly stillness
at the foot of thy cross I offer to you, my Lord, my Saviour...
And then I wait... for your Will to be done,
not mine, not mine....

Dubravka Williams-Podhraski

The Dream

I dream of a cottage somewhere out there,
Walls painted white, dark timbers bare.
Windows curtained against the night,
Sharp spears greeting the moon so bright.
A tiled path curls its way to the door
Through profusion of flowers, leaves on the floor.
Perfume so heady, filling the air,
Oh, how I wish ... I wish I was there!

I dream of how they'd be in the day,
Nodding and dancing in the sun's ray.
Marigolds, cornflowers and roses' hue,
A tapestry of colour, a new love for you.
A slight breeze rustles leaves in the tree
Causing my heart to flutter - but nothing to see
'Cept the gentle and warm presence of you,
Oh, how I wish ... I wish it was true!

Anne L. Daniels

The Tiger's Eyes No Longer Burn Bright

"The tiger's eyes no longer burn bright."
War in Vietnam was a catalyst.
Chemicals, lost their camouflage to light,
By maiming the shadows of the forest.
How must it feel for natural predators,
To be hunted; for its skin, claws and jaws?
Barbarism in pursuit of creditors.
Can our voice not be heard, invoking laws?
Prohibiting its furs and voodoo cures,
From mistakenly, accumulating wealth.
Sustain the tiger's habitat and lures;
Its tarnished grandeur, agility and stealth.
Lost in name of medicine and fashion.
Gone are the days of peaceful halcyon.

Chris King

Revolving Door — Selfridge's September 1995

Sun's slanting hand on summer's early morning dew
Warms not my heart as did one smile from you;
An unknown, un-named passer, who that day
Set small mischievous devils in my heart to play.
One glance, the curving of your lips,
The tilting of your head that set my feet amiss.
But strange; though not one word was said,
In that fleet time we met; we loved; then wed.
But I've not seen you since that fevered day
Though it well may my pounding heart allay,
But re-creation is a thing I must not make
For in the doing, fragile memory I may break
And in a second-seeing, may destroy
My moment of a bounding inward-breathing joy.

James Byron Archer

Interrupted Dreams

As I lay by the gently flowing stream
This is the place I laze and dream
The peace and quiet it's my domain
No people no cars just an occasional train
In the warm summer sun I lay for hours
Hypnotized by the water and scent of flowers
I think of my first love and the time we spent
Walking by the stream and what it meant
I remember days with fishing net and jar
At the stream edge, aren't lean to far
I dream of fame and my name in lights
Saying thank you to my public, how polite
No noisy phone to disturb my dreams
I've been here forever or so it seems
I Love these moments of solitude and peace
As I lay by the gently flowing stream
The silence is then broken, a voice says "Mam
Have any sandwiches other than boiled ham?"
Were out on a picnic at my favourite spot
As I lay there dreaming I nearly forgot.

Irene Witte

Time

Dedicated to my late father Selwyn Wells

I used to think that life itself
   Was full of ups and downs.
And every day meant more hard work
   To earn those extra pounds

And any chance of happiness
   You snatch at, if you dare
But keep an eye upon the clock
   There's just no time to spare

And then someone I dearly loved
   Was taken ill, and died
So for a while in my despair
   I cursed, I grieved and cried

Then I learnt that time alone
   Will show you how to find
The gift and pleasures left in life
   And give you peace of mind.

So now I make each moment count
   I look ahead and pray
That every soul will find the peace
   That I can feel today.

Christine Ash-Smith

The Best Things......

I'm sitting quietly on the river bank
Watching all the debris going by,
Remembering when I was a child
I could catch fish with a fly.

The river is now so polluted,
The fish couldn't even see the prey,
The water doesn't seem to be flowing,
It just lies there, murky and grey.

No more can I see my reflection
As I gaze into the water, so deep,
No tadpoles or minnows causing ripples
Just drops from my eyes as I weep.
I weep for the children of tomorrow,
Who will never experience the fun
Of jumping into fresh clear water
To get cool out of the hot mid-day sun.

This happiness didn't cost any money,
To the river there was no entrance fee,
We were happy with our own entertainment,
Which gave meaning to "The best things in life are free"

Elsie J. Speck

A Sleeping Babe

Softy, gently, the rain outside is falling,
Watching and waiting, her heart is beating fast,
She watches the headlights sweeping round the courtyard,
Breathless she waits, he is here at last.

She gazes at the bundle, asleep there in the corner,
An angel there sleeping, unaware of care.
She listens for his key turning in the door lock.
She strokes the tiny baby. Soon Daddy will be there.

The handle on the door turns, in steps a handsome figure.
Smiling, embracing, his kisses soft and sweet.
He greets with joy his woman, who all day has waited for him,
And gazes with tenderness at his baby there asleep.

Love is everlasting, growing more with parting,
Renewed and rekindled with every kiss they share.
The love they share together no-one could be doubting,
For it's there for all to see in the baby sleeping there.

Julie Freeman

Hidden Feelings

Yes, you have become an obsession with me,
Watching day and night to see.
Is the river high or low
Is the answer yes or no
You have ruined my life
Taken away all those years
All the precious things treasured, as time goes by
You have washed them away with your power and might
Leaving me to mourn, not forgetting that night
Over and over in my mind
The sound of the thunderous roar that awoke me.
The shiver of being cut off from the world
Watching the water take over and trap us
Controlling our lives
I want to forget the hurt you have left inside me
I want to look at you and see you calmness and beauty
As I did before
But as yet I cannot forgive and forget.
Chris Binner

People In The Streets

All day I sit in the streets
Watching people go by.
No friends
No feelings
No family I nearly cry.
People just stare at me as they go by.
When I was young I was happy
but that's in the past,
but this is reality
I just hope it goes fast
People don't care it's not fair
but it's just the way I am!
Katy Lambert

Silence

Silence is a black bird flying,
Water flowing down a river,
A big white swan swimming in a lake,
A time to think your thoughts,

Silence is a leaf falling from a tree,
The wind blowing the grass,
A pheasant asleep in a tree,
A time to close your eyes and think,

Silence is snow falling from the sky,
Rain tapping gently on the window,
Someone reading a book at night,
To lock out the noise of the world.
Danny Fennell

Hylas And The Nymphs

As the boat approached the wooded shore, the young boy,
Water-jug in hand,
With fearful heart and careful steps, slow made his way to land.
His ship-mates soon were left behind, they being older,
Cautious men,
But Hylas young and bold strode till he found a clearing
In the glen.
And what he saw then made him still, a group of girls were
swimming there,
Their lips of softest deepest red, and deeper red their trailing hair.
They coaxed him into waters green, and sang and begged him
there to stay.
His friends, grown hoarse from calling him, heartbroken sailed away.
So there he stays in dreamless sleep, while nymphs tend to his
every care,
And for his fate they gently weep, and kiss his face and comb
his hair.
But though from there he cannot go, and will sleep forever
amid the trees,
There never was one loved as he, by maids as fair as these.
Carol O'Dea

Lonely Watcher

Trawling for fish: But the catch is poor.
Waves are breaking on a polluted shore.
Lonely watcher looking out to sea —
Is it too late to change what has to be?
An empty space: With an empty skyline
A world away from that childhood bedtime
The world as we knew it has ceased to be —
Lonely watcher looking out to sea.
Pollution — and waste has taken over
No one looks at wild flowers, grass or clover
No one worries about diesel fumes
Around the town centre rising in plumes —
Every two seconds sees a plane in the air —
With noisy pollutants creating a nightmare
Lonely watcher looking out to sea
Turn back the pages of history
Do something now, before it's too late.
If everyone tries we can alter our fate.
Before earth movement in 2012 — let's say
Means the end of our world as we know it today.
Doreen Banas

Our World

Oh world you are but a symbol of our greed
We all exhaust your wealth, in order to succeed.
The bounteous gifts you offer are far beyond compare.
You are but a grain of sand, in the universe out there.

Hand in hand with the sun and moon, our days and nights are born
As you turn on your axis whilst we sleep, your journey will
greet the dawn.
The wonders that you have performed, mankind cannot perceive
Your elements beneath the ground have made us rich indeed.

The birth of mankind on your planet, shows what we are in a way
With knowledge gained through the ages, providing existence today.
But the powers you hold are far greater, than can ever be put
into rhyme
For you hold the key and the purpose, which creates all the
tides and Time.

This world of ours is so precious, can we appreciate what it is worth
Or through blindness destroy ourselves, as well as this
beautiful earth,
Can man put an end to destruction, by using his skills and his powers
Just by having a greater conception, we'd be saving this
planet of ours.

Out there in the universe, all the planets take their place
Each with their own dimension, all in the vastness of space.
Do they encounter the problems, that man has produced for you.
If there's to be an end of the world, will the universe end too?
Anne Seymour

Circle Of Life

There comes a day when life must change ...
We can no longer tread the way
That life has taken us day by day
For pastures new attract our gaze
And gates will open on fresh new days
To fill with joy and love most true -
Our hearts will tell us what to do.

Forget not the friends we've made,
Though at times we have disagreed.
Yet all we have learned,
We have learned through them -
For we have chosen the paths we've trod;
The paths we've trod with them.

So shut not the doors on those past days
But fling them open wide,
To let out old doubts and fears
And make way for new ideas
To boost us on our way.

There comes a day when life must change ...
Constance Osbourn

Mother (Through The Eyes Of A Son)

Of all the mothers in this world,
We certainly got the best.
I'm talking now through experience,
We've put you to the test.
You were the one who was always there
To help us when we were down,
You picked us up, and you put us right,
Always without a frown.
You feel the hurt, and you feel the pain,
When we've tripped up in life,
We're truly sorry for causing you
All this anguish and this strife.
You raised us well, and to do what's right,
And one day we might have to part,
But never in a lifetime, mother, will you
Ever leave our hearts.
David Crosbie

Sonnet To A Baby Niece

You were a long time coming my sweet girl
We had to wait what seemed a thousand years
Our hearts and arms were ready for this pearl
Who came to us after many prayers and tears
The joy of your arrival knew no bounds
Since we heard the sound of your first cry
The champagne corks were popping all around
As in your mother's arms asleep you lie
I can't believe the love I felt inside
When first I looked on your determined face
This child who is the family's pride
Who looked as though she owned the human race
I held you up for all the world to see
I little knew how changed my life would be
Doris I. Brown

In Your Comfort

In your comfort, I await, for your arms
to harbour my frailty;
Subtle glances, when in doubt of your
unyielding love for me.
Your soothing breath upon my face, as the
lilac she-moon bleeds the darkness;
Assuring my waking moments, of your
peaceful sleep, and not for Nirvana to repossess.
And when, in the oblivion of passionate release,
with your hand reaching out to clasp at mine,
The spiritual soul invokes within, and
eternally marks the eaves of time.
I await the comfort of your arms,
to harbour my frailty.
And the sweetness of your lips on
mine, to fill what once was empty.
Catherine Roberts

The Romany And The Burglar

One miserable Monday morning a Romany crossed my path,
told me many wonderful things
pierced my loneliness, released my smile, sold me a charm
and was arrested.

One bright Sunday evening a burglar entered my garden shed,
brazenly smirked, gave me his name
'No crime's been committed,' the policeman said.

The latter shattered my peace of mind.
The Romany's gentle, accurate, kind
words lifted me
for a while.

Her 'crime'? Selling the charm?
The burglar, with many convictions, doing such harm
walked free - smiling at me.
His eyes were steel; her gift was real.
I know which one I'd rather be!
Annette Borrill

Dogs

Do you like dogs? I do,
We have a poodle, whose name is Prue,
She's rather small, with soft, black curls,
And very fond of boys and girls.

She chases our cat. And barks at Tom
Who, frightened, runs quickly by,
And should he hiss and arch his back,
She's very hurt and wonders why?

She takes Dad's slipper, loves a nap
In his favourite, big arm-chair,
And if he calls, pretends not to hear,
Creeps under the cushion, shows she's not there.

But if I say, 'a walk in the park?'
The cushion's aside in a flurry,
And she's at the door, with barks of joy,
And begging me to hurry, please hurry!

I love the family very much,
My friends, and most of their pets, too.
But in my heart there's a special place,
For that lovely poodle, Prue!
Jean Jane

Destruction

We've caused so much destruction to the grasses oh so green
We have cut down several woodlands, and ruined most every scene
And what for? I want to ask, just what is it we've achieved
Is it true our lives have prospered, or have we been deceived

With the car to replace horses, and the roads cut through the land
Our seas are now polluted, with such debris on the sand
And the multi-storey buildings, used to house the human race
Are truly quite an eyesore, which is something we must face

For our day-to-day existence has changed throughout the years
The ozone layer's now threatening, it's one of the greatest fears
For the sole means of salvation is to revert back to the past
To get rid of cars and factories, then the world won't die as fast

For each species is diminishing, some are even now extinct
And it's the flourishing economy to which this destruction's linked
And even in those cities, which do appear to thrive
In the back streets there are people who are struggling to survive

It's true we're now more capable than a hundred years ago
But with the end approaching, something soon will have to go
For how can a father promise, and vow to his only son
That in life he's going to prosper: he can't, for death's begun
Jennifer Susan Dadds

Does Anyone Care

Have you forgot what we did for you?
We got rid of Hitler, Rommel too.
The cruel wars made us into men.
If the time came, we would do it again.

Food on ration, cloth's had to get.
Was it worth it? "You Bet."
Look at us, we have survived,
All due to men and woman that died.

Could someone please just give us a smile.
Stop for a chat, just for a little while.
Your time with us will not be a waste.
No, stop, don't go in haste.

It cost you nothing to be polite.
Oh how lonely we'll be tonight
Sitting alone in our old armchairs.
Someone please, show us you care.

I wonder what will become of me.
I've lost my hair, and can hardly see.
Please help the less fortunate than you.
Like us you can say, "I did this for you."
Ann Brown

Fledgling

Our Mother, Earth, She's crying,
We, Her children, are the best,
She doesn't want, but knows She must,
Drive us upwards, from our nest.

Oh! Mother Earth, our love is Yours,
We understand You now,
We will be strong, we must prevail,
Your mighty wondrous throng.

We'll take Your life and spread it out,
Among the stars, thro' space, and night,
And so across the cosmic palace,
Your light will shine so bright.

Our destiny with pride fulfilled,
Your purpose wrought eternal,
The universe so full of life,
And all from Earth's small kernel.
   C. Jolyss

Intruder

Ringing, buzzing, bleeping fiend,
we hide you deep behind our screens.

You shout and scream in different tones,
piercing through our very bones.

Plastic and wire your resilient form,
made by man you were never born.

Never to tire or water take,
you bare the cold and sun can bake.

I lift you up to quell your shriek,
a distant voice begins to speak.
Nerves already strained and tore,
the whisper changes fast to roar.

Warm lights and distant cheer,
when walking to my homely door,
frozen still in ridged fear,
the ghoulish scream begins once more.

Drifting, floating in sleeps dark bay,
my silent haven ejects the day,
no sharing of thoughts, I am alone,
intruder of dreams, uncaring phone.
   John Deacon

Our Search For Love

It's February and St Valentines has been revived
We hope to receive flowers- to brighten our everyday lives?
The shops are full of sugary hearts and cards with romantic verse
But does love last forever - or is it a bubble waiting to be burst?

As teenage girls we dream and plan
Ever longing for the day we meet the perfect man,
Like in the films he must be dashing, kind and fun
A bittersweet promise of wonderful things to come!

What is this feeling could we have found love it seems?
Our hearts flutter and race, as the telephone rings.
The emptiness and longing to be loved disappear
Our dreams have come true, at last a sweetheart so dear.

After the wedding, not quite like in the books
In sickness and in health we all loose our looks.
There are bills to pay even when we have no steady jobs
We worry and fret our offspring will become yobs?

The moral to this ode is to come down to earth
To live with each others shared moments of mirth.
If we forget the romantic notions taking life day by day
Then love really can shine through in its Mysterious Way!
   Catheryn Romano

Duane My Brother

You were so tiny and oh so small
We knew you were never going to be tall
You were so cuddly and so cute
Although you were a mute
We knew what you tried to say

"If only I could stay
Here in your arms
Safe in your palms
That's where I wanted to be
With the mum I still now see"

He's here in the house
As quiet as a mouse
The brother I loved dearly
Oh so close we were really
Although he passed away
I know I'll see him one day
My brother Duane
   Fay Bannister

Dad's Prayer

You were such a wonderful father
We know that we had the best
And words of comfort we send to you
Now the time has come for you to rest
You were our hero until the end
You were so courageous and brave
And if love had been the cure
Without a doubt you would have been saved.
And although we have lost our father
We have also lost our best friend
Because having you was the greatest gift
That life could ever send.
   God Bless.
   Lisa Richards

Ted

We married when we were young
We lived a life of fun
We always were together
Until last year
You turned to me and said
"Excuse me, could you tell me
Who are you and why you're in my bed?"
It's strange, to me you're still my Ted.
To you I'm no longer Meg!
I cry when I'm alone and
Wonder why it's so
I wish you could comfort me
And I you.
You seem to think I hurt you
You scream and shout at me
If only I could tell you
And you could understand
That I'm the lady you
Once loved and shared your hopes and dreams!!
   Jayne Moore

Mummy — Sheryl

Mummy always takes me to school
We often walk through the park
My dog likes coming with us
And we sometimes see a sky lark
If it rains, we go in the car
But the school is not very far.

I like my school, and all the teachers
Gymnastics, and cooking as well
And when I take my cakes home
My mum says they are real swell.

We are now getting ready for Christmas
Singing carols, and doing the school play
And when we do it in front of the people
My mummy will be there on that day.
   Elizabeth Ann Collis

The War Widow

Time will help you, all the comforters said.
We really are sad to know he is dead
But the buses still labour up the hill
And you must go forward — you are young still.

And time will heal, one young comforter sighed.
The anguish will lessen, the pain subside.
Right now your heart is heavy with sorrow
But it will lighten with each to-morrow

You'll surface in time, the comforters vowed.
Just don't sit on your own — mix with a crowd.
Grieve for a short while and then start anew.
He would not wish you to be always blue.

But I hear his laughter — the words he spoke.
His love wraps around me, warm like a cloak
He still walks beside me, handsome and tall.
Time isn't helping --
    not helping at all.
Joy Udell

Untitled

As through life, our ways we go
We reap benefits, we do not sow,
And many of these will always be,
Accepted without thanks - so naturally.

Friendship is that, which cannot be bought,
Its price is too dear, however sought,
And deserved it is, written in gold,
Of a place on our memories scroll.

We always find it and participate
It's wealth, but do not appreciate,
As blindly we tread along life's road,
A helping hand is sharing the load

With you, it has been found, sincere and true,
Very good wishes and thanks goes to you.
Fred Lewis

God's Velvet Glove

Nature's crust evolves the earth.
We too can have a second birth.
A second chance.
A second vision.
A chance again to look through the prism,
Of what mankind has done to man,
And has evolved a second plan.

A life lived through a vision screen,
Which seems to be in just a dream,
Without a metaphor it seems,
But just when no sense can be seen or heard,
Then comes the time of that hidden word,
Which gives advice so sure and true,
Which will help your life surrounding you.

Through that dark black hole you'll come.
Seeking justice in another tongue.
A sinner saved.
A heart re-born.
Rejoicing in that bright, new dawn.
Anne Hadley

Welcome Winter Arrgh

Summer's gone, if that's what it was
Welcome winter Arrgh and old jack frost
Winter intrudes with blizzard and storm
Wrap up well, try to keep warm
An adult's curse, a child's delight
Skating and sledging and snowball fights
Season of goodwill, carols to sing
Oh God — why wasn't your son — born in the spring
Cold and miserable, is this reason to celebrate
From November till April, we should all hibernate
David McGregor Bonhill

The 07.50 From Wolverhampton

An experience so often missed when swiftness is King
We travel quickly; no time to breathe
Without realizing what we are missing in our rushing
To accomplish without thinking each task and then leave
History, a subject left behind in the schoolroom
Skips by in our daily lives, though possible to see
We shield it, we cover it, lock it in the vacuum
Of memories, past fears; its importance not perceived
This day I witness the collusion of time
The frozen canal, the urban ponies that feed
The factories, now empty, still covered in grime
Clash with today and the clean commercial creed
As the cut disappears at Ash and Lacey
And the commuters flow out at Birmingham New Street
We have passed the old foundry, the memory now hazy
But what lingers, the vision, a taste of the life pre-concrete
Fiona Smith

Granddad

Going to see granddad was always great fun
We used to play cards, or look for worms in the sun
He'd always have time for my family and me
Even if it was just for a chat and some tea
He was the most generous, kind, loving person I knew
And I hoped someday I'd be like him too
He started to grow old, but he didn't stop smiling
He'd always told me not to be scared of dying
He became quite ill and his independence was lost
We told him we'd care for him no matter the cost
I went to visit, but it wasn't him there
I came to the conclusion he didn't really care
In the next few days he gave up and died
It really hurt, there was a part missing inside
It took me a long time to get over the pain
But I told myself we'd someday meet again
I'll never forget the time that we had
My memories of him will never be sad
He was the greatest granddad there ever could be
The number one granddad is what he was to me.
Helen Alderson

Nursing (The Old)

He was a child before
we were born
now he is helpless, old and unhappy
He walked with his wife,
their cheeks all aglow
His wife was a mother,
she had babes at her breast
caring for others, and giving her best

He was a man, salute him for this
now he is withered and harder to kiss
speak to him gently
and nurse him with pride
now as he waits to
sail with the tide
Our's are the last hands
he will ever hold
let him know love,
now he is old.
Caroline Foster

Agoraphobia

A poor wretched child, lost and distraught,
Wearing a noose of despair.
Soulless eyes stare back from a mirror,
I drown in a black hell hole.
Chased by an evil rampaging devil
That longs to devour my soul and sanity,
Leaving me snivelling, grovelling,
To lick my wounds till he returns again,
With a vengeance.
Evelyn Amos

The Good Old Days

We met and married a long time ago
We worked for long hours, wages were low
No T.V. no wireless, no bath, times were hard
Just a cold water tap and a walk in the yard
No holidays abroad, no carpet on the floor
We had coal on the fire, no locks on the door
Our children arrived, no pill in those days
We brought them all up without aid from the state
They were safe going out to play in the park
And old folks were safe to go out in the dark
No valium, no drugs, no LSD
We cured all ills with a good cup of tea.
No vandals, no mugging, there was nothing to rob,
We felt we were rich with a couple of bob
People were happier in those far off days,
Kinder and caring in so many ways.
Milkmen and paper boys would whistle and sing
A night at the pictures was our one mad fling
We all got our share of struggle and strife
We all had to face it, that's the pattern of life.

Hilda Morgan

" We met and we married a long time ago "

WE met and we married a long time ago
We worked for long hours when wages were low
No TV, no wireless, times were so hard
Just a cold water tap and a walk in the yard

NO holidays abroad, no carpets on floors
We had coal on the fires and we didn't lock doors
Our children arrived, no pill in those days
And 'we' brought them up, without any state aid

THEY were safe going out, to play in the park
And old folk could go for walks in the dark
No valium, no drugs and no LSD
We cured most of our ills, with a strong cup of tea

NO vandals, no muggings, there was nothing to rob
We felt we were rich with a couple of bob
People were happier in those far off days
Kinder and caring in so many ways

MILKMAN and paper boy would whistle and sing
A night at the pictures was our only made fling
We all got our share of troubles and strife
We just had to face it, 'twas the pattern of life'

D. R. Maskeen Gul

2 A.M.

2 a.m. and all the world is still
Weary limbs swing from well worn bed
Muffled thoughts swill in ruffled head
Nightly pilgrimage to bathroom unfurls
While silently my family curls, and
Nestles deeper under sheets.

Outside the January snow has lain
A pure silent blanket on the ground
Daytime cares now count for nought
As suddenly alone and fraught
One sees one as at time of birth
Stripped bare — of pretence
Little cause for mirth
But then again! maybe?

Quick flush and shiver
"On est on h'iver"
Goose pimpled flesh beats a hasty retreat
To the sanctuary of toasted feet.

John J. Flanagan

Isle Of The Mountains

Mountain of Blaven, rugged escarpment crudely etched
  against the sky,
Weird, enchanting, spewed up from the bowels of the earth
  long past,
Old man of Storr, with craggy finger pointing upwards ever high,
Like a monument set among the rocks that nature has cast.

The mighty Quirang, where somehow a sense of evil pervades,
Absorbed into the very depths of the rocks abounding,
What awful tales they could tell us of past decades,
Of fearful happenings, terrible deeds to set the heart a pounding,
The beauty of the Cuillins, oft wearing mist as a shroud,
Capricious, mercurial, with ever-changing moods and whims,
While in festive array, round their proud peaks, circlets of cloud,
Enticing climbers to ascend their slopes risking life and limbs.

This then is Skye, land of the mist and mountains,
A wondrous isle, set like a jewel in the deep blue sea,
Great waterfalls, cascading, tumbling, like myriads of fountains,
Mysterious, enchanting, and where I ever long to be.

Caroline M. Nicolson

Cousin Love

'Twas on a Winter's morning that Mother called me up,
We're going to see Auntie's baby, get dressed and hurry up.

When we arrived at Auntie's house, I then was shown the bed,
Wherein lay a baby girl, my Cousin Winifred.

The next ten years I watched her grow, and then I went abroad,
I went to farm in Canada, she went to Uncle Joe's.

Five years went by and back I came, my roaming days were through,
I knew that I loved this pretty girl, and that she loved me too.

I saw the Love-Light in her eyes, she saw the same in mine.
And from that very moment, our two hearts did entwine.

We never left each other's side, 'till she was just eighteen,
Until the Wedding-Knot was tied, and naught dare come between.

She made a perfect house-wife, she made me pies and buns,
She gave to me her perfect love, and four strong healthy sons.

As we approach Life's evening, we're very much alive,
Though Winnie now is Seventy-Six, and I am Eighty-Five.

Ernest Portman

Why

Were the women and children of Auschwitz to blame
Were the men at Dunkerque in the way
Was Pearl Harbour really at risk
Would Hiroshima's bomb make them desist

Did evacuee children miss their mums
Did women's land army work with their chums
Did our granddads join the home guard
Were the A R P wardens' lives hard

Was Coventry raised to the ground
Was Dresden in the same state found
When St. Paul's Cathedral remained
Were most cities of Europe horrifically maimed

Were Russia, Nagasaki and Poland involved
Were many more countries before peace resolved
Veteran's reflections we cannot discern
Will the world not listen and learn?

Jacky Hallett (c 24 August 1995)

The Environment

Keep the environment nice and clean,
Don't chop down trees or be mean,
Think of the animals point of view,
Lions and bears are turning extinct too,
People making things extinct,
Making furs using minks
Will there be tomorrow?

Natalie Johnson

'Warning'

Well, we've won!
We've beaten the Jap and the Hun;
We finished the war they begun.
So let all the world know, we won.

I can tell you, it's not been much fun,
There's been many a dirty job done;
And there's many a "Ma" lost her son;
Still, you can tell all the world that WE WON.

There's still quite a lot to be done
'Fore we all get a place in the sun
But, for the sake of the boys who are gone
Don't let them forget that WE WON.
Valentine Stealey

Absence Makes The Heart Grow Fonder

We started off so down and out, our lives both torn and tattered,
We've shown them all without a doubt, together still! That matters.
We're not quite where we want to be through work we live apart,
To earn, and save and then achieve, a new and happy start.

I miss you more than I can say, I wait for you to phone,
Your voice it thrills me through and through, I yearn for you to hurry home.
I'd like to think we'd be together, not just lovers but special friends,
Have happy times, grow old together, a full life till the bitter end.

Absence makes the heart grow fonder, these thoughts come from my heart,
There is a life for us out yonder, it's just we've had a busy start.
Because you are so wonderful, my lover and my friend,
My love for you is plentiful and it will never end.
Lorrain Skivington

Scottish From The Heart

It's hard to define in simple words,
What being Scottish means,
It isn't just the country,
Beautiful mountains, valleys and streams,
It isn't just the people,
Friendly and full of care,
And it isn't just the old Scots folk,
Hard-worked men with scraggy hair,
It's something much, much deeper,
Something that grows inside,
It's the whole idea of being a Scot,
The faith, the hope, the pride,
It began back in the days of old,
When men were loyal and true,
They died for the love of their country,
They died for me and you,
They fought to give us freedom,
To rid our land of foes,
and it's because of all this fighting
That the love inside us grows.
Jane E. Murdoch

After Edgehill

My sword is sheathed, the battle's done.
What cost in Blood? The count's begun.
Cromwell's hordes lay cut or slain;
A blood red sea where once green plain.
What women must this bleak day weep?
Sad tears will wash their eyes in sleep.
Poor widows all, for they must cry
For men of youth — too young to die.
But I'll return to greet my love,
Our thanks to give the Lord above;
But fight again I surely will,
The King's vile foes perchance to kill,
And when I fall, in honour deep,
Warm tears will bathe my love in sleep.
John C. Gallagher

Mirrors

When you look through a mirror,
What do you see.
It's a person so old, so young, it is me.
Through the glass is an image, only
few can conceive, only those very few can believe.
Life is a once, it doesn't happen again,
So let's make it real, yet really not to plain
There are highs and sometimes lows
There are joy's and then joe's.
These are people we know, we perhaps even love
This has all come from the man above,
He looks through just glass,
He doesn't even ask?
Are you happy?
Are you sad, he just say's be glad.
That the chance come your way,
It's a gift every day when we look through a mirror.
Carole Eunice Brown

Adonis

Why do looks, mean so much?
We're not all handsome with a bulging crutch,
Some just can't seem, to get ahead,
If you're ugly, then you're socially dead.
You get total rejections, from the beautiful sections,
As they laugh at your imperfections,
But then we all get old and ugly,
So just wait for the just corrections.
Maybe I should start another diet?,
Or should I maybe start to jog?,
Because I'm sure life is a riot,
But not when you're a dog, no, never as a dog.
James Connor

The Stranger On The Shore

The night was cold as toiled the fishermen,
Upon dark Galilee but work was all in vain,
Then through the dawn a sweet voice did implore
And when they looked they saw a stranger on the shore,
He listened to their tales of wasted energy,
Then at His word they reaped a harvest from the sea,
And then they knew the Christ of days of yore,
No longer was He now a stranger on the shore..

His hands and feet by cruel nails were scarred,
His bless'ed side was torn, His lovely brow was marred,
For wicked men upon dark Calvary had nailed Him to the cross,
His blood was shed for you,
They laid Him in the tomb, the third day He arose,
This mighty Christ of God had conquered all his foes,
O make this Christ the one that you adore,
Don't leave Him standing there a stranger on the shore.
Hugh Bailie

I Love You So

I wrote a verse a while ago,
To try to say I love you so,
You do so much for me I'll say,
Such things I never can repay
You're always there to lend a hand
To listen and to understand.
If you need me I'll be always there,
To love, to help, to show I care
For all the bad things we'll overcome
Because I'm your daughter, and you're my mum
You always protect me from things that are bad
So that I will be happy, and never feel sad
For how can I feel distress or despair
When I look around me and you're always there
So I say thank you to heaven above
For dad having found you, and falling in love,
Then nature took over and it's clear to see,
That without one another, there'd never have been me.
Andrea Bridgwood

The Ocean Of Reflection

Here I stand at the water's edge,
feet sinking in the shifting sands,
see the gull dive for his daily catch,
and feel the once angry wave caress my feet.

This blue savannah mirrors the life I lead,
with its tragedy, dreams and pearls,
oh, to ride its wave forever and a day, oh to stowaway.

Here alone I feel the breeze,
and hear tragic orchestral strings,
I watch the pebble skip and dance, then disappear,
only to reappear on shifting sands,
for one more lonely soul to throw and ponder.

Do I have a role or part to play
in this world some call a stage, am I the actor,
am I the clown, or am I just a freak of nature?

Time stands not still for any man,
so many years I dream awake,
of times gone by with virgin eyes,
oh, those times again to find.

Mark Westwood

Shot Down In Flames

Earthbound again
Feet heavy like clay
Drag through another day
Filled with loneliness
And other people's troubles.
I don't need them; I have my own
And I don't want them either.
Yesterday I was flying,
Orbiting your world
My thoughts soaring through your cosmos.
Moon, June, swoon
And all that love stuff.
But last night I crashed,
Brought to earth
Watching you kiss someone else.
I wanted to surprise you
But you shot me down in flames.
Now this wreckage, this broken heart
Is lost in no man's land.

Terry Brown

Life's Harvest

When you are sitting all alone
Feeling lonely and depressed,
Wondering if all the things you have done
Have turned out for the best,

Take stock of all the memories
You have treasured from the past
As time goes by, some things die
But they will always last.

We do not reap a harvest
From every seed we sow.
But life has its compensations
In the ones that flourish and grow.

Count the blessings that you have
They are around you everywhere,
The harvest of all the seeds that grew
When tended with loving care.

Forget the ones that failed
Take comfort from the rest
And you'll realize that all you have done
Has turned out for the best.

Florence E. Hardwidge

In A Crowded Room

In a crowded room — standing all alone,
feel so very out of place, should have stayed at home.
Seems every other person's so hale and bloody hearty.
No good at socializing, you don't know how to party.

In a crowded room — keeping to yourself,
with no-one in particular, just watch everyone else.
Seems every other person's heard a bloody funny joke.
Have no sense of humour? You don't drink, don't smoke.

In a crowded room — faking the good cheer,
don't even understand what you're doing here.
Seems every other person's having a bloody great time.
Release those inhibitions? You can't relax, can't unwind.

In a crowded room — outside looking in,
Way it always will be? The way it's always been.
Seems every other person's got the bloody awful knack.
Of manipulating the situation — a talent you sorely lack.

o. famojure

Untitled

Oh, the caress of the waves at sea
Far out from the jostling towns.
Only the gulls, the stars and me —
None of society's frowns.

Never to see dry land again,
Refusing to hear the cry.
Heart-rending keen of a world in pain —
Racing the wind I will fly.

Who knows if I'll miss the pleasures of Earth
Or if I will need the sight
Of the sighs of the groans of death of the birth
Or the tree-filtered, leaf-dappled light.

No! Head for salt spray, stick to my guns,
Wander the world as the tides
Sleep in the starlight, wake to strange suns —
Lost where the twin world divides.

D. Holmes

Dreams

Far away from the gaze of man
Far from the beaten track
Farther than the moon and back
Lies an isle so lush and green
Where gently swaying palms are seen
Upon a beach of golden hue
Surrounded by a sea of blue
Where cattle on the verdant fields to graze
Where man could find contentment all his days
And streams a constant, babble as they flow
And fruit and wheat in plenty grow
Silvery fish in the rivers swim
And song birds in the tree tops sing
This paradise, this shangri-la
Is so near and yet so far
How do I find it, how long does it take
I am there when I sleep till morning I wake.

T. D. Wigzell

Why!

Watching the falses of evil come down,
Faces of horror, emotion, no sound.
Moment stood still, way for the kill,
Powers of evil, this was for real.
Fearsome and gallant, raging fast,
The Almighty God, don't let us live past.
Give us a will that is strong to fight of the falses,
The evilness twisted, insanely distorted.
Thunder and lightning striking quick,
Time stopped, no second, no tick.
Breath released, falses have gone,
Now motionless people still battling on...

Marsha Shepherd

Borrowed Wings

If I had wings I'd fly away
Far far across the sea
I'd ride on a cloud so soft and white
And dream the time away

Then to the end of the rainbow I would go
I'd touch each colour bright
I'd find a star all sparkling white
That twinkles in the night

Then to the moon I'd wander
Its secrets to unfold
I'd sprinkle moon dust down to earth
and make it look like gold

On, on, I'd fly as far as I could go
I'd float on air, ride on the clouds
The wind would kiss my cheek,
As swiftly it passed me by

Then back I'd float out of my dream
Back down to earth again
I'll leave behind my borrowed wings
And settle down once more

M. Wilson

Thoughts For Everyone

Up above you — oh! So far,
Far beyond the evening star,
Up — where angels make the weather
To the right of Never-Never,
There's a land that knows no hate,
Where the key of love unlocks each gate,
Where there's no greed — and there's no self,
And the sick are succoured by a national elf!
Where children play, in constant sun
And each takes the hand of every one.
How d'you get there?.... what's the fare?....
Just tight shut eyes — and a whispered prayer.

A. Bath

A City At Night

From an attic window, I looked one night
Far across a city, that was ever so bright
It looked as if the stars, had fallen down
Because of the lights, that were twinkling all around

Oh! It was such a beautiful sight
From the attic window, I saw that night
The sky was covered, with shining stars
The city beautiful with lights from house and cars

I then heard the sounds of ships from a far
And as I looked up, I made a wish on a star
If I should ever end up, losing my sight
May I never forget, the beauty of a city at night

H. Stewart

Life Is Like A Burning Candle

Life is like a burning candle which can
Fade and flicker. Love is the match
That relights the wick.
Death comes after the last match
Has been struck. Or when the wick
Is all burned up.
Matches may appear quite easy
To find, but only one will make the flame
Burn bright.
The dripping wax is innocence that fades
With time, to expose the wick
That lies inside.
And the wick is the heart.

Melanie Bullivant

Deserted

Her final good-bye was apparent;
eyes of awareness,
half-smiling lips.....
As I lost a lifetime in our deserted love.

Abandoned, and all things I cared for
have turned up against me
leaving me less than myself.

Tears in my head
instead of brains;
my heart being squeezed as by slow, iron fists
while my soul is imprisoned
inside of my neck.

Reaching with hopeless hands into frightening emptiness,
trying to hold on to the nothing I am left with.

Too puzzled to cry,
too shaken to sleep,
too worn out to take it away from myself.

She had only been playing with fire
and decided to drown it
once and for all.

Thorsteinn Eggertsson

Armistice Hymn

They stand to attention for the last post chime,
Eyes moist, faces softened by the pumice of time,
Gathered here in a cold grey November,
Friends and comrades and loved ones remember.

Some battleworn, still defiant with pride,
These who returned with God on their side,
Give prayers to the fallen whose bodies still lay,
In some foreign land which seems so far away.

As the light catches the medals they wear,
One thinks of the sorrow that each has to bear,
But for their sorrow, their fight to be free,
Sacrificed for a good world for sinners like me.

Each bears no malice for their foes anymore
Just saddened by the horror and the waste of a war,
For what does it gain us to blow life away,
Like dead petals of a poppy at the end of the day?

Now they play the reveille, it resounds bright and shrill,
You imagine those souls who have slept long and still
Will rise in their glory and look down from above,
And see those who pray with their grief, pride and love.

Margaret Duffy

Seasons

Cloudy white breaths hang on the air in silent condemnation,
Eyes blinded by whiteness all around
Snow hanging heavy upon one's very soul;
Then slowly disappearing as warmth arrives
Turning the earth into a friendlier place once more.

Pushing their heads towards the sky, nodding in the breeze,
Tiny buds with green shirts tightly closed greet the dawn,
A new season heralding new life, a new beginning.
Gradually people begin to smile again, even in the rain,
Greeting the days which will free their spirits and souls.

The sun gets stronger day by day, warming all in her path
Long balmy evenings that go on forever
Gardeners mowing, cutting and watering,
Ice cold glasses of beer drunk in pockets of shade
But all too soon the sunshine fades, another season passes.

Mornings seem colder while evenings get darker
The earth hardens up, the ponds all freeze over
Life slows right down and envelops itself in blackness
Winter arrives, the forerunner of snowy days again
But take heart for spring is just around the corner.

Teri-Ann Taylor

"Birth of a Scientist"

For nine months we observed its growth in the womb
Expand and transform from quivering nothing,
And we listened to Miss Barker who'd calmly explain
That the daddy was the sperm
And the mummy was the egg.
And we accepted that.

And she'd patiently explain that in olden days
Our mummies and our daddies had done other things
Than science for us to be born,
Produced from her tummy. Strange, no talk of
Building with cells then.
And we accepted that.

And then one day, we heard the wail of a child
Kicking and screaming—the first new birth,
And we looked, and we cowered from this blathering mass,
Knowing that if we offered our fingers for it to suck
It would rip them off.
And we accepted that.
  Simon Judd

Old Pawky The Paternal

Nothing was missing way back then
Except a limb, which is minor
I think you would agree
Then laugh, and say something dryly.
Were cigarettes always on ration?
Though it was for health reasons I know
But you still hid them close.
I remember the budgerigar
But I forget the name,
Yellow and green
Like a water-colour scene,
Then a quick drag
Before margarita time,
You! You old devil
You make me smile.
  Pluto Moran

Of Ice And Snow

Just a short time ago
Everywhere was white with snow;
Trees and bushes were completely bare,
But cold sunshine was shining there;
No sign of life could be seen,
What happened to the fields of green?
Fragile flowers of ice and snow,
Were chased through the sky and down below;
And without a single sound
They then melted on the ground.
  Sheryl Williamson

"Into The Light"

Up the steps and into the light,
Everything shines so beautiful and bright,
Suddenly it seems, it is all so clear,
Nothing can harm me, I have nothing to fear.

In this garden, I feel safe and secure,
Everything around me is so clean and so pure,
Soft grass underfoot, bright sun in blue sky,
I want to stay here until the day that I die.

But I know very soon, I must return to my life,
Not peaceful of safe, just conflict and strife,
Always confused, I keep losing my way.
Can't show my true love or know the right things to say.

I long to find peace, I need to be free,
To find out what it means to really be me,
I look in the mirror and all that I see,
Are the sad eyes of a stranger, gazing back at me.
  Michelle Jeffrey

The Coming Of Spring

Looking out to a sky of blue
Everything is awakening anew
Trees that just looked like dead wood
Are now beginning to look good
Tiny flower buds opening wide
Revealing beauty they no longer can hide
Baby lambs skipping in the fields
Remind us all what the future yields
After months of being indoors
We all feel more like doing the chores
Sun through the windows revealing the dust
Showing us all that cleaning is a must
We work in the garden removing the weeds
Making way for our summer seeds
Of all the seasons spring is the best
It should give us all a feeling of zest
So after pondering this awhile
Feel 'Happy' friends and wear a smile.
  Margaret A. Emsden

Nature's Loss To Man

Where did the peaceful life go?
Everyone wishing it was already tomorrow.
Who sees now the baby hedgehog
Or even a small bewildered frog?
The once safe country road
Over-taken by Man's Highway code.

The air no longer pure and clear for birds
Rivers have become so murky to the fish,
Yet on goes the war of words
Will man always get his wish?
Houses shops, factories his priority
Mother Nature and her kind a poor minority.

Green pastures become fewer in number
The wild life has less time for slumber,
Leafy woods and busy Ponds were common place,
Yesterdays children had so much space
Long furrows were trod by gentle silent horses
Now Man's noisy machines do the same courses.
  P. M. H. Wood

Love And Feelings

Love is like a seed, that'll grow and grow,
Everyone in the world needs love as we know.

Love is loving someone, and they'll love you back.

Love and feelings are the same.
Love can be so painful, and hurting people's
feelings is no game.

Many people in a far off land, don't get much
love, but they have got feelings.
They feel hurt by what people say, so love
everyone day by day

Everyone and everything needs love as you'll understand.
So when you think that you're not loved,
you're wrong, a lot of people do.
So be prepared to love them as much as
they love you.
  Vicky Lee Jones

Concern

Dirty cars, ships and planes.
Excreting filth along their lanes,
Poisoning meadows, forests, seas,
Killing God's majestic trees.
The waves that lap this planet's shore
Are not just water anymore;
They're sewage, oil, filth and slime.
This planet's running out of time.
  J. L. King

Untitled

Isn't God's air a wonderful thing,
Every sound trapping then absorbing,
What a horrible world this would be
If all sound was allowed to go free.

More wonderful still is God's life force,
Which He gives free to Man, Insect, Horse,
There in that tiny swift moving speck
Is the same force that lets a bird peck.

What profuse things are found in the Earth
Ev'ryone with a purpose and worth.
Oh what a helpless creature is Man,
Without that force God gives for a span.

S. Finns

The Past Revisited

Visiting a place long since abandoned.
Every corner turned brings shadows of times long since passed.
Haunted by memories of old acquaintances and lovers.
The ghosts follow you every step you take.
You never wanted to leave at the time.
Heartache plagued you for ages after, never seeming to set you
Free.
Yet suddenly and unexpectedly, one day it did.
And here you find yourself again,
Back in the land you once loved and cherished.
You ask yourself, will you be able to let go for a second time?
Only this visit, it is not your home, you don't belong anymore.
You are a guest here now,
Visiting a place which will always remain in your thoughts and
Forever in your heart.
People you will always hold dear and memories that can never be
Taken from you.
You went back and left again, only this time contented and
Satisfied
You've set yourself free and laid the ghosts to rest.

Tamsin Wright

Alone

Surrounded by people, yet all alone,
Even with family, not feeling at home.
Heart full of sorrow,
Burdens to bare,
No one to listen,
Nobody cares.

Once you were happy and feeling secure,
There was mother and father to love and to care,
Always forgiving despite what you do,
Never despising, they always loved you.
At home you were happy, every one smiled,
There was nobody nagging, when you were a child.

But how things have changed with a home of your own,
There is nobody smiling,
They all just moan.

P. Willis

The Price Of Life

Too many pubs, too many clubs
Too many drinks, too many drugs
Too many drunks bothering me
Too many beggars needing money for tea
Too many murders, too many rapes
Too many do-gooders, too many fakes
Too many homeless, too many rich
Too many decisions made by hypocrites
Too many Governments producing weapons not food
Too many seas overflowing with crude
Too much land destroyed by greed
Too little food for the world to feed
Too many rivers choking to death
Too many peoples feeling bereft

Why is our planet's destruction so rife?
Just put it down to the price of life!

Lorraine R. Smith

V. E. Day

The Eighth of May, Nineteen Forty-Five,
Europe's hostilities came to an end;
When all nations of the Northern world,
Became allied in peace, if not in friends.

Now the victory celebrations,
The carefree dancing and singing;
With all lights on, and those silent bells,
Were so gloriously ringing.

This was the day — they had long awaited.

To release the tension, the fearful strain,
From what seemed an eternity to hoard;
For to have kept it in themselves,
Was a battle they all had to endure.

Yet somehow they had grown accustomed,
Like the bearing of some great weight;
Now as that burden was lifted,
Spirits were so ready to elate.

This was the day — they had long awaited.

N. R. J. Hutchings

Commemoration Day

What have we died for you young ones of today,
we hoped that you could have your say in the way the
world could thrive, helping each other,
and the weak ones to survive.
Not turning to pills and needles when life gets hard,
and tough, but pull yourself together,
and be made of sterner stuff.
You have a chance to live, we didn't have that chance,
our country needed us to fight, we had to go to France.
Now don't let us down, make this world fit for all,
live your life each day, and do not forget
the sacrifice that we all had to pay.
We landed on this shore so very long ago,
we fell upon this shore, guns blazing,
the sand all aglow.
The tide came in and washed the signs of war away,
now our friends are marching where we fell
ON THIS COMMEMORATION DAY,
their marching slower than before, then the tide came in
and washed their footprints from the shore.

Iris Tennent

Our Leisure (With Apologies To W. H. Davies)

What is this life if full of care
We must make time to stand and stare:

The time to stare at atom clouds
And aircraft flying low and loud:

The time to stand beneath bare boughs
And gaze at radioactive cows:

The time to see when woods we pass,
The lager cans and broken glass:

The time to see in broad daylight
Slimy streams and algae blight:

To heave a sigh and gaze askance
As new technologies advance:

The time to stop that ugly sprawl,
and slow that urban giant's crawl:

A good life this, though full of care,
Should we make time to stand and stare.

John Wallis

Underground

Down to the depths, drawn on with the crowd
Escalators, gusts of air, and noises loud.
The rumbling sound gains strength to a roar
And the monster arrives, the crowd surges more
Slowly the long train comes to a halt
Giving the passengers a final jolt
Doors slam back, with a hiss from the brake
Seemingly impatient of the people that make
A dive for the platform, spilling into the flow
Of people boarding the train before it can go.
And shoppers bereft of their usual jest
Push hardest to board, for home and a rest.
Doors close, rhythm and speed begins
And many coloured hands grasp the rings.
Jogging bodies stand in rhythmic sway
Match empty cans on the floor where they lay.
Strangers scan maps for the station they need
Others surge forward as the train slackens speed
A final jolt, then the yawn of the door takes place.
So this circle goes on, of this mechanical race.
Patricia Watson

Cup Of Eternity

There distilled black upon white
Equal in strength, equal in sight
Into the heavens enter the odour
And like sorcery it makes to conjure

Then from the heavens a gift is bestowed
Roared like a waterfall, down with its load
Meshed all the goodness and evil below
Confusing and losing life's open flow

There in new life, it awakens a thought
Dark and untamed. Its beckonings are short
As its loving father pours on his love
Just a little bit to make enough

Mixed a little dark, a little white
To make the eternal cup taste just right.
Oscar Gonzalez

Frosty Stars

Impoverished and deprived I till the soil in any weather and
endure misery and pain beyond most men's endurance.

I tread the clay with my gnarled bleeding feet.
The days spread out before me in my haste to meet
the approaching spring.

When I begin work in the morning, bright frosty stars
glow in the heavens. When I retire at night, nothing
has changed except the light and the sweat on my brow.

Love is the fuel that propels me forward. My family are
hungry. It will be this way until I can no longer see
those frosty stars that hang in the infinite heavens.

A rich man cannot know of such an existence.
Peter Reakes

Untitled

Loneliness thrives upon the tears I shed,
Empowered by the loss of someone real,
Alive, but dead. And, left inside my heart,
Death's features now reside, to laugh and jeer;
For my loss, her death, he now has won
Another place in which to make his home.
None again will fill this inner void;
A void that rots to widen with the years
Of a loss, stillborn, with maudlin thoughts depressed,
I sit and think my thoughts — to dust they turn
For Death encroaches on such memories;
O'ershadows them till darkness stifles life.
A baby lost, I feel her presence still,
But loneliness still calls aloud my name.
D. K. Ramsay

Child

Through the eyes of a child who could not express,
Emotional feelings that she knew best,
The amount of discomfort, distaste and distress,
Remained buried inside; where? No one could guess.

Where no-one dared to hope to find,
Invading thoughts controlling her mind,
Frozen actions in an eternal bind,
Her presence on earth, precious and timed.

Ceaseless horrors refusing to go,
Clouding her vision that would not show,
There is no escape, hide, lie low,
Until you justify friend or foe.

Unobserved in a room, the mocking door,
Condemning ceiling and cold hearted floor,
Peeling wallpaper, attractive no more,
Leaving behind the odour of war.

She looked around her, face perfectly dry,
Betrayed by her body, slipped a depressing sigh,
Restraining no longer, she began to cry,
Alone in the world, she whispered goodbye.
Sarah Willetts

Dewdrops

Pearls of early morning dew, along the linen line were strewn,
Embellishing October morn, autumn dewdrops newly born.
There stood I, as in a trance, caught in heaven's own high romance.
'Twas little I could do but stare, upon those dewdrops hanging there.
A sparrow chanced to pay a call, and landed near the pearly haul
Which made the chain of dewdrops shimmer, to give the line a pristine glamour.
By then the iridescent score, made hurried landing soft and sure
To settle on a full-blown rose, to nestle as in sweet repose.

The autumn morn was giving way, to sunshine and a pearly day.
Those sparkling dewdrops gave me this — the joy of nature's heaven-sent bliss.

> When skies are grey
> And leaves all gone
> I oft recall
> That radiant morn —
> The jewelled necklace
> That did shine
> Upon my little
> Linen line.

H. M. Hedley

Keen The Eye

Keen the eye and stealthy go, as if to kill a deer or no.
Earthly smells of leafy mould rise within the Greenwood old
To meet the rain from Heaven's care now sinking softly everywhere.
Broadleaf heavy hangs his head, in sorrow, for my love is dead
Or dying yet (I know not sure). Now lying in the waters pure
She stares into a distant place, the colour fresh has left her face
All horror! Open-mouthed in shock. Where once sweet
pillow now a rock.

Keen the eye and stealthy go, as if to kill a deer or no.
I followed here this woody path a-black of heart from pain and wrath
For sure my lover was deceiving. Truth it was and now I'm grieving.
Loosed the arrow from my bow and sent her to her death below.
Her other love has manly fled, abandoned her whom I would wed
Now pierced and smashed and bleeding still, her wounds
washed in the river chill.

Keen the eye and stealthy go, as if to kill a deer or no.
The rain is stopped though falling yet from canopy of green and wet,
A sparrow calls to greet the sun and tell the world of what I've done.
She lies down there, going colder. Soon her flesh and skin
will moulder.
But not before I feel the noose, for I have let my lover loose.

Keen the eye and stealthy go, as if to kill a deer or no.
Nicholas Robin Hood

Spring

At last the cold of winters gone
Earth lies basking in warming sun.
Fields once brown now a brilliant green
All around new life is seen.

Meadows ring with the cry of sheep
New lambs frolic around their feet..
Tiny feet beneath hedgerows scurry,
Birds above with full beaks hurry.

Hens are busy in the farmers yard,
Their yellow chicks are trying hard
To keep up with mum as she struts around,
Scratching and pecking where worms abound.

Hedgerows soon will burst with pride,
Wreathed in blossom, like a blushing bride.
All pink and white with upturned faces
Turning now to sun warmed breezes.

How beautiful this land of ours
Full of life and scent of flowers.
Where children's happy voices ring,
When winters gone, and in comes spring.

Marjorie Fovargue

Who Cares

Is it only I, that want to live on this
earth in peace, to work and enjoy this
paradise so sweet, to awake each day and
breath the air that it gives.

Is it only I, that see the trouble which
causes these terrible conflicts, between
the nations so rich.

Is it only I, that see dividing this earth
can only end, ceasing to exist, as a world
giving us life so that we may live.

Is it only I, that see the fear in the
eyes, upon the stricken faces of the
children of innocents.

Is it only I, that see the horrors that
creatures of this earth, conflicts upon
the creatures of its own kind.

Is it only I, that want my generation and
future generations to continue upon this
earth, within our universe.

Is it only I, that care?.

A. Randall

Someone

When you meet someone for the first time, and you think
  about him every night,
Alarm bells in your head start to chime,
But you ignore them and hope what you're feeling is right.
You know you have been here once before, and disaster is all
  you can recall,
But you shut your mind off and close the door,
Because if you didn't you would be a fool.
As if you were blind, you blunder a head, because you know
  it's the right thing to do,
A positive side you think of instead,
And hope that he feels the same way too.

A relationship takes time to grow into something worth having,
One false move and the ice will crack,
So build on something you feel is worth saving.
Don't just give up and throw in the sack.
Trust and understanding is what you need, and a little love
  and affection you should find
If trust isn't there, your heart will bleed,
And too much love turns you blind.

Sharon Smith

Hope Renewed

Dark winter holds the earth within its grasp
Earth frozen solid neath a coat of white.
The days are short with heavy laden skies,
The world somehow bereft of light.
Branches show stark and bare against a lowering sky.
The stars at night all hidden from view.
Winds whip a few dry shrivelled leaves
And everywhere seems lone and chill.

But wait, a robin suddenly appears-
Bright, confident in russet sheen,
Patrols his boundaries with joy,
And brings our hearts to life again.
Sharp points of green appear above the snow,
Promise of life renewed.
Snowdrops pushing their way through melted ice,
Pearl drops await the sun's first gleam.

M. Cain

To A Daughter On Her Wedding Day

To mothers all their children are special, set apart
Each one that comes commands a place, within the mother's heart.
She cares for and protects them as the children bloom and grow,
Then the day comes when she marries, and a mother must let go.

But darling please remember from this home you may depart
There's one place you will never leave and that is from my heart.
I've no need to say I love you that I know you realize
So darling do not get upset it tears come to my eyes

It's just that I'm so happy, a mother's dream come true
That I have raised successfully a daughter dear like you.
So go now and be happy with this new love in your life
If you carry on just being you you'll make the perfect wife.

Paula Gowan

Can't Get You Out Of My Head

I can't get you out of my head
Each night when I go to bed
I dream about you all the time
Praying one day that you'll be mine
I want to make a new selection
And to make the right connection
I'm glad I'm alive
I'm glad I'm not dead
Oh baby I can't get you out of my head

Your love is strong
It's never blind
Your love to me
Was hard to find
I searched my heart high and low
When you stood there
I don't know
"I love you"
Were the words you said
From that point I couldn't get you out of my head

Neil Rutter

Once Bitten

The sunset flames in the Whitby sky,
The wind in the trees begins to sigh,
The air grows cold, all is still —
A wolf appears upon the hill.
A wisp of fog, a bat, then DRACULA stands tall,
"Lucy — Lucy" you hear him call,
His hypnotic voice enfolds her soul,
She melts to the sounds and loses control.
Behind the abbey the sky grows dark.
Cruel sharp teeth, they leave their mark,
To the silent world she whispers a name,
His blood-red eyes turn to purple stain,
"I love you, master" and then she dies,
Now Lucy's the one to Vampirize.
God save her soul through eternity,
For only he can hold the final key.

Brenda Willison

Said The Spider To The Fly

Yum, Yum, said the spider to the fly,
Drop dead was the fly's smart reply.
The spider curled up and dropped off dead,
Good heavens said the fly, he did what I said!
The fly wriggled hard to free his wing,
Which was very well caught in that web thing.
At last he managed to get himself free,
And flew off buzzing, You're not clever like me!
Round and round the room he flew,
Narrowly missing some plates of stew.
That wretched fly is driving me mad,
Said a very annoyed and fed up Dad!
So he went and fetched a News of the World,
Where upon lay the dead spider curled.
He rolled the paper, took careful aim,
He wanted to kill, not just to maim!
One quick whack and the fly was no more,
Just like the spider, he was dead on the floor.

Yvette Evans

Clouds...

I watch the clouds as they drift along,
Driven by the winds from far beyond.
Dark ones, white ones, fluffy ones too,
All shapes and sizes from out of the blue.

Heavy with rain the low hills they cover,
The rain drops start and I head for cover.
Where do they come from I often ask,
Filled with moisture that wets the grass.

In summer they're high and dotted about,
But today they're low and carry a clout.
I stand here sheltering beneath the trees,
Hoping the rain will eventually ease.

The wind is rising, the clouds are hurrying,
The trees are wet, the leaves are turning.
The long wet winter lingers on.
With many more months before it's gone.

D. A. L. James

" Winter "

Snowflakes falling — softly — softly,
Drifting gently — deep — so deep.
I woke up one morning early
So light it was, I couldn't sleep.

Snow covered landscape
So strange — so white.
No cattle lowing — no sheep in sight.
Deadened all foot falls, quiet the lane.
High up a crow calls — a sad refrain.

Little brown birds, just balls of feather
Trying to keep warm in the wintry weather.
Waiting for scraps put on their table.
Just keeping alive so long as they're able.

Put out your scraps
Both crumbs and rind
They are sure to sing "thank you"
For being so kind.

Margaret Naylor

The Ozone

How long before time runs out
Don't you think it's time to shout
there's a hole in the ozone layer
chimneys smoking, people choking
People still spray CFC'S and
wood choppers are knocking down trees
cars are polluting, rubbish is building
oil and gas is pumped into seas
And someone catches a new disease
there's no time to waste
there's only one world, save it

Natalie Bill

Nosy Neighbours

Step out the door, breathe the air
Dressed up for a night on the town an occasion now rare.
Wander up the path into a dusky cool night,
Your friends to meet, better rush cutting it tight.
Twitch twitch twitch, something catches your eye
The nosy neighbours are starting to pry.
Net curtains sway from side to side,
People there unseen trying to hide.
Subtle they're not, though they may try
To hide their hobby of keeping a secret eye
On all that moves in the interest of safety.
Neighbourhood watch you'll be grateful one day.
But until that day of unwarranted gratitude arrives
You'll have no secrets you'll be able to hide.
So watch your step or you know what they'll choose,
To speculate your life and gossip your news.

Sarah Beecham

Rock Of Dreams

This, my rock of dreams upon sandy shore,
Dressed in cloth of weed, and moss coat velour.
Shrouded in shadows cast by an ivory moon,
Illuminating, magically, an ancient rune.
Salt liquid tongues lick at your craggy form,
Showing tender love, then punishing scorn.

Allow me, rock, to sit upon your granite back this eve,
And journey with you far away to a land of make-believe.
Show me the place where the mermaid sings,
And the angels fly with butterfly wings.
Take me to that mystical ivory moon, and the
flickering stars above...
A distant world overflowing with everlasting peace and love.

Nicola J. Cole

The Scars Of Love

Since you left, that day of treason
Dreams they pass like nature's seasons
Memories of you they fade each year
Drying up those hopeless tears
The scars of love they never heal
Knife wound deep for those who feel
I fail to reason how you hid it well
For it's in my face for all to tell

The scars of love are pain to me
Deep scars of love they will always be

If you had loved the way I did
The treachery and lies so often said
Would not be as easy to take as give
Do you realize how you made me live?
The path of life we clearly laid
Was destined to be broken paved
When cracks appeared I tried to hide
The cancer of love forming deep inside

The scars of love are pain to me
Deep scars of love they will always be

Stephen Walker

Dream Angel

Darling, dancing shadows, black and white.
Dreams of you, walking through the darkness into the light.
Like a butterfly with Gossamer wings.
Cloaked in your loveliness, visions of flowing silks it brings.
Your hand reaches out to mine.
Rough with soft skinned fingers intertwine
Pull you close, your warmth, your scent envelope me.
Brush my lips, onto yours, so gently.
You pull away, just one last glance.
Tomorrow night, perhaps, perchance.
Darling Dream Angel, come again to my arms.
As I miss your sweet face, by you I am charmed.

Susan Abdulrahman

Remembering

All my childhood lay before me
Dreaming summer days...
Of tickling trout in happy streams
Or helping with the hay.
The air was cool and nights were still,
We swam in silver pools
And climbed the trees that spread their shade
Where sunbeams lay like jewels
On lawns of velvet green...
Pim Claridge

Memories

I lay so still — so peaceful.
Dreaming of the love I lost,
Breathing the air....
Only that joins us together....
Or keeps us apart forever.

I've heard that tune somewhere before
Longing for that time again
Knowing it can never be....
Only wish I could return
The fire of love will always burn.

I looked away like a frightened horse.
Reliving memories would do no good
The clock has turned its fateful hand.
Only don't throw them away....
Keep them... for a rainy day.
Brenda Spong

Child Speak

Here I am and just seven
Dreaming of babies made in heaven,
I think!
Yet you describe HIV, Mummy's and Daddy's,
Then wink!
All I understand so much is new,
How my thoughts stray, unlike yours please realize,
Off onto white clouds, a beautiful sky full of surprise.
From rosy dawn to smoky dark night, charging my delight.
Give me days of smiles and free of pressure,
Leave me untouched to discoveries I will treasure.
Leave me innocent for yet awhile.
Growing up should come slowly, and not defile.
I am only seven, going towards eight.
Life and its problems surely can wait.
Let me be a child, let me be.
You have all been around so much longer than me.
It could all be so good, think back and you will agree,
It should.
I am innocent and so it will be.
If you stop trying to take childhood from me.
Mine are technicolour dreams.
Yours are black and white, it seems.
Myriam Forster

The Environment

Nature is living creatures (like you and me).
We all live in a circle called life in harmony.
But a few little things make it a spoil.
Things like traps, nets, litter, pollution and oil.
If only us humans and animals could live in peace.
Then all this destruction would definitely cease.
No cars, no cries of pain from animals, just peace and quiet.
Fireworks, factories and cars make too big a riot.
A busload full makes 20 animals die of the deadly fumes.
If those animals were reincarnated the bus would be in doom.
Things you wouldn't expect are harmful a cooker, bus station.
A gas fire and litter make some animals have major operations.
The animals in our environment are dropping like flies.
If it was the animals' way all humans would die.
The humans would be like rock crumbling with erosion.
The only thing to stop this happening is a magic potion
FOUND IN EVERYONE'S HEART.
Jade Hudson

Mystery Man

I feel the presence of you
Drawing, nearer and nearer
I see you, I tingle inside.
I feel the need to touch you, but decline
Then you pass me
Do I see a smile?
You are gone just as before
Lingering in my thoughts.

Feelings
They're getting stronger
four years worth
But now one look is all it takes
for you to move your soft lips
"Alright" are those magic words
My head feels funny
My stomach's all shaky
Maybe soon you'll be mine
Feelings mutual
I love you but...
do you love me?
Michelle Walker

Take My Hand

Take my hand and walk with me,
Down life's long, long road.
Take my hand and talk with me,
Let's lighten each other's load.
Take my hand, let's grow old together,
Down this well trodden way.
Take my hand, let's share our dreams,
Let neither of us dismay.
Take my hand and let us play
The games we played when young.
Take my hand, let's sing together
The songs that once we sung.
Take my hand and fill my heart
With the love I have for you.
Take my hand, fill my life
With the love that you have too.
Just take my hand.
A. M. Wood

Christmas Joy

It's the night that children sleep
Dreaming of present's, jelly and sweet's
The sleigh it fly's through the night
The moon aglow the star's alight
From house to house and town to town
Santa he fly's up and down
Through the eve and morn till dawn
When children awake with a yawn
Seeing on their beds and beneath the tree
Their face's are full of glee
Their toy's a plenty this joyous morn
For this is the day Jesus was born.
J. J. Sabin

Never Been The Same

What's it like in the Fast Lane
Do you have time to slow down
Do you recognize yourself in the daily frown
Are you really what they say
Is it as good as it seems
You're living the young child's dream — young adults too
One day they will take over from you
Will they have the same effect, as you had on me
From the screaming guitars, violins, choirs
The thought-provoking words to the quite absurd
The energy you breathe is still with me
I've never been the same
You won't put out the flame.
Tim Paul Sutton

Happiness Is

Happiness is watching children at play
Down by the sea on a Sunny Day.
Fair castles and Fortes they're making.
Waves rolling in on the rocks and breaking
Happiness Is
Skylarks singing hovering on Wings.
A distant church hear the choir sings
The trees all bright with new leaves.
Birds building nest as the spider weaves.
Happiness is picnics by the gurgling streams.
Watching silvery shimmers of trout and Bream
Paddling over the stepping stones.
The cows being led to milk with mooing tones.
Happiness is setting gazing in Firelight glow
Making imaginary picture of things we know
While the chestnuts are popping in the grate.
The children eager with waiting plate.
Happiness is holding a new born baby close to your breast
More precious than gold from a treasure chest
Thinking all the beauty and earth we've trod.
Everything made for us by the love of God.
  Thora J. Melling

Warwick

Flowers are trampled and fences are flattened,
Doors have been boarded, the steps are knocked down.
Fern hills I loved, overrun with cold echoes,
In front of the house I can hear not a sound.

No more sunshadows dance onto the garden,
No butterfly wings rest on cobblestone paths.
Nor dragonfly monsters we chased in those evenings,
Of spindly legged children with ice cream cold hands.

Yesterday casts its clouds over my memory,
The house I lived in stands barren and bleak
I probe for faces, I search for smiles,
I call for voices which no longer speak.

Lost in my young world I feel the pain
I smell the lupin I touch the rain.
Shielding my eyes from a sun which once shone,
I weep for days which now are long gone.
  Peter Birmingham

Heaven Or Hell?

When you see the sun in a blood-red sky.
Do you feel a tingle in your mind's eye?
Can you imagine what's happening out there?
The signs of life are everywhere.

The blood-red sky is a thing of beauty.
But so is the tiger, who is also quite deadly.
We're all given the signs so we might see,
Just what we are doing with our own destiny.

Our mind is a heaven, or hell on earth.
It is pure and clean on the day of our birth.
We do have the choice, is it heaven or hell?
If you live life for love, you'll be able to tell.

Just look at that sun in a blood-red sky.
Feel the tingle in your own mind's eye.
Can you tell what you see?
Do you see God bleeding?
Millions dying from want of a seedling?

Perhaps you see people dying in wars.
If you do you're in hell,

But the choice is yours.
  Peter Moring

To A Loved One

Don't by my bed weep as I drift into everlasting sleep
Don't pray for me to stay, for yet another day
It's time for me to go, to leave no footprints in the snow
To wander the lonely hills, and say goodbye to my pills
Don't look for me where we used to meet, or in a crowded street
When Christmas comes, I'll not be there
There will be an empty chair
I'll be in the gentle breeze, I'll travel the seven seas
I'll shine in the stars at night, I'll be just a bright white light
I'll be up in that clouded sky, please don't cry,
For I will not die.
  Margaret E. Wilson

Self-Love

HOPE you will be happy,
Don't fret be kind to yourself,
Still your mind — and I will come,
Peace, contentment, serenity.

If you call then I'll be there,
I'll come — you'll see,
Your thoughts are your internal power,
Use them well and you will see,
Hope, Beauty, Serenity,
I'll come you will see.

Be kind to yourself,
You are meant to be here, meant to be happy,
Meant to be free.
Love yourself and all your fears will evaporate,
You'll have fun, laughter, excitement.
All that you deserve and desire.

Have faith and hope — love yourself and you'll be free,
Free from the chains that hold you down,
From a life of Peace, Contentment, Beauty, and Serenity.
  Maureen Taylor

'Sagittarius'

Fairness and freedom — come follow me.
Don't confine or fool insincerely.
Tell me no lies, for my intuition is sound,
Or my love of the truth will more than astound.

Restrict me not, for I love to roam,
To travel around, away from home.
My aims are high — my hopes are too;
So much to see and hear and do!

Fun-loving and strong and so sincere.
I take life's challenges — gamble away fear.
Born to the blunt and honest and wise,
No airs, or graces, or any disguise.

Let me breathe and give me space
So my arrows can find a resting place.
Then-up and away, I wander once more,
There's so much left, for me to explore.
  Soulla E. Christou

Loving You Always

Don't cry for me when I am gone,
Don't be sad, not for long,
Remember all the good times that we had,
Laugh, smile, again be glad,
Don't give up, life is precious,
Life goes on.
I love you with all of my heart,
Because of this we will never part,
Take courage, look life in the face,
For you are part of me,
You must be strong.
You may think you stand alone,
  Remember!
By your side I will always stay, loving you
Always, till we meet again.
  Mavis Henderson (nee Taylor)

Society And The Rape Of Emotion

And so they shot him.
Didn't give him a second glance.
As the world looked by,
Leaving him to die,
On a sunny afternoon.
As he lay in the beam-drenched mud;
And his only crime was being human;
The last remnants of humane humanity;
But that died with his cry,
And fluttered to oblivion with the wind.
He was born an outcast.
Tortured by society, for being different,
Just the same as everyone else.
Nobody cried for him,
Nobody even buried him,
They just shrugged off the grief and sorrow.
For they are humane feelings,
Rarely used, scarcely known,
With no place in society today!

Peter Hall

Natural Performer

A natural empire of wealth and beauty
Developed from emptiness striving to please.
An expanse of richness unfolds, desperate to perform
Offering pleasure to an ungrateful audience.
In an endless theatre, millions watch the ever-altering stage
Where this modest actress performs
Playing the uncomplimented supporting role.
Enhancing each performance, revelling in anonymity,
She fears glory, wishing only to be noticed.
A well known play, unrehearsed and scriptless
Varies from day to day,
Scenes and cast are removed and replaced.
Overtures and finales interweave
Without interval.
But the unflinching actress plays on.
Dedicated to her post, she gives a spectacular performance.
Yet throughout,
She remains unapplauded.

S. J. Davies

Behind Closed Doors

Not many know, only few can see, the
despair, the tears, the torment we feel,
our lives have altered, since losing our son,
we're left with deep scars, and nowhere to run.
as time goes by, it is a fact, we've learned
to smile, and how to act, not all can
be expected to share, the pain and sadness
we have to share. You're aware of those,
who can take your grief, we're grateful to them
we get some relief. We can talk with
emotion, of the boy we have lost, not holding
back tears — that would be at our cost.
Unfortunately, with some, the mask must go on,
so we say! we're fine, we're getting along!
They haven't got time, and don't want to know,
their lives are so busy, there's no "open door"
we thank those dear friends, who give us
their time, to us the bereaved, it is
a lifeline.

Mildred Flett

That Day

I considered why I couldn't sleep,
Content to rest,
Churning thoughts,
The phone to hand minutely rang
Melody to my ears.
She's feeling fine now, my son announced,
Content to rest,
Churning thoughts
Your granddaughter too is waiting for you
My eyes welled up a tear.

Patricia I. Poskitt

The Rigours Of Life

In agony we are, as the joy of life disappears;
Deep in our hearts are a number of fears.
There's reason to wonder if anyone cares,
At times we are so unhappy, that we shed many tears;
In search for answers we make grave mistakes,
Trying to seek help by using the wrong ways; for, by
Believing that liquor can help us gain brave feelings,
We drink in excess and do not realize
It's ourselves we're hurting.

If only in our hearts, we can find some peace,
Most would be prepared for whatever life brings;
By accepting that life is not a bed of roses,
We learn today we're up while tomorrow we're down.

It is absolute unkindness to feel
That life has turned into a heel;
Regardless of the obstacles that you face daily,
Hope for good health and strength each day.

Osgood Browne

Death Is.....

In loving memory of Emiline Gordon

Death is... all around us and affects our lives
Death is... sudden and unkind: No one special is left behind
Death is... not partial as to favour another
Death changes one's life: Like bread is to butter
Death is... a sure thing: Simple and true
Death might seem slow: But catches up with you
Death is... just round the corner
Death looks you straight in the eye
Death knocks at your door
Death is... all this and much more
But whatever you do: You can be sure
Death is... something you can't ignore
Death is uncertain and not blind, not like love:
That is... long-suffering and kind
Death is... death dealing with no feeling
Death is...

J. Gordon

Untitled

Peace at last, my oh my
daydream on if I could fly
scattered wings sat perched high
above all trees I could fly
nestling branches with feathers on my wings,
Shattered dreams tears when I cry
plea for thy love not a single cry
your lips are sealed tho' face is dry
those shattered words with tensive cry
O long life let come
and then let die

Z. Graham

Holiday Fun

Summertime comes, and with it the sun,
We think of holidays, and having fun,
Going for a swim, in a big deep pool,
Cold drinks and ice-creams to keep us cool.

Lying on the beach, when it's nice and hot,
Playing in the water, splashing a lot,
Taking a boat trip across the sea,
Going for a walk, there's sights to see.

After dinner, the sun goes down,
Time to get dressed for a night on the town,
Will we go to a club, or maybe a bar,
My feet hurt in these shoes, we can't go far.

We'll go on a tour to see the sights,
I can't go up there, I'm scared of heights,
Time to go home, holiday's done,
But we'll come back next year, 'cause it was great fun!

Judith Scott

Poverty

Poverty happens each and every
day,
Another human life is wasting
away,
We take food for granted, we even
choose what to eat,
While there are poor frail people
Who can't manage to stand on two feet.
Food is the main ingredient-for living,
It can also help cause you to die
cases like anorexia;
bring a tear to your eye
The next time you have a sandwich,
or even a meal,
Just stop and think how other people
might feel.
This poem is to show just how much
I care,
And to spare a thought for the less
fortunate ones out there.
Sallyann Allen

Bloodshed

Murder, rape, beatings, thugs, riots, robbers, muggers, drugs
Darkness late, all alone, kick your head in, break a bone

Stranger, danger, hear a sound, walk faster, don't look 'round
Hand appears from behind, mouth open, screams are blind

Take your money, take your life, use a gun, use a knife
Rape your body, rape your mind, this is our world, our mankind

Violence, hate, cheating, lies, blood, torture, whispers, spies
Terrorist bombs killing lots, eating humans cooked in pots

Blood, horror, fear, dread, tears, pain, terror, dead
Pull the rubber, tight on arm, inject the drug, what's the harm

Aids, cancer, fever, rabies, HIV, typhoid, unwanted babies
Stick the knife in, twist and turn, cigarette in face, watch it burn

Disease swarming, spreading inside, in your body, in your mind
An eye for an eye, a tooth for a tooth, this is our world, this is
   the truth.

"Who so sheddeth man's blood. By man shall his blood be shed"
   — Genesis, Chapter 9, Verse 6
Tara Belinda Larouche

Wishing

The sun sets over the heat of Bombay.
Dark land against a back-drop of pink ribbon, blue sky and a
silver crescent. All is alive below — horns blare, people sing,
children play
And in here the fan gently blows stray hairs across my face.
I close my eyes and wish you were here. Soft images fill my
mind — a sheath of net, white sheets, cool air and the gentle
heat of your skin as you lie sleeping beside me. The wave of
emotion is overpowering. I clench my fist and heart against
the burning flame
I hear the laughter from showers, trains and buses,
See a shine of teeth as you grin,
Feel the fire in your hands as you pull me into you,
Your lips on mine, your hardness against my belly.
The wave gets stronger and the flame burns, threatening to
tear me apart. The final image is the worst — the bus, the
desperate grip on your hand, the fear I may never feel its
tenderness again.
The pain in your face as you turn away. Now the sun has
gone too.
The sky is black and the fan stirs my hair and dries my tears.
The flame still burns and it hurts and it scars.
As night sets in, alone I lay myself down on cool white sheets,
Close my eyes and wish you were here.
Tracey Louise Francis

Love's Death Dance

Round and round we go
Dancing through love's twilight
Such a pitiful sight
We loved each other once
We burnt our bridges long ago
Yet hung on by our fingertips
Staring down into that deep abyss
Remember we loved each other once
Before the bitterness showed in our eyes
Before those devious and stupid lies
I know we loved each other once
No deeper love
No! None so destructive
Like a knife through butter
those vicious words you utter
You cannot hate to that degree
What we had you must agree
Should not be thrown away so lightly
Surely, we loved each other once
At least I loved you
J. M. Hayton

Bitter Sweet Dreams

Little people with proud inches not with feet
Dancing through dreams that are kept so neat,
Their willowed hair and tortured skins
Fix crying lines to their hearts with pins.

Piercing subconscious thoughts like a knife
Their ignorant pupils of the lesson of life,
But yet they continue their meaningful dance
All the while their richness they truly enhance!

Little people with proud inches not with feet
Scattered like daisies in search of some heat,
And wakening at night wet with tears
Unable at rest to hide from their fears.

I have never walked there in their cloud
My possessions are my protective shroud,
But I do not dance through my nightmare dreams
For fear their reality may become my theme.
Sally Colgate

Winning

It's swirling in the snow,
Dancing in the rain,
Flowing through the water
Out of reach again.
It's hard to stand against despair --
A deeper, darkening day;
The wind's a-tangle with leaves
Like a dream that's lost its way.

Hard not to cry these bitter tears,
Hard not to close my eyes
But keep them open to possible breaks
In the moor swept skies.
Just to stand on this green earth
Without being blown away,
Or seeing the snow swirling still
Like a dream that's lost its way.
Natasha Marie Eyre

The New Blouse

Crisp and crunchy
crisp new wrappers,
Plastic sound and plastic smell.
Dreamy colours pink and silver.
This didn't come from a jumble sale.

Shiny, glitzy,
gaudy wrapping,
I know we should despise the packing,
and revise our wasted thinking.
Our plastic fix our plastic binging.
Patricia Walker

"Brief Encounter"

Blossoms from the cherry tree
Dainty clusters, falling free,
Lying there 'midst all the dust
Pick them up, I feel I must!

Cherry tree, in dainty splendour
Your blossoms pink, I will remember,
Petals thick upon the path
A fairy wedding aftermath!

Gently borne upon the breeze
That playfully caress and tease,
Then whoosh! you're whisked into the air
Swirling, twirling, everywhere.

Soon, there'll be no hint or trace
Of your once bewitching grace,
Only care boughs will remain
Until the spring returns again.

D. M. Salter

Untitled

Little Terry Copestake small and sweet,
Cute from head right down to feet,
Is this Angel face sincere,
Or is a little devil lurking near,
Although so young he can turn on the charm,
And that's the time to be alarmed,
What mischief has he been up to now,
Or what does he want, and when, and how,
Such a little tinker is he,
The tricks he gets up to still amaze me,
But when he looks at you with those big brown eyes,
You have to laugh or melt and sigh,
How can you stifle such a razor sharp mind,
That plots and plans yet is loving and kind,
That makes you laugh and fills your soul,
Who makes your life complete to help achieve your goal,
I'll never tire of watching you grow,
To help with all your new experiences, your highs and lows,
My lovely little boy, without you I'd never be,
For you truly mean the world to me.

Trina Copestake

Little Sue

Soft shining hair of raven hue
Curls round the face of little Sue,
And two bright eyes with lashes sweeping
Are quite closed, for she is sleeping!

Not long ago a babe in arms
Unaware of her infant charms!
A flow'ret very sweet and small
Captivating the hearts of all!

Come next spring she will be four
Our precious daughter, we adore!
Oh lovely and entrancing Sue,
Laughing, mischievous sprite are you!

Soft shining hair of raven hue
Curls round the face of little Sue;
Upon her rosy lips a smile
As she lies there and dreams awhile...

D. Townshend

First Meeting

My heart's been stolen clean away
by a dark haired stranger I met to-day
He looked at me with eyes of blue
and I enchanted surely knew.
He'd come into my life to stay
to grow more precious every day.
But unconcerned he gave a yawn,
my little grandson newly born.

Maureen Davison

Soundbite

"Royal flamingos killed by fox."
Cruel hunger in the night;
No more they lift above the lake,
Pink sunset-winged in flight.

Behind the palace walls they lived
In watery green embrace,
Like ancient boatmen stood and served,
The guardians of Her Grace.

Around the world the children cry,
The weak must hide in hell;
Still weep for these lost fairy tales,
Since how replace their spell?

Mary Mason

Black Shroud

Super-tanker cracked its hull, wedged across the rocks.
Crude black, oil spill, floating, as a shroud.
Steadfast tugs, anchor ropes, a David and Goliath stroke,
Ferocious powerful pounding sea, tossed the boats incessantly.
Leaking cargo flowing free, environmental catastrophe.
Marine-life, seals, sea-birds plight,
No air to breathe, no wings for flight.
Against the odds, some may survive, hundreds perish, washed aside.
Pollution encroaches on the shore, death, destruction, sad remorse.
Helicopter overhead, directs containment of oil-slick.
Detergent spray, laid down by planes, No lesson's learned from yesterdays.
Devastation; determination, of natures beauty to restore.

Patricia A. Barclay

Drifting

Souls of the dead adorn my existence,
Crowding my mind, the ghostly figures immense,
The screams of the entities pierce my spirit,
Floating souls, their pain and desire infinite,
Drifting in limbo eternally bound anguish,
Horrors from the past destined never to finish,
Never to reveal pain and sorrow, hatred non-existent,
Desire, horror and distress their only remnant,
Their bodies lain to rest, their souls an endless walk,
Do they dream, do they wish, an eternal stalk,
Death brings no peace, only a demonic burden,
Only to walk in deaths lifeless garden.

Neil Harvell

Apocalypse

Shapeless shadows 'cross the moonlit night
Creating fears of old,
Who can stand before such fright?
Or be he of the bold.
Stark bare forms of winter trees
Stare out on formless land,
Not even the slightest breath of breeze,
No sign of human hand,
Were they horses riding 'cross the sky?
Or fantasy I see?
Were four horseman riding by
And did they stop for me?
Should I reach to touch the sky
Or look the other way?
Would the horsemen pass me by
And leave me here to stay?
Four riders on their deadly course
Looking down on me.
But did I see one on a pure white horse
Smile down and set me free?

Margaret Cox

The Crested Waves

Can you not see the crested waves below,
crashing against the greyness of the rocks,
shimmering white heads of stormy glow,
weathering the stone, like hot water on ice-blocks?
Taking this land of ours with wilful intent,
caring not for gathered ancient Heritage,
nor from whence they came, if of Heaven sent,
but racing and roaring, like a Lion from its cage.
Watch them slide back, towards the angry Sea,
as if in need of breath, and after a slight pause
come crashing back, this time more hastily,
ready for all that's in their path, grabbing with their claws.
All part of the cruel Sea, yet, when becalmed,
how silently they swish, no more the need to crash,
No urgency, just gently, no need to be alarmed,
as now they've lost their thunderous dash.

Margaret G. Peacher

A Moment Past

The blackness of a lake asleep,
Cows mooing on distant hills,
The droning of a passing plane,
Two heart-beats sound as one.
Children's voices with happiness heard
Traffic noise is deadened
A gentle breeze blows new born leaves
Even daffodils made sounds,
A passing fly buzzed quietly by,
And a butterfly awoke
The songs of birds were those of love,
As their home they build with care,
Sitting on old grey stone steps,
Warmed gently by the sun,
In these silent minutes, sharing,
Peace of heart and mind,
Closing our eyes and listening together
To the sounds in our beautiful world.

Michaela Moxey

Dear Angel

A guardian angel guides me.
Courage, strength and faith is within.
Love's always presence, reaches,
forward from despair and unhappiness.
Hopeful stars scatter and touch the most vulnerable,
Seeking goodness and deserving needs.
I forever fight on;
Please open up your heart.
Set me free from impossibilities.
Keep goodness in my life, correct me.
Run a comb through my hair
Let there be neither anxiety nor fear
In this universe so harsh,
Tell me there's a light,
Dear Angel of the night
With hands outstretched to protect me.
There's nothing left to do
But keep my faith in you
Dear Angel, sweet angel
To be brave is to grow strong.

Sarita Wooten

A Timely Thought

What is life without hope
But what is hope without resolve
To make this world a happier place
For all who share God's gift of faith
The world itself he made for us all
To share and enjoy the fruits as they fall
But man must now stop and ponder each day
Upon how much our activities really do slay
The things we are meant to treasure for life
—— The beauty of nature
—— The wildlife delight

S. Hogarth

"Love's Era"

If only beauty, in your grace,
Could show the smile within your face.
And only time, that's passing by,
Could ease the ache within a sigh.

A sudden thought, a fleeting glance,
Could take in love, if just by chance.
It's not a wonder of this world,
An old beginning long unfurled.

Nor just a wonder of the heart
Where one can share, till death do part.
The grace and beauty in its style
Is granted to us once a while.

It's just a phase when time stands still
and hearts stop beating just at will.
Love's different in so many ways.
Some love for years, some for days.

But love, if really strong and true,
Could take the part of me of you.

M. Baird

Heritage

The murmur of innumerable bees
    Conversing with the flowers on either hand;
The frocks that gently rustle on the trees;
    And shadows stalking proudly on the sand.

A silent turmoil from the distant reef;
    Rainbows that arch their backs and sadly fade;
Beetles that conquer worlds upon a leaf -
    But this is not the world that we have made.

Complaining houses tightly packed in rows,
    Exuding poisonous vapours as they pant;
Grimy reminders of our past that pose
    In rusty metal, leaning at a slant;

A portly population slightly bald
    That wheezes over taxes never paid;
And over this, a sooty cloud, enthralled,
    That gazes wild-eyed on a gilt parade.

This heritage is left to us by you,
    Our parents - benefactors, if you wish-
And we shall hand it on down to our sons,
    A putrid meal upon a lovely dish.

Michael Odlum

Creator Of The Tides

Waking up, pulling the lids, thinking it is closed, one more tug.
Conscience at first hinting, then piercing, the pupils are exposed.
Assumption still asleep but conscience in a dream soon
    vanishes with the forms of sound.
Looking round without seeing anything except darkness,
    scream for the lights.
Adapting ears, comforting words help encourage to defy the
    emotion fight.
Thoughts logic accepting the happening with sadness and
    enormous might.
Tears indicating the understanding of the future always being night.
Long sighs, deep silences, internal friends saying, Do not
    worry, you have life,
Making excuses, making reasons of why what happened
    happened.
Nothing fulfils. Nothing is enough, not until this great wish is
    gained.
Oh yes the occurrence definitely enforces the respecting of
    life, no it should not be taken for granted.
Clenching the lips, tightening the eyes, slightest gesture of
    nearly unnoticeable multi nods and a shrugging smile.
For the river flows on, though many barriers arise.
Travelling on to the glorious Creator of the tides,
And behold all is harmonious and kind.

Shah-Alom

Paper Meal

Hostess, made to serve, made to please,
confronted by editorial consumption.
Glasses are thrown and in turn the gossip of the
moment of jealousy.
In turn each skeleton re-addressing the ghostly past
of each secret cupboard, bitten by the forgotten moment
eaten by embarrassed misfortunate laughter,
on our happy ever after.
Ridiculed and tortured, from those who hide their secrets,
fearful of self discovery.
While lamed and maimed in redemption of your recovery.
French cuisine, unbottled secrets of passion nights
of rose'wine, uncorked moments of drunken time
how we love to consume, do all these things
keep us satisfied,
to read from life's menu, and who pays the bill,
from an unsatisfied customer, unsatisfied meal.
Life's a dinner and I gave it to the dog.

Zara Frances Duke

Life Choices

Life strolls on day by day
coming and going come what may,
Work all week, means to an end.
Bills to pay — money to spend.
Happy at work? Happy at play?
or just the beginning and end of a day?
Meaning to life, purpose to live?
Is it all take and very little give?

Walk by the sea, stroll in the park,
Look at the sky and stars in the dark.
The answers lie in the heavens above
The answer lies in a world of love.
Open our eyes, look and see
The answers lie in you and me.
There is purpose to life, reason to live.
Happiness is within, not to own — but give.

V. A. Hamilton

Waiting

Waiting.
Comfortable chairs and for me a sofa,
The smell of polished wood and well worn leather,
Magazines and papers piled neatly together.

Waiting.
Burnished glints of gleaming brass,
Rainbows of sun through coloured glass,
Footstep outside as people pass.

Waiting.
The sibilant whisper of a glowing log,
The slow percussion of a clock,
Muffled sounds and then a knock.

Waiting over.

Pauline Mills

Mother Love

First breath of life, a world anew,
Comes from it born, a child so new,
Needing comfort, needing rest,
Nourishing its soul, from mother's breast,
Beating heart, the sound of time,
Sleepy eyes from voice and rhyme,
Cuddled, coddled, rocked and cradled,
Heavy arms full and laden,
  of life a child so new.

Growing stronger, learning fast,
Reaching out from worlds a past,
Wanting praise, here and yonder,
Searching eyes, full of wonder,
Needing love, needing laughter,
Throughout life, and here on after,
  of life, a child, so new.

D. Huxley

Oh My Sweet Auburn-Haired Lady Autumn

Oh my sweet auburn-haired lady autumn,
Come take a walk with me, through my green
September countryside.
Oh my sweet auburn-haired lady autumn,
Breath from your mouth, with cold red lips,
a chilling wind of change.
Oh my sweet auburn-haired lady autumn,
Gaze upon this fertile emerald land, and
with eyes of deepest ochre,
Give the withering autumn stare, to all
those lifeless eyes perceive.
Oh my sweet auburn-haired lady autumn,
Take summer's store of chlorophyll, now greens of every hue.
Now strip their warmth, with a frosty touch
from cold white hands.
Then give to me your autumn tones of yellows,
golds and browns.
Now give a loving icy kiss to brittle spiders' webs,
leaving them as jewelled starlight silver strands.

R. Marshall-Regan

War

I couldn't stand the loud, loud sound
Due to banging all around
as guns fired, bombs went boom
I hoped it would end very soon.

As I walked down the street
I saw a dead man on a seat
covered in blood, a pale sight
he really gave me such a fright

I now stand at the garden gate
I'm now going to stand and wait
for my dad is in the fight
I hope he is quite alright

I get very scared when the post arrives
in case it says my dad had died
it's a thought that's never true
he writes to say 'I miss you'

The war has stopped
The streets are safe, tomorrow I will see his face
for my dad has left his den
I hope the war won't start again

Rachel Kirk

Autumn Mist

Cold fingers of mist wreathed silently
Clammily
Along the river banks
Spreading their damp touch steadily
Gently
In rolling silvery ranks.

The black tracery sentinels stood stiffly
Damply
In the cold wet meadow ground,
Tendrils of ivy clinging tightly
Hardily
To the bark wrapped 'round.

The reddening autumn sun sank slowly
Lowly
Into the drifting and thickening veil
And the church spire melted softly
Vaguely
Like a distant horizon sail.

In the cold, wet grass a fox crept warily
Stealthily
His breath like smoke in the air,
And I turned away home thoughtfully
Musingly
As the fox slipped back to his lair.

Raymond G. White

Passing

Swimming in a dreary haze
Colours melting deep into themselves,
With them comes a cold wind
That blows inside.
And as the last moment melts away
A myriad of dreams and truths play,
Till they become a silent film
That rolls till the reel spins no more.
Then cold becomes ice
Colours become tones,
And sounds become nothing
But only a whisper.
Beat stops.
Eyes close.
Then black...

Then
Light...
Marc Goodall

Untitled

Dawn breaks in the garden, all is silent now,
Cobwebs on the bushes, sparkling bough to bough.
All the world seems silent, everything asleep.
I sit here in the soft light, to think of you and weep.
Suddenly your presence, surrounds me and I hear
The faintest movement of the breeze and know that you are near.
You knew that I was grieving and came to ease my pain,
The softest breeze upon my cheek, your kiss is mine again.
The comfort of your presence is in the very air;
You came to tell me you were at peace and I must not despair,
That always you watch over me and that you are always near,
To watch over those who love you and those who you hold dear.

Birds begin their chorus and the sun begins to rise,
I hear you softly leave me and the tears dry from my eyes,
For I know you will return again, to walk among the flowers,
When dew lies softly on the grass, in the early morning hours,
To hold me and to comfort me, to soothe and ease my pain.
So au revoir my darling, until we meet again.

Pauline Andersson

At Peace

A golden sunset ends his day and shrouds him with the night,
clothed in his finest robes and life's extinguished light,
through tranquil vales of peace as tearful eyes they gaze,
where mind and body once was life, now hid from sight they laze,
words are spoken beautifully, how handsome, honest, brave,
but virtues cannot keep him from his dark, cold grave,
hymns rang out in sad remorse lamenting for their dead,
but still he sleeps eternal in his silk lined bed,
slowly this heavy weight upon grieving shoulders borne,
is taken to the graveside for those who lost to mourn,
now he slips into the shade and memories fill the heart,
our last goodbye to one so dear as we watch his soul depart,
so we return to raise a glass and send him on his way,
and toast the memory that we lost
   on the sunset of this day.

J. L. Stanbury

Time Travellers

Do you sometimes hear a whisper - of - something in the air?
Do you sometimes see - a movement - but there's really no-one there?
Do you smell the faintest perfume, feel a touch upon your hair?
Hear the merest rustle - but - there's really no-one there?

Do you hear accompanying footsteps, when you are walking
  by yourself?
Has someone turned the pages of that book upon the shelf?
There's a flicker at the edge of sight, there's a tinkle on the air!
I'm conscious of a presence - but - there's really no-one there!

Do you often wake at midnight, having heard your name?
And in the early morning, do you sometimes hear the same?
Is there a sense you almost understand, a loss you can't quite bear?
A person you can almost touch - but - there's really no-one there!

J. M. Jones

Garden Schemes

We're doing rounds of the Centres,
Cissy, my dear wife, and me,
Whenever she sees one approaching
She leaps from the car in her glee.
Now Cissy has plans for her garden
(They're surely the best you will see)
With borders all bursting with flowers
Beneath the occasional tree.
So she plans and she picks and she chooses
'Til she knows where each plant ought to be,
Then it's off to the Centre we hurry
(The cost of it's quite ruined me.)

Now the flowers are all planted neatly
But there's one point where we disagree,
For whilst I am digging and raking
My Cissy sits down with some tea.

Margaret Clarke

In Remembrance Of Our Glorious Dead

In World War 2 England stood so tall,
Churchillian strength possessed by all,
No way would she be a stepping stone,
And decided to fight on alone.

But what has gone wrong since World War 2?
I'd like to ask every one of you,
Unemployment and inflation high,
Youngsters in London Strand doorways lie.

Old soldiers up in heaven on high,
Don't you ever ask yourselves oh why?
Did you give your lives for our new dawn,
And now our country's split, torn, and worn.

But I would still like to thank you all,
For scaling all those enemy walls,
And giving us all a chance in life.
Your sacrifice was as high as Christ's.

Paul Younger

Untitled

Winter came the day you left.
Chill mornings, evening curtains drawn.
The outside wining dining
Joyous sunshine sharing
Gone.

How was it so sudden?

The door that gave away your coming
Firmly shut against the cold.
The sound of gate, of beaded curtain
Each footstep on the path awakening
False hope.

An empty bed, to books and clothes
Forsaken, debris of the previous day.
The window overlooking trees and sky
Where we used to love to lie
Closed.

How was it so sudden?

Sarah Davies

Pass Out Sphinx Troop

Ten weeks of suffering, pain and grief,
But today there are only sighs of relief.
Our sergeant, he was as hard as nails,
He had to be the toughest of all the males
He took us all to hell and back,
Gave us more than our share of flack.
But thank you sergeant for what you've done,
You've made us feel like number one.
Fall out Sphinx Troop the order of the day,
Three weeks leave, yes I should say.
Well, congratulations to all you lads,
From the battery staff and especially the mums and dads.

A. Guerin

Love Unfulfilled

Now you have gone, I feel an emptiness
Chill like the draught from an open door
Stirring grey ashes of a dying fire.
I do not know how secretly you stole into my heart,
How silently you touched my soul, like a shadow in the night.
Why do I care so much when I have my own love and you
  have yours?
Two fires burning apart will flourish; together, will die,
  self-consumed.
But love is not fire nor its residue ash, so still I ask 'Why?'
Why these pangs at the thought of you, these heartaches
  unconsoled?'
Will time ever heal the remorse which inside,
As a cloud o'er the sun, blots some warmth from my life?
It is strange that such love, though it disturbs me with guilt,
Should plunder my conscience and my anguish prolong.
But stay on this thought; is it wrong thus to love
Through a friendship so deep but unwanted, unasked, unreturned?
What then do I seek? Is it jealous obsession tempered by ill-
  wrought desire?
Is honour vain, a strumpet in finery clad,
An apple with the worm, so low would I stoop?
Now you have gone, I would have peace of mind, but my
  conflict prevails.
Blow the flame, and the wick smoulders on.

Trevor Cox

Time

As I sit and ponder of days gone bye
Children grow doesn't time fly
When you think you are all alone.
Little Grandson eye's a shine
runs to me with open arms
Stories to tell song's to sing.
Oh where does time go when I play with him

As I look at him my eye's grow dim.
I'm taken back to another time
When his dad was small.
And all his hugs and kisses were mine
Oh the joy grandchildren bring
Everyday is just like spring

They make you forget those days gone bye
Some were happy some were sad
So now my time is full of love
My time to ponder has gone away
I just live in happy days.

Margaret Walker

Changes

All things change, alter with every passing day.
Children become adults, age, depart, nature's way
But nature may be cruel, a child this life must leave,
Parents stay behind and quietly "Why us?" they grieve.

Now in an empty room, which once was full of noise
An older woman dusts the long abandoned toys
A teddy, often glued to dirty sticky fingers,
Looks clean, forlorn, unneeded, and wistfully, she lingers.

Sitting heavily upon the old fashioned eiderdown
She thoughtfully fingers the hair of a multi-coloured clown.
The mirror shows flecks of grey in her once-dark curls,
Her boy, long gone, adored, although she loves their girls.

The time has come, let go, change this timeless room,
Only things, inanimate, she must lift the saddened gloom.
Remember happiness, the flame his short span brought.
Never be afraid to clutch at straws, was what his life had taught.

Life is rosier than it was, and easier in her mind,
She starts to pack the spotless toys, a new use she must find,
To ease the boredom, pass the time of another little one,
Just like that soul who still remains, her own beloved son.

Margaret Dent

Welcome

Welcome young friend trusting and free,
Chase the wind with mischief and glee.
Live life's rich pattern on our hill and moor,
There's always a welcome at my door.

Run free, run swift, my faithful hound,
The joys of spring in every bound.
Chase the wind o'er hill and moor,
Come back safely to my door.

Sleep in peace, dream sweet dreams,
Of sandy beaches and meadow streams.
My dear old friend although we're poor,
You are more than welcome at my door.

Into the twilight of your life you move,
More content to rest than rove,
Now watching wind o'er hill and moor,
Giving fond greeting at my door.

Go to sleep now head held high,
As you breathe out one last big sigh.
Soon you'll be running o'er heaven's sweet moor,
And guarding heaven's pearly door.

Martin Thompson

Day Dreams

I think I will just lie here,
Close my eyes, and dreams feel near,
Under the shade of this great tree,
Young again, change my life, a student I would be.

Languages of this world I'd learn,
Talking with life's people is what I yearn,
Meeting different faces, near and far,
Under the European Sun, or even the Eastern Star.

I'd study, day and night, to make this dream come true,
Conversing in life with many, not just only few,
Then off to travel, with pack upon my back,
I'd understand their culture and knowledge, I would not lack,

As the sun goes down, slowly I open my eyes.
Tomorrow I start, my language course, with the girls and guys.
No, I am not young, but I am quite bold, and up I rise,
As they say, you are never too old, or too wise.

There is a method in my madness, though,
I have another arrow in my bow,
The course is great, and the students fun,
But I want to live with others in the sun.

R. E. McCall

Seasons And Colours

Winter.
Cold and windy in the air.
Rivers frozen, robins hopping here and there.
Days are short, nights are long.
Black and white everywhere. These are the signs of winter.

Spring.
Snow melting, rivers running.
Seeds growing, colours coming to dress the
Big and beautiful world, after the dark and gloomy winter.

Summer.
Long and sunny golden days. Bright and colourful flowers blossom.
Shades of red, green, pink and yellow.
Butterflies playing in the meadow.
Birds singing high in the tree, as far as the eye can see.

Autumn.
The flowers drooping and wilting away.
Leaves falling with the colours of brown.

Gold and red.
Birds flying to warmer countries
And winter comes to us again.

Selim Granqvist-Ahmed

Countryside

When I go back to the country, I hope it hasn't
Changed, I hope the flowers smell the same, I hope
it doesn't rain.
East or West, which way is best? Just pick one,
go on, this one's on the motorway, the other, you
can go astray. Okay I pick this route.

This so-called route took us right through
Brooking brook. We once were lost but now we're
found and that's Amazing Grace's sound.

Lilylee was a very nice place that couldn't
afford to keep toxic waste, because John
Major and two MP's were visiting the next
town Seazelheaze.

So that's my story as you can see, of flowers
and routes and ever MP's!
Mellissa Warrender

Teach Them

Teach them, Teach them well
Cause what they know is what
They will show
Instill in them strength and courage
Understanding and care,
Instill in them the ability to share.
Teach them, teach them the lesson of wrong
And right
Let them understand it's God wish
That they must unite
When they are alone tell them to call
There is an anchor if they fall.
Prepare them, prepare them good
Cause on them entrust tomorrow
If they get it wrong then woe be to
Sorrow,
Teach them, teach them well.
Marie-Rose

Grandpa

Grandpa has left his home,
cause his mind began to roam.
He looks in the mirror as if someone was there,
he's losing his mind but he's not aware.
He's not aware of what's happening,
he doesn't know who's talking to him.
Now his mind has gone for good,
He's returning back to his childhood.

Oh grandpa why did you go this way?
Why do you look at me but not know what to say?
Grandpa I'm so full of rage,
why couldn't you be left to enjoy your old age?
They say you're content within yourself,
how do they know, did they ask someone else?
How do they know what's going on inside your head?
Just by quoting from the Books they read.

Grandpa, what's going on deep inside your head?
Grandpa do you listen to what the voices said?
Nick Dunbar

The Woman's Hand

The woman's hand with its gentle touch
Can be enlikened to a torch
That guides a ship
Through a storm without a slip.
The winds may blow unceasing,
Yet her hand will hold caressing,
Making things much brighter
And the storm seem lighter.
Yet when the storm has abated
They both will be underrated.
God Bless them both, for they are
  There when needed.
Seagreen

" Our Five Cats "

Cats here — cats there
Cats in the kitchen
Cats on the stair
Cats playing dodgems
with flashes of light
Sliding down bannisters — what a delight

Cats in the sunshine
Stretched out like a rug
cats curled up —
As snug as a bug
Sleeping and snoozing
the whole day through
cats everywhere — what a ta-doooo

When night time falls
and all is quiet
it's hard to believe
They've made such a riot,
fast asleep in corners galore,
Not a sound to be heard,
just the occasional 'snore'
Virginia Jarosz

Silent Arches

A stark imposing silhouette, stands silent in the night,
Dark ivy slowly sucks its life, in the full moon's silver light.
Nine arches built from cold grey stone, a structure from the past,
A viaduct from other days, when things were built to last.
The men who proudly raised it up, now dust beneath the clay,
This monolith they left for us, the finest of its day.
Once how proud it must have stood, in those distant days of yore,
Twin rails of steel then crossed its back, bound for the Western shore.
In prophecy it was foretold, the cargoes it would carry,
The death trains bound for Achill sound, the corpses for to ferry.
Young lives lost through tragedy, some by fire, some at sea,
The best of Achill Island's blood was lost so tragically.
It's many years since it last held a steam train on its back,
The whistle and the hiss of steam, that thundered down its track,
Yet who's to say what happens here, when mortals lie in slumber,
Its ghostly track might echo yet, with the sound of ghostly thunder.
There it stands, a cenotaph to those who passed its way,
I pray that it be standing still, when I'm long passed away.
Patrick J. Guthrie

Life As A Button

Here am I an object, taken for granted, I'm just there, nobody really cares. They say "All of them are the same" but little do they know we are all our own Individual, striving to have Identity. You people complain about being unloved, you know nothing of being unknown. It is only now I put forward my point as my youth has outgrown. It took time, but that is fine as patience is the answer. We may as well accept it, after all we have no say in the matter. Now if I were to pop off I'm sure my absence would remain unnoticed and only the gap would come to focus. The dreaded moment has come, she needs me no longer. I'm over and done. I'm now thrown on a shelf where lives a jug, some dust, a few dead beetles and of course myself. Split in half am I as if cursed to die, but she saves me as not know I. I yell from under the dust were I lie, you split me in two, you know I have some feelings too. You hurt my pride, please try see my side, as in the end it would benefit you. You know nothing of the favours I did for you. There was many a time when you ate your fill, the seams would be bursting and the threads they would pull, but struggling I hung on, I hung on for you. As if she were reading my mind she took me in her small soft hand and wiped me clean, until my four holes could be seen, she stuck me together. I am now one and no longer two. She looked down on me, and muttered my dear faithful friend, I almost forgot about you.
Michelle Docherty

Parents

Your immortal ambitions live on through me.
Can't you see I don't want success were you failed:
I have my own dreams.

You try to shape me to your angular society,
Masking suppression with care,
You strangle me with your ideals.

You try to scare me of the world I have to live in,
Can't you see I'm already frightened.

Patronizing hugs give false security,
Can you really love me?

You condemned me to this evil world,
Why do you keep punishing me?

I find it hard to love you
Like everyone says I should.
Who are you anyway?
S. L. Somerscales

Reflections On A Hospital Journey

Painfully, up to a sitting position
   can't find the button to call up the nurse
Foot finds the floor, with infinite caution
   transfer the weight to it - gently at first
Reach for the crutch - remember the drill
   crutch first - bad leg - good leg - rest
Step out in faith - the floor is real
   will the good leg - I wonder, stand up to the test
Two steps to the door - the floor ice cool
   crutch first - bad leg - mind that stool
Open the door - the hallway is clear
   bad leg - good leg - nothing to fear
One more door - stifle that groan
   that leg must weigh at least twenty stone
Stupid really to try this alone
   thank heavens for someone who left the seat down!
P. Morris

War — To Remember Or Not To Remember

Can we remember the victory and forget the horror?
Can we lose the past and live for tomorrow?
Can we remember our allies and forget our dead?
Who lost their lives while we slept safely in our beds.
Shall we live for what we gain and not for what we lose?
And completely forget the slaughter of the Jews.

Can you remember gas masks and powered eggs?
Can you forget soldiers returning without legs?
Can you remember evacuees and ration books?
Can you forget the camps, the showers, the haunted looks?
Can you remember the dead once in a while?
Can you forget they lost more than a smile?
If you can remember this now and then
Perhaps we'll forget to do it again.
Tina O'Neill

Clouds

Formations are resulting from the dark and stormy sky
Can I see him? Yes I can - a horseman riding by
Now I see what looks like a giant Polar Bear
Next a lady dark of face with long and curly hair
Lumps of fluffy cotton wool there above my head
Icebergs too and colours now - Orange - Yellow - Red
Puffs of smoke are rising so anxious to be free
Can another spot these things or is it only me?
The day is drawing to a close it's getting rather late
More storms are forecast through the week
More clouds to fascinate
As darkness falls the images are fading out of sight
My lovely clouds are lost awhile
As day gives way to night
Marjorie Fraser

The Wish Of A Child

A year ago life was different for me, I had no family and no
  place called 'home'
There were people about and things to do, but still I felt all alone.
I know that I wasn't a perfect child, but my deeds were not terribly bad.
Yet even though I was fed and clothed, I often would feel quite sad.

I wanted a family to call my own, to love me and show that they care.
And when I felt ill or I wanted to cry, there would always be
  someone there.
I know that you can't have all that you want, but I wasn't asking a lot.
I wanted someone to love me forever and at last that's just what I got.

I've now got some parents, the best in the world, at bedtime a
  story they tell.
I've got aunties and uncles, lots of friends, a Granny and
  Grandpa as well
I don't know why I was so lucky, why they chose me from all
  of the rest.
But I know after waiting such a long time, what I've got is the
  very best.
Patricia Fox

A Mother's Lament

In the sloughy mud of hopelessness,
Call my name, sweet love, flesh of my womb,
And soothe the raging tempest,
In the violent swells of my heart.

Bright eyes dimmed beneath their canopy,
See not my anguish and submission,
Purple lips refuse the kiss,
Silence, harbours our memories.

Heaving bosom, cradles lifeless joy,
You who suckled the potion, but now,
Drinks deep the eternal draught,
The delight of saints and angels.

Traverse the Stygian pool of gloom,
Through to the light of immortal keep.
Death cannot corrupt our wills,
Concur child, from the womb of Eve.
W. G. Heatley

The Parting

Kiss me no more my darling,
  By this I do not imply that your kisses
Are of the unwanted kind, but
  use your mind; and you will recall
How oft in the past I've said
  'Tis best that we know not
The last time for anything,
  'ere it befalls us.
The place of the last is here.
  And the time of the last is now.
Richard G. Berry

Seaside

I love to walk along the sand
Carrying a shoe in each hand
Watching the waves rushing in and out
Listening to gulls flapping about.

The rush of summer has now gone
And it makes the beach look really long
Empty and quiet apart from the tide
Long and spacious with nowhere to hide

Picking up shells as we shift our toes
Walking in water as it comes and goes
Feeling the wind, the winter breeze
See the beach getting ready to freeze.

Gone are the ice cream and lollipops
No more swimming or belly flops
Gone are the dingis and beach balls
Nothing left till summer falls.
J. T. Stevens

Thoughts

Thoughts inside my mind sentenced
By some Supreme Court,
Trapped inside an unknown world,
Never to be transcribed into words —
or music —
Never hitting that vital chord,
Seeking justice but never getting it,
Sentenced for some unknown sin,
These are my thoughts that roam within.

Olivia Dolan

Lost Inheritance

Hedgerows so dense, fields unkempt and wild
Buttercups and daisies, I remember when a child
Hawthorn, willow, hazel with buds bright like gems
Wild life's vibrant orchestra echoed in the glen

Dawn broke, such music the birds sang just for me
How I mourn for this past where I felt so free
Progress they call it, men with machines in a line
Roads weaving amid houses, motorways to save time

Harsh voices drown nature's chorus, how they decline
So I mourn not for men or flesh of mankind
But my wild secret garden axed by humans so cruel
Which to me was like a precious jewel

More thought from our superior race
Could have made the countryside a better place
My childhood garden gone forever, no recompense
So I mourn not for men but a child's lost inheritance

C. J. Johns

Untitled

I went to see my Mum today, I heard that something's wrong
But when I walked into the ward, she didn't know her son
It's been a long time since we spoke, two years, or so it seems
She looked at me with question eyes and said, "Is this a dream?"
"Who are you?" she asked of me, "It's your youngest son"
"I can't believe that", she replied, "you sure, but yet, which one?"
"Your youngest son", I said to her, "your baby who has grown"
Yet, still she looked with question eyes and deep inside I moaned
Whilst I have written of my mum harsh words in verses past
I realize as I write this, no feelings ever last
You only feel what you do feel just when you feel something
Anger, hatred, love or fear or joy our path can bring
Coming back to see her there confused and all alone
Not knowing what or where or why, I heard my mother's moan
So Mum, what can I say to you, you call for elder son
Still well caught up within his web, that's how your life has run
And as for me, I do not know, will you remember when
I have been gone, five minutes hence, when I have left you then?
My mother, Mum, I wish you peace and love and life and light
Your youngest son will still be here, may yet your path burn bright

Richard I. Baum

The Open Heart Surgery Lesson

The bottom line is money.
But today the subject is heartache.

There are those ill-fated souls
Who pay a price for life,
Cruel consequence — a heart of stone.
With that last drink
It rests its beat upon the slab,
To sing no more its rhythmic tune
Of love and blood — through twisting sinew.

In time the body hardens, like those arteries of steal.
Cadaver on its metal stage,
The 'learner surgeons' hesitate,
With glistening scalpels raised,
To slash at cold flesh of one 'Jon Doe',
In the hope of one day saving other 'would-be stiffs'.

Toni Rebecca Farmer

Seasons

Spring is not a season to cry,
but to laugh, jump and this is why,
blue skies are dawning and birds everywhere,
Sun sending rays like golden blonde hair.

Summer means holiday, home or abroad,
if you're not happy you're certainly odd,
and isn't it beautiful walking for hours,
Stopping to notice the lovely flowers.

Autumn is grey but not all the way,
On the eve of the 31st we cannot delay,
costumes to make, candy to buy,
no wonder the spirits don't want to die.

Winter is my favourite season of the year,
don't think of cold and wet,
there is no need to fear,
for Santa Claus is coming, coming on his sleigh,
then we can go ski-ing, ski-ing all the way!

Samantha Jane Craig

The Shallowness Of Death

The stench of death never seems to enter the chapel,
But to-day
While she lies alone and cold by the altar
Death saturates the air, like fog lingering on the valley floor.

Now she's not alone, but we who are left behind are
Alone — like sheep without a shepherd, a plant without
its roots.

The guardian angel of my life is now an angel of God,
in a world so distant — free from the riddles of Satan
relieved from the torture of pain.

Why is it that death cultivates negative fruitless emotions?
A time to be glad, to rejoice and recall, drowned by the
tears of jealously, created by Satan fuelled by debility
and ignorance.

Smile and inhale for one day; I know it will be my
turn to reach paradise and be contented.

Thomas Magill

Time

Time is the essence of life so they say
But time has a habit of slipping away
Sometimes a friend, sometimes a foe
To all it is given but how long we don't know.

Who was it divided the day with a clock
With a chime and a tick and a voice that could mock.
And on a day when life's busy would tick even faster
Make me the servant and gloat as the master.

Minutes that slip into hours don't last
The ones that we savour go only too fast
But then as we're waiting for some special day
I'm certain the clock stops to keep us at bay!

We're rushing and dashing and filling each minute
With hardly a thought for the quality in it
The clock waits for no man, devouring time
And takes without conscience what's yours and what's mine.

Time's freely given, also free to give
The way we divide it dictates how we live.
Share it with others though hard it may seem
But keep back an hour to dream your own dream.

Sheila E. Crathern

A Cottage In The Country

A cottage in the country is beyond my means,
But this card holds more than at first it would seem,
A house or a cottage is a wish or dream,
A dream in the future I hope can be seen,
But until your dreams are fulfilled and wishes come true,
Have a wonderful Christmas and New Year too.

Peggy Quinnell (dedicated to Reg)

Phantom Pains Of An Amputee

Sharp knife pains in his foot
But there's nothing there, no boot
Infantry man, best asset his feet
Only one leg, not much good on the retreat
He screams as his leg is being crushed
The invisible foot is getting bashed
Pins and needles in his stump
Children call him Mr Grump
Only an amputee knows this feeling
Is the pain real, or am I dreaming
Shall I put up with the aches and be brave
Will the pain be with me? Till I go to the grave
The nerve endings believe, my feet are still a pair
Please God tell them, only one foot is there.
M. Fuller

Old Father Nature

The sun has gone now
But the moon will still rise
Again to meet the slumbering sky
Finding the path to life's slow silver stream
Reflecting on fish fins that gleam
Frilling and fanning between the ragged rocks

High on the bank the green drake nestles
Nuzzling his bill below fluffed feathers
And in a black park beyond the earth turns around
As a giant horse nods on in the moonlight
Drawing its yolk picking its way
Through the unfurrowed ground
E. M. Thomson

Peace

Night has fallen, over all the country darkness
But the dark night has a shining brightness
The moon and stars in all their glory
Could tell tales to make a story -
Of when the earth was born and young
When only animals and the song of birds were sung,
Before the human forms became part of the world
And wars were fought and banners furled
When, once and the only time, peace reigned
And of all the creatures only the peacock fain,
The beasts bigger than hippos or elephants-
Roamed, and thick forest grew with many plants,
No one to chop or hinder, the trees grew strong
Till they nearly touched the sky, nothing wrong-
With Gods world-until man roamed
Never content, always after another home.
Oh! That men could learn to live a life
Full of peace - not wars and strife.
God grant that we one day, may see right
And keep us ever safe in the starry night.
Margaret Mohyla

The Year

Spring is here and the primrose is showing
Down in the wood where the windflowers are blowing
The buds on the trees are turning to green
And the earth's re-awakening all around can be seen

Now here comes summer - spring must give way
The flowers all bloom in their finest array
Long lingering twilights to close each day
And the farmers are busy making the hay

Russet and Gold tell us Autumn is here
The days grow shorter now I fear
But the beauty of autumn is there to behold
Try to think that the year's growing old

Icy fingers grip the earth
Cold winds blow for all they're worth
Mankind shivers now Winter is here
But spring will come - as it does each year.
E. Fisher

Sleepless Nights

From the moment they see you, you're sweetness and light,
But that's not the case in the middle of the night.

You look so helpless, cuddly and cute,
But at three in the morning, with a gun I could shoot.

After five years of trying you're finally here,
We stood at your cots with a smile and a tear.

The hard part was over, what else could go wrong?
But one week with you, and for my bed I do long.

One moment of silence, a hug and a kiss, till
You scream out again and your nappy you fill.

Time is a blur and night becomes day,
And after your bottle in your cots you will stay.

Look at their faces and that little button nose,
And between us we're thinking, yes, how little they know.

How beautiful and good, do they sleep through the night?
Your lying smile says, yes, they're doing alright.

But you're mine and I love you, and in old age I'll miss,
The sleepless nights and hunger pains from all the meals missed.

Goodnight and God bless you, now let yourself go,
Even if only for an hour or so.
Philip A. W. Tattersall

The Wave

In the distance the dark sea
Calm, yet within its depth
A great green God is gathering
Bending his back painfully, rising, coiling
Until he lies suspended.
In agony he opens his eyes
Where is his Beloved?

As he falls white tendrils
Rise to meet him
Thankfully he crashes upon her
Stabbing white fingers
Throb through him, every pore jangles
As their wedding dance
Propels them shouting through the sea
Until sated, spent
They fall exhausted on the shore
Content, clear and warm.

And I a watcher still
Cannot tell the male and female
The coupling was complete.
Rosemary Collingborn

The Changing Sea

I love the sea, never knowing what the next day will bring,
Certain only that the moon will control its ebbing and flowing.
One day it's as smooth as a sheet of smoky, grey glass,
Or rippling gently, gilded briefly where the sun's rays pass.
Next day, white horses gallop briskly towards the shore,
Each crest rides in more gracefully than the one before.
The ocean wears many colours, varying shades of grey, green, blue,
Far from land, maybe navy, in a sunlit cove a turquoise hue.
I dream of the Mediterranean, unbelievably, brilliantly blue,
Pure white villas with vivid orange shutters emphasizing the view.
At Corbière, where many currents meet, storm waves grow higher, troughs deeper.
As waves crash ferociously against the rocks, I'm glad I'm not the lighthouse keeper.
Close to the shipping lanes of the English Channel, near my home,
Beaches are almost unpolluted, safe to swim, free to roam.
On board an ocean liner during a gale, I try to balance a cup of tea.
There's only sky to starboard, the next moment—whoops!—only sea.
When the storm abates I watch the wake churning away.
It settles, unfolding an endless, pure white, highway.
Terrors of a hurricane I've not endured, so have no fear of the sea.
I enjoy its changing moods, for the cruel sea has been kind to me.
J. V. Moon

A Lover's Wish

I know my love is hard to bear
But surely you find comfort there
In passing time you could set me free
But then you would miss the inner me
The sadness of my broken heart
Would make you wonder why we had to part
Though I cannot live my life for you
Neither can I live on a pedestal
So my love let me go now
I don't know where and I don't know how
But this I know is the only way
To not hear the things we need to say
But I am compelled to wish you well
And also all the things you wish yourself
So here is to joy and here is to life
A wish from a lover not yet a wife

Mary Elizabeth McSephney

Outside?

It's warmer now the snow has gone,
    but still the snowman's hanging on,
A single pile of lonely snow
    he doesn't seem to want to go,
Perhaps he'll wait until the spring,
    and watch the birds as they begin
To dash around and search for food
    to feed an eager waiting brood,
The gardener he'll be out there too,
    to sow his seeds, and start anew,
To try and make the summer scene
    neat and tidy, bright and green,
And then to cooler days again,
    the summer colours drenched with rain,
The snowman may not stay here though,
    he'll disappear, where will he go?

William A. Dowse

Motor Malady

Busy mechanic I know you are,
But please spare a thought for my ailing car,
It rattles and rumbles each time it starts,
Because, perhaps, of faulty parts.

Take it to your garage and raise it on the ramp,
Give it a going over with your inspection lamp,
Use your skills to get it up and running,
Replace the rattling with purring and humming.

Fetch it back home as good as new,
Post me the bill, so I can pay you what's due.
Mend my car, I beg, I plead,
Please put right my trusty steed.

A. Saffery

Portrait Of Lockerbie

Oh little town, how still you lie, nestling beneath a silent sky but peaceful now your people dwell as they strive to forget your night of hell.
With unbelief I gaze on you, remembering the terror you came through, your poise, your stillness, all are right, as you put behind that awful night.

Strangers come and strangers go, painful details they want to know, but reluctantly you cannot part with what's engraved upon your heart.
What really happened no-one can see as they look on the town of Lockerbie, because inside your soul lie mem'ries so bleak, that you keep them all hidden from those who do seek to know all the details of your tortured mind, as you try to renew your faith in mankind.

Like mem'ries of war too painful to share, your heart keeps its secrets so much do you care, for silence is golden is the rule you apply and a measure of peace comes as time passes by, so have pride in your stillness quiet Lockerbie, as it's one of the things that endear you to me.

Margaret Marshall

Miscarriage

I'm sorry that I had to leave when all your plans were made —
But other voices beckon — and I in turn obeyed.
The vehicle was weary, I knew it from the start — I tried in vain
But could not hurt those closest to my heart.
Don't question why it was to be, there is no rhyme nor reason —
Like summer, spring and autumn, we too each have our season.
For certain mine will come again — it was written long ago —
That I'd return again to you, for God ordained it so.
The baby's warmth, the mother's love, so sacred and maternal —
But the fire that ignites them is both infinite and eternal.
So look for me in cooler days when trees are stiff and white —
When eager hearts await this elusive little mite.
But speak of me in days between and know me as I am —
No more or less a person, neither woman nor of man.
Just a cloud of dreams and wishes, simple, pure and kind — of
Love and understanding, from a world I'll leave behind.
For one day soon, this little star shining high above — will
Zoom to earth to shower you with all my heavenly love.
But know that it was me who came and me alone who went — just
As I will come again — because I'm heaven sent.

D. Miller

Untitled

Children of the mist, brought to this earth of ours.
But only for a little while, lent but not given.
Just here long enough, to bring happiness to someone.
Who whilst it lasted, brought memories of a love, that will be
    ever green,
Laughter that brought brightness to everyone who came in contact.
Little childish sayings and expressions will be forever remembered.
When family and friends gathered, on special occasions,
    presents were exchanged.
Then the love was seen as a living sunbeam.
Where are the children, who didn't live long enough to grow up.
Was it for the best to leave this world of ours?
Maybe! But at least, they will never grow old.
A living memory, which will stay forever young.
We who are left should not mourn,
Because we know they are in a perfect world,
Amongst beauty and unselfish love.
We pray they will now understand why they had to go,
    now they are in Paradise.

E. M. Findlay

Tears For Bosnia

We should learn to cry for treasures lost
but our tears have caught the breath of frost
and the greying sky over you and I
casts a black shadow on times gone by

We should learn to cry for pity of love
but tears of regret are not enough
for those who have to struggle on
when everything they loved is gone

We should learn to cry, but so often drink
too tired to speak or even think
as winter ravages the land
and all is too bleak to understand

And as blood and snow mingle on the ground
our souls weep softly with no sound
while nightmare gunfire haunts the night
and day brings little hope or light

And these eyes are too tired to cry
for love and beauty born to die
for music the heart no longer hears
and grief too deep for words or tears.

Sara Russell

Chances

You're a still a baby, so sweet and never moan
But now expecting a child of your very own
If he really cared for you
And wanted your relationship to be true
Then what was so wrong with using a condom
It's so easy
There's not even a big risk of HIV

But no, you thought later and acted first
Letting alcohol aid your thirst
Unprotected sex was bad enough
But too drunk to realise was very rough

Your situation could have been a lot worse, so there's still a lesson to be taught and to make: to me, there is only one easy and simple way to live
Life is too short to play with
From now on, with every chance that you are going to take
Make sure that all your decisions are completely thought through
Stand tall and decide carefully what it is that you really want to do
If you're unsure about anything, don't let anyone else pressure or force you
That way you can carry on learning from your own mistakes
Being extra careful with the chances that you choose to take.

Nicola Marie Harvey

Mother

Throughout the world there are Mothers rare,
But not one of them with you can compare,
All through my life you've always shown,
Great love and caring, that's yours alone.
And so Mother dear, on your special day,
May countless blessings come your way,
I pray that God will always bless
The path you tread with happiness
And that good health in fullest measure
Will be ever with the Mother I treasure,
I thank God above for your tender care --
God bless you forever, this is my prayer!

Olive Brookes

Perfunctory Thought

The victor in his silence starred,
But not before he left a card,
Whose source became a mystery,
Just like the boot of history:
A paradox of add/delete,
When ivy grew from ancient peat,
Reversed, in sight of cliffs that scarred
A landscape with perfection marred;
And rue the day when senses failed
To warn of future sense assailed,
By what would bring opacity,
Through routing, rapt voracity,
When all would bet he could not pat
The land's topography plane flat,
For linear trundling in the night
Towards a source of northern light.

D. J. Holdaway

Your Life

When you're born, you're nice and new
By the time you talk, you're almost two
When you're five, you stamp and scream
By the time you're ten, you really start to dream.

By the time you're twenty, you know it all
And when you're thirty, you want it all
By the time you're forty, life's done you proud
And when you're fifty, you want things quiet, not loud.

By the time you're sixty, you're like a setting sun
By three score and ten, all over and done
And that's when you think, was it all worthwhile
Of course it was, and you die with a smile.

J. R. Thorogood

Vacant Face

I see your face before me, a face I know and love
But it's not the face I knew so long ago of
Bright youth, laughter and hopefulness
A bond that held us both as one fades as
separate paths we take.

A vacant stare meets my eyes not knowing who I am
Many a request repeated, completed
Done all in vain
Just to be asked again, again and again.

At times the road seems so long and weary
The sorrow deep inside becomes so great
But carry on I must until the end
Because I have not changed
I love the 'man inside the man'
Beneath the vacant face.

J. A. Akester

Hug Us Hard, Down We Go Together

I was worried it was the changing clothes on the way to school.
But it was worse:
"No, we're perfect! I defy the world. I'm
willing to get up others' noses if that's what
it takes."

How did they know? — the daydreaming over dinner or the
missed bus stops?
I knew I shouldn't have dared risk going home so late,
And the way we used to sit on the wall till we forgot the time...
But I'd give up father's wake-me-ups for that.

What can I do? It was all I'd never expected,
And now they're going to take it away.

Michael Cerdan

I've Tried

I've tried so very hard to forget you,
But in my mind you still are - so what can I do?
I've tried so very hard to forget you,
But yet after so many months I'm still blue!

I've tried so very hard to forget you,
I look at other guys but none of whom compare.
I've tried so very hard to forget you,
When I close my eyes you're always there!

I've tried so very hard to forget you,
But I cared so much you don't have a clue.
I've tried so very hard to forget you,
But have I tried enough? That might not be true.

I've tried so very hard to forget you,
But I remember everything even what you wear.
I've tried so very hard to forget you,
But for some weird reason I still want you here!

I've tried so very hard to forget you,
Will I ever find someone else to be mine?
I've tried so very hard to forget you,
I'll be ok, I'll be ok, just a matter of time!

L. Mingo

Lament For A City

The tenements are coming down,
But only we Glaswegians frown;
Outsiders say it's for the best,
And Glasgow's heart is laid to rest,
Beneath concrete columns grey
Perhaps she'll rise another day.
And the hive will buzz once more,
Pubs, dairies and the old grain store,
The smell of hot bread in the air
That nostalgia at "ne'erday" and "the fair".
People hurrying through the streets
And chatting in the closes.
Oh God! To really live once more
And leave this "Bed of Roses?"

Patricia Russell

Terrorist's Bullet

They tell us there's a reason for the things they do
but I just can't understand, can you?
There's people murdered on the streets, more will die each day
How long can we turn our backs, you just can't walk away

The terrorist's bullet has taken too many lives, when is it going to end?
The terrorist's bullet comes to claim anyone, a relative or a friend!

Another blast, another burning street,
Makes me wonder what they're trying to achieve
Another death but life goes on, living in fear we carry on
Why do they fight in the name of religion, doesn't make any sense to me
Another victim feels the force of the bullet
Seems that blood spills so easily
and while gunmen shoot over terrorist's graves powerless police stand yards away
It's an indictment of society, when murderers can do as they please

They can bomb us, intimidate us, kill or maim us
But they'll never defeat us
The fight goes on, on every street
Violent acts done so cowardly
But if we break these chains, open misguided minds
we'll find peace somewhere in time

Peter Cosgrove

My Granddad

I don't remember my granddad much
but I do remember this,
he tossed me in the air and caught me
and called me his little princess.

He built me a slide for the garden
we played on it all summer long
when I was tired and sleepy
he'd cuddle me and sing me a song.

My aunty reminds me of him
always joking around
he was a great big strong man
but he was also a bit of a clown.

He was a very good decorator
he really loved his job
but he also loved his garden
I ate his peas from the pod.

I keep a photo of him
safely beside my bed
the photo is one at christmas
happy times kept safe inside my head.

Natalie Bright

Mum

I didn't want to lose you Mum,
But I couldn't keep you here.
Evelyn you were wonderful,
Evelyn you were great,
Evelyn I couldn't have wished for, a better Mother and mate.

And now that you have left me,
I feel so much alone,
I really need to see you smile,
I really need to see you laugh,
I need you more than ever Mum, now that you have gone.

If only I have told you, just before you died,
How much I loved and cared for you, I still would have cried,
But the pain would not be half as bad, As it's feeling right now,
Because I've lost a good mother, a good mother in you.

Evelyn, I feel heavy. Evelyn I feel blue,
Because I'm so alone, and really missing you.

Patricia Dommett

Never-Ending Flame

I wanted to tell you how I felt
But I couldn't find the words
I've kept my feelings to myself
Though I wanted to be heard.
You have your life — it's not with me
I'm trying to let go
I'll be a friend forever
I just wanted you to know.

I know the time will soon arrive
When we'll have to say goodbye
We'll have to go our separate ways
Though my love for you won't die.
The memories will stay with me
The photo's never fade
I have to live my life my way
Not acting a charade.
I may be an old romantic
My feelings are insane
My love for you burns deep inside
Like a never-ending flame.

Stuart Robb

He Does Not Cry

I took him from his mother,
but he did not cry
A tattered box to carry him home,
How can I assure him he is not alone,
A shiver, a scratch, I know he is there,
but he does not cry.

I open the door, we step inside,
a strange room, no-where to hide,
but he does not cry.

I pick him up, upon my knee,
So warm and soft, I cuddle thee,
I'm different I know,
but I do love you so,
I shall comfort you if you cry.

Time to sleep, the worst has passed.
A cry from behind the door at last,
A lonely kitten he is no more.
Safe and snug he hands me his paw.

Sandra Anne Hiles

The Need For Peace

My abhorrence of war is not born from reality
But fed by the images and testimonies of others
The stark pictures of human debris
The grief-stricken faces of war-torn mothers

My detached view is uncomfortable to bear
As the tears flow readily now
I pray for world peace to appear
But do I really believe in this vow?

Faith is the key
My conviction must be strong
That the basic need of humanity
Is a peaceful world in which to belong.

Maria Crawford

Taking Part

We know we are different in so many ways,
But are all the same when humanity plays,
It's a question of sport,
Not reason of race,
And how we are taught,
Not colour of face,
We all can compete for love of our land,
And at the end of it all, hold out our hand,
Not for accolades, medals, or bouquets of flowers,
But for friendship, love and all it empowers.

Sidney William Taylor

Prayers and Sacrifices

Not for you brave hearts do fears linger,
but fall by the wayside upon rock and stone.
Not to grow from seed but to become deeds of valour,
to urge a thought or meditation, to last for eternity.
On fields of emerald green your acts become
feats of the brave against the cold anger of your foe.
Come you brave hearts, come to heathered slopes,
willowed banks and remember days of
sunshine and sweet smells of flowered fields.
Await the turning of the season, see the light of the
sun and feel warm breezes on your souls again.
You lay in fields forever still but your spirits pass
to heaven's eternal summer.

G. Willoughby

Untitled

There are sweet memories, inside my mind.
But at times, your face, it's hard to find.
There are deep memories inside my heart.
All my love for you, I will never part.
The years have passed, and I have grown.
I now have children of my own.
They will never know your warm embrace,
but they do know
their granddad's face.

Nayereh Kelly

" Our Journey Through Life's Way "

We start our life most innocent, so pure, so young and true,
But as we grow from childhood, we're uncertain what we do,
The education that's received to help us in our quest,
To understand life's values, true needs, and all the rest.

For growing up is difficult, when choices must be made,
To overcome such problems, our courage can-not fade,
We learn as we grow older, much wiser now are we,
Surrounded by our loved ones, gives added strength you see.

But as we change to adult, commitments must be faced,
For making wrong decisions would only bring disgrace,
Now coping with a family brings memories back again,
Yes, when then a child, remembering the joy and even pain.

Our parents hold their grandson, granddaughter too in turn,
Believing in the code of life, that they must surely learn,
To grow up good and steadfast, will make their life worthwhile
And through the early years, reward us with a smile.

The twilight times are beckoning, our duty now complete,
But as we sit and ponder, the times that were so sweet,
To see the family prosper, grow strong, so firm and straight,
For life itself is precious, as we search for heaven's gate.

G. H. Carter

Reynard

My valley has changed into its winter garment.
But all beauty is not sleeping.
Light sunshine casts a radiance o'er
  the dark green leaves of a holly tree;
A great pine spreads out its branches
  filling the air with its sweet scent.
Silence broken only by the twittering of
  a few birds who remained with us,
There is a sacredness and peace in
  this enchanted valley.
Suddenly that peace is shattered
In the distance I can hear the cry of hounds.
Horse men are fast approaching and
  the hounds are in pursuit,
Collect all your strength Reynard
  and make a safe getaway.
Sly fox you may be, but no dumb
  animal should suffer death by mutilation.

Nora Cotter

The Path Of Life

This life is but a moment of time in eternity,
But a journey of learning it is meant to be.
Before our soul descended into this body on Earth,
We decided where and when we would have our birth;
What our lesson this time around would be,
The path of karma from a former life to decree.
But as the first few years of our life go by,
The third eye closes and our memories die.
We have to find our way alone
To seek and search until we can return home.
We meet other soulmates along the way
To whom we are drawn, close friends to stay.
How long this will take all depends on each incarnation,
It is like a train journey going from station to station.
With each life we stop at a different place in time,
So we can gain valuable experience along the line.
When the time comes to ascend into spirit once more,
We can assess our last life before we close the door.
To see how much progress we have made along the way,
And how much karma we have left next time to pay?

Katie Beardsley

Enough Of Dreaming

If I could just reach out my hand and with it heal,
Broken bodies, hearts and minds.
If my faith were the type to move mountains,
And my love within the power, which increased the more it
  outward flowed
To enhance the gift of seeing pain, hidden by a smile,
And take this burning fire within and put it to good use.
With open arms I could the whole world embrace,
But wasn't that done long ago on a hill outside a city gate?
What coward soul am I, I do not yearn for pain,
But that darkness surrender quietly, slipping silently away.
Enough of dreaming, the reality is such,
Still goes on the battle, that for centuries has been fought.
Put on your righteous armour, do not shirk duty or be afraid,
Absorb divine power, you idle feeble knave.

Margaret Ashfield

Despair

The sun rises, casting its light
But in my head it's not day — it's night

My light in the storm has faded and gone
My anchor, my lifeline, life's sweet song

Can't think — won't think,
Keeps me sane,
Can't feel — won't feel,
But still the pain.

Life marches on — no time to wane
Crushing its gifts with haughty disdain

Big timeless clock ticking away
Don't think, don't feel — don't want to stay.

Margaret Kortje

Aftermath

Twilight falling,
casting shadows
on a world that's dead and cold,

the song of birds no longer heard,
nor rustling leaves, or whispering grass,
as silence comes to pass,

no more laughter, no more love,
no more childhood; only hunger
and the whimpering cries of pain

as people shuffle through the darkness,
lost in the knowing
that their sun will never shine again

and that those twilight
casting shadows will forever reign.

K. Hengeveld

Wintertime

The darkest season with earth unfavourably tilted,
Brings snow and ice to England's wintry shores.
Some birds fly south, they seek a warmer climate,
The squirrel sleeps in hibernating snores.
   But people stay, equipped to brave the colder weather,
   With boots, galoshes, overcoat and glove.
   They spurn the icy winds and sleety showers,
   But grumble daily at the sky above.
The trees are bare, their leaves in soil have blended,
Red berries hang on holly trees still green.
And all too soon we find it is December,
With cards and presents and the Christmas scene.
   The old year dies, and January enters,
   A snowy carpet makes the earth seem white.
   Then snowdrops stir and crocus add their colour,
   Reminding us of Mother Nature's might.
The squirrel from his treetop nest is wakened,
He seeks his cache of hazelnuts below,
His fellow creatures stir, their winter rest is over,
For spring's new warmth has melted all the snow.

Norman Woodward

" Patience "

Patience is a virtue that's possessed by very few,
Bringing moderation to all we say and do,
To give to us reflection of the outcome of our deeds,
To help us think, and count the cost, before we then proceed.

So many things are said in haste, and bitterly resented,
That with a little patient thought may well have been prevented,
Loved ones hurt by ill thought words, sometimes hearts are broken,
Just because, in sudden rage, the wrong words have been spoken.

If we only had the strength of mind to patiently endure,
And leave things in the hands of God, whose love is ever sure,
Secure, and in the knowledge that he knows what's best for us,
Instead of running to and fro, and kicking up a fuss.

For God has endless patience, as he watches from above,
Gazing down eternally on the creation that he loves,
Regarding all our weakness, understanding all our fears,
Knowing all will be put right within the future years.

So let us patiently proceed to live our daily lives,
And play our part for the happiness of our children, husbands, wives,
Taking each day as it comes, contented with our lot,
Giving grateful thanks to God, for everything we've got.

Norman J. Edwards

Snow Frolic

The air is crisp and still.
Bright sunshine fills the place around us.
Rings of laughter pierce the air.
Everything has a silver counterpane, glittering in the sunlight.
A sharp, cold shock strikes my face.
Silver flakes before my eyes, tells me our snow frolic has begun.
I see before me your beautiful face, surrounded by a halo of fur.
Your eyes glitter like diamonds.
Your face beams with happiness,
As silver flakes fill the air and shower over you.
The sun sparkles on the flakes.
Like diamonds in your hair.
Hot breath, like steam escapes your lips,
To fade away like dreams.
We roll the cloudy covered ground.
Showering diamonds in our path,
Which melt away at a touch.
The thrill as the cold flakes touch our skin.
Those are our happy and carefree moments,
Of our frolic in the snow.

R. F. Tomes

Dream Of The Hills

O' to see Helvellyn, in the distance Striding Edge,
Bright sun between the storm clouds that form a darkening wedge.
The tree tops gently murmuring to the quickening wind and showers,
And darkness slowly covering the banks of grass and flowers.
Hillside tops bathed in glory no picture can unfold,
The summit of the mountain patterned blue and gold.
No matter what the season, the picture still I see,
I close my eyes just to recall its grandiose majesty.
Mist may mask their sharpness but memory will remain
Of peaks and valleys glistening after summer rain.
The softness and the harshness that each new view reveals,
The freshness of the springtime treading winter's heels.
And lorries climbing over Shap before the motorway,
Carrying tier on tier of huddled sheep whose woolly coats looked grey.
Cars following, not too close when mist is blanking all,
The hillside disappearing into the gathering pall.
And Shap on a sunny day when I could see for miles,
The farmyards in the valleys, wreathed suddenly in smiles.
Goodbye my hills and valleys, was all my love in vain?
When I am long forgotten you will remain the same.

F. Ronneback

The Windows Of My Soul

My soul is like the moon
Bright, shining and full of mystery
Mirroring romance
Thoughts and feelings winging their way across the sky
No matter how far away you are.

The sun is the warmth
That lies deep within me
Representing Love
Strong and full bodied, shining on everyone
We need it to warm the earth and our relationship with each other.
Then there are the stars
Points of light piercing the darkness
fanciful dreams
That brighten the soul as it sleeps
Stimulating surprises for the future.

My soul is a rainbow of colour
Spanning the sky
Reflecting my moods
Making me what I am and who I am
With infinite variations and nuances.

Sheena Christensen

Book Of Sorrow

The events in the book are no longer the same,
But he still feels familiar;
Although the hero has changed his name
And so the story is hard to understand.

He walks past and will wave,
Like the sea that's always there and somewhere else.
And like the fishes, he cannot be saved,
Even though the fishing net is not where he should be.

People try to find an explanation,
But hindsight offers no security from the past,
For the hero has no foundation;
He is crumbling away.

The book's end will be his end
With a final act of harsh tragedy,
And the readers will be his friends
Because the other characters couldn't reach his needs.

The pages had already been written for him;
He was just part of the wrong story.
And so he could never win;
Yet hero he deserves to be.

Sara Bearman

The Candle

Tall white virginal candle,
Breaking the darkness, shedding your light,
Probing the shadows, the curtain of night,
Bringing bright hope to a people bereft,
Giving them dreams of promises kept.

Small white humble candle,
In lowly cottage your light is so dim,
Where poverty reigns making life grim,
But your feeble flame in the cold pitiless air
Keeps the poor dweller just one step from despair.

Richly embossed, decorative candle,
In grand stately home your light is entrancing.
A hundred flames are flickering and dancing,
And the richness and grandeur are shown to perfection
In the gleaming of silver and the mirrored reflection.

Blessed holy altar candle,
It is in the church that your true beauty shows,
And your spiritual light with a purity glows.
The faithful believers see the presence of God
In the flame that burns as a sign of his love.

A. Summerbell

" Misunderstood "

All my life I've been grossly misunderstood,
Branded the black sheep, my intentions still good;
Never had a chance of proving my worth —
In dreary jobs, without music or mirth.

A thousand violins I've yearned to play —
Sadly, that good fortune escaped my way —
My grandpa taught music to anyone, free —
Father did likewise, only partly taught me.

Hymns, marches, and waltzes echoed thro' the land —
When grandfather founded "The Robin Hood Band".
Disappointed desires that still remain —
Won't melt on a trip — down memory lane.

There it's never too late to make amends;
With an artistic mind, the good Lord sends —
Tho' still cleaning, sewing, and having to cook.
Hurrah! I've even started to write a book —

Sev'ral poems I've written, and hope one day —
To get them all published, then earn some pay.

E. S. Clark

Thoughts For Mum And Dad
On Their Daughter's Wedding Day

You have nurtured her life since a seed in your womb
Both are so full of pride as she stands with her groom
So happy for them, yet so saddened inside
That with Life's Chapters—Time does not bide.

It is true her key seldom now your door will unlatch
And silence replaces the laughter of friends gathered for a chat
Her bedroom once so littered with fashions of the day
Orderly and neat now echoes "Nancy's gone away".

Parents are always needed, Dad is her Solomon—so wise
But only when requested must he be ready to advise
Mum's comfort too is required should storm clouds love e'er mask
For you are the solid rocks from which her life was cast.

School Reports, Ballet Shoes, Baby Dresses, Infant Art
Are stored away with programmes of plays in which she played a part
These have become beloved 'Treasures', from which sweet memories stem
And today is a brand new chapter making memories again.

Patricia Pitman

Guilt Of The Innocent

My life was sown as a seed of regret.
Born unwanted and at the wrong time.
Fathered by the wrong man,
No excellence or love acknowledged by the one who should be closest.
Nurtured in basic ways — but neglected in that which means most... a mother's unquestioning love.
To hear drumming in my ears over and over again —
"You walk like him, you talk like him",
And worst of all, "you look like him!"
Can any child be divorced from parental similarity?
The innocence of birth should overwhelm all else,
And flawless love be welcomed uppermost.
How can such blame be held against me for so long?
My heart aches, my mind exists in deepest anguish.
Can I never be seen in my own light?
The father of this child lives on — though dead and long since gone.
His guilt is to be mine — forever.

Wilma Jayne Gravenor

Who Will Forgive

So much anger, so much strife,
Bombs going off, loss of life.
Why does it happen — do we really know?
Who are these people who do it more and more?
Life is nothing to them, just candles
To blow out.
Flames that should burn brightly
Suddenly snuffed out.

How do you forgive them the heartache and the pain
God teaches us to be loving — but are these people sane?
This madness we do not understand,
How can they live with blood on their hands?
God can forgive them but can you, can I,
Who knows who will try?

E. Matthew

Just A Mom

Get up for work, rush to get dressed.
Bolt down your breakfast, put your nerves to the test.
Rush out the door and get in the car.
Sometimes you may wonder just who you are.
That's if you've got time to sit down and think
You can't stop for long, dirty dishes in the sink.
Squeeze in the ironing, put on the tea, tread on the cat, run up for a wee.
A read of the paper, a soak in the bath.
You're joking in this house peace, that's a laugh.
Being a mom is the hardest job of all, whatever you give them they always want more.
I wonder what would happen if I went on strike
That would wake them up and give 'em a fright.
Mom, you haven't been shopping, or been to work.
The bathroom's filthy and I've no clean shirts.
We're starving mom, but you've done no tea.
I smile, at last they've noticed me.
The look on their faces, concern in their voice.
Get back on the treadmill, I haven't much choice
I blend in the background, I'm just a mom.
But without me this house wouldn't be home.

P. Hodgkins

To Philip Larkin

Winged arrowhead entering targeted heart
Bloodflow of life slowed to lowering pulse
Regretted lessons laid in infinite hope pools
Unopened plans abandoned to mourned at past times
Revisited cold stone pathways of memory
Converging to open arm merciless eternity
Open soul sight ever focused on flight

Ray Waugh

Springtime

The wild, wild wind of Winter
Blows no more from the west
And Spring, at last, is with us
The time of year that I like best.
Winter wheat now growing, green shoots one inch high
The skylark rejoices, singing his up in the sky
The sound of rooks, discordant
I hear it every year
Fighting over old nests
That show Winter's wear and tear.
The promise of Spring is with us
There for all to see
And soon the buds are breaking
On the branches of every tree
Bird-song to entertain us, as they all begin to pair
Nest building taking place, in hedgerows everywhere.
And so we are in Springtime
When lambing soon begins
And I can listen to the music
That gladdens my heart strings.
   R. S. Thomson

Winter Day

Listen to the winter wind,
Blowing through the trees
The snow-flakes are falling fast,
They are dancing in the breeze.
So winter is upon us
Making it bleak and cold,
The air feels so crisp and chill
It keeps so quiet and still,
The winter's sun shines on the scene of white
Showing us it glistens, a pretty sight.
Beyond the beauty that looks so bare
The petals of the primrose peep,
They have awakened from their sleep.
   J. Walster

My Daughter

I have a daughter that has
bloomed through life, has grown
up and become a wife.
Any day now she will become a mother,
loving and caring for another,
Maybe a girl, maybe a boy,
She will love either with nothing but joy.

Either way it was meant to be,
To have a child upon her knee.
This is the reason for life, to become
A mother and a wife. So be it.
   A. McGhee

Leukaemia

There are so many things that break your heart
Cancer, death and the month of March
The child that we must live without
The anger that makes one want to shout
At God, at life, at the injustice of
A disease that takes away the love
The innocent love that children give
Children that have the right to live
So why on earth can't they find a cure
For the cancer that ends the lives so pure
Of the children to whom each Mother gives birth
In the hope that they'll live a full life on earth
And not have that precious life cut short
There's a lesson that grieving parents are taught
Don't take it for granted there's a God up above
And if there is, He's devoid of love
For how could a loving God be so cruel
As to take away the wonderful jewel
That was our child
   Mary Bernadette Evans

The Sacred Tree Of Wounded Knee

Wide and shallow were the valley wastes,
   black were the nights, the spital froze,
came the searing day in white ball glare,
   merciless the path the hunters chose.

A hundred thousand moons afore the cross,
   'twixt Chuckchi and Seward, a stark melting sea,
made captive the Mongul Indian
   as the last people on Earth that truly were free.

To reindeer hunt in the desolate whites
   and track in the grey murk of the dripping cedars,
to streamer worship the Northern lights,
   and dance to the drums before cross-legged leaders.

Canoeing the swamps and roaming the prairie
   to search and savour a bounteous fare,
to whoop through the buffalo and pronghorn herds
   to farm and war and crop their share.

They first welcomed the strangers, then a greed to unfold,
   swept by the Hotchkiss and cavalry scattered,
their beautiful dream, their sacred tree
   the hopes of their Nation, lay broken and shattered.
   D. W. Brown

Summer

Summer has come, spring has gone
Birds are singing their favourite song
The flowers on the trees are full of blossom
They fall to the ground and we've lost them
The eggs are cracking, a new life begins
The crows come down and search the bins
The onions in the garden, are just sprouting through
I planted six or seven or was it just two
The colours of the flowers, it's lovely to see
It's my favourite season, it's got to be
   J. S. Findlay

What Is Love?

Togetherness and tenderness, a feel for one another,
Bird song and the morning dew, a baby with its mother;
That's Love.

A painter with his canvas, a she-cat with her kittens,
A granny on a winter's day, knitting children's mittens;
That's Love.

A warm and languid summer's day, a pastor with his flock,
A father with his son at play, a sculptor and his rock;
That's Love.

Comradeship and honour, a promise to be true,
A tender feeling deep inside, just like I feel for you;
That's Love.
   J. Pat. King

Who Done It?

Who was it wrote the very first word
To teach our ancestors the secrets of the world?
Who was it made the first pane of glass,
That shields us from the rain and many an icy blast?
Who was it that discovered the use of wool from sheep,
Making clothes for everyone even as they sleep?
Who composed the first sweet musical tones
To tempt the feet to dance despite the bunions and corns?
Who made wine from fruit, flowers and grapes,
Bringing alcohol that destroys the soul and muddles up the brain?
Who made the first wheel to go round and round,
Helping man, woman and child to roam the world around?
Who distilled the first perfume that women so adore,
Teasing the senses of men and boys who always return for more?
Who found the information to make encyclopedias
That teach the young, old and always the press media?
There's only one true way to gain knowledge of this:
Pay attention at home, school and college to each Master and Miss.
   Eve Clucas

Thoughts Of A Lovelorn Squire

Would you in moments idle, I have wondered,
Bid me to you hasten through hostile crowd
Were I there deliberately to seek you
Search with diligence in dip and rise and then
Locate you
Look for pleasured recognition of me in your eyes
And would you then...in wishful muse of fancy
Smile with joy and not again as I have known it be
Meet my eyes only for a moment
Before your gaze is turned disdainfully from me
To cause once more all courage fail me
Be not the knight who won your colours valiantly
And know in truth too fair you are
And far you are above me
Whom I could never hope to reach or kiss, fair lady,
....but fancifully

Victor Stephen Maynard

Untitled

Beyond the darkness of the night
Beyond the stars all twinkling bright
Beyond man's senses, sound and sight
Into the everlasting light.

Some live for years, some just a day
But all life's forces fade away,
We're in God's hands, he holds the sway
How long we live, he has the say.

Why are we here? What reason? None?
But now my race on earth is run
I hope to claim the prize I've won
Everlasting life with the Eternal one.

Don't cry for me — I know I'm right
His promise true is now in sight
I see His love come shining bright
Beyond the darkness of the night.

J. G. Fowler

The Scream

I heard it first at close of day,
beyond the night, so far away.
A tiny, piercing, cat-like sound.
It seemed to come from underground.

The river waters tossed and churned.
Turbulent, crying, the wild tides turned.
I held my head to ease my fear,
but still the sound came ever near.

Louder still to deafening pitch,
like hanging pig or burning witch.
Higher, drowning out the rain.
Rising, frantic, filled with pain.

Then, like an instant flash of light.
Now feeling sweet, released from fright.
The scream, so eager to be free,
was coming from the heart of me!

Sonja Frances Mills

Growing Old

They sit around in old folks homes
bewildered and confused.
The zest for life they once all had they
find has all been used.
They should not need reminding,
there's no shame in growing old;
The shame is in the indifference of
people aloof and cold.
Kindness can work wonders,
so show a friendly face,
and help them spend their final years
with dignity and grace.

Ronald Coleman

The Old Fisherman

This tranquil scene, the peaceful waters here,
Beneath the sun and cleansing clouds above.
The whispered sounds that drift from brook and weir,
Where the trees caress the waters with their love.

This quiet haven far from crowded lock,
Where centuries past, this time of year have been.
And here a patient mother tends her flock,
So pleased to pass the dangers by unseen.

This docile floor that passes by my eyes,
My aged mind remembers long ago,
The blissful times away from people's lies,
When I cast my troubles in and watched them go.

This calm repose that makes me live thus far,
In deference, now that I must take my leave.
And though the gates of heaven be left ajar,
I judge it not the time for you to grieve.

This tranquil scene, the peaceful waters here,
Above the sun and cleansing clouds below.
Although my soul be happy, wandering near,
In comparison to thee it fills me so.

R. P. Gibson

Love Hurts

I see a woman, lady, mother, lover too, yet lift the thin veneer
Beneath its surface I did find a heart of gold so pure
Yet deeper still and deeper yet I simply had to go
To depth unplumbed I sought to find the sanctuary of the soul.
What sweetness dwelt in this secret place kept under lock and key
I pray to all the Gods this sleeping beauty's awaited kiss, this precious gift, this wondrous task is given unto me.
I love her with a flame so pure, the Gods, they envy me.
We are as one, I feel her pain, her every little mood, on
Emotion's crest she carries me.
I have no heart, I have no soul; they all belong to she.
The little things I see her do which means she thinks of me.
Or to catch perchance a passing glance from limped pools so clear
She engulfs my very being and holds me timeless there.
In lang'uor then I swim around in eyes I hold so dear.
Bathing in their beauty but strangely also fear.
This sweet love, this deadly barb of pain.
For all these things and all her love if I only had the keys
No jewel from any sceptre came that I would change for these.

J. Mount

Untitled

Our endless years of love in your eyes.
Beneath a million stars in our wonders skies.
Our love awakes, the birds serenade the sun.
Love yearning deep within as pure in depth and tone
I breathe a sigh I'll never be alone.

Rosalinda Yule

Bliss

The huge smooth stone at the side of the house
Used to warm through with the sun
I'd sit there and sing and dream away
After my chores were done
You're singing too high, my mother would say
You'll hurt your throat — you'll see
But it never it seemed to happen and
 I never did agree
As I dreamed and sang and sang and dreamed
How I loved to look around
At the yellow flowers of silverweed
Downy leaves spread on the ground
Those days were all sunny or so it seemed
When I was but just seven
But that lovely warm stone at the side of the house
To me — well it was heaven.

Lilian Jeffcock

Dear Mother

You loved me before I came into this world,
Before you even knew if I was a boy or a girl.
You nursed me all through my infant years,
Dirty nappies and nightmares, tantrums and tears.
You taught me everything that I know,
Tended me lovingly, helped me to grow,
And now that I've got a child of my own
I'll try to follow the path you have shown.
Dear Mother, you know that you are to me
Everything that I would love to be.
Maria Cornell

The Last Son

Alas today my youngest son
Becomes the ripe old age of twenty-one
No more tears to dry cut knees to plaster
No little voice to say Dad can't we go any faster
No more waiting for Father Christmas to excite
No more fireworks and sparklers to delight
No more hide and seek with Easter egg
No more for a bucket and spade will he beg
Now when he comes home through the door
Dirty muddy football boots upon the floor
Then to bath and groom and style
Out to enjoy himself for a while
Mum is left with dirty boots to clean
Wash and polish till they gleam
Then the hours go ticking by
Till suddenly bedtime is nigh
Mum and Dad drift off to sleep
A car arrives, Mum has a peep
Their son is home, safe and sound
Goodnight, sleep tight, till next time round
Rosalyn Cole

Into The Light

The light was so bright,
Beckoning me to follow
it through the darkness of the night.

I was floating high above,
Looking down upon the
crowd below and the ones I love.

Wrapped tightly in warm wings,
Keeping me safe and
welcoming me into the garden of Kings.

Then peace descended upon me,
My spirit once trapped
within my earthly body was now free.

Goodbye to those I've left behind,
Perhaps one day you too will find
the light that leads you on your way,
and we shall meet another day.
Pamela Dymott

If Only

If only I had let the last time I saw you be the first
because you are what I have been
searching for I need your thirst for life
I desire your breath in my mouth.

but I lost you and found out
if my life without you is just living
I would rather die.
But you saw through this subtle lie.

And now as I walk past your door at night I can
feel your inner fight I wish I had that
certain right to rush in and put your
fears to sleep if only?
Mark Donovan

Tabby

He came to us from another home
Because he was all alone
At first he wandered all around
In cupboards, boxes and corners found
Then almost to my surprise
He's under the blankets in disguise
Then down the stairs he follows me
And into the garden where he's free
Now he's chasing birds on high
Thinking that he can fly.

For now it's getting dark
And Tabby has made his mark
Now he curls around my legs
Then he sits up and begs
Food is left on his shelf
Where he can help himself
When he's finished all his scraps
He comes looking for his wraps
You see he's very much the family pet
To leave him now, he'd truly fret.
Maureen Hyam

London Town

London town with parks, trees and flowers aglow,
Beautiful buildings, museums of interest on show,
Shops in streets with great things to see,
Peoples of all nations walk around free.
A cry of 'have you any coins to spare?',
From those who have a home nowhere.
Commuters passing to catch their trains,
Have not the time to stop and care,
For those who cry out in despair.
What can we do to help these folk?
To give them comfort and some hope,
For better things to come,
I hear that cry oh, oh when,
Shall we see a glimpse of the sun?
Alice Grosse

Turbulent Times

What kind of world is this we live in?
be-set with greed and lust, strife and hunger,
both young and old not safe from murder,
even God himself is no reminder,
for ruthless, mindless, thoughtless plunder,
from mortals, whose only goal in life is turmoil.

What kind of life is this we're leading?
With endless wars, heartache and souls unfeeling,
we need to learn, and to discover,
the selflessness to love each other,
in finding this, we can make way,
for justice, and end all moral decay.
Pat Coleman

God's Peace

Majestic oaks and mighty pines,
Conifers of every hue,
River winding 'neath the hills
of heathers, mauve, red and blue.
Fields of green where rabbits play,
and birds are busy every day.
Picnickers are loathe to leave
The place where air is good to breathe.
Tranquil thoughts will come to mind
as tensions ease and thoughts are kind.
With so much beauty everywhere
People have some time to care.
But city people surging home,
Queues for buses, tubes, and phone.
Dull expressions mask the face
Of resignation to the pace,
and daily tensions stress the mind.
Where God's peace is hard to find.
Phyl Fry

America

Staring down the future with eyes of sun-narrowed steel,
Bat in hand.
The leap from discovered to discoverer.
You made my heart leap into my mouth. You moved me.
You shone and turned me on. Turned the world on.

You cradled fantasy.
You grew from the centre of the Earth,
Rose like a bizarre sun over our charted horizons.
Unmapped wonder, we pillaged you.

You warred and laughed.
You clattered and burned.
Inspirational folly.
Heart and soul of this crucible century.

You were our Heaven,
Our only universe.
We worked to be your burning stars.
Our idol through the decades.

We saw the proud nations,
And you stood proudest among those...
America will conquer the world.
Philip Laverty

The March Of Time

Could music ever return, do you think
Back to the way it used to be
Do other people long for the old sounds
Or does the thought belong only to me
Would you go along to witness
The nineties music execution
Then see and hear it replaced
With the sixties revolution
What days they were, what times we had
To see the artists shed inhibition
It's no wonder Oasis reign today
For they have no competition
But wait a minute, it's not all that bad
I suppose I'm being a little unfair
I'm still spending money on today's CDs
So I guess I still must care
There's music around to suit everyone
So my thoughts must not be the gauge
Was I just being cynical
At my approaching middle age
Philip Rowbottom

On This Earth

While on this earth I've seen many things
Births of my children for joy to bring
Society changes, same good same bad
Deaths of nations oh so sad

Monstrous people who kill and maim
Everyone else they try to blame
Innocent victims of a vicious mind
Then they pretend to be nice and kind

Countries at war for what?
Who wants to stand there and be shot
A few thousand dead and all is well
Are they under a disastrous spell

Famine, hunger, poor children die
While satellites are sent up to spy
Millions of pounds on useless inventions
Give to the poor they need the attention

Once in a while sit down and think
Someone dies as you blink
Could someone have healed that poor soul
Achieve some sort of goal.
C. P. Ward

Anyone Can Dream

A simple little paint-box, its colours bright and new,
awoke in me, to take a look at Nature's paint-box too.
And, so it was that I set out to seek — perhaps to share.
The lovely blends our good Lord takes, with loving tender care.

A blue sky in the Morning, but oh! so red, at night.
The rainbow's awesome glory, the snow, so clean and white.
Multi-coloured roses, a pansy mauve and blue,
Humble little buttercups, bluebells and violets, too.
Daffodils and tulips, poppies by the score,
cheeky little snowdrops — and lavender to store.
The trees stand in such glory, in every shade of green
which quickly turns to brown and red, when autumn is the scene.
I look down at my paint-box, and wonder if it's true,
If such colours I have seen, I must go paint them, too.
I shake my head, in disbelief, No! No! That's not for me,
I lack the skill, and what is more I'm just gone eighty-three.
R. Dowles

Take Care Of The Child

Take care of the child, my sorrow lures me
Away from his sweet face as fair as hers.
Into your hands I entrust his young life,
Neglect him not, no more to blame than I.
No sign of torment lies upon his brow,
Innocent of she who bore him this night.
My grief is like guilt of his mother's blood.
I know not how to endure this misery.

I did not take her by casual choice,
The wonder of her overwhelmed my soul.
From passion's seed his life has been thrust
And hers is all drained and mine is all lost.
Is not to live, unloved, a sorry state?
This my fear for the child should I remain.
Let him know not my awful confession,
My resentment of fate's cruel trade tonight!
Shelley Jones

Seasons

When we were young, the summer sun would last from morn
    til' night
Autumn leaves would fall knee deep, 'twas such a wondrous
    sight
Rain came down in sparkling drops, we longed to go outside
Snowflakes came yet while we slept, such fun to slip and slide
When we grow old, we hope the sun will last to warm our bones
The cursed leaves get everywhere and everybody moans
Another wet and soggy day, oh please dry up, we beg
And oh, the cold, cold snow, we'll surely fall and break a leg
And yet we're told, when we grow old, second childhood is
    the boss
This can't be so, because you know, all weathers make us cross
Rena Unwin

The 20's

Remember the days we lived on the farm
At 'Tile Barn' where we come to no harm
Running about — breathing fresh air
Spotting a Rabbit and maybe a Hare.

A large pot of stew on the kitchen stove
An apple pudding flavoured with clove
Freshly baked bread we spread with jam
Home boiled bacon, sandwiched with ham

We picked our flowers for daisy chains
On Sundays we strolled through the Country Lanes
No telly was needed, or expensive toys
For our own fun we made, us girls and boys

How I long for those days once more
Such laughter and fun never a bore
It's lovely to think back of those happy days
Everybody sociable with such lovely ways
V. R. Morris

My Little Friend

My dear black cat who brought me such pleasure
At the yard where I work and sell wood by the measure
Dragged his poor old body today through the door
And lay sadly down, he could take no more.

What's wrong, dear puss, I asked with distress,
And could see pretty soon his front leg was a mess.
Broken or fractured I could not tell yet
And quickly we hurried him off to the vet.

His shoulder is broken, his nerve severed too,
His leg is quite useless — what shall we do?
His life in the yard never would be the same
Whereas he was master he would soon be fair game.
A figure of fun to all other cats, and never
again would he chase the rats.

So farewell dear friend, I will miss you so much
As I sit in my office, no soft head to touch.
I loved you, and hope in the last long year
I made your life sweeter and free from fear.

Stephanie M. Jones

Summer Drought

I looked through the ghostly gums at eve,
At the scarlet glow in the west
While it slowly blackened its face to watch
O'er the day when it sank to rest.
The sun sped over the burning sand
And left the desert to cool:
While the tottering cattle,
Some already dead,
Stood around the drying pool.
Some limbs were dead.
Not a blossom nor bee.
No song from the perishing bird.
The cow-boys were absent;
They were over the hill
Pulling boughs for the hungry herd.
The dingoes came in thro' the dusty pall,
They seemed to want to be nigh.
The merit of catching a bird was gone;
They were scarcely able to fly.

Timothy A. P. Sexton

'An Angel's Rocking Chair'

"With Children's eyes you wonder as you gaze into the blue,
at the mystery of Creation and its message there for you.
Grown-up still you ponder, though the reason's clear and true
why eternal springs of wisdom generate each anew,
for amidst the maze up yonder lies the answer old but new.

There's an empty Cradle and a vacant rocking chair,
in the nursery now so silent, lonely, cold and bare.
Happy was the laughter, fitful were the tears,
the Children will remember oft in future years,
when they recall their childhood as they grapple with life's cares.

They'll draw again fresh succour from the Cradle well aware,
that the Gentle hand still rocks it
from an Angel's rocking chair."

R. P. Neave

Trusting

Trusting is the expectation of hope
Believing in truthfulness
To feel comfortable and safe, with no fear.
Confidentiality is the trusting of spoken words
Innermost thoughts, feelings and secrets, my soul.
You held my hope in one hand, my soul in the other
You held me up — then smashed me together
You wrote it down and I am hurting
My soul is crying out with incredible pain
So loud, it is far beyond any human tears.

Sandra Lunt

The Gate

I remember a little gate
At the end of a winding road
Where a loving grandmother used to wait
As the wagonette emptied its load.

I remember her welcome smile,
The table laid, fresh butter oatcake
Warmth and cosiness, prayers awhile
Good night kisses, then "still awake?"

I remember the gate of a little church
And came to the end of my youthful search
And seemed to hear a voice so sweet
"Take off thy shoes from off thy feet.

I remember our Dear King's voice
As he spoke of the "Gate of the Year"
How he gave us heart in the strife and noise
And gave us strength in our fear.

A gate is a thing of beauty
Be it wrought iron, carved, ornate,
Large one, small one, way to duty
"What a lovely thing is a gate!"

Murriel Barraclough

On Reflection

Suddenly you realize how much you've known in life
Being a loving daughter, a student then a wife
The miracle of babies and the trust they give to you
Sharing joys and sadness, the pride in things they do
Like being chosen for the choir, or coming first in Art.
The worry of exam time, you feel you're taking part.
Holidays by the seaside it only seemed to rain.
When going back at tea time — next morning fine again.
And then they've gone their own ways with loves and homes, careers.
Putting into practice all they've learned throughout the years.
The extended family growing, with you as their second Mum.
Nothing prepares you for the time when their own children come.
You look in their eyes and you'll know instantly.
This is your reason to be.

M. Allison

Twilight

The world is full of people who
Don't seem to care — do you?
When so much sadness fills the news
And daily tragedies ensue.
I wonder sometimes if just once
A stream of daylight could crack this dusk?

And, oh what joy we all could feel
If sweetness repelled the foulness here.
A happiness, engulfing us
To shed the cloak of sadness thus;
I wonder sometimes if just once
A stream of daylight could crack this dusk?

And if daylight wins I wonder then
Could this last, could we sustain?
If dusk were beat and we could know and
The depths to which we stoop could go.
Might we let this daylight in?
Might we crack this dusk's chagrin?

Tania Watson

My Boys, My Life

The zoo trips, the theme parks, days on the beach,
Bike rides and long walks all helping to teach
You that childhood is fun and something to treasure
When granny and grandpa gave you time without measure

When illness struck and my life looked bleak,
I was left with no hope, so tired and weak
Then I thought of you boys, and I fought to survive
To watch you grow up. Thank God I'm alive!

Val Cole

Hidden Love

Most pleasures in life are totally free.
At the drop of a hat and together we'll be,
in each other's arms canoodling quite blindly,
on that beautiful staircase all white, and so winding.

Not a care in the world, as we both know we're hidden,
and we're carried away with our lust so forbidden.
If those steps were a mattress — how we'd have loved!
And the view was stupendous in the hot midday sun.

Yes the scene was exquisite, we do not deny,
for two people, forever cannot stay entwined.
As a point will be reached when we both have to rest,
for if passion takes over, I'll be kissing his chest!

That wouldn't be fitting, if we're caught in daylight,
by some strangers just trying to get up those flights!
So we'll go for a drink, and maybe some lunch,
and return to the 'Main-Course' again in the sun.

When we have finished and done all we please,
we can go and find somewhere for afternoon tea.
Who knows after that, just where we could roam.....
But I waved at that staircase, on my way home!

M. Laela Spagnoli

And So

Sitting up there on a wishing stone for almost an hour
At least that how long it seemed to be
On this land of the brave the strong and the
Freedom, oh sweet freedom ninety five years
Would about suit me I reckon
But then again some leave at three
Or forty five, oh dear me their goes
Another one
Was it just a dream from a wishing stone

Here we go round and around don't seem like
I'm touching this fair isle
With these aching limbs that have stood the test of time
To rest awhile would be heaven sent
Whatever heaven is anyway
I'm sure there is a feeling to match the thoughts
of every being you care to imagine
Strange as it may seem to your so called advanced superiors
Maybe a wee dram of the water of life
Would cut as way through this tangled
Web of knowledge we've come to know and so

R. Jones

Snapshots

I'd seen a real bear in the bushes,
At least, I thought it was there,
But when I looked for it later,
The spot where I'd seen it was bare.

'Can I see you again', I asked the girl,
'Please', I added, in dread,
For fear that she'd snub me, as others had done,
'Of course you can', she said.

A crimson sky woke up the sleeping guns once more
And started up again the ever present sound
Of war as, ruby red-ochred on emerald core,
The scarlet poppies coloured the broken ground.

It seemed to me, it was a very subtle change,
This slow, inexorable, gradual, turning beige;
When colours, once so bold and bright and gay,
Gave way, eventually, to sombre shades of brown and grey.

Memories of things that once had been:
Discontinuity:
Snapshots and fragments of time and space:
Immortality.

Tony Webster

Frère Martin Meditates

Now candle-white he lies with candles high
At head and feet, Frère Jean, bird-brittle, dry.
I loved him, but his bees will miss him most
To them he talked as if the Holy Ghost
Perched on his shoulder. Yet he spoke to me
Of driftwood shore and darkly-swelling sea
Off Donegal; of fuchsia hedges wild
Where fleeces dry. He told me as he smiled
His mother once had woven him a spread
Of tweed, in colours of the sea, for bed.
A doubt he voiced to me as once we stood
By Loire's sleek, sluggard flowing and his mood
Was dim. He wondered if Saint John had seen
Aright on Patmos. How could he demean
Our future bliss by banishing the sea
From heaven? Had John forgotten Galilee?
I ventured humbly that the Saint had meant
All barriers should fall. He seemed content.
Now I, young Martin timidly must learn
To talk to bees, my Paradise to earn.

Doris M. H. Brownlee

You

Could I be you I wonder?
As you're everything I'm not,
You're confident and arrogant,
I admire this such a lot.

Could I be you I wonder?
You're not afraid to speak your mind,
While I skirt round life a timid mouse,
So afraid to be unkind!

Could I be you I wonder?
You're the leader of the pride,
While I'm the sickly weak one,
Afraid to chance the ride.

Would I be you I wonder?
If we could swap a time,
Maybe I couldn't live your kind of life,
Am I happier in mine?

Carole Richardson

The Milk Of Paradise

When you get to this place you feel alive
as you move to the beat of the drum.
The lights are dim, but the wheel gives forth
rainbow patterns that live in the mind.
If only the dance could last for ever
in a misty evasive eternity
we could forget the reasons for birth,
and our place on this earth.

The first time you meet your peers
in this strange world of shadow and form,
you forget your family left behind
as you contact the lights and laughter.
The push of the pill is just for you
when you pay your way to erotica.
Now you're part of the pack who dare.
Who will cry "Beware"?

Paula Le Cras

The Gifts Of Life

Oh what a joy it is to hear the early birds sing,
As they flutter back and forth upon the wing,
Oh what a sight it is to see clouds gently floating by,
Blown along swiftly across a bright blue sky.
What a bliss it is to smell the flowers as they grow,
Filling your nostrils with their scent when the gentle winds blow,
Oh what a joy it is to hear the voices of those you love
These gifts are given to us by our maker up above.
Other gifts he gave us with fellow people to share,
The gift of peace and forgiving, also the gift to care.

L. P. Cappell

" A Message To My First-Born Child "

A message to my first-born child
As you lie sleeping, so meek and mild
God giveth me a fine strong son
I thank him for the deed he's done.

Because son, I love and cherish you
My hopes and dreams are for you too
In times of joy and also despair
Then if you need me I'll be there
Waiting to hold and comfort you
Or to give praise and a smile or two

And as you grow to be proud and strong
Then I will teach you right from wrong
You will also learn how to love and hate
And see the world at its sorriest state.

I'll try to be a good father, my son
And give you a childhood full of fun
For the love that I will share with you
Is shared in life by very few,
Please keep these thoughts deep in your mind
You're my pride and joy, my first-born child.
Sean Joseph Carr

Absence

Absence makes the heart grow fonder, we wondered if it's true,
As we stood there on the quayside, before we kissed adieu,
The love we said would always burn, in your heart and mine,
Would it stand the test of time, all along the line,
The job that you were going to, so many miles away,
You prayed and hoped for all the while, now it's here today,
You shed a tear, a smile forlorn, then you were gone from me,
You waved a hand in fond farewell, my tears you could not see,
The regular letters that you sent, I answered by return,
I wondered if you knew from them, how my heart did yearn,
You wrote of all the wondrous things, that you had seen, and done
The marvellous people you had met, the blue skies, and the sun.
Then suddenly the message came, I had been waiting for
You'd had enough of foreign lands, you wanted me once more
I stood alone upon the quay, the skies above were blue.
The sun was shining down on me, as I waited just for you,
That look of joy on your face, made us both feel sure,
Absence made the love we shared, last forevermore.
B. Luffman

By The Lake

Sunlight, dancing on the ripples
As we skirt the water's edge,
Eyes of moorhen, quiet and watchful,
Nesting in the reeds and sedge.
In the distance, across the water,
See the pine trees, straight and tall,
Planted amongst the oaks and birches
Whose leaves will turn and start to fall.
We see a fish rise to the surface
Where gnats and midges make a meal
For a frog who waits and watches
On a rowboat's upturned keel.
Then as the sun sinks crimson,
And the distant trees stand stark,
We turn and walk home, slowly
Overtaken by the dark.
Mary Walker

Untitled

Your tender smile it shone on me
As we rested 'neath our own love tree,
The tree we planted so long ago
With young loves wish it would flower and grow,
Our folks they said our love won't last
But nigh on thirty years have passed,
I'm glad we proved our folks were wrong
For like our tree our love grows strong,
As I turn and look at my lovely wife
I thank the Lord for this wonderful life.
R. M. McCormick

Living Inside A Crystal Ball

Hand in lead, I explore the cultured wilderness,
As time allows.
Fields of green appear before me, miniature forests
Of the sticks of shed leaves — of which I
know every intimate secret.
As I block out the angry raving of the traffic,
And turn my back on the grey road of dull routine,
With naught but solitude and dog as company,
Dreams like cool rain flitter throughout with sun,
Fall for me.
How long I will stay in my closed oyster of a world
Is a mystery.
This was my past, is my present, may be my future.
How hard it is to let go of the familiar and dear.
I live in crystal ball
And wonder do I want to leave.
Sandra Nicholson

God Please Lift The Mist

Each day that you are gone I miss you till my body aches,
As though a mist were wrapped around my heart,
 without you I suffocate.

They say that soon this mist will lift and life will be beautiful
 once more,
How dare they try to tell the grieved that life can EVER be
 beautiful after war!

I fear for your life, my only son, and mine, that I might never
 see your smile, hear your voice or touch your cheek.
I watch other women passing by, talking, laughing, but hear
 the pain their laughter; like me, they too are weak.

I see their very souls beneath their smiles, empty, wanting,
 waiting scared, all so scared they daren't be still.
So they bake and they clean and they scrub and they sew, that they
 might stop these imaginings and let their minds become tranquil.

And you my son, who walked away with excitement in your
 soul, had no fear, like the others all so young.
How long before the excitement died, and the repugnant taste
 of war settled on your tongue?

That I could be there with you, fight your battles for you, keep
 you safe as I've always done.
Who is tending you now, holding your hand, who is loving
 you for me?
Oh God, PLEASE lift the mist and return me my son.
Pamela Frisch

To Be Or Not To Be

"The world is but a hole," said the penguin to the bear,
As they sat adjacent on the ice.
"A hole, a hole, but where does it lead?"
The bear scratched his ear as he made his reply.

"Why the Universe, of course, and all its twinkly stars,"
The penguin smiled and curled his beak.
The bear's face crumpled as he pondered.
"Why are you so clever and tell me how you know?"

The penguin blinked and waved his wing,
"From books of course, from what we learnt at school."
The bear fell upon his front paws and rested there his head.
This tricky bird was just too smart, or maybe he was dense.

"Books you say. I've never seen. Not much call you see,"
A cloud of snow caught his eye, "I think it's time to go."
The penguin laughed and then he cried,
"Don't rush, let's talk some more instead."

But as he turned he talked to space,
The bear had quickly gone,
The penguin fell in one foul swoop before the hunter's gun,
A learned bird, he died that day, whilst the earthwise bear
lived on.
Phillip G. Williams

I Sat Watching

I sat watching,
As the sun shone on the rippling water,
Creating shimmering shadows,
On the leaves of the willow.
A swan glided past,
Her white body reflected like a twin beside her.
The sun peeped through the arched leaves
And made everything dance.
It was like sitting in Aladdin's cave,
Surrounded by sparkling diamonds,
Hidden from the world by the leaf filled branches,
That hung limp around me.
There I sat,
Not really hearing the flow of traffic on the road behind.
Birds hopped about me,
Looking for scraps.
There it was like a dream,
Everything looked so beautiful,
And everyone was free.

Trudy Warman

The Lonely Neighbour

She looks through parted curtains,
As the man comes down the road.
He calls at all the houses,
With his heavy load.
Three doors away, then two, and now next door is he,
It's the postman on his rounds, humming happily.
He stops and hesitantly fingering the mail,
Carries on right past her house,
She who looks so frail.
Disappointed, oh so sad, she lets the curtain fall,
A card is all she wanted, a card from her son Paul.

In her chair she sits alone, on this Christmas Eve,
Feeling so unwanted, trying not to grieve.
A knock, oh yes, a knock she hears, and
Hurries to the door,
A dozen Christmas Roses was the sight she saw.
You see I had to send them, Paul died in the war.

Vera May Richardson

A Country Gent

I strolled into a sheltered spot
As the heat of the day was really quite hot
I wiped my brow as I lifted my cap
I sat down near a tree and just tried to relax
The shade was so cool it wasn't too long
As a gentle breeze blew the tree into song
The leaves shimmering the sun from outside
And gently persuaded a closing of eyes
My head dropped back on the trunk of the tree
As the whispering leaves got right through to me
I felt my body relax and then sigh
As my cap caught the bark and dropped over my eyes
A bird softly whistled as I woke from my sleep
An hour had passed I must have slept deep
I stood up and stretched thanking nature a lot
For providing me with this wonderful spot
You see I'm a man of no fixed abode
They call men like me, Gents of the road
I feel very grateful to nature you see
It's surprising what nature has provided for me.

J. M. J. Callaghan

The Footballer

There was a young man who played football
Who never got the ball when he'd call
He ran off the pitch
And fell in a ditch
And then he got paid by the dole.

Andy Brighouse

The Vampire Beauty

Summer tears falls from its open arms
as the colour of love shines onto its silk lip like petals
from the sea of stars above.

In the garden of matureness
a White Knight takes the delicate heart
to give to the princess.

To the girl it is a token of love,
but to an ant it is a skyscraper amongst the grass.

The flower dies as the flame grows cold,
and the sense of love is lost through a bitter
thunderstorm.

The Vampire Beauty is now awake
drawing blood from its love lost victims,
only it survives,
no petals,
just a lonely stalk of thorns.

Victoria Fullalove

Sandgate

The rising Sun is a glorious sight,
As it edges out the dark of night,
And the great Orb glows with a reddish light,
As it lifts and lifts to gain its height.

Then sometimes the wavelets sing and sigh,
When the tide is low and the shingle dry,
And the seabirds call as I pass by,
Then take to the air and away they fly.

And sometimes a most unwelcome guest,
A roaring storm comes out of the West,
And the spindrift flies from each wave crest,
And the seawall shudders, but stands the test.

Then the thunder roars like the crack of doom,
And a seabirds wail comes out of the gloom,
The waves crash down with a sullen boom,
Covering the shore with yellowish spume.

These things have been through Eternity,
Showing in all their majesty,
But you'll never see them unless, like me,
You rise up early and walk by the sea.

F. O. Green

Pleasurable Moments

What great pleasure it gave to me
As I walked through a quaint old village,
That had stood the test of time.
As I strolled along a river bank,
Swans majestically floating by,
Wary of the fisherman, as he cast his line.
I wandered carefree through a forest,
Watched squirrels scampering in the trees,
Some very timid, some quite bold.
Hearing a songbird sing a sweet melodious song,
As a small rodent scurried through the leafy mould.
As I stopped to listen to nature's sounds,
A fallow deer, fleet of foot ran by
And fluttering down to rest upon my shoulder,
Came a delicate and oh so beautiful blue butterfly.
Nature's beauty was all around me,
The sounds sweet music to my ears.
I pray these scenes and sounds
Will last forever, but if not,
Then at least, for many many years.

F. J. White

The Seaside

I walked along a sandy beach, the bright blue sky above me.
As I gazed across the sea, the rainbows high above me.
The sailing boats so far away, how lovely, I must say.
I think I'll head for home now, until another day.

Philomena Gobbett

In The Dark Of The Night

The night time's fallen, the moon is high,
As I stand and look at the open sky,
What a sphere, so big, so bright,
As shadows creep in the dark of the night.
I look into that big vast space,
Are we the only species, the human race?
So many stars, there, flickering light,
Like many candles in the night.
I look into that milky lace,
So many galaxies far out in space,
Then from deep out, from afar.
A flash of light, a shooting star!
Then something catches my eye,
That old owl that sits on by.
It sits with its head tucked down,
Snuggled into its feathered gown,
Then it swoops on its rodent prey,
Then with silent wings, just drifts away,
I thank the Lord that I've got sight,
To see it all in the dark of the night.
Terrence McIntyre

Mother Lanka

In my twilight years
As I sit by the window
I gaze at the stars
I dream many a dream

Oh my beloved Lanka
What made thee so fair
The skies, the mountains and the sea
The fields and the meandering streams

Where the fish dart to and fro
Swallowing rays of the silvery moon
The cool evening breezes
So gentle and so soothing
With the scent of many a flower
Jasmines and the Queen of the Night

I played many a game
Hugging your bosom soil
Chasing the dragonflies
That glided over the stream
In the corner of our garden
In your beautiful serendipity
Priya Wijesinghe

Whisper On The Sand

I wake up every morning
as I draw back the curtains I see
the sun shining, I immediately think
of you, this feeling I have inside
is like a whisper on the sand,

My heart is pumping fast and hard
my face is permanently smiling,
I close my eyes and think of you and
how wonderful you are, this feeling I have
inside me is like a whisper on the sand

I wish I could be near you and feel
your arms around me, I long for the touch of
your lips kissing mine, my heart is locked in
turmoil every time I think of you
you lips are like candy so sweet and fine

If only you knew how much I need you
by my side, but I guess you already know
oh this feeling I have for you
locked and flowing inside
is like a whisper on the sand.
Maria Domanic

Dreamscapes

I had forgotten the sharp intake of breath that comes
with high pleasure
but she brought it back to me, in other body, in dreams.
When he came he brought me to endless fallow fields
where the people ate mud, and thrived on it.
I ate too. And when a wise man turned and told me I
could not stomach what they survive on, I felt worms,
in my mouth alone.
Vile moment of naked lunch pushed sickness into my dry
mouth.
I shook and paled at the possibility of waking
meaning. And still perhaps there is none.
But my lost dream soul stumbled on,
and, as I stood at the edge of the world, before I
became somewhere else, I was struck by the coldness
and longed for the shameful warmth of her sweet smell.
Ann Jones

The Leprechaun's Secret

To see the arch of a rainbow,
With its colours bright and clear,
Vivid across a dull grey sky,
Just a ray of sunshine near.

The Leprechauns of Old Ireland,
Believe there, at the rainbow's end,
Is a crock of shiny gold pieces,
Just waiting for someone to spend.

But no-one knows where the rainbow ends,
Or where the gold can be found,
For once the sun begins to shine,
The rainbow melts into the ground.

Just for a while, "till the next time"
When the rays of the sun meet the rain,
When the arch of the rainbow appears once more,
Will the gold be there once again?

Only the Leprechauns know for sure,
For their stories of old seem to say,
It's the Leprechauns who hide it!
Each time the rainbow melts away.
Helene Tresadern

Travelling

"Oh! the world is a wonderful place to see
with its mountains and rivers, the bird and the bee
But the pathos of life in women and men
their sayings and doings, both now and then

The Kaleidoscope of humanity
with its changing, colourful pattern
Is a whirling, whirling satisfying thing
and enlivens the time of travelling."
Lois M. Cook

Soup

Mam made a pan of soup today
With lots of good things I say
Onions, carrots, pile of potato
Mutton bone and two ripe tomato

A pinch of fresh herbs will help
Tasting hot liquid made mam yelp
Salt and pepper added to taste
None of this will go to waste

Stir it gently with wooden spoon
Beautiful smell floats round the room
Everyone sits round kitchen table
Mam serves all with great big ladle

Happy faces with stomachs all full
No one can say Mam's soup is dull
Thank you Lord for our dear mam
Perhaps tomorrow she'll make jam
Audrey Shetland

Life's Store

Of tender years we visualize what life has in its store;
What friends and opportunities will come knocking at our door.
We see our life before us as a chance to make our mark,
But it all may be quite different and reality quite stark.

The partner that we chose for life and until death us part,
Has changed beyond all reason and has no place in our heart.
Careers have their ups and downs, we all expect a change;
Demands around us moving, all our goalposts re-arranged.

Babies bring a total change to everything we do.
Demanding shouts both day and night, how do we see it through!
They grow up fast, but still demand huge chunks of our emotions;
How quiet life at home would be without all their commotions

In later years we sit and think of what was in life's store,
What friends and opportunities came knocking at our door.
Our lives are spread before us; we see the marks we've made,
Each giving lasting memories of the special part we played.

Emma Kingscott

Back To Basics

Take away the tray cloth from my tea
What have the powers that be, bestowed on me
V.A.T. on electricity
Spreading gloom and deprivation
Throughout all our glorious nation
V.A.T. on electricity
No cloth to put on table laid
With fewer goodies to be made
No starched collars for our men
As they push paper and fountain pen
No crisp petticoats to wear oh! So pretty
Since the use in electricity
Our children won't be so clear and fresh
With this never ending mess
Back to coal fires and tea baths
With candles lighting our weary paths
Repeating the poverty of the past.
Back to basics it must be
We cannot afford the electricity
V.A.T. R.I.P.

Cheryll Bailey

Flying Is My Life

Flying is my life and so mating too, this is what I live for, this is what I do. I love all the seasons as I fly here and there. So I land upon a cliff top and I look out to the sea, my friends are flying above the water, and they look and shout at me. I take off from that cliff top and glide towards my friends, they tell me to be careful as this sea is now a plague, it's no longer safe to land in, it's no longer safe to feed.

I fly a little longer and I look down at that sea and there I see my friend, but my friend does not see me. I fly a little lower and there I see my friend, motionless in the water covered in black like tar. The pain I feel is sharp and the tears I cannot control, my feathers are wet from crying, where do I go? Our world is being polluted, all our seas are dying within, I feel lost and no longer treasured by these people who sin. I may be a bird with feathers, but I have feelings too, like my friend who will never be remembered, by you.

Julie Bolam

Guilt

Does the hangman feel guilty at the drop of the rope?
When does the innocent man give up hope?

Does the adulterer feel guilty when he climbs into bed?
When does suspicion enter his wife's head?

Does the mercenary feel guilty at the death of a child?
When does the mother feel her life's been defiled?

When will man feel guilty as poisons the Earth?
Does the Human Race know that they will cause their own death?

Eric L. Bailey

Thoughts

So many times I've wondered
What I should have done;
Did I do the right thing
For my daughter or my son?
But what is the right thing -
Is it not to do
What I think is right for them
So to themselves they're true?

They may not do quite what I want,
But just so long as they
Can think and act and love - for them,
That surely is the way;
And hope that some small traces
Of what I'd hoped they'd be
Lie buried deep within them,
That little piece of me!

Jill E. Hodge

I Only Asked!

Where shall I find
what is WHY?
Why is WHAT?
And the 'WHO' that knows... that very place?
What does it matter if
'WHY'... 'WHEN'... 'WHO'
come to the mind; then go,
Seeking an answer no-one else knows;
Finding a place where more questions grow?
Perhaps, in the face of a child,
or bark of a dog
there will glimmer a light to
comfort the fog,
and a sign-post 'finger-pointing'
to a place named
'BECAUSE'

Gordon Reid Johns

Our Belson

Close your eyes that you might see
What it feels to be such as me.
Pain, hunger, thirst, and little sleep,
Through the bars we try to peep
Smell the green grass after rain
And "wish" that we were free again,
Oh! what is happening to me?
I do not know the things I see
The dreadful noise, the moving ground,
Smell of fear is all around,
"Oh let us out! 'Please' let us go!"
Where we are we do not know
Fear and trembling, feel so weak
In our way we try to speak
"Why" treat us "gentle" creatures so?
"You" cause our pain, you cause our woe,
Look in our eyes, can't you see
I could be you, you could be me!

Evelyn Ann Livett

Oh Lovely Rose

Look at the Rose,
At the bud as it starts to unfurl,
And when in full bloom,
Behold a glorious ball gown of Crimson velvet,
Fit for a Queen.

Look at the petals,
How delicate and frilly they are,
The perfume is heaven,
Enough to lift up your soul.

Behold a garden of roses,
All in their gowns of different hue,
Their scent fills the air,
The raindrop falls like a jewel.

Maureen Thompson

Ghost On The Incline

Avaricious, avaricious, avaricious, avaricious!
  What's the ghostly loco say,
Snorting up a longish incline,
  Where the diesels now hold sway?

So pernicious, so pernicious, so pernicious, so pernicious!
  It's astonished at the fate
That befell a once-great railway,
  Now dismembered by the State.

Meretricious, meretricious, meretricious, meretricious!
  All those fingers in the pie.
All involved in bits of railway:
  Bureaucrats alone know why.

So suspicious, so suspicious, so suspicious, so suspicious!
  Giving voice to nagging fear.
Mighty shade of bygone glories,
  Vanished with rail's yesteryear.

Inauspicious, inauspicious, inauspicious, inauspicious!
  Not surprising, this dismay:
Since the ghost was on the incline,
  It's been downhill all the way.

John Slim

" Nae Time "

Nae time that's a' you ever hear, nae time
What's wrang wi' fowk that winna talk
that's ever runnin' never walk,
a constant race agin' the clock, nae time.

Nae time, guid day and cheerio, nae time
I used tae like a wee bit chat
wi' pals aboot, och, this and that
noo they're past afore you raise your hat, nae time

Nae time, we're racing tae our doom, nae time
the driver in his driving seat
on busy roads where bumpers meet
wont stop to let me cross the street nae time.

Nae time, a supersonic race, nae time
an hour by jet tae Timbuctoo
a rockets roond the world in two
of course you can't admire the view nae time.

Nae time, a could be fatal move, nae time
how it will end I cannae tell
I'd like tae leave this livin' hell
but cannae pause tae shoot ma'sel nae time.

Alexander B. Sinclair

True Friends

When you are down and feeling blue,
When all the World seems bright but you,
When each day's cup of woe descends,
How dearly loved are my true friends.

They cheer us up when we feel sad,
When things revert from good to bad,
When we are ill and feel much pain,
True friends come to our aid again

And when our cup of joy is full
When screams of happy laughter rule,
True friends are there to share that joy,
To help us the event enjoy.

When family members pass away,
And we stand numb in deep dismay,
True friends come rushing to our side,
And help to sweep our grief aside.
Then when our course of life run,
When death is nigh and hope is glum
True friends will come and be right there,
To close our eyes, to fight despair

John P. Murphy

The Forgotten Past

Once there was a first Christmas time, so very long ago,
When a baby boy was born, a king we all should know.
In a draughty stable, his mother did give birth, to the
to the humble baby boy whose life is what I'm worth.

Many years have passed since that first Christmas morn,
And slowly we're forgetting the baby king was born.
So Christmas is developing into a shopkeeper's dream,
Where the real meaning of Christmas is never really seen.

In not so many years to come, Christmas will be forgotten,
so when a child asks,
"Mummy, why?"
the parent will reply,
"My dear child I can but sigh, for I have no reason!"

Deborah Howison

Sonnet To Morphian Teasing

When with the blood of toil the east doth run,
When after moonlit labours I lie spent,
When dozing dreams from their warm beds are rent,
Then cry out at the oh-too-early sun;
When joining them on earliness to whine,
Wakeful laments in morning mode to sing,
Wing'd nestlings, daybreak's sharp air draweth in,
Then, with their inspiration, cometh mine;
When I float in Night's wake, not yet awake,
When Lethe waves still lap my buoyant brain,
When conscious sures my craft is yet to gain,
Then is the time when I my pen should take;
  Yet flying for that pen to note such song,
  Alas, I fall awake, the muse is gone.

Craig Cameron-Fisher

Spring Fever

Spring!
When daffodil trumpets gush and spurt
In golden splashes on wild landscapes.
When March winds whip away my winter woes.
When mowing motors rip ragged fields
In readiness for willing seed,
And blackbird sings in praise of longer day.

When bough and branch, finger-tipped with bud,
Beckon blossom and sweet perfume of the Spring.
When little lambs limply leap along with ewes,
And love awakens hope in longing hearts.

Spring!
Like a great dawning,
A long morning of promises unleashed.
Spring sprays the dew of hope and cheer,
And like a child I want to laugh
And dance,
And sing.

Carmel O'Shea

Solemn Night

In the solemn depths of night
When darkness ebbs, and voice is still
From secret bower on yonder hill
The brown owl takes to flight.

From darkened haven 'neath the soil
The field mouse from his slumbers stir,
Into the chill of night's dank air,
Through danger seeks a fruitful toil.

Beneath the bush of blackened thorn
In solitude the blackbird sleeps
And where the entwining ivy creeps
The wren awaits the brinking dawn.

Around my bed where darkness veils
Oh! Solemn night when voice is still
And howling winds my soul does chill
Through drifting thoughts my slumber fails.

Elizabeth Davey

Just A Thought

When leaves are dripping wet and bushes wear a shimmering gown,
When every blade of grass has little teardrops running down,
Then it is good to watch the watery sun at last appearing,
To kiss the tears away and coax the puddles into clearing.

When gutters run like rivers and a deluge sweeps the tiles,
Then it is fun to watch the transformation into smiles,
A summer breeze from nowhere sweeps the lanes and hurries by,
Catching at the corners of the leaves to shake them dry,

The air is drenched in perfume of a fragrant name unknown, and when
We look outside the plants and flowers seem to have grown.

Andrea Marrie Morton

Mother's Day

It's mothering Sunday, the first day of spring
When happy birds, come out to sing
The children buy mum floral posies
Then along comes dad with his long stemmed roses

All Mum wants is a nice quiet day
But she never seems to get her way
She's wakened up before it's light
To have an early morning bite

The house is cleaned, the beds are made
The dinner's prepared, the tables laid
The children try to be very good
But as usual, they play and pick at their food

The dinner's over, the kids are in bed
Mum sits back after being well fed
She's determined to make the most of her day
'Cause it means much more than she can say

At 12 o'clock she sheds a tear
Oh well, she says, there's always next year.

Georgina Curran

I May Have Got Wed

How can I tell you the way that I feel
When I am scared it will drive you away
The way you touch me has great sex appeal
And I want your body today

I may have got wed
A few years ago
But I want to take you to bed
And move to and fro

Now I know we have friendship
And known each other long
I want to kiss your lips
And believe me nothing is wrong

I'll always have feelings
Whatever I do
But I'm scared of not doing
What I want when I'm with you.

Elizabeth Bartlett

Bad Days

From the prison it has built
brief tunnels lead,
from whose dead ends my mind recoils
hysterically screaming.

Before the one remaining exit
it sits despairingly and weeps.

That last way out is sealed
by a wall,
carved and delicate,
through which streams morning sunlight,
sound and warmth;
a lovely thing in its own right
and a source of joy.
To leave the prison it must be part destroyed.

V. A. Meek

When The Bell Tolls

When my time on earth is over
When I have breathed my last breath,
I shall look back on this life
Then stand to face my death.
I'm not frightened of the dying
Nor frightened of the pain
For once the bell tolls, my life begins again.
When death washes over me
I will not stand to fight
I shall accept my responsibility and walk towards the light.
Yes, when the bell tolls
I shall accept with all good grace,
for I know we shall meet
another time another place.
Please do not mourn for me.
Hold your head up high each time you think of me
look towards the sky,
for I'll be looking over you in everything you do
Smile when you remember me and know I think of you.

D. Green

Not I, Lord, But We

Not I, Lord, but we, my soul wants to say
When I wake up each morning to start off the day
Not I, Lord, but we, as I dress to begin
Today it is us, Lord, please keep me from sin.
So often it's I, Lord, and despair quickly comes
And depression can smoulder like threatening drums
So if Thou be most willing, I beg teach my heart
To remember it's us, Lord, right from the start.
It's us, Lord, who walk through the moments of time
It's us, Lord, together each task do entwine
Not I, Lord, but we, when you each me to pray
So my footsteps are sure steps which we take today.
I'm tempted to say it is me, only me
When problems and insults and pain's all that I see
When my mind is confused and my heart wants to break
I'm tempted to feel that it's me You forsake.
Remind me, Sweet Saviour, that's just what You are
The hope of all hope and love's guiding star
Not I, Lord, but we, as my soul wants to say
Now and forever, Lord, to the end of my days.

Jane Roze

My Uncle

As I was growing up my Uncle wasn't always there,
When I was young I thought my Uncle was cruel,
As I grew into the person I am today,
I realized...
The rules my Uncle made were for me,
The person I am today is made from what I've learned,
Though to me he was strict I now know...
He loves me for me,
He's part of the reason I am who I am,
The qualities given to me through his love,
Will never fade,
So now I thank the Lord...
You were my Uncle.

Carly Thomas

Where Do The Resident Yardiges (Blackbirds) Go?

Where do the resident yardiges go
when all the grass is dry?
Where are they standing on one
leg, when the sun is high in the sky?
Do they converge on some half withered tree,
or fly up high to catch the
breeze? Who really knows? Not I!
You can hazard a guess where
the yardiges go, but alas it
might be in vain, 'cos the only
time I've seen a yardige in
summer is when it stood scrunched
in the rain.

Dawn A. Letting

The Night Sky

Have you ever looked at the sky at night,
when it's clear it's a beautiful sight.
Constellations of stars, many light years away,
invisible to the eyes in the light of day.
The moon is up there, whether full or part,
when learning Astronomy it's a good place to start.
Planets often appear in view,
Mars, Jupiter, Venus, to name but a few.
Flashing lights of the planes flying by,
disappear sometimes behind clouds so high.
Relaxing it is to look up above,
especially when with someone you love.
Dreams of wonder take over your mind,
one day the answers to out there we will find.

June Pagdin

Lost Love

The day dawned bright
When Love was young and felt
And everything was right —
Life fitted like a hand-in-glove
As hearts would melt
And love would weave its spell,
To dance and wend its way,
In all of its radiance — like blossoms of May.
So how then could we know?
That as it danced its own pure song --
The day could not ever last that long;
And must at sometime meet the night,
And blossoms must fade and blow away -
As ripples of doubts become loud sighs,
That ever louder, become loud cries,
And hearts that once loved so bold,
Were calmer now that truths were told. And realized
The dance was done and hearts
That once beat fast -
    run cold.

Julie Weller

Be With Me

Be with me Lord when love brings joy.
When love's pure perfume fills my heart
And every living thing becomes a part of me.
When every sense that I possess
Is travelling high upon the winds
And fills my body with perfect ecstasy.

Be with me Lord when love brings peace.
When seas of serenity sweep my soul
And a timeless state take over the whole of me.
When every minute of life that's lived
Contains the secret only love can give
A holy vision of heaven's eternity.

Be with me Lord when love brings pain.
When the agony's far too much to bear
And you, alone, can take such care of me.
When the heights are replaced with the depth of hell

And the mountains too rugged and steep to scale
Lift me high in your arms, my Lord, and carry me.

Helene Blick

Swimming

I see you watching me.
Yet I cannot read the ripples in those cool blue pools.
With those eyes, your smile is disembodied.
A lifelong prisoner, your key lies at the bottom of a moat.
Submerged. Silent. Cold.
I dive for it, flounder, panic, drift.
Breathe water and feel it trickle, seep.
I am helpless.
Poseidon beckons.

Kate Hargreaves

Time Out

In the hour of preoccupation
When moments are often missed
Thoughts elsewhere throughout the duration
And minutes only lightly kissed

Arrows of concern touch tender zones
Minds brim beyond capacity
Hearts ache for a lull in the mist
Souls break under adversity

Locks created without keys
Obstacles at every turn
Only time not in possession
Can build the key to learn

In the hour of preoccupation
When moments are often missed
Should we wonder at the elation
When peace is slowly kissed

Jacqueline Dredge

Untitled

Life must go on, so they say
When one's life partner is gone
So we're eating and sleeping and sometimes praying,
But who says this is living?
No joy to be had from the morning sun
Alas if only sleep could be long
But no, we mustn't give in,
we carry on
You'll have sad times they say,
truth is the only moments of peace
are during sleep
Lonely, sad, putting on a brave smile
But deep down our hearts are crying
Why did you leave me alone?
You know our love was everlasting,
But everyone feels this way
So they say.

Jean Gale

" The Cat "

The cat is an animal giving much pleasure
When sitting and resting and whenever at leisure
Very often it jumps and curls up on one's knees
One daren't move an inch let alone have a sneeze
The cat is an animal with soft sleeky fur
Soothing to watch and to hear its purr
It will sit very patiently by an empty dish
Waiting for scraps or a nice piece of fish
The cat is an animal highly intelligent
Doesn't expect its owner to be negligent
There are all kinds of breeds from "Alley" to Persian
It needs lots of sleep, not too much exertion.
The cat is an animal which gives off its best
Will give lots of love if put to the test
Giving lots in return if shown affection
But needs a good home and also protection
The cat is an animal giving much joy
Cuddly and warm but far from a toy
Not very practicable to take for a walk
But given one's love one can get it to talk!

Howard A. Latham

Comatose

If only they knew I'm still functioning inside
Would that dispel the fear that they hide?
Remorse and regret, of family and friends
That in this vegetative state they can't make amends,
For failing to keep a watchful eye
Over me — they knew I'd much rather die
Than remain in a world full of horror and hate
And abide by the rules of society and fate
So morosely I'll remain in this in-between place
And contemplate life or death — face to face.

Katherine Maria Kane

Seasons Of Love

Our love is like the Winter so beautiful to see
When snuggling to an open fire content as we can be
And each day seems like Christmas seeing your happy face
So warm and cosy in our world enwrapped in warm embrace
And when the Spring comes to the fore
Up sprouts each daffodil
The world seems such a better place
Our love is burning still
The Summer sun awakens life's passions to behold
Relationships grow stronger releasing joys untold
True colours come with Autumn and leaves begin to fall
The prettiest of seasons for lovers to recall
Throughout the year the seasons arrive and gently go
But each and every one of them just makes me love you so
Whatever time of year it is, whatever nature's scene
I know we'll be together for our love is evergreen
Jill Robinson

Untitled

Do you remember in days long since gone
when the skies seemed so blue and the Sun always shone?
Through the fields and meadows through woods we would roam
it didn't seem to matter if we strayed far from home.
With a bottle of water and some bread and jam
not for us sandwiches made with best ham.
We'd swim in the river and gaily we'd shout
that's what our childhood was all about.
But now its computers, television and things
and everything else that this Nuclear age brings.
There's muggings and murders, burglaries galore
and those woods fields and meadows just aren't safe anymore.
No more cowboys and indians in meadows of green
children play near their homes where they can always be seen.
But how did this happen why aren't things the same?
do we think sparing the rod is really to blame?.....
John Knight

Who Cares

Who cares about the homeless?
When the snow lays on the ground
Who cares about the homeless?
Do they just walk round and round
Do they still sleep in cardboard boxes
When the temperature drops below
Who cares about the homeless?
Does anybody know?
Is there enough room in all the shelters
For everyone to go
Or do some have to sleep outside
Amidst the freezing snow
So tonight when you're tucked up in bed
Think about the homeless
And the winter that's ahead.
Kathy Iley

The Dinner

Why did they tell me "dress optional"
When they sent me an invitational chit,
Everyone here's dressed up to the nines
And I feel the most out-of-place twit.

The men's hair is all down to their shoulders
And there's not a shaved face to be seen
And the women are bare to the small of their backs,
It's really on the verge of obscene.

And they all talk with superior accents,
I can hardly tell a word that they say
And they cluster together in tight little knots
So I'm always in somebody's way.

Now there is a waiter who's all by himself,
I'll ask him when dinner is due...
Oh God, it's a Poets' Convention
And I wanted the Old Boys of Renfrew.
Geoffrey J. Martin

Times In Our Lives

There are times in our lives
When things seem wrong,
When emotions fly like
Windswept kites
That dance and twirl,
Then fall to earth
Our minds filled with thoughts
In lonely nights.
Sometimes there is no reason,
No sense of tranquillity
Just hopeless, endless journeys through
Time — in all its unity.
Time passes,
Relenting not
Our thoughts in turmoil
Ramble on
Dark tunnels cloud
Our rosy hue
Till, time itself
Is all but gone.
Diane Murawa

The Home Coming

I believe it was somewhere near a quarter to seven,
When we arrived home at one one seven.
The journey home was not at all bad,
Although it was not the best we have had.

It's good to be home again I feel I must say,
Although Joyce and I enjoyed being away.
The lawn at the front could do with a cut,
And the flowers need some water from the water butt.

The fish seem alright, I am glad to say,
And are none the worse for us being away.
The Buddlea's out, but the weeds have grown too,
So I'm going to be busy for there's plenty to do.

We both know what a success the holiday has been,
As we come back inside and see it all clean.
But there is no place like home, it has often been said,
And there is nothing like sleeping in one's own bed.
Charles Waterman

Here, There And Everywhere

Our friends are not always at home,
When we have a joy or care to share,
There's just no-one here to love us,
And it seems there's no-one here to care.
We should not be down-hearted as we are always dear
To our Heavenly Father — He is always HERE

He cares when we are happy,
And when we're very sad,
And when we're being tempted,
Nearly more than we can bear,
He understands our needs and feels for us,
Oh, yes, He knows much more than us, because
Our Jesus has been THERE

When you feel sad and lonely,
And things seem just too hard to bear,
Just kneel and seek your Friend above,
He promises to be there.
He will gladly come to cheer you, 'cos
His love is EVERYWHERE
Barbara G. Brown

A Poem For Peter

There is a place more beautiful than this, our earth,
Where things are more miraculous than a woman giving birth,
Where peace, love and happiness surrounds one and all,
And emptiness and bitterness are not allowed to call.
This is where we go when we have done our best.
This is where we go when our time has come to rest.
Debra Newman

Golden Chair

I'll wait for you by the golden chair,
When you arrive I'll ruffle your hair.

And if you arrive I'll give you a key,
That key will be for eternity,
We'll be together till death do us part,
And we'll stick together, glued from the heart,
They'll be golden gates, fluffy clouds and white mist too,
And they'll also be me together with you,

I'll wait for you by the golden chair,
When you arrive I'll ruffle hair
But if you don't meet me at that golden chair,
I'll wait and wait until you are there.

Donna Worthington

Life And Feelings

Always look forward to good times
When you feel down and out
Don't let your emotions and feelings beat you
If necessary, don't be afraid to cry out.

Try and forget all the hard times
Remember one is always by your side
Think of those around you
After all, deep inside it's your respect and pride.

Sometimes you may feel happy
Sometimes even sad.
Other times you may feel you need to give to others
That your emotions and feelings are high.

At the end of the day
We're all human
After all it's natural to smile and to cry.

All that is left to say
Is my motto which is never give in
It's the love and affection from in your heart
That will see that you and others win.

Julian James Old

My Greatest Treasure

Who needs Gold and Silver?
When you have Christ in you,
Who needs riches and splendour?
It's to God we should be true.

Surely the gift of Jesus
Is more valuable than money,
Surely a taste of Jesus
Is more sweeter than honey.

The greatest gift in all my life,
Just has to be Jesus Christ living his life in me,
I don't care for diamonds or expensive Jewels,
All I need in my life is for Christ to reign and rule.

So first put your trust in Jesus,
He will look after you,
Then you will gain the greatest gift,
And Jesus will bless you!

Julie Mathers

Life Is A Book

When you pick up a book it wants to be read
When you have a child it wants to be fed
That's the start of life and social learning
It's the period when the plot starts turning

When you read a book, you turn each page
As you go through life you act your age
There is compromise and inter-relation
When you're making room for the next quotation

When you finish a book the story's complete
At the end of your life you don't have to compete
So close your eyes, lay down and rest
You've finished each chapter, having given your best.

Angus J. Fitchet

My Rebecca

When you hurt, I feel it too,
When you laugh, I laugh with you,
When you rest, I watch you sleep,
When you play, I watch you peep!

I feel a love I never knew,
My life, my love was made for you,
A cuddle gives me so much pleasure
And thoughts I will forever treasure.

I thank you for the sleepless nights,
The felt tip pen that's on your tights,
The endless nappies, shouts and screams
And wallpaper lifted at the seams!

So little one of mine I say,
I love you more and more each day,
An angel living on this earth —
You'll never know how much you're worth.

Lynn Clarke

To a dragonfly who drifted through The Marlborough Arms

I thought I'd written all I had to say
   When your travels brought you floating past my eyes,
Like a child whose only mode is but to play
   Your inquiring flight-path random in the skies.
And I've never seen a picture such as yours,
   Of innocence in nature — so portrayed
That when you circled round outside the doors,
   You'd clearly never seen life so arrayed.
And as you drifted off into the night,
   I'm sure I saw you bank around and call:
I watched you on your observation flight,
   And you said, "My friend, you'll never see at all."
If only you could write them down for me,
Then I could understand the things you see.

Andrew Davie

If

If only time and tide would stop
   whenever I did choose.
I could study the shine of sea-wet rocks
   with their myriad glowing hues.
I could watch the frozen flutter
   of a butterfly's gossamer wings,
And hear the endless, captured note
   as a lonely blackbird sings.
I could watch the sheen of sunlight
   through the spray of time-held waves,
And listen to endless echoes
   in many a sea-bound cave.
I could gain so many memories
   in one frozen second of time,
And all that I saw, and all that I heard,
   would be, forever, mine.

Jacqui Sherriff

Brief Encounter 1955-*

Ours was like the film 'Brief Encounter',
but I was single and you were a widower!
We first met at the hospital gates
where we both were workmates.
Within weeks we were going out together
to concerts, the theatre and the opera.
When my English lapsed into Cockney
you would correct me; it was so funny!
The difference of ages was enormous
although a marriage would have been harmonious.
But we were both sensible and talked it over
We decided to part and met once more.
We went to see 'Pygmalion', our favourite play,
which I'll remember till my final day!
You called me 'Eliza' and I called you 'Enery 'Iggins'
dropping 'H's for our last giggles!

Romana Bartosiak

The Squirrel

We have a lovely garden,
Where birds all fly amok.
They swoop down on the bird table,
In a very unruly flock.

We also have a funny bird,
All furry grey with a bushy tail.
Of course, it is a squirrel, but
It thinks it's a bird when it comes for a nut.

It jumps onto the bird table,
Then on the peanut holder;
Every moment growing bolder,
Eating as much as it is able.

When it fancies a change it sits up instead,
With its tail curled round up to its head.
In its paws it holds a piece of bread,
And nibbles it gently, like a lady well-bred.

Then it fancies a drink and skips off to the lawn,
And finds the pond, where the tadpoles are born.
It shins up a tree, which is not very tall;
Then leaps off the tree and runs away, well-fed and free.

Jean M. Senior

Bathroom Blues

My bathroom is a forsaken place,
Where I wait to wash my face.
Turn the tap on for hot water,
Bathe my young and lovely daughter.

Searching around for a bar of soap.
Staying clean, oh what a hope.
A whiff or two of expensive scent,
Value for money, a five p spent.

Out with a gurgle, the bath waters go.
Where it will end up, I don't even know.
I suppose it's the river, my usual wish,
Bodily poisons won't kill all the fish.

Leave the bathroom nice and tidy,
Won't wash again until next Friday.
Drip drying out before the fire,
Wife wonders why I'm an awful liar.

Rushing about to get dirty again,
This horrible affair is always a pain.
The total cost of ingredients must
Explain why bankers say I am bust.

Alan K. Maddison

Destiny?

Were we too old that fateful day
When you smiled at me in that sweet way?
Were we too old to learn to dance
Or fall in love and take a chance?

I lingered when you called my name
I'd often seen you come down the lane
You'd watched me too for more than a year
But couldn't speak because of your fear.

You full of fear that you'd be shunned
I was surprised and utterly stunned
You wanted us to share a life
But didn't know I was still a wife.

The lilting voice, the twinkling eyes
Carried me away to moonlit skies
We looked across the rippling sea
And knew forever 'twould be you and me

Now you've gone to wait for me
Was our time together meant to be?
Golden memories now flow free
And I still feel your love for me.

Eunice Doyle

The Mask

My heart spreads out for the fields unfold,
Where lies the souls, once given life,
They lie with masks, now changed with pain
No more to die — no more to fight
To lie and rest — where one was slain.

One's heart remembers their losing years
To think them young — their future dear
To them their shadow felt no fear
They fought with strength amid the vast
Where now they lie with ashen masks
Their souls had youth — they're now the past

Where lies the truth
 BEHIND THOSE MASKS.

Alice Lee Woods

'Bustle To Tranquillity'

From Monday to Friday I go to work in town
Where people bustle and hurry
Workmen continue to bang and shout
And no-one ever seems to worry
Buses cars and lorries toot and roar
And every time that I look out
The traffic seems to have grown even more
So when I do have some spare time
I like to walk and wonder
The beach is my favourite place
Where I can find a special space
I close my eyes and I feel fine
I hear the sea gulls cry for food
The waves splash up over the rocks
Sometimes the water comes up and over my socks
The soft sand blows over my knees
While I can listen to the wind blowing through the trees
Sometimes it sounds like a tune...
And then I realize that I must go home soon.

Linda Sweetland

Untitled

What sort of life is this that we're living,
Where everyone is taking and no-one is giving?
They take from the poor to give more to the rich
And the old and homeless get tossed in a ditch,

Where children are molested, slaughtered and slain,
And each is out for their own personal gain,
Where death is forever and "life" is ten years
Yet the family never gets over the heartbreak and tears.

What sort of future do we look forward to
When no-one cares what we say or do?
Where murder and rape are part of everyday living
Is this really the world that we want to be giving?

What sort of future do we look forward to, when no-one cares what we say or do,
When friends and family don't care anymore, and the world is rotten to the core?

Geraldine Anne McGinty

The Wind

The whistling wind whips through the wild wood,
Where the weeping willow weeps.
In the darkness of the night he sleeps,
Hidden in a valley deep.

When the clock strikes twelve,
Up he gets with forceful gust,
Sweeping up the sleeping dust,
Waking up the whole earth's crust.

The terrified trees tremble with fear,
Cold clouds cover the clear sky,
Flowers dwindle away and die,
And the dying night sadly sighs.

Emma Martin

Bluebell Woods

I love the pretty bluebell woods
Where ramblers often roam,
I stoop to pick the wild spring flowers
Before I head for home.

Grey squirrels jump from tree to tree
Whilst branches gently sway,
I call old Jess to come to heel
Before I wend my way.

I pass the seat upon the hill
Which overlooks the dell,
I stroll along the well trod path
Through woods I know so well.

The ground's a massive carpet,
In spring a glorious hue,
Large oak trees make a canopy
O'er zones of vivid blue.

As I head home with faithful Jess
Blue skies shine up above
But I feel sad whene'er I leave
Those bluebell woods I love.

Helen Locke

Searching

The blaze of summer stirs this pool,
   Where 'rushes stoop and faint,
And in the haze the heron drools,
   And cries his languid plaint.

'Neath red rimmed clouds the swallows swoop,
   To quench their savage thirst,
And dip their beaks in spreading loops,
   Of ripples soon dispersed.

But like the great kingfisher I,
   Who with a mighty sweep,
Grows weary of the frowning sky,
   And darts into the deep.

And otter sleek he does emerge,
   Beak filled with silver bream,
To settle on the grassy verge,
   Now keeper of the dream!

James Shillito

A Glimpse Of Peace

Six barbed wired counties above an Emerald Isle,
Where streets paved with khaki separate a red hand from a green shamrock.
I sit amidst a haze of blasting bombs and bullets and wonder of a peace.

And then it comes, a land bustling with calm,
the hours, days, weeks and months go by,
and then it leads to what!

Six barbed wired counties above an Emerald Isle,
Where streets paved with khaki separate a red hand from a green shamrock.
I sit amidst a haze of blasting bombs and bullets and wonder of a peace.

Gavin D'Arcy

I Remember

I remember the village where I used to live,
Where the neighbours motto was to give.
I remember the horses with their loads,
Struggling to cope with the dirt roads,
I remember the horses pulling the boats.
At the same time eating their oats,
I remember the fields that always looked green.
And the trees a toy to be seen,
I remember my mother at the tub,
Nothing to do but to scrub.
And as I sit here due to retire,
I see those pictures in the fire.

Ernest Smith

Hope Of Freedom

There is a place called "Tienamen Square",
Where students gathered in.
But for too long did linger,
Where peace of soul went out,
And heart of man came in.

With guns ablaze the tanks came,
And man with gun on arm.
They shot at random
And at will,
Gone all peace and calm.

The square awash with blood of man,
Of woman and of child.
The future youth no longer stand
Because of silent, screaming pride, and courage
Of one lone man, who stood before the tanks in line

O may the righteous heart of those
Who stood for peace that day,
Who died, gave their life,
Gave all for future's freedom way,
Be not lost, but burn in our hearts, always!

Julia Almond

A Cheshire Scene

Picturesque Cheshire is my home town,
Where the air is fresh and clean.
It has beautiful churches and village greens
And at nighttime a sly old fox can be seen.

There are stately homes museums and parks
Where people flock all year round,
The forests and woods are a squirrel's delight
And many wise owls can be heard at night.

The fisherman visit from far and wide
To fish in the waters so clean.
There are rivers, canals, meres and streams
To have a good catch is the angler's dream.

The Romans designed old worldly chester,
They built all the castles and roads.
Many tourists gather to see the sights
Of the ancient city which stands so bold.

Northwich, Middlewich and Nantwich are the home of the salt
With black and white buildings in view.
Many houses subsided in years gone by
Caused by pumping of brine which was new.

Evelyn Wilkins

The Torture Trade

It all begins on the farm
Where the animals are at no risk or harm

They graze amongst their fellow friends
And chew contentedly in their pens

The grass is lush, fresh and green
The animals unaware of the ordeal from the mean

They're the ones who've been born and bred
To travel far and soon be dead

On our plates, that's all it takes
For them to be tortured and soon for the bake

The hatches are opened far and wide
The calves shoved in and kicked aside

In they go, all squashed and cramped
There is no room to move, not even to stamp

People need to stop and listen,
To take a note of the terrible conditions

To say what is wrong and what is right,
To never give up their needy plight

And maybe soon the calves will be free
To see the outside world, how great that would be

Charlotte Ambrose

Shadows In The Glass

Before the glass a creation takes place
Where the studied face of her reflection
Will shed its age in metamorphosis,
In faith that all eyes will be blind to trace
The deliberate toil of her perfection:
A butterfly blooms from the chrysalis.

She paints her lips red like a good girl should
And she daubs a blush on her bloodless cheeks;
The loose silken dress drapes over each curve.
Each long tress falls like a river in flood
While vanity, beneath her skin so sleek,
Lies triggered and attentive on each nerve.

What is it that the glass does not reflect?
The secret it keeps, the knowledge it hides?
For sometimes when at the mirror a while
She shudders to find that youth is not kept,
She shrinks away at the malice inside,
The death in that bland, insidious smile.

Jim Newcombe

Dear Daddy

Where were you on my Birthdays Daddy!
Where were you at Christmas Daddy!
Where were you!
Dear, Dear Daddy.

When I was seven I longed for you so,
When I was Eleven I resented you so,
Now you are in Heaven I miss you so,
Dear, Dear Daddy.

You visited me when I was Twenty,
I made you a Granddad,
From then on I saw you plenty,
Dear, Dear Daddy.

Until the day there was no more,
You died when I was Twenty four,
Dear, Dear Daddy.

I long for you so,
I resent you so,
I miss you so,
I love you so,

DEAR DADDY.

Jane Atkins

The Autistic Child

I talk to rouse you from your land of dreams,
Where you live alone, in a shadowy space;
So remote, so still, unhearing, unseeing,
Unable to follow life's random pace.

I hear your words, Mother, but what do they mean?
Will they help make sense of the world out there?
Will they slow the world down, bring order from chaos
And entice me out of my solitary lair?

I smile to reach you beyond your walls
When your eyes look through me, glazed with pain.
Then fright follows anguish across your face
And you fall back into your void again.

I see your smile, Mother, but what is it for?
Will it lighten my dark and stem my tears?
Will it build a bridge to cross the chasms
And help me run from my nameless fears?

I hold you gently, within my love,
To bring you back from your private hell.
But you stiffen in fear whilst on my knee
And retreat in silence behind your shell.

Gillie Baerselman

Your Life And Mine

The gift of life should always be cherished,
Whether we're young or old,
The roads of life have many turns,
Not always with rainbows or gold,
It's hard when you're young to understand,
The good things in life are all free,
Good Luck, Good Health and Good Fortune,
Of the good things these are just three,
But if we have health and battle on,
We can wish for the others by doing no wrong,
Forget our misfortunes when they are passed,
And always be thankful that they don't last,
There are silver linings we don't always see,
The grass can be greener for you and for me,
We all get our share, have sorrows to bear,
And if we look forward,
We're sure to get there,
Try and be nice to friends and foe,
And life will be worth living wherever we go.

Anne B. Robertson

Shakespeare's Apprentice

I have spent my life saying goodbye
which as becomes, as easy as breathing air.

And then the spoken word is said in my past reminded time
the language, the language shall regress
into the precedence of thine self-opulence

And when born unto field of grey
from sheets that still cover may
for everyone and everything will make you twine
yourself... it may

And by silent screams from yelps to scoff
of unfold breaths contained back into pots.
There of life unlived, disposed of labours gained regiments
as wisdom shows, should not gauge a single miss life spent.

Trust not your eyes nor ears of words
that they the rhythm of mortal idleness.

Colin Mark Nixon

Ashes

Scatter me unto the brine
Which falls upon that land of mine

Let me drift amidst the waves
Passing by those poets' graves

Where I shall seep through every pore
Lying along that sacred shore

That land where words are spoken well
And sung with magic to increase their spell

For there I was born near the liffey's swell
Where the oulones trundled to the mass bell

That land of bottomless wombs
Where sons have left their unfilled tombs

Where horsemen ghosted the morning dew
And Normans brought a language new

Let me surge through that final tide
Where I shall land by my father's side

For you I could never disown
Though I fight every fight but my own

To finally be as one with blessed waters
And be the tears of my sons and daughters

Anthony Magee

Treasured Moments

I see a dear little face at the window
Which gives me such great pleasure,
It's my young friend peering through
And I find her a real treasure.

She's so full of life, and vitality,
And brings me down to reality
With her chirpy chatter, and toothless grin,
She'll breeze into my day with a smudgy chin.

She will call and see me if I'm not well,
And eagerly listen to tales that I tell
She's brightened the twilight of my years
She's a dear little girl, with lovely curls.

This dear child is growing up fast,
I must treasure each moment while it lasts.
Until that time comes, I'd like her to know
How she's brightened up my days, and I love her so.

Lorna Culshaw

The Four Seasons

Spring, Summer, Autumn, Winter.
Which one is the best
Could we separate one from the rest
They all have a purpose and try as they do.
Winter with its darkness, bitter winds and icy snow.
Would we like to hibernate. Some animals can
'Till spring appears and then
To see the trees, hedgerows and flowers sprout
But what's the old saying "about May
to never cast a clout"
Then we're into summer-long evenings,
holidays and sun
Sadly soon to end — into Autumn.
Almost back to where it all begun
But they are all wonderful — in a natural way
and 'Old Man Time' gave his reason
For these four seasons to continue and stay.

Daphne D. A. Newman

Autumn Leaves

The autumn clowns go dancing, spinning, dancing down the lane.
Whirling, chasing, prancing, a hold on life they claim. The colours
stun and sparkle, rebuff the darkling sky; they scintillate and
mesmerize the entranced watching eye. Their pseudo life is catching;
I want to dance and run, in memory of a summer when life was
full of fun.

The colours of the harlequin are dashed across their skins, yet
the deathly whispering rustle says there's little life within. Yet
well they show their colours as long as they do run; but,
whispery dry is every voice, the dying call - not their's by
choice; the augury of what's to come, but still they dance and
run, run, run!

A merry minuet, pavane, between the needle pricks of rain;
they settle stop and dance again. A passing breeze and off
they go, frenetic now as winter comes and darkness falls, and
stiff and still they all will crawl, into congregations heaped on
high - but, still, like all, they fade - and die.

Francis Drake

Dunkirk

..... And so in years to come
Will some future sun
Slant fiercely down upon that sandy shore
And will the generation then
Remember those heroic men
Who suffered hell, who joked and prayed and swore.

As suntanned bodies lie
'Neath a peaceful sky
Will ghosts of men find rest from toils of war
Or will the beach washed clean of stain
By pounding seas and driving rain
Recall the seeping warmth of blood once more.

Joan Rea

Sounds Of Summer

Summertime's gentle breeze
Whispers songs of love to all the trees
Flowers of every colour and size
Languish under clear blue skies

Bees flitter from flower to flower
Humming their tune in the daylight hour
Butterflies on gossamer wings
Ladybirds and crawling things

The blackbird gives us such delight
As he trills his song from morn till night
The cuckoo joins in with the rest
Giving of his very best

In waving rippling fields of corn
Where the skylark sings his songs from dawn
The lonely curlew's plaintive call
Is the saddest sound of them all

Away in the woodland where trees grow tall
You could hear the most beautiful sound of all
The nightingale's song so sweet and clear
Bringing the close of day very near.

Elsie Keeling

Enchanting Summer Days

Within a sleepy village a cottage stands
White walls with shutters blue
Climbing roses cascade softly to the floor
Partially covering the wooden door

Skies in shades of grey and blue
Fluffy white clouds breaking through
Swallows swoop and blackbirds sing
Butterflies flitter with delicate wings

Raindrops fall like silver pearls
Glistening in the morning dew
Gentle breeze brings scattered showers
Ripening buds to open fragrant flowers

Marigolds bloom in yellow and gold
Velvet petals on roses unfold
Blossom appears on an apple tree
Summers magic for all to see

Children playing, a faraway cry
Remembering childhood days gone by
Past memories we recall
Silently a teardrop falls

Claire Massingham

Your Selfish Ways

I spoke to a close friend last night
who was worried about His children,
insisting He had given His best,
despite few showing any gratitude.

He said that people should worship Him,
and worship nobody else but Him.
I asked what had caused such selfish ways,
but He told me to listen to what He had to say.

"Why do people work on the Sabbath Day?
Why do they use my name in vain?
I wonder if you have honoured your parents,
maybe killed; perhaps inflicted pain?"

He advised me to not commit adultery
or deviate to steal.
"With all respect my friend," I answered,
"Idealism is unreal."

He knew that I had lied to my neighbour,
but shouldn't desire his material gains.
And I listened and I thought:
Thank the Lord! (I haven't been caught...)

Jason Marlon

Laudamus Christus

Adore with me the much-anointed King,
Who by his cross our cross has helped to bear,
And eased to burden of our suffering,
And proved to us His Supreme Loving Care.
Pray let us not be haunted by remorse,
Or lose ourselves as Judas lost
By cowardly betrayal and a course
Which all the paths of righteousness hath crossed.
Abhor the hedonism of our age,
Which threatens to destroy immortal souls,
Tread carefully this planetary stage,
Excesses must exact excessive tolls.
With my mind's eye each day I live I see
That sacrifice He made on Calvary.

Arthur John Hindley

A Silicon Chip

I am a silicon chip
Who gives some people the 'pip',
By taking over their jobs
In no uncertain way, but
I'm part of the future,
I'm here to stay.
Such a minute little fellow
But when my programme is set,
I work watches, calculators and computers,
Indeed, I am everyone's pet.
For me the future is rosy,
I look to the next decade with glee!
For whatever your thoughts about silicon chips,
There's no future for you - without me!!!

Catherine Langdon

Conflict

Nations together, Nations apart
Who knows when Conflict will start.
Greed and seniority are the keys to game
For this reason alone, the world will never be the same.
The flurry of bombs rage one by one
The intense noise make the ears so numb.
Destruction and ruin rule the earth
The death of innocent women who haven't given birth.
Streets of fire, a portrait of hell
Smoke and death creating a terrible smell.
No time for anger, mourning or pain
It's survival of the fittest to avoid the black rain.
Mushroom type shapes dominate the sky
The time has come to say goodbye.
Man's technology given so evil thought
Remember a cost of a life can never be bought.
Why destroy the earth so beautiful and kind
Whatever made this race of people to be so blind.
And one day there will be silence and no more
Who knows, what the future holds in-store.

Abul Alam Kashem

The Love O' Ma Life

Oh shut yer mooth ya sickenin scunner,
Whit A saw in you A often wunner.
Yer harder tae cope wi than ony bairn,
Wi yer evil tongue an yer cursin an swearin.

God's gift tae earth just wisnae you,
Mair like tae be the devil's brew.
A ken Scots men are classed as dour,
But A niver met yin just sae sour.

Patience a virtue you're sadly lackin,
Appears like magic when rods yer packin.
Only content when the fishin comes oot,
A'd be better thocht o' if A wis a troot.

A hert o' stane nae will tae forgive,
Nae ither pair craitur wi' you could live.
But this wee angel wi hert o' corn,
Wis sent by God tae suffer yer scorn.

Eileen Irvine

The Meaning Of Love

Someone -
    who makes you feel good about living,
who brings out the you, who is joyful and giving -
    This is the meaning of love.

Something -
    that gives you a chance to be strong,
or trust in another to help you along -
    this is the meaning of love.

Somewhere -
    that you feel like you've been forever,
a place where you're growing and learning together -
    this is the meaning of love.

Lynette Ogden

Britannia Decimalized

Oh! Britannia, Britannia, imperial Britannia
Who ruled the waves and declared with majestic splendour
That Britons never ever would be slaves
You who didn't give a bushel or a peck
When hectored and heathed into metric
Not a nay or a yea, when you hear them say,
That you must pay
For your five foot eleven to become a mere one metre eight O
Or your regal four O, twenty eight, four O
Inflated to a feeble one O one, seventy one, one O one

Are events not a little overdone.

With not a pound between us
Or an ounce to spare
Our feet metred!
Our gallons litred!
Our miles kiloed!
Our inches millied!
Stoned without a gram
Why not just embalm

What say you Ma'am?

John Kilgallon

The Time Of Love

When we fell in love... it was Spring,
White clouds, lambs and catkins... just the thing.
And Summer was just fine with skies of blue,
And crisp-aired Autumn was lovely too.
But love in Winter time is less amusing,
The day to day of life can be confusing.
Eyes may grow dim and limbs are not so strong.
Sometimes it seems the pain goes on and on.
Health is not good.... what lies ahead tomorrow?
Still sharing happiness, but sometimes sharing sorrow.
Then... I see a look, a smile, I hear a name,
I feel a hand and know it's still the same.
I feel those ice cold fingers stealing
Along my spine, and get that shaky feeling.
No matter what the time: Spring, Summer, Autumn and Winter too,
No matter what, I'm still in love with you.

Anne Cooper

Race

I am a face, a normal face,
Why should it matter about my race.

I have two eyes a nose and mouth,
My blood is red, my limbs well-formed,
But still they don't see that at all.

In school she said:
"I don't want to be you friend
my daddy says to keep away from your kind."

Am I a threat,
I don't understand,
All I want is to play,
To walk hand-in-hand.

Ann Frederick

Untitled

There was a keen gardener called Ellis
Who swore that his fingers were green
He planted all manner of veg in his garden
But not a tomato was seen

His caules and marrows were marvellous
His peas were as sweet as could be
His lettuces spread, green and fat in their bed
But tomatoes he never did see

He sat all day long in his greenhouse
And he treated them ever so well,
Making sure they were warm, through the cold and the storm
Praying one little "Tommy" would swell

He did everything that he could think of
He tried all, but to take them to bed.
I think if it were me, I'd give up gracefully
And take up basket weaving instead!

Beryl MacKenzie

My Gran

Eeh Lad what's gonna happen to you, who's gonna fasten ya shoe,
Who's gonna sew ya buttons back on when I'm dead an gone,
Ya nearly nine, ya little swine, ya never do as ya told.
Go wash ya face ya damn disgrace, take ya finger out of ya nose,
Ya mam works all day for a machinist's pay
Gets home at six, she's out at seven, won't be back till gone eleven,
Be a good boy for ya Gran, she says, I won't be late,
Get to bed early 'cos it's school at eight,
Where's she gone, I say to me Gran, has she gone to meet a man?
I'll 'ave no men 'ere, 'ave no fear
But e'h lad when I'm gone, she'll marry first one
And then what'll 'appen to you
After all I'm only ya Gran, not ya Mam
Even though ya think I am, God gimme strength ya little sod
For a love ya more than life dear God.

Anthony James

Why

He doesn't like me
  WHY?
He doesn't know me
  WHY?
He doesn't want me living near him
  WHY?
He doesn't like me because
  I am black.
He doesn't know me because
  I am black.
He doesn't want me living near him because
  I am black.
Perhaps if we had met in my country,
The white man would like me.

Christine Dale

Peace Of Mind

I'd like to travel far away, to some far distant shore
Where feuding friends and angry words, can trouble me no more
Golden sunshine bathes the valleys, and warms me in its light
At night the moon and stars appear, I marvel at the sight

A bright and sparkling river, flowing gently to the sea
Its banks awash with colour, it seems to cry, I'm free
The wind is gently stirring, neath a canopy of trees
Flowers dance, and come alive, in answer, to the breeze

It is a tranquil quiet place, this island in the sun
Where harmony and peace prevail, no battles to be won
Up aloft the birds wing by, and sing their joyous song
Butterflies, amid the reeds, join in the happy throng

Oh! Why can't we, who live our lives, in hate and disarray
Be like this peaceful island, and go from day to day
With loving thoughts, and joyous hearts, and harmony of mind
Doves of peace, not birds of prey, and leave this mess behind

Janet Lowery

Sorry For Caring

Some people have yet to learn;
Why care, when you get nothing in return.

Why show respect and love,
When they open their wings and take off like a dove.

Why give out and get nothing back.
Why run yourself down and off the beaten track.

Why should you be thoughtful and think of others,
When they pretend not to care and hide under the covers.

Why try your hardest and give it your best,
When you're treated like rubbish, like an old dirty vest.

Why show how you feel, how much you really care;
When the cupboard inside their head is empty and bare.

Why bother letting them have their way each time,
Don't they know that we were next in line.

I'm sorry for caring, caring about you,
I'm sorry it might hurt, but all the above is just so true.

Kirsty Zoe Kirk

A Parent's Thoughts

Is there anything she/he wants and doesn't get?
Will sacrifice reward — or cause regret?
For watching life unfold through open eyes,
Can at times cause consternation and surprise.

It's not possible to harness someone's will,
And expect them to express themselves, but still!
Lessons taught and lessons learned I hope apply,
As no guarantees are issued from on high.

Only time will tell what destiny beholds,
It's a constant for us all, as life unfolds.
No good hindsight when you've given all you could,
But forgiveness for their ways if err they should.

David Brooks

" Dusk "

Drawn to the window, will see
Wind bending the branches,
The bark falling with its own sort of grace
From the dead "Elm",
Now looking grey, in the fading of the day.
Such "Girth" that Elm had,
Now dry and leafless,
As though a medal, overdue for an aged tree
Noticed now, because it died.
"A star" like, bracken "Nest" of a crow
No green leaves to hide in,
Will see flights to and fro, young birds fed.
This tree has died, why I do not know.
It's sad to behold its bareness of dress
But "Joy" of its inhabitants seen
If only by me, "At Dusk",
It died not in vain.

Lydia Milton

Winter In Lakeland

The magnificent tempestuous
Winter scene or magical stillness
When newly fallen snow the earth o'er lies.
Oyster shell lilac, pink and pale blue sunrise;
Orange and golden tints in the red sunset
Trees, their leafless boughs in lacy silhouette;
Clusters of snowdrops exquisite, dainty;
Robin redbreasts' perky personality;
Sting of the East wind — the raging mighty sea;
God's messengers on winged feet
Tread the earth through wind, rain, snow and sleet,
Blessings from the Divine Spirit they bring,
Renewing creation — proclaiming spring
To awaken, to rejoice and to sing.

Jane Carnill

Wintertime

Snow is falling thick and fast
Winter time is here at last.
Earth is covered in gleaming white
Glistening, sparkling in the starry night.

Dawn approaches and with the light
Our eyes behold a wondrous sight.
Trees and hedges bowed down so low
Seem to pay homage to the virgin snow.

Amidst this shimmering icy land
One lone robin makes his stands.
Red breast glowing, his song so bold
Quickly dispels the wintry cold

I gaze with awe upon this scene
Breathe in air so fresh and clean
And wonder whose mighty magical hand
Has turned this earth into wonderland.

Freda Brazil

London Weather

People shuffling, noses red
Wishing they had stayed in bed
Collars up, keeping out the breeze
Longer coats to cover blue knees
Unprepared, as usual, for our weather
Four seasons in one day — we're at our tether
Trains cancelled, airports closed
Lorries stranded, still full with loads

Wait, the sun shows from behind a cloud
Suddenly children's voices, laughter, loud
Skaters on ponds, children on sleighs
Giggles and screams echoing all ways
Snowballs thrown, there's so much fun
Quite different from how the day had begun
So remember, when things seem to be bad
Could turn out the best day you've ever had!

Jacqueline Lewington

Song In The Shelter

It's cold and dark, where a mother sings lullabies,
With a back-beat harmony from war in the skies.
The sad thing that she doesn't realise,
Is that her baby has died in the cries.

An old, old man is shaken by what he has seen,
Thinks of when the town was clean and the grass was green.
With all the bombings and deaths that have been,
He doesn't know why, or what it can mean.

It's under the shelter where people sing a song,
Singing because they all hope that it won't be long,
'Til the peace will come and take away the wrong.
Sing with those in the shelter, sing a song.

Jenny Sarah Harold

Trixie

I like to sit quietly when evening comes round
With a really good book on my knee,
There's nothing disturbing the silence at all
Save the rustling of wind in the trees

It's grand to relax and to feel all the cares
Of my work a day world left behind
But a certain little body behind the settee
Has other idea's on her mind.

Round about nine, there's a scratch and a thud
A steady tap, tap on the floor
Then my dear old dog brings her collar and lead
As she looks all the time at the door.

How she pleads with her eyes, you will never believe
That a dog is unable to talk
So I put on my coat get my hat and my stick
And my Trixie and I take a walk.

June MacDonald

In My Dream Last Night

A crashing thunder woke me in my sleep last night,
With a roar and a rattle and a flashing light.
My window flew open and there he stood,
A shadowy figure in a cloak with a hood.

"Get up and clean your room!" He said,
As he waved my stereo above his head.
All my things as usual were on the floor,
"Pick them up", he said, "Or they'll go to the poor."

I jumped up in terror out of my bed,
I had no choice but to do what he said.
I slaved and cleaned and tidied all night,
Until my bedroom became alright.

At last I had finished and could go back to sleep,
But before I did I wanted a peep.
This man had woken me and made me feel bad,
So I lifted his hood and there was my dad!

He was laughing so loud it hurt my ears,
This was a nightmare, all my worst fears.
I shouted and balled and started to scream,
Then I woke up — it was only a dream.

Jodie L. Richards

Pow Wow

Gazing down thro' the valley, discover the awesome Missouri River, with everlasting winding banks reaching into the distance. Deafening sounds of throbbing drums announce the Indians dancing fever. Intoxicating smell of cottonwood fires melts my resistance.

Lured by my senses, guides me to the jingle dancer's Pow Wow. Fiery in spirit, flamboyant in dress, time will never alter. Hidatsa woman's excitement of tribal Christening explains how her daughter takes her late grandmother's name, Running Water.

Big chief bows his magnificent headdress, holds a golden eagle's leg, with open claws held uppermost. Offers me cold buffalo meat, bitter chuck berry jam, with very little said. Honoured to be their solitary guest, and they my Host. Attractive squaw's bluish black plaits resting on her beaded dress, exposed tobacco-stained teeth, offering an unnerving smile. Extended hospitality now displayed at its very best. Paranoid, should they use me for their own amusement, in just a little while. Bewitched by the vibrating musical sounds of grass reed instruments. Listening to the whispering grasses, sweeping this way and the other. Changing winds carry sounds of howling coyotes and petrified skunks' scents. Their cultural pride was mine for a day as they named me, Brave Cloud Mother.

Deborah Lockwood

" Dream Wise "

In our dreams scenes are created,
Why do they tend to be exaggerated,
With situations of which we've no control,
The strangest part of the action is,
We see ourselves playing the leading role.

Have you ever managed to skate or ski,
Drive a golf ball off a tee,
Or do things to great extremes,
Events you would never try to attempt,
Are acted out in all our dreams.

Some dreams it's said can be a premonition,
Others, if danger threatens, a monition,
Romantic ones could cause heartbreak.
We see them clearly when deeply asleep.
But very little is remembered when awake.

Dreamland, is a state of another world,
It's like a new flag being unfurled,
With everything in disarray,
Experiences in our daily life,
Is what our dreams portray.

Harold Lamb

Mountain Reverie

Great lonely mountains, why do you call me
with an inaudible cry?
Why do you urge me to climb to your tops,
touching the blue of the sky?

Oh! to be happy and sit on a hill,
sniffing the pure highland air,
Watching the grace of a lovely bird fly,
feeling the wind in my hair.

When I am down in the valley below
Heavy, oppressive you seem
Up here my spirits mysteriously soar,
Up here I can dare to dream

Great lonely high hills, why do you call me?
Maybe we're all of a kind.
I also like to climb high up,
and leave the cares of the valley behind.

Jane Gilbert

Seasons

The winter brings the frost and snow
  with children playing to and fro;
The lovely snowballs on the grass
  make fun for all as they pass.

Now winter's gone and here comes spring
  it brings the flowers and birds will sing,
The clock rings out a merry tune, it
  tells us it is summer soon.

The summer sun is warm each day,
  the flowers in bloom, the month is May.
The holidays are here at last;
  Forget the cold, it's long since past.

As autumn leaves begin to fall,
  we feel at last it's getting cold;
But lovely colours on the ground
  Look like a carpet weaved in gold.

Dympna Slattery

Canine Devotion

I was gifted a dog with dumb dialogue
With dignity and grace which held me in place
Extended a love to plains well above
Woman purporting pure white of the dove
Psychopathic charismatic failure to give
A shell in my life without reason to live
But then my dog without malice or motive
Brought around calm to past life emotive

The years gone by bring a tear to my eye
In stability sound turned he tabled around
Not my love lost and not my love found
My beautiful dog my beautiful hound
A tumour it was that caused her to lose
Her fight in this life and unable to chose
I know that she save me my well loved canine
So hopelessly helpless when the next turn was mine

John S. Kitch

A Question Answered

The rain was soft and gentle as a wisp of silk against my skin.
With eyes narrowed and with fixed stare I drank the beauty in.
Soft greens, earthy browns, rocks majestic rising to meet the clouds -
But none of this tranquillity could ease the crease between my brows.

The hard core of anger and hurt rose like bile within
Until every pore oozed anguish and I felt the stiffening of every limb.
I raised my eyes to heaven in mute appeal, seeking an answer
  to the unspoken question - "why?"
"Why did he have to suffer so long? Why did he have to die?"

Then, as if from a long way off, his dear, dear voice replied,
"I'm not dead, I'm alive and well - but on the other side!"

Hazel Pavitt

Every Tear I Shed, I Shed It For you

The autumn leaves silently fall and fall,
With ever so much melancholy on the earth which is still warm.
My heart pounds and hurts so,
For nature died with you today, that I know.
Finally the time came that I tried to ignore,
But wouldn't get the thought out of my mind.
God had taken you away somewhere,
Far where I will once reach, or maybe never.
After all the pain and suffering you had to bear,
You suddenly disappeared into thin air.
But ever so silently and unnoticed,
To the long wished for welcoming arms of the gracious earth.
I know it's time to let you go tomorrow,
But I can't stop this aching sorrow.
Someone please help me to understand,
Why mankind has to be so fragile and ephemeral.
Maybe the only way I can let you go,
Is to make myself believe that you sensed how much I loved you so.
But my tears will never stop, they will always fall and fall,
With ever so much melancholy on my face which is still warm.

Andrea Zupan

Middle-Aged Spread

Some middle-aged people surround themselves
With families, friends, homes and gardens
And grow large and flabby, like friendly cacti,
Spawning growths at their tips.
They are round and surrounded, visibly content.

Other middle-aged people are great heavy tanks
Scattering family and friends as they pass.
They're impregnable and solid,
Hardly pausing for more than trivial chat,
Selfish and energetic, visibly aware

That others, for them, exist in time warps
Of their own past lives. When they meet
They will hardly recognize their old friends;
Ex-husbands will seem of a different species.
Stout and robust, they seem to thrive.

Harriet Jillings

The Bluebird

A tiny little bluebird sat way up in a tree.
With feathers preened and colourful he peeped at you and me.
He spread his wings and gently dipped-
His tiny body down — and slipped
To grass so green and luscious sweet.
His little frame just could not eat
All that he wished he could carry.
But time goes by. He could not tarry,
For peering at him with eyes so black
He saw a most ferocious cat.
Once again he spread his wings
And, as God is with tiny things,
He soared high, high, up in the air.
And me? Well, I could only stare,
Grateful the bluebird, which was so divine,
Had not been hurt by the cat, which was mine.

Doris M. Beal

New World

Life in a new world of only just peace,
Would be like having a new life lease,
Everyone happy, and no falling out.
This is the sort of thing to have about,

Just imagine, it would be like paradise.
Everyone happy, would that suffice.
To walk about freely, without any fear.
No more trouble, no shedding of tear.

No more suffering, no more pain.
A lovely gift for everyone to gain.
If we truly want to live in this world so new,
Let's have it for all, and not just a few.

Albert Thomas

An Insect's Lot

I'm glad I'm not an insect small
   with feelers and feet designed to crawl
to be on the ground never making a sound
   and to be always wary of those humans so scary,
with their feet so enormous, so clumsy and large
   and when crossing a road, well, you're crushed flat by cars.

No, I'm glad I'm not an insect, you haven't many friends,
   your life is just a short one and pretty soon it ends,
You're liable to be trod on and squashed flat underfoot
   by some short-sighted person who didn't even look.

Insect repellent is never very nice,
   It's not much good to spiders and certainly not to lice.
No, I don't want to be an insect, I'll stay just as I am,
   a scary human being, commonly known as man.
Colin Spicer

Pembrokeshire Lament

The Daffodils about to burst
With gay crocus interspersed
As worldly cares are washed away
Like pebbles on the shore
The seasons and our hopes renew, as many times before
Then suddenly, without warning
Just as first days of spring were dawning
A tanker spilled its filthy oil
The best of nature yet to spoil.
The beauty of the Pembroke coast
With golden beaches, wildlife rare
Besmirched with oil, her soul laid bare.
Our wealth does not with money lie
But with the seabirds you see die,
The fisherman would his trawler give
Once more to see his fish to live.
The wings of birds who cannot fly
They were not meant this way to die.
Tomorrow a grey day is dawning
What hope come morning.
Ann Shirley Cornish

Epithalamium

'Let's fly!' I cry, and at a bound
with hands entwined we leave the ground.

Above the teeming city's roar
into the silent air we soar,
to rest upon a wispy cloud,
secret, secluded from the crowd.

Beneath a cerulean sky
the witching moments sweetly fly,
as all the birds of earth take wing,
and in the hall of heaven sing.

With folded wings my lady lies,
until the strident cuckoo cries;
then gently falling, side by side,
back to the homely earth we glide.

Now slowly fades the cloud-borne dream...
and things again are what they seem.
Edward Benbow

The Love Of My Life

You are the love of my life,
You are my love
My one and only true love
You know you can knock on my hearts door
Whenever you want my heart galore.

You are the love of my life, my love.
I hope you know this more than ever before.
My hearts door is open only to you,
From now and beyond eternity.
My love the love of my life.
Joanne C. D. Mills

Our Mother Nature

As she walked through the shadows of the willowy trees,
With her soft golden tresses gently caressed in the breeze.
The silence was broken as the leaves on the ground,
So fresh with the morn — softly whispered around.

So beautiful was she, with the sun in her eyes,
Her heart all aglow, as the morning bird flies.
So gracefully floating with the clouds high above,
Blessing us all, so tenderly with Love.

As the trees reached up their branches to kiss with the sun,
She patiently waited, as the new day begun.
So silently still, with her arms open wide,
Gently feeling the warmth that was so radiant inside.

When she tells us to feel, we obey silently,
For she is the one who knows — what will be.
So listen to her carefully, and from her warning, take heed,
For she is Mother Nature — the Mystical "someone" we all need.
Carôle Diânè Pace

A Tramp

This man you see is not a hiker
   with no transport, he is not a biker,
He walks the highway every day
   he has no home in which to stay.

He wanders on from place to place
   travelling light, he needs no suitcase,
His clothes are all upon his back
   'cept for a billy can and ruck sack.

With greying beard and hair so long
   sometimes you'll hear him sing a song,
He is a tramp, he's not a crook
   don't judge him by the way he'll look.

Maybe he looks a bit remote
   wandering along in his shabby coat,
Much wisdom he gathered on the way
   so this is the role he has to play.

For him it will always be like this
   the open road and the sun to kiss,
No love for him, he's out in the cold
   but inside his breast beats a heart of gold.
Christine Farquhar

Starry Nights

On starry nights I could walk forever,
With or without company I feel an excited quiver.
It is said when you see a falling star a wish you should make.
I've watched a falling star and a wish I did take.

Starry nights are oh so romantic
I wonder does the moon go frantic,
Watching twinkling stars winking at me.
A starlight of a night makes it easier for me to see.

When the sky is a deep blue,
More stars come out to greet me and you.
Touching a star would be my delight.
In a glass jar I would keep it all night.

Studying the Milky Way,
As I walk through a field of hay,
Gives me great satisfaction,
Knowing the attraction of the constellation.

On starry nights my eyes look heavenward.
It isn't that I may feel scared.
It's the fascination of twinkly stars, especially their names,
That has me entranced when at night I am going home.
Biddy McAuley

From Ancient Egypt With Magic

I foresee by natural signs
With outward bodily movements that only the eye mimes
The powers that transcend such quality of human sense.
For now I pour out the knowledge you aspire to through mist so dense.

Reach out to me from the doorway, to a future age
That I shall only learn to touch the smallest manifestation lost in space.
I'm bound up with Sirius in magical references and connotations
That only my deeper state of mind will engage.
And the cosmic truth and nature will be what you want to make.
In my time capsule I'll wait and from this Siriun genetic strain I'll gravitate.
When you finally open the door, I'll vanish without trace.

Luisa Allan

Spring Awakening

Mother Nature awakes to welcome the Spring
With primroses and crocus and birds on the wing
A profusion of blossoms decks the trees
And golden heads of daffodils nod in the breeze
Out on the lake the proud swans glide
With their family of cygnets by their side
The blackbird is busy building her nest
Flying to and fro without any rest
Whilst out in the fields the little lambs play
And nearby the horses stand munching the hay
Deep in the thicket a baby fawn
Arrives to greet the springtime dawn
And in the hedgerows and gardens too
All new life comes in to view
The buds are bursting from winter sleep
And the tiny insects begin to creep
The yellow honeysuckle with its fragrant perfume
And red flowering currant are in full bloom
A chaffinch sings his sweet song to tell
Winter has passed, Spring is here, all is well

Jeanne Kiley

Ode To Peter

Walking on the windy downs
With raindrops in my hair
I thought of days that used to be
And wished that you were there...

Playing with the grandchildren
Their faces bright and fair
I thought how you would have loved them
And wished that you were there...

But in the quiet times at home
When no one else is near
My heart is filled with joyfulness -
I know that you are here!

Eileen M. Etheridge

Bertie

Bertie Bunny was a strange little fellow
with tail so white yet ears bright yellow.
"Ha,ha,ha," laughed Roger Rabbit
"yellow in ears, means yellow in habit".
Bertie Bunny was not amused
he felt so sad and most abused.
"I'm not afraid," he shouted loud,
"I'll show them all," he quietly vowed.
So away he hopped over hills and vale
trying to find grey ears for sale.
He showed magic tricks to earn the money,
all the baby bunnies thought him very funny.
Yet, no grey ears could he find,
although by now he did not mind.
"I'll stay here" he thought, "and live forever."
Because these new friends thought him very clever.

Joan Kirby

The Hunt

Ere my bit
With teeth I grit
As onward trudge my hooves
A hound, a sound, a horn blasts out!
Whipped! kicked! now quickly moves
Froth sweat body towards the rout;
'Tis not my choice to hurry so
But spurs dig deep, a voice yells 'Go!'
Wearied, pained, tired of chase,
I gallop on to keep the pace.
Astride my back and oh such weight
Grips leather booted huntsman's fate.
If I should defy his cruel whip
Throw him off or feign to trip,
He would say
Without delay,
'T'is damn stallion stableless beast
Knockers yard dogs meat to feast!'
So, each moment I think to defy
I think to slaughter and don't quite die.

John A. J. Rook

My Life Of Nature

Where the lochs lie deep and dark
with the song of the sky lark rising high
A woodpecker drums at a pine tree's bark
I catch a trout with my rod and fly

Poppies blowing in the breeze
I'll see hares jumping with glee
A flock of geese fly over with perfect ease
I look at a picture of my dog and me

Clipping the sheep in the heat
Whistling to the collie dogs
Unpacking the lunch for me to eat
Steering the sheep out of the mucky bogs

I go up the hills after stags
Along with a party including me.
Past lots of muddy peat hags
An adult kestrel flies by singing its song kee kee.

I eat up all my porridge oats,
then I ride up the hill on my quad bike
to feed the mountain goats
past the old stone dike.

Calum Gillies

Can This Be God?

Where is the God I seek to find
Within the darkness of my mind,
Is he the goodness that I seek —
The soundless voice that bids me speak
The truth, when oft my lips would stray,
And lie, to save another day.

And when I see a crippled form,
And find myself with pity torn,
And when my heart cries out in pain
At some poor creature cruelly slain!
And when I watch, with silent tear,
The suffering of a loved one dear...

Then, beholding a new day's dawn,
With soul refreshed, and hope new-born,
I watch each splendid morning ray
Proclaim to me another day,
And whisper to my wondering heart:
Of this, he surely must be part!

I remember the cross... and then I know
Oh yes! I know! All this is God!

J. Dinsley

"Finding The Way"

Ignorance is the charge for entering the fray,
Without any wisdom, well, not that first day.
You're taught to take part in the pattern of others,
Help may be around, a sister, no brothers.

Love was aplenty, no thought of a frown,
Everything was warm, life up, never down.
The conflict arrives you listen to others,
The knowledge best sought was always your mothers.

The crossroads a looming which one left or right,
One holds the sunshine, the other dark night.
The choice may seem clear, no problem to crack,
You've chosen the latter to run with the pack.

Your road was well marked "REBEL AT ALL COST",
No thoughts, at this stage, of the things you have lost.
The respect of your peers is nothing you seek,
Well everyone knows, no fun for the weak.

But time has a way of making you see,
That without any chains, you're not always free.
And wisdom will grow despite the wrong move,
To pull from the rut and back in life's groove.

Joe Atherton

Occluded Front

I knew not of him or of his
Worthy intentions. That man, obvious
Anticyclone, moves in circles, clockwise.
A powerful leadership, enough to hypnotise.

In my head hovers a rain cloud,
Black as my mind, a corpse, wrapped in shroud.
My anti-clockwise depression grows
Cold and wild; my temperament shows.

His warm self brings to me warm
Spells; my depression not always a slicing thorn,
But, I pay him nothing in return except
One thundering occluded front.

The winds of frustration blow furious,
In tight circles, around me. I am dubious
Toward anticyclone; he misinterpreted
My anger. All between us becomes defected.

My weathered mind, deteriorating
Over time, causes my winds to be prevailing.
Anticyclone is still here, remaining at
My side, not distracted by my unruly act.

Gillian Downie

Because I Am A Woman

Into the hospital she was rushed,
With pangs of pain here and there,
Pains of joy and happiness flushed,
Like the wind that fills the atmosphere.
"It is a girl", they shouted with joy,
Because I would be a woman.

Now I am a woman no one seems to notice,
Like time that comes and goes by,
No one bothered by what and who I am,
Because I am a woman.

A woman brought into the world to wear and tear,
To endure all the hustles and bustles,
For to be a woman is to bear and to rear,
To cook and to feed,
At home to stay to nurse the family,
Because I am a woman.

Born a woman I was,
Lived a woman I have,
Die a woman I will,
Because I am woman.

Harriet Nannyonga

"Just Another Day"

Legs numb
Without feeling.
Frost sparkles atop my cardboard home.
More misery this day,
perhaps death.
A happy release,
indeed.
God give me strength for another day,
or maybe two.
Crowds hurry across the station yard.
Kindly commuter
Hands me corned beef sandwich.
Glorious sun shines over station roof.
People start to greet me.
Perhaps life is still
worthwhile, after all.

Jack York

Wholesomeness

Forget not the one who means everything
Without which being cannot be
What flower competes to show its display
What thought has shown its ways
What violent thought its nurse
What payment whose purse
Whose limitation in earth's dimension
Amid poor sense and dissension
of words that but explain a wayward affair
And not one as life can dare
To unfold what scholarship has never explained
Nor any age of reason has ever ordained
The subtle dance passing through

The misshapen patterns that would undo
What is first complete and true
The shining being absorbing the darkness of mind
That opposite to reality the mote blind.

John Short

The Prison

Does anyone out there have the same problem as me?
Wondering when I will be set free.
In the same room hour upon hour,
Not looking up because I have no strength or power.
Speaking then scarred for saying one word,
Is this something one should be endured?

The teachers will tell them off once or twice,
But now I get threats to keep quiet like mice.
The pain, the strain, the mind-pounding confusion,
Now I plan to teach those people a lesson.
So as the lesson begins,
I wait for the day that they repay their sins.

Faye Stemp

Down Our Street

I wonder what goes on behind the closed doors in our street
With the pretty coloured curtains, and the gardens very neat
There's a cottage on the corner, where the twins are nearly three
You can hear their mother calling them, to wash their hands for tea
A lady watches from her window, curtains never still.
She only sees the postman, all he brings her is a bill.
A midwife, lives at number nine, she's out at night, and in the day
We hear her little mini start, she knows a baby's on the way.
A family of six moved in just the other day.
The mother takes in washing, it helps to pay the way.
The little man with silvery hair, who has the creaking gate
He'll have a chat with anyone who has the time to wait.
I stand and wonder what goes on
Behind the shuttered blinds.
It's no one's business but their own
I'll go away and mind my own.

Elsie Waring

Life

You brought so much joy into our lives
Without you we are lost
Taken so young, we don't know why
But us dearly, this has cost

God must have wanted you for a star
Because he knows you're special
Now we'll look up to the night sky afar
And watch you as you twinkle

Your favourite game was chase the balloon
In your mouth you'd swing it
Jumping round and round the room
Trying not to burst it

The best friend we could ever have
So faithful loyal and true
We've loved you ever since the day
We first set eyes on you

We never got to say goodbye
To our friend so full of 'Life'
You'll be forever in our hearts
God bless, dear 'Life,' Goodnight...

Kym Hadley

The Seventh One

In Cambridgeshire Behold! St. Ives with delightful pub' The Seven Wives',
Time was when wives were six,
Came the seventh, haughty, full of tricks,
Who sought to charm him, poking fun, knowing his dolly's dance was done,
Thought, 'If loving's your idea of heaven, I'll see they go not beyond seven.'
He was so hale and hearty, enjoyed a sup of beer,
So she laced it well with arsenic, which made him over queer.
Whilst his dear wives loved their pussy cats, He loved their pussies too.
But short lived were his pleasures. His joys became quite few.
His health fell to the seventh bride,
He lost his wealth and manly pride.
Thus the more he drank, his fond heart sank,
His head began to sway, 'Oh, woe is me'
So sad was he, he wasted fast away.
So woo not seven maidens,
Nor love and make them thine.
All things in moderation lads.
Take one wife at a time.

Betty Coupland

The Wolves

It's night-time and the wolves are here, the wolves come out to play,
With sharpened salivating teeth they look down on their prey,
The lambs and pigs go marching in to feel their knight's embrace,
Their ignorance will not detect the devil that they face.
The wolves will fester in disguise no sign of guilt or shame,
Manipulation, exploitation rule this evil game.
A lamb may squeak, a pig may squeal, a suicide, a death,
The truth will never be revealed, just guilt to the bereft.
Mingling amongst us now, their confidence will grow,
But feeble lambs and stupid pigs will never really know.

Laurie Yates

Life, The Quest

Looking for something of which we do not know
Wondering which is the way, the right way to go
Where will we find it, what will it be
A searing force willing thee.

Maturing years build up the fire
A fire of life and a desire
Crackling coals will not cease
Until it's found, the missing piece.

Restless roamings on the quest
Filled with serendipity nonetheless
Adding more fuel to the furnace
Torrid temperatures, with no egress.

Life itself may be the search
Until the day the two converge
When exalting feelings, reflecting stars
And spiritual beings reveal who you are.

Celestial magic uncovering the soul
Eternal existence becoming whole
The journey over, searching was requisite
Embracing fulfilment, becoming complete.

Diane Needham

My Daughter

You are every little miracle that there could possibly be,
   Words cannot describe how much you mean to me.
Your love is warmer than the golden sun,
   You are a thousand smiles rolled up into one.

Your hair is softer than that of a feather,
   Your scent is more beautiful than that of sweet heather.
Your eyes shine so blue like that of a cloudless sky,
   And they twinkle just like the stars so high.

The sound of your laughter touches every heart,
   You are even more beautiful than any work of art.
Your skin is so soft, smooth and delicate to the touch,
   It's difficult to explain emotions when the love is felt so much.

Your tiny little fingers are so eager to explore,
   And at every turning of a new day,
   I love you more and more.

Love always,
Mummy

Gillian Harvey

Untitled

I recall in years gone by, arm in arm my friend and I:
   Would wander off come rain or shine,
   She to her school, I to mine.

In Sunday bonnets, worn with pride, we'd skip to church side by side,
   We each would take a separate door,
   To meet again the service o'er.

The years elapsed, times were hard, but we would share all we had,
   A bowl of soup, some warming tea,
   I to her, she to me.

More years passed by, our families came, still our friendship did remain,
   She had two daughters, I had one,
   Then joy of joy, each had a son.

The bond grew strong from old to young, till hatred spewed from evil
   tongue,
   Wicked men o'er callow youth held sway,
   Some loyalist, some I.R.A.

Now my friend and I today, with heavy hearts pass on our way.
   No longer do our arms entwine,
   As she buries her son and I mine.

Anne Ellis

Despair

Another day, what will it bring,
yes to the streets, my voice will sing,
there's nothing else — the dole queue's long,
busking lets me sing my song.

It used to be a job was there,
life was good, with little care,
but now the hope has almost gone,
and all that's left is mournful song.

Why is this what people face,
why every job do hundreds chase,
does no one care, are they all blind,
why is progress so far behind?

I'm keen to work, and pay my way,
and in this land I want to stay,
but where's my hope, where is my hope,
can I survive, and can I cope?

Perhaps one day, hope will be here,
and all of us will have no fear,
perhaps one day, perhaps one day,
is that the best that one can say?
John G. Davidson

I Have Pleasure To Look On You

I have pleasure to look on you.
You assault my senses,
Storm my emotions,
Weaken the fortress of my principles.
Sensuality and innocence
Rising like tides, within your eyes,
Lifting my heart on magic waves,
carry it off
To the shameless shores of deep desire.
Leaving me aghast
and momentarily without direction.
I wish... and continents contract,
Shrivelling space gives way,
Two souls collide...
New stars are flung towards paradise.

Conniving Cupid aims his dart,
Brings my tears,
And long dead fires spring up again
And move my centre;
I have pleasure to look on you.
Emily Kerkosh

Lost In Love

Sweet love is lost but we are found,
You brought my feet back down to ground
We used to float with moon and stars,
Held hands as we danced on Jupiter and Mars.

Sweet love is lost but we are found,
A raging world with no sound
Too blind to see the final curtain
Peel back the layers to find we're hurting.

Sweet love is lost but we are found,
Two hearts together sealed and bound
No longer dancing with the stars,
But kept apart by invisible bars.

Once lost in love but now I'm found,
The stars came crashing to the ground
Where once we danced without a care,
Lay thousands of pieces in life's own snare.

Sweet love I've lost but now I'm found
The cloud has burst, the stars have drowned
Forever together in heart and mind,
But no longer are our paths entwined.
Loretta Roncone

Friendship

I first met you a decade ago
you came as a stranger to my home
friendly, yet uncertain you approached as I spoke
little did I know how our friendship would grow

Day after day you came
you asked for nothing yet gave everything
Never uncaring, never selfish
your nature always remained the same

How I looked forward to your visits
the love we shared was plain to see
as strangers we had met so long ago
Now inseparable friends forevermore

As I think of you I brush away the tears
alas you call no more
what fate befell you I know not
my feline friend of so many years
Ann O'Neill

Prayer

What a wonderful thing is prayer.
You can do it almost anywhere,
In the house or in the garden,
No need to ask the dear Lord's pardon.
For everywhere you are, your Lord's there too,
Seeing, hearing all you do,
So talk to him, confide in him,
He will keep you free from sin.
Our hearts can be lightened in a wonderful way,
When to him each day we earnestly pray.
Remember, thank our Lord for answered prayer,
In which family and loved ones can always share.
Set aside a time each day
To kneel to your Lord and sincerely pray.
You'll be surprised what your heart can convey
To the Lord, who loves and cares for you every day.
Freda Allan

Caribbean Breeze

You can smell the beauty of the colours in the sea air,
You can hear the laughter of the people as you stare,
You can feel the warmth of the endless summer sun,
Why can't this feeling go on and on?

The people, they have a lot to say,
Why did Bob Marley leave us this way?
Why did we have to fight against slavery?
We have every right now to be free.

Poverty is not an unusual sight,
Neither is the urge to have a fight.
These beautiful people find it hard to rest,
Even on Sunday, when they look their best.

Ganga is legal, the old rasta said,
Sit back now, he flicked his dreads,
Be Irie man, as life is too short,
Don't worry, respect, this world can't be bought.
Annabelle Lilly

Dreams

The joys of spring will shortly be within us,
with flowers adding beauty all around us,
but what of those dark spaces of our minds
where sunshine and beauty cannot be seen from out our eyes.
Those recesses where the trauma of our lives, hides
and only surfaces while we sleep and thrives
in our subconscious, bringing dreams of fear alive.

Engulfed in darkness we scream for help to no avail,
and on awakening find our sweat has been our tears,
falling as the rain yet not drowning our fears,
These nightmares then continue even in our waking hours
and we lay there knowing that this fate is always ours.
For we cannot understand the meaning that surely there must be
behind the sleep that brings such dreams to you and me.
Ann Crone

The Kick

You kick the boundary of your existence,
You flex each limb impatiently,
You push with greater and greater resistance,
Towards a world you cannot see.

You move under such restriction,
Fighting for your space,
So you kick out in all directions,
Against the protective interface.

And at the edge of your environment,
Through the barrier we touch,
And there is joy to sense your movements,
As you continue to kick and punch.

So you kick in my direction,
I can feel you're growing strong,
And we will build on our connection,
As I hold you when you're born!

Alison Bosi

Crossroad Of Life

I gave you love
You gave me a child
I gave you my life
You made me your wife.
I said I would love, cherish and obey
Until that solemn, hurtful day
The love I gave was from the heart
So why are we so far apart?
You believe so strongly in the ring
But that cannot protect you from the sin
That fragments you limb from limb.
But all I know is don't give in
I fought to keep you by my side
So degraded I wanted to hide.
So now I sit and still don't know
Was it right to let you go?
Abandoned, deserted, oh not I
Yet at the start all I could do was cry
But I am strong and have come alive
And yes my dear I shall survive

Jo Jackson

Softest Storms

Hush, little child, the darkness is falling,
you know that night comes with a purpose;
to steal the light that hurts your eyes
and wrap her blanket of comfort all around you.
So look now, across the angel's playground
and set your heart free,
to wander through the softest storms.
Look now, through the veil of sleep
and watch the faces that adore you
lit up, by the light, out in the street.

So lay your head down on the pillow
and dream your dreams.
Follow the whisper that travels with the dusk,
ride on the back of the lightest feather.
So look now, at the ten thousand diamonds
spread out across the nervous sky.
Yes, look now, for no-one can know
when the next tear will fall from God's eye.

J. MacKenzie

Life

Life is like an open book;
You set your own paragraphs,
You make your own stories.
As you turn a page,
You turn a corner in your life.
As you finish a chapter,
You start a new story.
The more stories,
The nearer you come to the meaning of life.

Claire Felix-Davies

" A Tribute To A Soldier "

You were prepared and ready to go when the day of your call up came,
You left us without any show, forgotten your childhood games.
As a soldier you had no choice but to train in the art of war,
To charge with a screaming voice, and act as a course of law.

Home for a period of leave, now training was given its best,
Proudly showing the flash on your sleeve, still just a boy in a soldier's vest.
A solemn affair the goodbyes, with a wave of farewell as you turned,
A trace of tears in our eyes and thoughts for your safe return.

The burden of war is a testing ordeal, fighting an enemy on foreign soil,
Gone is your youth in battles real, as for freedom you constantly toil.
Dawn breaks through the misty air and orders come for another raid,
To rout the enemy from his lair, for this the gift of life you paid.

Your death was a loss to us all, your laughter and smiles we all miss,
A tear will show, we recall, the last goodbye and the kiss.
Far away in a foreign place you lie, asleep and laid to rest.
Memories of you will never die, farewell my brother, you gave your very best.

Derek Tew

Life Begins At The End Of Your Nose

You look to the North, East, South and West
You look no farther than the end of your nose
You scream in despair
and find no-one there.

Didn't anyone tell you
that's the way the story goes?
But deep inside
you feel a tremor, you feel
the beginning of — what
you don't yet know,
and yet it grows!! And then it shows,
find the beginning to the
end of your nose.
And watch your life's
story as it grows!!
And thank God for the
end of your nose.....

Emma Saurino

" Mam "

A mam is a special person, but no other mam is as special as you,
you love me in a way no other could, if I could keep you forever I
honestly would.
You love me when I'm bad, you love me when I'm good, you know
me inside out like no one ever could.
Your love is unconditional, there is no price to pay, wouldn't it be
nice if everyone loved this way.
You know when I'm happy, you know when I'm sad, it's reassuring
to know you're there to take my hand.
You take away the pain and fill me with joy and warmth again, you
take me for whatever I am.
No need to wear a disguise, no need to hide with my mam.
You're loved by many, admired by most, I'm so very proud to have
you as my mam.
I'll love you forever no matter what.
When your time on earth is through please never forget how much
"I Love You."

Jacqui Charlton

Memories Of Better Times

When life begins to get you down
You need to smile but want to frown
When modern man becomes a bore,
Throws values, standards through the door.

Just close your eyes and do a span
To time when manners maketh man.
Where courtesy went hand in hand
with graciousness throughout the land.

An age of war, an age of strife,
Where value was so low on life,
Where each man was the next man's brother,
Respect and love for one another.

And now this world so full of greed,
On opulence the humans feed.
If love is self, then man will fail.
How sad to go beyond the pale.
Jill Neal

One More Time

I'd love to see you one more time
You said goodbye and walked away.
Now time has passed but nothings altered how I feel.
I'd love to see you one more time.
Your face I can't quite picture in my mind.
To ask you how you feel now time has soothed the
hurt I caused you.
Would you want me still?
Has time covered hurt and bitter feelings
Would you smile and take my hand and say you're
glad I came.
I'd love to see you one more time
To say I love you just the same
Brenda Mallett

Thoughts

I have laid here now for near a year just staring at the ceiling,
You see I've lost the power of speech, also my sense of feeling.
The nurses come in every day, they chatter and they laugh,
But do they really see me here when giving me my bath?
My mind is still as active as before I had the crash,
How long must I put up with all their condensing trash?
My lovely wife, she doesn't come, that I can understand,
It would be good though, just once more to have her hold my hand.
Maybe one day I'll learn to live again with dignity.
Dear Lord, you took my life away, please take my memory.
One day, maybe someone will stop as they pass by my bed,
And see the tears that mist my eyes,
You see, I'm not yet dead!
Alison Lee

Earth Tremor

In the darkness something stirred...
Writhing,
Twisting,
In a kaleidoscope of pain,
But not its own pain,
The pain of a dying breed rests upon its brow,
A forest of darkness crashes about it,
The blood of the broken rock spills across it,
The booming thud of a continent's collision,
Deafening,
Voices of the dead,
Too many to distinguish,
They moan and cry,
But not for their lives,
For those to follow,
In the devastation of a past era,
The creature knows all,
Sees all,
Screams.
In the darkness something stirred....
Kevin Outlaw

Feelings

It's like a candle starting to melt
You try to relight it, but no feelings are felt
You dig deep inside to pick up a smile
But it's no good the pain stands out a mile
You look out the window where children are glad
Your aching head thinks why am I sad
Tears trickle down your gentle face
Eye's filled with fear which spoils your grace
Your heart starts sinking, you don't know what to do
When you realize your life in depending on you
Your life is so lonely you attempt to grin
You realize that love comes from within
But it's too late you've cried and it's no good
You try to pull yourself together like you know that you should
When you realize that the candle's a flame
When you think life's turned into a game
That Monopoly board isn't so bad
You go and rejoin the people who are glad
Next time you cry it will come to a halt
You'll say to yourself it was the tears fault
Hayley Wilson

Spring To Opportunity

Take time for yourself to do what you want,
You will find it is very worthwhile.
The odd hour you spend, perhaps with a friend
Can really help broaden your smile.

Open up doors, embrace all ahead,
Soak up what life has to give.
Believe in yourself, aim for the top,
We only have one life to live.
Lesley Rowan

Love Lost

If I'd met you ten years ago
You would have loved me better
Ten years ago you'd have been on your knees
— I wouldn't be writing this letter

  The marks and lines that Time has left
  Deepened by melancholy
  Make us look in the mirror with remorse
  And bear witness to our folly

If I'd met you ten years ago
You'd still have all you've lost
Ten years ago you'd have given your heart
And never counted the cost

  We should have found love, both of us,
  But we haven't found it yet
  Perhaps it's still ahead of us
  With someone we haven't met

If I meet you in ten years' time
I hope we'll be able to smile
In ten years' time we'll be able to say
"I loved you for a while"
Deborah Preece

Blessed

When you can remember
Your mother and dad,
The house that you lived in,
The friends that you had,
Your school, and your teachers,
Your Sunday school days
The war and its traumas!
A lesson for all
Of sacrifice, sharing, and caring, re-called,
Afterwards! Marriage and children, and love
Trying our best to be worthy of all.
Then comes the time we enjoy most of all,
To notice the birds, and the trees, and the flowers,
And play with our Grandchildren, hour after hour,
  It's blessed we are.
Dorothy Peters

The Kids

The kids they drive me mad they do
You'll change his nappy then he'll poo
Give him a bottle and he'll still cry, oh dear God please let me die.

The kids they drive me mad they do
I'm sure to go grey in a year or two
She wants this, he wants that
I'm going crazy, no that's a fact.

The kids they drive me mad they do
Why can't I go to work, like you, no more crying, no more screaming
Oh pull yourself together and stop dreaming.

The kids they drive me mad they do
He's crying again and it's only two, oh my God he's poo'd again
That brings the happy count to 10.

The kids they drive me mad they do
She doesn't understand she's only two
I've finally cracked, he's pulling her hair
I won't tell you again, sit over there.

The kids they drive me mad they do
It doesn't take long to get to you
No-one listens, no-one care, oh this life isn't fair.

Angela Marlow

The Ages Of Man

Life is eternal, a cycle of stages repeating in different souls.
Your brain being wiped clean of memories from your former life,
Of rebirth, cleansing of the soul, a chance to change,
To feel the warmth once more of your mother's breast,
  secure, dependent, innocent,
The first faltering step into the age of the child
First achievements, first rejections, first independence,
  as the years pass, childhood fades
The stress of adolescence replaces the wonder years, experiencing love and lost ideals,
Experimenting with your life, all too soon that's gone,
Responsibility raises its head, mortgage, marriage, motherhood,
Decades of all consuming parenthood,
The house that bustled with noise now lies still, time to reminisce, rejoice, rest,
The days seem longer, the nights shorter, memory relives your childhood,
Yesterday's news a blur, time to make your entrance once more,
infinity a short step ahead, because all the world's a stage,
and all the men and woman merely players, all have exits and entrances,
one man in his time plays many parts.

Katie Leigh Hall

Pussy Cat

How does it feel pussy cat?
Your purr, your purr.
But when my fingers press hard,
And find your jugular,
How does it feel?

Clamped around your neck
They squeeze, they squeeze.
You twist and turn and twitch,
Faced with no life,
How does it feel?

And as you escape with a scared screech of triumph
My finger bleeds, my finger bleeds.
Split open by an angry claw,
Love gone when faced with extension,
How does it feel?

I push and probe and finger.
I blow, I blow
And as I spread my red hot blood across my mouth,
Like lipstick, I ask...
How does it feel pussy cat?

Christopher Smith

Standing Up To Life

A blurry kaleidoscope of mingled colour,
Your eyes see soft, unfixed shadows,
What you see then becomes duller,
Things are scattered randomly, not in the usual rows.

A spark of your vivid imagination plays havoc with your mind,
The darkness of this lonely world,
Seems to push away all thoughts of being kind.

As most people grow older,
Old memories slip away,
The world is no longer colder,
You have caught one of the sun's rays.

The mingled colour stretches,
It brings a clear cut picture out,
Your life sails from all the wretches,
You've stood up to all the doubt!

Catherine Freeman

Miscarriage

Anguish turns against the edge
your face white, smeared mascara,
assaulted tears, no hand outstretched,
bruised and bruised again a hundred times,
your bleeding extinguished then reality
unseen, unborn, unloved by all but you,
washed away unsung.
Biting on tears that spring to view,
as others tell of trivia,
Torment receding, slow the years;
Yet still the searing flame.

David C. Pattison

Fond Memories

Everybody loved you
Your goodness shining through
No harsh word or action
No badness part of you
And oh what laughs, what merriment
My stomach almost burst
As we shared a joke, a look, a smile
What joy; and you its source
That smile, those eyes, lit up my world
That voice it soothed my ears
Encouragement you gave me
You banished all my fears
But now you're gone, a lights gone out
And here's a darker place
Without your love, your kindness
I have an empty space

Ann DeMicheli

Confusion

Your mouth once small like a rosebud pink,
Without any teeth, all you did was drink,
Then after a while, before you know,
You fill it up with your baby toe.
They said growing up was so much fun,
With your mouth there were scores of things to be done,
Like scolding and shouting when you are displeased,
Bending down kissing two sore little knees,
Saying sweet nothings and whispering low,
To the one that you love, your very own beau,
Laughing and joking and eating ice-cream,
Panting and puffing as in a bad dream,
Singing with happiness when good luck abounds,
Sobbing with sadness when your dreams tumble down,
Some people say in fun no doubt, that your lips stop your mouth
From wearing out,
So you can see without a pout,
Total confusion without your mouth.

Jessica Roestenburg

A Blind Man's Message

You have your sight, yet fail to see
Your learning, knowledge could set us free,
If you see with your heart the gift of each day
All greed and corruption will soon pass away.
Open your eyes, what is there to gain
From power, wars, destruction and pain?
Let peace be your strength to banish all sorrows,
With kindness and love for all our tomorrows.

Annette Hayes

Message To Man

I feel as one with the wind and the soil
Your oceans polluted, your harvests par-boiled
I fear not the fires deep under your lands
Nor your darkness or storms or sunlight's elan
I know well your wildlife, the price that they pay
For all that is human, thief, taker, Earth-raper
There is only one danger on this world of blue-green
And its name is humanity, its taint to be seen
In the skies full of smoke and ash from the pyre
The furs and the pelts and the skins you admire
The woodlands destroyed, the species wiped out
To feed and amuse you, to nurture the lout
There's a future that only the humans deserve
But all will reap now, the bees and the birds
The sow and the bull, rare tiger and whale
What's left of the herds, now you doom to fail
Man is a vampire, a leech on the soil
You use and abuse, you break and despoil
The prey is your host and vengeance will come
For in destroying your planet, you murder your sons.

Lyn Harrild

Rest In Peace, My Friend

I believe perhaps you are getting stronger,
Your willpower has impressed one and all,
You will go on for so much longer,
The strength inside your body will not fall.

You are our sister, daughter, mum or our friend,
For all of us you have got a heart of gold,
For the sake of us you shall battle to the end,
Then for you, loving memories we shall hold.

You close your eyes to rest now and forever,
Knowing that this is the last goodbye,
The nurse appears and turns off the monitor,
As she watches you a tear forms in her eye.

You put your powers and your strength to the test,
Until you really knew it was the end,
All is silent in this Chapel of Rest,
I touch your hand and wish you peace, my friend.

Jane L. Howick

The Picture: Neville And Me

Here we are together, close.
You the big burly Granddad
And me the small child.
They tell me I was your favourite.
Now they tell me, not then.
"Now then!" you'd say and chuckle.
A big figure to us little children.
You sometimes intimidated but
You always cared and loved.
I wasn't there when you died.
That cup of coffee, I still feel guilty.
Now I see you in my dreams
As still alive somewhere.
The strange thing is I feel closer to you
Mourning now years later.
All I have is this picture —
Here we are together, close.
    Death is nothing at all... All is well.

Katie Tatterton

I Miss You!

I Miss You!
You're always on my mind
I always sit back and think about
all the good times we've had together,
I'm always surrounded by people,
But not the people I want to be with.
They try to make me happy
But how can I tell them
How lonely I feel without you?
I Miss You!
I miss all those cuddles,
The love and laughter we shared
Will be in my heart always....
I Miss You!
I miss all those short but sweet meetings.
Just yesterday we were together,
And today we're thousands of miles apart!
And now I live with your memories
Yet, I have no words to describe how much
"I Miss You!"

Gemini Vadgama

Not Dead Yet

It isn't very funny when your brain is still in gear but
you're sitting in a wheel chair every day.
When people just ignore you and ask somebody else to tell
them what you'd really like to say.
"Does your friend take sugar?" "How is he today?" Why do
they assume that he is dumb?
It doesn't stop him speaking when his legs no longer go.
And it doesn't mean he isn't really plumb.
So don't be condescending and treat him with respect,
it's a human being sitting in that chair.
He needs the same things you do: conversation, love and care,
not to be treated just as if he weren't there.
Tomorrow could be your turn to lose the power to walk;
would you like to sit and be ignored?
Or go into a corner where no-one knows you're there and be
lonely miserable and bored?
So speak to him for goodness sake,
go on he doesn't bite.
But then again ignore him and then perhaps he might.

Dorothy Illingworth

Did You Go To Heaven Or Hell?

From the moment you're born to the day that you die,
You're told what to think, what to feel, what to do.
They think it's the best advice that they can give,
But they are really trapping and deceiving you.

So many thoughts and images rushing through your mind,
You can't blacken out the pain because you're too tired to fight.
You just want to die, so you can be alone.
Will anyone mourn for your tortured soul?

So you lay still and numb in this fetid world
Amongst the reek of the inhabitant mould
Which spreads like wildfire across the earth.
You're hiding on your impulse, seeking refuge.

As you conceal yourself, stale sweat covers your face.
You hear faint impoverished weeping from a not so distant race.
You look up to see a refulgent light at the end of the wall,
Hope, no, an angry God coming to punish you all.
You start to smile at him but he doesn't seem the same.
It's then that you realize that your smile was in vain.
You can feel shapened red fingers tighten around your neck.
Your life slips away and you're finally dead.

Donna-Maria Friell

The Wind

The wind blows through the trees with ease,
as gently as a dream
and like a lily upon a stream,
it whispers through a valley with much tease.

It touches the clouds with a silvery glee
and lifts the birds so high.
Then with a peaceful sigh
rests with loving calm, upon the sea.

It creeps through quietly the dwellings of man
bringing their fires to rage
and quickly turning any page.
It will even breathe hard into the sails for man.

Yet, when Fate commands, the wind becomes her hand
to ravage and destroy any known land.

J. Wolverson

The Double Decker Bus

The wind whips dust into the air,
As for the bus we watch and wait.
At last a double decker bears
Down on us in its lordly state.

Its slipstream whisks warm air around.
With swish of brakes it comes to stand,
And shields us from the biting wind,
As fares are paid with outstretched hand.

The door slides shut, as moving limbs
Climb metal stairs to padded seats.
Past seated folk and ticket bins,
What views! What perambulating treats!

With lurching roar it ploughs along,
Now fast, now slow in traffic queues.
It sings its own warm, oily song,
Our bus with panoramic views.

M. Mitchell

" The Rise And Fall Of The Fantastic Four "
" The Beatles "

The Beatles were a fantastic four
As a group they don't perform anymore
Fame and fortune came their way
But oh the music they did play
Fans came swirling
Crowds galore
Just to see the fantastic four
Ain't it a shame what fame can do
Even to the Beatles that we once knew
Success ain't always a great old thing
At first it makes you feel like a king
Drugs and drink, women and bed
Next thing you know you're off your head
They mix you up, they get you down
You're wishing your feet were back on the ground
They say stardom and fame is always to blame
Or in this case,
Did they really blame,
Yoko.

Margaret Hanrahan

" Tahilla " A Dunkirk Little Ship

She was built of teak in the year twenty-two
And had classic lines, what a pleasure to view.
She had seen darker times and at Dunkirk was used
To pick up the troops with no time to lose.
And then she was left abandoned to rot,
A sad fate for a ship that had given a lot.
It seemed for a time that nobody cared
Till someone came by and she was repaired.
And now she's restored to her glory of old,
A lady of grace and a joy to behold.

M. Marshall

Imagination

Darkness brings fear, black shadows creep
around buildings, trees and pathways.
Why am I afraid? Sinister
shapes whisper in corners demon-like.
What was behind the oak tree?
Who is lurking in those bushes
waiting to pounce as I walk by?
Just a hedgehog snuffling for food,
yet I perspire with a cold sweat.
A dog barks, lips curled, hair on end.
Something padded across my path.
Stealthful footsteps mimic my own.
I hurry, then stop — so do they!
my pounding heart would fly my breast.
I try to scream; my throat constricts.
At mid-day the bush was in bloom,
the tree trunk, host to small insects,
friendly dogs barked to welcome me.
After dark — why am I afraid?

Margaret Aitken

Childhood

There's a little white bed where a boy kneels to pray
Are you listening, Lord Jesus, I've plenty to say
I went off to school, was my very first day,
Did you cry, Lord Jesus, when your mum walked away.
There were others just like me and girls with long hair
We were given our places, with Ben I've to share
Then we played. Such a very good game. Sorry, I just can't
  remember its name.
We sang a song about "Little Boy Blue" and one called
  "Paddy Wack", do you know that too?
Soon, Lord Jesus, I'll be learning to write; shall I send you a
  letter, will that be alright?
Then our teacher, she's so very nice, read us a story about
  "three little blind mice".
Will you heal them, dear Jesus, is all I can pray and thank you
  for this happy day.
I go again tomorrow, I'll meet up with Ben and I'll tell you
  about it when I come home again.

E. F. Merritt

In The Face Of Conflict

Both sides, fighting for what they believe in, or are they?
Perhaps no one really knows what they're fighting
for any more, and so it's just a senseless squander
of innocent lives.

Children brought up knowing nothing but anger and hate.
Plotting and killing on behalf of a cause, which belongs
to their parents or the generations which have gone before.

Always looking over our shoulders, being watchful of
who we are seen socializing with.
There's no need for uniforms in this war.
Your name, a simple thing can identify in a moment
which side of the fence you're on

When is it going to end, when will we be able to
walk where we want, and talk to whom we please?
Can't anyone see what this is doing to us?
It's a crying game, and the reason it all began
has been lost.

Sinead Hughes

" Layers Of Colour "

Layers of colour is the sky tonight — filling my mind
and eyes with delight — this time of the day making
ready to meet the night — whatever the speed or pace
of this life that can take our thoughts far away — always
remember to stop and look for the time of the day that
makes ready to surrender to the night.

Rowland Patrick Scannell

To My Candied Apple Of Ecstasy

Another stolen moment
Another veiled glance
Another share experience
of a life that cannot be

Just as the sun and moon
cannot share the open sky together
in equal brilliance
So we, less luminary satellites
can only share these transient moments
That quiver with promise
But wilt with the burden
Of consequence and responsibility

Yet asked to return and fight the battle
without hope of salvation
or glory
or recognition
there is only one answer:-

Willingly
Reuben Ayavoo

The Valley Of Broken Promises

The government detach themselves from it all
Another poverty stricken senseless war
The ones that lose have no food to eat
Trying to survive in the dry and dusty heat
Children's eyes covered in flies
One born every minute
As another one dies
Nurses and doctors try to give a helping hand
In this disease-ridden and barren land
Guerillas they call them, soldiers they are not
Fighting for something they haven't got
Food and medical supplies pour in from country to country
To save the lives of the weak and the hungry
But somehow it all seems a little too late
As evil and cruelty arrive to seal their fate
Food is stolen and taken away
It's never ending, and happens each and every day
This is the Africa no one wants to show
The one the African government doesn't want to know
Only God! can help them now
Michael Robinson

Bully's Epitaph

Another day, another dawn
Another page from life's diary torn
Who is this stranger in our yard?
So very worn and battle scarred
He has no meow or shrieking howl
But something tough in his lowly growl

No more a stranger or all alone
As he paced around his adopted home
An old Tom, maybe, or abandoned cruelly
But what's his name? We'll call him Bully

Very content as the family pet
But ways in which he was very set
His previous life from which he was sent
Always made him so independent

He travelled far from North to South
No word of complaint ever from his mouth
Bully was tough and that's no lie
But as with all there is a time to die
Another day, Another dawn
Another page from life's diary torn
Michael Pollard

Life After Love

When your heart seems withered like a winter flower,
and your mind is climbing an infinite tower;
When you struggle to sleep and struggle to wake,
and your soul is asking how much it can take;
When the pain travels with you wherever you go,
and you look twice at strangers — when deep down you know;
When the hurt seems eternal and peace is a dream,
and life has no meaning — or so it would seem;
Just look out the window and into the light,
and imagine the future when life will be bright;
Your heart will start healing and the hurt will fade,
and you'll think of the sunshine instead of the shade;
You'll smile with a meaning and laugh from your soul,
and the past will be memories — the future a goal;
You'll reach the end of that infinite tower,
and your heart will be bright like a summer flower.
Wendy Holloway

The Loch

The flowing loch so smooth
And yet relentless with whoe'er may cross her path
To swallow up her victim
And then ripple with a laugh.
Her beauty is as such
That no man can pass her by
That he does not look in admiration
With a contented sigh.
Cruelty and beauty, how oft has this been known
To fill them with delight
To make them venture
Then go on alone.
So does this lovely loch
Surrounded and protected
By her great mountain friends
She has no fears, but gambols on,
As other people's lives she ends.
B. Puddefoot

" Will Earth And Heaven Really Meet "

Each day we look up at the skies
  And wonder where our heaven lies.
Is it north, east, south, or west
  Maybe our minds know it best.
I believe my soul is in heaven
  But my body remains on earth.
Until I am dead, I will never know
  If I leave this earth, and to heaven I go.
It's hard to realize as a human being
  That we only live on earth.
For we speak of, and see, the heaven;
  Every day from birth,
Why cannot heaven see us
  For it can look down, as we look up
I wonder why we earthly bodies make such a fuss
  We know that heaven is really there.
Yet, each day we look up, and often stare
  Will earth and heaven really meet,
I don't think we will ever know
  until our death is complete.
H. F. Marshall

For Josephine

Did you ever look closely at a flower
And wonder at its perfection,
With dew, lightly formed like teardrops
  So beautiful.

Did you ever look closely at a new-born child
And wonder at its perfection,
With tears, lightly formed like dew
  So beautiful.

Who is it
That says nothing is perfect?
Marguerite J. Darken

Spring

When spring first shakes her mantle green o'er bush and tree,
And winds still fresh and cool raise tides at sea,
Earth stirs anew and each day brings
Pure wonders for the seeing eye to see.
A blade of grass glints with the early dew
Blackbird and thrush sing heavenward two by two
Small creepers climb and twist round trunk of tree
And busy creatures work where none can see.
In sprays the flowers glow jewel-like all around
Giving the earth a natural paradise aground
Light dappled clouds take turns with those of rain
Sprinkling the light on lambs exploring plain
The first fresh butterflies so rare test
Flimsy wings before they take to air

Open your eyes, it's there for all to see,
Enjoy the earth that God gave you and me.
C. Elliott

New Snow

From dark to palest grey
and white
Landscape of shades and sighs
but light.
Delicate tracery trees
Fields under down-like shrouds
of flakes that whirl in clouds
of kaleidoscope crystals that seize
with light
Into clotted folds of a blanket that lies
all white
from here to the edge of day.
H. K. Farrow

No Words Needed

The sparkling sunlight on the water reflects the love in your eyes.
And when your hand reaches out for mine,
It tells me you will always love me, and you'll always be there.
I feel the strength in your embrace, as you hold me ever so tightly.
With one simple smile, you light up my life.
You set my heart aglow, with a look that says you'll never leave me.
With a gentle loving kiss, I know my love for you will never die,
But keep on growing, till my life is through.
I will capture our treasured memories,
Each special moment we share,
And lock them deep within my heart.
For each new dawn brings a new day.
With you beside me, I feel safe.
You make me feel needed, you make me feel alive.
And without a word spoken, I know you will always love me.
With just a touch my world is so complete.
You fill my heart with true happiness.
You make my life worthwhile.
My love, my one and only,
I will love you forever, until the day I die.
Pauline Donoghue

A Winter's Day

The snow it falls on budding trees.
And there it stays, there is no breeze,
A blanket of white covers the ground,
It falls so silent, hear not a sound,
The rooftops high have its patches of snow,
The children laugh, their faces aglow,
The traffic still travels unsure of the road,
Are there icy patches? "be careful the mode",
A picture postcard of winter's day,
Nature is having once more her say,
The ducks on the pond are in their glory,
If it iced over it'd be a different story,
How long will it last? Who can tell?
Enjoy it all, we wish you well.
a Brenda Original

The Birds

I stood beneath the linden tree,
And watched the flying birds go by.
They flew in line towards the sun,
And made me wish I too could fly.

Some days ahead they would be gone
And settling on the warmer shores,
While I was left with snow and ice
With frosted trees and shuttered doors.

The leader dipped and led them on
Through fog and cloud and swirling wind.
Would they be killed by peasant guns
Before the warmer shores they find?

I rose and left my sheltered tree,
And stumbled on my homeward way.
Would I could fly away with them
And reach a world of sun and spray?

I looked towards the empty sky,
I must go home and get the tea
And watch the snowflakes nightly fall
Around the birds' deserted tree.
Mary Oakeley

Forever Be My Valentine

If I could hold the dream in my hand,
and try to make you understand.
For time too quickly passes by,
and like the Flowers, we wither and die.
But life is just so beautiful,
Loving you has made my life so full.
My love is yours till the end of time,
So forever be my valentine.
Words cannot express the way that I feel,
For loving you, is so wonderful and real.
You make me feel so special, with your warm and tender care,
being with you, is a loving and lasting affair.
So stay with me, and let our hearts entwine,
and forever be my valentine.
Love is for everyone, young or old,
two arms to embrace you, when you feel cold.
Life is so precious, don't throw it away,
Live every minute, of each and every day.
So may our love go beyond the end of time,
For you alone will forever be my valentine.
Margaret Smith

Relationships

Relationships are to be based on trust
And to know that each is caring,
to give and take from each other
I guess, it's known as sharing.

I've known you a good few years now
And I hope there'll be many more,
We've shared a lot together
I think we both now know the score.

I know that I really do love you
I guess I've known for quite a while,
My stomach still churns with butterfly's
Every time I see you smile.

We must put each other first sometimes
When things in life go wrong,
Just being there to offer guidance
Can make our love stay strong.

Maybe one day we'll share a home
And we'll build it up together,
but as long as I've still got you
I'd be happy to wait forever.
Teresa Webster

Judge Not

I thank thee, Lord, for all my friends,
And thoughts that they evoked —
Exchanged ideas — adventure too —
And the way they smiled and joked.
We learned each other's secret ways,
And exchanged so freely too,
And handshake — or upon the cheek,
A woman's kiss — in lieu.
Forgiving too, the odd harsh word,
And banter with a sting.
And when one's lot was bettered —
Words with a rancoured ring.
I forgive them Lord — I've known them long —
Man wins perfection never;
So in my mind, all failures locked —
It thus shall be forever.
And now I ask — How shall it be —
Perchance we dream — then die —
What Lord, shall thus become of me,
If my friends just cannot cry?
C. D. Wells

Memories

I stand in awe of all I see
and think of things that used to be
when as a boy I'd often roam
in wood and meadow all alone.

But now the scene is changing fast
no longer can I see the past
no lush green hedgerows in the lane
but open fields all filled with grain.

No horse and cart to rumble by
but cars and planes that fill the sky
the wild flowers in the meadow gone
oh how I miss the lark's sweet song.

Alas the years go fleeting by
but in my mind I can but try
to see it all just once again
the smell of spring, the falling rain.

The sun dips slowly out of sight
and creeping shadows fill the night
from all my memories I must part
but hold them ever in my heart.
D. V. Brooks

Rest In Peace

Why do people live their lives
and then leave us as they sadly die.

Why do people go up above
and leave the ones they dearly love!

Words cannot explain
The hate, the anger,
the numbness of the pain.

They may have reached
The Golden Gate
and travelled along the path
where they live without fear or hate.

If you keep them in your mind,
and remember everything
from the start
then they shall always remain
deep in your heart!

We shall never know what it's like up there
until our time has come,
So we shall not say good-bye
But instead, until we meet again!
Tarra Western

My Week Ahead

ON MONDAY: I might do math,
  and then come home to a bubble bath.
ON TUESDAY: I'll watch T.V. at school,
  and then go for a dip in the swimming pool.
ON WEDNESDAY: I might get a Valentine card,
  to work out who sent it might be a bit hard.
ON THURSDAY: I might do games,
  I might have some cousins 'round there a bag of pains.

ON FRIDAY: I'll do my tables,
  and after that I'll go to Granny Mable's.
ON SATURDAY: I might lie in,
  Oh! and watch the lottery and hope I win.
ON SUNDAY: I'll have a bit of a rest,
  and at my dance class I'll do my best.
Sarah Cronin

Judas Iscariot

The sky above me darkens
and the wind begins to moan.
I run through the street of Jerusalem
not knowing where is my father's home.
Is there not a person to grasp and hold
and stay my desperate speed?
Barrabas my friend, where are you?
it's your assurances that I need.
The streets are deserted and I am a desolate man
death is the only course left for the instigator of this
the most despicable of plans.

Will the Master forgive me when He sees the light?
Will my God judge me and set my soul to right?
You shake your head
and muttering have many words to say?
I tell you beloved reader
that it is in your daily life
the Son of Man you betray.
Rhona Muriel Renz

The Ghost Of A Young Drowned Girl

Tapping of rain shook the washed town,
And in her drenched attire
Came pattering down
Fallen from foggy moon breeze
Ghost-visible by her star-lit gown.

Now spirit she
Higher than the spire-spear
Of the chapel,
Which holds her dear.
M. Q. Pressman

Learn

We learn to love from a very young age
And we also learn to care
We learn what it means to control our rage
And we also learn to share
Very few people can express how they feel
And to me that's very sad
Some people think it's not a big deal
But showing your feelings can be very hard
If we all could think of others
Instead of ourselves for a change
Helping our sisters and brothers
To me it's not that strange
If everyone learned to think the same
We would not judge and pass the blame
For we are Gods children each and everyone
And I know we can learn to have some fun
So make this world a better place to be
And remember keep on learning that's the key.
Sharon Scott

Empty Nights

The nights are hollow now,
And the sound of my breath resounds into spaces
where you once stood.
The echoes shattering my eardrums!
Restless sleep presents me with cruel dreams,
Dreams of a time when you whispered gently to me.
Promising a lifetime of happiness.

The nights are lonely now,
And the quilt, magnified in its size, suffocates the life
from my body,
Stealing away my breath!
Fitful sleep brings harsh memories,
Memories of a time when you lay beside me
Keeping me safe in your embrace.

The nights are endless now,
And the spears of light plunge through the blind
to pierce my body like a knife.
Sharp, revengeful pain!
Feverish sleep carries upsetting thoughts,
Thoughts of a time when my pain was your pain,
My life was yours.

Please... come back to me.
Rescue me from the night.

Sue King

Above The Skies

Above the skies a starlight twinkles in my eyes
And the rhythm of my heart changes to many lies,
For the wind only blows where true love is found
And above the skies is that one promising sound,
For I look into your eyes and it's magic that I see
'Cause without you and me, nature would move blindly.

I look across the seas towards the distant rain
Then above the skies to a lonely star again,
And I remember you and me, no matter what I do
'Cause you're like the wind as our love passes through,
But more than that, you're special in your own way
For above the skies lies a glimpse of another day.

Above the skies my heart is buried in the earth
And I'm reaching out to you for what it's worth,
'Cause constantly I'm alone and that's all I know
Yet above the skies these feelings are hard to show,
Maybe you're a miracle that you let hide
Or maybe it's your pride that you've hidden inside.

Susan Thompson

The Dying Man

The clock has just struck midnight,
And the lonely passer-by
Stood and heard an eerie sound
And gave a long drawn sigh.

His chest is weak and racked with pain,
And as he cries and sighs.
He knows his time soon must come,
Then must bide.

One step and then another
This lonely fellow tried,
But he could only stagger on,
This man who cried.

Let us follow this poor fellow
Who walks so far and wide,
The one who listens for the chimes
The one who sighed.

He sat down upon a step
He knew that he had lied.
He prayed to God "Forgive Me Now"
And then lay down and died.

M. Martin

The Night

Whoosh goes the wind, howl goes the wolf
and the leaves bustle, but wait, I cannot
hear the sound of the ripples from the lake.
What has gone wrong? It is the bump in the
night that gives us the fright. Might be something
spooky that makes us all woolly. But all of
a sudden the sun comes up. Bye bye night
hello morning. But what has happened to the
lake? Nobody knows up to this day.

Marrisa Joseph

The End Of The Season

When the final drive has been driven,
And the last high bird been dropped,
When the last brave fox has been viewed away
And the last big earth been stopped;
Then, in the dusk of the evening,
As the lengthening shadows fall,
We think of each thrilling moment
At water and bank and wall;
And we see again that gallant cock
Swing over the whole long line
To be stopped by the last gun's "second" —
"Gad! that was a shot of mine!"
Now and again, in the nighttime,
We wake, with our hand gripped fast
On the ghostly rein — as we gripped it
On that run that must be the last;
Then there were many to see us,
But only the cold moon beams
Are watching those wonderful gallops —
As we live them again — in our dreams.

R. A. A. Dawes

Dreaming Dreams

What if I dreamt I was dreaming
And the dream of the dream that I dreamt
Was the dream that I dreamt I was dreaming
And a dream I already had dreamt

Could it mean that it meant
That the dream that I dreamt
Would mean that the dream would have meaning
Or would it just seem, that the meaning of dream
Was the fact of the dream
And the dream that I dreamt I was dreaming

For if this is so, and the answer is no
Then the dream that I dreamt I was dreaming
Was no more than a dream, seeming so to be seen
As a dream that I dreamt had a meaning
If the answer is yes, and it's only a guess
That the dreaming of dreams has no meaning
It can then only seem, that this poem of a dream
Was a meaningless dream, dreamt of dreaming

Marcus J. Jones

Free Runner

At ease now Wild Thing, the hunter is gone,
And taken the fear to the valley beyond.
Spared once again to run in the free,
The firestick of man is not yet for thee.

By stealth and by cunning escape came your way,
From two legged danger seeking to slay.
At ease now the muscle, the nerve and the eye,
Soon comes the night cloak to darken the sky.

At ease now Wild Thing alone in your lair,
The fur coat they covet is still yours to wear.
At ease now Wild Thing and hide 'til the day,
When enlightenment comes to the seekers who slay.

C. N. Newman

Where Is The Love?

We humans claim our heart is filled with love
And swear this love comes from above
We say our love is bigger than mountains
And pours out like waters from fountains
Then I die to ask
Perhaps to remove our pretentious mask

Where was this love when the slave trade started?
When Africans and their lands were parted
Where was this love, when the first and second world war began?
When everybody left their families and ran
And where is this love when racism still exist
with a very strong foundation in our midst?
Where is this love?
   Silver Talabi

A Sonnet

When darkness falls upon this troubled world,
And stillness grows,
I walk alone through quiet lanes and fields
Where no one goes.
And by myself in peace beyond compare
I stand and gaze
At silver stars so still and quiet
In their heavenly maze.
The tall dark trees standing as sentinels
Against the sky
Whisper a rustling secret message
As I pass by.
And as I stand my troubles melt away,
Leaving me free to meet another day.
   Margaret Waddington

Bread And Dripping

I promised to love you
And stay by your side
Because knowing I am with you
Fills me with pride
We will work hard together and build our home
We will always be there for each other
And never be alone
We will bring up our children and do our best
For when they are grown it is our time to rest
We will look back at things we used to do
Times were hard but we pulled through
We were happy and contented in our own little way
But we worked at things from day to day
A little bit of money it never went far
An occasional luxury was a chocolate bar
You kept the place clean and the children warm and fed
Sometimes you gave them dripping on bread
We sit by the fire with stories to tell
Fifty years on haven't we done well
   Marie Wilkinson

Peace

Peace comes at eventide. When all children are in bed at rest.
and the suns bright says fade, as it goes to sleep in the west.
Peace is a walk by the river, as it flows silently on towards the sea
The quiet now the last bird song is over, whilst they roost
'neath the leaves of a tree
Peace comes in the country, away from the bustle of town
where one is content to laze on a hillside.
Wearing a butter cup crown
Peace comes at the end of a battle.
When all weapons are laid on the ground.
And the air is disturbed by a whispering.
The echo of those no longer around.
So! Lets keep the peace of the country..
and the river that flows silently on.
Then our children can awake in the mornings.
To a world where hate and bitterness are gone.
   C. Worthington

Dream Of Argyll

The rugged mountains tower above the glen
And snowy wreaths bedeck each peak and ben in gaunt perfection
Echoes across the moor the curlew's lonely trill
As sunshine shimmers on the loch to spell a true reflection.

A single hiker breasts a ridge and stops
To gaze on heather clad in bright dewdrops in subtle shades
His eyes uplift to broad horizons island strewn
With granite rocks from ancient cliffs rough hewn in past decades.

Such splendid isolation in dreams I oft behold
A little croft among the braes to me worth more than gold or
   jewel bright
A fishing boat toward a stone built jetty gently sways
Her sails highlighted by the setting sun's last rays,
   a welcome sight.

The shadows lengthen, twilight now invades the sky
Peat smoke from the cottage chimney drifts on high in
   deepening haze
Contented cattle seek the sheltered lea replete
Here I too could find my happiness complete and end my days.
   Nan Park

Circle Of Life

The seasons come, the season's go.
And the circle of life goes on.
Birth and Death like a
contentious wheel, forever going around.
We live we die without knowing why
Our existence a complete mystery.
Until such a time when we all cross the line
from illusion to reality
   Patricia Whitehowe

Spring

The joy of Spring is everywhere,
And those of us who would dare
to step among the daffodils,
would find joy beyond compare.

The thrush alive with morning song,
The field fair in flocks around us throng.
The blue-tit nesting places find.
Even church bells herald ding dang dong.

The trees with buds are bursting.
The ash so black is thirsting
with the oak for warmer days.
The willow waves a welcome lasting.

The season of Spring, it is for youth.
New beginnings, fresh life within the earth.
Thank God for the return of Spring.
May all people realize its full worth.
   Sheila A. Brown

The Clock On The Wall

The clock on the wall ticks the hours away
And soon tomorrow will be today.
When our Life's work is done.
And Time's clock stops for everyone.
Forever and ever will be our today.
With no tomorrow or yesterday,
No clock to tick the hours away.

Eternity needs no clock on the wall
To tell the hours by day or when night falls.
Is forever a world of dazzling light
With rainbow colours shining bright,
Of Seraphim with gossamer wings,
Or none of these things?
We will never know.

'Til the clock on the wall
Stops for us all.
   Shirley Nel

Last Of The Sailormen

We've wallowed in the Wallet in a welter of spray and foam,
And slipped from misty Mistley, the East Anglian coast to roam.
Raw winters spent their rage on us as we carried heavy loads
Past Felixstowe and Orfordness bound for Yarmouth Roads.

We've run rampant round to Ramsgate, headed north through Hemsby Hole,
Past Spurn Point and the Dudgeons to fill up with Keadby coal.
Romped through Swin and Gunfleet, the Knock and Barrow Deep,
And brought up safe in London Pool whilst shore-folk were asleep.

We've shipped hay and straw from Suffolk to be pulped at Ridham Dock,
Been stranded up in Mersea strood with a load of Kentish rock.
On balmy summer evenings at anchor we would ride
Or ghost along in zephyr airs on a slowly flooding tide.

In lonely, quiet estuaries, in creeks, by wick and hard,
You would see our vanished topmasts and our staunch hulls, freshly tarred.
Or spy a pair of Sailormen surging through the sea,
Sailing hard, lee rails awash and canvas billowing free.

For many years we sailed the coast, a small and dwindling fleet,
In freezing cold north-easterlies, through rain, hail, snow and sleet.
The work was hard, the tricks were long, we battled winds and waves,
Until motor craft destroyed our trade and sent us to our graves.

Mike J. Thurbon

New York

People talk about Paris and London
and rave about Rome and Capri
the Magic of Norway in Winter
and Holland with its Zuider Zee.

Now travellers of all sorts will bore you
with tales of the Kremlin and Steppes
and Hong Kong is really quite passé
Whilst Prague one so easily forgets

But for me the most happy adventure
(a Columbus you don't need to be)
is a view of New York, from East River
Manhattan, the Battery, I see.

Times Square and Saint Patrick's and Wall Street
some history abounds for us all
remember it is an Old City
despite modern structures so tall.

Atlanta may have the Olympics
New England its glorious Fall
but New York is something real special,
As the Yankee would say, "it beats all".

Michael Kendall

Devonshire

Devonshire is the place I love,
And proudly call my home,
The place I return to, each and every time I roam.
I feel my roots are planted,
In its soil rich and red. I enjoy its patchwork landscape,
Like a tapestry is spread.

I wonder at its geology,
Its famous history too.
The forest and the woodland
Trees sparkling, with morning dew.
The hills in all their glory,
Not a thing, I'd rearrange.
I speak the Devonshire dialect,
To some it's rather strange.

But it's when I hear the ripple,
Of the little Devonshire stream.
I know I really am at home, I know it's not a dream.
It is only when I find this peace,
In the tranquillity of Devon.
It's then I know for sure, 'tis the nearest place to heaven.

M. I. Mountain

Clouds

Mountains and hills of another land
And oceans of turquoise blue.
I see these things when I look at clouds.
And wonder if you see them too.

A dragon's fiery breath hangs there,
Then disappears from view.
I spy a castle among the clouds,
And wonder if you see it too.

A magic realm, a distant world,
In a glow of golden hues.
I watch drama unfold within the clouds.
And wonder if you see it too.

C. A. Shapcott

Fond Memories And Anticipation Of Home

Where the hard rain falls, driven by the cold March wind,
and naked trees with branches outstretched
in anticipation of Spring.
Where a mad hare runs, and a plough share turns,
That's where I want to be.

Where spring lambs run to their mothers' side,
and the snowdrops give way to the crocus who
nod their heads as you pass,
where the cat kins sway in the hedgerows
That's where I want to be.

Where the chimney pots are a welcome sight
as the swirling smoke wisps lightly in the air
A young girl skips to her daddy's side,
A kiss from my wife and lover —
That's where I soon shall be.

Peter John Dalley

Fighting Spirit

I fought in that battle I thought I could win, with clenching fist and my heart of sin,
For I was a fighter of greatness I thought, till that fateful day, I found out I was not.

He hit me so hard I thought I would die, the blood came out of my bloody eye
I was in pain but I could not show it, for I was a fighter and I aimed him to know it.

I picked myself up from that floor I was downed, with my heart still beating
In that rhythmical sound, again and again he kept coming at me with such forceful power that proved the end to be.

Get up! Get up! I heard him cry, but my eyes did cease to be alive,
I tried to feel this body of mine so I could fight this one last time.
But it was gone and beyond my reach, my fighting spirit that he did breach.

I tried and tried to stay alive, to fight this last fight for my dream to survive.
For I was a fighter of greatness I thought, but to my dismay, I found out I was not.

I lay on my back with my dreams all gone, with lights shining on me fromabove and
beyond, I could feel no pain, no sorrow or grief, all that I cherished laid down and beneath.

This misty light that did shine on me from those misty depths of sincerity, was I dead or was I asleep? Were these dreams, nightmares, or has my life did so leap? From the hell of the canvas from the starch of the sheets, did I understand that this was for keeps. I am not dead, for I am a fighter who will never give in, for I am that fighter with the heart of sin, I will always, always win.

He fought with a vengeance his life was complete, for he was a fighter now heaven's to keep.

Stephen Maxwell

Two Pomes

My trusting nature often leads me into danger.
And, my blind folded wit prevents my heart from
warning. Now, the time has come for my old weary
heart to stop tearing apart and start loving once more.
So, my tender, weary heart, from you I'll never part.

My lead-weight heart lies in a house where night never
ends. It lies there awaiting for the love it once knew,
in a time long ago, when the smallest star in the sky
seemed bright in the darkest of nights.
It lies here trapped, for the need of know-how to rekindle its
fire starting its drum-like beat.
That's when night becomes day, once more.
Nora Galvin

Sky Contemplation

The colours of my pigments — rainbow hues
And mixed to perfect shade with morning dews
I'd use my mind for palette — thoughts for brush
In silence paint for Thee Thy twilight hush

Too sacred far that I commit to sound
Except such sound that is not mortal bound
That hush is sleep for some — but dawn for me
For in that silence is where I find Thee
Margaret Evans

The Lost Pipers

When darkness falls on castle walls
And mist cloaks deep the glen
There comes the sound of mournful calls
But I cannot tell from when
For many years have flown away
Brave battles lost and won
I heard the sounds from hill to brae
Lost pipers, piping on.
And some maintain at fullest moon
When thick mist clothes the land
There comes the sound of fearful doom
From the hill in where the pipers stand
Their kilts sway with the tune they play
As the mist swirls round and round
They all vanish at the light of day
And cease from mournful sound
But what sad fate, was that so strong
To draw them from deaths sleep
And bid them play the whole night long
And that sombre vigil keep.
Pamela D. Harris

To The One I Love

I love you more than words can say
And miss you so each passing day.
It's been six months since we've been together
But I know one day it will be forever.

I keep your photo beside my bed
And kiss your face before I rest my head.
I say good morning and good night to you
Hoping that you say it too.

I want one day to be your wife.
Knowing we'd be happy all our life.
Never again do I want us to part
It's like having a knife stuck in my heart.

I've never loved anyone like I love you
I'll always mean it, my love is true.
I promise I won't cause you sorrow
And always look forward to tomorrow.

I couldn't live' my life without you
And hope you feel the same way too.
I love you so much as you can see
So please come quickly back to me.
Mary E. Carr

Supra-National Man

Stand back from yourself, oh man,
And meditate; I know you can.
You are dust and ash, yes, and more,
Much more than dust upon the floor.
You've flesh and blood, and bone and hair,
Indeed, that with ass you share.
More sense has horse, the horse that runs,
Than senseless man who kills with guns.
More grace has beast and more aplomb
Than ruthless man who plants a bomb.
The beast is beast; let man be man
And not the one who also ran.
Alas! "Blot - hate" upon our race!
Why not try love and live in grace!
For only grace can change the brute
In brutish man, to live the truth,
Man, you can think and think you must;
There's more to you than mobile-dust.
You are the flower of creation!
Much more than someone of some nation.
Martin O'Quigley

Camelot To-day

In Camelot they grab a lot,
And leave me fairly raving.
I say why not and chance a shot
With cash I should be saving.

I promise you, should dreams come true
And a winner I should be,
My gold I'd share just everywhere,
Not keep it all for me.

It's quite obscene when winners mean
Just celebrate unthinking
Of poor unseen without a bean
And homeless cold and stinking.

Just speedy cars and private bars
And vacations yet undreamt,
Or mansions fine with food and wine
Until the fortune's spent.

Please spare a thought for those with naught
And help the poor and needy.
The cash you win is not a sin
Unless you're mean and greedy.
Tom Smyth

The Phone Call

The phone rang, Friday night,
And mortality entered
Suddenly, life became
A fragile wing of a butterfly,
Suspended the whole world,
Hanging, on one heartbeat.
My parents, my bastion
And my bulwark, ill the fear
Touches like the wing of a bird
And I wonder did I ever say I love you?
The world you gave and
The knowledge you taught me,
Was the embryo, the seed that gave me
The vision and the balance to be me;

All I give and do now, comes from you,
Please stay, for though
Flesh may be mortal,
My love is with you for all time,
And may you be with me for a lot more time.
Selma Abasy

The Blackbird

A male blackbird flew on to our lawn,
And landed where the grass was worn,
He stamped his feet on the ground,
Then stood and listened to every sound,
Suddenly he started forward and pulled out a worm,
Who around his beak did squirm and squirm,
He then flew off into a hedge,
And used a branch just for a ledge,
As he landed you could hear his young,
The song of spring is being sung,
He reached right up and did his best,
As he placed the worm into the nest,
From within came squeaks of delight,
To prove that nature was having its right,
This bird then flew off with his hen,
And commenced this ritual all over again.

W. J. B. Jones

Until

I hear familiar footsteps outside our cottage door
And know that you will soon come in, the one whom I adore
I see your sweet and smiling face, you take me in your arms
I feel so safe and well loved then, I know I'm free from harm
You whisper softly, I love you, a moment then you've gone.
A dream, a silent memory, a love which always stays
A warmth which dwells within my heart, since parting of our ways
I know we'll meet again one day, in heaven's eternal clime
And then we'll laugh and love anew, until the end of time

Patricia Woodcock

I Wonder

Oh for the days when the world was young
and innocence walked abroad,
when children could play by a running stream
free from the fear of the sword.
When the only thing that fell from the skies
was the gentle rain from God,
to wash the flowers and blush the rose
and quietly nurture the sod.
When the only noise was the crash of a storm
and the flash of the lightning bright,
when a man could walk beneath the stars
without any fear of the night.
When men could sail the oceans, to find the far off land,
and not end up on a beach somewhere, wasted on the sand.
If only we could turn the clock of time to start again,
would we have learned our lesson from remembrance of the pain?
Or would there always be one bad apple in the end,
to spoil again this lovely world?
I wonder this, my friend.

Marion Elkington

Strings

Let the music of another man's soul sweep over me,
And in it for a moment, let me lose my own,
And yet having lost it, rediscover
The most intimate feelings which are so seldom stirred.

Let chords and dischords wrung from another's
Happy or tortured mind, find answering chords
So long lain undisturbed.
Play soft music that I may see, rather than hear
Pictures of summer days... distant hills purple in fading light.
Let me feel all nature surrounding me
As the music flows on like a rippling stream

And then... bring me from my reverie with strong and vibrant chords
Shatter all my illusions with dischords that will make me
Want to beg for silence... and yet delight in the agony
They send through my whole being

I only become truly alive
Whilst listening to the strains of heart moving music
So for a while let me live... live life fully...
With deep feeling and perception... that composers from the past
Have left a heritage for me.

I. Spencer

Prophesy

I had a dream?
And in this dream I did see
A lonely world that was alien to me.
I saw a barren, windswept land,
with not a trace of vegetation.
And gone from it was the once proud human nation.
The sometimes placid,
sometimes violent oceans that I knew,
Gone from them all, the large and the small, their inhabitants too.
I cried aloud at mankind's stupidity,
To be members of this world, but too arrogant to see.
They were put upon this earth for great things to achieve,
Not to decimate, and not one trace to leave,
Of civilization, nature, even the lowliest creature that did strive,
To struggle to exist, is now no more alive.
To own the stars, and encompass the universe without restriction.
When all that they achieved was Mother Earth's extinction.

T. Penman

Land O' The Leal (Realm Of The Faithful)

If you have perception of others in your heart,
   And in giving of yourself, expect no praise or reward.
     You are ploughing a furrow through immortal earth.
Know then, you are sowing seeds for The Almighty Lord.

If your soul, mind and ears are listening,
   To every tiny whimpering sound of pain or fear.
     Should one tear of yours fall in sympathy.
Know then you have irrigated fields of compassion here.

If your heart and eyes see men, beasts and birds,
   Lost and floundering on forgotten untilled land.
     Should you stop and open wide your arms, just once!
Know then, you have reaped lost hope by your hand.

If the basis of your prayers to The Father is of love,
   The unification of all people to exercise good will.
     Know then, from where you issued and you will return
To the fertile soil of the Land o' the Leal.

Rhys Reese

Abstract Matters

'Where does he fit all his organs?' they asked
And I thought, 'but he can get away with anything',
He can swing his legs to an angle in mid air.
Look at him, so lithe and slim
His shoulders arched forward, his hair a whim,
Hands dug deep in pockets, but grace is his

Danger brushed past him and lifted his cap on the way
And received a wink in return.
He whistles at success and it runs to him,
Tongue dangling, tail wagging
Even his bragging is an accident of fate.

My admiration makes me blush.

'But no, let us speak seriously of him'.
I said, 'He is a tennis-playing, football-kicking,
Dancing-actor, biking-boy.'
'A bungy-jumping, guitar-playing, piano-thumping Rush.'
'Oh,' they said, glancing knowingly at each other, eyes twinkling.
'But can he discuss abstract matters?'

Vicky Akhras

From Time Beyond All Memory

I was naked
and naked I died in the bonfire
where the thorned birds fly to the south
lovers and mad
the reason of the chaos
the bells of the universe
the oniric voyage of
caressing your beloved body.

Rogerio Saviniano Telo

My Son

I held your hand when you were small
and I held it tight lest you should fall
I tried to make you proud and strong
and teach you the difference between right and wrong
your first days at school I walked by your side
and went home alone, and was alone when I cried
for you were out facing the world on your own
and oh how I longed for the time you were home
But a mum has to stand back, she has to let go
How else will her Sons be able to grow
to stand on their own feet with heads held high
With strength in their hearts and pride in their eyes.
So if I made mistakes, and all mothers can
I did all I did to make you a man,
and now you're all grown up and my job is done
I look at you and I'm proud you're my son.
A. L. Butler

The Weather

The snow has been so very cold
and I am not so very old
I'll be glad when the sunshine comes
then I'll be able to play with my garden gnomes
It's nice to know that Spring is coming
That all the flowers in the garden are blooming
I love the warm and sunny weather
So that my friends and I can play together
In the spring the daffodils will nod
and that's the time that I'll thank GOD
I hope the summer is not to dry
That water shortages make me cry
When summer comes I'll have a tan
and thank the Lord I have a fan.
Samantha Ward

To A Muse

Poets assert the length and breadth
And height of their emotion,
And lovers the intensity
And depth of their devotion;
So forgive me if I dare to mention
That I have found a new dimension:
The radiance from a loving-kindness
That strikes an old man's eyes with blindness.
Of course, young men have prior claim,
But have very few criteria,
And my regard's detached and cool,
Devoid of their hysteria.
Just what attracts the eye of youth?
The figure's slender grace,
The chin, the eyes, the lovely mouth,
And yet, that's just a face;
If they could look behind, they'd find,
And treasure till their dying day,
A beauty in the heart and mind
To take their breath away.
Maurice Ebbage

Pilgrimage

You are born to life's journey with nothing
And gain what you can on the way.
It matters little how much you spend travelling
With your life at the end you will pay.

So enjoy whatever is opporune
To work and play hard is a must
Even if you amass a great fortune
At the end you're a handful of dust.

Take heed my friends and pray really well
We each have a soul to be saved
Be it heaven or hell, nobody can tell
It could be down to the way you behaved.
Ron Long

Sandra

She loves to walk in meadows green
   And hear the birds in summer song.
She likes to sit and sketch, unseen,
   Unmindful of the city throng.

Where Sandra goes I'd also go,
And this is why I love her so.

Whilst wandering through a blue-bell wood,
   Her 'artist's' eye absorbs the splendour,
Appreciating how she could,
   In paint, this woodland vision render.

Where Sandra goes I'd also go,
And this is why I love her so.

And, should I see, in leafy glade,
   Her — more fair than any flower.
Whose beauty shines in nature's shade;
   I'd feel compelled, within my power,
To paint her graceful features, rare,
   As she rests and sketches there.

What Sandra does I do also,
And this is why I love her so.
Arthur Gilbert

The Hillside

I stood upon the hillside
and gazed across the fields,
I caught a glimpse of flowers
That bloomed amongst the trees.

The corn fields were so golden,
With poppies everywhere,
Even birds were twittering
As they were flying through the air.

I could hear the sound of buzzing bees
Even trickling in the streams,
Lambs that strayed across the fields,
Everything just seemed to beam.

As I turned to walk away,
I felt a gentle breeze.
I couldn't forget the beauty
Of everything I had seen.
Mauis E. Bulmer

Never Alone

I still see your face
And all the warmth you had to share
I live your life within me
To show you I still care

You whispered to me softly
I saw the tears well in your eyes
As the pain crept slowly through your veins
I prayed that you wouldn't cry

Eternal rest forever
Was only a heartbeat away
But you resisted the urge to take it
If only to stay for one more day

I heard your every whisper
And felt your pain in every sigh
Your kisses will stay with me forever
Although we never said goodbye

Even though I don't take it so hard now
And I try not to get sad
I am always thinking of you
Because I love you, Dad.
Sue Plant

Smile

Measure not, my age in years.
And for my passing, cry no tears.

For death itself, holds no pain.
Except for those, who do remain.

So let no tears, mist your eyes.
Nor depression, moans or sighs.

For how many men, as lucky as me.
Having had good friends, and family.

And if my life, I could re-arrange.
There's none of it, that I would change.

Although all I leave, as legacy.
Are the memories, you have of me.

So smile for good memories, they are worth.
More than all other treasures, man stored up of Earth.
J. E. M. Dodds

'Idiomanic' Advice

If your complicated life's an uphill struggle to endure,
And folk see you're going downhill at a fast rate,
Bear in mind we all encounter ups and downs throughout our days,
But we end up on a level at the last... late.

Should your present circumstances make you feel you're cracking up,
On the verge of being broken down and battered,
You must first pick up the pieces and repair to some resort
For a break before you're absolutely shattered.

When a freezing look from friend or foe is aimed at you direct,
First reaction is to boil with indignation,
But you must not let off steam; just simmer down and keep your cool.
A warm handshake should replace retaliation.

If you reckon it is high time that you had a high old time,
For you're feeling very low and close to real tears,
Seek a downtown dive and order double highball (soda-free).
Lift your glass on high and find your spirits raised. Cheers!
Wilfred Bruce Smith

The Gift Of Friendship

What is friendship? We all know in troubled times we need to go
And find some solace, shed a tear, grateful that someone lends an ear

A smile of welcome, clasp of hand, knowing that they understand,
No cold indifference, not ignored, with friendship's warmth, we're reassured

In happy times to share the wealth — untroubled mind, of perfect health
The joy of giving, seeing pleasure, on faces — happiness to treasure

Some friendships formed by word or deed, no colour bar, no class or creed. Teachings by a loving mother, sharing, caring for each other.

We all can share, throughout the land, with happy heart reach out your hand. Give grateful thanks to him above, for lasting friendship and his love.
E. A. Holmes

Yeats' Tower

The winds howled like a vengeance
across the stone-wretched land
whistling around the stone tower
scouring voices that seemed to shriek
'What then? What then?'
and Yeats flung down his pen

as he fitfully slept
velvet wings ushered in the dawn
mirroring over opaque pools
where the thunder clouds had wept
silver stepping-stones.
Patrick Sexton

We All

We all are sometimes down in health
and feel that earthly grind,
but soul will rest and charge with wealth
to give that newborn mind!

We all are sometimes out of depth
and don't know where to go,
but God is just and sends the rest
to give that newborn glow!

We all believe we are alone
but life renews that lease,
for man will find he's not forlorn
and finds that newborn peace!
Theo E. Kientsch

Memories Of Summer

I lie in the hammock 'neath blossoming trees
And feel myself rocked by a cool, gentle breeze.
The warm summer sunshine makes me want to doze.
Small insects fly round me and tickle my nose.
The buzz of the bees and the drone of a 'plane
Bring memories of childhood to me once again,
When I played in the fields of so long ago
And ran down the lanes where wild roses grow.
I picked lots of petals to make some perfume,
Then hid it in bottles in my special room.

The chattering of sparrows, the blackbird's loud song,
The scent of sweet lavender all summer long.
Walls covered in Ivy and Clematis too,
Snap Dragons and Lupins, red, yellow and blue.
The clinking of cups as we picnicked again.
The time that we took to make one daisy chain.
The scents and the sounds wrapped in mists of the past
Now seem far away, but I know they will last.
For each summer will dust the cobwebs away
And memories of summer will come back to stay.
S. M. St. Clair

Seasons

The are four seasons in the year
And each one brings a tear,
Of loved ones gone from this fair earth
To our heavenly God above

Springs comes with blossoms ever new
And lambs in the fields at play.
The Good Shepherd tends his flock
For everyone to see.

Summer follows on with glorious days ahead,
And colours of every hue.
Even the rainbow casts a spell,
On every living thing.

Autumn with leaves of Green, Red and Gold,
Tells of His handicraft true to behold.
As Winter draws near, with frost and the snow.
Sit down and think of long, long ago.

And each of these seasons have a story to tell.
With memories so dear to the Heart,
But time goes by and the scars they heal,
And we pick up the threads once more.
E. Ford

Grief

Another empty bottle and still your empty chair,
An empty heart to match it and a world that doesn't care
A mind that cannot take it, a dream that's gone away
I don't know how to face it or live another day
To me you were my everything, my life, my love, my guide
But now there isn't anything, and I am dead inside
The sun is cold, the rain is dry
Yet here I am and cannot answer why.
C. A. Palmer

Easter

Was I among those crowded streets of Old Jerusalem?
And did I see a lonely man, with thorns pressed like a diadem
Upon his weary Head?
Did my feet walk behind his feet along that stony way?
When all Heaven was weeping, on that drear and dreadful day,
Up on that green hill far away, they placed that Cross of Shame.
And nailed Our Saviour to it, for all to see who came.
Then as HE hung in agony, a sword thrust in his side,
"Forgive them Father" was His cry; then for our Sins, HE died,
But on that first great Easter Morn, new hope for all mankind
was born.
Our Lord from death arose alive,
And Life Eternal is the prize He offers now to me and you.
If only we will follow Him,
His love will free us from all sin.
Olive N. Sussex

" Surviving "

Facing the truth no hiding away on days so long
and cold.
When dark clouds above block the light and rays of
warmth from the golden heart of the sun.
Thoughts and feelings that flow like the river
meeting the sea.
Memories so vivid and clear, so easily bring a tear.
Time ticking by brings with it pain, that quickly
comes and so hastily goes.
Looking for the light at the end of the tunnel.
Trying to gain strength after the hurt.
Emotions that were eroded from day to day and
gradually crumbled like that of our coastal cliffs.
Surviving through the day and night
Holding on learning to be strong.
L. K. Cox

" The Forgotten World "

What a joy to hear birds singing at dawn.
And church bells ringing on a sunday morn.

What a joy to watch the flowers that are in bloom
And the sun shining on us in the afternoon.

A world so beautiful, yet so full of pain.
So much happening, so much unexplained!

Where has our trouble-free world gone?
Why can't we live where we yearn to belong?

Stop the guns in the distance, feed and clothe everyone
Please God help and show us what has to be done!

So we can all live in peace and be happy on this earth.
This earth full of beauty, this place of our birth.

What a joy to see winter, summer, autumn and spring.
And the changes that all these seasons bring.

Let's take each day to show someone we care!
Or this world full of beauty will become something rare!
Sally Masters

Untitled

I look into my forefathers' eyes
And see the anguish in their lives
The lines of experience across their faces
Pulled taut by the memories they once shared
So much has passed since the turn of their days
My life like a young bird
Waiting to take flight
Dwells on the memories of yesterday
How cold the doors of life would seem
If such great men did not pave the way for my future
And stand by me even in spirit as a tool of my existence
I pray and I wait for that day
When I can be like them
And hold the memories of life
Paul Thomas Lansley

Love Is

Love is all around,
and can be found everywhere I stare,

Love is all around,
It's there in the air, as the wind flows through my hair.

It's deep in my heart,
even when we are apart.

Love is all around,
It can sometimes get lost, but for no extra cost,
It can be found again.

It's right here in my lap, as my cat has a nap,
In its sound of purring, love keeps re-occurring.

Love is all around on the ground,
It can be found, everywhere I care.
J. Lindh

Winter Wind

It's very real, though never seen,
And can at times be very keen,
How it gets here no one knows,
But when winter comes its power grows,
Blowing, whistling, howling too,
Like noisy animals in the zoo,
We feel it, yet there's nothing there,
It's free and colourless, like the air,
Strong force may uproot many a tree
And make huge waves upon the sea,
Never welcome, it makes folk shiver,
While sailors on their ships do quiver,
It keeps the windmill's sails a 'turning'
Whilst in our homes bright fires are burning,
From gentle breeze to full blown gale,
Winds are part of a winters tale
May Dabrowiecki

Village Life

This des. res. Chiltern village has views of fields and hills
And busy village people, all drawing up their wills.
We've all got great big gardens and some have paddocks, too
By night, they're home to muntjacks. And a murderer or two.
Three murders in a decade may seem rather few;
But it makes you think a bit, however grand the view.

One man did his wife in, kept her head safe in his fridge,
In a postcard-pretty house, beside a hump-backed bridge.
The cops unearthed the torso, a hundred miles away.
He was pruning roses, but they wouldn't let him stay.
One man gave a girl a lift and took her to a barn.
She never lived to see the view from that pretty Listed farm.

The other month the cops came back. Not just PC Plod.
Scene of Crime. Forensic. Taking samples. Matching blood.
Another pretty farmhouse, in another lonely lane.
No-one's been arrested, but Number Three's been slain.
The ponies clip-clop down the lanes, riding two-by-two,
Tripping new intruder lights. Dusk-to-dawn curfew.

I'm relaxing in my garden, taking in the view,
Praying that the killer doesn't come to get me, too.
Tom Rayfield

For Paul And Rachel's Wedding

P is for the partnership you realized this May
A is for the altar where vows were took today
U is for united, together as you stand
L is for the love, that goes with your gold band

R is for romance, that blossomed into love
A is for all the joys, sent from up above
C is for caring, given like a mother
H is for happiness, you'll give to one another,
E is for each other, to share as man and wife
L is for the longing for a happy married life.
I. L. Camwell

Time To Forgive

There is always time to forgive
And a time to forget
In this old world where we live,
We seem to have regrets.

There is always a star up alive
Telling us which way to go
And there's that old word called love
Which we should really know.

So don't put off this tomorrow
What we must do today,
Then all our sadness and sorrow
Will surely pass away.

A. M. Smith

Monotony

One of these days I will leave this house
And
I will get myself into another house,
And that day
I will leave this name behind
And
I will get myself another name.
From one house
To another house
From one name
To another name
But a step on the same spot
One man to one woman
One mother one father
To one child life goes on
A step on the same spot
Cutting succulent orange-red ripe tomatoes
Into slices dicing onions
I listen to its sharp, sharp clear sound
Cutting into bits and pieces.

Sharmini Jayewardena

Timeless Love

Silence in a winter sky,
An owl disturbs the still,
The eerie fog descends across,
And settles around the hill.
Churchyard grass is sparkling,
The diamonds in the dew,
A bride and groom all dressed in white,
Are stood beneath the yew
Slowly, both, across the grass,
Hid by a misty veil,
Old man moon stares dimly down,
To light the hallowed trail.
Pausing at the wooden gate,
Between the ancient trees,
They kiss a kiss that never ends,
And melt within the breeze.

Owen Thomas

Random Thoughts On Valentines Day

In days of old when knights were bold,
An errant knight on charger white
Bore his lady fair to a castle where
   They lived happily ever after —
In the middle ages, when men were sages,
With bell, book and candle, and often scandal
On moor, hill and dell, or whatever befell
   They had their way with the ladies —
In more modern fare, when all is laid bare,
And nobody seems to care what they wear.
They fly on high, have pie in the sky,
   But St. Valentine still has his day —
We're all held in thrall, by a loving call
Of a soul mate with invite to date —
One's dreams of fulfilment don't always come true,
   Is it fate that's at fault — or just you?

E. J. Lawrence

The Desert Of Pain

A long time ago in the desert of pain,
an old man died and his knowledge remained.

A thousand years was the span of his life,
the knowledge was earned by dangerous plight.

A battle a day for a thousand years,
mind drain the dead, absorb all their tears.

A young man he came, the knowledge required,
a different battle, a battle of fears.

A defeat on his part, the old man was dead,
the knowledge was drained and in to his head.

A Messiah was born on that great day,
a world was saved, the darkness kept at bay.

A price to be paid the young man returned,
to the desert of pain, his freedom was burned.

Michael Anthony Wheatcroft

Disaster At Sea

A disaster struck on February fifteenth,
An oil tanker shedding its oil beneath.
People, frantic with terror, were all saved,
But surrounding wildlife in oil were bathed.
The thick black waves of death we see,
Engulfing the birds, struggling to be free.
Marine life colourful, as before we knew,
Now striving for breath, in thick black glue.
More oil pouring from the tanker, 'Sea Empress,'
How can one disaster cause such a mess!
They had many a warning, but took no heed —
So tell me why, they began to proceed.

E. S. Smith (nee Keeys)

Sunday Morning

Sunday morning the sun did rise
An inmate came out for exercise
He didn't know about the lies
He didn't last the exercise

He got stabbed twice in the back
The inmates say he deserved the attack
The officers came and picked him up
Took him to hospital to be stitched up

The rumour is he died that day
It was so sad to die that way
I had no choice but to walk away
For I want to live for another day

Take this advice and take it wise
If you go out on exercise
Use your head and not your eyes
Just keep on walking don't go talking
Keep them shut, that is your lips
Or you're the next one on their list
You won't get help, no matter what you can't go home
To end this poem you're all alone

Malcolm Gillett

Why The Bad Shepherd Lost A Sheep

The Government is my shepherd I shall
Always be in want; he maketh me to
Lie down on the pavement.
He leadeth me in the path of oppression for his
Own selfish sake. Yea, though I walk
Through fields, streets and factories, I
Obtain no labour and thou art with me.

The church and the state, they oppress me.
They prepare before me bombs in the presence
Of my distress; they anoint my small income
With inflation, my expense runneth over.
Surely, nakedness and hardship shall follow me
All the days of my life and I will dwell
In the house of poverty forever.

Paul Fairbank

" Imagine A World Without Trees "

I stood and gazed upon the land wonders to behold,
An Autumn breeze caressed my face and it was chill and cold.
The birds were singing in the trees and flying all around.
The autumn touch had turned the leaves from green to golden brown.
I wandered home along the lanes as dusk began to fall.
Shadows fell across my path from the trees, so strong and tall.
I hurried home and closed the door and sat down beside the fire.
The shadows flickered on the walls, it was time to retire.
I went to bed and dreamed about the beauty all around
When suddenly I awoke to hear a terrifying sound.
It was a wind so fierce and strong, it lashed with all its might.
It seemed to rush by like a train, it was a dreadful night.
I looked out in the morning and tears rolled down my face.
For everywhere was havoc, not a single thing in place.
The trees lay still upon the ground their roots towards the sky.
Their graceful boughs were broken and the fields were blown awry.
The starkness of the landscape without a single tree,
This tragedy would make this life an empty place to be.

O. E. Thomas

Untitled

Would it not be wonderful if all the wars would cease
And we could wake one morning to a world of peace
Where all the bombs and guns stop killing children women and their sons
To see the people walking down the tracks with the few possessions on their backs
They dare not even look around for fear of seeing their homes raised to the ground
On God please tell us what to do
We have always so relied on you
Why do men do such dreadful things
Only sadness and unhappiness does it bring
The men who cause these wars should fight
All women think this only right
Why do they have to take our men
Away from family and friends
What dreadful men who kill for greed
Oh God please help us this we plead.

I. F. Willshire

A Bird

A bird
a fragile being, delicately created,
with gentleness it must be treated.
Made not to speak, but forever sing,
to bring sounds of joy to everything.
A colourful, wond'rous sight
when wings a'spread out in flight.
Seen and heard by day
at dusk nestle within the trees do stay.
Upon the dawn, the singing starts,
the world awakens with chorus in its heart.
Thank you God for this gentle creature,
a bird must have been your favourite feature.

Ngaire G. M. Parker

The Garden

Our garden does not belong to us
Although we give it all lots of fuss
The fox and squirrel frogs birds and bees
All think they may use it as they please.

We plant our flowers and prune our shrubs
We try to remove unwanted grubs
We cut the grass and control the weeds
We tend to all the various needs.

But they will return from year to year
When we are all gone away from here
New people will come and tend this plot
And do all the things that we forgot.

M. E. Lee

William

He was our constant companion,
Always with us! — come what may!
Whatever the weather! — whatever the day!
A Westie, faithful and true,
Maybe an obstinate character! —
But a lovable darling too! —
He gave us both undemanding love!
And knew our every word! — and our every move!
He would answer every call! —
His gorgeous eyes said it all!
To-day our home is coldly silent,
Our cats wonder what we've done with him!
Oh dear! — How very much we shall miss him!
To-day, no longer will a loving paw reach out and push a door!
Or two adoring eyes gaze within,
Wondering when his pal will take a walk with him!
Now he has left us, filled with an aching heart!
He gave us all his love! —
And played his part! — Better than any Human would!
Well done, William, we will remember you always! — as we should!

Winifred F. Carter

My Friend

True friends are for life
always there through trouble and strife
but sadly now my friend has died
together when we laughed and cried
the little things I miss the most
like days when we shared cheese on toast.
the knitting patterns that we shared
choosing cloths we like to wear
planning diets we never kept
thanking God for the day we met
no more the laughter and the joy
in my life there is just a big void
You were so brave until the end
goodnight good bless my dearest friend.

Rika Lindsey

Eternal Friends

All through our lives we've been connected,
always there, never rejected.

The ones who put us on the road of life,
give us friends to rid the strife.

Friends who guide you in your spiritual
quest, answer the questions so you can rest.

These mysteries of life we try to solve,
will return when our lives revolve.

So let us be thankful for eternal friends,
because life with them never ends.

Mark Laurence Addison

Life

Programmed minds of robot people,
Always marching forwards on,
Sticking in the poisoned needle,
Revelling in the trip they're on,

Love is dead but not forgotten,
Peace is nowhere to be seen,
All their hearts are cold and frozen,
Nothing left is really clean

Looking for their lost horizons,
Will they ever find their goal,
Caring for their young and dear ones,
Giving up their very soul,

The time will come when they'll awaken,
And see the world as it should be,
When the spell is finally broken,
And they'll realize that they are free.

Ken Stephens

Desertion

The sight and smell of people dying
Always makes me feel like crying.
Wounded soldiers everywhere,
No one seems to really care.

Family news I wait to hear,
Day by day, it doesn't appear.
There's disease and infection in the air,
Fear of death is everywhere.

Afraid and lonely, cold as well,
Here I really am in hell.
Shots are fired, blood and gore,
I don't think I can take much more.

Misery and destruction not wanting to see,
I dream of home, it's where I should be.
Fresh air, clean clothes, food and a bed,
Not knowing if tomorrow I too could be dead.

"Why am I here?" I scream and shout,
Disgusted with war, what's it all about?
Ashamed! A coward, I have no doubt,
Desertion is the only way out.
Victoria Bolger

The Sneakybeaks

The sneakybeaks are tall but small
although they're fat they're thin
they quietly sneak around your house
yet make a terrible din.
You never hear them talking
but chatter they won't stop
and keep a guard on everything
including your favourite pop.

For sneakybeaks are naughty things
and when you've gone to bed
they'll pinch your sweet and drink all night
while painting your clothes bright red.
Then tie you up in cotton and hide your toys away
lock mum and dad in the shed and leave them there to stay.

And if you have a sister or a brother he would do
they'll cover them in custard and sell them to the zoo.

So, keep just one eye open, for when you go to bed
and tell your favourite dolly or your friendly Ted
to guard you very carefully and wake you very quick
if they see those sneakybeaks up to their awful tricks.
T. R. Slaney

An Empty Playground

Happy cries of children fade,
Along with the snow white clouds.
The peacefulness provides no aid,
Against the darkened shrouds.

This place once filled with laughter,
Is now a lonely place.
Filled with sadness and despair,
With none a joyful face.

A lone young boy strays across the field,
Where life was now governed by fear.
Not a ray of sunshine the clouds did yield,
The thudding rain was all to hear.

But as his feet gently struck the ground,
Something stirred in this bleak earth.
Flowers rose gracefully from the ground,
To meet a brand new birth.

If heaven on earth is really true,
Then this could be described as such.
Though we must strive to not be blue.
Only then can heaven be clutched
Phillip Sacramento

Our World

To be or not to be, Shakespeare bequeathed the quote,
Along with others talented, painters, those who wrote,
Musicians, artistes, men of learning, those who penned a score,
Isn't it a pity Satisfaction is no more?

They toiled under persecution, but faith came shining through,
Often penniless, plus scant o' comfort, just to name a few
Rewards they came in different ways, though not while they were living,
They left a sense of values for us, loveliness and giving.

Today, those who would govern us have lost some dedication,
Indeed, we oft feel let down together as a nation,
Surely they could find some answers, give us peace of mind,
What better tribute could there be, to those we'll leave behind

Stephenson supplied the steam, the apple man was Tell,
Then we had the telephone, Alexander Graham Bell,
There'll always be some clever men, of that there is no doubt,
But why can't men of brains today sort some of this lot out?

Our world is here for us to see, to love and to enjoy,
For every living creature, girl, woman, man and boy,
But if we cannot come to some conclusion very soon,
We will all be living on the Dark Side of the Moon.
Catherine M. Duguid

Untitled

Am I to wander forever, in this isle of mist,
Am I to be haunted forever, by the face and lips I once kissed.

The soft form of the one that betrayed me, betrays me still.
The one that punishes me, punishes with an iron will

I am not cleansed by the summer rain,
The caress of the sun does not ease the pain.

I cannot find a place to hide,
For the pain that I feel comes from deep inside.

I do not see the blue skies, or hear the singing lark,
I do not walk the green hills, or picnic in the park.

I do not see the blossom on the bough,
Or see my children play, where are they now?

To my torment is there no end,
I ask you my friend,
Must I suffer until my death,
Will the pain only cease with my last breath?

Tell me it will not be so, for along the road of life I must go,
To take my punishment as a man, and do the best I can.
Philip Storey

The Gypsy Girl

I espied a gypsy girl, riding on a caravan
And at her side there sat, a kind old gentle man.
Her aura was so fresh, as a rushing mountain spring
And as they trundled slowly past, I could hear her softly sing.

"I am a gypsy girl, and have travelled far and wide
But here I am at last, to be always by your side.
You are my country boy, and you've waited oh so long
And now that we're together, I sing for you this song.

Just a poor little gypsy girl, and a simple life I live
But so much love I have inside, and this treasure to you I give.
Come travel life's long road, in my van of yellow and red
And the first stop that we will make, is for us to be wed."

Her words danced sprightly on charmed red lips, and waltzed their way to me
And I heard the sweetest sounds, of an unknown symphony.
It was the pots and pans vibrating, to the tune of an old black kettle
And as they rhythmed to her verse, the chorus in my ears did briefly settle.

Like an inquiring moth that's drawn to a bright reflective light
I touched her silken hand, then held it oh so tight.
As she gazed into my face, with eyes as warm as a fire glow,
I was awakened from my dream, and now I miss her ever so.
B. Tallbot

I Wish I Knew Why

I wish I knew why I sometimes cry
Alone in the night, watching the stars sail by
Listening to the silence and the peace of the night
Wondering when it will be time to take flight

I wish I knew why I long to be free
Of pain and discomfort, just to be me
Welcoming the loneliness that comes with old age
Memories fading, remembered, gone in a haze.

I wish I knew why you left me alone
Did I do wrong, bringing you home
The house is the same, your presence has gone
What a pleasure it is to hear the old songs.

I wish I knew why I sit here tonight
So scared, so lonely, crippled with fright
The music is louder, the light hurts my eyes
I wish I knew why you had to die.

Sue Briggs

My Blackbird

My blackbird comes in the twilight,
Alone in the dusk of the day,
His special bough he sits upon.
And sings a roundelay.
With notes of untold memories,
Lost in the passage of time;
of long past joys - and joys to be.
Told in this life of mine.
He sings with the joy of living,
In the beauty of evening calm.
The shadows gather in whispers, held by natures arm.
I listen long to my blackbird (such a welcome bird).
While in the far off echoes,
An answering song is heard:
If only these moments would linger-
If I always could hear his song.
But darkness descends,_
The notes fade away.
Another day over and gone.!

Rosemary Goram

The Pit Pony

I am a pit pony way underground.
Alone in my stable I am bound.
When daylight comes it makes no difference to me,
as the light of day I'll never see.
Pulling heavy crates of coal,
I'd rather be free,
with other ponies just like me.
In the fields running around,
eating grass from the fresh, fertile ground.
All I want is the chance to see,
just what the world has to offer me,
I cannot bear being caged in this mine
and all I want is the chance to see the sun shine.
But my life's not my own, it's one I lend,
therefore I'll be trapped down here till my bitter end.

Steven Williams

Wishing

Sunday morning in the kitchen,
All alone and sadly wishing
Life could be like nursery rhymes
All filled with fun, not miserable times.

Always ending on a happy note
And filled with colour, like Joseph's coat.
No unkind word or dreadful deeds,
Sarcastic voices-Oh where it leads.

Keep the peace! How hard I try
But kind words disappear like
Smoke in the sky.

Patricia Cherrington

The Sculptor

I saw her image in the stone, asleep,
Alone, and gently waiting out of sight.
I longed to chip the shadows dark and deep,
To bring her beauty out into the light.
I chiselled and I hammered in the sun,
With my pulsating heart and stubborn will,
Till my creative hand and eye were one.
I wept for joy, and revelled in my skill.
But now and then, the frenzied chisel sped
To mar my figurine. I worked forlorn,
In fractious mood, through pangs of birth and dread.
I heard her cry! My Work of Art was born.!
I looked at her. I loved her! Could it be
She too displayed a secret love for me?

E. Blackbourn

Life's Love Lost

My mind awakens, the day begins
Alone and crying for many things
I failed to cherish enough, my life before,
Until it's gone, and the one I adore.

Live life to the full, and take care of each other.
Let no one destroy your love for one another
Enjoy what you have for as long as you can,
For tomorrow is cruel, no length to life's span
The birds still sing, but for me it's too late
God took him away, and with broken heart
I await my lone fate.

P. A. Bowen

My Family

There's Frankie George and Ann. That's three,
Allan, Mary and me.
Ann's husband is named Kenneth,
Frankie's wife is Kathleen.
Allan's wife is named Mary.
Georgie's wife is Pauline.
Mary's husband is named Wilmot.
Frank was married to me.
But he passed away some time ago.
I am now on my own you see.
I have ten grand children
I am as proud as can be.
There's six boys and four girls
The youngest's the same birthday as me.

There's Julia, Andrew, Andrea, Antony and Gary
Angela, Lynn, Ross, Adam and Rudi.

Some people are very lonely,
They have no family.
I am a lucky person,
Don't you agree.

E. M. Darlington

A Kitten Named Butch

At two weeks old I was put out in the cold
and left in a cardboard box.
On someone's step,
there I slept for half a day, there I lay.
Then. Oh what luck I was gently picked up
and given a hug and a kiss.
It's sheer bliss, to be feeling this
the love and warmth of her touch.

She took me in and gave me a drink
from a bottle with warm milk inside
I love my new home and to my mummy I owe
my friendship my love and a kiss.

Till death us do part with all of my heart.
I promise to stay by her side
through thick and through thin
I will never give in,
to my mummy I owe my life.

B. Tuffill

Everything

Everything you are I miss so much,
All through my life, I knew that sweet loving touch,
Re-birth of the pain the loss still brings,
When I think of so many wondrous things.

Be still! My heart, I feel your presence — there,
Just beyond my reach, yet it will forever bring,
The warmest glow to rise and ascend,
So deep this love its power transcends.

A mirrored image to see deep within my mind,
That thought to hold, always to find,
The wealth in reaches on a greater plain,
A place not of earth in man's domain.

To trust and hope we shall meet again,
To believe in this and in truth proclaim,
Love never endeth it is written thus
A greater 'being' love as all so much.

To meet once more as we did so oft,
All sense of time and space so soon forgot,
That step beyond not too far away,
To reach the Kingdom on that eternal day.

Sylvia E. Findlay

Some-One Loves You

Life can be a b****, even if you're very rich
All the time things go wrong, but most don't last very long.

Some problems can last forever, when will they go away, never
You can't get them out your head, they only go when you're dead.

This isn't a hint to take your life or be tempted with a knife
They might sort themselves out, but make sure you don't live in doubt.

Life does have its good times, maybe you should try writing rhymes
Let your feelings be known, before you are all alone.

Maybe you should get some friends before your life really ends
If they're good they'll treat you right, they won't argue, they won't fight.

You'd better listen to what I say, before down below is where you lay
Surely someone thinks you've got wit, someone loves you a little bit.

Stuart Welsh

Psychic's Secret World

Travelling faster than the speed of light I am getting younger
All the time.
Bodies aging everywhere, but not for me I haven't a care
Thanks to Einstein's dream, which he told to me last week.
Lying on my bed, he called my name, his voice was soft,
Told me why he came.
The room was dull and cold 'til he appeared, gave me a plan
To build a machine.
Who knows? I may become as famous as the Queen.
I worked all year and the craft was very weird.
Einstein's figure lit up the room, then he disappeared

J. McKillop

A Young Child's Happiness

"It makes the children happy,"
A young child said to me,
As with her sister she gathered
Fallen leaves from an autumn tree.

Tints, with a wealth of gold and rose;
The chestnut, oak and beech.
Spiders sailing on gossamer threads,
And little birds with twittering speech.

The splendour of Mother Nature,
On that autumn day so mild,
Revealed a precious gift in life -
The happiness of a Little Child.

Pamela M. L. Crisp

A Window To His Soul

His eyes a window to his soul, like a treasure chest to unfold,
all the magic that is bestowed, who holds the key, only he knows.

In acts performed his heart comes forth, the love in a gesture so
small, the love in a smile, or a touch, from so little comes so much.

I often dream of his body, calling to mine so deep, enchanted by
the atmosphere around me, drunk by the love I reap.

He creates auras to flow, memories to store in his treasure chest,
all precious items locked away, until he is laid to rest.

Clearly he is a mystery, God's serendipity, his life will make
history, in awe I watch him grow.

His lips as summer fruit, his face from Zeus he stole, his mind
to his life a root, his eyes a window to his soul.

Natasha Dayaramani

Gardening

Back breaking toil, enormous expense,
All that effort and little recompense,
Blackfly, greenfly, caterpillars and slugs,
Mildew and fungus and all sorts of bugs.
You nurture your plants through the hardest frost,
Talk to them nicely, don't think of the cost,
Transplant the seedlings to the vegetable plot,
Then Tiggs the cat digs them up, or snails eat the lot.
Then just as you think things might be alright,
A torrential storm rages all through the night,
The plants are all flattened and all washed away,
You have to start again, oh what a day!
You're out in the garden digging up weeds,
And carefully planting next season's seeds,
A neighbour walks past and stops to chat,
Says your garden's a picture and that's a fact,
There's nothing like seeing your own crops grow,
Or eating the fresh vegetables that you have sown,
On second thought you feel quite elated,
It's therapeutic after all, you're rejuvenated.

Susan Tina Maria Jackson

The Meaning Of Life

The twist of life, the trust of faith, revolves around
all our mistakes. The dogs that bark, the baby which cries,
all these things are true to life. The wind in the trees
that cat in the bin, all these things are never a sin.
The thunder and lightening, the wind in the sky,
 are all these things a cause to die.

The flowers in the garden, the trees in the park, two lovers kissing
alone in the dark, the beautiful lake, the ducks in the pond,
the meaning of this, it all corresponds.
Alone in the sky a bird flies by, where is it going.
I often wonder why, it all paints a picture, but what does it mean?
Is it reality or only a dream?
The death of a friend, a laugh or a cry
 the birds collide alone in the sky.

A new year comes, an old one goes;
 the meaning of life is still to be told.

Paul C. Slaney

" Love's Sweet Call! "

It sparks, ignites, then grows to a glow
a warmth inside that does not show.
It speeds the pulse and quickens the heart
illogical it seems to those who are smart.

Mountains are climbed, oceans are spanned
by the lucky few in their own dream land.
Emotions are gained but few are lost,
barriers of time and space are crossed.

To those who experience this wondrous delight
is given the gift of mutual insight.
To know the giving of one's heart, one's all
is to know the great joy of love's sweet call!

M. G. Friend

God's Free Gifts

Nature's beauties, and every one free,
All on display for you and for me.
The mountain waterfall with its shimmering cascade,
Like a ghostly figure, all in white arrayed.

Bright spring flowers after long winter days,
Song birds on tree blossom our spirits to raise,
Rocky coastline, tall cliffs and a turmoil sea,
Endlessly moving, like a spirit wishing to be free.

Big harvest moon with its mellow light,
The warm scented air of a summer's night,
Autumn's glorious tints of russet and red,
A colourful leafy carpet on which to tread,

Those sharp hoarfrosts, glisteningly bright,
Covering everything in gossamer white,
Winter's snow falls, a picturesque scene,
Obliterating ugly sights much best unseen

High mountain peaks against skyline.
Breathtakingly beautiful in fading sunshine,
How fortunate we are with nature's bounteous gift,
Brightening our lives, our spirits to uplift.

K. Jones

All Too Often

Ideas, ideals and longevity,
All facets of an inspired mind.
The 'birds' and the 'bees' and bottled beer,
All facets of a humdrum life.

Jobs taken to further a career,
Corrupted minds soon to appear.
Babies born to a frightening new world,
Many scarred with being throttled

Ideas, ideals and longevity,
All facets of a motivated mind,
The 'birds' and the 'bees' and bottled beer,
All common to a humdrum life.

Successful career, house and car,
Out of work, lost in love.
Happy career, checkout operator,
Family love demonstrated.

What is right?
What is wrong?
Is it right?
Is it wrong?
Life as life is lived

Susan Scott

Rest In Peace

The night has gone, the morning's here,
All be it far too soon,
With pulse rate taken, bed baths done,
It must be nearly noon!
But no, the day has scarce begun
And yet I'm fair worn out,
While still I wait.... and wait..... for news
Of when I'll be about.
The doctor comes, a nurse or two,
And students by the score,
They stand and whisper by the bed,
I still don't know the score!
"A few more days, and then we'll see,
'Till then you must have rest."
Have rest? In here? Well that's a joke,
Oh well, the Doc knows best.
So in between the x-ray folk,
The blood test, physio, scan,
I'll just lie here, do as they say,
"Oh nurse, I need a pan!"

C. A. Howard

The Clown

We know the whole world loves a clown,
All ages from one hundred down.
Babes and toddlers, round eyed, they look
At this magical figure from a story book.
Young school children shout with laughter,
At antics remembered long years after.
Old or young, almost every fan,
Just sees the clown and not the man.
We never look beyond the paint,
To the ordinary man, neither sinner nor saint.
But when the circus came to town,
There was a lady who looked at the clown.
She looked beyond the painted face,
And saw the man who stood in his place.
And now she's with him all year long,
This clown who entertains the throng.
Oh yes, the whole world loves a clown,
We're thrilled when he comes with the circus to town.
But Mary is his greatest fan,
She laughs with the clown, and loves the man.

I. L. Cowlbeck

Forward

Primitive (yet intricate in operation) electrical energy sparks synaptic shock,
Alivens muscle to hinge and lever
Inner frameworks of biologically stored power,
Released in forward movement,
Each foot placed in turn, shifting body weight in walk

The earth enlargens, promising wealth and enlightenment,
farther places intrigue,
Knowledge to absorb, opportunities to exploit,
Natural movement is no longer enough —
Too slow, too limited —
Vastness of space, lengthy journeys to be negotiated without fatigue

On pathway, via road, lifted by air, carried by sea,
Through age lie countless revised drawings,
Designs discarded as technology quickly evolves
Its offspring of machinery,
Taking forward Man the distance from points A to B

Imagination and practicality overview the carriage over water and land,
Vehicles harnessing beast, turning of wheel,
Creations that race, drive, drift, soar,
Bridging diverse cultural highways,
Allowing international relationships — the clenched fist, the shaking of hand

Scott McIntyre

Time's Corridor

Angry footsteps pounding
Along a deserted corridor;
  Before I appeared there were footsteps
  Marching through the stream of time,
Calling to the open sky
Cheering at the burning sun.
  Death to a troubled youth, Once sounding
  Deep in time's corridor:
Early in the light of former footsteps
Evening is lost to the rush of time.
Farewell to the rolling sky!
Follow the cheer of the burning sun.
  Growing light causes the dawn's founding,
  Giving origins in the empty corridor,
Hearing now those angry footsteps
Who have ancestors who are lost in time,
In the scope of the open sky,
In the sweat of the burning sun;
  A King is calling from the open sky,
  The Creator of the burning sun.

Rodney Taylor

Why?

Why the sorrow, why the pain.
A young man's body lying in the rain.
A single bullet through the chest.
A meaningless death like all the rest.
A mother's son his father's pride.
So many bitter tears were cried.
To join the Army was his dream.
Though things aren't always as they seem.
In a war zone he spent his first year.
Coming to terms with constant fear.
But he never saw the man that day.
Who cruelly stole his life away.
I ask myself what he'd have done.
Had he been forced to use his gun.
Killing a man couldn't be his scene.
For he was only just eighteen.
Time will slowly dull the pain.
Though the way he died will still remain.
Cold-blooded murder was the aim.
The target a Soldier with no Name.
Tracey Shapland

The Fisherboy

The white frosty ground, the darkening sky,
A young boy yearns to cast his line.
Alone by the river with Dad's cap on his head
And warm winter clothes to keep out the cold.

The water's like glass, a perfect reflection.
An upturned boat becomes a table.
The bread for bait, the book for hints,
The tub of hooks and other bits.

He casts his line. Where are his thoughts?
A picture of peace on a chill afternoon.
The air is now freezing, the grass is so crispy,
But still he continues to wait for a bite.

Such patience, contentment; a promise fulfilled.
It's time to go home to a warm fire and tea.
Who captured the moment? A memory for always.
His Mum whilst walking to pass the time.
Veronica Dunne

Farewell

What can I say?... farewell?
A word that hides the thought,
A word that serves as a parting knell
Revealing nought.

What of the thought?... unsaid?
So must it be, forgotten.
In depth of mind its truth must tread.
Remaining, never given.

And so?... we part
With nothing save a smile.
A smile that hides the tears, the heavy heart
That says farewell.
G. E. Roy

Accepting

Another scar begins to weep
A tear drop rolls upon my cheek
Another pain begins to swell
The hurt that's there, it just can't quell
I'd lay my life down and want to die
Another tear falls from my eye
Accepting defeat is hard to swallow
It make's ones life feel oh so hollow
Another tear, another nail
No one want's to try then fail
From now on I'll believe in fate
And not dwell on thoughts of late
Love and pain go hand in hand
I've cried, so what!, I'm still a man.
Nigel Tubb

Divided Nation - " A Greater Serbia "

A greater world; a stronger race; a new regime for them to face,
A wholesome land the future sees; filled with horror and atrocities,
His plan to rid his world of them; the ethnic cleansing starts again.

Triumphant song of bombs a blast; sounds of noxious shells wail past,
Filthy rats plagued with disease; starved of life's normalities,
An outstretched arm; yet prominent fear; will the end of the tunnel ever appear?

By dominant, potent leaders led; their prospects drowned in cruel bloodshed,
Triumphant march on blood-soaked soil; taunted nation in turmoil,
Exposed hatred; success nearer; pungent smell of death's grim reaper.

Broken body left twisting in breeze, around her starving refugees,
Yet no one knew or even cared, knowing her fate would soon be shared,
Now she lies in fields of clover; her Serbian holocaust days are over!

To escape the horrors of mass annihilation,
She left this bloody situation,
Her final wish; a prayer to be,
Free, from all this anarchy!
Nikola Jayne Bunyan

Three Kings From The East

Three kings journeyed from out of the east
Across the desert sands,
They came with hope and joy in their hearts,
And symbolic gifts in their hands.

They diligently searched through many a town
And many a palace fair,
But could not find the tiny king
Till they came to a stable bare.

They had followed a star and came to where
It stood over the infant king,
Brightly shining, way up high
Where heaven's angels sing.

Yes, there in a stable low and mean
Sleeping among the hay,
The new-born saviour of the world
In sweet contentment lay.

On bended knee they offered gifts
To him who had come to reign,
Gold for kingship, incense for God,
And myrrh for suff'ring and pain.
Margaret Collins

Madeira

White-painted houses shine bright in the sun —
A terracotta rooftop on every one;
Exotic flowers growing in bucket and tin,
Bottle green shutters for coolness within.

Pebbled paths and painted tiles,
Finished embroidery stacked in neat piles;
A skinny small dog barks and waits to be fed
By a wizened old man — woolly hat on his head.

The sweet taste of wine, the aroma of fish
And flambe bananas — a favourite dish;
Fruits to the market in baskets of wicker,
A sample of poncha — the strong local liquor.

Walk the levadas and hear tales of history,
Experience the folklore and unravel the mystery
Of roosters and music and ankle high boots;
Tracing the costumes back right to their roots.

Terraces, forests, valleys and peaks,
Long lazy days that drift into weeks;
A temperate climate that's summer all year —
The delight is Madeira, and we visited here.
Shirley Lynall

A Bride's Wish

The pretty frocks, the glitter and scent
A wedding day that's heaven sent
God's gift of love to cherish close
All shared with those we love the most

A glowing sun to enhance the shine
Of a special day — yours and mine
This day as I become your wife
A moment I will treasure for life

When this day passes our lives to share
To snuggle close when no ones there
Our love to last through laughter and tears
The ups and downs that come with years

This gift, these words, I write with love
May our marriage be blessed by the Lord above

C. Rees

Summer

Birds serenade us from the trees
A warm and gentle summer breeze
Butterflies flitting from flower to flower
Are so busy in this garden bower
Ants scurrying busy on some unknown chore
Making trails of black across the floor
Then all at once a dancing shower
And jewels shimmer on every flower
Out comes the sun once more on this wondrous scene
Just as if the rain had never been
In the meadow rabbits skip and jump
Playing hide and seek round the old tree stump
A little girl with hair of gold kissed by the sun
Is making daisy chains and having so much fun
Time travels so quickly, soon the day will be done
And the sun will set like a gigantic bun
It's a red sky tonight, so if the sayings true
Tomorrow will dawn with skies of blue

C. Kettle

The Miracle

A baby began, our wise men do know
A spec in a puddle, umpteen years ago
And then, for no apparent reason
Began changing shape a bit, season by season
Supping the water, and eating the mud
Doing instinctively all that it should
Because although there was no one to know it
It would one day grow perfect, with all things below it
All things apparently grew perfect too
And whatever was needed, the clever Earth grew
To a blind horse a wink is as good as a nod
But the rest will find truth in the Handbook of God.

Margaret Duffield

A Vision For Peace

We pray for a world without tears
A world that never hides in fear
A world in which no wars are fought
An only peace is always sought

We wish to see a world that's safe
A world in which children have no grief
A world covered by clouds above
Echoing the song of peace's dove

Let's live in a world where people can talk
A world in which it's safe to walk
A world where we can love one another
For we will all be sisters and brothers

Let this be our hearts speaking
For a world which we are wishing
A world that's not a dream
But a place where peace will gleam

I. M. Littlewood

Joy

Ricks of hay stand sentinel
A tribute to work done
Casting lengthening shadows
Over the golden meadow
A pungent fragrance fills the air
Warm and dry
Butterflies flutter over the
Plundered stalks
A shimmering crescendo into
The liquid blue horizon
She tramps across the field resplendent
In flowered apron
Bearing bread and cheese
And sweet lukewarm tea
Oblivious to the scratch
Of the violated stubble
We run to meet her the warm breath of her kiss
Profound rapturous joy.
Oh mo Mhuirnin, mo mhuirnin
The sunshine and the flowers.

Nuala Nodwell

The Under Achiever

The nearly man, a phone call that was never made,
A substitute, stand in, second in command.
The nearly man, a letter that was never mailed,
The article that showed promise was rejected
due to pressure of space.
Sitting thinking what might have been,
All that could have been achieved,
The time, money and energy you couldn't afford.
The nearly man, the brother she never had,
Always the best man, not the bridegroom.
A non-playing reserve, a message that didn't get passed on.
The uncompleted painting on an easel in your mind.
Sitting thinking what might have been,
An underachiever?
Yes indeed!
Just the black ball away from victory.
The nearly man — an unfinished novel under somebody's bed.

N. J. Usher

Memory

The mind, quietly ticking, is jerked awake.
A sound, a voice, a smell, a glance
Evocative of past emotions, shake
Through the dimness of memory, by chance,
And a potpourri of feelings take
Form, bringing long forgotten desolation and fear.

The dreadful sound, terrifying and shrill,
Of bombs, of blasts of hell on earth.
Our peaceful, loving life destroyed, the will
Of a foreign tyrant of no worth.
You're gone and yet I feel you still
Around me, beside me, through all the years.

I gathered the pieces, went on with a smile,
Fulfilled hopes and ambitions we'd spawned.
Success and good living came after a while
Traumas deep buried, hidden and mourned.
But a sound, a voice, a glance or a smile
And you're back, heralding both joy and tears.

Millicent E. Judson

Unborn

Farewell my precious to small and so weak
A life pure and simple is what you tried to seek.
If this could have happened what joy you would bring
But you must go now darling with the angels you'll sing.
The angels that greet you will take you into their home
They will love and they'll hold you, you won't be alone
Although I'm not with you, my loves not denied
So wait patiently sweetheart 'till I can walk by your side.
Your face and your smile is what I long to see
I love you my baby you are still part of me.

Vicki Lambourne

The Bird

I thought I heard a bird today.
A song that filled the air.
I looked at the skies with wide staring eyes
But I could not see it there.

The sky is so dark. The colours are strange.
Is it day? Is it night? Is it dusk? Is it dawn?
Where are the sights that I know — the sounds that I know
Where? — where have they gone?

Someone pressed the button somewhere.
In a land — was it near? — was it far?
Who caused this madness? Who scorched the earth?
Who? — Did they say who they were.

God, let me die — please — no more wondering why.
Let me rest in your care at last.......
.... My memory stirred. I did hear that bird
In a world — that was ours — that is past.

Sylvia Sivyer

Cotswold Country (Gloucestershire 1986-1993)

Amidst the loomed hills and winding lanes
A song bird sings her sweet refrain
An old thatched cottage here and there,
That's Cotswold Country I declare.

The village school and church yard too
Are memories that will cling to you,
The old oak trees stand sound and still
Surveying the land like silent sentinels.

A deserted farm where children once played
Remains untouched by time to this present day,
A ghostly shepherd at the rear
With his faithful dog standing near.

Flowers shrew the paths and lanes
Of Cotswold stone and Roman roads
And every church spire points the way
From a peaceful hamlet to a welcoming home,
Splendour and beauty gladdens the eye
Treasured memories that will never die.

Selena Pearce

Dying To Fly

If sea birds and others can fly so high, why can't I?
a slave forever to earth's gravity
up there; where there's freedom, I want to be.
With white wings, in ecstasy they soar and they tear
with no ties or worries that we humans must bear;
but then seabirds eventually come to an end
and not even a miracle their bones can mend.
For some crash into metallic things
that crush their frail bodies and buckle their wings;
so full is the sky of man made matter
that some seabirds can-not avoid the latter.
Whatever goes up, in time must come down
to shrinking fields and smoke filled towns;
to oil spills and polluted waters, that kill them off
and their sons and their daughters.
On second thoughts, I think I'll stay as I am
an ecology defunct, remote controlled man.

B. J. Young

Black

A panther's fur,
A raven's wing,
A starless sky at night,
The swirling depths of a cold, cold pool,
The hole within the eye.
The ebony hair of an Egyptian queen,
The heart and soul of evil,
A cavernous mine,
The end of time,
When death's dark cloak is yours and mine,
Black is Black is Black.

Stephanie Jane Scott

Night Shades

Above the cloud rack high in the skies
A silver disc on purple lies,
Illuminating the earth below
Bathing all in an eerie glow.
Moonbeams filled with luminous light
Enrich the darkened space of night.
Moonlight magic sets the scene
Viewed in abstract like a dream
Strange shapes by imagination form
Conjured in shadows before the dawn.
Soon these forms by morn beguiled
Will slink away like a wayward child,
All swept by rays of the rising sun
Moonlights magic its course now run.

B. Wilson

Grief

The funeral is over, the numbness is gone,
A sense of relief now important jobs are done.
Then feelings of unsettled quiet — despondency,
No light in my dark world, a bitterness in me.
I have nothing — no Christian spirit — emptiness.
Is my God out there? I can't even say 'God Bless'.
Give me faith to touch the hem of your garment, pray,
Please God, please do come down and show me the right way.
It's Mother's birthday — I take flowers to her grave.
Has this really happened? What love she always gave.
I arrange the lovely flowers on her headstone
And as I stand there silently gazing, alone,
I sense a presence by my side I cannot see
And a strange feeling of warmth steals quickly over me.
My chains fall off, I am free, I have faith anew,
My great depths of despair I'll no longer pursue.
I've touched the hem of His garment, my heart feels free
And now I'm ready once again to follow Thee.

M. Vaill Stockham

Greed For Love

Is greed for love an ill-got vice,
A selfish, childlike goal,
A canker born of craving lice
That riddles lonely souls?

If such it is, Devil take my core!
Strip it cleanly from my fruit!
For I could not crave for sweet love more
To quench my thirsting roots.

Romantic winds sweep o'er the brow
Of every passing hill,
And gently sway my stretching boughs
To beckon for loves fill.

Coarse it in! — through leaf and shoot,
To softly kiss my pith.
Join it with warm sun to moot
The growth of love herewith.

Mark Williams

Proud Voices

Smooth voices talking loud
A nation trying to stand proud.
A surface imitation,
A cover up, a lie of a true nation.

The people stand proud,
But they don't dare look down at the ground.
The whole world is the same,
The poverty might as well be slain.

At the feet of the world,
The air is still sweetly curled.
The atmosphere is one of stress and pain,
But few have cause to hang their head in shame.

Natalie Puxley

The River

I gazed upon the beauty of a valley,
A river winding through,
My eyes beheld a picture rare as
Instantly I knew that as I gazed my
Soul within me stirred in wonder at the view.

The river does not hurry quite content
To wend its way, not seemingly to
Care that in its shallows small fish
Leap and play.

The willow on its bank bends as if
To greet it as it glides whilst
At the water's edge a nervous vole plops
Into the water as it hides.
On through fields of wheat and barley and of clover.
Whilst here and there it covers water meadows over.

Through farms cows standing like a spectre
Lowing, bend their heads and sip of its clear nectar.

Then suddenly around a bend it
Widens to its estuary and is no
More as it mingles in the bosom of the sea.

S. T. Sweetman

A Teenager In Your Home

A cyclone blowing through the house,
A rhythmic thump in your head.
The sprint for the bathroom's under way,
Your teenager's out of bed.
"Mum where's my" — rivals the radio's din,
"I really must wash my hair",
"Oh look I've got spots, I can't go today",
"I'm ugly, but you don't care".
Just part and parcel of every day,
With more for years to come,
But when the chips are down, one things for sure,
She'll always need her mum.

Patricia J. Jarvis

A Poet's Dream

'I'll write a poem' I thought one day,
A poem that's jolly to keep frowns at bay,
I'd like to rhyme and to be quite witty,
The rhythm must flow so not to be bitty.

Next is the subject, of what shall I write?
So many ideas but none seem quite right,
It can't be too heavy or slushy and dreary,
But nothing too morbid, sad, bad or teary.

My mind overflows with ideas of all sorts,
This poem's a hit, even with all its warts,
I'm sat at my desk, pen ready to flow,
A blank sheet in front, right here I go.

My minds gone a blank, I don't know why,
My ideas have all gone, I let out a sigh,
Wordsworth I'm not so I'll just face the facts,
I'll read other people's, sit back and relax.

Tracy Ann Johnson

The Ship

Sailing along on a sun-kissed sea
   A poem of grace and majesty,
Queen of the ocean - she dips and sways
   In the spray and the spume of the restless waves;
Sails spread aloft - etched white against blue
   She ploughs her way homeward - stately and true;
Down through her rigging the suns shattered rays
   Dance on the water in brilliant displays;
Gulls swooping down to the white-capped sea
Follow her wake expectantly:
   Across the horizon when land is in sight
She'll head for safe harbour
   Sails furled for the night.

Patricia Surman

The Blue Room

Amid these ancient walls and rustic beams
A part of you and I we leave behind
Unlike the places in our far off dreams
This room holds memories of a different kind.
The patchwork on the bed has sung our song,
More softly now that time has played its part
In slowing down the once - young race for love
Bestowing deeper feelings on the heart.
These pictures on the wall of times gone by
Now celebrate new travellers not the same
For us the need to rush along replaced
By age - old dreams to live and love again.
The Inglenook is reaching out its arms
Enveloping and spreading warmth around
The table by the bed holds vessels grand
Now filled with wine from grapes plucked from a foreign ground.
With goblets raised to welcome in the new,
We watch the years long - past slip gently by,
And when we gaze on fields, white cliffs, cathedral spires,
Will we recall THE BLUE ROOM and ask why?

P. Pearce

Aircrews To Winco

He would not have us mourn him, this kind and gentle man.
A paragon amongst the things all good.
Who would not harm a fly, and yet in danger stood
with his comrades few, against an evil host
that would threaten this land of ours.
Hour upon hour they flung their fragile craft against the Hun's.
Day followed day, weeks into months,
Till the world's applause did drown the cannonfire of their guns.

He would not have us mourn him, who long outlived the strife
and seizing hard with both his hands on life,
did squeeze and shake it so, until from it he wrung
every last vestige of its joyfulness.
We shall mourn him, and grieve upon his pallor,
though we know there'll be rejoicing in Valhalla.
So, walk from here on with spring back in your stride,
Knowing full well our offspring oft will boast with pride,
My grand-dad flew with John Ashton.

J. Holloway

The Old Swimming Pool

Twisting through the mountains, far from all the towns.
A motorway of movement, and never ending sounds.
A symbol of our greatness and engineering skills,
Has robbed us of our treasure, much against our wills.

Fifty feet up from where the old pool lay,
You can buy an ice cream almost any time of day.
But that never will compare with the joy,
We all got from a dip in the old swimming pool.

Gone the quaint old school house, and the village store,
The winding country road doesn't wind any more,

And the peaceful swimming pool hears the sound of spinning wheel,
On a thick lair of concrete and a framework of steel.

William York

Yesterday's Tomorrow

Awakening up to the call of the sparrow
A new day brings memories, like yesterday's tomorrow.
Time to stir, to capture the dawn
A sight of all sights,
Remembering the sunsets of yesterday's nights.

Sleep has gone, now wake to a new day
Happiness fills my heart, but thoughts seem to stray
Once all alone, forgotten and lost
My childhood memories I treasure most.

Wakening up to the call of the sparrow
Such happiness like yesterday's tomorrow.
Recapture memories lost and forlorn
I linger on to my yesterday's dawn.

D. D. Eden

Our Neighbour

Let me tell you about our neighbour who lived next door to us,
a miserable man, a real mean man, who'd spit and swear and cuss,
if we were in the garden playing out our games,
he'd shout at us to keep it quiet and call us dreadful names.
One day we tried to talk to him, we'd hardly said a word
when he leaned across the garden fence and said
"Children should be seen not heard!"
We tried to ignore him 'coz we knew he wasn't fair
and we knew when he was cross with us because he'd stand
out there and glare,
Then one day we lost our Dad — my Mum said that he'd died,
I ran out to my tree house and just cried and cried and cried.
When I'd finished all my crying I climbed down from the tree
and there stood this old man looking down at me,
He put his arm around me and said "Son, the world's not come
to an end,
I can't replace your Daddy but I'd like to be your friend".
I'm older now but remember that day and I think I always will,
when the miserable man who lived next door
became my best friend Bill.
Patricia Rushton

One More Lonely Lifer

In Armley Jail, through the rails
A man is dying slowly
Swinging there, in deep despair
It's all because he's lonely.

He got the time, to fit the crime
And now it's nearly over
In his mind "Oh sweet release,
Like dancing through the clover".

Ten more minutes now to go
They'll be op'ning up his door
To find the nonce beast, hanging there
Blue faced, and in a coma.

So little can be said
'Bout a man who's nearly dead
'Cept to say "Oh Lord,
We should have watched him closer,
We should have took his belt,
When he really needed help
But to us he was...
One more lonely lifer."
Mark A. Barnes

BASIC TRAINING

I didn't know a BOLD from an ITALIC,
a KEYBOARD was an organ, so I thought,
to JUSTIFY was proving to the missus
that my FLOPPY DISC wasn't something that I'd caught.

I thought DELETE was hanging from de ceiling
a SHIFT was "6 to 2" or "2 to 10"
and of course I knew a CURSOR when I saw one
my wife at midnight, "where've you....been again."

A MONITOR was a great big ugly lizard
ALT was "stop at major road ahead",
and a FONT I well remember as a baby,
when some idiot poured water on my head.

BASIC was your training in the Army
when you queued in single FILE outside the Mess,
the MENU was the same from dawn to sunset,
and a MOUSE could not exist on any less.

So if you want to learn COMPUTER language
and like me, your MEMORY's like an empty shed
this LIST may HELP INPRINT it in your SYSTEM, then
like me you can ESCAPE and GO TO bed. — (In the DOS
house presumably)
B. Smith

Walking's Free

My friends come join me on this walk
A long walk through your mind
Your choice of destination, but be sure to read the signs
Make your decision, don't follow old lines
Walk further than we can see, no cost, no VAT
　All because walking's free

Walk to the sun, walk to the moon
Wherever we go, we'll be back soon
Singing our song and whistling our tune
We've been to where we wanted to be
We're going to where we want to go
　All because walking's free.

When we come to the end of the road
And we feel that we are wise
Nothing will hold our tears, or hide our cries
For sure enough, one of us dies
We've been what we wanted to be
We've seen what we wanted to see
　All because walking's free.
Scott Campbell-Cook

The Good And Bad Days

When I look back fifty years or more
A long time before the war
Some say they were the good old days
Maybe they were in many ways
Saturday night dance at the village hall
No drugs there as I recall
Couples married and stayed wed
No quickie divorce at the nod of a head
In the meadows children could play
Safe and sound in every way
Some say they were the bad old days
Maybe they were in many ways
Deadly diseases they were rife
Many lost their fight for life
For most hard graft was all they knew
Luxury was for the favoured few
Air was foul and reeked of pollution
No effort was made to find a solution
Were they good days or were they bad
Were they happy or were they sad
Margaret Teather

Mighty Oak Tree

I watch you in your majesty
A lofty tower portraying might.
Your vision held by years — surveying
Our green and felted Countryside.

In splendour standing serene and strong
The core of England deep swelled in pride.
You hold within — our heritage
Of freedom lands, with rivers flowing wild.

Within your mighty wisdom
Silent, strong and true,
Are memories past and present
Of the England we once knew.

Your pride is held on high,
Each branch withholds a dream
Fulfilled by those since gone
Who trod England's pleasant scene.

As I watch you mighty oak tree
And your countless years review
I sustain and hold an ambience
which from little acorns grew.
Maureen Breckell Stringer

To A Baby Sparrow

There, almost at my feet, a baby sparrow;
A little ball of fluff with fluttering wings.
Bright-eyed; its tiny beak, half-hardened,
A-gape for the food its patient mother brings.

I long to pick it up, to feel the softness
Of its baby-down, its warmth, the beating of its heart.
To feel the little claws grasping at my fingers;
To fondle it, and hold it in my hands awhile, apart.

Ah, little scrap of life, here in my garden,
Your journey's just beginning — mine's half done.
You're welcome to my corner of the Universe,
There's much to learn ere you fly to the sun.

The world is full of beauty, full of menace.
Your little life is such a fragile thing.
But God is watching over all His creatures,
The humblest peasant to the proudest king.

They say that there's a better place awaiting us
When, finally, we reach our journey's end.
They say His eye is even on the sparrow;
You'll finish up in Heaven, little friend.

E. M. Summers

Tuppenny

She came into our lives one night
  A little ball, all fluffy and white
We made the rules that she must keep
  Her own little basket, in which to sleep
No coming indoors with muddy paws
  Or using chairs to sharpen her claws

Just for a while, we made her obey
  But, very soon she got her own way
As, gradually into our hearts she crept
  We never worried where she slept
Wherever she went she left her white hairs
  The sitting room carpet and best armchairs

What fun she had as she played with our feet
  She was clever, pretty, playful and sweet
Our "Tuppenny" was no ordinary cat
  Content to lie on the fireside mat
She'd love to hide pounce and play
  With all her antics, she'd brighten our day
She ruled us all, and felt no shame
  Home without her, won't be the same.

Vilma Paget

The Ladder Home

On the twelfth hour we return to the sea
a watery grave for you and me,
where Darwin's theories interact
untouched by society.
Sunbeams are the slides for angels
that tumble to the waves,
smiling on a turbulent fever
caused by Satan's hellish slaves.
The octopus has arms to hold us
when the sky's weight pushes down,
reflecting back the innocent masses
where our daydreams never drown.
A benevolent eye shines down at night
where all sweet heaven's peeping through
the ocean writhes in sensuous ripples
a seductive moon moves with the blue.
The day mankind crawled from the sea
to talk so we could learn,
Neptune made the tide a ladder
and on it we will all return.

Sara Hulse

The Garden

The garden tools lie at the ready,
A kneeling mat to keep me steady.
Planting and weeding, much pruning and seeding,
No time for advice or informative reading.
Hacking and trimming the bushes to shape,
Topping trees and making the neighbours gape.
Some mowing and hoeing, raking and scraping
Neat and tidy garden in the making.
Filling the black bags by the score
A Dustman has a treat in store.
The child is effervescent, full of fun
Running at high speed in the sun,
Darting here, skipping there, with much delight.
Flowers blooming, colours blending, everything just right.
All is finished, energy and money spent
At last I sit and stare, content.
But wait, have I made a bungle?
Child is yelling, shrieking, "THIS IS JUNGLE."

J. L. Gillespie

A Little April Madness

Spring-heeled; amidst a field of dreams,
a hooves-breadth from the fallen and the tragic.
Jumping past
In silks of black and green,
Competing for a little April magic.

Bouncing off the hallowed, sunlit turf,
challenging the Gods who write the story.
Necks arched,
hearts beat for all their worth;
striving for a share of April glory.

Muscles straining, lungs ache with every breath.
Overpowered by the smell of sweat and leather.
Heavy limbs
defying pain and death,
striding onwards, in the heady April weather.

Crossing the line, saluted with a cheer,
hats tossed into the air with insane gladness,
grand applause
awarded every year;
the prize for a little April madness.

Roslyn Claire Robertson

She On A Pedestal

Brushed aside on flights of fancy
A goddess on my planet's surface
Around her sun my world revolves
A centre for my eyes to focus.
I watch her sit in climates of beauty
As my eyes pierce through her satin skin
To find what lies inside, within
For beauty in the eye of the beholder
Can leave you blind, forever scarred
As hearts are weak and easily broken.
Can hold together or fall to pieces
My head is ruled by mortal thoughts
Are they shared or just one-sided?
I fear not, as my sun has set already
Casting shadows on her light.

Michael J. Kane

From The Garden Gate

The Sun, not yet strong, sends its faint light across the hill.
A gentle breeze rustles the leaves on trees that were once still.
The lush green meadows meet the fields of golden corn, and
up the hill a rugged path, well worn.

An old stone farmhouse, white, stark against the clear blue sky
offers welcome rest to the weary passer-by.
Soft lowing sounds accompany the sight of cows and sheep,
whilst in the old, gnarled oak tree an owl is fast asleep.

Trudy French

Friendship

A friend is a friend in word and deed
A friend is someone who knows your needs,
One who is there to hear your moans
Even though they have their own.

Just to be there and sit and chat
And talk about just this and that,
Someone there to share our trouble
When our problems seem to double.

To discuss weather, topics and news
And over a cuppa to exchange views,
When you are ill, you soon can learn,
That to bring you an errand is such a good turn.

But most of all, it's the friendly smile,
The warmth and feeling for a while,
That someone's there, and someone cares,
And lets you know they are aware.

Of all your problems large and small
And be prepared to share them all.
God bless my friends for all they do,
For I will, Lord, my whole life through.

Nan Booth

Creation

A purpose, something to strive for: A task that is set as a goal.
A foolhardy ambition, when to reach it exposes your soul.
All the hopes that have held you together, when your world was breaking in two:
All the tears and the fears, and the memories, the essence of being just you.
To strip away slowly and painfully, each little piece, every part
To expose to all those who surround you, the central core of your heart.

Taking a clean sheet of paper — totally and utterly plain;
Taking a half empty ball point and starting all over again.
Waiting a long time for a subject when nothing will leap into your mind,
Chasing an elusive idea around until you eventually find —
That the only thing which enters your head is the knowledge that you need
To write something special that someone else will take and happily read.

To give of all that's inside you, then dig deep and give once again:
To transcend the surface confusion leaving you open to pain;
Surpassing the fear of rejection, to proffer for distant review.
Hoping that they don't read too profoundly and see every soul shade that makes you
Relief with the knowledge it is over and returning pensively home
Knowing you'll delve to your soul again in writing the very next poem.

Trudie Ann Hamadé

The Perfect Life

Give me a quiet spot beneath the trees,
A little sun and a little breeze.
And there I'll rest when day is done,
Reading quietly in the sun.

You may have your town life,
Dances gay and bright.
But give me the country side,
There in quietness to abide.

For when the trees their leaves do spread,
All around and above my head.
Content am I to sit and dream
Of flowers and birds and a running stream.

A running stream that gambles on,
Like the music of a song.
This the perfect life I say.
In the country at end of day.

M. Binns

"Auntie B"

"HELLO MRS. ELLIS, watcha having for tea?"
A fond recollection of our "Auntie B."
One happy existence you had to forsake
sorrow, unhappiness, feeling, heartache.
Such a terrible illness that ended your life
a kind, loving mother, a wonderful wife.
Although you're not here on earth anymore
I know you are waiting close by heaven's door
One day in the future we'll meet again
there will be no tears, there will be no pain
sharing the happiness and love that you gave
a wonderful lady from cradle to grave.
The memories of you are deep and sincere
words are no longer but the message is clear
from Family and friends and especially from me
oh, how we miss you, our dear Auntie B.

M. O'Donnell

A Fragile Life

Hidden away and hard to see
A flower plays host to a bumble bee
A glance skywards, a wondrous sight
A majestic bird, an eagle's flight
Droplets of water cavort with time
To hypnotize and enchant the human mind
A membrane, a veil, crisp and new
The sunshine highlights that morning dew
The power and flight they will abide
A crest of a wave the dolphins glide
A reflection, an image, a tranquil setting
The moon over water and its light projecting
A concerto, a play, for one and all
A river cascades over a waterfall
A crystal, a quartz, a paper of rice
So brittle, so delicate, a lake of thin ice
Our spirit, our soul, on an edge of a knife
Our state of existence, our fragile life.

Mark Ellis

Lazy Dreamy Day

The rippling water sparkled in the reflection of the sun.
A fishing boat passed by causing the ripples to get bigger.
Lazy dreamy day.
Siesta time. Quietness reigns throughout the white sleepy buildings.
Fishermen on rocks at the end of a working harbour.
Ferry boats coming and going.
Wind surfers playing in reflections of sun and water against volcanic scenery.
Sand dunes pressed against the coast.
Speed boats filled with people looking for a faster pace.
Wet-suited divers hoping for the unknown discovery.
Sun beating down upon red and brown bodies.
Ferry traffic coming and going.
Fishing rods in and out of the water with bait
Disappearing at an alarming pace.
Exotic species arriving on land only to be battered and eaten.
Shimmering water glowing like white diamonds.
Lazy Dreamy Day.

Wendy Simmonds

Winnie Hat

I look at you and what do I see,
A confused old woman of 83,
No longer do you know the date or day,
Or what to do, or what to say,
You sit the day through
In your chair by your bed
What thoughts are you thinking
What words left unsaid
You win the hearts of all you meet
As you watch the world from your bedside seat...

Suzanne Baker

Producing

The size of an elephant, heavy with child,
A few twinges, the hospital is dialled,
Spread eagle across the back seat of the car,
Oh, I wish the hospital wasn't so far!

Upon the trolley, full speed ahead,
Rushing towards my maternity bed,
A woman screaming at the top of her voice,
Quick decision, pain relief was now a choice!

"Do you want to push?" the midwife enquired.
Well actually I'm feeling rather tired,
The threat of the 'stirrups' soon changed my mind,
And I gave it my best with a grunt, groan and whine.

"I can see the head!" the midwife exclaimed.
My partner hit the deck, the heat he later claimed,
One last push and we're nearly done,
Out she pops and is placed on my tum.

So here I lay stroking my baby's head,
My partner coming round in the next bed,
A new life begun for all to see,
A new life for us, now we are three!

S. Mooney

Dream Of War

Asleep, a story unfolding, a pattern,
A dream of fear as I opened a door.
A dream of dread at what I saw.
A man so thin and with a gun.

I saw him, described his empty face,
Those eyes, fixed with shame and guilt,
those eyes which knew what walls had been built,
By those hands which held that gun.

I reached to touch his ragged clothes
tried to say I wanted to help his world,
But fear of knowledge of the people being
        killed,
I slammed that door shut.

I turned to the safety of my home,
But found him there, the gun poised
And I dared to guess this world had come
to tell me of the world of war.

Natalie Russell

The Thoughts Of Freddy Cat

When we come home, in our old ford
A dark brown flash, crossed o'er the road
When the door is unlocked, and opened wide
He's first o'er the step, running inside

When you come inside, you go where you wish
Everything's ignored, that's put in a dish
And climb on the sink, for water to drink
Oh Fred, tell us, what do you really think

What food is put down, I'll sniff decide
Whether to eat it, or to leave it aside
And come back later, when I wish to eat
And finish the crisp, and dried up old meat

I sit on the sill, in the warmth and observe
The world as it passes, this my preserve
And dare any moggy, to venture on land
Where I am the Lord, and master so grand

And when it suits, I'll sit on your lap
To curl in a ball, while I take a nap
To think and to ponder, on a significant fact
As I am a she, and not even your cat

J. J. Karn

Soaring Proud

You can be whatever shape you want to be.
A cloud that sits in valleys or floats on high
Over rocky territory or calm sea
Releasing all your rainfall with a long sigh.
Of course that's the secret to being carefree,
By giving yourself the permission to fly.

Being pushed along on the wind that blows
Never straining from your aerial pathway
Always accepting all of life's highs and lows.
Joining others in the sky that gently sway.
Naturally, that is the way that a cloud grows,
Living visibly, up there, on display.

Absorb all there is, don't droop or fall,
Inflate fully, fluffy and unbowed.
So if you're black or white, big or small,
Up, against the sky — be your own cloud.
It really makes no difference at all,
Just as long as you soar and stay proud.

Peter Adamson

Riverside

The only sound to be heard is silence
A clock strikes its melodic tune
A night boat passes, disturbing
Rippling waters, alight by the moon

The air is clear and fresh
Morning waiting to burst its way through
There is no other company for us
Just a stone laid years before, once unforgotten, once new

I look across the river to a busy contrast
Time seems to have no meaning on this side
A sense of freedom, the world could slip away
Perhaps taken out to sea by the deep moving tide

We cuddle closer, enjoying contentment
These moments could last forever, no words to be said
Thoughts and feelings are all we are now
Wishes to be made and held deep in the rivers bed

I look in his eyes, I see the love he holds for me
That special man who has found his way into my heart
What life holds for him has no bearing
I just want to play a part

S. Charles

Continuity Of Love

'Our little butterfly,' my dad called me,
A child, loved by all, for the world to see.
Plain, plump and freckly was my childhood.
Their love added a sparkle that made it good.

The love received begged release,
To blow free like an evening breeze.
By trial and error it reached its destination,
A man who received all my affection.

We nurtured our love and made a home,
Our spirits free, not under a dome.
For some years we grew older together
Joined to each other but free from tethers.

Then a great miracle our God did send.
A little child for us to lend.
Another followed just ten months later.
Our home for two others was to cater.

As boys, our little glow-worms they shall be,
Each a shining light for the world to see.
Our love made flesh with our God's aid.
Our future when to rest we are laid. Love never dies.

Odette Symonds

" Nocturnal View "

From my pillow I see a heavenly scene,
   a changing fascinating moving screen,
The clouds scud round a blackened sea,
   or a Satellite passes like a star broken free,
The Poplars are swaying with Angular grace,
   their dark arms in Winter weaving black lace.

A summer's night view is lighter and brief,
   A date with sunshine the sky wants to keep.
An Autumn scene is mystic and pure.
   While Greek ancient Gods don't seem false anymore.
Jupiter's low in the heavens these nights,
   He rises with lustrous robes of white light,
And reaches the top of the Poplar trees,
   to stare through the glass with hypnotic tease.

When gales tear in and pick a fight,
   The poplars dance with all their might.
The screaming shrieking fiend flies through,
   To tear their limbs and break their fingers too.
A moaning, sighing wind, seeking branches tall,
   Throwing moving shadows across the garden wall.
   C. E. Tatlow

Untitled

As dawn releases another day
A chance to begin something new
And time to stop and ponder
On the things we want to do

We grow and learn, we build our lives
And choose what has to be
Then we stop and ponder
And wish that we were free

For those we love and care for
And where commitments lie
We can always stop and ponder
When the years will break the tie

So now the chains have fallen
And sanctuary rings its bell
Don't just sit and ponder
Run like bloody hell!!
   K. M. Precious

Deep Sleep

A candle glowing in the night,
A candle glowing lonely and bright.
A cold wind blows the candles out,
The cold wind's blowing all about.
A child sleeping innocent and still,
Everything's quiet not a sound until,
Suddenly she gasps for her last breath,
The horrible reality of the Black Death.
A tear falls from the mothers face,
Hail Mary Full Of Grace.
   Marysia McSperrin

Oxford — The Narcissi Seed

Nature is but a book in Oxford.
A cold sterile page.
Here, dawn and dusk have long since lost their meaning.
There is no given hour of rest or rise.
Even the birds sing at confused times,
What little there are of them.
Instead there are many grey, foreboding walls.
Ancient, maybe even historical,
But they are equally as entrenched in the minds of the inhabitants.
Those who leave here are the earth's weakest.
Physical strength gnawed away by long hours of study.
Squinting, bespectacled eyes drowned by words.
This is the town of thought but no real reflection.
Pages and paper are the tirelessly used mirrors of worth.
Immortality cannot be achieved by endless reading however,
Nature inevitably draws the book to a close.
   Tamsyn Conroy

This Cannot Happen Anymore

Here in bonny Berkshire, with protests every day
A bypass in the making, felled trees along the way
Tears and frustration, the weather cold and cruel
The work force and protester, prepare to fight a duel

Houses in the branches there, paths a strand of wire
Hearts were near to breaking point, their spirits full of fire
They stood peacefully protesting, their point to get across
Hands off Berkshire countryside, we cannot take the loss

They try hard to outwit each other, the felling must be stopped
They have to find an answer, before more trees are lopped
But the work force has a job, to push the bypass through
The order has been given, there's nothing they can do

Coach loads of sympathisers and sightseers came to see
The protesters' hidden tunnels, and houses in the tree
With hearts heavy laden, at the destruction spread before
Their voices rang in harmony, this cannot happen anymore
   E. K. Harris

The Bond

There is a bond between a mother and son.
A bond that can never, ever be undone
There are times you want to squeeze him so tight
And you listen to his breath, in the quiet of the night
You listen intensely for every loving word
You feel the anger of pain when he is hurt
I know he loves me and he knows I love him
We don't need to say these words
We feel them deep within
I've cried tears of sadness and cried tears of joy
But nothing on this earth will come
Between this mother and her boy
   Pam Cook

The Truth Of Love And Understanding

When the eyes are first open of a baby child
A blear is seen from a distant world
Of a belief in its new world around
To the experience to come of this life,
From stage to stage of an age of understanding as we grow in life.
A belief in the self from a world from within
Searching through the corners of time itself
As each new understanding is truly found
Oceans and seasons change in an ever decreasing way
An understanding of beauty of our wonderful planets around us.
Nature sings in its glory each day of our life
In love with growth and its death and rebirth
Of times that come and go by itself
With its truth of lovely memories that go on and on
Till time stands still once again.
Our love of truth of understanding done
It is time to move on into another sun of other worlds beyond
When the eyes of a baby open in such wonderment of what is to become
The new experience of truth love and great understanding of the new soul within.
   J. Precious

Rainbow Moods

Red conjures passion, expressed by roses or in blood —
Orange — bright, burning sunsets — atavistic flames against the dark —
Yellow tossing daffodils — gaiety greeting new spring days —
Green lush abundance of summer meadows and lovers in the grass —
Blue of skies and seas and loving, brimming eyes — desolate tears of loss and pain —
Indigo — deep, deep blue of summer evenings — the lingering aftermath of magic times —
Violet — purple pomp and regal splendour; or the humble wayside flower promising spring —
White — all colours — all hopes and fears for new beginnings —
Black — merciful sleep and rest and no more pain.
   Patricia A. M. Webb

The Chestnut Tree

The village green is where I proudly stand.
A beck runs by close at hand.
Children come to play round me,
Because I have a swing you see.

I change as seasons come and go.
In spring among my leaves of green,
Many candles can be seen.
When summer comes along I'm sad.

Sticks and stones are thrown at me,
Because I am a conker tree.
Autumn with my coat of gold,
I'm admired by young and old.

When my leaves fall to the ground,
A golden carpet is spread all around.
Winter comes, I'm cold and bare,
Snowflakes falling, everywhere.

Though I am very old,
I still stand strong and bold.
I'm sure you'll all agree
That I'm a very lovely tree.
Wendy Anita Hutchinson

Salute The Crown

Far away on some foreign land
A battle fought on sea and sand
Whose glory never to grow old
No medals won of bronze or gold
They fought for me and you, no slave
The ultimate sacrifice, their lives they gave
To risk your life, to take a chance
The thrill of enemy in advance
A battle raged on land and sea
So to make this England free
Can you imagine what the scene
To live and die for King and Queen
And for those on land and sea
So bring them back in memory
And for those on foreign soil
Pushed on and on with no recoil
For king and country, a job well done
And in the end a battle won
These few words and what they say
Remember those on poppy day.
A. Sheard

The Horse

Each passing day a story to be told
A body of muscle a heart of gold
With their grace and dignity that abounds
Their power and strength, an aura that surrounds

Majestic they stand, like the wind they run
Their undying stamina like the ever burning sun
The horse is a creature of gentleness and beauty
Loyalty that is endless to do their duty

In years gone by their valour we saw
As they served without enmity when sent to war
Without the horse there would be no great nation
No industrial revolution no modernization

Our father's before us this legacy they gave
For us to inherit to cherish and save
But far to often in this world we find
The horse is treated cruelly when they should be treated kind

So regard the horse as something to treasure
As for years to come they will give us great pleasure
For remember my friend you may be in need
And a horse by your side will be a friend in deed
W. Lister

Smuggled Inn

Stepping out into the night, drunk with ale and evil, two of a kind.
On galloping horses; through windswept moorland, across crumbling cliffs,
MUST HURRY, if we're to make it in time!
Leaving behind covered coves, though just ahead, heavy seas in mind,
but wait; not a thought spared, for anyone who's about to die.
"Wrecking" this ship is our aim, hence, our legendary bad name.

Off shore, the ship's now sunk, with travellers ruined and died.
For now we make our way for home, weary, tested and tried.
The mystery and intrigue yet to follow,
for this unopened contraband, is our profit for tomorrow.
And turning a deaf ear to morning folk talk.
"Aye" let them talk, for our ghostly secret is with us here!
That of one, not been caught,
"SMUGGLING" into and out of the night.
Paula Harding

The Rape Of Mother Earth

The earth once full of life and riches now teeters on the edges of oblivion.
Like our forefathers we squander the wealth of this lonely liveable world.
We've sucked her black life's blood from her vines and eat away her warming fuels.
We borrow the power that her elements produce in order to fill our greedy pockets.
This world is dying and who is to care this planet's last days?

I've seen many wondrous things that Mother Earth had cherished for millennia.
I have seen the rocks as old as time itself and felt humbled to be alive. Who cares?
I have seen the never ending circle of life in action all around this world. Who cares?
I have seen the beauty and ugly live together until Man decided otherwise. Who cares?
I have seen the wrath and death that power has bestowed on us.

My children may never see what I have seen, alas what a loss.
They will never see the creation as it was meant to be, alas what a loss.
They may not know the seasons as we have known them, alas what a loss.
They will ask. Dad, what did a Blue Whale look like? Alas what a loss.
They will wonder, when they read, what is the great Albatross?

The unborn generations will wonder why Mother Earth was raped and sold.
The future will ask when we are old. Why did Man have to be so bold?
What can I say to them? Has man always been cold?
People must stand up now and be heard, if this world's future history is to be hold.
I pray I never see the end, or although it may be eons away, to Mother Earth it's only around the bend.
Russell J. Baxter

The Lifeboatmen's Girls

I spent my holidays a roving
Along a railroad track,
Stopping at places pleasant,
Till I winded my way back
To my cottage in the country
High up on the hill
But I left my heart with a big lifeguard
I hope he thinks of me still.

If I return there next year
Will he be waiting there for me
Or was it just a flirtation
For him another spree
One of the many maybe
To while away the time
But I left my heart with that big lifeguard
Without him I know I will pine
S. P. Day

The Watchers

Wand'ring spirits all are we, released from life now floating free.
Let loose upon this world to roam, as sea spray separates up from foam.
And we will hide among the shadows, travel with the moon,
Glide along in darkness, starlight festooned.

You may sometimes feel our presence for we are always there.
And some may take their courage up, to see us if they stare,
As we'll be hiding in the shadows, travelling with the moon,
Gliding in the darkness; starlight festooned.

Do not try to join us, for only we are free
To float among the ones that live, and see what we can see.
Only we can hide in shadows, and travel with the moon,
Festoon ourselves in starlight, but you might be with us soon!

You will escape your earthly bondage, leave all your cares behind,
Be free as wind, be light as air, released from human-kind,
To hide among the shadows, and travel with the moon,
Glide along in darkness, starlight festooned.

Susan Johnson

Spring

Fading stars, early dawn, an owl hoots softly in the fast growing light.
Birds awaken, pheasants call, small animals rest after the wild, haunting night.
Shepherd weary, walks the hill, the dog by his side, alert and bright.
Sun's rays, sky reddens, the fields are bathed in an eerie light.

Everything waits, anticipation, an ewe lies down and grunts and strains.
Dog stands, shepherd watches, her lamb is born to ease her pains.
She relaxes, lamb wriggles, she gets up and licks it clean from bloodstains.
Lamb suckles, ewe content, the man and his dog walk back along the lanes.

Birds sing, cows low, the sun melts the hoarfrost on the thorn,
Leaves drip, hedgehog stirs, snowdrops lift their heads to the morn,
Fox barks, vixen hunts, by the end of the day her cubs will be born.
Magpies chatter, cockerel crows, hens cackle, eagerly pecking their corn.

Frogs croak, tadpoles hatch, a blackbird flies off with a piece of string.
Fishes dart, moorhen busy, then the first swallow appears on the wing.
Earth warms, seeds sprout, toadstool soldiers guard the fairy ring.
Gentle breeze, fluffy clouds, life starts anew with each season of Spring.

Wendy Simpson

Seasonal Memories

Spring has come and blossoms deck the trees, mayfly teasing the trout.
As the sun lifts high in the sky, the breeze dusts the greening leaves.
The fisherman makes his way down to the water's edge,
Graceful movement, the straight arm places line across the wind-shimmered surface,
The heart pounding, the flash of silver, fish turns to crash and roll.
Line tightens with a crack, the hum of the reel.
The trout is on, the season has begun.

Summer brings the lengthening days, hot sun blazes high in the sky,
By day the river sleeps, fish down, deep water, waiting, waiting.
Early morning and dusk brings the rise, fish to feed,
In cooling top water delicately place the fly.
A whipping tail, the fish is on, the fish is on.

The year rolls on, September dawns the hatch,
Fry glittering, shimmering, sparkling, fill the shallows,
We cast and stretch, the prize moves in to feed,
Just a few more inches, out of reach, out of reach.
We talk long into the night as the season closes,
Left to ponder and just dream the winter away.

Margaret Wilson

S-O-S

Aggression is the scourge that has society in its grip.
A disease that's spread throughout the world. There's no escape from it.
With a countenance that's ugly, this Godforsaken breed
Spits out from each contorted mouth the slime of evil seed.

Safely well embedded, richly nurtured all the way
The seeds of poison flourish with encouragement each day.
No beauty can emerge, nor all that beauty can impart.
There's nothing but the thumping beat of venom in the heart.

Right from wrong. The difference? Too well they know the score.
Fostering evil intent firmly bolts the conscience door.
Imagine each new villain — once the miracle in a cot
Destined to become a rogue. Sans fear! Sans love! Sans God!

Existence is their privilege, but they've yet to get it right.
Murderers, rapists, thieving perverts mock the gift of life.
Ambassadors of Christ can't save them. Words are just a bore.
Dear God in your wisdom, help them free the conscience door.

Their next potential victim is a constant worry — WHO?
This ever present nightmare could be me. It could be you.
The world's become a breeding ground of hatred and ill will.
The power of thought is mighty — A CONSCIENCE mightier still!

S. M. Linney

Mother's Love

I look at you and feel inside
A love so deep, so hard to describe,
Then I see those innocent eyes
And a little voice that sometimes sighs,
Two tiny hands that can never keep still,
I love you darling and always will.

A thousand stars could never compete
This love in my soul so deep.
Millions of years could come and go,
I would feel the same I know.
It's so strange what love can do,
When it is a part of you.

Many things have passed my way,
But nature gave me you to stay.
With tiny lips that whisper low,
Mummy, I do love you so.
Those words mean more than anyone knows,
Because I've inscribed them deep in my soul.

Patricia D. Gray

The Waterfall

A vibrant mineral in a kinetic rage.
A vision of beauty at every stage,
The fall imitates lions roaring,
A clump of raindrops Synchronised falling,
A magnificent sight, a glimpse of a dream,
Alive and free the mother stream,
A draped blanket, embraced by mist,
Elegantly powerful, by nature kissed.

Dawn Emma Tricker

I And...

Who are you?
It is I.
What are you?
Man.
What do you want?
I do not know.
Why do you bother me, then?
I don't know.
What are you doing here?
Searching.
For what?
What I know not.
You won't know it when you find it.
I know.

Alicja Dryszko

The House that Jacques built

Without a care and more specific
"Let's do it in the South Pacific"
She thought he meant a new position
Instead he thought of nuclear fission

A silly, rather puny man
searching for a bigger bang
To raise his flag and give him "cred"
A region cried, he snored in bed

His dreams are filled with new clear spunk
and smelling like a dying skunk
His cancer deep below the coral
This sad, dark man just likes to quarrel

He leaves his mark on Muroroa
Each time it sank a little lower
In time the World will just agree
on Jacques sheer acts stupidity

Pierre Marcar

Public School

Boredom is a sin
said the man with authority
rocking back on his degrees
which could not be denied
being a rule
and a feeling
like nearly drowning when someone lets go
they learnt not to trust explanation
were terrified by the hands in the water
but passing the test early
an acceleration of words one-laned their progress
safely directed without choice they gave up steering
but kept staring ahead
expecting directions
if you drink more water your eyes will feel better
but it was cheap white wine behind the bush that helped
brush the leaves off and let them tow for a bit

Rosamund Hall

Night Colours

Some people think that night
is the opposite of light;
some say
the opposite of day
is blue;
now that — I think, is true,
yet not just deep — pale too,
with stars — mist moon-shine silver-bright
mapping the path of the glow-worms' flight
over the dew soaked lawn.
Watching the moon —
I let night colours keep
my eyes from sleep.
Counting stars, oh, how I hope that dawn
won't come too soon.

Sylvia Cole

Dangerous Times Of Childhood Days

A visit to Grand-Ma's garden, was a visit to Paradise
Bushes with red and black currants tempting the appetite
A sandpit and a swing and roses in bloom in June.
Across the road a little girl stood longingly
and I asked her, would shed like to come and play with me?
She was ready to come, but her mother came and took her away.
Sadly I asked Grand-ma why she couldn't play
Sadly Grand-Ma looked across the way
towards he house with the yellow star
and said: "May be it was her time for tea"
Only some years later I learned the reason WHY?
I was an Aryan girl and she was a jewish child.

Gusty Cotterell

Exams

And now, heads best, with furrowed brain
the concentration hangs like a thick curtain
upon the morning air.

The leaking fens squeak like complaining spiders,
slowly, steadily, despairingly across the endless page.
For how much longer?

Hopeful eyes turn towards the ticking clock,
like varnished, peeking on the classroom wall
no reassurance there.
Relief comes swiftly unexpected from 'Sin'
put down your pencils, time is up, he says.
The relief is probable, the curtain lifts.
Lightness fills the air.

Nancy Cameron

Time For Tea

With head bent against the storm,
The old woman goes home, to be in the warm,
Key in the lock, kettle on, feet up
With that warming cup of tea.

Sunday afternoon on the village green,
The cricket team play out this summer scene,
Last ones, game over, into the club house
For a winning cup of tea.

The new mother lay back with some relief
Three babies she's had, it's beyond belief!
Relax take stock, lay quietly
With a servicing cup of tea.

Last night he had drunk too much wine,
Mouth dry, head aching, always a bad sign,
So now it's that old remedy time
A thirst quenching cup of tea.

So now in praise of tea I say
Lemon, iced, mint, cool Grey,
Sip, savour, always enjoy,
That precious cup of tea.

Kay Chisholm

The Drawback Of Security

Walking down the corridors of life
The once open doors have now slammed shut,
Opportunity's door is locked and bolted,
Success is closed forever more.

The door to despair is vacant and wide,
It screams out its desire for your presence within it,
The temptation to surrender is immerse,
You walk on with painful ignorance.

Where does this winding corridor lead,
The twists and turns of this chequered path,
The constant struggle to continue the journey,
The last turn of a corner,
The terminal end to progress.

Sarah Findlay

The Search For Happiness!

Take time to consider when you want what is right,
The right might be wrong and the dark might be light.
Think about your choices when you want what you know,
The want might be need and he stop might be go!

Don't be afraid to say what you feel,
The fear might be power and the fake might be real.
Stand up for yourself and say that you're proud,
The confused might be plain and the silence might be loud!

Don't dwell on the past just lock straight ahead,
The past isn't future and your life isn't dead.
Try not to be doubtful, just let yourself live,
You'll find all your happiness is in what give!

Amanda Aldred

Lost Love

In the house upon a hill
A big grey cloud is hanging still
The old man sits there all alone
Feeling lonely on his own
Gloomy face big sad eyes
Really sad he's lost his wife
Thinking of the things he's done
All the time through his life
In his chair he gently sways
Going back to happy days
But time goes by that we know
Months and years they come and go
To pick up pieces is so slow
Fond memories last of loved ones so
Deep in our heart they always stay
In dreams there never far away
Many happy days spent together
But now he's on his own forever

Yvonne Gallagher

After Chernobyl

They call it China Syndrome;
A new phrase:
As man limps forward to an
Unknown phase.

Will it be the same hereon,
As before?
Or earth's fiery crumbling crust
Meet its core?

Shall we still have what we love
And cherish?
Will monuments to progress
Now perish?

A moment of truth, perhaps,
On the brink.
Time for explorer man to
Pause and think.

Albert Jackson

My Final Journey

I'm going on a journey
Along a dark, dark road.
The gates of death are opening
To welcome me inside.
My heart is beating faster
My eyes are growing dim.
I'm strolling through the garden
From which there's no retreat.
I stand before my maker
To repent for all my sins.
My weary life is over now,
My heart no longer beats.
With loved ones all around me,
My journey is complete.
I've made it through the garden
And found "Eternal Peace."

Daphne Mockridge

Island

My soul is an island,
amidst seas of despair,
cut off and forgotten,
from a world that no longer cares.

My mind a burning sun,
covered by the clouds,
yearning to be seen,
to be rid of this lonely shroud.

Of my heart I cannot say,
for this I no longer control,
my only wish is that,
I'd shielded it like my soul.

D. C. Amis

Together

Please help me live my dream
And share my joy with you,
Please help enjoy my happiness,
And help my dream come true.

Please help me share my wealth,
Unselfish in my pride,
And help to share my health,
Be ever by my side.

I need you more each day,
To share my everything,
And help me share my work and play,
And cares that this can bring,

There's no one I could choose,
To share these joys with me,
And nothing that I could refuse,
Which you could ask of me.

You are in all my dreams,
Please darling let them be,
Our future life and happiness,
So full of you and me.

Robert W. Moore

Shiver

As sharp as a vampires stare,
As blunt as witches hair,
As soft as skeletons liver,
As hard as Frankensteins bolts,
They all make me shiver.

Richard Kinslay

Don't Know How I'm Feeling

Don't know how I'm feeling
as time see's me by
I don't know how I'm feeling
as there ain't a reason why.

You left me with people
people I didn't know
please forgive me,
but I had to go.

Walking down the road
in the poring rain
arriving at the airport
and catching the first plane.

I need time to think
to think what I'm going to do
I don't know how I'm feeling
feeling towards you.

David A. B. McKay

Untitled

The wind of change
Blows hard and strong,
Its force so hard behind me.
Urging me forwards - onwards - away.

I'm relying on instinct,
My ever faithful friend.
For they must not see
'Tis with great fear I tread
    What does my future hold?

From my lonely troubled past
The sadness tears and sorrow
I look for light and love.

I am myself
Accept me please
My defences are down
I'm tired and can fight no more.

Julie Brown

Number 1

The pain is still there,
but the reason has gone.
There's no point in living
I just can't go on.

I think I might end it.
to break from my chain
from sadness and torment,
unbearable pain

The love that I once had,
has ceased to exist.
And If I live on.
You will ever be missed.

Louise Condie

The Tiff

These flowers of mine
Express a love so divine.
No words can match your charm.
As your beauty abounds
To capture our minds.
No words can express
Your beauty so enshrined.
These flowers are mine
To capture your mind
With words I could not find.
These flowers of mine
To help the mind
Understand my love so divine.

David Bruce Moffatt

Love

I'm in your hand
Following you forever
Through a loveland
But could never

It hurts to touch
As you can see
It hurts so much
Can't reach for me

Anger and pain
Leave me somehow
A crying shame
Just go now

A heart attack
Love is the way
I won't go back
I'm here to stay

Part of my soul
As was never
Is in control
Happiness for ever

Frances S. Lusty

Elizabeth Our Queen

On your seventieth birthday ma'am
We send our love and say.
Here's to joy and happiness
On this your special day.

Warm and gentle majesty
In all sincerity
We trust the future holds for you
Good health, long, and prosperity.
And may god give you always
The strength to reign supreme
E'er to be
Exclusively
The worlds most gracious queen.

Maurice I. Birch

The World

The world is very wicked
Full of death and sin
Wars, drought and famine
Killing everything

Cars, roads and chemical
Destroying, all the air
It doesn't need to be this way
If people really care

The world could be so different
With love and care and fun
The land, air and sea we have
Can share it all as one

The flowers will grow
The birds will sing
People will be happy
To live and laugh and sing

This would be much better
If only it come true
The world would be a better place
For him and me and you

Emma Dawson

Conventional Boredom

Rotate,
Go round and come back again.
Irate,
No pleasure gained from anything.
Template,
Stencilled into fit your every need.
Imitate,
That which already is.
Hate,
The lack of variety and enjoyment
Of routine.

Gavin Connor

" Pollution "

Under a tree
Grass in my mouth.
Sun on my skin
Warmth creeps in.
Haze from the heat,
Blossoms and sky.
Youth and my love,
The days go by.
Horizons will fade.
Green will be grey.
Death takes my child.
Life bows to decay.
Time and despair.
Stench from the sea.
Stark stands the tree
A crone is me
Hope is a star, fight is joy.
Live while the field is green
Ourselves we destroy.

Josephine Jessup

Free Spirit

A hot air balloon rises
Up into the sky,
The flames burning brightly
Colours blending together,
Stillness all around.
Tiny dots the people
Scattered on the ground,
Freshness of air and space
of gliding peacefully now.

C. A. Morris

Earth

The earth spins so very fast
How long can this truly last.
The trees vanish before our eyes
Yet they still tell us so many lies.
It is time to make a stand
Stop them killing our lovely land.
All to soon their will no longer be
Fresh green fields, deep blue seas.
Bird singing up in the sky
Much too late to ask them why?
So stop the murder and the pain
To make the earth their home again
With so many planets in the sky
Ours is dying, I wounder why?
This is our home, it's where we live
Respect is due, it's time to give,
Take, take, take, is all we do,
Don't blame other's, start with you!!

Kathy Laver

Brief Encounter

I've fallen for your charm
I crave the magic of your kiss,
But deep within I know
I'd not be satisfied with this.

One passing glance from you
Gives me a feeling deep inside,
A feeling of excitement
That I know I have to hide.

My ultimate desire
Would be making love with you,
A dangerous liaison
One which I must not pursue.

I dare not make advances
For the fear of wanting more.
I must resist temptation
I've been through all this before.

You've featured in my dreams
Where you have been my secret lover,
But waking up I find
In truth, I really love another.

Lydia Martin

Yours

What we have shared together,
I will never find again,
A love so rare and perfect,
Will in my heart remain.

For as long as I am living.
Both here, or in heaven above,
A feeling of completeness,
I got, from knowing your love,

You are an inner part of me,
I know that is so true,
You will always be my life,
For my love belongs to you.

Although it may be over,
You need to find your way,
You long for your freedom,
And away from me you'll stay.

But I know that you'll come back to me,
When your wondering days are through,
My love is with you, where you go,
And my heart, it waits for you.

June Cornish

In Years Gone By

As I sit here
in the winter sun
with my gloves
and barnet on
I think of all
the days to come
When winters done
when gardens with
there flowers bright
awaken in the
morning light
of summer days

It's times like these
we give thanks
to be able to see
old natures franks
and think of all
the things were missed
in years gone by.

Douglas Parley

The Garden

The garden is a private place
 it's red and blue and green.
The wildlife in its mattress
 is rarely to be seen.

The water keeps on flowing
 with a sparkle and a gleam and,
the sun beams shine upon, it,
but yet they stay unseen.

It watches.
 as we ponder and,
it see's our lives devour,
It's here long after us,
 No man is a lover, and
when our lives are over, and
people are all gone,
All things will be natural,
 as the garden ventures on.

S'phen Anderton

Longing For Peace

Echoes of wails,
Lingering sobs,
Heart-rending once more
Timorous yearning
Deep and thirsty,
Red-tinged with yesterdays.

Marianne W. Calderon

" Dancing — Free "

As I look upon the sea,
Sparkling, moving, dancing free,
Washing peoples, shifting sand,
Bringing seaweed, to the land,
Little pools you leave behind.
Filled with life, that are not mine,
You could tell of many things,
Of sea gulls nesting, on the wing,
How since time, and world began,
Your waves have washed, and shaped
The land.
Oh mighty sea, where do you go
When from these shore's you leave,
How free you are, you have no cares,
You travel far, I know not where,
But you'll come bark again to me,
Sparkling, moving, dancing free.
And I shall know, just as today,
That as with time, you can-not stay.

La'Verne Truscott

Alone

Being old and all alone,
no one there to call your own
a house of silence no one calls
I'm a prisoner in these four walls
Oh! Why does not one call?
I hear the people rushing by.
No one cares if I live or die.
No one to say goodbye,
when I take my final breath
How sad to be alone in death

Barbara Pinches

Urban Birds

In the early morning wake,
The birds the first to arise,
Filling the sky,
The silence of the city,
Awaits the sleeping madness,
As the birds fly fleetly,
Seizing a chance from repression,
To sing on the wing,
Before man starts his engines,
A hollow cry,
Through streets so virgin,
A mating call,
Is ever certain.

Paul Cruickshank

The Face

Do not ask to see
The face beneath the mask;
For why should we reveal
How we are made.
Do not remove the stars
or braid which hide
The filth beneath the gilt.
These are warm so we
May keep what we have got.
And seem what we are not.

J. M. MacAuslan

Untitled

Beauty is a sunset
The river as it rushes to the seas
A snow capped mountain top
With the sun like gold running down
Beauty is a proud black horse
Free has the day it was born
Galloping along happy
And free, splashing,
Through river and stream
Then a shake and a
Neigh has though to say
It's good to be alive
That's beauty

Jean Gill

Abduction

The taking of a body
The taking of a soul
The ruining of emotions
The cells of fear
The splitting of two souls
Sheds more than a tear
The endless searching
Never to be found
You'll never forget
When the bond of emotion
Has been wound.

Laura Mitchell

Untitled

Rain on my window
The world's way of crying
Despair in my heart
For the innocent dying
People who govern don't know
Where to start
Time and again they all
Play a part
Children are crying
And pleading for peace
What an insult to
Our future youth
Different religions
Different creeds
But always a few
Where hatred breeds
If I had a wand
I'd wave it about
And instead of the rain
The sun would shine bright.

R. Lamond

Snowdrops

They hold their heads high,
they fling their arms low,
like tall ballerina's,
they sway to and fro.

The curtains will open,
as each new dawn,
on their icy stage,
these ballerina's perform.

The breeze is their music,
choreographed by each bird,
pretty ballerina's, to the chorus,
pirouette, unheard.

Just one more finale,
these dancers can't stay,
till their debut next year,
hide their dresses away.

Andrea Palmer

Ponder This

It's funny how the clock beats
Time that never lasts
Seconds, minutes, hours
Now they are the past
Precious time is wasted
There's always more in store
What happens when the clock stops?
You're dead forever more
So grab every opportunity
Let nothing pass your way
Tomorrow's for the lucky
At least you've had today.

Heather Johnston

Untitled

Where did you go?
To your God's
To the spirit's sacred?
Who will know?

No more your own.
They took your lives.
As warriors you fight on,
No-one could take your pride.

When do our angels come?
Our guardians, our spirits,
The wise ones that taught?
They are still whispers, old shadows,
Our gift from Mother Earth.

K. May

Rina O'Roses

As I put pen to paper,
to write a poem,
I heard the 'phone ring.
My mind had been
on our blossoming love,
but now it was completely blown.
The voice in my ear
was telling me you'd gone,
That your restless breath
had finally flown.
It blows through me now
stilling my heart,
Scattering the blossoms wide apart.
Crushing their petals,
and releasing your scent.
The voice becomes an echo,
Mine becomes a scream.
Where will my love go now?
But into a scarlet dream.

Thomasin Penny

Wondrous Things

Do you ever stop to think of the
wondrous things you see,
The daisy white, the rosebud pink,
The lovely greenwood tree.
Do you ever stop to look at the
wondrous things around, the
soaring bird, the babbling brook
where marigolds abound.
You've often heard what people say,
That God moves in a mysterious way.
So just you stay a little while
To see HIS work in every mile,
For then I know what you will say
Where'er you go, GOD is the way!

May Allan

Optimism

Out of the sun,
And into the rain,
Out of the joy,
And into the pain.

Out of the day,
And into the night,
Out of the dark,
And into the light.

Once there was darkness,
For so many years,
So much sorrow,
And so many tears.

But this is the time,
To begin a new,
There is so much to change,
And so much to do.

Forget the past,
And what went wrong,
Think of the future,
And you can be strong.

Simon Taylor

Untitled

I'd like to be a flower.
I'd like to be a flower,
red in the face, alive.
I'd like to be a flower,
magnificent, oblong.
I'd like to be a flower,
alive, forever.

Diane White

Miracles

Tiny Baby
Born premature
So many problems...that's for sure!
Heart a bit dicky
Operation tricky
Chances of survival...poor!

Years ago
Now History
Hundreds of Babies died in Infancy
Lying there all bare
In modern Intensive Care
Being kept alive artificially!

Incubators
Special Ward
Overhead a Damoclesian Sword
Staff as a Team
Realizing a Dream
Full recovery will be their Reward

Mary Scott

Untitled

Whistling kettle, Frosted lawn
Early Morning, dark to dawn

Days of wonder, full of sun
Clouds and thunder, one by one,

Gutter puddles, dammed and muddy
Sticks for boats, watch them hurry.

Rides on horses falling leaves
Clifftop walks, creamy waves.

Blooms of beauty, open wide
Taste the tears when I cried.

Rainy evenings, where to go,
Flames and embers softly glow.

Know the love of folks who care
Remember always in your prayer.
Days of Childhood
I was there

G. Harrison

I Wonder Why?

I wonder why the sky is so high
I wonder why flowers blossom and die
I wonder why those tears that we cry
I wonder why birds fly so high

I wonder why stars shine so bright
I wonder why we have day and night
I wonder why life passes us by
I wonder why we live and die

I wonder why new born babies cry
I wonder why we say goodbye
I wonder why life is so great
I'm glad I wonder before it's too late

Marilyn Willats

Spring

The coming of spring
Is a wondrous thing
With bulbs springing up all round
The birds they are singing
And all of them wining
Back to their old resting ground
White clouds in the sky
Swans on the lake swimming by
Young children at play on the swing
The air filled with laughter
That hangs on every rafter
We can enjoy the coming of spring.

Daisy Wilson

That's Who He Is

I tell you he is....

He's the graceful bird up high
He's the coral of the deep
He's the colour of the crisp snow
He's the twinkling stars so high
He's the strawberries in the tort
He's the smooth silk chocolate
He's the speed of the cheetah
He's the guard, like a dog
He's the gem in a coal mine
He's the graceful swan swimming
He's the ripefulness of a deep red apple
He's the soft feathers of a tiny bird
He's the breeze on a galloping horse and
He's the only key to my heart

That's who he really is.

Cheryl Whyte

Untitled

Oh little Jumping Joan
Is your heart made of stone?
 You have not writ me!
Mail boats still plough the sea
No cards they bring for me,
Aeroplanes fly to and fro
But "letters for me?" No!
 Joan has not writ me!
This wife so wonderful
With heart so bountiful
And ways so dutiful
And face so beautiful
 She has not writ me!
But as I write I see
The post-clerk come to me
His pack is filled with mail
It falls on me like hail
 JOAN SHE HAS WRIT ME!

Colin Siddons

Jewels Of The North

Northumberland is beautiful
People come from near and far
From Canada, Australia
To see our jewelled stars
They come to see our castles
And also the Roman Wall
They come to see our Abbeys
The bridges and Keilder Dam

Have you ever stopped to wonder
How all these things were built?
The men of old, of yesteryear
They toiled from dawn to dust
So we must cherish all they did
Because they did it, just for us.

Audrey Turnbull

'Coming Of Age'

As a child, I lived at home
Went through many a phase,
Had an admiration for a Pop star,
But that was just a sudden craze,
As I grew older,
Wanted to do something new,
Parents interfered,
And replied, we tried telling you,
As I lived under the same roof,
I had to do as I was told,
Once I reached the coming of age,
On me, they no longer had any hold,
At the coming of age,
I could leave home, and go,
Of course I would keep in touch,
Because I love them so.

Jacqueline Esme Twine

The Galloping Major

In ninety-one the British nation
Travelled to their polling station
Back to basics was the theme
It turned out to be a dream

Public spending cuts increased
No more money was released
The lottery was introduced
Again the public was seduced

Cardboard cities were elected
A result of policies by the elected
Unemployment was allowed to rise
This was no surprise

With fewer policemen on the beat
Crime increased upon the street
as waiting lists began to swell
The sick suffered when unwell

Mr. Major was the modern day Robin Hood
The people believed he would be good
But he robbed the poor to help the rich
After taking over from the b****

A. D. Taylor

Grampy

"Make a cup of tea".
Was all Gran said to me
When she found old Grampy dead.

She stood and looked at him,
Lying there dead and thin.
She wiped her hands on her pinny,
From her pocket took two pennies.
Placed them gently over his eyes.

"He was a good old man", she said,
"Now he's dead."
"Chris, where's that cup of tea?"

I learned something of age;
Loss and resignation,
As we both sat there not crying.
"His watch is yours now lad,
Don't take it bad."

"Thank you for the tea."
Was all Gran said to me.
Then she turned, and straightened her dead.

Dee Whitman

A Granted Wish

Laughter, smiles and a happy face,
A room of books and toys,
A destined dream, a destined wish,
So full of girls and boys.

Every night beneath these stars,
I dream, I pray and wish,
that one day, someway somehow,
I will receive your kiss.

We were all the same at once,
in the nest we did all live,
but now I'm just all alone,
there's nothing to me you'll give

At night I cry and sit alone,
in tears of salt and dust,
but no one come to comfort me,
So my cry now turns to rust.

So now I lay asleep at night,
in my dream without a kiss,
Still praying to God above,
to send 'A granted wish.'

Ruth Elizabeth Price

You Can Always Count On Me

When the sunshine has gone from your life.
When you're down and filled with despair,
Don't ever forget you are never alone,
There's one certain someone who'll care.
I'll do all I can to help you along
And with you your heartache I'll bear.
There's one certain someone you can always turn to
And all of your troubles will share.
I'll give you my shoulder to cry on,
For your worries I'll lend you an ear,
I'll give you a smile to help make life worthwhile
And help soothe away that sad tear.
Yes! I'll do all I can to help you to see
That life is worth living and one day there
Will be, a beautiful rainbow, a life bright once more
I'll help you to knock upon futures door,
So don't despair if at present you're low, there's just
One thing I want you to know.
We can't control fate, what will be - will be
But you know you can always count upon me.
   B. Reynolds

A Birthday

I do like having birthdays,
for it gives us all the chance
to stop a little minute,
to be grateful for the past.
The pleasures we have had with friends,
are only just a few,
we should be very thankful for all the things they do.
We argue quite a bit at times,
When one is always wrong,
but make it up when the one who is right
is never very wrong. The time goes past so
very quick, when one is getting old.
What memories we all do have, and many
tales are told. The times have changed quite
a bit, since we were all so young, but
"Oh" dear me, I am so glad, we won't forget
the happy days, the laughter and the fun, as we
travel on the road, since our life begun.
   Frances Findlay

Marching Angels

We knew that they would go one day
And with them they would take
A little piece of each of us
In their golden suit-case.
The angels they will dine with
And fine wine they will drink,
And live in peace for eternity
And of them we shall think.
And every day of remembrance
We shall pray for you,
And hope one day the children will pray
For us as we did for you.
   Kelly Oakley

Paper, Chain

School began, you found me
life was cool, we were free
You took me in your arms
I was baffled by your charms
A paper chain you hung around my neck
And a worthless ring you placed on my finger,
And asked me to wait for our wedding day.
Still this paper chain hangs around my neck.
And this worthless ring on my finger
And the waiting is the dying
When you just feel like crying.
   Sarah Louise Spencer

The Lonely Child

Walking, walking,
Waiting, waiting,
Waiting for someone to ask
If I might play.
Find a friend
Meet them, greet them,
Loose them
When they choose
Another heart to be broken
   Tara Faruque

A Kissed Shadow

One friend in this world although only one,
A kiss forever held in my palm.

Forced to stay this one cannot leave,
Cry prays a voice in the wisp of a breeze.

He dances with me she hears all my dreams,
This shadow I told isn't all that it seems.

It understands me and all that I feel,
A secret disclosed his lips are thus sealed.

If a cry to a lover I entrust my whole heart,
Knowing not any other through she knew me from the start.

To hit her to cry to scorn with disgrace,
I feel not afraid for he has not a face.

I pour out my heart it understands me,
But answers me not and alone lets me be.

Figurative eye, sees more than sunbeams,
Beyond golden sunlight a shadow holds dreams.

Lazily cool and always to be,
A friend when I need one who understand me.
   Oneetta Reynolds

Bread — Stuff Of Life

Mother's baking! Sniff the air,
A warm and comfy smell is there.
Children run and wash their hands
Drag up chairs on which each stands.
Laughing faces all aglow,
Each is given a lump of dough.

The fun they have, the shapes they make,
Hedgehogs, mice and now a snake.
Hours pass before they're through
Dough takes on a greyish hue.
Works of art rising on a tray
What a tea they have that day.

Smells the same, all safe and warm.
Bread takes more conventional form.
Now I'm kneading all alone
But what a memory store I own,
I am content, my spirits rise
As suddenly I realize
I was shaping children's lives!
   Pat Stobbs

" Mum "

Mum, I want to thank you for the life you gave to me,
For the way you cared throughout my tender years.
Not only as my Mother, but also as my Friend,
Always there, to share my laughter, pain and tears.

Now you have left this world behind, you've found a better place,
And we on earth who love you can no longer see your face.
But we never will forget you Mum, our love will never die,
You'll always be a part of what we do,
Your memory and your influence will guide us through our days,
And in all our actions, we'll remember you.
   P. Gibson

Brief Encounter At 8-3 Hrs

I?
Am I?
Qui
You are you
Hand? Fist?
Non
Doigt!

A protest against France's
Decision to "press the button" testing
Nuclear warheads in the Pacific.
A.T. is the chemical symbol for astatine.
A radioactive element, half life 8-3 hours.
The natural element contrasts with France's
decision to play God.

Alan Warrander

Memories

I love the little village,
And house where I was born.
The old mill by the stream, alongside the waterfall.
The sound of rushing water,
And thud of the old mill wheel
Many happy hours and pleasant memories.

Autumn with her golden hue.
Harvest and the morning dew.
Leaves falling carpet the ground.
Squirrels I see scrambling around
Collecting their food for winter day
Scenes like these and many more
Are put away in my private store.

I remember the winters cold and grey,
The curtains drawn at the end of day,
The lamp was lit it was coy inside,
Brasses shone In looked with pride,
Around the room to the other side,
A china dog winked in the firelight glow,
These are the memories I will always know.

Muriel Hanson

Untitled

I gaze at the garden which mother planted with such love and care
And memories of my dear mother, come's floating along there.
I gaze at the chair, where mother used to sit.
The tear's in my eye's are hard to dismiss.

Whom would have thought when mother left us alone,
How much we would all miss mother so, the smile mother smiled
When I was there, whom could have thought
Of the pain that the cancer caused, that my dear mother bare.

Now it's a few years since mother has gone.
But the memories of my dear mother, still linger on.
Of the kindness and love that mother gave,
Silently went with mother to the grave.

So I pray to God above, that God will take care of our beloved.
In God's care mother has gone to rest.
In God's garden of love mother's laid down her head.
God had given us one of His best.

Brenda P. Spencer

My Fairy-God Mother

Always ready with a comforting word,
helping through everything that I have fared
Ready to take my troubles all away
Guiding me back to the road if gone astray.
Someone to tell my feelings and hopes to,
Someone who will never lie, and always be true
Someone who will always be there,
And that someone will always care.
Whatever I feel and whatever I think
I know that my heart will never sink,
as long as I've got you to help and offer cover,
no-one is dearer, kinder than you fairy god-mother.

Helen Seiga

Mud Lark

I stepped off the path in the marshes
And sank right up to my knee,
My dogs thought I was playing
and decided to follow me.
I thought they were ripe for disaster
For I was literally caught on the hop!
But being lighter than me (who isn't?!)
They scampered around on the top!
Whilst trying to pull my foot out,
My Wellie became quite stuck.
I hauled it out two-handed
Completely covered in muck!
As I balanced one-legged to clear it,
They gambolled around me with glee,
Then toppled me into the quagmire
And gave me a mud but for free!

Ann Harris

The Human Race

Created out of dust, the Universe unbleached
    And the Worlds; like beautiful jewels, floating
In a black wide void; were unleashed;
    Twisting, turning, falling, never ending.
Heaven, controller of this galaxy, you
    Your own computer commands: all obey.
Faultless: Except, for the Human race, who
    Live in a bottled up world of egoistic play.
From the day man is born, he exists
    For one thing. Perfection or destruction!
Himself, his maker, everything that subsists
    Within his own fulfilment or corruption!
Nature is for him, a creation of playfulness
    To love, destroy at will, its very eminence.
Not until his own strength and subtleness
    Has been matched against the fervent elements.
    Then will he see, the horror and futility.
    And rise triumphant: Atonement for all eternity.

Colin A. Shepherd

Memories

She sits alone on a summers day.
And watches the children as they play.
It seems that time has moved so fast
Leaving happy memories of the past

Those happy days when she was gay
And all things seemed to go her way
When she had thoughts of eternal youth
But soon found out it was not the truth

She hopes someone will call today
on this lovely morning in May
Listen someone comes up the stairs at last
What a disappointment they've gone straight past

She settles down in her old armchair
And tries to remember when he was there
He has been gone for a long time now
And had always been true and kept his vow

Thoughts of him just fill her mind
Oh to leave all this behind
She feels a flutter in her breast
And slowly settles down to rest.

Jean Seton

Disharmony

When you look at me, you do not see
your eyes are empty, distant.
When you are closed, I have no key
to open up old feelings once so instant.

I do not understand why we are not happy.
I do not believe this is true!
I look at you and I feel so snappy
I almost dislike the whole of you!

R. Sanders

Untitled

How about the guy, who swallowed a fly
As he was eating an apple pie
He started to cry
Thought he was going to die
The last thing he said was bye bye

Tom W. Styles

The Baby

At twelve o'clock we were of to line.
At three o'clock on the production line
At five o'clock little Ashley did cry.
At ten o'clock in the pub in July.

We go to bed with a hot cop of brew.
Knowing we'd be awake by two.
When dawn, arrives we realize
We just can't open our weary eyes.

I now think it's time for me to discover
Just how this birth has left her mother
As we lay in bed, I start to feel
That she does certainly still look ill.

We always went out and had a drink
But now it's sometimes we're always skint
Never mind, said the in laws with their little bit
We will always come around and baby sit

But now when all is said and done
Little Ashley's life has just begun
One thing we know all else above
We are devoted to her with all our love!

A. G. Harper

Scars

When some friend has proved untrue
Betrayed your simple trust
Used you for their selfish end,
And trampled in the dust
The past with all its memories and all its sacred ties
The light is blotted from the sky
For something in you dies.
Bless your false and faithless friend, just smile and pass along
God be the judge of it, he knows the right and wrong...
Life is too short,
Don't waste the hours by brooding on the past
His great laws are good and just,
Truth conquers at last.
Red and deep our wounds may be
But after all our pain
God's own fingers touched us and we are healed again
With faith restored and trust renewed,
We look towards the stars
The world will see the smiles we have
But God will see the scars.

June Walden

The Man In Black

At my back - the man in black - follows where I go, and every night by some street light - I see him laying low.

Just like a ghost - by some lamp post - I see him hanging round, he's never heard - don't say a word - and never makes a sound.

Sometimes small - sometimes tall - a master of disguise, he shadows me - but I can see - and wonder why he tries.

Thin or fat - just like a cat - he follows me around, left or right - he's there each night - like some tracking hound.

Side by side - in front behind - this phantom keeps space, I strain my eyes but sly and wise he wont reveal his face.

But one night - filled with fright - I stopped to lay him low, then turned to see - that it was me - casting my SHADOW.

Down on the street - out of my feet - this phantom seemed to grow, it was no SPY - only I - casting my SHADOW.

Tony Springham

Spring Morning

Virgin white snowdrops flecked with green,
Carpet the lawns with a luminous sheen.
A rosy dawn, a fairy mist,
And daffodils in a golden drift.
The violets shy, the primrose fair.
The trilling of birdsong filling the air.
A bristling hedgehog, a small furry vole
And dark earthly mounds from a burrowing mole.
Diamond dewdrops on gossamer webs
The sweet scent of morning as winter now ebbs.
Frothing pink blossom on apple trees tall,
These innocent pleasures I love above all
O happy heart, o glorious morn
Life spring anew and I am reborn

Pauline Williams

The Ways Of Sun

Leading me down a patch ever winding,
Chemical cadavers and celestial infusions
Swirl and frolic among the lilies;
Chasing their shadow makers
Where angels fear to head.

Floating through the milling cruds
Drowning in bloodstone finery and words unspoken,
I grease my lips with the sweat and tail
Of any souls I crass,
Where angels fear to head.

Ministers of darkened delight do haunt me,
Whispering words drenched in the wailing echoes
Of suppressed divinity,
Guiding the willing
Down that path ever widening....

Stacy Richardson

Just After Sunset...

Just after sunset on a bleak Norfolk
coast, with sky orange against the waves
I met a stranger on the beach
A moments hesitation then a second
of courage was all it took a quiet
excuse me, may I sit?"
to meet a stranger on the beach
The sea sounding upon the stones,
hungrily drawing them down, we spoke
of nothing.
Just two strangers on the beach
In an hour she was gone and I
sat alone, words and smells and the
sound of the water lingering
a memory of the stranger on the beach
How long will I remember her and her
me? It matters not, but we were there,
then and will always be
just two strangers who met on the beach.

D. N. Ring

'Pay Her Homage'

The mighty wrath of a turbulent night, sparing not a soul,
Cries unheard from shores nearby, drowning hopes and fears.
The enigma of a tragedy passed, concealed within the shallows.

Enshrouded in the ocean bed, she lies in deepest slumber,
Pieces of a greater form, the flow of time suppressing.
Those bygone days and distant lives shall all now be perceived.

High above, a shaft of light, the weather is permitting,
The beauty of her tranquil state, revealing all with ease.
The search begins, they touch and see, OH! This precious gift of wisdom!

Now, let her rest and pay her homage. Peace with all at last.

Cathie Whatmough

My Only Love

The rain was, pitter patter on window pane,
Darkest of days, looking out of the window
There was joy in my heart, war is over
Suddenly flowers in the garden was full of bloom
Then came my sweetheart soldier boy,
Coming slowly, down the path
In his hand, was a beautiful, bouquets of deep
Red roses he was limping, that did not matter
To me he was home, and I had waited so long
I ran towards him, arms outstretched, my
Undying love was hear at last, home to stay.

Elsie Wardle

404 Days

One day, one week, one month, one year, I thought we would last forever, but you felt stifled and I was the one who had to suffer your restlessness and discontent, we lived and laughed, learned and loved, weaving a myriad of memories for comfort in our absence. But somewhere beyond the love I thought you felt for me, came creeping doubt, nagging and gnawing at the tenuous threads that held our hearts together, until one night your discontent enveloped you, suffocated you and wrapped itself around you like a shroud, and you severed them completely.

When the stars chase of the last remnants of a summers day,
I remember walking hand in hand beneath the twin towers of the Pans, the rivers of silver cascading down the castles granite walls, the nights spent carousing at the Sorbonne then lying together in the dark listening to the Tyger's Cage, the sketch I treasure of two little creatures bathed in misty moonlight she was weeping, why was she weeping?
Did you know then how much you were going to hurt me?

Time has eased the pain of missing you, wanting you, needing you, my first, my only true true love, you drove me into the exile of another's embrace, then I had a taste of discontent, of feeling trapped and having no sense of self, and bitter it was, bitter it was.

Sandra Taylor

Painting

This evil substance, this bitter gall
Hath lain too long in my icy soul
Rejection, anger and loss
Festering in a murky pit possessed
Possessed by the shame and guilt
of a shattered childhood
Uncontainable no longer the abomination surfaced
Red blood lips spewed out a sickness of
bile-green hatred and yellow jealousy
Painting the devil out of my system
Every orifice overflowed
Blood letting and disgorging
spilling out an unwanted life
It fell onto the pristine paper
Begging for shape and brightness
Colours sobbing for release and explanation

Sandra Sandford

Entropy

Now I've travelled so far, I only desire
to travel back to where and whence I came.
Since creation where I was made, I was projected
out ward in the initial great beat.
Cyclic oscillation always the same.

Human endeavour to defeat my beloved,
wanting to go outward, to escape from gravity
even reality, or to bring about change.
My only desire to stay the same, to retrograde,
achieve wholeness, to escape from this game.

J. Manning

Down And Out

In a dark, cold alley lurks a mysterious man,
He lives in the cardboard, stealing food where he can.

He searches through bins for scraps of a lifestyle
Now removed from his own, but physically less than a mile.

He trudges the streets looking for some salvation,
Amongst world of people who still believe in their nation.

When winter draws in he steals wood for a fire,
Desperate for some warmth, his situation is dire.

Everyone sees him on their way to work.
They step over and around him ignoring the smells that lurk.

He's in a never-ending circle with little hope of escape.
This is what it comes to in his emotional rape.

Not criminally minded, just driven to despair.
Stealing to survive in a world that doesn't care.

He could die tomorrow but no one would know.
His body decomposing, death gives him a home.

Jill Simpson

The Watcher In The Woods

Crouched in the leaves of the yearly book,
Hidden to all in the forest of days,
Know that it waits there, haunting its nook,
Only thing real amongst shadowy ways.
Its form has long been known to us.
Clothed in seasons hues,
A mantle of April greens, or winter greys,
And summer azure blues.
Such everlasting beauty, in root and branch and buds
Hides the face of malice worn by
The watcher in the woods.

Along the dappled woodland pathway
We know the lurker waits,
And chance to meet it every year,
But fail to see its face.
Can we delay a final meeting?
Hide fear neath cloaks and hoods?
And teach our children well to ware the watcher in the woods.
Heedless we may seek it, but few dare to try,
That sleepless woodland watcher that we call the day we die.

Ivan Wolstenholme

Fragile Peace

The peace we are having here to-day
is in our hearts and minds
a peace that's filled with doubt's and fear's
and a hope for better times

We know not what this peace will bring
or what it will achieve
in our heart of heart's we want this peace
but we hope it won't deceive

Genuine peace is priceless
and sought for from the heart
if it is to stand a chance
we all must play our part

And to the pollution
be genuine in your stand
this peace is very fragile
that you hold within your hand

Treat it with respect
and handle with great care
like a wilderness gem
it is precious and rare

Frank Scott

My Winter's Dream

As I gaze into the garden on a cold grey winter's day
I look at all the dreary things that winter brings our way
Like fallen leaves, dead plants and weeds and trees that are so bare
It seems to shout, please help us, is there no one who will care.

So I close my eyes and dream about the bulbs that will appear
I see the plants and flowers grow and it soon becomes quite clear
The grass is green, old leaves have gone and the trees begin to sprout
In the garden life begins again and the birds are all about.

As days go by the sun comes out, the garden lives again
For all it takes is a little warmth and some very gentle rain
From white and pink and blue and green to yellow red and brown
The garden is alive again, wearing its summer crown.

And now that summers really here my dreams have all come true
For what was once a dreary grey is born a riotous hue
The bees are humming all around, the birds are singing clear
So now my dreams are put to bed, until Winter comes next year.

Judith Rogers

How Do I Love You?

How do I love you? Let me count the ways.
I love you more than you could ever know.
I love you like eternal break of days,
Sometimes the passion is too great to show.
My heart will race with the warmth of your touch
And your love for me makes the stars shine bright,
Like gleams of a glow-worm; never too much
To love you as far as distance of sight.
I love you as I need the warmth of sun
To warm and light up my life with such grace.
I love you like a knot; never undone.
I love every detail true to your face.
  As long as we are both here together
  Our love will live forever and ever.

Lynsey Provan

A Slob's Philosophy

Being clean and tidy is no thrill
I think it's making me quite ill
Fresh elegant life is such a job
So I'll laze around and be a slob
And tidiness is work and boring
So I'll stay in bed and keep on snoring
Get up at noon and have some tea
In a dirty mug then I'll watch T. V.
Some day I'll wash up, polish and clean
Can't find the vac. in this messy scene
Can't be bothered to wash and dress
I'm fed up with this smelly mess
Back to my bed. Woke up at dawn
My rain-washed garden made me reform
So spring clean, shower and shampoo
My house is now elegant and I am too
I think of my garden and the sweet-smelling flowers
And the time that I washed in lazy hours.

Kay Williamson

Lost

The moment I met you
Your eyes reached deep into my emotions.
The moment you touched me
The provocation disturbed my soul.
The moment you held me
My frozen boundaries melted.
I cannot begin to rationalize,
I cannot begin to understand
The breathlessness I'm feeling.
It's like stars have collided
And the rivers run dry,
The moon has fallen
But the sun's always high.
I'm losing my centre
I'm losing my mind
I've lost my heart.

Lynne Roberts

Life's Timepiece

A swinging pendulum moves the time
Introducing and hourly chime.
It counts the days, the months and seasons,
Has numerous numeric reasons.

If we keep it fast, do we live as long?
If we keep it slow, are we then still wrong?
Let's keep it right, it tells the truth,
That with each tick it spends our youth.

A face on every mantelpiece, in every bedroom dwells.
On every steeple holding back the tolling of the bells,
Ding dong, tick tock,
Sound away my life o' clock.

Slow or fast or running true,
Yours may run longer than it's due.
I hope it does, and mine as well,
How I hate the tolling of the bell.

J. B. Fowler

Grief

Silent grief and moments of sadness
Now I shall never see him no more
Fills my heart with aches and sadness
But I can still see my love at the door

On his face the worry is no more
Filled with tears mine eyes run over
At each change of wind I tremble
But still I see my love at the door
Of he would kiss my lips in parting
And as our bodies touched
We said I love you very much
But still I see him at the door.

For when God called my loved one
He had to go he cannot care for me no more
He is so special to me
But I can still see him at the door
I do hope one day we will meet in heaven
But I wish I could be sure
Then all my prayers would be answered
And we will both be at that door.

M. A. Clark

To Marc, A Most Devoted Son And Brother

There's so much we remember about your ways
  on all these long and lonely days,
your smiles and laughter to name a few
  our memories are endless when we think of you.

Day by day you thrived to give
  how we wish you'd been allowed to live,
there is one thing you'll never know
  how it broke our hearts when you had to go.

We'll never know the reason why
  oh we wish we could have said 'good-bye,'
we've cried so many endless tears
  you gave us seventeen wonderful years.

Were we being greedy expecting more
  wanting you to stay the eldest of four,
you were far too young to have to die
  so much more you had yet to try.

Our lives are empty now you're not here
  we will never forget you, that is clear,
nothing can mend this broken heart
  since that tragic day you had to part.

Barbara Skillen

Life

Life can be a weave of confusion,
one split second of joy can crumble
into a fragment of sorrow.
But this miracle of life will begin
a new tomorrow.

With eyes a wide, we absorb all around is.
The love, the joy, the pain surrounds us.

Life is to see a child in laughter
the eyes that tell a tale of a distant life yet untold.
We begin not knowing what comes before us.
All we hope is hope.

We often wonder why there is an end to our beginning
for this we are not yet wise.
I hope this precious gift from god to us.
will end with peace in paradise.

C. Rampello

Maggie's Message

Sitting in my rocking chair,
Rocking to and fro.
Quietly thinking to myself,
Where did the future go?
Past the age of sixty-three,
How much future's left for me?
So when I pop my clogs one day,
There's something I would like to say
Life is like the seasons of the year
It sometimes makes you shed a tear
So don't weep for me when I'm dead
I was happy in the life I lead
And when I'm gone remember me
With kindness and goodwill
I tried my very best to see
And your wishes to fulfil
To all I may leave behind me
Put past grievances behind thee
Look after one another
That will be the message from a loving wife and mother

M. B. Wright

The Lovers

Be it night or day,
Shades of twilight grey,
Shadowy lovers on bed entwined,
Rapturous movements in kind,
Soft spoken words of love,
Touches as light as a doves,
Filtered light gives off a hazy glow,
Music plays soft, so slow,
The song increases in speed,
As does the lovers passionate need,
Crescendo of heavenly delights,
An implosion of orgasmic delights,
The breathing stills, time to sleep.

R. Banham

Symphony Of Love

What is this, I'm feeling inside.
Is it power, or is it pain.
Or the passion, running through my veins,
The fire, in my soul.
Or the Beating, of my heart.
In dreams, at night.
And thoughts, in day.
Are rushing through, my head.
Is this the, symphony of love.
Or the symphony, of pain.
This the love, that will remain.
And won't tear, my soul apart.
Or the lonely, thoughts.
Wont rust, my heart.
The symphony, of love.
Will forever, last.

Colin Rowan

The Telephone

Silently you sit there on a seat of your own,
Silently I sit here feeling so alone,
There's nothing on the tale that I wish to see,
What wouldn't I give for some company,
Just a word or two would pierce the gloom,
But there you just sit as remote as the moon,
The nights are so long, when you're on your own,
I thought you would help me, not leave me alone,
I've tried all my friends, but no one is there,
The families away, so I can't try there,
Then loud is the ring, a summons at last,
Would you like new windows the caller asks,
Politely I say, sorry but no,
And reluctantly let the caller go,
Again it rings and I jump up to find,
It's a girl selling papers that's on the line,
Still it's a word or two so I can't complain,
Maybe I'll be lucky if it rings again.

M. G. Clements

2000 Years

I have lived my life among the heather,
Since I just saw light of day,
I've held this rugged heathen land,
In the bosom of my eye,
But now my days are numbered.
I look more closely on
The cruel and blind and vicious,
That natures wars have won,
The rising swell, white mountain tops,
Engulfs the splintering wood,
And night and day blend into one,
As tortuous deeds are done,
And yet does man for man's own sake,
Play God upon the land and sea
And did a fool or genius
Say war would set us free
Whatever man has said or done
Is lost along the way,
And when the next millennium come,
Will nature have to pay.

M. E. Boucher

The Grey Suit

All was fine when I tried to retire,
spending my time by the living room fire.
The books I'd save over many a year,
brought some joy and the odd little tear.
The coffee and cakes were ever handy,
life was great and I felt real dandy.
Over the months all the jobs got completed,
the coffee and cakes never depleted.
To a family wedding we got invited,
the wife and I were really excited.
On the day of the wedding I went to get dressed,
the grey suit I'd wear as that was the best.
I'd had a good shave and a nice hot shower,
the suit hung there, complete with a flower.
The shirt and tie were soon in place,
next the trousers, what a disgrace!
They slid up my legs without spoiling the crease,
on reaching my waist all movement did cease.
Coffee and cakes had caused this I know,
so back to work I know I must go.

Frank Reast

Kindness

Give a little kindness wear a gentle smile
These are the small things that make life worthwhile.
Take time to help neighbours listen to
Their troubles life doesn't pass you by but
Friendship doubles so spread a little
Kindness has you pass along life's way you
Will be rewarded you will need help yourself one day.

J. Skelland

Hostage

Can you imagine reaching for a telephone
Switch on a light that's not there
Squint with your eyes, in the darkness a sigh
On the map of the world you're somewhere
And you feel like you're stuck, left to rot in a hole
And wonder who cares, if you eat shrink or grow
You're sure they're asking questions
The friends that you knew
But there ain't no directions, no hidden clues
And you feel like a rat, in a hole
Don't you just know what freedom is
When you're tied in a cave, with a lift up lid
Where the darkness stays and there ain't no days.

Is that voices that you know, you feel like a rat in a hole
There's lenth on your finger, nails rough on your face
And a change of clothes wouldn't feel out of place
But you know there's salvation, and you know that there's right
And you squeeze your hands till the blood runs white
And you feel like a rat in a hole.

E. Skinner

Redundancy

Sixteen years overcome the fears
The anxiety the nerves and the politics
Starting again leaving the friends
The colleagues and the comfort zone
Feeling alone unsure and doubting
The knowledge the skills and the judgement
Achievements awards successes forgotten
Past glories distant memories fading

Hit by the axe had to make tracks
Facing the fear the facts
It happened it's true could happen to you
Sacred! Not any longer

Now made a start given me heart
Finding my feet feeling the part
Working again making new friends
Swelling with pride no need to hide
The memories inside

Dignity respect growing stronger
The past is the past the futures ahead
Life now worth living fears put to bed.

Paul Sainsbury

The Life Of Man

When man first ventured out from his cave,
Thinking himself so superior and brave,
He searched around for a better life,
Often only leading to trouble and strife,

The further he went, the stranger it got.
Meeting other cultures of a different lot.
Taking from those of another race or creed,
Only being concerned with feeding his greed.

Man began to think that it would possibly be,
Is more peaceful life in a land over sea,
Finding the reasons as before once again,
Bringing with him his destruction and pain.

Taking, not giving from life and the land,
Often only turning the soil into sand,
With dear mother nature he abused and toyed,
Will he only learn when the earth is destroyed?

To save himself he must forget the past,
The cost a worthy price if he finds at last;
A world out in space where the human race,
Can finally live together in a peaceful place.

D. Tonks

Untitled

I often sit and wonder, and look o'er the years I've trod.
Thinking I often could have done better, for my maker God.
I have done so many silly things, that I know was not quite right.
It makes me so down hearted, these regrets I have to fight
I have helped people in their troubles, and lent a helping hand.
But still, I feel I could do better, before I reach the promised land.
If all my little mistakes, was to make my life seem all uphill.
It would not be worth living, my life would be at a stand still.
What I have done is past with, I can't put back the hands of time.
There are people in this world, would give their life for mine,
Still I'll try to do much better yes! I hope, and I will try.
Take like as I find it, never crumble never cry.
Then I should be happy till I die.

Mary Winton

Born Again

Whilst the life that I lead is dark and so deep,
thoughts of a past life come flooding through.
How can I feel, how can I see, I live in the
past do you not see.
A stormy day in May or June, a raging sea
full of blackness and gloom.
Has I stand alone at the edge of my doom
The wind in my face, and my heart full of ache.
Why am I here? What have I done, I see
only shadows, that pass then are gone.
The past that I know is ascending, now also is gone.
I can see a light now at the end of a tunnel, coming
Nearer and nearer and ever so brighter.
No memories now for it is all over,
I am born again and live my life over.

Trevor Smillie

Getting Old

Section of people, reaching retirement, regard themselves as old.
Time to sit in their arm chair, not attempting anything bold
Watching the world go by, thinking they've done their share
Now it's time for them to rest, taking every care.

The other section, looks at life, in another sort of way
Getting up and above, enjoying themselves, every single day
Taking up dancing, which they never even attempted before
Never realizing, how lovely it was, gliding around the floor.

Getting old, doesn't mean dressing, the manner, your parents used to do
Wearing drab clothes, straw hats, even old fashion pantaloons.
Make sure you're dressing in the mode of the modern style
Keeping young at heart, being active and always completely agile

Make sure, you do the things, you've always dreamt of doing not
meaning, jumping out of planes, climbing mountains,
or even canoeing
Enjoy the travel, holidays, dances, and theatres, life being so short
Always remember, the principles of life, which you have been taught

Get out of that chair, still feeling you're young at heart
Show the younger generation, in this world, you're still a part
Enjoying every moment in your life, that you have led.
Life being not fair, and you are a long time dead.

F. W. Fricker

Untitled

Many troops came o'er the sea,
To help us keep our country free,
From a vicious enemy
I was proud to serve with them,
On a air force station
They were very good comrades,
A credit to their nation
We were bombed, both day and night,
But always felt victory was in sight
Many now lie in their grave,
They were the "Bravest of the Brave"

W. Hammond

Reflections

We walked through bracken, heather and stone
Walking together tho' our thoughts were our own
The sky was grey and heavy with cloud
So too was my heart, clothed in a shroud.

Wondered did we without any reason
The sun broke through betraying the season
Where are we bound on this journey thro' life
Me with my husband, he with his wife.

Freedom to live? Freedom to grow?
We reap the crops the seeds we sow.
Jennie Rumford

" This Life Of Ours "

Some folk just live from day to day,
Well maybe it is best that way,
And not to thinks about to morrow.
Only joy and not of sorrow.

For life is very short, you know
So lets be happy, wherever we go.
A friendly word, and a pleasant smile,
Will make this world, of ours, worthwhile.

So lets be thankful, and grateful too,
For this gift of life, He gave to you.
And as we journey, on our way,
Lets give thanks, for another day.
Catherine Watson

You Can Always Count On Me

When the sunshine has gone from your life.
When you're down and filled with despair,
Don't ever forget you are never alone,
There's one certain someone who'll care.
I'll do all I can to help you along
And with you your heartache I'll bear.
There's one certain someone you can always turn to
And all of your troubles will share.
I'll give you my shoulder to cry on,
For your worries I'll lend you an ear,
I'll give you a smile to help make life worthwhile
And help soothe away that sad tear.
Yes! I'll do all I can to help you to see
That life is worth living and one day there
Will be, a beautiful rainbow, a life bright once more
I'll help you to knock upon futures door,
So don't despair if at present you're low, there's just
One thing I want you to know.
We can't control fate, what will be - will be
But you know you can always count upon me.
B. Reynolds

Little Feet

A little Cottage by the Sea.
Where most folks would like to be.
To see the waves so high and strong,
coming in so fast
Feeling the water sweeping round your feet.
To feel free as a bird in song.
The breeze whistling past your face
Not a come in the world.
Only the sound of the Sea.
So peaceful, and yet so quiet
Maybe it's because, there's no pitter patter of little feet
Could it be, that's what makes the world to-day.
Little feet little laugh of children.
Who get under your feet.
Non one these only me. Alone
all the children are grown up now
with children of these own.
M. A. Turner

Everyday War

Why do they do it
Why don't they care.
About the leaves on our trees.
And the birds in the air.

Do they understand the fighting
Do they understand the war
They know it too well
For they've seen it before.

Why can't they stop this selfish greed.
For Power, Lust and Money
Everyone deserves a life
To cherish without worry

Will this war ever end
That we suffer everyday
Maybe now is too late.
The Doves have flown away.
Tina Price

Spring

A maid she is, so fair, so sweetly shy,
With golden hair, and crystal eye,
And joy she harbours in her breast
To warble from the blackbirds nest

Her hands so deft, so neat, her heart so pure.
Her gentle feet shed soft allure,
And sweet enchantment surely lingers
Beneath the spell of her green fingers.

Each night beneath the moon, she combs her tresses,
Pins there a golden star, the while she dresses,
And Jasmine and Daffodil
Capture the gold for my window-sill,

Her flimsy robe she spreads, like fairy queen,
Upon the sapling branch, all warm and green,
When fleecy clouds drift down to see
Her mantle on the willow tree.
Ivy Whitfield

That Special Corner

He stares at me, and smiles away,
With his rosy cheeks, sits day by day.
His gentle smile, his glowing face,
But never moves from his place.

A white shirt, always clean,
His striking tie, 'oh how he gleams.'
A glowing blue stays over his shirt,
Not one speck of dust, nor of dirt.

He stays in his corner, night and day,
He's handsome in his own little special way.
Not a movement, nor a sound,
Not a blink, or his heart to pound.

Just sits there smiling, forever and more,
Not a face as handsome or as sure.
His gold edge rim, his shining cover,
Yes, it's that picture of my little brother!
Marianne Sillick

Stardust

When handfuls of stardust cover the skies,
A lonely girl stands on a street corner,
Her outstretched hand reaching for happiness.

To touch the stars would wipe away the pain,
Her body strains with the effort,
But her plight is useless.

The expectant fingers that succeed
Are scolded for their trouble
And scarred with the reality of rejection.
Elanor Endersby

Recklessness

Can you tell me why people drink and drive?
Would then my Father be alive?
"I am sorry"
"I didn't mean it"
"What do you want me to do?"
"Can you bring back my Father?"
No can do
I miss him. I love him but who can I tell
'cause Daddy's not here through my misery and hell.
Just mummy and me left to get on with life.

As I was young. I was an award of the court
No money in this world can my Dad's life be brought.
If I get married who will give me away?
These are the questions I ask myself everyday.
So stop and think before you drink and drive;
Next time it could be someone you know either dead or alive.
As they all say "Life is too short"
For a life that is lost is lost forevermore.
Davina Williams

Brad

Today I asked you for a kiss
You said "No, sweeties."
I said "No, sweeties."
You said "No kisses."
And I laughed a lot.
You just smiled, but there were no kisses that night
Tracey Short

Increase The Peace

Increase the peace, the army say
You'll be back in Catterick, one sunny day
The war will have ended
The wounds will be mended
And children will be back at play.

Increase the peace, and live as one
Your lives can't be ruled by the bomb and the gun
So please stop the shooting
The fires and loathing
Remember the old and the young.

Increase the peace, the country is yours
Things never get solved by these terrible wars
So why do you fight
By day and by night
Two wrongs never make a thing right.

Increase the peace, the guns will fall silent
But things will not be as they were
The trust will have gone
From the old to the young
Because of this terrible war.
David Ratcliff

Football

Football is a game of passion,
a game of respect,
a game of pride,
this is something that a supporter will never forget.

To see your team perform well,
and to get a good result,
is like nothing you've ever wanted before,
it's as if you are part of a religious cult.

When you've witnessed one of our players score in the top corner,
you feel a cold shiver down your spine,
I can't explain the sheer delight,
it's just something out of mankind.

I choose never to forget,
the moment that you know you've one the game,
that's another three points on the table,
how I've never felt this way, of a restless day.
Anya Dunne

Forgive Them (They Know Not What They Do)

Last night I dreamt a dream of a black gulf of yearning.
A greying man stood on a solitary green hill in the depth of night.
He was alone, as he had been all His life: why no-one come to Him?
A blanket of once pure snow lay about Him.
How the birds had danced in joyful gaiety, leaving their imprints!
But in the gloom of night the savage wolves crept, baying for blood.
Now the gore hides their lacy patterns and beauty is diminished.
The man looks up in silent prayer.
The wind still whips about his waning bones.
So still he stands amongst a noisy world of haunting cries.
If only our decaying humanity knew this man,
How we would rejoice!
Yet, this man calls for his last day with unprecedented eagerness.
And so the skies grows stronger and whips at His humanity.
Slowly, but surely, the rain drops gush to earth
And He is free, at last.
I look back and see how the silent years have crept by.
I look to the heavens and whisper my humble repentance,
Safe in the knowledge that I am heard.
Clare H. E. Jenkins

Escapism

Drinking, escapism, that's what it is,
A way of coping, when things are a miss.
It lightens my mood, and eases the pain,
Of unfaced problems, it keeps me sane.

I can't be assertive, I'm weak and shy.
Drink gives me confidence, I don't know why.
It changes my persona, it makes me bold.
I'm a different person, I know, I've been told.

Anxieties subside quickly, when I'm tipsy in drink,
I'm carefree, relaxed and don't have to think,
About the pressures of life, that I feel everyday.
Temporarily, reality has faded away.
Kathleen Mcmahon

Love

Softer than silk, the plume on a feather in a dove's wing,
Yet wonderfully swift, the soft dark arrow on a wild sky:
Strumming the wind, coming plunging home.

Humble the worm in a squirming burrow in the pasture,
Silently turning the hard world over to be fruitful:
Which cannot resist the soft, persistent plough.

Wayward the tide, caressing the beach and leaving
Rhythms in the sand, to glisten, abandoned and listen
For gulls' cries urging the restless, surging return.

Soft is the shoot, sprung from the root in a grey town,
But marvellously strong, the long slow thrust to the sunlight —
Cleaving the stone, relieving the concrete siege.

Cool is the skin to the tip of a touching finger.
But eagerly within, the senses thrill into turmoil,
Rocking the sun, thundering over the edge.
Christopher Dandy

The Tempest

A distant days of thunder rolls incessantly
And lightening flash illuminates a threatening sky
The someone clouds await to unleash their fly an undulating waters
Dark storm clouds gather at enormous velocity
And break upon the waters shattering its serenity
Coercing to bend it to the will with ruthless savagery
Protracting, roaring, screaming waves with daunted melody
Whiplashes the forbidding rocks which gouge the leadened sky
Where screeching gulls re-echo with abandoned torturous cry
A misty mantle weaves its cloak wound the murphy creek
Where unseen dangers but among the foils of the deep
When ocean fathoms, mercies their inmost secrets heap
From waving souls upon their wakes
And challenge all who seek to be its master,
Alas, no one can tame its arrogant sway.
Until suddenly, the storm abates and dies away and all is peace
Wendy Holford

Untitled

Come here my brother, come and take my side,
All lo on the game and the fates are our to ride,
On this day we will surely taste success or defeat,
Dogs and cowards may run, but we shall stand and not retreat,
The skies are black and the power of the thunder can be felt throughout the ground,
And on the earth, blood and death lie nearly all around,
But come closer my brother, come brother take my hand,
A pact of strength let it be, for us to defend our land,
For I know you not, and have never seen your face,
But such strong silent actions define your nobility and grace,
Country men are we and I love you with all my heart,
Together then, together, and lot us into this bloody ballet depart,
And now as the noise of battle, its tortured song has begun,
My thoughts turn to death, has the race of my life finished its run,
For if death calls my name, and from this day on I will no longer live,
Then I will taste the bitter poison, and for my people, my life I will give,
For if, with my countrymen side by side together we will stand,
Then no death will I find finer, no resting place so grand,
So come here my brother, come and take my side,
All is on the game and the fates are our to ride.
Malcolm McAndrew

Escalator

Converging and closing in from every side
All races, black, white, yellow, brown.
High booted, long-haired moppets,
Men with the morning paper,
Women in head-scarves.
Conveying
downwards
Conveying downwards.
Perpetual
motion
perpetual
motion.
Drone like
to hive
Streaming
streaming spewing
faceless humanity
into the long, low labyrinth
Of sunless, subterranean passages
To meet the endless roar of the trains.
B. M. Coles

Will You Be There?

When clouds of evening cross the sea
And breeze of summer waves goodbye
Last lonely flights of humming bees
Go homeward with a dying sigh.

The golden haze of the amber sun
Lost to the warmth and firelight's glow
It's then those memories start to come,
Those thoughts of mine you'll never know.

Thoughts of pleasures, long since gone
Of childhood dreams and wandering ways.
Of falling leaves and shadows long
And happiness, - just sunny days.

Touching a raindrop on a grassy blade
While all of life reached to the sky.
Those gentle bells in woody glade
In blueness covered, light misty dye.

And if those times should come again
When evening falls on glistening sand.
When shadows paint the lonely lane
Will you be there to hold my hand?
Joy M. Baker

Why Me

Sometimes the road is heavy
And burdens there are many
We often think that life's unfair
And we've more troubles tan our share
We ask ourselves "Why Me"?
When maybe, our neighbours of troubles are free
Yet when were in trouble, and we feel in need
We take them to God, at considerable speed
And he gives us a gift, of a beautiful peace
We never ever want this peace to cease
The gift of peace is perfectly free
It's there for life if we could but see
The Troubles we have, is not our loss
It's a privilege to help Christ carry his cross
Winifred Finnigan

Pain

In my life I've always felt lonely
and down
no-one to play with
or run around
All I needed was a helping hand
they abused me more than I could stand
I had no-one who cared
my pain was never shared
no-one I could talk to, to say
how much I hurt every day
no-one to hear the secrets
that gave me all the pain
trapped in abuse
God only knows how I kept sane.
Elaine Barnard

The Innocent Of Youth

I see the children playing, with the innocence of youth
And it hurts me when I think, that someday they'll learn the truth
For now they look so happy, their little faces are alight
And though it causes pain, it is such a pretty sight

For their eyes are aglow, they have nothing to conceal
So they play and laugh and sing, and tell us what they feel
You can read each single dream, and they're so eager to learn
It's a shame things have to change, but the road will always turn

When young everything is easy, and hurt never seems to exist
So hence when a child smiles at you, it is so hard to resist
As once we all were young, our heads filled with foolish dreams
But as we grew up we learn, that life is rarely what it seems

Which is what will surely happen, to all those children in the park
Their zest will soon diminish, their eyes will lose that spark
For there's always a disaster, of that we're all living proof
But it's nice before it happens, to enjoy the innocence of youth
John Dadds

Stuck

All good see bad,
All bad are proven,
The proven are right, yet wrong.

Our lives spin to the beat of the core
Our hearts are as red as apples.

We disappear then return, like a Godot,
Are we real? Are there others waiting for us?

The chance that the clutch is cut is slight,
We are doomed by duress, the Goddess of destiny

The oracle ordains our path,
It is unavoidable
We are destined, doomed and drained.

We are all one bead upon a string,
We stand with the stamina of snails,
We fight with fortitude for freedom.
Samantha Jayne Watt

Promises

Now, the memories that we shared have been destroyed
And the promises we did not keep, I've cast them away as lies.
Is it true that all the good things which we possess aren't
    made to last
And that we lock away our childhood fears in the safety of the past.

So, now I've broken all the bonds we forged throughout time
And hidden all the sadness in the corners of my mind.
If only I'd have had the sense to cherish what was mine..
Instead, the good times that we could have shared have long
    been left behind.

If nature has the power to destroy her own children
And offer up their ashes to be blown upon the wind.
You know, it can't be right to call an end to our own dreams
And throw away the chances that lie waiting at our feet.

But when the dust has settled on my weary body
And my last breath fades alone into the crisp and cold night air.
Maybe then I'll rest and crush my own creations,
Resign myself to eternity, give up the fight and forsake my
    hopes and dreams.
   Jon Morris

Lost For Eight Years

Do you now cry for us,
as our hearts break for you?
As we walk close by,
tears from heaven fall.
Young and brave we know
nothing of your life.
Yet hire we stand with aching hearts,
Looking on your stone,

Can you see us, do you know
a grandson proud and tall?
Searched and found your dying place,
and homage came to show.
For many years you laid alone,
felt forgot, unloved, uncared,

You're wrong, we care, we're part of you.
Your sorrow we now share.
   Linda Anne Adams

Spring

The air is filled with the scents of spring
as the earth from its troubled sleep
push the tender green leaves to the sky above
where a waiting sun now peeps
For this awakening is a miracle that only God can make
so that everyone in this universe with eager hands can take,
a share of these joys that please the eye
and fill our hearts with love
makes everything in life worthwhile, has come from his above,
Like the tinkle of the laughter, from a child who is running free
From the cold dark days of winter, these belong to you and me
and to look on a tiny newborn life so fresh from its mother womb
is lent to us from the cycle of life, each year, but goes so soon
so enjoy this spring in its newest gown, and the earth in its
    sweet parade
hold out your hands and take your fill before this miracle fades.
   I. Gallimore

Tara

Bedraggled, starved, shadow of a hound
Attached herself to Susan Homeward bound
Pathetic look from hound, and Susan's copious tears
Allayed sue and the hound's greatest fears
Banishment off — adoption on
Rollicking, frolicking, pestilent hound
Loving the folks in the home she has found
Gone is the gentle, pathetic glance
She now leads everyone a dance
And dog and cat look on with horror
At this cheeky incomer causing all the bother
   Margaret M. Benny

Hopes Dreams And Wishes

Frozen raindrops caught in midstream
Ashes for wishes, lost are my dreams
A lifetime ago my dreams were young,
flowering bright in the promised sun.
Anticipation now vaporized,
as sun on the dew.
Lost in a whirlwind, all that was true.
Normality stolen, laughter all gone.
A star off its course,
is the hope that was strong.
Yet hope cannot die,
if it does, so shall I.
   Shirley Franklin

Untitled

A young boy lies bearing pain and cold
At home they say he is brave and bold
As he lies on his stomach in mod knee deep
His eyes are heavy through lack of sleep

His sight remains in just one eye
He looks around at boys who lie
In mod face down for their glory and fame
At home no ones hold of the pain

Of blood and shooting all around
of dead men next to them on the ground
Shoot to kill is their law
For there's no room for sentiment in this bloody war
   Tracy Joynes

My Tree

He stands against the bitter wind, battered, tired and grey,
bayyards howling all around. Day after endless day.
There's nothing to protect her, gone is her dress of gold.
It lies there in the dirt below.
Beauty turning to mould.

And then one morn it changes, the sun is bright and warm.
She lift her head and day by day a miracle is born
wondrously and slowly, she done dress of green.
With head held high she stands there regal and serene.
The days get hat, the winds die down.
There's not a breath of air
but standing tall in her wide green dress
there's shade for all to shore.
Then autumn comes and again her dress
turns to red and gold
she's flamboyant. She is brilliant
waiting for the cold, cold chill ah winter
when once again she will be.
A dark forbidding giant
my old oak tree.
   Olive Blanch

India

The pulsing rhythm of the tom-toms beat
Blends with the shuffle of the naked feet
While the shrill harsh cries of the dancing girls
Rise and fall as the wood smoke whirls

Faster and faster with ecstatic speed
Bodies writhing with primitive need
The men's set faces and staring eyes
Glimmer like stars in the blue black skies

On and on with unceasing tread
While madness of passion throbs in the head
On yet on and the glittering moon
Sweeping toward her own high noon
Sees man and maid as a throbbing mass
Black in the shadows of the swaying grass
Then India turns on her side again
Breathing a sigh of animal pain.
   George Crosby

A Love Dove

Guns a blazing, hells a raising,
bodies falling, souls a calling, from their graves
Warriors craving blood from mortal men.
Politicians safe in their dens.
In the noise.
a bomb it falls,
to bring with it the silence rules.

In a burning flash of light the bodies fall.

On the ruins of a building, a dove sits.
Flapping its wing, it rises into the air.
Higher and higher.
As it rises the destruction it increases.
Higher....
Buildings and bodies turned to dust higher....
The machines of man now crumble, turn to rust.
Higher.....
With every desperate flap of its wings, rises
Still their is destruction
with a final flap of its wings, its heart sinks,
for it can see no more.

Steven Fox

'Tis Here I Rest

'Tis here I rest, no comfort in the floor,
But in my company, I pour.
Embracing me, evoking dreams.
Precious, was how it all seemed.
The void induced allows my thoughts to reel.
My eyes close.
I roll back,
And all again I feel.
Days when lain beside me was a different form.
Different company. Sensitive. Soft. Warm.
Again that careful tender touch. The passion.
Emotional delight, found in such, caressing exploration.
Traced in tongue, this voyage of discovery.
Moistened lips, fragile fingers, to love each inch of me.
Seduced by memories,
I slip beneath the wave.
Until,
From this contented sleep,
I find, I have to,
Wake.

Julie M. Chivers

Seasons In The Garden

No matter what season, or what time
A garden is a place sublime.
It yields all sorts of wondrous things
And a sense of well being it brings.

In summer such wonderful colour
Carpets of flowers, making life seem fuller,
Green lawns and lovely trees,
Making shade and swaying in the breeze.

Autumn too is a lovely sight,
With rustic colours, a sheer delight
The garden is going to sleep for a while,
Until it's time to come forth in style.

Winter, that too is a lovely scene
A carpet of white, when once there was green
The frost on the branches sparkles and dances,
The whole winter scene, that sparkle enhances.

Then comes spring and bulb tips are showing
The grass is growing and so we start moving
The plants are fed, with soft warm rain,
And the whole year cycle has started again.

M. Kidman

Where Oceans Roll

I stand alone upon an empty shore,
Calling your name. A futile cry,
For you are now beyond my reach,
Intangible, obscure.
Pearly white pebbles slumber in the sand,
And sea birds fly.
I lift tearstained face to endless skies,
Hoping to glimpse you there, beyond the blue.
Nothing; but sun streaked cloud, currents of air.
Tangles of seaweed float beneath the waves,
And seagulls cry.
Capricious cool sea breezes touch my skin;
Familiar fingers in an unforgettable caress.
I feel your spirit borne upon the wind,
And clasp your memory close;
Comforted;
Where oceans roll,
And sea birds swoop and fly.

Barbara E. Martin

Garden Of Dreams

Walk up the pathway to the pink blossom beams
Cascading gracefully in the garden of dreams
Fragrance of roses the sweet smell of love
Towering to great heights in the trees up above

The silence of spring giving life all around
Parading its beauty without a sound
Summer madness arrives scorching everything in sight
Praying so hard for the coolness of night

Slowly it returns the gentle autumn rain
Giving back the smiles by removing the pain
Winter marches through spraying everything white
Pride and courage stand tall with all their might

Awaiting the season with the golden reams
To unwind itself around my garden of dreams

Julie Jackson

Our Gran

A born fighter-that's our gran
A tough one — now that's for sure
Even though there was no cure
Our gran will always remain so pure
She shined like a star
With a shine in her eyes
Because she is our star
Who fought so far
She fought to the end
With her own intend
Because she was determined
For her life not to end
Even then she still
Fought to the end
Because our gran
Was a fighter
Right to the end.

Gillian Tait

A Poem About My Mum

From her 30's she suffered pain.
But hardly ever did she complain.
She was so brave right to the end.
But I really thought that she would mend.
I now know why she had to go.
Even though it hurt me so.
It was best she only suffered for a short time.
But now it is such a hard climb.
Back to a life of happiness.
At this very moment life seems one big mess.
I know she would want me to carry on and cope.
Not just to sit around and more.
There's one consolation - you took her quick.
Because at the end she was oh so sick.

M. A. Dale

The Almighty One

I think things that always have been
Does it really matter where we have been
Cause all the things that we have become
Isn't greater than the almighty one
The almighty one being the earth we live
can also be the one that gives
If we don't treat it quite that well
it could become our living hell
for what it's become is our fault
so don't bloody shout, it's not its fault
I've seen the world and it's seen me
we've been so bad to it
it wants to be free
it's seen the misery of all we have caused
but what it's to gain is always our loss
it gives us air so we can breath
so why cut down all the trees
to cut down the trees we will not see
the a for the bus of eternity
Alex McMullen

The Family Tree

Families are like a fruit tree
Just waiting to be ripe to fall
The mother tree still standing
To keep an eye over all

But as the tree gets older,
And fruit itself starts to bear,
Baby fruits take over
And the old tree is left standing there

Now and again, it's replenished
With 'good tidings' from its yield
We all gave many 'good tidings'
To that tree, in the field.

But sooner or later, the tree has to fall
The fruit rise up, and we all stand tall,
We've cared for the tree for many a year
But now, quite sadly, it falls..... with a tear.
Pamela Margaret Pletts

Family Of Faith

Sisters of sole solace hold the Bible in their hands,
Knowing that their father is the one that understands,
Brothers of convention hold their crosses upon high,
Knowing that the answer lies way up above the sky,
Mothers of deception hold the secret deep within,
Knowing that the sinner is the man that has no sin,
Standing knowing nothing, faith is hope that when I die,
I will find the answer lying up above the sky.
Bill Bartlett

Sands Of Time

As on my pillow of rest I lie,
On wings of thought once more I fly,
Back again to those Gallant bands,
Who gave their "all" on those deathly sands,

They did not from their duty shrink,
Nor did they stop to say or think
But across the desert sped,
To meet the "hordes" that Rommel led,

They want no praise or gloried fame,
Their graves "doth seldom bear a name,

Their only wish I knew to be
That "England ever should be free'
And as the sand of time is spilled
'My span of life near fulfilled"
Alone I sit with time to spare,
My thoughts will flee back again
 To the old company.
A. Matthews

Roy

"Laugh clown, laugh
Even though your heart is breaking"
The words of a brave man,
Who knew his life was to be taken,
Although always a smile to show a friend,
From ear to ear until the end.
But don't be saddened by the present,
Only gladdened by the past,
And look forward to the future with joy not tears,
He's no longer in pain but in peace at last.

Although I did not know him,
I've read and heard and cried,
For the pain which he went through,
Should have been denied,
He was a caring man to others,
Even helping to the end,
No-one did not like him,
He was everybody's friend.
Sharon Clink

My Thoughts

As another teardrop falls from my eye,
Everything gets blurred,
Smudged into a world of unknowing
Waiting for someone to come and
Take them the right way.
For most go along the wrong road,
Of hurt deceit and pain
Wishing they could turn back
But they have come too far go on
What could get worse?
Night is drawing in
Time is running out
As our lives fade into the mist
Existence is unreal
All life is gone
Never to be seen again.
Natalie Mooney

Your Son

It's a boy, a precious gift, a joy,
For all to see, a perfect little boy.
Full of fun and laughter shining out,
Curious and giggling, running about.

Eyes sparkling and cheeks aglow,
Screaming and crying to let you know
He's teething now and it's a pain
It could almost drive you insane.

He's your baby, you love him dearly,
The best you want for him clearly.
He's growing fast, (Crash!), now what's he done,
Don't be angry, after all he's your son.
Christine Phillips

Ingratitude

By water's edge with rod and hook
All night I'll happ'ly wait
For fresh caught fish just cast and look
Till fishes take the bait.

By river flowing, moonlit, bright
I sat and stared and I did wish
Until at last they cared to bite
Some not so big fresh fish.

Walking home with giant strides
Great food she will prepare
My little basket breakfast hides
With wife and kids to share.

My wife delighted me once more
Of steaming fish a plateful.
The ones she purchased at the store,
At least the cat was grateful!
L. Wiszniewski

Unicorn

Is the sadness of your eye
For your own demise
Or is that tear for my breed
And the knowing of their need

It is my understanding that make
me so sad
To know the truth cannot be had

Why should you have such understanding
and not
Let me take your horn.
For my fake purity and blind eyes

To take purity means that the pureness is lost
To take beauty means that you are blind
To take innocence means that you are guilty
Forever seeking what you cannot find

Then show the eyes of my heart what their
have been shown always
And let my man's mind find what it already knows
That it dose not need to take what is already given,
And love is all that need be shown

Frank William Morrell

Oh Not Again

The lead, oh not again.
Doesn't she know it's going to rain,
My feet gets wet, my feet are cold,
It's just too much, I'm getting old,
I do not want to go for a walk,
She'll only stop and stand and talk.

It'll be the park, the shops or river,
And I except I'll just stand and shiver,
I'd rather lie beside the fire,
It's just too much to expect of me,
I'm much too old now, can't she see
My paws feel sore, my back just aches
And when it's cold, I get the shakes.
But no it's walk time again,
Through the sun, snow or rain,
If I could speak I'd let her know,
This walk business has got to go,
Just leave me here to lie and sleep,
Let her go out, all on her own,
While I stay here, and wait, at home.

Hazel Webb

Sometimes I Think You Really Don't Like Me!

Dad! Why oh why, do you get so stroppy with me?
    Don't you like me, or are you just angry?
    Mum wins when you argue, who do you blame?
    Me of course it's always the same!

Mum! Why oh why, is it me, that changes Lucy's diaper?
    After her bath it's me who has to dry her!
    Sometimes I think you should go to school, and I
    Stay at home, I even have to do her hair with the comb!

Nan! Why don't you ever come to visit me?
    It makes me feel kind of unhappy!
    Why doesn't Granddad come with you too?
    Doesn't he like me, or is he fed up with you!

Aunt Ju! Why are you so stroppy and you don't talk to me?
    I'll make you listen, just you wait and see!
    Why don't you bring Uncle Gary too?
    He's much more fun than you Aunt Ju!

Uncle Bill! Why oh why do you shout so loud?
    You're like Thunder coming from a bursting
    cloud! Why does everyone put the blame
    on me? I'll stop them someday, just you wait and see!

Lisa Amy Leonard

In " Loving Memory Of Sam "

Here I sit broken hearted.
From my SAM, I am de-parted.
Where he's gone, no-one knows,
perhaps a wee vodka will soften the blow.

It was last Monday, he went astray.
I just thought he'd went out to "play".
After all, it's near Halloween,
And to get a "girl", he'd be quite keen.

I'd let him out, his "oats" to scatter,
But he'd always re-appear, no matter.
It's plain to see, without "ifs" or "buts"
He's gone a little further, for his "nuts".

So if you're out there, SAM, take heed,
Forget about your lustful needs,
And stay well clear of that "brazen, hussy",
For the bottom line is, your "SALLY'S PUSSY'

B. McCormack

Watching You Grow

Sleeping baby, there you lie.
Full of love and adoration for you lying
there, so innocent and so true.
I look and watch over you
When you wake, your smiling face
As a pleasure to behold.
There are many words left untold
You look at me inquisitively.
Your beautiful soft eyes, that say so much.
You will always need a loving touch.
When you grow, I will be there.
There to share your hopes and dreams
There to share your heartaches and pain.
Yes I will be there, you can depend on me.
I could never leave you,
I could never break free,
Because watching you grow,
Means the world to me.

M. Flynn

Mountain Home

The gem green cleavage of the heaving hills
Accentuates the bosom of the swelling, fertile land
its sheep frecked face is smiling secrets to the sun,
eyes of fish flecked pools
Reflect a sky too beautiful to bear.
The breeze, flirtatious, invites me to the dance.
A distant river shakes mercurial hair
Plaited by the currents
Waved in locks of water weed.
The rounded skyline stretches out its arms
And trees gesticulate in languorous array
My soul responds, reposes,
And I become a part
of the land that holds my heart.

T. G. Jenkins

Untitled

The father's eyes that see no more
closed and gone to another place
with family could in hand they
will forever walk together

The children that can no longer been seen,
but can be felt in the heart and in your
memory forever and will be missed.

A the passing is the end of a great friendship,
And the passing of an even greater love and
friendship.

I miss you even though it cos been for a short time.
I cried my tears at your passing and I cried at the
good memories.

Thank you for being my father.

David Hall

Remember

Remember me, when I've been gone awhile
Gone far away into the heavenly land,
Where you can no longer gently hold my hand
When you no longer see my tender smile.

Remember all the things that used to be,
The things we did, the future that we'd planned
The memories, that only you can understand
And hold within your heart your thoughts of me.

And afterwards my dear, don't grieve for me,
I wouldn't want to know that you were sad,
Just remember the happiness we had,
Then I can rest in peace, eternally.

M. Farnworth

Untitled

If there's something so strong you can feel it inside
Hard on to it tight else away it will slide
If your heart is full of love and light
Don't chuck it away else you will feel plight
Love is life and life should be fun
But when it goes away so does your sun
When love disappears you're left like all shell
All dead inside which makes life all hell
Like last weeks rubbish you get chucked away
When instead you just want to stay
It's hard to let go of what is your life line
But when you do it hurts and you don't seem to shine
When something's so good you just can't let go
But it suddenly slips and you go down with a blow
You can't always give up what feels so right
Or at least not until you've put up a fight
When you've lost the battle you feel really bad
Inside you feel anger but mostly you're sad
When it's done, it's done, when it's gone, it's past
But that love inside will always last.

Sussie Porter

Old Times

This old man is helpless and frail
He starts to wonder and his mind starts to sail
Thinking about pastimes - his birthday, the war
He's sitting in a spitfire, as the engine starts to roar
Up in the air he soars, he soars
He's got a plane on his tail, with machine guns clacking
He's black in his house, underfed and lacking
Needing attention from his son or his daughter
It's just pure vicious human torture.

Lee Page

Daddy?

Daddy, Daddy don't leave us tonight
How can you say that things are alright?
Mummy is sobbing with tears in her eyes.
Daddy, why did you tell her those lies?

Daddy, daddy don't you love us anymore?
He picks up his bags and walks through the door.
Mummy's still crying and looking so sad.
Daddy, was it me? Was I bad?

Hush little baby your daddy has gone
The house is quiet, the two of us alone.
Sleep little baby, sleep in your cot.
Mummy won't leave you she loves you a lot.

Watching through tears, her child is still
Her pan turns to anger, yet her eyes fill.
The woman is younger, pretty and slim.
But how could SHE love, the way she loves him.

As night moves on, the crying departs
Mother and child, two broken hearts.
The child's face is lit by the first rays of dawn
Mother smiles, thank God you were born.

Peggy Johnson

A Visit To The U.S.A.

Ancestral land across the sea, I think of you,
I felt at home where eagles fly.

Autumn trees aglow as if on fire,
A carpet of golden leaves to walk upon,
Where once I stood long ago, a boy child.

Little warrior to be, proud of head,
Chiselled profile, a chief in the making

A memory, an awaking of another time,
Glimpses of family ties, a parting.
Remembrance of an abandoned family,
Turning my back and riding away,
To be with a fair skinned woman.

Great white spirit forgive me.

Many moons have passed, the warrior returns in disguise,
An English tea drinking grannie of three.

The balancing of the wheel is true and just,
In this life my husband deserted me.

Shirley Brown-Paul

Thoughts

I have not lived, I have survived.
I know it now what I have missed.
In this world of ours, I have a list.
Of places to see, things to do
Memories to erase, and some to keep.
The joyous times and learning times.
In my mind they are there to seep.
I must use all my senses, to see, to
Hear to smell and taste.
To take life more slowly
Never in haste.
Be thankful each day for what I have.
Keeping my family close,
And to always love.

Iris Lister

Untitled

The light goes on and you are there
  I look at you and smile
The curtains close the night is hidden
  I look at you and smile
I tell you how my day has gone
  You look at me and smile
The rooms so quiet as you smile at me
  And I look at you and smile
The photo captures you so well
  You look at me and smile
Your lips don't speak as I'd like them to
  You just look at me and smile
Your eyes so bright with happiness
  As they look at me and smile
They follow me all round the room
  And look at me and smile
And your love shines through and comforts me
  As we share our secret smile.

M. E. Dekoning

My Good Friend

There she sits on the window-sill
"Let me in" it seems she cries
Like limpid fools, her beautiful eyes.
I open the door, and in she trails
Even alert, with bushy tail.
With fluffy coat and paws like silk
She quite likes a saucer of milk
When I thought I had reached the end.
She came to me, I had found a friend
Now to her needs I do attend
My neighbour's cat, Estee'
My very good friend.

Flora M. Lunam

My Love For You

I love you, because you're you.
I love you, you make my sky the brightest blue.
I love you when you're fast asleep, to hug,
to hold, be mine to keep.
My love for you goes oh, so deep.

I'll love you when the spring bulbs push through to bloom.
I'll love you when the summer sun turns to a crystal
clear moon.
I'll love you when the leaves begin to fall and I'll love
you when the frost is crisp and the evenings are cool.
I'll love you when the snow is deep, when the open
fire is roaring and the snow keeps on falling.

I'll love you when I'm old and grey, until my eyes
grow dim and my soul floats away.

Amanda Marshall

Panic

I'm breathing so fast, there's not enough air
I want to get up but I'm strapped in this chair

My stomach is churning and my mouth is so dry
I'm telling myself 'You better not cry.'

If it wasn't for you I wouldn't be here
I knew when the time came I'd be full of fear.

You said you would pay and I would go free
You were always so good at persuading me.

I can't hear you speak now, my hearts in my ear
Thumping so loud I can't even think clear.

The door has been locked, the temperatures high
I'll wish on that star I can see in the sky.

I'll wish to live past this frightful night
Is everyone like this on their first flight?!

Suzanne Donald

My Long Lost Friend

The music is playing on the stereo
I wish you would and say hello.
My friend I miss you in my heart.
Please can we make another start.

Every time the memories are there
It hurts me dearly to know you're not here
What have I done to you, cause I care
I wish you would tell me and clear the air.

Please don't forget me
my dear friend
because, I will always be here
my long lost friend.

Lucy Doyle

" Disillusioned "

When the kids were small, I seemed to have no time at all.
I wished that they were grown, just so I could have some time alone.
I imagined how it would be to eat in peace and quiet,
instead of every meal time being turned into a riot.
Or just to switch the T.V. on and watch a programme of my choice,
to see a film right through without that interrupting little voice.
There would be tidiness in every room,
instead of chaos where toys where strewn.
No school books on the bedroom floor,
no dirty clothes behind the door.
Now I look back the years have flown,
my wish is granted the kids have grown.
The rooms are empty where once they played,
no books or fluffy toys displayed.
They've gone away, they've fled the nest,
I'm bored with silence, I'm sick of rest.
There's no laughter, no chatter, no noise, no fuss.
Oooh! How I wish that they were small and back at home with us.

Linda Hunter

Heart Of My Life

My son is very special. He means the world to me
If I had never known him how great my loss would be.
How proud of him I've always been, he is my pride and joy
Since the moment someone said 'you have a little boy.'

In truth, I think my life began when he was in my arms,
The sleeping face, the gentle cry, I fell for all his charms.
This little boy, my family now, the sweetest task of all
To love him and to care for him and pray no harm befalls.

It's been the greatest pleasure to know this son of mine,
I used to tell him as a child he was my sunshine.
He was a super little boy, so loving and so kind
The joy he'd get just showing me the treasures he would find.

Within my life he takes great part
He holds a portion of my heart.
I couldn't live without him, he doesn't know his worth
He's more than gold and silver, he is the best on earth.

So now I've put my thoughts in rhyme,
I thank you Robert, son of mine.
For being all that I hold dear
And I pray that you'll be always near.

Kate Brown

Don't Cry For Me (In Death)

Don't Cry for me I'm not far away,
I'm holding your hand when you have a bad day.
I'm kissing your cheek when you cry at night.
I'm holding you close when you're full of fright.
I'll always be near, right by your side.
I'll be around if you need a guide
So please don't cry now that I've gone away.
Because we will be together again one day.

Veronica Miskelly

Laughter

I wept in tide and rapture
In laughter of stupendous folly
Bleeding each orifice in succession
Hath been jolly to surrender

I beam in splendour I acquire
O'er tedious boredom awakened
Relieving each particle of desire
Dragging one's being out of the mire

In soul with powerless adventure
Uncontrollably released in gratitude
Uplifted the animal inside
Toward all measure of pleasure.

Cameron McIntyre

Skeletons To Hide

People all have skeletons to hide,
Even if it's only a matter of pride,
Deep inside an old dark closet,
Full of thoughts and deed they deposit,
Things they did along time ago,
Things no one ever needs to know,

People all have skeletons to hide,
Things to which the past is tide,
Good or bad no one knows,
Mixed with the highs are the lows,
Things they did along time ago,
Things no one ever needs to know,

People all have skeletons to hide,
Secrets hidden deep inside,
Things that you don't have to share,
Even with the people that really care,
Things they did along time ago,
Things no one should need to know.

Michelle Gledhill

That Final Computer

Will your name be debit or credit when that button is pressed.
In that great computer amongst the blessed
No one knows right how one's record is kept
Of all our sins and failings in retrospect
Surely in that city where the streets are paved with gold
The computers will be golden, so I am told
Advancement about science has opened our eyes about outer space
Planets can be visited by the human race
Our father in heaven he overseas it all
We come to him through his son the Redeemer overall
One can only believe and do one's best
Until we come to that final test
When the button is pressed and the debits and credits are noted down
We will know then if it be thorn or crown
James Duthie

Save Our Trees

Why are we destroying this planet we're on,
in the end very soon our world will be gone.

Our forests that once covered the lands,
are being destroyed by man's own hands.

Our wildlife soon will have nowhere to live,
now the forests are bear and have nothing to give.

The forests were once so fresh and green,
now if they could talk you would hear them scream.

We don't even care we're polluting the air,
it's our children that will suffer and that isn't fair.

Do you remember that story of Robin Hood
And His Men, in a forest he lived, in the story back then.

Very soon his forest in the end will be gone,
for our growing population to build houses on.

We're taking these trees, just out of pure greed,
and should think to the future, because the trees we will need.
Richard Glenn Burton

Wonders Of Nature

Snow fell over our village one night
It made a most delightful sight
In the early morn to see
The trees as white as they can be

No marks to mar the crisp white ground
And only the birds to make a sound
Looking through my bedroom window I see
Little robins on a tree

Now that I've got out of bed
And all the birds I have fed
I shall go for a walk and look around
At all the wonders to be found

Although it is still snowing, the sky is lighter now
Over the road across the way
I see sparrows on a bough
The snow will not be here for long
For it is nearly Spring
Soon the woodpecker will be seen
And the swallows on the wing.
O. Homer

Untitled

How I gaze out of a window
Patiently watching as the sun falls from a blanket of clouds
As the sky settles in for the night
I dare not leave my window for as I do the night grows darker
Whispering trees and talking leaves
A new world grows yet one that flourishes in its own right
Owls hooting foxes prowling know that this is their time
As the moon shines and stars twinkle
I leave my window to sleep to wake to a new world
   for everyday is different.
Kerrianne Dougan

" The Pavement Artist "

On the day Elvis Presley died
it rained (heavily) in Stultgard.

Standing once
Erect in youth, he called himself "believer"
Men laughed and spat, there called him dreamer.

He believed once, Once he believed
That he beheld the dynasties of beauty and precision
Now—— He curses his senses.

Falling to the ground
He acknowledges the laughter and the spit.
Falling to the ground
His eye changes upon the light behind his shadow.

Falling to the ground
He interprets dreams of yesterday's vision of tomorrow.

They were made up of so much coloured chalk
Mixed up and spread over one to many sidewalk.
From where he lay he beheld a pair of eyes gazing skywards.
Then the rain fell (heavily)

And the colours merged to be carried off on the
Soles of marching feet.
Daniel Michael Chapman

Who Am I?

Searching for clarity in my darkened soul, though black in depth.
It sees the harsh reality of light
eternally new light aged seven minutes.
People who look see only the surface
yet to me, even the observer's mind is transparent.
Like glass, distorting the values of life
as more they diffuse the light's truths.
If I wished to shatter the heart of their prism,
a moment's reality, glimpse of my what is
is all would suffice to shatter their angel
and insanity would overcome the shreds
gather them screaming, laughing.
People look at me and see whatever they don't want to be.
With effort I have shown them what they would not be.
And intentionally my good acts fade.
As time eats their memory as their games they play.
With futility I could try to be them.
But why try when they are only part of me
I judge my own court and find justification.
I exist.
Duncan Feeley

Lost Eden

The ideals we live by
Most of them aren't ours
They are forced upon us
By ruling powers

If we choose to dis-obey them
We are always oppressed
They say the forests need cultivating
In the name of progress

You see, I don't question our existence
Or the purpose of our lives
I just question the evolution
Of our so called modern times

When you look at our world today
And the destruction that swells within
The true guilty go unpunished
That is today's true sin.

If there's any change for mankind
We must not ignore our fears
Or earth's future, not measured in centuries
But sadly measured in years.
Nicholas Hinks

Prayer Before Birth

I am not yet born; O hear me;
let not the gremlins, goblins and witches
or the blood sucking snakes or ogres
come near me. Save me from
sinking sea, or in a car crash and also
save me from crashing in a plane.

I am not yet born; provide me
with family and friends, sunlight and darkness.
Provide me with food and water, creatures
and living things. Provide me with warm
shelter and a clean world,
teach me to read and write.
God keep me sake.

Sally Doleman

Flight To Eternity

Let us open the doors to a timeless eternity
let us run in their light and then feed upon our God's
They call us, it is time
to grow our wings and fly
to the safe haven of darkness
it will surround us
hold us warmly
In its secure, assuring hug of forgiveness
it is time for me to leave
may my heart blood in the name of love
may my soul grow strong
and protect thee forever.

Jonathan Chown

Karen Carpenter

Karen sings a voice-a-throbbing
Like a robin,
She sings even now
A pleasant and beautiful row.
She sings a pleasant song,
She sings not for long.

She sings of her beautiful island in the sun,
She sings of her beautiful one.
Why did you die, Karen, so tragically?
You gave us, Karen, your voice so magically.

I listen to your beautiful songs,
She sings a sweet and beautiful rhyme,
She doesn't sing off key and off time.
She even makes me believe
It's your first time in a nutshell,
She blossomed so well.

Karen went on a diet,
She died without causing a riot.

Shona Conroy

That Special Sound

Close your eyes real tight
Listen to the sound outside
The rain is falling to the ground
Making that real and special sound

See it fall through the leaves
Falls to the ground to rivers and seas
Hitting the window real fast
opening your imagination at last

Falling in the gutter down the drain
under the tunnel through the fields
Over stones were fish will play
Feeding the land running to the bay

Flowing down rivers taking all the fish
Running down canals through the towns
To the sea and every oceans in the world
That special sound we hear is called the rain

Sandra Hawkins

"Now Is The Date"

Floodlight pavements, children enshrouded in the suns ray's.
Little arms and legs, eager bright eyes, yet we worry and we
shout we protest!
We try to mould them in our little moulds;
how we miss the joy of loud happiness, laughter and fun.

Were we never young - have we forgotten - the joys of
our childhood?
Yes I fear - we have, we expect them - sensible - fair minded
do we not see their untamed beauty?

Let us leave them alone a while - let them reach out
with all their senses.
Now is the date - tomorrow is too late

How swift the tide of life turns; magic moments gone forever.
Each time it sweeps across a stretch of sand it changes
something in its path.
If only we could reach out & freeze the beautiful
moments in our life and hold them ever near.
When our children are young how quickly it slips away
how very dear time is; how very short!

Catherine Clements

A New Life

I've waited for mornings and afternoon
Measured my life in small teaspoons
Spat out the dog ends of my days
I've killed the fire in rainy days
The moon that gives the night its glow
I've watched it fade, I've watched it grow
The wind that blows the leaves away
To bring them back another day
The clouds that bring the sleet & snow
I've seen then care I've seen them go
My time I know will care to its end
Where freedom awaits me like a long lost friend
To hold me close and sigh relief
To release me of my torment, chains and grief.

E. P. Gorecki

Heat Wave Summer '95

The clay was a baked crust
Needing to plant some greenery
I probed with trowel first
But it refused to budge.

The addition of water
Enabled me to scoop a well.
Into proven ground sufficiently moistened
I placed my hopes.

As thoughts of famine and drought
In other places came to mind
I blessed our climate
Of seasonal mix.

Ita Kenny

Economy To The End

Matilda left her instructions
Of how to economize when she dies.
She doesn't want any fuss
Just a funeral of minimum size.
She has even cut out the hearse
And suggests a Salford Hire van
Which can sneak early to the Crematorium
Being in place before the funeral began.
Don't waste money on a coffin,
Surely you'll find a recycled cask!
Let everyone bring a few sandwiches
And a drop of coffee in a flask.
Then when the service is over
And the tears and "Goodbyes" said,
Just scatter my ashes in the wind
It won't worry me 'cos I'll be dead.

Val E. Patten

Waiting For Spring

The wind blows cold, and wild and free.
Over mountain, rill and lea.
Signs of autumn all around.
Leaves like carpets on the ground.

Time to check our roofs and walls.
See the chimney free of falls.
Make the windows all secure.
Lag the pipes and just make sure.

That when the winds of winter blow.
Bringing sleek and bringing snow.
We shall be all snug and warm.
No need to fear that awful storm.
At last when spring, though tardy, does arrive.
We're there to great it All Alive.
   B. Hirst

Alpha And Omega

Kaleidoscopic in my entity
   Part of the vortex of the rising sun
Winging the nimbus of the silent clouds
   Edged with the silver of the zenith star
Poised on the chasm of infinity.
   Then will I be the russet gold of sunset
Racing the planets amber void
   And purpled nothingness.
The green of deepest seas will know my touch,
   And mine the endless universe will be.
The glory of a thousand worlds will pass
   Within the orbit of my destiny,
When I this present life have left behind.
So will my soul joy in the waiting time
Before another life I must begin.
Forgetting sometimes, when I shall feel despair
   I hold the key to Paradise within.
   D. C. Deacon

Waiting For The Storm To Pass

Worn tears like wrung out socks
Past years like craggy rocks
I sat, knowing this night had passed me before,
I sat, with thoughts etherized like a perpetual sore.
The eternal monotony of daybreak lighting night,
Passing so rapidly as to portray no insight
Into any new glimmer, new distraction from pain,
The same wretched thoughts crop up again and again.
A new day cannot explode with a drizzle of rain.
New hope cannot emerge unless day and night explode with pain,
And exorcise feeble showers, vague mist
Comb memories from my hair, with a flick of the wrist,
Laugh unknown depths, unexpected and fresh
And knowingly cage pain in a gilded mesh.
So when the next storm brews and thunder crashes and roars
I'll be there, lifting up old wounds crusted into sores,
And I'll scream at the wind, and make the clouds part
And force a new morning to mean a new start.
   Tessa Dummett

Growing Old Disgracefully

He lies in his chair, for all the world dead
Skin sallow, mouth open, snoring like a pig unfed
Did I once love this wrinkly old geezer
Who wears old togs, a look-a-like Caesar
I, now feel thirty although my face belies that
With aches and pains brought by extra fat
My mother said wistfully, "why do we have to grow old?"
Now it's my turn to value that thought
To consider mortality from living to nought.
The figure opposite yawns and stirs, gazing into space
"You've let yourself go, you're a blooming disgrace
Why don't you buy yourself a new dress and make up your face?"
Ah well things are back to normal we're Darby and Joan
He's a grumpy old sod, but I love his old bones.
   Dael Ogilvie

Cardboard Dreams

Oh how I wish I had a home I wouldn't ask for more,
pretty curtains at the windows, carpets on the floor.
I'd have a little kitchen with cupboards full of food,
so I could cook a five-course meal if I was in the mood.
I'd have a lounge where I could sit, with my feet up, drinking tea,
listen to some music or maybe watch T.V.
My days would be full and happy, doing all my chores,
the polishing and dusting, washing dishes, cleaning floors.

I'd have a little bathroom with a big bath, gleaming white,
with gallons of hot water, I would bathe myself each night,
I'd have lots of perfumed oil and I'd smile as I got in,
with loads of soapy bubbles coming right up to my chin.
I'd have a pretty bedroom with a lovely little bed,
with feather quilt and pillows, somewhere soft to lay my head.
I'd be snuggled in the blankets feeling safe and warm.
I could sleep all through the night knowing I'd be free from harm.

Oh, but I must stop this dreaming, I'm getting wet from rain
   and sleet,
I'll find an alley or a doorway, somewhere to got to sleep,
huddled up inside my old coat, shivering to the bone,
praying to the Lord above, please, grant me a home.
   Violet Kelk

Beauty In Australia

The sky is of the deepest blue
Reflections in the sea are too,
Also the big jacaranda tree
Deep purple, blue as it can be,
These pretty flowers all come first
Before the green leaves form and burst.

Around the electric pole geraniums grow
Pale or deep pink make a lovely show,
In botanic say's "please do not touch,"
Parrots feed on the fig tree seed
There is plenty for every need.

Oranges and lemons grow next door
The biggest fruit I ever saw.
I still wake early every morn
And hear birds start to sing at dawn,
A blackbird from the top of a tree
Sounds like he's singing just for me.
   Lucy M. Johnson

Reach For The Sky

Ever wished that you could fly.
Sing like Streisand. Pavarotti.
Dance.
Play like Getz or Bream.
Listen to the Messiah, dream.

Ever thought how these things work.
An electric light bulb. Fork lifts.
Lasers. Computers.
CD Rom's. Oppenheimer's bomb.
Try to write a song. Or poems, like Yeats. Donne.

Ever wondered what happens when you die.
Is there a Heaven. Or is it
pie in the sky.
Can you visualize eternity. Oceans
from a distant star.

Ever thought about us. What we've become.
Years of greed.
Corruption. Lies.
Look around and see the fear.
Or is it tears behind the eyes. I do.
   Trudi Danks

Untitled

The night was long, I could not sleep, the pain was really bad.
So I sat by the window feeling lonely, low and sad.
I looked across the garden, the moon was high and bright
Something moved so furtively I thought I'd die of fright,
I then saw two huge frightened eyes looking straight at me
Those eyes were filled with fright and pain and Oh! such misery
The body was so sleek and thin, the ribs were showing through
She still stood there and looked at me deciding what to do.
My heart was filled with pity for this poor pathetic thing
As she slowly moved away from me towards the refuge bin
She ripped the bags and foraged, 'til she had a pile of food.
She made a noise "A signal" and with her bounty stoop.
I sat there fascinated as three pairs of eyes appeared.
These were the raider's babies for whose lives she was afeared.
She guarded them until the food was gone and all were fed.
Those frightened eyes were calmer now as with her brood she fled.
How long I sat there I'm not sure, it must have been 'till dawn.
The Mother and her babies were well and truly gone.
You see? I am disabled but I have love and warmth and food
Thank-you Madame Viven, today I'm feeling good.
Dawn Kinnon

War Is Death

Unmarked graves in far off fields.
So many lives to the grim reaper do yield.
Death looked on in a khaki shroud,
As millions died by the Hiroshima cloud.
Soldier's bodies are often not found,
But still both sides' machine guns fire off more rounds.
If war kills so many, how can it be right?
Yet plenty more warriors join up to fight.
Countries send in your loved ones to sort out their strife,
Fighting solves nothing;
It's just a great waste of life.
Everyone's lost so call a truce and wave a flag that's white,
Surely if we all share this world, our nations should unite?

War, what is it good for?
Absolutely nothing.
Say it again.
Teri-Louise Caterer

Inside Outside

When you walk through those prison gates
Sort from your mind your loves and hates
Though to me you ought to see
Just how much you mean to me
You would not trust me for a guide
And now you find yourself inside
Those prison gates

Though it hurt to see you cry
Take heart three years will soon pass by
And if you still feel as I do,
You know you have a love that's true
Viv, you'll find that a real love waits
For you outside
Those prison gates
Tony Gifford

The Past

When I sigh at the dark night sky
It makes me cry, and I wonder why
When I stare into the vast
Mindless landscape of the past,
My mind is filled with joy and laughter
And me, wanting it to last forever after
But then it blurs from my eye
And all I see is the skies black dye,
Dotted all over with spots of paint,
Then that to becomes so faint,
And then the sad, lonely memories of things gone by,
Reforms again in the back of my eye
And the dark, black memories become less coy,
And I start to see light, faint joy.
Nicholas Capehorn

'Lasting Peace'

We're a strange species, we humans,
Stockpiling arsenals of terrifying weaponry,
Kidding ourselves, that by this, all thoughts of war will cease,
We've only to look around the world
At 'trouble-spots' and 'war-torn Countries'
To be justifiably cynical when ave hear of 'Lasting Peace!

It seems we'd rather spend 'Billions'
On what are known as 'Deterrents',
Instead of giving the sick and poor what they need for the
their pain to ease,

if only we could learn to cherish our world,
And turn our resources towards Preserving and conserving it,
Then maybe we could all hope for a 'Lasting Peace'

I fear though, that, human nature being what it is
Interlaced with greed, envy, hate and all sorts of corruption
That countries to undermine society and bring the world to its knees,
For very many individuals; ordinary folk, like you and me,
The only true thing that we can depend on, is the inevitable end
That we all come to
And with it, our own 'Lasting Peace'
Richard J. Clarke

A Sick, Sick World

A world of unrest, at best, is this all we can hope for
Surely differences could be reasonably tolerated
instead of berated, which causes adversity.
People are entitled to different opinions
this is their right, no need to fight
agree to differ amiably.
The innocent suffer from political wars
where the heads of the land are behind closed doors
nothing can touch them
they make sure of that
Plenty of food, getting fat,
whilst their fellow men suffer starvation
for ordinary people,
there is no salvation
For some, no place to lay their head
crying, mourning for their dead.
still more infants are being born each day
in their mother's arms they lay
No food in their bellies, no milk in the breast
no end in sight to this world of unrest.
M. Black

Fighter Station: Mid November Morning

Tall, gaunt, and leafless poplars in the breeze;
The scent of wood smoke; pale blue sweeps of sky,
Cold, clear and sunny air that's fit to freeze,
And russet leaves that on the roadways lie..,
The hum of engines, revving up for speed,
A steady purr that grows into a roar
And nerves are steel - controlled, to tension keyed,
"They're off?" With angry scream the Spitfires soar
Fold up their wheels, and into steady flight
On the North wind the smooth-winged squadrons sail;
-And now they're gone. The winter sun is bright
The trees are silent - and the sky is pale...
Elizabeth Garrett Miller

Care!

People - All need someone to care -
Someone to talk too love or be there.

When out on a limb - there is nobody in -
Just a shell with its flame glowing dim.

Your light is shining bright, just ready to ignite-
and so it glows all through the night.

Accidents happen - everyone's there -
Full of attention, but do they really care?
Lesley Ann Mccarthy

The Golden Day

The light of heaven gently breaks
The sleep of dawn it softly wakes
As starry heavens fade away
Upon the mist of dawns hey day
Where sweet larks sing their tender song
On fields of green they fly upon
And on the dawns early mist
Sweet smell of wild flowers softly drifts
Across the fields of dewy moss
Their beauty blooms upon the dawns early frost
And soft winds blow their gentle breeze
Upon the weeping willow trees
With leaves of pearl that dance and swirl upon the summer breeze
And butterflies flutter by a lovely stream
Sunbeams dance as in a dream upon the shimmering stream
And sleep of dawn drifts away
Upon the mist of golden day.
David Richard Carey

Ode To Dalmatia

Softly shimmering sunshine sifts through leafy trees.
The soft air stirs around us, stirred by a gentle breeze.
The beauty of the songbird, high in the bough above,
His lilting voice so sweet, such joy,
Wonderful sounds of love.

White clouds high in a blue blue sky,
Look down on a turquoise sea.
Soft waves roll to a beautiful shore.
For such beauty Lord, we thank thee.
Joyce Port

" There Is Light "

There are times when grey skies are above far too long, so
The sun can never shine through.
There's sign that the right things are forever wrong and
The wrong things, so easy to do.
To wake in the morn, then to rise from your bed,
is so hard when you know what awaits.
To take of the corn, or break of the bread,
is a waste when your mind's in this state.
You question the light at the end of the road,
because darkness is all you can see.
There is no delight, in knowing the load,
is as heavy for you as for me.
Who cares that you worry, who cares where you go,
you wallow in all your self pity.
There's no need to hurry, just go with the flow,
then prepare to abandon tear city.
Once freed from depression, released from despair,
you can leap from the jaws of decay.
Change all false impression, stand tall if you dare,
there is light shining through from the grey.
Allan Hudd

My Pet

My dog was very big,
It was as white as snow,
And had a black patch on his ear,
Which was as black as coal.
His eyes were small round black balls
He had one ear that was like a leaf.
About to fall,
from a twig
And a tail like a ball of fluff.

He used to chase his tail,
Round and round,
Like a spinning top,
Never going to stop.
If anyone came to the door he would bark his head off.
Now he's gone
It took sometime getting used to that,
He would no longer bark,
If anyone came to the door.
Kirsty Galbraith

The Return

My heart lifts.
The wearisome worries of waiting vanish
At the sound of a horn and tyres on the wet drive.
Solemn brown eyes stare at me.
Starfish hands hurry to unloose the hated belt.
And quick jump a quicker kiss
And in she runs to survey her kingdom.
The books and toys are in their familiar places
As are the brasses in the inglenook.
Is the stool as usual beside the fridge?
Then - with a happy sigh and smile of pure joy
She throws her arms around me.
Zoe's back.
E. Allinson

Pity The Soldier

Welcome soldier, have a beer
There'll always be one here for our heroes.
He was tired but proud,
And made some friends.
Some months later he brought some mates.
They were still tired and not so proud.
Beer's not free for you lot now,
The desert looked much darker then.
They drank a lot and cheered up some.
Get out of here, you drunken squaddies!
Typical soldiers, who needs 'em?
Why do we go to war for them?
Said Private Atkins to his mate.
God knows, but I think the band's stopped playing.
Matthew Minshall

Says It All

The flowers stand up tall and proud
They don't need to shout out loud,
Their beauty says it all.

The powerful moon controls the tide
From shore to shore the waves abide,
Their obeyance says it all.

The mighty sun sits in the sky,
Gives warmth and light to all that pass by,
Its brightness says it all.

In this great plan, since time began,
Where is self-important man,
His smallness says it all.
S. A. Gregor

The Echo's Along The Grey Corridor Of Life Will Haunt You Forever More

He sees me here;
Though not me, but a mere shadow of troubled waters.
I think it not worth the humiliation;
Bat as the words fall from my tongue,
Like dew to the ground, I take myself to him,
It's the cold piercing sound of silence that breaks you.

Then as I walk out, to the darkened night,
I mirror myself by some past life,
To the river's moon-torched waters,
Flicker's of light, Fly to tear the heart,
That once beat so fiercely proud;
It once did beat,
Life weighed out by breaking waves.

A heart that now wanders in dark despair,
Through the phase of life's lights;
Only tears to break that silent death,
The years merge to this,
A whispered reflection of light;
The purest of love you never knew,
Whispers in my heart.
V. L. Fereday

Life Sentence

The familiar pounding soldiers on beside me as I
Thrash out into the watery darkness
In which I am securely engulfed.
I hear voices in another planet,
But am safe here
In my rumbling darkness.

Oddly rejected, I am pushed away in disgrace
Into obscure, orange openness.
I feel no walls. Is this Planet Voices?
I am a stranger here, in this light to which I am not accustomed.
I do not belong in this place of little charm
But I will bide my time.

I have served punishment for my crime,
And have been returned to eternal darkness.
But my warmth has vanished
And my rumbling water has been replaced,
I will never be safe in this cold hardness
But am left in peace to recall the happy times.

Nicola Coull

" As Flies To Wanton Boys "

Multi-coloured thread, entwined and twisted
To confuse the mind of simple mortal man,
Who sees every shadowy moment as hades enlisted
In this lengthlessness that is his life's span.

A piece of railway track called man's time;
Monotony in disguise as a graceful dance,
Totally lacking in rhythm, reason or rhyme,
With a touch of beauty that Chance might enhance.

Man scratches his head and politely asks,
"Why did it start, when must it end?"
The trees carry on swaying in their ever ending tasks,
No answer do they give, no assistance do they lend.

Man smiles for the question he wants left unanswered,
And retreats into obscurity unnoticed and unheard.

Robin Bendall

Why

To ask is not the reason why, to cry is just a form of expression.
To me the world is not so good, especially with this ongoing recession
So here we are so sad and down,
all we can do is look and frown.

WHY

To us the world is one sad face
with evolution vanishing without a trace.
The north pole is melting the rain forest has gone.
The man of distraction has won.

WHY

It's too late to change, so forget the rage.
Be thankful for the animals we have in the cage.
For they are all that is left
and all we can do is watch the death.

Sharon Brown

The Wind

Like a mad dog it rushes through the street
Turning over dustbins and rustling leaves
It screams and snarls at people rushing by
While knocking branches off trees.

It whacks the birds like bat and ball
And makes the waves crash off boats
Like a wolf howling on a hill,
While you feel uneasy.

It haunts the streets like a lost ghost
And knocks tiles off roofs
While knocking over bottles
As swift as an owl.

Leanne Dyer

Untitled

While I pondered slowly through my dreams and drift
upon the scented breeze.
I caught your smile that filled the sky with purple
clouds that pass me by,
And far away a small child cry's, then fades to
leave a warm bright sky.
Then shining brightly from the sun I see your
eyes that tell me life has not begun.
And drift I might upon the placid waves
until I float to shore, and there I find through
sands of time that gentle voice that calls
to me, and sets me free to roam through
fields of yellow flowers that let me see
that all is well.
Then contended in your laughter through
days that pass much faster.
I hold a daisy in my hand till all the
petals have blown away, but always in
my heart you'll stay.

Lynne Bridge

My Case Against E.C.T.

Captured by aliens? A prisoner of war?
What are these mindless experiments for?
In a room full of zombies, a waiting my turn
for electrical currents my memories to burn.
Treatment not fortune psychiatrists claim
Please ask your patients if they feel the same.

I imagine these currents have damaged my soul
Killing off pieces that were part of a whole
These are probably far-fetched and unfounded fears
But of my son's teenage life I've lose two or three years
Since the experience alone I can't be the same
To wake up, and not to know my own name.

Janet Craig

Ode To A Bombed City

Oh, noble city, so long our deepest pride,
What have you done this slaughter to deserve?
What would those hands, so crafted and so brave,
That laid your first foundations wish us now?

Those hands which set each stone, so carefully, so trim,
To last fore'er, their sons' sons to admire,
To shelter from life's tempest and from all
Of Nature's far more pardonable ways?

Would they despair to see their work undone?
Their city, made by man, by ma destroyed?
They'd lose no time, or will their sons, but build
A better place set in a better world.

Yes! First a better place in which to build their homes again
A better place for other humans, too.
Then let our leader's prophesy of what they'll say ring true.
"This was, indeed, their very finest hour!"

Stanley B. Jackson

Baby

A baby is a bundle of joy
Whether it be a girl or boy
A gift from God above
A human being for you to love,
Not always fun for Mum
It may be a crochet one
That means a disturbed night
In and out of bed, to comfort the mite,
You wouldn't want to change it though.
Because you know you love it so,
The comfort of your arms will soon send it to sleep
Then thankfully off to bed you creep
Praying that God his watch will keep
Till the dawn of another day, through the window will peep.

W. Ordidge

Housing Market Blues

Once upon a saddened tale
When our house went up for sale.
When we could not afford to pay,
The mortgage bills that came our way.

For many years we scrimped and saved,
We even had a patio made.
Now it will belong to someone else,
That is if it ever sells.

All demand is in a slump,
You'd think we'd offered some old dump.
Sometimes seen it may sell,
But then again you can never tell.

Until then we'll wait and see,
If someone will come and rescue me.
It's not a dream but a living hell,
But for that all else is well.

One thing alone will end my blues,
That is when I get some news.
To tell me that my house is sold,
Before I gets just damned to old!

Stephen McCluskey

The Ship That Slipped Its Moorings

Friendship-what does it mean,
Where does the ship come on to the scene.
The friend part was right, but where were the morals
All I seemed to gain was heartache and sorrows.

I had a friend, a friend so rare
but she stepped on my 'waters', how did she dare.
My minds still confused and in a terrible muddle,
My heart is torn and life's a dreadful struggle.

The 'ship' from my friend has sailed away,
It left its sage harbour, it ended that day.
That was the day that she broke my heart,
And from my life 'so sad' she must now depart.

I miss her now, I probably always will
my friendship and love she did kill,
She Trod on my 'waters' and my heart did drown
Can I smile again, or will I always grown.

Rekindle this friendship - I'm not so sure
The ship is still missing, maybe forever more.

Tracy Bessey

" My Daughter "

Who buys the sweets she loves to choose?
Who brushes her golden hair?
Who lays out her clothes to wear next day?
Who listens to her prayer?

I saw her with a friend today,
Laughing and skipping, free,
And I wondered in my lonely heart
If she ever thinks of me.

I longed to put my arms round her
Like mothers always do,
To hear those lovely words again,
"Mummy, I love you."

Who puts their arms round her these days?
Who comforts her when she cries?
Who whispers those soothing, tender words
As in her bed she lies?

I'd give the world to be back again
With my family, so precious to me,
But one foolish moment spoilt it all,
"Mothers, think twice, is my plea."

D. Hilda Peterson

The Panther

Panther, Panther of the night,
who shall give they such a fright.
With thy speed,
thy prey shalt lead.

Panther, Panther who does thou fear,
is it thy man with thy spear.
Does thy man kiss for thine skin,
yet after use is it in thy bin.

Panther, Panther tell me please,
what does thou do among thy trees.
Is thou listening with thine powerful ear,
is thou listening for a deer.

Panther, Panther please tell me do,
what does thou do if he sees a deer or two.
Does thou lurk in the shadows or
stalk for more and more and more.

Panter, Panther oh let me guess, thou tears and rips at thine
prey's skin, does thine prey scream with pain, fill me in.
Is thou free to run and kill,
why must thou hide in fear of the hand of man...

Lisa Marriott

Tomorrow

Close your eyes.
With a mere thought you can see everything
you ever dreamed.
The mind is filled with questions, and their answers,
yet the two never seem to meet.
The thinkers are the most pernicious.
Always searching. But to find what?
People do stupid things.
They hurt each other with no real reason.
The pain and anguish wells up inside so the
past can't but effect the future.
Grin and bear the world gracefully, after all the
pessimist is snubbed whilst the optimist
derided.
Hold tight your beliefs and if all else fails,
strive to change the world, not yourself.

Helen Louise Attisha

Welcome To Wales

In the hills there are daffodils,
Yellow and glowing like the sun
I go down to the river and throw stones
And I know that summer's just begun.
The castles on the rocks, very historic.
Fresh winds everywhere on the land
And the beautiful, beautiful bay.
The rushing rivers blue as ever
Our mountains are as high as the sky
And in the night when I go to bed
I think about our flag all white, green and red
And I hear our dragon saying welcome to Wales

Alex Davies

Deceit

Do you love me asked the young girl
Yes, the boys reply
In truth he does not love her
For lusts the reason why
Do you miss me asked the young girl,
Yes, I do my love.
He lies again, her prize to gain
How subtle is true love
Will you stay with me my lover
Will you hold me in your arms.
His answer's "Yes" his sweet caress, may only do her harm.
Don't leave me now my darling.
Please stay with me my love.
Silence replied her pleading cries.
He owes no debt to love.

Steve Kenyon

Flight To Romance

A plane will fly, away out of sight.
you and I on it some beautiful night.
We'll never be lonely, always be glad,
we are the best friends we ever had.

On a glorious morning our plane will land.
we'll climb down the steps and go hand in hand
skipping down the runway without a care,
hearts beating unable to bare.

In this foreign land our dreams will come true.
How lovely just me and you.
In this romantic island in the sun.
Wine and dine and have lots of fun.

Along the golden sunny beaches,
Love will grow and will reach us.
It shall be far to big to measure,
this holiday flight to treasure.

Eileen Kenyon

Dear...Happiness

You enter my life, but the times are so few,
You make me feel younger-refreshingly new.
You lighten my though, and loosen my grip,
And I feel like I'm on a spontaneous trip.
The world is then mine - I can do anything
I wish you would stay though - my ultimate fling.
I need you so much, yet you leave without warning,
You leave me distressed and obsessed with morning.
Your absence is hurtful - so cold and untrue,
It brings out the opposite - in me - of you.
My thoughts without you are so unappealing.
Yet you are my own individual feeling
Your coming-success - like a pass of exam
And I don't have to worry about who I am
Your visits are less now, you've shut all my doors
I see why you don't come - you haven't much cause
I'm dying without you - my hopes at a halt
I hardly know you and it's all my fault
You give me more hope than my brain will allow
I love you - need you - and want you here - Now.

Sarah Mursell

Spring

The snowdrop appears beneath its blanket of snow,
The weak sun strikes the petals that glow.
The old oak without its leaves still gaunt,
Its mighty trunk like a ghost the land haunts,
As snow and ice slowly melt from the aged pine
Its mature bark of orange in the sun does shine,
The delicate crocus flowers lift our spirits and hearts,
The early bird sings its joy imparts
A sign of spring's triumph as winter departs.

Barrie Lowe

Farewell

We never grew together,
But we were never far apart,
Although I didn't tell you,
You were always in my heart.

We Were never one for showing,
How we felt to those around,
But it didn't really matter,
What we had was very sound.

And as the time drew nearer,
When you knew you would depart,
You didn't have to tell me,
I felt it in my heart.

I knew you wouldn't go before,
I came to say goodbye,
You are my own dear brother,
Now you have seen me, you will die.

Beulah Williams

Ode To Sally - (My Dog)

Sally you make me happy, more than you'll ever know, -
Your knowing eyes and warm licks, they always comfort me
so. Through the night as I hold you close, I know right now I
love you most. People hurt and cause me pain, but your love
for me still stays the same, we're special friends as long as we
live, I guess we both know how to give. Giving to humans is
wasted I know, give to your dog and their joy it will show.
When I'm sad you so very near, it's you who licks away each
tear. Sally you are a gift from above, you've shown me
unconditional love. You are sensitive, my faithful friend, I
know on you I can depend. I hope you live a long long time,
Sal I'm so privileged, that you are mine. Like me you have had
a very sad life, but together we'll survive this strife, for a
special bond we do share, you understand that life's not fair
People say dogs lives are easy, and that still may be true,
But they are also tough and hard, for feeling dogs like you
I love to hold you in my arms, and lie right by your face -
To know before I fall asleep, you're locked in my embrace.
So Sal I'd just like to say, you'll always be my friend,
When your doggie life is nearly through, I'll be with you till the end.

Melanie Jane Baker

Untitled

I hate the thought of being old when my
poor old body feels the cold as I look
Through my window my eyes won't be clear
The world outside I'll begin to fear as
I sit in my rocking chair for hours on end
Without even a call from a passing friend
My mind will go back in time that has
Passed me by, sometimes I'll laugh, sometimes
I'll cry as I struggle to stand up with
The help of my simmer the whole of my
Future will look a little slimmer
As I take a few steps forward my
Face will show the pain I'll be
Thinking oh! What I would give to
To be young again but I will
Count my blessings and go to my
Bed as I am still very much alive
And it could be I was dead

G. Ottewell

Untitled

In my mind's eye last week I saw your face,
A face for years I had not seen.
In my mind's ear your voice, so clear it
spanned the years between.
I wondered why faint memories could return
without a reason,
was it the anniversary when first we met?
Was it the time of year, or day, or season
That filled my heart with sadness and regret?
    And then I knew that you had died.
Did that love we once had for each other,
Unconsciously unite us for all time?
That your dear spirit dying, leaving,
Reached out in search of mine?
Now death is all that stands between us,
No other lives and loves keep us apart,
When my own soul goes questing outwards,
I now know I'll find your loving,
waiting heart.

H. K. Tonkin

Life Through My Window

As I sit upon my chair
Gazing through my window
The little birds begin to stir
Down on the ground, they wander around,
Pecking at crumbs and bits they've found.
Gazing through my window.
The washing line is full of life
The dancing trousers that belong to my wife.
The socks all lined up in a row
The sheets hanging down and beginning to blow
There's life out there, didn't you know.
Looked up to the sky and stared at the clouds
The winds getting up and sounding quite loud.
The man next door was cutting his grass
Looked over to me shouted! I hope it won't last.
The children are playing in the road.
Skipping and jumping, oh it makes me feel old,
But happy to sit and watch the world go by.
Took a deep breath a gave a big sigh,
Gazing at life through my window
Elizabeth Ann Holt

Peel Life Boat

The wind it roared, the day was grey,
The sea ran fast, and waves were high
And as we peered o'er the wall we saw
The peel lifeboat come fighting for the shore.

"They have been out since eight" they said
"There are at least three fisherman dead"
Their bodies they searched for but in vain
And at three o'clock they returned again.

These brave men who brave the sea
They go out to save people like me,
They volunteer because they know
That sailors need then when winds blow.

They are often forgotten by folks ashore
For all their needs now and before.
But I will never, ever forget them
Or those tired faces of those brave men.
Thelma Prescott

Search For Freedom

Down into the depths,
Whirls a mother and her calf.
Below her, dark and safety.
Above her, pools of red. Thickened,
By the dreaded whalers' laugh.

How long will it be?
Before she joins her mate.
A question, she now asks herself,
In her frantic search for freedom - no element of escape.
A future - succumbed to fate.

Her calf under her belly,
Lured into shore by bait.
The whalers' tricks are plenty.
She strokes her calf - tears scream goodbye.
They no longer have to wait.
Beverly Fairweather

Mother Nature

When winter has laid her bare she does not care
For she has her beauty, and her pride
Under a blanket of soft snow she will hide
And she whispers stay, stay for the birds
That do sing about the sweetness of spring

Then with sweet perfume and sweet bouquets
She adorns herself, as a bride, for a groom
Or as a flower when in full bloom.
And she whispers stay, stay for dawns
Early light and the warm summer night

Where wild rose and honeysuckle fill the air
And cool breezes waft their soft sweet scent
Where many times her beauty and perfume
She has leant
And she whispers stay, stay for the leaves
That softly do fall from splendid trees tall
Stay for the sound of winter's cold call.
P. Britcher

Picture Of Health

O' the woes of a dietary plan
a minefield of disaster for the middle-aged man,
a catalogue of calories
that deflates the will.
"If only we had a super slim pill"
It took twenty years to put this lump on.
So where do I start to take the bits from?
If I could afford it I'd have surgery
but apart from the cost it terrifies me.
So it leaves me no choice, no options at all;
I'll just have to invest in a damn bicycle,
or maybe I'll jog like so many do, inhaling
the fumes on the A22.
O' it all seems so pointless
to inflict such pain,
for a picture of health
in a corpulent frame.
Marcus Taylor

Thankfulness

Walking my dog every day,
Along the river we like to play.
If I feel very sad
I think of these things and I feel glad.

Look at the wildlife and the trees,
See the flowers and the bees.
God made them all, also the river.
He is the taker, and He is the giver.

For when I have been near death's door,
It makes life more precious than ever before.
I can be busy like a beehive,
And very thankful to be alive.

As we head home to our abode,
I feel as if I've shed my load.
Thanks to God for my health.
With things like these, who needs wealth.
J. Vokes

Biographies of Poets

AARON, CLAUDINE
[b.] 18 December 1967, Watford; [ch.] Kasey Aaron; [ed.] Langley Bury School Hunton Bridge, Hertfordshire; [occ.] Hardware, Installation Computer Engineer; [hon.] City and Guilds 224 Electronic Servicing part 1-award winner 1991-92; [pers.] I like to think that technology is here to help improve our lives, but I often think it's here to take over; [a.] Watford, Hertfordshire, UK

AARONS, PAULINE
[b.] 22 June 1947, South London; [m.] Bernard Aarons, 16 October 1971; [ch.] (2) Girl - Gillian and Boy - David; [ed.] Notre Dame Primary School Waverley Secondary Girls School Rachel McMillan Teacher Training College; [occ.] Teacher - Nursery; [oth. writ.] 2 other poems Ping Pong, Abba Father. Have been published - but I've written many other poems.; [pers.] As a committed Christian I am strongly pro life and I am most concerned with the number of abortions carried out in this country.; [a.] Walthamstow, London, UK

ABBOTT, ARTHUR
[pen.] Arthur Abbott; [b.] 8 June 1920, Middlesbrough; [p.] Richard and Annie Abbott (Deceased); [ch.] Grandchildren: Melanie, Jennifer, Paul Abbott; [ed.] Kedleston Rd School, Derby.; [occ.] Retired 1965; [hon.] Many war service medals including the special "City of Caen" on behalf of the citizens of Caen, "To those who like yourself crossed the seas in the face of danger to restore peace and liberty to France and Europe"; [oth. writ.] "A Glimpse of Gold," publishers note: A Delightful Collection of poems recalling a lifetimes experiences of the author from life in orphanages to his time in the army, the author has been extensively featured in the press and radio throughout the North East.; [pers.] Since my retirement many years ago I tried my hand at poetry, writing for profile, and broadcasting my work in hospitals, to the sick and infirm and to all kinds of communities and societies including schools, the listeners enjoyed my talks as much as I.; [a.] Middlesbrough, Cleveland, UK

ADAIR, CONSTANCE
[b.] 2 July 1946, Belfast; [p.] Cecil and Martha Holmes; [m.] Harry, 13 June 1970; [ch.] Edward and Harry; [ed.] Finiston Primary, Belfast Girls Model Secondary; [occ.] Housewife; [pers.] I have always been interested in poetry and I have compiled a book of my own of "Poems I learnt at school and others." When I read a poem I often try to get into the mind of the poet and try to see things from their point of view.; [a.] Donaghadee, Down, UK, BT21 0HY

ADDISON, MARK LAURENCE
[pen.] Mark Laurence Addison; [b.] 14 April 1971, Aberdeen; [p.] William Addison and Mary Addison; [m.] Sarah Addison, 14 October 1995; [ed.] Hazlehead Academy; [occ.] Mail-Room Clerk; [memb.] Scottish Choi Kwan Do Association; [hon.] Purple Belt Red Tag or (5th grade) I.E. Belt Ranking System; [oth. writ.] Other various poems; [pers.] Poems involve very strong emotional feelings in us and I feel they are the keys to the understanding of life.; [a.] Aberdeen, Grampian, UK

ADIO, KAZEEM O.
[b.] 19 April 1975, Oyo State, Nigeria; [p.] Bulliameen Adio and Risqoat Adio; [ed.] St. Patricks Grammar School, Oyo State Hammersmith and West London College, London. University of Sheffield.; [occ.] Student; [hon.] Social Studies (Best student in year 1 of grammar school); [oth. writ.] Few other poems - unpublished Philosophical prose - unpublished.; [pers.] Everything happens for a reason, but not every reason is reasonable..; [a.] Sheffield, S. Yorkshire, UK

AFFORD, SUSAN MARIE (BROWN)
[p.] Susan Brown / Susan Marie; [b.] 06/05/70, Middlesex; [p.] Ruth and Mick (Michael) Swain; [m.] Stephen Afford, 03/05/96; [ch.] James Afford; [ed.] Mellow Lane Comp School; [occ.] Housewife; [memb.] St. Paul's Choir, Brentford, ex-member of St. Edmund's Choir; [hon.] Royal school of church music awards - holder of light blue, dark blue and red ribbons; [oth. writ.] I have just completed putting together a format of my poems and hope to get them published at a later date. Have had other poems published in local magazines, papers, etc.; [pers.] My poems are based on true emotions both personally and seen through the eyes of friends and family, whether affected by media stories, works of fiction or personal tragedies.; [a.] Brentford, Middlesex

AIDULIS, MICHAEL
[b.] 19 December 1972, Glasgow; [p.] John and Patricia Aidulis; [oth. writ.] Many songs as well as poems, having been brought up on Paul Simon and other great songwriters.; [pers.] Poetry is a reaching in to our private selves and a reaching out to each other.

AINSLEY, GEORGINA
[b.] 4 January 1953, Catchgate; [p.] Richard Grenfell, Elizabeth Grenfell; [m.] Graeme Morton Ainsley, 23 September 1989; [ch.] Honor Ainsley, Kerrie Ainsley; [ed.] Greencroft Secondary Modern School; [occ.] Housewife; [hon.] General Service Medal for Army Service in Northern Ireland; [a.] Stanley, Durham, UK

AIRD, KRIS ANTHONY
[b.] 12 August 1980, Ashford; [p.] Mr. B. K. Aird; [m.] Mrs. S. G. Aird, 14 September 1963; [ch.] Two Boys; [ed.] Secondary School, going to South Kent College; [occ.] Final time at school taking GCGE; [hon.] Skiing, Fishing Swimming and School Merit Awards English Achievement Award; [a.] Folkestone, Kent, UK

AISTROP, WILLIE
[b.] 20 April 1922, Sheffield; [p.] Willie - Doris May; [m.] Floremel Sheila (Deceased 1 May 1993), 2 April 1966; [ch.] Alan Stephen (stepson), Kathryn (step-daughter); [ed.] Council School; [occ.] Retired; [memb.] Wales Jubilee Social Club and Institute, Swallowhest Miners Welfare Club Stradbrook Community Centre (Sequlmer Dance Section.); [oth. writ.] Short verses for relatives and friends for social occasions, and for my later wife's Demise Anniversary. The longest and latest form, inspired by the Beauty of my First Climpse of the Scottish Highlands, January 8, 1996.; [pers.] My father and mother acquired a home on a new council estate when I become school and new school in Vicinity therefore I was considerably later starting school mother taught me to read via newspapers I left school one work prior to my fourteen birthday commences work in Polline Mill on fourteen birthday. Daring Love of my Life, courtesy is an admirable companion.; [a.] Sheffield, South Yorkshire, UK

AITCHISON, DEBORAH
[b.] 30 April 1972, Gloucester; [p.] Colin and Yolande Nixon; [m.] James Aitchison, 17 February 1990; [ch.] Naomi Yvonne, Natasja May; [ed.] Severn Vale Comprehensive; [occ.] Play Group Assistant 'Rising Fives'; [pers.] My work comes from inside. I endeavor to find words to express my deepest feelings.; [a.] Colerne, Wiltshire, UK

AITKEN, CHRISTINE
[b.] 4 May 1944, St. Albans, Herts; [p.] Harold Alexander Aitken and Lavinia May Barwood; [ed.] Belmont Sch. Chiswick, Iona Convent, Pretoria, S. Africa Hillview High, Pretoria, S. Africa, Loro Milner Sch. Farm, Settlers, S. Africa; [occ.] Sabbatical Leave; [memb.] Ex. Leading Dancer Royal Ballet (1966-1984), Founder Member Pact Ballet, S. Africa, (1963-64); [hon.] Professional Dance Teacher Certificate, at Royal Academy of Dancing; [oth. writ.] Articles, and reviews for 'Dance and Dancers' and 'The Dancing Times'. Poems, stories, and animal child/adult book (not published); [pers.] Our world of Fauna and Flora is our gift. Please let it exist, and flourish.; [a.] Brentford, Middx, UK

AITKEN, MARGARET
[b.] 4 January 1925, Stoke Hammond; [p.] Albert and Elizabeth Bonner; [m.] Andrew Aitken, 30 March 1946; [ch.] Gillian, Judith and Alison; [ed.] Stoke Hammond C of E and Bletchley Rd. Secondary Modern Schools; [occ.] Housewife; [memb.] S.H.W.I, Winslow, and Bletchley Indoor Bowls Clubs, Organist and fund raiser for SH Methodist Church, Stoke Hammond Garden Club - a keen gardener; [oth. writ.] 16 poems published in anthologies contribution in the Buckinghamshire WI Book Articles in village magazine. I am about to have my book of memories published.; [pers.] I enjoy writing poetry on almost any subject as an idea presents itself to me.; [a.] Stoke Hammond, Buckinghamshire, UK

ALEXANDER, KAY MIRIAM
[b.] 31 January 1956, Ham, Surrey; [m.] GPA; [ch.] Lauren Dutton; [ed.] Grey Court Secondary School; [occ.] Housewife (Mother); [oth. writ.] "Autumn" - Entered International Amateur Open Poetry Contest. (April, May 1996); [pers.] Our precious hearts! A basic key for life. Ambiguous in fragility of need and essential look into and life surrenders riches and treasures, like the hand of marriage. The warmth of the sun, the colour of flowers - say yes this is free. Say no and you are lost to love.; [a.] Andover, Hampshire, UK

ALEXANDER, ROSALIND
[b.] 5 March 1950, Birmingham; [p.] Ella and Alec; [ch.] 1 Daughter, Victoria Helen; [ed.] 1. Marsh Hill Girls Grammar/Tech., Erdington Birmingham, England, 2. Birmingham College of Food; [oth. writ.] Unpublished poetry for personal pleasure; [pers.] To my love and inspiration, Kevin your difficult work does not go unnoticed.; [a.] Den Haag, Netherlands

ALLAN, MAY
[pen.] May Allan; [b.] 2 May 1914, Great Harwood; [p.] Sarah and Robert Smithson; [m.] Stanley (Deceased), 1936; [ch.] Son Keith (died in 1991); [ed.] High School in Blackburn; [occ.] Retired; [hon.] Scholarship for Blackburn High School; [pers.] I am now 82 years of age. All my life I enjoyed music and poetry. I was a baker employed in our family bakery when I was 16 years of age.

In my spare time I played on my piano and sang my own songs, and recited my own poems in public. Now I live alone and have some health problems, but my visitors still enjoy my singing and my poems. I decided to get in touch with you hoping that maybe some of my work will give enjoyment to others.; [a.] Great Harwood, Lancashire, UK

ALLEN, BETTY
[b.] 27 November 1926, Walthamstow, London; [p.] Daisy and Ernest Allen; [ed.] William Morris Secondary School; [occ.] Retired and Enjoying each moment; [a.] Walthamstow, London, Essex, UK

ALLEN, D.
[b.] 30 May 1948, Hampstead; [p.] Ron and Iren; [m.] Lydia; [ch.] Claudine; [ed.] London School of Fashion; [occ.] Free Lance writer; [memb.] Conservative Club; [hon.] City and Guilds; [pers.] 'Twas in the night that inspired to write. For now the sleeper has awaken.; [a.] Edgware, Herts, UK

ALLEN, JOAN
[b.] 23 February 1917, Guildford, Surrey; [p.] Albert and Dorothy Larbey; [m.] Terence Carlyle Allen (Deceased 1965), 25 October 1939; [ch.] John, Roger, Rosalind, Margaret, Christopher, Andrew, Nigel; [ed.] Denehyrst School, Guildford Guuildford Central School. Further Education through numerous evening classes and courses.; [occ.] Busily Retired; [memb.] The Religious Society of Friends (Quakers), The John Muir Trust, Plantlife and other Conversation Groups; [oth. writ.] Local and Quaker histories - 'Heardred's Hill', 'Our George', 'Quakers of Hartshill'; [pers.] Writing, historical research and my family have been my chief interests in recent years. I have reached an age where I appreciate the blessings of every day.; [a.] Nuneaton, Warwickshire, UK

ALLEN, KENNETH ERNEST
[pen.] Ken Allen; [b.] 11 January 1927, Halesowen; [p.] Leonard and Doris Evelyn Allen; [m.] Maureen Allen, 30 August 1975; [ch.] Susan (Previous Marriage); [ed.] Halesowen Church School - and (old name) Halesowen County Modern School for boys; [occ.] Antiquarian book and record shop proprietor; [memb.] Honorary Life Membership of Cranley Heath Amateur Operatic Society, and Current Member of Brierley Hill Amateur Operator Society; [hon.] National Operatic and Dramatic Association Commendation Medal for services to the Amateur Theatre as a Producer, Actor, Singer, Writer, Choreographer; [oth. writ.] Five Full-Length Musical Shows, 6 Mini-Musicals, Biography Book of Mother, poems in local magazine, and short stories in local news papers.; [pers.] I strongly believe that poetry should rhyme, and that I agree with Robert Frost that writing free verse is like playing Tennis with the net down!; [a.] Twidale, Dupley, Sandwell, UK

ALLEN, LUCITA THERESA
[pen.] Topaz Bright; [b.] March 6, 1960, Kingston, Jamaica; [p.] Inez Allen, Leslie Allen; [m.] Dennis Porter; [ch.] Caroline Marie; [ed.] Tilton Rd Secondary, Solihull College, Sandwell College; [occ.] Bank Clerk -- large bank with international connections; [oth. writ.] Nothing else published as yet but have had several poems read out in church and several public functions; [pers.] My poems are based on everyday life and the lives of people around me and worldwide. I would like to think that they can be easily read with understanding by everyone, young or old.; [a.] Birmingham, West Mids

ALLEN, MARION ROSEMARIE
[p.] Nannie Norfolk; [b.] 23 April 1938, Wickford, Essex; [m.] Derrick Allen, 4 March 1980; [ch.] five; [ed.] Wickford Junior & Senior Schools, Chelmsford Technical College (pre-nursing course); [occ.] foster parent; [memb.] SSAAFA (Norfolk Fostering); [oth. writ.] "Summer of 1957", the struggle of a teenage girl to keep her child in the year 1957, was used to lobby MPs into the plight of the single mum.; [pers.] Young children and the elderly have played a big part in my life. I try to bring them to-gether in my writing. I write of what I have seen and the joy that I have known along with sadness.; [a.] Lakenheath, Suffolk

ALLO, THEODORE
[p.] Facques and Sarah Allo; [ed.] University of Abidjan (Ivory Coast); [oth. writ.] Several poems published in the Ivorian national newspaper, (fraternity matin) included this one which I've translated myself from French.; [pers.] I have been influenced early by the great french pet Baudelaive. But being an African poet I tend to be the voice of the wind or rather a voice in the wind which says loud the fears and anguish of African people.; [a.] London, UK, SE17 1HA

ALLUM, JUNE
[b.] 27 June 1935, Chieveley, Berks; [p.] William Perry, Winifred Perry; [m.] David Allum, 30 October 1987; [ch.] Ruth Stella, Mark John (both married); [ed.] Townsend Secondary Modern Girls School, St. Albans Herts; [occ.] Retired ex SRN and Relief Catering Assistant; [memb.] Calcot Country Music Club, Wagon Wheel (Reading) Country Music Club. I write reports for above Country Music Clubs in Southern Country Magazine; [hon.] Nursing Finals S-R-N 1958, Basic Food Hygiene 1992; [oth. writ.] Publication in "Voices On The Wind", poems printed in Southern Country Magazine poems written at Live Country Gigs given to bands written 2 poems to the queen; [pers.] I enjoy writing poetry as a hobby all my work is centered on life as I see it, as things that affect me, and my surroundings and family.; [a.] Reading, Berkshire, UK

AMA, GRACE
[pen.] 'Buchi'; [b.] London; [ed.] BSC Zoology University of Port Harcourt; [occ.] Civil Servant Benefits Agency; [pers.] I like to write my poems and stories in a way that everyone can relate to, sometimes bringing out perspectives that have never been looked at. Being very emotional, I potray a lot in my writing.; [a.] Nunhead, London

AMBROSE, CHARLOTTE
[b.] 15 August 1980, Trowbridge; [p.] Steve Ambrose, Vickie Ambrose; [ed.] Student; [a.] New Milton, Hampshire, UK

AMOS, EVELYN
[pen.] Annie Keylock; [b.] 25 July 1954, Banbury; [p.] Herbert Edward and Navana Beryl Marsh; [m.] Ronald George Amos, 22 July 1972; [ch.] Russell George, Rebecca Louise; [ed.] Brittania Rd, Primary School, Dashwood Rd School, Broughton Hall; [occ.] Learning Support Assistant; [pers.] I love writing poetry, but I would also love to write and illustrate children's books, and write short stories.; [a.] Banbury, Oxfordshire, UK

AMSBY, JOHN SAMUEL
[pen.] Fonda John Samuel; [b.] 20 February 1924, Leyton; [p.] Ernest and Lavinia Amsby; [m.] Anne McGrady (Deceased January 1980), 14 September 1957; [ch.] Son and their Daughter; [ed.] Elementary 1928-1938, University of Life, Italy 1943-1945, was service and London Blitz 1940-1941, 35 years Postal Service, Little Schooling after 12 1/2 years due to an accident; [occ.] Retired; [memb.] Royal British Legion, Postal Veteran's Assoc.; [hon.] Certified of Merit Royal British Legion (Manor Par Brch,) for Hospital Visitor in 1980's. (Stopped through ill health 1991); [oth. writ.] Occasional articles in Church and Work Magazines.; [pers.] Pleasing to be accepted as a poet.; [a.] Ford Essex, Essex, UK

AMSDEN, JOHN SELWYN
[b.] 31 July 1928, London; [p.] Frederick Henry Amsden, Ethel Sarina Amsden; [memb.] The Vegan Society; [oth. writ.] "Animal songs and Vegan verses."; [pers.] Against all ethical statement, higher thought to the humblest distress, the life or ecology of the world or beyond is even increasing as a matter of non-observance. The natural world of interdependance can be one of carnage and despair: Light, beauty and truth taken from the animals, too, who must not suffer and suffer persistent destruction.; [a.] Yarmouth, Isle of Wight, UK

ANDERSON, KATHLEEN
[pen.] Kaz; [b.] 9 July 1964, Johnstone; [p.] Billy and Ria; [m.] Neil, 1 September 1989; [ch.] Three girls, one boy; [ed.] Left Camphill High Comprehensive School (Age 16); [occ.] Housewife; [memb.] Anchor Book Ltd.; [hon.] Poem's published in magazines also poem published in another anthology; [oth. writ.] Putting a book together for my daughter Leighann (Eldest) who has disabilities. Other poems; [pers.] For the insight from a very special girl who has taught me so much passion to and for other lifes, otherwise I'd never have known true worth.; [a.] Paisley, Renfrewshire, UK

ANDERSON, LYNN
[pen.] Lynn Anderson; [b.] 16 August 1975, Edinburgh; [p.] Alan Anderson and Marion Anderson; [ed.] St. Davids High School - Dalkeith; [occ.] Purchase Ledger Clerk (Tarmac Topmix); [a.] Rosewell, UK

ANDERSON, SUSAN
[b.] 15 August 1977, Rochford; [p.] Mrs. Pamela Anderson, Mr. Robert George Anderson (Deceased); [ed.] Cornelious Vermuydan Secondary School; [occ.] Shop Assistant, Pounstrechers Southern-on-Sea; [hon.] Commendation for a short horror story for the local paper; [oth. writ.] A poem published in Go Green, a book about the environment, called Pains of a Mother; [pers.] I would like to think that my father is proud of my poem. May he rest in peace.; [a.] Canvey Island, Essex, UK

ANDERSON, TOM
[b.] 22 November 1965, Glasgow; [p.] Cyril and Betty Anderson; [ed.] Victoria College/Clinic Linthouse College (Electronics) Cardonald College (Heath Studies); [occ.] Chiropodist; [oth. writ.] Small selection of other poems as well as loads of songs. Nothing published as yet though.; [pers.] I just write what and how I feel; [a.] Belfast, Antrim, UK

ANDERTON, STEPHEN
[b.] 17 September 1961, Bolton; [p.] Joyce Ann Ronald; [m.] A loving Denise, not married; [ch.] Two stepsons - Gary and Alan, 2 daughters Cheryl

and Sara; [ed.] Basic education, passes include mathematics, English literature and English language; [occ.] Caterer; [memb.] Mainly of cycling clubs; [hon.] Various certificates concerned with cycling, certificates for catering and hygiene, certificate of merit from Mensa, prizes and trophies for winning rock 'n' roll diving competitions; [oth. writ.] Second poem I submitted was printed in the Bolton Evening News 28/5/96; [pers.] An open mind and a realistic view of life and everything natural around us, can create a basis for any kind of literature, serious or comical, like life itself.; [a.] Bolton, Lancs, UK

ANDREWS, KAYE
[b.] 8 November 1962, Devizes, Wiltshire; [p.] Geoff and Vilma Paget; [m.] Nick Andrews, 27 July 1985; [ch.] Stacey Michelle, Stephanie Katrina, Sophie Rose; [ed.] 'Bromham' St Nicholas primary school, then, John Bently (Calne, wiltshire); [occ.] Childminder; [memb.] Bromham Troupers, (Amateur Dramatic's); [oth. writ.] Poems published in 'Parish Magazine', also written for others for birthdays and special vents. My parents and Aunty write and I would love to published 'A family a poems'.; [pers.] I have written a poem called "The child with no name" based on the T.V. documentary - The dying rooms - I was asked if it could be published for the people working on a New orphanage in china, Newsletter) - I was honoured to say yes.; [a.] Chippenham, Wiltshire, UK

ANDREWS, RUTH M.
[b.] 14 December 1950, Nottingham; [m.] Kalian; [ch.] 1 son; [ed.] University of York; [occ.] Music Coordinator, Int'l. School of Amsterdam; [memb.] 1. European Music Educators' Association, 2. Music Educators' National Conference; [oth. writ.] Short story collection: "Leavings" (awaiting publication), poems, music/education articles: 1. "The Composing Process", 2. "The Use of Journals in Music" published in EMEA magazine; [pers.] Lived in Italy 10 years, The Netherlands 9 years. I choose mostly to explore real (mundane) situations, to pinpoint the beauty and sadness in the "ordinary".; [a.] Amsterdam, Netherlands

ANGELL, GRANVILLE STACEY
[pen.] Lord of Cannock; [b.] 13 November 1932, Cannock; [ed.] Severly Disrupted because of 2nd world war (1939-45) latent education development left school no qualifications; [occ.] Retired; [memb.] 46 Holder of Title since October '86. Lord of the Manor of Cannock.; [hon.] First non-commissioned officer in history of royal navy to get a degree entirely by correspondence courses - London University B. Sc. (Economics) 1971 B.A. Open University, M. Ed. 1981 University of Birmingham 1981.; [a.] Cannock, Staffs, UK, WS11 1AA

ANSTEE, SANDRA ANN
[pen.] Sandra Anstee - Brown; [b.] 21 June, Barnstaple, N. Devon; [p.] Alec, Donald, George, (known as Don) and Joan Helen; [m.] Christopher Anstee, 6 February 1993 and 18 May 1974; [ch.] Robert Davis, Louise Davis, Sally Davis, Deborah and Clare; [ed.] Georgeham Primary, Braunton Primary, Braunton Secondary Modern; [occ.] Warden of Elderly Sheltered Accomodation; [memb.] Founder member of S. A. Players (amateur Drama Group); [oth. writ.] Three Original plays a three pantomimes. Play Titles "Schools Out", "Who Cares Anyway", "Littles Big Story"; [pers.] I write to express my explorations and reflections on life.; [a.] Grantchester, Cambs, UK

ANTELL, BARRY
[b.] Leigh Orchard; [p.] Robert and Helen Antell; [m.] Patricia Antell; [ch.] Kathryn Claire and Sally Louise; [ed.] Queen Elizabeth's Grammar School Wimborne Dorset; [pers.] My philosophy recognizes need to treat every living thing with respect. I am deeply saddened by man's in humanity to the living world around him; [a.] Frome, Somerset, UK

ARMSTRONG, JOAN
[b.] 15 February 1926, Swansea; [p.] Florence and William Johnson; [m.] William Armstrong (Deceased, 1984), 2 February 1944; [ch.] Lyndon and Angela; [ed.] St. Thomas Girl's School and Tycoch College of further education Swansea (night classes); [occ.] Retired; [hon.] Obtained 0 levels in English language. Literature and religious instruction. At the age of 49. I obtained an a level in English literature when I was 50 years old.; [oth. writ.] Numerous articles for local paper whenever they request me to write for them.; [pers.] I hope that my writings evoke the imagination of the readers. The works of William Wordsworth have been my inspiration.; [a.] Swansea, West Glamorgan, UK

ARROWSMITH, STANLEY
[b.] 24 July 1941, Trowbridge, Wilts; [p.] Stanley and Phyllis; [m.] Ann Legget, 25 September 1965; [ch.] Darren John, Christine Ann; [ed.] County Primary, County Secondary; [occ.] Retired due to M.S. since 1991. Before Illness, Master Carpenter/Shopfitter; [memb.] Multiple Sclerosis Society (Northlands) Bromley Kent, Lledo, Vintage car collectors club, Gold plated models of cars.; [oth. writ.] M.S. Society Magazine, M.S. Society Newsletter, M.S. Charity Ashford Kent, including publishing a small book myself to raise money for Charity; [pers.] My work has since I started helped me to ease and endure the great pain I suffer each day there is no pill that can do this I call my work (A Pill Called.....Concentration) and have even written a poem entitled the same.; [a.] Sydenham, UK

ARTHUR, MR. CARL A.
[b.] 26 July 1950, Birkenhead; [p.] Alan, Joan Arthur; [m.] Angela Susan, 30 December 1994; [ch.] 5; [ed.] Secondary Modern; [occ.] Trainee Driving Instructor; [oth. writ.] This is first entry, although I have things written which I have things written which I have not yet entered into competition.; [pers.] Unlike some poets, I have not been influenced by there writing, I write from personal experiences of events that have taken place throughout my life, I have experienced life in all its form's feelings of love, happiness sadness.; [a.] Nallasey, Merseyside, UK

ASH, OLIVE FRANCES
[b.] 5 April 1927, Caerphilly, South Wales; [p.] Joseph Williams and Elizabeth Anne Williams; [m.] Late Michael H. Ash, 26 March 1949; [ch.] Guy Henry, Late Richard Henry and Simon Lawrence Henry; [oth. writ.] Letter published in "Letters Magazine" and poem in "Wiltshire Times."; [pers.] I prefer classic use of words and am fascinated with Shakespeare's sonnets, the couplets are brilliant and challenging.; [a.] Trowbridge, Wilts, UK

ASHBY, DOROTHY
[b.] February 27, 1920, Doncaster; [p.] Gustave and Ada Taylor; [m.] Raymond John Ashby, January 20, 1972; [ch.] David; [occ.] Retired Personnel Officer; [memb.] Towns Women's Guild Doncaster Women's Luncheon Club, Bridge Club; [oth. writ.] "Invitation to Doncaster" published in "A Taste of the North" "March Winds" - (awaiting publishing in amateur poets year book 1995).; [pers.] Have compiled rhymes since school days - mainly for friends - birthdays and works magazine - also special occasions - wedding anniversaries etc.; [a.] Doncaster, Yorkshire

ASHFIELD, MARGARET LORRAINE
[b.] 4 May 1953, West Bromwich; [p.] William E. Long, Irene Long Brettoner; [m.] James S. Ashfield, 26 April 1975; [ch.] James, Samantha and Emma; [oth. writ.] "Passing Stranger" poem published in Midland words, 1992; [pers.] I wish to dedicate, "If I could just reach out my hand" to my beloved mother who passed away from this earth on 14 May 1996. And to my grand mother who I never met. Two wonderful women.; [a.] Great Barr, B'ham, West Midlands, UK

ASHTON, BETTY
[b.] 3 July 1934, London; [p.] Jack and Ethel Gold; [m.] Raymond Ashton, 24 October 1954; [ch.] Elaine, Sandee and Rosalynn; [ed.] Fairclough Street, School, Whitechapel, London E.I.; [occ.] Professional Grandmother; [pers.] "There but for the Grace of God go I".; [a.] Dulwich, London, UK

ASKER, DEREK W. G.
[b.] 7 February 1932, Binfield, Berks; [p.] John Henry Asker and Violet Selina Asker; [m.] Janice Asker, 28 April 1996 (Recent); [ch.] Four boys, two girls (two including stepsons); [ed.] Farley Hill School, Reading, Berks; [occ.] Retired; [hon.] Renshaw Cup (Bakery), 1st Class City and Guilds (Int) (Bakery), passed 'O' level English when 4 yrs of age; [oth. writ.] The hospice poems book/romance is the star, other poems in anthologies. Songwriter; [pers.] I think youth and romance daily - my pen has humour, insight and tenderness, for I love people and love life.; [a.] Farnborough, Hants, UK

ASTON, DAVID SHAUN
[b.] 18 October 1954, Redruth; [p.] Ivy Aston, Gilbert Aston; [m.] Felicity Ann Aston, 24 July 1981; [ch.] Janine, Eleanor and Carlin; [ed.] Basset Road Boy's School Camborne, Redruth Grammar School; [occ.] Fitter for (Civil Engineer/Construction) Company; [pers.] I have written forty-one poems to date constantly striving to paint with words the kaleidoscope of emotions that permeate my mind; [a.] Pool Redruth, Cornwall, UK

ATKINS, ANNETTE
[pen.] Annie Atkins; [b.] 28 March 1961, Birmingham; [p.] Gerald and Rebecca O'Brien; [m.] Shaun Atkins, 18 August 1979; [ch.] Michaela and Lynnette; [ed.] Registered Nurse Dip/He Sir Gordon Roberts School of Nursing, University of Leicester; [occ.] School nurse; [oth. writ.] Various poems, inspired by nursing, and life experiences; [pers.] Leave behind you what happened yesterday, and look to the future with a smile.; [a.] Northampton, Northants, UK

AYER, JANE
[b.] 5 October 1923, Merthyrty Ofic; [p.] Edith Mary Smith; [pers.] This poem I dedicate to my husband Frederick Alexander Ayer a survivor of World War Two and to my father William James Smith a survivor of World War One.

BADER, SERENA LOUISE
[b.] 9 April 1974, Braintree; [p.] Jean Bader; [ed.] Bretton Hall, College of the University of Leeds; [occ.] Student; [hon.] BA (Hons) degree in English and Drama; [pers.] I feel poetry is a medium where unheard voices in society can be sensitively articulated.; [a.] Wakefield, W. Yorks, UK

BAGNALL, MRS. LINDA
[b.] 23 December 1958, Fulford, York; [p.] John and Irene Kemp; [m.] John Bagnall, 24 May 1980; [ch.] Rebecca and Lisa; [ed.] Popleton Road Primary School Dadcaster Grammar School York College of Arts and Technology; [occ.] "Little School" Pre-School Group Owner and Organizer (NNEB); [pers.] I am thrilled to have my first published poem which I would like to dedicate to my family who I love dearly.; [a.] Haxby York, N. Yorks, UK

BAIL, GEORGINA
[b.] 13 March 1979; [p.] Mother deceased and father Chris Bail; [ed.] Wildern Secondary, Brockenhurst College; [occ.] College Student; [oth. writ.] Own personal folder full of my own work. None have ever been published anywhere.; [pers.] I get inspired by my emotions and experiences. This poems is dedicated to my Mum who died. God Bless!; [a.] Southampton, Hampshire, UK

BAILEY, CHRISTINE
[b.] 26 September 1947, Cheshire; [p.] Harry and Susannah Knowles; [m.] W. P. Bailey; [ch.] Tanya Marie, Heidi Suzanne, Matthew Peter; [occ.] Housewife; [pers.] I have come to learn through struggling with illness, to grasp tightly to even the smallest ray of hope.; [a.] Hyde, Cheshire, UK

BAIRD, MAVIS
[b.] 5 August 1931, Newstead; [p.] George Gibson and Doris Gibson; [m.] Alexander Baird, 23 February 1952; [ch.] Linda, Christine, Gary, Arthur, Terry; [ed.] Blidworth, Junior, Infant mixed; [occ.] House wife; [memb.] Mansfield District Council Poetry Magazine Society; [oth. writ.] First Prize Local Paper, several-poems published. In local magazine; [pers.] Dedicated to my late husband, Alexander, who encouraged me in my writings.; [a.] Mansfield, Nottingham, UK

BAKER, ANTHONY
[b.] 7 June 1969, Dundee; [p.] Mrs. Carol Ann Baker; [ed.] Mewzieshill High School, Dundee. I'm currently studying with O.U. for an arts degree.; [occ.] Furniture restoration - currently unemployed, seeking employment; [memb.] Cooking Vinyl LTD - (Record Club), local libraries, (Audio LIbrary), Dundee Rep. Theatre; [oth. writ.] Short stories (various kinds) fact-based writings (fiction/songs -- have also attempted plays, need coaching though); [pers.] Poetry serves itself as an anchor for our innermost thoughts. Without poetry we would be adrift, floating wordless and sad.; [a.] Dundee, Tayside, UK

BAKER, CAMILLA ANGELA JENNETTA
[b.] 17 December 1943, Stokenchurch; [m.] Roy William Baker, 24 March 1962; [ch.] Jane Susannah; [occ.] Housewife; [memb.] Stokenchurch Parish Council 1983-1996 on going for four years, League of Jewish Women (Maidenhead Branch); [pers.] My poetical thoughts are of Jerusalem, precious everlasting memories, of silent moments thoughtful and yearning, finding my roots, the home of my soul and my foundation for life.; [a.] High Wycombe, Bucks, UK

BAKER, DAWN
[pen.] Twiggy; [b.] 13 September 1963, Plymouth; [p.] David Rogers and Betty Rogers; [m.] James Baker, 20 September 1986; [ed.] Efford Secondary, Modern School, Efford Plymouth; [occ.] Domestic Asst. 15, years; [oth. writ.] None, this is my first competition; [pers.] There's an old saying, no one can take our memories away. When I wrote this poem it was for someone to whom I worked with many years, we had laugh's also tears, but stayed friends for many years.; [a.] Plymouth, Devon, UK

BAKER, JANICE MAUREEN
[b.] 5 May 1950, Brighton; [p.] James Victor Clark and Marjory Lydia Clark; [m.] Keith John Baker, 16 December 1977; [ch.] Peter James, Melanie Angela, Melissa Jane, Mark David; [ed.] Elm Grove Comprehensive School; [occ.] Housewife; [memb.] Gardening Club, Music Society; [hon.] S.G.S.E. Subjects Maths, English, English-Literature, Art, Religious Studies; [oth. writ.] This will be my first published poem. I enjoy for pleasure and satisfaction.; [pers.] I gain great understanding of people and the world which reflects in all I write. I truly believe to read and write is a tree of knowledge. (Influenced by Wordsworth and Stevenson.; [a.] Littlehampton, W. Sussex, UK

BAKER, LESLEY
[b.] 24 June 1945, Hillingdon, Middx; [p.] Jean and Victor Cooper; [m.] Raymond, 31 July 1965; [ch.] Simon, Andrea and Lea; [ed.] Harlington S. M. School; [occ.] Administrative Assistant; [memb.] Psoriatic Anthropalthy Alliance; [oth. writ.] Several poems published in anthologies.; [pers.] In my writing I try to reflect on 60th the joys and sorrows of life.; [a.] Street, Somerset, UK

BAKER, MELANIE JANE
[b.] 4 February 1968, London; [ed.] Aieburth Vale High School, Mabelfletcher Technical College (Training) in Social Care; [occ.] Trainee Counsellor previously worked caring for children with special needs; [hon.] Royal schools of music, Piano Examinations up to and including grade 5; [oth. writ.] There's always hope, as the rain falls down, sad at Christmas option for silence, despair, pain, alone, love injustice, survival. (Some of my poems been in local papers); [pers.] My poems express true love from the heart I've learnt the hard way, that true love involves pain, but pain always has a purpose - and when you've come through it - there is always hope of a future; [a.] Liverpool, Merseyside, UK

BAKER, STEVEN
[b.] 4 September 1968, Colchester; [p.] Peter Baker, Gwen Baker; [m.] Vanessa Baker, 9 February 1991; [ed.] The Gilberd Comprehensive, The Joint Services School of Radiography; [occ.] Radiographer; [memb.] The Council for professions supplementary to medicine; [hon.] Diploma in Diagnostic radiography; [oth. writ.] Private collection of unpublished poems; [pers.] "Putting words to verse is my way of expression. I hope when I die I've left a lasting impression."; [a.] Aldershot, Hampshire, UK

BAKER, MRS. T.
[b.] 1 August 1968, Newcastle; [p.] Mrs. M. Devlin; [m.] Mr. S. Baker, 30 September 1994; [ch.] Four; [occ.] Housewife; [a.] Newcastle, Tyne and Wear, UK

BAKHURST, MAVIS JEAN MARY
[pen.] Havis; [b.] 25 January 1932, London; [p.] Maude and Leslie Bakhurst; [m.] Hugh Hasan-Ali (Deceased), 10 October 1953; [ch.] David (Deceased), Roxanna and Roselinda; [ed.] Schools in Cornwall during the war. Years send with mother because of bombing; [occ.] Ass'ts Sales Consultant Kurt Geiger Shoes Ltd; [oth. writ.] Short stories, children's stories and poems; [pers.] Live for the moment, not yesterday, not tomorrow, but now. Yesterday is gone, tomorrow might never come like Wortworh Omar Kyan poems.; [a.] London, UK

BALDERSTONE, BEV
[b.] 26 August 1964, Cornwall; [p.] Gordon and Maureen Rosevear; [m.] 19 September 1992; [ed.] Bodmin Secondary School; [occ.] Book Binder; [oth. writ.] None, this is my first attempt to get published; [pers.] Due to the seperation from my husband, I started to put my feelings into writing poetry.; [a.] Bodmin, Cornwall, UK

BALL, GEMMA
[b.] 23 June 1983, Cambridge; [p.] Joanne and Stephen Ball; [ed.] Saint Felix Primary School, Thurlow Primary School and Partway Middle School; [oth. writ.] I have written a number of poems but have not been published; [pers.] I do a lot of sport, and I love animals especially Whales and Dolphins, I have adopted my own Whale. I write my poems based on real life things.; [a.] Haverhill, Suffolk, UK

BALLARD, IRIS ROSEMARY MILDRED
[b.] 17 May 1929, Bottle, Sussex; [p.] Benjiman and Mildred Chesson; [m.] Alan Frank Ballard (Died 3 May 1985), 30 September 1950; [ed.] Four sons, one daughter; [occ.] In Hastings my home until 1961, I attend the local school I finished my education in the Sacred Heart college for girls in hastings; [memb.] I belong to a Christian Brotherhood, do healing. Meditation German Shepherd Societies, Reserve Societies; [hon.] Passed my Music Exams, for the piano, I was able to teach the piano, on my days of from Nursing when young, along with my husband, won several Sailing Awards, and awards for Cine Films, in the sixties, in Hastings Cine Club; [oth. writ.] Several poems about sailing and the sea, a few about my German Shepherd, poems concerning bereavement, religion world affairs, and nature, written about Iona, the two worlds of Iona, and several other thing, I've not bothered to get and think published.; [pers.] Except for a few, in Christ Waltons Books. I write, because it helps me to get things out my system, and express, my grief love, joys and sadnesses I was influenced by poets like long fellow, Robert Burns.; [a.] Lee on Solent, Hampshire, UK

BANGERT, NIGEL
[b.] 8 March 1965, Bishops Storford; [m.] Dawn Whiffin (Fiancee); [ed.] Newport Essex (free) Grammar School; [occ.] Stockroom Supervisor; [memb.] Subscribe to: Envoi and poetry now magazines; [oth. writ.] Poems published in envoi, and poetry now; [pers.] I write for peace love and harmony in the world. Failing that a million avid and a fast car will do; [a.] Harlow, Essex, UK

BANNISTER, CAROL
[pen.] Cass; [b.] 13 July 1948, Birmingham; [p.] Louise Higgs and Walter Higgs; [m.] Divorced; [ch.] Son age 22, Lee Bannister; [ed.] Harry Lucas Secondary Modern, Birmingham, St. Matthews Hospital Nursing College Burntwood Staffs; [occ.] Sales and Marketing and Investigations and Tracing Agency; [memb.] Local Operatic Society and Drama Group, Recently Toured Sweden in "Run for Your Wife"; [hon.] State Enrolled Nurse; [oth. writ.] Several poems in poetry anthology. Published many lyrics to songs awaiting melodies to accompany; [pers.] "Never lose sight of your dreams" I love all Wordsworth's work. So dreamily descriptive; [a.] Cannock Wood, Staffs, UK

BARCLAY, DR. JENNIFER M.
[b.] Lowell, Massachusetts; [p.] Mr. James and Mrs. Agnes Barclay; [ed.] St. Julian's School, Carcavelos, Portugal Dundee High School, Edinburgh University Medical School (Graduated 1983); [occ.] General medical practitioner; [memb.] Member of the College of General Practitioners (MRCGP), Christian Medical Fellowship, National Trust; [pers.] The main influences in my life and writing have been a warm Christian home, many colourful contacts with the public during my years in medical practice and a long-standing and enduring Christian faith.; [a.] Monifieth, Tayside, UK

BARKER, JOAN JULIA
[b.] 1 August 1920, London; [p.] Julia and John Barker; [ed.] St. Julianna's Convent London SW5; [occ.] Retired; [memb.] "Society of Amateur Artists" Newark, Notts: "Sidmouth Society of Artists" Sidmouth Devon, "International Fund for Animal Welfare" Crowborough E. Essex; [hon.] Award - Champion for Animals (IFAW); [oth. writ.] Three novels and a play (unpublished); [pers.] I have been influenced by patience strong, and I strive to write all that is good in this life.; [a.] Sidmouth, Devon, UK

BARKER, ROSAMUND JANE
[b.] 17 April 1946, Kirkby-in-Ashfield, Notts; [p.] Alan Lee and Barbara Lee; [m.] Roger Leslie Barker (Deceased), 17 October 1981; [ch.] Thomas Benjamin; [ed.] Sherwood Hall Grammar; [occ.] Civil Servant; [pers.] To be happy with my mind.; [a.] Lee on the Solent, Hants, UK

BARLOW, ALAN
[b.] 3 April 1935, Wolverhampton; [p.] Cyril and Ellen Barlow; [m.] Beryl Meek; [ch.] Ian Stuart, Alison Jane, Janet Isla; [ed.] Wednesbury County Commercial (Grammar) School, Wolverhampton Polytechnic; [occ.] Retired; [memb.] Labour Party, M.I.E.D. (Institute of Engineering Design); [hon.] School Cert, Higher National (MECH); [pers.] I suppose I am interested in what lies underneath the veneer. The Victorians I find particularly fascinating in this respect.; [a.] Chester, Cheshire, UK

BARLOW, LYN
[b.] 18 July 1963, Sheffield; [p.] Margaret and George Barlow; [ed.] Hillcroft Residential College for Women (Surrey), New Hall College (Cambridge University, Anglia Polythechnic University (Cambridge); [occ.] Student; [oth. writ.] 'Oh Father' and 'Feather' (Nineties poetry) 'Shadowland' (The West In Her Eye, Pyramid Press) several poems published in magazines. A couple of articles in the New Stateman.; [pers.] The chief aim of my work is that it is accessible to people from all backgrounds, I try to write with a view of what the reader will think upon reading. I love to write, especially poetry and hope it brings pleasure.; [a.] Cambridge, Anglia, UK

BARNES, MARK ANTHONY
[b.] 14 August 1964, Wendover, Hants; [p.] Lawrence Barnes, Valerie Barnes; [m.] Sharon Wheelhouse; [ch.] Richard Anthony, Samantha Gayle, Simon Christopher, Maegin Leah, Daniel Junior; [ed.] Intake High School, Bramley, Leeds; [occ.] Pallet Repair and Maintenance Technician; [hon.] N.V.Q. Level 1 Business Administration; [oth. writ.] Several poems, children's short stories, songs and music. So far unpublished. A short story based on a true life experience to be published around christmas in a popular magazine; [pers.] My work is influenced by read 'Hard' life, thoughts and day to day feelings. Also news and media. In a working class environment, general life is food for thought.; [a.] Leeds, W. Yorks, UK

BARRACLOUGH, MRS. MURIEL
[pen.] Muriel Sowerby, Muriel Barraclough; [b.] 12 February 1908, Emley Moor; [p.] Benjamin Sowerby and Ruth H. Sowerby; [m.] Roy Barraclough, 19 May 1934; [ch.] Antony Heywood-Holmes; [ed.] Darton Council School Barnsley Institute of Further Education, Wath-upon-Dearne; [occ.] Retired; [memb.] Teacher in Further Education (25 years) Methodist Church Steward Former Member of Samaritans (12 years) Helper in Local Gideons. Bible Society Committee. Barnsley Blind and Partially Sighted; [hon.] Bronze Medal (embroidery) Teaching Certificate, City and Guilds Embroidery, City and Guilds Soft Furnishing, City and Guilds Upholstery, Ockenden Venture Helper; [oth. writ.] Stars and Mist, Pen Portraits. Poems published in local magazines.; [pers.] I am a happy person and strive through my poems to reflect that happiness to those who read them.; [a.] Barnsley, S. Yorks, UK

BARRETT, CAROL
[b.] 14 June 1957, Jamaica; [p.] Delores Brown, Basil Brown; [m.] Joseph Barrett, 29 January 1982; [ch.] Gavin, Charlotte, Nadino; [ed.] Wood Green High; [occ.] Promotion Manager Hillingdon; [hon.] English Communication Skills; [oth. writ.] Several poems published in national news paper and a anthology; [pers.] A believes in the well bung of children, opportunity and justice for all. A true romantic at heart aim for such reflection in my writing.; [a.] Hillingdon, Middlesex, UK

BARRETT, SINEAD
[b.] 24 May 1978, Hammersmith, London; [p.] John Barrett and Rosemarie Barrett; [ed.] Sacred Heart High School, Hammersmith Loreto Convent, Letterkenny; [occ.] Student; [memb.] Letterkenny Writers Group; [hon.] Prize winner in the Letterkenny, Writers Group Short-Story, Competition and Winner of the Donegal Short Story Competition; [oth. writ.] Short-stories published in local newspaper.; [pers.] Peace and justice. I have been greatly influenced by W.B. Yeats; [a.] Letterkenny, Donegal, UK

BARRETT, ZELIA E. J.
[b.] 28 September 1913, Southfields; [p.] Mabel and Stanley Edwards; [m.] William Barrett, 29 July 1935; [ch.] Pauline and Colin; [ed.] Ashley Lodge, Wimbledon, Pk Rd and Wandsworth Technical. My work has been in magazines E.G. School and Kodak Ctd. I write about real life (events); [occ.] Housewife, Seaford, Sussex; [memb.] Civil Service Motoring Club

BARRY, ESTHER
[b.] Wicklow, Eire; [p.] Henry and Mary Watson; [m.] Alfred Barry, died 1990; [ed.] Convent of Mercy, Rathdrum, Wicklow, Eire; [occ.] retired nurse; [memb.] Life member of C.S.C.A.W., (Catholic Study for Animal Welfare); [oth. writ.] Published 14 times in various anthologies; [pers.] My poems reflect my feelings towards everyday situations, amusing incidents, grief of bereavement, and the folly of war. My interests are poetry, painting, music and reading 17th Century history.; [a.] Finchley, London

BARTLETT, HELEN
[pen.] Spyder; [b.] 12 January 1971, Windsor; [p.] Michael Wheeler, Jean Wheeler; [m.] Steven Bartlett, 11 May 1991; [ch.] Christopher, David, Liam James; [ed.] Ryde High; [occ.] Housewife; [oth. writ.] Many other works, as yet unpublished; [pers.] Much of my work has a double meaning, designed to be re-read and re-discovered.; [a.] Ryde, Isle of Wight, UK

BARWICK-WARD, LUCY
[b.] 12 August 1980, Harrogate; [p.] Robert Barwick-Ward, Laura Cowing Step-father, Malcolm Cowing; [ed.] Ashville College, Harrogate; [occ.] Student; [memb.] Katrina Hughes Dancers - Haroggate, England; [hon.] Lamda Grade 7 - Honours BB0-Grade 4 Tap, Grade 4 Ballet. Associated Board Music Exams Grade 4 Clarinet - Distinction; [pers.] "I would like to dedicate this poem to my Grandma - "Joan Marie Sutcliffe" although she is not here today, she is eternally loved and remembered by everyone who knew her.; [a.] Wetherby, England

BATCHELOR, PAMELA
[pen.] Pamela Frisch; [b.] 1 September 1956, Harrow-on-the-Hill, Middlesex; [p.] Edward Frisch (Deceased) Rose Frisch; [m.] Graham Batchelor, 9 July 1992; [ch.] Melissa; [ed.] St. Gregory's Comp (Kenton) Harrow 6th Form College; [occ.] Housewife and mother; [oth. writ.] Nothing published as yet; [pers.] Poetry to me has always been the most wonderful way of both expressing and sharing my inner thoughts and feelings with others.; [a.] Pinner, Middlesex, UK

BATES, ELIZABETH
[b.] 20 February 1955, Chichester, West Sussex; [ch.] (Two), one boy 21 years old and one girl 23 years old; [ed.] Petworth Secondary Modern School; [pers.] My poetry and writing at my main hobbies, I try to reflect a wide range of interests to suit all taste. I can lose myself in my work and enjoy it immensely.; [a.] Midhurst, West Sussex, UK

BAUNTON, MR. L. E.
[pen.] Lewis Baunton; [b.] 12 November 1926, East London; [p.] Rose Baunton, Henry Baunton; [m.] Violet May Baunton (Deceased), 17 March 1951; [ch.] Janette Rose Baunton, Lewis E. Baunton (Died age 39 1993); [ed.] Standard Local Education; [occ.] Retired ex-carpenter; [memb.] Bingo, Bereavement Club, British Diabetic Association; [hon.] A loving wife over forty years; [oth. writ.] A poem called 'Xmas' published in the 1996 British poem review. Also my story as a wartime evacuee was included in a book published.; [pers.] My poem 'is there a place' is one of many written in deep grief in memory of my dear wife who has now passed away. But it still seems like yesterday. Since 1992; [a.] Dagenham, Essex, UK

BAUTISTA, LOTIS
[pen.] Melisande; [b.] 6 August 1988, London; [p.] Melisande Bautista, Judith Redoble; [ed.] Barham School; [memb.] Girl Guide and Brownie; [hon.] For sharing good work at assembly from year 1-3; [a.] Wembley, Middlesex, UK

BEACHAM, BARBARA ANN
[pen.] Barbara Ann Beacham; [b.] 7 January 1944, Halifax; [p.] Vera and Kenneth Pearson; [m.] Divorced; [ch.] Andrew, Nicola and Simon Beacham; [ed.] Grammar School; [occ.] Secretary; [oth. writ.] None published I write poems for a hobby; [pers.] I adore romantic poetry my favourite being-Elizabeth Barrett Brownings 'I Love Thee' let me count the ways; [a.] Todmorden, Lancashire, UK

BEAMAN, BARBARA
[pen.] Barbara Pitter; [b.] 9 March 1934, Rochford; [p.] Neville Rhodes Pitter and Winifred Pitter; [m.] Ronald Beaman, 6 March 1954; [ch.] Kevin Paul, Trevor Martin, Jonathan James; [ed.] Southend-on-Sea High School for girls; [occ.] Art student; [oth. writ.] Numerous poems and stories as yet unpublished; [pers.] I like to write about human nature - its trials and humour. I think the most important thing in life is to be open, and true to oneself. However different this may be.; [a.] Benfleet, Essex, UK

BEARDSLEY, KATHLEEN
[pen.] Katie Beardsley; [b.] 25 April 1928, Kirkby-in-Ashfield; [p.] Arthur and Florence Tryner; [m.] Geoffrey Beardsley, Deceased, 21 April 1948; [ch.] Matthew; [occ.] Retired; [memb.] Homoeopathic Society, Astrological Association, National Federation of Spiritual Healers; [hon.] Ph D. (Hom.), DMS Astrol (Credit), DIP Psychology; [oth. writ.] Articles for the Astrology and Medicine Newsletter Children's Book - 'Katie's Magic Kite and other stories!; [pers.] My poem explains my philosophy of life - it is a journey in the pursuit of wisdom or knowledge leading to ultimate reality and spiritual enlightenment.; [a.] Mansfield, Notts, UK

BEATTIE, MARY LOUISE
[b.] 20 July 1946, Warwickshire; [p.] Violet and William Hams; [m.] Arthur William Beattie, 3 October 1970; [ch.] Samantha and Arthur; [ed.] Ashburnham Primary Kingsley Sec, Mod; [occ.] Receptionist; [memb.] Sutton Theatre Company F.E.B.S. Reg. Charity Fund Raiser; [hon.] Medals and Certificates in Athletics; [oth. writ.] Articles for school magazine; [pers.] I believe a sense of humour is the keyword to happiness; [a.] London, UK

BEAZLEIGH, GARY SCOTT
[b.] 16 May 1972, Gillingham; [p.] David J. H. Beazleigh, Christine Beazleigh; [ed.] Howard Grammar, Rainham, Kent; [occ.] Insurance Claims Negotiator; [pers.] I have been greatly influenced by family and friends all of whom have their own special quality.; [a.] Gillingham, Kent, UK

BECK, AUDREY
[b.] 26 February 1943, Wells, Somerset; [p.] Ronald Beck and Alice Beck; [m.] Dissolved; [ch.] Sarah, Simon, Suzanne; [ed.] Ansford Comprehensive Castle Cary Somerset; [occ.] Part Time Home Carer/Artist; [memb.] Westbury Art Society; [oth. writ.] Family/Friends Greeting Cards - Local paper; [pers.] My Westcountry background has been the inspirational subject of my writing, influencing a quiet observation of rural life and its characters; [a.] Westbury, Wiltshire, UK

BEER, DELPHIA
[pen.] Delphia Beer; [b.] 28 May 1918, Minsier, Kent; [p.] Fostered (Mr. and Mrs. Dennett); [m.] Raymond William Beer, 30 December 1971 (2nd Marriage); [ch.] Six girls, three boys, two of my boys are my grandsons, I brought up from birth, Simon is 26 and Autistic, I have 20 grandchildren and 10 great grandchildren.; [ed.] Church School, (Ordinary) but have educated myself, in reading English etc.; [occ.] Housewife. I lads from London used to foster teenage difficult; [memb.] Too old was a member of Committee on Duraeeu Social Club. Local, also member of Support Group at Wandsworth London, Foster Parents Association; [oth. writ.] I have written many poems. Some I call poetical stories. But just did not know where to send them. Years ago I wrote poems and recited them for my children's schools; [pers.] I feel greatly influenced by poets, like Kipling and Newbolts poetical stories, also by what I read and hear. And I try to tell how I feel. In some, sadness. Others wonderment, or warning about drugs; [a.] Crawley, Cifield, W. Sussex, UK

BEHESHTI, AFI
[b.] 27 May 1961, Yorkshire; [ed.] City of London, Polytechnic; [occ.] Managing Director of own sales promotion agency; [pers.] Lives in West London and has run own sales promotion agency for 7 years.; [a.] Ealing, London, UK

BELL, MAUREEN
[pen.] 'Jade'; [b.] 14 August 1942, Lancashire; [p.] Elsie Veronica and Robert Clegg; [ch.] Barrie, Lee, Christine and Donna; [ed.] Newhey Council School and Milnrow Church School; [occ.] Housewife; [memb.] Civic Trust, and International Songwriters Association; [hon.] Obtained Son Publisher; [oth. writ.] 'Summit Thro' They Eyes of Jade, book pf poetry published, and various other poems printed; [pers.] Try to be at one with nature in a rugged Pennine environment, believing that with the understanding of God, true poetry is drawn up from the depths of the soul.; [a.] Littleborough, Lancs, UK

BENACS, PHILIPPA CATHERINE
[b.] 7 May 1944, Birkenhead; [p.] William George and Ethel Townson; [m.] George Benacs, 14 June 1986; [ch.] Mark Edward and Kathryn Jane; [ed.] Secondary school and Carlet Park College; [occ.] Rest home proprietress, Bunkers Bounty Rest Home; [pers.] If I have been gifted enough to bring pleasure to others, my writings have been worthwhile.; [a.] Blackpool, Lancashire, UK

BENBOW, EDWARD
Senior Lecturer at Shenstone College of Education 1945-1974. Member of Education Board of Studies, Birmingham University, 1962-1970. Publications: Challenge Science International, Books 1-4 with Teachers' Guide, Books 1-4, Hamish Hamilton. Numerous Feature Programmes and children's stories for BBC. Books of verse, Odd Bods and Arkytypes. Many stories and articles published by World Books. Record of Shropshire dialect made for British Drama League. Contributor to Verse and Drama Anthologies published by Hamish Hamilton, Collins, and U.L.P. Numerous education articles in periodicals. 24 short stories in Shropshire Unfolded, 1992-1994. 100,000 word palindromic composition recorded in Guinness Book of Records, 1975-1992.

BENJAMIN, CAROLE
[b.] 18 April 1960, Exeter; [p.] David McManus, Jean McManus; [m.] John Benjamin, 26 May 1979; [ch.] Christina Emma; [ed.] Clyst Vale Community College; [memb.] Colchester Garrison Saddle Club; [a.] Wivenhoe, Essex, UK

BENJAMIN, CHRISTINA
[b.] 20 August 1982, Clacton-on-Sea; [p.] John Benjamin, Carole Benjamin; [ed.] The Colne Community School; [memb.] Colchester Garrison Saddle Club; [a.] Wivenhoe, Essex, UK

BENNETT, JEAN
[pen.] Jean McFall; [b.] 26 October 1957, Ireland; [p.] John McFall and Heather Mathison; [ch.] John and Kerrie Bennett; [ed.] Secondary to 'A' Level Secretarial; [occ.] Warden-Sheltered Housing for the Elderly; [oth. writ.] And May Your Time Rene Clelland, recent- Lady of Cambodia; [pers.] I have received a new spark of poetic inspiration through my daughter, Kerrie, aged 10, another poet whose writings I enjoy most of all.; [a.] Farnborough, Hampshire, UK

BIBI, AASIA
[pen.] Asia; [b.] 20 July 1976, Birmingham; [ed.] Hodge Hill Girls School, St. Phillips R.C. VI Form College; [occ.] Clerical Assistant; [hon.] A-levels in English Literature, law and general - studies NVQ II in Administration; [pers.] I have seen greatly influenced by the 'Bronte' sisters, and the 'Anne of Green Gables' series by Lucy Montgomery when I was a child.; [a.] Birmingham, UK

BILL, NATALIE
[b.] September 11, 1981, Cambridge; [p.] Barry Bill, Gaynor Bill; [ed.] Hinchingbrooke School Huntingdon; [memb.] Girl Guides Association; [pers.] Many of my poems were inspired by my personal thoughts and feelings.; [a.] Saint Neots, Cambridgeshire

BINNER, CHRIS
[pen.] Chris Binner; [b.] 16 March 1945, London; [p.] Albert Stagg, Beatrice Stagg; [m.] Gordon Binner, 26 March 1966; [ch.] Amanda, Bob, Laura; [ed.] Barnsbury Central School for girls, Kentish Town Polytechnic; [occ.] Nursery Nurse; [memb.] International Dolphin Watch; [hon.] N.N.E.B.; [oth. writ.] Several poems and short stories written for people I care about; [pers.] After therapy for post traumatic stress I found I had so many hidden deep feelings I needed to express. I needed to share my anger and experience with others.; [a.] Pitlochry, Perthshire, UK

BIRCH, EUNICE
[b.] 19 July 1940, Blackburn, Lancashire; [ch.] Justin and Ashley (2 sons); [ed.] B/Burn High, Leeds Teacher Training College; [occ.] Retired; [hon.] Junior Teacher N.N.E.B. Tutor, Church Pianist Foster Mother.; [oth. writ.] 'Deafness', 'War In The East' - published by Triumph House 1996; [pers.] I try to convey personal feeling re animals, and attitudes toward fellow men. Personal feelings after life's VPS and downs; [a.] York, North Yorks, UK

BIRCH, MAURICE IVOR
[pen.] Mog; [b.] 3 November 1941, Bloxwich; [p.] Wallace Edward Florrie Elsie; [m.] Beryl Lynne Birch (Nee Reaney), 13 March 1965; [ch.] Andrew Robert Melanie Reaney; [ed.] Aldridge, Cooper Jordan and Leighswood Secondary Modern; [occ.] Retired Audit Inspector; [memb.] BRD Sports and Social Club Aldridge, King Street

Progressive club and institute, walsall wood and the transport and general workers union.; [oth. writ.] 'Walsall Reminisce' - 'Aldridge in the Fifties' - The Snob - The anglers Needs Precious Mum - Closed in Love - So Did I - And quite - Published in Various Anthologies - Always Donkey in the Poetry now Magazine - And Who Cry For Help - In An Anthology Entitled - Animal Matters - With spike Milligan - James Streaker - Lyndsey De Paul - And Desmond Tarrant - Plus Many more in local newspapers and magazines.; [pers.] There are many accomplished writes of poetry and perhaps as many subjects that prompt the pen: But the reader who gains personal satisfaction from his or her own interpretation of another words is surely the ultimate poet.; [a.] Aldridge, Staffs, UK

BLACK, EILEEN
[pen.] Eileen Black; [b.] 31 August 1978, Downpatrick; [p.] Patrick Black and Bernedette Black; [ed.] Convent of Mercy Primary, St Mary's High School, East Down Institute further and higher education; [occ.] Student; [pers.] In my writing, I strive to ensure that my readers hear the voice of the 'unheard' and overwhelmed by this, I hope that they open their hearts and welcome 'Societies so-called outcasts' into their arms.; [a.] Downpatrick, Down, UK

BLACK, JEANETTE
[pers.] My first dedicated to my love, Gerald Marr, forever in my heart.; [a.] Livingston, UK

BLACK, MARGARET
[b.] 27 December 1948, Tillicoultry; [p.] Flora and John Philp; [m.] Robert J. Black, 15 February 1969; [ch.] Tracy Black; [ed.] Grange School Alloa; [occ.] Housewife; [pers.] We never pass this way again.; [a.] Tullibody, Clacks, UK

BLACKNELL, SIMON RICHARD
[b.] 5 February 1975, Gainsborough; [p.] Donald and Jennifer Blacknell; [ed.] Queen Elizabeth's High School, Gainsborough; [occ.] "Agricultural Parts Salesman" (Storeman) - Peacock and Binnington; [memb.] Nothing of Consequence; [oth. writ.] Nothing recognized or published (several potentials too long for the poetry contest.); [pers.] Never want for inspiration - it will come when it's ready. For me it's usually when I should be sleeping!; [a.] Gainsborough, Lincolnshire, UK

BLACKWELL, HAZEL ANN
[b.] 3 October 1944, N. Ireland; [p.] Samuel and Hester Thompson; [m.] Divorced; [ch.] Carl and Felicity; [ed.] Grammar School Open University Student Social Sciences; [occ.] Resettlement Officer for the Single Homeless; [memb.] Local History Group; [pers.] I have tried to put feelings on paper for the first time; [a.] Cookstown, Tyrone, N. Ireland

BLAKE, CLIVE
[b.] 30 January 1954, Redruth; [p.] Joan Blake, Arthur Rowse; [m.] Jennifer Distin, 24 May 1980; [ch.] Adrian, Amy; [ed.] Bodmin Secondary, Mid Cornwall College; [occ.] Accounts Manager, Fine Art Greetings Card Co.; [memb.] Poets and Writers Society; [oth. writ.] Song lyrics, several poems published in collective anthologies. I am currently working on a corroborative project with a photographer and a graphic artist.; [pers.] I am Cornish by a long line of descent and very proud of my deep celtic roots. I am registered as partially-sighted, but like to think of my poetic vision as crystal clear!; [a.] Wadebridge, Cornwall, UK, PL27 7JB

BLAMEY, ALICE
[b.] 28 July 1976, Truro, Cornwall; [p.] Mr and Mrs B. Blamey; [ed.] Penwith College Penzance, Bed Honours Degree, English Westminster College Oxford, Stendhal University, Grenoble; [occ.] Student; [memb.] Oxford Poetry Society, Oxford Union Society, Secretary of International Society, Westminster College Oxford; [oth. writ.] Several other poems including A World Apart, Broken Lines, The Old Woman, Pine Cone I have also written a sonnet and some prose writing.; [pers.] I started writing poetry at age five. Then experimented with various genres of writing at Westminster College Oxford. I wrote 'Traffic Jam' during my Eraserus Exchange in the mountainous region of Grenoble. My seminars with Joan Sidney taught me a technique; [a.] Penzance, Cornwall, UK

BLANCHARD, MAUREEN
[b.] 9 August 1942, Patrington Nr Hull; [p.] Caroline and Arthur Jobling; [m.] Michael Blanchard (Deceased 2 November 1995), 9 November 1963; [ch.] Denise and Elaine Lesley; [ed.] Withernsea High School, E. Yorks; [occ.] Print Company Manager Reading Berks; [memb.] Member of the Writers Bureau; [oth. writ.] Several poems published in local poetry magazine, and local post newspaper. Poem published in Nostalgia Magazine, short novel; [pers.] I have found, by expressing emotions through my writing, brings events wether sad, happy or funny/topical into the right perspective, it can be a great comfort, and satisfaction too.; [a.] Reading, Berkshire, UK

BLANCHFIELD, MRS. KATHLEEN
[b.] St. Lukes Hospital, Co Kilkenny; [p.] Catherine and John Glendon; [m.] Michael Blanchfield, 14 August 1969; [ch.] Four Daughters, Denise, Marie, Caroline, Michelle; [ed.] Primary, Bonnettestown National School, Secondary Education, Kilkenny City Vocational School; [occ.] Housewife and Mother, writing stories and poetry in my spare time; [memb.] Scribblers Avon, Writers Group, Kilkenny City Eire. Joined almost one year ago. I have had a great love of writing always.; [hon.] Achievement award for "National Letter Writing Competition" June 1995 from DN. Post the letter was published in a book which I was presented with at a special awards ceremony in the writers museum in Dublin; [oth. writ.] Writing some short stories and poetry at the moment. Typing course recently concluded.; [pers.] Writing means so much to me. When I sit down to write after my daily work, I feel so relaxed its like as if I'm in a completely different world; [a.] Acragar, Ballyragget, Co. Kilkenny, Eire

BLEACH, LINDA
[pen.] Linda Brock; [b.] 13 April 1969, Walthamstou; [p.] Violet Brock, Williams Brock; [occ.] Avon Rep; [memb.] Fellowship of Christian Writers; [oth. writ.] This is my first poem; [pers.] I became a born again Christian two years ago. I strive to reflect my love for the Lord in my poems.; [a.] Canvey Islands, Essex, UK

BLOW, JAN
[b.] 13 February 1935, Woolwich; [p.] Florence Hathaway, Rupert Legg; [m.] Widowed; [ch.] 5; [ed.] Cowplain Secondary School, Hants 1947-1952; [occ.] Housewife; [oth. writ.] Variety of items purely for the pleasure of friends and family. One favorable comment years ago from Godfrey Winn especially.; [pers.] Well...there's music in poetry and both enhance the quality of life, but King Solomon "sought to find delightful words" (Ecc. 12 v. 10) which is what appeals to me.; [a.] Lymington, Hants, UK

BLYTH, MARY
[p.] Yvonne O'Connor; [b.] 21/10/25, Clonlisk, Co. Offaly, Eire; [p.] Michael and Kathleen Killackey; [m.] Robert Blyth, 21/9/50; [ch.] 9, five boys and four girls; [ed.] Leaving Certificate and Commercial Course and Computer Course and 14 Historical conferences and courses in Liturature and History U.C.C. Fluent in Irish (Gaelic); [occ.] Homemaker; [memb.] The Irish Country Women's Association, The Country Markets, The Longh Gramophone Society, The Railway Record Society; [hon.] 3 Arts Awards I.C.A., 14 Crafts Awards I.C.A., several prizes for slogans, stories and essays; [oth. writ.] 1. Gypsy Child Poetry, 2. Poems of The Golden Years, 3. Happy Endings Children's Stories, 4. (unpublished) - "A Penny For Your Thoughts" (16 Stories for Adults); [pers.] I enjoy God in nature and hope my writings will reflect that sense of happiness to those who read it.; [a.] Cork, Eire

BODEN, CATH
[b.] December 1951, North Shields; [p.] Kenneth T. Yeelers and F. Agnes Hughes; [m.] Barry Boden, 11 July 1987; [ch.] Sally Elizabeth Clare; [oth. writ.] Personal Anthology "inside every hill is a submarine trying to get out"; [pers.] This poem marks a significant milestone for me in an extraordinary personal journey and is dedicated to all those people whose love and guidance helped to bring it about; [a.] Kirklevington, Cleveland, UK

BODEN, JULIE MAUREEN
[b.] 1 June 1960, Sutton Coldfield; [p.] Maureen and Stanley Davis; [m.] John Boden, 2 October 1982; [ch.] Nathaniel, Charlotte; [ed.] Sutton Coldfield Grammar School, Fairfax High School, West Midlands College, and University of Central England.; [occ.] Teacher and Hotelier and Mother; [a.] Wishaw, Warks, UK

BOLAND, MARY
[pen.] Matrent Bheollatn; [m.] Joe, 1965; [ch.] 3 sons and 2 daughters; [occ.] Have worked with 6-8 years old far 17 yrs as; [memb.] A member of The Scout Ass. of Ireland; [hon.]; [oth. writ.] Love writing poetry but haven't tried to have anything published before; [pers.] Our eldest son was killed in a motorbike accident in England in 1988. He was 21 yrs old. A lot of my work is about him. We still find it hard to accept Michael's death; [a.] Craignamanagh, Kilkenny, UK

BOND, GEORGINA
[b.] 4 October 1934, Gloucestershire; [p.] I was adopted; [m.] Mr. Leslie Bond, 21 December 1953; [ch.] Three; [ed.] Brimscombe, Secondary Modern; [occ.] Retired; [oth. writ.] Several poems published in local newspaper; [pers.] I find that I can express my feelings in many of my poems. Also I enjoy reading other peoples poem especially from my area.; [a.] Stroud, Glos, UK

BONES, STEPHANIE KAREN
[b.] 27 December 1960, Dartford; [p.] Patrick and Barbara Young; [m.] Kenneth Bones, 16 February 1991; [ch.] Marc David, Tracey Karen; [ed.] Uptergrove Public School and O.D.C.V.I (High School) in Orillia, Ontario, Canada; [occ.] Housewife; [memb.] Forresters; [pers.] Writing for me is a way to relax. To let my inner feelings escape.; [a.] Saint Leonards, E. Sussex, UK

BONNING, MRS. SOE
[pen.] Crystal Shannon; [b.] 1 September 1958, St. Asaph; [p.] Doreen and Frank Jones; [m.] Jeff, 15 September 1979; [ch.] Michael and Steven; [ed.] Ysgol Emmanuel, Rhyl High School, Llanorillo Technical College; [occ.] Self employed, gardener/landscaper; [memb.] Rhyl Cycling Club; [hon.] Swimming Medals, Cycling Medals, Hockey Medals; [oth. writ.] My Mam. P. -poems For Mom, Kath. P. - all kinds Of Love, Winter Training. P. - Poetry life, Cissy. P - Shared Lives, My Mate Angie P. - a Trooble Shared, Time Trialin G. P. - Metric Muscles You - P-Expressions Amour. Poems in Cycling Magazine; [pers.] I write from personal experience and from the heart. Poems often form in my head when the vibes of the soul are greatly moved.; [a.] Rhyl, Denbighshire, UK

BOOTH, JENNY
[b.] 21 March 1950, Hampstead; [occ.] Counselling; [oth. writ.] Some poetry, and short stories; [pers.] I am part of "The Ark" a lively Watford based church, whose aim is to glorify God. I like to write along these lines! People so need the hope God gives.

BOOTH, MARGARET PATRICIA
[b.] 24 October 1942, South African; [p.] Richard and Biddy De Wal; [m.] Clifford Burnard Booth, 2 June 1990; [ch.] Laurence, Yorden, Neilson, Heather, Margaret, Warrener; [ed.] Public School St. Marys Johannesburg; [occ.] Writer/Traveller; [oth. writ.] Never Again (Holocaust Fiction), Salute the Selous, both awaiting publishment; [pers.] Keep the earth green protect endangered spews and people, find contentment making it a better place for future generations.; [a.] Southampton, Hampshire, UK, SO15 2FZ

BOOTON, DONNA
[pen.] Donna Booton; [b.] 20 March 1976, Newport; [p.] John Booton, Marie Booton; [ed.] Oakdale Comprehensive School Crosskeys College Cardiff University; [occ.] Student of Sociology at Cardiff University; [memb.] Oakdale Youth Choir; [oth. writ.] Several other pieces which I have lacked confidence to publish.; [pers.] In my writing, my own hopes and fears are reflected. The poem reflects the universal feeling that others can bring both sadness and joy.; [a.] Blackwood, Gwent, UK, NP2 0JT

BORRILL, ANNETTE
[b.] 23 September 1946, Old Leake, Boston, Lincs; [m.] Michael Borrill, 24 October 1970; [ch.] Kate - 24 yrs; [ed.] I left school aged 15 - no qualifications I studied as a (Mature student and became a qualified reader at Boston College (through Nottingham University EG Certificate in Education (Adults) and other qualifications; [occ.] I worked at Boston College for 2 years, as a part-time lecturer (Communication Skills) until September 1995. I taught special needs student, GNVQ advanced, GCSE and was course tutor for A level student. I also worried with women returners and adult legacy classes I am currently Village Correspondent from the local newspaper, but not working. I have just undergone a major operation and hope to use the experience to help other women through my writing.; [oth. writ.] Articles for 'Lincolnshire Life' magazine, local newspapers and several poems published, one of which 'Bullied' was a acknowledged by 'Children' and used by the Anti-bullying Campaign in London. I have also won first prize of 100 pounds in a letter comp.; [pers.] Words are a powerful, often abused, tool. I would like to use my words to give a voice to those seldom listened to in society. My words are from 'one soul to another', rather than 'intellectually clever'. My late grandfather was my inspiration; [a.] Boston, Lincolnshire, UK

BOSTOCK, CLAIRE
[pen.] Sam Fox, Michele Keating; [b.] 30 October 1970, Manchester; [p.] Janice and Peter Duffy; [m.] 17 May 1995; [ch.] Dillon Shannon Wayne; [ed.] School School School my education is an army women my husband Darren's a DJ; [occ.] Help teacher and helper in army and a babysitter; [memb.] Boyzone Fan Club and 3rd's.; [hon.] Deplomer and Army Medals and a Katre Model.; [oth. writ.] I love my husband Darren very much and also my kids; [pers.] I love my husband Darren very much and also my kids and I've got another 2 coming called Kurt and Shane both twins.; [a.] Mesborough, S. Yorkshire, UK

BOWLER, LESLEY
[b.] 7 January 1947, Hathersage; [p.] Arnold and Nora Stocks; [m.] Separated, 11 May 1964; [ch.] Tracey Beet and Janice Birks; [ed.] Penistone Grammar School; [occ.] Payroll Manager; [oth. writ.] In the pipeline. This is my first publication, of which I hope to be the start of many more.; [pers.] My inspiration comes from various avenues. "The Pirates" was inspired by a very dear penpal, and dedicated thus. Many thanks. Ted.; [a.] Thurlstone, Sheffield, South Yorkshire, UK

BOWLEY, MARGARET L.
[pen.] Alice Emily Gracis; [b.] 22 January 19148, Croydon; [p.] Stanley and Grace Hazell (Both Deceased); [m.] Mr. Brian Bowley, 8 July 1967; [ch.] Belinda and Alexander; [ed.] St. Andrew de School The Open University Further Education.; [occ.] Station Officer with metropolitan police; [memb.] Buddy Holy Fun Club Church Chior; [hon.] Achievement Award For Higher Education.; [oth. writ.] None published yet I have a collection on different subjects.; [pers.] Live life to the full each day. To do serve people and places and weather moods-changes. Just feelings. I read all subjects. I listen and play all types of music. I love the theatre. I draw - I love the arts.; [a.] Coulsdon, Surrey, UK

BRACE, ROSEMARIE
[b.] 29 August 1927, London; [p.] Ellen Harbut, Alfred Harbut; [m.] Divorced; [ch.] Leslie, Philip, Christopher, Gillian, Mandy, Nicholas and Melanie; [ed.] Penge Central School for Girls; [occ.] Retired Civil Servant; [pers.] This being my first published poem was inspirational. I hope to continue in this vein.; [a.] Bromley, Kent, UK

BRACKEN, BEVERLEY ANN
[pen.] Beverley Ann Bracken; [b.] 2 February 1964, Manchester; [p.] Albert and Carole (Without Surname); [ed.] Chorlton Convent, Xaverian College; [occ.] R.G.N.; [memb.] Royal College of Nursing; [hon.] Social Studies; [oth. writ.] One poem published in local newspaper; [pers.] Poetry is the pathway to expression of emotion. I strive to reflect on humanistic feelings in my writing.; [a.] Manchester, UK

BRADBURY, DENNY
[b.] 1 February 1949, Winchester; [ch.] Pippa (20), Russell (17); [ed.] Winchester County High School and Life; [occ.] Manager - National Charity; [memb.] Speak easy writers group and MIIRSM (International Institute Risk and Safety Management); [oth. writ.] Poetry, plays, thoughts; [pers.] I have always loved poetry, plays film and theatre through my writing I try to portray human frailty, love, despair, hope.; [a.] Leighton Buzzard, Beds, UK

BRADLEY, DHE
[b.] 24 October 1927; [m.] Divorced; [occ.] Retired; [memb.] Probationary Member of The Human Race, I rest my case; [oth. writ.] "Taking the Epistle" 1985 Merlin Books Ltd., Braunton, Devon, "More Moronic Rubbish" 1986 Merlin Books Ltd.. "Random Ruminations" 1987 Vantage Press, Inc., New York, USA; [pers.] When your race is all-but run, biographies aren't much fun, retired, but not discarded, in mind and body, not retarded, living the thing, I've had my fling!; [a.] Cheltenham, Glos, UK

BRANDLEY, CLARE
[pen.] Clare Louise; [b.] 26 November 1976, Lambeth; [p.] Patricia Brandley, Kenneth Brandley; [ed.] Barstable Comprehensive School Basildon Essex; [occ.] Trainee Hairdresser Thurrock College Grams Essex; [oth. writ.] None published; [pers.] I have no influences, just my own personnel thoughts.; [a.] Basildon, Essex, UK

BRANDON, NICOLA
[pen.] Nicola Brandon; [b.] 25 November 1977, Chelmsford, Essex; [p.] David Brandon, Marion Brandon; [ed.] Bancroft's School, VI Form College, Westminster University (09/96); [occ.] Student; [oth. writ.] Several articles in local paper and magazines. Poetry also previous published.; [pers.] Always remember never forget where you have been and who you have met.; [a.] Buckhurst Hill, Essex, UK

BRANDRICK, NICOLA
[b.] 15 December 1966, London; [ed.] Access To Higher Education; [occ.] Student, B.A. Hons. Drama and Education at The Central School of Speech and Drama; [pers.] This poem is anexpression of a reality I have experienced within my self. This inspiration came from the prance of Sahajyoga which is taught of H.H. Shirmatasi Nir Mala Devi I would like to thank her for all the Joy she brings; [a.] Putney, UK

BRAY, RUTH
[b.] 9 June 1957, Barking; [p.] Dennis Pittman, Madeline Pittman; [m.] Terry Bray, 3 June 1978; [ch.] Nicholas Bray, Rebecca Bray; [ed.] Burleigh Secondary Modern, Plymouth; [occ.] State Enrolled Nurse, Endoscopy Unit, Derriford Hospital; [memb.] Plymouth and District Table Tennis, South West Nurses of Gastroenterology for Gastroenterology, United Reformed Church; [hon.] Diploma Orthopedic Nursing April 1976, State Enrolled Nursing, May 1977, Bachelor of Science Dec. 1993; [oth. writ.] Poem published in life in poetry book, poems currently being published by my church magazine.; [pers.] My poems are inspired through my personal life, from deep down and within. I feel at peace when I am writing and hope this poem will inspire others to write in the same way. Perhaps in this way one can bring out ones inner most thoughts or feelings of the past or future on paper. This will enable you to feel you have a more meaningful and purposeful life.; [a.] Plymouth, Devon, UK

BRAY, SELENA
[b.] 7 March 1981, Nottinghamshire; [p.] Maxine and Alan Bray; [ed.] John Cleveland College; [occ.] Student; [memb.] Fox Agility Dog Training Club, Beacon Dog Training Club, John Cleveland

College Hockey Club, Kennel Club (K.C.J.O.); [hon.] High gold medal awards in ballet, tap, disco dancing and swimming. Reaching the Kennel Club Dog Agility finals since 1990. Winning mini barbour pairs 1996 (dogs); [pers.] Always encouraged to write poetry, feelings, emotions, first time anyone has seen any poetry of mine, this poem is inspired by and dedicated to 'Fox' my border collie puppy; [a.] Hinckley, Leicestershire, UK

BRAY, SYLVIA
[b.] 26 January 1929, Christchurch, Dorset; [p.] Cecil Tuck and Amelia Tuck; [m.] Stanley Leonard Bray, 2 November 1985; [ch.] Son - Christopher; [ed.] Christchurch Priory School and Twynham Secondary School; [occ.] Housewife; [oth. writ.] Several - poems, written but never published; [pers.] My poems are always written spontaneously based on particular times in my life, either sad or happy. Sometimes, I'm influenced by a place I have visited.; [a.] Christchurch, Dorset, UK

BRAYSHAW, YVONNE
[pen.] Yvonne Jacques; [m.] Roger Spencer Brayshaw; [ch.] 2 children, 2 step children; [ed.] Qualified as Teacher 1972 (English, drama) Compelled to take early retirement 1996 because of sight loss; [occ.] Work for East Sussex assoc. for blind as a volunteer; [oth. writ.] Other poems. Collection children's poems. Composer, song writer. Collection of ideas-woman's thoughts on men and middle age-music, poetry composition - 7 Musical pieces - 6 poems Henry VIII's six wives (none published) written for pleasure. (A selection of songs have been performed on Radio Essex); [a.] Wadhurst, E. Sussex, UK

BRENNAN, TINA PATRICIA
[pen.] Tina Patricia Brennan; [b.] 30 April 1965, Hammersmith; [p.] Phyllis and Michael Moylan; [m.] Eamonn Michael Brennan, 28 May 1983; [ch.] Claire, Gemma, Rachael, Gary, Stacey, Justine, Leah-Jayne, Kayleigh; [ed.] Sion Manning, Ladbroke, Grove London; [occ.] Housewife; [oth. writ.] Have written other poems, but have never enter any before; [pers.] Inspired by thee simplicity of life itself; [a.] Willesden, London, UK

BRETT, RAYMOND
[pen.] Raymond Brett; [b.] 19 February 1931, Winlaton, Tyne and Wear; [p.] James Brett and Constance Brett; [m.] Irene Isabel, 4 July 1959; [ch.] Susan Patricia, Stephanie Anne, Jean Marie, Viviane Margaret; [ed.] St Cuthberts Grammar School, Wesgate road Newcastle upon Tyne Ruthford College, Newcastle College of Gurtuer Education, Harrogate; [occ.] Retired; [memb.] St Roberts Catholic Club, Harrogate Institute of Quarrying Quiz Teams, Billiards and Snogker Teams; [hon.] Fellow Institute of Quarrying Bronze Medallist; [oth. writ.] Several short stories including of over 6000 words a few other poems but printpass I'm a yarn-spinner; [pers.] I write to entertain avoiding PC. cliche and modern in-Jargon I admire the works of writers such as Henry Trecce, Ambrose Biercg Roald Dhal, Henry Williamson, Griezola Russel Braddon, Wilbur Smith, Kathleen Cookson, Ian Fleming and Francis Clifford; [a.] Harrogate, North Yorkshire, UK

BRICKNELL, ROY
[b.] 15 November 1946, London; [ed.] Harold Hill Grammar School; [occ.] Retired; [memb.] De Havilland Moth Club. Radio Society of Great Britain; [hon.] English language city and guilds radio amateurs examination; [oth. writ.] Several poems. One of which has been published short stories. A novel is also being written.; [pers.] Poetry is communication that requires the reader or listener to think and interpret. It is a means of opening one's mind to a higher level of understanding.; [a.] Leigh-on-Sea, Essex, UK

BRIDGWOOD, ANDREA
[pen.] A. M. B.; [b.] 24 June 1956, 10 Marlow Rd; [p.] Graham and Beryl Jean Barker; [m.] Kenneth, 24 November 1979; [ch.] Lee Kenneth; [ed.] Willfield High School; [occ.] Studio Sculpture Artist (Paintress); [pers.] My poetry is my way of expressing my true feelings from within, and I hope people who read them experience the same happiness or sadness that I have. They just give me so much pleasure.

BRIDLE, JOYCE
[pen.] Joyce Bridle (Oblate) OSB; [b.] 26 February 1941, West Yorkshire; [p.] Joseph Walker (Deceased), Vera Blacker; [m.] Donald Jack Bridle, 9 September 1982; [ch.] Andrew Bowler; [ed.] Stroud College of Further Education, (Access to Higher Education); [occ.] Carer, poet, writer, homemaker; [memb.] Poetry Society (Representative for Gloucestershire) R.C. (Convert) Lifelong Oblate (Order of St Benedict); [oth. writ.] Stroud College poetry prize - May 1996, Semi-finalist at Chelthenham Festival of Literature 1994 and 1995 Poems in 7anthologies published by Triumph House; [pers.] To change dreams into reality "Synthesis of Heart and Mind Poetry's born of this, I find."; [a.] Stroud, Glos, UK

BRIDSON, KWAI HEUNG
[pen.] Kwai Heung Bridson; [b.] 26 August 1959, Hong Kong; [p.] Shing Kong To (M), Shin Ho To (F); [m.] Roderick Bridson, 30 October 1981; [ed.] Park High Comprehensive; [occ.] Shop Manageress; [oth. writ.] Several letters published in National Press and magazine contributor.; [pers.] I'm an observer of the small details of everyday life.; [a.] Douglas, Isle of Man, UK

BRIGHT, MRS. EDNA CLARA
[pen.] Clare Bright; [b.] 11 December 1927, Bedfordshire; [p.] William Newman, Maud Newman; [m.] Derek Arthur Bright, 22 July 1950; [ch.] Beverly, Garrick, and Roland Bright; [ed.] Queens Square Infants, Langley Street Juniors, Surrey Street Seniors; [occ.] Retired; [hon.] Instructors Authorization to teach yoga for 'Yoga for Health Organization' also taught yoga for adults for 'Beds County Council'; [oth. writ.] Two poems published in our local paper, one poem accepted by 'anchor books'; [pers.] Enjoy life, this is not a rehearsal.; [a.] Ampthill, Bedfordshire, UK

BRIGHT, JOHN
[b.] 10 October 1970, Barnet, Herts; [p.] Mary Bright; [ed.] East Barnet Secondary School; [occ.] P/T Self employees Decorator/Gardener; [hon.] English Literature 'O' level Grade A; [pers.] My poems tend to express how I felt at the time of writing, and how personally I am affected by the subject.; [a.] Palmers Green, UK

BRISTON, VERA
[pen.] Vera Otto; [b.] 31 October 1929, London; [p.] Florence and Ernest Otto; [m.] Died 15 years ago (of cancer) his name Philip, June 1956; [ch.] Daniel, Jason and Paulette; [ed.] Luton High School for Girls. We spent a lot of time going into Air aid Shelters to avoid the bombing as the war was at it's worst then; [occ.] Housewife and also relaxation therapist. Bird keeping, teaching foreign students; [memb.] Relaxation Therapy Association, Eastbourne Bird Club, Sussex Wives Club, Sussex Dancing Group; [hon.] Diploma for Berlei Corsetierre also Spirella Corsetry. Sunday School superintendent at St. Mary's Church Eastbourne for five years; [oth. writ.] Children's stories published in local Parish Pump magazine. Articles on relaxation therapy also published.; [pers.] I have always thought that the saying. "Two wrongs don't make a right" is a very good code to live by.; [a.] Eastbourne, E. Sussex, UK

BROMHAM, MARGARET
[b.] 26 April 1945, Dorchester, Dorset; [p.] Howard Gawler, Betty Gawler (both Deceased); [m.] The Reverend Ivor Bromham (Deceased), 22 October 1988; [ed.] Rydal School, Weymouth (head girl) Weymouth Grammar School Cambridgeshire College of Arts and Technology South Dorset Technical College; [occ.] Professional accountancy assistant (retired). Degree student (Theology); [memb.] Trimar hospice trust; [pers.] I am trying to use my gifts and reach out to others: I would like especially to write hymns. I have been influenced by my late husband (an author) also by the work of Frances Ridley Havergal; [a.] Weymouth, Dorset, UK

BROOKES, BRENDA
[b.] 8 April 1943, Wigan; [p.] John and Annie Dawber; [m.] John Brookes, 6 February 1965; [ch.] Shelley and Simon; [ed.] Wigan Girls' High School; [occ.] Recently Retired District Nursing Sister; [memb.] Royal College of Nurses; [hon.] Registered Gen Nurse, Certificate of District Nursing, Community Practice Teacher Certificate; [oth. writ.] First poem published 1995 by the Poets Institute of the British Isles; [pers.] My poems put into words the feelings I have about the meaning of life and relationships; [a.] Wigan, Lancs, UK

BROOKES, OLIVE
[b.] Burnley; [pers.] My poem is a tribute to my wonderful mother, for a lifetime of love, care and devotion. A lady who it was a privilege to know!; [a.] Burnley, Lancs, UK

BROOKS, DEREK VICTOR
[b.] 20 June 1938, Stoke Mandeville; [p.] Cecil Brooks, Margaret Brooks; [ch.] Michael John, Caroline Ann; [ed.] Wendover C of E School; [occ.] Timber Yard Manager; [memb.] National Trust County Music Club Bicester Theatre Club; [pers.] I am a keen amateur gardener and nature lover which I like to reflect in my poems.; [a.] Bicester, Oxon, UK

BROOKS, JOAN
[pen.] Joan Brooks; [b.] Manchester; [p.] William and Elsie Struttman; [m.] John Brooks, 1963; [ed.] Lived and educated in Glasgow; [occ.] Retired Secretary, having worked in London over 20 years; [memb.] Yorkshire Countrywomen; [oth. writ.] Collection of various poems (not published), short stories - children's stories (not published); [pers.] My husband encouraged me in my desire to put my thoughts and experiences into rhyme. My poems are based on human response to humour, and serious aspects, covering such things as 'the hunt', dog fights etc. I try also to speak for others plus imagination.; [a.] Stamford Bridge, E. Riding, Yorkshire, UK

BROWN, ALISTAIR
[b.] 9 June 1946, Northern Ireland; [p.] William James and Elizabeth; [m.] Pearl Frances, 6 June 1984; [ch.] Two own and six adopted special wards; [ed.] Primary School at Warren Point Co. Down N. Ireland Till 12 yrs old then one year Wenry Technical School till 15 yrs old. Employed 24 yrs in Fish and Cliptrade; [occ.] Now full time house father.; [oth. writ.] Unpublished recent poems "I heard An Angel Sing" and "Lent Love".; [pers.] The thoughts that led to the writing of my first poem "Towards the Light" came from the inspiration of our beautiful special needs children and the hope that the words may be of comfort to others in troubled times.; [a.] High Wycombe, Bucks, UK

BROWN, CAROL
[b.] 17 June 1959, Hitchin; [p.] Barbara and Leonard Brown; [ed.] Stevenage Girls School; [occ.] Accountant; [memb.] ACCA, MAAT; [oth. writ.] Poems, articles and short stories; [pers.] I aim to produce work that inspires pictures in the imagination as I have been inspired.; [a.] Stevenage, Herts, UK

BROWN, DORIS IVY
[pen.] Jessica Brown; [b.] 2 February 1939, Nottingham; [p.] Thomas and Doris Brown (Both Deceased); [ed.] Mundella Grammar School Nottingham Clarendon College Nottingham I have recently taken two courses at the University of Nottingham Adult Education Centre. (Creative writing and Painting and Drawing); [occ.] I took early retirement last year after working as an education Welfare officer for the Notts County Council for twenty-eigth years; [oth. writ.] None published. I am presently writing a book of poems of children, which I am also illustration.; [pers.] I seem to have 'slid gently' into the world of Poetry which I believe can poetry life and can portray life and emotions in many different ways, whether it be with love, criticism or humour.; [a.] Village Langar, Nottinghamshire, UK

BROWN, MRS. KATE
[b.] 6 June 1945, Hayes, Middlesex; [p.] Edna Doris Huffer/Abel Lomas; [m.] Peter John Brown, 26 July 1986 (First marriage 1965 - 12 years); [ch.] Robert Darren (1966) - Wendy Michelle (1968); [ed.] Secondary Modern Hitchin High School for Girls 1956-1960; [occ.] Part-time Company Receptionist William Ransom and Son Hitchin (Pharmaceutical Company); [oth. writ.] Several other poems all personal dedications to loved ones.; [pers.] My children ar my inspiration - I want them to know, what is in my heart, and what they have meant to my life.; [a.] Lower Stondon, Beds, UK

BROWN, MANDY JANE
[pen.] Imogene Brown; [b.] 28 April 1965, Perth, Scotland; [p.] James Comrie Brown, Vera Alexander Brown; [occ.] Registered General Nurse; [oth. writ.] Recently published one other poem "My Clay Angel" in "Inspirations from Eastern England."

BROWN, PATRICIA M.A.
[b.] 25 July 1944, Rosyth; [p.] Elizabeth and Donald Black; [m.] Mr. Raymond George Brown, 24 December 1962; [ch.] Gary, Raymond and Melanie, Elizabeth; [ed.] Camdean Primary Rosyth Brown and Kings Road Secondary Rosyth; [occ.] Florist with my Husband in ou' own shop; [memb.] Rosyth Boiling Club, The Litvain Guild; [hon.] 2nd prize for essay in 1958 on the subject of a Imagine yourself a bird in a cage, and afterwards the same birds free!! Free lance and why!! 1st prize in essay in 1956-57 on the subject of Nature!! Awarded by "Dunfri-line Carnegie Trust for National History"; [oth. writ.] Poems for own personal and family enjoyment! In the middle of writing a children novel of my granddaughter Natalie Ines Connelly!; [pers.] Poems written today from the heart can be enjoyed by the mind for ever in the future!; [a.] Rosyth, Fife, UK

BROWN, RITA
[b.] 19 March 1954, London; [p.] Francis Henry Shepherd, Irene Josephine Shepherd; [m.] Peter William Brown, 19 March 1977; [ch.] Samantha and Steven; [ed.] St. Pauls Way, Secondary School; [occ.] Court Usher; [oth. writ.] Golf, falling in love, my children - Samantha and Steven and caring parents - published by Anchor books.; [pers.] My work is inspired by love, life, family and personal experience.; [a.] London, UK

BROWN, SUSAN
[pen.] Sue - Marie or Susan Brown; [b.] 6 May 1970, Harlington, Middlesex; [p.] Ruth and Mick Swan; [m.] Stephen Afford, 5 March 1997; [ch.] 1st due to 16 July 1976; [ed.] Mellow Lane Camp School; [occ.] Housewife; [oth. writ.] I have many more poems but I have you to get them published.; [pers.] I wrote my poems based on true feelings of myself and close friends/family. My favourite poets are Tennyson and Keats.; [a.] Brentford, Middlx, UK

BROWN, SYLVIA SHARON
[pen.] Syron; [b.] 17 January 1944, Middlesbrough; [p.] Mary McKittrick and Thomas McKittrick; [m.] Kenneth Brown, 3 April 1965; [ch.] Stephen and Janene; [oth. writ.] Wise One, Darkest Earth, Reflections, Last Gift, Sweetest Name, The Visitor; [pers.] I was inspired to write Unborn Dream on the forthcoming birth of my first grandchild Andrew-James born on 3rd May 1996.; [a.] Normanby, Cleveland, UK

BROWN, MR. TONY J.
[b.] 19 November 1968, Chasetown; [p.] Sylvia D. Averill and David J. Brown; [ed.] Chase Terrace High School; [occ.] Fork Lift Operator; [memb.] Black Star Aikido School of which I am the Chief Instructor. Also membership to British Aikido Board, Black Star Aikido School; [hon.] 3rd Dan Black Belt Teaching Diploma in "The Theory and Practice of Aikido; [oth. writ.] "The Way Of The Black Star" a unique instructional manual on learning the martial art of Aikido.; [pers.] A personal Quote from "The Way of The Black Star" "The Battle Within Oneself Must Be Conquered So The Enemy May Pass On By".; [a.] Cannock, Staffordshire, UK

BROWN, VALERIE
[pen.] Chapel Mary-Maria; [pers.] Society is the inward mirror of a soul as perceived by the individual.

BROWNE, OSGOOD
[pen.] Aubrey; [b.] 11 October 1960, St. Kitts, W.I.; [p.] St. Clair and Lauretta Browne; [m.] Hyacinth Browne, Nee Coates, 20 July 1991; [ch.] Louis, Frank Kellen; [ed.] Sandy Point High School, La Salle University (PHD candidate) International Career Institute, Brantridge University, Bilston College, G and E; [occ.] Mature Student, on Basic Skills Teaching Practice Placement (Bilston College); [hon.] Special Awarding in Civil procedure (Law), Legal Research, Contracts, Real Estate (Conveyancing) Law, Legal Writing and Corporations. All are Certified Paralegal special awards (5); [oth. writ.] Several self published poems and Social Commentaries; [pers.] Let's eliminate jealousy and hatred without delay, and make peace, love and community interest our goal and motto today, then exterminate all bad deeds-they won't take mankind no where.; [a.] Merridale, Wolverhampton, Staffordshire, UK

BROWNLEE, MISS DORIS M. H.
[b.] April 15, 1907, Lurgan; [p.] Deceased; [ed.] Victoria College, Belfast, Queen's University, Belfast; [occ.] Retired Teacher and Headmistress; [memb.] Queen Elizabeth's Girls' Grammar School, Barnet, Head - Grey House School in Stow-on-the-Wold; [hon.] Honours degree (BA) in French and German subsidiary subjects English and Spanish. Higher diploma in education; [oth. writ.] Winner of various competitions in literature.; [pers.] My philosophy is simple "Rejoice in the Lord always and again I say rejoice."; [a.] Stow-on-the-Wold, Gloucestershire

BRUCE, DORIS A.
[b.] 7 May 1913, Suffolk; [p.] C. Q. Linn and A. Linn; [m.] Cyril D. Bruce, 20 October 1934; [ch.] 1 Daughter; [ed.] Small Village School, Bury St. Edmunds County Grammar School and Pupil Teacher Centre; [occ.] Retired; [memb.] Ipswich Institute and Reading Rooms (Visiting Member); [hon.] Natural Science Dist, Art Needlework and English Credits, Qualified Assistant Teacher, Bishops Prize (Religious Knowledge), First Aid - St. Johns; [oth. writ.] Short poems and jingles for local magazines and press, 2 poems published by "Poetry Now", items in church magazines; [pers.] Teaching was my main interest, married to a country copper and later became matron of a boy's home. My hoppy seems to have been "people", patchwork and nature - good books and music.; [a.] Ipswich, Suffolk, UK

BRUNELL, GLADYS
[ed.] Graduate of London University B.A. (Hons) Psychology; [occ.] Teacher of English, Lecturer in Education Psychology; [memb.] Member of the English Speaking Union.

BRYAN, DOREEN V.
[b.] 2 April 1936, Rutland; [ch.] 3 Girls 1 Boy; [ed.] Grammer School; [occ.] Private Boarding School Housekeeper; [oth. writ.] Nothing of importance really, only to me. Have had a couple of poems published. Enjoy writing poems, pantomimes for special occasions, and friends requests.; [pers.] I admire Pam Ayers very much, and enjoy her poems; [a.] Abingdon, Oxon, UK

BUGLER, LOTTIE
[b.] 26 May 1929, Pontypool; [p.] Charles Sims, Lilian Sims; [m.] Anthony Bugler, 22 January 1949; [ch.] Diane Bugler; [occ.] Retired; [oth. writ.] Several poems published in day centre magazine also by forward press; [pers.] My poems are a gift from God after being very ill unable to do a thing for over eight years.; [a.] Wareham, Dorset, UK

BULL, RACHEL
[pen.] Rachel Bull; [b.] 16 March 1965, Eltham, SE London; [p.] James Tate, Maureen Tate; [m.] Laurence Bull, 8 April 1989; [ch.] James Bull, Grace Bull; [ed.] Haberdashers Askes Hatcham Girls School SE12, Camberwell School of Art and Crafts; [occ.] Visiting Music and Art Teacher; [oth. writ.] Nothing published write and sing

songs; [pers.] How can words convey the deep ache of losing a father. He has gone now, but his gift of creativity lives on in all who loved him.; [a.] Lee, London, UK

BULLEN, MARIANNE
[b.] 11 August 1965, Surrey; [p.] Ruth and Cliff Bullen; [ch.] Jamie (3), Daniel (9) years; [ed.] C & G Hair and Design Farnborough Tec, D.P.P. Diploma (Pre-school Education) Child Protection etc...; [occ.] Hairdresser and working with young children; [memb.] Member of the Freelance Press Services; [hon.] Anthologies: My work has appeared in 'Poetry Now 93-96' 'Poets Favorites', Poets of the 90's, 'Poets in London and the Home Countries', 'Poetic Letters', 'Point of No Return', 'To love and Be loved', 'State of the Nation', 'Women on Men, Men of Women', 'Encounters'. Various articles in women magazines and I contributed to a programme called 'First Sight' for BBC South in 1994 entitled 'Domestic Violence.'; [pers.] I strive to create images which are almost palpable, rich, evocative, powerful and thought provoking. If a statement can be made - 'I' want to make it!; [a.] Guildford, Surrey, UK

BURFOOT, JOHN DURKIN
[pen.] John Durkin; [b.] 1 September 1935, Harrow; [p.] James Burfoot, Honor Durkin Burfoot; [m.] Widowed; [ch.] Sally Ann Freeman; [ed.] Waterpark College, Waterfored. University of Hertfordshire; [occ.] Marketing Consultant; [memb.] Institute of Management; [hon.] Commendation of Air Officer Commanding in Chief, Strike Command, Royal Air Force, New Years Honours 1974; [pers.] Having lived on four continents, I came home to yeats country, and reflect life as I see it, not as I think it should be.; [a.] Castletown, Corballa, Sligo

BURGE, JOHN
[b.] 10 June 1915, Cwmcarn, Gwent; [p.] Herbert Burge, Elizabeth; [m.] Violet, 2 November 1940; [ch.] 6 Children; [ed.] Village School; [occ.] Retired; [memb.] S.S.A.F.A., N.U.M.; [oth. writ.] Several; [pers.] Fair play and true justice for all. Free the world from greed and lust ex. Miner, soldier, salesman, hospital, worker.; [a.] Aston, Sheffield, S. Yorkshire, UK

BURMAN, RAY
[b.] 16 January 1951, London, England; [p.] George Burman and Elizabeth Burman; [m.] Val Burman (Nee Skinner), 1 September 1973; [ch.] Matthew George, Mark Edward, Carly Ann; [ed.] Mary Hare Grammar School Newbury, Berks; [occ.] Micrographics Field Engineer; [memb.] Group Scout Leader, 1st Rudgwick, Hon. Member Old School Association; [hon.] Eric Shotts Memorial Trophy for Young Deaf Achiever; [oth. writ.] First poem published in local paper; [pers.] I enjoy writing poems as a release from the pressures of modern-day living. All the poems I have written over the past twenty years have been devoted to my wife, Val, for a wonderful marriage despite the both of us being profoundly deaf from a very young age. We are blessed with three loud, boisterous hearing children.; [a.] Horsham, West Sussex, UK

BURNS, JANET
[pen.] Jessie Hetherington; [b.] 23 July 1954, Stafford; [p.] Gerard and Jessie Burns; [ed.] Blessed Richard Gwyn Grammar; [occ.] Company Secretary; [hon.] Queen's Guide certificate; [pers.] I discovered great mental stimulation and spiritual gratification in my poetry of the love of life and eternity.; [a.] Buckley, Clwyd, UK

BURROWS, AILEEN
[pen.] Alene Kimm; [b.] 7 June 1959, Crook, Co. Durham; [p.] Albert Edward Hauxwell, Mary Hauxwell; [ch.] Lauren; [ed.] Sherwood Hall Grammar School; [occ.] Martial Arts Instructor; [memb.] International Combat Hapkido Federation (I.C.H.F.) American Womens Self Defense Association (A.W.S.D.A.); [hon.] 1st Degree Black Belt Combat Hapkido, Runner up in the Hilton House, Poet of the Year 1996; [oth. writ.] Articles published in several Martial Arts Magazines. School plays, poetic works published in ten anthologies to date. Poems on permanent display in Mansfield Library and various shops and cafes in Mansfield.; [pers.] With my poetry I can cut the air with bleeding wings a Nemesis of retribution or a seraphim of salvation a gemini angel.; [a.] Mansfield, Notts, UK

BURROWS, MARIE WEIR
[b.] 28 May 1960, Dalserf, Scotland; [p.] Isabella Weir, John Burrows; [ch.] Emma and Andrew; [ed.] Cherryhill Grammar Strathclyde; [occ.] Proprietor/Teacher Hair and Beauty School; [hon.] NVQ Assessor/Verifier; [oth. writ.] Local Magazines in process of writing children's book; [pers.] My work is all dedicated to a special person who made me realize that life itself is poetry just waiting to be written.; [a.] Acton, London, UK

BUSLEY, IRIS
[b.] 15 October 1923, Lichfield Staffs; [p.] Charles and Elsie Cope.; [m.] Harold Busley, 15 May 1963; [ch.] 4 Daughters; [ed.] West Riding Yorkshire; [occ.] Housewife; [oth. writ.] Written poetry for leavers court day centre. Arnold Nottm.; [pers.] I am disabled and love poetry sewing knitting and crotchet love and writing and making poetry up in my head.; [a.] Nottingham, Woodborough, UK

BUSUTTIL, GAIL JUNE
[pen.] Jessica Graham; [b.] 7 June 1962, Cardiff; [p.] Graham and Gloria Evans; [m.] Lawrence Busuttil; [ch.] Dean, Craig, Kirsti, Ryan and Kayleigh; [ed.] Radyr Comprehensive; [pers.] As a mother of 5 children, my first love is to write poetry, and also stories, that children can understand and enjoy. I have been greatly influenced by my children, who love to listen to my writings, and by my mother who was encouraged me enormously.; [a.] Cardiff, S. Glam, UK

BUTLER, IRIS MARGARET
[pen.] Judy Butler; [m.] Kenneth Butler; [ed.] Grammar School for Girls, Gravesend and Redland College, Bristol; [occ.] Student of Chiropody; [memb.] Mensa and Lindley Players, Whitstable; [oth. writ.] Poems and short stories in newspapers and magazines, also in 'South East Voices' (Ed: Glenn Jones, pub: Anchor Books); [a.] Whitstable, Kent, UK

BUTLER, JACQUELINE C.
[pen.] Jacqueline Butler; [b.] 10 September 1942, Leicester, England; [p.] John Charles and Esther Butler; [ch.] Daughter (28) and Son (26); [ed.] Sir George Williams University Montreal, Quebec Canada (Business) Daytona Beach Community College Daytona Beach, Florida U.S.A (Computer information systems); [occ.] Medical secretary to consultant forensic Psychiatrist Acknowledgements (preparation) "208 Water Quality Mgmt Plan" "Beach Management Plan" "Planning and zoning ordinance (1986)" for county of Volusia, Florida U.S.A.; [oth. writ.] "A moment in time" "The catalyst" "Home" "Dwelling Place", and more but unpublished at this time; [pers.] "The heart beat of man is only as rich as his search for his own spiritual growth"; [a.] Leicester, Leicestershire, UK

BUTLER, JENNIFER ANNE
[b.] 10 April 1951, Sri Lanka; [p.] Ronald Simpson M. B. E., Betty Simpson; [m.] 28 August 1979; [ch.] Elanor, Meri and Daniel Arthur; [ed.] Thorne Grammer, Bury St Edmunds County Grammar School Khormaksor Comprehensive (Aden), Madras College, St Andrews; [occ.] Housewife and Mother; [memb.] Resicrucian Order A.M.D.R.C; [oth. writ.] Small piece published in the Rosicrucian digest 1974; [pers.] My inspiration has come from poetry, music, art, literature, and personal experience. As others have inspired me so I offer my small contribution in return.; [a.] Carshalton, Surrey, UK

BUTLER, JULIE KAREN
[b.] 30 November 1960, Warrington; [p.] Walter and Barbara Butler; [ed.] Ulverston Victoria High School; [hon.] Diploma in Hypnotherapy; [oth. writ.] Articles in "The Home Miniaturist" and many poems as yet unpublished; [pers.] I enjoy listening to my intuition and gaining from my inspirational ideas; [a.] Ulverston, Cumbria, UK

BUTLER, PAULINE
[b.] 8 December 1925, Adlington; [p.] Wm Southworth, Josephine Southworth; [m.] Stanley Butler, 22 March 1975; [ed.] Notre Dame Convent Blackburn; [occ.] Retired Srn Scm. Rdn.; [memb.] Amnesty International S.P.U.C.; [oth. writ.] Poems only one ever submitted and published in nursing magazine; [pers.] Wrote majority in San Francisco, mostly 'occasion poems' birthdays 'leavings' - whatever mostly humorous - but find music and creation emotion.; [a.] Preston, Lancs, UK

BUTTERY, MIKE
[pen.] "Butts"; [occ.] Commercial Fisherman; [memb.] Commercial Fishing and Angling Societies, I.G.F.A. Various sporting Clubs; [oth. writ.] Besides poems, novels, short stories, lyrics for songs. I also paint in acrylics and oils and have sold numerous paintings, also make chess boards, decorative boxes, wall plaques etc from wood and slate.; [pers.] In my writings I try to paint and create pictures of sadness, laughter and especially life using only words. To give it depth, shadows, highlight and warmth.; [a.] Mousehole, Cornwall, UK

CADE, MR. LAWRENCE A.
[b.] 3 September 1962, Surry; [ed.] King Arthurs Secondary Modern, Wincanton; [occ.] Unemployed due to illness; [memb.] Tiger Trust, R.S.P.B., Green Peace, People Trust for Endangered Species; [pers.] I try to paint pictures of my feelings and emotions with words.; [a.] Wincanton, Somerset, UK

CAILE, SUSAN
[b.] 1 October 1954, Fulham, London; [p.] Billattwood Betty Attwood; [m.] Robert Caile, 4 September 1976; [ch.] Jason Robert, Grace-Marie, Claire Louise; [ed.] Hurlingham Secondary School for Girls; [occ.] Hair Dresser, Child Minder; [oth. writ.] In Home Counties, poets with Ryme Arrival 1995.; [pers.] My inspiration comes from the observation of life its self which is rich in variety and diversity.; [a.] North Cheam, Surrey, UK

CAIRNS, DIA VA
[b.] Banbridge; [p.] David Magill, Winifred Magill; [m.] George Cairns; [ch.] Glenn, Dean, Jane and Sarah-Ann; [ed.] Banbridge High School, Upper Bann Institute, Lurgan Campus, North Down and Ards Institute of Further and Higher Education; [occ.] Hairdresser/Skills Assessor; [memb.] Hairdressing Council of Great Britain; [hon.] Master Craftsman Award, State Registered Hairdresser (S.R.H.); [oth. writ.] "My Town," "Droicheadna-Banna," "Christ is in Christmas" were published through an advert in our local paper; [pers.] A dedication to peace, love and harmony worldwide.; [a.] Banbridge, Down, UK

CALDWELL, PATRICIA
[pen.] Patricia Caldwell; [b.] 27 May 1943, Stockton; [p.] Joseph and Mary Storey; [m.] Peter Caldwell, 25 October 1979; [ch.] James Andrew and Jonathan Lee; [occ.] House wife; [oth. writ.] Author of "Thoughts" published by Pentland Press in November 1992. Poem published in `Aspects Of Faith' 1992, poem published in `Fishers Of Men' 1993; [pers.] 'My own thoughts that have come to me when in need, simple words from the heart, thoughts from life, my faith in God.; [a.] Ineleby Barwick, Stockton, UK

CAMERON, PAUL
[pen.] P. A. Cameron; [b.] 10 January 1981, Belfast; [p.] Sandy and Anne; [ed.] St. Gabriels Secondary School year 5 Education; [memb.] Ardoyne Youth Club; [hon.] Award for cross community work.; [oth. writ.] Published in school magazine.; [pers.] I would like this dedicated to my beloved grandmother Mary Cameron. This is my greatest achievement to date. I have many other poem's and 1 day I hope to have my own book.; [a.] Belfast, Antrim, UK

CAMP, ELIZABETH
[b.] 13 April 1941, Hawick, Scotland; [p.] Deceased; [m.] Andrew, 29 September 1979; [ch.] Three grown sons, five grandchildren; [ed.] Hawick High School; [occ.] Seasonal Shop Work; [memb.] British Hedgehog Preservation Society, Secretary to Carnival, Committee of Princetown, Village Community Fund; [oth. writ.] Love writing children's stories. I published have had several poems accepted by Arrival Press to be included in their books.; [pers.] I love playing with words and as I work right out in the country seeing natures daily changing pictures, favorite poet Robert Burns.

CAMPBELL, GLENN
[pen.] Shrub; [b.] 9 December 1981, Omagh; [p.] Joe and Imelda Campbell; [ed.] St. John's Secondary School, Dromore. Year 10 No exam for two years; [memb.] Dromore St. Dympnas Gaelic Football Club.; [pers.] I like writing poems on real life I use my poems to tell a story I also like to write short stories.; [a.] Dromore, Tyrone, UK

CAMPBELL, JULIE
[pen.] J. Campbell; [b.] 12 June 1978, Ashton; [ed.] Fairfield High Loreto College; [occ.] 'A' Level Student; [pers.] I write with words I dare not speak aloud, and wish only that they be read and that they be enjoyed. Main influences, Keats, Wilfred Owen, Sylvia Plath.; [a.] Manchester, UK

CAMPBELL, KEITH KENNETH
[pen.] K.C.; [b.] 13 October 1937, Portsmouth; [p.] Molly Charlotte; [m.] Gillian Irene, 8 February 1975; [ch.] Kelly and Claudia; [ed.] Secondary and Purbrook High; [occ.] Material Controller; [hon.] English; [oth. writ.] First; [pers.] I love to observe life and people I write as I feel; [a.] Portsmouth, Hants, UK

CAMPBELL, MARY ELIZABETH
[b.] Glasgow; [p.] Thomas Wilson Mackay, Violet Mackay; [m.] Robert L. Campbell, 11 December 1970; [ed.] North Kelvinside Senior Secondary School, Langside College, Glasgow; [occ.] Housewife, Previously N.H.S. Administration: (Ill Health Forced Early "Retirement"); [memb.] Harbour Arts Society, Irvine, Ayrshire; [hon.] Business Administration Certificate of Proficiency. (Nothing of note Education Terminated at Early Age because of Shortage of Family Income, I had Intended Higher Education, then University - no need to Mention this, Really!); [oth. writ.] One limerick published in "loony toons limericks," an arrival press book! Several short poems and letters published in newspapers (for which payment was received, I mean!) Countless personalized greeting cards as `Favours' for people. I do the illustration then as well as the verse but mainly just for their pleasure - and mine!; [pers.] I value beauty, happiness and laughter and therefore endeavour to contribute to this as best I can.; [a.] Stevenston, Ayrshire, UK

CAMPBELL, NICHOLAS
[b.] 6 June 1969, Woolwich; [p.] Mr. D. G. Campbell; [ed.] St. Columba's Roman Catholic school, Bexleyheath, Kent; [occ.] General Builder; [oth. writ.] Many other poems as of yet unpublished; [pers.] Many of my poems are written through personal experiences, and I hope my verses touch the hearts of the readers.; [a.] Blackfen, Kent, UK

CANHAM, LAURENCE
[b.] 12 August 1971, Clermont, Ferrand; [p.] Christian and Margot Moncelet; [m.] Daniel Canham, 27 June 1992; [ch.] Matthew Ludovic and Dorian Alexander; [ed.] Lycee Blaise Pascal - University of Clermont - Ferrand; [occ.] Student; [hon.] Poetry Prize 1985; [oth. writ.] Several poems in French and a short story "Le Beret"; [pers.] Read a poem, and your heart and your mind will jubilate in harmony.; [a.] Fen Drayton, Cambridgeshire, UK

CANNON, JOHN
[b.] 2 December 1924, Aldershot; [p.] Annie Gertrode and John Thomas Cannon; [m.] Dorothy May Hellier, 6 January 1947; [ch.] 4; [ed.] Farnborough Grammar School Salesian College Farnborough; [occ.] Forced retirement to above residence; [oth. writ.] Many assorted poems/prose/licensed words; [pers.] My writings are purely (My thoughts transcribed); [a.] Penzance, Cornwall, UK

CANTWELL, EILEEN
[b.] 13 November 1942, Newbury; [p.] Benjamin Gore, Ruby Gore; [m.] Malcolm Cantwell, 15 October 1966; [ch.] Andrew John, Stephen Philip, Teresa Anne; [ed.] Housewife; [a.] Newbury, Berkshire, UK

CAPARELLI, LETIZIA ANGELA
[pen.] Letizia Alfieri; [b.] Avellino, Italy; [p.] Giuseppina and Aniello Alfieri; [m.] Severino Caparelli, 22 July 1978; [ch.] Francesca and Selina; [ed.] Westfield School, Bedford, Mander College, Bedford; [occ.] Export Sales Administrator; [oth. writ.] Have written poetry since the age of thirteen and have been greatly influenced by the poet Dylan Thomas.; [a.] Darwen, Lancs, UK

CAPEHORN, NICHOLAS
[b.] 29 December 1983, Surrey; [p.] Alan J. Capehorn and Sheila Capehorn; [ed.] Barrow Hills Prep School, Surrey; [occ.] School-boy; [memb.] Milford Pumas Boys FC. School Choir; [hon.] Keyboard Initial Grade and Grade 1; [oth. writ.] Several Poems Published in the School magazines

CAPENHURST, ARTHUR CHARLES
[b.] 11 April 1949, Leicester; [p.] Arthur, Trudi; [m.] Joanne, 29 June 1984; [ed.] Secondary Modern Took 'O' and 'A' Level English in my early 40's at night school, (Flexistudy); [occ.] Firefighter; [memb.] "Winter's Kramp" (Small Writers Club), 'The Writer BAU'; [oth. writ.] Stories published in 'Nautical Magazine', short story submitted to Radio 4: Articles published in local magazines; [pers.] As a practicing buddhist I continually strive to become a better human being. Any artistic talent or appreciation of the arts is an important aspect of human development which I try to nurture in myself in my writing.; [a.] Manchester, Lancs, UK

CARDNO, MAUREEN
[b.] 19 September 1955, Fraserburgh; [p.] Gilbert Stephen, Jess Stephen; [m.] Bobby Cardno, 2 December 1977; [ch.] James, Mark, Angela; [ed.] Inverallochy School; [occ.] Shop Keeper; [oth. writ.] Poem and story in school magazines; [pers.] I'll pass through this world but once, any good therefore that I can do or any kindness that I can show to any human being, let me do it now, for I shall not pass this way again. [a.] Inverallochy, Aberdeenshire, UK

CARPENTER, TRUDY
[b.] 8 January 1968, Roehampton; [m.] David Carpenter; [ch.] Chelsey, Lauren, Charly and Reiss; [occ.] Housewife; [oth. writ.] Three previous publications in various anthologies and the 2nd publications of "Lesliekins"; [pers.] My work is based on every day life situations and reflects my true feelings which is easy said in poetry.; [a.] Ewell, Surrey, UK

CARR, SEAN JOSEPH
[b.] 31 March 1967, Wolverhampton; [p.] Dorothy May and Pius Joseph Carr; [m.] Lorraine Michelle Carr, 19 September 1987; [ch.] Adam Joseph Carr; [ed.] St. Edmunds R.C. Comprehensive, Wolverhampton; [occ.] Steel Production Worker; [pers.] The love of a child is so pure and undemanding just one smile from my son makes my darkest hours seem so bright again, he is my strength, my reason, and my wealth, I love him so much.; [a.] Wolverhampton, West Mids, UK

CARRETT, ADA PICKERING
[b.] 26 November 1918, Dawdon, Seaham; [p.] Hannah Amelia and David High; [m.] Austin George Carrett (Deceased), 27 March 1948; [ch.] One son, one daughter; [ed.] Camden Square, Seaham, great interest in poetry. English, History and Cookery. Nine years, Nursing, Sick and Elderly.; [occ.] Retired, Catering, Maageress Metropolitan Police, London; [memb.] Salvation Army. My parents showed a wonderful example of Christian living. As I am one of ten children, we were taught about caring and sharing with others.; [hon.] Gateaux, competition, whilst in Metropolitan police. Certificate for best Gateax signed by, Sir Robert Mark.; [oth. writ.] Two poems published in local newspaper, three since writing to triumph house. Also in our monthly letter, (salvation army) written by our Corps Officer.; [pers.] Constant in seeking, after knowledge, wisdom and love of people. Love reading, works of others.

Thankful to God, for many blessings bestowed, and his wonderful gifts to us all; [a.] Washington, Tyne and Wear, UK

CARROLL, HELEN
[b.] 11 November 1966; [p.] Leonard Ivor Jones, Freda Jones; [m.] Ian William Carroll, 13 July 1991; [ch.] Scott Owen; [ed.] Pontlanfraitz Comprehensive School; [occ.] Housewife and mother; [pers.] I have always enjoyed reading poetry since I was young, my husband and family inspired me to write this poem, on the loss of our 1st child, Chelsea Elizabeth.; [a.] Blackwood, Gwent, UK

CARROLL, THOMAS F.
[pen.] Thomas F. Carroll; [b.] 14 July 1956, Port Glasgow; [p.] James, Susan; [ed.] St Stephen's High School Caledonia University; [occ.] Assembly Line Operator; [oth. writ.] Have had other poems published by mast publications, Birds, The Restarters, Summer Time, Rwanda at Christmas, "Wee Jinky" tribute, Adolescence, Trees, Mercedes, Thought of a Teenager in Summer; [pers.] The influence of the late Norman MacCaig (Modern Scottish) cannot be underestimated.; [a.] Port Glasgow, Inverclyde, UK

CARTER, ARTHUR GEORGE
[b.] 16 July 1921, Brownhills; [p.] Alfred and Edith May Carter; [m.] Phoebe Carter, 26 December 1945; [ch.] 4 Daughters, 1 Son; [ed.] Local Primary and Senior School; [occ.] Retired; [oth. writ.] 'Poems Of The Bible' Published 1994 (a copy accepted and personally acknowledged by her Majesty Queen Elizabeth II). Many poems of variety incl. local interest, Topical, wit, humour, secular etc. Selections published in local and national magazines.; [pers.] Poetry the art of verse in rhyme or otherwise to condense and yet enhance and magnify the illimitable themes of life, nature, humanity etc. The pleasure of inspiration to oneself that has mutual effect to any who will correctly interpret.; [a.] Brownhills, West Midlands, UK

CARTER, CYRIL B.
[b.] 3 November 1912, Penrhiwceiber; [p.] Eli James Carter Mary Carter; [m.] Sarah Elizabeth Carter Deceased, Jeanie Carter, 26 November 1936, 12 March 1983; [ch.] Alan Graham Joy Gareth Tony; [ed.] Comprehensive schools in South Wales short courses University of Warwick and Mid Warwickshire College; [occ.] Retired; [memb.] Anchor books arrival press; [oth. writ.] Eight poems published in eight books descriptive writings for magazine; [pers.] Creative writing is wonderful, and magical, creating something out of nothing; [a.] Leamington Spa, Warwicks, UK

CARTER, MR. GEORGE HENRY
[b.] 26 September 1936, West Bromwich; [p.] Albert and Margaret; [ed.] Secondary and Modern School, Icknield St. B'ham 19; [occ.] Unemployed; [memb.] Ex. National Service I was in R.E.M.E., which stands for Royal Electrical Mechanical Engineers. I am a member of the forget me not, club, and British Legion.; [hon.] I have wrote many poem's on various subjects, and several times been acknowledge for the High Quality that they posses; [oth. writ.] I enjoy ancient history other interests include reading old books concerning this Monarcy as far back as James 1st, classical music, and many more interests.; [a.] Kingstanding, Birmingham, UK

CARTER, MARIAN
[b.] 31 January 1924, Blackburn, Lancs; [p.] Deceased Arthur and Jane Hargreaves; [m.] Terence Carter, 4 September 1965; [ch.] Terence Jr., Diane Hurn, Vanessa Jane, David James; [ed.] Feniecowles Council School (when young), Technical College - Knott Street Darwen, Blackburn College - Feilden Street, Blackburn, Lancs; [occ.] Poet, Artist, Pianist; [hon.] Fellow of the International Academy of Poetry, Cambridge, England, Biographee "International Who's Who in Poetry", "Dictionary of Biography", "The World's Who's Who of Women", "Who's Who in Western Europe", "Certificate of Merit for Distinguished Contributions to Poetry (1969) Diploma - Companion of Honour (1980) to Western Europe; [oth. writ.] "Colourscope" Small Poetry Book "Kaleidoscope" Ditto have written short stories published in the newspapers, also articles. Played piano to public for 22 years!; [pers.] I have been blessed with writing poetical words on paper, and my right hand has painted over 200 pictures. Both hands are eager to play my piano, so I say once more, I have been blessed. If one thinks hard when quiet - wondrous things begin to happen!; [a.] Darwen, Lancashire, UK

CARTER, WINIFRED FLORENCE
[b.] 27 October 1900, Surrey; [ed.] Council School; [pers.] My only poems have been in reference to my family - I have also written a poem about a 10 week old baby and Cot Death.; [a.] Marham Church, Cornwall, UK

CASEY, RACHEL
[b.] 21 March 1985, Stoke-on-Trent; [p.] Karen Casey and Timothy Casey; [ed.] St. George and St. Martin's R.C (A) Primary School. Going up to St. Margaret Ward, R.C. (A) Secondary School; [occ.] Student at St. George and St. Martin's Primary School; [memb.] Port Vale, Junior Valiants Club, Drama Club, Athletics Club, Art Club.; [hon.] Winning a Long Jump Competition at Athletics, winning a medal at Cross Country, representing my school and town at relay spirit, Long Jump and Skipping.; [oth. writ.] Wrote to Blue Peter from the B.B.C, written to the local paper to be published. Wrote a leap year poem for my teacher at school.; [pers.] I have enjoyed writing poems since I was nine and I have been influenced by my mum, dad and my school and inspired by people and places from all over the world; [a.] Stoke-on-Trent, Staffordshire, UK

CATERER, TERI-LOUISE
[memb.] British Surfing Association, Fender Club, Surfers Against Sewage; [oth. writ.] Several poems published in Anthologies, articles in Local Press; [pers.] Not everyone will always believe in you so always believe in yourself; [a.] Lacey Green, Bucks, UK

CAVES, EMMA
[b.] 9 September 1966, Bedfordshire; [p.] Robert and Diana Caves; [ed.] Bedford High School; [occ.] Practice Nurse; [oth. writ.] Poem published in local magazine, aged 7; [pers.] My passion is the 'Arts' I believe we must take time to indulge in our passion, to feed our soul.; [a.] Belper, Derbyshire, UK

CAWFORD, MARIA JULIET
[b.] 24 May 1956, Dartford, Kent; [p.] William Harris, Kathleen Harris; [m.] Divorced; [ch.] Warren Anthony and Faye Maria; [ed.] Erith Grammar, University of Greenwich; [occ.] Under Graduate Student BA Hons (English); [memb.] SGI-UK (The Society for the Creation of Value - Buddhist Lay Society); [oth. writ.] Articles for UK express (SGI-UK monthly magazine); [pers.] My Buddhist philosophy has revolutionised my attitude to life, instilling hope and an earnestness to progress daily, fulfilling my ambitions whilst supporting others.; [a.] Erith, Kent, UK

CAZALY, IRIS
[b.] 28 September 1915, Manchester; [p.] Alice and Francis Crawshaw; [m.] Hedley Cazaly, 22 April 1946, in Beirut; [ch.] 1 Son, Hedley John Cazaly, 19 June 1947; [ed.] Ashby De La Zouch, Boy's Grammar School, Tudor Grange Boy's Grammar School, Solihull; [occ.] Retired; [hon.] Sgt. Served in the ATS/EFI, in the Middle East, 1945-7. In Cairo, Alexandria, Beirut, and Jerusalem - (received Palestine (King George VI) Campaign Medal - Worked as a recording operator of voices of the forces, Censored and dispatched discs to H.Q. in Cairo. Postal records closed down in June 1946. I took over as a forces beautician "Olivia's" when studio in Jerusalem was refurbished into Olivia's beauty parlor for service girls; [oth. writ.] No Birthday Card (Untitled) (Poetry how, Midlands, 1991, Volume 1). Poetry how - 1.e. "No Birthday Card" and "I Must Bread Like A Whisper" are the only two poems I have ever written to date; [a.] Solihull, West Midlands, Warwickwhire, UK

CHADWICK, GRAHAM
M.A. Creative Writing, Lancaster University; Currently working on epic prose poem history of the 20th century.; Published work takes in journalism for Peace News, Tribune etc., Herault; France; 34700

CHALMERS, WILLIAM
[b.] 5 October 1937, Stirling; [ed.] Kilsyth Academy; [oth. writ.] Thirty short stories unpublished. Several stage plays performed and poetry. Books one, two, three and four "Faces and Places" "O" Mice And Men" poem "Wee Scots Dracula". "Glasgow and Strathclyde Poetry Anthology", unabridged. Two poems "Nae Mair" and "The Guild Lord Cried Time"; [pers.] (Justice and freedom is the universal language of the world's people. Where it is suppressed, change it. Where you find it, share it). Inspired by Robert Burns, Abe Lincoln, Elizabeth Fry, Oscar Wilde and Rod McKuen.; [a.] Kilsyth, Stirling, UK

CHANDLER, D. E.
[b.] 1 March 1932, Lambeth; [p.] Charles and Claira Kight (Deceased); [m.] Fredrick M. Chandler (Deceased), 26 March 1956; [ed.] Secondary Modern, Dagenham Essex; [occ.] Retired; [memb.] Founder, Hom Member and President of Aveley Obedience and Working Trials Society Dog Club; [oth. writ.] A novel going to print; [pers.] My pen is my master. I do its bidding, only then am I free.; [a.] Tonbridge, Kent, UK

CHANDLER, SUSAN
[b.] 19 February 1951, Woking; [p.] Reginald and Rosemarie Chandler; [ed.] West Byfleet County Secondary School; [oth. writ.] First ever entry of my poetry; [pers.] My poems are based on my personal feelings, observations and life experience. It is an outlet for the emotion I feel. Having lost both parents at an early age, this achievement would be a tribute to them.; [a.] Walton-on-Thames, Surrey, UK

CHATWIN, DOROTHY
[b.] 6 January 1913, Kings Lynn, Norfolk; [p.] Walter Chaplin, Elizabeth Chaplin; [m.] William Chatwin (Deceased), 22 December 1955; [ed.] Kings Lynn High Sch., Ipswich Secondary Bognor Regis Teachers Training College - Mature Student (37); [occ.] Retired Teacher-Junior, also still Teach the Piano; [memb.] Methodist Church, Retired Teachers Association; [hon.] Nothing Outstanding, various certificate for odd thing, including Drawing and Piano Certifs: Ass. Board Grades I-VIII; [oth. writ.] Articles in various magazines over the years and a first poem accepted for an anthology. This spring for Autumn 1996! In addition to your kind offer!; [pers.] I become inspired by episodes in nature and use as parables. I see world of nature walking hand in hand with human nature. We both go through similar traumas of life death resurrection. The great oneness of creation sunshine-stronger. Joy-sorrow.; [a.] Norwich, Norfolk, UK

CHAUDHARI, MRS. SAMEENA
[b.] 20 July 1959, London; [ed.] O Levels; [occ.] Company Secretary; [oth. writ.] Many other poems written by myself as this is my favorite hobby, not yet published.; [a.] Hainault, Essex, UK

CHECKETTS, GILES
[b.] August 11, 1977, Worcester; [ed.] Worcester Royal Grammar, York University; [occ.] Student; [memb.] Mensa; [a.] Ombersley, Worcester

CHEW, DAWN
[b.] 20 June 1955, Birmingham; [p.] Joyce and John Lawrence; [m.] Ron Chew, 6 September 1975; [ch.] Adam and Matthew; [ed.] Yardley Grammer; [occ.] Typist-Burnsalls Metal Finishers; [memb.] Streetly Cricket Club; [pers.] Poetry for me is an ideal way to express feelings and thoughts.

CHILDS, JOAN SYLVIA
[pen.] Louise Walker; [b.] 11 October 1930, London; [p.] Walter Gibbered and Margaret Gibberd; [m.] Dennis Frederick Childs, 19 July 1952; [ch.] Sally Anne, Rosemary Jane, Robert Brian; [ed.] Convent of St. Francis De Sales, Tring, Herts; [occ.] Retired, housewife; [memb.] Guisborough Writers Group, Guisborough Rugby Club, Mothers Union At Nunthorpe; [hon.] Art, 'Typical English Girl' Competition for a portrait, four dancing competitions, Tennis doubles (not wimbledon!!!); [oth. writ.] Novel about my parents. A poem about each of our six grandchildren. Wartime true stories of our village. Poem for old peoples home at christmas.; [pers.] I endew our to help others enjoy 'Love Of Life.'; [a.] Middlesbrough, Middlesbrough, UK

CHRISTIAN, ROMA CADWGAN
[b.] 10 July 1914, Blaengarw, S Wales; [p.] Harry and Winifred Thomas; [m.] Albert James Christian, Deceased; [ed.] Garw Grammar School, Pontycymer Mid Glamorgan S. Wales, State Registered Nurse St. Alfeges Greenwich; [occ.] Retired; [memb.] Ledbury Baptist Church; [oth. writ.] Several poems published in church magazines; [pers.] Have always loved poetry inherited from my mother. Most poetry written is Christian based; [a.] Ledbury, Herefordshire, UK

CHRISTIE, JAMES RICHARD
[b.] 27 May 1935, Soho Dist. Thomas Jamaica, West Indies; [p.] Alexander Christie and Eliza Saunds; [m.] Edel Elsada McKenzie, 26 November 1961; [ch.] Pauline Angela, Richard Calvin and Yvonne Fay; [ed.] Fair Prospect Govt. Elementary School, Jam. Airy Castle Govt. Elementary school, Jam. Port Morant Govt. Elementary School, Jam. Kingsway High School, Kingston, Jam.; [occ.] Nursing Auxiliary; [pers.] My love of poetry comes from listening and reading it and I like to write about people and events.; [a.] Carlton, Nottingham, UK

CHRISTOPHER, MRS. DOREEN
[b.] 2 November 1928, Nottingham; [p.] Arthur and Annie Morley; [m.] (Divorced), 26 December 1955; [ch.] 2 boys and 1 girl; [ed.] Cowley St John Senior School Oxford; [occ.] Retired; [oth. writ.] 1 poem published in a book by arrival press remembering book called eastern works; [pers.] I had find an ordinary education, living school at 11 yrs old have always liked to write verse and have another to adapt called mind summer madness; [a.] Basildon, Essex, UK

CHRISTY, MICHAEL GERALD
[b.] 25 February 1973, St Asaphs; [p.] Violet Christy, Thomas P. Christy; [m.] Marian Lloyd Christy, 17 November 1994; [ch.] Aidan Wyn Christy; [ed.] Ysgol Syr Hugh Owen, Caernarfon; [oth. writ.] Poems published by triumph house and anchor books; [a.] Caernarfon, Gwynedd, UK

CHURCHILL, DANNY
[b.] 14 February 1944, Drogheda; [p.] Thomas and Elizabeth Churchill; [m.] Divorced; [ch.] One son and one daughter; [ed.] St. Mary Primary School, Drop lead, Cort Regional Locational College Cort; [occ.] Plamber; [hon.] Junior and Senior Trade's Exam's; [oth. writ.] Lyrics, Poems, Sonnets, Odes; [pers.] The older I get the younger old people get. The strong carry blame The weak apportion blame; [a.] Droylede, Louth, UK

CLACHRIE, JANE OSBORNE
[b.] 20 May 1908, Ayr, Scotland; [p.] Mr. and Mrs. J. Clachrie (Deceased); [ed.] Newton Academy, Ayr; [occ.] Retired; [oth. writ.] Two poems published in church magazine (a thank you after a spell in hospital) 1989 and (one of those days) 1991 one poem published in Hammondville Nursing home, magazine Australia (old age) 1992.; [pers.] I try to control my own human failings, and tolerate them in others, with the exception of cruelty either to human's animals or creatures. Hobbies reading writing poems, solving cross words.; [a.] Ayr, Ayrshire, UK

CLARIDGE, PIM
[b.] 16 December, Twickenham; [p.] Kenneth Ker, Eileen Ker; [m.] Tony Claridge, 23 December; [ch.] Marten, Mike, Salli, Rob; [ed.] Governess due to Polio; [occ.] Recently widowed and reshaping life; [memb.] R. S. Horticultural Soc., Friend of Festival Theatre and Scottish Chamber Orch., Born Free Foundation; [oth. writ.] Stuffed away in drawers!; [pers.] Son Marten has 3 books published first was short listed for Raymond Chandler Award.; [a.] Edinburgh, UK

CLARINGBOLD, SHARRON
[b.] 31 March 1972, Carlisle; [p.] Robert Fearon, Edith Fearon; [m.] Scott Claringbold, 25 June 1994; [ed.] Nelson Thomlinson School, Wigton, Cumbria; [occ.] Customer Service Assistant at 'Send the Light' (S.T.L.) Carlisle; [pers.] I believe my ability to write poetry is a gift from God many of my poems are centered around nature and God's marvellous creation.; [a.] Carlisle, Cumbria UK

CLARK, ANTONY G.
[b.] 16 March 1967, Woking; [p.] Ann Margaret Clark; [ed.] Highlands Secondary School, Woking Sixth form College; [occ.] Administration Officer, Nittan (UK) limited, old Woking, Surrey; [oth. writ.] Several poems published in "Iota", "Envoi" and "First Time" Magazines; [pers.] I feel strongly that poetry should be the moving, disciplined, artistic communication of thought and of feeling - feeling above all. Most of my poetry stems from thing I have seen/thought/ felt, also the media and other artists lives.; [a.] Woking, Surrey, UK

CLARK, MRS. DORIS ADA
[b.] 12 June 1910, Grays, Essex; [p.] Mr. and Mrs. W.T. King; [m.] James Clark (Deceased), 23 July 1932; [ch.] One son; [ed.] Grays Park School, Bridge Road, Grays; [occ.] Pensioner; [oth. writ.] Autobiography, "The Ups and Downs of a Lifetime", booklet, printed (not published); [pers.] I like to reflect the happy events in my life in verse.; [a.] Grays, Essex, UK

CLARK, EMILY SELINA CRIPPS
[pen.] Selina Styles, Cripps; [b.] 10 October 1911, High Wycombe; [p.] William Alfred Cripps, Sarah Ann Styles; [m.] Herbert Bannerman Clark (Deceased), 28 July 1945; [ch.] Son: Still Born. At almost forty; [ed.] Elementary Village School (Left aged 14) Haddenham Bucks Nr Aylesbury, Loved Poetry and Music always moved at Kipling's poems; [occ.] Housewife; [oth. writ.] (Local weekly newspaper. Christmas Poems) in small magazine. "The Bucks Free Press," "International Dolphin Watch" "Age Concern." The Peace Movement and others.; [pers.] Never waste your talents like me, persevere.; [a.] High Wycombe, Bucks, UK

CLARK, KELLY
[b.] 20 October 1978, Gravesend; [p.] David Clark, Elaine Whittaker; [ed.] The Appleton School; [pers.] Many thanks to Mr. Hamilton for all his encouragement throughout my school years, and for making me believe in my talent.; [a.] South Benfleet, Essex, UK

CLARK, MARGARET ANN
[pen.] Sandee Ainge; [b.] 24 September 1942, Northampton; [p.] Charles Merrey and Edna Merrey; [m.] Deceased; [ed.] Kingsthorpe Secondary School, Northampton College; [occ.] Professional; [memb.] WRUS Northampton Victory Services Club London; [oth. writ.] Written several poems but never had any published until now; [pers.] I have been writing poetry since the age of fourteen and I admire the great poets and read their poems often.; [a.] Northampton, Northants, UK

CLARK, MARY K.
[pen.] Mary K. Clark; [b.] 13 May 1950, Lincoln; [p.] Ernest Kirk, Nellie Kirk; [m.] David Dunn Clark, 26 November 1977; [ch.] Elliot Russel Clark; [ed.] Great Limber Primary Caistor Secondary; [occ.] Tempt School Supervisor Cleethorpes; [oth. writ.] Several poems published (competitions), shorts story published in Germany (newspaper). Various poems and short stories published in an amateur magazine for poets and writers.; [pers.] I very much appreciate the encouragement given to me by Mrs. Philo at the creative writing classes that I attended.; [a.] Cleethorpes, NE Lincs, UK

CLARK, PAUL
[b.] 11 December 1964, Ongar, Essex; [p.] Margaret Clark, Derek Clark; [m.] Sonia Clark; [ch.]

Charlotte Elizabeth, Adam Leigh; [ed.] Ongar Comprehensive, Harlow Technical College; [occ.] Care Assistant for the disabled at Lulworth Court; [oth. writ.] I have written over 50 other poems none of which have been seen by anybody other than family and very close friends.; [pers.] All the poetry I have written is a result of Jesus love and faithfulness throughout my life. The words are God's and the glory goes to him; [a.] Southend on Sea, Essex, UK

CLARK, STEVEN
[b.] 21 December 1955, Ely; [p.] Bernard, Margarete; [m.] 20 March 1980, 5 July 1992; [ch.] Karl Glen; [ed.] Soham Village College, Cambridge CTAD; [occ.] Self-employed; [hon.] Business Administration; [pers.] My writing is a reflection of what I have experienced and also impressions. Poetry conveys much in atmosphere and expression, in relatively few words. I like all poetry, especially early poetry.; [a.] Soham, Cambridgeshire, UK

CLARK, VALERIE
[b.] 23 March 1943, Nottingham; [m.] Alan Clark, 10 May 1985; [ch.] Daughter Melanie Jayne; [occ.] Housewife; [memb.] The Poetry Society; [pers.] This is my first published poem and my ambition for the future would be that maybe I could help others to find peace, strength and courage, hope and sometimes laughter through my poetry.; [a.] Long Bennington, Newark, Notts, UK

CLARKE, KIRSTY
[b.] 11 February 1974, Cardiff; [p.] Christine and Steve Clarke; [ed.] Nene College of Northampton; [hon.] Bachelor of Education (Hons) with English Literature major; [oth. writ.] First published work; [pers.] My writing reflects the reality of my life, the people I share it with, the world through my experiences.; [a.] Barry, S. Glamorgan, UK

CLARKE, MR. R. H.
[pen.] "Ramon"; [b.] 10 March 1928, Birmingham; [p.] Horace and Alice Clarke; [m.] Mary Clarke, 10 March 1956; [ch.] Martin Clarke; [ed.] Aston Commercial School Birmingham, 6 `R.S.A.' certs. Military Service - Army Apl '46-Feb '49; [occ.] Retired - Gen. Mgr. of Yorkshire Area of `RTZ' "Metals Group"; [memb.] Local Probus Club `Past Treasurer', Local `Unionist' Social Club; [hon.] "Paris" School of Art - `Portraits Landscapes', certificate; [oth. writ.] Nothing extra ordinary minor publications only; [pers.] Have always been interested in art and writing for mainly personal and family benefits. Most correspondence is in rhyme. Now opportunity to be more serious with poetry.; [a.] Burley-in-Wharfedale, Yorkshire, UK

CLARKE, MR. RICHARD J.
[pen.] Richard J. Clarke, John F. White; [b.] 10 June 1946, Derby; [p.] Not known - Orphaned at 1 year of age; [m.] Ann M. Clarke, 28 November 1987 (Second Marriage); [ch.] Jenni - 23, Danny - 21, Matthew - 17; [ed.] Hargrave House Infant School, Derby, Spondon Springfield School, Derby Spondon Park Grammar School, Derby; [occ.] Medically Retired, but part-time volunteer worker for methodist church; [memb.] Member of Institute of Advance Motorists; [hon.] Merit Passes in G.C.E. 'O' level in French, combined Sciences, History, Mathematics and English; [oth. writ.] Personal anthology of poems entitled 'Reflections' published to raise money for church youth group.; [pers.] I seek to encourage, by inspirational writings and personal involvement, others to cherish each other and their world.; [a.] Spondon, Derbyshire, UK

CLARKE, ROSE MARIE
[pen.] Marie; [b.] 6 March 1938, Ireland; [p.] Rose and Thomas White; [m.] Bernard Clarke; [ch.] (Three) Christine, Angela, Barry; [ed.] Saint Johns Convent School, Limerick City Ireland; [occ.] House Wife; [oth. writ.] Wrote a song once, it was accepted, but I never sent the money, to have it put to music, it was never recorded.; [pers.] Thoughts come to my mind I put them on paper, sometimes they make me laugh, sometimes sad, but being able to write, that makes me glad.; [a.] Hainault, Essex, UK

CLAYTON, DAWN
[b.] 22 November 1962, Derby; [p.] Hazel Heaney, Jack Heaney; [m.] Anthony Mark Clayton, 5 September 1987; [ch.] Christopher, Stephanie, Kirstie, Katie and Stacie; [ed.] Charles Read Secondary School; [occ.] Housewife; [pers.] With a large family, writing is my refuge.; [a.] Grantham, Lincs, UK

CLEGHORN, EVELYN
[b.] 6 May 1922, Berwick on Tweed; [ed.] Went to school in New Brunswick, Canada Trained as Signal Operator in A.T.S. 1941-1946; [occ.] Great Grandmother; [memb.] Part of "Atticus Writers Circle" - A group of Local Writing Enthosiasts; [pers.] Since retiring and moving to Lancaster, after working for police as civilian control - room assistant, has taken several adult education courses mostly in writing. Struggling to understand new computer system. Writes at home in spare time.; [a.] Lancaster, Lancashire, UK

CLEMENT, CHARLES REES
[pen.] Rhys Clement; [b.] 19 December 1915, Crickhowell; [p.] William Clement, Jeanette Clement; [m.] Mary Josephine Clement, 22 July 1950; [ch.] Timothy Charles, Janet Elizabeth; [ed.] Brynmawr Grammar School; [occ.] Retired (Local Gov't. Officer); [memb.] Herefordshire Art and Craft Society, Herefordshire Branch Newman Society, Herefordshire Golf Club; [pers.] In poetry I endeavour to convey my feelings concerning the certainty and growth of the spiritual in mankind.; [a.] Hereford, Worcester, UK

CLEMENTS, CATHERINE
[b.] 13 January 1950, Walsall; [p.] Joseph Evans and Irene Evans; [m.] John Clements, 1937 Divorced and re-married 10 years ago, same man; [ch.] Jonathan, Rachel, Susanne and Ildiko, granddaughter: Katie; [ed.] Joseph Leckie Comprehensive Stafford College, Cannock College "Life"; [occ.] Housewife, recently career; [memb.] Present: None/previously art group, writer's circle present none really - save "The fellow ship of man." And the ultimate membership of "Life And Death"; [hon.] None save the "Honour of Love" - and the rewards of infinite time spend adopting my daughter, Ildiko (Romanian) - and the "Re-Birth of my son from a "Head Injury"; [oth. writ.] Poems and beginning's of a book. Observations of life. Observations of life in Romania also - the new beginnings - after a severe head injury. "Ultimate to recovery," "Up and Running."; [pers.] Since writing this poem - "Life" has sorely stretched my patience and belief's due to my son Jonathan's R. T. Accident 1991, but I can now see definite things of light in a very dark tunnel. "Love is all consuming!"; [a.] Rugeley, Staffordshire, UK

CLEMENTS, GRACE M.
[b.] 30 September 1916, Shildon; [p.] Fred Wright, Edith Wright; [m.] Richard Clements, 25 January 1936; [ch.] Irene, Ronald; [ed.] Guisborough Providence Girls School; [occ.] Retired; [oth. writ.] Poems as presents none published; [pers.] I write for pleasure and from personal experience mostly; [a.] Guisborough, Cleveland, UK

CLEMENTS, JOY
JOYCE MARY DRACKETT-CASE
[pen.] Joy Drackett-Case, Joy De Case; [b.] Newmarket; [p.] Herbert and Mary Drackett-Case; [m.] Edgar Clements; [ch.] Maxwell and Susan Clements; [ed.] Kingston-on-Thames; [occ.] Artist and Housewife; [memb.] Associate Royal Ulster Academy, Past Pres. Ulster Society of Women Artists, Vice Pres and Chairman Ulster, Water Color Society, Student of School Philosophy; [hon.] Twice Recipient Perpetual Trophy-Ulster, Society Women Artists (Paint Under Joy Clements); [oth. writ.] Article published in local magazine "Mandalas" and poem attend creative writing class and am doing correspondence course.; [pers.] "No Man Is An Island" we are all part of the great universal consciousness but most of us are asleep and unaware. Poetry and art can awaken.; [a.] Newtownabbey, Antrim, UK

CLIFT, DONNA JUNE
[pen.] Constance, Dinky Berenger; [b.] 3 February 1964; [ch.] Charmain, Mark, Darren; [occ.] Housewife, Independent Knitted Toy Designer; [oth. writ.] None previously attempted for publication; [a.] Liskeard, Cornwall, UK

CLOUGH, ADELE-MARIE
[b.] 13 October 1976, Hull; [ed.] Archbishop Thurstan School, Wilberforce Sixth Form College, Beverly College; [occ.] Cultural and Graphic Fine Arts; [oth. writ.] I have completed a book of poems, which is now awaiting publication, and am presently writing my first novel.; [pers.] If you don't have a dream it can never come true! If you are determined, and strive to achieve something important to you, regardless of others views on it, you can and will succeed.; [a.] Hull, East Yorkshire, UK

CLOUGH, DENNIS VICTOR
[b.] 31 October 1939, Bradford; [p.] Theodore Clough, Constance Clough; [m.] Janet Rose Clough, 15 February 1992; [ed.] Hanson Boys Grammar School, Bradford; [occ.] Assistant Manager Social Services; [hon.] Council of Europe Medical Fellowship (1974); [oth. writ.] Articles for professional magazines. Subject material: Physically disabled and elderly, 'Council of Europe' report on physically disabled people in a community setting. (Sweden); [pers.] I use life's experience in my poetry to highlight a variety of moods and emotions.; [a.] Bradford, Yorkshire, UK

COCHRANE, JULIE
[b.] 31 July 1956, Leeds; [p.] Robert and Matilda Coleman; [m.] George Cochrane, 14 June 1976; [ch.] Robert and Alma Cochrane; [ed.] Ripon Secondary School, Ripon City Yorkshire; [occ.] Housewife, disabled; [pers.] I have written poems since I was at a young age. But never had any published.; [a.] Thornton, Fife, Scotland

COCK, MS. CHARLOTTE
[b.] 29 November 1973, Templecombe; [p.] Roger Harold Cock, Pearl Claire Hansford; [ed.] Arle Comprehensive, Gloscat, College of Arts and Technology - Cheltenham; [occ.] Office Administration; [memb.] Rounders Team member; [hon.] BTEC First Diploma in Business and Finance; [pers.] Observing and listening instead of talking as much is the key to creative poetry. I find it easier to write my poems from my own experiences.; [a.] Castle Cary, Somerset, UK

COGAR, MAUREEN
[pen.] Maureen Jean Cogar; [b.] 12 August 1941, Pontypool, Wales; [p.] Jean Stone and Henry Stone; [m.] Maurice Cogar, 28 October 1961; [ch.] Caroline; [ed.] Lower Compton School; [occ.] "Ducal" Pine Furniture Consultant, at a department store in Plymouth; [memb.] "Copthorn" Gym and Lesiure Club; [oth. writ.] Two poems published the change of love and middle age groupie.; [pers.] Dedicated to all my family and friends and grandchildren Jonathan, Mark, and with love.; [a.] Plymouth, Devon, UK

COLE, JACQUELINE MICHELLE JEAN
[b.] 13 April 1960, London; [m.] Steve; [ch.] Jamie, Katie; [pers.] Sometimes I awaken from my sleep to write thought's down, I love animals and have 15 cats, the calmness of their nature inspire me to write. I love art and sometimes express my thoughts in drawings and paintings; [a.] Colchester, Essex, UK

COLE, NICOLA
[b.] 19 March 1971, Fly; [p.] Graham Cole, Jean Cole; [ed.] Soham Village College, Ely Sixth Form, National Extension College, Open University; [occ.] Unable to work due to illness, part-time correspondence student; [hon.] Striving towards a degree in Psychology; [pers.] I love to drift into the place of dreams, to be back as imagination takes me on a journey where reality is but a distant notion. Poetry is the key that unlocks my mind, transporting me to a world free of physical restraints and pain.; [a.] Soham, Cambridgeshire, UK

COLE, ROSALEEN GWENLLIAN
[b.] 6 March, 1928, Bedwas, Gwent; [p.] Oliver Sherwood, Gwenllian Sherwood; [m.] Michael Cole, October 22, 1966; [ch.] William Jeffrey and Huw John; [ed.] Pagefield College, Newport, Gwent; [occ.] Retired; [memb.] South Wales Organ Society; [hon.] Three Honors Awards for Music; [oth. writ.] Letters published in Woman's Weekly, Woman's Realm, Family Circle Article in Essex Gazette.; [pers.] I enjoy writing poetry as it allows me greater freedom of expression.; [a.] Cefn Hengoed, Mid Glamorgan

COLE, SYLVIA
[b.] Portsmouth; [ed.] Professional training in speech and drama, piano and singing; [occ.] Piano Teacher; [memb.] British Actors Equity Association; [oth. writ.] Numerous poems in various anthologies, published by Anchor Books, Triumph House, and the Poetry Guild; [pers.] Music and poetry are kindred souls, born as a union of rhythm and sound conceived in the energy of silence.; [a.] Waterloo, Hampshire, UK

COLEMAN, LEONARD T.
[b.] 10 July 1916, Frant, Sx., Nr Turnbridge Wells; [p.] Thomas Coleman, Margaret Coleman; [m.] Pamela Coleman, 23 September 1972; [ch.] David aged 51 - by first wife Joan who died 1963; [ed.] Frant Church School Skinners Co School Turnbridge Wells 1928-1933; [occ.] Retired L.G. Officer 5 yrs Royal Air Force was service technician N.C.O.; [memb.] Bomber Command Assoc., Assoc. Memb. Welsh Academy; [hon.] Defence Medal Queens Silver Jubilee Medal; [oth. writ.] Anthologies poems - 'Anchor Books' poetry now - 'Voices' own book of poems 'A Procession of Words' (33 poems) Minerva Press/5.99/ West Sussex Gazette.; [pers.] Many single published poems in anthologies - hope to follow 'Procession of Words' 'Farther along the Procession' (in preparation) favorite poet - Georgina Christina Rossetti.; [a.] Crawley Down, W. Sussex, UK

COLEMAN, PAT
[pen.] "Tricia Paterson"; [b.] 4 July 1951, Inverness; [p.] Bing and Betty Paterson; [m.] Divorced; [ch.] Christopher and Jason-Paul; [ed.] Inverness High School; [occ.] Bank Cashier; [oth. writ.] Various unpublished poems and short stories, written purely for my personal enjoyment.; [pers.] Now that one of my poems "What Kind of World is This We..." has been published, it may give me the courage to release more. In the future... I find inspiration in all manner of humanity, more so now, as I grow older.; [a.] Inverness, Highland, UK

COLEMAN, STACEY-MARIE
[b.] 7 April 1981, Birmingham; [p.] Kevin Coleman, Carmen Coleman.; [ed.] St. George and St. Teresa Primary School, Dorridge, Solihull. Holy Child Senior School, Edgbaston (1992 to date); [occ.] Student; [memb.] Solihull Arden Tennis and Squash club.; [hon.] Application award ('94 and '95). Natwest UK Schools Mathematical Challenge - Silver award (1993) Bronze award (1994) Gold award (1995); [pers.] I prefer to write from emotions and experiences.; [a.] Solihull, West Midlands, UK

COLES, MARY
[b.] 12 August 1918, Yorkshire; [ed.] R1; [occ.] Retired; [memb.] Recorded Music Society W.I., Trefoil Guild Catholic women's League; [hon.] B.A. (Hons) English - 1970 London University (External); [oth. writ.] A few articles and poems in papers and magazine a book of poems (1985) 'A Path Work of poetry'; [pers.] I am fascinated by the diversity in nature and every aspect of life including poetic form; [a.] Bridport, Dorset, UK

COLGATE, SALLY
[b.] 26 July 1952, Redhill, SY; [p.] John and Kay Anderson; [m.] Peter Colgate, 10 August 1974; [ch.] Guy Thomas, Amy Louise; [ed.] 'Oxted County' Surrey, Carshalton Technical College; [occ.] Laboratory Technician (Biology); [oth. writ.] Five poems in other anthologies; [pers.] I would really like to see my name on the front of a book of poems one day. Published.; [a.] Felpham, W. Sussex, UK

COMERFORD, SINEAD
[b.] 5 April 1972, Dublin, Ireland; [p.] William and Elizabeth Comerford; [ed.] St. Patrick's College Maynooth Co Hildare, Ireland Newman College, Stillorgan, Co Dublin Ireland; [occ.] Cabin Crew Member with British Airways; [hon.] A University degree, Batchelor of Arts in German and Sociology, Postgraduate diploma in Journalism; [oth. writ.] I have had a large number of articles published in a main Irish newspaper dealing with social political issues. Currently writing a fictional novel myself.; [pers.] I enjoy voicing my thoughts, dreams and opinions. Putting words on a page is the perfect medium for relaxation. I strive to observe society, question its wrong - doing in the fight for world peace, justice and serenity.; [a.] Crawley, West Sussex, UK

CONCEPRIO, DOROTHY MARIA
[b.] 14 March 1924, Cardiff; [p.] Rosa and Octave Veillard; [m.] Celestino Conceprio, 26 November 1960; [ch.] Two; [ed.] High School Cardiff; [occ.] Retired; [memb.] Western Front Association; [oth. writ.] Sundry poems; [pers.] A consuming interest in World War One. visited battlefields of Picardy and Flanders since 1984. Not to glorify war but to pay tribute and remember.; [a.] Harrow, Middlesex, UK

CONLEY, JOYCE JOHNSON
[b.] 4 September 1978, Dulwich; [p.] Jenny Conley and Joseph Johnson; [ch.] Shanice Johnson; [occ.] College Student; [hon.] English Certificate Silver Running Plaque

CONLON, ANTHONY P. C.
[b.] 13 March 1960, Bristol; [m.] Michelle Jane Harding, 25 September 1993; [ch.] Gemma Victoria, Ashley James; [pers.] To my family I send my most heartfelt love and to John Denver my thanks for twenty years of hope and inspiration. Life is so good!; [a.] Chippenham, Wiltshire, UK

CONNOLLY, JAMES T.
[b.] 8 July 1944, Rochdale; [p.] Peter John and Mary Connolly; [ed.] St. Gabriels RC School, 49-59, Extension courses, Roman History Latin (at present); [occ.] Sales Consultant with the Canada Life Assurance Co; [memb.] Local Crown, Green Bowling Club, Previous Rochdale Cine Club, Local Interest, Civic History, Reading many Historical also Autobiography; [hon.] Rochdale Cine Club Metro Grown Green Competition 1986, various awards at workers exam's and others. Recent winner of a poetry competition, Council of Poetry; [oth. writ.] Sixty poems hoped to be published in the future. Complete history of both parents family (just finished and in print) many letters sent to the local paper (whom I got your details from). Short story; [pers.] I have been writing for a number of years. Having traveled the globe, I now enjoy gardening (pot-patios). In meeting people I love to discuss many topics. Listening to the manner which people often speak the poem 'Eloquence' was founded.; [a.] Rochdale, Lancs, UK

CONNOLLY, SARAH-JANE
[b.] 16 April 1996, Guys Hospital, South Wark; [p.] Terry and Christine Connolly; [ed.] St. Mary's RC Primary School, Eltham.; [memb.] Cherished Teddies Collectors Club; [pers.] My poems always reflect the way I feel.; [a.] Lee, London, UK

CONROY, TAMSYN
[b.] 4 January 1977, Gravesend; [p.] William and Barbara Conroy; [ch.] First Baby due September 1996; [ed.] Charles Darwin Mixed Comprehensive School - 1988-1995; [occ.] Awaiting Birth of First child; [hon.] 9 Higher Grade G.I.S.Es, 3 Higher Grade a Levels, Marjorie McClure Excellence Award, Gained a place at St High's College Oxford 1995; [oth. writ.] None published.; [pers.] There are two sides to every coin. Any event, object me person is perceived in a variety of ways according to the nature of the inner self. Poetry is my means of communication.; [a.] Biggin Hill, Kent, UK

COOK, DOREEN
[b.] 21 December 1929, Gillingham, Kent; [p.] Winifred Gillard, Sydney Gillard; [m.] (The Late) John William Cook, 12 May 1948; [ch.] Paul John, Wendy Doreen, Alan Paul; [ed.] General - owing to war years, and evacuation; [occ.] Retired; [memb.] Swarovski Crystal Society; [hon.] My honour is my three children who have made me very proud. All doing extremely well in their vocations.; [oth. writ.] Several children stories yet to be published, one or two poems in the company magazine, where I worked for 25 years, and played a part in its production.; [pers.] I like to do whatever I can for those near to me, who are less fortunate than I. I love interesting and joyful books and poetry.; [a.] Chatham, Kent, UK

COOK, PAMELA ANNE
[pen.] Pam Cook; [b.] 5 July 1965, Co. Durham; [m.] Edward Cook, 13 July 1991; [ch.] Adam William Cook; [occ.] Bus Driver; [pers.] I find the inspiration for my poetry in my family and surroundings. I am also inspired by down to earth poets like Frank O'Hara.; [a.] Peterlee, Durham, UK

COOKNEY, MARGARET
[pen.] Harriet Bridgman; [b.] 30 August 1952, Windsor, Berkshire; [p.] Michael Bridgman and Phyllis Bridgman; [m.] Paul Cookney, 27 February 1971; [ch.] Chad Daniel and Max Robert; [ed.] Windsor High School For Girls Ealing Grammar School for Girls, Swindon-Headlands Comprehensive School; [occ.] Office Administrator; [oth. writ.] First published poem - in fact, first submitted poem currently studying with London School of writing since Jan 96. I just love to write friends encouraged me to enter!; [pers.] Life s a kaleidoscope of emotion through experience by which we learn and grow.; [a.] Plymouth, Devon, UK

COOKSON, DANIEL THOMAS
[b.] 1 March 1973, Blackpool; [ed.] Arnold School Blackpool, Edinburgh University; [occ.] Medical Student; [a.] Edinburgh, UK

COOKSON, JOHN WILLIAM
[pen.] JC or JWC; [b.] 21 July 1948, Scunthorpe; [p.] Bill and Lily Cookson; [m.] Janice Elaine, 12 December 1972; [ch.] Rachel Louise, Katie Jane; [ed.] Westcliffe Secondary Modern, CSE General Science Army Ed Centre GSE 'O' Maths, Eng, Geography and Man Management GSE'A' Eng, Geog, and Management, Comm Skill; [occ.] Security Officer; [memb.] Royal Artillery Assoc, RNA Old Comrades Assoc; [hon.] GSM NI and Lsgc. medals; [oth. writ.] Poems published only in regimental magazine. This will be my first public publication for which I'm highly delighted and proud.; [pers.] Poetry to me should be a product of the heart and mind. I find it easier to express my feelings in this way. I have other poems with a military bent which I would value your professional opinions on.; [a.] Grimsby, NE Lincs, UK

COOMBES, NATASHA JAYNE
[pen.] Natasha Jayne Coombes; [b.] 10 December 1981, Chichester; [p.] Sally and Graham Coombes; [ed.] Student at Midhurst Grammar School; [memb.] Newsround Journalist Club; [hon.] Speech and Drama Exam - Grade 2 Merit Grade 3 Honours; [oth. writ.] None yet!!; [pers.] I don't usually write poems. I have an interest in drama and journalism so I do get enjoyment from writing and one day I would like to write my own successful play. I was inspired to write this poem last year by my teacher Mr. Mills at Midhurst intermediate School who made to a brilliant year. Also thanks to my Mom for sending the poem in!!; [a.] Midhurst, West Sussex, UK

COOPER, ANNE
[b.] 1 April 1938, Basingstoke; [m.] Gordon Cooper, 8 August 1959; [ch.] Rosemary, Christine Philip; [ed.] Basingstoke High School for Girls; [occ.] Retired Registered Nurse; [memb.] Royal Horticultural Society; [oth. writ.] Several short stories and other poems. None previously published.; [pers.] I write about the things that have meant a lot to me, and also so that my grandchildren will have some knowledge of the world during my life; [a.] Up Nately, Hampshire, UK

COOPER, AUDREY
[pen.] Audrey Cooper; [b.] October 5, 1929, Bovingdon; [p.] William Chales and Florance Jane; [m.] Reuben John Cooper, March 17, 1951; [ch.] Three; [ed.] Bovingdon Village School; [occ.] Retired widow; [oth. writ.] 1994 Poetry Anthology *24 hours in the life of Ayles Bury Vale* (my poem's called "The Visit"). 1995 *Voices from the Heart of England* (my Poem's "The Foundation of Life") by Anchor Books, (anthology) 1995 *My Dream* book poetry life anthology by Anchor Books, December 1995 year passed to be published also again by Anchor Books, book name *Sixty Something*.; [pers.] My love of poetry.; [a.] Maulden, Bedfordshire

COOPER, JOHN ERIC
[b.] 4 May 1922, Chesterfield, Pilsley; [p.] William and Jane Cooper; [m.] Mary Cooper (nee Bourne), 26 September 1945; [ch.] Elizabeth Marie and Charles Neville; [ed.] Pilsley Elementary School, Chesterfield Technical College, Metropolitan College (correspondence); [occ.] Retired Accountant; [memb.] Associate of the Chartered Institute of Cost and Management Accountants; [a.] Coalville, Leics, UK

COPE, MYFANWY ANN
[pen.] Mary Casey; [b.] 23 September 1972, Clwyd; [p.] Mervyn Williams, Ivy Williams; [m.] Paul Charles Cope, 6 October 1995; [ed.] Ysgol Bryn Elian, Colwyn Bay, Llandrillo College, Gwynedd; [occ.] Self-employe,d Craftworker, (Dried flowers); [memb.] Dr. Who Appreciation Soc, (DWAS). And the prisoner, fan club, (Six of one) landcrab 1800 club.; [oth. writ.] Poems published in local poetry magazine.; [pers.] Living in the country has made me realize the wave of life. I have become a more gentle person and my writing is better because of u-. I have only my husband to thank for this.; [a.] Pwllheli, Gwynedd, UK

CORICA, ELIZABETH
[pen.] Gem; [b.] 20 April 1916, Everton, Liverpool; [p.] Mattew Garrett Forshaw - Mary Anne Cooper Ne Forshaw; [m.] William Henry Corica, 3 September 1939 (Sunday War-declared); [ch.] Four (one daughter - three sons - one remaining); [ed.] Very basic - Marvellous Teachers all good on discipline - a council school, left at 14 years knowing nothing didn't know - a verb from an adjective, never bothered to listen or take lessons in.; [occ.] Senior Citizen living alone (widow), (late hairdresser); [memb.] The poetry Society 22 Betterton Street London WC 2H 9BY, Country Park Estate Friendship Group; [hon.] Several years ago won a Churchill - Wall Plate - for a poem published in a Scottish Anthology. My youngest son was emotionally badly effected by the death of his two brothers. (But has not cracking again works very hard.); [oth. writ.] 200 poems Something to Ponder Volume 1 - Volume II working on Volume III at the moment - also two half written books. Stranger than fiction - and gathering clouds.; [pers.] Sufficient unto the day is the evil thereof doubtful if the books ever get finished. After nursing my Parkasonian - Parkins disease husband I have 6 granddaughters - 3 grandsons - 2 great granddaughter many years - and death - quite untimely - of my two elder sons - feel like giving up the ghost.; [a.] Liverpool, Lancashire, UK

COSGROVE, LEIGH PAUL
[b.] 3 August 1973, Harpenden, Herts; [p.] John and Linda Cosgrove; [ed.] Roundwood Park School, Harpenden Barnfield College, Luton Leeds Metropolitan University; [occ.] Marketing and Systems Support Manager, City Catering Recruitment Services; [memb.] LMU, Tai Chi Club; [hon.] HND in Hotel, Catering and Institutional Management; [pers.] This was written in Mortonhampstead, Devon while on work experience at the White Hart Hotel. It describe the view from my window and my feelings at the time. I dedicate is to Annie Warren.

COTTERELL, AUGUSTA ANNA
[pen.] Known as Gusty; [b.] 19 July 1931, Hagen, Westphalia; [p.] Anna and Heinrich Biermann; [m.] David Cotterell, 22 October 1955; [ch.] Three Daughters only son died age 7 month at Great Ormond SW Hoop, London; [ed.] High School, Commercial Training, Nursing Training 2 years at Plater College Oxford; [occ.] Housewife Town Aln and District Aln and Town Major of Amershaw; [memb.] Life Member of National Trust, Life Member Oxford Union, Life Member Catholic Union, Fellow of Hughen of Society of London, Member or Amersham Society, Member of Chiltern Club of Arts; [oth. writ.] Contributions to press; [pers.] Amersham's Newtown mayor Gusty Cotterell promised she would be more than a "Queen of Hearts" at her inauguration this week. German-born Councillor Augusta Cotterell, known as Gusty, stamped her determined character on the new role from the start on Monday night. With Teutonic directness she said: "I don't want to be a Queen of Hearts. Only a listening ear for each and everyone in our community." The new mayor, who takes over from Councillor Tony Weedon, later said she would like to do something for Amersham teenagers and would also form a mayor's charity in her two years of office. "I would like something done for the 12 to 16-year olds who are roaming the streets and causing mischief - a skateboard ramp in King George V Field." And on charity she said: "I was thinking of the Red Cross but on a local level. I think charity begins at home." It was the Red Cross that brought Mrs. Cotterell, now 64, to Britain in 1954 to study as a nurse in London - she had volunteered for the Red Cross in Africa but, when she failed the medical, decided to study in the UK instead. She met her husband David, an insurance broker, and the couple moved to Amersham 36 years ago. They have three daughters and five grandchildren. Mrs. Cotterell was born in the ancient German Kingdom of Westphalia, in Hagen, the Gateway to the Sauerland, an area she described as similar to the Chiltern Hills. Now a British citizen, Mrs. Cotterell is a Roman Catholic and will be holding the mayor's civic service in St. Aiden's Catholic

Church, Little Chalfont, this year. Mrs. Cotterell has been an Amersham town councillor for five years and was elected to Chiltern District Council, representing Amersham-on-the-Hill ward for the Liberal Democrats, last year. "I'm not a learner any more," she told councilors this week. Councillor Derek Lodge was elected as Amersham's deputy mayor.; [a.] Amersham, Bucks, UK

COULL, NICOLA
[b.] 25 April 1980, Dundee; [p.] Irene Coull, Colin Coull; [ed.] Monifieth High School (Previously Seaview Primary School); [occ.] 1st Monifieth Girls Brigade, Badminton Club; [memb.] National Winner of Scottish Accident Prevention Council Public Speaking Competition, Certificate of Merit - Young Letter Writers Competition 1992; [a.] Dundee, Angus, UK

COUROUCLI, JENNIFER ROSEMARY
[b.] 22 August 1922, Watford, Herts.; [p.] William Clark and Molly Clark; [m.] Vangelis Couroucli, 1949; [ch.] Mary, Harry, Katerina and Theresa.; [ed.] Watford Grammar School. In A.T.S. during war. Worked in City of London for Stockbrokers. Met Vangelis and went out to Greece and married. Lived in Athens, still do but husband now dead.; [occ.] My children are married and have children themselves. They also live in a Athens and speak three languages. I see them very often but I live alone on the top floor of an apartment house and look after my beautiful garden. I still make poems and I have many friends, one is John Flynn who is a painter my chair. He has painted two of my girls and they are on eh wall, opposite my chair, currently, I am hoping to finish my present occupation, which is writing for the International Society of Poets.; [hon.] Awarded the Nobel Prize

COWIN, KATIE
[b.] 7 January 1982, Isle-of-Man; [p.] Phil Cowin, Edna Cowin; [ed.] Ashley Hill Primary School, Currently at St. Ninian's High School, Douglas; [hon.] Won a couple of short stories competitions; [oth. writ.] Poems published in the local paper; [pers.] I was inspired to write this poem by my brother, Jamie who is handicapped. I would just like to say how much I love him and that he will always have a special place in my heart.; [a.] Douglas, Isle of Man, UK

COWLEY, VIOLET
[pen.] Violet Cowley; [b.] 28 July 1920, London; [p.] Irish (father), Spanish (mother); [m.] Alfred (Deceased 1985), 24 April 1943; [ch.] Janet, John and Lynda; [ed.] Secondary Modern and Night School in Cheshire; [occ.] Retired night Nurse 19 3/4 years; [memb.] Church of England, Church Warden 22 yrs; [hon.] Night School Certificate 1935, English Literature, English - Language and Needle Work, Silver Medal 2nd Prize Needlework Bucks, County, Age, Concern, Festival; [oth. writ.] Words of two hymns my autobiography, published "Over My Shoulder."; [pers.] Having learned abou-ben-adhem at school. I've used it as my yard stick in life. I've always tried to help. My fellow men.; [a.] Buckingham, Bucks, UK

COX, MARGARET
[b.] 30 June 1940, Northfleet, Kent; [p.] Daisy Snelling and Ron Snelling; [m.] Geoffrey Cox, 25 January 1958; [ch.] Stephen Cox and Mark Cox, Debbie Cox; [ed.] Hall Rd School For Girls - 1 Northfleet. State enrolled nurse; [occ.] Retired/ Sen.; [oth. writ.] First submission other writing for personal pleasure and friendly reading.; [pers.] "Tragedy, deepens ones respect of life when sprinkled with hope" This I try believe.; [a.] Gravesend, Kent, UK

COX, SIMON
[b.] 21 April 1970, Dunstable; [p.] George Cox, Valarie Cox; [occ.] Systems Support Manager; [pers.] It take great strength to carry on, when lifes not going right. But it takes more courage to let it go, when no hope is left in sight.; [a.] Simpson Village, Buckinghamshire, UK

CRACKNELL, MARIA
[pen.] Marla Frank; [b.] 9 October 1975, Welwyn Garden City; [p.] Richard and Susan Cracknell; [ed.] Presdales Secondary School for girls, Didn't go on to further education; [occ.] Shop Assistant in home Town, Ware, Herts; [hon.] Other publications; [oth. writ.] I have written a book that I, one day, hope to get published. I have another poem published, and hope to get other work published too.; [pers.] Thanks to the continuous love and support of my loving family, I have persevered in putting my work forward, I thank them. I have been influenced by poets such as: W.B. Yeats, John Keats etc...The poetry that I write comes from deep within my heart, and I hope it will influence peoples lives.; [a.] Ware, Herts, UK

CRAMB, LINDA VIVIEN
[pen.] Lindz; [b.] 10 August 1981, Edinburgh; [p.] David T. E. Cramb and Linda Cramb; [ed.] Prestonfield Primary School, Gracemount High School; [occ.] School Girl; [memb.] Debra Ann School of Dancing Edinburgh, Highland and Jazz and Tap; [hon.] Several awards for Highland Dancing; [oth. writ.] Several poems not sent for publication; [pers.] My writing is important to me as it reflects my feelings at the time. Most things I have written as taken from personal experiences. I was influenced and encourage by my Nana Welsh; [a.] Edinburgh, Midlotian, UK

CRAMPTON, ROZ
[b.] 16 September 1961, Northampton; [p.] Henry John Crampton and Pamela Irene Crampton; [m.] Adi Scott; [ch.] Damien John; [ed.] Weston Favell Upper School, Kilburn Schools of dancing; [occ.] Fitness consultant (Founder and co-director of "Infinity Fitness"; [memb.] International Fund for Animal Welfare (I.F.A.W.), Vegetarian Society, Royal Academy of Dancing; [hon.] Associate of the Imperial Society of Teachers of Dancing; [oth. writ.] Poem in "The Path Of A Poet" (poetry now), philosophical addresses; [pers.] I hope some of my writings inspire people to search deep within...Find the divine light of which they truly are. To draw upon this to help them through all life's lessons, and grow infinitely towards their true potential.; [a.] Northampton, Northants, UK

CRAVEN, KATHRYN
[b.] 14 October 1959, Lowton; [p.] Arthur Smallman and Edna Smallman; [m.] Ken Craven, 19 March 1983; [ed.] Golborne Comprehensive School, Bradford University (78-82); [occ.] Previously Accountant - now recovering from Long-term illness; [hon.] B.A. Hons. Degree European Studies (German/Economics); [oth. writ.] Nothing published just write for personal pleasure.; [pers.] To me, poetry is a living experience where anything is possible!; [a.] Crewe, Cheshire, UK

CRAWSHAW, MOLLIE
[b.] 7 May 1935, Sheffield; [p.] Harry King and Maria King; [m.] Kenneth Crawshaw, 8 November 1958; [ch.] Kathryn N. Marie, Diane Rebecca; [ed.] Walkley County School, Chaucer Adult Education Centre Sheffield College; [occ.] Retired; [memb.] British Crown Green Bowling Ass. Longley Ladies Bowls Teams Trustee Crown Hill Ass.; [hon.] South Yorkshire Open Credits for English Language and Literature, making sense of Media and Women's History; [pers.] I write for pleasure and wish to share this pleasure with others.; [a.] Sheffield, Yorkshire, UK

CRELLIN, ELIZABETH MYRA
[pen.] E.M.C.; [b.] 30 October 1930, Workington; [p.] John and Maude Taylor; [m.] Clifford Rowland Crellin, 28 March 1953; [ch.] Rowland, Stephen, Christopher Andrea; [ed.] Cockermouth Grammar School - Cumbria; [occ.] Retired - Farmers wife; [oth. writ.] Numerous poems, prayers, verses and meditations to family and friends. Aiming to comfort and bring joy and laughter; [pers.] In my poems I aim to reflect God's precious Gifts and have been inspired by my love of the country side.; [a.] Newport, Gwent, UK

CRISP, ANITA RUTH
[pen.] Brucille Atkin; [b.] 24 February 1943, Welshpool, Powys, Wales; [p.] John Langford Watkin, Eleanor May Lee Watking; [m.] Malcolm John Crisp, 1 November 1969; [ch.] Gary, Helen, Ann; [ed.] Gungrog Rd Infantschool, Welshpool, Powys, Welshpool National School Berriew Rd, Welshpool Girl's Grammar School Powys, C.L.T.C. Scraptoft, Leicester; [occ.] Housewife; [oth. writ.] A personal anthology of approximately 90 poems and verse hopefully awaiting publication; [pers.] Inspired by the Poetical Works of Ella Wheeler-Wilcox, I enjoy writing about Nature and the 'Highs' and 'Lows' of everyday living.; [a.] Braunstone, Leicestershire, UK

CROFT, LESLEY
[b.] 19 February 1949, Nottingham; [p.] John Sheffield, Alice Sheffield; [m.] Richard Croft, 9 September 1989; [ch.] Stephen and Steina; [ed.] (Secondary Modern in Birmingham) Stockland Crew Bl-Lateral and Burcot Grange High School Sutton Coldfields; [occ.] Administrative Officer, Civil Service; [memb.] Local Art Club; [oth. writ.] I have many poems gathering dust, but this is my first submission; [pers.] As each page of my life is written - I am using more and more ink, and noticeably, less ink a lots are appearing!; [a.] Langtoft, Cambs, UK

CROFTS, JOHN
[b.] 23 February 1941, Bournemouth; [p.] Reginald Crofts, Gladys Crofts; [m.] Marika Crofts, 28 March 1992; [ch.] Sarah Jane, Clare Louise; [ed.] Secondary Modern School Building Technical College; [occ.] Care worker disturbed children; [memb.] Small Holders Association Ramblers Association Reiki Association; [hon.] Reiki One; [oth. writ.] Two published poems; [pers.] Changing the present into the future.; [a.] Combe, St Nicholas, Somerset, UK

CROOK, NETTY
[pen.] Netty; [b.] 9 May 1965, Exeter; [ed.] Launceston College Cornwall. My English Teacher for a time was the poet Charles Causley he was my main influence and introduced poetry to my education.; [occ.] Sales Assistant; [pers.] I just pick up a pen and write what's in my head, there is no planning and rarely changed my poem once written die never entered a competition before.; [a.] Taunton, Somerset, UK

CROOKE, PENELOPE HEATHER MARY
[pen.] Penelope Mary; [b.] 26 October 1947, Isleworth, Middx; [p.] Larry and Winne Sawyer; [m.] Raymond Crooke, 31 November 1988; [ed.] Secondary; [occ.] Managing Director; [pers.] All can be yours if you work at it!; [a.] Farnborough, Hampshire, UK

CROSBY, EDWARD LEE
[b.] 1 August 1970, Ipswich; [oth. writ.] Vision published February 1996. (Book of poems)

CROSS, ANNE
[b.] 31 July 1960, Banbury; [p.] Les and Barbara Bryan; [m.] Paul, 6 June 1981; [ch.] James and Emily; [occ.] Housewife; [pers.] I would like to dedicate my poem: "Becoming thirty something is a" to my best friend Kim.; [a.] Banbury, Oxon, UK

CROSSLAND, MR. COLIN LEE
[b.] 12 July 1962, Mansfield; [p.] Mr. C. A. and Mrs. J. Crossland; [m.] Mrs. Diane Crossland, 4 October 1989; [ch.] Baby due in August 1996; [ed.] Manor Comprehensive school formerly Manor Grammar; [occ.] Disabled but formerly employed as a sales Representative.; [oth. writ.] This is my first literary work to have been published, although I have been written several compositions which I have not attempted to get published.; [pers.] My poems are a reflection of how I see parts of life, and hope that they bring enjoyment to those that read them.; [a.] Mansfield, Notts, UK

CUFFLING, JOAN
[b.] 30 March 1939, Sheffield; [p.] Mr. and Mrs. A. Salter; [m.] Mr. Geoff G. Cuffling, 5 April 1980; [ch.] Five (all over 21); [ed.] Enrolled Nurse - 1972. ENB 941, Nursing Elderly People - 1988. ENB 934, Care and Management of Persons with AIDS/HIV Related Conditions - 1989. Registered General Nurse - 1992. UKCC PIN: 72G0347E. Courses/study days: Advanced Drug Assessment (1981), Parkinson's Disease (1985), BASE - Parkinson's Disease, the shape of things to come (1985), Elderly Mentally Infirm Patients Risk Choice (1986), BASE - Arranged/ spoke about Parkinson's Disease and Clinical Pathology (1986), Primary Nursing Implementation (1989), Development Course on Care Plans (1990), Pharmacy Placement, Two Weeks (1991), RGN Conversation Course (1991/92). In addition, I have completed a Management Course and attended regular in-service study days - Pain Control, Care of the Dying, Primary Nursing, Role of the Mentor, Drug Compliance, Blind and Deaf Patient Care, Incontinence, Diabetes, Alternative Medicine, Sensory Deprivation.; [occ.] Deputy Matron at Brook Home Nursing Home, Degbys; [memb.] 1972 to 1993: Sheffield Health Authority. 1982 to date - Primary Nurse (Grade 'E') frequently taking charge of a 28 bedded ward within the Stroke Rehabilitation Unit at Nether Edge Hospital. Responsible for teaching student nurses together with planning, implementing and evaluating patient care. 1981 - Acute Medical Care of the Elderly (Nether Edge Hospital). 1976 to 1980 - Acute Medical (Nether Edge Hospital). 1976 to 1977 - Young Disabled (Nether Edge Hospital). 1975 to 1976 - Rheumatology (Nether Edge Hospital). 1974 to 1975 - Stroke Rehabilitation (Nether Edge Hospital). 1972 to 1973 - Mental Handicap/Mental Subnormality, 0-16 years (Dronfield Hospital).; [oth. writ.] Yes - but none published to rate.; [pers.] I believe that sensitivity of the presence of life, is illustrated in my writing.; [a.] Sheffield, Yorks, UK

CURTIS, MR. BARRIE WALFORD
[pen.] Paper Mate; [b.] 10 July 1942, Wade Bridge, Cornwall; [p.] Fleeta; [m.] Susan Pamela Lowe, 2 August 1980; [ch.] Catherine, Victoria and Emma; [ed.] Durham University and Bristol University; [occ.] I am a sign language Tutor on British Sign Language and Examiner.; [memb.] I am member of He Bristol Deaf Association and the Cornwall Deaf Centre I am the Chair of the South West area council of British Deaf Association and President of the Cornwall Deaf Centre.; [hon.] I've the Oloman Ellis Award 1991 for my work to the Deaf people by the National Council of Social Workers with Deaf people of Great Britain.; [oth. writ.] I am writer of the Cornwall Deaf News. One of all for He Deaf and for the British news and writer of Deaf - Culture.; [pers.] I am a Strong believer in Deaf History and am Proud of the Deaf Community and their rights and also their very own language BSL - that all my poems I wrote are from the feelings in the Deaf Community in the past who have pasted on their culture to us today.; [a.] Camlome, Cornwall, UK

CUSACK, JOHN
[pen.] John - Joseph; [b.] 29 June 1925, Co. Clare, Ireland; [p.] Prish; [m.] Mary Francis, 15 May 1954; [ch.] 4 children; [ed.] Christian Bothers School, Limbricu, Preland; [occ.] Builder; [memb.] Master Builders, Radio Officer from 1942 to 1946 on Merchant Navy Ships; [hon.] Intermediate Cert.; [oth. writ.] Poem published by rhyme arrival, 1-2 Wainman Rd - Woodston, Peterborough PE2 7BU. "Pts Called", "The Earth", and small book called two small holes.; [a.] Plford, Essex, UK

D'ARCY, GAVIN
[b.] 25 August 1971, Dublin, Rep of Ireland; [p.] Michael and Mary D'Arcy; [m.] Elizabeth Lynch, Partner not married; [ed.] Sallynoggin Senior College, Country Dublin, Republic Of Ireland.; [occ.] Administrative Assistant.; [pers.] This poem was influenced by the struggle for peace by all of the people of Ireland.; [a.] Sallynoggin, Co Dublin, Rep of Ireland

DABROWIECKI, MAY
[b.] 14 March 1925, Otterton; [p.] Percy and Lilian Farrant; [m.] Michael (Deceased 22 December 1995), 29 March 1948; [ch.] Eight (1 Deceased); [ed.] Otterton Primary St. Peters Senior, Budleigh Salkerton; [occ.] Housewife; [oth. writ.] 1 poem published June 1995 (arrival press); [pers.] I turned to poetry in 1979 following the tragic death of my 18 years old son. Poetry gave me a sense of calm and I expressed my feelings in some of my writings which I never submitted for publications.; [a.] Budleigh Salkerton, Devon, UK

DALBY, YVONNE
[pen.] Yvonne Westbrook; [b.] Highgate; [p.] William Westbrook and May Westbrook; [m.] Peter Dalby, 20 February 1953; [ed.] Convent Lirsulines; [memb.] National Trust, Royal Society for the Protection of Birds, Enfield Preservation Society; [oth. writ.] Child and Pet Tales and poems, short stories; [pers.] Very interested in child and animal behaviour and all flora and fauna and comedy and theatre.; [a.] London, UK

DALE-PATTESON, RACHEL
[b.] 22 March 1969, Lincoln; [p.] Rosalind and Brian Dale-Patteson; [ed.] St Winefrides Convent School, Shrewsbury Mary Webb School, Pontesbury Radbrook College, Shrewsbury; [occ.] Reception Manager and Welcombe Hotel, Stratford on Avon; [hon.] Bitec Diploma in Hotel Management N.V.Q. Assessor Craft Trainer First Aider Welcome Host; [pers.] My poems are based on my fustrations, hopes, dreams and aspirations for the future. This poem is dedicated to my family without whose support and guidance I wouldn't be where I am today!; [a.] Stratford upon Avon, Warwickshire, UK

DALLIMORE, DEBRA
[b.] 20 August 1970, Penzance, Cornwall; [p.] William Pope and June Pope; [m.] Terry Dallimore, 9 July 1994; [ch.] William, Terri, Sean (Deceased); [ed.] Lescudjack Infants, Heamoor County Primary, Humphry Davy Comprehensive; [occ.] Housewife; [oth. writ.] Variety of unpublished poems; [pers.] My poems are written from my heart and personnel life experiences. I am also greatly influenced by the mystical of untouched Cornwall.; [a.] Penzance, Cornwall, UK

DALTON, ANNE
[b.] 13 June 1949, Lincoln; [p.] James Henry Livesey, Edith Livesey; [m.] David Dalton, 7 March 1970; [ch.] Joanne Marie, Rachel Anne and Gary David; [ed.] Christ's Hospital, Girls High School; [occ.] Housewife, Student; [memb.] World Books Club; [hon.] English Language and English Literature 'O' Levels Assertiveness Accreditation; [oth. writ.] Three poems published by Anchor Books. Latest poem published in poetry now Eastern 1996 Anthology; [pers.] I love to convey my thoughts and feelings in verse. I prefer writing humorous poems.; [a.] Lincoln, Lincolnshire, UK

DALY, EILEEN
[pen.] Eileen Eco-Irish/English; [b.] 26 August 1963, Birmingham, England; [p.] Sheila Daly, Paul, Patrick Daly; [ch.] Clair, Victoria 13 yrs, Joseph Francis 15 yrs; [ed.] Highgate Comprehensive School Sandwell College; [occ.] Part-time College Student Studying on a two year course in hairdressing; [hon.] English Study's, Counselling; [pers.] I continue to enjoy and learn through writing my own poems where I can freely explain self on its deepost level. I see poem writing as a 'stated' communication that gives valid insights into self expression and reflects the poets innermost thoughts and feeling; [a.] Warley, UK

DANCIGER, JASON L.
[b.] 2 March 1965, Surrey; [occ.] Wine buyer; [hon.] 1994 Sunday Telegraph Food Marketing Award, 1995 Routers Corps D'Elme Wire Award, 1994 Hotel and Caterer Acorn Award, nootery and Food Association Bronze Award; [oth. writ.] Various poems; [pers.] My philosophy comes from my favorite poem, "Laugh And The world Laughs With You" Weep And You Weep Alone."; [a.] Putney, London, UK

DANIELS, ANNE
[pen.] "Hannah Rose"; [b.] 29 July 1941, Holyborne, Hants; [p.] Laurence and Louisa Sibley; [m.] Thomas Daniels (Deceased, 1991), 23 March 1968; [ch.] Elizabeth, Sarah, Emma; [ed.] Northern Grammar School, Portsmouth 1952-59 Royal Portsmouth and Queen Alexandra Hospitals School of Nursing, 1960-63; [occ.] Early Retired (Ill Health) Ex-SRN, Ex-Secretary in NHS Worthing.; [oth. writ.] Short stories in progress and poems (Not Published) "Hannah Rose" is for the future"; [pers.] One is never too old to learn. Also and old school motto "be strong and very courageous" - in all adversity.; [a.] Worthing, West Sussex, UK

DANIELS, EDITH
[b.] 21 February 1939, Ashton-under-Lyne, Lancashire; [m.] Brian Daniels, 21 February 1959; [ch.] Christopher Mark and David Paul; [ed.] Ashton Grammar; [occ.] Artist and flower arranger (ex-Teacher of Pitman's Shorthand) Commerce, and ex-School Secretary); [memb.] I formed and run a local Art Group (N.A.G.) and am a member of a local flower-arranging group. Love the classic paintings of Rembrandt, da Vinci, etc.; [hon.] Hold painting exhibitions at local libraries and galleries. Take private commission for any type of picture - landscape, private dwellings, churches, portraits etc., although began with life drawing which I enjoy. My poetry started only recently since 1994, following part-disablement.; [oth. writ.] "The Rat Race", "My Life", Stop The World - I want To Get Off!"; [pers.] My varied interests coupled with many of life's experiences and travel, are reflected in my poetry. I hope one day to write a biographical novel. I particularly like the poems by Robert Browning.; [a.] Mottram, Cheshire, UK

DANIELS, MRS. THELMA
[pen.] Thelma Daniels; [b.] 24 November 1934, Guyana, South America; [p.] Deceased; [m.] (Deceased) 17 December 1966; [ch.] 10; [ed.] Government School I went up to form 4; [occ.] Pensioner; [hon.] My poems published with Triumph House; [oth. writ.] I am a Christian I just write that comes to me naturally. I have been influenced by God, this may not sound true but I want the whole world to know; [pers.] I think about the life I used to live before and the life I am living now, about my contemment my humbleness life is kinder to me because of my faith, I am stronger I think only about today; [a.] London, Lewisham, UK

DANSIE, MRS. J. M.
[pen.] Jean Dansie; [b.] 13 August 1945, Whitechapel, London; [p.] Arthur Rowland, Brenda Rowland; [m.] Ronald Henry Dansie, 14 September 1990; [ch.] Michelle Jeanette (first marriage) Kim Tye (stepson) Tony Dansie; [ed.] Red Coat C of E Secondary Modern Stepney London E1; [occ.] Retired, [memb.] Harmans Cross Women's Institute; [pers.] I still draw on the influence of my late beloved mother Brenda Rowland and her wonderful one liner pearls of wisdom; [a.] Wareham, Dorset, UK

DARLINGTON, MISS MARY
[b.] 8 June 1920, Halmerend, Stoke-on-Trent; [p.] George Riley and Lucretia Riley; [m.] Frank Darlington, 1 October 1938; [ch.] Frank, George, Ann, Allan, Mary; [ed.] Halmerend Grammar School; [occ.] Pensioner; [memb.] Derby and Joan Club, Open Door Club, Halmerend Pensioner Club, Halmerend Chapel; [hon.] Collect teapots, taken to teapots, to WI Club, chapels, churches, City General Therapy Class Hospital to give talks on them, also given poetry readings (some my own); [oth. writ.] Poems Alpha and Omega plus others. Frank George and Ann (first to be published); [pers.] I strive to be pleasant and helpful and above all I am a great lover of poetry. Worked at University of Keele for 13 years.; [a.] Stoke-on-Trent, Staffordshire, UK

DAVIDSON, JOYCE
[b.] 21 May 1942, Aberdeen, Scotland; [p.] James and Mabel Stuart; [ch.] 1 boy and 2 girls, 2 grandchildren; [ed.] Secondary education attended classes and gained 5 "O" levels; [occ.] Cook at a local night club; [oth. writ.] A short story published in a magazine many years ago. One poem published earlier in 1996; [pers.] I see myself as an incurable romantic and tend to show this in my writing. I write the way I feel so therefore most of my work reflects my mood.; [a.] Turriff, Aberdeenshire, UK

DAVIES, MRS. ADRIENNE
[b.] 27 January 1934, Pontardulais; [p.] Mrs. Ruby and Mr. Harry Coombes; [m.] Mr. Gareth Davies, 18 March 1954; [ch.] Robert Ian, Anthony Wayne, Jonathan Andrew; [ed.] Pontardulais Comprehensive School; [occ.] Retired Medical Receptionist; [memb.] Llanellie Arts Society, Gorseinon Bowling Club; [oth. writ.] Several poems published in "Collected Poems for 1982", by A.H. Stockwell Ltd, and magazines; [pers.] I try to impress upon people the beautiful things on this earth that should be appreciated, and the delight one gets from nature, I am greatly influenced by these things and the description in my poems comes straight from the heart.; [a.] Llanelli, Dyfed, UK

DAVIES, BRUCE
[pen.] 'BD'; [b.] 2 October 1936, Lambeth; [p.] Albert and Alice D.; [m.] Shirley Anne, 1960 and 1993; [ch.] Dawn Sara and Keith Michael; [ed.] Colfes Grammar 1948-1953; [occ.] Retired, Police Officer; [pers.] Words pile on words from morn till night.; [a.] Ilfracombe, Devon, UK

DAVIES, DAVID CARL
[pen.] David Davies; [b.] 2 March 1963, Middlesborough; [p.] Arthur Davies, Margaret Jeffels; [ed.] Vyne School Basingstoke University East Anglia; [occ.] Security officer soon to change to police officer; [memb.] Lifeguard R.L.S.S. English Civil War Society Kung Fu; [hon.] English History; [pers.] This world is full of evil and deception, but in everyone there is a flicker of hope for a better world. My writings try to fan flicker into, a flame.; [a.] Basingstoke, Hampshire, UK

DAVIES, DAWN JEAN
[b.] 25 September 1962, Cardiff; [p.] Hazel and John Davies; [m.] Martin James Preece (Fiance); [ch.] Eva, Martin, Davies; [ed.] High School Education (Whitcaurch High School, in Cardiff); [occ.] Training Manager For Tesco Stores Ltd.; [memb.] Worcester Dragon Boat Association; [hon.] "Just Plain Jane"; [pers.] I write about how I feel-when I cannot say how I feel. People should be able to say what they are thinking, and think about what they are saying! Life would be so much easier!!; [a.] Ledbury, Herefordshire, UK

DAVIES, ROBIN
[b.] Ceylon; [ed.] L.S.E. (London School of Economics); [occ.] Prof. of Economics Sarajevo; [oth. writ.] Academic Journals Newspaper Articles; [a.] Bellevue, Geneva, Switzerland

DAVIES, SALLY-ANN
[b.] 28 November 1963, Battersea, London; [p.] Edward Charles Davies, Ann Ellen Rossetta Davies; [ed.] Battersea County Comprehensive Sch. Battersea, London; [occ.] Disabled; [hon.] This is my first honour and award as previous and current scripts are yet to be submitted, my awards have been purely on a personal level; [oth. writ.] Working on Belief is Everything (book), working on Betrayed (book), working on Testimony of Love (poetry unpublished); [pers.] I must think my friend and constant companion Sharon Maria Kelly, my mum, sister Sharon Patricia Butler and husband Robert for their love, support and faith in my ability. To feel it is to know it, to know it is to feel it. Belief is everything.; [a.] Hove, E. Sussex, UK

DAVIES, SARAH
[b.] 21 July 1942, London; [ch.] Jonathan and Laura; [ed.] Architect; [occ.] Writer, Teacher, Group Facilitator, Natural Healing Therapist; [oth. writ.] Currently writing a book concerning the human, emotional side of Jesus and the impact of His life and teaching of his followers.; [pers.] My aim is to guide people towards reconnection with the spiritual aspect of themselves.; [a.] Northalleron, N. Yorks, UK

DAVIES, STEPHANIE FAITH
[b.] 15 July 1958, Nottingham; [ch.] Daniel 6 yrs., Ben 4 yrs.; [ed.] Bradfield Comprehensive, Stocksbridge College Richmond College, Sheffield Polytechnic, Wakefield College; [occ.] Housewife; [memb.] Bradfield Choral Soc for 2 yrs., Church Brigade for 2 yrs., Girl Guides for 5 yrs., Church Choir at Oughtibridge Sheffield for 14 yrs.; [pers.] I try to understand the sadness and reflect modern suffering in my writing, this enables me to give a positive outlook on an otherwise inward spiral of confusing situations.; [a.] Topmorden, Lancs, UK

DAVIES, TAMMY LOUISE
[b.] 19 August 1980, Rhondda; [p.] Graham and Gina Davies; [ed.] Porth County Comprehensive School; [occ.] Staying at School to do my A. Levels, O levels; [hon.] Gained compact certificate. Distinction award. In keyboard skills, also Religious Education Project has been submitted to W.J.E.C. due to work being of such a high standard.; [pers.] Writing poetry gives me a great sense of enjoyment and I hope the people who read them will also gain enjoyment from them.; [a.] Trealaw, Mid-Glam, UK

DAVIS, ANNE
[pen.] Anna Huntley; [b.] 10 April 1943, London; [m.] George (A wonderful husband) August 1960; [ch.] 3 daughters, 1 son, All married and now in New Zealand and Australia; [occ.] Foster parents.; [oth. writ.] This is the first poem I have ever entered anywhere. Although I have written many. I am thrilled it was chosen.; [pers.] We lived in New Zealand for 20 yrs. Hence "The Seasons" was inspired by my return to an English winter. I really enjoy writing, and try to express my thoughts on many subjects.; [a.] Guildford, Surrey, UK

DAVIS, LINDA
[b.] 17 July 1959, Plymouth; [p.] Joyce and David Collier; [m.] Kevin Davis, 6 June 1991; [ed.] Devonport High School for Girls, Plymouth Polytechnic; [occ.] Building Society Manager; [memb.] Member Institute of Personnel and Development (MIPD); [pers.] I enjoy trying to express my feelings in writing and sharing my thoughts.; [a.] Plymouth, Devon, UK

DAVIS, MELISSA S.
[b.] August 30, 1979, Harrow; [p.] Jonathan Davis, Roberta Davis; [ed.] Bushey Meads School, A-level student; [hon.] GCSE's (10) and L.A.M.D.A. certificates; [pers.] I can only express myself using poetry.; [a.] Watford, Hertsfordshire

DAVIS, SALLY
[b.] 19 November 1954, Cheltenham; [p.] Mr. and Mrs. H. I. Gintally; [ed.] Charlton Kings Secondary Modern; [occ.] Sales Assistant; [pers.] Writing is like music you feel with your heart.; [a.] Nr. Cheltenham, Glos, UK

DAVIS, WINIFRED M.
[pen.] Isabella Fagentees; [b.] 29 September 1921, Bishops Stortford, Herts; [p.] Thomas and Lilian Francis; [m.] Philp Seymour Davis (Retired Architect); [ch.] Son - Civil Engineer daughter- Nurse; [ed.] Essex and London 1920's - '36, Nursing Training "The London Hospital" and Training on Radar and Instrument Army; [occ.] Housewife and full-time hobbies, I.E. writing, reading, music; [memb.] Hon/Member A. E. Housman Guild (Ludlow-Shropshire); [hon.] Placed in the Shopshire Archives for writers, M.E.N.S.A. Certificate of Merit, 3rd place in International Writers of 1972, Poetry International; [oth. writ.] Poems published in ten anthologies over the past 25 years plus publication in county magazines and others. R.A.F. museum holds my "First of the Few".; [pers.] The inspirations for writing poetry came as a result of my service as a nurse in the London Blitz, and also from active service with the army 1942-1945. I felt a need to record my impressions for posterity - and would escape into the world of beautiful words.; [a.] Selsey-on-Sea, West Sussex, UK

DAWSON, KELLY-EMMA
[b.] 29/10/83, Many Gates, Wakefield; [p.] Bev Dawson; [ed.] Full Time Secondary School (age12); [pers.] I enjoy putting pen to paper and writing down my feelings. I hope that one day I will be a successful songwriter.; [a.] Castleford, W. Yorkshire

DAWSON, PHILLIP N.
[pen.] Phil D, Phil Dee; [b.] 25 August 1959, Stoke-on-Trent; [p.] John and Sylvia; [m.] Jacqueline, 25 August 1989; [ch.] Philip, Bernadette, Christina, Ann Louise, Wayne, Darren; [ed.] Berry Hill High; [occ.] Ceramic Placer; [oth. writ.] Several poems and articles published in various magazines and numerous poems published in various anthologies such as Louise published in 'Poets Favorites' Great Britain published in 'Voice Of The People' and A Penny Saved published in 'A Stitch Rhyme'; [a.] Stoke-on-Trent, Staffs, UK

DAWSON, WILLIAM MICHAEL
[pen.] Mike Dawson; [b.] 7 February 1940, Bradford, W Yorks; [p.] Elsie Elizabeth, William Thomas; [m.] Pauline Dawson, 16 August 1969; [ed.] Shaftesbury Society Boarding school, Northants, Southend Municipal College, Brentwood College of Teached training, Essex.; [occ.] Retired teacher; [memb.] Belfairs golf club, Leigh-on-Sea, Essex; [oth. writ.] Recently locally published book of numerous odes.; [pers.] In 1990 I was diagnosed as having renal failure but wanted to show one would overcome it via humour and wanted to use my love of language.; [a.] Leigh-on-Sea, Essex, UK

DAY, DAPHNE
[pen.] Daphne Day; [ed.] Painting and drawing Chelsea School of Art, Stone Carving and Modelling St. Martin's School of Art, Bronze Casting Camberwell School of Art; [occ.] Artist and writer; [memb.] Exhibitor and Archivist, Society of Graphic Fine Art (S.G.F.A.) 1986; [hon.] Professor of Fine Art - Academia Gentium Pro Pace - Rome 1979 (A.G.P.P.); [oth. writ.] Children's Author; [pers.] Extend charity, compassion and love to all creatures and our fellow travellers on the road to immortality.; [a.] Bedford Park, Chiswick, London, UK

DAY, MRS. PAULINE
[b.] 23 March 1945, Corbridge Land, Northumberland; [p.] Mr. and Mrs. A. R. Charlton; [m.] Divorced; [ch.] Marianne; [ed.] Shaftoe Trust School Haydon Bridge, Hexham Northumberland; [occ.] Kitchen Assistant; [memb.] Butlins Loyalty Club; [oth. writ.] This poem was my first one I have sent in to a competition; [a.] Newcastle, Tyne and Wear, UK

DE GRACIA, MARBILL
[b.] 12 June 1979, Guildford, Surrey; [p.] Mark De Gracia, Nonelita R. De Gracia; [ed.] Immaculate Heart of Mary College (Philippines), Quintin Kynshton School (London), City of Westminster College (London); [occ.] Student (A-Level); [hon.] 2nd Honours (IHMC 93-94); [oth. writ.] Several poems and short stories published in IHMC school paper. Poem published in Q.K. Yearbook; [pers.] Having studied in a catholic school (IHMC), most of my work reflect what I have been taught there. However, I also relish romantic poetry.; [a.] Saint John's Wood, Westminster, UK

DEAN, AMANDA
[pen.] Amanda Gray; [b.] 9 December 1964, Luton, Bedfordshire; [p.] Rowland Dean and Brenda Dean; [m.] Robert Janesies; [ch.] Kristina and Nichola; [ed.] Stockwood High (Luton) Barnfield College; [memb.] Taido Karate Club; [oth. writ.] Several poems published with another book company; [pers.] I would like to thank my boy friend Rob for having confidence in me where others failed. May my children Kristina and Nicholas enjoy reading my poetry when they get older. A message to all poets, it doesn't have to be shakespeare to be good. And I love you dad.; [a.] Barton-le-Clay, Bedford, UK

DEL RE, BELINDA TAGART
[b.] 6 June, London; [m.] A. Del Re; [occ.] Native Speaker Linguistic High School BG Italy; [memb.] Servas; [oth. writ.] Poems (Unpublished); [pers.] Belinda is simply me striving to relate to the 'Essential' in you. I am just a pilgrim in this fleeting terrestrial existence. (Interest Yoga)

DEL RIO, MICHAEL
[b.] 12 February 1955, Mexico, D.F.; [p.] Dr. Armando del Rio, Victoria del Rio; [m.] Darla Jean del Rio, 5 December 1987; [ch.] Michael Bernard del Rio; [ed.] Loyolla High School, NUU College, Cornell Univ. Med School; [occ.] Pediatric Cardiac Surgeon - Loma Linda Medical Center; [memb.] AMA, STS; [pers.] Inspired by the works of Dylan Thomas and Lord Byron; [a.] New York, New York

DELL, JEANE
[b.] 9 April 1912, Edinburgh; [p.] Jane and C. Cordon; [m.] Widow, 21 December 1937; [ch.] Jean, Ian; [occ.] Retired from Nursing; [a.] Wickford, Essex, UK

DEMEZA, CLIFFORD H.
[b.] 11 January 1939, Hastings; [p.] Thomas and Olive; [m.] Elizabeth, 1984; [ed.] Bal Edmund Independent School, St. Leonards Secondary Modern School, Medwar and Maidstone College of Technology Open University (Technology); [occ.] Traffic Officer with the Stagecoach Bus Company; [memb.] The Stables Theatre Trust, The National Trust, The Caravan Club, United Reformed Church; [hon.] Royal Society of Arts Diploma in Transport (6 subjects); [oth. writ.] Christian and humorous poems and short works; [pers.] I write for my own amusement, often with a humorous or evangelical christian theme. If others appreciate my work, may they be blessed by it.; [a.] St Leonards-on-Sea, East Sussex, UK

DENHAM, PHILIP ANTHONY
[b.] 21 June 1953, Scarborough; [p.] Raymond Denham, Rita Denham; [ch.] Simon, Nicola, Thomas; [ed.] Westwood C.M. School Scarborough Technical College; [occ.] P.C.V. driver (Passenger Carrying Vehicle); [memb.] Chairman of Harbour Lights Juvenile Jazz Band, Whitby.; [pers.] I am a very privileged to travel all over the country in my employment. I appreciate beautiful things of nature and like to express these feelings in words.; [a.] Whitby, N. Yorks, UK

DENNETT, CAROLINE
[pen.] Liza Warner; [b.] 7 April 1924, Leith; [p.] Henry Dennett, Marion Dennett; [ed.] Beellevues Tec/Commer School; [occ.] Retired Nursing Chiropody; [pers.] I have always loved nature, paintings, books, poetry. This year is my first attempt at writing; [a.] Edinburgh, Lothian, UK

DENNETT, MRS. MAUREEN CARLISLE
[pen.] Mrs. Maureen Carlisle Dennett; [b.] 28 November 1949, Manchester; [p.] Mary and Lawrence Carlisle; [m.] Alan Dennett, 13 November 1971; [ch.] Two both girls; [ed.] Secondary school for girls, Failsworth; [occ.] Housewife (Disabled); [oth. writ.] 'Children's Stories, never had any published; [pers.] I come from a family of eleven children, and we were very poor. I spent a lot of time telling stories to younger members of the family. I now suffer with arthritis. I love writing.; [a.] Manchester, Lancs, UK

DENYER, LISA MARIE
[b.] 25 March 1981, Portsmouth; [p.] Marilyn and Cliff Denyer; [ed.] Crookhorn School Waterlooville, Hants; [hon.] In 1994 I achieved the ABA boxing proficiency award and was the first girl in Britain to have past it.; [pers.] I have many of talents but my greatest love is writing poets.; [a.] Waterlooville, Hampshire, UK

DEVER, ANDIE
[pen.] Andie C. Dever; [b.] 14 April 1976, Birkenhead; [p.] Philomena Dever and Andrew Dever; [ed.] Plessington R.C. High, Wirral Met. College and North East Wales Institute; [occ.] Student Teacher; [pers.] My family, friends and my reflective nature are the source of my inspiration to write.; [a.] Bebington, Wirral, UK

DEVLIN, MISS HELEN
[b.] 17 February 1970, Chatham; [p.] Angela Devlin; [ed.] Rainham School for girls; [occ.] Photographer; [pers.] I feel poetry provides a window on the inner soul and I hope this poem touches the reader in the way that poetry I've read has touched me. Poetry to me is very special and well always hold a part of my being.; [a.] Rainham, Kent, UK

DEVONSHIRE, AZRA TEZIEN
[b.] 16 March 1964, Calcutta, India; [p.] Mohammad Hanif, Shanim Ara Hanif; [m.] Gillies John David Devonshire; [ch.] Kurt Iram Devonshire; [ed.] B.A. (Hons) English Literature, Hons: Diploma in Journalism; [occ.] Journalist/Writer; [hon.] Won the award "Most Commended Programme, 1994", WMTV, for producing, directing and script writing; [oth. writ.] Short stories and poems, some published in Indian newspapers; [pers.] "Don't let life rule you, rule it, and be always in control" This is my personal philosophy.; [a.] Maidenhead, Berkshire, UK

DHILLON, JAGROOP KAUR
[b.] 30 November 1977, Glasgow; [p.] Gurdarshaw Kaur; [ed.] 5 Highers, still in full-time Education at the University of Strathclyde; [occ.] Student; [oth. writ.] Written several poems, never been published before; [pers.] To me, life is all about painful ends and hopeful beginnings. This is what I try to express through my poetry. I have been influenced by several Asian poets who reflect the pain in life.; [a.] Glasgow, Scotland

DI-MAIO, HALA
[b.] 7 August 1966, Beirut, Lebanon; [p.] Nicolas Nahed, Victoria Kabani; [m.] Romolo Di-Maio, 5 June 1987; [ch.] One daughter, born 6 March 1994; [ed.] BA in Fashion Merchandising graduated in 1986; [occ.] Art Correspondent for a Radio Station (Voice of Lebanon); [pers.] I paint as well as write. I am currently writing a small book of poems with my drawings reflecting on my life as a woman and mother today, trying to combine my Lebanese upbringing with the English lifestyle.; [a.] London, UK

DIAMOND, SHELLEY
[pen.] Shelley Diamond; [b.] 19 January 1947, London; [ed.] Walpole Grammar; [occ.] Head of Administration Multi Media Company, London; [memb.] Social Clubs, London; [oth. writ.] Seasonal and greetings odes. Preparing books of odes. Currently book of reflective observations.; [pers.] There is humour in sadness and sadness in humour. Without either, there is nothing at all.; [a.] London, UK

DICKSON, ANNA
[b.] 11 August 1973, Leicester; [p.] Keith Dickson and Jo Dickson; [ed.] Leicester Grammar, Loughborough, College of Art and Design, Sheffield College; [pers.] I would like to dedicate my poem to my father, for whom it is written. And to thank my mother for being there for me throughout.; [a.] Stoneygate, Leicestershire, UK

DIGLIS, CHERYL KAREN
[b.] 13 March 1964, London; [p.] Andreas Dinglis, Iris Dinglis; [m.] Anthony Joyce, 18 June 1994; [ch.] Anthony Andreas Joyce III; [oth. writ.] Various poems, short stories, children's stories.; [pers.] I obtain inspiration from my surroundings. I try to reflect honesty and sincerity.; [a.] London, UK

DILKES, MRS. E. V.
[pen.] Eve de Silk; [b.] 4 May 1922, Scotland; [p.] Widow; [occ.] Retired; [hon.] 11 Poems, 2 short stories writer world. Queensland, Australia: 13 Award Certificates of Merit, all pertaining to above. (Highly commended); [oth. writ.] 1. Book of Poems "Rhythms of Life", 1. Book of Poems "Rhythms of Love"; [pers.] I strive to indicate the continuity of Life and the need for faith in one's self and our wonderful world.; [a.] Glenfield, Auckland 10, New Zealand

DINCALP, SIMON
[b.] November 11, 1968, Gloucester; [p.] Andrew and Jennifer Light; [occ.] Student; [pers.] "To fly the free trail", is a state of subconscious beauty, and experience of sublime freedom.; [a.] Grimsby, Sty-Hombershire

DINHAM, CAROL EVANGELINE
[pen.] Carol Dinham; [b.] 8 November 1950, Trinidad; [m.] Divorced; [ch.] 3 daughters, Hannah, Sara and Emma; [occ.] Previously Manager - Human Resources, currently Manager Offshore Business Development; [memb.] Institute of Employment Consultants, Trustee on the Board of Trustee Duke of Edinburgh's Award - Devon, Board Member - Engineering Training Services, Member Crediton Bonaface Rotary Club; [oth. writ.] None published; [pers.] Knowledge is the reward of life's experiences. Wisely used, it is the most powerful tool available to man. It is through experience that books are created. It is through books that knowledge is passed on.; [a.] Crediton, Devon, UK

DINSLEY, JENNY
[b.] 15 October 1914, Chester-le-Street, Co Durham; [p.] William George Bell and Mary Bell; [m.] (Deceased) Thomas Emerson Dinsley, 11 October 1941; [ch.] William (Son); [ed.] Chester-le-Street, Secondary; [occ.] Retired; [memb.] Flower Arranging Society, Church Sisterhood, Weekly Group Meeting (Bible Study); [hon.] Certificate of Merit for Short Story Writing; [oth. writ.] Articles and poem in "Peoples Friend (Magazine). Articles and letters in local papers and in church magazines.; [pers.] I aim for a high moral standard in my writing. And a love of my creator's goodness potrayed whenever possible; [a.] Chester-le-Street, Durham, UK

DIVERS, FLORA
[b.] Glasgow; [p.] John and Mary Meikle; [m.] James Divers, 4 July 1964; [ed.] Wellshot Road Primary School, Glasgow, Scotland East Bank Academy Glasgow, Scotland; [occ.] Free Lance Poet; [memb.] Spare time dedicated to my writing!!; [hon.] Blessed with a "Beautiful Disposition"!!; [oth. writ.] Several poems written for "Arrival Press" also for "Anchor Books" and "V.A Press" and "Poetry Now" and "Triumph House"; [pers.] When "The Miseries" have you feeling low. A "sense of humour" is like an in can descent candle glow!!; [a.] Denny, Stirlingshire, UK

DIX, CHERYL
[b.] 12 June 1973, Gloucester; [p.] Roy Dix and Sandra Dix; [ch.] Anthony Rhys; [ed.] The Castle Comprehensive; [occ.] Sales Co-ordinator New Venture; [pers.] Dedicated to Adam James Price who inspired my feelings; [a.] Risca, Gwent, UK

DIXON, SARAH
[pen.] Sadie; [b.] 19 May 1926, Barlow, Co. Durham; [p.] Clara and John William Bilcliff; [m.] Raymond Dixon, 5 October 1946; [ch.] Three; [ed.] Distington Junior School (came here as an evacuee) 1939; [occ.] Pensioner 70 yrs.; [memb.] B.A.S.C.A.; [hon.] I wrote words and music for the Carlisle Great Fair song contest (can't read music). And won by 52 votes "The Jubilee Pageant Fair Song", it was put on a record and sold at the Fair 1977.; [oth. writ.] Many songs (words and music) and various poems; [pers.] Got 1,000 records made of my songs "The Wedding of the Year" (for H.R.H. Prince Charles, Princess Di) with "The Wishing Well" on B. side; [a.] Workington, Cumbria, UK

DIXON, SUSAN
[b.] 30 May 1940, Southampton; [m.] Gordon, 30 March 1959; [ch.] Two Phillip and Craig; [ed.] Secondary Modern; [occ.] Fashions and part-time or previous model; [pers.] I am person who gains satisfaction from trying to achieve what appears to be the impossible.; [a.] Chandlers Ford, Hants, UK

DOBBINS, MARIAN D.
[b.] 30 July 1930, Childer Thorton, Wirral, Cheshire; [p.] John and Marian Esther Hyde,; [m.] Stanley Joseph Dobbins, 24 April 1957; [ch.] (Twins) Philip and Michael, Angela; [ed.] 'Our Lady, Star of the Sea' R.C. Primary School (Ellesmere Port). Then Rock Ferry Convent High School, Rock Ferry, Wirral, Cheshire.; [occ.] Retired Dinner Lady; [memb.] Old Time and Modern Sequence Dancing Club; [hon.] Oxford School Certificate; [oth. writ.] Twenty nine other poems both sad and amusing. One on Irish Ceilidh dancing published in an Irish magazines; [pers.] I like to write about the people I have loved or met who have inspired my admiration. I still love the poems I learnt at school!!; [a.] Sale, Cheshire, UK

DOCHERTY, MICHELLE
[b.] 29 September 1970, Scotland; [p.] Mary and James; [ed.] St. Gerards Secondary School, Govan Glasgow; [pers.] There are those who will encourage and those who will discourage, never rest until you have caught your star. It's the little things and the little people that make life a pleasure to live.; [a.] Glasgow, Scotland

DOIG, DAVID SIMON
[b.] 15 July 1972, Dundee; [ed.] Blairgowrie High School, Perth College; [occ.] Student; [oth. writ.] First work published; [pers.] I am influenced by the epic poems of Homer and Virgil and their simple relationships between man, nature and the supernatural. Over-explanation leads to confusion.; [a.] Coupar Angus, Perthshire, UK

DOLBY, NICOLA
[pen.] Nicola Dolby; [b.] 30 September 1978, Rotherham; [p.] Margaret Dolby and Terry Dolby; [ed.] Oakwood Comprehensive School; [occ.] Trainee Nursery Nurse; [memb.] Amateur Athletic's Club; [hon.] Seven GCSE's; [oth. writ.] Personal unpublished poems; [pers.] I looked in my heart and found my words to my poems.; [a.] Rotherham, South Yorkshire, UK

DOMANIC, MARIA
[b.] 13 August 1951, Birkenhead; [p.] Johnsaphine and John Steen; [ed.] Comprehensive School, South Kent College, Ashford Kent; [hon.] English Literature and Maths; [oth. writ.] Thoughts, Bolt of Love, Broken Hearted, First and Last, Crying Time, Moving On, Foolish Heart, Leaving, If I Were, How to Win Fair Madian, Babes Blue Eyes, These are Just a Few there is to marry to mention.; [pers.] Live life always I have been told that I am a romantic writer, I have almost a hundred poems I would like to have all my poems published in a book it's title would be "from then heart."; [a.] Overchurch, Upton, UK

DOMMETT, PATRICIA
[b.] 17 March 1944, Lostock, Bolton; [p.] Evelyn and Joseph McNulty; [m.] Divorced; [ed.] Secondary Modern; [occ.] Machine Opp Factory Worker; [oth. writ.] I've wrote several poems but I've never thought them good enough to be published, I've had two in the evening paper; [pers.] I've wrote eighteen poems and kept them in a book, because I feel very proud of what I've done and it's something of a hobby; [a.] Bolton, Lancs, UK

DONALD, SUZANNE
[b.] 21 September 1966, Whitehaven; [p.] Margaret Yip, Lam Tai Yip; [m.] Garnet Donald, 26 June 1992; [ch.] Catherine; [ed.] Parkview Compre-

hensive School, Barrow-in-Furness; [occ.] Guest House Manageress; [pers.] I am inspired by everyday events and if I can imagine the love or tear or hate of the subject, then the words will easily follow.; [a.] Barrow-in-Furness, Cumbria, UK

DOOGAN, FRANCES ANN
[b.] 25 August 1953, Scotland; [p.] Margaret McGee, Joseph Doogan; [occ.] Masterchef/Nutritionist; [memb.] Am member of the union and two noble Celtic families the Doogans. McGee, Ireland. "Faith has no fear". "I would rather die than be dishonoured" motto's Celtic blood runs strongly through me with its gifts of music, art, love of nature and fiery speech. Am closely associated with Carmelites motto. "I am burning with love for the glory of God, the Lord of Moses"; [oth. writ.] "Mary, Queen of Peace" poetry collection (Minerva Press), Treasures of Truth" commentary and poetry by (Headstart History); [pers.] To achieve the impossible, and live life to the full; [a.] Pollokshields, Glasgow, UK

DOUGAN, KERRIANNE
[b.] 28 October 1976, Bedford; [p.] Katrina and Michael Dougan; [ed.] Sharnbrook Upper School; [occ.] Nanny; [hon.] BTEC GNVQ Intermediate Health and Social Care Passed with Distinction; [pers.] This poem is dedicated to my family and friends, who have all helped me strive for the things, I most want and have always been there for me.; [a.] Lavendon, Bucks, UK

DOUGELA, K. M.
[b.] 11 March 1910, Mt. Ash, S. Glam; [p.] William and Margaret Glynn-Jones; [m.] John Dougela; [ed.] St. Margarets Primary Aberdare - Secondary, Aberdare High School, 7 years. Later St. Vincent's WestMinster; [occ.] Retired; [memb.] Town Women's Guild, (Chairlady) Church Society (Secretary) Various Choirs, Song Solo in West Minister Cathedral, Lead Singer in St. David's, Cardiff and others; [hon.] Poetry readings, wrote poetry from 7 yrs and still do! Many published 1st, 2nd and 3rd prizer over the years, art: 3rd prize for oil-painting-and others; [oth. writ.] Articles published over years, but only 1 short story published as few sent in my gifts lay in poetry, singing, writing, history, art, (I disliked math and science.); [pers.] My father was brilliant at figures (accountant) a good 'vaconteur' my mother wrote articles and had many natural gifts. Wonderful cook! And hostess my father had an copera voice and a sister.; [a.] Cardiff, S. Glam, UK

DOUGLAS, GWEN
[b.] 5 October 1948, Hull; [p.] Kenneth Hayzen, Jean Hayzen; [m.] Edward Douglas, 15 July 1995; [ed.] Estcourt High School for girls, Hull College of Technology, Hull College of Humberside.; [occ.] Chemical Analyst at Smith and Nephew Medical, Hull; [memb.] Leven Walking Club; [pers.] I tend to highlight strengths and weaknesses in my writings. Also environmental issues remain close to my heart. The greatest influence on my poetry has come from the lake land poets.; [a.] Hull, E. Yorkshire, UK

DOWDING, SHARON
[pen.] Phagos; [b.] March 1970, Paulton; [p.] Ruth Edditts, Francis Dowding; [occ.] Horticulturist; [hon.] 29 awards for Floral Displays from the Bath in Bloom Committee; [pers.] Influenced by the writings of Philip Carr-Gomm and of dragons my work reflects my knowledge of lore at its many stages.; [a.] Bath, Avon, UK

DOWNES, ALEXANDRA
[b.] 27 July 1978, Bury St. Edmunds; [occ.] Student; [pers.] This poem is a personal statement about the conflict between myself and the rest of my generation. My influences are my surroundings.

DOWNIE, GILLIAN
[b.] 12 September 1978, Irvine; [p.] Allan and Elizabeth Downie; [ed.] Arorossan Academy, currently in first year at the University of Paisley; [occ.] Physics Student; [hon.] Certificate of distinction in English; [oth. writ.] Other poems entered in local school competitions and for local radio broadcast; [pers.] Personal experiences are the greatest influence on my poetry. The human mind is complex, a poem in itself.; [a.] Saltcoats, Ayrshire, UK

DOWNIE, PAUL
[b.] 15 January 1964; [p.] Gil Downie, Margaret Downie; [ed.] Killingworth High School Wallsend College; [occ.] Lab Technician, Procter and Gamble; [hon.] Several poems published in local papers; [pers.] I endeavour to reflect the plight of nature, and the possible consequences of our actions. I am influenced by wordsworth, Coleridge, Keats.; [a.] Killingworth, Northumbria, UK

DOWSE, WILLIAM
[pen.] Arthur Relworg; [b.] 17 September 1959, Brigg; [p.] Dennis and Joan Dowse; [m.] Andrea, 16 December 1994; [ch.] Matthew, Sarah, Christopher, Rebekah; [ed.] Brigg Grammar; [occ.] Printer; [memb.] Local Sports Club; [hon.] English, Math, Physics, French, Additional Math; [oth. writ.] Several Articles in local magazine, other poems not yet published; [pers.] To take the reader deep into the time and place of my writing.; [a.] Brigg, N. Lincs, UK

DOYLE, GARY JAMES
[b.] 4 March 1975, Gateshead; [p.] Hazel Doyle and James Doyle; [ed.] St. Robert of Newminster R.C. Monkwearmouth College; [occ.] Actor, Classic Car Dealer; [memb.] M.G. Owners Club, Washington Arts Centre, Hyloton Castle Boxing Club; [pers.] Poetry, or any form of art, is for me, the only fulfilling way to express every feeling and emotion that may torment otherwise.

DOYLE, GAVIN
[b.] 21 March 1972, Dublin; [p.] Fergus and Maureen Doyle (nee Thomas); [ed.] Belvedere College, S.J., Dublin (1984-1990), Trinity College Dublin (1990-1994); [occ.] Administrative Assistant, European Training Foundation, Turin; [hon.] B.A. (hon) in European Studies (French, German, History and Political Science); [oth. writ.] Published weekly column in magazine of the "Stagiaires" of the European Commission. Letters published in the "Irish Times."; [pers.] A good writer is able to alter the way you look at the past. A great writer can even change the way you look at the future. I, however, write merely that I may take a fresh look at the present.; [a.] Via Lanfranchi, Torino, Italy

DOYLE, MARGARET
[b.] 22 February 1945, Manchester; [p.] Ernie and Bertha Roberts; [m.] 2 March 1974; [ch.] Marion, John, Robert; [pers.] I am often inspired to write when emotional. 'Precious memory' is a such inspiration for my late father Ernie Roberts.; [a.] Manchester, Lancs, UK

DRAKE, FRANCIS
[b.] 19 August 1940, Scotland; [p.] James and Ivy Drake; [m.] Tricia Drake; [ed.] Dartmouth Grammar, Exeter College; [occ.] Consultant in Strategic Human Resource Management and Development; [memb.] Fellow Institute of Personnel and Development, Member Institute of Management; [hon.] Hon Dsc, Hon PhD.; [oth. writ.] Various poems. Cheela The Whale Who Flew, First Holiday Neanderthal Genes, Professional Articles on People Development and stress; [pers.] An enthusiastic belief in the potential within all human beings waiting to be unlocked a striving for harmony in a wonderful universe of infinite possibilities.; [a.] Chichester, West Sussex, UK

DRAPER, LYDIA MILTON
[pen.] Lydia Milton; [b.] 5 April 1920, London; [p.] Bertha and Albert Milton; [m.] Widowed, 22 August 1940; [ch.] One son; [ed.] Church School; [occ.] Pensioner, Hardening, Craftwork; [pers.] "A Distance Away" is a "Wish".; [a.] Harrow, Middx, UK

DREDGE, CELIA
[b.] 19 September 1939, North Yorkshire; [p.] Arthur Fox - Mary Fox; [m.] Vic Dredge, 14 October 1959; [ch.] Timothy Catherine Steven; [ed.] Northallerton Secondary; [occ.] Sales Assistant; [pers.] In my writing I find calmness, I hope readers find calmness too.; [a.] Reading, Berks, UK

DREW, DIANA
[pen.] Di; [b.] 11 August 1959, West Yorkshire; [p.] Jean and Joseph Coupland; [m.] Kevin Mark Drew, 14 May 1982; [ch.] Katie 9 yrs, Jane and Simon 4yr Joseph; [ed.] Primary and secondary schools; [occ.] Housewife; [oth. writ.] I have 100, children's and adult poems, sat in a folder, crying to get out!! I write for fun, and to keep my mind active! Short children's - stories also.; [pers.] I have always loved to write, as I find it great therapy, as I suffer with Agoraphobia. Your letter has been of great encouragement to me. Made me feel worthwhile. Thank you.; [a.] Didcot, Oxon, UK

DREWERY, DENISE
[b.] 23 June 1982, Ballymena; [p.] Denis Drewery, Joan Drewery (nee Crawford); [ed.] Ardnaviegh High School; [occ.] At school; [a.] Antrim, Antrim, UK

DUFF, OLGA
[pen.] Olga Duffy; [b.] 22 January 1914, Iselworth; [p.] Both dead; [m.] Fredrick Duff, 16 September 1935; [ch.] Pru and Rosemary; [ed.] Secondary school where a wonderful English teacher taught me the love of poetry; [occ.] Housewife; [memb.] Member of Richmond Badminton Club, committee member of Iselworth Community Association and Badminton member; [oth. writ.] Poems in magazines and Poems of the North West by Anchor books; [pers.] Nothing exciting but a love of gardening and poetry has led to a happy life.; [a.] Congleton, Cheshire, UK

DUNBAR, NICHOLAS
[pen.] Nick Dunbar; [b.] 15 August 1976, Ballymoney; [p.] John and Rosemary Dunbar; [ed.] Dunluce Secondary School - Bushmills, Ballymena Tech, Northern Ireland Hotel and Catering College Portrush; [occ.] Student; [memb.] Member of a Local band which is hoping to release a tape in the near future; [oth. writ.] My desk in the

poetry now Compilation. Lyrics of songs for the group I'm in.; [pers.] I write poems about anything that influence me. I find it easier to write about personal feelings and final poetry and song writing to be good methods of expressing myself. My idol is the love John Lennon.; [a.] Bushmills, Antrim, UK

DUNCAN, ANNE
[b.] Dundee; [ed.] Morgan Academy, Dundee College of Education, Dundee College of Commerce, Dundee; [occ.] Library Assistant, European Documentation Centre, University of Dundee; [hon.] Dip. Pr.Ed, (Diploma in Primary Education), Dip. C.S. (Diploma for Graduate Secretaries); [oth. writ.] Children's stories, short spy-stories; [a.] Cupar, Fife, UK

DUNCAN, JOHN
[pen.] John; [b.] 22 December 1938, Belfast, Northern Ireland; [m.] Elizabeth, 29 August 1959; [occ.] Landscape Gardener; [memb.] "Old Campbellian", "Sports Club" (Honorary Member), Campbell College, Belfast, Northern Ireland; [pers.] Interest in theology and horticulture theologist, and horticulturist. Admirer of the works of Robbie Burns and wordsworth.

DUNLOP, DIDO
[b.] 1950, USA; [ed.] Oxford University; [occ.] Teacher of Tiberan Buddhist Meditation and creative art a potter; writing; [memb.] Various Buddhist Societies; [oth. writ.] Working on meditation workbook for women, and on stories of modern women following the spiritual path.; [pers.] For me, writing is a spiritual pursuit, like meditation. Creative work, can open up the depths, the opening is the most important thing.

DUNN, KEVIN SHAUN
[b.] 27 March 1974, Wolverhampton; [p.] Janet Dunn and John Lee; [ed.] Northicote High School, Sandwell College; [occ.] Supervisor, Rank Amusements, Haven Holiday Centre, Doniford, Somerset; [pers.] Poetry is the moment of experience, captured in verse, so we can look back at them, to remember to learn and to amuse.; [a.] Watchey, Somerset, UK

DUNNE, ANYA
[b.] 26 September 1978, Colchester; [p.] Mrs. Angela and Stephen Dunne; [ed.] Thomas, Lord Audley School/Colchester Institute; [occ.] Student; [memb.] Liverpool F.C., International Supporters Club/Essex Liverpool Reds Supporters Club; [hon.] Medals for Throwing Events in District Sports; [oth. writ.] Poems published in Liverpool Essex reds newsletter; [pers.] I aim to produce poems from the heart so other people can relate to them. Simple and straight to the point I hope this makes my poems an interesting read.; [a.] Colchester, Essex, UK

DUNNE, REV. JUDE MARTIN
[b.] 5 June 1948, Cork, Irl.; [p.] James (Deceased) and Margaret Dunne; [m.] Mary Dunne, 22 September 1990; [ch.] Jude Leslie and Jacinta Elizabeth; [ed.] B.TH. Jacksonville Theological Seminary, Florida, U.S. (Irish Satellite), M.A. candidate, candidate for Counsellor with Assoc. Christian Counsellors, Irl.; [occ.] Programme Mngr. J.T.S. Irish Satellite; [memb.] Association of Christian Counsellors (Irl) [oth. writ.] Currently preparing a booklet of Penned Poetry. A desire to publish penned short stories; [pers.] An expression of the heart is my intention through 'words' in poetry, so others may be lifted up and catch 'hope' to go on living fruitfully.; [a.] Cork, Ireland

DYER, PETER RICHARD
[b.] 8 July 1945, Harrogate, Yorks; [p.] Edward Dyer and Elizabeth Dyer; [ed.] Southport University School, Southport College of Art, Oasther College of Education Huddersfield; [occ.] Teacher, Film Scriptwriter; [memb.] Associate College of Preceptors, British Baseball Federation, Southport Amateur Rocket Group; [hon.] Diploma in the Advanced Study of Education (D.A.S.E) Children's Lit. Diploma in the Advanced Study of Ed. Urban Ed.; [oth. writ.] Contributions to the meantime History of N.W. (Skillcamp Lan Lancashire Mag/Lancashire Life, J.F.K. Classic American, present from Script project for U.S. maricet.; [a.] Southport, Merseyside, UK

DYMOND, NICOLA
[b.] 22 July 1975, Torquay; [p.] Mrs. V. Smart; [ed.] Audley Park School, South Devon Technical College; [occ.] General Assistant for Tesco's (Coffee Shop); [memb.] I am a member of the Devon and Cornwall Special Constabulary.; [oth. writ.] I have written many poems and short stories over the years although none of them have been read publicly.; [pers.] Most of my writing are about personal experiences or about when I try to imagine other people's situations and feelings.; [a.] Newton Abbot, Devon, UK

DYSON, MARY BISSET
[b.] 16 June 1936, Durban, South Africa; [p.] W. H. Dyson and U. W. Dyson; [m.] Jean Boutan; [ed.] Sara Paulos Abraham; [a.] Paris, France

EAGLES, CHRISTINE
[b.] 10 June 1945, West Bromwich; [p.] Mr. and Mrs. MacIntyre McGrotty; [m.] Anthony; [ch.] Shawn; [occ.] Retired on ill health ex auxiliary nurse; [memb.] Disabled Society Royal Doulton Club; [hon.] Open university in elderly care health and safety award training and instruction award.; [oth. writ.] For family and friends, passing away my own time this is my first poem I have let outsiders read they always have a meaning to myself.; [pers.] Caring for elderly and infirm was my occupation little things touch your heart so you write it down let everyone love, not hate and relieve your feelings.; [a.] Wednesbury, West Mids, UK

EDMEAD, ANN
[b.] 25 October 1941, London; [p.] Nell and Albert Edmead; [m.] John Folham, 14 December 1949, February 1984; [ch.] Paul Fordam, Ben Fordham; [occ.] Care Officer, Social Services; [memb.] Globe Centre Stepney, HIV Aids, Hackney Bing Club; [hon.] Social Care Diplomer Electrolysis Deplomer; [oth. writ.] Several poems not published. Book not published, life story not published.; [pers.] My love for John "Paul" Ben, Tony is so deep. So why do I feel "if only" my poems speak for me. As I can't speak for myself. I dedicate my poems to them and all poets.; [a.] London, Towerhamkets, UK

EDWARDS, GEORGE
[b.] 7 November 1916, Hendon; [p.] Mr. and Mrs. Edwards (Deceased); [m.] Deceased, 23 November 1940; [ch.] Three boys, and eight girls; [ed.] Primary Schools and Various Schools; [occ.] Retired Large Landscaping; [memb.] Served in the 2nd World War, was in hospital in india for nine months and for another 3 months England I used to write poems for Hospital Staff; [hon.] 2 school and Hendon Boxing Club, 8 Silver School Medals, 2 Boxing Silver Cups, 1 Award for capturing a burglar with gun and ammunition for police untidiness due to stroke; [pers.] My grand-father born in Scotland, lived and married in England, had a large collection of Burns Poetry books and knew every one of Burns poems, and taught me and my sister a lot of poetry when I was 5 yrs. and my sister 7 years, thus my liking for poetry in future years. I suffered a stroke 12 months ago.; [a.] Ashford, Kent, UK

EDWARDS, HELEN RUTH
[b.] 19 September 1981, Cambridge; [p.] Trevor and Jackie Edwards; [ed.] Droitwich High School; [occ.] Student; [memb.] Droitwich Theatre and Arts Club Ltd.; [oth. writ.] This is my first published work.; [pers.] I dedicate this poem to my brother, Matthew Edwards (31-12-75 to 19-1-94).; [a.] Droitwich Spa, Worcestershire, UK

EDWARDS, JEAN MARY
[b.] 12 May 1924, Norbury, London; [p.] Dr. William Edwards; [m.] Marjory Victoria Edwards; [ed.] Croydon High School, Parsons Mead School, Ashtead, St. Andrews Convent School, Leatherhead London University; [occ.] Retired Librarian (Civil Service); [memb.] Library Association, BCA Book Clubs, Britannia Music Club; [hon.] B.A. (Hons.), F.L.A.; [oth. writ.] Ed. "Old Portland", publ. by the Dorset Publishing Co., articles in the Meashan Motoring Magazine, etc. article on Edmund Spenser in the Cambridge Journal; [pers.] I believe in the "one-ness" of the world and of mankind. I find inspiration in nature and in the mysteries of nature and the past.; [a.] Ashtead, Surrey, UK

EDWARDS, JILL V. M.
[pen.] Tilly; [b.] 6 April 1953, Gloucester; [p.] Joan Mary Patterson; [m.] Stuart Hugh, 23 January 1971; [ch.] Andrew John - Paul Raymond; [ed.] Beverly Hills Girls High School Sydney - Australia; [occ.] Candlemaker; [hon.] The Bottle of Ouzo I won in Greece - for writing a poem - what else; [oth. writ.] Nothing published - yet!; [pers.] My writings are based on my own personal feelings and experiences.; [a.] Birkenhead, M'side, UK

EDWARDS, MARGARET
[pen.] Margaretta Williams; [b.] 11 April 1958, Jamaica; [p.] Dudley and Victoria Williams; [m.] Norman A. Edwards, 7 June 1980; [ch.] Jermaine, Andre, Omar and Devann; [ed.] Tom Hood Senior High Waltham Forest College; [occ.] Housewife; [memb.] Youth Club, Computer Op. Pen. Church.; [oth. writ.] Yes several none published us yet.; [pers.] Giving thanks to the king of Glory. I pray that these words will give pleasure, joy and hope to all who read them.; [a.] London, UK

EGGLETON, SUSAN
[b.] 9 February 1959, London; [p.] Dorothy and Peter Eggleton; [m.] Kimberly Eggleton, 31 January 1976; [ch.] Nichola Joanne and Wayne Ham; [ed.] Richard Jefferies Comprehensive School, Park High School; [occ.] Senior Customer Service, Representative; [pers.] As this is my first published piece I am hopeful that it will be the catalyst to my writing, both poetic and novelistic, career.; [a.] Swindon, Wiltshire, UK

EISENSCHMID, WENDY
[b.] 29 September 1959, Bristol; [p.] Richard and Sheila Yarnold; [m.] Claus Eisenschmid, 15 September 1995; [oth. writ.] Many poems written for family, friends and of course myself.; [pers.] I liken poetry to a vibrant ballerina skirting the edges of her stage with fine precision pointed steps, always leaving behind her a stir of emotion, an impression!; [a.] Berlin, Germany

ELEY, LINDA LOUISE
[b.] 25 August 1968, Morden, Surrey; [p.] John Hawkes and Ann Hawkes; [m.] Wayne Eley, 23 June 1990; [ch.] Kirsten Belynda and Sophie Ann; [ed.] Herbert Carter School; [occ.] Housewife; [oth. writ.] Only poems for personal pleasure and family and friends special occasions; [a.] Poole, Dorset, UK

ELLERSHAW, JEAN
[b.] 14 January 1946, Liverpool; [p.] Joseph Ball and Lily Ball (Deceased); [m.] Divorced; [ch.] Jon, Ben, Sara; [ed.] Childwall Valley High School; [memb.] Tangent Club; [pers.] Live life and care and life will came for you.; [a.] Birkenhead, Merseyside, UK

ELLIOTT, DAVE
[b.] 24 November 1948, Wolverhampton; [p.] Charles Raymond, Shelia Elizabeth; [m.] Lynn, 5 October 1974; [ch.] Victoria, Joanne, Robert; [ed.] Wolverhampton Municipal Grammar School, 1960-67 St Paul's College, Cheltenham 1968-71; [occ.] Primary Teacher Knavesmire C.P.S. York; [memb.] Goole Vermuyden Cycling Club, Howden Town Cricket Club, Goole Round Table 41 Club; [oth. writ.] Several poems published in various books, all titles beginning 'Dave On'; [pers.] I wrote this poem, Dave on 'Children of Hope', for the children of Knavesmire C.P. School Partial hearing Unit. I was so moved by their example of determination inspiration and pride.; [a.] Howden, E. Yorkshire, UK

ELLIS, CHRISTINA E.
[pen.] Christina Ellis; [b.] 26 July 1979, Gt. Yarmouth; [p.] Patricia and Michael Ellis; [ed.] Biggar High School; [occ.] Student at Biggar High School (6th form); [memb.] Biggar Theatre Workshop, Symington Youth Group, Line Dancing; [oth. writ.] Story published in 'Village Day' Booklet, article in school news letter.; [pers.] Don't ever compromise yourself - after all you're all you've got.; [a.] Symington, Lanarkshire, UK

ELLIS, MR. JOHN
[pen.] John Ellis; [m.] Ruth; [occ.] Retired; [memb.] Social: Phyllis Court Club, Henley Professional: Fellow of Institute of Bankers, Institute of Management, Institute of Administrators; [oth. writ.] Professional Management material only. Challenged by wife to try poetry competition. With wife, owns Brayville Irish Setters. Dog and two of five bitches are Show Champions, poem 'The Showdog' drawn from impressions at the ringside.; [pers.] Believes poetry, traditional or modern, must project a clear and worthwhile message of its own, as well as stimulating the imaginations of others.; [a.] Henley on Thames, Oxon, UK

ELLIS, MARY
[pen.] Edwina James; [b.] 6 June 1946, London; [p.] James and Inez Cannon; [m.] Ronald Ellis, 1 June 1968; [ed.] Harold Hill Grammar Open University; [occ.] Human Resources Manager; [memb.] Institute of Personnel and Development, British Institute of Graphology; [hon.] BA (Hons) Psychology; [oth. writ.] None in print; [pers.] I believe the essence of good poetry is inspiration: Language between souls.; [a.] Tunbridge, Wells, Kent, UK

EMSDEN, MARGARET
[b.] 23 March 1944, Eyke, Suffolk; [p.] Mr. and Mrs. Fordman; [m.] Mr. Richard Emsden, 1 April 1967; [ch.] 2 sons; [ed.] Hadleigh High School Ipswich College; [occ.] Doctor's Receptionist; [hon.] 2 SA Typing and Shorthand; [oth. writ.] Poems written for family and friends on special occasions; [pers.] I find it most satisfying to bring joy to others by writing a personal poem for them on special occasions.; [a.] Bildeston, Ipswich, Suffolk, UK

ENNIS, JOHN T.
[b.] 21 November 1969, Dublin; [p.] Michael and Carmel Ennis; [ed.] Holy Faith/De la Salle Community College Skerries; [occ.] Snooker Club Manager and Writer; [memb.] Republic of Ireland Billiard and Snooker Association, Irish Federation of Healing; [pers.] One law! Universal, communicate words are wisdom words, living things speak, share them see what they bring.; [a.] Skerries, Dublin, UK

ENTICKNAPP, DANIEL KEITH
[pen.] Daniel Enticknapp; [b.] 10 January 1959, Hove; [ed.] Was not educated, but went to the Knoll Boys School, Old Shoreham Road, Hove, East Sussex; [occ.] Caretaker at Cardinal Newman School, Hove, East Sussex; [oth. writ.] Only that I wrote a story in my spare time in which it taken almost three years to write, because of lack of English Education. The story is called two broken hearts.; [pers.] Only that I come from a large family of sixteen. Ten brothers and four sisters.; [a.] East Sussex, Hove, UK

EPPS, PEARL MOLVINA
[pen.] Molvina; [b.] 30 March 1921, Plymouth; [p.] John - Violet Simpson; [m.] John Epps, 13 December 1941; [ch.] Five; [ed.] St Johns School Plymouth; [occ.] Housewife widowed; [oth. writ.] A poem for the Queen of her Silver Jubilee it was published in the local press; [pers.] A romantic at heart in my day Wordsworth and Longfellow were my influence my philosophy is "if you can't do a good turn never do a bad one".; [a.] Swansea, Glam, UK

EPTON, KATRINA
[b.] 13 January 1957, West Yorkshire; [p.] Reginald and Lily Jukes; [m.] John Epton, 18 August 1984; [ch.] Sian, Dominique and Jade; [ed.] Airedale Highschool West Yorkshire; [occ.] Housewife extraordinary; [pers.] The time is now for everything, do it today tomorrow may be too late.; [a.] Bindlington, East Yorkshire, UK

ERANGEY, NELLY
[b.] 13 May 1905, Cork; [p.] Stephen and Catherine Erangey; [ed.] Primary and Secondary Schooling and Domestic Science course; [occ.] Retired Tailoress; [memb.] Former Member of Tennis Club and Drama School, St. Mary's Oratorio Society; [oth. writ.] Several poems unpublished, also short stories unpublished, one book of poems, published by friends; [pers.] I like to reflect life in a light hearted way.; [a.] Cork City, Cork, Ireland

EVANS, ANTHONY J.
[pen.] A. J. Evans, Tony James; [b.] 30 June 1954, Kingston-upon-Hull; [p.] Joseph J. Evans, Irene Evans; [m.] Carol Evans, 21 March 1981; [ed.] Saltshouse High; [occ.] Frozen Food Delivery Driver; [oth. writ.] At present I am doing research for my first novel; [pers.] I have been writing poetry for some years now, but only in the last 12 mths I have taken it more seriously; [a.] Kingston-upon-Hull, E. Yorkshire, UK

EVANS, CHRISTOPHER JOHN
[b.] 27 October 1958, Kibblesworth; [p.] Kathleen Jones, Thomas John (Deceased); [m.] Divorced; [ch.] Jennifer Maureen, Jo-Beth Marie; [ed.] Army Apprentices College, Harrogate, East Durham Community College, Peterlee; [occ.] Single father; [hon.] Community Education, Outstanding Achievement Award 1996; [oth. writ.] Rays of Sunshine, God's Gift To Me, An Eternal Pain, My Secret World, (all unpublished at present).; [pers.] I put my thoughts and feelings in writing, so that later on in life, my daughters can see how precious they are to me and how privileged I feel, for every moment I spend with them.; [a.] Horden, Durham, UK

EVANS, ERIC
[b.] 26 October 1929, Liverpool; [occ.] Retired; [pers.] The poem was written for the girl of my life Maria Davis we never made the special day.

EVANS, MARY BERNADETTE
[b.] 19 June 1950, Birmingham; [p.] Bert and Eileen Stevens (Both Dead); [m.] Kenneth, 6 June 1970; [ch.] Julie, Connie, Justin, Natalie; [ed.] Secondary modern education at John Wall R.C. I now spend a lot of time studying the after-life and am also doing an adult education course in hypnotherapy; [occ.] Housewife and mother, part time work in sales administration; [oth. writ.] Several other poems - all influenced by Natalie's death but this is my first poem to be published.; [pers.] I only started writing after my youngest daughter Natalie died from leukaemia, aged 13, in March 1995. All my poems are dedicated to her. My grief at her loss is indescribable.; [a.] Birmingham, West Mids, UK

EVANS, SHARON
[b.] 9 April 1966, Colchester; [p.] Sheila and Albert Evans; [m.] Christopher Shelley, 20 April 1985; [ch.] Twins, Boy Jayme, Girl Victoria - age 5; [ed.] Went to Secondary School Haishead Passed seven exams attended college for office skills plus two years cake decorating; [occ.] Apart from a house wife and mother of twins with production of perfume; [oth. writ.] Have have other poem published in small anthology and have a complete book of 76 poems waiting to be published in the near future.; [pers.] Every word in every poem comes straight from the heart being of an emotional nature find words easy to express on paper and put then across sincerely.; [a.] Witham, Essex, UK

EVANS, STELLA ANNE
[b.] 23 September 1957, Taunton; [p.] Charles Noel Page and Rosemary Page; [m.] Barry Evans (Now Widowed), 6 November 1982; [ch.] Dawn Marie and Paul Michael; [ed.] Hollywood comprehensive, Chard; [occ.] Accounts Clerk; [oth. writ.] Many family and factual poems, but this is the first one ever entered in a competition.; [pers.] Being very shy. God had given me the gift of poetry to help me communicate an express my feeling; [a.] Chard, Somerset, UK

EVEREST, JEAN
[b.] 13 July 1944, Crowborough; [p.] Thomas Silver and Ada Silver; [m.] Barrie Everest, 5 March 1966; [ch.] Anne Elizabeth; [ed.] Catford County School for girls; [oth. writ.] A book of prayer published several poems published in anthologies a few short stories published in magazines; [pers.] As a christian my faith influences my writing. Family life is very important to me. I enjoy reading a wide range of subjects.; [a.] Gravesend, Kent, UK

EVES, CLIVE A.
[b.] 20 June 1959, Preston; [p.] Roy Eves and Patricia Eves; [m.] Susan Eves, 14 March 1981; [ch.] Jack, Charlotte; [ed.] Queen Elizabeth Senior High School; [occ.] Betting Shop Manager; [hon.] Betting Shop Manager of The year 1990.; [oth. writ.] This is the first time I have submitted work for publication.; [pers.] I try to make people smile; [a.] Rochdale, Lancs, UK

EWART, BERTRAND
[pen.] Bertrand Ewart; [b.] 5 October 1925, South Wales; [ed.] Grammar School Edinburgh University; [occ.] RTD Flying Instructor; [memb.] British hang gliding Asc', British Microlight Aircraft Asc' Local Writers Group, Welsh Academy; [hon.] BSC Forestry Qual Light Aircraft Pilot. (Aged 70) student Helicopter Pilot (RTD) Hang glider and Microlight Aircraft Instructor Ocean going Yachtsman; [oth. writ.] Flying Magazines (articles) Novel "How Blue Was My Valley" satirical verse; [pers.] Tongue in cheek view of life hates, Political Cant. Snobbery.; [a.] Crickhowell, Powys, UK

FAGG, L.
[b.] 11 February 1978, Dover; [p.] Lesley Fagg; [occ.] Doing College Course in September, (Sociology and Psychology); [oth. writ.] My story (Past), for foster care, published in magazine; [pers.] I try to understand mankind motives, and I suppose understand why such a young life can be scared, by life's lessons. I am very strong through life's hick ups and live today as I will tomorrow!; [a.] Folkstone, Kent, UK

FAIRLEY, NORMAN
[b.] 2 February 1939, Gateshead; [m.] Frances Fairley, 22 December 1962; [ch.] Gloria and Norman; [ed.] Secondary Modern. (Brighton Avenue). Gateshead Tech. College Associate of London College music in subject Pianoforte (A. L. C. M.); [occ.] Music Teacher (private) Professional Musician Organ/Piano; [memb.] Member London College of Music Society. Musicians Union; [hon.] Diplomas A.L.C.M., A.V.C.M. (Hons.) in subject Pianoforte; [oth. writ.] Words and music for Gateshead schools to commemorate the 'Silver Jubilee'; [pers.] The poem 'Seldom Seen' is dedicated to all who have had the pleasure of seeing this part of Glencoyne and Lake Ullswater. Also those who may wish to in the future.; [a.] Gateshead, Tyne and Wear, UK

FALLA, JAN
[b.] 7 October 1945, Guernsey, CI; [ch.] 2 in their twenties; [ed.] Ladies College, Guernsey; [occ.] Secretary; [memb.] Member of Belles and Broomsticks Local Female Morris Side; [oth. writ.] Collection of serious/humorous poets-hoping to get them published as a book fairly soon.; [pers.] Other hobbies-playing the melodeon, tin whistle and boduran. Mom's dancing. Poetry writing started all with making up humorous verses to well-known tunes. Then went on to serious poetry. Ambition - to have poem back or novel published; [a.] St. Peter Pat, Guernsey, CI, UK

FALLA, MAUD
[b.] 9/11/27, Guernsey; [p.] John and Lilian Le Page; [m.] David Herbert Falla MBE, 19/8/54; [ch.] Diane and Colin; [ed.] Elementary School, Grammar School, Technical College; [occ.] Secretary of own company (Plant Nursery); [memb.] Women's Institute and various church committees; [oth. writ.] Poems for special events; [pers.] I enjoy writing poetry and finding out about words and I do a lot of crosswords; [a.] Guernsey

FARMER, CHRISTINE ELIZABETH
[b.] 14 September 1942, Stockport; [p.] Ernest and Elsie Element; [m.] Derek, 21 August 1965; [ch.] David 24, Andrew 22, Jonathan and Ian (twins) 21; [ed.] George Dixon Grammar School Edgbaston Birmingham; [occ.] Typist/Office Assistant; [memb.] Grange Choral Society, Christ Church, Dorset; [hon.] Winner Bournemouth Centenary Song; [oth. writ.] Poem - "Lying There" in inspirations from Southern England" (Anchor Press 1996), children's carols (words and music) not yet published!! At the moment working on an anthology of poems for nature lovers; [pers.] I am influenced by the beauty of the natural world around us and try to put some of my feelings into words.; [a.] Bournemouth, Dorset, UK

FARMER, TONI
[b.] 28 July 1971, Cardiff; [p.] Kenneth and Yvonne Farmer; [ed.] Bryn Hafren Girls School, Crosskeys College of Artland Design; [occ.] Support worker within an Intensive Support Team. I work with adults and children who have learning disabilities and challenging behavior.; [oth. writ.] Numerous unpublished poems.; [pers.] Poetry for me is an exploration of the inner self, the enigma of life and the way in which one affects the other. I am very interested in the use of poetry as a form of therapy.; [a.] Llanteg, S. Pembs, UK

FARNSWORTH, MARTIN STUART
[b.] 30 July 1971, Nottingham; [p.] Eunice and David Farnsworth; [ed.] 'O' level English, Woodwork, Music, Math, Business Studies 1st certificate; [occ.] Unemployed; [memb.] Breadsall Country Club Hotel, Fitness and Leisure, Karate Association; [hon.] Classical Guitar - Grades 5, 6, 7, and 8; [oth. writ.] Going to bed, nature poems printed in the Nottingham Evening Post; [pers.] I enjoy composing poems and I am currently writing a thriller. I find my experiences in life have inspired my poetry.; [a.] Wollation, Nottingham, UK

FARTHING, ANDREW
[b.] 24 December 1964, North Petherton; [p.] Margaret Farthing, Harry Farthing; [m.] Single; [ed.] Blare Comprehensive Bridgwater, Bridgwater College, St. Loyes College; [occ.] Maynards Bakeries; [memb.] Bridgwater Centurion Carnival Club; [hon.] City and Guilds Brickwork, NVQ 500 Wire and Cable Looming Electronics; [pers.] I have to enjoy what I'm doing otherwise I just won't do it. And poetry or should I say the poetry I write is a perfect example of that.; [a.] North Petherton, Somerset, UK

FAULKNER, BELINDA
[b.] 2 December 1979, Boston, Lincolnshire; [p.] Stephen and Linda Faulkner; [ed.] Richmond County Primary Skegness, Minster C of E Primary Beverly, Beverly High School; [occ.] Student; [memb.] Young leader with a local brownie pack. Did belong to the Sunday school before becoming a leader with the 2-5 year olds.; [hon.] Won a poetry competition by getting it published. Lifestyle '91-'94 winning 5 pounds gift vouchers and a trip to flamingo land. Lifestyle is a competition run by the local police in the summer holidays (for charities); [oth. writ.] 'The other side of the mirror' - in a local book called 'wot not humberside' (in 1994); [a.] Beverley, E. Yorkshire, UK

FAULKNER, HAZEL ROSALIE
[pen.] Emma Rose; [b.] 12 April 1939, Combe, St. Nicolas; [p.] George L-Abbe, Emma Amy; [m.] Fredrick Faulkner, 5 February 1957; [ch.] One son Brian; [ed.] Combe St. Nicolas Church of England School, then Williton S. Modern School; [occ.] Farmers wife; [oth. writ.] Of which I have a great many. (My words) Freedom.; [pers.] I am very happy, and find beauty and much pleasure in writing of which my late mother did in her young days in Jersey C.I. and won lots of prizes.; [a.] Wminster, Somerset, UK

FAULKNER, LORRAINE
[b.] 2 February 1954, Highgate, London; [p.] Ernest Faulkner, Sheila Faulkner; [ch.] Michelle-Alinka-Christian; [ed.] Collenswood Secondary Modern Stevenage Herts; [occ.] Self Employed in catering (Carnaby Street) London; [pers.] My poems was influenced by my love and affection for my wonderful father Ernie who passed away, after fighting very hard not to leave us, on 5th February 1996; [a.] London, UK

FAULL, CLAUDE
[b.] 29 June 1921, Beacon, Camborne, Cornwall; [p.] Deceased; [m.] Elizabeth Stella, 15 January 1947; [ch.] 1 son, 1 daughter; [ed.] Elementary left School at 14 joined the Royal Navy 7-9 1938, left the Royal Navy 7-3 1953; [occ.] Senior Citizen; [memb.] Manchester Unity Independent Order Of Odd Fellows, Masonic Institution; [hon.] None, apart from service medals including Russian Convoy Medal and Malta Star; [pers.] To endeavour to do unto others that which I might wish then should do unto me.; [a.] Redruth, Cornwall, UK

FEATHER, ROBERT JOHN
[b.] 11 August 1943, Exeter; [p.] Herbert, Dorothy, May; [m.] Divorced, 1968-86; [ch.] Alexia, Scott; [ed.] Ladysmith Sec. Med.; [occ.] Residential Social Worker; [oth. writ.] A few poems (Unpublished); [pers.] This poor have treasures unseen the rich are blinded by theirs.; [a.] Exeter, Devon, UK

FELIX-DAVIES, CLAIRE
[b.] 3 September 1972, Solihull; [p.] Dereck and Anne Felix-Davies; [ed.] Arden Secondary School, Knowle: Solihull 6th from college: Leeds Metropolitan University; [occ.] Final Year Engineering Student at Leeds Metropolitan University; [pers.] This was the first poem I wrote and the first to be entered into a competition it is dedicated to the memory of my father, a truly great man in my poetry, I aim to put real emotions onto paper in a simple, uncomplicated way, if what I write touches peoples thoughts and feelings then my aim has been achieved.; [a.] Solihull, West Midlands, UK

FENWICK, GIULIANA
[b.] 21 March 1971, Epping; [p.] Linda and Alfred Wheather; [m.] Nigel Oliver Fenwick, 22 April

1995; [ch.] 1 son - 2 weeks old; [ed.] Local Comprehensive - 9 O Levels, 3 A Levels, Exeter University and BA Hons French/Hist; [occ.] Antique dealer; [oth. writ.] I have written since the age of nine - novels and poetry. I have binbags full of the stuff; [pers.] I would not say I am influenced by any one particular person or movement- I just write what I feel at the time.; [a.] Urchfont Nr Devizes, Wiltshire, UK

FERGUSSON, DOREEN
[pen.] Doreen Clayton-Fergusson; [b.] 17 December 1931, Coventry; [p.] Doris and Josiah Stafford; [m.] Thomas Baden Fergusson, 6 November 1993; [ch.] Stephen George, Karen Susan, Jayne Marie and Richard John Clayton; [ed.] Windmill Road Secondary School Longford Coventry; [occ.] Retired; [hon.] Musical Honours with Victoria College of Music; [oth. writ.] Several poems in various books and readings on radio; [pers.] I am striving to get my complete book of poems published, for they reflect the beauty that is ours to enjoy if only we would realise this.; [a.] Honiton, Devon, UK

FIEBER, KEVIN
20-11-81, Scunthorpe; [p.] Mr. and Mrs. Allen; [ed.] Currently at Brumby Comprehensive School; [hon.] Have previously won school awards in English and Drama; [oth. writ.] "The Four Seasons", "My County -- Humberside", "Eat Your Greens", "Winter Thoughts"; [pers.] Main inspiration comes from anything I see or do around me. I hope one day to have my own book published.; [a.] Scunthorpe, N. Lincs

FIELD, KARIN
[b.] 19 July 1960, Exeter; [ed.] Priory High School, Exeter Tech; [occ.] Deputy Manager Hostel for people with mental health problems; [hon.] O/V degree BSC Hons Psychology. Counselling diploma; [oth. writ.] Article printed in Psychology magazine; [pers.] I am inspired spiritually and by the world I live in. Poetry helps me express my own feelings.; [a.] Exeter, Devon, UK

FINDLAY, JULIA SHAUN
[b.] 18 June 1957, White Lackington, Somerset; [p.] Percy and Doreen Larcome; [m.] Iain Findlay, 10 February 1979; [ch.] Robert Shaun and Shelley Francis; [ed.] Wadham Comprehensive Creukerne; [occ.] House keeper Hornsbury Mill, Nr. Chard; [pers.] I like my words to reflect the simple beauty of everyday life.; [a.] Chard, Somerset, UK

FINDLAY, SYLVIA EDNA
[pen.] Henrietta Valmore; [p.] Anne and Henry Morrell; [m.] Douglas Findlay; [ed.] Whickham County School, Wickham, Newcastle Tyne; [occ.] Local Government Clerk/Typist; [oth. writ.] Quite a number of poems, written. None published to date!; [pers.] A poem can personify and reveal the true feelings of the inner self. It can almost touch the soul!; [a.] New Castle, Tyne and Wear, UK

FISHER, ARCHIBALD P.
[b.] 9/1/1917, Kilsyth; [p.] Alexander Fisher, Agnes Fisher; [m.] Mary H. Fisher, 1st July 1953; [ch.] Helen Agnes (deceased); [ed.] Condorrat Preparatory and Cumbernauld Higher Grade Schools in Dunbartonshire; [occ.] Retired, (Shopkeeper), retail food trade; [memb.] Various church choirs, (Caravanning, walking), both clubs; [hon.] Excelled in English and French languages; [oth. writ.] Many witty & entertaining poems along with articles of a more informing nature.; [pers.] My aim is always to help the unfortunates and to applaud the triers, in all walks of life.; [a.] Denny, Stirling

FITCHET, ANGUS JOHN
[b.] 22 April 1956, Plymouth; [p.] Angus Fitchet, Valerie Fitchet; [ed.] Devonport High School, Plymouth School of Radiography; [occ.] Radiography; [memb.] Institute of Amateur, Cinematographers (IAC), Jersey Aero Club (JAC), College of Radiographers; [hon.] Health Care Quality Award, Diploma of the College of Radiographers; [oth. writ.] Poem published in the Marwell Zoological Magazine; [pers.] I love to live and live to love.; [a.] St. Helier, Jersey, UK

FLOCKHART, MOYA GRAY
[b.] 28 May 1942, Edinburgh; [p.] John Gray, Myrtle Gray; [m.] Hugh Stevenson Flockhart, 31 October 1964; [ch.] Andrew John, Laura June; [ed.] Leith Academy, Edinburgh; [occ.] Secretary, University of Edinburgh, Scotland; [oth. writ.] Collections of poems reflecting all aspects of life - humorous to sad. None sent for publication till now.; [pers.] Since learning Longfellow's "The Slave's Dream" off by heart in primary school, I have had a great love for poetry and try to write it as much as reed it.; [a.] Edinburgh, Midlothian, UK

FLOUNDERS, DENISE SCOTT
[b.] 21 September 1963, Gloucester; [p.] Arthur Thomas Scott and Helen Noelle Scott; [m.] Ian Flounders, 11 November 1989; [ch.] Daniel, Joshua, Gareth, Jack; [ed.] Linden Secondary School Gloucester; [occ.] Homemaker; [pers.] I have enjoyed writing poetry and stories for many years. Having a young family I have little time to spend on my pleasure. My writings are influenced by my own personal experiences and emotions from the past and for the future. I hope one day to achieve my ambition to have my own book published.; [a.] Gloucester, Glo'shire, UK

FLYNN, MONICA
[pen.] Bernadette Rosen; [b.] 23 April 1958, Manchester; [p.] James Flynn and Marjorie Flynn; [ch.] Narissa Tia, Naomi Asher; [ed.] Govt. Bank School Stockport, Whalley Range High School, Manchester; [hon.] English/Business Communications Certificate; [pers.] Life itself inspires me to write. I would like to think, through my writing I can inspire others.; [a.] Manchester, Lancs, UK

FORMAN, MARTIN
[b.] 13 March 1963, Dunfermline; [p.] Jane Forman, George Forman; [ed.] Woodmill High School, Lauder College, Halbeath, Fife College, Kirkcaldy; [occ.] General Assistant, Gardener-Merchant, HMS Caledonia, Rosyth; [memb.] Former Member of Fife Writers Group; [hon.] '0' level English (SCE) higher lever English (SCE); [oth. writ.] Several poems published by Dunfermline district arts festival, fife writers group, poetry now, anchor books and the people's poetry; [a.] Dunfermline, Fife, UK

FORSTER, MYRIAM
[b.] Northumberland, Oxford, Newcastle upon Tyne; [p.] William Jackson; [m.] Divorced; [ch.] Beautiful, generous, caring, courageous and I shall respect the decision of a fee paying Business College, guaranteed interview which led to employment; [occ.] Public Relation Director with a festival. Individual charity fund raising for a disabled child, Special School, and with Chris Brasher's help fulfilled a 70 yrs old dream of London Marathon. Organize a tour of day Centres/Hospitals annuals for disabled of all ages.; [memb.] NIL I never to have time for my own social life. My main concern is that the Three Tenors may we be duo or solo by time I fulfill my own dreams.; [hon.] As part of the festival we have been awarded several prestigious honours, The BBC's 'it's My City Award' 1989, European Year of Tourism Award 1990, Daily Telegraph ABSA Awards 1990, Arts Council/British Gas Awards 1991, Daily Telegraph ABSA Award 1991, The Foundation for Sports and the Arts Award 1992, Expo '92 Seville, 1993 ABSA/BSIS Award, Foundation for Sports and the Arts 1994, The High Sheriff of Tyne and Wear Awards 1994; [oth. writ.] Frequently prepare copy as PR and see it in print. One story written and returned. Poems usually direct to subject and thus personal; [pers.] Life is so fragile every moment counts. Tragedy has me value emotion and I find violence in word or deed abhorrent, wasteful. Poverty is iniquitous and should be a first priority of all governments. Poets, writers have always expressed needs, feelings which inspire and are within us all... We are meant to cry, laugh, sing, dance. A non-philosophy is 'stiff upper lip'.; [a.] Newcastle upon Tyne, Tyne and Wear, UK

FOSTER, CAROLINE
[b.] 3 April 1959, Chipping Norton; [ed.] NVQ Level 1 Business Administration; [pers.] I enjoy writing poetry and try to express my feelings about my experiences of everyday life.; [a.] Carterton, Oxfordshire, UK

FOULGER, MARGRET
[pen.] Mickey Mitch; [b.] 24 September 1949, Germany; [p.] Deceased; [m.] Divorced; [ch.] Silva Donges; [ed.] Grammer School Hamburg (Germany); [occ.] Tester of Electronic Equipment and Customer Service; [oth. writ.] Currently writing a series of childrens stories. No work previous published; [pers.] My work reflects my experiences and impressions felt during critical periods in my earlier life.; [a.] Norwich, Norfolk, UK

FOVARGUE, MARJORIE
[b.] 10 September 1937, Peterborough; [p.] Edward and Wily Fielding; [m.] Keith Norris, 6 October 1956; [ch.] Jane, Neil, Duncan; [ed.] South View School Crowland Spalding High School for Girls; [occ.] Warden in Sheltered Housing for the Elderly; [oth. writ.] Three poems published by a local "Printer Anchor Books"; [pers.] A piece in a local paper in November 1995 inspired me to submit a poem called "How times have changed". It was accepted for printing followed by two more. Before then I had written nothing; [a.] Crowland, Lincs, UK

FOWLES, ROBERT MICHAEL
[b.] 8 July 1969, Bedford; [p.] Judith and Helvyn Fowles; [ed.] John Howard Upper School (Bedford), Sheffield City Polytechnic (Materials Engineering), Open University (Engineering); [occ.] Student (Open University); [oth. writ.] Currently compiling anthology of own poems; [pers.] My poems are written photographs of situation I have seen, considered or experienced. I call them still reflections.; [a.] Bedford, Bedfordshire, UK

FOX, ANNA-MARIE
[b.] 1 July 1966, Derry City; [p.] Josephine Fox, John Fox; [ed.] Carnhill High School; [occ.] Student: Business Administration; [memb.] Team Co-Ordinator with 'Project Romania, (Charity Working with Abandoned Children with 'Aids' in Northern Romania), Member of 'City-Light' Christian-Fellowship; [oth. writ.] Poems compiled but not submitted to any other magazines before.; [pers.] The inspiration of mans heart is breath from the author of life.; [a.] Derry, UK

FOX, KATHLEEN
[b.] 11 March 1928, Harden, Bingley; [p.] Thomas and Ada Chamberlain; [m.] Eric Douglas (Deceased), 21 July 1951; [ch.] Barry Douglas, Tony Christopher; [ed.] Harden Junior, Mornington Rd, Bingley and Bingley Modern and Tech (now Bingley Grammar); [occ.] Retired; [hon.] Handwriting competitions (taken over schools in W Yorks) twice; [oth. writ.] Poems in local paper over different issues. Two other poems published over the last eight months.; [pers.] A very ordinary person who spent a lot of my children ill, so loosing a lot of schooling, I love the country-side through all seasons, and also my many friends. The world is a wondrous place full of beauty which I like to express.; [a.] Yeadon, Lees, W. York, UK

FOX, MAUDE DIXON
[b.] 9 April 1923, Gateshead; [m.] Percy Dixon Fox, 16 May 1946; [ch.] Pamela Ann Smith and Wendy Elizabeth Bell; [ed.] Marton Grove School (Head Girl 1937) Middlesbrough College of Art Middlesbrough; [occ.] Housewife, (retired nurse) ex. W.A.A.F. 1943-46 (Battle of Atlantic); [hon.] War Medal 1939-45, School Art Prize 1937; [oth. writ.] Various, while attending local branch 'writing class' of the University of Leeds Adult Education Programme 1994-5.; [pers.] I have a great love of life and nature, 'Feelings' play a large part in life, though are rarely thought about, by us. People, animals and plants deserve to voice their feelings. Hence my little poem.; [a.] Middlesbrough, Teesside, UK

FOX, ROBERT
[b.] 7 June 1951, West Bromwich; [p.] John Fox, and Hilda Fox; [m.] Rosey, 18 November 1978; [ch.] Johawwa, Adam; [ed.] Churchfields Secondary School; [occ.] Gardener; [oth. writ.] Three poems published in three other books. (Anthologies).; [pers.] I write my poetry in the hope if moving people deep enough for them to take action and strive for the simple goodness that can change so much.; [a.] Andover, Hants, UK

FOX, STEVEN
[pen.] Foxy; [b.] 12 March 1977, Cambridge; [p.] Eric, Pauline Fox; [ed.] Ramsey Ailwyn, Sawlry Village College; [occ.] Guitarist; [oth. writ.] "The Adventures of Karn", soon to be released; [pers.] "Look for God in everything you do".; [a.] Ramsey, Cambs, UK

FRANCIS, FAYE
[b.] 11 June 1980, Sidcup; [p.] Susan and Malcolm Francis; [ed.] Welling Secondary School, Elsa Road, DA16 1BL; [occ.] Student; [a.] Welling, Kent, UK

FRANKLAND, ROY
[b.] 22 July 1964, Newcastle-upon-Tyne; [m.] Divorced; [ch.] One son Daniel (5); [ed.] Gosforth High School, Sunderland University; [occ.] Project Manager - Powder Coatings; [memb.] Oxclose Writers Group - Washington, Belmont Writers Group - Durham; [hon.] BSC (Huns) Material Science Biddick Writers 2nd Prize in National Poetry Competition; [pers.] I have only been writing about 18 months and write from my own emotions and experiences. If just one person could gain inspiration or feel moved by my writing, I feel I would have achieved something.; [a.] Newcastle-upon-Tyne, Tyne and Wear, UK

FRANKLIN, SHIRLEY
[b.] Reading; [m.] Brian T. Franklin; [ch.] Lisa 29, Lawrence 21; [ed.] Church School then Sec Modern then Secretarial college; [occ.] Secretary; [memb.] Church; [oth. writ.] Have written a novel called "Seventh Son"; [pers.] Born again christian to glorify God. For my writings to encourage more love and forgiveness in the world; [a.] Weston, Wirral, UK

FREEMAN, JEAN
[b.] 17 March 1940, Alrewas, B-o-T; [p.] Thomas Swinfield, Dorothy Swinfield; [m.] Alan Freeman, 12 September 1959; [ch.] John, Paul, Janette, Jayne; [ed.] Church of England, School of Alrewas, Burton-on-Trent, Staffs; [occ.] House-wife, Ex-Foster Parent; [oth. writ.] I am greatly influenced by the beauty of nature and all of it stands for. I have several poems, I have wrote and no one has seen, yet or I would like to share with everyone.; [pers.] I listen to the troubles and happiness of others and put it all together to put my own version of fairytale, sadness or romance, for I feel I am that person in poems.; [a.] Burton-on-Trent, Staffs, UK

FREEMAN, JULIE
[b.] 11 June 1961, Blackhall; [p.] George and Edna Armstrong; [m.] Geoff Freeman, 16 March 1985; [ch.] Daniel and Sarah-Jayne; [ed.] Blackhall Secondary School, North Tees School of Nursing; [occ.] Aromatherapist; [oth. writ.] Other poems/ none published.; [pers.] The poems I write are write from the heart and are a window on my inner feelings.; [a.] Stockton-on-Tees, Cleveland, UK

FREEMAN, LEE KETH
[pen.] Stuart Nichols/Erik Kihlstedt; [b.] 23 September 1972, Shoreham, Sussex; [p.] Keith Freeman and Angela Freeman; [m.] 'Partner' Christine Butcher; [ed.] St. Andrews C of E School for boys, Northbrook College, both in working; [occ.] Security officer/publisher; [memb.] They are normal (Amateur Dramatics) Somniloquence Writers Guild; [oth. writ.] After The Cockoo, Nocturne, Reflections, MCMXCVI/Epitaph, the secret lives of Oswin Cady, clothes, but no cigar, all anthologies published by samniloquence publishing.; [pers.] All poetry is personal, so to label types of poetry, is to study it. To accept poetry, all that is needed is to read and understand. Labels are pretentious and I strive to outlaw all pretention; [a.] Worthing, Sussex, UK

FROST, BRIAN
[pen.] Bri; [b.] 24 December 1939, Uxbridge; [p.] Bought up by grandmother; [m.] Margaret Rose, 10 November 1982; [ch.] One step son; [ed.] C of E Grantham Lines (adopted Maybury High School Hull, Editor of School Magazine always Mid Class; [occ.] Retired Insurance Agent, due to epilepsy; [memb.] Writers Club, Sect, of Local Gardeng Club Leek Club; [hon.] Three half hour plays staged. 1 poem published "As Seen On T.V."; [oth. writ.] Press write up regarding book I have now been permitted to do by Health Authority "The Droppings Off A Living Tree" People with divorced unexpected brake downs drink-car accidents etc; [pers.] I love my country but dislike theft and mugging, smashing allotments up and our general taken for granted environment, so write to learn people everyday is a bonus, that is why curfew could be heaven to some!; [a.] Stakeford, Northumberland, UK

FTEROUDIS, MARGARET
[pen.] Margaret Settle; [b.] 2 January 1946, Barnsley, Yorks; [p.] Alfred and Joan Settle; [m.] Constantine Fteroudis, 1966; [ch.] 3 (2 Being Disabled); [ed.] Barnsley High School for Girls 'O' level Eng. Maths Latin French and German; [occ.] Homemaker and Carer; [memb.] Too busy caring.; [oth. writ.] Personal collection of unpublished poems.; [a.] Ferndown, Dorset, UK

FULLER, MRS. BETTY MAY
[pen.] B. M. Fuller; [b.] 29 December 1933, London; [p.] Lily Dean and John Shea; [m.] Leslie James Fuller (Husband), 14 July 1977; [ch.] One son, died 1986, age 23; [ed.] Church School London, back at school age 50, O'Level Art and Craft; [occ.] Retired; [memb.] The Society of Amateur Artists; [hon.] O'Level Art and Craft., Painting Hang in Westminster Gallery London, poems publish; [oth. writ.] Poems; [pers.] Started writing poems when my son died married in 1950 age 16 for 26 years then husband died on 2-12-76 age 47 remarried in 1977. Hobbies, cross stitch, art painting, sculpture, wood carving, and many other hobbies.; [a.] Walsall, West Midlands, UK

FULLER, MANDY
[b.] 21 June 1965; [p.] Mrs. Jean McWhirter; [m.] Andrew, 31 August 1985; [ch.] Stuart, Danny; [ed.] CE School (Moor Park Primary) Renfrew High School Renfrew Scotland; [occ.] Carer in my home for my husband; [pers.] My husband lost his leg in york on 16 June 1994 he was a Sgt in the army and I wrote the poem after listening to his experiences with phantom pains. I truly admire Robert Burns; [a.] Freckelton, Lancashire, UK, PR4 1RY

FURNER, KEITH
[b.] 11 February 1950, Croydon; [p.] Raymond Furner and Maude Furner; [ed.] Durham Univ. Hull Univ.; [occ.] Probation Officer; [memb.] International Friendship League, Local Poets Society; [hon.] BA (Hons) Social Policy. DIP SW-MA Social Work; [oth. writ.] Poem published in "Tranquil Echoes".; [pers.] I try to reflect the range of human emotions in my writing. Traditional folk music has influenced me.; [a.] Thrapston, Northants, UK

FURY, JUNE
[pen.] June Taylor; [b.] 15 February 1932, Dagenham; [p.] Ada (nee Gladwyn) Richardson, Arthur Richardson; [m.] Frank Fury, 21 March 1953; [ch.] Linda and Susan; [ed.] Private Chadwell Heath Romford Essex; [occ.] Housewife; [oth. writ.] This is my first effort; [pers.] I like to read Browning and Wordsworth and strive to be a good person doing good when I can love children and animals; [a.] Rochford, Essex, UK

GAFFNEY, JEANETTE
[b.] 24 August 1934, Plymouth; [p.] Vera and Jack McLeod; [m.] Laurence, 25 September 1974; [ch.] Janet, Robert, Colin, Steven, Samantha; [ed.] No High Flyer (Ford Secondary School); [occ.] Poetry writing, Housewife; [oth. writ.]

Several poems published in anthologies for Arrival Press Poetry Digest Magazine. Poem published in Stockwell Publishing Anthology, and Christian Anthology; [pers.] I started writing poetry in 93 after my elder brother died suddenly, and have continued in loops and bounds. I am inspired by life, love, and all thats wonderful in etc world; [a.] Plymouth, Devon, UK

GAILLARD, MOSTY

[b.] 3 July 1963, London; [p.] Hendrickson Gaillard and Elvira Gaillard; [ch.] Liam, Leona, Patrick; [ed.] St. Bernards R.C. School; [occ.] Silk Screen Printer; [memb.] Vechi Ryu Karate Club; [pers.] I worry about the world and what happens in it this sometimes reflects in my poetry. But still I am striving a produce a complete masterpiece.; [a.] London, Bow, UK

GALE, MRS. GLADYS

[b.] 26 February 1924, Farnham Royal, Bucks, Yorkshire; [m.] Ivo Gale (Now Widowed), 7 July 1947; [ch.] 3 sons David, Alan, John, 6 grandsons, 2 granddaughter; [ed.] 2 at University, I was educated at London schools; [occ.] Retired; [memb.] Served 10 yrs on committee at Caversham afternoon Tonns Woman Guild. Voluntary work for cancer care shop; [oth. writ.] Have wrote other poems first one published; [pers.] Enjoy writing poems usually ideas come on the spur of the moment.; [a.] Reading, Berks, UK

GALLIMORE, J.

[pen.] Ivy; [b.] 26 November 1923, Tunstall, S-o-T; [p.] Deceased; [m.] Dennis Gallimore, 25 July 1990; [ch.] 3, two son's and 1 daughter; [ed.] Council School; [occ.] House wife (retired), Home Held; [oth. writ.] Poems published local magazine been writing poems since teenager but I have only sent in one which was published I got my inspiration from cycling to my work each day to the home help job I was doing and watching the country changing each season.; [pers.] I believe in taking life as it comes and try to enjoy the simple things that God created with my family and friends around me I have never asked for much more I like to help out any of my family who needs our helping hands, with my husband.; [a.] Crewe, Cheshire, UK

GARDINER, GEOFFREY M.

[b.] 6/9/47, Birmingham; [p.] Allan F., F.N. Margaret Gardiner; [m.] divorced; [ch.] none; [ed.] King Edward's School, Birmingham; [occ.] Inventor; [memb.] Old Edwardians Association, Institute of Patentees & Inventors; [hon.] Royal Lifesaving Society Medallion; [oth. writ.] Several poems -- none published, considerable computer software; [pers.] When an Indian is lost, he must enter the Spirit world to read the signs and find the way.; [a.] Birmingham, W. Mids.

GARDNER, MARIANA

[pen.] Mariana Zavati; [b.] 20 January 1952, Bacau-Romania; [p.] Constantin Zavati, Iulia Bucur Zavati; [m.] John Edward Gardner, FRGS, 8 August 1980; [ch.] Fay Jacqueline and Philip Charles; [ed.] Master of Science in Philology University 'Alexandru Ioan Cuza', Iasi-Romania, PGCE - University of Leeds; [occ.] Teacher of Modern Languages in Norfolk; [memb.] The Poetry Society and the Literary Society - both before 1980; [hon.] First class honours in Philology; [oth. writ.] Poetry and literary criticism in various literary magazines before 1980; [pers.] I see myself as an apprentice...trying to reach and understand the intensity of life, transient and eternal.; [a.] East Dereham, Norfolk, UK

GARLICK, DOROTHY LILIAN

[b.] 30 December 1930, Oldbury, Worcs; [p.] Beatrice D. Gould, Harry W. Gould; [m.] F. W. Blount (Deceased), 13 June 1953, L. W. Garlick, 23 October 1982; [ch.] Colin P. Blount, Adrian F. Blount; [ed.] Albright S. Mod, Oldbury, Worcs; [occ.] Retired; [memb.] Shifnal Bowls Club, Rhyme Arrival, Parkinsons Disease Society; [oth. writ.] One published in "West Country Voices" by Anchor Books; [pers.] I love using words reflecting every day life, and try to add a little humour to make people smile. Inspired by patience strong. Life deals a blow, give something else a go in 1990 I was diagnosed with Parkinsons disease. I am still able to live a normal life.; [a.] Shifnal, Shropshire, UK

GARRATT, W. PEGGY FOLKARD

[b.] 31 October 1925, Georgetown, Dem.; [p.] Leon Harold H. R. Folkard, Thomanda L. Ward; [m.] Horace Ulric Garratt, 18 April 1949; [ed.] Kingston Methodist School Modern Educational High School; [occ.] Retired; [memb.] Invited to join Mensa I.Q. 147. various book and Music Clubs; [oth. writ.] Several poems, songs (lyrics and melodies) although I can not read or write music, hence the latter are on cassettes. Influenced by English poets especially those writings with military and patriotic flavours and Paul Robeson.; [pers.] My motto in life: "Love the Lord, Thy God, and Thy neighbour as Thyself."; [a.] Wisbech, Cambs, UK

GARRIOCK, JOLENE

[b.] 4 February 1983, Lerwick; [p.] John and Arlene Garriock; [ed.] Anderson High School; [occ.] Still at school; [oth. writ.] Everything, The Power Of Love, Funfairs, Danger Zone, Tearing Me In Half, Two Sides Of A Face, You'll Be The One To Cry and others; [pers.] I'm inspired by my own emotions and surroundings. I write about what I feel, see and hear.; [a.] Lerwick, Shetland, UK

GATE, HELEN FAY

[b.] 24 September 1973, Bulkington; [p.] Iris J. Harrison, David Harrison (Step-father), Thomas E. F. Miller (Father Deceased); [m.] Richard John Gate, 3 July 1993; [ed.] Stoke Park Senior School, Coventry Technical College for Dental Nursing Certificate; [occ.] Dental Nurse; [oth. writ.] I have been writing poetry for years, but until now, I have never sent any off her publishment.; [pers.] I strive to honor the good in the world, the love people have to offer. I share my grandfathers and my fathers love for literature and poetry. For the past three years it has been my husbands love and kindness that has encouraged and inspired me.; [a.] Coventry, West Midlands, UK

GATES, DORIS LAVINIA

[pen.] Doris L. Gates; [b.] 11 May 1916, Bromley, Kent; [p.] William and Elizabeth Ransom; [m.] William James Gates, 2 May 1936; [ch.] 3, 11 grandchildren and 16 great grandchildren; [ed.] Secondary school, Bromley Central School; [occ.] Widow; [oth. writ.] Poems published in local paper Basingstoke Gazette Extra; [pers.] I like my poems to reflect the way I view life; [a.] Hartley, Wintney, Hampshire, UK

GATFIELD, SHARON

[b.] 28 October 1961, London, UK; [p.] Mother: Maureen Gatfield; [ed.] Mount Grace School Church Road, Potters Bar, Hentfordshire; [occ.] Student; [oth. writ.] Numerous, Including: Dull Clouds, Half Smiling, Complete Peace, Gemma, (unpublished) Torment and The Dolphins; [pers.] I am studying english. I met a student 10 years ago studying english and education, I started to write small verses then and my interest great for poetry and reading in general.; [a.] Potters Bar, London, UK

GELLING, PATRICIA ANN

[pen.] Pat Gelling; [b.] 25 May 1943, Mexborough, S. Yorks; [p.] Emily and Horace (Bill) Toseland; [m.] Brian Gelling (Deceased), 30 August 1964; [ch.] Nicola and Sarah; [ed.] Ripon Girls' High School, Yorkshire Training College of Housecraft (Leeds); [occ.] Homemaker; [memb.] (Societies) Mananan Music Festival, Manx National Heritage Manx Astronomical Soc.; [oth. writ.] Several poems and songs, nothing previously submitted for publication.; [pers.] (Please include) My poems and songs are simply an expression of my love of God and his creation. I pray they may help others come to know Him.; [a.] Union Hills Nr Douglas, Isle of Man, UK

GEORGE, KATE-EMILY

[pen.] Kate-Emily George; [b.] 18 October 1979, Middlesex; [p.] Mrs. L. George and Mr. S. P. George; [ed.] Heathfield Infant and Junior School, Whitton Secondary School. Attending one of Two Colleges in September 1996; [hon.] School Bronze Certificate: Mathematical Challenge 1994, British Red Cross Certificate, Standard Course; [oth. writ.] Three poems in three separate books from 'anchor publishing.' One poem in a 'world vision' magazine in 1995 and chances of a poem in the 'National Anti - Vivisection Society' Magazine in July 1996, December 1996 edition; [pers.] I strive to help the world in all I write, mostly in my poems and short stories. I try to show my love for all things by capturing moments and keeping them on paper.; [a.] Whitton, Twickenham, Middlesex, UK

GEORGE, NICOLA

[b.] 12 November 1978, Aberystwyth; [p.] Roger George, Aneira George; [ed.] Tywyn School Gwynedd, took and passed 11 GCSE's. Currently studying for A levels in Ellesmere College. Geography music Business studies; [memb.] Chapel choir, Drama productions; [oth. writ.] I have a collection of poems, but this (Why Reality?) is the first entered into a competition; [pers.] In my writing I reflect life and how I see it during different situations.; [a.] Llwyngwril, Wales, UK

GIBBARD, ROSE E.

[pen.] Leoni Baker; [b.] 16 August 1920, Coventry, Warks; [p.] Edith and Major James Baker; [m.] Claud Gibbard (Deceased), 3 August 1940; [ch.] Two daughters, 1 son; [ed.] Holbrook Lane Elementary Girls, Coventry; [occ.] Retired Civil Servant; [memb.] Member of Choir, Artist (Amateur) Salvationist, Women's Group; [oth. writ.] I have had christian poems published in various church magazines locally and others.; [pers.] I like to write of things I experience or which I feel deeply about. I also like to introduce a touch of humour into my poetry.; [a.] Coventry, Warks, UK

GIBBS, FIONA ANITA
[pen.] Fiona Anita Gibbs; [b.] 22 October 1969, Taplow; [p.] Paul Dear, Joyce Dear; [m.] Paul Gibbs, 12 September 1992; [ch.] Hollie-Amy Doris; [ed.] Baylis Court Sec, Modern School for Girls, Slaigh-Langley College of FE Berkshire PCSC; [occ.] Healthcare Worker-Mental Health; [memb.] I.C.S., Home Study Courses (Student), Joint Helicopter Support Unit Army Wives Asso (U.K.), Whiteknight Dog Rescue; [hon.] Applicant of Mensa, Holder of Child Daycare - Child Psychology Diploma, Basic Ambulance Training Award-Diploma; [oth. writ.] Many poems written, most of which, express my innermost thoughts and feelings.; [pers.] To my Grandmother the late Doris Barker, from whom I gained much of my inspirations, to write. God bless her and may she rest in peace also a special thank you to my family for believing in me.; [a.] Odiham, Hants, UK

GIBSON, LILIAN
[b.] 22 September 1940, Glasgow; [p.] Agnes McBride, John McBride; [m.] Divorced 1971; [ch.] Angus Gibson; [ed.] North Kelvinside Secondary, Glasgow Scottish College of Commerce Jordanhill College of Education; [occ.] Retired Teacher; [memb.] Citizen's Theatre Society, Glasgow Charles Rennie Mackintosh Society, Glasgow; [oth. writ.] Short stories street/tenement poems; [pers.] Kindness, especially to other Partick Thistle supporters.; [a.] East Kilbride, Scotland

GIBSON, SHIRLEY
[pen.] Felicity Johnson; [b.] 8 December 1941, Essex; [oth. writ.] Many poems, also stories. This is first attempt at publication; [pers.] This poem was written for the marriage of my son and daughter-in-law.; [a.] Cranham, Essex, UK

GIBSON, SYLVIA M.
[pen.] Sylvia Colebourne, Esse Gee; [b.] 17 July 1926, Coalville; [p.] Alfred and May Colebourne; [m.] Edward Dennis, July 1947; [ch.] Beaulah Georgina; [ed.] 'Ladies of Mary' convent Sheffield University; [occ.] Writer; [hon.] L.R.A.M. Srn. Scm. Cups and Medals Singing; [oth. writ.] Short stories children's, present novel in progress; [pers.] Having been nurse/midwife - my writings tend to be about people, both humorous and factual. I people watch, and listen to conversations, for inspiration; [a.] Barrow-in-Furness, Cumbria, UK

GILBERT, MRS. S. V.
[pen.] Sandra Gilbert; [b.] 14 March 1942, Essex; [p.] Vera and Rena Atkins; [m.] Bob, 26 December 1961; [ch.] Mark; [pers.] This is dedicated to my first grand child. Bethany Jade Harriet Gilbert; [a.] Harwich, Essex, UK

GILDER, ROSE CARPENTER
Rose Carpenter, born of middle-class family, lived in average sized villa in Maidenhead, Berkshire. Started writing verse in Christmas cards and Birthday cards to relatives and friends whilst in her 20's. Married Mr. Stan Gilder in 1942. He was the driving force that encouraged her to carry her talents further. Friends who read her numerous poems call her "The Peoples' Poet" as they are easily understood by people in all walks of life. "Why Worry?" is a typical example of her writing. It is her first poem to be exhibited for the public everywhere to read.

GILES, MRS. PAULINE
[b.] 18 November 1959, Bishop Auckland; [m.] John Richard Giles, 26 August 1992; [ed.] Bishop Barrington Comp Bishop Auckland; [occ.] Residential Care Officer working with people with learning disabilities; [oth. writ.] Unpublished works; [pers.] I write on impulse, due to what and how I'm feeling. I have very strong feelings on what I write about.; [a.] Bishop Auckland, Durham, UK

GILL, PAMELA ELIZABETH
[pen.] Pamela E. Gill; [b.] 5 February 1942, Corbridge; [p.] George William - Elizabeth Ridley; [m.] Andrew Gill, 4 July 1964; [ch.] Michael Andrew - Carol Andrea; [ed.] Secondary Modern; [occ.] Retail Sales Manager; [memb.] Wylam and Ovingham Art Club; [oth. writ.] This is my first attempt to have any of my work published. Though I have put together a small book of poems with illustrations.; [pers.] I write about things that touch me inside about life itself and the beauty around me. I record them so my children/grandchildren will know how I felt.; [a.] Prudhoe, Northumberland, UK

GILL, SOPHIA
[b.] 3 May 1979, Kingston; [p.] Shamine Gill, Martin Gill; [ed.] Surbiton High School, Richmond College; [occ.] Student; [hon.] Regional Finalist in the Woolwich National Schools College Competition; [oth. writ.] Many other poems that reflect my life in general, which so far have been inspired by my family, friends and especially rue.; [pers.] I would never have made it without my friends and family, especially Morris Zwi who encouraged me to keep writing. Thank you. Life is but a meaning without a true way.; [a.] Teddington, Middlesex, UK

GILLIARD, SANDRA
[b.] 25 December 1966, Sidcup, Kent; [p.] Jean and Don Gilliard; [ed.] Hurst Primary School, Chislehurst and Sidcup Grammar, Avery Hill College; [occ.] Patient Admin. Officer in a Hospital; [memb.] Various mini owners clubs, Bat Groups, Falcon Archery Club; [hon.] B.Ed degree (in Education); [oth. writ.] None published as yet. Various poems and children's stories not yet submitted for publication; [pers.] The voyage has just begun - let it be at full sail.; [a.] Bexley, Kent, UK

GILLINGS, SONIA
[b.] 17 February 1964, Wanstead, Essex; [p.] Barbara and Colin Gillings; [ed.] West Hatch Technical High School, Harlow College, now doing C & G Photography at evening classes; [occ.] Psychotherapist/Hypnotherapist, p/t poet; [memb.] Mensa, Rushymead Sailing Club, Green Circle; [oth. writ.] Have had poems published in 29 anthologies (not including this one). I am just about to published a book of my own poetry. I have also written a poem for the Mensa Golden Anniversary concert this year. Have also had a couple of articles published in magazines.; [pers.] I write about life, as it is, as it was and as it should be. I write about the good and the bad, the happy and the sad. I take inspiration from life's experience, so that sometimes it is serious, sometimes comical.; [a.] Loughton, Essex, UK

GIRON, LEROY JESS
[V.I.P] #P0528151-031; [b.] 5 February 1950, Delta, CO; [p.] Silverio Giron, Margaret Vialpando; [ch.] Tanya, Jesse, and Darold; [occ.] Tax Accountant; [memb.] Church - New Hope Ministries; [oth. writ.] Essay on drug addiction title "My Affair"; [pers.] I'm a strong believer in Jesus Christ. Also a firm believer in family unity. They are only mistakes if we don't learn from them. Every one deserves a second chance.

GISSARA, ELISABETTE PUGLISI
[b.] 4 September 1945, Ragusa, Italy; [p.] Lusia and Bruno Puglisi; [m.] Aldo Gissara, 13 April 1966; [ch.] 2 Paola and Bruno; [occ.] Housewife, Poetess and Writer; [memb.] The Poetry Society, Manchester Poetry; [hon.] 1st prize in Italy in the "Anfors d'oro" competion held by ENdAS in Raguna in 1981; [oth. writ.] Several books of poems, one of it will be published next year in Italy. The title in English is: To You With Endless Love.; [pers.] I believe in love which is the enchantment of life my main source of inspiration in God; [a.] Didsbury, Manchester, UK

GIZMAN, MR. Z.
[b.] Istanbul; [p.] Deceased; [m.] Mrs. R. Gizman, 17 December 1953; [ed.] Italian Commercial College, Turkish High Studies in Economic and Commerces, Radio announcer of BBC Foreign Broadcasting; [occ.] Retired; [memb.] Competitors Companion; [hon.] One of my poem has been published in another anthology; [pers.] Poetry, in our day is a living and increasingly popular art. Most of the poems are rather reflective of the concerns people have for the disruptive and agitated worlds poems ought to be inspirational and not a fancy free rhyming.; [a.] London, Middlesex

GLASS, R.
[pen.] Ricci; [b.] 8 March 1935, Muirton-Drem; [p.] Deceased; [m.] Sarah, 23 March 1957; [ch.] 2 Boys, 1 Girl; [ed.] Higher and AEC Class I; [occ.] Semi Retired; [memb.] Royal Scots Dragoon Guards Association Ex Army Club; [oth. writ.] Other poems which have not been published; [pers.] Most of my work is based on real life romance and most of all how I see things happening. I am a very close person to my wife and all my family, also maybe a sentimentalist.; [a.] Haddington, Eastlothian, UK

GOLDSMITH, SHARON
[b.] 13 August 1959, Stevenage, Herts; [p.] Shirley Joyce; [m.] Michael Goldsmith, 15 October 1993; [ch.] Reece, Alan; [ed.] Comprehensive School Catering College; [occ.] Chef (working for special needs); [memb.] Active member of my local church; [pers.] I dedicate my poem to the memory of my beautiful daughter 'Elise'.; [a.] Stevenage, Herts, UK

GOLDSTEIN, EVE
[b.] 17 May 1946, Sunderland; [p.] Harry Cohen, Dorrie Cohen; [m.] Nat Goldstein, 25 May 1969; [ch.] Elizabeth, Laura, David, Stephanie; [ed.] Parliament Hill School, Goldsmith's College; [occ.] Teacher; [memb.] Creative Writing Class; [oth. writ.] Poetry for my own pleasure.; [pers.] I enjoy writing poetry, mainly to express my own feelings about personal events.; [a.] London, UK

GONSALVES, STELLA M.
[b.] 5 June 1965, London; [memb.] Mensa, The High IQ Society; [pers.] My influences are somewhat eclectic, ranging from the classics to rock music, whilst my writing tends to focus on the darker or more obscure aspects of life and beyond...; [a.] Waltham Cross, Hertfordshire, UK

GONZALEZ, OSCAR
[b.] 6 August 1976; [p.] Juan Jose Gonzalez, Maria Gonzalez; [ed.] Salvation College, St. Dominic's Sixth Form College; [oth. writ.] Several poems published in school magazine.

GOOCH, JOAN ELIZABETH
[pen.] Joan Elizabeth; [m.] Arthur William Gooch, 20 June 1964; [ch.] Two daughters both married; [occ.] Housewife; [a.] Norwich, Norfolk, UK

GOODALL, MARC
[b.] 14 July 1971, Wirksworth, Derbyshire; [p.] Carol, Christopher; [ed.] West Park Community School (Derby) 1982-1989, Wilmorton Further Education College 1990-92 (Derby), Arden School of Theatre 92-96 (Manchester); [occ.] Actor; [memb.] Good Companions Musical Society; [hon.] B.A. Hons in Acting; [a.] Manchester, Greater Manchester, UK

GOODEY, ELIZABETH GARRETT
[b.] 25 May 1918, Colombo, Ceylon (Sri Lanka); [p.] Muriel Garrett, Rev. Alfred Norton Garrett; [m.] Stanley Goodey, 9 December 1950; [ch.] Richard Geoffrey, Julian Francis; [ed.] Oxford University 1945-1948, St. Hilda's College; [occ.] Retired Teacher; [memb.] Sang in Operatic Society at Oxford (Gilbert and Sullivan and Mozart). Served in the WAAF during most of the war former member of the Oxford Author-Critic Club white at Oxford; [hon.] M.A. Oxon (English Language and Literature) Silver medal verse speaking - The poetry society; [oth. writ.] Several poems published in Oxford magazines between 1945-48. Have written a great deal of poetry and some music.; [a.] Livingston, West Lothian, UK

GOODSON, SHAUN
[b.] 4 February 1972, Freethorpe; [p.] Gordon Goodson, Pauline Goodson; [ed.] Acle High School, Great Yarmouth College of further Education; [occ.] Retail Cashier; [memb.] Freethorpe Football, Darts, Petanque Club, Halvergate Table Tennis Club; [hon.] Nine G.C.S.E., City and Guilds Communication Skills; [pers.] I hope that everyone enjoys my poems as much as I enjoy writing them I have been greatly influenced by my family to write poems.; [a.] Great Yarmouth, Norfolk, UK

GOODWIN, MARION IRENE
[b.] 9 September 1950, Bracknell; [p.] Elsie and Percy Rollett; [m.] Dennis Goodwin, 8 March 1969; [ch.] Nikki Jane and Terry Neil; [ed.] Sandy Lane Infant's and Junior School Bracknell Borbugh Green Secondary School, Bracknell; [occ.] Housewife; [oth. writ.] Nine poems, published by small publishers; [pers.] I inlay writing my poems and would like to share them with others.; [a.] Bracknell, Berkshire, UK

GORDON, MARY
[b.] 24 January 1948, Kent; [ch.] (Three) Liz, Julie and Paul; [occ.] Librarian at Local School; [oth. writ.] Lots of poems and some stories.; [pers.] I listen. I think. I feel then I write.; [a.] Ballinrobe, Co Mayo, UK

GOSLING, NANCY
[pen.] Nan Gosling; [b.] 2 June 1914, Longton, Stoke-on-Trent; [p.] James and Emily Bennett; [m.] William Ronald Gosling (Deceased); [a.] Dresden, Longton, Staffs, UK

GRAINGE, HARRY
[b.] 31 March 1921, Scotland; [p.] George and Jane Dowson Grainge; [m.] Kay Grainge (nee Cornish), 1 November 1950; [ch.] Andrew Dowson Grainge and Julia Margaret Palmour (Ne'e Grainge); [ed.] Bellshill Academy Scotland; [occ.] Retired; [memb.] Assoc. and International Accounts (Fellow) Institute of Management (Fellow) Chartered Institute of Arbitrators (Fellow), Wig and Pen Club (Life Member) City Livery Club; [hon.] Freeman Office of London Livery Man of the City of London, Founder-Member of the Worshipful company of Arbitrators (A City of London Livery Company); [oth. writ.] Novels (Seeking a publisher), "The Hallgarten Papers," "The Cookbook Test," "The Crime Of Marshall Wimberley," "Luckenbooth," short stories. Children's stories.; [a.] Brentwood, Essex, UK

GRANQVIST-AHMED, SELIM
[pen.] Selim; [b.] 17 March 1986, London; [p.] Dr. and Mrs. Granqvist-Ahmed; [ed.] Pupil (Chigwell School) Lower II; [occ.] Pupil; [oth. writ.] Short stories Young Times Magazine Bahrain; [a.] Westdown Rd, London, UK

GRANT, ELIZABETH
[b.] 1 February 1949, Birmingham; [p.] Arthur and Vera Bridger; [m.] Keith Grant, 20 September 1969; [ch.] Paul and Suzi; [ed.] Harborne Hill Comprehensive, Gastroent - Erology Course at Coventry University; [occ.] Senior Clinical Physiologist - London; [memb.] Until recently I was on the committee and sang in the massed hospitals choir raising funds for the Malcolm Sargeant Cancer Fund for Children; [oth. writ.] A selection of romantic poetry and I have recently begun my first novel which hopefully will be completed by the end of the year.; [pers.] My love of Greek Mythology inspired some of the earlier poems but more recently I have based the writings on fact which takes an enormous amount of interesting research.; [a.] Bridgnorth, Shropshire, UK

GRASSI, PETER
[b.] 26 October 1946, Bath, Avon; [m.] Fiance - Frances; [ch.] Oliver and Katie (Teenagers); [ed.] Oldfield Boys Schools, Bath; [occ.] Carpenter; [oth. writ.] Have written a book of humorous verse. (Unpublished as yet!) From my experiences while managing a restaurant in London from eight years.; [pers.] Only humans laugh and we're only human!; [a.] Mortlake, London, UK

GRASSICK, JAMES D. F.
[b.] 12 February 1973, Windsor; [p.] Brian and Annette; [ed.] Long and mostly unpleasant; [occ.] Constructor of TV stations, electric oranges and more; [oth. writ.] Now writing unusual verse, and science fiction shorts for those who dare.; [pers.] It will happen my poems included in this volume were written ten years ago when I was thirteen; [a.] Gerrards Cross, Bucks, UK

GRAVENOR, WILMA JAYNE
[b.] 11 June 1937, Barry, South Wales; [m.] Lewis Price Gravenor (Deceased 1974), December 1958; [ch.] Two daughters (Five grandchildren); [ed.] Barry Grammar School, Cardiff College of Art, University of Wales, Cardiff; [occ.] Retired Teacher; [hon.] Won several National Photographic competitions.; [oth. writ.] Short stories, poems and articles in magazines, newspapers and books.; [pers.] Have enjoyed writing since I was a small child, but the death of my husband in 1974 (when he was 39 yrs. old) has affected me deeply. I see the world more clearly now - and know it to be so fragile.; [a.] Taunton, Somerset, UK

GRAY, CHERYL
[pen.] Shelly Anne; [b.] 27 September 1980, Hartlepool; [p.] Mrs. P. Lodge; [ed.] Brierton Comprehensive Starting College in September CH, Pool; [occ.] Student; [memb.] Fishing Club. (H.M.S.C.A.C.); [oth. writ.] Poems written for people in the family; [pers.] I like to express my own personal feelings in my poems.; [a.] Hartlepool, H/pool, UK

GREEN, COLIN
[pen.] Sea Green; [b.] 6 July 1920, South Kirkby; [p.] Arthur Green and Alice Lowe; [m.] Margaret Buckley (died 6 July 1989), 11 August 1945; [ch.] Roger and Peter; [ed.] Elementary; [occ.] Retired; [memb.] South Elmsall Operatic Society, South Kirkby Sea Cadets. 'Elm Valley' Royal Naval Association. 'Burma Star' Association.; [hon.] Two merit awards from 'The Sir Arthur Markham Memorial Prize'; [oth. writ.] My autobiography 'Seagreen Flections'. Two extacts from this published in the local paper.; [pers.] Trying to reflect human nature.; [a.] South Elmsall, Yorks, UK

GREEN, MARJORIE E.
[pen.] Meg; [b.] 4 August 1921, London; [p.] Edith May Gamble, Frank Jabez Gamble; [m.] Norman Green, 15 September 1955; [ed.] State and Secondary Schools Courses during service with the Auxiliary Territorial Service. W.E.A. Creative Writing; [occ.] Retired Local Government Officer; [memb.] Various organizations covering youth work, animal and bird protection societies, Management Committee of Local Village Hall, Executive Committee of local Community Association. Amersham Dog Training Club. Women's Institute. Cruse. Amersham Society; [a.] Amersham, Buckinghamshire, UK

GREEN, RICHARD
[b.] 2 September 1953, Rinteln, Germany; [p.] Joseph Green and Jane Green; [m.] Petra Green, 30 December 1975; [ch.] Jerrie-Anne Green; [ed.] H. M. Forces School Leeds, Polytechnic (H.M.C.); [occ.] 'Regional Account Manager' Italy; [memb.] Olgiata Country Club; [oth. writ.] Selection of Poems; [pers.] "May The Force Be With You"; [a.] Chinnor, Oxon, UK

GREENOW, ALEX G.
[b.] 7 April 1956, Cardiff; [p.] Bobby Greenow, Rosemary Greenow; [m.] Julie Evans, 18 December 1976; [ch.] Kirsty Rhian, Kristy Anne, Kimberly Jane; [ed.] Hardye's School, Southampton Polytechnic, The Polytechnic of Wales; [occ.] Mineworker, Tower Colliery; [memb.] National Union of Mineworkers, Rhigos Fishing Club; [hon.] Runner up Cynon Valley strongest man event 1995 in Aid of local charities; [oth. writ.] Article published in Union Newsletter "Seren y Cwmoedd", during miners' strike; [pers.] The harsh reality of life experiences and observation have been the triggers and inspiration of my literary work to date. I enjoyed reading Chaucer at school.; [a.] Rhigos, Rhondda Cynon, Taff, UK

GRIEVE, ALISON SARAH
[b.] 25 May 1967, Harpender; [p.] Mr. and Mrs. M. B. Grieve; [ed.] Educate at Manland Primary, St George's Harpenden and John Mason Abingdon. Went to Bournemouth university and did HND catering and institutional management; [occ.] Duty Manager of the three thoughs hotel; [pers.] As a woman with dyslexia has a lot to battle through and just to be able to write for pleasure is a great achievement, through my love of nature and my strong christian faith, I love to bring cheer to the world even hope through my poems and short stories.; [a.] Yeovil, Somerset, UK

GRIFFIN, MARION
[b.] 2 March 1940, Bridport; [p.] Stanley and Bobbie Beer; [m.] Douglas Griffin, 21 November 1993; [ch.] Catherine, George, Lindsey and Sandra; [ed.] Bridport Grammar School; [occ.] Secretary/PA; [memb.] Exeter Library; [oth. writ.] Very many poems, mostly coming through from "The Other Side". All with good messages for our reading and following.; [pers.] Poems are written with love and hopeful advice for the readers.; [a.] Exeter, Devon, UK

GRIGGS, LYNNE
[b.] 9 September 1945, Herne Village; [p.] Muriel and Peter Hawkes; [m.] Tomy James Griggs, 19 January 1991; [ch.] Gary, Hayley, Natalie and Carly; [ed.] Archbishop of Canterbury School; [occ.] Dog breeding (boxers); [oth. writ.] First published poem; [pers.] My writing is inspired by all that stirs the soul, and is close to the heart. Nature, children, animals, love etc. My village up bringing lends a certain ease to my inspiration and I'm excited not so much by success but to see others truly enjoy my work.; [a.] Herne Bay, Kent, UK

GROVE, DIANA
[p.] Eric & Betty Empson; [m.] Barry Grove; [ch.] two: Mandy and Jane; [ed.] The Princess Margaret Boarding School for Girls, Woodford Bridge, Essex; Cheltenham College of Art; Cheltenham Technical College; [hon.] O Level History of Embroidery; [pers.] I write what I see and feel, in the hope of giving others, through writing, an awareness of what nature has to offer, since nature is what inspires me.; [a.] Coventry, Warwickshire

GUIBERT, ALEJANDRA
[b.] 3 October 1958, Buenos Aires; [p.] Fernando Guibert and Elba Riera de Guibert; [ed.] Instituto Nacional Superior En Lenguas Vivas, Buenos Aires; [occ.] Writer, Translator; [hon.] Fringe First Special Award at Edinburgh Fringe Festival 1988 with the play sideways glance; [oth. writ.] (All writings unpublished), Desire (Novel) 1995, Demons (Poetry Book) 1994, Poetry in two impossible loves (Poetry) 1993, Carmela (Play) 1991 Madeleine (Screenplay) 1991-1996, Sideways Glance (Play) 1987.; [a.] London, UK

GULLEY, MERILYN E. A.
[pen.] Merilyn Gulley; [b.] 23 February 1951, Hooe Nr. Plymouth; [p.] Lionel Lydon, Beryl Lydon; [m.] Geoffrey Gulley, 10 June 1972; [ed.] Plympton Secondary School; [occ.] Disabled Housewife; [oth. writ.] Two poems published.; [pers.] I love trying to write poetry as it feels so nice if I see other people getting as much pleasure out of reading my work as I did when writing it as I think that's how poetry should always be written to give as much pleasure to others as yourself.; [a.] Ivybridge, S. Devon, UK

GUNTER, GARY
[b.] 17 August 1939, Ebbw Vale, Gwent; [m.] Carol Anne Gunter, 27 July 1963; [ch.] Katharine and Michael; [ed.] Secondary School and Technical College; [occ.] Retired; [memb.] Local Drama Company; [oth. writ.] Newspaper stories, technical work; [pers.] Since retired, have taken up writing, as a hobby, and researching my uncle's squadron 12 Bonder Command. Also my family history.; [a.] Cumbran, Gwent, UK

GUPPY, SARAH
[pen.] Sarah Guppy; [b.] 26 January 1957, Auckland, New Zealand; [ed.] Diocesan School (NZ), Auckland Technical Institute (NZ), Morley College, London (UK); [occ.] Artist, Gilder, Poet; [memb.] Royal Academy, London (UK), Artist Alliance, Auckland NZ; [pers.] As an artist, poetry has become a word painting, a place to express metaphor with economy, flavour and imagery. I have a love of earth mystical writings and diverse religious philosophies, particularly jalal-up-din-ruini.

HACKLEY, JACQUELINE ANDREA
[pen.] Jackie Greenway; [b.] 6 September 1964, Keyworth, Nottingham; [p.] Christopher David Greenway, Carol Molly Greenway; [m.] Paul Anthony Hackley, 10 July 1993; [ed.] St. Robert of Newminster Comprehensive, Washington, Tyne and Wear, Teesside Polytechnic, Middlesbrough; [occ.] Admin./Finance Assistant, (Family Section), Hereford Magistrates' Court; [memb.] I am not a member of any societies as such but have recently completed a barn conversion together with my husband (we lived in ca caravan for 14 months whilst doing this I love films (cg Steel Magnolias, When Harry met Sally, Terms of Endearment) about 'people', love walking our dog (a beautiful German pointer called 'Teale'), listening to rock/pop music and Simon and Garfunkel and going to rock/pop concert and working in the garden. Also love going for a spin on the motorbike (one of my passions) - on the back of course!; [oth. writ.] Several poems written for friends and family (eg fathers 50th birthday) (I have written poetry since about the age of 10, but after losing my sister 6 years ago after the birth of her first baby I find myself feeling things very deeply and writing poetry is an easy way to 'empty out' some emotions. This particular poem is only part of a longer poem I actually wrote for a lady of work who lost her husband to cancer.); [pers.] I enjoy writing poetry and find it flows very fluently when writing for friends and family. I am always able to write when people have endured some sadness and try to express that everyone experiences the same emotions to some degree and a man is never alone in feeling any emotion - also try to keep it light-hearted.; [a.] Hereford, Hereford and Worcester, UK

HAGGER, CINDY
[pen.] Cindy Brewster; [b.] 13 October 1922, Dorking, Surrey; [p.] Frank Popplewell; [m.] Doris Popplewell, 19 August 1944; [ch.] Kenneth Jack, Ernest Ralph; [ed.] Village School Holmwood, Dorking, Surrey, no other education, have tried to educate myself further; [occ.] Housewife; [oth. writ.] Several essays and poems in magazines. Have six christian poems out in hardback books recently printed. Am in the process of completing a new poem called "Yester-Years"; [pers.] I try, by my poems, to reflect the wonder of God's creation. The seasons, the animals, birds and flowers, to bring to mankind the simple beauty of the world around us, that money cannot buy. I am inspired by these things.; [a.] Romford, Essex, UK

HAGGETT, PAULINE
[b.] 7 September 1942, Salisbury; [p.] Charles and Sylvia Arney; [m.] Gordon Haggett, 11 February 1978; [ch.] I have 2 daughters, 4 sons of former marriage; [ed.] Seconder School; [occ.] House wife can no longer work due to spine trouble; [oth. writ.] 1 poem published in a paper, 1 poem published in the sun's book for Dunblane's Angels; [pers.] A physical disability myself I find enjoyment in writing poems and thank a caring husband for his help and love.; [a.] Bridport, Dorset, UK

HAIGHTON, REV. MICHAEL E.
[b.] 10 October 1952, Nantwich, Cheshire; [p.] Edred and Maureen Haighton; [ed.] Nantwich Manor Rd School, Hampton House and Belmont Hall Boarding School. Cliff College (Bible training); [occ.] Minister of the Christian Church.; [hon.] None, only R.S.A. public speaking; [oth. writ.] (not in print yet) Numerous hymns, several poems and a couple of short stories; [pers.] Have always liked English, writing, etc. Become a Christian at 16 and love to write in verse and prose about my living faith. Currently a free church minister in the fens - Nr Wisbech; [a.] Tyddpoke Wisbeck, Cambs, UK

HALEY, MRS. SUSAN J.
[pen.] Sue J. Haley; [b.] 22 May 1958, Middlesex; [p.] Audrey May Budden (Maiden), Kenneth Victor Payne; [m.] Mr. Mark G. Haley, 18 April 1981; [ch.] Adam-Mark, Laura- Louise; [ed.] Longford Comp Tachbrook Rd, Feltham, Middx.; [occ.] Housewife; [hon.] Only this one! "So Proud"; [oth. writ.] Couple of poems published in womens magazines and have many more hopefuls; [pers.] Family life has a great influence in my work, and the pleasures of life as it unfolds "is life what you make it?...Or does fate lend a helping hand?"; [a.] Feltham Bedfort, Middx, UK

HALL, DAVID ANTHONY CLIFFORD
[b.] 9 October 1955, Isle of Wight; [p.] Fredrick William Hall, Florance Nelly Hall; [m.] Divorced; [ch.] Adam David, Patrick Hall, Leonie Susan Bridget Hall, Matthew Andrew, Simon Hall; [ed.] West Wight Secondary School no Qualification's; [occ.] (Disabled) Software Design Engineer; [hon.] BSC Software Design (first), B.A. Economic's (first), GCE History, Music and English Lit, GSC History, Math's, Music and English Lit, C and G's Levels 1/2/3 I.T., Advance Diploma I.T., C and G's Levels 1/2/3 Accounts, R.S.A Levels 1/2 I.T., C and G's Level's 1/2/3 Catering, OND. Hotel and Catering Management, IT Information Technology; [oth. writ.] None ever publish; [pers.] Since becoming disabled and after many set back's I am still standing and fighting.; [a.] Ryde, Hampshire, UK

HALL, MRS. JANET
[pen.] Janet Hall; [b.] Rossendale; [p.] Tom and Evelyn Eastwood; [m.] John Graham Hall, 22 October 1966; [ch.] Michael, Geoffrey and Julie; [ed.] St. Josephs School R.C. Bacup Lancs; [occ.] Housewife; [hon.] Poems published in two books, some in local newspaper; [oth. writ.] Write Verses on Request for Birthdays etc.; [pers.] I want to cheer up everyone with my poems in this hard going world.; [a.] W. Worth, Rochdale, Lancs, UK

HALL, JOY
[b.] May 20th 1930, Somersham; [p.] Milly Barlow, Percy Barlow; [m.] Marshall Hall (now deceased), married September 24th 1952; [ch.] Enid Gibbs, Vivienne Benton, Colin Hall; [ed.] Slepe Hall Private School for girls at St Ives in Huntingdonshire; [occ.] retired; [memb.] Agricultural Assoc., Somersham, Friendship Club, Somersham, Palace Social Club, Somersham, Ivy Leaf Club, St Ives; [oth. writ.] Arrival Press Poetry Institute of the British Isles, Ltd., local newspaper, Radio Cambridge; [pers.] I've been writing poems since 1983 and they have for the first time been published 1995 and now 1996. I enjoy writing poetry about everything in life.; [a.] Somersham, Cambs

HALL, KAREN GEORGINA
[pen.] Karen G. Hall; [b.] 17 June 1970, Luton, Bedfordshire; [p.] Miss Jacquiline Heighes; [ed.] Morris Secondary School Skegness, Lincolnshire; [occ.] Managers of "Holland and Barrett" Health Food/Natural Remedies; [oth. writ.] Several poem published for poetry now publications, articles in local news media, approx 800 personal poems written about life, love and the universe.; [pers.] "Believe...and so it shall be!", "The world is swamped by rules and regulations, writing is my freedom, it is my escape...; [a.] Boston, Lincolnshire, UK

HALL, KATIE LEIGH
[pen.] Katie Leigh Hall; [b.] 30 December 1976, Shepperton; [p.] Brian and Faye Hall; [ed.] Thamesmead Secondary School, Bournemouth University; [occ.] Student; [memb.] Member of Bournemouth University Student Union; [hon.] Award for English Literature at Thamesmead Secondary School; [oth. writ.] Various poems written at school and continued as a hobby; [pers.] Through poetry I can express my opinions, feelings and ideals poetry is my personal way of expressing my inner-most emotions.; [a.] Shepperton, Middlesex, UK

HALL, MICHAEL
[pen.] James Silver; [b.] 30 November 1976, Glasgow; [p.] Michael Hall, Helen Hall; [ed.] St. Andrew's Secondary School; [memb.] British Mensa Society; [hon.] Physics and Chemistry awards. Also an award from Mensa; [pers.] I believe in man's existential right to determine his own destiny. My greatest influence has been the poetry of Jim Morrison.; [a.] Springboig, Glasgow, UK

HALL, PETER
[b.] 13 August 1979, Cardiff; [p.] John Hall and Morna Hall; [ed.] Bishops of Llandaff Church in Wales High School; [occ.] VIth Form at Bishops of Llandaff; [memb.] Cardiff Wargames Club, Whitechurch Badminton Club; [hon.] Poetry prize at school speech day; [pers.] I wish to show the torture one soul can have for being original or different, for being themselves and influences include the early romantic and 20th century poets.; [a.] Cardiff, Cardiff, UK, CF4 7EL

HALL, RUBY PATRICIA MARY
[pen.] Ruby Hall; [b.] 28 December 1936, Upton Snodsbury; [p.] Edith and Thomas Camden MBE; [m.] Frederick James George Hall, 20 April 1957; [ch.] Carole-Ann and Martin (Ben and Tim) (Grandchildren); [ed.] Upton Snodsbury Coe School Pershore High School; [occ.] Housewife; [oth. writ.] One story forty poems one being published in "Voices of the Wind"; [pers.] Always lived in village. Married 39 years former village correspondent BBC. Hereford and Worcester radio 2 Worcester Berrow's Journal member of Upton Snodsbury branch Mother's Union and Correspondent Secretary. Takes an active part in village life. Started writing poems 2 years ago find it very relaxing; [a.] Worcester, Worcestershire, UK

HALLIDAY, BRENDA
[b.] 19 June 1945, Glasgow; [p.] Deceased; [m.] Stuart, 17 June 1988; [ch.] 2 grown up, 8 grandchildren; [ed.] In a Glasgow primary then Junior Sec Aberdeen never did too well; [occ.] Housewife; [memb.] Spiritualist church Bowling Club dollar Clackmaninshire Scotland on church committee fund raiser; [hon.] healing certificate 2nd year, honour of being part of the cycle of life; [oth. writ.] Some short stories though never any published and more poems writing hope we have more dealing in this sphere; [pers.] I have always fancied seeing my name on the front of a book even if it was only 1st and last time I reckon to me it would say yes you have done it I would be over the moon; [a.] Grangemouth, Stirlingshire, Scotland

HALLIDAY, CHRISTINE JAY
[pen.] Joy Holden; [b.] 5 January 1953, Sheffield; [p.] Florence and Leonard Townsend; [m.] Brian Halliday, 17 May 1988; [ch.] Stuart Leonard Halliday (3 1/2 yrs); [ed.] Silverdale Secondary, Sheffield Granville College, Sheffield; [occ.] Retired (Health Grounds), Ward Sister; [pers.] I often marvel at nature's creativity and find this fascinating topic. Writing comedy verse is particularly enjoyable.; [a.] Dundee, Tayside, UK

HAMILL, SANDRA
[b.] 24 July 1965, Lewisham; [p.] Arthur and Janet Page; [m.] Peter Hamill, 14 March 1986; [ch.] Leeann, Jack, Sarah-Kay; [ed.] Thomas Tallis Comp. School; [occ.] Housewife; [hon.] My three children are honours beyond words; [oth. writ.] Tool Box stories awaiting publication; [pers.] To create a humorous and fantasy world and achieve an ambition for myself and family.; [a.] Grove Park, London, UK

HAMMOND, CHRISTINE
[pen.] Christine Hammond; [b.] 11 October 1942, Stirling, Scotland; [m.] Divorced Douglas Hammond, November 1980; [ch.] Richard, Christine, Elizabeth; [ed.] Clydebank High School Scotland; [occ.] Nanny to a little girl in Jersey; [memb.] When I lived in Scotland, I was a member of Tayside Flying Club; [hon.] Played piano at the Glasgow Music Festival in my Teens (13); [oth. writ.] Several poems published in publishers 'Collected poems' 1994; [pers.] Influenced with the poems by Helen Steiner Rice. Simple but with so much meaning; [a.] St. Saviour, Jersey, Channel Islands, UK

HAMMOND, JOYCE
[b.] 14 May 1932, Gorleston-on-Sea, Norfolk; [p.] Alice and Sidney Farman; [m.] Frederick Brewster Hammond, 23 June 1951; [ch.] Keith and Susan; [ed.] Gorleston Secondary Girls School; [occ.] Housewife; [memb.] The Broadland Marquetry Club, The great Yarmouth, W.I., The Northgate Hospital, Retirement Fellowship; [oth. writ.] Have had other poems published; [pers.] I have been writing poetry since I was a child, I feel it is a gift, and like to share it with others.; [a.] Great Yarmouth, Norfolk, UK

HAMMOND, MARK
[b.] 6 February 1969, Northampton; [p.] Mike and Josie Hammond; [ed.] Wood Lane School, Ealing Green College Thames Valley Univ.; [occ.] Mature student (Thames Valley Univ.); [hon.] G.C.S.E English, G.C.S.E Psychology (Studying for BSC Psychology); [oth. writ.] First Piece Of Writing published; [pers.] Throughout my life I have experienced many 'sad times'. I find that if I write about these struggles it does not only give me the strength to carry on, but also allows me to express myself.; [a.] West Ealing, London, UK

HAMMOND, TINA LAURA
[b.] 9 December 1968, Bexley; [p.] Ronald Holland, Diane Holland; [m.] Antony John Hammond, 17 June 1989; [ch.] Daniel James Clark Hammond, 1 November 1995; [ed.] Howbury Grange Technology School, Erith College of Technology; [occ.] Beauty Therapist and hairdresser; [memb.] British Association of Beauty Therapist and Cosmetologist The Society of Genealogists; [hon.] Honours Electrolysis, honours Babtac Body Therapy; [pers.] My work is influenced by real things that matter with a touch of mystery and enchantment.; [a.] Headcorn, Kent, UK

HANCOCK, SIMON
[b.] 9 March 1964, Exeter; [p.] Eric, Enid Hancock; [m.] Louise, 4 May 1991; [ch.] Oliver, Gaia; [ed.] St Thomas High, Exeter College, University College London; [occ.] Manager of Training Dept.; [memb.] Institute of Financial Flaming Charterer Insurance Institute; [hon.] Psychology BSC; [oth. writ.] Various poems; [pers.] If I can tough one fellow traveller and make their journey less burdened I can sleep easier.; [a.] Punnetts Town, E. Sussex, UK

HANLEY, DEBORAH
[b.] 22 September 1966, West Midlands; [p.] Barbara Hanley, Frances Hanley; [ed.] Brownhills Community School, University of Central England; [occ.] District Manager, Norfolk Careers Services; [pers.] I write from the heart, using my own personal experiences of life and those around me; [a.] Norwich, Norfolk, UK

HANN, NATALIE PARSONS
[b.] 18 July 1964, Swindon, Wilts; [p.] Roy and Barbara Hinchliffe; [m.] David, 14 June 1986; [occ.] Part Time Revenue Officer for the Inland Revenue; [memb.] English Heritage; [pers.] If you don't try you never know what you might achieve.; [a.] Swindon, Wilts, UK

HANNEY, EMILY
[ed.] B.A.; [occ.] Teaching (Retired); [oth. writ.] About thirty poems, three or four put to music. Three plays-two of them for a Dublin theatre competition and one for Cafe theatre competition.; [pers.] We are in a hurry and we have no time to spare — to wander and to wonder at the beauty everywhere.

HANRAHAN, MARGARET
[b.] 8 April 1952, Stirling, Scotland; [p.] Deceased; [m.] Denis Hanrahan, 15 September 1995; [ch.] Kerry; [ed.] Denny High School Scotland; [occ.] Working in a Busy Dental Unit in Manchester Royal Infirmary; [oth. writ.] Had a few poems put into the local prospectus when attending the College of Adult Education but that's it really. Would like to write a book one day; [pers.] I think poetry is in a way like. Art, its something that comes from within, you can pick up techniques on the way. But the rest has to come from you.; [a.] Manchester, Lancashire, UK

HARDIE, MRS. JEAN
[b.] 22 March 1945, Lincoln; [p.] Thomas and Jessie Hunter; [m.] Michael John Hardie, 1 August 1990; [ch.] Jeremy K. Fish, Nicola J. Crane, Shan L. Hardle, Simon N. Hardle Richard M. H. Hardle; [ed.] St. Giles School for girls, Lincoln College of Technology; [occ.] Housewife; [memb.] British Diplomatic Spouse Association; [oth. writ.] Poems and editorials published in in-house magazine in India. Compilation of poems about to be sent to publishers. I am in the process of writing a novel.; [pers.] Everything I write is from the heart, what life is all about and what I would like life to be. Most of my poems are based on fact.; [a.] Altrincham, Cheshire, UK

HARDIE, MOIRA CHRISTINA
[b.] 25 June 1958, Aberdeen; [p.] Gordon Cameron, Marjory Cameron; [m.] Mitchell Hardie, 16 June 1989; [ch.] Martyn John, Steven James, Janine Louise, Tricia Leanne; [ed.] Hatton Cruden School, Peterhead Academy; [occ.] Housewife; [memb.] Brittania Music Club, Red House Book Club; [pers.] The beauty of nature nd its ever changing characteristics inspire me.; [a.] Ellon, Aberdeenshire, UK

HARE, VALERIE
[b.] 21 February 1953, York; [p.] Hazel Marsh and Bernard Hall; [m.] John Hare, 23 December 1975; [ch.] Two boys; [ed.] Educated in York and Cheltenham; [occ.] I illustrate; [oth. writ.] A children's fairy story; [pers.] I write about my thoughts on life.; [a.] Tunbridge, Wells, Kent, UK

HARLIN, SYLVIA MARIA
[pen.] Sylvia Maria Harlin; [b.] 9 April 1979, Northampton; [p.] Derek Hunt, Victoria Hunt; [ed.] Still in Education at Kingsthorpe Upper School and working towards entrance to College to study music; [occ.] A Level Literature/Music student. Also working as Songwriter/Singer; [memb.] Member of a few local music groups and choirs; [hon.] Due to young age has not received any honours. However, has in fact won a number of awards for songwriting.; [oth. writ.] Several poems (not yet published). But songwriting material professionally mastered, produced and recorded.; [pers.] Through my poetry and music I express feelings and circumstances close to me that I have personally felt, and I hope that people can relate to the specific feeling or circumstances and appreciate the imagery so that is turn they will have a greater understanding of themselves; [a.] Northampton, Northamptonshire, UK

HARMAN, EDINA
[b.] 10 August 1964, Maidenhead; [p.] Billee Harman; [ed.] Brackenhale Secondary; [occ.] Computer Operator Admin. Asst.; [memb.] R.S.P.C.A., W.D.C.S.; [hon.] City and guilds N.V.Q. Level 1 in Computer Studies; [oth. writ.] A couple of articles published in a local magazine in Australia, where I lived for a while.; [pers.] Do the best you can, no matter what it is, but remember nobody's perfect.; [a.] Bracknell, Berks, UK

HARMAN, JOY
[b.] 7 February 1931, London; [p.] Dorothy and Alexander Drummond; [m.] Gerry, October 1959; [ch.] Russell and Jacqueline; [ed.] Preston Manor Grammar and Pitmans College, London; [occ.] Legal Secretary; [oth. writ.] Poem published in an anthology "Voices of Love" in 1992 - entitled "Old Friends" also currently working on several short story ideas.; [pers.] My three grand-daughters, Natalie, Tania and Courtney are my inspiration.; [a.] Flackwell, Heath, Buckinghamshire, UK

HARMER, LOVEDAY
[b.] Southampton; [p.] Frank and Daisy Ramshaw; [m.] Ronald, 29 March 1947; [ch.] Tessa, Teacher in Australia; [ed.] Granville College, Southampton Girls College Southampton, London University, Phillipa Fawcett College of Education; [occ.] Retired Head Teacher of Purley Oaks Primary School, South Croydon, Governor of New Milton Infants' School; [memb.] Nat. Ass. Head Teachers (Retired) New Forest Mencap. Friends of Spencer Lodge (local Cheshire Home); [hon.] B.A. (Education) L.R.A.M. (Speech and Drama), Fellow of the College of Perceptors; [oth. writ.] Several poems and Articles on personal experiences. Articles on Education; [pers.] I write in order to deepen my own perception of life, education and philosophy and in the hope that others may benefit from reading my writings.; [a.] New Milton, Hampshire, UK

HARO, GARY
[b.] 7 September 1969, Irvine; [p.] Veronica Haro; [memb.] Yamaha School of Music; [oth. writ.] I have written many many songs. In 1986 I wrote my first song it called Never Ending Questions. I wrote the poem Never Ending Questions based on my very first written song. Never Ending Questions is my very first written poem; [pers.] For the rest of my life I will write songs, poems, and stories. My songs, poems have a message in them for you to read and listen. Our world is now a bad place to raise our kids. Have a smile and come together as we strive to make our world a better place.; [a.] Stewarton, Ayrshire, UK

HAROLD, JENNY SARAH
[b.] 3 September 1982, Bradford; [p.] Paul Harold and Kim Harold; [ed.] St Walburgas R.C. First, Whycliffe C.E. Middle School; [occ.] I am still in full time education, have a local baby-sitting job.; [memb.] I am a member of shipley Baptist Church, and also their youth fellowship.; [oth. writ.] Written many other poems and collated them to make two un-published anthologies, 'Poems for the jilted generation' and 'crystal clear'; [pers.] In many of my poems I try to project my inner-most thoughts and feelings. In my other poems I try to re-tell famous stories or memories, so that people won't forget our history.; [a.] Shipley, Yorkshire, UK

HARPER, J. E.
[pen.] John Harper; [b.] 4 July 1939, London; [p.] Elsie Harper, William Harper (Deceased); [ed.] Tylers Croft Secondary County Sca.; [occ.] Retired Taxi Driver; [pers.] Reflections on love, life and death. Influenced by Shelley and Shakespeare.; [a.] High Wycombe, Bucks, UK

HARRIS, ANN
[b.] Sutton, Norfolk; [p.] Sidney Woolston, Ivy Woolston; [m.] Ron Harris, 27 September 1982; [ed.] North Walsham High School for girls; [occ.] Housewife; [memb.] National Canine Defence League (Chairperson, Luton and District); [oth. writ.] "Best Friends" a collection of the best 100 poems entered in a competition in aid of guide dogs for the blind. Poems and articles in Staffordshire bull terrier news letters.; [pers.] I constantly get inspiration from my dogs and the comedy of everyday life; [a.] Luton, Beds, UK

HARRIS, MISS ELIZABETH G.
[pen.] Nil; [b.] 10 February 1920, Haddington; [occ.] Retired; [oth. writ.] Several poems published by Triumph House, I wainman road Peterborough. But just since July 1995.; [pers.] I do try to be helpful as well as numerous, to cheer folks up if possible.; [a.] Haddington, East Lothian, UK

HARRIS, GARY MICHAEL
[b.] 30 June 1971, Epsom; [p.] Mr. and Mrs. F. E. Harris; [ed.] Horsell High School, working sixth form College; [occ.] Security Officer; [oth. writ.] Poems published in 'Poetry Now' anthologies - Scared for Life, Is the World Round, My Life Your Game, A Word of Difference, Till I Don't Hurt; [pers.] My writing is born of the world I 'see', I strive to rumble the readers steady perch. Live to learn and learn to live.; [a.] Woking, Surrey, UK

HARRIS, LAVINIA MARY
[pen.] Polly (occasionally); [b.] 7 July 1954; [p.] Col Hugh Martin West Harris; [m.] Ann Varnish (Died) 3 others; [ed.] Wimdledon High School (GPDST), St Paul's Girls School (London) Sherbourne School for girls; [occ.] Sort of Secretary for Inter-Action Pear Tree Bridge MK Poetry Review; [memb.] 6 'O' levels other ballet and horse riding exams before 1967; [pers.] After writing this poem I cast myself off a bridge near Milton Keynes but am now fully recovered from that, thanks to Mr Milton.

HARRIS, MICHELLE
[b.] 19 March 1968; [p.] Jacqueline Harris and Heon Harris; [m.] Mr. Keith Mundy, 6 July 1996; [ch.] Darryl; [ed.] Howard of Effingham Secondary School; [occ.] Housewife; [memb.] Leatherhead Royal British Legion; [pers.] Live life for today, as tomorrow may never come; [a.] Fetcham, Surrey, UK

HARRIS, MR. ROY
[b.] 2 February 1920, Birmingham; [p.] Charles Frances Harris and Gertrude Harris; [m.] Widower; [ch.] Jacqueline Matthews and Suzanne Briggs; [ed.] Cardinal Vaughan School Kensington London, University of London; [occ.] Retired, Private Practice - Psychotherapy; [hon.] MA B.Sc. (Hons. Psych), Ch. Psych AFBPsS; [pers.] My many other poems are of a metaphysical nature inspired by places and events.; [a.] Hassocks, W. Sussex, UK

HARRISON, MARGARET
[pen.] Anne Garet; [b.] 19 July 1966, Royal Tonbridge Wells, Kent; [p.] Reginald Stevens, Doreen Stevens; [m.] Jason Harrison, 18 August 1992; [ch.] Charlotte Louise, James Anthony; [ed.] St. Barnabas Primary School Sandown Court Secondary School West Kent College of Further Education; [occ.] Mother/Housewife; [oth. writ.] One poem published in Local paper, poems just written for my own entertainment.; [pers.] I love writing poems. I hope people get enjoyment from reading them, as much as I get from writing them. I write how I feel, which I think poetry is all about. Just be you.; [a.] Eccles, Manchester, UK

HARRISON, MARK
[b.] 30 January 1958, Govan; [p.] Deceased; [occ.] Unemployed; [oth. writ.] Work in progress "Where Have Hugs Gone" A book of feelings - A journey of the soul; [pers.] I have watched people get lost within their world of emotions and my writing reflects the truth as it has never been said before, I believe in sharing an understanding which lies within the heart, feelings that every one try to tell someone but can't find the words-; [a.] Glasgow, Scotland

HART, PAULINE
[b.] 21 May 1957, Shropshire; [p.] Patrick and Kay O'Connor; [m.] Kevin W. Hart, 11 March 1978; [ch.] Katie Mary and William Patrick; [ed.] Blessed Robert Johnson Shropshire Cell High School Staffs Cauldon College Staffs.; [occ.] Marie Curie Nurse; [oth. writ.] Two poems in Linkwai writers Mag. poem in lifeline Mag. several Tips

and letters in magazines also reviews and tips in a local newspaper.; [pers.] Life alone provides the material for moving poetry, entertaining short stories and gripping novels. No one needs look any further than their own lives; [a.] Leek, Staffs, UK

HARTH, YVONNE ROCHE
[b.] 10 May 1995, Cork, Ireland; [p.] No longer living; [m.] Norbert Harth, 14 April 1978; [ch.] Two girls; [ed.] Diploma in the Theory and Methodology of Teaching English ELD (TESOL); [occ.] English Teacher lecturer at Bonn's University; [memb.] The British Embassy Players, Bonn (Theatre) Odoroka Mime Theatre, Bonn Lead Singer with "Ben Bulben" (traditional Irish folk Music) German - Irish Society, Bonn); [oth. writ.] "Poems for Outsiders" to be published in 1997 several poems published and exhibited with paintings/music/photos: Highly commended by New Prospects Poetry in 1991; [pers.] I'm blessed!; [a.] Sankt Agustin, Germany

HARVEY, GILLIAN KATE
[b.] 26 September 1974, Sudbury; [p.] David and Mary Harvey; [ch.] Shannon Mary; [hon.] Nominated Poet of Merit '95 in Washington, D.C., First Prize Winner in the John Kennedy Memorial Poetry Competition '96; [oth. writ.] Several poems published in England and U.S.A.; [pers.] This poem is dedicated to my daughter, Shannon. I will always love you.; [a.] Clackton-on-Sea, Essex, UK

HARVEY, VALERIE JOY
[pen.] Val Harvey; [b.] 18 March 1945, Amersham; [p.] William and Florence Podbury; [m.] Brian Alexander Harvey, 1 July 1967; [ch.] Belinda Louise; [ed.] Dr. Challoners Grammar School Amersham; [occ.] Residential Social Worker; [oth. writ.] Short story - "Pennies from Heaven" published in local paper; [pers.] I have a love of nature and I am an incurable romantic.; [a.] Chesham, Bucks, UK

HARWOOD, TRUDY
[pen.] Trudy French; [b.] 29 November 1947, Isleworth; [p.] Albert and Doreen Wheadon; [m.] Barry Anthony Harwood, 1 September 1990; [ch.] Dorian Michael Roald, Trudie Danyck; [ed.] Kennington Manor Secondary Modern Sunbury on Thames, Isleworth Polytechnic; [occ.] Receptionist - Southend Community Care NHS Trust; [memb.] B.H.S., (Blackwater) Leisure Centre; [oth. writ.] Short stories and poems for competitions and in-house magazines; [pers.] Light, Love and Happiness; [a.] Mundon, Maldon, Essex, UK

HASSETT, SINEAD
[b.] 5 April 1985, England; [p.] Bernadette and Philip Hassett; [ed.] Currently at Holy Family School but quite soon will be moving to Saint Bede's Secornady School. I have recently took my SATS; [memb.] Belong to a Browme pack and I am a member of my school drama group; [hon.] At school I have been honored many awards, for good writing; [oth. writ.] I have written many poems and the poem that I chose was my favorite I have also written other many stories.; [pers.] I am very honored that one of my poems is going to be published in a book. I have been greatly influenced by other famous poet writers.; [a.] Bristol, South Glos, UK

HATTON, MARION
[pen.] Maz; [b.] 16 October 1947, Bradford; [p.] Mr. and Mrs. W. Turton (Deceased); [m.] William Hatton, 6 March 1965; [ch.] Peter John and Steven Lesley; [ed.] School Certificate 1962, 2 City and Guilds Computing and Inform. Tech I am now doing a degree with the Open University on Information Technology; [occ.] Cook (for 30 years); [memb.] Ladies Forum (Eccleshill) Ladies Bowls Club (Bed); [hon.] Silver cup and Golden Hands Award 1986, (Bradford Telegraph and Argus) for Fund Raising Honours Certificate from Arthritis Research Presented by Bill-Whitely Bradford on behalf of Lady Patricia Hornsby Smith 1986; [oth. writ.] Several poems in local charity Magazines, Articles for local Exhibitions in Bradford Library Short Stories and poetry for local community centre productions.; [pers.] I am the youngest of eight children I strive to encourage local youth and friends and relatives to reflect my sincere christian upbringing on a large Bradford council estate. I have been influenced by my dear family and friends.; [a.] Bradford, W. Yorkshire, UK

HAUXWELL, COLIN FRANCIS
[b.] 24 February 1954, Stockton; [p.] Francis Hauxwell, Ethel Hauxwell; [m.] Karen Hauxwell (Nee Moore), 21 January 1978; [ch.] Lindsey, 12 July 1979; [ed.] Bowesfield Lane Primary School, Hardwick Secondary Modern, Stockton-on-Tees; [occ.] Career, for disabled wife; [oth. writ.] Poem published in regional anthology "Mind and Body, Life and Death" by poetry now 1995; [pers.] I have been inspired by the love of my wife and daughter, and my parents and my wifes parents, who are sadly no longer with us bodily, but remain with us in spirit.; [a.] Stockton, Cleveland, UK

HAWKINS, SANDRA
[b.] 30 October 1953, Edinburgh; [ed.] Gnoll Secondary School, NVQ Business Admin - Computers Typing; [memb.] Order of Bards, Ovatesy Druids, Order of Briehid Pagan Federation, Environment Centre, Swansea; [oth. writ.] Poems, short stories a soulful cry in - the drops of awen magazine.; [pers.] To find true enlightment with and to help our planet. I hope by writing poem and short stories to help people, children to better understand what is happening to our planet.; [a.] Swansea, W. Glam, UK

HAYES, KAREN D.
[pen.] Miss Tree.; [b.] 26 June 1967, Aldershot.; [p.] Kenneth D. Hayes and Patricia M. Hayes; [ed.] Vyne Comprehensive, Queen Mary's College, Basingstoke and Winchester School of Nursing.; [occ.] Student studying psychology at local college. (Retired Due To Injury.); [memb.] The Woodland Trust. Volunteer For Local Women's Group.; [hon.] Registered General Nurse-RGN. Registered Mental Nurse-RMN.; [oth. writ.] Several poems published in local paper.; [pers.] WE should all find our own way, by listening to what others have to say.; [a.] Basingstoke, Hampshire, UK

HAYNES, SIAN LOUISE
[b.] 20 January 1959, Tripoli, Libya; [ed.] Left school at 16, mainly educated by life! Trained Nurse, Secretary and Computer Programmer.; [oth. writ.] A number of my poems have been published in three anthologies: - "Poets Of The South East," "Dawn" and "Aeon."; [pers.] I use the practical philosophy of L. Ron Hubbard (Scientology) in my life. Greatest artistic influence on my writing was Jack Kezowalc. My poem reflect the beauty of England and spiritual aspects of life.; [a.] East Grinstead, W. Sussex, UK

HAYWARD, KITTY
[pen.] Kity Hayward; [b.] 18 August 1915, Wimbledon; [p.] Charles Rupert and Edith Mary Harding; [m.] Reginald Boyse Hayward, 6 March 1937; [ch.] One son Michael Boyse; [ed.] Pelham Central School Pelham Road Wimbledon SW19; [occ.] Widow - Senior Citizen; [memb.] Civil Service Association no others; [oth. writ.] Hundreds of what I call "Occasional" verses, is for `Births', `Engagements', Weddings, Retirement, etc. for friends, relatives and colleagues, for pure enjoyment! Also short stories in rhyme.; [pers.] My grandson fee persuaded me to enter my poem, fro which I thank him.; [a.] Portsmouth, Hants, UK

HEALE, TRIS FRANCES
[b.] 22 December 1913, New Malden; [p.] Jack and Mabel Pearson; [m.] Charles Heale, 24 August 1940; [ed.] Burlington Rod New Malden, the school I went to; [occ.] On a pension and I enjoy three days at a Day Centre and have been there since 1982; [oth. writ.] I have poem called Mickey he is my own cat which is published in a book called Hear my Voice Poetry Anthology Kingston-upon-Thames; [pers.] A born Christian with full belief in God word.; [a.] New Malden, Surrey, UK

HEASMAN, KATHLEEN WINIFRED MARGARET
[pen.] Katie; [b.] 14 August 1929, Ash; [p.] Florance and Jessie Stone; [m.] David James Heasman, 26 December 1948; [ch.] Three; [ed.] Church of England School; [occ.] Retired; [oth. writ.] About 25 yrs ago my first poetry published in "poetry Press Ltd" 4 poems under name of Margaret Stone. I've not written any more poems since until this contest. Published book Title's for the love of poetry/through the eyes of the poet; [pers.] I think everyone should read "the millennium and beyond" published free by the worldwide church of God.; [a.] Sittingbourne, Kent, UK

HEATH, R.
[b.] 29 October 1975; [pers.] If you do not wear, it is because you do not listen. If you do not see, it is because you do not look, where once there was grass, now there is concrete, where once there was air, now there is poisen, where once there was harmony, now there is humans.

HEATHWOOD, CELIA
[b.] 10 March 1933, Belfast; [p.] Pat and Jean Heathwood; [ed.] St. Peters Primary School, St. Malachys Convent Sussex Pl. Belfast. Rupert Stanley College. New towards Road Belfast; [occ.] Retired Dressmaker now full time writer; [memb.] London Poetry Society, Divis Writers Group, Linen Hull Historical Library, Linen Hall Writers Group; [hon.] Thames television book prize for short story for education section. Story title is, Store House 2 Anthology, Runner up in Belfast Telegraph's Centenary story for Central Library, runner up in BBI Radio Story, second in Point North Poetry competition; [oth. writ.] A collection of occult and mystery I strange tales of mystery and the paranormal' formerly published by 'Ireland's Eye' Mullingar, Eire stories in Belfast Telegraph, 'Ireland's Own', Ulster Tatler, West Belfast annual, poems: Irish weekly review; [pers.] From my own experience there are three elements needed for professional success in writing persistence, patience and practice; [a.] Belfast Nr. Ireland, Antrim, UK

HEATLEY, W. G.
[b.] 5 October 1934, Shoreditch; [p.] Millicent, William; [m.] Ruby, 27 February 1960; [ch.] Philip, John, Clare, Julian; [ed.] Convent Educated; [occ.] Retired; [memb.] SPUC; [oth. writ.] Short Stories (BBC), Newspaper Articles, Several Poems published; [pers.] Influenced by Keats, I attempt to encapsulate beauty cloistered in drama; [a.] Scunthorpe, N. Lincolnshire, UK

HEATON, CLARE LOUISE
[b.] 6 December 1976, Leeds; [p.] Wendy Ann Heaton; [ed.] Burley St Matthias Primary 82-86 Royal Park Middle School 86-90 Agnes Stewart Cofe School High 90-93; [occ.] Food Production line worker concept foods; [hon.] Diploma of Vocational Education C And G (Health and protective services); [pers.] My inspiration for this poem was the tragic loss of my dear friend Cecilia Waters whom I loved and lost.; [a.] Leeds, Yorkshire, UK

HEDLEY, BRENDA
[b.] 5 November 1933, Manchester; [p.] Alice and John Stephen Carter; [m.] Peter Stanley Hedley, 8 August 1959; [ch.] Jan and Jill; [ed.] Whalley Range High School. Matlock Teacher Training College; [occ.] Retired school teacher; [a.] Bowness-on-Windermere, Cumbria, UK

HEDLEY, HILDA MAY
[b.] 30 October 1910, Norwich; [p.] Ellen Austin and Cecil Arthur Mobbs; [m.] Joseph Johnson Hedley (Deceased), 1937; [ch.] Graham, Michael Austin, Patricia Jane; [ed.] Long Stratton Primary, Norwich Secondary, Norwich Studio Shorthand and Typing; [occ.] Retired civil servant; [memb.] Civil Service Retirement Association; [hon.] 1920 Bird and Tree Day Montagu Sharpe Prize, Medal for the Royal Society Protection of Birds - for Norfolk Pitman's Shorthand Certificates; [oth. writ.] Essay local Sunday Paper (Sunday Sun) - poems "Fiddler On The Roof" golden heirloom collection - "Unemployment" East Cleveland way magazine - various letters - poems and stories, local and national papers; [pers.] My early childhood in Norfolk, with nature all around me, and my success at age of 10 years to win a medal for an essay "Birds And Trees", sponsored by R.S.P.B. led me to write about nature in it's most succinct form "Poetry".; [a.] Framwellgate, Durham, UK

HELLEWELL, BARBARA
[b.] 6 March, 1940, Huddersfield; [p.] Isabella and Lewis Jebson (deceased); [m.] June 10, 1961; [ch.] Mark and Anne; [ed.] Scissett Secondary Modern School and Hudderfield Technical College; [occ.] Housewife, mature student; [memb.] Huddersfield Examiner Travel Circle; [hon.] Three Distinctions by the Poetry Institute of the British Isles; [oth. writ.] I have been writing 2 years and have had 23 poems published in 30 books (excluding this anthology) on various subjects. Also in local newspapers and second prize in local competition, Special Commendation Certificate by Hilton House (Publishers) Norwich, and Editor's Choice Award Certificate by International Society of Poets for this poem.; [pers.] The subject of my poem is about the beauty of the Rose while commemorating the memory of my Mother who died in April 1994 and holds great sentimental value to me. I hope it gives pleasure to the reader. Thank you for the honour of being able to share it in this anthology for generations to come.; [a.] Meltham, Huddersfield

HELM, KENNETH
[pen.] T.A.P; [b.] 11 February 1944, Lancashire; [p.] Thomas Helm, Hilda Helm; [m.] 22 July 1967; [ch.] One Daughter; [ed.] Primary Rossendale Grammer School; [occ.] Senior Officer in her Majesties Prison Service; [memb.] Various Book Clubs, Mostly Non-Fiction; [oth. writ.] My main hobby is compiling quiz's for various associations etc. (Military Meetings, Pubs Club - any charitable organization). I also compile treasure hunts.; [pers.] I have been writing poetry for approx 9 months this is my first attempt at publication.; [a.] Lincoln, Lincs, UK

HENDERSON, COLIN
[pen.] Colin Henderson; [b.] 26 October 1962, Edinburgh; [p.] Jack and Sheila Henderson; [m.] Irene Henderson, 27 June 1987; [ch.] Daniel James, Kayleigh; [ed.] Forrester High School Edinburgh; [occ.] Ministry of defence dog handler; [oth. writ.] My brother published in 'The Other Side Of The Mirror'; [pers.] The gift of life is dedicated to the memory of a courageous young lady and wife of a dear friend; [a.] South Queensferry, West Lothian, UK

HENDERSON, MRS. MAVIS TAYLOR
[b.] 21 May 1946, Hartlepool; [p.] Christopher, Carlton, Taylor; [m.] Freda Taylor nee Gaffney, 6 March 1965 (Divorced 1990); [ch.] Jeffrey, Elaine Henderson; [ed.] Elwick Road Secondary School For Girls Hartlepool; [occ.] Homemaker; [hon.] A Mother's child one of my poem's published by Anchor Book's in (word's from within) August 1994; [oth. writ.] Poems written to magazines, and local papers; [pers.] I try to put my inner most thoughts, and feeling's about life, and love, in a lasting testimony for others to read, and know that I have been there this is me!; [a.] Hartlepool, UK

HENDERSON, ROY CAMPBELL
[b.] 1 April 1966, Perth; [p.] Gordon and Kathella Henderson; [m.] Separated; [ed.] Alyth High School; [occ.] Student (again); [oth. writ.] Monarch Of The Glow, Old Wolf, Angels, Rose Of My Heart, Dreamers Hill, Just An Idiot, and many more.; [a.] Alyth, Perthshire, UK

HEPBURN, J.
[b.] 21 November 1965, St. Vincent, W.I.; [p.] Beluah Hepburn; [ed.] Hatters Lane Comprehensive School; [occ.] Student, studying mental health problems; [memb.] Wycombe Mind; [pers.] The beauty of words be shared by all and not kept to one's self; [a.] High Wycombe, Bucks, UK

HEWITT, MRS. ENID
[b.] 16 August 1929, Grantham; [p.] Tom and Alice Streather; [m.] Douglas Hewitt (Deceased), 24 March 1952; [ch.] Margaret, Christine, Colin, Alan and Hilary; [ed.] St. Anne's Junior, Girls Central School Grantham; [occ.] Retired former Grocery Shop Assistant; [memb.] District Church Council, Deanery Synod Representative Church Warden, Hospital Lay Assistant Chaplaincy Department; [oth. writ.] Poem "Perfection" bard of the year competition came 76th out of over two thousand; [pers.] I try to use my experiences of life's "Ups and Downs" to help and and advise others. I like reading Jeffery Farnal novels especially about days gone by.; [a.] Grantham, Lincs, UK

HICKMAN, MISS KATIE
[pen.] Katie Hickman; [b.] 31 May 1982, Sandwell; [p.] Josephine Frances and Graham Keith Hickman; [ed.] Blackheath Primary School, Rowley Regis. Heathfield G.M. High School, Cradley Heath; [occ.] School Girl; [oth. writ.] 'The Queens Square Rap' Sandwell poet of the year - local competition 1995 (1st prize); [pers.] 'Sun-Ray' due to be published August 1996 in book: Carousel West Midlands!; [a.] Cradley Heath, West Midlands, UK

HIDDLESTON, ERNEST IAN KERR
[b.] 23 March 1947, Poole, Dorset; [p.] Robert, Violet; [m.] Susan Anne Hiddleston, 2 April 1966; [ch.] 4 - Maxine, Mark, Ian, Sharon; [ed.] Henry Harbin Secondary Modern; [occ.] Cleaner Supervisor; [memb.] Hamworthy Royal British Legion; [oth. writ.] I am in the process of having a poem published in poets of the south in June, titled Heaven On Earth; [pers.] My father came from Dumfries. And took me to Robert Burns house on a few occasions, I have been back a few times since I've grown up, I think that must have inspired me.; [a.] Poole, Dorset, UK

HIGHFIELD, MRS. DORIS
[b.] 4 February 1946, Sheffield; [p.] Doris Gill and Willie Gill; [m.] Edward Highfield, 3 September 1966; [ch.] Donna Janine and Lee Edward; [ed.] Secondary Modern (Southey Green) Sheffield; [occ.] Housewife; [oth. writ.] None published, I just write poems for personal pleasure and to express emotions I am feeling at the time.; [pers.] Life, to me is all about living, not just being alive, Learing and growing from experiences, both good and bad. Without the bad times we couldn't appreciate the good; [a.] Sheffield, Yorkshire, UK

HILL, JOHN H.
[pen.] John H. Hill; [b.] 21 March 1909, Smethwick; [p.] John and Emily Hill; [m.] Daisy Elizabeth Hill, 19 May 1934; [ch.] One daughter, two great grandchildren, three grandchildren; [ed.] Elementary School, Bearwood Road, Smethwick; [occ.] Retired; [memb.] British Diabetic Association, Membership No 8516829; [oth. writ.] Several of my poems included in various published books of poetry.; [pers.] I have been interested in writing poetry since my school days but not until I lost my left leg in 1992 and became housebound did I take a keen interest in poetry but since then I have written over one hundred poems and it's a very relaxing hobby and hope my poems will give pleasure to lovers of poetry. I wrote the poem "The Passing of Time" on my 87th birthday 21-03-96 after reflections of my past life.; [a.] Llanfechain, Powys, UK

HILL, SYLVIA
[pen.] Sylvia Hill; [b.] 20 April 1908, Saintfield; [p.] Alfred and Agnes Kinghan; [m.] Samuel C. Hill (Deceased), 29 August 1929; [ch.] Three; [ed.] Saintfield Academy; [occ.] Retired; [memb.] Former member of Saintfield Heritage Society; [oth. writ.] Memories of Saintfield now in local libraries Sent may poems to Local Paper etc.; [pers.] I admired the works of Robert Burns.

HILLBECK, AMANDA
[b.] 8 May 1968, Barrow-in-Furness; [m.] Paul Hillbeck, 3 October 1987; [ch.] Stephanie and Caroline, Andrew; [occ.] Housewife; [pers.] I write how I feel at hat time to reflect on my inner emotions.; [a.] Barrow-in-Furness, Cumbria, UK

HILLS, JACKIE R.
[b.] East Sussex; [ch.] Steven and Darren; [ed.] Secondary School Education; [oth. writ.] 'Heaven Waits' is my first attempt at poetry and I have endeavoured to capture the imagination of those who read it.; [a.] Gravesend, Kent, UK

HIMMIGHOJEN, NADINE
[b.] 24 May 1976, Saarbricken, Germany; [p.] Ernst Himmighojen, Charlotte nee Dillschneider; [ed.] Johannes Kepler Grammar School, University of the Saarland, Saarbricken; [occ.] Student of English and German for a Teachers Degree; [memb.] Scheffelbund (Literary Society of Germany); [hon.] Scheffel Award; [oth. writ.] Several other poems, some published in a German poetry magazine; [pers.] Thanks to all people writers who have inspired me and kept me going. I never concentrate or a particular thing, I just bring my thoughts on paper in order to express what and how I feel.; [a.] Nalbach,, Germany

HIRST, STEVEN
[b.] 17 February 1971, Leeds; [m.] Lynsey Howick, 2 March 1996; [ch.] Baby due in June; [ed.] Royds Comprehensive Oviton; [occ.] Driver - Parcel Force; [pers.] As a beginner I was amazed to discover that I had enough talent to be published. It is a great honor for me and I hope many people will enjoy my work.; [a.] Rothwell-Leeds, W. Yorkshire, UK

HOBBS, CAROL
[b.] 17/5/1949, Swanage, Dorset; [p.] Liz Adams, the late Doug Adams; [m.] Christopher Hobbs, November 27, 1970; [ch.] Joanna and Nicola; [ed.] St. Mary's Convent School, Swanage; [occ.] Sales Assistant; [hon.] Creative Studies Flower Arranging; [oth. writ.] Several poems published in other books; [pers.] A few weeks after entering my poem into the competition, my dad sadly died; therefore, I would like to dedicate my poem to the memory of my dad.; [a.] Swanage, Dorset

HOBSON, PAUL
[b.] 13 May 1978, Liverpool; [p.] Helen and John Hobson; [ed.] Calday Grammar School; [occ.] Student Coxford University; [oth. writ.] Science - Fiction Comedy Novel (unpublished), poems and short stories; [pers.] Writing poems is a new and exciting pastime for me. I think it always will be.; [a.] Heswall, Merseyside, UK

HOCKLEY, JOYCE M.
[pen.] Occasionaly Joy Wilson for short stories; [b.] 26 July 1922, London; [p.] Albert and Elizabeth-Maude Killman; [m.] C. W. Hockley, 19 June 1948; [ch.] Michael and Sally-Anne; [ed.] St. Cuthbert's College, London; [occ.] Retired (Housewife); [hon.] 3rd place short play competition, one 1st and two 3rd places in songs contest for lyrics, one 3rd and one 4th places in Dutch-written poetry competitions; [oth. writ.] Poems in 19 Anthologies, 17 children's short stories, Weekly articles in local, South-West papers for (1) six years and (2) four years, two booklet on walking.; [pers.] Writing is my hobby - I just love to scribble! Poetry, short plays, comedies, short stories both for adults and children. Just give me a pen and paper, and I am in my element!; [a.] Stirling, Stirlingshire, UK

HODGE, NELLIE STANLEY
[pen.] Nell Hodge; [b.] 23 September 1913, Silverdale, Staffs; [p.] Albert and Jane Burgess; [m.] Robert Hodge, 9 February 1943; [ch.] Robert Stanley Hodge; [ed.] Underwood College; [occ.] Housewife (Ex Secretary); [oth. writ.] April, What Brings Me Joy, November Memories, and others written for special occasions including poems in the church magazine.; [pers.] Although I am a cancer patient and becoming increasingly physically handicapped I seem to be able to write my best verse during sleepless nights. My philosophy is to make the best of the bad days and enjoy the good ones and to help others.; [a.] Newcastle, Staffordshire, UK

HODGSON, E.
[b.] 15 March 1920, Sheffield; [p.] Joseph Kelly, Nellie Kelly; [m.] Husband Alan Hodgson, 23 March 1946; [ch.] No children; [oth. writ.] It was the war that inspired me, I went in the steel works and turned Propella Shafs for Airo planes and I had no doubt whatever that we would win the war.; [pers.] I wrote this poem in 1939 and I knew we would win the war then, I have not had my several education, but on my day, we were very proud of bring and everyone cared.; [a.] Sheffield, Yorkshire, UK

HOGG, BETTY
[b.] 20 October 1938, Greenwood; [p.] George Hogg, Jessie Hogg; [ed.] Morebattle Secondary School; [occ.] Unemployed; [oth. writ.] Several poems published in local papers and magazines; [pers.] I tend to reflect on nature and feelings, life in general, I greatly respect Tennyson, Milton and Robert Burns.; [a.] Denholm, Hawick, Roxburghshire, UK

HOLDCROFT, DAVID
[b.] 16 September 1978, Stoke-on-Trent; [p.] Philip Holdcroft, Cinnette Holdcroft; [m.] Stacey Legge; [ed.] Wolstanton High School, City of Stoke-on-Trent Sixth Form College; [occ.] Full time student at Sixth Form College; [oth. writ.] Poems and short stories on all subjects waiting to be published; [pers.] I write about what people notice but do not see, what they listen to but do not hear and what happens around them that they are both blind and deaf to.; [a.] Newcastle-under-Lyme, Staffordshire, UK

HOLDER, RANDOLPH
[pen.] Randolph; [b.] Barbados; [p.] Beryl and Oswal; [m.] Millie; [ch.] Four sons and daughter; [ed.] St. Judes Boys Comprehensive, St. Judes St. George Barbados W.T.; [occ.] Social Worker; [memb.] Social and Development Officer, Coventry Barbadian Community Association School Governor LEA; [hon.] Certificate in Sociology, Psychology and Welfare Studies, Humanitarian Award by then the City Lord Mayor of Coventry Arthur Waugh; [oth. writ.] No. of poems written and few printed in books and poems into songs; [pers.] I strive to bring people from all walks of life to read and enjoy the essence of my work I love writing poetry for all.; [a.] Coventry, West Midlands, UK

HOLLAND, VALERIE CAROL
[b.] 15 February 1938, Sheffield; [p.] Lawrence and Cecilia Dodds; [m.] Alan Holland, 7 April 1973; [ch.] Isabel Victoria, Simon David; [ed.] Hurlfield Grammar Sheffield; [occ.] Housewife; [oth. writ.] None published; [pers.] My life and the lives of those around me whom I love are the main influence in my poetry; [a.] Preston, Lancashire, UK

HOLLEY, MICHELLE L.
[b.] 1 May 1967, Henley-on-Thames; [p.] Christopher Bradford, Jacqueline Bradford; [m.] Simon M. Holley, 14 September 1991; [ch.] Natasha Leanne, Christopher Simon; [ed.] Silchester Primary, The Hurst Secondary School; [memb.] Aldermaston Primary School, Parent Teacher Association; [pers.] My poem is dedicated to a very special person, my grandma, Selina Broadhurts and to my family.; [a.] Aldermaston, Berkshire, UK

HOLLOWAY, JOSEPH
[b.] 24 May 1918, Stoke-on-Trent; [p.] George and Edith Mary Holloway; [m.] Lily Dorothy, 21 June 1941; [ch.] Sandra Dorothy, Coral Anne, Joy Yvonne; [ed.] Queens, Stoke on Trent, S.O.T College Mech. Eng. - R.A.F. Schools Elect. and Radio almost three P.O.W. years; [occ.] Retired Instrument Mech. (Power Station); [memb.] S.O.T. Chrysanthemum Society F.N.C.S., R.A.F. Association Air Gunners Ass. (Life); [hon.] Air Efficiency Medal R.A.F. Warrant Officer Aircrew Wireless of Air Gunner; [oth. writ.] Won Staffs Literature age 11 Industrial Revolution essay several poems published in Air Force Magazines etc. numerous anecdotes of P.O.W. life several humorous parodies, in particular of my namesake Stanley Holloway Albert Ramsbottom adventures; [pers.] Greatly influenced by the both were P.O.W. life taught me patience in all things. Like to think I have lost the man's to hate, in a personal way. Am deeply touched by humours, happiness, and sorrow, patriotic but not nationalistic.; [a.] Stoke-on-Trent, Staffs, UK

HOLT, DENIS NEIL
[b.] 3 December 1927, Chase Terrace, Staffs; [m.] Blodwyn Megan, 11 August 1951; [ch.] Nigel John (Decd), Simon (Decd), Madeline Elaine; [occ.] O.A.P., Ex Mining Electrical Engineer; [oth. writ.] Several unpublished poems and verse; [pers.] I write according to divine inspiration, when given by the holy spirit.; [a.] Slinfeld, Horsham, W. Sussex, UK

HOLYLAND, BETTY
[pen.] Betty Holyland; [b.] 16 September 1924, Leicester; [p.] Louisa Cooper, Arthur Cooper; [m.] Sidney Alfred Holyland, 18 November 1982; [ed.] Moat girls Intermediate school, Leicester; [occ.] Housewife; [oth. writ.] "Pendragon Tales" monthly serial when Editor of children's section in Local Village journal including several poems. Poetry accepted for open anthology! "Gone to Earth" a selection of poems in war and peace.; [pers.] I have tried to record factual events for future generations in poems. All based in real people, events and are a history of the vale of Belvoir.; [a.] Mowbray, Leics, UK

HOMFRAY, ANDREW GUY
[b.] 25 July 1943, Birmingham; [p.] Samuel Lawrence and Alfreda Homfray; [m.] Andrea Homfray, 18 August 1962; [ch.] Faith Dawn, Lorne Angela, Adam Jo Lyon; [ed.] King Edwards Grammar School, Aston, Birmingham; [occ.] Painter and Decorator; [oth. writ.] Several other poems written but to date not offered for publication; [pers.] Majority of poems written during period of time whilst serving aboard ship during and following the Falklands War, with the Royal Navy.; [a.] Play Blanca, Yaiza, Lanzarote, Canary Islands

HOPE, JONATHAN
[pen.] Cody Rhyback; [b.] 16 April 1973, Manchester; [p.] Mrs. Jackie Hope and Mr. David Hope; [ed.] Sir John Talbot's School; [occ.] Recently returned from working at sea for three years, including QE2 last year as silver service writer.;

[memb.] The Writer's Bureau; [hon.] John Sutch Award for commitment to art and drama.; [oth. writ.] 'One More for Dinner' unpublished.; [pers.] Make the most of the body you have now! Next time it's going to be different.; [a.] Ellesmere, Shropshire, UK

HOPES, HAZEL
[b.] 28 March 1969; [pers.] Don't be afraid to write, poetry can be a healing experience.; [a.] Avening, Glos, UK

HOPPS, JAMES RICHARD
[pen.] Richard James; [b.] 16 December 1949, Patrick, Isle of Man; [p.] Mrs. Evelyn Hopps, Mr. John Robert Hopps; [ed.] Brigham Junior School Lairthwaite Secondary Modern Keswick Cumbria; [occ.] Security Officer (Senator Security); [pers.] Had I not my dreams then I would be shackled to life as any other man. I dedicate my work to Annie forever apart of me.; [a.] Manchester, UK

HORAJOO, ANBARASI
[pen.] Amber De Winter; [b.] 17 March 1971, South India; [p.] Mr. R. Horajoo and Mrs. M. Horajoo; [ed.] Plashet School, Fiashet Road East Ham E-6; [occ.] Bank Officer Junior; [oth. writ.] Books (2) outcast first one badeler Duke second one both not published.; [pers.] I love people to be happy and be in love. Love mean lot to me. Not just a words but the feelings that goes with it.; [a.] Manor Park, London, UK

HORRELL, MR. ANTHONY
[pen.] Tony; [b.] 24 February 1948, Chelmsford; [p.] Frank and Margaret Horrell; [m.] Shelley, 16 February 1991; [ch.] Bradley, Kylie, Bridget, Dean; [ed.] Westlands Secondary Modern at Chelmsford; [occ.] Service Engineer; [oth. writ.] I have a collection of my own poems that have not been published. This is the first one I have sent for appraisal.; [pers.] My poetry reflects my innermost thoughts and emotions. I think all poetry should come from the heart, and poetry the writer's feelings to the reader.; [a.] Ipswish, Suffolk, UK

HORSEMAN, JANET D.
[pen.] Jan Horseman; [b.] 18 January 1942, Oadby, Leic.; [m.] Ronald Horseman, 21 July 1962; [ch.] Christopher, Robert, Peter; [ed.] Woodberry Down Comprehensive, North London; [occ.] Full Time Carer for Husband; [oth. writ.] Two articles on personal life story published. Also two short stories published. (All in women's magazines.); [pers.] Since giving up my career as a secretary to look after my husband, who has suffered two strokes and is now very disabled, I have found great pleasure in writing stories and poems. My way of coping with expressing how I feel.; [a.] Witham, Essex, UK

HORSFIELD, GORDON
[pen.] Gordon Barrie; [b.] 27 May 1926, Sheffield; [p.] George William Horsfield, May Horsfield; [m.] Divorced; [ed.] Elementary - plus private study; [occ.] Retired R.A.F. one year parachute regiment, 2 1/2 years fire service 32 years, fire advisor boots the chemists 11 years; [memb.] Member of Institution of Fire Engineers; [hon.] 1939-45 War Medal, General Service Medal (Palestine), Fire Brigade Long Service and Good Conduct Medal, Jubilee Medal; [oth. writ.] Numerous poems and short stories and number published; [pers.] Although influenced by early poets I constantly strive to do something different 'One Last Chance' was written whilst suffering a nervous breakdown - brought ex wife's on by divorce petition; [a.] Newhaven, E. Sussex, UK

HOUNSLOW, LOUISE
[b.] 19 July 1973, Redhill; [p.] Michael and Beverley Hounslow; [ed.] De Stafford Secondary School; [occ.] Legal Secretary; [a.] Sydenham, London, UK

HOUSTON, DON
[pen.] Don Spencer Fields; [b.] 13 March 1965, Scotland; [p.] Charles, and Frances Houston; [m.] Lady Wendy; [ch.] 1 girl (Toni); [occ.] Artist/Sculptor; [hon.] Diploma Arts/Graphics; [oth. writ.] Poem published in "Anthology Christian Verse", 1996. Several songs written for local musicians.; [pers.] I see my writing as an extension of my art, from abstract to contemporary, life moves me to create.; [a.] Dundee, Tayside, UK

HOWARD, CAROL ANN
[b.] 19 January 1943, Guernsey; [p.] Violet and Thomas Howard (1915 and 1911); [ed.] Amherst Primary and Junior, Ladies College, Guernsey; [occ.] Retired on health grounds since last June - was civil servant; [memb.] Zion Christian Fellowship (Evangelical church); [oth. writ.] Other poems which I have made into a small book - none published professionally; [pers.] All my poems are written out of my own experience of God in my life amidst many troubles - this particular one was during my latest stay in hospital.; [a.] St. Saviour's, Guernsey, UK

HOWE, MRS. JENNIE
[b.] 9/11/35, Co. Durham; [m.] John Howe; [ch.] David, Ian, Gavin, Peter and Tracy; [occ.] Accounts Clerk; [pers.] I like writing poems for family and friends on special occasions. My other hobbies are painting and drawing. I also enjoy the company of my six lovely grandchildren.

HUCKSTEPP, JULIE
[b.] 1 July 1979, Strood; [p.] Clive Huckstepp, Sally Huckstepp; [ed.] Chapter Secondary School; [occ.] Sixth form student; [pers.] In writing poems I hope to reach the inner feeling in each individual.; [a.] Rochester, Kent, UK

HUDD, ALLAN
[b.] 23 September 1965, Falkirk, Scotland; [p.] George Hudd, Mary Hudd; [m.] Linda Hudd, 24 May 1985; [ch.] Kerry Hudd, Allan Hudd, Falon Hudd; [ed.] Denny High School Scotland to O'Level Standard; [occ.] Security Officer; [hon.] English literature, Mathematics, Mensa Award, German Language; [oth. writ.] Several poems published in my youth, book of poetry yet to be published; [pers.] My inspiration for my writing comes from my family and from the love my wife and I will always share.; [a.] Clayton, Manchester, UK

HUDSON, CAROLYNE
[pen.] Anna May; [b.] 12 November 1964, Cardiff; [p.] Janice Richards; [m.] Richard Hudson, 5 November 1994; [ch.] Lorna, Felicity; [ed.] St. Brides Major Church in Wales Primary Brynteg Comprehensive Bridgend; [occ.] Childminder; [oth. writ.] First time I have had a poem published mostly write for pleasure.; [pers.] I observe life and find my inspiration to write from it. I try to write how a moment or an event in my life has made me feel.; [a.] Llandrindod, Wells, Powys, UK

HUDSON, IAN
[b.] 16 January 1940, Farmborough, Kent; [p.] George and Jessie Pasifull; [m.] Maureen Teresa, 5 October 1963; [ch.] Alan and Mark; [ed.] Charterhouse Secondary School, Orpington, Kent; [occ.] Industrial Cleaning Contractor; [oth. writ.] Plenty written, none published; [pers.] My one wish is to have my poems published in a book and this is an honour thank you.; [a.] Rochester, Kent, UK

HUDSON, TERESA
[b.] 6 April, 1964, Cornwall; [p.] William Pesterfield, Jill Pesterfield; [m.] Howard Hudson, 1 June 1987; [ch.] Christopher Hudson and Benjamin Hudson; [ed.] Chichester Girls' High School, King Edward VII Hospital Midhurst; [occ.] (Nurse) Sister in nursing home; [pers.] Poems are precious and should be individually interpreted and enjoyed, whether by the writer or by the reader. They should take you on a journey. This particular poem is dedicated to my grandmother, whom I loved dearly.; [a.] Littlehampton, West Sussex, UK

HUGHES, MARY E.
[b.] 6 November 1922, Port Talbot; [p.] Lewis John Jenkins and Mathilda Louisa Jenkins; [m.] Kenneth Hughes, 3 May 1947; [ch.] Keith, Jeanette; [ed.] Sandfields Elementary Port Talbot; [pers.] No record outer than from the school of life.; [a.] Port Talbot, West Glam, UK

HULL, WANITA
[b.] 21 March 1944, Jamaica; [p.] Deceased; [m.] Separated, 21 December 1968; [ch.] One, one grandson; [ed.] Guildhall University, London, Ecl. Modular Degree In Arts; [occ.] Unemployed at the moment; [pers.] The night does not wish to come so that you cannot come and I cannot go. Poet: Frederico Gracia Lorca

HUMFREY, MRS. JACQUELINE
[b.] 10 December 1955, Jersey; [p.] The Hon Louise and David Fellowes; [ed.] Brondesbury-at-Stocks, Tring, Herts, The Hilary Bradshaw Secretarial College Cambridge; [occ.] Journalist/song writer, (mostly comedy); [oth. writ.] Several poems published in various books and magazines. Articles in various magazines and newspapers.; [pers.] To much of a good thing is simply wonderful! My writing has been greatly influenced by Spike Milligan, Tommy Cooper and Morecambe and Wise.; [a.] Bury St. Edmunds, Suffolk, UK

HUNT, MRS. CAROLE
22 March 1944; Marjorie was my little grandson Billy's friendly neighbour. Whenever Billy saw her, he gave her a dandelion from his garden. Marjorie died, and on her rainy funeral day, I searched everywhere for a dandelion but they had all turned to seed. So, for his floral tribute, Billy blew the seeds of a dead dandelion onto Marjorie's grave. The following day the sun came out, as did all the dandelions.; Mitcham, Surrey, UK

HUNT, MARY BEATICE LEWIS
[pen.] Mary Hunt; [b.] 5 July 1914, Maida Vale, London; [p.] George Foss, Violet Foss; [m.] Albert Edward Hunt, 19 August 1960; [ed.] Maida Vale College Hillbrow School, Heathfield, Sussex Franciscan Convent, Soignies Belgium; [occ.] Retired Nursing Aid; [memb.] East Grinstead Justice/Peace Group, Mastermind Club, National/Film Theatre; [oth. writ.] "The Shepherds - a novel short story published in `Yours' Magazine

3 short stories in "Catholic Fire Side" (Now out of publication); [pers.] I am a Roman Catholic with ecumenical leanings was influenced in your by Theatre, Silent films and poetry.; [a.] East Grinstead, West Sussex, UK

HUNTER, MARY
[b.] 1 February 1924, Seaham Harbour; [p.] James Weir Andrews, Mary Andrews; [m.] James Hunter, 26 July 1947; [ch.] Gordon, Ian, Paul Stuart, Adrian, Lynne; [ed.] Byron Terrace Infant and Junior School Seaham Intermediate School Billingham Technical College; [occ.] Retired; [memb.] Englefield Green Gardeners Association, Art Classes; [oth. writ.] Several poems published in poetry anthologies; [pers.] Aim to set a good example to other prefer writing down to earth poems rather than romantics.; [a.] Egham, Surrey, UK

HURST, PAMELA
[b.] Over 21, Leek; [p.] Mary and Charles Butcher; [m.] Alan Hurst, 17 June 1967; [ch.] June (27), John (23); [ed.] Westwood Hall Girls' Grammar School, Leek; [occ.] Proofreader with the Leek Post and Times; [memb.] Leekemian Operatic Society and Leek Choral Society; [hon.] 5 'O' levels, 1 A level in English. Various certificates for 1-4 piano grades, shorthand and typewriting and business studies.; [oth. writ.] A full length novel called 'Angel of the Moorlands' which was locally published by Churnet Valley Books June 1995. It is a historical romance set in Leek.; [pers.] I regard life as a karmic journey and try to do unto others as I would have them do unto me.; [a.] Leek, Staffs, UK

HUTCHISON, MARION
[pen.] Black Douglas; [b.] 31 January 1919, Buckhaven; [p.] Christina Taylor, David Drysdale; [m.] John Hutchison (Deceased), 25 June 1937; [ch.] Three sons; [ed.] Stobswell School; [occ.] Retired; [hon.] Honours Cert. for Bible (COS) at age 13; [oth. writ.] One poem printed many others written; [pers.] When I'm sad or when I'm glad when I'm good or when I'm bad I must write it down I maybe old but my heart and mind are still growing; [a.] Tayport, Fife, UK

HYMAN, DAVID
[pen.] David Black; [b.] 15 May 1943, Isleworth; [p.] Emma Hyman, Andrew Hyman; [m.] Barbara Hyman, 17 October 1963; [ch.] Dean Vincent, Lynn Michelle; [ed.] Ashford Secondary (Middx); [occ.] Gardener, Imperial College, Ascot; [memb.] International Songwriters Association, Ireland; [oth. writ.] Several songs published; [pers.] I like to think that whatever my eyes see, my heart will feel.; [a.] Ascot, Berks, UK

ILOTT, PAULINE ANN
[b.] 27 August 1951, Beckingham; [m.] Paul Henry Ilott, 22 July 1972; [ch.] Three; [ed.] Secondary Modern Dorset and Oxford; [occ.] Phlebotomist; [memb.] Local Amateur Choir; [pers.] I feel both poetry and music is a very expressionable medium. Pleasure for all to give and receive.; [a.] North Hinksey, Oxford, UK

INDRAYAN, PRITI
[b.] 21 May 1969, India, Bombay; [p.] A. K. Lindrayen and Usha Indrayen; [ed.] University of Westminster, Secondary - Green School for Girls; [occ.] Business Analyst; [hon.] BSc Hons Science (Computing) class 2:1; [a.] London, UK

IRWIN, OLIVE
[pen.] Olive Irwin; [b.] 22 December 1972, Ireland, Leitrim; [p.] William and Emma Irwin; [ed.] Secretarial course (1992), Art and Design course (1994-95), Computer (Word Processing) City and Guilds Sligo Grammer (1996), Leaving cert (1992) School; [occ.] Doing art work painting; [memb.] The Book Club of Ireland; [hon.] Business Awareness Awards 1989 "Irish Life" received a certificate and plaque. Art: Dromahair show every year winning 1st and 2nd and 3rd places in some sections.; [pers.] I think all poetry school come from within our self. Listen to your heart and you will no.; [a.] Dromahair, Leitrim, UK

ISLAM, S. M. TAJUL
[b.] 25 January 1940, Chakhar, Bangladesh; [p.] Nurul Huda Syed and Tahera Syed; [m.] Rehana Islam Syed, 9 May 1963; [ch.] Munir, Shahed, Asif, Sonya, Tania; [ed.] F.H. School and F.H. College, Chakhar, and University of Dhaka, Dhaka, Bangladesh: B, A, (Honours) and M.A. in English; [occ.] Teaching part-time teacher of Bengali and English in two schools; [memb.] Bangladeshi Teachers' Association, National Council for Mother Tongue teaching, some other Bangladeshi Organizations.; [oth. writ.] Poems and lyrics, stories and articles in Bengali and English in Dhaka and London (including 2 poems in 2 anthologies published in the U.K.); [pers.] I often tend to delve into the metaphysical and spiritual depths of life in my obsession with time. I dream of a world of values—love, harmony, peace and so on, and my message is that of a good life of conscience and common sense. To some extent I may have been influenced by the romantics.; [a.] East Ham, London, UK

IZATT, LISA JANE
[b.] 11 November 1968, Huntingdon, Cambs.; [p.] Mr. Herbert James Izatt, Mrs. Betty Doreen Izatt; [ed.] St. Ivo Comprehensive School, Cambridge College of Further Education, Norfolk College of Art and Technology; [oth. writ.] There have been many pieces of writings and as of yet need to be copy written and hopefully published. [pers.] I wish for my writing, present and future, to not only become an appreciated inspiration to many people's lives, but to equally expand the mind and soul as mine has been through other writers. I thank both my parents for their encouragement and support.; [a.] West Town, Peterborough, Cambs, UK

JACKSON, MRS. DORIS M.
[b.] 13 November 1923, Wandsworth; [p.] Alice Glasspool, Francis Glasspool; [m.] Thomas E. Jackson, 21 December 1946; [ch.] Ian Jackson, Sue Jackson; [ed.] No special Education but after Education went on to do Business Studies at Pitmans College.; [occ.] Housewife; [oth. writ.] Poem in prize winning poetry by C. John Naylor "D.I.Y. on the National Health".; [pers.] Through poetry we can express our Philosophy of life, sometimes happy sometimes sad!; [a.] Crawley, W. Sussex, UK

JACKSON, HAZEL VALERIE
[pen.] Lettice Payne; [b.] 24 March 1951, Sunderland; [p.] John Payne Hudson, Margaret Hudson; [m.] George Jackson, 1 June 1974; [ch.] Sarah Lettice, Christopher George; [ed.] Chester Rd Senior School Thornhill Comprehensive Sunderland; [occ.] Housewife and Mother; [oth. writ.] I have written sixty something poems, but only submitted one for any form of competition; [pers.] I share my house with 4 cats and 2 dogs. And find my love for animals reflects in my poetry. Walking my dogs greatly influences my outlook of nature and the world in general; [a.] Sunderland, Tyne and Wear, UK

JACKSON, JULIE
[b.] 4 June 1970, Essex; [p.] Maureen Jackson, Eddie Jackson; [ed.] Parsloes Manor Comprehensive School; [occ.] Deputy Catering Manager, Westminster - London; [oth. writ.] I have had other poems published in books, and currently looking into some song and story writing.; [pers.] The most important thing in my life is my family and a special place in my heart for Paul who believes in me and my writing.; [a.] Dagenham, Essex, UK

JACKSON, KENNETH V.
[pen.] Kenneth V. Jackson; [b.] 14 March 1928, Nottingham; [p.] James Vincent Jackson, Alice Winifred Jackson; [m.] Gladys V. Jackson, 1 September 1951; [ch.] Sandrea Melodie, Clive Van, Stanley David; [ed.] London Rd, Elementary, Trent Bridge Senior Boys School, Mapperly Plains Rd, and Westdale Lane High School Nottingham, Nottm University, Army School of Catering Aldershot; [occ.] Retired; [memb.] Kingfisher Angling Club, Future Word, Worldwide Web Traders; [hon.] Catering City and Guilds various, Army Catering Certs 'A' and 'B'; [oth. writ.] Children's Stories Broadcast on British Forces Radio in Germany, several poems published by 'Arrival Press' and in Local Newspapers in National Press, articles and designs in 'Goodwoodworking Magazine X The Woodworker articles in 'Direction Mag.'; [pers.] I have been writing and publishing poems and songs since the age of seven. I have written stories and articles ever since I left school. I am an artist, designer aerospace.; [a.] Sheringham, Norfolk, UK

JACKSON, STUART DAVID
[b.] 31 March 1966, Wallsend; [p.] Doreen and Lawrence Jackson; [m.] Paula Alexander, 20 September 1997; [ed.] Burnside High School, Wallsend, North Tyneside College, Wallsend; [occ.] Merchandiser in D.I.Y. Retail; [memb.] Wallsend Cricket Club.; [pers.] I shall endeavour to write about reality, it is from this, that we learn. This poem is a tribute to all who lost their lives during the carnage that was world war I.; [a.] Wallsend, Tyne and Wear, UK

JACOBS, LEONIE KJT
[b.] 30 May 1970, Trinidad, West Indies; [p.] Dr. Franklyn Jacobs, Josephine Jacobs; [ed.] Girls High School (St. Vincent), Providence (Trinidad), Queen Elizabeth Girls School (London), Woolsey Hall Tutorial College (Oxford), Holborn College (London); [occ.] Pupil Barrister; [memb.] Member of the Honorable Society of the Middle Temple (Inn of Court); [pers.] I have recently come to understand the truth in, and power of, the ability of each individual to 'create his or her own reality.; [a.] London, UK

JAFFIER, MICHAEL
[pen.] Ridley Scott; [b.] 22 January 1961, Huddersfield; [p.] Winston Jaffier, Cynthia Jaffier; [ed.] Secondary school, Deighton High School; [occ.] Unemployed; [pers.] I write for the pleasure of it all.; [a.] Huddersfield, W. Yorkshire, UK

JAMES, D. A. L.
[pen.] Alwyn James; [b.] 28 December 1940, Swansea Valley; [p.] Bryn and Lilian James; [m.] Gillian James, 20 September 1978; [ch.] Marc James; [ed.] Comprehensive Education, attended Neath and Swansea Technical Colleges attaining, City and Guilds in woodworking; [occ.] Retired, Police Inspector, completed 27 yrs. Retired on Health; [memb.] St. Giles Gag Club Newtown, Handicap of 10 prior to my illness, have many trophies; [hon.] None, first poem written; [oth. writ.] Have written two Western novels, but up to now have been unable to get one published. Will keep trying.; [pers.] Have taken up writing since my retirement. With an illness known as M.E. had no previous difference.; [a.] Newtown, Powys, UK

JAMES, LINDA
[b.] 8 July 1951, South Shields; [p.] Hilda Bowman, Norman Bowman; [m.] Ernie James, 17 May 1975; [ed.] Brinkburn Comp. School; [occ.] Secretary; [oth. writ.] Several other poems, mainly done for family and friends, especially for special events e.g. retirements, leaving, birthdays etc.; [pers.] I have been greatly influenced by my father who also writes. It was from him I learnt the art of writing.; [a.] South Shields, Tyne and Wear, UK

JAPHET, RAYMOND BARUCH
[pen.] Raymond Japhet; [b.] 27 May 1909, Paris; [p.] Leon Judah Japhet, Esther Japhet; [ed.] Bronzesbury College; [occ.] Journalist; [memb.] West London Synagogue, National Union of Journalists, Guild of Jewish Journalists, Highgate Life-Buoys (Open-air swimmers), Clacton Swimming Club, YHA, Ramblers' Association, Tuesday Climbing Club; [oth. writ.] Reporter Islington and Holloway Press, Reporter Clacton Times, then Deputy Chief Sub-editor, Sub-editor East Anglian Daily Times, Sub-editor Daily Express, Sub-editor (part-time) Sunday Express; [pers.] I cannot kill, I cannot bomb a town, during world war II I opt for the National Fire Service in London. I am ready to lay my life down for the country and share the hardships of others.; [a.] Dollis Hill, London, UK

JARRAD, MARK
[pen.] Mark Jarrad; [b.] 18 September 1964, Birmingham; [p.] Maureen Norris, Joseph Burke; [ch.] Karl, Kurtis, Jamie, Kayley; [ed.] Various Schools; [occ.] Unemployed College Student (Studying Multimedia); [oth. writ.] I have written many other poems I hope to have published in the near future.; [pers.] Some of my poems are based on personal experience and are reflections of what I have thought and felt at the time life and the world are my inspiration.

JARVIS, ANGELA
[b.] 15 January 1947, Fenny Stratford; [p.] Rex Rhee, Dorothy Rhee; [m.] Bruce Jarvis, 24 September 1967; [ch.] Gareth Rex, Alun Charles, Robert Bruce; [ed.] Well St (First) School, Buckingham, County Secondary School Buckingham College Further Educ. High Wycombe; [occ.] (Housewife) Partner in Husband's Garage Business/secretary.; [hon.] County art competition (School) 1st. Brooke Bond Art Competition (school) 1st Speech Award (school) Buckingham Carnival Queen! (1968); [pers.] One should always, have faith but most important of all, one should always believe in oneself.; [a.] Buckingham, Bucks, UK

JARVIS, DOUGLAS
[b.] 15 December 1960, Mansfield, Notts; [m.] Julie, 4 November 1995; [ch.] Jamie and Jenna (Julie's 1st marriage); [ed.] Queen Elizabeths Grammar School at Mansfield, Later at Clowne College of F.E.; [occ.] Plater in Medium to heavy engineering; [hon.] Best student on CGLI 217 Course at clowne College 1979; [oth. writ.] Quite a lot but none published; [pers.] What ever you do, always enjoy your life, but try not to hurt anyone else, please dedicate the poem to Jason, he would have appreciated and known the meaning of it.; [a.] Bolsover, Derbyshire, UK

JARVIS, SALLY
[b.] 28 July 1941, Newchapel, Surrey; [p.] Alfred and Kathleen Cooper; [m.] John Jarvis (Deceased), 6 October 1959; [ch.] Stephen, John, Alan, Victoria, and Ellis; [ed.] St. Andrews Secondary Modern School, Old Town Croydon, Surrey; [occ.] Mother, Housewife and Widow; [pers.] The wonders of nature fascinate me, I've always liked nature and wildlife, and find it very therapeutic, and it makes you realize how wonderful life and nature really is. I have always read and enjoyed patience strong. So I believe she has influenced me.; [a.] London, UK

JAYAWARDENA, SHARMINI
[pen.] Rashmi Q, N.S.; [b.] 19 October 1957, Colombo, Sri Lanka; [p.] M.R. and Irene Jayawardena; [m.] Ismeth Magdon-Ismail; [ch.] Sumitra and Sunari Sooriaaratchi; [ed.] University of Kelaniya, Sri Lanka; [occ.] Company Director; [hon.] English language and literature; [oth. writ.] Poems published in the foll: University Poetry Publications. Phoenix - Sri Lanka Journal of English in the Commonwealth, 1991. Local Newspaper. The Great Sandy River by Darshini de Zoysa, 1995, Het Spienhuis Publishers. Amsterdam.; [a.] Middlesex, England

JEFFERIES, TIMOTHY C.
[b.] 05/03/70, Loughborough; [p.] Barbara and Trevor; [ed.] Manvers Pierrepont Comprehensive School, Forest Fields College, South Nottingham College; [occ.] Security Officer; [memb.] World Wide Fund for Nature, OXFAM; [oth. writ.] Poems published in numerous anthologies including: Sunlight and Shadows -- Poetry Institute of the British Isles, Simple Pleasures -- Arrival Press, Life as We Know It -- Anchor Books, Earthly and Divine Love -- Beehive Press; [pers.] To be inspired, inflamed with passion, to write as one's soul dictates, these are moments of triumph -- when the mind forms a union with the source of being and reflects onto a page an expression of vision.; [a.] Nottingham, Nottinghamshire

JEFFERSON, WILSON
[b.] 20 March 1923, Carlisle; [p.] Wilson and Sarah Jefferson; [m.] Gladys Jefferson, 19 June 1943; [ch.] Alan and Brian; [ed.] Elementary Newton Junior and Ashley Senior Carlisle; [occ.] Retired Heating-Engineer three years B.R. Fireman 1948-1951; [oth. writ.] Have other Railway poems, have had two on Radio Carlisle; [pers.] I try to keep the railway alive for future generations, both in poetry and pencil drawings.; [a.] Heysham-Morecambe, Lancs, UK

JENKIN, NICK S.
[b.] 15 August 1974, London; [p.] Graham Jenkin, Patricia Jenkin; [ed.] Fitzwimarc Secondary School, Seecat (Southend College); [hon.] BTEC OND in Construction, BTEC HNC in Construction; [oth. writ.] First novel: - 'Warlord: Vol 1 - The Resurrection' due to be published by Minerva Press late 1996!; [pers.] Everybody on this planet is supremely excellent at atleast one thing. The object of life is to find out personally what the hell it is.; [a.] Rayleigh, Essex, UK

JENKINSON, ANDREW
[b.] 6 May 1956, London; [p.] Edward Jenkinson and Dorothy Jenkinson; [m.] Sharon Jenkinson, 29 July 1978; [ch.] Warren, Lauren; [ed.] Furtherwick Park, Thurrock College; [occ.] Accountant; [pers.] I dedicate this poem to my late father who revealed in literature all of his life, and whom I miss dearly.; [a.] South Benfleet, Essex, UK

JENNINGS, MABEL VERA
[pen.] "Vee"; [b.] 16 April 1915, Bombay, India; [p.] George Jennings and Mabel Jennings; [ed.] Senior Cambridge in St. Marys Girls High School, Poona - Maharashtra, Diploma in Dress Making and Designing - Bombay; [occ.] Creating Exquisite Artifacts from Semi Precious Minerals; [memb.] Founder Member and Trustee of Society of All Saints Church School - Lonavla; [hon.] Highly Commended for the artifacts, Object De Art Exhibited at Bombay and Poona; [oth. writ.] Hundreds of "Four - Liners" poems on Every - day life situations, and printed in attractive booklets.; [pers.] Be firm yet kind - justice tempered with mercy - a philosophy I have tried to practice all my life.; [a.] Lonavla, Maharastra, India

JIACOUMI, PHYLLIS
[b.] 18 July 1952; [p.] Dorothy (Stiles) Jiacoumi and Procopis Jiacoumi; [m.] Divorced; [ed.] Secondary Alan International Hairdressing School Thanet Technical College Hildestone College Broadstairs; [occ.] Hair stylist; [memb.] Creature Writing Hildestone College Broad stars, Poetry Now; [hon.] H. W. F. Hairdressing diploma - Advanced City Guilds, Rodney's School Men's hairdressing; [oth. writ.] Poem published in 1991 - 'Poetry Now' South East. Title: 'What Would People Think'. Selection of poetry (Love Theme) Various short stories.; [pers.] I write to gain insight into humanity and my feelings about love and life.; [a.] Ramsgate, Kent, UK

JILLINGS, HARRIET
[b.] 25 May 1942, Emsworth, Hants; [p.] Douglas and Alice Carter; [m.] Guy Jillings, 21 September 1963, Fred Backrach, 26 October 1990; [ch.] Matthew (B-1967), Anna (B-1969); [ed.] Nonsuch High School, Cheam, University College, London; [occ.] Journalist/Lecturer Readers Digest/Richmond College; [memb.] Surrey Wildlife Trust.; [hon.] B.A. (Hon) History M.A. Dutch Golden Age Culture P.G.C.E. London (Distinction); [oth. writ.] Editor Our Island Heritage (Readers Digest Books) 1988. Writer Readers Digest College Guide 1989 and 1995, Articles in New Society, The Village Voice (New York), Evening Standard (London); [pers.] People matter more than things.; [a.] Twickenham, Middlesex, UK

JOHNS, ALICIA
[pen.] Alicia Johns; [b.] 1931, Cheshire; [m.] 1977; [occ.] Retired; [oth. writ.] Published - Anthology - 'Proud to be 50 +' by arrival press and various unpublished; [pers.] As a carer, I don't have a lot of spare time so I scribble a line here and there and then blend it together. Unorthodox but I need the outlet of writing; [a.] Northampton, UK

JOHNS, CYNTHIA JOAN
[pen.] Joan Johns; [b.] 15 May 1929, Saint Austell, Cornwall; [p.] Edward and Gwendoline Guy; [m.] Selbourne Johns, 30 October 1949; [ed.] Treverbyn Primary and County School Cornwall Technical College; [occ.] Retired; [memb.] Sussex Wildlife Trust; [oth. writ.] Award from Milk Marketing Board for Original Recipe Using Clotted Cream. Article about Treatment of Oiled Sea Birds published in Wildlife Magazine; [pers.] My first poem. Widowed and retired I now lead a fairly inactive life with my black Labrador Jet. Who is also getting on in years so maybe I will now continue to write more poetry; [a.] Chichester, West Sussex, UK

JOHNSON, DONNA
[b.] 9 June 1964, Bristol; [ed.] Aston Manor School, Handsworth Technical College; [occ.] Singer, songwriter; [memb.] The Presenter's Club, (BASCA) British Academy of Songwriters, Composers and Authors, and Equity; [oth. writ.] Songs performed on BRMB Radio and Jingles written for Radio WM.; [pers.] My aim is to express in words the emotions that we sometimes find hard to explain.; [a.] Kingstanding, Birmingham, UK

JOHNSON, JACQUELINE MARIE
[pen.] Marie Spencer; [b.] 24 April 1951, Rotherham; [p.] Katimierz and Joyce Donarski; [m.] John William Johnson, 24 March 1973; [ch.] Joseph, Benjamin, Alexis, Krysta; [ed.] Rotherham Girls High School Wolsey Hall, Oxford Correspondence College; [occ.] Freelance Translator/ Private Tutor (French, English, Maths); [memb.] Associate of Institute of Linguists, Member of British Mensa; [hon.] BA (Hons) Lond. French; [oth. writ.] Other poems and short stories, appreciations of other amateur literary works.; [pers.] While science seeks to solve the mysteries of the universe art transcends them thus we exist through science but we live through art.; [a.] Rotherham, S. Yorks, UK

JOHNSON, MISS JEAN
[pen.] Jean Johnson; [b.] 13 February 1967, Bristol; [ed.] Aston Mannor School, College of Food and Domestic Arts; [occ.] Singer, song writer; [memb.] B.A.S.C.A. the British Academy of Song Writer's Composers and Author's, Equity, P.A.M.R.A; [pers.] I am here for the children. My aim is to feed them knowledge for their survival.; [a.] Birmingham, UK

JOHNSON, JOY PATRICIA
[b.] 20 February 1962, Bristol; [occ.] Singer/ Songwriter, Artist (Painter), Poet; [memb.] BASCA (Bristish Academy of Songwriters Composers and Authors). Equity. Ebony eyes.; [pers.] Looking at my surroundings I feel like a traveller through time. My body is my spaceship and the only means of transport. It is the only way I can communicate with my species of this world. Our brains are the man source of power and exceeds our thoughts far greater than we realize or give it credit for.; [a.] Birmingham, UK

JOHNSON, SYLVIA
[b.] 1 May 1933, Northampton; [m.] Anthony, 25 April 1952; [ch.] Toni, Anne, Lynn, Nicola, Laurence; [ed.] Notre Dame High School Northampton College; [occ.] Retired Ass. Costing Manager; [oth. writ.] Poem published in 'Poetry Now' several poems and writings published in magazines.; [pers.] When one is feeling low or sad, the written word in poetry or prose can express the beauty and wonder of our world. It can transcend sadness into hopefulness.; [a.] Northampton, Northants, UK

JOHNSTON, JANIS
[b.] 14 April 1960, Birmingham; [m.] Cyril Johnston, 17 September 1984; [ch.] Peter, Daniel and Zoe; [ed.] Queensbridge Secondary School; [occ.] Housewife; [pers.] Patience brings it's own rewards, if you have the desire for success.; [a.] Birmingham, Warwickshire, UK

JONES, ANN
[b.] 4 October 1974, Ellesmere Port; [p.] John Richard Jones, Patricia Jones; [ed.] Ellesmere Port Catholic High, Blacon Arts Centre, University of Wolmerhampton; [occ.] Student, studying for BA Honours in English Literature and Philosophy; [memb.] Dudley Rag., Lourdes Hospitality; [pers.] I have stood at the edge of the world and in the silence and coldness I found there, lie the answers.; [a.] Ellesmere Port, Wirral, UK

JONES, CLAIRE
[b.] 5 June 1984, Llandloes, Mid-Wales; [p.] Gail and Huw; [ed.] Abermafesp County Primary School, Newtown High School; [occ.] School girl; [memb.] School Orchestra (violin); [oth. writ.] Poems published in "Poetry Now" 1996 anthology of Wales; [pers.] As I am only 12 years old, I hope to write many more poems, and hopefully have them published.; [a.] Newtown, Powys, UK

JONES, HELEN LOUISE
[b.] 18 September 1979, Caerphilly; [p.] Dawn and Paul Jones; [ed.] St. Martins Comprehensive School Ystrad Mynach College of Further Education; [oth. writ.] Story, titled we live in Wales, published by South Wales Reading Association for the 1988 writing competition.; [pers.] I enjoy writing poems in my spare time, and try to reflect the funny side of life is them. Pan eyes has been an inspiration to me.; [a.] Caerphilly, Mid-Glam, UK

JONES, MRS. HILDA
[pen.] Hilda Jones; [b.] 7 June 1923, Wrexham; [p.] Deceased; [m.] Deceased, 17 October 1942; [ch.] Douglas Seymour Jones - Alan Jones; [ed.] Holt Endowed School, Denbighshire Technical Institute; [occ.] Retired; [oth. writ.] Poems published in two anthologies, also poems published in "Tempo" and local press; [pers.] I pray for the strength to change the things I can. The courage to accept the things I can not change. And the wisdom to know the difference.; [a.] Runcorn, Cheshire, UK

JONES, JEANNETTE
[b.] 8 April 1940, Wroxall, Isle of Wight; [p.] Ethel and Albert Russell; [m.] John Jones, 13 May 1961; [ch.] Stephen, Nicholas, Matthew and David; [ed.] "The Fairway", Secondary Modern School, Sandown, I. of W.; [occ.] Housewife (and full-time granny)!!; [memb.] Regular member of the Bitterne Park Baptist Church; [oth. writ.] Constantly writing poetry and have had some published in church magazine. Often requested by others to write verses for special occasions.; [pers.] Poetry writing gives me great pleasures, I hope others will get as much pleasure from reading!; [a.] Southampton, Hants, UK

JONES, MARTIN
[b.] 20 December 1964, Cheshire; [oth. writ.] Poems, songs and several short stories; [pers.] To honestly share my experiences and to influence my generation in the descriptive beauty of words. Influenced by Shakespeare; [a.] Avoca Beach, N.S.W., Australia

JONES, MICHAEL
[b.] 25 January 1964, Nicosia, Cyprus; [ed.] Tabley House School Knutsford; [occ.] Writer; [pers.] You can never be free of those you are drawn to until you have nothing left to learn from them.; [a.] Warrington, Cheshire, UK

JONES, RACHEL AMANDA
[b.] 6 September 1980, Tywn; [p.] Glenys Jones and Rhyddarch Jones; [ed.] Tywyn Secondary and High School sitting my G.C.S.E's in the Summer Term of 1997; [occ.] Part-time Childminding and Restaurant Work; [oth. writ.] I love writing poetry and have written over 200 long and short poems in the past year. I also put rhythms to a few of my poems and my friends in a local band called 'Euphoria' write music to the words.; [pers.] Life inspires my poetry, everyday is so different. When inspiration touches me I like to write in the style of euphemism then people have to truly concentrate to understand my hidden thoughts.; [a.] Aberdovey, Gwynedd, UK

JONES, RUSSELL
[b.] 20 August 1962, Hartlepool; [occ.] Unemployed writer and Musician and Gardener; [pers.] They promised leisure time the pays just fine read between every line its a joke of the 90s crime times nearly up?; [a.] Hartlepool, Cleveland, UK

JONES, VIOLET
[pen.] Vee Jay; [b.] 9 March 1940, London; [p.] Charles and Jane Springett; [ch.] Trevor, Martin and Darron; [ed.] Keeble High School, Amberley Road London; [occ.] Cashier, Supervisor, Malton Leisure Centre; [hon.] Only a supermarket cake competition, only got a runners prize; [pers.] It was my great loss of you lady, that made me dedicate this poem to you.; [a.] Norton Malton, North Yorkshire, UK

JONES, MR. W. J. B.
[b.] 6 June 1924, Liverpool; [p.] Mary and Thomas Jones; [m.] Selina Florence Jones, 17 June 1950; [ch.] Keith, Valerie and Graeme; [ed.] Head Boy at Ellergreen Road School, Liverpool, II; [occ.] Retired (Footballer); [pers.] Bill was a devoted husband, father and grandfather. Who loved sport, especially football.; [a.] Chester, Cheshire, UK

JONES-MORRIS, VAUGHAN
[b.] 25 June 1959, Solihull; [hon.] None, but would like to have my own book published; [oth. writ.] I have one entry in an anthology; [pers.] I try to write what's inside most people's thoughts and dreams, poems that people can understand and relate to, and for Mandy my greatest love.; [a.] Solihull, W. Mids, UK

JORDAN, R. H.
[pen.] Gimi Jordan; [b.] 3rd November, 1913, Dovercourt, Essex; [p.] H. J. and F. L. Jordan; [m.] J. W. (Jo) Jordan, 25th December 1940; [ed.] Very little, mostly in the College of Longevity; [occ.] Retired; [oth. writ.] Plays and operettas for the schools in which I taught. "The Mees of Tre Boschi" (1995), "Bellocia" (1996), both tales of Italy, numerous verses in various publications.; [pers.] I am fired with am ambition to get as much as possible of my work into well-known channels. My father was a soldier and as he was moved to different stations, I attended 17 different schools and was therefore unknown in all of them!; [a.] Cromer, Norfolk

JOSEPH, MRS. MARY
[pen.] Mary Joseph; [b.] 18 January 1937, West Indies; [p.] Maria and Edgar Davis; [m.] A. S. Joseph, 21 June 1959; [ch.] Lorraine and Sharon; [ed.] All Saints School Antigua W.I.; [occ.] Retired lady; [memb.] The poetry society recently; [oth. writ.] Several poems published in Anchor Books, Arrival Press, Triumph House; [pers.] I am striving to reflect some goodness to mankind in all writing. I had this great influence of the love of poetry from my head master Mr. O'Mande. He gave us the urge also to love books.; [a.] London, UK

JUDD, SIMON ANDREW STUART
[b.] 19 September 1976, Singapore; [p.] Barry & Elizabeth Judd; [ed.] Tonbridge School, Kent, start English Literature at Leeds in September 96; [occ.] student on GAP year; [memb.] Burhill Golf Club, Walton-On-Thames, Surrey; [hon.] 4 'A' levels at A Grade, honorary scholar of Tonbridge School, awarded Senior Poetry Prize, House Praeposter, House Debating Team Captain, Member Elective Societies, English Society Secretary; [oth. writ.] Several poems published in school magazine, 2 poems published in "Tandem" magazine; [pers.] In my poetry, I try to induce action and thought by capturing experience. Poetry is the best medium for this as it shows words at their most powerful and persuades the reader to respond.; [a.] Weybridge, Surrey

JURY, SUSAN
[pen.] Sue; [b.] 9 December 1943, Patcham; [p.] Charles and Margery Parker; [m.] Alan Jury, 10 April 1992; [ch.] Jane, Alison and Katherine; [ed.] Secondary School; [occ.] Farmers wife; [oth. writ.] Being a milk lady for the last 10 years, I wrote a poem at Christmas for all my customers and sometimes they would write back in rhyme, or a die event in the village or on the farm would be put into verse.; [pers.] I love to write about the countryside, the farming way of life and animals.; [a.] Guestline, East Sussex, UK

KANE, ROMAINE
[pen.] Romaine Kane; [b.] 9 January 1968, Cookstown; [p.] Stanley and Shirley Smith; [m.] Robin Kane, 8 August 1992; [ed.] Cookstown High School, Dungannon F E College; [occ.] Civil Servant; [pers.] I adore painting pictures with words. I love their expression, power and effect. Immortalizing personal thoughts appeals greatly to me.; [a.] Cookstown, Tyrone, UK

KANWAR, RANJIT
[b.] Punjab, India; [m.] Mrs. Manjit Kanwar; [ch.] Three sons; [ed.] M.A., Ph. D. (Pol Sc.) Ph. D., (Metaphysics) M.A. (Jour.) Bsc. (Eng.), A.M.I.E.D. A.M.I.E.D. Associate member of Institution of Engineering Disfigures; [occ.] Editor - Newspaper; [memb.] (1) National Union of Journalists (UK). (2) Has been Chairman of Indian Punjabi writers Association Great britain. (3) Has been member International P.E.N. (Poet's essayists, Novelists) the English Centre (Award Association of Writers, London. (4) Life member of Kavi Mandal - Poets Circle Punjab India. (5) Has been General Secretary of Guild of Ethnic Minority Editors". (6) Has been Secretary of All India Literary Council. (7) Has been member of Rotary Club southall Greater London (8) Has been Chairman community relations Advisory Council Southall-London for 5 years. (9) Has been Governor of three Silvers in Greater London for 7 years.; [hon.] 1. Awarded first prize in poetry competition in India 2. Awarded first prize in short story contest in India 3. Awarded certificate of Merit in recognition of my contribution to the literature by the All India Literary Council India"; [oth. writ.] (1) Author and publisher "Who's who Indians in Britain (published in the U.K.), (2) Poem published in poetry now London 1996" (English) Anthology (3, 4, 5) Poem published in three books in Punjab Language Anthologies in India (6) Short story published in Punjab Language Anthology. (7, 8, 9) Three (of myself) poetry books under publication in Hindi Punjabu and Urdo languages (my original poems - about 300 Sonnets, songs and poems later to be translated in english language).; [per.] My original poems about 300, Sonnets, songs and poems, later to be translated in English language.; [a.] Hayes, Middlesex, UK

KARDAR, HELEN
[b.] Nr. Birmingham; [p.] Alec and Doreen Hastilow; [m.] A. H. Kardar (Dec.) former Pakistan Cricket Captain; [ch.] Julie Mariam; [ed.] Edgbaston Church of England College, Malvern Girl's College, Lady Margaret Hall, Oxford University; [occ.] Retired teacher of English and Classical Studies; [memb.] Atlanta Club, Oxford University, Cadbury and Northfield bridge clubs, Society Foe International Folk Dance, Birmingham Consumer Group; [hon.] MA (Oxon) English Literature Oxford "Blue" foe cricket; [oth. writ.] `Before I Forget' (Beldam Books) A semi-humorous description of life in a small village before the war and the effect of the war had on school children! Coventry Cavalcade and several magazine articles; [pers.] At the end comes understanding; [a.] Birmingham, W. Midlands, UK

KARIM, MINARA
[pen.] Mina Karim; [b.] 3 May 1974, London, UK; [p.] Mirja Monowara Begum and Late Haji Mohammed Abdul Karim; [occ.] Student; [oth. writ.] 'Bangladeshi Delights', 'Set The Bird Free' and many others, although have not been published, these poems are in my private collection.; [pers.] My poems are inspired by the experiences I have encountered in life so far, and the poem 'Dear Father' has been especially dedicated to my beloved late father Mohammed Abdul Karim who passed away on Sunday the 8th of August 1985.

KARRIE, PETER
[b.] 10 August 1946, Bridgend; [p.] Rex Alan and Jean Marjorie; [m.] Jane Elizabeth, 12 October 1984; [ch.] Alexandra (8) and Adam (6); [occ.] Entertainer (Singer/Actor), "Jean Val Jean" in "Les Miserables" Palace Theatre, London.; [hon.] Voted "Worlds Most Popular Phantom" twice 95/96; [oth. writ.] Yet to be published; [a.] Byfleet, Surrey, UK

KASHEM, ABUL ALAM
[b.] 1 July 1971, London; [p.] Abul Kashem, Aftara Banu; [m.] Rukshana Khanam, 17 December 1995; [ed.] Saint Pauls Way Comprehensive; [occ.] Financial Assistant, Imperial War Museum; [memb.] Whitechapel E.W. Taekwondo; [pers.] All my poems demonstrate feelings deep down from the heart whatever topic I'm writing about. My writing is direct, simple, yet constructive and carefully composed. All my work has meaning and can be read by young or old. I hope more of my work can be shared with the public.; [a.] Poplar, London, UK

KASRAIE, SHIREEN
[b.] 30 June 1978, Nottinghamshire; [p.] Behrouz Kasraie, Yvonne Kasraie; [ed.] Rodney School Kirlington, Clarendon College Nottingham; [occ.] Student; [oth. writ.] Several more poems, songs and short-stories. I am currently writing a novel.; [pers.] My writing reflects my deepest thoughts and feelings, of the issues which I hold closest to my heart.; [a.] Newstead, Abbey Park, Nottinghamshire, UK

KAY, MISS HEATHER LOUISE
[b.] 1 January 1985, Manchester; [p.] Lesley Kay and Dennis Kay; [ed.] St Mary's CE School Cadishead, Manchester; [occ.] Schoolgirl; [pers.] I enjoy writing poetry as a way of expressing myself, by letting what's in my mind just flow out on to a piece of paper.; [a.] Warrington, Cheshire, UK

KEELING, ELSIE
[b.] 29 August 1934, Chesterfield; [p.] Alice and Wilfred Wilkinson; [m.] Dennis Keeling, 23 July 1961; [ch.] Jacqueline Ann; [ed.] Pleasley Hill Secondary Modern School; [occ.] Housewife and Secretary; [oth. writ.] Several poems both serious and humorous. None up to date have been published. Because I have only just started to write for pleasure; [pers.] I find that my writing is a reflection of the way I perceive life. Always be true to yourself.; [a.] Chesterfield, Derby's, UK

KELLY, DENIS
[b.] 25 December 1951, Belfast; [occ.] Primary School Headteacher; [memb.] Cairde na N Gael (Friends of Ireland) National Association of Headteacher (NAHT); [hon.] B.Ed (Hons); [oth. writ.] Marjorie Matters (Minerva Press); [pers.] I write for pleasure and take delight when my work pleases others.; [a.] London, UK

KELLY, HELEN
[b.] 2 October 1957, Cork City, Ireland; [p.] Bernard and Kathleen Lynett; [m.] Brendan Kelly, 3 October 1983; [ch.] Tracy, Roy; [memb.] Satyananda Yoga Centre, Fitzpatricks Health Centre; [oth. writ.] This is my very first poem, and it is being published so maybe some of my others will be considered in the future.; [pers.] Life can never be lived happily or to its fullest, if there is anger or grief. Release these and everything else is secondary.

KELLY, MARGARET JEAN
[pen.] Jean Kelly; [b.] 6 July 1927, Swansea; [p.] Edward Sandy and Daisy Sandy; [m.] Royston Kelly, 10 May 1991 (2nd Marriage); [ch.] Victoria Margaret - Ian Victor; [ed.] Merrywood Grammar, Bristol Secretarial College; [occ.] Housewife Retired Local Govt Officer; [memb.] Townswomen's Guild National Trust Worldwide fund for nature int. fund for animal welfare royal sty. for the protection of birds; [oth. writ.] Over the years my poems have been for personal pleasure only. I have not considered publishing and have never entered a contest before.; [pers.] I try to reflect my personal observations on life, generally, and on the wonders of nature, which never cease to amaze me.; [a.] Bristol, UK

KELSEY, SIMON
[b.] 1 March 1965, Kingston, Surrey; [p.] Mr. Alan and Sally Kelsey; [m.] Donna Bodecott, Engaged; [ed.] Hinchleywood County, Secondary School Olaygate, Esher, Surrey; [occ.] Chief; [oth. writ.] I have written much poetry over the years, short stories, song lyrics, as yet nothing published.; [pers.] I feel poetry to be doorway to the soul of mankind. Often spiritual. It speaks a different language. More often expressing thoughts and feelings we cannot put into words.; [a.] Barnstaple, Devon, UK

KEMNA, INGRID
[b.] 4 May 1933, Wuppertal, Germany; [p.] Rolf and Hilde Kemna; [ed.] Municipal Grammar School for Girls Wuppertal - Barmen, Germany. Came to England in 1956 to learn English, private education; [occ.] Freelance translator and PA to Continental Law Consultant; [memb.] Fellow Institute of Linguists, Member Federal German Translators' Guild, Member British-German Assoc.; [pers.] I basically believe in "Life is what you make it" meaning that I take an active hand in shaping my life and try not to miss anymore opportunities. Expressing negative feelings in the succinct way of a poem puts them into perspective and allows me to put them behind me. I write poetry in German and English and sometimes mixing the two for fun.; [a.] London, UK

KEMPSTER, CHRISTINA
[b.] 28 February 1934, Manchester; [p.] Christina Roden, Stephen Perry; [m.] Bernard Kempster, 29 September 1956; [ch.] Mary Catherine, Paul Francis; [ed.] St. Charles Borromeo, (Hadfield, Derbyshire) Adelphi House Convent Salford; [occ.] Retired; [memb.] St. Vincent De Paul Society, St. Ann's Dramatic Society; [oth. writ.] Plays, Pantomimes hymns; [pers.] To love God and my neighbour. Striving to Be humble!!!; [a.] Ashton-under-Lyne, Lancs, UK

KEMPT, KEVIN KEITH
[b.] 10 March 1938, K.G.F. Mysore State, South India; [p.] Percival and Rosamund Kempt; [m.] Yvonne Philomena Kempt, 6 January 1968; [ch.] Two grown up daughters; [ed.] 6 "O" level G.C.E. passes Ex-Ecclesiastical Student with a Theological, Philosophical, Psychological Sociological and widely read background; [occ.] Retired Civil Servant after 24 years plus with the D.S.S.; [oth. writ.] Book-Living: Poetry and thoughts published by Minerva Press 1995, Poem: A Living Legend, Anthology: The New Voices Anthology published by Minerva Press 1994, Poem: Do This In Memory of Me, Book: Anthology, Christian Verse, Published by Triumph House from East Anglia; [pers.] This author is a Eurasian by Ethnic Origin and has been a British Citizen for the last 24 years. He has a deep interest in and an expanding knowledge of not only the Christian tradition, but also of all religions. East and West mystical truth and harmony are his life's way and work.; [a.] Tottenham, London, UK

KENNEDY, JOSEPH
[b.] 19/10/1935, County Carlow; [p.] Mary O'Byrne, Arthur Kennedy; [m.] Carmel Clarke, 9/9/59; [ch.] Paul, Ann, Joan, Shaun, Owen; [ed.] University College Dublin Dental Surgery Degree 1959; [occ.] Retired Dentist; [memb.] Irish Garden Plant Society, Alpine Gardening Society, Coleraine Art Society, Ballycastle Golf Club, Preservation of Countryside Society, Royal Society For Protection Of Birds; [hon.] Several gold medals for plant breeding, Golf Club Champion three times, Oil Painting awards; [oth. writ.] Some poems published by The Irish Times, gardening articles published, wildlife articles published; [pers.] Will only write poetry if moved by something. Very aware of the brevity of our lifespan; [a.] Ballycastle, Antrim

KENNEDY, MR. STEWART CRAIG
[pen.] Stewart Craig Kennedy; [b.] 19 November 1963, London-East; [p.] Eric Albert and Eileen Margaret Kennedy; [ed.] Langdon Comprehensive; [occ.] Retail; [hon.] Essential Food Hygiene Cert: The Royal Society of Health. November 1995; [oth. writ.] Poetry various, A few short stories, Working on Novel at present. Nothing published as yet.; [pers.] To Sue and Steph, For two finer friends, I could not wish. Happy 21st Steph, Stewart.; [a.] London, East-Ham, UK

KENYON, EILEEN
[pen.] Gabrielle; [b.] 27 May 1946, Dublin; [p.] The late: Michael and Katleen Eslin; [m.] Norman Kenyon, 13 October 1979; [ch.] Anthony James; [ed.] Convent School Dublin, Rossendale Secondary School. Further Education Runshaw College Leyland; [occ.] Filing Clerk; [oth. writ.] I have written several short stories, with none published as yet.; [pers.] I love writing - one day I hope to fulfill an ambition to write a book.; [a.] Leyland Preston, Lancashire, UK

KENYON, STEPHEN JAMES
[b.] 31 July 1962, Salford; [p.] Albert and Greta; [ed.] Castle Rushen High School, Castletown Isle of Man; [occ.] Welder; [oth. writ.] This poem is just one of several. But the first I have submitted for public reading or to any kind of Poetry Society.; [pers.] I have no explanation or profound insight into the reason for my writing. The only reason perhaps is to express feelings or emotional experiences through poetry. I would like to dedicate this poem to my fiance Lesley Dean and my good friend Phillip Callow. Both are in Gods hands.; [a.] Ballabey,, Isle of Man, UK

KENYON-SMITH, ANDREW J.
[pen.] Drew James; [b.] 8 December 1960, Lancashire; [p.] John and Brenda Smith; [ed.] Smithills Grammar School (Bolton, Lancs), Philosophy and Psychology Training at various locations; [occ.] Registered nurse and part-time Freelance Writer; [memb.] To various writers guilds, National Amateur Body Building Association (Life Member), and The R.A.C.; [hon.] S.B.C. (Subject of the British Commonwealth); [oth. writ.] Research papers, two novels, individualised personal poetry, several short stories.; [pers.] I would like to think my work may generate one of three things in the reader, more thoughts, greater emotion, or just a damned good laugh! My writing is greatly influenced by my ovedraft!; [a.] Lighthouse, Isle of Man, UK

KERR, SUSAN
[b.] 12 April 1945, Dacca, Bangladesh; [p.] Percy Trutwein and Peggy Trutwein; [m.] Andrew Kerr (Deceased), June 1973; [ed.] Abbey School, Reading Berkshire, Secretarial College, Various Secretarial Posts in Industry; [occ.] Verger, St. Andrews Church, Bradfield, Nr Reading, Berkshire; [memb.] Guild of Vercers (Oxford Diocese); [oth. writ.] Children's stories on church mice (not widespread publication) printed by local university for sale for church funds.; [pers.] I only write poems as and when the spirit moves. I write poems for friends to mark special occasions or generally if something I have read or seen has had a profound effect on me.; [a.] Reading, Berkshire, UK

KHAN, AHMED
[b.] 10 December 1965, Johannesburg, South Africa; [ed.] Burlington Danes School, Manchester University; [occ.] General Practitioner; [memb.] Royal College of General Practitioners; [oth. writ.] Several other poems as yet unforward for publication; [pers.] With my poems I am to overcome personal difficulties encourage a detachment from materialism and a reaching out to spiritual truths. My biggest influence has been Wayne Dyer's "You'll see it when you believe it".; [a.] Manchester, Lancashire, UK

KHURANA, JAG
[b.] 18 September 1974, Birmingham; [p.] Mr. H. Khurana and Mrs. R. Khurana; [ed.] Leasowes High School, King Edwards VI Sixth Form College, Stourbridge, University of Central Lancashire - Preston; [occ.] Student; [hon.] B.A. (Hons) English Literacy Studies; [pers.] Take the rules, the givens, the unrequested, and interrogate them until you transcend their limits. There is always more to be said, to be done, to be thought; [a.] Halesowen, Dudley, UK

KIDDELL, TINA
[b.] 5 September 1965, London; [p.] Brian and Sylvia Kiddell; [ed.] Broxbourne School; [occ.] Licensed London Taxi Driver; [memb.] Fareham Yacht Club; [oth. writ.] Several poems and short stories in school magazine; [pers.] My poems are visions of London and living as seen daily on the eternal wheel of life.; [a.] Cheshunt, Herts, UK

KIDMAN, MAURICE
[pen.] Maurice Kidman; [b.] 30 March 1923, Rotherham, Yorkshire; [occ.] Retired; [memb.] United Kingdom Alliance of Professional Teachers of Dancing; [hon.] Teacher of Dancing; [a.] Deal, Kent, UK

KIENTSON, THEO E.
[b.] 4 June 1928, Winterthur, Switzerland; [p.] Paul and Ernesta; [ch.] Michele, Russell, Evelyn; [ed.] St. Georg Gram W'Thur Switzerland, Sulzer Tech. Coll. W'Thur Switzerland, RTY University (Even.) Switzerland, B'Mouth Tech. Coll. England, Cambridge Univer. Corp. England.; [occ.] Chairman Aeroconsultants Ag.; [memb.] Fellow Inst. British Eng. Fellow Inst Eng. Designers, Memb Royal Astronaut Soc. C. Eng.; [hon.] Who is Who (USA Edit.); [oth. writ.] Another 30 poems both english and german.; [pers.] I have been greatly influenced by the ancient greek and 18th cent. german philos. I strife to be good to others as you are to yourself…but most of all..live and let live!; [a.] Hemingford, Abbots, Cambridgeshire, UK

KILGALLON, JOHN
[b.] 21 March 1924, Ballina, Co Mayo; [p.] J. J. and M. A. Kilgallon; [m.] V. A. Kilgallon, 30 August 1953; [ch.] Carmel, Kay, Nigel, Neil; [ed.] Ballina Nat. School, Ballina Vocational College, The Trades College, Charing Gross Road, London; [occ.] Chairman, Men's Wear Retailers; [memb.] House of Commons Dining Club, Chislehurst Golf Club; [hon.] As a young shop assistant served Queen Mary; [oth. writ.] Letters to the Press; [a.] Chislehurst, Kent, UK

KIMBER, MRS. JILL MAUREEN
[b.] 3 September 1930, Essex; [p.] Nora and Percival Carter; [m.] Basil Richard Kimber, 30 June 1951; [ch.] Karen and Gavin; [ed.] Loughton (then) High School College (now) London College of fashion; [occ.] Retired but still a housewife; [memb.] Seven Oaks Opera Company West Mallinc. Active Retirement Assn.; [hon.] 25 Years medal for singing in opera (N.O.D.A); [oth. writ.] Several poems published in various magazines (Inspired by John Bettamin) and wrote a magic moments, childrens poetry book.; [pers.] My poems are about life's experience and 'Happenings' (Spiritually based) which I hope helps others who find themselves in similar circumstances.; [a.] Borough Green, Kent, UK

KING, DAVID
[b.] 16 November 1956, Buckingham; [m.] Priscilla King, 25 March 1978; [ch.] Timothy (17), Philip (15), Michael (8); [ed.] Buckingham Secondary; [occ.] House husband; [memb.] Free Methodist Church Carnforth, Lancs; [pers.] As someone who has been so richly blessed. Having found a personal faith in Jesus, I long to share my faith with others in the hope that they will find Him too. Hence my poetry and song writing.; [a.] Carnforth, Lancs, UK

KING, MISS E. L.
[pen.] E. King; [b.] 29 September 1970, Bedford; [p.] Keith King and Anne McLean King; [m.] Dave Sarney; [ed.] Mark Rutherford Upper University of Plymouth, BSC (Hons) Biological Science; [occ.] Environment Agency Officer: Pollution Control; [oth. writ.] Published in "Inspiration from Central England"; [pers.] I write for my own pleasure and hope it gives pleasure to others; [a.] Bedford, Beds, UK

KING, JOHN LEONARD
[pen.] John Leonard King; [b.] 20 April 1923, Reading, Berks; [m.] Joyce King, 14 February 1946; [occ.] Retired; [pers.] My poem reflects how I feel about the environment; [a.] Reading, Berks, UK

KING, JOHN R.
[pen.] "Triptych"; [b.] 3 July 1944, Cardiff; [p.] Ronald Creed, Doreen Creed; [m.] Bunmee Rien King, 31 January 1989; [ch.] Michelle and Jason; [ed.] Secondary Education, Allensbank Secondary School; [occ.] Retired Disabled; [memb.] Mensa; [hon.] None sought. I've had a good life, and the love of my family and friends my greatest 'Honour' was to have experienced the 50's and 60's and time I feel will be remembered forever; [oth. writ.] This is my first poem to be published, though I have written many, this is the first poem that I've submitted. I also write lyrics for songs. And have started my first book.; [pers.] I try to express my feelings, and the inner, kinder thoughts of mankind, I feel that many people are unable to express their feelings, which can lead to frustration, and confusion I am inspired by the love of my wife Bunmee.; [a.] Cardiff, South Glamorgan, UK

KING, MELANIE VICTORIA
[b.] 5 November 1975, Leigh-on-Sea; [p.] Les and Jacqueline King; [ed.] Westcliff High School for Girls, Loughborough University; [occ.] Student: Reading mechanical engineering; [memb.] A member of the Leigh-on-Sea Leos Club, the junior division of Lions Club International; [pers.] "It's hard to be brave when you're only a very small animal."; [a.] Leigh-on-Sea, Essex, UK

KINGSTON, MR. RAYMOND
[b.] May 1925, Liverpool; [p.] Edward, Josephine; [m.] Emily May Critchley, December 1945; [ch.] Graham, Pauline, Linda; [ed.] Liverpool and Lancashire Secondary Schools; [occ.] Retired Newspaper and Agency Reporter; [a.] Huyton, Knowsley, Merseyside, UK

KINSLAY, RICHARD
[b.] 17 May 1985, Banbury, Oxon; [p.] Frank Kinslay and Sari Kinslay; [ed.] Hook Norton C of E Primary School; [memb.] Hook Norton Youth Club Manchester United Supporters Club; [hon.] National Cycling Proficiency, Swimming 25 Metre; [pers.] I like reading horror books. That's what I wrote this spooky poem.; [a.] Hook Norton Banbury, Oxon, UK

KIRBY, PAMELA
[b.] 3 August 1927, Wakefield, Yorks; [p.] Sarah I. Summers, Capt. Herbert Summers; [m.] Commander Rip Kirby R. N. (Deceased), 18 March 1950; [ch.] Jennifer Jane, Rosemary Gail; [ed.] Tutored in early years by Constance Heward, Childrens author, followed by Queen Mary's High School for girls, Lytham St. Annes, Lancs; [occ.] Retired; [memb.] Member of Plymouth Arts Club for several years, until leaving the area; [hon.] Winner of National Essay Competition on League of Nations, July 1939 aged eleven, unable to visit (as prize) their headquarters in Geneva until after the war - so cash prize awarded instead; [oth. writ.] After tentatively submitting my first poem in September 1995, I have had work published in several anthologies.; [pers.] Painting pictures in words, which hopefully arouse a response in whoever may read my work, is deeply satisfying and rewarding inspiration comes from poets who have always understood beautiful language.; [a.] Ruddington, Nottingham, UK

KIRK, KIRSTY
[b.] 23 August 1976, Bristol; [p.] Frank Kirk and Sarah Kirk; [ed.] Chichester College of Arts, Science and Technology, Middlesex University; [occ.] Student Nurse; [memb.] Amnesty International; [a.] Selsey, W. Sussex, UK

KITCH, JOHN STEPHEN
[pen.] Ashley Atkinson; [b.] 16 July 1940, Cardiff; [p.] Leonard and Beatrice Maude; [m.] Divorced; [ch.] 3 Stephen, Nicole and Dale - Ashley; [ed.] Whitchurch Infants and Primary. Whitchurch Church in Wales. Penarth County Grammar. Welsh School of Architecture - University of Wales Institute Science and Technology; [occ.] Involvement in Architecture and Writing; [memb.] Penarth Yacht Club; [oth. writ.] Father Dear Father, What Point, Flora, Case Dismissed, Injustice, Fodder all for the Judicial Machine, The Destruction of Great House Farm, War Child, Harry Dodds and Obediah, Canine Devotion, Special People, Peace Unattainable; [pers.] There has to be bureaucracy within the context of democracy but my aim is to do all I can to minimize it, set it off against reason and logic, and thereby hope to maximize the rights of the individual.; [a.] Penarth, S. Glamorgan, UK

KNELL, ANDREW
[b.] 6 July 1974, Barnet; [p.] Peter Kneel, June Knell; [ed.] Lochinver House School, Aldenham School, Dame Alice Owen School; [occ.] A level student; [memb.] Furzefield Sporting Asoc., Southgate County Football Club, Local Dramatic Society, Local Music Band; [hon.] Marshall prize at school for poetry, '92 and '95; [oth. writ.] Many other unpublished poems, a novel in the planning stage, journalist for local magazine; [pers.] I have been greatly influenced by the twentieth century poet Sylvia Plath who has inspired me beyond comprehension, James Dean Sums up life with the resounding words "Live past die young, and leave a good looking corpse"; [a.] Potters Bar, Hertfordshire, UK

KNIGHT, PATRICIA MARY
[b.] 16 January 1937, Leicester; [occ.] Legal Executive; [memb.] F. Inst. L. Ey; [hon.] Prizes, for high speed short hand writing; [oth. writ.] Articles reflecting childhood memories in local paper.; [pers.] I write poems inspired by photographs I have taken.; [a.] Leicester, Leics, UK

KNOWLES, CAROLINE ANNE
[b.] 3 November 1955, Farnham, Surrey Hospital; [p.] Hannah May and Frederick Preston; [m.] David Henry, 18 December 1980; [ch.] Laura (12) and Mark (14); [ed.] All Hallows R.C. Secondary Aldershot; [occ.] Assembly Worker Plasmecs Aldershot Hants; [oth. writ.] I have only written for enjoyment, this is my first ever poem, to be sent on.; [pers.] My own personal feelings always relate to my writing.; [a.] Crondall, Farnham, Surrey, UK

KOLACS, MISS VALERIE
[pen.] Val Harrison; [b.] Sept 7, 1969, Bradford; [p.] Maria Kolacs, John Kolacs; [ed.] St. Joseph's College, Bradford, Awarded B.A. Honours Degree from the University of Sunderland (1991); [occ.] Civil-Servant, the Office of Water Services, Leeds; [hon.] B.A. Honours Degree in English Literature; [oth. writ.] Articles published in National Cinema Magazines; [pers.] Inspired by the one thing that binds the universe, the power of love, my poetry seeks to convey the joy and pain, the agony and the ecstasy experienced through this all-encompassing emotion.; [a.] Bradford, West Yorkshire

KOUSPOYENIS, CONSTANTINA SAVVA
[pen.] Kouspoyenis; [b.] 28 September 1981, London; [p.] Christakis and Eleni Kouspoyenis; [ed.] Still at school (Saint Albans Cofe); [occ.] Student; [oth. writ.] Written more poems but not submitted for publication; [a.] Birmingham, West Midlands, UK

KRAVIS, CAROL-ANN
[b.] 30 March 1956, Grimsby; [p.] Viola Scholey, Terence Scholey; [ch.] Ramon Kravis, Carol-Ann Kravis; [ed.] Havelock School Grimsby, South Devon College, Dartington College of Arts; [occ.] Student; [pers.] I am currently studying for a B.A. degree in performance writing. This I believe will lead to career linked to the arts and writing; [a.] Torquay, Devon, UK

KRZYWORACZKA, KAZAMIERA
[pen.] Kate Edmunds; [b.] 3 October 1947, Penley, Wales; [p.] Kazimierz Pabian, Anna Pabian; [m.] Stanislaw Ryszard Krzyworaczka, 4 April 1967; [ed.] St. Gabriel's Secondary Modern School, Bury, Radcliffe Technical College; [occ.] Bookkeeper; [memb.] Polish folk Choir, Church Choir, Parish Prayer Group; [oth. writ.] Lyrics to songs, Reflections on the gospels, Reflections on life; [pers.] I strive to reflect goodness and hope and write mainly from personal experience.; [a.] Radcliffe, Gt. Manchester, UK

LAMBOURNE, PATRICIA MARY
[pen.] Pat Lambourne; [b.] 7 March 1937, Beenham, Berks; [p.] Ella and Frederick Welch; [m.] Terence C. Lambourne, 17 March 1956; [ch.] 4 Christine, Claire, Ian and Derek; [ed.] Shaw House Girls School, Newbury Berks; [occ.] Housewife; [memb.] Active member of The Caravan Club and West Hants Rally Club; [hon.] I devoted my life to being a wife and mother; [oth. writ.] Several poems published in small anthologies; [pers.] I started writing after the death of my son Ian (6 years ago). I write about things I see, things that interest me, and things that are in my heart.; [a.] Reading, Berkshire, UK

LAMDEN, T.
[b.] 29 February 1920, London; [m.] Deceased 14 February 1994, 12 October 1946; [ch.] 4; [ed.]

Council Sea at 16 years served 12 1/2 yrs Merchant Navy 1935-1947; [occ.] Retired; [memb.] Freemasonry, Arethusa Old Boys, Burma Star Ass; [oth. writ.] Poems printed in local press and my weekly magazine; [pers.] At my age 76 I try to depict life as it actually is.'; [a.] Wolverhampton, S. Staffs, UK

LANGSTON, IRIS
[b.] 6 December 1933, Brighton; [p.] Marjorie and Alexander McNeill; [m.] Brian Langston, 27 November 1956; [ch.] Richard, Gillian and David; [ed.] Convent of St. Josephs; [occ.] Retired; [memb.] Belong to 'Starliners' a local variety group; [pers.] When I was 5, my father who had been a regular soldier and one of the first to be called to dunkirk, was reported missing/pressured killed. This had a profound influence over me. I feel that poetry comes totally from the soul I am mostly motivated by the sadder side of life; [a.] Brighton, Sussex, UK

LANGTON, MARION
[b.] 16 August 1944, Chelmsford; [p.] Doris Forrest, John Forrest; [occ.] English Teacher, Hove, E Sussex; [memb.] Sussex Yacht Clubs, Sussex Downsmen Rambling Association, Mid-Sussex and Brighton Rambling Clubs; [oth. writ.] Several articles published in local newspapers/magazines abroad and in UK; [pers.] My mother taught me a great love of life. I left home when I was very young and traveled the world. I mixed with people of all races, from all walks of life and I think these experiences and my irrepressible gypsy spirit are the basis of my poems.; [a.] Hove, E. Sussex, UK

LATHAM, CAROL
[pen.] Carol Latham; [b.] 19 April 1961, Broomhill, Morpeth; [p.] Eric Parr, Maureen Parr; [m.] Adrian Latham, 2 December 1995; [ed.] Monkseaton Grammar School, Whitley Bay. Various College Courses; [occ.] Part-time Model and Aspiring poet; [memb.] Local creative writing group. And Assorted Arty Clubs in area; [hon.] English Language; [oth. writ.] Am at present collecting my assorted poetry and short stories together for a book; [pers.] I like to write poetry and short stories reflecting everyday life, depicting its humerus side, as life sadly is sometimes not.; [a.] Ribchester, Lancashire, UK

LATHAM, HOWARD
[b.] August 23, 1921, Acton, London W; [p.] Ernest Latham, Catherine Latham; [m.] Mary Blackwell, February 18, 1950; [ch.] Heather Allen, Paula Chapman, Sarah Latham, Clive Latham; [ed.] St. Pauls School, London; Regent Street Polytechnic; [occ.] Retired Office Manger/Accountant; [memb.] Royal British Legion; [oth. writ.] Poem in Wood Green Animal Shelters "Tips `n' Tales", Reader's Letters in national newspapers and local Brighton paper.; [pers.] Ex-"Desert Rat" Royal Engineers, 4th Field Squadron, 7th Armoured Division - ex Territorial 1939-1946.; [a.] Somersham Huntingdon, Cambridgeshire

LAWALL, CHRISTIAN DANIEL
[pen.] Chr. Lawall; [b.] 22 September 1966, Berlin; [p.] Peter and Ute Lawall; [m.] Eden Desta, Next year; [ed.] German Abitur, 1986 (Germ. Army) 1986-87, Joiver outfield 1987-89, University of Hamburg 1989-95, English and German Language and Literature, Goldsmith College English MA Course from Sept-96; [occ.] Receptionist in Cancer Laboratory; [oth. writ.] Rogen mund, short stories in German. ISBN Soldi - Verlog Hamburg.; [pers.] Love, Humanity, Christianity and the truth are very highest values. ('Twas born in Berlin, raised in Hamburg and I moved to London to study, work and many.) I was influenced by Schiller, Leasing, Shakespeare and T. S. Eliot.; [a.] London, UK

LAWRENCE, CAROLE E.
[b.] 1 March 1945, Abergavenny, South Wales; [p.] John Robert Barlow (Deceased), Nancy Muriel Barlow; [m.] Charles Bernard Lawrence, 18 February 1967; [ch.] Michelle Louise Lawrence; [ed.] Margaret Glenn-Bott Secondary School, Clarendon College (Both in the City of Nottingham); [occ.] Artist; [memb.] Wexford Arts Centre, Enniscorthy Golf Club; [hon.] Mathematics hon., English literature hon., Business/secretarial hon., swimming award, domestic science award, golf prizes; [pers.] Combined with the wonders of nature and my imagination I try and inspire thoughtfulness and hope to enrich the lives of people with the magic of the written word; [a.] Enniscorthy, Wexford, Eire, UK

LAWRENCE, EDNA J.
[b.] 13 January 1912, Long Sutton, Somerset; [p.] Sarah Ann and James C. Bryant; [m.] Widowed, (Married Twice); [ch.] Morena and William (1st marriage); [ed.] Friends Schools, Day-Long Sutton, Boarding-Sibford School Nr Banbury; [occ.] Retired Nurse; [memb.] W.I. Poetry Group Somerton Literary and poetical Society. Retired Member Somerton Amateur Dramatic Society also W.I. Drama Group; [hon.] (Mostly Derived from Crafts); [oth. writ.] Poems included in W.I. Anthologies. Children's stories songs to popular tunes limerick.; [pers.] Individuality - subtle humour. Greatly influenced by my school years and later A.A. Micne - Gilbert and Sullivan - the "Greats" like Kipling. Masefield. Shakespeare.; [a.] Somerton, Somerset, UK

LAWRENCE, NICOLA
[b.] 13 June 1978, Welwyn Garden, Herts; [p.] Malcolm, Christina Lawrence; [ed.] Collenswood School Stevenage, Ten G.C.S.E.'s currently studying A-level English Lit, French, Theatre Studies; [occ.] Student; [oth. writ.] A collection of unpublished poetry; [pers.] I write poetry purely for my own pleasure. My writing reflects people and situation I encounter every day. I have never before entered any of my work.; [a.] Stevenage, Herts, UK

LAWRENCE, RODNEY
[b.] 28 December 1970, Barnet; [p.] Ronald and Daphne Lawrence; [m.] Dawn Flashman, 3 December 1993; [ed.] Ashmole Comprehensive School, Southgate, London; [hon.] Six Years Service in her Majesty the Queens Royal Air Force Regiment and your Reading of this Poem; [oth. writ.] Several songs for personal enjoyment; [pers.] For my dearest dawn it was not today. Tomorrow however grows forever closer, as so do we.; [a.] Enfield, Middx, UK

LAWRENCE, MRS. SUSAN
[b.] 12 February 1960, London; [ch.] Alexis Donna; [ed.] The Dick Sheppard School, Basingstoke College of Technology; [occ.] Catering Assistant, aspiring Lyricist; [pers.] As with both my poetry and lyrics, I am inspired to write when listening to listening to beautiful music. I give thanks to the unknown force which guides my hand.; [a.] Basingstoke, Hampshire, UK

LAWRIE, ELIZABETH ANN
[b.] 14 July 1958, Cromer, Norfolk; [p.] James Surridge - Brenda Surridge; [m.] Divorced, 6 November 1976; [ch.] Richard Lawrie, Steven Lawrie; [ed.] Comberton Village College, National Extension College; [occ.] Doctor's Receptionist Cambridge; [memb.] Born Free Foundation; [hon.] GCE's - English Language and Literature (1992-3), 'A' level English Language and Literature (1995); [oth. writ.] This is my first attempt at entering a poetry competition; [pers.] I strive to portray the authenticity that lies within the innocence of life, thus highlighting the falsehood linked to the incomprehensible role of injustice; [a.] Great Eversden, Cambridge, UK

LAWSON, ALEXANDER JOHNSTON
[pen.] Alex J. Lawson; [b.] 26 June 1929, Edinburgh; [p.] John and Margaret Lawson (Dec'd); [m.] Christina D. Aneddon, 26 March 1955; [ch.] Yvonne Margaret Dewar Lawson; [ed.] Leith Academy, Edinburgh; [occ.] Retired from Scottish Widows Fund and Life Assurance Society Adinburgh; [memb.] Edinburgh Highland Reel and Strathspey Society, Dunfornline Caledonian Strathspey and Reel Society, Livingston Fiddlers Society; [hon.] Edinburgh Highland Reel and Strathspey Society McInroy Challenge CUP Winner 1991, 1993, 1994, for composing Strathspey Steel, Winner of Livingston Music Society Composition Competition 1995 with "Memories of Sarasejo" for Voilin with piano Accompaniment, Eckford Comrie Quaich Winner of Performance on Violin of slow slots air 11 March 1996; [oth. writ.] Exhibitor's Prize for short story called "Abdul" (Story of wolf cub exhibited at J. P. Taylor's Workshop at Seil Island Aprox. 30 years ago.; [pers.] After hearing in my youth mendelosokin's "On Wing of Song" play and by the Vionnes violinist. Frely Kreisler and also listening to the song a being sung of Robert Burn S. Foster, George G. and Jerome Keen involved that my rule of life would be to "aim at Beauty" whenever I camps I my music or wrote a poem a song by me.; [a.] Livingston, West Lothiam, UK

LECHNER, DOMINIQUE
[b.] 8 April 1960, South Africa; [p.] John Louth and Matty Louth; [ch.] Trish Lechner, 12 October 1982; [ed.] Graduated in Southfield Michigan, USA; [occ.] Fashion consultant; [hon.] Scholarship in Journalism to Michigan State University; [oth. writ.] Several poems and a short story unpublished as this is the first poem I have submitted to anyone.; [pers.] I have a deep love of nature and am very concerned about our planet. I draw on nature for inspiration when I write.; [a.] Marlow, Bucks, UK

LEE, JOHN MAURICE
[pen.] Jamel; [b.] 12 September 1942, Dartford, Kent; [p.] Frederick and Eileen Lee; [m.] Marion; [ch.] Allison Helen and Susanne Caroline; [ed.] Woolwich Polytechnic, University College, University of London; [occ.] Senior Lecturer, South Bank University, London; [memb.] Bexley Art Group Institute of Management; [hon.] Msc. (Architecture); [pers.] I write instinctively. The inspirational moments are fleeting and often it is as though someone else is telling me what to write - maybe ghosts from the past.; [a.] Blackheath, London, UK

LEE, RICHARD ARTHUR
[b.] 10 February 1937, Grimsby; [p.] Augustus Joseph and Jeanette May; [m.] Jean Allard, 28 September 1957; [ch.] Surrie Jean, Richard Anthony, Cindy Anne; [ed.] St Mary's Catholic School - Grimsby; [occ.] Security Supervisor Reliance Sec. Services; [oth. writ.] Many, and on various themes, mostly romantic, none published, and I have retained them. I have recently discovered I write in what is known as Picture Writing which nearly dies out but is now being revived. I do not know how I developed this style of poetry.; [pers.] As an aggressive young boy on the streets of Grimsby I was introduced to poetry by my teacher, Miss Relph. The first piece, The Highwayman, made such an impact on my mind that my aggression faded quickly. I joined the Merchant Navy and started to write when I discovered girls love poetry. I think that young people should be encouraged to indulge in poetry which may keep a number out of HM Prison and young offenders units. Music and words to soothe the savage breast.; [a.] Grimsby, Lincolnshire, UK

LENNOX, ELIZABETH
[b.] 23 February 1955, Curran; [p.] Robert Lennox, Ian Lennox; [m.] Thomas Lennox, 30 April 1976; [ch.] Robert, Ian; [ed.] Rainey Endowed School Magherafelt, Altnagelvin School of Radiography; [occ.] Radiographer Ultrasonographer Mid-Ulster Hosp., Magherafelt; [hon.] DCR (R), D.M.U.; [oth. writ.] Local magazines; [pers.] To find peace in life we must leave the past behind and look forward.; [a.] Magherafelt, Londonderry, UK

LETTING, MS. DAWN ADELE
[b.] 18 November 1959, Hyde, Cheshire; [p.] Roy Letting and Dorothy Letting; [ed.] Nine very different schools, private to comprehensive, two collages, studied! Computerized accounts and social work/care.; [pers.] Always keep an open mind.; [a.] Kings Lynn, Norfolk, UK

LEVETT-DARLING, MISS WENDY
[b.] 28 April 1947, Sevenoaks; [p.] Bunny and Pat; [ed.] Hatton Secondary Modern, Sevenoaks, Tunbridge Wells Technical College, Harrogate College of Arts and Technology.; [memb.] Society for Psychical Research (SPR), also, intended membership of Association of Speakers Clubs (ASC); [hon.] Honours and Awards as endowed by my peers at the University of Life!; [oth. writ.] Poems published in other anthologies as a new author.; [pers.] I write in the modern vernacular whilst wearing an 'L' plate. The realms of ESP, fantasy and the unknown are my sources of inspiration intermingled with a personal belief in God for good measure!; [a.] Harrogate, N Yorks, UK

LEWINGTON, JACQUELINE
[b.] 24 August 1949, Kent; [p.] John and Doris Johnson; [m.] Victor Lewington, 11 April 1970; [pers.] I wish to thank my husband Victor and my family for the love, support and encouragement they have given me; [a.] London, UK

LEWIS, BENJAMIN THOMAS
[b.] 8 January 1930, Sheffield; [p.] Ben and Eileen Lewis; [occ.] Retired; [pers.] Jesus said that the Kingdom of God would come on earth. When that happens, it will not be necessary to do battle with tyrants anymore.; [a.] Penarth, S. Glam, UK

LEWIS, MS. HEIDI
[pen.] Heidi Lewis; [b.] 14 April 1976, Chichester; [p.] John E. Lewis and Julie P. Lewis; [ed.] Springfield Park, Chichester College of Technology; [occ.] Insurance Technician; [memb.] Local Dance/Cabaret Group; [pers.] I write what I feel, I write to give freedom to the written work of art.; [a.] Horsham, W. Sussex, UK

LEWIS, JOAN E.
[pen.] Joan Lewis; [b.] 15 September 1921, Winnipeg, Canada; [p.] Walter Sparks, Annie Sparks; [m.] Bertie Richard Lewis, 17 September 1952; [ch.] Charles Douglas - Glyn Dowden; [ed.] Elementary; [oth. writ.] Children's short stories (not published); [pers.] I am nothing, but I have a big heart.; [a.] Lancing, West Sussex, UK

LEWIS, MARCIA CELESTINA
[pers.] To my mother, Violet Geraldine Lewis, who I loved dearly but is no here to see this day. She liked my poetry very much, I dedicate this to you Mum because this is one you did hear and like. Your ever loving daughter Marcia; [a.] Reading, Berkshire, UK

LIEGAUX, FRANCIS THEODORE
[pen.] Francis Theodore Liegaux; [b.] 4 November 1918, Coolham, Sussex; [p.] Arther Liegaux and Edith Liegaux; [m.] Phyllis Liegaux; [ch.] Three Daughters and one Son; [ed.] Never received one day of schooling. Self taught; [occ.] Lumber Jack Working in the woods every day still.; [oth. writ.] Lots of poems but never been shown to a publisher but has been printed in the local paper. Concerning Heathfield Park.; [pers.] I have had to do physical work all my life. Owing to failing eye sight. From the age of nine. Unfortunately glasses are to no avail. My daughter is writing this for me.; [a.] Heathfield, East Sussex, UK

LILLEY, CHRISTOPHER
[b.] 28 September 1960, Bournemouth; [p.] Gerald Edward (Deceased), Margaret Evlyn; [m.] Sandra (Partner); [ed.] Oakmead School for boys; [occ.] Typesetter; [oth. writ.] Over 100 poems none published.; [pers.] To my mother for her understanding and love.; [a.] Torquay, Devon, UK

LILLY, ANNABELLE
[pen.] Annabelle Lilly; [b.] 2 April 1973, Birmingham; [p.] Anthony Lilly and Shelia Lilly; [ed.] St. Bede's School, Hailshare Sussex King's College University, London; [occ.] Nursing Student; [oth. writ.] I have written several other poems and hope to put a book together soon. I am also writing a children's book about a little bear called "Barnaby."; [pers.] I never expect my poem to be published, I am glad other people like it. My poems reflects feelings and past experiences, I hope that people can relate well to them.; [a.] Seaford, Sussex, UK

LINES, DOROTHY
[pen.] Dorothy Lines; [b.] 11 February 1942, Hawkhurst, Kent; [p.] Frank Vine and Lodie Vine; [m.] Colin Lines, 23 April 1979; [ch.] Karen Paula, Robert William, Tristan Colin; [ed.] Australia, and Ashford School for Girls, Maid Stone College of Art, Brixton School of Building; [occ.] Architect; [a.] St. Leonards on Sea, East Sussex, UK

LINNEY, SYLVIA MAUD
[b.] 28 July 1921, Steyning, Sussex; [p.] Adeline Maud Camps, P. A. Harry Camps; [m.] H. John Linney, 7 July 1951; [ch.] Vanessa, Anthony; [ed.] Aldrington and Hove High School, Glebe Villas Hove, Sx. Miss Bollans Boarding School, Deal Kent; [occ.] Active interest occupying several hours weekly involving well being of elderly folk. By that I mean older than myself!; [memb.] Brighton and Hove Albion Football Team supporter. (Member) 69 years loyal support. Sadly after nearly 100 years, the ground has been sold. No home to go to!; [hon.] Brought up in a musical environment and sport of equal importance. School medals for many sports events, two brothers and parents all sporty and musical.; [oth. writ.] For personal pleasure only stories and poems; [pers.] Life proves in part to be a journey of personal injuries. 'Do as you would be done by' would lessen the bruising, bloodshed, and heartache -- en route.; [a.] Hove, Sussex, UK

LITTLE, JONATHAN
[b.] 14 October 1965, Box Hill South, Australia; [ed.] Camberwell Grammar, Melbourne University, (B. Mus.), Australian College of Theology (Th.A.), Monash University (Ph.D. on 'exotic' techniques in 19th and 20th century music and literature); [occ.] Musician/Writer; [memb.] Gothic Society, Wagner Society; [hon.] Lady Turner Exhibition in Music; [oth. writ.] Articles on aesthetics, short stories; [pers.] Founder 'Picturesque Archaism' school of poetry; [a.] Dymock, Glos, UK

LITTLEWOOD, IAN
[b.] 22 April 1967, Maldon; [ed.] The Plume School, Maldon; [memb.] All Saints Drama Guild; [oth. writ.] A variety of poetry, lyrics of which none has been published; [pers.] Most of my writing tends to reflect on what happens in our world, an our lives today.; [a.] Maldon, Essex, UK

LLOYD, DAVID
[b.] Plymouth; [pers.] My poem was written in memory of my great grandfather private William John Warden 8155 'A' Company 1st battalion Devonshire Regiment, who was killed in action on 13th May 1915, age 27, and lies forever at rest in Vlamertinghe, Belgium

LLOYD, RICHARD
[pen.] Richard Lloyd; [b.] 1 March 1908, Rhonda Valley, Maerdy; [p.] Lewis and Janet Lloyd (Deceased); [m.] Edith Anne Lloyd, 4 October 1938; [ch.] Four; [ed.] Maerdy Boy's School, Ferndale Secondary School, College Experience of Life; [occ.] Retired; [oth. writ.] Reflections, Quality Of Life, Just Tears, Appeared In Cynon Valley Leader; [pers.] Greatness comes from humility arrogance and ignorance leads to down fall of mankind. Remember the old adage only once we pass this way? So - Omah Kyam; [a.] Hirwain Aberdare, Mid-Glam, UK

LLOYD, ROBIN
[b.] 25 December 1924, Bangalore, India; [p.] Cecil George and Sybel Hope Lloyd; [m.] Sandra Ann Lloyd, 12 June 1986; [ch.] Susan Ann (from 1st marriage); [ed.] La Martiniere College Calcutta, Senior Cambridge. Various Journalistic and Short Story Courses; [occ.] Freelance journalist reviews racing software have own program; [memb.] Polygon Poets, Bristol but mainly go-it-aloner; [hon.] Short Listen BBC Radio 5 International Poetry Competition, Short Listed Strood Festival of Poetry, Won Filton Festival Poetry top award, Second Bristol WEA poetry prize, Won Bristol Asteddfod poetry prize etc.d Publishe in several poetry mags and anthologies; [oth. writ.] Like

poetry, short stories published for over 50 years write regular computer course column for various mans. Reviewing computer racing programs. Also reviews poetry, books, theatre etc.; [pers.] Much influenced by metaphysical poets and, stationary by Dylan Thomas, though I like to write tight - economy and evocation key elements. Short stories, DE Maupassont O. Henry, Saki, Sommerstet Marcham influences. Character - with good sting in tail; [a.] Bristol, Bristol, UK

LOCKWOOD, ALAN
[b.] 21 December 1946, Leeds; [p.] Jack Lockwood, Dorothy Lockwood; [m.] Separated, 1 October 1966; [ch.] Two Girls and One Boy; [ed.] Secondary School, Goldcotes Boys School, Leeds Yorks; [occ.] Scaffoldings Contractor; [pers.] People, and their feelings are what's important. Not to hurt, but to give, to others, confidence, support and love, is why we are here!; [a.] Leeds, Yorks, UK

LOGUE, JOSEPHINE ANN
[b.] 13 May 1962, Jersey; [p.] Francis and Margaret Gautier; [m.] Robert Logue, 25 February 1994; [ch.] James Logue; [ed.] Jersey College for girls; [occ.] Senior Trust and Company Administrator; [a.] Saint Saviour, Jersey, UK

LONGDEN, GRAHAM
[b.] 8 May 1937, Bournheath; [p.] James Longden, Minnie Longden; [m.] Doreen Longden, 14 September 1957; [ch.] Mark, Paul, James; [memb.] Woodland Trust; [a.] Bromsgrove, Worcs, UK

LONGLEY, KATHRYN
[pen.] Kathryn Longley; [b.] 11 April 1951, London; [p.] Stanley Major, Mary Major (Deceased); [m.] Martin Longley, 17 October 1970; [ch.] Michelle Amanda and Andrew Martin; [ed.] Garratt Green Comprehensive School, London SW17, Northampton College of further education; [occ.] Voluntary worker for Cancer Research Campaign Shop N'pton and Emmanuel Church Coffee Shop, Weston Favell; [memb.] Royal Society of Protection of Birds, Boothville Art Group; [oth. writ.] Poems published in six different anthologies. Power of Words. It's a Beautiful World. Poets for Peace - 'Destitute'. Poetry now (Central) Regional Anthology - 'New Life'. Sheltered from the Cold - 'Our Special Cat'. The Marching of Time - '1996'. Poets in the Heart of England - 'Mother' Visits Olney', plus poem published in local paper; [pers.] I have been influenced by many people through their music, Lennon and McCartney, Elton John and Bernie Taupin, Paul Simon, Andrew Lloyd Webber and Tim Rice, Cliff Richard and Eric Clapton. I care greatly about our environment and gain much pleasure from watching the birds. I am also fascinated by historical buildings through the ages and becoming interested in poet John Clare.; [a.] Northampton, Northants, UK

LOVE, SHEILA
[pen.] Sheila Love; [b.] 7 June 1943, Coseley; [p.] Betsy Priest, Frederick Priest; [m.] Kenneth Love, 28 January 1961; [ch.] 3 Boys and 2 girls, 4 grandsons and 2 granddaughters; [ed.] Christ Church Infants (Coseley), Mount Pleasant Junior (Coseley), Girls High School, Dudley; [occ.] Office Worker; [oth. writ.] Monthly poem for Church Magazine, also once in national daily and in local evening paper; [pers.] My work is influenced by family, friends associates lives and my personal issues and current affairs.; [a.] Dudley, West Midlands, UK

LOWDE, PAMELA ANN
[pen.] Ann Lowde; [b.] 2 October, 1956, Driffield; [p.] Margaret and Peter Hyde; [m.] Leslie John Lowde, April 5, 1980; [ch.] Amanda - 7, Christopher - 3; [ed.] Comprehensive School; [occ.] Housewife and Mother of 2 young children; [memb.] W.I.; [hon.] Certificate of Distribution; [oth. writ.] Titles of Books who have published my poems. Happiness - "An Invitation to Poetry" Mum "Dedicated to Mum". Love "Valentine Poets". What will be will be. "Expressions of faith", My love "In the heart of it". Children "Teddy Bears and Tears"; [pers.] I write my poems from the heart. My two children have inspired me.; [a.] Driffield, East Yorkshire

LUCK, JOSEPHINE M.
[pen.] Jessica James; [b.] Southlands Hs., Shoreham; [m.] Desmond James Luck; [occ.] Housewife; [oth. writ.] Many poems over a period at about eighteen years of write has been accepted your publication. "Others never entered for competition."; [pers.] I feel that my poetry is born from my love of nature, fellow man and God.; [a.] Windmill Hill, Hailsham, East Sussex, UK

LUND, MRS. S. E.
[pen.] Sue Lund; [b.] 4 February 1946, Accrington, Lancs; [p.] James and Betty Clegg; [m.] Richard A. Lund, 30 July 1966; [ch.] Nicholas - 29, Joanne - 26, Kathryn - 23, four grandchildren; [ed.] Paddock House Convent Grammar School, Oswaldtwistle 8 '0' levels, Counselling Qualifications mainly in N.L.P. (Neuro-Linguistic Programming); [occ.] Staff Welfare Officer for Education Department of North Lincs Council; [memb.] Fellow of Inst. of Welfare Officers, Members of Royal Society of Health, Member of British Assn for Counselling; [oth. writ.] Very few!; [pers.] For me poetry writing is a way of expressing the deep and powerful emotions which are brought to the fore during periods of intense sorrow or joy.; [a.] Scunthorpe, North Lincs, UK

LUNN, MELODIE
[b.] 25 December 1973, Leicester; [p.] Gaynor Reynold and A. Lunn; [occ.] Customer Advisor for Alliance and Leicester; [pers.] I have been writing poems since I was 9 years old, this is my first poem published, my aim is to get many more published. I enjoy writing romantic and meaningful poems.; [a.] Leicester, Leic'shire, UK

LUNNON, SANDRA
[b.] 1 July 1955, Midhurst; [p.] Florence Kathleen Tomsett and Dennis Tomsett; [m.] Clive Lunnon, 23 July 1977; [ch.] Kathleen Anne and Tony John; [ed.] Lancastrian School for Girls, Chichester Sussex, Chichester College of Arts, Science and Technology; [occ.] Housewife; [memb.] Working Association of Mothers, Liberal Democrats; [hon.] Computer Programming with Distinction; [oth. writ.] Several poems published in absent healer it is non Denominational and non-profit making and open to every one who has a desire to join in a circle of friends at their own time and place, who through prayers and spiritual union wish to alleviate suffering and help the flow of harmony in the world.; [pers.] My writing comes through personal experience but mostly from the heart.; [a.] Bognor Regis, Sussex, UK

LWANGA, CHARLES
[pen.] Ssenklingu; [b.] 12 February 1968, Mulajje, Uganda; [p.] Late Mr. Francis Xavier Lutaaya and Mrs. Deziderata Nabawanlika Lutaaya; [ed.] St. Bonaventure's P.S. Mulajje, NS Wanjere Junior Seminary, St. Joseph's Minor Seminary, Nyenga, Uganda Martyrs National Major Seminary Alokolum, obtained a Diploma in Philosophical and Higher Religious Studies (Alokolum), B.A. Philosophy (Urban University); [occ.] Currently, a second year Student at St. John's Seminary Wonersh pursuing at the Completion of the course hopes to be ordained as Roman Catholic Priest for Kampala Archdiocese (Uganda); [memb.] The Carolines, Uganda Martyrs Christian Association, NUS, ISOP; [hon.] Major work is 'Genocide in Luwero Triangle 1981-1985 and its consequences; [oth. writ.] Several poems and articles published in 'The Lily,' 'Star Herald' magazines and the New Vision Newspaper; [pers.] I revolve greatly on nature, politics, religion, morality and humanity in most of my writings. I have been motivated English Literature lessons at school and my rich Cultural Proverbial background.; [a.] Guildford, Surrey, UK

LYES, ARTHUR E.
[b.] 4 February 1941, Gloucester; [p.] Reginald Lyes, Edith Lyes; [m.] Elsie M. Lyes, 28 October 1961; [ch.] Susan, Philip, Alison; [ed.] Crypt Grammar School; [occ.] Security Officer; [oth. writ.] Several other poems written, but this is my first attempt to get one published. Another may possibly be published in a company magazine, sent in since entering this competition.; [pers.] Some things I feel I must write about, such as drugs, as a message needs to be sent out to the younger generation. Sometimes I just write for family and friends.; [a.] Gloucester, Glos, UK

LYTTON, EILEEN GRATTAN
[p.] Catherine Grattan Plunkett, Edward Lytton; [ed.] Abroad France; [occ.] In charge of the nurseries on P&O liners.; [hon.] I have won several competitions for poetry. Broadcast for 2 Countries Radio Bournemouth, also winning first prize in their short story competition.; [oth. writ.] Written many articles on psychology, spiritual healing etc. I am now retired and live in Hampshire.; [a.] London, Kensington, UK

MACDONALD, CATHERINE A.
[b.] 3 January 1968, Laxdale; [p.] John G. Graham, Maggie A. Graham; [m.] Hector M. MacDonald, 11 May 1989; [ch.] Kris and Ryan; [ed.] Nicolson Institute; [occ.] Housewife; [memb.] Stornoway Motor Cycle Club; [pers.] I wrote this poem with my husband Hector and best buddy Carol in mind.; [a.] Stornoway, Isle of Lewis, UK

MACDONALD, GAIL
[b.] 30 March 1977, Wick; [p.] Mr. and Mrs. R. G. MacDonald; [ed.] Wick High School 1989 - 1995, Currently at Central College of Commerce, Glasgow; [occ.] Student; [oth. writ.] Local publications, tribute to Tom Scott, School Magazine; [pers.] This is one of my first poems ot be published as I have only been writing creatively for a very short time, Hopefully it will continue this way for a long time to come.; [a.] Wick, Caithness, UK

MACKAY, REV. CANNON DOUGLAS BRYSSON
[b.] 20 March 1927, Glasgow; [p.] John and Violet; [m.] Catherine Elizabeth, 12 July 1952; [ch.] Jane and Catherine; [ed.] Possil Senior Secondary School, Edinburgh Theological College; [occ.] Minister of Religion; [memb.] Precentor, St. Andrew's Cathedral, Inverness, 1958, Rector,

Gordon Chapel, Fochabers, 1961 (also Priest-in-Charge, St. Margaret's Church, Aberlour, 1964), Canon St. Andrew's Cathedral, Inverness, 1965, Synod of Clerk, Diocese of Moray, Ross, Caithness, 1965, Honorary Canon, St. Andrew's Cathedral, Inverness 1972, Convenor of Youth, Moray Diocese, 1965, Brechin Diocese, Convernor, Social Service Board, 1974, Convenor, Joint Board, 1974, Convenor, Administration Board, 1982, President, British Red Cross, Carnoustie, 1874-82, President, British Legion, Carnoustie, 1981, Vice-Chairman, Carnoustie Community Care, 1981, Chairman, Carnoustie Community Council, 1979-81, President, Carnoustie Rotary Club, 1976; [hon.] Honorary Tutor - Community Studies, Tayside Centre for General Practice; [oth. writ.] Poems published 1992 Poetry Now 'Desert Highway', 1995 Poetry Now 'Mystical Union', 1995 Poetry Now 'Mourning', mag. articles various; [pers.] I try to keep the rumour of God alive.; [a.] Carnoustie, Angus, UK

MACKENZIE, JOHN A. S. F.
[b.] 19 December 1961, Glasgow; [ed.] University of Glasgow, University of Paisley, St. Andrews College of Education; [occ.] History and Modern, Studies Teacher (Secondary) St. Margaret Mary's Secondary, Castlemilk, Glasgow; [oth. writ.] Write lyrics for local band, several articles for local newspaper; [pers.] Influenced by the darker moods of the human experience. My poetry is eerie and sometimes tragic.; [a.] Glasgow, UK

MACLEOD, MAGGI L. THOMASON
[pen.] Maggi L. Thomason-MacLeod; [b.] 19 September 1945, Dudley, England; [p.] Ethel Hurst and Charles Leslie Thomason; [m.] Jim MacLeod, 1984; [ch.] Tess, Jenny; [ed.] Dudley Girls High School, Wolverhampton Art School, University of Victoria in Canada; [occ.] Hotel Proprietor and Craftsperson; [hon.] B.F.A. University of Victoria B.C. Canada; [oth. writ.] Many poems, some published in "poetry now" anthology; [pers.] North West Sutherland has been my home and inspiration for the last 22 years. I hope some of the magic of this place reaches other people through my poems; [a.] Bettyhill, Sutherland, UK

MADDISON, RICHARD
[pen.] Benjamin Richards; [b.] 23 May 1965, Newcastle-upon-Tyne; [p.] John Maddison and Marian Maddison; [m.] Alison Maddison, 31 October 1987; [ch.] Karen, Ann, Lauren and Amanda; [ed.] Seaton Burn Community High School; [occ.] Unemployed; [oth. writ.] None published, as this is my first attempt in competition; [pers.] I write these poems in the knowledge and hope that they bring comfort and happiness too all that may read them.; [a.] Cramlington, Northumberland, UK

MAGEE, ELEANOR
[pen.] Eleanor Magee; [b.] 24 January 1960, Motherwell; [p.] Michael Fallow, Jean Fallow; [m.] John Magee, 10 July 1981; [ch.] Caroline; [ed.] Dalziel High School, Bell College; [occ.] Road Safety Assistant; [memb.] Associate of the London College of Music - subject: Speech and Drama; [oth. writ.] 'Loving You' and 'Remember' poems both published in 1995 in publications "First Time Out" and "Worth Waiting For"; [pers.] Life is my inspiration, each day a new creation; [a.] Hamilton, Lanarkshire, UK

MAGILL, SARAH
[b.] 1 January 1931; [m.] Deceased; [ch.] Six sons, Three daughters; [occ.] Retired; [oth. writ.] Poems for my own pleasure. (Nothing ever published); [pers.] I strive to be of any help I can to my large family and their children. I have not been influenced by any other writers of poems; [a.] Randalstown, Antrim, UK

MAGILL, THOMAS A.
[b.] 11 May 1977, Larne, Northern Ireland; [p.] Tommy and Edith Magill; [ed.] St. Comgalls High School, Larne Grammar School; [occ.] Student - Southbank University - London; [memb.] Society for the Protection Unborn Child (SPUC); [pers.] I identify with the one thing we can all be sure about - death.; [a.] Larne, Co. Antrim, UK

MAGUIRE, MARY
[b.] 28 November 1941, Antrim, NI; [p.] John Kenyon, Hannah Kenyon; [m.] Patrick Maguire, 4 September 1969; [ch.] Patrick, Ann, Frances, Brian; [ed.] 13 Different schools through Ireland, England and Germany, finishing off at Our Lady of Mercy Secondary in Belfast, N.I.; [occ.] Partner in Soft Furnishings Manufacturing Business; [oth. writ.] I've never submitted any of my other work for competition or for publication. This is the first time.; [pers.] Poetry is the language I use to get something emotional out of my system. It's a therapy. Words have always fascinated me. They're a special fabric to create special personal pictures with.; [a.] Randalstown, Antrim, UK

MAHER, KELLY
[b.] 4 August 1971, Carmarthen; [p.] Roy Maher, Jean Maher; [ed.] Queen Elizabeth Maridunum Comprehensive School, Carmarthen, University College of North Wales, Bangor, Newcastle University School of Education.; [occ.] English Language Teacher; [oth. writ.] One other poem published in a welsh anthology.; [pers.] I have always loved poetry, especially because it has the power to connect with something deep inside of us, like an arrow piercing a target. The effect can be magnetic, electrifying. Poetry, ultimately, puts its finger on the pulse of life.; [a.] Carmarthen, Carmarthenshire, UK

MAHER, KEVIN
[b.] 22 October 1976; [p.] Michael Maher and Winnie Maher; [ed.] Archbishop Ilsley School; [occ.] Lighting Factory; [hon.] Medals and Trophies for playing Irish Traditional Music on The Button Accordion; [oth. writ.] My strong ambition is to be in a big rock band, like my heroes U2, and also to go far with my poetry; [pers.] I believe that no matter what anybody tells you, if you want something badly enough then you will get it through determination and dedication.; [a.] Birmingham, UK

MAHMUD, MANSUR
[pen.] Prince Mohamed; [b.] 7 August 1980, Aberdeen; [occ.] Still at school; [pers.] This is my first poem, I love writing songs of all sorts. I enjoy entertaining people through dance and music. This poems is dedicated to all the dead, dying and wanded children of the horrible war in Bosnia. I'm so sensitive to your pain. God hasn't given upon us yet.; [a.] Elgin, Moray, UK

MAIN, ANNETTE
[pen.] Spike; [b.] 19 February 1942, Aberdeen; [p.] Jeannie and Leonard I'Anson; [m.] Widow/New partner - John McMillan; [ch.] Elizabeth-Anne Hepburn; [ed.] Aberdeen Academy (1953-1959), Aberdeen University Dip. Ed- 1964, Aberdeen College of Education - Teaching qualification 1964-; [occ.] Semi-retired owner of photographic business, Primary school teachers for 30 years; [memb.] Retired Teacher's Association (Aberdeen Branch); [hon.] University graduate MA. Dip Ed.; [oth. writ.] I am currently engaged in writing a novel. Have written many poems in this part year only. Would be glad to submit them for appraisal. Usually fairly long pomes have been.; [pers.] Have written poetry for a year, never before felt inspire due to relationship with my new partner who has open the door to my soul. Mind dictates the poem, heart dictates the thought to do this whether or not I ought.; [a.] Aberdeen, Grampian, UK

MALING, LEE
[pen.] Cain; [b.] 17 June 1970, Solihull; [p.] Keith Alexander Maling, Eileen Patricia Maling; [oth. writ.] Began work on a debut anthology entitled 'Elegies of the Damned', in Feb 1992, hopes to be completed by the close of '96, if all goes to plan, shall be seeking publication 1997; [pers.] I never found poetry, poetry found me, from out of nowhere it came, and brought comfort in my darkest hours, a positive and constructive outlet for all the traumas that life's wretched hand tends to throw. "When life poses threat, let poetry be your guide", a guide for which I have developed a great love and respect.; [a.] Solihull, West Mids, UK

MALLIA, WALTER
[pen.] Walter Mallia; [b.] 30 June 1935, Msida, Malta; [p.] Emmanuel/Elizabeth (Both Deceased); [m.] Doris Ne' Bugeja, 12 April 1964; [ch.] Hilda, Fiona, Jonathan; [ed.] The Lyceum, Malta; [occ.] Night Manager/Day Controller; [memb.] Former Member, Dragonara Cultural Group, Malta Science-Fiction Society; [hon.] 1st. prize in Maltese Poetry Competition in Gozo. 2nd Prize Poetry, in Local Competition. Prize in Art, Dragonara Cultural Grp.; [oth. writ.] Poem Published in England. Currently publishing poems in different languages, in various local newspapers and magazines, usually with own illustrations.; [pers.] Greatly influenced by English, Maltese, Italian Literature in General and Art.; [a.] St. Julians, Malta

MALLPRESS, PHILLIP
[b.] 23 August 1923, Birkenshaw; [p.] Hubert and Annie Mallpress; [m.] Muriel, 26 November 1949; [ch.] Christopher, Joanna; [ed.] Hitchin Grammar School, Leeds University; [occ.] Retired Schoolmaster - Schools in Bradford and Batley Grammar School; [memb.] Scouting 1931-88 Birkenshaw Parish Church, Various Charities, C.A.B. Chairman, 4 years Leeds University Standing Committee of Convocation; [hon.] B.A. 1980, M.ED. 1961, M. Phil 1988 Silver Acorn, Silver Wolf Scouting Awards.; [oth. writ.] Local History - Birkernshaw The Birch Grove Published. Spen Valley Scouting the early years. Published. The Parish Church of St Paul Birkenshaw. Published. Two unpublished theses.; [a.] Birkenshaw, West Yorkshire, UK

MANNING, DANIEL
[b.] 15 April 1970, Jersey, CI; [ed.] D. Hautree Secondary School Jersey Channel Islands; [occ.] Security Guard; [memb.] Jersey Kai Shin Khi Aikido Association; [hon.] Aikido Award for dedication and effort; [oth. writ.] (Enhancing the ledgend) a collection of thirty poems and pilosophy's (The Black Epic) my second book consisting of Calligraphized poems and drawings currently being written) (Fifteen minutes worth of dreams (fantasy science fiction novel currently being written).; [pers.] Making your dreams into reality is the easy part one needs at special energy to fuel their progress. Using the laws of the universe there

is nothing you cannot accomplish.; [a.] Saint Helier, UK

MANNING, JOANNE PRITCHARD
[pen.] Joanne Manning; [b.] 2 November 1940, Dorchester; [ch.] Daughter, Claire, Joanne (Also interested in the arts); [occ.] Running a home and enjoying the occasional craft fair to exhibit, and writing poetry; [hon.] Various Cups as a commercial display artist (for my work)-Awards for my hobby as a "potter" and a gold medal cup in the swinging sixties for dancing Rock and Roll!!; [oth. writ.] Several poems published ref. Anthology, magazines and local papers; [pers.] Gentle reflections on inspiration-to nourish spirit and awareness of the world around us...; [a.] The Village of Hawkinge, Nr. Folkestone, Kent, UK

MANSFORD, CATHERINE
[b.] 30 October 1933, London; [p.] Norah and Dennis Jago; [m.] John Mansford, 30 April 1960; [ch.] John Patrick, Teresa Anne, Nicholas Paul; [ed.] Roman Catholic Secondary School and Technical College; [occ.] Housewife; [memb.] Several Local Choirs and Singing Groups; [hon.] Top Dancing and Singing; [oth. writ.] Lost of poems not yet published children's stories; [pers.] To make people happy; [a.] Frinton-on-Sea, Essex, UK

MARCAR, PIERRE
[pen.] Pierre Marcar; [b.] 26 October 1958, England; [p.] Maryse and Bill; [ed.] Alleyn's School, Dulwich and Brunel University; [occ.] Photographer, Scriptwriter and Poet; [hon.] LBIPP - Photography BSC - Metallurgy and Management Diploma of Advanced Hypnotherapy (Dip. A. Hyp.); [oth. writ.] A 26 part TV series, screened on sky TV, various articles for magazines in New York and a regular contributor to Valerie Austins books on Hypnotherapy; [pers.] From a spiritual base, I aim to share the little that I understand, with humour and an honest heart.; [a.] Thornton, Heath, Surrey, UK

MARKAC, YVONNE NEVENKA
[pen.] Nevenka Markac; [b.] 12 April 1986, Bells Hill; [p.] George Markac, Margaret Markac; [ed.] Kirkland Park Primary Scohool; [occ.] School Pupil (primary); [memb.] 1st Strathaven Brownies, Sunday School (Rankin Church); [hon.] Certificate for Anti Bullying Poster; [pers.] I am saddened by the suffering of children and adults in other parts of the world.; [a.] Strathaven, Lanarkshire, UK

MARSLAND, DAVID JOHN
[b.] 25 August 1983, Norwich; [p.] Robert and Dawn Marsland; [ed.] Stalham Middle School Broadland High School; [occ.] School Boy; [oth. writ.] Other poems published in school magazines; [pers.] Inspired by myths and legends hopes to be an actor; [a.] Catfield, Norfolk, UK

MARSTON, ANTHONY JOHN
[b.] 2 January 1951, Brighton; [ed.] Chichester High School for Boys, the University of Hard Knocks; [occ.] Computer Consultant; [memb.] Surrey Border Rifle and Pistol Club; [pers.] I wrote this poem in 1986 to express my love for Susan G., a special lady. Sadly, she did not return my love.; [a.] Sutton, Surrey, UK

MARTIN, MARY
[pen.] Fifi La Bon Bon; [b.] 10 August 1929, Wednesbury; [p.] Alice Gandy; [m.] Arthur Edward Martin, 21 April 1951; [ch.] Paul Terence; [ed.] George Dixon, Grammar School, Harborne Road, Birmingham, West Midlands; [occ.] Housewife; [hon.] Trophies for Latin American and Ballroom dancing. Honour for being married 45 years to a very special man; [oth. writ.] Many poems and short stories for personal pleasure. None published as this is my first attempt; [pers.] I am so proud to have been chosen as my family and friends have always told me to send my works up but didn't think they were good enough; [a.] Birmingham, West Mids, UK

MARTIN, PETER
[pen.] William Shackleton; [b.] 27 August 1952, Bishops, Stortford; [p.] Dories Alice (Deceased), William Stanley; [m.] Linda Martin, 10 February 1973; [ch.] Natasha 22 years, Aaron 16 years; [ed.] Stansted Secondary Modern School Essex; [occ.] Recovering from stroke and heart attack; [memb.] D.A.S. former equity B.F.P., N.U.J. Amateur Dramatics, R.S.P.B., R.S.P.C.A., B.C.A., M.B.S.; [oth. writ.] Filed at this time publication pending (books), Rancid Gang (children T.V. film), Bronze the Turkey (children), poem Days A Ground, Stormy Seas, Never a true Word, Ice Pack 2000, film (T.V.); [pers.] As a writer I disrelish the injustice of today's world! I aim for poignant compositions in my workings! When possible I try to reflect amnesty if and when appropriate.; [a.] Saffron, Walden, Essex, UK

MARTIN, WENVIS
[b.] 15 June 1925, Llangranog, Dyfed; [m.] George Martin, 1 September 1951; [ed.] Cardigan Grammar County School Cardiganshire; [occ.] Housewife; [memb.] Rumney Towns Women's Guild Rumney and District Local History Society; [hon.] Neither - But, have always tried to live up to my school motto - translated (from Welsh) to read - "Perseverance Wins!"; [oth. writ.] Many poems published in local magazines. Welsh Editions of Cardiganshire magazines. Appropriate poetry re different functions E.G. Golden Wedding etc.; [pers.] So much easier to express one's joy/sorrow by verse, letting your soul take over, to give a true message - be it sad or happy. Classical music floral arrangement. Research Welsh History; [a.] Cardiff, S. Glam, UK

MASON, CAROLYN
[pen.] Carolyn King; [b.] Windsor; [m.] Divorced; [ch.] Simon and Joely; [occ.] Special School for Language-Disorder Children; [hon.] 1996 Runner-up in Hilton House "Poet of the Year" Competition (3 poems); [oth. writ.] First Anthology "The Reunion" just completed and in search of a publisher!; [pers.] As one for whom imagination grows on trees, I find my most rewarding poetry that which unequivocally - and yet poetically - states a truth. This is one such poem.; [a.] Ventnor, Isle of Wight, UK

MASON, GWEN
[pen.] Gwen Mason; [b.] 16 July 1931, Southampton; [p.] Ernest Churcher, Elwyn Churcher; [m.] Philip Mason, 29 March 1956; [ed.] Bitterne Cope; [occ.] Retired; [oth. writ.] Twenty four poems in various anthologies, short story in travellers tales and article in poetry now.; [pers.] Simplicity I feel is missing this modern world so I strive to write in a simple way as did the "Greats" of yesteryear.; [a.] Petersfield, Hampshire, UK

MASON, MISS SELINA MARY
[pen.] Selina Mary; [b.] 18 October 1970, Stourport; [p.] John Mason and Marie Mason; [ed.] John Masefield High School, Herefordshire Worcester College of the Arts; [occ.] Dental Nurse; [memb.] ILPH International League for the Protection of Horses, British Association for Dental Nurse Assistants; [oth. writ.] Several poems all of which are un-published, this is my first entry and my first publication.; [pers.] I have written poetry for many years now and my inspiration comes from life's many ups and downs but mainly from love with all its joys and sorrows. I hope that my writing reflects the type of emotions that people feel at one time or another in their lives.; [a.] Wrexham, Clwyd, UK

MASTERS, MRS. SALLY
[pen.] Sally Russell; [b.] 22 December 1941, Rayners Lane Pinner Middx.; [m.] 18 November 1958; [occ.] Very busy housewife, mother, grandmother of 13, love writing poetry, singing, cooking.; [hon.] This is my first honour to have one of my poems published.; [oth. writ.] I have written many poems. Hoping to get them published in a book. Will continue to write them. I have written a funny poem that to me is Micheal Crawford material. He inspires me so. I have also written a poem for my special relations in Utah which I believe went into a magazine.; [pers.] When writing poetry I want to bring happiness and bring everyone together and to care fore each other. I have been influenced by many people and many things but especially Michael Crawford! I want to write an autobiography, can anyone help me to do this!; [a.] Greenford, Middx, UK

MATTHEW, ELIZABETH
[pen.] Betty; [b.] 25 March 1939, Cumbria; [p.] Anne Jane and David Hetherington; [m.] John William Matthew, 5 January 1961; [ch.] Three Daughters; [ed.] Infants School Primary School Secondary School; [occ.] Housewife; [oth. writ.] Just write for my own pleasure on any theme that comes into my mind; [pers.] After losing my husband last year I thought of all the killings going on all over the world all the love that could be swen to people wasted.; [a.] Whitehaven, Cumbria, UK

MATTHEWS, JOAN ALEXANDRA DUBICKI
[b.] 28 October 1922, Plymouth; [p.] Eleanor and Edward Matthews; [occ.] Retired; [hon.] Noted poet of the year in 1969 by Eagle Press, presented with Story "Inferno in Devonport" in book form. In a presentation by Lord Mayor of Exeter in 1995; [oth. writ.] "Leigham" published, "Beesands" inferno in Devonport published; [pers.] Greatly influenced by Wordsworths poem "Daffodils" my story "Inferno in Devonport." Published and placed in the archives for future generations; [a.] Plymouth, Devon, UK

MATTHEWS, JOAN
[b.] 3 November 1940, Birmingham; [p.] Edward and Violet Crook; [m.] Derek George Matthews, 29 March 1958; [ch.] Jacqueline, Annette, Philip. 5 grandchildren Katie, Lauren, Jay, Joseph and Jessica; [ed.] Sec/MOD/School; [occ.] (Worked from 15 yrs to 50 yrs) retired Sales Consultant. Registered now disabled with cervical spondylosis.; [memb.] Local Women's Institute, Patron Local Operatic Society; [hon.] School Diplomas in (Art and Design), (Elecution - Speech Choir) Elecution Handwriting School Reporter, Head Prefect House Captain, Painting in Local Art Gallery in 1952; [oth. writ.] (Written 10 poems recently) I have always loved to write from an early age and used to make up stories to tell my children.; [pers.] I believe that if you can put down on paper what you feel inside or what you see around you can be of benefit to others spiritually.; [a.] Swansea, Glam, UK

MATTHEWS, SUSAN
[b.] 18 September 1959, Rhymney; [p.] John Matthews, Valerie Matthews; [m.] Graham Thomas (Partner); [ch.] Stephen John; [ed.] Educated at Rhymney Comprehensive School, Further Education at Merthyr, Tydfil Technical College; [occ.] Residential Social Worker; [oth. writ.] 1 other poem recently published in a lovers anthology; [pers.] My poems are my memories to be passed on to others. They are what I call 'My Time', Favorite poet to date. William Wordsworth; [a.] Blackwood, Gwent, UK

MAUD, FALLA
[b.] 9 November 1927, Guernsey; [p.] John T. Le Page, Lilian Le Page; [m.] David H. Falla, 19 August 1954; [ch.] Diane, Colin; [ed.] Grammar School, Technical College; [occ.] Secretary of own business (Plant Nursery); [memb.] Woman's Institute, Church Committees; [oth. writ.] Poems written for special events; [pers.] I enjoy working with words, so I do crosswords and any competitions to do with the written word.; [a.] St. Sampsons, Guernsey, UK

MAWNAM-SMITH, FRANCES
[b.] 7 June 1946, Southwick, Hants; [m.] John Walker (Deceased), 8 January 1973; [ed.] St. Mary's Convent School, Worcester, Hereford College of Education, University of Birmingham; [occ.] Head Teacher Pendock Primary School; [memb.] College of Preceptors; [hon.] B. Phil (Ed) Birmingham University; [oth. writ.] "Love And Other Seasons". (Not submitted for publication) poems. "And hope to hear the Cuckoo," novel currently under production.; [pers.] Cornwall and Cornish Beginnings make strong word pictures for me. Robert graves, D. M. Thomas and sister Calista teased me into thought about words and their infinite shift of meaning. I seldom let a day pass without reading or writing about the puzzle of being: `Between A Laugh And A Tear'; [a.] Ledbury, Herefordshire, UK

MAWSTON, HARVEY GIBSON
[b.] 31-10-35, Co. Durham; [p.] Susannah & Sydney & (sister Lorna); [m.] Pamela Mawston, 1959; [ch.] Gary & Craig Mawston; [ed.] Rothwell Grammar School, Bretton Hall (Adult Educ. Course); [occ.] Residential Social Worker; [memb.] Methodist Church; [hon.] G.C.E.s, Certificate in Social Services (CSS); [oth. writ.] Various other anthologies & publications; [pers.] To be conscious of the present at all times, and its link with the past and future.; [a.] Shaw Cross, Dewsbury, West Yorks

MAXWELL, STEPHEN
[pen.] Doherty; [b.] 1 October 1967, Scotland; [p.] Joseph Maxwell, Cathrine Doherty; [ed.] Colston Sec., Glasgow College of Building and Printing; [occ.] Graphic Artist; [memb.] Scottish Karate Board, Taka-Kai Karate Association, Martial Arts Development Commission; [hon.] O.N.C., H.N.C., H.N.D. Graphic Art and Design; [pers.] It's not what you are that hold you back, it's what you think you are not.; [a.] Glasgow, Milton, UK

MAZZUCCATO, RACHAEL
[b.] 9 December 1971, Shrodells; [ch.] Danielle Mazzuccato; [ed.] Maple Cross Infants School; [occ.] Hairdresser; [oth. writ.] I have written many other poems. This is the first time I have tried to get any of them published; [pers.] All of my poems are written from personal experiences. I hope to enlighten the eyes of others through my writing.; [a.] Rickmansworth, Herts, UK

MCARTHUR, FRANK
[b.] 16 May 1938, N. Ireland; [p.] Sam and Martha; [m.] Sybil, 5 November; [ch.] 2, Ian and Michael; [ed.] Eyemouth High School, Berwickshire HIgh School Duns; [occ.] Landscape and Contact Garden Maintenance; [memb.] West Barns and Meadowmill Bowling Clubs; [hon.] Various sports champions plus Bowls Champion of Champions etc.; [oth. writ.] My Prayer (published), My Scotland, My Eagle etc. etc.; [pers.] I'm just a hardworking country man who enjoys all crafts and would like more time to devote to writing, drawing, painting, sculpting and woodworking; [a.] Dunbar, E. Lothian, UK

MCCARTHY, LESLEY ANN
[b.] 29 November 1956, Hammersmith; [p.] Frederick and Katleen Howick; [m.] Colin Michael McCarthy, 17 April 1993; [ch.] Step-childreen: Michael, Darren and Michelle; [ed.] Epsom Secondary Girls School, Leatherhead Secretarial College; [occ.] Unemployed due to Ill Health M.E. Sufferer; [hon.] Pitman's Shorthand and Typing, City and Guilds Make-Up and Manicure with credits; [oth. writ.] For pleasure on my feelings and like experiences; [pers.] I enjoy learning from the friendship and experiences of others and hope others may gain something of use from me.; [a.] London, UK

MCCLURE, MICHAEL JAMES SCHOFIELD
[b.] 10 June 1984, Bahrain; [p.] Sandra and Peter McClure, Step Dad - Roger Stevenson; [ed.] Bognor Regis Community College; [occ.] School Boy; [memb.] School Hockey, Cricket and Tennis Team, Middleton Sports Club Cricket, Squash, Hockey and Tennis Sections, Pagham Karate Club; [hon.] Green Belt Karate and Kata Competition. Trophy winner, Middleton Sports Club Squash u. 12's Plate, design and bake a cake trophy winner Nyewood Junior School and design a valentine card competition winner; [oth. writ.] First work; [pers.] I wrote this poem aged eleven.; [a.] Bognor Regis, West Sussex, UK

MCCLUSKEY, WINIFRED
[b.] 8 June 1914, Swall, Wells; [p.] Hugh Ried Hughes and Talbot; [m.] 4 February 1933, Deceased; [ch.] Three; [ed.] R. C. Blaydon Northumbert and; [occ.] Retired; [hon.] Honourable title; [oth. writ.] Irish Grand Parents; [a.] Mablethorpe, Lincs, UK

MCCORMACK, BERNADETTE
[b.] 9 February 1958, Ballyhena, Northern Ireland; [p.] The Late Patrick Kerr and Catherine Kerr; [m.] James Patrick McCormack, 30 August 1985; [ch.] Malachy James and Mairead-Anne; [ed.] Primary, Secondary and Technical Schools and College. R.S.A. Stage I English Language; [occ.] Cook Supervisor; [memb.] Unison Union at work; [hon.] "Only your recognition so far ie. The International Society of Poets.; [oth. writ.] Mostly about funny incidents and occurances which occured during my work routine some about myself, others about my friends and colleagues at work.; [pers.] I like to see the funny side of situations and to make people laugh. I also enjoy good jokes.; [a.] Randalstown, Antrim, UK

MCFARLANE, CATHERINE BROWNING
[pen.] C. Browning; [b.] 17 July 1928, London; [p.] Isa Hassen and Gavin Browning; [m.] Duncan McFarlane (Deceased), 4 November 1948; [ch.] 7; [ed.] Part London - Evaluated to the Bonny Banks at 11 yrs; [occ.] Retired; [oth. writ.] Book in the process I too have been influenced by the great poets; [pers.] As - Judge Rutherford - imprisoned in Aberdeen Castle - Said "It were a well spent journey - the sevens deaths lay between; [a.] Kilsyth, Nr Glasgow, Strathclyde, UK

MCFARLANE, MINETTE
[b.] 31 October 1961, Brighton, Sussex; [p.] Anna and Ian McFarlane; [ed.] Varndean Grammar School for Girls; [occ.] All around artist; [memb.] Tip Top Club; [hon.] Certificate for "Enthusiasm" in the Junior School; [oth. writ.] Plenty of poems, yet unpublished. This one's the only poem ever been shown.; [pers.] Never, ever, give up on your dreams.; [a.] Hove, Sussex, UK

MCGINTY, GERALDINE
[b.] 2 September 1966, Barrhead; [p.] Rosemary and Archie McGinty; [ed.] St. Lukes High School Reid Kerr College; [a.] Barrhead, Glasgow, UK

MCGOFF, ELAINE
[b.] 22 August 1978, Dublin, Ireland; [p.] Mary McGoff, Terry McGoff; [ed.] Killashee Primary School, Naas, Convent of Mercy Primary School, Naas, St. Mary's College Secondary School, Naas; [occ.] Student; [memb.] Irish Council Against Blood Sports, Alliance for Animal Rights; [hon.] Prize winner in 1994 School poetry competition; [oth. writ.] Several poems printed in my local newspaper; [pers.] I try to be honest, my influences include: Seamus Heaney, Patrick Kavanagh, Gerard Manley Hopkins and Emily Dickinson.; [a.] Naas, Kildare, UK

MCGOVERN, KENNETH
[pen.] Kenneth McGovern; [b.] June 25, 1938, Farnworth; [p.] George Hector McGovern and Bertha McGovern; [m.] Margaret McGovern, June 24, 1977; [ch.] 3 Sons, daughter, stepsons and daughter; [ed.] Queen Street Primary, Farnworth and Harper Green Secondary Modern Farnworth; [occ.] Retired Coal Miner; [hon.] Sir Arthur Markam, Memorial Awards for poetry, Sheffield University and three poems published in other books.; [oth. writ.] Indefinable love, You, Father. Phobias.; [pers.] To show mercy and tolerance to all mankind, no matter what race or creed and not to expect to much in return.; [a.] Leigh, Lancs, UK

MCGRATH, IAN
[b.] 23 June 1974, Dublin; [p.] May and Denis McGrath; [m.] Sharon Hynd (Engaged), 11 July 1997; [ed.] Ard Scoile La Salle (Raheny Dublins) and Napier University (Edinburgh); [occ.] Student; [hon.] BSC Civil Engineering; [oth. writ.] Plenty, none published; [pers.] I write for my own pleasure and relaxation, if other people enjoy my work, well great if not I'll still write.; [a.] Cowdenbeath, Fife, UK

MCGUIRE, NATHAN
[pen.] 20 November 1974, Birmingham; [b.] George and Carmel McGuire; [ed.] St. Thomas Aquinas R.C. School; [occ.] Currently Embarking on writing Freelance.; [memb.] Everton Fan Club; [hon.] Will be going to the University of Wales Lampeter in September to study English Literature; [oth. writ.] Currently writing poems and short stories which I hope will be published.; [pers.] I write about realism. It is a poets duty to inform others of what is truly wrong in society. Influenced by Auden and William Blake; [a.] Edgbaston, Warwicks, UK

MCINTOSH, CHRISTOPHER DAVID
[b.] 8 July 1965, St. Johns Hospital, Chelmsford; [p.] Mrs. C. A. McIntosh, Mr. H. G. McIntosh; [ed.] St. John Payne Comprehensive School, Patching Hall Lane, Chelmsford Essex; [occ.] Suffering from a form of Shrophreana since I was 18 yrs. old invalid; [hon.] 4 'O' levels Maths grade C Physics grade B Chemistry grade B, English language grade C achieve at night school around 1987; [oth. writ.] A flowing of Crimson was adapted from poetry story "The Phase of the Moon" other poetic story "Love With No Name", The Book Of Visions" poetic play called "A Traveller In Mind"; [pers.] When reality is demented thoughts stampeding don't let them succeed and give us a world, a world without meaning; [a.] Chelmsford, Essex, UK

MCINTYRE, CAMERON
[b.] 30 December 1959, Belfast; [p.] Thomas and Marion McIntyre; [m.] Diane, 14 November 1981; [ch.] Loren and Clare; [ed.] DunDonald Comprehensive School; [occ.] Plumbing and Heating Engineer.; [hon.] Twice North Down Plumber of the year.; [oth. writ.] Several poems published also British poetry review 1994 and 1996; [pers.] What I find in poetry I can not find without thats why it travels with me in every thought that I see; [a.] Newtownwards, Down, N. Ireland

MCINTYRE, SCOTT
[b.] 16 June 1970, Paisley; [ed.] Johnstone High School University of Stirling and Strathclyde (BSC/MSC); [occ.] Personnel/ Human Resource Work; [memb.] Graduate membership of institute of personnel and development, salvation army soldier; [oth. writ.] This poem is my first serious attempt at putting creative pen to paper; [pers.] To explore further my imagination and prove that it is always better to have a positive outlook on life's adventures; [a.] Lochwinnoch, Renfrewshire, UK

MCKAY, HENRY
[b.] 20 October 1932, Armadale, W. L.; [p.] John McKay and Mary McKay; [m.] Sadie Ousby, 20 September 1958; [ch.] Margaret, Thomson and Steward; [ed.] Armadale Primary; [occ.] Factory Services; [oth. writ.] Poems of a mainly humorous nature several tributes to Robert Burns Scotland's National Bard; [pers.] Favorite poem - Rudyard Kipling's 'if' I keep trying to look before I leap.; [a.] Bathgate, W. L., UK

MCKENDRY, JOYCE
[b.] 9 April 1959, Ballymoney; [ch.] Jason and Paul; [ed.] Dunseverick Primary School, Ballycastle High School; [occ.] Looking after my own children; [pers.] I always loved poetry and helping my children with it. I never entered any competitions before until I see yours in a magazine which I buy often at my local new agents.; [a.] Ballymoney, Antrim, UK

MCKEOWN, FRANCIS
[pen.] Frank McKeown; [b.] 30 March 1925, Belfast; [p.] Joseph McKeown, Mary McKeown; [m.] Lilian Hopkins, 2 April 1956; [ch.] Susan Jane, Beverly Ann; [ed.] Newport Boys Council School (Barton, Isle of Wight); [occ.] Retired; [memb.] Associate of the Society of Company and Commercial Accountants, Barton Boneheads (Old Boys Network); [oth. writ.] Humorous rhymes on everyday matters, historical and philosophical subjects, some translations from French and German poems, anti-war poems and songs; [pers.] "...Hill is now a comfortable four-tenths of a second in front of Schumacher"; [a.] Christchurch, Dorset, UK

MCKILLOP, JUNIRIS
[pen.] June or Juniris McKillop; [b.] (Gemini), Largs, Ayrshire; [p.] Samuel Alexander McKillop and Ella Angus MacLeod; [ed.] Hold a higher National Diploma in Business (very high I.Q., more than 97% of population); [occ.] Ex-Wraf Driver, Ex-Senior Manager in this ex-employer at the Royal Albert Hall presently career for Elderly Aunt; [hon.] Forst competition entered; [oth. writ.] Many poems - but have not offered any for publication before but was told by an F/E English teacher in Canterbury I should be writing books.; [pers.] Since childhood I have been a bit of Psychic and foresee good and bad events I believe everyone has an ancestor looking out for them on this earth, so should strive to develop the seed of happiness within themselves, a smile is always beautiful and free.; [a.] Largs, Ayrshire, UK

MCLEAN, CATHERINE M.
[pen.] Molly McLean; [b.] 29 April 1923, New Zealand; [p.] James and Mimie MacPherson; [m.] Maitland Naisby McLean, 28 August 1948; [ch.] Andrew McLean; [ed.] Thurso Academy, Aberdeen University; [pers.] I wrote "The Finality Of Death" one sad night a few months after my husbands death on 1 September 1995 (3 days after our 47th Wedding Anniversary). He was a unique person, who all his life was unstinting in his help to others less fortunate and less capable than himself. The poem is a tribute to him the Bathos crept in unintended but he would have enjoyed it.; [a.] Chorleywood, Herts, UK

MCMAHON, JANE LESLEY
[b.] 6 April 1959, Luton; [ch.] Sean James, David Michael, Laura Jane; [ed.] Rotheram High School; [occ.] Residential social worker caring for children with a learning disability; [oth. writ.] Various poems published mainly arrival press; [pers.] When I write, I find myself, I am myself I enjoy who I find.; [a.] Clophill, Beds, UK

MCNAMARA, BERNADETTE S. M.
[b.] 24 March 1958, Leeds; [p.] Deceased; [ed.] St. Benedicts R.C. Secondary School. Bramley, Leeds. (Now sadly no longer exists); [occ.] Data Controller V.D.U. Operator for a Ford Car Dealership; [memb.] Subscribing daily to the club of life!; [hon.] An honour to be able to get up every morning and run the gauntlet of living a life in this broken up old world!; [oth. writ.] Personal writings, thoughts and scribblings currently kept at home in a bottom drawer! Just waiting.; [pers.] My late father was my best friend and adviser. His love of books and Literature he has passed on to me over the years and it is only now since his death, that I fully appreciate what he was trying to tell me. Thanks also to Jim Morrison.; [a.] Leeds, West Yorks, UK

MCPEAKE, E.
[pen.] Caroline Carmel; [b.] 14 July 1982, Mid Ulster Hospital, Magherafelt; [p.] Seamus and Elizabeth McPeake; [ed.] Currently Attending Saint Mary's Grammar School Magherafelt; [occ.] Student; [memb.] School Choir, Local Sporting Teams; [hon.] Won an Acting Competition to meet a T.V. Star Helen Mirren out of Prime Suspect. I had to write a 200 word essay; [oth. writ.] "My most frightening experience." (C - McPeake) several small poems.; [pers.] I would like to thank my parents - Seamus and Elizabeth for giving me a place to stay and for putting up will me all these years. I would like them to know I love dearly.; [a.] Magherafelt, Derry, UK

MCTAGGART, THOMAS
[b.] North Ireland; [p.] Frank and Elizabeth McTaggart; [m.] Eileen McHugh, 23 February 1963; [ch.] Ian and Gary; [ed.] Holy Family School Mossend, Lanarkshire, Scotland, National School, Newtownstewart Co. Tyrone, St. Patrick's High Lanarkshire, Scotland; [occ.] Retired; [hon.] First prize at school for "God Hold The Key"; [oth. writ.] Included, Dream Stuff School Days, Pride of London, countless 'Words of Wisdom' have appeared in magazines and newspapers, the first in Ireland's own in 1946; [pers.] I feel you cannot write about life with understanding, unless you include good and evil. Once you can tell right from wrong, your education starts paying dividends.; [a.] Denham, Bucks, UK

MEADEN, MICHELLE
[b.] 17 April 1980, London; [p.] Paul Meaden and Maggie Everett; [ed.] St. Johns RC Comprehensive School Gravesend Kent; [occ.] Student; [memb.] Amateur Drama Group, Squash Club, Hockey Club; [hon.] Certificates of Merit and Achievement (school) sport trophies; [pers.] Writing poetry is a special hobby of mine and is a way I express my thoughts and feelings.; [a.] Gravesend, Kent, UK

MEADHURST, NEIL MICHAEL
[b.] 23 December 1971, Forest Gate; [p.] Dennis and Patricia Meadhurst; [ed.] Chingford School (Comprehensive) Nevin Drive, Chingford; [occ.] Purchasing Manager Design and Build Company; [oth. writ.] None published as yet although I am well on my way to completing 100 poems which I hope to get published.; [pers.] It is a hard world that we live in today and if my only salvation from today's steadily decaying society comes from drink, and your buying I'll have a large one!; [a.] Chingford, London, UK

MEARS, ROBERT H.
[b.] 1946, Derby; [ed.] Secondary Modern School and Trent Polytechnic Studied Engineering; [pers.] My poem is based on a real life incident although names are fictitious. The parkinson's victim was nursed by her loving husband for 11 years at the expense of his own health. He died 12 months later.

MEEK, DIANA
[b.] 10 May 1959, Kensington; [p.] Valentina and Dante Valentini; [m.] Gary Meek, 10 May 1994; [ch.] Giulia (Daughter); [ed.] Virgo Fidelis, Convent School; [occ.] Housewife; [oth. writ.] "Good Cooking" in "And" all that by arrival press - "Remember Me" in "The Book Of Life And Love" by arrival press - "My Life" in "Voices On The Wind."; [pers.] I try to write poems that everyone can enjoy and relate to in some way through their own lives.; [a.] Wembley, Middx, UK

MEGSON, ANDREW TIMOTHY
[b.] 20 April 1956, Hull; [p.] Wilfred Megson, Mary Megson; [ed.] Marist College (Hull), Hull College of Higher Education the open University; [occ.] Care Assistant; [hon.] B.A. (hons), Social Science (Lower Second), B.A. (hons) Psychology (Lower Second); [oth. writ.] A few other poems, short stories (no previous publication); [pers.] For someone who feels that he has many things to say, to share with and communicate to others about realities and various aspects of life, poetry would seem to be an appropriate and promising activity.; [a.] Hull, East Yorkshire, UK

MELBOURNE, PAULINE ROSE
[b.] 25 November 1951, Damerham; [p.] Eileen Elliott, Frederick Elliott; [m.] Divorced; [ch.] Paul Anthony, Michael George, Timothy David; [ed.] Twyham Comprehensive School; [occ.] Housekeeper at 3 Star Hotel; [pers.] I like reading also the classics like Bronte, George Eliot and Dickens. This has helped me greatly with my poetry. Also the things that happen around about me helps.; [a.] Ringwood, Hants, UK

MERCHANT, KENNETH
[b.] 28 December 1927, Bristol; [ch.] Two sons; [ed.] Carlton Park School; [occ.] Retired was in nursing for handicapped people.; [oth. writ.] I have had poems printed in "People" edited by Michelle Abbott "Under A Southern Sky" (An aural images anthology).; [pers.] Inspired by John Betjeman I commenced writing poetry on retirement at the age of 65.; [a.] Bristol, South Glos, UK

MERRIFIELD, SUSAN E.
[b.] 26 January 1961, Cornwall; [p.] Frederick (Deceased) and Margaret Parkyn; [m.] Gary Merrifield, 18 April 1981; [ch.] Samantha Louise, Darren James; [ed.] St. Stephen Comprehensive, St. Austell College of Further Education; [occ.] Clerical Officer; [oth. writ.] Several, poems published in new anthologies - all since summer 1995; [pers.] If my poetry pleases others it pleases me. Thanks to Daddy and Rebecca.; [a.] St. Austell, Cornwall, UK

MERTZIOS, GEORGIOS
[b.] 25 November 1962, Greece, Loannina; [p.] Antonios Mertzios, Beatrice Mertzios; [ed.] LLB, LLM (Sociology-Philosophy and History of law) Thessaloniki University (Greece) - Studies of law, Bari University (Italy) - Candidate for LLM (International Commercial law) Sussex University; [occ.] Lawyer, Bar Council of Loannina (Greece); [memb.] Artistic, LIterary Society of Loannina, Historical-Folkloric Society of Zagori, On The Committee Of Monthly Folkloric Review, Universal Association of Esperanto; [hon.] Ministry of Culture (Greece); [oth. writ.] Several poems and articles for monthly folkloric review - several Articles of International Affairs for local magazines - The publication of the historical book (1991) "Laista, Zagori, Loannina"; [pers.] In my writing I like to express the contrast between positive love laws, and the eternal conflict between positive laws and natural law. I have been greatly impressed and admire the surrealistic movement of poetry.; [a.] Hove, East Sussex, UK

METCALFE, HEIDI ELIZABETH
[b.] November 21, 1979, Preston; [p.] Isobel and David Metcalfe; [ed.] St. Micheal's Church of England High School, Blackburn College; [occ.] Student; [memb.] The Barn Players Theatre Company; [hon.] Grade 6A Speech and Drama (Guild Hall School of Music and Drama), Senior Shakespeare Certificate (Central School of Speech and Drama), Bronze medal LAMDA; [oth. writ.] Some short stories published in school magazine; [pers.] My poems are personal and reflects my moods and feelings although I hope they can be related to by others; [a.] Preston, Lancashire

MICHAEL, MRS. DOREEN
[b.] 22 January 1904, Birkenhead; [p.] Albert and Florence Postlethwaite; [m.] Alfred Michael, 4 September 1937; [ch.] David and Gaynor; [ed.] Church of England School; [occ.] Housewife (widow); [hon.] Won first prize in Poetry Competition Celebrating 21 years of the "Spastics Pool" now known as "Scope"; [oth. writ.] Have written another 40 poems which I hope to have published in due course; [pers.] My philosophy in life "Love and Laughter". Have cared for my celebrate palsied son for 50 years. "A labour of love." Have a wonderful daughter.; [a.] Birkenhead, Merseyside, UK

MIDDLETON, JANET
[b.] 22 September 1941; [m.] Robert Middleton (Divorced), 4 March 1961; [ch.] Esther, Peter, Michael; [ed.] Graeme High School Falkirk; [memb.] Musicians Union Song Writer's Club of America; [hon.] Semi finalist twice of the International Society of Poets, 2 songs one being published titled "What Country Means To Me" by country music U.S.A. Nashville one being published "Life's Window" by Tim Pay Alley Florida, U.S.A.; [oth. writ.] Lyrics for songs romance traditional old fashioned country western, ballads short stories. Inspired by the romance and adventure the picturesque old west; [pers.] I would like to see people being polite to each other and the return of honesty and integrity into human conduct and relationships again. Less violence, less swelling, in the home or street or on T.V.; [a.] Falkirk, Stirlingshire, UK

MILLEN, PATRICIA
[b.] 1 October 1930, Battersea; [p.] Albert and Marjorie Robertson; [m.] John Peter Millen, 16 March 1957; [ch.] Son and daughter; [ed.] Ordinary education at a L.C.C. School, was not accepted at a Secondary School owing to very bad writing. Subjects I did best was English and singing; [occ.] Retired formerly manages for sheltered scheme; [memb.] Since 1979 have been in Dartford Operatic Society also with Swanley Light Operatic Soc.; [hon.] Took a Tops course in 1980, passed for an R.S.A. in English, typing and office management.; [oth. writ.] Several small poems written over the years.; [pers.] I have dabbled in Poetry since I was 14 years old. I have never entered any of them for publication as I did not think them good enough. I do it for personal enjoyment.; [a.] Crayford, Kent, UK

MILLER, ANNA E.
[b.] 27 August 1966; [p.] Sara Lankester, Roger Miller; [ed.] Hatherop Castle School, Filton Technical College Spiro Institute; [occ.] Administration Manager; [oth. writ.] Anthology to be published later the year; [pers.] I believe to believing nothing to the exclusion of others right to believe. As long as those beliefs, shall not infringe the rights of any portion of society. The writings of Primo Levi have been my greatest personal influence.; [a.] London, UK

MILLER, SUSANNA
[pen.] Susanna Miller; [b.] 30 March 1978, Reading; [p.] Richard and Christine; [ed.] St. Bartholomews, Newbury; [occ.] Student; [oth. writ.] Countless other poems from my heart that I hope to share with people on a wider basis in the future.; [pers.] I thank God for the gift of poetry has given me, for everything he has done in my life and for the loving support of my family and friends who have inspired me.; [a.] Newbury, Berks, UK

MILLS, JANET
[b.] 5 July 1950, Manchester; [p.] Albert and Irene Wells; [m.] Clifford Johnson (Fiance); [ch.] Helen, Louise Anne; [ed.] Brownley Green, Sec. Med. Wythenshawe, M/Cr, C.S.E. English Lit. English Language Biology; [occ.] Pharmacy Assistant; [memb.] Parr Writers Group, Vol. Memb. Groundwork Trust, Environmental Group, St. Helens; [hon.] Won local poetry competitions.; [oth. writ.] Several short stories. Some being recorded for local blind groups.; [pers.] I try to write a reflection of life, hoping others may see theirs mirrored within.; [a.] Saint Helens, Lancs, UK

MILLS, JOANNE
[b.] 14/01/71, Plymouth; [p.] Mrs. Cindy Crews; [ed.] Devonport Secondary School, Plymouth, Devon; [occ.] Factory Worker; [oth. writ.] I have written other poems; [pers.] I believe that you only have one life, so make the most if you can, there's no time for arguments between one another.; [a.] Portsmouth, Hants

MILLS, PAULINE
[b.] 7 April 1937, London; [p.] The late Harold Dear, Iris Dear; [m.] Divorced; [ed.] Glendale Grammar School; [occ.] Retired BBC Registrar, Director of Property Management Co.; [memb.] Royal Horticultural Society, Consumers Association; [oth. writ.] Several poems published in various anthologies.; [pers.] Most of my poems reflect personal experiences and feeling and try to convey a strong sense of atmosphere. However I also enjoy waiting poems about amusing situations and events.; [a.] Croydon, Surrey, UK

MILNE, CAROL DIANE
[b.] 6 November 1942, Crayford, Kent; [p.] Thomas Wooderson and Wendy Wooderson; [m.] Alexander Milne, 5 July 1945; [ed.] Wrockwardine Wood Secondary Modern School, Shropshire and Oakeng Ates Technical College, Shropshire; [occ.] Housewife; [memb.] Chulmleigh Indoor, Short-Mat Bowls Club. "World Wide Fund for Nature," "Royal Society for Protection of Birds," and "Devon Wild Life Fund"; [oth. writ.] Three poems published in three different Books, this year.; [pers.] I try to convey my love of life, animals, and the wonder of nature around us in my poems.; [a.] Chulmleigh, Devon, UK

MILNE, CLAIRE
[b.] 26 March 1959, Linby, Notts; [p.] Edith Chambers and David Chambers; [m.] Alan Christopher Milne, 23 June 1984; [ch.] Jessica Elspeth; [ed.] Paddington and Maida Vale High School for girls - London; [occ.] Mail Order Buyer; [oth. writ.] Poems published in eight anthologies; [pers.] Without writers, we cannot read, without reading, we cannot reflect or contemplate. Without contemplation and thought, there is no depth of meaning to life. Through words there is communication nuturing peace in mankind.; [a.] Keighley, West Yorks, UK

MINSHALL, MATTHEW
[pen.] Iaian George; [b.] 10 January 1958, London; [p.] Merlin Minshall, Christina Minshall; [m.] Sharon Minshall, 26 August 1993; [ch.] George Charles, James McArthur; [ed.] Downham Grammar School Royal Military Academy Sandhurst; [occ.] Civilian Instructor, United Arab Emirates Armed Forces; [memb.] The Naval Club Institute of Supervisory Management; [oth. writ.] Articles for Military Journals.; [pers.] I look to reflect the futility, hypocrisy and horror of war. I am influenced by the war poets and personal experience.; [a.] King's Lynn, Norfolk, UK

MITCHELL, CATHERINE ANN
[pen.] Catherine Ann Mitchell; [b.] 13 July 1937, Thornaby, Teesside; [p.] Rose and Edward Conlin;

[m.] Kenneth Mitchell, 10 March 1956; [ch.] Kevin and Nigel Mitchell; [ed.] St. Patricks then Stockton Technical College; [occ.] Warden caring for pensioners; [memb.] Councillor for Cruse "Bereaved"; [hon.] "Ode To The Kennedy's Unborn Child" published in the American Times magazine still owned by me; [oth. writ.] Many controversial poems for my own satisfaction, I am also writing a biography on the life I have lived and experiences in my vocation of care.; [pers.] I find mankind can be a hard and sometimes a cruel establishment to the innocent of this world and am greatly influenced by far justice.; [a.] Stockton, UK

MITCHELL, RONNIE E.
[pen.] Frenchie; [b.] 3 November 1967, Lambeth; [p.] Granville Gayle and Carol Gayle; [m.] Rosemary Griffith; [ch.] Liam Sharp and Dean Griffith; [ed.] Sir Walter St Johns; [occ.] Laser Operator St Mary Cray Orpington, Kent; [memb.] Bingo, Snooker and The Librarie; [oth. writ.] I have had several poems and published in local magazines and a few newspapers; [pers.] If a man has money. Don't look up to him and if a man hasn't got any money don't look down on him the man with no shoes. Should cry for the man with no feet.; [a.] St. Mary Cray, Kent, UK, BR5 3PA

MOHAMMED, AMANDA
[b.] 19/02/76, Birmingham; [p.] Kamal and Jean Mohammed; [ed.] St. Providence Girl's (Trinidad), St. Joseph's Convent (Trinidad) and University of Birmingham; [occ.] student; [memb.] Birmingham University Dance Society, Catholic Society, Radio Society; [hon.] English trophy; Certificate of Excellence for Creative Writing; other smaller prizes for poetry; prizes for placing 1st, 2nd and 3rd for public speaking; [oth. writ.] Poems published in the local newspapers in Trinidad, many speeches for school functions; [pers.] The harmony of life is the poetry of love.; [a.] Edgbaston, Birmingham

MONJU, DELOWER HOSSAN
[b.] 30 November 1970, Bangladesh; [ed.] B.A. (Chittagong University, Bangladesh); [occ.] Journalist; [memb.] President, Bangladesh Welfare Association, North Wales, Member of Press Club, Sylhet, Bangladesh, Bangladeshis for Equil Right, U.K.; [oth. writ.] Story, Revolutionary Poetic Critics Specially on Post-Modernism. 1st Poetry Book Ispater Gulap (Still Rose) coming out soon on Bengoli.; [pers.] I believe in the limited man existing limitless life. Inside a person time life God existing together. Man is the totality of temporal, man is the abstract reality and absolute reason. About human relation I say in poetic way; [a.] Birmingham, UK, B19 1NT

MONTAGUE-THOMAS, LUCIE
[b.] Chelsea, London; [p.] Deceased; [m.] Deceased (Farmer), March 1950; [ch.] One daughter, two sons; [ed.] Annette-Daniel and Neville High Schools - London, High Schools - London, Exeter University - Devon; [occ.] Retired (to concentrate) with writing ambition in view; [memb.] Art society truro, many others when young, U.S.A. Truro (creative writers), C.U.F. Carrick; [hon.] Art-English and literature - Religion (certificates) first prize age five (poetry), Exhibitor - sculpture - pottery, paintings - oils and chinese inks.; [oth. writ.] Short stories - magazines, several poem - magazines articles (fact) - (newspapers) papers; [pers.] A committed christian, I feel deeply the pain of my fellow man, in atrocities of war, destruction of the environment, indifference to wildlife. Break up of family life with the effect on children.; [a.] Truro, Cornwall, UK, TR3 6TT

MOOLLAN, MARGARET
[b.] April 12, 1946, Peterhead, Scotland; [p.] Mary and Donald MacLeod; [m.] Died, June 12, 1969; [ch.] 1 Daughter - Reading University; [ed.] Studying Politics/International Relations; [occ.] Charge Nurse - RMN Working in the Community; [memb.] R.C.N., UKCC, Gaelic Society of London; [hon.] Diploma - Supervisory Management Studies, Diploma - Massage. Teaching Assessing - ENB 998, 910 Dying ENB 931. Teaching Assessing N.V.Q., All my awards are to do with nursing where I have spent all my working life; [oth. writ.] Personal poems written for relatives and friends - special occasions - birthday/retirement etc; [pers.] I have only recently started to write poetry. My greatest ambition is to be able to write poetry in my native language Gaelic.; [a.] Sutton, Surrey

MOORE, ANGELA
[b.] 22 June 1958, Stafford; [p.] C.W.L. Belcher, Monica M.G. Belcher; [m.] Cliff A. Moore, 23 July 1982; [ch.] Lee, Scott Leon; [ed.] Alleyne's Grammar School, Stone, Staffordshire University; [occ.] Electronic Meter, Test Operative; [pers.] Influenced by my mother, my poems are simply memories committed to paper, inspired by the activities of my family. We review them as one would a family album. It is a bonus to think that others can derive pleasure from them also.; [a.] Stone, Staffs, UK, ST15 0ED

MOORE, BRENDA ANN
[b.] 11 January 1941, Cuckfield; [p.] Mr. Ernest C. Manser and Emily; [m.] Michael Retis Keith Moore, 28 October 1961; [ch.] Shelley, Carole, Sarah, William; [ed.] Secondary School, Westham took O'level in English in 1978 A'Pass; [occ.] Assistant in Fashion store.; [hon.] Paul Harris Fellowship in Rotary International for easing 270.000 pounds to immunize children against Polio etc.; [oth. writ.] Unpublshed (The Adventures of Camelia the camel) in hymn, "The scored flower" a hymn called "O sing to save the world" lots of ode's poems and stories.; [pers.] An author I would love to be, my works to be known over land and sea, every night, I secretly pray, but what do the big wigs write back and say no, no, not listed today, this week next month, next year instead tear; [a.] Ringmer, E. Sussex, UK, BN8 5HU

MOORE, WENDY
[b.] 15 May 1952, Sunderland; [p.] John Thomas and Mary Ethel Johnson; [m.] James Moore, 19 June 1981; [ch.] James Jr.; [ed.] Bernard Gilpin Secondary Modern; [occ.] Bookkeeper; [memb.] Durham and Chester-le-Street, Alzheimer's Society; [pers.] This is the first time I have had the courage to put forward one of my poems which is based on life that is around us.; [a.] Leamside, Durham, UK, DH4 6SE

MORFITT, AUDREY
[pen.] Audrey Shetland; [b.] 15 January 1934, Grimsby; [p.] Hilda Beels - George Beels; [m.] Keith William Morfitt, 29 March 1952; [ch.] Raymond Morfitt, Karen Morfitt, Mark Morfitt; [occ.] Crofter/Retired; [oth. writ.] Only been writing one year 15 poems published to date; [pers.] I try to write about life as it is. Not how we want it to be.; [a.] Whalsay, Shetland, UK, ZE2 9AW

MORGAN, NIK
[b.] 31 March 1962, Norwich; [p.] David Morgan/Jean Morgan; [ed.] University of Wales; [occ.] Poet and Artist; [hon.] English Lit. B.A. 1983, English M.A. 1986, Exhibitions - St. David's Hall, Cardiff. Freuds, London/Oxford. Edinburgh Festival 1994. International Biennial of Humour and Satire, Bulgaria, 1995.; [oth. writ.] Poems published in various small press magazines. Poetry and illustrations appear in "Grandchildren of Albion", an anthology of contemporary poetry - 1992.; [pers.] In my work I am attempting to rediscover a sense of the magical. I have been influenced mainly by surrealism, Dylan Thomas, and Mervyn Peake.; [a.] Penarth, South Glamorgan, UK, CF6 2DA

MORLEY, KEVIN P.
[b.] 21 May 1958, Oldwindsor, Berks; [p.] Hugh Morley, Shirley Morley; [occ.] In Enforced retirement due to back injury; [oth. writ.] Amateur Theatre reviews for a local paper. A number of unpublished poems. I am currently working on my first novel.; [pers.] My poetry usually reflects my current emotional state and my personal view of the world in general, and my views on world conservation - particularly animal specifically. I also paint.; [a.] Gloucester, UK

MORRELL, FRANK WILLIAM
[b.] 14 April 1970, Notting Hill; [p.] Frank and Rose Morrell; [ed.] O'Level Art; [occ.] Bartender; [pers.] I write to understand the madness with in myself and with in the world and to seek its end if not it's meaning; [a.] Ventnor, Isle of Wight, UK, RO38 1LF

MORRIS, JOHN V.
[b.] 4 November 1949, Gwynedd; [ed.] 7 "O" Levels; [occ.] Sheep Farmer; [oth. writ.] Composing Welsh poetry; [a.] Caernarfon, Gwynedd, UK, LL55 3DR

MORRIS, MARK
[b.] 7 September 1962, Birmingham; [p.] Frank/Margaret; [ed.] Comprehensive School, Art and Design College; [occ.] Postman; [pers.] Try to write simply feelings and thoughts of a personal nature, whereby others may identify with.; [a.] Bromsgrove, Worcestershire, UK, B61 0TA

MORRIS, MARLENE
[b.] 4 June 1956, Guernsey; [p.] Henry and Doris Wilkins; [m.] Mick Morris, 10 April 1991; [ch.] Catherine Morris; [ed.] Les Beaucamps Secondary School, Guernsey Grammar School for Girls, Weymouth College of Further Education, Open University; [occ.] English and History Teacher, Dela Salle College, Jersey; [memb.] Member of the Baha'i Faith; [hon.] B.A. (Hon), Cert. Ed.; [oth. writ.] Contributed in, and helped edit "One Wing," am anthology of local (Quernsey) women's poetry. Helped edit "Another Wing" the men's companion anthology. Poems published in assorted anthologies. Recognition of poems and short story writing in Quernsey Eisteddford.; [pers.] To create an opportunity for silent writers to speak. To validate the local and the female voice in the world of humanity. To inspire identification, empathy and understanding.; [a.] St. Clements, Jersey, UK, JE2 6GF

MORRIS, MARY
[pen.] Mary Prescott Morris; [b.] 28 September 1929, Aspull; [p.] Wilfred and Dora Prescott; [m.] Harold Morris, 1 March 1952; [ed.] Council School

MORRIS, VALERIE
[b.] 18 May 1941, Horley, Surrey; [p.] Brought up by grandmother; [m.] Widow; [ch.] Carol; [ed.] Primary School; [occ.] Retired Bus Driver through arthritis; [oth. writ.] All different types of poetry, also a book, being written on my life, of which I am still only half way through.; [pers.] I have always loved poetry, from when I was a child, and bought my first book of poems, at a jumble sale for 1 penny old money.; [a.] Balham, London, UK

MORRIS, VERA ROSE ETHEL
[pen.] Greenfingers; [b.] 5 March 1920, Hoo Rochester, Kent; [p.] Ernest and Florence Harris; [m.] Ronald Jack, 28 July 1951; [ch.] Paul Philip (Deceased); [ed.] Hoo St Werberg and School for Girls, Greenwich; [occ.] Retired; [oth. writ.] One poem published.; [pers.] I wrote this poem to my two sisters, Florence Guy Dawey and Hilda Lilian Cook also my brother Ernest - now deceased.

MORRISON, DANETHEA DIANE
[b.] 1 January 1961, Uganda; [ed.] Oliver Lodge Primary School and Vaal High School in South Africa

MORTON, MRS. M. E.
[b.] 8 March 1923, South Shields; [p.] William, Esther Gibson; [m.] Capt. Albert Morton (M.N.) Decd., 19 April 1947; [ch.] Son - William Lloyd Morton; [ed.] Westoe High School For Girls (Private School); [occ.] Housewife, Retired Secretary; [memb.] So Shields Ladies Probus:, St. Stevens Church (South Shields):, The Friends of Bedes World (Jarrow) St. Chare's Hospice; [hon.] Prize Winner Jarrow Festival of Art and Literature 88 Oil Painting exhibited - Dovecote Art Centre Stockton on Tree: D.L.I. Museum Durham: Bede Art Gallery Jarrow: Jarrow Hall Examinations Senior Cambridge Examination - 8 Credits RSA Shorthand Typing; [oth. writ.] Several Poems for Anchor Books Arrival Press and Gyrwi Local Publications; [pers.] Be kind to one another; [a.] South Shields, Tyne and Wear, UK

MORTON-HOLMES, ROBERT
[pen.] Eugene Morton; [b.] 5 April 1913, East London; [p.] David and Mabel Morton-Holmes; [m.] Salina Coates, 28 July 1940; [ch.] Bernard and Brian; [ed.] Comprehensive; [occ.] Retired; [memb.] Devres Numismatic Society Chairman/Treasurer 6 years; [oth. writ.] Several poems in various numismatic society magazines. A monthly poem in local church magazine 1970-1990.; [a.] Devizes, Wiltshire, UK

MOSS, ANITA LARRAINE
[b.] 15 January 1947, Mansfield; [p.] Deceased; [m.] Roy Moss, 30 January 1965; [ch.] 4 Peter, Richard, Diane, Steven; [ed.] Revensdale Comprehensive; [occ.] Disabled; [oth. writ.] Poems published in local papers. Poem published in poetry anthology, Voices On The Wind.; [pers.] I find that nature often give me the inspiration, need for my poems. Perhaps because I grew up in the countryside.; [a.] Mansfield, Notts, UK

MOSS, ELLEN J.
[b.] 9 November 1959, Chelmsford; [p.] Lilian Roe and Ernest Roe; [m.] Brian Moss, 21 October 1978; [ed.] Maldon Plume School (Comprehensive); [occ.] Domestic Assistant in Elderly Persons Residential Home; [oth. writ.] Have several other poems written over past twenty years or so. None have ever been published.; [pers.] I find writing poetry a relief for tension and stress. Also a way of expressing feelings and emotions.; [a.] Maldon, Essex, UK

MOULDER, MAGGIE
[pen.] Maggie; [b.] 22 April 1931, Dunstew; [p.] William and Kathleen Brock; [m.] Patrick Moulder, 26 July 1952; [ch.] Andrew, Sarah, Nick, Caroline, (twins) Barry and Jeremy, Hayley, Emily, and Rosie; [ed.] Local school; [occ.] Housewife; [oth. writ.] A few poems through out my school years and for my children at their schools; [pers.] Country lover. Mother for much of my life not really religious although I believe in something. Humane. Never take more than you give; [a.] Banbury, Oxon, UK

MOUNTFORD, STUART GAVIN
[b.] 30 July 1948, Newcastle under Lyme; [p.] Denis Mountford and Mary Mountford; [m.] Jayne Elizabeth Mountford, 21 March 1987; [memb.] Royal Artillery Association American Civil War Society; [hon.] Studying Psychology with open University; [pers.] I believe writing should stimulate the readers imagination, just like re-enacting brings alive the period involved.; [a.] Bloxwich, West Midlands, UK

MOUNTNEY, CHRISTINE
[b.] 23 December 1952, East London; [p.] William Dovey, Lilian Dovey; [m.] David Mountney, 27 February 1971; [ch.] David James, Dawn Christine; [ed.] Pretoria Girls School; [occ.] Dental Receptionist; [pers.] I am inspired by my own, feelings. Of life and the world around me.; [a.] London, UK

MOUZO, EVELYN
[b.] 7 February 1970, London; [p.] Abel and Rosa Mouzo; [ed.] St Michael's Grammar and King's College London; [occ.] Hotelier; [pers.] Dedicated to my mother - whose grace and beauty will never fade.; [a.] London, UK

MOYA-GIL, LUCIA
[pen] Lucia 'Lulabelle' Moya-Gil; [b.] 15 April 1972, Evesham; [p.] Julie and Juan Moya-Gil; [ed.] Evesham High School, South Warwickshire College, Evesham College, Bournemouth and Poole College of Art and Design; [occ.] Student; [memb.] B.P.C.A.D.'s Drama Society; [oth. writ.] Articles for 'Internal' magazine-local What's on Magazine. Articles for 'Your Garden' monthly.; [pers.] Righteousness in the heart will save the world. Respect, love and laughter.; [a.] Bournemouth, Dorset, UK

MULDOWNEY, MARGARET
[b.] 1 June 1950, Meath, Ireland; [p.] Dolores and Jack Murtagh; [m.] Patrick Muldowney, 24 March 1979; [ch.] Aoife and Conor; [ed.] St. Marthas College of Domestic Science and Agriculture; [occ.] Home-maker; [oth. writ.] Short stories, and poetry published in "Tales form the Schoolhouse."; [pers.] I recognize my talents in the love of music and writing as a gift from God.; [a.] Dublin 22, Ireland

MULLAN, THERESE M. T.
[pen.] Theresa Mullan; [b.] 26 April 1987, Dublin; [p.] Don Mullan and Margaret Beatty; [ed.] Sister of Carl and Emma.; [occ.] Pupil at presentation convent - Dublin; [oth. writ.] Peace Poem, "Up the Dubs", "To a very nice teacher", "Go away"; [pers.] I dream of peace in Ireland and for all hungry people to have food.

MULLEN, SYLVIA ANN
[pen.] Ann Best; [b.] 28 April 1948, Tetbury, Glos; [p.] Alfred and Maureen Best; [ch.] Julian D. Gunton; [ed.] Sir William Romneys School, Tetbury, Glos., Memorial Hospital Cirencester, Glos; [occ.] Staff Nurse; [pers.] For my parents who's inspiration gave me strength.; [a.] Blackburn, Lancs, UK

MULLENS, NEIL
[b.] 7 March 1967, Bristol; [p.] Michael Mullens, Pauline; [ed.] Rodway Comprehensive, Bournemouth University, Abon Language School; [occ.] Private Tefl Teacher; [memb.] World Wildlife Fund, Greenpeace; [hon.] BA (Hons) Media Production. Trinity College Cert. (Tesol); [pers.] I'd like to remind people how much better a place the world would be if only we stopped to listen to each other every once in a while.; [a.] Wexford, Eire, UK

MULREAY, HOLLIE LOUISE
[b.] 19 May 1986, Chester; [p.] Gaynor Mulreay; [ed.] Brookside Infant Schoo, Sutton Way County Junior School; [occ.] School Girl; [memb.] Youth on Show; [hon.] Bronze, Silver, Gold Certificate of Achievement; [pers.] In school I was doing history on wars so I spoke to my nan about it and I wrote the poem.; [a.] Ellesmere Port, England

MUNDAY, JILL
[pen.] Jill Munday; [b.] 15 August 1949, Hertfordshire; [p.] William Tarlton, Ivy Tarlton; [m.] Barry Munday, 26 June 1971; [ch.] Barry Joseph Munday; [ed.] St. Pauls County Secondary Addlestone Surrey; [occ.] State Enrolled Nurse Ty' Mair Nursing Home Felinfoel Wales; [memb.] Elim Apostolic Church, Pontyetes; [hon.] City and Guilds Coach and Assessor for Care Workers; [oth. writ.] Several poems published in church magazines and Christian news papers; [pers.] As I read God's word, He teaches me to see life as it rarely is, from all different points of view. I then put them into poetry. Its truly a gift from God.; [a.] Llanelli, Dyfed, UK

MUNGAPEN, SHIRLEY
[b.] 9 December 1933, Boston, Lincs; [p.] William and Edith Johnson; [m.] Dana Mungapen (Mr), 30 March 1963; [ch.] Louise and Jerome (Mungapen); [ed.] Kesteven and Grantham Girls School, Nottingham College of Arts and Crafts. Portsmouth College of Art State Registered Nurse Peterborough Memorial Hospital; [occ.] Artist; [memb.] Society of Wood Engravers Women in Theology; [hon.] National diploma in Design and Wood Engravings, State Registered Nurse, Lay Reader Winchester; [oth. writ.] Religion and philosophical essays, art history (not published) poems on time themes articles in local magazine.; [pers.] I find writing is a creative direct way of getting ideas down in contrast with visual art work. I am interested in the writings of the Spanish Mystics. Life unfolds in a magical way.; [a.] Southampton, Hants, UK

MUNRO, ISMA
[b.] 24 May 1921, Braemar; [p.] Bert and Ella McAndrew; [m.] Joseph (Deceased), 4 January 1947; [ch.] Deirdre (Deceased); [ed.] Braemar Primary School, Banchory Secondary School, Aberdeen University, Aberdeen Teacher's Training College; [occ.] Retired Head Mistress; [memb.] National Trust for Scotland, Arthritis Care Association, Scottish Wildlife Trust, The Scots Lan-

guage Society, International Syna Esthesia Association, S.W.R.I. Committee, Tain Civic Trust Committee, Clan Munro Association Council; [hon.] Dux Prize Primary School, Proximeaccessit Prize Secondary School, M.A. Degree with First Class Certificates in Moral Philosophy and Botany, Teacher's Parchment; [oth. writ.] Poems in English and in Doric published in magazines and anthologies, one poem and one short story broadcast; [pers.] My life time motto: - "If you cannot have what you would like try to like what you have."; [a.] Milton, Invergordon, Ross-Shire, UK

MURPHY, AUDRA ANN
[b.] 22 November 1967, Berkshire; [p.] Michael Murphy; [ed.] St. Joan of Arc B-C Secondary; [occ.] Sale Assistant Mobrab Studio Cornwall; [memb.] Readers Union Embariting on Riding and Flying; [hon.] Mensa Certificate, Basic Stable Management, Diploma in Fitness and Nutrition, Diploma in Personnel Management, Diploma in Beauty and Personality; [oth. writ.] I am in the process of writing a novel. Under a pseudonym.; [pers.] Nature gave us the setting it's up to each individual to write their song. As it's the words we write, not the music which will remain when we've gone.; [a.] Truro, Cornwall, UK

MURPHY, JOHN P.
[b.] 31 March 1926, Toomebridge, Co Antrim; [p.] Jeannie and Bernard; [m.] Anna M. E. Murphy, 28 July 1958; [ch.] Katrina, Breige, Brian and Gerard; [ed.] BA (Uni. Dublin), H. Dip. Ed. (Queens, Belfast), Bed (Hons) University of Ulster, Coleraine, (Hons) Post Graduate Cert. St. Joseph's College of Education (Belfast); [occ.] Retired School Headmaster; [memb.] Maghera Bridge Club, Maghera Conference of St. Vincent De Paul Society P.T.T.A. - Pioneer Total Abstinence Association; [hon.] Academic Awards from four Universities and a college of education. Considerable number of football medals, including a 1947 national league medal; [oth. writ.] Footsteps in the night, "Reality" Dublin 1973. Widely published in St. Vincent De Paul Publications - "How's your Neighbor", "The Invisible Man" etc. and GAA publications - "Years of Glory" etc book of short stories presently with publishers - back cover will contain a salute by Seamus Heaney, Gaelic Athletic Association; [pers.] I take great pleasure in writing poems and short stories and if large numbers of other enjoy what I write that is certainly an extremely nice bonus.; [a.] Maghera, Derry, UK

MURRAY, HELENE FRIEDA HERMINE
[b.] 17 May 1923, Graz, Austria; [p.] Both deceased; [m.] Terry (Deceased), 18 November 1946, Henry Shaun Murray, 28 February 1992; [ch.] Two children; [occ.] Housewife; [oth. writ.] Short story published in a women's magazine. Creative writing classes for a number of years; [pers.] My philosophy has always been to help rather than hinder especially children, the old and needy; [a.] Chingford, London, UK

MUSKER, MRS. WENDY
[b.] 16 April 1960, Middlesex; [p.] Audrey Byford, Allan Byford; [m.] Peter Musker, 17 September 1988; [ch.] 4 Mad cats; [ed.] Harrow County Grammar School for girls, Lancaster University; [occ.] Civil Servant; [memb.] The Pagan Federation; [hon.] B.A. Hons. English Literature; [oth. writ.] Only poems for personal pleasure and friends; [pers.] Although I am a Pagan, and within that umbrella term of Wiccan, or 'White Witch', beyond and separate from that I have a healthy regard and respect for angels as beings of love and light.; [a.] Gloucester, Glos, UK

MUSLEH, MARIE
[pen.] Marie Maroc; [b.] 9 June, Glasgow; [p.] Mohammed and Mary Jane Musleh; [oth. writ.] Short story "Retribution" published (book); [pers.] Look beyond what others say and do. Look to the soul within them hiding behind a wall of pain; [a.] Glasgow, Lanarkshire, UK

MYTHEN, KATIE JAYNE
[b.] 19 November 1981, Stoke-on-Trent; [p.] Patricia and Michael Mythen; [ed.] St. Thomas a Beckett R.C., Primary School, Tutts Barn Lane Eastbourne; [occ.] At School; [hon.] Second in Eastbourne in Bloom Design Competition 1995; [oth. writ.] Nothing published; [pers.] I am eleven years old this will be the first poem I have had published. I write lots and lots at home because I enjoy it.; [a.] Eastbourne, East Sussex, UK

MYTHEN, PATRICIA ANN
[pen.] Mythen; [b.] 18 November 1943, Stoke-on-Trent; [p.] Robert and Agnes Kelsey; [m.] Michael John Mythen, 20 October, 1979; [ch.] Seven five girls, two boys; [ed.] Notre Dame Convent School for girls Sheffield; [occ.] Retired Nurse; [hon.] Graduated The Open College of writing 1972; [oth. writ.] First published work Nightmare "Thwaite Farm", numerous short stories and poetry.; [pers.] I am currently working on my first novel. Writing is my hobby, pursued mainly for my own gratification. There is so much I wish to commit to paper so much of myself.; [a.] Eastbourne, East Sussex, UK

NARRAMORE, GARTH R. G.
[b.] 15 March 1931, Plympton, Devon; [ed.] Plympton Grammar School, Towyn County School (Merionethshire N/Wiples) Seale Hayne Agricultural College, Weymouth College; [occ.] Retired (Farmer/Prison Officer); [memb.] Mensa, Weymouth Sailing Club, Society of Amateur Artists; [oth. writ.] Articles practical boat owner poem - a passage in time; [a.] Weymouth, Dorset, UK

NAYLOR, LISA
[b.] 15 February 1970, Blackpool; [ed.] Durham University, Open University; [occ.] Health and Education; [hon.] Lamda Speech and Acting B.A. (hons) Social Studies; [oth. writ.] Short stories for motorblue magazines; [pers.] Influenced by paganism and the power of positive thought.; [a.] Knott-end-on-Sea, Lancashire, UK

NEAL, EILEEN
[b.] September 12, 1916, Liverpool; [p.] John Dick, Christina Dick (both Dec.); [m.] September 2, 1939 to John William Neal (now deceased); [ch.] Jacqueline Wickham, Judith Cheney; [ed.] Intermediate School Underwood School of Commerce; [occ.] Housewife Prev. Dress Designer; [memb.] Prev. Member of Birstall Golf Club Leics.; [oth. writ.] 10 poems in 10 different poet anthologies and other books of poems. Autobiography (not published) compiling my own book of poems; [pers.] I took to writing poems after my husband died and what I have achieved so far has been done in just over 12 months at the age of 78-79.; [a.] Leicester, Leics

NEAL, JILL
[b.] 22 December 1942, Leamington Spa; [p.] Queenie and Leslie Keegan (Father Deceased); [m.] Trevor Horace Neal, 25 September 1965; [ch.] Katy and Piers; [ed.] St Mary's Priory Princethorpe Nr Rugby a Benedictine Convent with 60 pupils where I boarded for 10 years; [occ.] Receptionist; [oth. writ.] Many poems for family occasions and friends; [pers.] A romantic at heart poetry is my best medium for conveying my feelings.; [a.] Harrenden, Herts, UK

NEAVE, REGINALD PETER
[b.] 22 April 1918, Tunstead, Norfolk; [p.] Herold Neave and Namie Neave; [m.] Helen Beesley, 15 February 1958; [ch.] Step-Daughter 'Susan'; [ed.] Thorpe House School, Thorpe, Norwhich School Certificate 1934, Credits in Geography, French and General Science; [occ.] Retired Agricultural Engineer; [memb.] A Vice President Norfolk Cricket, Association, also various mainly, Hobby Clubs and Similar Organizations; [oth. writ.] One or two short semi-technical efforts to magazines: A few letters to the Local and National newspapers.; [pers.] A firm belief in the innate existence of goodness in all people. 'Truth is incorruptible and will always Triumph in the end.'; [a.] Mistley, Colchester, Essex, UK

NEEDHAM, JOAN
[pen.] Joan Needham; [b.] 29 October 1938, Bradford; [p.] Gilbert and Margaret Sedgwick; [m.] Basil Needham, 29 July 1958; [ch.] Beverley, Belinda, Beth, Sarah; [ed.] Belle Vue Girls Grammar School, Bradford; [occ.] Reflexologist and Trainee Healer; [memb.] Foundation of Spiritual Healing and Guidance; [oth. writ.] Poem in F.S.H.G. magazine; [pers.] After the suicide of my eldest daughter my search for answers led me to a greater awareness of, and empathy with the suffering of others.; [a.] Seaford, East Sussex, UK

NELSON, PETER W.
[b.] 22 May 1945, North Shields; [p.] Rose Nelson; [ch.] Mary-Anne Nelson; [ed.] Linskill Secondary Modern School. North Shields N/Land; [occ.] Retired through serious disability; [hon.] Gardener of the Year, Special Award National Competition 1993, Garden News and Thompson and Morgan Seeds; [oth. writ.] Love will survive poem and many more poems which have been read over local radio stations.; [pers.] It's said that gold and diamonds are a treasure to protect, the most valved treasure is our love for one another and a compassionate heart. I try to reflect this my writing.; [a.] Bellingham, Northumberland, UK

NETTLEFOLD, ELLA
[b.] Senior, Stevenston; [p.] Elizabeth and Thomas Hamilton (Deceased); [m.] Allan Nettlefold, 18 December 1940; [ch.] Brian, Pamela; [ed.] Ardeer Public School, Stevenson High School, Ardrossan Academy; [occ.] Retired, Civil Servant; [memb.] Retired, Commissioner Girl Guide Movement, retired, leader - Scottish Women's Keep Fit Association, Ardrossan, Bowling Club; [hon.] Four first class certificates, and a certificate of honour on religious instruction a special prize for General Excellence at school "Tales from Shakespeare"; [oth. writ.] Several poems, unpublished; [pers.] I find writing poetry a challenge, and I am delighted, and thrilled, to have my poem "The Storm" published.; [a.] Ardrossan, Ayrshire, UK

NEWCOMBE, JIM
[pen.] Ozymandias; [b.] 17 January 1976, Derby; [p.] Catherine and Reg Newcombe; [ed.] Ovid's 'Ars Amatoria'; [occ.] Hierophant; [oth. writ.] Poems published in previous anthologies; [pers.] I see poetry as a revelation of the self to the self, and it shall be my endeavour to summon up and capsulize the innermost part of myself in the metrical compression of poetry.; [a.] Derby, UK

NEWMAN, DEBRA
[b.] 7 July 1966, Otley, W. Yorks; [m.] Timothy Newman, 3 August 1991; [ch.] Melissa Newman; [ed.] Prince Henry's Grammer Otley, Downs School, Compton, Newbury College; [occ.] Wife and Mother; [memb.] British Redcross Society, National Canine Defence League, N.S.P.C.C.; [oth. writ.] Unpublished poems and short stories; [pers.] My work and my life are interwoven, each one depending upon the other.; [a.] Newbury, Berkshire, UK

NEWMAN, DOUGLAS TERENCE
[pen.] Mark Thyme; [b.] 6 March 1962, Carshalton, Surrey; [p.] Terry and Jean; [m.] Lesley, 12 August; [ch.] Robyn and Tanya; [ed.] Collingwood Comprehensive Farnborough Tech.; [occ.] Salesman/Franchise Partner; [oth. writ.] The Eternal Lovers, A Novel, The Edge Of A Dream, An Autobiography yet to be offered for publication; [pers.] Reaching the heart opens the curtains, letting in the light to show what we can truly be.; [a.] Camberley, Surrey, UK

NEWMAN, YASMIN TAARA
[b.] 17 July 1970; [m.] Bryan Newman, 15 July 1994; [ch.] Shane Thomson; [memb.] The White Eagle Lodge, London, W.W.F., Animal Aid, Vegan Society, Viva! Chelmsford; [pers.] When a man offers his love, as kindness to a woman abused, by every heart she's known. Carl Oakes has given me faith, to be myself.; [a.] Southminster, Essex, UK

NEWTON, DAVE
[b.] 22 January 1962, Newport; [p.] William and Ellen Newton; [ed.] Bedwas Comprehensive; [occ.] Sales Assistant, Newport; [oth. writ.] Several poems published locally, also published in poetry now Anthology (Wales) 1993 with "The Hunger" etc.; [pers.] I have been influence by many things, but need to find love and understanding on a greater level. I dedicate this writing to the lady who helped me find it! Yvonne Peters.; [a.] Newport, Gwent, UK

NICHOLSON, MINA
[pen.] S.W. Nicholson; [b.] 12 July 1949, Clare Tandragee, Co Armagh; [occ.] Housewife; [pers.] In writing down my thoughts, I set them free.; [a.] Kilkeel, Down, UK

NICOLLE, DENNIS PETER
[pen.] Dennis Nicolle; [b.] 11 February 1962; [p.] Dennis Henry and Mary Theresa; [m.] Tina Jane, 25 July 1987; [ch.] Two; [ed.] De La Salle College, Highlands College; [occ.] Dog Walker/Canine Cafe Assistant; [memb.] Jersey Pedigree Whippet, Racing Club, Tes Milles Golf Club, National Canine Defense League; [hon.] Painting and Drawing Honors Certificates; [oth. writ.] All dogs I regularly walk. Available on request.; [pers.] We all have choices to make, to be happy in what we do is a simple choice.; [a.] La Minoterie, St. John, UK

NICOLSON, PENNILUCK
[pen.] Penni-Luck; [b.] 16 February 1946, Dundee, Scotland; [p.] Margaret James McDinnis; [m.] John Nicolson, 30 August 1985; [ch.] 3 daughters - 6 sons; [ed.] Studying Social Science at open university other education Lawside Academy Dundee; [occ.] Disabled; [oth. writ.] This is my first published writing - but many are waiting already written in the wings have been too busy raising 9 children to try and publish.; [pers.] I dedicate this poem to my parents, both of whom are deceased, but who encouraged me to write since I was a child. Also to my husband John, and all my adorable children and grandchildren. Life is only a blink in time - So my advice is - Don't blink.; [a.] Redhill, Surrey, UK

NIMMO, MRS. MARGARET
[pen.] Margaret Nimmo; [b.] 11 June 1932, Muirkirk; [p.] John Hill, Margaret Hill; [m.] Robert Nimmo, 28 January 1952; [ch.] David, Robert, William, James, Kevin; [ed.] Muirkirk Junior Secondary and Higher Grade, Royal College of Nursing; [occ.] Retired; [hon.] State Enrolled Nurse, State Certified Midwife; [oth. writ.] Poems accepted for mags and books, religious works, Top Poets of 1968, (song poems) Buddy Bregman, T.V. programme, M.G.M. Studios Hollywood. Star Crest Recording Co, Nashville. (1960's); [pers.] I like to write about everything. I believe poetry is an expression of the soul, a bridge from heart to heart. Giving a sense of achievement to the writer and a sense of pleasure to the reader.; [a.] Kilwinning, Ayrshire, UK

NIXON, COLIN
[pen.] Nixon; [b.] 15 July 1964, Grenwich, London; [p.] Tom Nixon and Irene Nixon; [m.] Christine, 21 June 1986; [chi.] 2 Step Sons; [ed.] Infants primary and secondary ignitions. F.T. collage, C.A.D. level 3 C. G.; [occ.] Amateur poet, Lyre list - musician a of opposites on my expiration; [memb.] Of life, fully payable on my expiration.; [hon.] Honoured at being honored, but otherwise to notice.; [oth. writ.] Various unpublished poems, muses, song and prose.; [pers.] Constantly influenced by life, But its fascinations I try not to take seriously, "I leave that to those who judge".; [a.] Farnboruogh, Hampshire, UK

NKANSA, GRACE AGYAPOMA
[b.] 7 August 1967, Takoradi, Ghana; [p.] Albert and Nancy Nkansa; [ed.] Hatfield Girls High, Zimbabwe Bayero University Kano, Nigeria; [occ.] Media Researcher, film maker; [memb.] PAN African Writers' Association, Ghana Association of Writers; [hon.] English, Public Speaking, Music; [oth. writ.] Hassan, The Clever Beggar Boy, Vantage Publishers, Nigeria, Danger In The Palace, MacMillan, UK, Several articles and short stories in AWO - African Woman's Option - Ghanaian Women's Journal current work "Parables of a Woman" in progress.; [pers.] Nurturing positive feelings, self-awareness and understanding the sometimes painful cycle of life - towards a mental, emotional and spiritual balance.; [a.] Accra, Ghana

NODWELL, NUALA
[b.] 29 December 1958, Co. Donegal, Ireland; [p.] Mary and Tommy Gallagher; [m.] Robert Nodwell, 24 February 1989; [ch.] Ben, age - 6 yrs; [ed.] St. Columbus College, Stranorlar, Co. Donegal, Ireland; [occ.] Accounts Assistant; [memb.] The Fountain, Health Club; [oth. writ.] One poem published in local magazine have had many rejections.; [pers.] I love swimming, the idea of escape into the 'Big Blue'. I lived in Australia for two years, and worked in 'The Victorian' College of Arts in Melbourne.; [a.] Douglas, Isle of Man, UK

NOLAN, GRAINNE MICHELLE
[pen.] Michelle-Brigette Grace; [b.] 12 March 1979, Ireland; [p.] Frank Nolan and Mary Nolan; [ed.] Rockwell College; [occ.] Student; [hon.] Gold medal senior debating 1995. Silver medal 1996; [oth. writ.] Poems and short stories which have not learn printed; [pers.] I write for myself, in an attempt to express my deepest feeling on paper. My poems come from the heart and are inspired by events in my life.

NOLAN, MRS. LILIAN
[b.] 16 March 1926, Liverpool; [p.] John and Elizabeth Waring; [m.] Robert Nolan, 13 December 1993; [occ.] State Registered Nurse; [memb.] Border Fine Arts Society Member

NORTON, JAMES
[b.] 7 October 1995, Spalding; [p.] Leslie, Joan Mary; [ch.] Danny Norton; [ed.] Sr John Gleed Boys Secondary, Modern; [occ.] Draughtsman; [oth. writ.] Poems published in local competitions. Several short stories awaiting acceptance.; [pers.] To prove that by striving for what you believe in you can achieve it.; [a.] Spalding, Lincs, UK

NORTON, MARJORIE
[b.] 22/06/38, West Bromwich; [p.] Wilfred Hill m. Mabel Pearce; [m.] William Norton; [occ.] Retired; [memb.] ARP050 (Association of Retired People), A.T.L. (Association of Teachers and Lecturers), R.S.G.B. (Radio Society of Great Britain), and member of Pemberton Cottage Crafts; [oth. writ.] Poems in local magazines and anthologies by Triumph House Anchor Press and Arrival Press; [pers.] The philosophies of others guide me. But if it is true that for evil to triumph it only needs good men to do nothing, and if the pen is mightier than the sword, then the very least I can do is write.; [a.] Wigan

NOTON, VALERIE H.
[pen.] Val Noton-Wan; [b.] 17 June 1959, Yardley Gobion; [p.] Charles James and Margaret Hazel Bryan; [ch.] Dane John Charles, Rebecca Mary and Nathan Wan; [occ.] Company Director; [memb.] M.E.N.S.A. Challenge; [hon.] Business and Management Studies; [oth. writ.] Various publications in both local and national papers and magazines.; [pers.] My writing predominately reflects what my eyes see and my heart feels, since I am greatly influenced by all that happens around me, both personally and in general.; [a.] Kettering, Northants, UK

NWEKE, CHINYERE MBADIWE
[b.] 22 April 1938, Nigeria; [p.] Mrs. Celiya Mbadiwe and F. O. Mbadiwe; [ch.] Mr. Anthony and Uzo Nweke; [ed.] Westminster College, GCE 'O' Level Law and GCE 'A' Level Law; [occ.] Educated to 'LLB' Standard; [memb.] The Institute of Legal Executive; [oth. writ.] "God works in a" mysterious ways. His wonders yet to perform. His light shines upon those who believe in Him. And his foot leads us on."; [pers.] It will order another book on a laugh and fear when I must have received my first publication.

OATES, SYDNEY
[b.] 5-12-26, Cleckheaton W. Yorks; [p.] James George Oates, Hannah Ellen Oates; [m.] Jean; [ch.] Stephen, Martin, Julie, Vincent; [ed.] Whitcliffe Mount Grammar School, Cleckheaton; Technical College, Bradford; [memb.] FCIWEM - Fellow, Chartered Institution of Water and Environmental Management; [oth. writ.] poems in various anthologies; [pers.] "The spiritual world endures."

O'BRIEN, TESS GOOD
[b.] 25 June 1961, Ireland; [m.] Des O'Brien, 13 May 1988; [ed.] Convent of Mercy Dungarvan, Ireland; [occ.] Local Government Officer. Prev: Financial Co's Bournemouth and Southampton; [hon.] Diploma Social Studies U.C.C.; [pers.] "Without purpose, we float, like foam, Disintegrating further with each new impact"; [a.] Dungarvan, Waterford, Ireland

O'DONNELL, JASON
[pen.] Mr. Emotion; [b.] 24 September 1970, Luton; [p.] Olive O'Donnell and Eward O'Donnell; [ed.] Lea Manor High, Marshfarm, Luton, Beds; [occ.] Unemployed, was production operator; [oth. writ.] Five poems published by David Foskett editor- for anchor books, and one recently in the international society of poets in the other side of the mirror, road of dreams; [pers.] For better or worse, I put life's emotions into verse. My influences are of the song genre and motion picture's and themes that reflect on reality in our times; [a.] Luton, Bedfordshire, UK

O'DONNELL, JOHN PHILIP
[pen.] John Philip; [b.] 23 April 1967, London; [p.] Peter and Mercedes O'Donnell; [ed.] Chase School Comp Enfield, Middx; [occ.] Painter and Decorator; [pers.] My poem is a reflection of everybody's day to day life.; [a.] Enfield, Middx, UK

O'HARA, ROBERT EDWARD
[b.] 29 March 1996, Golborne; [p.] William O'Hara and Mona O'Hara; [m.] Vanessa Frances O'Hara, 27 June 1986; [ch.] Thomas and Stephanie; [ed.] St. Aelreds Catholic High School, Wigan and Leigh College; [occ.] Contracts Administration Supervisor; [memb.] National Trust International Guild of Music; [oth. writ.] Several other poems sermons for church; [pers.] The poem reflects situations within our lives and the "Circles of Time" will take us back to the beginning of the poem. Once we have evercome these obstacles hope and happiness will follow, just test the deepness.; [a.] Golborne, Lancs, UK

O'HENLEY, ANDREW ALEXANDER
[b.] 7 August 1976, Glasgow; [p.] Angus O'Henley, June O'Henley; [m.] Tanith Collins, 3 May 1996; [ed.] St. Luke's H.S.; [occ.] Undergraduate of English Literature at St. Andrews University; [oth. writ.] Completed several journals of unpublished poetry.; [pers.] All happiness is go aged on levels of sadness and through my poetry I discuss the entwining spectrum of emotion between.; [a.] Glasgow, Scotland

O'KANE, CATHERINE
[b.] 22 June, Strabane; [p.] Patrick McGranaghan, Rosaleen McGranaghan; [m.] Edward O'Kane, 3 July 1974; [ch.] Roisin, Patrick, Peter; [ed.] Our Lady of Mercy Secondary, 'Magee College' University of Ulster'; [occ.] Senior Clerical Officer Accounts; [memb.] Strabane History Society, Church of the Immaculate Conception Choir, CRAIC (Cultural Renual And Integrated Community) verbal arts; [hon.] Foundation studies for mature students (Commendation) and certificate in Counselling (Basic skills) with distinction; [oth. writ.] Variety of poems and stories, songs work on demand (Local), some work published in Anthologies and magazines. Letters and some advertising i.e. verse to promote CRAIC.; [pers.] I strive to reach people through my written expression and help especially the bereaved. I wish to help to rebuild the tradition of writing in poetry and stories. I wish you outside to enjoy my work as much as I do.; [a.] Strabane, Tyrone, UK

O'KEEFFE, ANN
[b.] Inverness; [m.] Maurice Joseph O'Keeffe (Deceased), 2 June 1947; [ch.] Mary, John, Monica, Clare, Bernard; [pers.] I thank God every day for my 5 gifted children. I believe nobody is good at everything, but everyone is good at something. I was encouraged by my daughter write this, my first poem in my seventy-plus years.; [a.] Weybridge, Surrey, UK

O'NEIL, HELEN
[b.] 4 December 1971, Ashington; [p.] Bernard, Sheila (O'Neil); [ed.] Edge Hill College, University of Newcastle upon Tyne, University of Northumbira, University of Cambridge; [occ.] Student, LLB Hons (currently Studying); [memb.] Poetry Society Yachting Club, Royal Shakespeare Company; [hon.] BSC Hons Sociology, Dip HE Diploma of TEFL, (CATS) RSC Eupides to Chehov, Wordsworth to Coleridge, History of the English Theatre; [oth. writ.] London school of journalism - poems.; [pers.] 'There is society, where none intrudes' (Byron), quote I have been greatly influenced by 19th, 20th century playwrights and poets.; [a.] Cramlington, Northumberland, UK

OAKLEY, MICHAEL
[b.] 12 December 1922, Barnet, Herts; [p.] Robert and Elsie O'Field Oakley; [ed.] Belmont Abbey School, Hereford; [occ.] Retired School Master; [memb.] Society for the protection of Ancient Buildings (Wind and Watermill Section; [oth. writ.] In The Dawning Light (poems), Haunted Ground (pounds), Verses and Versions (pomes) Translation: The Imitation of Christ (with Ronald Knox), Verse Translations: the poems of Horace (with Lord Dunsany), The Iliad of Homer, The Aeneid and the Eclogues of Virgil, the poems of Tibullus (unpublished): Sundry poems and articles in magazines.; [a.] Chart, Somerset, UK

OAKLEY, SIMON R.
[b.] 4 July 1969, Bath, Avon; [p.] David Oakley, Patricia Oakley; [ed.] Monkton Combe School, Portsmouth Grammar, Bournemouth University; [occ.] Sales Manager for Aegis Security, Southampton; [oth. writ.] Article published in Portsmouth news 'supplement' 1988; [pers.] In much of my poetry, I strive to capture suffering of the human soul, whilst also trying to expose its weaknesses when most vulnerable. All my poetry is based on people/places during my travels around the world.; [a.] Portsmouth, Hampshire, UK

ODGERS, JEANETTE MCILWAIN
[pen.] Jahnet McIlwain; [b.] 13 October 1953, Soho, London; [p.] Jeanette Violet McIlwain - Father unnamed Sikh; [m.] Brian Norman Odgers, 12 October 1978; [ch.] Daniella, Sammy Nicky Jane; [ed.] St. Mary's York St. W.I. Maida Vale High. W9 Hammersmith College W6.; [occ.] Aroma Therapist Counsellor writer teacher; [memb.] Paddi Diving Ass.; [oth. writ.] Articles in mags 200 poems and prose. Jack, Aspitual sci-fi; [pers.] I write and in writing I express life in all it's heaven and hell, to touch you with a oneness that says I understand.; [a.] London, UK

ORR, JEAN MARY
[pen.] Jean Mary Orr; [b.] 5 April 1916, Belfast; [p.] Fred C. Hughes, Hilda Hughes; [m.] Carl L. P. S. Orr, 3 October 1939; [ch.] 5 children 4 boys 1 girl; [ed.] Belfast Ashville House. Redmoor Boarding School, Bournemouth, England, Royal College of Music. London. Drama, Gate Thearne Dublin.; [occ.] Retired; [memb.] Director of Christian Healing Community Trust. "Columban Healing Community" Port Ballintride Co. Antrim, Trust. "Jesus Community and Healing, "Trust Donegal; [hon.] Certificates drama and education; [oth. writ.] Books of poems. "Autumn Leaves", poem "Cry for Peace" to be published in June 1990, "Finger Post" Derby magazine number of early poems published. "Poetry Review" England 1930's.; [pers.] I try to reflect the beauty I find in nature, in different seasons, and when moved by beauty found in places and people. Influenced by romantic poets, especially Irish, Yeats, etc.; [a.] Londonderry, Derry, UK

ORUC, AMNA
[b.] 27 April 1967, Sarajevo; [p.] Hamza Oruc and Edina Oruc; [ed.] University of Economics, Sarajevo, Southeastern University, London; [occ.] I work in finance dept. of ICA (Institute of Contemporary Art); [memb.] LSW (London Screenwriters group); [hon.] National award for Literary Criticism in Bosnia and Herzegovina (1985); [oth. writ.] TV Screenplay; [pers.] An artist must seduce God to create a piece of art, and then one must abandon both in order to prove and justify the existence of both.; [a.] London, Westminster, UK

OSBORN, MARIA
[b.] 10 January 1974, Bedford; [p.] Frank Osborn and Doris Osborn; [occ.] Office assistant; [oth. writ.] My first poem was published in the local paper when I was only 8 years old. I am now 22. I have many penpals all over the world. I have recently joined a penpal magazine called Jufle's Pals. Which will feature one of my poems.; [pers.] I love writing to all mt penfriends all over the world which I enjoy doing. I write many poems in my spare time, but have never entered any compitions like this before. When I heard that I had been entered into the finals, I was thrilled to bits; [a.] Milton Keynes, Buckinghamshire, UK

OSBORNE, JULIET
[pen.] Juliet West-Osborne; [b.] 9 June 1964, Watford; [p.] Kathleen West, James Edward West; [m.] Martin James Osborne (Ozzie), 20 July 1985; [ed.] Queens School, Bushey Herts; [occ.] Civil Servant, (Not working due to illness); [memb.] Me Association, National Trust; [pers.] My writing is influenced simply by life, my experiences, feelings and observation of others. Anything and anyone can inspire me places, people, events. It all makes for a rich tapestry from which to draw inspiration.; [a.] Eaton Ford, St. Neots, Cambs, UK

OTTEWELL, GAIL
[b.] 8 July 1944, Derby; [p.] Lilian Rose; [m.] Graham; [ch.] Lee and Dean; [ed.] Salford University; [occ.] Lee Senior Chartered Surveyor Dean Sign Engineer; [hon.] Carrying Certificate; [oth. writ.] I have a daughter in law Carole and a beautiful grandddson Thomas also, Lisa who is Deans Girlfriend; [a.] Derby, England

OUTLAW, KEVIN
[b.] 20 June 1979, Malmesbury; [p.] Geoffrey Outlaw, Margaret Outlaw; [ed.] Malmesbury Comprehensive; [occ.] A level student working towards English degree; [oth. writ.] No previous publications. Work in progress on fictional book; [pers.] In my works I strive to show the folly of mankind's destruction of the natural world. I have been greatly influenced by the works of J.R.R. Tolkien and Seamus Heaney.; [a.] Sherston, Wiltshire, UK

PACE, CAROLE DIANE
[pen.] Carrie-Anne; [b.] 17 August 1952, Stanmore; [p.] Bob and Ethel Lavender; [m.] John Stephen Pace, 22 November 1985; [ch.] Donna Marie Pace; [occ.] Housewife/P.A.; [memb.] Ealing School for Girls (Secondary Modern Education); [hon.] Certificates in History of interior design and draughtsmanship St. John Public First Aider; [oth. writ.] Have written poetry for special occasions and public affairs; [pers.] To express life's experiences through poetry, one must firstly have the courage to touch upon the inestimable depths of one's soul.; [a.] Ampleforth, York, UK

PACKETT, ALAN F. J.
[b.] 2 June 1934, Hastings, St. Leonards-on-Sea; [p.] Mr. A. C. Packett and Mrs. A. E. Packett; [m.] Joan M. Packett, 29 August 1959; [ch.] Son and daughter; [ed.] Secondary School Lower Stream Pupil Ex National Serviceman Stationed with M.E.L.F. in Egypt; [occ.] C.N.C. Machinest in Engineering Co.; [memb.] Sussex Family History Group, Member of the Salvation Army, A.A. Member various other interest History, Music, Reading, Walking; [oth. writ.] One other poem, in new poetry 1981 editors Anthony Wall, Victoria Beckett, page 187 "The Hunted."; [pers.] The inspiration for writing is in most everyone, although at times things don't flow with ease, as these few verses did, many thanks for offering me this opportunity to be read.; [a.] Rayleigh, Essex, UK

PADDOCK, GEMMA
[b.] 2 January 1984, Arrowe Park, Wirral; [p.] Michelle Paddock, Francis Paddock; [ed.] Glenview School, Alberton, South Africa, Weatherhead High School, Wallasey Wirral, England; [occ.] Student; [memb.] Parklane Liveries and Riding Centre, of Wirral; [oth. writ.] Several poems not yet published, but written for pleasure; [pers.] I find great pleasure in writing poetry. 'The Rose'. I was inspired by my father love of roses.; [a.] Wirral, Merseyside, UK

PADWICK, SYLVIE
[b.] 22 September 1942, Southampton; [p.] Eddie and Jessie Bowles; [m.] Divorced 1981, 6 February 1962; [ch.] Christopher Nicholas and Elizabeth, twin grandsons Robert and Michael; [ed.] Girls Grammar School Southampton, and the Technical College Southampton; [occ.] Residential Care Officer, Social Services; [oth. writ.] Published "Twenties and Later Divorce" "Ode to a would be Sylph" and "Make Sure You Care, You Could Be There"; [pers.] I write from personal experiences of my past life and now and reflections on the relationships, and outcomes of myself and others I encounter. I like to have experience of my poetic material. Its really feelings.; [a.] Southampton, Hants, UK

PAGET, VILMA
[b.] 31 December 1930, Bromham, Wilts; [m.] 6 September 1952; [ch.] Six (4 girls, 2 boys) (15 Grandchildren); [ed.] Grammar School; [occ.] Housewife; [oth. writ.] Poems published in parish magazine collection of poems in print entitled "feelings"; [a.] Bromham, Wiltshire, UK

PALAU, FRANCES L.
[b.] 24 June 1963, Queens, NY; [p.] Frances Mendez and Luis A. Palau; [m.] William J. Manderson Jr., 27 September 1996; [ed.] Bachelor of Arts Degree for English Literature from Queens College - CUNY, in New York City; [occ.] Production Coordinator for Parade Magazine, a national weekly magazine; [pers.] My fiance submitted my poem and told me of this afterwards. His belief in my talent, pride of my works and joy over my selection as a semi-finalist, are the greatest gifts to me. I had begun to look again at my talent because of him. Life motivates!; [a.] Bellerose, Queens, NY

PALFREY, LOUISE
[b.] 30 November 1981, Oxfordshire; [p.] Dennis and Jacqui Palfrey; [ed.] Cherwell Comprehensive; [oth. writ.] I have only written poetry as a hobby, and this is my first poem to be entered in a competition.; [pers.] I have been greatly encouraged to write poems by many people. But mainly my mother and english teacher (Mr. A. Hanlon) who I give great thanks too.; [a.] Oxford, Oxfordshire, UK

PALMER, ANDREA LOUISE
[occ.] Aroma Therapist Enchantress/Stress Councillor/Reflexology; [hon.] Guitar (an honour the only one I ever took); [oth. writ.] Magazines: Invictor/Workshop Anthology Village News/Bogg Publications poem and review/Northampton Life/Merry-Go-Round/Display window; [pers.] My poems are gentle and romantic or witty or sensuous I am a (very-very sensitive) romantic sensuous mystical lady - it shows in my writing and when I'm not working I have a poem in my head - or I'm always singing and playing back voice or I'm reading Spanish (painting pots and arranging dry flowers).; [a.] Wollaston, Northants, UK

PALMER, LILIAN ROSINA
[pen.] Lilian Rose Palmer; [b.] 29 November 1919, Wales; [p.] Rosina and William Gill (Deceased); [m.] Edward George Palmer, 12 April 1941; [ch.] Patricia and Roger (Recently deceased); [ed.] Elementary Avon Vale School Barton Hill, Bristol; [occ.] Pensioner; [oth. writ.] I write in my own name Lilian Rose Palmer I have had 2 books published thoughts in rhyme was the first and a booklet of poems entitled the treasure proceeds. From the treasure gave to cancer research several poems printed in local Mag's and also on local radio.; [pers.] I started writing at the age of 60 after writing a slogan for a local shoe and I try to make every happening into a poem of significance all my poems are true to life and seems of interest to most people, I have had 10 grand children and 6 great grandchildren.; [a.] Bristol, Bristol, UK

PANESAR, HARJIT
[b.] 23 September 1968, Birmingham; [ed.] Southbank University, London; [occ.] Electronics Engineer; [oth. writ.] Many yet unpublished; [pers.] Never talk down to a person and listen twice as much as you speak; [a.] Birmingham, West Midlands, UK

PARK, MAY
[pen.] May Park; [b.] 15 April 1942, Welling, Kent; [p.] Bill and Carrie Blowers; [m.] Divorced; [ch.] Michael and Jeffrey; [ed.] Secondary Modern Westwood School for Girls; [occ.] Warden Sheltered Housing.; [memb.] Speakers Club Spiritualist Church in the past 9 belonged to a writers group for 12 years and edited annual magazine comedian singer with Co. 80 Old Tyme Music Hall; [hon.] 'O' level English; [oth. writ.] Several poems and articles published in magazines and local papers 2nd prize in local writing comp. with story 'A need to belong' and several songs performed by local schools.; [pers.] I have 2 lovely grandsons Shawn and Ryan. For when I have written prayers I am a working medium and get most of my writing through inspirations. I give talks using my own poems and stories to local clubs.; [a.] Dartford, Kent, UK

PARKER, IRENE MARY
[p.] Passed away; [occ.] Retired; [oth. writ.] This is a Tribute to The Boys who fought The Battle of Britain. Many of the Graves of these young airmen in The Battle are now neglected and overgrown, forgotten. This poem is to remind us we must keep alive the memory of those who served and won the Battle of Britain

PARKER, J.
[pen.] Joan Anita; [b.] 13 April 1920, Woodlands; [m.] Peter Godfrey Parker, 23 August 1953; [ch.] Two; [ed.] Secondary Education; [occ.] Housewife; [pers.] I am a (retired) senior citizen, I am very interested in poems and writings or such.; [a.] Southampton, Hants, UK

PARKER, ROZ
[m.] Divorced; [ch.] Vicky; [oth. writ.] This 20 lines poem is taken from an original and longer composition; [pers.] Dedicated to my daughter Vicky who understood, gave me strength, supported me and is always there.; [a.] Stratford upon Avon, Warks, UK

PARKS, LINDA RAFOLA
[b.] 8 September 1962, Bath, Avon; [p.] Mr. and Mrs. Ronald Davis, Mrs. Ana and A. Davis; [m.] Single; [ed.] Malmesbury Comprehensive School, I had my own small printing firm. I write poetry all the time.; [occ.] Unemployed. Had my own printing business.; [oth. writ.] I have 400 poems and I am writing a romantic novel set in the 19th century. And two poetry books.; [pers.] I write from my heart and soul, I write about life. I feel that there is power and wisdom within the heart and soul of everyone and that we all have the ability to create the written words.; [a.] Malmesbury, Wiltshire, UK

PARLEY, DOUGLAS
[b.] 13 November 1943, Aberdeenshire; [m.] Second Marriage, 12 November 1994; [ch.] Son (28), Daughter (23); [ed.] Port Lethen Junior Secondary; [occ.] Factory Worker; [pers.] While off work for nearly a year with serious illness. Started to write poetry to pass time.; [a.] Aberdeen, Scotland

PARRATT, VICTOR
[b.] 8 June 1946, Bowes; [p.] C. E. Parratt, E. Parratt; [m.] R. E. Parratt, 10 July 1972; [ch.] R. M. Parratt, C. E. Parratt; [ed.] Ryhope Secondary Modern, Army Apprentice College, Chepstow; [occ.] Anti Nazi League Member; [memb.] Royal Engineers Association, Beachly Old Boys Asso-

ciation; [hon.] Freeman of the City of Winchester; [oth. writ.] Poem in Voices in the Wind, Articles in local paper Warning of Natzism; [pers.] God exists. Obey the Ten Commandments. Join the Anti Nazi League. 25 Life Membership. P.O. Box 2566, London, N4 2HG. Inform on crime. God exists.; [a.] Sunderland, Tyne and Wear, UK

PATERSON, ANTHONY
[ed.] University of North London; [pers.] I believe in individual initiative, however I cannot agree with excess individualism and reverence for wealth, one might say it is typical of liberty, I say it is conducive to injustice.

PATMORE, RICHARD
[pen.] Flakie; [b.] 3 August 1965, London; [occ.] Butcher, for Large Wholesale Factory; [memb.] Chelsea Football Club; [oth. writ.] 4 other poems published with anchor books called: Boot Camp, Designer Drugs, Battered Britain, Chelsea FC; [pers.] I've only been writing about a year, so it's still quite new to me yet, but I have my ideas on life, and the way I would like to be able to present my work in the future, given that opportunity. I get most of my inspiration from watching and being part of lifes merry go round; [a.] Eversholt, Beds, UK

PATTEN, MRS. VAL E.
[pen.] Val Patten; [b.] 3 January 1929, Welton, Yorkshire; [p.] Robina and Frank Pickering; [m.] Tom Patten (Deceased), 30 July 1948; [ch.] 2 (one now Deceased); [ed.] Hull College of Commerce; [occ.] P/T Church Register of Marriages, Retire Country Court Chief Clerk; [memb.] Past President Soroptimists, Vice President Knutsford Crosstown W.I.; [oth. writ.] Two books published - A Thought, A Smile, A Tear And More Thoughts More Smiles No Tears, several poems published in local papers, magazines etc; [pers.] All my ideas for poems stem from a chance remark, a snatch of conversation, at emotional experience or a related incident.; [a.] Knutsford, Chester, UK

PATTERSON, CYRIL DOUGLAS
[pen.] Salgoud; [b.] 24 September 1921, Rainhill, Lancs; [p.] Welsh; [m.] Margaret; [ch.] Two; [ed.] Morrison School Liverpool; [occ.] Retired; [memb.] Autumn Tints Cycling Club Fellowship, Ossie Dover Cycling Fellowship; [oth. writ.] Edited and wrote material for an outdoor and Camping Magazine Sheet (many years ago!); [pers.] Folk guitar music and regularly pen writings on topical affairs as they happen. Lifelong interests, camping, climbing, cycling. Ex-Sgnt St John Ambulance ex-worker for a political party vivid memory of wartime horrors.; [a.] Liverpool, Merseyside, UK

PEACH, CHRISTOPHER
[b.] 30 October 1941, Dorchester; [p.] Florrie and Stanley Peach; [ed.] Dorchester Grove School, Dorchester Primary Boys School, Dorchester Secondary Modern School; [occ.] Henry Ling Limited 23 High East Street Lithograhic Technician; [memb.] Dorchester Trinity Club, Dorchester Cricket Club (48 years), St. Marys Church Dorchester; [hon.] Service to Sport Award 25 years (Cricket) Voluntary Service for Dorchester Cricket Colts, (A Trophy) Rothman's, Dorset Echo Service Award, Television Performance Twice at London W. End; [oth. writ.] Poetry and Monologues for my stage act; [a.] Dorchester, Dorset, UK

PEARSON, LORRAINE
[pen.] Elle Pearson; [b.] 10 August 1967, Wembley; [p.] Stedman Pearson and Delores Pearson; [m.] Naji Simaan; [ed.] Robert Clack Comprehensive School, Hanault College; [occ.] Sales Manager; [memb.] Fitness First, Camberley Health Club and Library; [hon.] 'O' Level English and History - Art and Secretarial Course.; [oth. writ.] "Her, Me and Reality", published 1987; [pers.] My love for poetry from my heart. Every world I put down on paper ventures from heaven into my soul. I love for people to read my work - to touch them with enjoyment and everlasting love. Through writing I understand myself.; [a.] Blacknell, Berkshire, UK

PEARSON, ROSEMARY
[pen.] Rosemary Pearson; [b.] 25 May 1939, Birmingham; [p.] Doreen and Marry Evans; [m.] Stephen John (2nd man), 19 February 1988; [ch.] Son from 1st man, Mark; [ed.] State schooling; [occ.] Craft worker. Poems written to specification in calligraphy and framed; [memb.] Past member - Tamworth Cruising Club, Tennis Club; [oth. writ.] Poems published in local weekly paper and West Mids magazines - "Rhyme Arrival" and "Poetry Now" on numerous occasions; [pers.] I have found the words that are often difficult to say - can easily be set in poetry. They are usually words that should not be left unsaid. I enjoy offering this service, in the knowledge that it gives great pleasure to those who receive them.; [a.] Sutton, Coldfield, W. Mids, UK

PECK, IVAN JOHN
[pen.] Ivan J. Peck; [b.] 31 August 1962, London; [p.] John and Freda Peck; [ch.] Martin, Steven, Simon, Alan and Sarah; [ed.] A Level Standard Comprehensive School; [occ.] Disability Equality Trainer; [memb.] Maldon A.C., Halsted and Hedingham A.C, Disabled Options, Absal Park A.C. and Disabled People Forum of Essex; [oth. writ.] Beauty, Belong, Within Your Eyes, My Soul, Shower, My Sarah, and published works; [pers.] I have M.S. but refuse to accept that I have a problem. It only becomes a problem when others perceive it as such.; [a.] Felsted, Essex, UK, CM6 3DF

PEDEN, LYNN ANN
[pen.] Lynn Peden; [b.] 4 January 1977, Glasgow; [p.] Alyson Goldie, Robert Peden; [ed.] Queen's Park Secondary (Glasgow) Blackpool and Fylde College (St. Annes); [occ.] Beauty Therapist; [hon.] NVQ Level 2+3 Beauty Therapy and NVQ Level 2 Hairdressing; [pers.] All my poems come from the heart.; [a.] Glasgow, Scotland

PELL, GEOFFREY WILLIAM
[pen.] Pell Geoffrey William; [b.] 6 June 1938, Scunthorpe; [p.] William Pell and Constance Pell; [m.] Rita Pell, 4 August 1956; [ch.] Michael David and Karen Marie; [ed.] Brumby Secondary Modern; [occ.] Disabled - Heart Trouble Osteo Arthritis; [oth. writ.] Poems published in eastern anthology - Poetry now 1994, Regional anthologies - North East poetry now 1993; [pers.] I like to reflect to good and bad of mankind. I am influenced by current affairs, writing about life as I see it.; [a.] Scunthorpe, Lincolnshire, UK

PEMBERTON, MANDY
[b.] 12 March 1974, Nottingham; [p.] Phil Pemberton, Elly Pemberton; [m.] Partner - Paul Sherratt (Engaged to be married); [ed.] Manning Comprehensive Basford Hall College; [occ.] Typist/Deputy team leader, Serco Government Services Limited; [oth. writ.] None to date; [pers.] I have a number of people to thank for my poetry. They may never known it but I will be forever grateful. Apart from my loved ones they have been my greatest inspiration.; [a.] Nottingham, Nottinghamshire, UK

PENFOLD, CAROLINE MICHELE
[b.] 21 August 1970, Canterbury; [p.] Pamela Irene Smith; [m.] Michael A. McCall; [ch.] Bobby, Bonny, Billy, Cheyvonne; [ed.] Woodlands High School; [occ.] Housewife and mother; [oth. writ.] Poem published in a book called welcome to the jungle by anchor books; [pers.] This poem is dedicated to the parents of my best friend Yvonne 1970-1982 (Sheila and Graham), to my mum and children Bobby Bonny Bill and Cheyvonne all of whom mean the world to me.; [a.] Gillingham, Kent, UK

PENMAN, TERRENCE JOHN
[b.] 19 February 1928, Morton Connery, Co Durham; [p.] John George Penman, Fannie Penman; [m.] June Penman, 1 February 1964; [ch.] Terri, Sarah, Celia, Sadie; [ed.] St Josephs R.C. School Elementary West School at Fourteen and went down the Pit. joined R.N. 1947 Demob 1955; [occ.] Retired Bricklayer; [memb.] R.N.A.; [oth. writ.] Short Stories of poems purely for my own pleasure (none published); [pers.] I have always loved poetry and since I purchased a copy of "Robert Herricks" "Hesperides" and "only one moment", "By Lord Gorell", I was inspired to write two liners by "Robert Herrick" written in the fay leaf of the "Hesterings" was an inscription "To Ease Penman "from L.K.H. October 30, 1903. (Synchronisity at its very best.); [a.] Burnt Oak Edewake, Middx, UK

PENTY, AMANDA BONITA
[b.] 31 May 1978, Rochdale; [p.] Bonita and Brian Penty; [ed.] Oulder Hill Community School; [occ.] Varies, to finance my travel abroad; [pers.] If you cast your eyes across a field and in your mind it is just a field you have missed out on life. To have investigated the life which dwells with it blades of grass means you have no actually lived at all.; [a.] Rochdale, Lancs, UK

PERKINS, MS. AVERIL ANN
[b.] 2 July 1952, Reading; [p.] George and Phyllis, Perkins; [ch.] Paul, Jason, and Peter Haste; [ed.] Wilson, Reading Berks; [occ.] Hostess, London; [pers.] A special thank you to my boyfriend, Freddrick, James, Brady, (Born too Ivy and Fred), an influence and caring person towards my poetry, a very special person in my life.; [a.] Reading, Royal Berkshire, UK

PERKINS, GERALDINE
[b.] 19 February 1965, Wakefield; [p.] Janet Colton and Roy Colton; [m.] Roy Edward Perkins, 5 September 1986; [ch.] Two boys and one girl; [ed.] Cross Green High School Leeds; [occ.] Disabled Housewife; [memb.] A member of the Saville Road Gospel Hall, Skelmanthorpe; [oth. writ.] Several poems published in several anthology and several poems published for the local church magazine and several poems been distributed to several people; [pers.] My Inspiration came to me from the day I become a Christian. So from then on I thought I would like everyone to know how I felt and maybe have an experienced mine someday; [a.] Walcefield, West Yorkshire, UK

PERRY, BRENDA JOAN
[b.] 12 April 1942, Walsall; [p.] Mrs. Emily Hatfield (Widow); [m.] Mr. Barry Highfield, 9 October 1965 (now Widow); [ch.] One; [ed.] Edward Shelly High School; [occ.] Was a Beauty Consultant now disability; [memb.] Only Member of Church Our Lady of Perpetual Succour Cannock Road, Father Doyle; [hon.] Silver Circle Awards for Avon Cosmetics for Top Sales 1962 and 1965; [oth. writ.] I started writing poetry about nine months ago. This as become a great hobbies of mine, because of ill health I do not go out very often. It gives me pleasure to share it with other people, if this is published had none published so far.; [pers.] I have lots of poetry at home, and would like my own book of poetry. Many of my poems have a true meaning of what as happened in my life, some to show others of what life is all about. And to give upliftment to the sick and lonely.; [a.] Wolverhampton, West Mids, UK

PETERS, LISA
[b.] 13 March 1966, Hamilton, Ontario, Canada; [p.] Campbell and Elizabeth McClure; [m.] Andre Peters, 28 November 1992; [ed.] B.A. East European and Soviet Politics, McMaster University - Ontario, B.Ed. Mount Allison University, New Brunswick Canada; [occ.] Teacher; [memb.] Secondary Special Needs Timothy Eaton B.T.I., Toronto; [a.] Toronto, Ontario, Canada

PETERSON, D. HILDA
[b.] 14 September 1927, Lerwick; [p.] Thomas Spence, Dorothy Spence; [m.] George Peterson, 19 August 1953; [ch.] Dorothy, Eric, Ireen, Graham, Sylvia and Hazel; [ed.] Lerwick Central Public School, Edinburgh College of Domestic Science; [occ.] Housewife; [memb.] W.W.F., R.S.P.B., A.A. Shetland Anglers, Gideon's International; [oth. writ.] One poem published in Shetland Dialect. Also one story in Shetland Dialect - both in local magazine. One book to be published of life in a Shetland mansion 17-18th Century.; [pers.] Writing in the local dialect helps to keep it alive.; [a.] Lerwick, Shetland, UK

PHELAN, ROSEMARY
[b.] 21 May 1964, Waterford; [p.] Stephen and Joan Prendergast Murphy both Deceased; [m.] Eamonn Phelan, 29 August 1988; [ed.] Presentation Convent, Clonmel Co Tipperary, Ireland; [memb.] Tutor with Youghal Literacy Group; [pers.] Poetry satisfies the soul and the spirit in a way that prose never can.; [a.] Youghal, Cork, UK

PHILLIPS, ALAN JOHN
[pen.] Philip Allen; [b.] 10 May 1933, Manchester; [p.] Alan L. Phillips and Mary J. Phillips; [m.] Joyce Mary Phillips, 8 April 1982; [ed.] St. Anne's Secondary School, Crumpsall, Manchester Salford Technical College; [occ.] Professional dry cleaner; [memb.] Guild of dyers and cleaners; [oth. writ.] Several poems and verses, some for "over 60's clubs", one of which was sent to Buckingham palace and an appropriate reply was received; [pers.] Romantic words and phrases are always in my mind and I endeavour to express them through poetic writing. My influence has been the poetical works of Thomas Moore.; [a.] Atherton, Lancs, UK

PHILLIPS, MRS. DOROTHY M.
[pen.] Sally Branson; [b.] 27 March 1935, Stanpit, Christchurch, Dorset; [p.] Frank Webb and Evelyn Webb; [m.] Deryck Phillips, 12 August 1959; [ch.] Sally, Robin, Deborah, Mark, Derek, Rebecca, Simon and Ruth; [ed.] Leeds University, London Polytechnic, Private School, various infant, junior and comprehensive schools. The eldest two-degree in Psychology, and a fully trained chef (respectively.) The other six have various passes at A and O levels; [occ.] I'm now retired. An A.O.P. I'm a very busy grandma. I have 16 grandchildren; [oth. writ.] I've written probably around sixty poems. A few were created twelve years ago, but at last I can find time to write as I've always wanted to! I've written articles and essays, and I'm writing results of various entries into competitions.; [pers.] I have a strong Christian faith, and with God's help I've come through trials and tribulations. I love animals, birds, butterflies etc. all things green and beautiful, and like nothing better than to sit and describe I all... pat pen to paper.; [a.] Bournemouth, Dorset, UK

PHILLIPS, RACHAEL
[b.] 30 November 1981, Cardiff, Wales; [p.] David and Susan Phillips; [ed.] Home Tutored; [occ.] Student; [pers.] There is nothing you cannot achieve, all have to do is try, as disability is no handicap.; [a.] Blackwood, Gwent, UK

PHILP, STEPHEN
[b.] 17 March 1953, Louth, Lincolnshire; [p.] Sqn/Ldr Wilton Philp and Mrs. Pauline Doggins; [ed.] Stamford School and Various Colleges, but mainly Auto-Didactic; [occ.] Publishing Consultant; [memb.] British Chess Federation, West Bridgford Chess Club, Nottingham; [hon.] Chess awards, Pub Quiz awards; [oth. writ.] Poems published in an Anthology (Anti-Nuclear), currently working on a Philosophical Novel about the Immortal Principle; [pers.] Frequently my poems are written from the standpoint of a fictional character, or personal, whose views are different from mine; [a.] Nottingham, UK

PICKERSGILL, DENISE
[b.] 29 August 1962, Dewsbury; [p.] Alan Clayton and Joan Clayton; [m.] Stephen Gareth Pickersgill, 9 March 1991; [ch.] Nicola Marie, Kimberley Jayne and Daniel Gordon; [ed.] Roundhay High School, Leeds Sight and sound typing course, Yorkshire post, Leeds.; [occ.] Housewife, voluntary non-teaching assistant, headlands school, liversedge; [oth. writ.] I had a poem published in 1995 in a book titled "Yorkist Thoughts". I have written various poems for relatives anniversaries birthdays, etch and am at present writing a book of poetry for children which I hope to publish in the future; [pers.] My personal emotions influence me to write what I feel about certain subjects. To put personal feelings into writing can give pleasure to all who read it.; [a.] Liversedge, W. Yorks, UK

PICKUP, GARY
[pen.] Gary Pickup; [b.] 19 May 1977, Yeovil; [p.] William and Valerie Pickup; [occ.] Student; [hon.] A few bits mere and there; [oth. writ.] Lonely poems scribbled on bits of paper and left in a folder in a drawer somewhere; [pers.] Every body needs inspiration to do whatever it is they do. Be it writing poems or buying roses. I guess I owe this to my inspiration. My girlfriend Julie. I love you; [a.] Helston, Cornwall, UK

PILLAY, MR. RUBEN
[pen.] Para-Ma-Seven; [b.] 26 February 1933, Cape Town; [p.] Kistasamy and Naomi Pillay; [ed.] Educated at South African primary schools and Trafalgar High Cape Town and The Christian Brothers College, Crawford; [occ.] Business Broker; [oth. writ.] To be collated and published later; [pers.] I love life and appreciate humanity, especially foreign travel and meeting with people from all over the world. More over, Nature in its true beauty and texture of Godliness; [a.] Battersea, London, UK

PITT-KELLY, ROBERT
[b.] Scotland; [p.] M. S. Clare; [memb.] Life member Bridgeton Burns Club, The Scottish Music Hall Society Life member an Comunn Gladhealach, Society of Antiquaries of Scotland. Life member St. John Association of Scotland.; [hon.] Olj., F.S.A., Scot.; [oth. writ.] Foolish Man, Children Of The Light.; [pers.] Unknown unseen I reached and touched the sky.; [a.] Glasgow, UK

PLANT, PETER DAVID
[b.] 27 February 1968; [p.] William Plant and Irene Plant; [m.] Julie Allbutt (Fiancee); [ed.] Chawson first School, Witton Middle School, Droitwich High School; [occ.] Parts Technician Sealine International; [hon.] City and Guilds Maths Level 1, several Athletics Awards; [oth. writ.] Several unpublished poems; [pers.] I like to portray the real day to day life of mankind in my writing. Each poem tells its own true story; [a.] Droitwich, Dorcester, UK

PLANT, SUE
[b.] 27 January 1979, Stoke-on-Trent; [p.] Jean and David (Deceased) Plant; [ed.] Alleynes High School; [occ.] Student; [a.] Stone, Staffs, UK

PLATTS, MYRA
[b.] 11 March 1910, Wetheral, Cumbria; [p.] J. K. Miller and Florence England; [m.] A. W. Platts MA Oxon, 23 June 1947; [ch.] Alexander George, Florence Gillian; [ed.] Edinburgh School of Art. Glasgow College of Domestic Science.; [occ.] Housewife; [memb.] Bradford Writers Circle. International Poetry Society.; [hon.] M. B. E. Military Division (June 1967) Cordon Blue Cookery Medal (Glasgow); [oth. writ.] 2 Books published. Many verses published, (but not growing up). All in Northern Regional Anthologies. Articles published in press and magazines. Plays both published and performed.; [pers.] A reader, and lover, of poetry from childhood. First published in school magazines. 'Growing Up' inspired by, little daughter making some remark about what the future might hold for her.; [a.] Menston Nr Ilkley, W. Yorks, UK

PLEDGE, PATRICIA
[b.] 29 December 1944, Stapleford Abbotts, Essex; [m.] Peter John Pledge, 30 November 1962; [ch.] Peter Gary and Trevor John; [ed.] Stapleford Abbotts Primary, Ongar Comprehensive; [occ.] Home Assistant Night Care Officer for Springboard; [oth. writ.] Unpublished children's stories; [a.] Ongar, Essex, UK

PLETTS, PAMELA MARGARET
[b.] 5 August 1940, Chigwell Row; [p.] Mary Ann and Harry Earey; [m.] Robert Pletts, 6 May 1961; [ed.] No Educational Qualifications; [occ.] Civil Servant in Employment Service; [oth. writ.] Several poems written but have never attempted to have any published.; [pers.] 'The Family' was written 15/1/1996 as a tribute to my late mother who passed away on the 9/1/1996.; [a.] Ilford, Essex, UK

POLLITT, BRENDAN CARLTON
[pen.] Raven; [b.] 22 October 1974, Hannover, Germany; [p.] Raymond Pollitt, Teresa Pollitt; [m.] Katherine Pollitt, 14 February 1996; [ch.] None; [ed.] Sir Frank Markham Secondary, Milton Keynes College Leadenhall; [occ.] Merchandiser, House of Fraser; [memb.] The poetry Society Wargames Society; [oth. writ.] In excess of over 100 other poems, as yet unpublished; [pers.] Good and evil, which groups do they cover, and can you easily recognize one from the other. Taken from its opposite, could what remains exist.; [a.] Milton Keynes, Buckinghamshire, UK

PORT, MRS. JOYCE EVELYN
[b.] 16 January 1928, Reigate, Surrey; [p.] Mrs. and Mr. F. G. Clark; [m.] Major (QM) Sandy Port Deceased, 26 July 1948; [ch.] Trevor and Barry Port; [ed.] St. John's School Redhill, Surrey; [occ.] Widow, Retired; [oth. writ.] The MayFlower - (Poem), 'Joyce's Jolly Jotting's In The Bunde, North Germany - Weekly Army Magazine; [pers.] 'Ode To Dalmatia'. Inspired by bird-song and beauty of the isle of Korcula-Yugoslavia, while walking with my beloved walking with my beloved late husband Sandy.; [a.] Horley, Surrey, UK

PORTEN, RODERICK
[b.] 10 March 1940, Leicester, Royal Infirmary; [p.] Michael Porten, Elsie Ida Porten; [m.] Ann, 25 September 1965; [ch.] Ian, Neil, Graham; [ed.] South Wigston Secondary Modern, Leicestershire; [occ.] Quality Control Officer; [memb.] New Zealand Returned Services Association; [pers.] Since coming to live in New Zealand, in 1973, I have written a great deal of poetry, mainly for my own amusement. Like to write narrative verse, striving to create atmosphere, and reality.; [a.] Massey, Waitakere City, New Zealand

PORTER, PAM
[b.] 30 July 1947, Bristol; [p.] Gwen Southcott and George Southcott; [m.] John Porter, 10 July 1971; [ch.] Charlotte and Edward Porter; [ed.] Withywood Comprehensive School Bristol, (Brilliat at English Department!) and the Gloucestershire College of Education; [occ.] "Supply" Teacher, children 4-11 years; [memb.] Have spent many years in school P.A Work, and four years as a Secondary School Parent Governor; [hon.] Very little! Except the "Gold bar", the highest award then given, for exam. Work in the British Red Cross in the early `60's. I had 7 G.C.E.'s, and English `A' level; [oth. writ.] My last published poem was in a school anthology at seventeen, recently, I began writing again for myself, with the ambition to have it published, and have now quite a large collection of my own works.; [pers.] I have fulfilled one of my ambitions. The thing which is of greatest importance is to see Charlotte, 20, reading B.A. Hons English with Q.T.S, and Edward, 18, studying 3 Dimensional design, (B.T.E.C National), Through to their ultimate goals, through to their ultimate goals.; [a.] South Ockendon, Essex, UK

PORTER, SUSIE ROSE
[pen.] Susan Rose Porter; [b.] 3 October 1978, Aldershot, England; [p.] Sandy Porter, David Porter; [ed.] Presently attending Merrist Wood College for Land Based Industry.; [occ.] Student; [pers.] I love to write poems, they reflect how you feel and release emotions you are unable to express otherwise.; [a.] Farnham, Surrey, UK

PRATT, MRS. MARIANNE
[b.] 9 October 1943, London; [p.] Edmond and Katherine Pageot; [m.] Leonard Pratt, 20 August 1966; [ch.] Melanie (28) and Carolynne (26), (both married); [ed.] Finchley County Grammar School. F.E. College (London College of Fashion), University of Middx (Teacher's Cert Ed.); [occ.] Lecturer of Fashion at Southgate College, London; [memb.] Embroiderer's Guild (Institute), City and Guilds of London; [oth. writ.] Poems for family, friends when celebrating and remembering special occasions. I have written poems for retirements, weddings, funerals, farewells, etc. etc.; [pers.] Writing poetry is a way of putting ones feelings over to others particularly on special occasion, the poem "For Melanie" was written for our elder daughter when she converted to Islam.; [a.] Barnet, Herts, UK

PREEDY, SUSAN JAMES
[b.] 6 June 1966, Hereford; [p.] June Preedy and Gareth Preedy; [m.] Ted; [ch.] Gemma, Lee, Cassie and Keri-Emma; [ed.] Brecon High School; [occ.] Mother; [a.] Llandrindod Wells, Powys, UK

PRESCOTT, THELMA
[b.] 13 April 1934, Onchan, Isle-of-Man; [p.] Florence and Sidney Higgins; [m.] Eric John Prescott, 8 September 1962; [ed.] Onchan School and Douglas High School for girls; [occ.] Retired; [oth. writ.] None published but lots written. Only one article about childless marriages for which I received 10.; [pers.] I write my poems for pleasure and for friends to read and also enjoy. I write about things that are happening and people I care for. Also my feelings about world problems.; [a.] Onchan, Isle of Man, UK

PRESTON, ELIZABETH JANE
[pen.] Liz, Cissy Spaceship; [b.] 19 February 1961, Newton Abbot, Devon; [p.] Ron and Rosa Stickland; [m.] Divorced; [ch.] Emma Spry; [ed.] Coombes Head School Newtons Abbot; [occ.] Unemployed, due to Epilepsy; [memb.] None as yet but I have applied for a membership for U.F.O Investigation's; [hon.] C.S.E English Lit. Mathematics; [oth. writ.] Have written quite a bit at home but never entered any until now, I have also written a long prologue to a U.F.O Magazine of which I'm awaiting reply; [pers.] My art is in my writing and painting's, it is shown very strongly, within these talent's that I believe I've been gifted with. The truth as I see it and feel it, man is self destructing our planet and all the beauty that lay dying within it, unless we make a stand and recognize the help being off we'll blow it.; [a.] Newton Abbot, S. Devon, UK

PRICE, ANNIE LOUISA
[pen.] Luncy or Angie; [b.] 3 April 1914, Rhondda Vly, S. Wales; [p.] Mr. and Mrs. Hankey; [m.] John Price Smooker, Mad 143 Breat, 1936; [ch.] 3-2 Boys one Girl 19 Great Grandchildren; [ed.] Ordinary Schooling Left after 16 yrs old Worked as Housemaid for Powerger Lady Pennhyn Bucks; [occ.] Retired from various laundry rubber works; [memb.] Boewhouse arts and crafts center used to be little theatre in Burton 9 acted and song in many if their plays, won prizes for singing. If tried I would have been a coloritura sofrano cost voice at seventy none was member of Burton Municipal choir. Soprano section; [oth. writ.] I'm currently writing my life story. Finding writing difficult as I've never seen one before I bought it. But am improving will practice hand writing hopeless; [pers.] I am a great believe in being relaxed, and Philosophical I hardly ever show any emotion and Tend to not get equated in any crises. I suppose I may be called cold natured. But I like a joke and laugh with friends; [a.] Burton on Trent, Staffs, UK

PRICE, MRS. MARGARET OLIVE ELIZABETH
[pen.] Songbird; [b.] 28 June 1953, Lambeth, London; [p.] Mrs. Joyce Avard (Adopted Mother); [m.] Died (21 February 1989), 14 September 1986; [ch.] Sarah, Alice age 10; [ed.] Secondary School Qualifications - English R-Eligous - Education Spanish; [occ.] Housewife; [hon.] Have taken part and won in Carmantenshire Social Services "Eisleddfod" 1st Prize I won a Medal for Singing two Solo's without Music, 1 March 1996; [pers.] I enjoy writing poems as it is a way of expressing my true feelings.; [a.] Gorslas, Waneui, Carms, UK

PRICE, TINA
[pen.] Katrina Reardon; [b.] 9 February 1976, Abergavenny, South Wales; [p.] Frank Price, Joyce Price; [m.] Paul Roberts; [ch.] Kayla Louise; [ed.] Rhymney Comprehensive Pontypridd Technical College; [occ.] Mother; [pers.] The inspiration for my poems comes from the hope of world peace and a sake place for our children to grow up in.; [a.] Rhymney, Gwent, UK

PRINGLE, JOHN GERARD
[b.] 26 July 1978, Newcastle upon Tyne; [p.] James and Frances Pringle; [ed.] King Edward High School Morpeth Northumberland; [occ.] 6th Form Pupil; [memb.] Morpeth RFC Colts; [oth. writ.] I poem published in poetry now. Several poems published in local newspaper.; [pers.] Thought is what you see when you close your eyes; [a.] Rothbury Morpeth, Northumbria, UK

PRITCHARD, JAMES E.
[b.] 10 September 1920, Smethwick; [ed.] Council Schools, Smethwick 1925/1934, Smethwick Tech. College 1934/1958; [occ.] Retired but still Active Chairman of my Plastics Company; [memb.] P.R.O. for Bude Rotary Club (Paul Harris Fellow); [hon.] Award for Service to Rotary; [oth. writ.] Nothing published. Odd poems since war years, technical articles relating to plastics including Development of Chrom Plating of Plastics (1966); [pers.] "War Years" served in Rasc and Fire Service 1939/1945, have been involved with Plastics Industry since 1955. "You only gain experience by making a lot of mistakes, keep on trying"; [a.] Bude, Cornwall, UK

PROSSER, PHIL
[b.] 31 October 1949, Newport, Gwent; [ch.] Four; [ed.] Grammar School; [occ.] Self Employed; [oth. writ.] Articles for transport mag. (Published). (Written) battle for flume (Children Story) Written not published (Occasional, dress) Romance. Trader Menzzes.; [pers.] Self pity. Is a possessive companion, who will become your only friend. While self help, is the corner. Stone of an age of new friendships.; [a.] Newport, Gwent, UK

PROW, DONNA
[b.] 18 October 1965, Fleggburgh; [p.] Richard and Carole Cooper; [m.] Ivor Prow, 10 December 1983; [ch.] Leanne Heather, Natasha Kayleigh; [ed.] Flegg High School; [occ.] Temporary Disabled due to injury; [oth. writ.] Personal use only; [pers.] Dad, love is eternal. Smile for me.; [a.] Gt. Yarmouth, Norfolk, UK

PUDDEFOOT, BETTY
[pen.] Natahli Elspeth; [b.] 2 March 1914, Willdesden; [p.] Edith and William Booth Johnson; [m.] Arthur Puddefoot, 6 November 1938; [ch.] Gwen and Jenny; [ed.] Council School; [occ.] Housewife was a Chiropodist; [hon.] Spanish Dancing 1st Class Certificate; [oth. writ.] Children's stories not published; [pers.] Student of the Bible.

PURCELL, BRIGID
[pen.] Susan Shackleton; [b.] 10 March 1947, Norwich; [ch.] Rosalind Elaine; [ed.] Notre Dame High School, Norwich, Reading University; [occ.] Modern Languages, Teacher, Eaton (CNS) School; [pers.] My poems are an expression of my own personal and spiritual Odyssey, and of the constant process of change and adjustment I observe, both in myself and those around me.; [a.] Norwich, Norfolk, UK

QUADRI, OLAYINKA A.
[pen.] MayQ, Al-Asad, May-L-Quadri; [b.] 29 July 1965, Lagos, Nigeria; [p.] Babatunde Quadri and Ramota Abike Yesuf; [m.] Omobowale Oluyomi Quadri, 24 December 1994; [ch.] Olukorede Olamide Quadri; [ed.] HNC Business and Finance PGDip Marketing (DIPM), Masters of Business Administration (MBA); [occ.] Market Resource Executive; [memb.] Chartered Institute of Marketing; [oth. writ.] Several poems (unpublished), two novels (unpublished), various articles and short stories (published by the Punch in Nigeria and Africque in the UK). "Testimony" - filmed for video.; [pers.] We live in a world where it is fashionable to be someone else. When caught in this web we lose the ability to discover the treasure within, the beauty that is unique and a love everlasting. I am still getting to know me.; [a.] London, UK

QUANE, SISTER CATHERINE M.
[b.] 15 September 1938, Limerick, Ireland; [p.] Madge Liddy and Patrick Stephen Quane; [ed.] Certificate of Education at Manchester University BA Hons Degree at London University; [occ.] Retreat Ministry and Spiritual Direction also Superior of the convent.; [memb.] Sister of Mercy, Member of the Vicar for Reliousteam, Member of the National Retreat Association.; [hon.] BA Honours Degree. Diploma in Religious Studies; [oth. writ.] Eight Poems (not published); [pers.] My hope is that my poetry would enable people to discover the God that is within.; [a.] London, UK

QUINLAN, ROBERT JOHN
[b.] 28-8-42, Matlock; [p.] Amy Quinlan, Fred Quinlan; [m.] Pamela Quinlan, 4-8-96; [ch.] six; [ed.] Secondary Modern; [occ.] Professional Artist; [hon.] Achieved Black Belt in Ju - Jitsu - Martial Art. Also various medals in ballroom dancing. Plus I have received a certificate from MENSA; [oth. writ.] Work in about 14 books; [pers.] A year ago my God set my heart free to express and my hand with the pen, also courage to speak what I think is the truth and the way and word; [a.] Rotherham, South Yorkshire

QUINN, OLIVE R.
[pen.] O'R Quinn; [b.] 28 January 1914, Guernsey, Channel Islands; [p.] Deceased; [m.] Deceased, 29 August 1935; [ch.] One; [occ.] Housewife; [oth. writ.] One book called "The Long Goodbye," one poem "Rain Drops."; [a.] St. Peter Port, Guernsey, Channel Islands, UK

RACHEL, MARIE
[pen.] Marie Rachel; [b.] 12 October 1920, Menton, France; [m.] 18 August 1968; [ed.] Educated in France learn in England from the age of 13 in Boarding School in Brentwood Urshline Convent; [occ.] Retired, have been professional singer, have done voice over for television in French and English, still do an occasional concert and have been coaching students with their French oral examination.; [hon.] Left School with a 0 levels. French, Spanish and geography.; [oth. writ.] I have had an article published in "The People's War" I have written a novel "The Wild Nightingale" I have always loved poetry as the words come straight from the heart.; [pers.] I love Keats and Shelly and also Albert Camas! Poetic and philosophical essays (in French) nobel prize winner.; [a.] Goodmayes, Essex, UK

RAINE, DOUGLAS
[pen.] Will Stoney; [b.] 21 October 1930, Bishop, Auckland; [p.] George and Dora; [m.] Jane, 3 December 1955; [ch.] 5 Adults; [ed.] Disrupted during years of W.W. 2 basically 'Comprehensive' School then subsequent Adult Education Courses; [occ.] Retired; [memb.] West Sussex Writer's Club, Worthing; [oth. writ.] Poetry - usually drown from events experienced or witnessed, (but not always). Short stories around 2000 - 3000 words. Currently writing children stories. No previously published works in this field.; [pers.] As a child, I was greatly influenced by the writings of Kipling and R. L. Stevenson, but particularly W. Harrison Ainsworth. The degree of detail cautioned in this latters relatives, drew me into the story in ways few others can. In Pre-Raphaclife Faslisou, I endure to create word pictures of my subject in detail.; [a.] Angmering, West Sussex, UK

RANDALL, ARTHUR
[pen.] Liadnar; [b.] 5 November 1939, London; [p.] Arthur Randall, Doris Randall; [m.] Widower, 5 November 1962; [ch.] Irmgard, John Arthur, Clive; [ed.] Comprehensive; [occ.] Semi-retired; [memb.] Golf and Bowls (Enthusiast); [oth. writ.] Two poems published 1977. More poems and short stories awaiting to be discovered.; [pers.] The poem, is it only I, that want to live, I dedicate to my late wife, Elizabeth Wallace Randall.; [a.] Wembley, Middlesex, UK

RANKINE, JOY
[b.] 4 August 1972, Stirling; [p.] Tan Rankine, Sylvia Deans; [ed.] Lornstill Academy, Clackmannan College, Falkink Tech; [occ.] Carer; [hon.] N.C. in Health Care, N.C. in Drama and Theatre Arts.; [pers.] I am not a highly educated person who sweats over her writing, I'm just someone who feels more comfortable writing down how I feel.; [a.] Alva, Clackmannanshire, UK

RATCLIFFE, MARY
[b.] 25 February 1925, Brighton, Sx; [m.] Peter Ratcliffe (Deceased), 24 August 1946; [ch.] Jane, Peter and Kathy; [ed.] Boarding School and Commercial College Ex Wren, Category PV, German Enigma. Acupuncture - practitioner and various posts in institutions.; [occ.] The ageless power of the written word! Public speaking.; [memb.] Amnesty International (Mans inhumanity to man continues to influence my writing.); [oth. writ.] My book of dreams, and re-writing four children slaccis for publish Michael Twins of Child's Play. Some of my poetry has travelled far a wide, E.G. my "Tribute to Richard Burton", "The Ballad of Steam", and recently "Dunblane..." to the Sec: Of state for Scotland, and to George Hamilton M. P.; [pers.] I have also been portraying Queen Victoria for over 22 yrs. - invited to open venues and functions for charity! I have been invited to read several of my poems and Wiltshire sound. I contribute frequently to the evening advertiser.; [a.] Swindon, Wiltshire, UK

RAVENSCROFT, JILL T.
[pen.] Jill Stevens; [b.] 24 November 1952, Westgate, Kent; [p.] Elizabeth and Edgar Stevens; [m.] Divorced; [ch.] Sherena, Yvette and Natalie; [ed.] Charles Dickens Secondary Modern School Broadstairs; [occ.] Ass. Housekeeper for Hotel for Mental and Physically Handicapped; [memb.] Matchroom Snooker Club; [hon.] Trophies for Dart League since 1987-1996; [oth. writ.] Poem published a book called "Soap Suds." Won a comp. on the radio for poem I have written a children's book of poetry but not got it published so far.; [pers.] I love to write children's poetry and would love to write a couple more books to follow the one I have written.; [a.] Margate, Kent, UK

RAWLINGS, WILLIAM HENRY
[b.] 20 February 1932, Coven, Wolverhampton; [p.] Charles Rawlings and Florence Rawlings; [m.] Maureen Ann Merricks, 31 March 1987; [ch.] Sandra, Andrew, Sindy, Karl; [ed.] Brewood Grammar School; [occ.] Retired; [memb.] Brewood Old Boys Association, Uxbridge Flying Club; [hon.] C.I.T.B. Accredited Assessor; [oth. writ.] Previous contracts with E.M.I. and James McLane Recording Companies (gift of charm); [pers.] Any poetic knowledge whether read or heard proves the depth of understanding needed in putting any words to rhyme by the direction of its content in any language.; [a.] Cannock, Staffs, UK

REDFORD, DENISE
[b.] 6 April 1959, Burton Joyce, Nottingham; [p.] Derek, Sheila Burton; [m.] Simon Redford, 22 August 1987; [ch.] Katie (7), Michael (4); [ed.] Gedling Comprehensive Nottingham, Arnold and Carlton College of further Education Nottingham; [occ.] Housewife, former Care Assistant; [memb.] Nottingham Hospitals Radio, Nottingham Mencap - Care at home service, Fiex Fitness Club; [oth. writ.] Poetry for fiex fitness magazine; [pers.] If you can transfer any feelings from deep despair to sheer elation, onto paper, I feel there isn't anything in life. That you wouldn't be able to cope with. It has certainly helped me in this way.; [a.] Long Eaton, Derbyshire, UK, NG10 3QY

REEMAN, BRIAN HARVEY
[b.] 7 August 1952, Suffolk; [p.] Charles Reeman and Edith Reeman; [m.] Yvette Le Jeune; [ed.] Subdury Comprehensive, The Colchester Institute; [occ.] Director, Ad-Lib Advertizing and Marketing; [memb.] Penryn Gentlemans Club, Seahorse Petanque Club, Falmouth Arts Society; [oth. writ.] Many personalized odes and poems. Training tomorrow magazine; [pers.] I write from reflection on so much laughter and tears, influenced by characters and personalities from the words of hotels, advertising sales, and marketing-life.; [a.] Penryn, Cornwall, UK

REID, LISA
[b.] 31 December 1966, Margate; [p.] Margeret Pryor, Eric Pryor; [ch.] Catrina Lea, Robert Carl, Abbigayle Louise, Chloe Elizabeth; [ed.] The Charles Dickens School, Broadstairs; [occ.] Mother and housewife; [oth. writ.] I have written many

poems mostly for friends and family, and have been asked to write poetry on specific occasions.; [pers.] I find poetry a natural way of expressing my thoughts and feelings.; [a.] Margate, Kent, UK

RENDELL, A. E.
[b.] 25 July 1926, Cardiff; [ed.] Left School 1934, all pleasant knowledge from book reading, ect; [occ.] Retired Chef; [memb.] RAOB. Yacht Club Aberearon British Legion; [oth. writ.] The Sailors Grave published by International Society of Poets to be published in the summer? Plus others unpublished all ready over forty, invation North Africa (unpublished forty lines); [pers.] I try to reflect the goodness of life past and present.; [a.] Aberaeron, Dyfed, UK

RENZ, RHONA MURIEL
[pen.] Rhona Renz; [b.] 4 February 1951, Johannesburg; [p.] Petrus and Elizabeth; [ed.] Matriculated at St. Mary's Convent, Ballet Teachers Diploma with the Imperial Society of Dance Teacher/The Dance Teachers Society Teaching Diploma/Professor de Baile of Spanish Dance/Art Teacher/Liturgical Dance; [occ.] Classical Dance Teacher of the above; [memb.] Imperial Society of Dance Teachers, Dance Teachers Associated (affiliated in SA to British Ballet Organization)/Spanish Dance Teachers Society/Alianza Flamenca/National Society of Dance Teachers (Tester); [oth. writ.] The Chosen Ones in process of publication by Avon Books. England.; [pers.] I am greatly influenced by events and people in Ancient History, especially Biblical history. I believe in compassion and justice for all.; [a.] Randfontein, South Africa

REY, ANA-MARIA
[b.] 24 April 1972, Wallingford; [p.] Manuel and Lorraine Rey; [ed.] Gillott's School, Henley-on-Thames, Henley College, Henley-on-Thames; [occ.] Advertising Assistant/Part-time Vocalist; [memb.] MENSA, everything's Rosy local folk/rock Band; [pers.] To live each day to thee fullest tomorrow is an uncertainty.; [a.] Wallingford, Oxon, UK

REYNOLDS, BERNARDINE ANN
[b.] 12 January 1963, Liverpool; [p.] Joseph and Joan Cunningham; [m.] John Reynolds, 18 May 1985; [ch.] Mark Louis, Louise Ann, Sarah Elizabeth; [ed.] Warwick Bolam High School (comprehensive); [occ.] Housewife; [pers.] To my loving Mum, whose love of poetry inspired me to write from an early age.; [a.] Swinton, Manchester, UK

REYNOLDS, BERYL
[b.] 22 May 1940, Clowne; [p.] Kenneth and Grace Winifred Milner; [m.] Roy Reynolds, 1 October 1960; [ch.] Susan, Sandra, Roy; [ed.] Clowne Infants, Clowne Prinary, Boughton Lane Secondary, Modern (now called heritage); [occ.] Educational care officer for children with special needs; [hon.] At school I received a poetry book as a prize for efficiency leadership and excellent character. But I am honoured to have had my poem chosen as my poems just reflect my feelings for those I love; [oth. writ.] Monologues about the lives of my family and closest friends in rhyme from birth to the present day these are given as special birthday cards.; [pers.] My inspiration for writing poetry comes from the love of my family I express my feelings in verse. Writing about their lives trials tribulations and happiness. Being part of a large family who share all life's joys and sorrow is the greatest thing in life.; [a.] Chesterfield, Derbyshire, UK

REYNOLDS, GLORIA JEAN
[pen.] Gloria Jean; [b.] 12 October 1941, Chatham, Kent, England; [p.] Thomas E. Mason and Eileen J. Mason; [m.] John G. Raynolds, 15 December 1990; [ed.] Comprehensive School; [occ.] Housewife; [pers.] I am an ordinary housewife, who is interested in nature and the universe, I am a dedicated spiritualist. I write my poems from the heart.; [a.] Barry South Wales, South Glamorgan, UK

REYNOLDS, ONEETTA
[b.] 17 November 1970, Berkshire; [p.] Bruce and Garnet Reynolds; [ed.] Lister Community School; [occ.] Clerical Assistant (News Office); [pers.] Within me, a frustrated fire burns passion and pain, love and anger, my release comes from the words I express, and so I write, that I may breathe again.; [a.] London, Plaistow, UK

RICHARDS, GLADYS MURIEL SEYMOUR
[b.] 6 November 1914, Edmonton, London; [p.] Ethel Agnes and Phillip Bowes; [m.] Robert Shirley (Divorced), 2 January 1932; [ch.] Barry Frederick (one son), Cecil Shirley; [ed.] Secondary Edmonton County School; [occ.] Retired; [pers.] Although I was baptized by church of England at the moment, I do not belong to any organized faith. I love going into any church of any denomination. I also have poetry that makes a statement.; [a.] Broadstairs, Kent, UK

RICHARDS, HARVEY P. A.
[pen.] Pam Richards; [b.] 18 February 1925, Parkstone, Dorset; [p.] E. G. and D. A. Harvey (Deceased); [m.] G. Richards (Deceased), 2nd marriage (1951 and 1965); [ch.] Jocelyn Huwbert, Oks Sarah Green; [ed.] Talborhealth Higher S Club School Club (girls), introduce to St. Andrews, was interested. Worked, then in our own two hotels and was easily on my own like; [occ.] Retired Impecuniously; [memb.] Nat. Poet Society, M and M, HPB, Judge and Council Member. New Poster Poet Reading and Gentle Soc. Commerce Past President - Chairman N. Forest Enthuseirsk, Vice Ch. NF Association, Direction House Chairman Nr Haults and Shro and President Tect. for 1997. Breeds; [hon.] Committee RASE, International Writ Walive Breed Panels BHS (PIC); [oth. writ.] Poems published by Forestry Commission. Local papers Nat. P.S. Year Book and BDS Year Book. Abides our pony subject, for House and Pony publication (Holt, Riding and others).; [pers.] Money is imported to pay essentials but not the be-all and end-all of existence. Mostly people en-marie are disqualified, but most of is aren't thankful enough for what we have.; [a.] Bramshaw, Hampshire, UK

RICHARDS, JODIE LETITIA
[b.] 23 January 1983, Barnstaple Hospital; [p.] Jon and Penelope Richards; [ed.] Woolacombe Primary School, Edgehill College Bideford; [occ.] Student; [oth. writ.] Dunblane, Lolly Pop, Bag lady; [pers.] Although I am only thirteen, I get these really strong feeling that I have to put down on paper but despite this I like to have a good laugh in life.; [a.] Woolacombe, North Devon, UK

RICHARDS, LLOYD PRIDEAUX
[b.] 9 August 1968; [m.] Louise Jane Richards, 15 April 1989; [ch.] James, Harry, William; [ed.] Rugby School; [occ.] Unemployed; [oth. writ.] Too many to mention while none have been published. The attic is full to bursting, but nobody wants to look.; [pers.] I greatly admire the excesses of Dylan Thomas and the madness of William Blake. From being unemployed to a published poet is one dream realised. All editors and publishers are welcome.; [a.] Rugby, Warwickshire, UK

RICHARDS, PHIL
[b.] 6 November 1919, Cardiff; [p.] John Davies Richards and Maude Gordon R.; [m.] Margery, 7 June 1975, (Deceased) 30 January 1993; [ch.] Patricia Anne; [ed.] Cardiff High School, C.W.B. - London Matric; [occ.] Retired (Engineer) Long Associated with age concert Stafford and Starffordshire; [memb.] Labour Party, Coop Party, 12 years Boro Councillor, Hon. Director Stafford Unemployed Centre (Vol); [hon.] Not a lot except Deputy Mayor of Stafford Borough, 1984/5; [oth. writ.] Addnents over the years. Associated with Stafford Doledrums unemployed writing group; [pers.] I believe humanity is worthwhile, still has potential, but needs to value itself, and creation more highly; [a.] Stafford, Staffs, UK

RICHARDSON, DAVID
[pen.] David Richardson; [b.] 3 February 1975, Manchester; [p.] Brian Richardson, Margaret Richardson; [a.] Stretford, Gt. Manchester, UK

RICKARD, BEVERLEY MARIE
[pen.] Beverley Rickard; [b.] 7 October 1961 (age 34), Ealing, London; [p.] Ronald and Elizabeth Mosdall; [m.] Graham, 7 October 1982; [ch.] Carl 13, Gemma 11, Samantha 8 and Larissa 2 1/2; [ed.] Went to primary, middle and upper schools, didn't go to college; [occ.] I'm a housewife but I work part-time in the evenings.; [oth. writ.] Poems - A Child's Dream, A Teenage Dream, A Parent's Dream, Fond Memories; I also do personal poems for friends and family, for them to give to others.; [pers.] To be happy is to be content, and to be content is to be secure.; [a.] Brandon, Suffolk, UK

RIDDICK, MARY
[b.] 9 March 1936, Mary Port; [p.] William Parkin, Grace Parkin; [m.] Alan Riddick, 17 March 1954; [ch.] Susan, Alan, Paul, William, Dyane; [ed.] Ellenborough Secondary School, Mary Port, Cumbria; [occ.] Housewife; [oth. writ.] None previous though I have written many.; [pers.] I have always loved poetry and I find writing poems an ideal way to express the way I feel.; [a.] Blencogo, Wigton, Cumbria, UK

RIDGE, ANDREW
[b.] 14 November 1967, Rinteln, Germany; [p.] Bryan Ridge and Renate Garfield; [ed.] Umtali Grammar, Vainona Secondary in Zimbabwe, Paramatta University, Sydney Australia; [occ.] Analyst Programmer BCWA Bristol; [memb.] Royal Marines, Royal Navy Reserves Parachute Association, British Computer Society, South West England Theatre Club, British Chess Society; [hon.] Honours in Information Technology, Chess Masters Award; [oth. writ.] First published in Zimbabwe, 'Poetry for Africa' and a few articles for the local newspaper; [pers.] Live life to the full, blue skies forever. Big hello to my family who have always helped me. Thanks to all.; [a.] Bristol, Avon, UK

RIGBY, PAMELA JOYCE
[pen.] Pam Rigby; [b.] 17 June 1944, Manchester; [p.] Mr. and Mrs. Harry Greenhalgh; [m.] Ronald Rigby, 16 November 1983; [ch.] Three grown up sons; [ed.] Secondary School in Moston, Manchester; [occ.] Housewife; [memb.] I am very proud to be a committee member of our local guide dogs for the blind, and help at all the chasity events; [pers.] Since living in Thomas Hardy country I have been immensely interested in the background of this genius.

RIVETT, BETTY E.
[b.] 28 February 1908, Aldershot; [p.] Deceased; [m.] Deceased, 1 September 1934; [ch.] Two; [ed.] Five to Fourteen State School, 14 to 20 Training as an Army, School Mistress, twenty to 22 Diocesans Training Teacher College Salisbury; [occ.] Retired after Teaching in Army School Overseas then in rate schools until I was 70; [memb.] Queens Army School Mistress Association, Officer, Widow Associator; [oth. writ.] I am at present starting to write a book about my life as an army school Mistress, I was ask to write an after dinner speech in a friend attending our reunion of ex. Army School Pupils. This was the outcome of this speech.; [pers.] I should pay the 20 to have my poems published in your board of poems, as offered because I feel it may be comfort to your many readers, who have suffered a deep loss.; [a.] Nr. Ilchester, Kingston, Somerset, UK

RIXON, DANIEL
[pen.] Mr. Sunshine; [b.] 1 July 1975, Doncaster; [p.] Jonathan Rixon and Lynda Rixon; [ed.] Currently completing A Levels at Wem Adams College, Shropshire, hoping to go on to Liverpool John Moores University to study creative writing and journalism; [oth. writ.] Currently unpublished, but working on a book of short stories.; [pers.] Many people ask how I manage to remain 'loud back', it is due to four rules that I always keep in the back of my mind: Life happens, people is people, different eyes see different things and too much thinking always makes you depressed!; [a.] Shawbury, Shropshire, UK

ROBB, STUART
[b.] 18 August 1974, Alton, Hampshire; [p.] Mr. David Robb, Mrs. Margaret Robb; [ed.] The Grange School - Aylesbury, Aylesbury College; [hon.] B.T.E.C. National Diploma in Business and Finance; [oth. writ.] I've written several poems and song lyrics, none of which have been published as yet.; [pers.] To express my feelings and emotions through my writing for the pleasure of others. And "belief in oneself often holds the biggest key to success."; [a.] Aylesbury, Bucks, UK

ROBERTS, CATHERINE JULIE
[pen.] C. J. Roberts; [b.] 3 April 1963, Neath; [p.] Ronald Davies, Anita Davies; [ch.] Barry Francis, Natalie Louise; [ed.] Ysgol Gygun Ystalyfera, Neath Technical College; [occ.] Sales Telephonist; [hon.] City and Guilds Baker and Confectionist (Hons); [oth. writ.] Several other poems, mainly about wales and centic traditions.; [pers.] I am influenced by traditional romanticism, modern sexuality and spiritual senses in my writing; [a.] Swansea, W. Glam, UK

ROBERTS, ELAINE
[pen.] E. Roberts; [b.] 4 March 1958, Hemsworth; [p.] Michael and Muriel Jordan; [m.] John David Roberts, 25 November 1978; [ch.] 2 Boys 16, 18; [ed.] St. Wilfrid's RC High; [occ.] Housewife; [oth. writ.] Just write for leisure time; [pers.] Poetry was introduced to me by Mr. Harrison Junior School teacher, who very much encourage us in the arts.; [a.] South Elmsall, N. Yorks, UK

ROBERTS, FIONA
[pen.] Fiona Roberts; [b.] 12 October 1972, Bridgend; [p.] Mrs. Sylvia Roberts; [ed.] Lisnaskea High School Fermanagh College; [occ.] Senior - Care Assistant; [memb.] Drama Club at secondary school and an amateur comedy troop; [oth. writ.] A few poems published in school magazine.; [pers.] I strive to represent the purity and sickness of the human condition. My influences come from my mother who encouraged me to write and develop myself.; [a.] Birmingham, Warwickshire, UK

ROBERTS, JOYCE
[b.] 24 September 1935, Homa Point; [p.] Marguerite and Francis Kenya Verladue; [m.] John Roberts (Deceased), 21 July 1956; [ch.] Mandy Jane aged 26; [ed.] Kenya Preliminary Exam, Cambridge Overseas School certificate 1st Class; [occ.] Retired Secretary; [pers.] My first attempt at poetry. A few events and experiences have inspired me to capture them in verse.; [a.] Dinas Powys, S. Glamorgan, UK

ROBERTS, WILLIAM I. CLEATON
[pen.] William I. Cleaton Roberts; [b.] 30 January 1944, Stratford, London; [p.] Francis and May Louise Roberts; [m.] Margaret Alison Roberts, 10 September 1977; [ch.] Andrew and Sarah Roberts; [ed.] Chingfoul County Secondary School. Royal Society of Arts, (Technical Drowing).; [occ.] Writer/Painter and Driver.; [memb.] Mensa (Test score 133); [oth. writ.] Three unpublished short stories and many unpublished poems. Also two journals of Sea Travel unpublished (subject 14th century).; [pers.] I am something of a dreamer, but always strive to complete a task and follow my intuition when it comes to judging others.; [a.] Bristol, UK

ROBERTSON, IAN FORBES
[pen.] Robbie Robertson; [b.] 18 October 1952, Falkirk; [p.] James (Deceased), and Margaret; [m.] Ann Robertson, 29 April 1977; [ch.] Robbie, Angela and April-Ann; [ed.] Falkirk High School; [occ.] Singer/Songwriter; [memb.] Cabaret Band; [oth. writ.] Many songs for previous bands of which I was part; [pers.] We are all on earth to pass time. But it is better to be constructive or artistic than still or silent.; [a.] Falkirk, Stirlingshire, UK

ROBINSON, DREW
[b.] 17 January 1953, Dungannon; [p.] Johnston, Robinson, Martha Robinson; [m.] Anne Robinson, 5 April 1977; [ch.] Andrew, Edward, Thomas, John and Adam; [ed.] Royal School Dungannon, Loughry Agricultural College; [occ.] Farmer; [memb.] I hold office in several local religious and cultural organizations; [oth. writ.] Several poems published in various anthologies by arrival press and triumph house; [pers.] I like to write about my own personal experiences in life and to express my views in poems that contain rhythm and rhyme.; [a.] Dungannon, Tyrone, UK

ROBINSON, MRS. JILL
[pen.] Mrs Jill Robinson; [b.] 9 June 1937, Leeds; [m.] Mr Laurie Robinson, 6 September 1958; [occ.] Sales Administrator; [hon.] M.B.E.; [oth. writ.] Hundreds of poems mostly or other people or special occasions wrote also a Biblical alphabet in Rhyme; [pers.] I run an amateur show group for charity entertaining the less fortunate and earning money for charity. I used to be a John Tiller Girl you get out of life what you put in; [a.] Leeds, Yorkshire, UK

ROBINSON, KAY LOUISE
[pen.] Kitty Fisher (Children's Books only); [b.] 1 January 1971, Bolton; [p.] Mary Robinson; [ed.] Heathfield County Primary School Deane Comprehensive School, South Bolton 6th Form College - Bolton Institute of Higher Education.; [occ.] Private Tutor; [memb.] Voluntary work - Leukaemia (Christies Hospital - Manchester), Leukaemia Care (Organization), ALU (Organization) And Leukaemia Sufferers.; [hon.] BA (Hons) Degree, (Literature); [oth. writ.] Other poetry - Various 2 collections of poetry Harbour of Dreams, Ocean Paintings. Short Stories 'Till The End Of Time' (Semi-autobiographical - which one-day I would love to become a novel) and 'Life From A Window', Children's Reading.; [pers.] If my writing help someone to get through one of the "dark periods" in life - then it has been worthwhile. Some poems are auto - or semi-autobiographical but it isn't just that. Some cartoon my own emotions and feelings but it isn't just me lying to write my own life story. It's more me trying to capture an another thai I have felt and then pass on to someone else. That can limit the poem through. I mine me reader stood by and find their own thing in here. People should get what they want for it. We read to know we're not alone!; [a.] Bolton, Lancs, UK

ROBINSON, KEVIN
[pen.] Robin Sherwood; [b.] 20 November 1964, Hexham; [pers.] Life is a game that must be played.; [a.] Newcastle upon Tyne, Tyne and Wear, UK

ROBINSON, MICHAEL
[b.] 13 August 1958, Nottingham; [p.] Leonard Robinson, Edith Robinson; [ed.] William Lilly Infants School, Fairfield Primary School, Bramcote Hills Secondary School, South East Derbyshire of Further Education, Derby College; [occ.] Local Government, Attendant to the Lord Mayor of Nottingham.; [oth. writ.] Composing music and writing lyrics.; [pers.] The poems I produce are part of my own thoughts, and reflect my own personal beliefs about each given subject. With a element of a great imagination. But I feel as though there is a spiritual side to my writing, as if there is an hidden force guiding me to put pen to paper. Maybe it's just my imagination, sometimes I even surprise myself with my work; [a.] Stapleford, Nottingham, UK

ROBSON, SALLY L.
[pen.] Lucy Jordan-Meadows; [b.] Tetbury, Glos.; [p.] George Edward John/Alice Florence Jordan; [m.] Ray Robson, 22 May 1986; [memb.] (Farnborough and Cove) British Red Cross Society; [pers.] From a family of ten, (6 sisters, 1 brother) I appreciate the detail of life. Glorious childhood memories of daily country life living on a farm and the beauty it holds, which inspired me to write. I dedicate my poem to my Dad and sister Vanessa, (both departed) With Love.; [a.] Yateley, Hampshire, UK

ROESTENBURG, JESSICA
[pen.] Jay R.; [b.] 24 June 1925, Douglas, I.O.M.; [p.] Sarah, George Newsome; [m.] Anthony A. Roestenburg, 6 October 1945; [ch.] 4 boys, 1 girl, 8 grandchildren, 6 great grandchildren; [ed.] Hanover Street School Douglas Isle of Man; [occ.] Retired; [oth. writ.] Several poems and a book entitled "On A Clear Day; [pers.] I strive to improve my mind because indeed this is a virtue. Nature is as such - it compels us all to move through life. Not to remain stationary; [a.] Stafford, Staffs, UK

ROFFEY, KENNETH B.
[b.] 29 October 1942, Lee, London; [p.] Joseph Roffey and Theresa Roffey; [m.] I am now a widower; [ch.] Lee, Darren, Lisa, Emma; [ed.] Mixed Secondary School in Eltham SE9; [occ.]

London Bus Driver; [oth. writ.] I wrote a local news paper for an estate in new cross, London for about two years as a member of their tennants committee; [pers.] I lie to write as a from of passtime, infact my maine hobbies are writing words to music while I play key boards the poem that I entered was written for my daughter after the death of my wife.; [a.] Bellingham, London, UK

ROGERS, BETTE
[pen.] Beth Rogers; [b.] Yorkshire, England; [ed.] England/Australia (Citizen); [occ.] Retired (Writer); [memb.] Health Club, Cyprus I have been a member of the guide dogs for the blind and numerous dog show Club. These memberships have now capsed.; [hon.] Credit Pass Communication Skills (Australia); [oth. writ.] My first book is to be published October in U.S.A. I have written a series of 6 children stories. "Winibella the Winsome Wild is the first book being published.; [pers.] I retired to Cyprus to follow my love of writing children stories after the tragic death of my husband and three get over is living the environment and helping each other.; [a.] Limassol, Cyprus

ROGERS, JUDITH
[b.] 16 February 1943, Letchworth; [p.] Margaret and Nigel Seaward; [m.] John Brian Rogers, 30 June 1962; [ch.] David, Stephen, Belinda, Susan; [ed.] Norton Secondary Modern, Mullarkey's Secretarial College; [occ.] In Partnership with Husband and Eldest Son running a family Business; [memb.] Member of World Cancer Research Fund, Member of National Geographic Society, Past Secretary of Local Young Wives; [a.] Letchworth, Herts, UK

ROGERS, NICOLA
[b.] 26 January 1963, Wem, Shropshire; [p.] Arthur and Margaret Price; [m.] Stanley Rogers, 19 August 1989; [ch.] Marc Anthony John; [ed.] Sir John Talbots Grammar Witchurch, Shropshire, University of Kent. At Canterbury; [occ.] Publican - The Stanton Arms, Stanton, Shropshire; [hon.] B. A. (Hons.) History - Philosophy; [pers.] This poem was written for my son. It's content reflects my thinking that children certainly are the future.; [a.] Shawbury, Shropshire, UK

ROGERS, ROSEMARY
[b.] 2 January 1963, Strood, Kent; [p.] Len King, Betty King; [m.] Malcolm Rogers, 27 June 1987; [ed.] Blackfen Secondary; [occ.] Medical Administrator; [pers.] Life is so precious, complicated and dramatic, this is where I draw my inspiration from - life is just an open book waiting to be read, I hope my reflections make it clearer; [a.] Eltham, London, UK

ROLLE, MS. VEDA CHARMAINE
[b.] 7 December 1969, Nassau, Bah; [p.] Beryl Rolle; [ed.] A Bachelors degree in Communications, with a minor in Business Administration, from Auburn University at Montgomery, Montgomery, Alabama; [occ.] Banker, with Ansbacher (Bahamas) Limited; [memb.] A volunteer at the Christian Counselling Centre, member of the writers Society, member of Voices From My Backyard; [hon.] Won 2nd place in the Independence Poetry Competition 1996 (Nassau, Bahamas); [oth. writ.] Planned and organized several poetry readings and reads publicly upon request. Her book of poems, she hopes, will hit the Bahamian market no later than December 1996.; [pers.] Success is a bed that all can lay in, but bona fide success is ordained by God. A pen is the instrument of subtle revolution. [a.] Nassau, Bahamas

ROMANO, CATHERYN SPRING
[pen.] Cathy; [b.] 4 July 1956, Weymouth, Dorset; [p.] Sheila Laurence, John Spring; [m.] Carlo Aldo Romano, 15 October 1989; [ch.] Federico (5 1/2 yrs) Filippo (2 1/2 yrs); [ed.] Secondary Modern School Hotel and Catering School, Courses: Academy of Travel, Management (British Airways), Word Processing, Italian, French; [occ.] Busy mother of 2 small children; [oth. writ.] Essays for previous exams and other poems, have never thought of having been published!; [pers.] I adore nature and the countryside, those passions together with having travelled extensively, have gained lasting memories of countries and their populations - giving me, a lost of inspirations for my poems; [a.] Weymouth, Dorset, UK

ROOK, JOHN ANTHONY JAMES
[b.] 6 December 1943, London; [p.] Dr. Arthur Rook and Jane Rook; [m.] Sarah Rook nee Thicknesse, 14 April 1966; [ch.] William Rook, Edward Rook and James Rook; [ed.] The Leys School, Cambridge, Seale Hayne College; [occ.] Farming, writing, and frill-girdling; [memb.] British Institute of Management Chairman of the Lithium Club; [hon.] National Award from the R.S.P.C.A. for my writing concerning the welfare of animals; [oth. writ.] One novel "Grasping at Straw" published 1992 several poems published in local newspapers, articles in woman's own and farmers weekly; [pers.] "To be free in this world in a dream - so dream." There few lines engaged the mind of a young dancer. She smiled.; [a.] Birdbrook, Essex, UK

ROSAS, VERITY
[pen.] Melissa Gorton; [b.] Overton, Hampshire; [p.] Hugh and Rosemary Haydock-Wilson; [m.] Felix Rosas-Perez; [ch.] Carlos Miguel and Felicia; [ed.] Hamilton House School, Harrow College of F.E. (Ceramics) (DU) B.A. degree course in Art and technology.; [occ.] Artist - potter; [memb.] Lewis Carroll Society Northampton Contemporary Arts Society; [hon.] (1st Prize) Brooke Bond Tea Short Story Comp (9 yrs.) National; [oth. writ.] Poem published in Canterbury College of Art Magazine.; [pers.] Influenced by Shakespeare, Milton, Cahucer and the Victorian poets.; [a.] Northampton, UK

ROSCOE, MARGARET
[pen.] Margaret Roscoe; [b.] 15 December 1945, Birkenhead; [p.] William R. Wilson and Norah K. Wilson; [m.] Divorced; [ch.] Beverly, Carol Ine, Tracy; [ed.] Conway Secondary School; [occ.] Council worker; [oth. writ.] I have not had anything published until now. I have other poems and lyrics for 2 songs plus a short story and verses for greeting cards in a folder but have not done anything with them yet.; [pers.] I am a very romantic person so I like writing verses that have some sort of meaning, and that are true to life and people. I hope my poem helps many people to realise that life is too short to waste and to always strive for each target with inner strength and courage.; [a.] Leasowe, Merseyside, UK

ROSE, FRASER
[b.] 7 June 1982, Greenock; [p.] Daniel Rose and Mary Rose; [ed.] Highholm Primary School, Port Glasgow Presently, Park Mains High School, Erskine; [oth. writ.] A poem published by anchor books, "Parents: Grand and great."; [pers.] Being a 13 years old. I try to make poetry acceptable to other teenagers. Poetry is words that should produce emotions to its readers of laughter or tears.; [a.] Port Glasgow, Renfrewshire, UK

ROSEWALL, MARGARETTA
[pen.] Margaret; [b.] 14 November 1937, Penzance, Cornwall; [ed.] Private Boarding School Exam, Result in music, piano, and singing; [pers.] I enjoy writing. My late uncle Alfred Wallis, was a primitive painter I have a Salvation Army background, am an ex-salvation, army, officer. I am a uniformed salvationist and songster, mile cross salvation army corps Norwich; [a.] Norwich, UK

ROSS, SIAN
[b.] 14 October 1976, Eastbourne; [p.] Angela Ross, Albert Ross; [ed.] Bishopbell Cofe School; [occ.] Post Office Counter Clerk; [oth. writ.] Several poems published in various anthologies for poetry now magazine; [pers.] I strive to transport the contents of my spirit in my writing.; [a.] Eastbourne, E. Sussex, UK

ROSSER, ANDY
[pen.] Timothy Piers; [b.] 29 December 1960, Bristol; [p.] Trevor and Stella Rosser; [m.] Lorraine Rosser, 5 September 1987; [ch.] Tiana and Ashara Rosser; [ed.] Kingsfield Grammar Brunel Tech College UWE University of the West of England; [occ.] I.T. Engineer; [memb.] Guild of Weighing machine engineers; [hon.] Radio and television city and guilds, credits distinctions; [oth. writ.] Include "A Call From Afar" and "Within A Turmoil Of Change". Leading to a possible poetry book; [pers.] Poetry is the heart and soul of man. It kindles thoughts and aspirations beyond the norm to boundaries of life not yet born.; [a.] Bristol, Avon, UK

ROUNDHILL, LILIAN
[b.] 15 January 1937, Newcastle-upon-Tyne; [m.] John Roundhill, 1 October 1983; [ch.] Glenn, Angela, Val, Martin and Simon; [ed.] Secondary Modern Upper Wortley Leeds; [occ.] Sales Consultant; [oth. writ.] I often write poems for my family and friends. It gives me great pleasure to be able to put into words what they mean to me.; [pers.] I write from the heart. I am very fond of children, I see beauty in their innocence, being able to write about Gods greatest gift to mankind makes me so happy.; [a.] Leeds, Yorks, UK

ROWE, MARK
[b.] 11 November 1966, Newcastle; [p.] Jennifer and Michael Rowe; [ed.] Stonehouse High School Glos.; [occ.] Royal Engineer Signals Corporal, Army Physical Training Instructor; [memb.] Professional Association of Dive Instructors (PADI), Royal Engineers Mounteering Exploration Club; [hon.] Gulf War Medal and Rosette Northern Ireland Medal (GSM), United Nations Peace Keeping Medal (Bosnia); [oth. writ.] The book "Closet Poets" (1 poem) writings submitted to military publications; [pers.] Being separated from those I love or adversity due to commitments during my military career lead to good writing material; [a.] Stroud, Glocestershire, UK

ROWLAND, ERNEST D.
[b.] 23 April 1917, Holt.; [p.] Samuel and Elizabeth Rowland; [m.] Gladys May, 22 May 1945; [ch.] Anne Elizabeth; [ed.] Holt. Endowed School; [occ.] Retired Baker; [pers.] Granddaughter Charlotte, aged 5 inspires me to make up short stories, poems etc., and her quite frequent "say it again granddad" brings to mind. that well know phrase "play it again Sam". Indeed her remarks are a music to my ears.; [a.] Holt, Clwyd, UK

ROWLEY, BARBARA
[pen.] Julie Evans; [b.] Bordon, Hampshire; [p.] Tom and Minnie Evans; [m.] Deceased 1978; [ch.] One son, three grandchildren; [ed.] St. Michael's Church School, Aldershot, Hampshire; [occ.] Retired; [hon.] A.V.C.M. and L.V.C.M. (Pianoforte); [oth. writ.] Some poems published also short stories - one received a runner up prize in a national competition.; [pers.] Have always had a great love of words - both poetry and prose. Also, of course, music.; [a.] Woking, Surrey, UK

ROWSE, AMANDA JAYNE
[pen.] Amanda J. Rowse; [b.] 15 July 1975, Sheffield; [p.] Daphne Rowse and Donald Rowse; [ed.] Sheffield High School for girls Thomas Rotherham sixth form College Rotherham College of Art and Technology, Sunderland University Helsinki Business Poly (Finland); [occ.] Student; [memb.] The Poetry Club (Mid-Glamorgan), Sunderland Rag Society; [pers.] I attempt to reflect my inner feelings and thoughts via my poetry.; [a.] Rotherham, South Yorkshire, UK

ROWSE, DON
[b.] Sleaford, Lincs; [p.] William and Lily Rowse; [m.] Daphne, [ch.] Amanda Jayne; [ed.] Sleaford Sec. Mos.; [occ.] Retired Police Officer; [memb.] National Association Of Retired Police Officers Nentworth Angling Club; [hon.] Military - General Service Medal (Cyprus) Police - Long Service and Good Conduct Medal; [pers.] Always interested in poetry waiting but more so since liver transplant in 1991. Can express feeling better in poetry.; [a.] Rotherham, South Yorks, UK

ROZE, JANE
[b.] 26 October 1956, Blackpool, England; [ch.] Five children; [ed.] Lived in Iran until the age of 7 when returned to England.; [memb.] Roman Catholic; [oth. writ.] First book in print by Janus publishers called "Poems of Paradox" consists of 54 poems - to be released June 1996.; [pers.] All glory to God for poetry magnifies the things which touch the heart and soul, it captures moments of delight and despair, wonder and torment, it arrests the soul in a dance of love with God its creator. It is timeless in its essence......; [a.] Margate, Kent, UK

RUSHTON, PAT
[b.] 5 September 1948, Yorkshire; [p.] Ron and Joyce Degenhard; [m.] Michael, 9 May 1970; [ch.] Paul and Rebecca; [ed.] Ickneild Secondary School Luton; [occ.] Academic Secretary; [memb.] Volunteer Editor and Fundraiser for the Ampthill and Flitwick talking newspaper for the visually impaired; [oth. writ.] Have a collection of poems I have been writing since school days; [pers.] Poems are usually written from the heart and from own experiences; [a.] Westoning, Bedfordshire, UK

RYAN, ANDREW
[pen.] Andrew Ryan; [b.] 25 November 1965, Plymouth; [p.] Ken Ryan, Jean Ryan; [m.] Jean Jess, 6 February 1965; [ed.] Plymstock School, Plymouth; [occ.] Cook, Chef; [oth. writ.] I've had a poem published, in a Southwest anthology; [pers.] Most of the poems I've written have an autobiography touch to them, although I have written about other people. And places I've been too.; [a.] Plymouth, Devon, UK

RYAN, JOSEPH BENJAMIN
[b.] 27 September 1923, London, SE; [p.] George J. Ryan and Emily A. Ryan; [m.] Jessie Margaret Ryan, 7 January 1972; [ch.] John Philip, Janet, Beverly Joanne; [ed.] Stanley Sen. School, London, S.E. Goldmith's College, London, S.E.; [occ.] Retired; [memb.] The Burma Star Association, The Ponam Association N.R. (E.A.A.) Hon. District secretary, St. John's Ambulance Association London, N.W. area (Now retired); [hon.] Member of the M.V.D of the Hospital of St. John of Jerusalem; [oth. writ.] 'War in our Time' included in arrival press anthology 'Why'; [pers.] Having circumnavigated the world by sea and by air, visiting many countries, I still consider the United Kingdom, with all it's faults and failures, to be the finest country in which to live. Regretfully, I have become cynical of all political parties and deplore the current low standard of the Educational and Judicial systems.; [a.] Northampton, Northants, UK

RYDER, M. I.
[pen.] M. I. George Ryder; [b.] 14 January 1914, Littledean; [p.] Kate, Mary and Sidney Bayliss; [m.] T. K. Ryder (18 yrs), late T. L. George (40 yrs), 1934-1978; [ch.] Two; [ed.] South Bargoed, South Wales - Glam; [occ.] Housewife; [memb.] Various Local Organization Voluntary Work - Luncheon and Social Clubs; [hon.] Long service W.R.V.S. medal; [oth. writ.] Several poems published. Spring Poets 1972 West Country Poets; [pers.] I just have to write if something moves me deeply.; [a.] Popes Hill, Glos, UK

SABNER, JEFFREY
[pen.] Joshua Leigh; [b.] 15 August 1926, London; [p.] Samuel Sabner, Mildred Sabner; [m.] Leah Dora Sabner, May 1951; [ed.] William Alleyn Grammar School, London; [occ.] Retired Ex-Civil Servant; [memb.] Leeds Bridge Club, Leeds Poetry Workshop; [oth. writ.] Short stories, novel and autobiography, coming to poetry later mainly through influence of William Blake; [pers.] Courses at Arvon, foundation have helped me greatly; [a.] Leeds, West Yorks, UK

SACRAMENTO, PHILLIP
[pen.] James Marting; [b.] 4 July 1983, Belfast; [ed.] Our Lady and Saint Patricks College Knock; [occ.] Student; [hon.] School Bravery Cup 3 year running, Talent Show Winner; [oth. writ.] The Dark Ghost; [pers.] I write for the sad, lonely, angry and sick people in the world so they know they have a friend.; [a.] Bangor, Down, UK

SADZMAYA, KHATJUNA
[pen.] Katrina; [b.] 27 November 1963, Tbilisi, Georgia; [p.] Isabella Elsishvili and Gregori Sadzmaya; [m.] John Jezmon; [ed.] Modern Languages Tbilisi Technology; [occ.] Training and Support; [memb.] Business College Reading; [oth. writ.] Other "X" poems; [pers.] I had a green carpet in the flat and a picture on the wall. It was the deep lake and the pluz behind it on the picture that inspired me. It reflects my mood. I sensed what would happen I love the deep cabinet in a human soul.; [a.] Reading, Berkshire, UK

SAINSBURY, DAVID A.
[b.] 14 February 1957, Potterne Nr Devizes, Wiltshire; [p.] Don Sainsbury, Doreen Sainsbury; [m.] Patricia A. Sainsbury, 17 July 1976; [ch.] Abigail, Laura, Bethany; [ed.] Devizes Grammar, Devizes School; [occ.] Maint. Technician (Electrical); [memb.] Westbury (Wilts) Blue Circle Bowls Club, Devizes C.A.F. (Charity); [oth. writ.] Several poems relating to people I know and general environments I have lived in.; [pers.] I prefer to write humorous poems from the heart, of people, subjects I know well.; [a.] Frome, Somerset, UK

SALEEM, MEEKEL IBRAHIIM
[pen.] Meekel; [b.] 12 July 1958, East Dulwich, London; [p.] David Nicholson, Elma Jones; [m.] Magdelene Roberts, we are together for nine years; [ch.] Tamara, Jameel, Hamiyd, Layla, Saalima, Damiyr; [ed.] Primary School, Jamaica, WI Self-Thought, British Army Education, Thomas Calton Community Education Centre; [occ.] Unemployed; [memb.] Nubian Nation Freedom Federation, Pan African Congress Movement, Local Community Group; [hon.] Counselling, Hygiene Pest and R.P.C. Pegasus Award Mosqutto Control; [oth. writ.] Several poems published in local news letter and the alarm magazine. Several of my poems are hanging on people of different races and colour walls, drama and music.; [pers.] I strive to understand the difference in this world. John F. Kennedy, once said, victory has a hundred father and defeat is an orphan. I have been greatly influenced by the difference in this wonderful world.; [a.] Peckham, London, UK

SAMPSON, ALEXANDER KELLOCK
[b.] 1 November 1923, Cowdenheath; [p.] John Clayton Sampson, Elizabeth Kellock Sampson; [m.] Mary Grieve Wilson, 18 July 1953; [ch.] John Alexander, Elizabeth June; [ed.] Ballingry Public School: Salvation Army International Training College for Officers; [occ.] Retired from a) Electrical fitter, b) Salvation Army Officer, c) Civil servant; [memb.] Salvation Army Office Bearer, musician, and Press Officer for Dunfermline and district S.A. branch. (Still very active in my retirement).; [hon.] Diplomas - creative writing - Dunfermline and District Arts Council; [oth. writ.] 9 poems published in various anthologies (hardback): 3 poems published in creative writing anthologies (Annual magazine Dunfermline and District Arts Festival. One poem published in anthology of verse: Poetry Institute of the British Isles called 'Island Moods and Reflections': Pictorial Press. Local newspapers: And anthology of poetry called 'The Poems of Fife; [pers.] "I enjoy making poetry, especially when family and friends ask for special occasions to be recorded and aired in verse."; [a.] Rosyth, Fife, UK

SAMUEL, MISS JULIE E.
[b.] 9 March 1963, Gloucestershire; [p.] David Samuel (Deceased), Jane Samuel; [ed.] Newent Comprehensive School, Guildford College of Further and Higher Education; [occ.] Warden in Sheltered Housing; [memb.] Pirbright Players Amateur Dramatics; [oth. writ.] I have written several poems but nothing has ever been published, so this is an honour.; [pers.] I thank my dad and mum for their encouragement and support. Especially mum for the last ten years this poem is dedicated to her.; [a.] Stanford, Pirbright, Surrey, UK

SANDERS, MARIE
[b.] Tiverton, Devon; [ed.] Univ. of Bristol, B.A. Hons. (English); [occ.] Retired Teacher; [oth. writ.] "The Stranger" one act play (Pub. Morleys.) Many poems in magazines. Some articles.; [a.] Sixpenny Handley, Dorset, UK

SANDERS, MRS. SYLVIA
[b.] 3 November 1947, Carmarthen; [p.] Muriel and Trevor Jones; [m.] George Sanders, 27 April 1973; [ch.] Angela, Dean, Wendy, Cherylle, Michelle, Candy, Cindy; [ed.] Secondary Modern Carmarthen; [occ.] Housewife and well known Persian cat breeder; [hon.] I have won Silver and Bronze Award in breeding programmes in the great cats of Great Britain competition under my

Prefix Chermicican; [oth. writ.] 'The Cat And The Car' printed in an anthology of cats. Publishers arrival press.; [pers.] I would like people to think how a life can be changed in one single moment of madness; [a.] Swansea, Glamorgan, UK

SANDFORD, SANDRA
[b.] London; [m.] Divorced happily, 1 February 1965; [ch.] Three; [ed.] University of Sussex and Northwestern University Evanston, Illinois U.S.A., B.A. (Hons) and M.A. American; [occ.] (Undecided) studies working with deal students training for Educational Support Worker; [hon.] B.A (Hons) American Studies: (1989) social studies, M.A. Anglo- American (1991) Studies; [oth.writ.] Numerous poems dreams-made into short stories.; [pers.] My writings are influenced by recent personal tragedies I'm influenced by Sylvia Plath and Stevie Smith. "Drawing not waving"; [a.] Bristol, Somerset, UK

SAUNDERS, BARRY
[b.] 21 September 1976, Greenwich; [p.] Barry Saunders and Vikki Saunders; [ed.] Woolwich Polytechnic; [occ.] Unemployed; [pers.] I suffered for many years from an irrational hatred of myself. I finally found the cure, in the understanding of my deepest thoughts. I just hope that others can find their way through the darkness. Depression is a lonely place.; [a.] Abbeywood, London, UK

SAUNDERS, LEONARD
[b.] 17 August 1917, London; [p.] Deceased; [m.] 9 November 1946; [ed.] Post War - GCE in German French, Italian, Spanish and English; [occ.] Retired; [memb.] Member of Corby Male Voice Choir, Former Founder Member - Corby Writers Circle and Kettering Poetry Group; [hon.] Three Certificates of Merit - Scottish Open Poetry Comp. Gold Medal and Bar - Old Time Dancing: Euterpe Plaque - Eastbourne Music and Poetry Comp.; [oth. writ.] Excalibur Press London "All in a Lifetime" an autobiographical novel - 1992 short stories, articles and around 500 poems; [pers.] I changed direction about a year ago. I am a second tenor in the Corby Male Voice Choir and have appeared in VE Day celebrations in Hyde Park May 6, 1995 and Peterborough Cathedral with other choirs.; [a.] Corby, Northants, UK

SAURINO, EMMA CATHERINE
[pen.] Emma Kilduff; [b.] 23 May 1967, Cumbria; [p.] Alban (Deceased) and Maureen Kilduff, Stepfather - Edward Hillman; [m.] Vincenzo Saurino, 19 July 1989; [ch.] Francesca Bell Saurino; [ed.] St. Bernards R.C. Secondary School. Darlington College of Technology.; [occ.] Restaurant owner and mother; [oth. writ.] Poems and short stories, non published.; [pers.] I write as a release from the stress of everyday life. And I believe that everyone has in them a gift/ambition, which they should try to fulfil. But ultimately to be loved and to love is the end.; [a.] Darlington, Durham, UK

SAVAGE, JAMES CARL
[b.] 29 December 1932, Belfast; [p.] James Carl, Harriett Virginia; [m.] Kathleen Anne, 11 October 1965; [ch.] James Carl, Kerry Anne; [ed.] (Both Queens University), (Children's Education above) self: Seaview Primary School Belfast Tech. College; [occ.] Retired through Ill Health; [pers.] Favorite poems by Rudyard, Kipling; [a.] Green Island, Antrim, UK

SAVAN, ANNE
[b.] 30 May 1951, Pontypridd; [m.] Dr. Peter Savan, 6 April 1974; [ch.] Jamie, Emily, Jonathan, Rachael; [ed.] Pontypridd Girls Grammar School, University of Reading; [occ.] Science Teacher, Aberdare Boys School; [hon.] Physiology and Biochemistry; [oth. writ.] Several poems published in magazines and anthologies author of "Michael Meets Mozart" a study of music therapy with special needs children.; [pers.] My poetry reflects my feelings about personal experiences.; [a.] Hirwaun, S. Wales, UK

SAWDON, MARGARET
[b.] 4 August 1929, Burnley; [p.] Frank Marshall Thompson, Eveline Capstick; [m.] Frederick Clifford Sawdon, 18th June 1955 - Divorced January 1980; [ch.] Clifford Paul Sawdon, Karen Lesley Dacey; [ed.] Burnley Girls High School, Further Education in H.M. Forces ie. WAAF - WRAF, to school cert. standard. English - Eng Lit.; [occ.] Retired; [oth. writ.] Children's story, short stories and poems. Not yet offered for publication.; [pers.] I try to observe life in all it's facets, the forces and beauty of nature, plus humanity, or lack of , in my poems. I have been influenced by travel, meeting different nationalities and living amongst them, and also my own life experiences and beliefs.; [a.] Burnley, Lancashire, UK

SCARISBRICK, JOAN
[b.] 4 November 1928, Wrexham; [p.] Herbert and Ethel Tipton; [m.] 1st Marriage Allan Hughes, 15 August 1953, 2nd marriage Bernard Scarisbrick, 8 April 1982; [ch.] Of 1st marriage Anthony, Diane, grandchildren Katy, Emily, Kathryn, Edward, William; [ed.] Priory Girls Grammar Shrewsbury; [occ.] Retired Shropshire County Council 35 yrs. Generic/Psychiatric Social Worker; [memb.] WRVS; [oth. writ.] Several poems published in various anthologies; [pers.] First started to write poetry after retiring. I wanted my poems to express the emotions, joys and fears, experienced in later life.; [a.] Shrewsbury, Shrops, UK

SCOFIELD, BEATRICE MAY JENNINGS
[b.] 1 May 1907, Elmstead, Essex; [p.] Alfred and Jane Jennings; [m.] Henry Edward Scofield, 12 December 1931; [ch.] 1 son; [ed.] Myself C.E. Elmstead, Essex, son S.M. Brightlingsea, Essex. Did 5 years voluntary R.A.F. service, 2 1/2 years far east.; [occ.] Enjoy crochet, cross-stitch, water colour painting; [memb.] Was a founder member "Darby and Joan Club in November in 1956. A member of W.I. since 1956. A member of M.U. since 1955. This was in Alresford, No. Colchester.; [hon.] In 1966 won "The Blue Ribbon and medal in a local flower show. Best entry in show. I was also a W.R.V.S. member when it was first formed and have a long service medal.; [oth. writ.] Have written several, never had one published; [a.] Attleborough, Norfolk, UK

SCOTT, CHRIS
[b.] 1967, Belfast; [p.] James and Nancy; [m.] Gwen, 1990 - St. Lucia; [ch.] Kristin; [ed.] Wallace High School, Lisburn; [oth. writ.] Numerous poems published in anthologies and local newspapers; [pers.] I feel that poetry is a way of leaving something behind in this world for those who follow on.; [a.] Dundonald, Belfast, UK

SCOTT, FRANK
[b.] 18 April 1938, Bushmills; [p.] William Scott, Margaret Scott; [m.] Sadie Scott, 29 October 1959; [ch.] Gordon Scott; [occ.] Electrician; [memb.] Bushmills Folk Lore and History Group National Inspection Council for Electrical Contracting; [oth. writ.] Several poems published in various anthologies; [pers.] I wrote this poem to express my feelings of hope for the future and a deep longing for peace in Northern Ireland.; [a.] Bushmills, Antrim, UK

SCOTT, FRED
[b.] 26 April 1908, Fatfield; [p.] John James Scott and Margeret; [m.] Jane Scott; [ch.] Six; [ed.] Ordinary School; [occ.] Retired Miner; [memb.] Manchester Unity of Odd Fellows; [hon.] A letter of Congratulations from the Leader of the Mines rescue Station for my assistance to the Brigade during the Explosions in the Mines; [oth. writ.] Various poems with Anchors Aweigh Publishers.; [pers.] All that has been sent to you is the truth of my own work and dictation.; [a.] Newcastle upon Tyne, Northumberland, UK

SCOTT, JUDITH
[pen.] Judith Scott; [b.] 18 June 1965, Craigtoun, Saint Andrews; [p.] James Paton, Dorothy Paton; [m.] Alan Scott, 25 October 1985; [ch.] Kerri-Louise Scott, Gary Scott; [ed.] Grangemouth High School; [occ.] Housewife; [oth. writ.] Poems published in anthologies by arrival press; [pers.] To bring joy to the hearts of all who read my poems; [a.] Grangemouth, Stirlingshire, UK

SCOTT, SUSAN
[pen.] Soosan; [b.] 3 January 1971, Perth; [p.] Grace Scott and Robert Niven; [ed.] Glenwood High School, Glenrothes, Fife College of Technology, Aberdeen University; [occ.] Student at Aberdeen; [memb.] Young Scot, Perth Theatre; [hon.] Studying for MA English (Honours); [oth. writ.] Several Poems in young scot magazine, Article for 'Me' magazine article for Perth Theatre subscribers magazine article for young scot magazine; [a.] Bridge of Earn Perth, Tayside, UK

SEDDON, ANNE
[pen.] Le-Britton; [b.] 17 November 1939, Newcastle; [ch.] Paul, Steve and Mark; [pers.] This poem was written with a mixture of love and sadness following the death of my oldest son Paul who died in 1985 aged 25 years.; [a.] Newcastle, Tyne and Wear, UK

SEIGA, HELEN JOAN
[b.] 10 August 1983, Liverpool; [p.] Margaret and Joe; [ed.] Attends King David High School in Liverpool; [memb.] Enjoys reading, writing poetry, horse riding and looking after her numerous pets.

SELLEN, MARY BRIDGET
[b.] 15 May 1947, Eire; [m.] Reginald Sellen, 3 April 1965; [ch.] Shirley Elisabeth, Christopher Robert Edward Mark; [occ.] Martial Arts Instructor Writer; [oth. writ.] Several poems published in anthologies and martial arts magazine's; [a.] London, England

SEMMENS, GWYNIRIS
[b.] 11 January 1922, South Wales; [p.] William Lugg, Margaret Lugg; [m.] Stanley Semmens, 31 March 1956; [ch.] June, Linda, Stephen; [ed.] Bronllwyn, Ton Pentre; [occ.] Housewife; [memb.] Pendeen over fifty club; [hon.] Several awards from Cornish Gorsedd for Cornish Dialect verse. Poem published in Minach Theatre News Letter. Poems one a month published in local magazine short stories published locally. Plays enacted at local Chapel.; [oth. writ.] Children's stories.; [pers.] I aim to communicate with my fellow man, hopefully spreading beauty, joy and comfort that will maybe help when one has a Heavy load to carry.; [a.] Trewellard, Cornwall, UK

SETON, JEAN
[pen.] Notes; [b.] 15 October 1928, Scarborough; [p.] Harry Sellers and Beatrice Sellers; [m.] Herbert Seton, 13 September 1947; [ch.] David N. Seton and Kit Seton; [ed.] Central School (Elem) Scarborough, left School at 14 years of age during 1939-1945 war.; [occ.] Housewife; [memb.] Flower arranging club over the years I have done many crafts and still do.; [oth. writ.] Just for my own pleasure and people around me. I rhyme words to tunes for concerts we have where I live.; [pers.] I am interested in people of all ages and like to put my thoughts about them on paper.; [a.] York, Yorkshire, UK

SEWOKE, SAMMY VISHNU
[pen.] Lion Son; [b.] 27 December 1971, London; [p.] Anirood Sewoke, Jeeanwantee Sewoke; [ed.] Grinling Gibbons Primary School, Deptford Green Comprehensive School, Lewisham College, Goldsmoth's College (University of London); [occ.] Gardener; [memb.] Dennis The Menace Fan Club; [hon.] BSc Math's Studies; [oth. writ.] School magazine, letters in mask and transformers comics; [pers.] Always feed the birds in your garden; [a.] London, Deptford, UK

SEXTON, TIMOTHY A. P.
[b.] 10 August 1960, McLaren Vale, South Australia; [p.] Thomas Sexton (Deceased), Helen Madge Sexton (nee King); [m.] Suzanne Sexton (nee Walker); [ch.] 13 October 1984; [ed.] Gabrielle Emily (b. 24 May 1993); [occ.] Morphett Vale High School, Elder Conservatorium, University of Adelaide, completed degrees, Bachelor of Music (B. Mus.) Honours (Hons.) Diploma of Education (Dip. Ed.); [memb.] Freelance Composer, Conductor, Singer and Writer, Astronomical Society of South Australia, Malacological Society of Sth. Aust., Australian Music Centre, Arts Industry Council, Australian National Choral Association; [hon.] Co-winner Inaugural Henry Krips Memorial Conducting Scholarship; [oth. writ.] Several full length articles for operatic programmes, many lyrics for songs (classical). Many speeches and presentations, National Musicological Journals (Australian Music Centre/Kodaly Society) feature articles; [pers.] Much of my poetry reflects the beauty and the harshness of the Australian landscape. My poetry is influenced by the writings of the early bush poets, of whom my grandfather was one.; [a.] Birdwood, South Australia

SEYMOUR, ANNE
[b.] 11 November 1942, Sheffield; [p.] Mr. H. Moore, Mr. L. Moore (Both Deceased); [m.] Mr. N. Seymour, 29 January 1994; [ch.] Mark, Jane, and Karen Bletcher (Father Deceased); [ed.] Comprehensive; [occ.] Retired Nurse, Rotherham and Sheffield Hospitals; [oth. writ.] A poem in a Nursing magazine 1961; [pers.] Writing poetry has helped me to overcome many trials and tribulations. There are so many wonderful aspects to life. Giving, caring, loving and appreciating.; [a.] Rotherham, S. Yorkshire, UK

SHADARE, EDWIN OLUDOTUN
[b.] September 23, 1971, London, England; [p.] J. O. Shadare, Y. E. Shadare; [ed.] Egba High School, Ogun State, Abeokuta Nigeria, College of Northeast London, Tottenham London, Queenmary and Westfield College, University of London, London, U.K.; [occ.] Student; [memb.] Q.M.W. Music Society, Science Fiction Society, I'm a member of the choir of a church based in London; [pers.] That Jesus Christ is Lord and Saviour of all the Son of God's love, and through him, all mankind can come to experience the loving kindness of our selfless God, becoming selfless like him, and being out of their own way, make God known to others, through love.; [a.] Hackney, London

SHAH-ALOM
[pen.] Shalom; [b.] 20 October 1972, Bangladesh; [p.] Mr. Raja Miah and Mrs. Sarada Begum; [ed.] Haslingden St. James, Junior School and Haslingden High School; [occ.] Waiter; [oth. writ.] Dreamers write their dreams poets their poems. I writer your name and new one is born." An extract from a book I have begun writing "semi-biography"; [pers.] Being in the catering "World" for all of my working life, I'm appropriate expression of mine. - "Sometimes when the curry is too salty, it's unwise my view to think of throwing it away (regarding life) one should realise that everything happens in life according to each individual abilities.; [a.] Haslingden, Lancashire, UK

SHAPCOTT, CHRISTINE ANN
[pen.] Catya; [b.] 20 October 1948, Bristol; [p.] Doreen and James Heyward; [m.] David John Shapcott, 3 August 1987; [occ.] Insurance Clerk; [oth. writ.] Poems published in new age magazines; [pers.] I am greatly influenced by Celtic mythology and religion, particularly the Brythonic (Welsh) tradition, I enjoy writing poetry about the natural world and the ancient British gods and goddesses.; [a.] Yate, S. Gloucestershire, UK

SHAPLAND, TRACEY JANE
[b.] 14 September 1970, Barnstaple; [p.] Alan Isaac and Janet Isaac; [m.] Tim Shapland, 20 May 1995; [ed.] Park School Barnstaple; [occ.] Travel Consultant; [oth. writ.] I have written other poems for pleasure but as yet have never submitted any for publication.; [pers.] Poetry has been my hobby for some years now. For me it has always been a way of expressing my emotions. Having my poem published an honour and has given me greater confidence in my ability.; [a.] Barnstaple, Devon, UK

SHARMA, ARUN
[pen.] Alf; [b.] 21 November 1973, Barking; [p.] Mr. A. K., Mrs. I. K. Verma; [ed.] Eastbury Comprehensive school Barking Essex Barking Abbey School Barking Essex; [occ.] Retail; [oth. writ.] Name of poem: The Beast Within Name Of Book, The Other Side Of The Mirror published by The International Society of Poets.; [pers.] To want is not to have but to earn is to gain.; [a.] Barking, Essex, UK

SHARP, PETER
[b.] 14 January 1949, Worcester; [p.] Peter Sharp, Marjorie W. Sharp; [m.] Jean Monica Sharp, 17 July 1969; [ch.] Simon Peter, Dean, Paul Marcus, Melanie Patricia; [ed.] Claines Primary, Droitwich Secondary Modern, University of Life; [pers.] To share my perception puzzlement influences. My granddaughter Harlech (town in N. Wales) Him Morrison.; [a.] Worcester, Worcestershire, UK

SHATLIFF, ROSEMARY
[pen.] Rosa Day; [b.] 8 December 1946, Annesley, Notts; [p.] Lloyd Best and Rita Best; [m.] Divorced; [ch.] Dale and Marie/grandchildren Natasha and Judy; [ed.] Annesley Primary, Mowlands Secondary Modern Clarendon College; [occ.] Self employed mobile hairdresser; [memb.] Keep Fit Clubs; [hon.] City and Guild Hairdressing, many exams for ballet, tap, acrobat, musical comedy, modern musical; [oth. writ.] I have published a book of poems myself called 'From The Heart With Soul' and had several poems in local magazine 'Musings From Mansfield'; [pers.] Poetry should be written from the heart and reflect the soul within. One day I would love to write a novel.; [a.] Nuncargate, Kirkby-in-Ashfield, Notts, UK

SHAUGHNESSY, KATHRYN SUSAN
[b.] 7 February 1956, Stoke-on-Trent; [p.] Harold and Winnie Lowndes; [m.] Divorced - Soul Mate: Derek Edward Maddox; [ch.] Tamla, Emma, Matthew and Lucy-Ann; [ed.] Birches High School, Stoke-on-Trent; [occ.] Career/Housewife, 17 yrs. caring for disabled son; [memb.] I am a member of The Deaf Children Society; [hon.] 5 G.C.S.E. including Maths and English My love of poetry was kindled by my English teacher Mrs. Jacson when I was a young child; [oth. writ.] I have lots of poems that I keep in a drawer. Many were written as a child. Only ever read by members of my family and close friends.; [pers.] I like to write from the heart and bloodshed and tears was reflection of the troubles in Bosnia and Ireland.; [a.] Stoke-on-Trent, Staffs, UK

SHAW
[b.] 9 February 1954, Leeds; [p.] James Rawstron Shaw Edna (Shaw Nee Batten); [m.] Judith, 1 August 1992; [ch.] Emily Alice and Rebecca Louise, Andrew Anthony, Darryl James; [ed.] All Saints Catholic Secondary Mod (Boys) Blackpool/Fylde College (A Levels Nights School) Currently - Part Time MA York University (Mature Student); [occ.] DSS - Benefits Agency (Operations Manager) Preston; [memb.] Institute of Management; [hon.] Brooke Gond National School Poetry Prize (1968); [oth. writ.] Have written a dozen or more poems but never confident enough to attempt to have any published before.; [pers.] I am ordinary and unique, as we all are one important thing I can do is feel. My poetry reflects my feelings - happy, sad, angry I hope that some of it reflects your feelings too.; [a.] Thornton Cleveleys, Lancs, UK

SHAW, MRS. BERYLE
[pen.] Nan Bee; [b.] 12 July 1918, Rochdale; [m.] Bick Courcey Shaw, 25 September 1939; [ch.] Barry Dennis de Courcey Shaw; [ed.] Rochdale Higher Grade Central School for Girls specialized in book keeping short hand type, Comm, English French and Drama. 1938 did Management course and Floristry; [occ.] Retired Office Manageress; [memb.] Labour Party, Brooklands Trades and Labour Club, Brooklands over go (I am Secretary and Organizer.), Greater Interfriendship Force, Altringham Club Theatre, Voluntary Work for Wythenshawe Police Manchester - involving Economic Development and Encouraging children in Art and Drama and assisting in Police Crucial Crew, [oth. writ] Various poems and topical verses and the odd short story for children. I have been oil painting for 18 yrs and my 6th exhibition will be in November at Wythenshawe Forum. M/C also Public Speaker.; [pers.] I enjoy the work I do and hope to carry on into my 80's. Life is what you make it! I have also campaigned for better facilities for the homeless in connection with an appeal by Manchester Cathedral, some years ago.; [a.] Brooklands, Whythenshawe, Gt. Manchester, UK

SHEEHAN, SABRINA
[pen.] Sabrina Sheehan; [b.] 12 September 1978, Dublin; [p.] Michael Sheehan, Riona Sheehan; [ed.] St. Brigids Primary School, St. Mary's Secondary School 1st - 3rd year Institute of Education 5th - 6th year; [occ.] Student; [oth. writ.] I have written many poems but this is the first I've entered in a competition in the hope of publication.; [pers.] I write my poems in an effort to reflect the worries of teenagers in this day and age. In most of my poems I find that I look back in the past as a treasure and feel more united in my thoughts of it.; [a.] Dublin, Ireland

SHEEN, JOHN JAMES
[b.] 10 July 1933, Birkenhead; [p.] John Sheen, Janet Sheen; [m.] Irene Bibby, 26 July 1958; [ch.] Joanne Elizabeth, John David, Andrew Robert; [ed.] Birkenhead College York University; [occ.] Lecturer: Science and Mathematics, Wirral Metropolitan College; [memb.] Institution of Electrical Engineers, Royal Institute of Public Health and Hygiene; [hon.] Mathematics, English Literature.; [oth. writ.] GCSE Chemistry (1986); [pers.] Greatly influenced by the 'symbolist' poems. My writing attempts to express continuity between the temporal and the spiritual.; [a.] Birkenhead, Merseyside, UK

SHELVOCK, FREDA
[pen.] Freda Shelvock; [b.] 29 May 1910, Aldershot; [p.] Frederick J. Bailey; [m.] Dora Muscat, 10 September 1931; [ch.] Five Daughters; [ed.] Normal; [occ.] Retired; [a.] Leicester, Leics, UK

SHEPHERD, MARSHA BABETTE
[pen.] 1 March 1967, Hartley; [ch.] Patrick Shepherd and Angelo Shepherd; [occ.] Housewife; [pers.] Life itself inspired me to write. I like to reflect my poetry from the inner depth of thought.; [a.] Cranbrook, Kent, UK

SHEPPARD, PERCY FRANCIS SAMUEL
[b.] 1 February 1924, Bristol; [p.] George A. Sheppard, Gladys E. Sheppard; [m.] Mary Isobel, 26 March 1954; [ch.] Jane Mary, Paula Helen; [ed.] The Grange Smith Gloucestershire Kingswood, Bristol; [occ.] Service Layer and Plumber; [memb.] AMORC, Rosicrucian Order; [oth. writ.] A poem published in Rosicrucian magazine; [pers.] I am a painter and have had several exhibitions in London and was one of the top three artists that was chosen from entries from all over England in 1962 (The World is Perfect, Man Must Change).; [a.] Bristol, South Gloucestershire, UK

SHERIFF, DOREEN JEAN
[b.] 27 September 1938, Tysley, Birmingham; [p.] Ivy May and Henry Eustace; [ed.] Yarnfield Road Infants Hartfield Crescent, Juniors Furmans Road Senior School Monitor and Perfect; [occ.] Housewife; [oth. writ.] Poems to be entered in the Church Magazine this coming summer; [pers.] All my poems are inspirational and cover many aspects from humanity to nature.; [a.] Birmingham, West Midlands, UK

SHERLOCK, CHRISTINE ANNE
[pen.] Christine Anne Sherlock; [b.] 14 December 1953, New Malden, Surrey; [p.] Hilda Sherlock, Alfred Sherlock; [ed.] Burlington Rd Secondary Modern School, Himbledon Technical College; [occ.] Carer and voluntary (former secretary and travel consultant) worker; [memb.] Malden Arts Association, R.S.P.C.A., Liberal Focus Team; [hon.] Bronze and Silver Duke of Edinburgh's Awards, I.S.T.D. Bronze Ballroom and Latin American Dance Awards; [oth. writ.] Poem published in local Poetry Anthology; [pers.] I am inspired by personal experiences and observations.; [a.] New Malden, Surrey, UK

SHORT, JOHN
[pen.] Johnathan; [b.] 26 November 1929, Newcastle upon Tyne; [p.] Deceased; [m.] Divorced, June 1956; [ch.] One girl; [ed.] Elementary, Began work at 14 war service 1939 - 1946 Infantry man in Burma Various jobs to 1950 Merchant Navy to 1975 from then porter in N/C unions Soc. University 1985; [occ.] Retired; [oth. writ.] I wrote many poems at sea for a pass time some came spontaneously many ware of a religious content I never thoughts of publishing them my way of life not giving much chance for enduring earth contacts.; [pers.] I have come to understand life as one who someone that our acquisitive senses deny making it difficult for any individualization to accept true position in the part to be so played regarding other member of the one boy life.; [a.] Gateshead Tyne and Wear, Durham, UK

SHORT-WINDSOR, JANET
[pen.] Janet Short-Windsor; [b.] 9 November 1933, Brighton, E. Sussex; [p.] Kathleen and Sydney Short; [m.] 19 July 1958; [ch.] Stephen Philip; [ed.] Wistons Private School, Brighton; [occ.] Retired Library/Tourists Information Officer; [memb.] Hailsham Choral Society, Sussex Singers, Sussex Opera and Ballet Society, Hastings Opera, Canford Summer School of Music Choir, Eastbourne Sinfonia Choir; [hon.] True Short Story on my Memories of Ve Day. Three Short Fictional Stories. All published. Won a Holiday for Ve Day Memories; [oth. writ.] Several other poems published elsewhere. Wrote Christmas Carol and Friend set it to music. Often sing it at our Christmas Concert. Wrote words and music to a Lullaby for my son when he was small.; [pers.] Still do a lot of singing. Love and enjoy all classical music, opera, ballet and writing. Was a dancer on points and ice skater when younger. Danced and skated in many shows. Our Choral Society went to France in 1995 and are going to Belgium July 1996. Was an Extra in Film of "Half a Sixpence."; [a.] Hailsham, E. Sussex, UK

SILK, DORIS
[b.] 14 April 1924, London; [m.] Derrick Robert Silk, 9 December 1969; [ch.] David and Leslie Abberline; [occ.] Housewife; [memb.] National Federation of Womans Institutes, Ramble and Swimming Clubs; [hon.] Drama, swimming and long standing Service for Voluntary Work.; [oth. writ.] Children's stories; [pers.] I am privileged to be able to give. My support and commitment to children in need of help and care.; [a.] Hythe, Kent, UK

SILLICK, MARIANNE
[b.] 18 April 1982, Truro; [p.] Teresa Barnes, David Sillick; [ed.] Comprehension Student at Penrice School; [pers.] I write poetry to express my inner feelings towards many different things such as the environment, animals and my family and friends.; [a.] Saint Austell, Cornwall, UK

SIMMONDS, J.
[b.] 30 August 1934, Egham, Surrey; [p.] Charlie and Elizabeth Simmonds; [m.] Teresa Simmonds, 13 August 1957; [ch.] Two; [ed.] Technical College; [occ.] Maintenance Fitter; [hon.] Loads with Dogs; [pers.] Remember Rambo was my own feelings on losing "My Pal" My Champion, "Old English Sheep dog."

SIMMONDS, WENDY ANN
[b.] 11 August 1953, Clapham, London; [p.] Henry James Eileen, Evelyn Blenko; [m.] Keith Phillip Simmonds, 30 March 1974; [ch.] Rebecca, Clare, Victoria, Jane; [ed.] Pathfields Comprehensive School, Clacton-on-Sea, Essex; [occ.] Own business joint enterprise with husband; [oth. writ.] I have written many other poems in quiet moments; [pers.] When I write poems it helps me to understand my feelings and other peoples. It also enables me to put my thoughts into words. And gives me a clearer picture.

SIMMONS, GERALDINE
[b.] 9 February 1951, Dartford, Kent; [p.] Arthur and Thelma Hayter; [m.] Ian Graham Simmons, 6 February 1971; [ch.] Rachel Louise, Peter Graham, Kelly Anne; [ed.] Dartford West Secondary School for Girls; [occ.] Sole Proprietor, Furnishing Business; [oth. writ.] Several poems for my children none of which have been published; [pers.] I write on impulse; [a.] Brackley, Northants, UK

SIMPSON, CHARLES
[b.] 11 February 1915, Slatey Herham, Northumberland; [p.] John and Winifred Simpson; [m.] Gillian Hill-Lowe, 27 June 1945; [ch.] Two Daughter Fionn and Taya; [ed.] Ondle and (Pembroke) Cambridge, MA Cambridge, FR Met S; [occ.] Retired RAF; [memb.] Royal Yacht Squadra, Boodles, Hawkes, Achiles; [hon.] C.B.E.; [pers.] Was Au Atache Sweden '46-'48, Commander RAF East Africa '58-'61 Commander Cambridge University, Au Squadon 48-50.; [a.] Gerrard Cron Slough, Bucks, UK

SIMPSON, JILL BEVERLY
[b.] 3 September 1969, Norwich; [p.] David Simpson, Sheila Simpson; [ed.] BSc Psychology with American studies, 4 A-levels, 9 O-levels; [occ.] Administrator; [oth. writ.] This is the third occasion a poem has been published in an anthology.; [pers.] There is no philosophical statement, it is purely what I feel or see around me.; [a.] London, UK

SIMPSON, LEONORA ALISON
[b.] 17 June 1914, Newlyn, Cornwall; [p.] Charles Simpson R. I. and Ruth Simpson; [ed.] Kensington Garden School, Norland Place School London, Holland Park Avenue; [occ.] Retired D.A.P. Voluntary worker at Renter Museum and at Gallery Penyance Cornwall.; [memb.] Member of the Old Cornwall Society Penyance, Friend and Penlee Museum and Art Gallery Penyance Cornwall; [oth. writ.] Several other poems nothing published; [a.] Penyance, Cornwall, UK

SIMPSON, MARJORIE RUTH
[b.] 28 October 1941, Lechlade, Glos; [p.] Leslie and Winifred Smith; [m.] Joffre Leonard Simpson, 29 August 1970; [ch.] Shane, Katrina, Tanya and Natasha; [ed.] Brampton Down School Folkestone; [occ.] Assembler, Recently Retired from Department of Education; [oth. writ.] Fifty two poems poem published in school magazine; [a.] Wallington, Surrey, UK

SINCLAIR, NORAH
[b.] 16 April 1943, Swansea; [p.] John McGarry, Edna Nuttall; [m.] Mark Sinclair, 12 August 1967; [ch.] Ruth, Joanne; [ed.] Glenmor Grammar, Aldershot County High, La Sainte Union College Southampton; [occ.] Headmistress (Retired); [memb.] Founder Member St. David's Society, Lesotho; [oth. writ.] Club monthly magazine. Unpublished children's books and verse.; [pers.] God made the world with a twinkle in His eye.; [a.] Mytchett, Surrey, UK

SKILLEN, MRS. BARBARA
[b.] 4 June 1953, Liverpool; [p.] Richard Keill, Elsie Keill; [m.] Kenneth Skillen, 5 April 1973; [ch.] Colete Joanna, Gavin Lewis, Odette, Claudine; [ed.] Douglas, I.O.M. High School, Mid Devon College for further Education, I.O. Man College; [occ.] Highways Inspector for the Department of Transport; [oth. writ.] I write purely for pleasure; [pers.] Most of my inspiration has developed since the tragic death of our 17 year old son, who was killed in a car crash a few days before christmas in 1990. Expressing feelings and thoughts which are too painful to speak about.; [a.] Andreas, Isle of Man, UK

SKINNER, ERNEST EDWARD OLIVER
[b.] 4 February 1937, Wilton; [p.] Francis Edward and Olive Freda (Deceased); [m.] Margaret Skinner, 8 December 1962; [ch.] One girls and twin boys; [ed.] Last Two Schools, ATD., Purton - Broad town (Swindon); [occ.] Caretaker; [oth. writ.] A considerable amount in poems or song forms written after a span of 20 years, none of which are published.; [pers.] My general interest, is song writing, guitar. Playing, I love to turn a blank piece of paper into word, of rhyme, with meanings.; [a.] Swindow, Wilts, UK

SKINNER, JEAN FRANCES
[pen.] Lucy Laurie; [b.] Leicester; [occ.] Married with two daughter; [pers.] Has several poems published. Also writes under the pseudonym Lucy Laurie. Has three books published, 'A Way of Living' - a child's version of this - 'A Day in the Country' and 'A Way of Faith?'

SLADDEN, JULIA
[b.] 2 April 1946, London; [p.] Julia and David Moore; [m.] Malcolm Sladden, 30 September 1967; [ed.] Cardinal Pale R.C. Secondary School; [occ.] Retired Secretary; [oth. writ.] Several poems - none other submitted for publication; [pers.] I tend to write about the trials and tribulation of every day life; [a.] Romford, Essex, UK

SLADE, EVELYN
[b.] London; [p.] Rose and Harold Churley; [m.] William Kenneth Slade; [ch.] Paul and Susan; [occ.] Guest House Owner; [oth. writ.] Have had poems published by Anchor Books and Triumph House; [pers.] My writing come totally from inspirational influences this seems to give me a greater insight into the feelings of the average person - I strive to achieve the standard of Helen Stienra Rich.; [a.] Yeovil, Somerset, UK

SLANEY, CAROL
[pen.] Cazz; [b.] 16 September 1947, Withernsea; [p.] Mr. and Mrs. Francis Duncan; [m.] Ronald Slaney, February 1966; [ch.] Wayne and Jean; [ed.] Comprehensive Withernsea High School (Great winter not much else); [occ.] Shop Assistant; [hon.] Nursing the international society of poets - hold me my work is O.K.! that in itself is an honour (to me anyway); [oth. writ.] Zelda - Chronicals, diana - My Side, poems (Galore)!, (all published), small stories etc.; [pers.] I've gone through serious stages of life, and now I'm at the menopausal stage, but through all of them I've managed to laugh and put down my verse how I've felt. I helped! And the family understood my problems a lot better.; [a.] Wetherby, W. Yorks, UK

SLANEY, PAUL CHRISTOPHER
[b.] 26 March 1974, Mansfield, Notts; [p.] Mrs. Allegre Randall and Mr. Michael Randall; [ed.] "Shirebrook Comprehensive School" also "Chesterfield College of Technology and Arts"; [occ.] A "Rifleman" in the 1st Battalion "The Royal Green Jackets," "Army"; [hon.] Various Running Awards MENSA, Chalange Award - also Athletics Awards; [oth. writ.] Several poems published in "Folkland Islands Local," forces magazine; [pers.] I would like to thank all my family for all the support over the years on my career and also my poetry as it was always influenced by them and my friends. Love always.; [a.] Nether Heage, Derbyshire, UK

SLATTERY, DYMPNA
[b.] 14 May 1928, Ireland; [p.] Patrick and Marcella O'Reilly; [m.] John Slattery, February 8, 1958; [ch.] Three sons; [ed.] National School, Junior, Senior School, St. Louis Convent, Kiltimagh, Co. Mayo, Eire; [occ.] Retired, was manegress of Teashop for 10 years, Pub Landlady for 22 years.; [memb.] Hospital Visitor, Hospice Care, Member of Catholic Women's League; [hon.] One poem already published; [oth. writ.] Poems for pleasure (personal); [pers.] Writing poetry gives me pleasure and time to relax with my thoughts.; [a.] Weston-super-Mare, Avon

SMALL, ANNE
[b.] 2 October 1955, Hertfordshire; [ch.] Caroline Robert and Clementine; [ed.] North London Comprehensive School; [occ.] Mother and Housewife; [oth. writ.] My first ever poem sent, is now to be published in "The other side of the mirror".; [pers.] I enjoy reading and writing words. They express my real feelings.; [a.] Wickford, Essex, UK

SMALL, GLADYS
[pen.] David B. Small; [b.] 1 February 1916, Colne, Lancs; [p.] Clara Richardson, Varley Duckworth; [m.] David Bruce Small (now Deceased), 10 February 1953; [ch.] Daughter Sandra Elizabeth; [ed.] Ordinary Secondary Education left school at 14 to work in the cotton mill; [occ.] At present retired but involved in various activities; [memb.] Clubs of various kinds; [hon.] Awarded a certificate British History of Life story awards 1994; [oth. writ.] Has had various poems and anthologies published in local published books also an autobiography of 17,000 words still in manuscript formula.; [a.] Burnley, Lancs, UK

SMALL, JENNIFER B.
[pen.] J. R. Small; [m.] Sgt. Small L.S.G.C.; [ch.] Layne, Cassius, Gerson; [occ.] Housewifely mother; [memb.] "Musician's Union"; [oth. writ.] Song writing-released.; [pers.] "Sail in the ship of success and anchor in the harbour of fame, fortune and goodwill."; [a.] Mounslow, Middlesex, UK

SMART, CAROLE PATRICIA
[pen.] Carole Patricia Smart; [b.] 2 October 1957, Manchester; [p.] Anne Burton, Miles Daniels; [ed.] Chorlton High School O'Levels, Art English Literature, English Language; [occ.] Unpublished poet (A somewhat frustrating state of affairs); [oth. writ.] 1st book "Pashernate Oscars Eaten My Sweet William" (Poems 1), unpublished, 2nd book (Poem 2), unpublished short stories, songs; [pers.] If I can touch but one person with my incoherent scribblings, this will be my just reward. Many thanks to Oscar and Steven for giving me the inspiration, courage and sheer drive to carry on with the written word.; [a.] Manchester, Lancashire, UK

SMITH, ANDREA
[b.] 4/6/80, St. Mary's Hospital, Manchester; [p.] Karen and Victor Smith; [ed.] Reddish Vale School, Reddish, Stockport; [occ.] Secretary - Richard Chadwick Associates; [pers.] To my friends Joanne Bradburn, Nicola Smith (sister), Victoria Hillary, Carol Little, Louise Murphy, Lyndsey Ayres, Adele Brennan, Nicole Flannery, Lesley Newton; [a.] Reddish, Stockport

SMITH, ANTHONY ROBERT
[b.] 30 March 1959, South Wales; [p.] Janice Price; [ch.] Samantha Elizabeth, Geraint John; [ed.] Bryntirion Comprehensive, No 1 Radio School W-S-M, Life; [occ.] Computer Network Engineer - Freelance, Artist; [memb.] International Guild of Artists; [hon.] Published a christmas card in 1990 (for NATO HQ-Norway); [oth. writ.] Currently tackling a set of short novels, biography of a nobody. Various poems published in military magazines, regularly exhibit paintings - mixed poetry (my mothers) and painting.; [pers.] I followed a career in electronics only to find years too late it was a mistake. Financially it is rewarding but I feel trapped, there is an artists trying to escape. Follow your instincts and be satisfied!; [a.] Divonne-les-Bains, France

SMITH, BRIAN
[b.] 8 July 1934, Portsmouth; [p.] Arthur, Dorothy; [m.] Jane (nee Watts), 2 October 1965; [ch.] Lisa Jane; [ed.] Portsmouth Southern Grammar School; [occ.] Freelance writer since barely retirement from local government; [memb.] Portsmouth Music Club (Vice President); [oth. writ.] Poetry published in Dorset Poetry Magazine, Article for "Country Walking", Award from "Observer" for best sports letter.; [pers.] Life long love of the English language. Poetry mainly descriptive or metaphysical. Influenced by the romantic poets and those of the mid 20th century.; [a.] Portsmouth, Hants, UK

SMITH, CLAIRE LARAINE
[b.] 13 September 1961, London; [p.] Kenneth and Pauline Smith; [ed.] Northumberland Park Comprehensive; [occ.] Bank Clerk; [memb.] P.D.S.A. Cat Protection League; [oth. writ.] Personal poems for friends and family; [pers.] A sense of humour works wonders; [a.] Laindon, Essex, UK

SMITH, DONALD E.
[b.] 28 June 1951, Solihull, Warwickshire; [p.] Thomas Smith, Beatrice Smith; [ed.] Harold Malley Grammar, Solihull; [pers.] I have a great interest in the importance of humanities relationship to the world in which he lives and like to emphasize points relevant to this in items I write.; [a.] Mansfield, Nottinghamshire, UK

SMITH, JAMES COLIN
[pen.] Colin Smith; [b.] 31 May 1934, Featherstone; [p.] David and Violet; [m.] Patricia, 28 March 1959; [ch.] Robert, Adele, Elizabeth, five grandchildren; [ed.] Kings School Pontefract. Various

Further education establishments resulting, in ACIB. (Associate Of The Chartered Institute Of Bankers); [occ.] Retired Bank Manager; [memb.] Mensa Institute of Bankers Knottingley Conservative Club From time to time! - Singing, Acting Swimming and Rambling Associations.; [hon.] A.C.I.B Mensa (Army) G.S.M. Suez; [oth. writ.] Various small publication in magazines.; [pers.] I write from experience of life with all it vagaries, and free everything emanates from the mind including health, Artistry and inspiration.; [a.] Whitley, North Yorks, UK

SMITH, JOHN ALBERT
[pen.] Albert; [b.] 5 June 1949, London; [p.] Derek Lesley Smith and Rose Anne May Smith; [ed.] St. Edmunds College, Ware. Governsbury Grammar School, Leicester University, Notingham University; [occ.] Retired on health grounds; [hon.] B.A. (Hons.) Leicester University; [oth. writ.] 3 unpublished books of poetry; [pers.] I am particularly interested in philosophy and peace matters; [a.] Ealing Common, London, UK

SMITH, JOSEPHINE DOROTHY ANN
[pen.] Josie; [b.] 15 November 1943, Hammersmith; [p.] Violet May Shunn; [m.] Kenneth Smith, 16 March 1963; [ch.] Kenneth Edward, Trevor John; [ed.] Shiptoh Bellinger Primary Tidinorth Down Secondary Modern; [occ.] Vitacress, working on Hygiene; [memb.] Amesbury Baptist Church; [oth. writ.] Many poems, The King And I, Sloe Spring, Universes, Invisible Men, Thank You (All of these unpublished) Children's stories (all unpublished) believe, squiggle and peep, Ezra 1-2-3 series; [pers.] Since a young girl, I have always loved writing poems, Jesus Christ is my greatest love, since young. I find so much beauty in his work. When angry or concerned I write it down, sometimes in a prayer.; [a.] Shipton, Bellinger, Hampshire, UK

SMITH, KIRSTIN HELEN
[b.] 8 January 1961, Alloa, Scotland; [ch.] Stephanie Michala; [ed.] Leonard Stanley C. of E. and Maidenhill Schools Gloucs. Denes High Lowestoft, Gt. Yarmouth College; [occ.] Single mom and proud of it; [memb.] The Human Race; [hon.] Honours - The British Ballet Society, Award - City and Guilds; [oth. writ.] Just personal to myself or friends.; [pers.] We all realize how naive we can be and notice our own ignorance when we learn something new that we didn't know before, and when we start trusting our own natural instincts, reality takes over from fantasy. Even the most academic amongst us have those moment, nobody knows or can do everything, therefore nobody has the right to superiority, only individuality.; [a.] Lowestoft, Suffolk, UK

SMITH, MARTIN
[b.] 1 July 1959, Wolverhampton; [p.] Jean and Bernard Smith; [ed.] Penistone Grammar School, Huddersfield Technical Coll.; [occ.] Campsite Employee; [hon.] English Language Business Studies (O.N.D.); [oth. writ.] Lots, but none as yet published; [pers.] I found that writing things, (mainly thoughts) down, helped me through a bad patch, when I felt lonely, I just hope that I can continue now I'm not.; [a.] Argeles Sur Mer, South of France

SMITH, MELANIE JAYNE HEWSTONE
[b.] 20 October 1965, Rochford, Essex; [p.] May Adelaide Hewstone and Ronald Henry Hewstone; [m.] Paul Richard Hewstone Smith, 18 June 1988; [ch.] Grace Helen Hewstone Smith; [ed.] Colegio Maria Inmaculada, Davea, Spain until age 14, Westcliff High School for girls, Essex; [oth. writ.] Stories for young children, including "Moonbeam Wants To Paint" "Moonbeam And The Spotty Dog", Moonbeam's Christmas Party" and "A Giraffe called Grace" (In Rhyme).; [a.] Prittwell, Southend, Essex, UK

SMITH, MICHAEL ALEC
[pen.] Maesmith; [b.] 18 November 1945, Bushey, Herts, UK; [p.] Alec C. Smith, Gwenyth Rosamund (nee Jones); [m.] Dorothy Maguire, 23 July 1986; [ch.] Alexander Charles Nathaniel, Amelia Meridian Yolande; [ed.] Watford Technical High, King Edward VII Nautical College, Sir John Cass/City of London Hong Kong and Sydney Polytechnics; [occ.] Master Mariner (Foreign Going) Marine Superintendent and Consultant Company Director; [memb.] Nautical Institute, Society of Underwater Technology, Referendum Party, Gauge 'O' Guild (Model Railways) formerly British Institute of Management; [oth. writ.] Technical marine articles in 'Seaways' and 'Oil Asia' magazines. Descriptive MS on walking old railway lines. As yet unpublished non-fiction including 'Spunyarn' fiction 'Basrah Convention'. Various poems.; [pers.] 33 years at sea visiting almost 400 port in 70 odd countries worldwide, a truism learnt is that civilization is only skin deep and that people are much the same everywhere irrespective that still manages to assert itself through what is often a brutal oppressive fight for survival is the very essence of humanity which never cease to amaze me. Today the solar system, tomorrow the universe. And who knows, we may find ourselves already there.; [a.] Brynamman, Carmarthenshire, UK

SMITH, PAMELA
[b.] 8 September 1939, Bushey, Herts; [p.] Henry and Mavis Holder; [m.] John Brian Smith, 25 October 1958; [ch.] Kevin, Craig, Vance; [ed.] Secondary Modern School; [occ.] Nursing Assistant; [hon.] Certificate in English Language; [oth. writ.] Andy; [pers.] My poem was a dedication to my eight grandchildren who was born prematurely and lived for 2 1/2 weeks.; [a.] Watford, Herts, UK

SMITH, PAUL
[pen.] Ckle; [b.] 22 March 1973; [pers.] Through losing your presence I cannot gain achievement

SMITH, RACHEL ANNE
[pen.] Rachel Saebo; [b.] 10 October 1972, Prudhoe; [p.] Eric Francis Smith, Maureen McIver; [ed.] Prudhoe County High School, Newcastle School of Art and Design; [occ.] Freelance Photographer; [memb.] British Institute of Professional Photographers; [hon.] 3, city and guilds in photography, B-tec national diploma in design photography, B-tec higher national diploma in design photography; [pers.] My writings are a true reflection of my thoughts and feelings whilst dealing with life's traumas. It is these experiences which compel me to write, so that I can analyse my situation, I have always been moved by the writing of early romantic poets for they wrote with such passion and vigour, timeless in meaning.; [a.] Prudhoe, Northumberland, UK

SMITH, RONALD VINCENT
[b.] 8 January 1942, Kingston, Surrey; [p.] Ann and Thomas Smith; [m.] Maria Smith, 23 February 1993; [ch.] Three; [ed.] First Class (English) Subject, Tolworth Secondary Boys School, Tolworth Surrey; [occ.] Bus Driver; [hon.] No Honors or Awards as yet, but am Boosted to try as you have given me the inspiration to carry on and work harder?; [oth. writ.] None to date, but I have my own private collection of some fifty stories and poems I have done over the last 25 years.; [pers.] I try to write words of the countryside, which I reflect of the wildlife as I see them, I read a lot on war poets who can stress how they saw the world then, my favorite is "Runyard Kipling."; [a.] Kingston, Surrey, UK

SMITH, MISS SHARON
[p.] Mrs. Julie Giles, Mr. Brian Smith; [occ.] Secretary/Telephonist; [pers.] The only way I can escape, is through my poetry, my emotions and how I see life is reflected in what I write.; [a.] Canterbury, Kent, UK

SMITH, MRS. SHIRLEY ANNE
[pen.] Shirley Anne Smith; [b.] 10 March 1961, Torquary, S. Devon; [m.] Mr. Treavor Waller, live together; [ch.] Katrina/Katie Smith; [ed.] Swinton Comprehensive Swinton Kilnhurst Mexborough S. Yorkshire; [occ.] Housewife; [oth. writ.] This is my first poem I have shown to public or anyone else.; [pers.] As surely as night follows day I feel it's important to try to reflect and understand the inner darkness within mankind as well as the inner light (influenced by my own inner shadow); [a.] Wath upon Dearne, Rotherham, UK

SMITH, WILLIAM ARTHUR
[pen.] W. A. Smith; [b.] 13 January 1934, London; [ed.] Stroud Green Secondary Modern School; [pers.] Interests, metaphysics, sporting games, philosophy; [a.] Woking, Surrey, UK

SMOULT, ANNE LYNDA
[b.] 1 March 1954, Newcastle upon Tyne; [p.] George and Delia Douglas; [m.] Bob Smoult, 5 May 1973; [ch.] Robert Douglas Smoult and Beverley Anne Smoult; [ed.] Sacred Heart Grammar School. Newcastle upon Tyne Polytechnic; [occ.] Primary Teacher I enjoy cross-words, writing poetry and dancing of all kinds; [hon.] B Ed (Hons) 2:1 Specializing in math science and technology; [oth. writ.] Poem published in island moods and reflections - poetry institute of the British isles 1995 "You never never know"; [pers.] I live life to the full making the best of what I have and seeing good in all those I know; [a.] Newcastle upon Tyne, Tyne and Wear, UK

SOLLIS, DEBBIE
[b.] 21 June 1967, Birmingham; [p.] John and Alison Sollis; [ed.] Sutton Coldfield Girls School College of Food Birmingham South Devon Technical College; [occ.] Sales Advisor; [oth. writ.] Several poems unpublished just written for personal pleasure. This was my first poem submitted to anyone outside of my family; [pers.] I am influenced by events surrounding my life, all my poems are inspired by good, bad, happy or sad occurrences that affect me personally. Live each day as if it's your last, plan like you'll live forever.; [a.] Birmingham, West Mids, UK

SORRELL, MS. LAURA
[b.] 20 October 1956, Chelmsford; [ed.] Sandon Secondary School; [pers.] The pleasure I get to write and to be able to share it with others.; [a.] Chelmsford, Essex, UK

SOUTHALL, DOREEN J.
[b.] 20 July 1926; [p.] Anne Samuel Allen; [m.] Bernard William, 14 February 1945; [ch.] Seven; [ed.] Secondary Modern; [occ.] House wife; [oth. writ.] One poem published but have written eighty poems never sent any away only the two published; [pers.] Do a bit of painting, love cooking, flower arranging, writing; [a.] Northfield, Birmingham, UK

SOUTHERN, JOAN
[b.] 23 July 1929, Bristol; [p.] Stanley and Ellen Forse; [m.] John Southern, 7 August 1954; [ch.] Mike, Tim, Christopher, Dave; [ed.] Clifton High School (Scholarship from Cannaught Rd.) Bath Training College, Swansea University, London School of a Roma Therapy; [occ.] Aromatherapist, but Semi-Retired-work with HIV/AIDS; [memb.] Society of Friends (Quaker) Chapter Centre for Arts, Labour Party, Chair of Directors of Music Theatre Wales (Professional Contemporary Opera/Music Theatre); [hon.] When young a lot of prizes for piano exams: And Eistedofod. No notables recently! I was a city councillor from 1979-1987 does this count?; [oth. writ.] Short articles in 'The Friend' - quaker magazine. Publicity articles when employed by fringe theatre company after leaving teaching.; [pers.] I try to get my life speak my faith. Now that I have made time the words are pouring out in creative writing - making up for the years when this form of expression has been "on hold."; [a.] Cardiff, UK

SOUTHORN, MISS DENISE RACHEL
[b.] 6 November 1958, Parkgate Nr Rotherham; [p.] Edith Southorn, Dennis Southorn; [occ.] Sewing Machinist Claremont Garments Rotherham; [hon.] My parents are the best award I could ever own or receive; [pers.] People can relate to real life, that's why I write from the heart and experiences in my life.; [a.] Rotherham, South Yorkshire, UK

SPARKES, V. C.
[b.] 27 April 1951, Ireland; [p.] Dorothy, John Sparkes; [m.] Divorced; [ch.] James Fulcher; [ed.] Penang Institute Malay, (Father R.A.F.); [occ.] Secretary; [memb.] Recently returned from overseas; [hon.] Honor Pass Shorthand, Typing, (Commerce); [oth. writ.] Poems published local magazine in Australia. Won a competition for short story.; [pers.] Poetic truth always flows freely. Poetry comes from the heart, not the head - hence poetic truth.; [a.] Newhaven, E. Sussex, UK

SPEED, ROSINA DIAN
[b.] 28 May 1942, Shropshire; [p.] Francis and Edith Griffiths; [m.] David William Speed, 27 October 1962; [ch.] Julie, Tracy, Alison, Lesley Anne; [ed.] All Saints School, Monkmoor Girls School; [occ.] Severely disabled; [memb.] Shropshire Poetry Club; [oth. writ.] Poems published in local paper; [pers.] Being disabled my poetry is written strictly for pleasure and covers many subjects and areas.; [a.] Shrewsbury, Shropshire, UK

SPEER, HELEN M.
[pen.] Nella McCarney; [b.] 8 January 1943, Portlaoise, Eire; [p.] Una and Hugh O'Donnell; [m.] Ron (Speer), March 1964; [ch.] Alison (Business Woman), Rhonda (Dancer) and David (Multi-Media Artist); [ed.] Convent Education, BEd (Hons) as mature student; [occ.] Primary Teacher; [memb.] East Sussex Gliding Club; [oth. writ.] Story published in 1995, West Sussex Writer's Anthology; [pers.] Balance is important to me. I have a longstanding interest in integrating the inner and outer journeys of life and your anthology title 'Between a Laugh and a Tear' seems an appropriate setting for my poem 'Integration'; [a.] Billingshurst, West Sussex, UK

SPELLMAN, AGNES
[b.] Bradford; [p.] John, Elizabeth Gallagher; [m.] James Spellman, 29 March 1948; [ch.] Christopher, Moira; [ed.] Elementary - Saint Williams R.C. School; [occ.] Retired; [hon.] Good Conduct Medal, War Medal (W.A.A.F.) 1939/45; [pers.] Strive to combine everyday life with humour.; [a.] Bradford, W. Yorks, UK

SPENCER, BRENDA PATRICIA
[b.] 10 April 1936, Gainsborough; [p.] Mr. and Mrs. A. Hoo Ton; [m.] Mr. Leslie John Spencer, 12 May 1974; [occ.] Pensioner

SPERRING, PAT
[pen.] Pat Watt; [b.] 9 May 1937, Middlesex; [p.] Jo and Bill Watt; [ch.] Nicola, Maria, Evelyn, Robert; [ed.] Fairfield Grammar School Bristol; [occ.] Lab Technician Min of Agriculture fish and food now retired; [memb.] Rossetti Society Birchington, Commonwealth Society; [oth. writ.] Articles poems and short stories in local and national publications one act plays for Towns Woman's Guild; [pers.] In writing I am able to express my innermost feelings about what I have learned of life so far in this remarkable world.; [a.] Birchington, Kent, UK

SPIERS, STEPHANIE M.
[b.] 8 January 1952, Stafford; [ch.] Melanie Ann, Edward John; [ed.] Stafford Girls High School, Harlow Polytech - Stafford College of Art Stafford College; [occ.] Co-Founder: Milk for Schools, School Milk Champaign, Journalist and Campaign Spokesperson - Broadcaster - Public Speaker; [hon.] Co-Operative Local Community Award for Latest Report Dec '95: "The Sins of Omission," a Report into Lea School Milk Provision. Inadequacy; [oth. writ.] Several poems published - non-fiction two survey reports on school milk and the relationship is poverty and poor nutrition in deprived children.; [pers.] "Poetry is like music if you are not moved by it - it's no good."; [a.] Stafford, Staffs, UK

SPOONER, SARAH LOUISE
[b.] 7 January 1977, Mansfield; [p.] Philip Stephen Spooner and Elizabeth Anne Spooner; [ed.] The Bolsover School and The Bolsover Tertiary College; [occ.] Student; [pers.] It makes me happy to think that my poem may bring a smile to someones face and I hope that for as long as people exist, so will areas of natural beauty to provide such inspiration.; [a.] Chesterfield, Derbys, UK

SSAJJABBI, MARK RICHARDS
[b.] 29 November 1972, Entebbe; [p.] Paul and Matilda Ssewanziri; [ed.] Lake Vic. Kindergarten (Entebbe). St. Theresa's School (Entebbe) Christ the King's Seminary (Kisubi) St. Thomas' Major Seminary (Katigondo) Makerere University (Kampala).; [occ.] Student St. John's Seminary Wonersh, and Undergraduate Southampton Univ.; [hon.] Uganda advanced certificate of Education (UACE) Diploma in Higher Religious studies. Bachelor's degree in Philosophy B. PH Makerere Univ. Kampala Uganda.; [oth. writ.] A Philosophical Thesis. "Scholarly Education its impact on the roles and status of women. (Based in Entebbe - Uganda).; [pers.] "I am only alive if" I'm me, hear and now, more so when sensitive to my neighbour's need.; [a.] Entebbe, Uganda

STAINSBY, PETER THOMAS
[pen.] Peter Loughborough; [b.] 21 September 1935, Manchester; [p.] Thomas J. Stainsby, Phyllis Stainsby; [m.] Brenda Stainsby, 6 July 1957; [ch.] Lynn, Simon and Duncan; [ed.] Stretford Grammar School; [occ.] Retired; [a.] Loughborough, Leics, UK

STANBURY, JOHN
[b.] 3 July 1959, London; [p.] William and Elizabeth Joan, Stace; [m.] Charmaine Carol; [ch.] David, Stacy, Sarah, Danny-Lee, Carrie-Ann; [occ.] Interior Designer; [pers.] My poetry reflects the reality of life, from birth to death, as seen through cold hard eyes.; [a.] Bexhill on Sea, E. Sussex, UK

STANGE, MARK JAMES
[b.] 12 July 1964, Worcester; [p.] R. F. A. Stange and M. B. Stange; [m.] Jennifer Jane Dollmoze, 8 February 1993; [ch.] Jessica Zoe Michelle; [ed.] Evesham High School, Worcester Technical College, Evesham College of Futher Education.; [occ.] Security Officers, Force 3 Security Ltd.; [pers.] True wealth is not measured in money, it is measured in loved.; [a.] Evesham, Worcs, UK

STANLEY, ALAN
[b.] 23 November 1964, N. Ireland; [p.] James Stanley and Myra Stanley; [m.] Christine Stanley, 10 September 1994; [ch.] Tina Jane, Emma Clarissa; [ed.] Portadown Grammar University of Ulster; [occ.] Civil Engineer Isle of Man Government; [pers.] Can you hear the sound coming from all around, called the sound of silence, the world in its excellence.; [a.] Douglas, Isle of Man, UK

STANSFIELD, FRED
[b.] 17 August 1938, Annfield Plain; [p.] William and Elizabeth Stansfield; [m.] Valerie Parkin, 10 June 1961; [ch.] Graeme (Severely Handicapped); [ed.] Secondary Modern (Annfield Plain); [occ.] Unemployed; [hon.] County Caps for Durham Football and International Trial for England Football (Schools); [oth. writ.] A few other poems one published in local magazine; [pers.] I try to air my vies of life in general as I experience it.; [a.] Dipton Stanley, Durham, UK

STARKEY, ANN
[pen.] Silvia Ann Mawsell/Ann Hawkshaw; [b.] 28 January 1943, Birmingham; [p.] Arthur Hastilow/Dorothy (Fetriday); [m.] Frank Phillip Starkey, 25 September 1981; [ch.] Sarar Louise/ Ruth Elizabeth (previous marriage); [ed.] Basic Education till aged 15 at Great Barr Comprensive School Birmingham; [occ.] Housewife/Mother; [hon.] Isaac Pitman Secretarial 120 wpm shorthand/50 wpm typing when 18, no further awards; [oth. writ.] Short stories (unpublished) I have entered competitions but never successful till now; [pers.] I see life as a journey and that we come here to learn, many times, many lives. I love nature and animals. I try to help where I can. I like the poetry of Christina Rossetti and writing of Norah Lofts and Anya Seton.; [a.] Wednesbury, Staffordshire, West Midlands, UK

STEEL, LINDA
[b.] 8 January 1972, Kilmarnock; [p.] Jim Steel, Wilma Steel; [ed.] Loudown Academy, Galston; [occ.] Word Processor Operator; [oth. writ.] Personal collection; [pers.] My writing comes from the heights and depths of my heart.; [a.] Darvel, East Ayrshire, UK

STENHOUSE, BETTY
[pen.] Betty Stenhouse; [b.] 2 August 1931, Partick, Glasgow; [p.] Hugh Fox, Mary Fox; [m.] William Stenhouse, 15 February 1958; [ch.] Kevin Stenhouse; [ed.] St. Mungo's R. C. School Alloa; [occ.] Retired Textile Supervisor; [hon.] British Empire Medal; [oth. writ.] A few poems published in Church Magazines. Carmelite Nuns print my poems for me. i.e cards or small booklets for gifts.; [pers.] The first poem I wrote was for the alcoholic due to the illness of my young brother. Who died in a house fire. Through all this heart break I prayed to God to help me, and the sick. I pass my poems on within the community for comfort or pleasure.; [a.] Coalsnaughton, Tillicoulty, Slack Mannanshire, UK

STEVENS, MS. CHRISTINE
[pen.] Christine C. Stevens; [b.] 19 December 1956, Staffs; [p.] Francis Cooper, Harry Cooper; [m.] Divorced; [ch.] John James, Jodie Jayne, Trent, Stacey Dawn, Callum Thomas Robert Samuel; [ed.] Perrycrofts Girls School, Tamworth, British School of Yoga, Devon; [occ.] Writer, Past-life Therapist; [memb.] Celestine Experiential Exchange; [hon.] Diploma in Hypnology and applied Psychology; [oth. writ.] Trilogy of 'Past-Life" experiences collective name. 'Time-Wave' collection. Individual titled as yet I do not have a published but an N.S.A. Agent is interested, The Cornish Burning, The Bojey Principle (now being written), The Crow Totem (to be written on completion of); [pers.] It is not my intention to convert, but to make people aware of the alternatives. Nothing in this life is 'just' black and white. There is the full spectrum of the rainbows the explore - and more.; [a.] Thornton le Dale, North Yorks, UK

STEVENS, EDNA RUTH
[b.] 23 June 1923, Wrexham; [p.] Deceased; [m.] Walter Denis Stevens, 30 September 1950; [ch.] Ian Stevens; [occ.] Housewife

STEWART, CYNTHIA
[b.] 29-11-1920, Lahore, India; [p.] Mervyn and Olive (Johnson) Costello; [m.] Albert Stewart, 13-7-1943; [ch.] Pamela Mary Bevington; [ed.] Loreto Convent, Simla, Presidency General Hospital, Calcutta; [occ.] Retired Nursing Sister; [hon.] 1. Epic poem short-listed in South African National Competition, 2. Third Prize for a radio-play in a competition run by the "English Assn of S. Africa"; [oth. writ.] 1. Three published novels- *The Residency*, *Jethro's Daughters*, *Jigsaw*, 2. Two magazine serials - one in seven languages, 3. Radio Talks - delivered personally in S. Africa, 4. Articles, short stories and numerous poems in magazines and newspapers, and 2 poems in anthologies; [pers.] Writing poetry comes to me as a direct result of joyous inspiration, while prose remains a laboured perspiration. Nevertheless, each has brought a different kind of satisfaction/ reward in relation to psyche and soma! [a.] Whiteley Village, Surrey

STEWART, MRS. HILDA
[pen.] Hilda Stewart; [b.] 17 October 1936, Wolsingham, Co Durham; [p.] John George and Winifred Cooke; [m.] Divorced; [ch.] Seven (4 son - 3 daughters); [ed.] Small country school just basic education; [occ.] Disabled Housewife; [oth. writ.] Assorted poems and prayers none published; [pers.] I just write things I feel in my heart and memories P.S. never look back to what could of been. But forward to what can be.; [a.] Newcastle/Tyne, Tyne and Wear, UK

STEWART, UNA A.
[m.] Ed - Farming, Married nearly 52 years; [ch.] Audrey, David; [ed.] Primary to 10 yrs. old Cornwall, to 12 yrs. old Dunfermline, Secondary to 17 yrs. old Dunfermline, returned to become fully qualified (dundee) teacher to acting Head Arbroath; [occ.] Retired (1985); [hon.] Distinction in Teaching Diploma; [oth. writ.] 1 poem published 2 years ago in poetry now (Regional Anthology - Scotland) Edited by Kerrie Pateman - my first attempt, this is my second. I have own anthology. I love poetry. Handwritten for family.; [pers.] In woman's land army during war 1942 - 1945. In Angus. Committed to Girl Guide Association to District Commissioner 1961 - 1972. Painting since 1989 Sold approx. 150 interested in everything.; [a.] Arbroath, Angus, UK

STILL, SANDRA
[m.] Roger Still, 4 July 1981; [pers.] Dedicated to Flossie.

STIRK, MELVENE
[b.] 11 July 1936, Ansty, Dorset; [p.] Wilfred Thomas Reeve House and Lucy Alice; [m.] Derek John Stirk, 24 November 1956; [ch.] Richard John Reeve Stirk; [ed.] Dorchester County School For Girls; [occ.] Legal Secretary; [oth. writ.] Personal Diary of Safari and trip to Kenya, in memory of my father, very emotional and descriptive but, as yet, unpublished maybe one day; [a.] Dorchester, Dorset, UK

STONE, PAT
[pen.] Pat Stone; [b.] 7 February 1954, Bristol; [p.] June and Ivor Weaver; [m.] Robert Stone, 7 June 1975; [ch.] Richard and Robert; [ed.] Lockleaze Secondary School, Bristol; [occ.] School Secretary and School General Assistant (Juniors); [pers.] I began writing following the death of my daughter Leanne. I do not understand the source of my work - it just happens!; [a.] Bristol, Avon, UK

STRADLING, CAROL ANN
[b.] 28 December 1942, Treherbert, Rhondda; [p.] William Evans, Ivy Evans; [m.] David James Stradling, 4 September 1965; [ch.] Andrew James, Richard David; [ed.] Porth County Grammar School for Girls Rhondda; [occ.] Accounts Clerk; [oth. writ.] "The Little Shop" published in Poets At Work; [pers.] Both of my poems are based on personal experiences.; [a.] Carmarthen, Carms, UK

STREATFIELD, MARGARET
[pen.] Marika Stanley; [b.] 11 January 1937, Dartford; [p.] John Monk, Ada Whitehead-Monk; [m.] Reginald Streatfield, 28 March 1959; [ed.] Dartford West Secondary Modern School for Girls; [occ.] Housewife; [oth. writ.] Seven Years Wed, My Garden Fun. Also several short stories and slogans; [pers.] I love the written word. And hope to encourage others to share my passion.; [a.] Crayford, Kent, UK

STUART, TOM
[b.] 28 May 1981, London; [p.] Sue Stuart and Malcolm Stuart; [ed.] Currently studying for GCSE's at Brampton Manor Comprehensive whilst studying drama at Italia Conti stage school; [occ.] Part-time Actor/Student; [pers.] My poem is about anger and the effects of it it is not expressed. I owe my ability to laugh and smile to my best friend and sister Emma, and to my loving supportive family.; [a.] East Ham, London, UK

STYLES, JOHN W.
[b.] 15 March 1953, Bursscough; [p.] Mrs. Joan Styles; [occ.] Retired

STYLIANOO, PAMELA-JAYNE
[b.] 27 December 1962, Birmingham; [p.] Victor Cooper, Barbara Cooper; [m.] John Stylianoo, 29 September 1986; [ch.] Georgina Victoria, Cassie Elizabeth; [ed.] Bartley Green Girls School; [occ.] Housewife; [pers.] "Seldom do we write what we feel, often do we feel what we write."; [a.] West Bromwich, West Midlands, UK

SUCH, MAUREEN
[b.] 30 March 1942, Enfield; [m.] David William Such, 21 January 1961; [pers.] Dedicated to: My husband David, Daughter: Clancy and Graham, Children: Daniel and Samantha, Son: Ceri and Anita, Children: Tari, Lauren and Eve.; [a.] Cranbrook, Kent, UK

SULLIVAN, TONY
[b.] 15 May 1976, Tullamore; [p.] Lil and Joe Sullivan; [ed.] Lusmagh National School, Banagher Vocational School; [occ.] Student; [memb.] International Songwriters Association, Banagher United Football Club; [hon.] Certificate of excellence 1996 International Songwriters Association Lyric Contest, Championship Winners Medal with Banagher United 1991 to 92; [oth. writ.] Several poems published in local arts magazine, lyricist, currently in collaboration with several composers. Articles for "Midland Tribune" newspaper.; [pers.] I try to live every day as if it's my last, because someday, it will be. So, if I'm going to fall, I'm going to fall with my heart, no matter how hard that fall may be, because, once you're born, life's a chance you have to take.; [a.] Lusmagh, Offaly, UK

SURTEES, ALICE ELLEN
[pen.] Olga Surtees; [b.] 14 February 1920, Bisham, Berkshire; [p.] Arthur Frith, Ellen Frith; [m.] Charles Surtees, 27 December 1941; [ed.] Maidenhead County School for Girls; [occ.] Retired, Civil Servant; [memb.] Civil Service Fellowship, Local Communities; [oth. writ.] Many poems, and one short story, but never offered any for publication, previously; [pers.] I have always loved poetry, and I write my verses when an inspiration comes in my mind.; [a.] St. Mary's Bay, Kent, UK

SUTTON, HAYLEY MICHELLE
[b.] 10 November 1980, Southport; [p.] Pamela Wright and Epi Barry Sutton; [ed.] Meols Cop High School year 10 (presently) Southport; [occ.] Pharmacy Saturday Assistant; [memb.] Y.M.C.A. Climbing facilities member; [hon.] Music Award German Language Award; [oth. writ.] Book title - The Fast Lane of Life not been published in reviewed!; [pers.] I enjoy writing my poems in hope others enjoy reading them!; [a.] Southport, Merseyside, UK

SUTTON, JOANNE
[pen.] Joanne Sutton; [b.] 19 May 1969, England; [p.] Daniel Sutton, Veronica Sutton; [ed.] St. Ailbes Secondary School, Rossanna Rd., Tipperary Town, Ireland. I have achieved Intermediate Certificate and leaving Certificate with good results; [occ.] Full Time Sales Associate; [oth. writ.] I write for pleasure with a view to publishing; [pers.] I believe that my writing helps me escape the cruel and polluted society and world we are forced to live with and in today, my love for life inspires my love for poetry.; [a.] Tottenham, London, UK

SUTTON, VALERIE J.
[b.] 3 April 1948, Brighton; [p.] Reginald and Janet Payne; [m.] Tony B. Sutton, 12 July 1969; [ch.] Philippa and Simon Sutton; [ed.] Westlain Grammar School, Brighton, West Sussex College of Art and Design, Worthing; [occ.] Housewife and I help my daughter to run her dance and drama school; [memb.] Beeston Operatic Society; [oth. writ.] Various poems published in magazines, etc. I have been writing poetry for the last twenty years.; [a.] Nottingham, Notts, UK

SWEENEY, WILLIAM MICHAEL PATRICK
[pen.] Bill; [b.] 15 August 1921, Portsmouth; [p.] Agnus Vera, Daniel Christfor; [m.] Rita Joyce, 22 September 1947; [ch.] Son - Gary William, Daughters - Tracy, Rita and Sally Ann

SWEETMAN, LOIS
[b.] 22 December 1955, Isle of Man; [p.] Norma and Lynden Brandwood; [m.] Roy Sweetman, 20 September 1974; [ed.] Park Road High School Douglas, Isle of Man; [occ.] Lexicon Bookshop; [oth. writ.] I've been writing poem's for 12 months in that time, I've had three published in England; [pers.] My inspiration comes from the life and works of "Avatar Meher Baba", I share the deep love I have in my heart, to awaken and capture the hearts of mankind.; [a.] Onchan, Isle of Man, UK

SWEETMAN, SYDNEY THOMAS IRVING
[b.] 10 December 1916, Chessets Wood, Warwickshire; [p.] Charles Sweetman and Lilian Sweetman; [m.] Helen Naomi, 2 November 1939; [ch.] Jill Anne, Kay Christine; [ed.] Ladworth C.E. School; [occ.] Retired; [memb.] Ex. Royal Marines (February 1934 - December 1947), served in five ships of the Royal Navy, before and during 2nd World War; [hon.] 8 Campaign Medals; [oth. writ.] None; [pers.] Influenced by a country upbringing and inspired by the writings of the great poets. Wordsworth, Milton; [a.] Portsmouth, Hampshire, UK

SYKES, CYNTHIA ARNETT
[b.] 15 November 1938, Yorkshire; [m.] 12 October 1957; [ch.] 2; [ed.] SM; [memb.] EQ, ARC; [hon.] None except a certificate for singing; [oth. writ.] Song not published.; [pers.] The love of a good book is man's gateway to companionship.; [a.] Dundle, Northanes, UK

TADDEO, CAROLE ANN
[pen.] Carole Ann Taddeo; [b.] 6 January 1940, Nottm; [p.] Mr. and Mrs. Sims; [m.] Adamo Elio Taddeo, 18 January 1958; [ch.] Guiseppina, Maria, Alfonso, Nina and Adam; [ed.] Sycamore Sec, girls school Nottingham England; [occ.] Housewife; [memb.] I love all people of every race a country and love animals, and most all I love children, I love everyone.; [oth. writ.] I love romance and feelings I love God, music, songs a poetry and most of all I love my family.; [pers.] If everyone in this world. Love more cared more. Prayed more. We would all have a better, loving life.; [a.] Trowell, Notts, UK

TAIT, GILLIAN CHRISTINA
[b.] 9 March 1981, Middlesborough; [p.] Sam and Christine Tait; [ed.] Studying for my GCSE's; [occ.] At School; [memb.] Workshop for Drama; [hon.] Honours in Drama, History and European studies, I've got awards in Dancing English Literature, High Standard in Maths, Science and Health Education; [a.] Guisborough, UK

TALABI, GANIY K.
[pen.] Silver Talabi; [b.] 15 September 1971, England; [p.] David Talabi and Sada Talabi; [ed.] Lambeth College Para-Legal Student; [occ.] Students; [memb.] Poetry Society, Association of West African Young Writer, Reinshaki Karate Club; [oth. writ.] Poems and short stories being published by the West African Association of Young Writers; [pers.] Most of my writings reflect societal ills, while some reflects dust anything.

TALLBOT, BEVERLEY
[b.] 20 June 1954, Neath; [p.] Margaret, Mary (Father Deceased); [m.] Deborah Tallbot, 3 February 1978; [ch.] Rebekah Claire, Ebony Louise, Samuel Wesley; [ed.] Pencoed Secondary, Bridgend Tech. Coll., Hyde Tech. Coll.; [occ.] Accounts Manager; [memb.] Presently studying for I.A.B. of Bookkeepers; [oth. writ.] Poem published in "Sunlight and Shadows" anthology; [pers.] Although I am a realist, paradoxically I am an idealist also.; [a.] Bridgend, Vale of Glam, UK

TALWAR, RAMOLA
[b.] 6 May 1969, Bombay, India; [p.] Snehalata and Arvind Talwar; [ed.] B.A. Honours in Literature, University of Bombay, St. Xavier's College. M. Litt in Journalism, Scottish Centre for Journalism, Univ. of Strathclyde, Glasgow; [occ.] Journalist; [pers.] Forget, if you must, but learn from the past. Search for the human face behind the masks we have become comfortable with.; [a.] Glasgow, UK

TATTERSALL, PHILLIP A. W.
[b.] 26 June 1964, Oxford; [p.] Ralph Tattersall, Pearl Tattersall; [m.] Michael Tattersall, 18 August 1990; [ch.] Sophie Elizabeth (twins), Hanna, Frances; [ed.] Peers, Littlemore Comp. Naval Engineering Establishment, Fareham ICS, Home Learning; [occ.] Petty Officer, Weapons Engineering Mechanic, Radio; [memb.] Royal Navy, Racegoers Club of Great Britain; [hon.] Engineering diploma A.M.I.E.E.; [oth. writ.] Poems and short stories for local parish and school magazines electrical articles for naval handbooks.; [pers.] The best work comes from the heart and your eyes, write down your feelings and what is seen. The rest is just punctuation and the support of your loved ones.; [a.] Doncaster, S. Yorkshire, UK

TATTERTON, KATIE JANE
[b.] 15 February 1977, Harrogate; [p.] Judith and Keith Tatterton; [ed.] Boston SPA Comprehensive, De Montfort University - Leicester; [occ.] Student; [memb.] Leicester Poetry Society; [hon.] Clifford Youth in Art 1992 for poetry; [pers.] I wrote this poem about my grandad who I miss very much. I feel this poem will lay his spirit to rest in my heart and keep him there forever.; [a.] Leeds, Yorkshire, UK

TAYLOR, DAVID LEONARD
[b.] 16 July 1937, North Fawley, Berkshire; [p.] Percy Taylor and Daisy Taylor; [m.] Linda Joyce Adams, 4 August 1973; [ch.] Michael John Taylor; [ed.] Fawley, Church of England School and Wantage Secondary Modern; [occ.] Retired through ill Health; [oth. writ.] I have so far only submitted four of my poems and three have been published; [pers.] Through my poetry I try to look at the simple but important things in life, that are so easily overlooked.; [a.] Pewsey, Wilts, UK

TAYLOR, EILEEN
[b.] 28 July 1913, Wales; [m.] Deceased, 10 August 1938; [ch.] Three; [ed.] Primary School; [occ.] Pensioner; [oth. writ.] I have written poems. Before but never showed any.; [pers.] I enjoy expressing my feelings in poetry remembering the happy times in olden days and my youth.; [a.] London, UK

TAYLOR, JULIE TANIA
[b.] 26 April 1965, Limauady, N. Ireland; [p.] Derell Wynne, Sean Wynne; [m.] Barrie Taylor, 11 November 1989; [ed.] St. Felix School, Suffolk, Lincoln Technical College, Orsett School of Nursing, Angela University.; [occ.] Deputy Manager - Nursing Agency, Registered Nurse and Registered Midwife; [memb.] BSYA Diploma (Herbalism); [hon.] "A" Level English Literature 7 Ace's, Secretarial Skills, Registered Nurse, Registered Midwife (Diploma in Higher Education) BSY a Diploma (Herbalism); [pers.] I enjoy writing poetry which that lights my appreciation of daily loving, the beauty and the ugliness of the world around us.; [a.] Southend, Essex, UK

TAYLOR, MICHAEL J.
[pen.] Michael J. Taylor; [b.] 30.7.59, Bury; [p.] Mr. Jeff Taylor/Mrs. Joyce Taylor; [m.] Single, BUT LOVE OF MY LIFE BARBARA P. has HELPED me to realize what TRUE LOVE IS.; [ed.] St. James'C. of E. GCE'O' Level standard English Lang, Eng, Lit, Tec, Drawing, Art. CSE's Maths, French.; [occ.] Coach Driver endeavouring to bring JOY & LOVE to MANY. Have travelled for many years for my Soul felt so alone then on my return from Heaven's door a few years ago (after N.D.E.) realize we are never so alone. And Love is UPPERMOST TO US ALL.; [oth. writ.] Work in Anchor Books & Triumph Hse; [pers.] Love is most important in all we do and achieve. Love is forever in our hearts; if at times you're feeling low, listen to your heart's mind, for friends and loved ones are always by your side, and will be your guiding light. [a.] Banbury (at the Mo,) Oxon

TAYLOR, YVONNE
[b.] 2 September 1945, Warwickshire; [p.] Doris Gaywood and Bernard Gaywood; [m.] Frederick Taylor (Deceased), 3 September 1966; [ch.] Kelly Alan, Karen Marie, Samantha Anne; [ed.] Secondary Modern; [occ.] Senior Supervisor Polygram Record Company; [pers.] I enjoy writing poetry in my spare time I write mainly for family and friends, and try to look at every life and situations.; [a.] Dagenham, Essex, UK

TEASDALE, VALDA
[b.] 24 June 1950, Kendal; [p.] Richard Mooney and Eva Mooney; [m.] Ian Teasdale, 1 February 1969; [ch.] Julia and Kevin Teasdale; [ed.] Longland Girls Secondary Modern.; [occ.] Label Design and Printer For J. Cropper P.L.C. Paper Manufacturer.; [oth. writ.] Many poems for pleasure.; [pers.] To me - poetry is the language of perfection.; [a.] Kendal, Cumbria, UK

TELFER, IRENE
[pen.] Irene Telfer; [b.] 9 May 1939, Watford; [p.] Alex Forsyth, Mina Forsyth; [m.] George Telfer, 3 September; [ch.] George and Paul; [ed.] Strandaer High School; [occ.] Secretary in the Health Service; [memb.] Carnolistie Horticultural Society: 1986-1991; [hon.] 1987 The Norman Edward Trophy, 1988 The Norman Edward Trophy (both for best potted plant at Carnolistie Horticultural

Show); [oth. writ.] Poem published in local newspaper another poem broadcast on local radio after winning poetry competition 6 poems published in different poetry books.; [pers.] Having had a very happy childhood, spending many hours in the saddle, I like to recall the beauty and mystique of nature, through my writing.; [a.] Carnoustie, Angus, UK

TEMPLE, JOY
[b.] 12 February 1940, Burgess Hill; [p.] James P. Braysher, Ruby G. B. Braysher; [m.] Donald C. Temple, 18 January 1964; [ch.] Donna, Timothy, Jason; [ed.] Hove County Grammar; [occ.] Director/Housewife; [memb.] Haywards Heath Golf Club. West Sussex Bridge Club.; [pers.] My writing is totally inspirational and stems from my feelings towards everything around me; [a.] Burgess Hill, W. Sussex, UK

TENNENT, IRIS
[b.] 16 July 1928, Leven Shulme, MC; [p.] Robert Lowe, ELizabeth Lowe; [m.] James Young Tennent, 16 April 1949; [ch.] Stephen James, David Young, Paul Martin, Marks Scott; [ed.] Levenshulme Chapel Street School Manchester; [occ.] Was screen printer designer textiles now retired; [oth. writ.] Stories and poems none published; [pers.] I feel very strongly about each poem I write, especially this one. In memory of my brother-in-law who served in the army, in the desert "D Day he died before he could march with his friends."; [a.] Earby, Lancs, UK

THOMAS, JASON LEE
[b.] 8 September 1972, South Wales; [ed.] G.C.S.E. English mathematics craft and design-metal C.D.T. Design and Communication motor vehicle studies city and guilds basic and general engineering; [pers.] The poem in this book is dedicated to the first real love of my life, Miss Tara dawn Harris, for whom I shared a wonderful 4 years of my teenage life with. Thank you.; [a.] Caldicot, Gwent, UK

THOMAS, JOAN
[b.] 28 February 1922, Ballina, Australia; [p.] Frank and Jane Lee; [m.] Hugh Thomas (Deceased), 2 September 1943; [ch.] Thee girls and one boy; [ed.] In a small bush school till I was fourteen, 2 years postal course for higher education; [occ.] Retired Nurse; [hon.] A cup for nursing; [oth. writ.] Just a few poems and essays in newspapers; [pers.] As a young child my treasured possession was a book of verse by Banzo Paterson. It inspired me to write and my dream was to write beautiful poems.; [a.] Llandudno, Gwynedd, UK

THOMAS, NATALIE
[pen.] Ann Pageant; [b.] London; [p.] Charles Arnold and Minnie Arnold; [m.] Gil Thomas; [ch.] Debbie, Christopher; [ed.] Boarding School, Bexhill-on-Sea; [occ.] Retired (Foreign Office); [memb.] Wickwoods Country Club, West Sussex; [oth. writ.] Children's poem in Scottish Magazine. Short story woman's own short story my weekly articles, Kent life.; [pers.] I am fascinated by science fiction and fantasy. Alternatively, I find the writings of Colette Riveting and the early poets influential.; [a.] Rustington, W. Sussex, UK

THOMAS, OLIVE EDITH
[pen.] Olive Edith Thomas; [b.] 23 September 1914, Hornchurch, Essex; [p.] Mr. and Mrs. William Nash; [m.] John Helsdon Thomas (Deceased), 21 June 1947; [ch.] Four; [ed.] Romford County High School, Southend Art College, Bognor Regis Shorthand and Typing College; [occ.] Retired; [oth. writ.] "Childhood Memories of Hornchurch" 1914 - 1936 by Olive Edith Thomas (Published by the London Borough of Havering).; [a.] Hatfield, Herts, UK

THOMPSON, CHARLES ERNEST
[pen.] Chas Thompson; [b.] 15 January 1945, Bellshill, Scotland; [p.] Deceased; [m.] Kathleen Mary Thompson, 6 September 1969; [ch.] Craig (24), Rachel (21); [ed.] Raf Education English Math English Literature Civics (Central and Local Government); [occ.] Painter with Regional Electricity Board (Northern Electric); [hon.] Air Officer Commandings Commendation 1971 New Years Honours List. (For services to Youth); [pers.] Poem initially wrote in September 1969; [a.] Northallert, N. Yorkshire, UK

THOMPSON, DONALD GORDON
[b.] 18 June 1933, Newfort, G.O.W.; [p.] Ronald, Kathleen Thompson; [m.] Violet, 20 September 1958; [ch.] Steven and Donna; [ed.] West Wight Middle School Freshwater, Isle of Wight; [occ.] Self employed gardener; [oth. writ.] Comedy, Gags, Sketcher; [pers.] Enjoy life every day, work hard and play land; [a.] Hampshire, Hampshire, Isle of Wight, Scotland

THOMPSON, MARTIN
[pen.] Arfur Mo, Portia Thomas; [b.] 25 October 1953, Torquay; [p.] Iva and Fred Thompson; [m.] Pauline Anne, 22 April 1978; [ch.] Peter Michael and Benjamin Anthony; [ed.] Plympton County Secondary School Plymouth, Devon; [occ.] Security Officer; [memb.] The Dobermann Club The South West Dobermann Club, The Dobermann Welfare Association; [oth. writ.] Several poems published by arrival press; [pers.] Influences include: Charles Causley and Wendy Cope. Enjoys helping animals and children.; [a.] Taunton, Somerset, UK

THOMPSON, MAUREEN ELLEN
[pen.] Maureen Ellen; [b.] 4 September 1937, Erith, Kent; [p.] Lily and Sidney Thompson; [ed.] Saddle Worth Secondary Modern UMIST Manchester; [occ.] Occupational Health Nurse; [memb.] Greenfield Methodist Church. Parkinson's Disease Society Oldham Branch (Librarian); [hon.] State registered nurse. Part 1 certificate in occupational health.; [oth. writ.] Several poems type written in a brochure sold for parkinson's disease society 1990.; [pers.] I have been influenced by Helen Steiner Rice and Celia Haddon. I love the countryside, flowers, birds etc. and bring this out in poetry.; [a.] Oldham, Lancs, UK

THOMPSON, SUSAN ANGELA
[b.] 26 November 1966, Tottenham; [p.] Eunice and Emerson Thompson; [ed.] Suffolks Infant School, Chesterfield Junior School, Westbury Junior School (Barbados), Lynchs Secondary School (Barbados); [occ.] Student at Lewisham College; [memb.] B.C.A. Book Club; [hon.] I had one of my poems made into a song (country and western) the song was called 'Sunlight' it was produced in the U.S.A.; [oth. writ.] Poem published in 'Invitation to Poetry' I currently have 1,000 unpublished poems at home; [pers.] Writing poetry is something very beautiful for me. When I get pen to paper all the right words just come so naturally.; [a.] Eglinton Hill, Plumstead, UK

THORBURN, DUNCAN GLENN
[b.] 20 February 1957, Nigeria; [p.] Mrs. Ivy Lee Thorburn; [ed.] Duheris Comprehensive, no qualifications; [occ.] Coal Miner; [oth. writ.] Various songs; [pers.] I can make numerical chords which reflect a chosen vale and key. This theory I call "Structure in Sound" it is my life's ambition to promote this beautiful structure in Sound.; [a.] Ollerton, Nottingham, UK

THORN, EVELYN
[b.] 15 February 1938, London; [p.] Violet Thorn, Alfred Thorn; [ed.] University of Westminster; [occ.] Personnel Consultant; [memb.] Institute of Personnel and Development; [oth. writ.] Several poems about tigers, my nephews death and my experience of my mother's journey through senile dementia.; [pers.] I began writing following the "Road Rage" death of Andrew Wacey my 24 year old, poet nephew 2 years ago. My primary theme is about the creative spirit of humanity at one with nature.; [a.] Chingford, London, UK

THORNE, MRS. SHARON VICTORIA
[pen.] Victoria Webb; [b.] 28 December 1965, Sussex; [p.] Patricia Ball, Peter Ball; [m.] Ian Andrew Thorne, 11 May 1996; [ed.] Henley in Arden High School and Mid-Warwickshire College of further ed.; [occ.] "Housewife" suffering with multiple sclerosis.; [oth. writ.] (Unpublished material) "A New Day is Dawning" "Feel A Mountain Breeze"; [pers.] My inspiration comes from the beauty of nature and reflects my love for the simple things in life.; [a.] Camborne, Cornwall, UK

THORPE, DANYELLE LORRAINE
[pen.] Danyelle L. Thorpe; [b.] 12 January 1977, Ashton-under-Lyne; [p.] James Robert Thorpe, Lyne June Devenport; [ed.] Hathershaw Comprehensive, Oldham Sixth Form College, Salford University; [occ.] Student - Salford University Degree in English, Language and Literature; [memb.] Judy Garland Club; [oth. writ.] One previous Children's poem published in 'A vision of television' (Editor - Michelle Abbott) article in 'Rainbow Review' - Garland Club Magazine. Children's Story in school anthology.; [pers.] I particularly enjoy writing colloquial children's poetry I like to be amusing but sentimental in my writing.; [a.] Oldham, Lancashire, UK

THURBON, MICHAEL JOHN
[b.] 8 December 1946, Rutherhithe, London; [m.] Elizabeth Ann, 27 October 1973; [ch.] Owen, Sarah; [ed.] Raine's Foundation Grammar School for Boys; [occ.] Tax Inspector, Inland Revenue; [pers.] My writings have been influenced by my childhood which was set in London's Dockland and all it encompassed, as well as the Era of Steam Railways. These remain fascinations for me to this day.; [a.] Caerphilly, UK

TIERNEY, HARRIET
[pen.] Ann Beth; [b.] 9 December 1985, Shrewsbury; [p.] Mike and Ann; [occ.] School; [memb.] Saddle club, swimming club and Brownies; [hon.] Bronze, silver and gold in swimming.; [oth. writ.] Stories and poems in school.; [pers.] I love life to the full and help others, less fortunate, whenever I can.; [a.] Telford, Shropshire, UK

TIMMONS, MICHAEL FINBARR
[b.] 17 September 1940, Dublin; [p.] Sean Timmons, Ida Timmons; [m.] (Partner) Ana Barros; [ed.] Glenstal Abbey School (Ireland) University

of North London; [occ.] Art Gallery Assistant; [hon.] BA Hons Contemporary European studies; [pers.] I have been curious about the mind and the human spirit, the goodness and badness in us and how we cope. I have been influenced strongly by Eastern thinking.; [a.] Manchester, UK

TIMMS, TOM
[pen.] Tom Timms; [b.] 3 January 1925, Selston, Notts; [p.] Richard and Gerty; [m.] Eunice, 8 October 1949; [ch.] Roger and Rosemary; [ed.] Selston Cofe. West Notts Teg., started Work 14 Birthday Summit Pit. 1939 - Ret. Winding Engineman.; [occ.] Retired; [memb.] Society of Amateur Artists, Late. Sec. Notts, T.T. Association of Table Tennis Coach; [oth. writ.] The Gasman. The Past, First Love, Broken Promises, Retirement and Genociouz Fwinding Engines, Sanlem Hyms, Gypsy Maid, Yankee Missionaries D.H. Lawrench Progress, Granddad, Old Milk Jug; [pers.] Burdle Books prediction 2,010. Making first contact interstellar Space. Looking back two brothers. Porland Biac, Katy Keith Shine Man Scarborough, The Old Tavern. Grandmatimms 53 years a midwife "Someboyd's Mother". And Many more Etc.; [a.] Kirkby in Ashfield, Notts, UK

TINGEY, P. M.
[pen.] Primrose Tingey; [b.] 29 January 1937, Kingsbury; [p.] Morris and Mary Screen; [m.] Albert R. Tingey, 4 January 1984; [ed.] Tamworth Girls High School. Teaching Qualifications in English and Art; [occ.] Housewife; [oth. writ.] "My Warwickshire "published in "A Taste of Central England"; [pers.] Influenced by a wonderful English teacher who inspired me poetically and dramatically, reflected in the approach to my own students later. I left teaching to travel abroad with my husband continuing to write poems on every occasion. Holidays to have added to my collection-more graphic than a diary.; [a.] Nr Coleshill, Warwickshire, UK

TOMLINSON, TRACY JENKINS
[b.] 12 June 1970, Oxford; [p.] Lynne Woodrow, David Woodrow; [m.] Andy Tomlinson; [ch.] Vincent, Andrew; [ed.] Carterton Comprehensive; [occ.] Housewife; [pers.] My poems reflect life as I see it today, and hope there will be a better and brighter future for generations to come.; [a.] Chipping Norton, Oxfordshire, UK

TOOTAL, VALERIE
[b.] 19 August 1941, Aberdeen; [p.] Eva and Cyril Collins; [ch.] Natasha and Stuart; [ed.] Life; [occ.] Commercial Manager; [oth. writ.] Poetry, volume 1) Chaledony, 2) Moon Dust, 3) Cobblers Child, 4) River of Feelings, 5) Silver Apple of the Moon; [pers.] From adversity I wrote, wrote for me. When one door closes another one opens. Now I write for the sheer pleasure of writing.; [a.] Congleton, Cheshire, UK

TORTOLANO, ANTHONY
[pen.] Tony Tortolano; [b.] 17 April 1905, Bannockburn; [p.] Benedetto Tortolano and Maria Pizzi; [m.] Isabella McAllister, 19 June 1927; [ch.] Four, 1 girl and 3 boys; [ed.] St. Mary's Catholic School Bannockburn; [occ.] Retired; [hon.] Family Ice Cream Won First Prize for Ice Cream made in any Type of Freezer in Large Scotland 1953 held by Ice Cream Alliance; [oth. writ.] Area life from before the first war, horse transport to flying to the moon (from clop clop to mayhem and traffic madness.; [pers.] I remember when girls ambition was to be a mother and home maker. And boys were proud to be proud journeymen ship builders and makers of steam engines for the whole world.; [a.] Stirling, Central, UK

TOVELL, JANET
[b.] 17 January 1939, Bradwell, Gt. Yarmouth; [p.] Deceased, David; [m.] 1 March 1958; [ch.] Neil and Sally; [ed.] Gorleston High; [occ.] Home Carer, Norfolk County Council; [oth. writ.] Two poems published by Anchor Books Peterborough; [pers.] I enjoy writing poems of everyday life on the humours side.; [a.] Gorleston, Gt. Yarmouth, Norfolk, UK

TOWERSEY, MIA
[pen.] Mia Towersey; [b.] 5 February 1978, Toplow; [p.] Brian Towersey, Tina Towersey; [ed.] Newlands School East Berkshire College; [occ.] Business Student; [oth. writ.] I have many unpublished poems which I hope to have published in the future, and these poems reflect my various moods throughout my teenage years.; [pers.] I have been influenced by 3 certain poets, that put the true feelings and write from the depth of there heart about their life's and experiences; [a.] Maidenhead, Berkshire, UK

TRAN, PHUONG
[b.] 24 December 1977, Vietnam; [p.] Lan Tran and Sinh Tran; [ed.] Sept 89-91 The Elgar High School, Worcester. 91 - June 94, Lordswood Girl's School, Birmingham; [pers.] I wish to thank my good friend for the inspiration he has given me. I believe in love, you should forget your pride and always follow your heart.; [a.] Birmingham, W. Midlands, UK

TRAVIS, SHIRLEY
[b.] 14 December 1936, Derby; [p.] Norman and Phyllis Salt; [m.] Lewis Travis, 23 September 1978; [ch.] Carol Anne, David Philip, Wendy Louise; [ed.] Matlock Town St Giles, Church of England School; [occ.] Relief Warden at Two Senior Citizens Complex; [oth. writ.] I have had about 12 poems published by Anchor Books, Forward Press, S.B.K. Books; [pers.] I started writing poetry just under 2 years ago and find it very fulfilling; [a.] Matlock, Derbys, UK

TRAYNER, JUNE
[pen.] Jet; [b.] 23 August 1956, Rossendale; [p.] Wyn Pilling, Tom Pilling; [m.] Stephen Trayner, 20 February 1982; [ch.] Lisa, Donna, Steven and Scott; [ed.] Tunstead C/E School Fearns Sec School; [occ.] Housewife; [memb.] Former member of the St John Ambulance Brigade; [hon.] Ballet dancing, Tap dancing, Ball Room dancing, Various awards for Disco Dancing.; [oth. writ.] Quite a few verses about the family etc. I have never entered them in a competition before; [pers.] I would love to bring my children and grandchildren up in a more safer environment. And the world to be at peace.; [a.] Newquay, Cornwall, UK

TREVETT, CAROL
[pen.] Destiny Russell; [b.] 18 November 1946, Weymouth; [p.] Mr. Frederick R. Fall and Eva M. Fall; [m.] John Llewellyn, 27 August 1966; [ch.] 3 Paula, Scott-John Russell; [ed.] Secondary Modern Apprenticeships. As you see you don't have to be so educated to be able to unite (it can be a gift); [occ.] Retired nurse due to (disabled); [memb.] Manor Theatre Company Acting Stage Manager Producer. Writings Consumer forum; [hon.] I paint also; [oth. writ.] A book of poetry (Personal) Readings for my mother father funeral magazines (disabled) consumer forum. Compassion for all things is life.; [pers.] I believe we one masters of our own poetry we can let our feelings to known in our writings and above all you can only know others if your neatly known yourself and question that makes your soul and Heart Unquiet. I also believe that when we except death we can them short living. So them the spirit can find freedom. Mine has freedom to write and to observe and to go on.; [a.] Weymouth, Dorset, UK

TREVOR, ROGERS
[b.] 5 December 1939, Stockport; [p.] Fred and Lilian May; [m.] Joyce, June 6, 1964; [ch.] Tracey, Steve; [ed.] General; [occ.] Retired Bank Clerk; [memb.] Church Drama Group, Treasurer and Production Secretary, Treasurer Community Center and Scout Group and Rugby Club; [oth. writ.] 2 poems Pete Murrays Open House, 1 poem Charlie Chester (both radio 2), 1 poem local paper and church newsletter; [pers.] I decided to write a poem for a special card and since have been asked for special occasions. I write them for pleasure and to please people. Highlight - A poem in form of illuminated address for my daughter's wedding.; [a.] Stockport, Cheshire, UK

TREW, TERENCE JOHN
[pen.] T. J. Trew; [b.] 28 March 1933, Quetta; [p.] Harry Trew, Alice Trew; [m.] Doreen Mary, 26 December 1955; [ch.] Paul, Gerard, Terry, Karen-Lisa; [ed.] Secondary Modern School, Woolston Southampton, Military Education Certificates; [occ.] Security Officer; [oth. writ.] "First Steps" a book of poems 1992, a couple of poems published in another anthology and magazines.; [a.] Farnborough, Hants, UK

TUCKER, SHEILA
[pen.] Frances Ward; [b.] 26 December 1966, Northampton; [m.] Nigel Tucker, 18 June 1994; [ed.] None worth mentioning, unless I'm allowed to say - "Wonder'; [memb.] IFAW, Green Peace, Michael Jackson Fan club; [oth. writ.] Poems published in Women's magazines; [pers.] As we all know, truth can be as brutal as it is beautiful. I hope to express this through my poems, particularly in connection with subjects close to my heart, environmental, child and animal welfare issues.; [a.] Chudleigh, Devon, UK

TURNER, MRS. GAYNOR
[pen.] Mrs. Gaynor Cowell; [b.] 7 August 1961, Widnes; [p.] Mr and Mrs W.S. Cowell; [m.] Christopher D. Turner, 2 March 1995; [ch.] One boy, three girls; [edh.] 4 C.S.E's as a child 2 G.C.S.E's as an adult in English Language and English Literature also study Sign Language; [ed.] Disabled Mum; [oth. writ.] A Poem Entitled "Boredom" to be published in an anthology called "Symphonies of the Soul"; [pers.] I like to write about reality in everyday life, and of feelings and thoughts that most people keep locked inside I would like to thank my husband and children for their support, and encouragement.; [a.] Plymouth, Devon, UK

TURNER, JO
[pen.] Joanna Lawrence; [b.] 17 April 1954, Northampton; [ed.] St. Georges Secondary Modern School For Girls; [occ.] Auxiliary Nurse; [hon.] City and Guilds Communication Skills Levels I, II, III N.V.Q.2 Direct Care and Nursing R.S.A.I. Bookkeeping; [oth. writ.] Published in "an autumn anthology" 1974 (But I paid them so I don't think it counts.); [pers.] I have always felt deeply for the world around me and feel that there

is a wealth of love and untapped beauty in all things, that renews the spirit. If we would only acknowledge it, we would have a better, richer world.; [a.] Torquay, Devon, UK

TURNER, JOHN MARTIN
[pen.] John Martin Turner; [b.] 1 May 1938, Loughton, Essex; [p.] George Turner, Elenor Turner; [ed.] Secondary, Loughton, Essex; [occ.] Helping out in heaven; [pers.] John died on 29th Feb 1996 from lung cancer, he had been fighting it for quite sometime. Writing poems came to John late in his life but he said he loved it and enjoyed reading it - a surprise to himself.; [a.] Loughton, Essex, UK

TURNER, JOYCE MARGARET
[pen.] Joyce M. Turner; [b.] 22 January 31, Huddersfield, Yorkshire; [p.] Herbert Roy Turner, Christiana Mary Turner; [ed.] Royds Hall Grammar School, Huddersfield. Leeds school of Librarianship; [occ.] Retired music, drama and records librarian; [memb.] Cemetery road baptist church, sheffield, Y.M.C.A., sheffield, Y.M.C.A., women's auxiliary, sheffield, international association of music libraries, save the children, soroptimist international (Retired); [oth. writ.] Poems in anthologies published by: Anchor Books, Arrival Press, Poetry Now, Triumph House; [pers.] I am a born again christian who believes that Jesus Christ has the answers to the world's problems; [a.] Sheffield, Yorkshire, UK

TURNER, PETER WILLIAM PERCIVAL
[b.] 16 November 1936, Brighton; [p.] Harold Percival (F) and Marcia Victoria Alexandra; [ch.] Vanesa Janet; [ed.] Excelled in Art otherwise 'C's' in those Days! Secondary Modern; [occ.] School Caretaker; [memb.] National Trust Brighton and southdowns Centre Coastway Hospital Radio.; [oth. writ.] 'Odes' in Local paper (ARGUS) Poems in 'Smile' hospitals radio magazine; [per.] I strive to seek out my talent and if I find it? Use it for others pleasure and the betterment of the world.; [a.] Brighton, Sussex, UK

TUTON, HELEN ANN
[pen.] Carrie Prince; [b.] 10 September 1978, Hull; [p.] Paul and Christine Tuton; [ed.] Wolfreton School, Wolfreton Sixth Form College, University of Newcastle upon Tyne; [occ.] Student of English, Literature; [pers.] The tramp that my poem is based on had last his will to live, and he would have died with no one to remember him, too many people have been forgotten, and I would like to think that at least this one will be remembered.; [a.] Hull, East Yorks, UK

TUVEY, TERRY
[b.] 28 November 1934, East London; [p.] Alfred and Louisa Tuvey; [m.] Maureen; [ch.] Michael, Kim, Beverley; [ed.] Sec. Mod; [occ.] London Cab Driver; [oth. writ.] Two poems published in Round Britain Poets and East Anglian Poets; [pers.] I find my inspiration by leading a happy life, driving my cab around London and holidaying in Ireland.; [a.] Buckhurst Hill, Essex, UK

TWELLS, VERONICA ANN
[b.] 29 March 1941, Leicester; [p.] Archie White, Vera White; [m.] Ernest Twells, 28 April 1973; [ch.] Ian Christopher, Angeline; [ed.] Crown Hills (Secondary Modern), Gateway Girl's Grammar, Leicester, Leicester College of Art; [occ.] Housewife; [memb.] British Western Dance Association, Linford Rose Country Music Club; [oth. writ.] A few poems published in recent years.; [a.] Groby, Leicestershire, UK

TWINE, JACQUELINE
[b.] 1 May 1960, Kuala Lumpur, Malaysia; [p.] Mr. and Mrs. M. W. R. North-Coates; [m.] Phillip Michael Twine, 25 June 1988; [ed.] Hibaldstow County Primary School St. Francis School - Lincoln The National Star Centre - Ullenwood - Cheltenham Gloucestershire; [occ.] Assembly Operator at Gis Door and Windows, Cheltenham; [memb.] Phillip and myself are members of the Woodmancote Royal British Legion Club in Bishops Cleeve; [hon.] This has been an award for me, by entering a poem of mine in 'The International Society of Poets'; [oth. writ.] I enjoy writing poems, and I strive to continue writing, and I also have ambitions to write a hard back book, with a 'Collection of Poems' written by Jacqueline Esme Twine; [pers.] I was born in a Kuala Lumpur, Malaysia. My father was a rubber tree planter, in Kepogn Barhu, my parents married out in Malaysia on June 27, 1952. We came home to England when I was just nine months old. I have undergone a major heart operation and also after all my education in Lincoln, it was the National Star Centre, Ullenwood which brought me back to live in Cheltenham, where I now enjoy a happy married life with Phillip; [a.] Cheltenham, Gloucestershire, UK

TYLER, STACEY
[pen.] Bridget; [b.] 27 April 1979, Sydney, NSW, Australia; [p.] Maureen and Ronald Tyler; [ed.] North Manchester High School for Girls and the Radcliffe School; [occ.] Receptionist; [pers.] I like to write my poems on personal feelings and emotions.; [a.] New Moston, Manchester, UK

TYRRELL, DELPHINE
[pen.] Annie Elliott; [b.] 22 June 1963, London; [p.] Robert Edward Elliott; [m.] Alan Tyrrell, 28 November 1981; [ch.] Andrew Scott, Bryony Clare and Charis Alanah; [ed.] Notre Dame, Battersea and Archbishop Michael Ramsey Camberwell; [occ.] Housewife/mother Assistant Librarian; [memb.] New Eltham New Friends Voluntary Organization; [oth. writ.] A collection of poems regarding life's experiences; [pers.] Without my pen I would experience spiritual poverty, for it provides to stride on through life.; [a.] New Eltham, London, UK

VALE, GORDON
[b.] 12 January 1962; [p.] Denis Vale, Margaret Vale; [occ.] Choreographer; [memb.] British Amateur Gymnastics Association, RSPB, Manx Nature Conservation Trust; [hon.] English and European Literature, Moral Philosophy, (B.A. Hons. Degrees); [oth. writ.] Poems published locally in Wales, at University or in the Isle of Man. Award for poetry at Celtic In Chruinnaght Festival; [pers.] Prometheus is based upon Scriabin's music, his tone poem of that name, rising from dark silence to blinding ecstasy. As a choreographer, I enjoy blending various art forms.; [a.] Laxey Village, Isle of Man, UK

VALLIS, JUSTINE
[b.] 21 October 1970, Birmingham; [p.] K. T. Vallis, V. Bellis; [m.] Christopher J. D. Carter; [ed.] Hayley, Lewis, Domenic; [occ.] Park Hall School-Solihull; [memb.] Housewife; [pers.] I give my thanks to my son Domenic, for his love and inspiration for this poem.; [a.] Birmingham, West Midlands, UK

VANSFIELD, MARK EMILE
[b.] 2 June 1961, Canada; [p.] Patricia P. Frank; [ch.] Jake Emile; [ed.] Southbourg Boy School; [occ.] Woodcraft maker; [oth. writ.] Many poems never published.; [pers.] To live in harmony with the world; [a.] Surrey, UK

VANVIERE, ANDREW PAUL
[pen.] Kristian Michael; [b.] 21 October 1961, Harrow; [p.] Joseph Michael and Rose Anne; [m.] Lorraine Radford (Divorced), April 1991; [ch.] Two boys (11 and 9); [ed.] M.I.C.M. Member of the Institute of Credit Management; [occ.] Group Credit Management; [hon.] Poem published in secondary school about the dangers of smoking; [oth. writ.] I have a personal collection, yet unseen, read or published; [pers.] I wrote poetry in teenage years, some of which gained recognition. all lay dormant until 1992 when I met my girlfriend Lorraine after a long and painful divorce. She restored my faith in the human race. I devote my work to her.; [a.] Cippenham, Berkshire, UK

VEAL, SIMON J.
[b.] 4 June 1963, Belfast; [p.] John and Mildred Veal; [m.] Mary O'Friel, 30 July 1993; [ch.] Emily Frances; [ed.] Mixed: Too many to recall.; [occ.] Chef; [oth. writ.] Just completed first attempt at Novel. The sunshine flowers To be? Or not to be? T.I.T.Q. Numerous Lyrics to songs.; [pers.] Strive for humour when stress develops: Realise the short time we have: Open the undiscovered in my mind: Love the haunted: Release the Spiritual: Pray for the abused of the world: Revive empty poos where permitted get drunk at least once a week. Consider the possibilities.; [a.] Birmingham, West Midlands, UK

WADE, DI
[b.] 3 November 1971, Blackpool; [p.] Stuart and Jean Wade; [ed.] Exhall Grange School, Coventry Manchester Metropolitan University; [occ.] Unemployed; [a.] Blackpool, Lancs, UK

WADEY, NIC
[b.] 7 March 1975; [p.] Mr. D. J. and Mrs. A. P. Wadey; [ed.] Millfield School, Somerset Thames Valley University, Ealing; [occ.] Recently finished my degree; [oth. writ.] Currently writing my first novel; [pers.] Although in no way related, I wish to dedicate this poem to my cousin Neal, who sadly lost his life. My parents have always done everything possible to and my success and to them I am forever indebted. Thank you; [a.] Kingsbridge, S. Devon, UK

WAIN, APRIL
[b.] Born in Birmingham; [occ.] Just retired. Interests: gardening and flower arranging; [pers.] Relaxed in my garden I look to the sky. Feeling the transmatic powers on high. Magic, and enchantment I feel all around there's, solace, and tranquility, to be found. My inspirations flow so naturally-so no time to rehearse. But to rely on my "Clarity of thoughts" for composition in verse.; [a.] Nr. Stratford on Avon, Warwickshire, UK

WAINWRIGHT, PHYLLIS
[b.] 25 August 1957, Hereford Hospital; [p.] Frank Gwilliam, Doris Gwilliam; [ch.] Sarah Jane, Gregory Reece; [ed.] Ross Secondary Modern School; [occ.] Houswife; [oth. writ.] I have wrote several poems just for fun and on some occasions have replied to People's Letters in Poetry; [a.] Ross-on-Wye, Hereford, UK

WAKELIN, ROSEMARY ANN
[pen.] Teri-Ann Taylor; [b.] 8 July 1946, London; [m.] Anthony Wakelin, 4 August 1973; [ed.] Mountgrace Comprehensive Potters Bar, Hertfordshire; [occ.] Civil Servant; [memb.] Metropolitan Police Womens Association; [oth. writ.] Short stories published in "Shorts from Devon" and "Paper Clips" poems published in "Separate Lives" and "A Walk Down Memory Lane", poems and articles published in MPWA and other magazines; [pers.] I am influenced by the world around me and the many quirks of human nature. I find I am equally at home writing on opinions of others as I am my own.; [a.] Plymouth, Devon, UK

WALDRON, GEORGE
[b.] 29 April 1924, Birch Nr Heywood, Lancs; [p.] John and Cathrine Waldron; [m.] Jean (Deceased) 1987, Miriam married 1989; [ch.] Anthony, Christine Ann; [ed.] Primary School, Thornleigh Salesian College Bolton Lancs 1935-40, BA Degree Open University, BA Honours Degree Open University (Upper second); [occ.] Retired Civil Servant; [memb.] A.A., Civil Service Motoring Assn., Amnesty International, Bolton Road Cricket Club (of which I am President), The Labour Party, Whitworth Amateur Operatic Society; [hon.] Officer of the Order of the British Empire - conferred by H.M. the Queen - 1983, B.A. Degree (Open University), BA Honours Degree - OU Upper Second, Degree studies mainly Eng. Lit. and Philosophy; [oth. writ.] Numerous poems the latest of which is a long unfinished autobiographical poem based on the lives of my parents. None published but some broadcast on radio Merseyside; [pers.] I am a committed Christian, firmly believing in Christ's simple Doctrine of love. The greatest poetic influences in my life have been Yeats Thomas Hardy. My poems often reflect the despair I feel about my own imperfections and the materialistic society I inhabit.; [a.] Heywood, Rochdale, Lancs, UK

WALJI, ZAHARA
[b.] 21 September 1971; [p.] Mariam Walji; [ed.] Nunnery Wood High School (Worcester), St Francis Xavier Sixth Form College (London), Brighton University; [occ.] Chiropodist/Podiatrist North London.; [hon.] B.S.C. Pediatric Medicine.; [oth. writ.] Several poems/short stories published in local news papers. Award for poem entered into art/creative writing competition in liaison with Fay Weldon (author); [pers.] My writings seek to express personal experience of love, joy and sadness of those person who have held a special place in my heart, thoughts and affections.; [a.] Stockwell, London, UK

WALKER, DEBORAH JAYNE
[b.] 30 November 1968, Salisbury; [m.] Jason Walker, 23 March 1996; [ch.] First baby due January 1997; [ed.] Early private education, comprehensive finished; [occ.] Secretary; [a.] Salisbury, Wiltshire, UK

WALKER, JANET NADINE
[b.] 1 December 1936, Wimbotsham, Norfolk; [p.] Evelyn and Edward Gunns; [m.] Philip Walker, 20 November 1969; [ch.] Two Sons Robert and Dexter; [ed.] Kings Lynn Technical College; [occ.] Health Clinic Clerical Officer; [pers.] I discovered the beauty of poetry in my childhood and just enjoy writing for my own pleasure and the hope that I give pleasure to others when they read my poems in the local church magazine monthly.; [a.] Griston, Thetford, Norfolk, UK

WALKER, MARY
[b.] 18 January 1933, Chester; [m.] Ron Walker, 19 October 1952; [ch.] One son (Ronald); [ed.] Helsby Church of England Primary School. Runcorn Country Grammar School; [occ.] Housewife and Retired Hospital Worker; [hon.] Certificates for Pianoforte from Trinity College Of Music, London; [oth. writ.] Several poems published in other anthologies, and other poems unpublished as yet.; [pers.] I try to write how I feel about nature, wildlife, and other subjects which touch me deeply at the time.; [a.] Runcorn, Cheshire, UK

WALKER, MICHELLE
[b.] 10 May 1978, Falkirk; [p.] Peter Walker, Lynn Walker; [ed.] Graeme High School; [occ.] Part-time Kitchen Assistant; [pers.] I feel that I am influenced greatly by the lifes of people close to me.; [a.] Stenhousemuir, Stirlingshire, UK

WALKER, MYRTLE
[b.] 19 March 1933, JA, WI; [m.] 28 December 1958; [ch.] Five; [ed.] 6 grade in the W.I.; [occ.] Retired; [hon.] Credit 3 level one English/Communication, BTEC Adult Leaners Award; [oth. writ.] Short stories, sketches etc.; [a.] Sheffield, Yorks, UK

WALKER, NICOLA NATASHA G.
[b.] 11 February 1976, Middlesex; [p.] Geraldine Walker, Roy Walker; [ed.] The Douay Martyr's School (R.C.) Ickenham, London Guildhall University; [occ.] Politics Student; [hon.] Academic Awards, Water Skiing certificate and Bronze and Silver medals for skiing; [oth. writ.] Several other poems as yet unpublished; [pers.] Poetry is a means whereby one can capture a certain mood, or period of history. I hope my poetry both reflects and provokes comment on our present society.; [a.] Northolt, Middlesex, UK

WALKER, STEPHEN
[b.] 14 May 1956, Rochdale; [p.] William H. Walker, Annie Walker; [m.] Susan Walker, 9 August 1975; [ch.] Lee Anthony, Clare Louise, Nicola Lynsday; [ed.] Todmorden C.S, Salford Technical College, Manchester Polytechnic, University of Durham; [occ.] Managing Director of Colour Manufacturer; [memb.] Durham University Alumni Associate Society of Dyerse Colorists; [hon.] A.S.D.C. 19 M.B.A. 1994; [oth. writ.] Several unpublished Lancashire Dialect and Humour poetry. Love and Romantic poetry; [pers.] A belief that poetic verse should be enjoyable to all ages and class, whether in written or musical lyric ford. Influenced by B. Taupin and Elton John.; [a.] Rochdale, Lancs, UK

WALL, EMMA SARAH
[b.] 23 June 1978, London; [p.] Jacinta Watling, David Wall; [ed.] Our Lady of Grace, (London) R.C. Primary School Convent of Jesus and Mary, (London) RC Secondary School; [occ.] Legal Secretary; [a.] Bourne End, Bucks, UK

WALTON, PAULINE
[b.] 11 February 1957, Birmingham; [p.] Bezz Blackwell, John Walton; [ed.] Waverley Grammar Life; [occ.] Aspiring Writer; [oth. writ.] Unpublished (as yet) poetry, scripts; [pers.] My faith lies with human beings, I bow to no-one and nothing, I question everything and accept nothing.; [a.] Birmingham, W. Midlands, UK

WALUSIMBI, OLGAR
[pen.] Aubrey, Toma; [b.] 27 March 1977, Kampala; [p.] Y. Walusimbi, Solomy Naluwoza; [ed.] St. Teresa's School, Namasagali College School; [occ.] Student; [oth. writ.] 'Guy on Board', 'Fantasia', 'My World', 'Romance Flies In', 'Guy on Board'; [pers.] You only live once, so make the best out of life. But whatever you do, remembered to enjoy it!; [a.] Dorking, Surrey, UK

WANT, ELIZABETH LAVERS
[b.] 2 August 1939, Plumstead; [p.] Both deceased; [m.] Derek S. Want, 4 April 1959; [ch.] Sharon Hawkins, Raymond Want; [ed.] "Gypsy Hill", Comprehensive School, Upper Norwood, SE London; [occ.] Housewife; [memb.] Parish church choir "St Catherine of Sienna"; [oth. writ.] Several poems written for church magazine issued monthly; [pers.] I am a christian and I strongly feel that my writing is influenced by my faith. I developed cancer three years ago and I endeavour to bring words of true meaning into the lives of others.; [a.] Reading, Berkshire, UK

WARD, CHRIS
[b.] 16 January 1956, London; [p.] Michael Ward and Angela Taylor; [m.] Divorced; [ch.] Four - Kelly, Juliet, David and Stephanie; [ed.] St. Davids Sec. Mud. Windsor College; [occ.] Stock Keeper; [hon.] This is my first honour having my poems published; [pers.] My poems hopefully reflect the sadness of others who are alone in this world thanks to my four children - friends - Peter, Marion, Keli, Sara - Nikki - my special friend Luz, my grand-parents. Without those mentioned this would not be possible love you all.; [a.] London, UK

WARD, LISA
[b.] 26 July 1964, Leicester; [p.] Keith Ashton Bennett, Dorothy Ruth Bennett; [m.] Eric Ward, 4 March 1989; [ch.] Ashton Ward; [ed.] Sandown High School, Isle of Wight College of Arts and Technology; [occ.] Holiday Park Receptionist; [pers.] Life is like a note book, it is left to us what we write on to the pages.; [a.] Sandown, Isle of Wight, UK

WARD, LORAINE GILLIAN
[pen.] Loraine Ward; [b.] 13 September 1959, Clapton, London; [p.] Denis and Edna Staines; [m.] George Ward, 5 June 1982; [ch.] Daniel Curtis Ward, Richard Adam; [ed.] Walthamston Senior High School for Girls; [occ.] Special Needs, Teachers Assistant; [hon.] Various Dancing Awards, including Distinction Certificates for Modern, Tap, Stage Classical, and Cabaret Dancing. Also certificate of Merit for Plectrum Guitar, from the Federation of British Guitarists; [oth. writ.] Several poems and children's stories, as yet unpublished; [pers.] It is my ambition to have my children's stories published. The children I work with are a never ending source of inspiration, they never give up trying, so neither shall I.; [a.] Thundersley, Essex UK

WARDLE, ELSIE MARY
[pen.] Elsie Piary; [b.] 23 February 1924; [m.] 28 February 1964; [ch.] Three; [ed.] Ordinary School went to Hill Farm School Radford Coventry; [occ.] Housewife Retired; [oth. writ.] I am Senior Citizen and I have worked, hard all my life, I love writing and I have quite a few letters published in various papers I was born in Manchester Holme; [pers.] I worked for City Engineers Dept. Folshill Road Coventry 16 years we was first Lady Janitors to start at Gleaning City of Coventry up work was very hard before that 'twas inspector at Dunlop and Rothermans.; [a.] Daventry, Northants, UK

WARMAN, TRUDY
[b.] 29 March 1996, Cambridge; [ed.] Chesterton Community College, Cambridgeshire College of Agriculture and Horticulture; [oth. writ.] Two poems published, play the game and I'm in love with my car; [pers.] I write about the world and people the way they seem to me. There is always something hiding behind the norm.; [a.] Chatteris, Cambs, UK

WARNE, MISS HELEN
[b.] 27 December 1956, Oxford; [p.] Gladys and George Warne; [ch.] Daughter Natalie; [ed.] Grammar School Gibraltar; [occ.] Administrator; [oth. writ.] Poetry To Try and Reflect The Realities of Life; [a.] Basingstoke, Hants, UK

WARNER, MRS. DOROTHY ROWCROFT
[pen.] D. R. Payn Le Sueur; [b.] Victoria, V.I., B.C., Canada; [p.] Arthur William and Ruby Payn Le Sueur; [m.] David Moline Warner, 26 June 1964, (2nd marriage); [ch.] Lt. Col. Michael R. Goodliff, R.A. M.B.E.; [ed.] St. George's School for girls, Victoria, and Monterey, Oak Bay, Victoria, Van Couver Island, B.C. Canada; [memb.] National Trust, Concorde, C.P.L.; [pers.] Favourite occupations: gardening, drawing, tapestry and needle point, designing and hand sewing. Must have one or more cats. (Strays) writing letters. Reading ancient history, travel books, lives of explorers and artists, biographies and autobiographies. Letters and diaries. Travel: Semi-Cargo ships, no luxury liners, long train journeys. Flying if no alternative.; [a.] Warnham, W. Sussex, UK, RH12 3RF

WARNES, ANNETTE SARAH
[pen.] Annette; [b.] 9 June 1961, Norwich; [p.] Gerald and Klara Bishop; [ch.] Daughter Terri Colleen Warnes; [ed.] Sheringham High Norfolk; [pers.] My poetry comes from the heart and love is my inspiration.; [a.] Holt, Norfolk, UK

WARNES, SYLVIA
[b.] 3 December 1960, Grimsby; [p.] Frederick Camburn/Sylvia Camburn; [m.] Jonathan Warnes, 30 July 1994; [ch.] Marie (14), Zoe (8), Bradley and Brett (twins 1 yr); [ed.] Harold Street Secondary School; [occ.] Full time mother and wife; [oth. writ.] I have never written before in my life; [pers.] Would like a full book of my own poems published in the future. Poems to touch your hearts.; [a.] Cleethorpes, Humberston, South Humberside, UK

WARRANDER, ALAN
[pen.] Alan Warrander; [b.] 29 April 1958, Aberdeen; [ed.] Roberts Gordon's College Aberdeen University; [occ.] Mature Student at Aberdeen University 3rd year M.A, Degree Course; [oth. writ.] None, this is my first poem to be published; [a.] Aberdeen, Grampian, UK

WARWICK, PAUL
[b.] 12 January 1968, Lambeth, London; [occ.] Freelance Journalist; [oth. writ.] Have had a couple of articles on various social problems published in the guardian and observer newspapers and have written, directed and presented two short crime document car 'The Saher Cities' organization.; [pers.] Lots of us have got something to say, and as individuals have a unique way of expressing things, regardless of our education, status, or background; [a.] Upper Norwood, London, UK

WATERHOUSE, DONALD JOHN STANLEY
[pen.] John Stanley; [b.] 6 May 1922, Grantham, Lincs; [p.] Victor Waterhouse and Laura Hardy; [m.] Barbara (Deceased), 24 September 1949; [ch.] Madeleine Cordelia Pain; [ed.] Grantham King's School Leeds University; [occ.] Retired Dental Surgeon; [memb.] Food and Wine Society (Late President), Amateur Astronomy Society, Local Chess and Bridge Clubs; [oth. writ.] Various poems and short stories. Published booklet on Ophelia in Hemlet. Articles on wine and astronomy; [pers.] I love the stars too much to be frightened of the dark! Greatly influenced by the classics, especially latin; [a.] Wisbech, Cambs, UK

WATERS, CAROLE
[b.] 16 February 1943, Nr. Plymouth, Elburton; [p.] Jack Webber and Rosie Webber; [m.] Raymond George Waters, 16 February 1960; [ch.] Anita Rose, Keith Raymond, Patricia-Jane; [ed.] Plymstock, Secondary Modern School; [occ.] Owner of Green Grocer Shop; [pers.] My son Keith encouraged me to write poems, he said that I had a way with putting my thought's to paper. I have started doing this since Christmas 1995, I get a great pleasure from my writing.; [a.] Plymouth, Devon, UK

WATSON, MISS ANDREA CAROLINE
[b.] 12 February 1975, Croydon; [p.] Mary Bales, John Bales, Sandra Maynard, Trevor Watson.; [ed.] Selsdon High School, North Walsham High School, Paston Sixth Form College.; [occ.] Student; [memb.] Solomon Artistes management international. Photo FACTA modelling agency.; [hon.] Lamda Gold Medal, Bronze, Silver, Gold Dancing Medals.; [oth. writ.] The bloody Mary - A Novel to be published this coming autumn.; [pers.] To my foster - family - the Bales's - who have given me everything. Thank - you, I love you always.; [a.] North Walsham, Norfolk, UK

WATSON, BARBARA KATHLEEN
[pen.] B. K. Watson; [b.] 29 December 1946, Kent; [m.] Herbert Watson, 11 September 1965; [ch.] Two sons; [ed.] Secondary School; [occ.] Farm Worker; [oth. writ.] Poetry not published as yet.; [pers.] I love writing of the beauty of nature I particularly enjoy reading 'Patience Strong'.; [a.] Rainham, Kent, UK

WATT, SAMANTHA JAYNE
[pen.] Samantha Watt; [b.] 27 March 1977, Wolverhampton; [p.] David, Lesley Jones; [ed.] Lampeter Comprehensive School, 10 G.C.S.E.'s 'A Level English Level 1 Japanese; [occ.] Hotel Receptionist; [memb.] Lampeter Aqua Aerobics Club, Jay's Aerobics Club; [hon.] Received bronze medal in 1989 in the Welsh Schools Gymnastics Championships in Sophia Gardens, Cardiff. Also in the Dyfred Tea, which received overall silver medal. Numerous certificates and medals for dancing gymnastics, swimming and skating; [oth. writ.] One other poem published in December in the book titled: "Voices from Wales".; [pers.] It was one said, "That words are the only things that last forever". I hope with all my heart, that my work and all the works of others will never be forgotten.; [a.] Rhydcymerau, Dyfed, UK

WATTS, ROBERT
[b.] Chelmsford; [p.] Queenie and Leonard; [m.] Sheila; [ch.] One child Vernon; [memb.] Many years a member of a local writers club; [oth. writ.] Including three thriller novels, numerous short stories, poetry and quotations; [pers.] I enjoy reading science fiction, spy thrillers, traditional poetry. films including dramas, epics thrillers and sport.; [a.] Chelmsford, Essex, UK

WATTS, SHEILA
[b.] Barkingside; [p.] George and Lilian Ryall; [m.] Robert; [ch.] One son Vernon; [oth. writ.] I write for my own satisfaction which has included short stories and poetry; [pers.] I love to read romantic novels, films with a beginning, middle and ending. Dramatic films appeal strongly as do true stories.; [a.] Chelmsford, Essex, UK

WATTS, SUZY
[b.] 24 May 1952, Wallasey; [p.] John and Mavis McEvoy; [m.] Neil, 18 September 1982; [ch.] Daugthers Katrina, Johanne and Melanie Ages 18; [ed.] Walasey Girls Tec High School; [occ.] Local Aput; [hon.] Graduate of Mersey Common Purpose; [oth. writ.] For Personal use and Speeches; [pers.] Would like to write book or part book of poems of life experiences cradle to whatever tome is experienced; [a.] Wallasey, Merseyside, UK

WEAVER, AMANDA
[b.] 29 July 1971, Cambridge; [p.] Patricia and John Weaver; [m.] Stephen Stokes-Geddes; [ed.] Barclay School Stevenage, Stevenage College; [occ.] Benefits Agency Social fund Admin Officer; [pers.] The future can never escape the past that it will soon be; [a.] Stevenage, Hertfordshire, UK

WEBB, DAVID JOHN
[b.] 19 February 1913, S. Marden; [p.] David and Patricia Webb; [m.] Peggy Webb (Deceased), 21 August 1936; [ch.] Five; [ed.] Small R.C. School in Richmond taught by nuns, most of us were fatherless owing to the first world war.; [occ.] Retired; [memb.] Life honary membership of Twickenham Rifle Club; [oth. writ.] Novel but not published.; [pers.] During last war was down graded owing to crippled arm Drove ambulances in greater London area, joined Twickenham R.C. in 1948, 1960 was made club captain and club coach, have written coaching pamphlets which have been used by county coaches all over the country for which I only charged them the cost of photo copying, The Secretary of Hampton Rifle Club is currently printing them to sell in his club, of which I was a member as Coach, which since my 'stroke' I have had to cease.; [a.] Teddington, Middlesex, UK

WEBB, NIGEL
[b.] 8 February 1959, Cardiff; [p.] Mr. W. W. Webb and Mrs. P. G. Webb; [ed.] Barry Boys Comp. School, Port Road West, Barry South Glamorgan, South Wales; [occ.] Unemployed; [oth. writ.] I have had a previous poem published entitled "Cardiff Bay." This can be read in an anthology of Welsh poems called, poetry now Wales 1994. And it was published by arrival press, Peterborough

WEBB-JONES, KAREN
[b.] 14 June 1965, Cleethorpes; [p.] John Webb, Patricia Webb; [m.] David B. Webb-Jones, 27 April 1985; [ch.] Katie Antonia, Poppy Anastacia and Harvey David; [ed.] Humberston Comprehensive and Farnborough College; [occ.] Freelance Illustrator, Writer and Part-time Lecture; [memb.] Royal Lifesaving Society, Institute of Swimming Teachers and Coaches; [oth. writ.] Poems published in local magazines and 1 published in Poetry now Regional Anthology (South) exhibited artwork locally and London.; [pers.] I write poetry to capture the moment, the mood, to reflect the feelings from within myself.; [a.] Grimsby, South Humberside, UK

WEBSTER, ANTHONY
[pen.] Tony Webster; [b.] 23 August 1935, Ely, Cambridgeshire; [m.] Maureen, 30 March 1996; [ed.] Wellingborough Grammar School; [occ.] Retired Police Officer Freelance Proofreader - writer; [pers.] Served 12 yrs. fleet an arm prior to police service mentioned in dispatcher suez 1956 - chief constable's commendation for bravery 1987 - 'I like to write about what I see and feel'.; [a.] Dawlish, Devon, UK

WELBY, DOREEN MARY ANN
[b.] 6 September 1938, London; [p.] Lucy and Arther Hewitt; [m.] Charles Welby, 2 March 1957; [ch.] Four Boys, Two Girls; [ed.] Willesden London Comprehensive; [occ.] Housewife; [memb.] "Poetry Now" Magazine "Peterborough"; [hon.] City and Guilds in carework two poems excepted and printed in anthology's related to `Poetry now' Magazine, both 1995 joined 1995; [oth. writ.] Award of merit certificate from "world of poetry" sacramento California America 1991; [pers.] I am inspired by my own feelings within as to nature and the wonder of humanity; [a.] Harrow Weald, Mddx, UK

WELLER, JULIE
[b.] 19 September 1962, Beverley; [p.] George and Margaret Ingleson; [ch.] Emma Louise Weller; [ed.] South Holderness Secondary School, Hull College of Further Education, Hull District School of Nursing (S.E.N.); [occ.] Mother/Housewife; [pers.] I feel that poetry is the food and drink of the mind and soul. I have been inspired and influenced chiefly by the poetical works of rupert brook and wordsworth among others.; [a.] Scarborough, North Yorkshire, UK

WELLS, SANDRA
[b.] 11 May 1969, Slough; [p.] Moira and Mike Wells; [ed.] West Kent College of Further Education Liverpool University; [occ.] Teacher of English Barcelona; [hon.] Theatre Studies BA Hons.; [oth. writ.] Several short stories; [pers.] My poetry is direct. It is not and cannot be analysed. My poetry is to be read aloud and I try through my writing to ask questions, questions that many young people may ask.; [a.] Hadlow, Tonbridge, Kent, UK

WELNA, JANET
[b.] 11 June 1946, York; [p.] Mary and Walter; [m.] Henryk, 25 February 1972; [ed.] Secondary Modern; [occ.] Process Worker, Nestle Rowntree York; [oth. writ.] Two poems to my husband which he has framed and I am halfway through another to my sister who died.; [a.] York, North Yorkshire, UK

WELSH, MR. M. H.
[b.] 20 August 1947, Mauchline; [p.] Mr. and Mrs. M. P. Welsh; [m.] Johannah, 25 September 1970; [ch.] 2 girls; [ed.] University Deg.; [occ.] Manager BAE Prestwick; [oth. writ.] A book published by BAE for a charity (Mauchline Old Folks); [pers.] Write what I think, write what I see, write what I feel, write what I touch, write what I hear; [a.] Mauchline, Ayr, UK

WENN, REDFERN ARTHUR
[pen.] 'Wenn The Pen'; [b.] 19 December 1935, Friday Bridge, Cambs; [p.] Arthur and Agnes Wenn (Deceased); [m.] Divorced; [ch.] Julie, Andrew and Christopher; [ed.] Chatteris Cromwell School; [occ.] Disabled; [oth. writ.] One poem published in 'A Passage In Time', eight with Arrival Press, one with Rhyme Arrival and one with Peoples Friend.; [pers.] Since being disabled I raise funds for two brain damaged children Nicola and Richard, and any money made from my poetry goes into their funds. My main aim in life is to help others and strive to keep death off the roads.; [a.] Chatteris, Cambs, UK

WEST, DAVINA
[pen.] Debbie; [b.] 30 June 1967, Bristol; [p.] Mr. and Mrs. R. Gowing; [m.] Antony Charles West, 19 January 1991; [ch.] Anna Maria West; [occ.] Nursing; [pers.] Greatly influenced by my father my poem is dedicated to his memory.; [a.] Yate, Avon, UK

WEST, HELEN
[b.] 17 June 1914, Putney; [ch.] Sons, daughters, grandchildren; [ed.] Independent Schools, University of Wales, (University College of North Wales Bangor.); [occ.] Retired Maths Teacher. Have taught in English public schools in the Argentine. Travelled to many countries. Circumnavigated the world with stopovers in various countries. Am still travelling when countries. Am still travelling when possible to fill in the bits I have; [oth. writ.] Won a prize for a short story only recently begun offering for publication, after having a competition entry accepted. Since then have had several poems included in different collections have been writing since school days.; [pers.] Poems to me are thoughts and inspirations put into words. If they are not used at the time they vanish.; [a.] Whitstable, Kent, UK

WHEATER, RUTH
[pen.] Retna; [b.] 11 May 1953, Malaysia; [p.] Mr. and Mrs. Verutharajah; [m.] Divorce; [ch.] Kristian and Sonya; [ed.] GCSE, B. A. Social Studies, Diploma in social work; [occ.] Manager (children's home); [memb.] Brampton Health Club; [hon.] Literary prizes won at secondary school for writing short articles and poetry; [oth. writ.] Articles - school magazine; [pers.] Continually striving to improve personal actualization in terms of spiritual growth by practising various philosophical and religious perspectives is Buddhism.; [a.] Chesterfield, Derbyshire, UK

WHELER, AMANDA
[b.] Stratford-on-Avon, Warwickshire; [p.] Stephen and Annette Wheler; [m.] Robert B. Kenhard, pending Christmas '96!!; [ed.] Burgess Hill School for Girls; [occ.] Technical P.A. for Company Selling Flight Training Devices (Simulators); [memb.] Full member of the Institute of Advanced Motorists; [oth. writ.] None published but I do use a "Thought Recorder" in which I have written one or two short poems 2 some personal, philosophical observations about life in general!; [pers.] My father was a well-respected Free-lance journalist. He died 30 years ago and I hope I have inherited a small part of his talent for the written word. I am delighted my poem was chosen for publication. A small tribute to my letter.; [a.] Hassocks, W. Sussex, UK

WHITE, EMILY MARGARET
[pen.] Peggy White and Maggs Tyler; [b.] 15 December 1931, Ifield, Sussex; [p.] Rose Cooper, Frank Cooper; [m.] Godfrey White, 21 February 1953; [ch.] David Godfrey, Sandra Margaret; [ed.] Ifield C.E. left school at 14 went into service in 1949 to bluecoats school Christ Hospital; [occ.] Retired after 13 years at Gatwick airport as security supervisor for B.A.A.; [memb.] Adult education forest school Horsham for needle work and painting.; [hon.] Certificate of open learning Crawley College of further education; [oth. writ.] Children's short stories none put forward for publication yet. Some poems published one in Christian poets of the South East one more waiting publication.; [pers.] I try to take people at face value I try to put sincerity in my work and humor in some when you see me what you see is what you get I hate shallow people and I wish I'd learned more.; [a.] Horsham, West Sussex, UK

WHITE, FREDERICK J.
[b.] 17 May 1920, Kensington, London; [p.] Horace White, Minnie White; [m.] Pauline Joan (Toll), 4 August 1946; [ch.] Michael, Peter, Valerie; [ed.] Only Elementary; [occ.] (Electrician) Retired; [hon.] School Prizes. War Medals, Far Est Campaign; [pers.] I appreciate poems and songs that have feeling.; [a.] Fakenham, Norfolk, UK

WHITE, JOANNE
[b.] 28 April 1937, Bristol; [p.] Robert Burns and Rosalind Carey; [m.] Divorce; [ch.] Helen Irving, Neil Duncan, Melanie Jane; [ed.] St. George Grammar, Bristol; [occ.] Housewife/Artist; [memb.] Scottish Borders Arts Network, Galashiels Writers Group, Borders Family History Society, Soldiers, Sailors, Airmens Family Assocn.; [oth. writ.] Several poems published by Arrival Press and Poetry Now.; [pers.] An Anglo Scot I returned to the Borders 23 years ago. The history and beauty of the Cheviot Hills are an inspiration to my art and poetry; [a.] Village, Morebattle, Roxbs, UK

WHITE, JOHN GEORGE WILLIAM
[pen.] "Stagger The Bard", "The Benbow Bard" or "Bard Of Benbow"; [b.] 1 May 1926, Portsmouth; [p.] Hilda Clemett White (Nee Evans), George Thomas Albert White; [m.] Annie Patricia White (Nee Widdicombe), 20 March 1950 (Belfast); [ch.] Graham John White (43 yrs.), Trevor Michael White (38 yrs.); [ed.] Portsmouth Junior Technical School then Navalaircraft Apprenticeship (fleet air arm) also Borough Polytechnic (London); [occ.] Retired; [memb.] Society of friends of the Fleet Air Arm Museum (SoFFRAM) Civil Service Motoring Assoc. (C.S.M.A.); [hon.] Imperial Service Medal; [oth. writ.] 20 `Odes', eight of which were written for and about my ex Fleet Air Arm colleagues. One "A Benbow Catherine", published in SoFFRAM newsletter-magazine No 46 (April 1996) Other `Odes' about various happenings in my life or of people I've met. All unpublished.; [pers.] Not given to writing poetry. - This is my first attempt. Write humorous and topical odes, because they are not bound by conventional restrictions, which apple to poetry and limericks.; [a.] Gillingham, Kent, UK

WHITE, KATIE LOUISE
[pen.] Katie White; [b.] 7 March 1986, Leicester; [p.] Mark White and Anya White (nee Plucinski); [ed.] Holy Cross R.C. School Stonesby Ave, Leicester; [occ.] School girl; [memb.] Magpie Club; [hon.] 2 art competitions, 2 radio competitions; [pers.] Loves reading, writing and painting.; [a.] Leicester, Leics, UK

WHITE, PHILIP R.
[b.] 28 September 1965, Taunton; [p.] Marion White, Brian White; [m.] Tonia White; [ch.] Anthony, Brett, Stacey, Terri White; [ed.] Prior of Juniors/Heathfiled Comp. Secondary School; [occ.] Security Manager for McDonalds Fast Food Restaurant in Taunton; [memb.] Our Heritage DX Group GB Club; [hon.] It's nice to be important but it is also important to be nice my little saying with my

children are brought up with; [oth. writ.] This poem is dedicated to my wife, with out her love and support and the lovely children she has gives me, she has made me the man I am to day of which I am very proud all my love bird.; [pers.] Why must Governments fight for more power, why must people of all colours and creeds fight to have more than their neighbours to kill and main the innocent to get what they want can't we all share and live in peace with each other and get on with life.; [a.] Taunton, Somerset, UK

WHITE, RAYMOND
[b.] 10 December 1942, Plymouth, Devon; [p.] Charles White, Patricia White; [m.] Catherine Patricia Brush, 10 June 1972; [ch.] Dominic Piers (Ba Cantab!); [ed.] St Ignatius College, Norwood Adelaide Sth. Australia, professional training through Metropolitan College, St. Albans; [occ.] Training Officer for Financial Services Company; [memb.] Associate, Chartered Insurance Institute; [hon.] Awards and diplomas in professional studies; [oth. writ.] Several poems published in books produced by another publisher. Professional study course produced by the Chartered Insurance Institute.; [pers.] I love nature and God's beautiful creation. Living in the country I see the wonderful moods of nature and try to capture them in writing and in photography.; [a.] Wimborne, Dorset, UK

WHITE, STEPHEN GEORGE
[pen.] S. G. White; [b.] 5 June 1950, Sheerness, Kent; [p.] Leslie White, Dorothy White; [m.] Ann Elizabeth White, 11 October 1969; [occ.] Stevedore Kent United Contractors; [oth. writ.] Have been writing poems for 24 years, which are carefully recorded in a book. But this is the first time I have attempted to get anything published; [pers.] My poems document what has touched my life over the last 24 years. Be it political, personnel or just plain humour; [a.] Sheerness, Kent, UK

WHITE, SUSAN
[b.] 15 April 1947, Canvey Island; [p.] Iris White and George White; [ed.] Timberlog School Basildon Gray's Thurrock Technical Colleges Charlotte Mason Teachers Training College, Ambleside; [occ.] Proprietor book shop; [memb.] Canvey Island Sailing Club; [oth. writ.] Wrote and published book history of Canvey Island, five Generations; [a.] Canvey Island, Essex, UK

WHITELAW, ANDREW
[b.] 18 January 1972; [pers.] It is better to be heard only once, and understood than to be heard a thousand times, and never be.; [a.] Edinburgh, UK

WHITFIELD, CORIWAIANNA GEORGINA
[pen.] Georgina; [b.] 9 April, Co Down; [p.] Deceased; [m.] The Late Timothy (Kenya Farmer), 14 January 1948; [ch.] Deirdre, Roy, Pauline; [ed.] Ashleigh House School, Belfast, Edinburgh College of Domestic Science; [occ.] Psychic Medium; [memb.] Effingham Golf Club Silver Star Spiritual and Psychic Group.; [oth. writ.] Many poetical "jangles" previously assigned to the wastepaper basket.; [pers.] If I feel strongly about any thing I have always written about it in rhyme. Only recently, as a psychic I have been a ware of John, taking an interest in my endeavors.; [a.] Twiners Hill, W. Sussex, UK

WHITTAKER, SHIRLEY
[pen.] Shirley E. Whittaker; [b.] 5 March 1941, Bolton, Lancs; [p.] Harry Bulpitt, Phyliss Bulpitt; [m.] Leonard Whittaker, 28 March 1959; [ch.] Russell Barry, Peter Henry; [ed.] Secondary and Bolton Tec College; [occ.] Retired nursing sister/midwife; [memb.] Private; [oth. writ.] Various poems and numerous prose written for special occasions, when commissioned.; [pers.] Greatly influenced by the great English poet and essayist. Leigh Hunt.; [a.] Saint Marys, Isles of Scilly, UK

WICKHAM, GERALD PETER
[b.] 29 May 1974, Wexford, Ireland; [p.] Gerry Wickham, Helen Green; [ed.] Christian Brothers School, Wexford, Carlow Regional Technical College, University of Ulster, at Jordanstown; [occ.] Physical Education Student; [memb.] St. Mary's (Rosslare) G.A.A. Club; [pers.] Endeavour is the most powerful word I know. Help us due to those who are incapable of trying yet poorer are those who avoid endeavour. May God help us all.; [a.] Rosslare Harbour, Ireland

WILCOX, MRS. ENID KATHLEEN
[pen.] Enid; [b.] 7 October 1919, Monmouthshire; [p.] Oliver and Martha Young; [m.] Divorced; [ch.] Colin John; [occ.] Retired; [pers.] I strive to write what I see in the world around me.; [a.] Monmouth, Gwent, UK

WILD, KEVIN
[b.] 2 June 1956, London; [p.] Sylvia Charles; [m.] Jessica, 18 April 1982; [ch.] (3) Gemma, Lauren, Nathan; [ed.] Hailing Manor Secondary Modern Crydon; [occ.] Silver Smith - I work for Carrard the Crown Jeweller; [memb.] Freeman city of London playing in Local Band, the "Rhythm Club"; [oth. writ.] Several song lyrics published; [pers.] "Strange Days" was written, while the Berlin wall was being destroyed I was pondering of the consequences for the future, both sides of the imaginary line.; [a.] Redhill, Surrey, UK

WILDE, ALEX
[b.] 28/3/1946, Buxton, Derbyshire; [p.] Phyllis Audrey Whitwell, John Lawrence Whitwell; [m.] Robert Wilde (died 1989), were married in 1970; [ch.] Wendy; [ed.] Educated at St. Joseph's Convent, Dar-Es-Salaam; Loretto Convent, Nairobi; Durban Girls' Convent High School (South Africa); [occ.] Freelance Translator (German); part-time Singer (of Marlene Dietrich songs); [oth. writ.] I started writing short stories as a child and had my first success at the age of thirteen, with short stories appearing in the Kenya Weekly News. I have worked as a journalist and am currently working on a full-length novel.; [pers.] I have always believed it is important to live life to the full (this is not a rehearsal!); to be kind to others; and "to thine own self be true".; [a.] Norbury Hill, London

WILDISH, KEVIN ANTHONY
[b.] 22 October 1956, Chatham, Kent; [p.] Fredrick Wildish, Vera Wildish; [m.] Rosemary Beatrice Wildish, 27 October 1990; [ed.] Highfield Secondary Modern Chatham, Kent; [occ.] Security Officer since Oct 1993 previously H.M.F. 18 years with 1st Battalion Scots Guards; [memb.] R.S.P.B. (Royal Society Protection Birds), W.W.F. (World Wildlife Federation); [hon.] Northern Ireland medal, Gulf War medal, Kiwati Liberation medal; [oth. writ.] 1. Own biography not yet finished, 2. Short stories none yet published; [pers.] I'm greatly influenced by my past, for serving in H.M.F. Civi Street is my new beginning, my start in my new life. The West Chapter.; [a.] Dartford, Kent, UK

WILDY, ALEXANDRA
[b.] 15 September 1977, Burnley General; [p.] Alexandra Wildy and Joe Wildy; [ed.] SS J Fisher and T. More R.C. High School, Nelson and Colne College, A Levels Graphics and Fine Art; [occ.] Student; [pers.] I wish to dedicate this poem to my boyfriend Matthew Redwood, and tell Edward, Cindy, Jo-Ann, Samantha, Maria, Joseph, Poppy, and Bianca-Mercedes that I love them all.; [a.] Burnley, Lancashire, UK

WILKINSON, MARIE
[pen.] Marie Wilkinson; [b.] 7 June 1953, Paddington; [m.] Dave Wilkinson, 18 July 1992; [ch.] Michael Casey; [ed.] Secondary Modern School; [occ.] Plate Service, Waitress; [oth. writ.] I have had a poem published in the book called the winter medley 1992.; [pers.] I like children and animals, and do a lot of charity walks for them, and my writing, is based on what I are in everyday life.; [a.] London, UK

WILLETTS, SARAH MARIA
[b.] 30 November 1974; [ch.] Karrise Reanne; [hon.] One of four people selected as torchbearers, who represented great Britain in the 1994 Winter Olympics, Norway; [oth. writ.] A few poems published in local anthologies; [pers.] I wrote the poems 'Child' when I was fifteen; [a.] Sutton, Coldfield, West Midlands, UK

WILLIAMS, BEULAM
[b.] 6 May 1966, Paddington; [p.] Mr. and Mrs. Williams; [ch.] Michael Williams (age 7); [ed.] CSG English, French, Biology; [occ.] Housewife; [oth. writ.] This is my first piece of work.; [pers.] I was inspired to write poetry in my kitchen on a cold sunny day in January 1995 since then I feel as though it is something that fate wants me to do..; [a.] London, UK

WILLIAMS, CECIL
[b.] 24 October 1917, Trellech, Monmouth, Gwent; [p.] Cicelia and Albert; [m.] Irene, 20 August 1941; [ch.] Patricia, Sian; [ed.] Cofe Trellech Nr Monmouth; [occ.] Retired; [oth. writ.] 4 poems, world of verse 1975, one poem arrival press 1995, one poem "Island Moods and Reflections" an anthology of verse of the British Isles; [pers.] I like studying local history, photography, painting, walking, reading, music.; [a.] Crosskeys, Newport, Gwent, UK

WILLIAMS, ELWYN
[b.] 21 June 1929, Bangor, N Wales; [p.] John Williams, Elizabeth Williams; [m.] Mary Williams, 21 March 1959; [ch.] Clive and Peter; [ed.] Friars Grammar School, Bangor, N Wales, Liverpool College of Art; [occ.] Retired head of Education Services, Manchester Art Galleries; [memb.] Founder Member, Mountaineering Club of North Wales; [hon.] Art Dep't Visited by H.R.H. Princess Margaret and Lord Snowden C1963 Appointed first ever Chairman of Moderators to Supervise Art Examinations in Secondary Schools throughout Northern England. Responsible for 90,000 Candidates in 1987; [oth. writ.] Practicing artist Many works held in private collections throughout England, and some held in private collections in Ireland, the United States of America, Canada and Australia. Lectured at Several Universities and Art Galleries in the United Kingdom including the National Gallery London.; [pers.] My intention is to communicate ideas and images that will sometimes delight, sometimes amuse and sometimes influence in ways that I hope will be for the general good.; [a.] Tarleton, Lancashire

WILLIAMS, JOSIE
[b.] 5 June 1959, Kingsdown, Swindon; [p.] Edna and Douglas Williams; [m.] Victor Chamberlain, 30 June 1989; [ch.] Leanne, Calum, Floyd; [ed.] Headlands Comprehensive; [occ.] Writer/Photographer; [memb.] Licentiate member of Master Photographers Association; [oth. writ.] Book - The Wiltshire Hall of Fame. Articles in Wiltshire Life, my weekly, making music, Wiltshire Star, Swindon Messenger, several poems published. Photographic exhibition - Wiltshire Hall of Fame, Light Fantastic, Round the Bend. Also educational books and press.; [pers.] People of the world unite, and fight, fight dance to the light of unconditional love; [a.] Swindon, Wiltshire, UK

WILLIAMS, JULIE D.
[m.] David; [ch.] Richard, Janice, Helen, Suzanne, Michael; [occ.] Ward sister, St. James Hospital, Portsmouth; [oth. writ.] None. I have only just begun to write anything other than numerous rhymes for my family.; [pers.] My words are a reflection of my inner feelings and I write as an outlet for these. This poem is the first I have ever shared with anyone other than my family.; [a.] Southsea, Hants, UK

WILLIAMS, MARJORIE SHARPE
[pen.] Marjorie Sharpe; [b.] 2 November 1926, Henllan; [p.] G. A. Jones and Gladys Alice Jones; [m.] Elwyn Howatson Williams, 27 June 1953; [ed.] Henllan Primary School, Denbigh County School; [occ.] Retired; [a.] Henllan, Denbigh, Denbighshire, UK

WILLIAMS, NIGEL THOMAS
[b.] 26 May 1947, Ivybridge; [p.] Thomas Harold and Celia Mary; [m.] Twice divorced, Sadly; [ch.] David Neil Williams; [ed.] Ivybridge Secondary Modern (And Life!); [occ.] Was a storekeeper. Invalid Friday 13th May, 1994! (Manic Depression); [oth. writ.] Apart from letters and brief observations - nothing published. I write shortstories, (Sci-Fi and humour) and poems on any subject.; [pers.] I write what I observe in people, places and events and my own experiences/feelings. I try to be myself. Trust in God and keep my quill and parchment dry! Influenced by Dickens, Wells, Poe, Milligan, Bob Dylan, Milton, Gray.; [a.] Ivybridge, Devon, UK

WILLIAMS, PHILIP TREVOR
[b.] 8 November 1938, Hull, Yorks; [p.] William Williams, Dolly Williams; [m.] Rosina, 20 January 1973; [ed.] Grammar School; [occ.] Retired; [pers.] I was a policeman, I suffered from stress, as a result I began to write poetry. What a happy release!; [a.] Deal, Kent, UK

WILLIAMS, PHILLIP
[pen.] Phillip Gordon; [b.] 8 October 1959, Doveridge, Derbyshire; [m.] Teresa Williams; [ch.] Dan Williams; [ed.] Thomas Alleynes High School, Uttoxeter. Bradford and Ilkley Community College, Ilkley, West Yorkshire; [occ.] Craft/Retail Worker; [hon.] Cert. Youth and Comm.; [oth. writ.] Poems, short stories, as yet unpublished.; [pers.] Don't give up, even when times are hard. Grit your teeth, smile and get on with it!; [a.] Belper, Derbyshire, UK

WILLIAMSON, KAY
[pen.] Kay Williamson; [memb.] Interest, Art, Music, Literature, Poetry, Yoga, Travel; [pers.] Favourite song "Everyone's talking at me, I don't hear a word they're saying favourite words - 1 Corinthians chapter 13, verses 1-13.

WILLIAMSON, NATASHA
[b.] 20 March 1972, Saint Pauls, Hemel Hempstead; [p.] Andrew and Rosemary, Stothert; [m.] Michael Williamson, 7 December 1991; [ch.] Sophie Williamson; [ed.] Lord Williams School Thame; [occ.] Housewife; [oth. writ.] First attempt at professional poetry, although have written at home; [pers.] Due to my grandmothers death I felt I needed to write my grief down in poetry, I also very often show my emotions in writing poems, I have never really thought about sending them in to maybe published until now; [a.] Buckinghamshire, UK

WILLIAMSON, MRS. SHIRLEY
[b.] 29 November 1955, Huddersfield; [p.] Mr. and Mrs. C. Gilroy; [m.] Russell Scott Williamson, 18 November 1989; [ch.] Ruth, Emma-Louise, Jason; [ed.] Rawthorpe County Primary, Junior and Senior Secondary Schools; [occ.] Housewife; [pers.] I care about the world as a whole and the sufferings of all human beings.; [a.] Weston-super-Mare, Avon, UK

WILLISON, BRENDA
[pen.] Brenda Willison; [b.] 5 May 1954, Manchester; [p.] Neil Laurence Elthorpe, Martha Elthorpe; [m.] Peter Lawrence Willison, 9 December 1972; [ch.] Joanna Dawn Willison, Jeanette Claire Willison; [ed.] Whalley Range High School, Manchester; [occ.] Disney store cast member; [memb.] A.H.G.T.C., L.C.T.C. (Ancient and Honorable Guild of Town Criers) (Loyal Company of Town Criers - South West Committee Member); [hon.] Niagra Falls Town Criers Champion; [oth. writ.] None published (Never tried); [pers.] Kindness is the golden chain by which lives are bound together.; [a.] Peterborough, Cambridgeshire, UK

WILSHAW, J.
[pen.] Jay; [b.] 29 October 1951, Stoke-on-Trent; [p.] Vincent and Marion Wilshaw; [ed.] Woodhouse County Secondary School, North Staff's College of Further Education (Engineering); [occ.] Maint Technician; [hon.] Photographic awards in landscape still life photo essay, negative to positive printing colour photography; [pers.] When it flows, write it down.; [a.] Longton, S-o-T, Staff, UK

WILSON, ELIZABETH
[b.] 10 March 1954, Liverpool; [p.] Robert Wilson and Elizabeth Muriel Wilson; [ed.] Cuddington County Primary School Hartford Girls School, Cheshire School of Art; [occ.] Portrait Artist; [oth. writ.] Poem 'Pavement-Artist' published in the British poetry review, short story 'The Song Of A Chaffinch' for BBC Radio; [pers.] My poems reflect sensitive observations of life, from the beauty of nature to the harsh reality of a modern prosperous society, which too often ignores the needs of the disadvantaged, and animal welfare.; [a.] Chester, Cheshire, UK

WILSON, LEONARD
[b.] 31 October 1940, Yorkshire; [p.] Mary and Charli Wilson; [m.] Carol Wilson, 12 April 1960; [ch.] Angela and Susan; [ed.] Stainforth Secondary Modern; [oth. writ.] Several poems published local papers; [pers.] I strive to reflect what mankind is doing to the environment the good or bad in my writing I have been influenced by modern poets.; [a.] Scunthorpe, N. Lincs, UK

WILSON, MARGARET ELIZABETH
[b.] 16 March 1929, Birmingham; [p.] Emily Parker, Frederick Parker; [m.] Divorced; [ch.] Pamela, Ian, Alan (3 children); [occ.] Retired; [memb.] First Time Edited by Josephine Austin, also Birmingham, Midland Institute; [hon.] Highly Commended. Publication in "Travellers Joy." Printed by Birmingham, Midland Institute also Publications in "Poetry Now" anthologies Regional Central England. Midlands, Eastern England, South East Regional; [oth. writ.] I read and write my own work. Have written many poems.; [a.] Birmingham, West Midlands, UK

WINPENNY, RICHARD P.
[b.] 13 June 1969, Edinburgh; [p.] Brian and Olive Winpenny; [ed.] Merchiston Castle School, Edinburgh, Hertford College Oxford University. 1987-1990; [occ.] Administrator for Computer Training Company (Oxford Computer Applications LTD); [memb.] Oxford University Fencing Club; [hon.] Microsoft Certified Professional; [oth. writ.] No other published work at present; [a.] Oxford, Oxon, UK

WINTER, SUSAN JEAN
[b.] 24 July 1948, Kidderminster; [p.] John Cross, Beatrice May Cross; [m.] Anthony John Winter, 1 August 1964; [ch.] Teresa Jane Nigel John, Amanda Joy Timothy John, Joanne May; [ed.] Sladen Secondary Modern; [occ.] Canteen Assistant; [pers.] Everyday life is the basis for my poems, experience of which comes from life itself.; [a.] Stourport, Worcs, UK

WINTON, LINZIE NICOLE
[b.] 18 May 1981, Aberdeen; [p.] Elizabeth and Lewis Winton; [ed.] St Machar Academy; [occ.] School Girl; [pers.] I find it easy to express the way I feel through my writing. I enjoy writing poetry and reading other people's work. I think of my poems as a hobby but I am hoping to develop it in the future. Having my poem in print has encouraged me to write more.; [a.] Aberdeen, Scotland

WIRTH, HEIDI JANE
[pen.] Amber Cadelski; [b.] 2 November 1979, Edmonton; [p.] Elizabeth Wirth, Helmut Wirth; [ed.] Moulsham High School Brian Close Chelmsford Essex; [occ.] Doing GCSE'S; [pers.] Writing novels and poems gives me a sense of fulfillment and satisfaction. I am able to release strong emotions in this way, and feel better for it. It is a gift that everyone should feel; [a.] Chelmsford, Essex, UK

WITT, DANIELLE
[b.] 11 May 1966, Newport, Pagnell; [p.] Susan Holden and Peter John Witt; [ch.] Sky, Xien, Ishtar; [ed.] Local Primary, St. Dunstans Abbey, Plymouth, Tavistock, Comprehensive; [oth. writ.] Other poems as yet unpublished; [pers.] Being interested in human cultural developing, I am enjoying writing poetry that explores societies holding of human reactions.; [a.] Tavistock, Devon, UK

WOLSTENHOLME, IVAN
[b.] 14 July 1962, Rotherham; [p.] Ralph Burton and Marjorie May Wolstenholme; [ch.] 2 Children; [ed.] Secondary Modern; [occ.] Engineering Fitter; [pers.] Do what you wilt shall be the whole of the law.; [a.] Selby, N. Yorks, UK

WONG, YIN HENG
[b.] Malaysia; [p.] Chan Wong and Ah Moy Foo; [ed.] King George V Secondary School, Malaysia, Raja Melewar Teaching College, Malaysia, University of Strathclyde, Scotland.; [occ.] Student; [oth. writ.] One or Two poems in College Newsletters.

WOOD, AMALA ROSE
[pen.] "Amaqla"; [b.] 20th Century, Unsure; [p.] Seldom seen, but when so, it was fun and games.; [ch.] Two, a girl, later a boy, both infants by adoption.; [ed.] The 3 "R"s, with old style discipline U.K. Europe; [occ.] Writing/Former times S.R.N. Librarian, School Teacher; [memb.] Charities, Drama Horticultural; [hon.] Schools and Stage. Guildhall School of Music; [oth. writ.] Cookery Receipts. (Publ.) Puppet Plays for school and Royalty.; [pers.] Trust, faith. He who never takes a chance nothing much of ill will happen to him. But nothing much will ever happen - "Lord Halifax".; [a.] Dorchester, Dorset, UK

WOOD, JANE
[pen.] Jane Girlbert; [b.] 26 January 1934, Letham; [p.] Thomas and Jemima Morrison; [m.] 1953, Divorced 1989; [ed.] Letham Primary School Forfar Academy; [occ.] Retired Cleaner, Gardener, Farm Worker.; [memb.] Salvation Army Brechin Ramblers Club past member MENSA; [hon.] Certificates in theory of music up to grade 8, Royal schools of music London; [oth. writ.] Various poems; [pers.] I believe that God holds the whole universe, and I feel very close to nature. I think all things work together for good, and there is good in everyone, my favorite poets are Violet Jacob, and Max Ehrmann.; [a.] Forfar, Angus, UK

WOOD, MRS. LINDA
[b.] 24 February 1958, Mansfield; [p.] Mr. and Mrs. C. A. Bray; [m.] Mr. Kevin Geoffrey Wood, 5 June 1976; [ed.] Woodhill Secondary School, Collingham, Nr Newark, Notts; [occ.] Check-out Operative Morrisons; [pers.] Writing poetry makes me happy even when I'm sad. I am influenced grately by real life.; [a.] Newark, Nottinghamshire, UK

WOODHOUSE, LUNA
[pen.] Tina-Jane Woodhouse; [b.] 18 July 1965, Watford; [p.] Robin Woodhouse, Hilary Woodhouse; [ed.] Leggatts School, Watford and Patchetts Green Equestrian Centre, Aldenham; [occ.] Auxiliary Nurse; [hon.] B.H.S. Horsemastership Certificate, Proficiency in Nursing Certificate. Currently Studying for N.V.Q. level 2 in 'Direct Care'; [oth. writ.] Own book of spiritual poetry - Beyond the Rainbows End, in print very soon. Poems published in 'The Dragon Chronicle' magazine.; [pers.] I hope that my poetry opens up a gateway to a world of imagination, where people can receive the help they need to make their dreams come true.; [a.] St. Albans, Herts, UK

WOODS, BETTY
[pen.] Bett Wood; [b.] 6/1/36, Crohonaugh, Bally Bofey; [p.] Willie Armstrong, Kathleen Armstrong; [m.] Michael Woods, 24 Nov. 60; [ch.] 15 children: Michael, James, Mary, Kate, Joe, Caroline, Eilish, Sophia, Barbara, Delores, Anglia, John, Tess, Martin, Claire; [ed.] N.S. Community School, High School; [occ.] Dress Maker, Housekeeper; [oth. writ.] poems; [a.] Gortahork, Donegal

WOODS, SUSAN
[pen.] Harriet Hobbs; [b.] 2 January 1958, Bedford; [p.] Cyril Woods and Peggy Presland; [ed.] Roxton Primary School from '63 to '69 and Longsands Comprehensive until 1974 (left no qualifications); [occ.] Factory Worker Packer; [oth. writ.] I attended John Bunyan Community College, and learnt an awful lot about metering the tutor was wonderful! And full of praise. (I could never understand why really) I have my own book due out sometime this year 'insomniac's nightmare' and have a poem published in a book entitled 'Broken Resolutions' by the poetry now people.; [pers.] My writings are about animal welfare. I try to live my life free of cruelty to those creatures who share our world. I believe, whatever happens to us, is meant.; [a.] Bedford, Beds, UK

WOODTIME, MARTIN JAMES
[b.] 5 August 1959, Eastbourne; [ed.] Hastings Grammar School; [occ.] Accounts Supervisor; [memb.] Various private members clubs; [pers.] My writing is influenced by man's inability to cope with his own world.; [a.] Hastings, E. Sussex, UK

WOOTEN, SARITA
[b.] 29 January 1954, Swindon; [p.] Royden Fluck, Andre Fluck; [m.] Stuart Bunce, 24 June 1976; [ch.] Mandy, Elaine, Rachel, Lee, Alexander, Lisa, Frances, Richard, Michelle, Kerry-Anne, Louise; [ed.] Groundwell Road Infants, Lawns Infant and Junior, St. Joseph's Secondary and Comprehensive Schools, Judith Hockaday School of Dancing, Heath School of Dancing, College all in Swindon, Buxton School of Drama; [memb.] A 'Friend' of Anne Frank Educational Trust; [hon.] Academy award for 'Spoken English', Dancing medals, Karate yellow belt, GCE English French, Art, CSE Art, Extra in 1984 Richard Burton's film.; [oth. writ.] Write poems and essays, stories at home. I decided if I cannot write for people, I'd write for myself and children. Have an uncle abroad Gerard Lacourrege who's wrote several books.; [pers.] Would have liked to have become a journalist poet, direct films and write them. We were not promised success, its up to everyone to make it, aim with strength.; [a.] Chippenham, Wiltshire, UK

WOOTTON, JENNIFER DIANE
[b.] 24 December 1947, Sheffield; [p.] James Hill, Betina Hill; [m.] Edward Ian Wootton, 10 September 1966; [ch.] Victoria Helen, Sarah Elizabeth; [ed.] Abbeydale Grammar School for girls, Sheffield, Whiteley's Business of Sheffield; [occ.] Mature Student, due to graduate in June 1997; [memb.] Member of the Classical Association of Sheffield; [hon.] British Institute of Linguists certificates in French, Spanish and Italian, 'O' level in Latin, 'A' level in classical studies, reading at present for a degree in Biblical studies, graduating 1997; [oth. writ.] First poem published in 'Remember Hillsborough' - an anthology commemorating the Hillsborough disaster, several poems published in anthologies by forward press, poem published in Sheffield 'Gazette'; [pers.] The poetry I write reflects the changing seasons in nature and the similarly changing nature of humanity. It has been greatly influenced by my studies of the ancient Greek and Latin literature.; [a.] Sheffield, Yorkshire, UK

WORTHINGTON, CONNIE
[b.] 2 December, 1918, Rishton, Lancs; [p.] Thomas and Dorothy Wilson; [m.] William Worthington, 12 December, 1945; [ch.] Jean, Stephen, Catherine; [ed.] C of E. Elementary School, Whalley, Nr Blackburn, Lancashire; [occ.] Housewife; [oth. writ.] Three poems published in local papers.; [pers.] As a young girl I loved to read poetry. and wished I could write verse like. Claire Richie, and Noel Coward "The girl that I used to be." Then later Patience Strong.; [a.] Accrington, Lancashire

WRIGHT, ALAN
[b.] 18 November 1945, Fareham; [p.] William Wright and Agnes Wright; [m.] Sylvia Wright, 27 June 1970; [ch.] Michelle, Darren, Caroline, Sarah; [ed.] Funtley Primary, Fareham Secondary; [occ.] Storekeeper; [memb.] Locks Heath Free, Church, RSPB; [oth. writ.] Poems published in anthologies, mainly for triumph house, A Christian Poetry Publication.; [pers.] I try to write poetry that will inspire and help the people who read it, usually with a Christian flavour; [a.] Southampton, Hants, UK

WRIGHT, SHEILA PATRICIA
[b.] 5 January 1930, Moston, Manchester; [p.] Michael Killeen, Annie Killeen; [m.] Widow; [ed.] St Joseph's College, Bradford, Bradford Technical College; [occ.] Retired I; [memb.] Anchor Bowling Club, North Yorkshire Bowling League Pharmaceutical Society; [hon.] Pharmaceutical Chemist (PhC MPS); [oth. writ.] Several poems published with various publications. Article for bowling monthly paper; [pers.] I feel life around me offers so much to feel, ponder and write about.; [a.] Baildon, West Yorkshire, UK

WRIGHT, MISS TAMSIN
[pen.] Tottie; [b.] 15 March 1974, Cuckfield; [p.] Mara and Don; [ed.] Ardingly College, Haywards Heath, Sussex; [occ.] Travel Consultant; [oth. writ.] Several published in various anthologies both in the UK and USA; [pers.] "You cannot discover new oceans unless you have the courage to lose sight of the shore" "Success is a journey, not a destination"; [a.] Worthing, W. Sussex, UK

WYLDE, H. E.
[pen.] Penny Fielding Sherwood; [b.] 14 August 1943, Old Hill; [p.] Horace Fielding Sherwood; [m.] Dorthy Sherwood Wylde, 27 June 1962; [ch.] David and Philip; [ed.] Rowley Regis Secondary Girls School, Llandrillo Technical College; [occ.] Housewife; [memb.] Methodist Church, Mind User's Forum; [oth. writ.] None published; [pers.] Poetry was taught me by my grandmother she always told me it improves your ability to speak with rhythm on the philosophical side my father taught me to reason a matter through my mother had a love of kipling and words worth and Shakespeare so this came naturally to me.

YAI, HOC DENG DENG
[b.] 1 January 1965, Aweil, South Sudan; [p.] Deng Hoc Yai and Nyanjok Akot Deng; [ed.] Nyamlell Secondary School, (S. Sudan), Cairo University, Fac. of Arts, Dept. of English Language and Literature (Egypt), (BA) Luton University, Fac. of Humanities, Luton, England. (May); [occ.] Teacher of English as a second or foreign language (Unemployed); [memb.] Member, Materials Development Association (MATSDA), University of Luton, Fac. of Humanities 75 Castle St. Luton, Bed Fordshire LU1 3AJ; [oth. writ.] Unpublished anthology of poetry entitled "Songs of Joy and Sorrow", featuring The Silent Victims, Sacrifices, The Hollow Speech, The Mortal Split, The Freedom Fighter, Eve, The Secret passion and The Charming Idol.; [pers.] Sorrow, which has entombed the silent victims in the sudan prompted me to write poems as the sympathetic voice of the oppressed civilians. I wish mankind happiness and condemn anyone who makes their pursuit of this goal fruitless as much as I do condemn vice in general. I love and appreciate virtue and beauty of the human body and soul.; [a.] London, England

YATES, ELEANOR
[b.] 20 October 1912, Blackbury; [p.] Michial, Ada, Connell; [m.] Leslie A. Yates, 13 March 1934; [ch.] Five; [ed.] Convent; [occ.] Retired; [oth. writ.] Am, writing my life. Story, and had a couple of poems published in the local magazine. Free gratus.; [pers.] I started to get interested in writing poetry when my husband died in 1991 and my daughter said it would pass my time along.; [a.] Kirkby Lonsdale, Cumbria, UK

YATES, MR. LAURIE
[b.] Enfield, Middx; [p.] Edward Yates, Eileen Yates; [occ.] Merchant Banker; [pers.] To challenge existing views in my writing.; [a.] Beckenham, Kent, UK

YOUNG, BRENDA
[pen.] B. J. Young; [b.] 24 June 1953, Brighton; [p.] Sheila Young, Ronald Young; [ed.] Mouiscoombe Secondary Modern Ace 3 Her Majesty's Forces; [occ.] Prematurely retired by ill Health; [memb.] Royal Britism Legion; [oth. writ.] Other poems written and a novel awaiting completion soon; [pers.] If I can convey my innermost thoughts to strangers on paper, and they can understand my emotions, I have achieved my Aim.; [a.] Brighton, Sussex, UK

YOUNG, CATHERINE B.
[b.] 31 August 1964, Bushey; [m.] Nick Young, 2 May 1981; [ch.] Andrew, Kerry, Daniel, Laura, Michael; [occ.] Housewife and Primary School Volunteer Help; [memb.] Parent School Governer; [oth. writ.] I have written other poems and songs (unpublished). I am inspired by my heart and personal experiences.; [pers.] This poem was written for my daughter Laura and my niece Hayley, sadly lost, whose birthdays fall in March.; [a.] Hemel Hempstead, Herts, UK

YOUNGER, JOHN
[b.] 1 June 1930, Croydon, Surrey; [m.] Maureen Allen, 1967; [ed.] John Ruskill School, Croydon, Loyal College of Art (Painting School), University of Leeds (School of English); [occ.] Retd. University Lecturer; [hon.] A. R. C. A. and B.A. Honours; [oth. writ.] Poems published in various magazines including, Ariel, Circlings The Bound Spiral, Candelabrum, Envoi, Haiku Quart, Interactions, Iota, Poetry and Audience, Psychopoetica and Silver Wolf; [pers.] I trained and taught as a painter until blindness forced retirement. Read Eng. Lit. at Leeds Univ. gain lectureship, taught school of Eng. write poetry (about everything) full time, using computer with voice synthesizer.; [a.] Nr Market Rasen, Lincs, UK

YOUNGER, ROSE
[pen.] Rose Younger; [b.] 28 February 1918, London; [p.] Deceased; [m.] Deceased 1981, 28 November 1940; [ch.] Two Daughter, 4 Grandchildren, 1 Great Granddaughter; [ed.] Spent Seven Years in and out of Hospital from age 7 until 13, and so unable to receive Basic Education; [occ.] Retired; [memb.] Chairman of Cultural Society for Senior Citizens, Co-Ordinator of Class for Public Speaking, Self Expression, Retiring Editor of Journal J.A.C.S. (Jewish Association of Cultural Societies); [oth. writ.] Joined a local writers 1983 workshop, only person of my age wonderful rapport I had never written anything before, I found I had a natural flair, completed to date approx. 150 pieces of work poetry short stories and humour.; [pers.] I have given readings of my work to groups of people, in libraries, homes, for the disabled and blind in doing so I feel somewhat humble in my small way to give pleasure to so many people.; [a.] London, UK

YUEN, RITA
[pen.] Rita (Haines) Maiden Name; [b.] 21 June 1924, Middlesbrough; [p.] John George and Edith Haines; [m.] William James Yuen (Deceased), 6 December 1947; [ch.] Five, Three Boys and Two Girls, One Boy died in Infancy; [ed.] St. Paul's Elementary C of E School Short Period at Halton College of Further Education for Mature Students; [occ.] Retired; [hon.] English Language Grade A 'O' Level 1974; [oth. writ.] Poems short stories autobiography written 1978-83 about my early years 1924 up to 1947. (Nothing published to date).; [pers.] To find the strength within oneself to ride above life's knocks and unfairness to take what each day brings and as each day ends be thankful.; [a.] Middlesbrough, Yorks, UK

Index of Poets

A

Aaron, Claudine 208
Aarons, Pauline 119
Abasy, Selma 537
Abatagelos, J. C. A. 50
Abbott, A. 311
Abbott, Donald E. 460
Abdulrahman, Susan 478
Abrahams, Bruce 147
Abrey, Angela 227
Adair, Constance 392
Adams, Amanda 162
Adams, Gail 12, 460
Adams, Gareth M. 390
Adams, Julie 375
Adams, Julie 377
Adams, Linda Anne 574
Adams, Robert R. 279
Adams, Ruth 122
Adams, Seth 275
Adamson, K. F. 364
Adamson, Mark Anthony 114
Adamson, Peter 555
Addison, Mark Laurence 543
Adio, Kazeem O. 76
Adshead, John 240
Agege, Enoh 440
Agnes-Anne 453
Ahearne, B. Thomas 281
Aidulis, Michael 317
Aiken, Phillip Stephen 323
Ainsley, G. 350
Ainsley, John D. 54
Aistrop, Willie 46
Aitchison, D. 417
Aitchison, Jim 260
Aitken, Christine 184
Aitken, Margaret 530
Akester, J. A. 493
Akhras, Vicky 538
Akhter, Ayesha 69
Akram, Tahira 41
Alcobi, Colette 126
Alcraft, S. A. 331
Alder, Gwendoline 447
Alderson, Helen 469
Aldous, Beryl 22
Aldred, Amanda 559
Alexander, Kay 93
Alexander, Rosalind 419
Alfieri, Letizia 30
Allan, David 457
Allan, Elizabeth 296
Allan, Freda 17, 525
Allan, Jean 246
Allan, Jean 289
Allan, Luisa 522
Allan, May 562
Allan, Myra 411
Alldred, M. 363
Allen, A. F. 428
Allen, Alanna 251
Allen, Gordon S. 300
Allen, Joan 272
Allen, Kelly 157
Allen, Ken 29
Allen, Linda J. 226
Allen, Lucita 397
Allen, M. 193
Allen, Maggie 67
Allen, Sallyann 482
Allett, Fiona 151
Allinson, E. 584
Allison, M. 502
Allman, Justine 439
Allo, Theodore 309
Allum, June F. 171
Almond, Denise M. 233
Almond, Julia 514
Ama, Grace 11
Ambrose, Charlotte 514
Amis, D. C. 560
Amos, Evelyn 469
Amsden, John 218
Anderson, Angela D. 233
Anderson, Dianne 96
Anderson, Emma-Jayne 382
Anderson, Francis 3
Anderson, Jennifer Ann 167
Anderson, Kathleen 292
Anderson, Lisa 220
Anderson, Loraine 221
Anderson, Lynn 397
Anderson, Sheila 369
Anderson, Susan 340
Anderson, Susan Elizabeth 204
Andersson, Pauline 486
Anderton, S'phen 561
Andrew, Marie Louise 69
Andrew, Patricia 124
Andrews, Kaye 364
Andrews, Ruth M. 262
Ang, Jacqueline 304
Angell, Granville,
  Lord of Cannock 154
Angell, R. 365
Anibal, Thomas 277
Antell, B. J. 442
Antonietti, Janet 462
Anwar, Zarina 360
Appiah, Egya 32
Appleby, Eileen A. 98
Appleby, N. 53
Applegate, Craig 148
Archer, D. L. 428
Archer, James Byron 465
Archer, Robert D. 178
Arliss, Donna 297
Armitage, Anne 449
Armstrong, Helena S. 169
Armstrong, Jean 13
Armstrong, Joan 238
Arnett, Cynthia 253
Arnold, C. 406
Arnold, Eleana 462
Arnold, James 398
Arrowsmith, Jon 261
Arrowsmith, S. 181
Arter, George E. 284
Arthur, C. A. 330
Ash, Rosalind 318
Ash-Smith, Christine 465
Ashby, Dorothy 247
Ashe, Rose 322
Ashfield, Margaret 495
Ashton, Betty 93
Ashton, Dan 391
Ashton, G. M. 124
Asker, Derek 16
Aslam, Rukhsana 273
Aspinall, George 376
Assam, Carol 140
Atchison, Hilda 169
Atherton, Joe 523
Atkins, Annie 374
Atkins, Jane 515
Atkinson, C. E. 429
Atkinson, Rita 410
Atterton, Doreen 255
Attisha, Helen Louise 586
Austin, T. 339
Avery, June Margaret 236
Axworthy, Andrea 31
Ayavoo, Reuben 531
Ayer, Jane 28
Ayre, Alan 442
Ayre, Virginia Beryl 46
Azure 180

B

Bacon, Valerie M. 198
Baden, June 82
Bader, Serena 200
Baerselman, Gillie 515
Baetul, Charlotte 72
Bagnall, Linda 220
Bail, Georgie 255
Bailey, Cheryll 507
Bailey, Christine 450
Bailey, Eric L. 507
Bailey, Jan 99
Bailey, Joseph 304
Bailey, Lily 401
Bailey, M. 410
Bailey, Robert 282
Bailie, Hugh 471
Bainbridge, Jennifer 246
Baird, M. 484
Baker, Anthony 295
Baker, Brenda 4
Baker, Bruce Richard 243
Baker, Carole 241
Baker, Ivy E. 82
Baker, Janice M. 380
Baker, Joy M. 573
Baker, Kirstie 390
Baker, L. F. 315
Baker, M. D. 419
Baker, Melanie Jane 587
Baker, Richard Ian 269
Baker, Steve 330
Baker, Suzanne 554
Baker, Tracey 44
Bakhurst, Havis 219
Balch, Ivy 84
Baldam, C. 360
Balderstone, Beverly 254
Baldwin, L. 66
Bale, Enid 186
Ball, Jody 241
Ball, June 216
Ball, Lilian M. 375
Balla, Daya P. 395
Ballantyne, Kerry 293
Ballard, Iris 81
Ballinger, G. 268
Balmain, Catherine M. 22
Balmbra, Margaret 263
Balshaw, Peter P. 67
Bamber, Vivienne 325
Banas, Doreen 466
Bancroft, Mandy 184
Bangert, Nigel 329
Banham, M. 118
Banham, R. 569
Banks, Tracey 162
Bannister, Carol 298
Bannister, Fay 468
Barber, Grace 227
Barber, Olive E. 190
Barber, R. 184
Barclay, Jennifer 454
Barclay, Patricia A. 483
Barge, Patricia Ellen 174
Barker, Annette 143
Barker, Ian James 387
Barker, Iris 84
Barker, Jill 209
Barker, Joan 14
Barker, Julie 396
Barker, Rosamund Jane 326
Barlow, Alan 225
Barlow, Linda 349
Barlow, Lyn 301
Barnard, Elaine 573
Barnes, A. R. 119
Barnes, D. A. 315
Barnes, G. 360
Barnes, K. 262
Barnes, Mark A. 552
Barnett, Veronica 136
Baron, Patrick 333
Barr, Corrieanne 357
Barr, Kath 377
Barraclough, Murriel 502
Barrass, Allyson 215
Barratt, Jill 139
Barrett, Annabel 23
Barrett, Brian 155
Barrett, Carol R. 444
Barrett, Marie 126
Barrett, Sinead 321
Barrett, Victor S. 47
Barrett, Zelia E. J. 42
Barrie, G. 239
Barrington, Clare 371
Barron, M. 176
Barry, Esther 93
Bartholomew, C. S. 173
Bartlett, Bill 576
Bartlett, Elizabeth 509
Bartlett, Helen 458
Bartlett, Joy M. 33
Bartnik, Gregory 71
Barton, Clare 29
Barton, J. M. 201
Barton, Robert I. 192
Bartosiak, Romana 512
Barwick-Ward, Lucy 291
Barwood, Helen 153
Baskerville, Jenny 5
Bastin, Bernice 79
Bates, Elizabeth 445
Bates, L. 192
Bates, Robert E. 335
Bath, A. 473
Batho, Grace A. 302
Batten, Lisa 15
Battiscombe, B. 323
Baum, Richard I. 490
Baunton, Lewis E. 238
Bautista, Lotis 6
Baxter, M. J. 415
Baxter, Russell J. 557
Bayer, Ursula 310
Bayliss, Janet 243
Beacham, Barbara Ann 261
Beadle, Toni 363
Beal, Doris M. 520
Beardmore, C. A. 44
Beardsley, Katie 495
Beare, Molly 194
Bearman, Sara 496
Beaumont, A. D. 458
Beazleigh, Gary Scott 237
Beck, Audrey 458
Beddoes, Margaret 321
Beddow, Cynthia 277
Beech, Sarah 176
Beecham, Sarah 478
Beer, Catherine 223
Beer, Delphia 90
Beggs, Norman 422
Belafonte 197

Bell, Angela 455
Bell, Anthony 4
Bell, Dorothy 288
Bell, Margaret 312
Bell, Maureen 317
Bell, Rose 179
Bell, Terese 422
Benacs, Philippa C. 198
Benacs, Philippa C. 327
Benbow, Edward 521
Bendall, Robin 585
Benjamin, Carole 95
Benjamin, Christina 206
Bennet, Jane 440
Bennett, Jean 33
Bennett, Kerrie 243
Bennett, Moreene Adessa 358
Bennetts, G. R. 266
Benny, Margaret M. 574
Benson-Dare, Sandra 278
Bentley, A. 41
Benton, Toni-Marie 239
Benton, V. L. 191
Benz, Phil 316
Berry, Eileen Barbara 140
Berry, Helen 307
Berry, Richard G. 489
Berry, Sue 414
Bertram, Georgina 249
Bessey, Tracy 586
Best, Paula 107
Best, Sheena 325
Best, Sylvia Ann 423
Beswick, William 67
Bettinson, Charles 92
Bevan-Jones, Maureen 344
Bewers, Sylvia 282
Bhogal, Mandip 204
Bi, Aulfat 304
Bibby, Hilda J. 101
Bibi, Aasia 253
Bigg, Claude H. 230
Biggin, Susan 435
Bill, Natalie 478
Billups, Colin A. J. 212
Binner, Chris 466
Binns, Betty 13
Binns, M. 554
Birch, H. M. 345
Birch, Maurice I. 560
Birch, Raymond 141
Birchall, Christine W. F. 4
Birchall, Jenny 32
Birchall, Mark 414
Bird, A. J. 266
Bird, Nicola 187
Birke, Doris A. 163
Birmingham, Peter 480
Birtley, John N. 212
Bishenden, Maia 181
Bishop, Julia 250
Black, Anne 455
Black, David B. 26
Black, Eileen 211
Black, Jeanette 222
Black, M. 583
Black, Margaret 280
Black, Tania 423
Blackbourn, E. 545
Blackburn, Pamela 335
Blackburn, Peter 115
Blacknell, Simon 349
Blackwell, Hazel 73
Blair, Carole 306
Blake, Clive 391
Blake, V. C. 58

Blake, Walter N. 194
Blamey, Alice 237
Blanch, Olive 574
Blanchard, Maureen 326
Blanchfield, Kathleen 157
Blaney, David 302
Blasdale, Marjorie 323
Bleach, Linda 258
Bleasdale, G. 330
Blevins, Sharon 119
Blewitt, H. E. 332
Blick, Helene 510
Blomfield, Natalie 173
Bloodworth, T. G. 197
Bluck, Elizabeth 307
Blue, Elizabeth 148
Blundell, Laura 171
Board, Samantha 122
Boast, Joyce 380
Bocock, Dennis William L. 298
Boddy, Ian 213
Bode, Maggie 312
Boden, Cath 159
Boden, Julie M. 293
Boettcher, Kerry 25
Bolam, Julie 507
Bolger, Victoria 544
Bolwell, Marylynn 131
Bond, Georgina 163
Bones, Stephanie 125
Bonham, T. L. 41
Bonhill, David McGregor 469
Bonning, Sue 341
Boomsma-Williams, Muriel 108
Booth, B. M. 59
Booth, Gemma 463
Booth, M. P. 275
Booth, Nan 554
Booton, Donna 171
Borgeat, Bryan 28
Borowanski, Louise 385
Borrill, Annette 467
Bosi, Alison 526
Boss, Joan 149
Botteley, Gerald William 389
Botterill, Carol 372
Bottley, W. A. 367
Bottomley, Leane 248
Boucher, M. E. 569
Boucher, Penny 423
Boult, Karen 234
Boult, T. J. 431
Boulter, Chris D. 301
Boulton, Barbara 297
Boults, Ann 232
Bourge, Stephen 312
Bourne, K. A. 316
Bourne, Tracey 335
Bowden, Emily 251
Bowden, Emma 256
Bowen, P. A. 545
Bower, Eunice 138
Bowler, Lesley 148
Bowley, Margaret 269
Bowman, Margaret 347
Brace, Rosemarie K. 186
Bracken, Beverley Ann 149
Bradbury, Denny 87
Bradley, D. H. E. 266
Bradley, Jan 104
Bradshaw, Mark D. 356
Brady, Kathleen 24
Branch, Sheila 267
Brandley, Clare 306
Brandon, Cecily 392
Brandon, Nicola 202

Brandon-Smith, Angela J. 428
Brandrick, Nicola 351
Branford, Joyce 424
Bray, John 210
Bray, Patricia 415
Bray, Ruth 413
Bray, S. C. 107
Bray, Selena 420
Brayshaw, Yvonne 177
Brazier, Margery 43
Brazil, Freda 519
Breach, K. V. 188
Brealey, David 15
Breare, Alexandra Louise 242
Brenda, a Original 532
Brennan, Tina 136
Brennan, Tina 346
Brent, D. J. 211
Brent, Karen 255
Brent, Leanne 95
Brett, Raymond 318
Brew, Victoria 105
Brewe, Lena 13
Brewer, Elizabeth 377
Brewer, Enid 164
Brewster, Cindy B. 454
Bricknell, Roy 430
Bridge, Lynne 585
Bridgford, Stephanie C. 265
Bridgwood, Andrea 471
Bridle, Joyce 286
Bridson, K. 267
Briggs, Denis 449
Briggs, F. 332
Briggs, Peter Edward Waires 341
Briggs, Sue 545
Brighouse, Andy 505
Bright, Clare 82
Bright, Natalie 494
Brisco, Derek 385
Britcher, P. 588
Britton, C. 51
Britton, Joan 21
Broadbent, Thom 129
Brockway, Jacqueline 396
Brogan, Margaret 127
Bromham, Margaret R. 62
Bromley, Michael 125
Brookes, Brenda 221
Brookes, Dorothy 458
Brookes, Olive 493
Brooks, D. V. 533
Brooks, David 518
Brooks, Joan C. 390
Brown, Alistair 92
Brown, Ann 467
Brown, Barbara G. 511
Brown, Carol 231
Brown, Carol 294
Brown, Carole Eunice 471
Brown, Christine 104
Brown, D. L. 437
Brown, D. W. 498
Brown, Damion 24
Brown, Doris I. 467
Brown, E. B. 60
Brown, Eileen 223
Brown, H. 175
Brown, Jean 83
Brown, Jill 26
Brown, Joan Evelyn 270
Brown, Julie 560
Brown, Kate 579
Brown, Kathleen 381
Brown, Lavinia 155
Brown, M. A. 420

Brown, Mandy 367
Brown, Margaret 263
Brown, Marion 111
Brown, P. 59
Brown, Patricia M. A. 273
Brown, Paul Vincent 66
Brown, Rachel 353
Brown, Rita 59, 264
Brown, S. M. 189
Brown, Sharon 585
Brown, Sheila A. 535
Brown, Sylvia Sharon 281
Brown, Terry 472
Brown, Tony J. 283
Brown, V. P. 362
Brown-Paul, Shirley 578
Browne, Osgood 481
Browning, Catherine 246
Browning, Debbie 256
Browning, Dorothy 381
Brownlee, Doris M. H. 503
Brownlee, James 75
Bruce, Doris A. 306
Bruce, Helen 248
Bruce, Jane 446
Bruce, Marie 183
Brumel, Ben Herbert 407
Brumpton, B. I. 270
Brunell, Gladys Eileen 72
Bruno, Max 341
Bruton, Delia Mary Anne 160
Bryan, D. V. 364
Bryant, G. H. 60
Bryant, G. M. 345
Bryant, Pamela 183
Buchanan, Doreen 84
Buckley, I. 123
Buist, Barbara 16
Bull, Dee 300
Bullen, Marianne 334
Bullivant, Melanie 473
Bulmer, Mauis E. 539
Bulpin, Amy 263
Bunce, Lee Stuart 249
Bunch, C. J. 421
Bundey, Harold W. 4
Bunyan, Nikola Jayne 548
Burford, Andrew 74
Burge, J. 322
Burgess, Catherine 170
Burgess, G. E. 265
Burke, Sheila 351
Burks, Louise 258
Burley, Sarah 435
Burman, J. H. 354
Burman, R. G. 173
Burnett, Anne 222
Burns, Alan 214
Burns, F. 40
Burns, Janet Marian 438
Burns, Matthew L. 344
Burns, Stephanie 131
Burroughs, Eileen 285
Burroughs, P. 267
Burrows, Beverley 87
Burton, Gillian 209
Burton, Richard Glenn 580
Bush, Adam 76
Busley, I. 276
Busuttil, Gail 6
Butcher, C. 327
Butler, A. L. 539
Butler, George J. 211
Butler, Jacqueline 169
Butler, Jennifer Anne 76
Butler, Judy 278

Butler, Julie 261
Butler, May 273
Butler, Pauline 412
Butt, Leslie J. 167
Butt, Sarah 186
Buttery, Mike 56
Buxton, Daniel 241
Byford, Neal 328
Byford, Richard 128
Byrnes, Cynthia 33

C

Cade, Lawrence Andrew 399
Cadger, Katrina 290
Cadoux, Lilian 210
Cahill, Jeanne M. 162
Cahill, T. L. 323
Caile, Susan 310
Cain, M. 477
Caine, Rachel 406
Cairns, Diava 138
Cairns, Lynne 399
Cairns, Mary E. 310
Calderon, Marianne W. 561
Caldwell, Patricia 49
Callaghan, J. M. J. 505
Callum, Richard B. 336
Calvert, Susan 414
Cambridge, V. 48
Cameron, Claire 35
Cameron, Nancy 559
Cameron-Fisher, Craig 508
Camp, Elizabeth 251
Campbell, Catherine 311
Campbell, David 464
Campbell, Glenn 154
Campbell, Julie 372
Campbell, N. 264
Campbell-Cook, Scott 552
Campbell-Sturgess, Christine 18
Campisi, Cristian 448
Camwell, I. L. 541
Canham, Laurence 231
Cann, Sylvia 413
Cannan, Sharie 273
Cannings, Linda 138
Cantwell, Eileen 296
Capehorn, Nicholas 583
Capenhurst, Arthur 219
Capewell, Florice 212
Capon, Rosemary 412
Cappell, L. P. 503
Cardno, Maureen 426
Care, Hilda 134
Care, Jenny 207
Carey, David Richard 584
Carey, Joyce 77
Carkett, Gypsy 159
Carle, Louise D. 160
Carling, Jan 374
Carlton, E. 68
Carnill, Jane 518
Carpenter, Betty 397
Carpenter, Denise 235
Carpenter, Rowena P. 172
Carpenter, Trudy 127
Carr, Daniel 96
Carr, Mary E. 537
Carr, Sean Joseph 504
Carrigan, Erin-Marie 464
Carroll, Helen 292
Carroll, Jill 153
Carroll, Thomas 132
Carron, J. 264
Carrons, Marie 130
Carse, Venetia 281

Carter, Arthur George 87
Carter, Cyril 303
Carter, Delise 18
Carter, F. 128
Carter, G. H. 495
Carter, Janet 414
Carter, Violet 180
Carter, Winifred F. 543
Carthy, Duncan R. 103
Cartlidge, R. J. 356
Cartwright, Karen Jane 79
Caruso, Rosalind 331
Cary, Robert 123
Caryll, Leila 451
Casey, Barbara 29
Casey, Eileen 298
Cash, Janet 97
Cassidy, Deborah 292
Caswell, Julie 403
Caterer, Teri-Louise 583
Caton, Brian 294
Catterson, M. 188
Cave, Valerie J. 280
Cavender, Tracy 380
Caves, Emma 250
Cazaly, Iris 355
Cerdan, Michael 493
Chadwick, Graham 449
Chaggar, R. S. 327
Challis, D. R. 335
Chamberlain, Eileen 443
Chambers, M. J. 42
Chambers, Theresa 65
Champion, W. B. 365
Chandler, Faye 261
Chandler, Kate 156
Chandler, Mark D. 104
Chandler, Susan Rosemarie 60
Chanler, D. E. 342
Chant, Hamilton C. 392
Chapman, Amy G. 302
Chapman, Daniel Michael 580
Chapman, Elizabeth 171
Chapman, Eric 380
Chapman, Kate 229
Chapman, Nanette 346
Chapman, Shari Louise 191
Chapman, Steven 278
Charles, G. W. 54
Charles, S. 555
Charles, Sheila E. 265
Charlish, V. R. 67
Charlton, Bernadette 287
Charlton, Jacqui 526
Charlton, Lynne 288
Chatwin, D. M. 204
Checketts, Giles 286
Cheeseman, Michael T. 415
Chegwidden, Loretta 457
Chennell, Helen 388
Cherrington, Patricia 545
Chesterman, Maurice 412
Chestney, G. Y. 337
Chew, Dawn 10
Childs, Amy F. 91
Childs, Graham Peter 236
Childs, Joan S. 238
Chimutengwende, Seke 114
Chisholm, Kay 559
Chisnell, Sheena J. 370
Chittenden, Sharon 332
Chivers, Julie M. 575
Chorlton, Nigel 278
Chown, Jonathan 581
Christensen, Sheena 496
Christian, Roma C. 349

Christie, James Richard 301
Christie, Rosemary 272
Christmas, E. J. 278
Christou, Soulla E. 480
Christy, Michael Gerald 411
Churchill, Danny 446
Churton, Susan Evelyn 343
CKLE 435
Clachrie, Jane Osborne 32
Clack, Edi 159
Clapham, Sheila 175
Clapton, A. 114
Claridge, Pim 479
Claringbold, Sharron 426
Clark, Ann 451
Clark, Antony Gordon 98
Clark, Brenda 19
Clark, Catrina 295
Clark, Christina 21
Clark, Doris A. 167
Clark, E. S. 497
Clark, Elizabeth Harrington 228
Clark, Kelly 370
Clark, M. A. 568
Clark, Mary 311
Clark, Paul 339
Clark, Philip R. 106
Clark, Steven 40
Clark, Valerie 410
Clarke, B. 191
Clarke, Eleanor 299
Clarke, Kirsty 289
Clarke, Lynn 512
Clarke, Margaret 486
Clarke, Pat 312
Clarke, Phillip S. 135
Clarke, Ramon H. 123
Clarke, Richard J. 583
Clarke, Rose Marie 324
Clarke, Thomas Edwin 132
Claxton, Maureen 271
Clay, S. G. Brian 436
Clayton, Dawn 258
Clayton-Fergusson, Doreen 444
Cleaton-Roberts, William I. 327
Cleaver, A. V. 121
Clegg, Kurt 164
Clegg, Renee 318
Cleghorn, Evelyn 247
Clement, Rhys 53
Clements, Catherine 581
Clements, M. G. 569
Clench, A. G. 421
Cliff, Christine 248
Cliffe, Leagh 144
Clifford, Joyce 244
Clifford, M. 330
Clift, Donna June 78
Clifton, Hazel 377
Clink, Sharon 576
Close, Rebecca R. 39
Clough, Adele-Marie 226
Clough, Dennis V. 169
Clucas, Eve 498
Cobham, Catherine 75
Cochrane, Arma 228
Cochrane, J. 332
Cochrane, Mary 114
Cock, Charlotte 290
Cockerton, Guy 87
Codona, Iain 254
Cogar, Maureen Jean 405
Coker, Caroline 234
Coker, Mandy 177
Cole, Andrew 240
Cole, Gary 384

Cole, Jacqueline M. J. 259
Cole, Josephine 299
Cole, Nicola J. 478
Cole, Rosaleen G. 179
Cole, Rosalyn 500
Cole, Sylvia 559
Cole, Val 502
Colebourne, Sylvia 65
Colella, M. 339
Coleman, J. H. 178
Coleman, L. T. 131
Coleman, Pat 500
Coleman, Ronald 499
Coleman, Stacey 308
Coles, B. M. 573
Coleshill, Rosemary 356
Colgate, Sally 482
Colla, George 303
Collett, Steven 271
Collier, Janet 385
Colling, Diana 216
Collingborn, Helen 307
Collingborn, Rosemary 491
Collins, Amber 379
Collins, John 301
Collins, Margaret 548
Collins, Richard Paul 346
Collins, Wendy J. 112
Collinson, C. 282
Collis, Elizabeth Ann 468
Combellack, E. 334
Comerford, Sinead 330
Compitus, Alison L. 100
Conceprio, D. M. 61
Condie, Louise 560
Condron, Elizabeth Ann 445
Conesa-Ribera, Toni 279
Conlon, Tony 329
Connell, Coral 300
Connolly, Aiden 218
Connolly, James J. 214
Connolly, Sarah-Jane 44
Connor, Barry O. 102
Connor, Gavin 561
Connor, James 471
Conroy, Shona 581
Conroy, Tamsyn 556
Cook, Anna 85
Cook, D. 38
Cook, Dilys E. 438
Cook, Geoff P. 103
Cook, Heather E. 364
Cook, J. 68
Cook, Linda J. 457
Cook, Lois M. 506
Cook, Pam 556
Cook, Paul 37
Cook, W. A. 180
Cooke, Howard 223
Cooke, Stephen 185
Cookney, Margaret Ann 106
Cookson, Daniel Thomas 456
Cookson, John W. 256
Cooley, P. 331
Coombes, Natasha 340
Coon, H. 368
Coon, Margaret 417
Cooper, Anne 517
Cooper, Audrey 82
Cooper, Bridget 379
Cooper, Denise 256
Cooper, Emma Lee 256
Cooper, J. E. 55
Cooper, Michael 58
Cooper, Muriel P. 312
Cooper, Pamela 272

Cope, Myfanwy Ann 137
Copestake, Trina 483
Copland, Ann 373
Coppin, Doreen M. 241
Coppin, Jeffrey 86
Corcoran, Patrick 136
Corica, Elisabeth 74
Cornell, Maria 500
Cornish, Ann Shirley 521
Cornish, June 561
Corns, Rebecca 115
Corradi, Laura 82
Corradi, Selina 309
Cosaitis, Joy 332
Cosgrove, Leigh Paul 440
Cosgrove, Peter 494
Costello, Joanne 254
Costigan, H. A. 318
Cotter, Nora 495
Cotterell, Gusty 559
Cotterill, Brian D. 382
Cougill, Charlotte 15
Coull, Nicola 585
Coulter, Rosemary 360
Counihan, Kathleen B. 257
Coupland, Betty 524
Courtney-Thomas, Verity 129
Covey, Charles R. 462
Cowans, W. S. 333
Coward, Sylvia 199
Cowin, Katie 139
Cowin, Raymond M. 53
Cowlbeck, I. L. 547
Cowles, Nicolle 430
Cowley, Violet 333
Cowlin, S. 182
Cox, J. 404
Cox, L. K. 541
Cox, Lesley 247
Cox, Margaret 483
Cox, Paul 201
Cox, Simon 348
Cox, Trevor 487
Crabb, Jean B. 259
Craig, Alison M. 462
Craig, Angela 297
Craig, Janet 585
Craig, Richard 412
Craig, Samantha Jane 490
Craigie, Greta 104
Cramb, Linda V. 298
Cramp, Sarah 437
Crandon, Moyra 69
Crane, David 75
Crathern, Sheila E. 490
Craven, Kathryn 7
Crawford, Ian C. 373
Crawford, Jay-Bee 288
Crawford, Maria 494
Crawshaw, Mollie 134
Creagh, Elizabeth T. 389
Crellin, Elizabeth 316
Creswell, Elaine 24
Crewdson, Alex G. 306
Crisp, Anita 260
Crisp, Jenny 253
Crisp, Pamela M. L. 546
Crisp, Patricia 352
Critcher, S. L. M. 330
Croft, Jasmin 216
Croft, Lesley 20
Crofts, John 253
Crofts, Nigel 239
Cromie, Hazel 455
Crone, Ann 525
Cronin, Sarah 533

Crook, Annette 388
Crosbie, David 467
Crosby, Edward Lee 290
Crosby, George 574
Cross, Anne 257
Crowe, Rebecca 356
Crowe, Tracy 262
Cruickshank, Jim 73
Cruickshank, Paul 562
Crump, Graeme T. 456
Crumpton, Suzanne 318
Cuffling, Joan 232
Culmer, Marjorie B. 268
Culshaw, Lorna 516
Cundey, Betty E. 454
Cunnah, J. 317
Cunningham, J. 280
Cunningham, Moreen 276
Curley, Joan Anne 76
Curnow, Lindsay 138
Curran, E. 322
Curran, Georgina 509
Currie, Terence Craig 195
Curry, Kevin George 252
Curtis, B. W. 370
Curtis, Catherine 381
Curtis, Joanna 286
Cusack, John 163
Custerson, Malcolm 178
Cutner, Joan 245

D

Dabrowiecki, May 541
Dadds, Jennifer Susan 467
Dadds, John 573
Dalby, Yvonne 268
Dale, Christine 518
Dale, M. A. 575
Dale, Muriel L. 408
Dale-Patteson, Rachel 408
Dalley, Peter John 536
Dallimore, D. 408
Dalton, Elaine 78
Daly, Eileen 302
Daly, Mary 53
Danciger, Jason L. 439
Dandy, Christopher 572
Daniel, Martine Lara 131
Daniels, Anne L. 465
Daniels, Edith 89
Daniels, Kathleen M. 381
Daniels, Magdalen Mannion 277
Daniels, P. 179
Danks, Trudi 582
Dansie, Jean M. 243
Darch, Mark D. 280
D'Arcy, Gavin 514
Darken, Marguerite J. 531
Darlington, E. M. 545
Daubney, Brenda M. 12
Davenport, Donna 293
Davey, Elizabeth 508
Davey, Gillian 101
Davey, Sioux 324
Davidson, Iris A. 27
Davidson, John G. 525
Davidson, Nora M. 439
Davie, Andrew 512
Davies, Adrienne 224
Davies, Alex 586
Davies, Anthony 11
Davies, Bruce 87
Davies, Bryan 233
Davies, Cynthia 255
Davies, David 217
Davies, David J. 253

Davies, Dawn J. 264
Davies, Mark 368
Davies, Maureen 181
Davies, Morfydd 192
Davies, P. 275
Davies, Patricia 417
Davies, Paul 338
Davies, Ron C. 427
Davies, S. A. 309
Davies, S. J. 481
Davies, Sarah 486
Davies, Sian 318
Davies, Stephanie 111
Davis, Anne 379
Davis, B. 317
Davis, Chrissie 227
Davis, George S. C. 38
Davis, Kerry 163
Davis, Linda 149
Davis, Melissa 365
Davis, Paul V. 124
Davis, Sally 352
Davis, Shirley 331
Davis, Winifred 182
Davison, Maureen 483
Dawes, R. A. A. 534
Dawson, Emma 561
Dawson, Frank 93
Dawson, Kelly-Emma 245
Dawson, Phillip N. 70
Dawson, W. M. 315
Day, Daphne P. A. 379
Day, Derrick Alan 244
Day, S. P. 557
Dayaramani, Natasha 546
De Ath, Leslie 231
De Biasi, Kylie 284
De Gracia, Marbill 177
De Meza, Clifford H. 448
de Silk, Eve 206
De Voy, Jean 244
De-Whomes, Francesca 394
Deacon, D. C. 582
Deacon, John 468
Deakin, Wendy 198
Dean, Melodie 325
Dearie, Alan J. McGregor 211
DeBono, R. F. 51
Dedman, L. A. 419
Dekoning, M. E. 578
Delaney, Andrea J. 86
Delgaudio, Viola I. 177
Dell, J. 315
DeMeza, Elizabeth 376
DeMicheli, Ann 528
DeMontalt, Friar John D. 24
Demus, Ewa 80
Denham, Philip A. 313
Dennett, C. 46
Dennett, Maureen Carlisle 426
Dent, Margaret 487
Dent, Stephen 321
Denyer, Lisa 20
DeQuincey, J. 348
Derbyshire, J. 268
Desforges, Jane 104
DeSilva, Anno C. 236
Desney-Hudson, Sue 363
Devaney, T. M. 68
Dever, Andie C. 389
Dever, Andrea 6
Devine, Alison 304
Devine, Charles C. 225
Devine, R. J. 354
Devita, Alice 448
Devlin, Mary Josephine 315

Dewey, Jane 463
Dewhurst, Jo 289
Di-Maio, Hala 397
Diamond, Shelley 320
Diaper, Rob 276
Diglis, Cheryl Karen 103
Dillon, Doreen 447
Dillow, Dot, Biggin 378
Dincalp, Simon 349
Dinham, Carol 447
Dinner, Samantha 205
Dinsley, J. 522
Diplock, Jason 459
Divers, Flora 144
Dix, Cheryl 151
Dixon, Alice Marie 252
Dixon, Anthea 455
Dixon, J. J. S. 410
Dixon, Sadie 433
Dixon, Susan 329
Dobbins, Marian D. 64
Dobson, Claire 33
Dobson, J. M. 283
Docherty, Michelle 488
Docker, Sarah 343
Docker, W. 310
Dodds, J. E. M. 540
Doig, David 298
Dolan, Olivia 490
Dolan, P. A. 176
Dolby, Nicola 40
Doleman, Sally 581
Domanic, Maria 506
Dommett, Patricia 494
Donald, Suzanne 579
Donnell, Annamay O. 152
Donoghue, Jeffrey 21
Donoghue, Pauline 532
Donovan, Mark 500
Doogan, Frances Anne 163
Dorey, Jean 143
Dosunmu, Toheeb 36
Dotchon, S. M. 265
Dougan, J. G. 366
Dougan, Kerrianne 580
Doughty, Sylvia 310
Douglas, Gwen 164
Douglas, Rita 275
Douglas, Sandra 278
Dow, William W. 343
Dowding, Ann 237
Dower, Doreen 169
Dowie, Debra 376
Dowles, R. 501
Down, Tina E. 340
Downes, Alexandra 81
Downes, W. L. 363
Downey, D. 36
Downie, Gillian 523
Downie, Paul 105
Downs, Jean 143
Downs, Nan 367
Dowse, William A. 492
Doyle, Debra 153
Doyle, Eunice 513
Doyle, Gary 393
Doyle, Gavin 144
Doyle, Joseph 247
Doyle, Lucy 579
Doyle, Margaret 273
Doyle, Ruth 317
Drake, Francis 516
Dredge, Celia 295
Dredge, Jacqueline 510
Drew, Brian W. 216
Drew, Diana 305

Drewery, Denise 259
Driver, Kim 18
Drummond, Stacy 351
Dryden, Lynn 211
Dryszko, Alicja 558
Duff, David 243
Duff, Hettie 101
Duff, Mhorag 274
Duff, Olga 438
Duff-Pennington, Patrick 430
Duffield, Margaret 549
Duffy, Gabriel 464
Duffy, Margaret 473
Dugmore, Barry 228
Duguid, Catherine M. 544
Duke, Zara Frances 485
Dumbrill, Lucy 252
Dummett, Tessa 582
Dunbar, Charmaine 306
Dunbar, Nick 488
Dunbar, Sam 273
Duncan, Ann Craig 207
Duncan, Anne 292
Duncan, I. J. 338
Duncan, Jean Scott 398
Duncan, John 286
Dunkley, Jenny 153
Dunlop, Dido 306
Dunn, Kevin 163
Dunne, Anya 572
Dunne, Veronica 548
Dunstan, Catriona 88
Durkin, John 96
Durrant, Lesley 293
Duthie, James 580
Dutton, E. 421
Dyer, Leanne 585
Dyer, Peter R. 194
Dyer, Richard Gwyn 352
Dymond, Nicola 203
Dymott, Pamela 500
Dyson, Anne 452
Dyson, Mary 66
Dyson, Yvonne P. 238

E

Eagle, John 150
Eagles, C. 194
Earl, Mollie D. 270
Easterlow, Jeneane 84
Easton, Jim 14
Eaves, John 35
Ebbage, Maurice 539
Eccleston, T. 434
Ede, Ann 83
Eden, D. D. 551
Edmead, Ann 371
Edmonds, Jean 139
Edwards, Catherine A. 399
Edwards, Claire Michelle 284
Edwards, G. 332
Edwards, G. A. 341
Edwards, J. 52
Edwards, J. V. M. 180
Edwards, Jean Mary 378
Edwards, Jessie 217
Edwards, Laura 156
Edwards, M. 51
Edwards, Margaret 174
Edwards, Mary 333
Edwards, Nathan R. 113
Edwards, Norman J. 496
Edwards, Peggy 65
Egan, Beryl 74
Eggertsson, Thorsteinn 473
Eggleton, Susan 327

Eisenschmid, Wendy 177
Eisler, Paul 327
Eldred, J. P. 127
Eldridge, Jacqueline M. 7
Eley, Linda 18
Eliza 257
Elkington, Marion 538
Ellinger, M. 50
Elliott, C. 532
Elliott, Dave 164
Elliott, Elsie 158
Elliott, Graeme 297
Ellis, Anne 524
Ellis, John 81
Ellis, Linsey Sarah 81
Ellis, M. 436
Ellis, Mark 554
Elsmore, George 261
Elsworth, R. 55
Emary, John 381
Emsden, Margaret A. 474
Endersby, Elanor 571
English, Karen, aged 11 295
English, M. I. 326
Ennis, John 255
Enticknapp, Daniel 226
Escandell, Valerie J. 347
Etheridge, Eileen M. 522
Evan-Yates, M. J. 61
Evans, A. G. 275
Evans, A. J. 359
Evans, Bill 459
Evans, Brenda 25
Evans, Bruce J.W. 286
Evans, Christopher John 232
Evans, David Arthur 19
Evans, Dee 259
Evans, Garry I. G. 386
Evans, John 299
Evans, Keith 298
Evans, Margaret 537
Evans, Mary Bernadette 498
Evans, R. M. 329
Evans, Sharon 309
Evans, Stella 190
Evans, Tracy 326
Evans, Yvette 478
Everest, Jean 31
Evison, T. J. 429
Ewart, Bertrand 395
Eyre, Brenda 451
Eyre, Geoffrey Allan 264
Eyre, Natasha Marie 482

F

Fackerell, Diane (nee Spicer) 79
Fagg, L. 49
Fairbank, Paul 542
Fairhurst, P. F. C. 313
Fairish, Wendy 276
Fairley, Norman 202
Fairnington, Sarah Jane 202
Fairweather, Beverly 588
Falla, Jan 74
Falla, Maud 62
Fallon, Kaylea 38
famojure, o. 472
Fardon, S. 206
Farkhoy, Shireen 419
Farmer, Christine 404
Farmer, Toni Rebecca 490
Farmery, S. A. 310
Farnworth, M. 578
Farquhar, Christine 521
Farquhar, G. H. 107
Farrell, Joan 300

Farrington, Alan 245
Farrow, H. K. 532
Farrow, J. 363
Farthing, Andrew 259
Faruque, Brenda 221
Faruque, Tara 564
Faulds, Kirstie 289
Faulkner, Belinda 232
Faulkner, Hazel 234
Faulkner, Karen 248
Faulkner, Lisa 70
Faulkner, Lorraine 284
Faull, Claude 449
Fawcus, B. 112
Fay, Michael 308
Fay, Valerie 110
Fearnside, Alec 213
Fearon, Melford 206
Feather, Robert J. 269
Feeley, Duncan 580
Feeney, Sheila 59
Felix-Davies, Claire 526
Felstead, Beulah 242
Fendick, Edna 139
Fennell, Danny 466
Fenton, Minnie 202
Fenwick, Giuliana L. 400
Fereday, V. L. 584
Ferguson, Beryl 396
Ferrier, George 258
Ferrington, Thomas 197
Fiddes, M. 122
Fidler, Anthony 298
Fieber, Kevin 145
Field, Karin 253
Fields, Don Spencer 77
Fimognari, Elizabeth Anne 9
Finch, Tammy L. 417
Findlay, E. M. 492
Findlay, Frances 564
Findlay, J. S. 498
Findlay, Sarah 559
Findlay, Sylvia E. 546
Finn, H. Tracey 200
Finney, P. B. 181
Finnigan, Winifred 573
Finns, S. 475
Firn, Elizabeth Ann 3
Fisher, Arch P. 148
Fisher, Carole A. Thompson 402
Fisher, E. 491
Fisher, Ilona LaBouchardiere 73
Fisher, Leigh J. 15
Fishwick, D. 186
Fitchet, Angus J. 512
Fitzgeorge, Neil 426
Fitzgerald, Emma E. 296
Fitzsimons, Louise 374
Fixter, Cora 226
Flakie 279
Flanagan, John J. 470
Fleming, C. 325
Fleming, Natasha B. 276
Fletcher, A. 123
Fletcher, Doris 251
Fletcher, J. A. 70
Flett, Mildred 481
Flockhart, Moya Gray 365
Flynn, Joy 439
Flynn, M. 577
Fogg, Gillian 437
Foggin, Carolyn 403
Foley, T. G. 179
Folkard-Garratt, W. P. 70
Follett, John W. 35
Forbes, Bill 237

Ford, Beatrice 26
Ford, Craig 181
Ford, E. 540
Ford, Hannah 151
Ford, J. V. 321
Forder, Kaelin 374
Foreman, Daphne 74
Forman, Martin 320
Forrest, M. M. 419
Forrester, Charles 150
Forristal, P. M. 283
Forster, Ian G. 218
Forster, Myriam 479
Forsythe, Bronwen 144
Forteath, David 83
Foskett, R. T. 271
Foster, Caroline 469
Foster, Colin G. 10
Foster, J. J. 417
Foster, Jack 355
Foster, Ron 405
Foster, V. J. 263
Fotheringham, Dawn 247
Fotheringham, Lesley 71
Foulger, Margret 203
Foulkes, Christine 140
Fountain, Jo 223
Fountain, Sally 319
Fovargue, Marjorie 477
Fowkes, Clare 226
Fowler, Christina 155
Fowler, J. B. 568
Fowler, J. G. 499
Fowles, Robert M. 201
Fowles, Tanya 282
Fox, Anne-Marie 245
Fox, Jennifer 289
Fox, Kathleen 88
Fox, Margaret 321
Fox, P. A. 64
Fox, Patricia 489
Fox, Robert 325
Fox, Steven 575
Fox, Tommy 425
Foxall, Claire 224
Francis, Tracey Louise 482
Frankland, Roy 69
Franklin, Claudine 402
Franklin, Shirley 574
Franks, Roy B. 182
Fraser, Carolyn 375
Fraser, Doreen 299
Fraser, Keith Stephen 291
Fraser, Lynda 235
Fraser, Marjorie 489
Fraser, Yvonne 360
Frederick, Ann 517
Freeman, Catherine 528
Freeman, Clare 222
Freeman, Jean 208
Freeman, Julie 465
Freeman, Lee 405
Freeman, Robert A. 313
Freeman, Sadie 38
Freeman, T. G. 409
Freeman, Tracey 414
French, Deirdre 15
French, M. F. 280
French, Robert 202
French, Trudy 553
Fricker, Dulcie Veronica 75
Fricker, F. W. 570
Friell, Donna-Maria 529
Friend, M. G. 546
Frisch, Pamela 504
Frost, B. 363

Fry, Eileen 223
Fry, Phyl 500
Fudge, Pamela 308
Fulcher, Lana 298
Fullalove, Victoria 505
Fuller, B. M. 327
Fuller, M. 491
Funcy, P. 277
Fung, Allison E. P. 246
Furner, Keith 5
Fury, June 247

G

Gadd, Barbara 461
Gaffney, Jeanette 305
Gaillard, Mosty 336
Galbraith, Kirsty 584
Gale, G. 56
Gale, Jean 510
Gale, Margaret 133
Galforge, Linda 449
Gallagher, Elsie 140
Gallagher, John C. 471
Gallagher, Yvonne 560
Gallimore, I. 574
Galsworthy, Allan 404
Galvin, Nora 537
Gamble, Mandy Jane 427
Gander, Colin 379
Gannon, Linda 81
Gannon, Tracey 66
Gant, J. 435
Garbett, J. M. 147
Garbutt, Gill 402
Gardiner, Anne E. 146
Gardiner, Geoffrey M. 77
Gardiner, Rita 338
Gardner, Enid 290
Gardner, Mariana 313
Gardner, Marjorie 63
Garlick, Dorothy L. 142
Garner, Adele V. 90
Garner, G. 149
Garner, Pam 112
Garrod, I. 422
Garrud, Trevor 340
Garry, Linda 96
Gartside, S. 115
Gartside, Sandra 270
Garwell, Kirsty 244
Gaskell, Kathleen M. 12
Gaspar, Meg 276
Gaston, Lorn 226
Gate, Helen F. 34
Gates, D. L. 105
Gatfield, Sharon 405
Geatches, Anna 251
Gee, T. L. 271
Gelder, Lillian R. 453
Gelling, Pat 281
Genge, Sharon E. 269
George, Kate-Emily 147
George, Mary 311
George, Moira Patricia 328
George, Nicola 418
Gibbard, Rose E. 269
Gibbs, Fiona 457
Gibbs, Katherine M. 290
Gibbs, Melissa 347
Gibney, Linda 91
Gibney, Veronica 39
Gibson, Delia 245
Gibson, Dorothy Ann 219
Gibson, John 404
Gibson, June 161
Gibson, Kelly 157

Gibson, P. 564
Gibson, P. G. S. 265
Gibson, R. P. 499
Gibson, Shirley 274
Gibson-Barkess, Virginia 428
Gifford, Tony 583
Gil, Lucia Moya 291
Gilbert, Arthur 539
Gilbert, Jane 520
Gilbert, N. J. 359
Gilbert, S. V. 349
Gilbey, Paula 434
Gilchrist, Grace 440
Gilder, R. F. 360
Giles, Pauline 116
Gilhooly, Tracy 413
Gill, Andy 156
Gill, Jean 562
Gill, Joanne 440
Gill, Katie 170
Gill, Pamela E. 316
Gill, Sophia 52
Gillanders, Florence J. 160
Gillard, Philip 416
Gillespie, J. L. 553
Gillett, A. 153
Gillett, Malcolm 542
Gilliard, Sandra 279
Gillies, Calum 522
Gillingham, Paula 43
Gillings, Sonia 364
Gillions, J. 239
Gilliver, Joan 23
Giltnane, J. 366
Gissara, Elisabetta Puglisi 441
Gizman, Z. 121
Glass, R. 358
Glassbrook, Allan 210
Glasson, Andrew 400
Gleave, Wayne M. 204
Gleaves, Shirley 333
Gledhill, Michelle 579
Glendinning, Philip 313
Glikzeliger, Yvonne 181
Glover, Chris 391
Glover, Coral 19
Glover, Elizabeth Ann 76
Glozier, M. K. 115
Gobbett, Philomena 505
Godden, Peter 416
Golding, Charlotte 170
Goldsmith, Irene J. 144
Goldsmith, Sharon 133
Goldstein, Eve 158
Gonsalves, S. M. 325
Gonzalez, Oscar 476
Gooch, Joan 23
Good, Owen 319
Goodacre, Miriam Jean 183
Goodale, Anne 164
Goodall, D. 40
Goodall, Marc 486
Goodliffe, Leonard 299
Goodliffe, M. 127
Goodson, Shaun 307
Goodwin, Marja 430
Goram, Rosemary 545
Gordon, J. 481
Gordon, Mary 135
Gorecki, E. P. 581
Gormley, Albert H. 223
Gorton, Alison 154
Gosling, Kathleen 254
Gosling, Nan 238
Gosling, Rosa B. 420
Gosney, Enid 397

Gould, Christine 145
Gourlay, D. 428
Gowan, Paula 477
Gown, Debbie 402
Grace, Christopher 455
Grace, Enid 245
Graham, Carole 305
Graham, Christopher G. 373
Graham, Lillian 443
Graham, Marie 184
Graham, Sheila 411
Graham, Z. 481
Grainge, Harry 6
Granger, Linda 300
Granqvist-Ahmed, Selim 487
Grant, Elizabeth A. 383
Grassick, James Douglas 444
Gravenor, Wilma Jayne 497
Gray, Amanda 230
Gray, Cheryl 251
Gray, Christine N. 12
Gray, Kathy 224
Gray, L. E. 281
Gray, Patricia D. 558
Greason, Martin 191
Greathead, Elizabeth Anne 361
Green, C. 435
Green, Claire 244
Green, D. 509
Green, F. O. 505
Green, G. R. 333
Green, Geraldine 247
Green, Leslie 96
Green, Liza 83
Green, Margaret 351
Green, Margaret 358
Green, Nick 426
Green, Patricia 407
Green, Philippa 137
Green, Rose 326
Green, Tracy 433
Green, Valerie 189
Greenfield, Rosemary 46
Greenfield, Veronica J. 179
Greenhalgh, Kelli 454
Greenhow, Lawrence 97
Greenow, Alex 378
Greenwood, Joan G. 232
Greenwood, Vivienne 200
Gregor, S. A. 584
Gregory, Kathleen J. 445
Gregory, Vera 353
Greig, Brian 22
Grey, H. 116
Grey, John Adam 102
Gribble, Stephen 420
Grieve, A. S. 310
Grieve, Frances 461
Griffin, Marion 347
Griffith, Oonagh 362
Griffiths, Ben 83
Griffiths, Doreen 391
Griffiths, George A. 34
Griffiths, I. 48
Griffiths, Jackie A. 391
Griffiths, John 252
Griffiths, Leonard 165
Grinsted, Jean 24
Gross, Patricia-Mary 57
Grosse, Alice 500
Grounds, Heather 78
Grove, D. 272
Groves, Betty 291
Groves, Lynne 27
Guerin, A. 486
Guha, Sunil 359

Guile, Donita Lois 27
Gul, D. R. Maskeen 470
Gulley, Merilyn 271
Gunderson, M. 329
Gunter, G. 308
Gunther, Marilyn Faith 416
Guppy, Sarah 280
Gurl, Sarah 60
Gurr, L. 325
Guthrie, Patrick J. 488
Guy, Joan 401
Guy, Roland 43
Gwynn, V. 106

H

Hackley, Jacqueline A. 240
Hadley, Anne 469
Hadley, Kym 524
Haggett, Pauline 268
Haighton, Michael E. 353
Hailstones, Marion 267
Haines, Victoria 43
Hale, James 161
Hale, Lorna 68
Hales, Gordon Hereward 214
Haley, Susan J. 120
Hall, Alwyn 88
Hall, Carolyn 296
Hall, Chris M. 294
Hall, Constance 154
Hall, David 577
Hall, Frances 127
Hall, Ian 253
Hall, J. 315
Hall, Janet 377
Hall, Joy 398
Hall, Karen G. 215
Hall, Katie Leigh 528
Hall, Lal 227
Hall, Michael 323
Hall, Peter 481
Hall, Rosamund 559
Hall, Ruby 56
Hall, Stephanie 280
Hall, Susan 39
Hall-Baker, C. 116
Hallard, S. 435
Hallas, Eileen 379
Hallett, Jacky 470
Halliday, B. 206
Halliday, C. J. 104
Halligan, Pamela 409
Hallowes, Lucinda 22
Hamade, Trudie Ann 554
Hamblin, Pauline 369
Hamill, Kathryn 141
Hamill, S. 316
Hamilton, Jack 101
Hamilton, V. A. 485
Hamlin, Dena 98
Hammett, Reg 311
Hammond, B. 329
Hammond, Christine 143
Hammond, Denise 384
Hammond, Joyce 25
Hammond, Mark 416
Hammond, W. 570
Hampson, Barbara 247
Hampton, Delia 170
Hampton, J. 128
Hampton, Rachel A., age 10 131
Hancock, Denyse 89
Handel, Patricia Anne 343
Handy, Maureen L. 107
Hanley, Deborah 219
Hanna, B. M. 193

Hanna, Judith 142
Hannan, Norma G. 274
Hanrahan, Margaret 530
Hanrahan, Pat 426
Hanson, Eric 460
Hanson, M. 42
Hanson, Mavis 334
Hanson, Muriel 565
Hardie, Jean 215
Hardie, Moira C. 314
Harding, Amanda Jane 157
Harding, Emma 441
Harding, Paula 557
Harding, Peter 59
Hardman, A. 205
Hardstaff, Gina 387
Hardwick, Caroline 219
Hardwidge, Florence E. 472
Hardy, Doris 141
Hardy, Linda 383
Hare, Linda 249
Hare, Valerie 280
Hargreaves, Kate 510
Harker, Deborah 231
Harlin, Sylvia Maria 427
Harman, Edina 382
Harman, Joy 22
Harmer, Pauline 126
Haro, Gary 23
Harold, Jenny Sarah 519
Harper, A. G. 566
Harper, J. A. 313
Harper, J. E. 356
Harpham, S. M. 323
Harries, Vera 126
Harrild, Lyn 529
Harrill, D. 49
Harris, Ann 565
Harris, E. K. 556
Harris, Elizabeth G. 371
Harris, Gary Michael 13
Harris, Marni 194
Harris, Michelle 327
Harris, Pamela D. 537
Harris, Roy 178
Harris, Suzanne 105
Harris, W. Anne 421
Harrison, Anna 244
Harrison, Christopher 90
Harrison, David 34
Harrison, F. 286
Harrison, G. 563
Harrison, Margaret 275
Harrison, Mark 328
Harrison, May 346
Harrison, R. Jane 369
Harrison, S. J. 366
Harrison, Stephen R. 309
Harrison, Tom 56
Hart, Julie 329
Hart, Marjorie 274
Hart, Matthew 362
Hart, Pauline 324
Hartigan, N. 271
Hartley, Aimee 287
Hartley, C. 424
Hartley, Jacqueline 381
Hartley, Lesley 259
Hartley, Vera 315
Hartshorne, Michael 184
Hartwell, Alan 10
Harvell, Neil 483
Harvey, Gillian 524
Harvey, Jackie 447
Harvey, Ken 163
Harvey, Margaret 125

Harvey, Nicola Marie 493
Harvey, Sheila E. 410
Harvey, Val 332
Hassan, Salima 351
Hassett, Mairead 117
Hassett, Sinead 334
Hastie, Belinda 14
Hastie, Shona 278
Hathway, J. 174
Hatt, Jo 100
Hatton, Marion 415
Hatton, Tony 368
Haughey, C. 241
Haughey, Matthew J. 200
Haury, R. 205
Hauxwell, Colin Francis 298
Havard, K. J. 43
Hawes, Florence 27
Hawke, Lewis 213
Hawker, Lucy 7
Hawkes, Andrea 8
Hawkins, Alex 374
Hawkins, Sandra 581
Hayes, Annette 529
Hayes, Karen 257
Hayes, Ruth Mary 283
Haynes, John Roland 168
Haynes, Sian L. (c) 25/1/93 314
Hayton, J. M. 482
Hayward, Kitty 159
Hayward, Rosemary 436
Hayward, Susannah 110
Hazard, M. J. 182
Heach, John Vincent Michael 29
Heach, Lilian 20
Head, David 246
Heale, Iris 32
Heanley, Charles 445
Hearn, Alix 371
Hearn, Kathleen 19
Heasman, Kathleen W. 290
Heath, Alan 17
Heath, R., no one special 265
Heathwood, Celia 290
Heatley, W. G. 489
Heaton, Clare Louise 448
Hebberts, Valerie 309
Hedley, Brenda 395
Hedley, H. M. 476
Heenan, Lorraine 150
Heginbotham, John P. 15
Heinson, Katie 291
Hellawell, Mary Dale 133
Hellebrandt, Christina 69
Hellewell, Barbara 258
Helliar, Valerie 427
Hellon, Elsie M. 164
Helm, Kenneth 254
Hemingway, M. 205
Henderson, Colin 167
Henderson, Mavis 480
Henderson, Roy C. 433
Hendrie, Jean 100
Hengeveld, K. 495
Hennem, Janet L. 22
Hennessy, N. J. 199
Hennessy, Paul B. 275
Henning, Jane Elizabeth 7
Henry, Michael 429
Henwood, Suzanne 54
Hepburn, Jacqui 152
Hepton, Catherine 249
Heredge, Jeanne Clarke 297
Heron, Peter Giles 320
Herring, Irene 294
Herron, Mary N. 310

Hessey, Maurice 54
Hewitt, Enid 217
Hewitt, Tina 405
Hickman, Diana 161
Hickman, Katie 30
Hicks, Anthony J. 296
Higginbottom, M. G. 276
Higgins, Christopher 380
Higginson, Liam 307
Higgs, Joyce 375
Higgs, Rebecca 429
Highfield, D. 372
Hilditch, Elaine 146
Hiles, Sandra Anne 494
Hill, Adrian 292
Hill, Caroline 257
Hill, Heather 27
Hill, Helen Charlotte 215
Hill, John 233
Hill, Madeline 344
Hillbeck, Amanda 456
Hills, Jackie 4
Hilton, Anthony 292
Hilton, Karen 260
Himer, Catherine 253
Hindley, Arthur John 517
Hinds, Steven 316
Hindson, Alma 168
Hinkley, Vanessa 198
Hinks, Nicholas 580
Hinsley, Marie 47
Hinton, Sarah 61
Hinton, W. J. 345
Hirst, B. 582
Hirst, Steven 339
Hitchins, Samantha 308
Hobbs, Carol 109
Hobbs, Michelle 195
Hobson, Paul 297
Hockley, J. 54
Hodder, Miranda 133
Hodge, Jill E. 507
Hodge, Nellie Stanley 317
Hodgkins, P. 497
Hodgskin, R. H. 204
Hodgskins, Pamela 367
Hodgson, E. 312
Hodgson, Edna 146
Hogan, Amy 288
Hogarth, S. 484
Hogben, N. J. 355
Hogg, Michael 369
Hogg, Wilma 189
Holdaway, D. J. 493
Holdcroft, D. 48
Holder, Irene 140
Holder, Randolph 420
Hole, Adam 370
Holford, Wendy 572
Holland, Jennifer 451
Holland, Sarah 412
Holland, Valerie Carol 105
Holley, Michelle 273
Holliday, Albert W. 254
Holliday, Julia Ann 103
Hollier, L. 45
Holloway, J. 551
Holloway, Wendy 531
Holmes, D. 472
Holmes, E. A. 540
Holmes, S. G. 406
Holohan, Maria 121
Holsey, Claire 454
Holt, Denis N. 453
Holt, Elizabeth Ann 588
Holt, J. P. 316

Holt, Laura Louise 287
Holyland, Betty 370
Homer, O. 580
Honeysett, D. 328
Hood, Nicholas Robin 476
Hooper, Natalie 187
Hope, James 452
Hope, Julie 11, 151
Hopes, Hazel Deborah 242
Hopkin, Anne-Marie 234
Hopkins, G. A. 67
Hopkins, John 293
Hopkinson, Anthony 396
Hopkinson, Susan 321
Horajoo, Anbarasi 254
Horgan, Marjorie 319
Horn, Jennifer 243
Hornby, Elizabeth 457
Horpe, Olga 110
Horrell, Anthony 168
Horseman, Jan 303
Horth, Carmen 94
Horth, Michael 115
Horton-Rackstraw, Claire 143
Hough, Martyn J. M. 108
Hounslow, Louise 285
Housden, Sharon 47
Howard, A. J. 120
Howard, Barry 26
Howard, C. A. 547
Howard, Evelyn 335
Howard, Harrydan 27
Howarth, E. S. 437
Howarth-Hynes, Frank 292
Howe, Jennie 103
Howe, Tina 325
Howells, Stuart V. 262
Howes, Adrienne 447
Howick, Jane L. 529
Howison, Deborah 508
Howison, Louisa 140
Huckstepp, Julie 400
Hudd, Allan 584
Hudgell, Tanya 69
Hudson, Alan 30
Hudson, Carolyne 209
Hudson, Ian 102
Hudson, Jade 479
Hudson, Marjorie Joan 175
Hudson, Richard 370
Hudson, Teresa 362
Hudspith, Margaret 350
Huggett, M. P. 350
Huggins, A. 174
Hughes, Agneta 168
Hughes, Catherine 88
Hughes, Cheridan 349
Hughes, Christina 3
Hughes, Kenneth 7
Hughes, Lowri Rhiannon 10
Hughes, Mary 332
Hughes, Nicholas 51
Hughes, Rachael 63
Hughes, Sinead 530
Hughes, Theresa Elizabeth 337
Hull, W. 345
Hulme, Christine 292
Hulme, Lindsay Clair 250
Hulme, Mary 277
Hulse, Sara 553
Humfrey, Jacqueline 284
Humphries, Daniel 458
Hunaban, Jean 85
Hunt, B. J. 310
Hunt, Carole 285
Hunt, Linda 99

Hunt, Mary 130
Hunt, Thomas D. 122
Hunter, Alyson 371
Hunter, Andrew 29
Hunter, Elizabeth 84
Hunter, Linda 579
Hunter, Mary 437
Hunter, Peggy 60
Hunter, Reg 272
Huntington, Keith 255
Huntington, Norma G. 196
Huntly, Anne 287
Hurcombe, Robert 319
Hurley, George T. 72
Hurst, K. 114
Hurst, Pamela 348
Hutchings, Helena 462
Hutchings, N. R. J. 475
Hutchinson, Emma 459
Hutchinson, S. J. 114
Hutchinson, Wendy Anita 557
Hutchison, Marion 420
Hutt, P. A. 131
Huxley, D. 485
Hyam, Maureen 500
Hyde, Paul 266
Hyland, John 441
Hynes, Vera 327
Hyslop, James Norman A. 90

I

Ibbetson, Alice 301
Iley, Kathy 511
Illingworth, Dorothy 529
Ilott, P. A. 268
Imp. 392
Indrayan, Priti 311
Ing, Rosalind 272
Ingham, Joan 240
Ingle, Geoffrey 240
Insall, L. 318
Iqbal, Bushra 226
Irvine, Eileen 517
Irwin, Margaret 270
Irwin, Thomas E. 336
Isherwood, Janet Elizabeth 385
Ives, Gwen 5
Izatt, Lisa Jane 74

J

Jacklin, Tania 267
Jackman, W. G. 199
Jackopson, Ruth 314
Jackopson, Vic 323
Jackson, Albert 560
Jackson, David 402
Jackson, Doris M. 375
Jackson, Elaine 241
Jackson, Geoffrey H. 246
Jackson, Hazel V. 399
Jackson, Helen C. 298
Jackson, Jo 526
Jackson, Julie 575
Jackson, Ken 380
Jackson, Kenneth V. 398
Jackson, M. 57
Jackson, Pamela 176
Jackson, R. 423
Jackson, Stanley B. 585
Jackson, Stuart 132
Jackson, Susan Tina Maria 546
Jacobs, Leonie 12
Jacques, Susan Lesley 413
Jaffeir, Michael 274
Jakeway, Frances C. 20

James, Albert H. 401
James, Anthony 518
James, D. A. L. 478
James, Deborah 387
James, E. J. 309, 323
James, Georgina 166
James, N. T. 45
James, Richard 49
James, Susan 41
Jane, Jean 467
January, Delia 400
Japhet, Raymond 70
Jardine, John 221
Jarosz, Virginia 488
Jarrad, Mark A. 317
Jarvis, Angela 80
Jarvis, Annette 126
Jarvis, D. C. 354
Jarvis, Patricia J. 551
Jarvis, Sally K. 308
Jarwood, Alison 149
Jayewardena, Sharmini 542
Jeffcock, Lilian 499
Jefferies, Timothy C. 274
Jefferson, Wilson 347
Jeffery, P. N. 340
Jeffrey, Michelle 474
Jenkin, Anna 80
Jenkins, Clare H. E. 572
Jenkins, Joan Mavis 441
Jenkins, Stan 279
Jenkins, T. G. 577
Jenkins, T. J. 273
Jenkinson, Andrew 459
Jennens, Graeme Leslie 75
Jennings, Barbara 14
Jennings, Vera M. 124
Jensen, Susannah 111
Jepson, E. 330
Jessup, Josephine 561
Jillings, Harriet 520
Johanesen, Marjorie 350
John, Marion 136
Johns, C. J. 490
Johns, Gordon Reid 507
Johnson, A. J. 56
Johnson, Brian 17
Johnson, Constance 250
Johnson, Donna 307
Johnson, E. G. 314
Johnson, Jacqueline M. 93
Johnson, Jean Iona 382
Johnson, Joy Patricia 17
Johnson, Lucy M. 582
Johnson, Marjorie 120
Johnson, Natalie 470
Johnson, Peggy 578
Johnson, Susan 558
Johnson, Sylvia 426
Johnson, Tracy Ann 551
Johnson, Winifred 185
Johnson-Conley, Joyce 33
Johnston, Heather 562
Johnston, Janis 166
Johnstone, David 254
Jolyss, C. 468
Jones, Alan V. 172
Jones, Alyson Sian 102
Jones, Andrew 258
Jones, Ann 506
Jones, Averil 253
Jones, C. M. 345
Jones, Cathy 299
Jones, Christine 219
Jones, Claire (Age 10) 76
Jones, E. C. 110

Jones, Elizabeth 246
Jones, Glyn 463
Jones, Helen 143
Jones, Hilda 396
Jones, J. M. 486
Jones, Jeannette 98
Jones, Joan E. 447
Jones, K. 547
Jones, K. R. 336
Jones, Kathrine 401
Jones, La 84
Jones, Marcus J. 534
Jones, Martin Ashley 118
Jones, Matty 405
Jones, Michael 418
Jones, R. 503
Jones, R. I. 359
Jones, Rachel Amanda 432
Jones, Richard Towyn 185
Jones, Sara 187
Jones, Shelley 501
Jones, Stephanie M. 502
Jones, Terry 46
Jones, Tracey 55
Jones, Vicky Lee 474
Jones, Vie 184
Jones, W. J. B. 538
Jones-Morris, V. 334
Jordache, Bernie Jay 253
Jordan, Christine 295
Jordan, Jacqueline 389
Jordan, Patrick 270
Jordan, R. H. Gimi 106
Jordan-Meadows, Lucy 108
Joseph, M. 314
Joseph, Marrisa 534
Josling, P. G. 196
Joyce, Jacki 291
Joynes, Tracy 574
Judd, Simon 474
Judson, Millicent E. 549
Jury, Susan 134
Justice, Pam 200

K

Kane, Katherine Maria 510
Kane, Michael J. 553
Kane, Romaine 120
Kanwar, Ranjit 270
Kardar, Helen 211
Karim, Mina 407
Karn, J. J. 555
Karrie, Peter 196
Kashem, Abul Alam 517
Kasraie, Shireen 135
Kavanagh, Madeline 195
Kay, Heather Louise 31
Kay, M. 49
Kebby-Jones, Kay S. 458
Keeble, Dianne 250
Keeling, Elsie 516
Kelk, Violet 582
Kelly, Claire Elizabeth 223
Kelly, Helen 457
Kelly, Jean 131
Kelly, Lynsey 296
Kelly, N. 313
Kelly, Nayereh 495
Kelly, S. 36
Kelsey, Simon 279
Kemna, Ingrid 293
Kemp, Michelle 209
Kemp, Toni 44
Kempster, Christina 86
Kempster, Valerie 183
Kendall, Michael 536

Kennedy, Edith 252
Kennedy, Joseph 22
Kennedy, Kim 24
Kennedy, S. C. 434
Kenny, Ita 581
Kent, Faizan B. 228
Kent, Gwendolen M. 401
Kent, J. A. 197
Kent, Katie 248
Kenyon, Eileen 587
Kenyon, Steve 586
Kenyon-Smith, Andrew J. 35
Keogh, Julie 34
Kerfoot, B. 52
Kerkosh, Emily 525
Kerr, Emma 300
Kerr, James 235
Kerr, S. J. 279
Kerr, Sue 109
Kershaw, Gwendoline 445
Keswick, Charles 23
Kettle, C. 549
Keys, Chris 162
Khurana, Jag 372
Kiddell, Tina 322
Kidman, M. 575
Kientsch, Theo E. 540
Kilcoyne, E. J. 57
Kilduff, Emma 165
Kiley, Jeanne 522
Kilgallon, John 517
Kilminster, Alan 391
Kimber, Jill M. 292
Kimm, Alene 291
Kinch, Nicola 311
King, C. 137
King, Carolyn 393
King, Chris 465
King, Constance E. S. 90
King, David G. 9
King, E. L. 58
King, Emma 170
King, J. L. 474
King, J. Pat. 498
King, Jacqui 224
King, John R. 206
King, Kathy 268
King, Lorna 462
King, Lynette 231
King, Marie B. 117
King, Melanie Victoria 282
King, Michelle 281
King, Rhonda 119
King, Sheila 178
King, Sue 534
Kingscott, Emma 507
Kingston, Raymond 55
Kinnon, Dawn 583
Kinslay, Richard 560
Kirby, Emma 442
Kirby, Joan 522
Kirby, Pamela 427
Kirk, Kirsty Zoe 518
Kirk, Rachel 485
Kirkbright, B. 308
Kitch, John S. 520
Kitchin, Lilian 244
Kitson, Christine 379
Kluk, J. B. 129
Knaggs, M. I. 425
Knecht, Kathleen 26
Knell, Andrew 250
Knight, A. R. 38
Knight, Claude A. 241
Knight, J. W. 425
Knight, John 511

Knight, Patricia Mary 125
Knight, Philip 263
Knighton, Lianne 442
Knott, Helen 33
Knowles, Caroline 166
Knox, Jessie 372
Kolacs, Val 355
Konradsen, Betty C. 446
Korczynski, Samantha 413
Kortje, Margaret 495
Kouspoyenis, Constantina S. 16
Kravis, Carol 16
Krzyworaczka, Kazimiera 216
Kyriacou, Marina 332

L

Labancz, Erika Maria 454
Ladell, Kelly 402
Laing, Elizabeth 238
Lake, K. E. 331
Lake, Maureen 315
Lamb, Harold 519
Lamb, June 384
Lamb, Maureen 436
Lambe, Michael 99
Lambert, Doris 210
Lambert, John 253
Lambert, Katy 466
Lambert, Ron 70
Lambie, M. 57
Lambie, May 308
Lambourne, Pat 434
Lambourne, Vicki 549
Lambra, Jane B. 294
Lambton, Darin 390
Lamden, T. 343
Lamond, R. 562
Lampard, Nicola 135
Landau, Gita 75
Landon, Doreen 251
Lane, Ron 282
Lang, Raymond 62
Langbridge, John 376
Langdon, Catherine 517
Langdon, N. M. 173
Langford, E. M. 269
Langford, Joyce 251
Langley, Joy 94
Langshaw, Margaret 331
Langston, I. R. 425
Langton, Marion 129
Lansdell, Cynthia 387
Lansley, Paul Thomas 541
Larouche, Tara Belinda 482
Latham, Carol 142
Latham, Howard A. 510
Latham, Irene L. 73
Lathwood, Loretta 255
Lauder, J. 192
Laughton, F. M. 201
Laver, Kathy 561
Laverty, Philip 501
Lavery, Moira 280
Lavin, K. 353
Law, Celia 8
Law, Karen 345
Lawall, Christian Daniel 307
Lawlor, Deborah 438
Lawrence, Alison 447
Lawrence, Carole Elizabeth 214
Lawrence, E. J. 542
Lawrence, G. 201
Lawrence, Nicola 267
Lawrence, Rodney 330
Lawrence, Suzan 319
Lawrie, Elizabeth 284

Lawrie, Jean 376
Lawson, Alex J. 164
Lawson, S. 406
Lazarou, Maria 327
Le Cras, Paula 503
Le Pavoux, Christina 304
Le Stocker, Jacqueline 260
Le Sueur, D. R. Payn 422
Le-Britton, Anne 26
Leat, Terence W. 433
Leavold, Olive E. 432
Lechner, Dominique 295
Lee, Alison 527
Lee, D. E. 272
Lee, Diane F. 97
Lee, John 452
Lee, Julie 139
Lee, Kevin 260
Lee, M. E. 543
Lee, Richard A. 120
Lee, Samantha 312
Lee, Sandra Elizabeth 191
Leeming, Lillian 233
Lees, Hazel K. 258
Lees, Julie 256
Leeves, Ramon 45
Leighton, J. 335
Lennox, Elizabeth 288
Leonard, Lisa Amy 577
Leonard, Michael 130
Leonard, W. 329
Lester, Neil 319
Letting, Dawn A. 509
Levy, Gloria 9
Lewington, Jacqueline 519
Lewis, B. T. 203
Lewis, Fred 469
Lewis, Harriet 151
Lewis, Heather J. 376
Lewis, Heidi 396
Lewis, Joan E. 287
Lewis, Marcia Celestina 330
Lewis, Matthew 314
Lewis, Patricia 334
Lewis, Sonia 318
Lewis, Vera 54
Lewtas, Gillian 145
Leyland, James 214
Liegaux, Francis 446
Lightowler, Molly 352
Lilley, Chris J. 439
Lilly, Annabelle 525
Lima, Eithne Ryan 141
Lindh, J. 541
Lindop, George 257
Lindop, Michael Anthony 420
Lindop, Robert 263
Lindsay, Evelyn Davidson 454
Lindsey, Rika 543
Lineham, M. 136
Lines, D. L. 367
Linney, S. M. 558
Lister, Iris 578
Lister, W. 557
Little, Jonathan 451
Littlewood, I. M. 549
Livett, Evelyn Ann 507
Livingstone, David 445
Livingstone, Lyn 259
Llewellyn, Gladys 377
LLoyd, Beryl 160
Lloyd, Bryn 92
Lloyd, D. D. 109
Lloyd, Gillian 157
Lloyd, Richard 437
Lloyd, Valerie 320

Loader, Mary 332
Lock, A. E. 435
Locke, Helen 514
Lockey, Shirley 66
Lockington, Martie 355
Lockwood, Alan 30
Lockwood, Andrew 399
Lockwood, Deborah 519
Lockwood, Derek Morgan 19
Long, George Richard 385
Long, Howard 18
Long, L. C. H. 63
Long, M. E. 310
Long, Patricia 356
Long, Ron 539
Long, Wyn 131
Longden, Graham 89
Longley, Kathryn 258
Longrigg, Gail 254
Lord, C. E. 47
Lord, Sue 274
Losits, Beryl Joanne 255
Loughborough, Peter 407
Loughlin, G. A. 274
Love, Sheila 118
Lowde, Ann 306
Lowe, Barrie 587
Lowe, P. A. 436
Lowery, Janet 518
Lowsley, Lee 441
Lucas, Annie 11
Lucas, Paul 44
Luck, Clifford G. 146
Luck, J. M. 431
Luck, Sarah Jane 320
Luckham, Natalie 430
Luckhurst, Audrey 444
Luckhurst, Lynne Olivia 442
Luff, Karen 255
Luffman, B. 504
Lukan, Yewande 342
Lunam, Flora M. 578
Lund, Sue 310
Lund, Winifred 314
Lunn, Melodie 183
Lunnon, Sandra 410
Lunt, David 17
Lunt, Sandra 502
Lusty, Frances S. 560
Luton, David 22
Luxton, Cherry 100
Lyall, Kiran 207
Lyall, Priya 314
Lyes, A. E. 38
Lynall, Shirley 548
Lynas, Marlene 125
Lynch, Don 172
Lyne, Ruth 339
Lyon, M. 266

M

MacAuslan, J. M. 562
Macciolo, Anthony 74
Macdonald, Angela 92
MacDonald, Anita 395
MacDonald, Catherine A. 75
Macdonald, E. J. 129
MacDonald, Gail 34
MacDonald, J. C. 274
MacDonald, June 519
MacDonald, Katie Sarah 403
MacFadyen, Val 263
Machin, Bridget 144
Mackay, Canon D. 226
MacKenzie, Beryl 518
MacKenzie, J. 526

MacKenzie, Paul 335
Mackness, Noele 110
MacLachlan, Louisa Prince 384
MacLean, Joe 293
MacLeod, Benjamin 160
MacMahon, T. 316
MacPhail, Ian S. 242
MacPherson, Linda 100
MacPherson, Linda 383
Maddison, Alan K. 513
Magee, Anthony 515
Magee, Eleanor I. 463
Magill, Sarah 405
Magill, Thomas 490
Maguire, Mary 115
Maher, Danny 398
Maher, Kelly J. 306
Maher, Kevin 378
Mahmood, Haleema S. 284
Mahmud, Mansur 51
Mail, Kyle 243
Mainstone, Rebecca 36
Malcolm, Eleanor 102
Malcolm, Margaret 264
Malik, Mansurah 300
Maling, Lee 242
Mallett, Brenda 527
Mallpress, Phillip 129
Maloy, K. 431
Manley, Garry 29
Mannering, Shirley 319
Manning, Daniel 77
Manning, J. 279, 567
Manning, Joanne 151
Mannings, Eve 382
Mansell, Silvia Ann 93
Mansford, Catherine E. 209
Manuel, Stephanie 52
Mapp, Jonathan 210
Marcar, Pierre 559
Marie-Rose 488
Mark, Sylvia 313
Markac, Nevenka 239
Marlon, Jason 516
Marlow, A. 309
Marlow, Angela 528
Marlow, V. 408
Marriott, Dafydd 259
Marriott, Lisa 586
Marsh, Joanna 293
Marshall, Alastair 217
Marshall, Amanda 579
Marshall, Barry 456
Marshall, H. F. 531
Marshall, M. 530
Marshall, Margaret 492
Marshall, Margaret H. 133
Marshall, Michael 109
Marshall, V. A. 178
Marshall-Regan, R. 485
Marsters, S. C. 437
Marston, Alan 450
Marston, Anthony J. 166
Marten, Paula 333
Martin, Barbara E. 575
Martin, Claire 236
Martin, D. 419
Martin, Emma 513
Martin, Emma Victoria 152
Martin, Geoffrey J. 511
Martin, Lydia 561
Martin, M. 39
Martin, M. 534
Martin, Mary-Ann 351
Martin, Peter 205
Martin, Robert 433

Martin, Sheena-Rose 346
Martin, Wenvis 101
Mary, Penelope Heather 308
Mashongamhende, Rudy 264
Mason, Barbara 378
Mason, Brian 23
Mason, Catherine 25
Mason, Gwen 88
Mason, Jenny 225
Mason, M. K. 57
Mason, Mary 483
Massingham, Claire 516
Masters, A. J. 357
Masters, John 232
Masters, Sally 541
Mastin, Joyce 249
Mathers, Julie 512
Mathieson, Geraldine 286
Mathonsi, Davison 220
Matthew, E. 497
Matthews, A. 576
Matthews, C. 62
Matthews, Dawn 385
Matthews, Jenny 9
Matthews, Joan Dubicki 255
Matthews, Joan Y. 213
Matthews, Sheila 66
Matthews, Susan 190
Maudsley, Anne 294
Mawnam-Smith, Frances 225
Mawston, Harvey 260
Maxwell, Christine 303
Maxwell, Stephen 536
May, Beatrice 305
May, Brigitte 141
May, Caroline 464
May, James 379
May, K. 562
Mayers, Sian 360
Mayes, Anne R. 445
Maynard, Victor Stephen 499
Mayo, Mary 50
Mayoh, K. W. 70
Mazzuccato, R. 280
Mbadiwe, Chinyere 141
McAlpine, Jennifer 166
McAndrew, Malcolm 573
McArdle, Patrick 179
McArthur, Frank 11
McAuley, Biddy 521
McCabe, Ann 446
McCabe, Jean 459
McCabe, June 168
McCabe, May 52
McCairn, William 111
McCall, Cathie 246
McCall, Maisie 307
McCall, R. E. 487
McCamley, Peter M. 262
McCann, Jane Elizabeth 237
McCann, John 5
McCarroll, Alice 230
Mccarthy, Lesley Ann 583
McClune, B. A. 279
McClure, Michael 354
McCluskey, Bernadette 142
McCluskey, Stephen 586
McCluskey, Winifred 341
McConnochie, Chris 393
McCormack, B. 577
McCormick, Bernadette 213
McCormick, Fiona 225
McCormick, John J. 449
McCormick, R. M. 504
McCrea, Aureen 261
McCue, Jeff 161

McCutcheon, Elizabeth 386
McDermott, Laura 301
McDonald, Carol 395
McDonald, Fiona 148
McDonnell, Philip Anthony 264
McDuff, Sally-Ann 41
McEvoy-Morris, Simone 43
McFall, D. L. 188
McGaffin, Grace 209
McGarry, Paul 191
McGavock, Patricia 314
McGeeney, Stephen 271
McGeoch, Laura 4
McGhee, A. 498
McGill, Jacqueline 348
McGinty, B. 346
McGinty, Fiona 103
McGinty, Geraldine Anne 513
McGoff, Elaine 246
McGonnell, Eddie 25
McGovern, Kenneth 208
McGovern, Kenneth 296
McGowan, Frank 300
McGrath, Ian 212
McGrath, Tom 39
McGuigan, Caroline 247
McGuinness, P. 69
McGuire, Christina 221
McGuire, Nathan 37
McGuire, Sonia 324
McIlroy, James 288
McIntosh, Chris 240
McIntyre, Cameron 579
McIntyre, D. 126
McIntyre, Scott 547
McIntyre, Terrence 506
McKay, David A. B. 560
McKay, H. 344
McKeague, Robert 273
McKellar, Kim 245
McKendry, Joyce 26
McKenzie, Kathleen 89
McKeown, Frank 438
McKerchar, Cristina 460
McKillop, Euphemia 21
McKillop, J. 546
McKimmie, Annie 86
McLachlan, Margaret 358
McLaren-Gibbs, Carol 171
McLaughlin, D. F. 36
McLean, C. M. 134
McLean-Brown, Rebecca 268
McLeod, J. L. 361
McLuckie, William 196
McMahon, Desmond G. 450
Mcmahon, Kathleen 572
McMullen, Alex 576
McNally, E. J. 61
McNamara, B. S. M. 308
McNeil, Kay 443
McPeake, Caroline 391
McPhail, R. W. 358
McPherson, Delores 285
McRae, Christine 387
McSephney, Mary Elizabeth 492
McSperrin, Marysia 556
McTaggart, Thomas 263
McWilliams, Anne 152
Mead, Paul 49
Meaden, Michelle 417
Meader, June 297
Meadhurst, Neil 324
Meager, Susan 199
Meale, B. 329
Meek, Diana 302
Meek, Gillian 78

Meek, V. A. 509
Megginson, Shirley M. 263
Megson, Andrew T. 371
Meikle, Philip 362
Meja, Angela 218
Melbourne, Pauline R. 193
Meller, Louise 460
Melling, Thora J. 480
Mello, M. D. 409
Melville, Ada 27
Melville, Janis 150
Melville, Joyce 388
Melvin, Mabel 110
Mercalfe, Heidi E. 163
Mercer, Anna Caroline 296
Mercer, Deidre Gillian 287
Mercer, Margaret J. 370
Merchant, Kenneth 170
Merrick, Lorna 112
Merrifield, Susan 436
Merrill, Jean 448
Merritt, E. F. 530
Mertzios, Georgios A. 91
Metcalfe, Ann 307
Metcalfe, B. G. 327
Metcalfe, David 443
Metcalfe, Heidi E. 168
Meynell, Christine 459
Michael, Doreen 26
Michie, Agnes 21
Middleton, Janet 461
Miles, Reginald 107
Miles, Ronald William 320
Miles, Wenda 311
Miles-Berry, H. G. 422
Millband, Laurence 400
Millen, Marlyne A. 40
Millen, Patricia 178
Miller, Anna E. 211
Miller, Beverley 296
Miller, Christine 79
Miller, D. 492
Miller, Dorothy 252
Miller, Elizabeth Garrett 583
Miller, John 159, 393
Miller, Laura 152
Miller, Susanna 188
Millington, Dorothy 393
Mills, Janet 400
Mills, Joanne C. D. 521
Mills, Julie 79
Mills, Pauline 485
Mills, Sonja Frances 499
Milne, Carol Diane 77
Milne, Claire 148
Milne, Elenor 13
Milsom, G. 105
Milton, Lydia 518
Mingo, L. 493
Minish, Geoffrey 241
Minshall, Matthew 584
Miskelly, Veronica 579
Misra, Vidya 262
Mitchell, A. R. J. 174
Mitchell, Bridget Ann 305
Mitchell, Catherine 242
Mitchell, Ffyona 259
Mitchell, Kathleen 257
Mitchell, Laura 562
Mitchell, M. 530
Mitchell, R. 62
Mitchell, Ronnie 83
Mitchell, Sara 133
Mitchell, Winnie 264
Mitrega, Margaret 408
Mockridge, Daphne 560

Modinos, Antonis 156
Moffatt, David Bruce 242
Moffatt, David 560
Moffatt, Lorna 300
Mohammed, Amanda S. K. 171
Mohyla, Margaret 491
Moir, Michael W. 270
Moir, Patricia Ann 326
Moll, Valerie 312
Molyneux, Iris 87
Momber, Diana 444
Monger, A. J. 137
Monju, Delower Hossan 371
Monks, Steven 176
Monks, Wanda 432
Montague-Thomas, Lucie 303
Moody, Joyce 306
Moollan, M. 327
Moon, J. V. 491
Moon, Keith 160
Mooney, Doreen 136
Mooney, Natalie 576
Mooney, S. 555
Moore, Angela 81
Moore, Brenda Ann 206
Moore, G. D. 198
Moore, Grainne 169
Moore, Iain 464
Moore, Jayne 468
Moore, Jenny 458
Moore, Mary P. 320
Moore, Robert W. 560
Moore, Ronald 190
Moore, W. 59
Moran, Pluto 474
Moreland, Anne 285
Moreton, Sally 118
Morgan, C. R. P. 197
Morgan, D. T. 330
Morgan, Hilda 470
Morgan, Natalie 174
Moring, Peter 480
Morley, W. 351
Morosoli, Emily 88
Morrell, Frank William 577
Morris, C. A. 561
Morris, Eleanor M. 233
Morris, John V. 155
Morris, Jon 574
Morris, Mark 111
Morris, Mary 56
Morris, P. 489
Morris, Terry 192
Morris, V. R. 501
Morris, Valerie 280
Morris-Hague, Dorothy 87
Morrison, Alex 297
Morrison, Cheryl Ann 227
Morrison, D. 281
Morrison, Emma 86
Morrison, Jessie 453
Morrow, Marjorie E. 427
Morse, E. P. 172
Mortell, Jim 3
Mortimer, Janet 293
Mortlock, Carys 23
Mortlock, Lisa 451
Morton, Amanda 240
Morton, Andrea Marrie 509
Morton, M. E. 437
Morton-Holmes, R. S. 50
Moschoudi, Efrosini 448
Moseley, T. 123
Mosquera, Delia Viola 287
Moss, Anita Larraine 238
Moss, B. F. 324

Moss, E. J. 271
Moulder, Maggie 279
Mount, J. 499
Mountain, M. I. 536
Mountford, Roger D. 342
Mountford, Stuart G. 341
Mouzo, Evelyn 305
Mowat, G. A. 342
Moxey, Michaela 484
Moy, T. 36
Moyes, Jennie 285
Moynihan, Daniel 30
Mueen, Tasneem 188
Muende, Melanie 328
Muir, Ann 164
Muir, Helen B. 207
Mulcahy, Philip 277
Muldowney, Margaret 310
Mulla, Farooq 242
Mulreay, Hollie 235
Munday, Jill 140
Mungapen, Shirley 279
Munn, J. 128
Munro, Isma 302
Munro, Nora H. 203
Murawa, Diane 511
Murch, Joan 8
Murdoch, Eleanor 64
Murdoch, Jane E. 471
Murison, Deborah 248
Murphy, Audra Ann 322
Murphy, Doreen 244
Murphy, J. 353
Murphy, John P. 508
Murphy, Tracey Anne 70
Murray, Agnes 389
Murray, H. 330
Murrells, Cynthia 289
Mursell, Sarah 587
Musgrave, Lynda 215
Musker, W. 193
Musleh, Marie 432
Muxlow, S. 132
Mythen, Katie Jayne 218
Mythen, Patricia A. 42

N

Nabbs, T. F. 109
Nair, Jason Vinodh 103
Nancarrow, Rosalyn 65
Nannyonga, Harriet 523
Narramore, G. R. G. 404
Nash, Maria Patricia 133
Nation, Edna 82
Naylor, Margaret 478
Neal, Eileen 158
Neal, Jill 527
Neale, B. J. 412
Neale, Dorothy M. 404
Neale, Gordon 452
Neave, B. C. 408
Neave, R. P. 502
Need, Richard 63
Needham, Diane 524
Needham, Joan W. 71
Needham, Lily 31
Needham, M. 68
Neilson, Ruth Elisabeth 336
Nel, Shirley 535
Nelsey-Brown, Karenanne 451
Nelson, David 251
Nelson, Jacqueline 455
Nelson, P. W. 411
Netherton, Kathleen D. 250
Nettlefold, Ella B. M. 458
New, B. H. 415

Newall, George 388
Newbery, J. 364
Newcombe, Jim 515
Newell, D. K. 331
Newman, Bryan 303
Newman, C. N. 534
Newman, Daphne D. A. 516
Newman, Debra 511
Newman, Douglas T. 32
Newman, Heidi 293
Newman, Yasmin Taara 315
Newsham, Maureen 58
Newsome, D. 425
Newson, Gary 30
Newton, Dave 243
Newton, David 383
Newton, Esther 358
Newton-Edwards, Heidi 462
Nichols, Carmen Nicola 394
Nichols, M. E. 203
Nicholson, Joyce 258
Nicholson, S. W. 181
Nicholson, Sandra 504
Nicolle, Dennis Peter 140
Nicolson, Caroline M. 470
Nimmo, Margaret 187
Nissan, Helda 242
Nixon, Colin Mark 515
Nkansa, Grace Agyapoma 257
Noble, Jo 452
Nodwell, Nuala 549
Nolan, Grainne 101
Nolan, Lilian 237
Norfolk, Nannie 199
Norman, Joy 32
Norris, Agnieska 89
Norris, Andrew 160
North, Richard G. 45
Norton, Marjorie E. 132
Norton, Trevor 191
Noton, Val 353
Novotni, Maggie 334
Nutton, P. M. 336
Nwanosike, Amanda 383
Nyklewicz-Betney, Amy 304

O

Oakeley, Mary 532
Oakes, Gill 91
Oakley, Kelly 289, 564
Oakley, Michael 111
Oakley, Simon 49
Oates, Amy 71
Oates, Sydney 197
Oates-Smith, Denise 48
O'Brien, Constance 386
O'Brien, Margaret Angela 369
O'Brien, Michelle 175
O'Brien, Susan 123
O'Brien, Yvonne 311
O'Connell, P. 347
O'Connor, Bernadette 463
O'Dea, Carol 466
Odlum, Michael 484
O'Donnell, Jason 298
O'Donnell, John 87
O'Donnell, M. 554
O'Donnell, Mark 331
Ogden, Lynette 517
Ogilvie, Dael 582
O'Hara, Elizabeth 33
O'Hara, Robert 49
O'Hare, Seamus 431
O'Henley, Andrew Alexander 76
Ohlsson, Camilla 291
O'Kane, Catherine 305

O'Keeffe, Ann 146
Old, Julian James 512
Oldfield, Barbara 165
Oldfield, Maria E. 333
Oliver, Martin 363
Olley, Phyllis 188
O'Neale, Douglas J. 161
O'Neil, Helen 390
O'Neill, Ann 525
O'Neill, Tina 489
O'Quigley, Martin 537
Ordidge, W. 585
O'Reilly, T. M. 359
O'Riordan, Hayley 249
Ormerod, Sheila 326
Orpin, Allan 373
Orr, Jean Mary 18
Orr, Jenny 155
Orr, Julia 250
Orr, Peter 205
Orr, Rosanne 416
Orrey, Beverley Marie 210
Oruc, Amna 230
Osborn, Maria 312
Osborne, Cynthia 94
Osborne, Juliet 220
Osborne, Richard 39
Osbourn, Constance 466
O'Shea, Carmel 508
Osley, S. P. 130
Ottewell, G. 587
Otto, Vera 56
Outlaw, Kevin 527
Overbury, Don 6
Overson, Dawn 390
Owen, L. 122
Owen, M. C. 326
Owen, Matthew 324
Owen, Rebecca 185
Owens, Colette 150
Owens, Margaret 120

P

P., Sheily 262
Pace, Carole Diane 521
Packer, Ruth 312
Packett, Alan F. J. 296
Paddock, Gemma 441
Padmore, Jean 156
Padwick, Sylvie 317
Pagdin, June 510
Page, Lee 578
Page, Tanya 262
Paget, J. 175
Paget, Vilma 553
Pagett, F. T. 320
Palau, Frances L. 294
Palfrey, Louise 208
Palmer, Andrea 562
Palmer, C. A. 540
Palmer, Julie 249
Palmer, Lilian Rose 138
Pammenter, R. R. 186
Panesar, Harjit 307
Parish, H. 271
Parish, Hayley 14
Parish, Jean 102
Park, May 45
Park, Nan 535
Parker, Dorothy 288
Parker, Irene 98
Parker, J. 228
Parker, Kevin 99
Parker, Ngaire G. M. 543
Parker, Roz 37
Parker, Sally Annette 48

Parkes, Sadie 115
Parkin, Enid 218
Parkinson, Joan 8
Parkinson, Julie 376
Parkinson, Stuart George 325
Parks, Linda R. 153
Parks, S. M. 51
Parkyn, Wendy 341
Parley, Douglas 561
Parody, Caroline Ellul 266
Parr, Libby 233
Parratt, Victor 122
Parry, Kevin John 28
Parry, Ronnie 321
Parsons, Lora J. 290
Parsons-Hann, N. 331
Partington, H. M. 203
Partridge, Irene 231
Passant, Flora 256
Patching, Sandie 322
Patel, Naren Makan 350
Paterson, Anthony 85
Paterson, Erskine James 260
Paterson, Simon 433
Paton, Joy 94
Patten, Val E. 581
Patterson, Cyril Douglas 301
Patterson, G. 123
Pattison, David C. 528
Pattison, Kym 295
Paul, J. 209
Paul, Joan 453
Paus, Leslie 301
Pavitt, Hazel 520
Pawley, Leanora 89
Pay, Lisa 443
Payne, Geoffrey C. 387
Payne, Josephine 377
Peach, Christopher 294
Peacher, Margaret G. 484
Pearce 365
Pearce, Iona Mair 303
Pearce, P. 551
Pearce, Selena 550
Pearce, Sharon 425
Pearson, Christy 216
Pearson, Dorothy Iris 218
Pearson, Elle 225
Pearson, Kasy 440
Pearson, Len 381
Pearson, Rosemary 121
Peck, Iris 10
Peck, Ivan J. 99
Pedder, Jean 260
Pedlow, Shirley 106
Pell, Geoffrey W. 438
Pelling, Naomi 282
Penarski, Richard 59
Pendleton, P. A. 269
Pengelly, A. G. 112
Penlington, Austen A. 252
Penman, T. 538
Pennick, Leanne 32
Penny, Thomasin 562
Penty, Amanda 8
Percival, Claire Johanna 304
Perfit, Lauren 80
Perkins, Averil A. 94
Perkins, Geraldine 78
Perris, Suzanne 36
Perry, David 97
Perry, Jean 348
Perry, Lisa 461
Pescod, Elsie 460
Peters, Dorothy 527
Peters, Lisa 241

Peterson, D. Hilda 586
Phelan, Rosemary 278
Phillips, Alan J. 149
Phillips, B. M. 357
Phillips, Christine 576
Phillips, D. M. 132
Phillips, Dean (Age 8) 297
Phillips, Lucas Grant 464
Phillips, Philippa 202
Phillips, Samantha 417
Phillips, Sheila Salter 59
Physick, Suzanne 53
Pickering, Ada 384
Pickersgill, Denise 288
Pickford, O. B. 322
Pickup, Gary 150
Pierce, Daphne 28
Pigg, Sylvia 319
Pile, Shelagh R. 419
Pilgrim, Linda 4
Pilkington, Eileen M. 302
Pillar, Graham Roy 392
Pillay, Ruben 50
Pinches, Barbara 562
Pine, Edna F. 72
Pitman, Patricia 497
Pitt-Kelly, Robert 416
Pittam, Nadine 431
Pitter, Barbara 252
Plant, Peter D. 44
Plant, Sue 539
Platts, Moyra 185
Pledge, Julia 223
Pletts, Pamela Margaret 576
Plumley, Stuart 347
Podlipskaite, Laura 245
Pollard, Michael 531
Pollock, M. 63
Pomm, Elaine 219
Ponder, Brian 37
Poole, Dawn 11
Pope, Christina 380
Port, Joyce 584
Porten, Roderick 366
Porter, Ken 290
Porter, Kenneth A. 241
Porter, P. A. 176
Porter, Pamela C. 200
Porter, Sussie 578
Porter, William 173
Portman, Ernest 470
Poskitt, Patricia I. 481
Pothecary, Mrs. Belinda 7
Potter, Linda 251
Pottinger, Robert 320
Potts, Emily 146
Povey, Marjorie 338
Pow, Alan 15
Powell, Lucy Jane Elton 452
Power, J. 202
Poynter, Christopher Irwin 258
Pratchett, R. I. 64
Precious, J. 556
Precious, K. M. 556
Preece, Deborah 527
Preece, Thomas H. 44
Prentice, J. 129
Prentis, Vera 336
Prescott, Thelma 588
Pressman, M. Q. 533
Preston, A. Douglas 41
Preston, E. J. 358
Preston, Phil 265
Price, A. L. 119, 361
Price, Cynthia A. 88
Price, Leslie 96

Price, Margaret 277
Price, Maria 55
Price, N. 326
Price, Patricia Margaret 444
Price, Ruth Elizabeth 563
Price, Suzanne J. 187
Price, Tina 571
Priddle, Alan G. 101
Priest, Rodney George 62
Prigmore, Simone A. 275
Prime, Donna 389
Prince, Belinda 289
Pringle, John 93
Pritchard, Gwyneth 229
Pritchard, Jim 383
Probert, Gillian Mary 394
Protheroe, Clare 304
Provan, Lynsey 568
Prow, Donna 453
Puddefoot, B. 531
Pugh, Edward B. 97
Pummell, Gill 207
Purves, Gabrielle 291
Puxley, Natalie 550
Pyke, Juliet Louise 90

Q

Quadri, O. A. 117
Quane, Sister M. Catherine 130
Quayle, Ellen Marie 95
Quin, O. R. 281
Quinlan, D. C. 407
Quinlan, Robert John 61
Quinn, Jim 288
Quinn, John 286
Quinnell, Peggy 490
Quirk, Glenda 461

R

Rabjohns, Frederick Wilson 288
Raby, P. M. 148
Race, Katy 144
Rachel, Marie 42
Radcliffe, Renee D. 434
Radford, Angela 391
Radley, Beverley 104
Rae, Margaret C. 40
Rainbird, Rosemary 122
Rainbow, Lucy 306
Raine, Douglas 460
Rajgarhia, Prachi 364
Ramm, Sabrina 50
Rampello, C. 569
Ramsay, D. K. 476
Ramsay, Gladys 349
Ramshaw, Olga 359
Ramshaw, Tina 125
Randall, A. 477
Randall, Denise 142
Randall, E. H. 127
Randell, James R. 243
Rankine, Joy 155
Ratcliff, David 572
Ratcliffe, Mary 324
Ratcliffe, Mary Anne 116
Raven, Elizabeth 256
Rawlings, P. 265
Rawlings, William Henry 346
Ray, Nicola 344
Raybould, Mark 432
Rayfield, Tom 541
Rayment, Marjorie E. 134
Raymond, Pierre 38
Raynal, Keith 449
Rayner, Sheila 173

Rea, Joan 516
Rea, Mary 339
Read, Jean 98
Read, L. 309
Readman, Kelly Ann 298
Reakes, Peter 476
Reast, Frank 569
Redfern, Sonia 414
Redford, Denise A. 306
Reece, E. M. 277
Reed, Gemma Frances 297
Reeman, Brian H. 169
Rees, C. 549
Rees, T. B. 273
Reese, Rhys 538
Reeves, Margaret 189
Reeves, P. 115
Reeves, Tara Penny 366
Regan, L. F. 45
Rehill, Monica R. 309
Rehm, Carl R. 261
Reid, A. Brookes 193
Reid, Lisa 261
Reid, Michelle 277
Reid, V. J. 354
Rek, Diana C. 72
Rendell, A. E. 53
Rennie, Mary 113
Renshaw, Arthur 372
Renz, Rhona Muriel 533
Revell, Joan 295
Rey, Ana-Maria 157
Reynolds, B. 564, 571
Reynolds, B. A. 403
Reynolds, Cher 294
Reynolds, G. 176
Reynolds, Helen 254
Reynolds, Oneetta 564
Rhodes, Carrie-Ann 35
Rhodes, Claire 299
Rhodes, Stephanie 321
Ribera, Toni Conesa 324
Rice, Irene 237
Rich, C. G. 321
Richard, Beverley 34
Richards, Benjamin 410
Richards, Diane 71
Richards, Gladys 71
Richards, Jacqueline 461
Richards, Jodie L. 519
Richards, Lisa 468
Richards, Lloyd Prideaux 155
Richards, Pam Harvey 239
Richards, Pamela 340
Richards, Paul 366
Richards, Phil 205
Richards, Roxanne 443
Richards, Sharon C. 188
Richardson, Alexandra 210
Richardson, Anne 229
Richardson, Carole 503
Richardson, David 295
Richardson, J. 280
Richardson, Paula 270
Richardson, Stacy 566
Richardson, Vera May 505
Richmond-Bate, Christine 141
Rickard, Carol 3
Riddick, Mary 320
Ridge, Andy 409
Ridgway, M. 276
Rigby, Jennifer 35
Rigby, P. J. 274
Riley, Louise 212
Rimell, Ruth 421
Ring, D. N. 566

Ringham, Geoff 8
Ringrose, Freda 248
Rippingale, P. 40
Ritchie, Mark 67
Ritchie, Mary C. 415
Rivett, B. E. 339
Robb, Ian 294
Robb, Stuart 494
Robba, Ivan 20
Roberts, Alison 154
Roberts, Bill RCNVR (deceased) 447
Roberts, Carol 92
Roberts, Catherine 467
Roberts, Elaine 250
Roberts, J. 271
Roberts, J. D. 361
Roberts, Joyce 402
Roberts, June Relph 220
Roberts, Lynne 568
Roberts, Sandra 419
Roberts, Sarah E. 68
Roberts, Sylvia 192
Roberts, Wenda 409
Roberts, Winifred 194
Robertshaw, Dawn 307
Robertson, Anne B. 515
Robertson, Ian F. 220
Robertson, Roslyn Claire 553
Robey, Doris 31
Robey, Stuart 121
Robins, Carol 166
Robinson, Annette 247
Robinson, Drew 401
Robinson, H. 105
Robinson, J. 328
Robinson, Jill 511
Robinson, John Barry 249
Robinson, K. 63
Robinson, Kay Louise 453
Robinson, Lorraine 285
Robinson, Michael 531
Robinson, Philippa Louise 271
Robinson, Sean 124
Robshaw, David 9
Roche-Harth, Yvonne 433
Rock, M. 426
Roestenburg, Jessica 528
Roffey, Kenneth B. 236
Roge, Roger 266
Rogers, Beth 208
Rogers, David H. 256
Rogers, Jerry Layne Sr. 5
Rogers, Joanne 259
Rogers, Judith 568
Rogers, M. A. 129
Rogers, Nicola 271
Rogers, Rosemary A. 178
Rogers, Trevor 268
Roland, Christiane 299
Rolle, Veda C. 267
Romano, Catheryn 468
Romero, Joanna Mireles 166
Romero, Toni 414
Roncone, Loretta 525
Ronneback, F. 496
Rook, Georgina Irene A. 459
Rook, John A. J. 522
Rooney, E. 114
Roper, Maureen 322
Rosas, Verity 337
Roscoe, Margaret 195
Rose, Fraser 373
Rose, Lynn 257
Rose, Sandra Diana 415
Rose, Sylvia 135

Rosewall, Margaretta 342
Rosier, Mary 409
Ross, Jean Elizabeth 224
Ross, Muriel 196
Ross, Sian 278
Rosser, Andy 224
Rossington, David 398
Rothery, Christopher 383
Roundhill, Lilian 208
Rousell, Anthony 395
Rowan, Colin 569
Rowan, Lesley 527
Rowbottom, Philip 501
Rowe, G. B. 269
Rowland, Ernest D. 356
Rowland, George A. 15
Rowland, Lily 449
Rowlands, Liz 235
Rowley, Barbara 157
Rowse, Amanda Jayne 80
Rowse, Don W. 152
Rowsell, Bill 118
Roy, G. E. 548
Roze, Jane 509
Ruane, Kay F. 291
Rule, Eleanor 234
Rumford, Jennie 571
Rundle, D. 193
Rushton, Patricia 552
Rushworth, Antony A. 13
Rusmanis, Beryl Sylvia 388
Russell, Natalie 555
Russell, Nicola 182
Russell, Norman 106
Russell, Patricia 493
Russell, Pauline 424
Russell, Sara 492
Ruth 135
Rutter, Neil 477
Ryan, Andrew 240
Ryan, J. B. 422
Ryan, Shaun 322
Ryder, Irene 165
Ryder, K. 368
Ryland, Kevin 172

S

Sabin, J. J. 479
Sabner, Jeff 207
Sacramento, Phillip 544
Saddler, Jessica-Donna Marie 82
Sadzhaya, Katrina 288
Saffery, A. 492
Sage, Mollie 117
Sainsbury, D. A. 361
Sainsbury, Paul 570
Sale, Jo 79
Saleem, M. I. 424
Salisbury, Derek 208
Salmon, Emma 248
Salmon, P. D. 47
Salmon, P. E. 434
Salt, Beverley 413
Salter, D. M. 483
Sampson, Alexander K. 216
Sanders, Marie 197
Sanders, R. 565
Sanders, Sylvia 36
Sanderson, Eleanor Haydon 384
Sanderson, Jacqueline 382
Sanderson, Vanessa 323
Sandford, Christine 390
Sandford, Sandra 567
Sandiford, Phyllis 65
Sands, Robin 319
Saunders, Barry Alan 16

Saunders, Elizabeth 246
Saunders, Leonard 403
Saunders, Patricia 361
Saurino, Emma 526
Savage, Gerry 31
Savage, James Carl 392
Savage, Susan 276
Savan, Anne 440
Savigar, Sarah 264
Saville, Olga 200
Sawdon, Margaret 121
Saxon, L. Y. 171
Sayers, Glen 147
Scales, Jenny 222
Scannell, Rowland Patrick 530
Scarisbrick, Joan 302
Scoates, Eileen 294
Scofield, Beatrice May 84
Scone, C. M. 65
Scott, A. C. M. 411
Scott, Angela 95
Scott, Anne C. 285
Scott, Christopher 97
Scott, David M. N. 165
Scott, Ernest 162
Scott, F. 52
Scott, Frank 567
Scott, Jack 228
Scott, Jean B. 77
Scott, Judith 481
Scott, Juliet Elisabeth 230
Scott, Mary 563
Scott, Naomi 319
Scott, Sharon 533
Scott, Stephanie Jane 550
Scott, Susan 547
Scott, V. K. 183
Seagreen 488
Seaton, Raymond W. 357
Seeley, Scott 47
Seiga, Helen 565
Selby, Robert 429
Selkirk, Scott 199
Sell, Lucy Victoria 240
Sell, Maisie 48
Sellen, Denise 246
Sellen, M. B. 268
Semmens, Gwyniris 147
Senior, Jean M. 513
Seton, Jean 565
Settle, Margaret 184
Sewoke, S. V. 113
Sexton, Patrick 540
Sexton, Timothy A. P. 502
Seymour, Anne 466
Shackleford, Freda 455
Shackleton, Susan 388
Shadare, Edwin Oludotun 16
Shade, D. 337
Shah-Alom 484
Shapcott, C. A. 536
Shapland, Tracey 548
Sharma, Arun 3
Sharp, Bernard 81
Sharp, C. J. 9
Sharp, Peter 367
Sharp, Steve 128
Sharpe, D. R. 65
Sharpe, Marjorie 409
Shaughnessy, Kathryn Susan 86
Shaun, David Aston 85
Shaw, Andy 236
Shaw, B. 315
Shaw, Carole 5
Shaw, Dawn 102
Shaw, E. D. 187

Shaw, Lynda 222
Sheard, A. 557
Sheen, J. J. 277
Sheerin, May K. 308
Sheldrake, Helen Christine 30
Shelley, John F. 100
Shelvock, F. 185
Shepherd, Colin A. 565
Shepherd, Jacqueline Maria 89
Shepherd, Marsha 472
Sheppard, Percy 116
Shepstone, Jessica 261
Sheriff, Doreen 212
Sherlock, Christine Anne 305
Sherratt, Kate 23
Sherriff, Jacqui 512
Shetland, Audrey 506
Shevlin, Sherlene 317
Shier, Hester 139
Shillito, James 514
Short, Helen 438
Short, John 523
Short, Tracey 572
Short-Windsor, Janet 397
Shortall, Patrick 352
Shrimpton, Karen 461
Siddons, Colin 563
Sidhu, Raman Kaur 324
Silgram, G. 431
Silk, D. F. 279
Silk, Ricky 406
Sillick, Marianne 571
Simmonds, John 225
Simmonds, Katharine 221
Simmonds, Wendy 554
Simmons, A. 308
Simmons, Geraldine 456
Simpson, Albert 244
Simpson, Charles 303
Simpson, Elizabeth 99
Simpson, Janet 221
Simpson, Jill 567
Simpson, Leonora 99
Simpson, M. R. 265
Simpson, Wendy 558
Sims, Barbara 147
Sinclair, Alexander B. 508
Sinclair, Jean 13
Sivyer, Sylvia 550
Skelland, J. 569
Skillen, Barbara 568
Skinner, E. 570
Skinner, Jean F. 212
Skinner, Sarah 39
Skivington, Lorrain 471
Sladden, Julia 218
Slade, Evelyn 89
Slaney, Carol 300
Slaney, Paul C. 546
Slaney, T. R. 544
Slater, Julie 235
Slater, Vicki Ann 342
Slattery, Dympna 236
Slattery, Dympna 520
Slattery, J. 334
Sleigh, Rebecca 424
Slim, John 508
Sloyan, Noreen 342
Small, Anne 215
Small, Gladys 241
Small, Jennifer B. 159
Smart, Carole Patricia 290
Smart, Christopher 95
Smedley, B. 204
Smedley, Linda 80
Smillie, H. T. 356

Smillie, Trevor 570
Smith, A. M. 542
Smith, Alan Brett 245
Smith, Andrea 231
Smith, Anthony Robert 284
Smith, B. 552
Smith, Betty 162
Smith, Beverley Ann 303
Smith, Brian 165
Smith, C. A. 42
Smith, Carol P. 119
Smith, Cathryn 254
Smith, Charlie Boy 20
Smith, Christopher 528
Smith, Claire 158
Smith, D. M. 117
Smith, Daniel C. 85
Smith, Daphne 91
Smith, Donald E. 208
Smith, E. F. J. 198
Smith, E. S. (nee Keeys) 542
Smith, Ernest 514
Smith, Fiona 469
Smith, H. 363
Smith, H. A. 180
Smith, H. G. 428
Smith, Ian Woodward 9
Smith, Irene 463
Smith, Iris 304
Smith, J. Colin 197
Smith, Janine A. 142
Smith, John Albert 5, 290
Smith, John W. 12
Smith, K. D. 425
Smith, Kate 248
Smith, Kirstin Helen 207
Smith, Lorraine R. 475
Smith, Margaret 532
Smith, Margaret Butler 345
Smith, Martin 274
Smith, Michael A. 423
Smith, P. R. 52
Smith, Patrick — Padraig 60
Smith, Q. 183
Smith, Rachel 43
Smith, Robert G. 191
Smith, Ronald 352
Smith, Sharon 477
Smith, Shirley 362
Smith, Victoria 343
Smith, Violet 418
Smith, Wilfred Bruce 540
Smith, William A. 409
Smitherman, Lilian 457
Smoult, Lynda Anne 153
Smurthwaite, Danielle 143
Smyth, Angela Marie 155
Smyth, Rosemary Gowans 278
Smyth, Tom 537
Sneddon, F. L. 269
Snow, Dorothy 91
Snowman, Bertha 303
Soan, Aaron Marque 81
Sokolowski, Moira 350
Solley, Carol 215
Sollis, Debbie 285
Sollis, Leanne 217
Somers, Edna 389
Somerscales, S. L. 489
Somerville, Gertrude A. 243
Somerville, R. 432
Soppitt, N. 436
Sorbie, Elizabeth A. 161
Sorrell, Celia 260
Sorrell, Laura 224
Southall, Doreen 251

Southern, Joan 77
Southerton, M. 172
Southorn, D. R. 354
Sowerby, D. 266
Sowerby, G. E. 328
Sowerby, Jackie 3
Sowerby, Penlee A. 64
Spagnoli, M. Laela 503
Sparkes, V. C. 422
Sparks, L. J. 300
Speck, Elsie J. 465
Speed, Rosina Dian 210
Speer, Helen M. 351
Speirs, Karen 392
Spellman, Agnes 285
Spellman, Helen 242
Spencer, Alan 287
Spencer, Brenda P. 565
Spencer, Corrinne E. 450
Spencer, I. 538
Spencer, J. 349
Spencer, Jeff 374
Spencer, Sarah Louise 564
Sperring, Pat 431
Spicer, Colin 521
Spicer, Jane 249
Spiers, Stephanie M. 368
Spillane, C. M. 273
Spillett, C. R. 179
Spittle, R. R. 67
Splaine, Rosemary 65
Spong, Brenda 479
Spooner, Rita 134
Spooner, Sarah Louise 326
Spray, Roselynne 239
Spriggs, Patricia Anne 185
Spriggs, S. M. 365
Springham, Tony 566
Spurway, Linda 402
Ssajjabbi, Richard Mark 40
Ssenkungu, Charles Lwanga 12
St. Clair, S. M. 540
Stace, Mary 267
Stacey, Terence J. 113
Stack, Mary 206
Staff, W. H. 311
Stafford, Andrew 145
Stanbury, J. L. 486
Standen, Gary 293
Standen, Ivor F. 145
Stange, Mark 275
Stanley, Alan 230
Stanley, Eva 80
Stanley, Vera 320
Stansfield, Fred 138
Stanton, Fay 337
Staunton, E. 147
Stealey, Valentine 471
Stedman, Paula 338
Stedman-Polehampton, A. G. 116
Steel, Adrinia 213
Steel, J. K. 333
Steel, Linda 301
Steele, Ida 386
Steele, Peggy F. 417
Stemp, Faye 523
Stenhouse, Betty 5
Stephen, C. 190
Stephens, Ken 543
Stephens, Rowan 110
Stephenson, Christine 29
Stephenson, Eleanor 287
Stephenson, L. 406
Sterland, Abbe 11
Sterling, Ramona 432
Stevens, Christine C. 222
Stevens, Christine 450
Stevens, J. T. 489
Stevens, Susan 282
Stevenson, Charlene 254
Stewart, Cynthia 17
Stewart, H. 473
Stewart, Jean 95
Stewart, Josephine Ann 150
Stewart, Kim 143
Stewart, Lesley 92
Stewart, Una A. 311
Still, Sandra Kathleen 195
Stinson, Jean 168
Stirk, Melvene 172
Stirling, Emma 151
Stirling, John A. 14
Stirton, Michael 415
Stobbs, Pat 564
Stocker, Louise 233
Stockham, M. Vaill 550
Stoneman, Patricia 201
Stones, Hayley 250
Storer, Christine Anne 395
Storey, Philip 544
Stradling, C. A. 58
Strang, Kenneth 386
Strange, Kay E. 373
Stratton, Barbara M. 214
Stratton-Dresser, W. 418
Streatfield, M. J. 61
Stringer, Maureen Breckell 552
Stroud, Rachel 183
Stuart, Anne 31
Stuart, Ron 137
Stuart, Thomas 418
Stubberfield, Paul 268
Stuckey, Martin 272
Sturgess, Gwyneth 291
Styles, Keith 6
Styles, Tom W. 566
Such, Maureen 337
Sudders, Deneze 260
Sudworth, W. J. 428
Sullivan, Tony 434
Summer, Kathryn 12
Summerbell, A. 497
Summerfield, Patricia 196
Summers, E. M. 553
Summers, M. 315
Surman, Patricia 551
Surtees, A. E. 278
Sussex, E. 121
Sussex, Olive N. 541
Sutcliffe, Barbara 296
Sutcliffe, C. 357
Sutherland, Carole A. S. 293
Sutton, David Thomas 170
Sutton, Hayley M. 307
Sutton, Joanne 100
Sutton, Tim Paul 479
Sutton, Valerie 341
Swales, Pauline 317
Swann, R. 186
Swann, Stanley 407
Swann, W. M. 369
Sweeney, W. M. P. 418
Sweetland, Linda 513
Sweetman, Lois 245
Sweetman, S. T. 551
Swift, Alan 151
Swinburn, Linda 285
Sylana 37
Sylvan, Richard 44
Symonds, Jean 17
Symonds, Odette 555
Symons, Dennis 386

T

Taddeo, Carole 299
Tait, Gillian 575
Talabi, Silver 535
Talbot, George M. 8
Tallbot, B. 544
Tanner, T. 407
Tatlow, C. E. 556
Tattersall, Philip A. W. 491
Tattershaw, Ian 10
Tatterton, Katie 529
Tattum, John 249
Tavis, Jacqueline 32
Tayler, W. Helen 408
Taylor, A. D. 563
Taylor, David Leonard 457
Taylor, E. 277
Taylor, Emily 441
Taylor, Hayley 102
Taylor, Julie 165
Taylor, Marcus 588
Taylor, Marjorie 411
Taylor, Mark 283
Taylor, Maureen 480
Taylor, Michael J. 413
Taylor, Rodney 547
Taylor, Sandra 567
Taylor, Shaw 357
Taylor, Sidney William 494
Taylor, Simon 562
Taylor, Teri-Ann 473
Taylor, Tina 196
Taylor, Y. 46
Teasdale, Valda 335
Teather, J. E. 243
Teather, Margaret 552
Teece, M. A. 430
Telfer, Irene 158
Telford, Louise 285
Telo, Rogerio Saviniano 538
Templar-Smith, Hazel 232
Temple, Eyin 260
Temple, Joy Elizabeth 158
Tennent, Iris 475
Terry, Graham D. 76
Terry, J. 269
Tew, Derek 526
Tezien-Devonshire, Azra 286
Thaper, Kamla 142
Thatcher, Kellie 91
the, Wenn Pen 189
Theobald, Charlotte 301
Thomas, Albert 520
Thomas, Camilla 84
Thomas, Carly 509
Thomas, Carol 75
Thomas, Darren Paul 398
Thomas, Dennis 139
Thomas, Gwyneth 300
Thomas, Heather 72
Thomas, Jason 406
Thomas, Joan 73
Thomas, Natalie 42
Thomas, O. E. 543
Thomas, Owen 542
Thomas, Sarah C. 328
Thomas, Sharon Wyn 328
Thomas, V. P. 427
Thompson, A. 325
Thompson, Beulah 214
Thompson, Chas E. 161
Thompson, Chrissy 167
Thompson, D. G. 429
Thompson, Daniel 25
Thompson, Felicity 394
Thompson, Linda 14

Thompson, M. 128
Thompson, M. E. 125
Thompson, Margaret 48
Thompson, Margaret 406
Thompson, Martin 487
Thompson, Maureen 507
Thompson, Melvina Mary 125
Thompson, Nicoli 128
Thompson, Robert J. 355
Thompson, S. J. 190
Thompson, Sara-Jane 182
Thompson, Susan 117, 534
Thompson, Terry 113
Thompson-Scrivener, Saira 45
Thomson, Carole Anne 37
Thomson, E. M. 491
Thomson, Gillian M. 234
Thomson, Glynis Stuart 19
Thomson, Helen Smyth 159
Thomson, R. S. 498
Thomson, Serena K. 418
Thorburn, Duncan 214
Thorn, Evelyn 442
Thorogood, J. R. 493
Thorpe, Anthony 238
Thorpe, Danyele L. 161
Thorpe, Marina 362
Thorpe, Matthew 192
Thurbon, Mike J. 536
Thurley, Laura 217
Thwaites, E. R. 324
Thwaites, Rebecca 266
Thynne, John 261
Tickner, Jane 286
Tierney, Harriet 305
Tierney, Patrick 135
Timmons, Michael F. 313
Timms, Tom 118
Tindall, Richard 423
Tingey, Primrose 333
Tingley, S. 267
Tinker, Joanne 215
Todd, A. 325
Todman, M. K. 321
Toley, A. 52
Tomahawk 332
Tomblin, Gaynor 94
Tombs, Jean 158
Tomes, R. F. 496
Tompkins, Eileen 286
Tompsett, Cherry L. 381
Toms, Sheila 408
Tonkin, H. K. 587
Tonkins, Joanne 284
Tonks, D. 570
Tootal, Valerie Yvonne 281
Topalovic, Radmila 126
Toppin, Margaret 270
Topping, Rebecca Diane 409
Tortolano, Anthony 252
Tourle, M. 276
Towersey, Mia 361
Townsend, Winifred 361
Townshend, D. 483
Towse, Jennilea 301
Trace, W. C. 262
Trail, Charles 375
Tran, P. 318
Travis, Shirley 41
Trayner, June 257
Treasurer, Lorna E. P. 269
Tremble, Joyce 90
Tremblin, B. D. 61
Tresadern, Helene 506
Trevenelyn, Robina 314
Trevett, Carol 27

Trew, T. J.   117
Trewern, D. M.   369
Tricker, Dawn Emma   558
Trickett, K. J.   441
Trigg, M.   366
Trimmer, Kate   297
Tristram, Paul   431
Troke, Caroline   97
Trotter, Avril   443
Truscott, La'Verne   561
Tsang, Sai Kong   368
Tubb, Nigel   548
Tucker, Brenda   78
Tucker, Mark   352
Tucker, Sheila   312
Tuckett, Carol   256
Tuff, Deirdre   456
Tuffill, B.   545
Turk, Lisa   289
Turnbull, Audrey   563
Turner, Caroline   3
Turner, Dennis   18
Turner, Gaynor   173
Turner, Jo   213
Turner, Joyce M.   394
Turner, Joyce Margaret   292
Turner, Laira   289
Turner, M. A.   571
Turner, Maureen   418
Turner, Michael   274
Turner, Pauline   333
Turner, Peter W. P.   58
Tuson, Hannah   297
Tuton, Helen   242
Tutton, Phyllis   181
Tuvey, Terry A.   204
Tweedale, Lorna A.   251
Twells, Veronica   63
Twine, Jacqueline Esme   563
Twiss, Audrey   234
Tyldesley, Linda M.   222
Tyler, Stacey   424
Tyrrell, Delphine   154
Tyrrell, Nik J.   275

U

Uceda, Vicente   269
Udall, Stephanie   199
Udell, Joy   469
Udenkwo, Catherine   292
Underwood, R.   186
Unsworth, Emma   86
Unwin, Rena   501
Urwin, John   230
Usher, N. J.   549
Uttley, G. M.   110

V

Vadgama, Gemini   529
Vale, Gordon   145
Vallis, Justine   222
Vanes, Angela B.   249
Vansfield, M. E.   313
Vanstone, Simon   111
Vanviere, Andrew Paul   253
Vaughan, Marina   207
Veal, Simon J.   82
Venter, A. J.   117
Ventress, Jean   229
Ventris, Dorothy   229
Vince, Amanda   378
Vincent, Joan   304
Vincent, Patricia   56
Vincent, V.   116
Viney, C. M.   109

Voase, Ken   294
Vokes, J.   588
Voss, Barbara   217
Vyas, Anil   98

W

Waberski, Mark   278
Waddington, Margaret   535
Wade, Andrew   245
Wade, Di   399
Wade, Len S.   25
Wade, Malcolm R.   421
Wadhwani, Sneha   309
Wadsworth, Jinny   295
Wain, J.   425
Wainwright, P.   317
Waite, E. E.   275
Waite, Jane   252
Waite, Louise   227
Wakefield, Liz   462
Walden, June   566
Waldron, George   21
Wales, Dorothy   162
Walji, Zahara   262
Walkden, E. V.   263
Walker, C. G.   69
Walker, Daniel   377
Walker, Gail   171
Walker, Henrietta   86
Walker, Janet   261
Walker, Joyce   444
Walker, M.   283
Walker, Margaret   60
Walker, Margaret   487
Walker, Mariann   118
Walker, Mary   504
Walker, Michelle   479
Walker, Nicola   413
Walker, Patricia   482
Walker, Rachel   367
Walker, Stephen   478
Walker, V.   412
Wall, Emma   249
Wall, Lyndon T.   6
Wall, Trudy   316
Waller, Martina   178
Wallis, Alex   400
Wallis, David   301
Wallis, John   475
Wallis-Pattison, Marie   331
Walster, J.   498
Walter, Philippa   330
Walters, David   456
Walters, Emma   156
Walton, Laura   439
Walton, Maxine   321
Walton, Valerie   266
Ward, A. M.   108
Ward, Albert   303
Ward, Alisoun M.   227
Ward, C. P.   501
Ward, Dennis J.   149
Ward, Grace   393
Ward, Loraine   394
Ward, Mary L.   314
Ward, Samantha   539
Wardle, Elsie   567
Ware, Pamela K.   35
Waring, Edna   154
Waring, Elsie   523
Warman, Trudy   505
Warne, H.   334
Warnes, Annette   167
Warnes, Sylvia   119
Warrander, Alan   565
Warren, S. P.   50

Warrender, Mellissa   488
Warwick, Paul   132
Waterhouse, D. J. S.   180
Waterman, Charles   511
Waters, Carole   287
Watkins, Bruce   258
Watson, Andrea C.   7
Watson, Catherine   571
Watson, J. Burges   239
Watson, Joyce   450
Watson, K. J.   63
Watson, Patricia   476
Watson, S. Truda   185
Watson, Shelagh   202
Watson, Suzy Louise   66
Watson, Tania   502
Watt, Diane Mary   252
Watt, N. O.   130
Watt, Samantha Jayne   573
Watt, Sandra Mary   324
Watton, Sarah   429
Watts, F. W. C.   265
Watts, Natalia   124
Watts, Robert   106
Watts, Sheila   188
Watts, Suzy   348
Waugh, F. A.   334
Waugh, Laura   247
Waugh, Ray   497
Way, C.   124
Wayles, Florence J.   294
Weatherley, Emma   144
Weatherley, John   378
Weaver, A. C.   108
Weaver, Janet Elizabeth   257
Weaver, S. H.   50
Webb, Colin S.   255
Webb, D. J.   337
Webb, Hazel   577
Webb, Kerry   306
Webb, Nigel A.   318
Webb, Patricia A. M.   556
Webb, Percy   180
Webb, Susan   282
Webb, Violet M.   410
Webb-Jones, Karen L.   234
Webber, M.   355
Webster, Amanda-Louise   90
Webster, Teresa   532
Webster, Tony *(Devon)*   418
Webster, Tony *(Buckingham)*   503
Wedderburn, Joanna   221
Weedon, Mark   322
Weeks, Garry Royston   452
Weeney   112
Weir, Patricia E.   128
Weir-Burrows, Marie   118
Welby, Doreen   455
Weller, Iris E.   387
Weller, Julie   510
Weller, Naomi   343
Wells, C. D.   533
Wells, J. A.   284
Wells, Lesley   250
Wells, Sandra   137
Wells, Tina   175
Welna, J.   283
Welsh, Matthew   108
Welsh, Stuart   546
Wesson, H. P.   113
West, Amy   375
West, Anita   217
West, D.   46
West, H. J.   423
West, Helen   374
West, L. H.   344

West, Victor   353
Western, Tarra   533
Westley, Pamela   189
Weston, Brian Kenneth   85
Weston, Joan   21
Westwood, Mark   472
Westwood, Patricia   272
Wetton, A. E.   57
Wetton, Roger   112
Whalley, H. J.   267
Whatley, Christine   259
Whatley, Matthew   322
Whatmough, Cathie   566
Wheatcroft, Michael A.   542
Wheater, Ruth   357
Wheatley, Lynette   88
Wheler, Amanda   34
Whellans, Stuart   369
Whitchurch, Jill   72
White, Diane   562
White, Dorothy June   299
White, F. J.   505
White, J.   203
White, Jane A.   6
White, Joanne   384
White, John   16
White, Lisa   393
White, P.   329
White, Philip R.   190
White, Raymond G.   485
White, Stephen George   446
White, Winifred   264
Whitehead, Clare   33
Whitehouse, Stephen   424
Whitehowe, Patricia   535
Whitelaw, Andrew   101
Whitfeld, Georgina   244
Whitfield, Bryan William   439
Whitfield, Ivy   571
Whitford, Philip Howard   266
Whiting, Rose B.   121
Whitley, Dianne Elizabeth   28
Whitman, Dee   563
Whittle, Patricia   283
Whyles, C.   137
Whysall, Mary   323
Whyte, Brigid   92
Whyte, Cheryl   563
Wibberley, Brenda   256
Wicks, Ray   58
Wightman, June   450
Wigmore, R.   120
Wigzell, T. D.   472
Wijesinghe, Priya   506
Wilcox, David   145
Wilcox, Enid K. G.   385
Wild, D. J.   36
Wild, Kevin   446
Wilde, Alex   229
Wildish, Kevin   152
Wilford, Neal   64
Wilkins, Evelyn   514
Wilkins, John L.   220
Wilkinson, E.   39
Wilkinson, Gayle   156
Wilkinson, Gordon   399
Wilkinson, Ian Christopher   403
Wilkinson, Marie   535
Wilkinson, R.   107
Wilks, Pat   323
Willats, Marilyn   563
Willes, Carol   182
Willetts, Sarah   476
Williams, Beulah   587
Williams, Cecil   442
Williams, Davina   572

Williams, Dorothy 29
Williams, Elwyn 19
Williams, Gerol F. 291
Williams, Ian 229
Williams, Janice L. 405
Williams, Josie 289
Williams, Julie 371
Williams, K. 270
Williams, Kenneth J. 20
Williams, Lorraine 10
Williams, Mark 550
Williams, Patricia 127
Williams, Pauline 566
Williams, Peter 107
Williams, Philip Trevor 411
Williams, Phillip G. 504
Williams, Phyllis D. 281
Williams, R. T. 41
Williams, Steven 545
Williams, Sue 427
Williams, Teri 109
Williams, Tracey 314
Williams-Podhraski, D. 464
Williamson, Dorothy 305
Williamson, Dorothy 397
Williamson, Kay 568
Williamson, L. 200
Williamson, Linda 150
Williamson, N. 272
Williamson, Sheryl 474
Willis, Maibrooke 194
Willis, P. 475
Willis, Paula 263
Willison, Brenda 477
Willmore, Melanie 200
Willoughby, G. 495
Willox, Ethel 16
Wills, D. Pamela 335
Willshire, I. F. 543
Wilshaw, D'reen 302
Wilshaw, J. 189
Wilson, Adam 17
Wilson, Anne 289
Wilson, B. 550
Wilson, Daisy 563
Wilson, David Bain 373
Wilson, Elizabeth 454
Wilson, G. 248
Wilson, Hayley 527
Wilson, Irene Smith 145
Wilson, James A. 228
Wilson, Judith 78
Wilson, Kim 299
Wilson, Leonard 237
Wilson, Lorraine 85
Wilson, M. 473
Wilson, Margaret 318
Wilson, Margaret 558
Wilson, Margaret E. 480
Wilson, Mary 47
Wilson, N. 365
Wilson, S. 193, 354
Wilson, Sidney 368
Wiltshire, Anne 290
Wincentzen, Eileen 396
Winch, Sarah Louise 313
Wincup, Warrick G. 57
Windsor, S. M. 319
Wingate, Helen 389
Wingfield, Melanie 430
Winn, Christina 305
Winsborough, Lynne G. 287
Winter, S. J. 130
Winton, Mary 570
Winyard, P. 354
Wirth, Heidi Jane 296

Wisdom, Clemmie 240
Wisdom, Joanne 119
Wise, Jane 302
Wise, Susan 312
Wiseman, Sharon 55
Wiszniewski, L. 576
Witherington, G. 116
Withrington, Marion 412
Witt, D. S. 424
Witt, Sandra 187
Witte, Irene 465
Wolff, O. M. 267
Wollington, E. R. 339
Wolstenholme, Ivan 567
Wolstenholme, R. 199
Wolverson, J. 530
Wong, Yin Heng 109
Wood, A. M. 479
Wood, Alison 444
Wood, Amaqla 375
Wood, Angela 97
Wood, Elaine 209
Wood, Helen 73
Wood, Les 445
Wood, Linda 167
Wood, P. M. H. 474
Woodcock, M. 276
Woodcock, Patricia 538
Woodfine, Martin James 179
Woodhouse, Olive 28
Woodhouse, Patricia Anne 134
Woodhouse, Tina-Jane 328
Woodley, Nicola 195
Woods, A. Stella 127
Woods, Alice Lee 513
Woods, Betty 284
Woods, Gerard 240
Woods, Susan 329
Woodward, Andy 450
Woodward, E. 172
Woodward, Jeanne 385
Woodward, Norman 496
Woodward, P. R. 364
Woolcock, Tania 68
Wooldridge, Paul 346
Woolford, D. 287
Woolley, Sarah 51
Wooten, Sarita 484
Wootton, Jennifer D. 95
Worthington, C. 535
Worthington, Donna 512
Wren, Elizabeth 136
Wrenhurst, Roger 192
Wrenn, Kelly 24
Wright, Alan 98
Wright, C. J. 108
Wright, Ena 394
Wright, Hazel 373
Wright, M. B. 569
Wright, Margaret Jean 174
Wright, Mary 47
Wright, Michael 280
Wright, Rachel 262
Wright, Rosemary 352
Wright, Sheila P. 53
Wright, Tamsin 475
Wroe, Elsie 248
Wylde, H. E. 201
Wylie, S. 304

Y

Yai, Deng Deng Hoc 387
Yardley, E. 175
Yates, E. 362
Yates, Hannah 30
Yates, Laurie 524

Yates, Lisa 77
Yip, Wai-Ling 283
York, Jack 523
York, William 551
Young, B. J. 550
Young, C. 359
Young, J. W. 177
Young, Joanne 282
Young, P. 332
Young, Sally 311
Young, Violet M. 283
Younger, John 71
Younger, Paul 486
Younger, Rose 344
Yuen, Rita 338
Yule, Rosalinda 499

Z

Zupan, Andrea 520